Mobil Travel Guide®

2000

California and the West

Arizona • California • Nevada • Utah

ConsumerGuide™
Publications International, Ltd.

Acknowledgments

We gratefully acknowledge the help of our field representatives for their efficient and perceptive inspection of every lodging and dining establishment listed; the establishments' proprietors for their cooperation in showing their facilities and providing information about them; the many users of previous editions of the *Mobil Travel Guide* who have taken the time to share their experiences; and for their time and information, the thousands of chambers of commerce, convention and visitors bureaus, city, state, and provincial tourism offices, and government agencies who assisted in our research.

Published by Publications International, Ltd.
7373 N. Cicero Avenue
Lincolnwood, IL 60712

travel@pubint.com

Cover photo: SuperStock

California and the West
ISBN 0-7853-4157-9
ISSN 0076-9827

Printed in the United States of America.
10 9 8 7 6 5 4 3 2 1

Contents

A Word to Our Readers xxv
Welcome xxvi
How to Use This Book xxvii
Making the Most of Your Trip xxxii
Important Toll-Free Numbers xxxv
Four-Star and Five-Star Establishments in California and the West xxxvii

California and the West

Arizona 1
California 64
Nevada 325
Utah 350
Appendix A: Restaurant List 384
Appendix B: Lodging List 391
City Index 399

Maps

Interstate Highways .... iv-v
California and the West Region .... vi-vii
Distance/Driving Time .... viii-ix
Arizona .... x-xi
Phoenix xii
Tucson xiii
Las Vegas xiii
Nevada .... xiv-xv
California .... xvi-xvii
Los Angeles .... xviii-xix
San Francisco Bay Area xx
Fresno xxi
Monterey xxi
San Francisco xxi
Utah .... xxii-xxiii
Salt Lake City xxiv

Larger, more detailed maps are available at many Mobil service stations

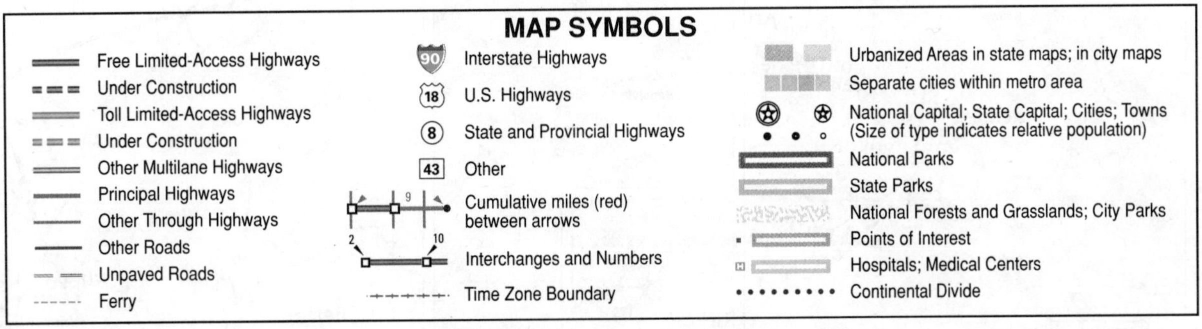

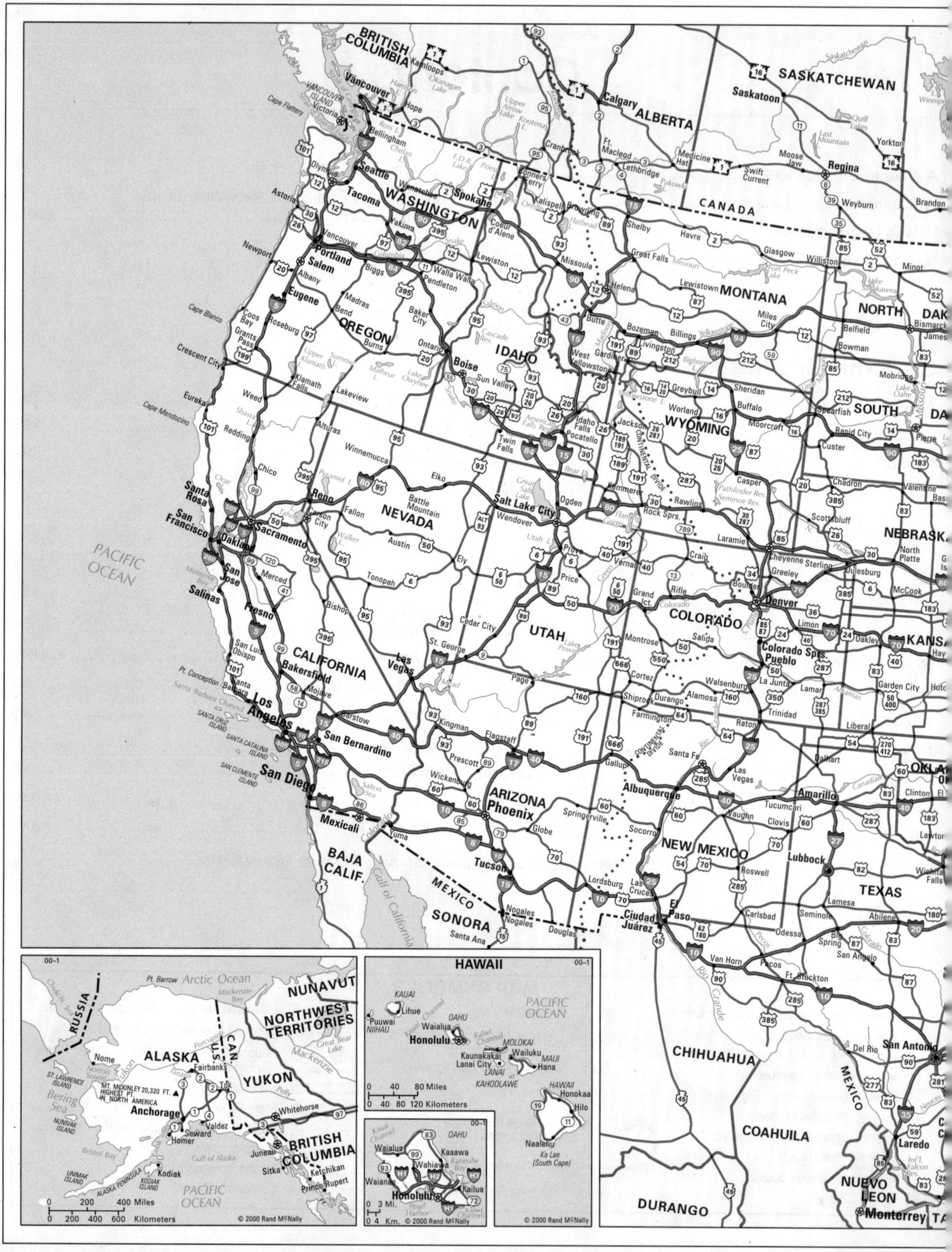
BRITISH COLUMBIA
SASKATCHEWAN
ALBERTA
CANADA
WASHINGTON
OREGON
IDAHO
MONTANA
NORTH DAK
SOUTH DA
WYOMING
NEVADA
UTAH
COLORADO
NEBRASKA
KANSA
CALIFORNIA
ARIZONA
NEW MEXICO
TEXAS
OKLA
PACIFIC OCEAN
BAJA CALIF.
SONORA
CHIHUAHUA
COAHUILA
DURANGO
NUEVO LEON
MEXICO
Gulf of California
Vancouver
Victoria
Kamloops
Hope
Calgary
Saskatoon
Regina
Moose Jaw
Yorkton
Brandon
Medicine Hat
Lethbridge
Swift Current
Cranbrook
Seattle
Tacoma
Olympia
Bellingham
Spokane
Yakima
Portland
Salem
Eugene
Coos Bay
Roseburg
Grants Pass
Crescent City
Eureka
Redding
Chico
Santa Rosa
San Francisco
Oakland
Sacramento
San Jose
Salinas
Fresno
Merced
Bakersfield
Los Angeles
San Bernardino
San Diego
Mexicali
Yuma
Reno
Carson City
Elko
Winnemucca
Tonopah
Austin
Ely
Las Vegas
Boise
Twin Falls
Pocatello
Idaho Falls
Missoula
Helena
Butte
Great Falls
Billings
Bozeman
Shelby
Havre
Glasgow
Williston
Minot
Bismarck
Salt Lake City
Ogden
Provo
St. George
Cedar City
Cheyenne
Casper
Laramie
Rock Sprs.
Rawlins
Sheridan
Denver
Boulder
Colorado Sprs.
Pueblo
Grand Jct.
Durango
Farmington
Gallup
Albuquerque
Santa Fe
Las Cruces
El Paso
Ciudad Juárez
Flagstaff
Kingman
Prescott
Phoenix
Tucson
Nogales
Amarillo
Lubbock
Odessa
San Angelo
San Antonio
Laredo
Monterrey
Del Rio
North Platte
Scottsbluff
Rapid City
Pierre
PACIFIC OCEAN
00–1
Arctic Ocean
RUSSIA
ALASKA
NUNAVUT
NORTHWEST TERRITORIES
YUKON
BRITISH COLUMBIA
Nome
Fairbanks
Anchorage
Juneau
Whitehorse
Kodiak
Sitka
Ketchikan
Prince Rupert
MT. MCKINLEY 20,320 FT. HIGHEST PT. IN NORTH AMERICA
Bering Sea
Gulf of Alaska
0 200 400 Miles
0 200 400 600 Kilometers
© 2000 Rand McNally
HAWAII
KAUAI
OAHU
MOLOKAI
MAUI
LANAI
KAHOOLAWE
HAWAII
Lihue
Honolulu
Wailuku
Hilo
0 40 80 Miles
0 40 80 120 Kilometers
© 2000 Rand McNally
Wahiawa
Kailua
0 3 Mi.
0 4 Km. © 2000 Rand McNally

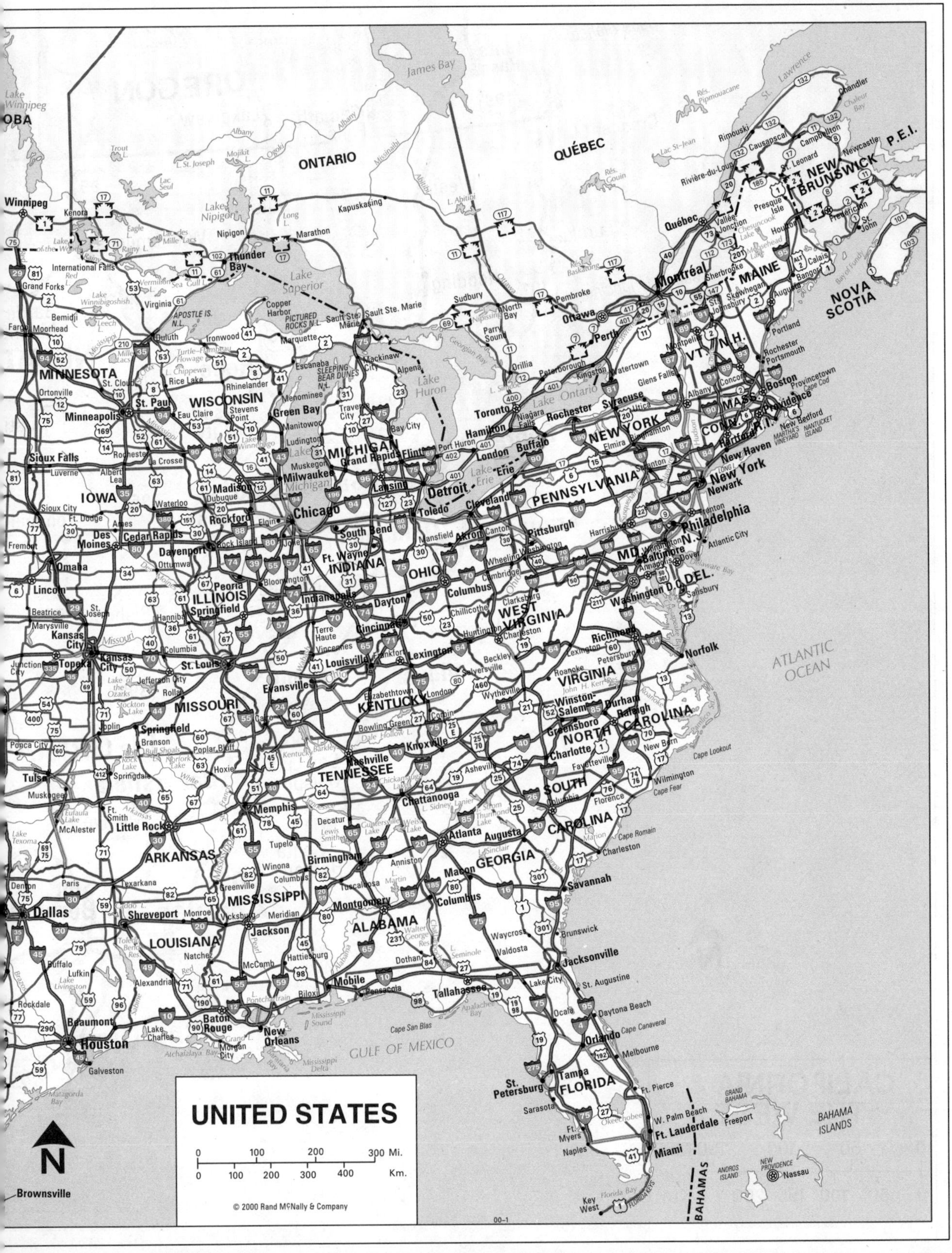
UNITED STATES
0 100 200 300 Mi.
0 100 200 300 400 Km.
© 2000 Rand McNally & Company
N
ONTARIO
QUÉBEC
NEW BRUNSWICK
P.E.I.
NOVA SCOTIA
James Bay
Lake Superior
Lake Michigan
Lake Huron
Lake Ontario
Lake Erie
ATLANTIC OCEAN
GULF OF MEXICO
BAHAMA ISLANDS
BAHAMAS
MINNESOTA
WISCONSIN
MICHIGAN
IOWA
ILLINOIS
INDIANA
OHIO
PENNSYLVANIA
NEW YORK
VT.
N.H.
MAINE
MASS.
CONN.
R.I.
N.J.
DEL.
MD.
WEST VIRGINIA
VIRGINIA
KENTUCKY
TENNESSEE
NORTH CAROLINA
SOUTH CAROLINA
GEORGIA
ALABAMA
MISSISSIPPI
LOUISIANA
ARKANSAS
MISSOURI
FLORIDA
Winnipeg
Thunder Bay
Sault Ste. Marie
Toronto
Ottawa
Montréal
Québec
Minneapolis
St. Paul
Milwaukee
Chicago
Detroit
Cleveland
Pittsburgh
Buffalo
New York
Boston
Providence
Philadelphia
Baltimore
Washington D.C.
Richmond
Norfolk
Indianapolis
Columbus
Cincinnati
Louisville
St. Louis
Kansas City
Omaha
Des Moines
Nashville
Memphis
Atlanta
Charlotte
Raleigh
Birmingham
Jacksonville
Orlando
Tampa
Miami
New Orleans
Houston
Dallas
Little Rock
Jackson
Savannah
Key West
Nassau
Brownsville

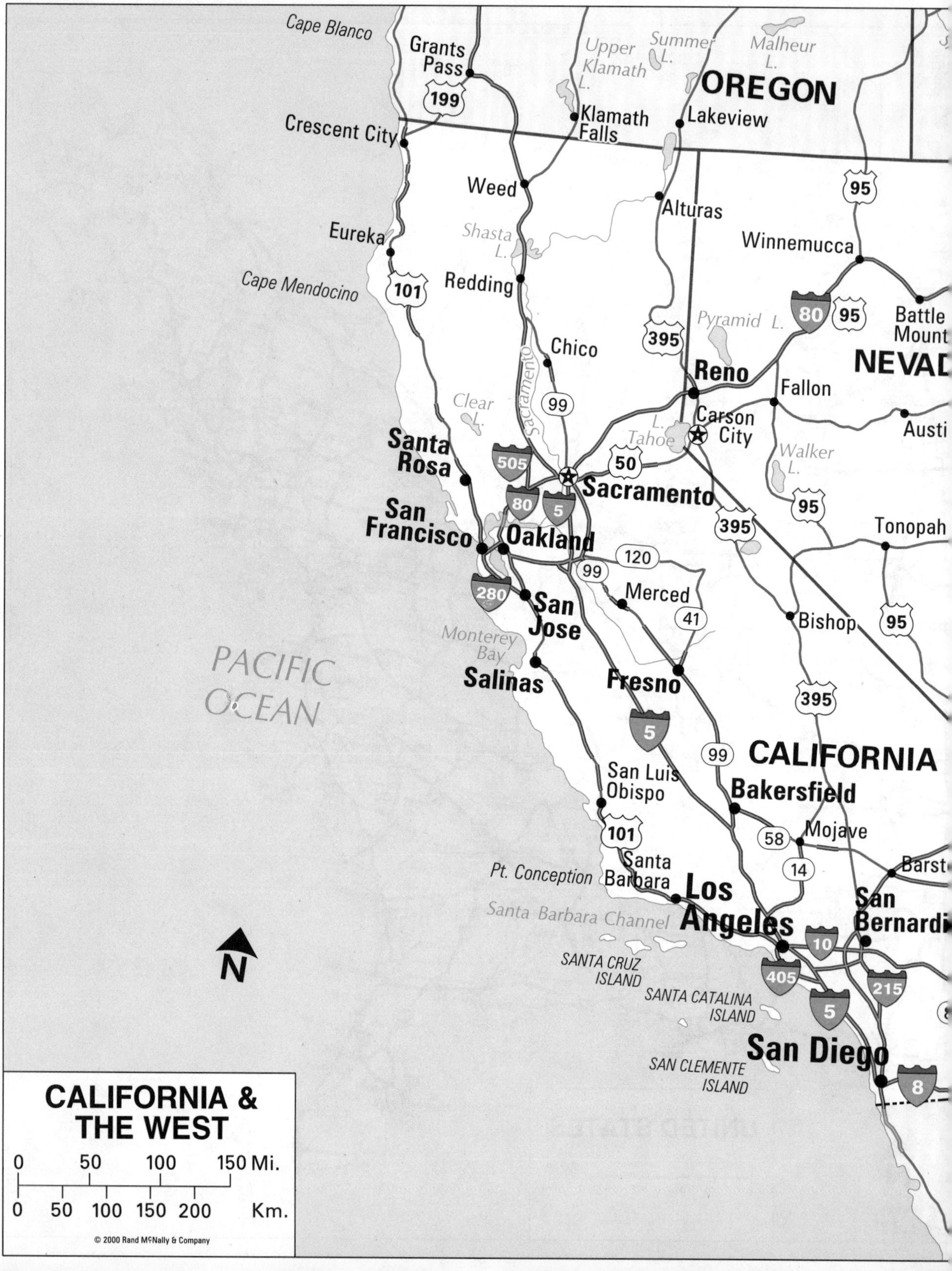
Cape Blanco
Grants Pass
199
Upper Klamath L.
Summer L.
Malheur L.
OREGON
Crescent City
Klamath Falls
Lakeview
Weed
95
Alturas
Shasta L.
Winnemucca
Eureka
Cape Mendocino
101
Redding
80
95
Battle Mount
Pyramid L.
395
Chico
NEVAD
Reno
Sacramento
Clear L.
99
Fallon
L. Tahoe
Carson City
Austi
Santa Rosa
505
50
Walker L.
Sacramento
80
5
95
San Francisco
Oakland
395
Tonopah
120
99
280
San Jose
Merced
41
Bishop
95
Monterey Bay
PACIFIC OCEAN
Salinas
Fresno
395
5
99
CALIFORNIA
San Luis Obispo
Bakersfield
101
58
Mojave
14
Pt. Conception
Santa Barbara
Barst
Los Angeles
San Bernardi
Santa Barbara Channel
10
SANTA CRUZ ISLAND
405
215
SANTA CATALINA ISLAND
5
San Diego
SAN CLEMENTE ISLAND
8
N
CALIFORNIA & THE WEST
0 50 100 150 Mi.
0 50 100 150 200 Km.

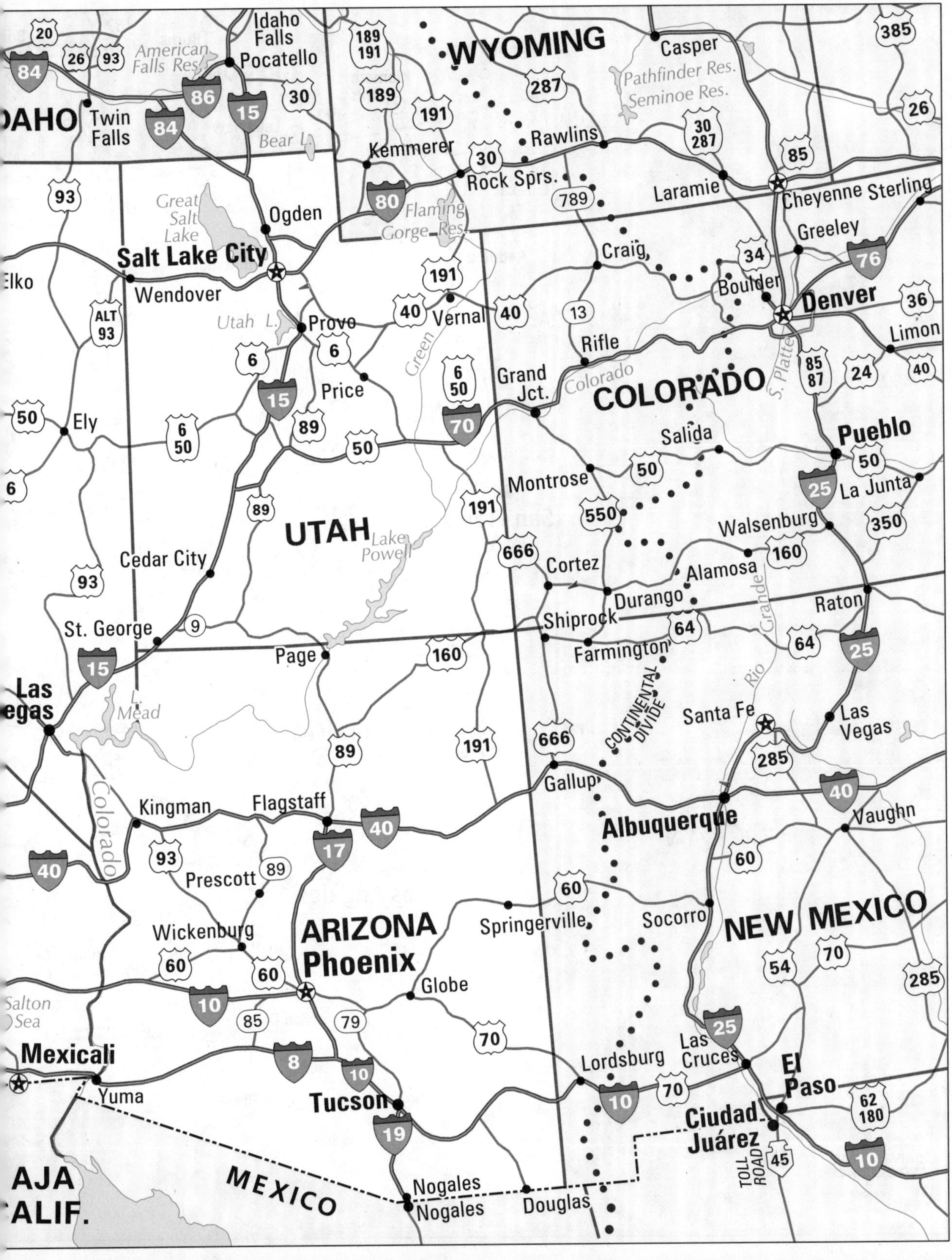
WYOMING
IDAHO
UTAH
COLORADO
ARIZONA
NEW MEXICO
MEXICO
BAJA CALIF.
Idaho Falls
Pocatello
American Falls Res.
Twin Falls
Bear L.
Casper
Pathfinder Res.
Seminoe Res.
Rawlins
Kemmerer
Rock Sprs.
Laramie
Cheyenne
Sterling
Flaming Gorge Res.
Great Salt Lake
Ogden
Salt Lake City
Elko
Wendover
Utah L.
Provo
Vernal
Craig
Boulder
Denver
Greeley
Limon
Rifle
Grand Jct.
Colorado
Green
S. Platte
Price
Ely
Pueblo
Salida
Montrose
La Junta
Walsenburg
Lake Powell
Cedar City
Cortez
Alamosa
Durango
Shiprock
Raton
Farmington
St. George
Page
Las Vegas
L. Mead
CONTINENTAL DIVIDE
Santa Fe
Rio Grande
Gallup
Kingman
Flagstaff
Albuquerque
Vaughn
Prescott
Springerville
Socorro
Wickenburg
Phoenix
Globe
Salton Sea
Mexicali
Yuma
Tucson
Lordsburg
Las Cruces
El Paso
Ciudad Juárez
TOLL ROAD
Nogales
Douglas

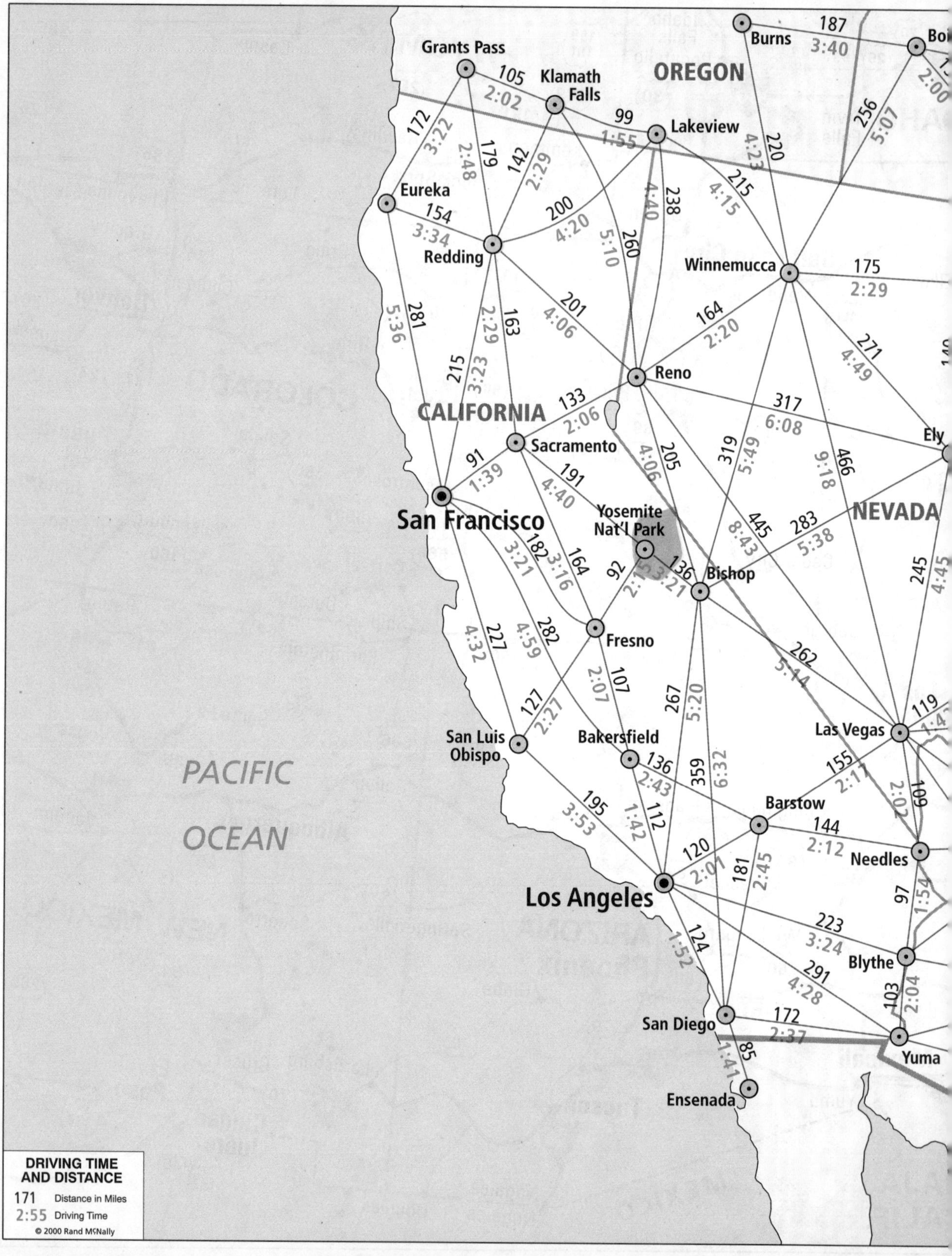
OREGON
CALIFORNIA
NEVADA
PACIFIC
OCEAN
Grants Pass
Klamath Falls
Lakeview
Burns
Eureka
Redding
Winnemucca
Reno
Ely
Sacramento
San Francisco
Yosemite Nat'l Park
Bishop
Fresno
San Luis Obispo
Bakersfield
Las Vegas
Barstow
Needles
Los Angeles
Blythe
San Diego
Yuma
Ensenada
187 3:40
105 2:02
99 1:55
172 3:22
179 2:48
142 2:29
220 4:23
256 5:07
215 4:15
154 3:34
200 4:20
260 5:10
238 4:40
175 2:29
281 5:36
163 2:29
215 3:23
201 4:06
164 2:20
271 4:49
133 2:06
317 6:08
91 1:39
191 4:40
205 4:06
319 5:49
466 9:18
445 8:43
283 5:38
245
182 3:21
164 3:16
92
136
227 4:32
282 4:59
107 2:07
262 5:14
127 2:27
267 5:20
119
136 2:43
359 6:32
155 2:17
109 2:02
195 3:53
112 1:42
120 2:01
181 2:45
144 2:12
97 1:54
223 3:24
124 1:52
291 4:28
103 2:04
172 2:37
85 1:41
DRIVING TIME AND DISTANCE
171 Distance in Miles
2:55 Driving Time
© 2000 Rand McNally

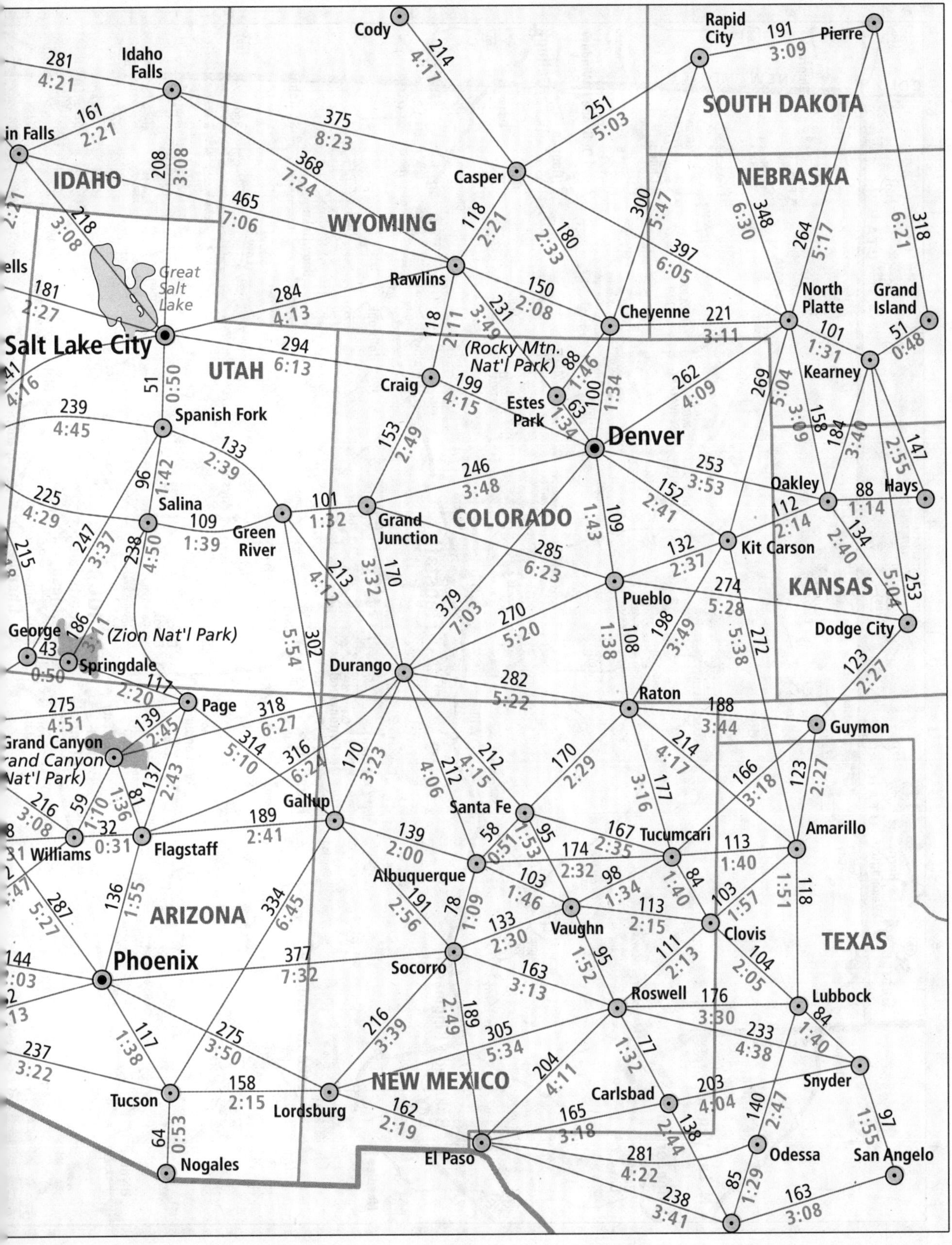

Cody
Rapid City
Pierre
SOUTH DAKOTA
Idaho Falls
Twin Falls
IDAHO
Casper
NEBRASKA
WYOMING
Great Salt Lake
Rawlins
North Platte
Grand Island
Cheyenne
Salt Lake City
UTAH
(Rocky Mtn. Nat'l Park)
Kearney
Craig
Estes Park
Denver
Spanish Fork
Oakley
Hays
Salina
Green River
Grand Junction
COLORADO
Kit Carson
KANSAS
Pueblo
Dodge City
St. George
(Zion Nat'l Park)
Springdale
Durango
Raton
Page
Guymon
Grand Canyon
(Grand Canyon Nat'l Park)
Gallup
Santa Fe
Amarillo
Williams
Flagstaff
Tucumcari
Albuquerque
ARIZONA
Vaughn
Clovis
TEXAS
Phoenix
Socorro
Roswell
Lubbock
Snyder
Tucson
Lordsburg
NEW MEXICO
Carlsbad
El Paso
Odessa
San Angelo
Nogales

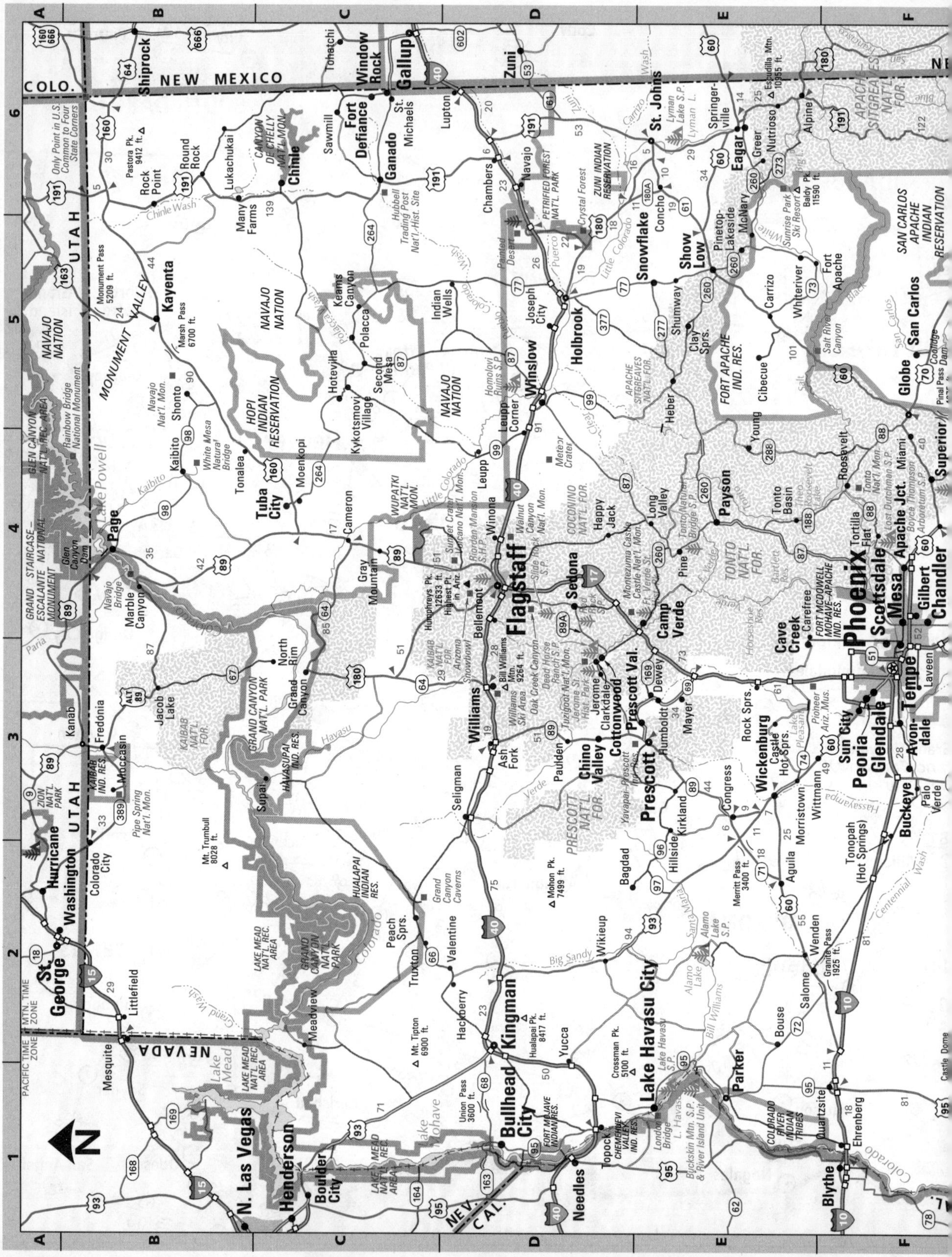
NEW MEXICO
UTAH
NEVADA
COLO.
CAL.
NEV.
Only Point in U.S. Common to Four State Corners
PACIFIC TIME ZONE
MTN. TIME ZONE
NAVAJO NATION
HOPI INDIAN RESERVATION
FORT APACHE IND. RES.
SAN CARLOS APACHE INDIAN RESERVATION
GRAND CANYON NAT'L. PARK
LAKE MEAD NAT'L. REC. AREA
KAIBAB NAT'L. FOR.
COCONINO NAT'L. FOR.
PRESCOTT NAT'L. FOR.
TONTO NAT'L. FOR.
APACHE SITGREAVES NAT'L. FOR.
PETRIFIED FOREST NAT'L. PARK
MONUMENT VALLEY
Lake Powell
Lake Mead
Lake Mohave
Colorado
Shiprock
Window Rock
Gallup
Zuni
St. Johns
Springerville
Eagar
Alpine
Fort Defiance
Ganado
Chinle
Kayenta
Page
Tuba City
Cameron
Flagstaff
Sedona
Williams
Winslow
Holbrook
Snowflake
Show Low
Payson
Globe
San Carlos
Superior
Prescott
Prescott Val.
Cottonwood
Camp Verde
Kingman
Bullhead City
Lake Havasu City
Parker
Wickenburg
Phoenix
Scottsdale
Mesa
Tempe
Chandler
Gilbert
Glendale
Peoria
Sun City
Buckeye
Blythe
Needles
Henderson
N. Las Vegas
Boulder City
St. George
Washington
Hurricane
Colorado City
Fredonia
Kanab
Mesquite
Littlefield

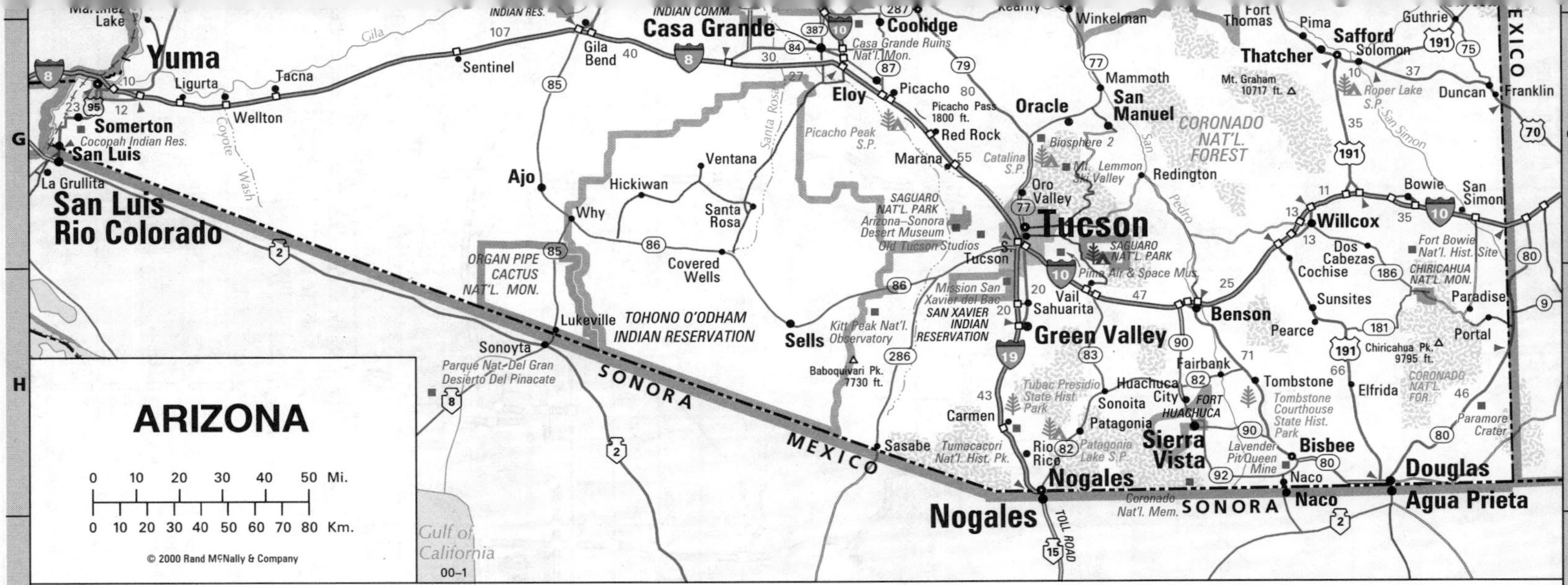

Cities and Towns

Arizona

Ajo G-3
Apache Junction . . . F-4
Aquila E-2
Ash Fork D-3
Benson H-5
Bisbee H-5
Bullhead City D-1
Cameron C-4
Camp Verde E-4
Carefree F-4
Casa Grande G-4
Chambers D-6
Chandler F-4
Chinle C-6
Clifton F-6
Cochise G-5
Congress E-3
Coolidge G-4
Cottonwood D-3
Douglas H-6
Duncan G-6
Eloy G-4
Flagstaff D-4
Florence F-4
Ganado C-6
Gila Bend F-3
Glendale F-3
Globe F-5
Grand Canyon C-3
Green Valley H-4
Greer E-6
Holbrook D-5
Huachuca City H-5
Jacob Lake B-3
Kayenta B-5
Kingman D-2
Lake Havasu City . . . E-1
Litchfield Park F-3
Many Farms B-6
Marble Canyon B-4
McNary E-5
Mesa F-4
Miami F-4
Nogales H-4
Oracle G-5
Oro Valley G-4
Page B-4
Parker E-1
Patagonia H-5
Payson E-4
Peach Springs C-2
Phoenix F-3
Picacho G-4
Pinetop-Lakeside . . . E-5
Prescott E-3
Prescott Valley D-3
Quartzsite F-1
Rio Rico H-4
Safford G-6
St. Johns E-6
Salome E-2
San Carlos F-5
San Manuel G-5
Scottsdale F-4
Second Mesa C-5
Sedona D-4
Seligman D-3
Sells H-4
Show Low E-5
Sierra Vista H-5
Snowflake E-5
Springerville E-6
Sun City F-3
Tempe F-4
Tombstone H-5
Tonalea B-4
Tucson G-4
Wickenburg E-3
Willcox G-5
Williams D-3
Window Rock C-6
Winslow D-5
Yucca D-2
Yuma G-1

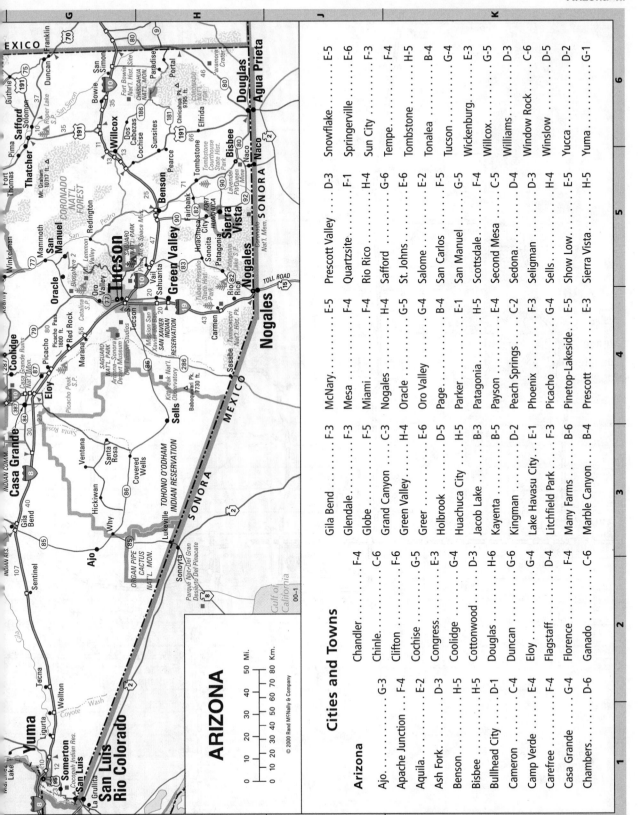

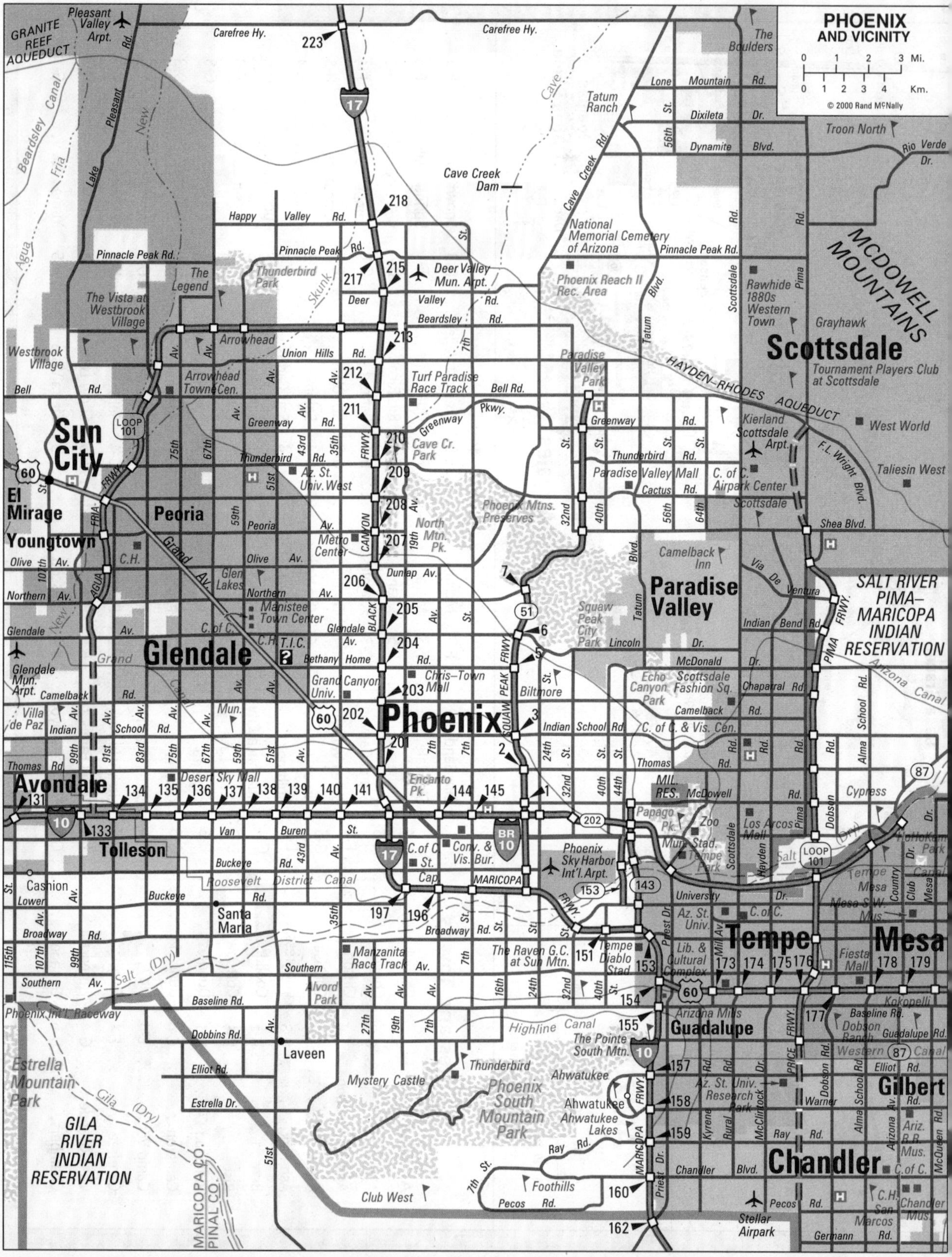

PHOENIX
AND VICINITY
0 1 2 3 Mi.
0 1 2 3 4 Km.
© 2000 Rand McNally
Pleasant Valley Arpt.
GRANITE REEF AQUEDUCT
Carefree Hy.
223
17
The Boulders
Lone Mountain Rd.
Tatum Ranch
Dixileta Dr.
Dynamite Blvd.
Troon North
Rio Verde Dr.
Beardsley Canal
Agua Fria
New
Lake Pleasant Rd.
Cave Creek Dam
Cave Creek Rd.
218
Happy Valley Rd.
National Memorial Cemetery of Arizona
Pinnacle Peak Rd.
MCDOWELL MOUNTAINS
The Legend
Thunderbird Park
Skunk
215
217
Deer Valley Mun. Arpt.
Deer Valley Rd.
Phoenix Reach II Rec. Area
Rawhide 1880s Western Town
Pima
Scottsdale Rd.
Tatum Blvd.
The Vista at Westbrook Village
Beardsley Rd.
Grayhawk
Arrowhead
213
Union Hills Rd.
Westbrook Village
Scottsdale
Paradise Valley Park
HAYDEN-RHODES AQUEDUCT
Tournament Players Club at Scottsdale
Bell Rd.
Arrowhead Towne Cen.
212
Turf Paradise Race Track
Sun City
LOOP 101
Greenway Rd.
211
Greenway Pkwy.
Kierland
Scottsdale Arpt.
West World
210
Cave Cr. Park
Thunderbird Rd.
43rd
35th
FRWY
F.L. Wright Blvd.
60
Az. St. Univ. West
209
Paradise Valley Mall
C. of C. Airpark Center
Taliesin West
El Mirage
Peoria
51st
59th
67th
75th
Cactus Rd.
Scottsdale
208
Phoenix Mtns. Preserves
32nd
40th
56th
64th
Shea Blvd.
Youngtown
Peoria Av.
Metro Center
CANYON
North Mtn. Pk.
19th
207
Olive Av.
107th
C.H.
Grand Av.
Glen Lakes
Dunlap Av.
Camelback Inn
Via De Ventura
SALT RIVER PIMA-MARICOPA INDIAN RESERVATION
Northern Av.
206
Manistee Town Center
7
Paradise Valley
205
51
Squaw Peak City Park
Indian Bend Rd.
Glendale Av.
C. of C.
C.H.
T.I.C.
Glendale
6
Lincoln Dr.
Bethany Home Rd.
204
5
McDonald Dr.
PIMA
Glendale Mun. Arpt.
Camelback Rd.
Grand Canyon Univ.
Chris-Town Mall
203
SQUAW PEAK FRWY
Biltmore
Echo Canyon Park
Scottsdale Fashion Sq.
Chaparral Rd.
Arizona Canal
Villa de Paz
Indian School Rd.
Mun.
60
202
Phoenix
3
Indian School Rd.
C. of C. & Vis. Cen.
School Rd.
201
2
24th St.
Thomas Rd.
99th
91st
83rd
Avondale
Desert Sky Mall
Encanto Pk.
MIL. RES.
McDowell Rd.
Cypress
87
131
134
135
136
137
138
139
140
141
144
145
1
10
133
Van Buren St.
BR 10
202
Papago Pk.
Zoo
Los Arcos Mall
Tolleson
C. of C.
St. Cap.
Conv. & Vis. Bur.
Phoenix Sky Harbor Int'l. Arpt.
Mun. Stad.
Tempe Park
HoHoKam Park
Cashion
Buckeye Rd.
Roosevelt District Canal
MARICOPA
153
143
Salt (Dry)
LOOP 101
Tempe Mesa
University Dr.
Country Club
Lower Buckeye Rd.
Santa Maria
197
196
Az. St. Univ.
Mesa S.W. Mus.
Broadway Rd.
Tempe
Mesa
The Raven G.C. at Sun Mtn.
151
Tempe Diablo Stad.
153
Lib. & Cultural Complex
Mill Av.
Fiesta Mall
Manzanita Race Track
173
174
175
176
178
179
Southern Av.
Phoenix Int'l. Raceway
154
Alvord Park
Baseline Rd.
Arizona Mills
177
Kokopelli
155
Guadalupe
Dobbins Rd.
Highline Canal
The Pointe South Mtn.
Dobson Ranch
Laveen
Estrella Mountain Park
Elliot Rd.
Thunderbird
Ahwatukee
157
PRICE FRWY.
Western Canal
Gilbert
Mystery Castle
Phoenix South Mountain Park
158
Az. St. Univ. Research Park
Warner Rd.
Estrella Dr.
Gila (Dry)
Ahwatukee Lakes
GILA RIVER INDIAN RESERVATION
MARICOPA CO.
PINAL CO.
Ray Rd.
159
Kyrene
Rural
McClintock
Ariz. R.R. Mus.
Chandler Blvd.
Chandler
C. of C.
Foothills
Club West
Pecos Rd.
160
Priest Dr.
Stellar Airpark
San Marcos
Chandler Mus.
162
Germann Rd.

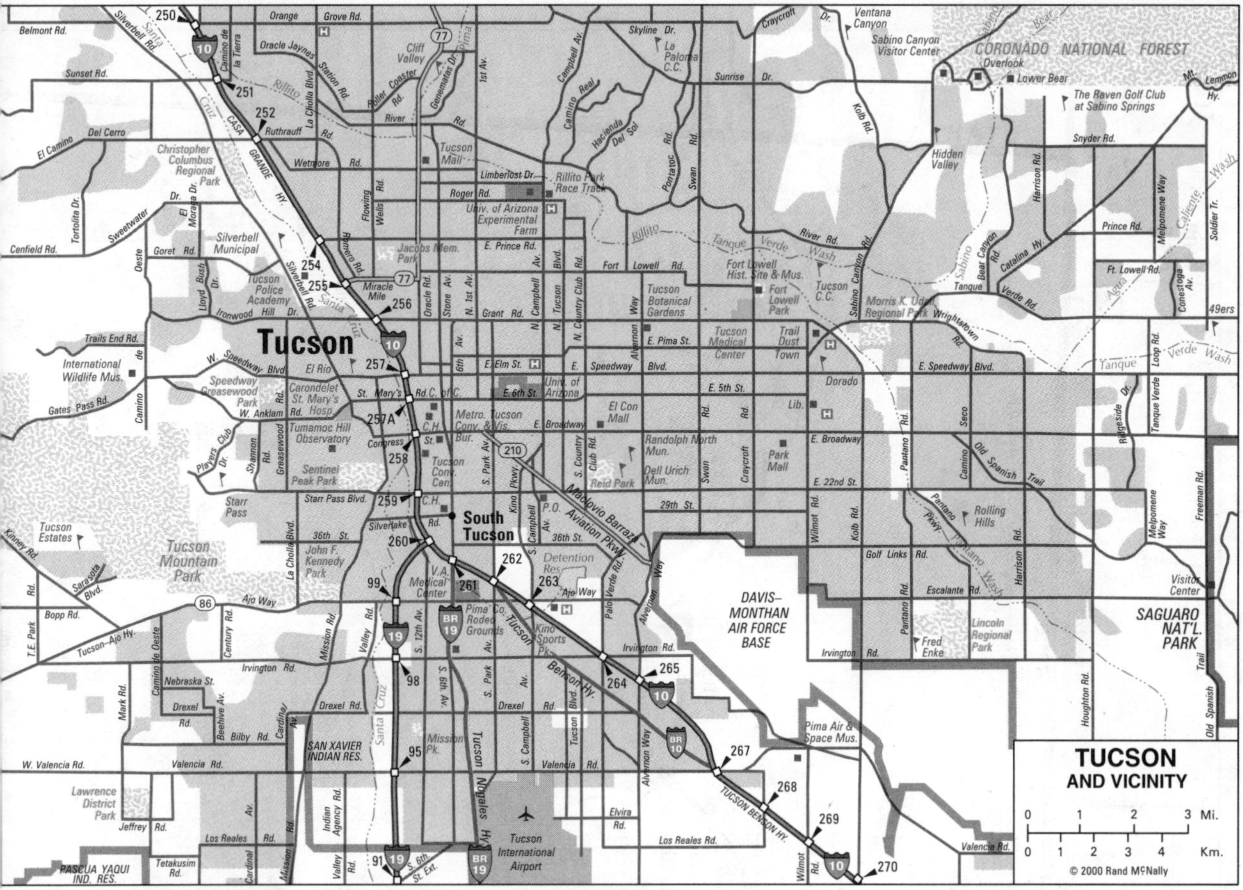
TUCSON
AND VICINITY
0 1 2 3 Mi.
0 1 2 3 4 Km.
© 2000 Rand McNally
Tucson
South Tucson
CORONADO NATIONAL FOREST
DAVIS-MONTHAN AIR FORCE BASE
SAGUARO NAT'L. PARK
Tucson Mountain Park
SAN XAVIER INDIAN RES.
PASCUA YAQUI IND. RES.
Tucson International Airport
Univ. of Arizona
TUCSON BENSON HY.

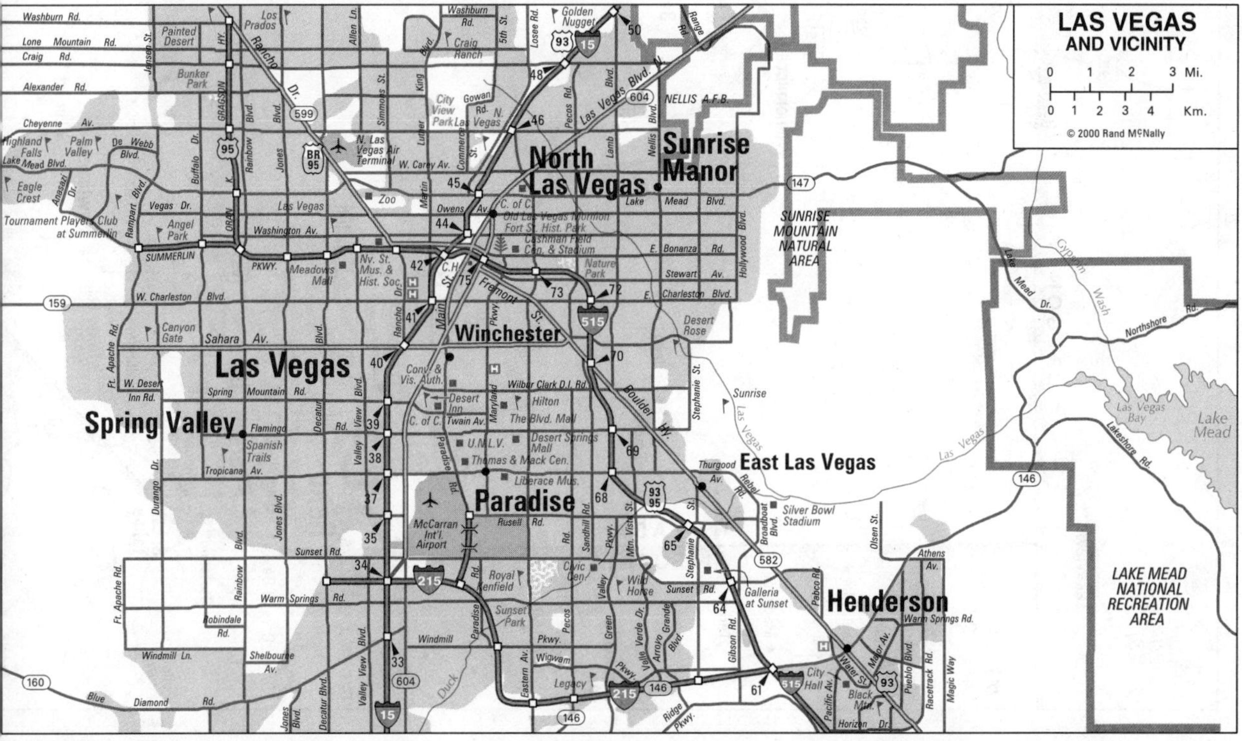
LAS VEGAS
AND VICINITY
0 1 2 3 Mi.
0 1 2 3 4 Km.
© 2000 Rand McNally
North Las Vegas
Sunrise Manor
Las Vegas
Winchester
Spring Valley
Paradise
East Las Vegas
Henderson
NELLIS A.F.B.
SUNRISE MOUNTAIN NATURAL AREA
LAKE MEAD NATIONAL RECREATION AREA
Lake Mead
Las Vegas Bay
McCarran Int'l. Airport

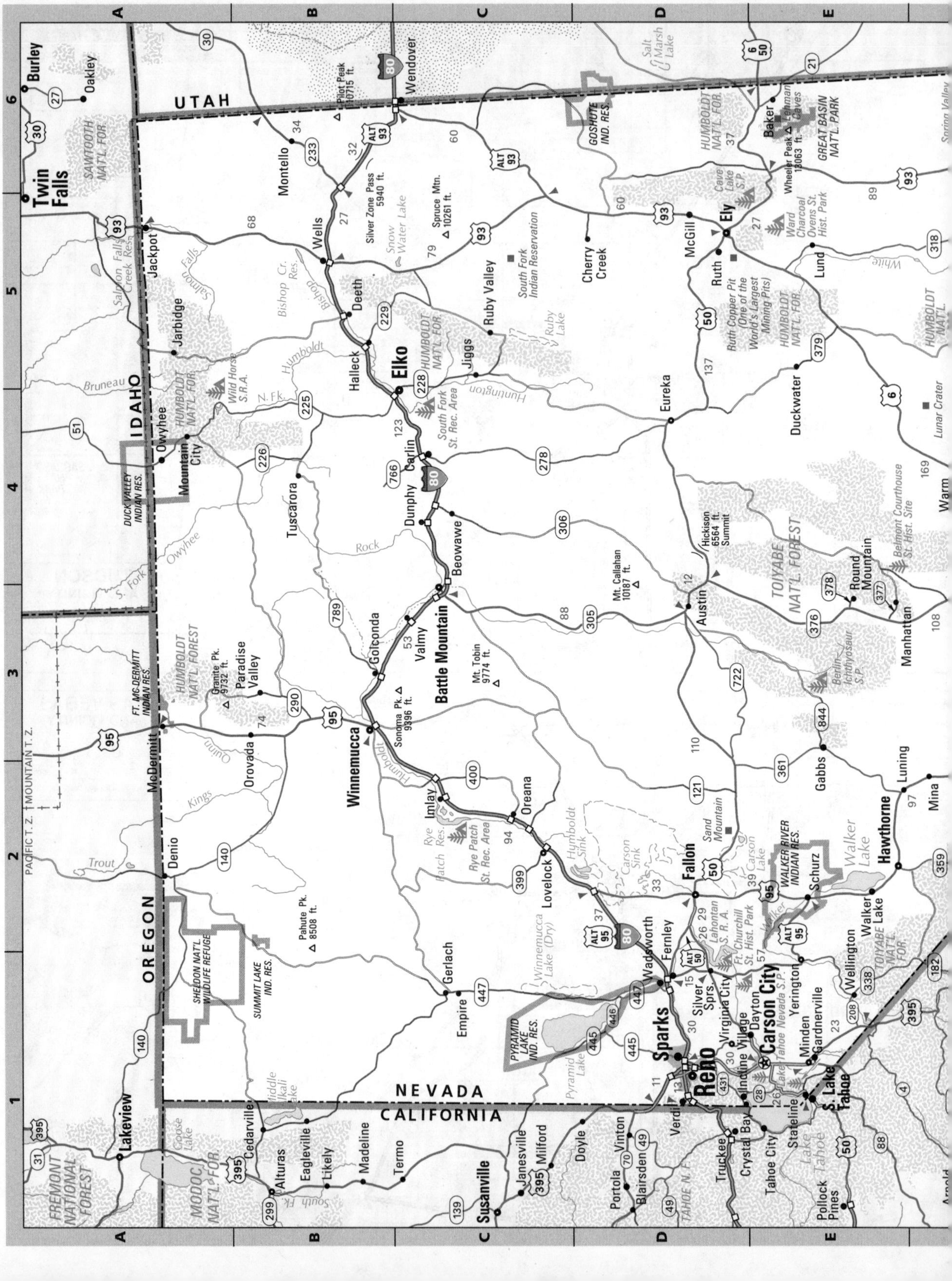

A
B
C
D
E
1
2
3
4
5
6
UTAH
IDAHO
OREGON
NEVADA
CALIFORNIA
PACIFIC T. Z.
MOUNTAIN T. Z.
Burley
Oakley
Twin Falls
SAWTOOTH NAT'L FOR.
Wendover
Pilot Peak 10715 ft.
Montello
Silver Zone Pass 5940 ft.
Spruce Mtn. 10261 ft.
Wells
Snow Water Lake
Jackpot
Salmon Falls Creek Res.
Jarbidge
Bishop Cr. Res.
Deeth
Halleck
Elko
HUMBOLDT NAT'L FOR.
Ruby Valley
Jiggs
South Fork Indian Reservation
Ruby Lake
Cherry Creek
GOSHUTE IND. RES.
Salt Marsh Lake
McGill
Ely
Ruth
Cave Lake S.P.
Baker
Lehman Caves
Wheeler Peak 13063 ft.
GREAT BASIN NAT'L PARK
Ward Charcoal Ovens St. Hist. Park
Lund
Ruth Copper Pit (One of the World's Largest Mining Pits)
Eureka
Duckwater
Lunar Crater
Owyhee
Mountain City
DUCK VALLEY INDIAN RES.
Wild Horse S.R.A.
South Fork St. Rec. Area
Carlin
Tuscarora
Dunphy
Beowawe
Hickison Summit 6564 ft.
Mt. Callahan 10187 ft.
Austin
TOIYABE NAT'L FOREST
Round Mountain
Belmont Courthouse St. Hist. Site
Manhattan
Warm
Battle Mountain
Valmy
Golconda
Mt. Tobin 9774 ft.
Berlin-Ichthyosaur S.P.
McDermitt
FT. MC DERMITT INDIAN RES.
Granite Pk. 9732 ft.
Paradise Valley
Orovada
Sonoma Pk. 9396 ft.
Winnemucca
Imlay
Oreana
Gabbs
Luning
Rye Patch Res.
Rye Patch St. Rec. Area
Humboldt Sink
Carson Sink
Sand Mountain
Hawthorne
Mina
Walker Lake
WALKER RIVER INDIAN RES.
Schurz
Denio
Lovelock
Fallon
Lahontan S. R. A.
Ft. Churchill St. Hist. Park
Pahute Pk. 8508 ft.
SHELDON NAT'L WILDLIFE REFUGE
SUMMIT LAKE IND. RES.
Gerlach
Empire
Winnemucca Lake (Dry)
Wadsworth
Fernley
Silver Sprs.
Virginia City
Dayton
Carson City
Yerington
Wellington
TOIYABE NAT'L FOR.
PYRAMID LAKE IND. RES.
Pyramid Lake
Sparks
Reno
Verdi
Incline Village
Lake Tahoe Nevada S.P.
Minden
Gardnerville
S. Lake Tahoe
Stateline
Lakeview
FREMONT NATIONAL FOREST
MODOC NAT'L FOR.
Goose Lake
Cedarville
Alturas
Eagleville
Likely
Madeline
Termo
Middle Alkali Lake
Susanville
Janesville
Milford
Doyle
Vinton
Portola
Blairsden
TAHOE N. F.
Truckee
Crystal Bay
Tahoe City
Lake Tahoe
Pollock Pines

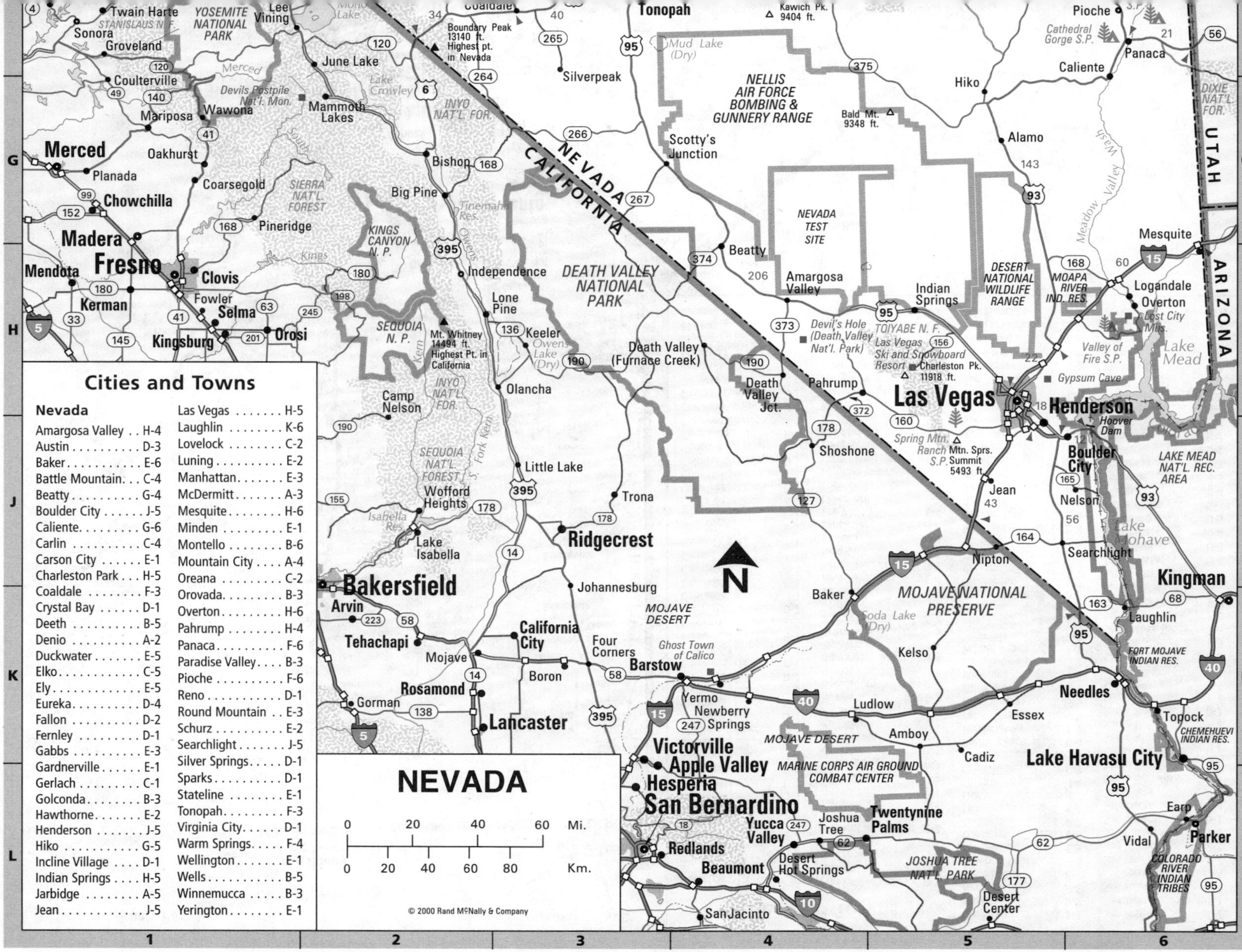

Cities and Towns

Nevada			
Amargosa Valley	H-4	Las Vegas	H-5
Austin	D-3	Laughlin	K-6
Baker	E-6	Lovelock	C-2
Battle Mountain	C-4	Luning	E-2
Beatty	G-4	Manhattan	E-3
Boulder City	J-5	McDermitt	A-3
Caliente	G-6	Mesquite	H-6
Carlin	C-4	Minden	E-1
Carson City	E-1	Montello	B-6
Charleston Park	H-5	Mountain City	A-4
Coaldale	F-3	Oreana	C-2
Crystal Bay	D-1	Orovada	B-3
Deeth	B-5	Overton	H-6
Denio	A-2	Pahrump	H-4
Duckwater	E-5	Panaca	F-6
Elko	C-5	Paradise Valley	B-3
Ely	E-5	Pioche	F-6
Eureka	D-4	Reno	D-1
Fallon	D-2	Round Mountain	E-3
Fernley	D-1	Schurz	E-2
Gabbs	E-3	Searchlight	J-5
Gardnerville	E-1	Silver Springs	D-1
Gerlach	C-1	Sparks	D-1
Golconda	B-3	Stateline	E-1
Hawthorne	E-2	Tonopah	F-3
Henderson	J-5	Virginia City	D-1
Hiko	G-5	Warm Springs	F-4
Incline Village	D-1	Wellington	E-1
Indian Springs	H-5	Wells	B-5
Jarbidge	A-5	Winnemucca	B-3
Jean	J-5	Yerington	E-1

NEVADA

0 20 40 60 Mi.
0 20 40 60 80 Km.

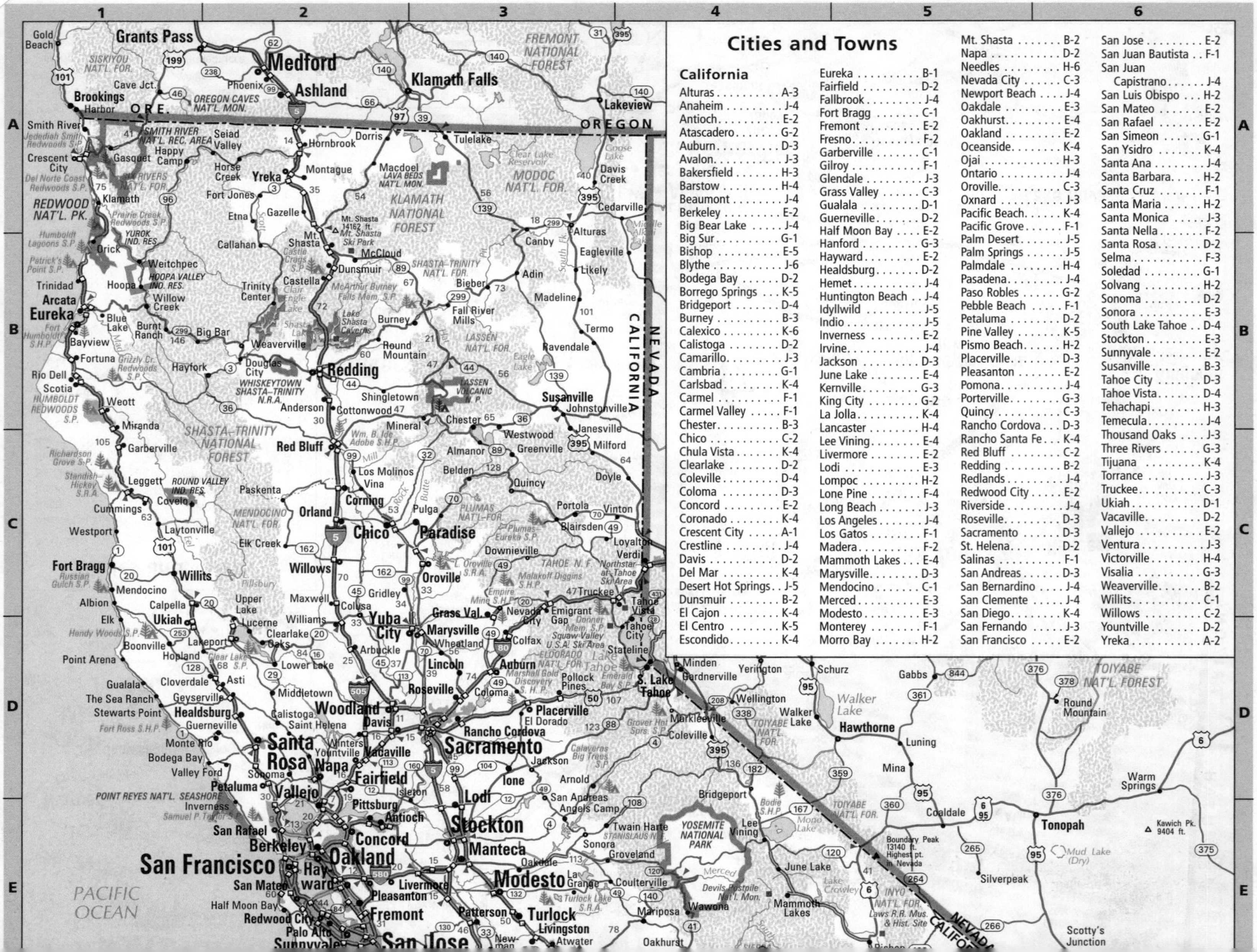

Cities and Towns

California

Alturas A-3
Anaheim J-4
Antioch E-2
Atascadero G-2
Auburn D-3
Avalon J-3
Bakersfield H-3
Barstow H-4
Beaumont J-4
Berkeley E-2
Big Bear Lake J-4
Big Sur G-1
Bishop E-5
Blythe J-6
Bodega Bay D-2
Borrego Springs K-5
Bridgeport D-4
Burney B-3
Calexico K-6
Calistoga D-2
Camarillo J-3
Cambria G-1
Carlsbad K-4
Carmel F-1
Carmel Valley F-1
Chester B-3
Chico C-2
Chula Vista K-4
Clearlake D-2
Coleville D-4
Coloma D-3
Concord E-2
Coronado K-4
Crescent City A-1
Crestline J-4
Davis D-2
Del Mar K-4
Desert Hot Springs J-5
Dunsmuir B-2
El Cajon K-4
El Centro K-5
Escondido K-4
Eureka B-1
Fairfield D-2
Fallbrook J-4
Fort Bragg C-1
Fremont E-2
Fresno F-2
Garberville C-1
Gilroy F-1
Glendale J-3
Grass Valley C-3
Gualala D-1
Guerneville D-2
Half Moon Bay E-2
Hanford G-3
Hayward E-2
Healdsburg D-2
Hemet J-4
Huntington Beach J-4
Idyllwild J-5
Indio J-5
Inverness E-2
Irvine J-4
Jackson D-3
June Lake E-4
Kernville G-3
King City G-2
La Jolla K-4
Lancaster H-4
Lee Vining E-4
Livermore E-2
Lodi E-3
Lompoc H-2
Lone Pine F-4
Long Beach J-3
Los Angeles J-4
Los Gatos F-1
Madera F-2
Mammoth Lakes E-4
Marysville D-3
Mendocino C-1
Merced E-3
Modesto E-3
Monterey F-1
Morro Bay H-2
Mt. Shasta B-2
Napa D-2
Needles H-6
Nevada City C-3
Newport Beach J-4
Oakdale E-3
Oakhurst E-4
Oakland E-2
Oceanside K-4
Ojai H-3
Ontario J-4
Oroville C-3
Oxnard J-3
Pacific Beach K-4
Pacific Grove F-1
Palm Desert J-5
Palm Springs J-5
Palmdale H-4
Pasadena J-4
Paso Robles G-2
Pebble Beach F-1
Petaluma D-2
Pine Valley K-5
Pismo Beach H-2
Placerville D-3
Pleasanton E-2
Pomona J-4
Porterville G-3
Quincy C-3
Rancho Cordova D-3
Rancho Santa Fe K-4
Red Bluff C-2
Redding B-2
Redlands J-4
Redwood City E-2
Riverside J-4
Roseville D-3
Sacramento D-3
St. Helena D-2
Salinas F-1
San Andreas D-3
San Bernardino J-4
San Clemente J-4
San Diego K-4
San Fernando J-3
San Francisco E-2
San Jose E-2
San Juan Bautista F-1
San Juan Capistrano J-4
San Luis Obispo H-2
San Mateo E-2
San Rafael E-2
San Simeon G-1
San Ysidro K-4
Santa Ana J-4
Santa Barbara H-2
Santa Cruz F-1
Santa Maria H-2
Santa Monica J-3
Santa Nella F-2
Santa Rosa D-2
Selma F-3
Soledad G-1
Solvang H-2
Sonoma D-2
Sonora E-3
South Lake Tahoe D-4
Stockton E-3
Sunnyvale E-2
Susanville B-3
Tahoe City D-3
Tahoe Vista D-4
Tehachapi H-3
Temecula J-4
Thousand Oaks J-3
Three Rivers G-3
Tijuana K-4
Torrance J-3
Truckee C-3
Ukiah D-1
Vacaville D-2
Vallejo E-2
Ventura J-3
Victorville H-4
Visalia G-3
Weaverville B-2
Willits C-1
Willows C-2
Yountville D-2
Yreka A-2

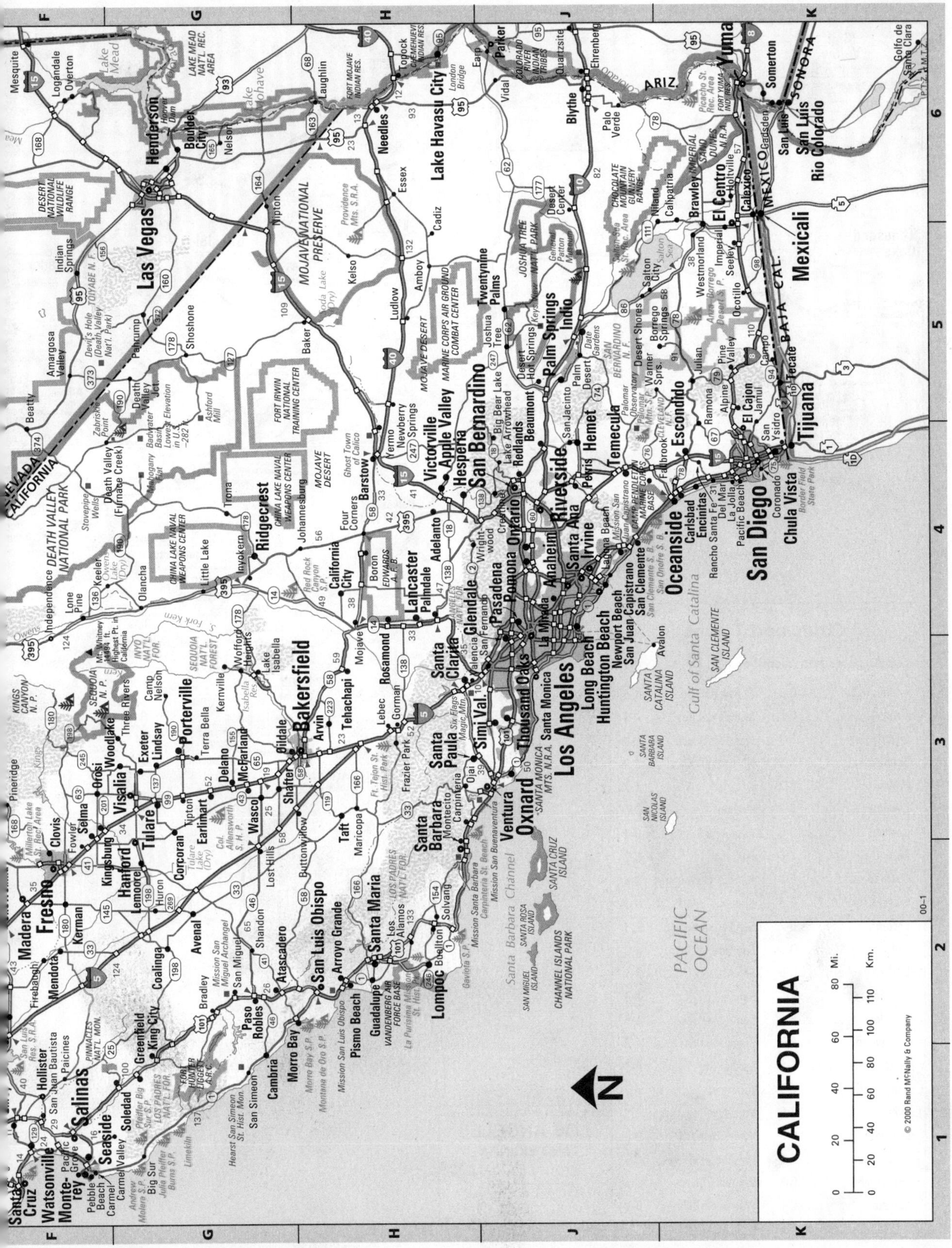
CALIFORNIA
PACIFIC OCEAN
NEVADA
CALIFORNIA
ARIZ.
MEXICO
BAJA CAL.
SONORA
Gulf of Santa Catalina
Santa Barbara Channel
CHANNEL ISLANDS NATIONAL PARK
SANTA CRUZ ISLAND
SANTA ROSA ISLAND
SAN MIGUEL ISLAND
SANTA CATALINA ISLAND
SAN CLEMENTE ISLAND
SAN NICOLAS ISLAND
SANTA BARBARA ISLAND
DEATH VALLEY NATIONAL PARK
MOJAVE NATIONAL PRESERVE
JOSHUA TREE NAT'L PARK
LAKE MEAD NAT'L REC. AREA
DESERT NATIONAL WILDLIFE RANGE
FORT IRWIN NATIONAL TRAINING CENTER
CHINA LAKE NAVAL WEAPONS CENTER
MARINE CORPS AIR GROUND COMBAT CENTER
MOJAVE DESERT
CHOCOLATE MOUNTAIN GUNNERY RANGE
EDWARDS A.F.B.
VANDENBERG AIR FORCE BASE
CAMP PENDLETON MARINE CORPS BASE
SANTA MONICA MTS. N.R.A.
LOS PADRES NAT'L FOR.
SEQUOIA NAT'L FOREST
SEQUOIA N.P.
KINGS CANYON N.P.
INYO NAT'L FOR.
ANGELES NAT'L FOR.
SAN BERNARDINO N.F.
CLEVELAND N.F.
Salton Sea
Lake Mead
Lake Mohave
Los Angeles
San Diego
Las Vegas
Henderson
Bakersfield
Fresno
Salinas
San Bernardino
Riverside
Anaheim
Santa Ana
Long Beach
Huntington Beach
Oxnard
Ventura
Santa Barbara
Santa Maria
San Luis Obispo
Lancaster
Palmdale
Victorville
Barstow
Ridgecrest
Palm Springs
Indio
Oceanside
Escondido
Chula Vista
Tijuana
Mexicali
Yuma
El Centro
Calexico
Blythe
Needles
Lake Havasu City
Visalia
Tulare
Porterville
Hanford
Madera
Monterey
Watsonville
Santa Cruz
Seaside
Pasadena
Glendale
Pomona
Ontario
Irvine
Thousand Oaks
Simi Val.
Santa Clarita
Temecula
Hemet
© 2000 Rand McNally & Company
0 20 40 60 80 Mi.
0 20 40 60 80 100 110 Km.

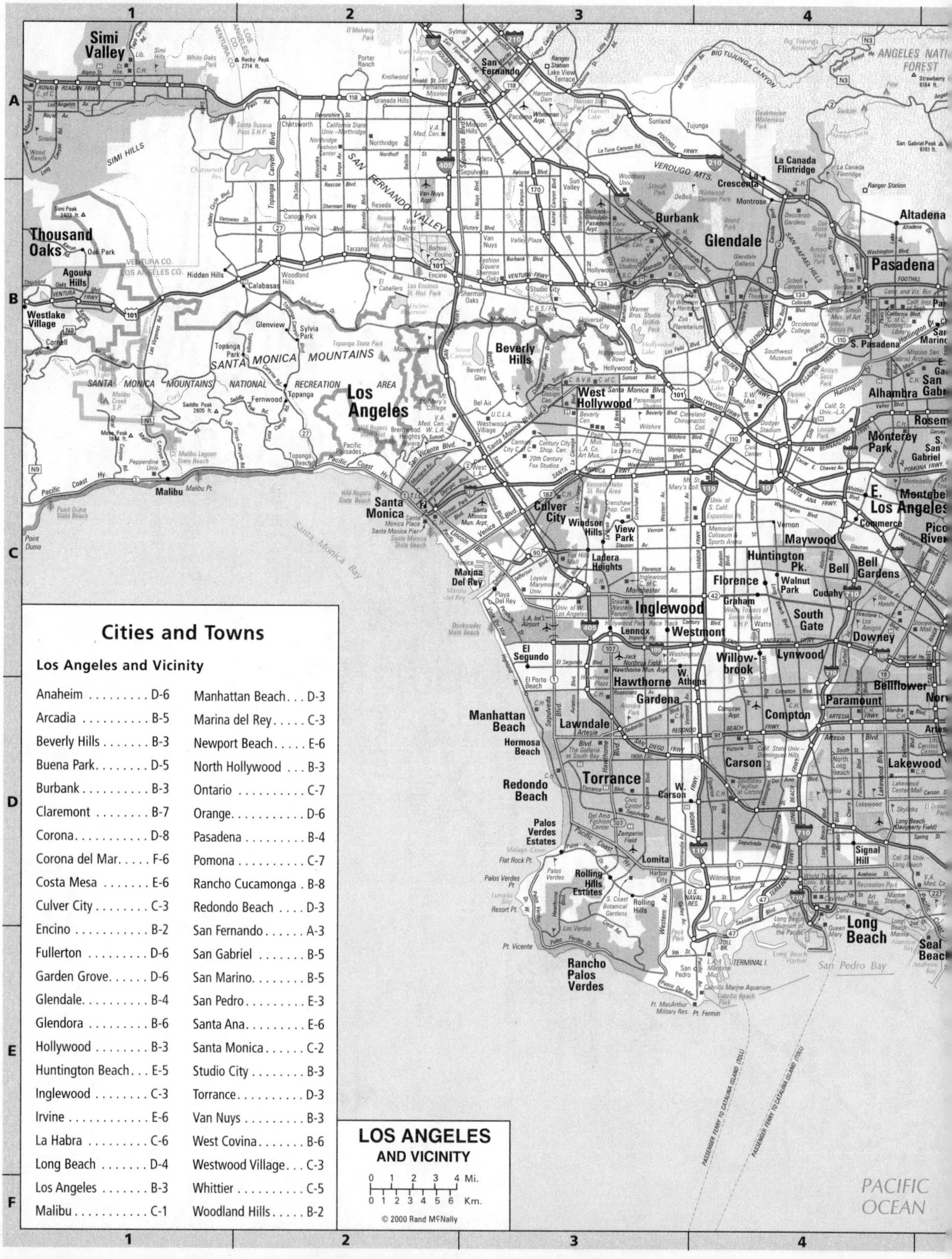

Cities and Towns

Los Angeles and Vicinity

Anaheim D-6	Manhattan Beach . . . D-3
Arcadia B-5	Marina del Rey C-3
Beverly Hills B-3	Newport Beach E-6
Buena Park D-5	North Hollywood . . . B-3
Burbank B-3	Ontario C-7
Claremont B-7	Orange D-6
Corona D-8	Pasadena B-4
Corona del Mar F-6	Pomona C-7
Costa Mesa E-6	Rancho Cucamonga . B-8
Culver City C-3	Redondo Beach D-3
Encino B-2	San Fernando A-3
Fullerton D-6	San Gabriel B-5
Garden Grove D-6	San Marino B-5
Glendale B-4	San Pedro E-3
Glendora B-6	Santa Ana E-6
Hollywood B-3	Santa Monica C-2
Huntington Beach . . . E-5	Studio City B-3
Inglewood C-3	Torrance D-3
Irvine E-6	Van Nuys B-3
La Habra C-6	West Covina B-6
Long Beach D-4	Westwood Village . . . C-3
Los Angeles B-3	Whittier C-5
Malibu C-1	Woodland Hills B-2

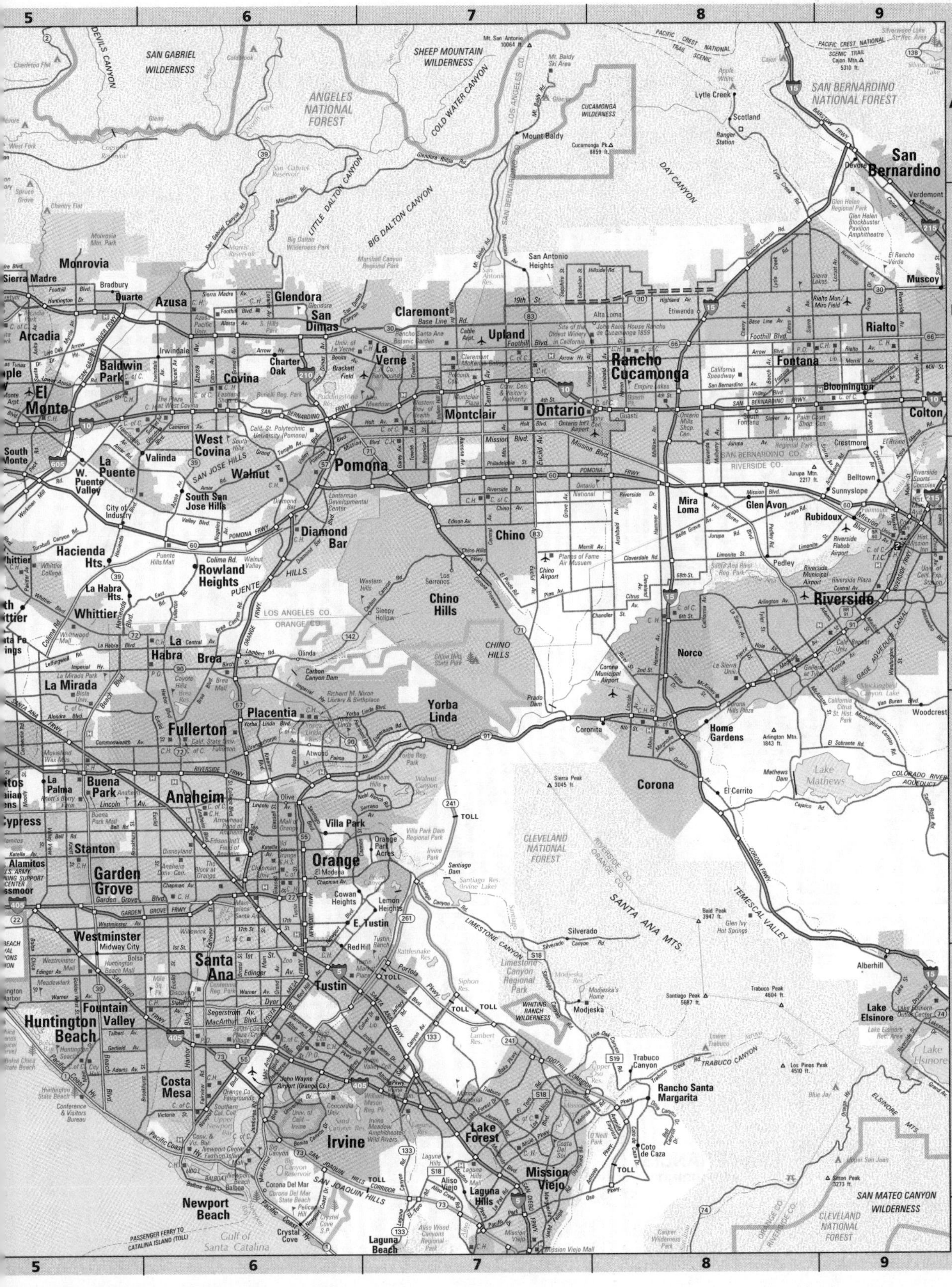
5
6
7
8
9
A
B
C
D
E
F
SAN GABRIEL WILDERNESS
SHEEP MOUNTAIN WILDERNESS
ANGELES NATIONAL FOREST
CUCAMONGA WILDERNESS
SAN BERNARDINO NATIONAL FOREST
PACIFIC CREST NATIONAL SCENIC TRAIL
Mt. San Antonio 10064 ft.
Mount Baldy
Lytle Creek
Scotland
San Bernardino
Verdemont
Muscoy
Rialto
Fontana
Bloomington
Colton
Monrovia
Sierra Madre
Arcadia
Duarte
Bradbury
Azusa
Glendora
San Dimas
Claremont
La Verne
Upland
Rancho Cucamonga
Alta Loma
Etiwanda
Ontario
Montclair
Pomona
Irwindale
Covina
Charter Oak
Baldwin Park
El Monte
West Covina
Walnut
La Puente
Valinda
South El Monte
W. Puente Valley
South San Jose Hills
City of Industry
Diamond Bar
Chino
Chino Hills
Mira Loma
Glen Avon
Rubidoux
Riverside
Hacienda Hts.
Rowland Heights
Whittier
La Habra Hts.
La Habra
Brea
Fullerton
Placentia
Yorba Linda
La Mirada
Buena Park
La Palma
Anaheim
Cypress
Stanton
Garden Grove
Orange
Villa Park
Westminster
Santa Ana
Tustin
Fountain Valley
Huntington Beach
Costa Mesa
Newport Beach
Irvine
Lake Forest
Mission Viejo
Laguna Hills
Laguna Beach
Norco
Corona
Home Gardens
El Cerrito
Lake Mathews
CLEVELAND NATIONAL FOREST
SANTA ANA MTS.
Silverado
Modjeska
Trabuco Canyon
Rancho Santa Margarita
Coto de Caza
Alberhill
Lake Elsinore
SAN MATEO CANYON WILDERNESS
Gulf of Santa Catalina
PASSENGER FERRY TO CATALINA ISLAND (TOLL)

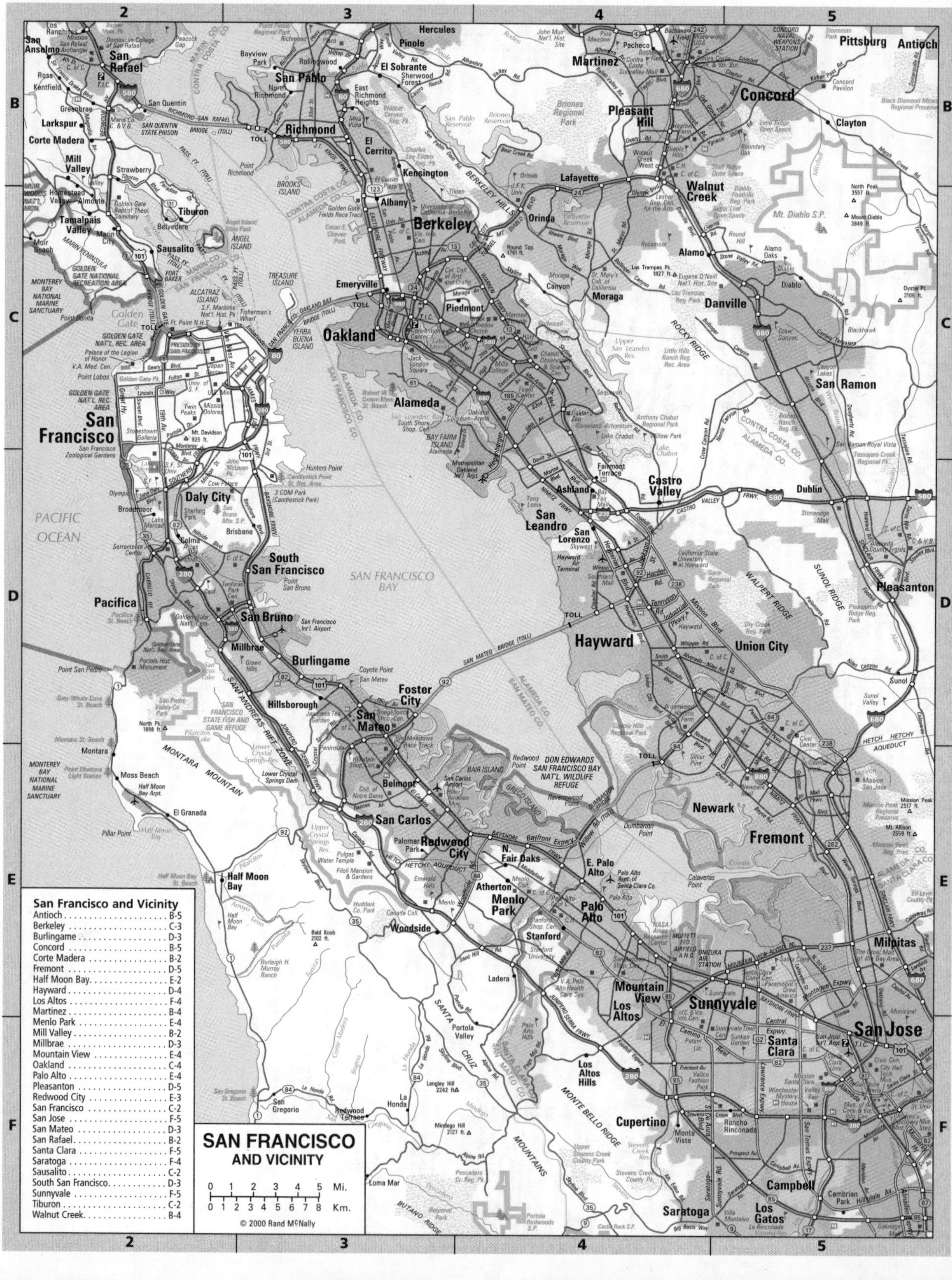
SAN FRANCISCO
AND VICINITY
0 1 2 3 4 5 Mi.
0 1 2 3 4 5 6 7 8 Km.
© 2000 Rand McNally
San Francisco and Vicinity
Antioch B-5
Berkeley C-3
Burlingame D-3
Concord B-5
Corte Madera B-2
Fremont D-5
Half Moon Bay. E-2
Hayward D-4
Los Altos F-4
Martinez B-4
Menlo Park E-4
Mill Valley B-2
Millbrae D-3
Mountain View E-4
Oakland C-4
Palo Alto E-4
Pleasanton D-5
Redwood City E-3
San Francisco C-2
San Jose F-5
San Mateo D-3
San Rafael B-2
Santa Clara F-5
Saratoga F-4
Sausalito C-2
South San Francisco D-3
Sunnyvale F-5
Tiburon C-2
Walnut Creek B-4
PACIFIC OCEAN
SAN FRANCISCO BAY
San Francisco
Oakland
Berkeley
San Jose
Hayward
Fremont
Concord

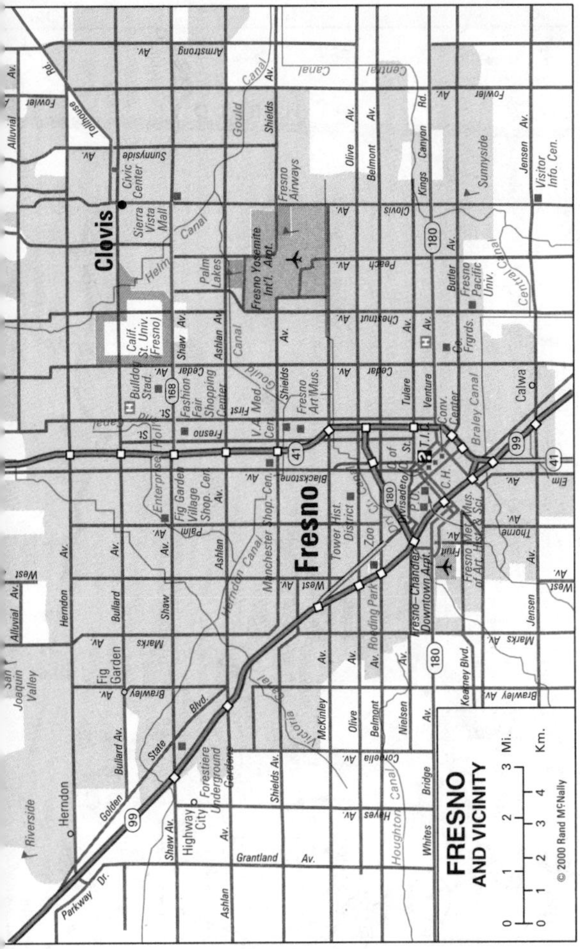
FRESNO
AND VICINITY
0 1 2 3 Mi.
0 1 2 3 4 Km.
© 2000 Rand McNally
Fresno
Clovis

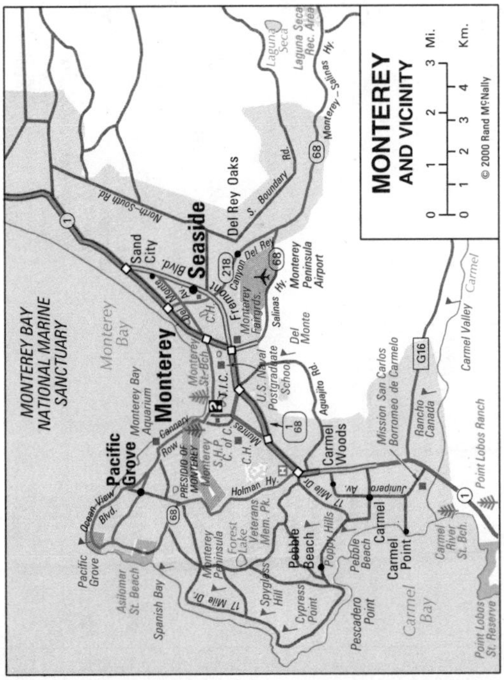
MONTEREY
AND VICINITY
0 1 2 3 Mi.
0 1 2 3 4 Km.
© 2000 Rand McNally
MONTEREY BAY
NATIONAL MARINE
SANCTUARY
Monterey
Seaside
Pacific Grove
Carmel

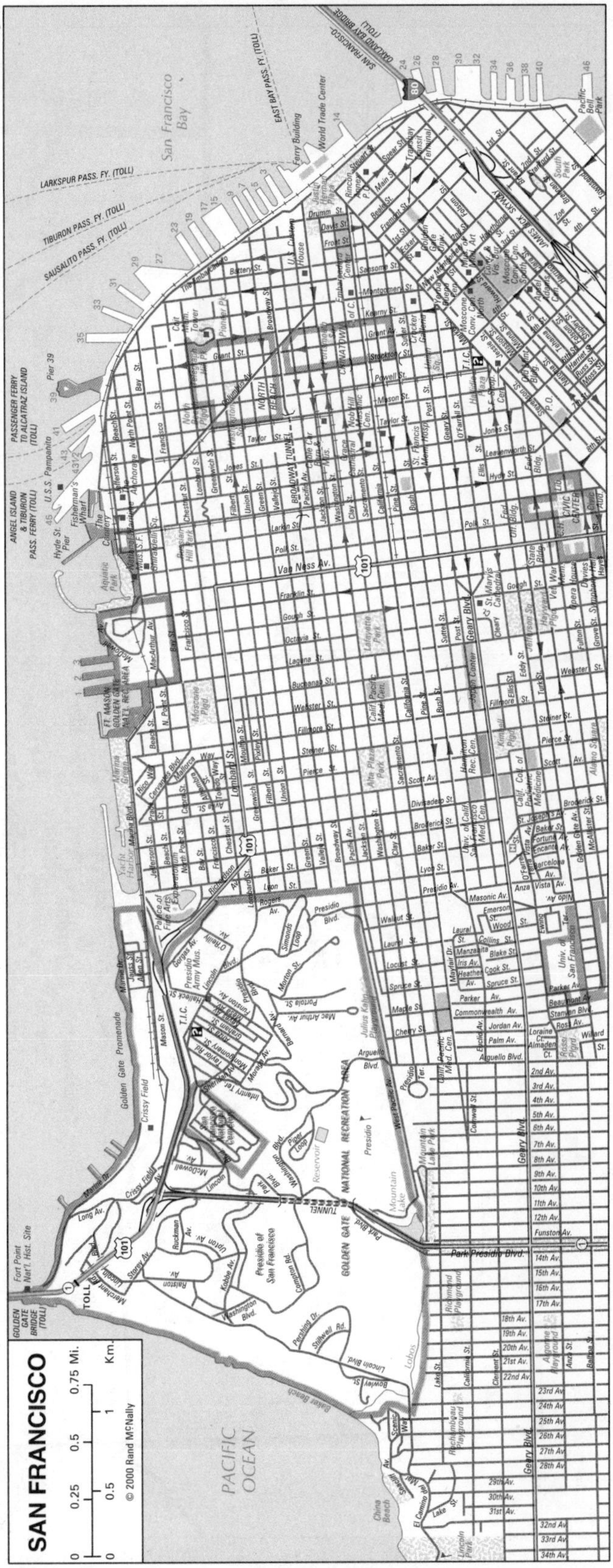
SAN FRANCISCO
0 0.25 0.5 0.75 Mi.
0 0.5 1 Km.
© 2000 Rand McNally
PACIFIC
OCEAN
San Francisco
Bay

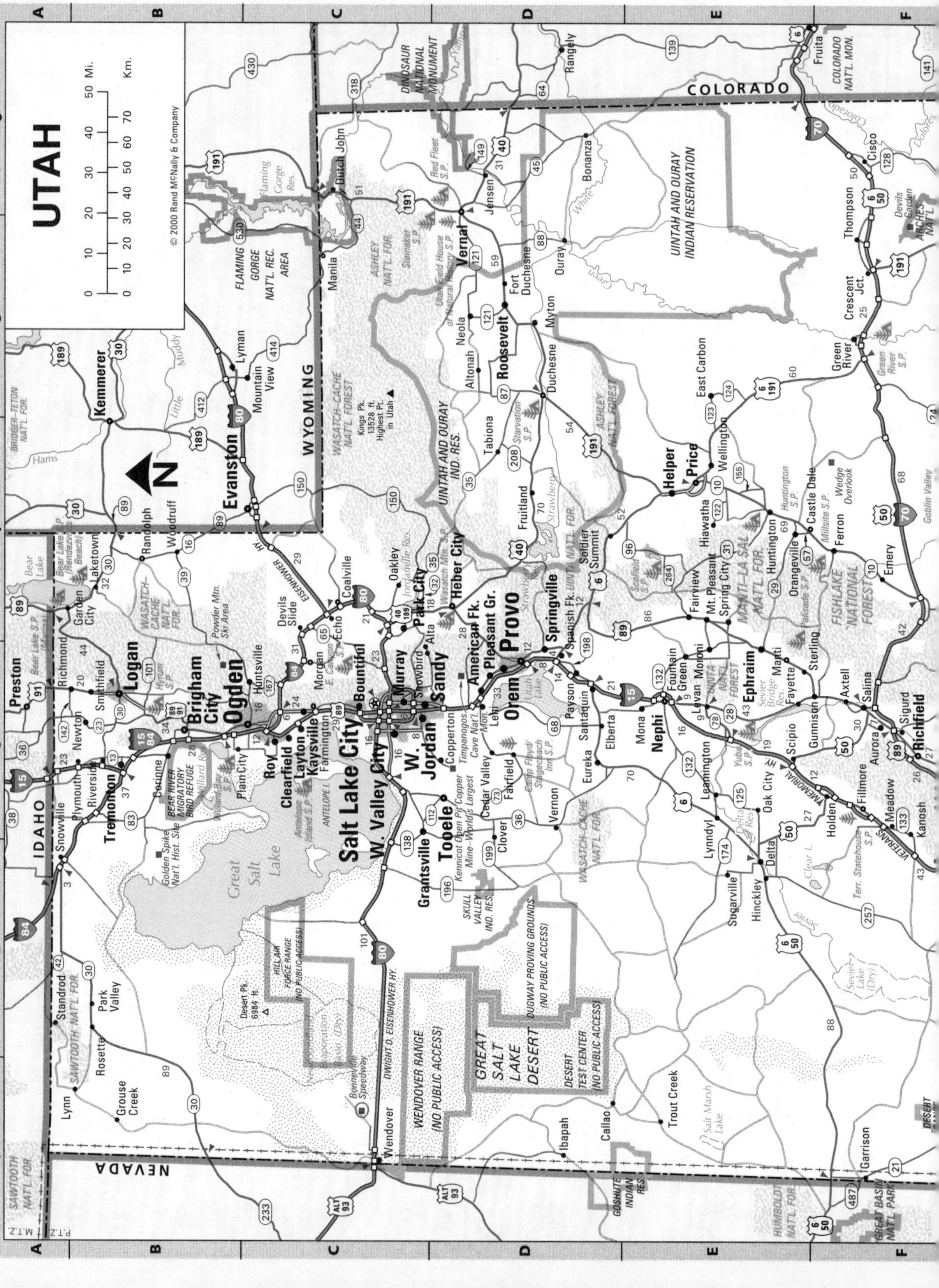
UTAH
© 2000 Rand McNally & Company
0 10 20 30 40 50 Mi.
0 10 20 30 40 50 60 70 Km.
N
IDAHO
NEVADA
WYOMING
COLORADO
Salt Lake City
W. Valley City
W. Jordan
Sandy
Murray
Bountiful
Ogden
Brigham City
Logan
Provo
Orem
Springville
American Fk.
Pleasant Gr.
Tooele
Grantsville
Layton
Clearfield
Roy
Kaysville
Farmington
Tremonton
Park City
Heber City
Evanston
Kemmerer
Vernal
Roosevelt
Price
Helper
Nephi
Ephraim
Richfield
Delta
Wendover
Great Salt Lake
Utah Lake
Flaming Gorge Res.
FLAMING GORGE NAT'L. REC. AREA
DINOSAUR NATIONAL MONUMENT
ASHLEY NAT'L. FOR.
WASATCH-CACHE NAT'L. FOREST
UINTAH AND OURAY IND. RES.
UINTAH AND OURAY INDIAN RESERVATION
MANTI-LA SAL NAT'L. FOR.
FISHLAKE NATIONAL FOREST
GREAT SALT LAKE DESERT
WENDOVER RANGE (NO PUBLIC ACCESS)
DUGWAY PROVING GROUNDS (NO PUBLIC ACCESS)
DESERT TEST CENTER (NO PUBLIC ACCESS)
HILL AIR FORCE RANGE (NO PUBLIC ACCESS)
BEAR RIVER MIGRATORY BIRD REFUGE
SKULL VALLEY IND. RES.
GOSHUTE INDIAN RES.
SAWTOOTH NAT'L. FOR.
Kings Pk. 13528 ft. Highest Pt. in Utah
Desert Pk. 6984 ft.
Bonneville Speedway
DWIGHT D. EISENHOWER HY.
Kennicott Open Pit Copper Mine–World's Largest
COLORADO NAT'L. MON.
ARCHES N.P.
Green River
Moab
Fruita
Cisco
Thompson
Crescent Jct.
Duchesne
Manila
Dutch John
Jensen
Bonanza
Rangely
Nephi
Fillmore
Salina
Gunnison
Castle Dale
Huntington
Ferron
Emery
Kanosh
Hinckley
Lynndyl
Eureka
Santaquin
Payson
Spanish Fk.
Lehi
Coalville
Morgan
Randolph
Woodruff
Garden City
Preston
Snowville
Grouse Creek
Park Valley
Ibapah
Callao
Trout Creek
Garrison
HUMBOLDT NAT'L. FOR.
GREAT BASIN NAT'L. PARK
P.T.Z. M.T.Z.

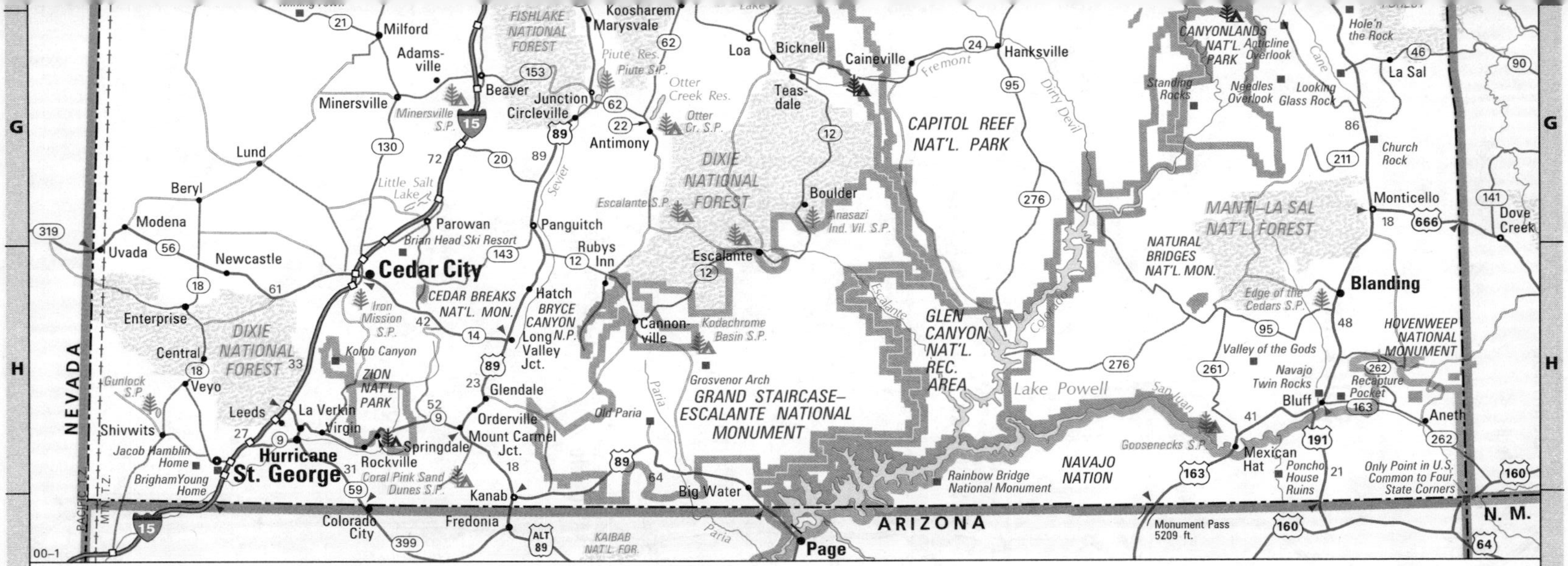

Cities and Towns

Utah

Alta C-3
American Fork D-3
Antimony G-3
Aurora F-3
Beaver G-2
Bicknell G-4
Big Water H-3
Blanding H-6
Bluff H-6
Bountiful C-3
Brigham City B-3
Castle Dale E-4
Cedar City H-2
Cisco F-6
Clearfield C-3
Copperton D-3
Crescent Junction F-5
Delta E-2
Duchesne D-5
Elsinore F-3
Emery F-4
Enterprise H-1
Ephraim E-3
Escalante H-3
Eureka D-3
Fairview E-4
Farmington C-3
Ferron F-4
Fillmore F-3
Fountain Green E-3
Fruitland D-4
Garden City A-4
Garrison F-1
Grantsville C-3
Green River F-5
Gunnison F-3
Hanksville G-4
Hatch H-3
Heber City D-4
Helper E-4
Holden F-3
Huntington E-4
Hurricane H-2
Junction G-3
Kanab J-2
Kaysville C-3
Laketown B-4
Layton C-3
Lehi D-3
Levan E-3
Loa G-3
Logan B-3
Lund G-2
Lynn B-1
Lynndyl E-3
Manila C-5
Manti E-3
Marysvale G-3
Mexican Hat H-5
Milford G-2
Minersville G-2
Moab F-6
Monticello G-6
Moroni E-3
Mount Carmel Junction H-2
Mount Pleasant E-4
Murray C-3
Nephi E-3
Oak City E-3
Ogden C-3
Orem D-3
Panguitch G-3
Park City C-4
Parowan G-2
Payson D-3
Pleasant Grove D-3
Price E-4
Provo D-3
Randolph B-4
Richfield F-3
Richmond B-3
Roosevelt D-5
Roy C-3
St. George H-1
Salina F-3
Salt Lake City C-3
Sandy C-3
Smithfield B-3
Snowbird C-3
Snowville A-2
Spanish Fork D-3
Springdale H-2
Springville D-3
Tabiona D-4
Tooele D-3
Tremonton B-3
Vernal D-6
Vernon D-3
Veyo H-1
Wellingrton E-4
Wendover C-1
West Jordan C-3
West Valley City C-3

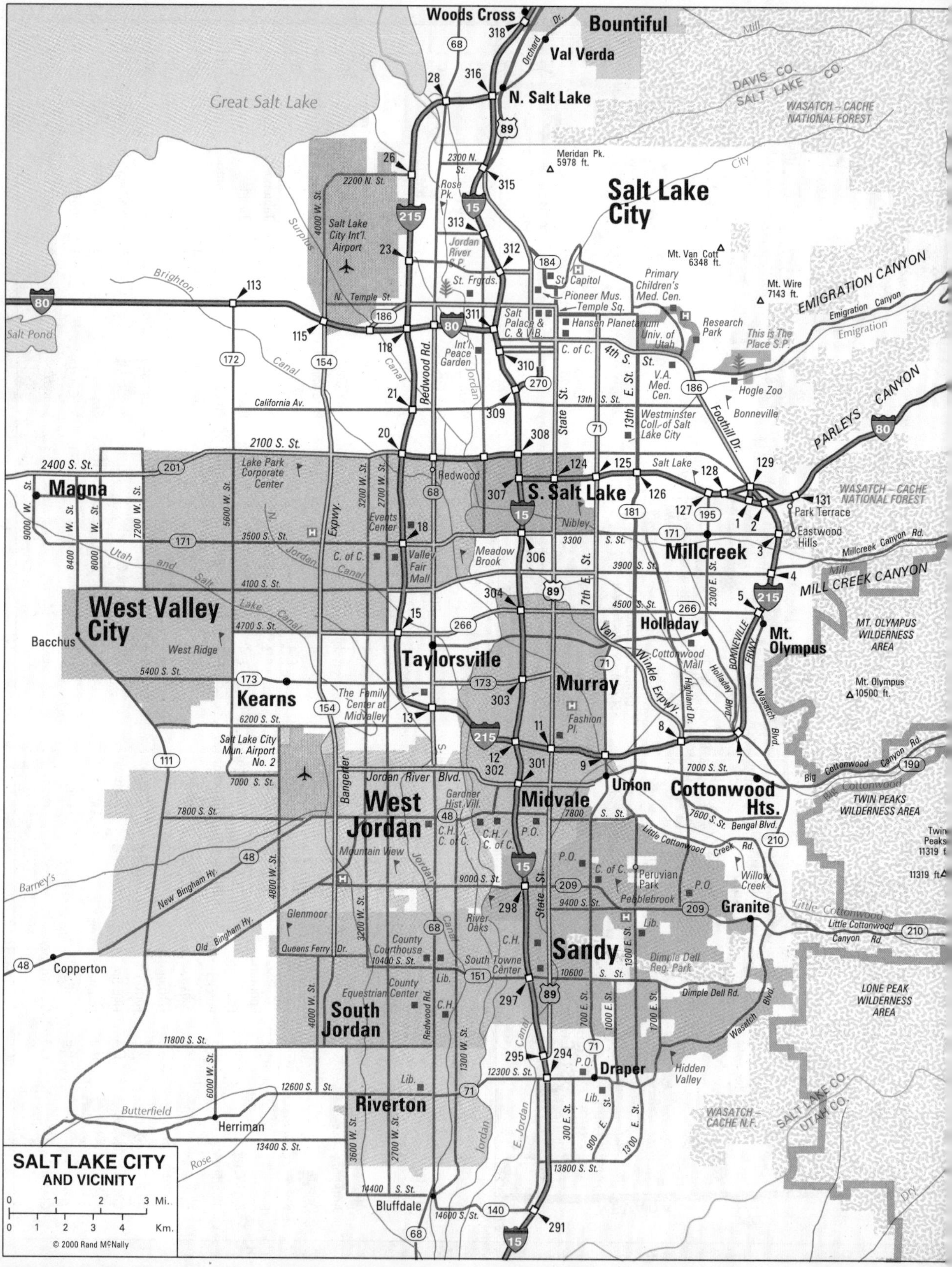
SALT LAKE CITY
AND VICINITY
0 1 2 3 Mi.
0 1 2 3 4 Km.
© 2000 Rand McNally
Woods Cross
Bountiful
Val Verda
N. Salt Lake
Great Salt Lake
DAVIS CO.
SALT LAKE CO.
WASATCH - CACHE NATIONAL FOREST
Meridan Pk. 5978 ft.
Salt Lake City
Mt. Van Cott 6348 ft.
Mt. Wire 7143 ft.
EMIGRATION CANYON
Emigration Canyon
Primary Children's Med. Cen.
Research Park
This is The Place S.P.
Hogle Zoo
Bonneville
PARLEYS CANYON
Salt Lake City Int'l. Airport
2200 N. St.
4000 W. St.
2300 N. St.
Rose Pk.
Jordan River S.P.
St. Frgrds.
St. Capitol
Pioneer Mus.
Temple Sq.
Hansen Planetarium
Univ. of Utah
Salt Palace & C. & V.B.
Int'l. Peace Garden
C. of C.
4th S. St.
13th E. St.
V.A. Med. Cen.
Westminster Coll. of Salt Lake City
Foothill Dr.
N. Temple St.
Brighton
Surplus
Canal
Salt Pond
California Av.
Redwood Rd.
13th S. St.
State St.
2100 S. St.
2400 S. St.
Magna
Lake Park Corporate Center
Redwood
S. Salt Lake
Salt Lake
Park Terrace
Eastwood Hills
WASATCH - CACHE NATIONAL FOREST
Millcreek Canyon Rd.
MILL CREEK CANYON
Millcreek
Nibley
Meadow Brook
Events Center
Valley Fair Mall
C. of C.
3500 S. St.
3300 S. St.
3900 S. St.
4100 S. St.
4500 S. St.
4700 S. St.
5400 S. St.
6200 S. St.
7000 S. St.
7800 S. St.
9000 W. St.
8400 W. St.
8000 W. St.
7200 W. St.
5600 W. St.
3200 W. St.
2700 W. St.
Expwy.
Utah and Salt Lake Canal
West Valley City
West Ridge
Bacchus
Kearns
Taylorsville
The Family Center at Midvalley
Murray
Fashion Pl.
Holladay
Cottonwood Mall
Holladay Blvd.
Highland Dr.
Van Winkle Expwy.
BONNEVILLE FRWY
Wasatch Blvd.
Mt. Olympus
MT. OLYMPUS WILDERNESS AREA
Mt. Olympus 10500 ft.
7th E. St.
2300 E. St.
Salt Lake City Mun. Airport No. 2
Bangerter
Jordan River Blvd.
West Jordan
Gardner Hist. Vill.
Midvale
Union
Cottonwood Hts.
Big Cottonwood Canyon Rd.
TWIN PEAKS WILDERNESS AREA
Twin Peaks 11319 ft.
7600 S. St.
Bengal Blvd.
Little Cottonwood Creek Rd.
Willow Creek
Mountain View
Jordan
C.H. / C. of C.
P.O.
Peruvian Park
Pebblebrook
Granite
Little Cottonwood Canyon Rd.
9000 S. St.
9400 S. St.
Barney's
New Bingham Hy.
Old Bingham Hy.
4800 W. St.
Glenmoor
Queens Ferry Dr.
River Oaks
County Courthouse
10400 S. St.
South Towne Center
10600 S. St.
Sandy
Dimple Dell Reg. Park
Dimple Dell Rd.
LONE PEAK WILDERNESS AREA
Copperton
Equestrian Center
County Center
Lib.
C.H.
South Jordan
11800 S. St.
700 E. St.
1000 E. St.
1700 E. St.
1300 E. St.
Draper
Hidden Valley
12300 S. St.
12600 S. St.
6000 W. St.
1300 W. St.
Riverton
Butterfield
Herriman
13400 S. St.
3600 W. St.
2700 W. St.
E. Jordan
300 E. St.
900 E. St.
WASATCH - CACHE N.F.
SALT LAKE CO.
UTAH CO.
Rose
13800 S. St.
14400 S. St.
Bluffdale
14600 S. St.
Dry

Would you like to spend less time buying gas?

With *Speedpass,* getting gas just got a little more exciting. All you have to do is wave it at the pump, gas up and go. Fast and easy. You can link it to a major credit card or check card that you *already* have. So call toll-free **1-877-MY MOBIL** or visit mobil.com/speedpass to enroll. Join the over 3 million people who already use *Speedpass.* It's safe, secure and best of all... it's free.

Mobil
Speedpass
The fastest way to get gas.

They all have 1 thing in common.

A Word to Our Readers

Some 50 years after the establishment of the U.S. interstate highway system, Americans continue to take to the roads in enormous numbers—for day trips, for extended family vacations, and for business. Airline travel, too, is ever-increasing. You, the traveler, deserve the best food and accommodations available in every city or town you visit. You could query local residents about quality places to stay and eat, but that time-consuming option is neither practical nor any guarantee of good advice.

Leave it to the *Mobil Travel Guide,* then, to direct you to satisfying places to eat and stay, as well as to events and attractions, in thousands of locations across America. Mobil Corporation has sponsored the *Mobil Travel Guide* since 1958. Now, in partnership with Consumer Guide, Mobil presents the latest edition of the annual Travel Guide series.

The information database that is the foundation of every title in the *Mobil Travel Guide* series is an astonishing resource: enormous, detailed, and continually updated to be as accurate and useful as it can be. Exhaustive, computerized inspection reports from highly trained field representatives spread out across the country are evaluated by senior staff, who also utilize the comments of *more than 100,000 readers* to arrive at fair, accurate, and useful assessments of hotels, motels, and restaurants. Valuable capsule descriptions of each site are highlighted by Mobil's respected and world-famous one- to five-star ratings system. All this, plus detailed information about thousands of attractions and things to do!

Space limitations make it impossible for us to include *every* hotel, motel, and restaurant in America. Instead, our database is comprised of a generous, representative sampling with information about places that are above-average of their type. In essence, you can patronize with confidence any of the restaurants, places of lodging, and attractions listed in the *Mobil Travel Guide* series.

You'll find that the *Mobil Travel Guide* books include information about a great variety of establishments. Perhaps you favor rustic lodgings and restaurants, or perhaps you're most comfortable with elegance and high style. Money may be no object or, like most of us, you may be on a budget. It's possible that you place a high premium on 24-hour room service or vegetarian menu items. Whatever your needs and desires, they will be reflected in the *Mobil Travel Guide* series.

Allow us to emphasize that no establishment is charged for inclusion in our guides. We have no relationship with any of the businesses and attractions we list, and act only as a consumer advocate. In essence, we do the investigative legwork so you won't have to.

When you look over the "How to Use This Book" section that follows, you'll discover just how simple it is to quickly obtain all the information you need. And for terrific tips on saving money, travel safety, and other ways to enjoy your traveling to the utmost, be sure to read our special section, "Making the Most of Your Trip."

Keep in mind that the "hospitality" business is ever-changing. Restaurants and places of lodging—particularly small chains or stand-alone establishments—can change management or even go out of business with surprising quickness. Although every effort has been made to double-check information during our annual updates, we nevertheless recommend that you call ahead to be sure a place you have selected is open and still offers all the features you want.

We hope that all your travel experiences are easy, fun, and relaxing. If any aspects of your accommodations or dining move you to comment, please drop us a line. We depend a great deal on our readers' remarks, so you can be assured that your comments will be read and assimilated into our research. General comments about our books are also welcome. You can write us at *Mobil Travel Guide,* 7373 North Cicero Ave., Lincolnwood, IL 60712, or send e-mail to travel@pubint.com.

Take your *Mobil Travel Guide* books along on every trip. You'll be pleased by their convenience, ease of use, and breadth of dependable coverage.

Happy travels in the new millennium!

THE EDITORS

Welcome

For over 40 years the *Mobil Travel Guide* has provided travelers in North America with reliable advice on finding good value, quality service, and the distinctive attractions that give a destination its special character. During this time our teams of culinary and hospitality experts have worked hard to develop objective and exacting standards. In so doing, they seek to fully meet the desires and expectations of a broad range of customers.

It is our hope, whether your travels are for business or leisure, over a long distance or a short one, that this book will be your companion, dependably guiding you to quality and value in lodging and dining. By including local attractions (both seasonal and year round) we are striving to provide you with experiences that will make your trip more interesting, pleasant, and memorable.

Because we continually update our attractions and evaluate our listings, we invite you to help us enhance the guides. Whether you wish to provide us with your reactions to the places you have visited or to make suggestions to improve the guides, we would consider it a privilege to hear from you. Please take the time to fill out the customer feedback form at the back of this book or contact us on the Internet at www.mobil.com/travel.

Thank you, and travel safely.

Lucio A. Noto
Chairman and Chief Executive Officer
Mobil Corporation

How to Use This Book

The *Mobil Travel Guide* is easy to use. Each state chapter begins with a general introduction that both provides a general geographical and historical orientation to the state and covers basic statewide tourist information, from state recreation areas to seat-belt laws. The balance of each chapter is devoted to the travel destinations within the state—cities and towns, state and national parks, and tourist regions—which, like the states themselves, are arranged alphabetically.

What follows is an explanation of the wealth of information you'll find within those travel destinations—information on the area, on things to see and do there, and on where to stay and eat.

Maps and Map Coordinates

The first thing you'll notice is that next to each destination is a set of map coordinates. These refer to the appropriate state map in the front of this book. In addition, there are maps of selected larger cities in the front section as well as maps of key neighborhoods within the sections on the cities themselves.

Destination Information

Because many travel destinations are so close to other cities and towns where visitors might find additional attractions, accomodations, and restaurants, cross-references to those places are included whenever possible. Also listed are addresses and phone numbers for travel-information resources—usually the local chamber of commerce or office of tourism—as well as pertinent vital statistics and a brief introduction to the area.

What to See and Do

More than 11,000 museums, art galleries, amusement parks, universities, historic sites and houses, plantations, churches, state parks, ski areas, and other attractions are described in the *Mobil Travel Guide.* A white star on a black background ★ signals that the attraction is one of the best in the state. Since municipal parks, public tennis courts, swimming pools, and small educational institutions are common to most towns, they are generally excluded.

Following the attraction's description are the months and days it's open, address/location and phone number, and admission costs (see the inside front cover for an explanation of the cost symbols). Note that directions are given from the center of the town under which the attraction is listed, which may not necessarily be the town in which the attraction is located. Zip codes are listed only if they differ from those given for the town.

Events

Events—categorized as annual, seasonal, or special—are highlighted. An annual event is one that's held every year for a period of usually no longer than a week to 10 days; festivals and fairs are typical entries. A seasonal event is one that may or may not be annual and that is held for a number of weeks or months in the year, such as horse racing, summer theater, concert or opera festivals, and professional sports. Special event listings occur infrequently and mark a certain date or event, such as a centennial or other commemorative celebration.

Major Cities

Additional information on airports and transportation, suburbs, and neighborhoods may be included for large cities.

Lodging and Restaurant Listings

ORGANIZATION

For both lodgings and restaurants, when a property is in a town that does not have its own heading, the listing appears under the town nearest its location with the address and town in parentheses immediately after the establishment name. In large cities, lodgings located within 5 miles of major commercial airports are listed under a separate "Airport" heading, following the city listings.

LODGING CLASSIFICATIONS

Each property is classified by type according to the characteristics below. Because the following features and services are found at most motels, lodges, motor hotels, and hotels, they are not shown in those listings:

- Year-round operation with a single rate structure unless otherwise quoted
- European plan (meals not included in room rate)
- Bathroom with tub and/or shower in each room
- Air-conditioned/heated, often with individual room control
- Cots
- Daily maid service
- Phones in rooms
- Elevators

Motels and Lodges. Accommodations are in low-rise structures with rooms easily accessible to parking (usually free). Properties have outdoor room entry and small, functional lobbies. Service is often limited, and dining may not be offered in lower-rated motels and lodges. Shops and businesses are found only in higher-rated properties, as are bellhops, room service, and restaurants serving three meals daily.

Lodges differ from motels primarily in their emphasis on outdoor recreational activities and in location. They are often found in resort and rural areas rather than in major cities or along highways.

Motor Hotels. Offering the convenience of motels along with many of the features of hotels, motor hotels range from low-rise structures offering limited services to multistory buildings with a wide range of services and facilities. Multiple building entrances, elevators, inside hallways, and parking areas (generally free) near access doors are some of the features of a motor hotel. Lobbies offer sitting areas and 24-hour desk and switchboard services. Often bellhop and valet services as well as restaurants serving three meals a day are found. Expanded recreational facilities and more than one restaurant are available in higher-rated properties.

The distinction between motor hotels and hotels in metropolitan areas is minor.

Hotels. To be categorized as a hotel, an establishment must have most of the following facilities and services: multiple floors, a restaurant and/or coffee shop, elevators, room service, bellhops, a spacious lobby, and recreational facilities. In addition, the following features and services not shown in listings are also found:

- Valet service (one-day laundry/cleaning service)
- Room service during hours restaurant is open
- Bellhops
- Some oversize beds

Resorts. These specialize in stays of three days or more and usually offer American plan and/or housekeeping accommodations. Their emphasis is on recreational facilities, and a social director is often available. Food services are of primary importance, and guests must be able to eat three meals a day on the premises, either in restaurants or by having access to an on-site grocery store and preparing their own meals.

Inns. Frequently thought of as a small hotel, an inn is a place of homelike comfort and warm hospitality. It is often a structure of historic significance, with an equally interesting setting. Meals are a special occasion, and refreshments are frequently served in late afternoon. Rooms are usually individually decorated, often with antiques or furnishings representative of the locale. Phones, bathrooms, and TVs may not be available in every room.

Guest Ranches. Like resorts, guest ranches specialize in stays of three days or more. Guest ranches also offer meal plans and extensive outdoor activities. Horseback riding is usually a feature; there are stables and trails on the ranch property, and trail rides and daily instruction are part of the program. Many guest ranches are working ranches, ranging from casual to rustic, and guests are encouraged to participate in ranch life. Eating is often family-style and may also include cookouts. Western saddles are assumed; phone ahead to inquire about English saddle availability.

Cottage Colonies. These are housekeeping cottages and cabins that are usually found in recreational areas. Any dining or recreational facilities are noted in our listing.

DINING CLASSIFICATIONS

Restaurants. Most dining establishments fall into this category. All have a full kitchen and offer table service and a complete menu. Parking on or near the premises, in a lot or garage, is assumed. When a property offers valet or other special parking features, or when only street parking is available, it is noted in the listing.

Unrated Dining Spots. These places, listed after Restaurants in many cities, are chosen for their unique atmosphere, specialized menu, or local flavor. They include delis, ice-cream parlors, cafeterias, tearooms, and pizzerias. Because they may not have a full kitchen or table service, they are not given a *Mobil Travel Guide* rating. Often they offer extraordinary value and quick service.

QUALITY RATINGS

The *Mobil Travel Guide* has been rating lodgings and restaurants on a national basis since the first edition was published in 1958. For years the guide was the only source of such ratings, and it remains among the few guidebooks to rate restaurants across the country.

All listed establishments were inspected by experienced field representatives or evaluated by a senior staff member. Ratings are based upon their detailed inspection reports of the individual properties, on written evaluations of staff members who stay and dine anonymously, and on an extensive review of comments from our readers.

You'll find a key to the rating categories, ★ through ★★★★★, on the inside front cover, All establishments in the book are recommended. Even a ★ place is above average, usually providing a basic, informal experience. Rating categories reflect both the features the property offers and its quality in relation to similar establishments.

For example, lodging ratings take into account the number and quality of facilities and services, the luxury of appointments, and the attitude and professionalism of staff and management. A ★ establishment provides a comfortable night's lodging. A ★★ property offers more than a facility that rates one star, and the decor is well planned and integrated. Establishments that rate ★★★ are professionally managed and staffed and often beautifully appointed; the lodging experience is truly excellent and the range of facilities is extensive. Properties that have been given ★★★★ not only offer many services but also have their own style and personality; they are luxurious, creatively decorated, and superbly maintained. The ★★★★★ properties are among the best in North America, superb in every respect and entirely memorable, year in and year out.

Restaurant evaluations reflect the quality of the food and the ingredients, preparation, and presentation as well as service levels and the property's decor and ambience, A restaurant that has fairly simple goals for menu and decor but that achieves those goals superbly might receive the same number of stars as a restaurant with somewhat loftier ambitions whose execution falls somewhat short of the mark. In general, ★ indicates a restaurant that's a good choice in its area, usually fairly simple and perhaps catering to a clientele of locals and families; ★★ denotes restaurants that are more highly recommended in their area; ★★★ restaurants are of national caliber, with professional and attentive service and a skilled chef in the kitchen; ★★★★ reflects superb dining choices, where remarkable food is served in equally remarkable surroundings; and ★★★★★ represents that rarefied group of the best restaurants in the country, where in addition to near perfection in every detail, there's that special something extra that makes for an unforgettable dining experience.

A list of the four-star and five-star establishments in each region is located just before the state listings.

Each rating is reviewed annually and each establishment must work to maintain its rating (or improve it). Every effort is made to assure that ratings are fair and accurate; the designated ratings are published purely as an aid to travelers.

In general, properties that are very new or have recently undergone major management changes are considered difficult to assess fairly and are often listed without ratings.

Good Value Check Mark. In all locales, you'll find a wide range of lodging and dining establishments with a ✔ in front of a star rating. This indicates an unusually good value at economical prices as follows:

In Major Cities and Resort Areas

Lodging: average $105-$125 per night for singles; average $115-$140 per night for doubles

Restaurants: average $25 for a complete lunch; average $40 for a complete dinner, exclusive of beverages and gratuities

Local Area Listings

Lodging: average $50-$60 per night for singles; average $60-$75 per night for doubles

Restaurants: average $12 for a complete lunch; average $20 for a complete dinner, exclusive of beverages and gratuities

LODGINGS

Each listing gives the name, address, directions (when there is no street address), neighborhood and/or directions from downtown (in major cities), phone number (local and 800), fax number, number and type of rooms available, room rates, and seasons open (if not year-round). Also included are details on recreational and dining facilities on property or nearby, the presence of a luxury level, and credit-card information. A key to the symbols at the end of each listing is on the inside front cover. (Note that Mobil Corporation credit cards cannot be used for payment of meals and room charges.)

All prices quoted in the *Mobil Travel Guide* publications are expected to be in effect at the time of publication and during the entire year; however, prices cannot be guaranteed. In some localities there may be short-term price variations because of special events or holidays. Whenever possible, these price charges are noted. Certain resorts have complicated rate structures that vary with the time of year; always confirm listed rates when you make your plans.

RESTAURANTS

Each listing gives the name, address, directions (when there is no street address), neighborhood and/or directions from downtown (in major cities), phone number, hours and days of operation (if not open daily year-round), reservation policy, cuisine (if other than American), price range for each meal served, children's meals (if offered), specialties, and credit-card information. Additionally, special features such as chef ownership, ambience, and entertainment are noted. By carefully reading the detailed restaurant information and comparing prices, you can easily determine whether the restaurant is formal and elegant or informal and comfortable for families.

TERMS AND ABBREVIATIONS IN LISTINGS

The following terms and abbreviations are used throughout the listings:

A la carte entrees With a price, refers to the cost of entrees/main dishes only that are not accompanied by side dishes.
AP American plan (lodging plus all meals).
Bar Liquor, wine, and beer are served in a bar or cocktail lounge and usually with meals unless otherwise indicated (e.g., "wine, beer").
Business center The property has a designated area accessible to all guests with business services.

Business serve avail The property can perform/arrange at least two of the following services for a guest: audiovisual equipment rental, binding, computer rental, faxing, messenger services, modem availability, notary service, obtaining office supplies, photocopying, shipping, and typing.
Cable Standard cable service; "premium" indicates that HBO, Disney, Showtime, or similar services are available.
Ck-in, ck-out Check-in time, check-out time.
Coin lndry Self-service laundry.
Complete meal Soup and/or salad, entree, and dessert, plus nonalcoholic beverage.
Continental bkfst Usually coffee and a roll or doughnut.
Cr cds: A, American Express; 0, Carte Blanche; D, Diners Club; DS, Discover; ER, enRoute; JCB, Japanese Credit Bureau; MC, MasterCard; V, Visa.
D Followed by a price, indicates room rate for a "double"—two people in one room in one or two beds (the charge may be higher for two double beds).
Downhill/x-country ski Downhill and/or cross-country skiing within 20 miles of property,
Each addl Extra charge for each additional person beyond the stated number of persons at a reduced price.
Early-bird dinner A meal served at specified hours, typically around 4:30-6:30 pm.
Exc Except.
Exercise equipt Two or more pieces of exercise equipment on the premises.
Exercise rm Both exercise equipment and room, with an instructor on the premises.
Fax Facsimile machines available to all guests.
Golf privileges Privileges at a course within 10 miles.
Hols Holidays.
In-rm modem link Every guest room has a connection for a modem that's separate from the phone line.
Kit. or kits. A kitchen or kitchenette that contains stove or microwave, sink, and refrigerator and that is either part of the room or a separate room. If the kitchen is not fully equipped, the listing will indicate "no equipt" or "some equipt."
Luxury level A special section of a lodging, covering at least an entire floor, that offers increased luxury accommodations. Management must provide no less than three of these four services: separate check-in and check-out, concierge, private lounge, and private elevator service (key access). Complimentary breakfast and snacks are commonly offered.
MAP Modified American plan (lodging plus two meals).
Movies Prerecorded videos are available for rental.
No cr cds accepted No credit cards are accepted.
No elvtr In hotels with more than two stories, it's assumed there are elevators; only their absence is noted.
No phones Phones, too, are assumed; only their absence is noted.
Parking There is a parking lot on the premises.
Private club A cocktail lounge or bar available to members and their guests. In motels and hotels where these clubs exist, registered guests can usually use the club as guests of the management; the same is frequently true of restaurants.
Prix fixe A full meal for a stated price; usually one price is quoted.
Res Reservations.
S Followed by a price, indicates room rate for a "single," i.e., one person.
Semi-a la carte Meals include vegetable, salad, soup, appetizer, or other accompaniments to the main dish.
Serv bar A service bar, where drinks are prepared for dining patrons only.
Serv charge Service charge is the amount added to the restaurant check in lieu of a tip.
Table d'hôte A full meal for a stated price, dependent upon entree selection; no a la carte options are available.
Tennis privileges Privileges at tennis courts within 5 miles.
TV Indicates color television.
Under certain age free Children under that age are not charged if staying in room with a parent.
Valet parking An attendant is available to park and retrieve a car.
VCR VCRs in all guest rooms.
VCR avail VCRs are available for hookup in guest rooms.

Special Information for Travelers with Disabilities

The *Mobil Travel Guide* symbol D shown in accommodation and restaurant listings indicates establishments that are at least partially accessible to people with mobility problems.

The *Mobil Travel Guide* criteria for accessibility are unique to our publication. Please do not confuse them with the universal symbol for wheelchair accessibility. When the D symbol appears following a listing, the establishment is equipped with facilities to accommodate people using wheelchairs or crutches or otherwise needing easy access to doorways and rest rooms. Travelers with severe mobility problems or with hearing or visual impairments may or may not find facilities they need. Always phone ahead to make sure that an establishment can meet your needs.

All lodgings bearing our D symbol have the following facilities:

- ISA-designated parking near access ramps
- Level or ramped entryways to building
- Swinging building entryway doors minimum 3′0″
- Public rest rooms on main level with space to operate a wheelchair; handrails at commode areas
- Elevators equipped with grab bars and lowered control buttons
- Restaurants with accessible doorways; rest rooms with space to operate wheelchair; handrails at commode areas
- Minimum 3′0″ width entryway to guest rooms
- Low-pile carpet in rooms
- Telephone at bedside and in bathroom
- Bed placed at wheelchair height
- Minimum 3′0″ width doorway to bathroom

- Bath with open sink—no cabinet; room to operate wheelchair
- Handrails at commode areas; tub handrails
- Wheelchair accessible peephole in room entry door
- Wheelchair accessible closet rods and shelves

All restaurants bearing our D symbol offer the following facilities:

- ISA-designated parking beside access ramps
- Level or ramped front entryways to building
- Tables to accommodate wheelchairs
- Main-floor rest rooms; minimum 3′0″ width entryway
- Rest rooms with space to operate wheelchair; handrails at commode areas

In general, the newest properties are apt to impose the fewest barriers.

To get the kind of service you need and have a right to expect, do not hesitate when making a reservation to question the management in detail about the availability of accessible rooms, parking, entrances, restaurants, lounges, or any other facilities that are important to you, and confirm what is meant by "accessible." Some guests with mobility impairments report that lodging establishments' housekeeping and maintenance departments are most helpful in describing barriers. Also inquire about any special equipment, transportation, or services you may need.

Making the Most of Your Trip

A few diehard souls might fondly remember the trip where the car broke down and they were stranded for a week, or the vacation that cost twice what it was supposed to. For most travelers, though, the best trips are those that are safe, smooth, and within their budget. To help you make your trip the best it can be, we've assembled a few tips and resources.

Saving Money

ON LODGING

After you've seen the published rates, it's time to look for discounts. Many hotels and motels offer them—for senior citizens, business travelers, families, you name it. It never hurts to ask—politely, that is. Sometimes, especially in late afternoon, desk clerks are instructed to fill beds, and you might be offered a lower rate, or a nicer room, to entice you to stay. Look for bargains on stays over multiple nights, in the off-season, and on weekdays or weekends (depending on location). Many hotels in major metropolitan areas, for example, have special weekend package plans, which offer considerable savings on rooms and may include breakfast, cocktails, and meal discounts. Prices change frequently throughout the year, so phone ahead.

Another way to save money is to choose accommodations that give you more than just a standard room. Rooms with kitchen facilities enable you to cook some meals for yourself, reducing restaurant costs. A suite might save money for two couples traveling together. Even hotel luxury levels can provide good value, as many include breakfast or cocktails in the price of the room.

State and city sales taxes as well as special room taxes can increase your room rates as much as 25% per day. We are unable to bring this specific information into the listings, but we strongly urge that you ask about these taxes when placing reservations in order to understand the total price to you.

Watch out for telephone-usage charges that hotels frequently impose on long-distance calls, credit-card calls, and other phone calls—even those that go unanswered. Before phoning from your room, read the information given to you at check-in, and then be sure to read your bill carefully before checking out. You won't be expected to pay for charges that weren't spelled out. (On the other hand, it's not unusual for a hotel to bill you for your calls after you return home.) Consider using public telephones in hotel lobbies; the savings may outweigh the inconvenience.

ON DINING

There are several ways to get a less-expensive meal at a more-expensive restaurant. Early-bird dinners are popular in many parts of the country and offer considerable savings. If you're interested in sampling a 4- or 5-star establishment, consider going at lunchtime. While the prices then are probably relatively high, they may be half of those at dinner and come with the same ambience, service, and cuisine.

PARK PASSES

While many national parks, monuments, seashores, historic sites, and recreation areas may be used free of charge, others charge an entrance fee (ranging from $1 to $6 per person to $5 to $15 per carload) and/or a "use fee" for special services and facilities. If you plan to make several visits to federal recreation areas, consider one of the following National Park Service money-saving programs:

Park Pass. This is an annual entrance permit to a specific unit in the National Park Service system that normally charges an entrance fee. The pass admits the permit holder and any accompanying passengers in a private noncommercial vehicle or, in the case of walk-in facilities, the holder's spouse, children, and parents. It is valid for entrance fees only. A Park Pass may be purchased in person or by mail from the National Park Service unit at which the pass will be honored. The cost is $15 to $20, depending upon the area.

Golden Eagle Passport. This pass, available to people who are between 17 and 61, entitles the purchaser and accompanying passengers in a private noncommercial vehicle to enter any outdoor NPS unit that charges an entrance fee and admits the purchaser and family to most walk-in fee-charging areas. Like the Park Pass, it is good for one year and does not cover use fees. It may be purchased from the National

Park Service, Office of Public Inquiries, Room 1013, US Department of the Interior, 18th and C Sts NW, Washington, DC 20240, phone 202/208-4747; at any of the 10 regional offices throughout the country; and at any NPS area that charges a fee. The cost is $50.

Golden Age Passport. Available to citizens and permanent residents of the United States 62 years or older, this is a lifetime entrance permit to fee-charging recreation areas. The fee exemption extends to those accompanying the permit holder in a private noncommercial vehicle or, in the case of walk-in facilities, to the holder's spouse and children. The passport also entitles the holder to a 50% discount on use fees charged in park areas but not to fees charged by concessionaires. Golden Age Passports must be obtained in person. The applicant must show proof of age, i.e., a driver's license, birth certificate, or signed affidavit attesting to age (Medicare cards are not acceptable proof). Passports are available at most park service units where they're used, at National Park Service headquarters (see above), at park system regional offices, at National Forest Supervisors' offices, and at most Ranger Station offices. The cost is $10.

Golden Access Passport. Issued to citizens and permanent residents of the United States who are physically disabled or visually impaired, this passport is a free lifetime entrance permit to fee-charging recreation areas. The fee exemption extends to those accompanying the permit holder in a private noncommercial vehicle or, in the case of walk-in facilities, to the holder's spouse and children. The passport also entitles the holder to a 50% discount on use fees charged in park areas but not to fees charged by concessionaires. Golden Access Passports must be obtained in person. Proof of eligibility to receive federal benefits is required (under programs such as Disability Retirement, Compensation for Military Service-Connected Disability, Coal Mine Safety and Health Act, etc.), or an affidavit must be signed attesting to eligibility. These passports are available at the same outlets as Golden Age Passports.

FOR SENIOR CITIZENS

Look for the senior-citizen discount symbol in the lodging and restaurant listings. Always call ahead to confirm that the discount is being offered, and be sure to carry proof of age. At places not listed in the book, it never hurts to ask if a senior-citizen discount is offered. Additional information for mature travelers is available from the American Association of Retired Persons (AARP), 601 E St NW, Washington, DC 20049, phone 202/434-2277.

Tipping

Tipping is an expression of appreciation for good service, and often service workers rely on tips as a significant part of their income. However, you never need to tip if service is poor.

IN HOTELS

Doormen in major city hotels are usually given $1 for getting you a cab. Bellhops expect $1 per bag, usually $2 if you have only one bag. Concierges are tipped according to the service they perform. It's not mandatory to tip when you've asked for suggestions on sightseeing or restaurants or help in making reservations for dining. However, when a concierge books you a table at a restaurant known to be difficult to get into, a gratuity of $5 is appropriate. For obtaining theater or sporting event tickets, $5-$10 is expected. Maids, often overlooked by guests, may be tipped $1-$2 per day of stay.

AT RESTAURANTS

Coffee shop and counter service wait staff are usually given 8%–10% of the bill. In full-service restaurants, tip 15% of the bill, before sales tax. In fine restaurants, where the staff is large and shares the gratuity, 18%–20% for the waiter is appropriate. In most cases, tip the maitre d' only if service has been extraordinary and only on the way out; $20 is the minimum in upscale properties in major metropolitan areas. If there is a wine steward, tip him or her at least $6 a bottle, more if the wine was decanted or if the bottle was very expensive. If your busboy has been unusually attentive, $2 pressed into his hand on departure is a nice gesture. An increasing number of restaurants automatically add a service charge to the bill in lieu of a gratuity. Before tipping, carefully review your check.

AT AIRPORTS

Curbside luggage handlers expect $1 per bag. Car-rental shuttle drivers who help with your luggage appreciate a $1 or $2 tip.

Staying Safe

The best way to deal with emergencies is to be prepared enough to avoid them. However, unforeseen situations do happen, and you can prepare for them.

IN YOUR CAR

Before your trip, make sure your car has been serviced and is in good working order. Change the oil, check the battery and belts, and make sure tires are inflated properly (this can also improve gas mileage). Other inspections recommended by the car's manufacturer should be made, too.

Next, be sure you have the tools and equipment to deal with a routine breakdown: jack, spare tire, lug wrench, repair kit, emergency tools, jumper cables, spare fan belt, auto fuses, flares and/or reflectors, flashlights, first-aid kit, and, in winter, a windshield scraper and shovel.

Bring all appropriate and up-to-date documentation—licenses, registration, and insurance cards—and know what's covered by your insurance. Also bring an extra set of keys, just in case.

En route, always buckle up!

If your car does break down, get out of traffic as soon as possible—pull well off the road. Raise the hood and turn on your emergency flashers or tie a white cloth to the roadside door handle or antenna. Stay near your car. Use flares or reflectors to keep your car from being hit.

IN YOUR LODGING

Chances are slim that you will encounter a hotel or motel fire. The in a listing indicates that there were smoke detectors and/or sprinkler systems in the rooms we inspected. Once you've checked in, make sure that any smoke detector in your room is working properly. Ascertain the locations of fire extinguishers and at least two fire exits. Never use an elevator in a fire.

For personal security, use the peephole in your room's door.

PROTECTING AGAINST THEFT

To guard against theft wherever you go, don't bring any more of value than you need. If you do bring valuables, leave them at your hotel rather than in your car, and if you have something very expensive, lock it in a safe. Many hotels have one in each room; others will store your valuables in the hotel's safe. And of course, don't carry more money than you need; use traveler's checks and credit cards, or visit cash machines.

For Travelers With Disabilities

A number of publications can provide assistance. The most complete listing of published material for travelers with disabilities is available from The Disability Bookshop, Twin Peaks Press, Box 129, Vancouver, WA 98666, phone 360/694-2462. A comprehensive guidebook to the national parks is *Easy Access to National Parks: The Sierra Club Guide for People with Disabilities* ($16), distributed by Random House.

The Reference Section of the National Library Service for the Blind and Physically Handicapped (Library of Congress, Washington, DC 20542, phone 202/707-9276 or 202/707-5100) provides information and resources for persons with mobility problems and hearing and vision impairments, as well as information about the NILS talking program (or visit your local library).

Traveling to Mexico

Proof of citizenship—passport or certified birth certificate—is required for travel into Mexico. Aliens must carry their alien registration cards, and naturalized citizens should carry their naturalization certificates. If you are planning to stay more than 24 hours or if you are a naturalized citizen or resident alien, get a copy of current border regulations from the nearest Mexican consulate or tourism office before crossing, and make sure you understand them. A helpful booklet, "Know Before You Go," may be obtained free of charge from the nearest office of the U.S. Customs Service.

If you take your car for the day, you may find it more convenient to unload all baggage before crossing than to go through a thorough customs inspection upon your return. You will not be permitted to bring any plants, fruits, or vegetables into the United States. Federal regulations permit each U.S. citizen, 21 years of age or older, to bring back one quart of alcoholic beverage, duty-free. However, state regulations vary and may be more strict; check locally before entering Mexico. New regulations may be issued at any time, so check further if you have any questions.

Your automobile insurance is not valid in Mexico; for short visits, get a one-day policy before crossing. U.S. currency is accepted in all border cities. Mexico does not observe Daylight Saving Time.

Important Toll-Free Numbers

and On-Line Information

HOTELS AND MOTELS

Adam's Mark 800/444–2326
www.adamsmark.com
Baymont Inns and Suites 800/428–3438
www.budgetel.com
Best Western .... 800/780–7234, TDD 800/528–2222
www.bestwestern.com
Budget Host 800/283–4678
www.budgethost.com
Clarion 800/252–7466
Comfort Inn 800/228–5150
www.choicehotels.com
Courtyard by Marriott 800/321–2211
www.courtyard.com
Days Inn 800/325–2525
www.daysinn.com
Doubletree 800/222–8733
www.doubletreehotels.com/
Drury Inns 800/325–8300
www.drury-inn.com
Econo Lodge 800/446–6900
www.econolodge.com
Embassy Suites 800/362–2779
www.embassy-suites.com
Exel Inns of America 800/356–8013
www.exlinns.com
Fairfield Inn by Marriott 800/228–2800
www.fairfieldinn.com
Fairmont Hotels 800/527–4727
www.fairmont.com
Forte 800/225–5843
www.forte-hotels.com
Four Seasons 800/819–5053
www.fourseasons.com
Friendship Inns 800/453–4511
www.hotelchoice.com
Hampton Inn 800/426–7866
www.hampton-inn.com
Hilton .... 800/445–8667, TDD 800/368–1133
www.hilton.com
Holiday Inn .... 800/465–4329, TDD 800/238–5544
www.holiday-inn.com
Howard Johnson .... 800/446–4656, TDD 800/654–8442
www.hojo.com
Hyatt & Resorts 800/233–1234
www.hyatt.com
Inns of America 800/826–0778
www.innsamerica.com
Inter-Continental 800/327–0200
www.interconti.com
La Quinta .... 800/531–5900, TDD 800/426–3101
www.laquinta.com
Loews 800/235–6397
www.loewshotels.com
Marriott 800/228–9290
www.marriott.com
Master Hosts Inns 800/251–1962
www.reservahost.com
Meridien 800/225–5843
www.forte-hotels.com
Motel 6 .... 800/466–8356
Nikko International 800/645–5687
www.nikkohotels.com
Omni 800/843–6664
www.omnirosen.com
Quality Inn 800/228–5151
www.qualityinn.com
Radisson 800/333–3333
www.radisson.com
Ramada .... 800/228–2828, TDD 800/228–3232
www.ramada.com
Red Carpet Inns 800/251–1962
www.reservahost.com
Red Lion 800/733–5466
www.redlion.com
Red Roof Inn 800/843–7663
www.redroof.com
Renaissance 800/468–3571
www.renaissancehotels.com
Residence Inn by Marriott 800/331–3131
www.marriott.com
Ritz-Carlton 800/241–3333
www.ritzcarlton.com
Rodeway 800/228–2000
www.rodeway.com
Sheraton 800/325–3535
www.sheraton.com
Shilo Inn 800/222–2244
www.shiloinns.com
Signature Inns 800/822–5252
www.signature-inns.com
Sleep Inn 800/753–3746
www.sleepinn.com
Super 8 .... 800/800–8000
www.super8motels.com
Susse Chalet 800/524–2538
www.sussechalet.com
Travelodge 800/578–7878
www.travelodge.com
Vagabond Inns 800/522–1555
www.vagabondinns.com
Westin Hotels & Resorts 800/937–8461
www.westin.com
Wyndham Hotels & Resorts 800/996–3426
www.travelweb.com

AIRLINES

Air Canada 800/776–3000
www.aircanada.ca
Alaska 800/252–7522
www.alaska-air.com
American 800/433–7300
www.americaair.com
America West 800/235–9292
www.americawest.com
British Airways 800/247–9297
www.british-airways.com
Canadian 800/426–7000
www.cdnair.ca
Continental 800/523–3273
www.flycontinental.com
Delta 800/221–1212
www.delta-air.com/
IslandAir 800/323–3345
Mesa 800/637–2247
www.mesa-air.com
Northwest 800/225–2525
www.nwa.com
SkyWest 800/453–9417
www.skywest.com
Southwest 800/435–9792
www.iflyswa.com
TWA 800/221–2000
www.twa.com
United 800/241–6522
www.ual.com
USAir 800/428–4322
www.usair.com

TRAINS

Amtrak 800/872–7245
www.amtrak.com

BUSES

Greyhound 800/231–2222
www.greyhound.com

CAR RENTALS

Advantage 800/777–5500
www.arac.com
Alamo 800/327–9633
www.goalamo.com
Allstate 800/634–6186
www.bnm.com/as.htm
Avis 800/831–2847
www.avis.com
Budget 800/527–0700
www.budgetrentacar.com
Dollar 800/800–3665
www.dollarcar.com
Enterprise 800/325–8007
www.pickenterprise.com
Hertz 800/654–3131
www.hertz.com
National 800/227–7368
www.nationalcar.com
Payless 800/729–5377
www.800-payless.com
Rent-A-Wreck 800/944–7501
www.rent-a-wreck.com
Sears 800/527–0770
Thrifty 800/847–4369
www.thrifty.com

Four-Star and Five-Star Establishments

in California and the West

ARIZONA

★★★★★ Lodging
Phoenician Resort, *Scottsdale*

★★★★★ Restaurant
Mary Elaine's, *Scottsdale*

★★★★ Lodgings
Arizona Biltmore Resort & Spa, *Phoenix*
The Boulders, *Carefree*
Canyon Villa Bed & Breakfast Inn, *Sedona*
Enchantment Resort, *Sedona*
Hyatt Regency, *Scottsdale*
The Lodge at Ventana Canyon, *Tucson*
Loews Ventana Canyon Resort, *Tucson*
Marriott Camelback Inn, *Scottsdale*
Omni Tucson National Golf & Conference Resort, *Tucson*
Ritz-Carlton Hotel, *Phoenix*
Royal Palms Hotel & Casitas, *Phoenix*
Scottsdale Princess Hotel, *Scottsdale*
Sheraton El Conquistador, *Tucson*
The Wigwam, *Litchfield Park*

★★★★ Restaurants
Arizona Kitchen, *Litchfield Park*
Gold Room, *Tucson*
Golden Swan, *Scottsdale*
Janos, *Tucson*
La Hacienda, *Scottsdale*
Latilla, *Carefree*
Marquesa, *Scottsdale*
The Tack Room, *Tucson*
The Terrace, *Scottsdale*
Ventana Room, *Tucson*

CALIFORNIA

★★★★★ Lodgings
Beverly Hills Hotel, *Beverly Hills*
Chateau du Sureau Hotel, *Oakhurst*
L'Ermitage, *Beverly Hills*
Mandarin Oriental, *San Francisco*
The Peninsula, *Beverly Hills*

★★★★★ Restaurants
The French Laundry, *Yountville*
Gary Danko's, *San Francisco*
Ginza Sushiko, *Beverly Hills*

★★★★ Lodgings
Auberge du Soleil, *St Helena*
Campton Place Hotel, *San Francisco*
Carmel Valley Ranch, *Carmel Valley*
The Fairmont, *San Jose*
Four Seasons Resort, *Carlsbad*
Four Seasons Hotel, *Los Angeles*
Four Seasons Newport Beach, *Newport Beach*
Four Seasons Biltmore, *Santa Barbara*
Hotel Bel-Air, *Los Angeles*
Hotel de Anza, *San Jose*
Hotel Nikko at Beverly Hills, *Los Angeles*
Hyatt Regency La Jolla at Aventine, *La Jolla (San Diego)*
Park Hyatt, *Los Angeles*
Hyatt Grand Champions, *Palm Desert*
Park Hyatt Hotel, *San Francisco*
Inn on Mt Ada, *Avalon (Catalina Island)*
L'Auberge Del Mar Resort & Spa, *Del Mar*
Marriott Coronado Island Resort, *Coronado*
Marriott's Desert Springs Resort & Spa, *Palm Desert*
Meadowood, *St Helena*
Old Monterey Inn, *Monterey*
Pan Pacific, *San Francisco*
Post Ranch Inn, *Big Sur*
Quail Lodge Resort & Golf Club, *Carmel*
Rancho Valencia, *Rancho Santa Fe*
The Regent Beverly Wilshire, *Beverly Hills*
Ritz-Carlton Hotel, *Laguna Beach*
Ritz-Carlton Hotel, *Marina del Rey*
Ritz-Carlton Hotel, *Palm Springs*
The Ritz-Carlton Huntington, *Pasadena*
Ritz-Carlton Hotel, *San Francisco*
Sheraton Grande Torrey Pines, *La Jolla (San Diego)*
Sheraton Marina, *San Diego*
The Sherman House, *San Francisco*
Simpson House Inn, *Santa Barbara*
Timberhill Ranch, *Fort Ross State Historic Park*
W Hotel, *San Francisco*
Westin Century Plaza Hotel & Tower, *Los Angeles*
The Willows, *Palm Springs*

★★★★ Restaurants
Aqua, *San Francisco*
Bay Club, *Pebble Beach*
The Belvedere, *Beverly Hills*
Boulevard, *San Francisco*
Campton Place Dining Room, *San Francisco*
Cielo, *Big Sur*
Club XIX, *Pebble Beach*
The Dining Room, *Laguna Beach*
The Dining Room, *Palm Springs*
The Dining Room, *San Francisco*
Downey's, *Santa Barbara*
Erna's Elderberry House, *Oakhurst*
Five Feet, *Laguna Beach*
Gardens, *Los Angeles*
The Grill, *Pasadena*
Gustaf Anders, *Santa Ana*
Hawthorne Lane, *San Francisco*
Jardienere, *San Francisco*
L'Orangerie, *Hollywood (L.A.)*
La Folie, *San Francisco*
Laurel, *San Diego*
Masa's, *San Francisco*
Patina Restaurant, *Hollywood (L.A.)*
Pavilion, *Newport Beach*
Postrio Restaurant, *San Francisco*
Sierra Mar Restaurant, *Big Sur*
Spago, *Beverly Hills*
Terra, *St Helena*
Valentino, *Santa Monica*
Wally's Desert Turtle, *Palm Springs*
Water Grill, *Los Angeles*

NEVADA

★★★★★ Restaurants
Picasso, *Las Vegas*
Renoir, *Las Vegas*

★★★★ Lodgings
The Bellagio Resort, *Las Vegas*
Caesars Palace, *Las Vegas*
Four Seasons Hotel Las Vegas, *Las Vegas*
Harrah's Hotel Casino, *Stateline*

★★★★ Restaurants
Aqua, *Las Vegas*
The First Floor Grill, *Las Vegas*
Le Cirque, *Las Vegas*
Napa, *Las Vegas*

UTAH

★★★★ Lodgings
Brigham Street Inn, *Salt Lake City*
Stein Eriksen Lodge, *Park City*

★★★★ Restaurants
Glitretind Restaurant, *Park City*
Riverhorse Cafe, *Park City*

Arizona

Population: 3,665,228
Land area: 113,510 square miles
Elevation: 70-12,633 feet
Highest point: Humphreys Peak (Coconino County)
Entered union: February 14, 1912 (48th state)
Capital: Phoenix
Motto: God enriches
Nickname: Grand Canyon State
State flower: Saguaro (sah-WAH-ro) cactus blossom
State bird: Cactus wren
State tree: Palo Verde
State fair: October 12-29, 2000, in Phoenix
Time zone: Mountain
Web: www.arizonaguide.com

This rapidly growing state has more than tripled its population since 1940. Its irrigated farms grow citrus fruits, cotton, vegetables and grain on lush green lands that contrast sharply with the surrounding desert. It also produces 60 percent of the nation's copper.

As a vacation state, its progress has been spectacular. In winter, the areas around Phoenix, Tucson and Yuma offer sunshine, relaxation and informal Western living. Air conditioning and swimming pools make year-round living pleasant. In summer, the northern mountains, cool forests, spectacular canyons, trout streams and lakes offer a variety of vacation activities, including hunting and fishing camps, ghost and mining towns, meadows filled with wildflowers, intriguing ancient Native American villages, cliff dwellings and dude ranches.

Francisco Vasquez de Coronado crossed the area in 1540 on his ill-fated search for the nonexistent gold of Cibola. Grizzled prospectors panned for gold in mountain streams and hit pay dirt. The missions built by Father Kino and his successors date back as far as 1692. Irrigation ditches, built by the Hohokam people hundreds of years earlier, have been incorporated into modern systems.

The state has 23 reservations and one of the largest Native American populations in the United States. More than half of the Native American population is Navajo. Craft specialties include basketry, pottery, weaving, jewelry and kachina dolls.

Arizona is a state of contrasts. It has modern and prehistoric civilizations; mountains, deserts and modern agriculture. Arizona offers fascinating adventures for everyone.

When to Go/Climate

We recommend visiting Arizona in the spring or fall, when temperatures are milder and the heavy tourist traffic is over.

AVERAGE HIGH/LOW TEMPERATURES (°F)

PHOENIX

Jan 66/49	**May** 94/64	**Sept** 98/73
Feb 71/45	**June** 104/73	**Oct** 88/61
Mar 76/49	**July** 106/81	**Nov** 75/49
Apr 85/55	**Aug** 104/79	**Dec** 66/42

FLAGSTAFF

Jan 42/15	**May** 67/33	**Sept** 74/41
Feb 45/18	**June** 78/41	**Oct** 63/31
Mar 49/21	**July** 82/51	**Nov** 51/22
Apr 58/27	**Aug** 79/49	**Dec** 43/16

Parks and Recreation Finder

Directions to and information about the parks and recreation areas below are given under their respective town/city sections. Please refer to those sections for details.

NATIONAL PARK AND RECREATION AREAS

Key to abbreviations. I.H.S. = International Historic Site; I.P.M.= International Peace Memorial; N.B. = National Battlefield; N.B.P. = National Battlefield Park; N.B.C. = National Battlefield & Cemetery; N.C. = National Conservation Area; N.E.M. = National Expansion Memorial; N.F. = National Forest; N.G. = National Grassland; N.H. = National Historical Park; N.H.C. = National Heritage Corridor; N.H.S. National Historic Site; N.L. = National Lakeshore; N.M. = National Monument; N.M.P. = National Military Park; N.Mem. = National Memorial; N.P. = National Park; N.Pres. = National Preserve; N.R. = National Recreational Area; N.R.R. = National Recreational River; N.Riv. = National River; N.S. = National Seashore; N.S.R. = National Scenic Riverway; N.S.T. = National Scenic Trail; N.Sc. = National Scientific Reserve; N.V.M. = National Volcanic Monument.

Place Name	Listed Under
Apache-Sitgreaves N.F.	SHOW LOW, SPRINGERVILLE
Canyon de Chelly N.M.	same
Casa Grande Ruins N.M.	same
Chiricahua N.M.	same
Coconino N.F.	FLAGSTAFF
Coronado N.F.	TUCSON
Coronado N.Mem.	SIERRA VISTA
Fort Bowie N.H.S.	WILLCOX
Grand Canyon N.P.	same
Glen Canyon N.R.	PAGE
Hubbell Trading Post N.H.S.	GANADO
Kaibab N.F.	WILLIAMS
Montezuma Castle N.M.	same
Navajo N.M.	same
Organ Pipe Cactus N.M.	same
Petrified Forest N.P.	same
Pipe Spring N.M.	same
Prescott N.F.	PRESCOTT
Saguaro N.P.	same
Sunset Crater Volcano N.M.	same
Tonto N.F.	PAYSON
Tumacacori N.H.	same
Tuzigoot N.M.	COTTONWOOD
Walnut Canyon N.M.	FLAGSTAFF
Wupatki N.M.	same

CALENDAR HIGHLIGHTS

JANUARY

Fiesta Bowl (Tempe). ASU Sun Devil Stadium. College football. Phone 602/350-0900.

Native American Festival (Litchfield Park). 100 Native American craft vendors. Native American dancing and other authentic entertainment. Phone West Valley Fine Arts Council 623/935-6384.

FEBRUARY

Winter Fest (Flagstaff). Features art contest and exhibit; theater performances; workshops; sled dog and other races, games; Winterfaire with arts and crafts; entertainment. Phone 520/774-4505.

PGA Tours Tucson Open. (Tucson). Tucson National Golf Course. $1.1-million tournament featuring top pros. Phone 800/882-7660.

Arabian Horse Show (Scottsdale). WestWorld. The largest Arabian horse show in the world. More than 2,000 champion horses. Barn parties and more than 300 commercial vendors. Phone 480/515-1500.

Arizona Renaissance Festival (Mesa). Hundreds of participants enjoy music, theater, crafts exhibits and games. Concessions. Jousting tournament at King's Jousting Arena. Phone 520/463-2700.

MARCH

Spring Festival of the Arts (Tempe). Downtown. Artists' exhibits, food, entertainment, family activities. Phone Mill Avenue Merchants Association 480/967-4877.

JULY

Flagstaff Festival of the Arts (Flagstaff).

SEPTEMBER

Navajo Nation Fair. (Window Rock) Navajo Nation Fairgrounds. Navajo traditional song and dance; Inter-tribal powwow; All-Indian Rodeo; parade; concerts; exhibits. Phone 520/871-6478.

Sedona Jazz on the Rocks (Sedona). More than 5,000 people attend this outdoor jazz festival, featuring internationally renowned artists. Phone 520/282-1985.

OCTOBER

Arizona State Fair (Phoenix). State Fairgrounds. Phone 602/252-6771.

Tucson Heritage Experience Festival (Tucson).

DECEMBER

Fiesta Bowl Block Party (Tempe). Includes games, rides, entertainment, pep rally, fireworks, food. Phone Fiesta Bowl Office 602/350-0911.

STATE PARK AND RECREATION AREAS

Key to abbreviations. I.P. = Interstate Park; S.A.P. = State Archaeological Park; S.B. = State Beach; S.C. = State Conservation Area; S.C.P. = State Conservation Park; S.Cp. = State Campground; S.F. = State Forest; S.G. = State Garden; S.H.A. = State Historic Area; S.H.P. = State Historic Park; S.H.S. = State Historic Site; S.M.P. = State Marine Park; S.N.A. = State Natural Area; S.P. = State Park; S.P.C. = State Public Campground; S.R. = State Reserve; S.R.A. = State Recreation Area; S.Res. = State Reservoir; S.Res.P. = State Resort Park; S.R.P. = State Rustic Park.

Place Name	Listed Under
Buckskin Mountain S.P.	PARKER
Catalina S.P.	TUCSON
Dead Horse Ranch S.P.	COTTONWOOD
Lake Havasu S.P. (Cattail Cove and Windsor Beach units)	LAKE HAVASU CITY
Lost Dutchman S.P.	MESA
Lyman Lake S.P.	SPRINGERVILLE
Patagonia Lake S.P.	PATAGONIA
Roper Lake S.P.	SAFFORD
Slide Rock S.P.	SEDONA

Water-related activities, hiking, riding, various other sports, picnicking, camping and visitor centers are available at all parks. There is a $5/car day-use fee at state parks; $35 and $65 annual day-use permits are available. Camping $8-$15/day. Arizona also has nine state historic parks ($4-$5; guided tours addl fee). For further information contact Arizona State Parks, Public Information Officer, 1300 W Washington, Phoenix 85007; 602/542-1996.

SKI AREAS

Place Name	Listed Under
Arizona Snowbowl	FLAGSTAFF
Mormon Lake Ski Center	FLAGSTAFF
Mt Lemmon Ski Valley	TUCSON
Sunrise Park Resort	McNARY
Williams Ski Area	WILLIAMS

FISHING & HUNTING

Both are excellent in a number of sections of the state. Nonresident fishing licenses: 1-day (exc Colorado River), $8; 5-day, $18.50; 4-month, $22; general, $38; Colorado River, all species, $32.50; trout stamp, $10. Urban fishing (for 14 lakes in 6 cities), $12.00. Inquire for fees to fish on Native American reservations. Nonresident hunting licenses: 3-day small game, $38; general, $85.50. Tags cost from $50.50 for turkey to $3,753 for buffalo. Permits for most big-game species available by drawing only. Combination nonresident licenses (fishing and hunting), $100 (incl trout stamp). Fees subject to change. For updated information contact the Arizona Game & Fish Department, 2222 W Greenway Rd, Phoenix 85023; 602/942-3000.

Driving Information

Safety belts are mandatory for all persons in front seat of vehicle. Children under 4 years or under 40 pounds in weight must be in an approved safety seat anywhere in vehicle. For further information phone 602/223-2000.

INTERSTATE HIGHWAY SYSTEM

Use the following list as a guide to access interstate highways in Arizona. You should always consult a map to confirm driving routes.

Highway Number	Cities/Towns within 10 miles
Interstate 8	Casa Grande, Gila Bend, Yuma.
Interstate 10	Casa Grande, Chandler, Glendale, Litchfield Park, Mesa, Phoenix, Scottsdale, Tempe, Tucson, Willcox.
Interstate 17	Cottonwood, Flagstaff, Glendale, Phoenix, Scottsdale, Sedona, Tempe.
Interstate 19	Nogales, Tucson.
Interstate 40	Flagstaff, Holbrook, Kingman, Seligman, Williams, Winslow.

Additional Visitor Information

Arizona Highways is an excellent monthly magazine; contact 2039 W Lewis Ave, Phoenix 85009. Several informative booklets may be obtained from the Arizona Office of Tourism, 2702 N 3rd St, Suite 4015, Phoenix 85004; 602/230-7733 or 888/520-3434.

Bisbee (H-5)

(See also Douglas, Sierra Vista, Tombstone)

Founded 1880 **Pop** 6,288 **Elev** 5,400 ft **Area Code** 520 **Zip** 85603
Information Greater Bisbee Chamber of Commerce, 7 Main St, Box BA; 520/432-5421

Nestled in the foothills of the Mule Mountains of southeastern Arizona, Bisbee once was a tough mining town known as "Queen of the Copper Camps." Today, Bisbee is rich in architecture and culture with many art galleries, period hotels and bed & breakfasts.

What to See and Do

Bisbee Mining and Historical Museum. Housed in the 1897 office building of the Copper Queen Consolidated Mining Co. Depicts early development of this urban center through displays on mining, minerals, social history and period offices; historical photographs. Shattuck Research Library. (Daily; closed Jan 1, Dec 25) 207B Youngblood Hill. ¢¢ Also operates **Muheim Heritage House** (early 1900s). (Thurs-Mon) 5 Copper Queen Plaza. Phone 520/432-7071 or -7848. ¢¢

Bisbee Restoration Association & Historical Museum. Local historical and pioneer artifacts; Native American relics. (Daily exc Sun; closed major hols) 37 Main St. Phone 520/432-4106 or -2386. **Donation.**

Mine tours. On US 80 near Old Bisbee. For information on all tours, Phone 520/432-2071. Tours include

Lavender Pit. A 340-acre open-pit copper mine, now inactive. Approx 1-hr van tour of surface mine and historic district (daily; closed Thanksgiving, Dec 25). Lavender Viewpoint (daily; free). ¢¢

Queen Mine. Approx 1-hr guided tour on mine train; takes visitor 1,800 ft into mine tunnel. Mine temperature 47°F-49°F; jacket recommended. (Daily; closed Thanksgiving, Dec 25). ¢¢¢

Hotel

★★ **COPPER QUEEN HOTEL.** *11 Howell Ave (85603). 520/432-2216; FAX 520/432-4298; res: 800/247-5829.* Web www.copperqueen.com. 47 rms, 4 story. S, D $70-$105; each addl $10. Crib $10. TV; cable. Heated pool. Restaurant 7 am-2:30 pm, 5:30-9 pm. Bar 11-1 am; entertainment Fri-Sat. Ck-out 11 am. Meeting rm. Business servs avail. Built in 1902. Cr cds: A, C, D, DS, MC, V.

D

Inns

✓★★ **CALUMET & ARIZONA GUEST HOUSE.** *608 Powell St (85603), off Bisbee Rd, left on Cole Ave to Powell. 520/432-4815.* 6 air-cooled rms, 4 share bath, 2 story. No rm phones. S $45-$55; D $60-$70; each addl $15. TV in sitting rm; cable, VCR (movies). Complimentary full bkfst. Restaurant nearby. Ck-out 11 am. Concierge serv. Totally nonsmoking. Patios. Cr cds: C, MC, V.

✓★ **HOTEL LAMORE BISBEE INN.** *45 Ok St (85603). 520/432-5131; FAX 520/432-5343; res: 888/432-5131.* 19 rms, 6 share bath, 2 story. S $45-$60; D $50-$75; each addl $15; wkly rates. Crib free. TV in sitting rm; cable. Complimentary full bkfst. Ck-out 11 am, ck-in after 3 pm. Restored 1917 hotel. Totally nonsmoking. Cr cds: A, C, D, DS, JCB, MC, V.

✓★ **SCHOOL HOUSE INN.** *818 Tombstone Canyon (85603), in Old Bisbee. 520/432-2996; FAX 520/432-2996.* 9 rms, 2 story, 3 suites. No A/C. No rm phones. S $50-$60; D $55-$65; each addl $10; suites $70-$75. Children over 13 yrs only. TV in den; cable. Complimentary full bkfst. Restaurant nearby. Ck-out 11 am, ck-in 3-5 pm. Concierge serv. Balconies. Totally nonsmoking. Cr cds: A, C, D, DS, JCB, MC, V.

D

Bullhead City (D-1)

(See also Kingman; also see Needles, CA, and Laughlin, NV)

Founded 1946 **Pop** 21,951 **Elev** 540 ft **Area Code** 520
Information Chamber of Commerce, 1251 US 95, 86429; 520/754-4121

Bullhead City was established in 1945 as a construction camp for Davis Dam, a reclamation facility located three miles to the north. The name is derived from its proximity to Bullhead Rock, now largely concealed by the waters of Lake Mojave. Bullhead City is across the Colorado River from Laughlin, NV (see) and its casinos.

What to See and Do

Davis Dam and Power Plant. Dam (200 ft high, 1,600 ft long) impounds Lake Mohave, which has a surface area of 28,500 acres and reaches 67 river miles upstream to Hoover Dam. Self-guided tour through power plant (daily). 4 mi N on Colorado River. Phone 520/754-3628. **Free**

Fishing, camping. Trout, bass, bluegill, crappie and catfish. Campsites, picnic grounds at Katherine, 5 mi N, a part of the Lake Mead National Recreation Area (see NEVADA). Standard fees.

Motels

★★ **BEST WESTERN.** *1126 Hwy 95 (86430). 520/754-3000; FAX 520/754-5234; res: 800/634-4463.* Web www.bestwestern.com. 88 rms, 2 story. S, D $45-$75; higher rates special events. Crib free. Pet accepted; $5. TV; cable (premium). Pool; whirlpool. Complimentary continental bkfst. Restaurant nearby. Ck-out noon. Business servs avail. Refrigerators; microwaves avail. Cr cds: A, C, D, DS, ER, JCB, MC, V.

D SC

★ **LAKE MOHAVE RESORT.** *Katherines Lndg (86442), 6 mi NE, 3½ mi N of AZ 68, N of Davis Dam. 520/754-3245; FAX 520/754-1125; res: 800/752-9669.* 51 rms, 1-2 story, 14 kits. S, D $60; each addl $6; kit. units $83; under 5 free. Crib $6. Pet accepted, some restrictions; $5. Restaurant 7 am-9 pm mid-Apr-Nov. Bar 4-10 pm. Ck-out 11 am. Business servs avail. In-rm modem link. Boat rental. Private patios, balconies. Spacious grounds. View of lake. Cr cds: C, DS, MC, V.

D SC

✓★ **LODGE ON THE RIVER.** *1717 Hwy 95 (86503). 520/758-8080; FAX 520/758-8283; res: 888/200-7855.* 64 rms, 2 story, 13 suites. S $30-$65; D $35-$78; each addl $6; suites $49-$95; under 12 free; wkly rates. Crib $6. TV; cable. Pool. Complimentary continental bkfst. Restaurant nearby. Ck-out 11 am. Some refrigerators; microwaves avail. On river. Cr cds: A, C, D, DS, MC, V.

D SC

Restaurant

✓★ **EL ENCANTO MEXICAN RESTAURANT.** *1884 S Highway 95 (86442), at the River Queen Resort. 520/754-5100.* Hrs: 11 am-11 pm. Closed some major hols. Res accepted. Mexican, Amer menu. Bar. Semi-a la carte: lunch $3-$5.25, dinner $5.60-$10. Child's meals. Specializes in Mexican cuisine. Outdoor dining. Mexican decor. Cr cds: C, MC, V.

D

Canyon de Chelly National Monument (C-6)

(See also Ganado)

Information Superintendent, Box 588, Chinle 86503; 520/674-5500
(In NE corner of state at Chinle)

The smooth red sandstone walls of the canyon extend straight up as much as a thousand feet from the nearly flat sand bottom. When William of Normandy defeated the English at the Battle of Hastings in 1066, the Pueblo had already built apartment houses in these walls. Many ruins are still here.

The Navajo came long after the original tenants had abandoned these structures. In 1864, Kit Carson's men drove nearly all the Navajo out of the area, marching them on foot 300 miles to the Bosque Redondo in eastern New Mexico. Since 1868, Navajo have returned to farming, cultivating the orchards and grazing their sheep in the canyon. In 1931, Canyon de Chelly (pronounced "de-SHAY") and its tributaries, Canyon del Muerto and Monument Canyon, were designated a national monument.

There are more than 60 major ruins, some dating from circa A.D. 300, in these canyons. White House, Antelope House and Mummy Cave are among the most picturesque. Most ruins are inaccessible but can be seen from either the canyon bottom or from the road along the top of the precipitous walls. The two spectacular, 16-mile rim drives can be made by car in any season. Lookout points, sometimes a short distance from the road, are clearly marked. The only self-guided trail (2½-miles round trip) leads to the canyon floor and White House ruin from White House Overlook. Other hikes can be made only with a National Park Service permit and an authorized Navajo guide (fee). Only four-wheel drive vehicles are allowed in the canyons; each vehicle must be accompanied by an authorized Navajo guide (fee) and requires a National Park Service permit obtainable from a ranger at the visitor center.

The visitor center has an archaeological museum and rest rooms. (Daily; free) Rim drive guides and White House Trail guides at visitor center bookstore. Picnic areas and campgrounds (free).

What to See and Do

Canyon Tours. Offered by Thunderbird Lodge (see MOTELS). Lodge personnel conduct jeep tours into the canyons; half-day (daily) and full-day (Apr-Oct, daily) trips. Phone 520/674-5841 or 800/679-2473. ¢¢¢¢¢

Motels

★★ **BEST WESTERN CANYON DE CHELL.** *100 Main St Rte 7 (86503), 3 blks E of AZ 191. 520/674-5288; FAX 520/674-3715; res: 800/528-1234.* 99 rms. Early May-Oct: S $108; D $112; each addl $4; lower rates rest of yr. Crib free. TV; cable. Indoor pool. Complimentary coffee in rms. Restaurant 6:30 am-10 pm; Nov-Mar to 9 pm. Ck-out 11 am. Gift shop. Picnic tables. Navajo decor. Cr cds: A, C, D, DS, JCB, MC, V.

D SC

★★ **THUNDERBIRD LODGE.** *Hwy 191 & RT 7 (86503), 3 mi SE of AZ 191 at entrance to monument. 520/674-5841; FAX 520/674-5844; res: 800/679-2473.* 72 rms in motel, lodge. Mar-Oct: S $85-$90; D $89-$94; each addl $4; lower rates rest of yr. Crib $6. TV; cable. Restaurant 6:30 am-9 pm; winter hrs vary. Ck-out 11 am. Meeting rm. Business servs avail. Airport transportation. Canyon tours avail. Cr cds: A, C, D, DS, MC, V.

D SC

Motor Hotel

★★ **HOLIDAY INN.** *RT 7 Box 1889 (63102), adj to entrance of monument. 520/674-5000; FAX 520/674-8264; res: 800/465-4329.* 108 rms, 2 story. May-Oct: S, D $95-$115; under 18 free; lower rates rest of yr. Crib free. TV; cable (premium). Heated pool. Restaurant 6 am-2 pm, 5-10 pm; winter hrs vary. Rm serv. Ck-out noon. Meeting rm. Business servs avail. Sundries. Gift shop. Balconies. Cr cds: A, C, D, DS, JCB, MC, V.

D SC

Carefree (F-4)

(See also Chandler, Mesa, Phoenix, Scottsdale, Tempe)

Pop 1,666 **Elev** 2,389 ft **Area Code** 602 **Zip** 85377
Information Carefree/Cave Creek Chamber of Commerce, 748 Easy St, Marywood Plaza, Box 734; 602/488-3381

The immense Tonto National Forest (see PAYSON) stretches to the north and east; the Ranger District office for the forest's Cave Creek District is located here. Located in the center of town is the largest and most accurate sundial in the Western Hemisphere.

Annual Event

Fiesta Days. PRCA rodeo, parade. Usually 1st wkend Apr.

Resort

★★★★ **THE BOULDERS.** *34631 N Tom Darlington Dr (85377). 480/488-9009; FAX 480/488-4118; res: 800/553-1717.* Web www.slh.com/slh. Ribbons of brilliant green fairways accentuate the natural desert flora and giant boulders from which this magnificent resort takes its name. Southwestern art adorns the walls and punctuates the understated elegance of the large guestrooms. Golf, tennis, swimming, and a world famous spa are among the activities available to guests.160 casitas, 1-2 story; also patio homes. Mid-Jan-Apr & late Dec: S, D $565; each addl $25; under 18 free; MAP avail; lower rates rest of yr. Serv charge $18/day. Crib free. Pet accepted, some restrictions; $50 deposit. TV; cable (premium), VCR. 3 heated pools; whirlpool, poolside serv. Dining rms (public by res) 7-10:30 am, noon-2:30 pm, 6-9:30 pm (also see LATILLA). Box lunches, snack bar. Rm serv. Bar 11-1 am. Ck-out noon, ck-in 4 pm. Grocery, package store 2 blks. Coin lndry 2 mi. Meeting rms. Business center. In-rm modem link. Gift shop. Airport transportation. Tennis, pro. 36-hole golf, greens fee $185, pro, putting green, driving range. Entertainment. Exercise rm; sauna, steam rm. Massage. Minibars, fireplaces. Private patios. Cr cds: A, C, D, MC, V.

D

Inn

★★★ **GOTLANDS INN CAVE CREEK.** *38555 N Schoolhouse Rd (85327). 480/488-9636; FAX 480/488-6879.* E-mail gotlands@inficad; web www.unleash.com/gotlands. 4 kit. units. Jan-Apr: S, D $140-$195; each addl $25; 2-day min hols, wkends. Closed mid-June-Aug. TV; cable (premium), VCR (movies). Complimentary continental bkfst. Complimentary coffee in rms. Restaurant nearby. Ck-out 11 am, ck-in 4-6 pm. Luggage handling. Concierge serv. Business servs avail. In-rm modem link. Microwaves. Picnic tables. Totally nonsmoking. Cr cds: A, C, DS, MC, V.

Restaurants

✓★★ **CANTINA DEL PEDREGAL.** *34631 N Tom Darlington Dr # G2 (85602), at el Pedregal, E on Carefee Hwy. 602/488-0715.* Hrs: 11:30 am-10 pm. Closed Thanksgiving, Dec 25. Res accepted. Mexican menu. Bar. Semi-a la carte: lunch $6-$12.50, dinner $8-$15.95. Child's meals. Specialties: Mexican Gulf shrimp, fajitas, chili rellenos. Patio dining. Colorful decor. Cr cds: A, C, D, MC, V.

D ♥

★★★★ **LATILLA.** *(See Boulders Resort) 480/488-9009.* Web www.slh.com/slh. The unique Southwestern cooking with subtle Asian influences is at home in the comfortable dining room with rich Southwestern decor. The polished, accommodating service is in keeping with the rest of the resort (see Boulders Resort).Contemporary Southwestern menu. Specializes in rack of lamb, Pacific salmon, grilled sea scallops. Own baking. Hrs: 6:30-10:30 am, 6-9:30 pm; Sun brunch 11:30 am-2 pm. Bar 11-1 am. A la carte entrees: bkfst $6.50-$9.75, dinner $22-$40. Sun brunch $36. Entertainment. Outdoor dining. Jacket. Totally nonsmoking. Cr cds: A, C, D, MC, V.

D ♥

Casa Grande (G-4)

(See also Florence, Gila Bend, Phoenix)

Pop 19,082 **Elev** 1,405 ft **Area Code** 520 **Zip** 85222
E-mail chamber@casagrande.com **Web** www.casagrandechamber.org
Information Chamber of Commerce, 575 N Marshall St; 520/836-2125 or 800/916-1515

Named for the Hohokam ruins 20 miles northeast of town, Casa Grande is situated in an agricultural and industrial area.

What to See and Do

Casa Grande Ruins National Monument (see). Approx 14 mi E on AZ 84, 287, then 9 mi N on AZ 87.

Casa Grande Valley Historical Society & Museum. Exhibits tracing Casa Grande Valley growth from prehistoric times to present with emphasis on farm, ranch, mining and domestic life. Gift shop. (Mid-Sept-Memorial Day wkend, daily exc Mon; closed major hols) 110 W Florence Blvd. Phone 520/836-2223. ¢

Factory outlet stores. Two different outlet malls: Factory Stores of America, 440 N Camino Mercado; phone 602/986-7616 and Tanger Factory Outlet Center, 2300 E Tanger Dr; 520/836-9663.

Picacho Peak State Park. This 3,400-acre park includes a sheer-sided peak rising 1,500 ft above the desert floor, which was a landmark for early travelers. The only Civil War battle in Arizona was fought near here. Colorful spring wildflowers; desert nature study. Hiking. Picnicking (shelter). Interpretive center programs (seasonal). 24 mi SE off I-10, Picacho Peak exit. Phone 520/466-3183. Per vehicle ¢¢

Annual Event

O'Odham Tash-Casa Grande's Indian Days. Rodeo, parades, ceremonial dances, arts & crafts, chicken scratch dance & bands; Native American foods, barbecue. Res advised. Phone 520/836-4723. Mid-Feb.

Resort

★★ **FRANCISCO GRANDE RESORT & GOLF CLUB.** *26000 W Gila Bend Hwy (85222), 4 mi W via AZ 84. 520/836-6444; FAX 520/836-5855; res: 800/237-4238.* E-mail sales@casagrande.com; web www.franciscogrande.com. 112 units, 8 story. Jan-Apr: S, D $109-$159; each addl $15; suites $189-$219; kits. $250; under 18 free; golf package plans; lower rates rest of yr. Pet accepted, some restrictions; $25. TV; cable (premium), VCR avail. Heated pool; wading pool, poolside serv. Coffee in rms. Dining rm 6:30 am-9 pm; Fri, Sat to 10 pm. Rm serv. Box lunches. Snack bar. Picnics. Bar 10-1 am, Sun from noon. Ck-out noon, ck-in 3 pm. Meeting rms. Business servs avail. Valet serv. Tennis. 18-hole golf, greens fee $55-$65 (incl cart), pro, putting green, driving range. Exercise equipt. Lawn games. Entertainment. Microwaves avail. Some balconies. Cr cds: A, C, D, MC, V.

D SC

Casa Grande Ruins National Monument (F-4)

(See also Casa Grande, Chandler, Florence, Phoenix)

(33 mi SE of Chandler on AZ 87, 1 mi N of Coolidge)

The Hohokam people existed in the Salt and Gila river valleys for hundreds of years before abandoning the region sometime before 1450. They built irrigation canals in order to grow beans, corn, squash and cotton. Casa Grande (Big House) was built during the 14th century.

Casa Grande was constructed of *caliche*-bearing soil (a crust of calcium carbonate on stony soil) and is four stories high (although the first story was filled in with dirt). The top story probably provided an excellent view of the surrounding country and may have been used for astronomical observations.

After being occupied for some 100 years, Casa Grande was abandoned. Father Kino, the Jesuit missionary and explorer, sighted and named it Big House in 1694.

Casa Grande is the only structure of its type and size in southern Arizona. It is covered by a large protective roof. There is a museum with archaeological exhibits (daily); self-guided tours. For further information contact Superintendent, 1100 Ruins Dr, Coolidge 85228; 520/723-3172. ¢

Chandler (F-4)

(See also Mesa, Phoenix, Scottsdale, Tempe)

Pop 90,533 **Elev** 1,213 ft **Area Code** 480 **Web** www.chandlerchamber.com

Information Chamber of Commerce, 218 N Arizona Ave, 85225; 480/963-4571 or 800/963-4571

Cotton, citrus fruits, pecans and sugar beets are grown in the surrounding area. A growing number of high-technology companies have facilities here including Intel, Motorola and Microchip Technologies.

What to See and Do

Casa Grande Ruins National Monument (see). 33 mi SE on AZ 87.

Gila River Arts & Crafts Center. Gallery featuring the works of outstanding Native American artists and artisans from more than 30 tribes. Restaurant features Native American food. Museum preserves cultural heritage of Pima and Maricopa tribes. Gila Heritage Park features five Native American villages. (Daily; closed major hols) 15 mi S via AZ 93 at jct I-10 (exit 175), on Gila River Indian Reservation. Phone 480/963-3981. **Free**

Seasonal Events

Chandler Ostrich Festival. Features ostrich racing, food, entertainment and arts & crafts. Early Mar.

ASA Amateur Softball National Tournament. Phone 480/782-2000. Sept.

Motel

★ **FAIRFIELD INN.** *7425 W Chandler Blvd (85226). 602/940-0099; FAX 602/940-7336; res: 800/228-2800.* 66 rms, 3 story, 18 suites. Jan-Apr: S $94.95; D $104.95; suites $104.95-$114.95; higher rates Fiesta Bowl; lower rates rest of yr. Crib free. TV; cable (premium). Heated pool; whirlpool. Complimentary continental bkfst. Restaurant nearby. Ck-out noon. Business servs avail. Coin lndry. Some refrigerators; microwaves avail. Cr cds: A, C, D, DS, MC, V.

D SC

Motor Hotels

★★ **HAMPTON INN.** *7333 W Detroit St (85226). 602/753-5200; FAX 602/753-5100.* 101 rms, 6 story. Jan-Mar: S $119; D $129; under 18 free; lower rates rest of yr. Crib free. TV; cable (premium). Complimentary continental bkfst. Complimentary coffee in rms. Restaurant adj open 24 hrs. Ck-out noon. Meeting rms. Business servs avail. In-rm modem link. Pool; whirlpool. Some in-rm whirlpools. Cr cds: A, C, D, DS, MC, V.

D SC

★★★ **WYNDHAM GARDEN HOTEL.** *7475 W Chandler Blvd (85226). 602/961-4444; FAX 602/940-0269; res: 800/996-3426.* 159 rms, 4 story, 19 suites. Mid-Jan-mid-May: S, D $129-$159; each addl $10; suites $149-$169; lower rates rest of yr. TV; cable. Heated pool; whirlpool, poolside serv. Coffee in rms. Restaurant 6:30 am-2 pm, 5-10 pm. Rm serv. Bar 4-11 pm. Ck-out noon. Coin lndry. Meeting rms. Business servs avail. Valet serv. Exercise equipt. Health club privileges. Some refrigerators. Cr cds: A, C, D, DS, ER, JCB, MC, V.

D SC

Resort

★★★ **SHERATON SAN MARCOS GOLF RESORT.** *One San Marcos Pl (85224), S of Arizona Ave, 1 blk W on Buffalo. 480/963-6655; FAX 480/963-6777; res: 800/528-8071.* E-mail ssmarcos@primenet.com; web www.sanmarcosresort.com. 295 rms, 4 story. Jan-May: S, D $225, suites $295; each addl $10; under 18 free; wkend, hol rates; golf plans; lower rates rest of yr. Crib free. Pet accepted; $50 deposit. TV; cable (premium). Complimentary coffee in rms. Restaurant 6:30 am-10 pm. Box lunches, snack bar, picnics. Rm serv 24 hrs. Bar 11-1 am. Ck-out noon, ck-in 3 pm. Grocery 1 blk. Coin lndry 2 blks. Package store 1 blk. Convention facilities. Business center. Bellhops. Valet serv. Concierge. Shopping arcade. Barber, beauty shop. Sports dir. Lighted tennis, pro. 18-hole golf, greens fee $90 with cart, pro, putting green, driving range. Bicycle rentals. Exercise equipt. Health club privileges. Pool; wading pool, whirlpool, poolside serv. Many balconies. Cr cds: A, C, D, DS, ER, JCB, MC, V.

D SC

Restaurants

✓★★ **C-FU GOURMET.** *2051 W Warner Rd (85224). 602/899-3888.* Hrs: 10 am-2:30 pm, 4:30-9:30 pm. Res accepted. Chinese menu. Bar. Semi-a la carte: lunch $5-$9, dinner $10-$25. Specializes in seafood, dim sum. Chinese decor. Live seafood tanks. Cr cds: A, C, D, DS, MC, V.

D

✓★ **YAMAKASA RESTAURANT.** *2051 W Warner Rd (85224). 602/899-8868.* Hrs: 11:30 am-2 pm, 5:30-10 pm; Sun 5-8:30 pm. Closed Mon; Thanksgiving, Dec 25. Res accepted (dinner). Japanese menu. Serv bar. Semi-a la carte: lunch $4.95-$9.95, dinner $11-$19.80. Specialties: sushi, tataki salad, saikyo yaki. Live seafood tank. Totally nonsmoking. Cr cds: A, C, D, DS, MC, V.

D

Chiricahua National Monument (H-6)

(See also Willcox)

(32 mi SE of Willcox on AZ 186, then 3 mi E on AZ 181)

This national monument features 20 square miles of picturesque natural rock sculptures and deep twisting canyons.

The Chiricahua (Cheer-a-CAH-wah) Apaches hunted in the Chiricahua Mountain range. Cochise, Geronimo, "Big Foot" Massai and other well-known Apaches undoubtedly found their way into this region during the 1870s and 1880s. A visitor center, two miles from the entrance, has geological, zoological and historical displays. (Daily) Per person (walk-in) **¢**; Per vehicle **¢¢**

At Massai Point Overlook, geologic exhibits explain the volcanic origin of the monument. The road up Bonita Canyon leads to a number of other outlook points; there are also 20 miles of excellent day-use trails to points of special interest.

Picnicking and camping sites are located within the national monument. Campground/night **¢¢¢**; 26-foot limit on trailers. For further information contact Superintendent, HCR #2, Box 6500, Willcox 85643; 520/824-3560.

Clifton (F-6)

(See also Safford)

Settled 1872 **Pop** 2,840 **Elev** 3,468 ft **Area Code** 520 **Zip** 85533

The scenic Coronado Trail (US 666) begins here and continues north 90 miles to Alpine. The Apache National Forest (see SHOW LOW) stretches north and east of Clifton; the Clifton Ranger District office of the Apache-Sitgreaves National Forest is located here.

What to See and Do

Old Jail & Locomotive. Jail blasted out of mountainside; first occupied by the man who built it. S Coronado Blvd.

Cottonwood (D-3)

(See also Flagstaff, Prescott, Sedona)

Pop 5,918 **Elev** 3,314 ft **Area Code** 520 **Zip** 86326
Information Chamber of Commerce, 1010 S Main St; 520/634-7593

This town is in the beautiful Verde Valley, an area offering many opportunities for exploration.

What to See and Do

Dead Horse Ranch State Park. This 320-acre park offers fishing, nature trails, hiking. Picnicking (shelter). Camping (dump station). Visitor center. Standard fees. At Verde River, N of town on 10th St. Phone 520/634-5283.

Fort Verde State Historic Park. Four original buildings of US Army fort, a major base during the campaigns of 1865-1890; museum; two furnished officers' quarters; post doctor's quarters; military artifacts. Picnicking. (Daily; closed Dec 25) 15 mi SE on AZ 279/260 in town of Camp Verde. Phone 520/567-3275. ¢

Jerome. Historic old copper-mining town with cobblestone streets and renovated structures now housing gift, jewelry, antique and pottery shops, art galleries, restaurants and hotels. Views of Verde Valley and the Mogollon Rim. 8 mi W on US 89A, 3,200-5,200 ft almost straight up. For information phone 520/634-2900. Also in Jerome is

Jerome State Historic Park. Douglas Memorial Mining Museum depicts history of Jerome, mining in Arizona; housed in former house of "Rawhide" Jimmy Douglas (fee). Picnicking. No overnight facilities. (Daily; closed Dec 25) Off US 89A. Phone 520/634-5381. ¢

Montezuma Castle National Monument (see). 20 mi SE on AZ 260, then N & E off I-17.

Tuzigoot National Monument. Excavated pueblo occupied from A.D. 1000-1450. Visitor center, museum with artifacts of Sinagua culture. (Daily) 2 mi NW via N Main St, follow signs. Phone 520/634-5564. ¢

Verde Canyon Railroad. Scenic excursion train takes passengers through the Verde Canyon on a 4-hr round trip from Clarkdale to Perkinsville. Panoramic views of rugged, high-desert area; Verde River; Native American ruins. Some open-air viewing cars. Starlight rides (summer). (Daily, schedule varies; closed Jan 1, Thanksgiving, Dec 25) 2 mi NW via US 89A. Contact 300 N Broadway, Clarkdale 86324; phone 520/639-0010 or 800/293-7245. ¢¢¢¢

Annual Events

Verde Valley Fair. Fairgrounds. 4th wkend Apr.

Paseo de Casas. In Jerome. Tour of unique old homes. 3rd wkend May.

Fort Verde Days. In Camp Verde. Parade, dancing, barbecue, reenactments. 2nd wkend Oct.

Motels

★★ **BEST WESTERN COTTONWOOD INN.** *993 S Main St (85222). 520/634-5575; FAX 520/634-5576; res: 800/528-1234; res: 800/350-0025.* E-mail cottonwoodinn@verdenet.com; web www.cottonwoodinn-az.com. 77 rms, 2 story. Mar-Oct: S, D $69-$109; each addl $6; suites $89-$109; under 12 free; lower rates rest of yr. Crib free. TV; cable. Heated pool; whirlpool. Complimentary continental bkfst. Coffee in rms. Restaurant 6 am-10 pm. Rm serv. Ck-out 11 am. Coin lndry. Meeting rm. Business servs avail. Some refrigerators. Cr cds: A, C, D, DS, MC, V.

D SC

★ **QUALITY INN.** *301 W Hwy 89-A (86004). 520/634-4207; FAX 520/634-5764; res: 800/228-5151.* 51 rms, 2 story. May-mid-Sept: S $66; D $78; each addl $5; under 18 free; lower rates rest of yr. Crib free. TV; cable (premium). Heated pool; whirlpool. Complimentary continental bkfst. Coffee in rms. Restaurant 11 am-9 pm. Bar. Ck-out 11 am. Meeting rms. Business servs avail. Cr cds: A, C, D, DS, MC, V.

D SC

Douglas (H-6)

(See also Bisbee)

Founded 1901 **Pop** 12,822 **Elev** 3,990 ft **Area Code** 520 **Zip** 85607
Information Chamber of Commerce, 1125 Pan American; 520/364-2477

Located on the Mexican border, this diversified manufacturing town is a warm, sunny place abounding in Western hospitality. A Ranger District office of the Coronado National Forest (see TUCSON) is located here.

What to See and Do

Agua Prieta, Sonora, Mexico, is just across the border. (For border crossing regulations, see MAKING THE MOST OF YOUR TRIP.) It is a pleasant place with shops, a historical museum of the days of Pancho Villa, restaurants and cabarets.

Annual Events

Cinco de Mayo. Mexican independence festival. Early May.

Douglas Fiestas. Mid-Sept.

Cochise County Fair & College Rodeo. Cochise County Fairgrounds. 3rd wkend Sept.

Seasonal Event

Horse races. Cochise County Fairgrounds, N on Leslie Canyon Rd. Mid-Apr-mid-Sept.

Flagstaff (D-4)

(See also Cottonwood, Sedona, Williams, Winslow)

Settled 1876 **Pop** 45,857 **Elev** 6,910 ft **Area Code** 520
E-mail visitor@flagstaff.az.us **Web** www.flagstaff.az.us
Information Visitors Center, 1 E Rte 66, 86001-5598, phone 520/774-9541 or 800/842-7293; or the Chamber of Commerce, 101 W Rte 66, 86001, phone 520-774-4505

In 1876, the Boston Party, a group of men who had been lured west, made camp in a mountain valley on the Fourth of July. They stripped a pine tree of its branches and hung a flag at its top. Afterward, the tree was used as a marker for travelers who referred to the place as the spring by the flag staff. In 1882, Flagstaff became a railroad town when the Atlantic and Pacific Railroad (now the Santa Fe) was built.

Flagstaff, home of Northern Arizona University (1899), is an educational and cultural center. Tourism is Flagstaff's main industry; the city is a good place to see the Navajo country, Oak Creek Canyon, the Grand Canyon (see) and Humphreys Peak (12,670 ft), the tallest mountain in Arizona, 14 miles north. Tall pine forests of great beauty abound in the surrounding area. A Ranger District Office of the Coconino National Forest is located here.

What to See and Do

Arizona Historical Society Pioneer Museum. History of northern Arizona. (Daily exc Sun; closed hols) 2½ mi NW on Fort Valley Rd (US 180). Phone 520/774-6272. **Free**

Arizona Snowbowl Ski & Summer Resort. Resort has 2 triple, 2 double chairlifts; patrol, school, rentals; restaurants, lounge; 2-day lodges. 32 trails, longest run over 2 mi; vertical drop 2,300 ft. (Mid-Dec-Mar, daily) Skyride (Memorial Day-Labor Day; fee) takes riders to 11,500-ft elevation. 7 mi NW off US 180 at Snowbowl Rd in Coconino National Forest. Phone 520/779-1951. **¢¢¢¢¢**

Coconino National Forest. Surrounds city of Flagstaff and the community of Sedona (see). Outstanding scenic areas include Humphreys Peak, Arizona's highest point; parts of the Mogollon Rim and the Verde River Valley; the red rock country of Sedona and Oak Creek Canyon, where Zane Grey wrote *Call of the Canyon;* the San Francisco Peaks; seven wilderness areas; the eastern portions of Sycamore Canyon and Kendrick wilderness areas and the northern portion of Mazatzal Wilderness area; extinct volcanoes; high country lakes. Fishing, hunting on almost 2 million acres. Winter sports. Picnicking. Camping (fee). Standard fees. Phone 520/527-3600.

Lowell Observatory. Established by Percival Lowell in 1894; the planet Pluto was discovered here in 1930. Guided tours; slide presentations; telescope viewing (seasonal). Museum, gift shop. Telescope domes are unheated; appropriate clothing advised. 1 mi W on Mars Hill Rd, off Santa Fe Ave. For hrs phone 520/774-2096. **¢¢**

Mormon Lake Ski Center. Terrain includes snowy meadows, huge stands of pine, oak and aspen, old logging roads and turn-of-the-century railroad grades. School. Has 19 mi of marked, groomed trails; restaurant, bar; motel, cabins. Rentals. Guided tours. 28 mi SE off Lake Mary Rd on Mormon Lake Rd. Phone 520/354-2240. **¢¢¢**

Museum of Northern Arizona. Exhibits on the archaeology, geology, biology, paleontology and fine arts of the Colorado Plateau; displays on contemporary Native American cultures of northern Arizona. Arts and crafts shop; bookstore. Research center. (Daily; closed Jan 1, Thanksgiving, Dec 25) 3 mi NW on US 180 (Fort Valley Rd). Phone 520/774-5213. **¢¢**

Oak Creek Canyon. This spectacular gorge may look familiar to you. It's a favorite location for western movies. The northern end of the road starts with a lookout point atop the walls and descends nearly 2,000 ft to the stream bed. The creek has excellent trout fishing. At the southern mouth of the canyon is Sedona (see), a resort town. 14 mi S on US 89A.

Riordan State Historic Park. Features a mansion built in 1904 by Michael and Timothy Riordan. The brothers played a significant role in the development of Flagstaff and northern Arizona. Original artifacts, handcrafted furniture, mementos. Picnic area; no overnight facilities. Guided tours. (Daily; closed Thanksgiving, Dec 24, 25) W on I-40, exit Flagstaff/Grand Canyon, then N on Milton Rd; turn right at sign past 2nd light. Phone 520/779-4395. **¢¢**

Sunset Crater Volcano National Monument (see). 15 mi N on US 89.

Walnut Canyon National Monument. A spectacular, rugged 400-ft-deep canyon with 300 small cliff dwellings dating back to around A.D. 1100. The dwellings are well-preserved because they are under protective ledges in the canyon's limestone walls. There are 2 self-guided trails and an educational museum in the visitor center. Picnic grounds. (Daily; closed Dec 25) 7 mi E on I-40 (US 66), 3 mi off exit 204. Phone 520/526-3367. **¢**

Wupatki National Monument (see). 30 mi N on US 89.

Annual Events

Winter Festival. Features art contest and exhibit; theater performances; workshops; sled dog and other races, games; Winterfaire, with arts and crafts; entertainment. Feb.

Zuni Artists' Exhibition. The Museum of Northern Arizona. Five days beginning Sat before Memorial Day.

Hopi Artists' Exhibition. The Museum of Northern Arizona. Late June-early July.

Navajo Artists' Exhibition. The Museum of Northern Arizona. Last wkend July-1st wkend Aug.

Flagstaff Festival of the Arts. Northern Arizona Univ campus, SW edge of city. Symphonic/pops concerts, chamber music; theater; dance; art exhibits; poetry; film classics. Phone 520/774-7750 or 800/266-7740. July-early Aug.

Coconino County Fair. Phone 520/774-5139. Labor Day wkend.

Motels

★ **ARIZONA MOUNTAIN INN.** *4200 Lake Mary Rd (86001), near Pulliam Field Airport. 520/774-8959; FAX 520/774-8837; res: 800/239-5236.* 20 units, 1-4 story, 17 kit. cottages, 3 suites. No A/C. No elvtr. No rm phones. S, D $75-$105; each addl $10; suites $90-$110; wkly rates. Pet accepted, some restrictions. Playground. Ck-out 11 am. Coin lndry. Business servs avail. Downhill/x-country ski 14 mi. Fireplaces. Porches. Picnic tables, grills. Rustic atmosphere. Cr cds: C, DS, MC, V.

D

✓★★ **BEST WESTERN PONY SOLDIER MOTEL.** *3030 E Rte 66 (86001). 520/526-2388; FAX 520/527-8329; res: 800/528-1234.* E-mail bwponyso@flagstaff.az.us. 90 rms, 2 story. Apr-Oct: S, D $69-$89; each addl $5; suites $99; under 18 free; lower rates rest of yr. Crib $5. TV; cable (premium). Indoor pool. Complimentary continental bkfst. Restaurant 11 am-9 pm; Fri, Sat to 10 pm. Ck-out 11 am. Business servs avail. Gift shop. Downhill ski 15 mi. Cr cds: A, C, D, DS, JCB, MC, V.

SC

★★ **COMFORT INN.** *914 S Milton Rd (86001), 1 mi N of I-40 exit 195B. 520/774-7326; FAX 520/774-7328; res: 800/228-5150.* 67 rms, 2 story. June-Aug: S, D $69-$95; each addl $5; under 19 free; lower rates rest of yr. Crib $2. Pet accepted, some restrictions. TV; cable (premium). Heated pool. Complimentary coffee. Restaurant nearby. Ck-out 11 am. Downhill ski 15 mi. Cr cds: A, C, D, DS, ER, MC, V.

D SC

★★ **DAYS INN.** *1000 W Rte 66 (86001). 520/774-5221; FAX 520/774-4977; res: 800/329-7466.* 157 rms, 2 story. Mid-June-mid-Sept: S, D $72-$82; under 18 free; higher rates: hols, special events; lower rates rest of yr. Crib free. Pet accepted, some restrictions. TV; cable (premium). Complimentary coffee in lobby. Restaurant 6-10 am, 5-9 pm. Bar from 5 pm. Ck-out 1 pm. Meeting rms. Business servs avail. Bellhops. Valet serv. Sundries. Gift shop. Coin lndry. Health club privileges. Pool. Cr cds: A, C, D, DS, ER, JCB, MC, V.

D SC

★ **DAYS INN-EAST.** *3601 E Lockett Rd (86004). 520/527-1477; FAX 520/527-0228.* 52 rms, 3 story. Mid-Mar-Oct: S, D $49-$99; under 18 free; higher rates: hols, special events; lower rates rest of yr. Crib free. TV; cable. Indoor pool. Complimentary continental bkfst. Restaurant adj 6 am-11 pm. Ck-out 11 am. Coin lndry. Business servs avail. Some refrigerators. Cr cds: A, C, D, DS, MC, V.

D SC

★★ **FAIRFIELD INN BY MARRIOTT.** *2005 S Milton Rd (86001). 520/773-1300; FAX 520/773-1462; res: 800/228-2800.* 135 rms, 3 story. Mid-May-Oct: S, D $65-$89; under 18 free; lower rates rest of yr. Crib free. TV; cable (premium). Pool. Complimentary continental bkfst. Ck-out noon. Meeting rm. Business servs avail. In-rm modem link. Downhill/x-country ski 15 mi. Health club privileges. Cr cds: A, C, D, DS, MC, V.

D SC

★★ **HAMPTON INN.** *3501 E Lockett Rd (86004). 520/526-1885; FAX 520/526-9885; res: 888/222-2052.* Web www.hamptoninn.com. 50 rms, 3 story. Mid-May-Sept: S, D $69-$99; under 18 free; higher rates: hols, special events; lower rates rest of yr. Crib free. TV; cable (premium).

Complimentary continental bkfst. Coffee in rms. Restaurant nearby. Business servs avail. Downhill ski 15 mi. Indoor pool; whirlpool. . Cr cds: A, C, D, DS, MC, V.

D SC

★★★ **HILTON GARDEN INN.** *350 W Forest Meadows St (86001). 520/226-8888; FAX 520/556-9059; res: 800/333-0785.* Web www.hilton.com. 90 rms, 3 story. May-Oct: S, D $89-$129; each addl $10; under 18 free; package plans; higher rates special events; lower rates rest of yr. Crib free. TV; cable (premium). Complimentary coffee in rms. Restaurant adj 6:30 am-10 pm. Rm serv 11 am-10 pm. Ck-out 1 pm. Meeting rms. Business servs avail. In-rm modem link. Valet serv. Coin lndry. Lighted tennis privileges. 18-hole golf privileges, greens fee $45-$55, pro, putting green, driving range. Downhill/x-country ski 15 mi. Exercise equipt. Indoor pool; whirlpool. Refrigerators, microwaves. Cr cds: A, C, D, DS, ER, MC, V.

D

★ **QUALITY INN.** *2000 S Milton Rd (86001). 520/774-8771; FAX 520/773-9382; res: 800/228-5151.* Web www.qualityinn.com. 96 rms, 2 story. June-Aug: S, D $79-$129; each addl $5; under 18 free; lower rates rest of yr. Crib free. TV; cable. Heated pool. Coffee in rms. Restaurant adj open 24 hrs. Ck-out 11 am. Business servs avail. Downhill ski 15 mi. Cr cds: A, C, D, DS, ER, JCB, MC, V.

D SC

★ **RAMADA INN.** *2755 Woodlands Village Blvd (85337). 520/773-1111; FAX 520/774-1449; res: 800/272-6232.* 90 suites, 2 story. May-Sept: S, D $59-$100; each addl $10; under 17 free; lower rates rest of yr. Crib free. Pet accepted; $25 refundable. TV; cable (premium), VCR avail. Heated pool; whirlpool. Complimentary continental bkfst. Restaurant nearby. Ck-out 11 am. Coin lndry. Meeting rms. Business servs avail. Sundries. Exercise equipt; sauna. Refrigerators, microwaves. Cr cds: A, C, D, DS, ER, JCB, MC, V.

D SC

Motor Hotels

★★ **AMERISUITES.** *2455 S Beulah Blvd (86004), I-40 exit 195B. 520/774-8042; FAX 520/774-5524.* Web www.canyon-country.com. 117 kit. suites, 5 story. May-Sept: S $109-$149; D $119-$159; each addl $10; under 18 free; ski plans; higher rates special events; lower rates rest of yr. Crib free. Pet accepted, some restrictions; $20. TV; cable (premium), VCR (movies). Indoor pool; whirlpool. Complimentary continental bkfst. Complimentary coffee in rms. Ck-out noon. Coin lndry. Business center. In-rm modem link. Valet serv. Free airport, RR station, bus depot transportation. Downhill/x-country ski 15 mi. Exercise equipt. Cr cds: A, C, D, DS, ER, JCB, MC, V.

D SC

★★★ **EMBASSY SUITES.** *706 S Milton Rd (86001). 520/774-4333; FAX 520/774-0216; res: 800/362-2779.* E-mail embassyflagstaff@thecanyon.com; web www.thecanyon.com/embassy flagstaff. 119 suites, 3 story. Mid-Apr-mid-Sept: suites $109-$164; each addl $10; ski, hol rates; lower rates rest of yr. Pet accepted, some restrictions; $25. TV; cable (premium). Heated pool; whirlpool. Complimentary full bkfst. Coffee in rms. Restaurant adj 11:30 am-10 pm. Rm serv 5-9 pm. Ck-out 1 pm. Meeting rms. Business servs avail. In-rm modem link. Gift shop. Game rm. Downhill ski 12 mi. Exercise equipt. Refrigerators, microwaves. Picnic tables. Cr cds: A, C, D, DS, ER, JCB, MC, V.

D

★★ **HAMPTON INN & SUITES.** *2400 S Beulah Blvd (86001). 520/913-0900; FAX 520/913-0800; res: 800/426-7866.* Web www.hampton-inn.com. 126 rms, 5 story, 39 suites, 33 kit. units. June-Sept: S, D $69-$109; suites, kit. units $89-$139; under 18 free; hols (2-3 day min); higher rates graduation; lower rates rest of yr. Crib free. Pet accepted. TV; cable (premium). Complimentary continental bkfst. Complimentary coffee in rms. Restaurant adj 10 am-10 pm. Ck-out noon. Meeting rms. Business servs avail. In-rm modem link. Bellhops. Valet serv. Sundries. Coin lndry. Downhill/x-country ski 15 mi. Exercise rm. Indoor pool; whirlpool. Many fireplaces; some in-rm whirlpools; refrigerator, microwave in suites. Cr cds: A, C, D, DS, MC, V.

D

★★ **HOLIDAY INN FLAGSTAFF.** *2320 Lucky Ln (86001). 520/526-1150; FAX 520/779-2610; res: 800/533-2754.* E-mail hiflag@aol.com. 157 rms, 5 story. Mid-May-mid-Oct: S, D $59-$119; each addl $10; under 18 free; lower rates rest of yr. Crib free. Pet accepted. TV; cable. Indoor pool; whirlpool. Coffee in rms. Restaurant 6-10 am, 5-10 pm. Rm serv. Bar 4 pm-1 am. Ck-out noon. Coin lndry. Meeting rms. In-rm modem link. Bellhops. Valet serv. Downhill ski 11 mi. Cr cds: A, C, D, DS, JCB, MC, V.

D SC

★ **HOWARD JOHNSON HOTEL.** *2200 E Butler Ave (86004), I-40 exit 198. 520/779-6944; FAX 520/774-3990; res: 800/446-4656.* Web www.traveler.net/htio/custom/service/0430.html. 100 rms, 3 story. June-Oct: S, D $79-$119; under 18 free; ski plans; higher rates special events; lower rates rest of yr. Crib free. Pet accepted, some restrictions. TV; cable, VCR avail. Indoor pool; whirlpool. Sauna. Coffee in rms. Restaurant open 24 hrs. Rm serv 7 am-10 pm. Bar 4:30 pm-1 am. Ck-out noon. Business servs avail. Bellhops. Sundries. Free airport, RR station, bus depot transportation. Downhill/x-country ski 15 mi. Game rm. Some refrigerators. Some balconies, patios. Cr cds: A, C, D, DS, ER, JCB, MC, V.

D SC

★★★ **LITTLE AMERICA HOTEL.** *2515 E Butler Ave (86003). 520/779-2741; FAX 520/779-7983; res: 800/352-4386.* Web www.lamerica.com/flagstaff.html. 248 rms, 2 story. May-Oct: S, D $109-$119; each addl $10; suites $119-$195; under 12 free; lower rates rest of yr. Crib free. TV; cable (premium), VCR avail. Heated pool; lifeguard. Playground. Restaurant open 24 hrs. Rm serv 6 am-11 pm; Fri, Sat to midnight. Bar 11-1 am; entertainment. Ck-out 1 pm. Coin lndry. Meeting rms. In-rm modem link. Valet serv. Concierge. Gift shop. Sundries. Tennis privileges. Golf privileges. Downhill ski 15 mi. Exercise equipt. Lawn games. Refrigerators; some fireplaces. Cr cds: A, C, D, DS, MC, V.

D

★★ **RADISSON WOODLANDS HOTEL.** *1175 W US Hwy 66 (86001). 520/773-8888; FAX 520/773-0597; res: 800/333-3333.* Web www.radisson.com. 183 rms, 4 story, 15 suites. Memorial Day-Mid-Oct: S, D $109-$119; each addl $8; suites $119-$129; under 12 free; ski plans; lower rates rest of yr. Crib $6. TV; cable (premium). Heated pool; whirlpool. Coffee in rms. Restaurant (see SAKURA). Rm serv. Bar. Ck-out noon. Coin lndry. Meeting rms. Business servs avail. In-rm modem link. Sundries. Gift shop. Downhill/x-country ski 11 mi. Exercise equipt; sauna. Microwaves avail. Refrigerator in suites. Cr cds: A, C, D, DS, MC, V.

D SC

Inns

★★★ **INN AT 410 BED & BREAKFAST.** *410 N Leroux St (86001). 520/774-0088; FAX 520/774-6354; res: 800/774-2008.* Web www.bbonline.com/az/at410. 9 rms, 1 with shower only, 2 story, 4 suites. No rm phones. S, D, suites $125-$175; each addl $10; min stay wkends, hols. Complimentary full bkfst; afternoon refreshments. Coffee in rms. Restaurant nearby. Ck-out 11 am, ck-in 4-6 pm. Concierge serv. Downhill ski 14 mi; x-country ski 7 mi. Refrigerators. Picnic tables. Built in 1907; antiques. Fireplaces. Totally nonsmoking. Cr cds: C, MC, V.

D

★★ **LAKE MARY BED & BREAKFAST.** *574 Lake Mary Rd (86001). 520/779-7054; FAX 520/779-7054; res: 888/241-9550.* Web www.bbonlinelkmary.com. 4 rms, 2 with shower only. No A/C. S, D $80; each addl $15; under 6 free. Crib free. TV in some rms; cable (premium), VCR avail (movies). Complimentary full bkfst. Restaurant nearby. Ck-out 11 am, ck-in 4-6 pm. Business servs avail. Luggage handling. Concierge serv. Free airport, RR station transportation. Some refrigerators; microwaves avail. Built in 1930; house moved from Jerome, AZ. Totally nonsmoking. Cr cds: C, MC, V.

Restaurants

★★ **BUSTER'S RESTAURANT & BAR.** *1800 S Milton Rd (86001). 520/774-5155.* Hrs: 11:30 am-10 pm; early bird dinner 4:30-6:30 pm. Closed Thanksgiving, Dec 25. Res accepted. Bar to 1 am. Semi-a la carte: lunch $5.50-$8.95, dinner $9.95-$18.95. Child's meals. Specializes in fresh fish, mesquite-grilled beef or chicken. Oyster bar. Casual dining. Cr cds: A, C, D, DS, MC, V.

D

★★★ **CHEZ MARC BISTRO.** *503 Humphreys St (86001). 520/774-1343.* E-mail dine@chezmarc.com; web www.chezmarc.com. Hrs: 11:30 am-3 pm, 5-9 pm; Fri, Sat to 10 pm (in season). Res required. French menu. Bar. Wine list. Semi-a la carte: lunch $5.50-$13.95, dinner $12.95-$29.95. Specialties: sterling salmon, trilogy of squab, duck confit. Outdoor dining. Country French bistro atmosphere. Cr cds: A, C, D, DS, MC, V.

D

★★ **COTTAGE PLACE.** *126 W Cottage Ave (86001). 520/774-8431.* Web www.tourists.com/cottage. Hrs: 5-9:30 pm. Closed Mon. Res accepted. No A/C. Continental menu. Wine, beer. Semi-a la carte: dinner $15-$25. Child's meals. Specialties: châteaubriand, scallops en croute, lamb chops. Own desserts. Intimate dining in 1908 cottage. Former residence of town mayor. Cr cds: A, C, MC, V.

D

★ **FIDDLER'S.** *702 Milton Rd (86001). 520/774-6689.* Hrs: 7 am-9 pm; Fri, Sat to 10 pm. Closed some major hols. Res accepted. Bar 2-9 pm; Fri-Sun to 10 pm. Semi-a la carte: bkfst, lunch, dinner $3.95-$28. Child's meals. Specializes in steaks, barbecue. Cr cds: A, C, MC, V.

D

✓★ **KACHINA DOWNTOWN.** *522 E Rte 66 (86001). 520/779-1944.* Hrs: 11 am-9 pm; Sun to 8 pm. Closed some major hols. Res accepted. Mexican menu. Bar. Semi-a la carte: lunch, dinner $4.25-$16.50. Specializes in fajitas, chimichangas. Cantina decor. Cr cds: A, C, D, DS, JCB, MC, V.

D

★ **MAMMA LUISA ITALIAN RISTORANTE.** *2710 N Steves Blvd (86004). 520/526-6809.* Hrs: 5-10 pm. Closed Thanksgiving, Dec. 25. Res accepted. Italian, vegetarian menu. Serv bar. Semi-a la carte: dinner $7.50-$16.50. Child's meals. Specialties: chicken rollantini, veal saltimbocca, fresh baked garlic bread. Cr cds: A, C, D, DS, MC, V.

✓★★ **MARC'S CAFE AMERICAIN.** *801 S Milton (86001). 520/556-0093.* Hrs: 11 am-9 pm, June-Sept to 10 pm. Res accepted. Bar. Semi-a la carte: lunch $6.95-$9.95, dinner $6.95-$15.95. Child's meals. Specializes in crêpes, rotisserie cooking. Outdoor dining in season. Wine bar; open kitchen. Cr cds: A, C, D, DS, MC, V.

D

★★ **SAKURA.** *(See Radisson Woodlands Hotel) 520/773-8888.* Hrs: 11:30 am-2 pm, 5-10 pm; Sun from 5 pm. Res accepted. Japanese menu. Bar to 1 am. Semi-a la carte: lunch $4.95-$9.95, dinner $5.95-$19.95. Child's meals. Specialties: hibachi salmon, flaming shrimp, sakura grill. Teppanyaki cooking, sushi bar. . Cr cds: A, C, D, DS, MC, V.

D

★ **SALSA BRAVA.** *1800 S Milton Rd (86001), in Greentree Village Shopping Center. 520/774-1083.* Hrs: 11 am-9 pm; Fri to 10 pm; Sat, Sun 8 am-10 pm. Closed Easter, Thanksgiving, Dec 25. Res accepted. Mexican menu. Bar. Semi-a la carte: bkfst $3.29-$6.95, lunch $4.95-$6.95, dinner $5.25-$7.95. Child's meals. Specialties: pollo asado, carnitas, fish tacos. Outdoor dining. Casual atmosphere. Salsa bar. Cr cds: A, C, MC, V.

D

Florence (F-4)

(See also Casa Grande)

Pop 7,510 **Elev** 1,490 ft **Area Code** 520 **Zip** 85232
E-mail info@florenceaz.org **Web** florenceaz.org

Information Chamber of Commerce, Box 929, phone 520/868-9433 or 800/437-9433; or the Pinal County Visitor Center, PO Box 967, phone 520/868-4331

Set in the desert amid multicolored mountains, the seat of Pinal County is the fifth oldest pioneer settlement in the state. Florence has many early houses still standing, making the town something of a living relic of pioneer days.

What to See and Do

Casa Grande Ruins National Monument (see). 10 mi W via AZ 287, then S on AZ 87.

McFarland State Historic Park (1878). First of 3 courthouses built here; restored adobe building with interpretive center, displays of early Arizona and US legal history, and the personal collections of Gov Ernest McFarland, also a US Senator and state supreme court justice. (Thurs-Mon; closed Dec 25) Ruggles Ave & Main St. Phone 520/868-5216. ¢

Pinal County Historical Society Museum. Exhibits depict early life in the area. (Wed-Sun; closed some major hols, also mid-July-Aug) 715 S Main St. Phone 520/868-4382. **Donation**

Annual Event

Junior Parade. Three-day celebration features parade and rodeo. Sat of Thanksgiving wkend.

Inn

✓★★ **RANCHO SONORA INN.** *9198 N Hwy 79 (85232). 520/868-8000; FAX 520/868-8000; res: 800/205-6817.* Web www.florenceaz.org. 10 rms, 5 with shower only, 3 casitas. Some rm phones. S, D $59-$69; casitas $95-$125; under 5 free. Pet accepted, some restrictions. TV; VCR avail (free movies). Complimentary continental bkfst. Restaurant nearby. Ck-out 11 am, ck-in 2 pm. Business servs avail. Coin lndry. Pool; whirlpool. Some refrigerators, microwaves. Picnic tables, grills. Built in 1930. Original adobe, western and traditional decor. Courtyard. Totally nonsmoking. Cr cds: A, C, D, MC, V.

D

Ganado (C-6)

(See also Canyon de Chelly National Monument, Window Rock)

Pop 1,257 **Elev** 6,386 ft **Area Code** 520 **Zip** 86505

What to See and Do

Hubbell Trading Post National Historic Site. The oldest continuously operating trading post (1878) on the Navajo Reservation; named for founder John Lorenzo Hubbell, who began trading with the Navajo in 1876. Construction of the present-day post began in 1883. The visitor center houses exhibits; Navajo weavers and a silversmith can be observed at work; tours of the Hubbell house, containing paintings, Navajo rugs and Native American arts & crafts; self-guided tour of the grounds (ranger-conducted programs in summer). (Daily; closed Jan 1, Thanksgiving, Dec 25) 1 mi W on AZ 264. Phone 520/755-3475 or 520/755-3477. **Free**

Gila Bend (F-3)

(See also Casa Grande)

Pop 1,747 **Elev** 736 ft **Area Code** 520 **Zip** 85337

Located on a desert plain near a sharp bend in the Gila River, Gila Bend was home to a flourishing Native American community prior to the arrival of Spanish explorers in the 17th century.

Motel

✓★★ **BEST WESTERN SPACE AGE LODGE.** *401 E Pima St (86023). 520/683-2273; FAX 520/683-2273; res: 800/528-1234.* 41 rms. Jan-Apr: S $60-$70; D $65-$85; each addl $4; under 17 free; lower rates rest of yr. Crib free. Pet accepted. TV; cable (premium). Pool; whirlpool. Coffee in rms. Restaurant open 24 hrs. Ck-out noon. Some refrigerators. Cr cds: A, C, D, DS, MC, V.

D SC

Glendale (F-3)

(See also Litchfield Park, Mesa, Phoenix, Scottsdale, Tempe)

Founded 1892 **Pop** 148,134 **Elev** 1,150 ft **Area Code** 623

Information Chamber of Commerce, 7105 N 59th Ave, Box 249, 85311; 623/937-4754 or 800/437-8669

Located just west of Phoenix in the beautiful and scenic Valley of the Sun, Glendale shares all of the urban advantages of the area. Luke AFB is located here.

Motels

★ **BEST WESTERN SAGE INN.** *5940 NW Grand Ave (85301). 602/939-9431; FAX 602/937-3137; res: 800/333-7172.* 85 rms, 2 story. Jan-Apr: S, D $59-$85; each addl $5; wkly rates; lower rates rest of yr. Crib $4. TV; cable (premium). 2 heated pools. Complimentary continental bkfst. Restaurant adj 6 am-9 pm. Ck-out 11 am. Coin Indry. Meeting rm. Business servs avail. Refrigerators. Cr cds: A, C, D, DS, JCB, MC, V.

D SC

★★ **FAIRFIELD SUITES.** *7810 W Bell Rd (85308). 602/878-6666; FAX 602/878-6611.* 89 suites, 4 story. Oct-Apr: suites $89-$139; under 18 free; lower rates rest of yr. Crib free. TV; cable (premium). Complimentary continental bkfst. Complimentary coffee in rms. Restaurant opp open 24 hrs. Ck-out noon. Business servs avail. In-rm modem link. Valet serv. Coin Indry. Lighted tennis privileges, pro. Pool; whirlpool. Refrigerators, microwaves, wet bars. Cr cds: A, C, D, DS, MC, V.

D SC

★★ **HOLIDAY INN.** *7885 W Arrowhead Towne Ctr (85308). 623/412-2000; FAX 623/412-5522.* 60 rms, 2 story. Mid-Jan-Mar: S, D $134-$139; each addl $10; under 18 free; lower rates rest of yr. Crib free. TV; cable (premium). Heated pool; whirlpool. Complimentary continental bkfst. Restaurant nearby. Ck-out 11 am. Business servs avail. Coin Indry. Exercise equipt. Many refrigerators; microwaves avail. Cr cds: A, C, D, DS, JCB, MC, V.

D SC

★★ **WINDMILL INN AT SUN CITY WEST.** *12545 W Bell Rd (85374), approx 7 mi E on Bell Rd. 602/583-0133; FAX 602/583-8366; res: 800/547-4747.* Web www.windmillinns.com. 127 rms, 3 story. Mid-Jan-mid-Apr: S, D $116-$145; each addl $6; under 18 free; lower rates rest of yr. Crib free. Pet accepted, some restrictions. TV; cable (premium). Heated pool; whirlpool. Complimentary continental bkfst. Restaurant adj 6 am-10 pm. Ck-out 11 am. Coin Indry. Meeting rms. Business servs avail. Golf privileges. Microwaves, refrigerators avail. Grills. Cr cds: A, C, D, DS, MC, V.

D SC

Motor Hotels

★★ **HAMPTON INN.** *8408 W Paradise Ln (85382), on AZ 101 exit Bell Rd. 602/486-9918; FAX 602/486-4842; res: 800/426-7866.* 112 rms, 5 story. Jan-mid-Apr: S $99-$159; D $109-$159; each addl $10; under 18 free; golf plans; lower rates rest of yr. Crib free. TV; cable (premium), VCR avail. Complimentary continental bkfst. Complimentary coffee in rms. Restaurant nearby. Ck-out noon. Meeting rms. Business servs avail. In-rm modem link. Valet serv. Coin Indry. Exercise equipt. Pool; whirlpool. Refrigerators, microwaves; some in-rm whirlpools, wet bars. Cr cds: A, C, D, DS, JCB, MC, V.

D SC

★★ **LA QUINTA INN & SUITES.** *16321 N 83 Ave (85382), adj to Peoria Sports Complex. 602/487-1900; FAX 602/487-1919; res: 800/687-6667.* Web www.laquinta.com. 108 rms, 5 story. Jan-Apr: S, D $109-$129; each addl $10; suites $175-$200; under 18 free; golf plans; lower rates rest of yr. Crib free. Pet accepted, some restrictions; $25 deposit. TV; cable (premium). Complimentary continental bkfst. Complimentary coffee in rms. Restaurant nearby. Ck-out noon. Meeting rm. Business servs avail. In-rm modem link. Valet serv. Coin Indry. Exercise equipt. Pool; whirlpool. Many refrigerators, microwaves. Cr cds: A, C, D, DS, ER, MC, V.

D SC

Restaurant

★★ **COUGAN'S AT ARROWHEAD.** *7640 W Bell Rd (85308). 602/878-8822.* E-mail norton@cougans.com. Hrs: 11 am-10 pm; Fri, Sat to 10:30 pm. Closed Thanksgiving, Dec 25. Bar. Semi-a la carte: lunch $5.95-$8.95, dinner $7.95-$16.95. Child's meals. Specialties: molasses brine pork chop, grilled salmon, smokehouse tomatoes and classic grilled meatloaf. Entertainment Wed. Outdoor dining. Brewery. Totally nonsmoking. Cr cds: A, C, D, DS, MC, V.

D

Globe (F-5)

(See also San Carlos)

Settled 1876 **Pop** 6,062 **Elev** 3,509 ft **Area Code** 520 **Zip** 85501

Information Greater Globe-Miami Chamber of Commerce, 1360 N Broad St, Box 2539, 85502; 520/425-4495 or 800/804-5623

A silver strike settled Globe, but copper made the town what it is today. One of the original copper mines, Old Dominion, is no longer worked; however, other mines are still in operation. Cattle ranching also contributes to the economy. A Ranger District office for the Tonto National Forest (see PAYSON) is located here.

What to See and Do

Besh-Ba-Gowah Indian Ruins. Ruins of a village inhabited by the Salado from 1225 to 1400. More than 200 rms. Visitor center, museum. (Daily; closed Jan 1, Thanksgiving, Dec 25) From end of S Broad St turn right across bridge, continue on Jess Hayes Rd. Phone 520/425-0320. ¢

Boyce Thompson Southwestern Arboretum. Large collection of plants from arid parts of world added to native flora in high Sonoran Desert setting at foot of Picket Post Mt; labeled plants in 39-acre garden. Picnicking. Visitor center features biological and historical displays. (Daily; closed Dec 25) 28 mi W on US 60; 3 mi W of Superior. Phone 520/689-2811. ¢¢

Gila County Historical Museum. Exhibit of artifacts of Gila County, including those of the Apache. (Mon-Fri; closed hols) 1 mi N on US 60. Phone 520/425-7385. **Donation**

Annual Events

Gila County Fair. 4 days mid-Sept.

Apache Days. 4th wkend Oct.

Motels

✓★ **HOLIDAY INN.** *2119 Old West Hwy 60 (85502). 520/425-7008; FAX 520/425-6410; res: 800/432-6655; res: 800/422-6655.* 45 rms, 2 story. S, D $56-$70; each addl $7; under 18 free. Crib free. Pet accepted. TV; cable (premium). Complimentary continental bkfst. Restaurant opp 11 am-9 pm. Ck-out noon. Meeting rms. Business servs avail. Coin Indry. Some refrigerators. Cr cds: A, C, D, DS, MC, V.

D SC

✓★ **RAMADA LTD.** *1699 E Ash St (85502), at jct US 60 & 70. 520/425-5741; FAX 520/402-8466; res: 800/256-8399.* 80 rms, 2 story. S $47-$62; D $53-$72, suites $60-$90; under 18 free. Crib free. Pet accepted, some restrictions; $20. TV; cable. Heated pool; whirlpool. Ck-out noon. Meeting rm. Business servs avail. Refrigerators. Cr cds: A, C, D, DS, MC, V.

D SC

Grand Canyon National Park (B-4 - C-2)

(See also Flagstaff, Williams)

Area Code 520

Every minute of the day, the light changes the colors and form of this magnificent spectacle. Sunrises and sunsets are particularly superb. In 1540, Spanish explorer de Cardenas became the first European to see this canyon of the Colorado River, but he and his party were unable to cross and soon left. In 1857, American Lieutenant Joseph Ives said the region was "altogether valueless.... Ours has been the first and will doubtless be the last party of whites to visit this profitless locality." As much as 18 miles wide and about a mile deep, the canyon has wildlife that includes at least 287 different species of birds, 76 species of mammals, 35 species of reptiles and 6 species of amphibians. The South Rim (see), open all year, has the greatest number of services and is the most popular to visit. The North Rim (see), blocked by heavy snows in winter, is open from approximately mid-May-mid-October. One rim can be reached from the other by a 220-mile drive. The South Rim has an altitude of about 7,000 feet; the North Rim is about 8,100 feet. The river is some 4,600 feet below the South Rim. It is seven miles via the South Kaibab Trail and nine miles via the Bright Angel Trail from the South Rim to the bottom of the canyon. The park encompasses more than one million acres. Of the Grand Canyon's 277-mile length, the first 50 or so miles along the Colorado River comprise what is known as Marble Canyon, where 3,000-foot, near-vertical walls of sandstone and limestone may be seen. US 89A crosses Navajo Bridge 467 feet above the Colorado River. Pets must be on a leash and are excluded from trails below the rim. For further information contact Trip Planner, Grand Canyon National Park, PO Box 129, Grand Canyon 86023; 520/638-7888. Per vehicle ¢¢¢¢¢

North Rim (Grand Canyon National Park) (C-3)

Zip 86052

(220 mi NW of Flagstaff: 116 mi N via US 89, 58 mi W via US 89A, then 46 mi S via AZ 67)

What to See and Do

Camping. Campsites, trailer parking space at North Rim Campground (7-day limit; no hookups). For camping reservations phone 800/365-2267. ¢¢¢ For lodging information at the North Rim phone 303/297-2757.

★ **Drive to Cape Royal.** About 23 mi from Bright Angel Point over paved road. Several good viewpoints along way. Many think the view from here is better than from the South Rim. Archaeology and geology talks in summer & fall.

Hiking. Six trails (¼ mi-10 mi); some are self-guided.

Muleback trips into canyon (daytime only). Also horseback trips (along rim only, not into canyon). Phone 520/638-9875 (summer) or 801/679-8665 (winter).

Programs by naturalists; occasionally other events. Consult information board at Grand Canyon Lodge for schedule. **Free**

Motel

★★ **GRAND CANYON LODGE.** *General Delivery (86052), at canyon rim, S on AZ 67. 520/638-2611; FAX 520/638-2554; res: 303/297-2757.* 201 units; 161 cabins, 40 motel rms. May-Oct: S, D $55-$91; each addl $5; under 13 free. Closed rest of yr. Crib $5. Restaurant 6:30-10 am, 11:30 am-2:30 pm, 5-9:30 pm. Bar 11:30 am-10:30 pm. Ck-out 11 am. Business servs avail. Bellhops. Sundries. Gift shop. Game rm. View of canyon. Cr cds: A, C, D, DS, MC, V.

D

South Rim (Grand Canyon National Park) (C-3)

Zip 86023

(Approx 80 mi NW of Flagstaff via US 180)

What to See and Do

Camping. Sites (no hookups) at Mather Campground (fee); reservations can be made through BIOSPHERICS by phone 800/365-2267. Adj is Trailer Village, with trailer sites (hookups; fee); for res phone 303/297-2757. ¢¢¢¢–¢¢¢¢¢

★ **Drives to viewpoints.** There are West Rim and East Rim drives out from Grand Canyon Village; each is rewarding. Grandview Point and Desert View on the East Rim Drive are especially magnificent. West Rim Drive is closed to private vehicles early Apr-early Oct. Free shuttle buses serve West Rim & Village area during this period.

Evening programs every night all year by Park Service ranger-naturalist in outdoor amphitheater; inside Shrine of the Ages Bldg during the colder months; daytime talks given all yr at Yavapai Observation Station and at Visitor Center. **Free**

Grand Canyon IMAX Theatre. Large screen film (35-min) highlighting features of Grand Canyon. (Daily) AZ 64/US 180, 1 mi S of park entrance. For schedule information Phone 520/638-2203. **¢¢¢**

Guided river trips. Res should be made well in advance.

Multi-day trips within the park. Phone 602/638-7888 (touch tone 1-4-6-2) for a written list of commercial outfitters.

One-day trips avail from Page to Lees Ferry, in Glen Canyon National Recreation Area; phone 520/645-3279.

Hiking down into canyon. Not recommended except for those in good physical condition, because heat and 4,500-ft climb back are exhausting. Consult Backcountry Office staff before attempting this. (**Caution:** always carry sufficient water and food; neither is avail along trails.) Res and fees required for camping below the rim; by mail from Backcountry Office, PO Box 129, Grand Canyon 86023, or in person at Backcountry, located adj to Maswik Lodge.

Kaibab National Forest. Adj to both North and South Rims are units of this 1.5 million-acre forest (see WILLIAMS). The Ranger District office for the Tusayan District is located in Tusayan, several mi S of the park. Phone 520/638-2443.

Mule trip into canyon. Easier than walking and quite safe; a number of trips are scheduled, all with guides. There are some limitations. Trips take 1, 2 or 3 days. Res should be made several months in advance (preferably one yr prior). For information phone 303/297-2757.

Scenic flights over Grand Canyon. Many operators offer air tours of the Canyon. Flights out of many different airports. For a partial list of companies contact the Grand Canyon Chamber of Commerce, PO Box 3007, Grand Canyon 86023.

Tusayan Museum. Exhibits on prehistoric man in the Southwest. Excavated pueblo ruin (ca 1185) nearby. (Daily, weather permitting) East Rim Dr, 22 mi E of Grand Canyon Village. **Free**

Visitor Center. National Park Service. Grand Canyon Village. Has information, maps, pamphlets and exhibits. (Daily) **Free**

Yavapai Observation Station. Scenic views, exhibits, information. (Daily) On rim, 1 mi E of Grand Canyon Village. **Free**

Motels

★★★ **BEST WESTERN SQUIRE INN.** *Highway 64 (86023), 7 mi S on AZ 64 just S of park entrance. 520/638-2681; FAX 520/638-2782; res: 800/622-6966.* E-mail bestwestern@thecanyon.com; web www.grandcanyonsquire.com. 250 rms, 3 story. Apr-Oct: S, D $150-$175; each addl $10; under 12 free; lower rates rest of yr. Crib free. TV; cable (premium). Heated pool; whirlpool. Restaurant 6:30 am-10 pm. Bar 10 am-midnight. Ck-out noon. Coin lndry. Convention facilities. Business servs avail. Concierge. Sundries. Gift shop. Beauty shop. Exercise equipt; sauna. Game rm. Rec rm. Bowling alley on premises. Cowboy museum, mural of Grand Canyon. Cr cds: A, C, D, DS, ER, JCB, MC, V.

D SC

✓★ **BRIGHT ANGEL LODGE.** *1 Main St (86023), 4 mi W on US 180 (AZ 64). 520/638-2631; FAX 520/638-9247.* Web www.amfac.com. 89 rms: 39 in lodge, 15 with bath; 50 cabins. No A/C. S, D $58-$114; each addl $7; suite $227. Crib free. TV in some rms. Restaurant 6:30 am-10 pm. Bar 11-1 am; Sun from noon. Ck-out 11 am. Bellhops. Sundries. Gift shop. Barber, beauty shop. Fireplace in some cabins. Some canyon-side rms. Canyon tour serv. Cr cds: A, C, D, DS, JCB, MC, V.

D

★ **GRAND CANYON PARK NATIONAL LODGES.** *1 Main St (86023), 4 mi W on US 180 (AZ 64). 520/638-2631; FAX 520/638-9247; res: 520/638-2401.* 278 rms, 2 story. S, D $72-$107; cabins $59; each addl $7-$9; under 16 free. Crib free. TV; cable. Restaurant 6 am-10 pm. Bar 11-1 am. Ck-out 11 am. Business servs avail. Bellhops. Sundries. Gift shop. Some private patios, balconies. Canyon tour serv. Cr cds: A, C, D, DS, JCB, MC, V.

D

★ **KACHINA LODGE.** *1 Main St (86023), 4 mi W on US 180 (AZ 64); register at El Tovar Hotel (see). 520/638-2631; FAX 520/638-9247.* Web www.amfac.com. 49 air-cooled rms, 2 story. S, D $107-$117; each addl $9. Crib free. TV; cable. Restaurant adj 6:30 am-2 pm, 5-10 pm. Ck-out 11 am. Bellhops. Canyon tour serv. Cr cds: A, C, D, DS, JCB, MC, V.

D

★★ **QUALITY INN.** *AZ 64 Grand Canyon (86023), near Grand Canyon IMAX Theatre. 520/638-2673; FAX 520/638-9537; res: 800/228-5151.* Web www.thecanyon.com/gcqual. 232 rms, 3 story. Apr-Oct: S, D $118-$178; each addl $10; under 18 free; lower rates rest of yr. Crib $10. TV; cable. Pool; whirlpool. Complimentary coffee in rms. Restaurant 6 am-10 pm. Ck-out 11 am. In-rm modem link. Gift shop. Some minibars. Balconies. Atrium. Cr cds: A, C, D, DS, ER, JCB, MC, V.

D SC

★ **RODEWAY INN RED FEATHER.** *AZ 64 (86023), US 180. 520/638-2414; FAX 520/638-9216; res: 800/538-2345.* Web www.gcanyon.com. 234 rms, 2- & 3-story. May-Oct: S, D $100-$175; each addl $10; under 18 free; lower rates rest of yr. Crib free. Pet accepted; $45. TV; cable. Restaurant adj 6 am-10 pm. Ck-out 11 am. Business servs avail. Exercise equipt. Cr cds: A, C, D, MC, V.

D

★ **THUNDERBIRD LODGE.** *1 Main St (86023), 4 mi W on US 180 (AZ 64); register at Bright Angel Lodge (see). 520/638-2631; FAX 520/638-9247; res: 303/297-2757.* Web www.amfac.com. 55 air-cooled rms, 2 story. S, D $102-$112; each addl $9. Crib free. TV; cable. Restaurant adj 6:30 am-10 pm. Ck-out 11 am. Meeting rms. Bellhops. Some canyon-side rms. Canyon tour serv. Cr cds: A, C, D, DS, JCB, MC, V.

D

★ **YAVAPAI LODGE.** *1 Main St (86023), 3 mi W of US 180 (AZ 64), opp visitor center. 520/638-2631; FAX 520/638-9247; res: 303/297-2757.* 358 rms, 2 story. No A/C. S, D $83-$98; each addl $9. Crib free. TV; cable. Restaurant 6 am-9 pm. Ck-out 11 am. Bellhops. Gift shop. Sundries. Canyon tour serv. . Cr cds: A, C, D, DS, JCB, MC, V.

D

Hotel

★★★ **EL TOVAR.** *1 Main St (86023), 4 mi W of entrance on US 180 (AZ 64). 520/638-2631; FAX 520/638-9247; res: 520/638-2401.* Web www.amfac.com. 78 rms, 4 story. S, D $112-$169; each addl $11; suites $192-$277. Crib free. TV; cable. Restaurant (see EL TOVAR DINING ROOM). Bar 11-1 am; Sun from noon. Ck-out 11 am. Concierge. Gift shop. Built 1905. Some suites with balcony overlooking canyon. Cr cds: A, C, D, DS, JCB, MC, V.

D

Restaurants

★★★ **EL TOVAR DINING ROOM.** *(See El Tovar Hotel) 520/638-2631.* Hrs: 6:30 am-2 pm, 5-10 pm. Res required. Bar. Wine cellar. Semi-a la carte: bkfst $2.50-$11.20, lunch $3.25-$17, dinner $14.75-$24.75. Child's meals. Specialties: shrimp toast with mango and prickly pear vinaigrette, smoked corn chowder, vegetable empanada with roasted pepper coulis. Stone fireplaces. Native American murals. Overlooks Grand Canyon. Totally nonsmoking. Cr cds: A, C, D, DS, JCB, MC, V.

D

★ **STEAKHOUSE AT THE GRAND CANYON.** *AZ 64 & US 180 (86023), across from IMAX theater. 520/638-2780.* Hrs: 11 am-10 pm. Bar. Semi-a la carte: lunch, dinner $6.95-$22.95. Child's meals. Specialty: beef, chicken cooked on open oak wood fire. Hayrides, stage coach rides Mar-Oct. Old West decor; brick fireplace. Covered wagon in front yard. Cr cds: C, MC, V.

D

Greer (E-6)

(See also McNary, Pinetop, Springerville)

Pop 125 (est) **Elev** 8,380 ft **Area Code** 520 **Zip** 85927

Within the Apache-Sitgreaves National Forests, this town is 18 miles southwest of Springerville (see) on AZ 273. Cross-country and downhill skiing are available nearby from December to March; fishing, hunting, backpacking, bicycling and camping are popular at other times of year.

Lodge

★ **GREER LODGE.** *44 Main St (85927), ½ mi S of post office. 520/735-7515; FAX 520/735-7720; res: 888/475-6343.* 8 rms in main lodge, 3 story, 9 kit. cabins. No A/C. No elvtr. No rm phones. S $90; D $120; each addl $15; kit. units $75-$110; each addl $15; package plans. Crib avail. Pet accepted in cabins; $10/day. TV in lobby & lounge. Restaurant (public by res) 7-10 am, 11:30 am-2:30 pm, 5-8:30 pm. Bar 10 am-10 pm. Ck-out 11 am. Meeting rm. X-country ski 5 mi. Ice-skating; skates provided. Sleigh rides. Stocked trout pond. Picnic tables, grills. Sun deck. Fireplace, piano in living room. On 9 acres; overlooks Little Colorado River. Cr cds: A, C, DS, MC, V.

D

Inn

★★★ **RED SETTER INN.** *8 County Rd 1120 (85927). 520/735-7441; FAX 520/735-7425; res: 888/994-7337.* 12 rms, 3 story. S, D $125-$195; each addl $25; wkends (2-day min); hols (3-day min). Children over 16 yrs only. TV in common rm; VCR (movies). Complimentary full bkfst; afternoon refreshments. Restaurant nearby. Ck-out 10:30 am, ck-in 3-7 pm. Business servs avail. Luggage handling. Concierge serv. Downhill ski 15 mi; x-country ski 5 mi. Some in-rm whirlpools, fireplaces. Many balconies. On river. Antiques; Irish Setter theme. Totally nonsmoking. Cr cds: C.

Restaurant

★ **MOLLY BUTLER.** *100 Main St (85927), Butler's Lodge. 520/735-7226.* Hrs: 5-9 pm. Res accepted. No A/C. Bar 8-1 am. Semi-a la carte: dinner $6.95-$32.50. Specializes in steak, seafood. Old West atmosphere; 2 dining areas; rustic decor. Scenic view of valley meadows, mountains. Cr cds: C, MC, V.

D

Holbrook (D-5)

(See also Hopi and Navajo Indian Reservations, Winslow)

Pop 4,686 **Elev** 5,083 ft **Area Code** 520 **Zip** 86025

Information Chamber of Commerce, 100 E Arizona St; 520/524-6558 or 800/524-2449

What to See and Do

Apache-Sitgreaves National Forests. 46 mi S on AZ 77 to Show Low (see).

Navajo County Historical Museum. Exhibits on Navajo, Apache, Hopi and Hispanic culture; petrified forest; local history; dinosaurs. (May-Sept, daily exc Sun; rest of yr, Mon-Fri; closed major hols) 100 E Arizona, in Old County Courthouse. Phone 520/524-6558. **Donation**

Petrified Forest National Park (see). North entrance, 26 mi E on US 66/I-40; south entrance, 19 mi E on US 180.

Annual Events

Old West Celebration. 1st wk June.

Gathering of Eagles. Native American art show and sale. Mid-July.

Navajo County Fair. Mid-Sept.

Motels

★★ **BEST WESTERN ARIZONIAN.** *2508 E Navajo Blvd (86025). 520/524-2611; FAX 520/524-2611; res: 800/528-1234.* 70 rms, 2 story. June-Aug: S $53-$66; D $58-$72; each addl $4; under 17 free; lower rates rest of yr. Crib $5. Pet accepted, some restrictions. TV; cable (premium). Heated pool. Complimentary coffee in lobby. Restaurant open 24 hrs. Ck-out 11 am. Some refrigerators, microwaves. Cr cds: A, C, D, DS, MC, V.

SC

★★ **COMFORT INN.** *2602 E Navajo Blvd (86025). 520/524-6131; FAX 520/524-2281; res: 800/228-5150.* 60 rms, 2 story. May-Sept: S $60; D $65; each addl $5; under 18 free; wkly, wkend rates; lower rates rest of yr. Crib free. Pet accepted, some restrictions. TV; cable (premium). Pool. Complimentary coffee in lobby. Restaurant adj open 24 hrs. Ck-out 11 am. Coin lndry. Some refrigerators, microwaves. Cr cds: A, C, D, DS, MC, V.

D SC

★★ **ECONO LODGE INN.** *2596 Navajo Blvd (86001), I-40 exit 289. 520/524-1448; FAX 520/524-1493; res: 800/553-2660.* 63 rms, 2 story. June-Aug: S $44; D $50; each addl $5; under 18 free; lower rates rest of yr. Crib free. Pet accepted. TV; cable (premium). Heated pool. Complimentary coffee in lobby. Restaurant adj. Ck-out 11 am. Coin lndry. Some refrigerators. Picnic table. Cr cds: A, C, D, DS, MC, V.

D SC

★★ **HOLIDAY INN.** *1308 E Navajo Blvd (86025), I-40 exit 286. 520/524-1466; FAX 520/524-1788; res: 800/465-4329.* Web www.cybertrails.com/nazguide. 59 rms, 2 story. Late May-late Aug: S $59; D $63; each addl $4; suites $69-$83; under 17 free; lower rates rest of yr. Crib $4. Pet accepted. TV; cable. Indoor pool; whirlpool. Complimentary continental bkfst. Restaurant nearby. Ck-out 11 am. Coin lndry. Meeting rm. Refrigerator, microwave in suites. Cr cds: A, C, D, DS, JCB, MC, V.

D SC

Restaurant

★★ **MESA ITALIANA.** *2318 N Navajo Blvd (86025). 520/524-6696.* Hrs: 11 am-9 pm. Closed Mon. Italian menu. Bar to 1 am. Semi-a la carte: lunch $3.50-$8.95, dinner $6.95-$14.95. Child's meals. Specialties: pasta primavera, chicken Jerusalem, pasta pescatore. Casual dining. Cr cds: C, DS, MC, V.

D

Hopi Indian Reservation (C-5)

(See also Canyon de Chelly National Monument, Holbrook, Kayenta, Page)

Completely surrounded by the Navajo Indian Reservation (see) is the 1.5 million-acre Hopi Indian Reservation. The Hopi are pueblo people of Shoshonean ancestry who have lived here for more than 1,000 years. The Hopi have a complex religious system. Excellent farmers, they also herd sheep, as well as craft pottery, silver jewelry, kachina dolls and baskets. They live in some of the most intriguing towns on the North American continent.

Both the Navajo and Hopi are singers and dancers—each in their own style. The Hopi are most famous for their Snake Dance, which may not be viewed by visitors. But there are dozens of other beautiful ceremonies that visitors are allowed to watch. However, the photographing, recording or sketching of any events on the reservation is prohibited.

All major roads leading into and across the Navajo and Hopi Reservations are paved. Do not venture off the main highways.

The Hopi towns are located, for the most part, on three mesas. On the first mesa is Walpi, founded around 1680, one of the most beautiful Hopi pueblos. It is built on the tip of a narrow, steep-walled mesa, along with its companion villages, Sichomovi and Hano, which are inhabited by the Tewa and the Hano. Hanoans speak a Tewa language as well as Hopi. You can drive to Sichomovi and walk along a narrow connecting mesa to Walpi. Only passenger cars are allowed on the mesa; no RVs or trailers. Individuals of Walpi and First Mesa Villages offer Hopi pottery and kachina dolls for sale; inquire locally.

The second mesa has three towns: Mishongnovi, Shipaulovi and Shongopovi, each fascinating in its own way. The Hopi Cultural Center, located on the second mesa, includes a museum and craft shops (daily); a restaurant serving both Hopi and American food and a motel; reservations (phone 520/734-2421) for May-August should be made at least three months in advance. Near the Cultural Center is a primitive campground (free). The third mesa has Oraibi, the oldest Hopi town, and its three offshoots, Bacabi, Kyakotsmovi and Hotevilla, a town of considerable interest. A restaurant, a small motel and tent & trailer sites can be found at Keams Canyon. There are not many places to stay, so plan your trip carefully.

Kayenta (B-5)

(See also Hopi and Navajo Indian Reservations)

Pop 4,372 **Elev** 5,641 ft **Area Code** 520 **Zip** 86033

Located in the spectacular Monument Valley, Kayenta's (Kay-en-TAY) surrounding area offers some of the most memorable sightseeing in the state; the great tinted monoliths are spectacular.

What to See and Do

Crawley's Monument Valley Tours, Inc. Guided tours in back-country vehicles to Monument Valley, Mystery Valley and Hunt's Mesa. Half- and full-day rates. (Daily) Phone 520/697-3734 or 520/697-3463. **¢¢¢¢¢**

Monument Valley Navajo Tribal Park. Self-guided tours of the valley (road conditions vary, inquire locally). Camping (at Park Headquarters only; fee). (Daily; closed Jan 1, Dec 25) 25 mi NE off US 163. Phone 801/727-3287. Park **¢¢**

Guided tours of the park are avail through **Bennett Tours,** phone 800/862-8270; **Daniel's Guided Tours,** phone 800/596-8427; **Totem Pole Tours,** phone 800/345-8687; **Goulding's Monument Valley Lodge,** phone 801/727-3231. Fees and schedules vary.

Navajo National Monument (see). 20 mi SW on US 160, then 9 mi N on AZ 564.

Motel

★★ **HOLIDAY INN.** *Jct US Hwy 160 & 163 (86033), jct US 160, 163. 520/697-3221; FAX 520/697-3349; res: 800/465-4329.* 160 rms, 2 story. Apr-Nov: S, D $110-$150; each addl $10; suites $120-$160; under 19 free; lower rates rest of yr. Crib free. TV; cable. Pool; wading pool. Restaurant 6 am-10 pm. Rm serv. Ck-out noon. Coin lndry. Sundries. Gift shop. Cr cds: A, C, D, DS, JCB, MC, V.

D SC

Kingman (D-2)

(See also Bullhead City, Lake Havasu City)

Pop 12,722 **Elev** 3,341 ft **Area Code** 520 **Zip** 86401
Web www.arizona guide.com/visitkingman

Information Chamber of Commerce, Box 1150, 86402; 520/753-6106

Kingman is the seat of Mohave County. It lies at the junction of two transcontinental highways, I-40 reaching from the East to the West coast, and US 93 from Fairbanks, Alaska, to Guatemala, Mexico. It is a convenient stop on the way to the Grand Canyon, Las Vegas or Los Angeles. Nearby are Lakes Mead, Mohave and Havasu, with year-round swimming, waterskiing, fishing and boating. To the south are the beautiful Hualapai Mountains. This city lies at the heart of historic Route 66 and once was a rich silver and gold mining area; several ghost towns are nearby.

What to See and Do

Bonelli House (1894). One of the earliest permanent structures in the city. Restored and furnished with many original pieces. (Thurs-Mon afternoons; closed hols) 430 E Spring St. Phone 520/753-1413 or 520/753-3195. **Free**

Mohave Museum of History & Art. Exhibits trace local and state history; portrait collection of US presidents and first ladies; Andy Devine display; turquoise display; rebuilt 1926 pipe organ; Native American displays. Local artists' gallery. (Daily; closed major hols) 400 W Beale St, ¼ mi E of I-40, Beale St/Las Vegas exit. Phone 520/753-3195. **¢**

Oatman. In the 1930s, this was the last stop in Arizona before entering the Mojave Desert in California. Created in 1906 as a tent camp, it flourished as a gold mining center until 1942, when Congress declared that gold mining was no longer essential to the war effort. The ghost town has been kept as authentic as possible; several motion pictures have been filmed here. Wild burros abound, many roaming streets that are lined with historic buildings, former mine sites, old town jail, old & modern hotel, museum, turquoise & antique shops. Gunfights staged (daily). 28 mi SW, located on old US 66. Contact the Oatman Chamber of Commerce, phone 520/768-7400.

Powerhouse Visitor Center. Renovated power generating station (1907). Houses Historic Route 66 Assn of Arizona, Tourist Information Ctr, Carlos Elmer Memorial Photo Gallery, model RR shop, gift shop, deli. (Daily; closed Jan 1, Easter, Thanksgiving, Dec 25) 120 W Andy Devine Ave. Phone 520/753-6106, ext 3. **Free**

Annual Events

Mohave County Fair. 1st wkend after Labor Day.

Andy Devine Days & PRCA Rodeo. Sports tournaments, parade, other events. 3 days early Oct.

Motels

★★ **BEST WESTERN WAYFARERS INN.** *2815 E Andy Devine Ave (86033). 520/753-6271; FAX 520/753-9608; res: 800/548-5695.* 100 rms, 2 story. Mid-May-Sept: S $60-$65; D $67-$70; suites $90; under 12 free; lower rates rest of yr. Crib $5. Pet accepted. TV; cable (premium). Complimentary full breakfast. Heated pool. Ck-out noon. Coin lndry. Refrigerators, microwaves. Cr cds: A, C, D, DS, ER, JCB, MC, V.

SC

★ **DAYS INN.** *3023 E Andy Devine Ave (86401). 520/753-7500; FAX 520/753-4686; res: 800/329-7466.* 60 rms, 2 story, 40 kit. units. May-Sept: S, D $55-$75; kit. units $60; higher rates hols; lower rates rest of yr. Crib free. Pet accepted; $3. TV; cable (premium). Heated pool; whirlpool. Coffee in lobby. Restaurant opp 6 am-11 pm. Coin lndry. Business servs avail. In-rm modem link. Microwaves avail. Cr cds: A, C, D, DS, ER, JCB, MC, V.

D SC

✓★ **HILL TOP MOTEL.** *1901 E Andy Devine (86401). 520/753-2198; FAX 520/753-5985.* E-mail stuglass@ctaz.com. 29 rms. May-Sept: S $25-$36; D $32-$44; each addl $5; higher rates hol wkends; lower rates rest of yr. Crib $5. Pet accepted, some restrictions. TV; cable (premium). Heated pool. Restaurant nearby. Ck-out 11 am. Coin lndry. Business servs avail. Refrigerators avail. Cr cds: C, DS, MC, V.

SC

★ **HOLIDAY INN.** *3100 E Andy Devine Ave (86401). 520/753-6262; FAX 520/753-7137; res: 800/465-4329.* 116 rms, 2 story. S, D $49-$89; each addl $5; under 12 free. Crib free. Pet accepted, some restrictions. TV; cable. Pool. Restaurant 6 am-10 pm. Rm serv. Bar 5 pm-1 am. Ck-out noon. Coin lndry. Meeting rms. Business servs avail. Valet serv. Sundries. Cr cds: A, C, D, DS, ER, JCB, MC, V.

D SC

✓★ **QUALITY INN.** *1400 E Andy Devine Ave (86401). 520/753-4747; FAX 520/753-4747; res: 800/869-3252.* 98 rms, 1-2 story. June-Aug: S, D, kit. units $54-$69; each addl $10; under 18 free; lower rates rest of yr. Crib free. Pet accepted. TV; cable (premium). Pool; whirlpool. Complimentary continental bkfst. Complimentary coffee in rms. Restaurant adj 7 am-10 pm. Ck-out noon. Meeting rm. Business servs avail. Free airport transportation. Exercise equipt; sauna. Cr cds: A, C, D, DS, ER, JCB, MC, V.

D SC

Restaurant

✓★ **HOUSE OF CHAN.** *960 W Beale St (86401). 520/753-3232.* Hrs: 11 am-10 pm. Closed Sun; Jan 1. Res accepted. Chinese, Amer menu. Bar. Semi-a la carte: lunch $3.95-$5.95, dinner $7.25-$14.95. Specializes in Cantonese cuisine, prime rib, seafood. Oriental decor. Cr cds: A, C, MC, V.

D

Lake Havasu City (E-1)

(See also Kingman, Parker; also see Needles, CA)

Founded 1964 **Pop** 24,363 **Elev** 600 ft **Area Code** 520 **Zip** 86403
E-mail lakehavasu@interworldnet.net
Web www.arizonaguide.com/lakehavasu

Information Lake Havasu Tourism Bureau, 314 London Bridge Rd; 520/453-3444 or 800/242-8278

This is the center of a year-round resort area on the shores of 45-mile-long Lake Havasu. London Bridge, imported from England and reassembled here as part of a recreational area, was designed by John Rennie and built in 1824-1831; it spanned the Thames River in London until 1968. It now connects the mainland city with a three-square-mile island that has a marina, golf course, tennis courts, campgrounds and other recreational facilities.

What to See and Do

Lake Havasu State Park. There are 13,000 acres along 23 mi of shoreline. **Windsor Beach Unit,** 2 mi N on old US 95 (London Bridge Rd), has swimming; fishing; boating (ramps). Hiking. Ramadas. Camping (dump station). Phone 520/855-2784. **Cattail Cove Unit,** 15 mi S, ½ mi W of US 95, has swimming; fishing; boating (ramps). Camping (incl some water-access sites; fee). Standard fees. Phone 520/855-1223.

London Bridge Resort & English Village. English-style village on 21 acres; home of the world-famous London Bridge. Specialty shops, restaurants; boat rides; 9-hole golf course; accommodations (see MOTOR HOTELS). Village (daily). 1477 Queens Bay. Phone 520/855-0888 or 520/855-0880. Parking **¢**

Sightseeing. Outback Off-Road Adventures, phone 520/680-6151; Lake Havasu Boat Tours, phone 520/855-7979; Bluewater Jet Boat Tours, phone 520/855-7171; Dixie Bell Boat Tours, phone 520/453-6776; London Jet Boat Tours, phone 888/505-3545. **¢¢¢-¢¢¢¢¢**

Topock Gorge. Scenic steep volcanic banks along Colorado River. Migratory birds winter here; herons, cormorants and egrets nest (Apr-May). Fishing. Picnicking. 10 mi N on lake (accessible only by boat), S boundary of Havasu National Wildlife Refuge. Phone 619/326-3853. **Free**

Motor Hotel

✓★ **HOLIDAY INN.** *245 London Brg Rd (85204). 520/855-4071; FAX 520/855-2379; res: 888/428-2465.* 162 rms, 4 story. Feb-Nov: S $49-$78; D $57-$84; each addl $8; suites $97-$135; under 18 free; wkly rates; golf plan; higher rates: hols, special events; lower rates rest of yr. Crib free. Pet accepted, some restrictions. TV; cable (premium). Heated pool. Restaurant 6 am-10 pm. Rm serv. Bar 11-1 am; Sun from noon. Ck-out noon. Coin lndry. Meeting rms. Business servs avail. In-rm modem link. Free airport transportation. Game rm. Refrigerators. Balconies. On lake; state park adj. Cr cds: A, C, D, DS, ER, JCB, MC, V.

D SC

Restaurant

★★ **SHUGRUE'S.** *1425 McCulloch Blvd (86403). 520/453-1400.* Hrs: 11 am-10 pm. Closed Dec 25. Res accepted. Bar to 1 am. Semi-a la carte: lunch $5.25-$7.95, dinner $9.95-$32.95. Child's meals. Specializes in fresh seafood, steak, chicken. Multi-level dining. Nautical decor. Overlooks London Bridge. Cr cds: A, C, MC, V.

D

Lake Mead National Recreation Area

(see Nevada)

Litchfield Park (F-3)

(See also Glendale, Mesa, Phoenix, Scottsdale, Tempe)

Pop 3,303 **Elev** 1,027 ft **Area Code** 602 **Zip** 85340
E-mail info@tricity westcofc.org **Web** www.tricitywestcofc.org

Information Tri-City West Chamber of Commerce, 501 W Van Buren, Suite K, Avondale 85323; 602/932-2260

In 1916, the Goodyear Tire and Rubber Company purchased and leased two tracts of land to grow Egyptian cotton. One tract was west of the Agua Fria River and was, for a short time, referred to as the Agua Fria Ranch. In 1926, the name was changed to Litchfield in honor of Paul W. Litchfield, vice president of the company.

What to See and Do

Duncan Family Farms. 2,000-acre working fruit and vegetable farm allows guests to pick their own organic produce. Petting zoo; farm play yard with "kittie kattle train," swings, giant maze. Country market & bakery. Seasonal festivals. (Fri-Sun; closed hols) 5 mi S in Goodyear; off of Cotton Ln at 17203 W Indian School Rd. Phone 602/853-9880. **Free**

Wildlife World Zoo. Houses a family of dromedaries (single-humped camels); exotic bird aviary; 3 species of rare antelope; monkeys; kangaroos, wallabies; leopards, tigers; all 5 species of the world's flightless birds. Petting zoo; concession. (Daily) 3 mi W on Northern Ave. Phone 602/935-WILD. ¢¢¢

Annual Events

Native American Festival. 387 E Indian School Rd. 100 Native American craft vendors. Native American dancing and other authentic entertainment both days. 3rd wkend Jan.

Goodyear Rodeo Days. In Goodyear. Includes entertainment, family games, dance. Late Feb.

Billy Moore Days. Held in Avondale and Goodyear. Carnival, entertainment, parade, other events. Mid-Oct.

Motel

★★★ **HOLIDAY INN EXPRESS.** *1313 N Litchfield Rd (85338), I-10 W exit 128. 623/535-1313; FAX 623/535-0950.* 90 rms, 3 story. Jan-May: S, D $129-$149; each addl $10; family rates; higher rates special events; lower rates rest of yr. Crib free. Pet accepted. TV; cable (premium). Complimentary continental bkfst. Restaurant adj 6:30 am-10 pm. Ck-out noon. Meeting rms. Business servs avail. In-rm modem link. Valet serv. Coin lndry. Exercise equipt. Pool; whirlpool. Game rm. Many in-rm whirlpools, refrigerators, microwaves, wet bars. Cr cds: A, C, D, DS, JCB, MC, V.

D

Resort

★★★★ **THE WIGWAM.** *300 Wigwam Blvd (85340), 2½ mi N of I-10 Litchfield Rd exit. 623/935-3811; FAX 623/935-3737; res: 800/327-0396.* E-mail wigwam@primenet.com; web www.wigwamresort.com. This beloved hotel is one of the original Arizona resorts inspired by the Southwestern aesthetic. Excellent dining is provided by the Arizona Kitchen. Expansive grounds feature 54 beautifully manicured holes of golf. 331 units in 1-2 story casitas. Jan-Apr: S, D $330-$390; each addl $25; suites $390-$1,800; under 18 free; golf plan; AP & MAP avail; family rates avail hol seasons; lower rates rest of yr. Crib available. Pet accepted, some restrictions. TV; movies on demand. 2 pools; whirlpool, poolside serv. Playground. Supervised child's activities (June-Sept & hols); ages 5-12. Dining rms (public by res) 6:30-10:30 am, 11:30 am-2:30 pm, 5-10 pm (also see THE ARIZONA KITCHEN). Rm serv 24 hrs. Box lunches, bkfst rides, steak fries. Bar 11-1 am. Ck-out 1 pm, ck-in 4 pm. Meeting rms. Business center. Concierge. Valet serv. Gift shop. Barber, beauty shop. Airport transportation. Lighted tennis, pro. 54-hole golf, greens fee $95-$130 (incl cart), pro, putting greens. Stagecoach, hayrides. Bicycles. Skeet, trapshooting. Indoor, outdoor games. Soc dir; entertainment, dancing; special hol programs for families. Exercise equipt; sauna, steam rm. Some refrigerators, minibars, wet bars, fireplaces. Library. Private patios. Cr cds: A, C, D, DS, ER, JCB, MC, V.

D

Restaurants

★★★★ **ARIZONA KITCHEN.** *(See The Wigwam Resort) 623/935-3811.* E-mail wigwam@primenet.com; web www.wigwamresort.com. A rustic early Arizona dining room with brick floors and an open kitchen with wood-burning oven provide the casual atmosphere of this innovative Southwestern restaurant. The food is wonderfully inventive and the service seamless. Southwestern menu. Specialties: smoked corn chowder, grilled sirloin of buffalo, pan seared sturgeon. Hrs: 6-10 pm. Closed Sun, Mon; also 8 wks in July-Aug. Res required. Bar 4 pm-midnight. Wine list. A la carte entrees: dinner $19-$29. Prix fixe $24-$31. Cr cds: A, C, D, DS, ER, JCB, MC, V.

D

★★ **LE RHONE'S BISTRO.** *12345 W Indian School Rd (85340). 602/535-1417.* Hrs: 5:30-8:30 pm. Closed Sun; also Mon mid-June-Aug. Res accepted. Continental menu. Bar. Complete meals: dinner $17.90-$26.75. Child's meals. Specialties: rack of lamb, chateaubriand, English Dover sole. Own baking. Outdoor dining. Totally nonsmoking. Cr cds: A, C, D, DS, MC, V.

D

Marble Canyon (B-4)

(See also Page)

Pop 150 (est) **Elev** 3,580 ft **Area Code** 520 **Zip** 86036

What to See and Do

Marble Canyon. Part of Grand Canyon National Park (see).

River-running trips. Multi-day trips on the Colorado River. For a list of commercial operators contact Grand Canyon National Park, PO Box 129, Grand Canyon 86023; phone 520/638-7888.

Motels

★ **CLIFF DWELLERS LODGE.** *Hwy 89A (85321), 10 mi W of Marble Canyon on US 89A. 520/355-2228; FAX 520/355-2229; res: 800/433-2543.* 20 rms. Apr-Nov: S, D $57-$74; lower rates rest of yr. Restaurant 6 am-11 pm (winter hrs may vary). Ck-out 11 am. Business servs avail. Gift shop. Hiking, fishing; river raft trips. Cr cds: C, DS, MC, V.

D

✓★ **MARBLE CANYON LODGE.** *Hwy 89A (86036), at Navajo Bridge. 520/355-2225; FAX 520/355-2227; res: 800/726-1789.* 58 rms, some kits. May-Aug: S $45; D $55-$60; suites $125; kit. units $55; under 12 free; some lower rates rest of yr. Crib free. Pet accepted. Complimentary coffee in rms. Restaurant 6 am-9 pm; Dec-Mar from 6:30 am. Bar 6 am-9 pm. Ck-out 11 am. Coin lndry. Meeting rms. Business servs avail. Sundries. Hiking. 4,500-ft paved landing strip. Shuttle serv for river rafting. Cr cds: C, DS, MC, V.

D SC

McNary (E-5)

(See also Greer, Pinetop, Show Low, Springerville)

Pop 355 **Elev** 7,316 ft **Area Code** 520 **Zip** 85930

McNary is in the northeastern section of the Fort Apache Indian Reservation. "Hon-dah" is Apache for "be my guest," and visitors find a warm welcome here. The White Mountain Apaches have a number of recreation areas on their reservation. Trout fishing, exploring and camping are available. For further information contact White Mountain Recreation Enterprise, Game & Fish Dept, Box 220, Whiteriver 85941; 520/338-4385.

What to See and Do

Hawley Lake. Summer activities include fishing, camping, hiking and cabin rental. (May-Oct.) 12 mi E on AZ 260, then S 11 mi on AZ 473. Phone 520/335-7511 or 520/338-4417.

Sunrise Park Resort. Resort has 2 quad, 4 triple, 2 double chairlifts, 3 rope tows; patrol, school, rentals; cafeteria, restaurants, bars. 62 runs. Also snowboarding. (Nov-mid-Apr, daily) Summer activities include swimming; fishing; canoeing. Hiking, horseback riding; tennis. Camping. 20 mi E on AZ 260, then S on AZ 273, on Fort Apache Indian Reservation. Phone 520/735-7669 or 800/55-HOTEL. **¢¢¢¢¢**

Mesa (F-4)

(See also Casa Grande, Chandler, Phoenix, Scottsdale, Tempe)

Founded 1878 **Pop** 288,091 **Elev** 1,241 ft **Area Code** 480
E-mail mesacvb@getnet.com **Web** www.arizonaguide.com/mesa

Information Convention & Visitors Bureau, 120 N Center, 85201; 480/827-4700 or 800/283-6372

Mesa, Spanish for "table," sits atop a plateau overlooking the Valley of the Sun and is one of the state's largest and fastest-growing cities. Mesa offers year-round golf, tennis, hiking and water sports. It also provides easy access to other Arizona and Southwest attractions.

What to See and Do

Arizona Mormon Temple Visitors' Center. Murals; 10-ft replica of Thorvaldsen's *Christus* statue; history of prehistoric irrigation; films; dioramas; information. Temple gardens (site of concert series) have large variety of trees, cacti and shrubs collected from all over the world; extensive light display during Christmas season. The Church of Jesus Christ of Latter-day Saints (Mormon) Arizona Temple is located just south of visitor center (not open to the public). Tours of the visitor center (daily). 525 E Main St. Phone 480/964-7164. **Free**

Arizona Museum for Youth. Fine arts museum with changing hands-on exhibits for children. (Daily exc Mon; closed major hols) 35 N Robson. Phone 480/644-2467. **¢**

Boyce Thompson Southwestern Arboretum. 300 acres of gardens and natural areas include cacti, streamside forest, desert lake, hidden canyon, herb garden. Miles of nature trails. (Daily; closed Dec 25) E via US 60 to Superior. Phone 520/689-2811. **¢¢**

Champlin Fighter Museum. Large vintage fighter aircraft collection of WW I, WW II, Korean and Vietnam War planes; also art gallery with paintings of aircraft in combat; display of automatic weapons; extensive collection of photos of fighter aces from WW I to Vietnam; fighter library. (Daily) Falcon Field, 4636 Fighter Aces Dr. Phone 480/830-4540. **¢¢¢**

Dolly Steamboat Cruises. Narrated tours and twilight dinner cruises of Canyon Lake, following the original path of the Salt River. For schedule and information phone 480/827-9144 (fax 480/671-0483). **¢¢¢¢-¢¢¢¢¢**

Lost Dutchman State Park. A 300-acre park in the Superstition Mts area. Hiking. Picnicking (shelter). Improved camping (dump station). Interpretive trails and access to nearby forest service wilderness area. (Daily; closed Dec 25) Standard fees. 14 mi E via US 60/89 to Apache Junction, then 5 mi NE via AZ 88 (Apache Trail Hwy). Phone 480/982-4485.

Mesa Southwest Museum. Displays trace Mesa history from dinosaurs to Space Age and emphasize Arizona history and archaeology. Participatory exhibits include panning for gold, "legendarium" and 1890s territorial jail cells. Changing exhibits; animated dinosaurs; Native American & pioneer celebrations; adobe schoolhouse. (Daily exc Mon; closed major hols) 53 N MacDonald. Phone 480/644-2230. **¢¢**

River tubing. Salt River Recreation Inc. Fee includes tube rental and shuttle bus service to various points on the Salt River. (Mid-Apr-Sept) 15 mi NE in Tonto National Forest (see PAYSON): E on US 60 to Power Rd, then N to jct Usery Pass Hwy. Phone 480/984-3305. **¢¢¢**

Annual Events

Mesa Territorial Days. Sirrine House, 160 N Center. Arizona's birthday party celebrated in Old West style. Western arts and crafts, music, food; rodeo. Phone 480/644-2760. 3rd wkend Feb.

Arizona Renaissance Festival. Phone 480/463-2700. Wkends mid-Feb-mid-Mar.

Seasonal Event

Baseball Spring Training. Ho Ho Kam Park. Chicago Cubs. Phone 480/964-4467. Late Feb-late Mar.

Motels

★★ **BEST WESTERN DOBSON RANCH INN & RESORT.** *1666 S Dobson Rd (85202). 602/831-7000; FAX 602/831-7000; res: 800/528-1356.* Web www.bestwest.com. 213 rms, 2 story. Jan-Apr: S $120-$145; D $130-$165; each addl $15; suites $180-$200; under 12 free; wkend rates; lower rates rest of yr. Crib $3. TV; cable (premium). Heated pool; whirlpool. Complimentary full bkfst. Restaurant 6:30 am-10 pm. Rm serv. Bar 10-1 am. Ck-out noon. Meeting rms. Valet serv. Sundries. Tennis privileges. Golf privileges. Exercise equipt. Health club privileges. Refrigerators avail. Cr cds: A, C, D, DS, ER, JCB, MC, V.

D SC

★★ **BEST WESTERN SUPERSTITION SPRINGS INN.** *1342 S Power Rd (85206). 480/641-1164; FAX 480/641-7253; res: 800/528-1234.* 59 rms, 2 story. Jan-mid-Apr: S, D $120-$139; each addl $10; under 18 free; lower rates rest of yr. Crib free. TV; cable (premium). Complimentary continental bkfst. Restaurant adj open 24 hrs. Ck-out 11 am. Meeting rms. Business servs avail. In-rm modem link. Coin lndry. 18-hole golf privileges, pro, putting green, driving range. Exercise equipt. Pool; whirlpool. Many refrigerators, microwaves. Cr cds: A, C, D, DS, JCB, MC, V.

D SC

★★★ **COURTYARD BY MARRIOTT.** *1221 S Westwood Ave (85210). 602/461-3000; FAX 602/461-0179; res: 800/321-2211.* Web www.courtyard.com. 149 units, 3 story. Jan-Apr: S, D $139-$149; suites $159-$169; wkend rates (off-season); lower rates rest of yr. TV; cable (premium). Heated pool; whirlpool. Complimentary coffee in rms. Restaurant 6-10 am, 5-9 pm; Fri to 10 am; Sat, Sun 7 am-noon. Bar 5-10 pm; closed Sun. Ck-out noon. Coin lndry. Meeting rms. Business servs avail. In-rm modem link. Valet serv. Sundries. Exercise equipt. Refrigerator, microwave in suites. Many balconies. Cr cds: A, C, D, DS, MC, V.

D

✓★ **DAYS INN.** *5531 E Main St (85205). 480/981-8111; FAX 480/396-8027; res: 800/329-7466.* E-mail dayseast@primenet.com; web www.daysinn.com. 61 rms, 2 story. Jan-mid-Apr: S, D $80-$95; under 12 free; lower rates rest of yr. Crib free. TV; cable. Heated pool; whirlpool. Complimentary continental bkfst. Restaurant nearby. Ck-out 11 am. Business servs avail. Cr cds: A, C, D, DS, JCB, MC, V.

D SC

★★ **DAYS INN.** *333 W Juanita Ave (85210). 602/844-8900; FAX 602/844-0973; res: 800/329-7466; res: 800/674-8429.* 124 units, 3 story. Mid-Jan-mid-Apr: S, D $86-$125; each addl $6; under 18 free; lower rates rest of yr. Crib free. Pet accepted. TV; cable (premium), VCR avail (movies). Heated pool; whirlpool. Complimentary continental bkfst. Ck-out 11 am. Coin lndry. Meeting rms. Business servs avail. Valet serv. Exercise equipt; sauna. Refrigerators. Cr cds: A, C, D, DS, MC, V.

D SC

★★ **FAIRFIELD INN.** *1405 S Westwood (85210). 480/668-8000; FAX 480/668-7313; res: 800/228-2800.* E-mail mesaffi@aol.com; web www.marriott.com/fairfieldinn. 66 rms, 3 story. Jan-Apr: S, D $99-$129; under 18 free; lower rates rest of yr. Crib free. TV; cable (premium). Complimentary continental bkfst. Restaurant nearby. Ck-out noon. Business servs avail. In-rm modem link. Pool; whirlpool. Some refrigerators, microwaves. Cr cds: A, C, D, DS, MC, V.

D SC

★★ **HAMPTON INN.** *1563 S Gilbert Rd (85204). 602/926-3600; FAX 602/926-4892; res: 800/426-7866.* 116 rms, 4 story. Jan-mid-Apr: S $119-$129; D $129-$139; under 18 free; lower rates rest of yr. Crib free. TV; cable (premium). Heated pool; whirlpool. Complimentary continental bkfst. Coffee in rms. Ck-out noon. Coin Indry. Meeting rms. Business servs avail. In-rm modem link. Health club privileges. Refrigerators. Cr cds: A, C, D, DS, MC, V.

D SC

★★ **LA QUINTA INN & SUITES.** *6530 E Superstition Springs Blvd (85206). 602/654-1970; FAX 602/654-1973; res: 800/687-6667.* Web www.laquinta.com. 107 rms, 6 story. Mid-Oct-mid-Apr: S, D $119-$129; suites $175; under 18 free; higher rates special events; lower rates rest of yr. Crib free. TV; cable (premium). Complimentary continental bkfst. Complimentary coffee in rms. Restaurant nearby. Ck-out noon. Meeting rms. Business servs avail. In-rm modem link. Valet serv. Coin Indry. Exercise equipt. Pool; whirlpool. Some refrigerators, microwaves. Cr cds: A, C, D, DS, MC, V.

D

★ **QUALITY INN ROYAL.** *951 W Main St (85201). 602/833-1231; FAX 602/833-1231; res: 800/228-5151.* 96 rms, 2 story. Mid-Jan-mid-Apr: S, D $99-$165; each addl $10; under 18 free; golf plans; higher rates Fiesta Bowl; lower rates rest of yr. Crib $5. TV; cable (premium). Heated pool; whirlpool. Complimentary continental bkfst. Coffee in rms. Ck-out noon. Guest Indry. Meeting rm. Business servs avail. Valet serv. Golf privileges. Exercise equipt; sauna. Some refrigerators, bathrm phones; microwaves avail. Private patios, balconies. Cr cds: A, C, D, DS, ER, JCB, MC, V.

D SC

✓★ **RAMADA INN SUITES.** *1410 S Country Club Dr (85210). 480/964-2897; FAX 480/461-0801; res: 800/272-6232.* 121 kit. units, 2 story. Jan-May: S, D $116-$155; each addl $10; studio rms $86; under 18 free; lower rates rest of yr. Crib free. TV; cable (premium). Heated pool; whirlpool. Complimentary continental bkfst. Restaurant nearby. Ck-out noon. Coin Indry. Meeting rms. Health club privileges. Tropical courtyard with gas grills. Cr cds: A, C, D, DS, MC, V.

D SC

★ **TRAVELODGE SUITES.** *4244 E Main St (85205). 480/832-5961; FAX 480/830-9274; res: 800/578-7878.* 75 rms, 60 kit. suites. Mid-Dec-Mar: S $73-$90; D $85-$110; each addl $3; suites $500-$600 wkly; higher rates special events; lower rates rest of yr. Crib $5. Pet accepted, some restrictions; $10. TV; cable (premium). Heated pool; whirlpool. Complimentary coffee in lobby. Restaurant adj 5 am-8 pm. Ck-out 11 am. Business servs avail. Some refrigerators, microwaves. Cr cds: A, C, DS, MC, V.

D SC

Hotels

★★★ **HILTON MESA PAVILION.** *1011 W Holmes Ave (85210). 480/833-5555; FAX 480/649-1886; res: 800/445-8667; res: 800/544-5866.* E-mail meshp_ds@hilton.com; web www.hilton.com. 263 rms, 8 story, 62 suites. Jan-May: S $150-$220; D $160-$230; each addl $10; under 18 free; some wkend rates; lower rates rest of yr. Crib free. TV; cable (premium), VCR avail. Heated pool; whirlpool, poolside serv (in season). Coffee in rms. Restaurant 6:30 am-10 pm. Bar 11-1 am; entertainment Tues-Sat. Ck-out noon. Convention facilities. Business center. In-rm modem link. Gift shop. Tennis privileges. Golf privileges. Exercise equipt. Refrigerators, wet bar in suites; some bathrm phones; microwaves avail. Luxury level. Cr cds: A, C, D, DS, JCB, MC, V.

D

★★ **SHERATON HOTEL.** *200 N Centennial Way (85201). 602/898-8300; FAX 602/964-9279; res: 800/456-6372.* Web www.sheraton.com. 273 rms, 12 story. Mid-Jan-Mar: S, D $119-$159; each addl $10; suites $225-$300; under 18 free; lower rates rest of yr. Crib free. TV; cable (premium), VCR avail. Heated pool; whirlpool. Coffee in rms. Restaurant 6 am-10 pm. Bar 11-1 am. Ck-out noon. Convention facilities. Business servs avail. 18-hole golf privileges, putting green, driving range. Exercise equipt. Refrigerators, minibars. Some balconies. Elaborate landscaping with palm trees, fountain. Luxury level. Cr cds: A, C, D, DS, JCB, MC, V.

D

Resorts

★★★ **ARIZONA GOLF RESORT & CONFERENCE CENTER.** *425 S Power Rd (85206), 1 mi N of Superstition Frwy. 480/832-3202; FAX 480/981-0151; res: 800/528-8282.* E-mail azgolfresrt@earthlink.net; web www.arizonaguide.com/arizona.golf. 187 kit. units, 1-2 story. Jan-Apr: S, D $185-$205; each addl $15-$25; suites $215-$440; under 16 free; golf package; lower rates rest of yr. Crib free. Pet accepted. TV; cable (premium), VCR avail. Heated pool. Coffee in rms. Dining rm 6 am-9 pm. Bar 10 am-midnight. Ck-out noon, ck-in 3 pm. Coin Indry. Meeting rms. Business servs avail. Valet serv. Lighted tennis. 18-hole golf, pro, putting green, driving range. Exercise equipt. Refrigerators, microwaves. Private patios, balconies. Picnic tables, grill. Cr cds: A, C, D, DS, ER, JCB, MC, V.

D

★★★ **GOLD CANYON GOLF RESORT LP.** *6100 S Kings Ranch Rd (85219), 7 mi E on US 60. 602/982-9090; FAX 602/983-9554; res: 800/624-6445.* 101 units. Jan-mid-May: S, D $160-$270; each addl $10; under 18 free; lower rates rest of yr. TV; cable, VCR avail. Heated pool; whirlpool, poolside serv. Dining rm 6:30 am-10 pm. Rm serv. Box lunches, cookouts, bkfst trail rides. Bar 10:30-1 am. Ck-out 11 am, ck-in 4 pm. Meeting rms. Business servs avail. In-rm modem link. Concierge. Valet serv. Lighted tennis. 36-hole golf, greens fee $80-$135 (incl cart), pro, driving range, putting green. Bicycle rentals. Refrigerators, fireplaces; many whirlpools. Private patios. In foothills of Superstition Mountains on 3,300 acres. Cr cds: A, C, D, DS, MC, V.

D

Restaurants

★★ **AMERICAN GRILL.** *1233 S Alma School Rd (85210). 602/844-1918.* Hrs: 11 am-4 pm, 5-10 pm; Sat from noon; Sun 5-9 pm. Closed Dec 25. Res accepted. Bar. Semi-a la carte: lunch $6.25-$9.95, dinner $9.95-$19.95. Child's meals. Specialty: Nawlins shrimp. Pianist Tue-Sat. Garage parking. Totally nonsmoking. Cr cds: A, C, D, DS, MC, V.

D

★★ **GIORDANO'S.** *2909 S Dobson Rd (85202). 602/831-9191.* Hrs: 11 am-10 pm; Fri, Sat to 11 pm; Sun 1-9 pm. Closed Thanksgiving, Dec 25. Res accepted. Italian menu. Bar. Semi-a la carte: lunch $2.99-$7.95, dinner $5.95-$14.95. Specializes in pizzas, own pasta. Cr cds: A, C, MC, V.

D

★★ **LANDMARK.** *809 W Main St (85201). 602/962-4652.* E-mail landmark@valuenet.net; web www.lmrk.com. Hrs: 11 am-9 pm, Sun to 7 pm. Closed July 4, Thanksgiving, Dec 25. Serv bar. Semi-a la carte: lunch $5.95-$8.95, dinner $9.95-$16.95. Child's meals. Specializes in seafood, beef, chicken. Salad bar. Parking. Former Mormon church (ca 1905). Antiques, original artwork. Totally nonsmoking. Cr cds: A, C, D, DS, MC, V.

D

✓★ **MATTA'S.** *932 E Main St (85203). 602/964-7881.* Hrs: 11 am-9 pm; Fri, Sat to 10 pm. Closed major hols. Res accepted. Mexican, Amer menu. Bar. Semi-a la carte: lunch $2.50-$6.95, dinner $6.50-$10.25. Child's meals. Specializes in tacos, chimichangas, chile rellenos. Mariachi band Fri, Sat. Family-owned. Cr cds: A, C, D, DS, MC, V.

D

Montezuma Castle National Monument (D-4)

(See also Cottonwood, Flagstaff)

(20 mi SE of Cottonwood on AZ 260, then N and E off I-17)

This 5-story, 20-room structure was built by Native Americans more than 800 years ago and is one of the most remarkable cliff dwellings in the United States. Perched under a protective cliff, which rises 150 feet, the dwelling is 70 feet straight up from the talus.

Visitors are not permitted to enter the castle, but there is a self-guided trail offering a good view of the structure and of other ruins in the immediate area. Castle "A," a second ruin, is nearby. Montezuma Well, about 11 miles northeast, is a 470-foot-wide limestone sinkhole, with a lake 55 feet deep. Around the rim are well-preserved cliff dwellings. An irrigation system built by the inhabitants about 800 years ago leads from the spring. Limited picnicking; no camping. The Castle Visitor Center and a self-guided trail are both accessible to wheelchairs. (Daily) For further information contact the Chief Ranger, Box 219, Camp Verde 86322; 520/567-3322. ¢

Navajo Indian Reservation (B-4 - C-6)

(See also Holbrook, Kayenta, Page, Winslow)

The Navajo Nation is both the largest Native American tribe and reservation in the United States. The reservation covers more than 25,000 square miles within three states: the larger portion in northeast Arizona and the rest in New Mexico and Utah.

More than 400 years ago, the Navajo people (the Dineh) moved into the arid southwestern region of the United States and carved out a way of life that was in harmony with the natural beauty of present-day Arizona, New Mexico and Utah. In the 1800s, this harmonious life was interrupted by westward-moving settlers and the marauding cavalry. For the Navajo, this conflict resulted in their forced removal from their ancestral land and the "Long Walk" to Fort Sumner, New Mexico. This forced removal of the Navajo was judged a failure; in 1868, they were allowed to return to their homeland.

Coal, oil and uranium have been discovered on the reservation. The income from these, which is handled democratically by the tribe, has helped improve its economic and educational situation.

The Navajo continue to practice many of their ancient ceremonies, including the Navajo Fire Dance and the Yei-bi-chei (winter) and Enemy Way Dances (summer). Many ceremonies are associated with curing the sick and are primarily religious in nature. Visitors must obtain permission to view these events; photography, recording and sketching are prohibited.

Most of the traders on the reservation are friendly and helpful. Do not hesitate to ask them when and where the dances take place. Navajo Tribal rangers, who patrol tribal parks, also are extremely helpful and can answer almost any question that may arise.

There are a number of paved roads across the Navajo and Hopi Reservations (see)—as well as some unpaved gravel and dirt roads. During the rainy season (mostly Aug-Sept), the unpaved roads are difficult or impassable; it is best to stay off them.

Some of the most spectacular areas in Navajoland are Canyon de Chelly National Monument (see); Navajo National Monument (see); Monument Valley Navajo Tribal Park, north of Kayenta (see); Four Corners Monument; and Rainbow Bridge National Monument (see UT). Hubbell Trading Post National Historic Site is in Ganado (see).

Accommodations on the reservation are limited; reservations are needed months in advance. For information contact the Navajoland Tourism Dept, Box 663, Window Rock 86515; 520/871-6436 or -7371

Navajo National Monument (B-5)

(See also Kayenta)

(19 mi SW of Kayenta on US 160, then 9 mi N on paved road AZ 564 to Visitors Center)

This monument comprises three scattered areas totaling 600 acres and is surrounded by the Navajo Nation. Each area is the location of a large and remarkable prehistoric cliff dwelling. Two of the ruins are accessible by guided tour.

Headquarters for the monument and the visitor center are near Betatakin, the most accessible of the three cliff dwellings. Guided tours, limited to 25 people (Betatakin tour), are arranged on a first-come, first-served basis (May-Sept; tours sometimes possible earlier in spring and late in fall; phone for schedule). Hiking distance is five miles round trip including a steep 700-ft trail and takes five to six hours. Because of hot temperatures, high elevations and rugged terrain, this tour is recommended only for those in good physical condition. Betatakin may also be viewed from the Sandal Trail overlook—a half-mile, one-way, self-guided trail. (Daily)

The largest and best preserved ruin, Keet Seel (Memorial Day-Labor Day, phone for schedule), is eight and a half miles one-way by foot or horseback from headquarters. A permit is required either way, and reservations can be made up to two months in advance. Primitive campground available for overnight hikers. The horseback trip takes all day; horses should be reserved when making reservations (fee for horses & for guide; no children under 12 unless previous riding experience).

The visitor center has a museum and film program. There are picnic tables, a campground and a craft shop at the headquarters area. (Daily; closed Jan 1, Thanksgiving, Dec 25) Contact the Superintendent, HC-71, Box 3, Tonalea 86044-9704; 520/672-2367. **Free**

Nogales (H-4)

(See also Patagonia, Tucson)

Founded 1880 **Pop** 19,489 **Elev** 3,869 ft **Area Code** 520 **Zip** 85621

Information Nogales-Santa Cruz County Chamber of Commerce, Kino Park; 520/287-3685

This is a pleasant city and port of entry directly across the border from Nogales, Mexico. (For Border Crossing Regulations, see MAKING THE MOST OF YOUR TRIP.) A Ranger District office of the Coronado National Forest (see TUCSON) is located here.

What to See and Do

Peña Blanca Lake and Recreation Area. Fishing; boating. Picnicking. 8 mi N on I-19 (US 89), then 9 mi W on AZ 289, Ruby Rd, in Coronado

National Forest (see TUCSON). Phone 520/281-2800. For camping information phone 520/281-2296.

Pimeria Alta Historical Society Museum. History of southern Arizona and northern Sonora, from A.D. 1000 to the present. Photo collection; library; archives; self-guided walking tours. (Tues-Sat; closed most major hols) 136 N Grand Ave, in former City Hall. Phone 520/287-4621. **Free**

Tubac Presidio State Historic Park. Arizona's first European settlement, where a presidio (military post) was built in 1752. Spanish colonial and territorial ruins. Picnicking, ramadas. Museum with exhibits and underground view of the remains of the presidio's main building. (Daily; closed Dec 25) 20 mi N off I-19. Phone 520/398-2252. ¢

Tumacacori National Historical Park (see). 18 mi N on I-19 (US 89).

Motel

✓★ **SUPER 8 MOTEL.** *547 W Mariposa Rd (85621), at I-19 exit 4. 520/281-2242; FAX 520/761-1898.* 116 rms, 3 story. No elvtr. S, D $46.88-$60.88; under 12 free. Crib $2. Pet accepted; $5/day. TV; cable. Pool; whirlpool. Restaurant 6 am-9 pm. Bar 3-11 pm; closed Sat, Sun. Ck-out noon. Coin lndry. Meeting rms. Valet serv. Refrigerators. Cr cds: A, C, D, DS, MC, V.

D SC

Resort

★★★ **RIO RICO RESORT & COUNTRY CLUB.** *1069 Camino Caralampi (85648), 12 mi N on I-19, exit 17. 520/281-1901; FAX 520/281-7132; res: 800/288-4746.* 180 units, 2-3 story. No elvtr. Jan-Apr: S, D $180; each addl $15; suites $250-$1,000; under 18 free; golf, tennis, horseback riding plans; lower rates mid-Apr-Sept. Crib free. Pet accepted; $50 refundable. TV; cable (premium). Heated pool; whirlpool, poolside serv. Coffee in rms. Dining rm 6 am-2 pm, 5-9 pm. Box lunches, picnics. Rm serv. Bar 11-1 am; entertainment wkends. Ck-out noon, ck-in 4 pm. Grocery ½ mi. Meeting rms. Business servs avail. Valet serv. Gift shop. Beauty shop. Airport transportation. Lighted tennis. 18-hole golf, $85 with cart, pro, putting green, driving range. Stables. Exercise equipt; sauna. Lawn games. Private patios, balconies. Western cook-outs. On mesa top with scenic view. Cr cds: A, C, D, DS, MC, V.

D SC

Restaurant

★ **MR C'S.** *282 W View Point Dr (85621), I-19 exit 4. 520/281-9000.* Hrs: 11:30-1 am. Closed Jan 1, Dec 25; also Sun. Res accepted. Bar. Semi-a la carte: lunch $6-$15, dinner $9.95-$30. Child's meals. Specialties: guaymas shrimp, fresh fish & steak. Salad bar. Entertainment. Hilltop location; supper club atmosphere. Cr cds: A, C, D, DS, MC, V.

Oak Creek Canyon

(see Flagstaff)

Organ Pipe Cactus National Monument (H-3)

(Park entrance 15 mi S of Ajo on AZ 85; Visitor Center 35 mi S of Ajo on AZ 85)

This 516-square-mile Sonoran desert area on the Mexican border is Arizona's largest national monument. The organ pipe cactus grows as high as 20 feet and has 30 or more arms, which resemble organ pipes. The plant blooms in May and June. Blossoms, usually at branch tips, are white with pink or lavender touches. Depending on the rainfall, during February and March, parts of the area may be covered with Mexican goldpoppy, magenta owl clover, blue lupine and bright orange mallow. Mesquite, saguaro, several species of cholla, barrel cacti, paloverde trees, creosote bush, ocotillo and other desert plants thrive here.

There are two graded scenic drives, which are self-guided: the 53-mile Puerto Blanco and the 21-mile Ajo Mountain drives. There is a 208-site campground near headquarters (May-mid-Jan, 30-day limit; mid-Jan-Apr, 14-day limit; 35-ft RV limit; fee), no reservations; groceries (5 miles). Information service and exhibits are at the visitor center (daily). Standard fees. For further information contact the Superintendent, Rte 1, Box 100, Ajo 85321; 520/387-6849.

Inns

★★ **GUEST HOUSE INN.** *700 W Guest House Rd (85321), 20 mi N on AZ 85, W on La Mina Rd to Guest House Rd. 520/387-6133.* 4 rms. No rm phones. Sept-May: S $69; D $79; each addl $10; lower rates rest of yr. TV in sitting rm; cable, VCR avail. Complimentary full bkfst. Restaurant nearby. Ck-out 11 am, ck-in 2 pm. Former executive guest house built in 1925; stately dining rm. Bird watching. Totally nonsmoking. Cr cds: C, D, MC, V.

★★ **MINE MANAGERS HOUSE BED & BREAKFAST.** *601 W Greenway Dr (85321), 15 mi N on US 85, W on La Mina to Greenway. 520/387-6505; FAX 520/387-6508.* 5 rms. S, D $72-$105; each addl $5-$10. TV in sitting rm. Complimentary full bkfst; afternoon refreshments. Ck-out 10 am, ck-in 2 pm. Coin lndry. Gift shop. Lighted tennis privileges. 9-hole golf privileges. Whirlpool. Library; sitting rm. Totally nonsmoking. Cr cds: C, MC, V.

D SC

Page (B-4)

(See also Marble Canyon, Navajo Indian Reservation)

Pop 6,598 **Elev** 4,000 ft **Area Code** 520 **Zip** 86040
E-mail chamber@page-lakepowell.com

Information Page/Lake Powell Chamber of Commerce, 644 N Navajo, Tower Plaza, Box 727; 520/645-2741 or 888/261-7243.

Page is at the east end of the Glen Canyon Dam, on the Colorado River. The dam, 710 feet high, forms Lake Powell, a part of the Glen Canyon National Recreation Area. The lake, 186 miles long with 1,900 miles of shoreline, is the second-largest man-made lake in the United States.

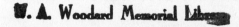

The dam was built for the Bureau of Reclamation for water storage and the generation of electric power. The lake is named for John Wesley Powell, the intrepid and brilliant geologist who lost an arm at the Battle of Shiloh, led an expedition down the Colorado in 1869 and was later director of the US Geological Survey.

What to See and Do

Boat trips on Lake Powell. One-hr to one-day trips, some including Rainbow Bridge National Monument. Houseboat and powerboat rentals. Res advised. 6 mi N on US 89 at Wahweap Lodge & Marina. Phone 602/278-8888 or 800/528-6154.

Glen Canyon National Recreation Area. More than one million acres including Lake Powell. Campfire program (Memorial Day-Labor Day). Swimming, waterskiing; fishing, boating (ramps, marina). Hiking. Picnicking, restaurants, lodge. Camping. Developed areas in Utah include Bullfrog, Hite, Halls Crossing, Dangling Rope (accessible by boat only); many of these have ranger stations, marinas, boat rentals & trips, supplies, camping and lodging. Lees Ferry on Colorado River (approx 15 mi downstream from dam, but a 45-mi drive SW from Page) has a launch ramp and camping. Visitor center on canyon rim, adj to Glen Canyon Bridge on US 89, has historical exhibits. Ranger station, 7 mi N of dam at Wahweap. (Daily; closed Jan 1, Dec 25) Guided tours (summer). Phone 520/608-6404. **Free**; Camping ¢¢¢

John Wesley Powell Memorial Museum. Fluorescent rock collection, Native American artifacts; books, videos; replica of Powell's boat. (Mar-Nov, schedule varies) 6 N Lake Powell Blvd. Phone 520/645-9496. **Free**

Rainbow Bridge National Monument (see UTAH). Approx 60 mi NE in Utah, NW of Navajo Mountain.

Scenic flights over area. Trips vary from 30 min to more than 2 hrs. (Daily; closed Jan 1, Thanksgiving, Dec 25) Page Airport, ½ mi NE on US 89. For fee information contact Scenic Air, Box 1385; phone 520/645-2494.

Wilderness River Adventures. Half-day smoothwater trip on the Colorado River in Glen Canyon in raftlike neoprene boats. (Mar-Oct) Phone 800/528-6154. ¢¢¢¢¢

Motels

★★★ **BEST WESTERN ARIZONA INN.** *716 Rim View Dr (86040). 520/645-2466; FAX 520/645-2053; res: 800/528-1234.* 103 units, 3 story. Apr-Oct: S $62-$92; D $79-$92; each addl $5; suites $125; under 18 free; lower rates rest of yr. Crib free. Pet accepted. TV; cable, VCR (movies). Pool; whirlpool. Restaurant 6 am-10 pm. Bar. Ck-out noon. Meeting rm. Business servs avail. Airport transportation. Overlooking Glen Canyon Dam & Lake Powell. Cr cds: A, C, D, DS, MC, V.

✓★ **BEST WESTERN WESTON INN & SUITES.** *207 N Lake Powell Blvd (86040). 520/645-2451; FAX 520/645-9552; res: 800/637-9183.* 100 rms, 1-3 story. S $58-$62; D $63-$150; each addl $5; under 18 free. Crib $3. TV; cable (premium), VCR avail (movies). Heated pool; whirlpool. Complimentary continental bkfst. Restaurant adj 5:30 am-10 pm. Ck-out 11 am. Business servs avail. In-rm modem link. Free airport transportation. Some rms with balconies & views of Lake Powell. Cr cds: A, C, D, DS, MC, V.

★ **WAHWEAP LODGE/LAKE POWELL MOTEL.** *100 Lakeshore Dr; 2505 US Hwy 89 (86040), 4 mi NW of Glen Canyon Dam on US 89 at Wahweap jct. 520/645-2477; FAX 520/645-1031; res: 800/528-6154.* 24 rms, 2 story. May-Oct: S, D $77; each addl $7; under 18 free; lower rates rest of yr. Crib free. Pet accepted. TV. Pool privileges. Ck-out 11 am. Free airport transportation. View of canyon, cliffs, Lake Powell. Cr cds: A, C, D, DS, MC, V.

★ **WESTON EMPIRE HOUSE MOTEL & RESTAURANT.** *107 S Lake Powell Blvd (86040), 107 S Lake Powell Blvd. 520/645-2406; FAX 520/645-2647; res: 800/551-9005.* 69 rms, 2 story. Apr-Oct: S $58; D $70; each addl $5; under 12 free with 2 adults; some lower rates rest of yr. Crib $4. Pet accepted. TV; cable. Pool. Restaurant 5:30 am-9 pm. Bar 3 pm-1 am; closed Dec-Mar. Ck-out 11 am. Gift shop. Free airport transportation. Balconies. Cr cds: C, MC, V.

Motor Hotels

★★ **RAMADA INN PAGE LAKE POWELL.** *287 N Lake Powell Blvd (86040). 520/645-8851; FAX 520/645-2523; res: 800/272-6232.* 130 rms, 3 story. Mid-Apr-Oct: S, D $85-$106; each addl $7; under 18 free; lower rates rest of yr. Crib free. Pet accepted. TV; cable. Heated pool. Restaurant 6 am-10 pm (summer); 6:30 am-2 pm, 5-9 pm (winter). Rm serv from 7 am. Bar 4 pm-1 am (summer). Ck-out 11 am. Coin Indry. Meeting rms. Business servs avail. Bellhops. Sundries. Gift shop. Private patios, balconies. Picnic tables, grills. Cr cds: A, C, D, DS, MC, V.

★★★ **WAHWEAP LODGE & MARINA.** *100 Lakeshore Dr (86040), 5 mi NW of Dam at Glen Canyon Recreation Area, 2½ mi SE of US 89. 520/645-2433; FAX 520/645-1031; res: 800/528-6154; res: 800/528-6134.* Web www.visitlakepowell.com. 350 rms in 8 bldgs, 2 story. May-Oct: S, D $125-$149; each addl $10; suites $227; under 18 free; lower rates rest of yr. Crib free. Pet accepted. TV; cable. 2 pools; whirlpool, poolside serv. Restaurants 6 am-10 pm. Bar 11-1 am; Sun from noon. Ck-out 11 am. Coin Indry. Meeting rms. Business servs avail. Bellhops. Concierge. Sundries. Gift shop. Free airport transportation. Golf privileges. Exercise equipt. Private patios, balconies. On lake. Boats, motorboats, scenic boat trips. Host for national bass fishing tournaments. Cr cds: A, C, D, DS, MC, V.

Restaurants

✓★★ **BELLA NAPOLI.** *810 N Navajo Dr (86040). 520/645-2706.* Hrs: 5-10 pm. Closed mid-Nov-Feb. Italian menu. Wine list. Semi-a la carte: dinner $7-$17. Specialties: shrimp scampi, chicken tetrazzini. Cr cds: A, C, DS, MC, V.

★ **KEN'S OLD WEST.** *718 Vista (86040). 520/645-5160.* Hrs: 4-11 pm. Closed Jan 1, Thanksgiving, Dec 25. Bar to 1 am. Semi-a la carte: dinner $5.95-$18.95. Child's meals. Specializes in steak, barbecued ribs. Salad bar. Country band. Patio dining. Cr cds: A, C, MC, V.

Parker (E-1)

(See also Lake Havasu City; also see Blythe, CA)

Founded 1908 **Pop** 2,897 **Elev** 413 ft **Area Code** 520 **Zip** 85344
E-mail parker.chamber@rivcom.net
Web www.coloradoriverinfo.com/parker
Information Chamber of Commerce, 1217 California Ave; 520/669-2174

Parker is located on the east bank of the Colorado River, about 16 miles south of Parker Dam (320 ft high, 856 ft long), which forms Lake Havasu. Popular recreational activities in the area include fishing, frogging, boating, jet and water skiing, hunting, golfing, rock hunting and camping. The town has become the trade center for surrounding communities and the Colorado Indian Reservation.

What to See and Do

Buckskin Mountain State Park. 1,676 acres. Scenic bluffs overlooking the Colorado River. Swimming; fishing; boating (ramp, marina). Nature trails, hiking. Picnicking (shelter), concession. Camping (electric hookups, dump station), riverside cabanas (fee). 11 mi NE on AZ 95. Phone 520/667-3231. **River Island Unit** has boating (ramp). Picnicking (shelter).

Camping. (Daily) Standard fees. ½ mi N of main unit. Phone 520/667-3386 or -3231.

★ **Colorado River Indian Tribes Museum, Library and Gaming Casino.** Museum contains exhibits that interpret the history of the four Colorado River Tribes: Mohave, Chemehuevi, Navajo & Hopi. Authentic Native American arts & crafts for sale. Bluewater Casino is open 24 hrs; slots, poker, bingo. Operated by the Colorado River Indian Tribes. (Daily exc Sun; closed hols) 2nd Ave at Mohave Rd. Phone 520/669-9211. **Free**
The museum is part of the

Colorado River Indian Tribes Reservation. More than 278,000 acres in Arizona and California. Fishing, hunting (tribal permit required); boating, waterskiing. Camping (fee).

La Paz County Park. A 540-acre park with 4,000 ft of Colorado River beach frontage. Swimming, waterskiing; fishing; boating (ramps). Tennis court, golf course, driving range. Picnicking (shelter), playground. Camping (electric hookups, dump station). Fee for some activities. 8½ mi N on AZ 95. Phone 520/667-2069.

Parker Dam & Power Plant. One of the deepest dams in the world, 65 percent of its structural height of 320 ft is below the riverbed. Only 85 ft of the dam is visible while another 62 ft of its superstructure rises above the roadway, across the top of the dam. (Daily) 17 mi N via AZ 95, Riverside Dr exit. **Free**

Annual Events

Parker 400 Off Road Race. Three Arizona loops. 400 mi of desert racing. Phone 520/669-2174. Late Jan.

Balloonfest. Hot air balloon racing. 1st wkend Mar.

La Paz County Fair. Carnival, livestock auction, farm olympics, entertainment. Mid-Mar.

Parker Enduro-Aquasports Weekend. Longest and oldest boat racing event in country. Phone 520/669-2174. May.

Holiday Lighted Boat Parade. Decorated boats parade on the 11-mi strip to selected site for trophy presentation; viewing from both sides of the river. Dec.

Motel

✓★ **KOFA INN.** *1700 S California Ave (85344). 520/669-2101; FAX 520/669-6902; res: 800/742-6072.* 41 rms, 1-2 story. S $37; D $41; each addl $4. TV; cable. Pool. Restaurant adj open 24 hrs. Ck-out noon. Sundries. Cr cds: A, C, D, MC, V.

D

Patagonia (H-5)

(See also Nogales, Sierra Vista)

Pop 888 **Elev** 4,057 ft **Area Code** 520 **Zip** 85624

Information Information/Visitors Center, Horse of a Different Color Emporium, Box 241; 520/394-0060 or 888/794-0060

A small cattle town with a distinct mining flavor, Patagonia is surrounded by beautiful mountains and Hollywood-style Western scenery.

What to See and Do

Patagonia Lake State Park. A 265-acre park with a lake. Swimming beach; fishing; boating (ramp, rentals, marina). Hiking. Picnicking, concession, ramadas. Camping (dump station). Standard fees. 8 mi S on AZ 82, then 4 mi N on Patagonia Lake Rd. Phone 520/287-6965.

Patagonia-Sonoita Creek Preserve. The 312 acres extend downstream along Sonoita Creek for more than 1 mi. Bordered by willows, cottonwoods and ash, it provides a perfect sanctuary for more than 250 species of birds. Along AZ 82; watch for directional signs to the entrance. For schedule and fee information phone 520/394-2400.

Motel

✓★ **STAGE STOP INN.** *303 McKeown Ave (85624), 1 blk S of AZ 82. 520/394-2211; FAX 520/394-2212; res: 800/923-2211.* 43 rms, 2 story, 11 kits. S $55; D $69; each addl $10; suites, kit. units $79-$125; under 9 $5. Pet accepted; $5. TV; cable. Heated pool. Restaurant 7 am-9 pm; Fri, Sat to 10 pm. Ck-out noon. Meeting rms. Business servs avail. Sun deck. Frontier atmosphere. Cr cds: A, C, D, DS, MC, V.

Payson (E-4)

(See also Phoenix)

Founded 1882 **Pop** 8,377 **Elev** 5,330 ft **Area Code** 520 **Zip** 85541
E-mail pcoc@netzone.com **Web** www.rimcountry.com

Information Chamber of Commerce, Box 1380, 85547; 520/474-4515 or 800/6-PAYSON

Payson, in the heart of the Tonto National Forest, provides many outdoor recreational activities in a mild climate.

What to See and Do

Tonto National Forest. This area includes almost three million acres of desert and mountain landscape. Six lakes along the Salt and Verde rivers provide opportunities for fishing, boating, hiking and camping. Seven wilderness areas are located within the forest's boundaries, providing hiking and bridle trails. The forest also features Tonto Natural Bridge, the largest natural travertine bridge in the world. Scenic attractions include the Apache Trail, Four Peaks, the Mogollon Rim and Sonoran Desert country. Phone 602/225-5200.

Annual Events

World's Oldest Continuous PRCA Rodeo. 3rd wkend Aug.

Old-Time Fiddler's Contest & Festival. Late Sept.

Motels

✓★★ **BEST WESTERN INN.** *1005 S Beeline Hwy (85541). 520/474-2382; FAX 520/474-1937; res: 800/528-1234; res: 800/772-9766.* 47 rms, 2 story. Late May-Aug: S, D $72-$130; each addl $10; family rates; hols (2-day min); higher rates special events; lower rates rest of yr. Crib $10. TV; cable (premium). Pool; whirlpool. Complimentary continental bkfst. Restaurant nearby. Ck-out noon. Business servs avail. Coin Indry. Refrigerators; some fireplaces. Cr cds: A, C, D, DS, MC, V.

D SC

★★ **HOLIDAY INN EXPRESS.** *206 S Beeline Hwy (85547), S of jct AZ 260 & AZ 87. 520/472-7484; FAX 520/472-6283; res: 800/465-4329.* Web www.holiday-inn.com. 44 rms, 3 story. June-Aug: S $89-$109; D $99-$119; each addl $10; suites $119-$169; under 19 free; higher rates special events; lower rates rest of yr. Crib free. TV. Indoor pool; whirlpool. Complimentary continental bkfst. Restaurant nearby. Ck-out 11 am. Coin Indry. Meeting rms. Business servs avail. Sundries. Refrigerator in suites; microwave avail. Cr cds: A, C, D, DS, JCB, MC, V.

D SC

★★ **INN OF PAYSON.** *801 N Beeline Hwy (85541), (AZ 87), ¼ mi N of AZ 260. 520/474-3241; FAX 520/472-6564; res: 800/247-9477.* 99 rms, 2 story. May-Sept: S, D $89-$149; each addl $10; apt (2-bedrm) $149; under 16 free; lower rates rest of yr. Crib $10. Pet accepted; $10/day. TV; cable (premium). Heated pool; whirlpool. Complimentary continental bkfst. Complimentary coffee in rms. Restaurant 11 am-2 pm, 5-9 pm, Fri-

Sat to 10 pm. Bar from 4 pm. Ck-out 11 am. Meeting rm. Business servs avail. Refrigerators; some in-rm fireplaces. Private patios. Cr cds: A, C, D, DS, JCB, MC, V.

D SC

★★ **MAJESTIC MOUNTAIN INN.** *602 E Hwy 260 (85541). 520/474-0185; FAX 520/472-6097; res: 800/408-2442.* 50 rms, 1 story. Feb-Nov: S, D $58-$140; each addl $6; lower rates rest of yr. Crib free. TV; cable (premium), VCR avail (movies). Pool. Complimentary coffee in rms. Restaurant adj 10:30 am-9 pm. Ck-out 11 am. Meeting rms. Health club privileges. Some fireplaces, in-rm whirlpools. Refrigerators. Picnic tables. Grills. Cr cds: A, C, D, DS, MC, V.

D

Restaurants

★ **LA CASA PEQUENA.** *911 S Beeline Hwy AZ 87 (85541). 520/474-6329.* Hrs: 11 am-10 pm. Closed Thanksgiving, Dec 25. Mexican, Amer menu. Bar to 1 am. Semi-a la carte: lunch $4.25-$7.95, dinner $5.50-$13.95. Specialties: La Casa chimichanga, chicken Acapulco, chicken fajitas. Entertainment Fri, Sat. Mexican decor; large collection of wheeled decanters. Surrounded by gardens. Cr cds: C, MC, V.

D

★ **MARIO'S RESTAURANT.** *600 E State Highway 260 (85541). 520/474-5429.* E-mail xmario@goodnet.com. Hrs: 10:30 am-9 pm; Fri, Sat to 10 pm. Closed Memorial Day, Dec 25. Italian, Amer menu. Bar. Semi-a la carte: lunch $3.25-$7, dinner $5.25-$13.25. Child's meals. Specializes in pasta, pizza. Own bread. Entertainment wkends. Cr cds: A, C, DS, MC, V.

D

Petrified Forest National Park (D-5)

(See also Holbrook)

(North entrance: 25 mi E of Holbrook on I-40. South entrance: 19 mi E of Holbrook on US 180)

These 93,532 acres include one of the most spectacular displays of petrified wood in the world. The trees of the original forest may have grown in upland areas and then washed down onto a floodplain by rivers. Subsequently, the trees were buried under sediment and volcanic ash, causing the organic wood to be filled gradually with mineral compounds, especially quartz. The grain, now multicolored by the compounds, is still visible in some specimens.

The visitor center is located at the entrance off of I-40. The Rainbow Forest Museum (off US 180) depicts the paleontology and geology of the Triassic Era. (Daily; closed Dec 25) Service stations and cafeteria at the north entrance; snacks only at south entrance. Prehistoric Pueblo inhabitants left countless petroglyphs of animals, figures and symbols carved on sandstone throughout the park.

The park contains a portion of the Painted Desert, a colorful area extending 200 miles along the north bank of the Little Colorado River. This highly eroded area of mesas, pinnacles, washes and canyons is part of the Chinle formation, a soft shale, clay and sandstone stratum of Triassic age. The sunlight and clouds passing over this spectacular scenery create an effect of constant, kaleidoscopic change. There are very good viewpoints along the park road.

Picnicking facilities at Rainbow Forest and at Chinde Point on the rim of the Painted Desert; no campgrounds. **Important:** It is forbidden to take even the smallest piece of petrified wood or any other object from the park. Nearby curio shops sell wood taken from areas outside the park. (Daily; closed Dec 25) Standard fees. Contact the Superintendent, Box 2217, Petrified Forest National Park 86028; 520/524-6228.

Phoenix (F-3)

Settled 1864 **Pop** 983,403 **Elev** 1,090 ft **Area Code** 602
Web www.arizonaguide.com/phoenix

Information Phoenix & Valley of the Sun Convention & Visitors Bureau, One Arizona Center, 400 E Van Buren St, Ste 600, 85004; 602/254-6500

Suburbs Glendale, Mesa, Scottsdale, Tempe. (See individual alphabetical listings.)

The capital of Arizona lies on flat desert, surrounded by mountains and green irrigated fields of cotton, lettuce, melons and alfalfa and groves of oranges, grapefruit, lemons and olives. It is a resort area, as well as an industrial area. It is also the home of Grand Canyon University (1949). The sun shines practically every day. Most rain falls in December, with some precipitation in summer. There is swimming, fishing, boating, horseback riding, golf and tennis. Phoenix, like Tucson, is a health center, known for its warm temperatures and low humidity. As a vacation spot, it is both sophisticated and informal.

Transportation

Car Rental Agencies. See IMPORTANT TOLL-FREE NUMBERS.

Public Transportation. Buses (City of Phoenix Transit System), phone 602/253-5000.

Rail Passenger Service. Amtrak 800/872-7245.

Airport Information

Phoenix Sky Harbor Intl Airport. Information 602/273-3300; lost and found 602/273-3307; weather 602/265-5550; cash machines, Terminals 2-4.

What to See and Do

Arizona Hall of Fame Museum. Changing exhibits focus on people who have made significant contributions to Arizona. Guided tours (by appt). (Mon-Fri; closed hols) 1101 W Washington; located in the restored Carnegie Library (1908). Phone 602/255-2110. **Free**

Arizona Mining & Mineral Museum. Collections of minerals, ores, gems; petrified wood; mining exhibits. Maintained by the Arizona Dept of Mines and Mineral Resources. (Mon-Fri, also Sat afternoons; closed state hols) 1502 W Washington. Phone 602/255-3791. **Free**

Arizona Science Center. Features energy, technology and life sciences exhibits. Visitor participation encouraged. (Daily; closed Thanksgiving, Dec 25) 600 E Washington St. Phone 602/716-2000. **¢¢¢–¢¢¢¢**

Arizona State Capitol Museum. Built of native stone with a landscaped area including a large variety of native trees, shrubs and cacti. Four-story restored Capitol Museum exhibits include re-creation of the original 1912 governor's office and the early House and Senate chambers and galleries. (Mon-Fri; closed hols) 1700 W Washington St. To arrange tours phone 602/542-4581 or -4675. **Free**

Desert Botanical Garden. Includes 150 acres of plants from the world's deserts; self-guided nature walk; public lectures; Cactus Show (Apr). (Daily; closed Dec 25) 1201 N Galvin Pkwy, in Papago Park. Phone 480/941-1217 or -1225. **¢¢¢**

Dog racing. Greyhound Park, 40th & E Washington Sts. (Daily) Phone 602/273-7181. **¢–¢¢**

Heritage Square. Historical city park has eight turn-of-the-century houses, including restored 1895 Victorian Rosson House (Wed-Sun; fee) and Arizona Doll & Toy Museum. Also open-air Lath House Pavilion. (Daily) 7th St & Monroe. Phone 602/262-5071 or -5029. **Free**

★ **Mystery Castle.** Unique stone and sand castle built by one man, over a period of 18 yrs, for his daughter. The castle features 18 furnished rms,

13 fireplaces, a cantilevered stairway and a chapel. Tours. (Oct-early July, daily exc Mon) 800 E Mineral Rd. 7 mi S via Central Ave, E on Baseline Rd, S on 7th St, then E on Mineral Rd. Phone 602/268-1581. **¢¢**

Phoenix Art Museum. Permanent and traveling exhibits; Western, contemporary, decorative arts, European galleries; Thorne miniature rms; Arizona Costume Institute; Oriental art; sculpture court. Tours avail. Special exhibits (fee). Store; cafe. (Daily exc Mon; closed major hols) 1625 N Central Ave. Phone 602/257-1880. **Free**

Phoenix Mountains Preserve. Located in both the northern and southern parts of the city, the parks offer more than 23,500 acres of unique desert mountain recreational activities. Hiking, riding and picnicking daily. Phone 602/262-6861. **Free**

Echo Canyon (Camelback Mountain). Hiking trails, including trail to top of Camelback Mountain. E McDonald & Tatum Blvd. Phone 602/256-3220.

North Mountain Recreation Area. Hiking on mountain trails. Picnicking (shelter). 10600 N 7th St. Phone 602/262-7901.

South Mountain. Offers 16,000 acres in a rugged mountain range. Hiking trails, park drives to scenic overlooks. Picnicking (shelter). 10919 S Central. Phone 602/495-0222.

Squaw Peak Park. Hiking trail (1¼ mi) offers panoramic view of city; park also offers access to other mountain trails. Picnicking (shelter). 2701 E Squaw Peak Dr (22nd St & Lincoln Dr). Phone 602/262-7901.

Phoenix Museum of History. More than 2,000 yrs of Arizona history; changing exhibits. (Daily; closed major hols) 105 N 5th St. Phone 602/253-2734. **¢¢**

Phoenix Zoo. A 125-acre zoo; home to more than 1,300 mammals, birds and reptiles, most in naturalistic exhibits. Features rare Sumatran tigers; Tropical Flights aviary; African savannah; Arizona Trail exhibit, with native animals; children's zoo; safari train tours; refreshment centers. (Daily; closed Dec 25) 455 N Galvin Pkwy, in Papago Park. Phone 602/273-1341. **¢¢¢**

Hall of Flame Firefighting Museum. The nation's largest collection of antique fire equipment, hand- and horse-drawn (from 1725) and motorized (1906-1961); fire communications, firemarks, artwork, models and memorabilia. (Daily; closed Jan 1, Thanksgiving, Dec 25) 6101 E Van Buren St. Phone 602/275-3473. **¢¢**

Professional sports.

National League baseball (Arizona Diamondbacks). Bank One Ballpark, 401 E Jefferson. Phone 602/514-8400.

NBA (Phoenix Suns). America West Arena, 201 E Jefferson. Phone 602/379-7900.

NHL (Phoenix Coyotes). America West Arena, 201 E Jefferson. Phone 602/379-7800.

Pueblo Grande Museum and Cultural Park. A Hohokam archaeological site and ruin, thought to have been occupied between A.D. 300-1450. Museum features permanent and changing exhibits. Interpretive trail. Tours (Sept-May). (Daily; closed hols) 4619 E Washington St, approx 1 mi NE of Sky Harbor Intl Airport. Phone 602/495-0901. **¢**

★ **The Heard Museum.** The arts and lifestyles of Southwest Native American culture, prehistoric to contemporary representation. Changing exhibits include primitive art from throughout the world and Native American art. Also features Goldwater kachina doll collection; artist demonstrations. (Daily; closed hols) 2301 N Central Ave. Phone 602/252-8848 or -8840. **¢¢¢**

Thoroughbred Horse Racing. (Late Sept-early May, Fri-Tues; closed some hols) Turf Paradise, 1501 W Bell Rd, 10 mi N on I-17 to Bell Rd exit. Phone 602/942-1101. **¢–¢¢**

Tonto National Forest. 20 mi NE on AZ 87. (See PAYSON)

Annual Events

Fiesta Bowl. College football classic game. Phone 480/350-0900. Early Jan.

Indian Fair and Market. Heard Museum (see). Native American artisans, demonstrations, dances, native foods. Phone 602/252-8840. 1st wkend Mar.

Yaqui Indian Holy Week Ceremonials. Phone 602/883-2838. Fri evenings prior to Easter, beginning 1st Fri after Ash Wed.

Arizona State Fair. State Fairgrounds. Phone 602/252-6771. Oct 12-29.

Cowboy Artists of America. Phoenix Art Museum (see). Phone 602/257-1880. Late Oct-mid-Nov.

Seasonal Events

The Phoenix Symphony. Symphony Hall, 455 N 3rd St, at 2nd St & Adams. For schedule, ticket information phone 602/495-1999. May.

Arizona Opera Company. Phoenix Symphony Hall, 4600 N 12th St. For schedule phone 602/266-7464. Thurs-Sun, Oct-Mar.

Arizona Theatre Company. Professional regional company performs both classic and contemporary works. 502 W Roosevelt. For schedule, ticket information phone 602/256-6899 or -6995. Nov-early June.

Additional Visitor Information

The Phoenix & Valley of the Sun Convention & Visitors Bureau has helpful information for visitors; contact them at One Arizona Center, 400 E Van Buren St, Suite 600, 85004; 602/254-6500; visitor information, 602/252-5588.

Phoenix Metro Magazine, available at newsstands, has up-to-date information on cultural events and articles of interest to visitors.

Motels

★★★ **COURTYARD BY MARRIOTT.** *2101 E Camelback Rd (85016). 602/955-5200; FAX 602/955-1101; res: 800/321-2211.* Web www.marr.com. 155 rms, 4 story. Jan-May: S, D $165-$175; suites $185-$195; under 13 free; wkend, wkly, hol rates; lower rates rest of yr. Crib free. TV; cable (premium). Heated pool; whirlpool. Complimentary coffee in rms. Restaurant 6:30-10:30 am; Sat, Sun 7 am-noon. Rm serv. Bar 4-11 pm. Ck-out noon. Coin lndry. Meeting rms. Business servs avail. In-rm modem link. Valet serv. Exercise equipt. Refrigerator, microwave in suites. Balconies. Cr cds: A, C, D, DS, MC, V.

D SC

★★ **COURTYARD BY MARRIOTT.** *2621 S 47th St (85034), near Sky Harbor Intl Airport. 602/966-4300; FAX 602/966-0198; res: 800/321-2211.* E-mail phxvc@aol.com; web www.marriott.com. 145 units, 4 story. Jan-early May: S, D $159-$169; each addl $10; suites $179-$189; wkend, wkly rates; lower rates rest of yr. Crib free. TV; cable (premium). Heated pool; whirlpool. Complimentary coffee in rms. Restaurant 6 am-2 pm, 5-10 pm; wkends 7 am-noon, 5-10 pm. Bar 4-11 pm. Ck-out noon. Coin lndry. Meeting rms. Business servs avail. In-rm modem link. Valet serv. Free airport transportation. Exercise equipt. Health club privileges. Refrigerator in suites. Many balconies. Cr cds: A, C, D, DS, MC, V.

D SC

★★ **FAIRFIELD INN AIRPORT.** *4702 E University Dr (85034). 480/829-0700; FAX 480/829-8068; res: 800/228-2800.* E-mail phxapt@aol.com; web www.marriott.com. 90 rms, 3 story, 22 suites. Jan-Apr: S, D $119-$139; suites $129-$149; under 18 free; higher rates special events; lower rates rest of yr. Crib free. TV; cable (premium), VCR avail. Complimentary continental bkfst. Restaurant adj from 6:30 am. Ck-out noon. Business servs avail. In-rm modem link. Valet serv. Coin lndry. Health club privileges. Pool; whirlpool. Refrigerator, microwave in suites; microwaves avail. Cr cds: A, C, D, DS, JCB, MC, V.

D

★★ **HAMPTON INN.** *8101 N Black Canyon Hwy (85021), I-17 exit Northern Ave on frontage rd. 602/864-6233; FAX 602/995-7503; res: 800/426-7866.* 149 rms, 3 story. Jan-mid-Apr: S, D $105-$120; under 18 free; higher rates special events; lower rates rest of yr. Crib free. Pet accepted, some restrictions. TV; cable (premium). Heated pool; whirlpool.

Complimentary continental bkfst. Ck-out noon. Meeting rms. Business servs avail. In-rm modem link. Coin Indry. Grills. Cr cds: A, C, D, DS, JCB, MC, V.

D SC

★★★ **HOMEWOOD SUITES.** *2001 E Highland Ave (85016). 602/508-0937; FAX 602/508-0854.* Web www.homewoodsuites.com. 124 kit. suites, 4 story. Jan-Apr: S $179-$189; D $189-$199; each addl $10; under 18 free; wkly, wkend, hol rates; lower rates rest of yr. Crib free. Pet accepted, some restrictions; $100. TV; cable (premium), VCR. Complimentary continental bkfst. Complimentary coffee in rms. Restaurant adj 11 am-11 pm. Ck-out noon. Meeting rm. Business center. In-rm modem link. Valet serv. Sundries. Coin Indry. Exercise equipt. Health club privileges. Pool. Refrigerators, microwaves; some fireplaces. Grills. Cr cds: A, C, D, DS, MC, V.

D SC

★★ **LA QUINTA INN.** *2725 N Black Canyon Hwy (85009), I-17 exit Thomas Rd. 602/258-6271; FAX 602/340-9255; res: 800/687-6667.* Web www.laquinta.com. 139 rms, 2 story. Jan-Apr: S, D $95-$110; each addl $10; under 18 free; lower rates rest of yr. Crib free. Pet accepted, some restrictions. TV; cable (premium). Heated pool. Complimentary continental bkfst. Coffee in rms. Restaurant adj open 24 hrs. Ck-out noon. Coin Indry. Business servs avail. In-rm modem link. Valet serv. Some refrigerators. Cr cds: A, C, D, DS, MC, V.

D SC

★★★ **PHOENIX NORTH COURTYARD BY MARRIOTT.** *9631 N Black Canyon Hwy (03264). 602/944-7373; FAX 602/944-0079; res: 800/321-2211.* 146 rms, 3 story. Jan-mid-Apr: S, D $129-$139, suites $149-$159; under 18 free; wkend rates; lower rates rest of yr. Crib free. TV; cable (premium). Heated pool; whirlpool. Complimentary coffee in rms. Restaurant 6:30-10 am, 5-9 pm. Rm serv. Ck-out noon. Coin Indry. Business servs avail. Valet serv. Exercise equipt. Some refrigerators; microwaves avail. Balconies. Cr cds: A, C, D, DS, MC, V.

D SC

✓★ **PREMIER INNS OF METRO CENTER.** *10402 N Black Canyon Hwy (85051), at I-17 Peoria Ave exit. 602/943-2371; FAX 602/943-5847; res: 800/786-6835.* 253 rms, 2 story. Jan-Apr: S, D $59.95-$89.95; suites $129.95; lower rates rest of yr. Crib $3. Pet accepted, some restrictions. TV; cable (premium). 2 pools, 1 heated; wading pool. Ck-out noon. Coin Indry. Meeting rms. Some refrigerators; bathrm phone in suites. Some private patios. Cr cds: A, C, D, DS, MC, V.

SC

Motor Hotels

★★ **BEST WESTERN GRACE INN AHWATUKEE.** *10831 S 51st St (85044), just S of I-10 Elliott Rd exit. 602/893-3000; FAX 480/496-8303; res: 800/528-1234.* 160 rms, 6 story. Jan-May: S, D $100-$132; each addl $10; suites $120-$175; under 17 free; lower rates rest of yr. Crib free. TV; cable (premium). Heated pool; poolside serv. Coffee in rms. Restaurant 6 am-10 pm. Rm serv. Bar 11:30-1 am; Sun from noon; entertainment. Ck-out noon. Meeting rms. Business servs avail. Bellhops. Valet serv. Sundries. Free airport transportation. Lighted tennis. Health club privileges. Lawn games. Refrigerators; microwaves avail. Many balconies. Luxury level. Cr cds: A, C, D, DS, JCB, MC, V.

D SC

★★ **BEST WESTERN INN SUITES.** *1615 E Northern Ave (85020). 602/997-6285; FAX 602/943-1407; res: 800/752-2204.* E-mail isphoenix@attmail.com; web www.arizonaguide. com/innsuites. 123 rms, 2 story, 4 kits. Jan-mid-Apr: S, D $119-$129; kit. suites $149-$169; under 19 free; lower rates rest of yr. Crib free. Pet accepted, some restrictions; $25 refundable. TV; cable (premium). Heated pool; whirlpool. Complimentary continental bkfst. Complimentary coffee in rms. Ck-out noon. Coin Indry. Meeting rms. Business servs avail. In-rm modem link. Exercise equipt. Health club privileges. Playground. Refrigerators, microwaves. Picnic tables, grills. Cr cds: A, C, D, DS, MC, V.

D SC

★★ **EMBASSY SUITES NORTH.** *2577 W Greenway Rd (85023). 602/375-1777; FAX 602/375-4012; res: 800/527-7715.* Web www.embassysuites.com. 314 suites, 2-3 story. Jan-mid-May: S, D $109-$199; under 18 free; lower rates rest of yr. TV; cable (premium). Heated pool; wading pool, whirlpool. Complimentary full bkfst. Coffee in rms. Restaurant 6 am-10 pm. Rm serv. Bar 11-1 am. Ck-out noon. Coin Indry. Meeting rms. Business servs avail. In-rm modem link. Bellhops. Valet serv. Lighted tennis. Exercise equipt; sauna. Lawn games. Refrigerators. Cr cds: A, C, D, DS, ER, JCB, MC, V.

D

★★★ **HILTON PHOENIX AIRPORT HOTEL.** *2435 S 47th St (85034), near Sky Harbor Intl Airport. 602/894-1600; FAX 602/921-7844; res: 800/728-6357.* E-mail pahilton@primenet.com; web www.hilton.com. 255 units, 4 story. Jan-May: S $149-$299; D $164-$314; each addl $15; suites $299-$425; under 18 free; lower rates rest of yr. Crib avail. TV; cable (premium), VCR avail. Pool; whirlpool, poolside serv. Coffee in rms. Restaurant 6 am-2 pm, 5-10 pm; Sun 5-9 pm. Rm serv to midnight. Bar 11 am-midnight. Ck-out noon. Convention facilities. Business center. In-rm modem link. Bellhops. Valet serv. Concierge. Sundries. Gift shop. Free airport transportation. Exercise equipt. Minibars. Many balconies. Luxury level. Cr cds: A, C, D, DS, ER, JCB, MC, V.

D

★ **LOS OLIVOS HOTEL AND SUITES.** *202 E McDowell Rd (85004). 602/258-6911; FAX 602/258-7259; res: 800/776-5560.* 48 rms, 3 story, 15 suites. Jan-Apr: S, D $99; each addl $10; suites $129; under 16 free; lower rates rest of yr. TV; cable (premium), VCR avail. Whirlpool. Complimentary coffee in rms. Restaurant Mon-Fri 6:30 am-3 pm; Sat to noon. Ck-out noon. Coin Indry. Meeting rms. Business servs avail. Sundries. Valet serv. Tennis. Health club privileges. Refrigerator in suites. Balconies. Picnic tables. Cr cds: A, C, D, DS, MC, V.

D SC

★★ **PHOENIX INN.** *2310 E Highland Ave (85016), adj to Biltmore Fashion Park. 602/956-5221; FAX 602/468-7220; res: 800/956-5221.* Web mmm.arizonaguide.com/phoenixinn. 120 rms, 4 story. Jan-May: S, D $119-$165; each addl $10; suites $209-$239; under 18 free; lower rates rest of yr. Crib free. TV; cable (premium), VCR avail. Heated pool; whirlpool. Complimentary continental bkfst. Complimentary coffee in rms. Restaurant nearby. Ck-out noon. Meeting rm. Business servs avail. In-rm modem link. Bellhops. Coin Indry. Free airport transportation. Exercise equipt. Health club privileges. Refrigerators, microwaves. Cr cds: A, C, D, DS, MC, V.

D SC

✓★ **QUALITY INN.** *5121 E La Puente Ave (85044). 480/893-3900; FAX 480/496-0815; res: 800/562-3332.* 193 rms, 4 story. Jan-Apr: S, D $99-$129; suites $135-$155; under 17 free; lower rates rest of yr. Crib free. Pet accepted; $15. TV; cable (premium). Heated pool; whirlpool. Coffee in rms. Restaurant 6:30-11 am, 5-9 pm. Rm serv. Ck-out 11 am. Coin Indry. Meeting rms. Business servs avail. Valet serv. Health club privileges. Some refrigerators; microwaves avail. Cr cds: A, C, D, DS, MC, V.

D SC

★★ **RADISSON AIRPORT.** *3333 E University Dr (85034), at I-10 & University Dr, near Sky Harbor Intl Airport. 602/437-8400; FAX 602/470-0998; res: 800/333-3333.* Web www.radisson.com. 163 rms, 6 story. Jan-Apr: S $159-$209; D $169-$219; each addl $10; under 18 free; hol rates; higher rates special events; lower rates rest of yr. Crib free. TV; cable (premium). Heated pool; whirlpool, poolside serv. Complimentary coffee in rms. Restaurant 6 am-2 pm, 5:30-10 pm. Rm serv. Bar 11-1 am. Ck-out noon. Meeting rms. Business servs avail. Bellhops. Valet serv. Sundries. Gift shop. Coin lndry. Free airport transportation. Exercise equipt; sauna. Some refrigerators; microwaves avail. Some balconies. Cr cds: A, C, D, DS, ER, JCB, MC, V.

D SC

✓★ **RAMADA INN.** *502 W Camelback Rd (85013). 602/264-9290; FAX 602/264-3068; res: 800/688-2021.* 166 rms, 4 story. Jan-Apr: S $91-$100; D $101-$110; each addl $10; suites $140-$150; lower rates rest of yr. Crib free. TV; cable (premium). Heated pool; whirlpool, poolside serv. Restaurant 6:30 am-2 pm, 5-9:30 pm. Rm serv. Bar 2-10 pm; wkends to 1 am. Ck-out noon. Coin lndry. Meeting rms. Business servs avail. Valet serv. Free airport transportation. Exercise equipt. Health club privileges. Refrigerators. Cr cds: A, C, D, DS, MC, V.

D SC

★★ **RAMADA PLAZA METROCENTER HOTEL.** *12027 N 28th Dr (85029). 602/866-7000; FAX 602/942-7512; res: 800/566-8535.* Web www.ramada.com. 172 rms, 4 story. Mid-Jan-mid-Apr: S $119; D $129; each addl $10; suites $159-$179; under 18 free; lower rates rest of yr; rates vary special events. Crib free. Pet accepted, some restrictions; $75 refundable. TV; cable. Heated pool; whirlpool, poolside serv. Complimentary coffee in rms. Restaurant 6 am-10 pm. Rm serv. Bar 4-11 pm. Ck-out noon. Meeting rms. Business servs avail. Some refrigerators, microwaves. Cr cds: A, C, D, DS, ER, JCB, MC, V.

D SC

★★★ **WYNDHAM GARDEN HOTEL.** *427 N 44th St (85008), near Sky Harbor Intl Airport. 602/220-4400; FAX 602/231-8703.* Web www.travelnet.com/wyndham. 210 rms, 7 story, 24 suites. Jan-May: S $197; D $207; each addl $10; suites $217; under 18 free; lower rates rest of yr. Crib free. TV; cable. Heated pool; whirlpool, poolside serv. Coffee in rms. Restaurant 6:30 am-2 pm, 5-10 pm; Sat, Sun from 7 am. Rm serv 5-10:30 pm. Bar 4 pm-midnight. Ck-out noon. Meeting rms. Business center. Valet serv. Sundries. Free airport transportation. Exercise equipt. Some bathrm phones. Cr cds: A, C, D, DS, ER, JCB, MC, V.

D SC

★★★ **WYNDHAM GARDEN HOTEL NORTH.** *2641 W Union Hills Dr (85027), at I-17 & Union Hills. 602/978-2222; FAX 602/978-9139; res: 800/822-4200.* Web www.wyndham.com. 166 rms, 2 story. Jan-Apr: S $149; D $159; each addl $10; under 18 free; lower rates rest of yr. Pet accepted, some restrictions; $25 refundable. TV; cable. Heated pool; whirlpool, poolside serv. Coffee in rms. Restaurant 6:30 am-10 pm. Rm serv 5-10 pm. Bar 4:30-11 pm. Ck-out noon. Meeting rms. Business servs avail. Valet serv. Sundries. Some refrigerators. Some private patios. Cr cds: A, C, D, DS, ER, JCB, MC, V.

D SC

Hotels

★★★ **BEST WESTERN EXECUTIVE PARK HOTEL.** *1100 N Central Ave (85004). 602/252-2100; FAX 602/340-1989; res: 800/528-1234.* Web www.bestwestern.com/best.html. 107 rms, 8 story. Jan-Apr: S, D $119-$135; each addl $10; suites $210; under 18 free; wkend rates; lower rates rest of yr. Crib free. TV; cable. Heated pool; whirlpool, poolside serv. Coffee in rms. Restaurant 6:30 am-10 pm. Bar 11 am-11 pm; Sun from noon. Ck-out noon. Meeting rms. Business servs avail. Free airport transportation. Exercise equipt; sauna. Health club privileges. Some bathrm phones, refrigerators, wet bars. Balconies. Panoramic mountain views. Cr cds: A, C, D, DS, ER, MC, V.

D SC

★★★ **DOUBLETREE GUEST SUITES-PHOENIX GATEWAY CTR.** *320 N 44th St (85008), near Sky Harbor Intl Airport. 602/225-0500; FAX 602/231-0561; res: 800/222-8733.* Web www.doubletree.com. 242 suites, 6 story. Jan-Apr: S $165-$265, D $175-$275; each addl $10; wkend rates; lower rates rest of yr. Crib free. TV; cable (premium), VCR avail. Heated pool; whirlpool, poolside serv. Complimentary coffee in rms. Restaurant 6 am-10 pm; Sat, Sun from 7 am. Bar 11 am-midnight. Ck-out noon. Meeting rms. Business center. Gift shop. Free airport transportation. Exercise equipt. Refrigerators, microwaves, minibars. Atrium. Cr cds: A, C, D, DS, MC, V.

D

★★ **EMBASSY SUITES.** *1515 N 44th St (85008), near Sky Harbor Intl Airport. 602/244-8800; FAX 602/244-8114; res: 800/362-2779.* Web www.embassy-suites.com. 229 suites, 4 story. Jan-Apr: S, D $185-$209; each addl $15; under 12 free; lower rates rest of yr. Crib free. TV; cable (premium). Heated pool; whirlpool, poolside serv. Complimentary full bkfst. Complimentary coffee in rms. Restaurant 11:30 am-10 pm. Bar. Ck-out noon. Coin lndry. Meeting rms. Business servs avail. Gift shop. Free airport transportation. Refrigerators, microwaves. Balconies. Grills. Glass-enclosed elvtr overlooks courtyard. Cr cds: A, C, D, DS, JCB, MC, V.

D

★★★ **EMBASSY SUITES.** *2630 E Camelback Rd (85016). 602/955-3992; FAX 602/955-6479; res: 800/362-2779.* Web www.embassy suites.com. 232 kit. suites, 5 story. Jan-May: S $250-$300; D $265-$325; each addl $15; under 13 free; lower rates rest of yr. Crib free. TV; cable (premium). Heated pool; whirlpool, poolside serv. Complimentary full bkfst; afternoon refreshments. Complimentary coffee in rms. Restaurant 11 am-10 pm. Bar to midnight. Ck-out 1 pm. Meeting rms. Business servs avail. In-rm modem link. Coin lndry. Gift shop. Tennis privileges. Golf privileges. Exercise equipt. Health club privileges. Refrigerators, microwaves. Private patios, balconies. Atrium with lush garden & fish pond. Cr cds: A, C, D, DS, ER, JCB, MC, V.

D

★★★ **HILTON SUITES.** *10 E Thomas Rd (85012), corner of Thomas Rd & Central Ave. 602/222-1111; FAX 602/265-4841; res: 800/932-3322.* Web www.hilton.com. 226 suites, 11 story. Jan-May: S, D $207-$239; each addl $15; under 18 free; wkend, hol rates; lower rates rest of yr. Crib free. Pet accepted. TV; cable (premium), VCR avail. Indoor pool; whirlpool. Complimentary full bkfst. Coffee in rms. Restaurant 11 am-2 pm, 5:30-10 pm; Sat, Sun from 5:30 pm. Bar 4 pm-midnight. Ck-out noon. Meeting rms. Business center. In-rm modem link. Concierge. Gift shop. Grocery. Exercise equipt; sauna. Health club privileges. Refrigerators, microwaves. Balconies. Cr cds: A, C, D, DS, ER, JCB, MC, V.

D

★★ **HOLIDAY INN.** *4300 E Washington St (85034), near Sky Harbor Intl Airport. 602/273-7778; FAX 602/275-5616; res: 800/465-4329.* E-mail phxea@aol.com. 301 rms, 10 story. Jan-mid-May: S $149-$189; D $159-$199; each addl $10; suites $198-$298; under 18 free; higher rates: hols (3-day min), special events, spring training; lower rates rest of yr. Crib $10. Pet accepted. TV; cable (premium), VCR avail. Heated pool; whirlpool, poolside serv. Coffee in rms. Restaurant 6 am-11 pm. Bar 11-1 am; entertainment Tues-Fri. Ck-out noon. Coin lndry. Convention facilities. Business servs avail. In-rm modem link. Valet serv. Gift shop. Garage parking. Free airport transportation. 18-hole golf privileges, greens fee $35-$120, pro. Exercise equipt. Game rm. Some refrigerators; microwaves avail. Cr cds: A, C, D, DS, JCB, MC, V.

D SC

★★ **HOLIDAY INN - WEST.** *1500 N 51st Ave (85043), I-10 exit 139. 602/484-9009; FAX 602/484-0108; res: 800/465-4329.* Web www.traveler.net/ht10/custom/servico/0410.html. 144 rms, 4 story. Jan-Apr: S, D $159; each addl $10; suites $259; under 18 free; higher rates special events; lower rates rest of yr. Crib free. TV; cable (premium), VCR avail. Pool; whirlpool, poolside serv. Coffee in rms. Restaurant 6 am-10 pm; wkend hrs vary. Bar 11 pm-1 am. Ck-out noon. Meeting rms. Business servs avail. Gift shop. Golf privileges, pro, putting green, driving range. Exercise equipt; sauna. Some refrigerators. Balconies. Cr cds: A, C, D, DS, ER, JCB, MC, V.

D SC

✓★ **HOTEL SAN CARLOS.** *202 N Central Ave (85004). 602/253-4121; FAX 602/253-6668; res: 800/678-8946.* E-mail sancarlos1 @aol.com. 132 rms, 7 story. Jan-Apr: S, D $119-$129; each addl $10; suites $169-$199; under 12 free; package plans. Crib free. Pet accepted, some restrictions. TV; cable (premium). Heated pool. Complimentary continental bkfst. Complimentary coffee in rms. Restaurant 11 am-11 pm. Ck-out noon. Meeting rms. In-rm modem link. Health club privileges. Refrigerators; microwaves avail. Cr cds: A, C, D, DS, MC, V.

SC

★★★ **HYATT REGENCY.** *122 N 2nd St (85004). 602/252-1234; FAX 602/254-9472; res: 800/233-1234.* E-mail concierge@hyatt.com; web www.hyatt.com. 712 rms, 24 story. Oct-Apr: S, D $225-$275; suites $350-$1,250; under 18 free; wkend rates; lower rates rest of yr. Crib free. Garage $10/day, valet $15. TV; cable (premium), VCR avail. Heated pool; whirlpool, poolside serv. Restaurant 6 am-midnight (also see COMPASS). Bar 11-1 am. Ck-out noon. Meeting rms. Business center. Concierge. Shopping arcade. Tennis privileges. Golf privileges. Exercise equipt. Health club privileges. Wet bar in some suites. Some balconies. Cr cds: A, C, D, DS, ER, JCB, MC, V.

D

★★ **LES JARDINS HOTEL & SUITES.** *401 W Clarendon Ave (85013), between Indian School Rd & Osborn Ave. 602/234-2464; FAX 602/277-2602; res: 800/333-3333.* Web www.radisson.com. 106 rms, 4 story. Jan-May: S, D $129-$149; each addl $10; suites $149; under 17 free; lower rates rest of yr. Crib free. TV; cable (premium). Heated pool; whirlpool, poolside serv. Coffee in rms. Restaurant 6:30 am-11 pm. Bar 11:30-1 am. Ck-out noon. Meeting rms. Business servs avail. Some refrigerators. Courtyard. Cr cds: A, C, D, DS, ER, JCB, MC, V.

SC

★★ **LEXINGTON HOTEL & SPORTS CLUB.** *100 W Clarendon Ave (85013). 602/279-9811; FAX 602/285-2932; res: 877/253-9749; res: 800/537-8483.* E-mail phxgm@attmail.com. 180 rms, 3 & 7 story. Jan-May: S, D $149-$169; under 18 free; wkend rates; lower rates rest of yr. Crib free. Pet accepted, some restrictions; $100 ($50 refundable). TV; cable (premium). Heated pool; whirlpool. Restaurant 6:30 am-10:30 pm; closed Sun. Bar. Ck-out noon. Business servs avail. Barber, beauty shop. Gift shop. Free valet parking. Exercise rm; sauna. Some microwaves, refrigerators. Some balconies. Cr cds: A, C, D, DS, ER, MC, V.

D SC

★★★★ **RITZ-CARLTON HOTEL.** *2401 E Camelback Rd (85016), in the Camelback Esplanade. 602/468-0700; FAX 602/468-0793; res: 800/241-3333.* Conveniently situated near the popular Biltmore Fashion Square, this handsome hotel has transported the feel of an elegant English manor house into the heart of the Sonoran Desert. Dark woods, fine marble and tapestries in the public areas are only a prelude to the richly furnished, technology-friendly guest rooms. 18th- and 19th-century European paintings and china collections decorate the large public rooms of this elegant hotel. 281 rms, 11 story. Jan-May: S, D $260-$325; suites $365-$500; under 12 free; lower rates rest of yr. Crib avail. TV; cable (premium), VCR avail. Pool; poolside serv. Restaurant (see BISTRO 24). Rm serv 24 hrs. Bar 5 pm-1 am; Sat, Sun from 11 am; entertainment. Ck-out noon. Convention facilities. Business center. Concierge. Gift shop. Covered parking. Airport, RR station, bus depot transportation. . Golf privileges. Exercise rm; sauna. Massage. Health club privileges. Bicycle rentals. Bathrm phones, minibars; microwaves avail. Luxury level. Cr cds: A, C, D, DS, ER, JCB, MC, V.

D

★★★ **SHERATON CRESCENT HOTEL.** *2620 W Dunlap Ave (85021), at I-17. 602/943-8200; FAX 602/371-2857; res: 800/423-4126.* E-mail dan_dickhart@ittsheraton.com; web www.arizonaguide.com/sheratoncrescent. 342 rms, 8 story. Early Jan-mid-May: S, D $165-$239; suites $400-$650; some wkend rates; lower rates rest of yr. Crib free. Pet accepted, some restrictions; $100 refundable. TV; cable (premium), VCR avail. Heated pool; whirlpool, poolside serv. Complimentary coffee in rms. Restaurant 6 am-10 pm. Bar 11-1 am; entertainment. Ck-out noon. Convention facilities. Business center. Gift shop. Free covered parking. Lighted tennis. Exercise rm; sauna, steam rm. Lawn games. Refrigerators, minibars. Balconies. Some fireplaces. Luxury level. Cr cds: A, C, D, DS, ER, JCB, MC, V.

D

★★★ **WYNDHAM HOTEL.** *10220 N Metro Pkwy E (85051), at Metrocenter Shopping Ctr, I-17 Peoria exit. 602/997-5900; FAX 602/997-1034; res: 800/822-4200.* Web www.travelweb.com. 284 rms, 5 story. Jan-May: S $149-$238; D $159-$248; each addl $10; suites $269-$349; under 18 free; wkend rates; lower rates rest of yr. Crib free. TV; cable (premium). Heated pool; whirlpool, poolside serv. Complimentary coffee in rms. Restaurant 6:30 am-11 pm. Bar 11-1 am; Sun from noon. Ck-out noon. Business center. Concierge. Shopping arcade. Lighted tennis. Exercise equipt; sauna. Heliport. Luxury level. Some refrigerators. Cr cds: A, C, D, DS, ER, JCB, MC, V.

D SC

Resorts

★★★★ **ARIZONA BILTMORE RESORT & SPA.** *24th Street and Missouri (85016), northeast of downtown. 602/955-6600; FAX 602/381-7600; res: 800/950-0086.* Designed by Frank Lloyd Wright's colleague, Albert Chase McArthur, and built in 1929, this historic hotel is set on 250 acres of lush gardens and lawns. The wide variety of rooms include secluded cottages. An outstanding spa and fitness center and championship golf top the list of amenities. 730 rms, 2-4 story. Jan-Apr: S, D $395-$495; each addl $30; suites from $620-$1,745; AP, MAP avail; golf plan; lower rates rest of yr. Crib avail. TV; cable (premium). 8 heated pools; wading pool, whirlpool, poolside serv. Supervised child's cabana club. Restaurants 5:30 am-midnight. Rm serv. Bar 10-1 am. Ck-out noon, ck-in 4 pm. Concierge. Shopping arcade. Barber, beauty shop. Lighted tennis. 36-hole golf, greens fee $150 (incl cart), putting greens, driving range. Bicycle rentals. Lawn chess, jeep tours and hot air ballooning. Rec rm. European spa w/salon and fitness center. Exercise rm; sauna. Refrigerators. Sun decks. Most w/private patios and mountain views, balconies. Paradise Pool w/92 waterslide and private cabana. Cr cds: A, C, MC, V.

D

★★★ **POINTE HILTON.** *11111 N 7th St (85020). 602/866-7500; FAX 602/993-0276; res: 800/932-3322.* E-mail phxrr_cro@hilton.com; web www.hilton.com/hotels/PHXTCPR. 585 suites, 6 story. Mid-Jan-May: S, D $219-$399; each addl $15-$25; under 18 free; wkend, hol rates; golf plan; lower rates rest of yr. Crib free. Pet accepted, some restrictions; $100 deposit. TV; cable (premium), VCR avail. Supervised child's activities May-Sept; ages 3-12. Complimentary coffee in rms. Restaurant (see DIFFERENT POINTE OF VIEW). Box lunches, snack bar, picnics. Bar 10-1 am; entertainment. Ck-out noon, ck-in 4 pm. Grocery 1 mi. Coin lndry. Package store 1 mi. Convention facilities. Business center. In-rm modem link. Bellhops. Valet serv. Concierge. Shopping arcade. Barber, beauty shop. Sports dir. Lighted tennis, pro. 18-hole golf, greens fee $130-$140, pro, putting green, driving range. Horse stables. Bicycle rentals. Game rm. Exercise rm; sauna, steam rm. Spa. Health club privileges. Pool; whirlpool, poolside serv. Refrigerators, minibars, wet bars; some bathrm phones, fireplaces. Balconies. Picnic tables. Luxury level. Cr cds: A, C, D, DS, ER, JCB, MC, V.

D

★★★ **POINTE HILTON RESORT.** *7677 N 16th St (85020). 602/997-2626; FAX 602/997-2391; res: 800/932-3322; res: 800/321-3232.* Web www.hilton.com/hotels/phxsppr. 563 suites, 4 story. Jan-Apr: S, D $159; suites $199-$319; under 18 free; golf plans; hols (4-day min); lower rates rest of yr. Crib free. TV; cable (premium), VCR avail. Complimentary coffee in rms. Restaurant 6 am-11 pm. Snack bar. Rm serv 6 am-midnight. Bar 11-2 am. Ck-out noon, ck-on 4 pm. Coin lndry. Convention facilities. Business center. Bellhops. Valet serv. Concierge. Shopping arcade. Barber, beauty shop. Airport transportation. Lighted tennis. 18-hole golf privileges, greens fee $119, pro, putting green, driving range. Bicycle rentals. Exercise rm; sauna, steam rm. Massage. Spa. Heated pool; wading pool, whirlpool, poolside serv. Supervised child's activities; ages 4-12. Many refrigerators, microwaves; minibar, wet bar in suites. Cr cds: A, C, D, DS, ER, JCB, MC, V.

D SC

★★★ **POINTE HILTON SOUTH MOUNTAIN RESORT.** *7777 S Pointe Pkwy (85935). 602/438-9000; FAX 602/431-6535; res: 800/876-4683.* E-mail phxsm_ns@hilton.com; web www.hilton.com. 638 suites, 2-4 story. Jan-mid-May: S, D $249-$339; each addl $15; suites $299-$495; under 18 free; lower rates rest of yr. TV; cable (premium). 6 heated pools; wading pool, whirlpool, poolside serv. Supervised child's activities; ages 5-12. Complimentary coffee in rms. Dining rm (see RUSTLER'S ROOSTE). Rm serv. Bar 11-1 am. Ck-out noon, ck-in 4 pm. Coin lndry. Convention facilities. Business center. Beauty shop. Sports dir. Lighted tennis, pro. 36-hole golf, greens fee $105 (incl cart), pro, putting green. Bicycles. Exercise rm, sauna. Massage. Rec rm. Minibars. Private patios, balconies. Cr cds: A, C, D, DS, ER, JCB, MC, V.

D SC

★★★★ **ROYAL PALMS HOTEL & CASITAS.** *5200 E Camelback Rd (85018). 602/840-3610; FAX 602/840-0233; res: 800/672-6011.* E-mail royalres@destinationtravel.com; web www.royalpalmshotel.com. A 1997 renovation restored this property to luxury status. The refurbished casitas have become designer showcases. Reflecting pools, outdoor fireplaces, and fountains accent the landscaped grounds. 116 rms, 1-2 story. Jan-May: S, D $345; each addl $25; suites $385-$3,500; under 18 free; ; lower rates rest of yr. Serv charge $16/day. Crib free. TV; cable (premium). Pool; poolside serv. Restaurant (see T. COOK'S). Rm serv 24 hrs. Bar 11 am-midnight; Fri, Sat to 1 am. Ck-out noon. Meeting rms. Business center. Valet serv. Airport transportation. Tennis, pro. Exercise equipt. Minibars. Some balconies. Spanish architecture; antiques. Totally nonsmoking. Cr cds: A, C, D, DS, MC, V.

D

Inns

★★ **HARMONY HOUSE INN.** *7202 N 7th Ave (35021). 602/331-9554; FAX 602/395-0528.* E-mail jfontaine@sprintmail.com; web www.bbonline.harmonyhouse.com. 5 rms, 2 with shower only, 2 story. Nov-May: S $90-$130; D $100-$140; each addl $5; suite $110-$145; under 12 free; lower rates rest of yr. TV in some rms; cable, VCR avail (movies). Complimentary full bkfst. Restaurant nearby. Ck-out noon, ck-in 3-6 pm. Business servs avail. Luggage handling. Concierge serv. Guest lndry. Picnic tables, grills. Built in 1934; Victorian decor. Totally nonsmoking. Cr cds: A, C, MC, V.

★★★ **LA ESTANCIA BED AND BREAKFAST.** *4979 E Camelback Rd (85018). 602/808-9924; FAX 602/808-9925; res: 800/410-7655.* E-mail laestancia@worldnet.att.net; web www.bbonline.com/az/laestancia. 5 rms, 2 story. No rm phones. Jan-May: S, D $175-$195; golf plan; lower rates rest of yr. Closed Aug. Children over 8 yrs only. TV in common rm; cable, VCR avail. Complimentary full bkfst; afternoon refreshments. Restaurant nearby. Ck-out 11 am, ck-in noon-4 pm. Business servs avail. Luggage handling. Concierge serv. Free airport transportation. Tennis privileges. Health club privileges. Pool. Lawn games. In-rm whirlpools. Built in 1929. Totally nonsmoking. Cr cds: A, C, D, DS, MC, V.

★★★ **MARICOPA MANOR.** *15 W Pasadena Ave (85013). 602/274-6302; FAX 602/266-3904; res: 800/292-6403.* E-mail mmanor@getnet.com. 6 rms, 1 kit. Sept-May: S, D, kit. unit $129-$189; each addl $25; lower rates rest of yr. TV; cable (premium). Pool; whirlpool. Complimentary continental bkfst in rms. Restaurant nearby. Ck-out 11 am, ck-in 4-6 pm. Business servs avail. Health club privileges. Many microwaves. Picnic tables. Restored Spanish mission-style mansion (1928); antiques, library/sitting rm. Gardens, fountains. Totally nonsmoking. Cr cds: A, C, DS, MC, V.

Restaurants

★★★ **AVANTI OF PHOENIX.** *2728 E Thomas Rd (85016). 602/956-0900.* Web www.avanti-az.com. Hrs: 11 am-2 pm, 5-10 pm; Sat, Sun from 5:30 pm. Closed Dec 25. Res accepted. Continental, Italian menu. Bar. Wine list. Semi-a la carte: lunch $8.95-$15.95, dinner $14.95-$28.95. Specializes in veal, fresh pasta, fresh seafood. Own desserts. Entertainment Wed-Sat. Valet parking. Patio dining in season. Cr cds: A, C, D, DS, MC, V.

D

★★ **BABY KAY'S CAJUN KITCHEN.** *2119 E Camelback St (85016), in Town and Country Shopping Center. 602/955-0011.* Hrs: 11 am-3 pm, 5-10 pm; Fri, Sat to 11 pm; Sun 11 am-9 pm. Closed major hols. Cajun menu. Bar. Semi-a la carte: lunch $6.95-$13.95, dinner $8.50-$19.95. Specialties: gumbo, crawfish etouffee, red beans and rice. Blues/jazz Tues-Sat. Outdoor dining. Casual dining. Cr cds: A, C, MC, V.

D

★★★ **BISTRO 24.** *(See The Ritz-Carlton Hotel) 602/952-2424.* Hrs: 6 am-11 pm; Fri, Sat to midnight; Sun brunch 11 am-2:30 pm. Res accepted. Bar. Wine cellar. Semi-a la carte: bkfst $6.25-$9.25, lunch $7.25-$17, dinner $14.50-$26. Sun brunch $27. Child's meals. Specialties: crab cakes, seafood risotto, crispy skin whitefish. Own baking. Valet parking. Outdoor dining on streetside patio. European-inspired bistro. Cr cds: A, C, D, DS, JCB, MC, V.

D

★★★ **CHRISTOPHER'S BISTRO.** *2398 E Camelback Rd (85016), in Biltmore Financial Center. 602/957-3214.* E-mail dine@christophers.com; web www.christophers.com. Hrs: 11 am-midnight; Sat, Sun from 5 pm. Closed some major hols. Res accepted. Bar. Wine cellar. A la carte entrees: lunch $8-$15, dinner $19-$30. Child's meals. Specializes in seafood, grilled veal chop, rack of lamb. Valet parking. Outdoor dining. Bistro-style dining room. Cr cds: A, C, D, DS, MC, V.

D

★★ **COMPASS ATOP HYATT REGENCY.** *(See Hyatt Regency) 602/440-3166.* Hrs: 11:30 am-2 pm, 5:30-10 pm; Sun brunch 10 am-2 pm. Res accepted. Bar to midnight. Semi-a la carte: lunch $7.50-$12, dinner $17-$23. Sun brunch $27. Child's meals. Specializes in prime rib. Own baking. Valet parking. Revolving dining area on 24th floor; panoramic view of city. Totally nonsmoking. Cr cds: A, C, D, DS, ER, JCB, MC, V.

D

★★★ **DIFFERENT POINTE OF VIEW.** *(See Pointe Hilton) 602/863-0912.* Hrs: 5:30-10 pm. Closed Sun, Mon (mid-June-Oct). Res accepted. Regional Amer menu. Bar 5 pm-1 am. Wine cellar. A la carte entrees: dinner $23-$36. Prix fixe: dinner (mid-June- mid-Sept) $29.95. Sun brunch (Oct-Father's Day) $34.95. Child's meals. Specializes in steak, seafood, regional dishes. Own baking. Entertainment Wed-Sat. Valet parking. Outdoor dining. On mountaintop, view of surrounding mountain ranges. Totally nonsmoking. Cr cds: A, C, D, DS, ER, JCB, MC, V.

D

★★ **EDDIE'S GRILL.** *4747 N 7th St (85014), S of Camelback. 602/241-1188.* Web www.savydiner.com. Hrs: 11:30 am-2:30 pm, 5-11 pm; Fri to midnight; Sat 5 pm-midnight; Sun 4-9 pm. Closed some major hols. Res accepted. Bar. Wine cellar. Semi-a la carte: lunch $9.95-$14.95, dinner $15.95-$21.95. Child's meals. Specialties: ginger cilantro-crusted salmon, seared filet mignon, baked meatloaf. Outdoor dining. Surrounded by Koi ponds. Totally nonsmoking. Cr cds: A, C, D, DS, MC, V.

D

★★ **FISH MARKET.** *1720 E Camelback Rd (85016). 602/277-3474.* Web www.fishmarket.com. Hrs: 11 am-9:30 pm; Fri, Sat to 10 pm; Sun noon-9:30 pm. Closed Thanksgiving, Dec 24 eve, Dec 25. Res accepted. Bar. Semi-a la carte: lunch $8-$20, dinner $10-$40. Child's meals. Specializes in fresh fish, live shellfish, smoked fish. Oyster bar. Outdoor dining. Nautical decor. Retail fish market. Sushi bars. Cr cds: A, C, D, DS, MC, V.

D

✓★ **GEORGE & DRAGON.** *4240 N Central Ave (85012). 602/241-0018.* Web www.georgeanddragon.com. Hrs: 11 am-10 pm; Fri, Sat to 11 pm. Res accepted. English menu. Bar to 1 am. Semi-a la carte: lunch $4.95, dinner $8.95. Child's meals. Specialties: fish and chips, shephard's pie, liver and onions. Authentic British pub. Cr cds: A, C, D, MC, V.

D

★★★ **GREEKFEST.** *1940 E Camelback Rd (85016). 602/265-2990.* E-mail grkfest@primenet.com; web www.arizonaguide.com/greekfest. Hrs: 11 am-2:30 pm, 5-10 pm; Fri, Sat to 11 pm; Sun 5-9 pm. Closed some major hols. Res accepted. Greek menu. Bar. Semi-a la carte: lunch $4.95-$12, dinner $8-$25. Child's meals. Specialties: lamb exohiko, rack of lamb, souvlaki. Parking. Outdoor dining. Greek decor; festive atmosphere. Cr cds: A, C, D, DS, MC, V.

D

★★★ **HARRIS'.** *3101 E Camelback Rd (85016). 602/508-8888.* Hrs: 11:30 am-2 pm, 5:30-10 pm. Closed Dec 25, also Sun (summer). Res accepted. Bar 11 am-10 pm; Sat, Sun 5-10 pm. Wine cellar. Semi-a la carte: lunch $8.95-$10.95, dinner $16-$29. Specializes in beef, lamb chops, Atlantic salmon. Pianist Thurs-Sat. Valet parking. Outdoor dining. Southwestern decor. Cr cds: A, C, D, DS, MC, V.

D

★★ **HAVANA CAFE.** *4225 E Camelback Rd (85018). 602/952-1991.* Web www.rapidax.com/havanacafe. Hrs: 11:30 am-10 pm; Sun 4-9 pm. Closed some major hols. Cuban, Spanish menu. Bar. A la carte entrees: lunch $4.95-$11.95, dinner $8.95-$25. Specialties: pollo Cubano, masas de puerco fritas, paella. Patio dining. Totally nonsmoking. Cr cds: A, C, D, DS, MC, V.

D

✓★★ **HOPS! BISTRO & BREWERY.** *2584 E Camelback Rd (85016). 602/468-0500.* E-mail alan@cougans.com. Hrs: 11 am-midnight. Closed Thanksgiving, Dec 25. Res accepted. Bar to 1 am Fri, Sat. Semi-a la carte: lunch, dinner $6.95-$18.95. Child's meals. Specialties: oven-roasted chicken, Chinese chicken salad, beer croutons. Valet parking. Outdoor dining. High-tech decor. Cr cds: A, C, D, DS, MC, V.

D ♥

✓★★ **HOUSTON'S.** *2425 E Camelback Rd Ste 110 (85016). 602/957-9700.* Hrs: 11 am-11 pm; Fri, Sat to midnight. Closed Thanksgiving, Dec 25. Bar. Semi-a la carte: lunch, dinner $7-$19. Specializes in ribs, fresh grilled fish. Outdoor dining. Cr cds: A, C, MC, V.

D

★★★ **LA FONTANELLA.** *4231 E Indian School Rd (85018). 602/955-1213.* Web www.lafontanella. Hrs: 11 am-2 pm, 4:30-9:30 pm; Sat, Sun from 4:30 pm. Closed Dec 25. Res accepted. Italian menu. Bar. Semi-a la carte: lunch $6-$9.50, dinner $10-$19.75. Child's meals. Entertainment Mon. Specialties: rack of lamb, osso bucco, pasta with seafood. Own desserts. Cr cds: A, C, D, DS, MC, V.

D

★★ **LE RHONE RESTAURANT BAR & CLUB.** *9401 W Thunderbird Rd (85381), US 101 exit Thunderbird Rd. 602/933-0151.* Hrs: 5:30-8:30 pm. Closed Mon; Jan 1. Res accepted. Swiss, continental menu. Bar. Complete meals: dinner $18.90-$27.95. Specialties: châteaubriand, jumbo gulf shrimp provençale, rack of lamb. Pianist. Cr cds: A, C, D, DS, MC, V.

D

✓★★ **LOMBARDI'S AT THE ARIZONA CENT.** *455 N 3rd St (85004), at the Arizona Center. 602/257-8323.* Hrs: 11 am-11 pm; Sun to 10 pm. Closed Thanksgiving, Dec 25. Res accepted. Italian menu. Bar. A la carte entrees: lunch $8-$14.95, dinner $9.50-$21.95. Specializes in homemade pasta, seafood. Patio dining. Open kitchen. Cr cds: A, C, D, MC, V.

D

✓★ **MARILYN'S.** *12631 N Tatum Blvd (85032). 602/953-2121.* Hrs: 11 am-10 pm; Sun, Mon to 9 pm; Fri, Sat to 10:30 pm. Closed Thanksgiving, Dec 25. Mexican menu. Bar. Semi-a la carte: lunch $4.95-$7.50, dinner $7-$14.95. Child's meals. Specialties: fajitas, spinach enchilada, pollo fundido. Southwestern decor; fiesta atmosphere. Cr cds: A, C, DS, MC, V.

D

★★ **MONTI'S.** *12025 N 19th Ave (85029), corner of 19th Ave and Cactus. 602/997-5844.* Hrs: 11 am-10 pm; Fri, Sat to 11 pm; early-bird dinner 3-6:30 pm. Closed Dec 25. Res accepted. Bar. Semi-a la carte: lunch $4.10-$8.80, dinner $5.30-$34.15. Child's meals. Specializes in sirloin, small filet. Parking. Outdoor dining. Western motif. Family-owned. Cr cds: A, C, D, DS, MC, V.

D

✓★★ **PIZZERIA BIANCO.** *623 E Adams St (85004), in Heritage Square. 602/258-8300.* Hrs: 11:30 am-2 pm, 5:30-10 pm; Sat, Sun from 5:30; Sun to 9 pm. Closed Mon; hols. Italian menu. Bar. A la carte entrees: lunch $4.50-$10.50, dinner $8-$11.50. Specializes in wood-fired pizzas, organic salads. Own dough, mozzarella. Totally nonsmoking. Cr cds: C, MC, V.

D

★ **PRONTO RISTORANTE.** *3950 E Campbell Ave (85018). 602/956-4049.* Web www.prontoristorante.com. Hrs: 11:30 am-2:30 pm, 5:30-10 pm; Fri, Sat to 10:30 pm. Closed Sun; Thanksgiving, Dec 25. Res accepted. Regional Italian menu. Bar. Semi-a la carte: lunch $5.95-$9.95, dinner $10.95-$17.95. Specialties: capellini alla pescarese, veal Marsala, gnocchi di patate. 3 dining areas. Dinner theater Fri, Sat. Stained-glass; antique instruments. Cr cds: A, C, D, DS, MC, V.

D

★★ **RAFFAELE'S.** *2999 N 44th St (85018). 602/952-0063.* Hrs: 11:30 am-10 pm; Fri to 11 pm; Sat 5-11 pm; Sun 5-10 pm. Closed Thanksgiving, Dec 25. Res accepted. Italian menu. Bar. Semi-a la carte: lunch $4.95-$11.95, dinner $9.50-$22. Specialties: osso bucco, vitello saltimbocca. Valet parking (Mon-Sat). Patio dining. Contemporary decor; view of fountain, courtyard. Cr cds: A, C, D, DS, MC, V.

D

★★★ **ROXSAND.** *2594 E Camelback Rd (85016), Biltmore Fashion Park. 602/381-0444.* Web www.roxsand.com. Hrs: 11 am-10 pm; Fri, Sat to 10:30; Sun noon-9:30 pm. Closed most major hols. Res accepted. Bar. Wine list. Semi-a la carte: lunch $8.25-$11.95, dinner $17.95-$25.95. Menu changes seasonally. Valet parking. Outdoor dining. Cr cds: A, C, D, MC, V.

D

★★ **RUSTLER'S ROOSTE.** *(See Pointe Hilton on South Mountain) 602/431-6474.* Hrs: 5-10 pm; Fri, Sat to 11 pm. Bar 4 pm-1 am. Semi-a la carte: dinner $9.95-$21.95. Child's meals. Specializes in steak, chicken, ribs. Entertainment. Valet parking. Outdoor dining. Rustic decor. Cr cds: A, C, D, DS, ER, JCB, MC, V.

D

★★ **RUTH'S CHRIS STEAK HOUSE.** *2201 E Camelback Rd (85016). 602/957-9600.* E-mail phoenix@ruthschris.com; web nt1.ruthschris.com. Hrs: 5-10 pm; Fri, Sat to 10:30 pm. Closed Thanksgiving, Dec 25. Res accepted. Bar. Semi-a la carte: dinner $18.95-$50. Specializes in steaks. Valet parking. Outdoor dining. Cr cds: A, C, D, MC, V.

D

★★ **STEAMERS OYSTER GRILL.** *455 N 3rd St #290 (85004), in Arizona Center. 602/252-6767.* Hrs: 11 am-10 pm; Fri, Sat to 11 pm. Closed Easter, Thanksgiving, Dec 25. Semi-a la carte: lunch, dinner $6-$25. Child's meals. Specializes in oysters, sushi, grilled fish. Colorful decor. Separate oyster bar area. Cr cds: A, C, D, MC, V.

D

★★ **STEAMERS SEAFOOD & RAW BAR.** *2576 E Camelback Rd (85016). 602/956-3631.* E-mail big4@infinet-is.com; web www.infinet-is.com/nbig4. Hrs: 11:30 am-10 pm; Fri, Sat to 11 pm. Closed Thanksgiving, Dec 25. Res accepted. Bar to 11 pm. Semi-a la carte: lunch $7.95-$14.95, dinner $16.95-$24.95. Child's meals. Specialties: stuffed crown of prawns, Jamaican BBQ escalar, sushi. Raw bar. Valet parking. Outdoor dining. Bright and colorful, spacious dining area. Cr cds: A, C, D, DS, MC, V.

D

★ **SUCH IS LIFE.** *3602 N 24th St (85016). 602/948-1753.* Hrs: 11:30 am-2:30 pm, 5:30-10 pm; Sat, Sun from 5 pm. Closed most major hols. Res accepted. Mexican menu. Bar. A la carte entrees: lunch $6-$12, dinner $10-$25. Specialties: fish Vera Cruz, pork, shrimp with garlic. Guitarist and singer Mon-Sat. Two dining areas with Mexican flair. Cr cds: A, C, D, DS, MC, V.

D

★★★ **T. COOK'S.** *(See Royal Palms Hotel and Casitas) 602/808-0766.* E-mail jbarba@destinationtravel.com; web www.royalpalmshotel.com. Hrs: 6 am-2 pm, 6-10 pm; Sun brunch 10 am-2 pm. Res accepted. Mediterranean menu. Bar 10 am-midnight; Fri, Sat to 1 am. Wine list. Semi-a la carte: bkfst $6-$14, lunch $9-$15, dinner $16-$27. Sun brunch $12-$28. Specialties: T. Cook's Mediterranean paella, mussels sauteed in Chardonnay thyme broth. Pianist. Valet parking. Outdoor dining. Mediterranean decor; handpainted walls. Cr cds: A, C, D, DS, MC, V.

D

★★★ **TARBELL'S.** *3213 E Camelback Rd (85018). 602/955-8100.* E-mail eat@tarbells.com; web www.tarbells.com. Hrs: 5-11 pm; Sun to 10 pm. Closed most major hols. Res accepted. Bar. Wine cellar. Semi-a la carte: dinner $15-$27. Specialties: grilled salmon, potato cake, veal chops. Own baking. Open kitchen with woodburning oven. Cr cds: A, C, D, DS, JCB, MC, V.

D

★★ **TIMOTHY'S.** *6335 N 16th St (85016). 602/277-7634.* Hrs: 11 am-11 pm; Fri to midnight; Sat 5 pm-midnight. Closed Sun; Labor Day, Thanksgiving, Dec 24, 25. Eclectic menu. Res accepted. Bar. Semi-a la carte: lunch $5-$10, dinner $12-$30. Jazz musicians nightly. Valet parking. Patio dining. Jazz theme. Cr cds: A, C, D, DS, MC, V.

★★★ **TOMASO'S.** *3225 E Camelback Rd (85016). 602/956-0836.* Hrs: 11:30 am-2:30 pm, 5-10:30 pm; Sat, Sun from 5 pm. Closed Thanksgiving, Dec 25. Res accepted. Italian menu. Bar. A la carte entrees: lunch $8-$14, dinner $12-$23. Child's meals. Specializes in pasta, veal, seafood. Cr cds: A, C, D, DS, MC, V.

D

★★ **TOP OF THE MARKET.** *1720 E Camelback Rd (85016), top floor of Fish Market. 602/277-3474.* Hrs: 5-9:30 pm; Fri, Sat to 10 pm. Closed Thanksgiving, Dec 24 & 25. Res accepted. Bar. A la carte entrees: dinner $15-$50. Child's meals. Specializes in seafood, pasta, pizza. Parking. Nautical decor. Wood-burning pizza oven. View of Squaw Peak Mountain. Cr cds: A, C, D, DS, MC, V.

D

✓★ **TUCCHETTI.** *2135 E Camelback Rd (85016), in Town & Country Shopping Center. 602/957-0222.* Hrs: 11:15 am-9:30 pm; Fri to 10:30 pm; Sat noon-10:30 pm; Sun 4:30-9 pm. Closed some major hols. Res accepted. Italian menu. Bar. A la carte entrees: lunch, dinner $6.95-$18.95. Child's meals. Specializes in pasta, chicken, pizza. Outdoor dining. Italian atmosphere. Cr cds: A, C, D, DS, MC, V.

D

★★★ **VINCENT GUERITHAULT ON CAMELBAK.** *3930 E Camelback Rd (85018). 602/224-0225.* Southwestern, Amer menu. Specializes in lamb, chicken, seafood. Own baking, ice cream. Hrs: 11:30 am-2:30 pm, 6-10:30 pm; Sat from 5:30 pm. Closed major hols; also on Sun during June-Sept. Res accepted. Bar. Wine list. A la carte entrees: lunch $7.50-$11.50, dinner $19.75-$24.50. Valet parking. Open-air market on Sat, mid-Oct-mid-Apr. Cr cds: A, C, D, MC, V.

D ♥

★★★ **WRIGHT'S.** *24th St & Missouri (85016). 602/954-2507.* Continental Cuisine. Hrs 11 am-2 pm; 6-10 pm; Sun brunch 10 am-2 pm. Prices lunch $10-$15; dinner $24-$34. A la carte entrees. Chef tasting menu $65. Brunch $37.95. Res reqd (dinner & brunch). Valet. Pianist & trio band Mon-Sun. Nonsmoking. Cr cds: C.

Unrated Dining Spots

CHOMPIE'S. *3202 E Greenway Rd, Greenway Park Plaza. 602/971-8010.* Hrs: 6 am-9 pm; Mon to 8 pm; Fri to 9:30 pm; Sun 6:30 am-8 pm. Kosher style deli menu. Wine, beer. Semi-a la carte: bkfst $2.50-$6, lunch $3.50-$7, dinner $5.95-$10.95. Child's meals. Specializes in beef, chicken, fish. Own baking. Family-owned New York-style, kosher deli, bakery & bagel factory. Cr cds: A, C, MC, V.

D SC

DUCK AND DECANTER. *1651 E Camelback Rd (85016). 602/274-5429.* Hrs: 9 am-7 pm; Thurs, Fri to 9 pm; Sun from 10 am. Closed some major hols. Bar. A la carte entrees: lunch, dinner $2.75-$5.95. Child's meals. Specialty: albacore tuna sandwich. Guitarist Fri-Sun evenings. Outdoor dining. Gourmet, wine shop. Totally nonsmoking. Cr cds: A, C, D, DS, MC, V.

D

ED DEBEVIC'S. *2102 E Highland Ave, in Town & Country Shopping Ctr, at 20th St & Camelback. 602/956-2760.* Hrs: 11 am-9 pm; Fri, Sat 10 pm. Closed Thanksgiving, Dec 25. Bar. A la carte entrees: lunch, dinner $2.75-$6.95. Child's meals. Specializes in hamburgers, malts, french fries. Nostalgic 50s-style diner; tabletop jukeboxes. Costumed servers improvise routine of songs, dances, skits, irreverent humor. Cr cds: A, C, D, DS, MC, V.

D

HARD ROCK CAFE. *2621 E Camelback Rd (85016). 602/956-3669.* Hrs: 11 am-midnight. Closed Dec 25. Bar to 1 am. Semi-a la carte: lunch, dinner $5.99-$14.99. Child's meals. Specializes in burgers, chicken. Outdoor dining. Rock and roll memorabilia. Cr cds: A, C, D, DS, MC, V.

D

PLANET HOLLYWOOD. *2402 E Camelback Rd, Ste 101 (85016), in Biltmore Fashion Park. 602/954-7827.* Hrs: 11 am-11 pm; Fri, Sat to midnight. Closed Dec 25. Bar to 1 am. Semi-a la carte: lunch, dinner $5.95-$17.95. Specialties: Captain Crunch chicken, margherita pasta, white chocolate bread pudding. Movie and Hollywood memorabilia; movie and TV screens throughout dining rm. Cr cds: A, C, D, MC, V.

D

Pinetop (E-5)

(See also McNary, Show Low)

Pop 2,422 **Elev** 6,959 ft **Area Code** 520 **Zip** 85935
E-mail plcofc@whitemtns.com **Web** www.pinetop.com/

Information Pinetop-Lakeside Chamber of Commerce, 674 E White Mt Blvd, PO Box 4220; 520/367-4290

Trout fishing, horseback riding, hiking, biking and golfing are popular summer activities here; skiing and snowmobiling draw many winter visitors.

Motels

✓★ **BEST WESTERN HOTEL.** *404 S White Mountain Blvd (85935). 520/367-6667; FAX 520/367-6672; res: 800/528-1234.* 42 rms, 2 story. June-mid-Sept, mid-Dec-Mar: S, D $99; suite $199; each addl $5; under 12 free; higher rates: hols, special events; lower rates rest of yr. Crib free. TV; cable (premium). Complimentary continental bkfst. Ck-out 11 am. Business servs avail. Whirlpool. Some refrigerators, microwaves. Cr cds: A, C, D, DS, MC, V.

D SC

★★ **COMFORT INN.** *1637 AZ 260 (85044). 520/368-6600; FAX 520/368-6600; res: 800/228-5150.* 55 rms, 2 story. May-Oct, Dec-Mar: S, D $60-$125; each addl $8; under 18 free; golf packages; higher rates hol wkends (2-day min); lower rates rest of yr. TV; cable, VCR avail. Complimentary continental bkfst. Ck-out 11 am. Meeting rm. Business servs avail. Whirlpool. Refrigerators; some fireplaces. Cr cds: A, C, D, DS, MC, V.

D SC

Restaurants

★★ **CHALET RESTAURANT & LOUNGE.** *348 White Mt Blvd AZ 260 (85929). 520/367-1514.* E-mail bigd@whitemtns.com. Hrs: 5-9 pm. Closed Sun; also Mon mid-Oct-Memorial Day; most major hols; last wk Mar, last 2 wks Nov. Res accepted. Bar. Serv bar. Semi-a la carte: dinner $9.99-$24.99. Child's meals. Specializes in ribs, seafood, chicken. Salad bar. Own baking. Hand-painted mural in chalet-style atmosphere. Cr cds: C, DS, MC, V.

D

★★ **CHARLIE CLARK'S STEAK HOUSE.** *1701 E White Mt Blvd AZ 260 (85935). 520/367-4900.* Hrs: 5-10 pm. Bar 11-1 am. Semi-a la carte: dinner $8.95-$19.95. Child's meals. Specializes in beef, seafood, steak. Cr cds: A, C, D, MC, V.

D

Pipe Spring National Monument (B-3)

(See also Kanab, UT)

(14 mi W of Fredonia on spur off AZ 389)

Located on the Kaibab-Paiute Indian Reservation, the focal point of this monument is a beautifully built sandstone Mormon fort, dating back to 1870. Several years earlier, Brigham Young had ordered the exploration of this region north of the Grand Canyon. According to legend, rifleman William "Gunlock Bill" Hamblin gave the place its name by shooting the bottom out of a smoking pipe at 50 paces.

The fort, actually a fortified ranchhouse, was built under the direction of Bishop Anson P. Winsor to protect the families caring for the church's cattle. Cattle drives, headed for the railroad in Cedar City, Utah, began here.

Guide service (daily); living history demonstrations (June-Aug). Kaibab Paiute Campground (fee), one-half mile N of access road to visitor center. Area closed Jan 1, Thanksgiving, Dec 25. Contact the Superintendent, HC 65, Box 5, Fredonia 86022; 520/643-7105. ¢

Prescott (E-3)

(See also Cottonwood)

Founded 1864 **Pop** 26,455 **Elev** 5,368 ft **Area Code** 520
E-mail chamber@prescott.org **Web** www.prescott.org

Information Chamber of Commerce, 117 W Goodwin St, PO Box 1147, 86302; 520/445-2000 or 800/266-7534

When President Lincoln established the territory of Arizona, Prescott became the capital. In 1867, the capital was moved to Tucson and then back to Prescott in 1877. After much wrangling, it was finally moved to Phoenix in 1889.

Tourism and manufacturing are now Prescott's principal occupations. The climate is mild during summer and winter. The Prescott National Forest surrounds the city; its headquarters are located here.

What to See and Do

Arcosanti. Architectural project by Paolo Soleri and the Cosanti Foundation. This prototype town is being constructed as a functioning example of "arcology," a fusion of architecture and ecology. Guided tours. (Daily; closed major hols) 36 mi SE on AZ 69 to Cordes Junction, then 2 mi E on unnumbered road (follow signs or inquire locally for directions). Phone 520/632-7135. ¢¢

Prescott National Forest. Minerals and varied vegetation abound in this forest (more than 1 million acres). Within the forest are Juniper Mesa, Apache Creek, Granite Mountain, Castle Creek, Woodchute and Cedar Bench wilderness areas, and parts of Sycamore Canyon and Pine Mt wilderness areas. Fishing (Granite Basin, Lynx lakes), hunting. Picnicking. Camping. 20 mi NE on US 89A or 1 mi SW on US 89. Phone 520/445-1762.

Sharlot Hall Museum. Period houses include the Territorial Governor's Mansion (1864), restored in 1929 by poet-historian Sharlot Hall; Fort Misery (1864); William Bashford house (1877); and John C. Frémont house (1875). Period furnishings. Museum, library & archives. Also on grounds are grave of Pauline Weaver; rose and herb garden; pioneer schoolhouse. All buildings (daily exc Mon; also open Memorial Day & Labor Day; closed Jan 1, Thanksgiving, Dec 25). 415 W Gurley St. Phone 520/445-3122. ¢

Smoki Museum. Native American artifacts, ancient and modern. (May-Sept, daily exc Wed, also Sun afternoons) 126 N Arizona St. Phone 520/445-1230. ¢

Annual Events

George Phippen Memorial Western Art Show. Dozens of artists. Memorial Day wkend.

Territorial Prescott Days. Courthouse Plaza, and throughout city. Art show, craft demonstrations, old-fashioned contests, home tours. Early June.

Bluegrass Festival. Courthouse Plaza. Mid-June.

Prescott Frontier Days Rodeo. Fairgrounds on Miller Valley Rd. Also parade & fireworks. July 4 wkend.

Motels

★★ **BEST WESTERN PRESCOTTONIAN.** *1317 E Gurley St (86301), at jct US 89, AZ 69. 520/445-3096; FAX 520/778-2976; res: 800/528-1234.* E-mail bwprescott@goodnet.com. 121 rms, 2-3 story. No elvtr. Apr-Oct: S $59-$93; D $79-$95; each addl $10; suites $125-$200; higher rates special events; lower rates rest of yr. Crib free. Pet accepted. TV; cable. Pool; whirlpool. Coffee in rms. Restaurant 6 am-10 pm. Bar 11 am-9:30 pm. Ck-out noon. Coin Indry. Business servs avail. Refrigerators. Some private patios, balconies. Cr cds: A, C, D, DS, ER, JCB, MC, V.

D SC

✓★ **COMFORT INN.** *1290 White Spar Rd (86303), US 89S, 1½ mi S from courthouse. 520/778-5770; FAX 520/771-9373; res: 800/228-5150; res: 800/889-9774.* 61 rms, 2 story, 11 kit. units. Apr-Oct: S, D $79-$119; each addl $7; kit. units $85-$115; under 12 free; higher rates: wkends, some hols; lower rates rest of yr. Crib free. TV; cable. Complimentary continental bkfst. Restaurant nearby. Ck-out 11 am. Whirlpool. Some refrigerators. Cr cds: A, C, D, DS, MC, V.

D SC

✓★★ **DAYS INN.** *7875 E State Rte 69 (86314). 520/772-8600; FAX 520/772-0942; res: 800/329-7466.* Web www.daysinn.com. 59 rms, 2 story. S $57-$67; D $67-$77; each addl $10; suites $99-$109; under 12 free; hols (2-day min); higher rates special events. Crib free. Pet accepted; $50. TV; cable (premium). Complimentary continental bkfst. Restaurant adj open 24 hrs. Ck-out 11 am. Meeting rm. Business servs avail. Pool; whirlpool. Some refrigerators; microwave, wet bar in suites. Cr cds: A, C, D, DS, JCB, MC, V.

D SC

★★ **HOLIDAY INN EXPRESS.** *3454 Ranch Dr (86303). 520/445-8900; FAX 520/778-2629.* E-mail holiday@bslnet.com; web us.worldpages.com/520-445-8900. 76 rms, 3 story. Mid-Apr-mid-Oct: S, D $89-$119; each addl $10; suites $109-$159; under 17 free; hols (2-day min); higher rates special events; lower rates rest of yr. Crib $10. TV; cable (premium). Complimentary continental bkfst. Restaurant nearby. Ck-out 11 am. Meeting rm. Business servs avail. In-rm modem link. Valet serv. Coin Indry. Exercise equipt. Indoor pool; whirlpool. Some refrigerators, microwaves; minibar, wet bar in suites. Cr cds: A, C, D, DS, JCB, MC, V.

D

★★ **HOTEL VENDOME - CLARION CARRIAGE HOUSE INN.** *230 S Cortez St (86303). 520/776-0900; FAX 520/771-0395; res: 888/468-3583.* E-mail vendome@mwaz.com; web www.vendomehotel.com. 21 rms, 2 story, 4 suites. May-Nov: S, D $79-$99; suites $99-$179; under 18 free; higher rates: major hols, special events; lower rates rest of yr. Crib free. TV; cable. Complimentary continental bkfst. Restaurant nearby. Bar 10-1 am. Ck-out 11 am. Business servs avail. Vintage (1917) lodging house. Cr cds: A, C, D, DS, MC, V.

D SC

Hotels

★★★ **FOREST VILLAS HOTEL.** *3645 Lee Cir (86301), E on AZ 69 to Lee Blvd. 520/717-1200; FAX 520/717-1400; res: 800/223-3449.* 62 rms, 2 story, 15 suites. Mid-Apr-Oct: S $85-$99; D $95-$109; each addl $10; suites $125-$185; under 13 free; wkly rates; lower rates rest of yr. Crib free. TV; cable (premium). Heated pool; whirlpool. Complimentary continental bkfst. Complimentary coffee in rms. Ck-out noon. Meeting rms. Business servs avail. In-rm modem link. Free garage parking. 18-hole golf privileges, greens fee $42 (incl cart), pro, putting green, driving range. Refrigerator in suites. Balconies. European decor with grand staircase. Cr cds: A, C, D, DS, MC, V.

D SC

★★ **HASSAYAMPA INN.** *122 E Gurley St (86301). 520/778-9434; FAX 520/445-8590; res: 800/322-1927.* E-mail inn@primenet.com. 68 rms, 4 story. Apr-Oct: S, D $109-$130; each addl $15; suites $150-$185; under 6 free; lower rates rest of yr. Crib free. TV; cable, VCR avail. Complimentary full bkfst. Restaurant 6:30 am-2 pm, 5-9 pm; Fri, Sat to 9:30 pm. Bar 11 am-11 pm. Ck-out noon. Convention facilities. Business servs avail. Maintained vintage hotel (1927); original wall stenciling, decorative tiles. In national register of historic places. Cr cds: A, C, D, DS, MC, V.

D SC

★★ **PRESCOTT RESORT CONFERENCE CTR & CASINO.** *1500 E State Rte 69 (86301). 520/776-1666; FAX 520/776-8544; res: 800/967-4637.* 160 rms, 5 story, 80 suites. Apr-Oct: S, D $159; suites $179; under 18 free; golf plans; lower rates rest of yr. Crib free. TV; VCR avail (movies). Indoor/outdoor pool; whirlpool, poolside serv. Restaurant 7 am-10 pm. Bar 11-12:30 am; entertainment Tues-Sat. Ck-out noon. Meeting rms. Business servs avail. Gift shop. Barber, beauty shop. Lighted tennis. Racquetball court. 36-hole golf privileges, pro. Exercise equipt; sauna. Bathrm phones, refrigerators. Balconies. Casino. On hill overlooking city. Cr cds: A, C, D, DS, JCB, MC, V.

D

Inns

★★ **MOUNT VERNON INN.** *204 N Mount Vernon Ave (85541), in historic district. 520/778-0886; FAX 520/778-7305.* E-mail mtvrnon@primenet.com; web prescottlink.com/mtvrnon/index.htm. 4 rms, 2 story, 3 cottages. No A/C. S, D, cottages $105-$125; each addl $15-$20; under 2 free; wkday, wkly, monthy rates. Crib free. TV; cable in cottages, sitting rm. Complimentary full bkfst (inn only); afternoon refreshments. Restaurant nearby. Ck-out 11 am, ck-in 3 pm. Concierge serv. Vintage (1900) Victorian house; front porch. Totally nonsmoking. Cr cds: C, DS, MC, V.

D

★★ **PLEASANT STREET INN.** *142 S Pleasant St (86303). 520/445-4774.* Web www.cwdesigners.com/pleasantstreet. 4 rms, 3 air-cooled, 2 with shower only, 2 suites. S $76.50-$85.50; D $85-$95; suites $108-$135; hols (2-day min). Complimentary full bkfst. Restaurant nearby. Ck-out 11 am, ck-in 2 pm. Street parking. Built in 1906; Victorian decor. Totally nonsmoking. Cr cds: C, DS, MC, V.

★ **PRESCOTT COUNTRY INN.** *503 S Montezuma St (86303), on US 89. 520/445-7991; FAX 520/717-1215; res: 888/717-0015; res: 888/757-0015.* 12 rms, shower only. S, D $79-$149; under 6 free; each addl $15. Crib $5. TV; cable. Complimentary continental bkfst. Coffee in rms. Restaurant nearby. Ck-out 11 am, ck-in 3-9 pm. Business servs avail. Grill. Individually decorated rms; handmade quilts. Totally nonsmoking. Refrigerators; some fireplaces. Cr cds: A, C, DS, MC, V.

SC

★ **THE MARKS HOUSE VICTORIAN BED & BREAKFAST.** *203 E Union St (86303), 1 blk S of Gurley St, 1 blk E of courthouse. 520/778-4632; res: 800/370-6275.* Web www.virtualcities.com. 4 suites. Some A/C. No rm phones. Suites $75-$135. Complimentary full bkfst; afternoon refreshments. Restaurant nearby. Ck-out 10 am, ck-in 3 pm. Queen Anne Victorian inn (1894). Elegant antique furnishings create a turn-of-the-century mood. Panoramic view from the veranda. Totally nonsmoking. Cr cds: C, DS, MC, V.

Restaurants

✓★★ **GURLEY STREET GRILL.** *230 Gurley St (86301). 520/445-3388.* Hrs: 11-1 am. Closed Dec 25. Bar. Semi-a la carte: lunch $4.95-$8.50, dinner $5.95-$13.99. Child's meals. Specializes in fresh pasta, pizza, chicken. Patio dining. Pub-style atmosphere. Open kitchen. In Arizona's 1st territorial capital bldg (ca 1890). Cr cds: A, C, DS, MC, V.

D

★★ **MURPHY'S.** *201 N Cortez (86301). 520/445-4044.* Hrs: Summer: 11 am-11 pm; rest of yr: 11 am-10 pm, Fri, Sat to 11 pm; early-bird dinner Sun-Thurs 4:30-6 pm; Sun brunch to 3 pm. Closed day after

Labor Day, Dec 25. Bar to 1 am. Semi-a la carte: lunch $5.25-$9.95, dinner $10.95-$20.95. Sun brunch $9-$15. Child's meals. Specialties: mesquite-broiled fresh fish, 21-day aged beef hand-cut steak, prime rib. Own bread. Memorabilia from turn-of-the-century on display. Restored (ca 1890) mercantile building. Cr cds: A, C, DS, MC, V.

D

✓★ **PINE CONE INN.** *1245 White Spar Rd (86303). 520/445-2970.* Hrs: 11 am-10:30 pm; Sun from 8 am; early-bird dinner 4-6 pm. Closed Dec 24-26. Res accepted. Bar to midnight. Semi-a la carte: bkfst $2.50-$5.25, lunch $4-$8.25, dinner $7-$18. Specializes in steak, seafood. Entertainment Tues-Sun. Family-owned. Cr cds: A, C, DS, MC, V.

D

★★ **THE PORTERHOUSE.** *155 Plaza Dr (86303). 520/445-1991.* Hrs: 4-9 pm; Sun to 8 pm; Sun brunch 11 am-3 pm; early-bird dinner 4-5 pm. Bar. Semi-a la carte: lunch, dinner $7.95-$24.95. Sun brunch $9.95. Child's meals. Specializes in steak, seafood, chicken. Piano Fri, Sat. Parking. Outdoor dining. Cr cds: A, C, DS, MC, V.

D

Safford (G-6)

(See also Willcox)

Founded 1874 **Pop** 7,359 **Elev** 2,920 ft **Area Code** 520 **Zip** 85546
E-mail chamber@safford.az.org **Web** www.safford.az.org

Information Graham County Chamber of Commerce, 1111 Thatcher Blvd; 520/428-2511

Safford is a marketplace for cotton, alfalfa, grain, vegetables and fruit produced on 35,000 acres irrigated by waters from the Gila River. It is the trade center for a wide area. Nearby is Aravaipa Canyon, a designated primitive area. A Ranger District office for the Coronado National Forest (see TUCSON) is located here.

What to See and Do

Roper Lake State Park. This 320-acre park includes a small man-made lake, a swimming beach and natural hot springs with tubs for public use; fishing (dock); boat launch (no gas-powered motors). Nature trails, hiking. Picnicking (shelter). Camping, tent & trailer sites (hook-ups, dump station). Fishing dock accessible to the disabled. **Dankworth Unit,** 6 mi S, is a day-use area with fishing and picnicking. Standard fees. 6 mi S, ½ mi E of US 666. Phone 520/428-6760.

The Swift Trail. AZ 366 snakes its way 36 mi SW from Safford to the high elevations of the Pinaleño Mountains in Coronado National Forest; splendid view from the top, where Mt Graham towers 10,713 ft. There are five developed campgrounds (mid-Apr-mid-Nov, weather permitting); trout fishing at Riggs Flat Lake and in the streams. The upper elevations of AZ 366 are closed from mid-Nov-mid-Apr. Phone 520/428-4150. Camping **¢¢¢**

Annual Events

Fiesta de Mayo. Mexican-American commemoration of *Cinco de Mayo* (May 5th), date of Mexican independence from Europe. 1st wkend May.

Pioneer Days. Commemorates Mormon settlement. Late July.

Graham County Fair. Mid-Oct.

Motels

★★ **BEST WESTERN DESERT INN.** *1391 Thatcher Blvd (85546). 520/428-0521; FAX 520/428-7653; res: 800/528-1234.* 70 rms, 2 story. S $59-$80; D $65-$85; each addl $6; under 17 free. TV; cable. Pet accepted. Heated pool. Coffee in rms. Restaurant adj 6 am-10:30 pm. Bar 11 am-11 pm; Sun from noon. Ck-out 11 am. Coin Indry. Business servs avail. Free airport, bus depot transportation. Refrigerators. Cr cds: A, C, D, DS, MC, V.

D SC

✓★ **COMFORT INN.** *1578 W Thatcher Blvd (85546). 520/428-5851; FAX 520/428-4968; res: 800/228-5150.* 45 rms, 2 story. S $58; D $68; each addl $5; under 18 free; golf plans. Crib $3. Pet accepted, some restrictions. TV; cable (premium). Heated pool. Complimentary continental bkfst. Coffee in rms. Ck-out 11 am. Business servs avail. Some refrigerators, microwaves. Cr cds: A, C, D, DS, ER, JCB, MC, V.

D SC

Restaurant

✓★ **CASA MANANA.** *502 1st Ave (85546). 520/428-3170.* Hrs: 11 am-9 pm; Fri, Sat to 10 pm. Closed Sun; Jan 1, Thanksgiving, Dec 25. Res accepted. Mexican, Amer menu. Beer, wine. A la carte entrees: lunch, dinner $3.50-$14. Specialties: green chili chimichangas, fajitas, fried ice cream. Spanish decor. Cr cds: C, MC, V.

D

Saguaro National Park (G-4 - G-5)

(See also Tucson)

(Rincon Mt District: 17 mi E of Tucson via Broadway and Old Spanish Trail. Tucson Mt District: 16 mi W of Tucson via Speedway and Gates Pass Rd)

The saguaro (sah-WAH-ro) cactus may grow as high as 50 feet and may live to be 200 years old. The fluted columns, spined with sharp, tough needles, may branch into fantastic shapes. During the rainy season, large saguaros can absorb enough water to sustain themselves during the dry season.

The suguaro's waxy, white blossoms (Arizona's state flower), which open at night and close the following afternoon, bloom in May and June; the red fruit ripens in July. The Tohono O'odham eat this fruit fresh and dried; they also use it to make jellies, jams and wines.

Wildlife is abundant. Gila woodpeckers and gilded flickers drill nest holes in the saguaro trunks. Once vacated, these holes become home to many other species of birds, including the tiny elf owl. Peccaries (piglike mammals), coyotes, mule deer and other animals are often seen. Yuccas, agaves, prickly pears, mesquite, paloverde trees and many other desert plants grow here.

The Rincon Mountain District offers nature trails, guided nature walks (winter), eight-mile self-guided drive (fee), mountain hiking, bridle trails. Picnicking (no water). Back-country camping. Visitor center with museum and orientation film.

The Tucson Mt District offers nature trails, a six-mile self-guided drive and hiking and bridle trails. Five picnic areas (no water). Visitor center; exhibits, slide program (daily). For further information contact the Superintendent, 3693 S Old Spanish Trail, Tucson 85730; 520/733-5100 or 502/733-5153. **Free**

San Carlos (F-5)

(See also Globe)

Pop 2,918 **Elev** 2,635 ft **Area Code** 520 **Zip** 85550

Information San Carlos Recreation & Wildlife Dept, PO Box 97; 520/475-2343

The San Carlos Apache Indian Reservation covers almost 2 million acres ranging from desert to pine forests. Many lakes, rivers and ponds offer fishing (fee) year-round for trout, bass and catfish. Hunting for small game, large game and waterfowl is also year-round. Camping (fee). Apache guides may be hired to lead visitors into the wilderness portions of the reservation. Sunrise ceremonial dances are held from time to time.

Scottsdale (F-4)

(See also Chandler, Glendale, Mesa, Phoenix, Tempe)

Pop 130,069 **Elev** 1,250 ft **Area Code** 602/480
Web www.arizonaguide.com/scottsdale

Information Chamber of Commerce, 7343 Scottsdale Mall, 85251; 480/945-8481 or 800/877-1117

Scottsdale is a popular resort destination located on the eastern border of Phoenix. It is renowned for outstanding art galleries, excellent shopping and dining, lush golf courses, abundant recreational activities and Western and Native American heritage.

What to See and Do

Cosanti Foundation. Earth-formed concrete structures and studios by Italian architect Paolo Soleri; constructed by Soleri's students. Soleri windbells made in crafts areas. (Daily; closed major hols) 6433 Doubletree Ranch Rd. Phone 480/948-6145 or 800/752-3187. **Free**

Gray Line sightseeing tours. Contact PO Box 21126, Phoenix 85036; phone 602/495-9100 or 800/732-0327.

Hot Air Expeditions. Hot-air balloon flights offer spectacular views of Sonoran Desert. Contact 2243 E Rose/Garden/Loop, Phoenix 85024. Phone 480/502-6999 or 800/831-7610.

McCormick Railroad Park. This 30-acre city park was created by civic support and volunteer labor. Displays include a full-size Baldwin steam engine, baggage car, and the Roald Amundsen Pullman car; exhibits by model railroad clubs; railroad hobby and artifact shops. Train rides aboard the steam-powered, nearly half-size *Paradise and Pacific* on 1 mi of 15-inch gauge track (fee). Museum, playground with 1929 carousel, picnic areas, desert arboretum; park office. (Daily; closed Thanksgiving, Dec 25) 7301 E Indian Bend Rd. Phone 480/312-2312. Train rides ¢

Rawhide 1880s Western Town. Town re-created in the image of the Old West; steakhouse and saloon; museum; 20 shops; Native American village; displays; rodeos; cowboy gunfights; stagecoach ride; petting ranch. (Daily; closed Dec 25) Fee for some attractions. 23023 N Scottsdale Rd. Phone 480/502-5600.

Scottsdale Center for the Arts. Offers theater, dance; classical, jazz and popular music; lectures; outdoor festivals and concerts. Sculpture garden; art exhibits (daily; closed major hols). 7380 E 2nd St. Phone 480/994-2787 or 480/994-2301.

★ **Taliesin West.** Winter house of Frank Lloyd Wright; now campus of the Taliesin Foundation; historic landmark of notable design. Tours; bookstore. (Daily; closed major hols) At Cactus Rd & Frank Lloyd Wright Blvd. Phone 480/860-2700 or 480/860-8810 (recording). ¢¢¢¢

WestWorld of Scottsdale. 360-acre recreation park & event facility at base of McDowell Mts. Trail Horse Adventure Stables provide trail & hay rides, riding lessons. Hosts concerts, sports competitions, special events. Restaurant with 5 western-themed rms & patio dining. (Daily) 16601 N Pima Rd. Phone 480/312-6802 for event & fee information.

Wild West Jeep Tours. Four-hr guided desert tour. Includes opportunity to shoot a pistol; see working gold mine and Native American petroglyphs; explore an ancient ruin. (Daily) Phone 480/922-0144. ¢¢¢¢¢

Annual Events

Parada del Sol & Rodeo. Phone 480/990-3179 (parade) or 480/502-5600 (rodeo). Parade, late Jan; rodeo, early Feb.

Arabian Horse Show. WestWorld, 16601 N Pima Rd. Phone 480/515-1500. One wk, mid-Feb.

The Tradition at Desert Mt. Cochise Golf Course at Desert Mt, 10333 Rockaway Hills. Senior PGA Tour golf tournament. Phone 480/595-4070. Early Apr.

Seasonal Event

Baseball Spring Training. Scottsdale Stadium. San Francisco Giants. Phone 480/312-2580. Late Feb-late Mar.

Motels

✓★★ **BEST WESTERN PAPAGO INN & RESORT HOTEL.** *7017 E McDowell Rd (85257). 602/947-7335; FAX 602/994-0692; res: 800/528-1234.* E-mail tewade1@juno.com; web www.bestwestern.com/best.html. 56 rms, 2 story. Jan-Apr: S, D $109-$179; each addl $5; under 18 free; lower rates rest of yr. Crib free. TV; cable (premium). Heated pool. Coffee in rms. Restaurant 7 am-1:30 pm, 5-9 pm. Rm serv. Bar 10-1 am. Ck-out noon. Coin Indry. Business servs avail. Valet serv. Free airport transportation. Exercise equipt; sauna. Bathrm phones, refrigerators; some microwaves. Shopping mall adj. Aviary in courtyard. Cr cds: A, C, D, DS, ER, JCB, MC, V.

D SC

★★ **COMFORT INN.** *7350 E Gold Dust Ave (85258). 602/596-6559; FAX 602/596-0554; res: 800/228-5150.* Web www.comfortinn.com. 124 rms, 3 story. Jan-Apr: S $112-$134; D $119-$141; each addl $10; suite $185; under 18 free; golf plans; lower rates rest of yr. Crib free. TV; cable (premium), VCR avail. Complimentary continental bkfst. Complimentary coffee in rms. Restaurant nearby. Rm serv 11 am-9 pm. Ck-out noon. Meeting rms. Business servs avail. In-rm modem link. Valet serv. Coin Indry. 18-hole golf privileges, pro, putting green, driving range. Health club privileges. Pool; whirlpool. Refrigerators; some in-rm whirlpools; microwaves avail. Cr cds: A, C, D, DS, MC, V.

D SC

★★ **COUNTRY INN & SUITES.** *10801 N 89th Pl (85260). 480/314-1200; FAX 480/314-7367; res: 800/456-4000.* E-mail cissscts@ix.netcom.com; web www.arizonaguide.com/countryinnscotts. 163 rms, 3 story, 90 suites. Jan-May: S, D $139-$159; each addl $10; suites $159-$189; under 18 free; lower rates rest of yr. Crib free. TV; cable (premium). Complimentary continental bkfst. Complimentary coffee in rms. Restaurant adj 7 am-11 pm. Rm serv. Ck-out noon. Meeting rms. Business servs avail. In-rm modem link. Bellhops. Coin Indry. Exercise equipt. Pool; wading pool, whirlpool. Refrigerator, microwave, wet bar in suites. Grills. Cr cds: A, C, D, DS, MC, V.

D SC

★★★ **COURTYARD BY MARRIOTT.** *17010 N Scottsdale Rd (85255). 602/922-8400; FAX 602/948-3481; res: 800/321-2211.* 153 rms, 3 story. Jan-Apr: S, D $159-$169; suites $179-$189; under 18 free; golf plans; higher rates special events; lower rates rest of yr. Crib free. TV; cable (premium), VCR avail. Complimentary coffee in rms. Restaurant 6 am-11 pm. Rm serv 6-11 am, 5-10 pm. Bar 4-11 pm. Ck-out noon. Meeting rms. Business servs avail. In-rm modem link. Bellhops. Valet serv. Coin Indry. 18-hole golf privileges. Exercise equipt. Pool; whirlpool. Some in-rm whirlpools; refrigerator, microwave, wet bar in suites. Some balconies. Cr cds: A, C, D, DS, MC, V.

D

★★★ **COURTYARD BY MARRIOTT MAYO CLINIC.** *13444 E Shea Blvd (85259), near Mayo Clinic. 480/860-4000; FAX 480/860-4308; res: 800/321-2211.* 124 rms, 2 story, 11 suites. Jan-mid-May: S, D $149-$159; suites $169-$179; lower rates rest of yr. Crib free. TV; cable (premium). Heated pool; whirlpool. Complimentary coffee in rms. Restaurant 6:30 am-9 pm; Sat, Sun 7 am-2 pm, 5-9 pm. Rm serv. Bar 4-11 pm. Ck-out noon. Coin Indry. Meeting rms. Business servs avail. Valet serv. Exercise equipt. Refrigerators, microwaves avail. Many balconies. Cr cds: A, C, D, DS, MC, V.

D

✓★★ **FAIRFIELD INN BY MARRIOTT.** *13440 N Scottsdale Rd (85254). 602/483-0042; FAX 602/483-3715; res: 800/228-2800.* 132 rms, 3 story. Jan-Apr: S, D $90-$140; under 18 free; lower rates rest of yr. TV; cable (premium), VCR avail. Pool; whirlpool. Complimentary continental bkfst. Restaurant nearby. Ck-out noon. Coin Indry. Business servs avail. Valet serv. Refrigerators avail. Picnic table. Cr cds: A, C, D, DS, MC, V.

D

★★ **FAIRFIELD SUITES.** *17020 N Scottsdale Rd (85255). 602/922-8700; FAX 602/948-2276.* 123 rms, 4 story. Jan-Apr: S, D $149-$169; under 18 free; golf plans; higher rates special events; lower rates rest of yr. Crib free. TV; cable (premium), VCR avail. Complimentary continental bkfst. Complimentary coffee in rms. Restaurant opp 11 am-10 pm. Rm serv 5-10 pm. Ck-out noon. Meeting rm. Business servs avail. In-rm modem link. Bellhops. Valet serv. Coin Indry. 18-hole golf privileges, greens fee $60-$120, pro, putting green, driving range. Pool; whirlpool. Refrigerators, microwaves, wet bars. Picnic tables. Cr cds: A, C, D, DS, MC, V.

D

★★ **HAMPTON INN.** *10101 N Scottsdale Rd (85253). 602/443-3233; FAX 602/443-9149; res: 800/426-7866.* Web www.hampton-inn.com/phoe-scottsdale. 132 rms, 2 story. Jan-mid-Apr: S $105-$160; D $112-$180; under 18 free; higher rates special events; lower rates rest of yr. Crib free. TV; cable (premium). Complimentary continental bkfst. Restaurant nearby. Ck-out noon. Meeting rms. Business servs avail. Coin Indry. Exercise equipt. Pool; whirlpool. Refrigerators, microwaves. Cr cds: A, C, D, DS, MC, V.

D SC

★★ **HAMPTON INN.** *4415 N Civic Center Plz (86001). 602/941-9400; FAX 602/675-5240; res: 800/426-7866.* Web www.hamptoninn.com. 126 rms, 5 story. Jan-Apr: S, D $120-$150; under 18 free; higher rates special events (3-day min); lower rates rest of yr. Crib free. Pet accepted; $50 deposit. TV; cable (premium). Complimentary continental bkfst. Restaurant adj 6 am-11 pm. Ck-out noon. Meeting rms. Business servs avail. Valet serv. Coin Indry. Health club privileges. Golf privileges. Tennis privileges. Pool. Cr cds: A, C, D, DS, MC, V.

D SC

★★ **HOMEWOOD SUITES.** *9880 N Scottsdale Rd (85253). 602/368-8705; FAX 602/368-8725; res: 800/225-5466.* Web www.homewood-suites.com/hws. 114 suites, 3 story. Dec-Apr: S $166; D $259; under 18 free; package plans; lower rates rest of yr. Crib free. TV; cable (premium), VCR avail. Complimentary continental bkfst. Complimentary coffee in rms. Restaurant nearby. Ck-out noon. Meeting rms. Business servs avail. In-rm modem link. Bellhops. Valet serv. Sundries. Grocery store. Exercise equipt. Pool. Refrigerators, microwaves. Picnic tables, grills. Cr cds: A, C, D, DS, MC, V.

D SC

★★ **HOSPITALITY SUITE RESORT.** *409 N Scottsdale Rd (85257). 602/949-5115; FAX 602/941-8014; res: 800/445-5115.* E-mail reservations@hospitalitysuites.com; web www.hospitalitysuites.com. 210 kit. suites (1-2 rm), 2-3 story. Mid-Jan-mid-Apr: S, D $169-$199; under 18 free; lower rates rest of yr. Crib $10. Pet accepted, some restrictions; $100 refundable. TV; cable (premium). 3 heated pools; whirlpool, poolside serv. Complimentary full bkfst. Coffee in rms. Restaurant 6:30 am-10 pm. Rm serv. Bar 11-1 am. Ck-out 11 am. Coin Indry. Meeting rms. Business servs avail. Bellhops. Valet serv. Free airport transportation. Lighted tennis. Lawn games. Health club privileges. Refrigerators, microwaves. Picnic tables; grills. Cr cds: A, C, D, DS, ER, JCB, MC, V.

D SC

★★ **LA QUINTA INN & SUITES.** *8888 E Shea Blvd (85260). 480/614-5300; FAX 480/614-5333; res: 800/687-6667.* 140 rms, 3 story. Jan-Apr: S, D $129-$134; each addl $10; under 18 free; lower rates rest of yr. Crib free. Pet accepted, some restrictions. TV; cable (premium). Complimentary continental bkfst. Complimentary coffee in rms. Restaurant adj 7 am-11 pm. Ck-out noon. Meeting rms. Business servs avail. Coin Indry. Exercise equipt. Pool; whirlpool. Some refrigerators, microwaves. Cr cds: A, C, D, DS, MC, V.

D SC

★★ **RESIDENCE INN BY MARRIOTT.** *6040 N Scottsdale Rd (85253). 602/948-8666; FAX 602/443-4869; res: 800/331-3131.* E-mail riscottsdale@marriott.com; web www.travelbase.com/destination scottsdale/residence-inn/guest.html. 122 kit. suites, 2 story. Jan-Apr: studio $186-$206; 2-bedrm $269-$289; wkly, monthly rates; lower rates rest of yr. Crib free. TV; cable (premium), VCR avail. Heated pool; whirlpool. Complimentary continental bkfst. Complimentary coffee in rms. Restaurant opp 6 am-10 pm. Ck-out noon. Coin Indry. Business servs avail. Valet serv. Lighted tennis privileges. 36-hole golf privileges, pro, putting green, driving range. Exercise equipt. Refrigerators, microwaves. Grills. Cr cds: A, C, D, DS, JCB, MC, V.

D

★ **RODEWAY INN.** *7110 E Indian School Rd (85251). 602/946-3456; FAX 602/874-0492; res: 800/228-2000.* 65 rms, 2 story. Jan-mid-Apr: S $99-$129; D $109-$139; each addl $8; suites $150; under 18 free; wkly rates; lower rates rest of yr. Crib free. TV; cable (premium). Heated pool; whirlpool. Complimentary continental bkfst. Restaurant nearby. Ck-out noon. Business servs avail. Refrigerators, microwaves. Cr cds: A, C, D, DS, ER, JCB, MC, V.

D SC

★ **SAFARI RESORT.** *4611 N Scottsdale Rd (85251). 602/945-0721; FAX 602/946-4703; res: 800/845-4356.* Web www.safari-resort.com. 187 rms, 2 story, 34 kits. Jan-mid-Apr: S $92-$150; D $102-$160; each addl $10; kit. units $130-$160; under 18 free; golf plans; lower rates rest of yr. Crib free. Pet accepted; $50 refundable. TV; cable, VCR avail (movies). 2 heated pools; whirlpool. Complimentary continental bkfst. Restaurant 11 am-11 pm. Rm serv. Bar 6-1 am. Ck-out noon. Coin Indry. Meeting rms. Business servs avail. Bellhops. Valet serv. Gift shop. Health club privileges. Lawn games. Many private patios, balconies. Cr cds: A, C, D, DS, MC, V.

D

★★★ **SOUTHWEST INN AT EAGLE MOUNTAIN.** *9800 N Summer Hill Blvd (85268), Shea E to Eagle Mt Pkwy to Summer Hill Blvd. 480/816-3000; FAX 480/816-3090; res: 800/992-8083.* E-mail eminfo@swinn.com; web www.southwestinn.com. 42 rms, 2 story, 11 suites. Jan-May: S, D $295-$325; each addl $25; suites $395-$445; under 13 free; package plans; lower rates rest of yr. Crib free. TV; cable (premium), VCR. Complimentary continental bkfst. Complimentary coffee in rms. Ck-out 11 am. Meeting rms. Business servs avail. In-rm modem link. Bellhops. Concierge. Gift shop. Lighted tennis privileges, pro. 18-hole golf privileges, pro, putting green, driving range. Heated pool; whirlpool. Bathrm phones, in-rm whirlpools, refrigerators, fireplaces. Balconies. Totally nonsmoking. Cr cds: A, C, DS, MC, V.

D

Motor Hotels

★★ **DOUBLETREE LA POSADA RESORT.** *4949 E Lincoln Dr (85253). 602/952-0420; FAX 602/840-8576; res: 800/222-8733.* 253 rms, 9 suites. Jan-May: S, D $264-$290; each addl $20; suites $375-$750; under 18 free; package plan; lower rates rest of yr. Crib free. Pet accepted, some restrictions. TV; cable (premium). 2 heated pools; whirlpool, poolside serv. Complimentary coffee in rms. Restaurant 6 am-10 pm; Fri, Sat to 11 pm. Rm serv. Bar noon-1 am. Ck-out noon. Convention facilities. Business servs avail. Bellhops. Valet serv. Sundries. Gift shop. Barber, beauty shop. Lighted tennis, pro. Golf privileges, 2 putting greens. Racquetball.

Exercise equipt; sauna. Lawn games. Bicycle rentals. Minibars; some refrigerators. Private patios. Multiple cascading waterfalls; lagoon-like pool. At foot of Camelback Mountain. Cr cds: A, C, D, DS, ER, JCB, MC, V.

D

★★★ **DOUBLETREE PARADISE VALLEY RESORT.** *5401 N Scottsdale Rd (85250). 602/947-5400; FAX 602/946-1524; res: 800/222-8733.* Web www.doubletreehotels.com. 375 rms, 2 story, 12 suites. Jan-mid-May: S, D $205-$300; each addl $10; suites $350-$2,000; under 18 free; wkend rates; golf plans; lower rates rest of yr. Crib free. TV; cable (premium). 2 heated pools; whirlpool, poolside serv. Coffee in rms. Restaurants 6:30 am-11 pm. Rm serv. Bar 11-1 am. Ck-out noon. Convention facilities. Business servs avail. Concierge. Gift shop. Barber, beauty shop. 2 lighted tennis courts. Golf privileges. Exercise rm; sauna, steam rm. Massage. Bathrm phones, minibars. Private patios, balconies. Grill. Extensive grounds elaborately landscaped; patio area overlooks courtyard. Cr cds: A, C, D, DS, ER, JCB, MC, V.

D

★★ **HAWTHORN SUITES.** *7445 E Chapparral Rd (85250). 602/994-5282; FAX 602/994-5625; res: 877/248-4348; res: 800/523-5282.* E-mail winhotel@aol.com; web www.winhotel. 108 rms, 2 story, 69 kit. units. Early Jan-Apr: S, D $129-$249; package plans; lower rates rest of yr. Crib free. Pet accepted, some restrictions; fee. TV; cable, VCR avail (movies). Complimentary bkfst buffet. Complimentary coffee in rms. Restaurant nearby. Ck-out noon. Meeting rms. Business servs avail. In-rm modem link. Valet serv. Tennis. 18-hole golf privileges, greens fee $60. Exercise equipt. Pools; whirlpools. Playground. Refrigerators, microwaves. Picnic tables, grills. Cr cds: A, C, D, DS, JCB, MC, V.

D SC

★★ **HOLIDAY INN HOTEL & SUITES.** *7515 E Butherus Dr (85260). 602/951-4000; FAX 602/483-9046; res: 800/528-1234; res: 800/334-1977.* Web www.holidayinn.com. 120 suites, 4 story. Mid-Jan-mid-Apr: S, D $115-$159; under 18 free; golf plans; lower rates rest of yr. Crib free. Pet accepted, some restrictions; $50 deposit. TV; cable. Heated pool; whirlpool, poolside serv. Complimentary full bkfst. Restaurant 6:30 am-10 pm. Rm serv. Bar 2 pm-midnight. Ck-out noon. Coin Indry. Meeting rms. Business servs avail. In-rm modem link. Valet serv. Exercise equipt. Refrigerators, microwaves. Some balconies. Cr cds: A, C, D, DS, MC, V.

D SC

★★ **INN SUITES HOTEL SCOTTSDALE RESORT.** *7707 E McDowell Rd (85257). 602/941-1202; FAX 602/990-7873; res: 800/898-9124; res: 800/238-8851.* E-mail isscottsdale@attmail.com; web www.innsuites.com. 121 rms, 2 story, 18 suites. Mid-Jan-Apr: S, D $109; suites $129-$149; kit. unit $169; under 18 free; family rates; higher rates special events; lower rates rest of yr. Crib free. Pet accepted, some restrictions; $25. TV; cable (premium). Complimentary bkfst buffet. Complimentary coffee in rms. Restaurant 6:30 am-9 pm. Rm serv noon-8:30 pm. Bar. Ck-out noon. Meeting rms. Business servs avail. In-rm modem link. Valet serv. Sundries. Gift shop. Coin Indry. Free airport, RR station, bus transportation. Exercise equipt. Health club privileges. Pool; whirlpool. Playground. Refrigerators, microwaves. Picnic tables, grills. Cr cds: A, C, D, DS, MC, V.

D SC

★★ **RESORT SUITES.** *7677 E Princess Blvd (85255). 602/585-1234; FAX 602/585-1026; res: 800/898-5768.* E-mail reserv@resortsuites.com; web www.resortsuites.com. 310 suites (1-4 bedrm), 3 story, 286 kits. Jan-Apr: S, D $210-$715; under 16 free; lower rates rest of yr. Crib free. TV; cable. 4 pools, 3 heated; whirlpools, poolside serv. Complimentary coffee in rms. Restaurant 6-1 am. Rm serv. Bar from 10 am. Ck-out 10 am. Coin Indry. Convention facilities. Business center. Bellhops. Concierge. Golf privileges. Exercise equipt. Refrigerators, microwaves. Balconies. Cr cds: A, C, D, MC, V.

D

Hotels

★★ **EMBASSY SUITES.** *5001 N Scottsdale Rd (85250). 602/949-1414; FAX 602/947-2675; res: 800/528-1456.* E-mail 1052153540@compuserv.com; web www.arizonaguide.com/embassy/scottsdale. 311 suites, 4 story. Jan-Apr: S $189; D $199; each addl $10; under 18 free; lower rates rest of yr. Crib free. TV; cable (premium), VCR avail (movies). 2 heated pools; poolside serv. Complimentary full bkfst. Coffee in rms. Restaurants 11 am-2:30 pm, 5-10 pm; Fri, Sat to 11 pm. Bars to 1 am. Ck-out noon. Coin Indry. Meeting rms. Business servs avail. Concierge. Gift shop. Free airport transportation. Lighted tennis. Golf privileges. Exercise equipt. Rec rm. Game rm. Refrigerators; some bathrm phones; microwaves avail. Cr cds: A, C, D, DS, ER, JCB, MC, V.

D SC

★★★ **MARRIOTT SUITES.** *7325 E 3rd Ave (85251). 602/945-1550; FAX 602/874-6095; res: 800/228-9290.* Web www.marriott.com. 251 suites, 8 story. Jan-May: S, D $209-$249; lower rates rest of yr. Crib free. TV; cable (premium). Heated pool; whirlpool, poolside serv. Complimentary coffee in rms. Restaurant 6:30 am-10 pm; Sat, Sun 7 am-11 pm. Bar 5-11 pm. Ck-out noon. Coin Indry. Convention facilities. Business center. Valet; covered parking. Tennis privileges. Golf privileges. Exercise equipt; sauna. Refrigerators; microwaves avail. Many private patios, balconies. Cr cds: A, C, D, DS, ER, JCB, MC, V.

D SC

Resorts

★★ **HOLIDAY INN.** *7601 E Indian Bend Rd (85250). 602/991-2400; FAX 602/951-7492; res: 800/364-9145.* E-mail sunspree@getnet.com; web www.arizonaguide.com/sunspree. 200 rms, 3 story. Jan-Apr: S, D $145; each addl $10; under 18 free; package plans; lower rates rest of yr. TV; cable (premium), VCR avail. Heated pool; poolside serv. Supervised child's activities (May-Aug). Coffee in rms. Dining rm 6:30 am-10 pm. Box lunches. Rm serv. Bar 11-1 am. Ck-out noon, ck-in 3 pm. Convention facilities. Business servs avail. Valet serv. Gift shop. Coin Indry. Lighted tennis, pro. 36-hole golf privileges, pro. Bicycles (rentals). Lawn games. Exercise equipt. Refrigerators. Some private patios. Cr cds: A, C, D, DS, ER, JCB, MC, V.

D SC

★★★★ **HYATT REGENCY.** *7500 E Doubletree Ranch Rd (85258), ½ mi E of Scottsdale Rd. 480/991-3388; FAX 480/483-5550; res: 800/233-1234.* Web www.hyatt.com. Perfect for family vacations, this comfortable hotel offers an extensive array of pool activities, including a large slide tower and a real sand beach. Excellent golf and tennis facilities await the sports minded guests. Dining options includes the highly regarded Golden Swan. Located on 640-acre Gainey Ranch, this resort features Sonoran desert landscaping; lagoons plied by gondolas, fountains, waterfalls and date palm trees. 486 units in main bldg, 4 story, 7 casitas (1-4-bedrm) on lake. Jan-mid-June: S, D $395-$500; suites $600-$3,000; under 18 free; golf plans; lower rates rest of yr. Crib free. TV; cable (premium), VCR avail. 10 pools; wading pool, poolside serv; clock tower with waterslide, sand beach. Playground. Supervised child's activities; ages 3-12. Restaurants (public by res) 6:30 am-10:30 pm (GOLDEN SWAN opens at 6 pm]. Rm serv 24 hrs. Bar noon-1 am. Ck-out noon, ck-in 4 pm. Meeting rms. Business center. In-rm modem link. Concierge. Gift shop. Free valet parking. Rec dir. 8 tennis courts, 4 lighted, pro. 27-hole golf, greens fee $135, pro, putting green, driving range. Bicycles. Exercise rm, sauna, steam rm. Massage. Minibars; microwaves avail. Fireplace, wet bar in casitas. Balconies. Luxury level. Cr cds: A, C, D, DS, ER, JCB, MC, V.

D SC

★★★★ **MARRIOTT CAMELBACK INN.** *5402 E Lincoln Dr (85253), Paradise Valley, northeast of downtown. 480/948-1700; FAX 480/951-8469; res: 800/242-2635.* Web www.camelbackinn.com. A popular resort with excellent meeting spaces, this perennial favorite offers spacious guest rooms in adobe-style casitas. Beautiful landscaping. 453 rms in 1-2-story casitas. Jan-May: S, D $389; suites $600-$2,000; AP addl $64/person; MAP addl $48/person; Camelback plan (bkfst, lunch) addl $29/person; under 18 free; wkend rates; golf, tennis, spa, package plans;

lower rates rest of yr. Crib free. Pet accepted. TV; cable (premium), VCR avail. 3 pools; whirlpool, poolside serv, lifeguards. Supervised child's activities on holidays only; ages 5-12. Dining rms 6:30 am-10 pm (also see CHAPARRAL DINING ROOM). Rm serv to midnight. Box lunches. Bars 11-1 am. Ck-out noon, ck-in 4 pm. Coin Indry. Business center. In-rm modem link. Valet serv. Concierge. Barber, beauty shop. Gift & sport shops. Lighted tennis, pro. 36-hole golf, greens fee $100-$115 (incl cart), pros, putting greens, driving range, golf school. Bicycle rental. Lawn games. Soc dir; entertainment; movies winter & spring hols. Extensive exercise rm; sauna, steam rm. Spa. Refrigerators, minibars. Wet bar, microwave; fireplace, private pool in some suites. Private patios; many balconies. Cr cds: A, C, D, DS, ER, JCB, MC, V.

★★ **MARRIOTT MOUNTAIN SHADOWS RESORT.** *5641 E Lincoln Dr (85253). 480/948-7111; FAX 480/951-5430; res: 800/228-9290.* Web www.marriott.com. 318 rms, 19 suites, 1-2 story. Jan-mid-May: S, D $249-$269; suites $300-$750; under 18 free; lower rates rest of yr. Crib free. TV; cable (premium). 3 heated pools; whirlpool. Dining rms 6:30 am-midnight. Rm serv. Box lunches. Snack bar. Bars 11-1 am. Ck-out noon, ck-in 4 pm. Convention facilities. Business center. Valet serv. Gift shop. Lighted tennis, pro. 54-hole golf, greens fee $60-$105 (incl cart), pro, putting greens, driving range. Lawn games. Playground. Exercise rm; sauna. Minibars; many bathrm phones; wet bar in suites; microwave avail. Private patios, balconies. On 70 acres; 3 acres of gardens. Cr cds: A, C, D, DS, ER, JCB, MC, V.

★★★ **ORANGE TREE GOLF & CONFERENCE RESORT.** *10601 N 56 St (85254). 480/948-6100; FAX 480/483-6074; res: 800/228-0386.* Web www.orangetree.com. 160 suites, 2 story. Jan-May: S, D $220-$249; under 18 free; golf plan; lower rates rest of yr. Crib free. TV; cable (premium), VCR (movies). Heated pool; wading pool, whirlpool, poolside serv. Supervised child's activities. Coffee in rms. Dining rm 6 am-10 pm. Box lunches. Snack bar. Picnics. Rm serv. Bar 11-1 am; entertainment Wed-Sat. Ck-out 11 am, ck-in 4 pm. Grocery 1 mi. Coin Indry. Package store 1 mi. Meeting rms. Business servs avail. Bellhops. Valet serv. Concierge. Gift shop. Airport transportation. Sports dir. Tennis privileges. 18-hole golf, greens fee $90 (incl cart), pro. Exercise equipt. Massage. Health club privileges. Bathrm phones, refrigerators, microwaves. Private patios, balconies. Golf resort with country club atmosphere. Cr cds: A, C, D, DS, MC, V.

★★★★★ **PHOENICIAN RESORT.** *6000 E Camelback Rd (85251), at 60th St. 480/941-8200; FAX 480/947-4311; res: 800/888-8234.* Web www.thephoenician.com. The luxuriously landscaped driveway winds past manicured fairways and pristine blue lakes to this world-class resort. Magnificent art and sculpture give the public spaces a museum quality. The huge rooms and baths open to balconies or patios and pamper guests with an endless list of amenities. Wonderful restaurants, terrific shopping, an incredible spa, multiple swimming pools, championship golf and tennis make this oasis in the desert Arizona's first address. 654 rms: 468 rms in main bldg, 4-6 story, 119 casitas. Sept-mid-Jan: S, D, casitas $525-$655; each addl $50; suites $1,225-$1,800; villas $3,100-$3,500; under 17 free; golf plans; lower rates rest of yr. Crib free. TV; cable (premium), VCR avail (movies). 7 pools; 2 wading pools, whirlpool, poolside serv. Supervised child's activities; ages 5-12. Dining rms (public by res) 6 am-10 pm (also see MARY ELAINE'S and WINDOWS ON THE GREEN). Rm serv 24 hrs. Bar 11-1 am; entertainment. Ck-out noon, ck-in 4 pm. Convention facilities. Business center. In-rm modem link. Bellhops. Valet serv. Concierge. Shopping arcade. Barber, beauty shop. Airport transportation. Sports dir. 12 lighted tennis courts, pro. 27-hole golf, greens fee $90-$170, pro, putting green, driving range. Hiking. Bicycle rentals. Lawn games. Exercise rm; sauna, steam rm. Spa. Bathrm phones, minibars; some refrigerators, wet bars; microwaves avail. Balconies. Picnic tables. Cr cds: A, C, D, DS, JCB, MC, V.

★★★ **RADISSON RESORT AND SPA SCOTTSDALE.** *7171 N Scottsdale Rd (85253). 480/991-3800; FAX 480/948-1381; res: 800/333-3333.* E-mail rhi_sctt@radisson.com; web www.radisson.com. 318 rms, 2 story, 35 suites (33 bi-level). Jan-May: S, D $255-$275; each addl $20; suites $375-$1,500; under 18 free; lower rates rest of yr. Crib free. TV; cable (premium), VCR avail. 3 heated pools; whirlpool, poolside serv. Supervised child's activities (Late June-mid-Sept); ages 4-12. Dining rms 6:30 am-10 pm. Rm serv 24 hrs. Snack bar. Bar 11-1 am. Ck-out noon, ck-in 4 pm. Coin Indry. Convention facilities. Business center. Valet serv. Concierge. Gift shop. Barber, beauty shop. Lighted tennis, pro. 36-hole golf privileges. Exercise equipt; sauna. Lawn games. Many refrigerators, minibars; some wet bars, fireplaces. Private patios, balconies. On 76 acres. Cr cds: A, C, D, DS, ER, JCB, MC, V.

★★★ **REGAL MCCORMICK RANCH.** *7401 N Scottsdale Rd (85253). 480/948-5050; FAX 480/948-9113; res: 800/243-1332.* E-mail regal@getnet.com; web www.regal-hotels.com/scottsdale. 125 rms, 3 story, 51 kit. villas (2-3 bedrm). Jan-Apr: S, D $195-$325; each addl $10; villas $350-$625; under 18 free; golf, tennis plans; lower rates rest of yr. Crib free. TV; cable. Heated pool; whirlpool, poolside serv. Coffee in rms. Dining rm 6:30 am-10 pm. Rm serv. Bar 11-1 am; entertainment Wed-Sat. Ck-out noon, ck-in 3 pm. Convention facilities. Business center. Valet serv. Valet parking. Concierge. Gift shop. Lighted tennis, pro. Golf privileges, pro, putting green, driving range. Dock; sailboats, paddleboats. Exercise equipt. Health club privileges. Sightseeing, desert trips. Lawn games. Soc dir. Minibars. Wet bar, fireplace in villas. Private patios, balconies. 10 acres on Camelback Lake; view of McDowell Mountains. Cr cds: A, C, D, DS, MC, V.

★★★ **RENAISSANCE COTTONWOOD RESORT.** *6160 N Scottsdale Rd (85253). 480/991-1414; FAX 480/951-3350; res: 800/468-3571.* Web www.renaissancehotels.com. 107 suites, 64 rms. Jan-May: S, D $245-$275; each addl $10; suites $285-$330; kit. units $345-$360; under 18 free; package plans; lower rates rest of yr. Crib free. Pet accepted, some restrictions. TV; cable (premium), VCR avail (movies). 3 heated pools; whirlpools, poolside serv. Complimentary continental bkfst. Restaurant 7 am-10:30 pm. Rm serv 24 hrs. Bar noon-11 pm. Ck-out noon. Meeting rms. Business servs avail. Bellhops. Concierge. Valet serv. Lighted tennis, pro. Golf privileges, putting green. Health club privileges. Lawn games. Bicycle rentals. Refrigerators, minibars; some bathrm phones, fireplaces; microwaves avail. Whirlpool on patios. Adj to Borgata shopping complex. Cr cds: A, C, D, DS, ER, JCB, MC, V.

★★★ **SCOTTSDALE PLAZA RESORT.** *7200 N Scottsdale Rd (85253). 602/948-5000; FAX 602/998-5971; res: 800/832-2025.* E-mail res@tspr.com; web www.tspr.com. 404 rms, 2 story, 180 suites. Jan-May: S, D $295-$325; each addl $10; suites $325-$3,500; golf, package plans; under 17 free; wkend rates; lower rates rest of yr. Crib $5. TV; cable, VCR avail. 5 heated pools; poolside serv. Dining rms 6 am-11 pm (also see REMINGTON). Rm serv. Bar 11-1 am; entertainment. Ck-out noon, ck-in 3 pm. Valet serv. Convention facilities. Business center. Concierge. Sundries. Gift shop. Beauty shop. Lighted tennis, pro. Racquetball. Putting green. Bike rentals. Lawn games. Exercise equipt, sauna. Refrigerators, minibars; many wet bars; microwaves avail. Spanish colonial-style buildings on 40 acres; waterfall. Cr cds: A, C, D, DS, ER, JCB, MC, V.

★★★★ **SCOTTSDALE PRINCESS HOTEL.** *7575 E Princess Dr (85255), off Scottsdale Rd just N of Bell Rd. 480/585-4848; FAX 480/585-0091; res: 800/344-4758.* Web www.princesshotels.com. Situated on 450 elaborately landscaped acres, with a waterfall in the central courtyard, this large resort offers airy rooms in a Spanish style. The golf course is the site of the Phoenix Open, a yearly stop on the PGA Tour. 650 rms, 3-4 story, 75 suites, 119 casitas. Jan-Mar: S, D $429-$689; each addl $30; suites $589-$2,900; casitas $539-$689; under 16 free; golf, tennis, spa, hol plans; lower rates rest of yr. TV; cable, VCR avail. 3 pools; whirlpool, poolside serv. Supervised child's activities (Memorial Day-Labor Day & hols); ages 5-12. Dining rms 6:30 am-11 pm (also see LA HACIENDA and MAR-

QUESA). Rm serv 24 hrs. Bars 11-1 am; entertainment. Ck-out noon, ck-in 4 pm. Convention facilities. Business center. Concierge. Shopping arcade. Barber, beauty shop. Valet parking. Lighted tennis, pro. 36-hole golf, greens fee $60-$180, pro, putting green, driving range. Lawn games. Basketball. Exercise rm; sauna, steam rm. Massage. Stocked lagoons; equipt avail for guests. Bathrm phones, refrigerators, minibars; some fireplaces. Private patios, balconies. Cr cds: A, C, D, DS, ER, JCB, MC, V.

D

★★★ **SUNBURST RESORT.** *4925 N Scottsdale Rd (85251). 602/945-7666; FAX 602/946-4056; res: 800/528-7867.* Web www.sunburstresort.com. 210 units, 7 with shower only. 2 story. Jan-Apr: S, D $200-$260; each addl $10; suites $425-$675; under 18 free; family, wkend, hol rates; golf plans; lower rates rest of yr. Crib free. TV; cable (premium). 2 heated pools; whirlpool, lifeguard, poolside serv. Complimentary coffee in rms. Restaurant 6 am-10 pm. Rm serv. Box lunches, snacks. Bar 10-1 am. Ck-out noon, ck-in 3 pm. Gift shop. Grocery, coin lndry 1 mi. Bellhops. Concierge. Valet serv. Meeting rms. Business servs avail. In-rm modem link. Tennis privileges, pro. 18-hole golf privileges, greens fee $95, putting green, driving range, pro. Exercise equipt. Refrigerators, minibars. Balconies. Cr cds: A, C, D, DS, JCB, MC, V.

D SC

Inns

★★★ **HERMOSA INN.** *5532 N Palo Cristi Rd (85253). 602/955-8614; FAX 602/955-8299; res: 800/241-1210.* 35 units, 5 suites, 4 houses, 13 kit. units. Jan-mid-Apr: S, D $245-$315; each addl $25; suites/houses $415-$595; under 6 free; lower rates rest of yr. Crib $25. TV; cable. Heated pool; whirlpool. Complimentary continental bkfst. Restaurant (see LON'S). Rm serv. Ck-out noon, ck-in 3 pm. Concierge serv. Luggage handling. Tennis, pro. Many fireplaces, wetbars. Cr cds: A, C, D, DS, MC, V.

★★★ **INN AT CITADEL.** *8700 E Pinnacle Peak Rd (85255), at Inn at the Citadel Complex. 602/585-6133; FAX 602/585-3436; res: 800/927-8367.* 11 suites. Jan-Mid-May: S, D $295-$335; lower rates rest of yr. Crib free. Pet accepted. TV; cable (premium). Complimentary continental bkfst. Coffee in rms. Restaurant adj 4 am-10 pm. Rm serv. Ck-out noon, ck-in 3 pm. Business servs avail. Golf privileges. Some balconies, minibars. Each rm individually decorated with antiques, artwork. View of Sonoran Desert, city. Cr cds: A, C, D, DS, MC, V.

D

Restaurants

★★★ **AVANTI'S OF SCOTTSDALE.** *3102 N Scottsdale Rd (85251). 602/949-8333.* E-mail tina@avanti-az.com; web www.avanti-az.com. Hrs: 5:30-10:30 pm; Fri, Sat to 11 pm. Res accepted. Northern Italian, continental menu. Bar 5:30 pm-1 am. Wine list. Semi-a la carte: dinner $16.50-$25.95. Specializes in seafood, veal. Own pasta. Pianist Tues-Sat. Valet parking. Outdoor dining. Black & white decor. Cr cds: A, C, D, DS, MC, V.

D

★★ **BANDERA.** *3821 N Scottsdale Rd (85251). 602/994-3524.* Web www.houstons.com. Hrs: 5-10 pm; Fri to 11 pm; Sat 4:30-11 pm; Sun from 4:30 pm. Closed Thanksgiving, Dec 25. Bar. Semi-a la carte: dinner $10.95-$19.95. Child's meals. Specialties: wood-fired, spit-roasted chicken; black bean chicken chili; millionaire's club filet. Parking. Totally nonsmoking. Cr cds: A, C, D, MC, V.

D

★★ **BUSTER'S RESTAURANT GRILL.** *8320 N Hayden (85258). 602/951-5850.* Hrs: 11:30 am-10 pm; June-Aug to 9 pm; early-bird dinner 4-6 pm. Closed most major hols. Res accepted. Bar. Semi-a la carte: lunch $6.45-$10.95, dinner $6.95-$18.95. Child's meals. Specialties: filet mignon, mesquite grilled seafood, chicken pasta. Parking. Outdoor dining. Overlooks Lake Marguerite. Cr cds: A, C, D, MC, V.

D

★★ **CAFE TERRA COTTA.** *6166 N Scottsdale Rd (85253). 602/948-8100.* Web www.cafeterracotta. Hrs: 11 am-10 pm; Fri, Sat to 11 pm. Closed Thanksgiving, Dec 25. Res accepted. Southwestern menu. Bar. Semi-a la carte: lunch $7.95-$13.95, dinner $10.95-$22.95. Specialties: prawns stuffed with goat cheese, chile relleno platter. Own desserts. Parking. Patio dining overlooking flower garden. Regional artwork displayed. Totally nonsmoking. . Cr cds: A, C, D, DS, MC, V.

D

★★★ **CHAPARRAL DINING ROOM.** *(See Marriott's Camelback Inn Resort) 480/948-1700.* Web www.camelbackinn.com. Hrs: 6-9 pm; Fri, Sat to 11 pm. Res accepted. Continental menu. Bar to midnight. Wine cellar. A la carte entrees: dinner $19-$32. Specialties: lobster bisque, Dover sole, rack of lamb. Own baking. Valet parking. Jacket (in season). Cr cds: A, C, D, DS, ER, JCB, MC, V.

D SC ♥

★★ **CHART HOUSE.** *7255 McCormick Pkwy (85258). 602/951-2550.* Hrs: 5-10 pm; Sun 4:30-9 pm. Res accepted. Bar. Semi-a la carte: dinner $10.95-$34.95. Child's meals. Specializes in seafood, fresh fish, steak. Salad bar. Parking. Outdoor dining. All dining areas have view of McCormick Lake. Cr cds: A, C, D, DS, MC, V.

D

★ **CHOMPIE'S.** *9301 E Shea Blvd (85260), Mercado del Rancho Center. 602/860-0475.* E-mail chompies@juno.com. Hrs: 6 am-9 pm; Sun, Mon to 8 pm. Closed Passover. Kosher deli menu. Wine, beer. Semi-a la carte: bkfst $1.75-$8.50, lunch $4.50-$10.95, dinner $7.50-$11.95. Specialties: Nova Scotia lox, matzo brie, mile-high sandwiches. New York-style decor. Cr cds: A, C, MC, V.

D

★★ **DON & CHARLIE'S AMERICAN RIB & CHOP HOUSE.** *7501 E Camelback Rd (85251). 602/990-0900.* Hrs: 5-10 pm; Fri, Sat to 10:30 pm; Sun 4:30-9 pm. Closed Thanksgiving. Res accepted. Bar. Semi-a la carte: dinner $11.95-$29.95. Child's meals. Specialties: barbecued ribs, prime center cut steak. Own pies, cakes. Parking. Photos of celebrities, sports memorabilia on walls. Totally nonsmoking. Cr cds: A, C, D, DS, MC, V.

D

★★ **EL CHORRO LODGE.** *5550 E Lincoln Dr (85253). 602/948-5170.* E-mail elchorro@aol.com; web www.elchorro.com. Hrs: 11 am-4 pm, 6-10 pm; Sat, Sun from 6 pm. Res accepted. Bar. Semi-a la carte: lunch $8-$16.25, dinner $13-$62. Specialties: châteaubriand, rack of lamb, prime beef. Piano, guitar Thurs-Sat. Valet parking. Outdoor dining. Western decor, paintings. Fireplaces. Family-owned. Cr cds: A, C, D, DS, MC, V.

D ♥

★★★★ **GOLDEN SWAN.** *(See Hyatt Regency) 602/991-3388.* The tiered room of this contemporary restaurant in the Hyatt Regency is comfortable and attractive. The creative Southwestern cooking uses local ingredients and the service is both warm and extremely helpful. Hrs: 6-10 pm; Sun brunch 9:30 am-2:30 pm. Closed Sun and Mon evenings from July 4th to Labor Day. Res accepted. Hispaña menu. Bar. A la carte entrees: dinner $25-$34.50. Sun brunch $34, $17 for children. Specialties: ranch chicken baked in red rock clay; grilled Pacific salmon filet with mesquite honey barbecue sauce; sauteed veal medallions. Own pastries. Valet parking. Braille menu. Totally nonsmoking. Cr cds: A, C, D, DS, ER, JCB, MC, V.

D

★★ **HOPS! BISTRO & BREWERY.** *8668 E Shea (85260), in Pima Crossing. 602/998-7777.* Hrs: 11 am-10 pm; Fri, Sat to 10:30 pm. Closed Easter, Thanksgiving, Dec 25. Res accepted. Bar to midnight; Fri, Sat to 1 am. Semi-a la carte: lunch, dinner $6.95-$19.95. Child's meals. Specializes in steak, seafood, pasta. Outdoor dining. Brewery. Cr cds: A, C, D, DS, MC, V.

D

★★ **HOUSTON'S.** *6113 N Scottsdale Rd (85250), in Hilton Village. 602/922-7775.* Hrs: 11 am-10 pm; Fri to 11 pm; Sat 11 am-11 pm. Closed Thanksgiving, Dec 25. Bar. Semi-a la carte: lunch, dinner $6.95-$20.95. Child's meals. Specializes in steak, chicken, barbecue ribs. Outdoor dining. Upscale casual dining. Cr cds: A, C, MC, V.

D

★ **KYOTO JAPANESE RESTAURANT.** *7170 Stetson Dr (85251). 602/990-9374.* Hrs: 11 am-2 pm, 5:30-10 pm; Fri, Sat to 11 pm. Closed most major hols. Res accepted. Japanese menu. Bar. Semi-a la carte: lunch $3.50-$5, dinner $11.95-$24.95. Specialties: sushi, teriyaki chicken. Parking. Tableside cooking. Cr cds: A, C, D, DS, MC, V.

D

★★★ **L'ECOLE RESTAURANT.** *8100 E Camelback Rd (85251). 602/990-7639.* E-mail learm@chefs.com; web www.chefs.com /culinary. Hrs: 11:30 am-1:30 pm, 6:30-8:30 pm. Closed Sat, Sun; major hols. Res required. Contemporary American menu. Serv bar. Wine list. Complete meals: lunch $7-$12, dinner $16-$22. Specializes in fish, poultry, beef. Own baking. Tableside cooking. Menu changes wkly. Parking. Primarily staffed by students of the Scottsdale Culinary Institute. Cr cds: C, DS, MC, V.

★★★★ **LA HACIENDA.** *(See Scottsdale Princess Resort) 480/585-4848.* Combine thick adobe walls, beautiful talavera tile, strolling mariachis, gracious service and a menu that has remained true to its Northern Mexican roots and you'll soon understand why La Hacienda continues to attract legions of faithful followers. Mexican menu. Specialties: filete al chipotle (char-broiled beef tenderloin), char-broiled lamb chops crusted with pumpkin seed, suckling pig. Own baking. Hrs: 6-10 pm; Fri, Sat to 11 pm. Res accepted. Bar from 5 pm. Wine list. A la carte entrees: dinner $19.50-$27.50. Child's meals. Strolling mariachis. Valet parking. Outdoor dining. Cr cds: A, C, D, DS, ER, JCB, MC, V.

D

★★ **LANDRY'S PACIFIC FISH COMPANY.** *4321 N Scottsdale Rd (85251), between Camelback & Indian School Rds, in multi-level structure at Galleria. 602/941-0602.* Hrs: 11 am-10 pm; Fri, Sat to 11 pm; Sun noon-10 pm; June-July hrs vary. Closed Thanksgiving, Dec 25. Res accepted. Bar. Semi-a la carte: lunch $7.95-$13.99, dinner $14.95-$23.95. Child's meals. Specialty: mesquite-broiled fish in Southwestern sauces. Entertainment wkends. Free valet parking. Outdoor dining. 2 floors of dining; nautical decor, memorabilia; open kitchen. Cr cds: A, C, D, DS, MC, V.

D

★★★ **LON'S AT THE HERMOSA INN.** *(See Hermosa Inn) 602/955-7878.* Hrs: 11:30 am-2 pm, 6-10 pm; Sun brunch 10 am-2 pm. Closed Jan 1, Memorial Day, July 4, Labor Day. Res accepted. Contemporary American menu. Bar. Wine list. Semi-a la carte: lunch $8.95-$14.95, dinner $16.95-$24.95. Sun brunch $7.95-$12. Specialties: seared breast of duck, wood grilled veal t-bone, seared Ahi tuna. Parking. Outdoor dining. Old Arizona adobe. Totally nonsmoking. Cr cds: A, C, D, MC, V.

D

★★★ **MANCUSO'S.** *6166 N Scottsdale Rd (85253), at the Borgata. 602/948-9988.* Hrs: 5-10:30 pm. Closed Thanksgiving, Dec 25. Res accepted. Northern Italian, continental menu. Bar. Complete meals: dinner $15.95-$26.95. Specializes in veal, pasta, seafood. Piano lounge. Valet parking. Ambiance of castle interior. Cr cds: C.

★★ **MARCO POLO SUPPER CLUB.** *8608 E Shea Blvd (85260). 602/483-1900.* Hrs: 5-10 pm; Fri, Sat to 11 pm. Closed some major hols. Res accepted. Continental menu. Bar to 1 am. A la carte entrees: dinner $11.95-$24.95. Child's meals. Specialties: gorgonzola New York strip, grilled veal chop, Hong Kong chicken. Musicians. Valet parking. Outdoor dining. Family photographs adorn walls. Cr cds: A, C, D, DS, MC, V.

D

★★★ **MARIA'S WHEN IN NAPLES.** *7000 E Shea Blvd (85254). 602/991-6887.* E-mail mshee@msn.com; web www.azbest.com. Hrs: 11:30 am-2:30 pm, 5-10 pm; Sat, Sun from 5 pm. Closed most major hols. Res accepted. Italian menu. Bar. Semi-a la carte: lunch $6.95-$10.95, dinner $12.95-$22.95. Specializes in pasta, veal. Own desserts. Parking. Outdoor dining. Open kitchen. Multi-tiered dining. Cr cds: A, C, D, DS, MC, V.

D

★★★★ **MARQUESA.** *(See Scottsdale Princess) 480/585-4848.* The decor of this restaurant combines the essence of a Spanish hacienda with the contemporary flair of a Barcelona restaurant. Classic Catalan cooking is augmented with contemporary touches such as curry seasonings and truffles. Hrs: 6-10 pm; Fri, Sat to 11 pm; Sun brunch 10:30 am-2:30 pm. Closed Sun & Mon. Res accepted. Bar. Wine cellar. A la carte entrees: dinner $27-$38. Sun brunch $45. Child's meals. Tapas bar. Flamenco guitarist Sun brunch. Valet parking. Outdoor dining. Cr cds: A, C, D, DS, ER, JCB, MC, V.

D

★★★★★ **MARY ELAINE'S.** *(See The Phoenician Resort) 602/423-2530.* Sitting regally atop the Phoenician Resort, Arizona's premier restaurant offers guests unobstructed sunset views of the Valley of the Sun. The elegant table settings and outstanding service make for gracious dining. The kitchen consistently produces innovative creations that are supported by the expansive wine list. Modern French menu. Specializes in fresh seafood from around the world, rack of lamb, veal. Hrs: 6-10 pm; Fri, Sat to 11 pm. Closed Sun; also Mon mid-June-Aug. Res accepted. Bar. Wine cellar. A la carte entrees: dinner $32-$45. Complete meals: dinner $70-$100. Child's meals. Entertainment. Valet parking. Jacket. Cr cds: A, C, D, DS, JCB, MC, V.

D

★★★ **MICHAEL'S.** *8700 E Pinnacle Peak Rd (85255). 602/515-2575.* Web michaelsrestaurant.com. Hrs: 6-10 pm. Closed Jan 1, Memorial Day. Res accepted. Contemporary Amer menu. Bar 4 pm-midnight. Wine cellar. A la carte entrees: dinner $18.95-$22.95. Child's meals. Specialties: seared Chilean sea bass, grilled medallions of beef tenderloin, pan-seared juniper duck and foie gras. Jazz Wed-Sun. Valet parking. Outdoor dining. Unique decor with waterfall. Totally nonsmoking. Cr cds: A, C, D, MC, V.

D

★★★ **P.F. CHANG'S CHINA BISTRO.** *7014 E Camelback Rd (85251), in Scottsdale Fashion Square. 602/949-2610.* Hrs: 11 am-11 pm; Fri, Sat to midnight. Closed Thanksgiving, Dec 25. Chinese menu. Bar. A la carte entrees: lunch, dinner $5.95-$12.95. Specialties: orange peel shrimp, Paul's catfish, Chang's spicy chicken. Valet parking. Outdoor dining. Cr cds: A, C, D, MC, V.

D

★★★ **PALM COURT.** *7700 E McCormick Pkwy (85258), in Scottsdale Conference Resort. 602/596-7700.* Hrs: 7-11 am, 11:30 am-2 pm, 5-10 pm; Sun 10:30 am-2 pm (brunch), 5-10 pm. Res accepted. Bar 10:30-1 am. Wine cellar. Semi-a la carte: bkfst $5.50-$10, lunch $7.50-$20, dinner $19-$35. Prix fixe: dinner $52. Sun brunch $26. Serv charge 18%. Child's meals. Specialties: duckling, lobster Lord Randolph, rack of lamb. Pianist brunch, evenings. Valet parking. Intimate dining; tableside cooking and preparation. Jacket (dinner). Totally nonsmoking. Cr cds: A, C, D, DS, MC, V.

D

★★ **PEAKS AT PINNACLE PEAK.** *8711 E Pinnacle Peak Rd (85255). 602/998-2222.* Hrs: 11:30 am-9 pm; Fri, Sat to 10 pm; early-bird dinner 4-6 pm. Res accepted. Bar to midnight. Semi-a la carte: lunch $5.99-$9.99, dinner $12.99-$21.99. Child's meals. Specializes in prime rib, steaks, seafood. Parking. Outdoor dining. Mission courtyard architecture with bell tower; antiques, art work. View of desert gardens. Cr cds: A, C, D, MC, V.

D

★ **PISCHKE'S PARADISE.** *7217 E 1st St (85251). 602/481-0067.* Hrs: 7 am-11 pm; Sun 8 am-10 pm. Closed most major hols. Bar. Semi-a la carte: bkfst $3-$9, lunch $5-$10, dinner $6-$18. Specialties: Cajun Caesar salad, six-egg omelettes. Outdoor dining. Colorful prints, photos above bar. Cr cds: A, C, DS, MC, V.

D

★★ **QUILTED BEAR.** *6316 N Scottsdale Rd (85253). 602/948-7760.* Hrs: 7 am-10 pm; Sun from 8 am. Res accepted. Semi-a la carte: bkfst $1.99-$7.95, lunch $4.95-$10, dinner $6.95-$18.95. Child's meals. Specializes in seafood, beef. Salad bar. Own soups. Outdoor dining. Colorful decor; stained-glass windows. Cr cds: A, C, D, DS, MC, V.

D

★★★ **RANCHO PINOT GRILL.** *6208 N Scottsdale Rd (85253). 602/468-9463.* Hrs: 5:30-10 pm. Closed Sun, Mon; major hols. Contemporary Amer menu. Bar. Wine cellar. Semi-a la carte: $17-$23. Specialties: Nonni's Sunday chicken, mesquite grilled seafood, steaks. Own baking, ice cream. Outdoor dining. Totally nonsmoking. Cr cds: C, DS, MC, V.

D

★★★ **RAZZ'S RESTAURANT & BAR.** *10321 N Scottsdale Rd (85253). 602/905-1308.* E-mail razzs@primenet.com. Hrs: 5-10 pm. Closed Sun, Mon; most major hols; also July-Aug. Res accepted, required Fri, Sat. Contemporary international menu. Bar. Semi-a la carte: dinner $15.95-$22.95. Child's meals. Specialties: duck cakes with nopalito cactus sauce, rack of lamb with tamarind, cashew and rosemary encrusted salmon filet. Own baking. Parking. Chef-owned. Cr cds: A, C, D, MC, V.

D

★★★ **REMINGTON.** *(See Scottsdale Plaza Resort) 602/951-5101.* Hrs: 11 am-2:30 pm, 5-10 pm; Sat, Sun from 5 pm. Res accepted. Bar 4:30 pm-midnight. Wine cellar. A la carte entrees: lunch $7.25-$16, dinner $18.50-$32. Specializes in seafood, lamb, mesquite-grilled steak. Jazz. Outdoor dining. Elegant Southwestern decor; columns, vaulted dome ceiling with sky mural. Cr cds: A, C, D, DS, MC, V.

D

★★★ **RESTAURANT HAPA.** *6204 N Scottsdale Rd (85253). 602/998-8220.* E-mail haparest@aol.com. Hrs: 11:30 am-2:30 pm, 5:30-10 pm. Closed Sun; most major hols; 2 wks in summer. Res accepted. Asian Amer menu. Bar to midnight. Wine list. Semi-a la carte: lunch $5-$12, dinner $14-$23. Specialties: fiery squid salad, caramelized Chinese mustard beef tenderloin, miso-marinated sea bass. Parking. Outdoor dining. Asian Amer decor. Cr cds: C, MC, V.

D

★★ **RESTAURANT OCEANA.** *8900 E Pinnacle Peak Rd (85255). 602/515-2277.* E-mail oceana2277@aol.com. Hrs: 5:30-10 pm. Closed most major hols; Sun (May-Aug); 1st 2 wks of Aug. Res accepted. Seafood menu. Bar. Semi-a la carte: dinner $13.95-$22.50. Complete meal: dinner $45-$59. Specialties: Casco bay cod, Dungeness crab cakes. Parking. Outdoor dining. Intimate atmosphere. Cr cds: A, C, D, DS, JCB, MC, V.

D

★★★ **ROARING FORK.** *7243 E Camelback Rd (85251). 602/947-0795.* Hrs: 11 am-3 pm, 6-10 pm; Fri to 11 pm; Sat 6-11 pm. Closed Sun; most major hols; hrs vary June-Aug. Res accepted. Bar. Wine cellar. Semi-a la carte: lunch $7-$12, dinner $13-$25. Child's meals. Specialties: sugar & chile-cured duckling, campfire-style salmon, grilled beef tenderloin with horseradish shellac. Valet parking wkends. Outdoor dining. Western artwork. Cr cds: A, C, D, DS, MC, V.

D

★★★ **RUTH'S CHRIS STEAK HOUSE.** *7001 N Scottsdale Rd (85253). 602/991-5988.* Hrs: 5-10 pm; Fri, Sat to 10:30 pm. Closed Thanksgiving, Dec 25. Res accepted. Bar. A la carte entrees: dinner $17.95-$43.50. Specializes in USDA prime-aged, corn-fed Midwestern beef; fresh seafood, live Maine lobster. Outdoor dining. Traditional steakhouse. Cr cds: A, C, D, MC, V.

D

★★ **SALT CELLAR.** *550 N Hayden Rd (85257). 602/947-1963.* Hrs: 5-11 pm; Fri, Sat to midnight. Closed Dec 25. Res accepted. Bar 4 pm-1 am. Semi-a la carte: dinner $15.95-$24.95. Child's meals. Specializes in seafood, prime steaks. Parking. Restaurant located underground, in former salt cellar. Rustic, nautical decor. Cr cds: A, C, MC, V.

✓★★ **SUSHI ON SHEA.** *7000 E Shea Blvd (85254). 602/483-7799.* Hrs: 11:30 am-2:30 pm, 5:30-10 pm; Fri, Sat to 11 pm; Sun from 5:30 pm. Closed most major hols. Japanese menu. Bar. Semi-a la carte: lunch $4.50-$10, dinner $8.25-$15. Child's meals. Specializes in chicken, sushi, tempura. Aquarium; sushi bar. Totally nonsmoking. Cr cds: A, C, D, DS, MC, V.

D

★★★★ **THE TERRACE.** *(See The Phoenician) 602/423-2530; FAX 602/947-4311.* Another jewel in the crown of The Phoenician Resort (see Mary Elaine's), this restaurant of marble and tapestries flows onto an expansive veranda set for alfresco dining. Innovative Italian cuisine and attentive service guarantee a memorable experience. Continental cuisine. Hours Mon-Sun. 6 am-10 pm. Closed for dinner Mon. Price (dinner) $30-$50. Sun brunch 10 am-2 pm $45. Valet. Child meals. Cr cds: C.

★★★ **WINDOWS ON THE GREEN.** *(See The Phoenician) 602/423-2530.* Hrs: 6-10 pm. Closed Mon; Tues (July-mid-Sept). Res accepted. Contemporary Southwestern menu. Bar. Wine cellar. Semi-a la carte: dinner $18-$32. Complete meals: dinner $39-$55. Child's meals. Specialties: achiote salmon, tortilla soup. Valet parking. Outdoor dining. View overlooking golf course. Totally nonsmoking. Cr cds: A, C, D, DS, JCB, MC, V.

D

Sedona (D-4)

(See also Cottonwood, Flagstaff)

Founded 1902 **Pop** 7,720 **Elev** 4,400 ft **Area Code** 520
Web www.sedonachamber.com

Information Sedona-Oak Creek Canyon Chamber of Commerce, PO Box 478, 86339; 520/282-7722 or 800/288-7336

Known worldwide for the beauty of the red rocks surrounding the town, Sedona has grown from a pioneer settlement into a favorite film location. This is a resort area with numerous outdoor activities—including hiking, fishing and biking—that can be enjoyed all year. Also an art and shopping destination, Sedona boasts Tlaquepaque (T-lock-ayPOCK-ay), a four-and-one-half-acre area of gardens, courtyards, fountains, galleries, shops and restaurants. A Ranger District office of the Coconino National Forest is here.

What to See and Do

Chapel of the Holy Cross. Chapel perched between 2 pinnacles of uniquely colored red sandstone. Open to all for prayer and meditation. (Daily) 2½ mi S on AZ 179. Phone 520/282-4069. **Free**

Jeep tours. Two-hr back country trips. (Daily) Other tours also avail. For details contact Pink Jeep Tours, phone 800/8-SEDONA; Red Rock Jeep Tours, 520/282-6826. ¢¢¢¢¢

Oak Creek Canyon. A beautiful drive along a spectacular fishing stream, N toward Flagstaff (see). In the canyon is

Slide Rock State Park. A 43-acre day-use park on Oak Creek. Swimming, natural sandstone waterslide; fishing. Hiking. Picnicking. Standard fees. 7 mi N on US 89A. Phone 520/282-3034. Per person ¢; Per vehicle ¢¢

Tlaquepaque. Consists of 40 art galleries and stores set in a Spanish-style courtyard; cafes. (Daily exc hols) On AZ 179. Phone 520/282-4838. **Free**

Verde Canyon Railroad. 20 mi SW via US 89A, in Clarkdale. (See COTTONWOOD)

Annual Events

Sedona Film Festival. 1st full wkend Mar.

Sedona Jazz on the Rocks. Late Sept.

Red Rock Fantasy of Lights. Late Nov-mid-Jan.

Motels

★★ **BEST WESTERN.** *1200 W Hwy 89A (37217). 520/282-3072; FAX 520/282-7218; res: 800/292-6344.* E-mail innofsedona@kachina.net; web www.innofsedona.com. 110 rms, 3 story. Mar-May, Sept-Oct: S, D $115-$155; each addl $10; under 12 free; hols (2-day min); lower rates rest of yr. Crib free. Pet accepted; $10. TV; cable (premium). Complimentary continental bkfst. Complimentary coffee in rms. Restaurant adj 11 am-9 pm. Ck-out 11 am. Meeting rms. Business servs avail. Bellhops. Exercise equipt. Pool; whirlpool. Many refrigerators; some fireplaces. Balconies. Cr cds: A, C, D, DS, JCB, MC, V.

✓★ **CANYON PORTAL MOTEL.** *280 N Hwy 89A (86336). 520/282-7125; FAX 520/282-1825; res: 800/542-8484.* 41 rms, 2 story. Mar-mid-Nov: S, D $59-$120; each addl $5; house (2-bedrm) $140; under 6 free; wkly rates; lower rates rest of yr. Crib $5. TV; cable (premium). Heated pool; whirlpool. Complimentary coffee in lobby. Restaurant nearby. Ck-out 11 am. Coin Indry. Meeting rms. Business servs avail. Some wet bars; microwaves avail. Many private patios, balconies. Cr cds: C, DS, MC, V.

✓★★ **DESERT QUAIL INN.** *6626 State Rte 179 (86351). 520/284-1433; FAX 520/284-0487; res: 800/385-0927.* E-mail quail@sedona.net; web www.desertquailinn.com. 32 rms, 9 suites, 2 story. S, D $54-$89; suites $100-$150; each addl $10; under 12 free; golf plan; higher rates: hols (2-day min), special events. Crib free. Pet accepted, some restrictions; $15. TV; cable (premium). Pool. Complimentary coffee in rms. Restaurant nearby. Ck-out 11 am. Guest Indry. Business servs avail. In-rm modem link. Tennis privileges. 18-hole golf privileges, greens fee $55-$89, putting green, driving range. Health club privileges. Jeep, bicycle rentals. Refrigerators; microwaves avail. Cr cds: A, C, D, DS, JCB, MC, V.

★★ **HAMPTON INN.** *1800 W Hwy 89A (86336). 520/282-4700; FAX 520/282-0004; res: 800/426-7866.* 56 rms, 2 story, 6 suites. Sept-Oct: S, D $109-$129; suites $139-$159; under 18 free; hols (2-3 day min); lower rates rest of yr. Crib free. TV; cable (premium). Complimentary continental bkfst. Complimentary coffee in rms. Restaurant nearby. Ck-out noon. Meeting rm. Business servs avail. In-rm modem link. Valet serv. Pool; whirlpool. Refrigerators, microwaves; in-rm whirlpool, wet bar in suites. Cr cds: A, C, D, DS, JCB, MC, V.

★★ **KOKOPELLI SUITES.** *3119 W Hwy 89 (86336). 520/204-1146; FAX 520/204-5851; res: 800/789-7393.* E-mail kokosuites@sedona.net; web www.sedona.net/hotel/kokosuites. 46 suites, 2 story. Mar-May, Sept-Nov: suites $79-$179; kit. suite $219; under 18 free; wkends (2-day min in season); lower rates rest of yr. Crib $10. TV; cable. Pool; whirlpool. Complimentary continental bkfst. Complimentary coffee in rms. Restaurant nearby. Ck-out 11 am. Business servs avail. Coin Indry. Health club privileges. Many refrigerators, microwaves; some in-rm whirlpools, fireplaces. Cr cds: A, C, D, DS, JCB, MC, V.

★★ **QUAIL RIDGE RESORT.** *120 Canyon Cir Dr (84767). 520/284-9327; FAX 520/284-0832.* E-mail info@quailridgeresort.com; web www.quailridgeresort.com. 14 kit. units, shower only, 2 story, 5 suites, 9 chalets. Mar-Nov: suites $69-$81; chalets $93-$136; wkly, wkend rates (2 day min); hols (3-day min); lower rates Jan, Dec, first 2 wks in Feb. Crib $9. Pet accepted; $10/day. TV; cable. Heated pool; whirlpool. Restaurant nearby. Ck-out 11 am. Business servs avail. Tennis. Microwaves avail. Picnic table, grills. Totally nonsmoking. Cr cds: A, C, DS, MC, V.

★★★ **SEDONA REAL INN.** *95 Arroyo Pinon Dr (85258). 520/282-1414; FAX 520/282-0900; res: 800/353-1239.* E-mail srealinn@sedona.net; web www.sedonareal.com. 47 suites, 2 story. Mar-May, Sept-Nov: S, D $140-$250; each addl $10; under 13 free; golf plans; lower rates rest of yr. Crib free. TV; cable (premium), VCR (movies avail). Complimentary continental bkfst. Complimentary coffee in rms. Restaurant nearby. Ck-out 11 am. Meeting rms. Business servs avail. Concierge. Exercise rm. Health club privileges. Pool; whirlpool. Refrigerators, microwaves, fireplaces. Some balconies. Cr cds: A, C, DS, MC, V.

★★ **SKY RANCH LODGE.** *Airport Rd (86339), S on AZ 89A to Airport Rd, 1 mi to lodge. 520/282-6400; FAX 520/282-7682; res: 888/708-6400.* E-mail skyranch@sedona.net. 94 rms, 1-2 story, 20 kit. units, 2 cottages. No A/C. S, D, kit. units $80-$130; each addl $8; cottages $160; under 12 free. Crib free. Pet accepted, some restrictions; fee. TV; cable. Heated pool; whirlpool. Complimentary coffee in lobby. Restaurant nearby. Ck-out 11 am. Coin Indry. Business servs avail. Gift shop. Some refrigerators. Cr cds: A, C, MC, V.

★★★ **SOUTHWEST INN.** *3250 W Hwy 89A (86301). 520/282-3344; FAX 520/282-0267; res: 800/483-7422.* E-mail info@swinn.com; web www.swinn.com. 28 rms, 2 story. Mid-Mar-May; Sept-Thanksgiving: S, D $135-$165; each addl $10; suites $195; under 13 free; wkends, hols (2-day min); lower rates rest of yr. Crib free. TV; cable (premium), VCR avail. Pool; whirlpool. Complimentary continental bkfst. Complimentary coffee in rms. Restaurant opp 11:30 am-9 pm. Ck-out 11 am. Bellhops. Concierge. Business servs avail. In-rm modem link. Tennis privileges. Health club privileges. Refrigerators, fireplaces; microwaves avail. Balconies. Totally nonsmoking. Cr cds: A, C, DS, MC, V.

Motor Hotel

★★ **BEST WESTERN ARROYO ROBLE HOTEL.** *400 N Hwy 89A (86339). 520/282-4001; FAX 520/282-4001; res: 800/528-1234; res: 800/773-3662.* E-mail arroyoroble@sedona.net; web www.bestwesternsedona.com. 59 rms, 5 story, 7 villas. Mid-Feb-Nov: S $125-$175; D $135-$185; each addl $10; studio rms $125-$145; villas $250-$300; under 12 free; lower rates rest of yr. Crib free. TV; cable (premium). Indoor/outdoor pool; whirlpool. Complimentary coffee in rms. Restaurant opp 7 am-9 pm. Ck-out 11 am. Coin Indry. Business servs avail. In-rm modem link. Tennis privileges. Exercise equipt; sauna. Microwave avail. Some private patios, balconies. Grills. Views of red sandstone buttes. Cr cds: A, C, D, DS, MC, V.

Hotel

★★★ **L'AUBERGE DE SEDONA.** *301 L'auberge Ln (86336). 520/282-1661; FAX 520/282-2885; res: 800/272-6777.* E-mail info@lauberge.com; web www.lauberge.com. 56 units, 2 story, 34 cottages. S, D $180-$270; cottage $255-$425; each addl $20; under 12 free. Crib free.

TV; cable (premium). Heated pool; whirlpool. Complimentary coffee in rms, library. Dining rm (see L'AUBERGE). Ck-out 11 am. Concierge. Business servs avail. In-rm modem link. Free airport transportation. Tennis privileges. Lawn games. Health club privileges. Refrigerators, minibars. Some balconies. Romantic atmosphere; on Oak Creek. Cr cds: A, C, D, DS, MC, V.

Resorts

★★★★ **ENCHANTMENT RESORT.** *525 Boynton Canyon Rd (86336). 520/282-2900; FAX 520/204-1267; res: 800/826-4180.* E-mail enchant@sedona.net; web www.enchantmentresort.com. Spectacularly situated amidst towering red rock cliffs in secluded Boynton Canyon. Balconies on the Pueblo-style casitas afford outstanding 360-degree views. Handsome Arizona territorial ranch furnishings create the perfect ambiance for this unique resort. 222 units, 56 kit. casitas (2-bedrm). Rooms: S, D $195-$325; suites $295-$425; kit. casitas $625-$725; lower rates rest of yr. Crib free. TV; cable (premium), VCR avail (movies). 4 heated pools; whirlpool, poolside serv. Supervised child's activities; ages 4-12. Complimentary coffee in rms. Restaurant (see YAVAPAI). Rm serv. Box lunches, snacks, picnics. Bar 11-1 am; entertainment Fri, Sat. Ck-out noon, ck-in 4 pm. Bellhops. Concierge. Valet serv. Guest Indry. Gift shop. Meeting rms. Business servs avail. In-rm modem link. Tennis, pro. Golf privileges. Hiking. Bicycle rentals. Lawn games. Exercise rm; steam rm, sauna. Spa. Massage. Patios; some balconies. Picnic tables. Cr cds: A, C, DS, MC, V.

★★★ **LOS ABRIGADOS RESORT.** *160 Portal Ln (85901). 520/282-1777; FAX 520/282-2614; res: 800/521-3131.* E-mail los abrigados@ilxinc.com; web www.ilxinc.com. 172 suites (1 & 2 bedrms), 1 cottage, 1-2 story. S, D $225-$410; each addl $20; cottage $2,000; under 16 free. Crib free. TV; cable (premium), VCR. 2 pools; whirlpool, poolside serv. Playground. Dining rm (see JOEY BISTRO). Box lunches; steak-fry area on Oak Creek. Rm serv. Bar 11-1 am. Ck-out noon, ck-in 4 pm. Coin Indry. Business servs avail. Valet serv. Concierge. Gift shop. Beauty shop. Sports dir. Tennis. Golf privileges. Lawn games. Exercise rm; sauna, steam rm. Fishing in Oak Creek. Refrigerators, microwaves; some fireplaces. Private patios, balconies. Grills. Spanish-style stucco & tile-roofed buildings set among buttes of Oak Creek Canyon. Former ranch site & early movie location. Cr cds: A, C, D, DS, MC, V.

★★ **POCO DIABLO RESORT.** *1752 S Hwy 179 (86336), 2 mi S on AZ 179. 520/282-7333; FAX 520/282-2090; res: 800/528-4275.* E-mail info@pocodiablo.com; web www.pocodiablo.com. 137 rms, 2 story. Mid-Mar-mid-Nov: S, D $115-$245; each addl $20; suites $240-$360; under 16 free; lower rates rest of yr. Crib free. TV; cable (premium). Heated pool; 2 whirlpools, poolside serv. Coffee in rms. Dining rm (public by res) 7 am-10 pm; Fri, Sat to 11 pm. Rm serv. Bar 11-1 am. Ck-out noon, ck-in 3 pm. Meeting rms. Business servs avail. Concierge. Gift shop. Free bus depot transportation. Lighted tennis, pro. 9-hole, par-3 golf, greens fee $10. Racquetball. Massage. Exercise equipt. Refrigerators; some in-rm spas, fireplaces. Some private patios, balconies. Views of Red Rock mountains. Cr cds: A, C, D, DS, MC, V.

Inns

★★ **A TOUCH OF SEDONA BED & BREAKFAST.** *595 Jordan Rd (86336), off AZ 89A. 520/282-6462; FAX 520/282-1534; res: 800/600-6462.* E-mail touch@sedona.net; web www.touchsedona.com. 5 rms, 1 kit. unit, 3 with shower only. No rm phones. Feb-June, Sept, Oct: S, D $119-$139; each addl $20; kit. unit $159; wkends, hols (2-3 day min); lower rates rest of yr. TV; cable (premium), VCR avail. Complimentary full bkfst. Restaurant nearby. Ck-out 11 am, ck-in 4-6 pm. Luggage handling. Concierge serv. Balconies. Picnic tables. Totally nonsmoking. Cr cds: A, C, DS, MC, V.

★★★ **APPLE ORCHARD INN.** *656 Jordan Rd (86336). 520/282-5328; FAX 520/204-0044; res: 800/663-6968.* E-mail appleorc@sedona.net; web www.appleorchardbb.com. 7 rms, 2 story. S, D $135-$225; each addl $20; hols 2-day min. Children over 10 yrs only. TV; VCR (movies). Complimentary full bkfst. Restaurant nearby. Ck-out 11 am, ck-in 3-6 pm. Business servs avail. Luggage handling. Concierge serv. Refrigerators; many in-rm whirlpools. Some fireplaces, patios. Totally nonsmoking. Cr cds: A, C, MC, V.

★★★ **BED & BREAKFAST AT SADDLE ROCK RANCH.** *255 Rock Ridge Dr (86336). 520/282-7640; FAX 520/282-6829.* E-mail saddle rock@sedona.net; web www.saddlerockranch.com. 3 rms. No rm phones. Mid-Mar-mid-June, mid-Sept-mid Nov (min stay required): S $125-$145; D $130-$150; each addl $20. Children over 14 yrs only. TV; cable, VCR avail. Pool; whirlpool. Complimentary full bkfst; afternoon refreshments. Ck-out 11 am, ck-in 4-6 pm. Luggage handling. Concierge serv. Business servs avail. Health club privileges. Original house (1926) was part of 6,000-acre ranch. Many antiques, Native American artifacts. Many Western movies filmed here. Cr cds: C.

★★ **BRIAR PATCH INN.** *3190 N Hwy 89A (86336), 3½ mi N on AZ 89A. 520/282-2342; FAX 520/282-2399; res: 888/809-3030.* E-mail briarpatch@sedona.net; web www.bbhost.com/briarpatch. 17 cottages, 15 with shower only. No rm phones. S, D $149-$295; each addl $25; wkend, hols (2-day min). Complimentary bkfst buffet. Ck-out noon, ck-in 2 pm. Business servs avail. Gift shop. Massage. Fireplaces; many refrigerators. Picnic tables. Some antiques. Library. Swimming hole on Oak Creek. Located on 9 acres. Cr cds: A, C, MC, V.

✓★★★★ **CANYON VILLA BED & BREAKFAST INN.** *125 Canyon Cr Drive (86351). 520/284-1226; FAX 520/284-2114; res: 800/453-1166.* E-mail convilla@sedona.net; web www.canyonvilla.com. Although the individually decorated guest rooms, landscaped grounds, and attentive service are impressive at this Southwestern-style inn, the stunning red rock views and magical sunsets are what take your breath away. Southwestern decor prevails here, and each guest room is individually decorated. 11 rms, 2 story. S $135-$215; D $145-$225; each addl $25. Children over 10 yrs only. TV; cable (premium). Heated pool. Complimentary full bkfst; afternoon refreshments. Restaurant nearby. Ck-out 11 am, ck-in 3-6 pm. Business servs avail. Tennis privileges, 18-hole golf privileges, greens fee $65-$75. Health club privileges. Patios, balconies. Totally nonsmoking. Cr cds: A, C, MC, V.

★★★ **CASA SEDONA BED & BREAKFAST.** *55 Hozoni Dr (86336). 520/282-2938; FAX 520/282-2259; res: 800/525-3756.* E-mail casa@sedona.net; web www.casasedona.com. 16 rms, 2 story. S $115-$195; D $125-$205; each addl $25; wkend, hols (2-day min). TV in sitting rm; cable, VCR avail. Complimentary full bkfst. Ck-out 11 am, ck-in 3-6 pm. Business servs avail. Concierge serv. Refrigerators, fireplaces. Balconies. Picnic tables. Each rm with view of red rocks. Totally nonsmoking. Cr cds: A, C, MC, V.

★★ **CATHEDRAL ROCK LODGE.** *61 Los Amigos Ln (86336). 520/282-7608; FAX 520/282-4505; res: 800/352-9149.* 4 air-cooled rms, 2 story, 1 kit. suite, 1 kit. cottage. Mid-Dec-Apr: S $80-$90; D $90-$100; each addl $10; suites $140-$150; wkends, hols (2-3 day min). Crib free. Some TVs; VCR avail (movies). Complimentary full bkfst; continental bkfst in cottage. Ck-out 11 am, ck-in 3-6 pm. Some refrigerators, balconies; microwaves avail. Picnic tables, grills. Totally nonsmoking. Cr cds: C, MC, V.

★★★ **LODGE AT SEDONA.** *125 Kallof Pl (86336), just off AZ 89A. 520/204-1942; FAX 520/204-2128; res: 800/619-4467.* E-mail lodge@sedona.net; web www.lodgeatsedona.com. 13 rms, 2 story. S, D

$120-$225; each addl $25. TV in sitting rm. Complimentary full bkfst; afternoon refreshments. Ck-out 11 am, ck-in 3-6 pm. Concierge serv. Business servs avail. Lawn games. Health club privileges. Some in-rm whirlpools, fireplaces. Picnic tables. Antiques. Library. Located on 2½ acres. Gardens, labyrinth. Totally nonsmoking. Cr cds: A, C, DS, MC, V.

D

★★★ **TERRITORIAL HOUSE BED & BREAKFAST.** *65 Piki Dr (86336). 520/204-2737; FAX 520/204-2230; res: 800/801-2737.* E-mail oldwest@sedona.net; web oldwestbb.sedona.net. 4 rms, 2 with shower only, 2 story, 1 suite. No A/C. 3 rm phones. S $105-$155; D $115-$165; each addl $20; suite $205; golf plans; min stay wkends, hols. Crib free. TV; VCR (free movies). Complimentary full bkfst; afternoon refreshments. Ck-out 11 am, ck-in 4-6 pm. Business servs avail. 18-hole golf privileges, greens fee $60, pro. Whirlpool. Refrigerators, microwaves avail. Balconies. Western ranch converted house; stone fireplace. Totally nonsmoking. Cr cds: A, C, DS, MC, V.

★★★ **THE GRAHAM BED & BREAKFAST INN & ADOBE VILLAGE.** *150 Canyon Circle Dr (86351), 6½ mi S via AZ 179, turn off onto Bell Rock Blvd. 520/284-1425; FAX 520/284-0767; res: 800/228-1425.* E-mail graham@sedona.net; web www.sedonasfinest.com. 6 rms in inn, 2 story; 4 kit casitas. Inn: S $154-$234; D $169-$249; each addl $20. Casitas: S $289-$349; D $309-$369; each addl $20; wkly rates; wkends 2-day min, hols 3-day min. Crib free. TV; cable (premium), VCR (movies). Pool; whirlpool. Complimentary drinks in casitas & sitting rm. Complimentary full bkfst; afternoon refreshments. Dining rm at opp 8-9:30 am. Ck-out 11 am, ck-in 3 pm. Business servs avail. Luggage handling. Concierge serv. Gift shop. Free lndry facilities. Bicycles avail. Fireplace, whirlpool in all rms. Bathrm phone, microwave, wet bar, fireplace in casitas. Balconies. Guest library. Totally nonsmoking. Cr cds: A, C, DS, MC, V.

D

★★★ **THE INN ON OAK CREEK.** *556 Hwy 179 (86336). 520/282-7896; FAX 520/282-0696; res: 800/499-7896.* E-mail theinn@sedona.net; web www.sedona-inn.com. 11 rms, 2 story, 2 suites. S $135-$220; D $150-$235; each addl $20; suites $180-$225; wkends, hols (2-day min). Children over 10 yrs only. TV; cable (premium), VCR (movies). Complimentary full bkfst; afternoon refreshments. Restaurant nearby. Ck-out 11 am, ck-in 3-6 pm. Business servs avail. In-rm modem link. Luggage handling. Valet serv. Concierge serv. In-rm whirlpools, fireplaces. Many balconies. On river. Views of Oak Creek and Red Rocks. Totally nonsmoking. Cr cds: C, DS, MC, V.

D

Restaurants

★ **ATRIUM.** *AZ 179 (86339), at Tlaquepaque. 520/282-5060.* Hrs: 8 am-3 pm. Closed Dec 25. Continental menu. Wine, beer. Semi-a la carte: bkfst $4-$7.50, lunch $5.95-$7.95. Child's meals. Specialties: Sedona frittata, grilled chicken Caesar salad, grilled vegetable pita. Outdoor dining. Atmosphere of greenhouse. Totally nonsmoking. Cr cds: C, MC, V.

D

★★ **COWBOY CLUB.** *241 N AZ 89A (86336). 520/282-4200.* E-mail cowboy@sedona.net. Hrs: 11 am-4 pm, 5-10 pm. Closed Thanksgiving, Dec 25. Res accepted. High desert menu. Bar. Semi-a la carte: lunch $5.95-$11.95, dinner $7.95-$29.95. Child's meals. Specializes in rattlesnake, buffalo, burgers. Parking. Cr cds: A, C, MC, V.

D

★★ **DYLAN'S.** *1405 W AZ 89A (86336). 520/282-7930.* E-mail zarry@sedona.net. Hrs: 11 am-9:30 pm; early-bird dinner 5-6 pm. Closed Thanksgiving, Dec 25. Res accepted. Bar. Semi-a la carte: lunch $5-$9, dinner $6-$21. Child's meals. Specialties: California wraps, prime rib, vegetarian dishes. Entertainment Fri, Sat. Parking. Southwestern art. Cr cds: C, MC, V.

D

✓★ **EL RINCON RESTAURANTE MEXICANO.** *336 State Route 179 # A112 (86336), Tlaquepaque Village, on the banks of Oak Creek. 520/282-4648.* Hrs: 11 am-9 pm; Sun noon-5 pm; winter hrs vary. Closed Mon; Jan 1, Thanksgiving, Dec 25; also Feb. Res accepted. Mexican menu. Bar. A la carte entrees: lunch, dinner $3.50-$14. Child's meals. Specializes in chimichangas, tamales, Navajo pizzas. Outdoor dining. Totally nonsmoking. Cr cds: C, MC, V.

D

★★★ **HEARTLINE CAFE.** *1610 W AZ 89A (86336). 520/282-0785.* E-mail heartline@sedona.net; web www.sedonanet.com/food/heartline. Hrs: 11:30 am-3 pm, 5-9:15 pm; Tues-Thurs from 5 pm. Res accepted. Eclectic menu. Bar. Wine cellar. Semi-a la carte: lunch $6.95-$13.50, dinner $12-$28. Child's meals. Specialties: mesquite crusted rack of lamb, pecan crusted local trout, crab cakes. Patio dining. Cottage surrounded by English garden. Smoking on patio only. Cr cds: A, C, D, DS, JCB, MC, V.

D

✓★ **HIDEAWAY.** *179 Country Square (86336). 520/282-4204.* E-mail hideaway@sedona.net; web www.sedona.net/hideaway. Hrs: 11 am-9 pm. Closed some major hols. Italian menu. Bar. Semi-a la carte: lunch $7.50-$9, dinner $8.50-$15. Specializes in pizza, antipasto salad, fettucine. Parking. Outdoor dining overlooking Oak Creek & Red Rock Mountains. Dining rm features stained-glass windows. Cr cds: A, C, D, DS, MC, V.

D

★★★ **JOEY BISTRO.** *(See Los Abrigados Resort) 520/204-5639.* Hrs: 5-10 pm; Sun brunch 10 am-2 pm. Res accepted. Southern Italian menu. Bar. Wine cellar. Semi-a la carte: dinner $10.95-$14.95. Sun brunch $15.95. Specialties: vitello mamma, tortellini and scampi, lobster ravioli. Decor features famous and infamous "Joes." Totally nonsmoking. Cr cds: A, C, D, DS, MC, V.

D

★★★ **L'AUBERGE.** *(See L'Auberge de Sedona) 520/282-1667.* E-mail info@lauberge.com; web www.lauberge.com. Hrs: 7:30-10:30 am, 11:30 am-2:30 pm, 5:30-10 pm; Sun 7:30-10 am, 11 am-3 pm (brunch), 6-10 pm. Res accepted; required dinner. French menu. Bar. Wine cellar. A la carte entrees: bkfst $8-$14, lunch $11-$18, dinner $28-$38.50. Complete meal: dinner $60-$80. Sun brunch $30. Child's meals. Specialties: grilled ahi tuna, sauteed duck breast with strawberry and black pepper sauce, chilled tomato consomme with shrimp. Parking. Outdoor dining. Elegant dining in French country atmosphere; many antiques. View of creek. Jacket (dinner). Totally nonsmoking. Cr cds: A, C, D, DS, MC, V.

D

★★★ **PIETRO'S ITALIAN RESTAURANT.** *2445 W Highway 89A # C (86336). 520/282-2525.* Hrs: 5:30-9:30 pm; Fri, Sat to 10 pm; Nov-Feb from 5 pm; early-bird dinner until 6:30 pm. Closed Dec 25. Res accepted. Northern Italian menu. Bar. Wine cellar. Semi-a la carte: dinner $8.75-$22.25. Specialties: veal Marsala, polenta with sausage. Totally nonsmoking. Cr cds: A, C, D, DS, MC, V.

D

★★ **RENE AT TLAQUEPAQUE.** *AZ 179 (86336). 520/282-9225.* Hrs: 11:30 am-2:30 pm, 5:30-8:30 pm, Fri & Sat to 9 pm. Closed Thanksgiving, Dec 25. Res accepted. Continental menu. Bar. Semi-a la carte: lunch $7.95-$11.95, dinner $17.95-$26.95. Outdoor dining. Casual, elegant dining. Totally nonsmoking. Cr cds: A, C, MC, V.

D

★ **ROSEBUDS RESTAURANT.** *320 N Highway 89A (86336), Sinagua Plz. 520/282-3022.* Hrs: 11 am-9:30 pm. Closed Dec 25. Res accepted. Bar to 10 pm. Semi-a la carte: lunch $6.95-$10.95, dinner $12.95-$20.95. Specializes in seafood, steak. Own desserts. Parking. Panoramic view of Sedona's red rocks. Cr cds: C, MC, V.

D

★★ **SEDONA SWISS RESTAURANT & CAFE.** *350 Jordan Rd (86336). 520/282-7959.* Hrs: 7:30 am-9:30 pm. Closed Sun. Res accepted. Complete meals: bkfst $3.25-$6.50. Buffet: lunch $1.95-$7.50. Semi-a la carte: dinner $9.95-$22.95. Child's meals. Specialties: veal emince Zurichois, rack of lamb Provençale, grilled salmon. Own pastries. Pianist Fri, Sat. Parking. Outdoor dining. Open kitchen. Stucco walls; fireplace. Original art on display. Totally nonsmoking. Cr cds: A, C, MC, V.

D

★★★ **SHUGRUE'S HILLSIDE GRILL.** *671 State Route 179 (86336). 520/282-5300.* E-mail mshugrue@sedona.net. Hrs: 11:30 am-3 pm, 5-9:30 pm. Closed Dec 25. Res accepted. Continental menu. Bar. Semi-a la carte: lunch $7-$13, dinner $12-$24. Child's meals. Specializes in steak, seafood, lamb. Jazz Fri-Sat. Parking. Outdoor dining. Located high upon a hill; commanding view of rock formations. Cr cds: A, C, DS, MC, V.

D

★★ **SHUGRUE'S WEST.** *2250 W AZ 89A (86336), 2 mi W on AZ 89A. 520/282-2943.* Hrs: 11:30 am-3 pm, 5-9 pm; Sun brunch 10 am-3 pm. Closed Dec 25. Res accepted. Bar to 11 pm. Semi-a la carte: lunch $3.50-$9.95, dinner $10.95-$20. Sun brunch $5.95-$10.95. Child's meals. Specializes in fresh seafood, steak, chicken. Parking. Patio dining. Dining rm overlooks garden. Cr cds: A, C, D, MC, V.

D

★ **WILD TOUCAN.** *6376 AZ 179 (86351), in village of Oak Creek. 520/284-1604.* E-mail toucan@sedona.net; web www.sedona.net/food/toucan. Hrs: 11 am-9 pm; wkends to 10 pm. Closed Thanksgiving, Dec 25. Res accepted. Mexican, Amer menu. Bar. Semi-a la carte: lunch $4.95-$14.95, dinner $5.95-$18.95. Child's meals. Specializes in hand-cut steaks, authentic Mexican dishes. Parking. Outdoor dining. Casual, colorful atmosphere with good view of Red Rocks. Cr cds: A, C, DS, MC, V.

D

★★★ **YAVAPAI.** *(See Enchantment Resort) 520/282-2900.* E-mail enchant@sedona.net; web www.enchantmentresort.com. Southwestern menu. Specialties: rack of Colorado lamb, pan roasted Maine lobster. Hrs: 6:30 am-2:30 pm, 5:30-9:30 pm; Sun brunch 10:30 am-2:30 pm. Res required. Bar. Wine cellar. A la carte entrees: bkfst $7.50-$12.50, lunch $7.50-$14.50, dinner $15.95-$35. Sun brunch $28.50. Child's meals. Entertainment Sat. Parking. Outdoor dining. Cr cds: A, C, DS, MC, V.

D

Seligman (D-3)

(See also Flagstaff, Williams)

Pop 950 (est) **Elev** 5,242 ft **Area Code** 520 **Zip** 86337
E-mail chamber@seligmannet.com

Information Chamber of Commerce, Box 65, 86337; 520/422-3939

What to See and Do

Grand Canyon Caverns. Includes the 18,000-sq-ft "Chapel of Ages" and other rms and tunnels; ¾-mi trail; temperature 56°F. Elevator takes visitors 210 ft underground; guided tours. Motel, restaurant; western-style cookouts (May-Sept). (Daily; closed Dec 25) Golden Age Passport accepted. 25 mi NW on AZ 66. Phone 520/422-3223. **¢¢¢**

Sells (H-4)

(See also Tucson)

Pop 2,750 **Elev** 2,360 ft **Area Code** 520 **Zip** 85634

Information Tohono O'Odham Nation Executive Office, Box 837; 520/383-2028

This is the headquarters of the Tohono O'Odham Indian Reservation (almost 3 million acres). The Papagos farm, raise cattle and craft pottery and baskets. The main road (AZ 86) passes through the reservation, and side roads lead to other villages. The older houses are made of saguaro ribs plastered with mud. More recently, burnt adobe (mud brick) construction and conventional housing have been adopted.

What to See and Do

Kitt Peak National Observatory. (National Optical Astronomy Observatories). Site of world's largest collection of ground-based optical telescopes; 36-, 50-, 84- and 158-inch stellar telescopes; world's largest solar telescope (60 in). Visitor center with exhibits. Tours. Observatory (daily; closed major hols). Approx 36 mi NE on AZ 86, then 12 mi S on AZ 386, in the Quinlan Mts of the Sonoran Desert (elev 6,882 ft). Phone 520/318-8600. **Donation**

Show Low (E-5)

(See also McNary, Pinetop)

Pop 5,019 **Elev** 6,347 ft **Area Code** 520 **Zip** 85901
E-mail slcofc@whitemtns.com **Web** www.showlow.com

Information Show Low Regional Chamber of Commerce, 951 W Deuce of Clubs, PO Box 1083, 85902; 520/537-2326 or 888-SHOW-LOW

This town, astride the Mogollon Rim on US 60, is a good stop for the golf enthusiast, fisherman, photographer or nature lover.

What to See and Do

Apache-Sitgreaves National Forests. Combined into one administrative unit, these two forests (see SPRINGERVILLE) encompass more than two million acres of diverse terrain. The Sitgreaves Forest (AZ 260) is named for Captain Lorenzo Sitgreaves, conductor of the first scientific expedition across the state in the 1850s; part of the General George Cook military trail is here. Fishing, hunting. Self-guided nature hikes. Picnicking. Camping (dump station; fee). Sat evening programs in summer. For camping reservations phone 800/280-2267. For other information phone 520/333-4301.

Fishing. Rainbow Lake. 8 mi SE on AZ 260. **Show Low Lake.** 4 mi SE off AZ 260. **Fool Hollow Lake.** 3 mi NW. Many others in area. Boat rentals at some lakes.

Hunting. Elk, deer, turkey, bear, mountain lion, big horn sheep, and antelope.

Motel

★ **DAYS INN.** *480 W Deuce Of Clubs Ave Hwy 60 (85615). 520/537-4356; FAX 520/537-8692; res: 800/329-7466.* 122 rms, 2 story. S $54-$65; D $69-$74; each addl $10; higher rates special events. Crib free. Pet accepted, some restrictions. TV; cable (premium). Heated pool. Complimentary full bkfst. Restaurant 6 am-10 pm. Ck-out noon. Coin Indry. Meeting rms. Business servs avail. Beauty shop. Free airport transportation. Refrigerators, microwaves. Cr cds: A, C, D, DS, MC, V.

D SC

Lodge

★★ **BEST WESTERN PAINT PONY LODGE.** *581 W Deuce Of Clubs (85901), near Municipal Airport. 520/537-5773; FAX 520/537-5766; res: 800/528-1234.* Web www.bestwestern.com. 50 rms, 2 story. Mid-May-mid-Sept: S $69-$79; D $74-$84; each addl $5; suites $129-$139; higher rates hols; lower rates rest of yr. Crib $5. TV; cable (premium). Complimentary continental bkfst. Restaurant 11 am-2 pm, 5-9 pm; wkend hrs vary. Rm serv. Bar. Ck-out 11 am. Meeting rms. Business servs avail. In-rm modem link. Sundries. Free airport transportation. X-country ski 17 mi. Refrigerators; some fireplaces; microwaves avail. Cr cds: A, C, D, DS, JCB, MC, V.

D SC

Restaurant

★ **BRANDING IRON STEAK HOUSE.** *1261 E Deuce Of Clubs (85901). 520/537-5151.* Hrs: 11 am-2 pm, 5-10 pm; early-bird dinner Sun-Fri 5-7 pm. Closed Dec 25. Res accepted. Bar. Semi-a la carte: lunch $4.50-$9, dinner $10-$28. Child's meals. Specializes in steak, beef, seafood. Salad bar. Western saloon. Cr cds: C, D, DS, MC, V.

D

Sierra Vista (H-5)

(See also Patagonia)

Pop 32,983 **Elev** 4,623 ft **Area Code** 520 **Zip** 85635
Information Chamber of Commerce, 21 E Wilcox; 520/458-6940

What to See and Do

Coronado National Forest (see TUCSON). One of the larger sections of the forest lies to the south and west of Fort Huachuca Military Reservation. Picnicking, camping (fee). Parker Canyon Lake offers boating, fishing and camping (fee). A Ranger District office is located in Sierra Vista. Phone 520/670-4552 for fees and information.

Coronado National Memorial. Commanding view of part of Coronado's route through the Southwest in 1540-1542. Hiking trails. Picnic grounds. Visitor center (daily; closed most hols). 16 mi S via AZ 92 to Coronado Memorial Rd then W on Montezuma Canyon Rd. Phone 520/366-5515. **Free**

Fort Huachuca. Founded by the US Army in 1877 to protect settlers and travelers from hostile Apache raids, the fort is now the home of the US Army Intelligence Center, the Information Systems Command and the Electronic Proving Ground. An historical museum is on the "Old Post," Boyd & Grierson Aves (daily; closed hols). The historic Old Post area (1885-1895) is typical of frontier post construction and is home to the post's ceremonial cavalry unit; open to public. Directions and visitor's pass at main gate, just W of Sierra Vista. Bronze statue of buffalo soldier. Phone 520/538-7111. **Free**

Motel

✓★ **SUPER 8 MOTEL.** *100 Fab Ave (85635). 520/459-5380; FAX 520/459-6052; res: 800/800-8000.* 52 rms, 2 story. S $42.88; D $52.88; each addl $5; under 12 free; golf plans. Crib $4. TV; cable. Pool. Complimentary continental bkfst. Restaurant nearby. Ck-out 11 am. Business servs avail. Coin Indry. Refrigerators. Cr cds: A, C, D, DS, MC, V.

D SC

Motor Hotel

★ **WYNDEMERE HOTEL.** *2047 S Hwy 92 (85635). 520/459-5900; FAX 520/458-1347; res: 800/825-4656.* E-mail windemere @windemere-hotel.com; web www.windemere-hotel.com. 149 rms, 3 story. S $78; D $86; each addl $8; suites $150-$200; under 18 free; golf plans. Crib free. Pet accepted, some restrictions; $50 refundable. TV; cable. Heated pool; whirlpool. Coffee in rms. Complimentary bkfst buffet. Restaurant 6 am-2 pm, 4:30-9 pm. Rm serv. Bar 4-9 pm; entertainment. Ck-out 11 am. Coin Indry. Meeting rms. Business servs avail. Valet serv. Health club privileges. Some refrigerators, microwaves. Cr cds: A, C, D, DS, ER, JCB, MC, V.

D SC

Inn

★★ **RAMSEY CANYON INN.** *29 E Ramsey Canyon Rd (85638), 6 mi S of Fry Blvd on AZ 92, then 3½ mi on Ramsey Canyon Rd, adj to Ramsey Canyon Preserve. 520/378-3010; FAX 520/803-0819.* 8 units: 6 rms in house, 2 cottages. No A/C. No rm phones. S, D $105-$135. Children under 16 yrs cottages only. Complimentary full bkfst (exc cottages); afternoon refreshments. Ck-out 11 am, ck-in after 3 pm. Charming country inn with antiques throughout; bounded on 2 sides by Coronado National Forest. Situated on a winding mountain stream, in a wooded canyon, this is a hummingbird haven; peak season is Mar-Oct (2-day min). More than 10 species visit the inn's feeders during the year. Totally nonsmoking. Cr cds: C, MC, V.

Restaurant

✓★★ **MESQUITE TREE RESTAURANT.** *S Hwy 92 & Carr Cyn Rd (85635), S AZ 92 & Carr Canyon Rd. 520/378-2758.* Hrs: 5-9 pm; Sun, Mon to 8 pm. Closed Thanksgiving, Dec 25. Res accepted. No A/C. Bar. Semi-a la carte: dinner $7.25-$17.95. Child's meals. Specialties: prime rib, steak, gulf shrimp scampi. Parking. Outdoor dining. Eclectic decor. Cr cds: A, C, DS, MC, V.

D SC

Springerville (E-6)

(See also Greer, McNary)

Pop 1,802 **Elev** 6,968 ft **Area Code** 520 **Zip** 85938
Information Round Valley Chamber of Commerce, 318 E Main St, PO Box 31; 520/333-2123

The headquarters for the Apache-Sitgreaves National Forests is located here.

What to See and Do

Apache-Sitgreaves National Forests. Combined into one administrative unit, these two forests (see SHOW LOW) encompass more than two million acres of diverse terrain. The Apache Forest (on US 180/666) features the Mt Baldy, Escudilla and Bear Wallow wilderness areas and Blue Range Primitive Area, which are accessible only by foot or horseback, and the Coronado Trail (US 666), the route followed by the explorer in 1540. Lake and stream fishing, big-game hunting. Picnicking. Camping (fee charged in some campgrounds). For information phone 602/333-4301.

Lyman Lake State Park. There are 1,180 acres bordering on a 1,500-acre reservoir near headwaters of the Little Colorado River; high desert, juniper country. Swimming, waterskiing; fishing (walleye, trout, channel & blue catfish); boating (ramps). Hiking. Picnicking (shelter). Tent & trailer sites (dump station). Standard fees. 18 mi N on US 180/666. Phone 602/337-4441.

Madonna of the Trail. Erected in 1927, the statue is one of 12 identical monuments placed in states along the National Old Trails Highway to commemorate pioneer women who trekked west. Main St.

Sunset Crater Volcano National Monument (D-4)

(See also Flagstaff)

(15 mi N of Flagstaff on US 89, then 2 mi E on Sunset Crater/Wupatki Loop Road)

Between the growing seasons of 1064 and 1065, violent volcanic eruptions built a large cone-shaped mountain of cinders and ash called a cinder cone volcano. Around the base of the cinder cone, lava flowed from cracks, creating the Bonito Lava Flow on the west side of the cone and the Kana'a Lava Flow on the east side. The approximate date of the initial eruption was determined by examining tree rings of timber found in the remains of Native American pueblos at Wupatki National Monument (see).

This cinder cone, now called Sunset Crater, stands about 1,000 feet above the surrounding terrain. Mineral deposits around the rim stained the cinders, giving the summit a perpetual sunset hue, thus the name Sunset Crater. Along the Lava Flow Trail at the base of the cone, visitors will find "squeeze-ups" and other geologic features related to lava flows.

Park rangers are on duty all year. Do not attempt to drive off the roads; the cinders are soft, and the surrounding landscape is very fragile. The US Forest Service maintains a campground (May-mid-Sept; fee) opposite the visitor center. Guided tours and naturalist activities are offered during the summer. Visitor center (daily; closed Dec 25). A 20-mile paved road leads to Wupatki National Monument (see). Phone 520/556-7042. **¢¢**

Tempe (F-4)

(See also Chandler, Glendale, Mesa, Phoenix, Scottsdale)

Founded 1871 **Pop** 141,865 **Elev** 1,160 ft **Area Code** 480
E-mail info@tempechamber.org **Web** www.tempechamber.org

Information Chamber of Commerce, 909 E Apache Blvd, PO Box 28500, 85285-8500; 480/967-7891

Founded as a trading post by the father of former Senator Carl Hayden, this city is now the site of Arizona State University, the state's oldest institution of higher learning.

What to See and Do

Arizona State University (1885). (47,000 students) Divided into 13 colleges. Included on the 700-acre main campus are several museums and collections featuring meteorites; anthropology and geology exhibits; the Charles Trumbull Hayden Library, the Walter Cronkite School of Journalism and the Daniel Noble Science and Engineering Library. In town center on US 60/80/89. For campus tour information phone 480/965-4980. Also on campus are

Nelson Fine Arts Center and **Matthews Center.** Exhibits of American paintings and sculpture; Latin American art; comprehensive print collection; American crockery and ceramics. Tours avail. (Matthews: Tues-Fri; Nelson: daily exc Mon; closed hols) Phone 480/965-ARTS. **Free**

Grady Gammage Memorial Auditorium (1964). Last major work designed by Frank Lloyd Wright. Guided tours (Mon-Fri). Phone 480/965-3434 (box office) or 480/965-4050 (tours). **Free**

Niels Petersen House Museum. Built in 1892 and remodeled in the 1930s. Restoration retains characteristics of both the Victorian era and the 1930s. Half-hr, docent-guided tours avail. (Tues-Thurs, Sat) 1414 W Southern Ave. Phone 480/350-5151. **Free**

Professional sports.

NFL (Arizona Cardinals). Sun Devil Stadium, Mill & University Dr, ASU campus. Phone 480/379-0101.

Tempe Historical Museum. Exhibits relating the history of Tempe from the prehistoric Hohokam to the present; artifacts, videos, interactive exhibits. Research library. Gift shop. (Daily exc Fri; closed major hols) 809 E Southern. Phone 480/350-5100. **¢¢**

Annual Events

Fiesta Bowl. ASU Sun Devil Stadium. College football. Early Jan.

Spring Festival of the Arts. Last wkend Mar.

Fall Festival of the Arts. First wkend Dec.

Fiesta Bowl Block Party. Includes games, rides, entertainment, pep rally, fireworks, food. Late Dec.

Seasonal Event

Baseball Spring Training. Tempe Diablo Stadium. Anaheim Angels. Phone 480/438-9300. Late Feb-late Mar.

Motels

★★ **COUNTRY SUITES BY CARLSON.** *1660 W Elliot Rd (85284). 480/345-8585; FAX 480/345-7461; res: 800/456-4000.* 139 kit. suites, 3 story. Jan-mid-May: kit. suites $99-$139, each addl $10; under 18 free; lower rates rest of yr. Crib free. Pet accepted, some restrictions; $50 deposit. TV; cable (premium). Pool; wading pool, whirlpool. Complimentary continental bkfst. Complimentary coffee in rms. Restaurant nearby. Ck-out noon. Coin lndry. Meeting rms. Business servs avail. Valet serv. Free airport transportation. Health club privileges. Refrigerators, microwaves. Cr cds: A, C, D, DS, MC, V.

D SC

✓★★ **HOLIDAY INN.** *5300 S Priest Dr (85283). 480/820-7500; FAX 480/730-6626; res: 800/465-4329.* 161 rms, 4 story. Jan-Apr: S $80-$130; D $90-$140; each addl $5; under 18 free; lower rates rest of yr. Crib free. Pet accepted. TV; cable (premium). Pool; whirlpool. Complimentary continental bkfst. Ck-out noon. Meeting rm. Business servs avail. Free airport transportation. Cr cds: A, C, D, DS, ER, JCB, MC, V.

D SC

★★ **LA QUINTA INN.** *911 S 48th St (85281), near Sky Harbor Intl Airport. 480/967-4465; FAX 480/921-9172; res: 800/687-6667.* Web www.laquinta.com/laquinta.html. 129 rms, 3 story. Jan-Apr: S, D $109-$119; each addl $10; suites $139-$149; under 18 free; lower rates rest of yr. Crib free. Pet accepted, some restrictions. TV; cable (premium). Heated pool. Complimentary continental bkfst. Restaurant adj open 24 hrs. Ck-out noon. Coin lndry. Business servs avail. Free airport transportation. Putting green. Cr cds: A, C, D, DS, MC, V.

D SC

★★ **RODEWAY INN AIRPORT EAST.** *1550 S 52nd St (85281), near Sky Harbor Intl Airport. 480/967-3000; FAX 480/966-9568; res: 800/228-2000.* 101 rms, 2 story. Jan-Apr: S, D $99-$129; suite $129-$149; under 18 free; lower rates rest of yr. Pet accepted, some restrictions. TV; cable (premium). Heated pool; whirlpool. Complimentary continental bkfst. Complimentary coffee in rms. Restaurant adj 6 am-10 pm. Ck-out noon. Coin lndry. Business center. Sundries. Free airport transportation. Health club privileges. Refrigerators, microwaves avail. Cr cds: A, C, D, DS, MC, V.

D SC

✓★ **TRAVELODGE.** *1005 E Apache Blvd (85281). 480/968-7871; FAX 480/968-3991; res: 800/578-7878.* 94 rms, 2 story. Jan-Apr: S, D $59-$89; under 16 free; lower rates rest of yr. Crib free. Pet accepted, some restrictions; $4/day. TV; cable (premium), VCR avail (movies). 2

pools. Complimentary continental bkfst. Complimentary coffee in rms. Restaurant nearby. Ck-out noon. Coin Indry. Business servs avail. Refrigerators, microwaves avail. Cr cds: A, C, D, DS, ER, MC, V.

D SC

Motor Hotels

★★★ **COURTYARD BY MARRIOTT DOWNTOWN.** *601 S Ash Ave (85281). 480/966-2800; FAX 480/829-8446; res: 800/321-2211.* Web www.marriott.com. 160 rms, 3 story. Jan-mid-May: S, D $149-$159; each addl $10; suites $169-$179; under 18 free; package plans; lower rates rest of yr. Crib free. TV; cable (premium). Complimentary coffee in rms. Restaurant 6-10 am; Sat, Sun 7-11 am. Bar 4-11 pm. Ck-out noon. Meeting rms. Business servs avail. In-rm modem link. Valet serv. Coin Indry. Exercise equipt. Heated pool; whirlpool. Some in-rm whirlpools; refrigerator, wet bar in suites. Some balconies. Cr cds: A, C, D, DS, MC, V.

D

★★★ **FIESTA INN.** *2100 S Priest Dr (85282). 480/967-1441; FAX 480/967-0224; res: 800/528-6481.* 270 rms, 3 story. Jan-May: S $150; D $160; each addl $10; suites $225-$275; under 18 free; lower rates rest of yr. Crib free. TV; cable (premium), VCR avail (free movies). Heated pool; whirlpool, poolside serv. Coffee in rms. Restaurant 6:30 am-10 pm. Rm serv. Bar 11-1 am. Ck-out 1 pm. Meeting rms. Business center. Bellhops. Valet serv. Concierge. Sundries. Free airport transportation. Lighted tennis, pro. 18-hole golf privileges, putting green, driving range, pro. Exercise equipt; sauna. Refrigerators. Mexican antiques. Cr cds: A, C, D, DS, MC, V.

D SC

★★ **HOLIDAY INN.** *915 E Apache Blvd (85281). 480/968-3451; FAX 480/968-6262; res: 800/465-4329; res: 800/553-1826.* E-mail hitempe@worldnet.att.net. 190 rms, 4 story. Jan-Apr: S $144-$154; D $154-$164; suites, studio rms $172; under 19 free; lower rates rest of yr. Crib free. Pet accepted. TV; cable (premium), VCR avail. Heated pool; whirlpool, poolside serv. Complimentary coffee in rms. Restaurant 6 am-10 pm. Rm serv. Bar 11-1 am. Ck-out 1 pm. Free Indry facilities. Meeting rms. Business servs avail. Bellhops. Valet serv. Gift shop. Free airport transportation. Tennis privileges. Golf privileges. Exercise equipt. Health club privileges. Refrigerators; microwaves avail. Some private patios, balconies. Cr cds: A, C, D, DS, JCB, MC, V.

D SC

★★ **INN SUITES HOTEL.** *1651 W Baseline Rd (85283), at I-10. 480/897-7900; FAX 480/491-1008; res: 800/841-4242.* 170 rms, 2-3 story, 79 kits. Jan-Apr: S, D $89-$129; suites, kit. units $99-$139; under 18 free; lower rates rest of yr. Crib free. Pet accepted; $25. TV; cable (premium). Heated pool; whirlpool. Playground. Complimentary continental bkfst. Complimentary coffee in rms. Restaurant 6 am-2 pm, 4-10 pm; Oct-Apr 6 am-10 pm. Ck-out noon. Coin Indry. Meeting rms. Business center. In-rm modem link. Valet serv. Free airport transportation. Lighted tennis. Exercise equipt. Health club privileges. Refrigerators, microwaves. Some private patios, balconies. Grills. Cr cds: A, C, D, DS, MC, V.

D SC

★ **SHERATON PHOENIX AIRPORT HOTEL.** *1600 S 52nd St (85281), at Sky Harbor Intl Airport. 480/967-6600; FAX 480/829-9427; res: 800/346-3049.* 214 rms, 4 story. Jan-Apr: S $165-$225; D $175-$235; each addl $10; under 18 free; lower rates rest of yr. Crib $10. Pet accepted, some restrictions; $100 deposit. TV; cable (premium). Pool; whirlpool, poolside serv. Coffee in rms. Restaurant 6 am-10 pm. Rm serv. Bar 11 am-midnight. Ck-out noon. Meeting rms. Business servs avail. Bellhops. Valet serv. Sundries. Free airport transportation. Bathrm phones. Private patios, balconies. Cr cds: A, C, D, DS, JCB, MC, V.

D

Hotels

★★ **EMBASSY SUITES HOTEL.** *4400 S Rural Rd (85282). 480/897-7444; FAX 480/897-6112; res: 800/362-2779.* E-mail embassy@getnet.com; web www.arizonaguide.com/embassytempe. 224 suites, 1-3 story. Jan-Apr: S, D $169-$189; each addl $10; under 18 free; wkend rates; higher rates Fiesta Bowl; lower rates rest of yr. Crib free. TV; cable (premium). Heated pool; whirlpool, poolside serv. Complimentary full bkfst. Coffee in rms. Restaurant 11 am-10 pm; Fri, Sat to 11 pm. Bar 11-1 am. Ck-out 1 pm. Meeting rms. Business servs avail. Free airport transportation. Exercise equipt; sauna. Game rm. Refrigerators, microwaves. Private patios, balconies. Cr cds: A, C, D, DS, JCB, MC, V.

D SC

★★★ **TEMPE MISSION PALMS HOTEL.** *60 E 5th St (85281). 480/894-1400; FAX 480/968-7677; res: 800/547-8705.* E-mail tempe@missionpalms.com; web www.missionpalms.com. 303 rms, 4 story. Jan-May: S, D $189-$239; each addl $10; suites $395-$495; under 18 free; golf packages; higher rates: Fiesta Bowl, art festival; lower rates rest of yr. Crib free. TV; cable (premium). Heated pool; whirlpool, poolside serv. Complimentary coffee in rms. Restaurant 6:30 am-9:30 pm. Bar 11-1 am. Ck-out noon. Convention facilities. Business center. In-rm modem link. Shopping arcade. Free airport transportation. Lighted tennis. Golf privileges. Exercise equipt; sauna. Health club privileges. Refrigerator in suites. Cr cds: A, C, D, DS, ER, JCB, MC, V.

D

★★ **TWIN PALMS HOTEL.** *225 E Apache Blvd (85281). 480/967-9431; FAX 480/968-1877; res: 800/367-0835.* Web www.inovate.com/hpmc/TwinPalms. 140 rms, 7 story. Jan-Apr: S $99-$129; D $109-$139; each addl $10; under 18 free; lower rates rest of yr. Crib free. TV; cable (premium). Complimentary coffee in rms. Restaurant adj open 24 hrs. Bar 4 pm-1 am. Ck-out noon. Meeting rm. Business servs avail. Coin Indry. Free airport transportation. Lighted tennis privileges. 18-hole golf privileges, pro, putting green, driving range. Health club privileges. Pool; whirlpool. Microwaves, refrigerators avail. Many balconies. Cr cds: A, C, D, DS, ER, MC, V.

D SC

★★ **WYNDHAM BUTTES RESORT.** *2000 Westcourt Way (85282), 1 mi S of I-10, exit 48th St from W, or Broadway from E. 480/225-9000; FAX 480/438-8622; res: 800/843-1986.* E-mail buttescone@aol.com; web www.arizonaguide.com/buttes. 353 rms, 4-5 story. Jan-May: S, D $275-$329; each addl $10; suites $475-$1,500; under 18 free; golf, wkend plans; lower rates rest of yr. Crib $10. TV; cable (premium). 2 pools; poolside serv. Complimentary coffee in rms. Restaurants 6 am-10 pm; Fri, Sat to 11 pm (also see TOP OF THE ROCK). Rm serv 5:30 am-midnight. Bar 5 pm-1 am. Ck-out noon. Meeting rms. Business center. Concierge. Gift shop. Lighted tennis. Golf privileges, pro. Exercise equipt; sauna. Massage. Minibars. Some private patios. Large resort built into mountainside. Heliport. Luxury level. Cr cds: A, C, D, DS, ER, JCB, MC, V.

D

Restaurants

✓★★ **BYBLOS RESTAURANT.** *3332 S Mill Ave (85282). 602/894-1945.* Web www.amdest.com/az/tempe/br/byblos.html. Hrs: 11 am-3 pm, 5-10 pm; Fri, Sat to 10:30 pm; Sun 4-9:30 pm. Closed Mon; Thanksgiving, Dec 25; 1st 3 wks July. Res accepted. Mediterranean menu. Bar. Semi-a la carte: lunch $3.95-$6.95, dinner $7.95-$15.95. Child's meals. Specializes in lamb, seafood, vegetarian dishes. Own baking. Belly dancing last Sun of month. Family-owned. Cr cds: A, C, D, MC, V.

D

✓★★ **HOUSE OF TRICKS.** *114 E 7th St (85281). 602/968-1114.* Hrs: 11 am-10 pm. Closed Sun; most major hols; also first 2 wks Aug. Res accepted. Contemporary Amer menu. Patio bar. A la carte entrees: lunch

$4.95-$8.50, dinner $12.75-$17. Specializes in beef, chicken, fish. Parking. Outdoor dining. Restored cottage (1918); hardwood and tile floors, stone fireplace. Cr cds: A, C, D, DS, MC, V.

D

★★ **HUNTER STEAKHOUSE.** *4455 S Rural Rd (85282). 602/838-8388.* Hrs: 5-9:30 pm; Fri to 10 pm; Sat 4:30-10 pm; Sun 4:30-9 pm. Closed July 4, Dec 25. Res accepted. Bar. Semi-a la carte: dinner $11.95-$18.95. Child's meals. Specializes in steak, beef, fresh seafood. Cr cds: A, C, D, MC, V.

D

★★ **LO CASCIO.** *2210 N Scottsdale Rd (85281). 602/949-0334.* Web www.amdest.com. Hrs: 11 am-2 pm, 5-10 pm; Fri, Sat 5-11 pm; early bird 5-6 pm. Closed hols; also Mon during summer. Res accepted. Southern Italian menu. Serv bar. Semi-a la carte: lunch $5.50-$7.95, dinner $7.95-$16.95. Child's meals. Specialties: penne alforno, mozzarella marinara. Cr cds: A, C, D, DS, MC, V.

D

✓★ **MACAYO MEXICAN RESTAURANT.** *300 S Ash Ave (85281). 602/966-6677.* Web www.macayo.com. Hrs: 11 am-11 pm; Fri, Sat to midnight. Closed Thanksgiving, Dec 25. Mexican menu. Bar. Semi-a la carte: lunch $4.50-$7.75, dinner $5.95-$12.95. Child's meals. Specializes in mesquite grilled items, fajitas. Entertainment Wed-Sat. Parking. Outdoor dining. Old Mexican-style cantina, located in a converted train station. Cr cds: A, C, D, DS, MC, V.

D SC

✓★★ **MARCELLO'S PASTA GRILL.** *1701 E Warner Rd (85284). 602/831-0800.* Hrs: 11 am-10 pm; Fri to 11 pm; Sat 4-11 pm; Sun 4-9 pm. Closed some major hols. Res accepted. Italian menu. Bar. Semi-a la carte: lunch $4.95-$7.50, dinner $8.95-$16.95. Child's meals. Specializes in veal, seafood, pasta. Outdoor dining. Italian decor. Cr cds: A, C, D, MC, V.

D

✓★ **SIAMESE CAT THAI RESTAURANT.** *5034 S Price Rd (85282), in Tempe Plaza shopping center. 602/820-0406.* Hrs: 11 am-2 pm, 5-9 pm; Fri, Sat to 10 pm. Closed some major hols. Res accepted. Thai menu. Wine, beer. Semi-a la carte: lunch $3.95-$9.95, dinner $4.95-$9.95. Specialties: pad ta lae, pad pak gratiem, prik Thai. Cr cds: A, C, MC, V.

D

★★ **TOP OF THE ROCK.** *(See Wyndham Buttes) 602/225-9000.* Hrs: 5-10 pm; Fri, Sat to 11 pm; Sun brunch 10 am-2 pm. Res accepted. Bar to 1 am. Semi-a la carte: dinner $18-$29. Child's meals. Specialties: New York steak, Top of the Rock salad, lobster Napoleon. Entertainment Fri, Sat. Valet parking. Outdoor dining. Comfortable dining with view of mountains and city. Cr cds: A, C, D, DS, ER, JCB, MC, V.

D

Tombstone (H-5)

(See also Bisbee)

Founded 1879 **Pop** 1,220 **Elev** 4,540 ft **Area Code** 520 **Zip** 85638
Information Office of Tourism, Box 917; 520/457-3421 or 800/457-3423

Shortly after Ed Schieffelin discovered silver, Tombstone became a rough-and-tumble town with saloons, bawdyhouses and lots of gunfighting. Tombstone's most famous battle was that of the O.K. Corral, between the Earps and the Clantons in 1881. Later, water rose in the mines and could not be pumped out; fires and other catastrophes occurred, but Tombstone was "the town too tough to die." Now a health and winter resort, it is also a museum of Arizona frontier life. In 1962, the town was designated a National Historic Landmark by the US Department of the Interior.

What to See and Do

Bird Cage Theatre. Formerly a frontier cabaret (1880s), this famous landmark has seen many of the West's most famous characters. In its heyday it was known as "the wildest and wickedest nightspot between Basin St and the Barbary Coast." The upstairs "cages," where feathered girls plied their trade, inspired the refrain, "only a bird in a gilded cage." Original fixtures, furnishings. (Daily) Allen & 6th Sts. Phone 520/457-3421. ¢¢

Boothill Graveyard. About 250 marked graves, some with unusual epitaphs, many of famous characters. NW on US 80W. Phone 520/457-9344.

Crystal Palace Saloon. Restored. Dancing Fri-Sun eves. (Daily) 5th & Allen Sts. Phone 520/457-3611.

Office of the Tombstone *Epitaph*. The oldest continuously published newspaper in Arizona, founded in 1880; it is now a monthly journal of Western history. Office houses collection of early printing equipment. (Daily) 5th St, near Allen St. Phone 520/457-2211. **Free**

O.K. Corral. Restored stagecoach office and buildings surrounding gunfight site; life-size figures; Fly's Photography Gallery (adj) has early photos. (Daily; closed Dec 25) Allen St, between 3rd & 4th Sts. Phone 520/457-3456. ¢¢

Rose Tree Inn Museum. Largest rose bush in the world, spreading over 8,000 sq ft; blooms in Apr. Museum in 1880 house (oldest in town); original furniture, documents. (Daily; closed Dec 25) Toughnut & 4th Sts. Phone 520/457-3326. ¢

St Paul's Episcopal Church (1882). Oldest Protestant church still in use in state; original fixtures. N 3rd & Safford Sts.

Tombstone Courthouse State Historic Park (1882). Victorian building (1882) houses exhibits recalling Tombstone in the turbulent 1880s. Tombstone and Cochise County history. (Daily; closed Dec 25) Toughnut & 3rd Sts, off US 80. Phone 520/457-3311. ¢

Tombstone Historama. Electronic diorama & film narrated by Vincent Price tell story of Tombstone. (Daily; hrly showings; closed Dec 25) Adj O.K. Corral. Phone 520/457-3456. ¢

Annual Events

Territorial Days. Commemorates formal founding of the town. Fire-hose cart races and other events typical of a celebration in Arizona's early days. 1st wkend Mar.

Wyatt Earp Days. Also fiddlers' contests. Memorial Day wkend.

Wild West Days and Rendezvous of Gunfighters. Labor Day wkend.

"Helldorado." Three days of reenactments of Tombstone events of the 1880s. 3rd Fri-Sun Oct.

Motel

✓★★ **BEST WESTERN INN.** *Hwy 80 W (85638), ½ mi NW on US 80. 520/457-2223; FAX 520/457-3870; res: 800/652-6772.* E-mail bwlookoutlodge@theriver.com; web www.tombstone1880.com/bwlookoutlodge. 40 rms, 2 story. S $58-$65; D $62-$69; each addl $5; under 12 free; higher rates special events. Crib free. Pet accepted, some restrictions; $50 & $5/day. TV; cable. Heated pool. Complimentary continental bkfst. Restaurant nearby. Ck-out 11 am. Business servs avail. Cr cds: A, C, D, DS, MC, V.

SC

Restaurants

✓★ **BIG NOSE KATE'S SALOON.** *417 E Allen St (85638). 520/457-3107.* E-mail bnkord@primenet.com; web www.bignosekates.com. Hrs: 11 am-8 pm. Closed Thanksgiving, Dec 25. Mexican menu. No A/C. Bar 10 am-10 pm; Thurs-Sat to midnight. Semi-a la carte: lunch, dinner $2.50-$16.95. Child's meals. Specializes in authentic Mexican entrees, burgers, pizza. Entertainment. Street parking. Outdoor dining. Original 1880 bldg; mine shaft at basement level; retail Western wear. Cr cds: C, MC, V.

D

★ **LONGHORN.** *501 E Allen (85638), in historic district. 520/457-3405.* E-mail bnkord@primenet; web www.bignosekates.com. Hrs: 7 am-8 pm. Closed Thanksgiving, Dec 25. Res accepted. Wine, beer. Semi-a la carte: bkfst $2.50-$10, lunch, dinner $5.95-$29.95. Specialties: hamburgers, mesquite smoked ribs, T-bone steak. Street parking. Western decor. Family-owned. Cr cds: C, MC, V.

D

★ **NELLIE CASHMAN'S RESTAURANT.** *117 S 5th (85638). 520/457-2212.* E-mail cashman1@mailexcite.com. Hrs: 7 am-9 pm. No A/C. Semi-a la carte: bkfst $3-$8, lunch $3.50-$7, dinner $9-$22. Specializes in chicken, pork, steak. Outdoor dining. In historic adobe building (1879); established in 1882 by Nellie Cashman, "the angel of Tombstone," at height of silver boom. Antique decor. Cr cds: A, C, DS, MC, V.

D

Tucson (G-4)

(See also Nogales)

Founded 1775 **Pop** 405,390 **Elev** 2,386 ft **Area Code** 520
E-mail mtcvb@azstarnet.com **Web** www.visittucson.org

Information Metropolitan Tucson Convention & Visitors Bureau, 130 S Scott Ave, 85701; 520/624-1817

Tucson (TOO-sahn) offers a rare combination of delightful Western living, colorful desert and mountain scenery and cosmopolitan culture.

It is one of several US cities that developed under four flags. The Spanish standard flew first over the Presidio of Tucson, built to withstand Apache attacks in 1776. Later, Tucson flew under the flags of Mexico, the Confederate States and, finally, the United States.

Today, Tucson is a resort area, an educational and copper center, a cotton and cattle market, headquarters for the Coronado National Forest and a place of business for several large industries. Health-seekers, under proper medical advice, nearly always find relief. The city's shops, restaurants, resorts and points of interest are varied and numerous.

What to See and Do

Arizona Historical Society Fort Lowell Museum. Reconstruction of commanding officer's quarters. Exhibits, period furniture. (Wed-Sat; closed hols) 2900 N Craycroft Rd; in Fort Lowell County Park, N end of Craycroft Rd. Phone 520/885-3832. **Free**

Arizona Historical Society Frémont House Museum (ca 1880). Adobe house restored and furnished in period style. Once occupied by John C. Frémont's daughter, Elizabeth, when he was territorial governor (1878-1881). Special programs all yr, including slide shows on Arizona history (Sat; free) and walking tours of historic sites (Nov-Mar, Sat; fee; registration in advance). Museum (Wed-Sat). 151 S Granada Ave, in the Tucson Community Center Complex, downtown. Phone 520/622-0956. **Free**

Arizona Historical Society Museum, Library and Archives. Exhibits depicting state history from the Spanish colonial period to present; Arizona mining hall; photography gallery; gift shop. Research library (daily exc Sun) contains collections on Western history; manuscripts. (Mon-Sat, also Sun afternoons; closed some major hols) 949 E 2nd St at Park Ave. Phone 520/628-5774. **Free**

Biosphere 2. An ambitious attempt to learn more about our planet's ecosystems began in Sept of 1991 with the first of a series of missions in this 3½-acre, glass-enclosed, self-sustaining model of Earth. Isolated from the outside, a rotating crew of researchers rely entirely on the air, water and food generated and recycled within the structure. It contains over 3,500 species of plants and animals in multiple ecosystems, including a tropical rain forest with an 85-ft-high mountain. Visitors are permitted within the biospherian living areas of the enclosure. They may also view the interior from outside as well as enjoy many other exhibits located throughout the campus. Because of variance in research schedule, the biospherian crew may not always be present. Walking tours (wear comfortable shoes) include multimedia introduction to Biosphere 2. Visitor center. Gift shop. Restaurant. (Daily; closed Dec 25) 35 mi N on US 89 to AZ 77 milepost 96.5, then ½ mi N to Biosphere 2 Rd. Phone 520/896-6200. **¢¢¢¢**

Catalina State Park. A 5,500-acre desert park with vast array of plants and wildlife; bird area (nearly 170 species). Nature & horseback riding trails, hiking, trail access to adj Coronado National Forest. Picnicking. Camping (dump station). Standard fees. 9 mi N on US 77. Phone 520/628-5798. Per vehicle **¢¢**

Colossal Cave. Fossilized marine life provides evidence of ocean that once covered Arizona desert. 70°F yr round. 45-min to 1-hr guided tours. (Daily) 19 mi SE on I-10 to Vail, exit 279, then 7 mi N on Colossal Cave Rd. Phone 520/647-7275. **¢¢¢**

Coronado National Forest. Mt Lemmon Recreation Area, part of this forest (almost 2 million acres), offers fishing, bird-watching. Hiking, horseback riding. Picnicking. Skiing. Camping (fee). Madera Canyon offers recreation facilities, lodge. Peña Blanca Lake and Recreation Area (see NOGALES) and the Chiricahua Wilderness area in the SE corner of the state are part of the 12 areas that make up the forest. The Santa Catalina Ranger District, located in Tucson (phone 520/749-8700), has its HQ at Sabino Canyon, 12 mi NE on Sabino Canyon Rd; a ¼-mi nature trail begins at the HQ, as does a shuttle ride almost 4 mi into Sabino Canyon (fee). NE, E & S of city. Phone 520/670-4552.

Gray Line bus tours. Contact PO Box 1991, 85702; phone 520/622-8811.

Greyhound racing. Parimutuel wagering. Tucson Greyhound Park, S 4th Ave at 36th St. For schedule information phone 520/884-7576. **¢-¢¢**

International Wildlife Museum. Includes hundreds of wildlife exhibits from around the world; hands-on, interactive computer displays; videos; cafe. (Daily; closed Jan 1, Thanksgiving, Dec 25) 4800 W Gates Pass Rd, on Speedway 5 mi W of I-10. Phone 520/617-1439. **¢¢**

Kitt Peak National Observatory. 44 mi SW on AZ 86, then 12 mi S on AZ 386. (See SELLS)

Mt Lemmon Ski Valley. Double chairlift, 2 tows; patrol, school, rentals; snack bar, restaurant. 15 runs, longest run 1 mi; vertical drop 900 ft. (Late Dec-mid-Apr, daily) Chairlift operates rest of yr (daily; fee). Nature trails. 35 mi NE via Mt Lemmon Hwy. Phone 520/576-1400. **¢¢¢¢¢**

Old Town Artisans. Restored adobe buildings (ca 1850s) in the historic El Presidio neighborhood are a marketplace for handcrafted Southwestern and Latin American art. Courtyard cafe. (Daily; closed most major hols) 186 N Meyer Ave. Phone 520/623-6024.

Picacho Peak State Park. 40 mi NW on I-10, Picacho Peak exit. (See CASA GRANDE)

Pima Air & Space Museum. Aviation history exhibits with an outstanding collection of more than 200 aircraft, both military & civilian. (Daily; closed Thanksgiving, Dec 25) 6000 E Valencia Rd; I-10 to exit 267 (Valencia Rd), then E. Phone 520/574-0462. **¢¢**

Reid Park. Fishing; picnicking; zoo; rose garden; outdoor performance center. (Daily exc Dec 25) 22nd & Country Club Rd. Phone 520/791-4873 or 520/791-3204 (zoo). Zoo **¢¢**

Titan Missile Museum. Deactivated Titan II missile on display; memorabilia, models, rocket engine that powered the missile, support vehicles, UH1F helicopter, various exhibits. A 1-hr guided tour begins with a briefing and includes visit down into the missile silo (may be strenuous; comfortable walking shoes required in the missile silo). The silo may also be viewed from a glass observation area located at the museum level. (Nov-Apr, daily; rest of yr, Wed-Sun) Located in Green Valley, approx 20 mi S via I-19, exit 69 (Duval Mine Rd), then W, past La Canada, turn right & follow signs. For information and res phone 520/625-7736. **¢¢¢**

Tohono Chul Park. A 37-acre preserve with more than 400 species of arid climate plants; nature trails; demonstration garden; geology wall; recirculating stream; ethnobotanical garden. Many varieties of wild birds visit the park. Exhibits, galleries, tea rm and gift shops in restored adobe house (daily; closed July 4). (Daily) Ina & Oracle Rds, entrance at 7366 N Paseo del Norte. Phone 520/575-8468. **Donation**

Tucson Botanical Gardens. Gardens include Mediterranean and landscaping plants; native wildflowers; tropical greenhouse; xeriscape/solar demonstration garden. Tours, botanical classes; special events. Picnic area (free). (Daily; closed major hols) 2150 N Alvernon Way. Phone 520/326-9255. ¢¢

Tucson Mountain Park. More than 18,000 acres of saguaro cactus and mountain scenery. Picnic facilities. Gilbert Ray Campground (electric hookups, dump station; fee). 12 mi W, via AZ 86 (Ajo Way) about 6 mi to Kinney Rd, turn right. Phone 520/883-4200 or 520/740-2690. Also here is

Arizona-Sonora Desert Museum. Live desert creatures: mountain lions, beavers, bighorn sheep, birds, tarantulas, prairie dogs, snakes, otters and many others. Nature trails through labeled desert botanical gardens. Underground earth sciences center with limestone caves; geological, mineral and mining exhibits. Orientation rm provides information on natural history of deserts. (Daily) Phone 520/883-2702. ¢¢¢

★ **Tucson Museum of Art.** Housed in 6 renovated buildings within the boundaries of El Presidio Historic District (ca 1800). Pre-Columbian, Spanish colonial and Western artifacts; decorative arts and paintings; art of the Americas; contemporary art and crafts; changing exhibits. Mexican heritage museum; historic presidio rm; 6,000-volume art resource library; art school. (Tues-Sat, also Sun afternoons; closed hols) Free admission Tues. 140 N Main Ave. Phone 520/624-2333. ¢

University of Arizona (1885). (35,000 students) The 343-acre campus is beautifully landscaped, with handsome buildings. Visitor center, located at University Blvd & Cherry Ave, has campus maps and information on attractions and activities. Tours (daily exc Sun). N Park Ave & E University Blvd. Phone 520/621-5130. On campus are

Arizona State Museum. Exhibits on the Native American cultures of Arizona and the Southwest from 10,000 yrs ago to the present. (Daily; closed major hols) N Park Ave & E University Blvd. Phone 520/621-6281. **Free**

Center for Creative Photography. Archives library, including archives of Ansel Adams and Richard Avedon, collection of works by more than 100 major photographers; changing exhibits. (Mon-Fri, also Sun afternoons; closed hols) S of pedestrian underpass on E Speedway Blvd, 1 blk E of N Park Ave. Phone 520/621-7968. **Donation**

Flandrau Science Center & Planetarium. Interactive, hands-on science exhibits (daily; closed major hols; free); planetarium shows (limited hrs). Nightly telescope viewing (Wed-Sat). N Cherry Ave & E University Blvd. Phone 520/621-7827. ¢¢; Laser light shows Wed-Sat ¢¢¢

Mineralogical Museum. Rocks, minerals, gemstones and cuttings; paleontological materials. Meteorite exhibit. (Mon-Fri, also Sat & Sun afternoons; closed major hols) Basement of Flandrau Science Center. Phone 520/621-4227. **Free**

Museum of Art and Faculty of Fine Arts. Art museum (free) with extensive collection, including Renaissance, baroque and contemporary art; changing exhibits. (Mon-Fri, also Sun afternoons; summer hrs vary; closed major hols) Music building and theater, in which plays are produced by students. Inquire locally for programs. N Park Ave & E Speedway Blvd. Phone 520/621-7567.

Annual Events

Gem & Mineral Show. Tucson Convention Center. Displays of minerals; jewelry; lapidary skills; Smithsonian Institution collection. Late Jan- Mid-Feb.

Tucson PGA Chrysler Classic. Tucson National Golf Course. $1.1-million tournament featuring top pros. Mid-Feb.

Tucson Heritage Experience Festival. Downtown. Commemorates Tucson's cultural and historic heritage with a torchlight pageant, Native American dances, children's parade, Mexican fiesta, frontier encampment and other events. Oct. Also included is

Fiesta del Presidio. Tucson Museum of Art Plaza. Low-rider car show, dancing, Mexican fiesta events, costumes, food.

Seasonal Events

Baseball. Hi Corbett Field, Reid City Park. Colorado Rockies, Chicago White Sox and Arizona Diamondbacks spring training. Late Feb-late Mar; AAA Arizona Diamondbacks' minor league team, Tucson Sidewinders. Apr-Sept. Phone 520/325-2621.

Tucson Symphony Orchestra. 2175 N 6th Ave. Phone 520/882-8585. Sept-May.

Arizona Theatre Company. The Temple of Music & Art. The State Theatre of Arizona performs both classic and contemporary works. Evening performances Tues-Sun; matinees Wed, Sat & Sun. Phone 520/622-2823. Sept-May.

Arizona Opera. Convention Center Music Hall. Phone 520/293-4336. Thurs, Jan & Nov; Fri-Sun, Oct-Mar.

City Neighborhoods

Many of the restaurants, unrated dining establishments and some lodgings listed under Tucson include neighborhoods as well as exact street addresses. Geographic descriptions of these areas are given.

Downtown. South of Speedway Blvd, west of Campbell Ave, north of 22nd St and east of US 10. **North of Downtown:** North of Speedway Blvd. **East of Downtown:** East of Kolb Rd. **West of Downtown:** West of US 10.

Foothills. South of Coronado National Forest, west of Bear Canyon Rd, north of River Rd and east of Oracle Rd.

Midtown. South of Ft Lowell Rd, west of Kolb Rd, north of 26th St and east of Campbell Ave.

Tanque Verde. South of Tanque Verde Rd, west of Pantano Rd, north of Speedway Blvd and east of Wilmot Rd.

Motels

★★ **BEST WESTERN INN SUITES.** *6201 N Oracle Rd (85704), in Foothills. 520/297-8111; FAX 520/297-2935; res: 800/554-4535.* E-mail isoracle@attmail.com. 159 rms, 2 story, 74 kit. suites. Jan-mid-Apr: S, D $109-$129; 2-rm suites $129-$179; under 18 free; wkend, wkly rates; higher rates special events; lower rates rest of yr. Crib free. Pet accepted, some restrictions; $25 refundable. TV; cable (premium). Heated pool; whirlpool. Complimentary bkfst buffet. Coffee in rms. Restaurant adj 6 am-midnight. Rm serv. Ck-out noon. Coin lndry. Meeting rms. Business servs avail. Valet serv. Lighted tennis. Exercise equipt. Refrigerators; some in-rm whirlpools. Some private patios, balconies. Grills. Microwaves avail. Cr cds: A, C, D, DS, MC, V.

D SC

★★ **BEST WESTERN ROYAL SUN INN.** *1015 N Stone Ave (85705), I-10 exit 257, downtown. 520/622-8871; FAX 520/623-2267; res: 800/545-8858.* 59 rms, 2 story, 20 suites. Sept-Apr: S, D $129-$149; each addl $10; suites $149-$179; higher rates gem show; lower rates rest of yr. Crib free. TV; cable (premium), VCR (movies). Heated pool; whirlpool, poolside serv. Coffee in rms. Restaurant 6 am-9 pm. Rm serv. Bar 4 pm-1 am. Meeting rm. Business servs avail. Valet serv. Bathrm phones, refrigerators; some wet bars. Balconies. Cr cds: A, C, D, DS, MC, V.

D SC

★★ **CLARION HOTEL AIRPORT.** *6801 S Tucson Blvd (85706), near Intl Airport, south of downtown. 520/746-3932; FAX 520/889-9934; res: 800/526-0550.* E-mail clarion@azstarnet.com; web www.arizonaguide.com/clarion-tucson. 189 rms, 2 story. Jan-Mar: S, D $85-$120; suites $210-$250; under 18 free; wkend rates; lower rates rest of yr. Crib free. TV; cable (premium). Heated pool; whirlpool, poolside serv. Complimentary bkfst buffet. Restaurant 6 am-11 pm; Fri, Sat to midnight. Rm serv. Bar. Ck-out noon. Coin lndry. Meeting rms. Business servs avail. Bellhops. Valet serv. Sundries. Free airport transportation. 18-hole golf privileges. Exercise equipt. Some refrigerators. Picnic tables, grills. Cr cds: A, C, D, DS, ER, JCB, MC, V.

D SC

★★ **COUNTRY INN & SUITES.** *7411 N Oracle Rd (85704), in Foothills. 520/575-9255; FAX 520/575-8671; res: 800/456-4000.* Web www.countryinns.com. 157 kit. suites, 3 story. Jan-Apr: S, D $89-$129; under 18 free; lower rates rest of yr. Crib free. TV; cable (premium). Heated pool; whirlpool. Complimentary continental bkfst. Coffee in rms. Restaurant opp 6 am-10 pm. Ck-out noon. Coin lndry. Meeting rm. Business servs avail. Valet serv. Free airport, RR station, bus depot transportation. Putting green. Health club privileges. Refrigerators, microwaves. Gazebo. Cr cds: A, C, D, DS, MC, V.

D SC

★★★ **COURTYARD BY MARRIOTT.** *201 S Williams Blvd (86336), east of downtown. 520/745-6000; FAX 520/745-2393; res: 800/228-9290.* Web www.marriott.com. 153 rms, 3 story. Mid-Jan-Mar: S, D $146-$151; higher rates special events (2-3-day min); lower rates rest of yr. Crib free. TV; cable (premium). Complimentary coffee in rms. Restaurant 6-10 am, 5-10 pm. Rm serv from 5 pm. Bar 4-11 pm. Ck-out noon. Meeting rms. Business servs avail. Bellhops. Valet serv. Sundries. Exercise equipt. Pool; whirlpool, poolside serv. Some balconies. Cr cds: A, C, D, DS, MC, V.

D SC

✓★★ **COURTYARD BY MARRIOTT AIRPORT.** *2505 E Executive Dr (85705), near Intl Airport, south of downtown. 520/573-0000; FAX 520/573-0470; res: 800/321-2211.* 149 rms, 3 story. Jan-mid-May: S, D $114-$140; under 12 free; lower rates rest of yr. Crib free. TV; cable (premium). Heated pool; whirlpool. Complimentary coffee in rms. Restaurant 6-10 am, 5-10 pm; Sat, Sun 7-11 am. Bar 4-11 pm. Ck-out noon. Coin Indry. Meeting rms. Business servs avail. Valet serv. Free airport transportation. Exercise equipt. Some microwaves; refrigerator in suites. Balconies, patios. Cr cds: A, C, D, DS, MC, V.

D SC

✓★★ **HAMPTON INN.** *6971 S Tucson Blvd (85706), near Intl Airport, south of downtown. 520/889-5789; FAX 520/889-4002; res: 800/426-7866.* Web www.hamptoninn.com. 126 units, 4 story. Jan-Apr: S $99; D $109; suites $119-$129; under 18 free; higher rates special events; lower rates rest of yr. Crib free. TV; cable (premium). Heated pool; whirlpool. Complimentary continental bkfst. Coffee in rms. Restaurant nearby. Ck-out noon. Coin Indry. Meeting rm. Business servs avail. Free airport transportation. Health club privileges. Some refrigerators. Some private patios, balconies. Cr cds: A, C, D, DS, ER, MC, V.

D SC

★ **HAWTHORN SUITES LTD.** *7007 E Tanque Verde Rd (85715), in Tanque Verde. 520/298-2300; FAX 520/298-6756; res: 800/527-1133.* Web www.hawthorn.com. 90 rms, 2 story, 60 kit. suites. Jan-Mar: S, D $100-$115; under 18 free; suites $120-$135; lower rates rest of yr. Crib free. Pet accepted, some restrictions; $75 ($50 refundable). TV; cable (premium). Heated pool; whirlpool. Complimentary continental bkfst. Complimentary coffee in rms. Restaurant adj 11 am-9 pm. Ck-out noon. Meeting rm. Business servs avail. In-rm modem link. Bellhops. Coin Indry. Bathrm phones; microwaves avail. Cr cds: A, C, D, DS, JCB, MC, V.

D

★ **RAMADA INN FOOTHILLS.** *6944 E Tanque Verde Rd (85715), in Tanque Verde. 520/886-9595; FAX 520/721-8466; res: 800/272-6232.* E-mail ramadafoothills@juno.com; web desert.Net/ramada. 113 units, 2 story, 61 suites. Jan-Apr: S, D $100-$120; each addl $10; suites $110-$140; under 18 free; lower rates rest of yr. Crib free. Pet accepted, some restrictions; $10. TV; cable (premium). Heated pool; whirlpool. Continental bkfst. Restaurant adj 24 hrs. Ck-out noon. Coin Indry. Meeting rms. Business servs avail. Sauna. Health club privileges. Some refrigerators. Cr cds: A, C, D, DS, ER, JCB, MC, V.

D SC

★ **RODEWAY INN NORTH.** *1365 W Grant Rd (85745), north of downtown. 520/622-7791; FAX 520/629-0201; res: 800/228-2000.* 146 rms, 2 story. Jan-Apr: S, D $60-$130; each addl $6; under 18 free; lower rates rest of yr. Crib free. Pet accepted; $10/day. TV; cable (premium). Heated pool; whirlpool. Coffee in rms. Restaurant 6 am-2 pm, 5-9 pm. Rm serv. Bar 3 pm-midnight. Ck-out noon. Coin Indry. Meeting rms. Business servs avail. Valet serv. Some refrigerators. Cr cds: A, C, D, DS, JCB, MC, V.

D SC

✓★★ **SMUGGLERS INN.** *6350 E Speedway Blvd (85710), in Midtown. 520/296-3292; FAX 520/722-3713; res: 800/525-8852.* E-mail smuggler@rtd.com; web www.arizonaguide.com/smuggler. 150 rms, 2 story, 28 kits. Jan-mid-May S $89-$119; D $99-$129; each addl $10; suites, kit. units $129-$145; under 15 free. Crib free. TV; cable (premium), VCR avail. Heated pool; whirlpool. Complimentary coffee in rms. Restaurant 6:30 am-10 pm. Rm serv. Bar 11:30-1 am; Sun from noon. Ck-out noon. Coin Indry. Meeting rms. Business servs avail. Valet serv. Lighted tennis privileges, pro. Health club privileges. Bathrm phones. Private patios, balconies. Some refrigerators; microwaves avail. Cr cds: A, C, D, DS, ER, JCB, MC, V.

D SC

★ **TRAVELODGE.** *1300 N Stone Ave (86336), north of downtown. 520/770-1910; FAX 520/770-0750; res: 800/578-7878.* Web www.travelodge.com. 80 rms, 2 story, 20 suites. Feb-Apr: S, D $72-$76; suites $82-$86; under 18 free; higher rates gem show; lower rates rest of yr. Crib free. Pet accepted, some restrictions; $50 deposit. TV; cable (premium). Heated pool; whirlpool. Complimentary continental bkfst. Complimentary coffee in rms. Restaurant nearby. Ck-out 11 am. Coin Indry. Meeting rms. Business servs avail. Health club privileges. Refrigerator, microwave in suites. Cr cds: A, C, D, DS, ER, JCB, MC, V.

D SC

★★ **TUCSON EAST.** *6404 E Broadway Blvd (85710), in Midtown. 520/747-1414; FAX 520/745-6903; res: 800/687-6667.* 140 rms, 2 story. Jan-Apr: S, D $99-$109; under 18 free; lower rates rest of yr. Crib free. Pet accepted, some restrictions. TV; cable (premium). Heated pool; whirlpool. Complimentary continental bkfst. Coffee in rms. Restaurant adj open 24 hrs. Ck-out noon. Coin Indry. Meeting rms. Business servs avail. Health club privileges. Some private patios, balconies. Cr cds: A, C, D, DS, MC, V.

D SC

Motor Hotels

★★ **BEST WESTERN INN AT THE AIRPORT.** *7060 S Tucson Blvd (85706), near Intl Airport, south of downtown. 520/746-0271; FAX 520/889-7391; res: 800/772-3847.* E-mail iaatucson@aol.com; web www.arizonaguide.com/bestwestern.air. 149 rms, 3 story, 3 suites. Jan-mid-Apr: S $119; D $129; each addl $10; suites $150; under 18 free; wkend rates; higher rates gem show; lower rates rest of yr. Crib free. TV; cable (premium). Heated pool; whirlpool. Complimentary continental bkfst. Restaurant 6 am-2 pm, 5-10 pm. Bar 4 pm-midnight; Sun to 10 pm. Ck-out noon. Meeting rms. Business servs avail. Bellhops. Sundries. Valet serv. Coin Indry. Free airport transportation. Lighted tennis. Refrigerators; some balconies; microwaves avail. Cr cds: A, C, D, DS, MC, V.

D SC

★ **CLARION HOTEL RANDOLPH PARK.** *102 N Alvernon Way (85711), at Broadway, in Midtown. 520/795-0330; FAX 520/326-2111; res: 800/227-6086.* 157 rms, 3 story. Jan-Mar: S, D $89-$119; each addl $10; suites $99-$149; under 18 free; lower rates rest of yr. Crib free. Pet accepted, $50. TV; cable (premium). Heated pool; wading pool. Complimentary continental bkfst. Coffee in rms. Ck-out noon. Meeting rms. Business center. Exercise equipt. Refrigerators, microwaves. Some balconies. Cr cds: A, C, D, DS, ER, MC, V.

D SC

★★ **DOUBLETREE HOTEL REID PARK.** *445 S Alvernon Way (85711), in Midtown. 520/881-4200; FAX 520/323-5225.* Web www.doubletree.com. 295 rms, 2-9 story. Mid-Jan-mid-Apr: S, D $149-$169; each addl $20; suites $290-$475; under 18 free; lower rates rest of yr. Crib free. Pet accepted, some restrictions; $50 refundable. TV; cable (premium), VCR avail. Heated pool; whirlpool, poolside serv. Restaurant 6 am-11 pm. Rm serv. Bars 11-1 am, Sun from noon. Ck-out noon. Meeting rms. Business servs avail. Bellhops. Valet serv. Gift shop. Beauty shop. Lighted tennis. 36-hole golf privileges. Exercise equipt. Some minibars. Some private patios. Cr cds: A, C, D, DS, ER, JCB, MC, V.

D SC

★★ **EMBASSY SUITES.** *5335 E Broadway (85711), in Midtown. 520/745-2700; FAX 520/790-9232; res: 800/362-2779.* Web www.embassy-suites.com. 142 suites, 3 story. No elvtr. Jan-Apr: S $179; D $189; each addl $10; under 18 free; lower rates rest of yr. Crib free. Pet accepted, some restrictions. TV; cable (premium). Heated pool; whirlpool. Complimentary full bkfst; evening refreshments. Coffee in rms. Restaurant opp 8 am-10 pm. Rm serv. Ck-out noon. Coin Indry. Meeting rms. Business servs avail. Bellhops. Gift shop. Valet serv. Sundries. Refrigerators, microwaves. Grills. Cr cds: A, C, D, DS, JCB, MC, V.

D SC

★★ **HOLIDAY INN PALO VERDE.** *4550 S Palo Verde Rd (85714), south of downtown. 520/746-1161; FAX 520/741-1170; res: 800/465-4329.* 301 rms, 6 story. Jan-mid-May: S, D $98-$175; each addl $10; suites $115-$185; under 18 free; lower rates rest of yr. Crib free. TV; cable (premium), VCR avail. Heated pool; whirlpool, poolside serv. Restaurant 6 am-2:30 pm; dining rm 5-10 pm. Rm serv. Bar 11 am-11 pm, Sun noon-10 pm. Ck-out noon. Coin Indry. Convention facilities. Business servs avail. Bellhops. Valet serv. Gift shop. Free airport transportation. Lighted tennis. Exercise equipt; sauna. Some refrigerators; microwaves avail. On 15 acres. Cr cds: A, C, D, DS, JCB, MC, V.

D

✓★★ **PLAZA HOTEL & CONFERENCE CENTER.** *1900 E Speedway Blvd (85719), I-10 exit Speedway Blvd E, in Midtown. 520/327-7341; FAX 520/327-0276; res: 800/843-8052.* 150 rms, 7 story. Jan-Apr: S $85-$159; D $95-$169; each addl $10; under 15 free; lower rates rest of yr. Crib free. TV; cable (premium). Heated pool; whirlpool, poolside serv. Restaurant 6:30 am-10 pm. Rm serv. Bar 11-1 am; Sun to 8 pm. Ck-out noon. Meeting rms. Bellhops. Some refrigerators. Cr cds: A, C, D, DS, MC, V.

D SC

★★ **WINDMILL INN AT TUCSON.** *4250 N Campbell Ave (85718), in Foothills. 520/577-0007; FAX 520/577-0045; res: 800/547-4747.* Web www.windmillinns.com. 122 suites, 3 story. Jan-Apr: suites $135-$395; each addl $10; under 18 free; lower rates rest of yr. Pet accepted, some restrictions. TV; cable (premium). Heated pool; whirlpool. Complimentary continental bkfst. Restaurant adj 11 am-11 pm. Ck-out 11 am. Coin Indry. Meeting rms. Business servs avail. Bathrm phones, refrigerators, microwaves, wet bars. Bicycles. Library. Cr cds: A, C, D, DS, MC, V.

D SC

Hotels

★★ **CLARION HOTEL & SUITES SANTA RITA.** *88 E Broadway Blvd (85701), downtown. 520/622-4000; FAX 520/620-0376.* E-mail choice121@aol; web www.clarionsantarita.com. 153 rms, 8 story, 31 suites. Mid-Jan-Easter: S, D $89-$119; each addl $10; suites $109-$139; under 18 free; golf plans; higher rates special events; lower rates rest of yr. Crib free. Pet accepted, some restrictions; $50 deposit. TV; cable (premium), VCR avail. Complimentary continental bkfst. Complimentary coffee in rms. Restaurant (see CAFE POCA COSA). No rm serv. Ck-out noon. Meeting rms. Business center. In-rm modem link. Coin Indry. 18-hole golf privileges, greens fee, pro, putting green, driving range. Exercise equipt. Pool; whirlpool. Refrigerators, microwaves. Some balconies. Cr cds: A, C, D, DS, JCB, MC, V.

D

★★ **DOUBLETREE GUEST SUITES.** *6555 E Speedway Blvd (85710), in Midtown. 520/721-7100; FAX 520/296-7896.* E-mail shore tucson@dtguestsuites.com; web www.dtguestsuites.com. 304 suites, 5 story. Jan-mid-Apr: suites $125-$250; under 18 free; package plans; lower rates rest of yr. Crib free. Pet accepted, some restrictions; $25. TV; cable (premium). Heated pool; whirlpool, poolside serv. Restaurant 6 am-11 pm. Bar. Ck-out noon. Coin Indry. Convention facilities. Business center. Gift shop. Indoor tennis privileges. Golf privileges. Exercise equipt. Health club privileges. Refrigerators; microwaves avail. Balconies. Picnic tables, grill. Cr cds: A, C, D, DS, ER, JCB, MC, V.

D

★★ **EMBASSY SUITES.** *7051 S Tucson Blvd (85706), near Intl Airport, south of downtown. 520/573-0700; FAX 520/741-9645; res: 800/362-2779; res: 800/262-8866.* 204 suites, 3 story. Jan-mid-May: S, D $139-$169; each addl $10; under 12 free; wkend rates; lower rates rest of yr. Crib free. Pet accepted, $15 refundable. TV; cable (premium), VCR avail. Heated pool; whirlpool, poolside serv. Complimentary full bkfst. Coffee in rms. Restaurant 11 am-10 pm; Fri, Sat to 11 pm. Bar to 1 am. Ck-out 1 pm. Coin Indry. Meeting rms. Business servs avail. Gift shop. Free airport transportation. Exercise equipt. Wet bars, refrigerators. Grills. Cr cds: A, C, D, DS, ER, MC, V.

D SC

★★★ **HILTON EAST.** *7600 E Broadway Blvd (85705), east of downtown. 520/721-5600; FAX 520/721-5696; res: 800/648-7177.* 233 rms, 7 story. Jan-Mar: S $140-$195; D $150-$205; each addl $14; suites $235-$425; under 18 free; some wkend rates; lower rates rest of yr. Crib free. TV; cable (premium). Heated pool; whirlpool, poolside serv. Complimentary coffee in rms. Restaurant 6 am-10 pm; Sat, Sun from 6:30 am. Bar 11-1 am, Sun from 10 am. Ck-out noon. Convention facilities. Business servs avail. Concierge. Gift shop. Some bathrm phones, minibars. Luxury level. Cr cds: A, C, D, DS, ER, JCB, MC, V.

D SC

✓★★ **HOLIDAY INN.** *181 W Broadway Blvd (85701), downtown. 520/624-8711; FAX 520/623-8121; res: 800/465-4329.* E-mail hitucson@aol.com; web www.holidayinntucson.com. 307 rms, 14 story. Late-Dec-Apr: S $89-$139; D $99-$139; each addl $10; suites $185; under 18 free; lower rates rest of yr. Crib free. Pet accepted, some restrictions; $25 refundable. TV; cable (premium). Heated pool; poolside serv. Complimentary coffee in rms. Restaurant 6 am-2 pm, 5-10 pm. Bar 2:30 pm-midnight; wkends to 1 am. Ck-out noon. Convention facilities. Business center. Concierge. Gift shop. Free garage parking. Exercise equipt. Health club privileges. Microwaves avail. Adj to Tucson Convention Center, music hall, theater, government offices. Cr cds: A, C, D, DS, ER, JCB, MC, V.

D SC

★★★ **MARRIOTT UNIVERSITY PARK.** *880 E 2nd St (85719), downtown. 520/792-4100; FAX 520/882-4100.* Web www.marriott.com. 250 rms, 9 story. Mid-Jan-Apr: S, D $149-$189; each addl $15; suites $174-$214; under 18 free; wkend rates; golf plans; higher rates special events; lower rates rest of yr. Crib free. TV; cable (premium). Complimentary coffee in rms. Restaurant 6 am-10 pm. Bar 10-1 am. Ck-out noon. Convention facilities. Business center. In-rm modem link. Concierge. Gift shop. 18-hole golf privileges, greens fee $35-$215, pro, putting green, driving range. Exercise equipt; sauna. Pool; whirlpool, poolside serv. Game rm. Many balconies. Refrigerator, microwave, wet bar in suites. Luxury level. Cr cds: A, C, D, DS, ER, JCB, MC, V.

D

★★ **SHERATON TUCSON HOTEL & SUITES.** *5151 E Grant Rd (85712), in Midtown. 520/323-6262; FAX 520/325-2989; res: 800/257-7275.* Web www.ittsheraton.com. 216 rms, 4 story. Mid-Jan-May: S, D $125-$175; under 18 free; wkend rates; lower rates rest of yr. Crib free. TV; cable (premium). Heated pool; poolside serv. Coffee in rms. Complimentary continental bkfst. Restaurant 11:30 am-11 pm. Bar 11-1 am. Ck-out noon. Coin Indry. Meeting rms. Business servs avail. Gift shop. Tennis privileges. Golf privileges. Exercise equipt; sauna. Refrigerators; microwaves avail. Glass-enclosed elevators. Cr cds: A, C, D, MC, V.

D SC

Resorts

★★★★ **LOEWS VENTANA CANYON RESORT.** *7000 N Resort Dr (85750), in Foothills. 520/299-2020; FAX 520/299-6832; res: 800/234-5117.* E-mail loewsventanacanyon@loewshotels.com. Some 3,000 feet above Tucson in the Santa Catalina mountains, this resort offers elegant accommodations and world-class golf. Visitors can expect friendly service from a knowledgeable, caring staff. 398 rms, 4 story. Jan-May: S, D $245-$385; each addl $25; suites $750-$2,100; under 18 free; lower rates rest of yr. Crib free. TV; cable, VCR avail. Heated pool; whirlpool, poolside serv. Playground. Supervised child's activities; ages 4-12. Dining rms (also see VENTANA ROOM). Afternoon tea. Rm serv 24 hrs. Bar 11-1 am. Ck-out noon, ck-in 3 pm. Meeting rms. Business center. In-rm modem link. Concierge. Shopping arcade. Beauty shop. Lighted tennis. Two 18-hole golf, greens fee $80-$157, putting green, driving range, pro shop. Bicycle rentals. Lawn games. Extensive exercise rm; sauna, steam rm. Spa. Bathrm phones, minibars; some refrigerators; microwaves avail. Private patios, balconies. Picnic tables. Cr cds: A, C, D, DS, JCB, MC, V.

✓★★★★ **OMNI TUCSON NATIONAL GOLF & CONFERENCE RESORT.** *2727 W Club Dr (85742), north of downtown. 520/297-2271; FAX 520/297-7544; res: 800/528-4856.* Web www.tucsonnational.com. Situated in the foothills of the Santa Catalina Mountains, this year-round resort offers a premier golf facility, pampering spa services, and elegant Southwestern decor. Occupies 650 acres dotted with 10 lakes. 167 units, 2 story. Jan-Apr: S, D $229-$274; each addl $10; suites $254-$390; under 18 free; golf plans; lower rates rest of yr. Pet accepted, some restrictions; $50 deposit. TV; cable (premium), VCR avail. 2 pools; whirlpool, poolside serv. Restaurants (also see CATALINA GRILLE). Dining rm 6:30-11 pm. Rm serv. Box lunches, snack bar. Bars 10-1 am; Sun from noon. Ck-out noon, ck-in 4 pm. Convention facilities. Business servs avail. Concierge. Gift shop. Barber, beauty shop. Sports dir. Lighted tennis, pro. 27-hole championship golf, greens fee $85-$150, pro, putting green, driving ranges. Soc dir. Entertainment. Exercise rm; sauna, steam rm. Massage. Lawn games. Wet bars, minibars; many fireplaces. Private patios, balconies. Cr cds: A, C, D, DS, MC, V.

✓★★★★ **SHERATON EL CONQUISTADOR.** *10000 N Oracle Rd (85737), 15 mi N, in Foothills. 520/544-5000; FAX 520/544-1228; res: 800/554-5064.* Web www.arizonaguide.com/sheraton_tucson. With the rugged Santa Catalina mountains towering in the background, the Sheraton El Conquistador offers extensive golf, tennis, and horseback riding for the adventurous. The beautifully landscaped central courtyard and large pool provide a quiet setting for those who wish to relax and enjoy the beauty of the Sonora desert. 428 rms. Jan-May: S, D $230-$300; suites, studio rms $275-$610; under 17 free; golf, tennis plans; lower rates rest of yr. Crib free. Pet accepted, some restrictions. TV; cable (premium), VCR avail. Pools; whirlpools, poolside serv. Supervised child's activities; ages 5-12. Coffee in rms. Dining rms 6 am-11 pm (also see LAST TERRITORY). Rm serv to 2 am. Bar to 1 am; Sun from 10:30 am; entertainment. Ck-out noon, ck-in 4 pm. Convention facilities. Business center. Bellhops. Valet serv. Concierge. Shopping arcade. Beauty shop. Pro shop. Sports dir. Lighted tennis, pro. 45-hole golf, greens fee (incl cart) $95-$135 ($48-$60 in summer), pro, putting green, driving range. Bicycles. Bkfst & evening horseback rides; hayrides. Exercise rm; sauna. Massage. Lawn games. Basketball. Hiking & nature trails. Minibars; some bathrm phones, wet bars, fireplaces; microwaves avail. Private patios, balconies. Cr cds: A, C, D, DS, ER, JCB, MC, V.

★★★★ **THE LODGE AT VENTANA CANYON.** *6200 N Clubhouse Lane (85750), in Foothills. 520/577-1400; FAX 520/577-4065; res: 800/828-5701.* This uniquely designed hotel has a spectacular setting in Ventana Canyon, an award winning golf course, and spacious suites furnished with Mission-inspired furniture and Anasazi cushions. The effect is a quintessential Southwestern Lodge. 50 kit. units, 2 story. Jan-Apr: 1-bedrm $345-$495; 2-bedrm $495-$695; each addl $25; under 16 free; family, wkly, wkend, hol, golf plans; lower rates rest of yr. Serv charge $15/day. Crib $10. TV; cable, VCR avail. Heated pool; wading pool, whirlpool, poolside serv. Complimentary coffee in rms. Restaurant 7 am-10 pm. Rm serv. Box lunches, snacks, picnics. Bar 3 pm-midnight. Ck-out noon, ck-in 4 pm. Gift shop. Guest lndry. Bellhops. Concierge. Valet serv. Meeting rms. Business servs avail. Lighted tennis, pro. 36-hole golf, greens fee $56-$167, pro, putting green, driving range. Bicycle rental. Jogging track. Exercise rm; sauna, steam rm. Lawn games. Massage. Minibars; microwaves avail. Balconies. Cr cds: A, C, D, DS, ER, MC, V.

★★★ **THE WESTIN LA PALOMA.** *3800 E Sunrise Dr (85718), foothills of Catalina Mountains, in Foothills. 520/742-6000; FAX 520/577-5877.* Web www.westin.com. The Westin La Paloma offers spectacular golf and world class tennis facilities. The extensive network of swimming pools, giant slide and dining options makes this a favorite destination for family getaways. 487 units, 3 story. Jan-May: S, D $350-$440; each addl $30; suites from $530; under 18 free; golf, tennis plans; lower rates rest of yr. Serv charge $7/day. Crib free. TV; cable (premium). 2 pools; whirlpool, poolside serv, waterslide. Supervised child's activities; ages 3-12 yrs. Coffee in rms. Dining rm 6:30 am-10 pm (also see JANOS). Box lunches, snack bar, picnics. Rm serv 24 hrs. Bar 11-1 am. Ck-out noon, ck-in 4 pm. Package store 2 mi. Convention facilities. Business center. Bellhops. Valet serv. Concierge. Shopping arcade. Beauty shop. Valet parking. Sports dir. 12 lighted tennis courts (4 clay), pro. 27-hole golf (Jack Nicklaus Signature Design), greens fee $145, pro, putting green, driving range. Lawn games. Horseback privileges 15 mi. Rec rm. Exercise rm; steam rm. Massage. Some fireplaces; microwaves avail; whirlpool, sauna in suites. Cr cds: A, C, D, DS, ER, JCB, MC, V.

★★★ **WESTWARD LOOK RESORT.** *245 E Ina Rd (85704), in Foothills. 520/297-1151; FAX 520/297-9023; res: 800/722-2500.* E-mail gm@westwardlook.com; web www.westwardlook.com. 244 rms, 2 story. Mid-Jan-Apr: S, D $169-$369; each addl $10; under 16 free; golf plans; hol rates; higher rates special events; lower rates rest of yr. Crib free. Pet accepted, some restrictions; $75. TV; cable (premium). 3 heated pools; whirlpools. Complimentary coffee in rms. Restaurants 7 am-2 pm, 5:30-10 pm (also see GOLD ROOM). Rm serv. Box lunches, snacks, picnics. Bar 4 pm-1 am; entertainment Thurs-Sat. Ck-out noon, ck-in 4 pm. Coin lndry 6 mi. Gift shop. Grocery ¼ mi. Bellhops. Valet serv. Concierge. Meeting rms. Business servs avail. Sports dir. Lighted tennis, pro. 18-hole golf privileges, greens fee $50-$150. Lawn games. Exercise rm. Some refrigerators, minibars. Some balconies. Bicycles. Cr cds: A, C, D, DS, MC, V.

Inns

✓★★ **ADOBE ROSE INN BED & BREAKFAST.** *940 N Olsen Ave (85719), in Midtown. 520/318-4644; FAX 520/325-0055; res: 800/328-4122.* E-mail aroseinn@aol.com; web www.arizonaguide.com/premier. 7 rms, 4 with shower only, 4 suites. No rm phones; phones in suites. Jan-mid-May: S $95-$105; D $95-$125; each addl $15; suites $115-$125; wkly rates; higher rates special events; lower rates rest of yr. Children over 12 yrs only. Pool; whirlpool. TV; cable, some VCRs. Complimentary full bkfst. Restaurant nearby. Ck-out 11 am, ck-in 3-6 pm. Luggage handling. Concierge serv. Refrigerators; microwaves avail. Picnic tables. Totally nonsmoking. Cr cds: A, C, D, DS, MC, V.

★★★ **ARIZONA INN.** *2200 E Elm St (85719), in Midtown. 520/325-1541; FAX 520/881-5830; res: 800/933-1093.* 71 rms, 2 story, 15 suites, 5 houses. Mid-Jan-mid-Apr: S, D $195-$245; suites $247-$300; houses $525-$1,500; each addl $15; under 2 free (summer); special events (2-day min); lower rates rest of yr. Crib free. TV; cable, VCR avail. Heated pool. Dining rm 6-10 am, 11 am-2 pm, 6-10 pm. Rm serv. Pianist 6-10 pm. Ck-out noon, ck-in 3 pm. Luggage handling. Concierge serv. Business servs avail. In-rm modem link. Exercise equipt. Lighted tennis. Refrigerators, microwaves avail. Some patios, balconies. Adobe-style bldgs (1930) on 14 acres of landscaped lawns and gardens. Individually decorated rms with antiques. Cr cds: A, C, MC, V.

★★★ **CAR-MAR'S SOUTHWEST BED & BREAKFAST.** *6766 W Oklahoma St (85735), west of downtown. 520/578-1730; FAX 520/578-7272; res: 888/578-1730.* E-mail carmarbb@aol.com; web members.aol.com/carmarbb.ntm. 4 rms, 2 share bath. Jan-Apr: S, D $65-$125; under 5 free; wkly rates; lower rates rest of yr. TV in some rms; cable (premium), VCR avail (movies). Complimentary full bkfst. Complimentary coffee in rms. Restaurant nearby. Ck-out 11 am, ck-in 4-6 pm. Business servs avail. Luggage handling. Concierge serv. Pool; whirlpool. Some refrigerators, microwaves. Picnic tables, grills. Antiques, hand-made furniture. Totally nonsmoking. Cr cds: C, MC, V.

SC

✓★★ **CASA ALEGRE BED & BREAKFAST INN.** *316 E Speedway Blvd (85390), north of downtown. 520/628-1800; FAX 520/792-1880; res: 800/628-5654.* E-mail alegre123@aol.com; web www.arizonaguide.com/premier. 5 rms, 2 with shower only. No rm phones. Jan-May: S $70-$105; D $80-$115; under 12 free; wkly, monthly rates; lower rates rest of yr. TV, VCR (free movies). Pool; whirlpool. Complimentary full bkfst. Restaurant nearby. Ck-out noon, ck-in 4 pm. Covered parking. Health club privileges. Bungalow (1915); period furnishings. Totally nonsmoking. Cr cds: A, C, DS, MC, V.

SC

★★ **CATALINA PARK INN.** *309 E 1st St (85705), in West University Historic District, downtown. 520/792-4541; res: 800/792-4885.* E-mail cpinn@flash.net; web www.catalinaparkinn.com. 6 rms, 2 story. Dec-May: S, D $95-$125; wkly, monthly rates; special events (2-day min); lower rates rest of yr. Children over 10 yrs only. TV; cable, VCR avail. Complimentary full bkfst; afternoon refreshments. Ck-out 11 am, ck-in 3-6 pm. Luggage handling. Concierge serv. House built in 1927 detailed with Mexican mahogany; unique antiques. Totally nonsmoking. Cr cds: C, DS, MC, V.

★★★ **EL PRESIDIO BED & BREAKFAST INN.** *297 N Main Ave (85701), downtown. 520/623-6151; FAX 520/623-3860; res: 800/349-6151.* 3 suites, 2 kit. suites. Sept-May: S, D (2-day min) $95-$115; wkly rates; lower rates rest of yr. TV; VCR avail (free movies). Complimentary full bkfst; afternoon refreshments. Restaurant adj 11 am-10 pm. Ck-out 11 am, ck-in 4-6 pm. Square, hipped-roof adobe house (1874) with balustrade & veranda; antiques. Courtyard, period landscaping. Totally nonsmoking. Cr cds: C.

★★ **LA POSADA DEL VALLE BED & BREAKFAST.** *1640 N Campbell Ave (85719), opp university medical center, in Midtown. 520/795-3840; FAX 520/795-3840.* Web www.arizonaguide.com/premier. 5 rms, 2 suites including 1 kit. cottage. Phones in suites only. Sept-May: S, D $90-$110; each addl $25; suites $115-$145; lower rates June-Aug. Crib free. TV; cable, VCR (movies). Complimentary full bkfst; afternoon refreshments. Restaurant adj 6-10:30 am, 11 am-2 pm, 5-10 pm. Ck-out 11 am, ck-in 3-6 pm. Concierge serv. Lighted tennis privileges. Picnic tables. Library. Totally nonsmoking. Cr cds: C, MC, V.

SC

★ **PEPPERTREES BED & BREAKFAST INN.** *724 E University Blvd (85719), in Historic District, downtown. 520/622-7167; FAX 520/622-7167; res: 800/348-5763.* Web travelassist.com/reg/az/102.html. 6 units, 1-2 story, 4 kit. units, 3 rms with showers only. 4 rm phones. Mid-Dec-Apr: S $98; D $108; suites $125-$175; higher rates special events; hols (2-day min); lower rates rest of yr. Crib free. TV in sitting rm; VCR. Complimentary full bkfst. Restaurant nearby open 24 hrs. Ck-out 11 am, ck-in 3-6 pm. Concierge serv. Refrigerators. Picnic tables. Totally nonsmoking. Cr cds: C, DS, MC, V.

★★★ **SUNCATCHER BED & BREAKFAST TUSCON DESERT RETREAT.** *105 N Avenida Javalina (85748), off Broadway, east of downtown. 520/885-0883; FAX 520/885-0883.* Web www.sun105.com. 4 rms, 1 with shower only. Sept-May (2-day min): S, D $140-$165; lower rates rest of yr. TV; VCR (movies). Heated pool; whirlpool. Complimentary full bkfst; evening refreshments. Ck-out noon, ck-in 3 pm. Business servs avail. Luggage handling. Concierge serv. Picnic table. Totally nonsmoking. Cr cds: A, C, D, DS, MC, V.

D SC

Guest Ranches

★★ **LAZY K BAR GUEST RANCH.** *8401 N Scenic Dr (85743), I-10 exit Cortado West, in Foothills. 520/744-3050; FAX 520/744-7628; res: 800/321-7018.* E-mail lazyk@theriver.com; web www.lazykbar.com. 23 rms in 8 buildings. AP, Feb-Apr, mid-Dec-Jan 1: S $145-$175; D $240-$275; suites $300; each addl $85; 6-17, $67.50; under 6, $25; weekly rates; lower rates rest of yr. Closed mid-June-mid-Sept. TV in lounge. Heated pool; whirlpool. Playground. Supervised child's activities (mid-June-mid-July). Family-style meals 8-9 am, 12:30-1:30 pm, 6:30-7:30 pm. Box lunches, picnics, cookouts. Private club open 24 hrs, setups. Ck-out 11 am, ck-in 2 pm. Coin Indry. Meeting rms. Business servs avail. Grocery, package store 2 mi. Gift shop. 2 lighted tennis courts. Basketball court. Trap-shooting. Mountain bikes. Lawn games. Hayrides, rodeos. Entertainment, movies. Rec rm. Some fireplaces. Picnic tables. Some private patios. Library. Children's summer camp. Adobe main house (1933). On 160 acres; beautiful desert and mountain trails. Cr cds: A, C, DS, MC, V.

★★★ **TANQUE VERDE GUEST RANCH.** *14301 E Speedway Blvd (85748), 18 mi E via Speedway Blvd, in Foothills. 520/296-6275; FAX 520/721-9426; res: 800/234-3833.* E-mail dude@tvgr.com; web www.tvgr.com. 75 rms in casitas. AP, mid-Dec-Apr: S $250-$320; D $295-$390; each addl $75-$85; lower rates rest of yr. Serv charge 15%. Crib $15. TV avail; VCR avail. 2 heated pools, 1 indoor; wading pool. Supervised child's activities; ages 4-11. Dining rm (public by res) 8-9 am, noon-1:30 pm, 6-8 pm. Box lunches, picnics, cookouts. Ck-out noon, ck-in 2 pm. Coin Indry. Package store. Meeting rms. Business servs avail. Gift shop. Free airport, RR station, bus depot transportation (4-night min). Sports dir. Tennis, pro. 18-hole golf privileges. Indoor, outdoor games. Soc dir; entertainment, dancing. Rec rm. Exercise equipt. Health club privileges. Sightseeing trips; overnight trail rides avail; rodeos. Full-time naturalist (2 walks/day). Refrigerators; many fireplaces. Private patios. Cr cds: A, C, DS, MC, V.

D

★★★ **WHITE STALLION RANCH.** *9251 W Twin Peaks Rd (85743), in Foothills. 520/297-0252; FAX 520/744-2786; res: 888/977-1624.* Web www.ranchweb.com/whitesr/glance.html. 32 rms in cottages & lodge. AP, mid-Dec-May: S $151; D $120-$140/person; suites $151-$170/person; wkly rates; lower rates Sept-mid-Dec. Closed rest of yr. Crib free. Heated pool. Family-style meals. Box lunches, cookouts. Bar. Ck-out 11 am, ck-in 2 pm. Coin Indry. Meeting rms. Business servs avail. Gift shop. Free airport, RR station, bus depot transportation. Tennis. Golf privileges. Trap, target shooting. Lawn games. Bkfst rides, hayrides, rodeos, bonfires with entertainment. Rec rm. Some refrigerators, fireplaces. Library. Informal ranch on 3,000 acres. Petting zoo. Team penning (working cattle in the arena). Cr cds: C.

Restaurants

✓★★ **BUDDY'S GRILL.** *4821 E Grant Rd (85712), in Crossroads Festival Shopping Center, in Midtown. 520/795-2226.* Web www.metrorestaurants.com. Hrs: 11 am-10 pm; Fri, Sat to 10:30 pm. Res accepted. Bar to 1 am. A la carte entrees: lunch, dinner $3.95-$13.95. Child's meals. Specializes in mesquite-grilled seafood, certified Black Angus beef steak. Parking. Exhibition kitchen; soda fountain. Cr cds: A, C, D, DS, MC, V.

D

✓★★ **CAFE POCA COSA.** *(See Clarion-Santa Rita) 520/622-6400.* Hrs: 11 am-9 pm; Fri, Sat to 10 pm. Closed Sun; most major hols; mid-July-early-Aug. Res accepted. Mexican menu. Bar. Semi-a la carte:

lunch $6.50-$9, dinner $11-$16. Specialties: mole negro, pastel de elote tropical. Menu changes daily. Outdoor dining. 3-tiered circular fountain. Totally nonsmoking. Cr cds: C, MC, V.

D

✓★ **CAFE SWEETWATER.** *340 E 6th St (85705), at 4th Ave, downtown. 520/622-6464.* Hrs: 11 am-10 pm; Fri to 11 pm; Sat 5-11 pm. Closed Sun; major hols. Res accepted. Bar to 1 am. A la carte entrees: lunch $6.25-$10.95, dinner $8.95-$15.95. Specializes in seafood, pasta. Entertainment Thurs-Sat. Parking. Multi-level dining rms. Cr cds: A, C, D, DS, MC, V.

D

★★★ **CAFE TERRA COTTA.** *4310 N Campbell Ave (85718), north of downtown. 520/577-8100.* Web www.cafeterracotta.com. Hrs: 11 am-9:30 pm; Fri, Sat to 10 pm. Closed Thanksgiving, Dec 25. Res accepted. Bar. Wine list. A la carte entrees: $5-$20. Specialties: prawns stuffed with goat cheese, black bean chili with sirloin, contemporary Southwestern cuisine. Own desserts. Patio dining. Light Southwestern atmosphere. Cr cds: A, C, D, DS, MC, V.

D

★★ **CAPRICCIO.** *4825 N 1st Ave (85718), north of downtown. 520/887-2333.* Hrs: 5:30-9:30 pm. Closed Sun; Jan 1, Thanksgiving, Dec 25; also Mon mid-May-Aug. Res accepted. Continental menu. Serv bar. Semi-a la carte: dinner $15-$24.50. Specialties: roast duckling with green peppercorn sauce, smoked chicken pâte, ravioli con vitello. Own pastries. Parking. Tableside appetizers & flambe. Cr cds: A, C, MC, V.

D

★★★ **CATALINA GRILLE.** *(See Omni Tucson National Golf Resort) 520/297-2271.* Hrs: 6-10 pm. Closed Sun & Mon June-mid-Sept. Res accepted. Bar. Wine list. A la carte entrees: dinner $16.95-$31.95. Specialties: pine nut crusted pork scallops, carrot dusted Chilean sea bass. Outdoor dining; view of mountains and golf course. Large murals; fireplace. Regional menu changes monthly. Cr cds: A, C, D, DS, MC, V.

D

✓★★ **CHAD'S STEAKHOUSE.** *3001 N Swan (85712), Midtown. 520/881-1802.* Hrs: 4-10 pm; Sun to 9 pm. Closed Thanksgiving, Dec 25. Res accepted. Bar. Semi-a la carte: dinner $8.95-$17.95. Child's meals. Specializes in steak, seafood. Parking. Family-owned. Cr cds: A, C, D, DS, MC, V.

D

★★★ **CHARLES.** *6400 E El Dorado Circle (85712), Tanque Verde. 520/296-7173.* Hrs: 4-10 pm; Sun brunch 11 am-3 pm; early-bird dinner 4-6 pm. Closed Mon. Res accepted. Continental menu. Bar. Wine cellar. Semi-a la carte: dinner $18.50-$29. Sun brunch $15.50. Child's meals. Specialties: rack of lamb, beef Wellington, duck l'orange. Entertainment Wed-Sat. Parking. Located in stone mansion. Cr cds: A, C, D, DS, MC, V.

D

✓★★ **CITY GRILL.** *6350 E Tanque Verde (85715), Tanque Verde. 520/733-1111.* Web www.metrorestaurants.com. Hrs: 11 am-10 pm; Fri, Sat to 11 pm; Sun to 9 pm. Closed most major hols. Res accepted. Bar to midnight; wkends to 1 am. Semi-a la carte: lunch, dinner $5.95-$15.95. Child's meals. Specialties: wood-fired pizza, Angus prime rib, spit-fired rotisserie. Outdoor dining. Cr cds: A, C, D, DS, MC, V.

D

✓★★★ **COTTONWOOD CAFE.** *60 N Alvernon Way (85711), north of downtown. 520/326-6000.* Hrs: 11:15 am-10 pm; Sun to 9 pm. Closed most major hols. Res accepted. Southwestern menu. Bar to 1 am. Wine list. Semi-a la carte: lunch $4.95-$9.95, dinner $10.95-$19.95. Child's meals. Specialties: Sonoran seafood paella, steak, snakebites. Entertainment. Parking. Outdoor dining. Historic farmhouse from 1920s. Totally nonsmoking. Cr cds: A, C, D, DS, MC, V.

D

★ **DAISY MAE'S STEAK HOUSE.** *2735 W Anklam (85745), west of downtown. 520/792-8888.* Hrs: 5-10 pm. Closed Thanksgiving, Dec 25. Res accepted. Semi-a la carte: dinner $9.95-$21.95. Child's meals. Specializes in Angus beef, mesquite-barbecued steak. Outdoor dining. Western memorabilia; rustic decor. Cr cds: A, C, DS, MC, V.

D

★★★ **DANIEL'S TRATTORIA.** *4340 N Campbell (85718), in St Phillip's Plaza, north of downtown. 520/742-3200.* Hrs: 5-10 pm. Closed July 4, Thanksgiving, Dec 25. Res accepted. Contemporary Northern Italian menu. Bar. Wine cellar. A la carte entrees: dinner $16-$27. Specializes in veal, seafood, pasta. Own desserts. Valet parking. Outdoor dining. Overlooks plaza. Cr cds: A, C, D, DS, MC, V.

D

✓★ **DELECTABLES.** *533 N 4th Ave (85705), downtown. 520/884-9289.* E-mail mjmock@rtd.com; web www.delectables.com. Hrs: 11 am-11 pm; Sun to 8 pm. Closed some major hols. Res accepted. Wine, beer. Semi-a la carte: lunch, dinner $4.95-$10.95. Specializes in crêpes, enchiladas, meat/cheese boards. Own desserts. Outdoor dining. Cr cds: A, C, D, DS, MC, V.

D

★★ **EL CHARRO.** *311 N Court Ave (85701), downtown. 520/622-1922.* E-mail elcharro@theriver.com; web www.arizonaguide.com/elcharro. Hrs: 11 am-9 pm; Fri, Sat to 10 pm. Closed most major hols. Res accepted. Mexican menu. Bar. Semi-a la carte: lunch $5-$6.95, dinner $4-$16.95. Child's meals. Specialties: carne seca, topopo. Own desserts. Patio/porch dining. Colorful Mexican decor. In historic house (1896); stained-glass windows; antiques. Cr cds: A, C, D, DS, MC, V.

D

★★★ **FUEGO RESTAURANT BAR & GRILL.** *6958 E Tanque Verde Rd (85715), in Tanque Verde. 520/886-1745.* Hrs: 5-10 pm; Fri, Sat to 11 pm; hrs vary June-Sept. Closed some major hols. Res accepted. Southwestern menu. Bar. Wine cellar. Semi-a la carte: dinner $6.95-$27.95. Child's meals. Specializes in fresh seafood, ostrich, Southwestern dishes. Outdoor dining. Southwestern decor. Cr cds: A, C, MC, V.

D

✓★★★★ **GOLD ROOM.** *(See Westward Look) 520/297-1151.* E-mail gm@westwardlook.com; web www.westwardlook.com. An inspired combination of regional ingredients and classic technique creates a unique variety of Southwestern dishes. Professional service, a good wine list, and an agreeable decor complete the overall experience. Hrs: 7 am-4 pm, 5:30-10 pm. Res accepted. Bar 4 pm-1 am; Sat from 11 am; Sun from 7 am. Semi-a la carte: bkfst $5-$12, lunch $7.50-$15, dinner $16-$38. Sun brunch $22.50. Child's meals. Specialties: medallions of buffalo, rattlesnake fritters, sliced filet of ostrich. Valet parking. Outdoor dining. Totally nonsmoking. Cr cds: A, C, D, DS, MC, V.

D

★ **GREAT WALL CHINA.** *2445 S Craycroft (85711), in Midtown. 520/747-4049.* Hrs: 11 am-10 pm; Fri to 10:30 pm; Sat, Sun 11:30 am-10:30 pm. Closed Thanksgiving. Chinese menu. Bar. Complete meals: lunch $3.75-$4.50; semi-a la carte: dinner $5.95-$21.95; buffet: lunch $4.95. Specialties: Peking duck, volcano beef. Parking. Outside resembles segment of Great Wall; waterfall, stream, wooden bridge at entrance. Antique, hand-painted furniture. Cr cds: A, C, MC, V.

D

★★★★ **JANOS.** *(See The Westin La Paloma) 520/884-1558.* E-mail janosrest@aol.com; web www.janos.com/janos. Situated in a new home on a bluff overlooking the city, this popular restaurant is decorated with a combination of colonial Spanish style and deep desert hues. The cuisine is an intriguing blend of French finesse and Southwestern boldness. French-inspired Southwest regional cuisine. Specialties: pepito-roasted venison, mushroom & brie relleno, lobster bisque. Grow own herbs, vegetables. Own baking, pastas, brioche. Hrs: from 5:30 pm. Closed Sun; Jan 1, Dec 25; also Mon mid-May-Nov. Res accepted. Bar. Wine cellar. Semi-a la carte: dinner $22-$35. Outdoor dining. Chef-owned. Cr cds: A, C, D, MC, V.

D

★★★ **KINGFISHER.** *2564 E Grant (85716), in Midtown. 520/323-7739.* Hrs: 11 am-midnight; wkends from 5 pm. Closed some major hols. Res accepted. Bar. Wine cellar. Semi-a la carte: lunch $5-$9.75, dinner $7-$18.75. Child's meals. Specialties: grilled baby back ribs, mixed grill pasta, mesquite-grilled salmon. Blues/jazz band Mon. Parking. Modern decor and artwork. Cr cds: A, C, D, DS, MC, V.

D

★★ **LA FUENTE.** *1749 N Oracle Rd (85705), north of downtown. 520/623-8659.* Hrs: 11 am-10 pm; Fri-Sun to 11 pm; Sat from noon; Sun brunch 11:30 am-2 pm. Closed most major hols. Res accepted. Mexican menu. Semi-a la carte: lunch $4.50-$17.95, dinner $6.75-$17.95. Sun brunch $9.95. Child's meals. Specialties: chicken mole poblano, pastel azteca, nopalitas. Entertainment. Family-owned. Cr cds: A, C, MC, V.

D

★★ **LA PLACITA CAFE.** *2950 N Swan Rd (85712), at the Plaza Palomino, in Midtown. 520/881-1150.* Hrs: 11:30 am-2:30 pm, 5-9:30 pm; Sun from 5 pm. Closed Jan 1, Thanksgiving, Dec 25. Res accepted. Mexican menu. Serv bar. Semi-a la carte: lunch $5.95-$7.25, dinner $5.95-$15.95. Specialties: bistec Mexicana al minuto, pescado cabrilla (estilo hermosillo), chiles rellenos. Own tortillas. Outdoor dining. Sonoran decor; turn-of-the-century Tucson prints, raised-hearth tile fireplace, serape drapes. Cr cds: A, C, D, DS, MC, V.

D

★★ **LANDMARK CAFE.** *7117 N Oracle Rd (85704), in Foothills. 520/575-9277.* Hrs: 10:30 am-10 pm; Sat, Sun from 9:30 am. Sun brunch 10:30 am-3 pm. Closed Mon; most major hols. Res accepted. Continental menu. Serv bar. A la carte entrees: lunch $5.95-$9.95, dinner $10-$25. Sun brunch $9-$14. Specialties: game, Dover sole, steak Diane. Parking. Patio dining under vine-draped trellis. Tableside cooking. Cr cds: A, C, D, DS, MC, V.

D

★★ **LAST TERRITORY.** *(See SHERATON EL CONQUISTADOR RESORT & COUNTRY CLUB) 520/544-5000.* Hrs: 5-10 pm; early-bird dinner to 7 pm (Sun-Tues, Thurs). Res accepted. Bar. Semi-a la carte: dinner $9.95-$19.95. Child's meals. Western musicians. Specialties: cowboy porterhouse steak, T-bone chili, rattlesnake. Outdoor dining. Cowboy motif. Cr cds: A, C, D, DS, ER, JCB, MC, V.

D

★★ **LE BISTRO.** *2574 N Campbell Ave (85719), in Midtown. 520/327-3086.* Hrs: 11 am-2:30 pm; 5-9:30 pm; Fri to 11 pm; Sat 5-11 pm; Sun from 5 pm. Closed Thanksgiving, Dec 25. Res accepted. Serv bar. A la carte entrees: lunch $5.95-$11.95, dinner $8.25-$18.95. Specialties: blackened scallops, crispy duck with raspberry vinegar sauce, salmon with ginger crust. Own desserts. Cr cds: A, C, DS, MC, V.

D

★★★ **LE RENDEZ-VOUS.** *3844 E Fort Lowell (85716), in Midtown. 520/323-7373.* Web www.ibs-net.com/rendez/htm. Hrs: 11:30 am-2:00 pm, 6-10 pm; Sat, Sun from 6 pm. Closed Mon; Jan 1, Dec 25. Res accepted; recommended on wkends. French menu. Serv bar. Semi-a la carte: lunch $4.50-$12.95, dinner $16.25-$29.95. Specialties: beef Wellington, salmon jalousie, steak au poivre. Enclosed patio dining. Cr cds: A, C, D, DS, MC, V.

D

★ **LOTUS GARDEN.** *5975 E Speedway Blvd (85712), in Midtown. 520/298-3351.* E-mail lotusgdn@aol.com. Hrs: 11:30 am-11 pm; Fri, Sat to midnight. Closed Thanksgiving, Dec 25. Res accepted. Chinese menu. Serv bar. Semi-a la carte: lunch $3.95-$6.50, dinner $7.75-$29. Specialties: sauteed spicy lobster, Mongolian beef, moo shu vegetables. Parking. Patio dining with unique Oriental fountain. Etched-glass panels separate dining areas. Family-owned. Cr cds: A, C, D, JCB, MC, V.

D

✓★★★ **METROPOLITAN GRILL.** *7892 N Oracle Rd (85704), in Foothills. 520/531-1212.* Hrs: 11 am-10 pm; Fri, Sat to 10:30 pm. Closed Dec 25. Res accepted. Bar to 1 am. Semi-a la carte: lunch $5.95-$9.95, dinner $8.95-$15.95. Child's meals. Specializes in beef, fresh fish, pork chops. Outdoor dining. Exhibition kitchen with wood-fired pizza oven. Cr cds: A, C, D, DS, MC, V.

D

★★★ **OLIVE TREE.** *7000 E Tanque Verde Rd (85715), in Tanque Verde. 520/298-1845.* Hrs: 5-10 pm. Closed Mon (June-Sept); also some major hols. Res accepted. Mediterranean, Greek menu. Bar. Wine list. Semi-a la carte: dinner $13.95-$26.95. Child's meals. Specializes in lamb, pasta, seafood. Courtyard dining. 2 intimate dining rms. Cr cds: A, C, MC, V.

D

★ **OLYMPIC FLAME.** *7970 E Broadway (85710), in Midtown. 520/296-3399.* Hrs: 5-9 pm. Closed Sun; some major hols. Res accepted. Greek menu. Bar. Semi-a la carte: dinner $6.95-$17.95. Child's meals. Specializes in Greek cuisine. Parking. Greek statuary. Cr cds: A, C, D, DS, MC, V.

D

★★ **PENELOPE'S.** *5837 E Rosewood St (85711), in Midtown. 520/325-5080.* Hrs: 11:30 am-2 pm, 5:30-8:30 pm; Fri, Sat to 9:30 pm. Closed Mon; some major hols; 2 wks in summer. Res accepted. French menu. Wine, beer. A la carte entrees: lunch $6.75-$11.95, dinner $12.95-$23.50. Complete meal: dinner $30.75-$46.75. Specialties: escargot a la bourguignonne, French onion soup, rack of lamb. Outdoor dining. Original artwork displayed in 4 small dining rms. Cr cds: A, C, D, JCB, MC, V.

D

✓★ **PINNACLE PEAK.** *6541 E Tanque Verde Rd (85715), in Tanque Verde. 520/296-0911.* Hrs: 5-10 pm. Closed Thanksgiving, Dec 25. Bar. Semi-a la carte: dinner $4.95-$13.95. Child's meals. Specializes in steak, ribs. Open mesquite grills. Old West atmosphere with gunfights Thurs-Sun. Family-owned. Cr cds: A, C, D, DS, MC, V.

D

★★ **PRESIDIO GRILL.** *3352 E Speedway (85716), in Midtown. 520/327-4667.* Web www.aznightlife.com/dining/presidio. Hrs: 11 am-10 pm; Fri, Sat to midnight; Sun from 10 am. Closed most major hols. Res accepted. Bar. Wine list. Semi-a la carte: bkfst $3.75-$7.95, lunch $5.95-$10.95, dinner $5.95-$19.95. Child's meals. Specialties: blackened prime rib, chicken pasta, roasted whole garlic with brie. Bistro atmosphere. Cr cds: A, C, DS, MC, V.

D

★ **SAGUARO CORNERS.** *3750 S Old Spanish Trail (85730), ¼ mi S of E section of Saguaro Natl Park, east of downtown. 520/886-5424.* Hrs: noon-2:30 pm, 5-9:30 pm; Sun noon-9:30 pm. Closed Mon; Dec 25. Res accepted. Bar. Semi-a la carte: lunch $4.75-$11.95, dinner $8-$22.50. Child's meals. Specializes in lamb, chicken, beef. Parking. View of desert wildlife. Family-owned. Cr cds: A, C, D, DS, MC, V.

D

★★★ **SCORDATO'S.** *4405 W Speedway Blvd (85745), west of downtown. 520/792-3055.* Web www.scordatos.com. Hrs: 5-10 pm; Sun 4-9 pm. Closed Sun, Mon (June-Aug); July 4, Thanksgiving, Dec 25. Res accepted. Italian, continental menu. Bar. Wine cellar. A la carte entrees:

dinner $15.95-$21.95. Child's meals. Specializes in veal, fresh seafood, steak. Own pastries. Outdoor dining. Desert, mountain view. Cr cds: A, C, D, DS, MC, V.

★ **SERI MELAKA.** *6133 E Broadway (85711), in Midtown. 520/747-7811.* Hrs: 11 am-9:30 pm; wkends to 10 pm; early-bird dinner Mon-Fri 4:30-6 pm. Res accepted. Malaysian, Chinese menu. Serv bar. Semi-a la carte: lunch $4.65-$6.95, dinner $6.95-$34.95. Buffet lunch $5.95. Specialties: sambal, satay, rendang. Malaysian and Chinese decor. Cr cds: A, C, D, DS, JCB, MC, V.

D

★★ **SOLARIUM.** *6444 E Tanque Verde (85715), in Tanque Verde. 520/886-8186.* Hrs: 11:30 am-2:30 pm, 5-10 pm; Fri, Sat 5-11 pm; early-bird dinner 5-7 pm. Closed most major hols. Res accepted. Bar. Semi-a la carte: lunch $5.50-$12.75, dinner $5.50-$24.95. Child's meals. Specializes in shrimp, pasta, beef. Guitarist Thurs-Sat. Outdoor dining. Multi-leveled dining in kidney bean shaped restaurant; decorated with mosaic tiles and greenery. Cr cds: A, C, D, DS, MC, V.

D

✓★★ **TERRA NOVA.** *6366 E Broadway (85710), in Midtown. 520/745-6600.* Hrs: 7 am-9 pm; Fri, Sat to 10 pm; Sun from 9 am. Closed day after Labor Day, Thanksgiving, Dec 25. Wine, beer. A la carte entrees: bkfst $2.45-$5.95, lunch $3.95-$6.95, dinner $6.95-$11.95. Child's meals. Specializes in fresh fish, pasta, vegetarian dishes. Cr cds: A, C, D, DS, MC, V.

D SC

★★★★ **THE TACK ROOM.** *7300 E Vactor Ranch Trail (85715), off Sabino Canyon Rd, in Foothills. 520/722-2800.* E-mail dvactor@azstarnet.com; web emol.org/emol/thetackroom. Located in a historic ranch house with views of the Catalina Mountains in the distance, this elegantly furnished restaurant serves sophisticated Southwestern cuisine. A fine wine list and superb service make for a delightful dining experience. Southwestern, Amer cuisine. Specialties: rack of lamb with mesquite honey & lime, roast duckling with pistachio crust & glaze of jalapeño and lime, Arizona four-pepper steak. Own baking. Hrs: from 6 pm. Closed Mon off-season; also first 2 wks of July. Res accepted. Bar from 5:30 pm. Wine cellar. A la carte entrees: dinner $28.50-$38.50. Child's meals. Valet parking. Family-owned. Cr cds: A, C, D, DS, JCB, MC, V.

D

★★★★ **VENTANA ROOM.** *(See Loews Ventana Canyon Resort) 520/299-2020.* Web www.ventanaroom.com. Perched atop the Loews Ventana Canyon Resort, this elegant restaurant offers views of downtown Tucson. Inspired, seasonal American cuisine is served in a plush setting—there are even harpists to set the mood—by a professional staff. Sophisticated, contemporary American seasonal cuisine featuring fresh local and imported ingredients. Specialties: pan-seared ahi tuna, grilled rack of lamb with toasted cumin sauce, mesquite-grilled game. Own pastries. Hrs: 6-9 pm; Fri, Sat to 10 pm. Res accepted. Bar. Wine cellar. A la carte entrees: dinner $22-$36. Valet parking. Totally nonsmoking. Cr cds: A, C, D, DS, JCB, MC, V.

D

Unrated Dining Spots

BLUE WILLOW. *2616 N Campbell Ave, in Midtown. 520/795-8736.* Hrs: 8 am-10 pm; Thur, Fri, Sat to midnight; Sun to 9 pm. Closed Thanksgiving, Dec 25. Wine, beer. Semi-a la carte: bkfst $2.25-$6.75, lunch $3.50-$7.95, dinner $3.50-$10.50. Specializes in omelettes, desserts. Outdoor dining. Totally nonsmoking. Cr cds: C, MC, V.

D

MILLIE'S WEST PANCAKE HAUS. *6530 E Tanque Verde Rd (85715), in Tanque Verde. 520/298-4250.* Hrs: 6:30 am-3 pm. Closed Mon; Jan 1, Thanksgiving, Dec 25. Res accepted. Semi-a la carte: bkfst $3.50-$5.50, lunch $4-$8. Child's meals. Specializes in pancakes. Country inn atmosphere; 2 dining rms. Fireplace; collection of plates & prints displayed. Cr cds: C.

D

TOHONO CHUL TEA ROOM. *7366 N Paseo Del Norte (85704), in Tohono Chul Park, north of downtown. 520/797-1222.* Hrs: 8 am-5 pm. Closed most major hols. Semi-a la carte: bkfst $1.75-$6.25, lunch $4.95-$9.95. Child's meals. Specializes in scones, salads, homemade soups. Own desserts. Outdoor dining. Adobe house in park dedicated to arid flora and landscape. Gift shop. Cr cds: A, C, MC, V.

D

Tumacacori National Historical Park (H-4)

(See also Nogales, Patagonia, Tucson)

(Exit 29 on I-19, 48 mi S of Tucson, 18 mi N of Nogales)

Father Kino, a Jesuit missionary, visited the Pima village of Tumacacori in 1691. Work began on the present historic mission church in 1800. It was completed in 1822, but was abandoned in 1848.

There is a beautiful patio garden and a museum with fine dioramas (daily; closed Thanksgiving, Dec 25). Self-guided trail; guided tours (Dec-Apr, daily; advance notice needed rest of yr). There is a fiesta held on the first weekend in December with entertainment, music and food. Contact the Superintendent, PO Box 67, Tumacacori 85640; 520/398-2341. ¢

Motel

★★ **TUBAC GOLF RESORT.** *1 Otero Rd (86046), on I-19, exit 40, 2 mi S on E Frontage Rd. 520/398-2211; FAX 520/398-9261; res: 800/848-7893.* Web www.arizonaguide.com/tubac. 46 rms, 9 kits. Mid-Jan-mid-Apr: S, D $135; each addl $15; suites $165-$225; lower rates rest of yr. Crib free. Pet accepted, some restrictions. TV. Heated pool. Complimentary coffee in rms. Restaurant 7 am-9 pm. Bar to 10 pm. Ck-out noon. Coin Indry. Meeting rm. Tennis. 18-hole golf, greens fee $59 (incl cart), pro, putting green, pro shop. Refrigerators. Many fireplaces. Many private patios. Mexican decor. Pool area has mountain view. Cr cds: A, C, MC, V.

SC

Walnut Canyon National Monument

(see Flagstaff)

Wickenburg (E-3)

(See also Phoenix)

Founded 1863 **Pop** 4,515 **Elev** 2,070 ft **Area Code** 520
E-mail wburgcoc@primenet.com **Web** www.wickenburgchamber.com

Information Chamber of Commerce, Santa Fe Depot, 216 N Frontier St, 85390; 520/684-5479 or 520/684-0977

Wickenburg was first settled by early Hispanic families who established ranches in the area and traded with the local Native Americans. The town was relatively unpopulated until a Prussian named Henry Wickenburg picked up a rock to throw at a stubborn burro and stumbled onto the richest gold find in Arizona, the Vulture Mine. His find began a $30-million boom and the birth of a town. Today Wickenburg is the oldest town north of Tucson and is well-known for its area dude ranches.

What to See and Do

Desert Caballeros Western Museum. Western art gallery; diorama rm; street scene (ca 1915); period rms; mineral display; Native American exhibit. (Daily; closed major hols) 21 N Frontier St. Phone 520/684-2272. **¢¢**

Frontier Street. Preserved in early 1900s style. Train depot (houses Chamber of Commerce), brick Hassayampa building (former hotel) and many other historic buildings.

Little Red Schoolhouse. Pioneer schoolhouse. 4 blks N of Wickenburg Way on Tegner.

Old 761 Santa Fe Steam Locomotive. This engine and tender ran the track between Chicago and the West. At Apache and Tegner, behind Town Hall.

The Jail Tree. This tree was used from 1863 to 1890 (until the first jail was built) to chain rowdy prisoners. Friends and relatives visited the prisoners and brought picnic lunches. Escapes were unknown. Tegner & Wickenburg Way.

Annual Events

Gold Rush Days. Bonanza days revived, with chance to pan for gold and keep all you find. Rodeo; parade. 2nd full wkend Feb.

Septiembre Fiesta. Celebration of Hispanic heritage. 1st Sat Sept.

Bluegrass Music Festival. Four-Corner States Championship. 2nd full wkend Nov.

Motels

★ **AMERICINN MOTEL.** *850 E Wickenburg Way (85358). 520/684-5461; FAX 520/684-5461; res: 800/634-3444.* 29 rms, 2 story. Nov-May: S $61-$72; D $66-$82; each addl $6; under 16 free; lower rates rest of yr. Crib free. TV; cable (premium). Heated pool; whirlpool. Complimentary coffee in lobby. Restaurant 7 am-1:30 pm, 5-8:30 pm; closed Mon. Rm serv. Bar (exc Mon). Ck-out 11 am. Business servs avail. Some microwaves. Private patios, some balconies. Cr cds: A, C, D, DS, MC, V.

D SC

✓★★ **BEST WESTERN RANCHO GRANDE MOTEL.** *293 E Wickenburg Way (85390). 520/684-5445; FAX 520/684-7380; res: 800/528-1234; res: 800/854-7235.* Web www.bestwestern.com. 80 rms, 1-2 story, 24 kits. Nov-Apr: S $63-$78; D $66-$80; each addl $3; suites $88-$99; higher rates special events; lower rates rest of yr. Crib $3. Pet accepted. TV; cable, VCR avail (movies). Heated pool; whirlpool. Playground. Complimentary coffee in rms. Restaurant nearby. Ck-out noon. Meeting rms. Business servs avail. Bellhops. Valet serv. Free airport transportation. Tennis. Golf privileges. Refrigerators; some bathrm phones, microwaves. Some private patios, balconies. Cr cds: A, C, D, DS, ER, JCB, MC, V.

D SC

Guest Ranches

★★ **FLYING E RANCH.** *2801 W Wickenburg Way (85390), 4 mi W on AZ 60W. 520/684-2690; FAX 520/684-5304; res: 888/684-2650.* E-mail flyinge@primenet.com; web www.guestranches.com/flyinge. 17 units. AP (3-day min), Nov-Apr: S $130-$170; D $210-$275; each addl $95; family rates. Closed rest of yr. TV; VCR avail. Heated pool. Family-style meals. Bkfst cookouts, chuckwagon dinners. Setups. Ck-out 11 am, ck-in varies. Business servs avail. Trail rides (fee); hay rides. Lighted tennis. Golf privileges. Shuffleboard. Exercise equipt; sauna. Occasional entertainment; square, line dancing. Refrigerators. On 20,000-acre cattle ranch in shadow of Vulture Peak. Cr cds: C.

★★★ **MERV GRIFFINS WICKENBURG INN & DUDE RANCH.** *34801 N Hwy 89 (85646), 8 mi NW on US 89. 520/684-7811; FAX 520/684-2981; res: 800/942-5362.* E-mail wickinn@primenet.com; web www.merv.com. 9 rms in lodge, 54 casitas. Feb-Apr, mid-Dec-early Jan AP: S $159-$279; D $239-$379; family rates; lower rates rest of yr. Serv charge 16%. Crib free. TV. 2 heated pools; whirlpool. Playground. Supervised child's activities; ages 3-12. Coffee in rms. Dining rm (public by res) 7-10 am, noon-2:30 pm, 6-8:30 pm. Box lunches, picnics, cookouts. Bar 11 am-11 pm. Ck-out noon, ck-in 3 pm. Coin lndry. Meeting rms. Business servs avail. Tennis. Exercise equipt. 3 trail rides. Nature program; movies. Crafts center, instruction. Refrigerators; fireplace, wet bar in casitas. Private patios; some sun decks. Many antiques, handcrafted furnishings. 4,700-acre wildlife area. Cr cds: A, C, D, DS, MC, V.

SC

★★★ **RANCHO DE LOS CABALLEROS.** *1551 S Vulture Mine Rd (85390). 520/684-5484; FAX 520/684-2267.* Web www.caballeros.com. 79 rms, 33 kit. units. AP, Feb-mid-May: S $219-$399; D $339-$499; under 5 free; golf plans; hol rates; lower rates Oct-Jan. Closed rest of yr. Crib free. TV. Pool; poolside serv. Playground. Free supervised child's activities; ages 5-12. Complimentary coffee in rms. Restaurant 7-9 am, 12:30 am-1:30 pm, 6:30-8:30 pm. Box lunches, snacks. Bar 10:30 am-midnight; entertainment Wed, Fri, Sat. Ck-out 1 pm, ck-in 4 pm. Grocery 2 mi. Coin lndry. Bellhops. Meeting rms. Business servs avail. Airport transportation. Tennis, pro 18-hole golf, greens fee $75, pro putting green, driving range, pro shop. Horse stables. Hiking. Bicycles. Hot air ballooning. Trap & skeet shooting. Soc dir. Health club privileges. Massage. Some refrigerators, microwaves. Cr cds: A, C.

D SC

Willcox (G-5)

(See also Safford)

Pop 3,122 **Elev** 4,200 ft **Area Code** 520 **Zip** 85643
E-mail willcoxchamber@vtc.net

Information Chamber of Commerce, Cochise Information Center, 1500 N Circle I Rd; 520/384-2272 or 800/200-2272

What to See and Do

Amerind Foundation. Amerind (short for American Indian) Museum contains one of the finest collections of archaeological and ethnological artifacts in the country. Displayed in art gallery are paintings by Anglo and Native American artists. Picnic area, museum shop. (Sept-May, daily; rest of yr, Wed-Sun; closed major hols) Approx 1 mi SW via I-10, exit 318 on Dragoon Rd in Dragoon. Phone 520/586-3666. **¢¢**

Chiricahua National Monument (see). 32 mi SE on AZ 186, then 4 mi E on AZ 181.

Cochise Information Center & Museum of the Southwest. Chiricahua Apache exhibits; mineral collection; photographic display of Southwestern historic sites; Heritage Park. (Daily; closed Jan 1, Thanksgiving, Dec 25) 1 mi N via Circle I Road just off Ft Grant Rd, exit from I-10. Phone 520/384-2272 or 800/200-2272. **Free**

Cochise Stronghold. Rugged canyon once sheltered Chiricahua Apache; unique rock formations provide protection and vantage points. Camping. Picnicking. Nature, hiking, horseback and history trails. (Daily) SW via I-10 to US 191S, then W on Ironwood Rd. Phone 520/364-3468.

Fort Bowie National Historic Site. Visitors pass ruins of Butterfield Stage Station, post cemetery, Apache Spring and the first Fort Bowie on the way to ruins of the second Fort Bowie. Visitor center. Carry water in summer, beware of flash floods and rattlesnakes. Do not climb on ruins or disturb any of the site's features. 22 mi SE on AZ 186, then 6 mi NE on graded road leading E into Apache Pass and 2 mi to trailhead, then walk 1½ mi on foot trail to the fort ruins. Phone 520/847-2500. **Free**

The Rex Allen Arizona Cowboy Museum & Cowboy Hall of Fame. Museum dedicated to Willcox-native Rex Allen, the "last of the Silver Screen Cowboys." Details his life from ranch life in Willcox to radio, TV and movie days. Also special exhibits on pioneer settlers & ranchers. Cowboy Hall of Fame pays tribute to real cattle industry heroes. Gift shop. (Daily; closed Jan 1, Thanksgiving, Dec 25) 155 N Railroad Ave. Phone 520/384-4583. **¢**

Annual Events

Wings Over Willcox/Sandhill Crane Celebration. Tours of bird-watching areas, trade shows, seminars, workshops. 3rd wkend Jan.

Rex Allen Days. PRCA Rodeo, concert by Rex Allen, Jr, parade, country fair, Western dances, softball tournament. 1st wkend Oct.

Motels

✓★★ **BEST WESTERN PLAZA INN.** *1100 W Rex Allen Dr (85643), I-10, exit 340. 520/384-3556; FAX 520/384-2679; res: 800/528-1234; res: 800/262-2645.* 92 rms, 2 story. S, D $59-$109; each addl $10; under 12 free. Crib free. Pet accepted, some restrictions; $8. TV; cable. Heated pool. Complimentary full bkfst. Coffee in rms. Restaurant 6 am-9 pm; Fri, Sat to 10 pm. Rm serv. Bar 4 pm-1 am. Ck-out noon. Coin lndry. Meeting rms. Business servs avail. Many refrigerators. Cr cds: A, C, D, DS, MC, V.

D SC

✓★★ **DAYS INN.** *724 N Bisbee Ave (85643). 520/384-4222; FAX 520/384-3785; res: 800/329-7466.* 73 rms, 2 story. June-Aug & Nov-Feb: S $38-$48; D $46-$56; each addl $5; under 13 free; lower rates rest of yr. Crib $5. Pet accepted, some restrictions; $5. TV; cable (premium). Heated pool. Complimentary continental bkfst. Restaurant opp open 24 hrs. Ck-out 11 am. Coin lndry. Business servs avail. Cr cds: A, C, D, DS, ER, JCB, MC, V.

D SC

Inn

★★ **CHIRICAHUA FOOTHILLS.** *6310 Pinery Canyon Rd (85643), 36 mi SE; AZ 186 to AZ 181, ¼ mi S of Chiricahua Natl Monument entrance. 520/824-3632.* 5 air-cooled rms. No rm phones. S $65; D $70; under 12 free. 2 TV rms; VCR avail (movies). Complimentary full bkfst. Ck-out 11 am, ck-in 3 pm. Picnic tables. Working cattle ranch. Totally nonsmoking. Cr cds: C.

D

Williams (Coconino Co) (D-3)

(See also Flagstaff, Seligman)

Settled 1880 **Pop** 2,532 **Elev** 6,750 ft **Area Code** 520 **Zip** 86046

Information Williams-Grand Canyon Chamber of Commerce, 200 W Railroad Ave; 520/635-4061

This town lies at the foot of Bill Williams Mountain (named for an early trapper and guide) and is the principal entrance to the Grand Canyon (see). It is a resort town in the midst of Kaibab National Forest, which has its headquarters here. There are seven small fishing lakes in the surrounding area.

What to See and Do

Grand Canyon National Park (see). Approx 50 mi N on US 180 (AZ 64) to South Rim.

★ **Grand Canyon Railway.** First operated by Santa Fe Railroad in 1901 as an alternative to the stagecoach, this restored line carries passengers northward aboard authentically refurbished steam locomotives and coaches. Full-day round trips include 3½-hr layover at canyon. At Williams depot, there is a museum of railroad history. Railway (June-Oct, daily; Mar-May, Wed-Sun; Nov, Jan-Feb, Fri-Sun; Dec, Sat & Sun; also Dec 25-Jan 1, daily). For reservations, Phone 800/843-8724. Railway **¢¢¢¢¢**

Kaibab National Forest. More than 1.5 million acres; one area surrounds Williams and includes Sycamore Canyon and Kendrick Mt wilderness areas and part of National Historic Rte 66; a second area is 42 mi N on US 180 (AZ 64) near South Rim of Grand Canyon; a third area lies N of Grand Canyon (outstanding views of the canyon from seldom visited vista points in this area) and includes Kanab Creek and Saddle Mountain wilderness areas, the Kaibab Plateau and the North Rim Parkway National Scenic Byway. The forest is home for a variety of wildlife unique to this area, including mule deer and the Kaibab squirrel. Fishing (trout), hunting. Picnicking. Camping (fee). Phone 520/635-2681. Also in forest is

Williams Ski Area. Pomalift, rope tow; patrol, school, rentals; snack bar. (Mid-Dec-Easter, daily exc Wed) Sledding slopes and cross-country trails nearby. 4 mi S of town, on the N slopes of Bill Williams Mt. Phone 520/635-9330. **¢¢¢¢¢**

Annual Events

Bill Williams Rendezvous Days. Black powder shoot, carnival, street dances, pioneer arts & crafts. Memorial Day wkend.

Labor Day Rodeo. Professional rodeo and Western celebration. Labor Day wkend.

Motels

★★★ **BEST WESTERN WILLIAMS.** *W Route 66 (86046). 520/635-4400; FAX 520/635-4488; res: 800/634-4445.* 79 rms, 2 story, 10 suites. Mid-May-Aug: S $79-$135; D $89-$135; each addl $10; suites $125-$181; under 12 free; ski plan; lower rates rest of yr. Crib free. TV; cable (premium). Complimentary full bkfst. Complimentary coffee in rms. Restaurant adj open 24 hrs. Bar 5-10 pm. Ck-out noon. Meeting rms. Business servs avail. In-rm modem link. Bellhops. Gift shop. Coin lndry. Downhill ski 5 mi. Pool; whirlpool. Bathrm phones. 1 mi to lake. Cr cds: A, C, D, DS, MC, V.

D SC

✓★ **EL RANCHO MOTEL.** *617 E Rte 66 (86046). 520/635-2552; FAX 520/635-4173; res: 800/228-2370.* E-mail elrancho@primenet.com. 25 rms, 2 story, 2 suites. Mid-May-Sept: S $57-$95; D $62-$95; each addl $5; suites $95-$105; lower rates rest of yr. Crib $3. TV; cable (premium). Heated pool. Complimentary coffee in rms. Restaurant opp 6 am-2 pm; 5-10 pm. Ck-out 11 am. Downhill ski 4 mi. Some refrigerators. Microwaves avail. Cr cds: A, C, DS, MC, V.

D SC

★ **IMA NORRIS MOTEL.** *1001 W Rt 66 (85365). 520/635-2202; FAX 520/635-9202; res: 800/341-8000.* E-mail ukgolf@primenet.com; web www.ima/lodging.com. 33 rms. May-Sept: S, D $59-$66; each addl $5; under 12 free; ski plans; lower rates rest of yr. Crib $7. TV; cable (premium). Pool. Complimentary coffee in lobby. Restaurant nearby. Ck-out 11 am. Business servs avail. In-rm modem link. Free RR station transportation. Golf privileges. Downhill ski 4 mi. Whirlpool. Refrigerators; microwaves avail. Grills. Cr cds: A, C, DS, MC, V.

★ **MOTEL 6.** *831 W Bill Williams Ave (86046). 520/635-9000; FAX 520/635-2300; res: 800/466-8356.* 52 rms, 2 story. June-Sept: S, D $45-$69; each addl $6; under 18 free; higher rates hols; lower rates rest of yr. Crib free. Pet accepted. TV, cable. Indoor pool; whirlpool. Restaurant opp 11 am-9 pm. Ck-out 11 am. Coin Indry. Business servs avail. Cr cds: A, C, D, DS, MC, V.

D SC

★ **MOUNTAINSIDE INN.** *642 E Rte 66 (86046). 520/635-4431; FAX 520/635-2292; res: 800/462-9381.* E-mail ramada@thegrandcanyon.com. 96 rms, 2 story. Apr-Oct: S, D $95-$125; each addl $10; under 18 free; 2-day min stay hols; lower rates rest of yr. Crib free. Pet accepted. TV, cable. Heated pool; whirlpool. Restaurant 6 am-2 pm, 4-10 pm. Rm serv (evening only). Bar. Ck-out noon. Gift shop. Downhill ski 4 mi. Microwaves avail. Picnic tables. Cr cds: A, C, D, DS, MC, V.

D SC

Motor Hotels

★★ **FRAY MARCOS HOTEL.** *235 N Grand Canyon Blvd (86046). 520/635-4010; FAX 520/635-2180; res: 800/843-8724.* Web www.thetrain.com. 89 rms, 2 story. Apr-mid-Sept: S, D $119; each addl $10; under 16 free; lower rates rest of yr. Crib free. TV; cable (premium). Complimentary coffee in lobby. Restaurant 4-10 pm. Bar. Ck-out 11 am. Business servs avail. Bellhops. Sundries. Gift shop. Cr cds: A, C, D, DS, MC, V.

D

★★ **HOLIDAY INN.** *950 N Grand Canyon Blvd (86046). 520/635-4114; FAX 520/635-2700.* 120 rms, 2 story, 12 suites. S, D $79-$99; each addl $10; suites $99-$119; under 19 free; higher rates hols; lower rates rest of yr. Crib free. Pet accepted. TV; cable. Complimentary coffee in lobby. Restaurant 6-10 am, 5-10 pm; summer hrs 6 am-10 pm. Rm serv. Bar from 5 pm. Ck-out 11 am. Meeting rm. Business servs avail. Bellhops. Gift shop. Coin Indry. Downhill ski 5 mi. Indoor pool; whirlpool. Some refrigerators. Wet bars in suites. Cr cds: A, C, D, DS, MC, V.

D SC

Inn

★★ **TERRY RANCH BED & BREAKFAST.** *701 Quarter Horse Rd (86046), 1½ mi E on Bill Williams to Rodeo then N on Quarter Horse. 520/635-4171; FAX 520/635-2488; res: 800/210-5908.* E-mail terryranch@workmail.com; web www.thegrandcanyon.com/terryranch. 4 rms. No A/C. No rm phones. May-Sept: S, D $90-$120; each addl $15; lower rates rest of yr. TV in common rm; cable (premium), VCR avail (movies). Complimentary full bkfst; afternoon refreshments. Restaurant nearby. Ck-out 10 am, ck-in 4-6 pm. Luggage handling. Concierge serv. Some in-rm fireplaces, whirlpools. Picnic tables, grills. Antiques. Country Victorian log house. Totally nonsmoking. . Cr cds: A, C, DS, MC, V.

D

Restaurant

★ **ROD'S STEAK HOUSE.** *301 E Bill Williams Ave (86046). 520/635-2671.* E-mail lawstel@infomagic.com; web www.rods-steakhouse.com. Hrs: 11:30 am-9:30 pm. Closed Thanksgiving, Dec 24, 25. Res accepted. Bar. Semi-a la carte: lunch $3.50-$7.50, dinner $7-$23. Child's meals. Specialties: mesquite-broiled steak, prime rib. Paintings of the Old West, stained-glass windows. Cr cds: C, MC, V.

Window Rock (C-6)

Pop 3,306 **Elev** 6,880 ft **Area Code** 520 **Zip** 86515
Web www.atiin.com/navajoland

Information Navajoland Tourism Department, PO Box 663; 520/871-6436 or 520/871-7371

This is the headquarters of the Navajo Nation. The 88-member tribal council, democratically elected, meets in an octagonal council building; tribal officials conduct tribal business from Window Rock.

Behind the town is a natural bridge that looks like a window. It is in the midst of a colorful group of sandstone formation called "The Window Rock."

What to See and Do

Canyon de Chelly National Monument (see).

Guided tours of Navajoland. Various organizations & individuals offer walking & driving tours of the area. Fees & tours vary; phone for information.

Hozhoni Tours. Contact PO Box 1995, Kayenta 86033; phone 520/697-8198.

Roland's Navajo Land Tours. Contact PO Box 1542, Kayenta 86033; phone 520/697-3524.

Stanley Perry, Step-On Tours. Contact PO Box 2381; phone 520/871-2484 (after 7 pm).

Navajo Nation Museum. Established in 1961 to preserve Navajo history, art, culture and natural history; permanent and temporary exhibits. Literature and Navajo information avail. (Mon-Fri; closed tribal & other hols) E of jct AZ 264 & Indian Rte 12, on AZ 264 in Navajo Arts & Crafts Enterprise Center. Phone 520/871-6673. **Donation**

Navajo Nation Zoological and Botanical Park. Features a representative collection of animals and plants of historical or cultural importance to the Navajo people. (Daily; closed Jan 1, Dec 25) E of jct AZ 264 & Indian Rte 12, on AZ 264. Phone 520/871-6573. **Free**

St Michaels. Catholic mission, established in 1898, which has done much for the education and health of the tribe. Original mission building now serves as a museum depicting history of the area. Gift shop. (Memorial Day-Labor Day, daily) 3 mi W. Phone 520/871-4172. **Donation**

Annual Events

Powwow and PRCA Rodeo. July 4.

Navajo Nation Fair. Navajo Nation Fairgrounds. Navajo traditional song & dance; Inter-tribal powwow; All-Indian Rodeo; parade; concerts; exhibits. Contact PO Drawer U; 520/871-6478. Five days beginning Wed after Labor Day.

Winslow (D-5)

(See also Holbrook, Hopi and Navajo Indian Reservations)

Founded 1880 **Pop** 8,190 **Elev** 4,880 ft **Area Code** 520 **Zip** 86047

Information Chamber of Commerce, 300 W North Rd, PO Box 460; 520/289-2434 or 520/289-2435

A railroad town, Winslow is also a trade center and convenient stopping point in the midst of a colorful and intriguing area; a miniature painted desert lies to the northeast. The Apache-Sitgreaves National Forests, with the world's largest stand of ponderosa pine, lie about 25 miles to the south.

What to See and Do

Homolovi Ruins State Park. This park contains 6 major Anasazi ruins dating from 1250 to 1450. Arizona State Museum conducts occasional excavations (June, July). Trails. Visitor center; interpretive programs. Standard fees. (Daily; closed Dec 25) 3 mi E on I-40, then 1 mi N on AZ 87. Phone 520/289-4106.

Meteor Crater. Crater is 4,150 ft from rim to rim and 560 ft deep. The world's best preserved meteorite crater was used as training site for astronauts. Museum, lecture; Astronaut Hall of Fame; telescope on highest point of the crater's rim offers excellent view of surrounding area. (Daily) 20 mi W on I-40, then 5 mi S on Meteor Crater Rd. Phone 520/289-2362 or 520/774-8350. **¢¢¢**

Old Trails Museum. Operated by the Navajo County Historical Society; exhibits and displays of local history, Native American artifacts and early Americana. (Apr-Oct, Tues-Sat; rest of yr, Tues, Thurs & Sat; closed hols) 212 N Kinsley Ave. Phone 520/289-5861. **Free**

Motels

★★ **BEST WESTERN ADOBE INN.** *1701 N Park Dr (86047). 520/289-4638; FAX 520/289-5514; res: 800/528-1234.* 72 rms, 2 story. June-Aug: S $50-$56; D $54-$58; suites $68; under 18 free; lower rates rest of yr. Crib $4. Pet accepted, some restrictions. TV; cable (premium), VCR avail. Indoor pool; whirlpool. Restaurant 6 am-2 pm, 4-10 pm; Sun to 9 pm. Rm serv. Bar 4-11 pm, Sun to 10 pm. Ck-out 11 am. Coin Indry. Meeting rms. Business servs avail. Free airport, RR station, bus depot transportation. Cr cds: A, C, D, DS, MC, V.

D SC

✓★ **ECONO LODGE.** *1706 N Park Dr (86047), N Park Dr & I-40 exit 253. 520/289-4687; FAX 520/289-9377; res: 800/228-5050.* 72 rms, 2 story. Late May-Sept: S, D $45-$59; under 18 free; lower rates rest of yr. Pet accepted; $5/day. TV; cable (premium), VCR avail. Pool. Complimentary coffee in rms. Ck-out 11 am. Coin Indry. Business servs avail. Some refrigerators, microwaves. Cr cds: A, C, D, DS, JCB, MC, V.

D SC

Restaurant

✓★ **FALCON RESTAURANT.** *1113 E 3rd St (86047). 520/289-2342.* Hrs: 6 am-8:30 pm. Closed Thanksgiving, Dec 25. Bar. Semi-a la carte: bkfst $3.75-$6.95, lunch $1.90-$4.90, dinner $4.90-$12.25. Child's meals. Specialties: chicken-fried steak, N.Y. steak sandwich, roast turkey. Family-owned. Cr cds: C, MC, V.

D

Wupatki National Monument (C-4)

(See also Flagstaff)

(35 mi N of Flagstaff on US 89)

The nearly 2,600 archeological sites of the Sinagua and Anasazi cultures were occupied between 1100 and 1250. The largest of them, Wupatki Pueblo, was three stories high, with about 100 rooms. The eruption of nearby Sunset Crater (see) spread volcanic ash over an 800-square-mile area and for a time made this an active farming center.

The half-mile ruins trail is self-guided; books are available at its starting point. The visitor center and main ruin are open daily (closed Dec 25). Rangers on duty. Wupatki National Monument and Sunset Crater Volcano National Monument (see) are located on a 35-mile paved loop off of US 89. Nearest camping at Bonito Campground (May-Oct; phone 520/526-0866). Contact the Superintendent, 6400 US 89A, Flagstaff 86004; 520/526-1157. ¢¢

Yuma (G-1)

Founded 1849 **Pop** 54,923 **Elev** 138 ft **Area Code** 520
E-mail yumacvb@primenet.com **Web** www.arizonaguide.com/yuma
Information Convention & Visitors Bureau, 377 Main St, PO Box 11059, 85366; 520/783-0071

Hernando de Alarcón, working with the Coronado Expedition, passed this point on the Colorado River in 1540. Father Kino came into the area in 1699. Padre Francisco Tomas Garces established a mission in 1780, which was destroyed a year later. The Yuma Crossing, where the Colorado River narrows between the Yuma Territorial Prison and Fort Yuma (one of Arizona's oldest military posts), was made a historic landmark in recognition of its long service as a river crossing for many peoples.

Yuma's air-conditioned stopping places are a great comfort to motorists crossing the desert. If the scenery looks familiar, it may be because movie producers have used the dunes and desert for location shots.

Irrigation from the Colorado River makes it profitable to raise cattle, alfalfa, cotton, melons, lettuce, citrus fruits and other crops here. A Marine Corps Air Station and an army proving grounds are adjacent to the town.

What to See and Do

Arizona Historical Society Century House Museum and Gardens. Former home of E.F. Sanquinetti, pioneer merchant; now a division of the Arizona Historical Society. Artifacts from Arizona Territory, including documents, photographs, furniture and clothing. Gardens and exotic birds surround museum. Historical library open by appt. (Tues-Sat; closed hols) 240 Madison Ave. Phone 520/782-1841. **Free**

Fort Yuma-Quechan Museum. Part of one of the oldest military posts (1855) associated with the Arizona Territory; offered protection to settlers and secured the Yuma Crossing. Fort Yuma is headquarters for the Quechan Tribe. Museum houses tribal relics of southwestern Colorado River Yuman groups. (Mon-Fri; closed hols) Fort Yuma. Phone 619/572-0661. ¢

Imperial National Wildlife Refuge. Bird-watching; photography. Fishing, hunting. Hiking. Interpretive center/office (Mon-Fri). 40 mi N via US 95. Phone 520/783-3371. **Free**

Saihati Camel Farm. Home to many animals native to the Arabian Desert: Arabian camels & oryx, African Pygmy goats, Asian water buffalo, Watusi cattle; also one of the largest camel herds in North America. (Oct-May, 2 tours Mon-Sat, 1 tour Sun afternoon) Ave 1E at County 16th St. Phone 520/627-2553 for information & reservations. ¢¢

Yuma River Tours. Narrated historical tours on the Colorado River; half- and full-day trips. Sunset dinner cruise. Also jeep tours to sand dunes. (Mon-Fri; fees vary) 1920 Arizona Ave. Phone 520/783-4400.

Yuma Territorial Prison State Historic Park. Remains of 1876 prison; museum, original cell blocks. Southwest artifacts and prison relics. (Daily; closed Dec 25) Off I-8, Giss Pkwy exit. Phone 520/783-4771. ¢¢ Nearby is

Yuma Quartermaster Depot. Established in 1864, the depot served as a supply distribution point for troops stationed at military outposts in the Arizona Territory. Tours. At Yuma Crossing off the Colorado River. (Daily; closed Dec 25) 2nd Ave & Colorado River, behind City Hall. Phone 520/329-0404. ¢¢

Yuma Valley Railway. Tracks run 12 mi through fields along the Colorado River levee and Morelos Dam. Two-hr trips; dinner trips. (Nov-Mar, Sat & Sun; Apr-May, Oct, Sat only; June by appt only; closed July-Sept) Levee at 8th St. Phone 520/783-3456. ¢¢¢

Annual Events

Midnight at the Oasis Festival. 1st wkend Mar.

Yuma County Fair. 5 days early Apr.

Motels

✓★★ **AIRPORT TRAVELODGE.** *711 E 32nd St (85365). 520/726-4721; FAX 520/344-0452; res: 800/835-1132.* 80 rms, 2 story. S $54; D $62; each addl $5; suites $78; under 14 free; higher rates special events (2-day min); lower rates rest of yr. Crib free. Pet accepted, some restrictions; $25 deposit. TV; cable (premium), VCR avail (movies). Complimentary continental bkfst. Complimentary coffee in rms. Restaurant 11 am-10 pm. Bar. Ck-out noon. Business servs avail. Coin Indry. Health club privileges. Pool; whirlpool. Refrigerators; microwaves avail. Wet bar in suites. Picnic tables, grills. Cr cds: A, C, D, DS, JCB, MC, V.

D SC

★★ **BEST WESTERN INN SUITES.** *1450 S Castle Dome Ave (92801). 520/783-8341; FAX 520/783-1349; res: 800/922-2034.* E-mail isyuma@attmail.com; web www.innsuites.com. 166 rms. Jan-Apr: S $84-$99; D $89-$119; 2-rm suites $94-$139; under 20 free; higher rates opening wk dove season; lower rates rest of yr. Crib free. Pet accepted. TV; cable (premium), VCR avail. Heated pool; whirlpool. Complimentary continental bkfst. Coffee in rms. Ck-out noon. Coin Indry. Business center. In-rm modem link. Valet serv. Lighted tennis. Exercise equipt. Refrigerators, microwaves. Library. Cr cds: A, C, D, DS, JCB, MC, V.

D SC

✓★ **INTERSTATE 8 INN.** *2730 S 4th Ave (85364). 520/726-6110; FAX 520/726-7711; res: 800/821-7465.* 120 rms, 2 story. Jan-Mar: S $34.95; D $56.95; each addl $6; under 13 free; higher rates special events; lower rates rest of yr. Crib free. Pet accepted, some restrictions. TV; cable (premium), VCR avail (movies). Complimentary coffee in lobby. Restaurant adj 6 am-11 pm. Ck-out 11 am. Business servs avail. Coin Indry. Pool; whirlpool. Refrigerators; microwaves avail. Picnic tables, grills. Cr cds: A, C, D, DS, ER, JCB, MC, V.

★★ **LA FUENTE INN.** *1513 E 16th St (85365). 520/329-1814; FAX 520/343-2671; res: 800/841-1814.* 50 rms, 2 story, 46 suites. Jan-May: S $66-$96; D $85; suites $95; under 12 free; higher rates special events; lower rates rest of yr. Crib free. TV; cable (premium), VCR avail (movies). Heated pool; whirlpool. Complimentary continental bkfst. Coffee in rms. Restaurant adj open 24 hrs. Ck-out noon. Coin Indry. Business servs avail. Exercise equipt. Health club privileges. Refrigerators; many wet bars, microwaves. Near Yuma Airport. Cr cds: A, C, D, DS, MC, V.

D SC

★★ **RADISSON HOTEL.** *2600 S 4th Ave (85364). 520/726-4830; FAX 520/341-1152; res: 800/333-3333.* Web www.radisson.com. 164 suites, 3 story. Oct-Apr: S $106; D $116; each addl $10; under 16 free; lower rates rest of yr. Crib free. Pet accepted. TV; cable (premium). Heated pool; whirlpool. Complimentary continental bkfst. Complimentary coffee in rms. Restaurant adj open 24 hrs. Ck-out noon. Meeting rms. Business servs avail. Bellhops. Valet serv. Free airport, RR station, bus depot transportation. Health club privileges. Refrigerators, microwaves, wet bars. Cr cds: A, C, D, DS, ER, JCB, MC, V.

D SC

Motor Hotel

★★★ **SHILO INN.** *1550 S Castle Dome Ave (85365), off I-8 exit 16th St. 520/782-9511; FAX 520/783-1538; res: 800/222-2244.* Web www.shiloinns.com. 135 rms, 4 story, 16 kits. S, D $85-$149; each addl $12; kit. units $109-$260; under 12 free. Crib free. Pet accepted, some restrictions; $7/day. TV; cable (premium), VCR. Heated pool; whirlpool, poolside serv. Complimentary full bkfst. Restaurant 6 am-10 pm. Bar to midnight. Ck-out noon. Coin Indry. Meeting rms. Business servs avail. Exercise equipt; sauna, steam rm. Refrigerators, microwaves avail. Private patios, balconies. Cr cds: A, C, D, DS, ER, JCB, MC, V.

D SC

Restaurants

★★ **HUNTER STEAKHOUSE.** *2355 S 4th Ave (85364). 520/782-3637.* Hrs: 11:30 am-2 pm, 5-9 pm; Sat, Sun from 4 pm. Early-bird dinner Mon-Sat 5-6 pm, Sun 4-6 pm. Closed Dec 25. Res accepted. Bar to 11 pm. Semi-a la carte: lunch $5-$8, dinner $10-$30. Child's meals. Specializes in beef, steak, fresh seafood. Cr cds: A, C, D, MC, V.

D

✓★★ **MANDARIN PALACE.** *350 E 32nd St (85364). 520/344-2805.* Hrs: 11 am-10 pm; Fri, Sat to 11 pm. Res accepted. Chinese, Amer menu. Bar. A la carte entrees: lunch $5.50-$6.95, dinner $7.25-$24.95. Specialties: crispy beef a la Szechwan, rainbow shrimp, crispy Mandarin duck. Elegant Oriental decor. Cr cds: A, C, D, MC, V.

D

★ **THE CROSSING.** *2690 S 4th Ave (85364). 520/726-5551.* Hrs: 11 am-9:30 pm; Sun to 8:30 pm. Res accepted. Italian, Amer menu. Margaritas, wine, beer. Semi-a la carte: lunch, dinner $3.95-$14.95. Child's meals. Specialties: prime rib, catfish, buffalo wings. Casual dining. Cr cds: A, C, D, DS, MC, V.

D

California

Population: 31,742,000
Land area: 158,693 square miles
Elevation: 282 feet below sea level-14,494 feet
Highest point: Mount Whitney (Between Inyo, Tulare Counties)
Entered union: September 7, 1850 (31st state)
Capital: Sacramento
Motto: *Eureka* (I have found it)
Nickname: Golden State
State flower: Golden Poppy
State bird: California Valley Quail
State tree: California Redwood
State fair: August 18-September 4, 2000, in Sacramento
Time zone: Pacific
Web: gocalif.ca.gov

California has the largest population of any state in the United States. Within it, only 80 miles apart, are the lowest and highest points in the contiguous US—Death Valley and Mount Whitney. It has ski areas and blistering deserts, mountains and beaches, giant redwoods and giant missiles, Spanish missions and skyscrapers. The oldest living things on earth grow here—a stand of bristlecone pine said to be 4,600 years old. San Francisco, key city of northern California, is cosmopolitan, beautiful, proud, old-worldly. Los Angeles, in southern California, is bright and brazen, growing, modern. California, with 1,264 miles of coastline and a width of up to 350 miles, does things in a big way.

Almost every crop of the US grows here. Prunes, huge oranges, bales of cotton and tons of vegetables roll out from the factory farms in the fertile valleys. California leads the nation in the production of 75 crop and livestock commodities including grapes, peaches, apricots, olives, figs, lemons, avocados, walnuts, almonds, rice, plums, prunes, dates and nectarines. It also leads in the production of dried, canned and frozen fruits and vegetables, wine as well as eggs, turkeys, safflower, beeswax and honey. Homegrown industries include Hollywood movies, television, electronics, aircraft and missiles.

Spaniards, Mexicans, English, Russians and others helped write the history of the state. The first explorer to venture into the waters of California was Portuguese—Juan Rodriguez Cabrillo, in 1542. In 1579, Sir Francis Drake explored the coastal waters and is believed to have landed just northwest of what is now San Francisco. Beginning in 1769, Spanish colonial policy sprinkled a trail of missions around which the first towns developed. The Mexican flag flew over California after Mexico won independence from Spain in 1821. American settlers later wrenched the colony from Mexico and organized the short-lived Bear Flag Republic. On July 7, 1846, Commodore John D. Sloat raised the US flag at Monterey. Under the Treaty of Guadalupe Hidalgo, California became part of what was to be the coastal boundary of the United States in 1848.

Perhaps the most important event in its history was the discovery of gold in January of 1848, setting off a sudden mass migration that transformed the drowsy, placid countryside and accelerated the opening of the Far West by several decades. The 49ers who came for gold found greater riches in the fertile soil of the valleys and the markets of the young cities.

During and after World War II, California grew at an astounding pace in both industry and population. Jet travel across the Pacific makes the state a gateway to the Orient.

When to Go/Climate

We recommend visiting California in the mid- to late spring or early to mid-fall, when the fog generally lifts and the heavy tourist traffic is over. Winter is rainy; summers are dry and hot in much of the state.

AVERAGE HIGH/LOW TEMPERATURES (°F)

LOS ANGELES

Jan 68/49	**May** 74/58	**Sept** 83/65
Feb 69/51	**June** 78/61	**Oct** 79/60
Mar 70/52	**July** 84/65	**Nov** 72/54
Apr 72/54	**Aug** 85/66	**Dec** 68/49

SAN FRANCISCO

Jan 56/46	**May** 63/51	**Sept** 69/56
Feb 60/49	**June** 64/53	**Oct** 69/55
Mar 61/49	**July** 65/54	**Nov** 63/52
Apr 62/50	**Aug** 66/55	**Dec** 56/47

Parks and Recreation Finder

Directions to and information about the parks and recreation areas below are given under their respective town/city sections. Please refer to those sections for details.

NATIONAL PARK AND RECREATION AREAS

Key to abbreviations: I.H.S. = International Historic Site; I.P.M. = International Peace Memorial; N.B. = National Battlefield; N.B.P. = National Bat-

CALENDAR HIGHLIGHTS

JANUARY

Tournament of Roses (Pasadena). Spectacular floral parade on Colorado Blvd attracts more than a million people. Culminates with the Rose Bowl in the afternoon. Phone 626/449-4100.

Bob Hope Chrysler Classic (Palm Desert). Golf pros and celebrities play at four country clubs at Bermuda Dunes, La Quinta, Palm Desert and Indian Wells. Phone 760/346-8184.

FEBRUARY

Chinese New Year (San Francisco). Chinatown. Largest and most colorful celebration of this occasion held in US. Week-long activities include Golden Dragon Parade, lion dancing, carnival, cultural exhibits. Contact Chinese Chamber of Commerce 415/982-3000.

MARCH

Whale Festival (Mendocino). Whale watching walks, wine tasting, chowder tasting. Contact Mendocino Chamber of Commerce 707/961-6300 or 800/726-2780.

APRIL

Toyota Grand Prix (Long Beach). International race held on downtown streets. Phone 562/981-2600.

Monterey Wine Festival (Carmel). Approximately 170 wineries participate in this food & wine-tasting festival. Phone 800/656-4282.

MAY

Cinco de Mayo (Los Angeles). El Pueblo de Los Angeles Historic Monument. Arts and crafts, music and dancing. Phone Hollywood Visitors Information Center 213/689-8822.

JULY

San Jose America Festival (San Jose). Food booths, arts & crafts; rides and games, entertainment. Phone 408/298-6861.

American Century Celebrity Golf Championship (Lake Tahoe Area). Edgewood Tahoe Golf Course. More than 70 sports and entertainment celebrities compete for a $500,000 purse. Phone 800/AT-TAHOE.

Mozart Festival (San Luis Obispo). Recitals, chamber music, orchestra concerts & choral music. Held at various locations throughout the county, including Mission San Luis Obispo de Tolosa and Cal Poly State University campus. Phone 805/781-3008.

AUGUST

California State Fair (Sacramento). California Exposition grounds. Includes traditional state fair activities; exhibits, livestock, carnival food, entertainment on 10 stages, Thoroughbred racing and 1-mile monorail. Phone 916/263-FAIR.

SEPTEMBER

Los Angeles County Fair (Pomona). Fairplex. Thoroughbred racing, carnival, exhibits, free stage shows, food booths, monorail. Phone 909/623-3111.

Monterey Jazz Festival (Monterey). County Fairgrounds. Reserved seats only. Oldest jazz festival in the US. Phone 831/373-3366.

NOVEMBER

Hollywood Christmas Parade (Hollywood). Largest celebrity parade in the world. Features floats, marching band; over 50 of Hollywoods famous stars. Televised worldwide. Phone Hollywood Chamber of Commerce 323/469-8311.

DECEMBER

Christmas-Light Boat Parade (San Diego). San Diego Harbor, Shelter Island Yacht Basin. Web www.sdparadeoflights.org

tlefield Park; N.B.C. = National Battlefield & Cemetery; N.F. = National Forest; N.G. = National Grassland; N.H. = National Historical Park; N.H.C. = National Historic Corridor; N.H.S. = National Historic Site; N.L. = National Lakeshore; N.M. = National Monument; N.M.P. = National Military Park; N.Mem. = National Memorial; N.P. = National Park; N.Pres. = National Preserve; N.R. = National Recreational Area; N.R.R. = National Recreational River; N.Riv. = National River; N.S. = National Seashore; N.S.R. = National Scenic Riverway; N.S.T. = National Scenic Trail; N.Sc. = National Scientific Reserve; N.V.M. = National Volcanic Monument.

Place Name	Listed Under
Angeles N.F.	PASADENA
Cabrillo N.M.	SAN DIEGO
Channel Islands N.P.	same
Cleveland N.F.	PINE VALLEY
Death Valley N.P.	same
Devils Postpile N.M.	same
El Dorado N.F.	PLACERVILLE
Eugene O'Neill N.H.S.	PLEASANTON
Fort Point N.H.S.	SAN FRANCISCO
Golden Gate N.R.	SAN FRANCISCO
Inyo N.F.	same
John Muir N.H.S.	MARTINEZ
Joshua Tree N.P.	same
King's Canyon N.P.	SEQUOIA & KINGS CANYON N.P.
Klamath N.F.	YREKA
Lassen N.F.	SUSANVILLE
Lassen Volcanic N.P.	same
Lava Beds N.M.	same
Los Padres N.F.	KING CITY
Mendocino N.F.	WILLOWS
Modoc N.F.	ALTURAS
Muir Woods N.M.	same
Pinnacles N.M.	same
Plumas N.F.	QUINCY
Point Reyes N.S.	INVERNESS
Redwood N.P.	CRESCENT CITY
San Bernardino N.F.	SAN BERNARDINO
Sequoia N.P.	SEQUOIA & KINGS CANYON N.P.
Sequoia N.F.	PORTERVILLE
Shasta-Trinity N.F.	REDDING
Sierra N.F.	FRESNO
Six Rivers N.F.	EUREKA
Stanislaus N.F.	SONORA
Whiskeytown-Shasta-Trinity N.R.	REDDING
Yosemite N.P.	same

For general information about national forests within California, contact USDA, Forest Service, 630 Sansome St, San Francisco 94111, phone 707/562-8737. For camping reservations only, phone 800/280-CAMP or phone the supervisor of any particular forest directly.

STATE PARK AND RECREATION AREAS

Key to abbreviations: I.P. = Interstate Park; S.A.P. = State Archaeological Park; S.B. = State Beach; S.C. = State Conservation Area; S.C.P. = State Conservation Park; S.Cp. = State Campground; S.F. = State Forest; S.G. = State Garden; S.H.A. = State Historic Area; S.H.P. = State Historic Park; S.H.S. = State Historic Site; S.M.P. = State Marine Park; S.N.A. = State Natural Area; S.P. = State Park; S.P.C. = State Public Campground; S.R. = State Reserve; S.R.A. = State Recreation Area; S.Res. = State Reservoir; S.Res.P. = State Resort Park; S.R.P. = State Rustic Park.

Place Name	Listed Under
Anza-Borrego Desert S.P.	same
Armstrong Redwoods S.R.	GUERNEVILLE

Place Name	Listed Under
Big Basin Redwoods S.P.	same
Carpinteria S.B.	SANTA BARBARA
Castle Crags S.P.	DUNSMUIR
Caswell Memorial S.P.	MODESTO
Clear Lake S.P.	CLEAR LAKE AREA
D.L. Bliss S.P.	LAKE TAHOE AREA
Del Norte Coast Redwoods S.P.	CRESCENT CITY
Donner Memorial S.P.	TRUCKEE
Emerald Bay S.P.	LAKE TAHOE AREA
Emma Wood S.B.	VENTURA
Folsom Lake S.R.A.	AUBURN
Forest of Nisene Marks S.P.	SANTA CRUZ
Fort Ross S.H.P.	same
Grizzly Creek Redwoods S.P.	REDWOOD HWY
Grover Hot Springs S.P.	LAKE TAHOE AREA
Henry Cowell Redwoods S.P.	SANTA CRUZ
Henry W. Coe S.P.	GILROY
Humboldt Redwoods S.P.	same
Indian Grinding Rock S.H.P.	JACKSON
Jedediah Smith Redwoods S.P.	CRESCENT CITY
Lake Oroville S.R.A.	OROVILLE
MacKerricher S.P.	FORT BRAGG
Malakoff Diggins S.H.P.	NEVADA CITY
Marshall Gold Discovery S.H.P.	PLACERVILLE
McArthur-Burney Falls Memorial S.P.	BURNEY
Mendocino Headlands S.P.	MENDOCINO
Millerton Lake S.R.A.	FRESNO
Morro Bay S.P.	MORRO BAY
Mt Diablo S.P.	same
Mt San Jacinto S.P.	IDYLLWILD
Mt Tamalpais S.P.	MILL VALLEY
Natural Bridges S.B.	SANTA CRUZ
Patrick's Point S.P.	TRINIDAD
Pfeiffer-Big Sur S.P.	BIG SUR
Prairie Creek Redwoods S.P.	CRESCENT CITY
Providence Mountains S.R.A.	NEEDLES
Richardson Grove S.P.	same
Russian Gulch S.P.	MENDOCINO
Salt Point S.P.	FORT ROSS STATE HISTORIC PARK
San Buenaventura S.B.	VENTURA
San Clemente S.B.	SAN CLEMENTE
Salton Sea S.R.A.	same
Samuel P. Taylor S.P.	INVERNESS
Seacliff S.B.	SANTA CRUZ
Silverwood Lake S.R.A.	CRESTLINE
Sonoma Coast S.B.	FORT ROSS STATE HISTORIC PARK
South Carlsbad S.B.	CARLSBAD
Sugar Pine Point S.P.	LAKE TAHOE AREA
Tahoe S.R.A.	LAKE TAHOE AREA
Tomales Bay S.P.	INVERNESS
Turlock Lake S.R.A.	MODESTO
Van Damme S.P.	LOS ANGELES
Will Rogers S.H.P.	LOS ANGELES

Water-related activities, hiking, riding, various other sports, picnicking, nature trails, and visitor centers, as well as camping, are available in many of these areas. Some parks limit camping to a maximum consecutive period of 7-30 days, depending on season and popularity of area. Campsite charges are $10-$29/night/vehicle; trailer hookups $9-$25. For campsite reservations phone 800/444-7275 from anywhere in the continental United States; out of country phone customer service at 800/695-2269. Day-use fee is $2-$6/vehicle; vehicle with sailboat over 8 ft & all motor vessels, $3-$5 addl; all other boats, $1 addl; annual pass for $75 includes unlimited day-use, $125 with boat; boat launching $3-$5. Fees may vary in some areas. There are also small fees for some activities at some areas. Pets on leash only, permitted in campground and day-use areas only, $1/night (camping), $1 (day-use). Reservations for Hearst-San Simeon State Historical Monument (Hearst Castle) (see) can be made by phone, 800/444-4445. For map folder listing and describing state parks ($2), contact the California State Parks Store, PO Box 942896, Sacramento 94296-0001; 916/653-4000. For general park information phone 916/653-6995.

SKI AREAS

The following ski areas are listed under What to See and Do; refer to the individual town for directions and information.

Place Name	Listed Under
Alpine Meadows	LAKE TAHOE AREA
Badger Pass	YOSEMITE NATIONAL PARK
Bear Mt	BIG BEAR LAKE
Bear Valley	SONORA
Boreal Ski Area	TRUCKEE
Dodge Ridge Ski Area	SONORA
Donner Ski Ranch	TRUCKEE
Heavenly Ski Resort	LAKE TAHOE AREA
June Mt	JUNE LAKE
Kirkwood Ski Area	LAKE TAHOE AREA
Mammoth Mountain	MAMMOTH LAKES
Mountain High Ski Area	SAN BERNARDINO
Mt Shasta Ski Park	MOUNT SHASTA
Northstar Ski Area	TRUCKEE
Royal Gorge Cross-Country Ski Resort	TRUCKEE
Sierra At Tahoe	LAKE TAHOE AREA
Sierra Summit	FRESNO
Snow Summit	BIG BEAR LAKE
Snow Valley Ski Resort	LAKE ARROWHEAD
Squaw Valley USA	LAKE TAHOE AREA
Sugar Bowl Ski Area	TRUCKEE
Tahoe Donner Ski Area	TRUCKEE

For skiing information contact the California Ski Industry Assn, 74 New Montgomery St, Suite 750, San Francisco 94105; 415/543-7036.

FISHING & HUNTING

Streams, rivers, canals and lakes provide a great variety of freshwater fish. Salmon and steelhead trout run in great numbers in major coastal rivers north of San Francisco. Everything from barracuda to smelt may be found along or off the shore.

Hunting for deer, bear and other big game is available in most national forests, other public lands and some private lands (by permission) except in national and state parks, where firearms are prohibited. Waterfowl, quail and dove shooting can be arranged at public management areas and in private shooting preserves. Tidepool collecting is illegal without special permit.

A fishing license is required for all persons 16 and older to fish in either inland or ocean waters. Some public piers in ocean waters allow fishing without a license (list available on request). A hunting license is required to hunt any animal. For information contact the California Department of Fish and Game, 3211 S St, Sacramento 95816. For general information phone 916/653-7664; for license information phone 916/227-2282.

Driving Information

Safety belts are mandatory for all persons anywhere in vehicle. Children under 4 years and under 40 pounds in weight must be in an approved safety seat anywhere in vehicle. For further information phone 916/657-7202.

INTERSTATE HIGHWAY SYSTEM

Use the following list as a guide to access interstate highways in California. You should always consult a map to confirm driving routes.

Highway Number	Cities/Towns within 10 miles
Interstate 5	Anaheim, Buena Park, Carlsbad, Costa Mesa, Del Mar, Dunsmuir, Fullerton, Garden Grove, Irvine, Lodi, Los Angeles Area, Mount Shasta, Oceanside, Orange, Rancho Santa Fe, Red Bluff, Redding, Sacramento, San Clemente, San Diego, San Fernando Valley Area, San Juan Capistrano, Santa Ana, Stockton, Valencia, Willows, Yreka.
Interstate 8	Calexico, El Cajon, El Centro, Pine Valley, San Diego.
Interstate 10	Beaumont, Blythe, Claremont, Desert Hot Springs, Indio, Los Angeles Area, Ontario, Palm Desert, Palm Springs, Pomona, Redlands, San Bernardino, Santa Monica, West Covina.
Interstate 15	Barstow, Corona, Escondido, Redlands, Riverside, San Bernardino, San Diego, Temecula, Victorville.
Interstate 40	Barstow, Needles.
Interstate 80	Auburn, Berkeley, Davis, Fairfield, Oakland, Sacramento, San Francisco, Truckee, Vacaville, Vallejo.
Interstate 110	Arcadia, Beverly Hills, Burbank, Culver City, Glendale, Long Beach, Los Angeles, Los Angeles Intl Airport Area, Marina del Rey, Pasadena, Redondo Beach, San Gabriel, San Marino, San Pedro, Torrance, Westwood Village.

Additional Visitor Information

For material on northern California, contact the San Francisco Convention & Visitors Bureau, 900 Market St, San Francisco 94102, phone 415/974-6900 or the Redwood Empire Assn, The Cannery, 2801 Leavenworth St, San Francisco 94133, phone 415/543-8334 (will send 64-page *Visitors Guide* to Northern Coast/Redwood area; enclose $3 for postage and handling). For southern California, contact the Los Angeles Convention and Visitors Bureau, 633 W 5th St, Suite 6000, Los Angeles 90071, phone 213/624-7300; the San Diego Visitor Information Center, 11 Horton Plaza, 1st & F Sts, San Diego 92101, phone 619/236-1212, is also helpful. Serious hikers should consult *Sierra North* or *Sierra South,* available from the Wilderness Press, 1200 5th St, Berkeley 94704 or phone 800/443-7227. For general information contact the California Division of Tourism, 801 K St, Suite 1600, Sacramento 95814, phone 916/322-2881 or 800/862-2543. The monthly magazine *Sunset* gives special attention to West Coast travel and life. Sunset Publishing Corp also publishes the Sunset Travel Books, among which are: *Northern California* and *Southern California.* Contact Sunset Publishing Corp, 80 Willow Rd, Menlo Park 94025-3691; phone 800/227-7346 outside California or 800/321-0372 in California.

Alturas (A-3)

Pop 3,231 **Elev** 4,366 ft **Area Code** 530 **Zip** 96101
Information Chamber of Commerce, 522 S Main St; 530/233-4434

What to See and Do

Modoc County Historical Museum. More than 4,000 Native American artifacts, including arrowheads, spear points and many other items; exhibits of local history, including antique gun collection. (May-Oct, daily exc Mon) 600 S Main St. Phone 530/233-6328. ¢

Modoc National Forest. Scene of the Modoc Indian Wars, this forest of nearly 2 million acres is famous for its scenic trails through the South Warner Wilderness. In Medicine Lake Highlands Area there is a spectacular flow of jumbled black lava surrounding islands of timber; craters, cinder cones and lava tube caves. For wildlife watchers, the Modoc National Forest is home to more than 300 species of wildlife; the Pacific Flyway for migratory waterfowl crosses directly over the forest, making this area a bird watcher's paradise. Swimming, stream and lake fishing, hunting. Winter sports area. Picnicking. Camping. Sections surrounding Alturas reached via US 395 & CA 139/299. Contact the Forest Supervisor, 800 W 12th St; Phone 530/233-5811.

Modoc National Wildlife Refuge. Nesting habitat for the Great Basin Canada goose; also ducks, sandhill cranes, other interesting birds. (Daily, daylight hrs; Dorris Reservoir Recreation Area closed during waterfowl hunting season; inquire about fees. Refuge closed to public fishing except Dorris Reservoir Recreation Area.) 2 mi S on County 115. Phone 530/233-3572. **Free**

Annual Events

Fandango Celebration. 1st Sat July.

Modoc-The Last Frontier Fair. In Cedarville. Phone 530/279-2315. 4 days mid-Aug.

Motels

★★ **BEST WESTERN TRAILSIDE INN.** *343 N Main St (96161). 530/233-4111; FAX 530/233-3180; res: 800/528-1234.* 38 rms, 2 story, 4 kits. May-Oct: S $50; D $50-$60; each addl $5; kit. units $10 addl; lower rates rest of yr. Crib $5. Pet accepted, some restrictions. TV; cable (premium). Pool. Complimentary coffee. Restaurant nearby. Ck-out 11 am. Business servs avail. In-rm modem link. Downhill/x-country ski 10 mi. Cr cds: A, C, D, DS, MC, V.

SC

✓★ **HACIENDA MOTEL.** *201 E 12th St (96101). 530/233-3459.* 20 rms, 2 kits. S $29; D $31-$49; each addl $3; kit. units $5 addl; under 8 free. Pet accepted; $3. TV; cable (premium). Complimentary coffee in rms. Restaurant nearby. Ck-out 11 am. Downhill/x-country ski 10 mi. Refrigerators. Microwaves avail. Cr cds: A, C, D, DS, MC, V.

SC

Anaheim (J-4)

(See also Buena Park, Corona, Los Angeles, Santa Ana)

Founded 1857 **Pop** 266,406 **Elev** 160 ft **Area Code** 714
E-mail mail@anaheimoc.org **Web** www.anaheimoc.org
Information Anaheim/Orange County Visitor & Convention Bureau, 800 W Katella Ave, PO Box 4270, 92803; 714/765-8999

Once part of a Spanish land grant, Anaheim was bought and settled by German colonists who came to this land to grow grapes and produce wine.

The town takes its name from the Santa Ana River and the German word for "home." Today, Anaheim is known as the home of Disneyland.

What to See and Do

Disneyland (see). On Harbor Blvd, off Santa Ana Frwy.

Pacific Coast Sightseeing (Gray Line Anaheim; A Coach U.S.A Company). For information contact 2001 S Manchester Ave, 92802; phone 714/978-8855 or 800/828-6699.

Professional sports.

American League baseball (Anaheim Angels). Edison Intl Field of Anaheim, 2000 Gene Autry Way. Phone 714/634-2000.

NHL (Mighty Ducks of Anaheim). Arrowhead Pond, 2695 Katella Blvd. Phone 714/704-2500.

Motels

★★ **BEST WESTERN STOVALL'S INN.** *1110 W Katella Ave (92802), 1 blk S & 1 blk W of Disneyland. 714/778-1880; FAX 714/778-3805; res: 800/854-8175.* E-mail stovalbw@aol.com. 290 rms, 3 story. S $60-$90; D $65-$100; each addl $6; under 18 free. Crib free. TV; cable (premium). 2 pools, 1 heated; wading pool, whirlpools. Complimentary coffee in rms. Restaurant adj 6 am-midnight. Bar 4 pm-midnight; closed Sun. Ck-out noon. Coin Indry. Meeting rm. Business servs avail. Gift shop. Free Disneyland transportation. Game rm. Refrigerators avail. Topiary garden. Cr cds: A, C, D, DS, JCB, MC, V.

D SC

★★ **CAROUSEL INN & SUITES.** *1530 S Harbor Blvd (92802), opp Disneyland. 714/758-0444; FAX 714/772-9965; res: 800/854-6767.* 131 units, 2-5 story, 26 suites. S, D $79-$89; suites $99-$139. Crib $5. TV; cable. Heated pool. Complimentary continental bkfst. Coffee in rms. Restaurant nearby. Ck-out 11 am. Coin Indry. Business servs avail. Gift shop. Valet serv. RR station, bus depot, Disneyland transportation. Game rm. Refrigerators, microwaves. Cr cds: A, C, DS, MC, V.

D SC

★★ **CASTLE INN & SUITES.** *1734 S Harbor Blvd (92802), opp Disneyland. 714/774-8111; FAX 714/956-4736; res: 800/227-8530.* Web www.castleinn.com. 198 rms, 4 story, 46 suites. S, D $72-$82; suites $92-$102. Crib $6. TV; cable (premium). Heated pool; wading pool, whirlpool. Restaurant nearby. Ck-out 11 am. Coin Indry. Business servs avail. Gift shop. Valet serv. Free Disneyland transportation. Refrigerators; microwaves in suites. Cr cds: A, C, D, DS, ER, MC, V.

D SC

✓★ **COMFORT INN.** *2200 S Harbor Blvd (92802), 1 mi S of Disneyland. 714/750-5211; FAX 714/750-2226; res: 800/479-5210.* 66 rms, 2 story. S, D $49-$104; each addl $5; under 18 free. TV; cable. Heated pool; whirlpool. Complimentary continental bkfst. Coffee in rms. Restaurant nearby. Ck-out 11 am. Coin Indry. Business servs avail. Valet serv. Free Disneyland transportation. Refrigerators, microwaves avail. Cr cds: A, C, D, DS, JCB, MC, V.

D SC

★★ **COMFORT SUITES.** *2141 S Harbor Blvd (92802), 3 blks S of Disneyland. 714/971-3553; FAX 714/971-4609; res: 800/526-9444.* Web www.hotelchoice.com. 94 units, 4 story, 73 suites. S, D $79-$119; each addl $5; under 18 free; wkly rates. Crib $5. TV; cable (premium), VCR avail (movies). Covered heated pool; whirlpool. Complimentary continental bkfst. Coffee in rms. Restaurant opp 6 am-midnight. Ck-out 11 am. Coin Indry. Business servs avail. Valet serv. Free Disneyland transportaion. Refrigerators, microwaves. Cr cds: A, C, D, DS, ER, JCB, MC, V.

D SC

★ **CONVENTION CENTER INN.** *2029 S Harbor Blvd (92802), 2 blks S of Disneyland. 714/750-0232; FAX 714/750-5676; res: 800/521-5628.* 122 units, 3 story, 34 suites. S $48-$68; D $58-$78; suites $68-$88. Crib $4. TV; cable (premium). Heated pool; whirlpool. Complimentary continental bkfst. Restaurant adj 7 am-10 pm. Ck-out 11 am. Coin Indry. Meeting rm. Business servs avail. Valet serv. Health club privileges. Refrigerator, wet bar in suites. Cr cds: A, C, D, DS, MC, V.

D SC

★ **DAYS INN.** *1604 S Harbor Blvd (92802), opp Disneyland. 714/635-3630; FAX 714/520-3290; res: 800/329-7466; res: 800/624-3940.* 58 units, 2 story, 8 suites. S $40-$99; D $49-$129; each addl $5; suites $99-$179; under 12 free. Crib $6. TV. Heated pool; whirlpool. Complimentary continental bkfst. Coffee in rms. Restaurant adj open 24 hrs. Ck-out 11 am. Coin Indry. Refrigerators, microwaves. Cr cds: A, C, D, DS, MC, V.

D SC

★★ **DAYS INN.** *1030 W Ball Rd (92802), near jct I-5 & Harbor Blvd. 714/520-0101; FAX 714/758-9406; res: 800/331-0055.* 45 rms, 3 story. June-Aug: S, D $56-$99; each addl $8; under 18 free; higher rates hols; lower rates rest of yr. Crib free. TV; cable (premium). Heated pool; whirlpool. Complimentary continental bkfst. Coffee in rms. Restaurant opp 6-1 am. Ck-out 11 am. Coin Indry. Business servs avail. Airport, RR station, Disneyland transportation. Some refrigerators, wet bars, in-rm whirlpools. Cr cds: A, C, D, DS, JCB, MC, V.

D SC

★★ **DOLPHIN'S COVE RESORT.** *465 W Orangewood Ave (92802). 714/980-0830; FAX 714/980-0943; res: 888/980-2843.* 136 suites, 2 story. Suites $150-$200. Crib $5. TV; cable, VCR (movies). Complimentary continental bkfst. Complimentary coffee in rms. Restaurant nearby. Ck-out 11 am. Business servs avail. In-rm modem link. Bellhops. Gift shop. Coin Indry. Exercise equipt. Pool; whirlpool. Playground. Refrigerators, microwaves, wet bars. Balconies. Picnic tables, grills. Cr cds: C, DS, MC, V.

D SC

✓★ **ECONO LODGE MAINGATE.** *1570 S Harbor Blvd (92802), opp Disneyland. 714/772-3691; FAX 714/635-0964; res: 800/638-7949; res: 800/334-7021.* 88 units, 2 story, 25 suites. S $49-$75; D $59-$79; suites $75-$130; under 14 free. Crib $5. TV; cable (premium). Heated pool; wading pool. Complimentary continental bkfst. Coffee in rms. Restaurant adj open 24 hrs. Ck-out 11 am. Coin Indry. Business servs avail. Gift shop. Refrigerators; wet bar, microwave in suites. Sun deck. Cr cds: A, C, DS, MC, V.

SC

★ **GRANADA INN.** *300 E Katella Way (92802), I-5 Brookhurst St exit, S to Lincoln Ave then ½ mi W. 714/772-8713; FAX 714/778-1235; res: 800/982-8239.* Web www.granadasuitesusa.com. 80 kit. units, 3 story. June-Sept: S, D $69-$89; wkly rates; lower rates rest of yr. Crib $5. TV; cable (premium). Pool. Complimentary continental bkfst. Restaurant 6:30 am-9:30 pm. Ck-out noon. Business servs avail. Free Disneyland transportation. Sightseeing tours. Golf nearby. Microwaves. Private patios, balconies. Cr cds: A, C, D, DS, JCB, MC, V.

SC

★★ **HANFORD HOTEL.** *201 N Via Cortez (92807), CA 91 Imperial Hwy exit, S to Santa Ana Canyon, E to Via Cortez. 714/921-1100; FAX 714/637-8790; res: 800/324-9909.* 163 rms, 4 story. S, D $69-$79; each addl $5; suites $109-$119; under 18 free. Crib free. TV; cable (premium). Heated pool; whirlpool. Complimentary continental bkfst. Coffee in rms. Restaurant adj 11-2 am. Ck-out noon. Coin Indry. Meeting rms. Business servs avail. Exercise equipt. Refrigerators avail. Cr cds: A, C, D, DS, JCB, MC, V.

D SC

✓★★ **PENNY SLEEPER INN.** *1441 S Manchester Ave (92802), 1 blk E of Disneyland. 714/991-8100; FAX 714/533-6430; res: 800/854-6118.* Web www.pennysleeperinn.com. 189 rms, 2 story. S, D $45-$79; suites $99-$119. Crib $6. TV; cable (premium). Heated pool. Complimentary continental bkfst. Restaurant nearby. Ck-out 11 am. Coin Indry. Business servs avail. Valet serv. Gift shop. Free Disneyland transportation. Game rm. Refrigerators, microwaves avail. Cr cds: A, C, DS, ER, MC, V.

D SC

★★ **RAMADA INN.** *921 S Harbor Blvd. (49770). 714/999-0684; FAX 714/956-8839; res: 800/235-3399.* 92 rms, 2 story. June-Aug: S, D $59-$79; each addl $6; suites $105-$145; under 16 free; higher rates hol wkends; lower rates rest of yr. Crib free. TV. Heated pool. Complimentary continental bkfst. Complimentary coffee in rms. Restaurant adj 6 am-11 pm. Ck-out noon. Coin Indry. Business servs avail. Valet serv. Free Disneyland transportation. Refrigerators; microwaves avail. Cr cds: A, C, D, DS, JCB, MC, V.

D SC

★★ **RAMADA INN MAINGATE/SAGA.** *1650 S Harbor Blvd (92802), opp Disneyland. 714/772-0440; FAX 714/991-8219; res: 800/854-6097.* E-mail earlgarr@aol.com. 185 rms, 2-4 story. S $69-$74; D $78-$83; each addl $5; suites $90-$120; under 17 free. Crib free. TV; VCR avail (movies). Heated pool; whirlpool. Complimentary continental bkfst. Restaurant adj 11 am-10 pm. Ck-out 11 am. Coin Indry. Business servs avail. Valet serv. Shopping arcade. Free Disneyland transportation. Some wet bars; refrigerators avail. Cr cds: A, C, D, DS, ER, JCB, MC, V.

D SC

★★ **RAMADA LIMITED.** *800 S Beach Blvd (92804). 714/995-5700; FAX 714/826-6021; res: 800/628-3400.* Web www.ramada.net. 72 rms, 3 story. S, D $55-$90; under 12 free. Crib $7. Pet accepted, some restrictions; $10/day. TV; cable (premium). Heated pool; whirlpool. Complimentary continental bkfst. Restaurant opp open 24 hrs. Ck-out noon. Meeting rm. Business servs avail. Coin Indry. Refrigerators, microwaves; some in-rm whirlpools. Cr cds: A, C, D, DS, JCB, MC, V.

D SC

✓★ **SUPER 8 MOTEL.** *915 S West St (92802), near jct I-5 & Harbor Blvd. 714/778-0350; FAX 714/778-3878; res: 800/800-8000; res: 800/248-4400.* 111 rms, 3 story. June-Aug: S, D $55-$65; under 12 free; lower rates rest of yr. TV; cable (premium). Heated pool; whirlpool. Complimentary continental bkfst. Restaurant opp 6-1 am. Ck-out 11 am. Coin Indry. Business servs avail. Free Disneyland transportation. Cr cds: A, C, D, DS, MC, V.

D SC

✓★ **TRAVELODGE.** *1700 E Katella Ave (92805). 714/634-1920; FAX 714/634-0366; res: 800/634-1920.* 72 rms, 2 story. S, D $42-$75; each addl (after 4) $5. Crib free. TV; cable (premium). Complimentary continental bkfst. Complimentary coffee in rms. Restaurant opp open 24 hrs. Ck-out 11 am. Business servs avail. Valet serv. Coin Indry. Free Disneyland transportation. Pool; whirlpool. Refrigerators; some wet bars; microwaves avail. Cr cds: A, C, D, DS, JCB, MC, V.

D SC

Motor Hotels

★★ **COUNTRY SIDE SUITES.** *22677 Oak Crest Cir (92887), 10 mi E on CA 91, Weir Canyon Rd exit. 714/921-8688; FAX 714/283-3927; res: 800/336-0632.* Web www.countryside inn.com. 112 rms, 4 story. S, D $97-$107; each addl $10; suites $127-$137; under 12 free. Crib free. TV; cable (premium). Complimentary full bkfst. Complimentary coffee in rms. Restaurant adj 11 am-10 pm. Ck-out noon. Meeting rms. Business servs avail. Valet serv. Sundries. Coin Indry. Exercise equipt. Pool; whirlpool. In-rm whirlpools, refrigerators, microwaves, wet bars. Cr cds: A, C, D, DS, MC, V.

D SC

★★ **FAIRFIELD INN BY MARRIOTT.** *1460 S Harbor Blvd (92802), opp Disneyland. 714/772-6777; FAX 714/999-1727; res: 800/447-4048; res: 800/854-3340.* 467 rms, 9 story. S, D $64-$94. Crib free. TV; cable (premium). Heated pool; whirlpool. Complimentary coffee in rms. Restaurant 6 am-midnight. Rm serv. Ck-out noon. Coin Indry. Meeting rm. Business servs avail. Bellhops. Valet serv. Sundries. Gift shop. Free Disneyland transportation. Health club privileges. Refrigerators. Cr cds: A, C, D, DS, ER, JCB, MC, V.

D SC

★★ **HOLIDAY INN.** *1221 S Harbor Blvd (92805), at jct I-5. 714/758-0900; FAX 714/533-1804; rres: 800/545-7275.* 254 rms, 5 story. S, D $109-$129; each addl $10; suites $175-$300; under 18 free. TV; cable. Heated pool; whirlpool, poolside serv. Coffee in rms. Restaurant 6:30 am-10 pm. Rm serv. Bar 5 pm-midnight. Ck-out noon. Coin Indry. Convention facilities. Business servs avail. Bellhops. Valet serv. Gift shop. Free Disneyland transportation. Game rm. Refrigerators avail. Cr cds: A, C, D, DS, ER, JCB, MC, V.

D SC

★★★ **HOWARD JOHNSON.** *1380 S Harbor Blvd (92802), opp Disneyland. 714/776-6120; FAX 714/533-3578; res: 800/446-4656; res: 800/422-4228.* E-mail info@hojoanaheim.com; web www.hojoanaheim.com. 318 rms in 6 bldgs, 2, 4 & 7 story. S, D $69-$99; suites $139-$149; under 18 free; package plans. Crib free. TV; cable. 2 heated pools; wading pool, whirlpool, poolside serv. Coffee in rms. Restaurant 6 am-11 pm. Rm serv. Ck-out noon. Coin Indry. Meeting rm. Business servs avail. Bellhops. Valet serv. Gift shop. Free Disneyland transportation. Game rm. Some refrigerators. Private patios, balconies. Cr cds: A, C, D, DS, ER, JCB, MC, V.

D SC

★★ **JOLLY ROGERS HOTEL.** *640 W Katella Ave (92802), 1 blk S of Disneyland. 714/772-7621; FAX 714/772-2308; res: 800/446-1555.* Web www.tarsadia.com. 238 rms, 2-4 story. S, D $99-$129; suites $250; under 17 free. Crib free. TV; cable (premium). 2 heated pools; wading pool, whirlpool. Coffee in rms. Restaurants 6:30 am-11 pm. Rm serv. Bar 11-2 am; entertainment Thurs-Sat. Ck-out 11 am. Coin Indry. Meeting rms. Business servs avail. Valet serv. Sundries. Gift shop. Barber, beauty shop. Airport, RR station, Disneyland transportation. Game rm. Refrigerators avail. Bathrm phone, wet bar in suites. Some patios, balconies. Cr cds: A, C, D, DS, MC, V.

D SC

★★ **PEACOCK SUITES HOTEL.** *1745 S Anaheim Blvd (92805), 2 blks E of Disneyland. 714/535-8255; FAX 714/535-8914; res: 800/522-6401.* 140 suites, 5 story. S, D $109-$179; under 16 free. Crib free. TV; cable (premium), VCR (movies). Covered heated pool; whirlpools. Complimentary continental bkfst. Complimentary coffee in rms. Restaurant opp 7 am-10 pm. Ck-out 11 am. Coin Indry. Business servs avail. Gift shop. Valet serv. Free garage parking. Free Disneyland transportation. Health club privileges. Game rm. Refrigerators, microwaves. Sun deck. Cr cds: A, C, D, DS, MC, V.

D SC

★★ **QUALITY HOTEL MAINGATE.** *616 Convention Way (92802), Anaheim Convention Center adj; 2 blks S of Disneyland. 714/750-3131; FAX 714/750-9027; res: 800/231-6217; res: 800/231-6215.* 284 units, 9 story, 100 suites. S $89.95-$139.95; D $99.95-$149.95; each addl $15; suites $99.95-$259.95; under 18 free. Crib free. Pet accepted. Parking $8. TV; cable (premium). Heated pool; poolside serv. Coffee in rms. Restaurants 6 am-2 pm; dining rm 5-10 pm. Rm serv. Bar 2 pm-midnight. Ck-out noon. Coin Indry. Convention facilities. Business servs avail. Bellhops. Free Disneyland transportation. Valet serv. Health club privileges. Gift shop. Barber, beauty shop. Game rm. Refrigerator, microwave in suites. Some balconies. Cr cds: A, C, D, DS, ER, JCB, MC, V.

D SC

★★★ **RADISSON MAINGATE HOTEL.** *1850 S Harbor Blvd (92802), 1 blk S of Disneyland. 714/750-2801; FAX 714/971-4754; res: 800/333-3333.* 314 rms, 5-8 story. S, D $119-$139; each addl $10; under 17 free; family rates. Crib free. TV; cable (premium). Heated pool; wading pool. Coffee in rms. Restaurant 6 am-2 pm, 5-10 pm. Rm serv. Bar noon-midnight. Ck-out noon. Coin Indry. Convention facilities. Business servs avail. Bellhops. Valet serv. Concierge. Gift shop. Airport, Disneyland transportation. Health club privileges. Game rm. Cr cds: A, C, D, DS, JCB, MC, V.

D SC

★★ **RAMADA INN CONESTOGA.** *1240 S Walnut St (92802), near jct I-5 & Harbor Blvd. 714/535-0300; FAX 714/491-8953; res: 800/824-5459.* 254 rms, 6 story. S, D $99-$129; each addl $10; suites $150-$295; under 17 free; package plans. Crib free. TV; cable (premium). Heated pool; whirlpool, poolside serv. Complimentary coffee in rms. Restaurant 6:30 am-1 pm, 5:30-9:30 pm. Rm serv. Bar. Ck-out 11 am. Coin Indry. Convention facilities. Business servs avail. Concierge. Bellhops. Valet serv. Gift shop. Free Disneyland transportation. Game rm. Refrigerator, wet bar in suites; microwaves avail. Disneyland ¼ mi. Cr cds: A, C, D, DS, JCB, MC, V.

SC

★★★ **SHERATON HOTEL.** *1015 W Ball Rd (92802), near jct I-5 & Harbor Blvd. 714/778-1700; FAX 714/535-3889; res: 800/544-5064.* Web www.sheraton.com/anaheim. 491 units, 3-4 story. June-Aug: S $170; D $190; each addl $20; suites $260-$280; under 18 free; lower rates rest of yr. Crib free. TV; cable (premium). Heated pool; whirlpool, poolside serv. Coffee in rms. Restaurants 6-1 am. Rm serv. Bar 11-1 am. Ck-out noon. Coin Indry. Convention facilities. Business servs avail. In-rm modem link. Concierge. Bellhops. Valet serv. Gift shop. Airport, Disneyland transportation. Game rm. Exercise equipt. Wet bar in suites. Disneyland 2 blks. Cr cds: A, C, D, DS, ER, JCB, MC, V.

D SC

Hotels

★★★ **DISNEYLAND HOTEL.** *1150 W Cerritos Ave (92802), opp Disneyland. 714/778-6600; FAX 714/956-6597; res: 800/642-5391.* Web www.disneyland.com. 1,036 rms, 11-14 story. S, D $170-$225; each addl $15; suites $350-$2,000; under 18 free. Crib free. Parking $10. TV; cable. 3 heated pools; whirlpool. Playgrounds. Restaurants 6:30-1 am. Bars 11-2 am. Ck-out 11 am. Convention facilities. Business center. Concierge. Shopping arcade. Airport, bus depot, Disneyland transportation. Exercise equipt. Game rm. Refrigerators avail. Private patios, balconies. On 30 acres. Tropical gardens, waterfalls, fish ponds. Beach. Fantasy light show. Luxury level. Cr cds: A, C, D, DS, JCB, MC, V.

D SC

★★★ **DISNEYLAND PACIFIC HOTEL.** *1717 S West St (92802), opp Disneyland. 714/999-0990; FAX 714/776-5763; res: 800/642-5391.* Web www.disneyland.com. 502 rms, 15 story. S, D $165-$225; each addl $15; suites $350-$1,000; under 18 free; seasonal packages. Parking $10. TV; cable, VCR avail. Heated pool; whirlpool, poolside serv. Restaurants 6:30 am-11 pm (also see YAMABUKI). Bars 11-1 am. Ck-out 11 am. Convention facilities. Business center. Concierge. Gift shop. Exercise equipt. Game rm. Refrigerators. Some private patios. Central atrium with skylight; observation elevator. Luxury level. Cr cds: A, C, D, DS, JCB, MC, V.

D SC

★★★ **EMBASSY SUITES ANAHEIM.** *3100 E Frontera St (92806), CA 91, Glassell St exit, S to Frontera St then 1 blk E. 714/632-1221; FAX 714/632-9963; res: 800/362-2779.* Web www.esanaheim.com. 222 suites, 7 story. S, D $149-$199; each addl $10; under 17 free. TV; cable (premium). Indoor pool; whirlpool. Complimentary full bkfst. Coffee in rms. Restaurant 11 am-10 pm. Bar to midnight. Ck-out noon. Meeting rms. Business servs avail. In-rm modem link. Gift shop. Free Disneyland transportation. Sauna. Health club privileges. Refrigerators, microwaves, wet bars. Private balconies. 7-story atrium courtyard with fountains, koi ponds, ducks, waterfalls. Cr cds: A, C, D, DS, ER, JCB, MC, V.

D SC

★★★ **HILTON & TOWERS.** *777 W Convention Way (92802), 2 blks S of Disneyland. 714/750-4321; FAX 714/740-4252; res: 800/222-9923.* Web www.hilton.com. 1,574 units, 14 story. S $89-$300; D $119-$330; each addl $30; suites $800-$1,600; under 18 free; family rates. Crib free. Pet accepted. Covered parking: valet $11, garage in/out $6. TV; cable (premium). 2 heated pools, 1 indoor; whirlpools, poolside serv. Coffee in rms. Restaurants 6 am-midnight. Bars 11-2 am; entertainment. Ck-out noon. Convention facilities. Business center. Concierge. Shopping arcade. Barber, beauty shop. Exercise rm; saunas, steam rms. Game rm. Some refrigerators. Some private patios, balconies. Luxury level. Cr cds: A, C, D, DS, ER, JCB, MC, V.

D SC

★★★ **HYATT REGENCY.** *100 Plaza Alicante (92840), jct Harbor & Chapman Blvds, 1 mi S of Disneyland. 714/750-1234; FAX 714/740-0465; res: 800/972-2929.* 396 rms, 17 story. S $99-$170; D $99-$195; each addl $25; suites $295-$895; under 17 free; Disneyland & Knott's Berry Farm packages. Parking $6, valet $8. Crib avail. TV; cable (premium), VCR avail. Heated pool; whirlpool, poolside serv. Restaurants 6 am-11:30 pm. Bars 3 pm-midnight. Ck-out noon. Convention facilities. Business center. Concierge. Shopping arcade. Airport, RR station, bus depot, Disneyland transportation. Lighted tennis. Golf driving range. Exercise equipt. Health club privileges. Game rm. Some bathrm phones, wet bars; whirlpool in suites. Some balconies. 17-story atrium with 60-ft palm trees provides tropical atmosphere. Cr cds: A, C, D, DS, JCB, MC, V.

D SC

★★★ **MARRIOTT HOTEL.** *700 W Convention Way (92802), adj to Anaheim Convention Center; Disneyland 2 blks. 714/750-8000; FAX 714/750-9100; res: 800/228-9290.* Web www.marriott.com. 1,033 rms, 19 story. S $103-$180; D $123-$210; each addl $10; suites $200-$1,300; under 18 free. Crib free. Garage parking $9; valet $12. TV; cable (premium). 2 heated pools, 1 indoor/outdoor; whirlpools, poolside serv. Continental bkfst in lobby. Restaurants 6:30 am-11 pm; Fri, Sat to midnight. Bar 11-2 am. Ck-out noon. Coin Indry. Convention facilities. Business center. Concierge. Shopping arcade. Barber, beauty shop. Airport, Disneyland transportation. Exercise equipt; sauna. Game rm. Bathrm phone, refrigerator, wet bar in suites; microwaves avail. Some patios, balconies. Luxury level. Cr cds: A, C, D, DS, JCB, MC, V.

D SC

Restaurants

★★ **CATTLEMAN'S WHARF.** *1160 W Ball Rd (92802), near jct I-5 & Harbor Blvd. 714/535-1622.* Hrs: 11 am-2 pm, 5-10 pm; Sat from 5 pm; Sun 5-9 pm; Sun brunch 10 am-2 pm. Res accepted. Bar. Semi-a la carte: lunch $6.25-$12.50, dinner $12.75-$24.75. Sun brunch $18.50. Child's meals. Specializes in steak, seafood. 6 dining rms: Wine, Garden, Fountain, Tara, Library, Paulette. Different design in each rm. Totally nonsmoking. Cr cds: A, C, MC, V.

D

★★ **FOXFIRE.** *5717 E Santa Ana Canyon Rd (92807), CA 91 Imperial Hwy exit S. 714/974-5400.* Hrs: 11:30 am-2:30 pm, 5-9 pm; Fri to 10 pm; Sat 5-10 pm; Sun from 5 pm; Sun brunch 10 am-2 pm. Closed most major hols. Res accepted. Eclectic menu. Bar. A la carte entrees: lunch $6-$11, dinner $16-$25. Sun brunch $16.95. Child's meals. Specializes in steak, seafood. Own baking. Entertainment. Outdoor dining. Cr cds: A, C, D, MC, V.

D

✓★★ **GUSTAV'S JAGERHAUS.** *2525 E Ball Rd (92806), CA 57 exit Ball Rd, W 1 blk. 714/520-9500.* Hrs: 7 am-9 pm; Fri to 10 pm; Sat 8 am-10 pm; Sun from 8 am. Closed Jan 1, Dec 25. Res accepted. German menu. Wine, beer. Semi-a la carte: bkfst $2.65-$6.50, lunch $4.50-$13.95, dinner $6.95-$15.75. Child's meals. Specializes in authentic German cooking. Own baking. Family-style neighborhood restaurant; many German knick-knacks displayed. Cr cds: A, C, D, DS, MC, V.

D

✓★ **HANSA HOUSE SMORGASBORD.** *1840 S Harbor Blvd (92802), 1 blk S of Disneyland. 714/750-2411.* Hrs: 7-11 am, noon-3 pm, 4:30-9 pm; Sun brunch noon-3 pm. Bar. Buffet: bkfst $5.50, lunch $6.25, dinner $9.95. Sun brunch $7.50. Child's meals. Specialty: Swedish-American smorgasbord. Salad bar. Own baking. Patio dining. Scandinavian country decor. Family-owned. Cr cds: A, C, DS, MC, V.

D

★★★ **MR. STOX.** *1105 E Katella Ave (92805), CA 57 Katella Ave exit, 1 mi W. 714/634-2994.* E-mail mrstox@mrstox.com; web www.mrstox.com. Hrs: 11:30 am-11 pm; Sat, Sun from 5:30 pm. Closed most major hols. Res accepted. Bar. Wine cellar. A la carte entrees: lunch $9.95-$15.95, dinner $15.95-$28.95. Specializes in fresh seafood, pasta. Own baking, herbs. Pianist. Valet parking. Family-owned. Totally nonsmoking. Cr cds: A, C, D, DS, MC, V.

D

★★ **THE CATCH.** *1929 S State College Blvd (92806). 714/634-1829.* Hrs: 11:30 am-2:30 pm, 5-9:30 pm; Fri to 10:30 pm; Sat 5-10:30 pm; Sun from 5 pm. Res accepted. Bar. Semi-a la carte: lunch $7.95-$15.95, dinner $13.95-$24.95. Child's meals. Specializes in fresh seafood, pasta, certified Angus beef. Oyster bar. Own desserts. Valet parking. Outdoor dining. Cr cds: A, C, D, MC, V.

D SC

★★★ **THEE WHITE HOUSE RESTAURANT.** *887 S Anaheim Blvd (92805), near jct I-5 & Harbor Blvd. 714/772-1381.* E-mail twhouse.earthlink.net; web www.imenu.com/theewhitehouse. Hrs: 11:30 am-2 pm, 5-10 pm; Sat, Sun from 5 pm. Closed major hols. Res accepted. Northern Italian menu. Bar. A la carte entrees: lunch $10.50-$25, dinner $17.50-$28. Specializes in veal, pasta, fresh fish. Own desserts. Outdoor dining. Built 1909; restored estate fashioned after the White House. Totally nonsmoking. Cr cds: A, C, MC, V.

D

★★ **YAMABUKI.** *(See Disneyland Pacific) 714/956-6755.* Web www.disneyland.com. Hrs: 11:30 am-2 pm, 5:30-10 pm; Sat, Sun from 5:30 pm. Res accepted. Japanese menu. Bar. Semi-a la carte: lunch $6.95-$12.95, dinner $9-$30. Child's meals. Specializes in sushi, tempura, teriyaki. Valet parking. Traditional Japanese decor; tatami rms avail. Original artwork. Cr cds: A, C, D, DS, JCB, MC, V.

D

Antioch (E-2)

(See also Concord, Martinez, Oakland, Vallejo)

Pop 62,195 **Elev** 25 ft **Area Code** 510 **Zip** 94509
E-mail acoc@ecis.com
Information Chamber of Commerce, 301 W 10th St, Ste 1; 510/757-1800

What to See and Do

Black Diamond Mines Regional Preserve. These 3,650 acres on flanks of Mt Diablo (see MT DIABLO STATE PARK) contain coal, silica sand mines and the Rose Hill Cemetery. Hiking, bicycle, bridle trails. Picnicking. Naturalist programs. Preserve (daily). From CA 4, S on Somersville Rd. Phone 510/757-2620. ¢

Contra Loma Regional Park. Approx 775 acres. Lake swimming (summer, daily), sand beach; fishing; boating. Hiking, bicycling. Picnicking, concession. (Daily) From CA 4, S on Lone Tree Way to Golf Course Rd then right on Frederickson Ln to park entrance. Phone 510/757-0404. Per vehicle ¢¢

Annual Event

Contra Costa County Fair. Fairgrounds, 10th & L Sts. Phone 510/757-4400. Late July.

Motels

★ **BEST WESTERN INN.** *3210 Delta Fair Blvd (94509), CA 4 exit Somersville Rd S. 925/778-2000; FAX 925/778-2000; res: 800/422-2340.* 73 units, 3 story. S $63-$77; D $67-$82; each addl $5; suites $81-$99; under 12 free. TV; cable (premium). Pool; whirlpool. Complimentary continental bkfst. Restaurant adj open 24 hrs. Meeting rms. Business servs avail. Some refrigerators; microwaves avail. Cr cds: A, C, D, DS, JCB, MC, V.

D SC

✓★ **RAMADA INN.** *2436 Mahogany Way (94509). 925/754-6600; FAX 925/754-6828; res: 800/272-6232.* E-mail antioch@soramanagement.com. 116 rms, 3 story, 10 suites. Apr-Sept: S, D $79-$99; each addl $10-$12; suites $115-$125; under 18 free; hol rates; lower rates rest of yr. Crib free. Pet accepted, some restrictions; $25. TV; cable (premium). Complimentary continental bkfst. Complimentary coffee in rms. Restaurant adj 6 am-midnight. Ck-out noon. Meeting rms. Business servs avail. Coin Indry. Pool; whirlpool. Refrigerators; microwave, wet bar in suites. Grills. Cr cds: A, C, D, DS, JCB, MC, V.

D SC

Anza-Borrego Desert State Park (K-5)

Approximately 600,000 acres of desert wilderness are preserved here, relieved by an occasional spring-fed oasis and colorful canyons. CA 78 bisects the park, with Borrego Springs (see), park headquarters and the visitor center to the north. Other improved roads are County S-2, S-3 and S-22. Anyone who wants to explore seriously must use a 4-wheel drive vehicle; road condition information is available at the visitor center. Driving across sand can be rough on vehicles and passengers. The best time to visit is November-mid-May. Six hundred species of flowering plants in the park soften the somewhat austere landscape during the spring months. Elephant trees reach the northernmost limits of their range in Anza-Borrego Park; rare smoke trees and fan palms grow here around natural seeps and springs. The park provides a refuge for wildlife, including roadrunners, rare bighorn sheep and kit foxes. There are nature, hiking and bridle trails and picnic grounds. Improved campsites (trailer hookups in Borrego Springs) are scattered in the park; primitive camping (fee) is allowed throughout the park and there is a horse campground. Naturalist programs, tours, campfire programs are offered weekends, November-May. Self-guided auto tour brochures are available at the visitor center (Oct-May, daily; rest of yr, wkends & hols), west of Borrego Springs (see). Standard fees. Phone 760/767-5311 or 760/767-4205 (visitor center). Day use ¢¢; Camping ¢¢

Arcadia (B-5 see Los Angeles map)

(See also Los Angeles, Pasadena)

Pop 48,290 **Elev** 485 ft **Area Code** 626 **E-mail** arcadiacc@earthlink.com
Information Chamber of Commerce, 388 W Huntington Dr, 91007; 626/447-2159 or 626/445-1400

Arcadia is known as the home of Santa Anita Park racetrack, a world-class Thoroughbred racing facility.

What to See and Do

Santa Anita Park. Thoroughbred racing. (Early Oct-early Nov & late Dec-late Apr, Wed-Sun; closed some major hols) 285 W Huntington Dr. Phone 626/574-7223.

The Arboretum of Los Angeles County. More than 200 peacocks roam 127 acres; plants from many parts of the world. Water conservation garden; aquatic gardens and waterfalls. Historical area with Hugo Reid Adobe (1839), Queen Anne Cottage (1885). Greenhouses, library, demonstration home gardens. Tram tours. (Daily) 301 N Baldwin Ave, 6 mi N of San Bernardino Frwy and just S of Foothill Frwy. Phone 626/821-3222. ¢¢

Motels

★★ **HAMPTON INN.** *311 E Huntington Dr (91006). 626/574-5600; FAX 626/446-2748; res: 800/426-7866.* Web www.hampton-inn.com. 131 rms, 4 story. S $75-$85; D $85-$95; under 18 free; higher rates Rose Bowl (3-day min). Crib free. Pet accepted; $5/day. TV; cable (premium). Heated pool. Complimentary continental bkfst. Complimentary coffee in rms. Restaurant nearby. Ck-out noon. Meeting rm. Business servs avail. Valet serv. Health club privileges. Refrigerators, microwaves avail. Cr cds: A, C, D, DS, MC, V.

D SC

★★ **RESIDENCE INN.** *321 E Huntington Dr (91006). 626/446-6500; FAX 626/446-5824; res: 800/331-3131.* Web www.marriott.com. 120 kit. suites, 2 story. Kit. suites $158-$188; higher rates Rose Bowl (4-day min). Crib free. Pet accepted; $50-$75 & $6/day. TV; cable (premium), VCR avail. Heated pool; whirlpool. Complimentary continental bkfst. Complimentary coffee in rms. Restaurant nearby. Ck-out noon. Coin lndry. Meeting rm. Business servs avail. Valet serv. Free airport transportation. Health club privileges. Refrigerators, microwaves; some fireplaces. Some balconies. Picnic tables, grills. Cr cds: A, C, D, DS, JCB, MC, V.

D SC

Motor Hotel

★★ **HOLIDAY INN.** *924 W Huntington Dr (91016). 626/357-1900; FAX 626/359-1386; res: 800/465-4329.* Web www.holiday-inn.com. 174 rms, 10 story. S, D $119-$139; wkly, wkend rates; higher rates Rose Parade (4-day min). Crib free. Pet accepted. TV; cable (premium). Heated pool; whirlpool. Complimentary continental bkfst. Complimentary coffee in rms. Restaurant 6 am-10 pm. Rm serv. Bar 3-11 pm. Ck-out noon. Meeting rms. Business servs avail. Bellhops. Valet serv. Sundries. Coin lndry. Health club privileges. Refrigerators, microwaves avail. Cr cds: A, C, D, DS, JCB, MC, V.

D SC

Hotel

★★★ **EMBASSY SUITES.** *211 E Huntington Dr (91006). 626/445-8525; FAX 626/445-8548; res: 800/362-2779.* Web www.embassy-suites.com. 192 suites, 7 story. S, D $129-$159; each addl $10; under 18 free. Crib free. TV; cable (premium). Indoor pool; whirlpool. Complimentary full bkfst. Coffee in rms. Restaurant 9:30 am-3 pm, 5-10 pm. Bar from noon. Ck-out 1 pm. Coin lndry. Meeting rms. Business servs avail. Gift shop. Free airport transportation. Sauna, steam rm. Health club privileges. Refrigerators, microwaves. 7-story atrium courtyard with fountains. Cr cds: A, C, D, DS, MC, V.

D SC

Restaurants

★★★ **CHEZ SATEAU.** *850 S Baldwin Ave (91007), near Santa Anita Park. 626/446-8806.* Hrs: 11:30 am-2:30 pm, 5:30-9 pm; Fri, Sat to 10 pm; early-bird dinner 5:30-6:30 pm; Sun brunch 10:30 am-2:30 pm. Closed Mon; Jan 1, July 4. Res accepted. Continental menu. Bar. Wine list. Semi-a la carte: lunch $6.95-$12.50, dinner $9.75-$22.50. Prix fixe: dinner (5:30-6:30 pm) $17.75. Sun brunch $15.75. Specializes in fresh fish, seasonal dishes. Own pastries. Valet parking. French country decor. Totally nonsmoking. Cr cds: A, C, D, DS, JCB, MC, V.

D

★★★ **LA PARISIENNE.** *1101 E Huntington Dr (91016), I-210 Mountain Ave exit, N to Huntington Dr, E 2 blks. 626/357-3359.* Hrs: 11:30 am-2 pm, 5:30-9:30 pm; Sat 5:30-10 pm. Closed Sun; most major hols. Res accepted. French menu. Bar. Wine list. Semi-a la carte: lunch $7.50-$16.95, dinner $16.95-$23.95. Specialties: bouillabaisse, duck with orange sauce, veal Normande. Own baking. French country atmosphere. Totally nonsmoking. Cr cds: A, C, D, MC, V.

★★ **THE DERBY.** *233 E Huntington Dr (91006). 626/447-8173.* Web www.thederby.com. Hrs: 11 am-10:15 pm; Fri to 11:15; Sat 4-11:15 pm; Sun 4-10:15 pm; early-bird dinner 4-6 pm. Closed Dec 25. Res accepted. Semi-a la carte: lunch $5.95-$16.95, dinner $10.50-$29.50. Child's meals. Specializes in steak, seafood, pasta. Own cheesecakes. Entertainment Wed-Sat. Free valet parking. Beamed ceiling, fireplaces. Portraits of famous thoroughbreds & jockeys. Family-owned. Cr cds: A, C, D, DS, MC, V.

D

Atascadero (G-2)

(See also Morro Bay, Paso Robles, San Luis Obispo)

Founded 1913 **Pop** 23,138 **Elev** 855 ft **Area Code** 805 **Zip** 93422
E-mail mready@atascaderocofc.com
Information Chamber of Commerce, 6550 El Camino Real; 805/466-2044

In the foothills of the Santa Lucia Mountains, Atascadero was founded by St Louis publisher E.G. Lewis, who also founded University City, Missouri. Lewis developed the town to be a self-sustaining community or colony.

What to See and Do

Atascadero Historical Society Museum. E.G. Lewis' original Atascadero Colony Administration Building (1918); Italian-Renaissance architecture. Houses displays on local history and Lewis' projects. (Daily exc Sun; closed hols) Fee for some special events. 6500 Palma Ave. Phone 805/466-8341. **Free**

Atascadero Lake. Fishing. Picnicking, playground. 2 mi W of US 101 on CA 41. Phone 805/461-5085. On premises is

Paddock Zoo. Assortment of domestic, native and exotic animals. (Daily; closed Jan 1, Thanksgiving, Dec 25) Phone 805/461-5080. ¢

Annual Event

Colony Days. Parade, activities, arts & crafts, displays, food booths. 3rd Sat Oct.

Auburn (D-3)

(See also Grass Valley, Placerville, Sacramento)

Settled 1848 **Pop** 10,592 **Elev** 1,297 ft **Area Code** 916 **Zip** 95603
Information Auburn Area Chamber of Commerce, 601 Lincoln Way; 916/885-5616

Here is a town with a split personality: the restored "old town" retains its gold rush boomtown flavor; the other Auburn, built on a hilltop, is a modern city. In 1848 a mining camp called North Fork Dry Diggins was renamed for Auburn, New York. It developed as a center for gold rush camps and survived when the railroad came through and orchards were planted after the gold gave out.

What to See and Do

Folsom Lake State Recreation Area. This 17,545-acre area offers swimming, waterskiing; fishing; boating (rentals, marina). Bicycle, hiking, bridle trails. Historic Folsom Powerhouse (Wed-Sun afternoons). Picnicking, concession; camping (dump station). Standard fees. Off Folsom-Auburn Rd, near the town of Folsom. Phone 916/988-0205.

Gold Country Museum. Exhibits depicting early days of Placer County; history of gold mining and lifestyle of gold miners. (Daily exc Mon; closed hols) 1273 High St, at the Gold Country Fairgrounds. Phone 916/887-0690. ¢ Admission includes

Bernhard Museum Complex. Restored 14-rm house (1851), winery (1874) and art gallery. Living history programs. Guided tours (daily exc Mon; closed hols). 291 Auburn-Folsom Rd. Phone 916/889-6500.

Old Town. Walk along Lincoln Way, Sacramento, Commercial & Court Sts. Restored area. Chamber of Commerce has information.

Annual Events

Wild West Stampede. Gold Country Fairgrounds. 3rd wkend Apr.

Placer County Fair. 2 mi N off I-80, on Washington Blvd in Roseville. Phone 916/786-2023. Early July.

Gold Country Fair. Thurs-Sun, wkend after Labor Day wkend.

Motel

★★ **AUBURN BEST INN.** *1875 Auburn Ravine Rd (95603), I-80 at Foresthill exit. 530/885-1800; FAX 530/888-6424; res: 800/272-1444.* 80 rms, 2 story. S $54-$60; D $60-$66; each addl $6; suites $75-$100; under 13 free. Crib $6. TV; cable. Pool; whirlpool. Complimentary continental bkfst. Restaurant opp open 24 hrs. Ck-out 11 am. Coin Indry. Meeting rms. Cr cds: C.

Restaurants

★★ **HEADQUARTER HOUSE.** *14500 Musso Rd (95603), NE off I-80 Bell exit. 530/878-1906.* Hrs: 11:30 am-10 pm; Sun 2-9:30 pm; Sun brunch 10 am-2 pm. Res accepted. Continental menu. Bar. Semi-a la carte: lunch $4.25-$8.95, dinner $8.95-$21.95. Sun brunch $6.95-$10.95. Specializes in fresh local foods. Own desserts. Pianist evenings and Sun brunch. Totally nonsmoking. Cr cds: A, C, D, DS, MC, V.

D

★ **LOU LA BONTE'S.** *13460 Lincoln Way (95603), CA 49 at Foresthill exit. 530/885-9193.* Hrs: 11 am-10 pm, Fri-Sun from 8 am. Continental menu. Bar. Semi-a la carte: bkfst $3.95-$9.95, lunch $5-$9.50, dinner $8.95-$21.95. Child's meals. Specializes in steak, seafood, beef. Dinner theater. Family-owned. Cr cds: A, C, D, DS, MC, V.

SC

Avalon (Catalina Island) (J-3)

(See also Laguna Beach, Long Beach, Newport Beach, San Pedro)

Pop 2,918 **Elev** 20 ft **Area Code** 310 **Zip** 90704
E-mail info@catalinas.net **Web** www.catalina.com

Information Catalina Island Visitors Bureau & Chamber of Commerce, PO Box 217; 310/510-1520

Avalon is the sportfishing and resort capital of 21-mile-long, 8-mile-wide Santa Catalina Island. The peaks of the island rise from the Pacific, 21 miles southwest of Los Angeles harbor. Scuba diving, kayaking, golf, tennis, horseback riding, swimming and hiking are popular.

Discovered in 1542 by Juan Rodriguez Cabrillo, the Portuguese navigator, it was named by the Spanish explorer Sebastian Viscaino in 1602. Later, Russians and Aleuts used the island as a base to hunt sea otter. The town experienced a brief miniature gold rush in 1863. In 1919, William Wrigley, Jr, chewing gum magnate and owner of the Chicago Cubs major league baseball team, bought controlling interest in the Santa Catalina Island Company from the Banning brothers, who had incorporated the island. Wrigley established a program of conservation that still applies; today, 86% of Catalina Island is protected by the Santa Catalina Island Conservancy. Tourism is the island's only industry and source of revenue today.

Daily air or boat service to the island is available all year from Long Beach (see) and San Pedro; boat service only from Newport Beach.

What to See and Do

Catalina Island Museum. Permanent exhibits on history of island; natural history and archaeology displays. (Daily) Casino Building. Phone 310/510-2414. ¢

Catalina tours and trips. Santa Catalina Island Company Discovery Tours offer boat and bus tours to several points of interest. Contact Box 737; phone 310/510-2500 or 310/510-8687. Catalina Adventure Tours offers boat and bus tours. Contact Box 797; 310/510-2888.

Wrigley Memorial and Botanical Garden. Native trees, cactus, succulent plants and flowering shrubs on 38 acres surround memorial to a man who contributed much to Catalina Island. (Daily) Tram may run here from Island Plaza (summer only; fee). 1400 Avalon Canyon Rd. Phone 310/510-2288. ¢

Motels

★ **EL TERADO TERRACE HOTEL.** *230 Marilla Ave (90704). 310/510-0831; FAX 310/510-1495; res: 800/540-0139.* 18 rms, 2 story, 2 townhouses. No A/C. No rm phones. May-Oct: S, D $75-$120; each addl $10; suites $120; townhouses $170; lower rates rest of yr. TV; cable, VCR avail. Complimentary coffee in rms. Restaurant nearby. Ck-out 11 am. Free shuttle from boat dock. Whirlpool. Refrigerators, microwaves. Cr cds: A, C, DS, MC, V.

★★ **HOTEL VILLA PORTOFINO.** *111 Crescent Ave (90704). 310/510-0555; FAX 310/510-0839; res: 800/346-2326; res: 888/510-0555.* E-mail hotelvp@catalinas.net; web www.catalina.com/vp.html. 34 rms, 3 story. No elvtr. June-Sept & wkends: S, D $95-$160; each addl $10; suites $200-$300; lower rates rest of yr. Crib $10. TV; cable (premium). Complimentary continental bkfst. Restaurant 5-10 pm. Bar to 11 pm. Ck-out 11 am. Sun deck. Some refrigerators. Some rms overlook bay. Cr cds: A, C, D, DS, MC, V.

SC

★★★ **HOTEL VISTA DEL MAR.** *417 Crescent Ave (90704). 310/510-1452; FAX 310/510-2917; res: 800/601-3836; res: 310/601-3836.* Web www.catalina.com. 15 rms. All rms on 3rd floor. May-Oct: S, D $95-$325; lower rates rest of yr. Crib $5. TV; cable (premium), VCR. Complimentary continental bkfst. Coffee in rms. Ck-out 11 am. Business servs avail. Refrigerators, fireplaces. Some in-rm whirlpools. Microwaves avail. Swimming beach. Atrium courtyard. Cr cds: A, C, DS, MC, V.

Motor Hotel

★★★ **HOTEL ST LAUREN.** *231 Beacon St (90704), jct Metropole. 310/510-2299; FAX 310/510-1369; res: 800/645-2471.* E-mail saintlaur@aol.com; web www.catalina.com/stlauren. 42 rms, 6 story. May-mid-Oct: S, D $90-$275; each addl $20; package plans; lower rates rest of yr. Crib free. TV; cable. Complimentary continental bkfst. Restaurant nearby. Ck-out 11 am. Meeting rm. Victorian-style architecture. Ocean 1 blk. Cr cds: A, C, MC, V.

D SC

Hotels

★ **GLENMORE PLAZA HOTEL.** *120 Sumner St (93301). 310/510-0017; FAX 310/510-2833; res: 800/422-8462.* 48 rms, 4 story, 2 suites. No elvtr. Apr-Oct: S, D $79-$175; suites $225-$450; wkends (2-day min); lower rates rest of yr. Crib avail. TV; cable. Complimentary continental bkfst. No rm serv. Ck-out 10:30 am. Free boat dock transportation. Built 1891. Cr cds: A, C, DS, MC, V.

★★★ **HOTEL METROPOLE.** *205 Crescent Ave (90704), in Metropole Marketplace. 310/510-1884; FAX 310/510-2534; res: 800/300-8528.* E-mail metropol@catalinas.net; web www.catalina.com/metropole. 48 rms, 3 story. May-Oct: S, D $110-$355; 2-bedrm suite $795; under 12 free; lower rates rest of yr. Crib free. TV; cable (premium). Complimentary continental bkfst. No rm serv. Ck-out 11 am. Coin Indry. Meeting rms. Business servs avail. Shopping arcade. Roof-top whirlpool, sun deck. Health club privileges. Minibars; many in-rm whirlpools, fireplaces. Microwaves avail. Balconies. Ocean view. Totally nonsmoking. Cr cds: A, C, MC, V.

D SC

Inns

★★ **CATALINA ISLAND SEACREST INN.** *201 Claressa Ave (92026). 310/510-0800; FAX 310/510-1122.* E-mail catisle@catalinas.net; web www.catalina.com/seacrest.html. 8 rms, 1 shower only, 2 story. No rm phone. May-Oct: S, D $105-$195; package plans; lower rates rest of yr. TV; cable (premium), VCR (movies). Complimentary continental bkfst. Restaurant nearby. Ck-out 11 am, ck-in 2 pm. Luggage handling. In-rm whirlpools. Victorian decor. Totally nonsmoking. Cr cds: C, D, DS, ER, JCB, MC, V.

★★★★ **INN ON MT ADA.** *398 Wrigley Road (90704). 310/510-2030; FAX 310/510-2237; res: 800/608-7669.* Occupying the historic Wrigley Mansion, this luxury inn offers elegantly decorated guest rooms and spectacular views of the ocean, harbor, and mountains. The property is decorated in a Georgian colonial style. Lunch and afternoon hors d'oeuvres are high quality. 6 rms, 2 story. MAP, June-Oct & wkends: S, D $310-$595; each addl $75; lower wkday rates rest of yr. are $210-$470, TV; cable (premium), VCR avail (movies). Afternoon refreshments. Ck-out 11 am, ck-in 2 pm. Many fireplaces. Balconies. Totally nonsmoking. Cr cds: C, MC, V.

Restaurants

★ **ANTONIO'S PIZZERIA & CATALINA.** *230 Crescent Ave (90704). 310/510-0008.* Hrs: 8 am-11 pm; Fri, Sat to midnight. Italian, Amer menu. Bar. A la carte entrees: bkfst $3.95-$6.95. Semi-a la carte: lunch $5-$8, dinner $5-$20. Specializes in pizza, pastas. Outdoor dining. Early 1950s decor. 1955 Seeberg juke box at each table. Overlooks harbor. Cr cds: A, C, MC, V.

D

★★ **ARMSTRONG'S FISH MARKET & SEAFOOD.** *306 Crescent Ave (90704), at harbor. 310/510-0113.* Hrs: 11 am-9:30 pm; Fri-Sun to 10 pm. Closed Thanksgiving, Dec 25. Bar. Semi-a la carte: lunch $5.95-$11.95, dinner $8.95-$24.95. Specializes in seafood cooked over mesquite wood. Outdoor dining. Deck overlooks harbor. Cr cds: A, C, DS, MC, V.

D

✓★★ **BLUE PARROT.** *205 Crescent Ave (90704), in Metropole Marketplace. 310/510-2465.* Hrs: 11 am-9 pm; Fri, Sat to midnight. No A/C. Bar. Complete meals: lunch $6.95-$7.95, dinner $11.95-$17.95. Child's meals. Specializes in steak, seafood, Cajun dishes. Polynesian decor. Harbor view. Cr cds: A, C, D, DS, MC, V.

★★ **CHANNEL HOUSE.** *205 Crescent Ave (90704), in Metropole Marketplace. 310/510-1617.* Hrs: 11 am-3 pm, 5-10 pm. Res accepted. Continental menu. Bar. Complete meals: lunch $6.95-$13.95, dinner $15.95-$24.95. Child's meals. Specializes in seafood, steak, lamb. Pianist Fri, Sat. Outdoor dining. Antique wooden bar. Cr cds: A, C, DS, MC, V.

D

Bakersfield (H-3)

Founded 1869 **Pop** 174,820 **Elev** 408 ft **Area Code** 805
Web www.bakersfield.org/chamber
Information Chamber of Commerce, 1725 Eye St, 93301; 805/327-4421

Surrounded by oil wells and fields of cotton and grain, Bakersfield is an important trading center—the hub of a network of highways that carry its produce and products to major cities. Founded by Colonel Thomas Baker, the town awakened in 1885 when gold was discovered in the Kern River Canyon. Overnight it changed from a placid farm town to a wild mining community, complete with gunfights and gambling halls. A fire in 1889 destroyed most of the old town and resulted in considerable modernization. The discovery of oil in 1899 rekindled the gold rush hysterics. Unlike gold, oil has remained an important part of the city's economy. Bakersfield is the seat of Kern County (8,064 square miles; third-largest county in the state). Nearby vineyards produce 25 percent of California wine, and surrounding fields provide a colorful flower display in spring. A Ranger District office of the Sequoia National Forest is located here.

What to See and Do

California Living Museum. Botanical garden and zoo house plants and animals native to California; natural history museum; interpretive tours. (Early May-late Oct, Tues-Sun; rest of yr, Wed-Sun; closed Thanksgiving, Dec 25) 10500 Alfred Harrell Hwy, 12 mi NE via CA 178. Phone 805/872-2256. ¢¢

Kern County Museum. Complete 16-acre outdoor museum of 60 restored or representational buildings including Queen Anne-style mansion (1891), log cabin, wooden jail, hotel, drugstore; 1898 locomotive, oil-drilling rig and horse-drawn vehicles. Main museum building contains changing exhibits on natural and cultural history of the area. (Daily; closed Jan 1, Thanksgiving, Dec 24, 25 & 31) Tickets avail through ticket office; phone 805/861-2132. ¢¢

Scenic drive. Many fine places for picnicking, camping and fishing along the road. Go E on CA 178 and follow the Kern River through a rock-dotted canyon.

Tule Elk State Reserve. This 969-acre reserve is home for a small herd of elk native only to California. Picnic shelters. (Daily) 20 mi W via Stockdale Hwy, then S on Morris Rd to Station Rd, then ¼ mi W. Phone 661/764-6881. Per vehicle ¢¢

Annual Event

Kern County Fair. Late Sept.

Motels

★ **BEST WESTERN.** *700 Truxton Ave (93301), near civic center. 805/327-4064; FAX 805/327-1247; res: 800/528-1234.* 99 rms, 2 story. S $50-$60; D $55-$65; each addl $5; under 12 free. Crib free. Pet accepted; $3. TV; cable (premium). Pool. Complimentary continental bkfst. Restaurant 6:30 am-8 pm. Bar. Ck-out noon. Meeting rms. Exercise equipt. Refrigerators. Balconies. Cr cds: A, C, D, DS, MC, V.

SC

✓★★ **CALIFORNIA INN.** *3400 Chester Ln (93309). 661/328-1100; FAX 661/328-0433; res: 800/707-8000.* 74 units, 3 story. S $39-$41; D $45-$49; each addl $4; suites $85; under 18 free. Crib $4. TV; cable (premium). Pool; whirlpool. Sauna. Complimentary continental bkfst. Complimentary coffee in rms. Restaurant adj 6 am-11 pm. Ck-out noon. Coin Indry. Refrigerators; in-rm whirlpool in suites. Cr cds: A, C, D, DS, MC, V.

D SC

★★★ **COURTYARD BY MARRIOTT.** *3601 Marriott Dr (93308). 661/324-6660; FAX 661/324-1185; res: 800/321-2211.* 146 rms, 3 story. S, D $82; suites $95; wkly, wkend rates. Crib free. TV; cable (premium). Heated pool; whirlpool. Complimentary coffee in rms. Restaurant 6-10:30 am. Serv bar 4-10 pm. Ck-out 1 pm. Coin Indry. Meeting rms. Valet serv. Exercise equipt. Health club privileges. Some balconies. Cr cds: A, C, D, DS, MC, V.

D SC

★★★ **FOUR POINTS HOTEL.** *5101 California Ave (93309). 661/325-9700; FAX 661/323-3508; res: 800/500-5399.* 198 rms, 2 story. S $95-$145; D $115-$145; each addl $10; suites $175-$300; under 17 free. Crib free. TV; cable (premium). Heated pool; whirlpool. Complimentary continental bkfst (exc Sat, Sun). Coffee in rms. Restaurant 6:30 am-10 pm. Rm serv. Bar 4-10 pm. Ck-out 1 pm. Meeting rms. Business servs avail. In-rm modem link. Bellhops. Valet serv. Airport, RR station, bus depot transportation. Exercise equipt. Some refrigerators. Private patios. Tropical decor; atrium. Extensive grounds. Cr cds: A, C, D, DS, JCB, MC, V.

D SC

★★ **HOLIDAY INN.** *4400 Hughes Ln (93304). 805/833-3000; FAX 805/833-3736; res: 800/465-4329; res: 800/636-1626.* Web www.holidayinnexpressbak.com. 108 rms, 4 story. S $81; D $86; each addl $5; under 18 free. Crib free. TV; cable (premium). Complimentary continental bkfst. Restaurant nearby. Ck-out 11 am. Meeting rms. Business center. In-rm modem link. Coin Indry. Pool; whirlpool. Game rm. Bathrm phones, refrigerators, microwaves; some in-rm whirlpools. Cr cds: A, C, D, DS, JCB, MC, V.

D SC

★ **LA QUINTA INN.** *3232 Riverside Dr (93308). 805/325-7400; FAX 805/324-6032; res: 800/687-6667.* 129 rms, 3 story. S $55-$65; D $62-$68; suites $110; under 18 free. Crib free. Pet accepted. TV; cable (premium). Heated pool. Complimentary continental bkfst. Complimentary coffee in rms. Restaurant adj 5:30 am-10 pm. Ck-out noon. Business servs avail. Free airport transportation. Health club privileges. Cr cds: A, C, D, DS, MC, V.

D SC

✓★★ **OXFORD INN.** *4500 Buck Owens Blvd (93308). 661/324-5555; FAX 661/325-0106; res: 800/638-7949.* 203 rms, 3 story. S $39-$52; D $46-$58; each addl $5; suites, kit. units $56-$64; under 18 free. Pet accepted; $10. TV; cable. Pool. Sauna. Ck-out 1 pm. Coin Indry. Meeting rms. Business servs avail. Valet serv. Sundries. Free airport, RR station, bus depot transportation. 9-hole golf course, $6 green fee. Refrigerator in suites. Some balconies. Cr cds: A, C, D, DS, MC, V.

D SC

★★ **QUALITY INN.** *1011 Oak St (93304). 805/325-0772; FAX 805/325-4646; res: 800/228-5050.* 90 units, 2 story. S $42-$60; D $50-$60; each addl $5; suites from $56; under 10 free. Crib free. Pet accepted, some restrictions. TV; cable (premium). Pool; whirlpool. Sauna. Complimentary continental bkfst. Complimentary coffee in rms. Restaurant adj 6 am-11 pm. Ck-out noon. Coin Indry. Valet serv. Some private patios, balconies. Cr cds: A, C, D, DS, ER, JCB, MC, V.

D SC

✓★ **SUPER 8 MOTEL.** *901 Real Rd (93309). 661/322-1012; FAX 661/322-7636; res: 800/800-8000.* 90 rms, 3 story. S $50-$54; D $54-$58; each addl $4; under 12 free. Crib free. TV; cable (premium). Pool. Complimentary coffee in lobby. Restaurant nearby. Ck-out 11 am. Cr cds: A, C, D, DS, MC, V.

D SC

✓★ **TRAVELODGE SOUTH.** *3620 Wible Rd (93309). 661/833-1000; FAX 661/832-3212; res: 800/578-7878.* 60 rms, 2 story. S $50; D $60; each addl $5; under 18 free. Crib free. TV; cable (premium). Complimentary continental bkfst. Complimentary coffee in rms. Restaurant adj 5 am-midnight. Ck-out 11 am. Business servs avail. In-rm modem link. Coin Indry. Pool; whirlpool. Refrigerators; some in-rm whirlpools, microwaves, wet bars. Cr cds: A, C, D, DS, JCB, MC, V.

D SC

Guest Ranch

★★ **RANKIN RANCH.** *23500 Walkers Basin Rd (93518), E on CA 58, N on rd to Caliente approx 3 mi E of Caliente where road forks; either 9½ mi on left branch on steep, narrow road over mountains, or 20 mi on right branch around mountains via scenic road. 805/867-2511; FAX 805/867-0105.* Web www.rankinranch.com. 14 rms, 7 cabins. No rm phones. AP: S $160/person; D $150/person; children $35-$100; wkly rates; lower rates Apr-May & Sept-Oct. Closed 1st Sun Oct-wk before Easter. Crib free. Heated pool. Playground. Free supervised child's activities (mid-June-Labor Day). Complimentary coffee in rms. Dining rm, 3 sittings: 7:30-9 am, 12:30 pm & 6:30 pm. Box lunches. Ck-out 1 pm, ck-in 3:30 pm. Grocery 5 mi. Meeting rms. Gift shop. Tennis. Boating. Hiking. Hay wagon rides. Lawn games. Soc dir. Square dancing. Rec rm. 31,000-acre working ranch (founded 1863) in Tehachapi Mountains. Cr cds: A, C, DS, MC, V.

D

Restaurants

★★ **MAMA TOSCA'S.** *6631 Ming Ave (93309), in Laurelglen Plaza. 805/831-1242.* Hrs: 11:30 am-2 pm, 5:30-10 pm; Sat from 5:30 pm. Closed Sun; major hols. Res accepted. Italian, Amer menu. Bar. Semi-a la carte: lunch $6.95-$19.95, dinner $9.95-$30. Specialties: veal scaloppini, eggplant Parmesan, rack of lamb. Vocalist, band Thurs-Sat. Parking. Cr cds: A, C, D, DS, MC, V.

D

✓★★ **ROSA'S ITALIAN RESTAURANT.** *2400 Columbus (93306). 805/872-1606.* Hrs: 11 am-1:45 pm, 4-9:30 pm; Fri to 10 pm; Sat 4-10 pm; Sun 4-9:30 pm. Closed most maj hols. Italian, Amer menu. Wine, beer. Semi-a la carte: lunch $3.85-$6.95, dinner $7.95-$14.95. Specialties: linguine with clams, fettucine Alfredo, lasagne. Patio dining. Italian village atmosphere. Family-owned. Totally nonsmoking. Cr cds: C, MC, V.

D

★ **WOOL GROWERS.** *620 E 19th St (93305). 805/327-9584.* Hrs: 11:30 am-2 pm, 6-9:30 pm. Closed Sun; Thanksgiving, Dec 25. Res accepted. Basque menu. Bar 10 am-11:30 pm. Complete meals: lunch $5.50-$11.50, dinner $10.50-$17.50. Child's meals. Specializes in French Basque dishes. Family-owned. Cr cds: A, C, DS, MC, V.

D

Barstow (H-4)

(See also Victorville)

Founded 1880 **Pop** 21,472 **Elev** 2,106 ft **Area Code** 760 **Zip** 92311

Information Desert Information Center, 831 Barstow Rd; 760/255-8760

In the heart of the beautiful high desert country, Barstow is a former frontier town that has become one of the fastest-growing cities in San Bernardino County. Once a desert junction for overland wagon trains and an outfitting station for Death Valley expeditions, Barstow thrives on nearby military installations and a $15-million tourist trade. It is the hub of three major highways that carry tourists into the Mojave Desert.

What to See and Do

Afton Canyon. Created in prehistoric times when Lake Manix broke through, chiseling a gorge through layers of multicolored rock. Primitive camping (fee). 40 mi E on I-15.

Calico Early Man Site. Archaeological digs; stone tool artifacts fashioned by early man approx 200,000 yrs ago are still visible in the walls of the excavations. Oldest evidence of human activity in the Western Hemisphere. Only New World site that Louis S. B. Leakey ever worked on; he served as project director until his death. Two master pits open for viewing; small museum. (Wed-Sun; closed hols) Guided tours. 18 mi E via I-15, Minneola Rd exit, then 2¾ mi on graded dirt road. For further information contact California Desert Information Center, 831 Barstow Rd; phone 760/255-8760. **Free**

Calico Ghost Town Regional Park. Restored 1880s mining town. For 6 decades a dust-shrouded ghost town; privately restored in 1954. General store, old schoolhouse, the Maggie Mine, collection of paintings in "Lil's Saloon," print, pottery, basket and leather shops; tramway, railroad, mine tours; shooting gallery. (See ANNUAL EVENTS) Nearby are the Calico Mts, which yielded $86 million in silver in 15 yrs. Camping (some hookups; fee). (Daily; closed Dec 25) 10 mi E via I-15, then 4 mi N on Ghost Town Rd. Phone 760/254-2122. E of Calico is

Odessa Canyon. Rock-studded landscape created by volcanic action. Erosion has etched striking rock formations. No cars.

Factory Merchants Outlet Mall. More than 90 outlet stores. (Daily) 2837 Lenwood Rd. Phone 760/253-7342.

Mojave River Valley Museum. Rock and mineral displays; photographs; archaeology and railroad displays; Native American exhibits. (Daily; closed major hols) 270 E Virginia Way. Phone 760/256-5452. **Donation**

Mule Canyon and Fiery Gulch. Cathedral-like rocks, S-shaped formations, crimson walls, natural arches. No cars. 14 mi NE.

Rainbow Basin. Colorful geologic display of a syncline and hogbacks on the 4-mi one-way drive. No motorhomes. 10 mi N on Old Irwin Rd.

Annual Events

Calico Hullabaloo. Calico Ghost Town. World tobacco-spitting championships, old miner's stew cook-off, flapjack races, horseshoe pitching championships. Palm Sunday wkend.

Calico Spring Festival. Calico Ghost Town. Fiddle and banjo contests, bluegrass music, gunfights, 1880s games, clogging hoedown. Mother's Day wkend.

Calico Days. Calico Ghost Town. Country music, Wild West parade, national gunfight stunt championship, burro race, 1880s games. Columbus Day wkend.

Calico Fine Arts Festival. Calico Ghost Town. Native American dance and works of art by many of the West's foremost artists displayed along Main St. 1st wkend Nov.

Motels

★★ **BEST WESTERN DESERT VILLA INN.** *1984 E Main St (92311). 760/256-1781; FAX 760/256-9265; res: 800/528-1234.* 95 rms, 2 story, 8 kit. units. S $68-$78; D $70-$80; each addl $5; kit. units $73-$76; under 12 free. Crib free. TV; cable (premium). Pool; whirlpool. Complimentary continental bkfst. Coffee in rms. Restaurant 5-9 pm. Ck-out 11 am. Coin lndry. Gift shop. Refrigerators, microwaves avail. Cr cds: A, C, D, DS, ER, JCB, MC, V.

D SC

✓★ **DAYS INN.** *1590 Coolwater Ln (92311). 760/256-1737; FAX 760/256-7771; res: 800/329-7466.* 113 rms, 2 story. S $26.90-$36.90; D $39-$49; under 12 free; wkly rates. Pet accepted. TV; cable (premium). Heated pool. Complimentary continental bkfst. Restaurant adj. Ck-out 11 am. Coin lndry. Some refrigerators. Cr cds: A, C, D, DS, MC, V.

D SC

Restaurant

★★ **IDLE SPURS STEAK HOUSE.** *690 W CA 58 (92311). 760/256-8888.* Web www.idlespurs.com. Hrs: 11 am-9 pm; Sat 4-9:30 pm; Sun 3-9 pm. Closed Jan 1, July 4, Thanksgiving, Dec 24-25. Res accepted. Bar to 11 pm. Semi-a la carte: lunch $6.50-$9.95, dinner $10.95-$24.95. Specialty: prime rib. Patio dining. Western decor. Cr cds: A, C, DS, MC, V.

D

Beaumont (J-4)

(See also Hemet, Palm Springs, Redlands, Riverside, San Bernardino)

Pop 9,685 **Elev** 2,573 ft **Area Code** 909 **Zip** 92223
E-mail bmtch@wmn.net

Information Chamber of Commerce, 450 E 4th St, PO Box 637; 909/845-9541

What to See and Do

Edward-Dean Museum of Decorative Arts. 17th- and 19th-century European and Asian furniture, bronzes, porcelains, rugs, paintings. (Daily exc Mon; closed hols, also Aug) 9401 Oak Glen Rd, in Cherry Valley. Phone 909/845-2626. ¢

Annual Event

Cherry Festival. Stewart Park. 1st full wkend June.

Motel

✓★★ **BEST WESTERN EL RANCHO MOTOR INN.** *550 Beaumont Avenue (92223), I-10 Beaumont Ave exit, 1 blk N. 909/845-2176; FAX 909/845-7559; res: 800/528-1234.* 52 rms, 2 story. S $50-$56; D $53-$59; each addl $3; suites $53-$75. Crib $6. TV; cable (premium). Heated pool. Restaurant 7 am-9 pm. Bar 11 am-11 pm. Ck-out noon. Meeting rm. Cr cds: A, C, D, DS, MC, V.

SC

Berkeley (E-2)

(See also Oakland, San Francisco, San Rafael, Sausalito)

Settled 1841 **Pop** 102,724 **Elev** 152 ft **Area Code** 510
E-mail chamber@dnai.com **Web** www.berkeleychamber.com

Information Berkeley Convention & Visitors Bureau, 2015 Center St, 94704; 510/549-7040

Berkeley is the home of the principal campus of the University of California. With an average monthly high temperature of 64°F, Berkeley regards itself as "one of America's most refreshing cities."

Named for George Berkeley, Bishop of Cloyne, an 18th-century Irish philosopher, the area was once a part of the vast Rancho San Antonio. Shortly after a group of developers bought the townsite, the College of California was founded—later to become the University of California.

The town's population was increased by refugees from the San Francisco earthquake and fire of 1906. In September of 1923, one-quarter of Berkeley was destroyed by fire. Quickly rebuilt, the city government instituted one of the most efficient fire-prevention systems in the country.

What to See and Do

Bade Institute of Biblical Archaeology. Devoted to archaeology of Palestine from 3200-600 B.C. Bible collection has documents from 5th-18th centuries (by appt only). Museum (Mon-Fri; closed hols). Pacific School of Religion, 1798 Scenic Ave. Phone 510/848-0528, ext 211. **Free**

Berkeley Marina. Public fishing pier (free); bait and tackle shop; sportfishing boat; 950 berths, 25 visitor berths; phone 510/644-6376. Protected sailing basin; 4-lane boat ramp (fee). Motel, restaurants. ½ mi W of Eastshore Frwy, I-80, at W end of University Ave, on San Francisco Bay.

Berkeley Rose Garden. Collection of 4,000 roses; 200 varieties. (Daily; best blooms mid-May-Sept) Euclid Ave & Eunice St. **Free**

Charles Lee Tilden Regional Park. The park's 2,078 recreational acres include swimming (fee), swimming beach, bathhouse; fishing at Lake Anza. Nature, hiking, bicycle, bridle trails. 18-hole golf (fee). Picnicking, concessions. Environmental Education Center, Little Farm, Jewel Lake. Merry-go-round, pony and steam train rides (fee); botanical garden of native California plants. Park connects with East Bay Skyline National Trail at Inspiration Point. (Daily) E on CA 24 to Fish Ranch Rd exit, then W to Grizzly Peak Blvd, right to park. Phone 510/562-7275. **Free**

Grizzly Peak Blvd. A winding drive along the crest of hills behind the city; it offers views of most of San Francisco Bay and the surrounding cities.

Judah L. Magnes Museum. Artistic, historical and literary materials, including ceremonial objects and textiles, trace Jewish life and culture throughout the world; Western Jewish History Center houses documentation of Jewish contributions to the history of the American West; research library of rare and illustrated Jewish books and manuscripts; permanent collection and changing exhibits of traditional and contemporary Jewish artists and themes. (Sun-Thurs; closed Jewish and legal hols) Guided tours (Sun & Wed; also by appt). 2911 Russell St, one blk N of Pine & Ashby. Phone 510/549-6950. **Free**

★ **University of California** (1873). (30,370 students) Covers more than 1,200 acres in the foothills of the E shore of San Francisco Bay. Instruction in fields of learning from agriculture to zoology. The oldest of nine campuses, its white granite buildings are surrounded by groves of oak trees; its 307-ft campanile can be seen from a great distance (elevator, fee). 2 mi E of Eastshore Frwy, I-80, at E end of University Ave. Phone 510/642-5215 for visitor information. On or near the campus are

Art Museum. Includes Hans Hofmann paintings, outdoor sculpture garden, Pacific Film Archive film program; 11 exhibition galleries. (Wed-Sun) 2626 Bancroft Way. Phone 510/642-0808. **¢¢¢**

Botanical Garden. Many unusual plants, including native, Asian, Australian and South American collections and a redwood grove; visitor center. (Daily; closed Dec 25) Tours (Sat & Sun). 200 Centennial Dr in Strawberry Canyon. Phone 510/642-3343. **Free**

The Greek Theatre. Gift of William Randolph Hearst; an amphitheater where leading pop and jazz artists perform. At E Gate. Phone 510/642-9988.

International House. This is a fine example of Mission-revival architecture. The dome is visible for miles. Built in 1930, this was the second such institution in the world. It serves as home and program center for 600 foreign and American students. (Daily) Bancroft Way & Piedmont Ave. Phone 510/642-9490.

Lawrence Hall of Science. Hands-on exhibits and activities for all ages. Classes, films, planetarium shows, discovery labs, special events and programs on a variety of scientific topics. (Daily; closed university hols) Centennial Dr, S of Grizzly Peak Blvd. Phone 510/642-5132. **¢¢¢**

Phoebe Apperson Hearst Museum of Anthropology. Changing exhibits on ancient and modern lands and people. (Daily; closed major hols) On Bancroft Way, at end of College Ave. In Kroeber Hall. Phone 510/642-3681. **¢**

Worth Ryder Art Gallery. Changing exhibits. (Sept-May, Wed-Fri afternoons) Hrs subject to change. 116 Kroeber Hall. Phone 510/642-2582. **Free**

Wildcat Canyon Regional Park. On 2,421 acres. Hiking, jogging, bicycle and bridle trails. Picnicking. Interpretive programs. Bird watching. (Daily) N of Tilden Regional Park, access from Tilden Nature Area. **Free**

Motel

✓★ **BERKELEY CAMPUS MOTEL.** *1619 University Ave (94703). 510/841-3844; FAX 510/841-8134; res: 800/447-8080.* 23 rms, 2 story, 1 kit. No A/C. S $50-$55; D $72-$80; suites $100.80; kit. unit $100.80. TV; cable (premium). Complimentary coffee in rms. Restaurant nearby. Ck-out 11 am. Business servs avail. Univ of CA 5 blks. Cr cds: A, C, MC, V.

Motor Hotel

★★★ **MARRIOTT.** *200 Marina Blvd (94710). 510/548-7920; FAX 510/548-7944; res: 800/243-0625.* Web www.radisson.com. 375 rms, 4 story. S, D $134-$180; each addl $15; suites $500-$750; under 12 free. Crib free. TV; cable (premium), VCR avail. 2 indoor pools; poolside serv. Restaurant 6 am-11 pm. Rm serv. Bar 11-2 am; Sun to midnight. Ck-out noon. Meeting rms. Business center. In-rm modem link. Gift shop. Exercise equipt; sauna. Dockage. Wet bar in suites; microwaves avail. Some balconies, private patios. Luxury level. Cr cds: A, C, D, DS, JCB, MC, V.

D SC

Hotels

★ **HOTEL DURANT.** *2600 Durant Ave (94709). 510/845-8981; FAX 510/486-8336; res: 800/238-7268.* E-mail hotdur@ix.netcom.com. 140 rms, 6 story. No A/C. S $99-$324; D $109-$324; each addl $15; suites $202-$324; under 12 free. Crib free. Limited covered valet parking $5/day. TV; cable (premium). Complimentary continental bkfst. Restaurant 11 am-10 pm. Bar. Ck-out noon. Meeting rms. Business servs avail. Airport transportation. Health club privileges. Some refrigerators, wet bars. City landmark (1928). Cr cds: A, C, D, DS, MC, V.

D SC

★ **SHATTUCK HOTEL.** *2086 Allston Way (94704). 510/845-7300; FAX 510/644-2088; res: 800/742-8825.* 175 rms, 5 story. No A/C. S $69-$90; D $79-$100; each addl $15; suites from $100; under 12 free. Crib $6. TV; cable (premium). Complimentary continental bkfst. Restaurant 7 am-3 pm; closed Sat, Sun. Ck-out noon. Meeting rms. Business servs avail. City landmark (1910). Cr cds: A, C, D, DS, JCB, MC, V.

D SC

Inns

★ **BANCROFT HOTEL.** *2680 Bancroft Way (94704). 510/549-1000; FAX 510/549-1070; res: 800/549-1002.* E-mail reservations@bancrofthotel.com; web www.bancrofthotel.com. 22 rms, 3 story. No A/C. S $99-$129; D $109-$139; under 12 free; higher rates special events (min stay). Parking $6. TV; cable, VCR. Complimentary continental bkfst. Restaurant nearby. Ck-out noon, ck-in 3. Business servs avail. Luggage handling. Many balconies. Built 1928. Totally nonsmoking. Cr cds: A, C, D, MC, V.

★★ **ROSE GARDEN INN.** *2740 Telegraph Ave (94705). 510/549-2145; FAX 510/549-1085; res: 800/992-9005.* 40 rms. No A/C. S, D $99-$165. TV; VCR avail. Complimentary full bkfst; afternoon refreshments. Complimentary coffee. Ck-out noon, ck-in 2 pm. Business servs avail. Many fireplaces. Some private patios. Some rms in 2 restored Victorian mansions; antiques. Some private decks; English country garden. Cr cds: A, C, D, DS, MC, V.

D SC

Restaurants

✓★ **AJANTA RESTAURANT.** *1888 Solano Ave (94707). 510/526-4373.* Hrs: 11:30 am-2:30 pm, 5:30-9:30 pm; Fri-Sun to 9:30 pm. Closed Thanksgiving, Dec 25. Res accepted. Indian menu. Wine, beer.

Semi-a la carte: lunch, dinner $11.25-$13.25. Complete meals: lunch, dinner $13.75-$14.75. Specializes in authentic Indian cuisine. Specials change monthly. Street parking. Indian artwork depicts scenes from Ajanta caves. Totally nonsmoking. Cr cds: A, C, D, DS, MC, V.

✓★★ **CAFE ROUGE.** *1782 4th St (94710). 510/525-1440.* Hrs: 11:30 am-9:30 pm; Mon to 3 pm; Fri, Sat to 10:30 pm. Closed most major hols. Res accepted. French bistro menu. Bar. Semi-a la carte: lunch $8-$13, dinner $8-$20. Specializes in meats, homemade charcuterie. Outdoor dining. Authentic meat market setting. Cr cds: A, C, MC, V.

D

★★★ **CHEZ PANISSE RESTAURANT & CAFE.** *1517 Shattuck Ave (94709). 510/548-5525.* Hrs: Cafe (upper level) 11:30 am-3 pm, 5-10:30 pm; Fri, Sat 11:30 am-4 pm, 5-11:30 pm; Restaurant dining rm (main floor) 6-9:15 pm. Closed Sun; Dec 25. Res accepted in cafe; required in dining rm. Contemporary Mediterranean menu. Beer. Wine list. A la carte entrees: lunch $15-$17, dinner $16-$20. Prix fixe: dinner $35-$65. Street parking. Cr cds: A, C, DS, MC, V.

D

★★ **GINGER ISLAND.** *1820 4th St (94710). 510/644-0444.* Web www.gingerisland.com. Hrs: 11:30 am-10 pm; Fri, Sat 10:30 am to 11 pm; Sun from 10:30 am. Res accepted. Bar. A la carte entrees: lunch $8.25-$14.50, dinner $8.50-$17. Specializes in American cuisine with Asian influences. Parking. Outdoor dining. Two dining rms; sky lights, light & airy feeling. Totally nonsmoking. Cr cds: A, C, D, MC, V.

D

★ **LALIME'S CAFE.** *1329 Gilman St (94706), 1 mi E of I-80. 510/527-9838.* Hrs: 5:30-9:30 pm; Fri, Sat to 10 pm; Sun 5-9 pm. Closed most major hols. Res accepted. Eclectic, Mediterranean menu. Bar. A la carte entrees: dinner $12.75-$19.95. Complete meals: dinner $22-$37. Specializes in unique lamb dishes, seasonal fresh produce. Own desserts. Street parking. Two-level dining area housed in a cottage. Cr cds: C, D, MC, V.

D

★★ **RIVOLI.** *1539 Solano Ave (94707). 510/526-2542.* Web www.rivolirestaurant.com. Hrs: 5:30-9:30 pm; Fri to 10 pm; Sat 5-10 pm; Sun 5-9 pm. Res accepted. A la carte entrees: dinner $13-$16. Specialties: portabella mushroom fritters, risotto cakes, braises. Street parking. Large window in rear dining room overlooks garden. Totally nonsmoking. Cr cds: A, C, DS, MC, V.

D

★★★ **SANTA FE BAR & GRILL.** *1310 University Ave (94702). 510/841-4740.* E-mail behjati@aol.com. Hrs: 11:30 am-3 pm, 5-11 pm; Fri, Sat to midnight. Res accepted. Bar to 1 am. A la carte entrees: lunch $5.95-$12.95, dinner $9-$19.95. Specializes in chicken, beef, fish. Own baking. Pianist. In turn-of-the-century Santa Fe Railroad depot; historic landmark. Cr cds: A, C, D, MC, V.

D

★★★ **SKATES ON THE BAY.** *100 Seawall Dr (94710). 510/549-1900.* Web www.citysearch.com. Hrs: 11:30 am-10 pm; Fri, Sat to 10:30 pm; Sun brunch 10:30 am-3 pm. Closed Thanksgiving, Dec 25. Res accepted. Bar. Semi-a la carte: lunch $6.95-$17.95, dinner $10.95-$28.95. Sun brunch $6.95-$15.95. Child's meals. Specializes in grilled meats, fresh seafood, pasta. Parking. Pier leads to entrance. View of Golden Gate Bridge. Cr cds: A, C, D, DS, MC, V.

D

Beverly Hills (C-3 see Los Angeles map)

(See also Hollywood, Los Angeles)

Pop 31,971 **Elev** 225 ft **Area Code** 310 **E-mail** admin@bhvb.org **Web** www.bhvb.org

Information Visitors Bureau, 239 S Beverly Dr, 90212; 310/248-1015 or 800/345-2210

Beverly Hills, an independent community 5.6 square miles in area, is conveniently located near downtown Los Angeles and many gorgeous beaches. It is famous for its exclusive residential districts, home to many movie and TV personalities. It boasts an international shopping area with the celebrated Rodeo Drive as its hub.

Hotels

★★★★★ **BEVERLY HILLS HOTEL.** *9641 Sunset Blvd (90210), at Rodeo Dr. 310/276-2251; FAX 310/281-2905; res: 800/283-8885.* Walking up the red carpet to the entrance of this legendary Beverly Hills hotel makes you feel like a movie star. Superior service and fine amenities, not to mention quirky touches like the hand-painted wallpaper with a giant palm motif, characterize the experience. Extensive grounds are well maintained. A welcome patina recalls old Hollywood. And the overall experience is nothing short of glamorous. 203 rms, 37 suites, 21 bungalows with 53 rms, 1-4 story, 12 kits. S, D $310-$390; suites $545-$4,700; 1-4 bdrm kit. bungalows $365-$3,595; under 12 free. Crib free. Valet parking $19. TV; cable (premium), VCR (movies). Pool; whirlpool, poolside serv. Restaurant (see POLO LOUNGE). Rm serv 24 hrs. Ck-out noon. Meeting rms. Business servs avail. In-rm modem link. Concierge. Beauty shop. Shopping arcade. Airport transportation. Lighted tennis, pro. Exercise equipt. Cr cds: A, C, D, JCB, MC, V.

D

★★★ **HILTON HOTEL.** *9876 Wilshire Blvd (90210). 310/274-7777; FAX 310/285-1313; res: 800/445-8667.* Web www.hilton.com. 581 rms, 8 story. S, D $195-$335; each addl $20; suites $500-$1,500; family rates. Crib free. Pet accepted. Garage parking $20, valet parking $21. TV; cable (premium), VCR avail. 2 heated pools; wading pool, poolside serv. Restaurant 6:30-11 pm; dining rm 5:30-11 pm. Rm serv 24 hrs. Bars 11:30-2 am. Ck-out noon. Meeting rms. Business center. In-rm modem link. Concierge. Shopping arcade. Barber, beauty shop. Exercise equipt. Some bathrm phones, refrigerators. Patio, balconies. Lanai rms around pool. Cr cds: A, C, D, DS, ER, JCB, MC, V.

D SC

✓★★★★★ **L'ERMITAGE.** *9291 Burton Way (90210). 310/278-3344; FAX 310/278-8247; res: 800/800-2113.* Web www.lermitagehotel.com. The sleek, modern design of this boutique hotel sets it apart from the other luxury properties in the Beverly Hills area. Understated but comfortable elegance describes the rooms, which boast state-of-the-art technology, spacious living areas, exquisite bathrooms, and French doors onto outdoor patios. Fine art and good taste abound. 124 rms, 8 story, 11 kit. suites. S, D, $385-$3,800. Crib free. Pet accepted, some restrictions. In/out garage parking $21. TV; cable (premium), DVD/CD (movies). Restaurant open 24 hrs. Rm serv 24 hrs. Bar 11-1 am. Ck-out 24 hrs/day. Meeting rms. Business servs avail. In-rm modem link. Concierge. Airport transportation. Exercise rm; sauna, steam rm. Massage. Pool; poolside serv. Bathrm phones, minibars. Balconies. Luxury level. Cr cds: A, C, D, DS, ER, JCB, MC, V.

D SC

★★★ **RENAISSANCE BEVERLY HOUSE HOTEL.** *1224 S Beverwil Dr at Pico (90035), at Pico Blvd. 310/277-2800; FAX 310/203-9537; res: 800/468-3571.* Web www.beverlyprescott.com. 137 rms, 12 story, 21 suites. S, D $175-$225; suites $350-$1,000; family, wkend rates. Crib free. Covered parking $17. TV; cable (premium), VCR. Heated pool; poolside serv. Restaurant 7 am-10 pm. Rm serv 24 hrs. Bar 11-2 am. Ck-out noon. Meeting rms. Business center. In-rm modem link. Concierge. Exercise equipt. Health club privileges. Minibars. Balconies. Cr cds: A, C, D, DS, ER, JCB, MC, V.

D

★★ **SUMMIT HOTEL RODEO DRIVE.** *360 N Rodeo Dr (90210). 310/273-0300; FAX 310/859-8730; res: 800/468-3541.* 86 rms, 3 story. S, D $185-$295; each addl $25; suites $350; under 17 free. Crib free. Valet parking $15, in/out $12. TV; cable. Complimentary coffee in rms. Restaurant 9 am-10:30 pm. Ck-out noon. Airport transportation. Tennis privileges. Health club privileges. Some refrigerators. Cr cds: A, C, D, DS, JCB, MC, V.

D SC

✓★★★ **THE BEVERLY HILLS PLAZA HOTEL.** *10300 Wilshire Blvd (90024). 310/275-5575; FAX 310/278-3325; res: 800/800-1234.* 116 suites, 5 story. S, D $155-$385. Crib avail. Pet accepted. TV; cable (premium), VCR avail. Heated pool; whirlpool, poolside serv. Restaurant 7 am-10 pm. Bar. Ck-out noon. Meeting rm. Business servs avail. In-rm modem link. Gift shop. Exercise equipt. Refrigerators, minibars. Many balconies. Garden; tropical plants. Cr cds: A, C, D, DS, JCB, MC, V.

SC

★★★★★ **THE PENINSULA.** *9882 Little Santa Monica Blvd (90212), at Wilshire Blvd. 310/551-2888; FAX 310/788-2319; res: 800/462-7899.* E-mail pbh@peninsula.com; web www.peninsula.com. This beautiful hotel is decorated like a fine home. The flowers are gorgeous, the couches are comfortable, and the lobby fireplace is always burning. Special touches like fresh fruit in the guest rooms and 24-hour checkout distinguish it from other hotels in its class. Newly renovated rooms are lavishly appointed, while the older rooms have large bathrooms and comfortable beds with fine sheets and down duvets. 196 units, 5 story, 32 suites, 16 villas (2 story, 1-2 bedrm). S, D $325-$450; each addl $35; suites, villas $600-$3,000; under 12 free; wkend rates. Crib free. Valet parking $21. TV; cable (premium), VCR (movies). Rooftop pool; whirlpool, poolside serv. Complimentary beverages on arrival. Restaurant (see THE BELVEDERE). Rm serv 24 hrs. Bar from 11:30 am; pianist. Meeting rms. Business center. In-rm modem link. Concierge. Gift shop. Clothing, jewelry stores. Airport transportation. Tennis privileges. 18-hole golf privileges, pro, putting green, driving range. Exercise equipt; sauna. Massage. Bathrm phones, minibars; many wet bars. Balconies. Cr cds: A, C, D, DS, ER, JCB, MC, V.

D

★★★★ **THE REGENT BEVERLY WILSHIRE.** *9500 Wilshire Blvd (90212). 310/275-5200; FAX 310/274-2851; res: 800/545-4000.* Web www.rih.com. Located at the foot of the world's most exclusive shopping street, Rodeo Drive, this fine hotel often serves as home to visiting celebrities and power brokers. 395 rms, 10 & 12 story, 120 suites. S, D $345-$460; suites $560-$7,500; under 16 free. Pet accepted. Covered parking, valet $21. TV; cable (premium), VCR avail (movies). Pool; whirlpool, poolside serv. Restaurant (see THE DINING ROOM). Rm serv 24 hrs. Bar 11-2 am; entertainment. Ck-out noon. Convention facilities. Business center. In-rm modem link. Concierge. Gift shops. Full Service salon. Fitness Center; sauna, steam rm. Massage. Bathrm phones, refrigerators. Some w/furnished balconies. Cr cds: A, C, D, DS, ER, JCB, MC, V.

D

Inn

★★ **CARLYLE INN.** *1119 S Robertson Blvd (90035), W on Wilshire Blvd to Robertson Blvd, then S; between Olympic & Pico Blvds. 310/275-4445; FAX 310/859-0496; res: 800/227-5953.* 32 rms, 5 story. S $110; D $120; each addl $10; suites $180-$200; under 10 free. Crib free. TV; cable, VCR (movies $3.50). Complimentary full bkfst; afternoon refreshments. Complimentary coffee in rms. Restaurant nearby. Ck-out noon, ck-in 2 pm. Business servs avail. In-rm modem link. Luggage handling. Valet serv. Concierge serv. Exercise equipt. Whirlpool. Rms are on 4 levels of circular terraces overlooking a lush courtyard, terrace and spa. Cr cds: A, C, D, DS, JCB, MC, V.

D SC

Restaurants

★★★ **CRUSTACEAN.** *9646 Little Santa Monica Blvd (90210). 310/205-8990.* Hrs: 11:30 am-10:30 pm; Fri to 11:30 pm; Sat 5:30-11:30 pm. Closed Sun; major hols. Res required. Asian, French menu. Bar. Wine list. A la carte entrees: lunch $11.95-$19.95, dinner $17.95-$34.95. Specialties: garlic-roasted crab, colossal royal prawns with garlic noodles, whole roasted dungeness crab. Pianist. Valet parking. Outdoor dining. Atmosphere is replica of 1930s French Colonial estate. Overlooks bamboo garden verandas. Cr cds: A, C, D, MC, V.

D

★★ **D A PASQUALE CAFE.** *9749 Santa Monica Blvd (90210). 310/859-3884.* Hrs: 11:30 am-3 pm, 5-10 pm; Fri to 11 pm; Sat 5-11 pm. Closed Sun; major hols. Res accepted; required wkends. Italian menu. Wine, beer. A la carte entrees: lunch $7-$15, dinner $15-$30. Specializes in pizza, pasta, fish. Patio dining. Italian atmosphere. Totally nonsmoking. Cr cds: A, C, D, DS, MC, V.

D

★★ **DA VINCI.** *9737 Little Santa Monica Blvd (90212). 310/273-0960.* Hrs: 11:30 am-2:30 pm, 5:30-10:30 pm; Sat, Sun from 5:30 pm. Res accepted. Italian menu. Bar. A la carte entrees: lunch $10-$15, dinner $15-$30. Specialty: osso bucco Milanese. Own pasta, desserts. Valet parking. Cr cds: A, C, D, JCB, MC, V.

D

★★★★★ **GINZA SUSHIKO.** *218 N Rodeo Dr (90210). 310/247-8939.* Although the tab is high, dinner at this traditional sushi restaurant costs less than a trip to Japan, and that's exactly where you'd have to go to sample fish as fresh or expertly prepared. The attentive service and extensive sake selection beautifully complement the dining experience. Japanese cuisine. Open Tues-Sat call for hours. Reserv reqd. Prices $300 per person. Valet. Jackets. Closed Sun & Mon. Cr cds: C.

★★★ **IL CIELO.** *9018 Burton Way, I-405 exit Wilshire Blvd E. 310/276-9990.* Hrs: 11:30 am-3 pm, 6-10:30 pm; Fri, Sat to 11 pm. Closed Sun; most major hols. Res accepted. Northern Italian menu. Beer. Wine list. A la carte entrees: lunch $10-$15, dinner $15-$25. Specializes in fresh seafood, veal. Own pasta, pastries. Valet parking. Outdoor dining. Gardens, fountains. Cr cds: A, C, D, DS, JCB, MC, V.

D

✓★★ **IL PASTAIO.** *400 N Canon Dr (90210). 310/205-5444.* Hrs: 11 am-11 pm; Sun 5-10 pm. Closed some major hols. Italian menu. Bar. A la carte entrees: lunch $8.50-$13, dinner $9.50-$15. Specializes in pasta. Valet parking. Patio dining. Contemporary decor, artwork. Cr cds: A, C, D, MC, V.

D

★★★ **JIMMY'S.** *201 Moreno Dr (90212). 310/552-2394.* Hrs: 11:30 am-3 pm, 5:30 pm-midnight; Sat from 5:30 pm. Closed Sun; major hols. French menu with California influence. Bar 11:30-2 am. Wine cellar. A la carte entrees: lunch $12-$18, dinner $22-$28. Specialties: peppered salmon, creme brulee Napoleon, Maryland crab cakes. Own pastries. Pianist. Elegant French decor with a California touch. Cr cds: A, C, D, MC, V.

D

★★★ **L'ERMITAGE.** *9291 Burton Way (90210). 310/278-3344; FAX 310/278-8247.* Distinct Mediterranean cuisine. Foie gras, house-smoked salmon, duck confit, lamb porterhouse, and venison. Hrs: 6-11:30 am; 11:30 am-2:30 pm; 6:30-10:30 pm. Prices $25-$38. Valet. Res pref. Child meal. Bar. Cr cds: A, C, D, DS, MC, V.

★★★ **LA SCALA RESTAURANT.** *410 N Canon Dr (90210). 310/275-0579.* Web www.menuserve.com. Hrs: 11:30 am-10 pm; Fri, Sat to 10:30 pm. Closed Sun; most major hols. Res accepted. Italian menu.

Bar. Wine list. A la carte entrees: lunch $10-$20, dinner $15-$30. Specialties: cannelloni alla gigi, minestrone soup, chopped salad. Valet parking. Outdoor dining. Totally nonsmoking. Cr cds: A, C, D, DS, ER, JCB, MC, V.

D

★★★ **LAWRY'S THE PRIME RIB.** *100 N La Cienega Blvd (90211), I-465 exit Wilshire Blvd E. 310/652-2827.* Hrs: 5-10 pm; Fri to 11 pm; Sat 4:30-11 pm; Sun 4-10 pm. Closed Dec 25. Res accepted. Bar. Semi-a la carte: dinner $19.95-$27.95. Specialties: prime rib, fish & lobster tails. Own desserts. Valet parking. Limited menu. Tableside serv. Cr cds: A, C, D, DS, JCB, MC, V.

D

★★★ **MAPLE DRIVE.** *345 N Maple Dr (90066). 310/274-9800.* Web www.restaurant-pages.com/mapledrive. Hrs: 11:30 am-2:30 pm, 6-10 pm. Closed Sun; major hols. Res accepted. Bar. A la carte entrees: lunch $15-$22, dinner $16-$32. Specialties: fried calamari, tuna tartar, grilled swordfish. Pianist. Valet parking (dinner). Terrace dining. Exhibition kitchen. Changing display of artwork. Cr cds: A, C, D, MC, V.

D

★★★ **MATSUHISA.** *129 N La Cienega Blvd (90211). 310/659-9639.* Japanese menu. Hrs: 11:45 am-2:15 pm, 5:45-10:15 pm; Sat, Sun from 5:45 pm. Closed most major hols. Res accepted. Japanese menu. Wine, beer. Semi-a la carte: lunch $20-$30, dinner $40-up. Omakase dishes $50-$100. Specializes in gourmet seafood, sushi. Valet parking. Totally nonsmoking. Cr cds: A, C, D, MC, V.

D

★★★ **OBACHINE.** *242 N Beverly Dr (90210). 310/274-4440.* Hrs: 11:30 am-3 pm, 5:30-10:30 pm. Res accepted. Asian menu. Bar. A la carte entrees: lunch $8.95-$12, dinner $12.95-$26. Complete meals: lunch $14-$22, dinner $32-$45. Specialties: sizzling catfish, Peking duck. Valet parking. Oriental decor. Cr cds: A, C, D, MC, V.

D

★★★ **POLO LOUNGE.** *(See Beverly Hills Hotel and Bungalows) 310/276-2251.* E-mail afarag@beverlyhillshotel.com. Hrs: 7-2 am; Sun brunch 11 am-3 pm. Res recommended. Bar. Wine cellar. A la carte entrees: bkfst $8-$14, lunch $14-$24, dinner $18-$28. Sun brunch $39. Specializes in Californian cuisine. Pianist. Valet parking. Outdoor dining. Cr cds: A, C, D, JCB, MC, V.

D

★★★ **PREGO.** *362 N Camden Dr (90201), I-405 exit Wilshire Blvd E. 310/277-7346.* Hrs: 11:30 am-11:30 pm; Sun 5-11 pm. Closed Thanksgiving, Dec 25. Res accepted. Northern Italian menu. Bar. A la carte entrees: lunch $8-$18, dinner $15-$28. Specializes in homemade pasta, fresh fish, chicken. Valet parking evenings. Oak-burning pizza oven & mesquite grill. Cr cds: A, C, D, ER, JCB, MC, V.

D

★★ **R J'S THE RIB JOINT.** *252 N Beverly Dr (90210). 310/274-7427.* Hrs: 11:30 am-10 pm; Sat to 11 pm; Sun 3-10 pm; early-bird dinner exc Sun 3-6 pm. Res accepted. Southwestern menu. Bar. Semi-a la carte: lunch $7.50-$12, dinner $10-$25. Child's meals. Specializes in ribs, chicken, fish. Parking. Totally nonsmoking. Cr cds: A, C, D, DS, ER, JCB, MC, V.

★★★★ **SPAGO.** *176 N Canon Dr. 310/385-0880.* The bright colors and geometric designs of the latest Spago outpost are merely a backdrop for the spectacle of diners—Hollywood celebrities, agents, sports heroes, and other followers of Wolfgang Puck and Barbara Lazaroff. In the hands of chef Lee Hefter, the creative French food with Asian accents has never been more elegant or refined. Cuisine American with Asian & French influence, Hrs (lunch) Mon-Sat 11:30 am-2:15 pm; (dinner) Mon-Sun 5:30 pm-10:30 pm. Prices lunch approx $20 dinner approx $28. Res pref. Valet. Outdoor dining. Cr cds: C.

★★ **STINKING ROSE.** *55 N La Cienega (90211), I-405 exit Wilshire Blvd E. 310/652-7673.* Hrs: 11 am-11 pm; Fri, Sat to midnight. Res accepted. Italian menu. Bar to 2 am. A la carte entrees: lunch $8-$11, dinner $8-$25. Specialties: 40-clove garlic chicken, bagna calda. Valet parking. Casual, eclectic decor. Cr cds: A, C, D, JCB, MC, V.

D

★★★★ **THE BELVEDERE.** *(See The Peninsula, Beverly Hills) 310/788-2306.* E-mail pbh@peninsula.com; web www.peninsula.com. Located in the posh Peninsula Beverly Hills Hotel, this formal dining room presents French/Continental fare. Hrs: 6:30 am-2:30 pm, 6-10:30 pm; Sun brunch 11 am-2:30 pm. Res highly recommended. Bar. Wine cellar. A la carte entrees: bkfst, lunch $16-$22, dinner $24-$31. Champagne brunch $52. Child's meals. Guitarist or harpist Sun brunch. Valet parking. Outdoor dining in partially covered terrace. Totally nonsmoking. Cr cds: A, C, D, DS, ER, JCB, MC, V.

D ♥

★★★ **THE DINING ROOM-BEVERLY WILSHIRE.** *(See Regent Beverly Wilshire Hotel) 310/275-5200.* Web www.rih.com. Continental menu. Specialties: egg white omelette with goat cheese, Maine lobster with tartar, Cowboy steak, loin of lamb, veal chop. Hrs: 6:30 am 2:30 pm, 6-10 pm; Sun 7 am-12 noon. Open hols. Res accepted. Bar 11-1:30 am. Pianist in both dining room and bar. Extensive wine list. A la carte entrees: bkfst $13-$18, lunch $17-$28, dinner $19-$36. Prix fixe: dinner $40. Valet parking. Jacket required wkends. Fri, Sat dancing. Res required. Cr cds: A, C, D, DS, ER, JCB, MC, V.

D ♥

★★★ **THE GRILL.** *9560 Dayton Way (90210). 310/276-0615.* E-mail thegrillonthealley@juno.com; web www.thegrill.com. Hrs: 11:30 am-11 pm; Fri, Sat to midnight; Sun 5-9 pm. Closed major hols. Res accepted. Bar. A la carte entrees: lunch $12-$20, dinner $15-$30. Specializes in fresh seafood, steak, chops. Valet parking. Turn-of-the-century decor. Cr cds: A, C, D, MC, V.

D

★★ **THE MANDARIN.** *430 N Camden Dr (90210). 310/859-0638.* Hrs: 11:30 am-10 pm; Fri to 11 pm; Sat 5-11 pm; Sun 5-10 pm. Closed most major hols. Res accepted. Chinese menu. Bar. A la carte entrees: lunch $15-$20, dinner $20-$25. Specialties: crispy chicken salad, Peking duck, steamed fillet of sea bass. Valet parking (dinner). Chinese decor. Totally nonsmoking. Cr cds: A, C, D, MC, V.

D

Unrated Dining Spots

ED DEBEVIC'S. *134 N La Cienega Blvd. 310/659-1952.* Hrs: 11:30 am-10 pm; Fri, Sat to midnight. Closed Thanksgiving, Dec 25. Bar. Semi-a la carte: lunch, dinner $4.50-$7.95. Specializes in meatloaf, hamburgers, chicken. Own desserts. Valet parking. 1950s-style diner; memorabilia of the era. Staff provides entertainment: singing, dancing. Cr cds: A, C, MC, V.

D

PLANET HOLLYWOOD. *9560 Wilshire Blvd (90212). 310/275-7828.* Hrs: 11 am-midnight; Fri, Sat to 1 am. Bar. A la carte entrees: lunch, dinner $7.50-$18.95. Child's meals. Specializes in pasta, pizza, salads. Valet parking. Movie posters and memorabilia. Totally nonsmoking. Cr cds: A, C, D, DS, JCB, MC, V.

D

Big Basin Redwoods State Park (F-1)

(See also Santa Cruz)

(23 mi N of Santa Cruz via CA 9, 236)

This 20,000-acre park is one of the most popular parks in California. The area was set aside as the state's first redwood preserve in 1902. Its redwood groves include trees 300 feet high. There are about 50 miles of hiking and riding trails, plus numerous picnic sites and campgrounds with full facilities (limit 8 persons per site; reservations required in summer). Ranger-conducted nature program, held in the summer, includes campfire programs and guided hikes. Flora and fauna of the park are on display in exhibits at the nature lodge. Supplies are available at a concession and a store. Standard fees. Phone 408/338-8860.

Big Bear Lake (J-4)

(See also Lake Arrowhead, Redlands, Riverside, San Bernardino)

Pop 5,351 **Elev** 6,754 ft **Area Code** 909 **Zip** 92315
E-mail bblra@bigbearinfo.com **Web** www.bigbearinfo.com

Information Big Bear Lake Resort Association, Box 1936; 909/866-6190, 909/866-7000 or 800/4-BIG-BEAR

This is a growing, year-round recreation area in the San Bernardino National Forest (see SAN BERNARDINO). Fishing, canoeing, parasailing, windsurfing, riding, golf, bicycling, picnicking, hiking and camping are available in summer; skiing and other winter sports are also popular in season.

What to See and Do

Alpine Slide at Magic Mountain. Includes Alpine bobsled-type ride (all yr), water slide (summer) and inner tubing (winter). Miniature golf (all yr). Video games; snack bar. (Daily) Approx ¼ mi W on CA 18. Phone 909/866-4626. ¢¢-¢¢¢¢

***Big Bear Queen* Tour Boat.** Paddlewheeler provides 90-min narrated tour of Big Bear Lake. Dinner and champagne cruises also avail. (May-Oct, daily) Big Bear Marina, Paine Rd at Lakeview Dr. Phone 909/866-3218. ¢¢¢-¢¢¢¢

Horseback riding. Contact PO Box 511; phone 909/878-4677.

Bear Mt. Riding Stables. 1- to 2-hr trail rides through San Bernardino National Forest; panoramic views of Big Bear Lake. Sunset hay rides avail (res required). (Memorial Day-Labor Day) Bear Mt Ski Resort (see) at top of Lassen Dr. ¢¢¢¢¢

Rockin' K Riding Stables. 1- to 4-hr trail rides through San Bernardino Natl Forest; views from highest elevations in Big Bear Valley. Sunset, Twilight, Moonlight and Overnight rides avail (res required for all). (May-Nov) 731 Tulip Ln. ¢¢¢¢¢

Skiing.

Bear Mt. 1 quad, 1 high-speed quad, 3 triple, 4 double chairlifts, 2 Pomalifts; patrol, school, rentals; snowmaking; cafe, 2 restaurants, bar. Longest run 2½ mi; vertical drop 1,665 ft. (Mid-Nov-Apr, daily) Hiking, 9-hole golf course (May-mid-Oct, daily). 2 mi S off CA 18. Phone 909/585-2519; for snow conditions phone 800/BEAR-MTN. ¢¢¢¢–¢¢¢¢¢

Snow Summit. 2 high-speed quad, 2 quad, 2 triple, 5 double chairlifts; patrol, school, rentals; snowmaking; 5 restaurants, 2 bars. Longest run 1¼ mi; vertical drop 1,200 ft. (Mid-Nov-Apr, daily) Night skiing, snowboarding. Chairlift also operates in summer (May-early Sept). ½ mi S off CA 18. Phone 909/866-5766; for snow conditions phone 909/866-4621. ¢¢¢¢-¢¢¢¢¢

Motels

★ **BIG BEAR LAKE INN.** *39471 Big Bear Blvd (92315), 2 mi W of Big Bear Lake Village. 909/866-3477; FAX 909/878-9187.* 52 rms, 2 story, 8 kit. units. S, D $89-$109; under 12 free. TV; cable. Heated pool; whirlpool. Complimentary continental bkfst. Restaurant nearby. Ck-out 11 am. Meeting rm. Downhill/x-country ski 3½ mi. Refrigerators. Picnic tables. Cr cds: A, C, DS, MC, V.

✓★ **DOC'S GETAWAY & GOLDMINE LODGE.** *42268 Moon Ridge Rd & 402 Georgia St (92315), 2 mi E of Big Bear Lake Village. 909/866-2139; FAX 909/866-3627.* 11 units, 2 story, 6 kit. suites. S, D $49-$89; kit. suites $69-$145; ski plans. Crib free. TV; cable (premium). Playground. Complimentary continental bkfst. Coffee in rms. Restaurant nearby. Ck-out 11 am. Downhill/x-country ski 1 mi. Whirlpool. Lawn games. Microwaves avail; fireplace in suites. Picnic tables, grills. Set amid pine forest in San Bernardino Mountains. Cr cds: A, C, DS, MC, V.

★★ **ESCAPE FOR ALL SEASONS.** *41935 Switzerland Dr (92321), at base of Snow Summit Ski Area. 909/866-7504; FAX 909/866-7507.* 60 kit. suites, 2 story. Nov-Mar: kit. suites $120-$360; wkly rates; lower rates rest of yr. Crib avail. TV; cable (premium), VCR (free movies). Ck-out 10 am. Business servs avail. Mountain biking. Downhill/x-country ski adj. Microwaves, fireplaces. Most balconies. Cr cds: A, C, DS, MC, V.

★★ **MARINA RIVIERA RESORT.** *40770 Lakeview Dr (92315), center of Big Bear Lake Village. 909/866-7545; FAX 909/866-6705; res: 800/600-6000.* 42 rms, 3 story, 3 kit. units. S, D $99-$135; each addl $8; kit. units $165-$295. Crib $6. TV; cable (premium). Heated pool; whirlpool. Complimentary continental bkfst. Complimentary coffee in rms. Restaurant adj 5 am-11 pm. Ck-out 11 am. Business servs avail. Downhill/x-country ski 1 mi. Driving cage, putting green. Refrigerators; some fireplaces, in-rm whirlpools. Balconies, patios. Picnic tables, grills. Lawn games. Rms overlook lake. Private beach. Cr cds: A, C, DS, MC, V.

★★ **ROBIN HOOD INN.** *40797 Lakeview Dr (92315), center of Big Bear Lake Village. 909/866-4643; FAX 909/866-4645; res: 800/990-9956.* E-mail robinhoodinn@bigbear.net; web www.robinhoodinn.com. 23 rms, 2 story, 5 suites. S, D $49-$159; suite $84-$199; higher rates hols. Pet accepted, some restrictions. TV; cable, VCR avail (free movies). Restaurant opp 6 am-11 pm. Ck-out 11 am. Meeting rm. Business servs avail. Downhill/x-country ski ½ mi. Whirlpool. Massage. Many refrigerators, some fireplaces, wet bars. Grill, picnic table, sun deck. Cr cds: A, C, MC, V.

✓★★ **WILDWOOD RESORT.** *40210 Big Bear Blvd (92315), ½ mi W of Big Bear Lake Village. 909/878-2178; FAX 909/878-3036; res: 888/294-5396.* Web www.wildwoodresort.com/cabinshtm. 5 rms in main bldg, 2 story, 14 kit. cottages. S, D $49-$85; kit. cottages $70-$180; wkly rates. Pet accepted; $10/day. TV; cable, VCR avail. Heated pool; whirlpool. Playground. Complimentary coffee in rms/cottages. Restaurant nearby. Ck-out 11 am. Downhill/x-country ski 3 mi. Many fireplaces. Lawn games. Picnic tables, grills. Cr cds: A, C, DS, MC, V.

Motor Hotels

★★★ **HOLIDAY INN BIG BEAR CHATEAU.** *42200 Moonridge Rd (92315), 2 mi E of Big Bear Lake Village. 909/866-6666; FAX 909/866-8988; res: 800/232-7466.* 80 rms, 3 story. S, D $79-$300; each addl $10; suites $150-$600. TV; cable. Heated pool; whirlpool. Restaurant 7 am-2 pm, 5-9 pm. Rm serv. Bar 5 pm-2 am; entertainment wkends. Ck-out noon.

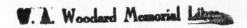

Meeting rms. Business servs avail. Bellhops. Downhill ski 1 mi. Fireplaces; microwaves avail. Balconies. European chateau-style decor. Cr cds: A, C, D, DS, JCB, MC, V.

D SC

★★★ **NORTHWOODS RESORT.** *40650 Village Dr (92315), W end of Big Bear Lake Village. 909/866-3121; FAX 909/878-2122; res: 800/866-3121.* E-mail info@northwoodsresort.com; web www.northwoods resort.com. 151 rms, 4 story, 9 suites. S, D $134-$194; each addl $10; suites $199-$499; under 18 free; ski plans; hol wkends (2-day min). Crib free. TV; cable. Heated pool; whirlpool, poolside serv. Coffee in rms. Restaurant 7 am-10 pm. Rm serv. Bar 3 pm-midnight. Ck-out noon. Meeting rms. Business servs avail. Bellhops. Concierge. Gift shop. Downhill/x-country ski 2 mi. Exercise equipt; sauna. Bicycles. Massage. Some fireplaces. Some wet bar, whirlpool, refrigerator in suites. Some patios, balconies. Cr cds: A, C, D, DS, MC, V.

D SC

Inns

★★★ **EAGLES NEST BED & BREAKFAST.** *41675 Big Bear Blvd (92315), E of Big Bear Lake Village. 909/866-6465; FAX 909/866-6025.* Web www.bigbear.com/enbb. 5 rms, 2 story, 5 cottages. S, D $75-$150; wkly rates. Pet accepted, some restrictions. TV. Full bkfst. Coffee in rms. Whirlpool. Ck-out 11 am, ck-in 2 pm. Downhill/x-country ski ¼ mi. Refrigerators, microwaves in cottages. Fireplaces. Western decor; antiques. Cr cds: A, C, DS, MC, V.

SC

★★★ **SWITZERLAND HAUS BED & BREAKFAST.** *41829 Switzerland Dr (92315). 909/866-3729; FAX 909/866-3729; res: 800/335-3729.* 5 rms, 4 with shower only, 2 story. No A/C. No rm phones. S, D $115-$145; each addl $20; suite $165-$175. TV; cable, VCR (movies). Complimentary full bkfst. Coffee in rms. Restaurant nearby. Ck-out 11 am, ck-in 2 pm. Downhill ski; x-country ski on site. Sauna. Fireplace. Refrigerator, microwave in suite. Totally nonsmoking. Cr cds: A, C, DS, MC, V.

Restaurant

★★ **BLUE WHALE LAKESIDE RESTAURANT.** *350 Alden Rd (92315), 2 blks E of Big Bear Lake Village. 909/866-5771.* Web www.cabiz.com. Hrs: 3-10 pm; Fri to 11 pm; Sat noon-midnight; Sun 9 am-10 pm; Sun brunch to 2 pm. Res accepted. Bar. Semi-a la carte: lunch $5.75-$7.50, dinner $13.95-$19.95. Sun brunch $9.95. Child's meals. Specializes in fresh seafood, beef, regional items. Oyster/sushi bar (summer). Salad bar. Pianist wkends. Parking. Outdoor dining. Late 19th-century building. Boat dock; view of lake. Cr cds: A, C, DS, MC, V.

Big Sur (G-1)

(See also Carmel, Carmel Valley, Monterey, Pacific Grove)

Pop 1,000 (est) **Elev** 155 ft **Area Code** 408 **Zip** 93920
Information Pfeiffer-Big Sur State Park, Big Sur Station #1; 408/667-2315

Big Sur is 30 miles south of Monterey on CA 1, with the Santa Lucia Range on the east and the Pacific Ocean on the west. **Pfeiffer-Big Sur State Park** contains a coast redwood forest. Recreational opportunities include swimming and hiking. Picnicking and camping facilities are available (fee for camping). There is also a lodge, gift shop and store. Naturalist programs are offered. Standard fees. Day use, per vehicle **¢¢¢**

Lodge

★★★★ **POST RANCH INN.** *Hwy 1 (93920), 26 mi S on CA 1. 831/667-2200; FAX 408/667-2824; res: 800/527-2200.* This architectural treehouse perched on the Big Sur coast offers dramatic ocean and mountain views. Rooms are luxuriously appointed with king-sized beds, fireplaces, and private porches with unsurpassed views. 30 rms. S, D $395-$695; each addl $50; 2-day min wkends. Heated pool. Complimentary continental bkfst. Complimentary refreshments in rms. Restaurant (see SIERRA MAR) serves regional California cuisine complemented with an excellent wine list. Rm serv. Ck-out 1 pm, ck-in 4 pm. Business servs avail. Luggage handling. Exercise equipt. Massage. In-rm whirlpools, refrigerators, fireplaces. Free wine tasting Sat. Cr cds: A, C, MC, V.

D

Inn

★★★ **VENTANA.** *CA 1 (93920). 831/667-2331; FAX 831/667-0573; res: 800/628-6500.* E-mail sabavnza@ventana.com; web www.ven tanainn.com. 62 rms, 1-2 story. S, D $340-$850; each addl $50; suites $525-$850. TV; cable, VCR (movies). 2 heated pools; poolside serv (summer). Complimentary continental bkfst; afternoon refreshments. Dining rm (see VENTANA). Picnics. Bar 11 am-midnight. Ck-out 1 pm, ck-in 4:30 pm. Luggage handling. Exercise equipt; sauna. Massage. Wet bars; many fireplaces; some whirlpools. Balconies. Sun deck. Cr cds: A, C, D, DS, MC, V.

D

Restaurants

★★★★ **CIELO.** *(See Ventana Inn) 831/667-2331.* E-mail sabaunzq@ventana.com; web www.go-dining.com. Contemporary California cuisine and friendly service, in additional to a remarkable view, are what make this restaurant overlooking the Pacific Ocean a lovely place to dine. Hrs: noon-3 pm, 6-9 pm; Fri-Sun & hols 11 am-3 pm, 6-9:30 pm; Grill menu 4-5 pm. Winter hrs vary. Res accepted (dinner). Bar to midnight; Mon-Thurs to 11 pm. A la carte entrees: lunch $9.50-$17, dinner $8.50-$30. Specializes in California dishes. Own baking. Outdoor dining (lunch). Totally nonsmoking. Cr cds: A, C, D, DS, MC, V.

D

★ **NEPENTHE.** *CA 1, 2½ Mi S Big Sur Riv (93920). 831/667-2345.* Hrs: 11:30 am-10 pm. No A/C. Bar. Semi-a la carte: lunch $9.75-$15.75, dinner $9.25-$24.50. Specializes in roast chicken, steak, fresh fish. Parking. Outdoor dining. 40-mile view of Pacific coastline. Family-owned. Cr cds: A, C, MC, V.

D

★★★★ **SIERRA MAR RESTAURANT.** *(See Post Ranch Inn) 831/667-2800.* Dangling off a cliff over the Pacific Ocean, this elegant restaurant serves contemporary American food, what some would call California cuisine, with an emphasis on fresh produce. The views are extraordinary. Ecletic California cuisine menu. Menu changes daily. Hrs: noon-4 pm, 5:30-9:30 pm. Res recommended dinner only. Bar. Extensive wine list. A la carte entrees: lunch $7-$18, dinner $29.50-$33.50. Prix fixe dinner $63 per person. Outdoor dining (lunch only). Totally nonsmoking. Cr cds: A, C, MC, V.

D

Bishop (E-5)

Pop 3,475 **Elev** 4,147 ft **Area Code** 760 **Zip** 93514
E-mail bishop@schat.com **Web** www.bishopvisitor.com

Information Bishop Area Chamber of Commerce and Visitors Bureau, 690 N Main St; 760/873-8405

What to See and Do

Ancient Bristlecone Pine Forest. These trees are estimated to be more than 4,600 yrs old, making them some of the oldest known living trees on earth. Naturalist programs. White Mt Rd District Visitor Center (July 4-Labor Day, Mon-Fri). In the White and Inyo mountains of the Inyo National Forest (see). CA 168 E from Big Pine to White Mt Rd to Schulman Grove & Patriarch Grove. Contact visitor center, 798 N Main St, phone 760/873-2500; or Supervisor, 873 N Main St, phone 760/873-2400.

Laws Railroad Museum & Historical Site. Laws Post Office with old-fashioned equipment, 1883 depot, narrow-gauge locomotive, restored station agent's five-rm house; hand-operated gallows-type turntable used 1883-1960, when Laws was the northern terminus of the Laws-Keeler Branch of the Southern Pacific RR; water tower, pumphouse; mining exhibits; library and arts building; Western building; pioneer building; firehouse; bottle house; doctor's office; country store; Native American exhibit. (Daily, weather permitting; closed Jan 1, Thanksgiving, Dec 25) 5 mi NE on US 6, then ½ mi E on Silver Canyon Rd. Phone 760/873-5950. **Donation**

Annual Events

Mule Days. Mule show and sale; concerts; barbecue; parade. Memorial Day wkend.

Tri-County Fair, Wild West Rodeo. Labor Day wkend.

Motels

★★ **BEST WESTERN HOLIDAY SPA LODGE.** *1025 N Main St (93514). 760/873-3543; FAX 760/872-4777; res: 800/528-1234.* 89 rms, 1-2 story. S $60-$87; D $84-$97; each addl $5; higher rates hols. Crib $10. Pet accepted, some restrictions. TV; cable (premium). Pool; whirlpool. Complimentary coffee in rms. Ck-out 11 am. Coin lndry. X-country ski 20 mi. Fish cleaning, freezer facilities. Refrigerators, microwaves. Cr cds: A, C, D, DS, JCB, MC, V.

D SC

✓★ **BISHOP THUNDERBIRD MOTEL.** *190 W Pine St (93514). 760/873-4215; FAX 760/873-6870; res: 800/828-2473.* 23 rms, 2 story. S $36-$55; D $44-$65; each addl $4. Crib $4. Pet accepted, some restrictions; $4. TV; cable (premium). Coffee in rms. Restaurant nearby. Ck-out 11 am. X-country ski 20 mi. Refrigerators, microwaves. Cr cds: A, C, D, DS, MC, V.

SC

★ **COMFORT INN.** *805 N Main St (93514). 760/873-4284; FAX 760/873-8563; res: 800/576-4080.* 52 rms, 2 story. S $64-$84; D $74-$84; each addl $5; suites $84-$90; higher rates hols. Crib $5. Pet accepted. TV; cable (premium). Heated pool; whirlpool. Complimentary continental bkfst. Complimentary coffee in rms. Restaurant nearby. Ck-out 11 am. Coin lndry. Fish cleaning, freezer facilities. Refrigerators, microwaves; some wet bars. Picnic tables, grill. Cr cds: A, C, D, DS, MC, V.

D SC

★ **MOTEL 6.** *1005 N Main St (93514). 760/873-8426; FAX 760/873-8060; res: 800/800-8000; res: 800/662-1162.* 52 units, 2 story, 2 kits. S $39.95-$46; D $54-$64.95; each addl $10; kit. units $10 addl; higher rates: wkends, hols. Crib free. TV; cable (premium). Heated pool; whirlpool. Complimentary coffee in lobby. Restaurant opp open 24 hrs. Ck-out 11 am. Business servs avail. Fish clean & store. Refrigerators. Cr cds: A, C, D, DS, MC, V.

D SC

Inns

✓★★ **CHALFANT HOUSE BED & BREAKFAST.** *213 Academy St (93514). 760/872-1790.* E-mail chalfantbb@gnet.com. 7 rms, 6 with shower only, 2 story, 2 suites, 1 kit. unit. No rm phones. S $55-$65; D $60-$70; each addl $15; suites $80-$90; kit. unit $90. Children over 8 yrs only. TV in some rms; cable, VCR avail (movies). Complimentary full bkfst. Restaurant nearby. Ck-out 7 am, ck-in 10 pm. Downhill/x-country ski 15 mi. Picnic tables. Built in 1898; antiques. Totally nonsmoking. Cr cds: A, C, DS, MC, V.

★ **THE MATLICK HOUSE BED & BREAKFAST.** *1313 Rowan Ln (93514). 760/873-3133; res: 800/898-3133.* Web www.innermind.net. 5 rms, 2 story. D $75-$85; under 6 free; wkly rates. Complimentary full bkfst. Restaurant nearby. Ck-out 11 am, ck-in 4 pm. Remodeled farmhouse built 1906; sitting rm with fireplace. Totally nonsmoking. Cr cds: A, C, DS, MC, V.

Restaurants

✓★★ **FIREHOUSE GRILL.** *2206 N Sierra Hwy (93514). 760/873-4888.* Hrs: 4:30-10 pm; early-bird dinner to 6 pm. Res accepted. Bar. Semi-a la carte: dinner $10-$18. Specializes in rack of lamb, fresh fish, choice of fresh meats. Cr cds: A, C, D, DS, MC, V.

D

✓★ **INYO COUNTRY STORE & RESTAURANT.** *177 Academy St (93514). 760/872-2552.* Hrs: 8 am-5 pm; Thurs-Sat to 9 pm. Closed Sun; Dec 25. Res accepted. Italian, Amer menu. A la carte entrees: bkfst, lunch $2.95-$8.95, dinner $4.95-$6.95. Semi-a la carte: dinner $7.95-$19.95. Specializes in lamb, steak, Northern Italian cuisine. Gift shop; deli. Totally nonsmoking. Cr cds: A, C, DS, MC, V.

★ **WHISKEY CREEK.** *524 N Main St (93514). 760/873-7174.* Hrs: 7 am-9 pm; June-Sept to 10 pm. Closed Dec 25. Res accepted. Bar. Semi-a la carte: bkfst $2.25-$9.95, lunch $4.50-$10.95, dinner $8.95-$19.95. Child's meals. Specializes in barbecue, beef, seafood. Outdoor dining. Country decor. Gift shop. Cr cds: A, C, D, DS, MC, V.

D SC

Blythe (J-6)

Settled 1910 **Pop** 8,428 **Elev** 270 ft **Area Code** 760 **Zip** 92225

Information Chamber of Commerce, 201 S Broadway; 760/922-8166 or 800/443-5513

Thomas Blythe, an Englishman, came here with an idea of turning this portion of the Colorado River Valley into another Nile River Valley. The techniques of modern irrigation have allowed that dream to come true as a series of dams has converted the desert into rich farmland and a vast recreational area. There is still some mining in the Palo Verde Valley and rockhounding is good in some nearby areas.

What to See and Do

Canoe trips. 1-5-day self-guided trips on lower Colorado River. Fishing, boating, waterskiing, camping. Canoe rentals; delivery and pickup. For schedule and fee information contact Desert Canoe Rentals, 12400 14th Ave; phone 760/922-8753.

Cibola National Wildlife Refuge. Large flocks of Canada geese, ducks, sandhill cranes and wintering passerine birds. Swimming; fishing, hunting; boating. Picnicking. Visitor center (Mon-Fri; closed hols). (Daily) 17 mi S of I-10, on Colorado River near Cibola, AZ. Contact PO Box AP; phone 520/857-3253.

Indian Lore Monument. Giant intaglio pictographs. 15 mi N on US 95.

Palo Verde Lagoon. A natural lake with fishing, picnicking and camping facilities. 20 mi S on CA 78.

Riverfront camping. There are 30 camps for sports enthusiasts along the banks of the Colorado, Mayflower Park among them. Approx 30,000-50,000 people visit here each winter to hunt deer, duck, pheasant, quail, doves and geese, and to fish for bass, crappie, bluegill and catfish.

Annual Events

Colorado River Country Music Festival. Bluegrass music. 3rd wkend Jan.

Colorado River Country Fair. Mid-Apr.

Motels

★★ **BEST WESTERN INN.** *825 W Hobson Way (92225). 760/922-7105; FAX 760/922-5836; res: 800/528-1234.* 47 rms. S $49-$66; D $54-$70; each addl $5; under 12 free; higher rates special events. Crib free. Pet accepted. TV; cable, (premium), VCR. Pool; whirlpool. Complimentary continental bkfst. Complimentary coffee in rms. Restaurant opp 5 am-11 pm. Ck-out noon. Refrigerators, microwaves. Cr cds: A, C, D, DS, ER, MC, V.

D SC

✓★ **COMFORT INN.** *903 W Hobson Way (92225). 760/922-4146; FAX 760/922-8481; res: 800/638-7949.* 48 rms, 2 story. S $48-$58; D $52-$65; each addl $5; under 18 free; higher rates special events. Crib free. Pet accepted. TV; cable (premium). Pool. Complimentary continental bkfst. Restaurant opp 5 am-11 pm. Ck-out noon. Refrigerators; microwaves avail. Cr cds: A, C, D, DS, ER, MC, V.

SC

★★ **HAMPTON INN.** *900 W Hobson Way (92225). 760/922-9000; FAX 760/922-9011.* 59 rms, 2 story. Jan-May: S $60-$95; D $68-$105; under 18 free; higher rates special events; lower rates rest of yr. Crib free. TV; cable (premium), VCR. Complimentary continental bkfst. Coffee in rms. Restaurant nearby. Ck-out 11 am. Meeting rm. Business servs avail. In-rm modem link. Coin lndry. Exercise equipt. Pool; whirlpool. Bathrm phones, refrigerators, microwaves. Cr cds: A, C, D, DS, MC, V.

D SC

★ **TRAVELODGE.** *850 W Hobson Way (92225). 760/922-5145; FAX 760/922-8422; res: 800/578-7878.* 50 rms, 34 with shower only, 2 story. S, D $46-$58; each addl $4; under 14 free; wkly rates. Crib free. Pet accepted, some restrictions; $25 deposit. TV; cable (premium). Pool. Complimentary continental bkfst. Complimentary coffee in rms. Restaurant adj 5 am-11 pm. Ck-out 11 am. Refrigerators; microwaves avail. Picnic tables, grills. Cr cds: A, C, D, DS, ER, JCB, MC, V.

D SC

Bodega Bay (D-2)

(See also Inverness, Santa Rosa)

Settled 1835 **Pop** 1,127 **Elev** 120 ft **Area Code** 707 **Zip** 94923

Motel

★★ **BODEGA COAST INN.** *521 Coast Hwy (94923). 707/875-2217; FAX 707/875-2964; res: 800/346-6999.* 45 rms, 3 story. Apr-Nov: S, D $109-$259; each addl $10; under 18 free; lower rates rest of yr. Crib free. TV; cable (premium), VCR (movies $4.50). Complimentary continental bkfst. Complimentary coffee in rms. Ck-out noon. Meeting rm. Business servs avail. Refrigerators; microwaves avail. Balconies. Bay view. Cr cds: A, C, D, DS, MC, V.

D SC

Motor Hotels

★★★ **BODEGA BAY LODGE RESORT & SPA.** *103 Coast Hwy 1 (94923), ½ mi S on CA 1. 707/875-3525; FAX 707/875-2428; res: 800/368-2468.* Web www.woodsidehotels.com. 78 rms, 2 story. No A/C. S, D $150-$375; each addl $10; under 18 free. Crib free. TV; cable. Heated pool; whirlpool. Complimentary coffee in rms. Restaurant (see DUCK CLUB). Ck-out 11:30 am. Meeting rms. Business servs avail. In-rm modem link. Exercise equipt; sauna. Refrigerators, fireplaces; some wet bars; microwaves avail. Private patios, balconies. Overlooks ocean, beach. Cr cds: A, C, D, DS, MC, V.

D

★★★ **INN AT THE TIDES.** *800 Coast Hwy # 1 (94923). 707/875-2751; FAX 707/875-2669; res: 800/541-7788.* 86 rms, 2 story. No A/C. S, D $139-$249; each addl $20; under 12 free; golf plan. Crib free. TV; cable (premium). Pool; whirlpool. Complimentary continental bkfst. Restaurant (see BAY VIEW ROOM). Rm serv 8-11 am, 5-9 pm. Bar from 5 pm; closed Mon, Tues. Ck-out 11 am. Meeting rms. Business servs avail. In-rm modem link. Exercise equipt; sauna. Refrigerators; some fireplaces. Some private patios. Opp Bodega Bay. Cr cds: A, C, DS, JCB, MC, V.

D SC

Inns

★★ **BAY HILL MANSION BED & BREAKFAST.** *3919 Bayhill Rd (94923). 707/875-3577; FAX 707/875-9456.* 5 rms, 3 share bath, 2 story. June-Sept: S, D $95-$200; each addl $20. Children over 12 yrs only. TV in sitting rm. Complimentary full bkfst; afternoon refreshments. Restaurant nearby. Ck-out 11:30 am, ck-in 4 pm. Business servs avail. In-rm modem link. Whirlpool. Decks with view of Bodega Bay and ocean. Gazebo. Totally nonsmoking. Cr cds: A, C, DS, MC, V.

SC

★★★ **INN AT OCCIDENTAL.** *3657 Church St (95465), E on CA 12, N on Bohemian Hwy for approx 4 mi . 707/874-1047; FAX 707/874-1078; res: 800/522-6324.* E-mail innkeeper@innatoccidental.com; web www.innatoccidental.com. 16 rms, 15 w/fireplaces all w/sitting rms, 1 w/private patio and hot-tub, 11 w/tub spa for 2, 2 bldgs, 8 with A/C. S, D $180-$270; 2-day min wkends, hols. Children over 12 yrs only. Complimentary full bkfst; afternoon refreshments, Sonoma County wine/hors d'oeuvres. Guest rooms offer feather beds, down comforters and garden views. Ck-out noon, ck-in 3 pm. Business servs avail. Luggage handling. Concierge serv. Rec rm. Many fireplaces. Totally nonsmoking. Cr cds: A, C, DS, MC, V.

D SC

★★★ **SONOMA COAST VILLA INC.** *16702 Coast Hwy 1 (94922). 707/876-9818; FAX 707/876-9856; res: 888/404-2255.* E-mail reservations@scvilla.com; web www.scvilla.com. 12 rms, 6 with shower only. No A/C. May-Nov: S, D $255-$295; under 12 free; wkends, hols (2-

day min). TV; VCR (free movies). Complimentary bkfst. Complimentary coffee in rms. Ck-out 11 am, ck-in 3-6 pm. Business servs avail. Concierge serv. Pool; whirlpool. Game rm. Putting green. Refrigerators, fireplaces. Some in-rm whirlpools. On 60 acres. Totally nonsmoking. Cr cds: A, C, DS, MC, V.

D

Restaurants

★★ **BAY VIEW RESTAURANT.** *(See Inn at the Tides) 707/875-2751.* Web www.innatthetides.com. Hrs: 5-10 pm. Closed Mon, Tues. Res accepted. Contemporary Amer menu. Bar. A la carte entrees: dinner $14.95-$26.50. Parking. View of bay. Cr cds: A, C, DS, JCB, MC, V.

D

★★ **DUCK CLUB RESTAURANT.** *(See Bodega Bay Lodge) 707/875-3525.* Web www.woodsidehotels.com. Hrs: 8-10 am, 6-9 pm. Res accepted. Wine, beer. Complete meal: bkfst $5-$12.95, dinner $10.95-$28.95. Child's meals. Specializes in seafood, duck. Casually elegant decor. Totally nonsmoking. Cr cds: A, C, D, DS, MC, V.

D

★★ **LUCAS WHARF.** *595 CA 1 (94923). 707/875-3522.* Hrs: 11 am-9:30 pm; wkends to 10 pm. Closed Thanksgiving, Dec 25. Bar. Semi-a la carte: lunch, dinner $6.95-$17. Child's meals. Specializes in fresh local seafood. Parking. Windows overlook bay and fishing boats. Totally nonsmoking. Cr cds: C, DS, MC, V.

D

Borrego Springs (K-5)

Pop 2,244 **Elev** 700 ft **Area Code** 760 **Zip** 92004
E-mail borspcoc@znet.com **Web** www.borregosprings.com
Information Chamber of Commerce, PO Box 420; 760/767-5555 or 800/559-5524.

Artifacts from the area show that nomadic tribes lived here at least 5,000 years ago. Although prospectors and cattle ranchers had driven through the desert in the late 19th century, it wasn't until 1906 that the first permanent white settler arrived.

In the winter and spring, wildflowers transform the desert's valleys, canyons and washes into a rainbow of colors, creating an oasis of this charming resort village in the midst of the desert.

What to See and Do

Anza-Borrego Desert State Park (see). Approx 600,000 acres surrounding Borrego Springs. Hiking, nature and bridle trails. Picnicking. Camping. Visitor center with underground desert museum. Phone 760/767-5311. Day use **¢¢**; Camping **¢¢¢¢**; Museum **Free**

Motels

★★ **BORREGO SPRINGS RESORT HOTEL.** *1112 Tilting T Dr (92004). 760/767-3330; FAX 760/767-5710; res: 888/264-6539; res: 888/826-7734.* E-mail borregospringsresorthotel@juno.com. 100 rms, 2 story, 36 suites. Nov-May: S, D $100; suites $125; under 10 free; golf plans; package plans; wkends 2-day min Nov-May; lower rates rest of yr. Crib free. Pet accepted; $100 deposit. TV; cable. Complimentary continental bkfst. Restaurant (See BORREGO SPRINGS COUNTRY CLUB). Ck-out noon. Meeting rms. Business servs avail. In-rm modem link. Sundries. Coin Indry. Free airport transportation. Lighted tennis. 18-hole golf, greens fee $49-$59, pro, putting green, driving range. Exercise equipt. Pool; whirlpool. Refrigerators, microwaves, wet bars. Many balconies. Picnic tables, grills. Cr cds: A, C, D, DS, MC, V.

D SC

★★ **PALM CANYON RESORT.** *221 Palm Canyon Dr (92004). 760/767-5341; FAX 760/767-4073; res: 800/242-0044.* 60 rms, 2 story. Nov-May: S, D $75-$150; under 12 free; lower rates rest of yr. Crib free. TV; cable; VCR avail. Pool; whirlpool. Complimentary coffee in rms. Ck-out noon. Coin Indry. Sundries. Gift shop. Grocery store. Some refrigerators. Cr cds: A, C, D, DS, MC, V.

D

Resort

★★★ **LA CASA DEL ZORRO.** *3845 Yaqui Pass Rd (92004), at Borrego Springs Rd, 5 mi SE of Christmas Circle. 760/767-5323; FAX 760/767-4782; res: 800/824-1884.* www.lacasadelzorro.com. 77 units, 19 cottages. Feb-Apr: S, D $105-$385; suites $260-$340; cottages $225-$825; under 8 free; lower rates rest of yr. Crib free. Valet Parking. TV; cable (premium), VCR avail, movies, Nintendo avail. Supervised child's activities (hols & special occasions by prior arrangement). Restaurant (see LA CASA DEL ZORRO). Rm serv. Bar 11-2 am; nightly entertainment. Ck-out noon, ck-in 4 pm. Conference facilities. Meeting rms. International teleconferencing. Business servs avail. Bellhops. Gift shop. 3 Heated pools; lap pool, exercise pool, whirlpools. 6 Lighted tennis cts, pro. Bicycles. Lawn games. Putting green. Fitness center. Salon, spa services. Massage. Some fireplaces; microwaves avail. 18-hole golf course nearby. Cr cds: A, C, D, DS, MC, V.

D SC

Inns

★ **BORREGO VALLEY INN.** *405 Palm Canyon Dr (92004). 760/767-0311; FAX 760/767-0900; res: 800/333-5810.* 14 rms. Feb-May: S, D $80-$155; wkends 2-day min; lower rates rest of yr. TV; cable, VCR avail. Complimentary continental bkfst. Restaurant nearby. Business servs avail. In-rm modem link. Free airport transportation. Outdoor pool; whirlpool. Many refrigerators, microwaves, wet bars. Some fireplaces. Picnic tables, grills. Totally nonsmoking. Cr cds: A, C, DS, MC, V.

D SC

★★ **PALMS AT INDIAN HEAD.** *2220 Hoberg Rd (92004). 760/767-7788; FAX 760/767-9717; res: 800/519-2624.* E-mail thepalms1@juno.com. 10 rms, 2 story. No rm phones. Nov-May: S, D $99-$139; lower rates rest of yr. TV; cable, VCR avail. Restaurant 11 am-2 pm, 5-9 pm. Ck-out noon, ck-in 3 pm. The former Hoberg Resort Hotel. Totally nonsmoking. Cr cds: C, D, DS, MC, V.

Restaurants

✓★ **BERNARD'S.** *503 The Mall (92004). 760/767-5666.* Hrs: 11 am-10 pm. Closed Sun. Res accepted. Continental menu. Bar. Semi-a la carte: lunch $4.25-$8.25, dinner $8-$14.95. Specialties: Wienerschnitzel, roast pork. Casual decor. Totally nonsmoking. Cr cds: C, DS, MC, V.

D

★★ **BORREGO'S KITCHEN.** *(See Borrego Springs Resort Hotel) 760/767-5173.* E-mail borregospringsresorthotel@juno.com. Hrs: 11 am-3 pm, 5-9 pm; Fri, Sat 5-10 pm. Closed Mon. Res accepted. Continental menu. Bar. Semi-a la carte: bkfst $9.95, lunch $5-$12, dinner $13-$21. Child's meals. Specializes in steaks, seafood. Entertainment Fri, Sat. Parking. Outdoor dining. Totally nonsmoking. Cr cds: A, C, D, DS, MC, V.

D

✓★ **D & E'S.** *818 Palm Canyon Dr (92004). 760/767-4954.* Hrs: 5-9 pm. Closed Sun; Dec 25; also July, Aug. Res accepted. Wine, beer. Semi-a la carte: dinner $5-$12.50. Specializes in pasta, seafood. Casual decor. Cr cds: C, MC, V.

★★★ **LA PAVILLION AT RAMS HILL.** *1881 Rams Hill Rd (92004). 760/767-5000.* Hrs: 11:30 am-3 pm, 5-9 pm; Mon to 2 pm; Sun to 2 pm (brunch). Res accepted. Continental menu. Bar 11 am-midnight. Semi-a la carte: lunch $5.95-$10.95, dinner $12.95-$28. Specialties: rack of lamb, filet mignon. Outdoor dining. Contemporary artwork. Cr cds: A, C, MC, V.

D

★★★ **PRESIDIO AT LA CASA DEL ZORRO.** *(See La Casa Del Zorro Resort) 760/767-5323.* Hrs: 7 am-10 pm; Res accepted. Bar 11 am-midnight; Fri & Sat to 2 am. Extensive wine list. Semi-a la carte: bkfst $3.50-$11, lunch $6-$14, dinner $16-$28. Child's meals. Specializes in steak, fresh seafood. Cr cds: A, C, D, DS, MC, V.

D

Bridgeport (D-4)

(See also Coleville, Lee Vining)

Pop 500 (est) **Elev** 6,473 ft **Area Code** 760 **Zip** 93517

A Ranger District office of the Toiyabe National Forest (see RENO, NV) is located here.

What to See and Do

Bodie State Historic Park. Unrestored ghost town of the late 1800s. Between 1879 and 1881 more than 10,000 people lived here. Fires in 1892 and 1932 took their toll and now only about 5 percent of the town remains. A self-guiding brochure takes you through the main part of town; church (ca 1880), jail, two-rm school, Miners Union Hall (now a museum), hillside cemetery with monument to James A. Garfield. Picnicking. 7 mi S on US 395, then 13 mi E on partially unpaved road; not cleared in winter (only accessible on foot). Phone 760/647-6445. Day use ¢¢

Yosemite National Park (see). Approx 20 mi S via US 395, then 8 mi W via CA 120.

Motels

✓★ **SILVER MAPLE INN.** *310 Main St (93517). 760/932-7383.* 20 rms. No A/C. S $60-$65; D $60-$70; each addl $10. Crib free. Pet accepted. TV; cable (premium). Complimentary coffee in rms. Restaurant opp 6 am-10 pm. Ck-out 11 am. Lawn games. Picnic tables. Grills. Cr cds: A, C, D, DS, MC, V.

D SC

★★ **WALKER RIVER LODGE.** *100 Main St (93517). 760/932-7021; FAX 760/932-7914; res: 800/388-6651.* 36 rms, 1-2 story. Mid-Apr-Oct: S $70-$135; D $75-$150; each addl $10; kit. units $95-$200; lower rates rest of yr. Crib free. Pet accepted. TV; cable (premium). Heated pool; whirlpool. Complimentary coffee in rms. Restaurant opp 6 am-2 pm. Ck-out 11 am. Business servs avail. Gift shop. Refrigerators. Some balconies. Picnic tables, grills. Fish freezer. X-country ski 12 mi. Cr cds: A, C, D, DS, MC, V.

D SC

Inn

★★★ **CAIN HOUSE.** *340 Main St (93517). 760/932-7040; FAX 760/932-7419; res: 800/433-2246.* 7 rms, 2 story. S, D $90-$140. TV; cable (premium). Complimentary full bkfst; afternoon refreshments. Complimentary coffee in rms. Restaurant nearby. Ck-out 11 am, ck-in 3 pm. Lawn games. Grills. Former residence of prominent local family. Totally nonsmoking. Cr cds: A, C, D, DS, MC, V.

Buena Park (D-5 see Los Angeles map)

(See also Anaheim, La Habra, Long Beach, Whittier)

Pop 68,784 **Elev** 74 ft **Area Code** 714 **E-mail** tourbp@buenapark.com **Web** www.buenapark.com

Information Convention & Visitors Office, 6280 Manchester Blvd, Suite 103, 90621; 714/562-3560 or 800/541-3953

What to See and Do

Knott's Berry Farm. Re-created town of gold rush days; focus on the history, heritage and culture of the West. Family entertainment park situated on 150 acres; includes rides, live entertainment, shops, food. This is the official home of Snoopy and the Peanuts characters. Farm is also noted for its berry preserves. (Daily; closed Dec 25) 8039 Beach Blvd, 2 mi S of Santa Ana Frwy (US 101, I-5) on CA 39. Phone 714/220-5200 (recording). ¢¢¢¢¢

Movieland Wax Museum. Museum houses more than 280 wax figures of Hollywood's greatest stars in more than 160 realistic movie sets; covers 70 yrs of movie history. Shop for favorite movie souvenirs and visit Chamber of Horrors. (Daily) 7711 Beach Blvd. Phone 714/522-1154. Combination ticket ¢¢¢¢¢ Includes admission to

Ripley's Believe It or Not Museum. Houses a collection of oddities and anthropological artifacts that allow visitors to experience first hand that truth is indeed stranger than fiction. (Daily) Opp Movieland. Phone 714/522-7045.

Motels

✓★ **BEST WESTERN.** *8580 Stanton Ave (90620), CA 91 Beach Blvd exit, S to Crescent Ave, E to Stanton Ave, then 2 blks S. 714/828-5211; FAX 714/826-3716; res: 800/828-1234; res: 800/646-1629.* Web www.bestwestern.com. 63 rms, 2 story, 3 suites. S, D $39-$59; suites $79-$99; under 18 free. Crib $5. TV; cable (premium). Heated pool. Complimentary continental bkfst. Restaurant adj 6 am-midnight. Ck-out noon. Coin Indry. Business servs avail. Some refrigerators; microwaves avail. Cr cds: A, C, D, DS, MC, V.

D SC

★ **COLONY INN.** *7800 Crescent Ave (90620), CA 91 exit Beach Blvd, S to Crescent Ave, 1 blk W. 714/527-2201; FAX 714/826-3826; res: 800/982-6566.* 90 units, 2 story, 8 suites. S, D $49-$54; each addl $10; suites, family units $65; under 12 free. Crib free. TV; cable (premium). Heated pool; wading pool. Complimentary continental bkfst. Restaurant adj 6 am-11 pm. Ck-out 11 am. Coin Indry. Meeting rm. Cr cds: A, C, D, DS, MC, V.

D SC

★★★ **COURTYARD BY MARRIOTT.** *7621 Beach Blvd (90620), CA 91 Beach Blvd exit, 2 blks S. 714/670-6600; FAX 714/670-0360; res: 800/321-2211.* Web www.courtyard.com. 145 rms, 11 suites, 2 story. S, D $79-$89; suites $104-$114; under 18 free; wkly rates. Crib free. TV; cable (premium). Heated pool; whirlpool. Complimentary coffee in rms. Restaurant 6-10:30 am, 5-10 pm. Bar 4-10:30 pm. Rm serv. Ck-out 1 pm. Coin Indry. Meeting rms. Business servs avail. Valet serv. Sundries. Exercise equipt. Health club privileges. Refrigerators in suites; microwaves avail. Some patios, balconies. Cr cds: A, C, D, DS, MC, V.

D SC

★★ **DYNASTY SUITES.** *13530 E Firestone Blvd (90670), approx 3 mi N on I-5, exit Carmenita Rd. 562/921-8571; FAX 562/921-2451; res: 800/842-7899.* E-mail info@dynastysuites. com; web www. dynastysuites.com. 49 rms, 2 story. S, D $49.95-$99.95, each addl $5. TV; cable (premium), VCR avail (movies). Heated pool. Complimentary continental bkfst. Restaurant adj 6 am-midnight. Ck-out noon. Coin Indry. Business servs avail. Refrigerators, microwaves. Cr cds: A, C, D, DS, MC, V.

D

✓★★ **FAIRFIELD INN.** *7032 Orangethorpe Ave (90621), CA 91 Knott Ave exit, N to Orangethorpe Ave then E 1 blk. 714/523-1488; FAX 714/523-1488; res: 800/228-2800.* Web www.marriott.com. 133 rms, 3 story. S, D $50-$60. Crib free. TV; cable (premium). Heated pool. Complimentary continental bkfst. Restaurant opp 6 am-midnight; Fri, Sat to 2 am. Ck-out noon. Business servs avail. Valet serv. Disneyland transportation. Health club privileges. Some refrigerators, microwaves. Cr cds: A, C, D, DS, MC, V.

D SC

★★ **INN SUITES HOTELS.** *7555 Beach Blvd (90620). 714/522-7360; FAX 714/523-2883; res: 888/522-5885.* Web www.innsuites.com. 185 rms, 2 story, 27 suites. S, D $69-$89; each addl $10; suites $79-$175; under 18 free. Crib free. TV; cable (premium). Heated pool; whirlpool. Playground. Complimentary coffee in lobby. Ck-out noon. Meeting rms. Business servs avail. Valet serv. Coin Indry. Free Disneyland transportation. Game rm. Exercise equipt; sauna. Some refrigerators, microwaves. Picnic tables, grill. Cr cds: A, C, D, DS, MC, V.

SC

★ **RED ROOF INN.** *7121 Beach Blvd (90620), CA 91 Beach Blvd exit, 1 blk N. 714/670-9000; FAX 714/522-7280; res: 800/538-0006.* 127 units, 4 story, 6 suites. S, D $49; each addl $4; suites $64-$70; under 19 free. Crib free. TV; cable (premium). Heated pool; whirlpool. Complimentary continental bkfst. Restaurant nearby. Ck-out 11 am. Meeting rms. Business servs avail. Health club privileges. Cr cds: A, C, D, DS, MC, V.

D SC

★★ **SUPER 8 MOTEL.** *7930 Beach Blvd (90620). 714/994-6480; FAX 714/994-3874; res: 800/800-8000; res: 800/854-6031.* 78 rms, 2 story, 40 kit. units. S $42-$50; D $44-$56; each addl $6; kit. units $42-$56; under 12 free; wkly rates. Crib free. TV; cable (premium). Heated pool; whirlpool. Complimentary continental bkfst. Complimentary coffee in rms. Restaurant adj 24 hrs. Ck-out 11 am. Business servs avail. Sundries. Coin Indry. Refrigerators; many wet bars. Some balconies. Picnic tables, grills. Cr cds: A, C, D, DS, ER, JCB, MC, V.

SC

★★ **TRAVELODGE.** *7039 Orangethorpe Ave (41101). 714/521-9220; FAX 714/521-6706; res: 800/578-7878; res: 800/854-8299.* E-mail tlbp@aol.com; web www.travelodge.com. 100 kit. units, 2 story, 12 suites. S $48-$58; D $52-$62; each addl $4; suites $115-$135; under 17 free; wkly rates. Crib free. TV; cable (premium). Pool; whirlpool. Sauna. Complimentary continental bkfst. Complimentary coffee in rms. Restaurant opp 8-1 am. Ck-out 11 am. Meeting rm. Business servs avail. Valet serv. Sundries. Coin Indry. Health club privileges. Game rm. Refrigerators; wet bars; some microwaves. Picnic tables, grills. Cr cds: A, C, D, DS, ER, JCB, MC, V.

D SC

Motor Hotels

★★★ **EMBASSY SUITES.** *7762 Beach Blvd (90620), I-5 Beach Blvd exit, 5 blks S . 714/739-5600; FAX 714/521-9650; res: 800/362-2779.* Web www.embassy-suites.com. 201 kit. suites, 4 story. S, D $129-$189; each addl $15; under 18 free. Crib free. TV; cable (premium). Heated pool; whirlpool. Complimentary full bkfst. Coffee in rms. Restaurant 11:30 am-10 pm. Rm serv. Bar 5:30-11 pm. Ck-out noon. Coin Indry. Meeting rms. Business center. In-rm modem link. Valet serv. Gift shop. Free Disneyland transportation. Game rm. Exercise equipt. Health club privileges. Refrigerators, microwaves, wetbars. Balconies. Grills. Knott's Berry Farm 1 blk. Cr cds: A, C, D, DS, JCB, MC, V.

D SC

★★★ **HOLIDAY INN.** *7000 Beach Blvd (90620), CA 91 exit Beach Blvd. 714/522-7000; FAX 714/522-3230; res: 800/465-4329.* Web www.holiday-inn.com. 245 rms, 4-5 story. S, D $99-$119; each addl $10; suites $175-$350; under 17 free. Crib free. TV; cable (premium). Heated pool; wading pool, whirlpool. Complimentary coffee in rms. Restaurants 6:30 am-10 pm. Rm serv. Bar 11 am-midnight. Ck-out noon. Coin Indry. Meeting rms. Business servs avail. In-rm modem link. Bellhops. Valet serv. Gift shop. Exercise equipt. Health club privileges. Refrigerator avail. Some patios. Cr cds: A, C, D, DS, JCB, MC, V.

D SC

Hotels

★★ **BUENA PARK HOTEL.** *7675 Crescent Ave (90620), CA 91 Beach Blvd exit, S to Crescent Ave then 1 blk W. 714/995-1111; FAX 714/828-8590; res: 800/422-4444.* E-mail bphotel@aol.com; web www.buenaparkhotel.com. 320 rms, 9 story, 8 suites. S, D $109; each addl $10; suites $199-$500; under 18 free. Crib free. TV; cable (premium). Heated pool; whirlpool, poolside serv. Coffee in rms. Restaurant 6 am-midnight. Bar 4 pm-2 am. Ck-out noon. Coin Indry. Convention facilities. Business servs avail. Concierge. Airport, Disneyland transportation. Game rm. Health club privileges. Some refrigerators. Cr cds: A, C, D, DS, JCB, MC, V.

D SC

★★★ **MARRIOTT.** *13111 Sycamore Dr (90650), N via I-5, Norwalk Blvd exit. 310/863-5555; FAX 310/868-4486; res: 800/228-9290; res: 800/442-4556.* E-mail marriott@dxnet.com; web www.marriott.com. 173 rms, 8 story, 27 suites. S, D $118-$139; suites $158-$178; wkend rates. Crib free. TV; cable (premium). Heated pool; whirlpool, poolside serv. Complimentary coffee in rms. Restaurant 6 am-10:30 pm. Bar 4-11 pm. Ck-out noon. Meeting rms. Business servs avail. In-rm modem link. Gift shop. Free Disneyland transportation. Exercise equipt. Refrigerators; microwaves avail. Cr cds: A, C, D, DS, ER, JCB, MC, V.

D SC

★★★ **SHERATON HOTEL.** *12725 Center Court Dr (90703), 4 mi W on CA 91, Bloomfield Ave exit S. 562/809-1500; FAX 562/403-2080; res: 800/544-5064.* Web www.sheraton.com. 203 units, 8 story, 23 suites. S, D $85-$180; each addl $15; suites $160-$400; under 18 free. Crib free. Pet accepted, some restrictions; $25. TV; cable (premium). Heated pool; whirlpool, poolside serv. Coffee in rms. Restaurant 6:30 am-10 pm. Rm serv 6 am-11:30 pm. Bar noon-1 am. Ck-out noon. Meeting rms. Business center. In-rm modem link. Concierge. Gift shop. Free Disneyland transportation. Exercise equipt. Refrigerators; some bathrm phones. Atrium. Cr cds: A, C, D, DS, ER, JCB, MC, V.

D SC

Restaurant

★★ **RAJDOOT INDIAN CUISINE.** *11833 Artesia Blvd (90701). 562/860-6500.* Hrs: 11:30 am-2:30 pm, 5:30-10 pm; Fri, Sat to 10:30 pm. Closed Thanksgiving, Dec 25. Res accepted. Northern Indian menu. Bar. A la carte entrees: lunch, dinner $7.95-$14.95. Specialties: samundri khazana, chicken methi, garlic chicken tikka. Entertainment Fri, Sat. Indian palace atmosphere. Totally nonsmoking. Cr cds: A, C, D, DS, MC, V.

D

Unrated Dining Spot

MEDIEVAL TIMES DINNER & TOURNAMENT. *7662 Beach Blvd (90620). 714/521-4740.* Web www.medievaltimes.com. Hrs: show at 7 pm; Fri 6:30 pm & 8:45 pm; Sat 6 pm & 8:15; Sun varies. Res required. Bar. Complete meals: adults $34.95-$35.95, children $22.95.

Medieval tournament competitions include ring piercing, javelin throwing, sword fighting, jousting. Reproduction of 11th-century castle; medieval decor. Hall of Banners and Flags. Museum of Torture. Cr cds: A, C, DS, MC, V.

D SC

Burbank (B-3)

Pop 93,643 **Elev** 598 ft **Area Code** 818

Motel

✓★★ **SAFARI INN.** *1911 W Olive Ave (91506), I-5 Olive Ave exit, SW approx 1 mi. 818/845-8586; FAX 818/845-0054; res: 800/782-4373.* 56 rms, 2 story. S,D $65-$90; each addl $5; kit. suites $84-$114; under 18 free. Crib free. TV; cable (premium). Heated pool; whirlpool. Complimentary continental bkfst. Coffee in rms. Restaurant nearby. Ck-out noon. Business servs avail. Airport transportation. Refrigerators, microwaves avail. Cr cds: A, C, D, DS, MC, V.

D SC

Hotel

★★ **HILTON.** *2500 N Hollywood Way (93010), I-5 Hollywood Way exit S 1½ mi, opp Burbank Airport. 818/843-6000; FAX 818/842-9720; res: 800/445-8667.* E-mail burhilton@aol.com; web www.hilton.com/hotels/burahhf/index.html. 486 rms, 8-9 story. S $120-$195; D $130-$205; each addl $15; suites $140-$480; under 19 free; family, wkend rates. Crib free. Pet accepted. TV; cable (premium). 2 heated pools; whirlpool, poolside serv. Complimentary coffee in rms. Restaurant 6 am-11 pm. Rm serv 24 hrs. Bar 11-2 am. Ck-out noon. Coin Indry. Convention facilities. Business center. Concierge. Gift shop. Free airport transportation. Exercise equipt; sauna. Health club privileges. Microwaves avail; refrigerator in suites. Cr cds: A, C, D, DS, ER, JCB, MC, V.

D SC

Restaurant

★★ **MI PLACE.** *801 N San Fernando Rd (91501). 818/843-1111.* Hrs: 11:30 am-11 pm; Fri, Sat to midnight. Closed Jan 1, Thanksgiving, Dec 25. Res accepted. Italian menu. Bar. A la carte entrees: lunch, dinner $5.75-$16.95. Specializes in southern Italian cuisine. Valet parking. Art deco decor. Totally nonsmoking. Cr cds: A, C, D, MC, V.

D

Burlingame

(see San Francisco Airport Area)

Burney (B-3)

(See also Mount Shasta, Redding)

Pop 3,423 **Elev** 3,130 ft **Area Code** 916 **Zip** 96013

Information Chamber of Commerce, 37088 Main St, PO Box 36; 916/335-2111

All the attractions of outdoor living are in the area surrounding Shasta Lake, Mount Shasta (see) and Lassen Volcanic National Park (see).

What to See and Do

Lassen National Forest. (See SUSANVILLE) S & E of town. In the forest is

Hat Creek Recreation Area. Fishing, picnicking, camping (fee). Geological sites include Subway Cave, a lava tube, and Spattercone, a guided volcanic nature trail. Camping and fishing facilities for the disabled. 17 mi SE on CA 89. Phone 916/336-5521.

McArthur-Burney Falls Memorial State Park. These 853 acres encompass Burney Falls (in season, water bubbles from underground springs, flows ½-mi, then drops over a precipice in 129-ft twin falls). Swimming; fishing, boat launching. Nature and hiking trails. Picnicking, concession. Camping. Naturalist program. Standard fees. 5 mi E on CA 299, then 6 mi N on CA 89. Phone 916/335-2777.

Calexico (K-6)

(See also El Centro)

Founded 1908 **Pop** 18,633 **Elev** 2 ft **Area Code** 760
Web www.calexico.com

Information Chamber of Commerce, 1100 Imperial Ave, PO Box 948, 92232; 760/357-1166

Once a tent town of the Imperial Land Company, this community at the south end of the Imperial Valley is separated from its much larger sister city, Mexicali, Mexico, by only a fence. The town represents the marriage of two diverse cultures. It serves as a port of entry to the US. (For Border Crossing Regulations see MAKING THE MOST OF YOUR TRIP.)

Motor Hotel

★★ **QUALITY INN.** *801 Imperial Ave (92231). 760/357-3271; FAX 760/357-7975.* 56 rms, 2 story. S, D $52-$59; each addl $6; suites $80; kit. units $55-$62; under 12 free. TV; cable (premium). Pool. Restaurant 6 am-10 pm. Rm serv. Ck-out noon. Meeting rms. Free covered parking. Some refrigerators. Cr cds: A, C, DS, MC, V.

D SC

Calistoga (D-2)

(See also Napa, Petaluma, Santa Rosa, Sonoma, St Helena)

Founded 1859 **Pop** 4,468 **Elev** 362 ft **Area Code** 707 **Zip** 94515
E-mail execdir@napanet.net **Web** www.napavalley.com/calistoga/

Information Chamber of Commerce, 1458 Lincoln Ave #9; 707/942-6333

Samuel Brannan, a wealthy San Francisco entrepreneur, came here in 1859 and recognized that the natural hot-water geysers, mineral springs and mineralized mud baths would support a resort community. Brannan considered the new resort the Saratoga of California; thus Calistoga. He was also among those who cultivated grape vines on the surrounding hillsides. As a result, Calistoga is a thriving resort town and center of an important wine-producing area.

What to See and Do

Mount St Helena. (4,344 ft). Extinct volcano where Robert Louis Stevenson honeymooned in 1880 and wrote "The Silverado Squatters." Robert Louis Stevenson State Park, on Mt St Helena, has monument (a statue of the author holding an open book) located near the site of the Silverado mine; ¾-mi hiking trail from parking lot. 8 mi N on CA 29.

Old Faithful Geyser of California. Approx 60-ft-high geyser is one of few, other than Yellowstone's Old Faithful, that erupts at regular intervals. Picnic area; snack bar; gift shop. (Daily; yrly avg eruption approx every 40 min) 1299 Tubbs Ln. Phone 707/942-6463. **¢¢**

Petrified Forest. Contains redwoods buried more than 3 million years ago by the eruption of Mt St Helena. The trees were knocked down by a volcanic explosion and then buried in volcanic ash. Discovered around 1860, some trees are as large as 80 ft long and 12 ft in diameter, with details excellently preserved. Picnic area. (Daily) 8 mi W on Petrified Forest Rd. Phone 707/942-6667. **¢¢**

Sharpsteen Museum and Sam Brannan Cottage. History of Calistoga in diorama and shadow box form; changing exhibits include hardware, hand mirrors, clothing, dolls, furniture. Restored cottage (1860) contains furniture of the period. (Daily; closed Thanksgiving, Dec 25) 1311 Washington St. Phone 707/942-5911. **Free**

Sterling Vineyards. Access to winery by aerial tramway; self-guided tour; shop; wine tasting. Tour includes a considerable amount of walking. Under 16 must be accompanied by adult. Roof-top terrace picnic area. (Daily; closed Jan 1, Thanksgiving, Dec 25) 1111 Dunaweal Ln. Phone 707/942-3344. Tramway **¢¢¢**

Annual Event

Napa County Fair. Fairgrounds, Oak St. July.

Motels

★ **CALISTOGA SPA HOT SPRINGS.** *1006 Washington St (94515). 707/942-6269; FAX 707/942-4214.* Web www.napavalley.com/calistoga. 57 rms with kits., 55 with shower only, 2 story. Mar-Oct: S $87; D $97-$132; each addl $7; min stay wkends, hols; lower rates rest of yr. Crib $5. TV; cable. Heated pool; wading pool, whirlpool, lifeguard. Complimentary coffee in rms. Restaurant nearby. Ck-out 11 am. Meeting rms. Business servs avail. Exercise equipt; sauna. Massage. Picnic tables. Cr cds: C, MC, V.

D

★★ **COMFORT INN.** *1865 Lincoln Ave (94515). 707/942-9400; FAX 707/942-5262; res: 800/228-5150.* Web www.comfortinn.com. 54 rms, 2 story. Mar-Oct: S $60-$150; D $75-$165; each addl $7; under 18 free; lower rates rest of yr. Crib free. TV; cable (premium). Pool; whirlpool. Sauna. Complimentary continental bkfst. Restaurant opp 5-10 pm. Ck-out 11 am. Meetings rms. In-rm modem link. Some refrigerators, microwaves. Cr cds: A, C, D, DS, JCB, MC, V.

D SC

✓★ **DR WILKINSON'S HOT SPRINGS.** *1507 Lincoln Ave (94515). 707/942-4102; FAX 707/942-6110.* Web www.drwilkinson.com. 42 units, 2 story, 16 kits. S, D $69-$139; each addl $12; kit. units $79-$149; package plans. Crib free. TV; cable. 3 heated pools, 1 indoor; whirlpool. Steam rm. Complimentary coffee in rms. Restaurant nearby. Ck-out noon. Meeting rm. Business servs avail. Massage. Many refrigerators. Victorian house (1877). Cr cds: A, C, MC, V.

SC

Hotel

★★ **MOUNT VIEW HOTEL & SPA.** *1457 Lincoln Ave (94515). 707/942-6877; FAX 707/942-6904; res: 800/816-6877.* 20 rms, 9 suites, 3 cottages. S, D $100-$225; each addl $25; suites, cottages $210-$225. TV; cable, VCR avail. Pool; whirlpool, poolside serv (summer). Complementary continental bkfst. Restaurant (see CATAHOULA). Bar 5 pm-2 am. Ck-out noon. Business servs avail. Health club privileges. Some in-rm whirlpools. Some suites with balcony. Restored hotel (1917); National Historic Monument. Old World decor. Some antiques. Cr cds: A, C, DS, MC, V.

Inns

★★ **BRANNAN COTTAGE INN.** *109 Wapoo Ave (94515). 707/942-4200.* 6 rms, 5 with shower only, 1-2 story, 2 suites. No rm phones. Apr-Nov: S, D $100-$160; each addl $25; suites $160; wkends (2-day min); lower rates rest of yr. Children over 12 yrs only. TV in common rm; cable. Complimentary full bkfst; afternoon refreshments. Restaurant nearby. Ck-out 11 am, ck-in 2 pm. Luggage handling. Refrigerators. Built by original developer of Calistoga in 1862. Totally nonsmoking. Cr cds: C, MC, V.

✓★ **CALISTOGA INN.** *1250 Lincoln Ave (94515). 707/942-4101; FAX 707/942-4914.* E-mail michael@nvbc.com. 18 rms, all share bath, 2 story. No A/C. No rm phones. S, D $49-$65. Complimentary continental bkfst. Restaurant (see CALISTOGA INN). Ck-out 11 am, ck-in 3 pm. Business servs avail. Street parking. Balconies. Built 1900. On-site brewery in old watertower. Beer garden. Totally nonsmoking. Cr cds: A, C, MC, V.

★★★ **CHRISTOPHER'S INN.** *1010 Foothill Blvd (94515). 707/942-5755; FAX 707/942-6895.* 22 rms, 5 with shower only, 2 story. Rm phones avail. S, D $125-$350; suite $165-$350. TV; cable, VCR. Complimentary continental bkfst. Restaurant nearby. Ck-out 11 am, ck-in 2 pm. Meeting rm. Business servs avail. Concierge. Some in-rm whirlpools. Fireplaces. Picnic tables. Lawn games. Built 1918; renovated to include modern amenities. English country decor; many antiques. Totally nonsmoking. Cr cds: A, C, MC, V.

★★★ **COTTAGE GROVE INN CALISTOGA.** *1711 Lincoln Ave (94515). 707/942-5500; FAX 707/942-2653; res: 800/799-2284.* Web www.cottagegrove.inn. 16 rms. S, D $195-$225; each addl $5; wkends, hols (2-day min). Children over 12 yrs only. TV; cable, VCR (movies). Complimentary continental bkfst; afternoon refreshments. Ck-out 11 am, ck-in 3-7 pm. Business servs avail. In-rm modem link. Gift shop. Refrigerators, microwaves, wet bars, fireplaces. Totally nonsmoking. Cr cds: A, C, D, DS, MC, V.

D

★★ **CULVER'S.** *1805 Foothill Blvd (94515). 707/942-4535; FAX 707/942-4535.* 4 rms, 2 story. No rm phones. S, D $140-$160. Children over 16 yrs only. Pool; whirlpool. Complimentary full bkfst; afternoon refreshments. Ck-out 11 am, ck-in 3-6 pm. Antiques. Built 1875. Totally nonsmoking. Cr cds: C.

D

★★★ **FOOTHILL BED & BREAKFAST.** *3037 Foothill Blvd (94515). 707/942-6933; FAX 707/942-5692.* Web www.foothillhouse.com. 3 rms, 1 cottage. Rm phones on request. S, D $150-$275; each addl $35. TV; cable, VCR avail (free movies). Complimentary full bkfst. Complimentary coffee in rms. Ck-out 11 am, ck-in 3 pm. Lndry facilities avail. In-rm modem link. Refrigerators, fireplaces; some in-rm whirlpools. Private patios. Remodeled turn-of-the-century farmhouse. Individually decorated rms with country antiques. Sun deck. Fish pond. Totally nonsmoking. Cr cds: A, C, D, MC, V.

SC

★★ **MEADOWLARK COUNTRY HOUSE AND INN.** *601 Petrified Forest Rd (94515). 707/942-5651; FAX 707/942-5023; res: 800/942-5651.* Web www.meadowlarkinn.com. 7 rms, 2 story. Mar-Nov: S, D $185. TV in sitting rm; cable, VCR. Pool. Complimentary full bkfst. Ck-out 11:30 am, ck-in 3:30 pm. Business servs avail. Picnic tables. English country antiques. Totally nonsmoking. Cr cds: C, MC, V.

★ **PINK MANSION.** *1415 Foothill Blvd (94515). 707/942-0558; FAX 707/942-0558; res: 800/238-7465.* Web www.pinkmansion.com. 6 rms, 3 story. Mar-Nov: S, D $135-$225; each addl $20; lower rates rest of yr. TV; VCR (free movies). Indoor heated pool, whirlpool. Complimentary full bkfst; afternoon refreshments. Restaurant nearby. Ck-out 11 am, ck-in 3 pm. Rec rm. Microwaves avail. Balconies. Antiques. Library/sitting rm. Built 1875. Country garden. Totally nonsmoking. Cr cds: C, MC, V.

SC

★★★ **SCOTT COURTYARD.** *1443 2nd St (94515). 707/942-0948; FAX 707/942-5102.* E-mail Jcourtyard@aol.com. 6 rms, 1 with shower only, 2 story, 3 kits. No rm phones. Apr-Oct: S, D $165-$185; each addl $20; wkends, hols (2-3 day min). Crib free. TV in main rm. Heated pool. Complimentary full bkfst; afternoon refreshments. Restaurant nearby. Ck-out 11:30 am, ck-in 3 pm. Business servs avail. Concierge serv. Game rm. Picnic tables. 1930s & '40s decor with many nautical items. Totally nonsmoking. Cr cds: A, C, MC, V.

★★★ **SILVER ROSE INN & SPA.** *351 Rosedale Rd (94515). 707/942-9581; FAX 707/942-0841; res: 800/995-9381.* Web www.silverrose.com. 20 rms, 2 story. S, D $165-$275; lower rates wkdays. 2 pools; 2 whirlpools. Complimentary continental bkfst; afternoon refreshments. Ck-out 11:30 am, ck-in 3-7 pm. Meeting rm. Business servs avail. In-rm modem link. Gift shop. Tennis. Putting green. Some in-rm whirlpools, fireplaces. Balconies. Picnic tables. Antiques. Library/sitting rms. Grounds surrounded by vineyards. Totally nonsmoking. Cr cds: A, C, DS, MC, V.

★★ **THE ELMS BED & BREAKFAST.** *1300 Cedar St (94515). 707/942-9476; FAX 707/942-9479.* E-mail 103702.1043@compuserve.com; web www.theelms.com. 7 rms, 5 with shower only, 3 story. No elvtr. No rm phones. Mid-Mar-mid-Jan: S, D $110-$180; lower rates rest of yr. TV; cable. Complimentary full bkfst; afternoon refreshments. Restaurant nearby. Ck-out 11 am, ck-in 3-6 pm. Concierge serv. Luggage handling. Some in-rm whirlpools. Built in 1871; antiques. Totally nonsmoking. Cr cds: C, MC, V.

D

★★ **WINE WAY INN.** *1019 Foothill Blvd (94515). 707/942-0680; res: 800/572-0679.* 6 rms, 4 with shower only, 2 story. No rm phones. S, D $90-$165; each addl $25. Crib free. Complimentary full bkfst. Restaurant nearby. Ck-out 11 am, ck-in 3 pm. Fireplace. Built 1915. Handmade quilts. Totally nonsmoking. Cr cds: A, C, DS, MC, V.

Restaurants

★ **ALEX'S RESTAURANT & PUB.** *1834 Lake St (94515). 707/942-6868.* Hrs: 4-10 pm; Sun from 3 pm; early-bird dinner Tues-Fri 4-6 pm. Closed Mon; Jan 1; also Dec. Res accepted. Bar from 3 pm. Semi-a la carte: dinner $7.50-$16.95. Child's meals. Specializes in beef, seafood. Large mural of California wine country landmarks. Family-owned. Cr cds: A, C, MC, V.

D

✓★★ **ALL SEASONS CAFE.** *1400 Lincoln Ave (94515). 707/942-9111.* Hrs: 11 am-3 pm, 6-10 pm. Closed Wed; Dec 24-25. Res accepted (dinner). Contemporary Amer menu. Bar 11 am-7 pm. A la carte entrees: lunch $5.95-$12.25, dinner $11.50-$19.50. Specializes in house-smoked poultry & fish. Own baking. Bistro-style cafe with rotating art display; wine shop on premises. Totally nonsmoking. Cr cds: C, MC, V.

D

★★ **BRANNAN'S GRILL.** *1374 Lincoln Ave (94515). 707/942-2233.* Hrs: 11:30 am-10 pm. Res accepted. Eclectic menu. Bar. A la carte entrees: lunch $7.95-$15.95, dinner $10.95-$22.95. Specialties: voodoo shrimp, creole spiced pork chop, rotisserie chicken. Own desserts. Piano Fri-Sun. Street parking. Local craftsmen & artisans works displayed. Totally nonsmoking. Cr cds: A, C, MC, V.

D

★ **CALISTOGA INN.** *(See Calistoga Inn) 707/942-4101.* E-mail michael@nvbc.com. Hrs: 11:30 am-10 pm. Wine, beer. A la carte entrees: lunch $5-$12, dinner $12-$18. Specializes in fresh seafood. Entertainment Tues-Sun. Outdoor dining. Totally nonsmoking. Cr cds: A, C, MC, V.

★★ **CATAHOULA.** *(See Mount View) 707/942-2275.* Hrs: noon-2:30 pm, 5:30-10 pm; Fri-Sun 8:30 am-3:30 pm, 5:30-10:30 pm. Closed Dec 25; also 2 wks in Jan. Res accepted. Bar. Semi-a la carte: lunch $10-$13, dinner $15-$24. Specialties: spicy gumbo yaya, braised beef short ribs with garlic mashed potatoes. Casual, contemporary dining. Cr cds: C, MC, V.

D

★ **HYDRO BAR & GRILL.** *1403 Lincoln Ave (94515). 707/942-9777.* Hrs: 7 am-11 pm; Fri, Sat to midnight. Closed Dec 25. Bar. A la carte entrees: bkfst $4.95-$7.95, lunch $5-$11.50, dinner $8-$16. Child's meals. Specialties: seared salmon on buckwheat noodles, spinach salad with roasted shallot. Own desserts. Musicians Wed-Sun. Contemporary decor. Totally nonsmoking. Cr cds: C, MC, V.

D

✓★ **PACIFICO.** *1237 Lincoln Ave (94515). 707/942-4400.* Hrs: 11 am-10 pm; Sat, Sun from 10 am; Sat, Sun brunch to 3 pm. Closed Thanksgiving, Dec 25. Mexican menu. Bar to 11 pm. Semi-a la carte: lunch $3.75-$7.50, dinner $5.95-$13.95. Sat, Sun brunch $3.75-$7.50. Child's meals. Specializes in authentic Mexican dishes. Cr cds: C, MC, V.

D

✓★★ **WAPPO BAR & BISTRO.** *1226 Washington St (94515). 707/942-4712.* Hrs: 11:30 am-2:30 pm, 6-9:30 pm. Closed Tues; Easter, Thanksgiving, Dec 25. Res required wkends. Wine, beer. A la carte entrees: lunch $10-$12, dinner $8-$17. Child's meals. Specialties: chili rellenos, duck carnitas with masa cakes, seared Chilean sea bass with mint chutney. Entertainment Sun. Outdoor dining on patio with fountain. Totally nonsmoking. Cr cds: A, C, JCB, MC, V.

D

Camarillo (J-3)

(See also Oxnard, Thousand Oaks, Ventura)

Pop 52,303 **Elev** 160 ft **Area Code** 805 **Zip** 93010
Web www.ci.camarillo.ca.us
Information Chamber of Commerce, 632 Las Posas Rd; 805/484-4383

What to See and Do

Camarillo Premium Outlets. Over 100 outlet stores. US 101, Las Posas Rd exit. Phone 805/445-8520.

Channel Islands Aviation. Offers trips to Santa Rosa Island, in the Channel Islands National Park; 1-day scenic trips (Daily; closed Jan 1, Dec 25) For information phone 805/987-1301. ¢¢¢¢¢

Motels

✓★★ **BEST WESTERN INN.** *295 Daily Dr (93921), US 101, exit Las Posas. 805/987-4991; FAX 805/388-3679; res: 800/528-1234.* 58 rms, 2 story. S $55; D $61-$63; each addl $5; under 12 free. Crib free. TV; cable (premium). Pool; whirlpool. Complimentary continental bkfst. Restaurant adj 6 am-10 pm. Ck-out 11 am. Meeting rms. Business servs avail. Cr cds: A, C, D, DS, ER, JCB, MC, V.

SC

★★★ **THE COUNTRY INN AT CAMARILLO.** *1405 Del Norte Rd (93010). 805/983-7171; FAX 805/983-1838; res: 800/447-3529.* 100 rms, 3 story. S, D $138; each addl $10; suites $159; under 12 free. TV;

VCR (movies $4). Heated pool; whirlpool. Complimentary full bkfst. Ck-out noon. Lndry facilities. Business servs avail. In-rm modem link. Valet serv. Health club privileges. Refrigerators. Cr cds: A, C, D, DS, JCB, MC, V.

D SC

Motor Hotel

★★ **HOLIDAY INN.** *4444 Central Ave (93010). 805/485-3999; FAX 805/485-1820; res: 800/447-3529.* 110 rms, 3 story. S, D $89-$109; each addl $10; suites $120; under 12 free. Crib free. Pet accepted. TV; VCR (movies $4). Heated pool; whirlpool. Complimentary continental bkfst. Restaurant adj 8 am-10 pm. Ck-out noon. Coin lndry. Business servs avail. Valet serv. Refrigerators. Balconies. Cr cds: A, C, D, DS, JCB, MC, V.

D SC

Restaurants

✓★★ **MONEY PANCHO.** *3661 Las Posas Rd (93010). 805/484-0591.* Hrs: 10 am-9 pm. Res accepted. Mexican menu. Semi-a la carte: bkfst $4.45-$7.95, lunch $3.95-$7.95, dinner $7.95-$13.95. Child's meals. Specialties: sea and earth, marina rey, fajitas chicken rey. Guitar. Parking. Formal Mexican-style atmosphere and decor. Family-owned since 1975. Totally nonsmoking. Cr cds: A, C, D, MC, V.

D

★★ **OTTAVIO'S.** *1620 Ventura Blvd (93010). 805/482-3810.* Hrs: 11 am-10 pm; Sun to 9 pm; early-bird dinner Sun-Thurs 3-6 pm. Closed some major hols. Res accepted. Italian menu. Bar. Semi-a la carte: lunch $5.50-$10.50, dinner $7.50-$16.95. Specializes in pasta, veal, pizza. Italian decor. Family-owned. Totally nonsmoking. Cr cds: A, C, DS, MC, V.

D SC

Cambria (G-1)

(See also Morro Bay, San Simeon)

Pop 5,382 **Elev** 65 ft **Area Code** 805 **Zip** 93428
E-mail cambriachamber@thegird.net
Web www.thegrid.net/cambriachamber

Information Chamber of Commerce, 767 Main St; 805/927-3624

Cambria's early commerce centered on lumbering, ranching, mining and shipping. However, the town's shipping and whaling volume declined as trade relied on the railroad extending to San Luis Obispo. Today, Cambria is known as an artists' colony on California's central coast; there are many art galleries and gift and antique shops throughout town.

What to See and Do

Beach recreation. Rock and surf fishing at Moonstone Beach. Whale watching late Dec-early Feb. The large rocks at Piedras Blancas are a prime refuge for sea lions and sea otters.

Hearst-San Simeon State Historical Monument (see). Approx 7 mi N on CA 1.

Motels

★★ **BEST WESTERN FIRESIDE INN.** *6700 Moonstone Beach Dr (93428). 805/927-8661; FAX 805/927-8584; res: 888/910-7100.* E-mail firesideinn@thegrid.com; web www.firesideinn.com. 46 rms. No A/C. S, D $69-$149; each addl $10; under 18 free; wkends, hols (2-day min). Crib free. TV; cable, VCR avail (movies). Heated pool; whirlpool. Complimentary continental bkfst. Complimentary coffee in rms. Restaurant nearby. Ck-out 11 am. Business servs avail. In rm modem link. Refrigerators, many fireplaces. Opp ocean. Cr cds: A, C, D, DS, ER, JCB, MC, V.

D SC

★ **CAMBRIA SHORES MOTEL.** *6276 Moonstone Beach Dr (93428). 805/927-8644; FAX 805/927-4070; res: 800/433-9179.* Web www.cambriashoresinn.com. 24 rms. No A/C. Memorial Day-Labor Day, wkends, hols: S, D $75-$115; lower rates rest of yr. Crib free. Pet accepted, some restrictions; $5. TV; cable. Complimentary continental bkfst. Complimentary coffee in rms. Ck-out 11 am. Business servs avail. Refrigerators; microwaves avail. Ocean view; beach opp. Cr cds: A, C, DS, MC, V.

✓★★ **CASTLE INN BY SEA.** *6620 Moonstone Beach Dr (93428). 805/927-8605; FAX 805/927-3179.* Web www.cambria-online.com/castleinnbythesea/. 31 rms. S, D $55-$125; each addl $5. Crib $5. TV; cable. Pool; whirlpool. Complimentary continental bkfst. Ck-out 11 am. Business servs avail. Many refrigerators. Ocean view; beach opp. Cr cds: A, C, DS, MC, V.

Inns

★★★ **J PATRICK HOUSE BED & BREAKFAST INN.** *2990 Burton Dr (93428), above East Village area just off CA 1. 805/927-3812; FAX 805/927-6759; res: 800/341-5258.* E-mail jph@jpatrickhouse.com; web www.jpatrickhouse.com. 8 rms, 2 story. No A/C. No rm phones. S, D $115-$180; wkends, hols (2-day min). Complimentary full bkfst. Ck-out 11 am, ck-in 3 pm. Health club privileges. Fireplaces. Each rm individually decorated; antiques, homemade quilts. Early American-style log house; garden with arbor; extensive grounds, landscaping. Totally nonsmoking. Cr cds: A, C, DS, MC, V.

★★★ **MOONSTONE INN.** *5860 Moonstone Beach Dr (93428). 805/927-4815; FAX 805/927-3944; res: 800/821-3764.* Web www.cambriasbest.com/moonstoneinn. 10 rms, 1-2 story. No A/C. May-Sept: S, D $110-$150; each addl $10; lower rates rest of yr. TV; cable, VCR (free movies). Complimentary continental bkfst. Complimentary coffee in rms. Restaurant nearby. Ck-out 11 am, ck-in 2 pm. Business servs avail. Whirlpool. Refrigerators, fireplaces. Antiques. On ocean; all rms with ocean view. Totally nonsmoking. Cr cds: A, C, D, DS, MC, V.

★★★ **SQUIBB HOUSE.** *4063 Burton Dr (93428). 805/927-9600; FAX 805/927-9606.* Web www.cambria-online.com/thesquibbhouse. 5 rms, 2 story. No A/C. No rm phones. S, D $95-$140. Complimentary continental bkfst. Restaurant adj 11 am-10 pm. Ck-out 11 am, ck-in 3-6 pm. Wine tasting. Built in 1877; antiques. Totally nonsmoking. Cr cds: C, MC, V.

★★★ **SYLVIA'S BURTON DRIVE INN.** *4022 Burton Dr (93428). 805/927-5125; FAX 805/927-9637; res: 800/572-7442.* Web www.burtondriveinn.com. 10 suites, 2 story. No A/C. S, D $85-$150; each addl $10; wkend, hols (2-day min). TV; cable (premium). Complimentary continental bkfst. Complimentary coffee in rms. Restaurant nearby. Ck-out 11 am, ck-in 2 pm. Refrigerators, microwaves. Comtemporary decor. Totally nonsmoking. Cr cds: A, C, MC, V.

D

Restaurants

✓★★ **BRAMBLES.** *4005 Burton Dr (93428). 805/927-4716.* Web www.bramblesdinnerhouse.com. Hrs: 4-9:30 pm; Sat to 10 pm; early-bird dinner Sun-Fri 4-6 pm, Sat 4-5:30 pm; Sun brunch 9:30 am-2 pm. Res accepted. Continental menu. No A/C. Bar. Semi-a la carte: dinner from

$7.95. Sun brunch $8.95-$12.95. Child's meals. Specialties: prime rib with Yorkshire pudding, oak-broiled fresh salmon. Outdoor dining. Victorian decor; antiques. Totally nonsmoking. Cr cds: A, C, D, DS, MC, V.

D

★★ **ROBIN'S RESTAURANT.** *4095 Burton Dr (93428), at Center St. 805/927-5007.* E-mail robins@robinsrestaurant.com; web www.robinsrestaurant.com. Hrs: 11 am-9 pm. Closed Thanksgiving, Dec 25. Res accepted. No A/C. Varied menu. Wine, beer. A la carte entrees: lunch $3.95-$10.95, dinner $7.95-$17.95. Specializes in vegetarian and Asian dishes with locally grown produce. Outdoor dining. Garden. Totally nonsmoking. Cr cds: C, MC, V.

Carlsbad (K-4)

(See also Escondido, La Jolla, Oceanside, San Diego, San Juan Capistrano)

Pop 63,126 **Elev** 39 ft **Area Code** 760 **E-mail** convis@carlsbadca.org **Web** www.carlsbadca.org/

Information Convention & Visitors Bureau, PO Box 1246, 92018; 760/434-6093 or 800/227-5722

Named for Karlsbad, Bohemia (now in the Czech Republic), a famous European spa, this beach-oriented community is a playground for golfers, tennis players, waterskiers and fishing enthusiasts.

What to See and Do

South Carlsbad State Beach. Swimming, surfing; fishing. Improved camping (dump station). Standard fees. 3 mi S on Carlsbad Blvd. Phone 760/438-3143 or 800/444-PARK.

Annual Events

Flower Fields at Carlsbad Ranch. Palomar Airport Rd. Phone 760/930-9123. Mid-Mar-Apr.

Carlsbad Village Fair. More than 800 art, craft and antique vendors; food, entertainment. 1st Sun May & 1st Sun Nov.

Motels

★★ **CARLSBAD INN BEACH RESORT.** *3075 Carlsbad Blvd (92008). 760/434-7020; FAX 760/729-4853; res: 800/235-3939.* Web www.carlsbadinn.com. 60 rms, 3 story, 27 kit. units. S, D $169-$195; each addl $15; suites $205-$238; under 12 free. Crib free. TV; cable, VCR (movies). Heated pool; whirlpools. Supervised child's activities; ages 6-12. Complimentary coffee in rms. Restaurant adj 6:30 am-10 pm. Ck-out 11 am. Coin Indry. Meeting rms. Business servs avail. Exercise equipt; sauna. Lawn games. Putting green. Refrigerators; microwaves avail. Bathrm phone in suites. Picnic tables. Near beach. Cr cds: A, C, D, DS, ER, JCB, MC, V.

D SC

★★ **HOLIDAY INN.** *850 Palomar Airport Rd (92008). 760/438-7880; FAX 760/438-1015; res: 800/266-7880.* 145 rms, 2 story. Mid-May-Sept: S, D $100-$130; under 12 free; lower rates rest of yr. Crib free. TV; cable (premium). Heated pool; whirlpool. Coffee in rms. Restaurant 6:30 am-10 pm. Rm serv. Bar 11 am-midnight; Fri, Sat to 2 am. Ck-out 11 am. Coin Indry. Meeting rms. Business servs avail. Valet serv. Free airport transportation. Some refrigerators. Private patios, balconies. Cr cds: A, C, D, DS, JCB, MC, V.

D SC

✓★ **INNS OF AMERICA.** *751 Raintree Dr (92009), W of I-5, Poinsettia Ln exit. 760/931-1185; FAX 760/931-0970; res: 800/826-0778.* 126 rms, 3 story. June-mid-Sept: S $63.90; D $68.90; lower rates rest of yr. Crib free. Pet accepted. TV; cable (premium). Heated pool. Complimentary continental bkfst. Restaurant adj 11:30 am-midnight; Sun brunch 9 am-1 pm. Ck-out 11 am. Coin Indry. Business servs avail. Cr cds: A, C, MC, V.

D SC

★ **OCEAN PALMS BEACH RESORT.** *2950 Ocean St (92008). 760/729-2493; FAX 760/729-0579; res: 888/802-3224.* 56 rms, 2 story, kit. suites. July-mid-Sept: S, D, kit. suites $84-$186; wkly rates; lower rates rest of yr. Crib $5. TV; cable, VCR avail (movies). Heated pool; whirlpool. Playground. Restaurant adj 7 am-10 pm. Ck-out 11 am. Gift shop. Coin Indry. Microwaves avail. Picnic tables, grills. Opp beach. Totally nonsmoking. Cr cds: A, C, D, DS, MC, V.

D SC

★★ **RAMADA INN & SUITES.** *751 Macadamia Dr (92009). 760/438-2285; FAX 760/438-4547; res: 800/644-9394.* E-mail carlsbad@soramanagement.com. 121 suites, 3 story. Suites $99-$139; under 18 free. Crib free. TV; cable (premium). Complimentary continental bkfst. Complimentary coffee in rms. Restaurant nearby. Ck-out noon. Meeting rms. Business servs avail. In-rm modem link. Valet serv. Coin Indry. Health club privileges. Pool; whirlpool. Refrigerators, microwaves. Opp beach. Cr cds: A, C, D, DS, MC, V.

D SC

Resorts

★★★★ **FOUR SEASONS RESORT.** *7100 Four Seasons Pt (92009). 760/603-6800; FAX 760/603-6878; res: 800/332-3442.* Web www.fshr.com. Located on the north shore of Batiquitos Lagoon, this thousand-acre resort has native wildflowers that bloom right up to the fairways that encircle the resort. Many spacious guest rooms have marble bathrooms and a balcony or landscaped terrace with a choice of view of the golf course, the lagoon, or the ocean. 331 rms, 5 story, 44 suites. S, D $355-$465; suites $500-$1,200; under 17 free; golf plans. Crib free. Pet accepted, some restrictions. TV; cable (premium), VCR avail. Pool; wading pool, whirlpool, poolside serv. Complimentary coffee in rms. Restaurants 6-10:30 pm (also see VIVACE). Rm serv 24 hrs. Bar to midnight; entertainment. Ck-out noon, ck-in 3 pm. Convention facilities. Business center. In-rm modem link. Bellhops. Valet serv. Concierge. Shopping arcade. Barber, beauty shop. Airport transportation. 6 lighted tennis courts, pro. 18-hole golf, greens fee $150; weekends $170. Putting green, driving range. Exercise rm; sauna, steam rm. Massage. Bathrm phones, minibars. Balconies. Cr cds: A, C, D, DS, JCB, MC, V.

D

★★★ **LA COSTA RESORT & SPA.** *2100 Costa Del Mar Rd (92009), 2 mi E of I-5 La Costa Ave exit. 760/438-9111; FAX 760/931-7585; res: 800/854-5000.* Web www.lacosta.com. 480 rms in hotel, 2-3 story, 2-3 bedrm houses. AP: S, D $320-$345; suites $535-$2,400; golf, tennis, spa plans; MAP avail. Crib free. TV; cable (premium), VCR avail. 2 pools; whirlpool, poolside serv. Supervised child's activities. Restaurants 6:30 am-10 pm. Rm serv to 1 am. Snack bar. Bar. Ck-out noon, ck-in 4 pm. Meeting rms. Business center. In-rm modem link. Valet serv. Concierge. Shopping arcade. Airport transportation. Lighted tennis courts including clay, composition & grass, pro. 36-hole golf, putting green, driving range. Soc dir. Exercise rm; sauna, steam rm. Spa. Minibars; wet bar in some suites. Some private patios. Cr cds: A, C, D, DS, JCB, MC, V.

D

Restaurants

★★★ **BELLEFLEUR.** *5610 Paseo Del Norte (92008). 760/603-1919.* 11 am-9 pm; Fri, Sat to 10 pm. Closed Jan 1, July 4, Dec 25. Res accepted. Contemporary Amer menu. Bar. Wine list. Semi-a la carte: lunch $9.25-$14.75, dinner $17-$22.75. Specializes in fresh, locally & regionally grown ingredients. Jazz & blues Tues, Thurs. Parking. Outdoor dining. Winery. Totally nonsmoking. Cr cds: A, C, D, DS, MC, V.

D

★★★ **BRASSERIE @ LA COSTA RESORT.** *5610 Paseo Del Norte.* 11 am-9 pm; Fri, Sat to 10 pm. Closed Jan 1, July 4, Dec 25. Res accepted. Contemporary Amer menu. Bar. Wine list. Semi-a la carte: lunch $9.25-$14.75, dinner $17-$22.75. Specializes in fresh, locally & regionally grown ingredients. Jazz & blues Tues, Thurs. Parking. Outdoor dining. Winery. Totally nonsmoking. Cr cds: C.

★★★ **FIGARO'S.** *La Costa Resort & Spa. 703/438-9111.* North American cuisine. Hours: 6:30-9:30 pm Tues, Thurs, Fri & Sat. Children meals. Prices approx $40. Restaurant is located in the La Costa Resort & Spa. Very elegant and quiet atmosphere. Cr cds: C.

★★★ **PISCES.** *La Costa Resort & Spa. 760/603-0674.* Seafood gourmet cuisine. Specialties: Dover sole, lobster, veal medallion. Hrs: 6:30-10 pm. Prices $25-$35. Reserv reqd. Jackets recommended. Bar. Entertainment upstairs. Cr cds: C.

✓★ **SPIRITO'S.** *300 Carlsbad Village Dr Ste 20 (92008). 760/720-1132.* Hrs: 11 am-9 pm; Fri, Sat to 10 pm. Closed Easter, Thanksgiving, Dec 24, 25. Italian menu. Wine, beer. A la carte entrees: lunch, dinner $5-$14. Specializes in fresh pasta, pizzas. Outdoor dining. Totally nonsmoking. Cr cds: A, C, MC, V.

D

★★ **TUSCANY RISTORANTE-BAR-CAFE.** *6981 El Camino Real (92009). 760/929-8111.* Hrs: 11:30 am-10:30 pm; Sat, Sun 4:30-11 pm. Closed Thanksgiving. Res accepted. Italian menu. Bar. Semi-a la carte: lunch $6.95-$12.95, dinner $8.95-$18.95. Specializes in pasta, seafood, Northern Italian dishes. Entertainment Fri, Sat. Parking. Italian villa-style decor. Cr cds: A, C, D, MC, V.

D

★★ **VIGILUCCI'S TRATTORIA ITALIANA.** *505 First St (92024), 10 mi S on I-5, exit Encinitas Blvd. 760/942-7332.* Hrs: 11 am-3 pm, 5-10 pm; Sat, Sun 11 am-10:30 pm. Closed Jan 1, Thanksgiving, Dec 25. Res accepted. Italian menu. Bar. Semi-a la carte: lunch $5.95-$13.95, dinner $7.95-$17.95. Child's meals. Specializes in fresh fish, pasta. Outdoor dining. Totally nonsmoking. Cr cds: A, C, D, DS, MC, V.

D

★★★ **VIVACE AT THE FOUR SEASONS.** *(See Four Seasons Aviara) 760/603-6999.* Hrs: 5:30-10:30 pm. Res accepted. Italian menu. Wine list. Semi-a la carte: dinner $14-$32. Child's meals. Specialties: osso bucco, wood grilled veal chop, lobster risotto. Valet parking. Outdoor dining. Cr cds: A, C, D, DS, JCB, MC, V.

D ♥

Carmel (F-1)

(See also Carmel Valley, Monterey, Pacific Grove, Pebble Beach)

Founded 1916 **Pop** 4,239 **Elev** 220 ft **Area Code** 831 **E-mail** carmel2@aol.com **Web** www.chambercarmel.ca.us

Information Carmel Business Assn, San Carlos between 5th & 6th Sts, PO Box 4444, 93921; 831/624-2522

Situated on the Bay of Carmel, the town sits at one of the loveliest spots along the California coast. A center for artists and writers since the turn of the century, Carmel fiercely protects its individuality. The architecture is a mixture of every style and whim of the literary and artistic populace, creating a unique and enchanting setting with endless activities for tourists.

What to See and Do

Antique & Art Galleries. More than 70 galleries display a wide variety of art and antiques in the Carmel area. A brochure, *The Guide To Carmel,* containing a list of galleries may be obtained from the Carmel Business Assn, PO Box 4444, 93921. Phone 831/624-2522.

Biblical Garden. Founded in 1904. Stained-glass windows in the sanctuary depict Biblical and local scenes. A Gaza St Galy mosaic, sundial on a granite boulder, mosaic cross in the garden. A 32-rank pipe organ provides quarterly concerts. Garden contains trees and plants mentioned in the Bible and indigenous to the Holy Land. (Daily) Church of the Wayfarer, Lincoln St & 7th Ave. Phone 831/624-3550. **Free**

Mission San Carlos Borromeo del Rio Carmelo. Basilica founded by Fr Junipero Serra in 1770; his burial place. Oldest church in Carmel. Headquarters for the California missions. (Daily; closed Thanksgiving, Dec 25) 1 mi S off CA 1, then W to 3080 Rio Rd. Phone 831/624-3600. **Donation**

Pacific Repertory Theatre. Company performs dramas, comedies and musicals in 3 venues: Golden Bough Playhouse, Circle Theatre and outdoor Forest Theatre. (May-Oct, schedule varies) For location, fees and schedule of plays, contact PO Box 222035, 93922; phone 831/622-0100.

Point Lobos State Reserve. Sea Lion Rocks, Bird Island just offshore. Natural grove of Monterey cypress. Picnic area (no fires or stoves), naturalist programs. No dogs. (Day use only) 3 mi S on CA 1. Phone 831/624-4909. Per vehicle **¢¢¢**

Rancho Cañada Golf Club. Two 18-hole championship courses; driving range. (Daily) Carmel Valley Rd, 1 mi E of CA 1. Phone 831/624-0111. **¢¢¢¢¢**

Seventeen-Mile Drive from Carmel to Monterey (see MONTEREY).

The Barnyard. Shopping area with 1½ acres of terraced flower gardens around rustic, old style California barns housing a number of shops, galleries and restaurants. CA 1, Carmel Valley Rd exit, then take 1st right and enter Barnyard from 26400 Carmel Rancho Blvd.

Annual Events

Monterey Wine Festival. Phone 800/656-4282. Early Apr.

Carmel Art Festival. Phone 831/625-2288. Mid-May.

Carmel Bach Festival. Sunset Center, San Carlos & 9th Sts. Concerts, recitals, lectures, special events. Contact PO Box 575, 93921; 831/624-1521. Mid-July-early Aug.

Sand Castle Building Contest. Phone 831/626-1255. Oct.

Motels

★★★ **ADOBE INN.** *Dolores & 8th (93921), between 7th & 8th Ave. 831/624-3933; FAX 831/624-8636; res: 800/388-3933.* Web www.adobeinn.com. 20 rms, 2 story, 1 suites. No A/C. S, D $116-$260; suites $240-$300. TV; cable, VCR avail. Heated pool. Sauna. Complimentary continental bkfst. Complimentary coffee in rms. Restaurant adj 11:30 am-11:30 pm. Ck-out noon. Meeting rm. Free covered parking. Refrigerators. Balconies. Cr cds: A, C, MC, V.

★ **BEST WESTERN.** *5th Avenue & San Carlos Street (93921), 5th Ave & San Carlos St. 831/624-1261; FAX 831/625-6783; res: 800/528-1234.* 28 rms. Apr-Oct: S, D $89-$160; each addl $6; lower rates rest of yr; under 12 free. TV; cable. Heated pool. Coffee in rms. Restaurant nearby. Ck-out 11 am. In-rm modem link. Some refrigerators. Sun deck. Cr cds: A, C, D, DS, MC, V.

SC

★★ **BEST WESTERN BAY VIEW INN.** *6th & Junipero St (93921), between 5th & 6th. 831/624-1831; FAX 408/625-2336; res: 800/528-1234; res: 800/343-1831.* 58 rms, 5 story. June-Oct: S, D $79-$209; suites $169-$299; under 12 free; lower rates rest of yr. Crib $5. TV; cable. Pool. Complimentary continental bkfst. Restaurant opp 11-2 am. Ck-out 11 am. Business servs avail. Some refrigerators. Cr cds: A, C, D, DS, MC, V.

D

★★ **BEST WESTERN MISSION INN.** *3665 Rio Rd (93923), 1 blk E of CA 1. 831/624-1841; FAX 408/624-8684; res: 800/348-9090.* 165 rms, 4 story. S, D $99-$199; each addl $10; suites $289-$359; under 13 free. Crib free. Pet accepted; $25. TV; cable (premium). Heated pool;

whirlpools. Restaurant 7-10 am; wkends to 11 am, 5:30-9:30 pm. Rm serv. Bar. Ck-out noon. Meeting rms. Business servs avail. Bellhops. Refrigerators. Many balconies. Picnic sites. Cr cds: A, C, D, DS, JCB, MC, V.

D SC

★★ **CANDLE LIGHT INN.** *San Carlos St (93921), between 4th & 5th Aves. 831/624-6451; FAX 831/624-6732; res: 800/433-4732.* E-mail concierge@carmelinns.com; web www.innsbythesea.com. 20 rms, 2 story, 5 kit. units. No A/C. June-Oct, wkends: S, D $149-$179; each addl $15; under 13 free; wkends (2-day min); lower rates rest of yr. TV; cable, some VCRs. Heated pool. Complimentary continental bkfst. Coffee in rms. Ck-out noon. Business servs avail. Refrigerators; some fireplaces; microwaves avail. Cr cds: A, C, DS, MC, V.

SC

✓★ **CARMEL RESORT INN.** *Carpenter & 1st Avenue (93921). 831/624-3113; FAX 831/624-5456; res: 800/454-3700.* 31 cottages, 2 kits. No A/C. June-Sept: S, D $89-$225; kits. $149-$225; under 6 free; lower rates rest of yr. Crib $10. TV; cable (premium). Complimentary continental bkfst. Coffee in rms. Ck-out 11 am. Whirlpool. Sauna. Refrigerators, microwaves; many fireplaces. Cr cds: A, C, D, DS, MC, V.

SC

★★ **DOLPHIN INN.** *San Carlos & 4th St (93921), at 4th Ave. 831/624-5356; FAX 831/624-2967; res: 800/433-4732.* E-mail concierge@carmelinns.com; web www.innsbythesea.com. 26 rms, 2 story. No A/C. June-Oct, wkends: S, D $99-$169 each addl $15; suites $219-$229; under 13 free; wkends (2-day min); lower rates rest of yr. TV; cable. Heated pool. Complimentary continental bkfst. Coffee in rms. Ck-out noon. Business servs avail. Refrigerators; many fireplaces; microwaves avail. Cr cds: A, C, DS, JCB, MC, V.

SC

★ **HOFSAS HOUSE.** *San Carlos & 4th Ave (05676). 831/624-2745; FAX 831/624-0159; res: 800/221-2548.* 38 rms, showers only, 4 story. No A/C. No elvtr. June-Sept: S, D $80-$150; suites $180; kit. units $110-$135; lower rates rest of yr. Crib $7.50. TV; cable, VCR avail (movies). Pool. Sauna. Complimentary continental bkfst. Restaurant nearby. Bar. Ck-out noon. Meeting rm. Cr cds: A, C, MC, V.

★★ **HORIZON INN.** *Junipero & 3rd St (93921). 831/624-5327; FAX 408/626-8253; res: 800/433-4732.* 29 rms, 1-2 story, 6 kits; 6 suites (1 bedrm) in bldg opp. No A/C. S, D $89-$169; each addl $15; suites $180-$209. TV; cable. Heated pool. Complimentary continental bkfst. Coffee in rms. Restaurant nearby. Ck-out noon. Coin Indry. Business servs avail. Refrigerators; many fireplaces; microwaves avail. Some private patios, balconies. Some rms with ocean view. Cr cds: A, C, DS, JCB, MC, V.

SC

★★ **INNS BY THE SEA- SVENDSGAARD'S INN.** *San Carlos & 4th (93921). 831/624-1511; FAX 831/624-5661; res: 800/433-4732.* E-mail concierge@carmelinns.com; web www.innsbythesea.com. 34 rms, 1-2 story, 14 kits. No A/C. June-Oct, wkends: S, D $119-$169; each addl $15; suites $199-$229; under 13 free; wkends (2-day min); lower rates rest of yr. TV; cable. Heated pool. Complimentary continental bkfst. Coffee in rms. Restaurant nearby. Ck-out noon. Business servs avail. Refrigerators; some fireplaces; microwaves avail. Country decor. Cr cds: A, C, DS, MC, V.

SC

✓★ **LOBOS LODGE.** *Ocean Ave & Monteverde St (93921), at Ocean Ave. 831/624-3874; FAX 831/624-0135.* 30 rms, 1-3 story. S, D $99-$129; each addl $25; suites $155-$195. TV; cable. Ck-out noon. Refrigerators, fireplaces. Private patios, balconies. Beach 4 blks. Cr cds: A, C, MC, V.

★★ **TALLY HO INN.** *Monte Verde St & 6th Ave (93921). 831/624-2232; FAX 831/624-2661.* Web www.tallyho-inn.com. 14 rms, 1-2 story. No A/C. May-Oct: S, D $115-$250; lower rates mid-wk. Crib free. TV; cable. Complimentary continental bkfst. Restaurant opp from 7 am. Ck-out noon. Business servs avail. In-rm modem link. Some fireplaces, whirlpools. Some private patios. Landscaped gardens. Cr cds: A, C, D, DS, JCB, MC, V.

SC

★★★ **TICKLE PINK COUNTRY INN CARMEL.** *155 Highlands Dr (93923), 4 miles S of Carmel on CA 1. 831/624-1244; FAX 831/626-9516; res: 800/635-4774.* E-mail mark@ticklepink.com; web www.ticklepink.com. 34 rms in 2 bldgs, 3, 4 story. No A/C. No elvtr. S, D $199-$269; each addl $25; suites $259-$309; cottage $259-$279; wkends (2-day min), special events (3-day min). TV; cable, VCR (movies). Complimentary continental bkfst. Coffee in rms. Restaurant adj 7 am-11 pm. Ck-out noon. Meeting rm. Business servs avail. Whirlpool. Refrigerators; some fireplaces, whirlpools. Many balconies. Scenic view of sea coast. Cr cds: A, C, MC, V.

D

★★ **VILLAGE INN.** *Ocean Ave & Junipero Ave (93921). 831/624-3864; FAX 831/626-6763; res: 800/346-3864.* 48 rms, 2 story. No A/C. May-Oct: S, D $79-$175; lower rates rest of yr. TV; cable (premium). Continental bkfst. Ck-out 11 am. Microwaves avail. Cr cds: A, C, MC, V.

★★ **WAYSIDE INN.** *Mission St & 7th Ave (93921). 831/624-5336; FAX 831/626-6974; res: 800/433-4732.* E-mail concierge@carmelinns.com; web www.innsbythesea.com. 21 rms, 2 story, 8 kits. No A/C. Mid-June-mid-Oct, wkends: S, D $149-$179; each addl $15; suites $219-$269; under 14 free; wkends (2-day min); lower rates rest of yr. Pet accepted. TV; cable. Complimentary continental bkfst. Coffee in rms. Restaurant nearby. Ck-out noon. Ck-in 3 pm. Business servs avail. Refrigerators; many fireplaces; microwaves avail. Some balconies. Colonial Williamsburg decor. Cr cds: A, C, DS, MC, V.

SC

Hotels

★★★ **HIGHLANDS INN.** *Highway 1 (93921), 4 mi S. 831/624-3801; FAX 831/626-1574; res: 800/682-4811.* E-mail gm@highlands-inn.com; web www.highlands.inn.com. 142 rms, 1-2 story, 100 spa suites. S, D $190-$350; each addl $25; spa suites $425-$575; 2-bedrm suites $550-$800; under 16 free. Crib free. TV; cable, VCR (movies). Heated pool; poolside serv. Coffee in rms. Restaurant 7 am-10 pm (also see PACIFIC'S EDGE). Bar 11-1 am; entertainment. Ck-out noon. Meeting rms. Business center. In-rm modem link. Concierge. Gift shop. Gourmet market. Free airport transportation. Exercise equipt. Bicycles. Minibars; some whirlpools, fireplaces; full kit. in suites. Microwaves avail. Private patios, balconies. On 12 wooded acres; views of Pacific Ocean and Big Sur coast. Cr cds: A, C, D, DS, JCB, MC, V.

D

★★★ **LA PLAYA HOTEL.** *Camino Real & 8th St (93921). 831/624-6476; FAX 831/624-7966; res: 800/582-8900.* Web www.monterey.infohut.com/laplayahotel. 75 rms, 3-4 story, 4 kit. cottages. S, D $135-$235; each addl $15; suites $235-$395; kit. cottages $235-$525; under 12 free. Crib free. TV; cable. Heated pool; poolside serv. Restaurant 7 am-10 pm. Bar 11 am-midnight. Ck-out noon. Meeting rms. Business servs avail. Concierge. Valet parking. Health club privileges. Private patios. Renovated Mediterranean-style villa (1904). Cr cds: A, C, D, MC, V.

D

★★★ **PINE INN.** *Ocean Ave And Monte Verde (93921). 831/624-3851; FAX 831/624-3030; res: 800/228-3851.* E-mail info@pine-inn.com; web www.pine-inn.com. 49 rms, 3 story, 6 suites. S, D $95-$200; each addl $10; suites $230; under 18 free. Crib free. TV; cable. Restaurant 7 am-10 pm; wkends 8 am-11 pm. Bar. Ck-out 1 pm. Concierge. Meeting rms. Business servs avail. Some refrigerators. In historic (1889) bldg. Cr cds: A, C, D, DS, JCB, MC, V.

SC

Resort

★★★★ **QUAIL LODGE RESORT & GOLF CLUB.** *8205 Valley Greens Dr (93923), 3 mi E of CA 1 on Carmel Valley Rd. 831/624-1581; FAX 831/624-3726; res: 800/538-9516.* E-mail qul@peninsula.com; web www.peninsula.com. Set amid 850 acres of impeccably landscaped grounds, the lodge is known for its gardens and its golf facilities. Guest rooms are done in a rustic California style. 100 units. S, D $225-$295; each addl $25; suites $405-$825; under 12 free; golf plan Sun-Thurs. Pet accepted. TV; cable (premium). 2 heated pools; whirlpool, poolside serv. Supervised child's activities by request (July-Sept). Complimentary afternoon refreshments. Complimentary coffee in rms. Restaurants 6:30-10 pm. Rm serv 7 am-11 pm. Bars 11 am-midnight; entertainment. Ck-out 1 pm. Meeting rms. Business center. Bellhops. Concierge. Airport transportation. Tennis, pro. 18-hole golf, greens fee $145-$175, putting greens, driving range. Bicycles. Health club privileges. Lawn games. Some fireplaces, wet bars. Private patios, balconies. Cr cds: A, C, D, JCB, MC, V.

D

Inns

★★ **BRIARWOOD.** *San Carlos St (93921), between 4th and 5th Sts. 831/626-9056; FAX 831/626-8900; res: 800/999-8788.* 7 rms, 1 with shower only, 2 story, 5 suites. No A/C. S, D $125-$185; each addl $20; suites $225-$450; wkends (2-day min). TV; cable, VCR (movies). Complimentary continental bkfst. Complimentary coffee in rms. Restaurant nearby. Ck-out 11 am, ck-in 2 pm. Refrigerators; some wetbars; microwaves avail. Totally nonsmoking. Cr cds: A, C, MC, V.

★★ **CARMEL GARDEN COURT INN.** *4th & Torres St (93921). 831/624-6926; FAX 831/624-4935.* 9 rms. No A/C. May-Oct: S, D $125-$245; suite $245-$425; wkends (2-day min). TV; cable, VCR (free movies). Complimentary continental bkfst; afternoon refreshments. Complimentary coffee in rms. Restaurant nearby. Ck-out 11 am, ck-in 4-9 pm. Business servs avail. Refrigerators. Garden. Totally nonsmoking. Cr cds: A, C, MC, V.

★★★ **CARRIAGE HOUSE INN.** *Junipero Avenue & 8th Avenue (93921), between 7th & 8th Aves. 831/625-2585; FAX 831/624-0974; res: 800/433-4732.* E-mail concierge@carmelinns.com; web www.innsbythesea.com. 13 rms, 2 story. No A/C. S, D $229-$249; suites $299; each addl $15; under 13 free; wkends (2-day min). TV; cable (premium), VCR. Complimentary continental bkfst; evening refreshments. Restaurant nearby. Ck-out noon, ck-in 3 pm. Business servs avail. Refrigerators, wet bars, fireplaces; some in-rm whirlpools. Antique furnishings. Totally nonsmoking. Cr cds: A, C, DS, MC, V.

SC

★★★ **COBBLESTONE INN.** *Junipero Ave, between 7th & 8th (93921). 831/625-5222; FAX 831/625-0478; res: 800/833-8836.* Web www.foursisters.com. 24 rms, 2 story. S, D $95-$200; each addl $15; suites $175. TV; cable. Complimentary full bkfst; afternoon refreshments. Ck-out noon, ck-in 2 pm. Business servs avail. Refrigerators, fireplaces. English country decor; cobblestone courtyard. Cr cds: A, C, D, MC, V.

★★ **CRYSTAL TERRACE INN.** *24815 Carpenter St (93921). 831/624-6400; FAX 408/624-5111; res: 800/600-4488.* 17 rms, 2 story. No A/C. May-Oct: S, D $150-$225; cottage $235-$275; higher rates special events; lower rates rest of yr. TV; cable (premium), VCR avail (movies). Complimentary continental bkfst; afternoon refreshments. Restaurant nearby. Ck-out 11 am, ck-in 3 pm. Business servs avail. Some refrigerators, microwaves, minibars, fireplaces. Some balconies. Built in 1927. Garden area. Totally nonsmoking. Cr cds: A, C, D, DS, JCB, MC, V.

SC

★★ **CYPRESS INN.** *Lincoln & 7th St (93921). 831/624-3871; FAX 831/624-8216; res: 800/443-7443.* E-mail hollace@cypress-inn.com. 34 rms, 2 story. S, D $110-$350; each addl $15; lower rates Dec-Jan. Pet accepted; $17. TV; cable (premium). Complimentary continental bkfst. Complimentary refreshments in rms. Bar 7 am-11 pm. Ck-out noon, ck-in 3 pm. Business servs avail. Luggage handling. Some refrigerators, fireplaces. Some verandas. Mediterranean facade; set in heart of Carmel Village. Cr cds: A, C, DS, JCB, MC, V.

★ **GREEN LANTERN INN.** *Casanova St & 7th Ave (93921). 831/624-4392; FAX 831/624-9591; res: 888/414-4392.* E-mail info@greenlanterninn.com; web www.greenlanterninn.com. 18 rms, 2 story, 3 suites. No A/C. June-Sept: S, D $120-$190; suites $165-$190; under 16 free; wkends, hols (2-3-day min); lower rates rest of yr. Crib free. TV; cable. Complimentary full bkfst; afternoon refreshments. Restaurant nearby. Ck-out 11 am, ck-in 2 pm. Business servs avail. Cottage-style units. Refrigerators; some fireplaces. Totally nonsmoking. Cr cds: A, C, D, DS, JCB, MC, V.

★★ **HAPPY LANDING INN.** *Monte Verde St (93921), between 5th & 6th Aves. 831/624-7917.* 5 rms, 2 suites. No A/C. No rm phones. S, D $90-$130; suites $165. Children over 12 yrs only. TV; cable. Complimentary full bkfst; afternoon refreshments. Restaurant nearby. Ck-out 11:30 am, ck-in 2 pm. Cathedral ceilings; antiques. Garden; gazebo; pond. 1925 Comstock cottage. Cr cds: C, MC, V.

★★★ **MISSION RANCH.** *26270 Dolores St (93923), CA 1, Rio Rd W, left on Lausen. 831/624-6436; FAX 831/626-4163; res: 800/538-8221.* 31 rms, 6 in farmhouse. No A/C. S, D $85-$225; each addl $15. TV; cable (premium). Complimentary continental bkfst. Complimentary coffee in rms. Restaurant (see MISSION RANCH). Bar; entertainment. Ck-out 11 am, ck-in 3 pm. Meeting rms. Business servs avail. Tennis, pro. Exercise equipt. Country decor; ranch atmosphere. Totally nonsmoking. Cr cds: A, C, MC, V.

D SC

★★ **NORMANDY INN.** *Ocean Ave & Monte Verde St (93921). 831/624-3825; FAX 831/624-4614.* 45 rms, 2 story, 2 kit. suites, 3 kit. cottages. June-Oct: S, D $98-$200; each addl $10; suites $165-$300; kit. cottages $250-$400; lower rates rest of yr. TV; cable. Heated pool. Complimentary continental bkfst. Ck-out 11 am, ck-in 2 pm. Some fireplaces; refrigerators, microwaves avail. French country garden atmosphere. Cr cds: A, C, MC, V.

★ **SANDPIPER INN AT THE BEACH CARMEL.** *2408 Bayview Ave (93923). 831/624-6433; FAX 831/624-5964; res: 800/633-6433.* Web www.sandpiper-inn.com. 16 rms, 2 story. No A/C. No rm phones. S, D $95-$200; each addl $20; hols, special events (3-day min), wkends (2-day min). TV in sitting rm; cable. Complimentary continental bkfst buffet; afternoon refreshments. Ck-out noon, ck-in after 3 pm. Business servs avail. Some fireplaces. Some rms with ocean view. Antiques. Cr cds: A, C, DS, MC, V.

SC

★ **STONEHOUSE INN.** *8th Ave & Monte Verde St (93921). 831/624-4569.* 6 rms, 5 share bath, 2 story. No A/C. No rm phones. S, D $99-$199. Children over 12 yrs only. Complimentary full bkfst; evening refreshments. Ck-out noon, ck-in 3 pm. Built 1906. Antiques. Garden. Cr cds: A, C, MC, V.

★★ **SUNSET HOUSE.** *Camino Real & Ocean Ave (93921), Camino Real, between Ocean & 7th Ave. 831/624-4884; FAX 831/624-4884.* E-mail sunsetbb@redshift.com; web www.sunset-carmel.com/. 5 rms, 4 with shower only. No A/C. S $150-$190; D $170-$210; each addl $20; under 5 free; wkly rates; wkends, hols (2-day min). Crib free. Pet accepted, some restrictions; $20. TV; cable (premium). Complimentary continental bkfst. Complimentary coffee in rms. Restaurant nearby. Ck-out 11 am, ck-in 3-6 pm. Business servs avail. In-rm modem link. Refrigerators, fireplaces. Picnic tables. Fountain. Totally nonsmoking. Cr cds: A, C, D, DS, JCB, MC, V.

✓★★ **VAGABOND'S HOUSE INN.** *Dolores St & 4th Ave (93921). 831/624-7738; FAX 831/626-1243; res: 800/262-1262.* 11 rms, 1-2 story. No A/C. S, D $85-$165; each addl $20. Pet accepted, $10. Children over 12 yrs only. TV; cable (premium). Complimentary continental bkfst. Ck-out noon, ck-in 3 pm. Many fireplaces. Antiques. Courtyard garden. Cr cds: A, C, MC, V.

Restaurants

★★★ **ANTON & MICHEL.** *Mission St (93921), between Ocean & 7th. 831/624-2406.* E-mail anton+michel@carmelsbest.com; web www.carmelsbest.com. Hrs: 11:30 am-3 pm, 5:30-9:30 pm. Res accepted. Continental menu. Bar 11 am-11 pm. A la carte entrees: lunch $7.75-$14.50, dinner $18.50-$39.50. Specialties: rack of lamb, fresh abalone, chicken Jerusalem. Garden view from main dining room. Cr cds: A, C, D, DS, JCB, MC, V.

D

★★ **CAFE BERLIN.** *Junipero Between 5th & 6th (93923). 831/626-8181.* E-mail pstuber723@aol.com. Hrs: 11:30 am-2 pm, 5:30-10 pm. Closed Mon. Continental menu. Wine, beer. Semi-a la carte: lunch $3.95-$14, dinner $6.95-$18.95. Child's meals. Specialties: veal rahmschnitzel, roasted duck. Outdoor dining. Cr cds: A, C, MC, V.

D

✓★★ **CAFFE NAPOLI.** *Ocean Ave & Lincoln (93923). 831/625-4033.* E-mail vedinapoli@aol.com; web caffenapoli.com. Hrs: 11:30 am-10 pm. Closed Thanksgiving, Dec 25. Res accepted. No A/C. Italian menu. Wine, beer. A la carte entrees: lunch, dinner $9-$15. Specializes in pasta, pizza. Italian decor. Totally nonsmoking. Cr cds: C, MC, V.

D

★★★ **CASANOVA RESTAURANT.** *5th Ave & Mission (93923). 831/625-0501.* E-mail casanova@mbay.net; web www.casanova-restaurant. com. Hrs: 11:30 am-3 pm, 5-10 pm; Fri, Sat to 10:30 pm; Sun brunch 9 am-3 pm, 5-10 pm. Closed Dec 25. Res accepted. No A/C. Wine cellar. Bar. French, Italian menu. Semi-a la carte: lunch $5.75-$13.75, dinner $19-$35. Sun brunch $7.25-$13.75. Specializes in southern French, northern Italian cuisine. Own baking, pasta. Outdoor dining. Cr cds: C, MC, V.

D

✓★ **COTTAGE RESTAURANT.** *Lincoln St (93921), between Ocean & 7th. 831/625-6260.* Hrs: 7:30 am-3 pm; Thurs-Sat also 5-9 pm. Closed Dec 25. Res accepted. No A/C. Wine, beer. Semi-a la carte: bkfst $5.50-$9, lunch $5.75-$10.50, dinner $6.25-$14.95. Child's meals. Specialties: eggs Benedict, artichoke soup, Caesar salad. Country-style decor; stained-glass windows. Totally nonsmoking. Cr cds: C, JCB, MC, V.

D

✓★★ **FLYING FISH CAFE-KENNYS.** *Carmel Plz (93923), between Ocean & 7th Aves. 831/625-1962.* Hrs: 5-10 pm. Closed Tues Nov-May. Res accepted. Semi-a la carte: dinner $13.75-$19.75. Specialties: black bean catfish, almond sea bass, seafood clay pot. Pacific Rim decor; fish motif includes artwork, papier mâche flying fish decorations. Cr cds: A, C, D, DS, MC, V.

★★★ **FRENCH POODLE RESTAURANT.** *Junipero & 5th Ave (93923). 831/624-8643.* Hrs: 5:30-9:30 pm. Closed Sun; Dec 25. Res accepted. Air-cooled. French menu. Semi-a la carte: dinner $16-$27. Extensive wine list. Specialties: sliced breast of duck in aged port wine sauce; les noisettes d'agneau au thym et a la moutarde de Dijon; abalone meuniere. Own desserts. Intimate dining. Chef-owned. Cr cds: A, C, D, MC, V.

D

★★ **GRILL ON OCEAN AVENUE.** *Ocean Ave (93921), between Dolores & Lincoln Sts. 831/624-2569.* Hrs: 11:30 am-10 pm. Res accepted. Bar. Semi-a la carte: lunch $7.75-$14.50, dinner $13.25-$20.75. Specializes in fresh seafood, grilled meats, pasta. Fireplace, artwork. Cr cds: A, C, D, DS, MC, V.

D

★★ **HOG'S BREATH.** *San Carlos Near 5th (93921). 831/625-1044.* Hrs: 11:30 am-3 pm, 5-10 pm; Sun brunch 11 am-3 pm. Closed Dec 25. Bar 11-1:30 am. Semi-a la carte: lunch $5.50-$13.50, dinner $9-$22. Sun brunch $4.75-$12.95. Specializes in fresh seafood, steaks. Outdoor dining. Family-owned. Cr cds: A, C, D, MC, V.

D

★★★ **LA BOHEME RESTAURANT.** *Dolores & 7th Ave (93923), between Ocean Ave & 7th Ave. 831/624-7500.* E-mail alan@laboheme. com; web www.laboheme.com. Hrs: 5:30-10 pm. Closed Easter, Thanksgiving, Dec 25. No A/C. European/country menu. Wine, beer. Semi-a la carte: dinner $21.75. Menu changes nightly. French village atmosphere. Cr cds: C, MC, V.

★★ **LE COQ D'OR.** *Mission St & 5th Ave (93923), between 4th & 5th. 831/626-9319.* Web www.lecoqdor.com. Hrs: 5-9 pm; Fri-Sat to 9:30 pm. Res accepted. No A/C. French, German menu. Wine, beer. Complete meals: dinner $18.25-$23.50. Child's meals. Specialties: confit de canard, jager schnitzel, scallops in orange buerre blanc. Outdoor dining. Intimate atmosphere; French & German pottery, artwork. Patio dining. Cr cds: C.

★★ **LITTLE NAPOLI.** *Dolores St (93921), between Ocean & 7th. 831/626-6335.* E-mail vedinapoli@aol.com; web www.caffenapoli.com. Hrs: 11:30 am-10 pm. Closed Thanksgiving, Dec 25. Res accepted. No A/C. Italian menu. Wine, beer. A la carte entrees: $9-$15. Specializes in pizza, pasta. Italian decor; ceramics, color prints. Totally nonsmoking. Cr cds: C, MC, V.

D

★★ **LUGANO SWISS BISTRO.** *3670 The Barnyard (93923). 831/626-3779.* E-mail lugano@swissbistro; web www.swissbistro.com. Hrs: 11:30 am-9 pm. Res accepted. Swiss, Continental menu. Bar. Semi-a la carte: lunch $5.75-$12.50, dinner $9.75-$17.50. Specializes in fondues. Outdoor dining. Alpine decor. Cr cds: A, C, MC, V.

D SC

★★ **MISSION RANCH.** *(See Mission Ranch) 831/625-9040.* Hrs: 4:30-10 pm; Sat 11 am-3 pm; Sun brunch 9:30 am-1:30 pm. Closed Dec 25. Res accepted. No A/C. Bar 4 pm-12:30 am. Wine list. A la carte entrees: lunch $6-$10, dinner $7.75-$26.95. Sun brunch $18.95. Child's meals. Specializes in prime rib, fish. Pianist; Jazz for Sun brunch. Parking. Outdoor dining. Rural ambiance with view of ocean, Ft Lobos. Totally nonsmoking. Cr cds: C, D, MC, V.

D

★★★ **PACIFIC'S EDGE.** *(See Highlands Inn) 831/622-5445; FAX 831/626-8105.* E-mail gm@highlands-inn.com; web www.highlands-inn.com. Contemporary regional cuisine. Specialties: Monterey Bay spot prawns, butter-poached Maine lobster, roasted prime Colorado rack of lamb, truffle roasted chicken breast. Hrs:11:30 am-2 pm, 6-10 pm; Fri, Sat to 10:30 pm; Sun brunch 10 am-2 pm. Res suggested. Sunset lounge/bar 11-2 am. Grand Master wine list. A la carte entrees: lunch $15-$18, dinner $23-$38. Prix fixe: dinner $56-$91. Sun brunch $29. Wed-Mon, pianist. Fri, Sat from 9 pm -12 midnight Jazz. Valet parking. Master Food & Wine Festival in February. Cr cds: A, C, D, DS, JCB, MC, V.

D

✓★ **PATISSERIE BOISSIERE.** *Carmel Plz (93923), between Ocean & 7th. 831/624-5008.* Hrs: 11 am-9 pm; Mon, Tues to 5 pm, Sat, Sun from 10 am. Closed Thanksgiving, Dec 25. Res accepted. California, French menu. Wine, beer. Semi-a la carte: lunch $6-$9.95, dinner $9.95-$16.95. Sat, Sun brunch $4.50-$7.95. Specialties: French onion soup, coquille Saint-Jaques, salmon baked in parchment paper. Own pastries. Louis XV dining room. Cr cds: C.

★★★ **RAFFAELLO CARMEL RESTAURANT.** *Mission & Ocean (93923), between Ocean & 7th Aves. 831/624-1541.* Hrs: 6-10 pm. Closed Tues; also first 2 wks Jan. Res accepted. Northern Italian menu. Beer. Wine cellar. Semi-a la carte: dinner $13.75-$23.50. Specialties: cannelloni alla Raffaello, fettucine alla Romana, salmone alle shallots. Own desserts. Paintings; fireplace. Family-owned. Cr cds: A, C, D, MC, V.

★★ **RED LION TAVERN.** *Dolores Between 5th & 6th (93921). 831/625-6765.* Hrs: 11:30 am-10 pm; wkends to 11 pm. Closed Dec 25. Res accepted. No A/C. Bar to 2 am. Semi-a la carte: lunch $4.95-$9.95, dinner $7.95-$16.95. Specializes in bangers & mash, cottage pie. Outdoor dining. English pub; casual atmosphere. Cr cds: A, C, DS, MC, V.

D

✓★★★ **RIO GRILL.** *101 Crossroads Blvd (93923), in Crossroads Shopping Ctr, CA 1 at Rio Road exit . 831/625-5436.* Hrs: 11:30 am-11 pm. Closed July 4, Thanksgiving, Dec 25. Res accepted. Bar to midnight. Wine cellar. A la carte entrees: lunch $9-$17, dinner $9-$17. Specializes in oakwood grilled chicken, fish, beef. Own pastries. Outdoor dining. Contemporary Southwestern adobe decor. Cr cds: A, C, DS, MC, V.

D

★★ **ROBATA GRILL & SAKE BAR.** *3658 The Barnyard (93923), at CA 1. 831/624-2643.* Hrs: from 5 pm. Closed Thanksgiving, Dec 25. Japanese menu. Bar. Semi-a la carte: dinner $10.95-$30.95. Specializes in open hearth cooking, sushi. Parking. Japanese farmhouse decor. Cr cds: A, C, D, MC, V.

D

★★★ **ROBERT KINCAID'S BISTRO.** *217 Crossroads Blvd (93923), in Crossroads Shopping Center. 831/624-9626.* Web www.spmag.com/robertkincaidsbistro. Hrs: 11:30 am-2 pm, 5:30-10 pm; Sat, Sun from 5:30 pm. Closed Thanksgiving, Dec 24, 25. Res accepted. French menu. Wine list. Semi-a la carte: dinner $17.95-$26.95. Complete meals: lunch $14.95. Specialties: rack of lamb, roast duckling, Holland Dover sole. Country-French atmosphere; fireplaces. Cr cds: A, C, D, DS, MC, V.

D

★ **ROCKY POINT.** *CA1 (93922), 12 mi S on CA 1. 831/624-2933.* Web www.rocky.point.com. Hrs: 9 am-9:30 pm. Res accepted. No A/C. Bar. Semi-a la carte: bkfst $4-$15, lunch $8-$15, dinner $19-$32. Specializes in steak, seafood. Parking. Full-window view of coastline; many outdoor tables and sitting benches. Totally nonsmoking. Cr cds: C, DS, MC, V.

D ♥

★★★ **SANS SOUCI RESTAURANT.** *Lincoln & 5th Ave (93923), between 5th & 6th Aves. 831/624-6220.* Hrs: 5:30-10 pm. Closed Wed. Res accepted. No A/C. French menu. Wine list. Semi-a la carte: dinner $16-$28. Specializes in lamb, duck, fresh seafood. French decor; fireplace. Family-owned. Cr cds: A, C, MC, V.

D

★★ **THE FORGE IN THE FOREST AND GENERAL STORE.** *5th & Junipero (93921). 831/624-2233.* E-mail theforge@mbay.net. Hrs: 11:30 am-11 pm; Sun brunch 11:30 am-3 pm. Bar to midnight. Semi-a la carte: lunch $8.75-$18.95, dinner $8.95-$21.95. Sun brunch $10. Child's meals. Specializes in rotisserie fowl. Outdoor dining. Cr cds: A, C, D, DS, MC, V.

D

★★ **WILL'S FARGO RESTAURANT.** *W Carmel Valley Rd (93924), in village. 831/659-2774.* E-mail tquilty@aol.com. Hrs: 5 pm to closing. Res accepted. No A/C. Bar from 5 pm. Semi-a la carte: dinner $13.95-$26.95. Specializes in steak, seafood, ribs. Own soups. Butcher shop. 1890s decor; old Western bar, fireplace. Cr cds: A, C, DS, JCB, MC, V.

D

Unrated Dining Spot

THUNDERBIRD BOOKSHOP CAFE. *3600 Barnyard (93923). 408/624-1803.* E-mail info@internet-books.com. Hrs: 10 am-8 pm. Closed some hols. No A/C. Wine, beer. Semi-a la carte: lunch, dinner $2.50-$8.95. Specializes in sandwiches, pot pies, popovers. Outdoor dining. Glass-enclosed garden rm. Cr cds: A, C, D, DS, MC, V.

D

Carmel Valley (F-1)

(See also Carmel, Monterey)

Pop 4,407 **Elev** 400 ft **Area Code** 408 **Zip** 93924

Hotel

BERNARDUS LODGE. *415 Carmel Rd (93924). 10 mi from Monterrey airport. 831/659-3131; FAX 831/659-3529; res: 888/648-9463.* Web www.bernardus.com. 57 rooms. Nov-Dec S,D $195-$525; Jan-Oct S,D $352-$650; suites up to $1,695. TV, cable. Bar. Refrig. Cribs. Valet. Concierge. Restaurants (2) indoor/outdoor dining. Bar. Beauty salon. Gift shop. Pool. Full spa. Tennis courts (2). Cr cds: A, C, D, DS, ER, JCB, MC, V.

D

Resort

★★★★ **CARMEL VALLEY RANCH.** *1 Old Ranch Rd (93923), Robinson Canyon Rd to Old Ranch Rd. 831/625-9500; FAX 831/624-2858; res: 800/422-7635.* Situated on 1,700 acres in the Santa Lucia Mountains, this exclusive resort offers beautiful ranch-style rooms, championship golf and tennis, and a chance to get away from it all. 144 suites. July-Oct: S, D $325-$850; each addl $25; under 16 free; lower rates rest of yr. Crib free. Pet accepted. TV; cable (premium), VCR avail (movies). 2 heated pools; 8 whirlpools, poolside serv. Restaurants 7 am-2 pm, 6-10 pm. Box lunches, snack bar. Rm serv 7 am-11 pm. Bar 11 am-midnight. Ck-out noon, ck-in 4 pm. Meeting rms. Business center. In-rm modem link. Concierge. Gift shop. Tennis, pro. 18-hole golf, pro, putting green, driving range, pro shop. Exercise rm; sauna. Entertainment Fri-Sat. Refrigerators, fireplaces. Private decks, balconies. Cr cds: A, C, D, DS, JCB, MC, V.

D

Inns

★★ **CARMEL VALLEY LODGE.** *8 Ford Rd (93924), Carmel Valley Rd at Ford Rd. 831/659-2261; FAX 408/659-4558; res: 800/641-4646.* Web www.valleylodge.com. 31 units, 1-2 story, 8 kits. No A/C. July-Sept: S, D $119-$142; each addl $15; studios $164; kit. units, cottages $186-$296; higher rates: hols, special events; wkends, hols (2-3-day min); lower rates rest of yr. Crib free. Pet accepted; $10/day. TV; cable, VCR avail. Heated pool; whirlpool. Complimentary continental bkfst. Complimentary coffee in rms. Ck-out noon, ck-in after 2 pm. Meeting rm. Business servs avail. Exercise equipt; sauna. Fireplace in studios, cottages; some wet bars. Private patios, balconies. Cr cds: A, C, MC, V.

D SC

★★ **LOS LAURELES.** *Carmel Valley Rd (93924). 831/659-2233; FAX 408/659-0481.* Web www.californiainns.com. 30 units, 5 suites. No A/C. Apr-Oct: S, D $110-$250; suites $150-$450; under 17 free; wkends, hols (2-day min); lower rates rest of yr. TV; cable (premium). Heated pool; whirlpool. Restaurant May-Oct: 7:30 am-11 pm. Ck-out noon, ck-in 3 pm. Luggage handling. Business servs avail. Refrigerators; microwaves avail. Main bldg built in 1890s; once home of Muriel Vanderbilt. Cr cds: A, C, MC, V.

SC

★★★ **STONEPINE ESTATE RESORT.** *150 E Carmel Valley Rd (93924). 831/659-2245; FAX 831/659-5160.* 14 suites, 2 story. No A/C. S, D $225-$750; each addl $50; 2-day min wkends, 3-day min hols. TV; cable. Heated pool. Children over 12 yrs only. Complimentary full bkfst; afternoon refreshments. Dining rm (by res). Rm serv. Ck-out noon, ck-in 3 pm. Business servs avail. Concierge serv. Luggage handling. Free airport transportation. Tennis. Exercise equipt. Lawn games. Refrigerators; some in-rm whirlpools. On 330 secluded acres with extensive equestrian facilities; built 1928. Cr cds: A, C, MC, V.

Catalina Island

(see Avalon)

Channel Islands National Park (J-2)

(Off the coast of southern California)

Eight islands, extending over a range of 150 miles in the Pacific Ocean, make up this chain, of which five have been set aside by the government as Channel Islands National Park. Visitors can reach the National Park by commercial boat (see SANTA BARBARA and VENTURA). Anacapa Island, 14 miles south of Ventura, is actually a slender chain of 3 islands, 5 miles long with average width of one-half mile; Santa Barbara Island, 38 miles west of San Pedro, is roughly triangular with its greatest dimension being 1¼ miles. Santa Cruz Island (30 miles offshore), Santa Rosa Island (40 miles offshore) and San Miguel Island (45 miles offshore) are also part of the park. Santa Rosa may be reached by commercial flights (see CAMARILLO).

On Anacapa Island in early spring there is a spectacular display of wildflowers; a yellow table of the giant coreopsis, with its large flowers, is visible from a great distance. Sea mammals, including the California sea lion and harbor seal, are observed around the island's rocky shores. From January through March the annual migration of gray whales passes close to Anacapa. The island also has a self-guided nature trail and a museum. Ranger-guided tours available all year. Scuba and skin diving are popular sports, since the islands are noted for their variety of marine life.

Santa Barbara Island is a marine terrace with steep cliffs, some rising to more than 500 feet. Numerous caves, coves, offshore pillars and blowholes are also found. Since Santa Barbara is so isolated, sea mammals, including the huge elephant seal, are occasional visitors. Bird watching is excellent on this island and numerous species may be observed, including Xantus' murrelet, American kestrel, brown pelican, black oystercatcher, orange-crowned warbler and others. Self-guided trails and ranger-conducted walking tours are available. Camping is permitted on Anacapa, Santa Barbara, Santa Rosa, Santa Cruz and San Miguel Islands. Permits are issued in advance and may be obtained by calling 800/365-2267. No pets are permitted on the islands.

San Miguel Island (14 square miles) contains an outstanding number of natural features, including "caliche" or "fossil forests," which give the island landscape an eerie, almost alien appearance. It is the only island where six pinniped (seals and sea lions) species are found, more than are found in any other single location in the world. In order to land on the island a permit must be acquired from park headquarters prior to your visit.

Santa Rosa Island (53 square miles) is now owned by Channel Islands National Park. Visitors to the island must be accompanied by a park ranger. For camping, a permit is required (phone 805/658-5711); a landing permit is required only for ranger-led walks & hikes (arranged by appt). Santa Cruz Island (96 square miles) is divided between the National Park Service, which owns and manages the eastern 10 percent, and the Nature Conservancy, which owns and manages the western 90 percent. Information about public access to this island may be obtained from the Santa Cruz Nature Conservancy, 213 Stearns Wharf, Santa Barbara 93101; 805/962-9111. A visitor center (open all year) at 1901 Spinnaker Dr in Ventura offers information, exhibits and audiovisual programs; phone 805/658-5730. For further information contact Park Superintendent, 1901 Spinnaker Dr, Ventura 93001; 805/658-5700 or -5730. **Free**; Camping **¢¢**

Chester (B-3)

(See also Quincy, Susanville)

Pop 2,082 **Elev** 4,528 ft **Area Code** 916 **Zip** 96020

Information Chester/Lake Almanor Chamber of Commerce, 529 Main St, PO Box 1198; 916/258-2426 or 800/350-4838

The Lake Almanor area offers both summer and winter sports. Mt Lassen is 30 miles north and west. Fishing is good in the lake and surrounding streams served by many boat landings and ramps. Deer, bear, waterfowl and birds are plentiful in season. There are many resorts, tent & trailer sites and two scenic golf courses around the lake and a number of improved campsites within five miles of Chester. Chester is also the home of the Collins Pine Sawmill, one of the largest in the state. A Ranger District office of the Lassen National Forest (see SUSANVILLE) is also located here.

Inn

✓★★ **BIDWELL HOUSE BED & BREAKFAST.** *1 Main St (96020). 530/258-3338.* 14 rms, 2 story, 1 cottage. No A/C. Rm phones avail. S, D $75-$150; cottage $150; hols (2-day min). TV avail. Complimentary full bkfst. Complimentary coffee in rms. Restaurant 5:30-8 pm. Ck-out 11 am, ck-in 3-6 pm. Game rm. Some fireplaces. Antiques. Built in 1901. Flower & vegetable gardens. Totally nonsmoking. Cr cds: C, MC, V.

D SC

Chico (C-2)

(See also Oroville)

Settled 1843 **Pop** 40,079 **Elev** 200 ft **Area Code** 530
E-mail visitor@chicochamber.com **Web** www.chicochamber.com

Information Chamber of Commerce, 300 Salem St, 95928; 530/891-5556 or 800/852-8570

Chico was originally settled in 1843 as Rancho Del Arroyo by General John Bidwell, a leading agriculturist of the 19th century as well as a gold-miner, statesman and a US congressman. Chico is now a city of diversified business, industry and agriculture in an area that is said to produce 20 percent of the world's almonds.

What to See and Do

Bidwell Mansion State Historic Park (1868). This is the 26-rm Victorian house of the founder of Chico (candidate for US president in 1892); 1st, 2nd & 3rd floors restored. (Daily; closed Jan 1, Thanksgiving, Dec 25) 525 Esplanade. Phone 530/895-6144. ¢

Bidwell Park. 10-mi-long, 3,700-acre city park with stream; site of location shots for many movies, including *The Adventures of Robin Hood.* Swimming pools; picnicking; 18-hole golf at NE end of park; bridle, foot and nature trails; kiddie playland. ½ mi E on E 4th St. Phone 530/895-4972.

California State University, Chico (1887). (15,000 students) On 115 tree-shaded acres; art galleries (daily exc Sat); "anthromuseum"; campus tour. Nearby is a 1,000-acre college farm. W 1st St. Phone 530/898-6116 or 530/898-5307.

Chico Museum. History museum housed in 1904 Carnegie Library; permanent and changing exhibits include local history artifacts and photos, Chinese Temple. Programs, activities. (Wed-Sun afternoons) 141 Salem St, at Second St. Phone 530/891-4336. **Donation**

Self-guided nature tours. Detailed brochures with tour maps avail from Chamber of Commerce, phone 530/891-5556.

Spring Blossom Tour. 40-mi tour allows participants to view the wealth of blooming orchards and wildflowers in Butte County. Blossoms include almond, prune, kiwi, pear and iris. (Mid-Feb-mid-Mar & mid-Apr-mid-May) **Free**

Winter Migratory Waterfowl Tour. 100-mi tour provides insight into importance of farmlands and wildlife preserves to migrating waterfowl in Butte County. Approx 150 bird species migrate here in winter. (Sept-Mar) **Free**

Annual Events

Bidwell Classic Marathon. 1st Sat Mar.

Silver Dollar Fair. Phone 530/895-4666. 5 days late May.

Chico Expo. Phone 530/891-5556. 1st wkend Oct.

Motels

★★ **BEST WESTERN HERITAGE INN.** *25 Heritage Ln (95926), on CA 99. 530/894-8600; FAX 916/894-8600; res: 800/446-4291.* 101 rms, 3 story. S $64-$74; D $71-$82; each addl $7; under 12 free; higher rates: university graduation wkend, auto races. Crib free. TV. Pool; whirlpool. Complimentary continental bkfst. Ck-out 11 am. Meeting rm. Business servs avail. In-rm modem link. Health club privileges. Some refrigerators, wet bars. Cr cds: A, C, D, DS, JCB, MC, V.

SC

✓★ **VAGABOND INN.** *630 Main St (95928). 530/895-1323; FAX 530/343-2719; res: 800/522-1555.* 42 rms, 2 story. S $34-$50; D $45-$75; higher rates special events; each addl $5; kit. units $8 addl; under 16 free. Crib free. Pet accepted. TV; cable (premium). Pool. Complimentary continental bkfst. Complimentary coffee in rms. Restaurant adj open 24 hrs. Ck-out 11 am. Meeting rm. Business servs avail. Health club privileges. Cr cds: A, C, D, DS, MC, V.

SC

Motor Hotel

★★ **HOLIDAY INN.** *685 Manzanita Ct (93923). 530/345-2491; FAX 530/893-3040; res: 800/310-2491.* 172 rms, 5 story. S, D $59-$75; each addl $6; suites $100-$160; under 19 free. Crib free. Pet accepted, some restrictions. TV; cable (premium). Pool; whirlpool. Restaurant 6 am-10 pm. Rm serv. Bar from 2 pm; entertainment. Ck-out 11 am. Coin Indry. Meeting rms. Business servs avail. In-rm modem link. Bellhops. Valet serv. Free airport, bus depot transportation. Health club privileges. Refrigerator in suites. Microwaves avail. Cr cds: A, C, D, DS, JCB, MC, V.

D SC

Chula Vista (K-4)

Pop 135,163 **Elev** 75 ft **Area Code** 619

The name Chula Vista is Spanish for "beautiful view." Set between the mountains and the sea, the city lives up to its name.

Motels

✓★★ **GOOD NITE INN.** *225 Bay Blvd (91910), I-5, E St exit. 619/425-8200; FAX 619/426-7411; res: 800/648-3466.* 118 rms, 2 story. Mid-May-mid-Sept: S $41; D $49; each addl $6; under 18 free; lower rates rest of yr. Crib free. Pet accepted, some restrictions. TV; cable (premium). Heated pool. Complimentary coffee in lobby. Restaurant 6 am-10 pm. Ck-out 11 am. Some refrigerators, microwaves. Cr cds: A, C, D, DS, MC, V.

D SC

★★ **HOLIDAY INN EXPRESS.** *4450 Otay Valley Rd (91911). 619/422-2600; FAX 619/425-4605; res: 800/628-2611.* 118 rms, 3 story. May-Sept: S $69-$79; D $79-$89; each addl $5; under 17 free; lower rates rest of yr. Crib free. TV; cable (premium). Heated pool; whirlpool. Complimentary continental bkfst. Restaurant adj open 24 hrs. Ck-out noon. Coin Indry. Meeting rm. Business servs avail. In-rm modem link. Valet serv. Refrigerators, microwaves avail. Cr cds: A, C, D, DS, JCB, MC, V.

D SC

★★ **RAMADA INN SAN DIEGO SOUTH.** *91 Bonita Rd (91910). 619/425-9999; FAX 619/425-8934; res: 800/272-6232.* 97 rms, 4 story. June-Sept: S $62-$72; D $70-$82; each addl $8; suites $72-$85; under 18 free; lower rates rest of yr. Crib free. TV; cable (premium). Heated pool; whirlpool. Restaurant adj 6:30 am-11 pm. Ck-out 11 am. Meeting rm. Business servs avail. Cr cds: A, C, D, DS, ER, JCB, MC, V.

D SC

✓★ **RODEWAY INN.** *778 Broadway (91910). 619/476-9555; res: 800/228-2000.* 49 rms, 3 story. May-Sept: S $60-$70; D $70-$80; each addl $5; under 18 free; wkly rates; lower rates rest of yr. Crib $5. TV; cable (premium). Pool; whirlpool. Complimentary coffee in lobby. Restaurant nearby. Ck-out 11:30 am. Refrigerators, microwaves avail. Cr cds: A, C, D, DS, JCB, MC, V.

D SC

Restaurants

★★ **BUON GIORNO.** *4110 Bonita Rd (91902). 619/475-2660.* Hrs: 11 am-10 pm; Fri, Sat to 11 pm; Sun 3-9 pm. Closed Jan 1, Thanksgiving, Dec 25. Res accepted. Italian menu. Bar to midnight. Semi-a la carte: lunch $5.95-$14.95, dinner $8.95-$22.95. Child's meals. Specializes in seafood, pasta. Pianist Thurs-Sat. Old-World Italian setting; prints of opera stars adorn walls. Cr cds: A, C, MC, V.

D

★ **BUTCHER SHOP.** *556 Broadway (91910). 619/420-9440.* Hrs: 11-1 am; Sun 2-10 pm. Closed Thanksgiving, Dec 25. Res accepted. Bar to 2 am. Semi-a la carte: lunch $7.95-$11.95, dinner $8.95-$25.95. Specializes in steak, prime rib. Entertainment Wed-Sat evenings. Family-owned. Cr cds: A, C, D, DS, MC, V.

D

Claremont (B-7 see Los Angeles map)

(See also Ontario, Pasadena, Pomona, Riverside)

Pop 32,503 **Elev** 1,169 ft **Area Code** 909 **Zip** 91711
Information Chamber of Commerce, 205 N Yale Ave; 909/624-1681

What to See and Do

The Claremont Colleges. A distinguished group of institutions comprised of Pomona College (1887) (1,500 students), Claremont Graduate School (1925) (1,800 students), Scripps College (1926) (550 students), Claremont McKenna College (1946) (900 students), Harvey Mudd College (1955) (650 students) and Pitzer College (1963) (700 students). College Ave between 1st St & Foothill Blvd (CA 66). Phone 909/621-8000. On campus are

Montgomery Art Gallery. Exhibits. (Tues-Sun afternoons; closed school hols & June-Aug) 330 N College Ave. Phone 909/621-8283. **Free**

Graduate School Art Building. Exhibits. (Daily, wkends by appt) 10th St & Columbia Ave. Phone 909/621-8071. **Free**

Rancho Santa Ana Botanic Garden. Native plants. (Daily; closed Jan 1, July 4, Thanksgiving, Dec 25) 1500 N College Ave, N of Foothill Blvd. Phone 909/625-8767. **Free**

Motel

★★ **RAMADA INN.** *840 S Indian Hill Blvd (91711), I-10 Indian Hill Blvd exit, 1 blk S. 909/621-4831; FAX 909/621-0411; res: 800/322-6559.* Web www.ramadaclar.com. 122 rms, 2 story. S, D $80; each addl $8; under 12 free. Crib free. Pet accepted. TV; cable (premium). Heated pool; wading pool, whirlpool. Complimentary continental bkfst. Restaurant opp open 24 hrs. Ck-out noon. Coin Indry. Meeting rms. Business servs avail. Valet serv. Lighted tennis. Health club privileges. Refrigerators. Picnic tables, grill. Cr cds: A, C, D, DS, JCB, MC, V.

D SC

Restaurant

✓★★ **YIANNIS GREEK RESTAURANT.** *238 Yale Ave (91711), I-10 Indian Hill Blvd exit. 909/621-2413.* Hrs: 11 am-10 pm. Closed Mon; major hols. Greek menu. Bar. Semi-a la carte: lunch $5.85-$7.55. Complete meals: dinner $10.75-$14.95. Sun brunch $6.75. Specialties: mousakka, souvlakia. Own bread, baklava. Outdoor dining. Greek artifacts; colorful lamps. Family-owned. Cr cds: A, C, MC, V.

Clear Lake Area (Lake Co) (D-2)

(See also Healdsburg, Ukiah)

Area Code 707
Information Chamber of Commerce, 290 S Main St, PO Box 295, Lakeport 95453; 707/263-5092

This is a popular recreation area for fishing, hunting, swimming, boating, golf and other sports.

What to See and Do

Clear Lake State Park. Pomo Native Americans once occupied this area. Swimming, waterskiing; fishing; boating (ramp). Nature, hiking trails. Picnicking. Camping (no hookups, dump station). Visitor center with wildlife dioramas, aquarium; nature films. Standard fees. 3 mi NE of Kelseyville on Soda Bay Rd. Phone 707/279-4293. Day use per vehicle ¢¢

Annual Events

Lake County Rodeo. Lake County Fairgrounds, Lakeport. July.

Lake County Fair and Horse Show. Lake County Fairgrounds. Phone 707/263-6181. Labor Day wkend.

Motels

★★ **ANCHORAGE INN.** *950 N Main St (95453). 707/263-5417; FAX 707/263-5453; res: 800/932-4031.* 34 rms, 2 story, 20 kits. S $54; D $62; each addl $10; 1-2 bedrm suites & kit. units $64-$115; hol wkends (2-3-day min). TV; cable. Pool; whirlpool. Complimentary coffee in rms. Restaurant opp 6 am-9 pm. Ck-out 11 am. Coin Indry. Business servs avail. In-rm modem link. Sauna. Private patios; some balconies. Picnic tables, grills. Dockage. On Clear Lake. Cr cds: A, C, D, DS, MC, V.

★ **HIGHLANDS INN.** *13865 Lakeshore Dr (95422). 707/994-8982; FAX 707/994-0613; res: 800/329-7466.* 20 rms, 2 story. S $45-$55; D $55-$65; each addl $5; suites $70-$80; higher rates hols. Crib $5. TV; cable. Pool. Complimentary continental bkfst. Complimentary coffee in rms. Ck-out 11 am. Coin Indry. Business servs avail. Refrigerators. Picnic tables. On lake. Grills. Cr cds: A, C, D, DS, MC, V.

D SC

Motor Hotel

★★★ **BEST WESTERN EL GRANDE INN.** *15135 Lakeshore Dr (95422). 707/994-2000; FAX 707/994-2042; res: 800/528-1234.* 68 rms, 4 story. S $67-$72; D $79-$95; each addl $7; suites $79-$95. Crib free. TV; cable (premium), VCR avail (movies). Indoor pool; whirlpool. Complimentary coffee in rms. Restaurant 7 am-1:30 pm, 5-9:30 pm. Bar 2 pm-midnight. Ck-out 11 am. Meeting rms. Business servs avail. In-rm modem link. Refrigerator in suites. Spanish-style lobby. All rms open to atrium. Cr cds: A, C, D, DS, MC, V.

D SC

Coleville (D-4)

(See also Bridgeport)

Pop 60 (est) **Elev** 5,400 ft **Area Code** 916 **Zip** 96107

Motels

✓★ **ANDRUSS MOTEL.** *106964 US Hwy 395 (96107), 5 mi S on US 395. 530/495-2216.* 13 air-cooled rms, 4 kits. S $36-$42; D, kit. units $42-$52; each addl $4. Crib free. Pet accepted; $5. TV; cable (premium). Heated pool. Playground. Complimentary coffee in rms. Restaurant opp 6 am-10 pm. Ck-out 11 am. Lawn games. Picnic tables, grill. Fish cleaning, freezing facilities. Cr cds: A, C, DS, MC, V.

D SC

Coloma

(see Placerville)

Concord (E-2)

(See also Martinez, Oakland, Vallejo)

Pop 111,348 **Elev** 70 ft **Area Code** 925 **E-mail** info@cccvb.com
Information Contra Costa Convention & Visitors Bureau, 1333 Willow Path Rd, Suite 204, 94520; 925/685-1184

What to See and Do

Concord Pavilion. Roofed, open-air performance and assembly facility, with lawn and reserved pavilion seating for 12,500; popular entertainment performances, sports and special events (Apr-Oct). 2000 Kirker Pass Rd. Phone 925/762-2277.

Waterworld USA. Twenty-acre park includes attractions such as Breaker Beach Wavepool, Treasure Island kid's area, Lazy River and The Big Kahuna, a 6-story raft adventure. Also here are a multi-level activity pool and waterslides. (Late May-early Sept, daily) 1950 Waterworld Pkwy. Phone 925/609-WAVE. ¢¢¢¢¢

Motels

★ **BEST WESTERN HERITAGE INN.** *4600 Clayton Rd (94521). 925/686-4466; FAX 925/825-0581; res: 800/528-1234.* E-mail bsoleil@aol.com. 126 rms, 2 story. S, D $65-$75; kit. units $85; under 18 free. Crib free. TV; cable (premium). Pool; whirlpool. Complimentary continental bkfst. Ck-out 11 am. Meeting rms. Business servs avail. In-rm modem link. Health club privileges. Refrigerators; some wet bars. Cr cds: A, C, D, DS, JCB, MC, V.

D SC

✓★ **COMFORT INN.** *1370 Monument Blvd (94520). 925/827-8998; FAX 925/798-3374; res: 800/638-7949.* 41 kit. units, 3 story. June-Sept: S, D $79-$94; each addl $5; wkly rates; lower rates rest of yr. TV; cable (premium), VCR (movies $4). Pool. Complimentary continental bkfst. Restaurant nearby. Ck-out 11 am. Coin Indry. Business servs avail. In-rm modem link. Exercise equipt. Patios, balconies. Cr cds: A, C, D, DS, JCB, MC, V.

D SC

Hotels

★★ **HILTON HOTEL.** *1970 Diamond Blvd (94520). 925/827-2000; FAX 925/827-2113; res: 800/445-8667.* E-mail beckywen@concordhilton.com; web www.concordhilton.com. 330 rms, 11 story. S $94-$152; D $94-$162; each addl $10; suites $375-$475; family, wkend rates. Crib free. TV; cable (premium), VCR avail (movies). Pool; whirlpool. Coffee in rms. Restaurant 6:30 am-10 pm, wkends from 7 am. Bar 11 am-midnight; entertainment Mon-Fri. Ck-out noon. Convention facilities. Business servs avail. In-rm modem link. Gift shop. Exercise equipt. Cr cds: A, C, D, DS, ER, MC, V.

D SC

★★★ **SHERATON CONCORD HOTEL & CONFERENCE CENTER.** *45 John Glenn Dr (94520), adj to Buchanan Airport. 925/825-7700; FAX 925/674-9567; res: 800/325-3535.* Web www.sheraton.com. 324 rms, 3 story. S $85-$139; D $85-$159; each addl $20; suites $175-$425; under 17 free. Crib free. Heated pool; whirlpool. TV; cable. Coffee in rms. Restaurant 6:30 am-2 pm, 5-10:30 pm. Bar noon-2 am; entertainment. Ck-out noon. Meeting rms. Business center. In-rm modem link. Concierge. Sundries. Gift shop. Indoor putting green. Exercise equipt. Health club privileges. Microwaves avail. Luxury level. Cr cds: A, C, D, DS, ER, JCB, MC, V.

D SC

Corona (D-8 see Los Angeles map)

(See also Ontario, Riverside)

Pop 76,095 **Elev** 678 ft **Area Code** 909
Information Chamber of Commerce, 904 E 6th St, 91719; 909/737-3350

A Ranger District office of the Cleveland National Forest (see PINE VALLEY) is located in Corona.

What to See and Do

Glen Ivy Hot Springs. Natural hot mineral spa. Swimming, 15 outdoor mineral baths, massage, sauna, clay bath, outdoor poolside dining. (Daily; closed Jan 1, Thanksgiving, Dec 25) 25000 Glen Ivy Rd, 8 mi S via I-15 at Temescal Canyon Rd exit. Phone 909/277-3529. ¢¢¢¢¢

Prado Basin County Park. 1,837-acre wildlife refuge area along the Santa Ana River has nature trail and picnicking. (Wkends only) 4½ mi N on River Rd. For general park information, phone 909/955-4310. Per vehicle ¢¢

Motels

★★ **BEST WESTERN KINGS INN.** *1084 Pomona Rd (91720), CA 91 Lincoln Ave exit, then 1 blk N . 909/734-4241; FAX 909/279-5371; res: 800/892-5464.* 87 rms, 2 story. S, D $59-$79; each addl $5; under 18 free. Crib free. TV; cable (premium), VCR avail (movies free). Heated pool; whirlpool. Complimentary continental bkfst. Restaurants adj 6 am-midnight. Ck-out noon. Meeting rm. Business servs avail. Health club priveleges. Valet serv. Some refrigerators. Microwaves avail. Cr cds: A, C, D, DS, MC, V.

D SC

✓★★ **DYNASTY SUITES.** *3735 Iowa Ave (92882). 909/371-7185; FAX 909/371-0401; res: 800/842-7899.* Web www.dynastysuites.com. 56 rms, 2 story. S, D $49.95; each addl $5. Crib free. Pet accepted, some restrictions; $10/day. TV; cable (premium), VCR avail (movies). Complimentary continental bkfst. Restaurant adj 5-1 am. Ck-out noon. Meeting rms. Business servs avail. Valet serv. Health club privileges. Heated pool; whirlpool. Bathrm phones, refrigerators, microwaves; some in-rm whirlpools. Cr cds: A, C, D, DS, MC, V.

D SC

★★ **THE COUNTRY INN.** *2260 Griffin Way (91719). 909/734-2140; FAX 909/734-4056; res: 800/448-8810.* Web www.countrysideinn.com. 102 rms, 2 story. S $79; D $89; each addl $10; under 12 free. Crib free. TV; cable (premium). Heated pool; whirlpool. Complimentary full bkfst. Restaurant opp 7 am-11 pm. Ck-out noon. Meeting rm. Business servs avail. Valet serv. Guest Indry. Refrigerators. Cr cds: A, C, D, DS, MC, V.

D SC

Corona del Mar (F-6 see Los Angeles map)

Elev 75 ft **Area Code** 714 **Zip** 92625

This community is part of Newport Beach (see).

Restaurants

★★★ **FIVE CROWNS RESTAURANT.** *3801 E Pacific Coast Hwy (92625). 714/760-0331.* Hrs: 5-10 pm; Sun 4-9:30 pm; Sun brunch 10:30 am-2:30 pm. Closed July 4, Dec 25. Res accepted. Bar. Wine list. A la carte entrees: dinner $14.50-$29.95. Sun brunch $11.50-$17. Specializes in beef, lamb, fresh fish. Valet parking. Patio, greenhouse dining. English-style inn, fireplaces. Cr cds: A, C, D, DS, JCB, MC, V.

D SC

★ **QUIET WOMAN.** *3224 E Pacific Coast Hwy (92625), 2 mi S of jct CA 1/73. 714/640-7440.* Hrs: 11:30 am-2:30 pm, 5-10 pm; Fri, Sat to 11 pm; Sun 5-11 pm. Closed major hols. Bar to 1:30 am. Semi-a la carte: lunch $8-$14, dinner $14.50-$32.50. Specializes in lamb, fresh seafood. Entertainment Wed-Sat. English pub decor. Cr cds: A, C, MC, V.

D

★★ **THE BUNGALOW.** *2441 E Coast Hwy (92625), 1 mi SE on Coast Hwy. 714/673-6585.* Hrs: 5-10 pm; Fri, Sat to 11 pm. Closed Memorial Day, July 4, Dec 25. Res accepted. Bar to 2 am. Semi-a la carte: dinner $13.95-$27.95. Specialties: fresh blackened rare ahi, fire-roasted Colorado rack of lamb. Valet parking. Outdoor dining. Garden patio; mahogany wood throughout. Totally nonsmoking. Cr cds: A, C, MC, V.

D

Coronado (K-4)

Pop 26,540 **Elev** 25 ft **Area Code** 619 **Zip** 92118

Known as the Crown City, Coronado lies across the bay from San Diego and is connected to the mainland by a long, narrow sandbar called the Silver Strand and by the beautiful Coronado Bridge. It is the site of the famous Hotel del Coronado (1888).

Motels

★ **CROWN CITY INN.** *520 Orange Ave (92118). 619/435-3116; FAX 619/435-6750; res: 800/422-1173.* 33 rms, 2 story. Mid-June-mid-Sept: S, D $106-$125; under 18 free; higher rates hols (3-day min); lower rates rest of yr. Crib $5. Pet accepted; $8. TV; cable (premium). Heated pool. Complimentary coffee in rms. Restaurant 8 am-2 pm, 5-9 pm. Rm serv. Ck-out 11 am. Coin Indry. Business servs avail. Health club privileges. Refrigerators, microwaves. Cr cds: A, C, D, DS, JCB, MC, V.

★★ **EL CORDOVA HOTEL.** *1351 Orange Ave (92118). 619/435-4131; FAX 619/435-0632; res: 800/229-2032.* 40 units, 2 story, 28 kits. Mid-June-mid-Sept: S, D $85-$95; suites $130-$295; studio rms $105-$135; wkly, monthly rates off-season; lower rates rest of yr. Crib free. TV; cable (premium). Heated pool. Restaurant 11 am-10 pm. Bar adj. Ck-out noon. Business servs avail. Health club privileges. Picnic tables, grills. Historic mansion (1902). Cr cds: A, C, D, DS, MC, V.

SC

★★ **GLORIETTA BAY INN.** *1630 Glorietta Blvd (92118). 619/435-3101; FAX 619/435-6182; res: 800/283-9383.* E-mail rooms@ gloriettabayinn.com; web www.gloriettabayinn.com. 100 units, 2 story, 33 kits. S, D $130-$195; each addl $10; suites, kit. units $185-$395. Crib free. TV; cable (premium). Heated pool; whirlpool. Complimentary continental bkfst. Ck-out 11 am. Coin Indry. Business center. In-rm modem link. Refrigerators; microwaves avail. Many private patios, balconies. Some rms overlook Glorietta Bay. Historic house (1908), part of Speckels mansion. Cr cds: A, C, MC, V.

D SC

★ **LA AVENIDA INN.** *1315 Orange Ave (92118). 619/435-3191; FAX 619/435-5024; res: 800/437-0162.* 29 rms, 2 story. July-Sept: S, D $105-$125; wkends (2-day min); lower rates rest of yr. Crib free. TV; cable (premium). Complimentary coffee in lobby. Restaurant adj 11 am-10 pm. Ck-out noon. Pool. Opp ocean. Cr cds: C.

Resorts

★★★ **HOTEL DEL CORONADO.** *1500 Orange Ave (92118). 619/435-6611; FAX 619/522-8262; res: 800/468-3533.* Web www.hoteldel. com. 692 rms, Room rates starting at $205 per night, under 18 free; Crib free. TV; VCR avail. 2 heated pools; whirlpool, poolside serv. Supervised child's activities. Fine dining available in various restaurants. Rm serv 24 hrs. Bar 7-2 am; entertainment. Ck-out noon, ck-in 4 pm. Convention facilities. Business center. In-rm modem link. Concierge. An elaborate spa and fitness center w/sauna and massage is available. Lighted tennis. Minibars. Many private patios, balconies. Swimming beach; sail and power boat rentals avail at hotel docks. Cr cds: A, C, D, DS, JCB, MC, V.

D

★★★ **LOEWS CORONADO BAY.** *4000 Coronado Bay Rd (92118). 619/424-4000; FAX 619/424-4400; res: 800/235-6397.* 440 guest rooms & suites. S, D $245-$285; each addl $20; suites $425-$1,300; under 18 free; tennis plans. Crib free. Pet accepted. TV; cable, VCR avail. Supervised child's activities. Restaurants (see AZZURA POINT and LA CANTINA BAR & GRILL). Rm serv 24 hrs. Bar 11-2 am; Entertainment (CAYS LOUNGE). Ck-out noon, ck-in 4 pm. Conference facilities. Meeting rooms. Business center. In-rm modem link. Bellhops. Valet serv. Concierge. Gift shop. Barber, beauty shop. Sports dir. 5 lighted tennis courts, pro. Beach, boats, water skiing, swimming. 3 pools; whirlpools, poolside serv. Bicycle rentals. Lawn games. Game rm. Health club, sauna. Massage. Bathrm phones. Minibars. Refrigerators, microwaves avail. Balconies. All rooms offer spectacular water views of the San Diego Bay, ocean, marina. Private marina. Private access to beach. Cr cds: A, C, D, DS, ER, JCB, MC, V.

D SC

★★★★ **MARRIOTT CORONADO ISLAND RESORT.** *2000 2nd St (92118). 619/435-3000; FAX 619/435-3032; res: 800/228-9290.* Flamingos greet you at the entrance to this luxury resort, and other exotic wildlife roam the 16 acres of landscaped grounds that include koi-stocked streams and lush lagoons. The interior of the hotel reflects its French heritage and California setting. 300 rms, 3 story, 28 villas. June-Sept: S, D $275-$325; suites, villas $325-$795; under 12 free. Crib free. Pet accepted. Covered parking $10; valet $14. TV; cable (premium), VCR avail. 3 pools; whirlpool, poolside serv. Restaurants 6:30 am-10 pm (also see L'ESCALE and MARIUS). Rm serv 24 hrs. Bar 11:30-1 am; entertainment Fri, Sat. Ck-out noon. Convention facilities. Business center. Concierge. Shops. Lighted tennis, pro, pro shop, tennis clinic. Scuba, snorkling, windsurfing classes. Bicycle rental. Exercise rm; sauna. Spa. Minibars; microwaves avail. Private patios. On bay; pier, 2 slips. Floral & wildlife tour. Cr cds: A, C, D, DS, MC, V.

D

Restaurants

★★★ **AZZURA POINT.** *(See Loews Coronado Bay Resort) 619/424-4000.* Hrs: 6-10:30 pm; Fri, Sat to 11 pm. Res accepted. Mediterranean, California, Mediterranean menu. Bar. Wine list. Semi-a la carte: dinner $22-$32. Child's meals. Specialties: scallop & prosciutto with porcini

& white truffle essence, pacific halibut with tomato-orange relish & garlic herbs. Valet parking. Panoramic view of the bay, ocean and city skyline. Jacket recommended. Cr cds: A, C, D, DS, JCB, MC, V.

D

★★ **BRIGANTINE.** *1333 Orange Ave (92118). 619/435-4166.* Hrs: 11:30 am-2:30 pm, 5-10:30 pm; Fri to 11:30 pm; Sat 5-11:30 pm; Sun 5-10:30 pm; early-bird dinner Sun-Thurs 5-7 pm. Res accepted. Bar to 2 am. Semi-a la carte: lunch $6.95-$12.95, dinner $8.95-$27.95. Child's meals. Specializes in fresh seafood, steak. Nautical decor. Family-owned. Cr cds: A, C, D, MC, V.

D

★★ **CHAMELEON CAFE.** *1301 Orange Ave (92118). 619/437-6677.* Hrs: 11 am-10 pm; Fri, Sat to 2 am. Closed Jan 1, Dec 25. Pacific Rim menu. Bar. Semi-a la carte: lunch $7.95-$14.95, dinner $8.95-$24.95. Child's meals. Specializes in fresh seafood. Street parking. Outdoor dining. Contemporary atmosphere. Totally nonsmoking. Cr cds: A, C, D, MC, V.

D

★★★ **CHEZ LOMA.** *1132 Loma Ave (92118). 619/435-0661.* Hrs: 5-10 pm; Sun brunch 10 am-2 pm. Closed some major hols. Res accepted. French menu. Bar. Wine cellar. Semi-a la carte: dinner $19-$29. Sun brunch $11.95. Specializes in duck, seafood. Own desserts. Historic landmark house (1889). Cr cds: A, C, D, MC, V.

★★★ **CROWN ROOM.** *(See Hotel del Coronado Resort) 619/435-6611.* Hrs: 7 am-9:30 pm; Fri, Sat to 10 pm; early-bird dinner Mon-Fri 5-6 pm. Res accepted. Serv bar. Wine cellar. Semi-a la carte: bkfst from $9.95, lunch from $10.95, dinner $18-$30. Prix fixe: dinner $26. Buffet: bkfst $14.95. Child's meals. Specializes in lamb, pasta, fresh fish. Own baking. Pianist Wed-Sat. Valet parking. Rotating menu. Historic 1888 structure; hand-tooled dome ceiling. Cr cds: A, C, D, DS, JCB, MC, V.

D

✓★★ **MEXICAN VILLAGE RESTAURANTE.** *120 Orange Ave (92118). 619/435-1822.* Hrs: 11 am-10 pm; Fri, Sat to 11 pm; Sun 8 am-noon. Mexican, Amer menu. Bar. Semi-a la carte: lunch $4.95-$8.95, dinner $5.95-$17.95. Child's meals. Specializes in Mexican pizza, romaine salad. Local landmark; opened 1945. Several dining rms; Mexican decor and artifacts. Cr cds: A, C, D, MC, V.

D

★★ **PEOHE'S.** *1201 1st St (92118). 619/437-4474.* Hrs: 11:30 am-2:30 pm, 5:30-9:30 pm; Sat 5-10:30 pm; Sun brunch 10:30 am-2:30 pm. Res accepted. Varied menu. Bar. Semi-a la carte: lunch $6.95-$14.95, dinner $17-$29. Sun brunch $8-$15. Child's meals. Specialties: coconut crunchy shrimp, fresh Hawaiian fish. Parking. Outdoor dining. Tropical atmosphere with waterfalls and running streams; lush plants; ponds stocked with tropical fish. View of San Diego Harbor and skyline. Cr cds: A, C, D, DS, MC, V.

D

★★ **PRIMAVERA.** *932 Orange Ave (92118). 619/435-0454.* Hrs: 11 am-2:30 pm, 5-10:30 pm; Sat, Sun from 5 pm. Closed Jan 1, Dec 25. Res accepted. Northern Italian menu. Bar. Semi-a la carte: lunch $7.25-$12.95, dinner $12.95-$26.95. Specialties: osso bucco Milanese, lamb chops al balsamico. Elegant, romantic Mediterranean decor; original artwork. Totally nonsmoking. Cr cds: A, C, D, DS, MC, V.

D

★★★ **PRINCE OF WALES.** *(See Hotel Del Coronado) 619/522-8818.* Hrs: 5:30-10 pm. Res accepted. Continental, contemporary Amer menu. Bar. Wine cellar. Semi-a la carte: dinner $21-$36. Specializes in seafood, pasta, lamb. Own baking. Valet parking. 1930s summer house atmosphere. Cr cds: A, C, D, DS, JCB, MC, V.

D

Corte Madera (B-2 see San Francisco map)

(See also San Francisco, San Rafael)

Pop 8,272 **Elev** 27 ft **Area Code** 415 **Zip** 94925

Motel

★★★ **BEST WESTERN INN.** *1815 Redwood Hwy (94925), at Madera Blvd. 415/924-1502; FAX 415/924-5419; res: 800/777-9670.* 110 rms, 2 story. S $89-$129; D $99-$139; each addl $10; suites $145-$185; under 18 free. Crib free. TV; cable (premium). Heated pool; wading pool, whirlpools; lifeguard. Playground. Complimentary continental bkfst in rms. Coffee in rms. Restaurant 8 am-11 pm; Fri, Sat 8:30 am-midnight. Ck-out noon. Coin Indry. Meeting rms. Business servs avail. In-rm modem link. Bellhops. Valet serv. Sundries. Exercise equipt. Massage. Refrigerators. Private patios, balconies. Picnic tables. Cr cds: A, C, D, DS, ER, JCB, MC, V.

D SC

Hotel

★★ **MARIN SUITES HOTEL.** *45 Tamal Vista Blvd (94925). 415/924-3608; FAX 415/924-0761; res: 800/362-3372.* 100 suites, 3 story. S, D $119-$199; under 17 free. Crib free. TV; cable (premium), VCR avail. Pool. Complimentary continental bkfst. Restaurant adj 11:30 am-10:30 pm. Ck-out noon. Coin Indry. Exercise equipt; sauna. Refrigerators. Cr cds: A, C, D, DS, JCB, MC, V.

SC

Restaurants

★★ **ATRIUM.** *1546 Redwood Hwy (94925). 415/927-8889.* E-mail royam@accountmate.com; web www.atriumcuisine.com. Hrs: 11:30 am-9 pm; Fri, Sat to 10 pm. Closed Dec 25. Res accepted (dinner). Chinese menu. Wine, beer. A la carte entrees: lunch, dinner $7.95-$28.50. Complete meal: dinner $26-$36. Parking. Family-style dining. Totally nonsmoking. Cr cds: A, C, D, DS, MC, V.

D

★★ **CALIFORNIA CAFE.** *1736 Redwood Hwy (94925). 915/924-2233.* Web www.calcafe.com. Hrs: 11 am-9:30 pm; wkends to 10 pm; Sun brunch 11 am-3 pm. Closed Dec 25. Res accepted. Bar. A la carte entrees: lunch $5.95-$12.95, dinner $12.95-$21.95. Sun brunch $7.95-$12.95. Child's meals. Specializes in steaks, fresh fish, pasta. Outdoor dining. Modern artwork. Totally nonsmoking . Cr cds: A, C, D, DS, MC, V.

D

★★ **IL FORNAIO CUCINA ITALIANA.** *223 Corte Madera Town Ctr (94925). 415/927-4400.* Hrs: 11:30 am-10 pm; Fri, Sat to 11 pm. Closed Thanksgiving, Dec 25. Res accepted. Italian menu. Bar. A la carte entrees: lunch, dinner $8.95-$21. Child's meals. Specialties: pollo tuscano, tiramisu. Own desserts. Parking. Outdoor dining. Bakery. Totally nonsmoking. Cr cds: A, C, D, MC, V.

D

★★★ **LARK CREEK INN.** *234 Magnolia Ave (94939), In Larkspur. 415/924-7766.* Farm fresh American cuisine. Hrs: Mon-Thurs 11:30 am-2 pm; Mon-Thurs 5:30-9 pm. Fri & Sat until 10 pm; Sun to 9 pm. A la carte. Prices $16-$28. Res pref. Valet. Child meals. Cr cds: C.

✓★★ **MCCORMICK & SCHMICK'S.** *55 Tamal Vista Blvd (94925). 415/924-6774.* Hrs: 11:30 am-10 pm; Sat, Sun 4-11 pm. Res accepted. Bar to midnight. A la carte entrees: lunch $6.95-$11, dinner $9.95-$15.50. Specializes in seafood. Outdoor dining. View of Mt Tamalpais. Cr cds: A, C, JCB, MC, V.

D

Costa Mesa (E-6 see Los Angeles map)

(See also Huntington Beach, Irvine, Newport Beach, Santa Ana)

Pop 96,357 **Elev** 101 ft **Area Code** 714
Web www.focusoc.com/cities/costamesa/chamber

Information Chamber of Commerce, 1700 Adams Ave, Ste 101, 92626; 714/885-9090

What to See and Do

California Scenario. This 1.6-acre sculpture garden is world renowned sculptor Isamu Noguchi's tribute to California's environment. Flanked by 2 reflective glass buildings and 2 40-ft-high concrete walls, the garden features tranquil walks, fountains, flowers and native grasses and trees. Noguchi's *The Spirit of the Lima Bean* is the centerpiece. (Daily) South Coast Plaza Town Center, San Diego Frwy at Bristol St. Phone 714/435-2100. **Free**

Annual Events

Highland Gathering and Games. Orange County Fairgrounds. Scottish games, dancing; soccer, rugby; piping, drumming competition. Memorial Day wkend.

Orange County Fair. Orange County Fairgrounds. Rodeo, livestock, exhibits, home arts, contests, photography, nightly entertainment, floriculture display, wine show, carnival, motorcycle races. Phone 714/708-3247. July.

Motels

★★ **BEST WESTERN INN.** *2642 Newport Blvd (92627), CA 55, exit Fair Dr. 949/650-3020; FAX 949/642-1220; res: 800/528-1234.* 97 rms, 3 story. S, D $54-$125; each addl $6; under 17 free; package plans. Crib free. TV; cable (premium). Heated pool; whirlpool. Sauna. Complimentary continental bkfst. Coffee in rms. Ck-out noon. Coin Indry. Meeting rms. Business servs avail. Some bathrm phones; some in-rm whirlpools. Some wet bars. Refrigerators avail. Balconies. Cr cds: A, C, D, DS, ER, JCB, MC, V.

✓★ **COZY INN.** *325 W Bay St (92627), CA 55 exit Victoria/22nd St. 949/650-2055; FAX 949/650-6281.* Web www.cozyinn.com. 29 rms, 2 story, 11 kits. June-mid-Sept: S $38-$48; D $42-$56; each addl $4; kit. units $10 addl; under 12 free; wkly rates; lower rates rest of yr. Crib $5. TV; cable (premium). Heated pool. Ck-out 11 am. Business servs avail. Refrigerators, microwaves avail. Cr cds: A, C, D, DS, MC, V.

★★ **RAMADA LIMITED.** *1680 Superior Ave (92627), Newport Blvd (CA 55) at 17th St. 949/645-2221; FAX 949/650-9125; res: 800/272-6232; res: 800/345-8025.* E-mail info@ramadalimitednewport.com; web www.ramdalimitednewport.com. 140 rms, 35 suites, 3 story. Mid-May-mid-Sept: S, D $89; each addl $5; suites $109-$169; under 17 free; lower rates rest of yr. Crib free. Pet accepted. TV; cable (premium). Heated pool; whirlpool. Complimentary continental bkfst. Restaurant nearby. Ck-out noon. Meeting rm. Valet serv. Coin Indry. Free airport transportation. Exercise equipt. Refrigerators; microwaves. Cr cds: A, C, D, DS, JCB, MC, V.

✓★ **VAGABOND INN.** *3205 Harbor Blvd (92626), I-405 exit Harbor Blvd S. 714/557-8360; FAX 714/662-7596; res: 800/522-1555.* Web www.vagabondinn.com. 127 rms, 2 story, 5 suites. May-Sept: S, D $50-$80; each addl $5; suites $75-$110; under 18 free; lower rates rest of yr. Crib free. Pet accepted, some restrictions; $5/day. TV; cable (premium). Heated pool; whirlpool. Complimentary continental bkfst. Coffee in rms. Restaurant opp 24 hrs. Ck-out noon. Meeting rm. Business servs avail. Valet serv. Free airport transportation. Exercise equipt. Health club privileges. Refrigerators, microwaves avail. Some balconies. Mission-style building. Cr cds: A, C, D, DS, MC, V.

Motor Hotels

★★★ **COUNTRY SIDE INN & SUITES.** *325 S Bristol St (92626), I-405 exit Bristol St S, near John Wayne Airport. 714/549-0300; FAX 714/662-0828; res: 800/322-9992.* Web www.countrysideinn.com. 290 units in 2 bldgs, 3 & 4 story, 32 suites. S, D $110-$150; each addl $10; suites $150-$160; under 13 free; wkly rates; lower rates some wkends. Crib free. TV; cable (premium), VCR avail. 2 heated pools; whirlpools. Complimentary bkfst buffet. Coffee in rms. Restaurant 6:30 am-10 pm. Rm serv. Bar 11:30 am-11 pm. Ck-out noon. Coin Indry. Convention facilities. Business center. Bellhops. Valet serv. Concierge. Gift shop. Free airport transportation. Exercise equipt. Health club privileges. Refrigerators; many in-rm whirlpools; some microwaves. Fireplace in lobby, many antiques; open air courtyard with imported tile fountain. Cr cds: A, C, D, DS, MC, V.

★★★ **DOUBLETREE HOTEL.** *3050 Bristol St (92626), I-405 exit Bristol St S. 714/540-7000; FAX 714/540-9176; res: 800/547-8010.* E-mail doubletreeoc@earthlink.net; web www.doubletreehotels.com. 484 rms, 7 story, 10 suites. S, D $89-$238; each addl $15; suites $425-$600; under 18 free. Crib free. Pet accepted. Self park $5. Valet parking $8. TV; cable (premium). Heated pool; whirlpool, poolside serv. Coffee in rms. 2 restaurants 6 am-midnight. Rm serv. Bar from 11 am; entertainment Fri-Sun. Ck-out noon. Convention facilities. Business center. In-rm modem link. Concierge. Gift shop. Barber, beauty shop. Free airport transportation. Tennis privileges. Golf privileges. Exercise equipt; sauna. Massage. Game rm. Refrigerators. Many private patios, balconies. Atrium lobby. Luxury level. Cr cds: A, C, D, DS, ER, JCB, MC, V.

★★ **HOLIDAY INN.** *3131 S Bristol St (92626), I-405 exit Bristol St S. 714/557-3000; FAX 714/957-8185; res: 800/465-4329; res: 800/221-7220.* 233 rms, 3-5 story. S, D $100-$175; under 18 free; family rates; family rates. Crib free. TV; cable (premium). Heated pool; wading pool. Coffee in rms. Restaurant 6 am-2 pm, 5-10 pm. Rm serv. Bar 4-11:30 pm. Ck-out noon. Coin Indry. Meeting rms. Business servs avail. Bellhops. Valet serv. Free airport transportation. Exercise equipt; sauna. Refrigerators avail. Balconies, patios. Picnic tables. Cr cds: A, C, D, DS, JCB, MC, V.

Hotels

★★ **MARRIOTT SUITES.** *500 Anton Blvd (92626), I-405 exit Bristol St N. 714/957-1100; FAX 714/966-8495; res: 800/228-9290.* 253 suites, 11 story. S, D $109-$139; wkend rates. Crib free. TV; cable (premium). Heated pool; whirlpool, poolside serv. Complimentary coffee in rms. Restaurant 6:30 am-10 pm. Rm serv 6 am-11 pm. Bar 11 am-11 pm. Ck-out noon. Coin Indry. Meeting rms. Business center. Gift shop. Free garage parking. Free airport transportation. Exercise equipt. Health club privileges. Refrigerators; microwaves avail. Wet bars. Many balconies. Cr cds: A, C, D, DS, ER, JCB, MC, V.

★★★ **WESTIN SOUTH COAST PLAZA.** *686 Anton Blvd (92626), I-405 exit Bristol St N. 714/540-2500; FAX 714/662-6695; res: 800/228-3000.* E-mail south@westin.com. 390 rms, 17 story. S, D $200-$240; each addl $20; suites $285-$960; under 18 free; wkend package plans. Crib free. Pet accepted, some restrictions. Parking $7, valet $13. TV; cable (premium). Heated pool; poolside serv. Complimentary coffee in rms. Restaurant 6:30 am-10 pm. Rm serv 24 hrs. 2 Bars noon-midnight; entertainment wkends. Ck-out 1 pm. Convention facilities. Business center. In-rm modem link. Gift shop. Free airport transportation. Lighted tennis.

Exercise equipt. Health club privileges. Minibars; wet bar in some suites. South Coast Plaza Retail Center & Village adj. Cr cds: A, C, D, DS, ER, JCB, MC, V.

D SC

★★ **WYNDHAM GARDEN HOTEL.** *3350 Ave Of The Arts (92626), I-405 exit Bristol St, N to Anton Blvd. 714/751-5100; FAX 714/751-0129; res: 800/966-3426.* Web www.wyndham.com. 238, 35 suites, 6 story. S, D $125-$135; each addl $10; suites $135-$145; under 12 free; wkly, wkend rates; higher rates special events. Pet accepted, some restrictions; $25. TV; cable . Heated pool; whirlpool. Coffee in rms. Restaurant 6:30 am-2:30 pm, 5-10 pm. Rm serv 5-10 pm. Bar 4:30 pm-midnight. Ck-out noon. Coin lndry. Meeting rms. Business servs avail. Free garage parking. Free airport transportation. Exercise equipt. Refrigerators, microwaves avail. Private patios, balconies. Fireplace in lobby; marble floors. Pool area overlooks lake. Cr cds: A, C, D, DS, JCB, MC, V.

D SC

Restaurants

★★ **DIVA RESTAURANT.** *600 Anton Blvd (92626), I-405 exit Bristol St N. 714/754-0600.* E-mail divascl@aol.com. Hrs: 11:30 am-3 pm, 5-10 pm; Mon 5-9 pm; Fri to 11 pm; Sat 5-11 pm. Closed Sun; most major hols. Res accepted. Continental, eclectic menu. Bar. A la carte entrees: lunch $6-$18.95, dinner $6.50-$24.95. Specialties: killer vegetable plate, ahi towers with tomatillo sauce, light chocolate grand marnier with raspberry sauce. Valet parking. Outdoor dining. Theater-style decor. Cr cds: A, C, D, JCB, MC, V.

D

✓★★ **EL TORITO GRILL.** *633 Anton Blvd (92626), I-405 exit Bristol St N. 714/662-2672.* Hrs: 11 am-10 pm; Fri, Sat to 11 pm; Sun brunch 10 am-2 pm. Closed Thanksgiving, Dec 25. Res accepted. Mexican, Southwestern menu. Bar to 11 pm; Fri, Sat to midnight. A la carte entrees: lunch, dinner $7.95-$16.95. Sun brunch $12.95. Specializes in grilled fresh fish, enchiladas, fajitas. Own tortillas, desserts. Valet parking. Southwestern decor. Totally nonsmoking. Cr cds: A, C, D, DS, MC, V.

D

★★★ **GOLDEN TRUFFLE.** *1767 Newport Blvd (92627), at 17th St. 949/645-9858.* Web www.goldentruffle.com. Hrs: 11:30 am-2:30 pm, 5:30-10 pm. Closed Sun, Mon; major hols. Res accepted. French, Caribbean menu. Bar. Extensive wine list. A la carte entrees: lunch $7-$18, dinner $7-$19. Complete meals: lunch $18-$24, dinner $32-$45. Specialties: Jamaican jerk chicken salad, chipolte barbeque duck legs with potatoes, grilled lamb loin with horseradish lasagna. Jazz Thurs (summer). Outdoor dining. Two distinct dining areas include semi-formal rm and a casual bistro-style cafe with champagne display case. Cr cds: A, C, MC, V.

D

★★ **HABANA.** *2930 Bristol St (92626). 714/556-0176.* E-mail hbana@pacbell.net. Hrs: 11:30 am-2:30 pm, 5-10 pm; Fri, Sat to 11 pm. Closed some major hols. Res accepted. Cuban, Caribbean menu. Bar. Semi-a la carte: lunch $7.95-$12.95, dinner $11.95-$17.95. Specialties: corn and black bean crab cakes, in-house smoked sea bass, plantain-crusted chicken breast. Own baking. Entertainment nightly. Outdoor dining. 1950s Caribbean decor. Cr cds: A, C, D, DS, MC, V.

D

✓★ **MEMPHIS SOUL CAFE.** *2920 Bristol St (92626). 714/432-7685.* Hrs: 11:30 am-2:30 pm, 5-10 pm; Fri, Sat to 10:30 pm; Sun from 5 pm; Sat, Sun brunch 10:30 am-2:30 pm. Closed most major hols. Res accepted. Bar. Semi-a la carte: lunch $4.50-$7.50, dinner $5.95-$16.50. Sat, Sun brunch $3.50-$11.75. Specialties: down home gumbo, southern crab cakes, center-cut pork chops. Jazz Thurs. Outdoor dining. Roadhouse cafe. Cr cds: A, C, D, MC, V.

★★★ **SCOTT'S SEAFOOD GRILL.** *3300 Bristol St (92626). 714/979-2400.* E-mail scottsscp@aol.com. Hrs: 11 am-10 pm; Fri, Sat to 11 pm; Sun from 10 am; Sun brunch 10 am-3 pm. Closed most major hols. Res accepted. Seafood menu. Bar. Wine list. Semi-a la carte: lunch $11.95-$35, dinner $11.95-$45. Sun brunch $21.95. Specializes in seafood, beef. Free valet parking. Outdoor dining. Southern plantation decor. Cr cds: A, C, D, DS, MC, V.

D

✓★ **TRATTORIA SPIGA.** *3333 Bear St (92626), in Crystal Court shopping mall. 714/540-3365.* Hrs: 11 am-9 pm; Fri, Sat to 10 pm; Sun 11:30 am-7 pm. Closed Jan 1, Easter, July 4, Dec 25. Res accepted. Italian menu. Bar. A la carte entrees: lunch, dinner $5.25-$13.95. Specialties: miniature ravioli with veal in a meat bolognese sauce; boneless breasts of chicken in a mushroom marsala wine sauce; Italian-style thin crust pizza. Patio dining. Trattoria-style dining in inner courtyard of mall. Cr cds: A, C, D, DS, JCB, MC, V.

D

Unrated Dining Spot

TEA & SYMPATHY. *369 E 17th St, at jct Tustin Ave. 714/645-4860.* Hrs: 11 am-6 pm; Sun brunch to 4 pm. Closed Dec 25. British menu. Wine, beer. Semi-a la carte: lunch $4.75-$12.50. Sun brunch $6.95-$12.95. Traditional English tea room. Cr cds: A, C, D, DS, JCB, MC, V.

Crescent City (A-1)

(See also Redwood Highway)

Founded 1852 **Pop** 4,380 **Elev** 44 ft **Area Code** 707 **Zip** 95531
E-mail ncolzerozero47@telis.org **Web** www.delnorte.org

Information Chamber of Commerce, Visitor Information Center, 1001 Front St; 707/464-3174 or 800/343-8300

The crescent-shaped beach that gives the city its name outlines a busy harbor. A party of treasure seekers discovered the harbor, and the city was laid out a year later.

What to See and Do

Battery Point Lighthouse (1856). On Battery Point, at the end of A St; accessible only at low tide; museum. (Apr-Sept, Wed-Sun) Phone 707/464-3089. **¢**

Del Norte County Historical Society Main Museum. Research center for local history; 2-story lighthouse lens (1892), Native American and pioneer exhibits housed in former county jail. (May-Sept, daily exc Sun) 577 H Street. Phone 707/464-3922. **¢**

Ocean World. Aquarium, shark petting tank, sea lion show. Gift shop. (Daily) 304 US 101S. Phone 707/464-3522. **¢¢¢**

Point St George. The *Brother Jonathan,* a side-wheeler, was wrecked here in 1865. Of 232 persons aboard, 203 died; they are buried in Brother Jonathan Cemetery, Pebble Beach Dr & 9th St. N of beach.

★ **Redwood National and State Parks.** Stretches 46 mi north and south, including 30 mi of coastline, and about 7 mi wide at its greatest width. Headquarters at 2nd & K Sts has exhibits, information. Established in 1968; the 113,200-acre park, home of what is said to be the world's tallest tree, offers hiking, biking and bridle trails; picnic areas; scenic drives; shuttle bus (summer); interpretive programs. S of town. Contact 1111 2nd St; phone 707/464-6101 for details. Exhibits and information at Hiouchi Information Center, 10 mi E or at Redwood Information Center, 2 mi S of Orick (daily). **Free** The three state parks located within the national park boundaries are

Del Norte Coast Redwoods State Park. Redwood trees grow on steep slopes just above the surf. Rhododendrons blanket the slopes, blooming in May and June. Nature, hiking trails. Picnicking. Camping (dump station). Standard fees. 7 mi S on US 101. Phone 707/464-6101 or 800/444-7275 (res). Day us. **¢¢**; Camping **¢¢¢¢**

Jedediah Smith Redwoods State Park. Stout Memorial Grove, at the center of Mill Creek Flat, is about 4 mi from park entrance. Swimming; fishing. Nature, hiking trails. Picnicking. Camping (dump station). Standard fees. 9 mi NE off US 101 on US 199. Phone 707/464-6101 or 800/444-7275 (res). Day use ¢¢; Camping ¢¢¢¢

Prairie Creek Redwoods State Park. These 14,000 acres are adorned by magnificent groves of coast redwoods. Gold Bluffs Beach was worked for gold in 1851, but most of it remained hopelessly mixed in vast amounts of sand and rock. Lush ferns cover the 50-ft walls of Fern Canyon and moss carpets the fallen tree trunks. Fishing. Hiking on 75 mi of nature trails. Picnicking. Educational displays in visitor center. Frequent campfire programs and ranger-conducted hikes in summer. Two campgrounds: **Elk Prairie,** tent & trailer (res recommended); **Gold Bluffs Beach,** approx 3½ mi S via US 101 to Davison Rd (unpaved road; vehicle size and weight restriction). Standard fees. 33 mi S on US 101. Information phone 707/488-2171; res phone 800/444-7275. Day use ¢¢; Camping ¢¢¢¢

Annual Event

World Championship Crab Races & Crustacean Festival. Del Norte County Fairgrounds. Phone 707/464-3174. President's Day wkend.

Motels

✓★★ **BAYVIEW INN.** *310 Us Hwy 101 S (95531). 707/465-2050; FAX 707/465-3690; res: 800/446-0583.* 65 rms, ½ with A/C, 3 story, 9 suites. S $45-$59; D $49-$64; suites $89-$99. TV; cable (premium). Complimentary coffee in rms. Restaurant open 24 hrs. Ck-out 11 am. Meeting rms. Business servs avail. Coin Indry. Some refrigerators, microwaves; in-rm whirlpool in suites. Opp harbor. Cr cds: A, C, D, DS, MC, V.

D

★★ **BEST WESTERN NORTHWOODS INN.** *655 Hwy 101 S (95531). 707/464-9771; FAX 707/464-9461; res: 800/528-1234; res: 800/557-3396.* 89 rms, 2 story. Late June-Sept: S $75-$99; D $79-$125; each addl $10; under 18 free; suites $150-$175; higher rates hols, special events; lower rates rest of yr. Crib $8. TV; cable (premium). 2 whirlpools. Complimentary full bkfst. Coffee in rms. Restaurant 6 am-9 pm. Bar 2 pm-midnight. Ck-out 11 am. Coin Indry. Meeting rms. Business servs avail. In-rm modem link. Sundries. Some refrigerators, microwaves. Cr cds: A, C, D, DS, MC, V.

D SC

★★ **CURLY REDWOOD LODGE.** *701 US Hwy 101 S (95531). 707/464-2137; FAX 707/464-1655.* E-mail curlyredwood@tehs.org. 36 rms, 1-2 story. No A/C. June-Sept: S $52-$60; D $56-$65; each addl $5; suites $75-$86; lower rates rest of yr. TV; cable. Complimentary coffee. Restaurants opp 7 am-10 pm. Ck-out 11 am. Business servs avail. Building constructed of wood from a single Curly Redwood tree. Harbor opp. Family owned. Cr cds: A, C, D, MC, V.

✓★★ **HOLIDAY INN.** *100 Walton St (95531). 707/464-3885; FAX 707/464-5311; res: 800/465-4329.* 46 rms, 2 story, 6 suites. June-Sept: S, D $80; suites $125; under 18 free; family rates; lower rates rest of yr. Crib free. TV; cable (premium). Complimentary continental bkfst. Restaurant opp 7 am-9 pm. Ck-out 11 am. Meeting rms. Business servs avail. In-rm modem link. Coin Indry. Refrigerators, microwaves; in-rm whirlpool in suites. Many balconies. Adj to bay. Cr cds: A, C, D, DS, MC, V.

D SC

★★ **PACIFIC MOTOR HOTEL.** *440 US Hwy 101 N (95531). 707/464-4141; FAX 707/465-3274; res: 800/323-7917.* 62 rms, 2 story. No A/C. May-mid-Oct: S $52; D $62-$65; each addl $5; suites $75; lower rates rest of yr. Crib $5. TV; cable, VCR avail (movies). Complimentary coffee. Restaurant noon-9 pm. Bar 3 pm-midnight. Ck-out noon. Meeting rms. Business servs avail. Sundries. Whirlpool. Sauna. Some refrigerators. Cr cds: A, C, D, DS, MC, V.

SC

✓★★ **SUPER 8 MOTEL.** *685 Hwy 101 S (95616). 707/464-4111; FAX 707/465-8916; res: 800/800-8000.* E-mail super8cc@northcoast.com; web www.visitdelnorte.com/super8. 49 rms, 2 story. No A/C. Mid-June-Labor Day: S $65; D $69-$74; each addl $5; under 13 free; lower rates rest of yr. Crib free. Pet accepted, some restrictions; fee. TV; cable (premium). Complimentary coffee in rms. Restaurant adj 7 am-9 pm. Ck-out 11 am. Business servs avail. Coin Indry. Ocean opp. Cr cds: A, C, DS, MC, V.

D SC

Restaurant

★★ **HARBOR VIEW GROTTO.** *150 Starfish Way (95531). 707/464-3815.* Hrs: 11:30 am-10 pm; winter to 9 pm. Closed Jan 1, Thanksgiving, Dec 24, 25. Bar. Semi-a la carte: lunch $3.75-$9.95, dinner $7.95-$20.50. Specializes in seafood, steak, prime rib. View of harbor, ocean. Totally nonsmoking. Cr cds: C, MC, V.

D

Crestline (J-4)

(See also Lake Arrowhead)

Pop 8,594 **Elev** 5,000 ft **Area Code** 909 **Zip** 92325
Web www.crestline.net

Information Chamber of Commerce, PO Box 926; 909/338-2706

What to See and Do

Lake Gregory Regional Park. Swimming beach (late June-Labor Day wkend); waterslide (fee); fishing, rowboats (rentals); picnicking, snack bars; park. Lake Dr & Gregory Rd, E of town. Phone 909/338-2233. Swimming (per person) ¢¢

Silverwood Lake State Recreation Area. Swimming; fishing; boating (rentals). Nature, bicycle trails. Picnicking, concession. Camping (dump station). Visitor center. Standard fees. 12 mi E off I-15 on CA 138. Phone 619/389-2303.

Cucamonga

(see Rancho Cucamonga)

Culver City (C-3 see Los Angeles map)

Pop 38,793 **Elev** 94 ft **Area Code** 213 or 310

Hotel

★★ **RAMADA PLAZA.** *6333 Bristol Pkwy (90230), I-405 exit Slauson St. 310/484-7000; FAX 310/484-7073; res: 800/321-5575.* E-mail ramada@earthlink.net; web www.ramada.com. 260 rms, 12 story. S, D $119-$134; suites $250; under 18 free; wkend rates. Crib free. TV; VCR avail. Heated pool; whirlpool, poolside serv. Complimentary coffee in rms. Restaurant 24 hrs. Rm serv 6 am-10 pm. Bar 11-1 am. Ck-out noon. Convention facilities. Business center. Gift shop. Free airport transportation. Exercise equipt. Health club privileges. Refrigerator in suites, wet bar. Cr cds: A, C, D, DS, JCB, MC, V.

D SC

Dana Point

(see Laguna Beach)

Davis (D-2)

(See also Napa, Sacramento, Vacaville)

Settled 1868 **Pop** 46,209 **Elev** 50 ft **Area Code** 530 **Zip** 95616
E-mail information@davischamber.com **Web** www.davischamber.com

Information Chamber of Commerce and Visitors Center, 228 B Street; 530/756-5160

The pioneer settler Jerome C. Davis planted 400 acres of wheat, barley, orchards and vineyards and pastured great herds of livestock here. Since then, Davis has remained the center of a rich agricultural area. The city is also known for its energy conservation programs and projects. A prime example is Village Homes Solar Village. Obtain a self-guided tour brochure at City Hall, 23 Russell Blvd.

What to See and Do

Davis Campus of the University of California (1905). (23,000 students) Nearly 5,200 acres with College of Agricultural and Environmental Sciences, College of Engineering, College of Letters and Science, School of Veterinary Medicine, School of Law, Graduate School of Management and School of Medicine. Art exhibits displayed in the Nelson and Union Memorial galleries and in the C.N. Gorman Museum. Tours. On CA 113, I-80. Phone 530/752-8111.

Annual Event

Picnic Day. Sponsored by Associated Students of Univ of California at Davis. Includes parade, floats, exhibits, aquacade, dachshund races, concerts, horse show, rodeo, sheepdog trials. Phone 530/752-1990. Mid-Apr.

Motels

★ **BEST WESTERN LODGE.** *123 B St (95616). 530/756-7890; FAX 530/756-0245; res: 800/528-1234.* 53 rms, 2 story, some kits. S $66-$70; D $72-$80; each addl $5. Crib $5. Pet accepted; $5. TV; cable (premium). Complimentary coffee in rms. Restaurant opp 6 am-11 pm. Ck-out noon. Exercise equipt. Whirlpool. Refrigerators. Univ of CA 1 blk. Cr cds: A, C, D, DS, JCB, MC, V.

D SC

★★ **HALLMARK INN.** *110 F St (95616). 530/753-3600; FAX 530/758-8623; res: 800/753-0035.* 135 rms, 2-3 story. S, D $75-$90; each addl $10; suites $90-$160; under 12 free; higher rates special events. Crib free. TV; cable (premium). Heated pool. Complimentary full bkfst. Restaurant adj open 24 hrs. Ck-out noon. Meeting rms. Valet serv. Some refrigerators. Balconies. Cr cds: A, C, D, DS, MC, V.

D SC

Restaurants

✓★ **CAFE BERNARDO.** *234 D St (95616). 530/750-5101.* Hrs: 7 am-10 pm; Fri, Sat, Sun to 11 pm. Closed Thanksgiving, Dec 25. Semi-a la carte: bkfst $2.75-$5.50, lunch $4.75-$6.50, dinner $5.25-$9.50. Specialty: pizzettas. Street parking. Outdoor dining. Cafe style. Totally non-smoking. Cr cds: C, MC, V.

D

★★ **SOGA'S RESTAURANT.** *222 D Street (95616). 530/757-1733.* Hrs: 11:30 am-2 pm, 5-9 pm; Fri to 10 pm; Sat from 5 pm. Closed Sun, Mon; most major hols. Res accepted. Wine, beer. Semi-a la carte: lunch $6-$9, dinner $12-$18. Specializes in roasted meats, seafood, pasta. Outdoor dining. Reminiscent of a 1930s home; fireplace. Totally non-smoking. Cr cds: A, C, DS, MC, V.

D

Death Valley National Park (F-4 - G-4)

(70 mi E of Lone Pine on CA 190)

Here, approximately 300 miles northeast of Los Angeles, are more than 5,200 square miles of rugged desert, peaks and depressions—an unusual and colorful geography. The park is one vast geological museum, revealing secrets of ages gone by. Millions of years ago, this was part of the Pacific Ocean; then violent uplifts of the earth occurred, creating mountain ranges and draining water to the west. Today, 200 square miles of the valley are at or below sea level; the lowest point on the continent (282 feet below sea level) is here; Telescope Peak (11,049 feet) towers directly above it. The valley itself is about 140 miles long and four to 16 miles wide. The average rainfall is less than two inches a year. From October until May the climate is very pleasant. In summer it is extremely hot; a maximum temperature of 134°F in the shade has been recorded. If considered altogether, this is the lowest, hottest, driest area in North America.

Death Valley was named in 1849 when a party of gold hunters took a short cut here and were stranded for several weeks awaiting help. The discovery and subsequent mining of borax, hauled out by the famous 20-mule teams, led to development of the valley as a tourist attraction.

The visitor center at Furnace Creek is open daily. Guided walks, evening programs and talks (Nov-Apr). Golden Age, Golden Eagle, Golden Access passports (see MAKING THE MOST OF YOUR TRIP). Phone 760/786-2331. Per vehicle ¢¢¢

What to See and Do

20-Mule-Team Canyon. Viewed from a twisting road; RVs and trailers are not allowed on this road. (This is an unpaved, one-way rd; watch carefully for the entrance sign.)

Artist's Palette. A particularly scenic auto drive (9 mi one way), with spectacular colors. Because of difficult roads, RVs and trailers are advised not to drive here.

Badwater. At 279 ft below sea level, near the lowest spot on the North American continent; look for sea level sign.

Camping. Developed and primitive camping in area; limited hookups. It is suggested that campers check with the visitors center for important information on camping facilities and road conditions. (Daily) ¢¢¢¢

Charcoal kilns. Beehive-shaped stone structures, formerly used to make charcoal for nearby mines. **Note:** The last mile of the access road is unpaved.

Dante's View. (5,475 ft). View of Death Valley with a steep drop to 279 ft below sea level at Badwater.

Devil's Golf Course. Vast beds of rugged salt crystals.

Golden Canyon. Offers a display of color ranging from deep red to rich gold. One-mi trail provides access.

Natural Bridge. A bridge spanning a rugged canyon in the Black Mountains; 1-mi walking trail.

Rhyolite Ghost Town. This was the largest town in the mining history of Death Valley in the early 1900s; 5,000-10,000 people lived here then. The town bloomed from 1905-1910; by 1911 it was a ghost town. One structure still left standing from that era is the "bottle house," constructed of 12,000-50,000 beer and liquor bottles (depending on who does the estimating).

Sand dunes. Sand blown by the wind into dunes 5 to 100 ft high.

Scotty's Castle. A desert mansion (ca 1922-1931), designed and built to be viewed as a work of art, as well as a house. The furnishings are typical of the period; many were especially designed and hand-crafted for this house. Living history tours are led by costumed interpreters. ¢¢¢

Telescope Peak. Highest point in the Panamint Range (11,049 ft). (Although there is a 14-mi round-trip hiking trail, it is inaccessible in the winter months.)

Ubehebe Crater. Colorful crater left by a volcanic steam explosion.

Visitor Center. It is recommended that visitors stop here before continuing on for an orientation film, day-trip suggestions, help in organizing sightseeing routes and important information on camping areas and road conditions. At Furnace Creek. Phone 760/786-2331.

Zabriskie Point. View of Death Valley and the Panamint Range from the rugged badlands of the Black Mountains.

NOTE: It can be very dangerous to venture off paved roads in this area in the summer months. Carefully obey all National Park Service signs and regulations. Make sure your vehicle has plenty of gas and oil. Carry water when you explore this park, especially in hot weather. For further information contact Superintendent, Death Valley National Park, Death Valley 92328; phone 760/786-2331.

Motel

✓★ **STOVE PIPE WELLS VILLAGE.** *State Hwy 190 (92240). 760/786-2387; FAX 760/786-2389; res: 800/236-7916.* Web www.placetostay.com. 83 rms, 5 buildings. No rm phones. S, D $58-$80; each addl $10; under 12 free. Crib $5. Pet accepted, some restrictions; $20 refundable. Heated pool. Restaurant 7 am-2 pm, 6:30-10 pm. Bar 4:30-11 pm. Ck-out 11 am. Sundries. Landing strip. Panoramic view of mountains, desert, dunes. Cr cds: A, C, DS, MC, V.

D

Hotel

★★★ **FURNACE CREEK RANCH.** *Hwy 190 (92328), ¾ mi S on CA 190. 760/786-2361; FAX 760/786-2514; res: 800/236-7916.* Web www.furnacecreekresorts.com. 66 units, 4 story. Feb-Apr S, D $230-$290; each addl $15; suites $325; under 18 free; lower rates rest of yr. TV; cable. Natural thermal spring water pool; poolside serv. Restaurant 7-10:30 am, 11:30 am-2 pm, 5:30-10 pm (also see INN DINING ROOM). Bar noon-11 pm. Ck-out noon. Concierge. Gift shop. Lighted tennis. Golf privileges, greens fee $40, pro, driving range. Exercise equipt; sauna. Lawn games. Refrigerators. Private patios, balconies. 1920s-30s decor; native stone in many areas. Cr cds: A, C, D, DS, JCB, MC, V.

D SC

Guest Ranch

★★ **FURNACE CREEK INN.** *Hwy 190 (92328), on CA 190, near monument headquarters. 760/786-2345; FAX 760/786-2514; res: 800/236-7916.* Web www.furnacecreekresorts.com. 224 rms, 1-2 story. S, D $90-$130; each addl $14; under 18 free. TV; cable. Bar noon-midnight. Natural thermal spring water pool. Playground. Dining rms 6 am-10 pm. Ck-out noon, ck-in 4 pm. Grocery. Coin Indry. Package store. Gift shop. Lighted tennis. Golf, greens fee $40, pro, driving range. Volleyball, basketball courts. Museum. Some refrigerators. Cr cds: A, C, D, DS, JCB, MC, V.

D

Restaurant

★★★ **INN DINING ROOM.** *(See Furnace Creek Inn Motor Hotel) 760/786-2361.* Hrs: 7-10:30 am, 11:30 am-2 pm, 5:30-10 pm; Sun brunch 11 am-2 pm. Res accepted. Continental menu. Bar noon-11 pm. Wine list. A la carte entrees: bkfst $9, lunch $8.50-$12.95, dinner $25. Sun brunch $17.95. Specializes in chicken, steak, seafood. Own baking. Valet parking. 1930s decor; beam ceilings. Jacket. Totally nonsmoking. Cr cds: A, C, D, DS, JCB, MC, V.

D

Del Mar (K-4)

(See also Carlsbad, La Jolla, San Diego)

Pop 4,860 **Elev** 100 ft **Area Code** 619 **Zip** 92014

Information Greater Del Mar Chamber of Commerce, 1104 Camino Del Mar; 619/793-5292

This village-by-the sea community offers beautiful white beaches and brilliant sunsets. It is also an attractive area for year-round ballooning.

Annual Event

Del Mar Fair. Fairgrounds. Name entertainment, carnival; livestock, trade, hobby and flower exhibits. Phone 619/755-1161. Mid-June-early July.

Seasonal Event

Del Mar Thoroughbred Club. County Fairgrounds. Thoroughbred horse racing. For prices, schedule and information phone 619/755-1141; for ticket reservations phone 619/792-4242. Late July-mid-Sept.

Motels

★★ **BEST WESTERN.** *710 Camino Del Mar (92014). 619/755-1501; FAX 619/755-4704; res: 800/446-7229.* 95 rms, 2 story, 29 suites. June-Sept: S, D $109-$139; suites $149-$169; under 18 free; lower rates rest of yr. Crib free. TV; cable (premium). 2 pools; whirlpool. Complimentary continental bkfst. Restaurant adj 11-2 am. Ck-out noon. Coin Indry. Valet serv. Health club privileges. Some refrigerators, microwaves. Some balconies. Cr cds: A, C, D, DS, MC, V.

D SC

★★ **CLARION CARRIAGE HOUSE DEL MAR INN.** *720 Camino Del Mar (92014). 619/755-9765; FAX 619/792-8196; res: 800/451-4515.* Web www.wimall.com/delmarinn. 81 rms, 3 story, 22 kits. Some A/C. June-Sept: S, D $115-$165; lower rates rest of yr. Crib $10. TV; cable (premium). Heated pool; whirlpool. Complimentary continental bkfst in rms; afternoon refreshments. Ck-out 11 am. Coin Indry. Meeting rm. Business servs avail. Health club privileges. Microwaves avail. Many balconies. Cr cds: A, C, D, DS, ER, JCB, MC, V.

D SC

★★ **COUNTRY SIDE INN.** *1661 Villa Cardiff Dr (92007), N via I-5, 1 blk E of Birmingham exit. 760/944-0427; FAX 760/944-7708; res: 800/322-9993.* E-mail csicardiff@aol.com; web www.countrysideinn.com. 102 rms, 2 story. S, D $68-$125; each addl $8; under 12 free. Crib free. TV; cable (premium). Heated pool; whirlpool. Complimentary full bkfst. Ck-out noon. Meeting rms. Business servs avail. In-rm modem link. Health club privileges. Refrigerators; microwaves avail. Country French decor. Cr cds: A, C, D, DS, MC, V.

D SC

Hotel

★★★ **HILTON DEL MAR NORTH SAN DIEGO.** *15575 Jimmy Durante Blvd (92014). 619/792-5200; FAX 619/792-9538; res: 800/833-7904.* 245 units, 3 story. S $139-$219; D $159-$229; each addl $20; suites $279-$699; family rates; package plans. Crib free. TV; cable (premium). Pool; whirlpools, poolside serv. Complimentary coffee in rms. Restaurant 6 am-2 pm, 5-11 pm. Bar 11-1 am. Ck-out noon. Convention facilities. Business servs avail. In-rm modem link. Gift shop. Valet parking. Tennis privileges. Exercise equipt. Some refrigerators, microwaves, minibars. Cr cds: A, C, D, DS, JCB, MC, V.

D SC

Resort

★★★★ **L'AUBERGE DEL MAR RESORT & SPA.** *1540 Camino Del Mar (92014). 619/259-1515; FAX 619/755-4940; res: 800/553-1336.* This resort in the village of Del Mar overlooks the Pacific Ocean, which is just a block away. Some rooms have coastal views and are named for the Hollywood luminaries who frequented the property in the 20s, 30s, and 40s. The resort still maintains an aura of California glamour. In addition to the luxurious spa treatments, there are 2 pools, tennis, golf, shopping and an acclaimed restaurant, serving California-style cuisine. 120 rms, 3 story. S, D $205-$395; each addl $25; suites $800-$1,300; package plans. Crib avail. Valet, underground parking (fee). TV; cable, VCR avail. 2 pools; poolside serv. Restaurant (see THE DINING ROOM). Bar 11-1 am. Ck-out noon, ck-in 4 pm. Concierge. Business servs avail. Shopping arcade. Lighted tennis. Exercise rm; sauna, steam rm. Spa. Minibars; some fireplaces. Cr cds: A, C, D, DS, JCB, MC, V.

D SC

Restaurants

★★★ **CILANTROS.** *3702 Via De La Valle (92014). 619/259-8777.* Hrs: 11:30 am-10:30 pm; Fri, Sat to 11 pm; Sun to 9:30 pm. Closed Dec 25. Res accepted. Southwestern menu. Bar to midnight. Semi-a la carte: lunch $3.95-$9.25, dinner $12.95-$19.95. Specializes in fajitas, chicken. Valet parking. Patio dining. Southwestern decor. Cr cds: A, C, D, MC, V.

D ♥

★★ **EPAZOTE.** *1555 Camino Del Mar (92014), in Del Mar Plaza. 619/259-9966.* Hrs: 11:30 am-10 pm; Fri to 11 pm; Sat 11 am-11 pm; Sun from 10:30 am. Closed Dec 25. Res accepted. Southwestern menu. Bar. Semi-a la carte: lunch $6-$12, dinner $9.95-$19.95. Specialties: spit-roasted chicken, char-broiled salmon. Jazz Wed evening. Valet parking. Outdoor dining. View of ocean. Cr cds: A, C, D, MC, V.

D

★★★ **IL FORNAIO.** *1555 Camino Del Mar (92014). 619/755-8906.* Hrs: 11:30 am-11 pm; Sat to midnight; Sun 10 am-11 pm. Closed Thanksgiving, Dec 25. Res accepted. Italian menu. Bar. Wine list. Semi-a la carte: lunch $12-$16, dinner $16-$26. Child's meals. Specializes in regional Italian dishes. Parking. Outdoor dining. Totally nonsmoking. Cr cds: A, C, D, MC, V.

D

✓★★ **JAKE'S DEL MAR.** *1660 Coast Blvd (92014). 619/755-2002.* Hrs: 11:15 am-2:30 pm, 5-9:30 pm; Mon from 5 pm; Fri, Sat to 10 pm; Sun brunch 10 am-2:30 pm. Closed Dec 25. Res accepted. No A/C. Continental menu. Bar to midnight. A la carte entrees: lunch $6.95-$10.95, dinner $10-$19.95. Sun brunch $6.95-$11.95. Specializes in fresh seafood, lamb, steak. Own desserts. Valet parking. Patio dining. Ocean view. Cr cds: A, C, DS, MC, V.

D

✓★★ **PACIFIC COAST GRILL.** *437 S Hwy 1 (92075), 2 mi N. 619/794-4632.* Hrs: 11:30 am-10 pm; Fri, Sat to 11 pm; Sun brunch 11:30 am-4 pm. Closed most major hols. Res accepted. Seafood menu. Bar. Semi-a la carte: lunch $6.95-$9.95, dinner $10.95-$18.95. Sun brunch $5.25-$9.95. Specialties: lobster tacos, steak cut ahi, spicy pork tenderloin. Parking. Outdoor dining. Eclectic atmosphere; bright mosaic tiles in floor. Cr cds: A, C, D, DS, MC, V.

D

★★★ **THE DINING ROOM.** *(See L'Auberge Del Mar Resort & Spa) 619/259-1515.* Hrs: 6:30-11 am, 11:30 am-2 pm, 5-10 pm; early-bird dinner 5-6:30 pm. Res accepted. Bar 11-1 am. Semi-a la carte: bkfst $4.95-$11.95, lunch $7-$12.95, dinner $12-$23. Prix fixe: dinner $29.95. Specializes in California cuisine with international flavor. Valet parking. Outdoor dining. Skylights. View of waterfall & gardens. Cr cds: A, C, D, DS, JCB, MC, V.

D

★★★ **TORREY PINES CAFE.** *2334 Carmel Valley Rd (92014). 619/259-5878.* Hrs: 11:30 am-2:30 pm, 5-9 pm; Fri to 10 pm; Sat 5-10 pm; Sun brunch 10 am-2 pm. Res accepted. Wine list. Semi-a la carte: lunch $4-$12.50, dinner $4-$19. Sun brunch $4.50-$8.50. Specialties: blackened catfish, lamb shank osso bucco. Outdoor dining. Overlooks Torrey Pines State Reserve Park. Totally nonsmoking. Cr cds: A, C, D, DS, MC, V.

D

✓★★ **TRATTORIA POSITANO.** *2171 San Elijo Ave (92007), 5 mi N on Hwy 101, exit Chesterfield. 760/943-1529.* Hrs: 11:30 am-3 pm, 5-10 pm; Sat, Sun from 12:30 pm. Closed most major hols. Res accepted. Italian menu. Bar. Semi-a la carte: lunch, dinner $7.95-$21.95. Specialties: agnello in crosta di herbe, maltagliati al granchio e asparagi. Outdoor dining. Family-style. Cr cds: A, C, D, DS, MC, V.

D

Unrated Dining Spot

TACO AUCTIONEERS. *1951 San Elijo (92007), N on I-5. 760/942-8226.* Hrs: 11 am-9 pm; wkends to 10 pm. Closed Thanksgiving, Dec 25. No A/C. Mexican menu. Bar. Semi-a la carte: lunch $5.95-$8, dinner $8.95-$14. Child's meals. Specializes in tacos, carnitas. Outdoor dining. Casual dining overlooks beach campground. Cr cds: A, C, D, DS, MC, V.

D

Desert Hot Springs (J-5)

(See also Idyllwild, Indio, Palm Desert, Palm Springs)

Pop 11,668 **Elev** 1,070 ft **Area Code** 760 **Zip** 92240
Web www.deserthotsprings.com

Information Chamber of Commerce, 11711 West Dr; 760/329-6403 or 800/346-3347

Motel

★★ **DESERT HOT SPRINGS SPA HOTEL.** *10805 Palm Dr (92240). 760/329-6495; FAX 760/329-6915; res: 800/808-7727.* E-mail dhs-spa@ix.netcom.com; web www.dhsspa.com. 50 rms, 2 story. Mid-Dec-May: S, D $99-$119; each addl $10; suites $109-$129; lower rates rest of yr. Crib $5. TV; cable (premium). 8 natural hot mineral pools (open to public); pool; 2 whirlpools, wading pool, poolside serv. Sauna. Restaurant 7 am-11 pm. Bar 10-1 am; entertainment Fri, Sat. Ck-out noon. Business servs avail. In-rm modem link. Sundries. Gift shop. Tennis privileges. 18-hole golf privileges. Refrigerators avail. Private patios, balconies. Cr cds: A, C, D, DS, MC, V.

SC

Resort

★★★ **TWO BUNCH PALMS RESORT & SPA.** *67-425 Two Bunch Palms Trl (92240). 760/329-8791; FAX 760/329-1317; res: 800/472-4334.* E-mail whiteowl@twobunchpalms.com; web www.twobunchpalms.com. 45 cottages. 2-day min: S, D $140-$415; suites $375-$570. Closed Aug. Adults only. TV; cable, VCR. 2 pools; whirlpool. Complimentary continental bkfst. Dining rm 8 am-9:30 pm. Box lunches, snacks. Bar. Ck-out noon, ck-in 3 pm. Business servs avail. Gift shop. Lighted tennis. Spa, sauna, massages. Bicycles avail. Refrigerators. Microwaves avail. 250-acres of rolling, wooded terrain include a lake and offer a secluded, private getaway. The rock grotto pools are fed from natural mineral hot springs. Cr cds: A, C, MC, V.

D

Inn

✓★★★ **TRAVELERS REPOSE BED & BREAKFAST.** *66920 1st St (92240). 760/329-9584.* 3 rms, 2 story. No rm phones. Sept-June: S $59-$75; D $65-$85; wkly rates. Closed rest of yr. Children over 12 yrs only. Whirlpool. Complimentary continental bkfst. Restaurant nearby. Ck-out 11 am, ck-in 2 pm. Parlor. Totally nonsmoking. Cr cds: C.

Devils Postpile National Monument (E-4)

(See also Mammoth Lakes)

(56 mi NW of Bishop, off US 395)

Just southeast of Yosemite National Park (see) and surrounded by Inyo National Forest (see) is Devils Postpile National Monument. The monument is among the finest examples of columnar basalt in the world, formed approximately 100,000 years ago when basalt lava erupted in the area. These columns, standing 40 to 60 feet high, are protected by the National Park Service. The formation is a half-mile hike from the ranger station. A short, steep trail leads to the top of the formation for a view of the ends of the columns, which have been polished by glaciers and resemble tile-like inlays. Pumice, a porous lava, and a nearby bubbling soda spring are evidence of recent volcanic activity.

Rainbow Falls is approximately two miles down the river trail from the Postpile. Here the San Joaquin River drops 101 feet—the foam-white water starkly contrasting with the dark cliffs. Its name was suggested by the rainbows that play across the falls in the afternoon. Fishing is permitted with license; hunting is prohibited. Picnic area on grounds. A campground is maintained in the northeast section. Park (mid-June-mid-Oct, daily; closed rest of yr). Ranger station (daily; hrs may vary). Campfire programs and guided walks available; call for schedule. For further information contact PO Box 501, Mammoth Lakes 93546; 760/934-2289 (June-Oct) or 760/872-4881 (Nov-May). Camping per day ¢¢¢¢

Disneyland (D-6 see Los Angeles map)

(See also Anaheim, Buena Park, Los Angeles, Orange)

(26 mi S of Los Angeles on Harbor Blvd, off Santa Ana Frwy in Anaheim)

The Walt Disney Company has sprinkled magic over 80 beautifully landscaped acres in Anaheim to create a fantasy that tantalizes adults as well as children. Park guests meet Mickey Mouse and the Disney characters and experience real-life adventures. Transportation ranges from horse-drawn streetcars to monorails; restaurant fare varies from pancakes to continental cuisine. Summer schedule includes name entertainment daily, dancing, fireworks and parades. You'll need a minimum of eight hours to see Disneyland. Plan to rest up the next day.

What to See and Do

The eight main sections of Disneyland are

Adventureland. Take a "Jungle Cruise" through tropical rivers of the world, with lifelike alligators, hippos, gorillas, monkeys, water buffalo and Indian elephants; Swiss Family Tree House; Enchanted Tiki Room shows musical fantasy with Audio-Animatronics: birds, flowers, talking and singing Tiki gods. The Indiana Jones Adventure thrill ride is also here.

Critter Country. Home of "Splash Mountain" log flume ride, Country Bear Playhouse, a 15-min country & western revue featuring musical Audio-Animatronic bears and Davy Crockett Explorer Canoes.

Fantasyland. Favorite Disney classics come to life in exciting adventures. Major attractions include It's a Small World, Pinocchio, Snow White, Dumbo, Peter Pan and Alice in Wonderland.

Frontierland. Relive the Old West and capture the pioneer spirit with the *Mark Twain* sternwheel riverboat, keel boats, the Golden Horseshoe Stage and Big Thunder Mountain Railroad. FANTASMIC! is a special effects and character presentation (nightly anytime Disneyland is open after dark) on the Rivers of America, which flow between Frontierland and Tom Sawyer Island.

Main St, U.S.A. Revives turn-of-the-century nostalgia with steam-powered Disneyland railroad, old-time cinema, Market House, 1900 emporium; an inspiring Audio-Animatronics presentation, "The Walt Disney Story," featuring "Great Moments with Mr. Lincoln."

Mickey's Toontown. A three-dimensional cartoon environment where guests can visit the homes of Mickey Mouse and his friends, including Goofy's Bounce House and Chip 'n Dale's Tree Slide and Acorn Crawl. Other attractions include The Jolly Trolley, Gadget's Go Coaster and Roger Rabbit's Car Toon Spin.

New Orleans Square. Shops, cafes, nostalgic courtyards, a "Pirates of the Caribbean" cruise and the Haunted Mansion.

Tomorrowland. This land of the future explores inner and outer space; features include Space Mountain rollercoaster, Autopia, Submarine Voyage, a 2½-mi monorail; rocket ride; Star Tours is an exciting out-of-this-world trip through the galaxy.

Disneyland Attractions are open daily (extended hrs during major hols). Passport to Disneyland good for unlimited use of rides and attractions (except arcades). Guided tours. Facilities for the disabled include wheelchair rentals, ramps; tape cassettes for the visually impaired. Contact 1313 Harbor Blvd, PO Box 3232, Anaheim 92803; phone 714/781-4565. Passport (individual) $36; children ages 3-11 $26; under 3 yrs fr.

Dunsmuir (B-2)

Pop 2,129 **Elev** 2,289 ft **Area Code** 530 **Zip** 96025
E-mail chamber@dunsmuir.com **Web** www.dunsmuir.com

Information Chamber of Commerce, 4118 Pine St, PO Box 17; 530/235-2177 or 800/DUNSMUIR

What to See and Do

Castle Crags State Park. On 4,250 acres. Named for nearby granite peaks up to 6,600 ft high. Fishing (exc in the Sacramento River and its tributaries). Picnicking. Camping. 6 mi S off I-5. Phone 530/235-2684. Day use per vehicle ¢¢; Camping per vehicle ¢¢¢¢¢

Annual Event

River Festival. Celebration of watershed stewardship. Exhibits, fishing clinics, demonstrations; art shows. Phone River Exchange Center, 530/235-2012. Late Apr.

Motels

✓★ **CEDAR LODGE MOTEL.** *4201 Dunsmuir Ave (96025). 530/235-4331; FAX 530/235-4000.* 16 rms, 6 kits. May-Oct: S $35-$39; D $38-$50; each addl $4; kit. units $10 addl; family units from $65; lower rates rest of yr. Crib $4. Pet accepted, some restrictions. TV; cable. Complimentary coffee in rms. Restaurant nearby. Ck-out 11 am. Downhill/x-country ski 16 mi. Private patios. Picnic tables, grill. Large exotic bird aviary. Near Sacramento River. Cr cds: A, C, DS, MC, V.

SC

★★ **RAILROAD PARK RESORT.** *100 Railroad Park Rd (96025). 530/235-4440; FAX 530/235-4470; res: 800/974-7245.* 28 rms, 4 cabins. S $55-$65; D $70-$85; each addl $8; cabins $70-$85. Pet accepted, some restrictions; $8. TV; cable. Pool; whirlpool. Complimentary coffee in rms. Restaurant 5-10 pm; closed Mon, Tues. Bar from 4 pm. Ck-out 11 am. Coin Indry. Business servs avail. Sundries. Gift shop. Game rm. Lawn games. Refrigerators. Picnic tables, grills. RV hookups. Rooms in authentic railroad cars; ¼ mi from Sacramento River. Cr cds: A, C, DS, MC, V.

El Cajon (K-4)

Pop 88,693 **Elev** 435 ft **Area Code** 619

Motels

★★ **BEST WESTERN CONTINENTAL INN.** *650 N Mollison Ave (92021). 619/442-0601; FAX 619/442-0152; res: 800/882-3781.* 97 rms, 2-3 story, 12 suites, 12 kits. Mid-June-mid-Sept: S, D $69-$105; each addl $5; suites $75-$150; kits. $75; under 18 free; lower rates rest of yr. Crib free. TV; cable (premium). Heated pool; whirlpool. Complimentary continental bkfst. Restaurant opp open 24 hrs. Ck-out 11 am. Coin Indry. Meeting rms. Business servs avail. Many refrigerators; some minibars, microwaves. Many balconies. Cr cds: A, C, D, DS, MC, V.

D SC

✓★ **THRIFTLODGE.** *1220 W Main St (92020). 619/442-2576; FAX 619/579-7562; res: 800/578-7878.* 28 rms, 10 with shower only, 2 story. S $42; D $49; suite $89-$99; under 18 free; higher rates hols. Pet accepted, some restrictions; $20. TV; cable. Complimentary coffee in rms. Restaurant adj open 24 hrs. Ck-out noon. Business servs avail. In-rm modem link. Pool. Some refrigerators. Cr cds: A, C, D, DS, MC, V.

D SC

✓★ **TRAVELODGE.** *471 N Magnolia Ave (92020). 619/447-3999; FAX 619/447-8403; res: 800/578-7878.* 48 rms, 3 story. S $35; D $70; each addl $5; under 17 free; higher rates hols. Crib free. Pet accepted, some restrictions; $15. TV; cable (premium), VCR avail. Complimentary continental bkfst. Complimentary coffee in rms. Restaurant opp 6 am-10 pm. Ck-out 11 am. Business servs avail. In-rm modem link. Coin Indry. Pool. Refrigerators, microwaves. Cr cds: A, C, D, DS, JCB, MC, V.

D SC

Resort

★★★ **SINGING HILLS RESORT.** *3007 Dehesa Rd (92019). 619/442-3428; FAX 619/442-9574; res: 800/457-5568.* E-mail lodge@singinghills.com; web www.singinghills.com. 102 rms, 1-2 story. S, D $84-$98; each addl $14; suites $109-$221; under 18 free. Crib free. TV; VCR avail. 2 heated pools; whirlpools. Complimentary coffee in rms. Restaurant 6 am-4 pm; dining rm 5:30-10 pm. Bar 10-2 am; entertainment Fri-Sat. Ck-out 1:30 pm. Coin Indry. Meeting rms. Business servs avail. Airport transportation. Lighted tennis, pro. 3 18-hole golf courses, greens fee $14-$45, 5 putting greens. Exercise equipt. Massage. Refrigerators; wet bar, some microwaves in suites. Private patios, balconies. View of mountains, valley and golf course. Cr cds: A, C, DS, MC, V.

D

El Centro (K-5)

(See also Calexico)

Settled 1901 **Pop** 31,384 **Elev** 40 ft below sea level **Area Code** 760 **Zip** 92243

Information Chamber of Commerce, 1100 Main St; 760/352-3681

This busy marketplace in the center of the Imperial Valley is the largest town entirely below sea level in the US. Water from the All-American Canal and Hoover Dam has turned arid desert into lush farmland, which produces great crops of sugar beets, melons and lettuce. The Imperial Valley was once part of the Gulf of California; mountains east of El Centro are ringed with coral reefs. Other points of geological interest are Fossil Canyon, north of town, and Painted Gorge, northwest off I-8.

Motels

★★★ **BARBARA WORTH GOLF RESORT & CONVETION CENTER.** *2050 Country Club Dr (92250), 8 mi E on CA 80. 760/356-2806; FAX 760/356-4653; res: 800/356-3806.* Web www.bwresort.com. 103 rms, 2 story. S, D $55-$70; each addl $6; kit. suites $140-$240; under 13 free; wkly, monthly rates; golf plans. Crib $6. TV; cable (premium). 2 heated pools; whirlpool. Coffee in rms. Restaurant (see BARBARA WORTH GOLF RESORT & CONVENTION CENTER). Rm serv. Bar 9 pm-midnight; Fri-Sun to 2 am. Ck-out noon. Meeting rms. 18-hole golf, greens fee $20-$28, putting green, driving range. Exercise equipt. Some refrigerators; microwaves avail. Private balconies. Cr cds: A, C, D, DS, JCB, MC, V.

D SC

✓★★ **CALIPATRIA INN.** *700 N Sorensen Ave (92233), 20 mi N on US 111. 760/348-7348; FAX 760/348-7348.* 40 rms, 5 with shower only, 5 suites. S, D $52-$59; each addl $5; suites $67-$121; under 12 free; higher rates special events. Crib free. Pet accepted. TV; cable (premium), VCR avail. Complimentary continental bkfst. Restaurant nearby. Ck-out noon. Meeting rms. Business servs avail. In-rm modem link. Pool; whirlpool. Many microwaves. Picnic tables, grills. Cr cds: A, C, DS, MC, V.

D SC

★★ **EL DORADO MOTEL.** *1464 Adams Ave (92243). 760/352-7333; FAX 760/352-4154; res: 800/874-5532.* 73 rms, 2 story, 6 kit. units. S, D $39-$45; each addl $4; kits. $39-$48; under 12 free; wkly rates. Pet accepted. TV; cable (premium). Pool. Complimentary continental bkfst. Restaurant adj 7 am-midnight. Ck-out 11 am. Some refrigerators. Cr cds: A, C, D, DS, MC, V.

SC

✓★ **EXECUTIVE INN.** *725 W State St (92243). 760/352-8500; FAX 760/352-1322.* 42 rms, 2 story, 5 kits. S, D $25-$50; kit. units $35-$50; each addl $2; suites $45-$60; under 12 free. Crib $5. Pet accepted, some restrictions. TV; cable. Pool. Complimentary continental bkfst. Restaurant nearby. Ck-out 11 am. Coin Indry. Some free covered parking. Some refrigerators; microwaves avail. Grills. Cr cds: C, DS, MC, V.

SC

★★ **RAMADA INN.** *1455 Ocotillo Dr (92243), I-8 & Imperial Ave. 760/352-5152; FAX 760/337-1567; res: 800/272-6232.* 147 rms, 2 story. S, D $52-$75; each addl $6; suites $75-$90; under 18 free. Crib free. Pet accepted. TV; cable (premium), VCR avail. Heated pool, whirlpool. Complimentary coffee in lobby. Restaurant open 24 hrs. Rm serv 6 am-2 pm, 5-10 pm. Bar 3:30 pm-midnight. Ck-out noon. Coin Indry. Meeting rms. Free airport, bus depot transportation. Exercise rm. Microwaves avail. Cr cds: A, C, D, DS, JCB, MC, V.

D SC

★★ **VACATION INN.** *2015 Cottonwood Cir (92243). 760/352-9523; FAX 760/353-7620; res: 800/328-6289.* 186 rms, 2 story. S, D $49-$54; suites $75-$95; higher rates special events. Crib free. Pet accepted; $25 deposit. TV; cable (premium). 2 heated pools; whirlpool, poolside serv. Restaurant (see SCRIBBLES). Bar 5:30 am-midnight. Ck-out noon. Coin Indry. Meeting rms. Business servs avail. In-rm modem link. Some refrigerators; microwaves avail. Exercise equipt. 31-space RV park adj. Cr cds: A, C, D, DS, MC, V.

D SC

Restaurants

★★ **BARBARA WORTH GOLF RESORT & CONVENTION CENTER.** *(See Barbara Worth Golf Resort & Convention Center) 760/356-2806.* Hrs: 6 am-10 pm; Sun brunch 10:30 am-2:30 pm. Closed Dec 25. Res accepted. Bar to midnight; Fri, Sat to 2 am. Semi-a la carte: bkfst $4.50-$6.25, lunch $3.50-$9.50, dinner $8.95-$19.95. Sun brunch $12.95. Child's meals. Specializes in beef, seafood. Outdoor dining. Garden atmosphere; large windows for outside view. Cr cds: A, C, D, DS, JCB, MC, V.

✓★★ **SCRIBBLES.** *(See Vacation Inn) 760/352-9523.* Hrs: 5:30 am-10 pm; Sun from 6 am. Closed Dec 25. Res accepted. Bar to 11 pm. A la carte entrees: bkfst $1.99-$8.95. Semi-a la carte: lunch $4.50-$8.50, dinner $9.95-15.95. Child's meals. Specialties: prime rib, filet mignon. Crayons at each table to mark bkfst & lunch menu choices. Totally nonsmoking. Cr cds: A, C, D, DS, MC, V.

D SC

Encino

(see Los Angeles)

Ensenada, Baja California, Mexico

Pop 175,000 (est) **Elev** 10 ft **E-mail** impamexicoinfo@worldnet.att.net

Information Tourism & Convention Bureau, 7860 Mission Center Court, Suite 202, San Diego 92108; 619/298-4105, 800/225-2786 outside CA or 800/522-1516 in CA, AZ & NV

Located on Todos Santos Bay, some 65 miles south of the border; Ensenada charms northern visitors with its good fishing, mild climate throughout the year and simple way of life. It is a favored vacation spot as well as the sports capital of Mexico. (For Border Crossing Regulations, see MAKING THE MOST OF YOUR TRIP.)

What to See and Do

Fishing. Giant white sea bass, yellow-tail, barracuda, bonita and other game fish in summer; bass in winter. Permit required for fishing and boating. Contact the Mexican Fish Commission in San Diego, phone 619/233-6956.

Hunting. Ducks, geese, quail, deer. Best S of town in mountains and plains region. Permit required. Contact the Mexican Consulate in San Diego, phone 619/231-8414.

Swimming. 5-mi beach along the bay.

Motels

★★ **HOTEL PARAISO LAS PALMAS.** *Av. Sangines #206. Col. Carlos Pacheco (22880).* 67 rms, 3 story, 13 suites. No A/C. Apr-Sept: S, D $38-$55; suites $60-$70; under 12 free; 2-day min hols; lower rates rest of yr. TV; cable. Pool; whirlpool. Complimentary coffee in rms. Restaurant 7 am-11 pm. Rm serv. Bar from 10 am; entertainment. Ck-out 1 pm. Meeting rms. Playground. Cr cds: A, C, MC, V.

★★ **PUNTA MORRO HOTEL SUITES.** *Km 106 Carretera Tijuana - Ensenada (02891), 2 mi N on Mexico 1 D; res: 800/526-6676.* E-mail pmorro@telnor.net; web www.punta-morro.com. 24 units, 21 kits. No A/C. S, D $70-$100; kit. suites $130-$300; wkly rates; 2-day min hols. TV; cable (premium). Pool; whirlpool, poolside serv. Restaurant (see PUNTA MORRO). Rm serv 8 am-11 pm. Ck-out noon. On ocean. Cr cds: A, C, MC, V.

★★ **TRAVELODGE.** *130 Avenida Blancarte (22800); res: 800/578-7878.* 52 rms. June-Sept: S, D $75-$83; under 12 free; 2-day min hols; higher rates special events; lower rates rest of yr. Crib free. TV; VCR avail. Pool; whirlpool, poolside serv. Complimentary coffee in rms. Restaurant adj 7 am-10 pm. Ck-out noon. Business servs avail. Sundries. Minibars. Balconies. Cr cds: A, C, MC, V.

SC

Motor Hotel

★★ **ESTERO BEACH RESORT.** *Tpmb 1186; 482 W San Ysidro Blvd; Mexico 1 (22785), 6 mi S, on Estero Bay.* 96 rms, 2 story. No A/C. No rm phones. Apr-Sept: S, D $75-$100; suites $400; under 5 free; 3-day min hols; higher rates hols, special events; lower rates rest of yr. TV; cable (premium). Pool; whirlpool, poolside serv. Playground. Restaurant 7:30 am-10:30 pm. Bar. Ck-out noon. Business servs avail. Shopping, arcade. Tennis. Rec rm. Some balconies. On beach. Cr cds: C, MC, V.

SC

Hotels

★ **CORONA.** *1442 Blvd Costero (22800), S of cruise boat terminal.* E-mail h.corona@microsol.com.mx. 93 rms, 4 story. S, D $38-$46; suites $100-$200; under 12 free; wkly rates; higher rates special events; TV; cable (premium). Pool. Restaurant adj 7 am-11 pm. Bar. Ck-out noon. Meeting rms. Business servs avail. Sundries. On ocean. Cr cds: A, C, MC, V.

★★★ **HOTEL CORAL & MARINA.** *Km 103; 3421 Zona Playitas. 619/523-0064; res: 800/946-2746.* 147 rms, 6 story. S, D $135-$150; each addl $15; kit. units $220; under 12 free; lower rates midwk. Crib free. TV; cable (premium), VCR avail. 3 pools, 1 indoor; whirlpool. Playground. Coffee in rms. Restaurant 7 am-11 pm. Bar. Ck-out 1 pm. Meeting rms. Business servs avail. Shopping arcade. Barber, beauty shop. Lighted tennis. Exercise equipt; sauna. Refrigerators, some microwaves. Balconies. Oceanfront overlooking marina. Cr cds: A, C, MC, V.

D SC

★★★ **LAS ROSAS BY THE SEA.** *K M 105 Tijuana-Ensenada Toll Rd (22800), 2 mi N on Mexico 1 D.* 32 rms, 4 story. No A/C. S, D $115-$120; kit. cottage $165. TV; cable. Pool; whirlpool, poolside serv. Restaurant 7 am-10 pm. Bar from 10 am; entertainment wkends. Ck-out noon. Business servs avail. In-rm modem link. Gift shop. Lighted tennis, pro. Exercise equipt; sauna. Massage. Balconies. On ocean. Cr cds: C, MC, V.

★★ **SAN NICOLAS RESORT HOTEL.** *Ave Adolfo Lopez Mateos (22800), at Avenida Guadalope.* 150 rms, 3 story. July-early Sept: S, D $68-$88; each addl $10; suites $130-$260; under 10 free; wkly, wkend rates; lower rates rest of yr. TV; cable (premium). 2 pools, 1 indoor; whirlpool, poolside serv. Complimentary coffee in rms. Restaurant 7 am-10:30 pm. Bar. Ck-out noon. Meeting rms. Business servs avail. Beauty shop. Health club privileges. Massage. Refrigerators avail. Balconies. Cr cds: C, MC, V.

SC

Resort

★★★ **BAJAMAR OCEAN FRONT GOLF RESORT.** *Carretera Escenica, Km 77.5 (92108), 20 mi S on Mexico 1 D. 619/299-1112; FAX 619/299-4344; res: 800/225-2418; res: 888/311-6076.* 81 units, 2 story. S, D $99-$118; each addl $20; suites $163-$185; under 12 free; golf plan. TV;

cable. Pool; whirlpool, poolside serv. Sauna. Restaurant 7 am-11 pm. Rm serv. Meeting rms. Business servs avail. Bellhops. Tennis. 27-hole golf course, greens fee $61-$71, pro, putting green, driving range. Massage. Microwave in suites. On ocean. Cr cds: A, C, MC, V.

Restaurants

★★ **CASAMAR.** *987 Blvd Lazaro Cardenas. 011-52-617/4-04-17.* Hrs: noon-11 pm. Closed Jan 1, Mar 21, May 1, Sept 16, Dec 25. Res accepted. Continental menu. Bar to 3 am. Semi-a la carte: lunch, dinner $5.75-$33. Specialties: seafood combination, abalone Casamar. Large picture windows offer view of marina. Family-owned. Cr cds: C, MC, V.

★★★ **CASINO ROYAL.** *Blvd Las Dunas & Ondinas #118. 011-52-617/7-14-80.* Hrs: noon-10:30 pm. Closed Sun; also Jan 1, Mar 21, Sept 16, Dec 25. Res accepted. Continental menu. Semi-a la carte: lunch, dinner $8.50-$35. Specialties: lobster Casino Royal, rack of lamb, abalone steak. Pianist wkends. Parking. French-style decor with rococo influence. Family-owned. Cr cds: A, C, MC, V.

★★★ **EL REY SOL.** *Ave Lopez Mateos & Blancarte 1000. 011-52-617/8-17-33.* Hrs: 7:30 am-10:45 pm. Res accepted. French, continental menu. Semi-a la carte: bkfst $4-$10, lunch, dinner $11-$35. Specializes in gourmet French cooking. Pianist exc Mon. Street parking. Beamed ceilings with chandeliers, antiques and statuary; elegant decor. Family-owned. Cr cds: A, C, MC, V.

★★ **HALIOTIS.** *179 Calle Delante. 011-52-617/6-37-20.* Hrs: 12:30-10 pm. Closed Jan 1, Dec 25. Seafood menu. A la carte entrees: lunch, dinner $4.75-$20. Child's meals. Specializes in seafood, abalone, lobster. Parking. Nautical decor with emphasis on fishing. Family-owned. Cr cds: A, C, MC, V.

★★★ **LA EMBOTELLADORA VIEJA.** *7th St & Miramar, in Bodega de Santo Tomas. 011-52-617/4-08-07.* Hrs: noon-midnight; Sun to 5 pm. Closed Tues; Jan 1, Dec 25. Res accepted. Mediterranean menu. Wine cellar. Semi-a la carte: lunch, dinner $7-$25. Specialties: marlin carpaccio, calamari Manchez, swordfish in black mole. Street parking. In converted winery; wine casks, antiques. Cr cds: A, C, MC, V.

★★ **PUNTA MORRO.** *(See Punta Morro) 011-52-617/8-35-07.* Hrs: noon-11 pm; Sat from 8 am; Sun 9 am-10:30 pm. Closed Jan 1, Dec 25. Res accepted. Continental menu. Bar. Semi-a la carte: bkfst $10-$15, lunch, dinner $8-$35. Sun brunch $12. Parking. Glassed-in dining room sits on ocean. Cr cds: A, C, MC, V.

Escondido (K-4)

(See also Carlsbad, La Jolla, San Diego)

Pop 108,635 **Elev** 684 ft **Area Code** 760 **E-mail** info@adnc.com **Web** www.sandiegonorth.com

Information San Diego North Convention and Visitors Bureau, 720 N Broadway, 92025; 760/745-4741 or 800/848-3336

A Ranger District office of the Cleveland National Forest (see PINE VALLEY) is located here.

What to See and Do

Escondido Heritage Walk. Escondido Historical Society history museum. Artifacts, books, preservation displays. Victorian ranch house; working blacksmith shop, early 1900s barn and windmill, 1888 Santa Fe RR depot, railroad car with model train replica of the Oceanside to Escondido run (ca 1920). (Thurs-Sat; closed major hols exc July 4) 321 N Broadway. Phone 760/743-8207. **Donation**

Palomar Observatory. Here are a 200-in Hale telescope (2nd-largest in the US) and 48-in and 60-in telescopes. There is a visitors' gallery in the dome of the Hale telescope; Greenway Museum has photography from telescopes, exhibits explaining equipment. Self-guided tours. Gift shop. (Daily; closed Dec 24, 25) 35 mi NE on County S6. Phone 760/742-2119. **Free**

San Diego Wild Animal Park. (See SAN DIEGO)

San Pasqual Battlefield State Historic Park & Museum. Interpretive displays of the Battle of San Pasqual, fought in Dec 1846, during the Mexican War. Fifty acres within deeply weathered granite foothills; self-guided native plant trail; hiking. Picnicking. (Fri-Sun; closed Jan 1, Thanksgiving, Dec 25) 8 mi E on CA 78. Phone 760/489-0076. **Free**

Welk Resort Center Theatre-Museum. Music Center houses memorabilia marking the milestones of Lawrence Welk's career. (Daily) Theater and dance performances (fee). At the Welk Resort Center (see RESORT). Phone 760/749-3448 or 760/749-3000. Museum **Free** .

Wineries.

Deer Park. Grape vineyard, winery, Napa Valley wine tasting rm (free) and deli; picnic areas. Also car museum with approx 90 antique convertibles and other vintage vehicles on display. (Daily; closed Thanksgiving, Dec 25) 8 mi N, at 29013 Champagne Blvd. Phone 760/749-1666. Museum **¢¢¢**

Ferrara. Producers of wine and grape juice. Self-guided tours, wine tasting. (Daily; closed Jan 1, Easter, Thanksgiving, Dec 25) 1120 W 15th Ave. Phone 760/745-7632. **Free**

Orfila. Guided and self-guided tours, wine tasting rm; picnic area beneath grape arbor overlooks the vineyards and San Pasqual Valley. (Daily; closed Jan 1, Thanksgiving, Dec 25) 13455 San Pasqual Rd. Phone 760/738-6500. **Free**

Motels

✓★★ **COMFORT INN.** *1290 W Valley Pkwy (92029). 760/489-1010; FAX 760/489-7847; res: 800/541-6012.* 93 rms, 3 story. S, D $89; under 18 free. Crib free. TV; cable. Pool; whirlpool. Complimentary continental bkfst. Restaurant adj 6 am-midnight. Ck-out noon. Meeting rms. In-rm modem link. Valet serv. Microwaves avail. Cr cds: A, C, D, DS, MC, V.

D SC

★★ **SHERIDAN INN.** *1341 N Escondido Blvd (92026). 760/743-8338; FAX 760/743-0840; res: 800/258-8527.* E-mail sheridan@sheridan-inn.com; web www.sheridan-inn.com. 54 rms, 2 story, 32 suites. S, D, suites $69-$86; wkly rates. Crib free. TV; cable (premium). Heated pool; whirlpool. Complimentary continental bkfst. Restaurant opp 7 am-midnight. Ck-out noon. Health club privileges. Some refrigerators; microwaves avail. Cr cds: A, C, D, DS, MC, V.

D SC

Motor Hotel

✓★★★ **QUAILS INN HOTEL.** *1025 La Bonita Dr (92069), W on CA 78 to Ranch Santa Fe Rd. 760/744-0120; FAX 760/744-0748; res: 800/447-6556.* 140 rms, 2 story. S, D $99-$149; each addl $10; suites, kit. cottages $199-$300; under 12 free; package plans. Crib $10. Pet accepted, some restrictions; $10. TV; cable (premium), VCR avail. 2 heated pools; whirlpool. Restaurant adj 6:30 am-10 pm. Rm serv 7 am-8 pm. Ck-out noon. Meeting rms. Tennis privileges. Golf privileges. Exercise equipt. Boat rental. Some refrigerators; microwaves avail. Many private patios, balconies. On Lake San Marcos. Extensive grounds. Cr cds: A, C, D, DS, MC, V.

D SC

Resort

★★★ **WELK RESORT CENTER.** *8860 Lawrence Welk Dr (92026). 760/749-3000; FAX 760/749-9537; res: 800/932-9355.* E-mail welk@2.com; web www.welkresort.com. 132 rms, 2-3 story. S, D $190; suites $160-$500; package plans. Pet accepted. TV; cable, VCR avail (movies). 2 heated pools; whirlpool. Supervised child's activities. Coffee in rms. Dining rm 7 am-9 pm. Bar 11 am-midnight. Ck-out noon. Meeting rms. In-rm modem link. Concierge. Shopping plaza. Beauty shop. 3 lighted tennis courts. 2 18-hole golf courses, putting green. Exercise equipt. Massage. Dinner theater. Semi-private patios, balconies. Some refrigerators. Cr cds: A, C, D, DS, ER, MC, V.

D SC

Inns

★★ **CASTLE CREEK INN RESORT & SPA.** *29850 Circle R Way (93955). 760/751-8800; FAX 760/751-8787; res: 800/235-5341.* E-mail cci@cadnc.com; web www.castlecreekresort.com. 30 rms, 2 story. S, D $119-$159; 3-bedrm cottage $500; under 18 free. Crib free. Pet accepted, some restrictions. TV; cable. Pool. Complimentary continental bkfst. Restaurant 5-9 pm. Rm serv. Ck-out noon, ck-in 3 pm. Meeting rms. Tennis. Golf privileges. Exercise equipt; sauna. Cr cds: A, C, DS, MC, V.

★★★ **ZOSA GARDENS BED & BREAKFAST.** *9381 W Lilac Rd (92026). 760/723-9093; FAX 760/723-3460; res: 800/711-8361.* Web www.zosagardens.com. 10 rms, 3 share bath, 1 guest house. No rm phones. S, D $100-$195; each addl $10; guest house $175-$250; hols 2-day min. Premium cable TV in some rms; VCR avail (movies). Complimentary full bkfst. Ck-out noon, ck-in 2 pm. Lighted tennis. Heated pool; whirlpool. Microwaves avail. Picnic tables, grills. Totally nonsmoking. Cr cds: A, C, D, DS, MC, V.

D SC

Restaurants

★★★ **150 GRAND CAFE.** *150 W Grand Ave (92029). 760/738-6868.* Web www.150grand.com. Hrs: 11:30 am-3 pm, 5-9 pm; Fri to 9:30 pm; Sat 5-9:30 pm. Closed Sun; most major hols. Res accepted. Bar. Semi-a la carte: lunch $6-$12, dinner $14-$22. Specialties: open faced seafood ravioli, roasted pork tenderloin. Guitarist Fri-Sat. Outdoor dining. Cr cds: A, C, D, MC, V.

D

★★ **SANDCRAB CAFE.** *2229 Micro Place (92029). 760/480-2722.* Hrs: 11 am-9 pm; Fri, Sat to 10 pm. Closed Dec 25. Seafood menu. Bar. Semi-a la carte: lunch $2-$9.95, dinner $10.50-$18. Child's meals. Specializes in shellfish. Totally nonsmoking. Cr cds: C, DS, MC, V.

D

★★ **SIRINO'S RESTORANTE.** *113 W Grand Ave (92025). 760/745-3835.* Hrs: 11:30 am-2 pm, 4:30-9:30 pm; Sat from 4:30 pm; early bird dinner 4:30-5:30 pm. Closed Sun, Mon; most major hols; last 2 wks Feb. Res required (dinner). Continental menu. Bar. Semi-a la carte: lunch $8-$18, dinner $14-$22. Specializes in lamb, duck. Outdoor dining. Cafe-style dining. Cr cds: A, C, D, DS, MC, V.

D

Eureka (B-1)

(See also Trinidad)

Founded 1850 **Pop** 27,025 **Elev** 44 ft **Area Code** 707 **Zip** 95501
E-mail eureka@northcoast.com **Web** www.eurekachamber.com

Information Chamber of Commerce, 2112 Broadway; 707/442-3738 or 800/356-6381

The largest fishing fleet north of San Francisco Bay makes the city of Eureka its main port. Lumbering is the city's major industry.

What to See and Do

Arcata Architectural Tour. Self-guided walking or driving tour to many Victorian structures, covering 35 city blocks. City of Arcata, 8 mi N on US 101. Obtain city map at Arcata Chamber of Commerce, 1062 G St, 95521; Phone 707/822-3619.

Clarke Memorial Museum. Regional history, collection of Karuk, Hupa, Wiyot and Yurok basketry and ceremonial regalia; firearms, Victorian furniture and decorative art. Guided tours by appt. (Tues-Sat afternoons & July 4; closed some hols, also Jan) Third & E St. Phone 707/443-1947. **Donation**

Ferndale Museum. Local history displays of "Cream City." (June-Sept, daily exc Mon; rest of yr, Wed-Sun; closed major hols, also Jan) 12 mi S on US 101, then 5 mi W in Ferndale, at 3rd & Shaw Sts. Phone 707/786-4466. **¢**

Fort Humboldt State Historic Park. Ulysses S. Grant was stationed at Fort Humboldt in 1854. Logging and military exhibits. Tours. Picnicking. (Daily; closed Jan 1, Thanksgiving, Dec 25) 3431 Fort Ave. Phone 707/445-6567. **Free**

Fortuna Depot Museum. Train memorabilia, barbed wire collection, fishing and logging displays. In 1893 train depot. (June-Aug, daily; rest of yr, Wed-Sun afternoons; closed Dec 25) 18 mi S on US 101 in Fortuna, Rohner Park. Phone 707/725-7645. **Free**

Humboldt Bay Harbor Cruise. 1¼-hr trips. (May-Sept, 3 departures daily: 2 afternoon, 1 evening) Special charter rest of yr. Foot of C St. Phone 707/445-1910. **¢¢¢**

Humboldt Bay Maritime Museum. Pacific and northcoast maritime heritage displays; marine artifacts. (Daily; closed some hols) 1410 Second St. Phone 707/444-9440. **Donation**

Old Town. Designated a National Historic District, this section of town has original buildings of early Eureka. Also here is a gazebo, cascading water fountain, sculptured benches, commercial and residential Victorian buildings; antique and specialty shops; horse and buggy rides (fee); restaurants. All situated on waterfront of Humboldt Bay. Cruises of the bay are avail. 1st, 2nd & 3rd Sts, C to G Sts.

Romano Gabriel Wooden Sculpture Garden. A colorful collection of folk art, constructed of wood in the mid-1900s. (Daily) 315 2nd St, in Old Town section. **Free**

Sequoia Park Zoo. Area surrounded by 46 acres of redwoods; duck pond, gardens, picnic facilities, snack bar, children's playground. (Daily exc Mon) Glatt & W Sts. Phone 707/442-6552. **Free**

Six Rivers National Forest. On 1,111,726 acres. The Klamath, Eel, Trinity, Van Duzen and Mad rivers provide excellent fishing. Hunting, camping, picnicking. Resorts and lodges located in and near forest. Standard fees. Reached via US 101, 199, CA 36, 96, 299. Contact Forest Supervisor's Office, 1330 Bay Shore Way; phone 707/442-1721. Located within the forest are

Smith River National Recreation Area. (305,337 acres) This is the heart of one of the largest wild and scenic river systems (315 mi) in the US. Offers whitewater rafting, wilderness hiking, bird watching, nature study, world-class steelhead fishing, hunting and camping. For information contact Gasquet Ranger Station, Box 228, 10600 US 199N, Gasquet 95543-0228; phone 707/457-3131.

Woodley Island Marina. Mooring for commercial fishing boats and recreational craft; cafe and shops; site of *The Fisherman* memorial statue and Table Bluff Lighthouse. 1 mi W via US 101, Samoa Bridge exit (CA 255).

Annual Events

Jazz Festival. Various locations in town. Last wkend Mar.

Rhododendron Festival. Varied events throughout Humboldt County include parades, races, art exhibits, contests, entertainment. Usually last wkend Apr.

Cross-Country Kinetic Sculpture Race. A 3-day, 35-mi cross-country race over land, water, beaches and highways. Participants race on their self-powered, artistically sculptured vehicles. Memorial Day wkend.

Motels

★★★ **BEST WESTERN THUNDERBIRD INN.** *232 W 5th St (95501). 707/443-2234; FAX 707/443-3489; res: 800/528-1234; res: 800/521-6996.* Web www.hotelswest.com/eureka/eureka.htm. 115 rms, some A/C, 2 story. Mid-May-mid-Oct: S $82-$97; D $86-$102; each addl $5; suites $90-$150; lower rates rest of yr. Crib free. TV; cable (premium), VCR avail (free movies). Heated pool; whirlpool. Coffee in rms. Restaurant 6 am-10 pm. Rm serv. Ck-out noon. Coin lndry. Meeting rms. Business servs avail. In-rm modem link. Sundries. Free bus depot transportation. Game rm. Some refrigerators. Cr cds: A, C, D, DS, ER, MC, V.

D SC

★★ **QUALITY INN.** *1209 4th St (95501). 707/443-1601; FAX 707/444-8365; res: 800/772-1622.* 60 rms, 2 story. No A/C. June-mid-Oct: S, D $75-$150; each addl $10; suites $100-$200; lower rates rest of yr. Crib $5. Pet accepted. TV; cable (premium). Heated pool; wading pool, whirlpool. Complimentary continental bkfst. Complimentary coffee in rms. Restaurant opp 7 am-11 pm. Ck-out noon. Meeting rms. Business servs avail. Sauna. Cr cds: A, C, D, DS, JCB, MC, V.

D SC

✓★ **TRAVELODGE.** *4 4th St (95501). 707/443-6345; FAX 707/443-1486; res: 800/578-7878.* 46 rms, 2 story. No A/C. S $37-$55; D $38-$73; each addl $5; under 12 free. Crib free. Pet accepted. TV; cable (premium). Heated pool. Coffee in rms. Restaurant nearby. Ck-out 11 am. Business servs avail. Sundries. Cr cds: A, C, D, DS, ER, JCB, MC, V.

SC

Motor Hotel

★★★ **DOUBLETREE HOTEL.** *1929 4th St (95501). 707/445-0844; FAX 707/445-2752; res: 800/547-8010.* 178 rms, 3-4 story. S, D $59-$95; suites $125-$175; under 18 free; wkend rates. Crib free. Pet accepted. TV; cable (premium), VCR avail. Heated pool; whirlpool. Coffee in rms. Restaurant 6 am-10 pm. Rm serv. Bar; entertainment wkends. Ck-out noon. Meeting rms. Business servs avail. In-rm modem link. Bellhops. Valet serv. Sundries. Free airport transportation. Balconies. Cr cds: A, C, D, DS, ER, JCB, MC, V.

D SC

Hotel

★★★ **EUREKA INN.** *518 7th St (95501). 707/442-6441; FAX 707/442-0637; res: 800/862-4906.* 104 rms, 4 story. No A/C. S, D $110-$140; each addl $10; suites $170-$250; under 16 free. Crib free. Pet accepted. TV; cable. Heated pool; whirlpool. Saunas. Restaurant 6:30 am-10 pm. Bar 11-2 am; entertainment Thurs-Sat. Ck-out noon. Meeting rms. Business servs avail. Free airport, bus depot transportation. Some bathrm phones. Fireplace in lobby. Historic Tudor-style building (1922). Cr cds: A, C, D, DS, MC, V.

D SC

Inns

★★★ **AN ELEGANT VICTORIAN MANSION.** *1406 C St (95501). 707/444-3144; FAX 707/442-5594.* Web www.bbonline.com/ca/abigails/. 4 rms, 3 share bath, 2 story, 1 suite. No A/C. Rm phones avail. June-Sept: S $85-$185; each addl $35-$50; suite $135-$185; MAP avail; lower rates rest of yr. Premium cable TV in common rm; VCR avail (movies). Complimentary full bkfst. Restaurant nearby. Ck-out 11 am, ck-in 3-6 pm. Business servs avail. Luggage handling. Valet serv. Coincierge serv. Guest lndry. Free RR station, bus depot transportation. Bicycles. Sauna. Massage. Game rm. Lawn games. Picnic tables. Built in 1886; Victorian decor, antiques. Totally nonsmoking. Cr cds: C, MC, V.

SC

★★★ **CARTER INN AND CARTER HOUSE BED & BREAKFAST.** *301 L St and 1033 3rd St (95501). 707/445-1390; FAX 707/444-8067; res: 800/404-1390.* E-mail carter52@carterhouse; web carterhouse.com. 25 rms, 3 story. S $79-$95; D $105-$165; suites $195-$250; cottage $500. Crib free. TV; cable, VCR (free movies). Complimentary full bkfst; afternoon refreshments. Dining rm 7:30-10 am; 6-9 pm. Ck-out 11 am, ck-in 3-6 pm. Meeting rms. Business servs avail. In-rm modem link. Valet serv. Golf privileges. Health club privileges. Massage. Some in-rm whirlpools; fireplace in suites. White pine antiques. Totally nonsmoking. Cr cds: A, C, D, DS, JCB, MC, V.

D SC

★★★ **CARTER INN AND CARTER HOUSE BED & BREAKFAST.** *301 L St and 1033 3rd St (95501). 707/445-1390; FAX 707/444-8067; res: 800/404-1390.* E-mail carter52@carterhouse; web carterhouse.com. 5 rms, 4 story. S, D $125-$145; suites $165-$275. TV; cable, VCR (free movies). Children over 10 yrs only. Complimentary full bkfst; afternoon refreshments. Ck-out 11 am, ck-in 3-6 pm. Business servs avail. In-rm modem link. Valet serv. Game rm. Golf privileges. Health club privileges. Massage. Suite with whirlpool, fireplace. Re-created 1884 San Francisco Victorian house. Antiques, Oriental rugs; marble fireplaces. Totally nonsmoking. Cr cds: A, C, D, DS, JCB, MC, V.

SC

★★★ **DALY INN.** *1125 H St (95501). 707/445-3638; FAX 707/444-3636; res: 800/321-9656.* E-mail dalyinn@humboldt1.com; web www.humboldt.com/~dalyinn. 5 rms, 2 share bath, 2 story, 2 suites. No A/C. No rm phones. May-Oct: S $70-$115; D $80-$125; each addl $20; suites $140-$150; hols (2-3-day min); lower rates rest of yr. TV in den; cable (premium), VCR (movies). Complimentary full bkfst; afternoon refreshments. Ck-out 11 am, ck-in 4-7 pm. Guest lndry. Business servs avail. Lawn games. Picnic tables. Built in 1905. Surrounded by gardens. Totally nonsmoking. Cr cds: A, C, DS, MC, V.

★★★ **GINGERBREAD MANSION.** *400 Berding St (95536), 20 mi S via US 101, 1 blk E of Main St. 707/786-9667; FAX 707/786-4381; res: 800/952-4136.* E-mail kenn@humboldt1.com; web gingerbread-mansion.com. 11 rms, 3 story. Some with rm phones. S, D $110-$310; each addl $40; suites $160-$350. TV in some rms. Complimentary full bkfst; afternoon refreshments. Ck-out 11 am, ck-in 2-7 pm. Business servs avail. Restored Victorian mansion (ca 1899); English gardens; in "Victorian Village; community setting. Elaborate bathrms; many fireplaces; formal dining rm. Totally nonsmoking. Cr cds: A, C, MC, V.

✓★★ **OLD TOWN BED & BREAKFAST INN.** *1521 3rd St (95501), at edge of Old Town District. 707/445-3951; FAX 707/268-0231; res: 800/331-5098.* E-mail otb-b@dreamwalkerusa.com; web www.dreamwalkerusa.com/otb-b. 6 rms, 2 share bath, 2 story. No A/C. S $70-$130; D $80-$140; each addl $20. Adults only. Complimentary full bkfst. Ck-out 11 am, ck-in 3-6 pm. Business servs avail. Airport, RR station, bus depot transportation. Whirlpool. Some fireplaces. Built 1871, oldest lodging in town; Greek revival Victorian home with antique furnishings. Garden. Bay 1½ blks. Totally nonsmoking. Cr cds: A, C, D, DS, MC, V.

Restaurants

★★★ **RESTAURANT 301.** *301 L St (95501). 707/444-8062.* E-mail carter52@carterhouse; web carterhouse.com. Hrs: 6-9 pm. Res accepted. Wine, beer. Semi-a-la carte: dinner $9.95-$24. Prix fixe: $39-$49, 8-course dinner $55. Child's meals. Wine cellar. Specialties: Humboldt Bay oysters, rack of lamb, Pacific salmon. Own desserts. Own garden vegetables. Original art; view of bay. Totally nonsmoking. Cr cds: A, C, D, DS, JCB, MC.

D

✓★★ **SEA GRILL.** *316 E St (95501). 707/443-7187.* Hrs: 11 am-2 pm, 5-9:30 pm; Mon & Sat from 5 pm. Closed Sun; some major hols; also 2 wks early Nov. Res accepted. Bar. Semi-a la carte: lunch $4.95-$10.95, dinner $12.95-$18.95. Child's meals. Specializes in fresh local seafood, steaks, prime rib. Salad bar. Restored Victorian building (ca 1870). Antique bar. Totally nonsmoking. Cr cds: C, D, DS, MC, V.

D

Fairfield (D-2)

(See also Vacaville, Vallejo)

Pop 77,211 **Elev** 15 ft **Area Code** 707 **Zip** 94533

This is the home of Travis Air Force Base and the seat of Solano County.

What to See and Do

Western Railway Museum. Take a 2-mi ride on electric streetcars and interurbans, with occasional steam and diesel operation. Museum collection includes 100 vintage railroad cars and trains operating on demonstration railroad; bookstore, gift shop; picnic area. (Early July- Labor Day, Wed-Sun; Sept-June, Sat, Sun & most hols; closed Jan 1, Thanksgiving, Dec 25) Museum admission includes unlimited rides. 12 mi E on CA 12. Phone 707/374-2978. ¢¢¢

Motels

✓★ **BEST WESTERN CORDELIA INN.** *4373 Central Pl (94585), I-80 Suisun Valley Rd exit. 707/864-2029; FAX 707/864-5834; res: 800/528-1234.* 60 rms, 2 story. S $58-$70; D $72-$80; each addl $6; under 18 free. Crib free. TV; cable. Pool; whirlpool. Complimentary continental bkfst. Complimentary coffee in rms. Restaurant nearby. Ck-out noon. Coin lndry. Business servs avail. In-rm modem link. Valet serv. Refrigerators, microwaves avail. Cr cds: A, C, D, DS, MC, V.

D SC

★★ **HAMPTON INN.** *4441 Central Pl (94585). 707/864-1446; FAX 707/864-4288; res: 800/426-7866.* Web www.hampton-inn.com/fairfield-napa. 57 rms, 3 story. S, D $69-$79; suites $145; lower rates winter. Crib free. TV; cable (premium), VCR avail (movies). Heated pool. Complimentary continental bkfst. Ck-out noon. Coin lndry. Meeting rms. Business servs avail. In-rm modem link. Exercise equipt. Microwaves avail. Cr cds: A, C, D, DS, MC, V.

D SC

Motor Hotel

★★ **HOLIDAY INN SELECT.** *1350 Holiday Ln (94533). 707/422-4111; FAX 707/428-3452; res: 800/465-4329.* 142 rms, 4 story. S, D $89-$99; each addl $10; suites $225; under 12 free; higher rates some special events. Crib free. TV; cable (premium). Pool; wading pool. Coffee in rms. Restaurant 6:30 am-2 pm, 5-10 pm. Rm serv. Bar 4 pm-midnight. Ck-out noon. Meeting rms. Business servs avail. In-rm modem link. Coin lndry. Bellhops. Valet serv. Exercise equipt. Health club privileges. Microwaves avail. Some patios, balconies. Cr cds: A, C, D, DS, JCB, MC, V.

D SC

Restaurants

★★ **FUSILLI RISTORANTE.** *620 Jackson St (94533). 707/428-4211.* Hrs: 11:30 am-2:30 pm, 5-9 pm; Sat 5-9:30 pm. Closed Sun; Easter, Thanksgiving, Dec 25. Res accepted. Italian menu. Wine, beer. A la carte entrees: lunch, dinner $8.25-$18. Specializes in wood-burning oven pizza. Own bread, pasta. Modern decor. Totally nonsmoking. Cr cds: A, C, MC, V.

D

✓★ **OLD SAN FRANCISCO EXPRESS.** *4560 Central Way (94585), I-80 Suisan Valley Rd exit. 707/864-6453.* Hrs: 11:30 am-9:30 pm; Fri, Sat to 10:30 pm. Closed Mon. Res accepted. Bar. Complete meals: lunch, dinner $5.95-$15.95. Child's meals. Specializes in pastas, seafood, beef. Comprised of 11 railroad cars connected together to form 2 large dining areas; some cars form private dining rms. Cr cds: A, C, MC, V.

D

Fallbrook (J-4)

(See also Temecula)

Settled 1880s **Pop** 22,095 **Elev** 685 ft **Area Code** 760 **Zip** 92028

Motels

★ **BEST WESTERN FRANCISCAN INN.** *1635 S Mission Rd (92028). 760/728-6174; FAX 760/731-6404; res: 800/528-1234.* 50 rms, 1-2 story, 27 kits. S, D $60-$75; each addl $5; kit. units $65-$80; under 12 free. Crib $5. TV; cable. Heated pool; whirlpool. Complimentary continental bkfst. Coffee in rms. Ck-out 11 am. Meeting rm. Microwaves avail. Cr cds: A, C, D, DS, MC, V.

SC

✓★ **TRAVELODGE.** *1608 S Mission Rd (92028). 760/723-1127; FAX 760/723-2917; res: 800/578-7878.* 36 units, 2 story, 8 kits. S, D $55-$60; each addl $5; kits. $60-$90; under 17 free; wkly rates. Crib free. TV; cable (premium). Complimentary continental bkfst. Restaurant opp 7:30 am-9 pm. Ck-out 11 am. Whirlpool. Some balconies. Cr cds: A, C, D, DS, JCB, MC, V.

D SC

Resort

★★★ **PALA MESA RESORT.** *2001 Old Hwy 395 (92028). 760/728-5881; FAX 760/723-8292; res: 800/722-4700.* E-mail teeup@palamesa.com; web www.palamesa.com. 133 rms, 1-2 story. S, D $110-$160; suites $250-$350; under 18 free; package plans. Crib free. TV; cable, VCR avail. Heated pool; whirlpool. Coffee in rms. Dining rm 6 am-10 pm. Rm serv to 11 pm. Bar 11-2 am; entertainment Fri-Sun. Ck-out noon, ck-in 4 pm. Meeting rms. Business servs avail. In-rm modem link. Lighted tennis. 18-hole golf, pro, putting green, driving range. Exercise equipt. Massage. Refrigerators. Cr cds: A, C, D, MC, V.

D SC

Restaurants

✓★★ **CASK 'N CLEAVER.** *3757 S Mission Rd (92028). 760/728-2818.* Hrs: 5-9 pm; Fri, Sat to 10 pm; Sun from 4:30 pm. Closed most major hols. Res accepted. Bar. Semi-a la carte: dinner $10-$19. Child's meals. Specialties: deep-fried avocado, mesquite pepper steak, prime rib. Music Sat. Parking. Outdoor dining. Totally nonsmoking. Cr cds: A, C, DS, MC, V.

D

✓★★ **PACKING HOUSE RESTAURANT.** *125 S Main St (92028). 760/728-5810.* Hrs: 11:30 am-9 pm; early-bird dinner 5-6 pm (Sun-Thurs). Closed July 4, Dec 25. Res accepted Fri, Sat. Bar. Semi-a la carte: lunch $6-$9, dinner $8-$18. Child's meals. Specialty: prime rib. Music Wed, Fri, Sat. Turn-of-the-century setting. Totally nonsmoking. Cr cds: A, C, DS, MC, V.

✓★ **SAU-HY'S CHINESE CUISINE.** *909 S Main Ave (92028). 760/728-1000.* Hrs: 11:30 am-10 pm. Closed July 4, Thanksgiving, Dec 25. Chinese menu. Wine, beer. A la carte entrees: lunch $4-$6, dinner $7.25-$10. Child's meals. Chinese decor, antiques. Cr cds: A, C, D, DS, MC, V.

Felton

(see Santa Cruz)

Fort Bragg (C-1)

(See also Mendocino, Ukiah, Willits)

Founded 1884 **Pop** 6,078 **Elev** 75 ft **Area Code** 707 **Zip** 95437
E-mail chamber@mcn.org **Web** www.mendocinocoast.com

Information Fort Bragg-Mendocino Coast Chamber of Commerce, 322 N Main St, PO Box 1141; 707/961-6300 or 800/726-2780

The town is a lumber, agricultural, recreational and fishing center that stands on the edge of the rocky coastline where the military post of Fort Bragg was set up in 1857. When the fort was abandoned in 1867, the land was opened for purchase and a lumber town sprang up. It was rebuilt after the earthquake of 1906. Driftwood and shell hunting are popular on nearby beaches.

What to See and Do

Forest Tree Nursery. Greenhouse with 2 million redwood and Douglas fir seedlings for reforestation on local timberland. Nature trail. Picnic tables. Visitor center (Mon-Fri; closed major hols). Georgia-Pacific Corp, foot of Walnut St on CA 1. Phone 707/964-5651. **Free**

Jughandle Ecological Staircase. Nature trail climbs from sea level to pygmy forest; 500,000 yrs of geological history. 5 mi S. For information phone 707/937-5804.

MacKerricher State Park. Approx 10 mi of beach and ocean access. Fishing (nonmotorized boat launching). Nature, hiking trails. Picnicking. Camping (dump station; fee). 3 mi N on CA 1. Phone 707/937-5804. Day use **Free;** Camping ¢¢¢¢

Mendocino Coast Botanical Gardens. Approx 47 acres of rhododendrons, heathers, perennials, fuchsias, coastal pine forest and ocean bluffs. Cafe; gift shop, nursery; picnic areas; self-guided tours. (Daily) 2 mi S on CA 1. Phone 707/964-4352. ¢¢

Noyo. Fishing village with picturesque harbor; public boat launching; charter boats avail. ½ mi S on CA 1 at mouth of Noyo River.

The "Skunk Train." Originally a logging railroad, the California Western Railroad train, affectionately known as "the Skunk," runs 40 mi through redwoods along the Noyo River and over the Coastal Range to Willits (see). Full-day round trips avail aboard either diesel-powered motor cars or a diesel-pulled train (all yr). Half-day round trips avail from Fort Bragg (Mar-Nov, daily; rest of yr, wkends). Half-day and full-day trips avail from Willits (2nd Sat June-2nd Sat Sept; inquire for schedule). Foot of Laurel St. Contact California Western RR, Box 907; phone 707/964-6371. Round trip ¢¢¢¢¢

Annual Events

Whale Festival. Whale watch cruises and walks; whale run; beerfest; chowder tasting. 3rd Sat Mar.

Rhododendron Show. More varieties of rhododendrons are grown here than anywhere else in the world. Last wkend Apr.

Salmon Barbecue. S Noyo Harbor. Sat nearest July 4.

Paul Bunyan Days. Logging competition, gem and mineral show; parade (Mon); fuchsia show, arts & crafts. Labor Day wkend.

Winesong. More than 20 vintners pour for wine tasting, food tasting, music, wine auction. Sat after Labor Day.

Seasonal Event

Whale Watch. Nov-Mar.

Motels

✓★★ **HARBOR LITE LODGE.** *120 N Harbor Dr (95437). 707/964-0221; FAX 707/964-8748.* E-mail stay@harborlitelodge.com; web www.harborlitelodge.com. 79 rms, 2-3 story, 9 suites. No A/C. May-Oct, hols, wkends: S, D $64-$86; each addl $6; suites $92-$110; lower rates rest of yr. Crib $6. TV; cable (premium). Complimentary coffee. Restaurant nearby. Ck-out noon. Meeting rms. Sauna. Refrigerator in suites. Balconies. Footpath to beach. Most rms with harbor view. Cr cds: A, C, D, DS, MC, V.

D

★★ **PINE BEACH INN & SUITES.** *16801 N Hwy 1 (95437), 4 mi S. 707/964-5603; FAX 707/964-8381; res: 800/341-8000.* E-mail pinebeach@pinebeach.com; web www.pinebeach.com. 50 rms, 1-2 story. No A/C. Apr-Oct: S, D $75-$120; suites $100-$160; lower rates rest of yr. Crib free. TV; cable. Restaurant 7-10:30 am, 5:30-9 pm; closed Nov-Feb. Bar from 5 pm. Ck-out noon. Meeting rms. Tennis. Private beach. Private patios, balconies. Some rms with ocean view. Cr cds: A, C, MC, V.

SC

★★ **SURF MOTEL.** *1220 S Main St (95437). 707/964-5361; FAX 707/964-3187; res: 800/339-5361.* E-mail surfmot@surfmotfortbragg.com. 54 rms, 2 kit. units. No A/C. Late May-mid-Oct: S $65; D $73-$90; each addl $6; kit. units from $90; lower rates rest of yr. Crib $6. TV; cable. Coffee in rms. Restaurant nearby. Ck-out 11 am. Business servs avail. Picnic tables, grill. Gardens. Cr cds: A, C, D, DS, MC, V.

SC

★ **TRADEWINDS LODGE.** *400 S Main St (95821). 707/964-4761; FAX 707/964-0372.* E-mail wmgchris@inreach.com; web mcn.org/a/tradewinds. 92 rms, 2 story. No A/C. Memorial Day-Sept. S $65-$75; D $69-$89; each addl $8; suites $120; under 12 free; lower rates rest of yr. Crib $8. TV; cable (premium). Indoor pool; whirlpool. Restaurant 4 am-midnight. Bar from noon. Ck-out 11 am. Coin Indry. Meeting rms. Business servs avail. In-rm modem link. Gift shop. Free RR station transportation. Some refrigerators. Bicycle rentals. Cr cds: A, C, D, DS, MC, V.

SC

Inns

★★ **CLEONE LODGE INN.** *24600 N Hwy 1 (95437), 2 mi N. 707/964-2788; FAX 707/964-2523; res: 800/400-2189.* E-mail cleonelodgeinn@mcn.org; web www.cleonelodgeinn.com. 10 rms, 1-2 story, 4 kits., 1 cottage. No A/C. Some rm phones. S, D $76-$140; each addl $10; kit. cottage $108. TV; cable. Pet accepted, some restrictions; $4. Ck-out 11 am, ck-in 1:30 pm. Business servs avail. Whirlpool. Health club privileges. Walking trails. Some refrigerators, fireplaces. Antiques. Private patios, balconies. Picnic tables, grills. On 9½ acres; gazebo. Near beach. Cr cds: A, C, DS, MC, V.

D

✓★★★ **GREY WHALE INN BED & BREAKFAST.** *615 N Main St (95437). 707/964-0640; FAX 707/964-4408; res: 800/382-7244.* E-mail stay@greywhaleinn.com; web www.greywhaleinn.com. 14 rms, 4 story. No A/C. S $80-$160; D $90-$180; each addl $25; hols, wkends (2-3-day min). TV; VCR avail. Complimentary bkfst buffet. Restaurant nearby. Ck-out noon, ck-in 1-8 pm. Meeting rm. Business servs avail. Game rm. Rec rm.

Some fireplaces. Some private patios, balconies. Library. Antiques. Some rms with ocean view. Mendocino coast landmark since 1915. Totally nonsmoking. Cr cds: A, C, DS, JCB, MC, V.

D

★★★ **LODGE AT NOYO RIVER.** *500 Casa Del Noyo (95437). 707/964-8045; FAX 707/964-9366; res: 800/628-1126.* Web www.mcn.org/a/noyoriver. 16 rms, 1-2 story, 8 suites. No A/C. No rm phones. S, D $105-$149; suites $149-$179. TV in suites; cable. Complimentary full bkfst. Ck-out 11 am, ck-in 3 pm. Balconies. Picnic tables. Sitting rm; antiques. Built 1868; located on 2½ acres overlooking Noyo River, Noyo Harbor Fishing Village. Totally nonsmoking. Cr cds: A, C, MC, V.

SC

Restaurants

★★★ **RENDEZVOUS.** *647 N Main St (95437). 707/964-8142.* E-mail kim@mcn.org; web www.rendezvousinn.com. Hrs: 5:30-8:30 pm; Fri, Sat to 9 pm. Closed Mon, Tues; also Dec 25. Res accepted. Country French menu. Wine cellar. Semi-a la carte: dinner $12.75-$19.75. Specialties: pepper steak Rendezvous, wild game. Music sat. Parking. In restored 1908 Redwood home; fireplace. Totally nonsmoking. Cr cds: C, DS, MC, V.

★★★ **RESTAURANT.** *418 N Main St (95437), opp Skunk Railroad. 707/964-9800.* Hrs: 5-9 pm; Thurs & Fri 11:30 am-2 pm, 5-9 pm; Sun brunch 10 am-1 pm. Closed Wed; Dec 25. Res accepted. No A/C. Continental menu. Beer. Wine list. Semi-a la carte: lunch $6.50-$8.50, dinner $9.75-$18.50. Sun brunch $4.50-$6.75. Child's meals. Specializes in seasonal dishes. Own baking. Jazz Fri, Sat evenings & Sun brunch. Totally nonsmoking. Cr cds: C, MC, V.

★★ **THE WHARF.** *780 N Harbor Dr (95437), at mouth of Noyo River Fishing Village. 707/964-4283.* E-mail thewharf@mcn.org; web www.mcn.org/a/wharf. Hrs: 11 am-10 pm. Res accepted. Bar to 2 am. Semi-a la carte: lunch $3.25-$8.95, dinner $9.25-$19.95. Child's meals. Specializes in fresh seafood, steak. Outdoor dining. View of harbor, fishing boats. Totally nonsmoking. Cr cds: C, DS, MC, V.

SC

Fort Ross State Historic Park (D-1)

(See also Bodega Bay, Guerneville, Healdsburg)

(12 mi N of Jenner on CA 1)

This was once an outpost of the Russian empire. For nearly three decades the post and fort set up by the Russian-American Company of Alaska was an important center for the Russian sea otter trade. The entire "Colony Ross of California" was purchased by Captain John A. Sutter in 1841.

Here are reconstructions of the Russian Orthodox chapel (ca 1825), the original seven-sided and eight-sided blockhouses, the Commandant's house, officers' barracks and stockade walls. Interpretive exhibits at Fort & visitor center. (Daily; closed Jan 1, Thanksgiving, Dec 25) Phone 707/865-2391 or 707/847-3286. Per vehicle ¢¢¢

What to See and Do

Salt Point State Park. Located here are Pygmy forest, Gerstle Cove marine reserve. Hiking, riding trails. Picnicking. Camping. Standard fees. 18 mi N of Jenner. Nearby is

Kruse Rhododendron State Reserve. Here are 317 acres of coastal vegetation. Trails. Rhododendrons bloom Apr-May. 2 mi N of park entrance.

Sonoma Coast State Beach. On 4,200 acres along coastline. Sandy beaches, rocky headlands, sand dunes. Diving, fishing, hiking, picnicking, camping. (Daily) 12 mi S, between Jenner & Bodega Bay. Phone 707/865-2391. Camping ¢¢¢¢–¢¢¢¢¢

Motels

★ **SALT POINT LODGE.** *23255 Hwy 1 (95450), 6 mi N of Fort Ross on CA 1. 707/847-3234; FAX 707/847-3354; res: 800/966-3437.* 16 rms. No A/C. S, D $50-$137; each addl $10. Crib free. TV; cable (premium), VCR avail. Restaurant 9 am-9 pm, wkends 9 am-10 pm; Dec-Apr hrs vary. Bar. Ck-out 11 am. Whirlpool. Sauna. Sun deck. Some fireplaces. Balconies. Ocean view. Cr cds: C, DS, MC, V.

★★ **TIMBER COVE INN.** *21780 N Coast Hwy 1 (95450). 707/847-3231; FAX 707/847-3704; res: 800/987-8319.* 51 rms, 26 with shower only, 2 story. No A/C. No rm phones. S, D $110-$390; wkends, hols (2-day min). Restaurant 7:30 am-3 pm, 4:30-9:30 pm; Fri-Sun to 10 pm. Rm serv. Ck-out 11 am. Gift shop. Many fireplaces; some in-rm whirlpools. Many balconies. Picnic tables. On ocean. Cr cds: A, C, MC, V.

SC

Inn

★★★★ **TIMBERHILL RANCH.** *35755 Hauser Bridge Rd (95421), 19 mi N of Jenner on Meyers Grade Rd to Hauser Bridge Rd. 707/847-3258; FAX 707/847-3342.* E-mail timber@mcn.org; web www.timberhillranch.com. At this secluded ranch on 80 wooded acres high on Hauser Ridge, the luxuriously appointed cedar guest cottages are positioned for maximum privacy. 15 cottages. No rm phones. MAP (Continental Breakfast & six-course dinner): S $345-$365; D $415-$435; each addl 50% of room rate; Higher rates: Jan 1, Thanksgiving, Dec 25. TV (see Common Rm). Pool; whirlpool, poolside serv. Complimentary coffee in rms. Dining room: 11:30 am-1:30 pm; 7-8:20 pm (Public by res only). Ck-out noon. ck-in 4 pm. Meeting rms. Business servs avail. In-rm modem link (commons rm). Luggage handling. Concierge. Gift shop. Minibars, fireplaces, private deck with furniture in all cottages. 2 Tennis surface cts. Hiking. Game room. Commons cottage for all guests has TV (satelite dish), phones, games, fireplace. Adjacent to 6,000 acres Salt Point State Park and the Sonoma Coastline. Cr cds: A, C, D, MC, V.

D

Restaurant

★★★ **TIMBERHILL RANCH.** *35755 Hauser Bridge Rd, 35755 Hauser Bridge Cazadero, CA 95421 (95421). 707/847-3258; FAX 707/847-3342; res: 707/847-3258.* Web www.timberhillranch.com. Located on a sunlit ridge high above the rugged Sonoma Coast, this Northern California restaurant offers from their highly acclaimed chef delectable six course dinners using locally-grown produce, fish, and fowl. Timberhill's own herb gardens supply many of the ingredients; and breads, pastries and desserts are created on the premises. California Haute Cuisine. Fresh Menu daily. Res required. Prix fixe: $45, six-course meal excl tax, bev, gratutity. Extensive wine list. Views from the dining room of lush hills, spectacular sunsets, and towering redwoods. Cr cds: C.

Fremont (E-2)

(See also Livermore, Oakland, San Jose, Santa Clara)

Pop 173,339 **Elev** 53 ft **Area Code** 510 **E-mail** fmtcc@infolane.com
Web www.infolane.fremontbusiness.com

Information Chamber of Commerce, 39488 Stevenson Pl #100, 94539; 510/795-2244

Lying at the southeast end of San Francisco Bay, this young town was created in 1956 from five Alameda County communities whose origin goes back to the days of the Ohlone.

What to See and Do

Mission San Jose (1797). The reconstructed adobe church was originally built in 1809 and destroyed by an earthquake in 1868. A portion of the padres' living quarters that survived holds a museum. Original baptismal font, historic vestments and mission-era artifacts. (Daily; closed Jan 1, Easter, Thanksgiving, Dec 25) 43300 Mission Blvd. Phone 510/657-1797. **Donation**

Regional parks. Contact East Bay Regional Park District, 2950 Peralta Oaks Court, PO Box 5381, Oakland 94605-0381; phone 510/635-0135.

Ardenwood Regional Preserve and Historic Farm. A 208-acre 1890s working farm. Patterson House (tours). Horse-drawn wagon, haywagon rides, farming demonstrations and rail car tour. Picnic area. (Apr-Nov, Thurs-Sun & Mon hols) I-880, CA 84 Decoto exit, right on Ardenwood Blvd to park entrance. Phone 510/796-0663. **¢¢¢**

Coyote Hills. Wetlands preserved on 966 acres. Hiking, bicycle trails. Picnicking. Guided tours of 2,000-yr-old Native American shell mounds (Sun); freshwater marsh; nature programs; access to Alameda Creek Trail, San Francisco Bay Natl Wildlife Refuge. (Daily) 8000 Patterson Ranch Rd. Phone 510/795-9385. Per vehicle **¢¢**

Sunol Regional Wilderness. Hiking trails. Picnicking. Camping (fee). Nature center and program; backpack area by reservation. Rugged terrain includes Maguire Peaks (1,688 ft), Flag Hill (1,360 ft). Connects with Ohlone Wilderness Trail (permit required). NE on I-680 to Calaveras Rd, then S to Geary Rd. Phone 925/862-2244. Per vehicle **¢¢**

Annual Event

Fremont Festival of the Arts. 4th wkend July.

Motels

★★ **BEST WESTERN.** *5400 Mowry Ave (94538). 510/792-4300; FAX 510/792-2643; res: 800/541-4909.* 122 rms, 2-3 story. S, D $129; under 14 free; wkend rates. Crib $10. Pet accepted, some restrictions; $50 ($25 refundable). TV; cable (premium). Pool; whirlpool. Complimentary continental bkfst. Restaurant 11:30 am-10 pm. Bar. Ck-out noon. Meeting rms. Business servs avail. Valet serv. Sauna. Health club privileges. Some private patios, balconies. Cr cds: A, C, D, DS, MC, V.

★★★ **COURTYARD BY MARRIOTT.** *47000 Lakeview Blvd (94538). 510/656-1800; FAX 510/656-2441; res: 800/321-2211.* 146 rms, 3 story. S, D $159; suites $179; under 12 free. Crib avail. TV; cable (premium). Indoor pool. Complimentary coffee in rms. Restaurant 6:30 am-2 pm, 5-10 pm, Fri from 5 pm, Sat to noon. Bar 4-11 pm. Ck-out 1 pm. Coin Indry. Meeting rms. Business servs avail. Sundries. Exercise equipt. Some refrigerators. Some balconies. Cr cds: A, C, D, DS, MC, V.

★★ **RESIDENCE INN BY MARRIOTT.** *5400 Farwell Pl (95450), E of I-880, Mowry Ave exit. 510/794-5900; FAX 510/793-6587; res: 800/331-3131.* 80 kit. suites, 2 story. Kit. suites $184-$204; wkly, monthly rates. Crib free. Pet accepted, some restrictions; $75 & $10/day. TV; cable (premium). Heated pool; whirlpool. Complimentary continental bkfst. Restaurant adj 6 am-midnight. Ck-out noon. Coin Indry. Meeting rms. Business servs avail. Valet serv. Health club privileges. Private patios, balconies. Picnic tables, grills. Cr cds: A, C, D, DS, JCB, MC, V.

Hotel

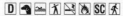

★★★ **HILTON HOTEL.** *39900 Balentine Dr (94560), on I-880, at Stevenson Blvd exit . 510/490-8390; FAX 510/651-7828; res: 800/445-8667.* 315 rms, 7 story. S $99-$189; D $109-$199; each addl $15; suites $199-$375; family rates; wkend rates. Crib free. Pet accepted. TV; cable (premium). Heated pool; poolside serv. Restaurant 6 am-10 pm. Bar 11-2 am; entertainment. Ck-out noon. Meeting rms. Business center. Gift shop. Exercise equipt; sauna. Massage. Some refrigerators. Some private patios, balconies. Cr cds: A, C, D, DS, ER, JCB, MC, V.

Inn

★★ **LORD BRADLEY'S INN.** *43344 Mission Blvd (94539), adj to Mission San Jose. 510/490-0520; FAX 510/490-3015; res: 877/567-3272.* 8 rms, 2 story. Some A/C. Some rm phones. S, D $75-$125. Children over 11 yrs only. Complimentary continental bkfst. Restaurant nearby. Ck-out noon, ck-in 3 pm. Free guest Indry. Built in 1868 as Solon Washington Hotel; survived earthquakes and fires that destroyed much of Mission San Jose; antique furnishings. Cr cds: A, C, D, DS, JCB, MC, V.

Fresno (F-2)

Founded 1874 **Pop** 354,202 **Elev** 296 ft **Area Code** 559
E-mail tourfresno@aol.com **Web** www.fresno-online.com/cvb

Information Convention & Visitors Bureau, 808 M Street, 93721; 559/233-0836 or 800/788-0836

Fresno was founded when the population of Millerton moved in a body from that town to the railroad line. In the geographic center of the state and heart of the San Joaquin Valley—the great central California "Garden of the Sun"—Fresno and Fresno County are enjoying tremendous growth. The county claims the greatest annual agricultural production of any in the United States, handling more than $3 billion annually. The world's largest dried fruit packing plant (Sun Maid) is here.

What to See and Do

California State University, Fresno (1911). (19,000 students) Farm, arboretum, California wildlife habitat exhibits; tours. Cedar & Shaw Aves, 9 mi NE of CA 99. Phone 559/278-2795.

Forestiere Underground Gardens. Former home of Italian immigrant Baldasare Forestiere has 10 acres of underground tunnels filled with citrus plants, grape vines, rose bushes and other flora. (Apr-Nov, Wed-Sun) 5021 W Shaw. Phone 559/271-0734. **¢¢**

Fresno Metropolitan Museum of Art, History and Science. Displays on the heritage and culture of the San Joaquin Valley; hands-on science exhibits; touring exhibits. (Wed-Sun; closed hols) 1555 Van Ness. Phone 559/441-1444. **¢¢**

Kearney Mansion Museum (1900-1903). Historic mansion has been restored; contains many original furnishings, including European wallpapers and art nouveau light fixtures. Servant's quarters adj houses ranch kitchen and museum gift shop. Narrated 45-min tour of mansion. (Fri-Sun afternoons; closed Jan 1, Easter, Dec 25) 7160 W Kearney Blvd, 7 mi W via CA 99, exit Fresno St, entrance is ½ mi on the right; located in 225-acre Kearney Park. Phone 559/441-0862. Park **free** with admission to mansion tour. **¢¢**

Kingsburg. Settled by Swedes, their colorful influence remains in this town. Swedish architectural design on buildings; dala horses and flags decorate streets. **Historical Society Museum** at 2321 Sierra St. 18 mi S via CA 99. Contact Kingsburg Chamber of Commerce, PO Box 515, Kingsburg 93631; Phone 559/897-1111.

Millerton Lake State Recreation Area. 14,107 acres. Swimming, waterskiing (lifeguards); fishing; boat launching. Hiking, riding trails. Picnicking, concession, store nearby. Camping (dump station). Standard fees. 21 mi NE via CA 41, Friant Rd. Phone 559/822-2332. Day use **¢¢¢**

Roeding Park. Variety of trees and shrubs on 157 acres ranging from high mountain to tropical species. Boating (rentals). Tennis. Camellia garden, picnic areas; children's storyland (fee); playland (fee/ride); amphitheater. (Daily) W Belmont Ave & CA 99. In the park is

Chaffee Zoological Gardens. This 18-acre zoo has more than 650 animals representing 200 species. Includes reptile house, elephant exhibit, humming bird and butterfly exhibits; also tropical rain forest exhibit containing plants and animal species found primarily in South American regions. (Daily) At the S end of the park, near Belmont Ave. Phone 559/498-2671. ¢¢

Sequoia and Kings Canyon National Parks (see). Approx 55 mi E on CA 180.

Sierra National Forest. Nearly 1.3 million acres ranging from rolling foothills to rugged, snow-capped mountains, 2 groves of giant sequoias, hundreds of natural lakes, 11 major reservoirs and unique geological formations. The topography can be rough and precipitous in higher elevations, with deep canyons and many beautiful meadows along streams and lakes; 5 wilderness areas. Rafting; boating, sailing; fishing, hunting. Downhill and cross-country skiing. Picnicking. Camping. Standard fees. Sections NE & E reached via CA 41, 99, 168. Contact Forest Supervisor, 1600 Tollhouse, Clovis 93611; phone 559/297-0706 or 877/444-6777 (res).

Sierra Summit Ski Area. 2 triple, 3 double chairlifts, 4 surface lifts; patrol, school, rentals; snowmaking; snack bar, cafeteria, restaurant, bar; lodge. (Mid-Nov-mid-Apr, daily) 25 runs; longest run 2¼ mi; vertical drop 1,600 ft. Half-day rates (wkends & hols). 65 mi NE on CA 168, in Sierra National Forest. Phone 559/233-2500; for ski report phone 559/443-6111. ¢¢¢¢¢

The Discovery Center. Participatory natural and physical science exhibits for families; outdoor exhibits, cactus garden; picnicking, Native American rm. (Daily) 1944 N Winery Ave. Phone 559/251-5533. ¢

Woodward Park. Approx 300 acres. Authentic Japanese garden (wkends only; summer wkday evenings, fee); fishing ponds for children under 16; jogging course; picnic area; bird sanctuary. (Daily) Audubon Dr & CA 41. Phone 559/498-1551.

Yosemite National Park (see). 89 mi NE on CA 41.

Annual Events

Clovis Rodeo. In Clovis, NE corner of Fresno. Parade. Phone 559/299-8838. Late Apr.

Swedish Festival. In Kingsburg. Parade, pancake bkfst, sm¨orgasbord, entertainment, arts & crafts, carnival, Maypole, folk dancing. 3rd wkend May.

Highland Gathering & Games. Coombs Ranch. Scottish athletics, dancing contests, bagpipe competition. Mid-Sept.

The Big Fresno Fair. Phone 559/453-3247. Oct.

Seasonal Event

Fresno County Blossom Trail. This 62-mi self-guided driving tour features the beauty of California agriculture during peak season (weather permitting). Highlights of the trail are fruit orchards, citrus groves, vineyards and historical points of interest. The Visitors Bureau has maps, information. Peak season late Feb-mid-Mar.

Motels

★★ **BEST WESTERN.** *3110 N Blackstone Ave (93703). 559/226-2110; FAX 559/226-0539; res: 800/722-8878.* 153 rms, 2 story. S $50-$54; D $56-$60; each addl $4; under 12 free. Crib $6. TV; cable (premium). Pool; whirlpool. Complimentary continental bkfst. Complimentary coffee in rms. Restaurant adj open 24 hrs. Ck-out noon. Business servs avail. In-rm modem link. Cr cds: A, C, D, DS, MC, V.

SC

✓★★ **CHATEAU INN BY PICCADILLY INNS.** *5113 E Mckinley Ave (93727), near Fresno Air Terminal Airport. 559/456-1418; FAX 559/456-4643; res: 800/445-2428.* 78 rms, 2 story. S $71; D $77; each addl $6; under 18 free. Crib free. TV; cable, VCR (free movies). Pool. Complimentary coffee in rms. Restaurant adj 6 am-10 pm. Ck-out 1 pm. Business servs avail. Free airport transportation. Bathrm phones; some refrigerators. Cr cds: A, C, D, DS, JCB, MC, V.

D SC

✓★ **ECONOMY INNS OF AMERICA.** *2570 S East St (93706). 209/486-1188; FAX 209/486-2743.* 121 rms, 2 story. S $31.90-$36.90; D $43.90-$47.90; each addl $5. Pet accepted. TV; cable (premium). Heated pool. Restaurant adj 24 hrs. Ck-out 11 am. Coin lndry. Cr cds: A, C, MC, V.

D SC

★★★ **PICCADILLY INN UNIVERSITY.** *4961 N Cedar Ave (93726), opp Fresno State. 559/224-4200; FAX 559/227-2382; res: 800/468-3587.* 190 rms, 3 story. S $94; D $104; each addl $10; suites $185-$195; under 18 free. TV; cable. Pool; whirlpool. Complimentary continental bkfst (exc Sat, Sun). Coffee in rms. Restaurant nearby. Ck-out 1 pm. Coin lndry. Meeting rms. Bellhops. Valet serv. Airport, RR station, bus depot transportation. Exercise equipt. Health club privileges. Bathrm phones; some refrigerators. Private patios. Cr cds: A, C, D, DS, ER, JCB, MC, V.

D SC

★★★ **THE SAN JOAQUIN SUITE HOTEL.** *1309 W Shaw Ave (93711). 209/225-1309; FAX 209/225-6021; res: 800/775-1309.* 68 suites, 3 story, 18 kit. units. Suites $89-$135; kit. units $135-$195; under 5 free; wkly, monthly rates. Crib free. TV; cable (premium), VCR avail. Pool; whirlpool. Coffee in rms. Restaurant nearby. Ck-out noon. Coin lndry. Meeting rms. Business center. In-rm modem link. Bellhops. Concierge. Free covered parking. Free airport, RR station transportation. Refrigerators, microwaves. Balconies. Cr cds: A, C, D, DS, MC, V.

D SC

Motor Hotels

★★★ **PICCADILLY INN.** *5115 E Mckinley Ave (93727), near Fresno Air Terminal Airport. 559/251-6000; FAX 559/251-6956; res: 800/468-3587.* 185 rms, 2 story. S, D $130; suites $235; under 18 free; wkend rates. Crib free. TV; cable, VCR avail. Pool; whirlpool; poolside serv. Complimentary coffee in rms. Restaurant 6 am-2 pm; dining rm 11 am-2 pm, 5-10 pm; Sat from 5 pm; Sun 5-9 pm. Rm serv. Bar 5-11 pm. Ck-out 1 pm. Coin lndry. Meeting rms. Bellhops. Valet serv. Gift shop. Free airport transportation. Exercise equipt. Health club privileges. Bathrm phones; some refrigerators. Private patios, balconies. Cr cds: A, C, D, DS, ER, JCB, MC, V.

D SC

★★★ **SHERATON FOUR POINTS HOTEL.** *3737 N Blackstone Ave (93726). 559/226-2200; FAX 559/222-7147; res: 800/742-1911.* 204 rms, 2 story. S $85-$96; D $90-$101; each addl $5; suites $175; wkend rates; under 17 free. Crib $5. TV; cable (premium), VCR avail. Heated pool; whirlpool, poolside serv. Complimentary coffee in rms. Restaurant 6:30 am-10 pm. Rm serv. Bar 10-1 am. Ck-out noon. Meeting rms. Business servs avail. In-rm modem link. Bellhops. Valet serv. Coin lndry. Free airport, RR station, bus depot transportation. Exercise equipt. Health club privileges. Refrigerators, bathrm phones. Private patios. Cr cds: A, C, D, DS, JCB, MC, V.

D SC

Hotels

★★ **DOUBLETREE HOTEL.** *1055 Van Ness Ave (93721). 209/485-9000; FAX 209/485-3210; res: 800/222-8733; res: 800/549-8549.* 193 rms, 9 story. S $74-$109; D $79-$129; each addl $10; suites $179-$525; wkend rates. Crib free. TV; cable (premium). Complimentary coffee in rms. Heated pool; whirlpool. Restaurant 11 am-10 pm. Bar. Ck-out noon. Meeting rms. Business servs avail. In-rm modem link. Free airport transportation. Cr cds: A, C, D, DS, MC, V.

D SC

★★ **RADISSON.** *2233 Ventura St (93721), opp Selland Arena. 559/268-1000; FAX 559/486-6625; res: 800/333-3333.* 321 rms, 8 story. S $79-$95; D $89-$105; each addl $10; suites $105-$205; under 18 free. Crib free. Pet accepted. TV; cable, VCR avail. Indoor/outdoor pool; whirlpool, poolside serv. Restaurant 6 am-2 pm, 5-10 pm. Bar noon-11 pm. Ck-out noon. Convention facilities. Business servs avail. Gift shop. Beauty shop. Free airport, RR station transportation. Exercise equipt; sauna. 8-story atrium lobby. Cr cds: A, C, D, DS, ER, JCB, MC, V.

D SC

Restaurants

✓★ **GEORGE'S.** *2405 Capitol St (93721), inside Galleria Shopping Mall. 209/264-9433.* Hrs: 6 am-3 pm; Sat from 7 am. Closed Sun; major hols. Armenian menu. Wine, beer. Semi-a la carte: bkfst $2.95-$7.50, lunch $3.50-$7.75. Specialties: lamb shank, shish kebab. Cr cds: C.

D

★★ **RIPE TOMATO.** *5064 N Palm Ave (93704), in Fig Garden Mall. 559/225-1850.* Hrs: 11:30 am-2:30 pm, 6-10 pm. Closed Sun, Mon; major hols. Res accepted. French Provençale menu. Bar. Semi-a la carte: lunch $8.95-$13.95, dinner $16.95-$27.95. Specializes in roast duck, salmon. Outdoor dining. Cr cds: A, C, MC, V.

D

Fullerton (D-6)

(See also Anaheim, Buena Park)

Pop 114,144 **Elev** 155 ft **Area Code** 714

Motel

✓★ **HOWARD JOHNSON EXPRESS INN.** *1000 S Euclid St (92832). 714/871-7200; FAX 714/871-3929; res: 800/225-7343.* E-mail hojorl@aol.com; web www.hojo.net. 59 rms, 2 story. S $49-$89; D $55-$95; each addl $6; under 18 free; wkly rates. Crib $10. TV; cable (premium), VCR avail (movies). Complimentary continental bkfst. Restaurant nearby. Ck-out 11 am. Business servs avail. Coin Indry. Disneyland transportation. Health club privileges. Heated pool. Many refrigerators; microwaves avail. Cr cds: A, C, D, DS, MC, V.

SC

Motor Hotels

✓★★ **FOUR POINTS HOTEL.** *1500 S Raymond Ave (92831), CA 91, Raymond Ave exit, 1 blk N. 714/635-9000; FAX 714/520-5831; res: 800/325-3535.* E-mail sales@fourpointshotel.com; web www.four-points-hotel.com. 256 rms, 3-6 story. S, D $120; each addl $10; suites $159-$300; under 13 free. Crib free. TV; cable (premium). Heated pool; poolside serv. Coffee in rms. Restaurant 6 am-10 pm. Rm serv. Bar 4 pm-midnight. Ck-out noon. Coin Indry. Convention facilities. Business center. Valet serv. Free Disneyland transportation. Exercise equipt. Refrigerators avail. Some balconies. Cr cds: A, C, D, DS, MC, V.

D SC

★★ **RADISSON HOTEL.** *222 W Houston Ave (92832), CA 91, Harbor Blvd exit, 1 blk N. 714/992-1700; FAX 714/992-4843; res: 800/553-3441.* E-mail fulca@aol.com. 289 rms, 4 & 7 story. S $115; D $125; suites $145; each addl $10; under 18 free. Crib free. TV; cable (premium). Heated pool; wading pool, poolside serv. Restaurant 6 am-2 pm, 4-10 pm. Rm serv. Bar 4 pm-midnight. Ck-out noon. Coin Indry. Convention facilities. Business servs avail. Bellhops. Gift shop. Free RR station, Disneyland transportation. Exercise equipt. Game rm. Some balconies. Cr cds: A, C, D, DS, JCB, MC, V.

D SC

Hotels

★★ **CHASE SUITE HOTEL.** *2932 E Nutwood Ave (92631). 714/579-7400; FAX 714/528-7945; res: 800/237-8811; res: 800/797-8583.* E-mail chasesuites@aol.com. 96 rms, 5 story. S, D $99-$159; each addl $10; under 18 free. Crib free. TV; cable (premium). Heated pool. Complimentary continental bkfst. Complimentary coffee in rms. Restaurant adj 6 am-11 pm. Ck-out noon. Coin Indry. Meeting rms. Business servs avail. Exercise equipt. Health club privileges. Bathrm phones, refrigerators, in-rm whirlpools; microwaves avail. Some balconies. Grill. Cr cds: A, C, D, DS, MC, V.

D SC

★★★ **MARRIOTT.** *2701 East Nutwood Ave (95445), CA 57, Nutwood Ave exit, 1 blk W. 714/738-7800; FAX 714/738-0288; res: 800/228-9290.* Web www.marriott.com. 224 rms, 6 story. S, D $119; suites $275. Crib avail. Pet accepted, some restrictions. TV; cable (premium). Heated pool; whirlpool, poolside serv. Coffee in rms. Restaurant 6:30 am-11 pm. Rm serv. Bar from 11 am. Ck-out noon. Meeting rms. Business center. Exercise equipt; sauna. Bathrm phone, wet bar, refrigerator in suites. Some patios. Luxury level. Cr cds: A, C, D, DS, JCB, MC, V.

D SC

Restaurants

★★★ **CELLAR THE CUISINE FRANCAISE.** *305 N Harbor Blvd (92832), CA 91, Harbor Blvd exit, 1½ mi N. 714/525-5682.* Web www.cellarthe.com. Hrs: from 5:30 pm. Closed Sun, Mon; major hols. Res accepted. French menu. Bar. Wine cellar. A la carte entrees: dinner $17.50-$33.50. Specializes in lamb, duckling, fresh seafood. Own baking, ice cream. Valet parking. Grotto decor. In cellar of former hotel (1922). Totally nonsmoking. Cr cds: A, C, D, DS, ER, JCB, MC, V.

★★★ **LA VIE EN ROSE.** *240 S State College Blvd (92821), 2 mi NE on CA 57, exit Imperial Hwy W. 714/529-8333.* E-mail lavnrose@earthlink.net; web www.imenu.com/lavnrose.htm. Hrs: 11:30 am-2 pm, 5:30-9 pm. Closed Sun; also major hols. Res accepted. French country menu. Bar. Wine list. A la carte entrees: lunch $9.75-$17.50, dinner $19.75-$31. Complete meal: 3-course dinner $35. Specialties: sauteed shrimp with lobster sauce, sauteed duck breast and leg confit with a dark cherry demi glace, grilled filet mignon with bearnaise sauce. Parking. French country decor; Norman (France) farmhouse replica. Totally nonsmoking. Cr cds: A, C, MC, V.

D

★★ **MULBERRY STREET.** *114 W Wilshire Ave (92832), CA 91, Harbor Blvd exit, 1½ mi N to Wilshire Ave then 1 blk W. 714/525-1056.* Hrs: 11 am-3 pm, 5-10 pm; Fri, Sat to 11 pm; Sun from 5 pm. Closed most major hols. Res accepted. Italian menu. Bar to 1 am; Fri, Sat to 2 am. Semi-a la carte: lunch $4.50-$10.95, dinner $8.95-$22.95. Specializes in fresh seafood, homemade pasta. Own baking. Cr cds: A, C, D, DS, MC, V.

D

★★★ **SUMMIT HOUSE.** *2000 E Bastanchury Rd (92835), CA 57 exit Yorba Linda Blvd, W to State College Blvd, then N. 714/671-4111.* Hrs: 11:30 am-2:30 pm, 5-9 pm; Fri to 10 pm; Sat 5-10 pm; Sun from 5 pm. Closed major hols. Res accepted. Continental menu. Bar. Wine list. Semi-a la carte: lunch $8.95-$16.95, dinner $17.95-$26.95. Specializes in roast prime rib, chef's creations. Own desserts. Pianist. Valet parking. Outdoor dining. Hilltop restaurant; Old-World English country-inn decor. View of Orange County. Cr cds: A, C, D, DS, MC, V.

D

Garberville (C-1)

Pop 900 (est) **Elev** 533 ft **Area Code** 707 **Zip** 95440

What to See and Do

Humboldt Redwoods State Park (see). Approx 15 mi W off US 101.

King Range National Conservation Area. Approx 60,000 acres on the coast including King Peak (4,087 ft). Saltwater fishing on 26 mi of coastline; inland stream fishing (subject to state regulations); hunting. Hiking. Picnicking. Improved camping (fee/car/night). 15 mi W off US 101. Phone 707/825-2300.

Richardson Grove State Park (see). 8 mi S on US 101.

Motels

★★ **HUMBOLDT REDWOODS INN.** *987 Redwood Dr (95542). 707/923-2451; FAX 707/923-2451.* 21 rms, 1-2 story. Memorial Day-Sept: S $42-$62; D. Cr cds: C.

★★ **SHERWOOD FOREST MOTEL.** *814 Redwood Dr (95542). 707/923-2721; FAX 707/923-3677.* 32 rms. May-Oct: S $56; D $60-$62; each addl $5; suites, kit. units $80-$88; lower rates rest of yr. Crib $6. Pet accepted. TV; cable (premium). Heated pool; whirlpool. Coffee in rms. Restaurant adj 6 am-3 pm. Ck-out 11 am. Coin lndry. Business servs avail. Free airport transportation. Refrigerators. Picnic tables, grills. Fish cleaning, fish storage facilities. Cr cds: A, C, DS, JCB, MC, V.

SC

Inn

★★★ **BENBOW INN.** *445 Lake Benbow Dr (95542). 707/923-2124; FAX 707/923-2897; res: 800/355-3301.* E-mail benbow@benbowinn.com; web www.benbowinn.com. 55 rms, 2-4 story. S, D $110-$195; each addl $20; suites $210-$295. Closed Jan-Mar. TV in some rms; cable, VCR avail (free movies). Pool privileges. Complimentary afternoon refreshments. Coffee in rms. Restaurant (see BENBOW INN). Bar 4 pm-midnight (seasonal); entertainment. Ck-out noon, ck-in 2 pm. Luggage handling. Business servs avail. Free airport, bus depot transportation. 9-hole golf, greens fee $18, putting green. Boats. Lawn games. Classic vintage movies nightly. Some refrigerators, fireplaces. On lake; private beach. Woodland setting. Tudor mansion resort hotel (1926); antiques. Totally nonsmoking. Cr cds: A, C, DS, MC, V.

SC

Restaurant

★★★ **BENBOW INN.** *(See Benbow Inn) 707/923-2125.* Hrs: 8-11 am, noon-1:30 pm (seasonal), 6-9 pm; Sun brunch 8 am-1:30 pm. Closed Jan-Mar. Res accepted. Wine cellar. A la carte entrees: bkfst $4.50-$8.50, lunch $6.50-$10, dinner $12.95-$22. Child's meals. Specializes in fresh pasta, fresh fish, lamb. Own desserts. Pianist. Patio dining. Tudor decor; antiques. Totally nonsmoking. Cr cds: A, C, DS, MC, V.

Garden Grove

(D-6 see Los Angeles map)

(See also Anaheim, Orange, Santa Ana)

Pop 143,050 **Elev** 90 ft **Area Code** 714

What to See and Do

Crystal Cathedral. The all-glass church resembles a 4-pointed crystal star. Designed by Philip Johnson; set on 36 acres of landscaped grounds. Guided tours. (Daily exc Sun; closed most hols) 12141 Lewis St. Phone 714/971-4013. **Donation**

Motel

★ **BEST WESTERN PLAZA INTERNATIONAL INN.** *7912 Garden Grove Blvd (92841), CA 22, Beach Blvd exit, 1 blk N. 714/894-7568; FAX 714/894-6308; res: 800/528-1234.* 100 rms, 2 story. Late May-late Sept: S $39-$79; D $44-$89; each addl $3; under 18 free; higher rates hols; lower rates rest of yr. Crib $8. TV; cable (premium), VCR avail. Pool. Sauna. Coffee in rms. Restaurant opp 7 am-11 pm. Ck-out 11 am. Meeting rm. Business servs avail. Refrigerators, microwaves avail. Cr cds: A, C, D, DS, JCB, MC, V.

D SC

Restaurant

★★ **LA FAYETTE.** *12532 Garden Grove Blvd (92843), CA 22 exit Harbor Dr. 714/537-5011.* Hrs: 11:30 am-2 pm, 6-10 pm. Closed Sun; some major hols. Res accepted. French menu. Bar. Semi-a la carte: lunch $8-$19, dinner $16-$28. Specializes in fresh fish, rack of lamb, veal. Pianist wkends. Classical French decor; original artwork. Family-owned since 1972. Totally nonsmoking. Cr cds: A, C, D, MC, V.

Gilroy (F-1)

(See also Salinas, San Jose)

Pop 31,487 **Elev** 200 ft **Area Code** 408 **Zip** 95020

What to See and Do

Fortino Winery. Small family winery. Tours, wine tasting rm, picnic area. (Daily; closed Easter, Thanksgiving, Dec 25) 5 mi W via CA 152, at 4525 Hecker Pass Hwy. Phone 408/842-3305. **Free**

Henry W. Coe State Park. Approx 68,000 acres. Highlights include unusually large manzanita shrubs and a botanical island formed of ponderosa pines. Hiking, backpacking, horseback riding and mountain biking. Primitive drive-in campsites (no electric). Pine Ridge Museum displays ranch life in the late 1880s (Sat, Sun). Guided walks and evening programs (Mar-June, wkends). Standard fees. 9 mi N on US 101, then 13 mi E of Morgan Hill on E Dunne Ave. Phone 408/779-2728.

Outlets at Gilroy. Approx 150 outlet stores. (Daily) 8155 Arroyo Circle. Phone 408/847-4155.

Annual Event

Gilroy Garlic Festival. Located at Christmas Hill Park. Features Gourmet Alley, a giant open-air kitchen; cooking demonstrations and contests; food & beverage booths; arts & crafts; entertainment. Phone 408/842-1625. Last full wkend July.

Glendale (J-3)

Pop 180,038 **Elev** 571 ft **Area Code** 626

Motels

★★ **BEST WESTERN.** *2911 Colorado Blvd (90041), at jct CA 2 & Colorado Blvd. 323/256-7711; FAX 323/255-6750; res: 800/528-1234.* Web www.bestwestern.com. 50 rms, 3 story. S $70-$90; D $80-$100; each addl $5; under 12 free; higher rates Rose Bowl activities. Crib $5. TV; cable (premium), VCR (free movies). Heated pool; whirlpool. Complimentary continental bkfst. Restaurant adj 11 am-10 pm. Ck-out noon. Business servs avail. Refrigerators, microwaves avail. Cr cds: A, C, D, DS, MC, V.

D SC

★★ **BEST WESTERN GOLDEN KEY MOTOR HOTEL.** *123 W Colorado St (91204), I-5 exit Colorado St, 1 mi E. 818/247-0111; FAX 818/545-9393; res: 800/528-1234; res: 800/651-1155.* E-mail bwgoldenkey@worldnet.att.net; web www.travelweb.com/thisco/bw/05257/05257_b.html. 55 rms, 3 story. S; D $99-$129; each addl $5; under 18 free; higher rates Rose Bowl. Crib $5. TV; cable (premium), VCR (free movies). Heated pool; whirlpool. Complimentary continental bkfst. Complimentary coffee in rms. Restaurant opp 6 am-10 pm. Ck-out noon. Meeting rms. Business servs avail. In-rm modem link. Valet serv. Sundries. Health club privileges. Refrigerators, microwaves. Cr cds: A, C, D, DS, MC, V.

SC

★ **VAGABOND INN.** *120 W Colorado St (91204), I-5 exit Colorado St, 1 mi E. 818/240-1700; FAX 818/548-8428; res: 800/522-1555.* 52 rms, 3 story. S, D $53-$85; each addl $5; under 18 free; higher rates: special events, Rose Bowl (3-day min). Crib $5. Pet accepted, some restrictions; $5/day. TV; cable (premium). Heated pool. Complimentary continental bkfst. Coffee in rms. Restaurant adj. Ck-out noon. Some refrigerators; microwaves avail. Cr cds: A, C, D, DS, MC, V.

SC

Restaurant

★★ **FAR NIENTE RISTORANTE.** *204 1/2 N Brand Blvd (91203), ½ mi S of CA 134. 818/242-3835.* Hrs: 11:30 am-10:30 pm; Sat 5:30-11 pm; Sun 5-9:30 pm. Closed major hols. Res accepted. Northern Italian menu. Bar. Semi-a la carte: lunch, dinner $7-$21. Specialties: penne Far Niente, ravioli. Own pasta, ice cream. Piano bar. Cr cds: A, C, D, DS, MC, V.

D

Grass Valley (C-3)

(See also Nevada City)

Settled 1849 **Pop** 9,048 **Elev** 2,411 ft **Area Code** 530
E-mail info@gvncchamber.org **Web** www.gvncchamber.org
Information Chamber of Commerce, 248 Mill St, 95945-6783; 530/273-4667 or 800/655-4667 (CA)

Immigrants followed their half-starved cattle to this spot, not knowing that under the thick grass were rich quartz deposits that were to make the Grass Valley area the richest gold mining region in California—the Mother Lode country. The stamp mills, cyanide tanks and shafts are no longer in operation. Located on the edge of the Tahoe National Forest, Grass Valley has become a recreation center and retirement haven.

A Ranger District office of the Tahoe National Forest is located here.

What to See and Do

Empire Mine State Historic Park. At one time, this historic hardrock gold mine was the largest and richest in California. Baronial cottage with formal gardens among 784 acres. Hiking. Picnicking. Visitor center, mining exhibits. Tours (daily; closed Dec 25). Standard fees. 10791 E Empire St. Phone 530/273-8522.

Lola Montez House. Facsimile of 1851 Grass Valley house once owned by Lola Montez; singer, dancer and *paramour* of the rich and famous. Now houses Grass Valley/Nevada County Chamber of Commerce. 248 Mill St. Phone 530/273-4667.

Mining Museum-North Star Powerhouse. Hard rock mining display and artifacts; 30-ft Pelton water wheel; stamp mill; largest operational Cornish pump in the US. (May-Oct, daily) Allison Ranch Rd. Phone 530/273-4255. **Free**

"Rough and Ready" Town. Gold strike named after General Zachary Taylor, "Old Rough and Ready." At one time the miners tried to secede from the Union and form the independent Republic of Rough and Ready. 4 mi W on CA 20.

Annual Events

Blue Grass Festival. Fairgrounds, McCourtney Rd. Mid-June.

Nevada County Fair. Fairgrounds, McCourtney Rd. Rodeo, horse show, livestock, loggers Olympics. 4 days mid-Aug.

Cornish Christmas. In Old Town. Street fair. Cornish treats, musicians, entertainment, vendors. Late Nov-early Dec.

Motel

✓★ **HOLIDAY LODGE.** *1221 E Main St (95945). 530/273-4406; FAX 916/477-2878; res: 800/742-7125.* 36 rms, 1-2 story. Mid-Apr-mid-Oct: S, D $48-$85; gold panning, hol rates; lower rates rest of yr. Crib $6. Pet accepted, some restrictions; $20 deposit. TV; cable. Pool. Continental bkfst. Coffee in rms. Restaurant nearby. Ck-out 11 am. Some balconies. Cr cds: A, C, D, DS, MC, V.

SC

Restaurants

★★ **SCHEIDEL'S.** *10100 Alta Sierra Dr (95949), off CA 49 at Alta Sierra exit. 530/273-5553.* Hrs: 5:30-8:30 pm; Sun 4-9 pm. Closed Mon, Tues; also Jan. German, Amer menu. Bar. Semi-a la carte: dinner $9.95-$18.95. Child's meals. Specialties: Wienerschnitzel, German marinated sauerbraten. Bavarian decor. Family-owned. Cr cds: C, MC, V.

D

★★ **STEWART HOUSE.** *124 Bank St (95945). 530/477-1559.* Hrs: 11 am-2 pm, 5-9 pm; Fri to 10 pm; Sat 5-10 pm. Closed Mon; also Dec 25. Res accepted. Continental menu. Bar. A la carte entrees: lunch $7.95-$10.95, dinner $15.95-$22.95. Specialties: rack of lamb, 22 oz lobster. Parking. Outdoor dining. In 4-story Victorian house. Cr cds: A, C, DS, MC, V.

D

Gualala (D-1)

Pop 1,200 (est) **Elev** 67 ft **Area Code** 707 **Zip** 95445
Information Redwood Coast Chamber of Commerce, PO Box 338; 800/778-5252

Because of its relative isolation and quiet atmosphere, the area attracts many visitors. Favorite local activities include steelhead, abalone and silver salmon fishing, canoeing and swimming in the Gualala River and camping. A debate on the origin of the name "Gualala" has persisted for more than 100 years. Some say it derived from the native Pomo word *qhawala-li,* meaning "water coming down place," while others maintain that it is a Spanish rendering of Valhalla.

What to See and Do

Point Arena Lighthouse and Museum. This 115-ft-tall lighthouse (1908) and Fog Signal Building (1869) houses historical artifacts and photographs. Viewing at top of lighthouse through a 2-ton lens. (Daily; closed Thanksgiving, Dec 25, also wkdays in Dec) 15 mi N on CA 1. Phone 707/882-2777. **¢¢**

Motel

★★ **SEA RANCH LODGE & GOLF LINKS.** *60 Sea Walk Drive (95497), 10 mi S off CA 1. 707/785-2371; FAX 707/785-2917; res: 800/732-7262.* Web searanchlodge.com. 20 rms, 2 story. No A/C. S, D $140-$205; each addl $15; under 6 free; package plans. Crib $5. Coffee in rms. Restaurant 8-10 am, 11:30 am-2:30 pm, 6:30-9 pm. Bar 11 am-midnight. Ck-out noon. Meeting rms. Business servs avail. Gift shop. 18-hole golf, greens fee $35-$55, pro, pro shop, putting green, driving range. Some fireplaces. On bluff overlooking ocean; 5,500 acres in historic Sea Ranch. Totally nonsmoking. Cr cds: A, C, MC, V.

Inns

★★★ **BREAKERS INN.** *39300 S Hwy 1 (95445). 707/884-3200; FAX 707/884-3400; res: 800/273-2573.* Web breakersinn.com. 27 rms, 3 story. No A/C. No elvtr. S, D $85-$235; under 5 free; lower rates mid-wk. Crib $10. TV; cable, VCR avail. Complimentary continental bkfst. Coffee in rms. Restaurant 8 am-2:30 pm, 5:30-9 pm. Ck-out 11 am, ck-in 3 pm. Luggage handling. Golf privileges. Some refrigerators. Some balconies. Fireplaces; some in-rm whirlpools. Cr cds: A, C, DS, MC, V.

D SC

★★ **NORTH COAST COUNTRY INN.** *34591 S Hwy 1 (95497). 707/884-4537; res: 800/959-4537.* 6 rms, 4 kit. units. No A/C. S, D $150-$195; hols, wkends (2-3-day min). Children over 12 yrs only. TV in common rm. Complimentary full bkfst. Ck-out 11 am, ck-in 2 pm. Gift shop. Free airport transportation. Whirlpool. Refrigerators, fireplaces. Private decks. Antiques, handmade quilts. Forested setting overlooking Mendocino coast. Totally nonsmoking. Cr cds: A, C, MC, V.

★★★ **ST ORRES RESTAURANT & INN.** *36601 S Highway 1 (95445), 2½ mi N on CA 1. 707/884-3335; FAX 707/884-1840.* E-mail rosemary@mcn.org; web www.saintorres.com. 8 rms, 3 baths, 15 cottages. No A/C. No rm phones. S, D $60-$75; cottages $85-$225. Complimentary bkfst. Restaurant (see ST ORRES). Ck-out noon, ck-in 3 pm. Whirlpool, sauna at cottages. Balconies. Fireplace in most cottages. Built by local craftsmen with local materials. The house is similar to Russian dacha, with onion-domed towers; stained glass, woodwork. Most rms with ocean view. Beach opp. Cr cds: C, MC, V.

★★★ **WHALE WATCH INN BY THE SEA.** *35100 S Hwy 1 (95445). 707/884-3667; FAX 707/884-4815; res: 800/942-5342.* E-mail whale@mcn.org; web whalewatchin.com. 18 rms, 1-2 story, 5 kits. No A/C. Some rm phones. S, D $170-$270. Complimentary full bkfst. Ck-out 11 am, ck-in 3 pm. Business servs avail. Many in-rm whirlpools. Fireplaces. Private patios. 2 acres on ocean bluff. Totally nonsmoking. Cr cds: A, C, MC, V.

D

Restaurant

★★★ **ST ORRES.** *(See St Orres Inn) 707/884-3335.* Hrs: 6-9 pm; Sat 5:15-10 pm. Closed Wed Oct-May. No A/C. Res accepted; required wkends. Wine, beer. Prix fixe: dinner $30. Specializes in lamb, fresh fish, wild game. Own baking. Natural wood, stained glass. Totally nonsmoking. Cr cds: C.

Guerneville (D-2)

(See also Bodega Bay, Healdsburg, Santa Rosa)

Pop 1,966 **Elev** 56 ft **Area Code** 707 **Zip** 95446
E-mail info@russian river.org **Web** www.russianriver.org

Information Russian River Region Visitors Bureau, 13250 River Rd, PO Box 255; 707/869-9212 or 800/253-8800

This scenic area is popular for recreational vacations, with swimming, golf, fishing, canoeing and hiking nearby.

What to See and Do

Armstrong Redwoods State Reserve. Named for Colonel James Boydston Armstrong of Ohio, who settled here with his family in 1874. Nature, hiking, riding trails. Picnicking. Standard fees. 2 mi N off CA 116. Phone 707/865-2391 or 707/869-2015. Per vehicle **¢¢**

Korbel Champagne Cellars. Produces wine, champagne and brandy. Guided tours; century-old cellars; champagne, wine tasting; garden tours in summer (1 in morning, 1 in afternoon). (Daily; closed Jan 1, Easter, Thanksgiving, Dec 25) 13250 River Rd. Phone 707/887-2294. **Free**

Annual Events

Russian River Blues Festival. Johnson's Beach. Phone 707/869-3940. Early June.

Russian River Jazz Festival. Johnson's Beach. Phone 707/869-3940. Wkend after Labor Day.

Inns

★★★ **APPLE WOOD.** *13555 Hwy 116 (95446). 707/869-9093; FAX 707/869-9170.* E-mail stay@applewoodinn.com; web www.applewoodinn.com. 16 rms, 3 story. A/C some rms. S, D $125-$185; suites $200-$250. TV; cable (premium). Pool; whirlpool. Complimentary full bkfst. Restaurant (see APPLEWOOD). Ck-out noon, ck-in 3 pm. Business servs avail. In-rm modem link. Library. Antiques. Some fireplaces. Private patios, balconies. Picnic tables. County historical landmark. Totally nonsmoking. Cr cds: A, C, DS, MC, V.

D

★★ **HIGHLAND DELL INN.** *21050 River Boulevard (95446), S on Bohemian Hwy, cross river, then left on River Blvd. 707/865-1759.* E-mail highland@netdex.com; web www.netdex.com/~highland. 8 units, 3 story, 4 suites. No A/C. May-Oct: S, D $100-$115; suites $140-$165; lower rates rest of yr. Adults only. Pet accepted, some restrictions; $100 deposit. TV; cable, VCR (free movies). Pool. Complimentary full bkfst; afternoon refreshments. Ck-out 11 am, ck-in 4-8 pm. Business servs avail. In-rm modem link. Refrigerator in suites. Grills. Built 1906. Stained-glass windows; fireplace in lobby; heirloom antiques and collection of historic local photos. Cr cds: A, C, DS, JCB, MC, V.

SC

★★ **RIDENHOUR RANCH HOUSE INN.** *12850 River Rd (95446), 7 mi E. 707/887-1033; FAX 707/869-2967.* E-mail frechberge@aol.com; web ridenhourranchhouseinn.com. 6 rms, 3 story, 2 cottages. D $95-$130; cottages $145. Complimentary full bkfst. Ck-out 11 am, ck-in 3-9 pm. Business servs avail. Dinner avail. Library. Antiques, handmade quilts. Balconies. Gardens. Picnic tables. Totally nonsmoking. Cr cds: A, C, MC, V.

D

Restaurant

★★ **APPLEWOOD.** *(See Applewood) 707/869-9093.* E-mail stay@applewoodinn.com; web www.applewoodinn.com. Sittings: 6:30 & 7:15 pm; Fri, Sat also 8 pm. Closed Sun, Mon. Res required. No A/C. Regional California menu. Wine, beer. Complete meals: dinner $40-$45. Specializes in fresh local meat, fowl, fish. In Mediterranean-style, historic inn; own vegetable and herb garden. Totally nonsmoking. Cr cds: A, C, DS, MC, V.

D

Half Moon Bay (E-2)

(See also San Mateo)

Pop 8,886 **Elev** 69 ft **Area Code** 650 **Zip** 94019

Motel

★ **HOLIDAY INN.** *230 Cabrillo Hwy S (94019). 650/726-3400; FAX 650/726-1256.* Web www.holiday-inn.com/hotels/hafca. 52 rms, 2 story. July-Aug: S, D $119-$139; each addl $10; under 18 free; higher rates: hols, special events; lower rates rest of yr. Crib free. Pet accepted; $10. TV. Complimentary continental bkfst. Restaurant nearby. Ck-out noon. Business servs avail. In-rm modem link. Cr cds: A, C, D, DS, JCB, MC, V.

D SC

Motor Hotel

★★★ **HALF MOON BAY LODGE & CONFERENCE CENTER.** *2400 S Cabrillo Hwy (94019), on CA 1, 2½ mi S of jct CA 1, 92. 650/726-9000; FAX 650/726-7951; res: 800/368-2468.* Web www.woodsidehotels.com. 81 rms, 2 story. No A/C. Mar-Nov: S, D $145-$200; each addl $10; suites $210; under 18 free; lower rates rest of yr. Crib free. TV; cable (premium). Heated pool; whirlpool. Complimentary continental bkfst. Complimentary coffee in rms. Restaurants adj 6 am-10 pm. Ck-out 11:30 am. Meeting rms. Business servs avail. Exercise equipt. Refrigerators; many wet bars; some fireplaces. Balconies. Overlooks golf course. Totally nonsmoking. Cr cds: A, C, D, DS, JCB, MC, V.

D SC

Inns

★★★ **CYPRESS INN.** *407 Mirada Rd (94019), 2½ mi N via CA 1, then Medio W to Mirada, at Miramar Beach. 650/726-6002; FAX 650/712-0380; res: 800/832-3224.* E-mail lodging@cypressinn.com; web www.cypressinn.com. 12 rms, 2-3 story. S, D $170-$275. TV; cable. Complimentary full bkfst; afternoon refreshments. Restaurants nearby. Ck-out 11:30 am, ck-in 3 pm. Meeting rm. Business servs avail. Massage. Health club privileges. Fireplaces. Balconies. Colorful collection of folk art. Oceanfront location with 5 mi of sandy beach. All rms have ocean view. Totally nonsmoking. Cr cds: A, C, DS, MC, V.

D

★★ **GOOSE & TURRETS BED & BREAKFAST INN.** *835 George St (94037), 8 mi N on CA 1. 650/728-5451; FAX 650/728-0141.* E-mail rhmgt@montara.com; web www.montara.com/goose.html. 5 rms, 2 shower only. No A/C. No rm phones. S, D $85-$120; each addl $20. Crib $20. Complimentary full bkfst; afternoon refreshments. Restaurant nearby. Ck-out noon, ck-in 4-7 pm. Concierge. Lawn games. Built in 1908; antiques. Totally nonsmoking. Cr cds: A, C, D, DS, MC, V.

SC

★★★ **MILL ROSE INN.** *615 Mill St (94019). 650/726-9794; FAX 650/726-3031; res: 800/900-7673.* E-mail millroseinn@msn.com; web www.millroseinn.com. 4 rms, 1 with shower only, 2 story, 2 suites. No A/C. S, D $165-$285; each addl $25; suites $255-$285; wkends (2-day min). TV; cable (premium), VCR (movies). Whirlpool. Complimentary full bkfst. Complimentary coffee in rms. Restaurants nearby. Ck-out 11 am, ck-in 3-9 pm. Meeting rm. Business servs avail. Luggage handling. Concierge serv. Exercise equipt. Health club privileges. Refrigerators. Picnic tables. English country gardens. Totally nonsmoking. Cr cds: A, C, D, DS, MC, V.

★★ **OLD SAW MILL LODGE.** *700 Ranch Road W (94060), 15 mi S on CA 1. 650/879-0111; FAX 650/879-0656; res: 800/596-6455.* E-mail innkeepers@oldsawmill.com; web www.oldsawmill.com. 5 rms, 1 with shower only. No rm phones. S, D $105-$175; wkends, hols (2-day min in summer). TV; VCR (movies). Indoor pool; whirlpool. Complimentary full bkfst. Restaurant nearby. Ck-out 11 am. Meeting rm. Business servs avail. Many balconies. Picnic tables. Totally nonsmoking. Cr cds: C, MC, V.

D SC

★★ **OLD THYME INN.** *779 Main St (94019). 650/726-1616; FAX 650/726-6394; res: 800/720-4277.* E-mail innkeeper@oldthymeinn.com; web www.oldthymeinn.com. 7 rms, 2 story. No A/C. No rm phones. S, D $90-$170; suite $165-$220. TV; VCR avail (free movies). Complimentary full bkfst; afternoon refreshments. Restaurants nearby. Ck-out 11 am, ck-in 3-7 pm. Business servs avail. Health club privileges. Some in-rm whirlpools, fireplaces. Picnic tables. Library/sitting rm. Herb garden. Built 1899. Totally nonsmoking. Cr cds: A, C, DS, MC, V.

★★ **RANCHO SAN GREGORIO.** *5086 La Honda Rd (94074), S via CA 1, then approx 5 mi E on La Honda Rd (CA 84) . 650/747-0810; FAX 650/747-0184.* E-mail rsgleebud@aol.com; web www.scruznet.com/~pranlestr/rancho/home.html. 4 rms, 2 story. No A/C. 1 rm with phone. S, D $85-$155; each addl $15. Crib free. Some VCRs (free movies). Complimentary full bkfst; afternoon refreshments. Ck-out noon, ck-in 3 pm. Business servs avail. Game rm. Lawn games. Picnic tables, grills. Overlooks historic San Gregorio Valley. Spanish mission-style home located on 15 acres; cactus courtyard; gazebo. Totally nonsmoking. Cr cds: A, C, D, DS, MC, V.

★★★ **SEAL COVE INN.** *221 Cypress Ave (94038), from US 101 or I-280, W on CA 92 to jct CA 1, then 6 mi N on CA 1 and left (W) on Cypress Ave. 650/728-4114; FAX 650/728-4116; res: 800/995-9987.* E-mail sealcove@coastside.net. 8 rms, 2 suites, 2 story. No A/C. S, D $190-$215; each addl $30; suites $270; 2-day min hols. TV; VCR (300 movies avail). Complimentary full bkfst; Wine & hors d' oeuvres afternoon refreshments. Restaurants nearby. Ck-out 11 am, ck-in 3 pm. Meeting rm. Business servs avail. Refrigerators, minibars. Balconies 2nd floor only. Nightly turn-down service. Picnic tables. Totally nonsmoking. Views of garden and Pacific Ocean. Cr cds: A, C, DS, MC, V.

D SC

★★ **ZABALLA HOUSE.** *324 Main St (94019). 650/726-9123; FAX 650/726-3921.* E-mail zaballa@coastside.com; web www.whistlere.com/zaballa.rooms.html. 9 rms, 2 story, 3 suites. No rm phones. S, D $140-$275; each addl $10. Pet accepted; $10. TV; cable in some rms. Complimentary bkfst buffet; afternoon refreshments. Restaurant nearby. Ck-out 11 am, ck-in 3-7 pm. Business servs avail. Oldest building in town still standing (1859); some antiques. Some in-rm whirlpools, fireplaces. Totally nonsmoking. Cr cds: A, C, DS, MC, V.

Restaurants

★★ **MOSS BEACH DISTILLERY RSTRNT.** *140 Beach Way (94038), 8 mi N on CA 1. 650/728-5595.* Hrs: noon-9 pm; Sun brunch 10 am-2:45 pm. California menu. Bar. Semi-a la carte: lunch $11.95-$16.95, dinner $16.95-$25. Sun brunch $22.95. Specializes in seafood, steaks. Terrace dining overlooking ocean. Displays on colorful history of restaurant (1927) include prohibition and resident ghost. Totally nonsmoking. Cr cds: C, D, DS, MC, V.

D

★ **PASTA MOON.** *315 Main St (94019). 650/726-5125.* Web www.pastamoon.com. Hrs: 11:30 am-2:30 pm, 5:30-9:30 pm; Fri to 10 pm; Sat noon-3 pm, 5:30-10 pm; Sun (brunch) 11 am-3 pm, 5:30-10 pm. Closed Thanksgiving, Dec 25. Res accepted. No A/C. Italian menu. Bar. A la carte entrees: lunch $8-$13, dinner $10-$20. Sun brunch $6-$13. Child's meals. Specializes in seafood, game. Own pasta, baking. Exhibition kitchen features wood-burning oven. Totally nonsmoking. Cr cds: A, C, DS, MC, V.

D

Hanford (G-3)

(See also Visalia)

Pop 30,897 **Elev** 246 ft **Area Code** 209 **Zip** 93230

Information Hanford Visitor Agency, 200 Santa Fe, Suite D; 209/582-5024 or for events 800/722-1114

China Alley, the century-old Chinatown, has been saved by Chef Wing's family. Two outstanding restaurants were the reason that presidents Eisenhower and Truman and Mao Tse-tung and Chiang Kai-shek suggested to others to eat in this historic town. One of these restaurants, Imperial Dynasty, remains open (see RESTAURANT).

Motel

★ **DOWNTOWN MOTEL.** *101 N Redington St (93230). 209/582-9036.* 29 rms, 2 story. S $36; D $38; each addl $2. TV; cable (premium). Restaurant nearby. Ck-out 11 am. Cr cds: A, C, D, DS, MC, V.

Motor Hotel

★★★ **INN AT HARRIS RANCH.** *24485 W Dorris (93210), 32 mi E on CA 198. 559/935-0717; FAX 559/935-5061; res: 800/942-2333.* 123 rms, 3 story. S, D $89-$104; each addl $8; suites $101-$250; under 12 free. Crib free. Pet accepted; $10/day. TV; cable (premium). Heated pool; whirlpools. Complimentary coffee in rms. Restaurant 6 am-11 pm. Bar from 11 am. Ck-out noon. Coin lndry. Meeting rms. Bellhops. Sundries. Exercise equipt. Minibars. Private patios, balconies. Private 2,800-ft paved and lighted airstrip on site. Cr cds: A, C, D, DS, MC, V.

D SC

Inn

★★ **IRWIN STREET INN.** *522 N Irwin St (93230). 559/583-8000; FAX 559/583-8793; res: 800/583-8080.* 30 rms in 4 Victorian-style buildings, 2 story, 3 suites. S, D $69-$92; suites $99-$125; under 14 free. Crib avail. TV; cable (premium), VCR avail. Pool; poolside serv. Continental bkfst. Restaurant 7 am-2 pm, 5-9 pm; Sun, Mon to 2 pm. Ck-out noon, ck-in 3 pm. Balconies. Historic buildings (late 1800s), restored; many antiques. Totally nonsmoking. Cr cds: A, C, D, DS, MC, V.

D SC

Restaurant

★★★ **IMPERIAL DYNASTY.** *406 China Aly (93230), 7th & Green Sts. 209/582-0196.* Hrs: 4:30-10 pm. Closed Mon; Jan 1, Thanksgiving, Dec 25; also 1 wk in Feb. Res accepted. Continental menu. Bar. Wine cellar. Complete meals: dinner $9.95-$29.95, gourmet dinner (1 wk advance notice) $60. Specialties: tournedos of beef bordelaise, escargots a la Bourguignonne, rack of lamb. Gourmet societies meet here; special meals prepared. In historic Chinese community; many original Chinese works of art, artifacts. Family-owned. Cr cds: A, C, MC, V.

Hayward (E-2)

(See also Fremont, Oakland, San Francisco Airport Area)

Pop 111,498 **Elev** 111 ft **Area Code** 510

What to See and Do

Garin Regional Park. Secluded 1,520 acres in the Hayward hills with vistas of south bay area. Birdwatching, fishing at Jordan Pond; hiking, riding trails. Picnicking. Interpretive programs at visitor center; historic farm equipment. (Mon-Fri) S on CA 238 to Garin Ave E. Phone 510/582-2206. Per vehicle (wkends & hols) ¢¢

Dry Creek Pioneer Regional Park. On 1,563 acres. Birdwatching; hiking, riding trails. Picnicking. Interpretive programs. Enter via Garin Regional Park. Phone 510/582-2206. Per vehicle (wkends & hols) ¢¢

Hayward Area Historical Society Museum. Displays include fire engines, costumes, California and local artifacts. Changing exhibits. (Tue-Fri; closed hols) 22701 Main St. Phone 510/581-0223. ¢

McConaghy Estate. (1886). 12-rm Victorian farmhouse with period furnishings; carriage house; tank house. During Dec, farm house is decorated for Christmas in 1886. Picnic and play areas in adj Kennedy Park. (Thurs-Sun; closed hols & Jan) 18701 Hesperian Blvd. Phone 510/276-3010. ¢¢

Motels

✓★ **COMFORT INN.** *24997 Mission Blvd (94544). 510/538-4466; FAX 510/581-8029; res: 800/835-6159.* 62 rms, 2 story. S, D $75-$125; each addl $5; suites $100-$125; under 18 free. Crib $5. TV; cable (premium). Complimentary continental bkfst. Restaurant nearby. Ck-out 11 am. Coin lndry. Meeting rms. Business servs avail. In-rm modem link. Refrigerators. Cr cds: A, C, D, DS, MC, V.

D SC

★★ **EXECUTIVE INN.** *20777 Hesperian Blvd (94541), 2 blks W of I-880, A St exit at Heperian. 510/732-6300; FAX 510/783-2265; res: 800/553-5083.* 146 rms, 3 story, 23 suites. S, D $79-$99; each addl $10; suites $105-$125; under 17 free; wkend rates. TV; cable (premium). Heated pool. Complimentary continental bkfst. Complimentary coffee in rms. Restaurant nearby. Ck-out noon. Coin lndry. Meeting rms. Valet serv. Sundries. Free airport transportation. Exercise equipt. Some balconies. Cr cds: A, C, D, DS, MC, V.

D SC

Restaurants

★★ **MANZELLA'S SEAFOOD LOFT.** *1275 W Winton Ave (94545). 510/887-6040.* Hrs: 11 am-9 pm; Fri to 10 pm; Sat from 5 pm; early-bird dinner 4:30-6 pm Mon-Fri. Closed Sun; most major hols. Res accepted. Italian, Amer menu. Bar. Semi-a la carte: lunch $7.95-$14.95, dinner $9.95-$25.95. Specializes in seafood. Cr cds: A, C, D, DS, MC, V.

D ♥

★★ **RUE DE MAIN.** *22622 Main St (94541). 510/537-0812.* Hrs: 11:30 am-2:15 pm, 5:30-10 pm; Mon to 2:15 pm; Sat from 5:30 pm. Closed Sun (exc Mother's Day); major hols. Res accepted. French menu. Semi-a la carte: lunch $9-$14. A la carte entrees: dinner $15-$22. Specialty: medaillons de veau. Own pastries. Contemporary French decor; murals of French city scenes. Cr cds: A, C, MC, V.

D

Healdsburg (D-2)

(See also Bodega Bay, Guerneville, Santa Rosa)

Pop 9,469 **Elev** 106 ft **Area Code** 707 **Zip** 95448
Web www.ci.healdsburg.ca.us

Information Chamber of Commerce & Visitors Bureau, 217 Healdsburg Ave; 707/433-6935 or 800/648-9922 (CA)

What to See and Do

Canoe trips. One-day to five-day trips on Russian River (Apr-Oct). Equipment and transportation provided. Contact Trowbridge Canoe Trips, 20 Healdsburg Ave; phone 707/433-7247 or 800/640-1386.

★ **Healdsburg area wineries.** More than 60 wineries are located in the northern Sonoma County region; most are open to the public for wine tasting. A map listing the wineries and other area attractions is avail from the Chamber of Commerce & Visitors Bureau. Among them are

Chateau Souverain. Wine tasting, restaurant (Fri-Sun). 5 mi N on US 101, Independence Ln exit, in Geyserville. Contact Box 528, Geyserville 95441; phone 707/433-8281. **Free**

Simi Winery. Winery dates from the turn of the century. Guided tours; wine tasting. (Daily; closed Jan 1, Easter, Thanksgiving, Dec 25) 16275 Healdsburg Ave. Contact PO Box 698; phone 707/433-6981. **Free**

Warm Springs Dam/Lake Sonoma. Earth-filled dam, anadromous fish hatchery operated by California Dept of Fish and Game and the Army Corps of Engineers; park overlook provides scenic views of lake and nearby wine country. Swimming, fishing; boating (marina). Hiking, bridle trails. Picnic facilities at marina, at Yorty Creek and near visitor center. Primitive and improved camping. Visitor center. (Thurs-Mon; closed major hols) 11 mi W via US 101, exit on Dry Creek Rd. Contact Visitor Center, 3333 Skaggs Springs Rd, Geyserville 95441; phone 707/433-9483. Camping ¢¢¢¢

Annual Event

Healdsburg Harvest Century Bicycle Tour. Road & mountain bikes tour through Alexander, Russian River & Dry Creek valleys. Phone707/433-6935. Mid-July.

Motels

✓★★ **BEST WESTERN DRY CREEK INN.** *198 Dry Creek Rd (95448). 707/433-0300; FAX 707/433-1129; res: 800/222-5784.* Web www.sonoma.com/lodging/drycreek/. 102 rms, 3 story. Apr-Oct: S, D $89-$99; each addl $10; under 12 free; lower rates rest of yr. Crib free. Pet accepted; $10. TV; cable (premium). Pool; whirlpool. Complimentary continental bkfst. Restaurant adj. Ck-out noon. Guest Indry. Business servs avail. In-rm modem link. Exercise equipt. Some refrigerators. Cr cds: A, C, D, DS, ER, JCB, MC, V.

D

★★ **GEYSERVILLE INN.** *21714 Geyserville Ave (95441), NE on Hwy 101 to Canyon Road exit. 707/857-4343; FAX 707/857-4411.* 38 rms, 2 story. Apr-Oct: S, D $99-$139; each addl $10; under 10 free; wkends (2-day min); lower rates rest of yr. Crib $10. TV; cable. Complimentary continental bkfst. Restaurant 9 am-5 pm. Ck-out 11 am. Business servs avail. In-rm modem link. Concierge. Gift shop. Pool; whirlpool. Many fireplaces. Some balconies. Surrounded by vineyards. Totally nonsmoking. Cr cds: A, C, DS, MC, V.

SC

Inns

★★★ **BELLE DEJOUR INN.** *16276 Healdsburg Ave (95448). 707/431-9777; FAX 707/431-7412.* 5 cottages. S, D $150-$250. Complimentary full bkfst. Ck-out 11 am, ck-in 4-7 pm. Business servs avail. In-rm modem link. Many refrigerators, in-rm whirlpools, fireplaces. Balconies. Picnic tables. Hilltop setting on 6 acres. Totally nonsmoking. Cr cds: C, MC, V.

★★ **CAMELLIA INN.** *211 North St (95448). 707/433-8182; FAX 707/433-8130.* E-mail info@camelliainn.com; web www.camelliainn.com. 9 rms, 2 story. No A/C. Some rm phones. S, D $75-$160. Crib free. Heated pool. Complimentary full bkfst; evening refreshments. Ck-out 11 am, ck-in 3-6 pm. Business servs avail. In-rm modem link. Valet serv. Some in-rm whirlpools, fireplaces. Victorian house; antique furnishings. Town's first hospital. Totally nonsmoking. Cr cds: A, C, MC, V.

★★★ **CAMPBELL RANCH INN.** *1475 Canyon Rd (95441), 7 mi N on US 101, exit Canyon Rd. 707/857-3476; FAX 707/857-3239; res: 800/959-3878.* Web www.campbellranchinn.com. 5 rms, 3 with shower only, 3 story. No rm phones. S $115-$215; D $125-$225; each addl $25; 2-3-day min wkends, hols. TV in main rm; cable, VCR avail. Pool; whirlpool. Complimentary full bkfst. Ck-out noon, ck-in 1 pm. Luggage handling. Concierge serv. Tennis. Game rm. Lawn games. Bicycles. Refrigerators. On 35-acre ranch. Totally nonsmoking. Cr cds: A, C, MC, V.

★★ **GRAPE LEAF INN.** *539 Johnson St (95448). 707/433-8140; FAX 707/433-3140.* E-mail suite@sonic.net; web www.grapeleafinn.com. 7 rms, 2 story. No rm phones. S, D $95-$165; each addl $35. Complimentary full bkfst; afternoon refreshments. Restaurant nearby. Ck-out 11 am, ck-in 4-6 pm. Some in-rm whirlpools. Picnic tables. Antiques. Sitting rm. Skylights. Victorian house (1900). Totally nonsmoking. Cr cds: C, DS, MC, V.

★★ **HAYDON STREET.** *321 Haydon St (95448). 707/433-5228; FAX 707/433-6637.* 8 rms, 2 story. No rm phones. S, D $95-$175; each addl $25. TV in sitting rm. Complimentary full bkfst; afternoon refreshments. Restaurant nearby. Ck-out 11 am, ck-in 3:30-6:30 pm. Business servs avail. Some in-rm whirlpools. Balconies. Picnic tables. Antiques. Sitting rm. Queen Anne/Victorian house (1912). Totally nonsmoking. Cr cds: C, MC, V.

★★★ **HONOR MANSION.** *14891 Grove St (95448). 707/433-4277; FAX 707/431-7173; res: 800/554-4667.* E-mail cathi@honormansion.com; web www.honormansion.com. 6 rms, 2 with shower only, 2 story. 1 rm phone. Mar-Dec: S, D $130-$250; each addl $25; 2-3-day min wkends, hols; lower rates rest of yr. TV in parlor; cable. Pool. Complimentary full bkfst; afternoon refreshments. Restaurant nearby. Ck-out 11 am, ck-in 3-7 pm. Luggage handling. Concierge serv. Lawn games. Minibars. Microwaves avail. Picnic tables. Italianate Victorian house built in 1883. Totally nonsmoking. Cr cds: C, DS, MC, V.

D

★★★ **MADRONA MANOR.** *1001 Westside Rd (95448). 707/433-4231; FAX 707/433-0703; res: 800/258-4003.* E-mail madronaman@aol.com; web www.madronamanor.com. 21 rms, 2-3 story, 3 suites. S, D $155-$250; suites $210-$250; under 6 free. Crib $15. Pool. Complimentary full bkfst. Restaurant (see MADRONA MANOR). Ck-out 11 am, ck-in 3 pm. Business servs avail. Luggage handling. Concierge serv. Many fireplaces. Balconies. Picnic area. Antiques. Sitting rm. Built 1881. Extensive gardens. Fountain. Cr cds: A, C, D, DS, MC, V.

D

★★★ **MAIN STREET DUPLEX.** *110 Matheson St (95448). 707/433-6991; FAX 707/433-9513; res: 800/431-8663.* Web www.healdsburginn.com. 10 rms. S, D $95-$245; each addl $35. TV; cable, VCR (free movies). Complimentary full bkfst; afternoon refreshments. Ck-out 11 am, ck-in 3 pm. Business servs avail. Many fireplaces. Former Wells Fargo Express Bldg, built 1901; antiques, artwork, stained glass. Enclosed solarium. Cr cds: C, MC, V.

Restaurants

★★ **BISTRO RALPH.** *109 Plaza St (95448), on plaza in center of town. 707/433-1380.* Hrs: 11:30 am-2:30 pm; 5:30-closing. Closed Thanksgiving, Dec 25. Res accepted. Wine, beer. A la carte entrees: lunch $6-$12, dinner $12-$18. Specialties: Campbell Ranch lamb, Caesar salad. Outdoor dining. Contemporary and casual atmosphere. Totally nonsmoking. Cr cds: C, MC, V.

D

★ **CATELLI'S THE REX.** *21047 Geyserville Ave (95441), 6 mi N on US 101, Independence Rd exit, N to Geyserville Ave. 707/433-6000.* Hrs: noon-2 pm, 5-9 pm; Fri to 9:30; Sat 5-9:30; Sun from 5 pm. Closed Mon; also major hols. Res accepted. Italian menu. Bar 11:30 am-9 pm. Semi-a la carte: lunch $6.95-$11.95, dinner $12.95-$19.95. Child's meals. Specialties: fresh seafood, lobster ravioli. Outdoor dining. Family-owned. Totally nonsmoking. Cr cds: C, DS, MC, V.

D

★★★ **CHATEAU SOUVERAIN.** *Alexander Valley (95441), 5 mi N on US 101. 707/433-3141.* Hrs: 11:30 am-2:30 pm, 5:30-8:30 pm. Closed Mon-Thurs; Thanksgiving, Dec 24, 25; also Jan. Res required. Country French menu. Wine cellar. A la carte entrees: lunch $10.75-$13.75, dinner $14-$19.95. Specialties: wild mushroom penne pasta with rock shrimp, roast leg of lamb, fresh ancho chile pepper tagliarini. Outdoor dining. View of valley, vineyards. Totally nonsmoking. Cr cds: A, C, DS, MC, V.

D

✓★ **EL FAROLITO.** *128 Plaza St (95448). 707/433-2807.* Hrs: 10:30 am-9 pm. Closed Jan 1, Easter, Thanksgiving, Dec 25. Res accepted. Mexican menu. Wine, beer. Semi-a la carte: bkfst $6-$7, lunch, dinner $6.50-$7.50. Child's meals. Specializes in carnitas. Cr cds: C, DS, MC, V.

D

★★ **FELIX & LOUIE'S.** *106 Matheson St (95448). 707/433-6966.* Hrs: 11:30 am-9 pm, Fri, Sat to 10 pm. Closed Dec 25. Italian, Amer menu. Bar to midnight. A la carte entrees: lunch $5.50-$14, dinner $7.50-$15. Child's meals. Specializes in wood-burning oven pizza. Own pasta. Parking. Outdoor dining. Totally nonsmoking. Cr cds: C, MC, V.

D

✓★ **LOTUS THAI RESTAURANT.** *109 Plaza St #A (95448). 707/433-5282.* Hrs: 11:30 am-2:30 pm, 5-9:30 pm. Closed Mon; Thanksgiving, Dec 25. Res accepted. Wine, beer. A la carte entrees: lunch $5.95-$8.50, dinner $8.50-$13.95. Specialties: pad thai, plamuk gapow. Thai decor. Totally nonsmoking. Cr cds: A, C, DS, MC, V.

D ♥

★★ **MADRONA MANOR.** *(See Madrona Manor) 707/433-4231.* E-mail madronaman@aol.com; web www.madronamanor.com. Hrs: 6-9 pm. Res accepted. Prix-fixe: dinner $40-$48. Specializes in wine country cuisine. Outdoor dining. Dining rms overlook extensive gardens. Formal dining in Victorian mansion. Totally nonsmoking. Cr cds: A, C, D, DS, MC, V.

D

★★ **MANGIA BENE.** *241 Healdsburg Ave (95448). 707/433-2340.* Hrs: 5-9 pm; Fri, Sat to 10 pm. Closed Jan 1, Thanksgiving, Dec 25. Res accepted. Italian menu. Bar. A la carte entrees: dinner $9.95-$15.95. Child's meals. Specialties: osso bucco, cannelloni, tiramisu. Street parking. Totally nonsmoking. Cr cds: A, C, MC, V.

D

✓★ **RAVENOUS.** *117 North St (95448). 707/431-1770.* Hrs: 11:30 am-2:30 pm, 5-9 pm; Fri, Sat to 9:30 pm. Closed Mon, Tues; Easter, Thanksgiving, Dec 25. Wine, beer. A la carte entrees: lunch $7.50-$11.50, dinner $12.50-$16. Specialties: roast pork tenderloin, Ravenous burger, duck breast. Totally nonsmoking. Cr cds: C.

D

★ **WESTERN BOOT STEAK HOUSE.** *9 Mitchell Lane (95448). 707/433-6362.* Hrs: 11:30 am-9 pm, Fri to 10 pm; Sat 4-10 pm, Sun 4-9 pm. Closed most major hols. Res accepted. Wine, beer. Semi-a la carte: lunch $4.95-$9.95, dinner $7.95-$23. Child's meals. Specializes in steak, ribs, seafood. Parking. Cr cds: A, C, MC, V.

D

Hearst-San Simeon State Historical Monument (Hearst Castle) (G-1)

(See also Cambria, San Simeon)

Web www.hearstcastle.org

Information Hearst Castle, 750 Hearst Castle Rd, San Simeon 93452; 805/927-2020 or 800/444-4445 (res)

Crowning La Cuesta Encantada—the Enchanted Hill—is a princely domain of castle, guest houses, theater, pools and tennis courts created by William Randolph Hearst as his home and retreat. After his death in 1951, the estate was given to the state as a memorial to the late publisher's mother, Phoebe Adderson Hearst. For years Hearst Castle could be glimpsed by the public only through a telescope at the nearby village of San Simeon, but today it is open to the public. A "carefully planned, deliberate attempt to create a shrine of beauty," it was begun in 1919 under the direction of noted architect Julia Morgan. An army of workers built the castle with its twin towers and surrounded it with formal Mediterranean gardens; construction continued for 28 years. And, though three guest houses and 115 rooms of the main house were completed, there was still much more Hearst had hoped to build.

Items collected by Hearst can be viewed in the castle and on the grounds. Features of the castle itself are the Refectory, an unbelievable "long, high, noble room" with a hand-carved ceiling and life-size statues of saints, silk banners from Siena and 15th-century choir stalls from a Spanish cathedral; the Assembly Room, with priceless tapestries; and the lavish theater where the latest motion pictures were shown.

The estate includes three luxurious "guest houses"; the Neptune Pool, with a colonnade leading to an ancient Roman temple facade and an array of marble statuary, an indoor pool, magnificent gardens, fountains, walkways and, of course, the main house of 115 rooms.

Visitors may explore an exhibit on the life and times of William Randolph Hearst inside the Visitor Center at the bottom of the hill. Also here is an iWERKS giant-screen theater showing "Hearst Castle: Building the Dream," a 40-min film detailing the rich history and architectural precedents of Hearst and his estate (phone 805/927-6811). Food and gift concessions are also located here. There is an area to observe artifact restoration in progress; entrance to the exhibit is free.

Parking is available in a lot near CA 1, where buses transport visitors to the castle. Access to the castle and grounds is by guided tour only. Tour 1 takes in the grounds, a guest house, the pools and the lower level of the main house; Tour 2 visits the upper levels of the main house, which include Hearst's private suite; Tour 3 covers the north wing and a guest house, and includes a video about the construction of the castle; Tour 4 (available Apr-Oct) is spent mostly outside in the gardens and around the pools but also includes behind-the-scenes areas such as the wine cellar and 2 floors of the largest guest house. Evening tours are available for selected evenings in the spring and fall; evening tours take in the highlights of the estate and include a living history program developed to give visitors a glimpse of life at the "Castle" in the early 1930s. All tours include the outdoor and indoor pools.

Day tours take approximately 1¾ hours; evening tours take approximately 2¼ hours. No pets. Reservations are recommended and are available up to eight weeks in advance by calling 800/444-4445. Tickets are also available at the ticket office in the visitor center. Tours entail much walking and stair climbing; wheelchairs can be accommodated under certain conditions and with 10 days advance notice by calling 805/927-2020; strollers cannot be accommodated. (Daily; closed Jan 1, Thanksgiving, Dec 25) For tour and reservation information, phone 800/444-4445. **¢¢¢¢**

Hemet (J-4)

(See also Palm Springs, Riverside)

Founded 1890 **Pop** 36,094 **Elev** 1,596 ft **Area Code** 909

Located in the beautiful San Jacinto Valley, Hemet was once the largest producer of alfalfa and herbs in the country. Today it is near the hub of an area that includes ocean, desert, mountains, lakes, health resorts and springs, along with neighboring historic Native American reservations and large cattle ranches, all within an hour's drive.

What to See and Do

San Jacinto Valley Museum. Permanent and temporary exhibits of genealogy, Native American archaeology and a variety of historical items of San Jacinto Valley. (Tues-Sat, afternoons; closed Jan 1, Thanksgiving, Dec 25) 181 E Main St, 3 mi N in San Jacinto. Phone 909/654-4952 or 909/654-7710. **Free**

Annual Events

Ramona Pageant. Ramona Bowl, a 6,662-seat outdoor amphitheater built into the side of a mountain. Beautiful setting among the rolling hills, where most of the action of Helen Hunt Jackson's story takes place. More than 350 persons participate in this romance of early California, presented annually since 1923. Contact Ramona Pageant Assn, 27400 Ramona Bowl Rd, 92544; 909/658-3111 or 800/645-4465. 3 wkends late Apr-early May.

Farmers Fair. Lake Perris Fairgrounds, 10 mi W on CA 74 in Perris. Competitions and exhibits, food, activities, entertainment. Phone 909/657-4221. Mid-Oct.

Motels

✓★★ **BEST WESTERN.** *2625 W Florida Ave (92545), I-215 exit CA 74, E 13 mi. 909/925-6605; FAX 909/925-7095; res: 800/605-0001.* Web www.bestwestern.com. 68 rms, 2 story, 29 kits. S $49; D $52-$100; each addl $6; suites $89; kit. units $52-$100; wkly, monthly rates; higher rates: Ramona Pageant, special events. Crib $4. Pet accepted, some restrictions; $10. TV; cable (premium). Heated pool; whirlpool. Complimentary bkfst. Coffee in rms. Restaurant adj open 24 hrs. Ck-out 11 am. Coin Indry. Business servs avail. Health club privileges. Lawn games. Refrigerators; microwaves avail. Grills. Cr cds: A, C, D, DS, ER, MC, V.

SC

✓★ **SUPER 8 MOTEL.** *3510 W Florida Ave (92545). 909/658-2281; FAX 909/925-6492; res: 800/800-8000.* 70 rms, 3 story. Oct-Apr: S $38.88; D $46.88; each addl $4; suites $54.88; under 12 free; lower rates rest of yr. Crib free. TV; cable (premium), VCR avail. Pool; whirlpool. Complimentary continental bkfst. Restaurant nearby. Ck-out 11 am. Business servs avail. Health club privileges. Refrigerators; microwaves avail. Cr cds: A, C, D, DS, JCB, MC, V.

D SC

✓★★ **TRAVELODGE.** *1201 W Florida Ave (92543). 909/766-1902; FAX 909/766-7739; res: 800/578-7878.* 46 rms, 2 story. S $38; D $43; suites $38-$43. Crib $5. Pet accepted, some restrictions; $5. TV; cable (premium), VCR avail. Pool; whirlpool. Complimentary continental bkfst. Restaurant opp 6 am-10 pm. Ck-out noon. Meeting rms. Coin Indry. Health club privileges. Refrigerators; microwaves avail. Cr cds: A, C, D, DS, JCB, MC, V.

D

Restaurant

★★ **DATTILO RISTORANTE.** *2288 E Florida Ave (92544). 909/658-4248.* Hrs: 11 am-9 pm; Sat from 4 pm; Sun to 8 pm. Closed Mon; hols. Italian menu. Bar. Semi-a la carte: bkfst $2.99-$5.99, lunch $3.99-$6.99, dinner $5.99-$19.99. Child's meals. Specialties: lasagna, ravioli, rack of lamb. Cr cds: A, C, D, MC, V.

D

Hollywood (L.A.) (B-3 see Los Angeles map)

(See also Los Angeles)

Elev 385 ft **Area Code** 213

Information Chamber of Commerce, 7018 Hollywood Blvd, 90028, phone 213/469-8311; or the Hollywood Visitors Information Center, 6541 Hollywood Blvd, phone 213/689-8822

Known as the "Entertainment Capital of the World," Hollywood is the birthplace of the motion picture industry and home to much of the movie and television industry today. Often thought of as a separate city, Hollywood is actually a neighborhood of Los Angeles.

What to See and Do

Barnsdall Art Park. Named after socialite Aline Barnsdall, who commissioned Frank Lloyd Wright to build her home and later gave the property to the city of Los Angeles. (Daily) 4800 Hollywood Blvd. Phone 213/485-8665. **Free** Within the park is

Hollyhock House. Built by Wright from 1919-1921, the house was given its name for Aline Barnsdall's favorite flower. Extensive outdoor courtyards and terraces were designed by Wright to extend living spaces to outdoors. Tours. (Daily exc Mon) Phone 213/662-7272. **¢**

Municipal Art Gallery. Features work by regional and local artists. (Daily exc Mon) Phone 213/485-4581. **¢**

Hollywood & Vine. One of the most famous intersections in the world.

Hollywood Blvd. "Main Street" of moviedom.

Hollywood Bowl. Huge outdoor amphitheater, where 250,000 hear "Symphony Under the Stars" each summer. 2301 N Highland Ave, just SW of Hollywood Frwy. Phone 213/850-2000.

Hollywood Entertainment Museum. Showcases contributions of film, TV, radio and recording industries through state-of-the-art exhibits and shows. Traces Hollywood's evolution as "Entertainment Capital." Includes complete set from *Cheers,* also the "bridge" from *Starship Enterprise.* (Daily exc Mon, closed major hols) 7021 Hollywood Blvd. Phone 213/465-7900. **¢¢¢**

Hollywood Memorial Park Cemetery Mortuary. Crypts of Tyrone Power, Cecil B. De Mille, Rudolph Valentino, Douglas Fairbanks, Sr, Nelson Eddy and Norma Talmadge, as well as other famous stars, statesmen and industrialists. (Daily) On the grounds at 6000 Santa Monica Blvd. Phone 213/469-1181. **Free**

Hollywood Studio Museum. Dedicated to preserving the history of Hollywood's silent film era. Site of Hollywood's first feature-length Western, *The Squaw Man,* in 1913. Costumes, props, photographs, early movie artifacts. Gift shop. (Sat & Sun; closed hols) 2100 N Highland Ave. Phone 213/874-2276. **¢¢**

Hollywood Wax Museum. More than 170 famous people of the past & present re-created in wax. Presidents, movie stars, Western scenes; theater. (Daily) 6767 Hollywood Blvd. Phone 213/462-8860. **¢¢¢**

Mann's Chinese Theatre. Historic movie palace; scene of spectacular opening nights for decades. Theatre's famous cement forecourt has stars' footprints, hand prints and autographs (since 1927). 6925 Hollywood Blvd, between Highland & LaBrea. Phone 213/464-8111. Forecourt **Free**

Universal Studios Hollywood (See LOS ANGELES)

Walk of Fame. The world's most famous sidewalk, with more than 2,000 stars embedded in charcoal and coral-colored terrazzo strip along Hollywood's main business district. Honors celebrities from film, television, radio, recording and live stage. From LaBrea to Gower along Hollywood Blvd, and from Yucca to Sunset along Vine St. For information on upcoming ceremonies phone 213/469-8311. **Free**

Westwood Memorial Cemetery (See WESTWOOD VILLAGE)

Annual Events

Easter Sunrise Services. Hollywood Bowl. Interdenominational service with music of select choral groups.

Hollywood Christmas Parade. Features floats, marching bands; over 50 of Hollywood's famous stars. Televised world wide. Sun after Thanksgiving.

Motels

✓★★ **BEST WESTERN INN.** *6141 Franklin Ave (90028), US 101 Gower St exit to Franklin Ave, then 1 blk W. 323/464-5181; FAX 323/962-0536; res: 800/528-1234; res: 800/287-1700.* Web www.bestwestern.com. 86 rms, 3-4 story. S $79-$89; D $89-$99; each addl $5; under 12 free; wkly rates; higher rates Rose Bowl. Crib $5. Pet accepted, some restrictions; $25. Heated pool. TV; cable (premium). Restaurant 7 am-10 pm. Ck-out noon. Business servs avail. Sundries. Coin Indry. Some refrigerators, microwaves, wet bars. Cr cds: A, C, D, DS, MC, V.

SC

✓★ **SUPER 8 MOTEL - HOLLYWOOD.** *1536 N Western Ave (90027). 323/467-3131; FAX 323/467-5258; res: 800/800-8000; res: 888/534-2298.* E-mail super8hlywd@stayanight.com; web www.stayanight.com/super8hlywd. 54 rms, 4 story. S $47-$57; D $57-$64; each addl $5. TV; cable (premium). Complimentary continental bkfst. Restaurant nearby. Ck-out 11 am. Business servs avail. Some refrigerators. Cr cds: A, C, D, DS, JCB, MC, V.

D SC

Motor Hotel

★★★ **RAMADA HOLLYWOOD LIMITED.** *1160 N Vermont Ave (90029). 323/660-1788; FAX 323/660-8069; res: 800/272-6232; res: 800/800-9733.* E-mail ramadahollywood@msn.com; web www.ramadahollywood.com. 130 rms, 8 with shower only, 4 story. S, D $79-$119; suites $99-$139; kit. units $159-$199; under 18 free; family rates; package plans. Crib free. Parking fee. TV; cable (premium). Complimentary continental bkfst. Restaurant 6:30 am-11 pm. Bar from 3 pm. Ck-out noon. Meeting rms. Business servs avail. Bellhops. Valet serv. Sundries. Gift shop. Coin Indry. Exercise equipt; steam rms, saunas. Heated pool. Game rm. Many refrigerators, microwaves. Many balconies. Cr cds: A, C, D, DS, ER, JCB, MC, V.

D SC

Hotels

★★ **HOLLYWOOD ROOSEVELT HOTEL.** *7000 Hollywood Blvd (90028), US 101 exit Highland Ave, S to Hollywood Blvd. 323/466-7000; FAX 323/462-8056; res: 800/333-3333; res: 800/950-7667.* E-mail reserv@hollywoodroosevelt.com; web www.hollywoodroosevelt.com. 320 rms, 2-12 story, 47 suites. S, D $159-$199; each addl $20; suites $299-$1,500; under 18 free. Crib free. Valet parking $9.90. TV; cable (premium), VCR avail. Heated pool; whirlpool, poolside serv. Coffee in rms. Restaurant 6 am-11 pm. Rm serv to 1 am. Bars 11-1 am; entertainment. Convention facilities. Business servs avail. Concierge. Gift shop. Exercise equipt. Massage. Minibars; some bathrm phones; refrigerators, microwaves avail. Site of first Academy Awards presentation. Cr cds: A, C, D, DS, ER, JCB, MC, V.

D SC

★★★ **LE MONTROSE HOTEL.** *900 Hammond St (90069), US 101 exit Sunset Blvd, W 4 mi to Hammond St. 310/855-1115; FAX 310/657-9192; res: 800/776-0666.* Web www.travel2000.com. 132 kit. suites, 5 story. Suites $270-$575; under 18 free. Crib free. Covered parking $15. Pet accepted. TV; cable (premium), VCR avail. Pool; whirlpool, poolside serv. Restaurant 5 am-10:45 pm. Rm serv 24 hrs. Ck-out noon. Meeting rm. Business servs avail. In-rm modem link. Concierge. Lighted tennis, pro. Exercise rm; sauna. Massage. Bathrm phones, refrigerators, fireplaces; many wet bars; microwaves avail. Some balconies. Art nouveau decor. Cr cds: A, C, D, DS, ER, JCB, MC, V.

D SC

★★★ **MONDRIAN HOTEL.** *8440 Sunset Blvd (90069), at La Cienega Blvd, in West Hollywood . 323/650-8999; FAX 323/650-9241; res: 800/525-8029.* 245 rms, 12 story. S, D $225-$445; under 12 free. Covered parking $20. TV; cable (premium), VCR. Heated pool; whirlpool, poolside serv. Restaurant 7 am-11:30 pm. Rm serv 24 hrs. Bar 11-2 am. Ck-out noon. Business center. In-rm modem link. Concierge. Exercise equipt; sauna. Minibars, wet bars. Some balconies. Contemporary decor. Cr cds: A, C, D, DS, MC, V.

D

★★ **RAMADA INN.** *8585 Santa Monica Blvd (90069), US 101 exit Santa Monica Blvd W. 310/652-6400; FAX 310/652-2135; res: 800/272-6232; res: 800/845-8585.* E-mail info@ramada-wh.com; web www.ramada-wh.com. 175 rms, 4 story, 44 suites. S, D $139-$145; each addl $15; suites $159-$279; under 16 free. Crib free. TV; cable (premium), VCR avail. Heated pool. Coffee in rms. Restaurant 6:30 am-11:30 pm. Bar. Ck-out noon. Coin Indry. Business servs avail. Shopping arcade. Airport transportation. Health club privileges. Bathrm phones, refrigerators; some wetbars; microwaves avail. Some balconies. Cr cds: A, C, D, DS, JCB, MC, V.

D SC

★★★ **SUNSET MARQUIS HOTEL & VILLAS.** *1200 Alta Loma Rd (91608), 1 blk W of LaCienega Blvd, 1 blk S of Sunset Blvd; west of downtown. 310/657-1333; FAX 310/652-5300; res: 800/858-9758.* E-mail smhsale@aol.com. 114 suites, 10 with kit, 3 story, 12 villas. Suites, kit. units $260-$450; each addl $30; villas $450-$1,200; under 12 free. Crib free. Valet parking $15. TV; cable (premium), VCR avail (movies). 2 heated pools; whirlpool, poolside serv. Restaurant 7 am-10 pm. Rm serv 24 hrs. Bar. Ck-out 1 pm. Meeting rm. Business center. In-rm modem link. Concierge. Butler serv avail. Exercise equipt; sauna, steam rm. Massage. Refrigerators; microwaves avail; some in-rm steam baths; wet bar in suites; bathrm phones in villas. Private patios, balconies. Recording studio. Cr cds: A, C, D, ER, MC, V.

D

★★★ **THE ARGYLE.** *8358 Sunset Blvd (90069). 323/654-7100; FAX 213/654-9287; res: 800/225-2637.* Web www.argylehotel.com. 64 rms, 15 story, 44 suites. S $250; D $275; suites $345-$850; wkend rates. Crib free. Valet parking $18. TV; cable (premium), VCR (movies). Heated pool; poolside serv. Complimentary coffee in lobby. Restaurant (see FENIX). Rm serv 24 hrs. Bar 11-1:30 am. Ck-out 1 pm. Meeting rms. Business servs avail. In-rm modem link. Concierge. Exercise rm; sauna. Massage. Bathrm phones, refrigerators, minibars; some in-rm whirlpools, wet bars; microwaves avail. Some balconies. Cr cds: A, C, D, JCB, MC, V.

D

★★★ **WYNDHAM BELL AGE HOTEL.** *1020 N San Vicente Blvd (90069), 1 block S of Sunset Blvd, in West Hollywood. 310/854-1111; FAX 310/854-0926; res: 800/996-3426.* Web www.wyndham.com. 200 suites, 10 story. S, D $205-$510; each addl $25; under 18 free; wkend rates. Valet parking $18. TV; cable (premium), VCR avail. Heated pool; poolside serv. Restaurants 7 am-11 pm (also see DIAGHILEV). Rm serv 24 hrs. Bar 11-2 am; jazz Thurs-Sat, Sun brunch. Ck-out 1 pm. Convention facilities. Business servs avail. In-rm modem link. Concierge. Shopping arcade. Barber, beauty shop. Exercise equipt. Bathrm phones, wet bars; microwaves avail. Private patios, balconies. Cr cds: A, C, D, DS, ER, JCB, MC, V.

D

Restaurants

★★ **ALTO PALATO TRATTORIA.** *755 N La Cienega Blvd (90069), US 101 Santa Monica Blvd exit, W 3 mi to La Cienega Blvd, then S. 310/657-9271.* Hrs: 6-11 pm; Fri noon-2:30 pm, 6-11 pm; Sun 5-10:30 pm. Closed Jan 1, Thanksgiving, Dec 25. Res accepted. Italian menu. Bar. A la carte entrees: lunch, dinner $9.50-$29. Specialties: wood-fired pizza, pumpkin gnocchi, sauteed breast of chicken. Own pasta, desserts. Valet parking. Outdoor dining. Two-story; Italian cafe atmosphere. Cr cds: A, C, D, MC, V.

D

✓★★ **ANTONIO'S.** *7472 Melrose Ave (90046), US 101 Melrose Ave exit, W 3 mi. 213/655-0480.* Hrs: 11 am-11 pm; Sat from noon; Sun noon-10 pm. Closed Mon; Thanksgiving, Dec 25. Res accepted. Mexican menu. Bar. A la carte entrees: lunch, dinner $8.50-$15.95. Specialties: pollo yucateco, blue corn tamales with spinach. Strolling musicians wkend evenings. Valet parking. Outdoor dining. Colorful Mexican decor. Family-owned. Cr cds: A, C, MC, V.

D

✓★★ **BOOK SOUP BISTRO.** *8800 Sunset Blvd (90069). 310/657-1072.* E-mail booksoup@aol.com. Hrs: noon-10 pm; Sat, Sun from 11 am. Closed Jan 1, Thanksgiving, Dec 25. Res accepted. Contemporary Amer menu. Bar. Semi-a la carte: lunch $6.50-$15.50, dinner $6.50-$22.50. Specialties: grilled Idaho trout, penne with grilled vegetables, sterling silver N.Y. steak. Own desserts. Outdoor dining. Casual dining. Adj large bookstore. Cr cds: A, C, D, DS, MC, V.

D

★★ **CA'BREA.** *346 S La Brea Ave (90036), I-10 La Brea Ave exit, N 2 mi. 323/938-2863.* Web www.calendarlive.com/cabrea. Hrs: 11:30 am-2:30 pm, 5:30-10 pm; Fri, Sat to 11:30 pm. Closed Sun. Res accepted. Northern Italian menu. Bar. A la carte entrees: lunch, dinner $8.95-$22.95. Specializes in authentic Venetian dishes. Own pasta, desserts. Valet parking. Patio dining. Italian cafe decor. Totally nonsmoking. Cr cds: A, C, D, DS, MC, V.

D

✓★ **CAIOTI.** *2100 Laurel Canyon Blvd (90046), N of Sunset Blvd at jct Kirkwood Dr. 213/650-2988.* E-mail caioti@earthlink.com; web www.caioti.com. Hrs: 4:30-11 pm. Closed some major hols. Res accepted. Italian, Californian menu. Wine, beer. Semi-a la carte: dinner $5.75-$14.25. Specializes in pizza, pasta, grilled entrees. Own pizza dough. Outdoor dining. Rural setting. Cr cds: A, C, MC, V.

★★★ **CHIANTI RISTORANTE & CUCINA.** *7383 Melrose Ave (90046), US 101 Melrose Ave exit, W 3 mi. 213/653-8333.* Hrs: Cucina 11:30 am-11:30 pm; Fri, Sat to midnight; Sun 4-11 pm. Chianti 5:30-11:30 pm; Fri, Sat to midnight; Sun 5-10:30 pm. Closed Thanksgiving, Dec 25. Res accepted. Northern Italian menu. Bar. A la carte entrees: Cucina: lunch, dinner $6.75-$18.95; Chianti: lunch, dinner $10.95-$24.50. Specializes in fresh seafood, pasta. Own baking. Valet parking. Two distinct dining areas. Totally nonsmoking. Cr cds: A, C, D, MC, V.

D

★★★ **CITRUS RESTAURANT.** *6703 Melrose Ave (90038), US 101 Melrose Ave exit, W 2 mi. 213/857-0034.* E-mail citrusinla@aol.com. Hrs: noon-2:30 pm, 6:30-10:30 pm; Sat 6-11 pm. Closed Sun; major hols. Res accepted. California, French cuisine. Bar. A la carte entrees: lunch $13-$17, dinner $25-$31. Complete meals: dinner $55-$65. Specialties: Chilean sea bass with black chanterelle crust, shiitake mushroom and vegetable tart with garlic cream. Own pastries. Valet parking. Open kitchen, garden setting. Totally nonsmoking. Cr cds: A, C, D, JCB, MC, V.

D

★★ **DAN TANA'S.** *9071 Santa Monica Blvd (90069), I-405 exit Santa Monica Blvd, E 4 mi. 310/275-9444.* Hrs: 5 pm-1 am; Sun to 12:30 am. Closed Thanksgiving, Dec 25. Res required. Northern Italian menu. Bar. A la carte entrees: dinner $15-$39. Specializes in NY prime steak, whitefish. Valet parking. 2 dining areas. New York-style Italian restaurant with fireplace. Family-owned. Totally nonsmoking. Cr cds: A, C, D, DS, MC, V.

★★★ **DRAI'S.** *4921 Onteora Way (90041), US 101 exit Santa Monica Blvd, W 3 mi to La Cienega Blvd, then S . 310/358-8585.* Hrs: 6:30-10:30 pm. Closed Sun; Thanksgiving, Dec 25. Res required. Southern French menu. Bar. Wine cellar. A la carte entrees: dinner $14-$28. Specialties: sashimi of ahi tuna layered on toasted filo; ravioli with fresh Maine lobster; glazed Chilean sea bass with soy sauce, garlic and ginger. Jazz Mon, Fri. Valet parking. Outdoor dining. Three distinct dining areas with modern decor; French doors lead to garden rm; landscape mural, original artwork. Cr cds: A, C, D, MC, V.

D

★★★ **FENIX.** *(See The Argyle) 323/848-6677.* French, California menu. Specializes in tuna in rice paper, gulf red snapper, duck. Hrs: 6:30 am-2:30 pm, 6-11 pm; Fri, Sat to midnight; Sun brunch 10 am-3 pm. Res accepted. Bar. Extensive wine list. A la carte entrees: bkfst $7.95-$10.50, lunch $7-$16.50, dinner $16.50-$25. Sun brunch $16-$21. Valet parking. Outdoor dining. Cr cds: A, C, D, JCB, MC, V.

D

★★★ **JOZU.** *8360 Melrose Ave (90069). 323/655-5600.* Pacific California with Asian influence. Specialties chillean sea bass; tomato & crab salad w/green mangoes & musaman curry vinaigrette, lobster w/ beet salad & chili lime vinaigrette. Hrs Mon-Fri 6-10 pm; Sat 5:30-11 pm; 5:30-9:30 pm. Prices $18-$27. Bar. Cr cds: C.

★★★ **L'ANGOLO RISTORANTE.** *6602 Melrose Ave (90038), US 101 Melrose Ave exit, W 2 mi. 323/935-4922.* Hrs: 5:30-10:30 pm. Closed Sun; most major hols. Res accepted. Contemporary Italian menu. Bar. Wine cellar. A la carte entrees: dinner $8.50-$19. Specialties: pumpkin ravioli in a white truffle butter sause with toasted almonds; almond crusted branzino in a lemon thyme sauce and mashed potato; parmesan crusted duckling crespella with a mild red onoin confit. Own baking. Valet parking. Balcony dining. Cr cds: A, C, MC, V.

D

★★★★ **L'ORANGERIE.** *903 N La Cienega Blvd (90069), US 101 Santa Monica Blvd exit, W 3 mi to La Cienega Blvd then S 2 blks. 310/652-9770.* E-mail loranger@pacbell.net; web www.orangerie.com. This romantic, flower-filled restaurant is a venerable Los Angeles institution. Whether you sit in the beautiful open-air patio or at one of the side-by-side tables that line the main dining room, the effective is enchanting. The creative

French cooking of Ludovic Lufevre combines unusual spices and ingredients to produce a thoughtful, personal cuisine. Contemporary French menu. Specialties: Eggs in the shell with caviar, whole roasted rock lobster, fides with small shellfish in cinnamon butter, lamb medallion with cardamon, paste of caper and grape, baby bell pepper stuffed with eggplant and artichokes, Peach Tart with Verbena ice cream. Hrs: 6-11 pm. Closed Mon. Res required. Extensive wine list. Bar. A la carte entrees: dinner $32-$45. Menu Degustation dinner $85, Vegetarian $50. Valet parking. Jacket required, tie optional. Terrace and patio dining on the courtyard. Cr cds: A, C, D, DS, JCB, MC, V.

D

★★ **LA MASIA.** *9077 Santa Monica Blvd (90069), US 101 Santa Monica Blvd exit, 3 mi W. 310/273-7066.* Web www.calendarlive.com/lamasia. Hrs: 6-11 pm; Fri, Sat to 12:30 am; Sun from 5:30 pm. Closed Mon, Tues; Jan 1, July 4, Dec 25. Res accepted. Spanish menu. Bar to 2 am. Semi-a la carte: dinner $14.50-$26.50. Specialties: paella, chuleta de ternera. Salsa, Latin jazz. Valet parking. Intimate dining. Tapas bar. Family-owned. Totally nonsmoking. Cr cds: A, C, D, DS, MC, V.

D

★★★ **LE DOME.** *8720 Sunset Blvd (90069), US 101 Sunset Blvd exit, 4 mi W. 310/659-6919.* Hrs: noon-midnight; Sat from 6 pm. Closed Sun; major hols. Res accepted. French, continental menu. Bar. Wine list. A la carte entrees: lunch $11.75-$19.75, dinner $14-$30. Specializes in fresh fish, prime beef. Own desserts. Valet parking. Outdoor dining. Art noveau decor. Cr cds: A, C, D, MC, V.

✓★ **LE PETIT FOUR.** *8654 Sunset Blvd (90069), US 101 Sunset Blvd exit, 4 mi W. 310/652-3863.* Hrs: 11-1 am; Sat 9-2 am; Sun from 9 am; Sun brunch to 6 pm. Closed Dec 25. Res accepted. Continental menu. Bar. A la carte entrees: lunch, dinner $5.50-$17.50. Sun brunch $4.50-$10.25. Specializes in fresh fish, pasta, salad. Own baking, ice cream. Outdoor dining. Sidewalk dining area has bistro atmosphere. Cr cds: A, C, D, MC, V.

✓★★ **LOLA'S.** *945 N Fairfax Ave (90046), US 101 exit Melrose Ave, W 3½ mi to Fairfax Ave, then N . 213/736-5652.* Hrs: 5:30 pm-2 am. Closed Thanksgiving, Dec 24, 25. Res accepted. Bar. Semi-a la carte: dinner $6-$16.50. Specialties: grilled pork chop, baked macaroni & cheese, chocolate kiss cake. Own desserts. Valet parking. Skylights, chandeliers. Totally nonsmoking. Cr cds: A, C, D, MC, V.

D

✓★★ **MI FAMILIA.** *8222 1/2 W Third St (90048), I-10 exit La Cieneca Blvd, N to Third St, then E . 323/653-2121.* Web www.calendarlive.com/MiFamilia/. Hrs: 11:30 am-12:30 pm, 5:30-10:30 pm. Closed major hols. Res accepted. Mexican menu. Bar. Semi-a la carte: lunch, dinner $9.25-$13.95. Specialties: al mojo de ajo estilo matador, el guisado de provincia, el tartin de berenjenas. Valet parking. Outdoor dining. Classic Mexican bistro; modern artwork. Cr cds: A, C, D, MC, V.

★★★ **MORTONS RESTAURANT.** *8764 Melrose Ave (90069), at Robertson Ave. 310/276-5205.* Hrs: noon-3 pm, 6-11 pm; Sat from 6 pm. Closed Sun; major hols. Res accepted. Bar to 1 am. Wine cellar. A la carte entrees: lunch $11-$19, dinner $20-$29. Specialties: tuna sashimi, grilled marinated lamb loin, free range lime grilled chicken. Own desserts. Valet parking. Modern decor. Totally nonsmoking. Cr cds: A, C, D, MC, V.

D

★ **MUSSO & FRANK GRILL.** *6667 Hollywood Blvd (90028). 323/467-5123.* Hrs: 11 am-11 pm. Closed Sun, Mon; major hols. Res accepted. Continental menu. Bar. A la carte entrees: lunch, dinner $4.95-$29.50. Specialties: Bouillabaisse Marseillaise, homemade chicken pot pie. Own desserts. Menu changes daily. Historic restaurant opened 1919. Famed Round Table of Saroyan, Thurber, Falkner and Fitzgerald met here. Totally nonsmoking. Cr cds: A, C, D, DS, MC, V.

★★ **PALM.** *9001 Santa Monica Blvd (90069), I-405 exit Santa Monica Blvd, E 3 mi. 310/550-8811.* Hrs: noon-10:30 pm; Sat from 5 pm; Sun 5-9:30 pm. Closed most major hols. Res accepted. Bar. A la carte entrees: lunch $10-$18, dinner $15-$30. Specializes in steak, lobster. Valet parking. Several dining areas. Hollywood celebrity caricatures cover walls. Totally nonsmoking. Cr cds: A, C, D, MC, V.

D

★★★★ **PATINA RESTAURANT.** *5955 Melrose Ave (90038), US 101 Melrose Ave exit, W 1½ mi. 213/467-1108.* Web www.patinapinot.com. The sparsely decorated dining room of this popular restaurant provides no distraction from chef/owner Joachim Splichal's extraordinary cooking. Drawing inspiration from France, Italy, Germany, and California, he produces a creative and highly personal cuisine. California french. $29-$34; hrs Mon-Sun 6-9:30 pm; Tues lunch from 12-2 pm. $16-$18. Reserv reqd. Jackets recom. Full bar. Cr cds: A, C, D, DS, MC, V.

D

★★★ **SONORA CAFE.** *180 S La Brea Ave (90036), I-10 to La Brea Ave exit, N 2 mi . 323/857-1800.* Web www.sonoracafe.com. Hrs: 11:30 am-10 pm; Fri to 11 pm; Sat 5:30-11 pm; Sun 5-9 pm. Closed major hols. Res accepted. Southwestern menu. Bar. Wine list. Semi-a la carte: lunch $9.95-$16.95, dinner $14.25-$24.95. Specialties: Prince Edward Island mussels, Texas barbecue pork chops, wood-grilled sea scallops. Own desserts. Valet parking. Outdoor dining. Southwestern decor; original Southwestern and early American artwork; fireplace. Cr cds: A, C, DS, MC, V.

D

★★★ **SPAGO.** *8795 W Sunset Blvd (90069), US 101 Sunset Blvd exit, approx 4 mi W. 310/652-4025.* California menu. Specializes in gourmet pizza, lobster ravioli, fresh fish. Own pasta. Hrs: 6-10 pm; Fri, Sat 5:30-11 pm. Closed Mon; some major hols. Res required. Bar. A la carte entrees: dinner $14.50-$34.50. Valet parking. View of Sunset Strip, West Hollywood. Totally nonsmoking. Cr cds: A, C, D, DS, MC, V.

D

★★★ **YUJEAN KANG'S.** *8826 Melrose Ave (90069). 310/288-0806.* Web www.ladining.com/yujeankangs. Hrs: noon-2:30 pm, 5:30-11 pm; Sat, Sun from 5:30 pm. Closed Thanksgiving. Res accepted. Chinese menu. Bar. Wine cellar. Semi-a la carte: lunch $8-$13, dinner $13.95-$18.95. Specialties: Chilean sea bass in spicy sesame sauce, crispy flank steak, lamb loin. Valet parking. Oriental decor; antiques. Totally nonsmoking. Cr cds: A, C, D, DS, JCB, MC, V.

D

Humboldt Redwoods State Park (B-1)

(See also Garberville, Redwood Highway)

(45 mi S of Eureka via US 101)

Park encompasses more than 52,000 acres, including 17,000 acres of old growth coast redwoods. The Avenue of the Giants parallels US 101 and passes through the park, site of redwoods over 300 feet tall. The South Fork of the Eel River follows the Avenue through the park. Recreation includes swimming, fishing; nature hiking, mountain biking and camping. Humboldt Redwoods State Park has a visitor center located next to park headquarters. Park headquarters is at Burlington, 2 mi S of Weott on the Avenue. Campfire and nature programs are offered (summer). Standard fees. Contact PO Box 100, Weott 95571; 707/946-2409.

Pacific Lumber Company. A cooperative agreement in the late 1920s between the Pacific Lumber Company and the Save-the-Redwoods League led to the establishment of Humboldt Redwoods State Park. A total of nearly 20,000 acres of magnificent groves once owned by Pacific Lumber are now permanently protected in parks. In Scotia, tour Pacific Lumber's mill, said to be the world's largest redwood operation (Mon-Fri);

phone 707/764-2222 for tour schedule. A museum (open summer months) features historic photographs and memorabilia from days gone by. **Free**

Huntington Beach (J-4)

(See also Costa Mesa, Newport Beach)

Pop 181,519 **Elev** 28 ft **Area Code** 714

Motels

✓★ **COMFORT SUITES.** *16301 Beach Blvd (92647). 714/841-1812; FAX 714/841-0214; res: 800/714-4040.* 102 suites, 3 story. S, D $59-$79; each addl $5; under 18 free. Crib free. TV; cable. Heated pool; whirlpool. Complimentary continental bkfst. Ck-out 11 am. Coin lndry. Meeting rm. Exercise equipt. Refrigerators. Balconies. Cr cds: A, C, D, DS, JCB, MC, V.

D SC

★★ **RAMADA LIMITED.** *17205 Pacific Coast Hwy (90742), N on Pacific Coast Hwy. 714/840-2431; FAX 562/592-4093; res: 800/654-8904.* 50 rms, 2 story. S, D $89-$119; each addl $10; under 12 free. TV; cable (premium). Complimentary continental bkfst. Ck-out 11 am. Business servs avail. Whirlpool. Refrigerators. Private patios, balconies. Beach opp. Cr cds: A, C, DS, MC, V.

D SC

Hotels

✓★★ **HOTEL HUNTINGTON BEACH.** *7667 Center Ave (92647), off Beach Blvd. 714/891-0123; FAX 714/895-4591; res: 800/465-4329.* 224 rms, 8 story. S, D $105-$115; each addl $10; suites $195; under 18 free. Crib free. TV; cable (premium). Indoor pool; whirlpool. Coffee in rms. Restaurant 6:30 am-10 pm. Bar 5-11 pm. Ck-out noon. Business servs avail. Gift shop. Airport transportation. Exercise equipt. Health club privileges. Cr cds: A, C, D, DS, JCB, MC, V.

D SC

★★★ **THE WATERFRONT HILTON BEACH RESORT.** *21100 Pacific Coast Hwy (92648). 714/960-7873; FAX 714/960-3791; res: 800/822-7873.* E-mail 74161.774@compuserve.com; web hilton.com. 290 rms, 12 story, 36 suites. S, D $159-$299; suites $339-$579; under 18 free; wkend rates. Crib free. Garage, valet parking $10. TV; cable (premium), VCR avail. Heated pool; whirlpool, poolside serv. Supervised child's activities (mid-June-Labor Day). Complimentary coffee in rms. Restaurant 6:30 am-11 pm. Bar 11-1:30 am; entertainment exc Sun. Ck-out noon. Meeting rms. Business center. In-rm modem link. Concierge. Gift shop. Free airport transportation. Lighted tennis. Golf privileges. Bicycle rentals. Exercise equipt. Minibars; bathrm phone in suites; microwaves avail. Balconies. All rms with ocean view. Luxury level. Cr cds: A, C, D, DS, JCB, MC, V.

D SC

Restaurants

✓★ **EL TORITO.** *16060 Beach Blvd (92647). 714/842-2541.* Hrs: 11 am-10 pm; Fri, Sat to 1 am; Sun 9 am-11 pm; Sun brunch to 2 pm. Closed Thanksgiving. Mexican menu. Bar. A la carte entrees: lunch $5.29-$8.99, dinner $7.49-$12.49. Sun brunch $9.99. Specializes in chimichangas, fajitas. Own sauces. Covered patio dining. Mexican decor. Cr cds: A, C, D, DS, MC, V.

D

★★★ **TROQUET.** *16060 Beach Blvd. 714/708-6865.* French cusine. Specialties: Foie Gras-apetizer, John Dory-fish, Angus strip steak, petit filet, chocolate souffle. Resv pref. Valet. Outdoor dining. Cr cds: C.

Idyllwild (J-5)

(See also Palm Desert, Palm Springs)

Pop 2,853 **Elev** 5,500 ft **Area Code** 909 **Zip** 92549
E-mail chamber@idyllwild.org **Web** www.idyllwild.org

Information Chamber of Commerce, Box 304; 909/659-3259 or 888/659-3259

Idyllwild, located in the San Jacinto Mountains amidst pine and cedar forests with towering mountains providing the backdrop, is a small alpine village at the gateway to thousands of acres of national forest, state and county parks. This popular resort and vacation area provides fishing in backcountry streams and lakes, hiking, rock climbing and riding. A Ranger District office of the San Bernardino National Forest (see SAN BERNARDINO) is located here.

What to See and Do

Mt San Jacinto State Park. On 3,682 acres. Nature and hiking trails. Picnicking. Camping (res recommended in summer). Interpretive programs. Standard fees. On CA 243. Phone 909/659-2607.

Riverside County parks. Phone 800/234-PARK.

Hurkey Creek. Camping (fee). Picnicking (fee), play area; hiking. Pets on leash. 6 mi SE via CA 243, 74, near Lake Hemet. Phone 909/659-2050.

Idyllwild. Camping (fee); res phone 909/659-2656. Picnicking (fee), play area; hiking. Pets on leash. Visitor center with museum. 1 mi W at end of County Park Rd. Phone 909/659-3850.

Motels

★★ **QUIET CREEK INN.** *26345 Delano Dr (92549). 909/659-6110; FAX 909/659-4287; res: 800/450-6110.* E-mail qci@pe.net; web quietcreekinn.com. 12 units, 5 suites, 5 studio rms, 2 cabins. No rm phones. Suites $88; studio rms $75, cabins $125-$150. TV, VCR avail. Complimentary coffee. Restaurant nearby. Ck-out 11 am. Meeting rms. Business servs avail. Game rm. Lawn games. Refrigerators, fireplaces; microwaves avail. Private patios, balconies. Picnic tables, grills. Cr cds: A, C, JCB, MC, V.

D

✓★ **WOODLAND PARK MANOR.** *55350 S Circle Dr (92549). 909/659-2657; FAX 909/659-2657; res: 877/659-2657.* Web www.idyl.com. 11 cottages, 6 with kit. No A/C. S, D $75; kit. units $95-$150; wkday rates. TV; VCR (free movies). Heated pool. Playground. Complimentary coffee in rms. Restaurant nearby. Ck-out 11 am. Lawn games. Fireplaces; microwaves avail. Picnic tables, grill. Sun decks. Scenic, mountainous area. Cr cds: C, MC, V.

Inns

★★ **FERN VALLEY INN.** *25240 Fern Valley Rd (92549). 909/659-2205; FAX 909/659-2630.* E-mail fernvalleyinn@idyllwild.com; web www.idyl.com. 11 cottage rms, 5 with kit. No A/C. S, D, studio rm $65-$105; each addl $10; kit. units $85-$105; wkday rates. TV; cable. Pool. Complimentary coffee in rms. Restaurant nearby. Ck-out 11 am, ck-in 2 pm. Refrigerators, fireplaces; microwaves avail. Private patios. Rms furnished with antiques, brass beds, handmade quilts. Totally nonsmoking. Cr cds: A, C, DS, MC, V.

SC

✓★★ **FIRESIDE INN.** *54540 N Circle Dr (92549). 909/659-2966; FAX 909/659-4286.* Web www.idyllwild.com. 8 rms, 4 with shower only, 2 suites, 1 cabin, 6 kit. units. 1 A/C rm. No rm phones. S, D $55-$75; each addl $10; suites $85; cabin $100; under 5 free. Pet accepted, some restrictions. TV; cable (premium), VCR. Complimentary coffee in rms. Restaurant nearby. Ck-out 11 am, ck-in 2 pm. Refrigerators; microwaves avail. Picnic tables. In wooded area near village center. Cr cds: A, C, D, DS, MC, V.

SC

★★ **PINE COVE INN.** *23481 Highway 243 (92549), 3 mi N on CA 243. 909/659-5033; FAX 909/659-5034; res: 888/659-5033.* Web www.idyllmtn.com.idyllwild. 10 rms, 3 with shower only, 2 story. No A/C. No rm phones. S, D $70-$100; each addl $10; under 12 free; wkly rates; wkends, hols (2-3-day min). TV and VCR in sitting rm. Complimentary full bkfst. Ck-out noon, ck-in 1 pm. Business servs avail. Refrigerators, microwaves. Picnic tables. Cr cds: A, C, DS, MC, V.

★★★ **STRAWBERRY CREEK INN.** *26370 Hwy 243 (92549). 909/659-3202; FAX 909/659-4707; res: 800/262-8969.* Web www.idyl.com. 9 rms, 5 in main house, 1 kit. cottage. Some rm phones. S, D $89-$109; kit. cottages for 2, $150; each addl (in cottage) $10-$20; wkends (2-day min); wkday rates. TV in some rms; VCR. Complimentary full bkfst; afternoon refreshments. Restaurant nearby. Ck-out 11 am, ck-in 2-6 pm. Business servs avail. Large rambling home nestled in the mountains, surrounded by pine and oak trees; Strawberry Creek is at edge of property. Totally nonsmoking. Cr cds: C, DS, MC, V.

D SC

Restaurants

✓★★ **GASTROGNOME.** *54381 Ridgeview (92549), adj to bank. 909/659-5055.* Web www.gastrognome.com. Hrs: 11:30 am-2:30 pm, 5-9 pm; Fri, Sat to 10 pm; Sun 4-9 pm; Sun brunch 11 am-4 pm. Res accepted. Bar. A la carte entrees: lunch $6.95-$9.95, dinner $10.95-$33.95. Sun brunch $14.95. Specializes in seafood, lamb, pastas. Outdoor dining. Cabin setting, fireplace, stained glass. Cr cds: C, D, DS, MC, V.

★★ **RIVER ROCK CAFE.** *26290 CA 243 (92549). 909/659-5047.* E-mail jt3026@pe.net.com; web www.pe.net.com. Hrs: 5-9 pm. Closed Mon-Wed; Dec 25; also Dec 1-15. Res accepted. Eclectic menu. Wine, beer. Semi-a la carte: $10.95-$25.95. Child's meals. Specialties: beef Wellington, New Orleans jambalaya, scampi linguini. Chef-owned. Cr cds: C, DS, MC, V.

D

Indio (J-5)

(See also Desert Hot Springs, Idyllwild, Palm Desert, Palm Springs)

Founded 1876 **Pop** 36,793 **Elev** 14 ft below sea level **Area Code** 760 **E-mail** indiochmbr@aol.com **Web** www.indiochamber.org

Information Chamber of Commerce, 82-503 Hwy 111, PO Box TTT, 92202; 760/347-0676 or 800/44-INDIO

Founded as a railroad construction camp, the town took its name from the large number of Native Americans nearby. Few settlers came until the All-American Canal and its 500 miles of pipeline turned the Coachella Valley into an area so fertile that it now produces 59 types of crops, including 95 percent of all American dates. The groves in the valley are the thickest in the Western Hemisphere. Today, Indio is a marketing and transportation hub for this agricultural outpouring. It is also known for its variety of festivals (see ANNUAL EVENTS).

What to See and Do

All-American Canal. Brings water 125 mi from Colorado River. N, E & W of the city.

Fantasy Springs Casino. Gaming and entertainment center offers off-track betting, video gaming machines, 1,200-seat bingo rm and more than 35 card tables. Also entertainment shows and dining. (Daily, open 24 hrs) 84-245 Indio Springs Dr. Phone 760/342-5000. Shows ¢¢¢¢

General George S. Patton Memorial Museum. Once the desert training headquarters on approx 18,000 square mi in the California, Arizona and Nevada deserts. Gen. Patton selected this site to prepare his soldiers for combat in North Africa. Patton memorabilia, artifacts; desert survival displays; natural science exhibits. (Daily; closed Thanksgiving, Dec 25) 30 mi E on US 60, I-10, at Chiriaco Summit. Phone 760/227-3483. ¢¢

Joshua Tree National Park (see). 25 mi E on I-10.

Salton Sea State Recreation Area (see). 24 mi S via CA 111 to nearest shoreline.

Annual Events

Indio Desert Circuit Horse Show. The largest hunter/jumper horse show west of the Mississippi River. Phone 800/44-INDIO. 6 wks Jan-Mar.

Riverside County Fair and National Date Festival. County Fairgrounds on CA 111 between Oasis & Arabia Sts. Fair and pageant done in Arabian Nights style. For schedule phone 760/863-8247. Mid-late Feb.

Indio International Tamale Festival. Celebration of traditional Latin American fare. Tamales prepared in various ways; traditional dance, music, entertainment. Carnival, petting zoo, arts & crafts, holiday parade. Phone 760/347-0676 or 800/44-INDIO. 1st wkend Dec.

Motels

★★ **BEST WESTERN DATE TREE HOTEL.** *81909 Indio Blvd (92714). 760/347-3421; FAX 760/347-3421; res: 800/292-5599.* Web www.bestwestern.com/thisco/bw/05215_b.html. 121 rms, 2 story. Jan-Apr: S, D $59-$98; each addl $6; suites, kit. units $79-$165; under 18 free; wkly rates; higher rates special events; lower rates rest of yr. Crib $10. Pet accepted, some restrictions. TV; cable. Heated pool; whirlpool. Playground. Complimentary continental bkfst. Restaurant adj open 24 hrs. Ck-out noon. Coin Indry. Business servs avail. In-rm modem link. Exercise equipt. Game rm. Lawn games. Refrigerators; microwaves avail. Balconies. Picnic tables, grills. Surrounded by palm trees, cactus gardens. Cr cds: A, C, D, DS, ER, JCB, MC, V.

D SC

✓★ **COMFORT INN.** *43505 Monroe St (92201). 760/347-4044; FAX 760/347-1287; res: 800/228-5150.* Web www.hotelchoice.com/cgi-bin/res/webres/sell.html. 63 rms, 2 story. Dec-May: S $59-$99; D $64-$129; under 18 free; higher rates: late Dec, Bob Hope Classic, Date Festival, Fri, Sat Dec-May; lower rates rest of yr. Crib $6. TV; cable (premium). Heated pool; whirlpool. Continental bkfst. Restaurant nearby. Ck-out 11 am. Business servs avail. Many refrigerators; microwaves avail. Cr cds: A, C, D, DS, MC, V.

SC

Inverness (E-2)

(See also Bodega Bay, San Rafael)

Pop 1,422 **Elev** 20 ft **Area Code** 415 **Zip** 94937

What to See and Do

Point Reyes National Seashore. More than 70,000 acres on Point Reyes peninsula. Shipwrecks and explorers, including Sir Francis Drake, who is believed to have landed here, brighten the history of this area; traders, whalers, fur hunters and ranchers followed. The weather is changeable—in winter, be prepared for rain in the inland areas; in summer, fog and brisk winds on the beaches. The area is especially beautiful during the spring flower season (Feb-June). Access is possible to most beaches; wading at Drakes Beach; surf fishing. There are more than 150 mi of trails to upland country. Picnic areas are scattered throughout the park. Four hike-in campgrounds with limited facilities (by res only, fee); no pets exc at some Point Reyes beaches. Visitor center at Drakes Beach (Sat, Sun & hols); interpretive programs and information at Bear Valley HQ (daily). For tours of the Point Reyes Lighthouse, phone 415/669-1534. Visitor area (Thurs-Mon). Park (daily). Guided tours (wkends). HQ ½ mi W of Olema on Bear Valley Rd. Contact Point Reyes National Seashore, Point Reyes 94956; 415/663-1092. **Free**

Samuel P. Taylor State Park. On 2,800 acres of wooded countryside with many groves of coastal redwoods. Historic paper mill site. Hiking and bridle trails. Picnicking. Camping (Mar-Oct, by res only; rest of yr, first come, first served). Standard fees. 2 mi S on CA 1 to Olema, then 6 mi E on Sir Francis Drake Blvd. Phone 415/488-9897. Per vehicle day use **¢¢**

Tomales Bay State Park. Virgin groves of Bishop pine and more than 300 species of plants grow on 1,018 acres. Swimming, sand beach; fishing. Hiking. Picnicking. Standard fees. 3 mi NW on Sir Francis Drake Blvd, 2 mi N on Pierce Point Rd. Phone 415/669-1140. Per vehicle day use **¢¢**

Inns

★★ **BLACKTHORNE.** *266 Vallejo Ave (94956), ¼ mi W off Sir Francis Drake Blvd. 415/663-8621; FAX 415/663-8635.* E-mail susan@blackthorneinn.com; web www.blackthorneinn.com. 4 rms, 4 story. S, D $175-$225. Complimentary buffet bkfst; afternoon refreshments. Ck-out 11 am, ck-in 4-7 pm. Business servs avail. Whirlpool. Balconies. Rustic structure resembles tree house; decks on four levels; wooded canyon setting. Totally nonsmoking. Cr cds: C, MC, V.

★★★ **INVERNESS LODGE.** *30 Callendar Way (94937). 415/669-1034; FAX 415/669-1598; res: 800/585-6343.* 14 rms, 4 with shower only, 2 story, 4 kit. cabins. No A/C. Rm phone in 3 cottages. S, D $135-$365; under 12 free; wkly rates; 2-day min stay wkends; lower rates winter wkdays. Crib free. Pet accepted, some restrictions; $50. TV; cable, VCR. Restaurant (see MANKA'S INVERNESS LODGE). Ck-out 11 am, ck-in 4 pm. Business servs avail. In-rm modem link. Hiking. Some refrigerators, some balconies, some fireplaces; microwaves avail. Turn-of-the-century hunting lodge & cabins. Totally nonsmoking. Cr cds: C, MC, V.

★★ **OLEMA INN.** *10000 Sir Francis Drake Blvd (94950), 5 mi S on CA 1. 415/663-9559; FAX 415/663-8783.* 6 rms, 2 with shower only, 2 story. No A/C. No rm phones. S, D $105-$115; lower rates wkdays. Complimentary continental bkfst. Restaurant (see OLEMA INN). Bar; entertainment Sun, Fri. Ck-out 11:30 am, ck-in after 2 pm. Country inn built in 1876. Totally nonsmoking. Cr cds: C, MC, V.

★★ **POINT REYES SEASHORE LODGE.** *10021 Hwy 1 (94950), 4 mi E on CA 1. 415/663-9000; FAX 415/663-9030; res: 800/404-5634.* E-mail prsl@worldnet.att.net; web www.placetostay.com. 21 rms, 7 with shower only, 3 suites. No A/C. Mar-Nov: S, D $105-$195; each addl over 12 yrs $15; under 13, $5; suites $175-$195; cottage $195-$250. TV in sitting rm; cable, VCR avail (free movies). Complimentary continental bkfst. Restaurant adj 11:30 am-9 pm. Ck-out noon, ck-in 3-6 pm. Business servs avail. Concierge serv. Rec rm. Many in-rm whirlpools, fireplaces. Some refrigerators, wet bars. Some balconies. Rustic; resembles turn-of-the-century lodge. Cr cds: A, C, DS, MC, V.

D SC

★★★ **SANDY COVE INN.** *12990 Sir Francis Drake Blvd (94937). 415/669-2683; FAX 415/669-7511; res: 800/759-2683.* E-mail innkeeper@sandycove.com; web www.sandycove.com. 3 rms, 2 with shower only, 1-2 story. No A/C. S, D $125-$225; each addl $50. Complimentary full bkfst; afternoon refreshments. Restaurant nearby. Ck-out 11 am, ck-in 4-5 pm. Business servs avail. In-rm modem link. Luggage handling. Refrigerators. Balconies. Picnic tables. Swimming beach. Modern Cape Cod-style house. Totally nonsmoking. Cr cds: A, C, DS, MC, V.

SC

★★ **TEN INVERNESS WAY.** *10 Inverness Way (94937). 415/669-1648; FAX 415/669-7403.* E-mail inn@teninvernessway.com; web www.teninvernessway.com. 5 rms, 3 story. No rm phones. S, D $145-$155; each addl $15; suite $180. Complimentary full bkfst; afternoon refreshments. Ck-out 11 am, ck-in 3-7 pm. Whirlpool. Refrigerator avail. Library. Antiques, handmade quilts. Built 1904. Totally nonsmoking. Cr cds: C, MC, V.

Restaurants

★ **GRAY WHALE PUB & PIZZERIA.** *12781 Sir Francis Drake Blvd (94937), in center of town. 415/669-1244.* Hrs: 11 am-9 pm; Sat, Sun from 8:30 am; fall hrs vary. Closed Thanksgiving, Dec 25. No A/C. Beer, wine. A la carte entrees: lunch, dinner $5.35-$19.30. Specializes in specialty pizzas, pasta, salads. Outdoor dining overlooking Tomales Bay. Small cafe atmosphere. Totally nonsmoking. Cr cds: C, MC, V.

D

★★ **MANKA'S INVERNESS LODGE.** *(See Manka's Inverness Lodge) 415/669-1034.* Hrs: 5:30-8:30 pm; Thurs, Fri 6-9 pm. Closed Tues, Wed. Res accepted. Wine, beer. Semi-a la carte: dinner $25-$35. Child's meals. Specializes in fish, wild game, regional foods. Built as a hunting lodge (1917). Totally nonsmoking. Cr cds: C, MC, V.

★★ **OLEMA INN.** *(See Olema Inn) 415/663-9559.* Hrs: 11:30 am-3 pm, 5-9 pm; Sun brunch 11 am-3 pm. Res accepted. No A/C. Wine, beer. Semi-a la carte: lunch $6.50-$13.50, dinner $14-$19.50. Specialties: rack of lamb, bouillabaisse. Classical guitarist Sun brunch, Fri. Outdoor dining on patio. Overlooks garden. Totally nonsmoking. Cr cds: C, MC, V.

D

✓★ **STATION HOUSE CAFE.** *11180 Main St (94956), approx 5 mi E via CA 1. 415/663-1515.* Hrs: 8 am-9 pm; Fri, Sat to 10 pm. Closed Thanksgiving, Dec 25. Res accepted. Bar; Fri, Sat to 11 pm. A la carte entrees: bkfst $4-$7.50, lunch $6-$9. Semi-a la carte: dinner $9-$18.50. Specializes in oysters, beef, chicken. Entertainment Fri-Sun, hols. Garden dining. Cr cds: C, DS, MC, V.

D ♥

Inyo National Forest (E-4 - F-4)

(See also Bishop)

(Sections E and W of Bishop, via US 395)

In this 2,000,000-acre area are 7 wilderness areas: John Muir, Golden Trout, Ansel Adams, Boundary Peak, South Sierra, Inyo Mountains and Hoover, with hundreds of lakes and streams. Impressive peaks include Mt Whitney (14,496 ft) and the famous Minarets, a series of jagged, uniquely weathered peaks in the Sierra Nevada. Devils Postpile National Monument (see) is also within the boundaries of the forest. The Ancient Bristlecone Pine Forest (4,600 years old), 600-million-year-old fossils, views of one of the world's great fault scarps (the eastern Sierra Nevada) and a unique high-elevation alpine desert (10,000-14,000 ft) are all east of US 395 in the White Mts. Palisade Glacier (the southernmost glacier in the US) is west of US 395 (west of the town of Big Pine), on the boundary of John Muir Wilderness and Kings Canyon National Park. There are 83 campgrounds; many of them are accessible to the disabled (inquire for details).

The Mammoth Lakes Area (see MAMMOTH LAKES) includes Mammoth Lakes Basin, Inyo Craters, Earthquake Fault, Hot Creek and many historic and archaeological features. Ranger naturalists conduct guided tours during the summer and offer ski tours during the winter; evening programs take place in the visitor center all year.

Deer, bear, tule elk, bighorn sheep, rainbow, brown and golden trout and a variety of birds abound in the forest. Swimming, fishing, hunting, boating, riding, picnicking, hiking, camping and pack trips are available. Winter sports include nordic skiing, snow play areas, snowmobiling and downhill skiing on Mammoth Mountain (see MAMMOTH LAKES) and June Mountain (see JUNE LAKE). For further information contact the White Mountain Ranger Station, 798 N Main St, Bishop 93514; 760/873-2500.

Irvine (J-4)

(See also Costa Mesa, Laguna Beach, Newport Beach, Santa Ana)

Pop 110,330 **Elev** 195 ft **Area Code** 949 **E-mail** icc@irvinechamber.com **Web** www.irvinechamber.com

Information Chamber of Commerce, 17755 Sky Park East, #101, 92614-6400; 949/660-9112

The land on which the community of Irvine lies was once the property of the Irvine Ranch. In the heart of Orange County, Irvine is a totally planned community.

What to See and Do

University of California, Irvine (1965). (17,000 students) Undergraduate, graduate and medical schools on 1,489-acre campus. Taped and guided tours of campus (daily). 2 mi W of I-405, closest off-ramp Jamboree. Phone 949/824-5011. **Free**

Motor Hotel

✓★★★ **ATRIUM HOTEL AT ORANGE COUNTY AIRPORT.** *18700 Macarthur Blvd (92612), ¼ mi S of I-405 MacArthur Blvd exit, opp Orange County Airport. 949/833-2770; FAX 949/757-1228; res: 800/854-3012.* E-mail info@atrium.com; web www.atriumhotel.com. 214 units, 3 story. S, D $138-$169; each addl $10; suites $179; under 18 free. Crib free. TV; cable. Heated pool; poolside serv. Complimentary coffee in rms. Restaurant 6 am-midnight. Rm serv. Bar 3:30 pm-2 am; entertainment. Ck-out 11:30 am. Coin Indry. Meeting rms. Business servs avail. Bellhops. Valet serv. Gift shop. Barber, beauty shop. Free airport transportation. Exercise equipt. Wet bar, refrigerator in suites; microwaves avail. Patios, balconies. Cr cds: A, C, D, DS, JCB, MC, V.

D SC

Hotels

★★ **CROWNE PLAZA.** *17941 Von Karman Ave (92614), I-405 MacArthur Blvd exit, near Orange County Airport. 949/863-1999; FAX 949/474-7236; res: 800/465-4329.* 335 rms, 14 story. S, D $179-$199; each addl $10; suites $300; family rates; lower rates wkends. Crib free. TV; cable (premium). Indoor pool; whirlpool, poolside serv. Coffee in rms. Restaurant 6 am-10 pm. Rm serv. Bar 11:30 am-midnight. Ck-out noon. Coin Indry. Convention facilities. Business center. Gift shop. Free airport transportation. Exercise equipt; sauna. Health club privileges. Refrigerators avail. Sun deck. Luxury level. Cr cds: A, C, D, DS, JCB, MC, V.

D SC

★★★ **EMBASSY SUITES ORANGE COUNTY AIRPORT.** *2120 Main St (92614), 1 blk NE of I-405 MacArthur Blvd exit. 714/553-8332; FAX 714/261-5301; res: 800/362-2779.* 293 suites, 10 story. S, D $115-$250; each addl $10. Crib free. TV; cable (premium). Indoor pool; whirlpool. Complimentary full bkfst. Coffee in rms. Restaurant 11 am-11 pm. Rm serv. Bar 11 am-11 pm. Ck-out 1 pm. Meeting rms. Business servs avail. Gift shop. Free airport transportation. Game rm. Exercise equipt; sauna. Health club privileges. Refrigerators; microwaves avail. Sun deck. 10 story triangular atrium. Cr cds: A, C, D, DS, JCB, MC, V.

D SC

★★★ **HYATT REGENCY.** *17900 Jamboree Blvd (95642), off I-405 Jamboree Rd exit, near Orange County Airport. 949/975-1234; FAX 949/852-1574; res: 800/233-1234.* Web www.hyatt.com. 536 units, 14 story. S, D $104-$198; each addl $25; suites $250-$3,000; under 18 free. Crib free. TV; cable (premium), VCR avail. Heated pool; whirlpool, poolside serv. Restaurants 6 am-11 pm. Bars 11-1 am. Ck-out noon. Convention facilities. Business center. Concierge. Gift shop. Free airport transportation. Lighted tennis, pro. Golf privileges. Exercise equipt; sauna. Massage. Health club privileges. Refrigerators avail. Some private patios, balconies. Luxury level. Cr cds: A, C, D, DS, ER, JCB, MC, V.

D SC

★★★ **MARRIOTT HOTEL.** *18000 Von Karman Ave (92612), in Koll Business Center, near Orange County Airport. 949/553-0100; FAX 949/261-7059; res: 800/228-9290.* 485 rms, 17 story. S, D $119-$199; suites $259-$789. Crib free. Pet accepted, some restrictions. Parking $5, valet $8. TV; cable (premium). Indoor/outdoor heated pool; whirlpool, poolside serv. Coffee in rms. Restaurants 6 am-midnight. Rm serv 6-1 am. Bars 11-2 am; Mon-Fri entertainment. Ck-out noon. Coin Indry. Convention facilities. Business center. Concierge. Barber, beauty shop. Free airport transportation. Lighted tennis, pro. Exercise equipt. Health club privileges. Massage. Game rm. Refrigerators avail. Some balconies. Luxury level. Cr cds: A, C, D, DS, ER, JCB, MC, V.

D SC

Restaurants

★★★ **CHANTECLAIR.** *18912 Macarthur Blvd (92612), ½ mi S of I-405, opp Orange County Airport. 949/752-8001.* Hrs: 11:30 am-2:30 pm, 6-10 pm; Sat from 5:30 pm; Sun 10 am-2 pm, 5-9 pm. Res accepted. Country French cuisine. Bar. Wine cellar. A la carte entrees: lunch $6.95-$15.95, dinner $21.95-$31.95. Sun brunch $21.95-$24.95. Specialties: herb-crusted rack of lamb with sweet mustard, sauteed imported Dover sole. Own desserts. Pianist. Free valet parking. Outdoor dining. Country French decor. 8 theme dining areas. Fireplaces; atrium; garden. Cr cds: A, C, D, DS, JCB, MC, V.

D

★★ **CHICAGO JOE'S.** *1818 N Main St (92614), I-405 exit MacArthur Blvd, N 1 blk. 949/261-5637.* Hrs: 11 am-midnight; Sun from 4:30 pm; early-bird dinner 4:30-6:30 pm. Closed some major hols. Res accepted. Bar. Semi-a la carte: lunch $7.95-$12.95, dinner $9.95-$25.95. Specialties: mesquite-grilled rack of lamb, Alberta beef. Own baking. Oyster bar. Turn-of-the-century Chicago decor. Totally nonsmoking. Cr cds: A, C, D, DS, MC, V.

D

★★ **MCCORMICK & SCHMICK'S SEAFOOD.** *2000 Main St (92614), 1 blk NE of I-405 MacArthur Blvd exit. 949/756-0505.* Web www.mccormickandschmicks.com. Hrs: 11 am-11 pm; Sat from 5 pm; Sun 5-10 pm. Res accepted. Bar. Semi-a la carte: lunch $4.90-$9.95, dinner $4.90-$21.95. Specializes in fresh seafood, salads, prime beef. Own desserts. Outdoor dining. Beveled, stained glass windows; wildlife artwork. Microbrewery. Cr cds: A, C, D, DS, JCB, MC, V.

D

Jackson (D-3)

(See also Lodi, Sacramento)

Pop 3,545 **Elev** 1,235 ft **Area Code** 209 **Zip** 95642

A Ranger District office of the El Dorado National Forest (see PLACERVILLE) is located in Jackson.

What to See and Do

Amador County Museum. Exhibits pertaining to gold country displayed in 1859 house; tours of Kennedy Mine model exhibit (fee). (Wed-Sun; closed major hols) 225 Church St. Phone 209/223-6386. **Free**

Indian Grinding Rock State Historic Park. Site of reconstructed Miwok village with Native American petroglyphs, bedrock mortars. Interpretive trail, picnicking; camping. Regional museum. Standard fees. 11½ mi NE via CA 88, Pine Grove-Volcano Rd. Phone 209/296-7488. Per vehicle **¢¢**

Motels

★★ **BEST WESTERN AMADOR INN.** *200 S State Hwy 49 (95642), SE of jct CA 49 & 88. 209/223-0211; FAX 209/223-4836; res: 800/543-5221.* E-mail bwamador@volcano.net. 118 rms, 2 story. S $54-$76; D $64-$86; each addl $10; kit. units $15 addl; under 16 free. Crib free. TV; cable (premium). Coffee in rms. Pool. Restaurant adj open 24 hrs. Bar 9 am-11 pm. Ck-out noon. Meeting rms. Business servs avail. In-rm modem link. Some refrigerators, fireplaces. Cr cds: A, C, D, DS, JCB, MC, V.

SC

✓★ **JACKSON LODGE.** *850 N Hwy 49 & 88 (93529). 209/223-0486; FAX 209/223-2905; res: 888/777-0380.* 36 rms, 2 story, 8 kits. S, D $48-$85; each addl $5; kit. units $79. Crib $5. Pet accepted, some restrictions; $10. TV; cable. Pool. Complimentary continental bkfst. Complimentary coffee in rms. Ck-out 11 am. Cr cds: A, C, D, DS, MC, V.

SC

Inns

★★★ **FOX ENTERPRISES INC.** *77 Main St. (95685), N on CA 49. 209/267-5711; FAX 209/267-0712; res: 800/726-4667; res: 800/987-3344.* E-mail foxes@cdepot.net; web www.foxesinn.com. 7 rms, 1-2 story. No rm phones. S, D $105-$170; wkends, hols (2-day min). Some TV; cable. Complimentary full bkfst. Ck-out 11 am, ck-in 3-6 pm. Covered parking. Former Brinn House, built during the Gold Rush (1857). Antique furnishings. Totally nonsmoking. Cr cds: C, DS, MC, V.

★★★ **GATE HOUSE INN.** *1330 Jackson Gate Rd (95642). 209/223-3500; FAX 209/223-1299; res: 800/841-1072.* E-mail info@gatehouseinn.com; web www.gatehouseinn.com. 5 air-cooled rms, 1-2 story, 1 cottage. No rm phones. S, D $100-$125; suite $145; wkly rates. Children over 12 yrs only. Pool. Complimentary full bkfst; afternoon refreshments. Restaurant nearby. Ck-out 11 am, ck-in 2:30 pm. Business servs avail. Gift shop. Some fireplaces. Victorian architecture and furnishings. Built 1903. Beautiful gardens. Totally nonsmoking. Cr cds: A, C, D, DS, MC, V.

SC

★★ **GREY GABLES BED & BREAKFAST INN.** *161 Hanford (95685), 4 mi N on CA 49. 209/267-1039; FAX 209/267-0998; res: 800/473-9422.* E-mail reservations@greygables.com; web www.greygables.com. 8 rms, 3 story. S, D $90-$145; each addl $20; wkends, hols (2-day min). Complimentary full bkfst; afternoon refreshments. Restaurant adj 5:30-9:30 pm. Ck-out 11 am, ck-in 3 pm. Business servs avail. Fireplaces. Picnic tables, grills. Built in 1897; renovated in 1994. Totally nonsmoking. Cr cds: A, C, DS, MC, V.

D

★★ **HANFORD HOUSE.** *61 Hanford St (95685), N on CA 49. 209/267-0747; FAX 209/267-1825; res: 800/871-5839.* E-mail bobkat@hanfordhouse.com; web www.hanfordhouse.com. 9 rms, 2 story. S, D $89-$149. Complimentary bkfst; afternoon refreshments. Restaurant nearby. Ck-out 11 am, ck-in 2:30 pm. In-rm modem link. Rooftop deck; shaded patio. Totally nonsmoking. Cr cds: C, DS, MC, V.

SC

★★ **IMPERIAL HOTEL.** *14202 Ca 49 (95601), 6 mi N on CA 49. 209/267-9172; FAX 209/267-9249; res: 800/242-5594.* E-mail host@imperialamador.com; web www.imperialamador.com. 6 rms, 2 story. Mar-Dec: S $85-$100; D $90-$105; each addl $15; wkends, hols 2-day min; lower rates rest of yr. Children over 5 yrs only. Complimentary full bkfst; refreshments. Restaurant 5-9 pm. Ck-out noon, ck-in 3 pm. In-rm modem link. Some balconies. Built in 1879 (goldrush era). Cr cds: A, C, DS, MC, V.

✓★★ **SUTTER CREEK INN.** *75 Main St (95685), 4 mi N on CA 49. 209/267-5606; FAX 209/267-9287.* Web www.suttercreekinn.com. 18 rms, 7 with shower only, 1-2 story, 2 suites. No rm phones. S, D $65-$140; each addl $25, suites $155-$175. TV in some rms; cable. Complimentary full bkfst; afternoon refreshments. Ck-out 11 am, ck-in 2:30 pm. Business servs avail. Some fireplaces. 1859 house; many antiques. Landscaped grounds; gardens. Totally nonsmoking. Cr cds: C, MC, V.

★★★ **WEDGEWOOD INN.** *11941 Narcissus Rd (95642). 209/296-4300; FAX 209/296-4301.* E-mail vic@wedgewoodinn.com; web www.wedgewoodinn.com. 6 rms, 1-2 story. Some rm phones. S $90-$155; D $100-$165. Complimentary full bkfst; afternoon refreshments. Ck-out 11 am, ck-in 3-6 pm. Whirlpool in suites. Microwaves avail. Lawn games. Some balconies. Picnic tables. Extensively furnished with antiques. Landscaped gardens; gazebo. Victorian replica building in scenic Sierra foothills. Totally nonsmoking. Cr cds: A, C, DS, MC, V.

SC

Unrated Dining Spots

CHATTER BOY CAFE. *39 Main St (95685), 4 mi N on CA 49. 209/267-5935.* E-mail mgillmgill@aol.com. Hrs: 6 am-3 pm; Sat, Sun 8 am-4 pm. Closed Thurs; also Jan 1, Thanksgiving, Dec 25. Semi-a la carte: bkfst, lunch $3.25-$6.75. Child's meals. Specializes in omelets, burgers. Own desserts. Totally nonsmoking. Cr cds: C.

ROSEBUD'S CLASSIC CAFE. *26 Main St (95642). 209/223-1035.* Hrs: 7 am-4 pm. Closed Dec 25. Res accepted. Semi-a la carte: bkfst $4-$10, lunch $5-$9. Child's meals. Specialties: omelets, Philly cheesesteak sandwich. Own pies. Street parking. Scottie dog motif. Totally nonsmoking. Cr cds: C, MC, V.

Joshua Tree National Park (J-5)

(See also Desert Hot Springs, Indio, Palm Desert)

(Entrances: 25 mi E of Indio on I-10 or S of Joshua Tree, Yucca Valley and Twentynine Palms on CA 62)

Covering more than 1,236 square miles, this park preserves a section of two deserts: the Mojave and the Colorado. Particularly notable is the variety and richness of desert vegetation. The park shelters many species of desert plants. The Joshua tree, which gives the park its name, was christened thus by the Mormons because of its upstretched "arms." A member of the Lily family, this giant yucca attains heights of more than 40 feet. The area consists of a series of block mountains, ranging in altitude from 1,000 to 5,800 feet and separated by desert flats. The summer gets very hot, and the temperature drops below freezing in the winter. Water is available only at the Black Rock Canyon Visitor Center/Campground, Cottonwood Campground, the Indian Cove Ranger Station and the Twentynine Palms Visitor Center. Pets on leash only; pets are not permitted on trails. Guided tours and campfire programs (Feb-May & Oct-Dec). Picnicking permitted in designated areas and campgrounds, but no fires may be built outside the campgrounds. For additional information contact 74485 National Park Dr, Twentynine Palms 92277; 760/367-5500. Per vehicle ¢¢¢

What to See and Do

Camping. Restricted to nine campgrounds with limited facilities; bring own firewood and water. 30-day limit, July-Sept; 14-day limit rest of yr. Cottonwood, Black Rock Canyon and Indian Cove Campgrounds (fee); other campgrounds free. Group camping at Cottonwood, Indian Cove and Sheeps Pass. Campgrounds are operated on a first come, first served basis except for Indian Cove and Black Rock Canyon; for res phone 800/365-2267.

Hidden Valley Nature Trail. One-mi loop; access from picnic area across Hidden Valley Campground. Valley enclosed by wall of rocks.

Keys View (5,185 ft). Sweeping view of Coachella valley, desert and mountain. A paved path leads off the main road.

Lost Palms Canyon. Eight-mi round-trip hike. Reached by 4-mi trail from Cottonwood Spring. Shelters largest group of palms (120) in the park. Day use only.

Oasis Visitor Center. Exhibits; self-guided nature trail through the Oasis of Mara, discovered by a government survey party in 1855. (Daily) Park HQ, just N of park at Twentynine Palms entrance.

Stands of Joshua trees. In Queen and Lost Horse valleys.

Motels

✓★★ **BEST WESTERN GARDEN INN & SUITES.** *71487 Twentynine Palms Hwy (92277), E on CA 62. 760/367-9141; FAX 760/367-2584; res: 800/528-1234.* 84 rms, 2 story, 12 kit. suites. S, D $65; each addl $10; kit. suites $85-$110; under 12 free. Crib free. TV. Heated pool; whirlpool. Complimentary continental bkfst. Restaurant nearby. Ck-out 11 am. Business servs avail. Health club privileges. Some refrigerators; microwaves avail. Grill. Cr cds: A, C, D, DS, MC, V.

D SC

★★ **CIRCLE C LODGE.** *6340 El Rey Ave (92277), E on CA 62. 760/367-7615; FAX 760/361-0247; res: 800/545-9696.* 12 kit. units. S $70; D $85; each addl $10. TV; cable (premium), VCR. Heated pool; whirlpool. Continental bkfst. Restaurant nearby. Ck-out 11 am. Meeting rm. Business servs avail. Refrigerators, microwaves. Picnic tables, grills. Cr cds: A, C, D, DS, JCB, MC, V.

SC

✓★ **DESERT VIEW MOTEL.** *57471 Primrose Dr (92284), 1 blk E of CA 247. 760/365-9706; FAX 760/365-6021.* E-mail desertview@thegrid.net; web rentor.com/ca/yucca/hotels/desert-view.html. 14 rms. S $40; D $45.50; each addl $5; under 12 free. Crib free. TV; cable (premium). Heated pool. Complimentary continental bkfst. Restaurant nearby. Ck-out 11 am. Business servs avail. Refrigerators avail. Cr cds: A, C, D, DS, MC, V.

SC

★★ **OASIS OF EDEN INN & SUITES.** *56377 Twentynine Palms Hwy (92284), W on CA 62. 760/365-6322; FAX 760/365-9592; res: 800/606-6686.* Web www.desertgold.com/eden.html. 39 rms, 1-2 story, 20 suites, 6 kit. units. Jan-May: S $44.75-$54.75; D $64.75-$106.75; each addl $5; suites, kit. units $54.75-$95.75; family, wkly, monthly rates; lower rates rest of yr. Crib free. Pet accepted, some restrictions; $10. TV; cable (premium), VCR (movies $3). Heated pool; whirlpool. Complimentary continental bkfst. Restaurant opp 7 am-10 pm. Ck-out 11 am. Meeting rms. Business servs avail. Golf privileges. Refrigerators; microwaves avail. Theme rms with in-rm whirlpools avail. Cr cds: A, C, D, DS, MC, V.

D SC

Inn

★★ **JOSHUA TREE INN.** *61259 29 Palms Hwy (92252). 760/366-1188; FAX 760/366-3805; res: 800/366-1444.* 10 rms, shower only, 1 with A/C, 2 suites. Oct-mid-June: S $55-$85; D $85-$95; suites $125-$150; each addl $10; under 10 free; wkly, monthly rates; lower rates rest of yr. Pet accepted, some restrictions; $10. TV; cable (premium), VCR avail. Pool. Playground. Complimentary full bkfst; afternoon refreshments. Dining rm by res. Ck-out noon, ck-in 2 pm. Business servs avail. In-rm modem link. Concierge serv. Luggage handling. Airport transportation. Some refrigerators; microwaves avail. Picnic tables. Cr cds: A, C, D, DS, MC, V.

SC

June Lake (E-4)

(See also Lee Vining, Mammoth Lakes)

Pop 425 (est) **Elev** 7,600 ft **Area Code** 760 **Zip** 93529

What to See and Do

June Mountain Ski Area. 2 detachable quad, 5 double chairlifts, 1 high-speed tram; patrol, school, rentals; snowboarding; cafeteria, bar; day care center. Longest run 2½ mi; vertical drop 2,590 ft. Half-day rates. (Mid-Nov-Apr, daily) W of US 395. Phone 760/934-2224. ¢¢¢¢¢

Motel

✓★ **BOULDER LODGE MOTEL.** *2282 Hwy 158 (93529), 2 mi W of US 395 on CA 158. 760/648-7533; FAX 760/648-7330; res: 800/863-5253.* 60 rms, 2 story, 8 suites, 30 kits., 10 cabins. No A/C. S, D $52-$78; each addl $8-$10; suites $90-$250; kit. units $75-$175; cabins $50-$105; 5-bedrm house $260-$300; wkly rates; ski plans; wkday rates in winter; higher rates: July-Labor Day & hols. Crib $8. TV; cable. Complimentary coffee in rms. Indoor pool; whirlpool. Sauna. Playground. Restaurant nearby. Ck-out 11 am. Business servs avail. Tennis. Downhill/x-country ski 1 mi. Game rm. Fish cleaning & freezing facilities. Overlooking June Lake. Picnic tables, grill. Cr cds: A, C, DS, MC, V.

SC

Restaurant

★★ **SIERRA INN.** *CA 158 (93529), 2 mi W. 760/648-7774.* Hrs: 5-10 pm. Closed Nov-mid-Dec & Easter to opening day of fishing season. Res accepted. Bar to midnight. Semi-a la carte: dinner $8.95-$19.95. Dinner buffet: (Sat) $14.95. Child's meals. Specializes in steak, fresh seafood. Salad bar. View of mountains, lake. Outdoor dining. Cr cds: A, C, DS, MC, V.

SC

Kernville (G-3)

Pop 1,656 **Elev** 2,650 ft **Area Code** 760 **Zip** 93238
E-mail kernvillechamber@lightspeed.net
Information Chamber of Commerce, 11447 Kernville Rd, PO Box 397; 760/376-2629 or 800/350-7393

A Ranger District office of the Sequoia National Forest (see PORTERVILLE) is located in Kernville. Trout fishing is enjoyed in nearby Kern River.

What to See and Do

Greenhorn Mountain Park. Park has 90 campsites with barbecue pits, 115 picnic tables, camping supplies. Camping limited to 21 days, no res; pets on leash only. 12 mi W via CA 155 in Sequoia National Forest. Phone 805/861-2345. Camping **¢¢¢**

Isabella Lake. Swimming, waterskiing; fishing; boating (marinas). More than 700 improved campsites with showers, rest rms (site/night). Camp 9 & Auxiliary (primitive) camp areas (free). S of town. For information contact Sequoia National Forest, Lake Isabella Visitors Center, PO Box 3810, Lake Isabella, 93240-3810; phone 760/379-5646 or 760/376-3781.

Annual Events

Whiskey Flat Days. Gold Rush days celebration. Mid-Feb.

Kernville Rod Run. Show for pre-1949 cars. 1st full wkend Oct.

Kernville Stampede. Usually Oct.

Motels

✓★★ **KERNVILLE INN.** *11042 Kernville Rd (93238). 760/376-2206; FAX 760/376-3735.* 26 rms, 1-2 story, 8 kit. units. S $49-$59; D $59-$74; each addl $10; kit. units $64-$99; wkends, hols (2-3 day min). TV; cable (premium). Complimentary coffee in lobby. Restaurant adj 6 am-9 pm. Ck-out 11 am. Coin Indry. Downhill/x-country ski 15 mi. Pool. Picnic tables. Cr cds: A, C, DS, MC, V.

SC

★★ **WHISPERING PINES LODGE.** *13745 Sierra Way (93238). 760/376-3733; FAX 760/376-6513; res: 877/241-4100.* 17 rms, 5 kit. units. S, D $99-$159; each addl $15. TV; cable; VCR (movies). Pool. Complimentary full bkfst. Complimentary coffee in rms. Ck-out 11 am. Downhill ski 14 mi. Some fireplaces, in-rm whirlpools. Balconies. Refrigerators. Picnic tables, grills. On river. Totally nonsmoking. Cr cds: A, C, DS, MC, V.

D SC

Inn

✓★★ **KERN RIVER INN BED & BREAKFAST.** *119 Kern River Dr (93238). 760/376-6750; FAX 760/376-6643; res: 800/986-4382; res: 800/376-6750.* Web www.virtualcities.com/ons/ca/s/cas3501.htm. 6 air-cooled rms, 2 story. No rm phones. Apr-Oct: S $79-$89; D $89-$99; each addl $15; wkends (Memorial Day-Labor Day: 2-day min); lower rates rest of yr. Cable TV in common rm; VCR avail (movies). Complimentary full bkfst; afternoon refreshments. Restaurant nearby. Ck-out 11 am, ck-in 3-6 pm. Business servs avail. Luggage handling. Downhill/x-country ski 15 mi. Some in-rm whirlpools, fireplaces. Opp river. Antiques. Totally nonsmoking. Cr cds: A, C, MC, V.

D

Restaurant

★ **JOHNNY MCNALLY'S FAIRVIEW LODGE.** *Star Rte 1, Box 95 (93238), 15 mi N on Kern River. 760/376-2430.* Hrs: 5-10 pm; Sun 4-9 pm. Closed Dec-Feb. Bar 4:30-11 pm. Complete meals: dinner $7.50-$29.95. Child's meals. Specializes in steak, seafood. Western decor. Hamburger stand mid-Apr-Sept, lunch. Totally nonsmoking. Cr cds: C, MC, V.

King City (G-2)

Pop 7,634 **Elev** 330 ft **Area Code** 408 **Zip** 93930

What to See and Do

Los Padres National Forest. Contains the Santa Lucia Mts, which feature the southernmost groves of coastal redwoods and the only natural stands of bristlecone fir. The 164,575-acre Ventana Wilderness was almost completely burned in a 1977 fire, but vegetation in the fire area reestablished itself and provides an excellent opportunity to witness the changing conditions. Fishing. Hiking. Camping. W of town is the forest's northernmost section. (Daily) For further information contact the District Ranger Office, 406 S Mildred, Phone 408/385-5434; or the Forest Supervisor, 6144 Calle Real, Goleta 93117, phone 805/683-6711. (See SANTA BARBARA) Camping **¢¢–¢¢¢¢¢**

Mission San Antonio de Padua. Founded in 1771 as the third in the chain of missions. Restoration includes gristmill, waterwheel, wine vat; tannery; museum; Padres Garden. (Daily; closed major hols) 24 mi SW on County G14 in Jolon. Phone 408/385-4478. **Donation**

Annual Event

Mission San Antonio de Padua Fiesta. Special Mass and music, barbecue, dancing. 2nd Sun June.

Motels

★ **COURTESY INN.** *4 Broadway Cir (92629), off US 101 Broadway exit. 831/385-4646; FAX 831/385-6024; res: 800/350-5616.* 28 rms, 35 suites. S, D $54-$110; each addl $6; suites $59-$135; under 14 free. Crib free. Pet accepted, some restrictions; $10. TV; cable (premium), VCR (movies $2.50). Pool; whirlpool. Complimentary continental bkfst. Coffee in rms. Restaurant adj 6 am-10 pm. Ck-out noon. Coin Indry. Meeting rm. Business servs avail. In-rm modem link. Refrigerators, microwaves; whirlpool suites avail. Grill. Cr cds: A, C, D, DS, MC, V.

D SC

✓★ **KEEFER'S INN.** *615 Canal St (93930). 831/385-4843; FAX 831/385-1254.* 47 rms, 1-2 story. S $43-$53; D $48-$58; each addl $5; under 12 free. Crib $5. TV; cable (premium). Pool; whirlpool. Complimentary continental bkfst. Restaurant 7 am-9:30 pm. Ck-out 11 am. Coin Indry. Business servs avail. Refrigerators; microwaves avail. Grill. Cr cds: A, C, D, DS, MC, V.

D

Kings Canyon National Park

(see Sequoia & Kings Canyon National Parks)

Laguna Beach (J-4)

(See also Costa Mesa, Irvine, Newport Beach, San Juan Capistrano)

Pop 23,170 **Elev** 40 ft **Area Code** 714

Information Chamber of Commerce, 357 Glenneyre St, 92652; 714/494-1018

Artists have contributed to the quaint charm of this seaside town. Curio, arts and crafts and antique shops make leisurely strolling a pleasure. There is swimming and surfing at beautiful beaches.

What to See and Do

Laguna Playhouse. Theater company presents dramas, comedies, musicals, children's theater. Main stage (Sept-May, daily exc Mon; closed Jan 1, Dec 25). 606 Laguna Canyon Rd. Phone 714/494-8021 (afternoons) for schedule.

Seasonal Events

Festival of Arts & Pageant of the Masters. 650 Laguna Canyon Rd. All pageant seats reserved. Exhibits by 160 artists; *tableaux vivants;* entertainment; restaurant. Grounds: daily. For information on ticket prices and reservations, contact festival box office, phone 800/487-FEST. July-Aug.

Sawdust Festival. 935 Laguna Canyon Rd. Nearly 200 Laguna Beach artists showcase their work. Phone 714/494-3030. Daily, July-Aug.

Motels

★★ **ALISO CREEK INN.** *31106 S Coast Hwy (92677). 949/499-2271; FAX 949/499-4601; res: 800/223-3309.* 62 suites, 1-2 story. No A/C. July-Aug: S, D $145-$290; each addl $10; lower rates rest of yr. Crib $5. TV; cable (premium). Heated pool; wading pool. Restaurant 11 am-10 pm. Bar to 1 am. Ck-out noon. Coin lndry. Meeting rms. Business servs avail. 9-hole golf, pro, putting green. Some in-rm whirlpools; microwaves avail. Private patios, balconies. In secluded area of Aliso Canyon. Near beach; fishing pier. Cr cds: A, C, D, DS, MC, V.

D SC

★★ **BEST WESTERN LAGUNA BRISAS SPA HOTEL.** *1600 S Pacific Coast Hwy (92651). 949/497-7272; FAX 949/497-8306; res: 800/624-4442.* Web www.bestwestern.com. 65 rms, 4 story. June-Sept: S, D $139-$359; each addl $10; under 16 free; 2-day min: wkends, July, Aug, hols; lower rates rest of yr. Crib free. Pet accepted, some restrictions. TV; cable (premium), VCR avail. Heated pool; whirlpool. Complimentary continental bkfst. Complimentary coffee in rms. Restaurant nearby. Ck-out noon. Coin lndry. Meeting rms. Business center. Health club privileges. Massage. In-rm whirlpools, refrigerators; microwaves avail. Balconies. Ocean view sun deck. Cr cds: A, C, D, DS, ER, JCB, MC, V.

D SC

✓★★ **BEST WESTERN LAGUNA REEF INN.** *30806 S Coast Hwy (92651). 949/499-2227; FAX 949/499-5575; res: 800/528-1234; res: 800/922-9905.* 43 rms, 2 story, 7 kits. July-Sept: S, D $120-$175; each addl $10; kit. units $175; wkly rates; lower rates rest of yr. TV; cable, VCR (free movies). Heated pool; whirlpool. Sauna. Complimentary continental bkfst. Restaurant nearby. Ck-out noon. Some refrigerators; microwaves avail. Botanical garden. Cr cds: A, C, D, DS, MC, V.

SC

★★ **HOLIDAY INN EXPRESS.** *34744 Pacific Coast Hwy (92624), S on I-5 exit Pacific Coast Hwy off at Coast Highway S left, ¾ mi S on left. 949/240-0150; FAX 949/240-4862; res: 800/465-4329; res: 800/266-3343.* E-mail hiexpress@net-star.net. 30 rms, 3 story. May-Sept: S, D $149-$199; each addl $10; under 18 free; lower rates rest of yr. Crib free. TV; cable (premium). Complimentary continental bkfst. Complimentary coffee in rms. Restaurant adj noon-10 pm. Ck-out 11:30 am. Business servs avail. Free covered parking. Health club privileges. Whirlpool. Sauna. Refrigerators, wet bars; microwaves avail. Some balconies. Most rms with ocean view. Cr cds: A, C, D, DS, JCB, MC, V.

D SC

★★ **LAGUNA RIVERA HOTEL.** *825 S Coast Hwy (92651). 949/494-1196; FAX 949/494-8421; res: 800/999-2089.* 41 rms, 5 story, 20 kits. No elvtr. Some A/C. Mid-June-mid-Sept: S, D $76-$160; each addl $10; suites $94-$177; studio rms, kit. units $81-$180; wkends (2-day min); lower rates rest of yr. Crib $5. TV; cable (premium). Indoor pool; whirlpool. Complimentary continental bkfst. Restaurant nearby. Ck-out noon. Sauna. Rec rm. Some fireplaces; microwaves avail. Balconies. Sun decks, terraces. Oceanfront. Cr cds: A, C, D, DS, JCB, MC, V.

Motor Hotels

✓★★ **COURTYARD BY MARRIOTT.** *23175 Avenida De La Carlota (92653), I-5, Lake Forest Dr exit to Carlota . 949/859-5500; FAX 949/454-2158; res: 800/321-2211.* 136 rms, 5 story. S, D $85-$99; suites $114-$129. Crib free. TV; cable (premium). Heated pool; whirlpool. Complimentary coffee in rms. Restaurant 6:30-10:30 am. Bar. Ck-out 1 pm. Coin lndry. Meeting rms. Business servs avail. In-rm modem link. Exercise equipt. Valet serv. Refrigerator in suites; microwaves avail. Balconies. Cr cds: A, C, D, DS, MC, V.

D SC

★★ **HOLIDAY INN.** *25205 La Paz Rd (92653), E on I-5 La Paz Rd exit. 949/586-5000; FAX 949/581-7410; res: 800/465-4329; res: 800/282-1789.* 147 rms, 4 story. S, D $89-$109; each addl $10; under 18 free. Crib free. TV; cable. Pool; poolside serv. Coffee in rms. Restaurant 6 am-10 pm. Rm serv. Bar; entertainment. Ck-out 1 pm. Meeting rms. Business servs avail. In-rm modem link. Bellhops. Valet serv. Free airport transportation. Health club privileges. Microwaves avail. Cr cds: A, C, D, DS, ER, JCB, MC, V.

D SC

★★★ **INN AT LAGUNA BEACH.** *211 N Coast Hwy (92651). 714/497-9722; FAX 714/497-9972; res: 800/544-4479.* E-mail info@innatlagunabeach.com; web www.innatlagunabeach.com. 70 rms, 5 story. Memorial Day-Labor Day: S, D $179-$459; each addl $20; under 18 free; wkday rates; lower rates rest of yr. Crib free. TV; cable, VCR (movies). Heated pool; whirlpool. Complimentary continental bkfst. Coffee in rms. Restaurant adj 8 am-10 pm. Ck-out noon. Meeting rms. Business servs avail. In-rm modem link. Bellhops. Massage. Health club privileges. Minibars; microwaves avail. Some private balconies. On ocean; beach. Cr cds: A, C, D, DS, MC, V.

D SC

✓★ **QUALITY INN & SUITES.** *34280 Pacific Coast Hwy (92629), 5 mi S of Laguna Beach. 949/248-1000; FAX 949/661-3136; res: 800/228-5151; res: 800/232-3262.* E-mail elites97@aol.com; web www.ocsouth-online.com/qualitysuites. 86 rms, 3 story, 60 suites. May-Sept: S, D $79; each addl $5; suites $85; under 16 free; higher rates hols; lower rates rest of yr. Crib $10. TV; cable (premium). Complimentary continental bkfst. Restaurant opp open 24 hrs. Ck-out 11 am. Meeting rms. Business servs avail. In-rm modem link. Coin lndry. Exercise equipt; sauna. Pool. Some in-rm whirlpools; refrigerators, microwaves avail. Many balconies. Cr cds: A, C, D, DS, JCB, MC, V.

D SC

★ **VACATION VILLAGE HOTEL.** *647 S Coast Hwy (92651). 714/494-8566; FAX 714/494-1386; res: 800/843-6895.* 133 rms in 5 bldgs, 3-5 story, 70 kits. July-Labor Day (2-day min): S, D $88-$235; each addl $10; suites $190-$325; kit. units $95-$205; family, wkly rates Sept-Memorial Day; winter wkends (2-day min); some lower rates rest of yr. Crib free. Pet accepted, some restrictions. TV; cable. 2 heated pools; whirlpool. Complimentary coffee in rms. Restaurant 8 am-10 pm. Bar. Ck-out 11 am. Meeting rm. Bellhops. Some covered parking. Health club privileges. Game rm. Refrigerators; microwaves avail. Some balconies. Sun deck. On beach. Cr cds: A, C, D, DS, MC, V.

SC

Hotels

★★ **DOUBLETREE GUEST SUITES.** *34402 Pacific Coast Hwy (92629), 5 mi S on Coast Hwy. 949/661-1100; FAX 949/489-0628; res: 800/634-4586.* Web www.doubletreehotels.com. 196 rms, 4 story. Mid-June-mid-Aug: S, D $220-$270; under 18 free; monthly rates; lower rates rest of yr. Crib free. Garage parking $5. Pool. Complimentary coffee in rms. Restaurant 6:30 am-10 pm. Bar. Ck-out noon. Meeting rms. Business servs avail. In-rm modem link. Gift shop. Valet serv. Exercise equipt. Massage. Refrigerators, microwaves. Cr cds: A, C, D, DS, ER, JCB, MC, V.

D SC

✓★ **HOTEL LAGUNA.** *425 S Coast Hwy (92651). 949/494-1151; FAX 949/497-2163; res: 800/524-2927.* E-mail hotellaguna@msn.com; web www.menbytes.com/hotellaguna. 65 rms, 3 story. No A/C. June-Labor Day: S, D $100-$220; lower rates rest of yr. Crib $10. TV; cable (premium). Complimentary continental bkfst; afternoon refreshments.

Restaurant 7 am-10 pm. Bar 11-2 am; entertainment. Ck-out noon. Meeting rms. Business servs avail. Barber, beauty shop. Massage. On ocean; private beach. Cr cds: A, C, D, DS, MC, V.

D SC

★★★ **SURF & SAND HOTEL.** *1555 S Coast Hwy (92651). 949/497-4477; FAX 949/494-2897; res: 800/524-8621.* E-mail rvanness@jcresorts.com. 164 rms, 9 story. No A/C. Mid-June-mid-Oct: S, D $285-$365; suites $500-$1,000; lower rates rest of yr. Crib avail. Covered parking, valet. TV; cable (premium). Heated pool; poolside serv. Supervised child's activities (July-Aug); ages 3-12. Restaurant 7 am-10 pm; Fri, Sat to 11 pm. Bar 11 am-midnight; Fri, Sat to 1 am. Ck-out noon. Meeting rms. Business servs avail. In-rm modem link. Concierge. Shopping arcade. Beauty shop. Massage. Health club privileges. Refrigerators, minibars; some in-rm whirlpools, fireplaces. Private patios; balcony rms overlook ocean. On beach. Cr cds: A, C, D, DS, MC, V.

D

Resorts

★★★ **MARRIOTT'S LAGUNA CLIFFS RESORT.** *25135 Park Lantern (92629), 5 mi S on Coast Hwy. 949/661-5000; FAX 949/661-5358; res: 800/545-7483.* 346 rms, 3 & 4 story. S, D $199-$269; suites $300-$1,200; under 16 free; seasonal rates avail. Crib free. TV; cable (premium), VCR avail. 2 heated pools; whirlpool, poolside serv. Coffee in rms. Restaurant 6 am-11 pm. Picnics. Rm serv. Bar 11-2 am; entertainment. Ck-out noon, ck-in 3 pm. Grocery, package store ¼ mi. Coin lndry ½ mi. Convention facilities. Business center. In-rm modem link. Bellhops. Valet serv. Gift shop. Lighted tennis, pro. Golf privileges, greens fee $80-$125, pro, putting green, driving range. Bicycle rentals. Exercise equipt; sauna. Health club privileges. Massage. Minibars; some wet bars. Some balconies. Opp beach. Park. Located on the cliffs above the bay, with 42 acres of lawn and parkland. Cr cds: A, C, D, DS, ER, JCB, MC, V.

D SC

★★★★ **RITZ-CARLTON HOTEL.** *33533 Ritz Carlton Dr (92629), 5 mi SW of I-5, Crown Valley Pkwy exit, 1 mi S on Pacific Coast Hwy . 949/240-2000; FAX 949/240-1061; res: 800/241-3333.* Set on a bluff overlooking a 2-mile Pacific Ocean beach, this luxury resort features sumptuous Mediterranean-style architecture, an imposing marble-columned entry, and colorful gardens. Traditionally furnished guest rooms boast double marble Italian vanities. 393 rms, 4 story. May-Sept: S, D $395-$595; suites $480-$3,700; lower rates rest of yr. Crib free. Valet parking $20. TV; cable (premium), VCR avail. 2 pools; poolside serv. Supervised child's activities; ages 6-12. Restaurants 6:30 am-midnight (also see THE DINING ROOM). Afternoon tea in library 2:30-5 pm. Rm serv 24 hrs. Bars; entertainment. Ck-out noon, ck-in 4 pm. Convention facilities. Business center. In-rm modem link. Bellhops. Valet serv. Concierge. Shopping arcade. Barber, beauty shop. International currency exchange. Airport transportation; shuttle serv to beach. Tennis, pro. 18-hole golf privileges, pro, putting green. Swimming beach. Lawn games. 2-mi bicycle path. Exercise rm; sauna, steam rm. Massage. Bathrm phones, refrigerators, minibars; microwaves avail; fireplace in some suites. Balconies. Luxury level. Cr cds: A, C, D, DS, JCB, MC, V.

D

Inns

★★★ **BLUE LANTERN INN.** *34343 St Of The Blue Lantern (92629), S on Coast Hwy, Blue Lantern exit. 949/661-1304; FAX 949/496-1483; res: 800/950-1236.* Web www.toursisters.com. 29 units, 3 story, 3 suites. S, D $140-$210; each addl $15; suites $275-$500; under 2 free; package plans. Crib free. TV; cable (premium). Complimentary full bkfst; afternoon refreshments. Restaurants nearby. Ck-out noon, ck-in 3 pm. Business servs avail. Luggage handling. Exercise equipt. In-rm whirlpools, refrigerators, fireplaces. Many rms have private sun decks. Located on a bluff overlooking yacht harbor; some rms have view of the coast. Park adj. Totally nonsmoking. Cr cds: A, C, D, MC, V.

D

★ **CASA LAGUNA INN.** *2510 S Coast Hwy (92651). 714/494-2996; FAX 714/494-5009; res: 800/233-0449.* 20 rms, 3 story, 6 kit. suites. S, D $105-$120; suites $175-$225; wkly rates. Crib $5. Pet accepted. TV; cable, VCR avail. Heated pool. Complimentary continental bkfst; afternoon refreshments. Ck-out 11 am, ck-in 2 pm. Some refrigerators; microwaves avail. Balconies. Elaborate grounds; garden. Spanish architecture, individually decorated rms. Panoramic ocean views. Cr cds: A, C, DS, MC, V.

SC

★★ **EILERS INN.** *741 S Coast Hwy (92651). 949/494-3004; FAX 949/497-2215.* 12 rms, 2 story. No A/C. No rm phones. May-Sept: S, D $120-$145; suites $195; lower rates rest of yr. Complimentary continental bkfst; afternoon refreshments. Restaurant adj 7 am-11:30 pm. Ck-out noon, ck-in 2 pm. Luggage handling. Business servs avail. Tennis privileges. Health club privileges. Totally nonsmoking. Cr cds: A, C, DS, MC, V.

★ **LAGUNA HOUSE.** *539 Catalina St (92651). 949/497-9061; res: 800/248-7348.* 8 kit. suites, 2 with shower only, 3 story. No A/C. Late May-mid-Sept: kit. suites $125-$185; under 18 free; wkly, wkend, hol rates; wkends (2-day min); lower rates rest of yr. Crib free. TV; cable, VCR (free movies). Complimentary coffee in rms. Restaurant nearby. Ck-out 11 am, ck-in 3 pm. Microwaves. Picnic tables. Beach cottage atmosphere; courtyard with fountain and outdoor furniture. Cr cds: A, C, MC, V.

D SC

Restaurants

★★ **BEACH HOUSE INN.** *619 Sleepy Hollow Lane (92651), adj Vacation Village. 949/494-9707.* Hrs: 8 am-9:30 pm; Fri, Sat to 10:30 pm. Closed Thanksgiving, Dec 25. Res accepted. No A/C. Bar. Semi-a la carte: bkfst $4.95-$9.95, lunch $7.95-$13.95, dinner $12.95-$26.95. Child's meals. Specializes in fresh fish, seafood, steak. Oyster bar. Valet parking. Outdoor dining. On beach; view of ocean. Cr cds: A, C, D, MC, V.

D

★★ **CEDAR CREEK INN.** *384 Forest Ave (92651). 949/497-8696.* Hrs: 11 am-11:30 pm; Sun brunch to 3 pm. Closed most maj hols. Res accepted. Bar. A la carte entrees: lunch $5.95-$12.95. Semi-a la carte: dinner $9.75-$23.95. Sun brunch $6.75-$12.95. Child's meals. Specializes in rack of lamb, beef, fresh fish. Own desserts. Entertainment Tues-Sun. Parking. Old World atmosphere; patio dining, skylit ceilings, stained-glass windows, stone fireplace. Family-owned. Cr cds: A, C, MC, V.

D

★★ **DELANEY'S.** *25001 Dana Dr (92629), approx 5 mi S on CA 1. 949/496-7859.* Hrs: 11:30 am-9:30 pm; wkends to 10:30 pm. Res accepted. Bar. Semi-a la carte: lunch $7.95-$14.95, dinner $9.95-$19.95. Specializes in seafood. Entertainment Fri-Sun. Patio dining. Pond, waterfall. View of marina, harbor. Cr cds: A, C, DS, MC, V.

D

★★★★ **FIVE FEET.** *25001 Dana Dr. 949/497-4955.* Hrs: Sun-Thurs 5-10 pm; Fri, Sat 5-11 pm. Entree $16-$30; dinner $40-$45. Beer, wine. Res accepted. The unique fusion cooking of Michael Kang combines California produce and Asian techniques with his own flavorful creative touches. The artsy, avant-garde dining room matches the eclectic menu perfectly. And the crowd is casually chic and patiently waits for the chance to sample the highly seasoned food. Cr cds: C.

★★★ **LAS BRISAS DE LAGUNA.** *361 Cliff Dr (92651). 949/497-5434.* Hrs: 8 am-3:30 pm; 5-10 pm; Sat 4:30-11 pm; Sun brunch 9 am-3 pm; June-Labor Day open 4-11 pm daily. Closed Dec 25. Res accepted. Mexican, continental menu. Bar 11-1 am. Semi-a la carte: lunch $8.50-$12.95, dinner $11.55-$24.95. Buffet: bkfst $7.25. Sun brunch $18.95. Specialties: marisco en banderilla, filete de calamar. Valet parking. Overlooks Laguna Beach and ocean. Cr cds: A, C, D, DS, MC, V.

D

✓★ **MARK'S RESTAURANT.** *858 S Coast Hwy (92651). 949/494-6711.* Hrs: 5-10:30 pm; Mon, Fri, Sat to 11 pm. Closed Dec 25. Res accepted. Bar. Semi-a la carte: dinner $11-$17.50. Specialties: basil garlic rigatoni, tournedos of salmon. Valet parking. Outdoor dining. Art-deco decor; local artists' works displayed. Cr cds: A, C, MC, V.

★★ **ODESSA RESTAURANT & BAR.** *680 S Coast Hwy (92651). 949/376-8792.* Hrs: 5:30-10 pm; Fri, Sat to 2 am; Sun brunch 11 am-2 pm (June-Sept). Closed Jan 1, Dec 24. Res accepted. Southern menu. Bar. A la carte entrees: dinner $16-$32. Sun brunch $6-$18. Specialties: herb-crusted catfish, pan-seared scallops with portabello mushrooms. Pianist. Valet parking. Contemporary decor; oversized stone fireplace, baby grand piano. Totally nonsmoking. Cr cds: A, C, MC, V.

D

★★★ **PARTNERS BISTRO.** *448 S Coast Hwy (92651). 949/497-4441.* Hrs: 5:30-10 pm; Fri to 10:30 pm; Sat to 11 pm; Sun from 5 pm. Closed Dec 25. Res accepted. French, Amer menu. Bar. Wine list. Semi-a la carte: dinner $11-$23. Specialties: rack of lamb, salmon en papillote, spinach en croute. Parking. Outdoor dining. Elegant decor. Totally nonsmoking. Cr cds: A, C, MC, V.

D

★★ **RUMARI RESTAURANT.** *1826 S Coast Hwy (92651). 949/494-0400.* Hrs: 5-9:30 pm; Fri, Sat to 10:30 pm. Closed Dec 25. Res accepted. Italian menu. Bar. Semi-a la carte: dinner $11-$25. Specialty: linguine nere del mare al cartoccio. Outdoor dining. Italian decor. Totally nonsmoking. Cr cds: A, C, D, DS, JCB, MC, V.

D

★ **SAN SHI GO.** *1100 S Coast Hwy Suite 303 (92651). 949/494-1551.* Hrs: 11:30 am-2 pm, 5-10 pm; Fri, Sat to 11 pm; Sun 3-10 pm. Closed July 4, Thanksgiving, Dec 25. Res accepted. Japanese menu. Wine, beer. A la carte entrees: lunch $5-$11.50, dinner $7.95-$16.95. Specializes in sushi. Parking. Ocean view. Cr cds: A, C, D, DS, MC, V.

★★★ **SAVANNAH CHOP HOUSE.** *32441 St Of The Golden Lantern (92677), 8 mi S on Coast Hwy, exit Golden Lantern. 949/493-7107.* Hrs: 5-10 pm. Res accepted. Bar 5 pm-midnight. Semi-a la carte: dinner $11.95-$26.95. Child's meals. Specializes in American cuisine with southwestern flair. Outdoor dining. View of ocean. Totally nonsmoking. Cr cds: A, C, D, MC, V.

★ **THE COTTAGE.** *308 N Coast Hwy (92651). 949/494-3023.* Hrs: 7 am-3 pm, 5-10 pm; Fri, Sat to 11 pm. Res accepted. Wine, beer. Semi-a la carte: bkfst $4.35-$9.95, lunch $4.95-$8.95, dinner $8.95-$16.95. Child's meals. Specializes in fresh seafood. Parking. Outdoor dining. Turn-of-century landmark home; many dining areas, fireplaces. Cr cds: A, C, D, DS, MC, V.

★★★★ **THE DINING ROOM.** *(See The Ritz-Carlton, Laguna Niguel Resort) 949/240-2000.* Alsatian-born chef Ivan Goetz creatively reinterprets the specialties of his native land, working wonders with game, in this sumptuous settng. The wine list and service are top notch, and ordering a tasting menu paired with wines is a treat. A world-class dining experience. Inside the Ritz-Carlton, Laguna Niguel. Hrs: 6:30-9:30 pm. Closed Sun, Mon. Res requested and required on Fri. and Sat. Contemporary, French mediterranean menu. Dinner: 3-course without wine $50/person. Prix fixe dinner: 5-course $85-$135, updated monthly. Specializes in fresh seafood, prime meats. Menu changes seasonally. Valet parking. Jacket required, tie optional. Cr cds: A, C, D, DS, JCB, MC, V.

D

Unrated Dining Spot

A LA CARTE. *1915 S Coast Hwy (92651). 949/497-4927.* Hrs: 10 am-8 pm; Sun 11 am-5 pm. Closed Jan 1, Dec 25. No A/C. A la carte entrees: lunch $4-$6.50, dinner $4.99-$8.99. Specializes in gourmet meals to go. Counter serv. Outdoor dining on patio. Cr cds: C, MC, V.

D

La Habra (C-6 see Los Angeles map)

(See also Buena Park, Whittier)

Pop 51,266 **Elev** 298 ft **Area Code** 562 **Zip** 90631

Restaurant

★★★ **CAT & THE CUSTARD CUP.** *800 E Whittier Blvd (90631), I-5 Beach Blvd exit N to Whittier Blvd, then ½ mi W. 562/694-3812.* Hrs: 11:30 am-2:30 pm, 5:30-9 pm; Sat to 10:30 pm; Sun 5-9 pm. Closed July 4, Dec 25. Res accepted. California cuisine. Bar. A la carte entrees: lunch $9.25-$14.75, dinner $15.75-$25.75. Specialties: North Atlantic salmon, sauteed venison. Own pastries. Pianist Tues-Sun. Patio dining. Antiques. Cr cds: A, C, D, MC, V.

D

La Jolla (San Diego) (K-4)

(See also San Diego)

Area Code 619 **Zip** 92037

Information La Jolla Town Council, 7734 Herschel Ave, Suite F; 619/454-1444

This resort community is known as the jewel of San Diego. Sandstone bluffs laced with white sand and sparkling ocean suggest the look of the French Riviera. La Jolla is also a recognized center for scientific research.

What to See and Do

Kellogg Park. Swimming, skin diving, surfing; bathing beach; small boat landing; boardwalk, picnic areas. (Daily) At La Jolla Shores Beach, foot of Avenida de la Playa.

Museum of Contemporary Art. Permanent collection and changing exhibits of contemporary painting, sculpture, design, photography and architecture. Sculpture garden; bookstore; films, lecture programs. (Daily exc Mon; closed Jan 1, Thanksgiving, Dec 25) 700 Prospect St. Phone 619/234-1001. ¢¢

Scripps Park at La Jolla Cove. Oceanfront landscaped park with swimming beach, scuba & skin diving areas, picnic areas. (Daily)

★ **Stephen Birch Aquarium-Museum.** At Scripps Institution of Oceanography, Univ of California, San Diego; situated on a hilltop, with a spectacular view of the ocean. Visitors can explore the "blue planet," from the depths of the ocean to the far reaches of outer space, at this impressive interpretive center. This facility presents undersea creatures in realistic habitats, and allows visitors to experience the frontiers of marine science through interactive museum exhibits. Tidepool exhibit. Bookshop. Beach and picnic areas nearby. (Daily; closed Thanksgiving, Dec 25) 2300 Expedition Way (entrance at N Torrey Pines). Phone 619/534-3474. ¢¢¢

University of California, San Diego (1960). (18,000 students) Scattered around campus is an outdoor collection of contemporary sculpture. Campus tours. On La Jolla Village Dr & N Torrey Pines Rd, near I-5. Phone 619/534-8273 (recording) or -4831 (tour information).

Wind'n'sea Beach. Surfing area; also bathing beach. (Daily) At foot of Palomar St.

Motels

★★ **ANDREA VILLA INN.** *2402 Torrey Pines Rd (92037). 619/459-3311; FAX 619/459-1320; res: 800/411-2141.* Web www.andreavilla.com. 49 rms, 2 story, 20 kits. Mid-June-mid-Sept: S, D $105-$125, kit. units $119-$165; monthly rates; lower rates rest of yr. Crib free. Pet accepted; $25. TV; cable (premium). Heated pool; whirlpool. Complimentary continental bkfst. Ck-out noon. Coin lndry. Business servs avail. Health club privileges. Microwaves avail. Sun deck. Cr cds: A, C, D, DS, MC, V.

SC

✓★★ **INN AT LA JOLLA.** *5440 La Jolla Blvd (92037). 619/454-6121; FAX 619/459-1377; res: 800/525-6552.* 44 rms, 1-2 story, 19 kit. suites. No A/C. Mid-June-mid-Sept: S, D $79-$99; each addl $10; kit. suites $99-$109; under 18 free; lower rates rest of yr. TV; cable (premium). Heated pool; whirlpool. Complimentary continental bkfst. Restaurant nearby. Ck-out 11 am. Putting green. Many refrigerators. Cr cds: A, C, D, DS, MC, V.

SC

★★ **LA JOLLA COVE SUITES.** *1155 Coast Blvd (92037). 619/459-2621; FAX 619/454-3522; res: 800/248-2683.* 90 rms, 6 story. No A/C. June-Aug: S, D $115-$195; each addl $15; suites $195-$325; under 18 free; lower rates rest of yr. Crib $15. TV; cable (premium). Pool; whirlpool. Complimentary coffee in rms. Restaurant nearby. Ck-out 11 am. Meeting rms. Business servs avail. Valet serv. Coin lndry. Health club privileges. Putting green. Refrigerators; microwaves avail. Cr cds: A, C, D, DS, MC, V.

D SC

✓★ **LA JOLLA SHORES INN.** *5390 La Jolla Blvd (92037). 619/454-0175; FAX 619/551-7520.* 39 rms, 2 story, 4 suites, 8 kits. No A/C. Mid-May-Sept: S, D $79-$99; each addl $10; suites $99-$119; kit. units $99-$109; under 18 free; lower rates rest of yr. Crib free. TV; cable (premium). Heated pool. Complimentary coffee. Restaurant nearby. Ck-out 11 am. Many refrigerators. Cr cds: A, C, D, DS, MC, V.

SC

★★ **RESIDENCE INN BY MARRIOTT.** *8901 Gilman Dr (92037). 619/587-1770; FAX 619/552-0387; res: 800/331-3131.* 287 kit. suites, 2 story. Kit. suites $180-$299; wkly rates. Crib free. Pet accepted; $100 & $10/day. TV; cable (premium). 2 heated pools; 5 whirlpools. Complimentary continental bkfst. Restaurant nearby. Ck-out noon. Coin lndry. Meeting rms. Business servs avail. In-rm modem link. Valet serv. Airport transportation. Health club privileges. Lawn games. Refrigerators, microwaves, fireplaces. Grills. Cr cds: A, C, D, DS, JCB, MC, V.

D SC

✓★★ **TRAVELODGE.** *6750 La Jolla Blvd (92037). 619/454-0716; FAX 619/454-1075; res: 800/578-7878.* 44 rms, 29 with shower only, 3 story. No elvtr. June-Sept: S $54-$89; D $64-$129; under 17 free; wkly rates; lower rates rest of yr. Crib free. TV; cable (premium). Heated pool; whirlpool. Complimentary coffee in rms. Restaurant adj 6 am-midnight. Ck-out noon. Coin lndry. In-rm modem link. Health club privileges. Refrigerators; microwaves avail. Cr cds: A, C, D, DS, ER, JCB, MC, V.

SC

★ **TRAVELODGE.** *1141 Silverado St (92037). 619/454-0791; FAX 619/459-8534; res: 800/578-7878.* 30 rms, 23 with shower only, 3 story. July-Aug: S, D $79-$150; wkly rates; higher rates hols, special events; lower rates rest of yr. Crib free. TV; cable (premium). Coffee in rms. Restaurant nearby. Ck-out noon. Refrigerators avail. Sun decks. Picnic tables. Cr cds: A, C, D, DS, JCB, MC, V.

SC

Motor Hotels

★★ **BEST WESTERN.** *7830 Fay Ave (92037). 619/459-4461; FAX 619/456-2578; res: 800/528-1234; res: 800/462-9732.* E-mail innbyseabw@aol.com. 132 rms, 5 story. July-Aug: S, D $119-$199; each addl $10; suites from $350; under 12 free; lower rates rest of yr. Crib free. TV; cable. Heated pool; whirlpool. Complimentary continental bkfst. Restaurant 6 am-10 pm. Rm serv from 7 am. Ck-out noon. Coin lndry. Meeting rms. Business servs avail. In-rm modem link. Bellhops. Valet serv. Health club privileges. Some refrigerators; microwaves avail. Balconies. Ocean view from some rms. Cr cds: A, C, D, DS, ER, JCB, MC, V.

D SC

★★★ **SEA LODGE OCEANFRONT HOTEL.** *8110 Camino Del Oro (92037). 619/459-8271; FAX 619/456-9346; res: 800/237-5211.* Web www.sealodge.com. 128 rms, 3 story. June-Sept: S, D $205-$339; each addl $15; suites $409-$479; under 12 free; lower rates rest of yr. TV; cable (premium). Heated pool; wading pool, whirlpool, poolside serv. Coffee in rms. Restaurant 7 am-10 pm. Rm serv. Bar 10:30 am-11 pm. Ck-out noon. Coin lndry. Meeting rms. Business servs avail. In-rm modem link. Bellhops. Valet serv. Covered parking. Tennis; pro. Exercise equipt; sauna. Massage. Refrigerators; microwaves avail. Private patios, balconies. On ocean. Cr cds: A, C, D, DS, MC, V.

D SC

Hotels

★★★ **EMBASSY SUITES LA JOLLA.** *4550 La Jolla Village Dr (92122). 619/453-0400; FAX 619/453-4226; res: 800/362-2779.* E-mail sales@eslajolla.com; web www.embassy-suites.com. 335 suites, 12 story. Suites $195-$295; each addl $10; under 18 free. Crib free. TV; cable (premium), VCR avail. Indoor pool; whirlpool. Complimentary full bkfst. Coffee in rms. Restaurant 11 am-11 pm. Bar to 1 am. Ck-out noon. Coin lndry. Meeting rms. Business servs avail. In-rm modem link. Gift shop. Exercise equipt; sauna. Health club privileges. Game rm. Refrigerators, microwaves, wet bars. Cr cds: A, C, D, DS, JCB, MC, V.

D SC

★★★ **EMPRESS HOTEL.** *7766 Fay Ave & Silverado St (92037). 619/454-3001; FAX 619/454-6387; res: 888/369-9900.* 73 rms, 5 story. S, D $119-$189; kit. suites $325; under 18 free. Crib free. Valet parking $5. TV; cable. Complimentary continental bkfst. Coffee in rms. Restaurant 11:30 am-2 pm, 5:30-10 pm. Bar 11:30-1:30 am. Ck-out noon. Meeting rms. Business servs avail. In-rm modem link. Exercise equipt; sauna. Whirlpool. Health club privileges. Refrigerators. Sun deck. Cr cds: A, C, D, DS, MC, V.

D SC

★★ **HOTEL LA JOLLA.** *7955 La Jolla Shores Dr (92037). 619/459-0261; FAX 619/459-7649; res: 800/666-0261.* 108 rms, 11 story. July-Aug: S, D $149-$189; each addl $20; suites $350; under 18 free; package plans; lower rates rest of yr. TV; cable (premium), VCR avail. Heated pool; whirlpool. Coffee in rms. Restaurant (see CRESCENT SHORES GRILL). Bar 11-1 am; entertainment wkends. Ck-out noon. Meeting rms. Business servs avail. Concierge. Exercise equipt; sauna. Refrigerators, minibars. Balconies. Cr cds: A, C, D, DS, MC, V.

D SC

★★★★ **HYATT REGENCY LA JOLLA AT AVENTINE.** *3777 La Jolla Village Dr (92122). 619/552-1234; FAX 619/552-6066.* Web www.hyatt.com. Noted architect Michael Graves designed this hotel, which mixes neoclassic, postmodern and Mediterranean elements. The spacious guest rooms feature cherry wood furnishings. 419 rms, 16 story. S, D $175-$250; each addl $35; suites $325-$2,500; under 18 free. Crib avail. Garage parking $12, valet $16. TV; cable (premium), VCR avail. Pool; whirlpool. Restaurant 6 am-midnight. Bar from noon. Ck-out noon. Convention facilities. Business center. In-rm modem link. Concierge. Gift shop. Tennis. Health club privileges. Massage. Minibars; microwaves avail. Luxury level. Cr cds: A, C, D, DS, JCB, MC, V.

D SC

★★★ **LA VALENCIA.** *1132 Prospect St (92037). 858/454-0771; FAX 858/456-3921; res: 800/451-0772.* 100 rms, 7 story, 7 kits. S, D $225-$475; each addl $15; suites $600-$900. Crib $10. TV; cable, VCR avail. Heated pool; whirlpool, poolside serv. Coffee in rms. Restaurant 6:30 am-11 pm. Rm serv 24 hrs. Bar; entertainment exc Sun. Ck-out noon. Meeting rms. Business servs avail. Exercise equipt; sauna. Health club privileges. Bathrm phones; many refrigerators, minibars. Some private patios, balconies. Gardens. Beach opp. Cr cds: A, C, D, DS, JCB, MC, V.

★★★ **MARRIOTT.** *4240 La Jolla Village Dr (92037). 619/587-1414; FAX 619/546-8518; res: 800/228-9290.* Web www.marriott.com. 360 rms, 15 story. S, D $119-$174; suites $275-$650; under 18 free; wkend rates. Crib free. Pet accepted. Covered parking $8/day, valet $12. TV; cable (premium), VCR avail. Indoor/outdoor pool; whirlpool. Complimentary coffee in rms. Restaurant 6:30 am-10:30 pm. Bar. Ck-out noon. Coin Indry. Convention facilities. Business servs avail. In-rm modem link. Exercise rm; sauna. Game rm. Tennis privileges. Refrigerators avail. Private patios, balconies. Luxury level. Cr cds: A, C, D, DS, ER, JCB, MC, V.

D SC

★★ **RADISSON HOTEL.** *3299 Holiday Ct (92037). 858/453-5500; FAX 858/453-5550; res: 800/333-3333.* 200 rms in 4 bldgs, 2 story. S, D $149-$199; each addl $10; under 18 free. TV; cable (premium), VCR (movies). Heated pool; whirlpool, poolside serv. Coffee in rms. Restaurant 6:30 am-10 pm. Rm serv. Bar; entertainment Tues-Sat. Ck-out noon. Meeting rms. Business servs avail. In-rm modem link. Bellhops. Free airport, RR station, bus depot transportation. Exercise equipt. Refrigerators; microwaves avail. Cr cds: A, C, D, DS, MC, V.

D SC

★★★★ **SHERATON GRANDE TORREY PINES.** *10950 N Torrey Pines Rd (92037). 619/558-1500; FAX 619/450-4584.* Web www.sheratontp.com. Set on a bluff above La Jolla, this luxury hotel overlooks the sea and the 18th fairway of the Torrey Pines golf course. 400 rms, 4 story. S, D $280; each addl $20; suites $450-$2,500; under 18 free. Crib free. Valet parking $12; in/out $9. TV; cable (premium), VCR avail. Pool; whirlpool, poolside serv. Supervised child's activities (Memorial Day-Labor Day); ages 3-12. Restaurant (see TORREYANA GRILLE). Rm serv 24 hrs. Bar 11-2 am; pianist. Ck-out noon, ck-in 3pm. Convention facilities. Business center. In-rm modem link. Concierge. Butler serv. Gift shop. Lighted tennis. Exercise equipt; sauna. Health club privileges. Bicycle rentals. Bathrm phones, minibars; microwaves avail. Wet bar in some suites. Balconies. Cr cds: A, C, D, DS, ER, JCB, MC, V.

D SC

★★ **THE GRAND COLONIAL.** *910 Prospect St (92037). 619/454-2181; FAX 619/454-5679; res: 800/826-1278.* 75 air-cooled rms, 4 story, 11 suites. S, D $164-$200; suites $200-$350. Crib free. Pet accepted. TV; cable. Pool. Complimentary coffee in lobby. Restaurant 7 am-2:30 pm, 5-10 pm; Fri, Sat to 11 pm. Ck-out noon. Meeting rms. Business servs avail. Health club privileges. Refrigerators avail. Cr cds: A, C, D, MC, V.

SC

Inns

★★★ **BED & BREAKFAST INN AT LA JOLLA.** *7753 Draper Ave (92037). 858/456-2066; FAX 858/456-1510.* Web www.innlajolla.com. 15 rms, 2 story. Rm phones avail. S, D $110-$250. TV in sitting rm & penthouse; VCR avail. Complimentary full bkfst; afternoon refreshments. Ck-out 11 am, ck-in 3-5 pm. Some refrigerators. Beach nearby. Cubist-style house built 1913; gardens. Cr cds: A, C, MC, V.

D

★★ **PROSPECT PARK INN.** *1110 Prospect St (92037). 619/454-0133; FAX 619/454-2056; res: 800/433-1609.* Web www.tales.com/ca/prospectparkinn. 22 units, 4 story, 6 kits. S, D $120-$185; suites $275-$325; wkly, monthly rates off season. Crib free. TV; cable (premium). Complimentary continental bkfst. Complimentary coffee in rms. Restaurant adj 7 am-11 pm. Ck-out 11 am, ck-in 3 pm. Business servs avail. In-rm modem link. Health club privileges. Refrigerators; microwaves avail. Balconies. Library. Most rms have ocean view. Totally nonsmoking. Cr cds: A, C, D, DS, ER, JCB, MC, V.

SC

Restaurants

★ **ASHOKA CUISINE OF INDIA.** *8008 Girard Ave (92037), La Jolla Cove Plaza, 2nd floor. 619/454-6263.* Hrs: 5:30-9:30 pm; Fri, Sat to 10:30 pm. Closed Mon. Res accepted. Indian menu. Wine, beer. Semi-a la carte: dinner $8.95-$17.95. Specializes in tandoori dishes, curries, authentic Indian cuisine. Dining rm overlooks La Jolla Cove. Cr cds: A, C, D, DS, ER, JCB, MC, V.

✓★★ **BIRD ROCK CAFE.** *5656 La Jolla Blvd (92037). 619/551-4090.* Hrs: 5-10 pm. Closed July 4, Thanksgiving, Dec 25. Res accepted. Bar. Semi-a la carte: dinner $8-$19. Specializes in seafood. Outdoor dining. Casual decor. Totally nonsmoking. Cr cds: A, C, D, DS, MC, V.

D

★★ **BROCKTON VILLA.** *1235 Coast Blvd (92037). 619/454-7393.* Hrs: 8 am-9 pm; Mon to 5 pm; Sun brunch to 3 pm. Closed Thanksgiving, Dec 25. Res accepted. No A/C. Beer, wine. Semi-a la carte: bkfst $2-$8, lunch $5-$8, dinner $11-$19. Sun brunch $4.50-$7.50. Specialties: coast toast, shrimp and chicken salad, rack of lamb. Outdoor dining. Hillside cottage overlooking cove and Scripps Park; abalone shell fireplace. Totally nonsmoking. Cr cds: A, C, DS, MC, V.

★★★ **CAFE JAPENGO.** *8960 University Center Lane (92122). 619/450-3355.* Hrs: 11:30 am-2:30 pm, 5:30-10:30 pm; Fri to 11:30 pm; Sat 5:30-11:30 pm; Sun 5:30-10:30 pm. Closed Easter, Thanksgiving, Dec 25. Res accepted. Pacific Rim menu. Bar. Wine list. A la carte entrees: lunch $10-$16, dinner $10-$30. Specializes in fresh seafood. Sushi bar. Valet parking. Japanese art and designs adorn walls. Cr cds: A, C, D, DS, JCB, MC, V.

D

★★ **CINDY BLACK'S.** *5721 La Jolla Blvd (92037). 619/456-6299.* Hrs: 5:30-10 pm; Sun 5-8 pm. Closed Mon. Res accepted. French country menu. Bar. A la carte entrees: dinner $10.50-$25. Prix fixe: Sun dinner $15.95. Specialties: whole Dover sole meuniere, provençale chicken stew, grilled duck. Valet parking Fri, Sat. Original art. Cr cds: A, C, D, DS, MC, V.

D

★★ **CRAB CATCHER.** *1298 Prospect St (92037), in Coast Walk Mall. 619/454-9587.* Hrs: 11:30 am-3 pm, 5:30-10 pm; Fri, Sat to 10:30 pm; Sun brunch 10:30 am-3 pm. Res accepted. Bar 11:30 am-midnight. A la carte entrees: lunch $8-$17, dinner $15-$30. Sun brunch $11-$18. Child's meals. Specializes in fresh fish, steak, pastas. Outdoor dining. View of cove. Cr cds: A, C, D, DS, MC, V.

★★ **CRESCENT SHORES GRILL.** *(See Hotel La Jolla) 619/459-0541.* Hrs: 6:30 am-10 pm; Fri, Sat to 11 pm; Sun brunch 10:30 am-2:30 pm. Res accepted. Regional Amer menu. Bar 11:30 am-midnight. Semi-a la carte: bkfst $4.75-$9.95, lunch $7.50-$13.50, dinner $12-$25 Sun brunch $4-$16. Specializes in grilled swordfish, grilled paillard of veal. Entertainment Thurs-Sat. On 11th floor overlooking ocean; open bistro kitchen. Cr cds: A, C, D, DS, MC, V.

D

★★★ **GEORGE'S AT THE COVE.** *1250 Prospect Place (92037), Prospect Place Mall. 619/454-4244.* Web www.georgesatthecove.com. Hrs: 11:30 am-2:30 pm, 5:30-10 pm; Fri, Sat 11:30 am-3 pm, 5-11 pm. Res accepted. Extensive wine list. Semi-a la carte: lunch $8.95-$14.50, dinner $19.50-$30. Specializes in fresh seafood, California cuisine Own baking. Valet parking. Outdoor dining. View of cove. Cr cds: A, C, D DS, MC, V.

★★★ **JAPENGO.** *Hyatt Hotel. 858/450-3355.* Closed for renovation. Cr cds: C.

✓★★★ **LA BRUSCHETTA.** *2151 Avenida De La Playa (92037). 619/551-1221.* Hrs: 11:30 am-3 pm, 5:30-11 pm. Closed Jan 1, Thanksgiving, Dec 25. Res accepted. Italian menu. Wine, beer. Semi-a la carte: lunch $4.95-$15, dinner $8.95-$22.95. Child's meals. Specializes in regional Italian cuisine. Parking. Outdoor dining. Italian decor. Totally nonsmoking. Cr cds: A, C, D, MC, V.

D

★★★ **MARINE ROOM.** *2000 Spindrift Dr (92037). 619/459-7222.* Hrs: 11:30 am-2:30 pm, 6-10 pm; Sun brunch 10 am-2 pm. Res accepted. Bar to midnight. A la carte entrees: lunch $7-$14, dinner $19.50-$35. Sun brunch $24.95. Specializes in fresh seafood. Entertainment. On beach; view of ocean, cliffs. Family-owned. Cr cds: A, C, D, DS, MC, V.

D

✓★★★ **PIATTI RISTORANTE.** *2182 Avenida De La Playa (92037). 619/454-1589.* Hrs: 11:30 am-10 pm; Fri, Sat to 11 pm; Sat, Sun brunch 11 am-3 pm. Res accepted. Italian menu. Bar. A la carte entrees: lunch $9.95-$13.95, dinner $9-$17. Sat, Sun brunch $7-$9. Specialties: il pollo arrosto, pappardelle fantasia, cannelloni "Mamma Concetta"; Outdoor dining. Patio area has fountain. Cr cds: A, C, D, MC, V.

D

★★★ **ROPPONGI.** *875 Prospect St (92037). 858/551-5252.* Asian fusion. Hrs: lunch Mon-Fri 11:30 am, Sat & Sun 10:30 am. Dinner Sun-Thurs until 10 pm. Fri & Sat 11pm. Prices lunch $6-$14; dinner $14-$25. Bar. Reserv pref. Valet. Outdoor dining. Cr cds: C.

✓★★ **SAMMY'S CALIFORNIA WOODFIRED P.** *702 Pearl St (92037). 619/456-5222.* E-mail sammys@connectnet.com. Hrs: 11:30 am-10 pm; Fri, Sat to 11 pm. Closed Thanksgiving, Dec 25. Bar. Semi-a la carte: lunch, dinner $5.95-$9.95. Child's meals. Specializes in woodfired pizzas. Outdoor dining. Casual dining. Totally nonsmoking. Cr cds: A, C, D, MC, V.

D ♥

★★★ **SANTE RESTAURANT.** *7811 Herschel Ave (92037). 619/454-1315.* Web www.santeristorante.com. Hrs: 11:30 am-2:30 pm, 5-11:30 pm; Sat, Sun from 5 pm. Closed Jan 1, Dec 25. Res accepted (dinner). Italian menu. Bar. Wine list. Semi-a la carte: lunch $8.95-$15, dinner $10-$24. Specialties: veal with marsala wine and shittake mushroom sauce, fresh Dover sole. Pianist Thurs-Sat. Street parking. Outdoor dining. Gated entry; Italian decor. Cr cds: A, C, D, DS, MC, V.

D

✓★★★ **ST JAMES BAR.** *4370 La Jolla Village Dr (92122). 619/453-6650.* Hrs: 11:30 am-10 pm. Closed Jan 1, Thanksgiving, Dec 25. Res accepted. Continental, California menu. Bar. Wine list. Semi-a la carte: lunch, dinner $8-$26. Specializes in fresh seafood, meats, vegetables. Cr cds: A, C, D, MC, V.

D

★★★ **TAPENADE.** *7612 Fay Ave (92037). 858/551-7500.* French cuisine. Hrs: Tues-Fri 12-2:30 pm; Tues-Sun 5:30-10 pm. Closed Mon & maj hol. $9-$16; dinner $10-$26. Resv reqd. Nonsmoking. Summer entertainment. Full bar. Cr cds: C.

★★★ **TOP O' THE COVE.** *1216 Prospect Place (92037). 619/454-7779.* Web www.topofthecove.com. Hrs: 11:30 am-10:30 pm; Sun brunch 10:30 am-2:30 pm. Res accepted. No A/C. Bar. Wine cellar. A la carte entrees: lunch $10-$18, dinner $25-$32. Specializes in Pacific Rim & European cuisine. Own pastries. Pianist Sat, Sun. Valet parking. Outdoor dining. In converted cottage (1896); rare Moreton fig trees at front entrance. 2nd-floor cafe overlooks La Jolla cove. Cr cds: A, C, D, MC, V.

D

★★★ **TORREYANA GRILLE.** *(See Sheraton Grande Torrey Pines) 619/450-4571.* Hrs: 6:30 am-10:30 pm; Sun brunch 10:30 am-2 pm. Res accepted. Bar 11-2 am. Semi-a la carte: bkfst $4.95-$14.50, lunch $8.95-$14.75, dinner $11.50-$29. Sun brunch $28.95. Child's meals. Specialties: filet mignon, steamed shelled Maine lobster. Entertainment Thurs-Sat. Valet parking. Outdoor dining. Elegant atmosphere. Cr cds: A, C, D, DS, JCB, MC, V.

D

★★★ **TUTTO MARE.** *4365 Executive Dr (92121). 619/597-1188.* Hrs: 11:30 am-10:30 pm; Tues-Thurs to 11 pm; Fri to midnight; Sat 5 pm-midnight; Sun 5-10 pm. Closed July 4, Thanksgiving, Dec 25. Res accepted. Italian menu. Bar. Semi-a la carte: lunch $8-$16, dinner $8-$18. Specializes in wood-fired oven-baked fish, charcoal-grilled meat and fish. Entertainment. Open cooking area. Cr cds: A, C, D, MC, V.

D

Unrated Dining Spots

DAILY'S FIT AND FRESH. *8915 Towne Centre Dr (92122). 619/453-1112.* Hrs: 10:30 am-9 pm; Sun 11 am-8 pm. Closed some major hols. Semi-a la carte: lunch, dinner $3.89-$5.89. Child's meals. Specializes in low-calorie and low-fat entrees. Outdoor dining. Casual dining with emphasis on nutritional food. Totally nonsmoking. Cr cds: C, MC, V.

D SC ♥

FRENCH PASTRY SHOP. *5550 La Jolla Blvd (92037). 619/454-9094.* Hrs: 7:30 am-11 pm. Closed Jan 1, Dec 25. Continental menu. Semi-a la carte: bkfst $3.25-$6.75, lunch $3.50-$11.95, dinner $6.75-$14.95. Specializes in pâte, chocolates. Own baking. Outdoor dining. Cr cds: C, MC, V.

Lake Arrowhead (J-4)

(See also Big Bear Lake)

Pop 6,539 **Elev** 5,191 ft **Area Code** 909 **Zip** 92352
E-mail lachamber@ js-net **Web** www.lakearrowhead.net
Information Chamber of Commerce, PO Box 219; 909/337-3715

This area specializes in year-round sports with water sports in the summer and snow skiing in the winter. The lake, which is 2½ miles long and about one mile wide, is slightly north of the breathtaking Rim of the World Highway (CA 18), which is a Scenic Byway, in the San Bernardino National Forest (see SAN BERNARDINO).

What to See and Do

Arrowhead Queen. Enjoy a 50-min narrated boat cruise on Lake Arrowhead, past architectural points of interest and historical sites. (Daily; hrly departures) On the waterfront at Lake Arrowhead Village. Phone 909/336-6992. ¢¢¢

Lake Arrowhead Children's Museum. Offers a hands-on interactive setting for children; learning through play and activities. (Daily; closed Thanksgiving, Dec 25) Lower Peninsula, Lake Arrowhead Village. Phone 909/336-1332 (recording) or 909/336-3093. ¢¢

Snow Valley Ski Resort. 5 triple, 8 double chairlifts; patrol, school, rentals; snowmaking; cafeteria, restaurant, bar. 25 runs; longest run 1¼ mi; vertical drop 1,141 ft. (Mid-Nov-Apr) Snowboarding. Summer activities include hiking, mountain biking, backpacking; camping; outdoor concerts. Indoor playland for children. 14 mi SE on CA 18, 30; 5 mi E of Running Springs. For information phone 909/867-2751; snow conditions, 909/625-6511. ¢¢¢¢¢

Motel

✓★ **LAKE ARROWHEAD TREE TOP LODGE.** *27992 Rainbow Dr (92352), at jct CA 173, near Lake Arrowhead Village. 909/337-2311; FAX 909/337-1403; res: 800/358-8733.* Web www.lakearrowhead.com/treetop. 20 rms, 1-2 story, 7 kits. S, D $59-$108; suites, kit. units $80-$139; fireplace units $74-$129. Pet accepted, some restrictions; $8/day. TV; cable, VCR avail (movies $2). Heated pool. Complimentary coffee in lobby. Ck-out 11 am. Refrigerators; some fireplaces. Patios, balconies. Picnic tables, grill. Private nature trail. Cr cds: A, C, D, DS, JCB, MC, V.

Motor Hotel

★★★ **LAKE ARROWHEAD RESORT.** *27984 Hwy 189 (92352), W of jct CA 173. 909/336-1511; FAX 909/336-1378; res: 800/800-6792.* E-mail lakearrowheadresortsales@dreamsoft.com; web www.lakearrowheadresort.com. 177 rms, 3 story. S, D $89-$189; each addl $15; suites $299-$399; under 18 free; package plans. Crib free. TV; cable. Heated pool; whirlpools, poolside serv. Supervised child's activities (June-Aug daily, Sept-May Fri evening, Sat & Sun only); ages 4-12. Complimentary coffee in rms. Restaurants 7 am-11 pm. Rm serv. Bar 4-11 pm, wkends to 1 am. Ck-out noon. Meeting rms. Business servs avail. Bellhops. Concierge. Gift shop. Barber, beauty shop. Valet parking. Airport transportation. Lighted tennis. Downhill/x-country ski 20 mi. Exercise rm; sauna, steam rm. Massage. Boating, waterskiing; fishing equipt avail. Game rm. Racquetball courts. Lawn games. Bicycle rentals. Minibars; many refrigerators; fireplace in some suites. Many balconies. On lake with private beach. Cr cds: A, C, D, DS, MC, V.

Inns

★★ **CHATEAU DU LAC.** *911 Hospital Rd (92352), 3 mi E. 909/337-6488; FAX 909/337-6746; res: 800/601-8722.* E-mail chateau@js-net; web www.lakearrowhead.com. 5 rms, 1 with shower only, 3 story. S, D $125-$250. TV; cable, VCR (free movies). Complimentary full bkfst. Restaurant nearby. Ck-out 11 am, ck-in 2 pm. Downhill ski 15 mi; x-country ski 12 mi. Some in-rm whirlpools, fireplaces. Some balconies. Country French decor. Totally nonsmoking. Cr cds: A, C, D, DS, JCB, MC, V.

★★ **ROMANTIQUE LAKEVIEW LODGE.** *28051 Hwy 189 (92352), W of jct CA 173 & 189. 909/337-6633; FAX 909/337-5966; res: 800/358-5253.* Web www.lakeviewlodge.com. 9 units, 2 story, 2 suites. No rm phones. Late June-early Jan: S, D $75-$160; suites $110-$225; lower rates rest of yr. Adults only. TV; cable, VCR (free movies). Complimentary continental bkfst. Restaurant nearby. Ck-out 11 am, ck-in 2-9 pm. Downhill ski 10 mi; x-country ski 10 mi. Many fireplaces. Reconstructed lodge was once a private home; antique furnishings; Victorian-style decor. Lush pine garden. Lake nearby. Totally nonsmoking. Cr cds: A, C, DS, MC, V.

Restaurant

★★ **ROYAL OAK.** *27187 CA 189 (92317), Blue Jay town center, 1½ mi SW of Lake Arrowhead Village. 909/337-6018.* Hrs: 11:30 am-2:30 pm, 5-9 pm; Sun, Mon from 5 pm. Closed Easter, Thanksgiving, Dec 25. Res accepted. Bar to 11 pm; Fri, Sat to midnight. Semi-a la carte: lunch $6.50-$12.95, dinner $14.95-$29.95. Specializes in beef, seafood, veal. Own desserts. Pianist Wed, Fri, Sat; jazz Thurs. English Tudor decor. Family-owned. Totally nonsmoking. Cr cds: A, C, DS, MC, V.

Lake County

(see Clear Lake Area)

Lake Tahoe Area (D-4)

Area Code 530 (CA), 702 (NV) **E-mail** ltva@sierra.net
Web www.virtualtahoe.com

Information Lake Tahoe Visitors Authority, 1156 Ski Run Blvd, South Lake Tahoe 96150; 530/544-5050 or 800/AT-TAHOE (reservations)

Lake Tahoe is one of the most magnificent mountain lakes in the world, with an area of about 200 square miles, an altitude of approximately 6,230 feet and a maximum depth of more than 1,600 feet. Mostly in California, partly in Nevada, it is circled by paved highways edged with campgrounds, lodges, motels and resorts. The lake, with some fine beaches, is surrounded by forests of ponderosa, Jeffery and sugar pine, white fir, juniper, cedar, aspen, dogwood, cottonwood, many other trees and a splendid assortment of wildflowers.

The Sierra Nevada, here composed mostly of hard granite, is a range built by a series of roughly parallel block faults along its eastern side, which have tipped the mountainous area to the west, with the eastern side much steeper than the western. Lake Tahoe lies in a trough between the Sierra proper and the Carson Range, similarly formed and generally regarded as a part of the Sierra, to its east.

There are spectacular views of the lake from many points on the surrounding highways. Eagle Creek, one of the thousands of mountain streams that feed the lake, cascades 1,500 feet over Eagle Falls into Emerald Bay at the southwestern part of the lake. Smaller mountain lakes are scattered around the Tahoe area; accessibility varies. Tahoe and El Dorado National Forests stretch north and west of the lake, offering many recreational facilities.

Public and commercial swimming (there are 29 public beaches), boating and fishing facilities are plentiful. In winter the area is a mecca for skiers. There is legalized gambling on the Nevada side.

What to See and Do

Boat rides.

Hornblower Cruises. *Tahoe Queen,* paddlewheeler, cruise boat to Emerald Bay (all yr, 3 departures daily, res required). Foot of Ski Run Blvd in South Lake Tahoe. Phone 530/541-3364. ¢¢¢¢-¢¢¢¢¢

MS *Dixie II* Cruises. Tours of Lake Tahoe and Emerald Bay aboard paddlewheeler; sightseeing, bkfst and dinner cruises avail. Champagne brunch cruise (Sun). Leaves Zephyr Cove marina, 4 mi NE of Stateline, NV on US 50. Res recommended. Phone 702/588-3508 or 702/882-0786 (in CA). Sightseeing. ¢¢¢¢; Other cruises ¢¢¢¢¢

Lake Tahoe Historical Society Museum. Displays of Lake Tahoe's Native American history, Frémont's discovery and development as a resort center. (Late June-Labor Day, daily; rest of yr, wkends) 3058 US 50. Phone 530/541-5458. ¢

Ponderosa Ranch (see INCLINE VILLAGE, NV).

Riding. Camp Richardson Corral. 1- & 2-hr rides, bkfst & steak rides (May-Oct, daily); pack rides (July-Sept, daily); sleigh rides (Dec-Mar). For further information contact PO Box 8335, South Lake Tahoe 96158; phone 530/541-3113. ¢¢¢¢¢

Skiing.

Alpine Meadows. Quad, 2 triple, 7 double chairlifts, 1 Pomalift; patrol, school, rentals; snowmaking; children's snow school; snack bar, cafeteria, restaurant, bars. Longest run 2½ mi; vertical drop 1,800 ft. Snowboarding. (Mid-Nov-late May, daily) 6 mi NW of Tahoe City off CA 89. Phone 530/583-4232; for snow information, 530/581-8374. ¢¢¢¢¢

Heavenly Ski Resort. Aerial Tramway to 8,250 ft. 2 detachable quad, 7 triple, 10 double chairlifts, 6 surface lifts; patrol, school, rentals; snowmaking; snack bar, cafeteria, restaurant, bars; 6 lodges. Longest run 5½ mi; vertical drop 3,600 ft. (Mid-Nov-mid-Apr, daily) Cross-country trails nearby. Tramway also operates May-Sept (fee). Observation platform, sun deck; hiking trail; picnic area; restaurant, bar. 1 mi E of US 50 in South Lake Tahoe. Phone 702/541-1330 or 702/586-7000; for 24-hr ski conditions, 702/541-7544. Summer ¢¢¢¢; Winter ¢¢¢¢¢

Kirkwood. 4 triple, 6 double chairlifts, 1 Pomalift; patrol, school, rentals; cafeteria, 4 restaurants, 4 bars. Longest run 2½ mi; vertical drop 2,000 ft. (Mid-Nov-mid-May, daily) Cross-country skiing. Rentals, lessons; machine-groomed trails. (Nov-May; daily) Half-day rates. 30 mi S off CA 88. Phone 209/258-6000; for snow conditions, 209/258-3000. **¢¢¢¢¢**

Sierra at Tahoe. 3 high-speed detachable quads, 1 triple, 4 double chairlifts; patrol, school, rentals; cafeterias. Longest run 3½ mi; vertical drop 2,212 ft. (Nov-Apr, daily) Shuttle bus service. 12 mi W of South Lake Tahoe on US 50. Phone 530/659-7453 or 530/659-7474; snow information 530/659-7475. **¢¢¢¢**

Squaw Valley USA. 3 high-speed quads, 8 triple, 15 double chairlifts, aerial cable car, gondola, 5 surface lifts; patrol, school, rentals; snack bars, cafeterias, restaurants, bars. Longest run 3½ mi; vertical drop 2,850 ft. (Mid-Nov-mid-May, daily) Cross-country skiing (25 mi); rentals (Mid-Nov-Apr, daily). Tram also operates late May-Oct (daily & eve). Also bungee jumping. 5 mi NW of Tahoe City off CA 89. Phone 530/583-6985; for 24-hr snow information, 530/583-6955. **¢¢¢¢¢**

State parks/recreation areas. Tahoe State Recreation Area. Pier, picnicking, camping. Near Tahoe City on CA 28. Phone 530/583-3074 (general information). **Sugar Pine Point State Park.** Cross-country skiing. Camping (fee). Pine Lodge is refurbished turn-of-century summer home (Ehrman Mansion), tours (July-Labor Day). Fee/vehicle day use. 10 mi S of Tahoe City on CA 89. Phone 530/525-7982. **D.L. Bliss State Park.** Beach, camping. 17 mi S of Tahoe City on CA 89. Phone 530/525-7277. **Grover Hot Springs State Park.** Hot mineral pool, swimming. Camping. 29 mi S of South Lake Tahoe on CA 89. Phone 530/694-2248. **Emerald Bay State Park.** Swimming; fishing. Picnicking. Camping. Closed in winter. Standard fees. 22 mi S of Tahoe City on CA 89. Phone 530/525-7232. In Emerald Bay State Park is

Vikingsholm. Old Scandinavian architecture and furnishings. Tours (mid-June-Labor Day, daily). Steep 1 mi walk from parking lot (CA 89). **¢¢**

US Forest Service Visitor Center. Information, campfire programs, guided nature walks; self-guided trails and auto tape tours. Visitors look into Taylor Creek from the Stream Profile Chamber; exhibits explain life cycle of trout. (Mid-June-early Sept, daily; Stream Profile Chamber open after Memorial Day-Oct, days vary) On CA 89, 3 mi NW of South Lake Tahoe. Contact US Forest Service, 870 Emerald Bay Rd, Suite 1, South Lake Tahoe 96150; phone 530/573-2600. **Free**

Annual Event

Isuzu Celebrity Golf championship. Edgewood Tahoe Golf Course. More than 70 sports and entertainment celebrities compete for a $500,000 purse. Phone 530/544-5050. July.

Note: Accommodations around Lake Tahoe are listed under South Lake Tahoe, Tahoe City and Tahoe Vista. See also, under Nevada: Incline Village, Stateline. In this area many motels have higher rates in summer and during special events and holidays. Reservations advised.

Lancaster (H-4)

(See also Palmdale)

Pop 97,291 **Elev** 2,355 ft **Area Code** 661 **E-mail** lcoc@hughes.net
Web www.lancasterchamber.org
Information Chamber of Commerce, 554 W Lancaster Blvd, 93534; 661/948-4518

What to See and Do

Edwards Air Force Base. Landing site for the NASA space shuttle program. Free 90-min walking tours (2 departures daily 7:30 am-4 pm, exc Sat & Sun); res required, phone 661/258-3460 (NASA info line). Also 1½-hr bus tours (Fri only; phone 661/277-3517). 10 mi N via CA 14 to Rosamond, then 10 mi E on Rosamond Blvd. For general information phone 661/258-3460.

Annual Event

Antelope Valley Fair and Alfalfa Festival. Fairgrounds. 11 days. (Mon-Fri, 8 am-5 pm) Phone 805/948-6060. Usually late Aug-Labor Day.

Seasonal Event

Wildflower Season. California State Poppy Reserve. 15101 W Lancaster Rd. Phone 661/942-0662. Usually late Mar-May.

Motel

★★ **BEST WESTERN ANTELOPE VALLEY INN.** *44055 N Sierra Hwy (93534). 661/948-4651; FAX 661/948-4651; res: 800/810-9430.* E-mail avinn@aol.com. 148 units, 1-3 story. S $65; D $73; each addl $7; suites $125; under 12 free. Crib free. Pet accepted. TV; cable. Heated pool; poolside serv, whirlpool. Playground. Complimentary full bkfst. Restaurant 5 am-11 pm. Rm serv 6 am-10 pm. Bar 5 pm-1:30 am. Ck-out 1 pm. Meeting rms. Business servs avail. In-rm modem link. Valet serv. Barber, beauty shop. Health club privileges. Many refrigerators. Cr cds: A, C, D, DS, ER, JCB, MC, V.

D SC

Restaurant

✓★ **EL TAPATIO.** *1006 E Avenue J (93535). 661/948-9673.* Hrs: 11 am-10 pm; Sun brunch 10 am-2 pm. Closed Thanksgiving, Dec 25. Res accepted. Mexican, Amer menu. Serv bar. Semi-a la carte: lunch $4.75-$6.45, dinner $4.95-$12.95. Sun brunch $7.25. Child's meals. Specialties: fajitas, tamales, rellenos. Mexican decor. Cr cds: A, C, D, MC, V.

D SC

Lassen Volcanic National Park (B-3)

(See also Chester, Red Bluff, Redding)

(44 mi E of Redding via CA 44; 51 mi E of Red Bluff via CA 36, 89)

This 165-square-mile park was created to preserve the area including Lassen Peak (10,457 feet), a volcano last active in 1921. Lassen Park, in the southernmost part of the Cascade Range, contains glacial lakes, virgin forests, mountain meadows and snow-fed streams. Hydrothermal features, the Devastated Area and Chaos Jumbles can be seen from Lassen Park Road. Boiling mud pots and fumaroles (steam vents) can be seen a short distance off the road at Sulphur Works. At Butte Lake, colorful masses of lava and volcanic ash blend with the forests, meadows and streams. The peak is named for Peter Lassen, a Danish pioneer who used it as a landmark in guiding immigrant trains into the northern Sacramento Valley.

The Devastated Area, after being denuded in 1915 by a mudflow and a hot blast, is slowly being reclaimed by small trees and flowers. The Chaos Crags, a group of lava plugs, were formed some 1,100 years ago. Bumpass Hell, a colorful area of mud pots, boiling pools and steam vents, is a three-mile round-trip hike from Lassen Park Road. Clouds of steam and sulfurous gases pour from vents in the thermal areas. Nearby is Lake Helen, named for Helen Tanner Brodt, first white woman to climb Lassen Peak (1864). At the northwest entrance is a visitor center (late June-Labor Day, daily) where one may find information on the park's human, natural and geological history. There are guided walks during the summer; self-guided nature trails and evening talks at some campgrounds. Camping (fee/site/night) at eight campgrounds; two-week limit except at Lost Creek and Summit Lake campgrounds (seven-day limit); check at the Ranger Stations for regulations.

Lassen Park Road is usually open mid-June to mid-October, weather permitting. Sulphur Works (south) and Manzanita Lake (northwest) entrances are open during winter months for winter sports.

Some facilities for the disabled (visitor center, comfort station & amphitheater at Manzanita Lake; other areas in park). For information and descriptive folder contact the Superintendent, PO Box 100, Mineral 96063; 530/595-4444.

Lava Beds National Monument (A-3)

(30 mi SW of Tulelake, off CA 139)

Seventy-two square miles of volcanic formations are preserved here in the extreme northeast part of the state. Centuries ago rivers of molten lava flowed here. In cooling, they formed a strange and fantastic region. Cinder cones dot the landscape—one rising 476 feet from its base. Winding trenches mark the collapsed roofs of lava tubes, an indicator of the 380 caves beneath the surface. Throughout the area are masses of lava hardened into weird shapes. Spatter cones may be seen where vents in the lava formed vertical tubelike channels, some only three feet in diameter but reaching downward 100 feet.

Outstanding caves include Sentinel Cave, named for a lava formation in its passageway; Catacombs Cave, with passageways resembling Rome's catacombs; and Skull Cave, with a broad entry cavern reaching approximately 80 feet in diameter. (The name comes from the many skulls of mountain sheep that were found here.) The National Park Service provides ladders and trails in the 24 caves easily accessible to the public.

In this rugged, other-world setting one of the most costly Native American campaigns in history took place. The Modoc War of 1872-1873 saw a small band of Native Americans revolt against reservation life and fight a series of battles with US troops. Although obliged to care for their families and live off the country, the Modocs held off an army almost 10 times their number for more than five months.

There is a campground at Indian Well (fee/site/night, water avail mid-May-Labor Day) and picnic areas at Fleener Chimneys and Captain Jacks Stronghold (no water). Guided walks, audiovisual programs, cave trips and campfire programs are held daily, mid-June-Labor Day. Headquarters has a visitor center (daily). No gasoline is available in the park—fill gas tank before entering. Golden Eagle, Golden Age and Golden Access passports accepted (see MAKING THE MOST OF YOUR TRIP). For further information, contact PO Box 867, Tulelake 96134; 530/667-2282. Per vehicle **¢¢**

Lee Vining (E-4)

(See also Bridgeport, June Lake)

Settled 1923 **Pop** 600 (est) **Elev** 6,781 ft **Area Code** 760 **Zip** 93541

A Ranger District office of the Inyo National Forest (see) is located here.

What to See and Do

Mono Lake. Located in the Mono Basin National Forest Scenic Area, Mono Lake is one of North America's oldest lakes. It contains 250 percent more salt than the ocean, and millions of migratory waterfowl feed on brine shrimp and brine flies. Stratified limestone rock formations, or tufa, surround the lake. Samuel Clemens wrote about the lake and its islands, volcanoes and gulls in *Roughing It.* (Daily) South Tufa area offers a visitor center with exhibits, movie; guided tours of lake area (all yr, 1 tour Sat & Sun; fee). Summer interpretive programs (July & Aug). NE of town. Lake access on W side. For more information contact the Visitor Center, PO Box 429, phone 760/647-6595. **Free** South Tufa area & tour **¢**

Yosemite National Park (see). W on CA 120.

Motel

★ **YOSEMITE GATEWAY MOTEL.** *85 Hwy 395 (93541), on US 395. 760/647-6467; FAX 760/647-6467; res: 800/282-3929.* 18 rms, 6 A/C, 1-2 story. May-Oct: S, D $69-$95; lower rates rest of yr. Crib $3. TV; cable. Whirlpool. Complimentary coffee in rms. Restaurant opp 6 am-10 pm. Ck-out 10 am. Downhill ski 11 mi; x-country ski 4 mi. Sun deck. View of Mono Lake. Cr cds: A, C, DS, MC, V.

Livermore (E-2)

(See also Fremont, Oakland, Pleasanton, San Jose, Santa Clara)

Pop 56,741 **Elev** 486 ft **Area Code** 925 **Zip** 94550
E-mail lcc@trivalley.com **Web** www.livermorechamber.com
Information Chamber of Commerce, 2157 First St; 925/447-1606

What to See and Do

Del Valle Regional Park. Centerpiece of these 3,997 acres is a 5-mi-long lake. Swimming, windsurfing, lifeguards in summer; fishing; boating (launch, rentals; 10 mph limit). Nature trails. Picnicking. Camping (all yr, fee; 150 sites; dump station, showers, 20 water/sewage hookups). Visitor center. From I-580, S on N Livermore, E on Tesla Rd, right on Mines Rd, S on Del Valle Rd to park entrance. For res phone 510/373-0332. Per vehicle **¢¢**; Camping **¢¢¢¢–¢¢¢¢¢**

Lawrence Livermore National Laboratory's Visitor Center. Research center operated by Univ of California for the US Dept of Energy. Multimedia presentation of the laboratory's major programs. Interactive and audio displays and computers allow for hands-on activities. (Mon-Fri, afternoons; closed major hols) 5 mi E via East Ave to Greenville Rd. Phone 510/423-3272. **Free**

Shadow Cliffs Regional Recreation Area. Formerly a gravel quarry on 255 acres. Swimming, bathhouse; fishing; boating (rentals). Hiking, riding trails. Picnicking. Giant water slide (Apr-Labor Day; fee). Between Livermore and Pleasanton; from I-580, S on Santa Rita Rd, left onto Valley Ave, then left onto Stanley Blvd to park entrance. Phone 510/846-3000. Per vehicle **¢¢**

Wineries.

Concannon Vineyard (1883). Picnic facilities. Tours; wine tasting. Horse carriage tours avail; inquire for details. (Daily; closed Jan 1, Easter, Thanksgiving, Dec 25) 4590 Tesla Rd, 3 mi S of I-580 via N Livermore Ave. Phone 510/455-7770. **Free**

Wente Bros Winery. Guided tours, tasting (daily; closed Jan 1, July 4, Thanksgiving, Dec 25). Picnic facilities by request. 5565 Tesla Rd, 2½ mi SE via S Livermore Ave. Phone 510/447-3603. A second location, at 5050 Arroyo Blvd, has restaurant (see), visitors center (daily) and guided tours on the hr. Phone 510/447-3694. **Free**

Annual Events

Wine and Honey Festival. Celebration focusing on wine, honey and bees. Early May.

Rodeo. PRCA sanctioned. 2 wkends June.

Restaurants

★★★ **WENTE BROTHERS.** *5050 Arroyo Rd (94550). 510/447-3696.* Hrs: 11:30 am-2:30 pm, 5:30-9:30 pm; Sat, Sun 10:30 am-2:30 pm, 5-9:30 pm; Sun brunch to 2:30 pm. Res accepted. Wine cellar. A la carte entrees: lunch $9.75-$16.75, dinner $15-$29. Sun brunch $9.75-$16.50. Complete meals Mon-Fri: lunch $16, dinner $28. Child's meals. Specializes in local meat and produce. Menu changes daily. Valet parking. Outdoor dining with view of grounds. California mission decor. Cr cds: A, C, D, MC, V.

D

★★★ **WENTE VINEYARDS.** *5050 Arroyo Rd.* Continental cuisine. Hrs: Mon-Sun 11:30 am-2:30 pm; 5:30-9:30 pm. Dinner prices $16-$30. Resv pref. Serv bar. Valet. Cr cds: C.

Lodi (E-3)

(See also Sacramento, Stockton)

Pop 51,874 **Elev** 51 ft **Area Code** 209

Information Lodi District Chamber of Commerce, 35 S School St, PO Box 386, 95241; 209/367-7840

Located in the northernmost county in the San Joaquin Valley, Lodi is surrounded by vineyards and a rich agricultural area. Lodi is home to the flame Tokay grape and more than 10 wineries.

What to See and Do

Camanche Recreation Area, South Shore. Swimming, waterskiing; fishing; boating (rentals, marina); tennis. Picnic facilities, concession, groceries. Camping (fee; hookups); cottages. 24 mi E off CA 12. Phone 209/763-5178. Day use ¢¢¢; Camping ¢¢¢¢

Lodi Lake Park. Major recreational facility for a wide area. Swimming beach; boating (rentals, ramp); nature area; discovery center; picnicking. (Daily) 1 mi W of US 99 on Turner Rd. Phone 209/333-6742 or 209/333-6888. Per vehicle ¢¢

Micke Grove Park & Zoo. Japanese garden, camellia and rose gardens; picnicking; historical museum. Zoo and park (daily; closed Dec 25). 11793 N Micke Grove Rd, 5 mi S, just off CA 99, Armstrong Rd exit. Phone 209/953-8800, 209/331-7400 or 209/331-7270 (zoo). Park per vehicle ¢–¢¢; Zoo ¢

Annual Events

Lodi Spring Wine Show & Food Faire. Festival Grounds, 413 E Lockeford St. Wine and food tastings from California wineries and food establishments. Art & flower shows; cooking demonstrations. Phone 209/369-2771. Late Mar.

Lodi Grape Festival and Harvest Fair. Festival Grounds, 413 E Lockeford St. County fair with exhibits, entertainment, carnival. Phone 209/369-2771. Late Sept.

Motels

✓★ **BEST WESTERN ROYAL HOST INN.** *710 S Cherokee Ln (95240). 209/369-8484; FAX 209/369-0654; res: 800/720-5634.* 48 rms, 2 story. S $45-$52; D $50-$62; each addl $8; suites $75. Crib $6. TV; cable (premium). Heated pool. Complimentary continental bkfst. Complimentary coffee in rms. Restaurant adj 8 am-11 pm. Ck-out 11 am. Refrigerators; some microwaves. Cr cds: A, C, D, DS, JCB, MC, V.

D SC

★★ **HOLIDAY INN.** *1140 S Cherokee Ln (95241). 209/334-6422; FAX 209/368-7967; res: 800/432-7613.* 95 rms, 2 story. S, D $70-$80; each addl $6; under 12 free. Crib free. TV; VCR avail. Pool; whirlpool. Complimentary continental bkfst. Restaurant nearby. Ck-out 11 am. Coin lndry. Meeting rms. Exercise equipt; sauna. Some refrigerators. Cr cds: A, C, D, DS, MC, V.

D SC

Inn

★★ **WINE & ROSES COUNTRY INN.** *2505 W Turner Rd (95242), jct Lower Sacramento Rd. 209/334-6988; FAX 209/334-6570.* E-mail info@winerose.com; web www.winerose.com. 10 rms, 2 story. S, D $125; each addl $15; suite $165; under 4 free. Crib free. TV; VCR avail. Complimentary full bkfst; afternoon refreshments. Restaurant (see WINE & ROSES). Rm serv. Ck-out 11 am, ck-in 3 pm. Business servs avail. Lawn games. Some balconies. Picnic tables. Historic inn, built 1902; individually decorated rms; fireplace in sitting rm. Situated on 5 acres, with shade trees and flower & herb gardens. Approx 1 mi from lake; swimming. Totally nonsmoking. Cr cds: A, C, D, DS, MC, V.

D

Restaurant

★★ **WINE & ROSES.** *(See Wine & Roses) 209/334-6988.* Hrs: 11:30 am-1:30 pm, 6-9 pm; Tues to 1:30 pm; Sat from 6 pm; Sun brunch 10:30 am-2 pm. Closed Mon; Dec 25. Res accepted. Serv bar. Semi-a la carte: lunch $7.25-$11.95, dinner $13.95-$23.95. Sun brunch $13.95. Specialties: fresh poached salmon with citrus salsa, rack of lamb. Entertainment Fri & Sat (summer). Garden dining. Totally nonsmoking. Cr cds: A, C, D, DS, MC, V.

D

Lompoc (H-2)

(See also Santa Maria, Solvang)

Settled 1874 **Pop** 37,649 **Elev** 104 ft **Area Code** 805 **Zip** 93436
E-mail chamber@lompoc.com **Web** www.lompoc.com

Information Chamber of Commerce, 111 South I St; 805/736-4567

Lompoc is known as "The City of Murals in the Valley of Flowers." Its more than two dozen murals showcase the works of internationally acclaimed muralists such as Roberto Delgado and Dan Sawatsky. Lompoc is also the flower seed capital of the world; most of the world's flower seeds come from here. From May through September, the city is bordered by over a thousand acres of vivid zinnias, marigolds, sweet peas, petunias, stock and other blossoms. Vandenberg AFB is ten miles west of here.

What to See and Do

La Purísima Mission State Historic Park. The 11th in a chain of 21 Franciscan missions. Founded in 1787, moved in 1812. Restored in current setting. Native American artifacts, mission relics. Guide map at museum. Craft demonstrations in summer. Picnicking. Living history tours summer and fall; write for schedule, fees. (Daily, mid-morning-mid-afternoon; closed Jan 1, Thanksgiving, Dec 25) 3 mi NE at jct Purisima Rd & Mission Gate Rd. For further information contact 2295 Purísima Rd; phone 805/733-3713. Per vehicle ¢¢

Mural Walk. More than 24 giant murals, painted by world class artists, adorn the exterior walls of buildings in old downtown. Contact Chamber of Commerce for brochure.

Annual Events

Greenhouse Tour. Spectacular display of flowers by Bodger Seed Company. Phone 805/737-0595. 2nd Sat Apr.

Flower Festival. Floral parade, flower exhibits, arts and craft show, entertainment, bus tours of 1,200 acres of flower fields. June.

Harvest Arts Festival. Features Mural-in-a-Day project—12 professional artists paint 12-ft x 48-ft mural in 9 hrs. Arts, music, entertainment, food. 2nd Sat Oct.

Motor Hotel

✓★★ **QUALITY INN.** *1621 N H St (90802). 805/735-8555; FAX 805/735-8566; res: 800/638-7949; res: 800/224-6530.* 218 rms, 4 story, 92 kits. S, D $74-$84; suites $85-$129; each addl $6; under 18 free. Crib free. Pet accepted; $25. TV; cable (premium). Heated pool; whirlpool. Full bkfst buffet. Coffee in rms. Ck-out noon. Coin lndry. Meeting rm. Business servs avail. Valet serv. Driving range. Health club privileges. Massage. Many refrigerators. Cr cds: A, C, D, DS, MC, V.

D SC

Hotel

★★★ **EMBASSY SUITES.** *1117 N H St (93436). 805/735-8311; FAX 805/735-8459; res: 800/362-2779; res: 800/433-3182.* E-mail gmlomca@aol.com. 155 suites, 3 story. Suites $107-$199; each addl $10; under 18 free. Crib free. TV; cable (premium), VCR avail. Heated pool; whirlpool. Complimentary full bkfst; evening refreshments. Coffee in rms. Ck-out noon. Coin lndry. Meeting rms. Business servs avail. In-rm modem link. Valet serv. Exercise equipt. Refrigerators. Balconies. Cr cds: A, C, D, DS, JCB, MC, V.

D SC

Lone Pine (F-4)

Pop 1,818 **Elev** 3,733 ft **Area Code** 760 **Zip** 93545
E-mail lpcc@cris.com **Web** www.cris.com/lpcc

Information Chamber of Commerce, 126 S Main, PO Box 749; 760/876-4444

Dating from the early 1860s, Lone Pine has catered to tourists and outfits hiking trips to nearby Mt Whitney (14,495 ft, tallest peak in the contiguous US). A 13-mile drive due west to the base of Mt Whitney leads through the unusual Alabama Hills.

A Ranger District office of the Inyo National Forest (see) is located here.

What to See and Do

Alabama Hills Recreation Area. Site of Indian Wars in the 1860s; named for Southern warship *Alabama.* These hills are a favorite film location for TV and movie companies because of the unique rock formations and Sierra backdrop. Contact Chamber of Commerce for details. 2 mi W via Whitney Portal Rd.

Death Valley National Monument (see). 70 mi E on CA 190.

Eastern California Museum. Little Pine Village; Native American baskets & artifacts; pioneer artifacts, photographs; natural history. (Daily exc Tues; closed major hols) 16 mi N via US 395, W on Center St in Independence. Phone 760/878-0364 or 760/878-0258. **Donation**

The Commander's House (1872). Victorian house, built for commander of Camp Independence and moved to present location in 1889; eight rooms of antique furniture, some made by soldiers at camp. (Late May-early Sept, Sat & Sun afternoons, also by appt) 16 mi N on US 395, 303 N Edwards in Independence. Phone 760/878-0364 or 760/878-0258. **Donation**

Annual Event

Lone Pine Film Festival. Celebration of movies made on location in Lone Pine. Fri eve concert; bus tour of movie locations; films; movie memorabilia; arts & crafts. Phone 760/876-4444 or 760/876-4314. Columbus Day wkend.

Motel

✓★★★ **DOW VILLA MOTEL.** *310 S Main St (93545). 760/876-5521; FAX 760/876-5643; res: 800/824-9317.* Web www.touringusa.com. 39 rms, 2 story. S, D $70-$80; each addl $5; suites $75; golf packages. Crib free. Pet accepted, some restrictions. TV; cable (premium), VCR avail. Heated pool; whirlpool. Complimentary coffee in rms. Restaurant open 24 hrs. Ck-out noon. Refrigerators. Some in-rm whirlpools. Motel for motion picture casts since the early 1920s. Cr cds: A, C, D, DS, MC, V.

D SC

Inn

✓★ **WINNEDUMAH COUNTRY INN.** *310 S Main St (93526), 15 mi on US 395. 760/878-2040; FAX 760/878-2833.* E-mail winnedum@cris.com; web www.cris.com/~winnedum. 24 air-cooled rms, 7 share bath, 2 story. Many rm phones. May-Oct: S $47-$57; D $55-$65; each addl $5-$8; wkend rates; lower rates rest of yr. Cable TV in common rm. Complimentary continental bkfst. Restaurant nearby. Ck-out 11 am, ck-in after 2 pm. Business servs avail. Luggage handling. Valet serv. Concierge serv. Downhill/x-country ski 10 mi. Built in 1927; movie stars and crews used this inn in the 1920s and 1940s. Totally nonsmoking. Cr cds: C, MC, V.

D SC

Long Beach (J-3)

(See also Anaheim, Buena Park, Los Angeles, Santa Ana)

Founded 1881 **Pop** 429,433 **Elev** 29 ft **Area Code** 562

Information Long Beach Area Convention & Visitors Bureau, One World Trade Center, #300, 90831; 562/436-3645 or 800/452-7829

A multibillion-dollar redevelopment program helped Long Beach become one of southern California's most diverse waterfront destinations, recapturing the charm it first attained as a premier California seaside resort in the early 1900s. Projects involving hotels and major attractions, along with shopping, commercial and residential area development, contributed to the revitalization of both the downtown and the waterfront. A 21.5-mile light rail system, the Metro Blue Line, connects Long Beach and Los Angeles.

Founded by British-born W.E. Willmore as the "American Colony" of Willmore City, the name change to Long Beach was prompted by a desire to advertise its 5½-mile-long, 500-foot-wide beach. Earlier in this century, prosperity came with the elegant hotels and summer houses of the wealthy, and later with the discovery of oil. Today, the state's largest beach city derives its economic security from the aerospace, harbor, oil and tourism industries. McDonnell Douglas is its largest employer.

What to See and Do

Alamitos Bay. 7 mi of inland waterways for swimming, sunning, windsurfing, boating.

California State University, Long Beach (1949). (32,000 students) On the 320-acre campus are monumental sculptures created by artists, from here and abroad, who participated in the first International Sculpture Symposium held in the US (1965); art museum with displays and exhibits; the Earl Burns Miller Japanese Garden. 1250 Bellflower Blvd. For campus tours (Mon-Fri, by appt) phone 562/985-5358.

El Dorado East Regional Park and Nature Center. A 450-acre park with four fishing lakes, boat rentals, archery range, nature and hiking trails, picnicking. Museum and visitors center (free). (Daily; closed Mon) 7550 E Spring St, at I-605. Phone 562/570-1745. Per vehicle **¢¢**

General Phineas Banning Residence Museum. Restored Greek-revival house (1864); exhibits tell of Banning's role in the development of Los Angeles. Docent tours (Tues-Thurs, Sat & Sun). 401 E M St in Wilmington. **Donation**

Long Beach Convention & Entertainment Center. A 111-acre multi-purpose complex houses major sporting arena, convention/exhibition complex and two traditional performing theaters. Terrace Theater has proscenium stage and Center Theater. Resident companies include Long Beach Symphony, Opera, Civic Light Opera and Classical Ballet. 300 E Ocean Blvd, at end of Long Beach Frwy. Phone 562/436-3636.

Long Beach Museum of Art. (Closed until June, 2000) Changing contemporary exhibitions housed in 1912 mansion overlooking the Pacific Ocean. Permanent collection includes American art, German expressionists, video art. Facilities include contemporary sculpture garden; education gallery; Media Arts Center (located in Station/Annex at 5373 E 2nd St, phone 562/439-0751; video production and post-production access). (Wed-Sun, mid-morning-mid-afternoon; extended hrs Fri; closed hols) 2300 E Ocean Blvd. Phone 562/439-2119. ¢

Long Beach Sport Fishing. Entertainment/fishing complex with full range of sportfishing vessels for half-day, three-quarter-day, full-day and night fishing excursions; restaurants; fish market; bar. Whale watching (Jan-Mar). 555 Pico Ave, in port of Long Beach. Phone 562/432-8993. ¢¢¢¢¢

Marinas. Downtown Shoreline Marina. Long Beach Marine Bureau. Slips for 1,824 pleasure craft; guest docking (fee). 450 E Shoreline Dr. Phone 562/570-1815. Shoreline Village has restaurants, shops. Fishing piers, five launching ramps, biking trails.

Alamitos Bay Marina. Slips for 2,005 pleasure craft; guest docking. On grounds is Seaport Village; restaurants, shops. (Daily) 205 Marina Dr. Phone 562/570-3215.

Municipal Beach. S of Ocean Blvd from Alamitos Ave to city limits. Lifeguards at many areas in summer. (Daily)

★ ***Queen Mary Seaport.*** This historic ship, which made more than 1,000 transatlantic crossings, is permanently docked here. Now a 365-rm hotel and tourist attraction, it is the centerpiece of a 55-acre site that includes the MegaBungee, one of the tallest free-standing bungee towers, and the Queen's Marketplace, with a number of eateries open for bkfst, lunch and dinner and opportunities for shopping. Guided and self-guided tours avail; res accepted for dining and guided tours (addl fee). (Daily) Located at the S end of the Long Beach Frwy (710), at 1126 Queens Hwy. Phone 562/435-3511. Admission ¢¢¢¢; Parking ¢¢

Rancho Los Alamitos. Guided tours of adobe ranch house (ca 1800) with antique furnishings; 6 barns and outbuildings, including a blacksmith shop; 5 acres of gardens. (Wed-Sun afternoons; closed hols) 6400 Bixby Hill Rd. Phone 562/431-3541. **Donation**

Rancho Los Cerritos (1844). One of original California land grants that became Long Beach. Renovated Monterey colonial-style adobe building served as headquarters for sheep ranchers in 1870s; historic garden; orientation exhibit. Special events throughout the yr (fee). Picnic area. (Wed-Sun afternoons; closed hols; guided tours on the hr, wkends) 4600 Virginia Rd. Phone 562/570-1755. **Free**

Shoreline Village. This 7-acre shopping, dining and entertainment complex recaptures the look and charm of a turn-of-the-century California seacoast village. Special features include a collection of unique shops, galleries and restaurants, a historic carousel and a complete marine center with daily harbor cruises and seasonal whale watch excursions. Alternative transportation to Shoreline Village is avail via the free Promenade Tram from downtown Long Beach, the Runabout Shuttle (also from downtown Long Beach) and the Water Taxi that transports passengers between Shoreline Village and the downtown marina. (Daily) Adj to the Downtown Shoreline Marina at the foot of Pine Ave, just S of the Convention Center. 419 Shoreline Village Dr. Phone 562/435-2668. **Free**

Sightseeing cruises.

Catalina Island. Daily excursions via Catalina Cruises. Departs from 320 Golden Shore Blvd. For schedule and fare information phone 800/228-2546. ¢¢¢¢¢

Catalina Channel Express. Departs from *Queen Mary.*

Annual Events

Toyota Grand Prix. International race held on downtown streets. Phone 562/981-2600. Apr 14-16.

Jazz Festival. Rainbow Lagoon Park. Festival info 562/436-7794. Aug 11-13.

Long Beach Blues Festival. Aug or Sept.

Boat Parades. Dec.

Motels

★★ **GUEST HOUSE.** *5325 E Pacific Coast Hwy (90804). 562/597-1341; FAX 562/597-1664; res: 800/272-6232.* 143 rms, 2 story. S, D $89-$149; each addl $10; suites $109-$149; under 18 free; wkly rates; higher rates Grand Prix. Crib free. Pet accepted. TV; cable (premium), VCR avail. Heated pool. Coffee in rms. Restaurant 7 am-10 pm. Bar to 2 am. Ck-out noon. Coin Indry. Meeting rms. Business servs avail. In-rm modem link. Valet serv. Airport transportation. Health club privileges. Some in-rm whirlpools, refrigerators; microwaves avail. Cr cds: A, C, D, DS, ER, JCB, MC, V.

D SC

✓★ **THE INN OF LONG BEACH.** *185 Atlantic Ave (90802), at Broadway. 562/435-3791; FAX 562/436-7510; res: 800/230-7500.* 46 rms, 2 story. S $48-$62; D $55-$70; each addl $5; suite $125; under 12 free; higher rates Grand Prix. Crib free. TV; cable (premium), VCR avail. Heated pool; whirlpool. Complimentary continental bkfst. Restaurant nearby. Ck-out noon. Business servs avail. In-rm modem link. Refrigerators avail. Balconies. Cr cds: A, C, D, DS, MC, V.

D SC

Motor Hotels

★★ **BEST WESTERN GOLDEN SAILS HOTEL.** *6285 E Pacific Coast Hwy (90803). 562/596-1631; FAX 562/594-0623; res: 800/762-5333.* E-mail goldsail@ix.netcom.com. 172 rms, 4 story. S, D $118-$138; each addl $10; under 12 free. Crib free. TV; cable (premium), VCR avail. Pool; whirlpool, poolside serv. Complimentary full bkfst. Restaurant 6 am-10 pm. Rm serv. Bar 10-2 am; entertainment. Ck-out noon. Coin Indry. Meeting rms. Business servs avail. In-rm modem link. Valet serv. Free airport transportation. Exercise equipt. Refrigerators; some in-rm whirlpools; microwaves avail. Private patios, balconies. Marina adj. Cr cds: A, C, D, DS, MC, V.

SC

★★ **COURTYARD BY MARRIOTT.** *500 E 1st St (90802). 562/435-8511; FAX 562/901-0296; res: 800/321-2211.* Web www.courtyard.com. 216 rms, 9 story. S, D $74-$94; wkend rates; higher rates: Grand Prix, special events. Crib free. TV; cable (premium). Heated pool; whirlpool. Restaurant 6:30-10 am, 5-10 pm. Rm serv 5-10 pm. Ck-out 1 pm. Coin Indry. Meeting rms. Business servs avail. In-rm modem link. Free garage parking. Valet serv. Exercise equipt. Balconies. Near beach, convention center. Cr cds: A, C, D, DS, MC, V.

D SC

Hotels

★★★ **HILTON.** *2 World Trade Ctr (90049), adj World Trade Center. 562/983-3400; FAX 562/983-1200; res: 800/445-8667.* Web www.hilton.com. 393 rms, 15 story. S $135-$200; D $155-$220; each addl $25; suites $450-$1,400; family rates; higher rates Grand Prix. Crib free. Pet accepted, some restrictions. Garage parking $8, valet $10. TV; cable (premium). Pool; whirlpool. Restaurant 6 am-midnight. Bar 4 pm-2 am. Ck-out noon. Convention facilities. Business center. In-rm modem link. Concierge. Gift shop. Beauty shop. Free airport transportation. Exercise rm; steam rm. Minibars; some wet bars; refrigerators avail. Balconies. Opp ocean; most rms have ocean view. Cr cds: A, C, D, DS, ER, JCB, MC, V.

D SC

★★★ **HYATT REGENCY.** *200 S Pine Ave (90831), adj Convention Center at Long Beach Marina. 562/491-1234; FAX 562/432-1972; res: 800/233-1234.* Web www.hyatt.com. 521 rms, 17 story. S $109-$218; D $109-$235; each addl $25; suites $325-$1,000; under 18 free. Crib free. Covered, garage, valet parking $10; self-park $8. TV; cable (premium), VCR avail. Heated pool; whirlpool, poolside serv. Restaurant 6 am-11 pm.

Bar 11-2 am. Ck-out noon. Convention facilities. Business center. In-rm modem link. Concierge. Gift shop. Exercise equipt. Opp harbor. Luxury level. Cr cds: A, C, D, DS, ER, JCB, MC, V.

D SC

★★★ **MARRIOTT.** *4700 Airport Plaza Dr (90815), at Municipal Airport. 562/425-5210; FAX 562/425-2744; res: 800/228-9290.* Web www.marriott.com. 311 rms, 8 story. S, D $99-$180; each addl $15; suites $350; under 13 free; wkend rates. TV; cable (premium), VCR avail. 2 pools, 1 indoor; whirlpool, poolside serv. Coffee in rms. Restaurants 6:30 am-11 pm. Bar noon-2 am. Ck-out noon. Convention facilities. Business center. In-rm modem link. Concierge. Gift shop. Free airport transportation. Golf privileges. Exercise equipt. Massage. Luxury level. Cr cds: A, C, D, DS, JCB, MC, V.

D SC

★★★ **RENAISSANCE HOTEL.** *111 E Ocean Blvd (90802). 562/437-5900; FAX 562/499-2509; res: 800/HOTELS1; res: 800/228-9898.* Web www.renaissancehotels.com. 374 rms, 12 story. S, D $109-$125; each addl $15; suites $175-$1,250; under 18 free; wkly rates; higher rates Grand Prix. Valet parking $8, garage $6. TV; cable (premium). Heated pool; poolside serv. Restaurant 6 am-11 pm. Bar to midnight. Ck-out noon. Convention facilities. Business center. In-rm modem link. Concierge. Gift shop. Free airport transportation. Exercise equipt; sauna. Minibars. Balconies. Luxury level. Cr cds: A, C, D, DS, ER, JCB, MC, V.

D SC

★★ **WESTCOAST HOTELS LONG BEACH.** *700 Queensway Dr (90802), I-710 exit Queensway Bay. 562/435-7676; FAX 310/437-0866; res: 800/426-0670.* Web www.westcoasthotels.com. 195 rms, 5 story. S $120-$140; D $140-$160; each addl $10; under 16 free. Crib free. TV; cable. Heated pool. Complimentary coffee in rms. Restaurant 6:30 am-10 pm; Fri-Sun 7 am-11 pm. Bar 11 am-11 pm. Ck-out noon. Meeting rms. Business servs avail. Gift shop. Free airport transportation. 2 lighted tennis courts. Exercise equipt. Health club privileges. Massage. Private patios, balconies. City, ocean view, bayside rms avail. Cr cds: A, C, D, DS, MC, V.

D SC

★★★ **WESTIN HOTEL.** *333 E Ocean Blvd (90802). 562/436-3000; FAX 562/436-9176; res: 800/228-3000.* 460 rms, 16 story. S, D $199-$209; each addl $20; suites $359-$1000; under 17 free; wkend rates; higher rates Grand Prix. Crib free. Pet accepted. Garage $8, valet parking $10. TV; cable (premium), VCR avail. Heated pool; whirlpool, poolside serv. Complimentary coffee in rms. Restaurant 6:30 am-10:30 pm. Rm serv 24 hrs. Bar 11-2 am. Ck-out noon. Convention facilities. Business center. In-rm modem link. Concierge. Gift shop. Exercise equipt; sauna. Minibars; some bathrm phones. Opp ocean. Cr cds: A, C, D, DS, JCB, MC, V.

D SC

Inns

★★★ **SEAL BEACH COUNTRY INN & GARDENS.** *212 5th St (90740), at Central Ave, near downtown. 562/493-2416; FAX 562/799-0483; res: 800/443-3292.* Web www.sealbeachinn.com. 24 rms, 2 story, 14 kits. S, D $155-$325. Crib $5. TV. Pool. Complimentary full bkfst. Restaurants nearby. Ck-out 11 am, ck-in 4-10 pm. Meeting rms. Business servs avail. Some in-rm whirlpools, fireplaces; microwaves avail. Some balconies. Ocean 300 yds. Restored inn (1923). Totally nonsmoking. Cr cds: A, C, D, DS, JCB, MC, V.

D SC

★★ **THE TURRET HOUSE VICTORIAN BED & BREAKFAST.** *556 Chestnut Ave (90802). 562/983-9812; FAX 562/437-4082; res: 888/488-7738.* E-mail innkeepers@turrethouse.com; web www.turrethouse.com. 5 air-cooled rms, 3 story. S, D $90-$150; higher rates special events. Premium cable TV in common rm. Complimentary full bkfst. Restaurant nearby. Ck-out 11 am, ck-in 3-9 pm. Street parking. Built in 1906; Victorian decor. Totally nonsmoking. Cr cds: C, D, MC, V.

Restaurants

✓★ **ANNELIESE'S BAVARIAN INN.** *5730 E 2nd St (90803). 562/439-4089.* Hrs: 11 am-2 pm, 4-9 pm; Sat, Sun from 4 pm. Closed Tues; major hols. Res accepted. German menu. Wine, beer. Semi-a la carte: lunch $5.95-$11.95, dinner $12.95-$14.95. Specialties: sauerbraten, Wienerschnitzel, rouladen. Bavarian decor. Cr cds: A, C, MC, V.

★★ **KING'S FISH HOUSE.** *100 W Broadway (90802). 562/432-7463.* Hrs: 11:15 am-10 pm; Fri, Sat to 11 pm; Sun to 9 pm; Sat, Sun brunch to 4 pm. Closed Thanksgiving, Dec 25. Res accepted. Seafood menu. Bar. Semi-a la carte: lunch $11-$13, dinner $15-$20. Sat, Sun brunch $9-$11. Child's meals. Specialties: sake-kasu Chilean sea bass, New Orleans barbecue shrimp. Blues music Wed, Sun. Street parking. Outdoor dining. Cr cds: A, C, D, DS, MC, V.

D

★★★ **MUM'S.** *144 Pine Ave (90802). 562/437-7700.* Hrs: 11:30 am-midnight; Fri, Sat to 2 am; Sun to 11 pm. Closed Thanksgiving, Dec 25. Res accepted. Bar 11:30-1 am. A la carte entrees: lunch $6.95-$13.95, dinner $8.95-$20.95. Specializes in California cuisine. Sushi bar. Jazz Tues-Sun. Valet parking. Patio dining. Cr cds: A, C, D, DS, MC, V.

D

★★★ **PARKER'S LIGHTHOUSE.** *435 Shoreline Dr #1 (90802), Shoreline Village. 562/432-6500.* Hrs: 11 am-11:30 pm; Fri, Sat to 1 am; Sun 10 am-11 pm; Sun brunch to 1 pm. Closed Dec 25. Res accepted. Bar. Wine list. Semi-a la carte: lunch $6.95-$13.95, dinner $11.95-$19.95. Sun brunch $17.95. Specializes in mesquite-grilled fresh fish, seafood platter, prime black Angus beef. Blues Sun. Patio dining. Landmark building overlooks Queen Mary and marina. Cr cds: A, C, D, DS, MC, V.

D

★★★ **THE YARD HOUSE.** *401 Shoreline Dr (90802), Shoreline Village. 562/628-0455.* Web www.yardhouse.com. Hrs: 11:30 am-midnight; Thurs-Sat to 2 am; Sun from 11 am. Closed Dec 25. Res accepted. Bar. Wine list. Semi-a la carte: lunch $5-$15, dinner $7-$30. Child's meals. Specializes in pizza, steak, seafood. Outdoor dining. One dining area is formal, the other is casual and features the world's largest selection of draft beer. Totally nonsmoking. Cr cds: A, C, D, MC, V.

D

Los Angeles Area (J-3 - J-4)

Occupying a land area of 463½ square miles, Los Angeles has spilled over from the plain into the canyons and foothills. Like an empire in miniature, it boasts mountains and deserts, canyons formed by skyscrapers and by rock, a Mediterranean climate and working ranches. The city has spread out and around the independent communities of Beverly Hills, Santa Monica, Culver City, Universal City and Inglewood. The Los Angeles city limits are twisting and confusing. Street maps are available at any Mobil service station.

Los Angeles Area Suburbs

The following suburbs and towns in the Los Angeles area are included in the *Mobil Travel Guide*. For information on any one of them, see the individual alphabetical listing. SURROUNDED BY LOS ANGELES: Beverly Hills, Culver City. NORTH OF LOS ANGELES: Burbank, Glendale, San Fernando. NORTHEAST OF LOS ANGELES: Arcadia, Pasadena, San Gabriel, San Marino. EAST OF LOS ANGELES: Fullerton, La Habra, Pomona, Whittier. SOUTHEAST OF LOS ANGELES: Anaheim, Buena

Park, Corona del Mar, Costa Mesa, Garden Grove, Huntington Beach, Irvine, Laguna Beach, Newport Beach, Orange, Santa Ana; also see Disneyland. SOUTH OF LOS ANGELES: Long Beach, Torrance. WEST OF LOS ANGELES: Malibu, Marina del Rey, Redondo Beach, Santa Monica. NORTHWEST OF LOS ANGELES (San Fernando Valley): San Fernando, Studio City, Valencia, Van Nuys, Woodland Hills.

Los Angeles Neighborhoods

The following neighborhoods in the city of Los Angeles are included in the *Mobil Travel Guide*. For information on any one of them, see the individual alphabetical listing. Hollywood, North Hollywood, San Pedro, Studio City, Van Nuys, Westwood Village and Woodland Hills.

Los Angeles (J-4)

Founded 1781 **Pop** 3,485,398 **Elev** 330 ft **Area Code** 213, 310, 569 or 818 (San Fernando Valley)

Information Convention and Visitors Bureau, 633 W Fifth St, Suite 6000, 90071; 213/624-7300

Imagine a sprawling formation made up of a thousand pieces from a thousand different jigsaw puzzles. Illuminate it with klieg lights and flashing neon signs, garnish it with rhinestones, oranges and oil wells—and you have Los Angeles.

The city has many faces: excitement, tranquility, tall buildings, cottages, ultramodern electronics plants, off-beat religious sects, health fads, sunshine, smog, movie stars and would-be stars, artists, writers, libraries, museums, art galleries, super highways and real estate booms.

Los Angeles presents a distilled, concentrated picture of the United States. People are drawn to its glamour, riches, excitement and sunshine—all of which have encouraged a general informality. Beneath the glitter and salesmanship there is a pioneer spirit. Although no further geographic frontiers exist, many writers, researchers, scientists and artists have settled in this area to explore scientific and intellectual frontiers.

Los Angeles is a young city with ancient roots. Along with modern architecture, exuberant growth and a cultural thirst, it has retained a Spanish serenity and historical interest. On September 4, 1781, Don Felipe de Neve, Governor of California, marched to the site of the present city and with solemn ceremonies founded El Pueblo de Nuestra Señora La Reina de Los Angeles de Porciuncula "The Town of Our Lady the Queen of the Angels of Porciuncula"—now popularly shortened to "Los Angeles."

The little pueblo slumbered until 1846, when the seizure of California by the United States converted it into a vigorous frontier community. The gold rush of 1849 fanned its growth; for a time lawlessness became so prevalent that the city was referred to as Los Diablos—The Devils. The railroads reached it in 1885 and 1886 and, helped by a fare war, brought a tidal wave of new settlers. By 1890 a land boom developed and the population figure reached 50,000, with oil derricks appearing everywhere. The piping in of water from the Owens Valley in 1913 paved the way for expansion and doubling of the population in the 1920s. In the half century between 1890 and 1940, the city grew from 50,395 to 1,504,277—a gain of more than 2,000 percent. The war years added new industries and brought new waves of population which continued throughout the 1980s. Currently, the city's economic assets are invested in "growth" industries such as electronics, machinery, chemicals, oil, printing, publishing, tourism and entertainment.

The city's geographic scope makes it almost essential that visitors drive their own car, or rent one, for sightseeing in areas other than the downtown section and Westwood. Parking facilities are ample.

Transportation

Airport. See LOS ANGELES INTL AIRPORT AREA.

Car Rental Agencies. See IMPORTANT TOLL-FREE NUMBERS.

Public Transportation. Buses (Metropolitan Transit Authority), phone 213/626-4455.

Rail Passenger Service. Amtrak 800/872-7245.

What to See and Do

Amateur Athletic Foundation. Resource Center contains more than 35,000 print and non-print volumes, multipurpose pavilion, audio and video exhibits, Olympic awards and memorabilia. (Mon-Fri; closed hols) 2141 W Adams Blvd; 5 mi SW via Santa Monica Frwy, Western Ave exit. Phone 323/730-9600. **Free**

Beach areas. There are miles of oceanfront in Los Angeles County within 35 mi of downtown Los Angeles. Beaches include Malibu, Santa Monica, Ocean Park, Venice, Manhattan, Redondo, Long Beach and others. Redondo Beach has a horseshoe pier and yacht harbor.

Descanso Gardens. On 165 acres with 10-acre native plant garden. Ornamental camellia gardens, more than 100,000 plants in bloom Dec-Mar, peaking in mid-Feb. Azalea and rhododendron display Mar-Apr; 5-acre rose garden in bloom May-Oct; iris and lilacs in spring; annuals in summer. (Daily 9-4:30, exc Dec 25) Tram tours (daily exc Mon). Hospitality House with changing artwork (daily). Oriental Pavilion with teahouse (Sat, Sun). 1418 Descanso Dr, just S of Foothill Blvd in La Cañada/Flintridge. Phone 818/952-4401. ¢¢

Downtown. Contains, among others, these facilities:

ARCO Plaza. Bi-level, subterranean shopping center; art shows, exhibits; restaurants, specialty & service shops. 505 S Flower St.

Broadway Plaza. Designed after an Italian Renaissance shopping galleria. 7th & Hope Sts.

Chinatown. Quaint shops and Chinese restaurants on "Street of the Golden Palace." N Broadway near College St.

City Hall. First tall building constructed in southern California. Observation deck (27th floor) in the tower. (Mon-Fri; closed hols) 200 N Main St. Phone 213/485-2121.

Grand Central Market. City' s oldest (1917) and largest open-air market offers fresh produce and goods from California and around the world. Parking at Hill & 3rd Sts.

Hall of Justice. County law enforcement headquarters. 211 W Temple St.

Little Tokyo. Japanese restaurants, art and crafts shops, flower exhibits. 1st St between Main & San Pedro Sts.

Los Angeles Children's Museum. "Hands-on" exhibits and programs designed to help children satisfy their curiosity about the world in which they live; includes "City Streets," where children drive a bus and ride a policeman's motorcycle, recording and TV studios and "H-2-O," a participatory look at how to use and conserve water. (Sat & Sun) 310 N Main St. Phone 213/687-8800. ¢¢

Los Angeles Mall. Mall complex; shops, restaurants; triforium; music and light presentation. Spring St across from City Hall.

Museum of Contemporary Art (MOCA). Seven-level museum devoted to art created since the early 1940s. The building, most of which is below street level, features 11 pyramidial skylight forms and a 53-ft barrel-vaulted structure housing the library and boardrm and serving as the entrance to the exhibits below. Paintings, photographs, drawings, sculptures and "transmedia." (Daily exc Mon; closed Jan 1, Thanksgiving, Dec 25) Free admission Thurs eves. 250 S Grand Ave, at California Plaza. Phone 213/621-2766. ¢¢¢

Music Center of Los Angeles County. Performing arts center contains Dorothy Chandler Pavilion, Ahmanson Theatre, Mark Taper Forum. Daily performances by renowned music, dance and theater companies. (See SEASONAL EVENTS) Free guided tours. 135 N Grand Ave, at First St. Phone 213/972-7211 for ticket information.

Wells Fargo History Museum. More than 140 yrs of Wells Fargo history depicted by displays and exhibits, including Dorsey gold collection, stagecoaches, treasure boxes, reward posters, 19th-century tools, archival documents, photographs, Western art objects and a reproduction of a Wells Fargo office (ca 1860); audiovisual presentations. (Mon-Fri; closed hols) 333 S Grand Ave, Plaza Level. Phone 213/253-7166. **Free**

World Trade Center. Retail stores, restaurants, banks, golf driving ranges, tennis center, travel and tour services. Concourse mural depicts the history of world trade. 350 S Figueroa St. Phone 213/489-3337.

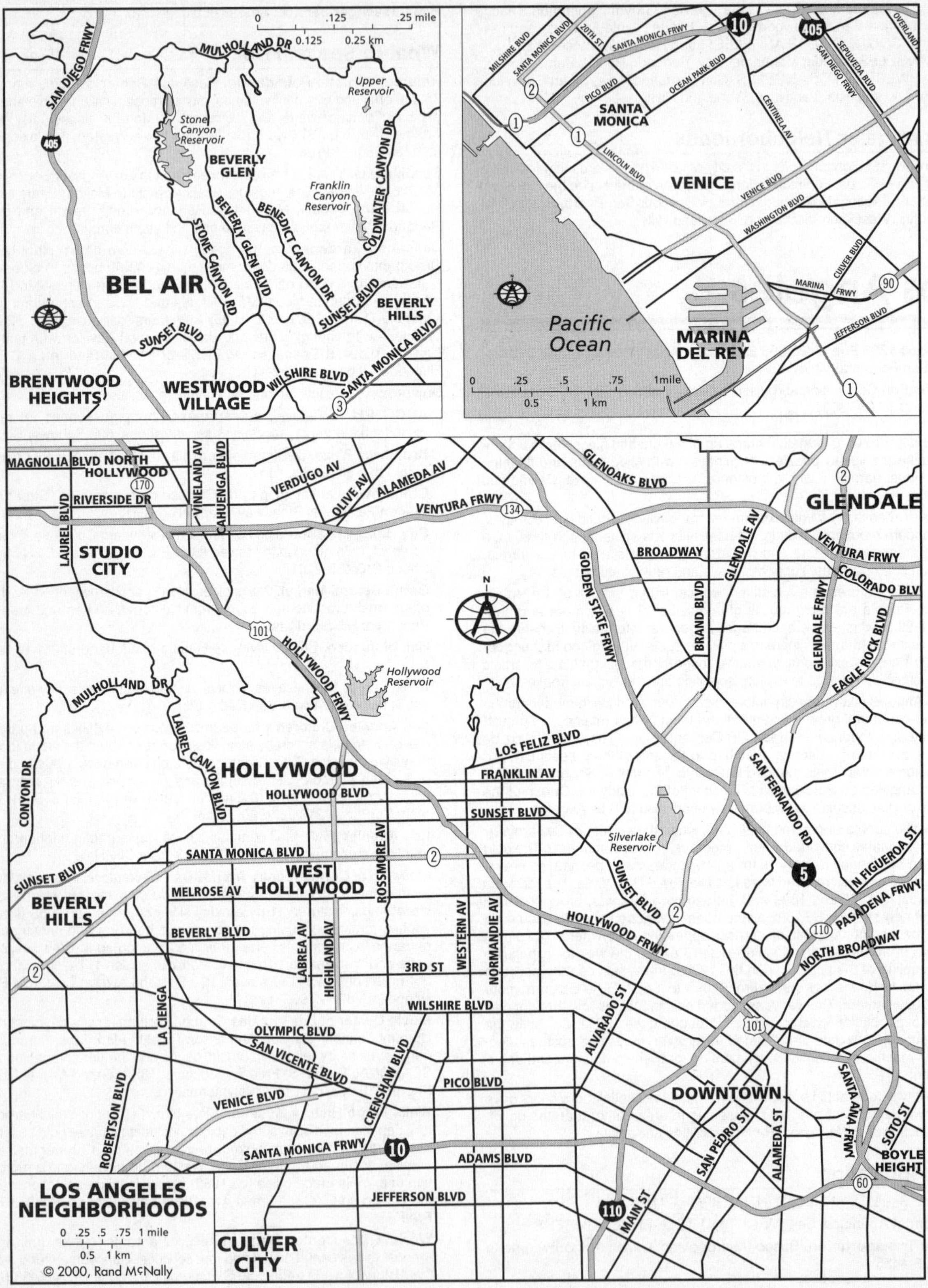

LOS ANGELES NEIGHBORHOODS
0 .25 .5 .75 1 mile
0.5 1 km
© 2000, Rand McNally
0 .125 .25 mile
0.125 0.25 km
BEL AIR
BEVERLY GLEN
BEVERLY HILLS
BRENTWOOD HEIGHTS
WESTWOOD VILLAGE
Stone Canyon Reservoir
Upper Reservoir
Franklin Canyon Reservoir
MULHOLLAND DR
SAN DIEGO FRWY
405
BEVERLY GLEN BLVD
STONE CANYON RD
BENEDICT CANYON DR
COLDWATER CANYON DR
SUNSET BLVD
WILSHIRE BLVD
SANTA MONICA BLVD
3
SANTA MONICA
VENICE
MARINA DEL REY
Pacific Ocean
0 .25 .5 .75 1mile
0.5 1 km
10
MILSHIRE BLVD
SANTA MONICA BLVD
20TH ST
SANTA MONICA FRWY
OCEAN PARK BLVD
PICO BLVD
LINCOLN BLVD
CENTINELA AV
SAN DIEGO FRWY
SEPULVEDA BLVD
OVERLAND
VENICE BLVD
WASHINGTON BLVD
CULVER BLVD
MARINA FRWY
90
JEFFERSON BLVD
1
2
MAGNOLIA BLVD
NORTH HOLLYWOOD
170
RIVERSIDE DR
LAUREL BLVD
VINELAND AV
CAHUENGA BLVD
VERDUGO AV
OLIVE AV
ALAMEDA AV
VENTURA FRWY
134
GLENOAKS BLVD
GLENDALE
STUDIO CITY
BROADWAY
GLENDALE AV
GOLDEN STATE FRWY
BRAND BLVD
VENTURA FRWY
COLORADO BLV
GLENDALE FRWY
EAGLE ROCK BLVD
101
HOLLYWOOD FRWY
Hollywood Reservoir
MULHOLLAND DR
LAUREL CANYON BLVD
LOS FELIZ BLVD
FRANKLIN AV
HOLLYWOOD
HOLLYWOOD BLVD
SUNSET BLVD
CONYON DR
SAN FERNANDO RD
Silverlake Reservoir
SANTA MONICA BLVD
WEST HOLLYWOOD
ROSSMORE AV
MELROSE AV
SUNSET BLVD
BEVERLY HILLS
5
N FIGUEROA ST
PASADENA FRWY
110
NORTH BROADWAY
BEVERLY BLVD
LABREA AV
HIGHLANDAV
WESTERN AV
NORMANDIE AV
3RD ST
LA CIENGA
WILSHIRE BLVD
ALVARADO ST
OLYMPIC BLVD
SAN VICENTE BLVD
CRENSHAW BLVD
PICO BLVD
VENICE BLVD
ROBERTSON BLVD
DOWNTOWN
SANTA ANA FRWY
SOTO ST
SANTA MONICA FRWY
ADAMS BLVD
SAN PEDRO ST
ALAMEDA ST
BOYLE HEIGHT
60
JEFFERSON BLVD
MAIN ST
CULVER CITY

El Pueblo de Los Angeles Historic Monument. Marks area close to where original pueblo of Los Angeles was founded in 1781. Much of the park has been restored; addl building restorations are underway that will also reflect the history and atmosphere of old Los Angeles. Exhibit on "History of Water in Los Angeles." 125 Paseo de la Plaza. For tour res phone 213/680-2525. **Free** The park includes

Avila Adobe. The oldest existing house in Los Angeles (ca 1820), damaged by an earthquake in 1971, now restored as an example of 1840s lifestyle in honor of Los Angeles' Hispanic heritage. (Daily) **Free**

Guided walking tours leave from Sepulvada House (see).

Nuestra Señora La Reina de Los Angeles (Our Lady Queen of the Angels) (1818-1822). The restored Old Plaza Catholic Church is still an active parish. Contains fine old statuary. (Daily) Phone 213/629-3101. **Free**

Old Plaza Firehouse. Built as Los Angeles' first firehouse in 1884; restored as a museum with photographs and fire-fighting equipment of 19th century. (Tues-Sun) 134 Paseo de la Plaza. Phone 213/625-3741. **Free**

Olvera Street. Preserved as a picturesque Mexican street market with stalls, shops and restaurants selling traditional food and merchandise. It has several annual celebrations, which include Blessing of the Animals (Sat before Easter), Cinco de Mayo (May 5), the city's birthday (Sept 4), Mexican Independence Day (Sept 15) and Los Posadas (Dec 16-24). (Daily) **Free**

Sepulveda House (1887). Partially restored Victorian business block; also houses **Visitors Center** (daily exc Sun). Offers 18-min film on early history of Los Angeles and the park (shown upon request). 622 S Main St. Phone 213/628-1274.

Elysian Park. Covers 575 acres with beautiful landscaping. Picnicking, playground, tennis courts and ballfields. Dodger Stadium, home of L.A. Dodgers baseball team, is located here. (Daily) Near intersection of Pasadena & Golden State Frwys. **Free**

Exposition Park. Park includes sunken rose garden, picnic grounds. Sports arena, Los Angeles Swimming Stadium. Figueroa St & Exposition Blvd. Park is also the setting for

California Museum of Science and Industry. Hands-on exhibits on science, mathematics, economics, the urban environment, energy and health. Hall of Health; Aerospace Hall; earthquake simulator; IMAX theater offers films (fee). (Daily; closed Jan 1, Thanksgiving, Dec 25) 700 State Dr, adj to the Coliseum. Phone 213/744-7400. **Free**

Los Angeles Memorial Coliseum and Sports Arena. Home field for USC teams and Clippers basketball. Also scene of soccer, concerts, track events and many others. Seating capacity of 92,516. Tours (Tues, Thurs, Sat). 3911 S Figueroa St. Phone 213/747-7111 or 213/765-6347 (res). Tour. **¢¢**

Natural History Museum of Los Angeles County. Permanent science exhibits feature mammal, bird, insect and marine life as well as dinosaurs, other prehistoric fossils and extinct creatures. Minerals and metals display includes extensive collection of cut gems. History gallery includes features on US history; 400 yrs of life in California; displays of pre-Columbian cultures. Docent tours (1 tour every afternoon exc 1st Tues of each month). Cafeteria. Parking fee. (Daily exc Mon; closed Jan 1, Thanksgiving, Dec 25) Free admission 1st Tues of month. 900 Exposition Blvd. Phone 213/763-3466 (recording). **¢¢¢**

Farmers Market. Historic landmark with outdoor food stalls, restaurants and shops. (Daily; closed hols) Corner of 3rd & Fairfax Ave. Phone 323/933-9211.

George C. Page Museum of La Brea Discoveries. Houses more than one million prehistoric specimens recovered from the La Brea asphalt deposits or "tar pits." More than 30 exhibits, including reconstructed skeletons; murals, theaters. (Daily exc Mon; closed Jan 1, July 4, Thanksgiving, Dec 25) Free admission 1st Tues of each month. 5801 Wilshire Blvd, in Hancock Park. Phone 323/857-6311 or 323/936-2230 (recording). **¢¢¢**

★ **Griffith Park.** More than 4,000 mountainous acres with swimming pool (fee); bridle paths; 4 golf courses (fee); tennis courts (fee), baseball fields and many picnic grounds. (Daily) N end of Vermont Ave, bordered by Ventura Frwy on N, Golden State Frwy on E, Los Feliz Blvd entrances on S. Also in the park are merry-go-round, miniature railroad, refreshment stands and

Greek Theatre. Scene of summer season of musical events in open-air setting. 2700 N Vermont Ave. Phone 323/665-5857.

Griffith Observatory and Planetarium. Includes Hall of Science (summer, daily; winter, daily exc Mon; closed Thanksgiving, Dec 24, 25; fee). Planetarium has frequent shows (daily exc Mon in winter; under age 5 admitted only 1:30 pm shows and special children's shows). Telescope (nightly exc Mon in winter). Laserium Light concerts (phone 818/901-9405); bookshop. 2800 E Observatory Rd. Phone 323/664-1191 (recording) for planetarium show schedule. Planetarium shows **¢¢**; Light concerts **¢¢¢**

Los Angeles Zoo. On 113 landscaped acres; animals grouped by continental origin; reptile house, aviary, aquatic section; koala house; children's zoo; animal rides. Tram service. Picnic areas, concessions. (Daily; closed Dec 25) 5333 Zoo Dr, in center of park. **¢¢¢**

Travel Town. Transportation museum with antique trains, steam engines, planes, fire engines, cable cars. Picnic areas, concession. (Daily; closed Dec 25) 5200 W Zoo Dr. Phone 213/662-5874. **Free**

In the area are

Cabrillo Marine Aquarium (see SAN PEDRO).

Disneyland (see). 26 mi SE via Santa Ana Frwy in Anaheim.

Hollywood (see). Reached via Hollywood Frwy.

Knott's Berry Farm (see BUENA PARK).

Los Angeles Maritime Museum (see SAN PEDRO).

Mission San Fernando Rey de España (see SAN FERNANDO).

Ports o'Call Village (see SAN PEDRO).

Six Flags California (see VALENCIA).

Trips to Catalina Island (see LONG BEACH). Also from Los Angeles International Airport.

Los Angeles County Museum of Art. This outstanding museum consists of 5 buildings. The Robert Anderson Bldg houses the 20th-century art collection and traveling exhibitions; the Ahmanson Bldg houses small changing exhibits and the museum's permanent collection, including paintings, sculptures, graphic arts, costumes, textiles and decorative arts of different cultures and periods, dating from prehistoric to modern times; the Hammer Bldg has major changing exhibits; the Leo S. Bing Center has music, film and theater programs; 2 cafes and educational services; and the Pavilion for Japanese Art displays Japanese paintings, sculpture, lacquerware, screens, scrolls and prints. (Daily exc Mon; closed Thanksgiving, Dec 25) Free admission 2nd Wed each month. 5905 Wilshire Blvd, 2 blks E of Fairfax Ave. Phone 323/857-6000. **¢¢¢**

★ **Los Angeles State and County Arboretum** (see ARCADIA).

Lummis Home and Garden State Historical Monument. Picturesque stone-faced house of Charles F. Lummis (1859-1928), author, historian, librarian and archaeologist; surrounded by model 2-acre water-conserving garden. Also HQ for Historical Society of Southern California. (Fri-Sun afternoons; closed hols) 200 E Ave 43, adj to Pasadena Frwy (CA 110). Phone 323/222-0546. **Free**

Mulholland Drive. Runs along crest of Santa Monica Mts. For a look at the Los Angeles hills and canyons and views of the city and San Fernando Valley, this drive is unsurpassed. Reached by Laurel Canyon Blvd, Hollywood Blvd, Coldwater Canyon Dr, Beverly Glen Blvd and other roads.

Museum of Tolerance. Unique museum focuses on 2 central themes: the Holocaust and the history of racism and prejudice in the American experience. (Daily exc Sat) 9786 W Pico Blvd, The Simon Wiesenthal Center. For schedule and fee information phone 310/553-8403. **¢¢¢**

Paramount Film and Television Studios. Two-hr walking tour of studios (Mon-Fri; no tours hols) and tapings of situation comedies and talk shows (seasonal; usually Tues or Fri eves). Walking tour given 2 times daily. Minimum age 10 yrs for studio tour and 18 yrs for television tapings. For taping schedule write to Paramount Promotional Services, 5555 Melrose Ave. (Mon-Fri) 5555 Melrose Ave, between Van Ness Ave & Gower St. Phone 323/956-1777. Tour **¢¢¢¢**; Tapings **Free**

Professional sports.

National League baseball (Los Angeles Dodgers). Dodgers Stadium, 1000 Elysian Park Ave. Phone 213/224-1500.

NBA (Los Angeles Clippers). LA Memorial Sports Arena, 3939 Figueroa St. Phone 213/745-0400.

NBA (Los Angeles Lakers). Great Western Forum, 3900 W Manchester Blvd, Inglewood. Phone 310/419-3100.

NHL (Los Angeles Kings). Great Western Forum, 3900 W Manchester Blvd, Inglewood. Phone 310/419-3160.

San Antonio Winery. Winery, gift shop, wine tasting; restaurant. Self-guided tours. (Daily; closed major hols) 737 Lamar St. Phone 323/223-1401. **Free**

South Coast Botanic Garden. Hillside and coastal plants on 87 acres of filled land. (Daily; closed Dec 25) 26300 Crenshaw Blvd, 1 mi S of Pacific Coast Hwy in Palos Verdes Peninsula. Phone 310/544-6815. **¢¢**

Southwest Museum. Prehistoric to contemporary Native American art and artifacts; research library. (Daily exc Mon; closed major hols) 234 Museum Dr, at Marmion Way, Pasadena Frwy, Ave 43 exit. Phone 323/221-2163. **¢¢**

State historic parks.

Los Encinos. Early California ranch; exhibits of ranch life contained in 9-rm adobe. Blacksmith shop, spring and small lake. Picnicking. Grounds (Wed-Sun 10 am-5 pm). 16756 Moorpark St, in Encino. Phone 818/784-4849. **Free**

Will Rogers. Home contains Rogers memorabilia, western art, Native American artifacts; audio tour and film. Hiking and riding trails (horses not avail). Picnicking. (Daily; closed Jan 1, Thanksgiving, Dec 25) Polo games (Sat afternoons, Sun mornings, weather permitting; phone 310/573-5000). 15 mi W, 1501 Will Rogers State Park Rd, in Pacific Palisades. Will Rogers polo club phone 310/454-8212. Per vehicle (per day) and tour **¢¢¢**

★ **The Getty Center.** 110-acre campus dedicated to visual arts and humanities situated in the Santa Monica Mts. Tram takes visitors up hill to central plaza with grand staircase leading to J. Paul Getty Museum, which features six 2-story pavilions; an open courtyard with changing exhibits; and a permanent collection of pre-20th-century European paintings, drawings, illuminated manuscripts, sculpture and decorative arts, and 19th- and 20th-century American and European photographs. The campus also has an auditorium, museum bookstore, restaurant, cafes, and extensive gardens and terraces with views of city and ocean. (Daily; closed major hols) Parking res required. 1200 Getty Center Dr, Suite 1000. For information and res, phone 310/440-7300. **¢¢**

"The Stack" is a 4-level junction of freeways. Motorists are likely to arrive in central Los Angeles on one of them. The high-speed, 6- and 8-lane roads cut across town: Hollywood Frwy to Hollywood and San Fernando Valley; Harbor Frwy to the south; Santa Ana Frwy to the southeast; San Bernardino Frwy to the east; Pasadena Frwy to Pasadena.

TV production studios.

CBS Television City. West Coast studios of CBS-Television and source of many of its network telecasts. Write for free tickets well in advance (specify dates and shows preferred) and enclose a stamped, self-addressed envelope. Tickets may also be picked up at Information Window (daily) on a first come, first served basis. Age limits for admittance vary and are specified on tickets; children under 12 not admitted to any broadcast; ages 12-15 with adult only. (Mon-Fri) 7800 Beverly Blvd, at Fairfax Ave, 90036. **Free**

NBC Studios Tour. Free tickets to a taping of one of NBC's TV shows; free parking. Age limits are specified on face of tickets. For tour information phone 818/840-3537 (24 hrs). 3000 W Alameda Ave, Burbank 91523. For general information phone 818/840-4444. Tours (Mon-Fri) **¢¢¢**

UCLA Mildred Mathias Botanical Garden. Collection of plants, trees and shrubs. Parking (fee). (Daily; closed univ & federal hols, also Jan 2, day after Thanksgiving, Dec 24) Guided tour of campus from visitors center (wkdays). Hilgard & Le Conte Aves. Phone 310/825-3620. **Free**

Universal Studios Hollywood. Offers a full day of behind-the-scenes views of Hollywood's largest and busiest studio; 45-min tram ride through 420-acre production area where motion pictures and television films are made. Experience the excitement of Jurassic Park—The Ride, *Backdraft* Live, fly with *E.T.*, face *King Kong,* and feel Earthquake, the Big One; also, take "the greatest ride in history" on *Back to the Future,* The Ride. Tours (daily; closed Thanksgiving, Dec 25). 100 Universal City Plaza, ½ blk N of Hollywood Frwy in Universal City. Phone 818/508-9600 (recording) or 818/622-3750. **¢¢¢¢¢**

Universities.

Fowler Museum of Cultural History, UCLA. Changing exhibits on cultures around the world. Museum store. (Wed-Sun afternoons, also Thurs eves) Free admission Thurs. Parking (fee). Enter campus from Sunset Blvd, at the Westwood Plaza entrance, and inquire about parking availability at the information kiosk. Located near the center of the campus. For information phone 310/825-4361. **¢¢**

University of California, Los Angeles (UCLA) (1919). (34,000 students) Tours (Mon-Fri). Art gallery, botanical garden, Franklin D. Murphy Sculpture Garden. Parking (fee). 405 Hilgard Ave. Phone 310/825-4321. Also here is

University of Southern California (1880). (29,500 students) This is the oldest and largest private university in the western US. Points of interest on campus include Fisher Gallery, 823 Exposition Blvd (Sept-Apr, Tues-Sat; May-Aug, by appt) phone 213/740-4561; Hancock Memorial Museum (Mon-Fri by appt). 3551 University Ave. For tour information, phone 213/740-1616 or 213/740-6605.

Watts Towers. Eight spires made of reinforced steel covered with cement, assembled without welding, nuts or bolts and encrusted with 70,000 bits of tile, crockery and bottles. Built solely by the late Simon Rodia over a 33-yr period, described as "paramount achievement of 20th-century American folk art." Two of the towers rise 100 ft. No tours due to restoration. Also art center (free) at 1727 E 107th St (Tues-Sun). Tower (Sat & Sun). 1765 E 107th St, S of Century Blvd, E of Harbor Frwy in Watts. Phone 213/847-4646.

Annual Events

Chinese New Year. Phone 213/617-0396. Feb.

Cinco de Mayo Celebration. El Pueblo de Los Angeles Historic Monument. Arts and crafts, music and dancing. May 5.

Lotus Festival. Echo Park Lake, Park & Glendale Ave. Celebrates various Asian and Pacific Island Cultures. 3900 Chevy Chase Dr. Phone 213/485-1310. Mid-July.

Nisei Week. Little Tokyo. Japanese cultural exhibits. Phone 213/687-7193. July 29- Aug 6.

Los Angeles County Fair. Fairplex, 1101 W McKinley Ave in Pomona (see). Largest in the nation. Early-late Sept.

Seasonal Events

Horse racing.

Santa Anita Park (see ARCADIA).

Hollywood Park. Century Blvd & Prairie Ave in Inglewood. Phone 310/419-1500. Late Apr-late July & early Nov-late Dec.

Greek Theatre in Griffith Park. Musical events. Mid-June-late Sept.

Los Angeles Music Center Opera. Music Center of Los Angeles County, Dorothy Chandler Pavilion, 135 N Grand Ave. Phone 213/972-7211. Early Sept-June.

Additional Visitor Information

The Los Angeles Convention and Visitors Bureau, 633 W Fifth St, Suite 6000, 90071; 213/624-7300, handles written inquiries and has general information brochures available in English, French, German, Japanese and Spanish. Printed tourist guides are available at two visitor information centers: downtown at 685 S Figueroa St, phone 213/689-8822; and in Hollywood, 6541 Hollywood Blvd, phone 213/236-2311. In addition, multilingual counselors are on staff at each information center to assist visitors.

Los Angeles Magazine, available at newsstands, has up-to-date information on cultural events and articles of interest to visitors.

Los Angeles Area Suburbs

For Los Angeles area suburbs listed in the *Mobil Travel Guide*, see LOS ANGELES AREA, which precedes LOS ANGELES.

Los Angeles Intl Airport Area

For additional accommodations, see LOS ANGELES INTL AIRPORT AREA, which follows LOS ANGELES.

City Neighborhoods

Many of the restaurants, unrated dining establishments and some lodgings listed under Los Angeles include neighborhoods as well as exact street addresses. Geographic descriptions of these areas are given.

Bel Air. West of Downtown; south of Mulholland Dr, west of Beverly Hills, north of the University of California Los Angeles (UCLA) campus and east of the San Diego Frwy (I-405).

Chinatown. Directly north of Downtown; south of Bernard St, west of N Broadway, north of College St and east of Hill St.

Downtown. South of the Hollywood Frwy (US 101), west of the Golden State Frwy (I-5), north of the Santa Monica Frwy (I-10) and east of the Pasadena Frwy (CA 110). **North of Downtown:** North of US 101. **South of Downtown:** South of I-10. **West of Downtown:** West of the Pasadena Frwy (CA 110).

Hollywood (see): Area northwest of Downtown; south of Mulholland Dr, Universal City and the Ventura Frwy (CA 134), west of the Golden State Frwy (I-5) and Alvarado St (CA 2), north of Wilshire Blvd and east of La Cienega Blvd.

Little Tokyo. Area of Downtown south of 1st St, west of Central Ave, north of 3rd St and east of San Pedro St.

Venice. Oceanfront area south of Santa Monica, west of Lincoln Blvd (CA 1) and north of Washington St.

West Hollywood. Area south and north of Santa Monica Blvd, between Doheny Dr on the west and La Brea Ave on the east.

(For full description, see alphabetical listings under Restaurants; also see restaurants listed under HOLLYWOOD.)

Note: When a listing is located in a town that does not have its own city heading, it will appear under the city nearest to its location. In these cases, the address and town appear in parenthesis immediately following the name of the establishment.

Motel

★★ **RESIDENCE INN BY MARRIOTT.** *1700 N Sepulveda Blvd (90266), CA 405 to Rosecrans exit. 310/546-7627; FAX 310/545-1327; res: 800/331-3131.* Web www.residenceinn.com. 176 kit. suites, 2 story. S $99-$178; D $150-$218; each addl $10; under 12 free; wkly, monthly rates. Crib free. Pet accepted, some restrictions. TV; cable (premium). Heated pool; whirlpool. Complimentary continental bkfst. Restaurant nearby. Ck-out noon. Meeting rm. Business servs avail. In-rm modem link. Valet serv. Free airport transportation. Microwaves. Balconies. Cr cds: A, C, D, DS, JCB, MC, V.

D SC

Motor Hotels

★★ **COURTYARD BY MARRIOTT.** *10320 W Olympic Blvd (90064), Century City, I-405 exit Santa Monica Blvd E, west of downtown. 310/556-2777; FAX 310/203-0563; res: 800/321-2211.* Web www.courtyard.com. 134 rms, 4 story. S, D $129-$139; each addl $10; suites $139-$159; wkend rates. TV; cable (premium). Coffee in rms. Restaurant 6-10:30 am. Bar 4:30 pm-midnight. Ck-out noon. Guest lndry. Meeting rm. Business servs avail. In-rm modem link. Bellhops. Valet serv. Free covered parking. Exercise equipt. Whirlpool. Health club privileges. Minibars; microwaves avail. Balconies. Cr cds: A, C, D, DS, JCB, MC, V.

D SC

✓★★ **HOLIDAY INN- DOWNTOWN.** *750 Garland Ave At 8th St (90017), downtown. 213/628-5242; FAX 213/628-1201; res: 800/628-5240.* E-mail laxdt@aol.com; web www.holiday-inn.com/hotels/laxdt/. 205 rms, 6 story. S, D $89-$129; under 18 free. Crib free. Pet accepted. TV; cable (premium), VCR avail. Pool. Complimenatry coffee in rms. Restaurant 6 am-2 pm, 5-10 pm. Rm serv. Bar 4:30-midnight. Ck-out noon. Coin lndry. Meeting rms. Business servs avail. In-rm modem link. Gift shop. Bellhops. Valet serv. Airport transportation. Exercise equipt. Cr cds: A, C, D, DS, JCB, MC, V.

D SC

✓★ **HOLIDAY INN EXPRESS.** *10330 W Olympic Blvd (90064), Century city, west of downtown. 310/553-1000; FAX 310/277-1633; res: 800/553-1005.* E-mail hiexpress@earthlink.net. 47 rms, 3 with shower only, 4 story, 14 suites. S $99; D $109; suites $119; under 18 free. Crib free. Valet parking $7.50, in/out $7.50. TV; cable (premium), VCR (movies). Complimentary continental bkfst. Complimentary coffee in rms. Restaurant nearby. Ck-out noon. Meeting rms. Bellhops. Refrigerators, microwaves. Cr cds: A, C, D, DS, JCB, MC, V.

D SC

Hotels

★★ **CHATEAU MARMOUNT HOTEL.** *8221 W Sunset Blvd (90046), in West Hollywood. 323/656-1010; FAX 323/655-5311; res: 800/242-8328.* E-mail chateaula@aol.com. 63 rms, 7 story, 54 kits. S, D $190; suites $240-$1,200; cottages, kits. $260; villas $600; monthly rates. Pet accepted. TV; cable (premium), VCR. Heated pool; poolside serv. Restaurant 6-2 am. Rm serv 24 hrs. Ck-out noon. Meeting rm. Business servs avail. In-rm modem link. Garage, valet parking. Exercise equipt. Refrigerators, minibars. Private patios, balconies. Neo-Gothic chateau-style building; old Hollywood landmark. Cr cds: A, C, D, MC, V.

D

★★★★ **FOUR SEASONS HOTEL.** *300 S Doheny Dr (90048), west of downtown. 310/273-2222; FAX 310/859-3824; res: 800/332-3442.* E-mail williammcckay@fourseasons.com; web www.fourseasons.com. Hollywood insiders enjoy this modern, high-rise hotel. Landscaped gardens, a terrace pool, and open-air gym distinguish the outside. Large floral arrangements, an airy atmosphere, and elegantly appointed guest rooms distinguish the inside. 285 rms, 16 story. S, D $325-$455; suites $525-$4,300; family, wkend rates. Pet accepted. TV; cable (premium), VCR avail. Pool; whirlpool, poolside serv. Restaurant 6:30 am-11 pm (also see GARDENS). Afternoon tea. Rm serv. Bar 11-1 am; pianist. Ck-out noon. Convention facilities. Business center. In-rm modem link. Concierge. Gift shop. Underground parking. Exercise equipt. Massage. Bathrm phones, refrigerators. Balconies. Cr cds: A, C, D, DS, ER, JCB, MC, V.

D

★★ **HOLIDAY INN.** *1020 S Figueroa St (90015), opp Convention Center, downtown. 213/748-1291; FAX 213/748-6028; res: 800/465-4329.* Web www.socalcol.com/la. 195 rms, 9 story. S, D $109-$169; each addl $10; under 18 free. Crib free. Pet accepted, some restrictions. TV; cable (premium), VCR avail. Heated pool. Restaurant 6:30 am-1 pm, 5-10 pm. Bar noon-midnight. Ck-out noon. Coin lndry. Meeting rms. Business servs avail. Gift shop. Exercise equipt; sauna. Cr cds: A, C, D, DS, JCB, MC, V.

D SC

✓★★ **HOLIDAY INN BRENTWOOD- BEL AIR.** *170 N Church Ln (90069), I-405 Sunset Blvd exit, west of downtown. 310/476-6411; FAX 310/472-1157; res: 800/465-4329.* E-mail hibelair@deltanet.com; web www.holiday-inn.com. 211 rms, 17 story. S, D $119-$169; each addl $10; suites $210; under 19 free; hol, wkend, wkly rates; higher rates special events. Crib free. TV; cable (premium), VCR avail. Pool; whirlpool. Coffee in rms. Restaurant 6:30 am-11 pm. Bar 11 am-midnight. Ck-out noon. Coin lndry. Meeting rms. Business servs avail. In-rm modem link. Concierge. Exercise equipt. Refrigerators avail. Balconies. Cr cds: A, C, D, DS, JCB, MC, V.

D SC

★★★★ **HOTEL BEL-AIR.** *701 Stone Canyon Rd (90077), I-405 to Sunset Blvd exit, in Bel Air. 310/472-1211; FAX 310/476-5890; res: 800/648-4097.* The service and amenities make for a delightful stay. The individually decorated guest rooms afford privacy and serenity and the overall experience is top notch. 92 rms, some kits. S, D $325-$525; suites $550-$2,500. TV; cable (premium), VCR (movies). Pool; poolside serv.

Restaurant (see THE RESTAURANT). Rm serv 24 hrs. Bar 10-2 am; entertainment. Ck-out 1 pm. Meeting rms. Business servs avail. In-rm modem link. Concierge. Valet parking. Airport transportation. Exercise equipt. Massage. Health club privileges. Bathrm phones; most wood-burning fireplaces. Private patios. Cr cds: A, C, D, JCB, MC, V.

★★★ **HOTEL INTER-CONTINENTAL.** *251 S Olive St (90012), I-110 exit 4th St, downtown. 213/617-3300; FAX 213/617-3399; res: 800/442-5251; res: 800/327-0200.* E-mail losangeles@interconti.com; web www.interconti.com. 434 rms, 17 story. S, D $220-$290; each addl $30; suites $395-$1650; under 14 free; package plans; higher rates special events. Crib free. Pet accepted, some restrictions. Valet parking $21. TV; cable (premium), VCR avail (movies). Restaurant (see GRAND CAFE). Rm serv 24 hrs. Bar 1 pm-1 am; piano. Ck-out noon. Convention facilities. Business center. In-rm modem link. Concierge. Shopping arcade. Barber, beauty shop. Exercise equipt; sauna. Massage. Heated pool; poolside serv. Bathrm phones, minibars; microwaves avail. Luxury level. Cr cds: A, C, D, DS, ER, JCB, MC, V.

★★★★ **HOTEL NIKKO AT BEVERLY HILLS.** *465 S La Cienega Blvd (90048), N of Wilshire Blvd, at Burton Way, west of downtown. 310/247-0400; FAX 310/247-0315; res: 800/645-5687.* Web www.nikkohotels.com. A striking blend of contemporary American architecture and traditional Japanese simplicity set this technology-friendly hotel apart. The lobby is filled with fine art and the rooms are spacious. 310 units, 7 story. S $310-$330; D $315-$415; each addl $25; suites $600-$1,800; under 12 free. Crib $25. Pet accepted. Valet parking $16. TV; cable (premium), VCR avail. Pool. Complimentary coffee in rms. Restaurants 6 am-10 pm (also see PANGAEA). Rm serv 24 hrs. Bar 3 pm-1 am; entertainment. Ck-out 1 pm. Business center. In-rm modem link. Concierge. Gift shop. Exercise equipt. Massage. Bathrm phones, Japanese soaking tubs, minibars. Balconies. Cr cds: A, C, D, DS, ER, JCB, MC, V.

★★★ **HOTEL SOFITEL.** *8555 Beverly Blvd (90048), at La Cienega, west of downtown. 310/278-5444; FAX 310/657-2816; res: 800/521-7772.* E-mail sofireserv@aol.com; web www.sofitel.com. 311 rms, 10 story. S, D $280-$320; each addl $30; suites $375-$500; under 18 free; wkend rates. Crib free. Valet parking $17.50. TV; cable (premium), VCR avail. Heated pool; poolside serv. Restaurant 6:30 am-11 pm. Rm serv 24 hrs. Bar 11-2 am; entertainment. Ck-out 1 pm. Convention facilities. Business servs avail. In-rm modem link. Concierge. Shopping arcade. Exercise equipt; sauna. Bathrm phone, minibar, wet bar in suites. Some balconies. Contemporary Mediterranean-style hotel features a blend of French and Californian cultures. Cr cds: A, C, D, ER, JCB, MC, V.

★★★ **HYATT REGENCY.** *711 S Hope St (90017), I-110 exit 6th St, downtown. 213/683-1234; FAX 213/629-3230; res: 800/233-1234.* Web www.hyatt.com. 485 rms, 26 story. S $175-$215; D $200-$240; each addl $25; suites $225-$750; under 18 free; wkend rates; package plans. Crib free. Garage parking; valet $15. TV; cable (premium), VCR avail. Restaurants 6 am-11 pm. Bar 11:30-1 am; entertainment. Ck-out noon. Convention facilities. Business center. In-rm modem link. Concierge. Shopping arcade. Barber, beauty shop. Exercise equipt. Some minibars. Luxury level. Cr cds: A, C, D, DS, ER, JCB, MC, V.

★★★ **NEW OTANI HOTEL & GARDEN.** *120 S Los Angeles St (90012), in Little Tokyo. 213/629-1200; FAX 213/622-0980; res: 800/421-8795.* Web www.newotani.com. 434 rms, 21 story. S $165-$280; D $190-$305; each addl $25; suites $475-$1,800; under 12 free. Crib free. Covered parking $13.75/day, valet $18.15/day. TV; cable (premium), VCR avail. Restaurants 6 am-9:30 pm. Bars 10-1 am. Ck-out noon. Meeting rms. Business center. Concierge. Shopping arcade. Barber. Exercise equipt. Japanese health spa. Bathrm phones, minibars. Japanese-style decor, garden. Cr cds: A, C, D, DS, ER, JCB, MC, V.

✓★★ **OXFORD PALACE.** *745 S Oxford Ave (90005), I-10 exit Western Ave, 2 mi N, west of downtown. 213/389-8000; FAX 213/389-8500.* Web www.oxfordhotel.com. 86 rms, 4 story, 9 suites. S $89-$139; D $94-$149; each addl $20; suites $110-$239. TV; cable, VCR (movies $3). Restaurants 7 am-2:30 pm, 5:30-10:30 pm. Bar 9-2 am. Ck-out 11 am. Meeting rms. Business center. Shopping arcade. Garage parking. Health club privileges. Minibars. Some balconies. Cr cds: A, C, D, MC, V.

★★★★ **PARK HYATT.** *2151 Ave Of The Stars (90067), I-405 exit Santa Monica Blvd to Ave of the Stars, west of downtown. 310/277-1234; FAX 310/785-9240.* Web www.hyatt.com. Located on the Avenue of the Stars in Century City, Los Angeles' west side business and financial district, this hotel is conveniently just minutes from several L.A. attractions such as Fox Studios, Beverly Hills, Rodeo Drive and Universal Studios. 367 rms, 17 story, 189 suites. S $299-$349; D $324; suites $349-$2,500; under 18 free; wkend rates. Valet parking $17. TV; cable (premium), VCR avail (movies). 2 pools, 1 indoor; whirlpool, poolside serv. Restaurant (see PARK GRILL). Rm serv 24 hrs. Bar 11:30-1:30 am; pianist. Ck-out noon. Meeting rms. Business center. In-rm modem link. Concierge. Shopping arcade. Tennis privileges. Golf privileges. Exercise equipt; sauna, steam rm. Massage. Bathrm phones, refrigerators, minibars; microwaves avail. Private patios, balconies. Cr cds: A, C, D, DS, JCB, MC, V.

★★ **RADISSON HOTEL.** *3515 Wilshire Blvd (90010), west of downtown. 213/381-7411; FAX 213/386-7379; res: 800/333-3333.* E-mail rwph@ix.netcom.com. 380 rms, 12 story. S, D $169-$209; each addl $10; suites $275-$575; under 18 free. Crib free. Valet parking $13. TV; cable (premium). Heated pool; poolside serv. Restaurants 6 am-11 pm. Bar 11-1 am; entertainment Mon-Fri. Ck-out noon. Convention facilities. Business center. In-rm modem link. Concierge. Barber, beauty shop. Exercise equipt. Minibars. Cr cds: A, C, D, DS, ER, JCB, MC, V.

★★★ **REGAL BILTMORE HOTEL.** *506 S Grand Ave (90071), I-110, 4th St, downtown. 213/624-1011; FAX 213/612-1545; res: 800/245-8673.* Web www.regal-hotels.com/losangeles. 683 rms, 12 story. S, D $225-$275; each addl $30; suites $390-$2,000; under 18 free; wkend rates. Valet parking $17.60. Pool; whirlpool. TV; cable (premium), VCR avail. Restaurants 6:30 am-11 pm (also see BERNARD'S). Rm serv 24 hrs. Bars 11-2 am. Ck-out noon. Convention facilities. Business servs avail. In-rm modem link. Shopping arcade. Beauty shop. Exercise rm; sauna. Massage. Health club privileges. Wet bar in most suites; some bathrm phones. Luxury level. Cr cds: A, C, D, DS, ER, JCB, MC, V.

★★ **SUMMERFIELD SUITES HOTEL.** *1000 Westmount Dr (90069), I-405 exit Santa Monica Blvd, in West Hollywood. 310/657-7400; FAX 310/854-6744; res: 800/833-4353.* E-mail sshollywood@attmail.com. 95 kit. suites, 4 story. S, D $210-$255; under 12 free; monthly rates. Crib free. Pet accepted. Covered parking $12. TV; cable (premium), VCR (movies $5). Pool. Complimentary continental bkfst. Ck-out noon. Coin Indry. Meeting rm. In-rm modem link. Exercise equipt; sauna. Health club privileges. Refrigerators, microwaves, fireplaces. Balconies. Cr cds: A, C, D, DS, JCB, MC, V.

★★ **SUMMIT HOTEL BEL AIR.** *11461 W Sunset Blvd (90049), in Bel Air. 310/476-6571; FAX 310/471-6310; res: 800/468-3541.* 162 rms, 2 story. S, D $149-$239; each addl $20; suites $199-$499; under 18 free; wkend rates. TV; cable (premium), VCR avail. Heated pool; poolside serv. Restaurant 6:30 am-11 pm. Bar. Ck-out noon. Meeting rms. Business servs avail. In-rm modem link. Gift shop. Valet parking. Airport transportation. Tennis, pro. Exercise equipt. Bathrm phones, refrigerators, minibars; microwaves avail. Private patios, balconies. Cr cds: A, C, D, DS, JCB, MC, V.

★★★ **THE BEVERLY PLAZA HOTEL.** *8384 W 3rd St (90048), west of downtown. 323/658-6600; FAX 323/653-3464; res: 800/624-6835.* E-mail info@beverlyplazahotel.com; web www.beverlyplazahotel.com. 98 rms, 5 story. S, D $192-$249; under 18 free. TV; cable (premium), VCR avail. Valet parking $13. Heated pool; whirlpool, poolside serv. Restaurant (see CAVA). Rm serv 24 hrs. Bar 11 am-midnight. Ck-out noon. Exercise equipt; sauna. Cr cds: A, C, D, MC, V.

D SC

★★★ **WESTIN BONAVENTURE.** *404 S Figueroa St (90071), downtown. 213/624-1000; FAX 213/612-4800; res: 800/228-3000.* Web www.westin.com. 1,354 rms, 35 story. S $170-$190; D $190-$230; suites $195-$2,500; under 18 free. Crib free. Garage $18.15/day. TV; cable (premium), VCR avail. Heated pool; poolside serv. Restaurants 5:30 am-midnight. Rm serv 24 hrs. Bars 11-2 am. Ck-out noon. Convention facilities. Business center. In-rm modem link. Concierge. Shopping arcade. Barber, beauty shop. Exercise equipt. Health club privileges. Six-story atrium lobby. Cr cds: A, C, D, DS, ER, JCB, MC, V.

D SC

★★★★ **WESTIN CENTURY PLAZA HOTEL & TOWER.** *2025 Ave Of The Stars (90067), in Century City, west of downtown. 310/277-2000; FAX 310/551-3355; res: 800/228-3000.* E-mail westincp@aol.com; web www.centuryplaza.la.com. The rooms in this modern, high-rise hotel have views of the city and the ocean. The 10-acres of property are landscaped with tropical plants and reflecting pools, 1,046 rms, 19-30 story. S $290; D $295; each addl $25; suites $500-$3,000. Tower: S $320; D $345; suites $750-$5,400; each addl $25; under 18 free. TV; cable (premium), VCR avail. Pet accepted. Pool; whirlpool, poolside serv (summer). Restaurant (see THE TERRACE), (Cafè Plaza in the Plaza bldg) Rm serv 24 hrs. Bars 11-2 am; entertainment. Ck-out 1 pm. Lndry facilities. Convention facilities. Business center. In-rm modem link. Concierge. Barber, beauty shop. Valet parking. Tennis privileges. Exercise equipt. Health club privileges. Massage. Bathrm phones. Balconies. Cr cds: A, C, D, DS, ER, JCB, MC, V.

D SC

★★★ **WILSHIRE HOTEL AND CENTRE.** *930 Wilshire Blvd (90017), downtown. 213/688-7777; FAX 213/612-3987; res: 888/773-2888.* 900 rms, 16 story. S $169-$209; D $189-$229; each addl $25; suites $375-$1,200. Crib free. Garage $18.50. TV; cable (premium). Heated pool; whirlpool, poolside serv. Coffee in rms. Restaurants 6:30 am-11 pm (see also SEOUL JUNG). Bar 10 am-midnight; pianist. Ck-out noon. Convention facilities. Business center. In-rm modem link. Concierge. Shopping arcade. Barber, beauty shop. Exercise equipt. Minibars. Luxury level. Cr cds: A, C, D, DS, ER, JCB, MC, V.

D SC

★★★ **WYNDHAM CHECKERS HOTEL.** *535 S Grand Ave (90071), downtown. 213/624-0000; FAX 213/626-9906; res: 800/ WYNDHAM.* Web www.travelweb.com. 188 rms, 12 story. S, D $179-$229; each addl $20; suites $380-$950; under 18 free; wkend rates. Crib free. Valet parking $20. TV; cable (premium), VCR avail. Heated pool; whirlpool, poolside serv. Restaurant (see CHECKERS). Rm serv 24 hrs. Bar 11:30 am-11:30 pm. Meeting rms. Business center. In-rm modem link. Concierge. Airport transportation. Exercise equipt; sauna, steam rm. Massage. Bathrm phones, minibars. Library. Opened in 1927. Cr cds: A, C, D, DS, ER, JCB, MC, V.

D SC

Restaurants

★★★ **AL AMIR.** *5750 Wilshire Blvd (90036), in the Wilshire Courtyard Complex, west of downtown. 213/931-8740.* E-mail mafito@aol.com. Hrs: 11:30 am-10 pm; Fri to 1 am; Sat 5:30 pm-1 am. Closed Sun; most major hols. Res accepted. Middle Eastern menu. Bar. Semi-a la carte: lunch $8-$12, dinner $11.95-$17.95. Complete meals: dinner $27.95. Specialties: chicken kabob, kafta kabob. Arabic band, belly dancing Fri, Sat. Valet parking. Outdoor dining (lunch). Overlooks courtyard with fountains. Cr cds: A, C, D, DS, MC, V.

D

★ **ANNA'S ITALIAN RESTAURANT.** *10929 W Pico Blvd (90064), west of downtown. 310/474-0102.* Hrs: 11:30 am-11 pm; Fri to midnight; Sat 4 pm-midnight; Sun from 4 pm. Closed Thanksgiving, Dec 25. Res accepted. Italian menu. Bar. Semi-a la carte: lunch $5.50-$13, dinner $6.95-$22. Specialties: chicken cacciatore, linguine Sorrento. Valet parking. Family-owned. Totally nonsmoking. Cr cds: A, C, D, DS, JCB, MC, V.

D

★★★ **ARNIE MORTON'S OF CHICAGO.** *435 S La Cienega Blvd (90048), I-405, E at Santa Monica Blvd exit, west of downtown. 310/246-1501.* Web www.mortonsofchicago.com. Hrs: 5:30-11 pm; Sun 5-10 pm. Closed major hols. Res accepted. Bar. Wine cellar. A la carte entrees: dinner $18-$30. Specializes in steak. Valet parking. Patrons select fresh cuts of meat brought tableside by waitstaff. Cr cds: A, C, D, JCB, MC, V.

D

★★★ **BERNARD'S.** *(See Regal Biltmore) 213/612-1580.* Web www.thebiltmore.com. Hrs: 11:30 am-2:30 pm, 6-10 pm; Fri to 10:30 pm; Sat 6-10:30 pm. Closed Sun; major hols. Res accepted. Continental menu. Wine cellar. A la carte entrees: lunch $13-$21, dinner $17-$30. Specializes in seafood. Own baking. Entertainment. Valet parking. Cr cds: A, C, D, DS, ER, JCB, MC, V.

D

★★★ **CAFE PINOT.** *700 W 5th St (90071), downtown. 213/239-6500.* Hrs: 11:30 am-2:30 pm, 5:30-9 pm; Sat, Sun 5-10 pm. Closed most major hols. Res accepted. Seasonal menu. Bar. Wine list. Semi-a la carte: lunch $13-$20, dinner $15.75-$19.95. Specialties: rotisserie chicken, suckling pig, Peking duck ravioli. Valet parking (dinner). Outdoor dining. French bistro atmosphere. Cr cds: A, C, D, DS, JCB, MC, V.

D

★★ **CAMPANILE.** *624 S La Brea Ave (90036), west of downtown. 213/938-1447.* Hrs: 11:30 am-2:30 pm, 6-10 pm; Fri to 11 pm; Sat 8 am-1:30 pm, 5:30-11 pm; Sun 8 am-1:30 pm. Closed Memorial Day, Thanksgiving, Dec 25. Res accepted. California, Italian menu. Bar. Semi-a la carte: bkfst $6-$15, lunch $12-$18, dinner $20-$35. Specialties: seared wild salmon, risotto, prime rib. Own baking. Valet parking. Charlie Chaplin's original offices. Malibu tile, fountain; skylights. Cr cds: A, C, D, DS, MC, V.

D

★★ **CAVA RESTAURANT.** *(See Beverly Plaza) 213/658-8898.* Hrs: 6:30 am-11 pm; Fri, Sat to midnight. Res accepted. Contemporary Spanish menu. Bar. A la carte entrees: bkfst $4.50-$9.75, lunch, dinner $7.50-$17.95. Specialties: pescado Vera Cruz, pollo diablo, paella Valenciana. Jazz Tues, Fri, Sat evenings. Valet parking. Outdoor dining. Contemporary decor. Cr cds: A, C, D, DS, MC, V.

D

★★★ **CHECKERS.** *(See Wyndham Checkers Hotel Los Angeles) 213/624-0000.* Hrs: 6 am-9 pm; Sat, Sun brunch 10 am-2 pm. Res accepted. Bar. Wine list. Semi-a la carte: bkfst $8-$15, lunch $10-$25, dinner $25-$40. Sat, Sun brunch $10-$18. Specializes in fresh seafood dishes. Valet parking. Outdoor dining. Intimate dining in formal setting. High tea. Totally nonsmoking. Cr cds: A, C, D, DS, ER, JCB, MC, V.

D

★★★ **CIAO TRATTORIA.** *815 W 7th St (90017), at Figueroa, downtown. 213/624-2244.* Hrs: 11 am-10 pm; Sat, Sun from 5 pm. Closed major hols. Res accepted. Italian menu. Bar. A la carte entrees: lunch

$10.95-$15.50, dinner $14.50-$22. Specialties: chicken cacciatore, farfalle gustose, veal saltimbocca. Valet parking. In historic Fine Arts Bldg. Intimate, European atmosphere. Cr cds: A, C, D, JCB, MC, V.

D

★★★ **DIAGHILEV.** *(See Wyndham Bel Age) 310/854-1111.* Web www.wyndham.com. Hrs: 6-11 pm. Closed Sun, Mon; Jan 1. Res accepted. Franco Russian menu. Bar. A la carte entrees: dinner $20-$50. Complete meal: dinner $75. Specialties: braised leg of duck, filet of salmon with sturgeon mousse, braised veal chop. Elegant dining. Jacket. Cr cds: A, C, D, DS, ER, JCB, MC, V.

D

★★ **EL CHOLO RESTAURANT.** *1121 W Western Ave (90006), west of downtown. 213/734-2773.* Hrs: 11 am-10 pm; Fri, Sat to 11 pm; Sun to 9 pm. Closed July 4, Thanksgiving, Dec 25. Res accepted. Mexican menu. Bar. Semi-a la carte: lunch, dinner $6.45-$13.95. Specialties: fajitas, green corn tamales, margaritas. Valet parking. Family-owned since 1927. Casual dining. Cr cds: A, C, D, MC, V.

D

★★★ **FOUR OAKS.** *2181 N Beverly Glen (90077), in West Hollywood. 310/470-2265.* Hrs: 11:30 am-2 pm, 6-10 pm; Sun, Mon from 6 pm; Sun brunch 10:30 am-2 pm. Closed some major hols. Res accepted. Modern French, Amer menu. Bar. A la carte entrees: lunch $15-$22, dinner $22-$27. Sun brunch $32. Menu changes seasonally; emphasizes natural ingredients. Own desserts. Valet parking. Patio dining. Mediterranean decor. Built 1890. Cr cds: A, C, D, MC, V.

D

★★★★ **GARDENS.** *(See Four Seasons Hotel) 310/273-2222.* Web www.fourseasons.com. This quiet and romantic restaurant in the Four Seasons Hotel is known for inspired Mediterranean food and a fabulous Sunday brunch. Professional service and a good wine list are added bonuses. Hrs: 7 am-11 pm; Sun brunch 10 am-2:30 pm. Res accepted. Mediterranean menu. Bar 11-1 am. Wine cellar. A la carte entrees: bkfst $5.95-$18, lunch $8.95-$18, dinner $18-$35. Sun brunch $42. Child's meals. Specializes in steak, lamb, seafood. Own baking, ice cream. Valet parking. Outdoor dining. Cr cds: A, C, D, ER, JCB, MC, V.

D ♥

★★★ **GRAND CAFE.** *(See Inter-Continental) 213/617-3399.* E-mail losangeles@interconti.com; web www.interconti.com. Hrs: 6:30-10:30 pm; early-bird dinner 5:30-7:30 pm (seasonal). Res accepted. Pan-Asian menu. Bar 1 pm-1 am. Wine list. A la carte entrees: bkfst $10-$15, lunch $14-$17, dinner $20-$30. Buffet: bkfst $17.95, lunch $14.95. Child's meals. Specialties: Dungeness crab cake salad, proscuitto and grab cheese wrapped tiger prawns, pecan-crusted halibut. Valet parking. Outdoor dining. Cr cds: A, C, D, DS, ER, JCB, MC, V.

D

★★★ **GRILL ON THE ALLEY.** *9560 Dayton Way (90210). 310/276-0615; FAX 310/276-0284.* E-mail info@thegrill.com; web www.thegrill.com. American cuisine. Hrs: Mon-Thurs 11:30 am-11 pm, Fri & Sat open til midnight; Sun 5 pm-9 pm. Avg lunch is $22, dinner $30. Child menu Sat & Sun. Valet (dinner). Resv pref. Cr cds: C.

★★ **LA CACHETTE RESTAURANT.** *10506 Santa Monica Blvd (90025), west of downtown. 310/470-4992.* E-mail lacachette@aol.com; web www.restaurant.pages.com.lacachette. Hrs: 11:30 am-2:30 pm, 6-10 pm; Fri to 10:30 pm; Sat 5:30-10:30 pm; Sun 5:30-9 pm. Closed most major hols. Res accepted. French menu. Bar service. A la carte entrees: lunch $12-$18, dinner $18-$29. Specialties: shellfish bouillabaisse, double-roasted muscovy duck, grilled swordfish. Intimate dining. Totally nonsmoking. Cr cds: A, C, D, MC, V.

D

✓★★ **LA GOLONDRINA MEXICAN CAFE.** *17 Olvera St (90012), north of downtown. 213/628-4349.* Hrs: 10 am-9 pm; Fri, Sat to 10 pm; Sun from 9 am. Closed Jan 1, Dec 25. Res accepted. No A/C. Mexican menu. Bar. Semi-a la carte: bkfst $4.25-$8.95, lunch, dinner $4.25-$13.95. Child's meals. Specialties: carnitas, costillas en adobado. Own breads. Mexican guitarists. Outdoor dining. Historical landmark; 1st brick bldg in Los Angeles (1855). Family-owned since 1924. Cr cds: A, C, D, DS, MC, V.

SC

★★ **LITTLE JOE'S.** *900 N Broadway (90012), in Chinatown. 213/489-4900.* Hrs: 11 am-9 pm; Sat from 3 pm. Closed Sun; major hols. Res accepted. Italian, Amer menu. Bar. Semi-a la carte: lunch $7.50-$12.50, dinner $8.50-$19.95. Child's meals. Specialties: homemade ravioli, butterflied halibut. Valet parking. Near Dodger Stadium, Civic Center. Family-owned since 1910. Cr cds: A, C, D, DS, JCB, MC, V.

★★ **LOCANDA VENETA.** *8638 W Third St (90048), opp Cedars Sinai Hospital, west of downtown. 310/274-1893.* Hrs: 11:30 am-2:30 pm, 5:30-10:30 pm; Fri to 11 pm; Sat 5:30-11 pm. Closed Sun. Res accepted. Northern Italian menu. Beer. Wine list. A la carte entrees: lunch, dinner $10-$25. Specializes in seafood, pasta. Own baking. Valet parking. Patio dining. Windows open to street; open kitchen. Cr cds: A, C, D, DS, MC, V.

★★★ **LUCQUES.** *8474 Melrose Ave. 323/655-6277.* Open Tues, Sun. for dinner. Entrees $18-$25. Full bar until 10 pm. Limited bar menu available after 10 p.m. Valet parking. AE, VISA, MC. Menu changes every 2 months. Cr cds: C.

★★ **MADEO RESTAURANT.** *8897 Beverly Blvd (90048), west of downtown. 310/859-0242.* Hrs: noon-3 pm, 6:30-11 pm; Sat, Sun from 6:30 pm. Closed Dec 25. Res accepted. Italian menu. Bar. A la carte entrees: lunch $10-$30, dinner $30-$50. Specialties: branzino, leg of veal. Own pastries. Valet parking. Wood-burning oven. Cr cds: A, C, D, MC, V.

D

★★★ **PANGAEA.** *(See Hotel Nikko at Beverly Hills) 310/246-2000.* Web www.nikkohotels.com. Hrs: 6:30 am-2:30 pm, 6-10:30 pm; Sun 11 am-3 pm (brunch), 6-10:30 pm. Res accepted. Pan Asian menu. Bar. Wine cellar. Semi-a la carte: bkfst $8.75-$13, lunch $11-$22, dinner $18-$29. Sun brunch $35. Specialties: sushi, sauteed Alaskan halibut. Jazz band Sun brunch. Valet parking. Elegant dining. Totally nonsmoking. Cr cds: A, C, D, DS, JCB, MC, V.

D

★★★ **PANGAEA.** *(See Nikko Hotel) 310/246-2100.* Asian American. Mon-Sun 6:30 am-2:30 pm; 6-10 pm. (Sun brunch 10:30 am-3 pm) breakfast $4.50-$24; lunch $5.00-$22.00; dinner $6.00-$31.00. Child meal. Reser pref. Non smoking. Jazz trio on Sunday. Cr cds: C.

★★★ **PARK GRILL.** *(See Park Hyatt Los Angeles) 310/277-1234.* Web www.hyatt.com. Hrs: 6:30 am-10:30 pm; Sat, Sun from 7 am; Sun brunch 10:30 am-2 pm. Res accepted. Continental menu. Bar 11:30 pm-1:30 am. Wine cellar. A la carte entrees: bkfst $8-$17, lunch $12-$20, dinner $17-$30. Buffet: bkfst $17. Sun brunch $25. Seasonal menu; changes monthly. Own baking. Valet parking. Cr cds: A, C, D, DS, JCB, MC, V.

D

✓★ **PATINETTE AT MOCA.** *250 S Grand Ave (90012), at Museum of Contemporary Art, downtown. 213/626-1178.* Hrs: 11 am-4:30 pm; Thurs to 8 pm. Closed Mon; major hols. A la carte entrees: lunch, dinner $5.95-$9.25. Specializes in salads, sandwiches, light entrees. Outdoor dining on terrace. Totally nonsmoking. Cr cds: A, C, D, DS, JCB, MC, V.

D

✓★★★ **PINOT HOLLYWOOD.** *1448 N Gower St (90028), north of downtown. 323/461-8800.* Web www.patinapinot.com. Hrs: 11:30 am-10:30 pm; Sat 5:30-11 pm. Closed Sun; most major hols. Res accepted. French menu. Bar to 1:30 am. Extensive wine list. Semi-a la carte: lunch $7.25-$16.50, dinner $14.25-$19.95. Child's meals. Specializes in beef, chicken. Valet parking. Outdoor dining. French bistro decor. Cr cds: A, C, D, DS, ER, JCB, MC, V.

D

★★★ **POSTO RESTAURANT.** *14928 Ventura Blvd (91403), 2 blks E of I-405 at US 101. 818/784-4400.* Hrs: 11:30 am-2:30 pm, 5-10 pm; Sat from 5 pm. Closed Sun; major hols. Res accepted. Italian menu. Bar. Wine cellar. A la carte entrees: lunch, dinner $8-$26. Specialties: veal osso bucco, risotto lobster, filet mignon with onions. Valet parking. Original artwork. Cr cds: A, C, D, MC, V.

D

★★★ **PRIMI RISTORANTE.** *10543 W Pico Blvd (90064), west of downtown. 310/475-9235.* E-mail primi@aol.com. Hrs: 11:30 am-2:30 pm, 5:30-10:30 pm; Sat from 5:30 pm. Closed Sun. Res accepted. Italian menu. Bar. A la carte entrees: lunch $10-$20, dinner $16-$22. Specializes in homemade pasta. Own baking. Valet parking. Outdoor dining. Cr cds: A, C, D, MC, V.

D

★★★ **SEOUL JUNG.** *(See Omni) 213/688-7880.* Hrs: 11:30 am-2 pm, 5:30-9:30 pm. Res accepted. Korean menu. Bar. Wine list. A la carte entrees: lunch, dinner $12-$25. Specialties: marinated short ribs, noodle casserole. Valet parking. Elegant dining; many Korean artifacts. Totally nonsmoking. Cr cds: A, C, D, DS, JCB, MC, V.

D

✓★ **SISLEY ITALIAN KITCHEN.** *10800 W Pico Blvd (90064), in Westside Pavilion Shopping Center, west of downtown. 310/446-3030.* Hrs: 11:30 am-10 pm; Fri, Sat to 10:30 pm; Sun to 9 pm. Res accepted. Italian, California menu. Bar. A la carte entrees: lunch $5.95-$10.95, dinner $7.50-$12. Specialty: cioppino. Valet parking. Italian cafe decor. Cr cds: A, C, MC, V.

D

✓★★★ **TAIX.** *1911 Sunset Blvd (90026), north of downtown. 213/484-1265.* Hrs: 11 am-10 pm; Sun noon-9 pm. Closed most major hols. Res accepted. Country French menu. Bar. Wine list. Complete meals: lunch $6.95-$16.95, dinner $7.95-$24.50. Child's meals. Specialty: escargots a la Bourguignonne. Own soups. Valet parking. Family-owned since 1927. Cr cds: A, C, D, DS, MC, V.

D

★★★ **TAM-O-SHANTER INN.** *2980 Los Feliz Blvd (90039), 5 blks E of I-5, north of downtown. 323/664-0228.* Hrs: 11 am-3 pm, 5-10 pm; Fri, Sat to 11 pm; Sun 10:30 am-2:30 pm (brunch), 4-10 pm. Closed Dec 25. Bar. A la carte entrees: lunch $8.95-$14.95, dinner $9.95-$22.95. Sun brunch $9.50-$17.95. Child's meals. Specialties: prime rib & Yorkshire pudding, creamed spinach, roast duckling. Free valet parking. Scottish motif. Family-owned since 1922. Cr cds: A, C, D, DS, MC, V.

D SC

★★★ **THE RESTAURANT.** *(See Hotel Bel-Air) 310/472-1211.* Hrs: 7-10:30 am, 11:30 am-2:30 pm, 6:30-10:30 pm; Sun brunch 11 am-2:30 pm. Res accepted. French, Californian menu. Bar. Complete meals: bkfst $8-$13. A la carte entrees: lunch $15-$26.50, dinner $28-$36. Sun brunch $37.50. Specializes in seasonal dishes. Own pastries. Valet parking. Herb garden. Chef's tableside dining. Cr cds: A, C, D, JCB, MC, V.

D

★★★ **THE TERRACE.** *(See Westin Century Plaza Hotel & Tower) 310/277-2000.* E-mail westincp@aol.com; web www.centuryplaza.com. Hrs: 6:30 am-2:30 pm, 5:30-10:30 pm; Sun brunch 10 am-2:30 pm. Res accepted. Mediterranean menu. Bar 4:30-1:30 am. A la carte entrees: bkfst $12-$18, lunch $14-$23, dinner $18-$42. Sun brunch $29. Child's meals. Specialties: potato-crusted sea bass, corn chowder with smoked shrimp, filet of beef with shallot and shiitake ragout. Guitarists Tues-Sun. Valet parking. Outdoor dining. In garden setting. Totally nonsmoking. Cr cds: A, C, D, DS, ER, JCB, MC, V.

D

★★★ **THE TOWER.** *1150 S Olive St (90015), on top of Trans-America Center, downtown. 213/746-1554.* Hrs: 11:30 am-2 pm, 5:30-10 pm; Fri to 11 pm; Sat 5:30-11 pm; early-bird dinner 5:30-6:30 pm. Closed Sun; major hols. Res accepted. Continental menu. Bar. Wine cellar. A la carte entrees: lunch $15-$30, dinner $23-$29. Specializes in contemporary dishes. Harpist (lunch), pianist (dinner). Valet parking. 360°; view of city from 32nd floor. Jacket. Cr cds: A, C, D, MC, V.

D

★★★★ **WATER GRILL.** *522 S. Grand Ave (90071). 213/891-0900.* The sleek modern design of this bustling restaurant attracts a fashionable crowd. The sophisticated seafood menu, which features everything from the freshest oysters on the half shell to artfully presented, Mediterranean-inspired dishes, keeps them coming back. American seafood. Hrs: Mon & Tues 5-9 pm, Wed-Fri 10 am-11 pm. Sat 5-10 pm; Sun 4-9 pm. Prices $24-$34. Reserv pref. Bar. Jackets pref. Valet. Cr cd: C.

Unrated Dining Spots

CASSELL'S. *3266 W 6th St (90020), west of downtown. 213/480-8668.* Hrs: 10:30 am-4 pm. Closed Sun; major hols. A la carte entrees: lunch $4.60-$5.80. Specializes in prime beef hamburgers. Old-style hamburger diner. Cr cds: C.

D

HARD ROCK CAFE. *8600 Beverly Blvd, in Beverly Shopping Center, west of downtown. 310/276-7605.* Hrs: 11:30-12:30 am. Closed Labor Day, Thanksgiving, Dec 25. Bar. Semi-a la carte: lunch, dinner $5.95-$15. Child's meals. Specialties: lime barbecued chicken, grilled hamburgers. Valet parking. Extensive rock 'n roll memorabilia collection. Cr cds: A, C, D, MC, V.

D

PHILIPPE THE ORIGINAL. *1001 N Alameda St (90012), downtown. 213/628-3781.* E-mail philippe@philippes.com; web www.philippes.com. Hrs: 6 am-10 pm. Closed Thanksgiving, Dec 25. Wine, beer. A la carte entrees: bkfst $1-$4.50, lunch, dinner $4-$7. Specializes in French dip sandwiches, salads, baked apples. Own baking. Since 1908; old-style dining hall. Totally nonsmoking. Cr cds: C.

D

ROAST TO GO. *317 S Broadway, #C-8 (90013), in Grand Central Market, downtown. 213/625-1385.* Hrs: 9 am-6 pm; Sun from 10 am. Closed most major hols. Mexican menu. Semi-a la carte: bkfst, lunch, dinner $1.50-$7. Child's meals. Specializes in tacos, charbroiled chicken. Parking. Family-owned since 1952. Cr cds: C.

D

UNCLE BILL'S PANCAKE HOUSE. *1305 Highland Ave (90266), S on Pacific Coast Hwy. 310/545-5177.* Hrs: 6 am-3 pm; wkends, hols from 7 am. Closed Jan 1, Thanksgiving, Dec 25. Semi-a la carte: bkfst $3.25-$5.95, lunch $3.50-$6.50. Specializes in potatoes Stroganoff, strawberry waffles, homemade muffins. Small, cozy atmosphere. Converted 1908 house. Cr cds: C.

Los Angeles Intl Airport Area

(C-3 see Los Angeles map)

(See also Los Angeles, Los Angeles Area)

Services and Information

Information: 310/646-5252.

Lost and Found: 310/417-0440.

Airlines: Aero California, Aerolineas Argentinas, Aeromexico, Aeroperu, Air Canada, Air France, Air New Zealand, Air Pacific, Alaska Airlines, Alitalia, All Nippon, American West, American, American Trans Air, AOM French Airlines, Asiana Airlines, Avianca, Aviateca, British Airways, Canadian Airlines Intl, Carnival Air Lines, Cathay Pacific, China Airlines, China Eastern, Continental, Delta, EgyptAir, El Al, EVA Airways, Frontier, Garuda Indonesia, Hawaiian Airlines, Iberia, Japan Airlines, KLM, Korean Air, LACSA, Lan Chile, LTU, Lufthansa, Malaysia Airlines, Mexicana, Midwest Express, Northwest, Philippine Airlines, Qantas, Reno Air, Singapore Airlines, Southwest, Swissair, TACA, Thai Airways, Tower Air, Transaero Airlines, TWA, United, USAir, Vanguard, Varig, Virgin Atlantic, Western Pacific Airlines.

Heliport: Helitrans, LA Helicopter.

Motels

✓★★ **HAMPTON INN.** *10300 La Cienega Blvd (90304), ¾ mi E on Century Blvd, then S on La Cienega Blvd. 310/337-1000; FAX 310/645-6925; res: 800/992-0825.* Web www.hampton-inn.com. 148 rms, 7 story. S, D $69-$99; under 18 free. Crib free. Pet accepted, some restrictions. TV; cable (premium). Complimentary continental bkfst. Restaurant nearby. Ck-out noon. Meeting rms. In-rm modem link. Valet serv. Free airport transportation. Exercise equipt. Cr cds: A, C, D, DS, ER, JCB, MC, V.

D SC

✓★★ **TRAVELODGE.** *5547 W Century Blvd (90045), ½ mi W off I-405, at Century Blvd & Aviation Blvd. 310/649-4000; FAX 310/649-0311; res: 800/421-3939.* E-mail aci@chms.net; web www.chms.net. 147 rms, 2 story. S $64-$74; D $69-$88; each addl $8; under 18 free. Crib $4. Pet accepted. TV; cable (premium), VCR. Pool. Coffee in rms. Restaurant open 24 hrs. Rm serv 6 am-10 pm. Bar 10-2 am. Ck-out noon. Coin lndry. Bellhops. Valet serv. Gift shop. Free airport transportation. Exercise equipt. Some private patios, balconies. Cr cds: A, C, D, DS, ER, JCB, MC, V.

Hotels

★★ **BARNABEY'S HOTEL.** *3501 Sepulveda Blvd (90266), S via I-405 exit Rosecrans W. 310/545-8466; FAX 310/545-8621; res: 800/552-5285.* Web www.barnabeys-hotel.com. 120 rms, 3 story. S $155; D $170-$185; under 12 free; hol, wkend rates. Crib $15. Overnight valet parking $8. TV; cable (premium), VCR avail. Pool. Complimentary full bkfst. Coffee in rms. Restaurant 6:30 am-10 pm. Bar 11 am-midnight; entertainment. Ck-out noon. Meeting rms. In-rm modem link. Gift shop. Free airport transportation. Health club privileges. Microwaves avail. European-style decor; antiques. Cr cds: A, C, D, DS, MC, V.

D SC

★★★ **CROWNE PLAZA HOTEL.** *5985 W Century Blvd (90045), ¼ mi E on Century Blvd. 310/642-7500; FAX 310/417-3608; res: 800/465-4329; res: 800/315-3700.* E-mail laxales@crowneplazalax.com; web www.crowneplaza.com. 615 rms, 15 story. S $139-$169; D $154-$185; suites $350-$550; under 12 free; wkend rates. Crib free. Garage $9. TV; cable (premium). Heated pool; whirlpool. Coffee in rms. Restaurant 6 am-11 pm. Bar 11-2 am; entertainment Tues-Thurs. Ck-out noon. Coin lndry. Business servs avail. Concierge. Gift shop. Free airport transportation. Exercise equipt; sauna. Luxury level. Cr cds: A, C, D, DS, JCB, MC, V.

D SC

★★ **DOUBLETREE CLUB HOTEL LAX.** *1985 E Grand Ave (90245), 1½ mi S of airport on Sepulveda Blvd, in business park. 310/322-0999; FAX 310/322-4758; res: 800/222-8733.* E-mail dtclax@aol.com. 215 rms, 7 story. S $102; D $112; each addl $10; suites $125; under 12 free. Crib $10. TV; cable (premium). Heated pool; whirlpool, poolside serv. Restaurant 6-10 am, 11 am-2 pm, 5-10 pm. Bar. Ck-out 1 pm. Meeting rms. Business servs avail. In-rm modem link. Free airport transportation. Exercise equipt. Cr cds: A, C, D, DS, JCB, MC, V.

D SC

★★★ **EMBASSY SUITES.** *1440 E Imperial Ave (90245), ½ mi S on Sepulveda Blvd, then 1 blk W on Imperial Ave. 310/640-3600; FAX 310/322-0954; res: 800/362-2779.* E-mail @eslaxsouth.com; web www.embassy-suites.com. 349 suites, 5 story. S, D $119-$169; each addl $15; under 18 free; wkend rates. Pet accepted, some restrictions. Parking $6/day. TV; cable (premium). Indoor pool; whirlpool. Complimentary full bkfst. Restaurant 11 am-10 pm. Bar to 2 am. Ck-out noon. Meeting rms. Business center. In-rm modem link. Gift shop. Free airport transportation. Exercise equipt. Refrigerators, microwaves. Balconies. Sun deck. Spanish mission architecture. Near beach. Cr cds: A, C, D, DS, JCB, MC, V.

D SC

✓★ **FURAMA HOTEL LOS ANGELES.** *8601 Lincoln Blvd (90045), jct Lincoln Blvd & Manchester Ave, NW edge of Intl Airport. 310/670-8111; FAX 310/337-1883; res: 800/225-8126.* E-mail fhla@furama-hotels.com; web www.furama-hotels.com. 760 rms, 12 story. S, D $99-$119; each addl $10; suites $250-$350; under 18 free. Crib free. TV; cable (premium). Pool. Restaurants 6 am-11 pm. Bar 3 pm-2 am; entertainment. Ck-out noon. Meeting rms. Barber, beauty shop. Free airport transportation. Exercise equipt. Some private patios. Garden patio. Golf, tennis opp. Luxury level. Cr cds: A, C, D, DS, ER, JCB, MC, V.

D SC

★★★ **HILTON.** *5711 W Century Blvd (90045), ¾ mi W of I-405. 310/410-4000; FAX 310/410-6250; res: 800/445-8667.* 1,234 rms, 17 story. S $119-$169; each addl $20; suites $150-$900; family, wkend rates. Valet parking $14, garage $10. Pet accepted. TV; cable (premium), VCR avail. Heated pool; whirlpools, poolside serv. Restaurants open 24 hrs. Bar 11-2 am. Ck-out noon. Convention facilities. Business center. In-rm modem link. Gift shop. Coin lndry. Free airport transportation. Exercise rm; sauna. Some bathrm phones; refrigerators avail. Some private patios. Luxury level. Cr cds: A, C, D, DS, ER, JCB, MC, V.

D SC

★★★ **MARRIOTT.** *5855 W Century Blvd (90045), I-405 exit Century Blvd W. 310/641-5700; FAX 310/337-5353; res: 800/228-9290.* 1,010 rms, 18 story. S, D $135-$160; suites from $189; family, wkend rates. Crib free. Pet accepted, some restrictions. Parking $10, valet $12. TV; cable (premium), VCR avail. Heated pool; whirlpool, poolside serv. Restaurants 6 am-midnight. Bars; entertainment. Ck-out 1 pm. Coin lndry. Convention facilities. Business center. In-rm modem link. Concierge. Shopping arcade. Beauty shop. Free airport transportation. Exercise equipt. Some bathrm phones, refrigerators. Balconies. Luxury level. Cr cds: A, C, D, DS, JCB, MC, V.

D SC

★★★ **MARRIOTT.** *1400 Parkview Ave (90266), I-405 exit Rosecrans W. 310/546-7511; FAX 310/546-7520; res: 800/228-9290.* Web www.marriott.com. 385 rms, 7 story. S, D $170-$185; suites $250-$1,000; under 16 free; higher rates special events. Crib free. Valet parking $10; garage $9. TV; cable (premium), VCR avail. Complimentary coffee in rms. Restaurant 6 am-10 pm. Bar noon-midnight. Ck-out noon. Convention facilities. Business center. In-rm modem link. Concierge. Gift shop. Free airport transportation. 9-hole golf par 3, greens fee $7, pro, putting green. Exercise equipt; sauna. Massage. Heated pool; whirlpool, poolside serv. Minibars; some bathrm phones. Some balconies. Luxury level. Cr cds: A, C, D, DS, ER, JCB, MC, V.

D SC

✓★★ **QUALITY INN.** *5249 W Century Blvd (90045), I-405 exit Century Blvd W. 310/645-2200; FAX 310/641-8241; res: 800/638-7949; res: 800/266-2200.* 278 rms, 10 story. S, D $89-$129; each addl $10; under 18 free; wkend rates. Pet accepted. TV; cable (premium), VCR avail. Pool; poolside serv. Restaurant 6 am-10 pm. Bar 5-11 pm. Ck-out noon. Convention facilities. Business center. Free airport transportation. Exercise equipt. Cr cds: A, C, D, DS, ER, JCB, MC, V.

D SC

★★★ **RENAISSANCE HOTEL.** *9620 Airport Blvd (90045), 1 mi N. 310/337-2800; FAX 310/216-6681; res: 888/293-0523; res: 800/468-3571.* Web www.renaissancehotels.com. 499 rms, 11 story, 56 suites. S, D $160-$200; each addl $10; suites $225; under 16 free; wkend rates. Valet parking $14, garage $11. TV; cable (premium), VCR avail. Heated pool; whirlpool, poolside serv. Restaurants 6-10:30 am, 11:30 am-2:30 pm, 5-11 pm. Rm serv 24 hrs. Bar. Meeting rms. Business center. In-rm modem link.

Concierge. Gift shop. Free airport transportation. Tennis privileges. Golf privileges. Exercise equipt; sauna. Massage. Health club privileges. Minibars. Cr cds: A, C, D, DS, ER, JCB, MC, V.

D SC

★★★ **SHERATON GATEWAY HOTEL LAX.** *6101 W Century Blvd (90045), ¼ mi E on Century Blvd. 310/642-1111; FAX 310/410-1267; res: 800/445-7999.* E-mail greg_moon@ittsheraton.com; web www.ittsheraton.com. 804 rms, 15 story. S $150-$190; D $170-$210; each addl $20; suites $185-$505; under 18 free; wkend rates. Crib free. Valet parking $15. TV; cable (premium), VCR avail. Heated pool; whirlpool, poolside serv. Restaurants 6-11 pm. Bar 11-2 am; entertainment. Ck-out noon. Convention facilities. Business center. In-rm modem link. Concierge. Gift shop. Free airport transportation. Exercise equipt. Minibars; microwaves avail. Luxury level. Cr cds: A, C, D, DS, ER, JCB, MC, V.

D SC

★★ **SUMMERFIELD SUITES.** *810 S Douglas Ave (90245), I-405 exit Rosencrans W. 310/725-0100; FAX 310/725-0900; res: 800/833-4353.* 122 kit. suites, 3 story. Jan-Aug: kit. suites $150-$220; family rates; package plans; lower rates rest of yr. Crib free. Pet accepted, some restrictions; $75-$250. TV; cable (premium), VCR (movies). Complimentary continental bkfst. Complimentary coffee in rms. Restaurant nearby. Bar. Ck-out noon. Meeting rms. Business servs avail. In-rm modem link. Concierge. Gift shop. Grocery store. Drugstore. Coin Indry. Free airport transportation. Exercise equipt. Health club privileges. Pool; whirlpool. Playground. Picnic tables, grills. Cr cds: A, C, D, DS, ER, JCB, MC, V.

D SC

★★★ **THE WESTIN HOTEL AT LOS ANGELES AIRPORT.** *5400 W Century Blvd (90045), 1 mi E on Century Blvd. 310/216-5858; FAX 310/645-8053; res: 877/216-1504.* E-mail westinlax@earthlink.net; web www.westin.com. 723 rms, 12 story. S, D $129-$159; each addl $20; suites $275-$1,500; under 18 free; wkend rates. Covered parking $10. Pet accepted. TV; cable (premium). Heated pool; whirlpool. Restaurant (see CHARISMA CAFE). Rm serv 24 hrs. Bar 10-2 am; entertainment. Ck-out noon. Convention facilities. Business center. In-rm modem link. Gift shop. Free airport transportation. Guest Indry. Exercise equipt; sauna. Minibars; bathrm phones in suites; microwaves avail. Balconies. Luxury level. Cr cds: A, C, D, DS, ER, JCB, MC, V.

D SC

★★ **WYNDHAM HOTEL.** *6225 W Century Blvd (90045), at entrance to Intl Airport. 310/670-9000; FAX 310/670-8110; res: 800/ WYNDHAM.* Web www.travelweb.com. 591 rms, 12 story. S $129-$159; D $139-$179; each addl $20; suites $350-$600; under 18 free; wkend rates. TV; cable (premium). Heated pool; whirlpool, poolside serv. Restaurant 6 am-11 pm; dining rms 11 am-10:30 pm. Bars 11-2 am, entertainment exc Sun. Ck-out noon. Convention facilities. Business center. In-rm modem link. Concierge. Gift shop. Garage parking. Free airport transportation. Exercise equipt. Sun deck. Luxury level. Cr cds: A, C, D, DS, ER, JCB, MC, V.

D SC

Restaurants

✓★★ **CHARISMA CAFE.** *(See Westin-L.A. Airport) 310/216-5858.* Web www.westin.com. Hrs: 6 am-11 pm. Res accepted. Eclectic menu. Bar. Semi-a la carte: bkfst $4.95-$14.50, lunch $10.50-$14.50, dinner $12.50-$22.50. Child's meals. Specialty: fire-roasted chicken. Salad bar. Valet parking. International decor; large windows. Totally nonsmoking. Cr cds: A, C, D, DS, ER, JCB, MC, V.

D SC

★★ **LIDO DI.** *1550 Rosecrans (90266), on I-405, exit Rosecrans. 310/536-0730.* Hrs: 11 am-10:30 pm; Sat, Sun 5-10:30 pm. Closed most major hols. Res accepted. Italian menu. Bar. A la carte entrees: lunch $9-$11.50, dinner $9-$22. Child's meals. Specialties: filet mignon; charbroiled chicken, sundried tomato and spinach pasta; baked halibut. Parking. Outdoor dining. Casual dining; Italian atmosphere. Cr cds: A, C, D, DS, ER, JCB, MC, V.

D ♥

★★★ **MANGIAMO.** *128 Manhattan Beach Blvd (90266), on I-405, exit Inglewood Ave. 310/318-3434.* Hrs: 5:30-10:30 pm. Closed most major hols. Res accepted. Italian menu. Bar. Wine cellar. A la carte entrees: dinner $12-$21. Child's meals. Specialties: rack of lamb, swordfish, penne with vodka sauce. Street parking. Italian decor; Italian atmosphere. Totally nonsmoking. Cr cds: A, C, D, DS, ER, JCB, MC, V.

D

★★ **MANHATTAN BAR & GRILL.** *1019 Manhattan Beach Blvd (90266), I-405 exit Inglewood, 1 blk W of Sepulveda Blvd. 310/546-4545.* Web www.southbayguide.com. Hrs: 11:30 am-2:30 pm, 5-9:30 pm; Fri, Sat to 10:30 pm. Closed Sun; also major hols. Res accepted. Italian menu. Bar to midnight. A la carte entrees: lunch $6.95-$11.95, dinner 48.95-$20. Child's meals. Specializes in seafood, veal, pasta. Piano Thurs-Sat. Parking. Outdoor dining. Intimate dining. Family-owned since 1978. Totally nonsmoking. Cr cds: A, C, MC, V.

D

★★★ **MCCORMICK & SCHMICK'S.** *2101 Rosecrans Ave (90245), on I-405 exit Rosecrans (W). 310/416-1123.* Web www.mccormickandschmick's.com. Hrs: 11 am-11 pm. Res accepted. Seafood menu. Bar to 1 am. Wine list. A la carte entrees: lunch $4.95-$9.95, dinner $9.95-$19.95. Child's meals. Specialties: crab cakes, cedar plank salmon, stuffed halibut. Valet parking. Outdoor dining. Victorian/art deco decor. Cr cds: A, C, MC, V.

D

✓★★★ **REEDS RESTAURANT.** *2640 N Sepulveda Blvd (90266), I-405 exit Rosencrans W. 310/546-3299.* Hrs: 11:30 am-2:30 pm, 5:30-10 pm. Closed most major hols. Res accepted. French menu. Wine list. Semi-a la carte: lunch $7.95-$17.95, dinner $12.95-$19.95. Child's meals. Specialties: filet mignon, rack of lamb with rosemary sauce, sea bass with potato crust in miso sauce. Piano Tues-Sun. Parking. Outdoor dining. Intimate atmosphere. Totally nonsmoking. Cr cds: A, C, D, MC, V.

D

★★ **TALIA'S ITALIAN RESTAURANT.** *1148 Manhattan Ave (90266), on I-405, exit Inglewood Ave . 310/545-6884.* Hrs: 5:30-10:30 pm; Sun brunch 8 am-2 pm. Closed most major hols. Res accepted. Italian menu. A la carte entrees: dinner $12-$18. Sun brunch $4-$7. Child's meals. Specialties: osso bucco, seared ahi, tortellini vico. Intimate dining. Family-owned since 1977. Cr cds: A, C, D, DS, ER, JCB, MC, V.

D

★★★ **WOLFGANG PUCK CAFE.** *2121 E Rosecrans (90245). 310/607-9653.* Hrs: 11 am-10 pm; Fri, Sat to 11 pm; Sun brunch 11 am-3 pm. Closed Jan 1, Thanksgiving, Dec 25. Res accepted. Contemporary Amer menu. Bar. Semi-a la carte: lunch $15-$18, dinner $18-$22. Sun brunch $13.50. Child's meals. Specialties: wood-burning pizzas, chinois chicken salad, sesame ahi tuna. Valet parking. Outdoor dining. Totally nonsmoking. Cr cds: A, C, D, MC, V.

D

Los Gatos (F-1)

(See also San Jose, Saratoga)

Founded ca 1870 **Pop** 27,357 **Elev** 385 ft **Area Code** 408 **Zip** 95030

Information Town of Los Gatos Chamber of Commerce, 180 S Market St, San Jose 95113; 408/354-9300

Free-roaming wildcats inspired the name "La Rinconada de Los Gatos," the corner of the cats. Today, two sculptured cats, Leo and Leona, guard the town entrance at Poets Canyon.

What to See and Do

Los Gatos Forbes Mill History Museum. Historic landmark; former grain mill. (Wed-Sun) 75 Church St. Phone 408/395-7375. **Donation**

Los Gatos Museum. Natural history exhibits; art displays, art history. In restored firehouse. (Wed-Sun afternoons; closed hols & Dec 24, 31) Tait & Main. Phone 408/354-2646. **Free**

Old Town. Shops, restaurants, art galleries, flowered garden walkways, housed in what was once an elementary school (1921). 50 University Ave.

Youth Science Institute-Vasona Discovery Center. Located in Vasona Lake County Park, this Junior Museum houses aquaria with local and native fish, reptiles and amphibians. Native plant trail. Museum (daily); park (daily). Parking fee. 296 Garden Hill Dr. Phone 408/356-4945. **Free**

Motels

★★ **LA HACIENDA INN HOTEL.** *18840 Saratoga Los Gatos Rd (95030). 408/354-9230; FAX 408/354-7590; res: 800/235-4570.* 20 rms, 3 kits. S $100; D $125; each addl $10; suites, kit. units $105-$150; under 6 free. Crib free. TV; cable (premium), VCR avail (free movies). Pool; whirlpool. Complimentary continental bkfst. Restaurant 11 am-2:30 pm, 5-11 pm. Ck-out noon. Meeting rm. Business servs avail. In-rm modem link. Guest lndry. Refrigerators; some fireplaces. Private patios. Beautifully landscaped grounds. Totally nonsmoking. Cr cds: A, C, D, DS, JCB, MC, V.

SC

★★ **LODGE AT VILLA FELICE.** *15350 S Winchester Blvd (95030). 408/395-6710; FAX 408/354-1826; res: 800/662-9229.* 33 rms, 2 story. S, D $130-$150; each addl $10; suites $160-$240 under 16 free. Crib free. TV; cable (premium), VCR avail. Heated pool; whirlpool. Complimentary continental bkfst. Ck-out noon. Meeting rms. Business servs avail. Sundries. Refrigerators; some in-rm saunas. Private patios, balconies. On mountain; view of Lake Vasona. Cr cds: A, C, D, MC, V.

D SC

Motor Hotels

★★ **LOS GATOS LODGE.** *50 Los Gatos-Saratoga Rd (95032), Hwy 17, E Los Gatos exit, first light turn rt. 408/354-3300; FAX 408/354-5451; res: 800/231-8676.* 129 rms, 2 story. S, D $109-$169; under 16 free. Crib free. Pet accepted, some restrictions. TV; cable. Heated pool; whirlpool. Coffee in rms. Restaurant 7 am-2 pm, 5-10 pm. Bar 10:30-2 am; entertainment Fri, Sat. Ck-out noon. Coin lndry. Meeting rms. Business servs avail. Sundries. Putting green. Lawn games. All rms have private patio or deck. Cr cds: A, C, D, DS, MC, V.

D SC

★★★ **TOLL HOUSE HOTEL.** *140 S Santa Cruz Ave (95030). 408/395-7070; FAX 408/395-3730; res: 800/238-6111.* 97 rms, 3 story. S $159; D $169; suites $250; under 16 free. Crib free. TV; cable (premium). Coffee in rms. Complimentary continental bkfst. Restaurant 6:30-9:30 pm; Fri, Sat to 10 pm. Rm serv 5-10 pm. Bar. Ck-out noon. Meeting rms. Business center. In-rm modem link. Garage parking. Free airport transportation. Exercise equipt. Health club privileges. Some refrigerators. Private patios, balconies. Cr cds: A, C, D, DS, MC, V.

D SC

Restaurant

★★ **LOS GATOS BREWING CO.** *130 N Santa Cruz Ave (95030). 408/395-9929.* Hrs: 11:30 am-10 pm; Fri, Sat to 11 pm; Sun brunch 11:30 am-3 pm. Closed Dec 25. Res accepted. Contemporary Amer menu. Bar. A la carte entrees: lunch $7.50-$12.95, dinner $7.95-$18.95. Sun brunch $6.95-$10.50. Child's meals. Specialties: spit-roasted chicken, fusilli pasta. Parking. In microbrewery. Totally nonsmoking. Cr cds: A, C, D, DS, MC, V.

D

Madera (F-2)

(See also Fresno)

Pop 29,281 **Elev** 270 ft **Area Code** 209 **Zip** 93637

Motor Hotel

★★ **BEST WESTERN.** *317 N G St (93637). 559/673-5164; FAX 559/661-8426; res: 800/528-1234.* 93 rms, 5 story. S $65; D $75; each addl $4; suites $85; under 12 free. Crib free. TV; cable (premium). Complimentary coffee in rms. Restaurant 6 am-9 pm. Rm serv. Bar 11:30-2 am. Ck-out noon. Meeting rms. Bellhops. Health club privileges. Free airport transportation. Refrigerators. Cr cds: A, C, D, DS, JCB, MC, V.

D SC

Restaurant

✓★ **FRUIT BASKET.** *117 S Gateway Dr (93637). 209/674-2805.* Hrs: 6 am-9:30 pm. Closed some major hols. Wine, beer. A la carte entrees: bkfst $1.49-$9.49. Complete meals: lunch $3.99-$11.99, dinner $5.29-$11.99. Child's meals. Specialties: pot roast, chicken-fried steak, soups. Opp city park. Cr cds: A, C, DS, MC, V.

Malibu (C-1 see Los Angeles map)

Pop 7,000 (est) **Elev** 25 ft **Area Code** 310 **Zip** 90265

What to See and Do

Pepperdine University (1937). (2,300 students) 830-acre campus includes School of Law as well as college of arts, sciences and letters; cultural arts center and Weisman Museum of Art (Tues-Sun; phone 310/456-4581). 24255 Pacific Coast Hwy. Phone 310/456-4000.

Motels

★★ **CASA MALIBU INN ON THE BEACH.** *22752 Pacific Coast Hwy (90265). 310/456-2219; FAX 310/456-5418; res: 800/831-0858.* 21 rms, 1-2 story, 6 kits. Some A/C. June-Sept: S, D $99-$329; each addl $15; kit. units $12 addl (3-day min); lower rates rest of yr. Crib $15. TV. Coffee in rms. Restaurant nearby. Ck-out noon. In-rm modem link. Valet serv. Health club privileges. Golf privileges. Tennis privileges. Refrigerators. Some balconies, fireplaces. Cr cds: A, C, MC, V.

★★ **MALIBU COUNTRY INN.** *6506 Westward Beach Rd (90265), off Pacific Coast Hwy. 310/457-9622; FAX 310/457-1349.* Web www.malibu.com. 16 rms, 1 story. No A/C. Apr-Sept: S, D $165; under 7 free; lower rates rest of yr. Crib free. TV; cable. Heated pool. Complimentary continental bkfst. Complimentary coffee in rms. Restaurant. Rm serv. Business servs avail. Ck-out noon. Refrigerators. Balconies. 1940s Cape Cod-style building with 3 acres of garden; located on a bluff overlooking Zuma Beach. Cr cds: A, C, D, DS, MC, V.

D

Motor Hotel

★★ **MALIBU BEACH INN.** *22878 Pacific Coast Hwy (90265). 310/456-6444; FAX 310/456-1499; res: 800/462-5428.* Web www.malibubeach.com. 47 rms, 3 story. June-Sept: S, D $160-$209; each addl $15; suites $275-$325. TV; cable, VCR (movies $5). Complimentary continental bkfst. Complimentary coffee in rms. Restaurants nearby. Ck-out noon. Business servs avail. In-rm modem link. Gift shop. Health club privileges. Minibars, fireplaces; some in-rm whirlpools. Balconies. Tile-roofed, Mediterranean-style hotel on beach. Cr cds: A, C, D, JCB, MC, V.

D SC

Restaurants

★★★ **GEOFFREY'S.** *27400 Pacific Coast Hwy (90265). 310/457-1519.* E-mail jlamarca@earthlink.net. Hrs: noon-10 pm; Sat 11 am-11 pm; Sun 10:30 am-9:30 pm. Res accepted. Bar. Wine list. A la carte entrees: lunch $8-$20, dinner $30-$45. Specialties: grilled stuffed lamb chop, grilled Norwegian salmon, eggs benedict en croissant. Valet parking. Patio dining. Panoramic view of ocean. Cr cds: A, C, MC, V.

D

★★★ **GRANITA.** *23725 W Malibu Rd (90265), N on Pacific Coast Hwy. 310/456-0488.* Hrs: 6-10 pm; Sat, Sun 11 am-2 pm, 5:30-10 pm. Closed Jan 1, Thanksgiving, Dec 24, 25. Res accepted; required wkends. California cuisine. Bar. Wine list. A la carte entrees: brunch $11-$19, dinner $22-$32. Specialties: grilled big-eye tuna, crisp potato galette with gravlax, dill cream and fresh chives. Entertainment Wed. Outdoor dining. Unique interior with underwater ocean fantasy theme. Cr cds: A, C, D, DS, MC, V.

D

★ **MOONSHADOWS.** *20356 W Pacific Coast H (90265). 310/456-3010.* Hrs: 11 am-11 pm; Fri, Sat to midnight; Sun to 10 pm. Closed Thanksgiving, Dec 25. Bar. Semi-a la carte: lunch $4.95-$12.95, dinner $15.95-$22.95. Specializes in steak, lobster, fresh fish of the day. Salad bar. Valet parking. Overlooks ocean. Cr cds: A, C, D, DS, MC, V.

D

Mammoth Lakes (E-4)

(See also Bishop, June Lake)

Pop 4,785 **Elev** 7,800 ft **Area Code** 760 **Zip** 93546
Web www.visitmammoth.com

Information Mammoth Lakes Visitor Bureau, PO Box 48; 760/934-2712 or 888/GO-MAMMOTH. The Visitor Center is located on CA 203

Spectacular scenery and a variety of recreational opportunities are found in this region of rugged peaks, numerous lakes, streams and waterfalls, alpine meadows and extensive forests. Much of the outstanding scenery was created by volcanos or carved by glaciers.

What to See and Do

Devils Postpile National Monument (see).

Fishing, boating, rentals. Crowley Lake, 6 mi S on US 395. **Sherwin Creek** (fishing, camping), 3 mi SE of ranger station. **Convict Lake,** 4 mi SE of Mammoth Junction, 2 mi W of US 395. SW on Lake Mary Rd are **Twin Lakes** (camping), **Lake Mary** (camping), **Coldwater** (camping), **Lake George** (camping), **Pine City** (camping). Fees charged at recreation sites. All campgrounds first come, first served basis (self-registration). For further details and information on other areas contact the Mammoth Ranger District, Box 148; phone 760/924-5500. Camping ¢¢¢

Mammoth Adventure Connection. In the summer, the Mammoth Mountain is transformed into a bike park. Park activities also include hiking, ropes course and rock climbing. Ride the gondola to the top of the mountain and bike down on a variety of trails, suited to various skills and ages. Helmets are required within park boundaries. (July-Sept, daily, weather permitting) Fee for activities. Phone 760/934-0606.

Mammoth Mountain Ski Area. 8 quad, 7 triple, 11 double chairlifts, 2 gondolas, 1 surface lift; patrol, school, rentals; cafeterias, restaurants. More than 150 runs; longest run 3 mi; vertical drop 3,100 ft. (Nov-June, daily) Gondola ride (daily). In Inyo National Forest. Phone 760/934-2571; snow conditions, 760/934-6166. ¢¢¢¢¢

Mammoth Visitor Center Ranger Station. Visitor summer activities (July 4-Labor Day wkend) include interpretive tours, evening programs, and Jr-Ranger programs (6-12 yrs). Visitor center (yr-round). Phone 760/924-5500 for details, -5531 (TDD). All family campgrounds (exc ½ of Sherwin Creek, which requires reservations) on first come, first served basis; group camping and Sherwin Creek camping reservable through National Forest recreation reservations, 800/280-CAMP. Shady Rest campground open in winter (tent camping only). Self-registration for backpackers during non-quota season; wilderness permits required all yr. Quota season last Friday in June-mid-Sept. Reservations may be made 6 months to 2 days in advance by contacting Wilderness Reservations, PO Box 430, Big Pine 93513; 888/374-3773. At the edge of town, surrounded by Inyo National Forest. Contact Mammoth Ranger District, Box 148; 760/924-5500. Camping ¢¢¢

Pack trips for wilderness camping.

Mammoth Lakes Pack Outfit. 4 mi SW on Lake Mary Rd near Lake Mary. Contact PO Box 61; phone 760/934-2434.

McGee Creek Pack Station. 12 mi SW. Contact Rte 1, Box 162 M; phone 760/935-4324 (summer) or 760/878-2207.

Red's Meadow Pack Station and Resort. 15 mi W on Minaret Hwy. Contact Box 395; phone 760/934-2345 (summer), 760/873-3928 (winter) or 800/292-7758.

Motels

✓★ **ECONO LODGE WILD WOOD INN.** *3626 Main St (93546), ¼ mi W of Old Mammoth Rd on Main St (CA 203). 760/934-6855; FAX 760/934-3626; res: 800/228-5050.* 32 rms, 2 story. No A/C. S $49-$99; D $59-$99; ski plans. Pet accepted. TV; cable (premium). Heated pool; whirlpool. Continental bkfst. Coffee in rms. Restaurant nearby. Ck-out 10 am. Business servs avail. Downhill/x-country ski 3 mi. Some refrigerators, microwaves. Mountain view from some rms. Cr cds: A, C, D, DS, MC, V.

SC

✓★★ **QUALITY INN.** *3537 Main St (CA 203) (93546). 760/934-5114; FAX 760/934-5165; res: 800/228-5050.* 59 rms, 2 story. No A/C. S, D $69-$150; each addl $10; under 18 free. Crib free. TV; cable (premium). Complimentary continental bkfst. Complimentary coffee in rms. Restaurant nearby. Ck-out 11 am. Business servs avail. Garage parking. Downhill/x-country ski 2 mi. Whirlpool. Refrigerators, microwaves. Cr cds: A, C, D, DS, MC, V.

D SC

★★ **SHILO INN.** *2963 Main St (93546). 760/934-4500; FAX 760/934-7594; res: 800/222-2244.* 70 rms, 4 story. Mid-Nov-mid-Apr: S, D $85-$150; under 12 free; lower rates rest of yr. Crib free. Pet accepted, some restrictions; $7. TV; cable (premium), VCR avail. Indoor pool. Complimentary continental bkfst. Complimentary coffee in rms. Restaurant adj 5 am-10 pm. Ck-out noon. Coin lndry. Meeting rm. Business servs avail. Garage parking. Free airport transportation. Downhill/x-country ski 5 mi. Exercise equipt; sauna. Bathrm phones, refrigerators, microwaves, wet bars. Cr cds: A, C, D, DS, ER, JCB, MC, V.

D SC

Lodge

★★★ **MAMMOTH MOUNTAIN INN.** *1 Minaret Rd (93546). 760/934-2581; FAX 760/934-0701; res: 800/228-4947.* Web www.mammoth-mtn.com. 213 rms, 3 story, 50 kit. condos. Nov-Apr: S, D $115-$210; suites $195-$490; family, mid-wk rates; ski plans; lower rates rest of yr.

Crib $10. TV; cable (premium). Supervised child's activities; ages 1-12. Complimentary coffee in rms. Restaurant 7:30 am-9:30 pm. Box lunches. Snack bar. Barbecues. Rm serv. Bar from 10 am. Ck-out 11 am. Grocery store. Coin lndry. Meeting rms. Business servs avail. Bellhops. Concierge. Gift shop. Covered parking. Free airport transportation. Downhill/x-country ski on site. Sleighing. Horseback riding. Haywagon rides. Bicycles. Entertainment. Whirlpools. Game rm. Fish/hike guides. Some balconies. Picnic tables. Cr cds: A, C, MC, V.

D SC

Motor Hotel

✓★★ **TRAVELODGE.** *6209 Minaret Rd (93546). 760/934-8576; FAX 760/934-8007; res: 800/578-7878.* E-mail travelodge@qnet.com; web www.mammothweb.com/travelodge. 131 rms, 3 story, 12 kit. cottages. No A/C. Nov-Apr: S, D $100-$116; lower rates rest of yr. Package plans. Complimentary coffee in rms. Crib free. TV; cable (premium). Restaurant nearby. Ck-out 11 am. Business servs avail. Downhill/x-country ski 1 mi. Whirlpool. Sauna. Some refrigerators. Some balconies. Cr cds: A, C, MC, V.

SC

Inns

★ **CINNAMON BEAR INN.** *113 Center St (93546). 760/934-2873; FAX 760/924-2873; res: 800/845-2873.* 18 rms, 2 story. No A/C. Some rm phones. Nov-Mar: S, D $49-$139; ski plans; higher rates hols; lower rates rest of yr. TV; cable (premium). Complimentary full bkfst; afternoon refreshments. Restaurant nearby. Ck-out 10 am, ck-in 2 pm. Business servs avail. Downhill ski 10 mi; x-country ski on site. Some refrigerators. Built in 1955. Cr cds: A, C, DS, MC, V.

SC

★ **SNOW GOOSE INN.** *57 Forest Trl (93546). 760/934-2660; FAX 760/934-5655; res: 800/874-7368.* E-mail snowgoose@qnet.com; web www.mammothweb.com. 19 rms, 2 story, 4 suites, 2 kits. No A/C. Nov-Apr: S, D $58-$98; each addl $12; suites $148-$168; ski plans; lower rates rest of yr. Pet accepted, some restrictions; $7/day. TV; cable (premium). Complimentary full bkfst; refreshments. Ck-out 10 am, ck-in 2 pm. Business servs avail. Downhill/x-country ski 3 mi. Balconies. Library/sitting rm; antiques. Snow goose motif throughout. Cr cds: C, DS, MC, V.

Restaurant

✓★ **GRINGO'S.** *On Main St (93546), ½ blk W of Old Mammoth Rd. 760/934-8595.* Hrs: 10 pm. Mexican menu. Bar midnight. Semi-a la carte: dinner $6.45-$12.95. Specialties: fajitas, rotisserie-cooked chicken. Outdoor dining. Colorful Mexican decor. Totally nonsmoking. Cr cds: A, C, DS, MC, V.

Manhattan Beach

(see Los Angeles)

Marina del Rey

(C-3 see Los Angeles map)

(See also Los Angeles, Santa Monica)

Pop 7,431 **Elev** 10 ft **Area Code** 310 **Zip** 90292
E-mail marina@ix.netcom.com **Web** www.itlnet.com/marina

Information Chamber of Commerce, Oakwood Corporate Center, 4111 Via Marina; 310/821-0555 or 800/919-0555

With its name, could this community next to Venice be anything but boat-oriented? The 6,000-slip facility attracts many boating and sportfishing enthusiasts. Sail and power boat rentals, ocean cruises and fishing expeditions are available. In addition, there are waterfront biking and jogging trails.

What to See and Do

Fisherman's Village. Modeled after a turn-of-the-century New England fishing town and located on the main channel of the largest man-made small craft harbor in the country, this area and its well-known lighthouse have appeared in many television and movie productions. Cobblestone walks complement the nautical atmosphere and provide a panoramic view of the marina; boat rentals, fishing charters, harbor cruises; shops, boutiques and restaurants. Entertainment throughout the yr (weather permitting), including free jazz concerts (Sun). (Daily) 13755 Fiji Way. Phone 310/823-5411.

Motel

★★ **FOGHORN HOTEL.** *4140 Via Marina (90066), 5 mi N of Intl Airport. 310/823-4626; FAX 310/578-1964; res: 800/423-4940.* 23 rms, 2 story. June-Aug: S, D $119-$139; each addl $10; under 10 free; lower rates rest of yr. Crib free. TV; cable (premium), VCR (movies). Complimentary continental bkfst. Restaurant adj 11:30 am-midnight. Ck-out 11:30 am. Free airport transportation. Refrigerators; microwaves avail. Swimming beach. Cr cds: A, C, D, DS, MC, V.

Motor Hotels

★★★ **COURTYARD BY MARRIOTT.** *13480 Maxella Ave (90292), 5 mi N of LAX off Lincoln Blvd. 310/822-8555; FAX 310/823-2996; res: 800/321-2211.* E-mail imdr2@attmail.com; web www.courtyard.com/laxcm. 276 rms, 5 story. S, D $129; each addl $10; suites $179; under 12 free; wkend rates. Crib free. TV; cable (premium), VCR avail. Heated pool; whirlpool, poolside serv. Restaurant 6:30-11 am. Rm serv. Bar 11-1 am. Ck-out noon. Meeting rms. Business servs avail. In-rm modem link. Bellhops. Tennis opp. Exercise equipt. Health club privileges. Minibars; microwaves avail. Private patios, balconies. Cr cds: A, C, D, DS, JCB, MC, V.

D SC

★★ **MARINA DEL REY HOTEL.** *13534 Bali Way (90292), I-405 to I-90W, Lincoln Blvd. 310/301-1000; FAX 310/301-8167; res: 800/882-4000.* 160 rms, 3 story. S $139-$210; D $149-$220; each addl $20; suites $350-$400; under 18 free. TV; cable (premium), VCR avail. Heated pool; poolside serv. Restaurant 6 am-11 pm. Rm serv 24 hrs. Bar 10-2 am. Ck-out noon. Meeting rms. Business center. In-rm modem link. Gift shop. Free airport transportation. Charter boats. Some bathrm phones. Private patios, balconies. On waterfront; view of marina. Cr cds: A, C, D, MC, V.

D SC

Hotels

★★★ **MARINA BEACH MARRIOTT HOTEL.** *4100 Admiralty Way (90292), 5 mi N of LAX on I-1. 310/301-3000; FAX 310/448-4870; res: 800/228-9290.* Web www.marriott.com. 370 rms, 9 story. S, D $225-$250; suites $268-$1,200; under 18 free; wkend packages. Valet parking $10. TV; cable (premium), VCR avail. Pool; poolside serv. Restaurant 6 am-11 pm. Bar 10-1:30 am; entertainment. Ck-out noon. Convention facilities. Business center. In-rm modem link. Concierge. Gift shop. Tennis privileges. Exercise equipt. Health club privileges. Bathrm phones, refrigerators. Balconies. Opp beach. Luxury level. Cr cds: A, C, D, DS, ER, JCB, MC, V.

D

★★★★ **RITZ-CARLTON HOTEL.** *4375 Admiralty Way (90292), I-405 to I-90W, N on Lincoln Blvd. 310/823-1700; FAX 310/823-2403; res: 800/241-3333.* Web www.ritzcarlton.com. Situated on a basin with panoramic views of the Pacific Ocean from most balconies, this deluxe high-rise offers well-appointed contemporary guest rooms, access to a marina, and a selection of opulent lounges and dining rooms. 306 rms, 12 story. S, D $280-$470; suites $550-$2,500; wkend rates. The Ritz-Carlton Lounge offers 5 food and beverage presentations daily and a private concierge. Crib free. TV; cable (premium), VCR avail. Valet parking $21. Pool; whirlpool, poolside serv. Supervised child's activities; ages 5-13. Restaurant (see THE TERRACE RESTAURANT). Rm serv 24 hrs. Bar 11-1 am; pianist evenings. Ck-out noon. Convention facilities. Business center. In-rm modem link. Concierge. Shopping arcade. Lighted tennis, pro. Golf privileges. Basketball. Bicycle rental. Exercise rm. Massage. Bathrm phones, refrigerators, minibars. Balconies. Luxury level. Cr cds: A, C, D, DS, ER, JCB, MC, V.

D SC

Inn

★★★ **INN AT PLAYA DEL REY.** *435 Culver Blvd (90293), I-90, S on Lincoln Blvd, W on Jefferson. 310/574-1920; FAX 310/574-9920.* E-mail playainn@aol.com. 21 rms, 3 story. S, D $95-$245; under 18 free. Crib avail. Garage parking. TV; cable (premium), VCR (free movies). Complimentary full bkfst. Restaurant adj 7 am-11 pm. Ck-out noon. Meeting rm. Business servs avail. In-rm modem link. Concierge serv. Some in-rm whirlpools; microwaves avail. Some balconies. Overlooks Ballona Wetlands bird sanctuary. Cr cds: A, C, DS, MC, V.

D

Restaurant

★★★ **THE DINING ROOM.** *(See The Ritz-Carlton, Marina Del Rey) 310/823-1700.* Web www.ritzcarlton.com. Unrated for 2000. Cr cds: A, C, D, DS, ER, JCB, MC, V.

D

Martinez (B-F see San Francisco map)

(See also Concord, Oakland, Vallejo)

Pop 31,808 **Elev** 23 ft **Area Code** 510 **Zip** 94553

What to See and Do

Briones Regional Park. Covers 5,484 acres of rolling hills and wooded ravines. John Muir Nature Area at north end. Hiking on many trails including 2 self-guided nature trails, horseback riding. Picnicking. Archery range. Connects with Briones to Mt Diablo Trail. (Daily) N entrance 2 mi S of Arnold Industrial Hwy (CA 4) via Alhambra Valley Rd. Phone 510/635-0135. Per vehicle (seasonal) **¢¢**

John Muir National Historic Site. House built in 1882 was the home of the conservationist, author and advocate of the National Park system. Visitor center, film, self-guided tours (Wed-Sun; closed Jan 1, Thanksgiving, Dec 25). Guided tour (1 departure daily, Wed-Sun). Martinez Adobe (1849) is also on the grounds. 4202 Alhambra Ave. Phone 510/228-8860. **¢**

Marysville (D-3)

(See also Oroville)

Settled 1842 **Pop** 12,324 **Elev** 63 ft **Area Code** 916 **Zip** 95901

Information Yuba-Sutter Chamber of Commerce, 429 10th St, PO Box 1429; 916/743-6501

Marysville is at the confluence of the Yuba and Feather rivers. The river town was once the third-largest community in the state. Hydraulic mining has raised the Yuba River bed so that it is above, rather than below, the city. The river is contained by huge levees. Named for a survivor of the Donner Party, the town was the head of river navigation—the point where miners continued upriver by foot to the gold diggings.

What to See and Do

Bok Kai Temple. Chinese temple, built in 1879, honors Bok Kai, river god of good fortune. Caretaker will open temple for visitors; guided tours may be arranged by appt (daily). D St on the Levee. Phone 916/742-2787. **Donation**

Annual Events

Bok Kai Festival. Parade, street entertainment, Lion Dances; martial arts demonstrations; 1-mi run; climaxed by firing of the "Lucky Bombs." Mar.

Stampede Days. Riverfront Park. Stampede and rodeo sponsored by the Flying U Rodeo; parade, activities. Memorial Day wkend.

California Prune Festival. Yuba-Sutter Fairgrounds in Yuba City. Food, wine tasting, music, art displays, children's activities. Usually 2nd wkend Sept.

Beckwourth Frontier Days. In commemoration of when James Beckwourth passed through here in the 1850s. Costumed participants re-create life as it was then; events including muzzle loaders; wagon train. Late Sept-early Oct.

Motel

★★ **BEST WESTERN INN.** *1001 Clark Ave (95991), 1 blk N of CA 20, ½ mi E of CA 99. 530/674-8824; FAX 530/674-0563; res: 800/562-5706; res: 800/562-5700.* 125 rms, 2-3 story. S $64-$75; D $64-$85; each addl $4; suites $89-$150. TV; cable. Pool; whirlpool. Complimentary coffee in rms. Restaurant 6 am-10 pm. Bar 4 pm-midnight. Ck-out noon. Meeting rms. Business servs avail. Some refrigerators, in-rm whirlpools, fireplaces, balconies. Cr cds: A, C, D, DS, MC, V.

D SC

Mendocino (C-1)

(See also Fort Bragg, Ukiah, Willits)

Founded 1852 **Pop** 1,100 (est) **Elev** 125 ft **Area Code** 707 **Zip** 95460 **E-mail** chamber@mcn.org **Web** www.mendocinocoast.com

Information Fort Bragg-Mendocino Coast Chamber of Commerce, 332 N Main St, PO Box 1141, Fort Bragg 95437; 707/961-6300 or 800/726-2780

Once a remote lumber port, Mendocino has evolved into a cultural center and popular vacation spot. The town's 19th-century legacy is reflected in its Cape Cod/New England architecture.

What to See and Do

Kelley House Museum & Library (1861). Displays feature antique photographs, exhibits of local artifacts and private collections. (June-Sept, daily; Oct-May, Fri-Mon) 45007 Albion St. Phone 707/937-5791. **¢**

Mendocino Art Center. Classes in ceramics, textiles, painting, drawing, printmaking and sculpture. Exhibition/sales gallery, art library, gardens; theatrical productions and arts and crafts fairs. (Daily; closed Jan 1, Dec 25) 45200 Little Lake St. Phone 707/937-5818. **Free**

State parks.

Mendocino Headlands. Includes 1850s building (Ford House Visitor Center) containing exhibits on town and local history (daily; fee); phone 707/937-5397. Bluff areas/headlands offer ocean view, sandy beach; fishing. Surrounds town; on 347 acres. Phone 707/937-5804. **Free**

Russian Gulch. Swimming beach; entry point for skin divers; fishing. Hiking, bicycle trails. Picnicking. Camping. Standard fees. (Apr-Nov, daily) 2 mi N via CA 1. Phone 707/937-5804.

Van Damme. In the SE portion of this 2,190-acre park is Pygmy Forest, where poor soil conditions inhibit tree growth. Some trees, nearly 200 yrs old, have trunks only ¼ inch in diameter. Fishing; beach with access for divers & boaters. Nature, hiking trails. Picnicking. Camping, environmental camping. (Daily) 3 mi S via CA 1. Phone 707/937-5804. Camping ¢¢¢¢

Annual Events

Whale Festival. Whale watching walks, wine tasting, chowder tasting. 1st wkend Mar.

Mendocino Music Festival. Chamber, symphonic, choral, opera and jazz concerts. 10 days July.

Mendocino Christmas Festival. Tour of inns; events. First 2 wks Dec.

Inns

★★★ **ALBION RIVER INN.** *3790 N Hwy 1 (95410), at the mouth of the Albion River. 707/937-1919; FAX 707/937-2604; res: 800/479-7944.* E-mail albionriverinn@mcn.org; web www.albionriver.com. 20 rms. No A/C. S, D $170-$260. Complimentary full bkfst. Complimentary coffee, wine in rms. Restaurant (see ALBION RIVER INN). Ck-out noon, ck-in 3 pm. Business servs avail. Fireplaces, refrigerators; some in-rm whirlpools. 10 landscaped acres on cliff above ocean; flower gardens. Individually decorated rms; antiques. View of ocean. Totally nonsmoking. Cr cds: A, C, MC, V.

D

✓★★★ **BLACKBERRY INN.** *44951 Larkin Rd (95460). 707/937-5281; res: 800/950-7806.* E-mail blackber@mcn.org; web www.innaccess.com/bbi. 17 rms, 2 kit. units. No A/C. Some rm phones. S $90-$140; D $95-$145; each addl $5; kit. units $145; mid-wk rates in winter. TV; cable. Complimentary continental bkfst. Coffee in rms. Ck-out 11 am, ck-in 2 pm. Many fireplaces; some refrigerators, in-rm whirlpools. Ocean view. Cr cds: C, MC, V.

★★★ **ELK COVE INN.** *6300 S Hwy One (95432), 15 mi S on CA 1. 707/877-3321; FAX 707/877-1808.* E-mail elkcove@mcn.org; web www.elkcoveinn.com. 14 rms. No A/C. No rm phones. D $108-$218; suites $248-$278; lower mid-wk rates (winter). Children over 12 yrs only. TV in sitting rm; VCR (free movies). Complimentary full bkfst. Coffee in rms. Bar. Ck-out 11 am, ck-in 2-6 pm. Business servs avail. Library; sitting rm. Antiques. Some fireplaces. Picnic tables, grills. Gazebo. Former executive guest house (1883). Overlooks ocean; private beach access. Totally nonsmoking. Cr cds: A, C, MC, V.

D

★★★ **HEADLANDS INN.** *Albion & Howard Sts (95460). 707/937-4431; FAX 707/937-0412; res: 800/354-4431.* Web www.headlandsinn.com. 7 rms, 3 story. No A/C. No rm phones. S, D $90-$195; lower rates winter mid-wk. TV in cottage; VCR. Complimentary full bkfst; afternoon refreshments. Restaurant nearby. Ck-out 11 am, ck-in 3-6 pm. Business servs avail. Street parking. Fireplaces. Sitting rms; antiques. Victorian house (1868) built as town barber shop overlooks English garden, ocean. Totally nonsmoking. Cr cds: A, C, MC, V.

★★★ **HERITAGE HOUSE.** *5200 N Hwy 1 (95456), 5 mi S in Little River. 707/937-5885; FAX 707/937-0318; res: 800/235-5885.* Web www.heritage-house-inn. 66 rms, 1-2 story, 10 suites. No A/C. No rm phones. S, D $125-$350; each addl $20; suites $225-$350; under 6 free; wkends, hols (2-3 day min). Complimentary coffee in rms. Restaurant 8-11 am, 6-8:30 pm. Ck-out noon, ck-in 2 pm. Business servs avail. Luggage handling. Concierge serv. Gift shop. Many fireplaces, refrigerators; some wet bars. On ocean. Built in 1877; on 37 acres. Cr cds: C, MC, V.

★★★ **HILL HOUSE INN.** *10701 Palette Dr (95460). 707/937-0554; FAX 707/937-1123; res: 800/422-0554.* 44 rms, 2 story, 4 suites. No A/C. S, D $110-$175; suites $195-$300. TV; cable. Complimentary coffee in rms. Dining rm 7:30-10:30 am, 11:30 am-9 pm. Bar. Ck-out noon, ck-in 3 pm. Meeting rms. Business servs avail. Private patios, balconies. Picnic tables. Library. Victorian decor. Overlooks ocean. On 2½ acres. Cr cds: A, C, D, DS, MC, V.

D SC

★★ **INN AT SCHOOLHOUSE CREEK.** *7051 N Hwy 1 (95456), 3 mi S. 707/937-5525; FAX 707/937-2012; res: 800/731-5525.* E-mail innkeeper@binnb.com; web www.binnb.com. 13 rms, 4 suites, 3 kit. units, 1 guest house. No A/C. Some rm phones. Mid-May-Sept: S, D $85-$135; each addl $10-$15; suites $115-$150; kit. units $140-$175; guest house $150-$180; wkends, hols (2-3 day min); lower rates rest of yr. Crib $10. Pet accepted, some restrictions; $15-$25. TV; cable (premium), VCR (movies). Complimentary continental bkfst. Complimentary coffee in rms. Restaurant nearby. Ck-out 11 am, ck-in 2 pm. Business servs avail. Concierge serv. Gift shop. Lawn games. Fireplaces; some refrigerators. Balconies. Built in 1862; on 8½ acres; gardens, meadows, forests. Totally nonsmoking. Cr cds: A, C, DS, MC, V.

SC

★★★ **JOSHUA GRINDLE INN.** *44800 Little Lake Rd (95460), at jct CA 1. 707/937-4143; res: 800/474-6353.* E-mail info@joshgrin.com; web www.joshgrin.com. 10 rms, 1 guest house, 1-2 story. No A/C. Rm phones avail. S, D $100-$195; guest house $200-$250; wkly rates; wkends (2-day min). Complimentary full bkfst; afternoon refreshments. Ck-out 11 am, ck-in 1 pm. Free airport transportation. Lawn games. Antiques. Many fireplaces. New England country atmosphere. 2 acre English-style garden. Antique pump organ. Built 1879 by local banker. Overlooks ocean. Totally nonsmoking. Cr cds: C, MC, V.

✓★★★ **MENDOCINO.** *45080 Main St (95460). 707/937-0511; FAX 707/548-0513; res: 800/548-0513.* 51 rms, 38 with bath, 1-3 story. S, D $85-$185; each addl $20; suites $190-$275; lower rates wkdays. TV in some rms; cable. Dining rm 8 am-9:30 pm. Rm serv. Bar. Ck-out noon, ck-in 4 pm. Meeting rms. Business servs avail. Luggage handling. Some fireplaces. Some balconies. Antiques. Built 1878. Some rms with ocean view. Cr cds: A, C, MC, V.

D

★★★ **STANFORD INN BY THE SEA.** *44850 Comptche Ukiah Rd (95460), S on CA 1. 707/937-5615; FAX 707/937-0305; res: 800/331-8884.* Web www.stanfordinn.com. 40 rms, 2-3 story, 2 kits. No A/C. S, D $215-$275; kit. suites $275-$365. Crib $5. Pet accepted; fee. TV; cable (premium), VCR (movies $4). Indoor pool; whirlpool. Complimentary full bkfst. Coffee in rms. Restaurant 8-10 am; Thurs-Sat 8-10 am, 6-8:30 pm; Sun 8 am-1 pm, 6-8:30 pm. Ck-out noon, ck-in 4 pm. Business center. In-rm modem link. Luggage handling. Concierge. Free airport transportation. Exercise equipt; sauna. Refrigerators, fireplaces. Private patios, balconies. Bike, canoe rentals. Antiques. Big River llamas on grounds. Tropical greenhouse. Organic gardens, nursery. On 10 acres of meadow, forest overlooking ocean, river. Totally nonsmoking. Cr cds: A, C, D, DS, ER, JCB, MC, V.

D

★★★ **THE HARBOR HOUSE INN.** *5600 S Highway 1 (95432), 14 mi S on CA 1. 707/877-3203; FAX 707/877-3452; res: 800/720-7474.* 10 rms, 2 story, 4 cottages. No A/C. No rm phones. MAP: S $144.50-$244.50; D $185-$285; each addl $55; mid-wk rates Jan-Mar. Children over 12 yrs only. Ck-out noon, ck-in 2 pm. Lawn games. Many fireplaces. Library. Antiques, original artwork, piano. Gardens, private beach. Built in 1916 for lumber company executive. Totally nonsmoking. Cr cds: C.

★★★ **WHITEGATE INN.** *499 Howard St (95460). 707/937-4892; FAX 707/937-1131; res: 800/531-7282.* E-mail staff@whitegateinn.com; web www.whitegateinn.com. 7 rms, 2 story, 1 guest house. No A/C. No rm phones. July-Oct & wkends: S, D $119-$249; each addl $25; guest house $189-$229; under 10 free (in cottage); wkends, hols 2-3 day min; lower rates rest of yr. Children over 10 yrs only (in inn). TV; cable. Complimentary full bkfst. Restaurant nearby. Ck-out 11 am, ck-in 3-6 pm. Business servs avail. Luggage handling. Concierge serv. Gift shop. Street parking. Fireplaces. Picnic tables. Built in 1883; old world atmosphere; antique organ. Totally nonsmoking. Cr cds: A, C, DS, MC, V.

Restaurants

★★★ **ALBION RIVER INN.** *(See Albion River Inn) 707/937-1919.* E-mail albionriverinn@mcn.org; web www.albionriverinn.com. Hrs: 5:30-9:30 pm; wkends 5-10 pm. Res accepted. No A/C. Coastal country menu. Bar 4:30 pm-midnight. Semi a la carte: dinner $14-$21. Specializes in fresh seafood, pasta, local produce. Pianist Fri, Sat. Original art. On ocean. Totally nonsmoking. Cr cds: A, C, MC, V.

D

★★★ **CAFE BEAUJOLAIS.** *961 Ukiah St (95460). 707/937-5614.* E-mail cafebeau@mcn.org; web www.cafebeaujolais.com. Hrs: 5:45-9 pm. Closed Dec 25. Res accepted. No A/C. French, California menu. Beer. Wine list. Semi-a la carte: dinner $16.95-$18.50. Specializes in French cuisine. Own bread. Victorian atmosphere. Totally nonsmoking. Cr cds: C, DS, MC, V.

Menlo Park (E-4 see San Francisco map)

(See also Palo Alto, Redwood City, San Francisco, Santa Clara, Saratoga)

Founded 1854 **Pop** 28,040 **Elev** 70 ft **Area Code** 650 **Zip** 94025

What to See and Do

Allied Arts Guild. Unique complex of shops set on a portion of the once vast Rancho de las Pulgas. Original barn and sheep sheds were preserved and new buildings constructed in Colonial Spanish design; formal gardens, paths and courtyards. (Daily exc Sun; closed hols) 75 Arbor Rd, at Cambridge. Phone 650/325-3259; for lunch & tea res phone 650/324-2588.

★ **Filoli House and Gardens** (1917). This 654-acre estate contains the Georgian-style residence built for William B. Bourn II and 16-acre formal gardens. The gardens are an Italian Renaissance-style of parterres, terraces, lawns and pools. The house was featured in the television series "Dynasty." House and garden: guided tours (mid-Feb-early Nov, Tues-Sat), res required exc Fri; self-guided tours (Fri & Sat), no res required. 3-mi guided nature hike (daily exc Sun). N on El Camino Real to Woodside Rd (CA 84), then 4 mi W to Cañada Rd, then 5 mi N, in Woodside. Phone 650/364-2880 for res. Tour of house and garden ¢¢¢; Nature hike ¢¢¢

Stanford Linear Accelerator Center (SLAC). This 426-acre national facility houses a 2-mi-long linear accelerator that generates the highest energy electron beams in the world. 2½-hr tour consists of orientation, slide show and bus tour. (Limited hrs; res required) 2575 Sand Hill Rd, E of I-280. Phone 650/926-2204. **Free**

Sunset Publishing Corporation and Gardens. Publishers of *Sunset* magazine and books. Self-guided tour of gardens. (Mon-Fri; closed hols) Willow & Middlefield Rds. Phone 650/324-5479 or 650/324-5481. **Free**

Motel

★★ **MENLO PARK INN.** *1315 El Camino Real (94025). 650/326-7530; FAX 415/328-7539; res: 800/327-1315.* 30 rms, 2 story. S $105-$115; D, suites $115-$125; each addl $7; under 18 free. Crib free. TV; cable (premium), VCR. Complimentary continental bkfst. Restaurant nearby. Ck-out 11 am. Business servs avail. In-rm modem link. Refrigerators. Cr cds: A, C, D, DS, MC, V.

D SC

Motor Hotel

★★★ **STANFORD PARK.** *100 El Camino Real (94025). 650/322-1234; FAX 650/322-0975; res: 800/368-2468.* Web www.woodsidehotels.com. Located near Stanford University, the Stanford Park Hotel sets the lodging standard for the San Francisco Penisula and Silicon Valley. 155 rms, 8 suites. 3-4 story. Standard room $295-$335; each addl $15; suites $360-$400; under 12 free. Crib free. Valet parking. TV; cable, VCR avail. Restaurant (see DUCK CLUB). Rm serv 24 hrs. Bar 11 am-midnight. Ck-out noon. Complimentary coffee, tea, apples each morning in the lobby. Evening Wine Hour, Mon-Thurs, 5-6 pm. Freshly baked cookies in lobby nightly at 9 pm. Coincerge. Meeting rms. Business center. In-rm modem link. Bellhops. Heated swimming pool, whirlpool. Fitness center, sauna. Two plush terry robes and full-size ironing boards and irons in all rooms. Bathrm phones, minibars; some refrigerators. Some balconies. Turn-down service. Guest Library stocked with recent best sellers & literary classics. Many granite fireplaces, courtyard views. Suites with wet bars, refrigerators and separate bedrooms. Cr cds: A, C, D, DS, JCB, MC, V.

D SC

Restaurants

★ **DUCK CLUB.** *(See Stanford Park Motor Hotel) 650/322-1234.* Hrs: 6:00 am-2 pm, 6-10 pm; Sun brunch 10 am-2 pm. Res accepted. Bar 11 am-midnight. Wine list. Semi-a la carte: bkfst $6.75-$14, lunch $8.95-$15.75, dinner $9.50-$24.95. Sun brunch $26.99. Child's meals. Specializes in fresh seafood, pasta, American regional cuisine. Own baking. Piano bar. Valet parking. Cr cds: A, C, D, DS, JCB, MC, V.

D ♥

★★ **LE POT AU FEU.** *1149 El Camino Real (94025). 650/322-4343.* Hrs: 5:30-9:30 pm; Sun to 9 pm. Closed Mon; Jan 1, July 4, Thanksgiving, Dec 24 & 25. Res accepted. Country French menu. Wine, beer. A la carte entrees: dinner $15.95-$19.95. Specialties: brie puff pastry with Riesling wine sauce & onion marmalade, beef Wellington, filet mignon with truffle cognac sauce. Patio dining. Two dining rms; country inn ambience. Cr cds: A, C, D, MC, V.

D

Merced (E-3)

Pop 56,216 **Elev** 172 ft **Area Code** 209
E-mail mercedvb@yosemite-gateway.org **Web** www.yosemite-gateway.org
Information Conference & Visitors Bureau, 690 W 16th St, 95340; 209/384-3333 or 800/446-5353

The Gateway to Yosemite National Park (see), Merced is the center of a rich agricultural area with dairy and beef production as well as peach, almond, tomato and alfalfa crops. Publishing, canneries, metal and plastic manufacturers contribute to its economic base.

What to See and Do

Castle Air Museum. Displays 44 vintage military aircraft; indoor military museum; inquire for guided tours. Restaurant. Museum (daily; closed Jan

1, Easter, Thanksgiving, Dec 25) 8 mi N, adj to Castle aviation park at Sante Fe & Buhach Rd. Phone 209/723-2178. ¢¢

Lake Yosemite Park. Swimming, sailing, waterskiing; fishing; boating. Picnicking. (Daily for sightseeing and fishing) Fee for group facility use & boat launching. 5714 N Lake Rd, 5 mi NE on G St, 2 mi E on Bellvue Rd, then ½ mi N on N Lake Rd to park entrance. Phone 209/385-7426. Per vehicle ¢¢

Merced County Courthouse Museum. Restored courthouse with collection of antique dolls, quilts, historical exhibits. (Wed-Sun afternoons) Courthouse Park, N & 21st Sts. Phone 209/723-2401. ¢

Merced Multicultural Arts Center. Three-story bldg contains theater, lobby & retail galleries, photo gallery, traveling exhibits and 6 visual & performing arts studios. (Mon-Fri; wkends by appt; closed major hols) 645 W Main St. Phone 209/388-1090. **Free**

Merced River Development Project. S of CA 132. **Exchequer Dam.** Rises 490 ft to impound Lake McClure (82-mi shoreline). **McClure Point, Barrett Cove, Horseshoe Bend and Bagby Recreation Areas. McSwain Dam** stands 80 ft high; impounds Lake McSwain (12½-mi shoreline). All areas offer swimming, showers, rest rms, waterskiing; fishing; boating (launching facilities; fee), marinas. Picnicking, concessions. Camping (fee; electricity addl). Contact Merced Irrigation District, Parks Dept, 9090 Lake McClure Rd, Snelling 95369; phone 209/378-2611. Camping ¢¢¢¢

Annual Events

West Coast Antique Fly-in. Antique & experimental aircraft. 1st full wkend June.

Merced County Fair. County Fairgrounds. Mid-July.

Central California Band Review. High school & junior high school band competitions. 1st Sat Nov.

Motel

✓★★ **BEST WESTERN INN.** *1213 V St (95340). 209/723-3711; FAX 209/722-8551; res: 800/735-3711.* 98 rms, 2 story. S $59-$64; D $64-$69; each addl $5; under 18 free. Crib free. Pet accepted. TV; cable (premium). Pool. Complimentary continental bkfst. Complimentary coffee in rms. Restaurant 6 am-11 pm. Rm serv. Bar noon-11 pm, wkends to midnight. Ck-out noon. Meeting rm. Business servs avail. Some refrigerators, microwaves. Cr cds: A, C, D, DS, JCB, MC, V.

D SC

Restaurant

✓★★ **EAGLES NEST.** *2000 E Childs Ave (95340). 209/723-1041.* Hrs: 6 am-10 pm; Sun brunch 9 am-2 pm. Res accepted; required some hols. Bar 10 am-midnight. Semi-a la carte: bkfst $1.95-$7, lunch $5.95-$8.95, dinner $5.49-$15.95. Sun brunch $9.95. Child's meals. Specialties: angel hair pasta, stuffed teriyaki chicken. Outdoor dining. Nature themed decor; etched glass depicts nature scenes. Cr cds: A, C, D, DS, ER, JCB, MC, V.

D SC

Mexico

(see Ensenada, Tijuana)

Mill Valley

(B-2 see San Francisco map)

(See also San Francisco, San Rafael)

Pop 13,038 **Elev** 80 ft **Area Code** 415 **Zip** 94941

What to See and Do

Mt Tamalpais State Park. This park is one of the favorite retreats of San Franciscans. The mountain rises 2,571 ft above sea level and provides a spectacular view of the entire bay area. A winding road climbs to a spot near the summit. Trails and bridle paths wind through the woods to attractive picnic areas; hike-in camping (fee; no vehicles). Muir Woods National Monument (see) is at the foot of the mountain. The Mountain Theatre, located just N of the park, presents plays in a natural amphitheater (May-June). Standard fees. 6 mi W on Panoramic Hwy. Phone 415/388-2070. Day use per vehicle ¢¢; Camping ¢¢¢¢

Motel

★ **HOLIDAY INN EXPRESS.** *160 Shoreline Hwy (94941). 415/332-5700; FAX 415/331-1859; res: 800/258-3894.* E-mail steventeed@marinternet.com; web www.hiexmv.com. 100 rms, 2 story. June-Oct: S, D $100-$130; each addl $8; under 18 free; lower rates rest of yr. Crib free. TV; cable (premium), some VCRs. Pool; wading pool. Complimentary continental bkfst. Ck-out noon. Meeting rms. Business servs avail. In-rm modem link. Valet serv. Exercise equipt. Private patios, balconies. Cr cds: A, C, D, DS, ER, JCB, MC, V.

D SC

Inns

★★★ **CASA DEL MAR CORPORATION.** *37 Belvedere (94970), N on CA 1. 415/868-2124; FAX 415/868-2305; res: 800/552-2124.* E-mail inn@stinsonbeack.com; web www.stinsonbeach.com. 6 rms, 4 with shower only, 3 story. No A/C. No elvtr. No rm phones. S, D $140-$235; each addl $20. Complimentary full bkfst; afternoon refreshments. Restaurant nearby. Ck-out 11 am, ck-in 4 pm. Concierge serv. Game rm. Refrigerators. Some balconies. Totally nonsmoking. Cr cds: A, C, MC, V.

★★★ **MILL VALLEY INN.** *165 Throckmorton Ave (94941). 415/389-6608; FAX 415/389-5051; res: 800/595-2100.* Web www.millvalleyinn.com. 25 rms, 3 story, 2 cottages. S, D, cottages $135-$240; each addl $20; under 18 free; wkly rates; spa plans; wkends, hols (2-3-day min). Crib free. TV; cable. Complimentary continental bkfst. Restaurant nearby. Ck-out 11 am, ck-in 4 pm. Concierge serv. Meeting rm. Business servs avail. In-rm modem link. Health club privileges. Some balconies, fireplaces. Stucco bldg, sun terrace in back. Original pieces in guest rms by North Bay craftspeople. Totally nonsmoking. Cr cds: A, C, MC, V.

D SC

★★ **MOUNTAIN HOME INN.** *810 Panoramic Hwy (94941). 415/381-9000; FAX 415/381-3615.* 10 rms, 3 story. No A/C. S, D $139-$259; each addl $29. Complimentary full bkfst. Dining rm 11:30 am-3:30 pm, 5:30-9:30 pm. Ck-out 11 am, ck-in 3 pm. Business servs avail. Some fireplaces. Private patios, balconies. Scenic view. On road to Mt Tamalpais. Cr cds: A, C, MC, V.

D

Restaurants

✓★★ **BISTRO ALSACIENNE.** *655 Redwood Hwy (94941), off US 101 at Seminary Dr exit. 415/389-0921.* Hrs: 5-10 pm. Closed Mon, also Tues (July-Sept); major hols. Res accepted. Beer, wine. A la carte entrees: dinner $12-$14. Specializes in Alsatian cuisine. Parking. Outdoor dining, views of Shelter Bay and Mt Tamalpais. Totally nonsmoking. Cr cds: A, C, MC, V.

D

★★ **BUCKEYE ROADHOUSE.** *15 Shoreline Hwy (94941). 415/331-2600.* Hrs: 11:30 am-10:30 pm; Fri & Sat to 11 pm; Sun brunch 10:30 am-3 pm. Closed Dec 25. Res accepted. No A/C. Bar. Semi-a la carte: lunch, dinner $7-$25. Sun brunch $7-$12. Child's meals. Specializes in steak, fresh crab, ribs. Free valet parking. Outdoor dining. Roadhouse first opened in 1937; flower gardens. Totally nonsmoking. Cr cds: C, D, DS, MC, V.

D

★★ **FRANTOIO.** *152 Shoreline Hwy (94941). 415/289-5777.* E-mail frantoio@slip.net; web www.frantoio.com. Hrs: 11:30 am-10 pm; Fri, Sat to 11 pm; Sun from 5 pm. Closed July 4, Thanksgiving, Dec 25. Res accepted. Italian menu. Bar. Semi-a la carte: lunch $7.95-$18, dinner $10-$20. Specializes in grilled meat and fish, pasta. Outdoor dining. Pianist. Contemporary decor, olive oil press operating Oct-Mar. Totally nonsmoking. Cr cds: A, C, D, DS, MC, V.

D

✓★ **MOUNTAIN HOME INN.** *810 Panoramic Way (94941). 415/381-9000.* Hrs: 11:30 am-3:30 pm, 5:30-9:30 pm; Sat, Sun from 8 am; Sat, Sun brunch 11:30 am-3:30 pm. Closed Mon Nov-Apr; Dec 25. Res accepted; required Fri, Sat. No A/C. Bar. Semi-a la carte: bkfst, lunch $7.50-$12.25, dinner $11.50-$18. Sat, Sun brunch $7-$12. Specialties: lamb shanks, teriyaki-marinated flank steak. Outdoor dining (exc dinner). Views of bay and mountains. Cr cds: A, C, MC, V.

★★ **ROBATA GRILL & SUSHI.** *591 Redwood Hwy (94941), US 101 to Seminary exit. 415/381-8400.* Hrs: 11:30 am-2 pm, 5:30-9:30 pm; Fri to 10 pm; Sat 5:30-10 pm; Sun from 5:30 pm. Closed major hols. Res accepted. Japanese menu. Wine, beer. Semi-a la carte: lunch, dinner $10-$25. Specializes in sushi, robata grilled dishes. Japanese decor; sushi bar. Totally nonsmoking. Cr cds: A, C, JCB, MC, V.

D

Millbrae

(see San Francisco Airport Area)

Modesto (E-3)

(See also Oakdale, Stockton)

Founded 1870 **Pop** 164,730 **Elev** 91 ft **Area Code** 209
E-mail mcvb@modestocvb.org **Web** www.modestocvb.org

Information Convention & Visitors Bureau, 1114 J Street, PO Box 844, 95353; 209/571-6480, ext 112 or 800/266-4282

A processing, shipping and marketing center for the rich farmlands of the central San Joaquin Valley and Stanislaus County, Modesto was named for a San Francisco banker who was too modest to publicize his own name. Nearby Don Pedro Dam provides the irrigation and power that is the key to the area's prosperity. Modesto is a gateway to Yosemite National Park (see) and the Gold Country.

What to See and Do

Caswell Memorial State Park. On 274 acres. Swimming; fishing. Nature, hiking trails. Picnicking. Camping. Standard fees. 15 mi N via CA 99, S on Austin Rd. Phone 209/599-3810.

Don Pedro Lake Recreation Area. Approx 37 mi E, N of CA 132 (see SONORA).

Great Valley Museum of Natural History. Exhibits of natural plant and animal habitats and complete ecosystems. Also children's discovery rm. (Tues-Sat) 1100 Stoddard Ave. Phone 209/575-6196. ¢

McHenry Museum. Historical exhibits in period rms; schoolrm, doctor's office, blacksmith shop. (Tues-Fri, afternoons) 1402 I Street. Phone 209/577-5366. **Free** One blk NE is the

McHenry Mansion (1883). Restored Victorian mansion built for one of Modesto's first families. Period furnishings. (Tues-Thurs & Sun; closed hols) 15th & I Streets. Phone 209/577-5367. **Free**

Turlock Lake State Recreation Area. On 3,000 acres. Swimming, waterskiing; fishing; boating. Picnicking. Camping. Standard fees. 23 mi E on CA 132, just off 132 on Lake Rd. Phone 209/874-2008.

Annual Events

International Festival. Graceada Park. 1st wkend Oct.

Riverbank Cheese & Wine Exposition. 6 mi E on CA 108 in Riverbank. Street festival with food booths, arts & crafts, antiques, entertainment. Tasting of local wines and cheeses. Phone 209/869-4541. 2nd wkend Oct.

Motels

★★ **BEST WESTERN MALLARDS INN.** *1720 Sisk Rd (95350), US 99 Briggsmore Ave exit (N). 209/577-3825; FAX 209/577-1717; res: 800/294-4040.* 126 units, 2 story, 11 suites. S $75-$105; D $80-$110; each addl $10; suites $105-$195; under 18 free. Crib $5. TV; cable (premium). Heated pool; whirlpool, poolside serv. Complimentary coffee in rms. Restaurant 6:30-9:30 am, 5-9 pm. Rm serv 5-9 pm. Ck-out noon. Meeting rms. Business servs avail. Free airport transportation. Exercise equipt. Some refrigerators. Wet bar in suites. Cr cds: A, C, D, DS, ER, JCB, MC, V.

D SC

★ **SUNDIAL LODGE & RESTAURANT.** *808 McHenry Ave (95350). 209/524-4375; FAX 209/521-2692.* 45 rms, 2 story. S $44-$48; D $48-$52. Crib free. TV; cable (premium). Pool. Restaurant 5 am-10 pm. Rm serv. Bar 10-2 am. Ck-out noon. Meeting rms. Valet serv. Private patios, balconies. Cr cds: A, C, MC, V.

SC

✓★ **VAGABOND INN.** *1525 McHenry Ave (95350). 209/521-6340; FAX 209/575-2015; res: 800/522-1555.* 99 rms, 2 story. S $43-$65; D $53-$78; each addl $5; under 18 free. Crib free. Pet accepted; $5. TV; cable (premium). Heated pool. Complimentary continental bkfst. Restaurant adj open 24 hrs. Ck-out noon. Business servs avail. Cr cds: A, C, D, DS, MC, V.

D SC

Motor Hotel

★★ **HOLIDAY INN.** *1612 Sisk Rd (95350), US 99 Briggsmore Ave exit (N). 209/521-1612; FAX 209/527-5074; res: 800/465-4329.* E-mail holiday@netfeed.com. 186 rms, 2 story. S, D $95-$100; suites $150; under 19 free. Crib free. TV; cable. Complimentary coffee in rms. 2 pools, 1 indoor, whirlpool. Playground. Restaurant 6:30 am-2 pm, 5-10 pm. Rm serv. Bar noon-1:30 am; entertainment. Ck-out noon. Meeting rms. Business servs avail. Coin Indry. Lighted tennis. Putting green. Exercise equipt. Rec rm. Cr cds: A, C, D, DS, JCB, MC, V.

D SC

Hotel

★★★ **DOUBLETREE HOTEL.** *1150 9th St (95354). 209/526-6000; FAX 209/526-6096; res: 800/222-8733.* 258 rms, 10 story. Jan-Nov: S $79-$135; D $79-$150; each addl $15; suites $250-$500; under 18 free; family rates; package plans; lower rates rest of yr. Crib free. Pet accepted; $100 deposit. Valet parking $7. TV; cable. Complimentary coffee in rms. Restaurant 6 am-midnight. Bar 11-2 am; entertainment Fri, Sat. Ck-out noon. Convention facilities. Business servs avail. In-rm modem link. Gift shop. Beauty shop. Free airport, RR station, bus depot transportation. Exercise equipt; sauna. Pool; whirlpool. Bathrm phones; some in-rm whirlpools. Some balconies. Cr cds: A, C, D, DS, JCB, MC, V.

D SC

Monterey (F-1)

(See also Carmel, Pacific Grove, Pebble Beach, Salinas)

Founded 1770 **Pop** 31,954 **Elev** 40 ft **Area Code** 831 **Zip** 93940

Information Monterey Peninsula Chamber of Commerce and Visitors & Convention Bureau, 380 Alvarado St, PO Box 1770, phone 831/649-1770; or the Visitors Center, 401 Camino El Estero, phone 831/649-1770

The calm harbor, red-roofed white stucco houses, white sand beach, Monterey cypress and Monterey pine all existed in the days when Monterey was the Spanish heart of California. A mélange of Mexican, New England, sea, mission and ranch makes Monterey uniquely Californian in its culture and history. The Spanish explorer Sebastian Vizcaino sailed into the bay in 1602 and named it for the Count of Monte-Rey, Viceroy of Mexico. The spot was rediscovered in 1770 when Fray Crespi, Fray Junipero Serra and Gaspar de Portola took possession, founding the Presidio and the Mission San Carlos Borromeo del Rio Carmelo (see CARMEL). The King of Spain recognized it as the capital of California in 1775, but in 1822 it became part of the Mexican Republic. Soon after, American whalers and traders began to arrive. Commodore Sloat raised the American flag in 1846, ending years of opposition to Mexican rule. Delegates to a constitutional convention in 1849 met in Monterey and drew up California's first constitution. The city became a whaling center; fisheries, canneries and specialized agriculture developed. The sardine fisheries and canneries, in particular, inspired the novels *Cannery Row* and *Sweet Thursday* by John Steinbeck. Now, with the sardines gone and the canneries silent, the row has been taken over by an aquarium, gourmet restaurants and art galleries while Fisherman's Wharf offers fishing and sightseeing trips and the bay's famous sea otters; nearby is the Maritime Museum of Monterey.

What to See and Do

Colton Hall Museum (1849) and **Old Monterey Jail** (1854). Built as a town hall and public school by the Reverend Walter Colton, alcalde (mayor or judge) of Monterey Dist during the American occupation of California, 1846-1848. Classic Revival design of stone and adobe mortar. The first constitution of California (in Spanish and English) was written here. Changing exhibits. The jail, a single-story addition of granite, was added to the building in 1854 at which time Colton Hall served as the Monterey County Courthouse. (Daily; closed Jan 1, Thanksgiving, Dec 25) Pacific St, between Madison & Jefferson Sts, in Civic Center, 2nd fl. Phone 831/646-5640. **Free**

Fisherman's Wharf. Restaurants, shops, tour boat departure area. On Monterey Harbor.

La Mirada. Original residence of Jose Castro, prominent Californian during the Mexican period, and later Frank Work, who added a collection of art and antiques to the 2½-acre estate. Garden and house tours (Thurs-Sun). 720 Via Mirada. Phone 831/372-3689. **¢¢**

Marina. Berths for 420 vessels up to 50 ft long; 2 launching ramps. Municipally owned. (Office closed Jan 1, Thanksgiving, Dec 25) Foot of Figueroa St. Phone 831/646-3950.

Maritime Museum of Monterey. Seven major theme areas provide exhibits on maritime and naval history of the area, including sailing ship era and whaling industry; ship models, maritime artifacts, interactive exhibits; paintings; research library; model workshop for restoration and building replicas of historic vessels. The jewel of the museum collection is the 16-ft-tall intricately crafted first order Fresnel Lens from the old lighthouse at Point Sur. Also here is a 100-seat theater featuring an orientation film and re-enactments. (Daily; closed Jan 1, Thanksgiving, Dec 25) Located in the Stanton Center at #5 Custom House Plaza, adj to Fisherman's Wharf. Phone 831/373-AHOY (2469). **¢¢**

Monterey Bay Aquarium. One of the largest aquariums in the US; 100 exhibits of the sea life and habitats along the shores of California's Monterey Bay include sea otters, sharks and a 3-story-tall kelp forest. The Outer Bay exhibit has twice wkly live video broadcasts, "Live from Monterey Canyon," of work in progress transmitted from waters up to 3,300 ft deep to a screen in the aquarium auditorium (Mon & Tues afternoons). (Daily; closed Dec 25) 886 Cannery Row. Phone 831/648-4888. **¢¢¢¢**

Monterey Peninsula Museum of Art. Displays early California and American art, folk, ethnic and tribal art, Asian art. Photography exhibits; changing exhibitions of major American artists. Docent-guided tour avail (Sun afternoon). (Wed-Sun; closed Jan 1, Thanksgiving, Dec 25) 559 Pacific St. Phone 831/372-7591. **Donation**

Monterey State Historic Park. Day ticket valid in all historic buildings in state historic park. Single tickets also avail. (Park and building hrs may vary, Phone 831/649-7118. Day ticket good for 2 days **¢¢**

Boston Store (1845). Restored general store built by Thomas Larkin and operated by Joseph Boston & Co. Houses a general merchandise store operated by the Monterey History and Art Assn. (Thurs-Sun; closed Jan 1, Thanksgiving, Dec 25) Scott & Olivier Sts. **Free**

Casa Soberanes (1842). Adobe house containing displays of Monterey history from 1840-1970. Excellent example of adobe construction; walls are 38 inches thick. Local art collection. (Mon, Wed & Fri-Sun) Guided tours (inquire for schedule). Admission included in 2-day ticket. 336 Pacific St.

Cooper-Molera House (1827). Largest complex in the park. Built by John Rogers Cooper, half-brother of Thomas Larkin. (Tues & Thurs-Sun; inquire for hrs) Admission included in 2-day ticket. Corner of Polk & Munras.

Custom House (1827). Old Mexican custom house exhibit re-creates a cargo of the 1840s. Commodore Sloat raised the American flag over this adobe building in 1846, bringing 600,000 sq mi into the Union. (Daily, inquire for hrs; closed major hols) Custom House Plaza. **Free**

Larkin House (1830s). Consulate for Thomas Larkin, first and only US consul to Mexican California (1843-1846). Large collection of antiques. (Mon, Wed & Fri-Sun) Guided tours (inquire for schedule). Admission included in 2-day ticket. 510 Calle Principal, at Jefferson St.

Pacific House (1847). A museum of California history and Holman Native American artifact collection. (Daily, inquire for hrs; closed major hols) Custom House Plaza. **Free**

Robert Louis Stevenson House. Preserved as a state historic monument with large collection of Stevenson memorabilia. Stevenson lived here for 4 months while visiting his future wife. (Tues & Thurs-Sun) Guided tours (hrs vary, inquire for schedule). Admission included in 2-day ticket. 530 Houston St.

"Path of History" tour. Leads to many old buildings of distinction. These are marked with a plaque explaining the history and architecture. Several buildings are open to the public. Some of these buildings and a number of others are part of the Monterey State Historic Park. Obtain map at the Monterey Peninsula Chamber of Commerce and Visitor & Convention Bureau, 380 Alvarado St, or at the Monterey Visitors Center, Camino El Estero & Franklin Sts.

Presidio of Monterey. Home of Defense Language Institute. Developed in 1902 as cantonment for troops returning from the Philippine Insurrection. Monument to John Drake Sloat, commander of American troops that captured Monterey (1846); statue in honor of Fray Junipero Serra. There are 12 historic sites and monuments on Presidio Hill; brochure and map avail. Pacific St, N of Scott St. Hrs vary, phone 831/242-5104. **Free**

Royal Presidio Chapel. Founded June 3, 1770, the only presidio chapel remaining in California; in continuous use since 1795. Façade is considered most ornate of all California missions. (Daily) San Carlos Cathedral, 550 Church St, between Camino El Estero & Figueroa St. Phone 831/373-2628. **Free**

★ **Seventeen-Mile Drive.** A famous scenic drive between Monterey and Carmel (see) along Pacific Coast past Seal Rock, Lone Cypress, Cypress Point and Spyglass Hill and Pebble Beach golf courses. This private community in Del Monte Forest is known around the world for its natural beauty. Road may be entered at several points; follow the red-and-yellow center lines and the 17-Mi Drive signs. Toll **¢¢¢**

Sightseeing tours.

Gray Line bus tours. Contact 350 8th St, San Francisco 94103; phone 415/558-9400 or 800/826-0202.

Annual Events

AT&T-Pebble Beach National Pro-Amateur Golf Championship. Takes place on Pebble Beach, Cypress and Spyglass courses. Late Jan or early Feb.

Adobe Tour. Sponsored by the Monterey History & Art Assn. Self-guided walking tour visits approx 25 historic adobes and gardens. Contact 5 Custom House Plaza; 831/372-2608. Last Sat Apr.

Monterey County Fair. Fairgrounds & Exposition Park. 2004 Fairground Rd, corner of Fairground Rd & Garden Rd. Phone 831/372-1000. 3rd wk Aug.

Monterey Jazz Festival. County Fairgrounds. Reserved seats only. Contact PO Box JAZZ; 831/373-3366. Mid-Sept.

Laguna Seca Raceway. 8 mi E on CA 68. International auto and motorcycle races. Includes ISMA races, historic races, and Indy cars. For specific dates and details phone 800/327-SECA. Late Sept.

Motels

★★ **BAY PARK HOTEL.** *1425 Munras Ave (93940). 831/649-1020; FAX 408/373-4258; res: 800/338-3564.* E-mail baypark@montereybay.com. 80 rms, 3 story. No elvtr. June-Sept: S, D $99-$155; each addl $10; under 18 free; lower rates rest of yr. Crib free. Pet accepted; $5/day. TV, cable. Heated pool; whirlpool. Coffee in rms. Restaurant 7 am-9 pm. Rm serv. Bar 4-10 pm; entertainment Sat. Ck-out noon. Meeting rms. Business servs avail. Sundries. Some refrigerators. Cr cds: A, C, D, DS, ER, MC, V.

D SC

✓★ **CANNERY ROW INN.** *200 Foam St (93940). 831/649-8580; FAX 831/649-2566; res: 800/876-8580.* 32 rms, 2 story. No A/C. S, D $79-$240. TV; cable. Complimentary continental bkfst. Complimentary coffee in rms. Ck-out noon. Business servs avail. Covered parking. Whirlpool. Refrigerators, fireplaces. Balconies. Cr cds: A, C, DS, MC, V.

D SC

★★ **CYPRESS GARDENS INN.** *1150 Munras Ave (93940). 831/373-2761; FAX 831/649-1329; res: 800/433-4732.* E-mail concierge@carmelinns.com; web www.innsbythesea.com. 46 rms, 2 story. No A/C. Late June-Oct: S, D $99-$129; each addl $10; suite $199; under 13 free; lower rates rest of yr. Crib free. Pet accepted. TV; cable (premium). Heated pool; whirlpool. Coffee in rms. Complimentary continental bkfst. Ck-out noon. Business servs avail. Refrigerators; fireplace in suite; microwaves avail. Private patios, balconies. Cr cds: A, C, DS, MC, V.

SC

✓★ **CYPRESS TREE INN.** *2227 N Fremont St (93940). 831/372-7586; FAX 831/372-2940.* E-mail meyercti@aol.com. 55 rms, 2 story, 12 kits. No A/C. S, D, kits. $48-$99; each addl $6; suites $95-$180. Crib $6. TV; cable. Ck-out 11 am. Coin lndry. Business servs avail. Whirlpool. Sauna. Refrigerators; some whirlpools, fireplaces in suites. Private patios, some balconies. Grill. Cr cds: C, MC, V.

D

★ **EL ADOBE INN.** *936 Munras Ave (93940). 831/372-5409; FAX 831/375-7236; res: 800/433-4732.* E-mail concierge@camelinn.com; web www.innsbythesea.com. 26 rms, 2 story. No A/C. Late June-Oct: S, D $89-$129; each addl $10; under 13 free; lower rates rest of yr. Crib free. Pet accepted. TV; cable (premium). Swimming privileges. Whirlpool. Complimentary continental bkfst. Coffee in rms. Ck-out noon. Business servs avail. Refrigerators. Sun deck. Cr cds: A, C, DS, MC, V.

SC

★★ **HOLIDAY INN EXPRESS.** *443 Wave St (93940). 831/372-1800; FAX 831/372-1969; res: 800/465-4329.* 43 rms, 3 story. No A/C. May-Oct: S, D $95-$229; each addl $10; under 19 free; higher rates Fri, Sat; lower rates rest of yr. Crib free. TV; cable (premium). Complimentary continental bkfst. Complimentary coffee in rms. Ck-out noon. Business servs avail. Covered parking. Whirlpool. Totally nonsmoking. Cr cds: A, C, D, DS, JCB, MC, V.

D SC

★★ **MARIPOSA INN.** *1386 Munras Ave (93940). 831/649-1414; FAX 831/649-5308; res: 800/824-2295.* 50 rms, 3 story. No A/C. S, D $79-$125; each addl $10; suites $89-$195; under 18 free; golf plans. TV; cable (premium). Heated pool; whirlpool. Coffee in rms. Complimentary continental bkfst. Restaurant nearby. Ck-out noon. Business servs avail. Refrigerator in suites; microwaves avail. Cr cds: A, C, D, DS, MC, V.

D SC

★★ **MONTEREY BAY INN.** *242 Cannery Row (93940). 831/373-6242; FAX 831/373-7603; res: 800/424-6242.* Web www.montereybay.com. 47 rms, 4 story. No A/C. May-Oct: S, D $199-$349; under 12 free; lower rates rest of yr. Crib free. TV; cable, VCR (movies). Whirlpools. Complimentary continental bkfst in rms. Complimentary coffee in rms. Restaurant nearby. Ck-out noon. Meeting rms. Business servs avail. Covered parking. Exercise equipt; sauna. Minibars. Balconies. On bay. Cr cds: A, C, D, DS, JCB, MC, V.

D SC

★ **OTTER INN.** *571 Wave St (93940). 831/375-2299; FAX 831/375-2352; res: 800/385-2299.* 33 rms, 4 story. No A/C. July-Aug: S, D $89-$249; suites $179-$269. Crib free. TV; cable. Complimentary continental bkfst. Complimentary coffee in rms. Restaurant nearby. Ck-out noon. Business servs avail. Whirlpool. Covered parking. Refrigerators. Near beach. Cr cds: A, C, DS, MC, V.

D SC

★★ **SAND DOLLAR INN.** *755 Abrego St (93940). 831/372-7551; FAX 831/372-0916; res: 800/982-1986.* 63 rms, 3 story. June-Sept: S, D $95-$125; each addl $10; suites $115-$125; under 12 free; wkends (2-day min); higher rates special events; lower rates rest of yr. Crib free. TV; cable, VCR avail (movies). Heated pool; whirlpool. Complimentary continental bkfst. Coffee in rms. Restaurant nearby. Ck-out noon. Business servs avail. Coin lndry. Some refrigerators, fireplaces. Some private patios, balconies. Cr cds: A, C, D, MC, V.

D SC

★★ **WAY STATION MOTEL.** *1200 Olmsted Rd (93940). 831/372-2945; FAX 408/375-6267; res: 831/858-0822.* 46 rms, 2 story. No A/C. S $99-$189; D $79-$209; each addl $10; suites $99-$239. TV; cable. Complimentary continental bkfst. Restaurant 11 am-10 pm. Bar. Ck-out 11 am. Meeting rms. Refrigerators. Cr cds: A, C, D, DS, MC, V.

D SC

Motor Hotels

★★ **BEST WESTERN.** *2600 Sand Dunes Dr (93942). 831/394-3321; FAX 831/393-1912; res: 800/528-1234; res: 800/242-8627.* Web www.montereybeachhotel.com. 196 rms, 4 story. June-Oct: S, D $99-$199; under 13 free; lower rates rest of yr. Crib free. Pet accepted; $25. TV; cable (premium). Pool; whirlpool. Coffee in rms. Restaurant 7 am-1:45 pm, 5:30-10 pm. Rm serv. Bar 4-11 pm. Ck-out noon. Meeting rms. Business servs avail. Bellhops. Exercise equipt. Some refrigerators. Ocean view; beach access. Cr cds: A, C, D, DS, MC, V.

D SC

★★ **BEST WESTERN VICTORIAN INN.** *487 Foam St (93940). 831/373-8000; FAX 831/373-4815; res: 800/232-4141.* Web www.victorianinn.com. 68 rms, 3 story. S, D $139-$309; each addl $10; under 18 free; higher rates special events. Pet accepted; $100 deposit, $25 fee. TV; cable, VCR (movies). Complimentary continental bkfst. Coffee in rms. Ck-out noon. Meeting rm. Business servs avail. Whirlpool. Bathrm phones, refrigerators, fireplaces. Private patios, balconies. Victorian furnishings. 2 blks from bay. Cr cds: A, C, D, DS, JCB, MC, V.

D SC

★★★ **HILTON.** *1000 Aguajito Rd (93940). 831/373-6141; FAX 831/655-8608; res: 800/234-5697; res: 800/234-5697.* Web www.monterey.hilton.com. 204 rms, 3 story. May-Oct: S, D $115-$225; each addl $10; suites $250-$500; kit. unit $250-$450; under 18 free; higher rates special events; lower rates rest of yr. Crib free. TV; cable (premium), VCR avail. Complimentary coffee in rms. Restaurant 6:30 am-2 pm, 5-10 pm. Rm serv. Ck-out noon. Business servs avail. In-rm modem link. Bellhops. Valet serv. Concierge. Gift shop. Coin lndry. Free airport transportation. Tennis. Exercise equipt; sauna. Pool. Some refrigerators, microwaves. Balconies. Picnic tables, grills. Cr cds: A, C, D, DS, ER, JCB, MC, V.

D

Hotels

★★★ **DOUBLETREE HOTEL AT FISHERMAN'S WHARF.** *2 Portola Plz (93940), at Fisherman's Wharf. 831/649-4511; FAX 831/649-4115; res: 800/222-8733.* E-mail doubletree@monterey.com; web www.monterey.com. 380 rms, 7 story. No A/C. June-Oct: S, D $125-$275; each addl $20; suites $250-$750; under 18 free; lower rates rest of yr. Crib free. TV; cable (premium). Heated pool; whirlpool, poolside serv. Restaurants 6 am-10 pm; Fri, Sat to 11 pm. Bar 11-1:30 am. Ck-out noon. Convention facilities. Business center. Concierge. Shopping arcade. Valet, self-parking. Exercise rm. Cr cds: A, C, D, DS, ER, JCB, MC, V.

D SC

★★★ **EMBASSY SUITES.** *1441 Canyon Del Rey Blvd (86351), CA 1, exit Del Rey. 831/393-1115; FAX 831/393-1113; res: 800/362-2779.* Web www.embassy-suites.com. 225 suites, 12 story. Apr-Oct: S, D $150-$286; each addl $20; under 18 free; higher rates special events; lower rates rest of yr. Crib free. TV; cable. Indoor pool; whirlpool. Complimentary full bkfst. Coffee in rms. Restaurant 11 am-2 pm, 5-10 pm. Bar to midnight. Ck-out noon. Meeting rms. Business center. Coin lndry. Gift shop. Free airport transportation. Exercise equipt; sauna. Game rm. Refrigerators, microwaves. Cr cds: A, C, D, DS, MC, V.

D SC

★★★ **HYATT REGENCY.** *1 Old Golf Course Rd (93940). 831/372-1234; FAX 831/375-3960; res: 800/233-1234; res: 800/824-2196.* E-mail hyattmon@redshift.com; web www.montereyhyatt.com. 575 rms, 4 story. No A/C. S, D $89-$300; suites $275-$2,500; higher rates special events. Crib free. TV; cable (premium), VCR avail. 2 heated pools; whirlpool, poolside serv. Supervised child's activities (summer & hols; rest of yr on request). Coffee in rms. Restaurant 6:30 am-10 pm. Bar 4 pm-1 am; wkends from noon. Ck-out noon. Convention facilities. Business center. Concierge. Beauty salon. 6 tennis courts, pro. 18-hole golf, greens fee $70-$90, putting green. Bicycles. Exercise equipt. Refrigerators avail. Situated on 23 landscaped acres. Luxury level. Cr cds: A, C, D, DS, JCB, MC, V.

D SC

★★★ **MARRIOTT.** *350 Calle Principal (93940). 831/649-4234; FAX 831/372-2968; res: 800/228-9290; res: 800/892-4789.* E-mail brendon@ montereymarriott.com; web www.marriott.com. 341 rms, 10 story. July-Sept: S, D $209-$300; suites $250-$600; under 18 free; lower rates rest of yr. Crib free. Pet accepted, some restrictions; $10/day. Valet parking $12. TV; cable (premium). Heated pool; whirlpool. Coffee in rms. Restaurants 6:30-1 am. Ck-out noon. Meeting rms. Business center. Concierge. Gift shop. Barber, beauty shop. Exercise equipt. Refrigerators, microwaves avail; bathrm phone in suites. Cr cds: A, C, D, DS, ER, JCB, MC, V.

D SC

★★★ **MONTEREY PLAZA HOTEL.** *400 Cannery Row (93940). 831/646-1700; FAX 408/646-5937; res: 800/334-3999.* Web www.woodsidehotels.com. 285 rms, 4 story. S, D $175-$350; each addl $30; suites $385-$800; under 12 free; package plans. Garage, valet parking $12. TV; cable. Coffee in rms. Restaurant (see THE DUCK CLUB). Bar 11:30 am-midnight. Ck-out noon. Business center. Concierge. Exercise equipt. Minibars. Some bathrm phones. Some private patios, balconies. Library on Monterey Bay; beach access. Located on oceanfront on historic Cannery Row. Totally nonsmoking. Cr cds: A, C, D, DS, JCB, MC, V.

D SC

Inns

★★★ **HOTEL PACIFIC.** *300 Pacific St (93940). 831/373-5700; FAX 831/373-6921; res: 800/554-5542.* 105 suites, 4 story. May-Oct: S, D $199-$349; each addl $10; under 12 free; lower rates rest of yr. Crib avail. TV; cable, VCR (movies). Whirlpools. Complimentary continental bkfst; evening refreshments. Coffee in rms. Ck-out noon, ck-in 4 pm. Meeting rms. Business servs avail. Luggage handling. Covered parking. Refrigerators, fireplaces. Private patios, balconies. Spanish decor; original art, antiques, fireplace in lobby. Gardens; fountains. Cr cds: A, C, D, DS, JCB, MC, V.

D SC

★★★ **JABBERWOCK.** *598 Laine St (93940), at Hoffman St. 831/372-4777; FAX 831/655-2946; res: 888/428-7253.* 7 rms, 2 share bath, 3 story. No A/C. No rm phones. S, D $110-$200. Complimentary full bkfst; afternoon refreshments. Ck-out noon, ck-in 3 pm. Business servs avail. Some fireplaces; 1 in-rm whirlpool. Library; antiques. ½-acre gardens; waterfalls. Former convent. Cr cds: C, MC, V.

D

★★★ **MERRITT HOUSE INN.** *386 Pacific St (93922). 831/646-9686; FAX 831/646-5392; res: 800/541-5599.* E-mail merrhouse@aol.com; web www.monterey.com. 25 rms, 2 story. Mar-Nov: S, D $135-$200; each addl $15; suites $195-$220; under 10 free; lower rates rest of yr. Crib avail. TV; cable (premium). Continental bkfst. Restaurants nearby. Ck-out noon, ck-in 3 pm. Business servs avail. Refrigerators. Some patios, balconies. Suites in adobe house (1830). Garden. Totally nonsmoking. Cr cds: A, C, D, DS, MC, V.

D SC

★★★★ **OLD MONTEREY INN.** *500 Martin St (93940). 831/375-8284; FAX 831/375-6730; res: 800/350-2344.* This English country house was built in 1929 on an oak-studded hillside near Monterey Bay. Guest rooms are individually decorated with antiques. 9 rms, 1 cottage. No A/C. No rm phones; cordless phone avail. S, D $200-$280, cottage $350; each addl $50. TV avail. Complimentary full bkfst; afternoon refreshments. Ck-out noon, ck-in 3-7 pm. Business servs avail. Many fireplaces. Totally nonsmoking. Cr cds: C, MC, V.

★★★ **SPINDRIFT INN.** *652 Cannery Row (93940). 831/646-8900; FAX 831/373-3984; res: 800/232-4141.* Web www.spindriftinn.com. 42 rms, 4 story. No A/C. May-Oct: S, D $219-$429; under 12 free; higher rates special events; lower rates rest of yr. Parking $6. TV; cable, VCR (movies). Complimentary continental bkfst; afternoon refreshments. Restaurant adj. Rm serv 11 am-9:30 pm. Ck-out noon, ck-in 4 pm. Business servs avail. Luggage handling. Concierge serv. Valet parking. Bathrm phones, refrigerators, honor bars, fireplaces. Some balconies. Roof-top garden; views of Monterey Bay. Cr cds: A, C, D, DS, JCB, MC, V.

D SC

★★★ **THE MONTEREY HOTEL.** *406 Alvarado St (93940). 831/375-3184; FAX 831/373-2899; res: 800/727-0960.* Web www.montereyhotel.com. 39 rms, 4 story, 6 suites. No A/C. S, D $119-$169; suites $199-$279; seasonal rates avail. Crib free. Valet parking $10. TV; cable (premium). Complimentary continental bkfst; afternoon refreshments. Ck-out noon, ck-in 3 pm. Meeting rms. Some refrigerators, wet bars. Fireplace in some suites. Cr cds: A, C, D, DS, MC, V.

D SC

Restaurants

✓★ **ABALONETTI SEAFOOD TRATTORIA.** *57 Fisherman's Wharf (93940). 831/373-1851.* Hrs: 11 am-10 pm; wkends to 11 pm. Closed Dec 25. Res accepted. No A/C. Italian, seafood menu. Bar 11 am-10 pm. A la carte entrees: lunch $6.95-$14.95, dinner $10.95-$21.95. Child's menu. Specializes in grilled fish, seafood pasta, pizza baked in wood-burning oven. Outdoor dining. Exhibition kitchen. Harbor view. Cr cds: A, C, D, DS, JCB, MC, V.

D

✓★ **AMARIN THAI CUISINE.** *807 Cannery Row (93940), on 2nd floor. 831/373-8811.* Web www.eureka1.com/amarinthai. Hrs: 11 am-9 pm. Closed Thanksgiving, Dec 25. Res accepted. No A/C. Thai menu. Wine, beer. Semi-a la carte: lunch $5.95-$7.95, dinner $8.95-$12.95. Specialties: pad Thai, masaman, basil squid. Contemporary Thai decor. Totally nonsmoking. Cr cds: A, C, DS, MC, V.

★★ **CAFE FINA.** *47 Fisherman's Wharf (93940). 831/372-5200.* Hrs: 11:30 am-2:30 pm, 5-10 pm; Sat & Sun 11:30 am-3 pm, 5-10 pm. Closed Thanksgiving, Dec 25. Res accepted. No A/C. Seafood menu. Bar. A la carte entrees: lunch $7.25-$17.95, dinner $10-$35. Specializes in fresh Monterey Bay seafood, pasta, meat dishes. Collection of family photos displayed. View of bay. Cr cds: A, C, D, DS, JCB, MC, V.

D

★★ **CHART HOUSE.** *444 Cannery Row (93940). 831/372-3362.* Hrs: 5-10 pm; Fri to 11 pm; Sat 4-11 pm; Sun from 4 pm. Res accepted. Bar. Semi-a la carte: dinner $12.95-$34.95. Specializes in fresh seafood, steak, prime rib. Salad bar. Parking. Bay view. Cr cds: A, C, D, DS, MC, V.

D

★★★ **CIBO RISTORANTE ITALIANO.** *301 Alvarado St (93940). 831/649-8151.* E-mail cibo@netpipe.com; web www.cibo.com. Hrs: 5-10 pm; Fri, Sat to 10:30 pm. Res accepted. Italian menu. Bar to 1 am; Sat, Sun to 1:30 am. Semi-a la carte: dinner $8.25-$19.95. Specializes in veal, seafood, pasta. Entertainment Tues-Sun from 9 pm. Neo-classic decor. Cr cds: A, C, D, MC, V.

D

✓★ **CLOCK GARDEN.** *565 Abrego (93940). 831/375-6100.* Hrs: 11 am-10 pm; early-bird dinner 5-7 pm; Sun brunch 10 am-3 pm. Closed Thanksgiving, Dec 25. Res accepted. No A/C. Bar to midnight. Semi-a la carte: lunch $5.50-$8.25, dinner $9.25-$16.25. Sun brunch $4.50-$8.95. Specializes in steaks, seafood, pasta. Own soups. Live jazz at Sun brunch. Outdoor dining. Gardens, fountains, fully stocked Koi pond. Clock collection. Cr cds: A, C, DS, MC, V.

D

★★ **DOMENICO'S.** *50 Fisherman's Wharf (93940). 831/372-3655.* E-mail jpisto@redshift.com; web www.gpmag.com. Hrs: 10:30 am-10:30 pm. Closed Dec 25. Res accepted. Bar. A la carte entrees: lunch $7.95-$20.95, dinner $14.95-$25.95. Child's meals. Specializes in seafood, pasta. Lobster tank. Oyster bar. Casual decor. Overlooks harbor. Cr cds: A, C, D, DS, JCB, MC, V.

★★★ **DUCK CLUB.** *(See Monterey Plaza) 831/646-1706.* Web www.woodsidehotels.com. Hrs: 6:30-11 am, 5:30-10 pm; Sat, Sun 6:30 am-noon, 5:30-10 pm. Res accepted. Contemporary Amer menu. Wine list. A la carte entrees: bkfst $7.25-$14, dinner $19-$32. Child's meals. Specializes in duck, seafood, pasta. Valet parking. Large windows provide ocean views. Totally nonsmoking. Cr cds: A, C, D, MC, V.

D SC

✓★ **EL TORITO.** *600 Cannery Row (93940). 408/373-0611.* Hrs: 11 am-10 pm; Fri, Sat to 11 pm; Sun 9 am-10 pm; Sun brunch 10 am-2 pm. Closed Thanksgiving, Dec 25. Res accepted. Mexican menu. Bar. Semi-a la carte: lunch $3.59-$10.99, dinner $3.59-$12.99. Sun brunch $10.99. Child's meals. Specializes in fajitas. Parking. Overlooks Monterey Bay. Totally nonsmoking. Cr cds: A, C, D, DS, MC, V.

D SC

★★★ **FRESH CREAM.** *100 C Heritage Harbor (93940). 831/375-9798.* E-mail dining@freshcream.com; web www.freshcream.com. Hrs: 6-10 pm. Res accepted; required wkends. French menu. Bar. Wine cellar. Semi-a la carte: dinner $22.95-$32.95. Specialties: roast duck, rack of lamb. Street parking. Five dining rms, all with harbor view. Cr cds: A, C, D, DS, MC, V.

D

★★ **JOHN PISTO'S WHALING STATION.** *763 Wave St (93940). 831/373-3778.* E-mail jpisto@redshift.com; web www.gpmag.com. Hrs: 5-10 pm. Closed most major hols. Res accepted. Bar. A la carte entrees: dinner $15-$40. Child's meals. Specializes in prime steak, seafood. Totally nonsmoking. Cr cds: A, C, D, DS, JCB, MC, V.

D

★★★ **MONTRIO.** *414 Calle Principal (93940). 831/648-8880.* Hrs: 11:30 am-10 pm; wkends to 11 pm. Closed Thanksgiving, Dec 25. Res accepted. Bar. Wine list. Semi-a la carte: lunch $6-$11, dinner $6-$22. Child's meals. Specializes in chicken, beef, lamb. Eclectic decor in former firehouse (1910); open kitchen features wood-burning rotisserie. Totally nonsmoking. Cr cds: A, C, DS, MC, V.

D

✓★★ **PARADISO TRATTORIA.** *654 Cannery Row (93940). 831/375-4155.* E-mail jpisto@redshift.com; web www.gpmag.com. Hrs: 11 am-10 pm; Fri, Sat to 10:30 pm. Closed Dec 25. Res accepted. Mediterranean menu. Bar. A la carte entrees: lunch $8-$14, dinner $10-$20. Child's meals. Specializes in steak, local seafood, pasta. Oyster bar. Casual decor. Large fish tanks. Wood burning pizza oven. Cr cds: A, C, D, DS, JCB, MC, V.

D

★ **RAPPA'S SEAFOOD RESTAURANT.** *101 Fisherman Wharf St (93940), at end of wharf #1. 831/372-7562.* Hrs: 11 am-9:30 pm; Fri, Sat to 10 pm; winter hrs vary. Closed Thanksgiving, Dec 25. Res accepted. Italian menu. Bar. A la carte entrees: lunch $5.95-$14.75, dinner $8.95-$28.50. Specialties: cioppino, bouillabaisse, fresh fish. Casual dining. Scenic view of bay. Family-owned. Cr cds: A, C, D, DS, JCB, MC, V.

D

★ **SANDBAR & GRILL.** *Fisherman's Wharf #2 (93940). 831/373-2818.* Hrs: 11:30 am-10:30 pm; wkends 10:30 am-11 pm. Bar to 2 am. Semi-a la carte: lunch $6.95-$12, dinner $9.95-$19.95. Sat & Sun brunch $6.95-$9.95. Specializes in seafood. Pianist in bar Tues-Sat. At waterfront; seals, otters often swimming in view. Cr cds: A, C, D, DS, JCB, MC, V.

★★★ **SARDINE FACTORY.** *701 Wave St (93940). 831/373-3775.* E-mail mz@sardinefactory.com; web www.sardinefactory.com. Hrs: 5-10:30 pm; Fri, Sat to 11 pm; Sun 5-10 pm. Closed wk of Dec 25. Res accepted. Bar. Wine cellar. A la carte entrees: dinner $17-$29. Specializes in fresh seafood, pasta, steak. Parking. Four separate dining rms; two wine cellar rooms. Historic building was originally built as a canteen for sardine workers. Cr cds: A, C, D, DS, JCB, MC, V.

D

★★★ **STOKES ADOBE.** *500 Hartnell St (93940). 831/373-1110.* E-mail stokes@mbay.net. Hrs: 11:30 am-10 pm; Fri, Sat to 10:30 pm. Closed Dec 25. Res accepted. No A/C. California, Mediterranean menu. Bar to midnight. Wine list. Semi-a la carte: lunch $3-$11, dinner $3-$18.25. Child's meals. Specialties: lavender-infused pork chop, pan-roasted halibut with spring-vegetable risotto, cassoulet with duck confit. Historic mission-style building. Totally nonsmoking. Cr cds: A, C, MC, V.

D

★★★ **TARPY'S ROADHOUSE.** *2999 Monterey-Salinas Hwy CA (93940), at Canyon Del Rey, near Monterey Peninsula Airport. 831/647-1444.* Web www.tarpys.com. Hrs: 11:30 am-10 pm; Sun brunch 11:30 am-3 pm. Closed July 4, Thanksgiving, Dec 25. Res accepted. Bar. A la carte entrees: lunch $6.55-$23.95, dinner $6.55-$29.95. Sun brunch $6-$12.

Specializes in game, chicken, steak. Parking. Outdoor dining. Located in historic country stone house; dining area is former wine tasting room. Fireplaces. Cr cds: A, C, DS, MC, V.

D

★★★ **TRIPLES.** *220 Olivier St (93940). 831/372-4744.* Hrs: 6-10 pm. Closed Mon. Res accepted. No A/C. California, French menu. Bar. A la carte entrees: dinner $10.95-$25.95. Specialties: crab cakes, rack of lamb, baked Alaska. California historic building. Outdoor dining in garden. Cr cds: A, C, D, DS, MC, V.

D

Morro Bay (H-2)

(See also Atascadero, Paso Robles, Pismo Beach, San Luis Obispo)

Pop 9,664 **Elev** 200 ft **Area Code** 805 **Zip** 93442
Web www.morrobay.com

Information Chamber of Commerce, 880 Main St, PO Box 876; 805/772-4467 or 800/231-0592

At the harbor entrance to this seaport town is Morro Rock, a 576-foot volcanic dome discovered by Juan Rodriguez Cabrillo in 1542. A large commercial fishing fleet sails from here and many boats dock along the Embarcadero. Morro Bay is a designated State and National Estuary; other natural features are Morro Bay Heron Rookery, Montana de Oro State Park, Morro Strand State Beach and Los Osos Oaks Reserve.

What to See and Do

Harbor cruises. One-hr narrated tours of bay on sternwheeler *Tiger's Folly II,* departing from Harbor Hut Dock. 1205 Embarcadero. Phone 805/772-2257 or -2255. ¢¢¢

Morro Bay Aquarium. Displays 300 live marine specimens. (Daily) 595 Embarcadero. Phone 805/772-7647. ¢

Morro Bay State Park. Approx 2,400 acres on Morro Bay. Fishing, boating. 18-hole golf course (fee). Picnicking, cafe. Hiking. Tent & trailer camping (showers, dump station; water & electric hookups). Standard fees. S of town. Phone 805/772-7434. On White Point is

Museum of Natural History. Films, slide shows, displays; nature walks. (Daily; closed Jan 1, Thanksgiving, Dec 25) State Park Rd. Phone 805/772-2694. ¢

Annual Event

Winter Bird Festival. Celebration of migrating birds includes birding and natural history field trips; workshops, guest speakers; banquet, ice cream social; art exhibit. Phone 800/231-0592. 4 days mid-Jan.

Motels

✓★ **ASCOT INN & SUITES.** *845 Morro Ave (93442). 805/772-4437; FAX 805/772-8860; res: 800/887-6454.* E-mail ascotinn@aol.com; web www.ascotinn.com. 25 rms, 2 story, 3 suites. No A/C. May-Oct: S, D $48-$95; each addl $5; suites $65-$168; under 15 free; lower rates rest of yr. TV; cable (premium). Complimentary continental bkfst. Complimentary coffee in rms. Restaurant adj 7 am-10 pm. Ck-out 11 am. Business servs avail. In-rm modem link. Beauty shop. Some refrigerators. Cr cds: A, C, D, DS, MC, V.

SC

★★ **BAY VIEW LODGE.** *225 Harbor St (93442), at Market St. 805/772-2771; res: 800/742-8439.* 22 rms, 2 story. No A/C. June-Sept, wkends: S $60-$80; D $65-$92; each addl $6; higher rates graduation wkend; lower rates rest of yr. Crib $4. TV; cable (premium), VCR (movies $2). Coffee in rms. Restaurant nearby. Ck-out 11 am. Coin Indry. Whirlpool. Refrigerators, fireplaces. Ocean view from some rms. Bay 1 blk. Cr cds: A, C, MC, V.

✓★★★ **BEST WESTERN MOTEL EL RANCHO.** *2460 Main St (93442). 805/772-2212; FAX 805/772-2212; res: 800/528-1234; res: 800/628-3500.* 27 rms. S, D $49-$89; each addl $7; under 12 free. Crib $5. Pet accepted; $10. TV; cable, VCR (free movies). Heated pool. Restaurant 7 am-10 pm. Ck-out 11 am. Coin Indry. Business servs avail. Refrigerators; microwaves avail. Grill. Redwood lobby, etched glass door. Ocean view. Cr cds: A, C, D, DS, MC, V.

SC

★★ **BLUE SAIL INN.** *851 Market Ave (93442). 805/772-7132; FAX 805/772-8406; res: 800/336-0707; res: 888/337-0707.* Web www.morrobay.com/bluessailinn/. 48 rms, 1-2 story. No A/C. S, D $65-$90; suites $95-$115. Crib $6. TV; cable (premium). Complimentary coffee in rms. Restaurant adj 7 am-10 pm. Ck-out 11 am. Business servs avail. In-rm modem link. Covered parking. Whirlpool. Refrigerators. Some wet bars, fireplaces. Balconies. Bay view. Cr cds: A, C, D, DS, MC, V.

D

★★ **BREAKERS MOTEL.** *780 Market Ave (96067), at Morro Bay Blvd. 805/772-7317; FAX 805/772-4771.* Web www.morrobay.com/breakersmotel/. 25 rms, some A/C, 2-3 story. No elvtr. S, D $70-$110; each addl $10. Crib $4. TV; cable (premium). Heated pool; whirlpool. Complimentary coffee in rms. Restaurant opp 7 am-10 pm. Ck-out noon. Business servs avail. Refrigerators; some fireplaces. Bay view from many rms. Cr cds: A, C, D, DS, MC, V.

SC

★★ **DAYS INN.** *1095 Main St (93442). 805/772-2711; FAX 805/772-2711; res: 800/329-7466.* 46 rms, 2 story. No A/C. Memorial Day-Sept: S, D $60-$125; each addl $6; lower rates rest of yr. Pet accepted, some restrictions; $10. TV; cable (premium). Complimentary continental bkfst. Coffee in rms. Restaurant opp open 24 hrs. Ck-out 11 am. Business servs avail. Whirlpool. Some refrigerators. Patios, balconies. Cr cds: A, C, DS, MC, V.

D SC

★★ **LA SERENA INN.** *990 Morro Ave (93442). 805/772-5665; FAX 805/772-1044; res: 800/248-1511.* Web www.laserenainn.com. 37 rms, 3 story, 5 suites. S, D $79-$104; each addl $10; suites $125-$160. Crib $10. TV; cable (premium). Complimentary continental bkfst. Restaurant nearby. Ck-out 11 am. Meeting rm. Business servs avail. In-rm modem link. Covered parking. Sauna. Refrigerators, microwaves. Balconies. Ocean view. Cr cds: A, C, D, DS, MC, V.

D SC

✓★ **SUNSET TRAVELODGE.** *1080 Market Ave (93442). 805/772-1259; FAX 805/772-8967; res: 800/578-7878.* 31 rms, 1-2 story. No A/C. S, D $45-$98; each addl $8; under 18 free; higher rates wkend, hols, special events. Crib free. Pet accepted; deposit required. TV; cable (premium). Heated pool. Complimentary continental bkfst. Coffee in rms. Restaurant nearby. Ck-out 11 am. Business servs avail. In-rm modem link. Refrigerators. Microwaves avail. Sundeck. Cr cds: A, C, D, DS, ER, JCB, MC, V.

SC

★★ **TWIN DOLPHIN.** *590 Morro Ave (93442). 805/772-4483; FAX 805/771-9775.* 31 rms, 3 story. S, D $65-$130; each addl $10. Crib $6. TV; cable (premium). Complimentary continental bkfst. Restaurant nearby. Ck-out 11 am. Meeting rm. Covered parking. Whirlpool. Refrigerators avail. Balconies. Cr cds: C, DS, MC, V.

D

Hotel

★★★ **INN AT MORRO BAY.** *60 State Park Rd; 19 Country Club Rd (93443), adj to Morro Bay Golf Course. 805/772-5651; FAX 805/772-4779; res: 800/321-9566.* Web innatmorrobay.com. 98 rms, 2 story. No A/C. S, D $95-$275; cottage $350. Crib free. TV; cable (premium). Heated pool; poolside serv. Restaurant 7 am-2 pm, 5-9 pm; summer to 10 pm. Bar 11 am-midnight; entertainment wkends. Ck-out noon. Meeting rms. Business servs avail. Health club privileges. Golf privileges. Massage. Many refrigerators, fireplaces. Private patios, balconies. Guest bicycles. On Morro Bay. Cr cds: A, C, D, DS, JCB, MC, V.

SC

Inn

★★★ **BEACHWALKER INN.** *501 S Ocean Ave (93430), N on CA 1. 805/995-2133; FAX 805/995-3139; res: 800/750-2133.* E-mail beachwalkerinn@fix.net; web www.beachwalkerinn.com. 24 rms, 2 story, 12 kit. units. No A/C. Mid-June-mid-Sept: S, D $90-$110; each addl $10; kit. units $105-$225; under 12 free; family rates; package plans; wkends, hols (2-3 day min); higher rates hols; lower rates rest of yr. Crib free. TV; cable (premium), VCR avail (movies). Complimentary continental bkfst. Complimentary coffee in rms. Restaurant nearby. Ck-out 11 am, ck-in 2 pm. Business servs avail. Gift shop. Fireplaces. Some balconies. Picnic tables. Opp beach. Totally nonsmoking. Cr cds: A, C, D, DS, JCB, MC, V.

D SC

Restaurants

✓★★★ **GALLEY RESTAURANT.** *899 Embarcadero (93442). 805/772-2806.* Hrs: 11 am-9 pm. Closed late Nov-Dec 25. Res accepted. Beer. Wine cellar. Semi-a la carte: lunch $3.95-$11. Complete meals: dinner from $13.75. Child's meals. Specializes in fresh fish. Overlooks Morro Bay and Morro Rock. Family-owned since 1966. Totally nonsmoking. Cr cds: A, C, DS, MC, V.

★★ **ROSE'S LANDING.** *725 Embarcadero (93442). 805/772-4441.* Hrs: 11:30 am-9 pm; Fri, Sat 11 am-10 pm; Sun 11 am-9 pm. Res accepted. Bar 11:30 am-10 pm; Fri, Sat to midnight. Semi-a la carte: lunch $5.95-$9.95, dinner $9.95-up. Child's meals. Specializes in steak, seafood, pasta. Entertainment (summer). Patio dining. View of bay. Cr cds: A, C, D, DS, MC, V.

Mother Lode Country (C-3 - D-3)

(See also Auburn, Grass Valley, Jackson, Nevada City, Placerville, Sonora, Truckee)

Three hundred eighteen miles long and only a few miles wide, this strip of land stretching through nine counties from the Sierra foothills was the scene of the gold rush of the mid-19th century. Discovery of gold at Coloma in 1848 touched off a wave of migration to the West that accelerated the development and population of all the western states by several decades. The enormous gold-bearing quartz vein was surface-mined until the end of the century; a few mines still exist, but it is now necessary to penetrate deep into the earth. In this narrow stretch of country have developed frontier and mining camp legends that are part of the warp and woof of the American West.

Today the scenic Mother Lode country is dotted with ghost towns, old mine shafts, rusting machinery and ancient buildings. Recreational gold panning is a favorite pastime. CA 49, a delightful but not high-speed highway, connects many of the towns where the 49ers panned for gold. Many picnic and camping areas can be found here. Map available from Chamber of Commerce offices throughout Mother Lode Country. For further information, contact the El Dorado County Chamber of Commerce, 542 Main St, Placerville 95667 or phone 530/621-5885.

Mount Shasta (B-2)

(See also Dunsmuir, Redding, Yreka)

Pop 3,460 **Elev** 3,554 ft **Area Code** 530 **Zip** 96067
E-mail o-msvisb@inreach.com
Web www.mtshasta.com/chamber/chamber.html
Information Chamber of Commerce 530/926-6212 or the Visitors Bureau, 300 Pine St 530/926-4865 or 800/926-4865

Set in Strawberry Valley, Mt Shasta offers a central location to fishing in nearby lakes and streams and year-round outdoor activities in the surrounding area. City water from a nearby spring is so pure that it is untreated.

A Ranger District office of the Shasta-Trinity National Forest (see REDDING) is located in Mount Shasta.

What to See and Do

Campgrounds. The US Forest Service maintains the following

Castle Lake. 6 units. Swimming; fishing. Picnicking. No trailers. 12 mi SW, ½ mi from Castle Lake. **Sims Flat.** Fishing. 20 mi S, 1 mi E of I-5. 19 units. **McBride Springs.** 9 units. 5 mi E of Mt Shasta. All closed winters. Fee at Sims and McBride. For additional information on these and other campgrounds contact the Shasta-Trinity National Forest, 204 Alma St; phone 530/926-4511.

Lake Siskiyou. Box Canyon Dam impounds the Sacramento River, creating a 430-acre lake for fishing and swimming. 2½ mi SW, off I-5. On W shore of lake is

Lake Siskiyou Camp-Resort. Swimming beach; fishing; boating (rentals, ramp, marina). Hiking. Picnicking. Snack bar; store. Camping (tent & RV sites; hookups, rentals; dump station). Contact PO Box 276; phone 888/926-2618. Day use per person **¢**; Camping **¢¢¢¢¢**

Mt Shasta. Perpetually snow-covered double peak volcano towering to 14,162 ft. Five glaciers persist on the slopes, feeding the McCloud and Sacramento rivers. A scenic drive on Everitt Memorial Hwy climbs from the city of Mt Shasta up the slope to 7,840 ft for a magnificent view. White pine, the famous Shasta lily and majestic stands of red fir are found at various elevations. E of I-5, in Shasta-Trinity National Forest (see REDDING).

Mt Shasta Ski Park. Three triple chairlifts, 1 surface lift; patrol, school, rentals; cafeteria, bar. 25 runs; longest run 1.2 mi; vertical drop 1,400 ft. (Thanksgiving-mid-Apr, daily) Night skiing (Wed-Sat), snowboarding. Park open for mountain biking, chairlift rides, climbing tower and volcanic exhibit (mid-June-Labor Day, daily). 10 mi SE on CA 89. Phone 530/926-8610 or 530/926-8686 (snow conditions). **¢¢¢–¢¢¢¢¢**

State Fish Hatchery. Raises trout; in continuous operation since 1888. Self-guided tour of trout ponds. Picnic tables, restrms. (Daily) ½ mi W off I-5, Central Mt Shasta exit. Phone 530/926-2215. **Free** Adj is

Sisson Museum. Features exhibits on area history, mountain climbing, fish hatchery and local Native American culture. (Daily; closed Easter, Dec 25, also Jan-Feb) Also annual quilt show. Phone 530/926-5508. **Free**

Motels

★★★ **BEST WESTERN.** *111 Morgan Way, Hwy I-5 & Lake St (96067). 530/926-3101; FAX 530/926-3542; res: 800/545-7164.* 95 rms, 2-3 story. S $69-$79; D $79-$94; each addl $5; suites $89-$154. Crib free. TV; cable. Indoor pool; whirlpool. Restaurant 5:30 am-10 pm; Sun to 9 pm. Bar from 10 am. Ck-out noon. Meeting rms. Business servs avail. In-rm modem link. Downhill/x-country ski 10 mi. View of Mt Shasta. Cr cds: A, C, D, DS, MC, V.

D SC

✓★★ **FINLANDIA MOTEL.** *1612 S Mt Shasta Blvd (96067). 530/926-5596.* 23 rms, 14 A/C, 1-2 story, 3 kits. S $34; D $38-$56; suites $48-$75. Crib $4. TV; cable. Whirlpool. Ck-out 11 am. Free bus depot transportation. Downhill ski 9 mi; x-country ski 8 mi. Picnic table, grill. Many lake, mountain views. Cr cds: A, C, D, DS, MC, V.

D

✓★★ **STRAWBERRY VALLEY INN.** *1142 S. Mount Shasta Blvd. (96067). 530/926-2052; FAX 530/926-0842.* 25 rms, 7 suites. No A/C. S $45.50-$52.50; D $55.50-$72.50; each addl $6; suites $67-$75; under 10 free; ski plans. TV; cable. Complimentary continental bkfst. Restaurant nearby. Ck-out 11 am. In-rm modem link. Downhill/x-country ski 10 mi. Picnic tables. Totally nonsmoking. Cr cds: A, C, D, DS, MC, V.

D SC

✓★ **SWISS HOLIDAY LODGE.** *2400 S Mount Shasta Blvd (96067), S Mt Shasta Blvd, 2 mi S at jct CA 89, I-5 McCloud exit . 530/926-3446; FAX 530/926-3091.* 21 air-cooled rms, 2 story. S $36-$42; D $42-$62; each addl $5; suite $95. Crib $5. Pet accepted; $5. TV; cable (premium). Heated pool; whirlpool. Complimentary continental bkfst. Complimentary coffee in rms. Ck-out 11 am. Downhill/x-country ski 10 mi. Refrigerators avail. Picnic tables, grills. View of Mt Shasta. Cr cds: A, C, DS, MC, V.

SC

Resort

★★★ **MOUNT SHASTA RESORT.** *1000 Siskiyou Lake Blvd (96067). 530/926-3030; FAX 530/926-0333; res: 800/958-3363.* E-mail msresort@inreach.com; web www.mountshastare sort.com. 50 cottages, 2 story. May-Sept: S $108-$128; D $155-$178; package plans; wkends, hols 2-3 day min; lower rates rest of yr. Crib free. TV; cable. Complimentary coffee in rms. Restaurant 7 am-9 pm; winter hrs from 11 am. Bar 11 am-9 pm. Ck-out 11 am, ck-in 3 pm. Meeting rms. Business servs avail. In-rm modem link. Lighted tennis, pro. 18-hole golf, greens fee $42, putting green, driving range. Downhill/x-country ski 10 mi. Tobogganing. Camping. Spa. Refrigerators, microwaves, fireplaces. Totally nonsmoking. Cr cds: A, C, D, DS, MC, V.

D

Inn

★★ **MCCLOUD HOTEL BED & BREAKFAST.** *408 Main St (96057), I-5 exit E on Hwy 89. 530/964-2822; FAX 530/964-2844; res: 800/964-2823.* E-mail mchotel@snowcrest.net; web www.mchotel.com. 17 rms, 2 story, 4 suites. No rm phones. S, D $74-$94; each addl $10; suites $134-$148; package plans; hols 2-day min. Adults only. TV in common rm. Complimentary full bkfst. Restaurant adj 5-9 pm. Ck-out 11 am, ck-in 3-7 pm. Business servs avail. Luggage handling. Concierge serv. Gift shop. Downhill/x-country ski 4 mi. Massage. In-rm whirlpool in suites. Picnic tables. Built in 1915. Totally nonsmoking. Cr cds: A, C, DS, MC, V.

Restaurant

★★ **PIEMONT RESTAURANT.** *1200 S Mount Shasta Blvd (96067). 530/926-2402.* Hrs: 5-9:30 pm; Fri, Sat to 10 pm; Sun from 1 pm; winter hrs vary. Closed Mon; Thanksgiving, Dec 24-25; also Tues Jan & Feb. Res accepted. Italian, Amer menu. Bar. Complete meals: dinner $8.25-$16.50. Child's meals. Specializes in pasta, chicken, steak. Own pasta. Family-owned since 1940. Totally nonsmoking. Cr cds: C, DS, MC, V.

Mountain View (E-4 see San Francisco map)

(See also Palo Alto, Santa Clara)

Pop 67,460 **Elev** 97 ft **Area Code** 650

Motels

★★ **COUNTY INN.** *850 Leong Dr (94043). 650/961-1131; FAX 650/965-9099; res: 800/828-1132.* 52 rms, 2 story. S $149; D $159; each addl $10; under 12 free; wkend, hol rates. Closed Dec 24-Jan 2. Crib free. TV; cable (premium), VCR (free movies). Heated pool. Complimentary continental bkfst. Complimentary coffee in rms. Restaurant adj open 24 hrs. Ck-out noon. Coin lndry. Business servs avail. In-rm modem link. Sundries. Valet serv. Health club privileges. Minibars. Cr cds: A, C, D, DS, JCB, MC, V.

SC

★★ **HOLIDAY INN.** *93 W El Camino Real (94040). 650/967-6957; FAX 650/967-4834.* 58 rms, 2 story. May-Dec: S, D $129; each addl $10; suites $145-$160; under 12 free; higher rates special events; lower rates rest of yr. Crib free. TV; cable (premium), VCR (movies). Heated pool; whirlpool. Complimentary continental bkfst. Complimentary coffee in rms. Restaurant adj open 24 hrs. Ck-out 11 am. Coin lndry. Valet serv. Exercise equipt. Refrigerators. Cr cds: A, C, D, DS, JCB, MC, V.

D SC

★ **MOUNTAIN VIEW INN.** *2300 W El Camino Real (94040). 650/962-9912; FAX 415/962-9011; res: 800/528-1234.* 72 units, 2-3 story, 2 suites. No elvtr. S $125; D $135; each addl $5; suites, kit. units $235; under 12 free. TV; cable (premium). Pool; whirlpool. Complimentary continental bkfst. Complimentary coffee in rms. Restaurant nearby. Ck-out 11 am. Coin lndry. Meeting rm. Business servs avail. In-rm modem link. Exercise equipt; sauna. Refrigerators. Cr cds: A, C, D, DS, MC, V.

D SC

★★ **RESIDENCE INN.** *1854 W El Camino Real (94040). 650/940-1300; FAX 650/969-4997; res: 800/331-3131.* 112 kit. suites, 2 story. S, D $229-$259; wkly, wkend, monthly rates. Pet accepted; $50-$75 & $10/day. TV; cable (premium). Heated pool; whirlpool. Complimentary continental bkfst. Restaurant nearby. Ck-out noon. Coin lndry. Meeting rm. Business servs avail. Valet serv. Health club privileges. Refrigerators. Picnic tables, grills. Cr cds: A, C, D, DS, JCB, MC, V.

D SC

Restaurants

★★ **AMBER INDIA.** *2290 El Camino Real (94040). 650/968-7511.* Hrs: 11:30 am-2:30 pm, 5-10 pm; Sun brunch 11:30 am-2:30 pm. Closed Thanksgiving, Dec 25. Res accepted. East Indian menu. Bar. A la carte entrees: lunch, dinner $7.25-$24.95. Complete meal: lunch, dinner $17.95-$22.95. Lunch buffet $8.95. Sun brunch $9.95. Parking. Indian decor. Cr cds: A, C, D, DS, MC, V.

D

★★★ **CHEZ T.J.** *938 Villa St (94041). 650/964-7466.* Web www.cheztj.com. Hrs: 5:30-9 pm. Closed Sun, Mon; Jan 1, Thanksgiving, Dec 25. Res required. No A/C. French, California menu. Complete meals: dinner $50-$65. Specializes in choice beef, fresh seafood. Outdoor dining. Intimate dining in Victorian house; original art, wood-burning fireplace. Totally nonsmoking. Cr cds: A, C, D, DS, JCB, MC, V.

Mt Diablo State Park
(C-5 see San Francisco map)

(See also Fremont, Livermore, Pleasanton, Santa Clara)

(5 mi E of I-680, Danville, on Diablo Rd)

A spiraling road leads to the summit of Mt Diablo (3,849 ft), the highest peak in the San Francisco Bay region. From here, on a clear day, one can see 200 miles in each direction. The mountain is dotted with rock formations containing fossilized shells. Hiking trails wind from ridge to ridge throughout the more than 19,000 acres of the park. Near the south entrance are unusual rock formations known as the Devil's Slide and the Wind Caves. There are more than 100 miles of unpaved roads and 68 miles of trails available to hikers and horseback riders. Also available are picnic and camping facilities. Standard fees. Phone 510/837-2525.

Muir Woods National Monument
(B-2 see San Francisco map)

(See also Corte Madera, Mill Valley, San Francisco, Sausalito)

(17 mi N of San Francisco, off CA 1)

This was the first area in the National Park system to preserve an old growth stand of redwoods *(Sequoia sempervirens)*, the tallest species of tree on earth. Every effort has been made to preserve this area as close as possible to what it was when the first European settler saw it in 1850. The monument lies at the south foot of Mt Tamalpais. Two parcels of land, totaling more than 465 of the monument's 553 acres, were donated to the United States by William and Elizabeth Thacher Kent and named in honor of John Muir, famous traveler and naturalist. The first parcel of land was donated in 1908.

Charred stumps and deep scars on living trees are proof that fires regularly occurred prior to 1850. During mid-December to mid-March, depending on winter rains, visitors may see mature salmon and steelhead trout fighting their way up Redwood Creek to spawn. There are 6 miles of trails; visitors must stay on trails. The following are not permitted: pets, picnicking, fishing, camping, hunting and possession of firearms. There are 1½ miles of flat, asphalt trail suitable for wheelchairs and strollers. The park is open every day, 8 am to sunset. Visitor Center, snack bar and gift shop (daily). Because the area is so popular, during the summer months it is best to drive there before 11 am or after 5 pm. Limited parking for oversize vehicles and large RVs. Contact the Site Manager, Muir Woods Natl Monument, Mill Valley 94941; 415/388-2595. Park ¢

Napa
(D-2)

(See also Calistoga, Sonoma, St Helena, Yountville)

Pop 61,842 **Elev** 17 ft **Area Code** 707

Information Chamber of Commerce, 1556 First St, 94559, phone 707/226-7455; or the Conference & Visitors Bureau, 1310 Napa Town Center, 94559, phone 707/226-7459

As gateway to the fertile Napa Valley, an area renowned for its fine wines, the town of Napa is a popular stopping-off point for tourists.

What to See and Do

★ **Napa Valley Wine Train.** Scenic trips aboard turn-of-the-century Pullman cars and 1950s diesel Steamliners. The 3-hr, 36-mi round-trip journey departs from Napa to St Helena and passes through Napa Valley vineyards. Lunch, brunch and dinner also served (fee). Res for wkends recommended one month in advance. Contact 1275 McKinstry St, 94559; phone 707/253-2111. ¢¢¢¢¢

Wineries. For tour map showing area wineries contact the Conference & Visitors Bureau, 1310 Napa Town Center; phone 707/226-7459.

Motel

★ **CHABLIS INN.** *3360 Solano Ave (94558). 707/257-1944; FAX 707/226-6862; res: 800/443-3490.* 34 rms, 2 story, 7 kits. Apr-Oct: S, D $100-$125; kit. units $75-$85; each addl $5; under 14 free; higher rates Fri, Sat, hols; lower rates rest of yr. Crib $5. TV; cable (premium). Heated pool; whirlpool. Complimentary continental bkfst. Complimentary coffee in rms. Restaurant nearby. Ck-out noon. Business servs avail. Refrigerators. Picnic tables. Cr cds: A, C, D, DS, MC, V.

D

Motor Hotels

✓★★ **BEST WESTERN INN.** *100 Soscol Ave (94559). 707/257-1930; FAX 707/255-0709; res: 800/528-1234.* 68 rms, 3 story. Apr-Nov: S $95-$150; D $110-$150; each addl $10; suites $175-$200; lower rates rest of yr. Crib free. TV; cable (premium). Heated pool; whirlpool. Coffee in rms. Restaurant open 24 hrs. Ck-out 11 am. Business servs avail. Meeting rm. Health club privileges. Refrigerators. Private patios, balconies. Cr cds: A, C, D, DS, ER, JCB, MC, V.

D SC

★ **CHATEAU HOTEL.** *4195 Solano Ave (94558). 707/253-9300; FAX 707/253-0906; res: 800/253-6272.* 115 rms, 2 story. Apr-Oct: S $115; D $120; each addl $10; suites $155-$190; under 12 free; lower rates rest of yr. Crib free. TV; cable (premium). Heated pool; whirlpool. Coffee in rms. Restaurant nearby. Ck-out noon. Meeting rms. Business servs avail. Some refrigerators. Cr cds: A, C, D, DS, JCB, MC, V.

D SC

★★ **JOHN MUIR INN.** *1998 Trower Ave (94558). 707/257-7220; FAX 707/258-0943; res: 800/522-8999.* Web www.toc.com/johnmuirinn. 59 units, 3 story. Apr-Oct: S, D $100-$170; each addl $10; suites $120-$160; kits. $95-$110; under 14 free; mid-wk rates. Crib free. TV; cable (premium), VCR avail (movies). Pool; whirlpool. Complimentary continental bkfst. Complimentary coffee in rms. Restaurant nearby. Meeting rms. Business servs avail. In-rm modem link. Valet serv. Some refrigerators. Microwaves avail. Cr cds: A, C, D, DS, MC, V.

D SC

★★★ **MARRIOTT.** *3425 Solano Ave (94558). 707/253-7433; FAX 707/258-1320; res: 800/228-9290.* 191 rms, 2 story. Mar-Nov: S, D $125-$193; suites $260-$470; lower rates rest of yr. TV; cable (premium). Heated pool; whirlpool, poolside serv. Coffee in rms. Restaurant 6:30 am-10 pm. Rm serv. Bar. Ck-out noon. Meeting rms. Business center. In-rm modem link. Bellhops. Valet serv. Sundries. Gift shop. Lighted tennis. Refrigerators avail. Some private patios, balconies. Cr cds: A, C, D, DS, ER, JCB, MC, V.

D SC

Hotel

★★★ **EMBASSY SUITES.** *1075 California Blvd (94559). 707/253-9540; FAX 707/253-9202; res: 800/433-4600.* E-mail suitenapa@aol.com. 205 suites, 3 story. May-Oct: S, D $184-$254; each addl $10; under 18 free; lower rates rest or yr. Crib free. TV; cable (premium). 2 pools, 1 indoor; whirlpool. Sauna, steam rm. Complimentary full bkfst. Complimentary coffee in rms. Restaurants 11 am-10 pm. Bar to 1 am;

entertainment. Ck-out noon. Meeting rms. Business servs avail. In-rm modem link. Health club privileges. Concierge. Refrigerators, wet bars. Cr cds: A, C, D, DS, ER, JCB, MC, V.

D SC

Resort

★★★ **SILVERADO COUNTRY CLUB RESORT.** *1600 Atlas Peak Rd (94558). 707/257-0200; FAX 707/257-2867; res: 800/532-0500.* E-mail resv@silveradoresort.com. 420 rms, 1 & 2 story, 280 suites. Mar-late Nov: S, D $155-$290; kit. suites $290-$1,300; each addl $15; hol, golf, tennis packages; lower rates rest of yr. Crib free. TV; cable (premium), VCR avail. 9 pools, some heated; whirlpool. Restaurant 5:30 am-5 pm; dining rms 5:30-11 pm (also see VINTNERS COURT). Bar 11-1 am; Fri, Sat to 2 am; entertainment. Ck-out noon, ck-in 4 pm. Coin Indry. Conference facilities. Business center. In-rm modem link. Concierge. Sundries. Valet parking. Golf, tennis pro shops. Lighted tennis $13, pro. 36-hole golf, greens fee $120 (includes cart), pro, putting greens, driving range. Refrigerators, minibars, fireplaces. Private patios, balconies. Cr cds: A, C, D, DS, JCB, MC, V.

Inns

★★★ **BEAZLEY HOUSE.** *1910 1st St (94559). 707/257-1649; FAX 707/257-1518; res: 800/559-1649.* E-mail jbeazley@napanet.net; web www.napavalley.com/beazley. 11 rms, 2 story. S $112.50-$222.50; D $125-$250; each addl $25. Complimentary full bkfst; evening refreshments. Ck-out 11:30 am, ck-in 3:30-6:30 pm. Meeting rm. Business servs avail. Health club privileges. Built 1902; antiques; library. Totally nonsmoking. Cr cds: A, C, MC, V.

SC

★★★ **COUNTRY GARDEN INN.** *1815 Silverado Trl (94558). 707/255-1197; FAX 707/255-3112.* E-mail innkeep@countrygardeninn.com; web www.countrygardeninn.com. 10 rms, 2 story. No rm phones. Apr-Nov, wkends: D $150-$225; each addl $25; lower rates rest of yr. Children over 16 yrs only. Complimentary full bkfst; evening refreshments. Ck-out 11:30 am, ck-in 3 pm. Business servs avail. Meeting rm. Lawn games. Fireplaces; some in-rm whirlpools. Private patios, balconies. Picnic tables. View of river. Built 1855; antiques. On 1½ acres of woodland; rose garden; aviary. Totally nonsmoking. Cr cds: A, C, MC, V.

D

★★★ **LA RESIDENCE COUNTRY INN.** *4066 Saint Helena Hwy (94558). 707/253-0337; FAX 707/253-0382.* 20 rms, 2-3 story. Mar-Nov: S, D $175-$195; each addl $20; suites $225-$275; lower rates rest of yr. TV avail. Heated pool; whirlpool. Complimentary full bkfst. Ck-out 11 am, ck-in 2 pm. Meeting rm. Business servs avail. In-rm modem link. Luggage handling. Balconies. Antiques, fireplaces. Gothic-revival architecture. Built 1870. Cr cds: A, C, D, MC, V.

D

★★ **OLD WORLD INN.** *1301 Jefferson St (94559). 707/257-0112; FAX 707/257-0118.* Web www.napavalley.com/oldworld. 8 rms, 2 story, 1 cottage. S, D $125-$160; cottage $215. Complimentary full bkfst; afternoon refreshments. Ck-out 11:30 am, ck-in 3-6 pm. Whirlpool. Some fireplaces. Built ca 1900; Scandinavian country decor; antiques. Garden. Totally nonsmoking. Cr cds: A, C, DS, MC, V.

Restaurants

★★★ **BISTRO DON GIOVANNI.** *4110 St Helena Hwy CA 29 (94558), between Salvador Ave & Oaknoll. 707/224-3300.* Web www.bistrodongiovanni.com. Hrs: 11:30 am-10 pm; wkends to 11 pm. Closed Jan 1, Thanksgiving, Dec 25. Res accepted. Italian, French menu. Bar. A la carte entrees: lunch, dinner $8.95-$16.95. Child's meals. Specialties: fritto misto, grilled portabello mushrooms, seared filet of salmon. Parking. Outdoor dining. Terrace overlooking vineyard. Mexican tile floors, original artwork. Cr cds: A, C, D, DS, MC, V.

D

★★ **CELADON.** *1040 Main St #104 (94559). 707/254-9690.* Hrs: 11:30 am-2 pm, 5-9 pm; Sat 5-9 pm. Closed Sun; also most major hols. Continental menu. Wine, beer. A la carte entrees: lunch $12-$15, dinner $15-$28. Specialties: flash-fried calamari with spicy chipotle chili glaze, steak frites, Asian-inspired noodle bowl. Parking. Outdoor dining. On creek. Totally nonsmoking. Cr cds: A, C, D, MC, V.

D

★★ **CHANTERELLE RESTAURANT.** *804 1st St (94559). 707/253-7300.* Hrs: 11 am-4 pm, 5-9:30 pm; Sun to 9 pm; Sun brunch 10:30 am-2:30 pm. Closed Jan 1. Res accepted. Mediterranean menu. Bar. Semi-a la carte: lunch $5.50-$12.95, dinner $11-$19. Complete meals: dinner $34. Sun brunch $15.50-$18.50. Specializes in beef, chicken. Cr cds: A, C, MC, V.

D

★ **JONESY'S FAMOUS STEAK HOUSE.** *2044 Airport Rd (94558). 707/255-2003.* Hrs: 11:30 am-9 pm; Sun to 8 pm. Closed Mon; Dec 25. Res accepted. Bar. Semi-a la carte: lunch, dinner $6.75-$16.95. Child's meals. Specializes in steak, seafood, salads. View of planes landing and taking off at airport. Totally nonsmoking. Cr cds: A, C, D, DS, MC, V.

D

★★ **LA BOUCANE.** *1778 2nd St (94559). 707/253-1177.* Hrs: 5:30-10:30 pm. Closed Sun; major hols; also 2 wks in Jan. Res accepted; required wkends. Semi-a la carte: dinner $14-$21. Specialties: salmon poached in cream & champagne, rack of lamb, roast duckling. Parking. House built 1885. Cr cds: C, MC, V.

★★★ **NAPA VALLEY WINE TRAIN.** *1275 Mckinstry St (94559). 707/253-2111.* E-mail wtres@napanet.net; web www.napavalley.com/winetrain.html. Sittings: 11 am & 6 pm; Sat, Sun noon & 5:30 pm; Mon 11 am; Sat, Sun brunch 8:30 am. Closed Dec 25; also 1st wk Jan. Res required. Bar. Wine list. A la carte entrees: lunch $27.50. Prix fixe: lunch $65-$77, dinner $70-$85. Sat, Sun brunch $57. Child's meals. Specializes in beef, chicken, fish. Eight vintage (ca 1915) railroad cars carry diners 36 mi through vineyards to St Helena and back to Napa; turn-of-the-century decor. Totally nonsmoking. Cr cds: A, C, D, DS, JCB, MC, V.

D SC

✓★★ **RUFFINO'S.** *645 1st St (94559). 707/255-4455.* Hrs: 5-10 pm; Sun 4-9:30 pm. Closed Mon; Jan 1, Thanksgiving, Dec 24-25. Res accepted. Italian menu. Bar. Semi-a la carte: dinner $7.95-$16.95. Child's meals. Specializes in steak, veal, pasta. Totally nonsmoking. Family-owned. Cr cds: A, C, D, JCB, MC, V.

D

★★ **VINTNERS COURT.** *(See Silverado) 707/257-0200.* E-mail resv@silveradoresort.com. Hrs: 6-10:30 pm; Fri to 9:30 pm; Sun brunch 10 am-3 pm. Closed Mon. Res accepted. Bar. A la carte entrees: dinner $21-$27. Fri seafood buffet $33.50. Sun brunch $23.50. Child's meals. Specialties: wok-fried Chilean sea bass, brasied lamb shank. Pianist nightly. Valet parking. Overlooks golf course. Totally nonsmoking. Cr cds: A, C, D, DS, JCB, MC, V.

D

Needles (H-6)

Founded 1882 **Pop** 5,191 **Elev** 488 ft **Area Code** 760 **Zip** 92363

Information Chamber of Commerce, 100 G Street, PO Box 705; 760/326-2050

Founded as a way station for the Santa Fe Railroad, this town took its name from the needlelike peaks visible 15 miles away in Arizona. The town has a variety of trees and desert plant life. Nearby are many mines and ghost towns. With marinas on the Colorado River and recreational areas under development, the area is attracting anglers, boaters and campers.

What to See and Do

Moabi Regional Park. Swimming beach and lagoon, waterskiing; fishing; boating (boat rentals, launches, marina). Camping (fee; hookups, hot showers); lndry, general store. Peninsula, riverfront camping. Pets on leash only. Water, rest rms only. Fee per vehicle. 11 mi SE via I-40, on the Colorado River. Contact Park Moabi Rd; phone 760/326-3831.

Providence Mountains State Recreation Area. Spectacular scenery including 300-sq-mi area of desert. Two of the Mitchell Caverns are open to the public—El Pakiva and Tecopa; both contain fine examples of stalactites and stalagmites. El Pakiva has rare shields or palettes (round plate-like protrusions from the walls). Cavern tours (daily; fee). Visitors are advised to bring adequate clothing, food and water. There are trails to the surrounding area near the visitor center. Developed & RV camping (fee). Park open all yr. 40 mi W on I-40, then 17 mi NW on Essex Rd. Contact the Ranger Office, Box 1, Essex 92332; or 1051 W Ave M, Suite 201, Lancaster 93534; phone 760/928-2586. Parking per vehicle ¢¢; Camping ¢¢¢¢; Cavern tours ¢¢

Annual Event

Colorado River Round-Up Rodeo. S to Lilly Hill Dr, Clary Dr exit at New Needles Rodeo Grounds. Apr.

Restaurant

✓★ **HUNGRY BEAR.** *1906 W Needles Hwy (92363). 760/326-2988.* Hrs: 5:30 am-10:30 pm. Closed Dec 25. Bar noon-2 am. Semi-a la carte: bkfst $3-$7, lunch $3.95-$7, dinner $4.95-$14.95. Child's meals. Specializes in steak, seafood. Own desserts. Salad bar. Route 66 motif in dining rm. Cr cds: A, C, D, JCB, MC, V.

Nevada City (C-3)

(See also Auburn, Grass Valley, Marysville, Oroville)

Settled 1849 **Pop** 2,855 **Elev** 2,525 ft **Area Code** 530 **Zip** 95959
E-mail ncchamber@oro.net **Web** www.ncgold.com

Information Chamber of Commerce, 132 Main St; 530/265-2692 or 800/655-6569 (CA & NV)

Two years after gold was discovered here, 10,000 miners were working every foot of ground within a radius of three miles. The gravel banks are said to have yielded $8 million in gold dust and nuggets in two years. Of the major gold rush towns, Nevada City remains one of the most picturesque, its residential areas dotted with multigabled frame houses. Principal occupations are lumbering, tourism, government, electronics and craft shops. The gold mines were closed in 1956.

A Ranger District office of the Tahoe National Forest is located here.

What to See and Do

Firehouse No. 1 (1861). On display are Donner Party relics, Joss House altar, Maidu artifacts and furniture, clothing and photos of early settlers. (Daily; closed Jan 1, Thanksgiving, Dec 25; also Wed in winter) 214 Main St. Phone 530/265-5468 or 530/265-5179. **Donation**

Historic Miners Foundry (1856). Group of stone, brick and frame buildings. The Pelton Wheel was originally tested and manufactured here (1878). Special events, theater and concerts are held here. 325 Spring St. Phone 530/265-5383 or 530/265-5040.

Malakoff Diggins State Historic Park. Gold mining town on 3,000 acres. Museum with hydraulic mining exhibits (Apr-Oct). Swimming; fishing. Hiking, bridle trails. Picnicking. Camping, cabins. Standard fees. 15 mi NE off CA 49 at Tyler-Foote Crossing. Phone 530/265-2740. Day use per vehicle ¢¢

National Hotel. Three stories, with balconies and balustrades reaching over the sidewalks. Victorian furnishings. Conducted a prosperous bar business during 1860s and 1870s. Still operates dining rm (see RESTAURANT) and saloon. 211 Broad St. Phone 530/265-4551.

Nevada Theatre (1865). The Foothill Theatre Company performs several productions in this historic theater. (Mar-Dec) 401 Broad St. For schedule, res contact PO Box 1812; phone 530/265-8587.

Walking tours. Booklets describing historical buildings and sites may be obtained at the Chamber of Commerce.

Annual Events

International Teddybear Convention. Phone 530/265-5804. 2nd wkend Apr.

Nevada City Classic Bicycle Tour. A 40-mi senior race and a 20-mi junior race through the city's hilly streets. Phone 530/265-2692. June.

Constitution Day Parade. Phone 530/265-2692. 2nd wkend Sept.

Seasonal Events

Fall Color Spectacular. Colorful maples, aspens, fruit trees, poplars, firs, cedars and pines. Phone 530/265-2692. Mid-Oct-mid-Nov.

Victorian Christmas. Street fair with costumes, crafts, music, entertainment. For details phone 530/265-2692. 3 Wed nights & 1 Sun preceding Christmas.

Inns

★★ **EMMA NEVADA HOUSE.** *528 E Broad St (95959), ¼ mi W of CA 49 on Broad St. 530/265-4415; FAX 530/265-4416; res: 800/916-3662.* E-mail emmanev@oro.net; web www.riese.com/emma.htm. 6 rms, 2 story. S, D $100-$150; each addl $20; wkends, hols (Apr-Dec: 2-day min); higher rates special events. Children over 10 yrs only. TV in some rms. Complimentary full bkfst. Restaurant nearby. Ck-out 11 am, ck-in 3-6 pm. Luggage handling. Concierge serv. Some in-rm whirlpools, fireplaces. Built in 1856; antiques. Totally nonsmoking. Cr cds: A, C, D, MC, V.

★★ **FLUMES END BED & BREAKFAST.** *317 S Pine St (95959). 530/265-9665; res: 800/991-8118.* 6 rms, 3 story. S, D $80-$140. TV in lobby; cable. Complimentary full bkfst; afternoon refreshments. Restaurant nearby. Ck-out 11 am, ck-in 2-6 pm. Balconies. Picnic tables. Victorian inn built 1861. On stream; historic water flume on property. Gold rush ambience. Totally nonsmoking. Cr cds: C, MC, V.

★★ **GRANDMERES BED & BREAKFAST INN.** *449 Broad St (95959). 530/265-4660; FAX 530/265-4411.* Web www.gvnet.com/~histinns/grand.htm. 7 rms, 4 with shower only, 3 story. S, D $100-$165; wkends, hols (Apr-Dec: 2 day min). Adults only. Complimentary full bkfst; afternoon refreshments. Restaurant nearby. Ck-out 11 am, ck-in 3-6 pm. Luggage handling. Concierge serv. Some balconies. Picnic tables. Built in 1856; country French decor; large garden. Totally nonsmoking. Cr cds: A, C, MC, V.

★★ **RED CASTLE.** *109 Prospect St (95959). 530/265-5135; res: 800/761-4766.* Web www.gv.net/~histinns/red.htm. 7 rms, 4 story. No rm phones. S, D $70-$150; higher rates wkends (2-day min). Children over 12 yrs only. Complimentary full bkfst; afternoon refreshments. Restaurant nearby. Ck-out 11 am, ck-in 2-4 pm. Balconies. Built in 1860, historic inn is fine example of domestic Gothic; restored and furnished with antiques and period pieces. Terraced gardens; fountain pool. Totally nonsmoking. Cr cds: C, MC, V.

SC

Restaurants

★★ **FRIAR TUCK'S.** *111 N Pine St (95959). 530/265-9093.* Hrs: 5-9 pm. Closed most major hols. Res accepted. Continental menu. Bar. Semi-a la carte: dinner $16-$23. Child's meals. Specialties: fondue dinners, rack of lamb, roast duck. Guitar. Street parking. Totally nonsmoking. Cr cds: A, C, DS, MC, V.

★ **KIRBY'S CREEKSIDE.** *101 Broad St (95959). 530/265-3445.* Hrs: 11:30 am-2:30 pm, 5-9:30 pm; Fri, Sat to 10 pm; Sun (brunch) 10:30 am-2:30 pm, 5-8:30 pm. Closed Jan 1, Dec 25. Res accepted. French menu. Bar 4:30 pm-midnight. A la carte entrees: lunch $6-$12, dinner $11-$25. Complete meal: dinner $33-$60. Child's meals. Specialties: veggie sampler, free range chicken, culinary adventures. Sun brunch $6-$13. Parking. Outdoor dining. On creekside. Totally nonsmoking. Cr cds: A, C, MC, V.

★★ **NATIONAL HOTEL VICTORIAN DINING ROOM.** *211 Broad St (95959). 530/265-4551.* Hrs: 7 am-2:30 pm, 5:30-9:30 pm; Sat to 3 pm; Sun brunch 7 am-3 pm. Res accepted. Continental menu. Bar 10-2 am. Semi-a la carte: bkfst, lunch $3.95-$8.95, dinner $11.95-$18.95. Sun brunch $7.25-$14.95. Child's meals. Specialty: prime rib. Own desserts. Entertainment Fri, Sat; pianist Sat, Sun in summer. Victorian decor. In historic hotel (1852). Totally nonsmoking. Cr cds: A, C, MC, V.

Newport Beach (J-4)

(See also Huntington Beach, Irvine, Laguna Beach, Long Beach)

Pop 66,643 **Elev** 25 ft **Area Code** 714 **Web** www.newportbeach.com

Information Newport Harbor Area Chamber of Commerce, 1470 Jamboree Rd, 92660; 714/729-4400

This seaside community, sometimes referred to as the American Riviera, is famous for elegant waterfront villas, smart shops and restaurants, and beautiful Pacific Coast scenery. With a six-mile-long beach and a fine harbor, it offers a variety of water activities. Vacation attractions are largely clustered around the Balboa peninsula, a six-mile finger of land running east and west. Behind it is Newport Harbor, with 12 miles of waterways and eight islands.

What to See and Do

O.C. Museum of Arts. Permanent and changing exhibits of modern and contemporary art, with an emphasis on California art since the second World War. Bookshop; Sculpture Garden Cafe (Mon-Fri). Museum (daily exc Mon; closed hols). 850 San Clemente Dr. Phone 714/759-1122. ¢¢

Sherman Library & Gardens. Botanical gardens set amidst fountains and sculpture. Historical library has a research center for the study of Pacific Southwest. (Daily; closed Jan 1, Thanksgiving, Dec 25) 5 mi S via Pacific Coast Hwy, Dahlia Ave exit to 2647 E Coast Hwy in Corona del Mar. Phone 714/673-2261. ¢

Annual Events

Newport SeaFest. Mid-Sept.

Christmas Boat Parade. Newport Beach Harbor. Late Dec.

Motel

✓★★ **BEST WESTERN BAY SHORES INN.** *1800 W Balboa Blvd (92663). 949/675-3463; FAX 949/675-4977; res: 800/222-6675.* 21 rms. Mid-June-early Sept: S, D $159-$219; each addl $10; suite $369-$389; under 10 free; lower rates rest of yr. Crib free. TV; VCR (free movies). Complimentary continental bkfst. Restaurant nearby. Ck-out 11 am. Business servs avail. In-rm modem link. Sun deck. Some ocean, bay views. Cr cds: A, C, D, DS, MC, V.

SC

Hotels

★★★★ **FOUR SEASONS NEWPORT BEACH.** *690 Newport Center Dr (92660). 949/759-0808; FAX 949/759-0568.* This luxury, high-rise hotel features a soaring marble lobby and elegant guest rooms, many with views of the harbor and ocean. A lively weekend bar scene keeps the restaurant hopping. 285 rms, 96 suites, 20 story. S, $375-$415; each addl $30; suites $485-$3,300; under 18 free; wkend rates; Pet accepted, some restrictions. Valet parking $14.50/day. TV; cable (premium), VCR avail (movies), Nintendo. Outdoor heated Pool, whirlpool, poolside serv. Restaurants 6:30 am-10 pm (see PAVILION and Gardens Lounge & Cafe). Rm serv 24 hrs. Bar 11-1 am; nightly entertainment. Ck-out noon. Ck-in 3 pm. Complimentary coffee in lobby. Conference facilities. Meeting rms. Business center. In-rm modem link. Fax machine avail. Concierge. Gift shop. Beauty shop. Airport transportation to John Wayne Orange County Airport. 2 lighted tennis courts, pro avail. Golf privileges. Bicycles. Fitness center, spa, sauna. Massage. Bathrm phones. Minibars. Microwaves in suites. Balconies. Ocean front views avail. Cr cds: A, C, D, ER, JCB, MC, V.

D SC

★★★ **MARRIOTT HOTEL & TENNIS CLUB.** *900 Newport Center Dr (92660), at Fashion Island. 949/640-4000; FAX 949/640-5055; res: 800/228-9290.* Web www.marriott.com. 578 rms, 16 story. S, D $139-$180; 1-2-bedrm suites $350-$750; under 12 free; wkend, tennis package plans. Crib free. Pet accepted. TV; cable (premium). 2 heated pools; whirlpool, poolside serv. Restaurant 6:30 am-10 pm. Bar 4 pm-2 am. Ck-out noon. Coin Indry. Convention facilities. Business center. In-rm modem link. Gift shop. Valet parking. Free airport transportation. 8 lighted tennis courts, pro, tennis club. Exercise rm. Health club privileges. Refrigerators avail. Private patios, balconies. Beautiful landscaping. Shopping center opp. Luxury level. Cr cds: A, C, D, DS, JCB, MC, V.

D SC

★★★ **MARRIOTT SUITES.** *500 Bayview Cir (92660), off Jamboree Rd. 949/854-4500; FAX 949/854-3937; res: 800/228-9290.* Web www.marriott.com. 250 suites, 9 story. S, D $115-$189; wkend rates mid-Sept-mid-May. Crib free. Pet accepted. TV; cable (premium). Pool; whirlpool, poolside serv. Coffee in rms. Restaurant 6:30 am-10 pm. Bar 6 am-11 pm. Ck-out noon. Meeting rms. Business servs avail. In-rm modem link. Free airport transportation. Exercise equipt; sauna. Refrigerators; microwaves avail. Private balconies. Cr cds: A, C, D, DS, JCB, MC, V.

D SC

✓★★ **SHERATON NEWPORT BEACH HOTEL.** *4545 Macarthur Blvd (92660). 949/833-0570; FAX 949/833-3927; res: 800/325-3535.* Web web163b.bbnplanet.com/sheraton/html/property/hotelsandresorts/857.html. 334 rms, 7 & 10 story. S, D $129-$139; suites $350-$400; under 18 free. Crib free. TV; cable (premium). Heated pool; whirlpool, poolside serv. Restaurant 6:30 am-10 pm. Bar 5 pm-midnight; Fri, Sat to 2 am. Ck-out 1 pm. Convention facilities. Business servs avail. In-rm modem. Gift shop. Free airport transportation. 2 lighted tennis courts. Health club privileges. Balconies. Luxury level. Cr cds: A, C, D, DS, JCB, MC, V.

D SC

★★★ **THE SUTTON PLACE HOTEL.** *4500 Macarthur Blvd (92660). 949/476-2001; FAX 949/476-0153; res: 800/810-6888.* E-mail res@npb.suttonplace.com; web www.travelweb.com/sutton.html. 435 rms, 10 story. S, D $190-$250; each addl $25; suites $310-$875; under 16 free; wkend rates. TV; cable (premium), VCR avail (movies). Pool; whirlpool, poolside serv. Restaurant 6:30 am-10:30 pm. Rm serv 24 hrs. Bars 4 pm-2 am; entertainment. Ck-out noon. Meeting rms. Business center. In-rm modem link. Concierge. Gift shop. Free airport transportation. Lighted tennis, pro. Exercise equipt; sauna. Massage. Health club privileges. Bathrm phones, minibars. Some balconies. European decor. Luxury level. Cr cds: A, C, D, DS, ER, JCB, MC, V.

D

Resort

★★★ **HYATT NEWPORTER.** *1107 Jamboree Rd (92660). 714/729-1234; FAX 714/644-1552; res: 800/233-1234.* E-mail kathy@hyatt newporter; web www.hyattnewporter.com. 410 rms, 2 & 3 story, four 3-bedrm villas. S, D $179-$234; each addl $25; suites $250-$400; villas for 1-6 $750-$900; under 18 free. Crib free. Pet accepted, some restrictions. TV; cable (premium). 3 pools, 1 heated; whirlpools, poolside serv. Dining rm 6 am-10:30 pm. Rm serv 24 hrs. Bar 11-2 am; entertainment. Ck-out noon, ck-in 4 pm. Convention facilities. Business center. In-rm modem link. Valet serv. Concierge. Gift shop. Barber, beauty shop. Free airport transportation. Lighted tennis privileges, pro. 18-hole golf privileges, 9-hole golf. Exercise equipt. Health club privileges. Bicycle rentals. Lawn games. Wet bar in suites. Villas have fireplaces, private pool. Private patios, balconies. 26 acres, beautiful landscaping, lush gardens, overlooking bay and harbor. Ocean 1 mi. Cr cds: A, C, D, DS, MC, V.

D SC

Inns

★★★ **DORYMAN'S OCEANFRONT INN.** *2102 W Ocean Front (92663), at foot of Newport Pier. 949/675-7300; FAX 949/675-7300; res: 800/634-3303.* 10 rms, 4 suites. S, D $160-$180; suites $220-$300. TV; cable, VCR avail. Complimentary continental bkfst. Complimentary coffee in rms. Ck-out noon, ck-in 3 pm. Business servs avail. In-rm modem link. Fireplaces; microwaves avail. French and American antiques; sitting rm; sun deck. On ocean with pier opp. Cr cds: A, C, MC, V.

SC

★★ **PORTOFINO BEACH HOTEL.** *2306 W Ocean Front (92663), 2 blks N of Newport Pier. 949/673-7030; FAX 949/723-4370; res: 800/571-8749.* E-mail portofino@newportbch.com. 15 rms, 5 villas, 2 story, 3 suites. D $125-$175; suites $250-$275; under 16 free. TV. Complimentary continental bkfst. Dining rm 5:30-11 pm. Rm serv from 6 pm. Ck-out noon, ck-in 3 pm. Business servs avail. Some fireplaces. Restored oceanfront hotel; library/sitting rm; many antiques. Cr cds: A, C, D, DS, MC, V.

Restaurants

★★★ **21 OCEANFRONT.** *2100 W Oceanfront (92663), at pier. 949/673-2100.* Hrs: 5:30-10 pm; Fri, Sat to 11 pm. Closed major hols. Res accepted. Bar from 4 pm. Wine list. A la carte entrees: dinner $22-$60. Specializes in seafood, pasta, prime meats. Valet parking. Elegant dining overlooking ocean and pier. Jacket. Totally nonsmoking. Cr cds: A, C, D, DS, MC, V.

✓★★ **AMELIA'S SEAFOOD & ITALIAN.** *311 Marine Ave (92662), take Jamboree across bridge to island. 949/673-6580.* Hrs: 11:30 am-2:30 pm, 5-10 pm; Sun brunch 10 am-3:30 pm. Closed some major hols. Res accepted. Italian, seafood menu. Wine, beer. Semi-a la carte: lunch $5-$9, dinner $9-$18. Sun brunch $4-$9. Specialties: crab-stuffed abalone, baby calamari with fresh bay scallops. Wood-beamed ceilings; antique mirrors. One of the original restaurants in Orange County. Cr cds: A, C, D, DS, JCB, MC, V.

D

✓★★ **BISTRO 201.** *3333 W Coast Hwy (92663). 714/631-1551.* Hrs: 11:30 am-10 pm; Fri to 11 pm; Sat 5-11 pm; Sun from 5 pm; Sun brunch 10:30 am-3 pm. Closed Jan 1, Labor Day. Res accepted. Bar. Semi-a la carte: lunch $8.95-$18, dinner $11.95-$23.95. Child's meals. Specialties: rack of lamb, roasted sea bass, grilled duck. Flemenco Thurs-Sat; Caribbean music Sun brunch. Outdoor dining. On marina. Totally nonsmoking. Cr cds: A, C, D, JCB, MC, V.

D

★★ **CANNERY RESTAURANT.** *3010 Lafayette (92663). 949/675-5777.* E-mail cannery@newportbeach.com; web www.newport beach.com/cannery. Hrs: 11:30 am-3 pm, 5-10 pm; Sun brunch 10 am-2:30 pm. Closed Thanksgiving, Dec 25. Res accepted. Bar to 2 am. Semi-a la carte: lunch $6.95-$12.95, dinner $17-$23. Sun brunch $9.25-$12.50. Child's meals. Specializes in steak, abalone, fresh fish of the day. Seafood bar. Entertainment. Valet parking. Outdoor dining. Converted cannery (1934). View of harbor, fishing boats. Brunch, dinner cruises avail. Cr cds: A, C, D, DS, JCB, MC, V.

D

★★ **CHIMAYO GRILL.** *327 Newport Center Dr (92660). 714/640-2700.* Hrs: 11:30 am-10 pm; Fri, Sat to 11 pm. Closed Thanksgiving, Dec 25. Southwestern menu. Bar. A la carte entrees: lunch $4.45-$15.45, dinner $5-$21. Child's meals. Specializes in beef, chicken. Outdoor dining. Several fireplaces, original artwork. Totally nonsmoking. Cr cds: A, C, D, DS, JCB, MC, V.

D

★★ **EL TORITO GRILL.** *951 Newport Center Dr (92660). 714/640-2875.* Web www.eltoritogrill.com. Hrs: 11 am-10 pm; Fri, Sat to 11 pm; Sun brunch 10 am-2:30 pm. Closed Thanksgiving, Dec 25. Res accepted. Southwestern menu. Bar to midnight. Semi-a la carte: lunch $6.95-$10.95, dinner $7.95-$15.95. Sun brunch $11.95. Child's meals. Specializes in tortillas, mesquite-grilled items. Valet parking. Outdoor dining. Southwestern atmosphere. Cr cds: A, C, D, DS, MC, V.

D

★★ **KOTO JAPANESE RESTAURANT.** *4300 Von Karman Ave (92660). 714/752-7151.* Hrs: 11:30 am-2:30 pm, 5:30-10:30 pm; Fri to 11 pm; Sat 5:30-11 pm; Sun brunch 11 am-2:30 pm. Closed July 4, Thanksgiving, Dec 25. Res accepted. Japanese menu. Bar. A la carte entrees: lunch $12-$15, dinner $15-$25. Complete meals: lunch $38, dinner $26-$50. Sun brunch $18.95. Specializes in sushi. Japanese tea house overlooking lake, gardens. Totally nonsmoking. Cr cds: A, C, D, DS, JCB, MC, V.

D

✓★★ **NEWPORT BEACH BREWING CO.** *2920 Newport Blvd (92663). 714/675-8449.* Web www.nbbcmicrobrew.com. Hrs: 11:30 am-11:30 pm; Fri to 1 am; Sat 9:30-1 am; Sun 9:30 am-11:30 pm. Closed Thanksgiving, Dec 25. Bar. Semi-a la carte: bkfst $2.99-$9.99, lunch $3.95-$9.95, dinner $5.85-$12.99. Child's meals. Specializes in salads, wood-fired oven pizzas. Brewery in historic Cannery Village. Cr cds: A, C, D, DS, MC, V.

D

★★★ **PASCAL FRENCH PROVENCAL.** *1000 N Bristol St (92660). 949/752-0107.* Hrs: 11:30 am-2:30 pm, 6-9:30 pm; Fri to 10 pm; Sat 6-10 pm; Mon to 2:30 pm. Closed Sun; most major hols. Res accepted. French Provençal menu. Bar. Wine cellar. A la carte entrees: lunch $7-$14, dinner $11-$25. Prix fixe: dinner $46. Specialties: Chilean sea bass, New York steak, mustard rabbit. Outdoor dining. Cr cds: A, C, D, MC, V.

D

★★★★ **PAVILION.** *(See Four Seasons Hotel) 949/760-4920.* Web www.fshr.com. The sophisticated decor of the elegant, formal dining room of the Four Seasons Hotel is matched by the interpretive Mediterranean cooking. Fine service and an excellent wine list complete the experience. California cuisine with Mediterranean accent. Specializes in fish, lamb, grilled veal chop. Housemade pastries and bread. Hrs: 6:30 am-2:30 pm, 6-10:30 pm. Res accepted. Bar 11:30-2 am. A la carte entrees: bkfst $12-$19.75, lunch $9.75-$15.95, dinner $24.95-$28.50. Prix fixe: dinner $32.50-$39.50. Valet parking. Outdoor dining. Overlooks garden. Cr cds: A, C, D, DS, ER, JCB, MC, V.

D ♥

✓★★ **PF CHANG'S CHINA BISTRO.** *1145 Newport Center Dr (92660). 714/759-9007.* Hrs: 11:30 am-11 pm; Fri, Sat to midnight. Closed Thanksgiving, Dec 25. Chinese menu. Bar. A la carte entrees: lunch $6.95-$12.95, dinner $8.95-$14.95. Specialties: spicy chicken, orange peel chicken, dan dan noodles. View of bay. Totally nonsmoking. Cr cds: A, C, MC, V.

D

✓★★ **ROYAL KHYBER.** *1000 Bristol St N (92660). 714/752-5200.* Hrs: 11:30 am-2 pm, 5:30-9:30 pm; Fri to 10 pm; Sat 5:30-10 pm, Sun brunch 11 am-2:30 pm. Res accepted. Indian menu. Bar. Lunch buffet $8.75. Complete meals: dinner $12-$15. Sun brunch $10.95. Specialties: moughlai, tandoori. Exotic east Indian decor, fountains. Cr cds: A, C, D, DS, MC, V.

D

★★ **SAPORI.** *1080 Bayside Dr (92660). 714/644-4220.* Hrs: 11:30 am-10 pm; Fri, Sat to 11 pm. Closed some major hols. Res accepted. Italian menu. Bar. A la carte entrees: lunch $7.50-$17.95, dinner $8.50-$22. Specializes in seafood, gourmet pizza, pasta. Outdoor dining. Cr cds: A, C, D, DS, MC, V.

D

★ **TALE OF THE WHALE.** *400 Main St (92661), at Balboa Peninsula. 949/673-4633.* Web www.taleofthewhale.com. Hrs: 7 am-11 pm; Sat, Sun brunch to 3:45 pm. Closed Dec 25. Bar 10-2 am. Semi-a la carte: bkfst, lunch $4.95-$11.95, dinner $10.95-$29.95. Sat, Sun brunch $3.95-$11.95. Specializes in seafood. Entertainment Thurs-Sun. Valet parking. In historic Balboa Pavilion (1905) overlooking bay. Cr cds: A, C, D, DS, MC, V.

D

★★★ **THE RITZ.** *880 Newport Center Dr (92660), at Fashion Island. 949/720-1800; FAX 949/720-1886.* Hrs: 11:30 am-3 pm, 6-10 pm; Fri, Sat 5:30-11 pm; Sun 5-9 pm. Res accepted. Continental menu. Bar. Wine cellar. A la carte entrees: lunch $8-$14, dinner $18-$34. Specialties: bouillabaisse, roast duck, rack of lamb. Own baking. Pianist. Valet parking. Elegant decor. Cr cds: A, C, D, MC, V.

D

★★ **TUTTO MARE.** *545 Newport Center Dr (92660), in Fashion Island Shopping Center. 714/640-6333.* E-mail specfoods@aol.com. Hrs: 11:30 am-11 pm; Fri, Sat to midnight; Sun to 10 pm; Sun brunch to 3 pm. Closed some major hols. Res accepted. Italian menu. Bar. A la carte entrees: lunch, dinner $4.95-$22.95. Sun brunch $18.95. Specializes in seafood. Guitarist Thurs, Sun brunch. Outdoor dining. Tropical atmosphere; fresh floral arrangements. Totally nonsmoking. Cr cds: A, C, D, JCB, MC, V.

D

★★★ **TWIN PALMS.** *630 Newport Center Dr (92660), in Fashion Island Shopping Center. 714/721-8288.* Hrs: 11:30 am-3 pm; Thurs-Sat to 10 pm; Sun 5-10 pm; Sun brunch 10:30 am-3 pm. Closed Dec 25. Res accepted. Continental menu. Bar to 10 pm; Thurs-Sat to 2 am. Wine list. A la carte entrees: lunch $8.95-$14.95, dinner $8.95-$25. Sun brunch $7.75-$14.95. Child's meals. Specialty: prime rib cheesesteak sandwich. Jazz; gospel Sun brunch. Valet parking. Outdoor dining. Tropical decor. Cr cds: A, C, D, DS, JCB, MC, V.

D ♥

★★★ **VILLA NOVA.** *3131 W Coast Hwy (92663). 949/642-7880.* E-mail villanovarestaurant@msn.com. Hrs: 5 pm-midnight; Fri to 1 am; Sat 4 pm-1 am; Sun 4 pm-midnight. Closed Thanksgiving, Dec 25. Res accepted. Italian menu. Bar. Wine cellar. A la carte entrees: dinner $9.95-$25. Child's meals. Specializes in veal, homemade pasta, seafood. Entertainment. Valet parking. Outdoor dining. Courtyard entry; resembles Italian villa. Original artwork; autographed celebrity photos. Cr cds: A, C, D, DS, JCB, MC, V.

D

★★ **WINDOWS ON THE BAY.** *2241 W Pacific Coast Hwy (92663). 714/722-1400.* Web www.windowsonthebay.com. Hrs: 11:30 am-2:30 pm, 5-10 pm; Fri, Sat to 11 pm; Sun brunch 10:30 am-2:30 pm. Res accepted. Semi-a la carte: lunch $7-$15, dinner $9-$22. Sun brunch $7-$15. Specializes in seafood, pasta, steaks. Valet parking. Overlooks Newport Harbor. Mediterranean decor. Cr cds: A, C, D, DS, MC, V.

D

North Hollywood (L.A.)

(B-3 see Los Angeles map)

(See also Hollywood, Los Angeles)

Elev 385 ft **Area Code** 818

This community is a neighborhood of Los Angeles, but is regarded by many as a separate entity.

Motor Hotels

★★★ **BEVERLY GARLAND'S HOLIDAY INN.** *4222 Vineland Ave (91602), US 101 Vineland Ave exit, ½ mi S. 818/980-8000; FAX 818/766-8387; res: 800/238-3759.* E-mail beverly 600@loop.com; web www.beverlygarland.com. 255 rms, 6-7 story. S, D $99-$159; each addl $10; suites $215-$395; under 18 free; wkend rates. Crib free. TV; cable (premium). Heated pool; wading pool, poolside serv. Playground. Coffee in rms. Restaurant 6 am-11 pm. Rm serv. Bar 11 am-11 pm. Ck-out noon. Convention facilities. Business servs avail. Bellhops. Valet serv. Concierge. Gift shop. Airport transportation. Lighted tennis, pro. Health club privileges. Private patios, balconies. Cr cds: A, C, D, DS, ER, JCB, MC, V.

D SC

★★ **MIKADO BEST WESTERN HOTEL.** *12600 Riverside Dr (91607), US 101 Laurel Canyon Blvd exit, N to Riverside Dr, then W. 818/763-9141; FAX 818/752-1045; res: 800/433-2339; res: 800/826-2759.* Web www.bestwestern.com. 58 rms, 2 story. S, D $89.99; suite $150; each addl $10; under 12 free. Crib free. TV; cable (premium). Pool; whirlpool. Complimentary full bkfst. Restaurant 11:30 am-2 pm, 5:30-9:30 pm; Fri, Sat 5:30-10 pm; Sun 5-9 pm. Rm serv. Bar. Ck-out 1 pm. Business servs avail. Bathrm phones; refrigerators avail. Some balconies. Cr cds: A, C, D, DS, ER, JCB, MC, V.

SC

Hotels

★★★ **HILTON & TOWERS HOTEL.** *555 Universal Ter Pkwy (91608), US 101, exit Lankershim Blvd. 818/506-2500; FAX 818/509-2031; res: 800/727-7110.* Web www.hilton.com. 469 units, 24 story. S, D $155-$215; each addl $30; suites $250-$1,395; under 18 free. Crib free. Garage parking $10, valet $14. TV; cable (premium), VCR avail. Heated pool; whirlpool, poolside serv. Coffee in rms. Restaurant 6:30 am-11 pm; pianist Fri-Sun. Rm serv 24 hrs. Bar 11-1:30 am. Ck-out noon. Convention facilities. Business servs avail. In-rm modem link. Gift shop. Exercise equipt. Bathrm phones, minibars. Some suites with vaulted, skylit ceiling panoramic view of city. Luxury level. Cr cds: A, C, D, DS, ER, JCB, MC, V

D SC

★★★ **SHERATON UNIVERSAL HOTEL.** *333 Universal Ter Pkwy (91608), US 101, exit Lankershim Blvd. 818/980-1212; FAX 818/985-4980; res: 800/325-3535.* Web www.sheraton.com. 442 rms, 20 story. S, D $190-$275; each addl $20; suites $250-$2,000; under 18 free. Crib free. Garage $14; valet parking $16. TV; cable (premium), VCR avail. Heated pool; whirlpool, poolside serv. Coffee in rms. Restaurant 6 am-10:30 pm. Bar 11-2 am. Ck-out noon. Convention facilities. Business center. In-rm modem link. Concierge. Exercise equipt. Game rm. Minibars. Some private patios, balconies. Overlooks San Fernando Valley and Hollywood Hills. Luxury level. Cr cds: A, C, D, DS, ER, JCB, MC, V.

D SC

Restaurant

✓★★ **WOLFGANG PUCK CAFE.** *1000 Universal Center Dr (91608), US 101, Lankershim Blvd exit. 818/985-9653.* Hrs: 11 am-11 pm; Fri, Sat to 11:30 pm. Wine, beer. A la carte entrees: lunch $7.95-$9.50, dinner $9.95-$18.95. Specializes in wood-burning oven pizza, rotisserie chicken. Patio dining. Ultramodern decor; kinetic wall art. Cr cds: A, C, D, MC, V.

D

Oakdale (E-3)

(See also Modesto)

Pop 11,961 **Elev** 155 ft **Area Code** 209 **Zip** 95361
E-mail bertalotto@worldnet.att.net
Web www.cwebpages.oakchamber/hom.html

Information Chamber of Commerce, 590 N Yosemite Ave; 209/847-2244

Oakdale's birth is linked to gold and the railroad. An important town along the freight lines to the Mother Lode towns, it was founded by the Stockton & Visalia Railroad Co in 1871. Beef and dairy cattle and a variety of produce support the area now, as do major industries Hershey Chocolate and Hunt-Wesson Foods.

What to See and Do

Hershey Chocolate USA. Visitors' Reception Center and 30-min factory tours. (Mon-Fri; closed major hols) No cameras. 120 S Sierra Ave, SE corner of jct CA 108 & 120. Phone 209/848-5100. **Free** Opp is

Oakdale Cowboy Museum. Pays tribute to local rodeo champions, farmers, ranchers and working cowboys. Housed in historic Depot Bldg. Tours. (Mon-Fri) 355 F St #1. Phone 209/847-7049. **Free**

Woodward Reservoir. Swimming, waterskiing; fishing, duck hunting; boating (moorings, marina). Picnicking, concession (Apr-mid-Sept). Camping, showers. (Daily) 5 mi N at 14528 26 Mile Rd. Phone 209/847-3304. Per vehicle (day use) **¢¢¢**; Camping **¢¢¢¢-¢¢¢¢¢**

Annual Events

PRCA Rodeo. 2nd wkend Apr.

Chocolate Festival. 3rd wkend May.

California Dally Team Roping Championships. Oakdale Saddle Club Rodeo grounds, CA 120. 3rd wkend Sept.

Motel

★★ **RAMADA INN.** *825 E F St (94612). 209/847-8181; FAX 209/847-9546; res: 800/272-6232.* 70 rms, 2 story. Apr-Sept: S $71-$91; D $77-$97; each addl $6; suites $126-$197; under 18 free; lower rates rest of yr. Crib free. TV; cable (premium), VCR avail (movies). Heated pool; whirlpool. Coffee in rms. Restaurant 5:30 am-11 pm. Bar 11 am-midnight. Ck-out noon. Meeting rms. Cr cds: A, C, D, DS, JCB, MC, V.

D SC

Oakhurst (E-4)

Pop 8,051 **Elev** 2,300 ft **Area Code** 209 **Zip** 93644
E-mail ysvb@sierranet.net **Web** www.yosemite-sierra.org

Information Yosemite-Sierra Visitors Bureau, 41729 CA 41; 209/683-4636Oakland (E-2)

Motels

★★ **BEST WESTERN.** *40530 Hwy 41 (93644), 1 mi N of jct CA 49, CA 41 . 559/683-2378; FAX 209/683-3813; res: 800/545-5462.* 118 rms, 2 story, 16 suites, 11 kits. Early May-mid-Oct: S, D $84-$94; each addl $6; suites $129; kit. units $5-$10 addl; wkly rates off-season; higher rates late Dec; lower rates rest of yr. Crib $2. Pet accepted. TV; cable (premium), VCR avail (movies). Indoor pool; whirlpool. Sauna. Restaurant adj 7-10:30 am, 5-9:30 pm. Bar. Ck-out 11 am. Coin lndry. Meeting rm. Some refrigerators. Balconies. Picnic table, grill. Cr cds: A, C, D, DS, ER, JCB, MC, V.

D SC

★ **COMFORT INN.** *40489 Hwy 41 (93644). 559/683-8282; FAX 559/658-7030; res: 800/228-5150.* 114 rms, 2 story. Apr-Nov: S $80; D $85; each addl $6; suites $125; kit. unit $225; under 18 free; lower rates rest of yr. Crib $5. Pet accepted, some restrictions; $6. TV; cable (premium), VCR avail (movies). Complimentary continental bkfst. Complimentary coffee in rms. Restaurant adj 11-2 am. Ck-out 11 am. Gift shop. Pool; whirlpool. Refrigerators. Cr cds: A, C, D, DS, MC, V.

D SC

★★ **SHILO INN YOSEMITE.** *40644 Hwy 41 (93644). 559/683-3555; FAX 559/683-3386; res: 800/222-2244.* 80 rms, 4 story. Apr-Sept: S, D $79-$115; each addl $10; under 13 free; lower rates rest of yr. TV; cable (premium), VCR avail. Pool; whirlpool. Complimentary continental bkfst. Coffee in rms. Restaurant adj 7 am-9 pm. Ck-out noon. Coin lndry. Exercise equipt; sauna, steam rm. Bathrm phones, refrigerators. Some patios, balconies. Cr cds: A, C, D, DS, ER, JCB, MC, V.

D SC

Inns

★★★★★ **CHATEAU DU SUREAU HOTEL.** *48688 Victoria Ln (93644), ¼ mi S of jct CA 49 & 41. 559/683-6800; FAX 559/683-0800.* E-mail chateau@sierranet.net; web www.jans-journeys.com/chateau. Like stumbling on a chateau in the French countryside, this elegant ten-room inn in the Sierra Nevada forest, four hours from San Francisco near Yosemite, is enchanting. The rooms are outfitted with genuine antiques (many have canopied beds) and the seven-acre estate is grand. Dinner in Erna's Elderberry House, prepared by proprietress Erna Kubin-Clanin, is equally exquisite. 10 rms, 2 story. S, D $325-$525 and 12% serv charge. TV in sitting rm; cable, VCR avail. Pool. Complimentary full bkfst. Complimentary coffee in rms. Restaurant (see ERNA'S ELDERBERRY HOUSE). Ck-out noon, ck-in 2 pm. Luggage handling. Concierge serv. Exercise equipt. Lawn games. Balconies. Totally nonsmoking. 2 rms also available in adjoining bldg (Villa Sureau) $2,500, w/24 hr butler service. Cr cds: A, C, MC, V.

D

★★ **HOUNDS TOOTH INN.** *42071 State Hwy 41 (93644). 209/642-6600; FAX 559/658-2946; res: 888/642-6610.* E-mail robray@sierranet.net; web www.sierranet.net/net/tooth/. 12 rms, 8 with shower only, 2 story. S, D $85-$145; each addl $20; under 12 free; hols 2-day min. TV; cable (premium). Complimentary full bkfst; refreshments. Restaurant nearby. Ck-out noon, ck-in 3-5 pm. Business servs avail. Concierge serv. X-country ski 10 mi. Some in-rm whirlpools. Totally nonsmoking. Cr cds: A, C, DS, MC, V.

D SC

Restaurant

★★★★ **ERNA'S ELDERBERRY HOUSE.** *(See Château du Sureau) 209/683-6800.* E-mail chateau@sierranet.net. The elegant dining rooms of this charming restaurant are in tune with the splendid French chateau in which it is located. Oil paintings, tapestries and imported Provencal furnishings set the tone. The kitchen takes full advantage of fine local ingredients. An extensive wine list and polished service complete the experience. French, California menu. Menu changes daily. Menu recited. Own baking. Hrs: Wed-Sat 11:30 am-1 pm, 5:30-8:30 pm; Sun brunch 11 am-1 pm. Res accepted. Bar. Wine cellar. Complete meals: lunch $4.50-$14.50; 6-course prix fixe dinner $68/person. Sun brunch $28.50. Cr cds: A, C, MC, V.

D

Oakland (E-2)

(See also Berkeley, Hayward, San Francisco, San Francisco Airport Area, San Mateo, Sausalito)

Founded 1850 **Pop** 372,242 **Elev** 42 ft **Area Code** 510
Web www.ocva.com

Information Oakland Convention & Visitors Bureau, 475 14 St, Suite 120; 510/839-9000 or 800/262-5526

Oakland lies just across the bay from San Francisco. The port of Oakland has excellent facilities and caters to heavy Pacific trade. More than 1,500 factories help make Alameda County a leading manufacturing center. The Bay Area Rapid Transit system (BART) links suburban areas and Oakland with San Francisco. Once part of the Rancho San Antonio, 48,000-acre domain of former Spanish cavalry sergeant Luis Maria Peralta, it was acquired as a townsite by Horace W. Carpentier, who named it for the evergreen oaks that marked the landscape.

What to See and Do

Camron-Stanford House (1876). Once the home of the Camron family and later the Stanford family, this building served as the Oakland Public Museum from 1910 until 1967. Today the house operates as a resource center and museum with authentic period furnishings, sculpture and paintings. Slide program; library. Guided tours. (Wed & Sun) Free admission 1st Sun of each month. 1418 Lakeside Dr, on the shores of Lake Merritt. Phone 510/444-1876. **¢**

Dunsmuir House and Gardens (1899). A 37-rm Colonial-revival mansion; 40 acres of trees, lawns, shrubs and gardens; special events (Apr-Dec). Guided tours (Apr-Sept, Wed & Sun). 2960 Peralta Oaks Ct. Phone 510/562-0328. **¢¢**

East Bay Regional Park District. Organization maintains more than 75,000 acres in 50 parks and recreation areas in Alameda and Contra Costa counties. Facilities include swimming, fishing, archery, boating, riding, picnic grounds, campgrounds and other pastimes. Most parks are open daily. Headquarters at 2950 Peralta Oaks Court. Phone 510/635-0135 or 510/562-PARK. The park system includes

Anthony Chabot Regional Park & Lake Chabot. Park offers 4,927 acres for hiking and riding, horse rentals; marksmanship range for rifle, pistol and trapshooting; 18-hole golf course. Camping: motor home and tent camping (fee); for res phone 510/562-2267. Park entrances along Skyline Blvd, between Redwood & Golf Links Rd and along Redwood Rd E of Skyline Blvd; stables and hiking along Skyline Blvd. At Lake Chabot there are fishing and boating facilities (rentals); bicycle trails and picnic areas. Park: E & S via 35th Ave & Redwood Rd; Lake Chabot: S on I-580 to Fairmont Ave, then E to Lake Chabot Rd and left to parking area. Per vehicle **¢¢** Adj is

Martin Luther King, Jr Regional Shoreline. On 1,219 acres, near Oakland Intl Airport. Sunning beach; fishing; boating (2-lane launching ramp). Hiking trails, bird watching. Picnicking, children's playfields, beach cafe. Nature study. S on I-880 to Hegenberger exit, then NW on Doolittle Dr. **Free**

Redwood Regional Park. Redwood groves, evergreens, chaparral and grassland on 1,830 acres. Hiking; nature study. Picnicking, playfields, children's playground. Creek with native rainbow trout. E of Skyline Blvd on Redwood Rd. Per vehicle **¢¢**

★ **Jack London Square.** Colorful waterfront area where the author worked. **Heinold's First and Last Chance Saloon,** 56 Jack London Square, at the foot of Webster St, is where London spent much of his time and wrote his most famous novels. Several restaurants and the reconstructed cabin in which the author weathered the Klondike winter of 1898 reflect characters and situations from his life and books. Adj is **Jack London Village,** foot of Alice St. Shops, restaurants, marina area. (Daily) Formed by Clay, Franklin, Embarcadero and the Oakland Estuary. Phone 510/814-6000.

Joaquin Miller Park. Site of the "Hights," former house of Joaquin Miller, "Poet of the Sierras." Four monuments erected by Miller to Moses, General Frémont, Robert & Elizabeth Browning and a funeral pyre for himself. Fountain and statuary from 1939 World's Fair. Park is also site of Woodminster Amphitheater, scene of Woodminster Summer Musicals (see SEASONAL EVENT). Hiking and picnic areas. (Daily) Joaquin Miller Rd. Phone 510/238-3187. **Free**

Kaiser Center. This complex was founded by industrialist Henry J. Kaiser and remains the home of Kaiser Aluminum & Chemical Corporation. The Kaiser Bldg is of aluminum and glass construction. Changing art exhibits on mezzanine; remarkable 3½-acre rooftop garden with trees, shrubs, flowers, pool and fountains. Cafeterias, restaurants. (Mon-Fri; closed major hols) 300 Lakeside Dr. Phone 510/271-6146. **Free**

Lake Merritt. In heart of downtown Oakland. Largest natural body of saltwater in the world completely within any city (155 acres), surrounded by drives and handsome buildings. Boat rentals (daily; fee), sightseeing launch (wkends, some hols). Sailing lessons, day camps. Special events include sailing regattas. 568 Bellevue. Phone 510/444-3807. Per vehicle (wkends) **¢** Adj lake is

Children's Fairyland. Everything child-size, with tiny buildings depicting fairyland tales. Many contain live animals and birds. Carousel, Ferris wheel, train and trolley rides, children's bumper boats and puppet theater (fee for some activities). (Summer, daily; spring & fall, Wed-Sun; winter, Sat & Sun; closed Jan 1, Thanksgiving, Dec 25) Bellevue & Grand Aves. Phone 510/452-2259. **¢¢**

Lakeside Park. Approx 120 acres. Picnic areas, free children's play area; lawn bowling, putting greens; trail and show gardens, duck-feeding area; bandstand concerts (summer, Sun & hols). Parking free (exc Feb-Oct, wkends & hols). Vehicle entrance at Bellevue & Grand Aves. Phone 510/238-3187. Also here are

Rotary Nature Center. North America's oldest wildlife refuge (1870); nature and conservation exhibits; native birds; films, illustrated lectures or walks (wkends); animal feeding area. (Daily) Phone 510/238-3739. **Free**

Trial and Show Gardens. Demonstration Gardens; includes cactus, fuchsia, dahlia, chrysanthemum, Polynesian, palm, herb and Japanese gardens. (Daily; closed Jan 1, Thanksgiving, Dec 25) 666 Bellevue Ave. **Free**

Northern California Center for Afro-American History and Life. Artifacts, photographs, exhibit and archive on black history in the US, with emphasis on California. (Tues-Sat; closed major hols) 5606 San Pablo Ave. **Free**

Oakland Museum of California. Galleries, gardens cover 4 city blocks; exhibits on natural science, history and art interpret land and people of California. Great Hall exhibits. (Wed-Sun; closed major hols) 1000 Oak St, near Lake Merritt. Phone 510/238-2200. For tour information phone 510/238-3514. **¢¢**

Oakland Zoo in Knowland Park. Situated on 525 acres, the zoo houses 330 native and exotic animals, a children's petting zoo and "Simba Pori," a 1½-acre habitat with a pride of 6 lions, and Siamang Island. Also here are children's rides and picnic areas. Free parking 1st Mon of each month exc hols. (Daily; closed Thanksgiving, Dec 25) 9777 Golf Links Rd. Phone 510/632-9523. **¢¢**

Paramount Theatre. Impressive, restored 1931 art-deco movie palace, home of Oakland Ballet. Hosts organ pops series and a variety of musical performances. 90-min tours start from Box Office (1st & 3rd Sat of each month; no tours hols). 2025 Broadway. Phone 510/465-6400 (box office, event information, tours). Tours **¢**

Professional Sports.

American League baseball (Oakland Athletics). Oakland Coliseum, 7000 Coliseum Way. Phone 510/638-4900.

NBA (Golden State Warriors). Oakland Coliseum, 7000 Coliseum Way. Phone 510/986-2200.

NFL (Oakland Raiders). Oakland Coliseum, 7000 Coliseum Way. Phone 510/864-5000.

Skyline Blvd. On top of Berkeley-Oakland Hills; superb views of entire East Bay area.

The Oakland Museum Sculpture Court at City Center. One-person exhibitions by contemporary California sculptors are mounted quarterly. (Daily; closed hols) 1111 Broadway, at 12th St. Phone 510/238-3401. **Free**

USS *Potomac*. Originally built in 1934 as the Coast Guard cutter *Electra*, this was Franklin D. Roosevelt's beloved "Floating White House." The fully restored, 165-ft steel vessel is now owned and operated as a floating museum by the Potomac Association; it is a National Historic Landmark. Dockside tours (Apr-Oct, Wed-Sun; groups by appt only). Narrated 90-min educational cruises around Treasure Island & San Francisco Bay (Apr-Oct, 2 departures 2nd Thurs & 4th Sun of each month). Expanded 3-hr educational cruises with gourmet lunch (Apr-Oct, 1 departure, 3rd Sat every month exc Sept). Res required for cruises. Franklin D. Roosevelt Pier, Jack London Sq. Phone 510/839-7533, ext 1. Tour ¢¢; Cruises ¢¢¢¢¢

Seasonal Event

Woodminster Summer Musicals. Joaquin Miller Park. For information phone 510/531-9597. June-Sept.

Motels

★★ **BEST WESTERN INN AT THE SQUARE.** *233 Broadway (94607), at 3rd St. 510/452-4565; FAX 510/452-4634; res: 800/528-1234.* Web www.hotelswest.com. 102 rms, 50 with shower only, 2-3 story, no ground floor rms. S, D $95-$129; each addl $10; under 12 free. Crib free. TV; cable (premium). Heated pool. Complimentary continental bkfst. Restaurant nearby. Ck-out noon. Business servs avail. In-rm modem link. Exercise equipt; saunas. Health club privileges. Garage. Refrigerators avail. Some balconies. Cr cds: A, C, D, DS, JCB, MC, V.

D SC

✓★ **CORAL REEF MOTEL & SUITES.** *400 Park St (94501), I-880 exit 23rd Ave. 510/521-2330; FAX 510/521-4707; res: 800/533-2330.* E-mail coral@ix.netcom.com; web www.alamedaca.com. 93 kit units, 1-2 story. S $81; D $88; each addl $7; suites $89-$96; under 6 free; wkly, monthly rates. Crib free. TV; cable. Heated pool. Complimentary continental bkfst. Restaurant opp. Ck-out 11 am. Coin Indry. Business servs avail. Balconies. Cr cds: A, C, D, DS, MC, V.

★★ **HAMPTON INN.** *8465 Enterprise Way (94621), near Intl Airport. 510/632-8900; FAX 510/632-4713; res: 877/547-7667.* 152 rms, 3 story. S, D $89-$99; under 18 free. Crib free. TV; cable (premium). Heated pool; whirlpool. Complimentary continental bkfst. Restaurant nearby. Business servs avail. In-rm modem link. Valet serv. Sundries. Free airport transportation. Health club privileges. Refrigerators avail. Cr cds: A, C, D, DS, MC, V.

D SC

★★ **MARINA VILLAGE INN.** *1151 Pacific Marina (94501), I-880 Webster Tube exit to Alameda. 510/523-9450; FAX 510/523-6315; res: 800/345-0304.* 51 rms, 2 story. S $83-$123; D $91-$133; each addl $8; under 12 free; wkend rates. Crib free. TV; cable (premium). Heated pool. Complimentary continental bkfst. Complimentary coffee in rms. Restaurant adj 11 am-9:30 pm. Ck-out noon. Business servs avail. In-rm modem link. Sundries. Valet serv. Refrigerators; microwaves avail. Balconies. On waterfront; berthing avail. Cr cds: A, C, D, DS, MC, V.

D SC

Motor Hotels

★★★ **HILTON HOTEL.** *1 Hegenberger Rd (94621), 5 mi SW, I-880 Hegenberger-Coliseum exit, at Intl Airport. 510/635-5000; FAX 510/729-0491; res: 800/ HILTONS.* 363 rms, 3 story. S $129-$149; D $149-$169; each addl $20; suites $350-$500; wkend rates. Crib free. TV; cable (premium), VCR avail. Heated pool; poolside serv. Coffee in rms. Restaurants 6 am-10 pm. Rm serv. Bar 10:30-2 am; entertainment. Ck-out noon. Meeting rms. Business center. In-rm modem link. Bellhops. Gift shop. Free airport transportation. Exercise equipt. Some bathrm phones; refrigerators avail. Private patios. Cr cds: A, C, D, DS, ER, JCB, MC, V.

D SC

★ **HOLIDAY INN.** *500 Hegenberger Rd (94621). 510/562-5311; FAX 510/636-1539; res: 800/465-4329.* E-mail hioakair@msn.com. 293 rms, 2-6 story. S, D $169; each addl $10; suite $199-$249; under 18 free. Crib free. TV; cable (premium), VCR avail. Pool. Restaurant 6 am-1:30 pm, 5-10 pm. Bar 4 pm-midnight. Ck-out noon. Coin Indry. Meeting rms. Business servs avail. In-rm modem link. Bellhops. Sundries. Gift shop. Airport transportation. Exercise equipt. Cr cds: A, C, D, DS, JCB, MC, V.

D SC

Hotels

★★ **CLARION SUITES.** *1800 Madison St (94612), at Lakeside Dr. 510/832-2300; FAX 510/832-7150.* 50 units, 6 story, 41 suites. S, D $109; each addl $10; suites $149-$179; under 17 free. Valet parking $9. Pet accepted; $150. TV; cable, VCR avail. Complimentary continental bkfst. Complimentary coffee in rms. Restaurant 11 am-10 pm; Sat, Sun by res. Bar. Ck-out 11 am. Meeting rms. Business servs avail. In-rm modem link. Concierge. Health club privileges. Refrigerators, microwaves. Restored Mediterranean/art deco landmark (1927) offers views of Lake Merritt. Cr cds: A, C, D, DS, MC, V.

SC

★★★ **MARRIOTT.** *1001 Broadway (94607). 510/451-4000; FAX 510/835-3466.* 479 rms, 21 story. S, D $178; each addl $20; suites $325-$750; wkend plans. Crib free. TV; cable. Heated pool; whirlpool. Restaurants 6:30 am-10:30 pm. Bar 4:30 pm-1 am. Convention facilities. Business servs avail. In-rm modem link. Concierge. Gift shop. Exercise equipt. Health club privileges. Refrigerator in suites. Cr cds: A, C, D, DS, ER, JCB, MC, V.

D SC

★ **WASHINGTON INN.** *495 10th St (94607), opp Oakland Convention Center. 510/452-1776; FAX 510/452-4436.* Web www.thewashingtoninn.com. 47 units, 4 story, 8 suites. S, D $119; suites $159-$179. Valet parking $17. TV; cable. Complimentary bkfst. Restaurant 7 am-9:30 pm. Bar 11 am-11 pm; closed Sun. Ck-out noon. Meeting rm. Business servs avail. In-rm modem link. Health club privileges. Wet bars. Renovated 1913 hotel with turn-of-the-century bar. Cr cds: A, C, D, DS, JCB, MC, V.

D SC

★★★ **WATERFRONT PLAZA HOTEL.** *10 Washington St (94607), at Jack London's Waterfront. 510/836-3800; FAX 510/832-5695; res: 800/729-3638.* E-mail wfp@ix.netcom.com; web www.waterfrontplaza.com. 144 rms, 5 story, 27 suites. S, D $175-$195; suites $250-$325; under 16 free; wkend packages. Crib free. Valet parking, in/out $10. TV; cable (premium), VCR. Heated pool. Coffee in rms. Restaurant (see JACK'S BISTRO). Rm serv 6:30 am-midnight. Bar 10-2 am. Ck-out noon. Meeting rms. Business center. In-rm modem link. Concierge. Exercise equipt; sauna. Bathrm phones, minibars; some fireplaces. Balconies. Many rms with view of San Francisco skyline. 2 boat slips avail. Cr cds: A, C, D, DS, JCB, MC, V.

D SC

Inn

★★ **GARRATT MANSION.** *900 Union St (94501), E on US 880, S on 23rd St (Park St). 510/521-4779; FAX 510/521-6796.* E-mail garratt@packbell.net. 7 air-cooled rms, 2 share baths, 3 story. No elvtr. Some rm phones. S, D $80-$130; each addl $10-$15; suite $130. Complimentary full bkfst; afternoon refreshments. Restaurant nearby. Ck-out 11 am, ck-in 3 pm. Concierge. Game rm. Microwaves avail. Built in 1893; antiques, stained-glass windows. Totally nonsmoking. Cr cds: A, C, D, MC, V.

Restaurants

★★ **BAY WOLF.** *3853 Piedmont Ave (94611). 510/655-6004.* Hrs: 11:30 am-2 pm, 6-9 pm; Sat, Sun from 5:30 pm. Closed most major hols. Res accepted. No A/C. Mediterranean menu. Bar. A la carte entrees: lunch $9-$13, dinner $14-$18. Specializes in duck, regional dishes. Street parking. Outdoor dining. Contemporary decor with several dining areas, including front porch. Family-owned. Totally nonsmoking. Cr cds: A, C, MC, V.

★★★ **CHEF PAUL'S.** *4179 Piedmont Ave (94611). 510/547-2175.* Hrs: 5 pm-midnight. Closed Mon. Res accepted. Eclectic French-Swiss menu. Wine list. A la carte entrees: dinner $8-$14. Complete meal: dinner $29-$36. Specializes in seafood, tasting menu, vegetarian menu. Outdoor dining. Elegant atmosphere. Chef-owned. Cr cds: A, C, DS, MC, V.

D

✓★ **EL TORITO.** *67 Jack London Square (94607). 510/835-9260.* Hrs: 11 am-11 pm; Fri & Sat to midnight; Sun 9:30 am-10 pm; Sun brunch to 2 pm. Closed Thanksgiving, Dec 25. Res accepted. Mexican menu. Bar 11 am-11:30 pm, Sun 10 am-midnight. Semi-a la carte: lunch $6-$9, dinner $7-$13. Sun brunch $10.99. Child's meals. Specializes in tacos, fajitas, chili rellenos. Outdoor dining. Spanish decor. Cr cds: A, C, D, DS, MC, V.

D

★★ **IL PESCATORE.** *57 Jack London Square (94607). 510/465-2188.* Web www.pescatore.com. Hrs: 11:30 am-10 pm; Sat from 11 am; Sun 3-9 pm, Sun brunch 10:30 am-3 pm. Closed Jan 1, Thanksgiving, Dec 25. Res accepted. Italian menu. Bar. Semi-a la carte: lunch $10.25-$14, dinner $10.25-$22. Sat & Sun brunch $10-$17. Specializes in pasta, seafood. Outdoor dining. On waterfront. Cr cds: A, C, D, MC, V.

D

✓★★ **JACK'S WATERFRONT RESTAURANT.** *(See Waterfront Plaza) 510/444-7171.* E-mail wfp@ix.netcom.com; web www.waterfrontplaza.com. Hrs: 6:30 am-10 pm; Sun brunch 7 am-2:30 pm. Res accepted. Mediterranean menu. Bar 10-2 am. Semi a-la carte: bkfst, lunch, dinner $8.25-$19.95. Sun brunch $6.50-$12.75. Specializes in pasta, pizza, rotisserie chicken. Own baking. Pianist; musicians Fri, Sat. Valet parking. Outdoor dining. Waterfront views; murals. Totally nonsmoking. Cr cds: A, C, D, DS, JCB, MC, V.

D ♥

★ **L.J. QUINN'S LIGHTHOUSE.** *51 Embarcadero Cove (94606). 510/536-2050.* Hrs: 11:30 am-2 pm, 5:30-9 pm; Fri to 10 pm; Sat 5:30-10 pm; Sun 11:30 am-3 pm, 4:30-9 pm. Closed Jan 1. Res accepted. No A/C. Bar. Semi-a la carte: lunch $5.95-$13.95, dinner $5.95-$15. Sun brunch $5.95-$11. Child's meals. Specializes in prawn dishes, pasta, steak. Parking. Outdoor dining. In historic Oakland Harbor Lighthouse (1890); nautical decor. Cr cds: C, MC, V.

D ♥

★★ **OLIVETO.** *5655 College Ave (94618). 510/547-5356.* Northen Italian menu. Menu changes daily. Specialities: Arista pork loin cooked on a spit, house-made pastas. Hrs: 11:30 am-2 pm, 5:30-10 pm; Sun 5-9 pm, Mon 5:30-9 pm. Closed most major hols. Res suggested. Bar. A la carte entrees: lunch $10-$16, dinner $16-$25. Some patio dining. Totally nonsmoking. Cr cds: A, C, D, MC, V.

D ♥

✓★ **OVERLAND HOUSE GRILL.** *101 Broadway (94607), at Jack London Square. 510/268-9222.* Hrs: 11 am-10 pm; Fri, Sat to 11 pm; Sun brunch 9:30 am-3 pm. Closed some major hols. Res accepted. Bar to midnight. Semi-a la carte: lunch $6.95-$17.75, dinner $7.50-$17.75. Sun brunch $6.25-$15. Specializes in steak, fresh pasta, sandwiches. Parking. Antiques. Family-owned. Cr cds: A, C, D, MC, V.

D

★★ **SCOTT'S SEAFOOD GRILL & BAR.** *2 Broadway, at Jack London Square. 510/444-3456.* Hrs: 11 am-10 pm; Fri, Sat to 11 pm; Sun to 9 pm; Sun brunch to 3 pm. Closed Dec 25. Res accepted. Bar. Semi-a la carte: lunch, dinner $12.95-$29. Sun brunch $12.95-$19.95. Specialties: grilled petrale sole, Norwegian salmon. Pianist. Jazz trio Sun brunch. Valet parking. Patio dining. On estuary; view of harbor, San Francisco. Cr cds: A, C, D, DS, MC, V.

D

★ **SILVER DRAGON.** *835 Webster St (94607). 510/893-3748.* Hrs: 11:30 am-9 pm. Closed Thanksgiving, Dec 25. Cantonese menu. Bar. Semi-a la carte: lunch $5-$8, dinner $12-$18. Specialties: Peking duck, stuffed crab claws, crispy-skin chicken. Cr cds: A, C, MC, V.

D

★ **SOIZIC RESTAURANT.** *300 Broadway (94607). 510/251-8100.* Hrs: 11:30 am-2:30 pm, 5:30-9 pm; Sat from 5:30. Closed Mon; some major hols. Res accepted. No A/C. Modern French menu. Bar. A la carte entrees: lunch, dinner $9.50-$15. Specializes in fresh fish, seasonal sorbets, ginger custard. Own desserts. Street parking. Bistro-style atmosphere in former warehouse bldg; eclectic art collection. Totally nonsmoking. Cr cds: C, MC, V.

D

★★★ **TRADER VIC'S.** *9 Anchor Dr (94608), 3 mi NW, ½ mi W of I-80 Powell St, Emeryville exits . 510/653-3400.* Hrs: 11:30 am-2:30 pm, 5-9:30 pm; Fri & Sat to 10:30 pm; Sun 4:30-9:30 pm. Closed some major hols. Res accepted. Bar. A la carte entrees: lunch $11-$17, dinner $15-$25. Specialties: peach blossom duck, fresh seafood, Indonesian rack of lamb. Entertainment. Valet parking. Tropical decor. Bay view. Family-owned. Cr cds: A, C, D, MC, V.

D

Oceanside (K-4)

(See also Carlsbad, Escondido, San Clemente)

Pop 128,398 **Elev** 47 ft **Area Code** 760
E-mail info@oceanside chamber.com **Web** www.oceansidechamber.com
Information Chamber of Commerce, Visitor Information Center, 928 N Coast Hwy, 92054; 760/721-1101

Camp Pendleton, a US Marine base, borders this city on the north. I-5 goes through the camp property for about 18 miles.

What to See and Do

Antique Gas & Steam Engine Museum. Agricultural museum on 40 acres of rolling farmland, featuring early farming equipment, steam and gas engines. Special shows 3rd & 4th wkends in June & Oct (fee). (Daily; closed Dec 25) 2040 N Santa Fe Ave. 7 mi E via Oceanside Blvd, in Vista. Phone 760/941-1791. **Free**

California Surf Museum. Learn about the sport and lifestyle of the surfer through various exhibits and presentations. Tours (by appt). (Thurs-Mon; closed major hols) 223 N Coast Hwy. Phone 760/721-6876. **Free**

Mission San Luis Rey de Francia (1798). Founded by Father Lasuén, it was named for Louis IX, crusader and ruler of France from 1226 to 1270. It was 18th of the chain. "King of Missions," largest of the 21 early California missions, it has a large collection of Spanish vestments, cloister gardens, Native American cemetery, first pepper tree (1830) and other historic artifacts. Picnicking. Self-guided tours. Museum (daily; closed Jan 1, Thanksgiving, Dec 25). 4050 Mission Ave. 4½ mi E on CA 76 in San Luis Rey. Phone 760/757-3651. **¢¢**

Oceanside Harbor and Marina. Mecca for sportfishing, whale watching, boating and other water-oriented activities. Marina has slips ranging in length from 25 to 51 ft. Transient moorings and limited RV beach camping avail. Seaport Village offers restaurants and gift shops. 1540 Harbor Dr N. Phone 760/966-4580.

Motels

★★ **BEST WESTERN INN.** *1680 Oceanside Blvd (92054). 760/722-1821; FAX 760/967-8969; res: 800/443-9995.* E-mail osideinn@aol.com. 80 rms, 2 story. S, D $79-$99; each addl $10; suites $99-$119. Crib free. TV; cable (premium), VCR avail (movies). Heated pool; whirlpool. Complimentary continental bkfst. Complimentary coffee in rms. Ck-out noon. Guest lndry. Meeting rms. Business servs avail. Valet serv. Sundries. Exercise equipt; saunas. Some bathrm phones; refrigerator in suites. Private patios, balconies. Cr cds: A, C, D, DS, JCB, MC, V.

SC

✓★★ **BEST WESTERN MARTY'S VALLEY INN.** *3240 Mission Ave (92054). 760/757-7700; FAX 760/439-3311; res: 800/528-1234; res: 800/747-3529.* E-mail bwmartys@inetworld.net; web www.bwmartys.com. 111 rms, 2 story. June-mid-Sept: S, D $69-$99; each addl $5; suite $125; under 12 free; lower rates rest of yr. Crib $7. TV; cable (premium). Pool. Complimentary continental bkfst. Restaurant adj 11 am-11 pm. Bar to 2 am. Ck-out noon. Meeting rms. Business servs avail. In-rm modem link. Refrigerators, microwaves avail. Cr cds: A, C, D, DS, JCB, MC, V.

D SC

✓★ **DAYS INN.** *3170 Vista Way (92056). 760/757-2200; FAX 760/757-2389; res: 800/458-6064.* 44 rms, 2 story. S, D $69-$79; each addl $5; wkly rates. Crib $5. TV; cable (premium). Heated pool. Complimentary continental bkfst. Ck-out 11 am. Tennis. 18-hole golf, greens fee $72, pro. Refrigerators, microwaves avail. Private patios, balconies. Cr cds: A, C, D, DS, JCB, MC, V.

SC

Restaurant

✓★ **LA PALOMA.** *116 Escondido Ave (92084), 5 mi E on Rte 78, exit Escondido Ave . 760/758-7140.* Hrs: 11 am-10 pm; Sat, Sun from 1 pm; early-bird dinner Sun-Thurs 4-7 pm. Closed Jan 1, Dec 25. Res accepted. Mexican menu. Bar. Semi-a la carte: lunch $5.95-$9, dinner $7.95-$18.95. Specializes in innovative gourmet Mexican cuisine. Parking. Outdoor dining. Intimate atmosphere and dining. Cr cds: A, C, DS, MC, V.

D

Ojai (H-3)

(See also Oxnard, Santa Barbara, Ventura)

Pop 7,613 **Elev** 746 ft **Area Code** 805 **Zip** 93023
E-mail the-ojai@jetlink.net **Web** www.the-ojai.org/

Information Ojai Valley Chamber of Commerce & Visitors Center, 150 W Ojai Ave, PO Box 1134, 93024; 805/646-8126

The Ojai Valley was first farmed by citrus and cattle ranchers after the Civil War. In the 1870s, publicity in Eastern newspapers initiated its popularity as a tourist haven and winter resort. Attracted by its quiet, rural beauty and proximity to urban centers, many artists, writers and other creative people make their home in the Ojai Valley.

A Ranger District office of the Los Padres National Forest (see SANTA BARBARA) is located here.

What to See and Do

Lake Casitas Recreation Area. Fishing; boating (rentals, trailer rentals). Picnicking, concession. Camping (fee; for res phone 805/649-1122; hookups); trailer storage (fee). Pets on leash only (fee); no firearms. Nearby are beaches, golf courses and tennis courts. (Daily) 5 mi W on CA 150. Contact 11311 Santa Ana Rd, Ventura 93001; 805/649-2233.

Ojai Center for the Arts. Rotating exhibitions of local artists; live theater productions. (Daily exc Mon) 113 S Montgomery. Phone 805/646-0117.

Ojai Valley Museum. Permanent & changing exhibits explore environmental, cultural and historical factors that shaped the Ojai Valley; research library. (Wed-Mon afternoons; closed Jan 1, July 4, Thanksgiving, Dec 25) 130 W Ojai Ave. Phone 805/640-1390. **Free**

Annual Events

Tennis Tournament. Libbey Park. Oldest amateur tennis tournament in the same location in the US (since 1895). Phone 805/646-7241. Late Apr.

Ojai Festivals. Libbey Park. Outdoor concerts. Phone 805/646-2094. Wkend after Memorial Day.

Ojai Shakespeare Festival. Libbey Park. Outdoor evening and matinee performances of two Shakespeare plays, with pre-show Madrigal entertainment. Phone 805/646-9455. Aug.

Ojai Studio Artists Tour. Recognized artists open their studios to the public. Phone 805/646-8126. Oct.

Motels

★★ **BEST WESTERN CASA.** *1302 E Ojai Ave (93023). 805/646-8175; FAX 805/640-8247; res: 800/528-1234.* 45 rms, 2 story. Mid-May-mid-Sept: S $75-$120; D $80-$120; each addl $10; under 12 free; lower rates rest of yr. TV; cable, VCR avail (movies $1). Heated pool; whirlpool. Complimentary continental bkfst. Coffee in rms. Restaurant nearby. Ck-out noon. Business servs avail. In-rm modem link. Some refrigerators; microwaves avail. Cr cds: A, C, D, DS, MC, V.

D SC

★★ **LOS PADRES INN.** *1208 E Ojai Ave (93023), I-101 exit I-33. 805/646-4365; FAX 805/646-0625; res: 800/228-3744.* 31 rms, 2 story. June-Oct: S, D $54-$115; under 12 free; higher rates special events; lower rates rest of yr. Crib free. Pet accepted, some restrictions; $10. TV; cable (premium). Complimentary continental bkfst. Restaurant nearby. Ck-out 11 am. Pool; whirlpool. Refrigerators, microwaves avail. Cr cds: A, C, D, DS, MC, V.

D

Resort

★★★ **OJAI VALLEY INN.** *Country Club Rd (93024). 805/646-5511; FAX 805/646-7969; res: 800/422-6524.* Web www.ojairesort.com. 209 units, 3 story. S, D $210-$290; suites, cottages $345-$850; family rates. Pet accepted; $25. TV; cable (premium). 3 heated pools; whirlpools, poolside serv. Playground. Supervised child's activities; ages 3-12. Coffee in rms. Restaurant (public by res): 6:30 am-10 pm. Box lunches, snack bar, picnics. Rm serv 24 hrs. Bar 11:30 am-midnight. Ck-out noon, ck-in 4 pm. Meeting rms. Business center. In-rm modem link. Concierge. Sports dir. Lighted tennis, pro. 18-hole golf, greens fee from $80, pro, putting green, driving range. Bicycles. Lawn games. Hiking, horseback riding, mountain biking. Aviary. Children's petting zoo. Soc dir; entertainment. Exercise rm; sauna, steam rm. Refrigerators, minibars; some fireplaces. Many private patios, balconies. On 220 acres. Mountain views. Cr cds: A, C, D, DS, MC, V.

D SC

Restaurants

★★★ **L'AUBERGE.** *314 El Paseo St (93023), at Rincon St. 805/646-2288.* Web www.tales.com/ca/l'aubergerestaurant. Hrs: 5:30-9 pm; Sat, Sun brunch 11 am-2:30 pm. Res accepted. Country French, Belgian menu. Beer. Wine list. A la carte entrees: dinner $16.50-$21. Sat, Sun brunch $8.75. Child's meals. Specializes in frogs' legs, sweetbreads, fish. Own desserts. Outdoor dining. In old house; country French decor. Cr cds: A, C, MC, V.

★★★ **RANCH HOUSE.** *102 Besant Rd (93023). 805/646-2360.* E-mail OjaiRanchH@aol.com; web www.TheRanchHouse.com. Hrs: dinner sittings 6-8:30 pm; Sun sittings 11 am-7:30 pm; Sun brunch to 2 pm. Closed Mon, Tues; Jan 1, Dec 24, 25. Res accepted. Continental menu. Beer. Wine cellar. A la carte entrees: dinner $18.95-$24.95. Sun brunch

$18.95. Child's meals. Specializes in garden dining, grilled fish. Own baking. Outdoor dining. Wine terrace. Bakery. Family-owned. Cr cds: A, C, D, DS, MC, V.

D

Ontario (J-4)

(See also Claremont, Pomona)

Founded 1882 **Pop** 133,179 **Elev** 988 ft **Area Code** 909
Web www.ontariocvb.org

Information Convention and Visitors Authority, 2000 Convention Center Way, 91760; 909/937-3000 or 800/455-5755

What to See and Do

California Speedway. 2-mi asphalt track is home to professional auto racing, including NASCAR Winston Cup Series and PPG CART World Series races. (June-Oct, dates vary) I-10 W to Cherry Ave, N to Randall Ave entrance. Phone 888/849-7223 for ticket information.

Industrial tour. Graber Olive House. Tour of sorting, canning, packaging areas. Mini-museum, gourmet food and gift shop. (Daily; closed major hols) 315 E 4th St. Phone 909/983-1761. **Free**

Museum of History and Art, Ontario. Regional history and fine arts exhibits. (Wed-Sun afternoons; closed major hols) 225 S Euclid Ave. Phone 909/983-3198. **Free**

Ontario Mills. California's largest entertainment & outlet mall; 1.7 million sq ft with over 200 shops, including an enormous Dave & Buster's with Million Dollar Midway, Special Events Theater, D & B Speedway, casino, billiards, golf simulator and dining room. Also here are IMAX theater (fee); 30 standard movie theaters (fees); American Wilderness zoo & aquarium (fee), featuring 5 regions, each with native plants and animals in indoor recreations of their natural ecosystems. Also adventure simulator ride; large food court; California Welcome Center. (Daily) 1 Mill Circle. Phone 909/484-8300 or 888-LA-MILLS. **Free**

Planes of Fame Air Museum. Exotic collection of more than 60 operable historic military aircraft, including Japanese Zero, ME-109G, B-17. Aircraft rides. (Daily; closed Thanksgiving, Dec 25) 5 mi S from I-10 via Euclid Ave, 7000 Merrill Ave in Chino. Phone 909/597-3722. **¢¢¢**

Prado Regional Park. Fishing; nonpower boat rentals. Horseback riding (rentals; fee), golf. Picnicking. Camping. (Daily; closed Dec 25) 8 mi S from I-10 via Euclid Ave; 6 mi S of Pomona Frwy. Phone 909/597-4260. Per vehicle **¢¢–¢¢¢**

Motels

★★ **BEST WESTERN AIRPORT.** *209 N Vineyard Ave (91764), I-10 Vineyard Ave exit S, near Intl airport. 909/937-6800; FAX 909/937-6815; res: 800/528-1234.* Web www.bestwestern.com. 150 rms, 2 story. S $55-$60; D $60-$70; each addl $5; under 12 free. Crib free. Pet accepted; $10. TV; cable (premium). Heated pool; whirlpool. Complimentary continental bkfst. Complimentary coffee in rms. Restaurant adj open 24 hrs. Ck-out noon. Coin lndry. Meeting rms. Valet serv. Free airport transportation. Exercise equipt. Some refrigerators; microwaves avail. Cr cds: A, C, D, DS, MC, V.

D SC

★★ **COUNTRYSIDE INN.** *204 N Vineyard Ave (91764), I-10 exit Vineyard Ave S, near Intl Airport. 909/937-9700; FAX 909/937-2070; res: 800/248-4661.* Web www.countrysideinn.com. 107 units, 2 story, 2 suites. S, D $69-$150; suites $150-$250; under 13 free; wkly rates. Crib free. TV; cable (premium), VCR avail (movies). Heated pool; whirlpool. Complimentary full bkfst. Complimentary coffee in rms. Restaurant adj open 24 hrs. Ck-out noon. Coin lndry. Meeting rms. Business servs avail. Valet serv. Free airport transportation. Exercise equipt. Refrigerators; wet bars, microwaves. Cr cds: A, C, D, DS, MC, V.

D SC

★★ **FAIRFIELD INN.** *3201 Centre Lake Dr (91761), I-10 exit Haven Ave S, near Intl Airport. 909/390-9855; FAX 909/390-9835; res: 800/228-2800.* Web www.marriott.com. 117 rms, 3 story. S, D $59.64; under 18 free. Crib free. TV; cable (premium). Heated pool. Complimentary continental bkfst. Restaurant adj 11 am-9 pm. Ck-out noon. Meeting rm. Business servs avail. In-rm modem link. Valet serv. Free airport transportation. Cr cds: A, C, D, DS, MC, V.

D SC

★★ **RESIDENCE INN AIRPORT.** *2025 Convention Center Way (91764), I-10 Vineyard Ave exit S, near Intl Airport. 909/937-6788; FAX 909/937-2462; res: 800/331-3131.* Web www.marriott.com. 200 kit. units, 2 story. Kit. units $145-$165. Pet accepted; $50-$75 & $6/day. TV; cable (premium), VCR avail. Heated pool; whirlpool. Complimentary continental bkfst. Coffee in rms. Restaurant nearby. Ck-out noon. Coin lndry. Meeting rm. Business servs avail. Valet serv. Free airport transportation. Exercise equipt. Health club privileges. Paddle tennis. Refrigerators, microwaves; some fireplaces. Some balconies. Picnic tables, grills. Cr cds: A, C, D, DS, MC, V.

D SC

✓★ **SUPER 8 LODGE.** *514 N Vineyard Ave (91764), I-10 Vineyard Ave exit S, near Intl Airport. 909/937-2999; FAX 909/937-2978; res: 800/800-8000.* 130 rms, 3 story. S, D $55-$65; each addl $5; under 12 free. Crib free. TV; cable (premium). Pool; whirlpool. Complimentary continental bkfst. Restaurant adj open 24 hrs. Ck-out 11 am. Free airport transportation. Health club privileges. Cr cds: A, C, D, DS, MC, V.

D SC

Motor Hotels

★★★ **COUNTRY SUITES.** *1945 E Holt Blvd (91761), I-10 exit Vineyard Ave, S to Holt Blvd, near Intl Airport . 909/390-7778; FAX 909/937-9718; res: 800/248-4661.* Web www.countrysideinn.com. 167 units, 3 story, 2 suites. S, D $70-$165; each addl $15; suites $150-$250; wkly rates. Crib free. TV; cable (premium). Heated pool; whirlpool. Complimentary full bkfst. Complimentary coffee in rms. Restaurant 11:30 am-2:30 pm, 4:30-10 pm; Sat, Sun from 4:30 pm. Rm serv from 4:30 pm. Ck-out noon. Meeting rms. Business servs avail. Bellhops. Valet serv. Coin lndry. Free airport transportation. Exercise equipt. Refrigerators, microwaves, wet bars; some in-rm whirlpools. Grills. Cr cds: A, C, D, DS, MC, V.

D SC

★★★ **DOUBLETREE.** *222 N Vineyard Ave (91764), I-10 Vineyard Ave exit S, near Intl Airport. 909/937-0900; FAX 909/937-1999.* E-mail dtontario@msn.com. 339 rms, 3-4 story. S, D $124-$144; each addl $15; suites $375-$650; under 18 free; wkend rates. Crib free. TV; cable (premium), VCR avail. Heated pool; whirlpool, poolside serv. Coffee in rms. Restaurants 6 am-11 pm; dining rm 11:30 am-2 pm, 5-10 pm; Sat 5-11 pm; Sun 9 am-2 pm, 5-10 pm. Rm serv. Bars 11-2 am; entertainment. Ck-out 1 pm. Convention facilities. Business servs avail. Bellhops. Valet serv. Gift shop. Free airport transportation. Exercise equipt. Microwaves avail. Balconies, patios. Luxury level. Cr cds: A, C, D, DS, ER, JCB, MC, V.

D SC

★★★ **HOLIDAY INN.** *3400 Shelby St (91764), I-10 Haven Ave exit N, near Intl Airport. 909/466-9600; FAX 909/941-1445; res: 800/642-2617; res: 888/668-2746.* E-mail hio@gte.net; web www.holiday-inn.com. 150 kit. suites, 3 story. Suites $99-$119; 1-bedrm suites $109-$129; each addl $10; under 18 free; wkly rates. Crib free. Pet accepted, some restrictions. TV; cable (premium), VCR avail. Heated pool; whirlpool. Complimentary full bkfst. Complimentary coffee in rms. Restaurant 6:30-10 am, 11 am-2 pm, 6-10 pm; Rm serv. Bar 4-10 pm. Ck-out noon. Coin lndry. Meeting rms. Business servs avail. Valet serv. Sundries. Gift shop. Free airport transportation. Exercise equipt; sauna. Game rm. Microwaves. Some patios. Grill. Cr cds: A, C, D, DS, MC, V.

D SC

Hotels

★★ **DOUBLETREE CLUB HOTEL.** *429 N Vineyard Ave (91764), I-10 Vineyard Ave exit S, near Intl Airport. 909/937-8000; FAX 909/937-8028; res: 800/582-2946.* Web www.double treehotels.com. 170 units, 6 story, 3 suites. S, D $138-$150; each addl $10; suites $175; under 12 free. Crib free. TV; cable (premium). Heated pool; whirlpool. Complimentary full bkfst. Complimentary coffee in rms. Restaurant 5-10 pm. Bar. Ck-out 1 pm. Meeting rms. Business servs avail. In-rm modem link. Free airport transportation. Exercise equipt. Refrigerators; microwaves avail. Cr cds: A, C, D, DS, ER, JCB, MC, V.

D SC

★★★ **HILTON AIRPORT.** *700 N Haven (91764), I-10 Haven Ave exit N, near Intl Airport. 909/980-0400; FAX 909/941-6781; res: 800/654-1379.* Web www.hilton.com. 309 rms, 10 story. S, D $129-$159; suites $265. Crib free. TV; cable (premium). Heated pool; whirlpool, poolside serv. Complimentary coffee in rms. Restaurant 5 am-midnight. Bar 11-1 am. Ck-out noon. Convention facilities. Business servs avail. In-rm modem link. Concierge. Gift shop. Free airport transportation. Exercise equipt. Some balconies. Luxury level. Cr cds: A, C, D, DS, JCB, MC, V.

D SC

★★★ **MARRIOTT.** *2200 E Holt Blvd (91761), I-10 Vineyard Ave exit, S to Holt then 2 blks E, near Intl Airport. 909/975-5000; FAX 909/975-5050; res: 800/228-5050.* 299 rms, 3 story. S, D $89-$169; suites $250; wkend rates. Crib free. TV; cable (premium). Heated pool; whirlpool, poolside serv. Restaurants open 24 hrs. Bars 11 am-midnight. Ck-out noon. Convention facilities. Business servs avail. In-rm modem link. Concierge. Gift shop. Free airport transportation. Lighted tennis. Exercise rm; sauna, steam rm. Racquetball, basketball courts. Cr cds: A, C, D, DS, JCB, MC, V.

D SC

Restaurant

★★★ **ROSA'S RESTAURANT.** *425 N Vineyard Ave (91764), I-10 Vineyard Ave exit S. 909/937-1220.* Web www.rosasitalian.com. Hrs: 11:30 am-10 pm; Sat from 5 pm; Sun 5-9 pm. Closed some major hols. Res accepted. Italian menu. Bar. Wine cellar. A la carte entrees: lunch $7-$18, dinner $11.50-$24. Specializes in fresh fish, pasta. Own pasta, desserts. Pianist. Mediterranean villa atmosphere. Cr cds: A, C, D, MC, V.

D

Orange (D-6 see Los Angeles map)

(See also Anaheim, Santa Ana)

Founded 1868 **Pop** 110,658 **Elev** 187 ft **Area Code** 714

Information Chamber of Commerce, 531 E Chapman Ave, Ste A, 92866; 714/538-3581

What to See and Do

Tucker Wildlife Sanctuary. 12-acre refuge for native plants and birds, including several species of hummingbirds (seasonal); observation porch, nature trails, museum displays. Picnic areas. (Daily; closed Dec 25) 29322 Modjeska Canyon Rd. Phone 714/649-2760. ¢

Motels

★★ **HAWTHORN SUITES.** *720 The City Dr S (92868), CA 22 The City Dr exit, 1 blk S. 714/740-2700; FAX 714/971-1692; res: 800/278-4837.* Web www.winhotel.com. 123 suites, 3 story. Suites $160-$230. Crib free. TV; cable (premium). Heated pool; whirlpool. Complimentary full bkfst. Complimentary coffee in rms. Ck-out noon. Coin lndry. Meeting rms. Business center. Valet serv. Sundries. Gift shop. Health club privileges. Refrigerators, microwaves, wet bars. Grill. Cr cds: A, C, D, DS, JCB, MC, V.

D SC

★★ **RESIDENCE INN BY MARRIOTT.** *201 N State College Blvd (92868), off I-5 Chapman Ave exit. 714/978-7700; FAX 714/978-6257; res: 800/423-9315.* 104 kits, 2 story. S, D $99-$218; family, wkly rates. Crib free. Pet accepted, some restrictions; $75. TV; cable (premium), VCR avail. Heated pool; whirlpool. Complimentary continental bkfst. Complimentary coffee in rms. Restaurant nearby. Ck-out noon. Coin lndry. Meeting rms. Business servs avail. Valet serv. Airport, RR station, bus depot transportation. Free Disneyland transportation. Health club privileges. Basketball, volleyball. Microwaves. Some balconies, fireplaces. Picnic tables, grills. Cr cds: A, C, D, DS, JCB, MC, V.

D SC

Motor Hotel

★★★ **COUNTYSIDE INN.** *3737 W Chapman Ave (92868). 714/978-9168; FAX 714/385-1528; res: 800/268-7946.* Web www.countrysideinn.com. 129 rms, 6 story. S, D $99-$109; wkend rates. Crib free. TV; cable (premium). Complimentary full bkfst. Complimentary coffee in rms. Restaurant 11:30 am-2:30 pm, 5-9 pm. Rm serv. Ck-out noon. Meeting rms. Business servs avail. Bellhops. Valet serv. Sundries. Coin lndry. Free Disneyland transportation. Exercise equipt. Pool; whirlpool. Cr cds: A, C, D, DS, MC, V.

D SC

Hotels

★★★ **DOUBLETREE HOTEL.** *100 The City Dr (92868), CA 22, The City Dr exit, then ½ mi N. 714/634-4500; FAX 714/978-3839; res: 800/528-0444.* E-mail anaheimdtree@earthlink.com; web www.doubletreehotels.com. 454 units, 20 story. S, D $190; each addl $10; suites $250-$575; under 18 free. Crib free. Parking $6, valet $8. TV; cable (premium). Heated pool; whirlpool, poolside serv. Coffee in rms. Restaurants 6 am-10 pm. Bar from 4 pm. Ck-out noon. Convention facilities. Business center. Concierge. Free Disneyland transportation. Lighted tennis. Exercise equipt. Bathrm phone, refrigerator in some suites. Cr cds: A, C, D, DS, ER, JCB, MC, V.

D SC

★★★ **HILTON SUITES.** *400 N State College Blvd (92868), off I-5 Chapman Ave exit (N) or I-5 The City Dr or State College Blvd (S). 714/938-1111; FAX 714/938-0930; res: 800/445-8667.* Web www.hilton.com. 230 suites, 10 story. Suites $140-$180; each addl $20; family rates. Crib free. TV; cable (premium), VCR (movies free). Indoor pool; whirlpool. Complimentary full bkfst. Complimentary coffee in rms. Restaurant 11:30 am-1:30 pm, 5:30-10 pm; wkend hrs vary. Rm serv 5:30-10 pm. Bar 4 pm-midnight. Ck-out noon. Meeting rms. Business center. In-rm modem link. Gift shop. Free Disneyland transportation. Exercise equipt; sauna. Refrigerators, microwaves. Some balconies. 10-story triangular atrium. Cr cds: A, C, D, DS, ER, JCB, MC, V.

D SC

Restaurants

★★★ **HOBBIT.** *2932 E Chapman Ave (92869). 714/997-1972.* One sitting: 7:30 pm; Sun 7 pm. Closed Mon; most major hols. Res required. Contemporary continental menu. Bar. Wine cellar. Complete meal: 7-course dinner $55. Menu changes wkly. Own baking. Parking. Two dining rms in Spanish-style house; mahogany staircase, antique fireplace. Jacket. Family-owned. Cr cds: C, MC, V.

★★ **LA BRASSERIE.** *202 S Main St (92868), CA 22 exit Main St N. 714/978-6161.* Hrs: 11:30 am-2 pm, 5-10 pm; Sat from 5 pm. Closed Sun; some major hols. Res accepted. Continental menu. Bar. Wine list. Semi-a la carte: lunch $8.95-$13.95, dinner $16.95-$28.95. Specializes in veal, fresh fish. Own desserts. Parking. French country-style decor; many antiques, fireplace. Totally nonsmoking. Cr cds: A, C, D, MC, V.

✓★★ **YEN CHING.** *574 S Glassell St (92666), CA 22, Glassell St exit, 1 blk N. 714/997-3300.* Hrs: 11:30 am-2:30 pm, 4:30-9:30 pm; Fri to 10:30 pm; Sat noon-10:30 pm; Sun noon-9:30 pm. Res accepted. Chinese menu. Wine, beer. Semi-a la carte: lunch $5.99-$7.80, dinner $8.75-$14.30. Complete meals: dinner $14.95. Specializes in Mandarin dishes. Parking. Totally nonsmoking. Cr cds: A, C, DS, MC, V.

Oroville (C-3)

(See also Chico, Marysville)

Settled 1850 **Pop** 11,960 **Elev** 174 ft **Area Code** 916 **Zip** 95965

Information Chamber of Commerce, 1789 Montgomery St; 916/538-2542

Water-oriented recreation, tourism and hunting predominate in Oroville—where the lure of gold once held sway and "too many gambling houses to count" catered to the wants of miners. Miners' Alley is a historic remnant of those days when Oroville was the second-largest city in California.

Oroville, in addition to being the portal to the Sierra's great watershed, the Feather River, also has orange and olive groves, which thrive in the area's thermal belt. Fruit and olive processing, as well as lumber, contribute much to the community's economy.

A Ranger District office of the Plumas National Forest (see QUINCY) is located in Oroville.

What to See and Do

Chinese Temple (1863). The "Temple Beside the River," largest of the authentic temples in California, has a tapestry hall and display rm. It is all that remains of a Chinatown that was second in size only to San Francisco's. (Daily; closed mid-Dec-Jan) 1500 Broderick St, at Elma. Phone 916/538-2496. ¢

Feather Falls. Sixth-highest in US. 3½-mi trail leads to a 640-ft drop of the Fall River into the canyon just above the Middle Fork of the Feather River in Feather Falls Scenic Area. Allow 4-6 hrs for round trip and carry drinking water. 25 mi NE in Plumas National Forest (see QUINCY). Phone 916/538-2200.

Feather River Fish Hatchery. Raises salmon and steelhead. Underwater viewing chamber (Sept-Jan); hatchery (daily). 5 Table Mountain Blvd, on N bank of Feather River. Phone 916/538-2222. **Free**

Historic Judge C. F. Lott House (1856). Authentically restored; period furnishings. Picnic area. (Sun, Mon & Fri, afternoons; closed mid-Dec -Jan) 1067 Montgomery St, in Lott-Sank Park. Phone 916/538-2497. ¢

Oroville Dam & Reservoir. This 770-ft-high earth-filled dam impounds Lake Oroville with a 167-mi shoreline. The dam is a vital part of the $3.2-billion California State Water Project. 7 mi E on CA 162, then 3 mi N on Canyon Dr. Phone 916/538-2200. For tours of Power Plant contact Dept of Water Resources, PO Box 939; 916/534-2306. **Free**

Visitor Center & Overlook. Exhibits, slide shows, films; observation tower. (Daily; closed Jan 1, Thanksgiving, Dec 25) 9 mi E on CA 162, 2½ mi N on Kelly Ridge Rd. Phone 916/538-2219. **Free**

Lake Oroville State Recreation Area. In several sections. **Forebay-South.** Powerboats allowed (fee for boat launch); no camping. (Daily; fee) 3 mi W, CA 70 Grand Ave exit. **Forebay-North.** Swimming, bathhouse; no powerboats. (Daily; fees) 1 mi W, CA 70 Garden Dr exit. **Loafer Creek Campground.** Swimming; camping (fee). (Daily, Apr-Oct) All three recreation areas have fishing; boat ramps; hiking trails; picnicking. Standard fees. 9 mi E via CA 162. Two marinas: **Lime Saddle** and **Bidwell Canyon.** Also camping facilities at Bidwell Canyon (campground all yr; full RV hookup; fees). **Spillway.** Wayside camping; launch ramp. (Daily; fees) 7 mi E via CA 162, N via Canyon Dr, 3 mi W across dam. Res for both campgrounds avail through DESTINET phone 800/444-7275. Contact park headquarters for swimming and launching status; phone 916/538-2200.

Annual Events

Old Time Fiddlers' Contest. Northern California Regional Championship. Phone 916/589-4844. Usually late Mar.

Dam Days. Parades. Car show. Pancake bkfst. Phone 916/534-7690. Early May.

Bidwell Bar Days. Gold panning, pioneer arts & crafts. Phone 916/538-2219. 1st Sat May.

Motels

★★ **BEST WESTERN GRAND MANOR INN.** *1470 Feather River Blvd (95965). 530/533-9673; FAX 530/533-5862; res: 800/528-1234.* 54 rms, 3 story. S, D $64-$84; suites $87-$125; under 12 free. Crib $6. Pet accepted, some restrictions. TV; cable. Pool; whirlpool. Complimentary continental bkfst. Complimentary coffee in rms. Restaurant nearby. Ck-out 11 am. Coin Indry. Meeting rm. Business servs avail. In-rm modem link. Exercise equipt; sauna. Refrigerators. Many balconies. Cr cds: A, C, D, DS, MC, V.

D SC

✓★ **VILLA MOTEL.** *1527 Feather River Blvd (95965). 530/533-3930.* 20 rms. S $50; D $55-$60; each addl $5. Crib free. TV; cable. Pool. Coffee in rms. Restaurant nearby. Ck-out 11 am. Cr cds: A, C, D, MC, V.

SC

Inn

★★★ **LAKE OROVILLE BED & BREAKFAST.** *240 Sunday Dr (95916), CA 70 to CA 162, E 1½ mi to Olive, S to Bell Rd, W to Sunday Dr. 530/589-0700; FAX 530/589-4761; res: 800/589-4761.* E-mail lakeinn@cncnet.com; web www.now2000.com/lakeoroville. 6 rms. S, D $75-$135; each addl $10; hols (2-3 day min). Pet accepted, some restrictions. TV avail; VCR avail (movies). Complimentary full bkfst. Restaurant nearby. Ck-out 11:30 am, ck-in 3-6 pm. Business servs avail. Luggage handling. 18-hole golf privileges. Bicycles avail. Game rm. Rec rm. Many in-rm whirlpools; microwaves avail. Some balconies. Picnic tables, grills. Lake view. Hiking trails. On 40 acres. Totally nonsmoking. Cr cds: A, C, D, MC, V.

D SC

Restaurant

✓★★ **DEPOT.** *2191 High St (95965). 530/534-9101.* Hrs: 11 am-2:30 pm, 4-9:30 pm; Fri to 10 pm; Sat 4-10 pm; Sun 3:30-9 pm; early-bird dinner Mon-Sun 4-5:30 pm. Closed Dec 25. Bar 11-2 am. Semi-a la carte: lunch $4.75-$8.50, dinner from $5.95. Child's meals. Specialties: chicken Cordon Bleu, prime rib. Salad bar. Outdoor dining. In 1908 Western Pacific railroad depot. Family-owned. Cr cds: A, C, D, DS, MC, V.

D

Oxnard (J-3)

(See also Ventura)

Pop 142,216 **Elev** 52 ft **Area Code** 805 **Zip** 93030
E-mail oxtour@west.net **Web** www.oxnardtourism.com

Information Tourism Bureau, 200 W Seventh St; 805/385-7545 or 800/2-OXNARD

What to See and Do

Carnegie Art Museum. Regional and international visual and fine arts. (Thurs-Sun) 424 South C St. Phone 805/385-8157 (recording). **¢¢**

CEC/Seabee Museum. Enter on Ventura Rd at Sunkist St, S of Channel Islands Blvd. Memorabilia of the US Navy Seabees, who are the construction battalions of the Navy; uniforms, Antarctic display, South Pacific artifacts, underwater diving display, outrigger canoes, World War II dioramas, weapons, flags. (Daily; closed hols) Naval Construction Battalion Center, Channel Islands Blvd & Ventura Rd, SW off US 101 in Port Hueneme. Phone 805/982-5165. **Free**

Channel Islands Harbor. Public recreation includes boating, fishing, swimming, beaches; parks, barbecue & picnic facilities; playgrounds, tennis courts; charter boat and bicycle rentals. Also here is

Fisherman's Wharf. A New England-style village with specialty shops, restaurants and transient docking for pleasure boaters.

Channel Islands National Park (see). HQ at 1901 Spinnaker Dr, Ventura 93001.

Gull Wings Children's Museum. 418 W 4th St. Phone 805/483-3005. **¢¢**

Ventura County Maritime Museum. (Thurs-Mon) 2731 S Victoria Ave. Phone 805/984-6260. **Donation**

Annual Events

Point Mugu Airshow. Pacific Coast Hwy (CA 1) or I-101 (Ventura Frwy) W to Las Posas exit. Military aircraft demonstration, parachutists & displays; civilian/foreign aerobatics. Phone 805/989-8094. Late Apr.

California Strawberry Festival. Strawberry Meadows at College Park. Waiters' race, wine tasting, entertainment, crafts, strawberry foods. 3rd wkend May.

Motel

★★★ **THE COUNTRY INN AT PORT HUENEME.** *350 E Hueneme Rd (93041), CA 1 Hueneme Rd exit, E to Ventura Rd; or US 101 to Ventura Rd exit, then 6 mi S to Hueneme Rd. 805/986-5353; FAX 805/986-4399; res: 800/447-3529.* 135 kit. units, 3 story. S, D $128; each addl $10; suites $138-$168; under 12 free. Crib avail. Pet accepted. TV; cable, VCR (movies $4). Pool; whirlpool. Complimentary full bkfst. Ck-out noon. Coin lndry. Business servs avail. In-rm modem link. Refrigerators. Near ocean. Nautical decor. Cr cds: A, C, D, DS, MC, V.

D SC

Motor Hotel

★★ **CASA SIRENA HOTEL & MARINA.** *3605 Peninsula Rd (93035). 805/985-6311; FAX 805/985-4329; res: 800/447-3529.* 273 rms, 2-3 story. Some A/C. S, D $120-$149; each addl $10; suites $179-$275; kit. units $179; package plans. Crib free. Pet accepted. TV; cable. Heated pool; whirlpool. Playground. Coffee in rms. Restaurant 6:30 am-10 pm. Rm serv to 9:30 pm. Bar 10-1:30 am; Sun to 11:30 pm. Ck-out noon. Convention facilities. Business servs avail. In-rm modem link. Valet serv. Sundries. Barber, beauty shop. Free airport, RR station, bus depot transportation. Lighted tennis. Putting green. Exercise equipt; sauna. Game rm. Refrigerators. Private patios, balconies. Marina. View of harbor. Park adj. Cr cds: A, C, D, DS, MC, V.

D SC

Hotels

★★★ **EMBASSY SUITES.** *2101 Mandalay Beach Rd (93035). 805/984-2500; FAX 805/984-8339; res: 800/362-2779.* Web www.embassy-suites/mandalaybeach.com. 250 suites, 3 story. S, D $159-$750; each addl $15; under 18 free. TV; cable (premium). Pool; whirlpool, poolside serv. Complimentary full bkfst. Coffee in rms. Restaurant 11:30 am-2:30 pm, 5-10 pm. Bar 11-2 am. Ck-out noon. Guest lndry. Convention facilities. Business servs avail. In-rm modem link. Garage parking. Gift shop. Free airport transportation. Exercise equipt. Lighted tennis. Bicycle rentals. Refrigerators. Some private patios, balconies. 8 acres; on beach. Cr cds: A, C, D, DS, MC, V.

D SC

★★★ **RADISSON HOTEL.** *600 Esplanade Dr (93030), adj to US 101 Vineyard exit. 805/485-9666; FAX 805/485-2061; res: 800/333-3333.* Web www.hilton.com. 160 rms, 6 story. S, D $109; each addl $10; suites $129-$169; under 18 free. Crib free. Pet accepted; $25. TV; cable (premium). Pool; whirlpool. Restaurant 6:30 am-10 pm. Bar 11-2 am; Fri, Sat to midnight; entertainment. Ck-out noon. Meeting rms. Business servs avail. In-rm modem link. Valet serv. Shopping arcade. Barber, beauty shop. Free airport transportation. Health club privileges. Refrigerators. Some balconies. Cr cds: A, C, D, DS, ER, JCB, MC, V.

D SC

★★★ **RESIDENCE INN AT RIVER RIDGE BY MARRIOTT.** *2101 W Vineyard Ave (93030). 805/278-2200; FAX 805/983-4470; res: 800/331-3131.* Web www.residenceinn.com. 250 kit. suites, 1-2 story. S $109; D $139; under 17 free; golf, tennis packages. Crib free. TV; cable (premium). 2 heated pools; whirlpools, poolside serv. Complimentrary bkfst buffet. Complimentry coffee in rms. Ck-out noon. Coin lndry. Convention facilities. Business servs avail. In-rm modem link. Free airport, RR station, bus depot transportation. Lighted tennis, pro. 18-hole golf, pro, greens fee, driving range. Exercise equipt. Some wood-burning fireplaces. Balconies. Picnic tables, grills. Located on 15 acres; gazebo. Cr cds: A, C, D, DS, ER, MC, V.

D SC

Restaurant

✓★ **MONEY PANCHO.** *155 E 7th St (93030). 805/483-1411.* Hrs: 8 am-10 pm. Res accepted. Mexican menu. Semi-a la carte: bkfst $4.45-$7.95, lunch $3.95-$7.95, dinner $7.95-$13.95. Child's meals. Specialties: sea & earth, marina rey, fajitas chicken rey. Guitar Mon, Fri, Sat. Parking. Mexican-style atmosphere and decor. Totally nonsmoking. Cr cds: A, C, D, MC, V.

D

Pacific Beach (San Diego) (K-4)

Area Code 619 **Zip** 92109

This community is an integral part of San Diego, but is regarded by many as a separate entity.

Motel

★★ **OCEAN PARK INN.** *710 Grand Ave (92109). 619/483-5858; FAX 619/274-0823; res: 800/231-7735.* Web go-explore.com/opinn. 73 rms, 3 story. May-Sept: S $134-$184; D $124-$204; each addl $10; suites $179-$219; under 12 free; lower rates rest of yr. Crib free. TV; cable (premium). Heated pool; whirlpool. Complimentary continental bkfst. Restaurant adj 7 am-9 pm. Ck-out 11 am. Business servs avail. Valet serv. Refrigerators; microwave in suites. Balconies. On beach. Cr cds: A, C, D, DS, MC, V.

D

Motor Hotel

★★★ **PACIFIC TERRACE INN.** *610 Diamond St (92109). 619/581-3500; FAX 619/274-3341; res: 888/723-3569.* E-mail bkingery@pacificterrace.com; web www.pacificterrace.com. 73 rms, 3 story, 42 kits. S, D $195-$255; each addl $10; suites, kit. units $255-$560. Crib free. TV; cable (premium). Heated pool; whirlpool. Complimentary continental bkfst. Coffee in rms. Restaurant nearby. Rm serv 6:30 am-11 pm. Ck-out 11 am. Meeting rm. Business servs avail. In-rm modem link. Bellhops. Covered parking. Health club privileges. Refrigerators; microwaves avail. Bathrm phone in suites. Private patios, balconies. On beach. Cr cds: A, C, D, DS, JCB, MC, V.

D SC

Hotel

★★★ **CATAMARAN RESORT HOTEL.** *3999 Mission Blvd (92109). 619/488-1081; FAX 619/539-8601; res: 800/288-0770.* 313 rms, 2-12 story, 120 kits. S, D $150-$275; each addl $15; suites $315-$400. Crib free. TV; cable (premium). Supervised child's activities (June-Labor Day). Heated pool; whirlpool, poolside serv. Complimentary coffee in rms. Restaurant 6:30 am-10 pm; Fri, Sat to 11 pm. Bar 11-2 am; entertainment. Ck-out noon. Meeting rms. Business center. In-rm modem link. Concierge. Exercise equipt. Sailboats. Beach activities. Many refrigerators. Private patios, balconies. Opp ocean. On Mission Bay. Cr cds: A, C, D, DS, MC, V.

D SC

Restaurants

★★ **CHATEAU ORLEANS.** *926 Turquoise (92109). 619/488-6744.* Web www.sddt.com. Hrs: 6-10 pm. Closed Sun; most major hols. Res accepted. Cajun menu. Wine, beer. Semi-a la carte: dinner $10.95-$22. Child's menu. Specializes in Creole and Cajun dishes. Blues/jazz Thurs-Sat evenings. Intimate, casual dining. Cr cds: A, C, D, MC, V.

D

★ **GREEN FLASH.** *701 Thomas Ave (92109). 619/270-7715.* Hrs: 8 am-10 pm; Sat, Sun from 7:30 am; Sun brunch to 3 pm; early-bird dinner Sun-Thurs exc hols 4:30-6:30 pm. Bar to 2 am. Semi-a la carte: bkfst $2.50-$9.95, lunch $5.95-$12.95, dinner $8.95-$39.95. Sun brunch $2.50-$12.95. Child's meals. Specializes in fresh seafood, prime rib. Outdoor dining. Intimate dining with view of beach and boardwalk. Family-owned. Cr cds: A, C, D, DS, JCB, MC, V.

D

★★ **LAMONT ST GRILL.** *4445 Lamont St (92109). 619/270-3060.* Hrs: 5:30-10 pm; Fri, Sat to 11 pm; Sun 5-10 pm. Closed Jan 1, July 4, Dec 24, 25. Res accepted. Bar. Semi-a la carte: dinner $9.95-$18.95. Specializes in beef, pork, fresh fish. Outdoor dining. Converted bungalow with intimate dining; garden courtyard. Totally nonsmoking. Cr cds: A, C, DS, MC, V.

D

✓★★ **OLD OX.** *4447 Mission Blvd (92109). 619/275-3790.* Hrs: 11:30 am-2 pm, 5-9 pm; Fri, Sat to 10 pm; Sat, Sun brunch 10 am-2 pm. Closed Dec 25. Res accepted. Bar to 1:30 am. Semi-a la carte: lunch $5.95-$10.95, dinner $10.95-$18.95. Sat, Sun brunch $6-$12. Specializes in prime rib, steak, fresh fish. Parking. Outdoor dining. Cr cds: A, C, MC, V.

Pacific Grove (F-1)

(See also Carmel, Carmel Valley, Monterey, Pebble Beach)

Pop 16,117 **Elev** 0-300 ft **Area Code** 831 **Zip** 93950
E-mail chamber@pacificgrove.org
Information Chamber of Commerce, Central & Forest Aves, PO Box 167; 831/373-3304 or 800/656-6650

What to See and Do

Asilomar State Beach and Conference Center. A 105-acre beach-front conference center, historical landmark and park. Recreational facilities, meeting rms, accommodations. (Daily) 800 Asilomar Blvd. Contact PO Box 537; phone 831/372-8016 for details on the conference center.

Ocean View Blvd. Five-mile scenic road along rocky, flower-bordered shoreline.

Pacific Grove Museum of Natural History. Natural history of Monterey County, including birds, shells, mammals, Native American exhibits; native plants garden. (Daily exc Mon; closed most major hols) (See ANNUAL EVENTS) 165 Forest Ave. Phone 831/648-3116 or 831/648-3119 (recording). **Free**

Point Piños Lighthouse (1855). Oldest continuously operating lighthouse on Pacific Coast. (Jan-late Nov, Sat & Sun afternoons) Asilomar Ave at Lighthouse Ave. Phone 831/646-8540, 831/648-3116 or -3119 (recording). **Free**

Annual Events

Good Old Days. Parade, fair, entertainment, quilt show, contests. Mid-Apr.

Wildflower Show. Pacific Grove Museum of Natural History. 3rd wkend Apr.

Feast of Lanterns. Lantern-lit processions on land and sea, barbecue; pageant. Late July.

Butterfly Parade. Celebrates arrival of thousands of Monarch butterflies. Mid-Oct.

Marching Band Festival. Parade, field show; competition of statewide high school championship bands. Early Nov.

Christmas at the Inns. Tour of old Victorian inns decorated for the holidays. Usually 2nd Tues Dec.

Motels

★★ **BEST WESTERN.** *1111 Lighthouse Ave (93950). 831/646-8885; FAX 831/646-5976; res: 800/638-7949; res: 800/232-4232.* 49 units, 2 story, 5 suites. S, D $70-$200; each addl $10-$20; suites $140-$550; under 18 free; higher rates: hols, special events. Crib $10. TV; cable (premium). Heated pool; whirlpool. Sauna. Complimentary continental bkfst. Complimentary coffee in rms. Restaurant nearby. Ck-out noon. Meeting rms. Business servs avail. Refrigerator in suites; microwaves avail. Cr cds: A, C, D, DS, ER, JCB, MC, V.

D SC

★ **DAYS INN AND SUITES.** *660 Dennett St (93950). 831/373-8777; FAX 408/373-2698; res: 800/329-7466.* 30 rms, 3 story, 11 kits. No A/C. May-Nov: S, D $135-$225; each addl $10; children under 17 free; wkends (2-day min); higher rates special events; lower rates rest of yr. Crib free. TV; cable (premium). Complimentary continental bkfst. Complimentary coffee in rms. Ck-out 11 am. Microwaves. Cr cds: A, C, D, DS, MC, V.

D SC

★★ **DEER HAVEN INN.** *740 Crocker Ave (93950). 831/373-1114; FAX 408/655-5048; res: 800/525-3373.* 27 rms, 2 story. No A/C. July-Oct: S, D $79-$139; each addl $10; 2-day min wkends; higher rates special events; lower rates rest of yr. Crib $10. TV; cable. Complimentary continental bkfst. Complimentary coffee in rms. Restaurant nearby. Ck-out 11 am. Coin lndry. Business servs avail. Cr cds: A, C, DS, MC, V.

SC

★★ **ROSEDALE INN.** *775 Asilomar Blvd (93950). 831/655-1000; FAX 831/655-0691; res: 800/822-5606.* 16 rms, 3 kit. units. No A/C. June-Sept: S, D $115-$195; under 18 free; lower rates rest of yr. Crib free. TV; cable (premium), VCR (movies $2). Complimentary continental bkfst. Complimentary coffee in rms. Restaurant nearby. Ck-out 11 am. In-rm whirlpools, refrigerators, microwaves, fireplaces. Cr cds: A, C, D, DS, MC, V.

D SC

★ **THE LARCHWOOD-DEER HAVEN INN.** *740 Crocker Ave (93950). 831/373-1114; FAX 408/655-5048; res: 800/525-3373.* 22 kit. units, 2 story. No A/C. July-Oct: S, D $89-$229; under 6 free; lower rates rest of yr. Crib $10. TV; cable. Whirlpool; sauna. Complimentary continental bkfst. Restaurant nearby. Ck-out 11 am. Coin lndry. Totally nonsmoking. Cr cds: A, C, DS, MC, V.

SC

Inns

★★★ **CENTRELLA INN.** *612 Central Ave (93950). 831/372-3372; FAX 408/372-2036; res: 800/433-4732.* 26 rms, 11 with shower only, 3 story, 9 suites; 5 guest houses. No A/C. No rm phones. June-Oct: S, D $139-$169; each addl $15; suites $189-$199; guest houses $209-$229; under 13 free; wkends, hols (2-day min); lower rates rest of yr. Children over 12 yrs only in main house. TV; cable, VCR avail (movies). Complimentary continental bkfst; afternoon refreshments. Restaurant nearby. Ck-out noon, ck-in 3 pm. Business servs avail. Concierge serv. Street parking. Refrigerator in suites; wet bar, fireplace in guest house. Cr cds: C.

★★ **GATEHOUSE INN.** *225 Central Ave (93922). 831/649-8436; FAX 831/648-8044; res: 800/753-1881.* 9 rms, 2 story. No A/C. S, D $110-$165. Complimentary full bkfst; afternoon refreshments. Ck-out noon, ck-in 2 pm. Business servs avail. Victorian inn (1884) with view of Monterey Bay. Totally nonsmoking. Cr cds: A, C, DS, MC, V.

★★★ **GOSBY HOUSE INN.** *643 Lighthouse Ave (93942). 831/375-1287; FAX 831/655-9621.* Web www.foursisters.com. 22 rms, 20 with bath. No A/C. S, D $90-$160; each addl $15. Complimentary bkfst buffet; evening refreshments. Picnic lunches. Ck-out noon, ck-in 2 pm. Business servs avail. Some fireplaces. 2-story Queen Anne/Victorian mansion built in 1887 by cobbler from Nova Scotia. Wine cellar. Cr cds: A, C, D, JCB, MC, V.

★★★ **GREEN GABLES INN.** *104 5th St (93950). 831/375-2095; FAX 831/375-5437.* Web www.foursisters.com. 11 rms, 7 with bath, 2 story, 6 rms in main bldg, 5 rms in carriage house. No A/C. S, D $110-$225. TV in some rms; VCR avail. Complimentary full bkfst; afternoon refreshments. Ck-out noon, ck-in 2 pm. Business servs avail. In-rm whirlpools avail. Victorian mansion (1888); on Monterey Bay. Cr cds: A, C, MC, V.

D

★★ **PACIFIC GROVE INN.** *581 Pine Ave (93950). 831/375-2825; res: 800/732-2825.* 16 rms, in 2 houses, 3 story. June-Oct: S, D $99.50-$169.50; lower rates rest of yr. TV; cable. Complimentary continental bkfst. Ck-out noon, ck-in 3 pm. Refrigerators, fireplaces; microwaves avail. Restored Queen Anne-style house (1904). Totally nonsmoking. Cr cds: A, C, D, DS, MC, V.

D SC

★★★ **SEVEN GABLES INN.** *555 Ocean View Blvd (94105). 831/372-4341.* 10 rms, 3 story. No A/C. No rm phones. S, D $155-$275; wkends, hols (2-3-day min). Children over 12 yrs only. Complimentary full bkfst; afternoon refreshments. Restaurant nearby. Ck-out noon, ck-in 2:30-10 pm. At edge of Monterey Bay overlooking Lover's Point beach. Cr cds: C, MC, V.

★★★ **SEVEN GABLES INN.** *555 Ocean View Blvd (93950). 831/372-4341.* 14 rms, 2-3 story. No A/C. No rm phones. S, D $155-$350. Children over 12 yrs only. Complimentary full bkfst; afternoon refreshments. Restaurant nearby. Ck-out noon, ck-in 2:30-10 pm. Some refrigerators. Oceanfront Victorian mansion (1886) with antiques. Totally nonsmoking. Cr cds: C, MC, V.

★★★ **THE MARTINE INN.** *255 Ocean View Blvd (93950). 831/373-3388; FAX 831/373-3896; res: 800/852-5588.* 23 rms, 3 story. S, D $150-$295; each addl $35. Complimentary full bkfst; afternoon refreshments. Ck-out 11 am, ck-in 2 pm. Meeting rms. Business servs avail. Game rm. Refrigerators; some fireplaces. Victorian, Mediterranean-style home built 1899. Antiques. On Monterey Bay. Cr cds: A, C, DS, MC, V.

D

Restaurants

✓★★ **CROCODILE GRILL.** *701 Lighthouse Ave (93950). 831/655-3311.* Hrs: 5-10 pm. Closed Tues; Thanksgiving, Dec 25. Res accepted. Californian menu. Wine, beer. A la carte entrees: dinner $9-$14. Specializes in seafood, slow-roasted meats, vegetarian dishes. Tropical, Southwestern atmosphere. Cr cds: A, C, D, DS, MC, V.

D

★★ **CYPRESS GROVE.** *663 Lighthouse Ave (93950). 831/375-1743.* Hrs: 11 am-3 pm, 5-10 pm; Sat, Sun brunch 11 am-3 pm. Closed Mon. Res accepted. French, Californian menu. Semi-a la carte: lunch $8.95-$11.95, dinner $14.95-$24.95. Specializes in sauteed foie gras, roasted quail with morels, ahi tuna tartar. Own pastries. French provincial decor; fireplace. Totally nonsmoking. Cr cds: A, C, MC, V.

★★★ **FANDANGO.** *223 17th St (93950). 831/372-3456.* Hrs: 11 am-3:30 pm, 5-9:30 pm; Sun 10 am-2:30 pm, 5-9:30 pm. Res accepted. No A/C. Mediterranean menu. Bar. Semi-a la carte: lunch $8.25-$14.75, dinner $11.75-$28.75. Specializes in fresh seafood, paella, rack of lamb. Outdoor dining. Casual southern European decor; fireplaces. Cr cds: A, C, D, DS, JCB, MC, V.

D

✓★ **FISHWIFE.** *1996½ Sunset Dr (93950), at Asilomar State Beach. 831/375-7107.* E-mail cocofish@cocofish.com. Hrs: 11 am-10 pm; Sun from 10 am; Sun brunch to 4 pm. Closed Thanksgiving, Dec 25. Res accepted. Caribbean menu. Wine, beer. Semi-a la carte: lunch $5.95-$9.25, dinner $8.25-$13.25. Sun brunch $5.95-$8.95. Child's meals. Specialties: sea garden salad with Cajun spices, prawns Belize. Caribbean decor. Cr cds: A, C, DS, MC, V.

D

★★★ **GERNOT'S VICTORIA HOUSE.** *649 Lighthouse Ave (93950). 831/646-1477.* Hrs: 5:30-9 pm. Closed Mon; Dec 25. Res accepted. No A/C. Wine, beer. Semi-a la carte: dinner $18-$24. Specializes in veal, game, local seafood. Restored Queen Anne-style Victorian mansion (1894). Cr cds: A, C, MC, V.

★★★ **OLD BATH HOUSE.** *620 Ocean View Blvd (93950). 831/375-5195.* Hrs: 5-10:30 pm; Sat, Sun from 4 pm. Res accepted. No A/C. Continental menu. Bar 4 pm-midnight. Semi-a la carte: dinner $16.50-

$28.50. Specializes in unique seafood, game, beef dishes, fresh Dungeness crab. Own pastries. In 1930s Victorian-style building overlooking Lover's Point. Cr cds: A, C, D, DS, MC, V.

✓★ **PEPPERS MEXICALI CAFE.** *170 Forest Ave (93950). 831/373-6892.* Hrs: 11:30 am-10 pm; Fri, Sat to 10:30 pm; Sun 4-10 pm. Closed Tues; some major hols. Res accepted. Mexican, Latin Amer menu. Beer, wine. Semi-a la carte: lunch, dinner $5.75-$10.95. Specializes in fresh seafood, fajitas. Own tamales, chips, salsa. Southwestern decor; Latin Amer artifacts. Cr cds: A, C, D, DS, MC, V.

D

★★ **TASTE CAFE & BISTRO.** *1199 Forest Ave (93950). 831/655-0324.* Hrs: 5-9 pm; Fri, Sat to 10 pm. Closed Mon; Easter, July 4, Thanksgiving; also mid-Dec-early Jan. Res accepted. Semi-a la carte: dinner $15-$25. Child's meals. Specializes in fish, lamb, chicken. Contemporary bistro decor. Totally nonsmoking. Cr cds: C.

D

★ **TINNERY AT THE BEACH.** *631 Ocean View Blvd (93950). 831/646-1040.* Hrs: 8 am-midnight; Sat, Sun to 1 am. No A/C. Bar. Semi-a la carte: bkfst $5.50-$9.99, lunch $6.50-$12.99, dinner $10.99-$23.99. Child's meals. Specializes in seafood, pizza, steak, ribs. Parking. Outdoor dining. Entertainment Wed-Sat. Ocean view. Cr cds: A, C, D, DS, MC, V.

D

✓★ **VITO'S ITALIAN RESTAURANT.** *1180 Forest Ave (93950). 408/375-3070.* Hrs: 5-10 pm. Closed Thanksgiving, Dec 25. Res accepted. Italian menu. Wine, beer. Semi-a la carte: dinner $10.50-$14.95. Child's meals. Specialties: seafood pasta, lasagna. Totally nonsmoking. Cr cds: A, C, D, DS, MC, V.

D

Palm Desert (J-5)

Pop 23,252 **Elev** 243 ft **Area Code** 760 **Zip** 92260

Information Chamber of Commerce, 72-990 CA 111; 760/346-6111 or 800/873-2428

What to See and Do

Palms to Pines Highway. Scenic CA 74 goes S & W toward Idyllwild and Hemet (see both).

The Living Desert. This 1,200-acre wildlife and botanical park contains interpretive exhibits from the world's deserts. Animals include mountain lions, zebras, bighorn sheep, coyotes, cheetas, reptiles and birds. Native American exhibits; picnic areas, nature trails; gift shop; cafe; nursery. Special programs on wkends. (Sept-July, daily; closed Dec 25, also Aug) 47-900 S Portola Ave. Phone 760/346-5694. ¢¢¢

Annual Event

Bob Hope Chrysler Classic. Golf pros and celebrities play at four country clubs at Bermuda Dunes, La Quinta, Palm Desert and Indian Wells. Phone 760/346-8184. Mid-Jan.

Motels

✓★★ **FAIRFIELD INN BY MARRIOTT.** *72 322 US Hwy 111 (92260). 760/341-9100; FAX 760/773-3515; res: 800/633-8300.* 112 rms, 3 story. Mid-Jan-May: S, D $85-$95; each addl $7; suites $130; under 18 free; lower rates rest of yr. Crib free. TV; cable (premium). Heated pool; whirlpool. Complimentary continental bkfst. Restaurant nearby. Ck-out 11 am. Meeting rm. Business servs avail. Free airport transportation. Putting green. Some refrigerators. Private patios, balconies. Cr cds: A, C, D, DS, MC, V.

D SC

★★ **HOLIDAY INN EXPRESS.** *74675 US Hwy 111 (92260). 760/340-4303; FAX 760/340-3723; res: 800/465-4329.* 131 rms, 3 story. Jan-May: S, D $79-$159; suites $95-$209; under 18 free; lower rates rest of yr. Crib free. TV; cable (premium), VCR avail (movies). Heated pool; whirlpool. Coffee in rms. Complimentary California bkfst. Restaurant adj. Ck-out noon. Coin lndry. Business servs avail. In-rm modem link. Valet serv. Tennis. Exercise equipt. Health club privileges. Lawn games. Some refrigerators. Balconies. Picnic tables. Cr cds: A, C, D, DS, MC, V.

D SC

★ **INN AT DEEP CANYON.** *74470 Abronia Trl (92260). 760/346-8061; FAX 760/341-9120; res: 800/253-0044; res: 800/253-0004.* E-mail innkper@msn.com; web www.desertgold.com/inn/inn.html. 32 rms, 2 story, 15 kit. units. Mid-Dec-May: S, D $69-$119; kit. units $109-$129; wkly rates, golf plans; lower rates rest of yr. Crib free. Pet accepted, some restrictions; $20 deposit. TV; cable. Complimentary continental bkfst. Complimentary coffee in rms. Restaurant nearby. Ck-out noon. Business servs avail. Golf privileges. Pool. Refrigerators. Cr cds: A, C, DS, MC, V.

D

★★ **INTERNATIONAL LODGE.** *74380 El Camino (86023). 760/346-6161; FAX 760/568-0563; res: 800/874-9338.* Web www.quikpage.com/i/interdesert. 50 kit. units, 50 with shower only, 2 story. Jan-Mar: S, D $110; under 3 free; wkly, monthly rates; hols (2-day min); lower rates rest of yr. TV; cable, some VCRs. 2 heated pools; whirlpool. Complimentary coffee in rms. Restaurant nearby. Ck-out noon. Coin lndry. Business servs avail. Balconies. Cr cds: A, C, DS, MC, V.

SC

★★ **VACATION INN.** *74715 US Hwy 111 (92260). 760/340-4441; FAX 760/773-9413; res: 800/231-8675.* Web www.vacationinn.com. 130 rms, 3 story. Jan-May: S, D $99-$116; each addl $10; under 17 free; lower rates rest of yr. Crib free. TV; cable (premium). Heated pool; whirlpool. Continental bkfst. Complimentary coffee in rms. Restaurant nearby. Ck-out noon. Meeting rm. Business servs avail. Free airport transportation. Tennis. Putting green. Refrigerators; microwaves avail. Private patios, balconies. Cr cds: A, C, D, DS, JCB, MC, V.

D SC

Motor Hotel

★★★ **EMBASSY SUITES.** *74-700 US Hwy 111 (92260). 760/340-6600; FAX 760/340-9519; res: 800/362-2779.* Web www.embassy-suites.com. 198 suites, 3 story. Jan-May: S, D $189-$249; each addl $15; exec suites $259-$289; under 12 free; lower rates rest of yr. Crib free. TV; cable (premium), VCR avail (movies). Heated pool; whirlpool, poolside serv. Complimentary full bkfst. Coffee in rms. Restaurant 11:30 am-2:30 pm, 5-10 pm. Rm serv. Bar to 2 am; entertainment. Ck-out noon. Meeting rms. Business servs avail. In-rm modem link. Exercise equipt. Health club privileges. Lighted tennis. Putting green. Gift shop. Refrigerators; microwaves avail. Some balconies. Courtyard. Cr cds: A, C, D, DS, MC, V.

D SC

Resorts

★★★★ **HYATT GRAND CHAMPIONS.** *44-600 Indian Wells Lane (92210), I-10, exit Washington. 760/341-1000; FAX 760/568-2236.* Web www.hyatt.com. Set on 35 elaborately landscaped acres, this Moorish-style resort has guest rooms and villas. The rooms have scenic views of the Ocean. 318 rms in main bldg, 5 story, 19 Italian-style garden villas, 1- & 2-bedrm. Jan-May: S, D $305-$380; each addl $25; villas $810-$1,020; under 18 free; golf, tennis plans; lower rates rest of yr. Crib free. Valet parking (fee). TV; cable (premium), VCR avail. 4 pools; whirlpool, wading pool, poolside serv. Supervised child's activities; ages 3-12. Complimentary coffee in rms. Dining rm 6:30 am-10 pm. Box lunches, snack bar, picnics. Rm serv 6am-2 am. Bar 11-1 am. Ck-out 1 pm, ck-in 4 pm. Convention facilities. Business center. In-rm modem link. Beauty shop. Sports dir. 12 tennis courts including 2 clay, 2 grass, 8 hard surface, pro, pro shop. 36-hole golf, greens fee $130-$180, pro, putting green, driving range, pro shop. Bicycles. Lawn games. Entertainment. Exercise rm; sauna, steam rm. Spa. Some refrigerators, minibars, fireplaces. Private patios, balconies. Butler serv in villas 6am-11 pm. Luxury level. Cr cds: A, C, D, DS, ER, JCB, MC, V.

D SC

★★★ **INDIAN WELLS RESORT HOTEL.** *76-661 Hwy 111 (89122), S on CA 111, at Club Dr. 760/345-6466; FAX 760/772-5083; res: 800/248-3220.* Web www.desert-resorts.com. 155 rms, 3 story. Mid-Jan-Apr: S, D $189-$249; suites $390-$430; under 18 free; golf plans; wkend, long-stay rates; lower rates rest of yr. Crib avail. TV; VCR avail (movies). Heated pool; whirlpool, poolside serv. Restaurant 6:30 am-2 pm, 5-10 pm; wkends to 11 pm. Rm serv. Box lunches. Bar 10:30 am-midnight; entertainment wkends. Ck-out noon, ck-in 3 pm. Gift shop. Grocery 1 mi, coin Indry 3 mi. Bellhops. Valet serv. Concierge. Meeting rms. Business servs avail. In-rm modem link. Airport transportation. Tennis. 27-hole golf privileges, greens fee $175, putting green, driving range. Bicycles. Exercise equipt; bicycles, treadmill. Health club privileges. Massage. Minibars. Balconies. Cr cds: A, C, D, DS, JCB, MC, V.

D SC

★★★★ **MARRIOTT'S DESERT SPRINGS RESORT & SPA.** *74855 Country Club Dr (92260). 760/341-2211; FAX 760/341-1872; res: 800/331-3112.* Web www.marriott.com/marriott/ctdca. Situated on 420 landscaped acres crisscrossed by waterways and dotted with lakes, this resort has an eight-story atrium lobby with a dramatic waterfall. Boats transport guests to the restaurants and bars. 884 rms, 8 story. Late Dec-Memorial Day: S, D $350-$450; suites $600-$2,000; golf, tennis, spa plans; lower rates rest of yr. Crib free. Garage, valet parking (fee). TV; cable (premium). 5 heated pools; whirlpools, poolside serv. Supervised child's activities; ages 4-12. Dining rms 6:30 am-10 pm (see TUSCANY). Box lunches, snack bar, picnics. Bar 11-2 am. Ck-out noon, ck-in 4 pm. Convention facilities. Business center. In-rm modem link. Concierge. Shopping arcade. Jose' Eber Salon. Sports dir. 20 hard tennis courts, 7 lighted, 3 clay, 2 grass. 36-hole golf, greens fee $145, pro, championship putting course, putting green, driving range. Boats. Lawn games. Act dir; entertainment. Exercise rm; 30,000 sq ft European Health Spa. Minibars; microwaves avail. Private patios, balconies w/view. Cr cds: A, C, D, DS, ER, JCB, MC, V.

D SC

★★★ **RENAISSANCE ESMERALDA.** *44-400 Indian Wells Lane (92210), 1 blk S of CA 111. 760/773-4444; FAX 760/773-9250.* Web www.renaissancehotels.com. 560 units, 7 story. Jan-May: S, D $300-$400; each addl $25; suites $600-$2,500; under 18 free; packege plans; lower rates rest of yr. Crib free. Pet accepted, some restrictions. TV; cable (premium). 2 pools; whirlpool, wading pool, poolside serv. Supervised child's activities; ages 3-12. Dining rms 6:30 am-10 pm (also see SIROCCO). Rm serv 6am-1am. Bar noon-2 am; entertainment. Ck-out noon, ck-in 3 pm. Coin Indry. Meeting rms. Business center. In-rm modem link. Bellhops. Valet serv. Concierge. Gift shops. Airport transportation. Sports dir. Lighted tennis, pro. 36-hole golf, greens fee $100-$110, pro, putting green, driving range. Tennis & golf clinics; equipt rentals. Private beach. Hiking. Lawn games. Game rm. Exercise rm; sauna, steam rm. Massage. Bathrm phones, minibars; some wet bars. Some suites with woodburning fireplace. Balconies. Cr cds: A, C, D, DS, ER, JCB, MC, V.

D SC

★★★ **SHADOW MOUNTAIN RESORT.** *45750 San Luis Rey (92260). 760/346-6123; FAX 760/346-6518; res: 800/472-3713.* Web www.shadow-mountain.com. 125 units, 1-2 story. Mid-Feb-mid-Apr, maj hols: S, D $155-$195; each addl $15; condos & villas $240-$520; under 18 free; lower rates rest of yr. Crib $15. TV; cable, VCR avail (movies $4). 4 heated pools; whirlpools, poolside serv. Supervised child's activities (wkends Dec-May), ages 5-12. Ck-out 11 am, ck-in 3 pm. Coin Indry. Meeting rms. Business center. In-rm modem link. Valet serv. Concierge. 16 tennis courts, 6 lighted, pro, pro shop. 18-hole golf privileges. Exercise equipt; sauna. Massage. Lawn games. Bicycle rentals. Private patios, balconies. Home of the Desert Tennis Academy. Cr cds: A, C, D, MC, V.

SC

Inn

★★★ **TRES PALMAS BED & BREAKFAST.** *73-135 Tumbleweed Ln (92260). 760/773-9858; FAX 760/776-9159; res: 800/770-9858.* Web www.innformation.com/ca/trespalmas. 4 rms. No rm phones. Mid-Oct-mid-June: S, D $110-$185; each addl $20; wkly rates; wkends, hols (2-day min); lower rates rest of yr. Children over 10 yrs only. TV; cable. Pool. Complimentary continental bkfst. Restaurant nearby. Ck-out 11 am, ck-in 3-8 pm. Southwestern decor. Totally nonsmoking. Cr cds: A, C, MC, V.

Restaurants

★★★ **A TOUCH OF MAMA'S.** *74063 US Highway 111 (92260). 760/568-1315.* Hrs: 5-10:30 pm; hrs may vary. Closed Dec 24. Res accepted. California Italian menu. Bar. Semi-a la carte: dinner $11.95-$23.95. Specialties: osso bucco, veal piccata, chicken basilica. Guitarist. Mural of Lago de Como. Cr cds: A, C, D, MC, V.

D

★★ **CEDAR CREEK INN.** *73-445 El Paseo (92260). 760/340-1236.* Hrs: 11 am-10 pm. Closed Dec 25. Bar. Semi-a la carte: lunch $7.95-$11.95, dinner $11.95-$22.95. Specializes in fresh fish, prime rib, steak. Own soups. Outdoor dining. Extensive dessert menu. Cr cds: A, C, D, MC, V.

D

★★★ **CLUB 74.** *73-061 El Paseo (92260). 760/568-2782.* Hrs: 11:30 am-2:30 pm, 5:30-10 pm; Sun from 5:30 pm. Res accepted. French menu. Bar. A la carte entrees: lunch $9.50-$14, dinner $16-$28. Specialties: L.I. duckling, escargot, salade Montrachet. Pianist. On 2nd floor, overlooking El Paseo, with view of valley. Jacket. Cr cds: A, C, D, DS, MC, V.

D

★★ **CUISTOT.** *73-111 El Paseo (92260). 760/340-1000.* Hrs: 11:30 am-2:30 pm, 6-10 pm. Closed Mon, some major hols, also Aug. Res accepted. French California menu. Bar. Wine cellar. A la carte entrees: lunch $8.75-$18.95, dinner $17.95-$28.75. Specializes in veal chop, rack of lamb, fresh fish. Cr cds: A, C, D, MC, V.

D

★★★ **HAMILTON'S @ THE HYATT.** *73-111 El Paseo. 760/340-4499.* Cuisine Mediteranian. Specialties lamp chops, lobsters, steaks. Hrs Mon - Sun 6:00 pm -10:00 pm. Bar open until 2am. Currently closed Mon & Sun. call to confirm. Prices $18 -$32 Great ambience of Casablanca. Very exotic. Outdoor seating. View of the moutains. Fireplaces. Cr cds: C.

★★★ **JILLIAN'S.** *74-155 El Paseo (92260). 760/776-8242.* Hrs: 6 pm-close. Closed Jan 1, Dec 25; also mid-June-Sept. Res required. Bar. Wine cellar. Semi-a la carte: dinner $17-$31. Specializes in rack of lamb, salmon in parchment, pasta. Pianist, vocalist. Valet parking. Outdoor dining in courtyard. Semi-formal decor in 4 dining areas. Cr cds: A, C, D, MC, V.

D

★★ **KAISER GRILLE.** *74-225 CA 111 (92260). 760/779-1988.* Hrs: 5-9:30 pm; early-bird dinner 5-6 pm. Closed some major hols. Res accepted. Bar. A la carte entrees: dinner $8.95-$19.50. Specialties: hazelnut salmon, blackened prime rib, pasta. Valet parking. Outdoor dining. Open kitchen. Cr cds: A, C, D, DS, MC, V.

D

★★ **LA QUINTA CLIFFHOUSE.** *78-250 CA 111 (92260). 760/360-5991.* Hrs: 11:30 am-2 pm, 5-9 pm; Fri, Sat to 9:30 pm; Sun brunch (seasonal) 10 am-2 pm. Closed Dec 25, July 4. Res accepted. Bar. Semi-a la carte: lunch $5.95-$11.95, dinner $12.95-$19.95. Child's meals. Specializes in fresh seafood, steak, pasta. Valet parking. Outdoor dining. Situated on a hillside. 3 separate dining ares, 2 with valley view. Southwestern decor, western artifacts, memorabilia. Cr cds: A, C, MC, V.

D ♥

★★ **LE DONNE CUCINA ITALIANA.** *72-624 El Paseo (92260). 760/773-9441.* Hrs: 5-9:30 pm. Closed Sun; Jan 1, Dec 25. Res accepted. Italian menu. Wine. A la carte entrees: dinner $8.50-$15.95. Child's meals. Specialties: veal masala, linguine with mussels and clams, fettuccine with lobster tail. Own baking. Outdoor dining. Italian decor; murals. Totally nonsmoking. Cr cds: A, C, MC, V.

D

★★★ **LE PAON.** *45640 CA 74 (92260). 760/568-3651.* Web www.desertconcierge.com. Hrs: 6-10 pm; wkends to 11 pm. Closed Thanksgiving. Res accepted. French, continental menu. Bar to 2 am. Wine cellar. A la carte entrees: dinner $16-$35. Specializes in veal, poultry, seafood. Pianist, vocalist. Valet parking. Outdoor dining. Elegant dining; rose garden. Cr cds: A, C, D, DS, MC, V.

D

★ **LE SAINT GERMAIN.** *74985 US Highway 111 (92210). 760/773-6511.* Hrs: Lunch 11:30-2:30, Dinner 5:30-10:00 pm. Res preferred. French menu. Bar. Wine cellar. Semi-a la carte: dinner $18-$32. Specializes in seafood, lamb, veal. Pianist. Valet parking. Oil painting of Paris. Cr cds: A, C, D, DS, MC, V.

D

★★ **LG'S PRIME STEAKHOUSE.** *74225 US Highway 111 (92260). 760/779-9799.* Hrs: from 5:30 pm. Res accepted. Bar. A la carte entrees: dinner $18.95-$45.95. Specializes in 6 varieties of steak, fresh fish, chicken. Valet parking. Pueblo-style structure with 4 separate dining areas; Southwestern decor, artifacts. Cr cds: A, C, D, DS, MC, V.

D

★ **LOUISE'S PANTRY.** *111 Town Center Way (92260). 760/346-1315.* Hrs: 7 am-8:30 pm. Closed Dec 25. Wine, beer. Semi-a la carte: bkfst $1.95-$5.50, lunch $4.95-$7.25, dinner $5.95-$10.95. Child's meals. Specializes in chicken dumplings, meat loaf, leg of lamb. Own desserts. Parking. Outdoor dining. Diner atmosphere. Cr cds: C, DS, MC, V.

D ♥

★ **NEST.** *75-188 CA 111 (92210), E of Cook St. 760/346-2314.* Hrs: 5-10:30 pm. Closed major hols. Continental menu. Bar to 12:30 am. Semi-a la carte: dinner $9.50-$21.95. Specializes in fresh fish, pasta. Entertainment. Parking. Newspaper menu. Bistro atmosphere, Parisian decor. Cr cds: A, C, D, DS, MC, V.

D

★★ **PALOMINO EURO BISTRO.** *73-101 CA 111 (92260). 760/773-9091.* Hrs: 5-10 pm; Fri, Sat to 11 pm. Closed July 4, Dec 25. Res accepted. Mediterranean menu. Bar. Wine list. A la carte entrees: dinner $7.95-$24.95. Child's meals. Specialties: grilled salmon, spit roasted garlic chicken, oven-roasted garlic prawns. Valet parking. Outdoor dining. Cr cds: A, C, D, DS, MC, V.

D

✓★ **PASTA ITALIA.** *44-491 Town Center Way (92260). 760/341-1422.* Hrs: 11:30 am-2:30 pm, 5-10 pm; Fri, Sat to 10:30 pm; Sun 5-10 pm. Res accepted. Italian menu. Bar. Semi-a la carte entrees: lunch $5.95-$8.95, dinner $6.95-$15.95. Specializes in pasta, non-cholesterol dishes, tiramisu. Own desserts. Entertainment. Parking. Outdoor dining. Old World trattoria atmosphere. Family-owned. Cr cds: A, C, D, MC, V.

D ♥

★★★ **RISTORANTE MAMMA GINA.** *73-705 El Paseo (92260). 760/568-9898.* Hrs: 11:30 am-2 pm, 5:15-10 pm; Fri, Sat to 10:30 pm; Sun from 5:15 pm. Closed Easter, Thanksgiving, Dec 25. Res accepted. Northern Italian menu. Bar. A la carte entrees: lunch $6.90-$13.90, dinner $12.90-$26.90. Specializes in pasta, veal. Valet parking. Contemporary and Italian decor. Cr cds: A, C, D, MC, V.

D

★★ **SESAME RESTAURANT.** *50981 Washington St (92253). 760/771-4040.* Hrs: 11:30 am-2:30 pm, 5:30-10 pm. Closed Sun; Thanksgiving, Dec 25. Res accepted. Bar. A la carte entrees: lunch $5.95-$8.95, dinner $10.50-$19.50. Child's meals. Specialties: veal piccata, lamb shank with couscous, monkfish with lobster cream sauce. Outdoor dining. Totally nonsmoking. Cr cds: A, C, D, DS, MC, V.

D

★★★ **SIROCCO.** *(See Renaissance Esmeralda Resort) 760/773-4444.* Hrs: 11:30 am-2:30 pm, 6-10 pm; Sat, Sun from 6 pm. Closed June-Sept. Res accepted. Mediterranean cuisine. Bar. Wine cellar. A la carte entrees: lunch $8.95-$16.95, dinner $12-$36. Specialties: shellfish cioppino, sauteed Maine lobster. Own baking. Valet parking. Classical Mediterranean decor. Two display wine rooms at entry. Overlooks golf course. Cr cds: A, C, D, DS, ER, JCB, MC, V.

D ♥

★★ **TUSCANY.** *(see Marriott's Desert Springs Resort) 74855 Country Club Dr. 760/341-2211.* Northern Italian. Hrs: Sun-Thurs 5:30-10, Fri & Sat until 11 pm. $19-$36. Res reqd. Child meals. Outdoor dining by request. Bar. Wine Cellar (dine in/wine tasting). Valet. Cr cds: C.

Palm Springs Area (J-5)

Area Code 760

What was once one of the country's favorite vacation towns has become one of America's most popular resort regions. Tourism experienced a remarkable boom in the years since the first Hollywood celebrities built their winter houses here. The beautiful scenery and ideal weather that attracted those first vacationers are still present, but as the area's popularity has increased they have been accompanied by an ever growing number of hotels, inns, resorts, shopping malls, golf courses, recreation sites and performing arts facilities. No longer is the area solely a retreat for the famous and wealthy. Although there are more luxurious restaurants, resorts and stores than ever before, it is now also quite easy to take full advantage of the area's attractions while on a restricted budget. The more than three million people who visit each year come mostly to relax, soak up the sun and enjoy the climate. It is also possible to enjoy everything from cross-country skiing atop Mt San Jacinto to camping among the tall cactus at Joshua Tree National Park (see). The following towns, all within a short distance of the city of Palm Springs, provide this great variety of recreation: Desert Hot Springs, Idyllwild, Indio, Palm Desert and Palm Springs (see all).

Palm Springs (J-5)

Founded 1876 **Pop** 40,181 **Elev** 466 ft **Area Code** 760
Web www.desert-resorts.com

Information Palm Springs Desert Resort Convention and Visitors Bureau, 69-930 CA 111, Ste 201, Rancho Mirage, 92270; 760/770-9000 or 800/417-3529

Discovered in 1774 by a Spanish explorer, this site was dubbed Agua Caliente (hot water). One hundred years later it was the location of a stagecoach stop and a drowsy, one-store railroad town. Today, after a second hundred years, Palm Springs is known as "America's premier desert resort." Originally the domain of the Cahuilla, the city has been laid out in a checkerboard pattern, with nearly every other square mile still owned by the tribe.

What to See and Do

Gray Line bus tours. Contact 333 S Indian Canyon Rd, Ste C, 92262; phone 760/325-0974.

Moorten's Botanical Garden. Approx 3,000 varieties of desert plants; nature trails. World's first "cactarium" contains several hundred species of cactus and desert plants from around the world. Guide maps to desert wildflowers. (Daily; closed some major hols) 1701 S Palm Canyon Dr. Phone 760/327-6555. ¢

Oasis Waterpark. This 22-acre water park has 13 water slides, inner tube ride, wave pool and beach sand volleyball courts. (Mid-Mar-early Sept, daily; early Sept-late Oct, wkends) 5 mi S off I-10, at 1500 Gene Autry Trail. Phone 760/325-7873 or 760/327-0499. ¢¢¢¢¢ Also here is

Uprising Rock Climbing Center. The only outdoor rock-climbing gym in the US. Offers training and climbing for all ages. Night climbing. (Daily) 1500 S Gene Autry Trail. Phone 760/320-6630. ¢¢¢¢¢

Palm Canyon. Approx 3,000 native palm trees line a stream bed. Magnificent views from the canyon floor or from points above the canyon. Picnic tables. (Early Sept-June, daily) 6½ mi S on S Palm Canyon Dr, in the Palm Springs Indian Canyons. Phone 760/325-5673. ¢¢

★ **Palm Springs Aerial Tramway.** World's longest double-reversible, single-span aerial tramway. Two 80-passenger cars make 2½-mi trip ascending to 8,516-ft elevation on Mt San Jacinto. Picnicking, camping in summer; cafeteria at summit. (Daily; closed 2 wks beginning 1st Mon Aug) 2 mi N on CA 111, then 4 mi W on Tramway Rd. Phone 760/325-1391 (recording). ¢¢¢¢¢

Palm Springs Desert Museum. Natural science and art exhibits; performing arts; features art of the American West, contemporary art and Native American basketry, film retrospectives. (Mid-Sept-June, daily exc Mon; closed Jan 1, Thanksgiving, Dec 25) Free admission 1st Tues each month. 101 Museum Dr. Phone 760/325-7186 or 760/325-0189. ¢¢

Tahquitz Creek Palm Springs Golf Resort. There are 87 other courses within a 15-mi radius of the city, making this area the "Winter Golf Capital of the World." (Daily) 1885 Golf Club Dr, 3 mi SE on CA 111. Phone 760/328-1005 or 760/328-1956. ¢¢¢¢¢

Village Green Heritage Center. Consists of two 19th-century houses exhibiting artifacts from early Palm Springs. **McCallum Adobe** (ca 1885) is the oldest building in city and houses extensive collection of photographs, paintings, clothes, tools, books and Native American ware. **Miss Cornelia's "Little House"** (ca 1890) was constructed of rail ties from the defunct Palmdale Railway and is furnished with authentic antiques. (Mid-Oct-May, Wed-Sun; rest of yr, by appt; closed major hols) 221 S Palm Canyon Dr. Phone 760/323-8297. Per house ¢

Motels

★★ **BEST WESTERN INN.** *1633 S Palm Canyon Dr (92264). 760/325-9177; FAX 760/325-9177; res: 800/528-1234; res: 800/222-4678.* Web www.bestwestern.com/thisco/bw/05466/05466_b.html. 72 rms, 3 story. Late Dec-mid-June: S, D $78-$138; each addl $10; under 12 free; higher rates: hols, wkends; lower rates rest of yr. Crib $10. TV; cable. Heated pool; whirlpool. Complimentary continental bkfst. Restaurant nearby. Ck-out noon. Business servs avail. In-rm modem link. Health club privileges. Refrigerators; some microwaves. Cr cds: A, C, D, DS, ER, JCB, MC, V.

SC

★ **CHANDLER INN.** *1530 N Indian Canyon Dr (92262). 760/320-8949; FAX 760/320-8949.* 21 rms, 2 story, 5 kit. units. Nov-May: S, D $79-$98; kit. units $98; wkly rates; golf plans; wkends, hols (2-, 3-day min). Pet accepted, some restrictions; $20 deposit. TV; cable, VCR avail (movies). Complimentary continental bkfst. Restaurant nearby. Ck-out 11 am. Business servs avail. Golf privileges. Pool; whirlpool. Refrigerators. Cr cds: A, C, D, JCB, MC, V.

SC

★★ **CHUCKAWALLA MANOR.** *269 E Chuckwalla Rd (92262). 760/325-2567; FAX 760/864-6208; res: 800/700-8075.* E-mail vilorleans@aol.com; web www.ernestallen.com:80//tr/ca/ville'orleans/html3. 14 units, 1-2 story, 6 suites. Sept-May: S, D $69-$89; suites $105-$225; monthly, wkly rates; higher rates major hols; lower rates rest of yr. Adults only. TV; cable, VCR (free movies). Heated pool; whirlpool. Complimentary coffee in rms. Restaurant nearby. Ck-out noon. Business servs avail. Bellhop. Concierge. Free airport transportation. Tennis privileges. 18-hole golf privileges. Refrigerators; microwaves avail. Cr cds: A, C, MC, V.

SC

★★★ **COURTYARD BY MARRIOTT.** *1300 E Tahquitz Canyon Way (92262), near Municipal Airport. 760/322-6100; FAX 760/322-6091; res: 800/321-2211.* 149 rms, 3 story. Mid-Dec-May: S, D $149; suites $169; under 18 free; lower rates rest of yr. Crib free. TV; cable (premium). Heated pool. Complimentary coffee in rms. Restaurant 6:30-10:30 am. Bar 4-11 pm. Ck-out noon. Coin Indry. Meeting rms. Business servs avail. In-rm modem link. Valet serv. Free airport transportation. Exercise equipt. Refrigerators, microwaves avail. Balconies. Cr cds: A, C, D, DS, MC, V.

D SC

★★ **DAYS INN.** *69-151 E Palm Canyon Dr (92234), 1 blk E of Date Palm Dr on CA 111. 760/324-5934; FAX 760/324-3034; res: 800/329-7466.* E-mail cathcity@soramanagement.com; web www.soramanagement.com. 94 kit. suites, 3 story. Jan-May: kit. suites $95-$159; under 16 free; higher rates wkends; lower rates rest of yr. Crib free. Pet accepted. TV; cable (premium). Heated pool; whirlpool. Complimentary continental bkfst. Restaurant opp open 24 hrs. Ck-out noon. Coin Indry. Meeting rms. Business servs avail. Valet serv. Free airport transportation. Golf privileges. Cr cds: A, C, D, DS, JCB, MC, V.

D SC

★★ **EL RANCHO LODGE.** *1330 E Palm Canyon Dr (92264). 760/327-1339.* 19 rms, 5 kit. suites. Oct-May: S, D $61-$80; kit. suites $131; lower rates rest of yr. TV; cable. Heated pool; whirlpool. Complimentary continental bkfst. Restaurant opp open 24 hrs. Ck-out noon. Coin Indry. Refrigerators; many microwaves. Some private patios. Cr cds: A, C, DS, MC, V.

✓★★ **HAMPTON INN.** *2000 N Palm Canyon Dr (92262). 760/320-0555; FAX 760/320-2261; res: 800/732-7755.* Web www.hampton-inn.com. 96 rms, 2 story. Jan-May: S, D $79-$99; under 18 free; higher rates: special events, hols, wkends; lower rates rest of yr. Crib free. TV; cable (premium). Heated pool; whirlpool. Complimentary continental bkfst. Restaurant nearby. Ck-out noon. Meeting rms. Business servs avail. In-rm modem link. Valet serv. Health club privileges. Some refrigerators; microwaves avail. Spanish-style architecture. Cr cds: A, C, D, DS, MC, V.

D SC

✓★ **HOWARD JOHNSON HOTEL.** *701 E Palm Canyon Dr (92264). 760/320-2700; FAX 760/320-1591; res: 800/854-4345.* 205 rms, 2 story. Mid-Dec-May: S $65; D $70; higher rates: Easter, Memorial Day, Labor Day; lower rates rest of yr. Crib free. TV; cable. Heated pool; whirlpool. Restaurant open 24 hrs. Bar 10 am-midnight. Ck-out noon. Coin Indry. Business servs avail. Cr cds: A, C, D, DS, JCB, MC, V.

SC

★★ **L'HORIZON GARDEN HOTEL.** *1050 E Palm Canyon Dr (92264). 760/323-1858; FAX 760/327-2933; res: 800/377-7855.* 22 rms, 19 with shower only, 7 kit. units. Mid-Dec-early July: S, D $115; kit. units $140; monthly rates; wkends (2-day min); lower rates rest of yr. TV; cable, VCR avail. Complimentary continental bkfst. Restaurant opp open 24 hrs. Ck-out noon. Business servs avail. Tennis privileges. Golf privileges. Pool; whirlpool. Picnic tables, grills. Totally nonsmoking. Cr cds: A, C, D, DS, MC, V.

★★★ **LA SIESTA VILLAS.** *247 W Stevens Rd (92262). 760/325-2269; FAX 760/778-6533.* E-mail sscolt@aol.com; web www.adpark.com/lasiestavillas. 10 villas (1-2-bedrm). Mid-Dec-May: villas $125-$225 (2-day min); wkly, monthly rates; lower rates rest of yr. Adults only. TV; cable, VCR. Heated pool; whirlpool. Restaurant nearby. Ck-out noon. Business servs avail. Concierge. Covered parking. Fireplaces. Private patios. Tropical setting. Cr cds: A, C, MC, V.

★★ **LE PALMIER INN.** *200 W Arenas Rd (89402). 760/320-8866; FAX 760/323-1501; res: 888/826-8866.* 24 kit. units, 16 with shower only, 1-2 story. Mid-Dec-early June: S, D $75-$125; each addl $15; wkends, hols (2-day min); higher rates: hols, special events; lower rates rest of yr. TV. Complimentary continental bkfst. Restaurant adj 7 am-10 pm. Ck-out noon. Business servs avail. Bellhops. Concierge. Tennis privileges. Pool. Lawn games. Refrigerators; many microwaves. Some balconies. Cr cds: A, C, DS, MC, V.

✓★★ **MIRA LOMA HOTEL.** *1420 N Indian Canyon Dr (92262). 760/320-1178; FAX 760/320-5308.* E-mail jmrook@ix.netcom.com; web www.prinet.com/miraloma. 14 rms, 6 kits. Oct-May: S, D $50-$90; kit. units $90; monthly rates; lower rates rest of yr. Adults only. TV; VCR avail. Heated pool. Complimentary continental bkfst. Ck-out noon. Refrigerators, microwaves. Cr cds: C, DS, MC, V.

✓★ **MOTEL 6.** *660 S Palm Canyon Dr (92264). 760/327-4200; FAX 760/320-9827; res: 800/466-8356.* 148 rms, shower only, 3 story. Sept-mid-Apr: S $34.99; D $40.99; each addl $3; under 17 free. Crib free. Pet accepted, some restrictions. TV; cable (premium). Heated pool. Restaurant nearby. Ck-out noon. Coin Indry. Business servs avail. Cr cds: A, C, D, DS, MC, V.

★★ **PLACE IN THE SUN.** *754 E San Lorenzo Rd (87123). 760/325-0254; FAX 760/327-9303; res: 800/779-2254.* 16 kit. units, 3 with shower only, 11 suites. Mid-Dec-May: S, D $59-$79; each addl $12; suites $99-$149; higher rates hols (2-day min); lower rates rest of yr. Crib $10. Pet accepted, some restrictions; $10. TV; cable. Heated pool. Restaurant nearby. Ck-out noon. Coin Indry. Meeting rms. Free airport transportation. Health club privileges. Lawn games. Refrigerators, microwaves. Cr cds: A, C, MC, V.

★★ **QUALITY INN.** *1269 E Palm Canyon Dr (92264). 760/323-2775; FAX 760/416-1014; res: 800/228-5050.* 145 rms, 2 story, 8 suites. Late Dec-May: S, D $65-$105; suites $95-$155; under 18 free; lower rates rest of yr. Crib avail. TV; cable. Heated pool; wading pool, whirlpool. Complimentary coffee in rms. Restaurant adj open 24 hrs. Ck-out noon. Coin Indry. Meeting rm. Business servs avail. In-rm modem link. Free airport transportation. Many refrigerators. Grill. Cr cds: A, C, D, DS, ER, JCB, MC, V.

★★ **SHILO INN.** *1875 N Palm Canyon Dr (92262). 760/320-7676; FAX 760/320-9543; res: 800/334-1049; res: 800/222-2244.* 124 rms, 2 story. Jan-May: S, D $90-$139; each addl $12; kit. units $140-$155; under 12 free; wkly, monthly rates; lower rates rest of yr. Crib free. TV; cable, VCR avail (movies). Heated pools; whirlpool. Complimentary continental bkfst. Coffee in rms. Ck-out noon. Coin Indry. Meeting rm. Business servs avail. Valet serv. Free airport transportation. Exercise equipt; sauna, steam rm. Health club privileges. Bathrm phones, refrigerators; microwaves avail. Private patios, balconies. Cr cds: A, C, D, DS, ER, JCB, MC, V.

★★★ **SUNDANCE VILLAS.** *303 W Cabrillo Rd (92262), 1 blk E of Palm Canyon Dr & 1 blk N of Racquet Club Rd. 760/325-3888; FAX 760/323-3029; res: 800/455-3888.* E-mail sundanceps@aol.com. 19 kit. villas. Mid-Dec-May: villas $295-$450; wkly rates; lower rates rest of yr. Crib $80/wk. TV; cable (premium), VCR. Pool; whirlpool. Restaurant nearby. Ck-out noon. Business servs avail. Valet serv. Concierge. Free airport transportation. Lighted tennis. Golf privileges. Wet bars, microwaves, fireplaces. Patios. Grills. Cr cds: A, C, D, DS, JCB, MC, V.

✓★★ **SUPER 8 LODGE.** *1900 N Palm Canyon Dr (92262). 760/322-3757; FAX 760/323-5290; res: 800/800-8000.* Web www.super8motels.com. 61 rms, 2 story. Late Dec-May: S $68; D $73; each addl $5; suites $90-$110; under 12 free; lower rates rest of yr. Crib $4. Pet accepted; $10. TV; cable. Heated pool; whirlpool. Complimentary continental bkfst. Restaurant nearby. Ck-out 11 am. Coin Indry. Business servs avail. Refrigerators. Cr cds: A, C, D, DS, MC, V.

★★ **TRAVELODGE.** *333 E Palm Canyon Dr (92264). 760/327-1211; FAX 760/320-4672; res: 800/578-7878.* E-mail langmann@aol.com; web www.ids2.com/motels/palmspringstl/. 157 rms, 2 story. Jan-mid-June: S, D $69-$89; each addl $10; higher rates: special events, hols, wkends; lower rates rest of yr. Crib free. TV; cable (premium). Heated pools; whirlpool. Complimentary coffee in rms. Restaurants nearby. Ck-out noon. Coin Indry. Business servs avail. Lawn games. Many refrigerators; microwaves avail. Private patios, balconies. Cr cds: A, C, D, DS, ER, MC, V.

✓★★ **VAGABOND INN.** *1699 S Palm Canyon Dr (92264). 760/325-7211; FAX 760/322-9269; res: 800/522-1555.* E-mail pavagabond@aol.com. 120 rms, 3 story. Jan-May: S, D $39-$99; higher rates: hols (2-day min), date festival, golf classics; lower rates rest of yr. Crib $6. TV. Heated pool; whirlpool. Sauna. Complimentary coffee in rms. Restaurant nearby. Ck-out noon. Business servs avail. Refrigerators avail. Cr cds: A, C, D, DS, ER, MC, V.

Motor Hotels

★★ **BEST WESTERN LAS BRISAS.** *222 S Indian Canyon Dr (92262). 760/325-4372; FAX 760/320-1371; res: 800/528-1234.* E-mail lbrisas@ix.netcom.com; web www.lasbrisashotel.com. 90 rms, 3 story. Jan-May: S, D $85-$159; each addl $10; suites $99-$169; under 17 free; lower rates rest of yr. Crib free. TV; cable. Pool; whirlpool, poolside serv. Complimentary full bkfst. Coffee in rms. Restaurant nearby. Bar noon-midnight. Ck-out noon. Coin Indry. Business servs avail. Health club privileges. Refrigerators; microwaves avail. Cr cds: A, C, D, DS, MC, V.

★★★ **PALM SPRINGS RIVERIA RESORT.** *1600 N Indian Canyon Dr (92262). 760/327-8311; FAX 760/327-4323; res: 800/444-8311.* E-mail riviera@thegrid.net; web desert-resorts.com. 477 rms, 2-3 story. Mid-Jan-mid-May: S, D $139-$189; each addl $20; suites $215-$860; under 18 free; lower rates rest of yr. Crib free. Pet accepted. TV; cable. 2 heated pools; whirlpools, poolside serv. Restaurant 6:30 am-10 pm. Rm serv. Bar 11 pm-2 am; entertainment. Ck-out noon. Convention facilities. In-rm modem link. Bellhops. Valet serv. Concierge. Sundries. Gift shop. Beauty shop. Free valet parking. Free airport transportation. Lighted tennis. Golf privileges. Exercise equipt. Massage. Health club privileges. Bicycle rentals. Lawn games. Bathrm phones, refrigerators; microwaves avail. Some wet bars. Balconies. Cr cds: A, C, D, DS, JCB, MC, V.

★★★ **SPA HOTEL & CASINO RESORT & MINERAL SPRINGS.** *100 N Indian Canyon Dive (92262), near Municipal Airport. 760/325-1461; FAX 760/325-3344; res: 800/854-1279.* Web www.desertresorts.com/facilities/hotels/spa/spa.html. 230 rms, 5 story. Jan-mid-June: S, D $129-$174; each addl $20; suites from $250; under 18 free; lower rates rest of yr. Crib $10. TV; cable, VCR avail (movies). 3 pools; 2 hot mineral pools; whirlpool, poolside serv. Restaurant 7 am-10 pm. Rm serv 24 hrs. Bar 10 pm-2 am. Ck-out noon. Meeting rms. Business center. Bellhops. Concierge. Sundries. Gift shop. Barber, beauty shop. Free airport transportation. Tennis privileges. 18-hole golf privileges. Exercise equipt; sauna, steam rm. Solarium. Some bathrm phones, refrigerators; microwaves avail. Private patios, balconies. Cr cds: A, C, D, DS, MC, V.

Hotels

★★★ **HILTON.** *400 E Tahquitz Canyon Way (92262), near Municipal Airport. 760/320-6868; FAX 760/320-2126; res: 800/445-8667.* E-mail pshilton@aol.com; web www.desertresorts.com. 260 rms, 3 story. Dec-May: S, D $205-$305; each addl $20; suites $265-$685; studio rms $155; kit. condos $235-$345; under 18 free; lower rates rest of yr. Crib free. Pet accepted. TV; cable (premium), VCR avail (movies). Heated pool; 2 whirlpools, poolside serv. Child's activities (Sept-May, some hols); ages 3-12. Coffee in rm. Restaurant 6 am-10 pm. Bar 4 pm-2 am. Ck-out noon. Convention facilities. Business center. In-rm modem link. Concierge. Gift shop. Barber, beauty shop. Valet parking. Free airport transportation. Exercise equipt; sauna. 6 lighted tennis courts, pro, pro shop. Golf privileges. Refrigerators, minibars; microwaves avail. Private patios, balconies. Cr cds: A, C, D, DS, ER, JCB, MC, V.

★★★ **HYATT REGENCY SUITES PALM SPRINGS.** *285 N Palm Canyon Dr (92262). 760/322-9000; FAX 760/322-6009.* Web www.hyatt.com. 192 suites, 6 story. Jan-Apr: suites $205-$425; under 18 free; mid-wk rates; lower rates rest of yr. Crib free. TV; cable (premium), VCR avail (movies). Pool; whirlpool, poolside serv. Restaurants 7 am-10 pm; Fri-Sun to 11 pm. Bar 11-1 am; entertainment Fri, Sat. Ck-out noon. Meeting rms. Business servs avail. Concierge. Valet parking. Airport transportation. Tennis privileges. Golf privileges. Exercise equipt. Massage. Bathrm phones, refrigerators, wet bars; microwaves avail. Private patios, balconies. Cr cds: A, C, D, DS, JCB, MC, V.

★★★ **PALM SPRINGS MARQUIS RESORT.** *150 S Indian Canyon Dr (92262), near Municipal Airport. 760/322-2121; FAX 760/322-2380; res: 800/223-1050.* Web www.desertresort.com. 166 rms, 101 kit. suites, 3 story. Jan-Apr: S, D $169-$210; suites $199-$750; wkly, monthly rates; golf, tennis packages; lower rates rest of yr. Underground, valet, overnight parking $7.50. Crib free. TV; cable, VCR avail (movies). 2 pools; wading pool, whirlpool, poolside serv. Supervised child's activities; ages 2-12. Restaurants 6:30 am-11 pm. Rm serv 24 hrs. Bar 11-2 am; entertainment wkends. Ck-out noon. Convention facilities. Business center. In-rm modem link. Concierge. Gift shop. Free airport transportation. Lighted tennis, pro. Golf privileges. Exercise equipt. Massage. Bathrm phones; microwaves avail. Private patios, balconies. View of San Jacinto Mountains. Eight-acre resort. Cr cds: A, C, D, DS, ER, JCB, MC, V.

★★ **RAMADA RESORT INN PALM SPRINGS.** *1800 E Palm Canyon Dr (92264), at Sunrise Way. 760/323-1711; FAX 760/327-6941; res: 800/245-6904.* 254 rms, 3 story. Feb-May: S, D $79-$139; each addl $15; suites $125-$200; under 18 free; higher rates: wkends, hols; lower rates rest of yr. Crib free. Pet accepted. TV. Heated pool; whirlpools, poolside serv. Coffee in rms. Restaurant 7 am-10 pm. Bar 11 am-midnight; entertainment wkends. Ck-out noon. Coin Indry. Meeting rms. In-rm modem link. Gift shop. Free airport transportation. Tennis privileges. Golf privileges. Exercise equipt; sauna. Refrigerators; wet bar in suites. Microwaves avail. Balconies. Cr cds: A, C, D, DS, MC, V.

★★★ **WYNDHAM HOTEL.** *888 Tahquitz Canyon Way (92262), near Municipal Airport. 760/322-6000; FAX 760/322-5351; res: 800/996-3426.* Web www.travelweb.com. 410 units, 5 story, 158 suites. Jan-June: S, D $210-$240; each addl $25; suites $230-$250; under 17 free; lower rates rest of yr. Crib free. Pet accepted; $25. TV; cable. Pool; wading pool, whirlpool, poolside serv. Coffee in rms. Restaurant 6:30 am-11 pm. Bar 11-1:30 am. Ck-out noon. Convention facilities. Business center. In-rm modem link. Concierge. Gift shops. Barber, beauty shop. Free valet parking. Free airport transportation. Tennis privileges. Golf privileges. Exercise equipt; sauna. Private patios, balconies. Covered walkway to convention center. Cr cds: A, C, D, DS, ER, JCB, MC, V.

Resorts

★★★ **DOUBLETREE RESORT HOTEL.** *67967 Vista Chino at Landau Blvd (92263). 760/322-7000; FAX 760/322-6853; res: 800/637-0577; res: 888/386-4677.* 285 rms, 4 story, 45 condos (1-3 bedrm). Jan-late Apr: S, D $125-$240; each addl $15; suites $150-$400; condos $135-$350; under 18 free; wkly, monthly rates in condos; golf plans; higher rates wkends; lower rates rest of yr. Crib free. TV; cable (premium). Heated pool; whirlpool, poolside serv. Dining rm 6:30 am-11 pm. Rm serv. Bar 10-2 am; entertainment. Ck-out noon, ck-in 3 pm. Grocery, package store 1 mi. Convention facilities. Concierge. Gift shop. Barber, beauty shop. Free airport transportation. Lighted tennis, pro. 27-hole golf, greens fee $85-$95, pro, putting greens, driving range. Lawn games. Exercise equipt; sauna. Massage. Health club privileges. Refrigerators. Private patios, balconies. On 347 acres; panoramic mountain view. Cr cds: A, C, D, DS, MC, V.

★★★ **LA MANCHA PRIVATE CLUB & VILLAS.** *444 N Avenida Caballeros (92262), near Municipal Airport. 760/323-1773; FAX 760/323-5928; res: 800/255-1773.* E-mail reservations@la-mancha.com; web www.la-mancha.com. 53 kit. villas, 1-2 story, 13 minisuites. Dec-Apr: minisuites $195-$225; villas $250-$895; extended-stay rates; tennis, golf, plans; lower rates rest of yr. Crib $25. TV; cable, VCR avail (movies). Pool; whirlpool, poolside serv. Dining rm 7:30 am-2:30 pm, 5:30-9:30 pm. Box lunches, picnics. Rm serv. Bar 8 am-9:30 pm. Ck-out noon, ck-in 3 pm. Grocery, coin Indry, package store 1 mi. Meeting rms. Business center. In-rm modem link. Concierge. Gift shop. Free airport transportation. Lighted tennis, pro. Golf privileges, putting green. Bicycles. Lawn games. Exercise rm; sauna. Microwaves avail. Some fireplaces. Private patios, balconies. Grills. Most villas with private pool, whirlpools and/or spa; some villas with private tennis court. Extensive landscaped grounds; Spanish-colonial decor. Cr cds: A, C, D, DS, JCB, MC, V.

★★★ **MARRIOTT RANCHO LAS PALMAS.** *41000 Bob Hope Dr (92270), SE on CA 111. 760/568-2727; FAX 760/568-5845; res: 800/458-8786.* E-mail rlpbus@earthlink.com; web www.marriott.com/marriott/pspca. 450 rms, 2 story. Jan-Apr: S, D $280-$300; suites $330-$1,000; under 18 free; golf, tennis plans; lower rates rest of yr. Pet accepted, some restrictions. TV; cable (premium), VCR avail (movies). 2 pools; whirlpool, wading pool, poolside serv. Playground. Supervised child's activities; under age 12. Restaurants 6:30 am-11 pm. Box lunches, snack bar. Bar 11-2 am. Ck-out noon, ck-in 4 pm. Convention facilities. Business center. In-rm modem link. Concierge. Gift shop. Barber, beauty shop. Lighted tennis, pro. Tennis school. 27-hole golf, greens fee $99-$109, pro, putting green, driving range. Bicycle rentals. Soc dir. Exercise equipt. Health club privileges. Some refrigerators, minibars; microwaves avail. Private patios, balconies. Cr cds: A, C, D, DS, ER, JCB, MC, V.

★★★★ **RITZ-CARLTON HOTEL.** *68-900 Frank Sinatra Dr (92270), CA 111 & Frank Sinatra Dr. 760/321-8282; FAX 760/321-6928; res: 800/241-3333.* Resting on a 650-foot plateau in the Santa Rosa mountain foothills, guest rooms at this luxury resort have spectacular views of the Coachella Valley and distant San Jacinto mountains. Conveniently located near the Palm Springs Airport (15 minutes) and downtown Palm Desert. 240 rms, 3 story. Jan-mid-Apr: S, D $295-$495; each addl $25; suites $425-$1,000; lower rates rest of yr. TV; cable (premium), VCR avail (movies). Pool; whirlpool, poolside serv. Supervised child's activities; ages 4-12. Restaurants 7 am-11 pm (also see THE DINING ROOM). Afternoon tea 2:30-5 pm. Rm serv 24 hrs. Bar 10:30-1 am. Ck-out noon, ck-in 3 pm. Convention facilities. Business center. In-rm modem link. Shopping arcade. Barber, beauty shop. Valet serv. Concierge. Underground valet parking. Lighted tennis, pro, pro shop. 18-hole golf privileges, greens fee $65-$170.

Lawn games. Exercise rm; sauna. Massage. Spa. Bathrm phones, minibars. Private patios, balconies. Luxury level. Cr cds: A, C, D, DS, ER, JCB, MC, V.

D

★★★ **THE WESTIN MISSION HILLS.** *71333 Dinah Shore Dr (92270), at Bob Hope Dr. 760/328-5955; FAX 760/321-2955.* Web www.westin.com. 512 units in 16 bldgs, 2 story. Jan-May: S, D $335-$475; each addl $25; suites $430-$1,250; under 18 free; golf, tennis plans; lower rates rest of yr. Crib free. TV; cable (premium), VCR avail (movies). 3 pools; whirlpool, poolside serv, lifeguard (main pool); 60-ft waterslide. Playground. Supervised child's activities; ages 4-12. Dining rms 6 am-11 pm. Box lunches, snack bar. Rm serv 24 hrs. Bars 10-2 am; entertainment. Ck-out noon, ck-in 4 pm. Convention facilities. Business center. In-rm modem link. Bellhops. Valet serv. Concierge. Shopping arcade. Beauty shop. Sports dir. 7 lighted tennis courts, pro, pro shop. Pete Dye & Gary Player championship 18-hole golf courses, pro, 6 putting greens, 2 double-sided practice ranges, pro shop. Bicycle rentals. Lawn games. Soc dir. Game rm. Exercise equipt; steam rm. Health and fitness center. Massage. Minibars; refrigerators avail. Cr cds: A, C, D, DS, ER, JCB, MC, V.

D SC

Inns

★★ **CASA CODY BED & BREAKFAST COUNTRY INN.** *175 S Cahuilla Rd (92262). 760/320-9346; FAX 760/325-8610; res: 800/231-2639.* Web palmsprings.com/hotels/palmsprings/historic/casacody. 23 rms, 21 kit. suites. Late Dec-late Apr: S, D $79-$199; each addl $10; monthly, wkly rates; lower rates rest of yr. Crib $10. Pet accepted. TV; cable, VCR avail (free movies). 2 heated pools; whirlpool. Complimentary continental bkfst. Restaurant nearby. Ck-out 11 am, ck-in 2 pm. Business servs avail. Health club privileges. Refrigerators, microwaves; many fireplaces. Many private patios. Cr cds: A, C, D, DS, MC, V.

★★★ **ESTRELLA INN.** *415 S Belardo Rd (92262). 760/320-4117; FAX 760/323-3303; res: 800/237-3687.* E-mail info@estrella.com; web www.estrella.com. 67 rms, 6 shower only, 2 story, 8 suites. Jan-Apr: S, D $150; each addl $15; suites $225-$275; villas $250-$275; under 12 free; wkly rates; tennis, golf plans; lower rates rest of yr. Crib free. Pet accepted; $10. TV; VCR avail. 3 heated pools. Complimentary bkfst. Complimentary coffee in rms. Restaurant nearby. Ck-out noon, ck-in 3 pm. Business servs avail. Luggage handling. Concierge serv. Free airport transportation. Health club privileges. Lawn games. Refrigerators, microwaves. Patios, balconies. Built 1929. Cr cds: A, C, D, MC, V.

SC

★★★ **INGLESIDE INN.** *200 W Ramon Rd (92264). 760/325-0046; FAX 760/325-0710; res: 800/772-6655.* E-mail ingleside@earthlink.net; web www.inglesideinn.com. 30 rms. Oct-May: S, D $95-$385; suites $295-$600; villas $125-$375; lower rates rest of yr. TV; cable, VCR avail. Heated pool; whirlpool, poolside serv. Complimentary continental bkfst. Complimentary coffee in rms. Restaurant (see MELVYN'S AT THE INGLESIDE). Rm serv. Bar; entertainment. Ck-out noon, ck-in 2 pm. Business servs avail. Valet serv. Concierge serv. In-rm whirlpools, refrigerators; some fireplaces; microwaves avail. Some private patios. Hacienda atmosphere; courtyard, fountain. Rms individually decorated; many antiques. Cr cds: A, C, D, DS, MC, V.

★★★ **KORAKIA PENSIONE.** *257 S Patencio Rd (92262). 760/864-6411; FAX 760/864-4147.* 20 rms, 15 with kits, 6 with shower only, 2 story. Sept-July: S, D $79-$239; each addl $30; 2-day min wkends. Heated pool. Complimentary continental bkfst. Restaurant nearby. Ck-out noon. Business servs avail. Luggage handling. Concierge serv. Tennis privileges. Golf privileges. Refrigerators; some fireplaces. Balconies. Picnic tables. Moorish-style architecture; built 1924, set against San Jacinto Mountains, antiques. Cr cds: C.

★★★ **ORCHID TREE INN.** *261 S Belardo Rd (92262). 760/325-2791; FAX 760/325-3855; res: 800/733-3435.* E-mail info@orchidtree.com. 40 rms, 19 with shower only, 1 & 2 story, 33 kit units. Nov-May: S, D $99-$125; each addl $15; suites $135-$295; lower rates rest of yr. TV; cable, VCR avail. 3 pools; 2 whirlpools. Complimentary continental bkfst. Ck-out noon, ck-in 3 pm. Luggage handling. Concierge serv. Business servs avail. Health club privileges. Game rm. Tennis, shuffleboard. Many refrigerators, microwaves avail. Cr cds: A, C, DS, MC, V.

SC

★★★★ **THE WILLOWS.** *412 W Tahquitz Canyon Way (92262). 760/320-0771; FAX 760/320-0780.* E-mail innkeeper@thewillowspalmsprings.com; web www.thewillowspalmsprings.com. This Mediterranean villa is nestled in the Palm Springs desert at the foothills of Mount San Jacinto. Mahogany beams, frescoed ceilings and stone floors punctuate the imposing architectural style. Rooms feature antique furniture, sumptuous linens, and stone fireplaces. 8 rms, 2 story. Oct-May: S, D $275-$525; wkends, hols 2-day min; lower rates rest of yr. TV; VCR avail. Pool; whirlpool. Complimentary full bkfst; afternoon refreshments. Restaurant nearby. Ck-out noon, ck-in 4 pm. Business servs avail. In-rm modem link. Luggage handling. Valet serv. Concierge serv. Bathrm phones, refrigerators; some fireplaces. Totally nonsmoking. Cr cds: A, C, D, DS, MC, V.

★★★ **VILLA ROYALE BED & BREAKFAST INN.** *1620 Indian Trl (92270), near Municipal Airport. 760/327-2314; FAX 760/322-3794; res: 800/245-2314.* E-mail info@villaroyale.com; web www.villaroyale.com. 33 rms, 19 suites. Oct-May: S, D $95-$295; each addl $25; suites $150-$295; lower rates rest of yr. Adults only. TV; cable. 2 pools; whirlpool. Dining rm (see EUROPA). Rm serv. Bar 5-11 pm. Ck-out noon, ck-in 2 pm. Meeting rms. Business servs avail. Health club privileges. Massage. Many refrigerators; some fireplaces. Private patios. Located on 3½ acres with series of interior couryards. Rms decorated with objets d'art from Morocco, France, England, Holland, Spain and Greece. European atmosphere. Cr cds: A, C, D, DS, MC, V.

SC

Restaurants

★★ **BLUE COYOTE.** *445 N Palm Canyon Dr. 760/327-1196.* Hrs: 11 am-10 pm; Fri, Sat to 11 pm. Closed Thanksgiving, Dec 25. Mexican, Southwestern menu. Bar. Semi-a la carte: lunch $5.50-$14.95, dinner $8.95-$20.95. Specialties: pollo cilantro, filete jalapeño. Parking. Outdoor dining. Cantina ambiance. Cr cds: A, C, D, MC, V.

D

★★ **CEDAR CREEK INN.** *1555 S Palm Canyon Dr (92264). 760/325-7300.* E-mail cashimire@aol.com. Hrs: 11 am-10 pm. Res accepted. Bar to 11 pm. Semi-a la carte: lunch $6.95-$12.95, dinner $11.95-$24.95. Specialties: chicken papaya salad, rack of lamb, homemade desserts. Entertainment Wed-Sun. Parking. Outdoor dining. Old World country garden atmosphere. Cr cds: A, C, D, MC, V.

D

★★★ **EUROPA RESTAURANT.** *(See Villa Royale) 760/327-2314.* E-mail info@villaroyale; web www.villaroyale.com. Hrs: 5:30-10 pm; Sun brunch 11:30 am-2 pm. Closed Mon. Res accepted. Continental menu. Bar. Wine cellar. A la carte entrees: dinner $13-$28. Sun brunch $20. Specialties: salmon in parchment, roast rack of lamb. Parking. Outdoor dining. Intimate setting. Cr cds: A, C, D, DS, MC, V.

D

★★ **FLOWER DRUM.** *424 S Indian Canyon Dr (92262). 760/323-3020.* Hrs: 11:30 am-3 pm, 4:30-10 pm; Fri, Sat to 10:30 pm; early-bird dinner 4:30-6:30 pm. Res accepted. Chinese menu. Bar to 10 pm. A la carte entrees: lunch $4.95-$12.95, dinner $8.95-$28. Specializes in chicken, duck, seafood. Chinese costumed dancing. Hosts Chinese New Year's Celebration (Jan-Feb). Goldfish stream. Rock gardens. Cr cds: A, C, MC, V.

✓★★ **GREAT WALL.** *362 S Palm Canyon Dr (92262). 760/322-2209.* Hrs: 11:30 am-3 pm, 4:30-10 pm. Res accepted. Chinese menu. Bar. A la carte entrees: lunch $4.95-$6.95, dinner $6.25-$14.95. Specialties: Chinese chicken salad, house pan-fried noodle, sesame chicken. Outdoor dining. Oriental decor; authentic Chinese watercolors; large tapestry of the Great Wall. Cr cds: A, C, D, DS, MC, V.

D

★★ **KOBE JAPANESE STEAK HOUSE.** *69838 US Highway 111 (92270), On CA 111. 760/324-1717.* Hrs: 5 pm-midnight; early-bird dinner to 6 pm. Closed Thanksgiving. Res accepted. Teppan cooking. Bar. Complete meals: dinner $12.25-$27.90. Child's meals. Specializes in steak, seafood, chicken. Sushi bar. Entertainment Thurs-Sat (seasonal). Valet parking. Tableside preparation. Japanese farmhouse decor. Cr cds: A, C, D, JCB, MC, V.

D

★★ **LAS CASUELAS NUEVAS.** *70050 US Highway 111 (92270). 760/328-8844.* Hrs: 11 am-9:30 pm; Fri, Sat to 10 pm; Sun brunch 10 am-2 pm. Closed Thanksgiving, Dec 25. Res accepted. Mexican menu. Bar. Semi-a la carte: lunch $6.50-$11.50, dinner $9.50-$16.95. Sun brunch $15.95. Child's meals. Specialties: crab enchiladas, pollo en mole, chicken fajitas. Entertainment wkends. Valet parking. Patio dining. Cr cds: A, C, D, DS, MC, V.

D ♥

✓★★ **LAS CASUELAS TERRAZA.** *222 S Palm Canyon Dr (92262). 760/325-2794.* Hrs: 11 am-closing; Sun from 10 am. Closed Thanksgiving, Dec 25. Res accepted. Mexican menu. Bar. Semi-a la carte: lunch $5.75-$11, dinner $6.95-$14.95. Child's meals. Specialties: Oaxacan black bean tostada, shrimp enchiladas, fajitas. Nightly entertainment. Parking. Outdoor dining. Antique bar. Mexican decor. Cr cds: A, C, D, DS, MC, V.

D ♥

★★★ **LE VALLAURIS.** *385 W Tahquitz Canyon Way (92262). 760/325-5059.* E-mail vallauris@aol.com; web www.levallauris.com. Hrs: 11:30 am-2:30 pm, 5:30-11 pm. Res accepted. French/California menu. Bar to midnight. Wine cellar. A la carte entrees: lunch $10-$18.50, dinner $22-$30. Specializes in veal, lamb, seafood. Own pastries. Pianist. Valet parking. Menu changes daily. Outdoor dining. Cr cds: A, C, D, DS, MC, V.

D

★★ **LORD FLETCHER INN.** *70385 US Highway 111 (92270). 760/328-1161.* Hrs: 5:30-9 pm. Closed Sun, Mon; also July-Aug. Res accepted. Continental menu. Bar. Complete meals: dinner $17.50-$22. Specializes in short ribs, prime rib with Yorkshire pudding, chicken dumplings. Valet parking. In authentic English inn. Family-owned. Cr cds: A, C, D, MC, V.

D

★★ **LYONS ENGLISH GRILLE.** *233 E Palm Canyon Dr (92264). 760/327-1551.* Hrs: 4-11 pm; early-bird dinner 4:30-6 pm. Res accepted. English menu. Bar. Semi-a la carte: dinner $10.95-$21.95. Specializes in steak, prime rib, fresh seafood. Own desserts. Pianist. Valet parking. Old English decor; stained glass. Family-owned. Cr cds: A, C, D, MC, V.

D

★★★ **MELVYN'S AT THE INGLESIDE.** *(See Ingleside Inn) 760/325-2323.* E-mail ingleside@earthlink.net; web www.prinet.com/ingleside/. Hrs: 11:30 am-3 pm, 6-11 pm; Sat, Sun brunch 9 am-3 pm. Res accepted. Continental menu. Bar 10-2 am. Wine cellar. Semi-a la carte: lunch $8.95-$16, dinner $16.95-$28. Sat, Sun brunch $13.95-$16.95. Specialties: veal Ingleside, chicken Charlene, steak Diane. Pianist, vocalist. Valet parking. Historic building; 2 main dining areas, garden rm. Jacket (dinner). Cr cds: A, C, D, DS, MC, V.

♥

★ **PALMIE FRENCH RESTAURANT.** *276 N Palm Canyon Dr (92262). 760/320-3375.* Hrs: from 5:30 pm. Closed Sun; Jan 1-2; Aug-mid Sept. Res accepted. French menu. Bar. A la carte entrees: dinner $14.50-$23. Specialties: lamb shank, ravioli, cheese souffle. Outdoor dining. Cr cds: A, C, D, MC, V.

★★ **ROCK GARDEN CAFE.** *777 S Palm Canyon Dr (92264). 760/327-8840.* Hrs: 7 am-midnight; early-bird dinner 5-8 pm. Res accepted. Bar. Semi-a la carte: bkfst $3.50-$5, lunch $5-$7, dinner $7-$15. Child's meals. Specializes in seafood, ribs, Greek salad. Pianist Wed-Sun. Parking. Outdoor dining. Cr cds: A, C, D, DS, MC, V.

D SC

★★ **SORRENTINO'S SEAFOOD HOUSE.** *1032 N Palm Canyon Dr (92262). 760/325-2944.* Hrs: 5-10 pm; off-season 5:30-10 pm. Closed Thanksgiving. Res accepted. Italian/seafood menu. Bar. Complete meals: dinner $10.95-$25. Specializes in seafood, veal, steak. Pianist. Parking. Outdoor dining. Family-owned since 1944. Cr cds: A, C, D, MC, V.

D

★★ **ST JAMES AT THE VINEYARD.** *254 N Palm Canyon Dr (92262). 760/320-8041.* Web palmsprings.com/dine/stjames. Hrs: 5-10 pm; Fri, Sat to 11 pm. Closed Aug. Eclectic menu. Bar. A la carte entrees: dinner $16-$32. Specializes in seafood, pasta, curries. Cr cds: A, C, D, DS, MC, V.

D

★★★★ **THE DINING ROOM.** *(See The Ritz-Carlton, Rancho Mirage) 760/321-8282.* The formal dining room with Victorian accents is awhirl with tuxedoed waiters. Classic French food is skillfully prepared and served with care. French, Mediterranean menu. Specialties: Chilean Sea Bass (seasonal), Dover Sole, Foie Gras, Rack of Lamb, Duck. Hrs: 6:30-10 pm. Closed Mon, Tues. Res accepted. Bar 10:30-1 am. Extensive wine list. Prix fixe: 2-course dinner $39, 3-course dinner $49, 4-course dinner $56. Child's meals. Pianist. Valet parking. Oil paintings; crystal chandeliers. Jacket, tie. Cr cds: A, C, D, DS, ER, JCB, MC, V.

D

★★ **TRILUSSA.** *123 N Palm Canyon Dr (92262). 760/323-4255.* Web palmsprings.com. Hrs: 11:30 am-10:30 pm; Fri, Sat to 11 pm. Closed Dec 25. Res accepted. Italian menu. Bar. A la carte entrees: lunch $12-$14, dinner $14-$20. Specializes in pasta, beef, seafood. Entertainment Thurs-Sun. Parking. Outdoor dining. Cr cds: A, C, D, DS, MC, V.

D

★★★★ **WALLY'S DESERT TURTLE.** *71-775 CA 111 (92270), W on CA 111. 760/568-9321.* Like a throwback to another time, this thoroughly enjoyable restaurant offers a serious and professional, if somewhat dated, dining experience. The haute continental cuisine and attentive service caters to affluent seniors with a taste for the familiar and a desire to be pampered.Hrs: 6-10 pm; Fri 11:30 am-2 pm, 6-10 pm. Closed mid-June-Sept. Res accepted. Continental menu. Bar. Wine cellar. A la carte entrees: lunch $13-$20, dinner $18-$36. Specializes in Dover sole, rack of lamb, duck. Pianist. Valet parking. Two-level dining with elevated terrace. Jacket. Cr cds: A, C, D, DS, MC, V.

D

★★★ **WILDE GOOSE.** *67-938 E Palm Canyon Dr (92234). 760/328-5775.* E-mail dkq673d@prodigy.com; web www.palmsprings.com/dine/wildgoose. Hrs: from 5:30 pm. Res accepted. Continental menu. Bar. Semi-a la carte: dinner $12.95-$34.95. Specializes in beef, seafood, wild game. Pianist Fri, Sat. Valet parking. European country inn decor. Cr cds: A, C, D, DS, JCB, MC, V.

D

★★ **ZORBA'S GREEK RESTAURANT.** *42434 Bob Hope Dr (92270), in Las Palmas Shopping Center. 760/340-3066.* Hrs: 11:30 am-2 pm, 5-10 pm. Closed July-Aug. Res accepted. Greek, continental menu. Bar. Semi-a la carte: lunch $5.95-$9.95, dinner $11.95-$25.95. Specialties: rack of lamb, moussaka, shrimp a la Mykonos. Belly dancer. Greek decor. Cr cds: A, C, D, DS, MC, V.

D

Palmdale (H-4)

(See also Lancaster)

Pop 68,842 **Elev** 2,659 ft **Area Code** 805 **Zip** 93550

The Angeles National Forest is west and south of town (see PASADENA).

Motor Hotel

✓★★ **RAMADA INN.** *300 W Palmdale Blvd (93551). 805/273-1200; FAX 805/947-9593; res: 800/272-6232.* 135 rms, 4 story. S, D $53-$75; each addl $5; under 13 free. Crib free. Pet accepted, some restrictions; $50. TV; cable (premium), VCR avail. Pool; whirlpool. Complimentary full bkfst. Restaurant 6 am-9 pm; wkends from 7 am. Rm serv. Bar 5 pm-1 am; Fri, Sat to 1:30 am; closed Sun. Ck-out noon. Coin Indry. Meeting rms. Business center. Valet serv. Exercise equipt. Refrigerators avail. Cr cds: A, C, D, DS, MC, V.

D SC

Palo Alto (E-4 see San Francisco map)

(See also Fremont, Redwood City, Santa Clara, Saratoga)

Founded 1889 **Pop** 55,900 **Elev** 23 ft **Area Code** 650
Web www.city.palo-alto.ca.us/palo/chamber

Information Chamber of Commerce, 325 Forest Ave, 94301; 650/324-3121

A tall and ancient redwood tree stands at the northwest entrance to the city. Nearly two centuries ago, Spanish explorers used it as a landmark, calling it El Palo Alto ("tall tree"). Stanford University is a major economic factor. The city is also one of the nation's most important electronics development and research centers.

What to See and Do

Junior Museum & Zoo. Displays introduce children to art, science, history and anthropology through a variety of media; hands-on exhibits and workshops. Zoo on grounds. (Daily exc Mon; closed some hols) 1451 Middlefield Rd. Phone 650/329-2111. **Free**

Lucy Evans Baylands Nature Interpretive Center. Nature preserve at edge of salt marsh. Naturalist-guided walking tours; slide shows; bicycling; bird-watching. (Daily exc Mon; closed Thanksgiving, Dec 25) 2775 Embarcadero Rd, E of US 101. Phone 650/329-2506. **Free**

★ **Stanford University** (1891). (13,549 students) Founded by Senator and Mrs. Leland Stanford in memory of their only son, it has become one of the great universities of the world. Near El Camino Real (CA 82). Phone 650/723-2300. Features of the campus include

Hoover Tower. Library houses collection begun by President Herbert Hoover during the First World War. At 250 ft high, the carillon platform on 14th floor offers panoramic view of campus and peninsula (daily; closed school breaks). Information desk (daily; closed school breaks). Phone 650/723-2053. Observation platform ¢

Stanford Guide Service. Located in Memorial Hall and in Hoover Tower (daily; closed hols, school breaks). Free 1-hr campus tours leave information booth (twice daily; closed some hols, school breaks). Maps and brochures are at both locations. Phone 650/723-2560 or 650/723-2053 during office hours.

Stanford Medical Center. A $21-million cluster of buildings on a 56-acre site, designed by internationally famous architect Edward Durell Stone. Tours (1st & 3rd Thurs of month). Phone 650/723-7167.

Stanford Stadium. Home of Stanford Cardinals football.

Thomas Welton Stanford Art Gallery. Changing exhibits. (Daily exc Mon; closed major hols) Phone 650/723-2842. **Free**

Trees for which Palo Alto is famous. **El Palo Alto** "The Tall Tree" that gives city its name. Palo Alto Ave near Alma St. Also, 60 varieties along Hamilton Ave, blocks between 100 & 1500.

Winter Lodge. Only outdoor ice rink in the US west of the Sierra Nevada Mountains. Skate rentals. (Oct-mid-Apr; closed Easter, Thanksgiving, Dec 24, 25) 3009 Middlefield Rd. Phone 650/493-4566. ¢¢¢

Motels

✓★ **COUNTRY INN MOTEL.** *4345 El Camino Real (94306). 650/948-9154; FAX 415/949-4190.* 27 rms, 12 A/C, 1-2 story, 13 kits. S, D $50-$70; each addl $6; kit. units $10 addl. Crib $5. TV; cable (premium). Heated pool. Complimentary continental bkfst. Restaurant adj open 24 hrs. Ck-out 11 am. In-rm modem link. Cr cds: A, C, DS, MC, V.

D

★★ **STANFORD TERRACE INN.** *531 Stanford Ave (94306). 650/857-0333; FAX 650/857-0343; res: 800/729-0332.* Web www.stanfordterraceinn.com. 80 units, 2-3 story, 14 kits. S, D $150-185; each addl $10; kit. suites $190-$310; under 12 free. TV; cable (premium). Pool. Complimentary continental bkfst. Coffee in rms. Restaurant nearby. Ck-out noon. Coin Indry. Meeting rms. Business servs avail. Free garage parking. Exercise equipt. Refrigerators, minibars. Stanford Univ opp. Cr cds: A, C, D, DS, JCB, MC, V.

D SC

✓★★ **TOWN HOUSE INN.** *4164 El Camino Real (94306). 650/493-4492; FAX 415/493-3418; res: 800/458-8696.* 38 rms, 15 with shower only, 2 story, 7 suites, 9 kit. units. S $69; D $85; each addl $6-$10; suites $89-$170; kit. units $90-$100; under 12 free; wkly rates. Crib free. TV; cable (premium), VCR. Whirlpool. Complimentary continental bkfst. Complimentary coffee in rms. Restaurant nearby. Ck-out 11 am. Exercise equipt. Refrigerators. Cr cds: A, C, D, MC, V.

D SC

Motor Hotels

★★★ **CREEKSIDE INN.** *3400 El Camino Real (94306). 650/493-2411; FAX 415/493-6787; res: 800/492-7335.* 136 rms, 2-4 story, 14 kits. S, D $125-$155; each addl $5; kit. units $165-$200. Crib avail. TV; cable (premium), VCR avail (movies $5). Heated pool. Coffee in rms. Restaurant 6:30 am-10:30 pm; Sat, Sun from 7 am. Bar 11 am-10:30 pm. Ck-out noon. Coin Indry. Business servs avail. In-rm modem link. Valet serv. Convenience store. Exercise equipt. Refrigerators. Private patios, balconies. Totally nonsmoking. Cr cds: A, C, D, DS, ER, JCB, MC, V.

D SC

★★★ **DINAH'S GARDEN HOTEL.** *4261 El Camino Real (94306). 650/493-2844; FAX 650/856-4713; res: 800/227-8220.* 107 rms, 1-3 story, 41 suites. D $154-$265; suites $180-$430. Crib free. TV; cable (premium), VCR avail. 2 pools, heated; poolside serv. Coffee in rms. Restaurant 6:30 am-11 pm. Rm serv. Ck-out noon. Coin Indry. Business servs avail. Valet serv. Sundries. Exercise equipt; sauna. Refrigerators. Many private patios, terraces. On 9 acres; lagoons. Cr cds: A, C, D, DS, JCB, MC, V.

★★★ **SHERATON HOTEL.** *625 El Camino Real (94301), at University Ave, opp Stanford Univ. 650/328-2800; FAX 650/327-7362; res: 800/465-4329.* 343 units, 4 story, 6 kits. S, D $199-$239; each addl $10; suites $259-$399; kit. units $179; under 18 free; wkend rates. Crib free. TV; cable (premium). Pool. Coffee in rm. Restaurant 6 am-11 pm. Rm serv. Bar 11 am-midnight. Ck-out noon. Coin Indry. Meeting rms. Business center. Bellhops. Valet serv. Concierge. Exercise equipt. Some bathrm phones, in-rm whirlpools; refrigerators avail. Some private patios, balconies. Cr cds: A, C, D, DS, JCB, MC, V.

D SC

Hotels

★★★ **GARDEN COURT HOTEL.** *520 Cowper St (94301), downtown. 650/322-9000; FAX 650/324-3609; res: 800/824-9028.* E-mail ahotel@gardencourt.com; web www.gardencourt.com. 62 rms, 4 story, 13 suites. S, D $250-$300; each addl $20; suites $300-$475. Crib free. Valet parking $12. TV; cable (premium), VCR (free movies). Restaurant 7 am-11 pm. Rm serv 24 hrs. Bar 11:30 am-midnight. Ck-out noon. Meeting rms. Business servs avail. In-rm modem link. Concierge. Exercise equipt. Bicycles. Minibars; some in-rm whirlpools, fireplaces. Balconies. Open-air, flower-laden courtyard reminiscent of a European village square. Cr cds: A, C, D, DS, JCB, MC, V.

D

★★ **HYATT RICKEYS.** *4219 El Camino Real (94306). 650/493-8000; FAX 650/424-0836; res: 800/233-1234.* 344 units, 1-6 story. S $229-$259; D $254-$284; suites $280-$650; under 18 free; wkend rates. Crib free. TV; cable (premium). Pool. Coffee in rms. Restaurant 6:30 am-10 pm. Bar 11-1:30 am. Ck-out noon. Convention facilities. Business center. In-rm modem link. Exercise equipt. Barber, beauty shop. Lawn games. Putting green. Fireplace in many suites; refrigerators avail. Some balconies. On 22 acres with gardens, pond. Cr cds: A, C, D, DS, JCB, MC, V.

D SC

Inn

★★ **COWPER INN.** *705 Cowper St (94301). 650/327-4475; FAX 650/329-1703.* 14 rms, 6 with shower only, 2 share bath, 3 A/C, 3 story, 2 suites, 2 kit. units. S, D, suites, kit. units $65-$130; each addl $10. TV; cable. Complimentary continental bkfst. Restaurant nearby. Ck-out 11 am, ck-in 2 pm. Business servs avail. Victorian house built in 1893. Totally nonsmoking. Cr cds: A, C, MC, V.

Restaurants

✓★ **BLUE CHALK CAFE.** *630 Ramona St (94301). 650/326-1020.* Hrs: 11:30 am-2:30 pm, 5-10 pm. Closed Sun; Jan 1, Thanksgiving, Dec 25. Res accepted. Southern regional menu. Bar. A la carte entrees: lunch $5.95-$11.50, dinner $6.95-$16.25. Child's meals. Specialties: pan-seared catfish, grilled jumbo prawns over grits, Carolina fritters. Outdoor dining. Casual dining; billiards and shuffleboard avail. Totally nonsmoking. Cr cds: A, C, D, MC, V.

D

★★ **EVIVA.** *420 Emerson St (94301). 650/326-0983.* Hrs: 11:30 am-2:30 pm, 5:30-10 pm; Fri to 11 pm; Sat 5-11 pm; Sun 5-9 pm. Closed most major hols. Res accepted. Greek menu. Bar. A la carte entrees: lunch $9.95-$15.95, dinner $13.50-$26.95. Specialties: lamb chops, whole striped bass, moussaka. Valet parking. Greek, Mediterranean decor. Totally nonsmoking. Cr cds: C, D, MC, V.

D

★★ **L'AMIE DONIA.** *530 Bryant St (94301). 650/323-7614.* Hrs: 5:30-10 pm; Fri, Sat to 10:30 pm. Closed Mon, Sun; major hols; also Jan, last wk June-1st 2 wks in July. Res accepted. French menu. Wine, beer. A la carte entrees: dinner $15-$25. Complete meal: dinner $30. Specialties: beef tongue salad, rabbit, tarte tatin. Street parking. Outdoor dining. French bistro atmosphere; rotating artworks by one artist. Totally nonsmoking. Cr cds: A, C, DS, MC, V.

D

★★ **SCOTT'S SEAFOOD GRILL & BAR.** *2300 E Bayshore Rd (94303), US 101 exit Embarcadero E to Bayshore Rd. 650/856-1046.* Hrs: 7 am-9:30 pm; Sat from 5 pm; Sun 5-9 pm; early-bird dinner 4-6 pm. Closed some major hols. Res accepted. Bar. A la carte entrees: lunch, dinner $7.95-$51. Specializes in seafood, steak. Parking. Patio dining. Cape Cod decor. Family-owned. Cr cds: A, C, D, DS, MC, V.

D

★★★ **SPAGO.** *265 Lytton Ave (94301). 650/833-1000.* Hrs: 11:30 am-10 pm; Sat, Sun 5:30-10:00 pm. Closed most major hols. Res accepted. Continental, contemporary and mediterranean menu. Bar. Wine list. A la carte entrees: lunch $9-$16.50, dinner $19.50-$29.50. Valet parking. Outdoor dining. Totally nonsmoking. Cr cds: A, C, D, DS, MC, V.

D

★★ **ZIBIBBO.** *430 Kipling St (94301). 650/328-6722.* Hrs: 11:30 am-10:30 pm; Mon to 10 pm; Fri to 11 pm; Sat 11 am-11 pm; Sun 11 am-10 pm. Closed some major hols. Res accepted. Mediterranean menu. Bar 11 am-1 am. A la carte entrees: lunch $5.95-$13.95, dinner $9.95-$19.95. Sun brunch $4.95-$11.95. Specialties: rotisserie chicken rosemary, non-skillet mussels. Valet parking (dinner). Outdoor dining. Totally nonsmoking. Cr cds: A, C, D, MC, V.

D

Pasadena (J-4)

(See also Claremont, Glendale, Los Angeles Area, Pomona, San Marino)

Founded 1874 **Pop** 131,591 **Elev** 865 ft **Area Code** 626
E-mail kfagan@pasadenacal.com **Web** www.pasadenacal.com

Information Convention & Visitors Bureau, 171 S Los Robles, 91101; 626/795-9311

Home of the world-famous Tournament of Roses, Pasadena was first chosen as a health refuge for weary Midwesterners and later as a winter retreat for Eastern millionaires. Today it is a cultural center and scientific and industrial frontier because of its many research, development and engineering industries, including NASA's Jet Propulsion Laboratory. The name "Pasadena" comes from the Chippewa dialect; it means "Crown of the Valley."

What to See and Do

Angeles National Forest. Approx 700,000 acres, including San Gabriel and Sheep Mt wildernesses. More than 100 camp and picnic grounds; many streams and lakes for fishing; hiking, winter sports. N, E & S via US 210, CA 2, 118, 39, I-5. Contact Office of Information, 701 N Santa Anita Ave, Arcadia 91006; phone 626/574-5200. Fee charged for some activities, also some campsites. Per vehicle per day ¢¢ Also here is

Crystal Lake Recreation Area. Fishing. Nature, hiking trails. Picnicking, store. Tent & trailer camping (fee). Amphitheater programs (summer). Visitors Center has maps and interpretive materials (Sat, Sun). Long trailers (over 22 ft) and recreational vehicles not recommended (steep roads). Phone 626/910-2848.

Norton Simon Museum of Art. Paintings, tapestries and sculpture from Renaissance to mid-20th century; sculptures of Southeast Asia and India. (Thurs-Sun, mid-afternoon-early evening; closed Jan 1, Thanksgiving, Dec 25) 411 W Colorado Blvd. Phone 626/449-6840. ¢¢

Pacific Asia Museum. Changing exhibits of traditional and contemporary Asian and Pacific Basin art; Chinese Imperial Palace-style building and

Chinese courtyard garden; research library; bookstore. Docent tours avail. (Wed-Sun) 46 N Los Robles Ave. Phone 626/449-2742. ¢¢

Pasadena Historical Society. Housed in 18-rm Fenyes Estate (1905); contains original furnishings, antiques, paintings and accessories. The mansion gives a glimpse of the elegant lifestyle that existed on Orange Grove Blvd at the turn of the century. Mansion, Finnish Folk Art Museum and library archives have extensive photo and San Gabriel Valley historic collections. Tours. (Thurs-Sun afternoons; closed major hols) 470 W Walnut St. Phone 626/577-1660. ¢¢

Rose Bowl. One of the country's most famous football stadiums, seats 98,636. Home of UCLA Bruins football team; scene of annual Rose Bowl game and other events throughout the yr. Rosemont Ave off Arroyo Blvd between I-210 & CA 134. Phone 626/577-3100.

The Gamble House (1908). Exemplary of the mature California bungalow designs of American architects Greene & Greene; interiors of teakwood, mahogany, maple and cedar; gardens. One-hr guided tour. (Thurs-Sun afternoons; closed major hols) 4 Westmoreland Pl. Phone 626/793-3334. ¢¢

Annual Event

Tournament of Roses. Spectacular floral parade on Colorado Blvd attracts more than a million people. Afternoon capped at the Rose Bowl. Special tournament events during preceding wk. Jan 1.

Motels

✓★ **BEST WESTERN COLORADO INN.** *2156 E Colorado Blvd (91107). 626/793-9339; FAX 626/568-2731; res: 800/528-1234.* Web www.bestwestern.com. 77 rms, 3 story. S $52-$60; D $60-$65; each addl $8; under 12 free; Rose Parade (3-day min). Crib free. TV; cable (premium). Heated pool; whirlpool. Complimentary continental bkfst. Restaurant nearby. Ck-out 11 am. Coin lndry. Meeting rm. Business servs avail. Refrigerators; some bathrm phones; microwaves avail. Some balconies. Cr cds: A, C, D, DS, JCB, MC, V.

SC

★★ **COMFORT INN.** *2462 E Colorado Blvd (91107), I-210 exit Sierra Madre Blvd S. 626/405-0811; FAX 626/796-0966; res: 800/228-5150.* Web www.citycent.com/comfort. 50 rms, 3 story. S, D $63-$70; each addl $6; under 18 free; Rose Parade 3-day min. Crib free. TV; cable (premium), VCR (free movies). Heated pool; whirlpool. Sauna. Complimentary continental bkfst. Complimentary coffee in rms. Ck-out noon. Coin lndry. Business servs avail. Valet serv. Refrigerators, microwaves. Cr cds: A, C, D, DS, ER, JCB, MC, V.

D SC

✓★★ **SAGA MOTOR HOTEL.** *1633 E Colorado Blvd (91106), I-210 exit Hill St S. 626/795-0431; FAX 626/792-0559; res: 800/793-7242.* 70 rms, 3 story. S $53-$79; D $55-$89; each addl $6; suites $69-$99; Rose Parade (3-day min). Crib free. TV; cable (premium). Heated pool. Complimentary continental bkfst. Ck-out noon. Business servs avail. Valet serv. Cr cds: A, C, D, DS, MC, V.

SC

Motor Hotel

★★★ **HOLIDAY INN.** *303 E Cordova St (91101), I-210 exit Marengo Ave S. 626/449-4000; FAX 626/584-1390; res: 800/457-7940; res: 800/465-4329.* E-mail hipasadena@aol.com; web www.holidayinn.com. 320 rms, 5 story. S $99-$139; D $114-$154; each addl $15; suites $229-$350; under 19 free; Rose Parade (4-day min). Pet accepted, some restrictions. Garage $5. TV; cable (premium). Heated pool; poolside serv. Coffee in rms. Restaurant 6 am-2 pm, 5-10 pm. Rm serv. Bar 2 pm-1 am. Ck-out noon. Convention facilities. Business servs avail. Bellhops. Gift shop. Lighted tennis. Health club privileges. Some patios, balconies. Cr cds: A, C, D, DS, JCB, MC, V.

D SC

Hotels

★★★ **DOUBLETREE HOTEL.** *191 N Los Robles Ave (91101), I-210 exit Lake St S to Union St W. 626/792-2727; FAX 626/792-3755; res: 800/222-8733.* Web www.doubletreehotels.com. 350 rms, 12 story. S, D $169-$299; each addl $20; suites $300-$1,200; under 16 free; wkend rates. Crib free. Garage parking $5; valet $10. TV; cable (premium). Heated pool; whirlpool, poolside serv. Coffee in rms. Restaurants 6:30 am-11 pm. Rm serv 24 hrs. Bars 11-1 am; entertainment Tues-Sat. Ck-out noon. Convention facilities. Business servs avail. Concierge. Gift shop. Airport transportation. Exercise rm; sauna, steam rm. Refrigerators, microwaves avail. Some balconies. City hall adj. Luxury level. Cr cds: A, C, D, DS, ER, JCB, MC, V.

D SC

★★ **HILTON.** *150 S Los Robles Ave (91101), ½ mi S of I-210. 626/577-1000; FAX 626/584-3148; res: 800/445-8667.* E-mail pasphhh@hilton.com; web www.hilton.com/hotels/pasphhh/index.html. 291 rms, 13 story. S $120-$180; D $135-$195; each addl $15; suites $200-$500; under 18 free; family, wkend rates; Rose Parade (4-day min). Crib free. Valet $10/day, garage $5/day. TV; cable (premium). Heated pool; whirlpool. Coffee in rms. Restaurant 6 am-10 pm. Bar 11-1 am. Ck-out noon. Convention facilities. Business center. Gift shop. Barber, beauty shop. Exercise equipt. Minibars; some bathrm phones. Some balconies. Cr cds: A, C, D, DS, ER, JCB, MC, V.

D SC

★★★★ **THE RITZ-CARLTON HUNTINGTON.** *1401 S Oak Knoll Ave (91106), I-210 Lake Ave exit, 2 mi S to Oak Knoll Ave. 626/568-3900; FAX 626/568-3700.* Web www.ritzcarlton.com. Built in 1907 as a fashionable resort and now restored and lavishly decorated with fine art and antiques, this landmark hotel occupies 23 elaborately landscaped acres in the foothills of the San Gabriel Mountains. On the property are themed gardens, such as the Japanese and Horseshoe gardens, and the celebrated Picture Bridge, decorated with murals that depict California scenes. 392 rms, 3-8 story, 16 suites, 7 cottages. S, D $245-$2,000; suites, cottages $350-$5,000; under 18 free; package plans. Crib free. Valet parking $19. TV; cable (premium), VCR avail. Heated pool; whirlpool, poolside serv. Restaurant (On the Terrace) 6 am-10 pm; (The Grill) M-W 6-9 pm, Th-Sat 6-10 pm, Sun 6:30-11:30 am [bkfst], 11:30 am-2:30 pm [lunch]. Rm serv 24 hrs. Bar wkdys till 1 am, wknd till 2 am, entertainment. Ck-out noon. Convention facilities. Business center. Concierge. Gift shop. Full service spa. Lighted tennis, pro. Golf privileges. Lawn games. Bicycle rental. Bathrm phones, minibars; many balconies. Luxury level. Cr cds: A, C, D, DS, ER, JCB, MC, V.

D SC

Inn

★★★ **ARTIST'S INN.** *1038 Magnolia St (91030), I-210 exit Fair Oaks Ave S. 626/799-5668; FAX 626/799-3678; res: 888/799-5668.* 5 rms, 1 with shower only, 2 story. S, D $110-$165; each addl $20; wkends (2-day min); higher rates Rose Parade (4-day min). Children over 9 yrs only. TV avail. Complimentary full bkfst; afternoon refreshments. Restaurant nearby. Ck-out noon, ck-in 3-6 pm. 1890s Victorian style; antiques. Cr cds: A, C, DS, MC, V.

Restaurants

★★ **BECKHAM PLACE.** *77 W Walnut St (91103), I-210 exit Fair Oaks Ave S. 626/796-3399.* Hrs: 11:30 am-2:30 pm, 5-9:30 pm; Fri, Sat 5-10 pm; Sun 5-9:30 pm. Closed some major hols. Res accepted. Bar 11 am-11:30 pm; Fri, Sat 5 pm-midnight. Semi-a la carte: lunch $6.95-$13.75, dinner $11.95-$17.95. Specializes in prime rib, fresh seafood. Own baking. Valet parking. Outdoor dining. English inn decor; antiques. Cr cds: A, C, D, MC, V.

D

★★★ **BISTRO 45.** *45 S Mentor Ave (91106), I-210 exit Lake Ave S to Colorado Blvd E. 626/795-2478.* Web www.bistro45.com. Hrs: 11:30 am-2:30 pm, 6-10 pm; Sat 5:30-11 pm; Sun 5-9 pm. Closed Mon; Jan 1, Thanksgiving, Dec 25. Res accepted. French menu. Bar. Wine list. A la carte entrees: lunch $11.45-$15.45, dinner $16.45-$25.45. Own pastries. Valet parking. Patio dining. Seasonal menu. Art deco atmosphere. Cr cds: A, C, D, MC, V.

D

★★ **CAFE SANTORINI.** *64-70 W Union St (91103), I-210 exit Fair Oaks Ave S. 626/564-4200.* Web www.citysearch.com/pas/cafesantorini. Hrs: 11 am-11 pm; Fri, Sat to midnight. Closed some major hols. Italian, Mediterranean menu. Bar. Semi-a la carte: lunch $6.50-$9.95, dinner $8.95-$17.95. Specialties: grilled calamari, red curry paella. Own baking. Top-40, salsa music Fri & Sat. Outdoor dining on rooftop with garden terrace. Relaxed Mediterranean atmosphere. Cr cds: A, C, D, DS, MC, V.

✓★ **CROCODILE CAFE.** *140 S Lake Ave (91101), I-210 exit Lake Ave S. 626/449-9900.* Hrs: 11 am-10 pm; Fri, Sat to midnight. Closed Thanksgiving, Dec 25. California eclectic cuisine. Bar. A la carte entrees: lunch, dinner $6.75-$16.95. Specializes in pizza, salads, grilled items. Patio dining. Contemporary room open to kitchen. Cr cds: A, C, D, MC, V.

D

★★ **MI PIACE.** *25 E Colorado Blvd (91105), I 210 exit Fair Oak Ave S. 626/795-3131.* Web www.citysearch.com/pas/mipiace. Hrs: 11:30 am-11 pm; Fri, Sat to midnight. Closed Thanksgiving, Dec 25. Res accepted. Italian menu. Bar. A la carte entrees: lunch, dinner $5.50-$15.95. Specializes in traditional Southern Italian dishes. Valet parking. Outdoor dining. Casual trattoria atmosphere. Cr cds: A, C, D, MC, V.

D

★★ **MIYAKO RESTAURANT.** *139 S Los Robles Ave (91101), lower level of Livingstone Hotel. 626/795-7005.* Hrs: 11:30 am-2 pm, 5:15-9 pm; Fri, Sat 5:15-9:30 pm; Sun 4-9 pm. Closed July 4, Thanksgiving, Dec 25. Res accepted. Japanese menu. Bar. Semi-a la carte: lunch $6.95-$13.95, dinner $7.95-$17.95. Child's meals. Specializes in shrimp tempura, beef sukiyaki, teriyaki dishes. Parking. Japanese & Western seating. Boat dinners. Family-owned. Totally nonsmoking. Cr cds: A, C, MC, V.

★★★ **OYE RESTAURANT.** *69 N Raymond Ave (91103). 626/796-3286.* Hrs: 5:30-10:30 pm. Closed some major hols. Res accepted. Asian-Cuban menu. Bar. Wine list. A la carte entrees: dinner $15-$18. Specialties: calle zanja eggroll, crispy seabass la charada, pa'-canton giant prawns. Valet parking. Supper club atmosphere; tropical decor. Totally nonsmoking. Cr cds: A, C, D, DS, MC, V.

D

★ **PEPPER MILL.** *795 E Walnut St (91101), I-210 exit Lake Ave S. 626/449-1214.* Hrs: 11:30 am-9:30 pm; Mon to 9 pm; Fri, Sat to 10 pm; Sun 10:30 am-9 pm; early-bird dinner 3-5:30 pm; Sun brunch 10:30 am-3 pm. Closed Thanksgiving, Dec 25. Res accepted. Continental menu. Bar. Semi-a la carte: lunch $6.25-$14.50, dinner $7.95-$21.95. Sun brunch $9.50-$10.95. Child's meals. Specializes in prime rib, steak, seafood. Salad bar. Own desserts. Patio dining. Cr cds: A, C, D, DS, JCB, MC, V.

D SC

✓★★★ **PINOT.** *897 Granite Dr (91101), I-210 exit Lake Ave S. 626/792-1179.* Web www.patina-pinot.com. Hrs: 11:30 am-2:30 pm, 6-9:30 pm; Fri to 10:30 pm; Sat 5:30-10:30 pm. Closed Sun; some major hols. Res accepted. French menu. Bar. Extensive wine list. A la carte entrees: lunch $8.95-$12.50, dinner $13.95-$21.95. Prix fixe: lunch $15.95. Specializes in grilled items, fresh seafood. Valet parking. French bistro decor, artwork. Totally nonsmoking. Cr cds: A, C, D, DS, MC, V.

D

★★★ **RAYMOND RESTAURANT.** *1250 S Fair Oaks Ave (91105), I-210 exit Fair Oaks Ave S. 626/441-3136.* Hrs: 11:30 am-2:30 pm, 6-9:30 pm; Fri to 10 pm; Sat 5:45-10 pm; Sun 4:30-8 pm; Sat brunch 11 am-2:30 pm; Sun brunch 10 am-2:30 pm. Closed Mon; Jan 1, July 4, Dec 25. Res accepted. Bar. Wine cellar. A la carte entrees: lunch $10-$17, dinner $28-$32. Complete meals: lunch $15, dinner $28-$45. Specialties: Long Island roast duckling, grilled king salmon. Menu changes weekly. Own desserts. Patio dining. Turn-of-the-century caretaker's cottage; wood floors, lace curtains, fireplace. Cr cds: A, C, D, DS, JCB, MC, V.

D

★★ **SALADANG.** *363 S Fair Oaks Ave (91105), I-210 exit Fair Oaks Ave S. 626/793-8123.* Hrs: 10 am-10 pm. Closed some major hols. Res accepted. Thai menu. Wine, beer. Semi-a la carte: lunch, dinner $5.95-$15.95. Complete meals: lunch $6.95. Specialties: miang salmon, Saladang spicy noodles. Parking. Work by local artists is displayed in this casual restaurant that features art deco decor. Totally nonsmoking. Cr cds: A, C, D, JCB, MC, V.

D

★★★ **SHIRO.** *1505 Mission St (91030), I-210 exit Fair Oaks Ave S. 626/799-4774.* Hrs: 6-9 pm; Fri, Sat to 10 pm; Sun 5:30-9 pm. Closed Mon; major hols; also 3 wks in Sept. Res accepted. Continental menu. Wine, beer. Semi-a la carte: dinner $16-$25.50. Specialties: tuna steak with shimeji and shiitake mushrooms in sesame sauce, whole sizzling catfish with ponzu sauce and fresh cilantro. Daily menu. Bistro atmosphere. Totally nonsmoking. Cr cds: A, C, MC, V.

D

★★★★ **THE GRILL.** *1505 Mission St. 626/568-3900.* Start your meal in this clubby restaurant with one of two dozen creative martinis. Follow up with fine contemporary cooking and attentive service. A serious wine list has many intriguing bottles. French. Hrs 6:30-11:30 am; 11:30 am-2:30 pm; 2:30-5 pm; 5-10 pm. Valet. Res pref. Child meal. Outdoor seating. Cr cds: C.

✓★★ **TWIN PALMS.** *101 W Green St (91105), I-210 exit Fair Oaks Ave S, in Old Town. 626/577-2567.* E-mail twinpalms@earthlink.net; web www.twin-palms.com. Hrs: 11:30 am-midnight; Fri, Sat to 1:30 am; Sun brunch 10:30 am-3 pm. Closed Dec 25. Res accepted. California coastal menu. Bar. A la carte entrees: lunch $8-$14, dinner $9-$29. Sun brunch $21.95-$24.95. Extensive salad selection. Own baking. Entertainment. Patio dining. In converted warehouse; California resort atmosphere. Cr cds: A, C, D, DS, MC, V.

D ♥

★★★ **XIOMARA.** *69 N Raymond Ave (91103), I-210 exit Fair Oak Ave S, in Old Town. 626/796-2520.* Web www.citysearch.com/pas/xiomara. Hrs: 11:30 am-2:30 pm, 5:30-10:30 pm; Sat, Sun from 5:30 pm. Closed some major hols. Res accepted. Continental menu. Bar. A la carte entrees: lunch $9-$15, dinner $17-$25. Complete meals: 3-course lunch $9.50, dinner (Mon) $20. Specialties: rock shrimp tamal, Chilean sea bass, churrasco Nicaraguense. Valet parking. Outdoor dining. Bistro atmosphere. Original artwork. Cr cds: A, C, D, DS, MC, V.

D

★★★ **YUJEAN KANG'S.** *67 N Raymond Ave (91103), I-210 exit Fair Oaks Ave S, in Old Town . 626/585-0855.* Web www.ladinig.com/yujeankangs. Hrs: Sun.- Thurs. 11:30 am-2:30 pm, 5-9:30 pm. Fri, Sat to 10 pm. Closed Thanksgiving. Res accepted. Chinese menu. Beer, wine. Semi-a la carte: lunch $6.95-$8.50, dinner $7.95-$17.95. Specialties: tea-smoked duck, crisp beef with chinese baby bok choy. Own ice cream. Totally nonsmoking. Cr cds: A, C, D, DS, MC, V.

D

Paso Robles (G-2)

(See also Atascadero)

Pop 18,600 (est) **Elev** 721 ft **Area Code** 805 **Zip** 93446
Web www.pasoroblaschamber.com

Information Chamber of Commerce, 1225 Park St; 805/238-0506 or 800/406-4040

Franciscan Fathers named this city for the great oak trees in the area, at the southern end of the fertile Salinas River Valley. Lying between mountains on the west and barley and grape fields on the east, Paso Robles is also noted for its almond tree orchards.

What to See and Do

Lake Nacimiento Resort. Swimming, waterskiing; fishing; boating (dock, landing, dry storage, rentals), marina (all yr, daily). Picnicking, lodge, cafe, general store. Camping (fee). Park (daily). 17 mi NW on Lake Nacimiento Dr (G14), off US 101. Phone 805/238-3256 or 800/323-3839 (CA). **¢¢¢-¢¢¢¢¢**

Lake San Antonio Recreation Area. Swimming, waterskiing; fishing; boating (marina, launching, rentals). Picnicking, snack bar, grocery; lndry. Camping (fee); trailer facilities (off-season rates mid-Sept-mid-May). Pets on leash only; fee. Fee for activities. (Daily) 28 mi NW off US 101, between Nacimiento & Lockwood on Interlake Rd. Phone 805/472-2311. Per vehicle **¢¢**

Mission San Miguel Arcángel (1797). Sixteenth in chain of 21 Franciscan missions; interior is in excellent condition; frescoes by Esteban Munras and his Native American helpers (1821); museum. Picnic facilities. (Daily; closed Jan 1, Easter, Thanksgiving, Dec 25) 7 mi N via US 101, Mission St in San Miguel. Phone 805/467-3256. **Donation**

Wineries. For a brochure describing many of the 35 wineries in the Paso Robles appellation, tours and tasting rms, contact the Chamber of Commerce.

Annual Events

Wine Festival. Wine tasting, winemaker dinner concerts and open houses. 3rd Sat May.

California Mid-State Fair. Rodeo, horse show, amusements, entertainment. Aug.

Motels

✓★★ ADELAIDE MOTOR INN. *1215 Ysabel Ave (93446), at 24th St. 805/238-2770; FAX 805/238-3497.* Web www.centralcoast.com/adelaideinn/. 67 rms, 1-2 story. May-mid-Oct: S, D $45-$60; each addl $5; lower rates rest of yr. Crib $3. TV; cable (premium), VCR avail (movies). Heated pool; whirlpool. Playground. Complimentary coffee in rms. Restaurant nearby. Ck-out noon. Coin lndry. Meeting rm. Business servs avail. In-rm modem link. Valet serv. Sundries. Free airport, RR station, bus depot transportation. Health club privileges. Putting green. Refrigerators; microwaves avail. Picnic tables, grills. Cr cds: A, C, D, DS, MC, V.

D SC

★★★ BEST WESTERN BLACK OAK MOTOR LODGE. *1135 24th St (93446). 805/238-4740; FAX 805/238-0726; res: 800/528-1234.* 110 units, 2 story. May-mid-Oct: S, D $58-$76; each addl $6; suites $104-$115; lower rates rest of yr. Crib $3. TV; cable, VCR avail (movies $2). Pool; whirlpool. Sauna. Playground. Complimentary coffee in rms. Restaurant 6 am-10 pm. Ck-out noon. Coin lndry. Business servs avail. In-rm modem link. Valet serv. Free airport transportation. Refrigerators. Picnic table, grills. Cr cds: A, C, D, DS, MC, V.

D SC

✓★ MELODY RANCH MOTEL. *939 Spring St (93446). 805/238-3911; res: 800/909-3911.* 19 rms. May-mid-Sept: S $36-$44; D $42-$50; higher rates special events; lower rates rest of yr. Crib $2. TV; cable. Heated pool. Complimentary coffee in rms. Restaurant adj 7 am-10 pm. Ck-out noon. Picnic table. Cr cds: A, C, D, DS, MC, V.

Restaurant

✓★ F. MCLINTOCKS SALOON. *1234 Park St (93446). 805/238-2233.* Hrs: 11:30 am-9 pm; Fri to 10 pm; Sat 8 am-10 pm; Sun 8 am-9 pm. Closed Jan 1, Thanksgiving, Dec 25. Bar. Semi-a la carte: bkfst $3.75-$8.25, lunch $4.50-$9.25, dinner $5-$16.50. Child's meals. Specializes in steak. Street parking. Unique ranch era decor. Totally nonsmoking. Cr cds: A, C, DS, MC, V.

D

Pebble Beach (F-1)

(See also Carmel, Monterey, Pacific Grove)

Pop 5,000 (est) **Elev** 0-37 ft **Area Code** 408 **Zip** 93953

Pebble Beach is noted for its scenic beauty, the palatial houses of its residents and the Pebble Beach golf courses, where the annual National Pro-Amateur Golf Championship is held (see MONTEREY).

Resorts

INN AT SPANISH BAY. *2700 Seventeen Mile Dr (93953). 831/647-7500; FAX 831/644-7955; res: 800/654-9300.* Web www.pebble-beach.com. Unrated for 2000. Cr cds: A, C, D, DS, JCB, MC, V.

D

THE LODGE AT PEBBLE BEACH. *Seventeen Mile Dr (93953), 3 mi N of Carmel on Seventeen Mile Dr. 831/624-3811; FAX 831/625-8598; res: 800/654-9300.* Web www.pebble-beach.com. Unrated for 2000. Cr cds: A, C, D, DS, JCB, MC, V.

D

Restaurants

★★★★ BAY CLUB. *(See Inn at Spanish Bay) 831/647-7500.* Cathedral ceilings and stunning floral arrangements accent the views of sand dunes, links, and the Pacific Ocean. An attentive staff assures you enjoy the regional Italian menu. Hrs: 6-10 pm. Res accepted. Northern Italian menu. Bar 4 pm-2 am. Wine cellar. A la carte entrees: dinner $23-$29. Specializes in fresh seafood, pasta. Own baking. Entertainment. Valet parking. Views of ocean, golf course. Cr cds: A, C, D, DS, JCB, MC, V.

D

★★★★ CLUB XIX. *(See The Lodge at Pebble Beach) 831/624-3811.* Web www.pebble-beach.com. Overlooking the infamous 18th hole of the Pebble Beach Golf Course and the bay, this clubby restaurant offers serious California French cooking under the supervision of Hubert Keller of San Francisco's Fleur de Lys. Hrs: 11:30 am-3:30 pm, 6-10 pm. Res accepted. Contemporary French menu. Bar. Wine cellar. A la carte entrees: lunch $10-$19, dinner $27-$38. Specialties: filet mignon, sea bass, rack of lamb. Own baking. Parking. Outdoor dining. Cr cds: C.

✓★★★ ROY'S AT PEBBLE BEACH. *(See Inn at Spanish Bay) 831/647-7423.* Hrs: 6:30 am-10 pm. Res accepted. Eclectic menu. Bar 11 am-11 pm. Wine list. A la carte entrees: bkfst $7.95-$11.95, lunch $8.25-$22.95, dinner $13.95-$25.95. Child's meals. Specializes in seafood, steak, pasta. Valet parking. Outdoor dining. Modern decor. View of ocean, golf course. Cr cds: A, C, D, DS, JCB, MC, V.

D

★★★ STILLWATER BAR AND GRILL. *(See The Lodge at Pebble Beach) 831/625-8524.* Web www.pebble-beach.com. Hrs: 7 am-2:30 pm, 6-10 pm; Sun brunch 10 am-2:30 pm. Res accepted. Bar 10 am-midnight. Wine cellar. A la carte entrees: bkfst $10-$14, lunch $9.95-$19, dinner $18-$28. Sun brunch buffet $30. Child's meals. Specializes in seafood from Pacific Northwest. View of golf course, Carmel Bay. Totally nonsmoking. Cr cds: A, C, D, DS, JCB, MC, V.

D

Petaluma (D-2)

(See also Guerneville, Napa, Santa Rosa, Sonoma)

Pop 43,184 **Elev** 12 ft **Area Code** 707 **Zip** 94952
E-mail pacc@petaluma.org **Web** www.petaluma.org

Information Petaluma Visitors Program, 799 Baywood Dr, Ste #1, 94954; 707/769-0429

What to See and Do

The Great Petaluma Mill. Refurbished historic grain mill housing shops intermingled with remnants of the riverboat era of the building. (Daily; closed Dec 25) 6 Petaluma Blvd N. Phone 707/762-1149. **Free**

Marin French Cheese Company. Manufacturer of soft ripening cheeses, including Camembert, Brie, Breakfast and Schloss. Guided tours (daily; closed Jan 1, Thanksgiving, Dec 25). 7500 Red Hill Rd, ¼ mi S of jct Novato Blvd & Petaluma-Point Reyes Rd. Phone 800/292-6001. **Free**

Petaluma Adobe State Historic Park. Restored adobe ranch house, built 1834-1845 for Gen. M. G. Vallejo, combines Monterey Colonial style with the traditional Spanish-Mexican plan. (Daily; closed Jan 1, Thanksgiving, Dec 25) 3325 Adobe Rd, 3 mi E of US 101 on CA 116. Phone 707/762-4871. **¢**

Petaluma Historical Museum & Library. Built with a grant from Andrew Carnegie in 1906, the museum contains one of California's only free-standing glass domes. Permanent and changing exhibits of Petaluma history. (Thurs-Mon; closed major hols) 20 Fourth St. Phone 707/778-4398. **Free**

Petaluma Village Factory Outlets. More than 50 name brand outlet stores in village-style setting. (Daily) 2200 Petaluma Blvd N. Phone 707/778-9300.

Annual Events

Sonoma-Marin Fair. Agricultural fair, carnival, rodeo, entertainment. Phone 707/763-0931. 5 days late June.

World Wrist Wrestling Championships. Mystic Theatre, 23 Petaluma Blvd N. Phone 707/778-1430. 2nd Sat Oct.

Motels

✓★★ **BEST WESTERN INN.** *200 S Mcdowell Blvd (94953). 707/763-0994; FAX 707/778-3111; res: 800/528-1234.* 75 rms, 38 with shower only, 2 story. S $68-$100; D $92-$116; each addl $6; under 12 free; higher rates special events. Crib free. TV; cable (premium). Heated pool. Complimentary coffee in lobby. Restaurant adj 6:30 am-11 pm. Ck-out 11 am. Coin lndry. Business servs avail. In-rm modem link. Cr cds: A, C, D, DS, MC, V.

D SC

★★ **QUALITY INN.** *5100 Montero Way (94954), US 101 Penngrove exit. 707/664-1155; FAX 707/664-8566; res: 800/228-5151.* 110 rms, 2 story, 4 suites. S $79-$114; D $84-$122; each addl $5; suites $110-$180; under 18 free. Crib $5. TV; cable (premium). Heated pool; whirlpool. Sauna. Complimentary continental bkfst. Coffee in rms. Restaurant adj open 24 hrs. Ck-out noon. Coin lndry. Meeting rm. Business servs avail. Valet serv. Refrigerators; microwaves avail. Cr cds: A, C, D, DS, ER, JCB, MC, V.

D SC

Restaurants

★★ **BUONA SERA.** *148 Kentucky St (94952). 707/763-3333.* Hrs: 5-9 pm; Fri, Sat to 10 pm. Closed some major hols. Res accepted. Italian menu. Wine, beer. Semi-a la carte: dinner $13.95-$19.95. Child's meals. Specializes in pasta, fresh seafood. Italian trattoria decor. Cr cds: A, C, MC, V.

D

★ **DE SCHMIRE.** *304 Bodega Ave (94952). 707/762-1901.* Hrs: 5:30-10 pm; Sun to 9 pm. Closed most major hols. Res accepted. No A/C. Continental menu. Wine, beer. A la carte entrees: dinner $14-$20. Child's meals. Specialties: ahi baked in nut crust, chicken Zanzibar, chicken Dijonaise. Parking. European bistro atmosphere; open kitchen. Eclectic mix of European, California, Pacific rim cuisine. Cr cds: A, C, MC, V.

D

✓★ **FINO CUCINA ITALIANA.** *208 Petaluma Blvd N (94952). 707/762-5966.* Hrs: 11:30 am-2 pm, 5-9 pm; Fri to 10 pm; Sat 5-10 pm; Sun 10:30 am-2:30 pm. Closed some major hols. Res accepted. Italian menu. Wine, beer. A la carte entrees: lunch, dinner $8.25-$15.95. Specialty: canneloni della casa. Parking. Totally nonsmoking. Cr cds: A, C, MC, V.

D

★ **GRAZIANO'S.** *170 Petaluma Blvd North (94952). 707/762-5997.* Web www.sterba.com/graziano. Hrs: 5-9:30 pm; Fri, Sat 5:30-10 pm. Closed Mon; most major hols. Res accepted. Italian menu. Bar. Semi-a la carte: dinner $10-$25.50. Specializes in fresh fish, rack of lamb. Open kitchen. Totally nonsmoking. Cr cds: A, C, MC, V.

D

Pine Valley (K-5)

(See also El Cajon, San Diego)

Settled 1869 **Pop** 1,297 **Elev** 3,736 ft **Area Code** 619 **Zip** 92062

What to See and Do

Cleveland National Forest. Surrounds town. Nearly 420,000 acres; dense chaparral environment with conifers at higher levels, tree-like manzanitas, Palomar Observatory (see ESCONDIDO). Fishing. Hiking, riding, nature trails, guided walks. Picnicking. Camping. Includes Laguna Mountain Recreation Area, 10 mi NE of I-8 on County S1. Fees at developed recreation sites. Contact Forest Supervisor, 10845 Rancho Bernardo Dr, Suite 200, San Diego 92127-2107; phone 619/673-6180.

Pinnacles National Monument (F-1)

(See also King City, Salinas)

(35 mi S of Hollister, off CA 25 or 35 mi NE of King City, off US 101; also 11 mi E of Soledad, off US 101)

Geologic activity formed a large volcano 23 million years ago—Pinnacles is the eroded remnant. The volcano formed where two plates of the earth's crust grind together along the San Andreas fault; one portion has remained near the point of origin, while the other has shifted 195 miles northward. The former section now lies between Gorman and Lancaster; the latter section, traveling at a rate of two centimeters a year, is the Pinnacles—an area of three square miles eroded by wind, rain, heat, frost and chemical action. Also here are the canyons of Bear Gulch and Chalone Creek, containing talus caves or "covered canyons," formed by large blocks of rock that have slipped from the steep walls. In all, the monument covers 25 square miles, is four miles wide and seven miles long. It has a variety of bird life, including the prairie falcon, turkey vulture and golden eagle.

Hiking is the main activity, with well-defined trails (some strenuous). High Peaks Trail follows the spectacular cliffs and pinnacles; the North Chalone

Peak Trail reaches 3,305 feet, the highest point in the monument. Trails in the caves area are shorter but equally interesting.

There are picnic areas with barbecue grills on both the east and west sides. Visitors must bring their own fuel. No wood fires permitted during high fire season (usually June-Oct). Pets on leash only; not permitted on trails. There is limited camping on west side (June-Jan only) and there is a private campground outside east entrance (phone 408/389-4462). A service station and camper store are also available there. Interpretive programs on east side (mid-Feb-Memorial Day, wkends). There is no through road; access to the east entrance is via Hollister, off CA 25 or via King City, off US 101. The west entrance is reached via Soledad, off US 101. Visitor center on east side. For campground and visitor information phone 408/389-4485. Golden Eagle Passport (see MAKING THE MOST OF YOUR TRIP). Per vehicle ¢¢

Pismo Beach (H-2)

(See also San Luis Obispo, Santa Maria)

Pop 7,669 **Elev** 33 ft **Area Code** 805 **Zip** 93449
E-mail pismobeach@aol.com **Web** www.pismobeach.org

Information Conference & Visitors Bureau, 760 Mattie Rd; 805/773-7034 or 800/443-7778 (CA)

This town is famous for its 23 miles of scenic beach. Ocean fishing, dunes, swimming, surfing, diving, golf, horseback riding and camping make the area popular with vacationers. Pismo Beach is also in a growing wine region. It is the last Pacific oceanfront community where autos can still be driven on the beach (access ramps are at two locations along the beach). A more dramatic and rugged coastline is found at Shell Beach, to the north, which has been incorporated into Pismo Beach.

What to See and Do

Lopez Recreational Area. On lake created by Lopez Dam. Swimming, waterskiing, water slide, windsurfing; fishing; boating. Hiking trail. Picnicking. Primitive camping, tent & trailer sites (hookups, dump station; fee). Summer campfire programs, boat tours. 12 mi SE via US 101, Grand Ave exit. Phone 805/489-1122. Day use, per vehicle ¢¢

Monarch Butterfly Grove. The state's largest winter site for Monarch butterflies; they can be seen in the grove located at the North Beach Campground (Nov-Mar, daily; dependent on butterfly migration). Pismo State Beach, 1 mi S via CA 1, North Beach Campground exit. Phone 805/489-1869. **Free**

Oceano Dunes State Vehicular Recreation Area. Operated by the state park system to provide location for off-highway vehicle use (vehicle access to the beach is not common in California). (Daily) 2 mi S via CA 1, Pier Ave exit. Phone 805/473-7220. Per vehicle ¢¢

Wineries of the Edna Valley & Arroyo Grande Valley. Several wineries, many with public tasting rms and offering tours, may be found along the county roads of Edna Valley and Arroyo Grande Valley; approx 5-8 mi NE & SE via CA 227 off US 101. Many are free; fee at some. Contact the Chamber of Commerce for winery maps; phone 805/541-5868.

Motels

★★★ **BEST WESTERN CASA GRANDE INN.** *850 Oak Park Blvd (93420). 805/481-7398; FAX 805/481-4859; res: 800/475-9777.* 113 rms, 2-3 story, 21 suites. June-mid-Sept: S $75-$90; D $85-$120; each addl $10; suites $100-$140; family rates; hols (2-day min); lower rates rest of yr. Crib free. TV; cable (premium), VCR avail. Pool; whirlpool. Complimentary continental bkfst; afternoon refreshments. Restaurant noon-10 pm. Bar. Ck-out 11 am. Meeting rms. Business servs avail. Coin Indry. Exercise equipt; sauna. Game rm. Many refrigerators; some wet bars; microwaves avail. Some balconies. Adj shopping mall. Cr cds: A, C, D, DS, MC, V.

★★★ **SEA CREST RESORT MOTEL.** *2241 Price St (93449). 805/773-4608; FAX 805/773-4525; res: 800/782-8400.* Web www.seacrest.com. 160 rms, 4 story. Memorial Day-Labor Day: S, D $79-$109; each addl $10; suites $125-$175; lower rates rest of yr. Crib $5. TV; cable (premium). Heated pool; whirlpools. Coffee in rms. Restaurant 8 am-10 pm. Ck-out noon. Coin Indry. Meeting rms. Business servs avail. Lawn games. Refrigerators. Private patios, balconies. Picnic tables, grills. On beach; ocean view from some rms, walkway to beach. Sun deck. Cr cds: A, C, D, DS, JCB, MC, V.

✓★★ **SEA GYPSY MOTEL.** *1020 Cypress St (93449), at Wadsworth St. 805/773-1801; FAX 805/773-9286; res: 800/592-5923.* Web www.pismobeach/seagypsy. 77 units, 3 story, 47 kits. S $35-$105; D $40-$105; each addl $10; suites $75-$190. Crib free. TV; cable. Heated pool; whirlpool. Complimentary coffee in lobby. Ck-out noon. Coin Indry. Business servs avail. In-rm modem link. Refrigerators. Private patios, balconies. On ocean, sand beach. Cr cds: A, C, DS, MC, V.

★★★ **SEA VENTURE RESORT.** *100 Ocean View Ave (93449). 805/773-4994; FAX 805/773-0924; res: 800/662-5545.* E-mail seaventure@fix.net; web www.seaventure.com. 51 rms, 3 story. Memorial Day-Labor Day: S, D $139-$349; each addl $15; 3-bedrm cottage $300-$650; under 18 free; wkends, hols (2-day min); higher rates: hols, special events; lower rates rest of yr. Crib free. TV; cable, VCR (movies). Pool. Complimentary continental bkfst. Complimentary coffee in rms. Restaurant 4-9 pm; Sun 9 am-2 pm. Rm serv. Bar. Ck-out noon. Meeting rms. Business servs avail. In-rm modem link. Bellhops. Valet serv. Concierge. Gift shop. Free garage parking. 18-hole golf privileges, greens fee $20. Massage. Health club privileges. Bathrm phones, refrigerators, minibars, wet bars, fireplaces; many in-rm whirlpools. Many balconies. On beach. Totally nonsmoking. Cr cds: A, C, D, DS, JCB, MC, V.

Motor Hotels

★★★ **KON TIKI INN.** *1621 Price St (93449). 805/773-4833; FAX 805/773-6541; res: 888/566-8454.* E-mail kontiki@thegrid.net; web www.kontiki.com. 86 rms, 3-4 story. Mid-Mar-early Oct: S, D $86-$100; each addl $7; lower rates rest of yr. Crib $7. TV; cable (premium). Heated pool; whirlpools. Complimentary continental bkfst. Restaurant 11:30 am-2 pm. Bar. Ck-out noon. Coin Indry. Meeting rms. Business servs avail. In-rm modem link. Lighted tennis. Exercise rm; sauna. Massage. Refrigerators; some fireplaces. Private patios, balconies. On ocean; stairway to beach. Cr cds: A, C, DS, MC, V.

★★★ **OXFORD SUITES RESORT.** *651 Five Cities Dr (93449). 805/773-3773; FAX 805/773-5177; res: 800/982-7848.* 133 suites, 2 story. S, D $79-$129; each addl $10; under 10 free. Crib free. Pet accepted; $10. TV; cable, VCR (movies $3). Heated pool; wading pool, whirlpool. Complimentary full bkfst. Ck-out noon. Coin Indry. Meeting rm. Business servs avail. Valet serv. Gift shop. Refrigerators, microwaves. Cr cds: A, C, D, DS, ER, MC, V.

★★ **SANDCASTLE INN.** *100 Stimson Ave (93449), at beach. 805/773-2422; FAX 805/773-0771; res: 800/822-6606.* E-mail sandcastle@thegrid.net; web www.sandcastleinn.com. 60 rms, 3 story. Memorial Day-Labor Day: S, D $110-$189; suites $175-$250; under 12 free; lower rates rest of yr. Crib free. TV; cable, VCR (movies). Complimentary continental bkfst. Complimentary coffee in rms. Ck-out 11 am. Business servs avail. Whirlpool. Refrigerators; some fireplaces. Patios, balconies. On beach. Cr cds: A, C, D, DS, MC, V.

★★★ **SPYGLASS INN SHELL BEACH.** *2705 Spyglass Dr (93449). 805/773-4855; FAX 805/773-5298; res: 800/824-2612.* E-mail spyglass.inn@thegrid.net; web www.spyglassinn.com. 82 rms, 1-2 story.

S, D $59-$159; each addl $6; suites, kit. units $89-$179; under 12 free; higher rates wkends. TV; cable, VCR (movies $3). Pool; whirlpool. Coffee in rms. Restaurant 7 am-2 pm, 4-9:30 pm. Bar 10-2 am; entertainment Fri-Sat. Ck-out 11 am. Meeting rm. Business servs avail. Refrigerators. Many private patios, balconies with ocean view. Cr cds: A, C, D, DS, ER, JCB, MC, V.

D SC

Hotel

★★★ **CLIFFS AT SHELL BEACH.** *2757 Shell Beach (91765). 805/773-5000; FAX 805/773-0764; res: 800/826-7827.* 165 rms, 5 story, 27 suites. S, D $145-$200; suites $275-$375; under 18 free; wkend packages; golf plans. Crib free. TV; cable, VCR avail. Heated pool; whirlpool, poolside serv. Complimentary coffee in lobby. Restaurant 7 am-9:30 pm; Fri, Sat to 10 pm. Bar 11-2 am; entertainment. Ck-out noon. Coin lndry. Meeting rms. Business servs avail. In-rm modem link. Valet serv. Gift shop. Valet parking. Free airport, RR station, bus depot transportation. Exercise rm; sauna. Lawn games. Some refrigerators. Whirlpool in suites. Private patios, balconies. On cliff overlooking beach. Cr cds: A, C, D, DS, JCB, MC, V.

D SC

Inn

★★★ **THE CRYSTAL ROSE INN.** *789 Valley Rd (93420), approx 3 mi S on US 101. 805/481-1854; FAX 805/481-9541; res: 800/ ROSEINN.* E-mail stay@callamer.com; web www.centralcoast.crystalroseinn.com. 8 rms, 2-3 story, 3 suites. No A/C. S, D $95-$165; each addl $35; suites $185; hols (2-day min). Crib free. TV in parlor; cable, VCR avail (movies). Complimentary full bkfst; afternoon refreshments. Restaurant 11:30 am-2 pm, 5-9 pm, Sun from 5:30 pm; closed Mon. Rm serv. Ck-out 11 am, ck-in 2 pm. Business servs avail. In-rm modem link. Luggage handling. Gift shop. Exercise equipt. Picnic tables. Victorian mansion built ca 1890. Totally nonsmoking. Cr cds: A, C, DS, MC, V.

D

Restaurants

★★ **F. MCLINTOCKS.** *750 Mattie Rd (93449). 805/773-1892.* Web www.mclintocks.com. Hrs: 4-10 pm; Sat 3-10:30 pm; Sun 9 am-9:30 pm; early-bird dinner Mon-Fri 4-6 pm, Sat 3-5 pm; Sun noon-5 pm; Sun brunch 9-11:30 am. Closed some major hols. Res accepted Sun-Thurs. Bar. Complete meals: dinner $9.50-$30.95. Sun brunch $9.95-$13.95. Child's meals. Specializes in steak, seafood, oak pit barbecue. Guitarist (seasonal). Unique ranch-era decor includes 6-foot-high stuffed buffalo, old farm implements, blacksmith and branding iron gear. Cr cds: A, C, DS, MC, V.

D

✓★★ **ROSA'S ITALIAN RESTAURANT.** *491 Price St (93449). 805/773-0551.* Web www.rosaristoranteitaliano. Hrs: 11:30 am-2 pm, 4-9:30 pm; Sat, Sun 4-10 pm. Closed Thanksgiving, Dec 25. Italian menu. Bar. Semi-a la carte: lunch $5.45-$10.25, dinner $7.95-$17.45. Child's meals. Specializes in pasta, seafood, chicken. Parking. Patio dining. Extensive floral display. Totally nonsmoking. Cr cds: A, C, D, DS, MC, V.

D

Placerville (D-3)

(See also Auburn, Sacramento)

Founded 1848 **Pop** 8,355 **Elev** 1,866 ft **Area Code** 530 **Zip** 95667
E-mail tourism@eldoradocounty.org **Web** www.eldoradocounty.org

Information El Dorado County Chamber of Commerce, 542 Main St; 530/621-5885 or 800/457-6279

This one-time rough-and-tough gold town was first known as Dry Diggin's (because the gravel had to be carried to water to be washed for gold) and later as Hangtown (because of the number of hangings necessary to keep law and order). At one time the town rivaled San Francisco and nurtured three notables: Mark Hopkins, railroad magnate; Philip D. Armour, meat-packing magnate; and John Studebaker, automobile magnate. A few mines still function, but lumbering, agriculture and recreation are the main industries.

What to See and Do

El Dorado County Historical Museum. Displays and exhibits of early Gold Rush days, when Miwok, Maidu and Washoe inhabited the area. (Wed-Sat; closed hols) 104 Placerville Dr. Phone 530/621-5865. **Free**

El Dorado National Forest. Approx 786,000 acres. Includes the 105,364-acre Mokelumne Wilderness, located between CA 4 & CA 88, and the popular 63,475-acre Desolation Wilderness, located immediately W of Lake Tahoe. Campgrounds have varying fees and facilities; all are closed in winter. 25 mi E via US 50. Contact the Information Center, 3070 Camino Heights Dr, Camino 95709; phone 530/644-6048.

Gold Bug Mine. Municipally owned double-shaft gold mine with exposed vein; restored gold stampmill. Picnic area. Guided tours avail (res required). (May-mid-Sept, daily; mid-Mar-Apr & mid-Sept-Nov, wkends) In Hangtown's Gold Bug Park. Phone 530/642-5232. **¢**

Marshall Gold Discovery State Historic Park. Marks place where James Marshall found flecks of gold in tailrace of Sutter's Mill in Jan of 1848. By the next year more than $10 million in gold had been taken from the American River's South Fork. Park includes Gold Discovery Museum (daily; closed Jan 1, Thanksgiving, Dec 25), Marshall's cabin and monument where he is buried, Thomas House Museum, operating replica of Sutter's mill, blacksmith shop and several other buildings. Fishing. Nature and hiking trails. Picnicking, concession. Park (daily). 8 mi NW on CA 49 in Coloma. Phone 530/622-3470. Per vehicle **¢¢**

Annual Events

El Dorado County Fair. Fairgrounds, SW on US 50. Early June.

Wagon Train Week. Celebrations each night along wagon train trek (US 50) from Nevada to Placerville. Sat celebrations at fairgrounds; parade on Sun. Mid-June.

Motels

✓★ **BEST WESTERN.** *3361 Coach Ln (95682). 530/677-2203; FAX 530/676-1422; res: 800/601-1234.* E-mail mac@foothill.net. 62 rms, 1-2 story. S $51-$65; D $56-$70; each addl $5; suites $75-$104; under 16 free; family rates. Crib free. Pet accepted. TV; cable (premium), VCR avail. Complimentary continental bkfst. Complimentary coffee in rms. Restaurant adj 6-2 am. Ck-out noon. Meeting rms. Business center. Coin lndry. Golf privileges. Health club privileges. Outdoor pool. Some refrigerators, microwaves. Some balconies. Grills. Cr cds: A, C, D, DS, ER, MC, V.

D SC

★★ **BEST WESTERN INN.** *6850 Greenleaf Dr (95667), S of US 50 at Missouri Flat Rd. 530/622-9100; FAX 530/622-9376; res: 800/528-1234; res: 800/854-9100.* 105 rms, 3 story. No elvtr. S $60-$70; D $71-$82; each addl $10; suites from $138; under 12 free. Crib free. Pet accepted; $10. TV; cable. Heated pool; whirlpool. Coffee in rms. Restaurant adj. Ck-out 11 am. Meeting rms. Business servs avail. Some patios, balconies. Cr cds: A, C, D, DS, MC, V.

D SC

Inn

★★ **COLOMA COUNTRY INN.** *345 High St. (95613), 8 mi NW on CA 49. 530/622-6919; FAX 530/622-1795.* E-mail alancci@innercite.com; web www.gonative.com. 6 rms, 2 share bath, 2 story, 2 suites, 1 guest house. No rm phones. S, D $90-$110; suites $130-$180; guest house $310; package plans; hols (2-day min). Complimentary full bkfst; afternoon refreshments. Restaurant nearby. Ck-out 11 am, ck-in 4 pm. Playground. Lawn games. Refrigerator in suites. Picnic tables, grills. Built in 1852. Totally nonsmoking. Cr cds: C.

Restaurant

✓★ **LYON'S RESTAURANT.** *1160 Broadway (95667). 530/622-2305.* Hrs: open 24 hrs; Sat, Sun brunch 9 am-3 pm. Bar. Semi-a la carte: bkfst $2.99-$8, lunch $5.99-$8.99, dinner $8.99-$12.99. Sat, Sun brunch $6.99-$8.99. Child's meals. Specialties: prime rib, Yankee pot roast, sizzling steak platters. Parking. Children eat free on Tuesdays. Totally nonsmoking. Cr cds: A, C, DS, MC, V.

D SC

Pleasanton (E-2)

(See also Fremont, Hayward, Livermore, Oakland)

Settled 1851 **Pop** 50,553 **Elev** 352 ft **Area Code** 925 **Zip** 94566

Information Tri-Valley Convention & Visitors Bureau, 260 Main St; 925/846-8910 or 888/874-9253

Named for the friend of an early settler, Pleasanton was once called "the most desperate town in the West," for its many bandits and desperados. Phoebe Apperson Hearst founded the PTA in Pleasanton.

What to See and Do

Alameda County Fairgrounds. Exhibit area; 9-hole golf course. Events and activities. Oldest racetrack west of the Mississippi River. Thoroughbred racing during county fair (see ANNUAL EVENT); satellite-broadcast races yr-round. 4501 Pleasanton Ave, I-680 at Bernal Ave. Phone 925/426-7600.

Behring Auto Museum. Display of 110 classic and rare automobiles, many custom-built. Modern sculpture building; library. (Wed-Sun) 7 mi N on I-680 to Crow Canyon Rd in San Ramon, then 4 mi E to Camino Tassajara, then 1 blk E, turn left on Blackhawk Plaza Dr. Phone 925/736-2277. **¢¢¢** Admission includes

Berkeley Museum of Art, Science and Culture. Houses university collections of anthropology, paleontology and changing art exhibits. (Wed-Sun) Combination ticket with Auto Museum. Phone 925/736-2277.

Eugene O'Neill National Historic Site. Winner of the Nobel Prize and four Pulitzer Prizes, O'Neill wrote some of his finest works at Tao House, including the autobiographical *Long Day's Journey Into Night* and *A Moon For the Misbegotten.* A blend of Chinese philosophy and Spanish-style architecture, Tao House was to be O'Neill's "final home and harbor." The house commands a spectacular view of the hills and orchards of the San Ramon Valley and Mt Diablo. Tours (Wed-Sun, morning & afternoon; by res only). Shuttle service provided from Danville. 7 mi W of I-680, near Danville. Contact Superintendent, PO Box 280, Danville 94526; phone 925/838-0249. **Free**

Annual Event

Alameda County Fair. Fairgrounds, jct I-680 & I-580, Bernal Ave exit. Horse racing, exhibitions, carnival, theatrical shows. Phone 925/426-7600. Late June-mid-July.

Motel

★★ **COURTYARD BY MARRIOTT.** *5059 Hopyard Rd (94588). 925/463-1414; FAX 925/463-0113; res: 800/321-2211.* E-mail cy.oakpl.gen@marriott.com; web www.courtyard. com-oakpl. 145 rms, 2-3 story, 14 suites. S $129; D $139; each addl $10; suites $149; wkly, wkend rates. Crib free. TV; cable (premium). Heated pool; whirlpool. Complimentary coffee in rms. Restaurant 6:30-10 am; wkends 7-11:30 am. Bar 5:30-10:30 pm. Ck-out 1 pm. Coin Indry. Meeting rms. Business servs avail. Valet serv. Sundries. Exercise equipt. Refrigerator in suites. Some balconies. Cr cds: A, C, D, DS, MC, V.

D SC

Motor Hotel

★★ **CANDLEWOOD SUITES.** *5535 Johnson Dr (94588). 925/463-1212; FAX 925/463-6080; res: 800/946-6200.* 126 suites, 4 story. S, D $109-$129; under 18 free; package plans. Crib free. Pet accepted; $75 & $10/day. TV; cable (premium), VCR (movies). Complimentary coffee in rms. Restaurant adj open 24 hrs. Rm serv 5-9 pm. Ck-out noon. Business servs avail. In-rm modem link. Sundries. Guest Indry. Exercise equipt. Pool privileges; whirlpool. Refrigerators, microwaves. Cr cds: A, C, D, DS, ER, JCB, MC, V.

D SC

Hotels

★★★ **CROWNE PLAZA.** *11950 Dublin Canyon Rd (94588), just W of jct I-580, I-680, Foothill Rd exit. 925/847-6000; FAX 925/463-2585; res: 800/227-6963.* 244 rms, 6 story. S $149-$169; D $159-$179; each addl $10; under 18 free; wkend rates. Crib free. Pet accepted, some restrictions; $50 deposit. TV; cable (premium). Heated pool; whirlpool. Complimentary coffee in rms. Restaurant 6 am-10 pm. Bar noon-midnight. Ck-out noon. Coin Indry. Convention facilities. Business servs avail. Gift shop. Exercise equipt. Refrigerators avail. Cr cds: A, C, D, DS, JCB, MC, V.

D SC

✓★★★ **HILTON AT THE CLUB.** *7050 Johnson Dr (94588), at jct I-580, I-680, Hopyard exit off I-580. 925/463-8000; FAX 925/463-3801; res: 800/445-8667.* Web www.pleasantonhilton.com. 294 rms, 5 story. S, D $135-$235; each addl $10; suites $300-$600; family, wkend rates. Crib free. Pet accepted, some restrictions; $15. TV; cable (premium), VCR avail. Heated pool; poolside serv. Restaurant 6:30 am-10:30 pm. Bar 11-1:30 am. Ck-out noon. Meeting rms. Business center. Gift shop. Barber, beauty shop. Valet parking. Indoor tennis, pro. Exercise rm; sauna. Bathrm phones. Luxury level. Cr cds: A, C, D, DS, ER, JCB, MC, V.

D SC

★★★ **WYNDHAM GARDEN HOTEL.** *5990 Stoneridge Mall Rd (94588), just S of I-580, Foothill Rd exit. 925/463-3330; FAX 925/463-3315; res: 800/996-3426.* 171 rms, 6 story. S $255; D $265; each addl $10; suites $550; under 18 free; wkend, hol rates. TV; cable (premium). Heated pool; whirlpool. Complimentary coffee in rms. Restaurant 6:30 am-10 pm; Fri, Sat 7 am-10 pm. Bar. Ck-out noon. Meeting rms. Business servs avail. In-rm modem. Exercise equipt; sauna. Refrigerator in suites. Cr cds: A, C, D, DS, ER, JCB, MC, V.

D SC

Inn

★★ **EVERGREEN BED & BREAKFAST.** *9104 Longview Dr (94588). 925/426-0901; FAX 925/426-9568.* Web www.evergreen-inn.com. 4 rms, 1 with shower only, 2 story. S, D $135-$225; each addl $20. TV; cable, VCR avail. Whirlpool. Complimentary full bkfst. Restaurant nearby. Ck-out 11 am, ck-in 3 pm. Guest Indry. Luggage handling. Concierge serv. Some in-rm whirlpools. Totally nonsmoking. Cr cds: A, C, MC, V.

Restaurants

✓★★ **GIRASOLE.** *3180 Santa Rita Rd (94566). 925/484-1001.* Hrs: 11 am-9 pm; Fri, Sat to 10 pm; Sun 4-9 pm. Closed most major hols. Res accepted. Italian, Amer menu. A la carte entrees: lunch $5.50-$14.95, dinner $9.50-$18.95. Child's meals. Specialties: scoozzi, absolut prawns, Tuscan pork. Parking. Outdoor dining. Totally nonsmoking. Cr cds: A, C, D, MC, V.

D

★★ **PLEASANTON HOTEL.** *855 Main St (94566). 925/846-8106.* Hrs: 11:30 am-2 pm, 5-9 pm; Fri, Sat to 10 pm; Sun 10 am-2 pm (brunch), 4:30-9 pm. Closed Memorial Day, Labor Day, Dec 25. Res accepted. Bar. A la carte entrees: lunch $7.50-$13.50, dinner $12-$19.75. Sun brunch $18.95. Specializes in fresh fish, pasta, beef. Band Thurs-Sun; blues Thurs, swing band Sun. Heated patio dining. Victorian dining room in 1864 hotel that was once a stagecoach stop and gambling house. Totally nonsmoking. Cr cds: A, C, D, DS, MC, V.

D

Pomona (J-4)

(See also Claremont, Ontario, Pasadena)

Pop 131,723 **Elev** 850 ft **Area Code** 909

Information Pomona Valley Latino Chamber of Commerce, 142 Third St, 91766; 909/469-0702

What to See and Do

Historical Society of Pomona Valley (1850-1854). Grounds, furnished 13-rm adobe house illustrate romantic "Days of the Dons." Native American artifacts, baskets. (Sun 2-5 pm or by appt; closed major hols) 491 E Arrow Hwy, 1 mi N on Garey Ave off San Bernardino Frwy. Phone 909/623-2198. **Donation**

Adobe de Palomares. 491 E Arrow Hwy, 1 mi N on Garey Ave off San Bernardino Frwy.

La Casa Primera. Corner of Park & McKinley Ave S.

California State Polytechnic University, Pomona (1938). (19,000 students) Kellogg West Continuing Education Center has conference facilities (daily). 3801 W Temple Ave. Phone 909/869-7659. On campus is the renowned

Kellogg Arabian Horse Center. Also houses Equine Research Center. One-hr performances (Oct-June, 1st Sun each month; no shows Easter). Stable (daily; free). Phone 909/869-2224. Shows ¢¢

Pomona School of Fine Arts. Classes in fine arts, exhibits. 242 S Garey Ave. Phone 909/868-0900.

Annual Event

Los Angeles County Fair. Fairplex, 1101 W McKinley Ave. Thoroughbred racing, carnival, exhibits, free stage shows, food booths, monorail. Contact PO Box 2250, 91769; 909/623-3111. Mid-Sept-early Oct.

Motel

★★ **BEST WESTERN HOTEL.** *259 Gentle Springs Ln (91765), at jct CA 57 & 60. 909/860-3700; FAX 909/860-2110; res: 800/528-1234.* 97 rms, 2 story. S, D $55-$61; each addl $5; suites $125; under 12 free; family, wkly rates. Crib $5. TV; cable (premium). Pool; whirlpool. Complimentary continental bkfst. Restaurant nearby. Ck-out noon. Meeting rms. Business servs avail. Valet serv. Coin Indry. Health club privileges. Some wet bars. Cr cds: A, C, D, DS, MC, V.

D SC

Motor Hotel

★★★ **SHILO INN HILLTOP SUITES.** *3101 Temple Ave (91768), CA 57 exit Temple Ave. 909/598-7666; FAX 909/598-5654; res: 800/222-2244.* Web www.shiloinns.com. 129 units, 69 suites, 3 story. S, D $133; suites $159; each addl $15; under 12 free. Crib free. TV; cable (premium), VCR (movies). Heated pool; whirlpool, poolside serv. Complimentary full bkfst. Complimentary coffee in rms. Restaurant 6 am-10 pm; Fri, Sat to 11 pm. Rm serv. Bar 11-2 am; entertainment Tues-Sat. Ck-out noon. Coin Indry. Meeting rms. Business servs avail. In-rm modem link. Bellhops. Valet serv. Sundries. Free airport transportation. Exercise equipt; sauna, steam rm. Health club privileges. Bathrm phones, refrigerators, microwaves, wet bars. Cr cds: A, C, D, DS, ER, JCB, MC, V.

D SC

Hotel

★★ **HOLIDAY INN SELECT.** *21725 E Gateway Dr (91765), CA 57 Grand Ave exit to Golden Springs Dr, then SW to E Gateway Center Dr. 909/860-5440; FAX 909/860-8224; res: 800/988-3587.* 176 rms, 6 story. S, D $79-$115; each addl $10; under 18 free. Crib free. TV; cable (premium). Heated pool; whirlpool, poolside serv. Restaurant 6 am-10 pm. Bar 4-10 pm. Ck-out noon. Meeting rms. Business servs avail. Some balconies. Cr cds: A, C, D, DS, MC, V.

D SC

Restaurant

★★ **D'ANTONIO'S RISTORANTE.** *808 N Diamond Bar Blvd (91765), CA 57 exit Temple Ave E, then S on Diamond Bar Blvd. 909/860-3663.* Web www.athand.com. Hrs: 11 am-10 pm; Fri to 11 pm; Sat noon-11 pm; Sun noon-10 pm. Closed some major hols. Res accepted. Italian menu. Wine, beer. Semi-a la carte: lunch $5.95-$13.95, dinner $8.45-$22.95. Specializes in steak, seafood, chicken. Own desserts. Outdoor dining. Cr cds: A, C, D, DS, JCB, MC, V.

D

Porterville (G-3)

Pop 29,563 **Elev** 459 ft **Area Code** 209 **Zip** 93257

What to See and Do

Sequoia National Forest. Precipitous canyons, spectacular views of the Sierra Nevada and more than 30 groves of giant sequoias on 1,139,000 acres. Largest tree of any National Forest is here; the Boole Tree stands 269 feet and is 90 feet in circumference. (The General Sherman Tree in Sequoia National Park is a few feet taller.) The forest contains the 303,290-acre Golden Trout, 130,995-acre Dome Land, 10,610-acre Jennie Lake, 63,000-acre South Sierra, 88,290-acre Kiavah and the 45,000-acre Monarch wilderness areas. Activities include swimming; lake and stream fishing for trout; hunting; whitewater rafting in the Kern and Kings rivers. Hiking, riding and backpacking trails in wilderness areas (permit required). Cross-country skiing, snowshoeing and snowmobiling in winter. Picnicking. Camping (for res phone 800/280-2267) at 50 areas; 14-day/month limit; no electric hookups or other utility connections; campgrounds (fees vary). 20 mi E via CA 190. Contact Forest Supervisor, 900 W Grand Ave; 209/784-1500, ext 1232.

Quincy (C-3)

(See also Chester)

Pop 4,271 **Elev** 3,432 ft **Area Code** 916 **Zip** 95971
Information Plumas County Visitors Bureau, PO Box 4120; 916/283-6345 or 800/326-2247

What to See and Do

Plumas County Museum. Period rms, changing historical displays, artifacts and photographs featured in main gallery; permanent exhibit of baskets woven by area's native Maidu. Mezzanine gallery features contemporary cultural displays by county artisans, historical exhibits and Western Pacific and local RR collections. Archival collection of Plumas County documents. (May-Sept, daily; rest of yr, Mon-Fri) 500 Jackson St. Phone 916/283-6320. ¢

Plumas National Forest. Beautiful 1½ million-acre forest in Feather River Country. Feather Falls (640-ft drop), sixth-highest waterfall in US, accessible by 3.5-mi trail (see OROVILLE). CA 70, which runs approx 150 mi through the forest, is a designated National Scenic Byway. Groomed cross-country skiing, snowmobile trails. Interpretive trails; hiking, backpacking. Fishing, boating; hunting (deer, bear, game birds). Picnicking. Camping (May-Oct, fee); res for some campsites can be made by phoning 800/280-2267. Contact the Forest Supervisor, 159 Lawrence St, PO Box 11500; 916/283-2050.

Annual Event

Plumas County Fair. Plumas County Fairgrounds. Held annually since 1859. Horse shows, stock car races, Pacific Coast Loggers Championship Show, country/western entertainment; parade, pageant; 4-H livestock auction. Phone 916/283-6272. 2nd wk Aug.

Motels

★ **LARIAT LODGE.** *2370 E Main St (95971). 530/283-1000; FAX 530/283-2154; res: 800/999-7199.* 20 rms. 12 A/C. S, D $42-$54; each addl $6; family units $58-$68. TV; cable (premium). Heated pool. Complimentary continental bkfst. Complimentary coffee in rms. Restaurant nearby. Ck-out 11 am. X-country ski 17 mi. Some refrigerators, microwaves. Cr cds: A, C, DS, MC, V.

SC

✓★ **RANCHITO MOTEL.** *2020 E Main St (95971). 530/283-2265; FAX 530/283-2316.* 30 rms, 4 kits. No A/C. S $44; D $51-$56; each addl $9; kit. units for 1-5, $53-$90. Crib free. TV; cable. Complimentary coffee in rms. Restaurant nearby. Ck-out 11 am. X-country ski 17 mi. Private patios. Picnic tables. Some adobe buildings; Spanish decor. Shaded gardens, brook, 2 wooded acres. Cr cds: A, C, DS, MC, V.

SC

Restaurants

✓★★ **MOON'S RESTAURANT.** *497 Lawrence (95971). 530/283-0765.* Hrs: 4-10 pm. Closed Mon; most major hols. Res accepted. Italian, Amer menu. Wine, beer. Semi-a la carte: dinner $8.25-$17.95. Specializes in fresh fish, vegetarian dishes, Angus beef. Own desserts. Patio dining. Restored early 1900s building. Totally nonsmoking. Cr cds: A, C, DS, MC, V.

★★★ **OLSEN'S CABIN RESTAURANT.** *589 Johnsville Rd (96103), ¼ mi W of Graeagle on Johnsville Rd. 530/836-2801.* Hrs: 6-9:30 pm; Closed Sun, Mon; also Tue, Wed Nov-Apr. Res accepted. Bar. Complete meals: dinner $16-$19. Child's meals. Specializes in seafood, steaks, chops. Salad bar. Own baking. In historic log cabin. Gift shop. Family-owned. Totally nonsmoking. Cr cds: C, MC, V.

D

Rancho Bernardo

(see San Diego)

Rancho Cordova (D-3)

(See also Sacramento)

Pop 48,731 **Elev** 126 ft **Area Code** 916 **Web** www.blacksand.com/~rccc
Information Cordova Chamber of Commerce, 3328 Mather Field Rd, 95670; 916/361-8700

Motels

★★ **BEST WESTERN HERITAGE INN.** *11269 Point East Dr (95742), SE of jct US 50 & Sunrise Blvd. 916/635-4040; FAX 916/635-7198; res: 800/528-1234.* 123 rms, 3 story. S $60-$75; D $65-$80; each addl $5; under 12 free. TV; cable (premium). Pool. Complimentary full bkfst. Restaurant 6-9:30 am, 5-10 pm. Rm serv. Bar 5-9:30 pm. Ck-out 11 am. Meeting rms. Business servs avail. Valet serv. Some in-rm whirlpools, refrigerators. Cr cds: A, C, D, DS, ER, JCB, MC, V.

D SC

★ **COMFORT INN.** *3240 Mather Field Rd (95670), S of jct US 50 & Mather Field Rd. 916/363-3344; FAX 916/362-0903; res: 800/638-7949.* 110 rms, 4 story. S $65; D $70; suites $90-$95; under 14 free. Pet accepted; $100 deposit. TV; cable (premium). Pool; whirlpool. Complimentary continental bkfst. Coffee in rms. Restaurant nearby. Ck-out noon. Coin Indry. Meeting rms. Some refrigerators. Cr cds: A, C, D, DS, ER, JCB, MC, V.

D SC

★★ **COURTYARD BY MARRIOTT.** *10683 White Rock Rd (95670), SW of jct US 50 & Zinfandel Dr. 916/638-3800; FAX 916/638-6776; res: 800/321-2211.* 144 rms, 3 story. S, D $109; suites $124; under 18 free; wkend rates. TV; cable (premium). Heated pool; whirlpool. Restaurant 6:30-10 am. Rm serv 5-10 pm. Bar 4-11 pm. Ck-out noon. Coin Indry. Meeting rms. Valet serv. Sundries. Exercise equipt. Some refrigerators. Private patios, balconies. Cr cds: A, C, D, DS, JCB, MC, V.

D SC

✓★ **ECONOMY INNS OF AMERICA.** *12249 Folsom Blvd (95742), SW of jct US 50 & Hazel Ave. 916/351-1213; FAX 916/351-1817; res: 800/826-0778.* 124 rms, 3 story. S $50-$60; D $59-$65; each addl (up to 4) $5. Pet accepted, some restrictions. TV; cable (premium). Pool. Complimentary continental bkfst. Restaurant adj 11 am-11 pm. Ck-out 11 am. Coin Indry. Cr cds: A, C, MC, V.

D SC

Motor Hotel

★★ **HALLMARK SUITES.** *11260 Point East Dr (95742), SE of jct US 50 & Sunrise Blvd. 916/638-4141; FAX 916/638-4287; res: 800/444-1089.* Web www.hallmarksuites.com. 159 suites, 32 kit. units, 3 story. S, D $92-$179, kit. units $95-$199; under 18 free; wkend rates. Crib free. TV; cable. Heated pool; whirlpool. Complimentary full bkfst. Restaurant nearby. Rm serv (lunch, dinner). Bar 5-11 pm. Ck-out noon. Coin Indry. Meeting rms. Valet serv. Gift shop. Exercise equipt. Bathrm phones, refrigerators. Some private patios. Cr cds: A, C, D, DS, ER, JCB, MC, V.

D SC

Hotel

★★★ **SHERATON HOTEL.** *11211 Point East Dr (95742), S of jct US 50 & Sunrise Blvd. 916/638-1100; FAX 916/638-5803; res: 800/544-5064; res: 800/851-2400.* 262 rms, 11 story. S $80-$150; D $90-$160; each addl $10; suites $250-$300; under 17 free; wkend rates. TV; cable (premium). Heated pool; whirlpool, poolside serv. Complimentary coffee in rms. Restaurant 6 am-10:30 pm. Bar 11-2 am; Sun to 11 pm. Ck-out noon. Convention facilities. Business center. In-rm modem link. Concierge. Gift shop. Airport, RR station, bus depot transportation. Exercise equipt. Luxury level. Cr cds: A, C, D, DS, JCB, MC, V.

D SC

Restaurants

✓★ **BROOKFIELD'S.** *11135 Folsom Blvd (95670), SW of jct US 50 & Sunrise Blvd. 916/638-2046.* Hrs: 6:30 am-11 pm; Fri, Sat to midnight. Closed July 4, Thanksgiving, Dec 25. Wine, beer. Semi-a la carte: bkfst, lunch $4-$7, dinner $6-$11. Child's meals. Specializes in own baking. Coffee shop atmosphere. Totally nonsmoking. Cr cds: A, C, D, DS, MC, V.

D SC

★★★ **SLOCUM HOUSE.** *7992 California Ave (95628), 3 mi N on Sunrise Blvd, opp Community Center. 916/961-7211.* Hrs: 11:30 am-2 pm, 5:30-10 pm; Sun brunch 10:30 am-2 pm. Closed Mon; Jan 1. Res accepted. Contemporary Amer menu. Bar. Wine list. A la carte entrees: lunch $8.50-$12.95. Semi-a la carte: dinner $17.95-$23.95. Sun brunch $13.95. Specializes in seafood, wild game. Jazz quartet Fri & Sat in summer. Outdoor dining. Historic 1920s luxury house; art deco decor; original marble/oak fireplace. Hillside setting, among trees and flowers. Cr cds: A, C, D, DS, MC, V.

D

Rancho Cucamonga (B-8 see Los Angeles map)

(See also Claremont, Ontario, Pomona)

Pop 101,409 **Elev** 1,110 ft **Area Code** 909 **Zip** 91730

Information Chamber of Commerce, 8280 Utica Ave, Suite 160; 909/987-1012

The original residents, the Serrano, called this area Cucamonga or "sandy place." Later, it was part of the vast Rancho de Cucamonga. Violent deaths and long legal battles caused the eventual sale of the land to several wine and citrus industries in 1871.

What to See and Do

Casa de Rancho Cucamonga (Rains House). Oldest burned-brick house in San Bernardino County (ca 1860); was home to wealthy and socially prominent John and Merced Rains. (Wed-Sun) 8810 Hemlock St, just north of vineyard. Phone 909/989-4970. ¢

Annual Event

Grape Harvest Festival. Wine tasting, grape stomping contest, carnival, displays, entertainment. Early Oct.

Motor Hotels

✓★★ **BEST WESTERN HERITAGE INN.** *8179 Spruce Ave (91730), I-15 exit Foothill Blvd (US 66) W. 909/466-1111; FAX 909/466-3876; res: 800/528-1234; res: 800/682-7829.* 116 rms, 6 story. S $79-$89; D $84-$94; each addl $8; suites $99-$104; under 13 free. Crib free. TV; cable (premium). Heated pool; whirlpool. Complimentary continental bkfst. Coffee in rms. Restaurant nearby. Ck-out noon. Meeting rms. Business servs avail. Valet serv. Exercise equipt. Refrigerators; wet bars in suites; microwaves avail. Cr cds: A, C, DS, MC, V.

D SC

Restaurants

★★ **MAGIC LAMP INN.** *8189 E Foothill Blvd (91730), I-10 exit Vineyard Ave N to Foothill Blvd. 909/981-8659.* Hrs: 11:30 am-2:30 pm, 5-10 pm; Sat & Sun from 5 pm; early-bird dinner Tues-Thurs 4:30-6:30 pm. Closed Mon; Dec 25 & 26. Res accepted. Continental menu. Bar. Semi-a la carte: lunch $6.95-$11.95, dinner $9.95-$26.50. Lunch buffet (Tues-Fri): $8.25. Child's meals. Specializes in prime rib, fresh seafood. Own soup. Entertainment Wed-Sat. Parking. Family-owned since 1955. Cr cds: A, C, D, MC, V.

D SC

★★★ **SYCAMORE INN.** *8318 Foothill Blvd (91730), I-10 exit Vineyard Ave N. 909/982-1104.* Web www.citivw.comirc/sycamore. Hrs: 5-10 pm; Sat to 11 pm; Sun 4:30-8:30 pm. Closed most major hols. Res accepted. Continental menu. Bar. Wine cellar. Semi-a la carte: dinner $13.95-$25.95. Specializes in prime rib, certified black Angus steak, fresh seafood. Parking. Historic stagecoach inn/stop (1848), surrounded by sycamore trees. Cr cds: A, C, D, DS, MC, V.

Rancho Santa Fe (K-4)

(See also Del Mar)

Pop 5,000 (est) **Elev** 245 ft **Area Code** 619 **Zip** 92067

Resorts

★★★ **INN AT RANCHO SANTA FE.** *5951 Linea Del Cielo (92067), Lomas Santa Fe Dr, Solana Beach. 858/756-1131; FAX 858/759-1604; res: 800/843-4661.* 89 units in lodge, cottages. S, D $95-$210; each addl $20; suites $275-$520. Crib $20. Pet accepted. TV; VCR avail. Heated pool; poolside serv. Restaurant 7:30-10:30 am, noon-2:30 pm, 6:30-9:30 pm. Rm serv. Box lunches. Bar 11 am-11 pm. Ck-out noon, ck-in 3 pm. Grocery 2 blks. Meeting rms. Business servs avail. Bellhops. Tennis. 18-hole golf privileges. Exercise equipt. Massage. Lawn games. Some in-rm whirlpools; refrigerators, wet bars, fireplaces; microwaves avail. Many private patios. On 22 acres of landscaped grounds. Beach house in Del Mar avail for day use. Cr cds: A, C, D, MC, V.

D

★★★★ **RANCHO VALENCIA.** *5921 Valencia Circle (92067). 619/756-1123; FAX 619/756-0165; res: 800/548-3664.* E-mail ranchv@aol.com; web www.ranchovalencia.com. Nestled amidst the rolling hills of Rancho Santa Fe, this resort is just 25 miles from San Diego and minutes from the beautiful communities of Del Mar and La Jolla. It is the perfect place for a retreat to refresh and restore one's mind and body offering a plethora of spa services and recreational activities. 43 suites. S, D $420-$4,000; 2-bedrm suites $900-$1,050; 3-bedrm hacienda from $4,000; tennis clinic, golf plans. Crib free. Pet accepted; $75/day. TV; cable (premium), VCR. Pool; poolside serv. Complimentary coffee in rms. Restaurant (see VALENCIA). Box lunches, picnics. Bar from 10 am. Ck-out noon, ck-in 4 pm. Guest lndry. Meeting rms. Business servs avail. In-rm modem link. Bellhops. Valet serv. Gift shop. 18 tennis courts, pro. 18-hole golf privileges, Bicycle rentals. Lawn games. Soc dir. Exercise equipt. Massage. Bathrm phones, refrigerators, minibars, wet bars, fireplaces; microwaves avail. Cr cds: A, C, D, MC, V.

D

Restaurants

★★★ **DELICIAS.** *6106 Paseo Delicias (92067). 619/756-8000.* Hrs: noon-2 pm, 6-10 pm; Tues from 6 pm. Closed Sun, Mon; Jan 1, July 4, Dec 25. Res accepted. Contemporary Amer menu. Bar to 11 pm. Wine list. A la carte entrees: lunch $8-$15, dinner $16-$30. Specialties: smoked salmon pizza, Chinese duck. Outdoor dining. French country-style decor. Outdoor fireplace. Cr cds: A, C, D, DS, MC, V.

D

★★★ **MILLE FLEURS.** *Country Squire Courtyard (92067). 619/756-3085.* French menu. Menu changes daily. Own pastries. Hrs: 11:30 am-2 pm, 6-10 pm; Sat from 5:30 pm; Sun from 6 pm. Closed Jan 1, Dec 25. Res required Fri, Sat. Bar 11:30 am-midnight; Sat from 5:30 pm; Sun from 6 pm. Wine list. Semi-a la carte: lunch $9-$25, dinner $28-$35. Pianist Tues-Sat. Outdoor dining. Cr cds: A, C, D, MC, V.

D

★★★ **VALENCIA.** *(See Rancho Valencia) 619/759-6216.* Hrs: 7 am-10 pm. Res sugested. Bar. A la carte entrees: bkfst $10-$17, lunch $12-$17, dinner $20-$32. Sun brunch $11-$15. Child's meals. Specialties: sauteed ahi tuna roll, roasted rack of lamb. Classical guitarist Fri, Sat. Valet parking. Outdoor dining. Overlooks gardens & tennis courts. Cr cds: A, C, D, JCB, MC, V.

D

Red Bluff (C-2)

(See also Redding)

Pop 12,363 **Elev** 340 ft **Area Code** 530 **Zip** 96080
E-mail rbtccofc@tehama.net **Web** www.redblufftehamacntyinfo.com

Information Red Bluff-Tehama County Chamber of Commerce, 100 Main St, PO Box 850; 530/527-6220

A marketing center for the products of the upper Sacramento Valley, the town is named for the reddish sand and gravel cliffs in the vicinity. The first settlers came for gold, but found wealth in wheat fields and orchards instead. As river steamers discharged passengers and freight, the city also became a transportation center for the mines around it. Now lumbering, agriculture and wood products are important industries. One notable pioneer of Red Bluff, William Ide, led the Bear Flag Revolt against Mexico.

What to See and Do

City River Park. Swimming pool (June-Aug, daily exc Sun; fee); boat ramp. Picnic areas, playgrounds. Band concerts (summer, Mon). On the Sacramento River, between Reeds Creek Bridge & Sycamore St. Phone 530/527-8177. **Free**

Fishing. In Sacramento River. Steelhead, salmon, trout. Sam Ayer Park and Dog Island Fishing Access, 1 mi N on Sacramento River. Footbridge to 11-acre island; nature trails, picnicking. Phone 530/527-8177. **Free**

Kelly-Griggs House Museum (1880s). Renovated Victorian house with period furnishings; Pendleton Gallery of Art; Chinese and Native American artifacts; historical exhibits. Map of auto tours of Victorian Red Bluff avail (fee). (Thurs-Sun, afternoons; closed major hols) 311 Washington St, at Ash St. Phone 530/527-1129. **Free**

Lassen Volcanic National Park (see). 45 mi E on CA 36.

William B. Ide Adobe State Historic Park. Restored version of adobe house of William B. Ide, only president of the California Republic. Collection of household artifacts. Picnicking. Demonstrations on process of adobe brickmaking, pioneer crafts in summer. (Daily; closed Jan 1, Thanksgiving, Dec 25) 21659 Adobe Rd. 2 mi NE off I-5 Wilcox Rd exit. Phone 530/529-8599. **¢¢**

Annual Events

Red Bluff Roundup. PRCA approved. One of the biggest 3-day rodeos in the West. 3rd wkend Apr.

Tehama County Fair. 4 days late July.

Motel

✓★★ **LAMPLIGHTER LODGE.** *210 S Main St (96080). 530/527-1150; FAX 530/527-5878; res: 800/521-4423.* 51 rms, 1-2 story, 3 family units. S $34-$38; D $44-$48; each addl $4; family units, suites $56-$65. Crib $4. TV; cable (premium). Pool. Complimentary continental bkfst. Restaurant 6:30 am-9 pm. Ck-out 11:30 am. Business servs avail. In-rm modem link. Cr cds: A, C, D, DS, MC, V.

SC

Inn

★★ **JETER VICTORIAN INN.** *1107 Jefferson St (96080). 530/527-7574.* 5 rms, 2 share bath, 4 story, 1 guest house. Some rm phones. S, D $65-$140; guest house $95-$115; special events 2-day min. Children over 14 yrs only. Cable TV in some rms. Complimentary full bkfst; refreshments. Restaurant nearby. Ck-out 11:30 am, ck-in 3:30 pm. Luggage handling. Street parking. Picnic tables. Built in 1881; Victorian decor and atmosphere; antiques. Garden. Totally nonsmoking. Cr cds: C, MC, V.

Restaurant

✓★ **PEKING CHINESE RESTAURANT.** *860 Main St (96080). 530/527-0523.* Hrs: 11 am-10 pm; Sat, Sun from noon. Closed Thansgiving, Dec 25. Res accepted. Chinese, Amer menu. Bar. Semi-a la carte: lunch $3.95-$5.50, dinner $5.50-9. Complete meals: dinner $6.50-$9.95. Specialties: Mongolian beef, lemon chicken, Kung Pao chicken. Chinese decor. Cr cds: A, C, DS, MC, V.

Redding (B-2)

(See also Burney, Mount Shasta, Red Bluff, Weaverville)

Founded 1872 **Pop** 66,462 **Elev** 557 ft **Area Code** 530
Web www.ci.redding.ca.us/convb/welcome.htm
Information Convention and Visitors Bureau, 777 Auditorium Dr, 96001; 530/225-4100 or 800/874-7562

The hub city of northern California's vast scenic Shasta-Cascade Region is located at the top of the Sacramento Valley, in the shadow of Mount Shasta—with the rugged Coast Range on the west, the Cascades on the north and east, and the Sierra Nevada to the southeast. The city was founded when the California and Oregon Railroad chose the site as its northern terminus; it became the county seat in 1888. Lumber and tourism are its principal industries. The Sacramento River flows directly through the city, providing popular pastimes such as fishing, rafting and canoeing.

What to See and Do

Coleman National Fish Hatchery. Chinook (king) salmon and steelhead trout are raised here to help mitigate the loss of spawning area due to construction of Shasta Dam. (Daily) S on I-5 to Cottonwood, 5 mi E on Balls Ferry Rd to Ash Creek Rd, 1 mi to Gover Rd, 2½ mi to Coleman Fish Hatchery Rd. Phone 530/365-8622. **Free**

Lake Redding-Caldwell Park. An 85-acre park; boat ramp, swimming pool. Picnic facilities. Falls of the lake are lighted in summer. Rio Dr, N on Market St, on N shore of Sacramento River. Phone 530/225-4095. (See ANNUAL EVENTS) **Free** In Caldwell Park is the

Redding Museum of Art & History. Rotating fine arts and regional history exhibits. (Daily exc Mon; closed major hols) 56 Quartz Hill Rd. Phone 530/243-8801. **Free**

Lake Shasta Caverns. Stalactites, stalagmites, flowstone deposits; 58°F. Guided tour includes boat ride across McCloud Arm of Lake Shasta and bus ride up mountain to cavern entrance. (Daily; closed Dec 25) 16 mi N on I-5, then 1½ mi E on Shasta Cavern Rd. Phone 530/238-2341 or 800/795-CAVE. **¢¢¢¢**

Lassen Volcanic National Park (see). 44 mi E on CA 44.

Shasta State Historic Park. Remains of gold rush town with several well-preserved original buildings; historical museum; art gallery. Picnicking. (Thurs-Mon; closed Jan 1, Thanksgiving, Dec 25) 6 mi W on CA 299. Phone 530/243-8194. **¢**

Shasta-Trinity National Forest. More than 2 million acres contain portions of the Trinity Alps Wilderness, Mt Shasta Wilderness, Castle Crags Wilderness, Chanchelulla Wilderness and the Yolla Bolly-Middle Eel Wilderness. Picnicking; camping (fee). N, E & W via CA 299, I-5. For recreation information phone 530/246-5338. For further information contact the Forest Supervisor, 2400 Washington Ave, 96001; 530/246-5222. **Free**

Waterworks Park. Water theme park with 3 giant serpentine slides, Raging River inner tube ride, activity pool, kiddie water playground. (Memorial Day-Labor Day, daily) Jct I-5 & CA 299E. Phone 530/246-9550. **¢¢¢¢**

Whiskeytown-Shasta-Trinity National Recreation Area, Whiskeytown Unit. Water sports; fishing; boating (marinas). Picnicking, snack bars. Camping (fee), campfire programs. 8 mi W via CA 299. Phone 530/241-6584. **Free** Contains areas surrounding

Clair A. Hill Whiskeytown Dam and Whiskeytown Lake. Part of the Central Valley Project; forms lake with a 36-mi shoreline. Camping (mid-May-mid-Sept, 14-day limit; rest of yr, 30 days; fee). Information center NE of dam at jct CA 299 & Kennedy Memorial Dr; phone 530/246-1225. Contact Box 188, Whiskeytown 96095; 530/241-6584.

Lewiston Dam and Lake. Regulator and diversion point for water to Whiskeytown Dam near Shasta. 17 mi NW on CA 299, then 6 mi N on unnumbered roads.

Shasta Dam and Power Plant. Three times as high as Niagara Falls: 602 ft high, 3,460 ft long. Roadway and sidewalks along the crest; view of Mt Shasta. Visitor center. Waters of 3 rivers back up to form Shasta Lake, 35 mi long with a 365-mi shoreline. (Memorial Day-Labor Day, daily; rest of yr, Mon-Fri) 5 mi W of I-5. Schedule may vary; phone 530/275-4463. **Free.**

Trinity Dam and Clair Engle Lake. Large earthfill dam (465 ft high) creates lake, known locally as Trinity Lake, 20 mi long with 145-mi shoreline. 22 mi NW via CA 299 W. (For information on Shasta and Trinity areas, contact US Forest Service, 2400 Washington Ave, 96001; phone 530/246-5222.).

Annual Events

Children's Lawn Festival. Caldwell Park. Children and adults participate in various activities including weaving, bread baking, cow milking and acorn grinding; also Native American games. Phone 530/225-4095. Late Apr or early May.

Rodeo Weekend. 3rd wk May.

Shasta District Fair. 11 mi S on US 99, I-5 in Anderson. Phone 530/378-6789. 3rd wkend June.

Renaissance Festival & Jousting Tournament. Aug 7 & 8.

Motels

★★★ **BEST WESTERN HILLTOP INN.** *2300 Hilltop Dr (96002). 530/221-6100; FAX 530/221-2867; res: 800/336-4880.* Web www.hotelswest.com/redding/redding.htm. 115 rms, 2 story. S $79-$99; D $89-$109; each addl $10; suites $95-$150; under 18 free. Crib free. TV; cable (premium), VCR avail. Heated pool; wading pool, whirlpool. Complimentary full bkfst buffet. Complimentary coffee in rms. Restaurant 11 am-11 pm. Bar 11 am-midnight. Ck-out noon. Coin Indry. Meeting rms. Business servs avail. In-rm modem link. Valet serv. Health club privileges. Many refrigerators. Cr cds: A, C, D, DS, MC, V.

D SC

✓★★ **BEST WESTERN HOSPITALITY HOUSE.** *532 N Market St (96003). 530/241-6464; FAX 530/244-1998; res: 800/700-3019.* 62 rms, 2 story. S $44-$64; D $50-$70; each addl $6; suite $99; under 18 free. TV; cable. Pool. Complimentary full bkfst. Complimentary coffee in rms. Restaurant 6:30 am-8:30 pm. Ck-out 11 am. Coin Indry. Business servs avail. Cr cds: A, C, D, DS, MC, V.

SC

★★ **BRIDGE BAY RESORT.** *10300 Bridge Bay Rd (96003). 530/275-3021; FAX 530/275-8365; res: 800/752-9669.* Web www.sevencrown.com. 40 rms, 1-2 story, 8 kit. suites; 2-day min suites. May-Sept: S $89; each addl $6; suites $120-$160; under 12 free; lower rates rest of yr. Crib $5. Pet accepted; $25 deposit, $5/day. TV; cable. Complimentary coffee in lobby. Restaurant 7 am-2 pm, 5-9 pm. Bar 4 pm-midnight. Ck-out 11 am. Meeting rms. Business servs avail. Gift shop. Grocery store. Pool. Cr cds: C, DS, MC, V.

SC

✓★★ **RIVER INN MOTOR HOTEL.** *1835 Park Marina Dr (96001). 530/241-9500; FAX 530/241-5345; res: 800/995-4341.* 79 rms, 2-3 story. No elvtr. S, D $55-$65; each addl $5; under 12 free. Crib $5. Pet accepted; $5. TV; cable (premium). Pool; whirlpool. Coffee in rms. Restaurant 7 am-7 pm. Bar 11-2 am. Ck-out 11 am. Business servs avail. Sauna. Refrigerators; some wet bars. Private patios, balconies. Picnic tables. Cr cds: A, C, D, DS, MC, V.

D SC

Motor Hotels

★★★ **DOUBLETREE HOTEL.** *1830 Hilltop Dr (96002). 530/221-8700; FAX 530/221-0324; res: 800/733-5466.* 193 rms, 2 story. May-Sept: S, D $79-$105; each addl $15; suites $250; under 18 free; package plans; lower rates rest of yr. Crib free. Pet accepted. TV; cable, VCR avail (movies). Pool; wading pool, whirlpool, poolside serv. Complimentary coffee in rms. Restaurant 6 am-11 pm; dining rm 11:30 am-1:30 pm, 5-10 pm; Fri, Sat to 11 pm. Rm serv. Bar 11-2 am; entertainment Thurs-Sat. Ck-out 1 pm. Meeting rms. Business servs avail. In-rm modem link. Bellhops. Valet serv. Sundries. Free airport, RR station, bus depot transportation. Exercise equipt. Health club privileges. Private patios, balconies. Cr cds: A, C, D, DS, ER, MC, V.

D SC

★★★ **LA QUINTA INN.** *2180 Hilltop Dr (96002). 530/221-8200; FAX 530/223-4727; res: 800/687-6667.* Web www.laquinta.com. 141 rms, 3 story. S, D (up to 4) $60; suites $99; under 18 free. Crib free. Pet accepted, some restrictions. TV; cable. Pool; whirlpool. Complimentary continental bkfst. Coffee in rms. Restaurant 5 pm-midnight. Ck-out noon. Coin Indry. Meeting rms. Business servs avail. In-rm modem link. Valet serv. Exercise equipt. Private patios, balconies. Cr cds: A, C, D, DS, MC, V.

D SC

Inn

★★★ **OBRIEN MOUNTIAN INN.** *18026 Obrien Inlet Rd (96051), 17 mi N of Redding, on I-5 . 530/238-8026; FAX 530/238-2027; res: 888/799-8026.* E-mail obrienmt@snowcrest.net; web www.obrienmtn.com. 4 rms, 2 shower only. No rm phones. S, D $95-$125; each addl $25; hols 2-day min. Complimentary full bkfst. Complimentary coffee in rms. Restaurant nearby. Ck-out 11 am, ck-in 4-6 pm. Business servs avail. Luggage handling. Concierge serv. Game rm. Lawn games. Built in 1963; antiques. On 47 acres. Totally nonsmoking. Cr cds: A, C, DS, MC, V.

Redlands (J-4)

(See also Big Bear Lake, Lake Arrowhead, Ontario, Riverside, San Bernardino)

Founded 1888 **Pop** 60,394 **Elev** 1,302 ft **Area Code** 909 **Web** www.redlandschamber.org

Information Chamber of Commerce, One E Redlands Blvd, 92373; 909/793-2546

Named for the color of the earth in the area and known for many years as the Navel Orange Center, Redlands still handles a large volume of citrus fruits, but has diversified its industry in recent years to achieve greater economic prosperity and stability.

What to See and Do

Asistencia Mission de San Gabriel (1830). Restored adobe with Native American and early pioneer exhibits, historic scenes of the valley; cactus garden; wishing well, bell tower, wedding chapel and reception rm. (Wed-Sat, also Sun afternoons; closed Jan 1, Thanksgiving, Dec 25) 26930 Barton Rd, 2 mi W. Phone 909/793-5402. **Free**

Kimberly Crest House and Gardens (1897). French chateau-style house and accompanying carriage house on 6.5 acres. Former house of John Kimberly, forefounder of the Kimberly-Clark Corporation. Structure is representative of the "Mansion Era" of Southern California; 1930s furnishings. Italian gardens and citrus grove on grounds. Guided tours. (Thurs-Sun afternoons; closed Easter, Dec 25, also Aug) 1325 Prospect Dr. Phone 909/792-2111. **¢¢**

Lincoln Memorial Shrine. George Grey Barnard's Carrara marble bust of Lincoln; murals by Dean Cornwell; painting by Norman Rockwell; manuscripts, books, artifacts relating to Lincoln and the Civil War. (Tues-Sat, afternoons; closed most hols) 125 W Vine St, in Smiley Park. Phone 909/798-7632. **Free**

Pharaoh's Lost Kingdom. Family theme park features race car complex with Indy, Grand Prix and kiddy cars; water park with wave pools and multiple water slides and flumes; 14 amusement rides; miniature golf; arcade, indoor playground, gift shop, restaurant, amphitheater. (Daily) 1100 California St, at I-10. Phone 909/335-PARK. **¢¢¢¢**

Prosellis Bowl. Also known as the Redlands Bowl; the free concerts held here every Tues and Fri in summer have earned it the name Little Hollywood Bowl. Eureka & Vine Sts.

San Bernardino County Museum. Mounted collection of birds & bird eggs of Southern California; reptiles, mammals. Pioneer and Native American artifacts; rocks & minerals; paleontology. Changing art exhibits. On grounds are steam locomotive, garden of cacti and succulents. (Daily exc Mon; closed Jan 1, Thanksgiving, Dec 25) 2024 Orange Tree Ln. Phone 909/798-8570. **¢¢¢**

Motels

✓★★ **BEST WESTERN SANDMAN MOTEL.** *1120 W Colton Ave (92374), I-10 Tennessee St exit, 1 blk S. 909/793-2001; FAX 909/792-7612; res: 800/528-1234.* Web www.bestwestern.com. 65 rms, 2 story, 6 kits. S $40-$55; D $44-$60; each addl $4; kit. units $5 addl; under 12 free. Pet accepted, some restrictions. TV; cable (premium). Heated pool; whirlpool. Complimentary continental bkfst. Restaurant adj 6 am-midnight. Ck-out 11 am. Business servs avail. Some refrigerators; microwaves avail. Cr cds: A, C, D, DS, MC, V.

D SC

✓★ **SUPER 8 MOTEL.** *1160 Arizona St (92374). 909/335-1612; FAX 909/792-8779; res: 800/848-8888.* Web www.super8motels.com/super8.html. 78 rms, 2 story. S $35-$55; D $38-$60; each addl $5; under 12 free. Crib $5. TV; cable (premium), VCR avail. Complimentary continental bkfst. Restaurant opp open 24 hrs. Ck-out 11 am. Meeting rm. Business servs avail. Valet serv. Coin Indry. Pool. Some refrigerators, microwaves. Cr cds: A, C, D, DS, JCB, MC, V.

D SC

Restaurant

★★★ **JOE GREENSLEEVES.** *220 N Orange St (92374), I-10 exit Orange St S. 909/792-6969.* Hrs: 11:30 am-2 pm, 5-9:30 pm; Sun from 5 pm. Closed some major hols. Res accepted. Wine list. Semi-a la carte entrees: lunch $5.95-$11.75, dinner $13.25-$25. Specializes in fresh fish, steak, chops. Own desserts. Nautical atmosphere; large, cedar-carved replica of sloop on display. Totally nonsmoking. Cr cds: A, C, D, DS, MC, V.

D

Redondo Beach (D-3 see Los Angeles map)

Pop 60,167 **Elev** 59 ft **Area Code** 310 **E-mail** uvisitrb@southbay.com **Web** www.visit.redondo.com

Information Visitors Bureau, 200 N Pacific Coast Hwy, 90277; 310/374-2171 or 800/282-0333

This is a recreation and vacation center featuring a 2½-mile beach and the popular King Harbor, which houses 1,700 craft.

What to See and Do

Redondo Beach Pier. Largest pier on California coast (72,000 sq ft). Fishing, cruises, collection of shops and restaurants featuring goods and food from all over the world. Western end of Torrance Blvd.

Motels

★★ **BEST WESTERN SUNRISE AT REDONDO BEACH MARINA.** *400 N Harbor Dr (90277). 310/376-0746; FAX 310/376-7384; res: 800/334-7384.* Web www.bestwestern.com. 111 rms, 3 story. S, D $82-$114; each addl $10; suites $135-$145; under 12 free; wkend rates. Crib free. TV; cable. Heated pool; whirlpool. Complimentary coffee in rms. Restaurant 6:30 am-10:30 pm. Rm serv. Ck-out noon. Meeting rms. Business servs avail. Valet serv. Refrigerators. Opp ocean. Cr cds: A, C, D, DS, JCB, MC, V.

D SC

★★ **HERMOSA HOTEL.** *2515 Pacific Coast Hwy (90254), Pacific Coast Hwy and Artesia Blvd. 310/318-6000; FAX 310/318-6936; res: 800/331-9979.* 81 units, 3 story, 8 suites. S, D $69-$125; each addl $10; suites $99-$109; under 12 free. Crib free. TV; cable (premium). Heated pool. Complimentary continental bkfst. Complimentary coffee in rms. Restaurant nearby. Ck-out 11 am. Coin Indry. Meeting rms. Business servs avail. In-rm modem link. Free garage parking. Exercise equipt. Bathrm phones, refrigerators; some wet bars. Attractive landscaping; Japanese garden. Cr cds: A, C, D, DS, MC, V.

D SC

✓★ **REDONDO PIER LODGE.** *206 S Pacific Coast Hwy (90277), 8 mi S of Intl Airport. 310/318-1811; FAX 310/379-0190; res: 800/841-9777.* 37 rms, 3 story, 2 suites. S $66-$67; D $70-$85; each addl $6; suites $90-$98; under 17 free. Crib free. TV; cable (premium). Heated pool; whirlpool. Complimentary continental bkfst. Coffee in rms. Restaurant nearby. Ck-out 11 am. Refrigerators. Cr cds: A, C, D, DS, ER, JCB, MC, V.

D SC

Motor Hotels

★★ **PALOS VERDES INN.** *1700 S Pacific Coast Hwy (90277), 9 mi S of Los Angeles Intl Airport. 310/316-4211; FAX 310/316-4863; res: 800/421-9241.* E-mail pv11700s@aol.com; web www.redondo.com. 110 rms, 4 story. May-Sept: S, D $110-$130; each addl $10; under 12 free; lower rates rest of yr. Crib free. TV; cable (premium). Heated pool; whirlpool. Restaurant 7 am-midnight (see CHEZMELANGE). Rm serv. Bar from 10 am. Ck-out noon. Meeting rms. Business servs avail. In-rm modem link. Bellhops. Valet serv. Health club privileges. Refrigerator in suites. Many balconies. Cr cds: A, C, D, DS, JCB, MC, V.

D SC

★★★ **THE PORTOFINO HOTEL & YACHT CLUB.** *260 Portofino Way (90277). 310/379-8481; FAX 310/372-7329; res: 800/468-4292.* Web www.nhhr.com. 163 rms, 3 story, 23 suites. S, D $165-$210; each addl $10; suites $245-$275; under 12 free; wkend, package plans. Crib free. TV; cable (premium), VCR avail. Heated pool; whirlpool, poolside serv. Restaurant 6 am-10 pm. Rm serv. Bar 11-1:30 am. Ck-out noon. Meeting rms. Business center. In-rm modem link. Bellhops. Valet serv. Gift shop. Exercise equipt. Refrigerators, minibars; microwaves avail. On ocean. Cr cds: A, C, D, DS, JCB, MC, V.

D SC

Hotel

★★★ **CROWNE PLAZA REDONDO BEACH.** *300 N Harbor Dr (90277), 7 mi S of Intl Airport. 310/318-8888; FAX 310/376-1930; res: 800/465-4329; res: 800/277-6963.* Web www.geninc.com. 340 rms, 5 story. S, D $169-$189; each addl $20; suites $275-$625; under 19 free. Crib free. Valet parking $9. TV; cable (premium). Pool; poolside serv. Restaurant 6 am-10 pm. Rm serv 24 hrs. Ck-out noon. Coin lndry. Convention facilities. Business center. In-rm modem link. Concierge. Gift shop. Lighted tennis. Exercise equipt. Health club privileges. Refrigerators. Private patios, balconies. Opp ocean. Large deck overlooks harbor. Luxury level. Cr cds: A, C, D, DS, ER, JCB, MC, V.

D SC

Restaurants

★★ **CHEZ MELANGE.** *(See Palos Verdes Inn) 1716 S Pacific Coast Hwy (90277). 310/540-1222.* Web www.chezmelange.com. Hrs: 7-11:15 am, 11:30-2:30 pm, 5-10 pm; Sun from 8 am; Fri, Sat to 11 pm. Res accepted. Bar 11 am-11 pm. Semi-a la carte: bkfst $4.50-$9, lunch $4.95-$10.95, dinner $7.95-$21.95. Sun brunch $4.95-$11.95. Champagne, oyster bar. Specializes in California eclectic cuisine. Own baking. Cr cds: A, C, D, MC, V.

D ♥

★★★ **CUCINA PARADISO.** *1611 S Catalina Ave (90277), I 405, Turrance Blvd exit. 310/792-1972.* Hrs: 11:30 am-2:30 pm, 5:30-10:30 pm. Closed some major hols. Res accepted. Italian menu. Bar. Wine cellar. Semi-a la carte: lunch $10-$20, dinner $15-$35. Specialties: osso bucco alla Milanese, ravioli con la zucca, bread pudding. Own pasta. Valet parking. Grappas display. Cr cds: A, C, D, MC, V.

D

★★ **LE BEAUJOLAIS.** *522 Pacific Coast Hwy (90277), 8 mi S of Intl Airport. 310/543-5100.* Web www.quickpages.com. Hrs: 11:30 am-3 pm, 5-10 pm; Fri, Sat to 11 pm; Sat, Sun brunch 10 am-3 pm. Res accepted. French menu. Serv bar. Semi-a la carte: lunch $5.95-$15.95, dinner $16.95-$26.95. Sat, Sun brunch $10.95. Specializes in rack of lamb, duck, fresh fish. Harpist Thur, Fri, Sun. Intimate dining. Elegant decor. Cr cds: A, C, D, DS, MC, V.

D

Redwood City (E-2)

(See also Palo Alto, San Francisco Airport Area, San Mateo)

Settled 1854 **Pop** 66,072 **Elev** 15 ft **Area Code** 650

Information Chamber of Commerce, 1675 Broadway, 94063,; 650/364-1722; or the San Mateo County Convention and Visitors Bureau, 111 Anza Blvd, Suite 410, Burlingame 94010, 650/348-7600

In the center of the booming commercial and industrial peninsula area, Redwood City has the only deepwater bay port south of San Francisco on the peninsula. Once a Spanish ranch, it was settled by S.M. Mezes, who called it Mezesville; lumbermen who cut the nearby virgin redwoods renamed it Redwood City. It was incorporated in 1867 and is the seat of San Mateo County.

What to See and Do

Lathrop House. Victorian house and furnishings. (Tues-Thurs; closed hols, Aug, late Dec) 627 Hamilton St. Phone 650/365-5564. **Free**

Marinas. Port of Redwood City Yacht Harbor, 675 Seaport Blvd, phone 650/306-4150. **Docktown Marina,** foot of Maple St, phone 650/365-3258. **Pete's Harbor,** Uccelli Blvd, at foot of Whipple Ave, phone 650/366-0922.

Methuselah Redwood. Tree more than 1,500 yrs old, measures 55 ft in circumference. Trunk has been blackened by repeated fires. Junipero Serra Frwy via Woodside Rd exit, W on CA 84 to Skyline Blvd, 4 mi N.

Annual Event

San Mateo County Fair & Floral Fiesta. Phone 650/574-FAIR. Aug.

Motels

★★ **BEST WESTERN EXECUTIVE SUITES.** *25 5th Ave (94063). 650/366-5794; FAX 650/365-1429; res: 800/386-7377.* 28 rms, 2 story, 5 suites. S $99; D $110; each addl $10; suites $145. TV; cable (premium), VCR. Complimentary continental bkfst. Complimentary coffee in rms. Restaurant nearby. Ck-out 11 am. Coin lndry. Business servs avail. Exercise equipt. Bathrm phones, refrigerators, microwaves; some minibars. Cr cds: A, C, D, DS, MC, V.

D SC

★★ **COMFORT INN.** *1818 El Camino Real (94063). 650/599-9636; FAX 650/369-6481; res: 800/638-7949.* 52 rms, 3 story, 11 kit. suites. May-Nov: S $118; D $128; each addl $10; suites $145-$155; under 16 free; lower rates rest of yr. TV; cable (premium), VCR. Pool. Sauna. Complimentary full bkfst. Restaurant nearby. Ck-out 11 am. Meeting rm. Business servs avail. In-rm modem link. Free garage parking. Refrigerators, microwaves. Cr cds: A, C, D, DS, JCB, MC, V.

D SC

✓★ **DAYS INN.** *2650 El Camino Real (94061). 650/369-9200; FAX 650/363-8167; res: 800/329-7466.* 68 rms, 2 story. S, D $70-$80; each addl $5. Crib free. TV; cable (premium), VCR avail. Heated pool; whirlpool. Complimentary continental bkfst. Restaurant nearby. Ck-out 11 am. Coin lndry. Meeting rm. Business servs avail. Exercise equipt. Refrigerators, microwaves. Some private patios, balconies. Picnic tables. Gazebo. Cr cds: A, C, DS, MC, V.

D SC

Lodge

★★★ **THE LODGE AT SKYLONDA.** *16350 Skyline Blvd (94062), 280 to 84 exit Woodside, to 35 N. 650/851-4500; FAX 650/788-7872; res: 800/851-2222.* 16 rms, 3 story. No A/C. Rm phones on request. S $425-$525; D $298-$362; package plans; wkends 2-day min. Complimentary full bkfst. Restaurant nearby. Meeting rms. Business servs avail.

Bellhops. Gift shop. Airport transportation. Exercise rm; sauna. Indoor pool; whirlpool. Game rm. Rec rm. Lawn games. Balconies. In Redwood forest. Totally nonsmoking. Cr cds: A, C, DS, MC, V.

D

Hotel

★★★ **HOTEL SOFITEL.** *223 Twin Dolphin Dr (94065). 650/598-9000; FAX 650/598-0459; res: 800/763-4835.* 319 units, 9 story. S $290; D $310; each addl $20; suites $329-$470; under 12 free. Crib free. TV; cable (premium), VCR avail. Pool. Restaurant 6 am-11 pm. Rm serv 5:30-2 am. Bar 10-2 am; entertainment exc Sun. Ck-out noon. Convention facilities. Business servs avail. In-rm modem link. Concierge. Gift shop. Free airport transportation. Exercise equipt. Minibars. Elegant atmosphere; Baccarat chandeliers. Cr cds: A, C, D, JCB, MC, V.

D SC

Redwood Highway (A-1 - C-1)

(See also Crescent City, Eureka)

E-mail tourism@redwoodempire.com **Web** www.redwoodempire.com

Information Redwood Empire/North Coast Visitors Services, 2801 Leavenworth, 2nd floor, San Francisco 94133; 415/394-5991 or 888/678-8509

US 101 runs for 387 miles from San Francisco to the wine country of Sonoma and Mendocino counties, through scenic countryside where 97 percent of the world's coastal redwoods grow. Redwoods can be seen in Marin County at Muir Woods National Monument (see), which has 6 miles of hiking trails and no vehicle access. The bulk of the giant redwood trees, *Sequoia sempervirens,* are from Leggett north to the Oregon state line. The Humboldt Redwoods State Park (see) runs on both sides of the highway; many of the major groves are here, including the spectacular Avenue of the Giants north of Phillipsville, south of Pepperwood. A guidebook with maps is available from the Redwood Empire/North Coast Visitors Services (fee). Other concentrations of redwoods are at **Grizzly Creek Redwoods State Park,** 18 miles E of US 101 on CA 36, camping (standard fees), picnicking, swimming, fishing; and at Redwood National and State Parks (see CRESCENT CITY), which takes in Prairie Creek Redwoods State Park, 6 miles north of Orick on US 101, Del Norte Coast Redwoods State Park, 7 miles south of Crescent City, and Jedediah Smith Redwoods State Park, 9 miles northeast of Crescent City. The highway has several spectacular overlooks of the Pacific Ocean and the north coast of California.

The Redwood Highway, a major thoroughfare from the Golden Gate Bridge north, has four lanes for more than 260 miles and two lanes with many turnabouts for the remainder. Lodging is usually available, but heavy summer traffic makes it wise to plan ahead.

Richardson Grove State Park (C-1)

(See also Garberville)

(8 mi S of Garberville on US 101)

One of California's beautiful redwood parks, Richardson Grove covers a 1,000-acre tract along the south fork of the Eel River. Swimming; fishing (Oct-Jan). Hiking trails. Picnicking, store (summer). Camping. Visitor center (summer); nature programs offered daily in summer. Standard fees. Phone 707/247-3318.

Riverside (J-4)

(See also San Bernardino)

Founded 1870 **Pop** 226,505 **Elev** 858 ft **Area Code** 909

Information Convention Bureau, 3737 Sixth St, 92501; 909/222-4700 or Visitor's Center & Convention Center, 3443 Orange St, 92501; 909/684-4636

In 1873, a resident of the new town of Riverside obtained from the US Department of Agriculture two cuttings of a new type of orange, a mutation which had suddenly developed in Brazil. These cuttings were the origin of the vast navel orange groves that make this the center of the "Orange Empire."

What to See and Do

California Museum of Photography. Large collection of photographic equipment, prints, stereographs, memorabilia. Interactive gallery, walk-in camera; library. (Wed-Sat, also Sun afternoons; closed major hols) Free admission Wed. 3824 Main St. Phone 909/787-4787. ¢

Castle Amusement Park. Features 80-yr-old Dentzel carousel with hand-carved animals; antique cars. Ride Park with 30 rides & attractions (Fri-Sun). Four 18-hole miniature golf courses and video arcade (daily). Fee for activities. 3500 Polk St, 92505, CA 91 between Tyler & La Sierra exits. Phone 909/785-4140.

Chinese Memorial Pavilion. Dedicated to Chinese pioneers of the West and those who contributed to the growth of Riverside. 3581 7th St, on Riverside Public Library grounds.

Heritage House (1891). Restored Victorian mansion. (Sept-June, Thurs, Fri & Sun; rest of yr, Sun) 8193 Magnolia Ave. Phone 909/689-1333. **Free**

Mount Rubidoux Memorial Park. According to legend, the mountain was once the altar of Cahuilla and Serrano sun worship. A cross rises on the peak in memory of Fray Junipero Serra, founder of the California missions. The World Peace Tower stands on the side of the mountain. Hiking. (Daily, weather permitting: vehicular traffic prohibited) W end of 9th St at Mount Rubidoux Dr ½ mi W. Phone 909/715-3440. (See ANNUAL EVENT) **Free**

Orange Empire Railway Museum. More than 150 rail vehicles and pieces of off-rail equipment; railroad and trolley memorabilia; picnicking. Trolley rides (Sat, Sun & major hols; fee). (Daily; closed Thanksgiving, Dec 25) 2201 South A Street, 14 mi S via I-215 in Perris. Phone 909/657-2605. **Free**

Parent Washington Navel Orange Tree. Propagated from one of the 3 original trees from Bahia, Brazil. Planted in 1873, all navel orange trees stem from this tree or from its offspring. Magnolia & Arlington Aves.

Riverside Art Museum. Changing exhibits of historical and contemporary sculpture, painting and graphics; lectures, demonstrations, juried shows, sales gallery. Housed in 1929 Mediterranean-style YWCA building designed by Julia Morgan. (Daily 10-4 exc Sun; closed major hols) Corner of Lime St & Mission Inn Ave. Phone 909/684-7111. ¢

Riverside Municipal Museum. Area history, anthropology and natural history displays; changing exhibits. (Daily exc Mon; closed major hols) 3580 Mission Inn Ave. Phone 909/782-5273. **Free**

University of California at Riverside (1954). (8,800 students) Centers around 161-ft Carillon Tower; Botanic Garden featuring flora from all parts of the world. 900 University Ave. For tours of campus and other inquiries phone 909/787-1012.

Annual Event

Easter Sunrise Pilgrimage. Mt Rubidoux Memorial Park. First nonsectarian sunrise service in US; continuous since 1909. Easter Sun.

Motels

✓★★ **DYNASTY SUITES.** *3735 Iowa Ave (92507), I-295 (CA 50) exit University Ave W. 909/369-8200; FAX 909/341-6486; res: 800/842-7899.* Web www.dynastysuites.com. 34 rms, 2 story. S, D $42.95-$47.95; each addl $5; suites $89.95. TV; cable (premium), VCR avail (movies). Heated pool. Complimentary continental bkfst. Restaurant nearby. Ck-out noon. Business servs avail. Refrigerators; microwaves avail. In-rm whirlpool in suites. Cr cds: A, C, D, DS, MC, V.

D SC

★★ **HAMPTON INN.** *1590 University Ave (92507), CA 60/I-215, exit University Ave, ½ mi W. 909/683-6000; FAX 909/782-8052; res: 800/426-7866.* 116 rms, 2 story. S, D $45-$50; under 18 free. Crib free. TV; cable (premium). Heated pool. Complimentary continental bkfst. Coffee in rms. Restaurant nearby. Ck-out noon. Meeting rms. Business servs avail. Health club privileges. Valet serv. Refrigerators, microwaves avail. Cr cds: A, C, D, DS, MC, V.

D SC

Hotels

★★ **COURTYARD BY MARRIOTT.** *1510 University Ave (92507), CA 60/I-215 exit University Ave, ½ mi W. 909/276-1200; FAX 909/787-6783; res: 800/321-2211.* 163 rms, 6 story. S, D $69-$75; under 18 free. Crib free. TV; cable (premium). Heated pool; whirlpool. Complimentary coffee in lobby. Bkfst avail 6:30-10 am. Bar 5-11 pm. Ck-out 1 pm. Meeting rms. Business servs avail. In-rm modem link. Valet serv. Exercise equipt. Refrigerators avail. Some balconies. Cr cds: A, C, D, DS, MC, V.

D SC

★★ **HOLIDAY INN.** *3400 Market St (92501), adj convention center. 909/784-8000; FAX 909/369-7127; res: 877/291-7519.* 292 rms, 12 story. S, D $99-$129; each addl $10; suites $129-$236; under 18 free. Crib free. TV; cable (premium). Heated pool; whirlpool, poolside serv. Coffee in rms. Restaurant 6:30 am-11 pm. Rm serv. Bar 11:30 am-midnight. Ck-out noon. Convention facilities. Business center. Gift shop. Free covered parking. Free airport transportation. Exercise equipt. Health club priveleges. Some wet bars; refrigerators, microwaves avail. Some balconies. Cr cds: A, C, D, DS, JCB, MC, V.

D SC

★★★ **MISSION INN.** *3649 Mission Inn Ave (92501), CA 91 University Ave exit N. 909/784-0300; FAX 909/782-7197; res: 800/843-7755.* Web www.missioninn.com. 236 rms, 15 with shower only, 5 story. S, D $120-$210; each addl $15; suites $400-$800; under 15 free; package plans. TV; cable (premium), VCR avail. Heated pool; whirlpool, poolside serv. Restaurants 6:30 am-10 pm. Bars 11-2 am; entertainment Thurs-Sat. Meeting rms. Business center. In-rm modem link. Concierge. Gift shop. Beauty shop. Free airport transportation. Exercise equipt. Massage. Minibars; some balconies. Gazebo. Historic building was originally a 2-story, 12-rm boarding house (1876); expanded over the years. Renovated, unique Spanish-style architecture; courtyard fountains, gardens; stained-glass windows; many antiques. 2 wedding chapels, mission bells. Cr cds: A, C, D, DS, MC, V.

D SC

Restaurants

★★ **CIAO BELLA.** *1630 Spruce St (92507), jct CA 60, CA 91, east of downtown. 909/781-8840.* Hrs: 11:30 am-10:30 pm; Fri to 11 pm; Sat 5-11 pm; Sun 5-10 pm. Res accepted. Northern Tuscany menu. Bar. Wine list. A la carte: lunch $6.95-$13.95, dinner $7.25-$15.50. Specializes in fresh pasta, seafood. Parking. Outdoor dining. Cr cds: A, C, DS, JCB, MC, V.

D

★★ **GERARDS FRENCH RSTRNT.** *9814 Magnolia Ave (92503), CA 91 Tyler St exit N, 4 blks E on Magnolia . 909/687-4882.* Hrs: 5-9:30 pm; Sun to 8:30 pm. Closed Mon; most major hols. Res accepted. French, continental menu. Wine, beer. Semi-a la carte: dinner $12.95-$21.95. Specialties: pepper-steak/filet mignon flambe, bouillabaise/shellfish stew au safran. Own desserts. Country French decor; intimate dining area. Family-owned since 1969. Totally nonsmoking. Cr cds: A, C, D, DS, MC, V.

✓★★ **MARKET BROILER.** *3525 Merrill St (92506). 909/276-9007.* E-mail broiler@aol.com. Hrs: 11 am-10 pm; Fri, Sat to 11 pm. Closed Thanksgiving, Dec 24, 25. Bar. Semi-a la carte: lunch $4.95-$8.95, dinner $6.95-$21.95. Child's meals. Specializes in mesquite-grilled fresh seafood, chicken, steaks. Nautical decor, tropical fish aquariums; seafood market on premises. Totally nonsmoking. Cr cds: C.

Roseville (D-3)

(See also Rancho Cordova, Sacramento)

Pop 44,685 **Elev** 160 ft **Area Code** 916 **Zip** 95678

What to See and Do

Folsom Premium Outlets. More than 60 outlet stores. (Daily) US 50, Folsom Blvd exit, 13000 Folsom Blvd, in Folsom. Phone 916/985-0312.

Motor Hotel

★★ **FIRST CHOICE INN.** *4420 Rocklin Rd (95677), W on I-80 exit Rocklin Rd N. 916/624-4500; FAX 916/624-5982; res: 800/462-2400.* 129 rms, 3 story. Apr-Sept: S, D $70-$100; each addl $7; suites, kit. units $85-$125; under 12 free; lower rates rest of yr. Crib free. Pet accepted; $20/wk ($100 deposit). TV; cable (premium), VCR avail. Pool; whirlpool. Complimentary full bkfst; afternoon refreshments. Complimentary coffee in rms. Restaurant adj open 24 hrs. Ck-out noon. Coin Indry. Meeting rms. Business center. In-rm modem link. Valet serv. Exercise equipt. Refrigerators, microwaves; minibar in suites. Picnic tables. Grill. Cr cds: A, C, D, DS, MC, V.

D SC

Hotel

★★★ **ROCKLIN PARK HOTEL.** *5450 China Garden Rd (95677). 916/630-9400; FAX 916/630-9448; res: 888/630-9400.* Web www.rocklinpark.com. 33 rms, 2 story. S, D $155-$175; suite $225; wkend rates. Crib free. TV; cable (premium), VCR avail (movies). Complimentary continental bkfst. Restaurant 11 am-10 pm. Bar; jazz Fri (summer). Ck-out noon. Meeting rms. Concierge. Airport transportation. Pool; whirlpool, poolside serv. Refrigerator, microwave in suite. Some balconies. Cr cds: A, C, D, DS, ER, JCB, MC, V.

D SC

Restaurant

✓★ **ROSY'S.** *4950 Pacific St (95677), 2 mi W on I-80 exit Taylor. 916/624-1920.* Hrs: 7 am-3 pm; Fri, Sat to 9 pm. Closed Dec 25. Res accepted. Bar. Wine, beer. Semi-a la carte: bkfst $4-$7.50, lunch $6-$9, dinner $6-$15. Child's meals. Specializes in burgers, omelettes, sandwiches. Parking. Outdoor dining. Football memorabilia. Totally nonsmoking. Cr cds: A, C, D, DS, ER, JCB, MC, V.

D SC

Sacramento (D-3)

(See also Davis, Rancho Cordova)

Settled 1839 **Pop** 369,365 **Elev** 25 ft **Area Code** 916
Web www.sacramentocvb.org/cvb/

Information Convention & Visitors Bureau, 1303 J St, Ste 600, 95814; 916/264-7777

Capital of the state since 1854, Sacramento is known to flower lovers as the "Camellia Capital of the World." It is the marketing center for 11 counties in the Sacramento Valley, producing a cash farm income approaching 11 percent of the state's income.

Modern Sacramento started when Captain John A. Sutter established New Helvetia, a colony for his Swiss compatriots. Sutter built a fort here and immigrants came. He prospered in wheat raising, flour milling, distilling and in a passenger and freight boat service to San Francisco. The discovery of gold at Coloma in 1848 (see PLACERVILLE) brought ruin to Sutter. Workers deserted to hunt gold, and he soon lost possession of the fort. The next year his son, who had been deeded family property near the boat line terminus, laid out a town there, naming it Sacramento City. At the entrance to the gold rush country, its population rocketed to 10,000 within seven months. Chosen as California's capital in 1854, the new capitol building was constructed at a cost of more than $2.6 million over a 20-year period.

Transportation facilities were important in the city's growth. In 1860, the Pony Express made Sacramento its western terminus. Later, Sacramento's "Big Four"—Mark Hopkins, Charles Crocker, Collis P. Huntington and Leland Stanford—financed the building of the Central Pacific Railroad over the Sierras. Deepwater ships reach the city via a 43-mile-long channel from Suisun Bay. Sacramento's new port facilities handle an average of 20 ships a month carrying import and export cargo from major ports around the world.

What to See and Do

Blue Diamond Growers Visitors Center & Retail Store. 20-min video (daily exc Sun). 1701 C Street at 16th St. Phone 916/446-8439. **Free**

Cal Expo. Multipurpose facility for variety of activities including various consumer shows, auto racing and concerts. (See ANNUAL EVENTS) 5 mi NE at 1600 Exposition Blvd, borders Business Loop I-80. Phone 916/263-FAIR.

California State University, Sacramento (1947). (25,000 students) A replica of the Golden Gate bridge serves as a footbridge across the river. 6000 J St, on the banks of the American River on the E side of campus. Take Hwy 50 to exit Power Inn and follow the signs. Phone 916/278-6156.

Crocker Art Museum. Original restored Victorian Gallery (1872), reconstructed Mansion Wing and Herold Wing housing E.B. Crocker collection; European and American paintings; master drawings; Asian art; decorative arts; changing exhibits. Museum bookstore/gift shop. (Wed-Sun; closed Jan 1, July 4, Thanksgiving, Dec 25) 216 O St at 2nd St. Phone 916/264-5423. **¢¢**

Discovery Museum. Regional history exhibits, including gold ore specimens and restored artifacts; hands-on exhibits; video computers; working print shop. (Daily exc Mon; closed some major hols) 101 I St, in Old Sacramento. Phone 916/264-7057. **¢¢**

Governor's Mansion. Once owned by Joseph Steffens, father of Lincoln Steffens, a turn-of-the-century journalist. Every governor from 1903 through 1967 lived here. Guided tours (daily 10 am-5 pm; closed Jan 1, Thanksgiving, Dec 25). 16th & H Sts. Phone 916/324-7405. **¢¢**

Gold Rush District State Park (ca 1850-1870). Adj central business district between I-5 & I St bridge. This 28-acre area of historic buildings along the banks of the Sacramento River, known as the old Sacramento Historic District, has been restored to its 1850-1870 period of the Pony Express, the arrival of the Central Pacific Railroad and the gold rush. Special events held throughout the yr. The area also has shops and restaurants. Most buildings closed Jan 1, Thanksgiving, Dec 25. For recorded information, including the Governor's Mansion and Sutter's Fort State Historic Park, State Indian Museum, State Railroad Museum, the Leland Stanford Mansion, and Woodland Upper House State Park. Phone 916/324-0539. **Free** Includes

California State Railroad Museum and Railtown State Historic Park. The largest part of this complex is the **Museum of Railroad History**, which houses 21 pieces of rolling stock and a total of 40 exhibits covering all aspects of railroading. (Daily; closed Jan 1, Thanksgiving, Dec 25) 125 I St in Old Sacramento. Phone 916/445-6645 or -7387 (business office). **¢¢¢** Also part of the State Railroad Museum, and included in museum admission fee, is the

Central Pacific Passenger Depot. 930 Front St. (Same days as railroad museum)

Hastings Building. Western terminus of the Pony Express and original home of the California Supreme Court. 2nd & J Sts.

Old Eagle Theatre. Guided tours (by appt). Front & J Sts.

Professional sports.

NBA (Sacramento Kings). ARCO Arena, One Sports Pkwy, 95834. Phone 916/928-0000.

State Capitol. The Capitol provides a unique combination of past and present under one roof. It has been the home of California's lawmaking branch of government since the Capitol opened in 1869. The main building has been restored to recreate its turn-of-the-century ambience and to ensure its safety. The Legislature still meets in the restored Senate and Assembly chambers. Nine historic offices include exhibits from the State Library and State Archives. The more modern east annex contains the offices of the legislators and the governor. The building is surrounded by a 40-acre park with hundreds of varieties of trees, shrubs and flowers. Free guided tours of building (daily, on the hour). Park tours (June-Sept, daily). Capitol (daily; closed Jan 1, Thanksgiving, Dec 25). 10th & L Sts. Phone 916/324-0333. **Free**

★ **Sutter's Fort State Historic Park.** Restored in the late 1800s. Exhibits depict Sutter's life; kitchen. Special craft and living history demonstration days. (Daily; closed Jan 1, Thanksgiving, Dec 25) Admission includes self-guided audio tour. 2701 L St at 27th St. Phone 916/445-4422. **¢** Also here is the

State Indian Museum. Displays include dugout canoes, weapons, pottery, basketry; changing exhibits. (Hrs same as park) Films (Sat & Sun). 2618 K St at 26th St. Phone 916/324-0971. **¢**

Towe Ford Museum. Extensive collection of American automobiles. (Daily; closed Jan 1, Thanksgiving, Dec 25) 2200 Front St. Phone 916/442-6802. **¢¢**

William Land Park. Wading pool (summer, daily); fishing (children under 16 only). Nine-hole golf course. Picnic facilities, supervised playground, ballfields. Amusement area near zoo has pony, amusement rides (summer, daily). **Sacramento Zoo,** in the park at Land Park Dr & Sutterville Rd, has more than 340 specimens representing more than 150 species of exotic animals displayed in a 15-acre botanical garden setting (daily, mid-morning-mid-afternoon; closed Dec 25). Fairytale Town children's theme park (daily). Fee for activities. Freeport Blvd between 13th Ave & Sutterville Rd. Phone 916/277-6060 or 916/264-5200; Sacramento Zoo 916/264-5888; Golf Course 916/455-5014; Fairytale Town 916/264-7462. **¢¢**; Fairytale Town **¢¢**

Annual Events

Sacramento Jazz Jubilee. Venues throughout city. Cabaret, concert and jam sessions. Phone 916/372-5277. Memorial Day wkend.

California State Fair. California Exposition grounds. Includes traditional state fair activities; exhibits, livestock, carnival food, entertainment on 10 stages, Thoroughbred racing and 1-mi monorail. Phone 916/263-FAIR. Aug 18-Sept 4.

Seasonal Event

Music Circus. Music Circus Tent at 15th & H Sts, box office at 1419 H St. Community Center Theatre at 14th & L Sts. Summer professional musical theater. Phone 916/557-1999. July-Sept.

Motels

★★ **BEST WESTERN HARBOR INN AND SUITES.** *1250 Halyard Dr (95691), S off I-80 Business, Harbor Blvd exit. 916/371-2100; FAX 916/373-1507; res: 800/528-1234; res: 800/371-2101.* 138 rms, 2-4 story, 19 suites. S, D $69-$79; each addl $5; suites $84-$94; under 12 free. Crib free. Pet accepted; $10. TV; cable (premium). Heated pool; 2 whirlpools. Complimentary continental bkfst. Complimentary coffee in rms. Restaurant adj 7 am-11 pm. Ck-out 11 am. Meeting rms. Business servs avail. Valet serv. Some refrigerators, in-rm whirlpools. Private patios, balconies. Cr cds: A, C, D, DS, MC, V.

D SC

★ **DAYS INN DISCOVERY PARK.** *350 Bercut Dr (95814). 916/442-6971; FAX 916/444-2809; res: 800/329-7466.* 99 rms, 2 story. S $69-$99; D $79-$109; each addl $5; under 12 free. Crib free. TV; cable (premium). Pool; whirlpool. Complimentary continental bkfst. Coffee in rms. Restaurant adj open 24 hrs. Ck-out 11 am. Meeting rms. Coin Indry. Valet serv. Some refrigerators, wetbars. Some private patios & balconies. Cr cds: A, C, D, DS, MC, V.

D SC

✓★ **LA QUINTA INN.** *200 Jibboom St (95814). 916/448-8100; FAX 916/447-3621; res: 800/531-5900.* 165 rms, 3 story. S, D $70-$75; under 18 free. TV; cable (premium). Pool. Complimentary continental bkfst. Complimentary coffee in rms. Restaurant nearby. Ck-out noon. Guest Indry. Meeting rms. Business servs avail. In-rm modem link. Free airport, RR station, bus depot transportation. Exercise equipt. On Sacramento River. Cr cds: A, C, D, DS, MC, V.

D SC

★★ **LA QUINTA INN.** *4604 Madison Ave (95841), at I-80. 916/348-0900; FAX 916/331-7160; res: 800/687-6667.* 127 rms, 3 story. S, D $59-$79; each addl $5; suites $131; under 18 free. Crib free. Pet accepted, some restrictions. TV; cable (premium). Pool. Continental bkfst. Restaurant adj open 24 hrs. Ck-out noon. Coin Indry. Meeting rms. Business servs avail. In-rm modem link. Health club privileges. Fireplace in lobby. Cr cds: A, C, D, DS, MC, V.

D SC

★★ **RESIDENCE INN BY MARRIOTT.** *1530 Howe Ave (95825). 916/920-9111; FAX 916/921-5664; res: 800/331-3131.* 176 kit. units, 2 story. Kit. units $129-$149; each addl $10; under 12 free; wkly rates. Crib free. Pet accepted; $60-$100 & $10/day. TV; cable (premium). Pool; whirlpools. Complimentary continental bkfst. Ck-out noon. Coin Indry. Meeting rm. Business servs avail. In-rm modem link. Valet serv. Sundries. Health club privileges. Balconies. Cr cds: A, C, D, DS, JCB, MC, V.

D SC

✓★ **SUPER 8 MOTEL.** *9646 Micron Ave (95827). 916/361-3131; FAX 916/361-9674; res: 800/800-8000.* 93 rms, 3 story. S $39; D $45-$50; each addl $5; under 13 free; higher rates special events. Crib $5. TV; cable. Complimentary coffee in lobby. Restaurant opp 6 am-10 pm. Ck-out 11 am. Coin Indry. Pool. Cr cds: A, C, D, DS, MC, V.

D SC

✓★ **VAGABOND INN.** *1319 30th St (95816), at N Street. 916/454-4400; FAX 916/736-2812; res: 800/522-1555.* 81 rms, 3 story. S, D $45-$65; each addl $5; under 18 free. Crib free. Pet accepted, some restrictions; $5/day. TV; cable. Pool. Coffee in lobby. Restaurant adj open 24 hrs. Ck-out noon. Cr cds: A, C, D, DS, MC, V.

SC

★ **VAGABOND INN.** *909 3rd St (95814). 916/446-1481; FAX 916/448-0364; res: 800/522-1555.* 108 rms, 3 story. S $73-$83; D $83-$93; each addl $5; under 17 free. Crib free. Pet accepted, some restrictions; $5/day. TV; cable (premium). Heated pool. Complimentary continental bkfst. Complimentary coffee in rms. Restaurant adj open 24 hrs. Ck-out noon. Meeting rm. Valet serv. Free airport, RR station, bus depot transportation. Some refrigerators, microwaves. Cr cds: A, C, D, DS, MC, V.

D SC

Motor Hotels

★★ **CLARION HOTEL.** *700 16th St (95814). 916/444-8000; FAX 916/442-8129; res: 800/443-0880.* 238 rms, 2-4 story. S $89-$109; D $109-$119; each addl $20; suites $135-$265; under 18 free; wkend rates. Crib free. Pet accepted; $50 deposit. TV; cable (premium), VCR avail. Pool; poolside serv. Complimentary coffee in rms. Restaurant 6:30 am-2 pm, 5-10 pm. Rm serv. Bar 11-1 am. Ck-out noon. Meeting rms. Business servs avail. In-rm modem link. Bellhops. Valet serv. Sundries. Airport transportation. Health club privileges. Some refrigerators. Some private patios, balconies. Cr cds: A, C, D, DS, ER, JCB, MC, V.

D SC

★★★ **DOUBLETREE HOTEL.** *2001 Point West Way (95815). 916/929-8855; FAX 916/564-7006; res: 800/547-8010.* 448 rms, 4 story. S, D $119-$199; each addl $15; suites $200-$500; under 18 free. Crib free. Pet accepted, some restrictions; $50. TV, cable (premium); VCR avail. Pool; poolside serv, whirlpool. Restaurant 6 am-midnight. Rm serv. Bar 11-2 am. Ck-out noon. Meeting rms. Business center. In-rm modem link. Bellhops. Valet serv. Gift shop. Free airport, RR station, bus depot transportation. Exercise equipt. Health club privileges. Bathrm phone, refrigerator, minibar, whirlpool in suites. Balconies. Cr cds: A, C, D, DS, ER, JCB, MC, V.

D SC

✓★★ **GOVERNORS INN.** *210 Richards Blvd (95814). 916/448-7224; FAX 916/448-7382; res: 800/999-6689.* E-mail gov.inn@juno.com. 133 rms, 3 story. Jan-Nov: S $79; D $89; each addl $10; suites $96-$106; under 12 free; higher rates jazz festival; lower rates rest of yr. Crib $5. TV; cable (premium). Complimentary continental bkfst. Complimentary coffee in rms. Restaurant opp open 24 hrs. Ck-out 11 am. Meeting rms. Business servs avail. In-rm modem link. Valet serv. Free airport, RR station, bus depot transportation. Exercise equipt. Pool; whirlpool. Refrigerator, wet bar in suites. Balcony in suites. On river. Cr cds: A, C, D, DS, MC, V.

D SC

★★★ **HAWTHORN SUITES HOTEL.** *321 Bercut Dr (95814), E off I-5 Richards Blvd exit. 916/441-1200; FAX 916/441-6530; res: 800/767-1777.* 272 suites, 3 story. S $129; D $139; each addl $10; under 12 free; wkend rates. Crib free. Pet accepted, some restrictions. TV; cable (premium), VCR avail. Heated pool; whirlpool. Complimentary full bkfst. Complimentary coffee in rms. Restaurant 7 am-11 pm. Rm serv. Bar 4 pm-1 am. Ck-out noon. Coin Indry. Convention facilities. Business servs avail. Bellhops. Valet serv. Sundries. Free RR station, bus depot transportation. Exercise equipt. Health club privileges. Refrigerators, microwaves. Cr cds: A, C, D, DS, MC, V.

D SC

★★★ **RADISSON HOTEL.** *500 Leisure Ln (95814). 916/922-2020; FAX 916/649-9463; res: 800/333-3333.* 307 rms, 2 story. S, D $119-$159; each addl $10; suites $159-$448; under 18 free; wkend rates. Crib avail. Pet accepted, some restrictions; $100 deposit. TV; cable, VCR avail. Pool; whirlpool, poolside serv. Complimentary coffee in rms. Restaurant 6:30 am-10 pm. Rm serv 24 hrs. Bar 11-2 am; entertainment. Ck-out noon. Convention facilities. Business center. Bellhops. Valet serv. Concierge. Sundries. Gift shop. Exercise equipt. Some refrigerators, minibars. Balconies. On small, private lake. Cr cds: A, C, D, DS, ER, JCB, MC, V.

D SC

★★ **RED LION INN.** *1401 Arden Way (95815). 916/922-8041; FAX 916/922-0386; res: 800/547-8010.* 376 rms, 2-3 story. S, D $125-$148; each addl $15; suites $150-$395; under 18 free. Crib free. Pet accepted, some restrictions; $25. TV; cable (premium). 3 pools, whirlpool, poolside serv. Restaurant 6 am-10 pm. Rm serv. Bar 11-2 am; entertainment Tues-Sat. Ck-out noon. Coin Indry. Meeting rms. Bellhops. Sundries.

Gift shop. Valet parking. Putting green. Exercise equipt. Some bathrm phones, in-rm whirlpools, refrigerators. Private patios, balconies. Cr cds: A, C, D, DS, JCB, MC, V.

D SC

Hotels

★★★ **HILTON.** *2200 Harvard St (95815). 916/922-4700; FAX 916/922-8418; res: 800/445-8667; res: 800/344-4321.* E-mail sachilton@aol.com; web www.sacramentohilton.com. 330 rms, 12 story. S $89-$179; D $89-$189; each addl $10; suites $275-$525; wkend rates. Crib free. TV; cable (premium), VCR avail. Heated pool; whirlpool, poolside serv. Coffee in rms. Restaurant 6 am-10 pm. Bar noon-midnight. Ck-out noon. Convention facilities. Business servs avail. In-rm modem link. Gift shop. Exercise equipt; sauna. Some balconies. Luxury level. Cr cds: A, C, D, DS, ER, JCB, MC, V.

D

★★★ **HOLIDAY INN.** *300 J St (95814). 916/446-0100; FAX 916/446-0117; res: 800/465-4329.* 364 rms, 16 story. S $122; D $132; each addl $10; suites $225-$550; under 12 free. Crib free. TV; cable (premium), VCR avail. Pool; sauna. Coffee in rms. Restaurant 6 am-2 pm; dining rm 6-11 pm. Bar 11-1 am; entertainment Tues-Sat. Ck-out noon. Convention facilities. Business servs avail. In-rm modem link. Concierge. Gift shop. Exercise equipt. Health club privileges. Some refrigerators. Luxury level. Cr cds: A, C, D, DS, JCB, MC, V.

D SC

★★★ **HYATT REGENCY.** *1209 L St (95814), opp State Capitol. 916/443-1234; FAX 916/321-6699; res: 800/233-1234.* 500 rms, 15 story. S $190; D $215; each addl $25; suites $225-$895; under 18 free; wkly, wkend rates. Crib free. Valet parking $12/day, garage $7/day. TV; cable (premium), VCR avail. Heated pool; poolside serv. Complimentary coffee in rms. Restaurant 6 am-midnight. Bar 11-2 am; entertainment Tues-Sat. Ck-out noon. Convention facilities. Business servs avail. In-rm modem link. Concierge. Airport, RR station, bus depot transportation. Exercise equipt; whirlpool. Minibars. Balconies. Luxury level. Cr cds: A, C, D, DS, JCB, MC, V.

D SC

Inns

★★★ **AMBER HOUSE BED & BREAKFAST INN.** *1315 22nd St (95816). 916/444-8085; FAX 916/552-6529; res: 800/755-6526.* E-mail innkeeper@amberhouse.com; web www.amberhouse.com. 14 rms in 3 houses, 2 story. S, D $119-$249. TV; cable (premium), VCR. Complimentary full bkfst. Rm serv. Ck-out noon, ck-in 4 pm. Business servs avail. In-rm modem link. Whirlpool in most rms. Bicycles. Health club privileges. Houses built 1895 and 1913; rms individually decorated; antiques; library. Totally nonsmoking. Cr cds: A, C, D, DS, MC, V.

★★★ **THE INN AT PARKSIDE.** *2116 6th St (95818). 916/658-1818; FAX 916/658-1809; res: 800/995-7275.* E-mail gmcgreal@2extreme.net; web www.innatparkside.com. 7 rms, 3 story, 2 suites. No elvtrs. S, D $79-$120; each addl $10; suites $120. TV; cable, VCR (movies). Complimentary full bkfst. Restaurant nearby. Ck-out noon, ck-in 3-8 pm. Business servs avail. In-rm modem link. Concierge serv. Microwaves avail; in-rm whirlpool, fireplace in suites. Picnic tables. Built in 1936 by Chinese ambassador and used as cultural center. Totally nonsmoking. Cr cds: A, C, MC, V.

D

★★★ **THE STERLING HOTEL.** *1300 H St (95814), 2 blks N of Sacramento Convention Center, downtown. 916/448-1300; FAX 916/448-8066; res: 800/365-7660.* 16 rms, 3 story. S, D $145-$225. Crib free. TV; cable (premium). Complimentary coffee in sitting rm. Dining rm (see CHANTERELLE). Rm serv. Serv bar. Ck-out 11 am, ck-in 3 pm. Meeting rms. Business servs avail. In-rm modem link. Health club privileges. In-rm whirlpools. Some refrigerators. Some balconies. Individually decorated rms. Totally nonsmoking. Cr cds: A, C, D, JCB, MC, V.

D SC

★★ **VIZCAYA.** *2019 21st St (95818). 916/455-5243; FAX 916/455-6102; res: 800/456-2019.* Web www.sleepingsacramento.com. 9 rms, 3 story. S, D $110-$225. TV; cable (premium). Complimentary full bkfst. Ck-out 11 am, ck-in 3 pm. Business servs avail. Street parking. Some in-rm whirlpools, fireplaces. Picnic tables. Landscaped gardens, Victorian gazebo. Built 1899; Italian marble in bathrms. Sitting rm; antiques. Brick patio. Totally nonsmoking. Cr cds: A, C, D, MC, V.

Restaurants

★★★ **ALDO'S.** *2914 Pasatiempo Lane (95821). 916/483-5031.* Hrs: 11:30 am-10:30 pm; Fri & Sat to 10:30 pm; Sun 4 pm-10 pm. Res accepted. French, Italian, Amer menu. Bar 11-1 am. Semi-a la carte: lunch $6.50-$15, dinner $12-$25.50. Specialties: chicken Jerusalem, flaming entrees & desserts, tournedos Rossini. Pianist 6:30 pm-1 am. Lavish decor; art display. Family-owned. Totally nonsmoking. Cr cds: A, C, D, DS, MC, V.

★★★ **BIBA.** *2801 Capitol Ave (95816). 916/455-2422.* Web www.ristorante-biba.com. Hrs: 11:30 am-2:30 pm, 5:30-9:30 pm; Fri to 10:30 pm; Sat 5:30-10:30 pm. Closed Sun; also major hols. Res accepted. Italian menu. Bar. Wine cellar. Semi-a la carte: lunch $8-$14, dinner $16-$20. Specializes in pasta, veal, rabbit. Pianist Tues-Sat. Street parking. Totally nonsmoking. Cr cds: A, C, MC, V.

D

★★ **CHANTERELLE.** *(See Sterling Hotel Inn) 916/442-0451.* Hrs: 5:30-8:30 pm. Res accepted. California, French menu. Setups. Wine list. Semi-a la carte: dinner $12.50-$21. Specialty: veal with chanterelle mushrooms. Own baking. Totally nonsmoking. Cr cds: A, C, D, JCB, MC, V.

D

★★★ **FIREHOUSE.** *1112 2nd St (95814). 916/442-4772.* Hrs: 11:30 am-2 pm, 5:30-9 pm; Fri to 10 pm; Sat 5-10 pm; Sun 5-9 pm. Closed major hols. Res accepted. Contemporary American menu. Bar 11:30 am-10 pm. A la carte entrees: lunch $6.95-$14.95, dinner $12.95-$34.95. Specialties: filet mignon, artichokes and asparagus. Courtyard dining (lunch). Antiques, crystal. In Old Sacramento; restored landmark firehouse (1853). Family-owned. Cr cds: A, C, MC, V.

★★★ **FRANK FAT'S.** *806 L St (95814). 916/442-7092.* E-mail frantfats@pacbell.com. Hrs: 11:30 am-2 pm, 5:30-10 pm; Sat 5:30-10 pm; Sun 5-10 pm. Closed July 4, Thanksgiving, Dec 25. Res accepted. Chinese menu. Bar. Wine cellar. Semi-a la carte: lunch $10-$15, dinner $15-$25. Specialties: honey-cured walnut prawns, clams in black bean sauce, Frank Fat's NY steak. Parking. Totally nonsmoking. Cr cds: A, C, MC, V.

D

✓★★ **LEMON GRASS.** *601 Munroe St (95825). 916/486-4891.* Hrs: 11:30 am-2 pm, 5:30-9:30 pm; Fri, Sat 5-10 pm; Sun 5-9 pm. Closed some major hols. Vietnamese, Thai menu. Bar. Semi-a la carte: lunch $5-$15, dinner $9-$18. Specializes in grilled seafood. Parking. Outdoor dining. Original art. Cr cds: A, C, D, MC, V.

D

★★★ **MORTON'S OF CHICAGO.** *521 L St (95814). 916/442-5091.* Hrs: 5:30-11 pm; Sun 5-10 pm. Closed most major hols. Res accepted. Bar. Wine cellar. A la carte entrees: dinner $20-$30. Specializes in prime aged beef, live Maine lobster, fresh seafood. Valet parking. Chicago-club atmosphere. Totally nonsmoking. Cr cds: A, C, D, JCB, MC, V.

D

✓★★ **MUMS VEGETARIAN RESTAURANT.** *2968 Freeport Blvd (95818). 916/444-3015.* Hrs: 11:30 am-2 pm, 5:15-9 pm; Mon 11:30 am-2 pm; Fri to 9:30 pm; Sat 5:15-9:30 pm; Sun 4-8 pm; Sat, Sun brunch 9:30 am-2 pm. Closed Jan 1, Dec 25. Res accepted. Vegetarian menu. Bar. Semi-a la carte: lunch $4.50-$7.50, dinner $9.75-$12.50. Sat, Sun brunch $5.75-$8. Child's meals. Specialties: Mum's shepherd's pie, avocado rarebit, herbed polenta torta. Parking. Outdoor dining. Totally nonsmoking. Cr cds: A, C, MC, V.

★★ **PILOTHOUSE.** *1000 Front St (95814), aboard historic Delta King paddlewheeler. 916/441-4440.* Web www.deltaking.com. Hrs: 11:30 am-2 pm, 5-10 pm; Sun brunch 10 am-2 pm. Res accepted. Bar. A la carte entrees: lunch $5.95-$10.95, dinner $11.95-$21.95. Sun brunch $16.95. Child's meals. Specializes in fresh fish, grilled meats, pasta. Valet parking. Authentic period decor. Totally nonsmoking. Cr cds: A, C, D, DS, MC, V.

D

✓★★ **RISTORANTE PIATTI.** *571 Pavilions Lane. 916/649-8885.* Hrs: 11 am-10 pm; Fri & Sat to 11 pm. Closed Dec 25. Res accepted. Italian menu. Bar. A la carte entrees: lunch, dinner $7.50-$17.95. Child's meals. Specializes in roasted chicken, wood-fired pizza, fresh pasta. Valet parking. Outdoor dining. Mediterranean decor. Totally nonsmoking. Cr cds: A, C, D, MC, V.

D

★ **RUSTY DUCK.** *500 Bercut Dr (95814), I-5 & Richards Blvd. 916/441-1191.* Web www.rustypelican.com. Hrs: 11:30 am-10 pm; Fri to 11 pm; Sat 4:30-11 pm; Sun 10 am-3 pm, 4:30-10 pm; early-bird dinner 4:30-6:30 pm. Res accepted. Bar; Fri, Sat to 1:30 am. Semi-a la carte: lunch $5.95-$12.95, dinner $9.95-$32.95. Child's meals. Specializes in fresh fish, prime rib, pasta. Own pies, cheesecake. Parking. Rustic hunting lodge decor; fireplace. Cr cds: A, C, D, DS, MC, V.

D SC

★★ **SILVA'S SHELDON INN.** *9000 Grant Line Rd (95624), 8 mi S on CA 99, left on Elk Grove Blvd to Grant Line Rd, NE 2 mi. 916/686-8330.* Hrs: 5-9:30 pm; Fri & Sat to 10 pm; Sun 5-8:30 pm. Closed Mon; some major hols; also wk of Jan 1 & wk of July 4. Bar from 5 pm. Complete meals: dinner $10-$17. Child's meals. Specializes in fresh fish, steak, Portuguese bean soup. Parking. Outdoor dining. In turn-of-the-century building. Totally nonsmoking. Cr cds: C, MC, V.

D

Unrated Dining Spot

RICK'S DESSERT DINER. *2322 K St. 916/444-0969.* Hrs: 10 am-11 pm; Fri, Sat to 1 am; Sun from noon. Closed Jan 1, Easter, Thanksgiving, Dec 25, 26. A la carte: $.90-$3.95. Specializes in desserts. Specialties: Chocolate OD, white chocolate almond torte. Outdoor dining. 1950s decor. Totally nonsmoking. Cr cds: C.

Salinas (F-1)

(See also Big Sur, Carmel, Monterey, Pacific Grove)

Pop 108,777 **Elev** 53 ft **Area Code** 831
E-mail salinas@salinas chamber.com **Web** www.salinaschamber.com

Information Salinas Valley Chamber of Commerce, 119 E Alisal St, PO Box 1170, 93902; 831/424-7611

Birthplace of novelist John Steinbeck, many of whose works, including *East of Eden* (1952), *Tortilla Flat* (1935) and *Of Mice and Men* (1937), are set in the Salinas Valley area.

What to See and Do

Hat in Three Stages of Landing. Sculpture by Claes Oldenburg. Concept of a straw hat tossed out of the rodeo grounds (adjacent) in 3 stages of landing on the field. Community Center, 940 N Main St.

National Steinbeck Center/Museum. (Daily, 10-5) One Main St. Phone 831/796-3833.

Pinnacles National Monument (see). Approx 25 mi S via US 101, then 11 mi E via CA 146.

Steinbeck House. Former home of famous Salinas native John Steinbeck. Gift shop. Lunch open 11:30-2 (2 seatings daily). (Daily; closed 3 wks late Dec-early Jan) 132 Central Ave. Phone 831/424-2735. Lunch ¢¢¢

Annual Events

California Rodeo. Rodeo Grounds, 1034 N Main St, ¼ mi N off US 101. Parades, dancing, entertainment, competitions, barbecue. Phone 831/757-2951 or 800/771-8807. 3rd wk July.

Steinbeck Festival. Sponsored by National Steinbeck Center Foundation. Bus and walking tours of Steinbeck country; films, plays, readings and lectures about the author. Phone 831/796-3833. Early Aug.

California International Airshow. Airport Blvd exit off US 101, at airport. Aerobatic displays, formation parachute jumping, precision close-formation flying by top US and international performers, including the US Navy's Blue Angels. Early Aug or Oct.

Motels

★★ **COMFORT INN.** *144 Kern St (93905). 831/758-8850; FAX 831/758-3611; res: 800/228-5150.* 32 rms, 2 story. S $59-$149; D $69-$149; suite $89-$149; each addl $8; under 16 free; higher rates some wkends. Crib $8. TV; cable (premium). Complimentary continental bkfst. Complimentary coffee in rms. Restaurant nearby. Ck-out 11 am. Business servs avail. Refrigerators, microwaves avail; bathrm phones. Cr cds: A, C, D, DS, ER, JCB, MC, V.

D SC

✓★★ **LAUREL INN MOTEL.** *801 W Laurel Dr (93906). 831/449-2474; FAX 831/449-2476; res: 800/354-9831.* 145 rms, 2 story, 4 suites. S $52-$130; D $58-$130. Crib $4. TV; cable (premium). Heated pool; whirlpool, sauna. Coffee in lobby. Restaurant adj 5:30 am-midnight. Bar from 11 am. Ck-out noon. Meeting rms. Business servs avail. Some refrigerators, fireplaces. Cr cds: A, C, D, DS, MC, V.

D SC

✓★ **VAGABOND INN.** *131 Kern St (93905). 831/758-4693; FAX 831/758-9835; res: 800/522-1555.* Web www.vagabondinns.com. 70 rms, 2 story. S $52-$65; D $62-$85; each addl $5; under 18 free. Crib free. Pet accepted, some restrictions; $5. TV; cable (premium). Heated pool. Complimentary continental bkfst. Restaurant adj. Ck-out noon. Cr cds: A, C, D, DS, ER, MC, V.

SC

Restaurants

★ **PUB'S PRIME RIB.** *227 Monterey St (93901). 831/424-2261.* Hrs: 11 am-10 pm; Sat noon-10 pm; Sun 3-9 pm. Closed major hols. Res accepted. Bar. Complete meals: lunch $7-$10, dinner $12.95-$20.95. Child's meals. Specialties: prime rib, skirt steak, sweetbreads. Own desserts. Cr cds: A, C, D, DS, MC, V.

D

★ **SMALLEY'S ROUNDUP.** *700 W Market St (93901). 831/758-0511.* Hrs: 11:30 am-1:30 pm, 5-8:30 pm; Sat 5-9 pm; Sun 4-8:30 pm. Closed Mon; major hols; also wk of July 4, wk of Dec 25. Res accepted. Wine, beer. Semi-a la carte: lunch, dinner $5.99-$20.99. Child's meals. Specializes in steak, chicken, ribs. Totally nonsmoking. Cr cds: C, MC, V.

✓★★ **SPADO'S.** *66 W Alisal (93901). 831/424-4139.* Hrs: 11 am-2:30 pm, 5-9 pm; Sat 5-9 pm; Sun 4-8 pm. Closed Jan 1, July 4, Dec 25. Res accepted (dinner). Italian menu. Wine, beer. A la carte entrees: lunch $5.50-$9.50, dinner $7.95-$12.95. Child's meals. Specializes in lamb, brick-oven pizzas. Outdoor dining. Contemporary decor. Totally nonsmoking. Cr cds: A, C, DS, MC, V.

D

Salton Sea State Recreation Area (J-5)

(See also Indio)

(N shore of Salton Sea, CA 111 at State Park Rd)

The Salton Sea, located in the Colorado Desert, is a popular inland boating and fishing area. In 1905, the Colorado River flooded through a broken canal gate into the Salton Basin, creating a vast new lake. Fishermen catch corvina, croakers, sargo and tilapia year round. A launch ramp is available and can accommodate any trailer boat. The recreation area covers 17,913 acres and has areas for swimming and waterskiing. There are nature trails for birdwatching, interpretive programs (Nov-May), picnic grounds and 148 developed campsites (dump station, hookups), plus two miles of primitive camping at Corvina Beach, Salt Creek and Bombay Beach campgrounds. Standard fees. (Daily) Phone 760/393-3052 or 760/393-3059.

San Bernardino (J-4)

(See also Anaheim, Lake Arrowhead, Redlands, Riverside)

Founded 1810 **Pop** 164,164 **Elev** 1,049 ft **Area Code** 909

Information San Bernardino Area Chamber of Commerce, 546 W 6th St, 92410; or PO Box 658, 92402; 909/885-7515

Set amid mountains, valleys and deserts, San Bernardino is a mixture of Spanish and Mormon cultures. The city takes its name from the valley and mountains discovered by a group of missionaries in 1810 on the feast of San Bernardino of Siena. In 1851, a group of Mormons bought the Rancho San Bernardino and laid out the city, modeled after Salt Lake City. The group was recalled by Brigham Young six years later but the city continued to thrive. The area has a vast citrus industry. In April the fragrance and beauty of orange blossoms fill the nearby groves.

What to See and Do

Big Bear Mountain Resort. Skiing, seasonal passes; also golf course & driving range; resort. N on I-215 (US 395), exit E on 10 freeway, exit Orange Ave in Redlands, left at Hwy 38 (Lagonia Ave), left on Big Bear Blvd, left on Moonridge Rd. Phone 909/585-2517. Web www.bearmtn.com. ¢¢¢¢¢

Glen Helen Regional Park. Approx 500 acres. Swimming (fee), 2 flume water slides (fee); fishing (fee). Nature trail. Picnicking, playground. Group camping (fee). (Daily; closed Jan 1, Dec 25) 2555 Glen Helen Pkwy, 10 mi N, 1 mi W of I-215. Phone 909/880-2522. Per vehicle ¢¢

Rim of the World Highway (CA 18). Scenic 45-mi mountain road leading to Big Bear Lake, Snow Summit, Running Springs, Lake Arrowhead, Blue Jay and Skyforest. Beaches on the lakes, fishing, hiking and riding trails, picnic grounds.

San Bernardino National Forest. One of the most heavily used national forests in the country; stretches east from San Bernardino to Palm Springs. Includes the popular San Gorgonio Wilderness at the forest's east edge by Redlands, the small Cucamonga Wilderness in the west end of the San Bernardino Mountains and the San Jacinto Wilderness in the San Jacinto Mountains (permits required for wildernesses). Fishing, hunting; boating. Hiking. Horseback riding. Skiing. Off-road vehicle trails. Picnicking. Camping (fees charged; res for camping accepted, as well as first come, first served basis). 10 mi N via I-215, CA 18, 30, 38, 330. Contact Forest Supervisor, 1824 S Commercenter Circle, 92408; phone 909/383-5588. Camping res 877/444-6777 (toll free). Camping ¢¢¢-¢¢¢¢¢

Annual Event

National Orange Show. Fairgrounds, Mill & E Sts. Marks completion of winter citrus crop harvest. Held annually since 1915. Exhibits, sports events, entertainment. Contact Natl Orange Show Fairground; 909/888-6788. Apr or May.

Seasonal Event

Renaissance Faire. Glen Helen Regional Park, 10 mi N on I-215, exit Devore Rd. Re-creates an Elizabethan experience with costumed performers, booths, food and games. Late Apr-mid-June, wkends.

Motels

★★ **LA QUINTA INN.** *205 E Hospitality Ln (92408), I-10 exit Waterman Ave N. 909/888-7571; FAX 909/884-3864; res: 800/687-6667.* Web www.laquinta.com. 153 rms, 3 story. S $65-$70; D $73-$78; suites $120-$150; each addl $8; under 18 free. Crib free. Pet accepted, some restrictions. TV; cable (premium). Heated pool. Complimentary continental bkfst. Coffee in rms. Restaurant adj 11 am-midnight. Ck-out noon. Business servs avail. Valet serv. Health club privileges. Refrigerators, microwaves avail. Cr cds: A, C, D, DS, MC, V.

D SC

✓★ **LEISURE INN & SUITES.** *777 W 6th St (92410), 1 blk E of I-215. 909/889-3561; FAX 909/884-7127; res: 800/800-8000.* 57 rms, 2 story. S $38-$41; D $40-$42; each addl $4; suites $48-$52. Crib $4. TV; cable (premium). Pool; whirlpool. Sauna. Complimentary continental bkfst. Restaurant nearby. Ck-out 11 am. Meeting rm. Guest lndry. Refrigerators; microwaves avail. Grills. Cr cds: A, C, D, DS, JCB, MC, V.

SC

Hotels

★★ **RADISSON HOTEL CONVENTION CENTER.** *295 N East St (92108), I-215 exit 2nd St E, downtown. 909/381-6181; FAX 909/381-5288; res: 800/333-3333.* E-mail radisson@earthlink.net. 231 units, 12 story, 24 suites. S $130; D $150; each addl $10; suites $220-$350; under 17 free. Crib free. TV; cable (premium). Coffee in rms. Restaurant 6:30-9 am, 11:30 am-2 pm, 5-10 pm. Bar from 4 pm; Sat from 5 pm; closed Sun. Ck-out noon. Meeting rms. Business center. Gift shop. Florist. Garage parking. Free airport, RR station, bus depot transportation. Exercise equipt; whirlpool. Some refrigerators. Convention center adj. Cr cds: A, C, D, DS, JCB, MC, V.

D SC

★★ **SAN BERNARDINO HILTON.** *285 E Hospitality Lane (90020), I-10 exit Waterman Ave N. 909/889-0133; FAX 909/381-4299; res: 800/445-8667.* Web www.hilton.com. 250 rms, 6-7 story. S, D $99-$175; each addl $10; suites $175-$325; under 18 free. Crib free. TV; cable (premium). Heated pool; whirlpool, poolside serv. Coffee in rms. Restaurant 6:30 am-3 pm, 5-10 pm; Sun 7 am-3 pm, 5-9 pm. Bar 11:30-1 am. Ck-out noon. Convention facilities. Business servs avail. Gift shop. Free airport transportation. Exercise equipt. Health club privileges. Bathrm phones, refrigerators; whirlpool in some suites. Cr cds: A, C, D, DS, MC, V.

D SC

Restaurant

✓★★ **LOTUS GARDEN.** *111 E Hospitality Lane (92408), I-10 exit Waterman Ave N. 909/381-6171.* Hrs: 11:30 am-9:30 pm; Fri, Sat to 10:30 pm. Res accepted. Chinese menu. Bar. A la carte entrees: lunch, dinner $7.25-$14.95. Complete meals: lunch $5.95-$8.75, dinner $10.55-$14.75. Buffet: lunch $5.75. Child's meals. Specializes in Mandarin dishes. Parking. Chinese decor; exterior resembles a Chinese temple. Totally nonsmoking. Cr cds: A, C, D, DS, MC, V.

D

San Clemente (J-4)

(See also Anaheim, Laguna Beach, San Juan Capistrano)

Pop 41,100 **Elev** 200 ft **Area Code** 949 **Zip** 92672
E-mail chamber@fia.net **Web** www.scchamber.com

Information Chamber of Commerce, 1100 N El Camino Real; 949/492-1131

What to See and Do

San Clemente State Beach. Swimming, lifeguard; fishing; hiking trail, picnicking; trailer hookups, camping. Camping res necessary. (Daily) Califia Ave, off I-5. Phone 949/492-3156. Day use per vehicle **¢¢¢**; Camping **¢¢¢¢¢**

Swimming. Municipal Pier & Beach. Swimming, surfing; picnicking, playground; fishing, bait and tackle shop at end of pier. (Daily; lifeguards) ½ mi W of I-5. For information contact Division of Marine Safety, 100 Avenida Presidio; phone 949/361-8219. **Free**

Annual Event

San Clemente Fiesta. Street festival. 2nd Sun Aug.

Motel

✓★ **TRAVELODGE.** *2441 S El Camino Real (92672). 949/498-5954; FAX 949/498-6657; res: 800/578-7878; res: 800/843-1706.* 19 rms, 3 suites. June-mid-Sept: S $55-$89; D $65-$105; each addl $4; suites $95-$145; lower rates rest of yr. Crib $4. TV; cable (premium), VCR avail (movies). Complimentary continental bkfst. Restaurant nearby. Ck-out 11 am. Free covered parking. Refrigerators, microwaves. Many private patios, balconies. Cr cds: A, C, D, DS, MC, V.

D SC

Motor Hotel

★★ **HOLIDAY INN RESORT.** *111 S Avenida De Estrella (92672). 949/361-3000; FAX 949/361-2472; res: 800/469-1161.* Web www.sanclemente.com/holidayinn. 72 rms, 3 story, 19 suites. S, D $99-$129; suites $139-$199; under 18 free; wkly, monthly rates. Crib free. Pet accepted; $10. TV; cable (premium), VCR avail. Heated pool. Restaurant 7 am-2 pm, 6-9 pm. Rm serv. Bar. Ck-out noon. Meeting rms. Business servs avail. In-rm modem link. Bellhops. Free garage parking. Health club privileges. Massage. Refrigerators; some wet bars; microwaves avail. Balconies. Cr cds: A, C, D, DS, JCB, MC, V.

D SC

San Diego (K-4)

Founded 1769 **Pop** 1,110,549 **Elev** 42 ft **Area Code** 619 **E-mail** sdinfo@sandiego.org **Web** www.sandiego.org

Information Convention & Visitors Bureau, 401 B St, Suite 1400, 92101; 619/232-3101 or Visitors Center 619/236-1212

Suburbs Carlsbad, Chula Vista, Coronado, Del Mar, El Cajon, Escondido, Oceanside, Rancho Santa Fe, San Ysidro. (See individual alphabetical listings.)

The southernmost city in California gains a Mexican flavor from its proximity to Mexico's border town of Tijuana (see; for Border Crossing Regulations see MAKING THE MOST OF YOUR TRIP). Like many California cities, San Diego stretches from the Pacific Ocean eastward over lovely rolling hills of 1,591 feet. It is a warm city where the sun nearly always shines; this balmy year-round climate encourages outdoor living. Within San Diego County are mountains as high as 6,500 feet, 70 miles of beaches, a desert area, resorts, flowers, palm trees and a lively cultural program. Several universities are located here.

For many years San Diego has been an important Navy center. Many Navy personnel, as well as others, retire here. It is a growing oceanography center and is also noted for avocado producing, electronics, ship, aircraft and missile building, manufacturing, education, health and biomedical research and tourism.

San Diego was "the place where California began" when the Portuguese conquistador Juan Rodriguez Cabrillo landed here in 1542. Since the first mission in California was built in San Diego in 1769, the city has grown steadily under the Spanish, Mexicans and North Americans.

Transportation

Car Rental Agencies. See IMPORTANT TOLL-FREE NUMBERS.

Public Transportation. Buses, trolleys downtown, to East County and to Tijuana (San Diego Transit), phone 619/233-3004.

Rail Passenger Service. Amtrak 800/872-7245.

Airport Information

San Diego Intl Airport/Lindbergh Field. Information 619/231-2100; lost and found 619/686-8002; weather 619/289-1212; cash machines, East Terminal.

What to See and Do

★ **Balboa Park.** Center of city on 1,200 acres. Art galleries, museums, theaters, restaurants, recreational facilities and miles of garden walks, lawns, flowers, subtropical plants and ponds. Off Park Blvd are

House of Pacific Relations. Thirty-one nations offer cultural and art exhibits in 15 California/Spanish-style cottages. (Sun; also 1st Tues of month) Phone 619/234-0739 or visitors center 619/239-0512. **Free**

San Diego Aerospace Museum. An International Aerospace Hall of Fame. Portraits, memorabilia and special exhibits honoring the men and women around the world who have made significant contributions to aerospace progress. (Daily; closed Jan 1, Thanksgiving, Dec 25) Phone 619/232-8322.

Mingei International Museum of World Folk Art. The museum moved into this 14,000-sq-ft facility in July 1996. Seven galleries contain exhibits of arts of people from all cultures of the world. Many art forms are shown in different collections and changing exhibitions such as costumes, jewelry, dolls and toys, utensils, painting and sculpture. Also here is a theater, library, collections research center and educational facilities. (Daily exc Mon; closed hols) 1439 El Prado, in Central Plaza (Plaza de Panama) Phone 619/239-0003. **¢¢**

Museum of Man. Exhibits on California and Hopi Native Americans, ancient Egypt, Mayan culture, early man, mummies; human reproduction; changing exhibits. (Daily; closed Jan 1, Thanksgiving, Dec 25) 1350 El Prado. Phone 619/239-2001. **¢¢**

Museum of Photographic Arts. Changing exhibitions featuring 19th century, early-mid-20th century and contemporary works by world-renowned photographers. (Daily; closed hols, also Mon & Tues between each exhibition) Free guided tours (wkends). 1649 El Prado, Casa de Balboa. Phone 619/238-7559. ¢¢ In same building is

Natural History Museum. Exhibits of flora and fauna and minerology of southwestern US and Baja California; seismograph, Foucault pendulum; traveling exhibits; classes, nature outings. (Daily; closed Jan 1, Thanksgiving, Dec 25) Eastern end of Balboa Park near intersection of Park Blvd and Village Place. Phone 619/232-3821. ¢¢-¢¢¢

Old Globe Theatre. One of 3 unique theaters of the Simon Edison Centre for the Performing Arts; productions staged include classical and contemporary comedy and drama of diverse styles in the 581-seat Old Globe Theatre, the 225-seat Cassius Carter Centre Stage and the 612-seat outdoor Lowell Davies Festival Theater. Performances (nightly exc Mon, also Sat & Sun matinees). For information on schedules and ticket prices contact Old Globe Theatre, PO Box 122171, 92112; phone 619/239-2255. ¢¢¢¢¢

Reuben H. Fleet Science Center and Space Theater. Space Theater features Omnimax theater with large-format, educational science films and multimedia shows. Science Center is a museum of natural phenomena; more than 50 permanent exhibits engage the visitor in active exploration. Admission includes participatory exhibits in Science Center. (Daily) On Park Blvd at Bay Theater Way. Phone 619/238-1233. ¢¢¢

San Diego Aerospace Museum. Aerospace Historical Center. Full-scale original and reproduction aircraft; moon rock exhibit. (Daily; closed Jan 1, Thanksgiving, Dec 25) 2001 Pan American Plaza, in Balboa Park. Phone 619/234-8291. ¢¢ Admission includes

San Diego Hall of Champions Sports Museum. Exhibits on more than 40 sports in the area; theater; gift shop; Breitbard Hall of Fame and San Diego sports archives. (Daily; closed Jan 1, Thanksgiving, Dec 25) 2131 Pan American Plaza. Phone 619/234-2544. ¢¢

San Diego Museum of Art. European and American paintings and decorative arts; Japanese, Chinese and other Oriental art, contemporary sculpture. (Daily exc Mon; closed Jan 1, Thanksgiving, Dec 25) Free admission 3rd Tues of month. 1450 El Prado in Balboa Park at the Plaza de Panama. Phone 619/232-7931. ¢¢¢

San Diego Zoo. More than 3,200 rare and exotic animals representing 800 species, many of which are displayed in natural habitats such as Polar Bear Plunge, Hippo Beach, Tiger River, Sun Bear Forest and Gorilla Tropics. **Children's Zoo** features petting paddock, animal nursery, animal exhibits at children's eye level. Walk-through aviaries. Animal shows daily; 40-min guided tour aboard double-deck bus; Skyfari aerial tramway. (Daily) In Balboa Park off Park Blvd. Phone 619/231-1515 or 619/234-3153. ¢¢¢¢¢

N off Laurel St (El Prado), on Village Place is

Spanish Village Arts and Crafts Center. Artists and craftspeople work here with amateur critics observing. Studios surrounding patios (daily; closed Jan 1, Thanksgiving, Dec 25) 1770 Village Place in Balboa Park, 92101-4792Phone 619/233-9050. **Free**

Spreckels Outdoor Organ Pavilion. One of the largest in the world; 4,400 pipes. (Concerts: Sun, hols; also Tues-Thurs in July-Aug) **Free**

On Laurel St (El Prado) are

Starlight Bowl. Setting for musical, dance and theater events.

Timken Museum of Art. Collection of European Old Masters, 18th- and 19th-century American paintings and Russian icons. Docent tours (Tues-Thurs or by appt). (Tues-Sat, also Sun afternoons; closed major hols, also Sept) 1500 El Prado. Phone 619/239-5548. **Free**

Recreational facilities in the park include

Golf. Municipal courses. 18- & 9-hole courses; pro shop, restaurant, driving range, 3 putting greens; rental carts. (Daily) Near 26th & A Sts.

Cabrillo National Monument. Commemorates arrival on what is now the west coast of the US by explorer-navigator Juan Rodriguez Cabrillo. From the most southwesterly point in the continental US, the view stretches north to La Jolla, west to the Pacific, south to Mexico, east into San Diego County. The old lighthouse (1855) is a feature of the monument and vantage point for observing annual migration of gray whales (Dec-mid-Mar). Visitor center and museum; slide and film programs. (Daily) 10 mi W of I-8 on Catalina Blvd (CA 209), at tip of Point Loma. Phone 619/557-5450. (See ANNUAL EVENTS) Per vehicle ¢¢

Gaslamp Quarter. A 16½-block national historic district bordered by Broadway on the north, 6th Ave on the east, Harbor Drive on the south and 4th Ave on the west. This area formed the city's business center at the turn of the century. Many Victorian buildings under restoration. Walking tours (Sat). Downtown. Contact Gaslamp Quarter Association at 619/233-5227. Walking tours ¢¢

Maritime Museum Association. Restored bark *Star of India* (1863) built at Ramsey on the Isle of Man and launched as the *Euterpe;* sailed under the British, Hawaiian (before it was part of the US) and United States flags. It sailed for the first time in 50 yrs on July 4, 1976. Also here are the steam ferry *Berkeley* (1898), with nautical exhibits and the luxury steam yacht *Medea* (1904). (Daily) 1306 N Harbor Dr (Embarcadero). Phone 619/234-9153. ¢¢¢

Mission Basilica San Diego de Alcala. (1769). First California mission. Restored, still used for services. Museum has relics of early days of mission; audio tours include mission and grounds. (Daily; closed Thanksgiving, Dec 25) 10818 San Diego Mission Rd. Phone 619/281-8449. Museum ¢

Mission Bay Park. Aquatic park on 4,600 acres. Swimming, lifeguards (summer, daily), waterskiing in Fiesta and Sail bays; fishing; boating, sailing (rentals, ramps, landings, marinas); sportfishing fleet. Golf. Picnicking. Camping. (Daily) N of San Diego River, reached via I-5. For details, res and regulations, send self-addressed, stamped envelope to Visitor Information Center, 2688 E Mission Bay Dr, 92109; phone 619/221-8901 also 619/276-8200 for Visitor Information Center. **Free** In park is

Sea World. This 150-acre marine park on Mission Bay features several shows and more than 20 exhibits and attractions. Special Shamu show. (Daily) Sea World Dr, exit W off I-5. Phone 619/226-3901 or 800/325-3150 (CA), 800/SEA-WRLD (exc CA). ¢¢¢¢¢

Museum of Contemporary Art, San Diego. Permanent and changing exhibits of contemporary painting, sculpture, design, photography and architecture. Bookstore. (Daily exc Mon; closed Jan 1, Thanksgiving, Dec 25) 1001 Kettner Blvd. Phone 619/234-1001. ¢¢

Naval ship tour. The public is invited to tour a ship as guests of the Commanding Officer. (Sat & Sun, when ships are in port) (May be temporarily closed when military deems security measures are necessary.) Broadway Pier, Broadway & Harbor Dr. For availability contact the Naval Base Public Affairs Office, phone 619/532-1430. **Free**

Old Town. Historic section of city with many restored or reconstructed buildings; old adobe structures, restaurants, shops. Guided walking tours (daily). Around the plaza at Mason St & San Diego Ave. Old Town includes Old Town San Diego State Historic Park and

Junipero Serra Museum. Landmark of San Diego; the museum stands on top of the hill recognized as the site where California's first mission and presidio were established in 1769. The museum interprets the Spanish and Mexican periods of San Diego's history. (Daily exc Mon; closed major hols) In Presidio Park. Phone 619/297-3258. ¢¢

Presidio Park. Site of the first mission in California. Mounds mark the original Presidio and fort. Presidio Dr off Taylor St. Inside is

Whaley House (1856). Once housed "The Tanner Troupe" theater company, and later served as the San Diego County Courthouse until the records were transferred to "New Town" on Mar 31, 1871. Restored and refurnished; on grounds are replica of Old Town drugstore; herb and rose gardens. (Daily; closed major hols) 2482 San Diego Ave, at Harney St. Phone 619/298-2482. ¢¢

Old Town San Diego State Historic Park. This is an area within Old Town that is bounded by Congress, Wallace, Twigg & Juan Sts. Visitor center, 4002 Wallace St (daily; closed Jan 1, Thanksgiving, Dec 25). Use Hwy 5 & Hwy 8. Park off Pacific Hwy between Taylor and Twig Sts. Phone 619/220-5422. **Free** Includes

Casa de Estudillo (1820-1829). Restored example of one-story adobe town house; period furnishings. (Daily; closed Jan 1, Thanksgiving, Dec 25) 40001 Mason St.

San Diego *Union* Historical Restoration. Restored birthplace of the San Diego newspaper that first came off the press in 1868. (Daily exc Mon; closed Jan 1, Thanksgiving, Dec 25) 2626 San Diego Ave. **Free**

Seeley Stable. Restoration of stables built in 1869 to serve US mail stage line; display of horse-drawn vehicles, historic Western artifacts. (Daily; closed Jan 1, Thanksgiving, Dec 25) Calhoun St. ¢

Professional Sports.

National League baseball (San Diego Padres). Qualcomm Stadium, 9449 Friars Rd. Phone 619/881-6500. Web www.padres.com.

NFL (San Diego Chargers). Qualcomm Stadium, 9449 Friars Rd. Phone 619/874-4500.

San Diego Bay and the Embarcadero. Port for active Navy ships, cruise ships, commercial shipping and tuna fleet. Sailing, powerboating, waterskiing and sportfishing at Shelter Island, Harbor Island, the Yacht Harbor and America's Cup Harbor.

San Diego Wild Animal Park. Operated by the Zoological Society of San Diego as a preservation area for endangered species. More than 2,400 African & Asian animals roam freely on the 2,100-acre preserve; 5-mi guided Wgasa Bush Line monorail tour; Africa-inspired Nairobi Village featuring animal shows, hiking trail, animal and botanical exhibits. (Daily) 30 mi NE via I-15 to Via Rancho Pkwy exit, follow signs, in Escondido (see). Phone 619/234-6541 or 760/796-5621 for upcoming events. ¢¢¢¢¢

Seaport Village. A 14-acre shopping, dining and entertainment complex on San Diego Bay. Includes 75 specialty shops and restaurants; restored 1890 Looff Carousel; horse-drawn carriage rides; ¼-mi boardwalk along the waterfront. (Daily) Market St at Kettner Blvd, adj to Embarcadero Marina Park. Phone 619/235-4014.

Sightseeing.

Corporate Helicopters of San Diego. Sky tours offer views of city's attractions and natural beauty. For tours, fees and schedules, phone 619/291-4356.

Gray Line bus tours. Contact 1775 Hancock, Ste 130, 92110; phone 619/491-0011 or 800/331-5077 (exc CA).

San Diego-Coronado Ferry. Hourly departures from Broadway Pier to Ferry Landing Marketplace in Coronado. (Daily)Phone 619/234-4111. ¢¢

San Diego Harbor Excursion. One-hr (12-mi) narrated tour highlights Harbor Island, Coronado and the Navy Terminals at North Island and 32nd St. Two-hr (25-mi) narrated tour includes the above plus Shelter Island, Ballast Point (where Cabrillo is believed to have first landed in 1542), the harbor entrance, the ship yards and the Navy's submarine base. (Daily) 1050 N Harbor Dr. Phone 619/234-4111. One-hr tour ¢¢¢; Two-hr tour ¢¢¢¢

San Diego Scenic Tours. Narrated bus and harbor tours. Choose from 4-hr San Diego City Tour, City & Harbor Tour, San Diego-LaJolla Tour, Tijuana Tour. Also Full-Day Tijuana Tour, and the ultimate full-day San Diego, Harbor & Tijuana Tour or Tijuana-San Diego-LaJolla Tour. (Daily) For res and to arrange hotel pickup, phone 619/273-8687. ¢¢¢¢¢

San Diego Trolley. The 15-mi South Line takes visitors to the United States/Mexico border; 17-mi East Line takes visitors to El Cajon. Lines merge at the Imperial & 12th Transfer Center. Departures every 15 min from Santa Fe Depot at Kettner Blvd & C St; tickets also avail at 5th & Broadway. (Daily)Phone 619/233-3004 or 619/685-4900. ¢-¢¢

Scenic drive. Many of the attractions noted above may be seen on a 59-mi loop marked by blue and yellow seagull signs. The drive takes 2½-3 hrs, includes waterfront, Shelter Island, Cabrillo National Monument, Point Loma, Old Town, and the top of Mt Soledad, which has a magnificent view of entire area.

Southwest Coaches. 1601 Newton Ave, 92113.

Villa Montezuma/Jesse Shepard House (1887). Lavish Victorian mansion built for Jesse Shepard, musician and author, during the city's "Great Boom" (1886-1888). More than 20 stained glass windows reflect Shepard's interest in art, music and literature; includes restored kitchen, antiques. Guided tours (Sat & Sun afternoons, last tour leaves at 3:45 pm; at 20th and K Sts) Phone 619/239-2211. ¢¢

Whale-watching trips. For 3 months each yr (mid-Dec-mid-Feb), California gray whales make their way from Alaska's Bering Sea to the warm bays and lagoons of Baja, passing only a mile or so off the San Diego shoreline. As many as 200 whales a day have been counted during the peak of the migration period. Trips to local waters and Baja lagoons are scheduled by the San Diego Natural History Museum, PO Box 1390, 92112; phone 619/232-3821, ext 203. For information on other whale-watching trips, inquire at local sport fishing companies or at the International Visitors Information Center; 619/236-1212. ¢¢¢¢¢

Annual Events

Corpus Christi Fiesta. Mission San Antonio de Pala. 41 mi N via CA 163, I-15, then 7 mi E on CA 76. Open-air mass, procession; games, dances, entertainment; Spanish-style pit barbecue; held annually since 1816. 1st Sun June.

Festival of Bells. Mission Basilica San Diego de Alcala. Commemorates July 16, 1769 founding of mission. Phone 619/281-8449. Wkend mid-July.

Admission Day. Commemoration of California's entry into United States. Mariachi bands, singers, dancers, food. Phone 619/297-1183. Early Sept.

Cabrillo Festival. Cabrillo National Monument. Celebration of discovery of the west coast. Phone 619/557-5450. Last wkend Sept-early Oct.

Christmas on the Prado. Spreckels Outdoor Organ Pavilion and throughout Balboa Park. Fifty-ft-tall lighted tree, Nativity scenes; special programs. First wkend Dec.

Christmas-Light Boat Parade. San Diego Harbor, Shelter Island Yacht Basin. Mid-late Dec.

Additional Visitor Information

The San Diego Convention & Visitors Bureau, International Visitor Information Center, 401 B St, Ste 1400, 92101, phone 619/236-1212, offers general information brochures in English, French, German, Japanese, Portuguese and Spanish. *San Diego Magazine* may be obtained at newsstands and has up-to-date information on cultural events and articles of interest to visitors.

Note: For towns in the San Diego area see map. These towns and their accommodations are listed alphabetically.

City Neighborhoods

Many of the restaurants, unrated dining establishments and some lodgings listed under San Diego include neighborhoods as well as exact street addresses. Geographic descriptions of these areas are given.

Balboa Park. Northeast of downtown; south of Upas St, west of 28th St, north of St Russ Blvd and east of 6th Ave.

Downtown. South and west of I-5 and north and east of the San Diego Bay. **North of Downtown:** North of US 5.

Mission Bay. South of Garnet Ave, west of I-5, north of I-8 and Mission Bay Channel and east of the Pacific Ocean.

Old Town. South of I-8, west of CA 163, north of I-5 and Washington St and east of I-5.

Point Loma. Peninsula west of San Diego Bay and east of the Pacific Ocean.

Motels

★★★ **BALBOA PARK INN.** *3402 Park Blvd (92103), adj to Balboa Park. 619/298-0823; FAX 619/294-8070; res: 800/938-8181.* Web www.balboaparkinn.com. 26 rms, 2 story, 17 kit. suites. S, D $80; kit. suites $99-$200; under 11 free. Crib $5. TV; cable (premium). Complimentary continental bkfst. Complimentary coffee in rms. Ck-out noon. Free guest lndry. Refrigerators; some in-rm whirlpools, microwaves. Many patios, balconies. Sun deck. Each rm has a distinctly different "theme; and decor. Cr cds: A, C, D, DS, MC, V.

★★ **BEST WESTERN ISLAND PALMS.** *2051 Shelter Island Dr (92106), in Point Loma. 619/222-0561; FAX 619/222-9760; res: 800/922-2336.* E-mail res@islandpalms.com; web www.islandpalms.com. 97 rms, 80 with shower only, 2 story, 29 kit. units. S, D $129-$169; each addl $10; kits. $209-$269; under 18 free; wkly rates. Crib free. TV; cable (premium). Pool; whirlpool, poolside serv. Complimentary coffee in rms. Restaurant 6:30 am-10 pm. Bar 10:30 am-midnight; Fri, Sat to 2 am. Ck-

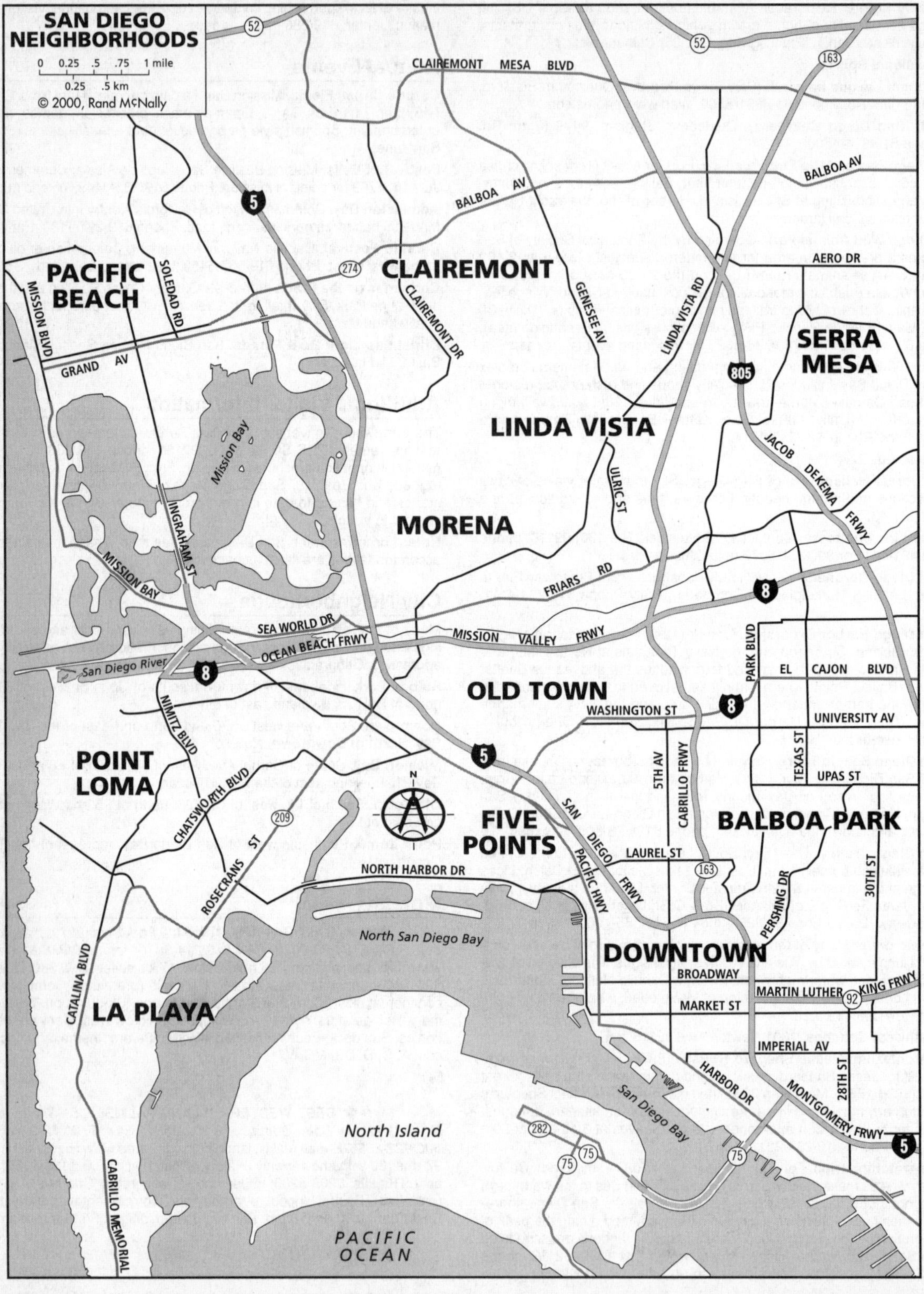
SAN DIEGO NEIGHBORHOODS
0 0.25 .5 .75 1 mile
0.25 .5 km
© 2000, Rand McNally
CLAIREMONT MESA BLVD
BALBOA AV
BALBOA AV
AERO DR
PACIFIC BEACH
CLAIREMONT
SERRA MESA
MISSION BLVD
SOLEDAD RD
CLAIREMONT DR
GENESEE AV
LINDA VISTA RD
GRAND AV
LINDA VISTA
Mission Bay
JACOB DEKEMA FRWY
ULRIC ST
INGRAHAM ST
MORENA
MISSION BAY
FRIARS RD
SEA WORLD DR
MISSION VALLEY FRWY
OCEAN BEACH FRWY
San Diego River
PARK BLVD
EL CAJON BLVD
OLD TOWN
NIMITZ BLVD
WASHINGTON ST
UNIVERSITY AV
POINT LOMA
5TH AV
CABRILLO FRWY
TEXAS ST
UPAS ST
CHATSWORTH BLVD
N
FIVE POINTS
BALBOA PARK
SAN DIEGO FRWY
PACIFIC HWY
ROSECRANS ST
LAUREL ST
NORTH HARBOR DR
PERSHING DR
30TH ST
North San Diego Bay
DOWNTOWN
BROADWAY
MARTIN LUTHER KING FRWY
MARKET ST
CATALINA BLVD
LA PLAYA
IMPERIAL AV
HARBOR DR
28TH ST
MONTGOMERY FRWY
San Diego Bay
North Island
CABRILLO MEMORIAL
PACIFIC OCEAN
52
52
163
5
274
805
8
8
8
5
209
163
92
282
75
75
75
5

out noon. Coin Indry. Meeting rms. Business servs avail. In-rm modem link. Valet serv. Exercise equipt. Refrigerators; microwaves avail. Many balconies. On bay. Near airport. Cr cds: A, C, D, DS, MC, V.

D SC

✓★★ **BEST WESTERN SEVEN SEAS LODGE.** *411 Hotel Cir S (92108), north of downtown. 619/291-1300; FAX 619/291-6933; res: 800/328-1618.* 307 rms, 2 story, 9 kit. units. S, D $69-$129; under 18 free. Crib free. TV; cable (premium). Heated pool; whirlpool, poolside serv. Playground. Complimentary coffee in rms. Restaurant 6 am-10 pm. Rm serv. Bar noon-2 am. Ck-out noon. Coin Indry. Meeting rms. In-rm modem link. Bellhops. Valet serv. Free airport, RR station, bus depot transportation. Some refrigerators; microwaves avail. Some balconies. Cr cds: A, C, D, DS, JCB, MC, V.

D SC

★★ **COMFORT INN & SUITES.** *2485 Hotel Circle Pl (92108), north of downtown. 619/291-7700; FAX 619/297-6179; res: 800/511-3537; res: 800/274-7127.* 200 rms, 4 story. July-early Sept: S, D $89-$109; suites $99-$139; under 18 free; lower rates rest of yr. Crib free. TV; cable (premium). Heated pool; whirlpool. Complimentary continental bkfst. Complimentary coffee in rms. Restaurant nearby. Ck-out noon. Coin Indry. Business servs avail. In-rm modem link. Free covered parking. Exercise equipt. Some refrigerators, in-rm whirlpools; microwaves avail. Cr cds: A, C, D, DS, MC, V.

D SC

★★ **DANA INN & MARINA.** *1710 W Mission Bay Dr (92109), in Mission Bay. 619/222-6440; FAX 619/222-5916; res: 800/445-3339.* E-mail wkblum@danainn.com; web www.danainn.com. 196 rms, 2 story. S, D $95-$149; each addl $10; under 18 free. Crib free. TV; cable (premium). Heated pool; whirlpool, poolside serv. Coffee in rms. Restaurant 7 am-10 pm. Rm serv. Bar. Ck-out noon. Coin Indry. Business servs avail. Bellhops. Valet serv. Free airport, RR station, bus depot transportation. Tennis. Marina. Boat launch adj. Cr cds: A, C, D, DS, MC, V.

SC

✓★★ **DAYS INN.** *543 Hotel Cir S (92108), in Old Town. 619/297-8800; FAX 619/298-6029; res: 800/345-9995.* E-mail sales@daysinnhc.com; web www.daysinnhc.com. 280 rms, 3 story, 49 kit. units. S, D $75-$149; kit. units $85-$109; under 18 free; wkly rates; higher rates wkends, special events. Crib free. TV; cable (premium). Heated pool; whirlpool. Coffee in rms. Restaurant 6:30 am-9 pm. Ck-out noon. Coin Indry. Business servs avail. Bellhops. Valet serv. Sundries. Barber, beauty shop. Health club privileges. Free airport, RR station, bus depot transportation. Refrigerators; microwaves avail. Cr cds: A, C, D, DS, JCB, MC, V.

D SC

✓★ **GOOD NITE INN.** *4545 Waring Rd (92120), NE of downtown. 619/286-7000; FAX 619/286-8403; res: 800/648-3466.* Web www.good-nite.com. 94 rms, 2 story. S, D $39-$55; each addl $6; under 18 free. Crib free. Pet accepted. TV; cable (premium). Heated pool. Restaurant adj 10 am-9 pm; Sat-Sun from 7 am. Ck-out 11 am. Coin Indry. Meeting rm. Refrigerators, microwaves avail. Private patios, balconies. Cr cds: A, C, D, DS, JCB, MC, V.

D SC

★★ **HAMPTON INN KEARNY MESA.** *5434 Kearny Mesa Rd (92111), north of downtown. 858/292-1482; FAX 858/292-4410; res: 800/292-1482.* Web www.hampton-inn.com. 150 rms, 5 story. June-Aug: S, D $84-$99; under 18 free; lower rates rest of yr. Crib free. TV; cable (premium). Heated pool. Complimentary continental bkfst. Coffee in rms. Restaurant adj 7 am-11 pm. Ck-out 11 am. Coin Indry. Meeting rms. Business servs avail. In-rm modem link. Valet serv. Health club privileges. Some refrigerators; microwaves avail. Cr cds: A, C, D, DS, MC, V.

D SC

★★★ **HUMPHREY'S HALF MOON INN.** *2303 Shelter Island Dr (92106), in Point Loma. 619/224-3411; FAX 619/224-3478; res: 800/345-9995.* E-mail sdavies@halfmooninn.com; web www.halfmooninn.com. 182 rms, 2 story, 30 kit. units. Late May-early Sept: S $139-$189; D $149-$199; each addl $10; kit. suites $219-$299; under 18 free; lower rates rest of yr. Crib free. TV; cable (premium), VCR avail. Heated pool; whirlpool, poolside serv. Complimentary coffee in rms. Restaurant 6:30 am-10 pm. Rm serv. Bar 11-2 am; entertainment. Ck-out noon. Coin Indry. Meeting rms. Business servs avail. In-rm modem link. Bellhops. Concierge. Sundries. Free airport, RR station transportation. Bicycles. Health club privileges. Lawn games. Refrigerators. Many private patios, balconies. South Sea island decor. Gardens. Cr cds: A, C, D, DS, MC, V.

D SC

★★ **LA QUINTA INN.** *10185 Paseo Montril (92129), north of downtown. 858/484-8800; FAX 858/538-0476; res: 800/687-6667; res: 800/531-5900.* 120 rms, 4 story. S, D $58-$69; each addl $8; under 18 free. Crib free. Pet accepted. TV; cable (premium). Heated pool. Complimentary continental bkfst. Complimentary coffee in rms. Restaurant adj 6 am-midnight. Ck-out noon. In-rm modem link. Cr cds: A, C, D, DS, MC, V.

D SC

★ **OLD TOWN INN.** *4444 Pacific Hwy (92110), near Lindbergh Field Intl Airport, north of downtown. 619/260-8024; FAX 619/296-0524; res: 800/643-3025.* 84 rms, 41 with shower only, 1-3 story. June-Sept: S, D $39-$62; each addl $5; suites $111; kit units $62-$77; under 12 free; wkly rates; higher rates hols (3-day min); lower rates rest of yr. Crib $5. Pet accepted; $5. TV; cable (premium). Complimentary continental bkfst. Restaurant nearby. Ck-out 11 am. Coin Indry. Refrigerators avail. Cr cds: A, C, D, DS, JCB, MC, V.

D SC

★ **RAMADA LIMITED.** *641 Camino Del Rio S (92108), north of downtown. 619/295-6886; FAX 619/296-9661; res: 800/624-1257.* 170 rms, 3 story, 58 kit. suites. May-Sept: S $89; D $109; each addl $10; kit. suites $99-$129; under 18 free; higher rates special events; lower rates rest of yr. Crib free. TV; cable (premium), VCR avail (movies). Complimentary continental bkfst. Complimentary coffee in rms. Restaurant nearby. Ck-out 11 am. Meeting rms. Business servs avail. In-rm modem link. Sundries. Coin Indry. Free airport, RR station, bus depot transportation. Health club privileges. Many refrigerators; microwave, minibar in kit. suites. Cr cds: A, C, D, DS, ER, JCB, MC, V.

D SC

★ **TRAVELODGE.** *1201 Hotel Cir S (93420), north of downtown. 619/297-2271; FAX 619/542-1510.* 101 rms, 2 story. June-Sept: S $69; D $79; each addl $10; under 18 free; higher rates special events; lower rates rest of yr. Crib free. TV; cable (premium), VCR avail (movies). Complimentary coffee in rms. Restaurant 6:30 am-11 pm, Sun 7 am-1 pm. Ck-out noon. Business servs avail. In-rm modem link. Health club privileges. Pool. Cr cds: A, C, D, DS, MC, V.

D SC

✓★★ **TRAVELODGE.** *16929 W Bernardo Dr (92127), north of downtown. 619/487-0445; FAX 619/673-2062; res: 800/578-7878.* 49 rms, 2 story. Mid-May-mid-Sept: S, D $59-$75; each addl $7; under 16 free; lower rates rest of yr. Crib free. TV; cable (premium). Complimentary continental bkfst. Complimentary coffee in rms. Restaurant nearby. Ck-out 11 am. Pool. Refrigerators, microwaves avail. Cr cds: A, C, D, DS, JCB, MC, V.

D SC

✓★ **VAGABOND INN.** *625 Hotel Cir S (92108), north of downtown. 619/297-1691; FAX 619/692-9009; res: 800/522-1555.* 88 rms, 2 story. Mid-May-mid-Sept: S, D $65-$100; each addl $5; under 18 free; lower rates rest of yr. Crib free. Pet accepted; $10. TV; cable (premium). 2 heated pools; whirlpool. Complimentary continental bkfst. Restaurant adj open 24 hrs. Ck-out noon. Business servs avail. In-rm modem link. Cr cds: A, C, D, DS, MC, V.

SC

Motor Hotels

★★★ **BAY CLUB HOTEL AND MARINA.** *2131 Shelter Island Dr (92106), in Point Loma. 619/224-8888; FAX 619/225-1604; res: 800/672-0800.* Web www.bayclubhotel.com. 105 rms, 2 story. S $119-$189; D $129-$199; each addl $10; suites $199-$299; under 12 free; package plans. Crib $10. TV; cable (premium), VCR avail. Heated pool; whirlpool, poolside serv. Complimentary full bkfst. Coffee in rms. Restaurant 6:30 am-10 pm. Rm serv. Bar 10 am-midnight. Ck-out noon. Meeting rms. Business servs avail. Bellhops. Valet serv. Concierge. Sundries. Covered parking. Free airport, RR station, bus depot transportation. Exercise equipt. Refrigerators; microwaves avail. Private patios, balconies. On bay; marina. Fishing from nearby pier. Cr cds: A, C, D, DS, ER, JCB, MC, V.

D SC

★★★ **BEST WESTERN HACIENDA HOTEL.** *4041 Harney St (92110), in Old Town. 619/298-4707; FAX 619/298-4771; res: 800/528-1234; res: 800/888-1991.* Web www.haciendahotel-oldtown.com. 169 suites, 2-3 story. June-Aug: S, D $135-$150; each addl $10; under 16 free; lower rates rest of yr. Crib free. TV; cable, VCR (movies). Heated pool; whirlpool, poolside serv. Complimentary coffee in rms. Restaurants 6:30 am-10 pm. Rm serv. Bar 11 am-midnight. Ck-out noon. Meeting rms. Business servs avail. Bellhops. Valet serv. Concierge. Covered parking. Free airport, RR station, bus depot transportation. Exercise equipt. Refrigerators, microwaves. Some private patios, balconies. Grills. Spanish architecture. Cr cds: A, C, D, DS, JCB, MC, V.

D SC

★★ **DOUBLETREE CLUB HOTEL.** *11611 Bernardo Plz Ct (92128), north of downtown. 858/485-9250; FAX 858/451-7948; res: 800/528-0444.* 209 rms, 4 story. S, D $200-$280; each addl $10; suites $400; under 10 free; wkend rates. Crib free. TV; cable. Heated pool; whirlpool. Restaurant 6-9 am, 5-10 pm; Sat, Sun from 7 am. Rm serv. Bar from 5 pm. Ck-out 1 pm. Meeting rms. Business servs avail. In-rm modem link. Exercise equipt. Microwaves avail. Cr cds: A, C, D, DS, ER, JCB, MC, V.

D SC

★★★ **HANDLERY HOTEL RESORT.** *950 Hotel Circle N (92128), I-8 Hotel Circle exit, north of downtown. 619/298-0511; FAX 619/298-9793; res: 800/676-6567; res: 800/843-4343.* E-mail sales@handlery.com; web www.handerly.com. 217 rms, 2 story. S, D $109-$139; each addl $10; suites $175-$250; under 14 free. Crib free. Pet accepted, some restrictions, $25. TV; cable. 3 pools (1 lap pool); whirlpool, poolside serv. Coffee in rms. Restaurant 6:30 am-10 pm. Rm serv 7 am-9 pm. Bars 11-2 am. Ck-out noon. Lndry facilities. Meeting rms. Business center. In-rm modem link. Bellhops. Valet serv. Sundries. Gift shop. Barber, beauty shop. Tennis, pro. Exercise rm. Massage. Some balconies. Cr cds: A, C, D, DS, JCB, MC, V.

D SC

✓★★ **HOLIDAY INN.** *4875 N Harbor Dr (92106), near Lindbergh Field Intl Airport, north of downtown. 619/224-3621; FAX 619/224-3629; res: 800/662-8899.* Web www.bartellhotels. com/holinnbayside. 237 rms, 2-5 story. S, D $109-$149; each addl $10; suites $179-$219; under 18 free. Crib free. TV; cable (premium). Heated pool. Complimentary coffee in rms. Restaurant adj 6 am-10 pm. Bar 2 pm-2 am. Ck-out noon. Coin lndry. Meeting rms. Business center. In-rm modem link. Bellhops. Valet serv. Sundries. Free airport, RR station, bus depot transportation. Exercise equipt. Putting green. Lawn games. Refrigerators. Some private patios, balconies. Opp marina. Cr cds: A, C, D, DS, JCB, MC, V.

D SC

★★ **HOLIDAY INN MISSION VALLEY STADIUM NORTH.** *3805 Murphy Canyon Rd (92123), north of downtown. 619/277-1199; FAX 619/277-3442; res: 800/465-4329; res: 800/666-6676.* E-mail sandyt@inetworld.net; web www.holidayinnsandiego.com. 174 rms, 4 story, 19 suites. S, D $89-$129; each addl $10; suites $119-$149; under 18 free. Crib free. TV; cable (premium). Pool; whirlpool. Coffee in rms. Restaurant 6:30 am-2 pm, 5-10 pm. Rm serv. Bar. Ck-out noon. Coin lndry. Meeting rms. Business servs avail. In-rm modem link. Free garage parking. Exercise equipt. Refrigerators; microwaves avail. Wet bar in suites. Most suites with balcony. Cr cds: A, C, D, DS, ER, JCB, MC, V.

D SC

★★★ **HOLIDAY INN RANCHO.** *17065 W Bernardo Dr (92127), north of downtown. 619/485-6530; FAX 619/485-7819; res: 800/465-4329; res: 800/777-0020.* 179 rms, 2-3 story, 16 kits. S, D $99-$119; each addl $10; suites $119-$179; under 19 free. Crib free. TV; cable (premium). Heated pool; whirlpool. Complimentary full bkfst. Coffee in rms. Restaurant opp 11 am-midnight. Rm serv. Ck-out noon. Coin lndry. Meeting rms. Business servs avail. In-rm modem link. Some covered parking. Exercise equipt; sauna. Health club privileges. Some refrigerators, in-rm whirlpools; microwaves avail. Many private patios, balconies. Cr cds: A, C, D, DS, JCB, MC, V.

D SC

★★ **QUALITY RESORT.** *875 Hotel Circle S (92108), north of downtown. 619/298-8282; FAX 619/295-5610; res: 800/362-7871.* E-mail qualrst@adnc.com; web www.qualityresort.com. 202 rms, 2 story. June-Aug: S, D $109-$129; suites $139-$169; under 18 free; lower rates rest of yr. Crib free. TV; cable. Pool; poolside serv. Coffee in rms. Restaurant adj open 24 hrs. Bar 11 am-11 pm. Ck-out noon. Meeting rms. In-rm modem link. Beauty shop. Valet serv. Coin lndry. Lighted tennis. Exercise equipt; sauna. Massage. Lawn games. Microwave in suites. Some balconies. Cr cds: A, C, D, DS, MC, V.

D SC

★★ **QUALITY SUITES.** *9880 Mira Mesa Blvd (92131), at jct I-15, north of downtown. 619/530-2000; FAX 619/530-0202; res: 800/822-6692.* 132 suites, 4 story. Early June-mid-Sept: suites $105-$199; each addl $10; under 18 free; lower rates rest of yr. Crib free. TV; cable (premium), VCR. Heated pool. Complimentary continental bkfst. Coffee in rms. Ck-out noon. Meeting rms. Business servs avail. In-rm modem link. Health club privileges. Microwaves. Cr cds: A, C, D, DS, JCB, MC, V.

D SC

★ **RAMADA INN.** *5550 Kearny Mesa Rd (92111), north of downtown. 619/278-0800; FAX 619/277-6585; res: 800/272-6232; res: 800/447-2637.* 150 rms, 2 story. June-Sept: S $79; D $129; each addl $10; suites $99-$159; under 17 free; lower rates rest of yr. Crib free. Pet accepted; $75. TV; cable. Complimentary continental bkfst. Complimentary coffee in rms. Restaurant 6-2 am. Rm serv. Bar; entertainment Sat. Ck-out noon. Meeting rms. Business servs avail. Valet serv. Coin lndry. Pool; whirlpool. Refrigerators; some microwaves. Cr cds: A, C, D, DS, MC, V.

D SC

★★ **RAMADA LIMITED.** *3900 Old Town Ave (92110), in Old Town. 619/299-7400; FAX 619/299-1619; res: 800/272-6232.* 125 rms, 3 story. Mid-May-mid-Sept: S, D $99-$109; each addl $10; suites $129-$169; under 18 free; lower rates rest of yr. Crib free. TV; cable (premium). Heated pool; whirlpool. Complimentary continental bkfst. Complimentary coffee in rms. Restaurant opp 11 am-10 pm. Ck-out noon. Coin lndry. Meeting rms. Business servs avail. In-rm modem link. Covered parking. Free airport, RR station transportation. Health club privileges. Refrigerators, microwaves; some wet bars. Some balconies. Cr cds: A, C, D, DS, JCB, MC, V.

D SC

✓★★ **RAMADA PLAZA HOTEL.** *2151 S Hotel Cir (92108), north of downtown. 619/291-6500; FAX 619/294-7531; res: 800/532-4241; res: 800/405-9102.* 182 rms, 4 story. S $79-$129; D $89-$139; each addl $5; under 18 free. Crib free. TV; cable (premium). Heated pool; whirlpool. Complimentary coffee in rms. Restaurant 6:30 am-2:30 pm, 5-10 pm. Rm serv. Bar 5-11 pm. Ck-out noon. Coin lndry. Meeting rms. Business servs avail. In-rm modem link. Bellhops. Valet serv. Some covered parking. Exercise equipt. Health club privileges. Game rm. Refrigerators avail. Cr cds: A, C, D, DS, ER, JCB, MC, V.

D SC

✓★★ **RODEWAY INN.** *833 Ash St (92101), downtown. 619/239-2285; FAX 619/235-6951; res: 800/228-2000; res: 800/522-1528.* E-mail rodeway@flash.net; web www.flash.net/rodeway. 45 rms, 4 story. S, D $69-$109; each addl $5-$15; under 18 free. Crib free. TV; cable (premium). Complimentary continental bkfst. Restaurant opp 6 am-3 pm. Ck-out noon. Coin Indry. Business servs avail. In-rm modem link. Valet serv. Sauna. Whirlpool. Health club privileges. Some refrigerators; microwaves avail. Some balconies. Cr cds: A, C, D, DS, ER, JCB, MC, V.

D SC

Hotels

★★ **BEST WESTERN BAYSIDE INN.** *555 W Ash St (92101), near Lindbergh Field Intl Airport, downtown. 619/233-7500; FAX 619/239-8060; res: 800/341-1818.* E-mail tichotels@sandiego. com; web www.bay side.com. 122 rms, 14 story. July-early Sept: S, D $89-$129; each addl $10; under 12 free; lower rates rest of yr. Crib $6. TV; cable (premium). Pool; whirlpool. Complimentary continental bkfst. Complimentary coffee in rms. Restaurant adj 6 am-2 pm, 5-9 pm. Ck-out noon. Business servs avail. In-rm modem link. Free airport, RR station tranportation. Health club privileges. Cr cds: A, C, D, DS, ER, JCB, MC, V.

D SC

★★★ **CLARION HOTEL BAY VIEW.** *660 K St (92127), downtown. 619/696-0234; FAX 619/231-8199; res: 800/766-0234.* E-mail reser vations@clarionbayview.com; web www.clarionbayview. com. 312 rms, 21 story, 48 suites. Late May-early Sept: S $109-$169; D $119-$179; each addl $15; suites $159-$189; under 18 free; lower rates rest of yr. Crib free. Covered parking $9/day. TV; cable, VCR avail. Coffee in rms. Restaurant 6:30 am-10 pm. Bar 11-2 am; entertainment Fri, Sat. Ck-out noon. Coin Indry. Meeting rms. Business center. In-rm modem link. Gift shop. Exercise equipt; whirlpool. Sauna. Massage. Game rm. Some bathrm phones. Balconies. View of San Diego Bay. Cr cds: A, C, D, DS, JCB, MC, V.

D SC

★★★ **DOUBLETREE HOTEL.** *7450 Hazard Center Dr (92108), Mission Valley, north of downtown. 619/297-5466; FAX 619/297-5499; res: 800/222-8733.* Web www.doubletreehotels.com. 300 rms, 11 story. S, D $210; each addl $10; under 18 free. Crib free. Pet accepted. TV; cable. 2 pools, 1 indoor; whirlpool, poolside serv. Complimentary coffee in rms. Restaurant 6:30 am-10:30 pm. Bar 5 pm-2 am; entertainment. Ck-out noon. Convention facilities. Business servs avail. In-rm modem link. Gift shop. Garage parking; valet. Free airport, RR station, bus depot transportation. Lighted tennis. Exercise equipt; sauna. Minibars. Microwaves avail. Some bathrm phones, wet bars in suites. Some balconies. Luxury level. Cr cds: A, C, D, DS, JCB, MC, V.

D SC

★★★ **EMBASSY SUITES.** *601 Pacific Hwy (92101), near Seaport Village, west of downtown. 619/239-2400; FAX 619/239-1520; res: 800/362-2779.* E-mail es_sdb@ix.netcom.com. 337 suites, 12 story. Mid-June-mid-Sept: suites $189-$269; under 18 free; lower rates rest of yr. Crib free. Covered parking $10. TV; cable (premium). Indoor pool; whirlpool. Complimentary full bkfst. Coffee in rms. Restaurant 11 am-midnight. Bar to midnight. Ck-out noon. Coin Indry. Meeting rms. Business center. In-rm modem link. Concierge. Gift shop. Barber, beauty shop. Free airport transportation. Exercise equipt; sauna. Refrigerators, microwaves. Some balconies. Cr cds: A, C, D, DS, JCB, MC, V.

D

★★★ **HANALEI HOTEL.** *2270 Hotel Circle N (92108), downtown. 619/297-1101; FAX 619/297-6049; res: 800/882-0858.* E-mail sales@hanalei.hotel.com; web www.hanalei.com. 416 rms, 8 story. June-Sept: S, D $79-$169; suite $225-$375; under 18 free; hols (2-day min); lower rates rest of yr. Crib free. Pet accepted, some restrictions; $25 deposit. TV; cable (premium). Pool; whirlpool, poolside serv. Restaurant 6:30 am-10 pm; Sat, Sun to 11 pm. Bar. Ck-out noon. Coin Indry. Meeting rms. Business center. In-rm modem link. Concierge. Tennis privileges. Golf privileges. Exercise equipt. Health club privileges. Lawn games. Some refrigerators. Balconies. Cr cds: A, C, D, DS, ER, JCB, MC, V.

D SC

★★★ **HILTON BEACH & TENNIS RESORT.** *1775 E Mission Bay Dr (92109), in Mission Bay. 619/276-4010; FAX 619/275-7991; res: 800/345-6565.* E-mail contact@hiltonsandiego.com; web www.hilton.com. 357 rms, 8 story. S $160-$280; D $195-$300; each addl $20; suites $450-$710; family, wkend rates. Crib free. Pet accepted; $50. TV; cable (premium), VCR avail. Heated pool; wading pool, whirlpool, poolside serv. Playground. Supervised child's activities; ages 6-12. Complimentary coffee in rms. Restaurant 6:30 am-10 pm. Bar 10:30-1 am; entertainment. Ck-out noon. Coin Indry. Convention facilities. Business center. In-rm modem link. Gift shop. Beauty shop. Valet parking. Lighted tennis, pro. Putting greens. Exercise rm; sauna. Massage. Rec rm. Lawn games. Many bathrm phones, refrigerators, minibars; microwaves avail. Private patios, balconies. Dock; boats. On beach. Cr cds: A, C, D, DS, ER, JCB, MC, V.

D SC

★★ **HOLIDAY INN.** *1617 1st Ave (92101), downtown. 619/239-9600; FAX 619/233-6228; res: 800/465-4329; res: 800/366-3164.* 218 rms, 16 story. Late Mar-Sept: S $129; D $169; under 18 free; hols 2-day min; lower rates rest of yr. Crib free. Garage parking $3. TV; cable (premium). Complimentary coffee in rms. Restaurant 6 am-10 pm. Bar. Ck-out noon. Meeting rms. Business servs avail. In-rm modem link. Concierge. Coin Indry. Free airport transportation. Exercise equipt. Pool; poolside serv. Refrigerators, microwaves avail. Luxury level. Cr cds: A, C, D, DS, JCB, MC, V.

D SC

★★ **HOLIDAY INN.** *3737 Sports Arena Blvd (92110), in Point Loma. 619/226-3711; FAX 619/224-9248; res: 800/511-6909.* 316 rms, 3 story, 192 suites. May-Sept: S $109; D $149; each addl $10; suites $149-$189; under 19 free; hols 2-day min; higher rates bowl game; lower rates rest of yr. Crib free. TV; cable (premium). Complimentary coffee in rms. Restaurant adj 6 am-10 pm. Ck-out noon. Meeting rms. Business servs avail. In-rm modem link. Concierge. Gift shop. Coin Indry. Health club privileges. Heated pool; whirlpool, poolside serv. Many bathrm phones; microwaves avail; refrigerator, microwave in suites. Cr cds: A, C, D, DS, ER, JCB, MC, V.

D SC

★★ **HOLIDAY INN ON THE BAY.** *1355 N Harbor Dr (92101), downtown. 619/232-2861; FAX 619/235-4239; res: 800/877-8920.* E-mail hionthebay@aol.com; web www.hionline.com. 600 rms, 14 story. S, D $169.95-$189.95; each addl $10; suites $250-$800; under 18 free. Crib free. Pet accepted, some restrictions. Parking $12/day. TV; cable (premium). Heated pool. Coffee in rms. Restaurant 6:30 am-11 pm. Bar 11-2 am. Ck-out noon. Convention facilities. Business center. In-rm modem link. Shopping arcade. Free airport transportation. Exercise equipt. Health club privileges. Some bathrm phones; refrigerators avail. Balconies. Many bay view rms. Outside glass-enclosed elvtr. Cruise ship terminal opp. Cr cds: A, C, D, DS, JCB, MC, V.

D SC

★★★ **HORTON GRAND HOTEL.** *311 Island Ave (92101), downtown. 619/544-1886; FAX 619/239-3823; res: 800/542-1886.* 132 rms, 4 story. S, D $119-$200; each addl $20; suites $189-$259; under 12 free. Crib $20. Some covered parking, valet $10. TV; cable. Restaurant 7 am-10 pm. Tea 2:30-5:30 pm. Bar 4 pm-midnight. Ck-out noon. Meeting rms. Business servs avail. Free airport transportation. Health club privileges. Fireplaces; refrigerator, microwave in suites. Some balconies. Victorian building; built 1886. Antiques, oak staircase. Chinese Museum & Tea Room. Skylight in lobby; bird cages. Oldest building in San Diego. Cr cds: A, C, D, MC, V.

D SC

★★★ **HYATT ISLANDIA HOTEL.** *1441 Quivira Rd (92109), on Mission Bay. 619/224-1234; FAX 619/224-0348; res: 800/228-9000.* Web www.hyatt.com. 422 rms, 17 story. S, D $159-$304; suites $359-$3,300;

under 18 free. Crib free. TV; cable (premium). Heated pool; whirlpool, poolside serv. Supervised child's activities (June-Sept). Restaurant 6 am-10 pm; Fri-Sun to 11 pm. Bar 11:30-2 am; entertainment Thurs-Sat. Ck-out noon. Convention facilities. Business center. In-rm modem link. Concierge. Exercise equipt. Some refrigerators. Many private patios, balconies. Bicycle rentals. Marina; sport fishing; sailboat charters. Whale watching (Dec-Mar). Cr cds: A, C, D, DS, ER, JCB, MC, V.

D SC

★★★ **HYATT REGENCY.** *1 Market Place (92101), adj to Convention Center and Seaport Village, downtown. 619/232-1234; FAX 619/233-6464; res: 800/233-1234.* E-mail hrsandiego@lanz.com; web www.hyatt.com. 875 units, 40 story, 56 suites. S, D $265-$290; suites from $500; under 18 free. Crib free. Garage parking $12-$18. TV; cable (premium), VCR avail. Pool; whirlpool, poolside serv. Coffee in rms. Restaurants 6 am-10 pm (also see SALLY'S). Rm serv 24 hrs. Bar noon-1:30 am. Ck-out noon. Convention facilities. Business center. In-rm modem link. Concierge. Shopping arcade. 4 tennis courts. Exercise rm; sauna, steam rm. Massage. Some refrigerators, minibars. Located on San Diego Bay; panoramic view of harbor and marina. Luxury level. Cr cds: A, C, D, DS, ER, JCB, MC, V.

D SC

★ **J STREET INN.** *222 J St (92101), downtown. 619/696-6922; FAX 619/696-1295.* 221 rms, 4 story. Rm phones avail. S, D $39.95-$60; under 10 free; package plans. Parking $5. TV; cable. Complimentary coffee in rms. Restaurant nearby. Ck-out 1 pm. Exercise equipt. Refrigerators, microwaves. Balconies. Near bay, airport. Cr cds: A, C, D, DS, MC, V.

D

★★★ **MARRIOTT HOTEL & MARINA.** *333 W Harbor Dr (92101), adj to Seaport Village & Convention Center, downtown. 619/234-1500; FAX 619/234-8678; res: 800/228-9290.* Web www.sdmarriott.com. 1,355 rms, 26 story. S, D $290-$310; each addl $20; suites from $425; under 18 free. Crib free. Pet accepted, some restrictions. TV; cable (premium). Pool; whirlpool, poolside serv. Coffee in rms. Restaurant 6:30 am-11 pm. Rm serv 24 hrs. Bar 11-2 am; entertainment. Ck-out noon. Coin lndry. Meeting rms. Business center. In-rm modem link. Concierge. Shopping arcade. Barber, beauty shops. 6 lighted tennis courts, pro. Exercise rm; sauna. Game rm. Bathrm phones; some refrigerators. Some balconies. Luxurious; large chandeliers in lobby. Bayside; marina. Luxury level. Cr cds: A, C, D, DS, ER, JCB, MC, V.

D SC

★★★ **MARRIOTT SUITES DOWNTOWN.** *701 A Street (92101), downtown. 619/696-9800; FAX 619/696-1555; res: 800/228-9290; res: 800/962-1367.* E-mail sdsuites@aol.com; web www.marriott.com. 264 suites, 27 story. S, D $259-$269; under 18 free. Crib free. Pet accepted, some restrictions; $50. Garage $10, valet parking $15. TV; cable (premium). Indoor pool; whirlpool. Coffee in rms. Restaurant 6:30 am-10 pm. Bar 11:30 am-midnight. Ck-out noon. Meeting rms. In-rm modem link. Gift shop. Exercise equipt; sauna. Health club privileges. Minibars; refrigerators, microwaves avail. Cr cds: A, C, D, DS, ER, JCB, MC, V.

D SC

★★★ **MISSION VALLEY HILTON.** *901 Camino Del Rio S (92108), off I-8 Mission Center Rd exit, north of downtown. 619/543-9000; FAX 619/543-9358; res: 800/733-2332.* Web www.hilton.com. 350 rms, 14 story. S $189-$219; D $199-$229; each addl $10; suites $250-$450; under 18 free. Crib free. Pet accepted, some restrictions; $25. TV; cable (premium). Heated pool; whirlpool, poolside serv. Coffee in rms. Restaurant 6:30 am-10:30 pm. Bar 11-1 am. Ck-out noon. Convention facilities. Business center. In-rm modem link. Some covered parking. Exercise equipt; sauna. Health club privileges. Refrigerators. Large entrance foyer. Cr cds: A, C, D, DS, MC, V.

D SC

★★★ **RADISSON HOTEL.** *1433 Camino Del Rio S (92108), Mission Valley, north of downtown. 619/260-0111; FAX 619/497-0813; res: 800/333-3333.* E-mail radse@aol.com; web www.radisson.com. 260 rms, 13 story. S, D $215; each addl $15; under 18 free; wkend rates. Crib free. TV; cable, VCR avail. Heated pool; whirlpool. Restaurant 6:30 am-10 pm. Bar 4 pm-1:30 am. Ck-out noon. Convention facilities. Business servs avail. In-rm modem link. Free airport transportation. Exercise equipt. Health club privileges. Some balconies. Luxury level. Cr cds: A, C, D, DS, ER, JCB, MC, V.

D SC

★★★ **RADISSON SUITE HOTEL RANCHO BERNARDO.** *11520 W Bernardo Ct (92127), north of downtown. 619/451-6600; FAX 619/459-0253; res: 800/333-3333.* Web www.radisson.com. 176 suites, 3 story. S, D $119-$179; each addl $10; under 12 free; golf plans. Crib free. Pet accepted, some restrictions. TV; cable (premium), VCR (movies). Heated pool; whirlpool. Complimentary full bkfst. Complimentary coffee in rms. Restaurant 6-9:30 am, 5-11 pm. Bar 5-11 pm. Ck-out noon. Coin lndry. Meeting rms. Business servs avail. In-rm modem link. Tennis privileges. Golf privileges. Exercise rm. Health club privileges. Minibars, microwaves. Cr cds: A, C, D, DS, ER, JCB, MC, V.

D SC

★ **RAMADA INN & SUITES.** *830 6th Ave (92101), downtown. 619/531-8877; FAX 619/231-8307; res: 800/664-4400.* E-mail rooms@stjameshotel.com; web www.stjameshotel.com. 99 rms, 35 with shower only, 10 story. June-mid-Sept: S $119; D $139; under 18 free; some hols 2-day min; lower rates rest of yr. Crib free. Valet parking $8. TV; cable (premium). Complimentary continental bkfst. Complimentary coffee in rms. Restaurant 7 am-10 pm. Bar from 10 am. Ck-out noon. Meeting rms. Business servs avail. In-rm modem link. Concierge. Exercise equipt. Refrigerator, microwave, minibar in suites. Totally nonsmoking. Cr cds: A, C, D, DS, ER, JCB, MC, V.

SC

★★ **REGENCY PLAZA HOTEL.** *1515 Hotel Cir S (92108), north of downtown. 619/291-8790; FAX 619/260-0147; res: 800/228-8048; res: 800/619-1549.* 217 rms, 8 story, 32 suites. June-Sept: S $99; D $159; each addl $10; suites $119-$179; under 18 free; higher rates special events; lower rates rest of yr. Crib free. TV; cable (premium), VCR avail (movies). Complimentary coffee in rms. Restaurant 7 am-2 pm, 5-10 pm; Fri, Sat to 11 pm. Bar. Ck-out noon. Meeting rms. Business servs avail. In-rm modem link. Concierge. Gift shop. Coin lndry. Lighted tennis privileges, pro. 48-hole golf privileges. Exercise equipt. Health club privileges. Pool; whirlpool, poolside serv. Game rm. Bathrm phones, refrigerators; microwave, wet bar in suites. Balconies. Cr cds: A, C, D, DS, JCB, MC, V.

D SC

★★★ **SHELTER POINTE HOTEL & MARINA.** *1551 Shelter Island Dr (92106), in Point Loma. 619/221-8000; FAX 619/221-5953; res: 800/566-2524.* 211 rms, 3 story, 32 suites, 5 kit. units. May-Sept: S $165; D $185; each addl $20; suites $195-$225; kit. units $450; under 12 free; hols 3-day min; higher rates bowl games; lower rates rest of yr. Crib free. TV; cable (premium). Complimentary coffee in rms. Restaurant (see EL EMBARCADERO). Bar 11 am-11 pm. Ck-out noon. Meeting rms. Business servs avail. In-rm modem link. Concierge. Gift shop. Coin lndry. Free airport transportation. Lighted tennis, pro. Exercise rm; sauna. Massage. Pools; whirlpools, poolside serv. Playground. Supervised child's activities (May-Sept); from age 5. Some microwaves, wet bars; refrigerator in suites. Balconies. Picnic tables, grills. On ocean. Cr cds: A, C, D, DS, MC, V.

D SC

★★★★ **SHERATON MARINA.** *1380 Harbor Island Dr (92101), near Lindbergh Field Intl Airport, north of downtown. 619/291-2900; FAX 619/692-2337.* E-mail sheratonsandiego@sheraton.com; web www.ittsheraton.com. Set on the edge of San Diego Bay, this large hotel is perfect for both business and leisure travelers. The health and recreation facilities are extensive and well maintained. Rooms are warmly decorated and comfortable. Rooms are warm and casual; all have water views. 1,044 rms in 2 bldgs, 12 story. S, D $300-$365; each addl $20; suites $375-$1,100; under 18 free. Crib free. TV; cable (premium), VCR avail. 3 pools; whirlpool, 2 wading pools, poolside serv. Complimentary coffee in rms. Restaurant 6 am-10 pm. Rm serv 24 hrs. Bar 11-1 am. Ck-out noon. Coin lndry. Convention facilities. Business center. In-rm modem link. Concierge.

Shopping arcade. Free airport transportation. Lighted tennis, pro. Exercise rm; sauna. Spa. Massage. Bicycle rentals. Minibars; microwaves avail. Bathrm phone in suites. Balconies. Cr cds: A, C, D, DS, ER, JCB, MC, V.

★★★ **THE WESTGATE HOTEL.** *1055 Second Ave (92101), downtown. 619/238-1818; FAX 619/557-3737; res: 800/221-3802.* 223 units, 19 story, some kits. S, D from $194; each addl $10; suites from $500; under 18 free; wkend rates. Valet parking $12/day. Crib free. TV; cable (premium), VCR avail. Irons and ironing boards in every rm. Complimentary coffee in lobby. Restaurants 6 am-11 pm (also see LE FONTAINEBLEAU). Rm serv 24 hrs. Bar 11-1 am; entertainment. Ck-out noon. Meeting rms. Business servs avail. In-rm modem link. Concierge. Free airport, RR station, bus depot transportation. Exercise equipt. Bathrm phones, minibars; microwaves avail. Cr cds: A, C, D, DS, MC, V.

★★★ **TOWN & COUNTRY HOTEL.** *500 Hotel Cir N (92186), north of downtown. 619/291-7131; FAX 619/291-3584; res: 800/772-8527.* E-mail consales@towncountry.com; web www.towncountry.com. 964 rms, 1-10 story. S $95-$175; D $110-$190; each addl $15; suites $350-$675; under 18 free. Crib free. Parking $8. TV; cable (premium). 4 pools, 1 heated; whirlpool, poolside serv. Coffee in rms. Restaurant 6-1 am. Bar 11-2 am; entertainment. Ck-out noon. Convention facilities. Business center. In-rm modem link. Concierge. Barber. Lighted tennis privileges, pro. Golf privileges; driving range adj. Health club privileges. Some refrigerators; microwaves avail. Some private patios, balconies. On 35 acres. Cr cds: A, C, D, DS, MC, V.

✓★★ **TRAVELODGE.** *1960 Harbor Island Dr (92101), near Lindbergh Field Intl Airport, north of downtown. 619/291-6700; FAX 619/293-0694; res: 800/578-7878.* 207 rms, 9 story. S, D $119-$139; each addl $10; suites $225-$375; under 18 free. Crib free. TV; cable (premium). Heated pool; whirlpool. Complimentary coffee in rms. Restaurant 6:30 am-2 pm, 5:30-10 pm. Bar 11-1 am. Ck-out noon. Meeting rms. Business servs avail. In-rm modem link. Concierge. Gift shop. Free airport transportation. Exercise equipt; sauna. Some in-rm whirlpools, refrigerators. Balconies. Cr cds: A, C, D, DS, ER, JCB, MC, V.

★★★ **U S GRANT HOTEL.** *326 Broadway (92101), downtown. 619/232-3121; FAX 619/239-9517; res: 800/237-5029.* 280 rms, 11 story, 60 suites. S, D $175-$235; each addl $20; suites $215-$1,500. Crib free. Pet accepted. Valet parking $14. TV; cable (premium), VCR avail. Coffee in rms. Restaurant 6:30-10:30 pm. Bar 11-2 am; entertainment Fri, Sat. Ck-out noon. Business center. In-rm modem link. Concierge. Gift shop. Free airport transportation. Exercise equipt. Massage. Bathrm phones, minibars. Antiques, artwork, period chandeliers and fixtures. 1910 landmark has been restored to its original elegance. Luxury level. Cr cds: A, C, D, DS, JCB, MC, V.

★★★ **WESTIN HOTEL AT HORTON PLAZA.** *910 Broadway Cir (92101), downtown. 619/239-2200; FAX 619/239-0509; res: 800/222-8733; res: 800/993-7846.* E-mail hashley@starlodge.com; web www.westin.com. 450 rms, 16 story. S, D $129-$289; each addl $15; suites $250-$1,500; under 18 free; wkend, wkday packages. Crib free. Covered parking $12; valet $18. TV; cable (premium), VCR avail. Heated pool; whirlpool, poolside serv. Restaurant 6:30 am-11 pm. Rm serv 24 hrs. Bar to 2 am. Ck-out noon. Convention facilities. Business center. In-rm modem link. Concierge. Exercise equipt; sauna. Bathrm phones, refrigerators, minibars; microwaves avail. Some balconies. Connected to Horton Plaza. Luxury level. Cr cds: A, C, D, DS, ER, JCB, MC, V.

★★★ **WYNDHAM EMERALD PLAZA.** *400 W Broadway (92101), downtown. 619/239-4500; FAX 619/239-3274; res: 800/327-8585; res: 800/626-3988.* 436 rms, 25 story. S, D $194-$248; each addl $20; suites $380-$2,000; under 18 free. Crib free. Garage $16. TV; cable (premium), VCR avail. Heated pool; whirlpool, poolside serv. Restaurant 6 am-10 pm. Bar 11-1 am; entertainment Wed-Sat. Ck-out noon. Convention facilities. Business center. In-rm modem link. Concierge. Shopping arcade. Free airport transportation. Exercise rm; steam rm, sauna. Massage. Bathrm phones, minibars. Cr cds: A, C, D, DS, ER, JCB, MC, V.

Resorts

★★★ **DOUBLETREE CARMEL HIGHLAND RESORT.** *14455 Penasquitos Dr (92129), north of downtown. 619/672-9100; FAX 619/672-9187; res: 800/622-9223.* E-mail carmel@highland.doubletreehotels.com; web www.highlanddoubletreehotels.com. 172 rms, 3 story, 6 suites. S, D $119-$189; each addl $10; suites $189; under 12 free; golf, tennis, fitness plans. Crib free. Pet accepted, some restrictions; $150. TV; cable (premium). 2 pools; whirlpool, poolside serv, lifeguard (summer). Supervised child's activities (June-early Sept); ages 6-12. Complimentary coffee in rms. Dining rms 6:30 am-10 pm. Rm serv. Bar 11-1 am. Ck-out noon, ck-in 3 pm. Convention facilities. Business servs avail. In-rm modem link. Bellhops. Beauty shop. 5 lighted tennis courts, pro. 18-hole golf, greens fee $48-$60, pro, putting green. Exercise rm; saunas, steam rm. Microwaves avail. Private patios, balconies. On 130 acres. Cr cds: A, C, D, DS, ER, JCB, MC, V.

★★ **RANCHO BERNARDO INN.** *17550 Bernardo Oaks Dr (92128), north of downtown. 619/675-8500; FAX 619/675-8501; res: 800/542-6096.* E-mail ranchobernardoinn@jcresorts.com. 285 rms, 3 story. Mid-Sept-mid-May: S, D $239-$260; suites $289-$800; under 12 free; golf, tennis plans; lower rates rest of yr. TV; cable (premium), VCR avail. 2 pools; 7 whirlpools, poolside serv. Supervised child's activities (Aug & major hols); ages 5-15. Complimentary afternoon refreshments Wed & Sat. Dining rms 6 am-10 pm (also see EL BIZCOCHO). Snack bar. Rm serv to midnight. Bars 11-1 am. Ck-out 1 pm, ck-in 4 pm. Convention facilities. Business center. In-rm modem link. Concierge. Sundries. Gift shop. Airport transportation. Lighted tennis, pro. Three 18-hole, one 27-hole golf courses, pro, putting green, driving range. Volleyball. Bicycles. Exercise equipt; sauna, steam rm. Massage. Many minibars; some bathrm phones; microwaves avail. Private patios, balconies. Cr cds: A, C, D, DS, MC, V.

★★★ **SAN DIEGO PARADISE POINT RESORT.** *1404 W Vacation Rd (92109), on island, in Mission Bay. 619/274-4630; FAX 619/581-5929; res: 800/344-2626.* Web www.princessresort.com/princess. 462 cottage rms, 153 kits. May-Aug: S, D $180-$230; each addl $15; suites $245-$395; kit. units $190-$240; lower rates rest of yr. Crib free. Pet accepted. TV; cable (premium). 5 pools, 2 heated; wading pool, whirlpool, poolside serv. Supervised child's activities (June-Aug); ages 3-18. Complimentary coffee in rms. Dining rms 7 am-11 pm. Rm serv. Bars 11-2 am; entertainment Tues-Sun. Ck-out noon, ck-in 4 pm. Coin Indry. Convention facilities. Business center. In-rm modem link. Valet serv. Concierge. Gift shop. Lighted tennis, pro. Putting green. Exercise equipt; sauna, steam rm. Health club privileges. Bicycles. Game rm. Lawn games. Boats. Some bathrm phones, refrigerators; microwaves avail. Private patios. On beach. Botanical walk. Cr cds: A, C, DS, ER, MC, V.

Inns

★★ **ELSBREE HOUSE BED & BREAKFAST.** *5054 Narragansett Ave (92107), north of downtown. 619/226-4133; FAX 619/224-4133; res: 800/510-6975.* E-mail ktelsbree@juno.com; web www.oceanbeach-online.com/elsbree/b&b. 6 rms, 1 condo, 2 story. No A/C. No rm phones. 2-4-day min: S, D $95-$105 (2-day min); condo $285 (4-day min); wkly rates. TV in sitting rm. Complimentary continental bkfst. Restaurant nearby. Ck-out 11 am, ck-in 3 pm. Balconies. New England-style house near ocean. Totally nonsmoking. Cr cds: A, C, MC, V.

★★★ **HERITAGE PARK INN.** *2470 Heritage Park Row (92110), in Old Town. 619/299-6832; FAX 619/299-9465; res: 800/995-2470.* E-mail Innkeeper@HeritageParkInn; web www.heritageparkinn.com. 12 rms, 5 with shower only, 2 story, 1 suite. No A/C. S, D $90-$200; each addl $20; suite $250; under 12 free; wkends, hols (2-day min). TV; VCR (movies avail). Complimentary full bkfst; afternoon refreshments. Restaurant nearby. Ck-out 11 am, ck-in 3 pm. In-rm modem link. Free airport transportation. Victorian house (1889) moved to this site. Many antiques. Totally nonsmoking. Cr cds: A, C, D, DS, MC, V.

D SC

★★★ **JULIAN GOLDRUSH HOTEL INC.** *2032 Main St (92036), 35 mi E on US 8, turn N on US 79 for 22 mi. 760/765-0201; FAX 760/765-0327; res: 800/734-5854.* E-mail b&b@julianhotel.com; web www.julianhotel.com. 14 air-cooled rms, 12 with shower only, 2 cottages. Sept-May: S, D $82-$125; cottages $120-$175; wkends 2-day min; lower rates rest of yr. Complimentary full bkfst; refreshments. Restaurant adj 7 am-9 pm. Ck-out noon, ck-in 2 pm. Street parking. Built in 1897. Totally nonsmoking. Cr cds: A, C, MC, V.

SC

★★ **JULIAN WHITE HOUSE BED & BREAKFAST.** *3014 Blue Jay Dr (92036), I-8 E to I-79, N to Julian. 760/765-1764; FAX 760/765-1764; res: 800/948-4687; res: 800/948-4687.* E-mail stay@julian-whitehouse-bnb.com; web www.julian-whitehouse-bnb.com. 4 rms, 1 with shower only; 1 suite. No rm phones. S, D $90-$135; each addl $25; suite $145; under 5 free; wkends, hols (2-day min). Closed Dec 24, 25. Complimentary full bkfst. Ck-out noon, ck-in 4 pm. Business servs avail. In-rm modem link. Some fireplaces. Totally nonsmoking. Cr cds: C, MC, V.

SC

★★★ **ORCHARD HILL COUNTRY INN.** *2502 Washington St (92036), E on I-8, 15 mi N on CA 79. 760/765-1700; FAX 760/765-0290; res: 800/716-7242.* Web www.orchardhill.com. 22 rms, 2 with shower only, 12 deluxe rooms. S, D $160-$170; each addl $25; deluxe rms $210-$265; 2-day min wkends. TV; cable, VCR (movies). Complimentary full bkfst; afternoon refreshments. Complimentary coffee in rms. Ck-out noon, ck-in 3 pm. Business servs avail. Gift shop. Some in-rm whirlpools; refrigerator, wet bar, fireplace in deluxe rms. Balconies on deluxe rms. Totally nonsmoking. Cr cds: A, C, MC, V.

D SC

Restaurants

★★ **A CELADON THAI RESTAURANT.** *3628 5th Ave (92103), north of downtown. 619/295-8800.* Hrs: 11:30 am-2 pm, 5-10 pm; Sat from 5 pm. Closed Sun; some major hols. Res accepted. Thai menu. Wine, beer. A la carte entrees: lunch $6.25-$10, dinner $8.25-$15. Specializes in shrimp, chicken, beef. Cr cds: A, C, MC, V.

D

✓★★ **AFGHANISTAN KHYBER PASS.** *4647 Convoy St (92111), north of downtown. 619/571-3749.* Hrs: 11 am-2:30 pm, 5-10 pm; Sun from 5 pm. Res accepted. Afghan menu. Wine, beer. Semi-a la carte: lunch $6.95-$11.95, dinner $10.95-$15.95. Specializes in shish kebab, curries. Interior designed as an Afghan cave. Cr cds: A, C, DS, MC, V.

★★ **ANTHONY'S FISH GROTTO.** *11666 Avena Place (92128), off Bernardo Center Dr in Rancho Bernardo, north of downtown. 619/451-2070.* Web www.gofishanthonys.com. Hrs: 11:30 am-8:30 pm. Closed major hols. Res accepted. Bar. Semi-a la carte: lunch $4.75-$8.95, dinner $7.50-$26. Child's meals. Specializes in fresh seafood. Parking. Outdoor dining. Overlooks Webb Lake Park. Family-owned. Cr cds: A, C, D, DS, MC, V.

D

★★★ **ANTHONY'S STAR OF THE SEA ROOM.** *1360 Harbor Dr (92101), downtown. 619/232-7408.* Web www.gofishanthonys.com. Hrs: 5:30-10:30 pm. Closed major hols. Semi-a la carte: dinner $16-$34. Specialties: Pacific abalone piccata, grilled swordfish. Valet parking. Harbor view. Family-owned. Cr cds: A, C, D, DS, MC, V.

D

★★ **ATHENS MARKET TAVERNA.** *109 W F Street (92101), downtown. 619/234-1955.* Hrs: 11:30 am-10 pm; Sat, Sun from 5 pm. Closed some major hols. Res accepted. Greek menu. Bar to midnight. Semi-a la carte: lunch $5.50-$14.50, dinner $11.75-$22.75. Specializes in lamb, fish, vegetarian specials. Cr cds: A, C, D, DS, MC, V.

★★★ **BACI RISTORANTE.** *1955 W Morena Blvd (92110), Mission Bay. 619/275-2094.* Hrs: 11:30 am-2 pm, 5:30-10 pm; Sat from 5:30 pm. Closed Sun; major hols. Res required Fri, Sat. Northern Italian menu. Bar. Wine list. A la carte entrees: lunch $7.95-$16.95, dinner $11.95-$23.50. Specializes in seafood, veal, pasta. Own baking, pasta. Intimate atmosphere; many art pieces, prints. Cr cds: A, C, D, DS, MC, V.

D

★★ **BAYOU BAR & GRILL.** *329 Market St (92101), downtown. 619/696-8747.* Hrs: 11:30 am-3 pm, 5-10 pm; Fri, Sat to 11 pm; Sun brunch 11:30 am-3 pm. Closed Jan 1, Thanksgiving, Dec 25. Res accepted. Cajun, Creole menu. Bar. Semi-a la carte: lunch $5.95-$11.95, dinner $11.95-$16.95. Sun brunch $12.95. Specializes in beef, chicken. Outdoor dining. Casual dining in New Orleans atmosphere. Cr cds: A, C, D, DS, MC, V.

D

★★★ **BELGIAN LION.** *2265 Bacon St (92107), Mission Bay. 619/223-2700.* Hrs: 5-10 pm. Closed Sun-Wed; major hols. Res accepted. French, Belgian menu. Beer. Wine list. A la carte entrees: dinner $18.50-$24.50. Specialties: fresh fish, classic duck confit. Own pastries. Parking. Outdoor dining. Country Belgian decor. Cr cds: A, C, D, DS, MC, V.

★★ **BELLA LUNA.** *748 5th Ave (92101), downtown. 619/239-3222.* Hrs: 11:30 am-2:30 pm, 5-11 pm; Fri & Sat to midnight. Closed Jan 1, Dec 25. Res accepted. Italian menu. Bar. Semi-a la carte: lunch $4.95-$12.95, dinner $5.95-$18.95. Specializes in pasta, seafood. Valet parking. Patio dining. Original artwork with moon motif; ceiling painted to look like sky. Cr cds: A, C, MC, V.

D

★★ **BENIHANA.** *477 Camino Del Rio South (92108), north of downtown. 619/298-4666.* Hrs: 11:30 am-2 pm, 5-10 pm; Fri to 11 pm; Sat 1-11 pm; Sun 1-10 pm. Res accepted. Japanese menu. Bar. Semi-a la carte: lunch $6.75-$15.75, dinner $14-$35.75. Child's meals. Specializes in Japanese steak & seafood. Sushi bar. Valet parking. Japanese village settings. Cr cds: A, C, D, DS, JCB, MC, V.

D

★★★ **BLUE POINT.** *565 Fifth Ave (92101), downtown. 619/233-6623.* Hrs: 5-10 pm; Fri, Sat to 11 pm; Sun to 9 pm. Closed Dec 25. Res accepted. Bar. Extensive wine list. Semi-a la carte: dinner $15.95-$23.95. Specialties: miso marinated bass, fresh Maine lobster with macadamia nut butter, grilled Hawaiian ahi. Oyster bar. Valet parking. Outdoor dining. Oil paintings. Cr cds: A, C, D, DS, MC, V.

D

★★★ **BUSALACCHI'S.** *3683 5th Ave (92103), north of downtown. 619/298-0119.* Hrs: 11:30 am-2:15 pm, 5-10 pm; Fri & Sat to 11 pm. Closed most major hols. Res accepted. Italian menu. Bar. A la carte entrees: lunch $7.25-$19.95, dinner $10.95-$26.95. Specializes in Sicilian dishes. Valet parking. Outdoor dining. Victorian-style house. Cr cds: A, C, D, DS, MC, V.

✓★ **CAFE COYOTE.** *2461 San Diego Ave (92110), in Old Town Esplanade, in Old Town. 619/291-4695.* Hrs: 7:30 am-10 pm; Fri, Sat to 11 pm. Closed Dec 25. Res accepted. Mexican, Amer menu. Bar. Semi-a la carte: bkfst $3.50-$6.95, lunch, dinner $3.95-$9.95. Child's meals.

Specialties: blue corn pancakes, carnitas, carne asada. Own tortillas. Entertainment Thurs-Sun on patio. Parking. Outdoor dining. Pictures, statues of Southwestern wildlife. Cr cds: A, C, D, DS, MC, V.

D

★★★ **CAFE PACIFICA.** *2414 San Diego Ave (92110), in Old Town. 619/291-6666.* Hrs: 5:30-10 pm; Sun from 5 pm; early-bird dinner 5:30-6:30 pm. Res accepted. Bar. Semi-a la carte: dinner $14-$22. Specializes in fresh fish. Near Old Spanish Cemetery. Cr cds: A, C, D, DS, MC, V.

D

★★★ **CALIFORNIA CUISINE.** *1027 University Ave (92103), north of downtown. 619/543-0790.* E-mail calcuisine@aol.com. Hrs: 11 am-10 pm; Sat, Sun from 5 pm. Closed Mon; Jan 1, Thanksgiving, Dec 25. Res accepted. California menu. Wine, beer. Semi-a la carte: lunch $7-$14, dinner $12.75-$19.75. Specializes in fresh seafood, pasta, salad. Outdoor dining. Menu changes daily. Original paintings. Cr cds: A, C, D, DS, MC, V.

★★ **CASA DE BANDINI.** *2660 Calhoun St (92110), in Old Town. 619/297-8211.* Hrs: 11 am-10 pm; Sun from 10 am; winter to 9 pm. Closed Thanksgiving, Dec 25. Mexican menu. Bar. Semi-a la carte: lunch, dinner $5.95-$15.50. Child's meals. Specializes in seafood. Mariachi band. Parking. Outdoor dining. Early California atmosphere, garden patio with fountain. Adobe bldg (1829) once served as headquarters for Commodore Stockton. Cr cds: A, C, D, DS, MC, V.

D

✓★★ **CHIEU-ANH.** *16769 Bernardo Center Dr (92128), north of downtown. 619/485-1231.* Hrs: 11 am-2 pm, 5-9 pm; Sat, Sun 5-9:30 pm. Closed Mon; Dec 25. Res accepted. Vietnamese menu. Wine, beer. Semi-a la carte: lunch $5.95-$7.45, dinner $9.50-$14.95. Specializes in rice noodles, clay pot dishes. Contemporary decor. Cr cds: A, C, D, MC, V.

D

★★ **CROCE'S.** *802 5th Ave (92101), downtown. 619/233-4355.* Web www.croce.com. Hrs: 5 pm-midnight. Closed Thanksgiving, Dec 25. Res accepted. Contemporary Amer menu. Bar to 2 am. Semi-a la carte: dinner $12.95-$21.95. Specializes in seafood. Jazz. Valet parking. Outdoor dining. Tribute to famous singer, composer Jim Croce. Cr cds: A, C, D, DS, MC, V.

D

✓★★★ **DAKOTA GRILL & SPIRITS.** *901 5th Ave (92101), downtown. 619/234-5554.* Hrs: 11:30 am-2:30 pm, 5-10 pm; Fri, Sat to 11 pm, Sun 5-9 pm. Closed Thanksgiving, Dec 25. Res accepted. Bar. Semi-a la carte: lunch $5.95-$10.95, dinner $10.95-$21.95. Specializes in barbecue ribs, mesquite-broiled meat, seafood. Pianist Wed-Sat. Valet parking. Balcony, patio dining. Original artwork. Cr cds: A, C, D, DS, MC, V.

D

★★★ **DOBSON'S BAR & RESTAURANT.** *956 Broadway Circle (92101), downtown. 619/231-6771.* Hrs: 11:30 am-3 pm, 5:30-10 pm; Thur, Fri to 11 pm; Sat 5:30-11 pm. Closed major hols. Res accepted. Continental menu. Bar to 1:30 am. Semi-a la carte: lunch $7-$11.25, dinner $15-$26. Prix fixe: dinner $21.95. Specializes in fresh seafood, veal. Own sourdough bread. Covered parking. Cr cds: A, C, D, MC, V.

★★ **EDGEWATER GRILL.** *861 W Harbor Dr (92101), in Seaport Village, downtown. 619/232-7581.* Hrs: 11 am-10 pm; Fri, Sat to 10:30 pm. Res accepted. Seafood menu. Bar. Semi-a la carte: lunch $6.95-$22.95, dinner $8.25-$22.95. Child's meals. Specialties: pan-roasted salmon, ruby red ahi. Parking. Outdoor dining. View of harbor. Cr cds: A, C, DS, MC, V.

D

★★★ **EL BIZCOCHO.** *(See Rancho Bernardo Inn) 619/675-8500.* Hrs: 6-10 pm; Fri, Sat to 10:30 pm; Sun brunch 10 am-2 pm. Res accepted. Classical French menu. Bar. Extensive wine list. A la carte entrees: dinner $23-$40. Sun brunch $24. Specializes in seasonal cuisine. Pianist. Valet parking. Jacket required (exc brunch), tie optional. Cr cds: A, C, D, DS, MC, V.

★★★ **EL EMBARCADERO.** *(See Shelter Point Hotel & Marina) 619/221-8000.* Hrs: 6:30 am-10:30 pm, Fri, Sat to 11 pm; Sun brunch 10 am-2:30 pm. Res accepted. Continental menu. Bar. Semi-a la carte: bkfst $4.25-$8.95, lunch $7.95-$13.95, dinner $12-$21.95. Sun brunch $19.95. Child's meals. Specialties: blackened halibut, pasta fruta del mar. Parking. Outdoor dining. View of marina; romantic atmosphere. Totally nonsmoking. Cr cds: A, C, D, DS, MC, V.

D

✓★ **EL TECOLOTE MEXICAN RESTAURANT.** *6110 Friars Rd (92108), north of downtown. 619/295-2087.* Hrs: 11 am-10 pm; Sun 4-9 pm. Mexican menu. Bar. Semi-a la carte: lunch $2.40-$10.55, dinner $7.35-$11.50. Child's meals. Specialties: cheese-filled zucchinis, mole poblano, fish fillet ensenada. Parking. Outdoor dining. Mexican artifacts, photographs, original art. Totally nonsmoking. Cr cds: A, C, D, DS, MC, V.

D

✓★ **FAIROUZ CAFE & GALLERY.** *3166 Midway Dr (92110), in Point Loma. 619/225-0308.* Hrs 11 am-9 pm; Fri, Sat to 10 pm. Closed Jan 1. Res required Fri, Sat. Mediterranean menu. Bar. Semi-a la carte: lunch $3.95-$7, dinner $5-$13.95. Buffet: lunch $5.25, dinner $10.95. Specialties: hommos, taboleh, kabobs. Parking. Cr cds: A, C, D, DS, MC, V.

D

★★★ **FIO'S.** *801 5th Ave (92101), downtown. 619/234-3467.* Hrs: 5-10:30 pm; Fri, Sat to 11:30 pm; Sun to 10 pm. Closed Dec 25. Res accepted. Italian menu. Bar. Wine cellar. Semi-a la carte: dinner $11.95-$24.95. Specializes in pasta. Outdoor dining. European decor; original artwork depicting Palio of Siena. Cr cds: A, C, D, DS, MC, V.

D

✓★★ **FORTUNE COOKIE.** *16425 Bernardo Center Dr (92128), north of downtown. 619/451-8958.* Hrs: 3-9 pm; Fri, Sat to 10 pm; Sun from 4 pm. Closed Thanksgiving. Res accepted. Chinese menu. Bar. Semi-a la carte: lunch $6.45-$12.95, dinner $8.95-$19.95. Specialties: kung pao chicken, stir-fried sea bass, Taiwanese rib-eye steak. Parking. Totally nonsmoking. Cr cds: A, C, D, DS, JCB, MC, V.

D

★★★ **FOUNTAINBLEU @ WESTGATE HOTEL.** *Westgate Hotel. 619/238-1818.* American cuisine. Filet salmon, fresh seafood. Hrs; Mon-Sat 11:30-2; 6-10. Sun brunch 10-2. Price lunch $12-$18. Dinner $25-$29. Bar. Harpist lunch; pianist dinner; Sat opera. Valet. Cr cds: C.

✓★★ **FRENCH MARKET GRILLE.** *15717 Bernardo Heights Pkwy (92128). 619/485-8055.* Hrs: 11 am-10 pm; Sun 9 am-9 pm. Res accepted. French, Amer menu. Semi-a la carte: lunch $8-$12, dinner $15-$20. Specialties: coq au vin, beef bourguignon, lamb shank on artichoke ravioli and white beans. Opera Tues. Outdoor dining. Intimate dining. Cr cds: A, C, D, MC, V.

D

★★ **HARBOR HOUSE.** *831 W Harbor Dr (92101), in Seaport Village, downtown. 619/232-1141.* Hrs: 11 am-11 pm. Res accepted. Bar from 11 am. A la carte entrees: lunch $8.95-$22.95, dinner $14.95-$23.95. Child's meals. Specializes in fresh seafood. Oyster bar. Parking. View of harbor, boat docks, Coronado Bay Bridge. Cr cds: A, C, DS, MC, V.

D

✓★★ **HOB NOB HILL.** *2271 1st Ave (92101), adj to Balboa Park. 619/239-8176.* Hrs: 7 am-9 pm. Closed Dec 25. Res accepted. Wine, beer. Semi-a la carte: bkfst $2.35-$10.95. Complete meals: lunch $5.65-$8.55, dinner $5.65-$13.45. Child's meals. Specializes in Eastern fried scallops, lamb shanks, roast turkey. Family-owned. Cr cds: A, C, D, DS, MC, V.

D

★★ **HUMPHREY'S BY THE BAY.** *2241 Shelter Island Dr (92106), in Point Loma. 619/224-3577.* Hrs: 6:30 am-2 pm, 5:30-10 pm; Fri 5:30-11 pm; Sat 7 am-3 pm, 5:30-11 pm; Sun 7 am-2 pm, 5:30-10 pm; Sun brunch 10 am-2 pm. Res accepted. Seafood menu. Bar 11 am-midnight. Semi-a la carte: bkfst $3.95-$7.95, lunch $6.95-$12.95, dinner $14.95-$24.95. Sun brunch $24.95. Child's meals. Specializes in seafood, prime beef, pasta. Entertainment. Parking. View of bay. Cr cds: A, C, DS, MC, V.

D

★★ **IMPERIAL HOUSE.** *505 Kalmia St (92101), north of downtown. 619/234-3525.* Hrs: 11 am-4 pm, 5-9 pm; Mon to 2 pm; Fri, Sat to 11 pm; early-bird dinner Tues-Fri 5-6:30 pm. Closed Sun; most major hols. Res accepted. Continental menu. Bar to 11 pm; Fri, Sat to 12:30 am. A la carte entrees: lunch $7-$11, dinner $11-$22. Specializes in rack of lamb, pepper steak, seafood. Pianist Wed-Sat. Valet parking. Old-world decor. Family-owned. Cr cds: A, C, D, MC, V.

★★ **ITRI ITALIAN RESTAURANT.** *835 4th Ave (92101), downtown. 619/234-6538.* Hrs: 11 am-3 pm, 5-11 pm; Sat, Sun 5-11 pm. Closed most major hols. Res accepted. Italian menu. Wine, beer. Semi-a la carte: lunch $9-$11, dinner $10-$25. Specialties: lamb shank, portobello itrano, pollo al profumi di bosco. Street parking. Outdoor dining. Italian country atmosphere and decor. Totally nonsmoking. Cr cds: A, C, D, DS, MC, V.

D

✓★ **JACK & GIULIO.** *2391 San Diego Ave (92110), in Old Town. 619/294-2074.* Hrs: 11:30 am-2 pm, 5-9:30 pm; Fri, Sat to 10:30 pm. Closed Easter, Thanksgiving, Dec 25. Italian menu. Wine, beer. Semi-a la carte: lunch, dinner $4.95-16.95. Child's meals. Specialties: scampi guilio, tortellini verdi. Outdoor dining. Italian bistro atmosphere. Cr cds: A, C, DS, MC, V.

D

★★ **JASMINE.** *4609 Convoy St (92111), north of downtown. 619/268-0888.* Hrs: 10 am-11 pm. Res accepted. Chinese menu. Bar. Semi-a la carte: lunch $5.95-$18, dinner $9-$25. Specializes in dim sum, live seafood. Parking. Large dining rm with movable walls. Cr cds: A, C, MC, V.

✓★ **KARL STRAUSS' BREWERY & GRILL.** *1157 Columbia St (92101), downtown. 619/234-2739.* E-mail karlstrauss@downtown.com; web www.karlstrauss.com. Hrs: 11:30 am-10 pm; Thur-Sat to 1 am. Closed most major hols. Res accepted. Bar. Semi-a la carte: lunch $6-$11, dinner $7-$16. Specializes in hamburgers, fresh fish, German-style sausage. Brew own beer; some seasonal varieties. View of microbrewery from restaurant. Cr cds: C, MC, V.

D

★★ **KELLY'S STEAKHOUSE.** *500 Hotel Circle N, north of downtown. 619/291-7131.* Hrs: 4-10 pm; Fri, Sat to 11 pm; early-bird dinner 4-6 pm. Closed Easter, Thanksgiving, Dec 25. Bar to 2 am; Sat, Sun from 4 pm. Semi-a la carte: dinner $10.50-$23.95. Specializes in barbecued ribs, steak, prime rib. Entertainment. Parking. Waterfalls. Cr cds: A, C, D, DS, MC, V.

✓★★ **LA VACHE & CO.** *420 Robinson St (92103), north of downtown. 619/295-0214.* Hrs: 11:30 am-2:30 pm, 5-10 pm; Fri-Sat to 11 pm. Closed Dec 25. Res accepted. Country French menu. Wine, beer. Semi-a la carte: lunch $5-$10, dinner $5-$18.50. Specializes in beef, chicken. Outdoor dining. Casual European decor. Totally nonsmoking. Cr cds: A, C, D, DS, MC, V.

D

★★★★ **LAUREL.** *505 Laurel St (92101), downtown. 619/239-2222.* E-mail Laurelrb@aol.com; web www.winesellar.com. This contemporary restaurant offers upscale French/Mediterranean cuisine by executive chef Douglas Organ and an excellent selection of domestic and international wines under the congenial stewardship of manager Jack Jaeger. French-Mediterranean menu. Specialities: Moroccan spiced braised lamb shank, pan-roasted venetian with sauteed red grapes, grilled yellowfin tuna with warm green lentil salad, warm peach tart with raspberry sorbet. Hrs: 5-10 pm; Fri, Sat to 11 pm; Sun 5-10 pm. Res accepted. Bar. A la carte entrees: dinner $15-$28. Extensive Wine list. Nightly Entertainment. Valet parking $6. Contemporary decor. Cr cds: A, C, D, DS, MC, V.

D

★★★ **LE FONTAINEBLEAU.** *(See The Westgate Hotel) 619/238-1818.* Hrs: 6-10 pm; Sun brunch 10 am-2 pm. Res accepted. Continental menu. Bar. Wine cellar. Semi-a la carte: dinner $16-$30. Sun brunch $28.95. Child's meals. Specializes in seafood, veal. Pianist. Valet parking. Lavish French period setting; antiques. Cr cds: A, C, D, DS, MC, V.

D

✓★★ **LINO'S.** *2754 Calhoun St (92110), in Old Town. 619/299-7124.* Hrs: 11 am-9 pm; Fri, Sat to 10 pm. Closed Jan 1, Thanksgiving, Dec 25. Res accepted. Italian menu. Bar. Semi-a la carte: lunch $4.50-$8.95, dinner $5.50-$14.95. Specializes in veal, chicken, shrimp. Own pasta. Parking. Outdoor dining. Cr cds: A, C, D, DS, ER, JCB, MC, V.

♥

★★★ **MISTER A'S.** *2550 5th Ave (92103), on 12th floor of Financial Center, north of downtown. 619/239-1377.* Hrs: 11 am-2:30 pm; 5:30-10:30 pm; Sat, Sun from 5:30 pm. Closed some major hols. Res accepted. Continental menu. Bar 11-2 am; Sat, Sun from 5 pm. Wine list. Semi-a la carte: lunch $6.95-$13.95, dinner $16.95-$35.95. Specialties: chateaubriand, rack of lamb, fresh fish. Entertainment Fri-Sat. Valet parking. Rococo decor; oil paintings. Rooftop dining; panoramic view. Family-owned. Jacket (dinner). Cr cds: A, C, D, DS, JCB, MC, V.

D

★★ **MIXX.** *3671 5th Ave (92103), north of downtown. 619/299-6499.* Hrs: 5-10 pm; Fri, Sat to 11 pm. Closed Jan 1, Thanksgiving, Dec 25. Res accepted. Contemporary Amer menu. Bar. Semi-a la carte: dinner $9.95-$17.95. Specialties: pan-roasted trout, grilled lamb rack chops. Entertainment Wed-Sat. Intimate dining. Unique dish presentation. Totally nonsmoking. Cr cds: A, C, D, DS, MC, V.

D

✓★★ **MONTANA'S AMERICAN GRILL.** *1421 University Ave (92103), north of downtown. 619/297-0722.* Hrs: 11:30 am-10 pm; Fri to 11 pm; Sat 5-11 pm; Sun 5-9 pm. Closed most major hols. Res accepted. Bar. Semi-a la carte: lunch $7.95-$10.95, dinner $8.95-$19.95. Specializes in BBQ ribs, skirt steak. Valet parking. Contemporary decor. Totally nonsmoking. Cr cds: A, C, D, DS, MC, V.

D

✓★ **NATI'S MEXICAN RESTAURANT.** *1852 Bacon St (92107), north of downtown. 619/224-3369.* Hrs: 11 am-9 pm; Sun to 8 pm; winter to 8 pm. Closed some major hols. Mexican menu. Bar. Semi-a la carte: bkfst $3.95-$6.75, lunch, dinner $4.95-$8.75. Specializes in chiles rellenos, sour cream tostadas, carne asada. Parking. Outdoor dining. Cr cds: C, MC, V.

★★ **NICK'S AT THE BEACH.** *809 Thomas Ave (92109), downtown. 619/270-1730.* Hrs: 11-2 am; Sun brunch 10 am-2 pm. Closed Dec 25. Bar. Semi-a la carte: lunch, dinner $5.95-$14.95. Sun brunch $4.95-$9.95. Child's meals. Specializes in fresh seafood. Casual atmosphere. Totally nonsmoking. Cr cds: A, C, D, DS, MC, V.

D

✓★ **OLD TOWN MEXICAN CAFE & CANTINA.** *2489 San Diego Ave (92110), in Old Town. 619/297-4330.* Hrs: 7 am-11 pm. Closed Thanksgiving, Dec 25. Mexican menu. Bar to 2 am. A la carte entrees: bkfst $2.95-$7.25, lunch, dinner $2.75-$13. Specialties: carnitas, Old Town pollo, Mexican-style ribs. Own tortillas. Child's meals. Parking. Patio dining. Cr cds: A, C, D, DS, MC, V.

D

✓★★ **OSTERIA PANEVINO.** *722 5th Ave (92101), downtown. 619/595-7959.* Hrs: 11:30 am-midnight. Closed Thanksgiving, Dec 25. Res accepted. Italian menu. Bar. Semi-a la carte: lunch $9-$14, dinner $13-$20. Specializes in wood-burning pizza, wild game. Valet parking. Outdoor dining. Mural of Florence on walls. Cr cds: A, C, D, DS, MC, V.

D

★★ **PANDA INN.** *506 Horton Plaza (92101), on top floor, downtown. 619/233-7800.* Hrs: 11 am-10 pm; Fri, Sat to 10:30 pm. Closed Thanksgiving. Res accepted. Mandarin menu. Bar. Semi-a la carte: lunch $6.25-$10.45, dinner $6.50-$19.95. Specialties: sweet & pungent shrimp, orange-flavored beef. Parking. Outdoor dining. Several dining areas, all with Chinese art pieces, 1 with entire ceiling skylight; pandas depicted in stained-glass windows. Cr cds: A, C, D, DS, JCB, MC, V.

D

★★★ **PREGO.** *1370 Frazee Rd (92108), north of downtown. 619/294-4700.* Hrs: 11:30 am-11 pm; Fri to midnight; 5 pm-midnight; Sun 5-10 pm. Closed most major hols. Res accepted. Italian menu. Bar. Wine list. A la carte entrees: lunch, dinner $8.50-$21.50. Specialties: grilled veal chops, lobster/prosciutto filled pasta, fresh fish of the day. Valet parking. Outdoor dining. Italian artwork. Cr cds: A, C, D, MC, V.

D ♥

★★★ **RAINWATER'S.** *1202 Kettner Blvd (92101), near train depot, downtown. 619/233-5757.* Hrs: 11:30 am-midnight; Sat from 5 pm; Sun 5-11 pm. Closed July 4, Thanksgiving, Dec 25. Res accepted. Bar. Wine list. Semi-a la carte: lunch $7-$15, dinner $19-$40. Specializes in fresh seafood, prime steaks. Own pastries. Valet parking. Outdoor dining. Cr cds: A, C, D, MC, V.

D

★ **RED SAILS INN.** *2614 Shelter Island Dr (92106), in Point Loma. 619/223-3030.* Hrs: 7 am-11 pm; early-bird dinner Sun-Thurs 5-7 pm. Closed Dec 25. Res accepted. Bar. Semi-a la carte: bkfst $1.95-$8.95, lunch $5.95-$9.95, dinner $9.95-$21.95. Child's meals. Specializes in steak, seafood. Street parking. Outdoor dining. On marina; boating memorabilia. Family-owned since 1975. Cr cds: A, C, D, MC, V.

★★★ **RUTH'S CHRIS STEAK HOUSE.** *1355 N Harbor Dr (92101), downtown. 619/233-1422.* Web www.ruthschris.com. Hrs: 5-10 pm; Fri, Sat to 10:30 pm. Closed Thanksgiving, Dec 25. Res accepted. Bar. A la carte entrees: dinner $18.95-$29.95. Specializes in steak, lobster. Contemporary decor. Cr cds: A, C, D, DS, MC, V.

D

★★★ **SALLY'S.** *(See Hyatt Regency) 619/687-6080.* Hrs: 11:30 am-11 pm. Closed Dec 25. Res accepted. Mediterranean menu. Bar. Semi-a la carte: lunch $8-$15, dinner $18-$32. Specializes in seafood. Outdoor dining. Contemporary decor. Cr cds: A, C, D, DS, ER, JCB, MC, V.

D

★★★ **SALVATORE'S.** *750 Front St (92101), downtown. 619/544-1865.* Hrs: 5-10 pm. Res accepted. Italian menu. Bar. Wine list. A la carte entrees: dinner $15-$24. Specializes in Northern Italian dishes. Parking. Original artwork. Cr cds: A, C, D, MC, V.

D

★★ **SAN DIEGO PIER CAFE.** *885 W Harbor Dr (92101), in Seaport Village, downtown. 619/239-3968.* Hrs: 7 am-10 pm; Fri, Sat to 11 pm. Serv bar. Semi-a la carte: bkfst $4.25-$8.95, lunch $5.50-$13.95, dinner $9.95-$18.95. Child's meals. Specializes in fresh fish broiled. Outdoor dining. On harbor pier. Cr cds: A, C, DS, MC, V.

★★ **TAKA RESTAURANT.** *614 5th Ave # M (92101), north of downtown. 619/338-0555.* Hrs: 5:30-10 pm; Fri, Sat to 11:30 pm. Closed Jan 1, Dec 25. Res accepted. Japanese menu. Bar. Semi-a la carte: dinner $6-$24. Specializes in seafood, sushi. Valet parking. Outdoor dining. Japanese decor. Totally nonsmoking. Cr cds: A, C, MC, V.

D

★★★ **THEE BUNGALOW.** *4996 W Point Loma Blvd (92107), north of downtown. 619/224-2884.* Hrs: 5:30-9:30 pm; Fri, Sat 5-10 pm; Sun 5-9 pm. Closed July 4, Dec 26. Res accepted. Extensive wine list. Continental menu. Semi-a la carte: dinner $9.95-$22. Specializes in roast duck, rack of lamb, fresh seafood. Parking. In converted house. Many special wine dinners planned throughout the year. Cr cds: A, C, D, DS, MC, V.

★★ **TOM HAM'S LIGHTHOUSE.** *2150 Harbor Island Dr (92101), north of downtown. 619/291-9110.* E-mail tomhams@juno.com. Hrs: 11:15 am-3:30 pm, 5-10:30 pm; Sat 4:30-11 pm; Sun 4-10 pm; early-bird dinner Mon-Fri 5-6 pm, Sun 4-6 pm; Sun brunch 10 am-2 pm. Closed Jan 1, Dec 25. Res accepted. Bar 11-2 am. Semi-a la carte: lunch $6.95-$14.95, dinner $9.95-$24.50. Sun brunch $11.95. Child's meals. Specializes in steak, seafood. Salad bar (lunch). Entertainment Wed-Sat. Parking. Early California, Spanish decor. View of bay, San Diego skyline. Official Coast Guard No. 9 beacon. Family-owned. Cr cds: A, C, D, DS, MC, V.

SC

★★ **TOP OF THE MARKET.** *750 N Harbor Dr (92101), downtown. 619/232-3474.* Web www.thefishmarket.com. Hrs: 11 am-10 pm; Sun brunch 10 am-2 pm. Closed Thanksgiving, Dec 25. Res accepted. Bar to 10 pm. Semi-a la carte: lunch $9.50-$31.75, dinner $13-$34.25. Sun brunch $16.50. Child's meals. Specializes in seafood. Oyster, sushi bar. Parking. Outdoor dining. Pictures of turn-of-the-century fishing scenes. Retail fish market lower floor. Cr cds: A, C, D, DS, MC, V.

D

★★ **TRATTORIA FANTASTICA.** *1735 India St (92101), downtown. 619/234-1734.* Hrs: 11:30 am-2 pm, 5-10 pm; wkends to 11 pm. Closed some major hols. Res accepted. Italian menu. Wine, beer. Semi-a la carte: lunch $6-$14.95, dinner $8-$19.95. Specializes in family-style cooking. Patio dining. Casual atmosphere. Italian decor. Cr cds: A, C, D, DS, MC, V.

D

★★ **TRATTORIA LA STRADA.** *702 5th Ave (92101), downtown. 619/239-3400.* Web www.trattorialastrada.com. Hrs: 11 am-11 pm. Res accepted. Italian menu. Bar. Semi-a la carte: lunch $10.95-$19.95, dinner $11.95-$21.95. Specialties: osso buco alla milanese, salmone ai carciofi e basilico. Outdoor dining. Italian bistro atmosphere. Cr cds: A, C, D, DS, MC, V.

D

✓★★ **VINCINO MARE.** *1702 India St (92101), downtown. 619/702-6180.* Hrs: 11:30 am-2 pm, 5-10 pm; Fri to 11 pm; Sat 5-11 pm; Sun 5-10 pm. Closed major hols. Res accepted. Italian, seafood menu. Wine, beer. Semi-a la carte: lunch $9.50-$15.95, dinner $12.95-$18.95. Specialties: involtini di pesce spada, blackened ahi, paella. Valet parking. Outdoor dining. Italian seaside trattoria decor. Totally nonsmoking. Cr cds: A, C, D, DS, MC, V.

D

★★★ **WINESELLAR & BRASSERIE.** *9550 Waples St (92121), north of downtown. 619/450-9576.* E-mail winesellar@aol.com; web www.winesellar.com. Hrs: 5:30-10 pm; Sun to 9 pm. Closed Mon; most major hols. Res accepted; required Fri-Sun. Contemporary French menu. Wine list. A la carte entrees: dinner $20-$38. Menu changes seasonally. Intimate, formal dining. Cr cds: A, C, D, DS, MC, V.

Unrated Dining Spots

AESOP'S TABLES. *8650 Genesee Ave (92122), in Costa Verde Center, north of downtown. 619/455-1535.* Hrs: 11 am-10 pm; Sun from 4 pm. Closed major hols. Greek, Middle Eastern menu. Bar. Semi-a la carte: lunch $4-$9.95, dinner $5-$12.95. Patio dining. Cr cds: A, C, D, DS, MC, V.

D

CITY DELICATESSEN. *535 University Ave (92103), north of downtown. 619/295-2747.* Hrs: 7 am-midnight; Fri, Sat to 2 am. Closed Dec 25; Yom Kippur. Jewish-style delicatessen. Wine, beer. A la carte entrees: bkfst, lunch $4.50-$8.50, dinner $4.50-$9.95. Child's meals. Own baking. Delicatessen and bakery. Cr cds: A, C, D, DS, MC, V.

CORVETTE DINER BAR & GRILL. *3946 5th Ave, downtown. 619/542-1001.* Hrs: 11 am-11 pm; Fri, Sat to midnight. Closed Jan 1, Dec 24 eve, 25. Bar. Semi-a la carte: lunch $4.85-$7.95, dinner $5.50-$9.95. Specializes in hamburgers, chicken-fried steak. DJ. 1950s-style diner with soda fountains. Corvette in center of room. Cr cds: A, C, DS, JCB, MC, V.

D.Z. AKIN'S. *6930 Alvarado Rd, north of downtown. 619/265-0218.* Hrs: 7 am-9 pm; Fri, Sat to 11 pm. Closed July 4, Thanksgiving, Dec 25; some Jewish hols. Semi-a la carte: bkfst $3.50-$6, lunch $6-$8, dinner $8-$12. Specializes in delicatessen items. Own pastries. Parking. Cr cds: C, MC, V.

DICK'S LAST RESORT. *345 5th Ave (92101), downtown. 619/231-9100.* Hrs: 11-1:30 am. Closed Dec 25. Res accepted. Bar to 2 am. Semi-a la carte: lunch $3.25-$8.95, dinner $6.95-$14.95. Child's meals. Specialties: beef & pork ribs, crab, chicken. Entertainment. Valet parking Fri, Sat. Outdoor dining. Large warehouse setting. Casual dining. Cr cds: A, C, D, DS, MC, V.

D

EL INDIO MEXICAN. *3695 India St (92103), north of downtown. 619/299-0333.* Hrs: 7 am-9 pm. Mexican menu. Semi-a la carte: bkfst $3-$4, lunch, dinner $5-$7. Outdoor dining. Cafeteria-style. Tortilla factory in kitchen. Family-owned. Cr cds: C, MC, V.

D SC

GREEK CORNER. *5841 El Cajon Blvd, north of downtown. 619/287-3303.* Hrs: 11 am-9:30 pm. Greek, Middle Eastern menu. Wine, beer. Semi-a la carte: lunch, dinner $4-$10. Specializes in Greek dishes, Middle Eastern vegetarian dishes. Parking. Outdoor dining. Greek cafe-style dining. Cr cds: C, MC, V.

LORNA'S ITALIAN KITCHEN. *3945 Governor Dr (92122), north of downtown. 619/452-0661.* Hrs: 11 am-9:30 pm; Fri to 10:30 pm; Sat 4-10:30 pm; Sun 4-9 pm. Closed most major hols. Italian menu. Wine, beer. Semi-a la carte: lunch $4.50-$8.50, dinner $6.50-$14.50. Child's meals. Specializes in pasta, salad. Italian bistro decor. Totally nonsmoking. Cr cds: A, C, D, DS, MC, V.

SAFFRON. *3737 India St (92103), north of downtown. 619/574-0177.* Hrs: 11 am-9 pm. Closed Sun; Jan 1, Thanksgiving, Dec 25. Thai menu. A la carte entrees: lunch, dinner $3.75-$12. Specialties: Thai grilled chicken. Picnic baskets avail. Cr cds: C, MC, V.

San Fernando (J-3)

Pop 22,580 **Elev** 1,061 ft **Area Code** 818 **E-mail** sfcc@sfvalley.org
Information Chamber of Commerce, 519 S Brand Blvd, 91340; 818/361-1184

A Ranger District office of the Angeles National Forest (see PASADENA) is located here.

What to See and Do

Mission San Fernando Rey de España (1797). Restored 17th mission of chain; collections of Native American artifacts, furniture, woodcarvings, gold-leaf altars. A 35-bell carillon rings with an ancient melody sung by Native Americans in mission days. Guided tours (Sat afternoons). (Daily; closed Thanksgiving, Dec 25) 15151 San Fernando Mission Blvd. Phone 818/361-0186. ¢¢ Also here, and included in admission, is the

Archival Center. Located in the west garden of the mission, the center houses ecclesiastical and historical documents; medals and mitres; relics of early California missionaries; changing exhibits. (Mon & Thurs, afternoons)

San Fernando Valley Area (A-2 - B-3 see Los Angeles map)

North and west of Los Angeles (see) and bounded by the Santa Monica, Santa Susana and San Gabriel mountains is the area known as the San Fernando Valley. The Los Angeles River, which flows through the valley, has its source in the mountains. Once primarily an agricultural area, the San Fernando Valley has diversified into a haven for light industry and commuters to Los Angeles.

The valley was explored by the Spanish in 1769; they found "a very pleasant and spacious valley with many live oaks and walnuts." The arrival of the Southern Pacific railroad in 1876, linking Los Angeles to San Francisco, temporarily boosted agricultural production. However, production decreased following the Second World War, when the land was divided into housing tracts. At one time, the valley gained 15,000-20,000 new residents per year, rivaling the spectacular growth of Los Angeles.

The following towns and Los Angeles neighborhoods in the San Fernando Valley area are included in the *Mobil Travel Guide.* For additional information on any of them, see the individual alphabetical listing: North Hollywood, San Fernando, Studio City, Van Nuys, Woodland Hills.

San Francisco (E-2)

Founded 1776 **Pop** 723,959 **Elev** 63 ft **Area Code** 415
Web www.sfvisitor.org
Information Convention & Visitors Bureau, 900 Market St for Visitor's Information Center; or PO Box 429097, 94102-9097; 415/391-2000

Suburbs Berkeley, Corte Madera, Hayward, Mill Valley, Oakland, San Mateo, San Rafael, Sausalito, Tiburon. (See individual alphabetical listings.)

Nearly everyone who comes to San Francisco falls in love with it. A city of sea, hills and parks, cable cars, a bustling waterfront, bridges that span mighty spaces—all freshened by clean Pacific breezes and warmed by a cooperative sun and a romantic fog—San Francisco is alive and lovely. Heart of a great Pacific empire, it is the true capital of the West.

This city of precipitous hills stretches seven miles across in each direction, rimmed on three sides by water. Its awe-inspiring bay, 500 square miles, equal in beauty to the Bay of Naples, constitutes one of the most nearly perfect natural harbors on earth. Rome has its 7 hills; San Francisco was built on 43 hills. The city encompasses a total of 129.4 square miles of which only 46.6 square miles are land. Within its boundaries are islands—Yerba Buena, Treasure and Alcatraz—plus the Farallon group 32 miles west, part of the city since 1872.

San Francisco is one of nature's few "air-conditioned cities"—relatively warm in winter and cool in summer. Weather Bureau statistics show sunshine in 66 out of every 100 possible hours. The average mean temperatures for San Francisco are 50°F in winter; 55°F in spring; 62°F in summer and 60°F in fall.

Gateway to the Orient, San Francisco is a melting pot of cultures. Its population is descended from peoples of almost every nation of the world and every state of the Union. Leading national groups are Italian, German, Irish, Chinese, English, Russian, Latin American, Japanese, Korean and Filipino. More than 500 churches, temples and meetinghouses conduct services in 23 different tongues. Fifty periodicals are published in 13 languages.

San Francisco is an important financial center and headquarters of one of the largest banks in the world (Bank of America). Although no longer considered the air hub of the West (Los Angeles now holds that title), the city still plays a major role in the nation's air travel; San Francisco Interna tional Airport, a $250-million air gateway to the world, is located 14½ miles south off Bayshore Freeway and US 101. The San Francisco Bay Area ranks second on the West Coast in waterborne commerce. The Port of San Francisco is a $100-million public utility with a 7½-mile stretch of shipberthing space, 229 acres of covered and open wharf area and a total of 43 piers. More than 1,500 San Francisco firms engage in international trade.

Hellenic in its setting and climate, European in its intellectual and cultural scope, American in its vigor and informality and Oriental in its tranquility, San Francisco is indeed an exciting "Baghdad by the Bay." Author and raconteur Gene Fowler said, "Every man should be allowed to love two cities—his own and San Francisco."

San Francisco's lusty history began with early Portuguese, English and Spanish explorers penetrating the Bay. In 1775 the Spanish ship *San Carlos* sailed through the Golden Gate to drop the first anchor off San Francisco. On March 28, 1776, a mission site was selected and dedicated to St Francis of Assisi. The little village of Yerba Buena developed near the mission, but slumbered until 1836, when the port grew into an important trading post.

In 1846, the USS *Portsmouth* dropped anchor in the cove; Captain John B. Montgomery and 70 men came ashore and hoisted the Stars and Stripes, marking the end of Mexican rule. The next year, the village changed its name to San Francisco, taking its cue from the mission.

A year later, gold was discovered in Sutter's millrace on the American River at Coloma. This had tremendous impact on San Francisco; few of the inhabitants remained, and, as the news spread around the world, a torrent of people and ships descended on the city. A year later, 6,000 miners were digging and San Francisco was a wild tent city of 20,000 rough, tough transients. An average of 50 sailing ships a month anchored in San Francisco Bay; many were deserted by crews eager for gold.

A few farsighted men realized that fortunes could be made in San Francisco as well as in the gold camps. Their foresight is reflected today in many of the city's distinguished stores.

Meanwhile, thirsty for gold, the East was migrating to California. With the aid of imported Chinese labor, 2,000 miles of railroad track crossed the nation's two greatest mountain ranges to join East and West. Shipping to the Orient flourished and small industries prospered.

Young and raw, San Francisco spent the last half of the 19th century as an exciting mix of growing metropolis, frontier and boom town. Then, on April 18, 1906, came the great earthquake (8.6 on the Richter scale) and fire. Raging unchecked for three days, the fire wiped out the entire business area and burned out 497 blocks of buildings in the heart of the city. Losses amounted to some 2,500 lives and nearly $350 million. With the ashes still warm, the city started rebuilding; it was largely completed by 1915, when the city celebrated the opening of the Panama Canal with the Panama Pacific International Exposition.

The opening of the San Francisco-Oakland Bay Bridge in 1936, followed by the Golden Gate Bridge in 1937 and the completion of the Bay Area Rapid Transit System (BART) have tied the cities of the Bay Area together.

A significant historical event took place April 25-June 26, 1945, when delegates from the nations of the world assembled here to found the United Nations. San Francisco became the birthplace of the UN—another facet of its cosmopolitan personality.

In sightseeing, dining, nightlife, shopping and all other tourist adventures, San Francisco is rivaled—and perhaps not exceeded—only by New York City.

From the Twin Peaks area, the center of the city, Market Street bisects the eastern segment of San Francisco, ending at the Ferry Building and the Embarcadero. The business section, "the Wall Street of the West," is a cluster of skyscrapers extending from Kearny Street to the waterfront and south of Market Street from New Montgomery Street north to Jackson Street. Chinatown, Nob Hill, Telegraph Hill and Fisherman's Wharf fan out north of Market Street. Russian Hill gives a panoramic view of San Francisco Bay. Here is Lombard Street, known as "the crookedest street in the world"—lined by hydrangea gardens and handsome residences, it makes nine hairpin turns in a single block. The Presidio, several museums and Golden Gate Bridge are on the northwest side of the peninsula.

One formula for a systematic exploration is to start with a guided three-and-a-half-hour "around San Francisco" sightseeing bus tour. (These tours can be booked through your hotel.) Note the places you want to visit at greater length, then explore in detail. Use your own car or rent one to reach outlying areas and to explore across the bridges. The San Francisco hills are not for fainthearted drivers, but they're not as bad as they look. Be sure to turn your wheels in toward the curb and set your brake when parking.

San Francisco also has its scenic "49-Mile Drive," marked with blue and white seagull signs. This begins at City Hall in the Civic Center (Van Ness Ave & McAllister St), then twists around the entire city and leads to most of the spectacular sights. You can pick this up and follow its signs at any point or obtain a map of the drive from the San Francisco Visitor Information Center, lower level of Hallidie Plaza, Powell & Market Sts.

San Francisco's famous cable cars (designated a National Historic Landmark) were the brainchild of Andrew Hallidie. The inaugural run was made down Clay from Jones Street on August 2, 1873. The century-old cable car system was temporarily shut down in 1982 for renovations. The $60-million project was completed in June 1984.

These cable cars offer a thrilling roller-coaster experience (fare $2). The natives hop on and off with abandon, but visitors are advised to be more cautious. Also, avoid rush hours. There are three lines: Powell-Mason and Market Streets goes up Powell, over Nob Hill, along Columbus Avenue to Taylor and down to Bay Street at Fisherman's Wharf; the Powell-Hyde cable runs from Powell and Market Streets, up Powell to Jackson Street, west on Jackson to Hyde, north on Hyde over Russian Hill to Beach Street at Aquatic Park; the California cable runs from California and Market Streets to Van Ness Avenue, through the financial district, past Chinatown and over Nob Hill.

The city's diverse restaurants number nearly 3,300. The gold of the mining camps attracted some of the finest chefs in the world to San Francisco and this heritage persists today. Chinatown features the exotic cuisine of Asia; Fisherman's Wharf is famous for seafood. Mexican, Italian, French, Armenian, Russian, Japanese, Vietnamese, East Indian, American are all here—you can make a culinary trip around the world without leaving San Francisco.

Nightlife in San Francisco is only partly carried on in the tradition of the "Barbary Coast" days. One of the most famous cocktail lounges in the world is "The Top of the Mark" (Mark Hopkins Inter-Continental Hotel). The Fairmont, across the street, offers an equally fine view of the city, as do several other high-rise hotels and office buildings. The theaters have long, successful seasons. In sports, the San Francisco Giants play in spring and summer and both college and professional football are played in the fall.

Transportation

Airport. See SAN FRANCISCO AIRPORT AREA.

Car Rental Agencies. See IMPORTANT TOLL-FREE NUMBERS.

Public Transportation. In San Francisco—cable cars, streetcars, subway trains, buses (San Francisco Municipal Railway), phone 415/673-6864; from San Francisco across bay—ferries (Golden Gate Bus Transit), phone 415/923-2200; from San Francisco to Bay Area towns—buses (AC Transit), phone 510/839-2882.

Rail Passenger Service. Amtrak 800/872-7245.

What to See and Do

"A World of Oil." Plaza has trees, shrubs, fountains and flowers. Petroleum exhibit in lobby of building tells how oil is found, produced and refined. Self-guided tours (Mon-Fri; no tours hols). Chevron USA Inc, 555 Market St. Phone 415/894-7700. **Free**

Acres of Orchids (Rod McLellan Co). Largest orchid & gardenia nursery in the world; scientific laboratories show cloning. Guided tours (twice daily: mid-morning & early afternoon). Visitor center (daily; closed major hols). 1450 El Camino Real (CA 82), in South San Francisco. Phone 415/362-1520. **Free**

Cable Car Museum. Three antique cable cars, including the world's first. Also features machinery that powers the cables. Underground viewing area, artifacts, mechanical explanation of operations, vintage photographs, 16-min film on cable car operation. Museum shop. (Daily; closed Jan 1, Thanksgiving, Dec 25) 1201 Mason St. Phone 415/474-1887. **Free**

California Academy of Sciences, Natural History Museum & Aquarium. Includes Morrison Planetarium (shows daily; closed Thanksgiving, Dec 24, 25); Steinhart Aquarium and the Fish Roundabout; African Safari

Hall, Cowell Hall (main entrance), Wild California, Earth & Space Hall, Hall of Human Cultures, Gem & Mineral Hall and "Life Through Time," a hall devoted to the evidence for evolution. Also Far Side of Science Gallery, featuring more than 160 cartoons by Gary Larson. Cafeteria. (Daily) Admission free 1st Wed of month. Golden Gate Park. Located on Music Concourse Dr. Phone 415/750-7145 (recording). ¢¢¢; Planetarium shows ¢¢

Civic Center. 11-sq-blk cluster of buildings bounded by Franklin, 7th, Golden Gate & Hayes Sts. Includes

Bill Graham Civic Auditorium. Seats 7,000. Opp is

Brooks Hall. Under Civic Center Plaza; connected to Civic Auditorium by ramp and escalators; 90,000 sq ft of exhibit space.

City Hall. Classic building with dome more than 13 ft taller than that of the Capitol in Washington, DC.

The Federal and State Buildings are also part of the Civic Center group.

Louise M. Davies Symphony Hall. This $30-million concert hall opened in 1980; capacity of 2,743. (See SEASONAL EVENTS) Van Ness Ave & Grove St. Phone 415/864-6000.

Performing Arts Center. Second-largest performing arts center in US, with a total seating capacity of 7,233. Also here is Van Ness Ave & Grove St.

San Francisco Public Library. In Apr 1996, the library opened its expanded 7-story facility across the street from its previous location. Special Collections Dept features rare books and many volumes on California and San Francisco (tours daily). (Daily; closed hols) 100 Larkin St between Grove & Fulton Sts, housed in the Civic Center. Phone 415/557-4400.

War Memorial/Opera House. Opened in 1932, it was here that the UN was established in 1945 and the Japanese Peace Treaty Conference was held in 1951. First civic-owned opera house in the country. (See SEASONAL EVENTS) Van Ness Ave & Grove St. Phone 415/864-3330. Adj is

Cow Palace. World famous exhibit center and arena, seating 14,700. Used for sports events, exhibits and concerts. (See ANNUAL EVENTS) Geneva Ave, 1 mi W off Bayshore Blvd. For schedule phone 415/469-6000 or 415/469-6065 (box office).

Exploratorium. Hands-on museum dedicated to providing insights into scientific and natural phenomena. More than 700 participatory exhibits on science, art and human perception. Changing exhibits. (Memorial Day-Labor Day, daily; rest of yr, daily exc Mon; closed Thanksgiving, Dec 25) Free admission 1st Wed of month. 3601 Lyon St, housed in the Palace of Fine Arts. Phone 415/561-0360. ¢¢¢

Ferry Building. Ferries to Sausalito and Larkspur leave from Ferry Plaza end of building (Pier ½); ferries to Oakland, Alameda, Vallejo and Tiburon leave from terminal at N end. Also here is a waterfront promenade. Embarcadero at the foot of Market St. Ferries ¢¢–¢¢¢

★ **Golden Gate National Recreation Area.** Within the 74,000 acres of the recreation area are most of the shoreline of San Francisco, the countryside extending 20 mi N in Marin County and a 1,047-acre parcel in San Mateo County to the S. The Golden Gate Bridge connects the 2 segments of the park. The most popular visitor areas are the former penitentiary on Alcatraz Island, the historic Cliff House, Ft Point National Historic Site, Muir Woods National Monument (see) and the cultural-entertainment center, Ft Mason Center. The area has 28 mi of shoreline with many beaches, lagoons, rugged headlands, meadows, fortifications, valleys, hillsides, picnic facilities and 100 mi of trails within the area Congress and designated in 1972 as one of the first urban national parks. (Hrs vary, but most areas are always open during the day) For general recreation area information, phone 415/556-0560 ext. 1, or write Golden Gate National Recreation Area, Ft Mason, Bldg 201, San Francisco 94123. Some of the park areas include

Alcatraz Island. Once a famous maximum security federal penitentiary, closed in 1963. Former inmates include Al Capone, "Machine Gun" Kelly, public enemy #1 Al Karpis and Robert Stroud, the "Birdman of Alcatraz." Boats leave Pier 41 near Fisherman's Wharf every ½-hr (all-yr). Tours include long uphill walk. Self-guided tour; slide show; taped audio tour (fee). In San Francisco Bay, 1¼ mi from shore. Ferry ¢¢¢; With audio tour ¢¢¢¢

Baker Beach. Sandy beach on the western shore of the Presidio. **Free**

China Beach. Wind-protected cove with swimming beach. **Free**

Ft Mason Center. Two piers and other buildings of the former Army port of embarcation are a cultural and entertainment center with restaurants (Phone 415/441-5706). Bldg E houses the J. Porter Shaw Library of the National Maritime Museum (Tues eves & Wed-Fri afternoons, also Sat; phone 415/556-9870). The last surviving intact Liberty ship, the SS *Jeremiah O'Brien,* is moored at Pier 45; phone 415/441-3101.

Ft Mason. Old Army Post, once the Army's western headquarters, is now headquarters for the Golden Gate National Recreation Area. Jogging, bicycling and exercise courses.

Ft Point National Historic Site. This restored Civil War-era fort houses an exhibit explaining story of the fort; also a museum with military artifacts. Guided tours. (Wed-Sun; closed Jan 1, Thanksgiving, Dec 25) Long Ave & Marine Dr, under southern end of Golden Gate Bridge in the Presidio. For information contact PO Box 29333, Presidio of San Francisco 94129; phone 415/556-1693. Web www.nps.gov/fopo **Free**

Golden Gate Promenade. Bay shoreline between Ft Point and Ft Mason provides an area to walk, run and observe; also off-leash dog walking permitted.

Mt Tamalpais State Park. (See MILL VALLEY) (Daily) Some day-use parking fees. 4 mi N via CA 1, then right turn on Panoramic Hwy, 5 mi to park headquarters. Phone 415/388-2070. **Free**

Muir Beach. Protected cove in the ocean coastline, picnicking. (Daily) Phone 415/388-2596 or 415/331-1540. **Free**

Muir Woods National Monument. (see). Adj to Mt Tamalpais State Park, at the base of the mountain. Phone 415/388-2596. ¢

Ocean Beach. 3½ mi of beach on San Francisco's Pacific shore. **Free**

Seal Rocks & Cliff House. Restaurants at the Cliff House (1909) overlook the ocean, the Marin Coast to the north and the Seal Rocks habitat of sea lions. Visitor information center (limited hrs). **Free**

Stinson Beach. North to Bolinas. (Daily) Phone 415/868-0942. **Free**

Tennessee Valley and Beach and Bonida Cove. Secluded, protected beach on ocean. Approx 1½-mi walk from parking. (Daily) Phone 415/331-1540. **Free**

Golden Gate Park. Once a 1,017-acre sand waste, from 1887 the area was developed by John McLaren, master botanist and landscaper, into one of the most beautiful parks in the world. Park contains more than 10,000 trees and shrubs, a restored Dutch windmill, statues and monuments, 11 gardens, 2 waterfalls, 11 lakes and 40 picnic areas. Also, McLaren Rhododendron Dell (free), a conservatory on Kennedy Dr near Arguello Blvd (daily; fee), a Music Concourse near Fulton St & 8th Ave entrance (band concerts: Sun, hols, weather permitting), the Strybing Arboretum and Botanical Garden, King Dr & 9th Ave (daily, free). Fee for some activities. Bounded by Lincoln Way, Stanyan & Fulton Sts & Great Hwy. Phone 415/831-2700; Golden Gate Park Store 415/984-0640. Other park attractions include

Buffalo paddock. A 10-acre enclosure with bison.

Japanese Tea Garden. Oriental landscaping; includes a teahouse, gift shop, pagoda, Buddha, several ponds, streams, footbridges. In spring, cherry blossoms, azaleas and flowering shrubs are in bloom. (Daily). ¢¢

Mary Connolly Children's Playground. Innovative play equipment, Herschel Spillman Carrousel (1912-1914) (fee); picnic area. Near King Dr & 3rd Ave.

Prayerbook Cross (1894). Commemorates first prayer service in English language held on Pacific Coast, conducted by Sir Francis Drake's chaplain. Kennedy Dr.

Sports. 9-hole golf course (fee), 47th Ave off Fulton St, phone 415/751-8987; 3 lawn bowling greens, 21 tennis courts (fee), 3 fly and plug casting pools; 2 indoor and 2 outdoor handball courts; archery field, horseshoe courts; trotting track, bicycle track, running trails, baseball diamonds (fee).

Spreckels Lake. Used primarily for sailing model boats. Kennedy Dr & 36th Ave.

Stow Lake. Surrounds Strawberry Hill. View of park and city. One-hr boat rentals (fee): electric motorboat, rowboat, pedal boat. Stow Lake Dr off Kennedy Dr, near 16th Ave.

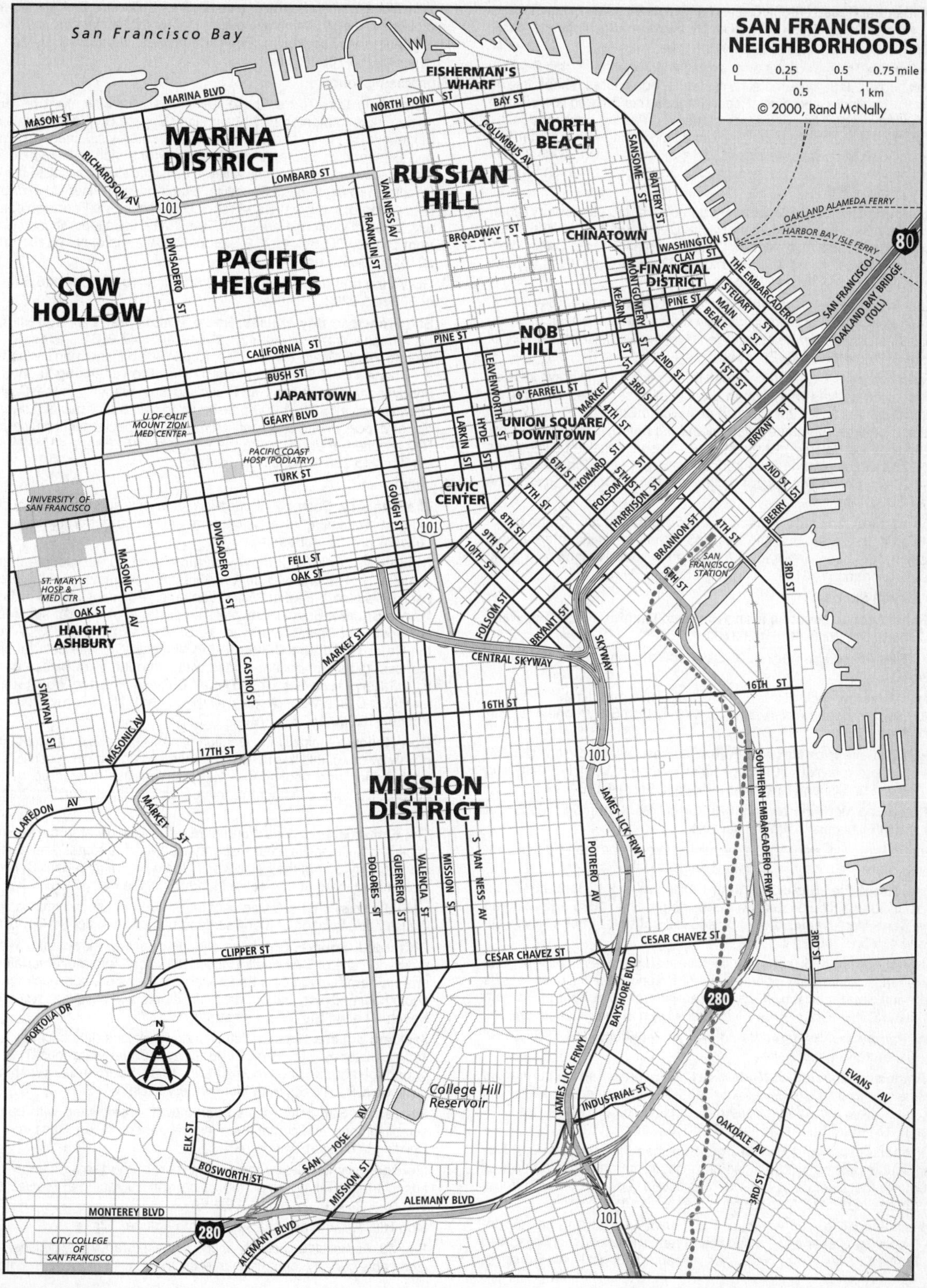
SAN FRANCISCO NEIGHBORHOODS
0 0.25 0.5 0.75 mile
0.5 1 km
© 2000, Rand McNally
San Francisco Bay
FISHERMAN'S WHARF
MARINA DISTRICT
NORTH BEACH
RUSSIAN HILL
CHINATOWN
PACIFIC HEIGHTS
COW HOLLOW
FINANCIAL DISTRICT
NOB HILL
JAPANTOWN
UNION SQUARE/ DOWNTOWN
CIVIC CENTER
HAIGHT-ASHBURY
MISSION DISTRICT
U OF CALIF MOUNT ZION MED CENTER
PACIFIC COAST HOSP (PODIATRY)
UNIVERSITY OF SAN FRANCISCO
ST. MARY'S HOSP & MED CTR
SAN FRANCISCO STATION
College Hill Reservoir
CITY COLLEGE OF SAN FRANCISCO
OAKLAND ALAMEDA FERRY
HARBOR BAY ISLE FERRY
SAN FRANCISCO-OAKLAND BAY BRIDGE (TOLL)
MARINA BLVD
MASON ST
RICHARDSON AV
LOMBARD ST
NORTH POINT ST
BAY ST
COLUMBUS AV
VAN NESS AV
FRANKLIN ST
DIVISADERO ST
BROADWAY ST
SANSOME ST
BATTERY ST
WASHINGTON ST
CLAY ST
MONTGOMERY ST
KEARNY ST
PINE ST
THE EMBARCADERO
STEUART ST
MAIN ST
BEALE ST
CALIFORNIA ST
BUSH ST
O' FARRELL ST
GEARY BLVD
LEAVENWORTH ST
LARKIN ST
HYDE ST
MARKET ST
2ND ST
3RD ST
4TH ST
1ST ST
BRYANT ST
TURK ST
6TH ST
5TH ST
HOWARD ST
FOLSOM ST
HARRISON ST
7TH ST
8TH ST
9TH ST
10TH ST
BRANNON ST
BERRY ST
GOUGH ST
MASONIC AV
FELL ST
OAK ST
CASTRO ST
CENTRAL SKYWAY
SKYWAY
16TH ST
17TH ST
STANYAN ST
CLAREDON AV
SOUTHERN EMBARCADERO FRWY
JAMES LICK FRWY
POTRERO AV
DOLORES ST
GUERRERO ST
VALENCIA ST
MISSION ST
S VAN NESS AV
CESAR CHAVEZ ST
CLIPPER ST
BAYSHORE BLVD
PORTOLA DR
EVANS AV
INDUSTRIAL ST
OAKDALE AV
ELK ST
SAN JOSE AV
BOSWORTH ST
MONTEREY BLVD
ALEMANY BLVD
101
80
280
N

Haas-Lilienthal House (1886). Queen Anne-style Victorian house. One-hr guided tour (Wed, Sun). 2007 Franklin St, between Washington & Jackson Sts. Phone 415/441-3004 (recording). **¢¢**

Japan Center. The focal point of an expanding Japantown, this 3-sq-blk complex houses Japanese restaurants, baths, bookstores, shops; movie complex, art galleries and hotel. Peace Pagoda has 5-tiered roof. Peace Plaza, paved in slate, has Japanese gardens, reflecting pools and is the site of traditional Japanese entertainment during spring and summer festivals. (Daily; most businesses closed Jan 1-3, Thanksgiving, Dec 25) On Post St, between Fillmore, Geary & Laguna Sts, 1 mi W of Union Square. Phone 415/922-6776.

M.H. deYoung Memorial Museum. Features 17th- to 20th-century American art. Paintings from collection of John D. Rockefeller III; British art; tribal rugs from Central Asia; African, Oceanic and ancient art. Cafe. (Wed-Sun) Free admission 1st Wed of month. Golden Gate Park. Phone 415/863-3330. **¢¢¢** In the W wing is the

Asian Art Museum. The Avery Brundage Collection; art from China, India, Japan, Korea and southeast, central and western Asia; traveling exhibitions; displays rotate often. (Wed-Sun) Free admission 1st Wed of month. Phone 415/668-8921. **¢¢¢**

Mission Dolores (1776). Fountainhead from which the city grew. Mission San Francisco de Asís was sixth in a chain of missions established by Franciscan fathers under the direction of Junipero Serra. (It is now known as Mission Dolores, the name being taken from nearby Laguna de Nuestra Señora de los Dolores.) Cornerstone of present mission building was laid in 1782. Many pioneers are buried in ancient cemetery beside the church. (Daily; closed Thanksgiving, Dec 25) 16th & Dolores Sts. Phone 415/621-8203. **¢**

Palace of Fine Arts. Monumental Greco-Romanesque rotunda with Corinthian colonnades; built for the 1915 Panama-Pacific International Exposition; has been restored. Surrounded by duck lagoon and park. Houses Exploratorium. 3601 Lyon St. Grounds. **Free**

Professional Sports.

National League baseball (San Francisco Giants). Pacific Bell Park, at China Basin. Phone 415/468-3700.

NFL (San Francisco 49ers). 3COM Park, at Candlestick Pt. Phone 408/562-4949.

Randall Museum. Includes live animal rm (Tues-Sat, limited hrs) 199 Museum Way, between Roosevelt Way, 14th & 17th Sts. Phone 415/554-9600. **Free**

Ripley's Believe It or Not Museum. Oddities collected from US and abroad; video displays; walk-through kaleidoscope. (Daily) 175 Jefferson St, at Taylor St & Fisherman's Wharf. Phone 415/771-6188. **¢¢¢**

San Francisco Maritime National Historical Park. Adj to Ft Mason, at the N end of Fisherman's Wharf. Includes

Aquatic Park. Cove contains a swimming beach and municipal pier for fishing. Here are most of the historic ships and the

Hyde Street Pier Historic Ships. Collection of 5 historic merchant ships, including SV *Balclutha,* a sailing ship built in 1886 and restored as a Cape Horn trader. (Daily; closed federal hols) Foot of Hyde St. Phone 415/556-3002. **¢**

National Maritime Museum. Collection of ship models, relics & gear; figureheads, scrimshaw, photographs of historic Pacific Coast vessels and early San Francisco. (Daily; closed federal hols) Foot of Polk St. Phone 415/556-3002. **Free** Included as part of the museum are

USS *Pampanito.* Restored World War II fleet submarine. (Daily) Pier 45, Fisherman's Wharf. **¢¢**

San Francisco Museum of Modern Art. 20th-century art on permanent exhibit, also traveling exhibitions; concerts, lectures, special events. Gift shop, cafe. (Daily exc Wed; closed major hols) Free admission 1st Tues of month. 151 Third St. Phone 415/357-4000. **¢¢¢**

San Francisco-Oakland Bay Bridge. Stretches 8½ mi to the East Bay cities. Double-decked, with 5 lanes on each; the upper deck is one-way westbound, the lower deck one-way eastbound. Tunnels through Yerba Buena Island in midbay. Auto toll collected westbound only.

San Francisco Zoo. Zoo with over 1,000 animals, including unique Primate Discovery Center with 14 species of rare and exotic monkeys. Also here, Prince Charles, a rare white tiger, African wild dogs; Koala Crossing, Gorilla World, African Scene and Insect Zoo. Children's Zoo with barnyard and nursery (fee); 25-min train tour on the Zebra Zephyr; carousel. Nature trail in summer. Zoo (daily). Fee for activities. Sloat Blvd at 45th Ave. Phone 415/753-7080. **¢¢¢**

Sightseeing tours.

CCInc Auto Tape Tours. These 90-min cassettes offer mile-by-mile self-guided tours to Monterey (139 mi) along Skyline Blvd, atop Santa Cruz Mountains, to Henry Cowell Redwoods, Monterey's Fisherman's Wharf and Cannery; to Sacramento (166 mi) with a visit to Sausalito, Muir Woods, wineries in the Napa Valley, the historic state capital; to the Wine Country (160 mi) through Sausalito, Muir Woods, a winery tour, dramatic re-creation of the great San Francisco earthquake. Fourteen different tour tapes of California are avail. Tapes may also be purchased directly from CCInc, PO Box 227, 2 Elbrook Dr, Allendale, NJ 07401; phone 201/236-1666. **¢¢¢¢**

Gray Line bus tours. Contact 350 8th St, 94103; phone 415/558-9400 or 800/826-0202.

San Francisco Bay cruises. Red & White Fleet. Bay cruises. (Daily) Fisherman's Wharf, at Pier 43½. Phone 415/447-0591. **¢¢¢¢¢; Blue & Gold Fleet.** Offers 1¼-hr cruise. (Daily) Adj to Fisherman's Wharf, Pier 41. Phone 415/705-5444. **¢¢¢¢¢; Hornblower Dining Yachts.** Luxury dining yachts cruise San Francisco Bay. Flagship is the *California Hornblower,* a 183-ft, 1,000-passenger vessel with 3 decks. Luncheon, dinner/dance, wkend champagne brunch and special event cruises avail. Res required. Pier 33, along the Embarcadero. Phone 415/394-8900, ext 7 or 415/788-8866, ext 7. **¢¢¢¢¢**

Special areas.

The Cannery. Complex of shops, restaurants and markets housed in old fruit-processing factory; informal entertainment on the mall. 2801 Leavenworth St, at Beach St.

Chinatown. A "little Cathay" with more than 80,000 people. Largest community of its kind outside Asia. Grant Ave, its main thoroughfare, has been called the "Street of 25,000 Lanterns." Points of interest include **St Mary's Square,** Bufano's stainless steel statue of Sun Yat-sen, founder of Republic of China. Nearby is Old St Mary's Church (1853). Also see the **Chinese Culture Center.** Art exhibitions, Chinese cultural performances, gift shop; docent-guided walks through the Chinese community. Gallery (Tues-Sat; closed hols). Chinese Heritage Walk (Tues-Fri; fee). Also Culinary/Luncheon Walk (Wed; fee). 750 Kearny St, 3rd floor. Phone 415/986-1822. **Free**

Cow Hollow. Originally the location of a milk-producing area populated mostly by cows, this has been developed into an area of specialty shops, art galleries and bookshops. Many shops are in restored Victorian houses. Numerous restaurants in area. Union St between Van Ness Ave & Lyon St.

The Embarcadero. Wide thoroughfare paralleling waterfront behind the docks from China Basin to Fisherman's Wharf, about 3½ mi. Between Montgomery St and the Ferry Bldg is the new Embarcadero Center. On the Embarcadero at the foot of Market St is the Ferry Bldg.

Fisherman's Wharf. Center of multimillion-dollar commercial fishing industry and location of many seafood restaurants. Foot of Taylor St.

Ghirardelli Square. Charming shopping-restaurant complex with live theater on site of Ghirardelli Chocolate factory. Informal entertainment arts and crafts, women's and children's fashions, sports clothes, sk equipment and many other interesting stores and buildings. North Point Beach & Larkin Sts, W of Fisherman's Wharf.

Jackson Square. Historic District; many buildings date back to the mid-1800s. Includes 1 Jackson Pl (formerly a paper warehouse)—a compound of shops, showrooms, and gaslit courtyards. Washington Jackson & Pacific Sts from Montgomery to Battery St.

Market St. San Francisco's best-known street, lined with business establishments and center for municipal transportation. Runs from Ferry Building to base of Twin Peaks.

Montgomery St. Called the "Wall Street of the West," it's the West's financial hub. Tall buildings form a canyon beginning at Market St and extending to within a block of the Embarcadero.

Nob Hill. A 376-ft crest at Sacramento & Jones Sts.

Pier 39. Approx 110 specialty shops, 10 restaurants, bay cruises, motorized cable car, city tours, free entertainment, waterfront park, 350-bertl marina. Re-creates early San Francisco Barbary Coast. Shops (daily); restaurants (daily). On Embarcadero 2 blks E of Fisherman's Wharf. Phone 415/981-7437.

The Presidio. Wooded tract of 1,450 acres, fortified since 1776 and now a national park. The present Officer's Club contains sections of the first building to be erected in San Francisco. Markers indicate points of historical interest; hiking. Museum (Wed-Sun afternoons); Lincoln Blvd. 102 Montgomery St. Phone 415/561-4323. **Free**

Sigmund Stern Memorial Grove. Natural amphitheater enclosed by eucalyptus trees. Free outdoor concerts in summer (see SEASONAL EVENTS). Picnic tables and barbecue pits nearby. Sloat Blvd & 19th Ave.

Telegraph Hill (284 ft). Topped by 210-ft Coit Memorial Tower, monument to Volunteer Firemen of 1850s and 1860s. Murals decorating 1st and 2nd floors can also be seen from the outside. Elevator to top. (Daily; closed Thanksgiving, Dec 25) The hill itself is occupied by artists' studios and expensive homes. Lombard above Kearny St. **Free.**

Union Square. Public park above four-story subsurface parking garage, first of its kind in the nation. Square is in midst of city's fashionable downtown shopping center. Stores (daily). Bounded by Geary, Powell, Post & Stockton Sts.

★ **The Golden Gate Bridge.** Connecting San Francisco with Marin County. One of famous sights of the world, conceded to be the most beautiful bridge on the globe because of its setting and design. Auto toll collected southbound only.

The Mexican Museum. Pre-Hispanic, Colonial, Folk, contemporary Mexican and Mexican-American art. Permanent and changing exhibits. Gift shop. (Wed-Sun, afternoons; closed some hols & late Dec) Free admission 1st Wed of month. Fort Mason Center, Bldg D, Laguna St & Marina Blvd. Phone 415/441-0404 or 415/202-9700. **¢¢**

Twin Peaks. The breathtaking view it provides comes not only from the panorama, but also from the breezes that whip the hilltops. The north peak is 903 ft, the south peak 910 ft. Many apartment buildings and homes dot the hillsides. Near center of city.

Wells Fargo Bank History Museum. Artifacts and displays dating from the Gold Rush to the 1906 earthquake to present-day banking; Concord Stagecoach. (Mon-Fri; closed hols) 420 Montgomery St. Phone 415/396-2619. **Free**

Annual Events

Chinese New Year. Chinatown. Largest and most colorful celebration of this occasion held in US. Wk-long activities include Golden Dragon Parade, lion dancing, carnival, cultural exhibits. For more information, contact Chinese Chamber of Commerce, 730 Sacramento St, 94108; 415/982-3000. Late Jan-mid-Feb.

Cherry Blossom Festival. Japan Center. Japanese music, dancing, flower arranging, doll & sword exhibits, bonsai show, martial arts, calligraphy, origami, Akita dog exhibit, tea ceremony, children's village, arts & crafts, films, food bazaar, parade. Phone 415/563-2313. 2 wkends Apr.

Carnival. Mission District. Phone 415/826-1401. Memorial Day wkend.

Grand National Rodeo, Horse & Stock Show. Cow Palace. On Geneva Ave at Old Bay Shore. Phone 415/469-6005. Late Oct-early Nov.

Seasonal Events

San Francisco Ballet. War Memorial/Opera House, opera house on corner of Van Ness Ave & Grove St. For information phone 415/864-3330. Repertory season early Feb-early May; *Nutcracker,* Dec.

Stern Grove Midsummer Music Festival. Sigmund Stern Memorial Grove, 19th Ave & Sloat Blvd. Sun afternoons. Phone 415/252-6252. Mid-June-late Aug.

Pop concerts. Bill Graham Civic Auditorium, Grove St at Larkin St. Check newspapers for schedule. Phone 415/974-4000. July.

San Francisco Opera. War Memorial/Opera House, corner of Van Ness Ave & Grove St. Contact Box Office, Opera House, 94102; 415/864-3330. Some summer presentations and 14 wks beginning early Sept.

San Francisco Symphony Orchestra. Louise M. Davies Symphony Hall, Van Ness Ave & Grove St. Obtain tickets in lobby and at major ticket agencies. Phone 415/864-6000 (box office). Also special events. Sept-July.

Additional Visitor Information

The San Francisco Convention & Visitors Bureau, PO Box 429097, 94102-9097, phone 415/391-2000, handles written inquiries. Tourist guides may be obtained by mail (postage & handling fee) or at the San Francisco Visitor Information Center, Hallidie Plaza, Powell & Market Sts on lower plaza level. Phone 415/391-2001 for a daily recording of events.

San Francisco Magazine, available at newsstands, has up-to-date information on cultural events and articles of interest to visitors.

San Francisco Airport Area

For additional accommodations, see SAN FRANCISCO AIRPORT AREA, which follows SAN FRANCISCO.

City Neighborhoods

Many of the restaurants, unrated dining establishments and some lodgings listed under San Francisco include neighborhoods as well as exact street addresses. Geographic descriptions of these areas are given.

Chinatown. South of Broadway, west of Kearny St, north of California St and east of Stockton St; along Grant Ave.

Civic Center. South of Golden Gate Ave, west of 7th St, north of Hayes St and east of Franklin St.

Cow Hollow. Area along Union St between Van Ness Ave on the east and Lyon St on the west.

Financial District. South of Jackson St, west of San Francisco Bay, north of Market St and east of Chinatown (Kearny St).

Fisherman's Wharf. On San Francisco Bay, west of Powell St, north of Bay St and east of Hyde St; at foot of Taylor St.

Haight-Ashbury. Between University of San Francisco and University of California San Francisco; south of Oak St (Panhandle of Golden Gate Park), west of Buena Vista Park, north of Waller St and east of Golden Gate Park.

Japantown. South of Pine St, west of Laguna St, north of Geary Blvd and east of Fillmore St.

Marina District. South of Marina Blvd, west of Webster St, north of Lombard St and east of the Palace of Fine Arts and Lyon St.

Mission District. Area around Mission Dolores; south of Market St and I-101, west of Potrero Ave, north of Army St and east of Castro St.

Nob Hill. On and around crest at Sacramento and Jones Sts.

North Beach. South of Fisherman's Wharf, west of Telegraph Hill, north of Chinatown and east of Russian Hill.

Pacific Heights. South of Lombard St, west of Lyon St, north of Pine St and east of Van Ness Ave.

Richmond District. South of the Presidio, west of Arguello Blvd, north of Golden Gate Park and east of the Pacific Ocean.

Russian Hill. South of Jefferson St, west of Mason St, north of Pacific Ave and east of Van Ness Ave.

Union Square. South of Post St, west of Stockton St, north of Geary St and east of Powell St. **North of Union Square:** North of Post St. **South of Union Square:** South of Geary St. **West of Union Square:** West of Powell St.

Motels

★ **BEST WESTERN.** *364 9th St (94103), in Civic Center area. 415/621-2826; FAX 415/621-0833; res: 800/528-1234.* 57 rms, 2 story. No A/C. May-Oct: S, D $99-$109; each addl $10; under 18 free; lower rates rest of yr. Crib free. TV; cable. Heated pool. Complimentary coffee in rms. Restaurant 7 am-2 pm. Ck-out noon. Coin lndry. Business servs avail. In-rm modem link. Refrigerators; microwaves avail. Cr cds: A, C, D, DS, ER, JCB, MC, V.

SC

★★ **BUENA VISTA MOTOR INN.** *1599 Lombard St (94123), at Gough, in Cow Hollow. 415/923-9600; FAX 415/441-4775; res: 800/835-4980.* 50 rms, 3 story. Mid-Apr-mid-Oct: S, D $119; under 12 free; suite $175; lower rates rest of yr. Crib free. TV. Complimentary coffee in rms. Ck-out noon. Business servs avail. Cr cds: A, C, D, DS, MC, V.

D SC

★★ **CHELSEA MOTOR INN.** *2095 Lombard St (94123), at Fillmore St, in Marina District. 415/563-5600; FAX 415/567-6475.* 60 rms, 3 story, no ground floor rms. S $88-$92; D $92-$120; each addl $10; under 5 free. Crib free. TV; cable. Complimentary coffee in rms. Restaurant nearby. Ck-out noon. Free covered parking. Health club privileges. Cr cds: A, C, D, MC, V.

D

★ **COLUMBUS MOTOR INN.** *1075 Columbus Ave (94133), in North Beach. 415/885-1492; FAX 415/928-2174.* 45 rms, 5 story. Mid-May-mid-Oct: S, D $110-$130; each addl $10; suites $155; lower rates rest of yr. Crib free. TV; cable. Complimentary coffee in rms. Restaurant nearby. Ck-out noon. Business servs avail. Free covered parking. Cr cds: A, C, D, MC, V.

★ **COVENTRY MOTOR INN.** *1901 Lombard St (94123), in Marina District. 415/567-1200; FAX 415/921-8745.* 69 rms, 3 story. S $84-$96; D $88-$116; each addl $10; under 6 free. Crib free. TV; cable. Complimentary coffee in rms. Restaurant nearby. Ck-out noon. Business servs avail. Free covered parking. Cr cds: A, C, D, MC, V.

D

★ **COW HOLLOW MOTOR INN & SUITES.** *2190 Lombard St (94123), in Marina District. 415/921-5800; FAX 415/922-8515.* 117 rms, 2-4 story, 12 suites. Mid-May-mid-Oct: S $92; D $96-$120; each addl $10; suites $185-$265; under 5 free; lower rates rest of yr. Crib free. TV; cable. Coffee in rms. Restaurant adj 7 am-2:30 pm. Ck-out noon. Business servs avail. Free covered parking. Health club privileges. Cr cds: A, C, D, MC, V.

D

★ **DAYS INN.** *2600 Sloat Blvd (94116), opp zoo, south of Union Square. 415/665-9000; FAX 415/665-5440; res: 800/350-3297.* 33 rms, 2 story. July-mid-Sept: S $70-$90; D $85-$95; suites $95-$130; under 12 free; lower rates rest of yr. Crib free. TV; cable. Complimentary continental bkfst. Restaurant nearby. Ck-out 11 am. Business servs avail. Refrigerators, microwaves. Cr cds: A, C, D, DS, JCB, MC, V.

D SC

✓★ **FRANCISCO BAY MOTEL.** *1501 Lombard St (94123), in Marina District. 415/474-3030; FAX 415/567-7082; rres: 800/410-7007.* 39 rms, 4 story. Mid-May-mid-Sept: S $75-$85; D $85-$95; each addl $10; lower rates rest of yr. TV; cable, VCR avail. Complimentary continental bkfst. Complimentary coffee in rms. Restaurant nearby. Ck-out 11 am. Some refrigerators. Cr cds: A, C, D, DS, ER, JCB, MC, V.

★ **LOMBARD MOTOR INN.** *1475 Lombard St (94123), at Franklin, in Cow Hollow. 415/441-6000; FAX 415/441-4291; res: 800/835-3639.* Web www.citysearch7.com. 48 rms, 3 story. May-Sept: S $88-$92; D $88-$108; each addl $5; under 5 free; lower rates rest of yr. Crib free. TV. Complimentary coffee in rms. Ck-out noon. Business servs avail. Cr cds: A, C, D, MC, V.

✓★ **NOB HILL MOTEL.** *1630 Pacific Ave (94109), in Pacific Heights. 415/775-8160; FAX 415/673-8842; res: 800/343-6900.* 29 rms, 12 with shower only, 2 story. Mid-May-Oct: S $75-$85; D $85-$105; each addl $15; suites $160-$185; hols (2-3-day min); higher rates: hols, special events; lower rates rest of yr. TV; cable, VCR avail. Complimentary continental bkfst. Restaurant adj 5-10:30 pm. Ck-out 11 am. Concierge. Free garage parking. Refrigerators; some microwaves. Cr cds: A, C, D, DS, MC, V.

SC

★ **PACIFIC HEIGHTS INN.** *1555 Union St (94123), in Marina District. 415/776-3310; FAX 415/776-8176; res: 800/523-1801.* 40 rms, 2 story, 17 kits. No A/C. S, D $69-$95; suites $95-$150; family rates. Crib free. TV; cable. Complimentary continental bkfst. Complimentary coffee in rms. Restaurant opp open 24 hrs. Ck-out noon. Business servs avail. In-rm modem link. Bellhops. Refrigerators; some in-rm steam and whirlpool baths. Microwaves avail. Cr cds: A, C, D, DS, MC, V.

SC

✓★ **ROYAL PACIFIC MOTOR INN.** *661 Broadway (94133), in Chinatown. 415/781-6661; FAX 415/781-6688; res: 800/545-5574.* 74 rms, 12 A/C, 5 story. Apr-Nov: S, D $75-$93; each addl $5; suites $95-$105; lower rates rest of yr. Crib $10. TV. Complimentary coffee in rms. Restaurant nearby. Ck-out noon. Coin Indry. Business servs avail. Parking. Sauna. Refrigerators avail. Some balconies. Cr cds: A, C, D, MC, V.

★★ **THE PHOENIX INN.** *601 Eddy St (94109), at Larkin St, in Civic Center area. 415/776-1380; FAX 415/885-3109; res: 800/248-9466.* Web www.sftups.com. 44 rms, 2 story. No A/C. May-Oct: S, D $119; suites $149-$159; under 12 free. Crib free. TV; cable, VCR avail (free movies). Heated pool; poolside serv. Complimentary continental bkfst. Restaurant 6 pm-midnight. Bar to 2 am. Ck-out noon. Business servs avail. Concierge. Sundries. Free parking. Health club privileges. Some refrigerators. Private patios, balconies. Cr cds: A, C, D, DS, MC, V.

✓★ **THRIFTLODGE.** *2011 Bay Shore Blvd (92507), south of Union Square. 415/467-8811; FAX 415/468-3097; res: 800/525-9055.* 103 rms, 27 with shower only, 2 story. No A/C. S $60; D $85-$98; each addl $8; under 5 free. TV; cable. Complimentary coffee in lobby. Restaurant open 24 hrs. Ck-out 11:30 am. Meeting rms. Business servs avail. Coin Indry. Indoor/outdoor pool. Sauna. Some balconies. Cr cds: A, C, D, JCB, MC, V.

SC

★ **VAGABOND INN.** *2550 Van Ness Ave (94109), in Russian Hill. 415/776-7500; FAX 415/776-5689; res: 800/522-1555.* 132 rms, 5 story. No A/C. S, D $89-$159; each addl $5; suites, kit. units $109-$195; under 19 free; higher rates special events. Crib free. TV; cable (premium). Heated pool. Complimentary continental bkfst. Complimentary coffee in rms. Ck-out noon. Meeting rm. Business servs avail. In-rm modem link. Valet serv. Some refrigerators. Some balconies. Cr cds: A, C, D, DS, MC, V.

D SC

★★ **WHARF INN.** *2601 Mason St (94133), at Fisherman's Wharf. 415/673-7411; FAX 415/776-2181; res: 800/548-9918.* 51 rms, 3-4 story. No A/C. June-Oct: S, D $119-$179; kit. suite $275-$375; lower rates rest of yr. Crib free. TV; cable (premium). Complimentary coffee in lobby. Restaurant nearby. Ck-out 11 am. Concierge. Some balconies. Cr cds: A, C, D, DS, MC, V.

Motor Hotels

★★ **BEST WESTERN AMERITANIA.** *121 7th St (94103), in Civic Center area. 415/626-0200; FAX 415/863-2529; res: 800/444-5816.* E-mail americania@reneson.com. 143 rms, 4 story, 17 suites. No A/C. Apr-Oct: S $129-$169; D (up to 6) $139-$199; each addl $10; suites $159-

$229; under 17 free; lower rates rest of yr. Crib free. TV; cable (premium). Heated pool. Coffee in rms. Restaurant 6:30 am-10 pm. Rm serv. Bar 11 am-midnight. Ck-out noon. Coin lndry. Meeting rms. Business servs avail. In-rm modem link. Valet serv. Exercise equipt; sauna. Some refrigerators; microwaves avail. Cr cds: A, C, D, DS, ER, JCB, MC, V.

SC

★★ **BEST WESTERN CANTERBURY HOTEL.** *750 Sutter St (94109), near Taylor St, west of Union Square. 415/474-6464; FAX 415/474-5856; res: 800/227-4788.* 250 rms in 2 bldgs, 4 & 10 story. S, D $125-$175; each addl $15; suites $200-$250; under 4 free; wkend, honeymoon plans. Valet parking $22. TV; cable (premium). Pool privileges. Restaurant (see MURPHY'S). Rm serv. Bar. Ck-out noon. Meeting rms. Business servs avail. In-rm modem link. Gift shop. Health club privileges. Cr cds: A, C, D, DS, JCB, MC, V.

D SC

★★ **BEST WESTERN MIYAKO INN.** *1800 Sutter St (94115), in Japantown. 415/921-4000; FAX 415/923-1064; res: 800/528-1234.* E-mail miyakoin@ix.netcom.com. 125 rms, 8 story. S $99-$109; D $109-$119; each addl $10; suites $175-$275; under 18 free. Crib free. TV; cable. Garage parking $10. TV. Restaurant 7 am-10 pm. Bar to midnight. Ck-out noon. Business servs avail. Bellhops. Valet serv. Gift shop. Health club privileges. Balconies. Cr cds: A, C, D, DS, JCB, MC, V.

SC

★★ **HOLIDAY INN.** *1300 Columbus Ave (94133), at Fisherman's Wharf. 415/771-9000; FAX 415/771-7006; res: 800/465-4329.* Web www.holiday_inn.com. 585 rms, 2-5 story. June-Nov: S, D $174-$235; each addl $15; suites $400-$500; lower rates rest of yr. Crib free. Parking $13. TV; cable (premium), VCR avail. Heated pool; poolside serv. Restaurants open 24 hrs. Bar 4-11:30 pm. Rm serv. Ck-out noon. Coin lndry. Meeting rms. Business center. In-rm modem link. Bellhops. Valet serv. Sundries. Some refrigerators. Cr cds: A, C, D, DS, JCB, MC, V.

D SC

★ **HOLIDAY LODGE.** *1901 Van Ness Ave (94109), in Pacific Heights. 415/441-4000; FAX 415/474-7046; res: 800/367-8504.* E-mail holidaylodge@worldnet.att.net; web www.joiede vivre.sf.com. 77 rms, 3 story. No A/C. May-Oct: S $99; D $119; each addl $10; suites $150-$165; kit. units $109; under 16 free; hol rates; lower rates rest of yr. Crib free. TV; cable (premium). Complimentary continental bkfst. Restaurant opp 5:30 pm-midnight. Ck-out noon. Meeting rms. Business servs avail. Bellhops. Concierge. Pool. Microwaves avail. Picnic tables. Cr cds: A, C, D, DS, JCB, MC, V.

SC

★★ **RAMADA PLAZA HOTEL.** *590 Bay St (94133), at Fisherman's Wharf. 415/885-4700; FAX 415/771-8945; res: 800/272-6232; res: 800/228-8408.* Web www.ramada.com. 232 rms, 4 story. May-Oct: S $190-$260; D $190-$270; each addl $15; suites $275-$500; under 17 free; lower rates rest of yr. Crib free. Garage in/out $10. TV; cable, VCR avail. Restaurant 6:30-11 am, 5-10 pm. Rm serv. Bar 5 pm-midnight. Ck-out noon. Meeting rms. Business servs avail. In-rm modem link. Valet serv. Sundries. Gift shop. Refrigerator in suites. Cr cds: A, C, D, DS, ER, JCB, MC, V.

D SC

★★★ **SHERATON FISHERMANS WHARF.** *2500 Mason St (94133), at Fisherman's Wharf. 415/362-5500; FAX 415/956-5275; res: 800/544-5064.* Web www.ittsheraton.com. 524 rms, 4 story. S, D $150-$280; each addl $20; suites from $400-$600; under 17 free; package plans. Crib free. Garage $14. TV; cable (premium), VCR avail. Heated pool. Restaurant 6:30 am-10 pm. Rm serv to midnight. Bar to 11:30 pm, Fri, Sat to midnight; entertainment Sat. Ck-out noon. Convention facilities. Business center. In-rm modem link. Valet serv. Concierge. Gift shop. Barber, beauty shop. Health club privileges. Luxury level. Cr cds: A, C, D, DS, ER, JCB, MC, V.

D SC

★★ **THE SUITES AT FISHERMANS WHARF.** *2655 Hyde St (94109), at Fisherman's Wharf. 415/771-0200; FAX 415/346-8058; res: 800/227-3608.* 24 kit. suites, 3 story. No A/C. S $219-$259, D $319; each addl $10; under 12 free. Garage in/out $15. TV; cable, VCR avail. Complimentary continental bkfst. Ck-out 10 am. Coin lndry. Business servs avail. Concierge. Refrigerators, microwaves avail. Private rooftop patio; some balconies. Ghirardelli Square 1 blk. Totally nonsmoking. Cr cds: A, C, D, DS, JCB, MC, V.

D SC

Hotels

★★★ **ARGENT HOTEL.** *50 3rd St (94102), south of Union Square. 415/974-6400; FAX 415/543-8268; res: 800/543-4300.* Web www.ananet.or.ip/anahotels/e/. 667 rms, 36 story. S, D $230-$285; each addl $25; suites $380-$1,500; under 12 free. Crib free. Valet, garage parking $27. TV; VCR avail. Coffee in rms. Restaurant 6:30 am-10 pm; Fri, Sat to 10:30 pm. Bar 11-1:30 am. Ck-out noon. Convention facilities. Business center. In-rm modem link. Concierge. Gift shop. Tennis privileges. Exercise equipt; sauna. Health club privileges. Massage. Bathrm phones, minibars; microwaves avail. Cr cds: A, C, D, DS, ER, JCB, MC, V.

D SC

✓★★ **ATHERTON HOTEL.** *685 Ellis St (94109), at Larkin St, west of Union Square. 415/474-5720; FAX 415/474-8256; res: 800/474-5720.* E-mail reservations@hotelatherton.com. 74 rms, 6 story. No A/C. S, D $79-$129; each addl $10; under 12 free. Crib free. TV; VCR avail. Complimentary coffee in lobby. Restaurant 7 am-11 pm. Bar 5 pm-2 am. Ck-out noon. Meeting rm. Business servs avail. Cr cds: A, C, D, DS, ER, JCB, MC, V.

★★ **BERESFORD ARMS HOTEL.** *701 Post St (94601), west of Union Square. 415/673-2600; FAX 415/929-1535; res: 800/533-6533.* E-mail beresfordsfo@delphi.com; web www.beresford.com. 96 rms, 8 story, 40 kit. units. No A/C. S, D $114-$124; each addl $10; suites $140-$175, under 12 free. Crib free. Pet accepted, some restrictions. Valet parking $16 in/out. TV; cable, VCR (movies $5). Complimentary continental bkfst. Ck-out noon. Business servs avail. In-rm modem link. No rm serv. Health club privileges. Refrigerators; some bathrm phones, in-rm whirlpools, minibars; microwaves avail. Cr cds: A, C, D, DS, JCB, MC, V.

D SC

★ **BERESFORD HOTEL.** *635 Sutter St (94102), north of Union Square. 415/673-9900; FAX 415/474-0449.* E-mail beresfordsfo@delphi.com; web www.beresford.com. 114 rms, 7 story. No A/C. S $109; D $119; each addl $10; family units $129-$139; under 12 free. Crib free. Pet accepted, some restrictions. Garage parking $16 in/out. TV; cable, VCR avail. Complimentary continental bkfst. Restaurant 7 am-2 pm, 5:30-10 pm; Sun, Mon to 2 pm. No rm serv. Bar 7-1 am, Sun to 2 pm. Ck-out noon. Business servs avail. In-rm modem link. Health club privileges. Refrigerators, minibars. Cr cds: A, C, D, DS, JCB, MC, V.

SC

★★★ **BEST WESTERN TUSCAN INN.** *425 Northpoint St (94133), at Fisherman's Wharf. 415/561-1100; FAX 415/561-1199; res: 800/648-4626.* Web www.tuscaninn.com. 221 rms, 4 story. S, D $188-$218; each addl $10; suites $238-$258; under 16 free; package plans. Crib free. Garage $17/day. TV; cable, VCR avail. Complimentary coffee. Restaurant 7 am-10 pm. Bar. Ck-out 11 am. Meeting rms. Business servs avail. Concierge. Health club privileges. Minibars. European-style "boutique hotel" following the tradition of a classic inn. 3 blks from Pier 39. Cr cds: A, C, D, DS, JCB, MC, V.

D SC

★★★★ **CAMPTON PLACE HOTEL.** *340 Stockton St (94108), on Union Square. 415/781-5555; FAX 415/955-5536; res: 800/235-4300.* E-mail reserve@campton.com. This small, luxurious, boutique hotel is hidden behind a simple facade.The lavish decor is punctuated with antiques and artwork. A fine restaurant garners raves.110 rms, 9 suites, 17 story. S,

D $295-$415; suites $550-$2,000. Rate change Sept-Dec. Pet accepted, some restrictions $35. Valet parking $26/day. Complimentary coffee in lobby. TV; cable, VCR avail (movies). Restaurant (see CAMPTON PLACE). Rm serv 24 hrs. Bar 10 am-11 pm; Fri, Sat to midnight. Ck-out noon. Ck-in 3 pm. Meeting rms. Business servs avail. In-rm modem link. Concierge. Valet serv. Health club avail. Bathrm phones, minibars. Views of Union Square and Financial District. Cr cds: A, C, D, JCB, MC, V.

D

★ **CARLTON HOTEL.** *1075 Sutter St (94109), west of Union Square at Larkin. 415/673-0242; FAX 415/673-4904; res: 800/922-7586.* E-mail carlton@carltonhotel.com; web www.carlton.com. 165 rms, 9 story. No A/C. S, D $160; each addl $20; under 12 free. Crib free. TV; cable. Complimentary afternoon refreshments. Coffee in rms. Restaurant 7-11 am, 5-9 pm. Ck-out 1 pm. Meeting rm. Business servs avail. Health club privileges. Minibars. Cr cds: A, C, D, DS, JCB, MC, V.

SC

★ **CARTWRIGHT HOTEL.** *524 Sutter St (94102), at Powell St, north of Union Square. 415/421-2865; FAX 415/398-6345.* 114 rms, 34 A/C, 8 story. S, D $129-$169; suites $189-$229; under 3 free. Crib free. Valet parking in/out $21. TV; cable, VCR avail. Complimentary afternoon refreshments. Ck-out noon. Meeting rm. Business servs avail. In-rm modem link. Health club privileges. Game rm/library. Many refrigerators. Antiques. Originally opened 1915. Cr cds: A, C, D, DS, ER, JCB, MC, V.

★★ **CATHEDRAL HILL HOTEL.** *1101 Van Ness Ave (94109), at Geary Blvd, west of Union Square. 415/776-8200; FAX 415/441-1174; res: 800/622-0855.* 400 rms, 8 story. S $105-$149; D $125-$200; each addl $20; suites $200-$400; under 18 free; wkend rates. Crib free. Garage parking $15 in/out. TV; cable, VCR avail. Heated pool. Restaurant 6:30 am-10 pm. Bar 11-1 am. Ck-out noon. Convention facilities. In-rm modem link. Concierge. Shopping arcade. Barber, beauty shop. Health club privileges. Bathrm phones; some refrigerators. Balconies; some private patios. Cr cds: A, C, D, DS, JCB, MC, V.

D SC

★★ **CHANCELLOR HOTEL.** *433 Powell St On Union Sq (94102), north of Union Square. 415/362-2004; FAX 415/362-1403; res: 800/428-4748.* E-mail chnclrhtl@aol.com; web www.globescope.com/chancellor. 137 rms, 16 story. No A/C. S $124; D $139; each addl $15; suites $230. Crib free. TV; cable (premium). Restaurant 7 am-3 pm, 5-9:30 pm. Bar 11-1 am. Ck-out noon. Meeting rm. Business servs avail. In-rm modem link. Health club privileges. Gift shop. Tallest building in the city when constructed (1914) after the San Francisco earthquake in 1906. Cr cds: A, C, D, DS, ER, JCB, MC, V.

SC

★★ **CLARION HOTEL.** *761 Post St (94109), west of Union Square. 415/673-6040; FAX 415/563-6739; res: 800/227-5642.* E-mail bedfordhotel@compuserv.com. 144 rms, 17 story. No A/C. S, D $129; each addl $10; 2-bedrm family unit $179; under 18 free. Crib free. Valet parking $18. TV; cable. Coffee in rms. Restaurant 6 am-midnight. Bar. Ck-out noon. Meeting rms. Business servs avail. In-rm modem link. Refrigerators, minibars. Cr cds: A, C, D, DS, ER, JCB, MC, V.

SC

✓★★ **COMFORT INN.** *2775 Van Ness Ave (94109), at Lombard St, north of Union Square. 415/928-5000; FAX 415/441-3990; res: 800/228-5150.* Web www.hotelchoice.com. 138 rms, 11 story. Mid-June-Oct: S, D $119-$189; each addl $10; under 19 free; lower rates rest of yr. Crib free. Garage parking in/out $15. TV; cable. Complimentary continental bkfst. Ck-out noon. Business servs avail. In-rm modem link. Microwaves avail. Cr cds: A, C, D, DS, ER, JCB, MC, V.

D SC

★★ **COMMODORE INTERNATIONAL HOTEL SAN FRANCISCO.** *825 Sutter St (94109), west of Union Square. 415/923-6800; FAX 415/923-0177; res: 800/338-6848.* E-mail commodorehotel@worldnet.att.net. 113 rms, 6 story. No A/C. July-Oct: S, D $99-$129; each addl $10; under 12 free; hols (2-day min); lower rates rest of yr. Crib free. Garage, in/out parking $15. TV; cable, VCR avail. Restaurant 7 am-2 pm. No rm serv. Bar 5 pm-2 am. Ck-out noon. Meeting rm. Business servs avail. In-rm modem link. Concierge. Health club privileges. Some refrigerators. Cr cds: A, C, D, DS, JCB, MC, V.

SC

★★★ **CROWNE PLAZA UNION SQUARE.** *480 Sutter St (94108), north of Union Square. 415/398-8900; FAX 415/989-8823; res: 888/218-0808.* 400 rms, 30 story. S $179-$239; D $195-$255; each addl $15; suites $250-$750; under 19 free; wkend rates. Crib free. Parking in/out $23. TV; cable (premium), VCR avail. Restaurant 6:30-11:30 am, 5-11 pm. Bar. Ck-out noon. Convention facilities. Business center. Valet serv. Gift shop. Exercise equipt. Refrigerator in suites. Cr cds: A, C, D, DS, JCB, MC, V.

D SC

✓★★ **ESSEX HOTEL.** *684 Ellis St (94109), at Larkin St, west of Union Square. 415/474-4664; FAX 415/441-1800.* 96 rms, 7 story. No A/C. S $69; D $79; each addl $10; suites $99; under 12 free. TV. Complimentary coffee in lobby. Ck-out noon. Some balconies. Civic Center 3 blks. Cr cds: A, C, MC, V.

★★★ **FAIRMONT HOTEL.** *950 Mason St (94108), California & Mason Sts, on Nob Hill. 415/772-5000; FAX 415/837-0587; res: 800/527-4727.* Web www.fairmont.com. 596 rms, 8 & 24 story. S, D $229-$319; each addl $30; suites $350-$8,000; under 13 free; wkend rates. Crib free. Garage, in/out $27/day, valet. TV; cable, VCR (movies). Restaurant 6 am-11 pm. Rm serv 24 hrs. Bars; entertainment. Ck-out 1 pm. Convention facilities. Business center. In-rm modem link. Concierge. Shopping arcade. Barber, beauty shop. Free financial district transportation. Exercise rm; sauna. Whirlpool. Massage. Bathrm phones, minibars; microwaves avail. Some suites with private patio. Outside glass-enclosed elvtr to Fairmont Crown Room. Panoramic view of city; rooftop garden. Cr cds: A, C, D, DS, JCB, MC, V.

D

★★★ **GRAND HYATT.** *345 Stockton St (94108), on Union Square. 415/398-1234; FAX 415/391-1780; res: 800/233-1234.* Web www.gohyatt.com. 683 rms, 36 story, 33 suites. S, D $199-$300; each addl $25; suites $450-$1,550; under 18 free; package plans. Crib free. Valet parking, garage in/out $25. TV; cable (premium), VCR avail. Restaurant 6:30 am-10 pm. Bar 11-2 am; entertainment. Ck-out noon. Convention facilities. Business center. In-rm modem link. Concierge. Shopping arcade. Barber, beauty shop. Exercise equipt. Health club privileges. Massage. Refrigerators, minibars, bathrm phones; some wet bars; microwaves avail. Luxury level. Cr cds: A, C, D, DS, ER, JCB, MC, V.

D SC

✓★ **GRANT PLAZA HOTEL.** *465 Grant Ave (94111), in Chinatown. 415/434-3883; FAX 415/434-3886.* E-mail grantplaza@worldnet.att.net; web www.smarttraveler.com/grantplaza.htm. 72 rms, 6 story. S $52-$55; D $62-$69; each addl $10; under 10 free. Crib $10. Garage $14.50. TV; cable (premium), VCR avail. Restaurant adj open 24 hrs. No rm serv. Ck-out noon. Business servs avail. Microwaves avail. Cr cds: A, C, D, JCB, MC, V.

★★★ **HANDLERY UNION SQUARE HOTEL.** *351 Geary St (94102), west of Union Square. 415/781-7800; FAX 415/781-0216; res: 800/843-4343.* E-mail hushres@handlery.com; web handlery.com. 377 rms, 8 story. S, D $140-$185; each addl $10; suites $170-$370; under 16 free. Crib free. Garage in/out $20. TV; cable, VCR avail. Heated pool. Sauna. Coffee in rms. Restaurant 7 am-11 pm. Rm serv 7-10:30 am, 5-10 pm. Bar 10 am-11:30 pm. Ck-out noon. Meeting rms. Business servs avail. In-rm modem link. Concierge. Gift shop. Barber, beauty shop. Luxury level. Cr cds: A, C, D, DS, ER, JCB, MC, V.

D SC

★★★ **HILTON & TOWERS.** *333 O'Farrell St (94102), south of Union Square. 415/771-1400; FAX 415/771-6807; res: 800/445-8667.* Web www.hilton.com. 1,896 rms, 19, 23 & 46 story. S $185-$265; D $205-$275; each addl $20; suites $300-$2,500; wkend rates. Garage, in/out $28. TV; cable (premium), VCR avail. Pool on 16th floor in garden court. Restaurants 6-1 am. Bars 10:30-1:30 am. Ck-out noon. Convention facilities. Business center. In-rm modem link. Shopping arcade. Barber, beauty shop. Exercise equipt; sauna. Health club privileges. Massage. Balconies. Some penthouse suites with solarium. 16th floor lanai rms. 46-story tower with distinctive rms and rooftop dining. Luxury level. Cr cds: A, C, D, DS, JCB, MC, V.

D

★★ **HOLIDAY INN.** *1500 Van Ness Ave (94109), at California St, in Russian Hill. 415/441-4000; FAX 415/776-7155; res: 800/465-4329.* Web www.holiday-inn/holiday.html. 499 rms, 26 story. May-Oct: S, D $115-$220; each addl $15; suites $185-$460; under 19 free; lower rates rest of yr. Crib free. Parking in/out $16. TV; cable. Heated pool. Restaurant 6 am-10:30 pm. Bar. Ck-out noon. Convention facilities. Business servs avail. In-rm modem link. Gift shop. Exercise equipt. Some refrigerators. On cable car line. Cr cds: A, C, D, DS, JCB, MC, V.

D SC

★★ **HOLIDAY INN-CIVIC CENTER.** *50 8th St (94103), at Market St, in Civic Center area. 415/626-6103; FAX 415/552-0184; res: 800/465-4329.* 394 rms, 14 story. S $109-$189; D $119-$189; each addl $15; suites $250-$350; under 19 free; wkend rates. Garage $16. Crib free. TV; cable (premium). Heated pool. Restaurant 6-11 am, 5-10 pm. Bar 5 pm-midnight. Ck-out noon. Coin lndry. Meeting rms. Business servs avail. In-rm modem link. Gift shop. Health club privileges. Balconies. Cr cds: A, C, D, DS, JCB, MC, V.

D SC

✓★ **HOTEL BIJOU.** *111 Mason St (94102), south of Union Square. 415/771-1200; FAX 415/346-3196; res: 800/771-1022.* 65 rms, 6 story. No A/C. S, D $99-$129; each addl $10; under 14 free; hol rates. Crib free. Garage in/out parking $14. TV. Complimentary coffee in lobby. Restaurant opp open 24 hrs. No rm serv. Ck-out noon. Concierge. Cr cds: A, C, D, DS, JCB, MC, V.

✓★ **HOTEL BRITTON.** *112 7th St (94103), near Civic Center area. 415/621-7001; FAX 415/626-3974; res: 800/444-5819.* 79 rms, 5 story. Apr-Oct: S, D $109-$129; each addl $10; suites $139-$159; lower rates rest of yr. Crib free. TV; cable (premium). Coffee in rms. Restaurant 6 am-10 pm. Ck-out noon. Coin lndry. Business servs avail. In-rm modem link. Microwaves avail. Convention Center 3 blks. Cr cds: A, C, D, DS, ER, JCB, MC, V.

D SC

★★ **HOTEL DIVA.** *440 Geary St (94102), west of Union Square. 415/885-0200; FAX 415/346-6613.* 111 rms, 7 story. S, D $149; each addl $10; suites $169-$450; under 12 free. Crib free. Valet parking, in/out $17. TV; cable (premium), VCR (movies). Complimentary continental bkfst. Restaurant 11:30 am-10 pm; Fri, Sat to 11 pm; Sun 1-9 pm. Rm serv 7 am-10 pm. Ck-out noon. Meeting rm. Business center. Concierge. Exercise equipt. Bathrm phones, refrigerators, minibars. Cr cds: A, C, D, DS, ER, JCB, MC, V.

D SC

★★ **HOTEL GRIFFON.** *155 Stewart St (18612), south of Union Square. 415/495-2100; FAX 415/495-3522.* 62 rms, 5 story. S, D $215-$315; suites $315; under 18 free. Crib free. Garage parking $15. TV; cable. Complimentary continental bkfst. Restaurant 11:30 am-10 pm; Sat, Sun from 5:30 pm. Ck-out noon. Meeting rms. Business servs avail. Concierge. Cr cds: A, C, D, DS, ER, JCB, MC, V.

D

★★★ **HOTEL MILANO.** *55 5th St (94103), south of Union Square. 415/543-8555; FAX 415/543-5843; res: 800/398-7555.* 108 rms, 8 story. S $169-$189; D $169-$259; each addl $20; under 12 free; wkend, hol rates. Crib free. Parking $19. TV; cable (premium). Restaurant (see M POINT). Bar 5-11 pm. Ck-out noon. Meeting rms. Business servs avail. Concierge. Exercise equipt. Minibars. Cr cds: A, C, D, DS, MC, V.

D

★★★ **HOTEL MONACO.** *501 Geary St (94102), west of Union Square. 415/292-0100; FAX 415/292-0111; res: 800/214-4220.* Web www.hotelmonaco.com. 201 rms, 7 story, 34 suites. S, D $189-$279; suites $299-$439; under 16 free; hol rates. Crib free. Pet accepted. Valet parking; in/out $24. TV; cable (premium), VCR avail. Complimentary coffee in rms. Restaurant (see GRAND CAFE). Bar 11:30-1:30 am. Ck-out noon. Meeting rms. Business servs avail. In-rm modem link. Concierge. Exercise rm. Massage. Minibars. Cr cds: A, C, D, DS, ER, JCB, MC, V.

D SC

★★★ **HOTEL NIKKO.** *222 Mason St (94102), west of Union Square. 415/394-1111; FAX 415/421-0455; res: 800/645-5687.* 523 rms, 25 story, 33 suites. S $250-$340; D $280-$370; each addl $30; suites $525-$2,000; under 18 free; wkend rates. Crib free. Covered parking, in/out $27; valet. TV; cable, VCR avail. Indoor pool; whirlpool, poolside serv. Complimentary bkfst, refreshments. Restaurant 6:30 am-10 pm. Rm serv 24 hrs. Bar 11-2 am. Ck-out noon. Convention facilities. Business center. Concierge. Sundries. Barber, beauty shop. Exercise rm; sauna, steam rm. Minibars. 2-story marble staircase in lobby frames cascading waterfall. Luxury level. Cr cds: A, C, D, DS, ER, JCB, MC, V.

D SC

★★★ **HOTEL REX.** *562 Sutter St (94102), north of Union Square. 415/433-4434; FAX 415/433-3695; res: 800/433-4434.* E-mail hotelrex@pop.sfo.com. 94 rms, some A/C, 7 story. S, D $165-$295; each addl $20; suites $575. Crib free. Valet $25 in/out. TV; cable. Complimentary coffee in lobby. Restaurant 7-10 am; Sat, Sun to 11 am. Bar 5 pm-midnight. Ck-out noon. Business servs avail. In-rm modem link. Concierge. Health club privileges. Minibars. Microwaves avail. Renovated hotel with 1920's atmosphere. Cr cds: A, C, D, DS, JCB, MC, V.

D SC

★★★ **HOTEL TRITON.** *342 Grant Ave (94108), east of Union Square. 415/394-0500; FAX 415/394-0555.* Web www.tritonsf.com. 140 rms, 7 story. S, D $159-$229; suites $245-$299; under 16 free. Crib free. Valet, in/out parking $24. Pet accepted; $15. TV; cable, VCR avail. Complimentary afternoon refreshments. Restaurants 6:30 am-10 pm. Bar from 11 am. Ck-out noon. Meeting rm. Business servs avail. Concierge. Exercise equipt. Health club privileges. Minibars. Cr cds: A, C, D, DS, ER, JCB, MC, V.

D SC

★★ **HOTEL UNION SQUARE.** *114 Powell St (94102), west of Union Square. 415/397-3000; FAX 415/399-1874; res: 800/553-1900.* 131 rms, 6 story. S, D $115-$169; each addl $10; suites $159-$350; under 12 free. Garage in/out $18. TV. Complimentary continental bkfst. Restaurant adj 11 am-11 pm. Bar 11 am-9 pm. Ck-out noon. Business servs avail. Health club privileges. Refrigerators avail. Penthouse suites with deck. Cr cds: A, C, D, DS, ER, JCB, MC, V.

SC

★★ **HOTEL VINTAGE COURT.** *650 Bush St (94108), north of Union Square. 415/392-4666; FAX 415/433-4065; res: 800/654-1100.* Web www.vintagecourt.com. 106 rms, 65 A/C, 8 story. S, D $129-$179; each addl $10; under 12 free. Crib free. Valet parking in/out $21. TV; cable (premium), VCR avail. Complimentary coffee in lobby. Restaurant (see MASA'S). Ck-out noon. Meeting rm. Business servs avail. In-rm modem link. Health club privileges. Refrigerators. Built 1912. Cr cds: A, C, D, DS, JCB, MC, V.

D SC

★★★ **HUNTINGTON HOTEL.** *1075 California St (94108), top of Nob Hill. 415/474-5400; FAX 415/474-6227; res: 800/227-4683.* 100 rms, 12 story, 40 suites. S $230-$350; D $255-$375; suites $425-$990; under 6 free. Crib free. Garage, in/out $19.50. TV; cable, VCR avail. Restaurant (see BIG FOUR). Rm serv 6 am-11:30 pm. Bar 11:30-12:30 am; pianist. Ck-out noon. Meeting rms. Business servs avail. Concierge. Health club privileges. Minibars; many wet bars; microwaves avail. Cr cds: A, C, D, DS, JCB, MC, V.

★★★ **HYATT FISHERMAN'S WHARF.** *555 N Point St (94133), at Fisherman's Wharf. 415/563-1234; FAX 415/749-6122; res: 800/233-1234.* 313 rms, 5 story. S $175-$265; D $190-$290; suites $375-$800; under 18 free. Crib free. Garage $23 in/out. TV; cable (premium), VCR avail. Heated pool; whirlpool. Restaurant 6:30 am-11 pm; Fri, Sat to 2 am. Rm serv. Bar noon-11 pm, Fri, Sat to 2 am. Ck-out noon. Coin lndry. Meeting rms. Business center. In-rm modem link. Concierge. Gift shop. Exercise equipt; sauna. Some bathrm phones. Cable car line opp. Cr cds: A, C, D, DS, ER, JCB, MC, V.

D

★★★ **HYATT REGENCY.** *5 Embarcadero Ctr (94111), Market & Drumm Sts, in Financial District. 415/788-1234; FAX 415/398-2567; res: 800/233-1234.* 803 rms, 15 story. S $179-$300; D $204-$325; each addl $25; suites $425-$1,400; under 18 free. Crib free. Covered parking, valet $27. TV; cable (premium), VCR avail. Coffee in rms. Restaurant 6-10 pm. Rm serv 6 am-midnight. Bars; entertainment; revolving rooftop restaurant/bar. Ck-out noon. Convention facilities. Business center. In-rm modem link. Concierge. Shopping arcade. Exercise equipt. Health club privileges. Refrigerators; microwaves avail. Balconies. Spacious 17-story atrium in lobby. Luxury level. Cr cds: A, C, D, DS, JCB, MC, V.

D

★★★ **INN AT THE OPERA.** *333 Fulton St (94102), in Civic Center area. 415/863-8400; FAX 415/861-0821.* 30 rms, 7 story, 18 suites. A/C in suites only. S $140-$215; D $165-$230; suites $240-$315. Crib $15. Parking $22. TV; cable (premium), VCR avail. Complimentary bkfst. Restaurant 5-10 pm. Bar; Fri, Sat to 1 am; entertainment exc Mon. Ck-out noon. Business servs avail. In-rm modem link. Concierge. Health club privileges. Refrigerators, microwaves, minibars. Elegant European decor. In Performing Arts district. Cr cds: A, C, D, DS, JCB, MC, V.

D

★★ **JULIANA HOTEL.** *590 Bush St (94108), north of Union Square. 415/392-2540; FAX 415/391-8447; res: 800/328-3880.* 107 rms, 9 story. S, D $135-$185; suites $165-$245; monthly rates. Crib free. TV; cable (premium). Complimentary coffee in lobby; afternoon refreshments. Ck-out noon. Business servs avail. In-rm modem link. Health club privileges. Refrigerators, honor bars. Cr cds: A, C, D, DS, ER, JCB, MC, V.

D SC

★★ **KENSINGTON PARK HOTEL.** *450 Post St (94102), west of Union Square. 415/788-6400; FAX 415/399-9484; res: 800/553-1900.* 87 rms, 12 story. S, D $150-$190; each addl $10; suites $255-$550; under 13 free. Crib free. Valet parking $17. TV; VCR avail. Complimentary continental bkfst; afternoon refreshments. Ck-out noon. Meeting rms. Business servs avail. In-rm modem link. Exercise equipt. Bathrm phones; some refrigerators. Renovated 1924 hotel, guest rms on floors 5-12. Grand piano in lobby. Traditional English decor. Theater in building. Cr cds: A, C, D, DS, JCB, MC, V.

D

★★ **KING GEORGE HOTEL.** *334 Mason St (94102), west of Union Square. 415/781-5050; FAX 415/391-6976; res: 800/288-6005.* E-mail kgeorge@ix.netcom.com; web www.kinggeorge.com. 141 rms, 9 story. No A/C. S, D $95-$160; each addl $10; suites $225; package plans. Crib free. Garage, in/out $16.50. TV; cable. Restaurant 7-10 am, 3-6:30 pm. Rm serv 24 hrs. Bar; entertainment. Ck-out noon. Meeting rms. Business servs avail. In-rm modem link. Concierge. Health club privileges. Union Square 1 blk. Cr cds: A, C, D, DS, ER, JCB, MC, V.

D SC

✓★★★★★ **MANDARIN ORIENTAL.** *222 Sansome (94104), between Pine & California Sts, in Financial District. 415/885-0999; FAX 415/433-0289; res: 800/622-0404.* E-mail mandarinsfo@mosfo.com; web www.mandarin-oriental.com. This business travelers' paradise is perched on the top 11 floors of San Francisco's third tallest building. Views from the large rooms are spectacular and the service is attentive and professional. Asian accents include complimentary tea service upon arrival. 158 rms, 11 story; on floors 38-48 of the twin towers in the California Center. S, D $415-$610; suites $950-$2,000; under 12 free; wkend rates. Crib free. Covered parking $30. TV; cable (premium), VCR avail. Restaurant (see SILKS). Rm serv 24 hrs. Bar 11 am-11 pm; entertainment exc Sun. Ck-out noon. Meeting rms. Business center. In-rm modem link. Concierge. Exercise equipt. Health club privileges. Bathrm phones, refrigerators, minibars. Cr cds: A, C, D, DS, JCB, MC, V.

D

★★ **MARK HOPKINS INTER-CONTINENTAL.** *1 Nob Hill (94108), on Nob Hill. 415/392-3434; FAX 415/421-3302; res: 800/327-0200.* 390 rms, 19 story. S, D $240-$340; each addl $30; suites $425-$1,600; under 17 free; wkend rates. Crib free. Garage Parking $26/day. TV; cable, VCR avail. Restaurant 6:30 am-11 pm (also see NOB HILL). Bars noon-1:30 am. Ck-out noon. Conference facilities. Business center. Concierge. Exercise equipt. Health club privileges. Minibars. Some balconies. Luxury level. Cr cds: A, C, D, DS, ER, JCB, MC, V.

D

★★★ **MARRIOTT.** *55 4th St (94103), opp Moscone Convention Center, south of Union Square. 415/896-1600; FAX 415/777-2799; res: 800/228-9290.* Web www.marriott.com/sfodt. 1,500 rms, 39 story, 141 suites. S, D $195-$249; each addl $20; suites $280-$2,400; under 18 free. Crib free. Garage $27, in/out 24 hrs. TV; cable (premium), VCR avail. Indoor pool; poolside serv. Restaurant 6:30 am-11 pm; Fri, Sat to midnight. Bar 10:30-2 am. Ck-out noon. Convention facilities. Business center. In-rm modem link. Concierge. Gift shop. Sundries. Exercise equipt; sauna, steam rm. Minibars; some bathrm phones. Refrigerator, wet bar in suites. Some balconies. Six-story atrium lobby. Luxury level. Cr cds: A, C, D, DS, ER, JCB, MC, V.

D SC

★★★ **MARRIOTT FISHERMAN'S WHARF.** *1250 Columbus Ave (94133), at Fisherman's Wharf. 415/775-7555; FAX 415/474-2099; res: 800/228-9290.* Web www.marriott.com/marriott/sfofw. 285 rms, 5 story. S, D $139-$300; suites $300-$800; under 18 free; wkend rates. Crib free. Valet parking in/out $19. TV; cable (premium), VCR avail. Restaurant 6 am-10 pm. Bar 11-1 am. Ck-out noon. Meeting rms. Business center. In-rm modem link. Gift shop. Exercise equipt; sauna. Bathrm phones. Marble floor in lobby. Cr cds: A, C, D, DS, ER, JCB, MC, V.

D SC

★★ **MAXWELL HOTEL.** *386 Geary St (94102), west of Union Square. 415/986-2000; FAX 415/397-2447; res: 888/734-6299; res: 888/574-6299.* Web www.joiedevivre-sf.com. 153 rms, 12 story. Apr-mid-Nov: S, D $145-$215; each addl $10; under 18 free; some wkends, hols (2-day min); lower rates rest of yr. Crib free. Garage, in/out parking $18. TV; cable. Restaurant 7-1 am. Bar. Entertainment Fri, Sat. Ck-out noon. Meeting rms. Business servs avail. In-rm modem link. Concierge. Health club privileges. Bathrm phones; refrigerators avail. Cr cds: A, C, D, DS, JCB, MC, V.

SC

★★★ **MONTICELLO INN.** *127 Ellis St (94102), south of Union Square. 415/392-8800; FAX 415/398-2650; res: 800/669-7777.* E-mail montinn@aol.com; web www.monticelloinn.com. 91 rms, 5 story, 28 suites. S, D $115-$195; suites $165-$255. Crib free. Valet parking $20. TV; cable (premium). Complimentary continental bkfst. Restaurant 11:30 am-10 pm.

Ck-out noon. Business servs avail. In-rm modem link. Concierge. Health club privileges. Minibars. 18th-century decor. Renovated hotel built 1906. Cr cds: A, C, D, DS, ER, JCB, MC, V.

D SC

★★ **NOB HILL LAMBOURNE HOTEL.** *725 Pine St (94108), on Nob Hill. 415/433-2287; FAX 415/433-0975; res: 800/274-8466.* E-mail nobhilllambourne@att.net. 20 kit. units, 3 story, 6 suites. No A/C. S, D $190-$210; suites $295; family, monthly rates. Crib avail. Garage; valet, in/out $24. TV; cable, VCR (free movies). Complimentary continental bkfst. Complimentary coffee in rms. Restaurant nearby. Ck-out noon. Business center. In-rm modem link. Concierge. Exercise equipt. Health club privileges. Microwaves, wet bars. Balconies. Totally nonsmoking. Cr cds: A, C, D, DS, JCB, MC, V.

SC

★★★ **PALACE HOTEL.** *2 New Montgomery St (94105), at Market St, south of Union Square. 415/512-1111; FAX 415/543-0671; res: 800/325-3535.* Web www.sheraton.com. 550 rms, 8 story. S $310-$380; D $330-$400; each addl $20; suites $475-$2,900; family, wkend rates. Crib free. Valet parking $22. TV; cable (premium), VCR avail (movies). Indoor pool; whirlpool, poolside serv. Restaurant (see GARDEN COURT). Rm serv 24 hrs. Bar from 11 am; entertainment. Ck-out noon. Convention facilities. Business center. In-rm modem link. Concierge. Shopping arcade. Exercise rm; sauna. Health club privileges. Bathrm phones, refrigerators. Cr cds: A, C, D, DS, ER, JCB, MC, V.

D SC

★★★★ **PAN PACIFIC.** *500 Post St (94102), west of Union Square. 415/771-8600; FAX 415/398-0267; res: 800/533-6465.* E-mail vulrich@sfo.pan-pacific.com; web www.panpac.com. This centrally located hotel features a third-floor atrium lobby, decorated mostly in marble (with commissioned sculpture) and highlighted by a spectacular 17-story skylight. 330 units, 21 story. S, D $320-$420; suites $460-$1,800; under 18 free; wkend rates. Crib free. Garage, in/out $27; valet parking. Pet accepted, some restrictions. TV; cable (premium), VCR avail. Restaurant 6:30 am-10:30 pm (also see PACIFIC). Rm serv 24 hrs. Bar 11 am-11:30 pm; pianist. Ck-out noon. Meeting rms. Business center. In-rm modem link. Personal valet serv. Concierge. Exercise equipt. Health club privileges. Minibars, bathrm phones. Cr cds: A, C, D, DS, JCB, MC, V.

D

★★★★ **PARK HYATT HOTEL.** *333 Battery St (94111), at Clay St, in Financial District. 415/392-1234; FAX 415/421-2433; res: 800/233-1234.* Located in the Ebarcadero Center in downtown San Francisco, this hotel is convenient to the financial district. It is connected by a landscaped pedestrian mall to the historic Federal Reserve Building, and is near the waterfront, Chinatown and California Street cable cars. 360 rms, 24 story, 37 suites. S, D $315-$390; each addl $25; suites $415-$3,350; under 18 free; wkend rates. Crib free. Pet accepted, some restrictions. Covered valet parking; in/out $26. TV; cable (premium), VCR avail (movies). Afternoon refreshments. Restaurant (see PARK GRILL). Rm serv 24 hrs. Bar 11-1 am; entertainment. Ck-out noon. Meeting rms. Business center. Concierge. Exercise equipt for in-rm use. Health club privileges. Bathrm phones, minibars; microwaves avail. Some balconies. Cr cds: A, C, D, DS, ER, JCB, MC, V.

D SC

★★★ **RADISSON HOTEL.** *1625 Post St (94115), in Japantown. 415/922-3200; FAX 415/921-0417; res: 800/333-3333.* E-mail miyakosf@slip.net; web www.mim.com/miyako/. 218 rms, 5 & 16 story. S $139-$179; D $159-$199; each addl $20; suites $179-$299; under 18 free. Crib free. Garage in/out $10. Valet $15. TV; cable, VCR avail. Restaurant (see YOYO BISTRO). Bar 10-1 am. Ck-out 1 pm. Meeting rms. Business center. In-rm modem link. Concierge. Exercise equipt. Health club privileges. Massage. Refrigerator, sauna in suites. Balconies. Japanese decor; authentic Japanese furnishings in some rms. Cr cds: A, C, D, DS, JCB, MC, V.

D SC

★★★ **RENAISSANCE PARC 55 HOTEL.** *55 Cyril Magnin St (94102), Market at 5th St, south of Union Square. 415/392-8000; FAX 415/403-6602; res: 800/697-8103.* E-mail p55sales@aol.com. 1,009 rms, 32 story. S, D $155-$195; each addl $15; suites $340-$1,200; under 19 free. Crib free. Garage $25. TV; cable (premium), VCR avail. Restaurants 6:30 am-10 pm. Bar 11-1 am; pianist. Ck-out noon. Convention facilities. Business center. In-rm modem link. Concierge. Drugstore. Exercise equipt; sauna. Health club privileges. Massage. Bathrm phones. Luxury level. Cr cds: A, C, D, DS, ER, JCB, MC, V.

D SC

★★★ **RENAISSANCE STANFORD COURT.** *Nob Hill (94108). 415/989-3500; FAX 415/391-0513; res: 800/227-4736.* Web www.renaissancehotels.com. 393 rms, 8 story. S $255-$400; D $275-$420; each addl $30; 1-bedrm suites $675-$750; 2-bedrm suites $875-$4,500; under 18 free. Crib free. Valet parking, in/out $27/day. TV; cable (premium), VCR avail. Restaurant (see FOURNOU'S OVENS). Afternoon tea in lobby. Rm serv 24 hrs. Bars 11-1 am. Ck-out noon. Meeting rms. Business center. In-rm modem link. Concierge. Shopping arcade. Exercise equipt. Health club privileges. Marble bathrms with phone. Microwaves avail. Cr cds: A, C, D, DS, JCB, MC, V.

★★★ **RENAISSANCE STANFORD COURT HOTEL.** *905 California St (94108). 415/989-3500; FAX 415/986-8195; res: 800/468-3571.* FOURNOU'S specialities: veal, lamb & duck. Breakfast 6:30 -2:30 pm, 5:30 -10 pm. Brkfst $8 - $32.50, Dinner $8. -$21.50; Child meals; Old world Mediterranian. Cr cds: C.

★★★★ **RITZ-CARLTON HOTEL.** *600 Stockton St (94108), at California St, on Nob Hill. 415/296-7465; FAX 415/291-0147; res: 800/241-3333.* This magnificent hotel atop Nob Hill was designated a city landmark in 1984. The grand entrance and antique-filled lobby ready you for the luxury of the spacious rooms with marble ensuites. It's a pity the service no longer lives up to the quality of the property itself. 336 rms, 9 story, 44 suites. S, D from $400; suites $525-$3,800, rates may vary; under 18 free; package plans. Crib avail. Garage; valet, in/out $30. TV; cable (premium), VCR avail. Indoor pool; whirlpool. Restaurants 6:30 am-11 pm (also see THE DINING ROOM). Rm serv 24 hrs. Bar; entertainment. Ck-out noon. Convention facilities. Business servs avail. In-rm modem link. Concierge. Gift shop. Exercise rm; sauna. Spa. Bathrm phones, minibars; some wet bars. Luxury level. Cr cds: A, C, D, DS, ER, JCB, MC, V.

D SC

★★★ **SAVOY HOTEL.** *580 Geary St (94102), west of Union Square. 415/441-2700; FAX 415/441-0124; res: 800/227-4223.* 83 rms, 7 story, 13 suites. Apr-Oct: S, D $125-$145; each addl $15; suites $195-$245; under 12 free; wkends, hols (2-day min); higher rates special events; lower rates rest of yr. Crib free. Valet, in/out parking $18. TV; cable (premium). Complimentary coffee in rms; afternoon refreshments. Restaurant (see BRASSERIE SAVOY). Bar; piano wkends. Ck-out noon. Meeting rms. Business servs avail. Concierge. Health club privileges. Minibars. Cr cds: A, C, D, DS, MC, V.

SC

✓★ **SHEEHAN HOTEL.** *620 Sutter St (94102), west of Union Square. 415/775-6500; FAX 415/775-3271; res: 800/848-1529.* E-mail sheehot@aol.com; web www.citysearch.com/sfo/sheehanhotel. 65 rms, 60 with bath, 6 story. No A/C. S $59-$89; D $75-$125; each addl $10; under 12 free. Crib free. Garage $16. TV; cable. Indoor pool; lifeguard. Complimentary continental bkfst. No rm serv. Ck-out 11 am. Meeting rms. Business servs avail. Beauty shop. Exercise equipt. Cr cds: A, C, D, DS, JCB, MC, V.

D SC

★★★ **SIR FRANCIS DRAKE HOTEL.** *450 Powell St (94102), north of Union Square. 415/392-7755; FAX 415/391-8719; res: 800/227-5480.* E-mail sfdsf@aol.com; web www.citysearch. com/sfo/sirfrancisdrake. 417 rms, 21 story. S, D $169-$229; each addl $20; suites $350-$600; under 18 free; package plans. Crib free. Valet parking in/out $24. TV; cable (premium), VCR avail. Restaurant (see SCALA'S BISTRO).

Bar 11:30-1 am. Ck-out noon. Meeting rms. Business servs avail. In-rm modem link. Concierge. Shopping arcade. Exercise equipt. Cr cds: A, C, D, DS, JCB, MC, V.

D SC

★ **SUPER 8 HOTEL.** *1015 Geary St (94109), at Polk St, west of Union Square. 415/673-5232; FAX 415/885-2802; res: 800/800-8000.* Web www.superhotel.com. 101 rms, 6 story. No A/C. S, D $99.88; each addl $10; under 12 free. Crib free. Valet parking in/out $15/day. TV; cable (premium). Complimentary coffee. Restaurant 7-11 am. Ck-out noon. Meeting rm. Business servs avail. Game rm. Some refrigerators. Cr cds: A, C, D, DS, ER, JCB, MC, V.

SC

★★★ **THE CLIFT HOTEL.** *495 Geary St (94102), at Taylor St, west of Union Square. 415/775-4700; FAX 415/441-4621; res: 800/652-5438.* 329 rms, 17 story. S, D $255-$305; each addl $30; suites $395-$905; under 18 free; wkend rates. Crib free. Pet accepted. Valet parking $25. TV; cable (premium), VCR avail. Restaurant (see FRENCH ROOM). Rm serv 24 hrs. Bar 11-2 am; pianist 5:30 pm-1:30 am. Ck-out 1 pm. Valet serv 24 hrs. Concierge. Business center. In-rm modem link. Exercise equipt. Bathrm phones, refrigerators, minibars; microwaves avail. Cr cds: A, C, D, DS, JCB, MC, V.

D

★★★ **THE DONATELLO.** *501 Post St (94102), west of Union Square. 415/441-7100; FAX 415/885-8891; res: 800/227-3184.* E-mail sfd-ntlo@aol.com. 94 rms, 14 story. S, D $189-$239; each addl $25; suites $325-$525; under 12 free; wkend rates. Crib free. Garage, in/out $24. TV; cable (premium), VCR avail (movies $2). Restaurant 6:30 am-11 pm (also see ZINGARI). Bar 11 am-midnight. Ck-out noon. Meeting rms. Business center. In-rm modem link. Concierge. Exercise equipt; sauna. Whirlpool. Bathrm phones; some refrigerators. Italian Renaissance decor; antiques; classic elegance. Cr cds: A, C, D, DS, JCB, MC, V.

D

★★ **THE GALLERIA PARK HOTEL.** *191 Sutter St (94104), in Financial District. 415/781-3060; FAX 415/433-4409; res: 800/792-9639.* E-mail galleria@sirius.com. 177 rms, 8 story. S, D $175-$225; suites $250-$450; family, wkend rates. Garage in/out $25. TV; cable (premium). Restaurant 7 am-11 pm. Bar. Ck-out noon. Meeting rms. Business center. In-rm modem link. Concierge. Shopping arcade. Exercise equipt. Refrigerators, mini bars. Atrium lobby with unique sculptured fireplace. Cr cds: A, C, D, DS, ER, JCB, MC, V.

D SC

★★ **THE HARBOR COURT MOTEL.** *165 Stewart St (94105), in Financial District. 415/882-1300; FAX 415/882-1313; res: 800/346-0555.* 131 rms, 5 story. Apr-mid-Nov: S, D $135-$245. Crib free. Parking in/out $24. TV; cable (premium). Indoor pool; whirlpool, lifeguard. Complimentary coffee, evening refreshments. Restaurant 11:30 am-10 pm. Bar to 2 am; entertainment. Ck-out noon. Meeting rm. Business center. In-rm modem link. Concierge. Exercise rm; sauna. Refrigerators, minibars. On waterfront. Cr cds: A, C, D, DS, ER, JCB, MC, V.

D SC

★★★ **THE HOTEL MAJESTIC.** *1500 Sutter St (94109), at Gough St, in Pacific Heights. 415/441-1100; FAX 415/673-7331; res: 800/869-8966.* Web www.expedia.msn.com. 57 rms, 5 story. S, D $135-$175; each addl $15; suites $215-$350. Covered parking $18; valet parking. TV; VCR avail. Restaurant 7-10:30 am, 5:30-10:30 pm; Sun brunch 7 am-2 pm. Rm serv 24 hrs. Bar 11 am-midnight; pianist. Ck-out noon. Lndry serv. Meeting rms. Business servs avail. Concierge. Health club privileges. Many fireplaces, refrigerators. Each rm individually decorated with antiques, custom furnishings. Restored Edwardian hotel (1902); antique tapestries. Cr cds: A, C, D, DS, JCB, MC, V.

D

THE WESTIN ST FRANCIS. *335 Powell St (94102), on Union Square. 415/397-7000; FAX 415/774-0124.* E-mail sfhotel@aol.com; web www.westin.com. Unrated for 2000. Cr cds: A, C, D, DS, JCB, MC, V.

D SC

★★★ **VILLA FLORENCE.** *225 Powell St (94102), south of Union Square. 415/397-7700; FAX 415/397-1006; res: 800/553-4411.* E-mail villaflo@aol.com; web www.citysearch.com/sfo/villaflorence. 183 rms, 7 story, 36 suites. S, D $135-$199; suites $165-$199; under 16 free. Crib free. Valet parking, $23. TV; cable, VCR avail. Coffee in rms. Restaurant 7 am-11 pm. Bar. Ck-out noon. Meeting rms. Business servs avail. In-rm modem link. Concierge. Health club privileges. Refrigerators, minibars. Cr cds: A, C, D, DS, ER, JCB, MC, V.

D SC

★★★★ **W HOTEL.** *181 3rd St (94103). 415/777-5300; FAX 415/817-7823; res: 800/946-8357.* Web www.whotels.com. This new hotel with a natural focus is one of the hottest hang outs in town. The strikingly beautiful design is augmented by high-tech amenities. Intended to provide a calming respite from the busy city, the effect is soothing and restorative. 423 rms, 31 fl; S,D $289-$319. Call for wkend & hol rates; kids under 17 free; AARP rate avail. Crib $20. Handicap accesible. Pet allowed. TV, CD, in room modem link, digital wireless phone. Restaurant 6:30 am-10 pm, res reqd. Exercise room 24 hrs; massage, indoor pool. Business center. Cr cd: C.

★★★ **WARWICK REGIS HOTEL.** *490 Geary St (94102), west of Union Square. 415/928-7900; FAX 415/441-8788; res: 800/827-3447.* 80 rms, 8 story. S, D $109-$239; each addl $15; suites $150-$239; under 15 free. Crib free. Valet parking in/out $25. TV; cable (premium), VCR avail. Restaurants 7-10 am, 6-10 pm. Bar 11-2 am. Ck-out 1 pm. Meeting rms. Business center. In-rm modem link. Health club privileges. Refrigerators; some fireplaces. Balconies. Louis XVI decor. Built 1911. Cr cds: A, C, D, DS, ER, JCB, MC, V.

D SC

★★ **YORK HOTEL.** *940 Sutter St (94109), on Nob Hill. 415/885-6800; FAX 415/885-2115; res: 800/808-9675.* 96 rms, 7 story. S, D $95-$137; each addl $10; suites $210; under 12 free; lower rates Nov-mid-Apr. Crib $10. Parking $14-$25. TV; cable. Complimentary continental bkfst. Complimentary coffee in rms. Ck-out noon. Meeting rm. Business servs avail. In-rm modem link. Exercise equipt. Health club privileges. Minibars; some refrigerators. Renovated 1922 hotel; marble floors, ceiling fans. Hitchcock's Vertigo filmed here. Cr cds: A, C, D, DS, ER, JCB, MC, V.

SC

Inns

★★ **ALAMO SQUARE INN.** *719 Scott St (94117), west of Union Square. 415/922-2055; FAX 415/931-1304; res: 800/345-9888.* E-mail wcorn@alamoinn.com; web www.alamoinn.com. 14 rms in 2 bldgs, 10 with shower only, 3 story. No A/C. S, D $85-$195; each addl $25; suites $195-$295; wkly rates; wkends (2-day min). Crib free. TV in some rms; VCR avail. Complimentary full bkfst; afternoon refreshments. Restaurant nearby. Ck-out noon, ck-in 2-9 pm. Business servs avail. Concierge. Some balconies. Picnic tables. Inn complex includes two restored Victorian mansions, 1895 Queen Anne and 1896 Tudor Revival, located in historic district. Antique furnishings, some wood-burning fireplaces; stained-glass skylight. Garden. Overlooks Alamo Square; panoramic view of city skyline. Totally nonsmoking. Cr cds: A, C, MC, V.

✓★ **ALBION HOUSE INN BED & BREAKFAST.** *135 Gough St (94102), west of Union Square. 415/621-0896; FAX 415/621-3811; res: 800/625-2466.* 8 rms, 2 story. S, D $95-$155; suite $195-$235. TV. Complimentary full bkfst; afternoon refreshments. Ck-out noon, ck-in 4 pm. Business servs avail. Built 1906; individually decorated rms, antiques; piano in parlor. Cr cds: A, C, D, DS, MC, V.

SC

✓★★ **AMSTERDAM HOTEL.** *749 Taylor St (94108), west of Union Square, between Sutter & Bush. 415/673-3277; FAX 415/673-0453.* 34 rms, 3 story. No elvtr. S $89-$99; D $99-$109; each addl $10; under 11 free. Crib free. Garage $13 in/out. TV; cable. Complimentary continental bkfst. Restaurant nearby. Ck-out 11 am, ck-in noon. Business servs avail. Garden/patio for guests. Cr cds: A, C, MC, V.

★★★ **ARCHBISHOP'S MANSION.** *1000 Fulton St (94117), at Steiner St, south of Union Square. 415/563-7872; FAX 415/885-3193; res: 800/543-5820.* Web www.joiedevivre.com. 15 rms, 3 story. S, D $129-$199; each addl $20; suites $215-$385; under 12 free. TV; cable, VCR (free movies). Complimentary continental bkfst; afternoon refreshments. Restaurant nearby. Ck-out 11:30 am, ck-in 3 pm. Business servs avail. Concierge serv. Health club privileges. Stained-glass skylight over stairwell. Built 1904; antiques. Individually decorated rms. Cr cds: A, C, D, DS, MC, V.

★★ **HOTEL BOHEME.** *444 Columbus Ave (94133), in North Beach. 415/433-9111; FAX 415/362-6292.* E-mail BA@hotelboheme.com; web www.hotelboheme.com. 15 rms, 2-3 story. S, D $115-$140; each addl $10; under 2 free. TV; cable. Restaurant adj 7-1 am. Ck-out noon, ck-in 2 pm. Concierge serv. Business servs avail. In-rm modem link. Cr cds: A, C, D, DS, JCB, MC, V.

✓★★★ **INN AT UNION SQUARE.** *440 Post St (94102), west of Union Square. 415/397-3510; FAX 415/989-0529; res: 800/288-4346.* E-mail inn@unionsquare.com; web www.unionsquare.com. 30 rms, 6 story. No A/C. S, D $175-$220; each addl $15; suites $220-$350. Crib free. Valet parking in/out $22. TV; cable, VCR avail. Pool privileges. Complimentary afternoon refreshments. Rm serv 5am-10 pm. Bar. Ck-out noon, ck-in 2 pm. Business servs avail. In-rm modem link. Luggage handling. Concierge serv. Health club privileges. Sitting area, fireplace most floors; antiques. Robes in all rms. Penthouse suite. Totally nonsmoking. Cr cds: A, C, D, DS, JCB, MC, V.

D SC

★★★ **INN SAN FRANCISCO.** *943 S Van Ness Ave (94110), in Mission District. 415/641-0188; FAX 415/641-1701; res: 800/359-0913.* 21 rms, 18 baths, 3 story. No A/C. S, D $85-$235; each addl $20; suites $175-$235. Limited parking avail; $10. TV. Complimentary full bkfst. Restaurant nearby. Ck-out noon, ck-in 2 pm. Business servs avail. Whirlpools. Refrigerators. Balconies. Library. Italianate mansion (1872) near Mission Dolores; ornate woodwork, fireplaces; antique furnishings; garden with redwood hot tub, gazebo; view of city, bay from rooftop sun deck. Cr cds: A, C, D, DS, MC, V.

★★ **JACKSON COURT.** *2198 Jackson St (94115), in Pacific Heights. 415/929-7670; FAX 415/929-1405.* 10 rms, shower only, 3 story. No A/C. S, D $139-$195; each addl $25; under 12 free; wkends (2-day min). TV; cable (premium). Complimentary continental bkfst; afternoon refreshments. Restaurant nearby. Ck-out 11 am, ck-in 2 pm. Concierge serv. Street parking. Some fireplaces; microwaves avail. Brownstone mansion built in 1900. Totally nonsmoking. Cr cds: A, C, MC, V.

★★ **MANSIONS HOTEL.** *2220 Sacramento St (94115), in Pacific Heights. 415/929-9444; FAX 415/567-9391.* Web www.themansions.com. 21 rms, 3 story. No A/C. S, D $139-$279; suites $225-$299. Pet accepted. Complimentary full bkfst. Dining rm (res required) dinner only. Rm serv 7:30 am-midnight. Ck-out noon, ck-in 3 pm. Business servs avail. Parking $15. Luggage handling. Game rm. Music rm. Evening magic concerts. Some balconies. Built in 1887; Victorian memorabilia, antiques, art; Presidential letter collection; Jack London's typewriter used to write Call of the Wild. Cr cds: A, C, D, DS, MC, V.

✓★★ **MARINA INN.** *3110 Octavia St (94123), at Lombard St, north of Union Square. 415/928-1000; FAX 415/928-5909.* 40 rms, 4 story. S, D $65-$115; each addl $10. TV; cable. Complimentary continental bkfst; afternoon refreshments. Ck-out noon, ck-in 2 pm. Business servs avail. Luggage handling. Barber, beauty shop. Restored 1928 bldg; English country ambiance. Cr cds: A, C, MC, V.

D

★★★ **PRESCOTT HOTEL.** *545 Post St (94102), west of Union Square. 415/563-0303; FAX 415/563-6831; res: 800/283-7322.* Web www.prescott.com. 166 rms, 7 story. S, D $195; each addl $10; suites $250-$1,200; hol rates. Crib free. Covered valet parking, in/out $24. TV; cable, VCR avail. Pool privileges. Dining rm (see POSTRIO). Complimentary coffee; afternoon refreshments. Rm serv 6 am-midnight. Bar 11-2 am. Ck-out noon, ck-in 3 pm. Business servs avail. In-rm modem link. Concierge serv. Health club privileges. Minibars; some wet bars. Union Square shopping 1 blk. Luxury level. Cr cds: A, C, D, DS, ER, JCB, MC, V.

D SC

★★ **QUEEN ANNE HOTEL.** *1590 Sutter St (94109), west of Union Square. 415/441-2828; FAX 415/775-5212; res: 800/227-3970.* E-mail queenanne@sfo.com; web www.queenanne.com. 48 rms, 4 story. No A/C. S, D $110-$175; each addl $10; suites $175-$275; under 12 free. Parking in/out $12. TV; cable (premium). Crib free. Complimentary continental bkfst; afternoon refreshments. Ck-out noon, ck-in 3 pm. Meeting rm. Business servs avail. In-rm modem link. Luggage handling. Health club privileges. Bathrm phones; some wet bars, fireplaces. Restored boarding school for young girls (1890); stained glass, many antiques, carved staircase. Cr cds: A, C, D, DS, JCB, MC, V.

D

✓★ **SAN REMO HOTEL.** *2237 Mason St (94133), in North Beach. 415/776-8688; FAX 415/776-2811; res: 800/352-7366.* E-mail info@sanremohotel.com; web www.sanremohotel.com. 62 rms, shared baths, 2 story. No rm phones. Apr-Oct: S $55-$65; D $65-$80; lower rates rest of yr. Bar 5-11 pm. Parking $10. Ck-out 11 am, ck-in 2 pm. Business servs avail. Lndry facilities. Health club privileges. Italianate Victorian bldg; antiques, art. Cr cds: A, C, D, JCB, MC, V.

★★★ **SPENCER HOUSE.** *1080 Haight St (94117), at Baker St, in Haight-Ashbury. 415/626-9205; FAX 415/626-9230.* Web www.spencerhouse.com. 8 rms, shower only, 2 story. No A/C. S, D $120-$170; wkends (2-day min). Complimentary full bkfst. Restaurant nearby. Ck-out noon. Business servs avail. Victorian house built in 1887; original light fixtures, many antiques. Totally nonsmoking. Cr cds: A, C, MC, V.

★★ **STANYAN PARK HOTEL.** *750 Stanyan St (94117), in Haight-Ashbury. 415/751-1000; FAX 415/668-5454.* E-mail info@stanyanpark.com; web www.stanyanpark.com. 36 rms, 3 story, 6 kits. No A/C. S, D $99-$145; suites $185-$225. Municipal parking $5. TV, cable. Complimentary continental bkfst; afternoon refreshments. Ck-out noon, ck-in 3 pm. Business servs avail. In-rm modem link. Luggage handling. Refrigerator in suites. Restored Victorian hotel. Cr cds: A, C, D, DS, MC, V.

D

★★ **THE ANDREWS HOTEL.** *624 Post St (94109), west of Union Square. 415/563-6877; FAX 415/928-6919; res: 800/926-3739.* E-mail andrews-hotel@mcimail.com; web www.joledevivre-sf.com. 48 rms, 7 story. No A/C. S, D $89-$119; each addl $10; suites $132. Parking adj, $15 in/out. TV. Complimentary continental bkfst. Dining rm 5:30-10 pm. Ck-out noon, ck-in 3 pm. Business servs avail. European decor; impressionist prints. Former Turkish bathhouse built 1905. Totally nonsmoking. Cr cds: A, C, D, JCB, MC, V.

★★★★ **THE SHERMAN HOUSE.** *2160 Green St (94123), in Pacific Heights. 415/563-3600; FAX 415/563-1882; res: 800/424-5777.* Tucked away in the exclusive residential neighborhood of Pacific Heights, this 1876 landmark mansion offers 14 rooms, each individually appointed with period antiques (several have marble fireplaces and canopied beds).14 rms, 4 story. No elvtr. S, D $385-$445; suites $675-$850; under 12 free. TV; cable (premium), VCR (movies). Dining rm (by res) 7 am-2 pm, 5:30-9 pm. Rm serv 24 hrs. Ck-out noon, ck-in 4 pm. Business servs avail. In-rm modem link. Concierge serv. Butler serv. Health club privileges. Bathrm phones; many wet bars. Private patios, balconies. Totally nonsmoking. Cr cds: A, C, D, MC, V.

★★ **VICTORIAN INN ON THE PARK.** *301 Lyon St (94117), in Haight-Ashbury. 415/931-1830; FAX 415/931-1830; res: 800/435-1967.* E-mail vicinn@aol.com; web www.citysearch.com/sfo/victorianinn. 12 rms, 4 story. No A/C. No elvtr. S, D $124-$174; each addl $20; suites $174-$345. Parking $13. TV in lounge, rm TV avail. Complimentary continental bkfst; afternoon refreshments. Ck-out 11:30 am, ck-in 2 pm. Business servs avail. In-rm modem link. Health club privileges. Some fireplaces; microwaves avail. Historic building (1897); Victorian decor. Cr cds: A, C, D, DS, JCB, MC, V.

★★ **WASHINGTON SQUARE INN.** *1660 Stockton St (94133), in North Beach. 415/981-4220; FAX 415/397-7242; res: 800/388-0220.* 15 rms, 2 story. No A/C. S, D $125-$210; each addl $15. Valet parking $20. TV; cable, VCR avail. Complimentary continental bkfst; afternoon refreshments. Ck-out noon, ck-in 3 pm. Business servs avail. In-rm modem link. Luggage handling. Concierge serv. Health club privileges. Individually decorated rms with English & French country antiques. Opp historic Washington Square. Totally nonsmoking. Cr cds: A, C, D, DS, JCB, MC, V.

D

Restaurants

★★ **42 DEGREES.** *235 16th Ave (94118), south of Union Square. 415/777-5558.* Hrs: 11:30 am-3 pm, 6:30-11:30 pm; Mon, Tues to 3 pm. Closed Sun; major hols. Res accepted. Mediterranean menu. Bar. Semi-a la carte: lunch $5-$11, dinner $5-$20. Specialties: pan seared sea bass, Iberian sausage, slow roasted lamb shank. Entertainment Wed-Sat. Outdoor dining. Casual decor. Totally nonsmoking. Cr cds: A, C, MC, V.

D

★★★ **A. SABELLA'S.** *2766 Taylor St (94133), at Fisherman's Wharf. 415/771-6775.* E-mail fresh_fish@compuserv.com; web www.asabella.com. Hrs: 11 am-10:30 pm; Sat to 11 pm. Closed Dec 25. Res accepted. Bar. Wine list. A la carte entrees: lunch $7.50-$15, dinner $11.75-$46.75. Child's meals. Specializes in fresh local seafood. Own desserts. Dinner theater Fri & Sat (7:30 pm). 1,000-gallon crab, abalone, and lobster tanks. Overlooks wharf, bay. Family-owned. Cr cds: A, C, D, DS, JCB, MC, V.

D

✓★★ **ACE WASABI'S ROCK & ROLL SUSHI.** *3339 Steiner St (94123), in Marina District. 415/567-4903.* Web www.citysearch.com/sfo/acewasabis. Hrs: 5:30-10:30 pm; Fri, Sat to 11 pm; Sun 5-10 pm. Closed Jan 1, July 4, Dec 25. Japanese menu. Bar. Semi-a la carte: dinner $4.95-$9.50. Specialties: ahi and Hamachi pot stickers, flying kamikaze roll. Modern Japanese decor. Totally nonsmoking. Cr cds: A, C, D, MC, V.

D

★★★ **ACQUERELLO.** *1722 Sacramento St (94109), in Russian Hill. 415/567-5432.* Web www.acquerello.com. Hrs: 5:30-10:30 pm. Closed Sun, Mon; most major hols. Res accepted. Northern Italian menu. Wine, beer. A la carte entrees: dinner $22-$28. Prix fixe dinner: $55/person. Menu changes seasonally. Totally nonsmoking. Cr cds: A, C, D, DS, MC, V.

D

★ **ALAMO SQUARE SEAFOOD GRILL.** *803 Fillmore St (94117), west of Union Square. 415/440-2828.* Web www.citysearch.com/sfo/alamosquare. Hrs: 10 am-2 pm, 5:30-10 pm; Sun (brunch) 10 am-2 pm. Seafood menu. Wine, beer. A la carte entrees: dinner $8.50-$13.50. Sun brunch $5.50-$6.95. Specialties: crab cake, blackened swordfish with beurre blanc sauce, grilled tuna with beurre rouge sauce. Cr cds: C, MC, V.

D

★★ **ALBONA RISTORANTE ISTRIANO.** *545 Francisco St (94133), in North Beach. 415/441-1040.* Hrs: 5-10 pm. Closed Sun, Mon; Thanksgiving, Dec 25. Res accepted. Northern Italian menu. Wine, beer. A la carte entrees: dinner $12.50-$16.75. Specializes in Italian cuisine with Austrian-Hungarian influence. Free valet parking. Intimate dining. Chef-owned. Totally nonsmoking. Cr cds: A, C, D, DS, MC, V.

★ **ALEGRIA'S FOODS FROM SPAIN.** *2018 Lombard St (94123), in Marina District. 415/929-8888.* Hrs: 5:30-11 pm. Res accepted. Spanish menu. Bar. A la carte entrees: dinner $12.50-$14.95. Specialties: zarzuela de mariscos, tapas, paella. Entertainment Thurs-Sun. Spanish decor. Totally nonsmoking. Cr cds: A, C, D, JCB, MC, V.

D

★★ **ANJOU.** *44 Campton Pl (94108), off Stockton St, north of Union Square. 415/392-5373.* Web www.citysearch7.com/arjou. Hrs: 11:30 am-2:30 pm, 5:30-10 pm. Closed Sun, Mon. Res accepted. French menu. Bar. A la carte entrees: lunch $8-$17, dinner $12-$18. Prix fixe: lunch $12.50. Specialties: Chilean sea bass, confit of duck leg, honey-roasted chicken. Bi-level dining area, high ceiling. Cr cds: A, C, D, DS, JCB, MC, V.

★ **ANNABELLE'S BAR & BISTRO.** *68 4th St (94103), south of Union Square. 415/777-1200.* Hrs: 7 am-10:30 pm. Closed Dec 25. Res accepted. No A/C. Bar. Semi-a la carte: bkfst $5.95-$10.50, lunch, dinner $6-$14.95. Specializes in rotisserie cooking. Streetfront cafe was once a bank; teller cages from 1900s. Totally nonsmoking. Cr cds: A, C, MC, V.

D

★ **ANTICA TRATTORIA.** *2400 Polk St (94109), on Russian Hill. 415/928-5797.* Hrs: 5:30-10 pm; Fri, Sat to 10:30 pm. Closed Mon; most major hols. Res accepted. No A/C. Italian menu. Wine, beer. A la carte entrees: dinner $8-$15. Child's meals. Specializes in pasta. Casual corner cafe. Totally nonsmoking. Cr cds: A, C, D, MC, V.

D

★★★★ **AQUA.** *252 California St (94111), in Financial District. 415/956-9662.* This sophisticated restaurant at the foot of Nob Hill serves innovative cuisine to rival any in town. That seafood is the main attraction almost comes as a surprise, what with the intricate preparations, daring presentations, and long wine list. The dining room is modern and sleek. And the service is friendly and helpful. Stylish crowd. Hrs: 11:30 am-2:15 pm, 5:30-10:30 pm; Fri, Sat to 11 pm. Closed Sun; most major hols. Res accepted. Bar. A la carte entrees: lunch $14-$19, dinner $27-$45. Complete meals: lunch $35, dinner $65. Specialty: medallions of ahi tuna (rare) with foie gras in wine sauce. Cr cds: A, C, D, MC, V.

D

★ **AVENUE 9.** *1243 9th Ave (94122), in Civic Center. 415/664-6999.* Hrs: 11:30 am-10 pm; Fri, Sat to 11 pm; Sun from 10 am; Sun brunch 10 am-3 pm; early-bird dinner 5:30-7 pm (seasonal). Closed July 4, Thanksgiving, Dec 25. Res accepted. Contemporary Amer menu. Bar. A la carte entrees: lunch $7-$15, dinner $10-$18. Sun brunch $5-$10. Child's meals. Specializes in hand-crafted cuisine. Street parking. American bistro decor. Totally nonsmoking. Cr cds: A, C, D, DS, V.

D

✓★ **BAKER STREET BISTRO.** *2953 Baker St (94123), between Lombard & Greenwich, in Cow Hollow. 415/931-1475.* Hrs: 10 am-2 pm, 5:30-10:30 pm; Sun 5-9:30 pm; Sat, Sun brunch 10 am- 2:30 pm. Closed Mon. Res accepted. No A/C. Country French menu. Wine. Semi-a la carte: lunch $4.75-$7.50, dinner $8.75-$13.50. Prix fixe: dinner $14.50. Sat, Sun brunch $4.75-$7.50. Specializes in rabbit, duck, escargot. Street parking. Outdoor dining. Bistro atmosphere; trompe l'oeil painting on front of building. Cr cds: C, MC, V.

D

✓★★ **BALBOA CAFE.** *3199 Fillmore St, in Marina District. 415/921-3944.* Hrs: 11 am-10 pm; Sun brunch 10:30 am-4 pm. Bar to 2 am. A la carte entrees: lunch, dinner $8-$16. Sun brunch $7-$14. Specializes in beef. Built 1897. Cr cds: A, C, D, MC, V.

D

★★ **BASIL THAI RESTAURANT & BAR.** *1175 Folsom St (94103), in Civic Center area. 415/552-8999.* Web citysearch7.com/sfo/basilthai. Hrs: 11:45 am-3 pm, 5-10 pm; Fri to 10:30 pm; Sat 5-10:30 pm; Sun 5-10 pm. Thai menu. Bar. A la carte entrees: lunch, dinner $7.50-$14. Specializes in curries. Street parking. Totally nonsmoking. Cr cds: A, C, MC, V.

D

✓★★ **BASTA PASTA.** *1268 Grant St (94133), at Vallejo St, in North Beach. 415/434-2248.* Hrs: 11:30-1:45 am. Closed some major hols. Res accepted. Italian menu. Bar. Semi-a la carte: lunch, dinner $7.95-$16.50. Specializes in pizza baked in wood-burning oven, pasta, veal. Valet parking. Outdoor (rooftop) dining. Main dining rm on 2nd floor. Cr cds: A, C, D, DS, JCB, MC, V.

D

★★ **BETELNUT PEJIU WU.** *2030 Union St (94123), in Cow Hollow. 415/929-8855.* Web www.citysearch.com. Hrs: 11:30 am-11 pm; Fri, Sat to midnight. Closed Thanksgiving, Dec 25. Res accepted. Southeast Asian menu. Bar. A la carte entrees: lunch $8-$13, dinner $14-$20. Specializes in multi-regional Pacific Rim cuisine. Outdoor dining. Asian decor. Totally nonsmoking. Cr cds: C, D, DS, MC, V.

D

★★★ **BIG FOUR RESTAURANT.** *(See Huntington Hotel) 415/771-1140.* Hrs: 7-10 am, 11:30 am-3 pm, 5:30-10:30 pm; Sat & Sun 7-11 am, 5:30-10:30 pm. Res accepted. Bar 11:30 am-midnight. Contemporary American cuisine. A la carte entrees: bkfst $5-$12.95, lunch $9.50-$18.50, dinner $18-$28.50. Complete meal: bkfst $15. Specialties: seasonal wild game dishes, lamb sausage with black pepper papardelle noodles. Pianist eves. Valet parking. Traditional San Francisco club atmosphere. Cr cds: A, C, D, DS, JCB, MC, V.

★ **BISCUITS & BLUES.** *401 Mason St (94102), at Geary, west of Union Square. 415/292-2583.* E-mail sfblues@pacbell.net; web www.sanfrancisco/citysearch.com. Hrs: 5 pm-1 am. Southern, New Orleans cuisine. Bar. A la carte entrees: dinner $9.95. Specializes in biscuits, catfish, jambalaya. Entertainment. Casual decor. Cr cds: A, C, MC, V.

D

★★ **BIX.** *56 Gold St (94133), in Financial District. 415/433-6300.* Hrs: 11:30 am-11 pm; Fri to midnight; Sat 5:30 pm-midnight; Sun 6-10 pm. Closed major hols. Res accepted. Bar to 1:30 am. A la carte entrees: lunch $10-$15, dinner $18-$28. Specializes in classic American dishes with California influence. Jazz nightly. Valet parking (dinner). Modernized 40's supper club with grand piano. Cr cds: A, C, D, DS, JCB, MC, V.

D

✓★★ **BIZOU.** *598 Fourth St (94107), at Brannan, south of Union Square . 415/543-2222.* Hrs: 11:30 am-2:30 pm, 5:30-10 pm; Fri to 10:30 pm; Sat 5:30-10:30 pm. Closed Sun; most major hols. Res accepted. No A/C. French, Italian menu. Bar. Semi-a la carte: lunch $5.50-$14.50, dinner $11.50-$19. Specialties: batter-fried green beans, beef cheek, bittersweet chocolate and coffee vacherin. Street parking. Totally nonsmoking. Cr cds: A, C, MC, V.

D

★★ **BLUE POINT.** *2415 Clement St (94121), in Richmond District. 415/379-9726.* Hrs: 5-10 pm. Closed Tues; Dec 25. Res accepted. Wine, beer. A la carte entrees: dinner $7.95-$11.75. Specializes in cioppino, salmon cakes. Contemporary decor. Totally nonsmoking. Cr cds: C, MC, V.

D

★ **BOBBY RUBINO'S.** *245 Jefferson St (94133), at Fisherman's Wharf. 415/673-2266.* Hrs: 11:30 am-11 pm. Res accepted. No A/C. Bar. A la carte entrees: lunch $4.95-$12.95, dinner $6.95-$17.95. Child's meals. Specializes in steak, baby back ribs, fresh seafood. Casual, family dining, on two levels. View of fishing fleet. Cr cds: A, C, D, DS, JCB, MC, V.

★★ **BOCCA ROTIS RESTAURANT.** *1 W Portal Ave (94127), south of Union Square. 415/665-9900.* Hrs: 7 am-10 pm; Sat from 11 am; Sun from 9 am. Closed Thanksgiving, Dec 25. Italian, French menu. Bar. A la carte entrees: bkfst $7-$12, lunch $7-$14, dinner $7-$16. Child's meals. Specialties: rotisserie chicken, pork chops. Own desserts. Street parking. Totally nonsmoking. Cr cds: C, MC, V.

D

✓★★ **BONTA RISTORANTE.** *2223 Union St (94123), in Cow Hollow. 415/929-0407.* Web www.citysearch.com/sfo/bontaristorante. Hrs: 5:30-10:30 pm; Fri, Sat to 11 pm; Sun 5-10 pm. Closed Mon; some major hols. Res accepted. No A/C. Italian menu. Wine, beer. A la carte entrees: dinner $10.50-$18.75. Child's meals. Large vegetarian selection. Storefront dining rm. Totally nonsmoking. Cr cds: C, MC, V.

D

★★★★ **BOULEVARD.** *1 Mission St (94105), south of Union Square at Embarcadero. 415/543-6084.* E-mail kking@kuleto.com; web www.kuleto.com/boulevard. Chef Nancy Oakes serves innovative New American cuisine at this busy restaurant in the historic Audiffred Building near the Embarcadero waterfront. Art-nouveau inspired decor is stunning. Hrs: 11:30 am-2:15 pm, Sun - Wed 5:30-10 pm; Thurs-Sat to 10:30 pm. Closed major hols. Res accepted. Contemporary Amer menu. Bar. Semi-a la carte: lunch $20-$30, dinner $45-$60. Specialties: roasted chicken breast, pork loin, pan-roasted halibut. Valet parking. Totally nonsmoking. Cr cds: A, C, D, DS, MC, V.

D

★★ **BRASSERIE SAVOY.** *(See Savoy Hotel) 415/441-8080.* Hrs: 7 am-noon, 5-10 pm; Wed, Thurs to 10:30 pm; Fri, Sat to 11 pm. Closed July 4, Labor Day. Res accepted. French menu. Bar. A la carte entrees: bkfst $4-$13, dinner $16-$20. Complete meal: dinner $28. Specialties: coulibiac of salmon, beef cheeks, oysters in champagne sauce. Pianist wkends. Valet parking. Elegant decor. Totally nonsmoking. Cr cds: A, C, D, DS, MC, V.

D

✓★★ **CAFE AKIMBO.** *116 Maiden Lane (94108), in Union Square. 415/433-2288.* Hrs: 11:30 am-3 pm, 5:30-9 pm; Fri, Sat to 10 pm. Closed Sun; most major hols. Res accepted. Contemporary menu. Wine, beer. Semi-a la carte: lunch $8.95-$12.95, dinner $9.95-$15.95. Specialties: akimbo roll, sauteed prawns with pine nuts. Contemporary decor. Totally nonsmoking. Cr cds: A, C, DS, JCB, MC, V.

✓★ **CAFE BASTILLE.** *22 Belden Place (94104), in Financial District. 415/986-5673.* Web www.cafebastille.com. Hrs: 11 am-11 pm. Closed Sun; also most major hols. Res accepted. French menu. Bar. Semi-a la carte: lunch, dinner $8-$13. Child's meals. Specializes in crepes, mussels. Entertainment Thurs-Sat. Outdoor dining. French bistro decor. Totally nonsmoking. Cr cds: A, C, D, MC, V.

D

✓★ **CAFE KATI.** *1963 Sutter St (94115), in Pacific Heights. 415/775-7313.* Hrs: 5:30-10 pm. Closed Mon; some major hols. Res accepted. Eclectic menu. Wine, beer. Semi-a la carte: dinner $15-$19. Specialties: vegetarian risotto, miso marinated chicken, sea bass, cider-marinated tenderloin of pork. Valet parking Fri, Sat. Contemporary Asian decor. Totally nonsmoking. Cr cds: C, MC, V.

★ **CAFE MARIMBA.** *2317 Chestnut St (94123), in Marina District. 415/776-1506.* Hrs: 11:30 am-10 pm; Mon from 5:30 pm; Fri, Sat to 11 pm; Sat, Sun brunch 11:30 am-2 pm. Closed Thanksgiving, Dec 25. Res accepted. Mexican menu. Bar. A la carte entrees: lunch, dinner $6.25-$11.95. Sun brunch $6.75-$8.25. Child's meals. Specialties: chicken breast with mole sauce, Veracruz-style fresh fish, margaritas. Brightly colored restaurant with papier mache figures and Mexican folk art. Cr cds: A, C, MC, V.

D

★★ **CAFE PESCATORE.** *2455 Mason St (94133), at Fisherman's Wharf. 415/561-1111.* Hrs: 7 am-10 pm; Fri & Sat to 11 pm. Closed Dec 25. Res accepted. Italian, Amer menu. Bar. A la carte entrees: bkfst $5.95-$9.95, lunch $6.95-$16.95, dinner $8.75-$16.95. Child's meals. Specializes in fresh seafood, oak burning oven pizza. Outdoor dining. Trattoria-style dining with maritime memorabilia. Cr cds: A, C, D, DS, JCB, MC, V.

D

✓★★ **CAFE RIGGIO.** *4112 Geary Blvd (94118), in Richmond District. 415/221-2114.* Hrs: 5-10 pm; Fri, Sat to 11 pm; Sun from 4:30 pm. Closed some major hols. Italian menu. Bar. A la carte entrees: dinner $7.95-$14.50. Child's meals. Specializes in veal, fish, pasta. Casual atmosphere. Cr cds: C, MC, V.

D

★★ **CAFE TIRAMISU.** *28 Belden Place (94104), in Financial District. 415/421-7044.* Hrs: 11:30 am-3 pm, 5-10 pm; Sat 5-11 pm. Closed Sun; some major hols. Res accepted. Italian menu. Wine, beer. Semi-a la carte: lunch $8.50-$16.50, dinner $11-$25. Specialties: rack of lamb, risotto. Outdoor dining. Italian decor. Totally nonsmoking. Cr cds: A, C, D, MC, V.

★★★★ **CAMPTON PLACE DINING ROOM.** *(See Campton Place Hotel) 415/955-5555.* E-mail reserve@campton.com. Although chef Todd Humphries has gone to Napa (see The Wine Spectator Restaurant at Greystone), this contemporary American restaurant continues to impress. The food is creative and artfully presented, and the service is serious and attentive. Hrs: 7-10:30 am, 11:30 am-2 pm, 6-10 pm; Fri to 10:30 pm; Sat 8-11 am, noon-2 pm, 5:30-10:30 pm; Sun 8 am-2 pm, 6-9:30 pm. Res accepted. French cuisine. Bar 10 am-11 pm; Fri, Sat to midnight. Wine list. A la carte entrees: bkfst $9-$16, lunch $9.50-$16.50, dinner $23-$36. Prix fixe: lunch $21.50, dinner $48-$69. Sun brunch $9-$14.50. Child's meals. Own baking. Valet parking. Cr cds: A, C, D, JCB, MC, V.

D

★★★ **CARNELIAN ROOM.** *555 California St (94104), in Financial District. 415/433-7500.* Hrs: 6-10 pm; Sun brunch 10 am-2 pm. Closed some major hols. Res accepted. Bar from 3 pm; Sun from 10 am. Wine cellar. A la carte entrees: dinner $21-$39. Prix fixe: dinner $35. Sun brunch $27. Child's meals. Vintage 18th-century decor; antiques. 11 dining rms. Panoramic view of city. Jacket. Cr cds: A, C, D, DS, JCB, MC, V.

D

★★ **CARTA.** *1772 Market (94102), in Civic Center area. 415/863-3516.* E-mail carta@creative.net; web www.creative.net/~carta. Hrs: noon-3 pm, 5:30-10:30 pm; Fri to 11 pm; Sat 5:30-11 pm; Sun brunch 10 am-3 pm. Closed Mon; Thanksgiving, Dec 25; also 1st wk Jan & 1st wk Aug. Res accepted. Continental menu. Bar. A la carte entrees: lunch $5-$12, dinner $6-$20. Sun brunch $2-$10. Menu changes monthly. Street parking. Outdoor dining. Totally nonsmoking. Cr cds: A, C, D, DS, MC, V.

★ **CHA CHA CHA.** *1801 Haight St (94117), in Haight-Ashbury. 415/386-5758.* Hrs: 11:30 am-4 pm, 5-11 pm; wkends to 11:30 pm. Closed Dec 25. Caribbean, Cuban menu. Wine, beer. A la carte entrees: lunch $4.75-$7, dinner $5.25-$13.50. Specializes in tapas. Casual dining in colorful atmosphere. Totally nonsmoking. Cr cds: C, MC, V.

D

★★★ **CHARLES NOB HILL.** *1250 Jones St (94109), at Clay, on Nob Hill. 415/771-5400.* Hrs: 5:30-10 pm; Fri, Sat to 10:30 pm. Closed Mon. Res accepted. French menu. Bar. Semi-a la carte: dinner $19-$32. Complete meals: dinner $65. Specialties: lobster, squab, loin of lamb. Formal decor. Cr cds: A, C, MC, V.

D

★★★ **CHEZ MICHEL.** *804 North Point St (94109), in Russian Hill. 415/775-7036.* Hrs: 5:30-10:30 pm. Closed Mon; some major hols. Res accepted. French menu. Bar. A la carte entrees: dinner $19-$24. Specialties: rabbit, sweetbread scallops, lamb. Intimate and sophisticated atmosphere. Totally nonsmoking. Cr cds: C, MC, V.

D

★★ **CHIC'S SEAFOOD.** *Pier 39 (94133), at Fisherman's Wharf. 415/421-2442.* Web www.citysearch.com/sfo/chicsseafood. Hrs: 9 am-11 pm. Res accepted. Bar. Semi-a la carte: bkfst $5.95-$7.50, lunch $5.95-$10.95. A la carte entrees: dinner $9.95-$19.95. Specializes in seafood. Own desserts. Parking. View of bay, Alcatraz, Golden Gate Bridge. Cr cds: A, C, D, DS, JCB, MC, V.

D

★★★ **CYPRESS CLUB.** *500 Jackson St (94133), in Financial District. 415/296-8555.* Hrs: 5:30-10 pm; Fri, Sat to 11 pm. Closed major hols. Res accepted. Contemporary Amer menu. Bar 4:30 pm-2 am. Wine list. A la carte entrees: dinner $20-$29. Menu changes daily. Jazz nightly. Whimsical, 1940s-style design. Cr cds: A, C, D, MC, V.

D

✓★ **DAME A RESTAURANT.** *1815 Market St (94103), in Mission District. 415/255-8818.* E-mail kjdame@earthlink.net; web www.citysearchch7.com/damearestaurant. Hrs: 11:30 am-2 pm, 5-9:30 pm; Fri to 10:30 pm; Sat 5-10:30 pm; Sun 10 am-2 pm, 5-9:30 pm. Closed Mon; July 4, Thanksgiving, Dec 25. Res accepted. Italian menu. Wine, beer. Semi-a la carte: lunch $6.50-$9, dinner $10-$14.50. Sun brunch $6.50-$9.50. Specialties: polenta-crusted chicken breast, potato and parmesan-crusted salmon, roasted chicken. Contemporary decor. Totally nonsmoking. Cr cds: A, C, D, MC, V.

D

★ **EL TOREADOR.** *50 W Portal (94127), south of Union Square. 415/566-2673.* Hrs: 11 am-9 pm; Fri, Sat to 10 pm. Closed Mon; Easter, Dec 25. No A/C. Mexican menu. Wine, beer. Semi-a la carte: lunch, dinner $7.25-$12.95. Child's meals. Specialties: mole poblano, mole de cacahuate, el pipian de pollo. Eclectic, brightly colored decor. Totally nonsmoking. Cr cds: A, C, MC, V.

D SC

✓★★ **ELEVEN.** *374 11th St (94103), at Harrison St, in Civic Center area. 415/431-3337.* Web www.sfstation.com/live/eleven.htm. Hrs: 11 am-5 pm, 5:30-11 pm; Fri & Sat to midnight. Closed Sun; major hols. Res accepted. Continental menu. Bar. A la carte entrees: lunch $6-$7, dinner $10-$19. Specializes in pasta, pizza, fresh seafood. Live Jazz from 7 pm. Rustic Italian courtyard atmosphere; faux stone walls, trompe l'oeil grapevines, antique wrought-iron gates. Cr cds: A, C, D, MC, V.

D

✓★ **ELIZA RESTAURANT.** *1457 18th St (94107), south of Union Square. 415/648-9999.* Hrs: 11 am-3 pm, 5-10 pm; Sat 11 am-10 pm; Sun noon-10 pm. Closed Thanksgiving, Dec 25. Res accepted. Chinese menu. Bar. Semi-a la carte: dinner $5.25-$10.15. Specialties: lotus root with prawns, Mongolian beef, Hunan salmon. Modern Chinese decor. Cr cds: C, MC, V.

D

★★ **EMPRESS OF CHINA.** *838 Grant Ave (94108), Top floor of China Trade Center Bldg, in Chinatown. 415/434-1345.* Hrs: 11:30 am-3 pm, 5-11 pm. Chinese menu. Res accepted. Bar. A la carte entrees: lunch $7.50-$10.50, dinner $12.50-$29. Complete meals (for 2 or more persons): lunch $9.50-$16.95, dinner $16.95-$33.95. Specialties: regional delicacies of China. Oriental decor; ancient art objects. View of city, Telegraph Hill. Jacket (dinner). Cr cds: A, C, D, JCB, MC, V.

D

✓★ **ENRICO'S SIDEWALK CAFE.** *504 Broadway (94133), in North Beach. 415/982-6223.* Hrs: 11:30 am-11 pm; Fri, Sat to midnight. Closed Jan 1, Dec 25. Res accepted. No A/C. Mediterranean menu. Bar. A la carte entrees: lunch $8-$10, dinner $8-$19. Live jazz. Outdoor dining. Bistro with glass wall, large terrace. Local artwork. Cr cds: A, C, MC, V.

D

★★ **EOS.** *901 Cole St (94117), in Haight-Ashbury. 415/566-3063.* Hrs: 5:30-close; Sun from 5 pm. Closed major hols. Res accepted. No A/C. Eclectic, Asian menu. Bar. Semi-a la carte: dinner $18-$30. Specialties: shiitake mushroom dumplings, Peking duck breast. Street parking. Corner cafe. Cr cds: A, C, MC, V.

D

★★★ **FARALLON.** *450 Post St (94102), in Union Square. 415/956-6969.* Web kuleto.com. Seafood menu. Specialties: housemade caviar, seafood indulgence, fresh fish speciality, fresh sorbet. Hrs: Sun-Wed 11:30 am-2:30 pm, 5:30-10:30 pm; Thurs-Sat 5:30-11 pm. Closed most major hols. Res accepted. Bar. Wine list. A la carte entrees: lunch $11-$15, dinner $22-$32. Prix fixe lunch $22. Valet parking. Underwater theme; unique decor with painted mosiac, jellyfish lamps. Totally nonsmoking. Cr cds: A, C, D, DS, MC, V.

D

✓★ **FATTOUSH.** *1361 Church St (94114), in Mission District. 415/641-0678.* Hrs: 11:30 am-2:30 pm, 5:30-9:30 pm; Fri to 10 pm; Sat 9 am-3 pm, 5:30-10 pm; Sun 9 am-3 pm, 5:30-9 pm. Closed Mon. Res accepted. Middle Eastern menu. Wine, beer. Semi-a la carte entrees: lunch $4.50-$9.95, dinner $9.95-$14.95. Sat, Sun brunch $4.50-$8.95. Specialty: sesame chicken. Patio dining. Built 1903. Totally nonsmoking. Cr cds: C, DS, MC, V.

★★ **FAZ RESTAURANT & BAR.** *161 Sutter St (94104), in Financial District. 415/362-0404.* Hrs: 11:30 am-3 pm, 5-10 pm. Closed Sat, Sun; most major hols. Res accepted. Italian, Mediterranean menu. Bar. A la carte entrees: lunch, dinner $8.95-$19.95. Specializes in fresh pasta. Jazz Mon-Fri 5-9 pm. Outdoor dining. Elegant fine dining. Cr cds: A, C, D, MC, V.

D

✓★ **FIGARO.** *414 Columbus Ave (94133), in North Beach. 415/398-1300.* Hrs: 10 am-midnight. Closed Dec 25. Res accepted. Italian menu. Bar. A la carte entrees: bkfst $4.50-$8.25, lunch, dinner $7.50-$16.95. Specializes in pizza, pasta, oversize salads. Outdoor dining. Murals on ceiling. Cr cds: A, C, DS, MC, V.

D

★★ **FINO RESTAURANT.** *632 Post St (94109), south of Union Square. 415/928-2080.* Web www.jocedevivre.com. Hrs: 5:30-10 pm. Closed major hols. Res accepted. Italian menu. Bar. Semi-a la carte: dinner $8.95-$16.95. Specializes in fresh seafood, fresh pasta. Descending staircase leads to dining area; marble fireplace. Totally nonsmoking. Cr cds: A, C, D, MC, V.

★★ **FIOR D'ITALIA.** *601 Union St, in North Beach. 415/986-1886.* Web www.fior.com. Hrs: 11:30 am-10:30 pm. Res accepted. Northern Italian menu. Bar. A la carte entrees: lunch, dinner $11-$22. Specializes in veal, risotto. Own pasta. Valet parking. On Washington Square Park; Tony Bennett memorabilia. Family-owned. Totally nonsmoking. Cr cds: A, C, D, DS, JCB, MC, V.

D

★ **FIREFLY RESTAURANT.** *4288 24th St (94114), in Mission District. 415/821-7652.* Hrs: 5:30-9:30 pm; Fri, Sat to 10 pm. Res accepted. Contemporary menu. Bar. Semi-a la carte: dinner $11.50-$16. Specializes in seafood, organic produce and meats. Contemporary decor. Totally nonsmoking. Cr cds: A, C, MC, V.

D

★★★ **FLEUR DE LYS.** *777 Sutter St (94109), north of Union Square. 415/673-7779.* French menu. Specialties: Maine lobster tail & salsify en tartelete, boneless quail, grand finale dessert. Hrs: 6-9:15 pm; Fri, Sat 5:30-10:30 pm. Closed Sun, New Year's Eve. Res required. Bar. Extensive wine list. A la carte entrees: dinner $28-$36. Prix fixe: dinner $70, vegetarian $58. Valet parking. Jacket required. Totally nonsmoking. Cr cds: A, C, D, JCB, MC, V.

D

★★ **FLY TRAP RESTAURANT.** *606 Folsom St (94107), between 2nd & 3rd, south of Union Square. 415/243-0580.* Hrs: 11:30 am-10 pm; Fri to 10:30 pm; Sat, Sun 5:30-10:30 pm. Closed major hols. Res accepted. No A/C. Continental menu. Bar. A la carte entrees: lunch, dinner $8-$18. Specialties: chicken coq au vin, oysters Rockefeller, celery Victor. Own pasta, desserts. Jazz Sun. Valet parking. Courtyard entrance; named after 1898 restaurant. Totally nonsmoking. Cr cds: A, C, D, MC, V.

D

★★ **FOG CITY DINER.** *1300 Battery St (94111), in Financial District. 415/982-2000.* E-mail 103422.3235@compuserve.com. Hrs: 11:30 am-11 pm; Fri, Sat to midnight. Closed Thanksgiving, Dec 25. Res accepted. Bar. A la carte entrees: lunch, dinner $10-$24. Specializes in cocktails, seafood. Oyster bar. Railroad dining car atmosphere. Cr cds: C, D, DS, MC, V.

D

✓★ **FOUNTAIN COURT.** *354 Clement St (94118), in Richmond District. 415/668-1100.* Hrs: 11 am-3 pm, 5 pm-midnight; Fri, Sat to 2 am. Closed Thanksgiving. Res accepted. Chinese menu. Wine, beer. A la carte entrees: lunch $4-$4.50, dinner $6-$10. Specializes in Shanghai cuisine, catfish, chicken. Modern decor. Cr cds: A, C, D, MC, V.

D

★★ **FOURNOU'S OVENS.** *(See Renaissance Stanford Court) 415/989-1910.* Web www.renaissancehotels.com. Hrs: 6:30 am-2:30 pm, 5:30-10 pm; Fri, Sat to 10:30 pm; Sat and Sun brunch 11 am-2:30 pm. Res accepted; required hols. Mediterranean setting with continental cuisine. Bar. Wine cellar. A la carte entrees: bkfst, lunch $9.75-$17.95, dinner $9-$28. Table d'ote: dinner $25-$45. Sun brunch $12-$18.50. Child's meals. Specializes in rack of lamb, farm-raised meats, fish selections. Own pasta. Valet parking. Cr cds: A, C, D, DS, JCB, MC, V.

D

★★★ **FRANCISCAN.** *Pier 4 1/2 (94133), at Fisherman's Wharf. 415/362-7733.* Hrs: 11 am-10 pm; Fri & Sat to 10:30 pm. Closed Thanksgiving, Dec 25. Res accepted. Bar. A la carte entrees: lunch, dinner $6.95-$39. Child's meals. Specializes in California contemporary cuisine. Own desserts. View of bay, city, Alcatraz, Golden Gate Bridge. Cr cds: A, C, D, MC, V.

D

★ **FRASCATI.** *1901 Hyde St (94109), in Russian Hill. 415/928-1406.* Hrs: 5:30-10 pm; Fri, Sat to 10:30 pm. Closed Mon; Dec 25. Res accepted. No A/C. Contemporary Amer menu. Wine list. A la carte entrees: dinner $13-$17. Monthly menus of new American cuisine. Valet parking. Outdoor dining. Storefront location; bistro atmosphere. Cr cds: C, MC, V.

★★★ **FRENCH ROOM.** *(See The Clift Hotel) 415/775-4700.* Hrs: 6:30-10:30 am, 5:30-10 pm; Mon to 10:30 am; Sat, Sun 7-11 am, 5:30-10 pm; Sun brunch 10 am-2 pm. Res accepted. California, continental menu. Bar. Wine list. A la carte entrees: bkfst $9-$17, dinner $19-$34. Prix fixe: 5-course dinner $75. Sun brunch $40. Child's meals. Specializes in beef, veal, lamb. Pianist. Valet parking. Classic decor. Jacket. Cr cds: A, C, D, DS, ER, JCB, MC, V.

D

✓★★ **FRINGALE.** *570 Fourth St (94107), south of Union Square. 415/543-0573.* E-mail beastro@aol.com. Hrs: 11:30 am-3 pm, 5:30-10:30 pm; Sat from 5:30 pm. Closed Sun; some major hols. Res accepted. No A/C. French menu. Bar. A la carte entrees: lunch $7.50-$14, dinner $11-$17. Upscale bistro fare. Atmosphere of European country cafe. Totally nonsmoking. Cr cds: A, C, MC, V.

D

★★ **GABBIANOS.** *1 Ferry Plaza (94111), at foot of Market St, in Financial District. 415/391-8403.* E-mail gabbiano@hooked.net; web www.hooked.net/~gabbiano. Hrs: 11 am-10 pm; Sun brunch 10:30 am-2 pm. Res accepted. Italian, Amer menu. Bar. A la carte entrees: lunch $7.50-$15.25, dinner $9.75-$19.50. Sun brunch $24.95. Specializes in fresh seafood, pasta. Valet parking. Patio dining. Waterfront with views of Alcatraz, Oakland and Mt Tamalpais. Cr cds: A, C, D, DS, JCB, MC, V.

D

★★★ **GARDEN COURT.** *(See Palace Hotel) 415/392-8600.* Web www.sheraton.com. Hrs: 6:30 am-2 pm, 6-10 pm; Sun (brunch) 6:30-10 am, 11:30 am-1:30 pm; Mon to 2 pm. Res accepted. Californian menu. Bar. A la carte entrees: bkfst $11-$19.75, lunch $13.50-$18.25, dinner $14-$28. Complete meals: lunch $15, dinner $39. Bkfst buffet $18.75. Sun brunch $36. Entertainment. Formal decor. Totally nonsmoking. Cr cds: A, C, D, DS, JCB, MC, V.

D

★★★★★ **GARY DANKO'S.** *2 New Montgomery. 415/749-2060.* This outstanding restaurant, named for its chef/owner, is the most exciting newcomer to the San Francisco dining scene. Danko's modern California cuisine demonstrates a perfect balance between respect for fresh ingredients and creativity. Though relatively new, this restaurant is already one of the best in the country. California French. Specialty: table-side cheese cart. Hrs: Mon-Sun 5:30-9:30 pm. Prix fixe: 3 course $48, 4 course $57, 5 course $66, 6 course $75. Closed some hol (call). Valet. Reser pref. Jacket & tie pref. Cr cds: C.

★★ **GAYLORD INDIA.** *900 North Point St (94109), in Ghirardelli Square, at Fisherman's Wharf. 415/771-8822.* Web www.gaylords.com. Hrs: 11:45 am-1:45 pm, 5-10:45 pm; Sun brunch noon-2:45 pm. Closed Thanksgiving, Dec 25. Res accepted. Indian menu. Bar. Semi-a la carte: lunch $9.75-$13.25, dinner $9.95-$21. Complete meals: dinner $22.70-$28.75. Specializes in tandoori dishes, Indian desserts. Parking. View of bay. Totally nonsmoking. Cr cds: A, C, D, DS, JCB, MC, V.

★★ **GLOBE.** *290 Pacific (94111), in Financial District. 415/391-4132.* Hrs: 11:30-1 am; Sat 6 pm-1 am. Closed Sun; Thanksgiving, Dec 25. Res accepted. Contemporary Amer menu. Bar. A la carte entrees: lunch $8-$13, dinner $14-$20. Specialties: double cut t-bone for 2 with potato gratin; grilled salmon on baccacino pasta; baked mussels with scallops and rock shrimp with Thai basil and garlic butter. Street parking. Outdoor dining. Totally nonsmoking. Cr cds: A, C, MC, V.

★★ **GOLDEN GATE PARK BREWERY.** *1326 9th Ave (94122), in Civic Center. 415/665-5800.* Web www.goldengatepark.com. Hrs: 4:30-10 pm; Thurs, Fri to midnight; Sat 11:30 am-midnight; Sun 11:30 am-10 pm; Sat, Sun brunch 11:30 am-3 pm. Closed most major hols. Res accepted. Contemporary Amer menu. Bar. Semi-a la carte: dinner $16.95. Sat, Sun brunch $1.95-$8.95. Child's meals. Specialties: wasabi-crusted salmon, pan-seared Asian shrimp salad. Bingo Wed. Street parking. In brewery. Totally nonsmoking. Cr cds: C.

★★★ **GRAND CAFE.** *(See Hotel Monaco) 415/292-0101.* Hrs: 7 am-10:30 pm; wkends to 11:30 pm; Sat, Sun brunch 9 am-2 pm. Closed July 4, Thanksgiving, Dec 25. Res accepted. Continental menu. Bar 11:30-1:30 am. A la carte entrees: bkfst $7.95-$9.95, lunch $8.95-$16.50, dinner $11.95-$22.95. Sat, Sun brunch $7.95-$12.95. Specialties: polenta souffle, roasted rack of lamb, veal sweetbread fricassee. Valet parking. Chandeliers and bronze sculpture add elegance to this hotel dining rm. Totally nonsmoking. Cr cds: A, C, D, DS, ER, JCB, MC, V.

D

✓★★ **GREENS.** *Building A At Fort Mason (94123), in Marina District. 415/771-6222.* Hrs: 11:30 am-2 pm, 5:30-9:30 pm; Sat 11:30 am-2:30 pm, 5:30-9:30 pm; Sun brunch 10 am-2 pm; Mon-Sat 9:30-11 pm (dessert only). Closed most major hols. Res accepted. Vegetarian menu. Wine, beer. A la carte entrees: lunch $7-$12, dinner $11-$15. Prix fixe: dinner (Sat) $40. Sun brunch $7-$11. Parking. View of bay. Totally nonsmoking. Cr cds: C, DS, MC, V.

D

★★ **HARRIS'.** *2100 Van Ness Ave (94109), in Pacific Heights. 415/673-1888.* Hrs: from 5:30 pm; Sat, Sun from 5 pm. Closed Jan 1, Dec 25. Res accepted. A la carte entrees: dinner $24-$34. Specializes in beef, fresh seafood, Maine lobster. Jazz Thur-Sun. Valet parking. Cr cds: A, C, D, DS, JCB, MC, V.

D

★★ **HARRY DENTON'S.** *161 Steuart St (94105), in Financial District. 415/882-1333.* Hrs: 11:30 am-2:30 pm, 5:30-10 pm. Cover charge Thurs-Sat $10. Closed most major hols. Res accepted. Bar. A la carte entrees: lunch $7.25-$15.95, dinner $7.95-$25. Specializes in steaks, fresh seafood, pasta. Entertainment. Valet parking (dinner). Jazz club atmosphere. Cr cds: A, C, D, DS, MC, V.

D

★★★★ **HAWTHORNE LANE.** *22 Hawthorne St (94105), south of Union Square. 415/777-9779.* Web www.hawthornelane.com. Ann and David Gingrass have created a beautiful, bustling home for their creative American cooking, which draws on the flavors of the Mediterranean and Asia. A friendly and attentive staff make the experience thoroughly enjoyable. Hrs: 11:30 am-2 pm, 5:30-10 pm; Fri, Sat to 10:30 pm. Closed some major hols. Res accepted. Continental menu. Valet parking. Modern decor. Bar to midnight. A la carte entrees: lunch $8.50-$14, dinner $18-$26. Child's meals. Specialties: miso-glazed black cod, fresh spot prawns, glazed quail. Cr cds: C, D, DS, JCB, MC, V.

D

★★ **HAYES STREET GRILL.** *324 Hayes St (94102), in Civic Center area. 415/863-5545.* Hrs: 11:30 am-2 pm, 5-9:30 pm; Fri to 10:30 pm; Sat 5:30-10:30 pm; Sun 5-8:30 pm. Closed major hols. Res accepted. Seafood menu. Bar. A la carte entrees: lunch $9.50-$17, dinner $13-$25. Specializes in fresh seafood, salads, charcoal-grilled fish. Cr cds: A, C, D, DS, MC, V.

D

✓★★ **HELMAND RESTAURANT.** *430 Broadway (94133), in North Beach. 415/362-0641.* Hrs: 5:30-10 pm; Fri, Sat to 11 pm. Res accepted. Afghanistan menu. Wine, beer. Semi-a la carte: dinner $9.95-$15.95. Specialties: shish kebab, mantwo, rack of lamb. Paintings and photos of Afghani scenes. Cr cds: A, C, MC, V.

D

★ **HONG KONG FLOWER LOUNGE RSTRNT.** *5322 Geary Blvd (94121), at 17th Ave, in Richmond District. 415/668-8998.* Hrs: 11 am-2:30 pm, 5-9:30 pm; Sat, Sun from 10 am. Res accepted. Chinese menu.

Bar. A la carte entrees: lunch $8-$10, dinner $15-$25. Complete meals: dinner (for 4) $88. Street parking. Oriental decor. Cr cds: A, C, D, DS, JCB, MC, V.

D

✓★★ **HOUSE.** *1230 Grant Ave (94133), in North Beach. 415/986-8612.* Hrs: 11:30 am-3 pm, 5:30-10 pm; Fri to 11 pm; Sat 5-11 pm. Closed Sun. Continental menu. Wine, beer. Semi-a la carte: lunch $5.95-$15.95, dinner $8.95-$16.95. Specializes in fish, rack of lamb, noodles. Contemporary decor. Totally nonsmoking. Cr cds: A, C, MC, V.

D

★★★ **HOUSE OF PRIME RIB.** *1906 Van Ness Ave (94109), at Washington St, in Russian Hill. 415/885-4605.* Hrs: 5:30-10 pm; Fri, Sat from 4:30 pm; Sun from 4 pm; hols vary. Res accepted. Bar. Wine list. A la carte entrees: dinner $19.65. Semi-a la carte: dinner $18.75-$23.95. Child's meals. Specializes in corn-fed, 21-day aged prime rib of beef. Prime rib carved at table. Valet parking. English decor. Cr cds: A, C, D, MC, V.

D

✓★ **HUNAN RESTAURANT.** *924 Sansome St (94111), in Financial District. 415/956-7727.* Hrs: 11:30 am-9:30 pm. Closed July 4, Thanksgiving, Dec 25. Res accepted. No A/C. Chinese menu. Bar. A la carte entrees: lunch, dinner $5-$9.95. Specializes in smoked Hunan dishes. Chinese decor. Cr cds: A, C, D, JCB, MC, V.

D

★★ **I FRATELLI.** *1896 Hyde St (94109), at Green, in Russian Hill. 415/474-8240.* Web www.citysearch.com/sfo/ifratelli. Hrs: 5:30-10 pm. Closed major hols. Italian menu. Bar. A la carte entrees: dinner $11-$18. Child's meals. Specializes in homemade pasta. Piano bar Tues, Thurs. Cafe atmosphere; photos of Italian street scenes. Cr cds: A, C, MC, V.

D

✓★ **INFUSION BAR & RESTAURANT.** *555 Second St (94107), south of Union Square. 415/543-2282.* E-mail infusn@aol.com; web www.citysearch.com/sfo/infusion. Hrs: 11:30-2 am; Sat, Sun from 5 pm. Closed most major hols. Res accepted. No A/C. Bar. Semi-a la carte: lunch $5-$13, dinner $12-$20. Specialties: peppered filet mignon, fresh fruit-infused vodkas. Musicians Thurs-Sat. Street parking. Modern lighting, artwork. Totally nonsmoking. Cr cds: A, C, D, MC, V.

D

★★★★ **JARDIENERE.** *300 Grove St (94102), in Civic Center area. 415/861-5555.* The striking design of this popular bi-level restaurant—deep colors, exposed brick, plush banquettes, sculpted railings—evokes an elegant supper club. Chef/owner Traci Des Jardins' Mediterranean-inspired menu features regional ingredients simply prepared. Hrs: 5:30-10:30 pm, Mon-Fri. Closed most major hols. Res accepted. French Californian menu. Latenight menu available. Bar. Wine list. A la carte entrees: dinner $19-$27. Complete meal (6-course): dinner $75. Menu changes seasonally. Jazz duet. Valet parking. Cr cds: A, C, D, MC, V.

D

★ **JASMINE HOUSE.** *2301 Clement St (94121), in Richmond District. 415/668-3382.* Hrs: 11 am-10 pm; Mon from 5 pm; Fri, Sat to 11 pm. Res accepted. Vietnamese menu. Wine, beer. Semi-a la carte: lunch $4.50-$6.50, dinner $5.95-$23.95. Specializes in seafood, beef, chicken. Casual decor. Totally nonsmoking. Cr cds: A, C, D, JCB, MC, V.

D

★★ **JULIUS CASTLE.** *1541 Montgomery St (94133), on Telegraph Hill, in North Beach. 415/362-3042.* E-mail jcastle@ix.netcom.com. Hrs: 5-10 pm. Res accepted. No A/C. Italian menu. Bar. A la carte entrees: dinner $19-$39. Specializes in veal, rack of lamb, seafood. Own pastries, pasta, ice cream. Valet parking. Turreted castle overlooking San Francisco Bay. Historic landmark (1922). Totally nonsmoking. Cr cds: A, C, D, DS, MC, V.

★ **KABUTO SUSHI.** *5116 Geary Blvd (94118), in Richmond District. 415/752-5652.* Hrs: 5:30-11 pm. Closed Mon; some major hols. Res accepted. Japanese menu. Semi-a la carte: dinner $9-$18. Specializes in sushi. Street parking. Fish tanks. Cr cds: C, MC, V.

★ **KATIA'S RUSSIAN TEA ROOM.** *600 5th Ave (94118), in Richmond District. 415/668-9292.* Web www.citysearch.com/sfo/katias. Hrs: 11:30 am-2:30 pm, 5-9 pm; Fri, Sat to 10 pm; Sun from 5 pm. Closed Mon; most major hols. Res accepted. No A/C. Russian menu. Wine, beer. Semi-a la carte: lunch, dinner $9-$14.50. Child's meals. Specializes in Russian pastries. Accordianist, guitarist nightly. Intimate corner cafe. Totally nonsmoking. Cr cds: A, C, D, DS, JCB, MC, V.

D

★★ **KHAN TOKE THAI HOUSE.** *5937 Geary Blvd (94121), in Richmond District. 415/668-6654.* Hrs: 5-11 pm. Closed Labor Day, Thanksgiving, Dec 25. Res accepted. Thai menu. Wine, beer. A la carte entrees: dinner $4.95-$10.95. Complete meal: dinner $16.95. Specialties: pong pang (seafood), choo chee goong (prawn in coconut milk curry). Thai classical dancing performance Sun (8:30 pm). Thai decor and furnishings. Family-owned. Street parking. Totally nonsmoking. Cr cds: C, MC, V.

D

★★ **KULETO'S RESTAURANT.** *221 Powell St (94102), south of Union Square. 415/397-7720.* E-mail kuletos96@aol.com. Hrs: 7-10:30 am, 11:30 am-11 pm; Sat, Sun from 8 am. Closed Labor Day, Thanksgiving, Dec 25. Res accepted. Northern Italian menu. Bar 11 am-midnight. Complete meals: bkfst $4.50-$8.95. A la carte entrees: lunch, dinner $8.25-$17.50. Specializes in grilled fish, chicken, pasta. Italian decor. Cr cds: A, C, D, DS, ER, JCB, MC, V.

D

★★★ **KYO YA.** *2 New Montgomery St (94105). 415/512-1111.* japanese Menu. Specialities: Sukiyaki, Shabu Shabu, Yosinabi. Hrs: Tues-Fri 11:30 am-2 pm, 6-10 pm; Sat, 6-10 pm, closed Sun, Mon. Res suggested for Sushi Bar. Private Party res accepted. Bar. Lunch $15-$24, Dinner $27-$37, Specialities from $40. Valet Parking. Totally nonsmoking. Cr cds: C.

★★★★ **LA FOLIE.** *2316 Polk St (94109). 415/776-5577.* Clouds dance on the ceiling of this casually elegant restaurant, where French native Roland Passot mans the stove. The seasonal menu is artfully presented and the service is attentive. French cuisine. Hrs 5:30-9:45 pm. Mon-Sat. Closed Sun & maj hol. Reserv reqd. Prices: $30-$40. Valet. Cr cds: C.

★ **LA VIE VIETNAMESE RESTAURANT.** *5830 Geary Blvd (94121), in Richmond District. 415/668-8080.* Hrs: 11 am-10 pm; Fri, Sat to 10:30 pm. Res accepted. Vietnamese menu. Wine, beer. A la carte entrees: lunch $4.65-$5.25, dinner $6.95-$10.95. Street parking. Family-style dining. Totally nonsmoking. Cr cds: C, D, MC, V.

★ **LAGHI.** *2101 Sutter (94115), in Richmond District. 415/386-6266.* Hrs: 4-11 pm. Res accepted. Northern Italian menu. Bar. A la carte entrees: dinner $10.75-$19.50. Specializes in pasta. Own baking, pasta. Street parking. Totally nonsmoking. Cr cds: A, C, D, JCB, MC, V.

D

★★ **LE CHARM FRENCH BISTRO.** *315 5th St (94107), south of Union Square. 415/546-6128.* Hrs: 11:30 am-2:30 pm, 5:30-9:30 pm; Sat 5:30-10 pm. Closed Sun; some major hols; also 3 wks in August. Res accepted. No A/C. French menu. Wine, beer. A la carte entrees: lunch $6.50-$9, dinner $11-$14. 3-course prix fixe: dinner $20-$33. Specialties: onion soup, escargot, roasted salmon. Street parking. Outdoor dining. French bistro atmosphere. Totally nonsmoking. Cr cds: A, C, MC, V.

D

✓★ **LHASA MOON.** *2420 Lombard St (94123), in Marina District. 415/674-9898.* Hrs: 5-10 pm; Thurs 11:30 am-2:30 pm, 5-10 pm; Fri, Sat to 10:30 pm; Sun 4:30-9:30 pm. Closed Mon; Dec 25. Tibetan menu. Bar. Semi-a la carte: lunch, dinner $7.50-$12.50. Specializes in curries, steamed pie. Tibetan decor. Totally nonsmoking. Cr cds: A, C, MC, V.

D

★★ **LOLLI'S CASTAGNOLA.** *286 Jefferson St (94133), at Fisherman's Wharf. 415/776-5015.* Hrs: 9 am-11 pm. Closed Dec 25. Bar. Semi-a la carte: bkfst $3.95-$9.95, lunch, dinner $7-$30. Child's meals. Specializes in seafood. Outdoor dining. View of fishing fleet. Cr cds: A, C, D, DS, JCB, MC, V.

D

★★ **LULU.** *816 Folsom St (94107), south of Union Square. 415/495-5775.* Web www.citysearch.com/sfo/lulu. Hrs: 11:30 am-2:30 pm, 5:30-10:30 pm; Fri, Sat to 11:30 pm. Res accepted. French, Italian menu. Bar. Semi-a la carte: lunch $6:50-$14, dinner $9-$18.50. Cr cds: A, C, D, MC, V.

D

★★ **M POINT BAR-SUSHI & GRILL.** *(See Hotel Milano) 415/543-7600.* Hrs: 7-10:30 am, 11:30 am-2:30 pm, 5-10 pm. Res accepted. Bar. A la carte entrees: bkfst $5.50-$7.50, lunch $11.25-$13.50, dinner $18-$26. Specializes in sushi. Valet parking. Mural stretching full length of restaurant. Totally nonsmoking. Cr cds: A, C, DS, JCB, MC, V.

D

★★ **MAC ARTHUR PARK.** *607 Front St (94111), in Financial District. 415/398-5700.* Hrs: 11:30 am-3:30 pm, 5-10 pm; Fri to 11 pm; Sat 5-11 pm; Sun 4:30-10 pm. Closed Thanksgiving, Dec 25. Res accepted. Bar. A la carte entrees: lunch, dinner $7.95-$24.95. Specializes in barbecued ribs, mesquite-grilled fish. Complimentary valet parking (dinner). Cr cds: A, C, D, MC, V.

D

★★ **MANDARIN.** *900 North Point St (94109), in Ghirardelli Square, at Fisherman's Wharf. 415/673-8812.* Web www.themandarin.com. Hrs: 11:30 am-11 pm. Res accepted. Northern Chinese, mandarin menu. Bar. Semi-a la carte: lunch $8.95-$13, dinner $13-$35. Complete meals: dinner $16-$38. Mandarin banquet for 8 or more, $25-$58 each. Specialties: minced squab, beggar's chicken (1-day notice), Peking duck (1-day notice). Chinese decor; artifacts. 19th-century structure. View of bay. Cr cds: A, C, D, DS, JCB, MC, V.

D

★ **MANGIAFUCCO.** *1001 Guerrero St (94110), in Mission District. 415/206-9881.* Hrs: 5:30-10:30 pm; Fri, Sat to 11 pm. Closed major hols. Res accepted. No A/C. Italian menu. Wine, beer. A la carte entrees: dinner $7.50-$16. Specializes in regional Italian grilled meats. Own pasta. Valet parking. Rustic Italian decor; countryside atmosphere. Totally nonsmoking. Cr cds: C, MC, V.

D

★★ **MARRAKECH MOROCCAN.** *419 O'farrell St (94102), south of Union Square. 415/776-6717.* Hrs: 6-10 pm. Res accepted. Moroccan menu. Bar. Prix fixe: dinner $24.95. Specialties: chicken with lemon, lamb with honey, couscous fassi. Belly dancing. Seating on floor pillows or low couches. Moroccan decor. Cr cds: A, C, DS, MC, V.

★★★★ **MASA'S.** *(See HOTEL VINTAGE COURT) 415/989-7154.* Chef Chad Callahan has ably filled Julian Serrano's shoes, and this elegant restaurant has retained its place among the city's best. Highly stylized French cooking is served in a formal setting by a knowledgeable and attentive staff. An exceptional wine list features many hard-to-find bottles. French menu. Specialties: Foie Gras saute with Madeira truffle sauce, Lobster Salad with crispy leeks and truffle vinaigrette, sauteed medallions of New Zealand Fallow Deer. Hrs: 6-9:30 pm. Closed Sun, Mon; First 2 wks in Jan & week of July 4. Res suggested. Bar. Wine cellar and Private Dining in Wine Cellar for 8-12 persons. Prix fixe: 4 or 5 course dinner $75-$80. Valet parking $9/day. Cr cds: A, C, D, DS, JCB, MC, V.

D

✓★★ **MATTERHORN SWISS.** *2323 Van Ness (94109), in Russian Hill. 415/885-6116.* E-mail mathorn@aol.com. Hrs: 5-10 pm. Closed Mon. Res accepted. Swiss menu. Bar. Semi-a la carte: dinner $13-$22. Specialties: fondue, wienerschnitzel, veal cordon bleu. Valet parking. Casual dining; hand-carved woodwork. Cr cds: A, C, D, DS, MC, V.

D

★★★ **MC2.** *470 Pacific Avenue (94133). 415/956-0666; FAX 415/956-6461.* French Californian cuisine. Specialties: Seared tuna & tart flambee'. Hrs: Mon - Fri 11:30-2 pm; Mon-Wed 5:30-9:30 pm; Thurs-Sat 5:30-10:30 pm. Prices: lunch $12-$16; dinner $23-$28. Bar. Valet for dinner. Res reqd. Cr cds: C.

★★ **MCCORMICK & KULETO'S.** *900 N Point St (94109), on Ghirardelli Square, in Fisherman's Wharf. 415/929-1730.* Hrs: 11:30 am-11 pm; Sun from 10:30 am. Res accepted. Bar. A la carte entrees: lunch, dinner $5-$50. Child's meals. Specializes in fresh seafood. Parking. Crab Cake Lounge has open kitchen. View of bay. Cr cds: C.

★★ **MECCA.** *2029 Market St (94114), in Mission District. 415/621-7000.* Web www.sfmecca.com. Hrs: 6-11 pm; Thurs-Sat to midnight. Closed Thanksgiving, Dec 25. Res accepted; required Fri, Sat. Mediterranean, Amer menu. Bar. A la carte entrees: dinner $14-$24. Own baking. Valet parking. Ultra-modern ambience. Totally nonsmoking. Cr cds: A, C, D, MC, V.

D

✓★★ **MEETING HOUSE.** *1701 Octavia St (94109), in Pacific Heights. 415/922-6733.* Web www.citysearch.com. Hrs: 5:30-9:30 pm. Closed Sun, Mon; July 4, Dec 25. Res accepted. Wine, beer. A la carte entree: dinner $13-$20. Specialties: hominy crusted catfish, rock shrimp and scallion johnnycakes. Totally nonsmoking. Cr cds: A, C, D, MC, V.

★★★ **MOOSE'S.** *1652 Stockton St (94133), between Union & Filbert Sts, in North Beach. 415/989-7800.* E-mail Dolly@mooses.com. Mon-Wed closed for lunch, 5:30-10 pm; Thurs and Fri 11:30 am-2:30 pm, 5:30-10 pm, 10-11 pm with a lighter menu; Sat 10 am-2:30 pm, 5:30-11 pm; Sun brunch 9:30 am-2:30 pm, 5-10 pm. Closed some major hols. Res accepted. Bar. Wine cellar. A la carte entrees: lunch $4.95-$14.50, dinner $7.50-$28. Sun brunch $2.95-$12.95. Child's meals. Jazz evenings start at 8pm. Valet parking. Cr cds: A, C, D, JCB, MC, V.

D

★★ **MORTON'S OF CHICAGO.** *400 Post St (94102), in Union Square. 415/986-5830.* Hrs: 5-11 pm; Sun to 10 pm. Closed most major hols. Res accepted. Bar. A la carte entrees: dinner $20.95-$30.95. Specializes in steak. Club atmosphere. Totally nonsmoking. Cr cds: A, C, D, JCB, MC, V.

D

★★ **MURPHY'S.** *(See Best Western Canterbury Hotel) 415/474-6478.* Hrs: 6:30-11 am, 5-10:30 pm. Res accepted. Bar. Buffet: bkfst $11.95. Semi-a la carte: dinner $13.95-$29.95. Child's meals. Specializes in organic cuisine. Valet parking. Tropical decor. Totally nonsmoking. Family-owned. Cr cds: A, C, D, DS, JCB, MC, V.

D SC

★★ **NEW GOLDEN TURTLE RESTAURANT.** *2211 Van Ness Ave (94109), at Broadway, in Russian Hill. 415/441-4419.* Hrs: 5-10:30 pm. Closed Mon. Res accepted. Vietnamese menu. Wine, beer. A la carte entrees: dinner $8.95-$18.95. Specialties: spicy calamari saute, chili chicken, pan-fried Dungeness crab. Carved wooden panels depict scenes of Vietnamese culture. Cr cds: A, C, D, MC, V.

D

★★ **NEW JOE'S.** *347 Geary St (94102), west of Union Square. 415/397-9999.* Hrs: 7 am-11 pm. Res accepted. Contemporary Italian menu. Bar. A la carte entrees: bkfst $5-$8.75, lunch $6-$14, dinner $9-$16. Child's meals. Specialties: linguine Portofino, chicken Luciano, pizza Margharita. Mahogany paneling and moldings. Mural of city. Cr cds: A, C, D, DS, JCB, MC, V.

D

★★★ **NOB HILL.** *(See Mark Hopkins Inter-Continental Hotel) 415/616-6944.* Hrs: 11:30 am-11 pm. Res accepted. Bar. A la carte entrees: lunch $9-$21, dinner $18-$26.50. Child's meals. Specialties: steamed or grilled salmon, sauteed duck foie gras, grilled lamb. Pianist. Jazz trio Fri, Sat. Valet parking. Cr cds: A, C, D, DS, ER, JCB, MC, V.

D ♥

★★★ **NORTH BEACH.** *1512 Stockton St, at Columbus, in North Beach. 415/392-1700.* Hrs: 11:30-1 am. Closed some major hols. Res accepted. Northern Italian menu. Wine cellar. A la carte entrees: lunch $8.50-$24, dinner $11.75-$19.75. Specializes in fresh fish, veal, pasta. Valet parking. Cr cds: A, C, D, DS, JCB, MC, V.

D

★★ **NORTH INDIA.** *3131 Webster St, at Lombard St, in Marina District. 415/931-1556.* Web www.citysearch7.com. Hrs: 11:30 am-2:30 pm, 5-10:30 pm; Sat from 5 pm; Sun 5-10 pm. Res accepted. Northern Indian menu. Bar. Semi-a la carte: lunch $7.95-$11.95, dinner $12.95-$24.50. Prix fixe: $12.95. Child's meals. Specializes in tandoori seafood, lamb, poultry. Own desserts. Paintings of Moghul and Bengal lancers. Kitchen tours. Cr cds: A, C, D, DS, MC, V.

D

✓★ **O'REILLY'S.** *622 Green St (94133), in North Beach. 415/989-6222.* Hrs: 11-2 am; Sat, Sun from 8 am. Res accepted. Irish menu. Bar. Semi-a la carte: lunch, dinner $5.95-$16. Specializes in corned beef & cabbage, cottage pie. Outdoor dining. Photos and memorabilia from Ireland. Cr cds: A, C, D, MC, V.

D

★★★ **ONE MARKET.** *1 Market St (94105), in Financial District. 415/777-5577.* Hrs: 11:30 am-2 pm, 5:30-9:30 pm; Fri to 10 pm; Sat 5-10 pm. Closed Sun; some major hols. Res accepted. Contemporary Amer menu. Bar. A la carte entrees: lunch $12-$18, dinner $20-$30. Child's meals. Specialties: ahi tuna rossini, Hudson Valley foie gras two ways. Own desserts. Pianist. Totally nonsmoking. Cr cds: A, C, D, MC, V.

D

★★ **OSAKA GRILL.** *1217 Sutter St (94109), in Russian Hill. 415/440-8838.* Hrs: 11:30 am-2 pm, 5:30-10 pm. Closed most major hols. Res accepted. Hibachi cuisine. Wine, beer. Complete meal: lunch $6.50-$10, dinner $14-$30. Specialties: Chilean sea bass, grilled king prawns, center-cut filet mignon. Street parking. Dinner prepared at table. Totally nonsmoking. Cr cds: A, C, D, JCB, MC, V.

D

★★★ **PACIFIC.** *(See Pan Pacific Hotel) 415/929-2087.* E-mail vulrich@sfo.pan-pacific.com; web www.panpac.com. Hrs: 6:30 am-11 pm; Sun brunch 10 am-2 pm. Res accepted. Bar 3-11:30 pm. Wine list. A la carte entrees: bkfst $5-$14, lunch $9.50-$16, dinner $18.50-$26. Sun brunch $9-$16. Specializes in Pacific Rim cuisine with French accent. Pianist. Valet parking. Modern decor; atrium setting in lobby of hotel. Cr cds: A, C, D, DS, JCB, MC, V.

D

★★ **PALIO D'ASTI.** *640 Sacramento St (94111), at Montgomery St, in Financial District. 415/395-9800.* Hrs: 11:30 am-2:30 pm, 5:30-10 pm. Closed Sat, Sun; major hols. Res accepted. Italian menu. Bar. A la carte entrees: lunch $15-$20, dinner $19-$25. Specialties: risotto, mezzelune alla monferrina. Exhibition pasta-making and pizza-making kitchens; wood-burning ovens. Cr cds: A, C, D, DS, MC, V.

D

★★ **PANE E VINO RESTAURANT.** *3011 Steiner St (94123), in Cow Hollow. 415/346-2111.* Hrs: 11:30 am-2:30 pm, 5-10 pm; Fri, Sat 11:30 am-10:30 pm. Closed major hols. Res accepted. Italian menu. A la carte entrees: lunch, dinner $8.25-$19.95. Specialties: osso bucco, branzino. Italian decor. Totally nonsmoking. Cr cds: A, C, MC, V.

D

★★★ **PARK GRILL.** *(See Park Hyatt Hotel) 415/296-2933.* Hrs: 6:30 am-9:30 pm; Sun brunch 10 am-2:30 pm. Res accepted. Bar 11 am-9:30 pm. Wine list. A la carte entrees: bkfst $9.75-$17.50, lunch $9.75-$19, dinner $17-$23. Sun brunch $22.50. Child's meals. Specializes in mixed grills. Own baking. Pianist. Valet parking. Outdoor dining. Club rm atmosphere; original art. Cr cds: A, C, D, DS, ER, JCB, MC, V.

D

★★ **PASTIS.** *1015 Battery St (94111), in Financial District. 415/391-2555.* Hrs: 11:30 am-3 pm, 5:30-10:30 pm. Closed Sun; most major hols. Res accepted. French menu. Bar. A la carte entrees: lunch $7-$12, dinner $8-$19. Specialties: oxtail rouelle with gribiche, roast magret of duck, warm banana and chocolate pannequet. Street parking. Outdoor dining. Original artwork. Cr cds: A, C, MC, V.

★ **PERRY'S.** *1944 Union St (94123), in Cow Hollow. 415/922-9022.* Hrs: 9 am-10 pm; Wed, Thurs to 11 pm; Fri, Sat to midnight. Closed Thanksgiving, Dec 25. Res accepted. Bar. A la carte entrees: bkfst $5.95-$13.95, lunch, dinner $8.50-$19.95. Child's meals. Specializes in steaks, chops, salads. Street parking. Outdoor dining. Family-owned since 1969. Totally nonsmoking. Cr cds: A, C, MC, V.

D

★ **PERRY'S DOWNTOWN.** *185 Sutter St (94104), in Financial District. 415/989-6895.* Hrs: 7 am-9:30 pm. Closed Sun; major hols. Res accepted. Bar to midnight. A la carte entrees: lunch, dinner $5.50-$17.95. Specializes in lobster, pasta. Casual decor. Cr cds: A, C, D, DS, MC, V.

D

★ **PICKLED GINGER.** *100 Brannan St (94107), in Financial District. 415/977-1230.* Hrs: 11:30 am-2 pm, 5-10 pm; Fri to 11 pm; Sat 5-11 pm; Sun 5-10 pm. Closed major hols. Res accepted. Pacific Rim menu. Bar. A la carte entrees: lunch $8.50-$11, dinner $11-$15.50. Child's meals. Specialties: seared pork & scallops gyozas, chopstick salads, tea-spiced smoked salmon. Street parking. Outdoor dining. Totally nonsmoking. Cr cds: A, C, D, MC, V.

D

✓★ **PLOUF.** *40 Belden Pl (94104), in Financial District. 415/986-6491.* Hrs: 11:30 am-3 pm, 5:30-10 pm; Sat from 5:30 pm. Closed Sun; major hols. Res accepted. No A/C. French, seafood menu. Bar. Semi-a la carte: lunch $12-$15, dinner $12-$17. Specializes in seafood. Outdoor dining. Totally nonsmoking. Cr cds: A, C, D, MC, V.

D

✓★★★ **PLUMPJACK CAFE.** *3127 Fillmore St (94123), in Marina District. 415/563-4755.* Hrs: 11:30 am-2 pm, 5:30-10 pm; Sat from 5:30 pm. Closed Sun; most major hols. Res accepted; required dinner. Extensive wine list. Semi-a la carte: lunch $8-$15, dinner $15-$20. Specializes in duck, risotto, seasonal dishes. Street parking. Henry VIII decor; intimate dining. Totally nonsmoking. Cr cds: A, C, MC, V.

D

★★★★ **POSTRIO RESTAURANT.** *(See The Prescott Hotel) 415/776-7825.* Web postrio.com. Past the bustling bar and down the dramatic staircase you enter into a chic, sophisticated restaurant. Chef/brothers Mitch and Steve Rosenthal interpret American cooking through a Mediterranean lens from their post in the open kitchen. A favorite spot for power breakfasts. American contemporary menu. Specialties: Chinese duck, roasted salmon. Own baking. Hrs: 7-10 am, 11:30 am-2 pm, 5:30-10 pm; Sat 11:30 am-2 pm; Sun from 5:30 pm; Sun brunch 9 am-2 pm. Closed July 4, Thanksgiving, Dec 25. Res required. Bar 11:30-12 am. Wine list. A la carte entrees: bkfst $5-$12, lunch $25-$30, dinner $55. Sun brunch $12-$22. Valet parking. Totally nonsmoking. Cr cds: A, C, D, DS, JCB, MC, V.

D

★ **POT STICKER.** *150 Waverly Place (94108), in Chinatown. 415/397-9985.* Hrs: 11 am-10 pm. Res accepted. No A/C. Hunan/Mandarin/Szechwan menu. A la carte entrees: lunch, dinner $5.25-$18. Complete meals: lunch $4.50-$5, dinner $6.50-$9.95. Specialties: pot stickers, Szechwan crispy fish, orange spareribs. Cr cds: A, C, MC, V.

★★ **PREGO RISTORANTE.** *2000 Union St (94123), in Cow Hollow. 415/563-3305.* Hrs: 11:30 am-midnight. Closed Thanksgiving, Dec 25. Res accepted. Northern Italian menu. Bar to midnight. A la carte entrees: lunch, dinner $8.95-$17.95. Specialties: carpaccio, agnolotti d'aragosta, pizza baked in wood-burning oven. Outside dining. Cr cds: A, C, D, MC, V.

D

✓★★ **PUCCINI & PINETTI.** *129 Ellis St (94102), south of Union Square. 415/392-5500.* Hrs: 11:30 am-10 pm; Fri, Sat to 11 pm; Sun 5-10 pm. Closed July 4, Thanksgiving, Dec 25. Res accepted. Italian menu. Bar. A la carte entrees: lunch $5.25-$12.95, dinner $6.95-$14.95. Specializes in spaghetti putanesca, wood-fired pizza. Open kitchen with wood burning oven. Totally nonsmoking. Cr cds: A, C, D, DS, MC, V.

D

★★★ **RESTAURANT AT SHERMAN HOUSE.** *2160 Green St (94123). 415/563-3600.* Open for in-house guests only. California cuisine. Cr cds: C.

✓★ **RISTORANTE IDEALE.** *1315 Grant Ave (94133), in North Beach. 415/391-4129.* Hrs: 11:30 am-2 pm, 5:30-10:30 pm; Fri, Sat to 11 pm; Sun to 10 pm. Closed Mon; Dec 25. Res accepted. Italian menu. Bar. Semi-a la carte: lunch $4.50-$9, dinner $9-$17.50. Child's meals. Specialties: fettuccine alla Norcina, saltimbocca alla Romana. Contemporary decor. Cr cds: C, DS, JCB, MC, V.

D

★★ **ROCCO'S SEAFOOD GRILL.** *2080 Van Ness Ave (94109), on Russian Hill. 415/567-7600.* Hrs: 5-10 pm; Fri, Sat to 11 pm. Closed Jan 1, Dec 25. Res accepted. Bar to midnight. A la carte entrees: dinner $13-$19.50. Child's meals. Specializes in seafood, oyster bar. Valet parking. Contemporary decor. Cr cds: A, C, D, DS, MC, V.

D

★★★ **ROSE PISTOLA.** *532 Columbus Ave (94133), in North Beach. 415/399-0499.* Hrs: 11:30 am-10:30 pm; Fri, Sat to 1 am. Closed some major hols. Res accepted. Northern Italian menu. Bar. A la carte entrees: lunch, dinner $9-$23. Child's meals. Specialties: cioppino, zucchini chips, gnocci. Entertainment. Outdoor dining. Contemporary decor. Totally nonsmoking. Cr cds: A, C, D, MC, V.

D

✓★★ **ROSE'S CAFE.** *2298 Union St (94123), in Cow Hollow. 415/775-2200.* Hrs: 7 am-10 pm; Fri to 11 pm; Sat 8 am-11 pm; Sun from 8 am. Closed July 4, Thanksgiving, Dec 25. Res accepted (dinner). Italian menu. Bar. Semi-a la carte: bkfst $5-$9, lunch $5-$10, dinner $7-$13. Specialties: iron skillet roast mussels, salmon sandwich, Italian-style pizzas. Street parking. Outdoor dining. Totally nonsmoking. Cr cds: A, C, D, MC, V.

D

✓★ **ROSTI RESTAURANTS.** *2060 Chestnut St (94123), in Marina District. 415/929-9300.* Hrs: 11:30 am-10 pm; Sat, Sun to 10:30 pm. Closed Thanksgiving, Dec 25. Italian menu. Wine, beer. Semi-a la carte: lunch, dinner $4.50-$12.95. Child's meals. Specialties: pollo al mattone, rollati, tiramisu. Street parking. Imported Italian tile flooring; Tuscan decor. Totally nonsmoking. Cr cds: C, DS, MC, V.

D

★★ **ROTI RESTAURANT.** *155 Stewart St (94105), in Hotel Griffon, in Financial District. 415/495-6500.* Web www.citysearch7.com. Hrs: 11:30 am-10 pm; Fri, Sat 5:30-11 pm. Closed Memorial Day, Labor Day, Dec 25. Res accepted. Bar. A la carte entrees: lunch, dinner $10.95-$23.95. Specialties: spit-roasted chicken, spit-roasted duck, fresh fish. Valet parking (dinner). Rustic atmosphere, American rotisserie grill. Totally nonsmoking. Cr cds: A, C, D, DS, MC, V.

D

★★★ **RUBICON RESTAURANT.** *558 Sacramento (94111), in Financial District. 415/434-4100.* E-mail interactivegourmet@cuisine.com; web www.cuisine.com. Hrs: 11:30 am-2:30 pm, 5:30-10 pm; Sat from 5:30 pm. Closed Sun. Res accepted. French Californian menu. Bar. Wine cellar. Semi-a la carte: lunch $12.50-$15, dinner $19-$25. Prix fixe: $31-$45. Menu changes seasonally. Totally nonsmoking. Cr cds: A, C, D, MC, V.

D

★ **RUE LEPIC.** *900 Pine St (94108), at Mason St, on Nob Hill. 415/474-6070.* Hrs: 11:30 am-2:30 pm, 5:30-10 pm; Sat, Sun from 5:30 pm. Closed most major hols. Res accepted; required wkends. French menu. A la carte entrees: lunch $6-$17, dinner $17-$21. Complete meals: dinner $35-$38. Specialties: roast medallion of veal with mushroom sauce, lobster tail, roasted rack of lamb with garlic. Totally nonsmoking. Cr cds: A, C, MC, V.

✓★★ **RUMPUS.** *1 Tillman Place (94108), in Union Square. 415/421-2300.* Hrs: 11:30 am-2:30 pm, 5:30-10 pm; Fri, Sat to 11 pm; Sun from 5:30 pm. Closed most major hols. Res accepted. Contemporary menu. Bar. Semi-a la carte: lunch $6-$16, dinner $10-$19. Specialties: pan-roasted chicken, risotto. Outdoor dining. Open kitchen; modern art. Totally nonsmoking. Cr cds: A, C, D, JCB, MC, V.

D

★★ **RUTH'S CHRIS STEAK HOUSE.** *1601 Van Ness Ave (94109), on Russian Hill. 415/673-0557.* Hrs: 5-10:30 pm; Sun to 10 pm. Closed Thanksgiving, Dec 25. Res accepted. Bar. A la carte entrees: dinner $18.95-$29.95. Specializes in steak. Club atmosphere. Totally nonsmoking. Cr cds: A, C, D, JCB, MC, V.

D

✓★ **SAJI JAPANESE CUISINE.** *3232 Scott St (94123), in Marina District. 415/931-0563.* Hrs: 5:30-10:30 pm; Fri, Sat to midnight; Sun to 10 pm. Closed Jan 1-2, Thanksgiving, Dec 25. Res accepted. Japanese menu. Complete meals: dinner $9-$14. Specializes in sushi. Japanese decor. Totally nonsmoking. Cr cds: A, C, D, DS, JCB, MC, V.

D

★ **SAM'S GRILL.** *374 Bush St (94104), in Financial District. 415/421-0594.* Hrs: 11 am-9 pm. Closed Sat, Sun; major hols. Res accepted. Seafood menu. Bar. A la carte entrees: lunch, dinner $7-$25. Specializes in fresh fish. Outdoor dining (lunch). 1867 building with original wooden booths. Family-owned. Cr cds: A, C, D, MC, V.

★★ **SCALA'S BISTRO.** *(See Sir Francis Drake Hotel) 415/395-8555.* Hrs: 7-10:30 am, 11:30 am-midnight; Fri, Sat from 8 am. Closed most major hols. Res accepted. Italian menu. Bar. A la carte entrees: bkfst $7-$12; lunch, dinner $8.75-$24. Specialties: persillade tagliatelle, seared salmon. Own baking. Contemporary decor. Cr cds: A, C, D, JCB, MC, V.

D

★ **SCHROEDER'S.** *240 Front St (94111), in Financial District. 415/421-4778.* Hrs: 11 am-9 pm; Fri, Sat to 9:30 pm. Closed Sun; major hols. Res accepted. German, Amer menu. Bar. Semi-a la carte:

lunch $5.95-$14, dinner $9.50-$16.50. Child's meals. Specializes in baked chicken & noodles, sauerbraten, Wienerschnitzel. German decor, murals. Established 1893. Family-owned. Cr cds: A, C, D, DS, JCB, MC, V.

D

★★ **SCOMA'S.** *Pier 47 (94133), at Fisherman's Wharf. 415/771-4383.* Web www.scomas.com. Hrs: 11:30 am-10:30 pm; Fri, Sat to 11 pm. Closed Thanksgiving, Dec 24, 25. Italian, seafood menu. Bars. A la carte entrees: lunch, dinner $14.95-$54.95. Child's meals. Specialties: calamari, cioppino, sauteed shellfish. Complimentary valet parking. View of fishing fleet. Originally fisherman's shack. Family-owned. Cr cds: A, C, D, DS, JCB, MC, V.

D

★★★ **SILKS.** *(See Mandarin Oriental Hotel) 415/986-2020.* E-mail mandarinsfo@mosfo.com; web www.mandarin-oriental.com. Hrs: Mon-Fri 6:30-10 am; 11:30-2 pm; 6-9:30 pm. Sat & Sun 7-11 am; 6-9:30 pm. Res accepted. California cuisine. Bar 11 am-11 pm. Wine list. A la carte entrees: bkfst $10.95-$16, lunch $18-$23, dinner $19-$32. Prix fixe: dinner $75 & $95. Specializes in contemporary American cuisine with Asian accents. Own pastries. Valet parking. Cr cds: A, C, D, DS, JCB, MC, V.

D

★★ **SLANTED DOOR.** *584 Valencia (94110), between 16th & 17th Sts, in Mission District. 415/861-8032.* E-mail eat@slanteddoor.com; web www.slanteddoor.com. Hrs: 11:30 am-3 pm, 5:30-10 pm; Fri, Sat to 10:30 pm. Closed Mon; most major hols. Res accepted. No A/C. Vietnamese menu. Bar. A la carte entrees: lunch $5.50-$7, dinner $8.50-$18.50. Specialties: Shaking beef, steamed sea bass, spring rolls. Street parking. Modern Asian decor. Totally nonsmoking. Cr cds: C, MC, V.

D

★ **SOCCA RESTAURANT.** *5800 Geary (94121), in Richmond District. 415/379-6720.* Web www.citysearch.com/sfo/socca. Hrs: 5:30-9:30 pm; Fri, Sat to 10 pm. Closed Mon; also Jan 1, Dec 25. Res accepted. French Provencal menu. Bar. A la carte entrees: dinner $8.25-$20. Child's meals. Specialties: braised lamb shanks, sauteed skate, bouillabaisse. Valet parking. Totally nonsmoking. Cr cds: A, C, D, DS, MC, V.

★★★ **SPLENDIDO.** *101 California St # 4 (94111), promenade level, in Financial District. 415/986-3222.* Web www.citysearch.com.sfo. Hrs: 11:30 am-2:30 pm, 5:30-10 pm. Closed major hols. Res accepted. Contemporary Italian menu. A la carte entrees: lunch $11-$18, dinner $11-$28. Specializes in fresh seafood, game, baked goods. Own baking, ice cream. Outdoor dining. Cr cds: A, C, D, DS, MC, V.

D

★★★ **STARS.** *555 Golden Gate (94102), at Van Ness Ave, in Civic Center area. 415/861-7827.* Hrs: 11:30 am-2 pm, 6-10 pm; Fri, Sat from 5:30 pm. Closed Dec 25. Res accepted. Bar from 11 am; wkends from 4 pm. A la carte entrees: lunch $8-$15, dinner $19-$30. Pianist. Changing menu. Bistro decor. Cr cds: A, C, D, JCB, MC, V.

D

★★ **SUNNY JIM'S.** *500 Van Ness Ave (94102), in Civic Center area. 415/546-7050.* Hrs: 11:30 am-11 pm; Mon to 10 pm; Sat to midnight. Closed July 4, Dec 25. Res accepted. Bar. A la carte entrees: lunch $10-$14, dinner $14-$18. Specialties: grilled fish, pot au feu, chops. Modern, 1930s atmosphere. Totally nonsmoking. Cr cds: A, C, MC, V.

D

★★ **SWISS LOUIS.** *Pier 39 (94133), at Fisherman's Wharf. 415/421-2913.* Hrs 11:30 am-10 pm; Sat & Sun brunch 10:30 am-4 pm. Closed Thanksgiving, Dec 25. Res accepted. No A/C. Italian menu. Bar. Semi-a la carte: lunch $9.50-$15, dinner $11.50-$25. Sat, Sun brunch $10.50. Child's meals. Specializes in veal dishes, seafood. Own desserts. View of bay, Golden Gate Bridge. Cr cds: A, C, D, DS, JCB, MC, V.

D

★ **TADICH GRILL.** *240 California St (94111), in Financial District. 415/391-1849.* Hrs: 11 am-9:30 pm; Sat from 11:30 am. Closed Sun; major hols. Bar. A la carte entrees: lunch, dinner $12-$25. Child's meals. Specializes in fresh seafood. Also counter serv. Turn-of-the-century decor. Established in 1849. Family-owned since 1928. Cr cds: C, MC, V.

D

★★ **THE CAPITAL GRILLE.** *121 Spear St (94105), in Financial District. 415/495-4109.* Hrs: 11:30 am-3 pm, 5-10 pm; Sat, Sun 5-11 pm. Res accepted. Steak, seafood menu. Bar. A la carte entrees: lunch $7.95-$16.95, dinner $16.95-$29.95. Specializes in dry-aged beef, lobster. Own desserts. Valet parking. Club-like atmosphere; presidential portraits. Totally nonsmoking. Cr cds: A, C, D, DS, MC, V.

D

★★★★ **THE DINING ROOM.** *(See Ritz-Carlton Hotel) 415/296-7465.* The antique-filled dining room of this grand hotel affords all the substance of a formal French restaurant without stuffiness. Chef Sylvain Portay's prix-fixe menu invites you to sample several courses. An outstanding wine list and excellent service complete the experience. Specializes in contemporary French cuisine. Hrs: 6-10 pm. Closed Sun. Res accepted. Bar. Extensive wine list. Prix fixe: dinner $61-$75. Child's meals. Entertainment. Valet parking. Totally nonsmoking. Cr cds: A, C, D, DS, ER, JCB, MC, V.

D

★★★ **TOMMY TOY'S.** *655 Montgomery St (94111), in Financial District. 415/397-4888.* Hrs: 11:30 am-2:30 pm, 5:30-9:30 pm; Sat and Sun open 5:30-9:30 pm. Closed Jan 1, Dec 25. Res required. Chinese menu. Bar. A la carte entrees: lunch $11.95-$15.95, dinner $14-$18.95. Table d'hôte: lunch $18.50-$32.50. Prix fixe: 6-course dinner $55/person. Specializes in seafood, Peking duck. Valet parking (dinner). Jacket and tie required. Cr cds: A, C, D, DS, JCB, MC, V.

D

✓★★ **TUBA GARDEN.** *3634 Sacramento Ave (94118), in Pacific Heights. 415/921-8822.* Hrs: 11 am-2:30 pm; Sat, Sun from 10 am. Closed Dec 25. Res accepted. Continental menu. Wine, beer. Semi-a la carte: lunch $8-$12. Child's meals. Specializes in chicken salad Hawaii, cheese blintzes, Belgian waffles. Own desserts. Outdoor dining. Victorian house with original art. Cr cds: A, C, D, DS, JCB, MC, V.

✓★ **UNIVERSAL CAFE.** *2814 19th St (94110), in Mission District. 415/821-4608.* Hrs: 7:30 am-10 pm; Sat from 9 am; Sun 9 am-9:30 pm. Closed Mon; most major hols. Res accepted (dinner). Wine, beer. Semi-a la carte: bkfst $5-$8.50, lunch $5-$12, dinner $5-$20. Outdoor dining. Contemporary decor. Totally nonsmoking. Cr cds: A, C, D, MC, V.

★★★ **VERTIGO RESTAURANT.** *600 Montgomery St (94111), in Trans America Pyramid, in Financial District. 415/433-7250.* Hrs: 11:30 am-2:30 pm, 5:30-10 pm; Fri, Sat to 10:30 pm. Closed Sun; most major hols. Res accepted. California menu. Bar to 12:30 am. Wine list. A la carte entrees: lunch $12-$20, dinner $16-$26. Prix fixe: lunch $22, dinner $60. Valet parking (dinner). Outdoor dining. Multi-level dining, avant-garde decor. Cr cds: A, C, D, MC, V.

D

★★ **WATERFRONT.** *Pier 7 (94111), the Embarcadero at Broadway, in Financial District. 415/391-2696.* Hrs: 11:30 am-10 pm; Sun from 5:30 pm. Res accepted. Bar. A la carte entrees: lunch $9-$22, dinner $9-$32. Specializes in seafood with Asian influences. Valet parking. View of bay. Cr cds: A, C, D, DS, MC, V.

D

✓★★ **YABBIES COASTAL KITCHEN.** *2237 Polk St (94109), in Russian Hill. 415/474-4088.* Hrs: 6-10 pm; Fri, Sat to 10:30 pm. Closed most major hols. Res accepted. No A/C. Seafood menu. Bar. Complete meals: dinner $14-$21 Specialties: tuna pokee, oyster bar feast. Contemporary decor. Totally nonsmoking. Cr cds: C, MC, V.

D

✓★★ **YANK SING.** *427 Battery St (94111), in Financial District. 415/781-1111.* Web www.yanksing.com. Hrs: 11 am-3 pm; Sat & Sun 10 am-4 pm. Res accepted. Bar. Semi-a la carte: lunch $14-$16. Specialties: dim sum cuisine. Tableside carts in addition to menu. Cr cds: A, C, D, MC, V.

D

★★ **YOSHIDA-YA.** *2909 Webster St (94123), in Cow Hollow. 415/346-3431.* Web www.citysearch.com. Hrs: 11:30 am-2 pm, 5-10:30 pm; Fri to 11 pm; Sat 5-11 pm; Sun 5-10:30 pm. Closed most major hols. Japanese menu. Bar. Complete meals: dinner $20-$25. Specialties: sushi, yakitori. Oriental decor; traditional dining upstairs. Totally nonsmoking. Cr cds: A, C, D, DS, JCB, MC, V.

D

★★ **YOYO BISTRO.** *(See Miyako Hotel) 415/922-7788.* E-mail miyakosf@slip.net; web www.mim.com/miyako/. Hrs: 6:30 am-10 pm. Res accepted. Asian bistro. Bar. A la carte entrees: lunch $7-$10, dinner $12-$20; buffet: bkfst $12.50. Mix of modern American and Asian decor. Cr cds: A, C, D, DS, JCB, MC, V.

D

✓★ **ZARZUELA.** *2000 Hyde St (94109), on Russian Hill. 415/346-0800.* Hrs: 5:30-10:30 pm; Fri, Sat to 11 pm. Closed Sun, Mon; most major hols. Spanish menu. Wine, beer. Semi-a la carte: dinner $8.95-$13.95. Specialties: zarzuela, tapas, paella. Spanish decor. Totally nonsmoking. Cr cds: C, DS, MC, V.

D

✓★★ **ZAX.** *2330 Taylor St (94133), in North Beach. 415/563-6266.* Hrs: 5:30-10 pm. Closed Sun, Mon; wk of July 4, Thanksgiving, Dec 25. Res accepted. Mediterranean menu. Wine, beer. Semi-a la carte: dinner $14-$19.50. Specialties: goat cheese souffle. Contemporary decor. Totally nonsmoking. Cr cds: C, MC, V.

★★ **ZINGARI.** *(See The Donatello) 415/885-8850.* Hrs: 6:30 am-10:30 pm; Fri, Sat to 11 pm. Res accepted. Italian menu. Wine, beer. Semi-a la carte: bkfst $8-$13.95, lunch $7-$12.95, dinner $11.50-$22.50. Specializes in filet mignon, pork chop, veal. Italian decor. Totally nonsmoking. Cr cds: A, C, D, DS, JCB, MC, V.

D

★★ **ZUNI CAFE.** *1658 Market St (94102), in Civic Center area. 415/552-2522.* Hrs: 11:30 am-midnight; Sun to 11 pm; Sun brunch 11 am-3 pm. Closed Mon; some hols. Res accepted. Italian, French menu. Bar. A la carte entrees: lunch $8-$14, dinner $10-$18. Sun brunch $5.50-$14.50. Own desserts. Pianist Fri, Sat. Outdoor dining. Changing art displays. Cr cds: A, C, MC, V.

D

Unrated Dining Spots

CAFE LATTE. *100 Bush St, 2nd floor, north of Union Square. 415/989-2233.* Hrs: 8 am-2:30 pm. Closed Sat, Sun; major hols. No A/C. Nouvelle California/northern Italian menu. Wine, beer. Avg ck: bkfst $3.50, lunch $7. Specializes in fresh fish, fresh pasta, salads. Stylish cafeteria in landmark art deco skyscraper; mirrored deco interior with marble counters, tray ledges, floors. Cr cds: A, C, D, MC, V.

DAVID'S. *474 Geary St, west of Union Square. 415/771-1600.* Open 24 hrs. Closed Jewish high hols. Jewish deli menu. Beer, wine. Semi-a la carte: bkfst $3.35-$9.75, lunch $4.95-$9.95, dinner from $6.95. Complete meal: dinner $16.95. Specializes in chopped chicken liver, stuffed cabbage, cheese blintzes. Cr cds: A, C, D, JCB, MC, V.

DOTTIE'S TRUE BLUE CAFE. *522 Jones St (94102), west of Union Square. 415/885-2767.* Hrs: 7:30 am-2 pm. No A/C. Wine, beer. Semi-a la carte: bkfst $4-$7.95, lunch $4-$8.50. Specializes in all-American bkfst. Own breads. Cr cds: C, DS, MC, V.

GHIRARDELLI CHOCOLATE MANUFACTORY. *900 North Point St, on grounds of Ghirardelli Square, at Fisherman's Wharf. 415/771-4903.* Hrs: 9 am-11 pm; Fri, Sat to midnight. Closed Thanksgiving, Dec 25. Soda fountain & chocolate shop. Specializes in ice cream sundaes, premium chocolates. Own candy making, ice cream toppings. Parking. Located in former chocolate factory; built in late 1890s. Totally nonsmoking. Cr cds: C, JCB, MC, V.

D

ISOBUNE. *1737 Post St, in Japantown. 415/563-1030.* Hrs: 11:30 am-10 pm. Closed Jan 1-3, Thanksgiving, Dec 25. Japanese sushi menu. Wine, beer. A la carte entrees: lunch $5-$8, dinner $10-$12. Specializes in sashimi. Dining at counter; selections pass in front of diners on small boats. Cr cds: C, MC, V.

JUST DESSERTS. *3 Embarcadero Center, in lobby, in Financial District. 415/421-1609.* Hrs: 6:30 am-7 pm; Sat 11 am-5 pm; Sun noon-5 pm. Closed most major hols. A la carte entrees: pastries, cakes, muffins $2.50-$4. Specializes in cheesecake. Own baking. Outdoor dining. Modern cafe atmosphere. Cr cds: C, MC, V.

D SC

LA BODEGA. *1337 Grant Ave (94133), in North Beach. 415/433-0439.* Hrs: 5 pm-midnight. Res accepted. Spanish menu. Bar. Semi-a la carte: dinner $4-$9. Specialties: tapas, paella. Entertainment. Spanish decor. Totally nonsmoking. Cr cds: A, C, DS, MC, V.

D

MIFUNE. *1737 Post St, in Japantown. 415/922-0337.* Hrs: 11 am-10 pm. Closed Jan 1-3, Thanksgiving, Dec 25. Japanese menu. A la carte entrees: lunch, dinner $3.50-$13. Specializes in noodle dishes. Own noodles. Validated parking. Cr cds: A, C, D, DS, MC, V.

MO'S GOURMET HAMBURGERS. *1322 Grant Ave (94133), in North Beach. 415/788-3779.* Hrs: 11:30 am-10:30 pm; Fri, Sat to 11:30 pm. Closed Dec 25. Wine, beer. Semi-a la carte: lunch, dinner $4.75-$7.75. Specializes in grilled or charbroiled hamburgers. Casual dining with art deco design. Kitchen with rotating grill over lava rocks at front window. Cr cds: C, MC, V.

D

SEARS FINE FOODS. *439 Powell St (94102), in Union Square. 415/986-1160.* Hrs: 6:30 am-2:30 pm. Closed Jan 1, Thanksgiving, Dec 25. Semi-a la carte: bkfst, lunch $7-$15. Child's meals. Specialties: 18 Swedish pancakes, sourdough French toast. Casual decor. Totally nonsmoking. Cr cds: C.

D

SWAN OYSTER DEPOT. *1517 Polk St (94109), in Russian Hill. 415/673-1101.* Hrs: 8 am-5:30 pm. Closed Sun; most major hols. No A/C. Seafood menu. Wine, beer. A la carte entrees: dinner $6.50-$13.95. Child's meals. Specializes in seafood salads, fresh fish, oysters. Street parking. Family-owned since 1912. Totally nonsmoking. Cr cds: C.

TITANIC CAFE. *817 Sutter St (94109), west of Union Square. 415/928-8870.* Hrs: 7 am-2 pm. Semi-a la carte: bkfst, lunch $3.50-$6. Specializes in omelets, applewood smoked bacon. Casual decor. Cr cds: C.

D

TRIO CAFE. *1870 Fillmore St, in Pacific Heights. 415/563-2248.* Hrs: 8 am-6 pm; Sun 10 am-4 pm. Closed Mon; Easter, Thanksgiving; also Dec 24-Jan 2. Eclectic menu. Bar. A la carte entrees: bkfst, lunch $4-$6. Outdoor dining in cafe setting. Store front entrance. Totally nonsmoking. Cr cds: C.

San Francisco Airport Area (D-3 see San Francisco area map)

(See also Hayward, Oakland, Redwood City, San Francisco, San Mateo)

Services and Information

Information: 650/761-0800.

Lost and Found: 650/876-2261.

Weather: 831/656-1725.

Cash Machines: South Terminal, business center.

Airlines: Aeroflot, Air Canada, Air China, Air France, Air Jamaica, Alaska Arlns, American West, American, American Trans Air, Asiana Arlns, Austrian, British Airways, Canadian Arlns Intl, China Arlns, Continental, Delta, EVA Airways, Frontier, Hawaiian Arlns, Japan Arlns, KLM, Korean Air, LACSA, Lufthansa, Mexicana, Northwest, Philippine Arlns, Qantas, Reno Air, Singapore Arlns, Southwest, Swissair, TACA, Tri Star, TWA, United, USAir, Vanguard, Virgin Atlantic, Western Pacific Arlns.

Motels

★★ **COMFORT INN & SUITES.** *121 E Grand Ave (94080), 2 mi N on US 101, E Grand Ave exit. 650/589-7766; FAX 650/589-7766.* 169 suites, 3 story. S $129; D $139; each addl $10; under 18 free. TV; cable (premium). Complimentary continental bkfst. Coffee in rms. Ck-out noon. Business servs avail. In-rm modem link. Valet serv. Free airport, RR station transportation. Whirlpool. Health club privileges. Refrigerators, microwaves. Grill. Cr cds: A, C, D, DS, JCB, MC, V.

D SC

★★★ **COURTYARD BY MARRIOTT.** *1050 Bayhill Dr (94066), 1½ mi N on US 101 to jct I-380 W, then 1 mi W to El Camino Real South (CA 82), then 1 blk S to Bayhill Dr. 650/952-3333; FAX 415/952-4707; res: 800/321-2211.* 147 rms, 3 story. S, D $159; each addl $10; suites $179; under 13 free. Crib free. TV; cable (premium). Indoor pool; whirlpool. Complimentary coffee in rms. Restaurant 6-11 am, 5-10:30 pm. Ck-out 1 pm. Coin lndry. Meeting rms. Business servs avail. Free airport transportation. Exercise equipt. Refrigerators, microwaves avail. Some balconies. Cr cds: A, C, D, DS, MC, V.

D SC

✓★★ **MILLWOOD INN.** *1375 El Camino Real (94030), 1 mi SE on US 101, then ½ mi W on Millbrae Ave to El Camino Real (CA 82), then 1 mi NW. 650/583-3935; FAX 650/875-4354; res: 800/345-1375.* 34 rms, 2 story. S $65-$100; D $75-$110; suites $85-$160. Crib $4. TV; cable (premium), VCR. Complimentary continental bkfst. Coffee in rms. Restaurant nearby. Ck-out 11 am. Coin lndry. Business servs avail. In-rm modem link. Exercise equipt. Bathrm phones, refrigerators, microwaves. Cr cds: A, C, D, DS, ER, JCB, MC, V.

D SC

★ **RAMADA INN - SAN FRANCISCO AIRPORT NORTH.** *245 S Airport Blvd (94080), 2 mi N on US 101, off S Airport Blvd exit. 650/589-7200; FAX 650/588-5007; res: 800/272-6232.* 323 rms, 2 story. S $139; D $169; each addl $10; under 18 free; wkend rates. Crib free. Pet accepted, some restrictions. TV; cable (premium). Pool; whirlpool. Coffee in rms. Restaurant 6:30 am-1:30 pm, 5-10 pm. Rm serv. Bar 4 pm-midnight; Sat, Sun from 11 am. Ck-out noon. Coin lndry. Meeting rms. Business servs avail. Bellhops. Gift shop. Barber shop. Free airport transportation. Exercise equipt. Health club privileges. Cr cds: A, C, D, DS, ER, JCB, MC, V.

D SC

★ **TRAVELODGE.** *326 S Airport Blvd (94080), 2 mi N on US 101, exit S Airport Blvd. 650/583-9600; FAX 650/873-9392; res: 800/578-7878.* 197 rms, 100 with shower only, 2 story. S $79; D $115; each addl $7; under 17 free. Crib free. TV; cable (premium). Heated pool. Complimentary coffee in rms. Restaurant open 24 hrs. Ck-out 1 pm. Meeting rms. Business servs avail. Valet serv. Sundries. Free airport transportation. Picnic tables. Cr cds: A, C, D, DS, JCB, MC, V.

D SC

Motor Hotels

★★ **BEST WESTERN.** *1100 El Camino Real (94030), 1 mi SE on US 101, then ½ mi W on Millbrae Ave to El Camino Real (CA 82), then 1 mi NW. 650/588-8500; FAX 650/871-7150; res: 800/826-5500.* 306 rms, most A/C, 1-3 story. S $115-$145; D $120-$150; each addl $10; kit. units, suites $135-$160; under 18 free. Crib free. TV; cable (premium). Heated pool; whirlpool. Coffee in rms. Restaurant 6:30 am-10 pm. Rm serv. Bar. Ck-out 1 pm. Coin lndry. Meeting rms. Business servs avail. In-rm modem link. Bellhops. Valet serv. Free airport transportation. Exercise equipt. Some refrigerators. Cr cds: A, C, D, DS, ER, JCB, MC, V.

D SC

★★ **BEST WESTERN GROSVENOR HOTEL.** *380 S Airport Blvd (94080), 2 mi N on US 101, exit S Airport Blvd. 650/873-3200; FAX 415/589-3495; res: 800/528-1234.* 207 rms, 9 story. June-mid-Oct: S, D $99-$169; each addl $15; suites $175; under 12 free; lower rates rest of yr. Crib free. TV; cable (premium). Heated pool. Complimentary continental bkfst. Complimentary coffee in rms. Restaurant 6 am-2 pm, 5-10 pm. Rm serv. Bar 4 pm-midnight. Ck-out noon. Meeting rms. Business servs avail. Bellhops. Valet serv. Sundries. Free airport transportation. Health club privileges. Some refrigerators. Cr cds: A, C, D, DS, JCB, MC, V.

D SC

Hotels

★★ **DOUBLETREE HOTEL SF AIRPORT.** *835 Airport Blvd (94010), 2 mi S on US 101. 650/344-5500; FAX 650/340-8851; res: 800/222-8733.* 292 rms, 8 story. S, D $179-$239; each addl $10; suites $229-$300; under 18 free. Crib free. TV; cable (premium), VCR avail. Coffee in rms. Restaurant 6:30 am-10 pm. Bar 2:30 pm-1:30 am. Ck-out noon. Meeting rms. Business center. In-rm modem link. Gift shop. Free airport transportation. Exercise equipt. Refrigerator, wet bar in suites. Cr cds: A, C, D, DS, JCB, MC, V.

D SC

★★★ **EMBASSY SUITES.** *250 Gateway Blvd (94080), 2 mi N on US 101, E Grand Ave exit, then N on Gateway Blvd. 650/589-3400; FAX 650/876-0305; res: 800/433-4600; res: 800/362-2779.* 312 suites, 10 story. S, D $219-$249; each addl $10; under 18 free; wkend rates. Crib free. TV; cable (premium), VCR avail. Indoor pool; whirlpool. Sauna. Complimentary full bkfst. Complimentary coffee in rms. Restaurant 11 am-11 pm. Bar 11-1 am; entertainment. Ck-out 1 pm. Coin lndry. Meeting rms. Business servs avail. Gift shop. Free airport transportation. Health club privileges. Refrigerators. Balconies. Atrium courtyard. Cr cds: A, C, D, DS, JCB, MC, V.

D SC

★★★ **HOLIDAY INN CROWNE PLAZA.** *600 Airport Blvd (94010), 1½ mi S on US 101 to Broadway exit, then E to Airport Blvd, then 1 mi along bay. 650/340-8500; FAX 650/343-1546; res: 800/827-0880.* 404 rms, 15 story. S, D $229-$269; each addl $10; suites $450-$650; under 18 free; wkend rates. Crib free. TV; cable (premium). Indoor pool; whirlpool. Restaurant 6 am-midnight. Bar 11-1:30 am; entertainment. Ck-out noon. Meeting rms. Business servs avail. Gift shop. Free covered parking. Free airport transportation. Exercise equipt; sauna. Refrigerators avail. Luxury level. Cr cds: A, C, D, DS, JCB, MC, V.

D SC

★★★ **HYATT REGENCY SAN FRANCISCO AIRPORT.** *1333 Bayshore Hwy (94010), off US 101 Broadway exit. 650/347-1234; FAX 650/696-2669; res: 800/233-1234.* Web www.hyatt.com. 793 rms, 9 story. S, D $255-$270; each addl $25; suites $249-$750; under 18 free; wkend rates. Crib free. Valet parking $15. TV; cable (premium). Heated pool; whirlpool. Restaurant 6:30 am-11 pm. Rm serv 24 hrs. Bar 11-1 am. Ck-out noon. Convention facilities. Business center. Concierge. Gift shop. Free airport transportation. Exercise equipt; sauna. Some bathrm phones, wet bars; refrigerators avail. Atrium. Luxury level. Cr cds: A, C, D, DS, ER, JCB, MC, V.

D SC

★★ **PARK PLAZA HOTEL SAN FRANCISCO.** *1177 Airport Blvd (94010), 1½ mi S on US 101 to Broadway exit, then E to Airport Blvd. 650/342-9200; FAX 650/342-1655; res: 800/411-7275.* 302 rms, 10 story. S, D $180; each addl $10; suites $250-$395; wkend rates. Crib avail. TV; cable (premium), VCR avail. Indoor/outdoor pool; whirlpool. Restaurant 6 am-11 pm. Bar; entertainment. Ck-out noon. Coin Indry. Convention facilities. Gift shop. Barber, beauty shop. Free airport transportation. Exercise equipt. Cr cds: A, C, D, DS, MC, V.

D SC

★★★ **SAN FRANCISCO AIRPORT MARRIOTT.** *1800 Old Bayshore Highway (95035), 1 mi SE on US 101, then E on Millbrae Ave to Old Bayshore Hwy, then SE on San Francisco Bay. 650/692-9100; FAX 650/692-8016; res: 800/228-9290.* 684 rms, 11 story. S, D $229-$249; suites $450-$600; under 18 free; wkend, wkly rates. Crib free. Pet accepted, some restrictions. Valet parking $13. TV; cable (premium), VCR avail. Indoor pool; whirlpool, poolside serv. Restautant 6 am-11 pm. Rm serv to 1 am. Piano bar. Ck-out noon. Coin Indry. Convention facilities. Business center. In-rm modem link. Concierge. Gift shop. Free airport transportation. Exercise equipt; sauna. Health club privileges. Some bathrm phones, refrigerators. Luxury level. Cr cds: A, C, D, DS, JCB, MC, V.

D SC

★★★ **WESTIN HOTEL.** *1 Old Bayshore Hwy (94030), 1 mi SE on US 101, then E on Millbrae Ave to Old Bayshore Hwy. 650/692-3500; FAX 650/872-8111; res: 800/228-3000.* Web www.westin.com. 393 rms, 7 story. S, D $219-$254; each addl $20; suites $400-$600; under 18 free; wkend rates. Crib free. Pet accepted, some restrictions. Valet parking $14; self-park $10. TV; cable (premium), VCR avail. Indoor pool; whirlpool, poolside serv. Restaurant 6 am-10 pm. Rm serv 24 hrs. Bar noon-1 am; entertainment. Ck-out 1 pm. Convention facilities. Business center. Concierge. Gift shop. Free airport transportation. Exercise equipt. Refrigerators, minibars. Cr cds: A, C, D, DS, ER, JCB, MC, V.

D

Restaurants

✓★ **STACKS'.** *361 California Dr (94010). 650/579-1384.* Hrs: 7 am-2:30 pm. Closed Thanksgiving, Dec 25. Complete meals: bkfst $2.95-$7.95, lunch $4.95-$8.25. Specializes in pancakes, skillet breakfast. Casual decor. Totally nonsmoking. Cr cds: C, MC, V.

D

★★ **YAKINIKU HOUSE JUBAN.** *1204 Broadway (94010), S on US 101 to Broadway exit. 650/347-2300.* Hrs: 11:30 am-2 pm, 5-10 pm; Sat 11:30 am-10 pm; Sun 4:30-10 pm. Closed Jan 1, Thanksgiving, Dec 25. Res accepted. Japanese menu. Wine, beer. Semi-a la carte: lunch, dinner $5-$38. Specialties: wagyu loin, short ribs. Street parking. Tableside preparation of dinner. Totally nonsmoking. Cr cds: A, C, MC, V.

D

San Gabriel (B-5 see Los Angeles map)

(See also Arcadia, Pasadena)

Pop 37,120 **Elev** 430 ft **Area Code** 626

Restaurant

★★ **CLEARMAN'S STEAK 'N STEIN INN.** *7269 N Rosemead Blvd (91775), at Huntington Dr. 626/287-1424.* Hrs: 5-10 pm. Closed Mon, Tues; July 4, Thanksgiving, Dec 25. Res accepted. Bar. Semi-a la carte: dinner $12.50-$34.95. Specializes in prime rib, seafood, chicken. Parking. Fireplace in lounge; stained-glass windows; art display. Totally nonsmoking. Cr cds: A, C, D, MC, V.

San Jose (E-2)

(See also Fremont, Livermore, Santa Clara, Santa Cruz, Saratoga)

Founded 1777 **Pop** 782,248 **Elev** 87 ft **Area Code** 408
E-mail visitorinfo@sanjose.org **Web** www.sanjose.org

Information Convention & Visitors Bureau, 333 W San Carlos St, Suite 1000, 95110; 408/977-0900, 408/295-2265 (24-hr recording) or 888/VISIT-SJ

At the south end of San Francisco Bay, 50 miles from San Francisco, San Jose is known as the "Capital of Silicon Valley." San Jose was founded as "Pueblo de San Jose de Guadalupe" in the name of Charles III of Spain; the first American flag was raised above the town hall in 1846. The city was one of the first to be incorporated in California. Before California was even a state, San Jose became the first state capital; the first state legislature assembled here on December 15, 1849. In recent years it has become an important electronic and aerospace center. It is also the home of San Jose State University.

What to See and Do

Alum Rock Park. These 720 acres are known as "Little Yosemite" because of the natural formations. Hiking, bicycle, bridle trails. Picnic grounds, playground. (Daily) 16240 Alum Rock Ave, 6 mi E. Phone 408/259-5477. Parking fee per vehicle **¢¢** Also in park is

Youth Science Institute. Natural science classes, exhibits and nature trips. (Tues-Sat) 16260 Alum Rock Ave. Phone 408/258-4322. **¢**

The Children's Discovery Museum. Provides children and their families with "hands-on" exhibits that explore the relationships between the natural and created worlds, and among people of different cultures and times. Exhibits include the Streets, a ⅝ scale replica of an actual city, with street lights, parking meters, fire hydrants; Waterworks allows operation of pumps and valves to move water through a reservoir system. (Tues-Sat, also Sun afternoon) 180 Woz Way, in Guadalupe River Park. Phone 408/298-5437. **¢¢¢**

J. Lohr Winery. Producer of J. Lohr varietal wines. Tasting rm (daily; closed hols). Tours (wkends, 2 departures: late morning & early afternoon). 1000 Lenzen Ave. Phone 408/288-5057. **Free**

Kelley Park. Keyes St at Senter Rd. Phone 408/277-4191. Includes

Happy Hollow Park and Zoo. On 12 acres. Themed children's rides; creative play areas; zoo and contact area; special events. (Daily; no admittance during last hr open; closed Dec 25) 1300 Senter Rd. Phone 408/295-8383. **¢¢**

Historical Museums of San Jose. Original and replica structures have been placed on the grounds to re-create most elements of early San Jose. Outdoor exhibits include original pioneer houses, doctor's office, print shop, fruit barn, 1927 gas station; replicas of early landmarks, including hotel, stables, trolley barn, firehouse, bank, 117-ft electric light tower, operating ice cream store and 1880 Chinese Temple with original altar. Indoor hotel exhibits trace history of area's Native American, Spanish, Mexican and Chinese background. Museum (daily; closed Jan 1, Thanksgiving, Dec 25). At South Kelley Park, 1650 Senter Rd. Phone 408/287-2290. ¢¢

Japanese Friendship Garden. A 6½-acre Japanese Stroll Garden patterned after Korakuen Park in Okayama, Japan; on 2 levels with a waterfall dropping from lake on upper level into one of two lakes on lower level; 22 symbolic features include bridges and lanterns; teahouse; ¾-mi paved walkway trail. (Daily) 1500 Senter Rd. Phone 408/277-5254. **Free**

Lick Observatory. Main building has astronomical exhibits, guide lectures and 36-inch refracting telescope. At a 120-inch reflecting telescope there is a Visitors Gallery with a self-guided tour. Maintained by the Univ of California at Santa Cruz. (Daily; closed Thanksgiving & day after, Dec 24, 25) 25 mi SE on CA 130 at Mt Hamilton. Phone 408/274-5061. **Free**

Mirassou Winery. Produces vintage wines and champagnes. Wine tasting and tours. (Mon-Sat, also Sun afternoons; closed some hols) 3000 Aborn Rd. Phone 408/274-4000. **Free**

Municipal Rose Garden. Approx 5,000 rose plants on 6 acres, peak blooming in late Apr-May. Picnicking. (Daily) Naglee & Dana Aves. Phone 408/277-4191. **Free**

Overfelt Gardens. This 33-acre botanical preserve includes extensive natural areas, a formal botanic garden and a wildlife sanctuary. Migratory waterfowl and other wildlife inhabit 3 lakes; wooded areas with wild flowers; Chinese Cultural Garden has a bronze and marble statue of Confucius overlooking a reflecting pond, an ornate Chinese gate and 3 Chinese pavilions—all a gift from the Chinese community. (Daily) No pets, skates, skateboards or bicycles. McKee Rd, at Educational Park Dr, W of Jackson Ave, via US 101 & I-680. Phone 408/251-3323. **Free**

Paramount's Raging Waters. Water theme amusement park with more than 35 water park attractions, including the Shark, a double tube ride; river rides; Wacky Water Works, a children's activity area; water slides; lagoon and a beach. (Mid-June-late Aug, daily; mid-May-mid-June & late Aug-Sept, Sat & Sun) 2333 S White Rd, in Lake Cunningham Regional Park. Phone 408/654-5450. ¢¢¢¢¢

Peralta Adobe and Fallon House. Built in 1797, the Peralta adobe is the last remaining home of the first pueblo (city) in California. The Fallon house is a Victorian home built for a wealthy resident. Both homes are furnished in the period. (Daily exc Mon) 175-186 W St John St. Phone 408/993-8182. ¢¢¢

Professional Sports.

NHL (San Jose Sharks). San Jose Arena, 525 W Santa Clara St. Phone 408/998-2277.

Rosicrucian Park. Headquarters of the English Grand Lodge of the Rosicrucian Order, AMORC; worldwide philosophical fraternity. (Daily; closed Jan 1, Thanksgiving, Dec 25) Park & Naglee Aves. Phone 408/947-3636. ¢¢¢

Egyptian Museum. One of largest collections of Egyptian antiquities west of the Mississippi; mummy collection includes those of children, adults and animals; replica of a nobleman's tomb. Also art gallery with contemporary works on display. (Daily; closed Jan 1, Thanksgiving, Dec 25) Phone 408/947-3636. ¢¢¢ On grounds are

Planetarium & Science Center. The feature exhibit "Geological Gems" looks at mineral properties, crystals, quartz, gemstones and rock types. (Daily; closed Jan 1, Thanksgiving, Dec 25) Children under age 5 not admitted to planetarium shows. Phone 408/947-3636. **Free**; Planetarium shows ¢¢

San Jose Museum of Art. International exhibits featuring contemporary art; multimedia resource center. Book & gift shop. Cafe. (Daily exc Mon; closed most hols) 110 S Market St. Phone 408/294-2787. ¢¢¢

San Jose Museum of Quilts & Textiles. Regularly changing exhibits feature quilts and other textiles from around the world. Museum's collection includes quilts and coverlets from the 19th century. Explores the role of quilts in cultural traditions, the lives of their makers, and their significance as historical documents. (Daily exc Mon; closed most major hols) 110 Paseo de San Antonio. Phone 408/971-0323. ¢¢

The Tech Museum of Innovation. 132,000-sq-ft facility offers visitors 4 themed galleries: Innovation, Exploration, Communication and Life Tech. See how a microchip is made, design a roller coaster or make a movie in the Digital Studio. Also IMAX Dome Theater (fee). (Daily exc Mon; closed Jan 1, Thanksgiving, Dec 25) 201 S Market St. Phone 408/279-7150. ¢¢¢

Winchester Mystery House. Started in 1884 by widow of the firearms manufacturer. Told by a medium that she would never die as long as she kept building, Sarah Winchester kept a crew of carpenters busy 24 hrs a day until her death in 1922, 38 yrs later. The expenditures cost more than $5 million. The mansion includes 160 rms, thousands of doors and windows, 40 stairways (most with 13 steps, many that go nowhere), blank walls, blind chimneys, trapdoors and secret passageways. Sixty-five-min guided mansion tour; behind-the-scenes-tour; self-guided gardens and outlying buildings tour. Guided tours (daily; closed Dec 25); admission to Historic Museum of Winchester Rifles included in tour. 525 S Winchester Blvd, at I-280 & CA 17. Phone 408/247-2101 (24-hr info). ¢¢¢¢

Annual Events

San Jose America Festival. Food booths, arts & crafts; rides, games, entertainment. Phone 408/294-2100 ext 444. Early July.

Obon Festival. Japanese-American outdoor celebration with hundreds of costumed dancers and Taiko drummers; games, food, crafts. Phone 408/293-9292. Early or mid-July.

Santa Clara County Fair. Santa Clara County Fairgrounds, 344 Tully Rd, 3 mi S off US 101. Phone 408/494-FAIR. Late July-early Aug.

Tapestry in Talent's Festival of the Arts. Downtown. Multi-cultural arts festival celebrates the arts and ethnic diversity of Santa Clara County. Phone 408/293-9728. Labor Day wkend.

Motels

✓★★ **BEST WESTERN GATEWAY INN.** *2585 Seaboard Ave (95131), near Intl Airport. 408/435-8800; FAX 408/435-8879; res: 800/528-1234.* 146 rms, 2 story. S, D $129-$159; each addl $5; under 18 free; wkend rates. Crib free. TV; cable (premium), VCR avail (movies). Pool; whirlpool. Complimentary continental bkfst. Ck-out noon. Meeting rms. Business servs avail. Valet serv. Sundries. Free airport transportation. Health club privileges. Refrigerators; microwaves avail. Totally nonsmoking. Cr cds: A, C, D, DS, MC, V.

D SC

★ **COMFORT INN AIRPORT SOUTH.** *2118 The Alameda (95126). 408/243-2400; FAX 408/243-5478; res: 800/423-6184.* 40 rms, 2 story. S, D $115-$125; suites $135; under 18 free. Crib avail. TV; cable (premium), VCR (free movies). Heated pool; whirlpool. Complimentary continental bkfst. Coffee in rms. Restaurant nearby. Ck-out 11 am. Business servs avail. In-rm modem link. Some bathrm phones, in-rm whirlpools; refrigerators, minibars in suites. Cr cds: A, C, D, DS, MC, V.

D SC

★★★ **COURTYARD BY MARRIOTT.** *10605 N Wolfe Rd (95014), 12 mi N on I-280 exit Wolfe Rd, 1 blk N. 408/252-9100; FAX 408/252-0632; res: 800/321-2211.* 149 rms, 3 story, 12 suites. S, D $184; suites $204; under 18 free. Crib free. TV; cable (premium). Heated pool; whirlpool. Continental bkfst. Complimentary coffee in rms. Ck-out noon. Coin lndry. Meeting rms. Business servs avail. Exercise equipt. Some refrigerators. Balconies. Cr cds: A, C, D, DS, MC, V.

D SC

★★ **RESIDENCE INN BY MARRIOTT.** *2761 S Bascom Ave (95008), off I-880 exit Camden Ave. 408/559-1551; FAX 408/371-9808; res: 800/331-3131.* 80 kit. suites, 2 story. Kit. suites $169-$189. Crib free. Pet accepted, some restrictions; $75 & $10/day. TV; cable (premium). Heated pool; whirlpool. Complimentary continental bkfst. Ck-out noon. Coin lndry. Meeting rm. Business servs avail. Free airport transportation. Health club privileges. Refrigerators, fireplaces. Balconies. Grills. Cr cds: A, C, D, DS, MC, V.

D SC

★★ **SUMMERFIELD SUITES HOTEL.** *1602 Crane Ct (95112), off US 101, 1st St exit, then right on Brokaw Rd, ¼ mi NE to Bering Dr, then S to Crane Ct, near Intl Airport. 408/436-1600; FAX 408/436-1075; res: 800/833-4353.* 98 kit. units, 2-3 story. S, D $209-$259. Pet accepted, some restrictions; $75 & $10/day. TV; cable (premium), VCR (movies). Heated pool; whirlpool. Complimentary continental bkfst. Complimentary coffee in rms. Restaurant nearby. Ck-out noon. Coin Indry. Meeting rms. Business servs avail. Valet serv. Sundries. Free airport transportation. Exercise equipt. Health club privileges. Some fireplaces. Picnic tables, grills. Cr cds: A, C, D, DS, JCB, MC, V.

D

Motor Hotels

★★★ **CAMPBELL INN.** *675 E Campbell Ave (95008), W off I-880, CA 17 at Campbell Ave. 408/374-4300; FAX 408/379-0695; res: 800/582-4449.* 95 rms, 2 story, 8 suites. S, D $185-$225; suites $275-$325; under 12 free; wkend rates. Pet accepted, some restrictions; $10 per night. TV; VCR (free movies). Heated pool; whirlpool. Complimentary full buffet bkfst. Ck-out noon. Business servs avail. Valet serv. Free airport, RR station, bus depot transportation. Lighted tennis. Health club privileges. Bathrm phones, refrigerators; steam bath, fireplace in suites. Private patios, balconies. Cr cds: A, C, D, DS, MC, V.

D SC

★★ **CROWNE PLAZA.** *777 Bellew Dr (95035), E on US 237, at I-880. 408/321-9500; FAX 408/321-9599; res: 800/465-4329; res: 800/838-5827.* 305 rms, 12 story. S $209; D $259; each addl $10; suites $280-$325; under 18 free; wkend, hol rates. Crib free. TV; cable (premium). Heated pool; whirlpool, poolside serv. Restaurant 6 am-2 pm, 5-10 pm. Rm serv. Bar 11-1 am; entertainment Mon-Thurs. Ck-out noon. Coin Indry. Convention facilities. Business servs avail. In-rm modem link. Bellhops. Valet serv. Sundries. Gift shop. Free airport transportation. Exercise equipt; sauna. Refrigerator avail. Cr cds: A, C, D, DS, JCB, MC, V.

D SC

★★★ **CROWNE PLAZA.** *282 Almaden Blvd (95113), at San Carlos St. 408/998-0400; FAX 408/289-9081; res: 800/465-4329.* 231 rms, 9 story. S, D $219; each addl $10; suites $239-$249; under 18 free. Crib free. TV; cable (premium), VCR avail. Restaurant 6 am-midnight. Bar 11:30-1:30 am; entertainment. Garage. Ck-out noon. Meeting rms. Business servs avail. In-rm modem link. Gift shop. Airport, RR station, bus depot transportation. Exercise equipt. Cr cds: A, C, D, DS, JCB, MC, V.

D SC

★★ **HOLIDAY INN.** *399 Silicon Valley Blvd (95138). 408/972-7800; FAX 408/972-0157; res: 800/465-4329.* 210 rms, 3 story, 24 suites. S, D $209-$249; each addl $10; suites $229-$309; under 18 free. Crib free. TV; cable (premium). Pool. Complimentary coffee in lobby. Restaurant adj 6 am-10 pm. Rm serv. Bar. Ck-out noon. Meeting rms. Business servs avail. In-rm modem link. Valet serv. Free airport, RR station, bus depot transportation. Exercise equipt. Refrigerator in suites. Cr cds: A, C, D, DS, JCB, MC, V.

D SC

★★★ **PRUNEYARD INN.** *1995 S Bascom Ave (95008), Off I-880 (CA 17) Hamilton Ave exit, in Pruneyard Shopping Center. 831/559-4300; FAX 408/559-9919; res: 800/559-4344.* 118 rms, 3 story, 11 kits. S $179; D $189; each addl $10; suites $265; kits. $189; under 12 free; wkend rates. Crib free. TV; cable (premium), VCR (free movies). Heated pool; whirlpool. Complimentary continental bkfst. Ck-out noon. Meeting rms. Business servs avail. In-rm modem link. Bellhops. Valet serv. Free airport, RR station, bus depot transportation. Some in-rm whirlpools. Bathrm phones, refrigerators, minibars; some fireplaces. Cr cds: A, C, D, DS, MC, V.

D SC

Hotels

★★★ **BEVERLY HERITAGE HOTEL.** *1820 Barber Ln (95035), just off I-880, on Montague Expy in Oak Creek Business Pk. 408/943-9080; FAX 408/432-8617; res: 800/443-4455.* 196 rms, 3 story, 67 suites. S $189; D $269; each addl $10; suites $199-$500; under 18 free; wkend package plans. Crib free. TV, cable (premium). Heated pool; whirlpool, wading pool, poolside serv. Complimentary continental bkfst (wkdays). Restaurant 6:30 am-10 pm. Bar from 11 am. Ck-out noon. Meeting rms. Business servs avail. Free airport transportation. Exercise equipt. Health club privileges. Bathrm phones. Mountain bikes avail. Cr cds: A, C, D, DS, JCB, MC, V.

D SC

★★★ **DOUBLETREE HOTEL.** *2050 Gateway Pl (95110), off US 101, 1st St exit/Brokaw Rd, near Intl Airport. 408/453-4000; FAX 408/437-2899; res: 800/547-8010.* 505 rms, 10 story. S, D $265-$285; each addl $20; suites $495-$695; under 17 free; wkend rates. Crib free. Pet accepted, some restrictions; $15 refundable. TV; cable (premium), VCR avail. Heated pool; poolside serv. Restaurants 6 am-midnight. Bar to 1:30 am; entertainment. Ck-out noon. Convention facilities. Business center. In-rm modem link. Concierge. Gift shop. Barber, beauty shop. Free airport, RR station transportation. Exercise equipt; sauna. Refrigerator in suites. Balconies. Luxury level. Cr cds: A, C, D, DS, ER, JCB, MC, V.

D SC

★★★ **EMBASSY SUITES SILICON VALLEY.** *901 E Calaveras Blvd (95035), 10 mi N on I-880. 831/942-0400; FAX 408/262-8604; res: 800/362-2779.* 266 suites, 9 story. S $109-$219; D $119-$229; each addl $10; under 18 free; wkend rates. TV; cable (premium). Indoor pool; whirlpool. Complimentary full bkfst. Coffee in rms. Restaurant 11 am-10 pm. Bar. Ck-out 1 pm. Convention facilities. Business servs avail. In-rm modem link. Gift shop. Sauna. Health club privileges. Refrigerators. Some private patios, balconies. Atrium. Cr cds: A, C, D, DS, JCB, MC, V.

D SC

★★★ **HAYES CONFERENCE CENTER.** *200 Edenvale Ave (95136). 831/226-3200; FAX 408/362-2388; res: 800/420-3200.* Web www.hayesconferencecenter.com. 135 rms, 2-3 story. S $245; D $260; suites $325; wkend rates. Crib free. TV; cable (premium), VCR avail (movies). Complimentary coffee in rms. Restaurant 11:30 am-2 pm, 5:30-9:30 pm. Meeting rms. Business center. In-rm modem link. Concierge. Gift shop. Airport, RR station transportation. Tennis privileges. Exercise equipt; sauna. Massage. Heated pool; poolside serv. Playground adj. Rec rm. Lawn games. Bathrm phones, refrigerators; microwaves, wet bars avail. Balconies avail. Cr cds: A, C, D, DS, JCB, MC, V.

D

★★★ **HILTON & TOWERS.** *300 Almaden Blvd (95110). 408/287-2100; FAX 408/947-4489; res: 800/445-8667.* Web www.sjhilton.com. 355 rms, 16 story. S $119-$259; D $134-$274; each addl $15; suites $395; under 18 free; wkend rates. Crib free. Pet accepted, some restrictions. Valet parking $11; garage parking $7. TV; cable (premium). Complimentary coffee in rms. Restaurant 6 am-10 pm. Bar 10-2 am. Ck-out noon. Convention facilities. Business center. In-rm modem link. Concierge. Gift shop. Coin Indry. Exercise equipt. Massage. Heated pool; whirlpool, poolside serv. Many minibars; refrigerator, wet bar in suites; microwaves avail. Luxury level. Cr cds: A, C, D, DS, JCB, MC, V.

D SC

✓★★★★ **HOTEL DE ANZA.** *233 W Santa Clara St (95113), at Almaden Blvd. 408/286-1000; FAX 408/286-0500; res: 800/843-3700.* E-mail deanza@ix.netcom.com; web www.hoteldeanza.com. Built in 1930 and recently restored, this Art Deco hotel is an excellent value in downtown San Jose. This hotel was built in Art-Deco style in 1930 and has been restored. 101 units, 10 story. S, D $105-$279; each addl $15; suites $195-$1,300; under 16 free; wkend rates. Valet parking $11.50. TV; cable (premium), VCR (movies). Restaurant 7 am-10 pm, closed from 2-5 pm. Bar 11-2 am; entertainment Wed-Sat. Ck-out noon. Meeting rms. Business servs avail. In-rm modem link. Exercise equipt. Health club privileges. Bathrm phones, refrigerators, minibars; some wet bars. Some balconies. Cr cds: A, C, D, DS, JCB, MC, V.

D SC

★★ **HYATT.** *1740 N 1st St (95112), near Intl Airport. 408/993-1234; FAX 408/453-0259; res: 800/233-1234.* 508 rms, 2-3 story. S, D $180-$250; each addl $25; suites $199-$599; under 18 free; wkend rates. Pet accepted. TV; cable (premium), VCR avail. Heated pool, whirlpool; poolside serv. Coffee in rms. Restaurant 5:30 am-midnight. Bar 11-2 am. Ck-out noon. Meeting rms. Business servs avail. In-rm modem link. Gift shop. Free airport transportation. Exercise equipt. Some refrigerators; wet bar in suites. Many private patios, balconies. Cr cds: A, C, D, DS, JCB, MC, V.

D SC

★★★ **HYATT SAINTE CLAIRE.** *302 S Market St (95113). 408/885-1234; FAX 408/977-0403; res: 800/233-1234.* 170 rms, 6 story, 18 suites. Feb-Oct: S, D $235-$265; each addl $20; suites $300-$900; under 12 free. Crib free. Valet, garage parking $11. TV; cable (premium). Restaurants 6:30 am-11 pm. Bar 11:30 am-11 pm. Ck-out noon. Meeting rms. Business servs avail. In-rm modem link. Bellhops. Exercise equipt. Bathrm phones, refrigerators. Renovation of 1926 hotel. Cr cds: A, C, D, DS, JCB, MC, V.

D SC

★★★ **RADISSON PLAZA HOTEL.** *1471 N 4th St (95112), near Intl Airport. 408/452-0200; FAX 408/437-8819; res: 800/333-3333.* 185 rms, 5 story. S, D $234. each addl $10; suites $250-$325; under 17 free. Crib free. TV; cable (premium). Heated pool; whirlpool, poolside serv. Complimentary coffee in rms. Restaurant 6:30 am-11 pm. Bar 10:30-1 am. Ck-out noon. Meeting rms. Business servs avail. In-rm modem link. Covered parking. Free airport transportation. Exercise equipt. Refrigerators; in-rm whirlpool in suites. Luxury level. Cr cds: A, C, D, DS, ER, JCB, MC, V.

D

★★★ **SHERATON SAN JOSE.** *1801 Barber Ln (95035), N on I-880, exit Montague Expy, W on Montague, N on McCarthy, E on Barber Lane. 408/943-0600; FAX 408/943-0484; res: 800/325-3535.* 229 rms, 9 story, 60 suites. S $220; D $229; each addl $10; suites $260; under 18 free; wkend rates, packages. Crib free. TV; cable (premium). Heated pool; whirlpool, poolside serv. Complimentary coffee in rms. Restaurant 6 am-10 pm. Bar 11-2 am; entertainment. Ck-out 1 pm. Meeting rms. Business center. Concierge. Gift shop. Free airport transportation. Exercise equipt. Health club privileges. Bathrm phones. Refrigerator, wet bar in suites. Balconies. Luxury level. Cr cds: A, C, D, DS, JCB, MC, V.

D SC

★★★★ **THE FAIRMONT.** *170 S Market St (95113). 408/998-1900; FAX 408/287-1648; res: 800/527-4727.* E-mail sanjose@fairmont.com; web www.fairmont.com. Located in the heart of downtown San Jose, this local landmark is adjacent to the Convention Center. Among the thoughtful amenities is a fully automated mini bar. 541 rms, 20 story. S, D $229-$259; each addl $25; suites $329-$1,000; hol plans. Covered parking $15/day. TV; cable (premium). Heated pool; poolside serv. Restaurants 6:30 am-10:30 pm; Fri, Sat to 11pm (also see GRILL ON THE ALLEY). Rm serv 24 hrs. Bar 11-1:30 am; entertainment. Ck-out 1 pm. Convention facilities. Business center. In-rm modem link. Concierge. Shopping arcade. Barber, beauty shop. Exercise equipt; sauna, steam rm. Massage. Bathrm phones, minibars. Some private patios. Cr cds: A, C, D, DS, JCB, MC, V.

D

★★★ **WYNDHAM HOTEL.** *1350 N 1st St (95112), near Intl Airport. 408/453-6200; FAX 408/437-9558; res: 800/538-6818.* 355 rms, 9 story. S, D $229-$249; each addl $20; suites $249-$350; under 12 free; wkend rates. Crib free. TV; cable (premium). Pool; poolside serv. Restaurant 6 am-11 pm. Bar. Ck-out 3 pm. Convention facilities. Business servs avail. Gift shop. Free airport transportation. Exercise equipt. Refrigerator in suites. Cr cds: A, C, D, DS, JCB, MC, V.

D SC

Inn

✓★★ **BRIAR ROSE BED & BREAKFAST.** *897 E Jackson St (95112). 408/279-5999; FAX 408/279-4534.* Web www.briar-rose.com. 6 rms, 4 baths, 2 story. S, D $85-$140; each addl $20; under 5 free. TV. Complimentary full bkfst. Restaurant nearby. Ck-out 11 am, ck-in after 4-6 pm. Street parking. Restored Victorian farm house (1875); antique furnishings; garden with pond, fountain. Totally nonsmoking. Cr cds: A, C, D, MC, V.

Restaurants

★★★ **EIGHT FORTY NORTH FIRST RSTRNT.** *840 N 1st St (95112). 408/282-0840.* Web www.840.com. Hrs: 11:30 am-10 pm. Closed Sun; also major hols. Res accepted. Contemporary Amer menu. Bar. Wine list. A la carte entrees: lunch $8.95-$15.95, dinner $9.95-$24.95. Specializes in game, seafood, pasta. Valet parking. Jacket. Totally nonsmoking. Cr cds: A, C, D, DS, JCB, MC, V.

D

★★★ **EMILE'S.** *545 S 2nd St (95112). 408/289-1960.* Hrs: 6-10 pm; Fri 11:30 am-2 pm, 6-10 pm. Closed Sun, Mon; most major hols. Res accepted. Contemporary French menu. Bar. Wine cellar. A la carte entrees: lunch $14.95-$18.95, dinner $25-$35. Specialties: salmon filet in potato crust, rack of lamb, cappucino souffle. Valet parking. Cr cds: A, C, D, DS, JCB, MC, V.

D

★★ **EULIPIA.** *374 S 1st St (95112). 408/280-6161.* Web www.eulipia.com. Hrs: 11 am-2:30 pm, 5:30-10 pm. Closed Mon; major hols. Res accepted. Bar. A la carte entrees: lunch $8.95-$13.50, dinner $7.95-$22. Specializes in pasta, steaks, fish. Cr cds: A, C, D, DS, MC, V.

D

★★ **FUNG LUM.** *1815 S Bascom Ave (95008), 2 mi S on CA 17. 408/377-6956.* Hrs: 11:30 am-2 pm, 5-9:30 pm; Fri, Sat to 10 pm; Sun 11 am-3 pm (brunch), 4:30-9 pm. Closed Thanksgiving. Chinese menu. Bar. A la carte entrees: lunch $5-$8.25, dinner $5.25-$30. Complete meals: lunch $10.50-$20.50, dinner $14.50-$32.50. Sun buffet, brunch $10.95. Specialties: lemon chicken, Fung Lum spareribs. Chinese decor. Totally nonsmoking. Cr cds: A, C, D, MC, V.

D

★ **GERMANIA AT THE HOCHBURG.** *261 N 2nd St (95112), at Julian. 408/295-4484.* Hrs: 11:30 am-2 pm, 5-9:30 pm; Sat, Sun from 5 pm. Closed Mon; major hols. Res accepted. German menu. Bar. Semi-a la carte: lunch $5-$12, dinner $11-$24.50. Specializes in veal, pork, beef. Outdoor dining. German setting; medieval decor. Cr cds: A, C, D, DS, MC, V.

★★ **GRILL ON THE ALLEY.** *(See The Fairmont) 408/294-2244.* Mon-Fri: 11:30 am-11 pm; Sat-Sun from 4:30-11 pm. Res accepted. Bar. Wine cellar. A la carte entrees: lunch $7.75-$18.75, dinner $14.50-$32.50. American cuisine specializing in crab Louis, USDA prime beef, lamb chops. Valet parking. Cr cds: A, C, D, DS, JCB, MC, V.

D

★★★ **LA PASTAIA.** *233 West Santa Clara (95113). 408/286-8686.* Hrs: 11 am-10 pm; Fri to 10:30 pm; Sat noon-2 pm, 5-10 pm; Sun noon-2 pm, 5-9 pm. Closed some major hols. Res accepted. Italian menu. Wine list. A la carte entrees: lunch $9.95-$24.95, dinner $10.25-$24.95. Specialties: carpaccio, osso bucco, linguine vongole. Valet parking. Outdoor dining. Cr cds: A, C, D, DS, JCB, MC, V.

D

★★★ **LOU'S VILLAGE.** *1465 W San Carlos St (95126). 408/293-4570.* Hrs: 11:30 am-10 pm; Sat 5-11 pm; Sun 4:30-9 pm. Closed Jan 1, Dec 25. Res accepted. Semi-a la carte: lunch $9.95-$19.95, dinner $13.95-$32.95. Child's meals. Specializes in seafood, pasta. Own desserts. Nautical decor. Family-owned. Cr cds: A, C, DS, MC, V.

D

★★ **ORIGINAL JOE'S.** *301 S 1st St (95113). 408/292-7030.* Hrs: 11-1:30 am. Closed some major hols. Italian, Amer menu. Bar. A la carte entrees: bkfst $4.95-$16.95, lunch $6.95-$12.95. Semi-a la carte: dinner $8.95-$26.95. Child's meals. Family-owned. Cr cds: A, C, DS, MC, V.

D

San Juan Bautista (F-1)

(See also Gilroy, Salinas)

Pop 1,570 **Elev** 150 ft **Area Code** 408 **Zip** 95045 **Web** www.sanjuanbautista.com

Information Chamber of Commerce, 402 3rd St, PO Box 1037, 95045-1037; 408/623-2454

The San Andreas Fault intersects this little town, providing residents with a few minor tremors and a topic of speculation, but little worry; most of the buildings have been standing more than 150 years. San Juan Bautista began in 1797 with the Spanish mission. The town that spread around the mission prospered as a center of cattle ranching and commerce from a nearby lode of quicksilver. However, in 1870 the Southern Pacific Railroad ran the region's first tracks through a nearby town and San Juan Bautista began to decline. Today, tourists and artists contribute to the economy of the town.

What to See and Do

Pinnacles National Monument (see). 8 mi E on CA 156, then 35 mi S on CA 25.

San Juan Bautista State Historic Park. 2nd St, 3 mi E of US 101. Phone 408/623-4881 or -4526. Here are

Mission San Juan Bautista (1797). Fifteenth and largest mission church built by the Franciscans. Church, finished in 1812 and still in use, contains many original items. The museum has old vestments, music books, barrel organ, relics and original kitchen and dining rm. Cemetery has graves of 4,300 Native Americans. (Daily; closed most major hols) 2nd & Mariposa Sts. Phone 408/623-4528 or -4542. **Donation**

Plaza Stable (1861), houses collection of restored horse-drawn carriages, blacksmith and wagonwright equipment and tools; **Castro-Breen House** (1841) (self-guided tours); **Plaza Hall** (1868), used as a residence, assembly place and dance hall; **Plaza Hotel**, restored. Picnicking. (Daily; closed Jan 1, Thanksgiving, Dec 25) All buildings ¢

Annual Events

Early Days Celebration. Commemorates founding of mission; food, entertainment, history demonstrations. Mid-June.

San Benito County Saddle Horse Show, Parade & Rodeo. 8 mi W on CA 156 to Hollister, then 8 mi S on CA 25. Phone 408/628-3421. Late June.

Motel

✓★ **SAN JUAN INN.** *410 Alameda St & Hwy 156 (95045), jct CA 156. 831/623-4380; FAX 408/623-0689.* 42 rms, 2 story. S $45-$65; D $55-$85; each addl $6. Crib $5. TV; cable. Pool; whirlpool. Restaurant nearby. Ck-out noon. Microwaves avail. Cr cds: A, C, D, MC, V.

SC

Restaurants

✓★ **DONA ESTHER MEXICAN RESTAURANT.** *25 Franklin St (95045). 831/623-2518.* Hrs: 9 am-10 pm. Closed Easter, Thanksgiving, Dec 25. Res accepted. Mexican menu. Bar. Semi-a la carte: bkfst $3-$7.45, lunch $3.95-$6.95, dinner $4.50-$9.95. Buffet: Sun lunch $7.75. Specializes in fish, authentic Mexican dishes. Guitarist, vocalist Thurs-Sun. Outdoor dining. Cr cds: A, C, DS, MC, V.

D SC

★ **JARDINES DE SAN JUAN.** *115 3rd St (95045). 831/623-4466.* Hrs: 11:30 am-9 pm; Fri, Sat to 10 pm. Closed Thanksgiving, Dec 25. Res accepted. No A/C. Mexican menu. Bar. A la carte entrees: lunch, dinner $2.95-$9.75. Semi-a la carte: lunch, dinner $8.50-$9.75. Complete meal (dinner Fri-Sun): $13. Child's meals. Specialties: carne asada, crab and shrimp tostada, red snapper Veracruz. Outdoor dining. Extensive garden area; Mexican decor. Family-owned. Totally nonsmoking. Cr cds: C, MC, V.

D

★ **JT'S BRANDING IRON.** *206 4th St (95045). 408/623-4841.* Hrs: 11 am-2 pm, 5-8 pm; Fri to 9 pm; Sat 11 am-1:30 pm, 5-9 pm; Sun 9 am-8 pm. Closed Mon; also Thanksgiving, Dec 25. Res accepted. Bar. Semi-a la carte: bkfst $4.95-$7.95, lunch $4.95-$8.95, dinner $9.95-$24.95. Child's meals. Specialties: barbecue steak, calamari, prime rib. Street parking. Outdoor dining. Western theme; family-dining. Totally nonsmoking. Cr cds: C, DS, MC, V.

D

San Juan Capistrano (J-4)

(See also Anaheim, Laguna Beach, San Clemente)

Founded 1776 **Pop** 26,183 **Elev** 104 ft **Area Code** 714 **Zip** 92675 **Web** www.sanjuanchamber.com

Information Chamber of Commerce, 31781 Camina Capistrano, Suite 306; 949/493-4700

Because of its colorful mission and its euphonious name, this town has been romanticized in song, legend, short stories and movies. Perched between mountains and ocean, San Juan Capistrano developed around the mission and today is occupied, in part, by descendants of early Mexican settlers. At one time the village declared war on Mexico.

What to See and Do

Mission San Juan Capistrano. Famous for its swallows, which depart each yr on St John's Day, Oct 23, and return on St Joseph's Day, Mar 19. Founded by Fray Junipero Serra in 1776 and named for St John of Capistrano, the Crusader, the church was built in the form of a cross and was one of the most beautiful of all California missions. The arched roof, five domes, nave, cloister and belfry collapsed during the 1812 earthquake. Pillars, arches, the garden and quadrangle remain. Self-guided tour includes the Serra Chapel (still in use), oldest building in California, ruin of the Great Stone Church, padres' living quarters, soldiers' barracks and 3 museum rms exhibiting artifacts from Native American and early Spanish culture. Also the site of a major North American archaeological dig. (Daily; closed Easter, Thanksgiving, Dec 25) 2 blks W of I-5, Ortega Hwy exit. Phone 949/248-2048. ¢¢

O'Neil Museum. Housed in a restored Victorian house, museum features collections of historical photographs, rare books, period furniture and clothing, Native Americans artifacts; also genealogical information. (Tues-Fri & Sun; closed major hols) 31831 Los Rios St. Phone 949/493-8444. ¢

Regional Library and Cultural Center. Architecturally noteworthy post-modern building, designed by Michael Graves, combines Spanish, Egyptian, Greek and pre-Columbian American influences in its design.

(Mon-Thurs, Sat; tours by appt) 31495 El Camino Real. Phone 949/493-1752. **Free**

Ronald W. Caspers Wilderness Park. Wilderness on 8,060 acres. Riding and hiking trails, nature center. Camping (fee). Inquire in advance for camping and trail use information and restrictions. (Daily) No pets. No one under age of 18 yrs allowed in park. 33401 Ortega Hwy, I-5 Ortega exit, approx 8 mi E on Ortega Hwy. Phone 949/728-0235 or 949/831-2174. Day-use per vehicle ¢–¢¢

Tour of old adobes. Sponsored by the San Juan Capistrano Historical Society. (Tues-Sat) Contact the Historical Society, 31831 Los Rios St, PO Box 1878; phone 949/493-8444. ¢

Annual Events

Festival of Whales. Dana Point Harbor, in Dana Point. Educational and entertainment events saluting visit of California gray whales. Phone 949/496-1555. Late Feb-mid-Mar, wkends.

Fiesta de las Golondrinas. Celebrates the return of the swallows to the mission; dance pageant, art exhibits. Mar 19.

Motel

★★ **BEST WESTERN CAPISTRANO INN.** *27174 Ortega Hwy (92675). 949/493-5661; FAX 949/661-8293; res: 800/441-9438.* 108 rms, 2 story. Mar-Sept: S, D $74-$89; each addl $6; kit. units $79-$84; under 18 free; lower rates rest of yr. Crib $5. Pet accepted; $250 deposit. TV; cable (premium), VCR avail. Heated pool; whirlpool. Complimentary full bkfst (Mon-Fri). Complimentary coffee in rms. Restaurant adj open 24 hrs. Ck-out noon. Meeting rm. Business servs avail. In-rm modem link. Health club privileges. Microwaves avail. Some balconies. Cr cds: A, C, D, DS, ER, JCB, MC, V.

D SC

Restaurants

★★ **EL ADOBE DE CAPISTRANO.** *31891 Camino Capistrano (92675). 949/493-1163.* Hrs: 11 am-9 pm; Sat to 10 pm; Sun from 10 am. Res accepted. Mexican, Amer menu. Bar. Semi-a la carte: lunch $5.75-$15.50, dinner $9.50-$18.50. Sun brunch $6.25-$12.95. Child's meals. Specialty: President's choice. Entertainment Fri-Sun. Patio dining. Spanish adobe courthouse (1776). Cr cds: A, C, D, DS, MC, V.

★★★ **L'HIRONDELLE.** *31631 Camino Capistrano (92675), opp Old Mission. 949/661-0425.* Web www.onlineguide.com/l'hirondelle.html. Hrs: 11:30 am-2 pm, 5-9 pm; Fri, Sat to 10 pm; Tues 5-9 pm; early-bird dinner Tues-Thurs, Sun 5-6:30 pm; Sun brunch 11 am-2 pm. Closed Mon; Jan 1, Dec 25. Res accepted. French, Belgian menu. Wine, beer. Semi-a la carte: lunch $6.75-$8.95, dinner $11.95-$18.95. Sun brunch $12.50. Specializes in braised duckling, rabbit, sweetbreads. Own baking. Patio dining. Many antiques. Cr cds: A, C, MC, V.

★★ **SARDUCCI'S CAFE & GRILL.** *31751 Camino Capistrano (92675). 714/493-9593.* Hrs: 7 am-10 pm; early-bird dinner Mon-Fri 4-7 pm; Sun brunch 7 am-4 pm. Closed Jan 1, Thanksgiving, Dec 25. Res accepted. Wine, beer. Semi-a la carte: bkfst $3-$6.95, lunch $5.25-$9.95, dinner $5.50-$16.95. Sun brunch $8.95-$9.95. Child's meals. Specializes in pasta, seafood. Outdoor dining on large patio. Cr cds: A, C, D, DS, MC, V.

D

✓★ **WALNUT GROVE.** *26871 Ortega Hwy (92675), adj to Mission. 949/493-1661.* Hrs: 6:30 am-9 pm; Fri, Sat to 9:45 pm; early-bird dinner 3-6 pm. Closed Dec 25. Wine, beer. Semi-a la carte: bkfst $2.45-$10.50, lunch $3.95-$7.95, dinner $7.75-$10.95. Child's meals. Specializes in home-style cooking. Patio dining. Family-owned. Cr cds: A, C, D, DS, MC, V.

SC

San Luis Obispo (H-2)

(See also Morro Bay, Pismo Beach)

Founded 1772 **Pop** 41,958 **Elev** 315 ft **Area Code** 805
E-mail www.slochamber@slochamber.org **Web** www.slochamber.org

Information Chamber of Commerce, 1039 Chorro St, 94301-3278; 805/781-2777

Father Junípero Serra, who established the mission in 1772, saw a resemblance to a bishop's mitre in two nearby volcanic peaks and named the mission San Luis Obispo de Tolosa (St Louis, Bishop of Toulouse). After the thatched mission roofs burned several times, a tilemaking technique was developed that soon set the style for all California missions. Located in a bowl-shaped valley, the town depends on government employment, tourism, agriculture, retail trade and its university population.

What to See and Do

Ah Louis Store (1874). Leader of the Chinese community, Ah Louis was an extraordinary man who achieved prominence at a time when Asians were given few opportunities. The two-story building, which served as the Chinese bank, post office and general merchandise store, was the cornerstone of the Chinese community. (Daily afternoons exc Sun; closed hols) 800 Palm St. Phone 805/543-4332.

California Polytechnic State University (1901). (17,000 students) On campus are 3 art galleries, working livestock and farm units, horticultural, architectural and experimental displays. Campus tours (Mon, Wed & Fri; res required). N edge of town. Phone 805/756-5734. **Free** Also here are

Performing Arts Center of San Louis Obispo. 91,500-sq-ft center offers professional dance, theater, music and other performances all year. The 1,350-seat Herman Concert Hall is JBL Professional's exclusive North American test & demonstration site. Grand Ave. For event schedule and fee information, phone 805/756-2787.

Shakespeare Press Printing Museum. Collection of 19th-century printing presses, type and related equipment; demonstrations for pre-arranged tours. (Mon-Fri, by appt; closed hols) Graphic Arts Bldg. Phone 805/756-1108. **Free**

Children's Museum. A "hands-on" museum for children pre-school through elementary school (must be accompanied by an adult); houses many interactive exhibits; themes change monthly. (Mid-June-Aug, daily exc Wed; rest of yr, Thurs-Sat & Mon, hrs vary; closed most major hols) 1010 Nipomo St, jct Monterey St. Phone 805/544-KIDS. ¢¢

Mission San Luis Obispo de Tolosa. Fifth of the California missions, founded in 1772, still serves as the parish church. Eight-rm museum contains extensive Chumash collection and artifacts from early settlers. First olive orchard in California planted here; two original trees still stand. (Daily; closed Jan 1, Easter, Thanksgiving, Dec 25) 782 Monterey St, between Chorro & Broad Sts. Phone 805/543-6850. **Donation**

San Luis Obispo County Historical Museum (1905). Local history exhibits; decorative arts; turn-of-the-century parlor re-creation. (Wed-Sun; closed major hols) 696 Monterey St, near mission. Phone 805/543-0638. **Free**

Annual Events

I Madonnari Italian Street Painting Festival. Mission San Luis Obispo de Tolosa. Local artists canvas the streets around the mission with chalk drawings. Also music, Italian cuisine and open-air market. Apr.

Renaissance Faire. Celebration of the Renaissance; period costumes, food booths, entertainment, arts & crafts. July.

Mozart Festival. Recitals, chamber music, orchestra concerts & choral music. Held at various locations throughout the county, including Mission San Luis Obispo de Tolosa and Cal Poly State University campus. Contact PO Box 311; 805/781-3008. Late July-early Aug.

SLO International Film Festival. Downtown. Showcases history & art of filmmaking. Screenings of new releases & classics. Phone 805/546-FILM. 4 days Nov.

Motels

★★★ **APPLE FARM TRELLIS COURT.** *2015 Monterey St (93401). 805/544-2040; FAX 805/546-9495; res: 800/374-3705; res: 800/255-2040.* Web www.applefarm.com. 34 rms, 1-2 story. July-mid-Sept: S, D $89-$129; each addl $20; under 18 free; higher rates: wkends, hols; lower rates rest of yr. Crib free. TV; cable (premium). Restaurant (see APPLE FARM). Ck-out noon. Business servs avail. Bellhops. Valet serv. Gift shop. Free airport, RR station, bus depot transportation. Pool; whirlpool. Fireplaces. Cr cds: A, C, DS, MC, V.

SC

★★ **BEST WESTERN OLIVE TREE INN.** *1000 Olive St (93405). 805/544-2800; FAX 805/787-0814; res: 800/777-5847.* 38 rms, 2 story, 6 kits. S $55-$58; D $62-$95; each addl $6; suites $85-$125; kits. $85-$95; higher rates: wkends, special events. Crib free. Pet accepted. TV; cable (premium). Heated pool. Complimentary continental bkfst. Restaurant 7 am-9 pm; Mon, Tues to 2 pm. Ck-out 11 am. Coin Indry. Business servs avail. In-rm modem link. Sundries. Sauna. Many refrigerators; microwaves avail. Balconies. Cr cds: A, C, D, DS, MC, V.

SC

★★ **BEST WESTERN ROYAL OAK.** *214 Madonna Rd (93405). 805/544-4410; FAX 805/544-3026; res: 800/545-4410.* Web www.hotelswest.com. 99 rms, 2 story. May-mid-Nov: S, D $69-$99; each addl $7; under 12 free; higher rates: special events, some hols; lower rates rest of yr. Crib free. Pet accepted, some restrictions. TV; cable (premium). Heated pool; whirlpool. Complimentary continental bkfst. Complimentary coffee in rms. Restaurant 6 am-10 pm. Rm serv. Ck-out noon. Coin Indry. Meeting rms. Business servs avail. In-rm modem link. Valet serv. Some refrigerators; many microwaves. Balconies. Cr cds: A, C, D, DS, ER, JCB, MC, V.

D SC

★ **ECONO LODGE.** *950 Olive St (93405). 805/544-8886; FAX 805/543-1611; res: 800/578-7878.* 32 rms, 2 story. Mid-June-late Sept: S $55-$125; D $65-$130; each addl $8; suites $80-$165; under 12 free; higher rates: hols (2-day min), graduation, county fair; lower rates rest of yr. Crib free. TV; cable (premium). Complimentary coffee in rms. Restaurant adj 6:30 am-9 pm. Ck-out 11 am. Business servs avail. Whirlpool. Refrigerators avail. Cr cds: A, C, D, DS, ER, JCB, MC, V.

D SC

✓★★ **GUESTHOUSE INN AND SUITES.** *1604 Monterey St (93401). 805/547-7777; FAX 805/547-7787.* Web www.lamplighterinn.com. 40 rms, 2-3 story, 2 cottages. No elvtr. S $42-109; D $45-$139; each addl $10; suites $75-$225; higher rates special events. TV; cable (premium), VCR avail. Heated pool; whirlpool. Complimentary bkfst. Complimentary coffee in rms. Restaurant nearby. Ck-out 11 am. Coin Indry. Business servs avail. In-rm modem link. Refrigerators. Cr cds: A, C, D, DS, MC, V.

SC

★★★ **SANDS MOTEL & SUITES.** *1930 Monterey St (93401). 805/544-0500; FAX 805/544-3529; res: 800/441-4657.* Web www.sandssuites.com. 56 rms, 1-2 story, 14 suites. May-Sept: S, D $59-$99; each addl $7; suites $69-$139; under 12 free; higher rates: special events, hols; lower rates rest of yr. Crib $5. Pet accepted, some restrictions; $5. TV; cable, VCR (free movies). Heated pool; whirlpool. Complimentary continental bkfst. Restaurant adj 6-1 am. Ck-out 11 am. Coin Indry. Meeting rms. Business servs avail. In-rm modem link. Sundries. Some covered parking. Free airport, RR station, bus depot transportation. Refrigerators. Some private patios, balconies. Picnic tables, grill. Delicatessen. Cr cds: A, C, D, DS, MC, V.

D SC

✓★★ **VILLA MOTEL.** *1670 Monterey St (93401). 805/543-8071; FAX 805/549-9389; res: 800/554-0059.* 14 rms, 1-2 story. S $35-$79; D $36-$99; each addl $4; higher rates: university events, major hols. Crib free. TV; cable (premium), VCR avail. Heated pool in season. Complimentary continental bkfst. Coffee in rms. Restaurant nearby. Ck-out 11 am. Refrigerators; some microwaves. Cr cds: A, C, D, DS, JCB, MC, V.

SC

Motor Hotels

★★ **HOLIDAY INN EXPRESS.** *1800 Monterey St (93401). 805/544-8600; FAX 805/541-4698; res: 800/544-0800.* E-mail hiexpsl0@fix.net; web www.holiday-inn.com/hotels/sbpex. 100 rms, 3 story. June-Sept, wkends: S $110-$120; D $120-$130; each addl $10; suites $130-$150; under 18 free; higher rates: special events, hols (2-day min); lower rates rest of yr. Crib free. TV; cable (premium), VCR avail (movies). Heated pool; whirlpool. Complimentary continental bkfst. Complimentary coffee in rms. Restaurant (see IZZY ORTEGA'S). Bar 11:30 am-9 pm. Ck-out noon. Meeting rm. Business servs avail. In-rm modem link. Valet serv. Refrigerators avail. Cr cds: A, C, D, DS, JCB, MC, V.

D SC

★★★ **MADONNA INN.** *100 Madonna Rd. (93405). 805/543-3000; FAX 805/543-1800; res: 800/543-9666.* Web www.madonnainn.com. 109 rms, 1-4 story. Some A/C. No elvtr. S $87; D $97-$145; suites $160-$240. Crib free. TV; cable (premium). Complimentary coffee in rms. Restaurant 7 am-10 pm, dining rm from 5:30 pm. Bar noon-midnight; entertainment Tues-Sat. Ck-out noon. Meeting rms. Business servs avail. Sundries. Gift shops. Free airport transportation. Some refrigerators; fireplace in suites. Some balconies. Individually decorated rms, each in motif of different nation or period. On hill with mountain view. Totally nonsmoking. Cr cds: A, C, JCB, MC, V.

D

★★★ **QUALITY SUITES.** *1631 Monterey St (93401). 805/541-5001; FAX 805/546-9475; res: 800/228-5050.* E-mail newlandg@aol.com; web www.qualitysuites.com. 138 suites, 3 story. May-Labor Day: S $115-$155; D $119-$155; each addl $10; under 18 free; higher rates special events; lower rates rest of yr. Crib free. TV; cable (premium), VCR (movies $6). Heated pool; wading pool, whirlpool. Complimentary full bkfst. Coffee in rms. Restaurant 6:30-9:30 am; wkends 7-10 am. Ck-out noon. Coin Indry. Meeting rm. Business servs avail. In-rm modem link. Valet serv. Sundries. Gift shop. Free airport, RR station, bus depot transportation. Health club privileges. Refrigerators, microwaves. Private patios, balconies. Library. Grill. Cr cds: A, C, D, DS, ER, JCB, MC, V.

D SC

Hotel

★★★ **EMBASSY SUITES HOTEL.** *333 Madonna Rd (93405). 805/549-0800; FAX 805/543-5273; res: 800/864-6000.* E-mail sloca1@aol.com; web www.embassy-suites.com. 196 suites, 4 story. S, D $109-$174; each addl $10; under 18 free. Crib free. TV; cable (premium). Indoor pool; whirlpool. Complimentary full bkfst. Coffee in rms. Restaurant 11:30 am-2 pm, 5-10 pm. Bar 11 am-11 pm. Ck-out noon. Coin Indry. Meeting rms. Business servs avail. In-rm modem link. Shopping arcade. Free airport, RR station, bus depot transportation. Exercise equipt. Refrigerators, microwaves. Balconies. Atrium lobby; glass elevators. Cr cds: A, C, D, DS, MC, V.

D SC

Inns

✓★ **ADOBE INN.** *1473 Monterey St (93401). 805/549-0321; FAX 805/549-0383; res: 800/676-1588.* E-mail JTowles@aol.com; web www.adobeinns.com. 15 rms, 2 story, 7 kit. units. Some A/C. May-Sept: S, D $55-$115; each addl $6; lower rates rest of yr. TV; cable. Complimentary full bkfst. Restaurant nearby. Ck-out 11 am, ck-in 2 pm. Meeting rm. Business servs avail. In-rm modem link. Southwestern decor. Totally nonsmoking. Cr cds: A, C, DS, MC, V.

★★★ **APPLE FARM TRELLIS COURT AND INN.** *2015 Monterey St (93401). 805/544-2040; FAX 805/546-9495; res: 800/374-3705.* Web www.applefarm.com. 69 rms, 3 story. July-mid-Sept, wkends, hols: S, D $119-$239; each addl $20; under 18 free; lower rates rest of yr. Crib free. TV; cable. Pool; whirlpool. Restaurant (see APPLE FARM). Ck-out noon. Business servs avail. In-rm modem link. Gift shop. Free airport, bus depot, RR transportation. Fireplaces. Sitting rm. Antiques. Bakery, millhouse. Cr cds: A, C, DS, MC, V.

D

★★★ **GARDEN STREET INN.** *1212 Garden St (93401). 805/545-9802; FAX 805/545-9403; res: 800/488-2045.* E-mail garden@fix.net; web www.fix.net/garden. 13 rms, 2 story, 4 suites. S, D $90-$130; suites $150-$175; hols (2-day min). Children over 16 yrs only. Complimentary full bkfst; afternoon refreshments. Restaurant nearby. Ck-out 11 am, ck-in 3-7 pm. Business servs avail. Free airport, RR, bus depot transportation. Some in-rm whirlpools, fireplaces. Restored Victorian house (1887) furnished with antiques. Totally nonsmoking. Cr cds: A, C, MC, V.

SC

Restaurants

✓★ **APPLE FARM.** *(See Apple Farm Inn) 805/544-6100.* Web www.applefarm.com. Hrs: 7 am-9:30 pm; Fri, Sat to 10 pm; early-bird dinner Mon-Fri 2:30-5 pm. Wine, beer. Semi-a la carte: bkfst $3.25-$8.95, lunch $3.95-$8.95, dinner $6.95-$16.95. Specialties: prime rib, apple dumplings, homemade ice cream. Salad bar. Patio dining. Gift shop, bakery; water-powered grist mill. Totally nonsmoking. Cr cds: A, C, DS, MC, V.

D

★★ **CAFE ROMA.** *1020 Railroad Ave (93401). 805/541-6800.* E-mail caferoma@fix.net; web www.fix.net/~caferoma. Hrs: 11:30 am-2:30 pm, 5:30-9:30 pm. Closed Mon; major hols. Res accepted. Italian menu. Bar. Semi-a la carte: lunch $6-$11.75, dinner $6.75-$19. Specialties: canelloni Maria Rosa, scampi alla diavolo, ravioli della casa. Outdoor dining. Italian murals. Romantic dining. Totally nonsmoking. Cr cds: A, C, D, DS, MC, V.

D

✓★ **IZZY ORTEGA'S.** *(See Holiday Inn Express) 805/543-3333.* Hrs: 11:30 am-9 pm; Fri, Sat to 9:30 pm. Closed Jan 1, Thanksgiving, Dec 24, 25. Res accepted (lunch). Mexican menu. Bar. Semi-a la carte: lunch $4.50-$10.95, dinner $5.95-$10.95. Child's meals. Specialties: fajitas, chili relleños, nachos. Parking. Outdoor dining. Authentic Mexican decor; cantina atmosphere. Totally nonsmoking. Cr cds: A, C, DS, MC, V.

D

San Marino (B-5 see Los Angeles map)

(See also Arcadia, Los Angeles)

Pop 12,959 **Elev** 566 ft **Area Code** 626 **Zip** 91108 **Web** www.smnet.org/comm_group/smcofc

Information Chamber of Commerce, 2304 Huntington Dr; 626/286-1022

What to See and Do

El Molino Viejo (ca 1816). First gristmill to be operated by water in southern California. Changing exhibits of paintings and prints of California and the West. (Daily afternoons exc Mon; closed hols) 1120 Old Mill Rd. Phone 626/449-5450. **Free**

Huntington Library, Art Collections and Botanical Gardens. Comprehensive collection of British and French 18th- and 19th-century art and American art. Home of Gainsborough's *Blue Boy,* a Shakespeare First Folio, Ellesmere manuscript of Chaucer's *Canterbury Tales* and manuscript of Franklin's autobiography; 150-acre botanical gardens. (Daily exc Mon; closed hols) Free admission 1st Thurs of month. 1151 Oxford Rd. Phone 626/405-2141 (recording) or 626/405-2100. ¢¢¢

Restaurant

✓★ **COLONIAL KITCHEN.** *1110 Huntington Dr (91108), 2 mi W of City Hall. 626/289-2449.* Hrs: 7 am-9 pm. Semi-a la carte: bkfst $2.95-$7.95, lunch $3.50-$6.35, dinner $3.65-$12.95. Child's meals. Specializes in home-style cooking, puddings. Colonial decor. Totally nonsmoking. Cr cds: C, DS, MC, V.

San Mateo (E-2)

(See also Redwood City, San Francisco Airport Area)

Settled 1851 **Pop** 85,486 **Elev** 28 ft **Area Code** 650
E-mail info@sanmateocountycvb.com
Web www.sanmateocountycvb.com

Information San Mateo County Convention & Visitors Bureau, 111 Anza Blvd, Suite 410, Burlingame 94010; 650/348-7600 or 800/288-4748

Once a stop between the chain of missions established by Fray Junipero Serra, San Mateo is now a busy suburban area within easy access to both the coast and the bay.

What to See and Do

Coyote Point Museum. Museum features 4-level exhibition including ecological concepts, dioramas, computer games, live insect colonies, aquarium displays. Two-acre Wildlife Center features native bay area animals, walk-through aviaries and native plants. (Daily exc Mon; closed Jan 1, Thanksgiving, Dec 24 & 25) Free admission 1st Wed of month. 1651 Coyote Point Dr, 1 mi E via US 101; northbound exit Dore Ave; southbound exit Poplar Ave. Phone 650/342-7755. ¢¢

Horse racing. Bay Meadows Racecourse. Turf club, clubhouse, grandstand and infield park. Thoroughbred racing (late Aug-mid-Nov, Wed-Sun). Parking fee. Bayshore Frwy (US 101), CA 92 & Hillsdale Blvd. Phone 650/574-7223. ¢¢

Japanese Garden. Collection of *koi* (carp), bonsai specimens; pagoda from Toyonaka, Japan; teahouse. (Daily; closed Dec 25) In Central Park, 5th & Laurel Aves. Phone 650/377-4640. **Free**

Woodside Store (1854). First store between San Jose and San Francisco. The building, once used as a post office and general store, still contains original equipment and furnishings. (Tues, Thurs, Sat & Sun afternoons) Tours by appt. 10 mi SW via I-280 then E on CA 84 (Woodside Rd) to Kings Mt & Tripp Rds in Woodside. Phone 650/851-7615. **Free** Also in Woodside is

Filoli Gardens. This was a filming location for *Dynasty* TV program. Georgian-style mansion and 16 acres of gardens. Guided tours of mansion (Feb-Nov, Tues-Sat; res required; no children under 12 yrs). Cañada Rd. Phone 650/364-2880. ¢¢¢¢

Annual Event

San Mateo County Fair & Floral Fiesta. Expo Center. Phone 650/574-FAIR. Aug.

Motel

★★ **HOLIDAY INN EXPRESS.** *350 N Bayshore Blvd (94401), US 101 N, exit Dore Ave. 650/344-6376; FAX 650/343-7108; res: 800/465-4329.* 110 rms, 4 story. S $89; D $99; suites $109-$135; under 18 free. Crib free. TV; cable (premium). Complimentary continental bkfst. Restaurant adj 6:30 am-9:30 pm. Ck-out 11 am. Coin Indry. Meeting rm. Business servs avail. In-rm modem link. Valet serv. Sundries. Free airport, RR station transportation. Health club privileges. Refrigerator in suites. Cr cds: A, C, D, DS, JCB, MC, V.

D SC

Motor Hotel

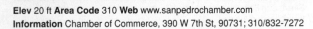

★★ **VILLA HOTEL.** *4000 S El Camino Real (94403). 650/341-0966; FAX 650/573-0164.* 285 rms, 2-5 story. S $89-$109; D $99-$119; each addl $10; suites $139-$269; under 18 free. Crib free. Pet accepted, some restrictions; $50 refundable. TV; cable (premium). Pool; poolside serv. Complimentary coffee in rms. Restaurant open 24 hrs. Rm serv. Bar 10-2 am. Ck-out 1 pm. Convention facilities. Business servs avail. Bellhops. Gift shop. Barber, beauty shop. Massage. Free airport transportation. Exercise equipt. Some refrigerators. Some balconies. Cr cds: A, C, D, DS, ER, JCB, MC, V.

D SC

San Pedro (L.A.)

(E-3 see Los Angeles map)

(See also Los Angeles)

Elev 20 ft **Area Code** 310 **Web** www.sanpedrochamber.com

Information Chamber of Commerce, 390 W 7th St, 90731; 310/832-7272

Nestled in the Palos Verdes hills, this community is a neighborhood of Los Angeles, but is regarded by many as a separate entity.

What to See and Do

Cabrillo Marine Aquarium. Extensive marine life displayed in 34 seawater aquaria; interpretive displays, environmental conservation, multimedia shows, "Touch Tank." (Daily exc Mon; closed Thanksgiving, Dec 25) Seasonal grunion programs, whale-watching, tidepool tours. Access to beaches, picnic areas, fishing pier, launching ramp (beach parking fee). 3720 Stephen White Dr. Phone 310/548-7562. **Free**

Los Angeles Maritime Museum. Features scale models of ships, numerous displays and artifacts from sailing vessels of all types. Models include the *Titanic* and movie studio models from the films *The Poseidon Adventure* and *Mutiny on the Bounty.* (Daily exc Mon; closed hols) Berth 84, foot of 6th St at Los Angeles Harbor. Phone 310/548-7618. **Donation**

Ports o'Call Village. Area with many specialty shops and a number of restaurants, all with waterfront dining. E at Berth 77.

Motel

★★ **BEST WESTERN.** *525 S Harbor Blvd (90731). 310/548-1080; FAX 310/519-0380; res: 800/356-9609.* 112 rms, 3 story. S, D $65-$78; each addl $4; suites $99; under 12 free. Crib free. TV; cable (premium). Pool; whirlpool. Complimentary continental bkfst. Ck-out noon. Meeting rms. Bellhops. Valet serv. Some bathrm phones, refrigerators, wet bars. Shuttle to nearby cruise terminal; harbor view. Cr cds: A, C, D, DS, JCB, MC, V.

D SC

Hotels

★★★ **HILTON PORT OF LOS ANGELES.** *2800 Via Cabrillo Marina (90731). 310/514-3344; FAX 310/514-8945; res: 800/HILTONS.* Web www.hilton.com. 226 rms, 3 story. S, D $99-$159; each addl $10; suites $180-$325; under 18 free; wkend rates. Crib free. Pet accepted. TV; cable (premium). Pool; whirlpool. Restaurant 6:30 am-11 pm. Bar. Ck-out noon. Meeting rms. Business center. Gift shop. Barber, beauty shop. Free parking. Lighted tennis. Exercise equipt; sauna. Refrigerators avail. On marina. Cr cds: A, C, D, DS, ER, JCB, MC, V.

D SC

★★★ **SHERATON LOS ANGELES HARBOR.** *601 S Palos Verdes St (90731). 310/519-8200; FAX 310/519-8421; res: 800/835-2525; res: 888/890-9888.* 244 rms, 10 story, 54 suites. S, D $148-$158; each addl $20; suites $225-$500; under 18 free. Crib free. TV; cable (premium). Heated pool; whirlpool. Restaurant 6:30 am-2:30 pm, 5-10 pm. Rm serv 24 hrs. Bar; entertainment. Ck-out noon. Coin Indry. Meeting rms. Business servs avail. Gift shop. Exercise equipt; sauna. Luxury level. Cr cds: A, C, D, DS, JCB, MC, V.

D SC

Restaurants

★★ **22ND STREET LANDING SEAFOOD.** *141 W 22nd St # A (90731). 310/548-4400.* Hrs: 11 am-10 pm. Closed Dec 25. Res accepted. Bar. Semi-a la carte: lunch $9.95-$14, dinner $14.95-$39.95. Specializes in grilled seafood. Outdoor dining. Waterfront fish house overlooking harbor. Cr cds: A, C, D, DS, MC, V.

D SC

★★ **SIMON'S.** *1050 Nagoya Way (90731), Berth 80. 310/514-1050.* Hrs: 11:30 am-2 pm, 5:30-9:30 pm; Sat, Sun from 5:30 pm. Closed July 4, Thanksgiving, Dec 25. Res accepted. Bar. Semi-a la carte: lunch $4.50-$15, dinner $6.95-$35. Chef specials daily. Jazz Tues-Thurs. Parking. Outdoor dining. Elegant dining on the harbor. Cr cds: A, C, D, DS, MC, V.

D ♥

San Rafael

(E-2)

(See also San Francisco)

Founded 1817 **Pop** 48,404 **Elev** 34 ft **Area Code** 415 **E-mail** srcc@ix.netcom.com **Web** www.sanrafael.org

Information Chamber of Commerce, 817 Mission Ave, 94901; 415/454-4163 or 800/454-4163

Built around an early Spanish mission, San Rafael is a busy residential community across the Golden Gate Bridge, north of San Francisco. It is the commercial, cultural and governmental hub of scenic Marin County.

What to See and Do

Marin County Civic Center. Complex designed by Frank Lloyd Wright; one of his last major projects. Tours (res required). (Mon-Fri; closed hols) 2 mi N on N San Pedro Rd off US 101. Phone 415/499-6104. **Free**

Mission San Rafael Arcángel. The 20th in a chain of California missions; built in 1817 and rebuilt in 1949. Gift shop. Chapel (daily). 1102 5th Ave at A St, 3 blks W of US 101. Phone 415/456-3016. **Free**

Motel

★ **VILLA INN.** *1600 Lincoln Ave (94901). 415/456-4975; FAX 415/456-1520; res: 888/845-5246.* 60 rms, 2 story, 9 kits. S $69-$75; D $71-$83; kit. units $10 addl (3-day min); suite $112; under 12 free. Crib free. Pet accepted. TV; cable. Pool; whirlpool. Complimentary continental bkfst. Restaurant 11:30 am-2 pm, 5:30-9:30 pm; closed Sun. Rm serv. Bar 11:30 am-11 pm. Ck-out noon. Coin Indry. Business servs avail. Refrigerators; microwaves avail. Cr cds: A, C, DS, MC, V.

D SC

Motor Hotel

★★ **BEST WESTERN NOVATO OAKS INN.** *215 Alameda Del Prado (94949), 2 mi N on US 101. 415/883-4400; FAX 415/883-4128; res: 800/625-7466.* E-mail novaks@reneson.com; web www.travelweb.com/thisco/bw/05548/05548b_html. 106 rms, 3 story. S $79-$104; D $84-$109; each addl $8; family rates. Crib free. TV; cable, VCR avail. Pool; whirlpool. Complimentary bkfst. Coffee in rms. Restaurant nearby. Ck-out noon. Meeting rms. Business servs avail. In-rm modem link. Valet serv. Exercise equipt. Some refrigerators; microwaves avail. Balconies. Cr cds: A, C, D, DS, JCB, MC, V.

D SC

Hotel

★★★ **WYNDHAM GARDEN HOTEL.** *1010 Northgate Dr (94903), off US 101 at Freitas Pkwy exit. 415/479-8800; FAX 415/479-2342; res: 800/822-4200.* 235 rms, 4 story. S $218; D $226; each addl $10; suites $238-$248; under 18 free; wkend rates. Crib free. TV; cable (premium). Heated pool; whirlpool, poolside serv. Restaurant 6:30 am-10 pm; wkends from 7 am. Rm serv 4-10 pm. Bar 4 pm-midnight. Ck-out noon. Meeting rms. Business servs avail. In-rm modem link. Valet serv. Exercise equipt. Some refrigerators. Cr cds: A, C, D, DS, JCB, MC, V.

D SC

Inn

★★★ **GERSTLE PARK INN.** *34 Grove St (94901). 415/721-7611; FAX 415/721-7600; res: 800/726-7611.* E-mail gerstle@wenet.net; web www.wenet.net/~gerstle. 12 rms, 2 with shower only, 4 kit. units. No A/C. S, D $139-$199; each addl $15; kit. units $169-$189; wkly rates; wkends, hols (2-day min). TV; VCR (free movies). Complimentary full bkfst. Restaurant nearby. Ck-out noon, ck-in 3 pm. Business servs avail. In-rm modem link. Concierge serv. Free bus, ferry transportation. Tennis privileges. Some in-rm whirlpool. Balconies. Picnic tables. Built in 1895. Elegant decor with garden, antiques. Totally nonsmoking. Cr cds: A, C, MC, V.

D

Restaurants

✓★ **ADRIANA'S RISTORANTE.** *190 Andersen Dr (94901), off US 101, Francisco Blvd exit. 415/454-8000.* Hrs: 11:30 am-2:30 pm, 5-9:45 pm. Closed Jan 1, Memorial Day, Dec 25. Res accepted. Italian menu. Wine, beer. A la carte entrees: lunch $8.50-$14.50, dinner $9.50-$15. Child's meals. Specialties: linguine tutto mare, caciucco (bouillabaise), grilled seafood. Own pasta. Parking. Outdoor dining. Totally nonsmoking. Cr cds: A, C, D, MC, V.

D

★★ **CACTI RESTAURANT.** *1200 Grant Ave (94945), De Long exit off US 101. 415/898-2234.* E-mail cacti4food@aol.com. Hrs: 11:30 am-2 pm, 5-9 pm; Fri, Sat 5-10 pm. Closed Jan 1, Thanksgiving, Dec 25. Res accepted. Southwestern menu. Bar. A la carte entrees: lunch $9.95-$14.95, dinner $10.95-$18.95. Specialties: steaks, crab cakes, grilled mahi mahi with tropical salsa. Formerly a mission-style church; white stucco walls, open kitchen. Cr cds: A, C, D, DS, MC, V.

D

★★ **KASBAH MOROCCAN RESTAURANT.** *200 Merrydale Rd (94903), US 101, exit San Pedro Rd N. 415/472-6666.* Hrs: 5:30-10 pm. Closed Mon. Res accepted Fri, Sat. Moroccan menu. Wine, beer. A la carte entrees: dinner $10-$13. Complete meal: dinner $25.75. Specialty: couscous. Belly dancing Thurs-Sun. Moroccan decor; Persian-carpeted walls, inlaid patterned wood tables, tented ceiling. Totally nonsmoking. Cr cds: A, C, MC, V.

D

San Simeon (G-1)

(See also Cambria, Morro Bay, Paso Robles)

Pop 250 (est) **Elev** 20 ft **Area Code** 805 **Zip** 93452
Web www.sansimeon-online.com

Information Chamber of Commerce, 9255 Hearst Dr, PO Box 1; 805/927-3500 or 800/342-5613 (recording)

San Simeon is an historical old whaling village. About 100 years ago, death-defying forays took place off these rocky shores when whales were spotted. Sea lion, sea otter and whale-watching is popular during northward migration in March, April and May; and also during December and January, when southward migration occurs. Deep-sea fishing is especially popular all year.

What to See and Do

Hearst-San Simeon State Historical Monument (see).

Motels

★★★ **BEST WESTERN CAVALIER OCEANFRONT RESORT.** *9415 Hearst Dr (93452). 805/927-4688; FAX 805/927-0497; res: 800/826-8168.* Web www.cavalierresort.com. 90 rms, 2 story. No A/C. May-Oct: S, D $89-$179; each addl $6; lower rates rest of yr. Crib free. Pet accepted, some restrictions. TV; cable (premium), VCR (movies avail). 2 heated pools; whirlpool. Restaurant 7 am-10 pm; summer to 11 pm. Rm serv. Serv bar. Ck-out noon. Coin lndry. Meeting rms. Business servs avail. In-rm modem link. Shopping arcade. Exercise equipt. Refrigerators, minibars; many wet bars, fireplaces. Many private patios, balconies. On ocean. Cr cds: A, C, D, DS, ER, JCB, MC, V.

SC

★★ **SAN SIMEON PINES RESORT.** *7200 Moonstone Beach Dr (93428). 805/927-4648.* Web www.smarttraveler.com/usa/ca/bigsur/bsurh10.htm. 60 rms, 1-2 story. No A/C. S, D $74-$98. TV; cable. Pool. Complimentary continental bkfst. Complimentary coffee in rms. Restaurant nearby. Ck-out 11 am. Meeting rm. 9-hole par 3 golf course. Hiking. Lawn games. Many fireplaces. Some patios. 8 wooded acres on ocean. Cr cds: A, C, MC, V.

D

San Ysidro (San Diego) (K-4)

Area Code 619

Information Chamber of Commerce, 663 E San Ysidro Blvd, 92173; 619/428-1281 or 888/767-4376

Just across the border from Tijuana, San Ysidro reflects the combined influences of the United States and Mexico. (For Border Crossing Regulations see MAKING THE MOST OF YOUR TRIP.)

This community is an integral part of San Diego, but is regarded by many as a separate entity.

Motels

★★ **AMERICANA INN & SUITES.** *815 W San Ysidro Blvd (92173), just off I-5, 2 mi N of border. 619/428-5521; FAX 619/428-0693; res: 800/553-3933.* 125 units, 2 story, 15 suites. July-Sept: S, D $35-$42; each addl $5; suites $59-$89; under 16 free; lower rates rest of yr. Crib free. TV; cable (premium). Heated pool; whirlpool. Complimentary continental bkfst. Restaurant adj open 24 hrs. Ck-out noon. Coin lndry. Refrigerators, wet bars; microwaves avail. Cr cds: A, C, D, DS, MC, V.

D SC

✓★ **ECONOMY INN.** *230 Via De San Ysidro (92173). 619/428-6191; FAX 619/428-0068; res: 888/884-7440.* 121 rms, 2 story. S, D $28-$50; family rates; higher rates: wkends, special events. Pet accepted; $10/day. TV; cable (premium). Heated pool. Complimentary coffee in lobby. Restaurant adj open 24 hrs. Ck-out 11 am. Coin lndry. Cr cds: A, C, D, DS, MC, V.

D SC

★★ **INTERNATIONAL MOTOR INN.** *190 E Calle Primera (92173). 619/428-4486; FAX 619/428-3618.* 92 rms, 2 story, 35 kit. units. S, D $52; each addl $3; kit. units $50-$56; under 18 free. Crib free. Pet accepted. TV; cable (premium), VCR avail. Complimentary coffee in rms. Restaurant adj open 24 hrs. Ck-out 11 am. Business servs avail. Sundries. Coin lndry. Pool; whirlpool. Refrigerators. Cr cds: A, C, D, DS, MC, V.

D SC

Santa Ana (J-4)

(See also Anaheim, Irvine, Long Beach, Newport Beach, Orange)

Pop 293,742 **Elev** 110 ft **Area Code** 714 **Web** www.santaanacc.com
Information Chamber of Commerce, PO Box 205, 92702; 714/541-5353

What to See and Do

Santa Ana Zoo at Prentice Park. Playgrounds, picnic area; zoo. (Daily; closed Jan 1, Dec 25) 1801 E Chestnut, I-5 to 1st St exit. Phone 714/836-4000. ¢¢

The Bowers Kidseum. For children ages 6-12. Focuses on art and culture of the Americas, Pacific Rim and Africa. (Wed-Fri afternoons, also Sat & Sun; closed some major hols) 1802 Main St. Phone 714/480-1520. ¢¢

The Bowers Museum of Cultural Art. Over 80,000 objects in its collection, which focuses on the artworks of pre-Columbian, Oceanic, Native American, African and Pacific Rim cultures. (Daily exc Mon; closed Jan 1, Thanksgiving, Dec 25) 2002 N Main St. Phone 714/567-3600. ¢¢

Motor Hotels

★ **COMFORT SUITES JOHN WAYNE AIRPORT.** *2620 Hotel Ter Dr (92705). 714/966-5200; FAX 714/979-9650; res: 800/592-4776.* 130 suites, 3 story. S $65; D $85; each addl $10; under 18 free. Crib free. TV; cable (premium). Heated pool; whirlpool. Continental bkfst. Ck-out noon. Coin lndry. Business servs avail. In-rm modem link. Free airport transportation. Health club privileges. Refrigerators; microwaves avail. Cr cds: A, C, D, DS, MC, V.

D SC

✓★★ **HOLIDAY INN ORANGE COUNTY AIRPORT.** *2726 S Grand Ave (92705). 714/966-1955; FAX 714/966-1889; res: 800/522-6478.* 175 rms, 3 story. S, D $69-$89; under 18 free. Crib free. TV; cable. Heated pool; whirlpool, poolside serv. Coffee in rms. Restaurant 6:30 am-1:30 pm, 5-9:30 pm. Rm serv. Bar 5-10 pm. Ck-out noon. Coin lndry. Meeting rms. Business center. In-rm modem link. Valet serv. Free airport, Disneyland transportation. Exercise equipt. Many refrigerators. Microwaves avail. Some private patios. Cr cds: A, C, D, DS, JCB, MC, V.

D SC

★★ **QUALITY SUITES.** *2701 Hotel Ter Dr (92705). 714/957-9200; FAX 714/641-8936; res: 800/638-7949.* 177 suites, 3 story. S $129; D $139; each addl $10; under 18 free; wkend rates. Crib free. TV; cable (premium), VCR (movies). Heated pool; whirlpool. Complimentary full bkfst; evening refreshments. Coffee in rms. Ck-out noon. Coin lndry. Business servs avail. In-rm modem link. Gift shop. Free airport, RR station, bus depot, Disneyland transportation. Health club privileges. Minibars, microwaves. Private patios, balconies. Cr cds: A, C, D, DS, ER, JCB, MC, V.

D SC

Hotels

★★ **DOUBLETREE CLUB HOTEL AT ORANGE COUNTY AIRPORT.** *7 Hutton Centre Dr (92707), near Orange County Airport. 714/751-2400; FAX 714/662-7935; res: 800/528-0444.* Web www.gus.net/doubletree.com. 167 rms, 6 story. S $99-$109; D $109-$119; each addl $10; suites $150-$200; under 12 free; wkend rates. Crib free. TV; cable (premium). Heated pool; whirlpool. Coffee in rms. Restaurant 6-9 am, 11 am-2 pm, 5-10 pm; Sat, Sun 7-10 am, 5-10 pm. Bar 5-11 pm. Ck-out noon. Meeting rms. Business servs avail. In-rm modem link. Free airport transportation. Exercise equipt. Refrigerators. Microwaves avail. Cr cds: A, C, D, DS, JCB, MC, V.

D SC

★★ **EMBASSY SUITES ORANGE COUNTY AIRPORT.** *1325 E Dyer Rd (92705). 714/241-3800; FAX 714/662-1651.* E-mail staes1@aol.com; web www.winhotel.com. 301 suites, 10 story. S, D $119-159; each addl $10; under 16 free; wkend rates. Crib free. TV; cable (premium). Pool; whirlpool. Coffee in rms. Restaurant 11 am-11 pm. Bar to 1 am; entertainment. Ck-out noon. Meeting rms. Business servs avail. In-rm modem link. Gift shop. Free airport transportation. Exercise equipt; sauna. Refrigerators, microwaves. Balconies. Cr cds: A, C, D, DS, JCB, MC, V.

D SC

Restaurants

★★★ **ANTONELLO.** *1611 Sunflower (92704), in South Coast Plaza Village. 714/751-7153.* Hrs: 11:30 am-2 pm, 5:45-10 pm; Fri to 11 pm; Sat 5:30-11 pm. Closed Sun; major hols. Res accepted. Northern Italian menu. Bar. Wine list. A la carte entrees: lunch $6.75-$16.50, dinner $12-$32. Specializes in seafood, veal, pasta. Own breads, pasta. Valet parking. Jacket. Cr cds: A, C, D, JCB, MC, V.

D

★★★★ **GUSTAF ANDERS.** *1651 Sunflower (92704), opp South Coast Plaza on the Bear St side. 714/668-1737.* E-mail hunduzn@aol.com web imenu.com. The food in this polished restaurant ranges from Scandinavian to continental to almost-retro American, and the home-baked breads are terrific. Hrs: 11:30 am-2 pm, 5:30-10 pm; Sun from 5:30 pm Closed Mon; also Memorial Day, July 4, Labor Day. Res accepted. Continental menu with Swedish flair. Bar. Extensive wine list. A la carte entrees lunch $10-$20, dinner $20-$45. Specialties: gravad lax, parsley salad with sun-dried tomatoes, filet of beef with Stilton/red wine sauce. Outdoor dining. Totally nonsmoking. Cr cds: A, C, D, MC, V.

D

✓★★ **TOPAZ CAFE.** *2002 N Main St (92706). 714/835-2002* Hrs: 11:30 am-3 pm; Thurs-Sat 11:30 am-3 pm, 5-9 pm; Sun brunch 10 am-3 pm. Closed Memorial Day, July 4, Dec 25. Res accepted. Southwestern menu. Bar. Semi-a la carte: lunch $7.95-$11.95, dinner $7.95-$15.95. Sun brunch $13.95. Child's meals. Specialties: Chinese chicken salad, sweet corn chicken tamale, rack of lamb. Entertainment Sun. Outdoor dining. Contemporary Mexican decor. Totally nonsmoking. Cr cds: A, C, D, JCB, MC, V.

D

Santa Barbara (H-2)

(See also Ojai, Solvang, Ventura)

Founded 1769 **Pop** 85,571 **Elev** 37-850 ft **Area Code** 805
E-mail sbcvb@silcom.com **Web** www.santabarbaraca.com

Information Conference & Visitors Bureau & Film Commission, 12 E Carrillo St, 93101; 805/966-9222 or 800/676-1266

Spanish charm hangs over this city, with its colorful street names, Spanish and Moorish-style architecture, adobe buildings and beautiful houses and gardens on the slopes of the Santa Ynez Mountains. It faces east and west on the Pacific Ocean along the calmest stretch of the California coast. Although the Spanish explorer Vizcaino entered the channel on Saint Barbara's Day, December 4, 1602, and named the region after the saint, a Portuguese navigator, Juan Rodriguez Cabrillo, is credited with the discovery of the channel in 1542. Its large harbor and breakwater can accommodate many boats and offers boat rentals and excursions. A Ranger District office of the Los Padres National Forest is located in Santa Barbara.

What to See and Do

Carpinteria State Beach. Swimming, lifeguard (summer), fishing. Picnicking. Camping (some hookups, dump station). (Daily) 12 mi SE on US 101. Phone 805/684-2811. Camping ¢¢¢¢¢

El Paseo. Courtyards and passageways similar to old Spain. Shops, art galleries, restaurants. Opp City Hall, de la Guerra St.

El Presidio de Santa Barbara State Historic Park. Original and reconstructed buildings of the last presidio (military & government outpost) built by Spain in the New World. Museum displays, slide show. (Daily; closed some hols) 123-129 E Cañon Perdido. Phone 805/965-0093. **Free**

Island & Coastal Fishing Trips. Scuba diving trips, fishing, dinner cruises; whale-watching in season. For further information phone 805/963-3564. ¢¢¢¢¢

Los Padres National Forest. Forest of 1,724,000 acres encompassing the La Panza, Santa Ynez, San Rafael, Santa Lucia and Sierra Madre Mountains. The vegetation ranges from chaparral to oak woodlands to coniferous forests, which include the Santa Lucia fir, the rarest and one of the most unusual firs in North America. Also contains the mountainous 149,000-acre San Rafael Wilderness, the 64,700-acre Dick Smith Wilderness and the 21,250-acre Santa Lucia Wilderness. There is also the Sespe Condor Refuge. Fishing for trout in 485 mi of streams; hunting. Hiking and riding on 1,750 mi of trails. Camping. N of town. Contact the District Ranger Office, HC 58, Paradise Rd, 93105; phone 805/967-3481. (See KING CITY).

Mission Santa Barbara. Founded in 1786, the present church was completed in 1820. Known as "Queen of the Missions" because of its architectural beauty, the 10th California mission stands on a slight elevation and at one time served as a beacon for sailing ships. Its twin-towered church and monastery represent the earliest phase of Spanish Renaissance architecture. Self-guided tours. Display rms exhibit mission building arts, mission crafts and examples of Native American and Mexican art. (Daily; closed some hols) E Los Olivos & Upper Laguna Sts, 2 mi N. Phone 805/682-4713. ¢¢

Moreton Bay fig tree. Believed to be largest of its kind in the US. Planted in 1877, it is considered possible for the tree to attain a branch spread of 160 ft. A Santa Barbara city engineer estimated that 10,450 persons could stand in its shade at noon. Chapala & US 101.

Santa Barbara Botanic Garden. Native trees, shrubs and wild flowers of California on 65 acres; Old Mission Dam (1806). Guided tours. (Daily) 1212 Mission Canyon Rd, 1¼ mi N of Mission. Phone 805/682-4726. ¢¢

Santa Barbara County Courthouse. Resembles a Spanish-Moorish palace. Considered one of the most beautiful buildings in the West. (Daily; closed Dec 25) Guided tours (Mon, Tues, & Fri at 10:30 am. Mon-Sat at 2:00 pm). 1100 Anacapa St. Phone 805/962-6464. **Free**

Santa Barbara Historical Museum. Documents, paintings, costumes and artifacts from 3 cultures: Spanish, Mexican and American. Large, gilded Chinese *Tong* shrine. Library (Tues-Fri). Museum (daily exc Mon; closed some hols). 136 E de la Guerra St. Phone 805/966-1601. **Free**

Santa Barbara Museum of Art. Collections of ancient and Asian art; 19th-century French art; American and European paintings and sculpture; 20th-century art; photography collection; changing exhibits; lectures; guided tours. (Daily exc Mon; closed most hols) 1130 State St. Phone 805/963-4364. ¢¢

Santa Barbara Museum of Natural History. Exhibits of fauna, flora, geology and prehistoric life of the Pacific coast; lectures, shows, planetarium. (Daily; closed Thanksgiving, Dec 25) 2559 Puesta del Sol Rd, beyond Mission. Phone 805/682-4711. ¢¢

Santa Barbara Zoo. Zoo with walk-through aviary, monkeys, big cats, elephants and other exhibits; miniature railroad (fee); snack bar; picnic, barbecue sites. (Daily; closed Thanksgiving, Dec 25) 500 Niños Dr, just off US 101. Phone 805/962-6310 or 805/962-5339. ¢¢¢

Stearn's Wharf. Oldest operating wharf on the West Coast. Restaurants, shops, sport fishing pier, beautiful view of harbor and city. Wharf open 24 hrs. 3 blk extension of State St.

Truth Aquatics. Direct boat service to Channel Islands National Park (see). (1 departure daily) For fee information and res, Phone 805/962-1127 or 805/658-5725.

University of California, Santa Barbara (1944). (18,500 students) An 815-acre seaside campus. For tours (Mon-Fri) phone 805/893-2485. Approx 10 mi N on US 101, in Goleta. For current performing arts activities on campus phone 805/893-3535. On campus is

Art Museum. Sedgwick collection of Old Master and Baroque period paintings; Morgenroth collection of Renaissance medals and plaques; Dreyfus collection of Mid-Eastern and pre-Columbian artifacts; changing exhibits. (Daily exc Mon) Arts Bldg. Phone 805/893-2951. **Free**

Annual Events

Santa Barbara International Orchid Show. Earl Warren Showgrounds, US 101 & Las Positas Rd. Early Mar.

Summer Sports Festival (Semana Nautica). More than 50 land and water sports. Late June or early July.

Santa Barbara National Horse Show. Earl Warren Showgrounds. Mid-July.

Old Spanish Days Fiesta. City-wide. Recreates city's history from Native American days to arrival of American troops. Late July-early Aug.

Motels

★ **BEACHCOMBER INN.** *202 W Cabrillo Blvd (93101). 805/965-4577; FAX 805/965-9937; res: 800/965-9776.* Web www.oceanpalm.com. 32 rms, 2 story. S, D $55-$300. Pet accepted. TV; cable. Heated pool. Complimentary continental bkfst. Restaurant nearby. Ck-out 11 am. Business servs avail. In-rm modem link. Sun decks. Large fountain patio. Beach opp. Cr cds: A, C, D, DS, ER, MC, V.

★★★ **BEST WESTERN ENCINA LODGE & SUITES.** *2220 Bath St (93105). 805/682-7277; FAX 805/563-9319; res: 800/526-2282.* Web www.sbhotels.com. 121 rms, 2 story, 33 kit. units. S $116-$126; D $126-$136; each addl $10; kit. units $134-$154; under 12 free; wkly rates. Crib free. TV; cable (premium). Heated pool; poolside serv, whirlpool. Sauna. Complimentary coffee in rms. Restaurant 6:30 am-10:30 pm. Rm serv. Bar. Ck-out noon. Coin Indry. Business servs avail. Bellhops. Gift shop. Barber, beauty shop. Valet serv. Free airport, RR station transportation. Health club privileges. Refrigerators; microwaves avail. Balconies. Cr cds: A, C, D, DS, ER, JCB, MC, V.

D SC

★★★ **BEST WESTERN PEPPER TREE INN.** *3850 State St (93105). 805/687-5511; FAX 805/682-2410; res: 800/528-1234; res: 800/338-0030.* E-mail pepper@silcom.com; web www.sbhotels.com. 150 rms, 1-2 story. S $122-$142; D $132-$162; each addl $10; under 12 free. Crib free. TV; cable (premium). 2 heated pools. Complimentary coffee in rms. Restaurant 6 am-9:30 pm. Rm serv. Bar 10-2 am. Ck-out noon. Coin Indry. Meeting rms. Business servs avail. In-rm modem link. Concierge.

Sundries. Gift shop. Barber, beauty shop. Valet serv. Free airport, RR station transportation. Exercise equipt; sauna. Health club privileges. Refrigerators. Private patios, balconies. Cr cds: A, C, D, DS, ER, JCB, MC, V.

D SC

★★ **CASA DEL MAR.** *18 Bath St (93101). 805/963-4418; FAX 805/966-4240; res: 800/433-3097.* Web www.casadelmar.com. 21 rms, 2 story, some kits. June-Sept: S, D $79-$129; each addl $10; suites $114-$199; under 13 free; lower rates rest of yr. Pet accepted, some restrictions; $10/day. TV; cable. Complimentary continental bkfst; evening refreshments. Ck-out noon. Business servs avail. In-rm modem link. Whirlpool. Many fireplaces. Near ocean. Cr cds: A, C, D, DS, MC, V.

D SC

★★ **COAST VILLAGE INN.** *1188 Coast Village Rd (93108). 805/969-3266; FAX 805/969-7117; res: 800/257-5131.* E-mail cvi@mi.com. 27 rms, 1-2 story, 2 kits. No A/C. Mid-May-Sept: S, D $115-$145; suites, kit. units $155-$165; higher rates hols, wkends; lower rates rest of yr. TV; cable. Heated pool. Complimentary continental bkfst. Ck-out noon. Business servs avail. Totally nonsmoking. Cr cds: A, C, D, DS, ER, MC, V.

SC

★★ **EL PRADO INN.** *1601 State St (93101). 805/966-0807; FAX 805/966-6502; res: 800/669-8979.* 68 rms, 1-2 story, 6 suites. Mid-May-Sept: S, D $75-$160; each addl $10; suites $120-$160; 2-day min stay wkends, hols in season; lower rates rest of yr. Crib free. TV; cable (premium). Heated pool. Complimentary continental bkfst. Restaurant nearby. Ck-out noon. Meeting rm. Business servs avail. In-rm modem link. Valet serv. Beauty shop. Garage parking. Some refrigerators; microwaves avail. Cr cds: A, C, DS, MC, V.

D SC

★★ **FRANCISCAN INN.** *109 Bath St (93101). 805/963-8845; FAX 805/564-3295.* 53 rms, 2 story, 25 kit. suites. S, D $80-$109; each addl $8; kit. suites $99-$140; monthly, wkly rates; lower rates rest of yr. Crib free. TV; cable (premium), VCR avail (free movies). Heated pool; whirlpool. Complimentary continental bkfst; afternoon refreshments. Restaurant nearby. Ck-out noon. Coin Indry. Business servs avail. Valet serv. Many refrigerators. Balconies. Beach, marina 1 blk. Cr cds: A, C, D, ER, MC, V.

D

★ **HARBOR SIDE INN.** *433 W Montecito St (93101). 805/963-7851; FAX 805/962-9428; res: 800/626-1986.* 43 rms, 2 story, 23 kit. suites. No A/C. S, D $79-$104; each addl $5; kit. suites $99-$160; under 3 free; wkly rates; wkends, hols (2-day min). Crib free. TV; cable. Heated pool; whirlpool. Complimentary continenal bkfst. Restaurant nearby. Ck-out noon. Coin Indry. Business servs avail. Valet serv. Microwaves; refrigerator in suites. Totally nonsmoking. Cr cds: A, C, D, DS, JCB, MC, V.

SC

★★★ **HARBOR VIEW INN.** *28 W Cabrillo Blvd (93101). 805/963-0780; FAX 805/963-7967; res: 800/755-0222.* Web www.santabarbaraca.com. 80 rms, 3 story. S, D $150-$350; each addl $10; under 16 free; 2-day min stay wkends. Crib free. TV; cable (premium). Heated pool; wading pool, whirlpool. Coffee in rms. Restaurant 7 am-9 pm. Bar. Ck-out noon. Meeting rms. Business servs avail. In-rm modem link. Valet serv. Concierge. Health club privileges. Refrigerators. Balconies. Opp beach. Cr cds: A, C, D, MC, V.

D SC

✓★★ **MAUINA BEACH MOTEL.** *21 Bath St (93101). 805/963-9311; FAX 805/564-4102.* 32 rms, 18 kits. Some A/C. Mid-May-mid-Sept: S, D $68-$275; lower rates rest of yr. TV; cable. Complimentary continental bkfst. Coffee in rms. Restaurant nearby. Ck-out noon. Business servs avail. Bicycles. Beach ½ blk. Cr cds: A, C, D, DS, MC, V.

D

★★★ **PACIFICA SUITES.** *5490 Hollister Ave (93111), near Municipal Airport. 805/683-6722; FAX 805/683-4121; res: 800/338-6722.* Web www.pacificasuites.com. 87 suites, 2 story. Memorial Day-Labor Day: S, D $160-$200; each addl $10; under 11 free; lower rates rest of yr. Crib free. TV; cable, VCR (movies $6). Heated pool; whirlpool. Complimentary full bkfst. Complimentary coffee in rms. Ck-out noon. Meeting rms. Business servs avail. In-rm modem link. Valet serv. Sundries. Gift shop. Free airport transportation. Health club privileges. Refrigerators; microwaves avail. Balconies. Cr cds: A, C, D, DS, ER, JCB, MC, V.

D SC

★★ **RAMADA LIMITED.** *4770 Calle Real (93110), at US 101 exit Turnpike Rd. 805/964-3511; FAX 805/964-0075; res: 800/654-1965.* 126 rms, 2 story. S $75-$115; D $85-$130; each addl $10; suites $120-$160; under 12 free. Crib free. TV; cable (premium). Heated pool; whirlpool. Complimentary continental bkfst. Coffee in rms. Ck-out noon. Coin Indry. Meeting rms. Business servs avail. Valet serv. Airport, RR station transportation. Refrigerators avail. Private patios, balconies. Cr cds: A, C, D, DS, MC, V.

D SC

★★ **TRAVELODGE.** *22 Castillo St (93101). 805/965-8527; FAX 805/965-6125; res: 800/578-7878.* E-mail bchtrvl@west.net. 19 rms, 1-2 story. May-mid-Sept: S, D $95-$150; each addl $10; under 17 free; higher rates: special events, wkends; lower rates rest of yr. Crib free. TV; cable (premium). Complimentary coffee in rms. Restaurant nearby. Ck-out 11 am. Business servs avail. Some refrigerators. Some private patios. Park opp; beach ½ blk. Cr cds: A, C, D, DS, ER, JCB, MC, V.

D SC

★★ **TROPICANA INN & SUITES.** *223 Castillo St (93101). 805/966-2219; FAX 805/962-9482; res: 800/468-1988.* 31 rms, 2 story, 16 suites. No A/C. S, D $102-$132; each addl $5; suites $122-$218; under 3 free; wkly rates; wkends, hols (2-day min). Crib free. TV; cable. Heated pool; whirlpool. Complimentary continental bkfst. Restaurant nearby. Ck-out noon. Coin Indry. Business servs avail. Valet serv. Garage parking. Refrigerators, microwaves. Bicycles (rentals). Totally nonsmoking. Cr cds: A, C, D, DS, JCB, MC, V.

SC

Lodge

★★★ **EL ENCANTO HOTEL.** *1900 Lasuen Rd (93103). 805/687-5000; FAX 805/687-3903; res: 800/346-7039.* E-mail elencanto@aol.com. 84 cottages. Some A/C. S, D $179-$199; cottage suites $239-$999. Crib avail. TV; cable, VCR avail (movies). Heated pool. Coffee in rms. Restaurant (see EL ENCANTO DINING ROOM). Rm serv. Bar 11 am-midnight; entertainment. Ck-out noon. Coin Indry. Meeting rm. Business servs avail. Bellhops. Concierge. Free valet parking. Tennis, pro. Golf privileges. Health club privileges. Minibars; some fireplaces; microwaves avail. Private patios, balconies. Formal gardens. Ocean view. Cr cds: A, C, D, MC, V.

SC

Motor Hotels

★★★ **BEST WESTERN INN.** *4558 Carpinteria Ave (93013), I-101 exit Santa Monica N to Reynolds S. 805/684-0473; FAX 805/684-4015; res: 800/528-1234.* Web www.bwcarpinteriainn. com. 145 rms, 3 story. S, D $89-$135; each addl $10; suites $200; under 18 free; hols (2-day min). Crib free. Pet accepted, some restrictions. TV; cable (premium). Complimentary coffee in rms. Restaurant 7-11 am, 5:30-10:30 pm. Bar 4:30 pm-midnight. Ck-out noon. Business servs avail. In-rm modem link. Health club privileges. Heated pool; whirlpool. Many balconies. Cr cds: A, C, D, DS, MC, V.

D SC

★★★ **HOLIDAY INN.** *5650 Calle Real (93117), US 101, Patterson exit. 805/964-6241; FAX 805/964-8467; res: 800/465-4329.* 160 rms, 2 story. S, D $79-$149; each addl $10; under 18 free; higher rates special events; lower rates rest of yr. Crib free. Pet accepted; $25. TV; cable. Complimentary coffee in lobby. Restaurant 6:30 am-9 pm. Rm serv. Ck-out noon. Meeting rms. Business servs avail. In-rm modem link. Free airport transportation. Pool. Cr cds: A, C, D, JCB, MC, V.

D SC

★★ **HOTEL SANTA BARBARA.** *533 State St (93101). 805/957-9300; FAX 805/962-2412; res: 888/259-7700.* E-mail hotelsb@aol.com; web www.hotelswest.com. 75 rms, 4 story. June-Sept: S, D $89-$199; hols (2-day min); higher rates special events; lower rates rest of yr. Crib free. Valet parking $5. TV; cable (premium). Complimentary continental bkfst. Complimentary coffee in rms. Restaurant nearby. Meeting rms. Business servs avail. Valet serv. Refrigerators, microwaves. Cr cds: A, C, D, DS, MC, V.

D SC

Hotels

★★★ **FESS PARKER'S DOUBLETREE RESORT.** *633 E Cabrillo Blvd (93101). 805/564-4333; FAX 805/564-4964; res: 800/879-2929.* E-mail info@fessparkersdoubletree.com; web www.fessparkers-doubletree.com. 360 rms, 3 story. S, D $279-$389; each addl $15; suites $429-$849; under 18 free; package plans. Pet accepted, some restrictions. TV; cable (premium), VCR avail (free movies). Heated pool; poolside serv. Coffee in rms. Restaurants 6:30 am-11 pm. Rm serv 24 hrs. Bar 11-1 am; entertainment. Ck-out noon. Coin Indry. Convention facilities. Business servs avail. In-rm modem link. Valet serv. Concierge. Barber, beauty shop. Valet parking. Free airport transportation. Lighted tennis, pro. Exercise equipt. Massage. Game rm. Lawn games. Minibars; microwaves avail. Private patios, balconies. Atrium lobby. On 24 acres; ocean opp. Cr cds: A, C, D, DS, ER, JCB, MC, V.

D SC

★★★★ **FOUR SEASONS BILTMORE.** *1260 Channel Dr (93108). 805/969-2261; FAX 805/565-8323; res: 800/332-3442.* Web www.fshr.com. Depending on their orientation, guest rooms at this beautiful hotel have views of the ocean, mountains, or manicured gardens. Professional service and spacious guest rooms distinguish the hotel from others in the area. 217 rms, 1-2 story. S, D $270-$500; suites from $795; under 18 free. Crib free. Pet accepted. Valet parking $16. TV; cable (premium), VCR. 2 heated pools; wading pool, whirlpool, poolside serv. Supervised child's activities (June-Aug, rest of yr wkends); ages 5-12. Restaurants 7 am-10 pm (also see LA MARINA). Rm serv 24 hrs. Bar 11:30 am-midnight; Fri, Sat to 2 am; entertainment. Ck-out noon. Meeting rms. Business center. In-rm modem link. Concierge. Gift shop. Beauty salon. Lighted tennis, pro. Golf privileges, putting green. Exercise rm; sauna. Massage. Bicycles. Lawn games. Bathrm phones, minibars; many fireplaces. Many private patios, balconies. Cr cds: A, C, D, ER, JCB, MC, V.

D

★★★ **MONTECITO INN.** *1295 Coast Village Rd (93108). 805/969-7854; FAX 805/969-0623; res: 800/843-2017.* E-mail info@montecitoinn.com. 60 rms. Some A/C. May-Sept: S, D $185-$225; suites from $265; 2-night min wkends, 3-night min hols; lower rates rest of yr. Crib $10. TV; cable (premium), VCR (free movies). Heated pool. Complimentary continental bkfst. Restaurant 11:30 am-2:30 pm, 5:30-10 pm. Ck-out noon. Guest Indry. Meeting rm. Business servs avail. Free valet parking. Exercise equipt; sauna. Bicycles. Refrigerators avail. Established in 1928 by Charlie Chaplin & Fatty Arbuckle; inspiration for Richard Rodgers' "There's a Small Hotel." Beach 3 blks. Cr cds: A, C, DS, ER, MC, V.

D SC

★★★ **RADISSON HOTEL.** *1111 E Cabrillo Blvd (93103). 805/963-0744; FAX 805/962-0985; res: 800/643-1996; res: 800/643-1994.* Web www.radisson.com. 174 rms, 3 story. July-early Oct: S, D $209-$259; each addl $20; suites $275-$775; under 17 free; lower rates rest of yr. Crib free. TV; cable (premium). Heated pool; poolside serv. Coffee in rms. Restaurant 6:30 am-10:30 pm. Bar 11-1 am; entertainment Thurs-Sat. Ck-out noon. Meeting rms. Business servs avail. In-rm modem link. Concierge. Gift shop. Beauty shop. Free covered parking. Exercise equipt. Massage. Minibars. Balconies. Ocean opp. Cr cds: A, C, D, DS, JCB, MC, V.

D SC

★★★ **SANTA BARBARA INN.** *901 E Cabrillo Blvd (93103). 805/966-2285; FAX 805/966-6584; res: 800/231-0431.* Web www.sbinn.com. 71 rms, 4 story. Some A/C. July-Aug: S, D $179-$259; each addl $15; kit. units $15 addl; suites $225-$375; lower rates rest of yr. Crib free. TV; cable. Heated pool; whirlpool, poolside serv. Coffee in rms. Restaurant (see CITRONELLE). Bar 11 am-9 pm. Ck-out noon. Meeting rms. Business servs avail. Valet parking. Health club privileges. Massage. Bathrm phones, refrigerators. Balconies. Adj to beach, ocean. Cr cds: A, C, D, DS, MC, V.

D SC

Inns

★★★ **CHESHIRE CAT INN.** *36 W Valerio St (93101), off US 101 Mission exit. 805/569-1610; FAX 805/682-1876.* E-mail cheshire@cheshirecat.com; web www.cheshirecat.com/cat. 17 rms, 2 story, 5 suites, 3 cottages. S, D $140-$180; suites $190-$270; cottages $300; wknds 2-day min. TV, VCR (free movies) in 5 rms. Complimentary full bkfst; afternoon refreshments. Restaurants nearby. Ck-out noon, ck-in 3-6 pm. Business servs avail. Some in-rm whirlpools, microwaves. Lawn games. Balconies. Sitting rm; antiques. Built 1880s. Alice in Wonderland theme. Totally nonsmoking. Cr cds: A, C, DS, MC, V.

D SC

★★ **GLENBOROUGH INN.** *1327 Bath St (93101). 805/966-0589; FAX 805/564-8610; res: 800/962-0589.* E-mail glenboro@silicom.com; web www.silicom.com/~glenboro. 12 rms in 4 houses, 2 story. Some A/C. Mid-May-mid-Sept: S, D $100-$225; each addl $30; suites $170-$250; lower mid-wk rates rest of yr; wkends, hols (2-day min). Complimentary full bkfst. Ck-out 11 am, ck-in 3-6 pm. Business servs avail. Whirlpool. Some fireplaces. Turn-of-the-century home; antiques; garden. Totally nonsmoking. Cr cds: A, C, D, DS, JCB, MC, V.

★★★ **INN ON SUMMER HILL.** *2520 Lillie Ave (93067), S on US 101, exit Summerland, right on Lillie Ave. 805/969-9998; FAX 805/565-9946; res: 800/845-5566.* E-mail denisel@innonsummerhill.com. 16 rms, 2 story. S, D $170-$200; each addl $25; suite $295; package plans. TV; cable, VCR (free movies). Complimentary full bkfst; afternoon refreshments. Complimentary coffee in rms. Restaurant nearby. Ck-out 11 am, ck-in 3 pm. Business servs avail. Whirlpool. Bathrm phones, refrigerators, fireplaces. Balconies. New England-style inn with view of ocean or landscaped grounds. Totally nonsmoking. Cr cds: A, C, DS, MC, V.

SC

★★ **OLD YACHT CLUB INN.** *431 Corona Del Mar Dr (93103). 805/962-1277; FAX 805/962-3989; res: 800/676-1676.* E-mail oyci@aol.com; web www.clia.com/members/oldyachtclubinn. 12 rms, 2 story. No A/C. D $105-$185; mid-wk rates in winter. Complimentary full bkfst; evening refreshments. Ck-out 11 am, ck-in 2-6 pm. Business servs avail. Some in-rm whirlpools. Bicycles. Former headquarters of Santa Barbara Yacht Club (1912); antiques, Oriental rugs. Totally nonsmoking. Cr cds: A, C, DS, MC, V.

SC

★★ **OLIVE HOUSE.** *1604 Olive St (93101). 805/962-4902; FAX 805/962-9983; res: 800/786-6422.* E-mail olivehse@aol.com; web www.sbinns.com. 6 rms, 2 story. No A/C. S, D $110-$180. TV in sitting rm; cable. Complimentary full bkfst; afternoon refreshments. Restaurant nearby. Ck-out 11 am, ck-in 3-7 pm. Built in 1904; antiques. Totally nonsmoking. Cr cds: A, C, DS, MC, V.

★★ **PRUFROCKS GARDEN BED & BREAKFAST.** *600 Linden Ave (93013), I-101 exit Casitas Pass. 805/566-9696; FAX 805/566-9404; res: 877/837-6257.* 7 rms, 2 air-cooled rms, 2 share bath, 2 suites. No A/C. S, D $69-$169; each addl $25; suites $150-$229; higher rates special events. Complimentary full bkfst. Complimentary coffee in rms. Restaurant nearby. Street parking. In-rm whirlpool in suites. Picnic tables. Built in 1904; seaside village. Totally nonsmoking. Cr cds: C, DS, MC, V.

★★★★ **SIMPSON HOUSE INN.** *121 E Arrellaga St (93101), I-101 to Garden St exit. 805/963-7067; FAX 805/564-4811; res: 800/676-1280.* E-mail 105031.243@compuserve.com; web www.simpsonhouseinn.com. Built in 1874, this inn is one of the oldest wooden buildings in Santa Barbara. The inn rooms, barn suites and English garden cottages all feature unique art, antiques, fine Oriental carpets and handprinted Victorian wall papers. Single or Double occupancy $175-$295; suites $400; cottages $425. TV in all rms. Complimentary full bkfst; afternoon refreshments. Ck-out 11 am, ck-in 3 pm. Business servs avail. In-rm modem link. Massage. Heath club privileges. Lawn games. Sitting rm with fireplace. Microwave avail. Balconies. Picnic tables. Totally nonsmoking. Cr cds: A, C, DS, MC, V.

★★★ **TIFFANY INN.** *1323 De La Vina St (93101). 805/963-2283; FAX 805/962-0994; res: 800/999-5672.* Web www.sbinns/tiffany. 6 rms, 3 story, 1 suite. S, D $125-$225; suite $225; mid-wk rates off-season. TV and VCR in suite. Complimentary full bkfst; afternoon refreshments. Ck-out 11 am, ck-in 3:30-7 pm. Business servs avail. Whirlpool in suites. Restored Victorian house (1898); antique furnishings; many fireplaces. Garden. Totally nonsmoking. Cr cds: A, C, DS, MC, V.

★★★ **UPHAM HOTEL.** *1404 De La Vina St (93101). 805/962-0058; FAX 805/963-2825; res: 800/727-0876.* 50 rms, 1-2 story. No A/C. S, D $130-$205; each addl $10; suites $205-$370; under 12 free. Crib $10. TV; cable, VCR avail. Complimentary continental bkfst. Dining rm 11:30 am-2 pm, 6-10 pm. Ck-out noon, ck-in 3 pm. Meeting rms. Business servs avail. Valet serv Mon-Fri. Health club privileges. Whirlpool in master suite. Fireplace in cottages. Some private patios. Historic Victorian hotel established 1871. Period furnishings include antique armoires, beds. Garden with roses, camellias. Cr cds: A, C, D, DS, ER, JCB, MC, V.

★★★ **VILLA ROSA INN.** *15 Chapala St (93101). 805/966-0851; FAX 805/962-7159.* 18 rms, 2 story, 3 kits. July-Sept, wkends (2-day min): S, D $100-$210; suite, kit. units $85-$185; mid-wk, winter rates; lower rates rest of yr. Children over 14 yrs only. TV avail; cable. Heated pool; whirlpool. Complimentary continental bkfst. Ck-out noon, ck-in 3 pm. Business servs avail. Health club privileges. Some refrigerators, fireplaces. Balconies. Spanish architecture; southwestern decor. Near beach. Totally nonsmoking. Cr cds: A, C, MC, V.

Guest Ranch

★★★ **SAN YSIDRO RANCH.** *900 San Ysidro Ln (93108), I-101, San Ysidro Rd exit. 805/969-5046; FAX 805/565-1995; res: 800/368-6788.* E-mail jansyr@west.net; web www.sanysidro.com. 38 cottages units. S, D $335-$625; suites $750-$3,500. Crib free. Pet accepted; $75. TV; cable (premium), VCR (movies). Heated pool; wading pool, poolside serv. Playground. Coffee in rms. Dining rm (see STONEHOUSE). Rm serv 24 hrs. Box lunches. Bar 5 pm-midnight, wkends to 1 am; entertainment Thurs, Fri. Ck-out noon, ck-in 3 pm. Grocery 1 mi. Meeting rms. Business servs avail. In-rm modem link. Bellhop. Gift shop. Tennis. Driving range. Summer activities. Exercise rm. Massage. Lawn games. Refrigerators, fireplaces; some in-rm whirlpools; microwaves avail. 550 acres in mountains. Cr cds: A, C, D, MC, V.

Restaurants

★★ **ANDRIA'S HARBORSIDE.** *336 W Cabrillo Blvd (93101), I-101 exit State St to Cabrillo. 805/966-3000.* Hrs: 8 am-11 pm. Res accepted. Bar. Wine list. Semi-a la carte: bkfst $3.95-$7.95, lunch $5.95-$8.95, dinner $10.95-$19.95. Specializes in mesquite charbroiled fresh seafood, steak, chicken. Own desserts. Entertainment. Parking. Oyster bar. Cr cds: A, C, DS, MC, V.

✓★★ **BIG YELLOW HOUSE.** *108 Pierpont Ave (93067), I-101 exit Evans Ave, S to Summerland exit. 805/969-4140.* E-mail bigyellowhouse@sb.net; web www.bigyellowhouse.com. Hrs: 8 am-9 pm; Fri, Sat to 10 pm; Sun brunch 8 am-2:30 pm. Closed Dec 24, 25. Res accepted. Bar. Semi-a la carte: bkfst $4.95-$11, lunch $5.95-$12, dinner $8.95-$16.95. Sun brunch $4.95-$12. Child's meals. Specializes in fried chicken, pot roast. Parking. In Victorian house. Totally nonsmoking. Cr cds: A, C, DS, MC, V.

★★★ **BLUE SHARK BISTRO.** *21 W Victoria St (93101), on I-101 exit Garden. 805/564-7100.* Hrs: 5-9:30 pm; Fri, Sat to 10 pm; Sun to 9 pm. Closed Mon; Jan 1, Dec 25. Res accepted. Bar. Wine list. A la carte entrees: dinner $8.95-$19.95. Child's meals. Specializes in seafood, steak, soups. Outdoor dining. In turn-of-the-century Victorian house. Cr cds: A, C, D, MC, V.

✓★★ **BRIGITTE'S RESTAURANT CAFE.** *1325 State St (93101). 805/966-9676.* Hrs: 11:30 am-2:30 pm, 5-10 pm; Fri, Sat to 11 pm; Sun 5-10 pm. Closed some major hols. Bar. A la carte entrees: lunch, dinner $8.75-$18.95. Specialties: smoked salmon with caviar, fresh fish. California-style bistro. Totally nonsmoking. Cr cds: A, C, D, DS, MC, V.

★★★ **CITRONELLE.** *(See Santa Barbara Inn) 805/963-0111.* Web www.sbinn.com. Hrs: 7 am-10 pm; Sun brunch 10:30 am-2:30 pm. Res accepted. Bar. Award of excellence wine list. Semi-a la carte: bkfst $10.50-$12, lunch $12-$18, dinner $21-$31. Sun brunch $17-$25. Specialties: Roasted duck w/cider sauce, grilled swordfish. Valet parking. 3rd flr of Santa Barbara Inn; view of ocean. Totally nonsmoking. Cr cds: A, C, D, DS, MC, V.

★★★★ **DOWNEY'S.** *1305 State St (93101), I-101 exit Garden St. 805/966-5006.* The serious food at this charming restaurant belies the casual bistro atmosphere. Service is super friendly and helpful. Hrs: 5:30-9 pm; Fri, Sat to 9:30 pm. Closed Mon; some major hols. Res accepted. Wine, beer. A la carte entrees: dinner $21.95-$26.95. Specialties: grilled lamb loin, fresh Dungeness crab, local swordfish with fresh papaya vinaigrette. Cr cds: A, C, DS, MC, V.

★★★ **EL ENCANTO DINING ROOM.** *(See El Encanto Hotel) 805/687-5000.* E-mail elencanto@aol.com. Hrs: 7 am-10 pm. Res accepted. French, Amer menu. Bar 11 am-midnight. Wine cellar. A la carte entrees: bkfst $8.75-$12.50, lunch $8.75-$14.50, dinner $16-$28. Child's meals. Specialties: El Encanto pagella, cioppino, roasted sea bass. Piano Thurs-Sun. Valet parking. Outdoor dining. Ocean view; romantic decor. Cr cds: A, C, D, MC, V.

★★ **EL PASEO RESTAURANT.** *10 El Paseo Place (93101). 805/962-6050.* Hrs: 11:30 am-10 pm; Fri to midnight; Sat to 2 am; Sun from 10:30 am; Sun brunch 10:30 am. Closed Dec 25. Res accepted. Mexican menu. Bar. A la carte entrees: lunch $5.95-$10.95, dinner $7.95-$24.95. Sun brunch $16.95 & $21.95. Specialties: Mexican-stuffed porkchop, shrimp espanoles, filet al chipotle. Latino music Sat. Valet parking. Outdoor dining. In historic courtyard. Opened over 70 yrs ago. Cr cds: A, C, MC, V.

★★ **HARBOR AND LONGBOARD'S GRILL.** *210 Stearns Wharf (93101). 805/963-3311.* Hrs: 11 am-midnight; Fri to 1 am; Sat 8-1 am; Sun 8 am-11 pm; Sun brunch 10:30 am. Res accepted. Bar. Semi-a la carte: bkfst $7.50-$11.95, lunch $7.95-$19.95, dinner $12.95-$39.95. Sun brunch $19.95. Child's meals. Specializes in fresh seafood. Valet parking. Outdoor dining. Mountains & islands view. On ocean. Cr cds: A, C, MC, V.

D

★★★ **LA MARINA.** *(See Four Seasons Biltmore Hotel) 805/969-2261.* Web www.fshr.com. California contemporary menu. Specialties: roasted Maine lobster, angel hair pasta with prawns, chocolate grand marnier souffle. Hrs: 6-10 pm; Sun brunch 10 am-2 pm. Res suggested. No A/C. Bar 11:30 am-midnight; Fri, Sat to 2 am. Extensive wine list. A la carte entrees: dinner $17-$35. Sun brunch with outside dining avail $49.95. Complimentary valet parking. Ocean view. Cr cds: A, C, D, DS, ER, JCB, MC, V.

D ♥

✓★★ **LEFT AT ALBUQUERQUE.** *803 State St (93101), I-101 N exit Garden St to State St. 805/564-5040.* Web www.1spot.com/left. Hrs: 11:30 am-10 pm; Fri, Sat to 11 pm. Closed Thanksgiving, Dec 25. Res accepted. Southwestern menu. Bar. Semi-a la carte: lunch $6-$10, dinner $8-$13. Child's meals. Specializes in enchiladas, burritos, fajitas. Outdoor dining. Southwestern motif; large tequila collection. Totally nonsmoking. Cr cds: A, C, D, MC, V.

D

★★★ **PALACE GRILL.** *8 E Cota St (93101), I-101 exit Garden St. 805/963-5000.* Web www.palacegrill.com. Hrs: 5:30-10 pm; Fri, Sat to 11 pm. Res accepted. Cajun, Creole menu. Bar. Semi-a la carte: dinner $9-$24. Child's meals. Specialties: crawfish etouffee, blackened redfish, Louisiana bread pudding souffle. New Orleans Mardi Gras atmosphere. Totally nonsmoking. Cr cds: A, C, MC, V.

D

✓★★★ **PALAZZIO.** *1151 Coast Village Rd (93108). 805/969-8565.* Web www.palazzios.com. Hrs: 11:30 am-2:30 pm, 5:30-11 pm; Fri, Sat to midnight; Sun from 5:30 pm. Closed Thanksgiving, Dec 25. Res accepted. Italian menu. Bar. A la carte entrees: lunch, dinner $7-$16. Specialties: capellini shrimp, tiramisu, fusilli roasted eggplant. Parking. Outdoor dining. Murals. Totally nonsmoking. Cr cds: C, MC, V.

D

★★ **PALAZZIO-DOWNTOWN.** *1026 State St (93101). 805/564-1985.* Web www.palazzios.com. Hrs: 11:30 am-3 pm, 5:30-11 pm; Fri to midnight. Closed Thanksgiving, Dec 25. Res accepted. Italian menu. Bar. A la carte entrees: lunch, dinner $8.95-$15.95. Child's meals. Specialties: penne al fumo, capellini shrimp, capellini grilled chicken. Parking. Outdoor dining. Family-style. Cr cds: C, MC, V.

D

★★ **SANTAS KITCHEN.** *3805 Santa Claus Ln (93013). 805/684-3338.* Hrs: 7 am-3 pm, 3-9:30 pm; early-bird dinner 4-6 pm. Res accepted. bar. Semi-a la carte: bkfst $3.75-$7.50, lunch $5.50-$7.95, dinner $6.95-$19.95. Child's meals. Specialties: prime rib, oak-grilled steak & chicken, fresh salmon. Parking. Outdoor dining. Park-like setting. Cr cds: C, MC, V.

✓★ **STATE & A BAR & GRILL.** *1201 State St (93101). 805/966-1010.* Hrs: 11 am-midnight. No A/C. Bar. Semi-a la carte: lunch, dinner $4.25-$10.95. Specializes in steak, international salads, seafood. Salad bar. Entertainment Thurs-Sat. Outdoor dining. Cr cds: A, C, DS, MC, V.

D

★★★ **STONEHOUSE.** *(See San Ysidro Ranch) 805/969-5046.* E-mail ressyr@west.net; web www.sanysidro.com. Specialties: lobster, caviar, veal chop. Hrs: 8 am-9:30 pm; Fri, Sat to 10:30 pm; Sun brunch 11:30 am-2:30 pm. Res accepted. Bar to midnight. Wine cellar. Semi-a la carte: bkfst $9.95-$14.95, lunch $10.45-$17.95, dinner from $23. Prix fixe: lunch $22.95. Sun brunch $29.95. Child's meals. Entertainment Thurs, Fri. Valet parking. Adobe walls, Spanish tile floors and antiques create a contemporary rustic atmosphere. Totally nonsmoking. Cr cds: A, C, D, MC, V.

D

★★ **TEE OFF.** *3627 State St (93105). 805/687-1616.* Hrs: 4-11 pm; Fri, Sat to midnight; Sun to 10 pm. Res accepted. Bar. Semi-a la carte: dinner $8.95-$29.95. Specialty: prime rib. Parking. Cr cds: A, C, MC, V.

D

★★★ **WINE CASK.** *813 Anacapa St (93101). 805/966-9463.* E-mail winecask@winecask.com; web www.winecask.com. Hrs: 11:30 am-3 pm, 5:30-10 pm; Fri to 11 pm; Sat, Sun 5:30-10 pm; Sat, Sun brunch 10 am-3 pm. Closed some major hols. Res accepted. Bar. Wine cellar. A la carte entrees: lunch $7-$14, dinner $19-$27. Sat, Sun brunch $7-$13. Child's meals. Specializes in seafood, chicken, pasta, grilled meat. Seasonal menu. Valet parking. Patio dining. Fine dining. Totally nonsmoking. Cr cds: A, C, D, MC, V.

D

Santa Clara (F-5 see San Francisco map)

(See also Fremont, Livermore, San Jose, Saratoga)

Founded 1777 **Pop** 93,613 **Elev** 88 ft **Area Code** 408 **Web** www.santaclara.org

Information Convention & Visitors Bureau, 1850 Warburton Ave, PO Box 387, 95052; 408/244-9660

Santa Clara, the "Mission City," is in the heart of Silicon Valley, just 50 minutes south of San Francisco.

What to See and Do

Intel Museum. A 3,500-sq-ft museum that explores the computer chip industry. Hands-on exhibits describe the differences between various types of chips, how they are used and how they are constructed. (Mon-Fri; closed hols) 2200 Mission College Blvd, at the headquarters of Intel Corporation. Phone 408/765-0503. **Free**

Paramount's Great America. In this 100-acre park is a blend of movie magic and theme park thrills. Features an array of thrilling rides, live stage shows and entertainment; among Paramount's Great America's premier attractions are "Top Gun," a mind boggling inverted roller coaster and "Invertigo," a face-to-face roller coaster. Also featured are Star Trek, Nickolodeon and Hanna Barbera characters. Also spectacular is the IMAX theater, and the world's tallest double-decker carousel, Carousel Columbia, which is near the park's entrance. There is a Nicklodeon area for children called "Splat City." (Mid-Mar-Oct; inquire for schedule) Admission includes rides and attractions. Great America Pkwy, off I-101. Phone 408/988-1776. ¢¢¢¢¢

Santa Clara University (1851). (7,900 students) Oldest institution of higher learning in California, founded in 1851. Self-guided tour of the Mission Gardens, which includes the Adobe Lodge and Wall (restored) from the 1822-1825 mission. Olive trees and grinding stones in the gardens also date to the early mission period. On both sides of The Alameda between Bellomy & Franklin Sts. Phone 408/554-4000. On campus are

De Saisset Museum. Rotating exhibits (all-yr); California Historical Collection focuses on pre-contact Native American period, Mission period, and early yrs of the university. (Daily exc Mon) 500 El Camino Real. Phone 408/554-4528. **Free**

Mission Santa Clara de Asís (1777). The modern mission, dedicated in 1928, is an enlarged and adapted replica of the original mission. The present roof contains 12,000 cover tiles salvaged from earlier missions. Of the 4 mission bells in the tower, one was a gift from Carlos IV of Spain in 1798, and survived the 1926 fire; another was a gift from Alfonso XIII of Spain in 1929. Surrounded by beautiful gardens and restored Adobe Lodge and Wall; part of the 1822 mission quadrangle. (Mon-Fri) Phone 408/554-4023. **Free**

Triton Museum of Art. Permanent and changing exhibits of 19th- and 20th-century American and contemporary works; sculpture garden; landscaped grounds on 7 acres. (Daily exc Mon; closed some hols) 1505 Warburton Ave, opp Civic Center. Phone 408/247-3754. **Free**

Annual Event

Santa Clara Art & Wine Festival. Sept.

Motels

✓★ **BEST WESTERN INN.** *4341 El Camino Real (95051). 408/244-3366; FAX 408/246-1387; res: 800/528-1234.* 52 rms, 1-2 story. S $70-$135; D $75-$135; each addl $6. Crib $4. TV; cable (premium), VCR. Pool. Continental bkfst. Coffee in rms. Restaurant nearby. Ck-out 11 am. Coin Indry. Business servs avail. In-rm modem link. Refrigerators; microwaves. Cr cds: A, C, D, DS, MC, V.

D SC

★ **GUESTHOUSE INN & SUITE.** *2930 El Camino Real (95051). 408/241-3010; FAX 408/247-0623; res: 800/334-3928.* 69 units, 2 story, 16 kits. S $89-$200; D $99-$200; each addl $10; kit. units $149-$250; under 17 free. Crib $10. Pet accepted; $10. TV; cable, VCR (movies). Heated pool. Complimentary continental bkfst. Complimentary coffee in rms. Restaurant nearby. Ck-out 11:30 am. Business servs avail. In-rm modem link. Valet serv. Health club privileges. Refrigerators. Some balconies. Cr cds: A, C, D, DS, JCB, MC, V.

SC

★★ **HOWARD JOHNSON.** *5405 Stevens Creek Blvd (95051). 408/257-8600; FAX 408/446-2936; res: 800/446-4656.* 96 rms, 2 story. S, D $145-$185; under 18 free. Crib free. TV; cable (premium). Pool; wading pool. Restaurant adj 6 am-10 pm. Ck-out noon. Meeting rms. Business servs avail. Coin Indry. Health club privileges. Some refrigerators. Some balconies. Cr cds: A, C, D, DS, JCB, MC, V.

D SC

★★ **MARIANI'S INN.** *2500 El Camino Real (95051). 408/243-1431; FAX 408/243-5745; res: 800/553-8666.* 143 units, 1-2 story, 53 kits. S $99; D $120; each addl $8; kit. suites $109-$125; under 12 free. Crib free. TV; cable (premium), VCR avail. Heated pool; whirlpool. Complimentary continental bkfst. Restaurant 6:30 am-11 pm. Rm serv. Bar 11-12:30 am; entertainment. Ck-out 11 am. Coin Indry. Meeting rms. Business servs avail. In-rm modem link. Valet serv. Free airport transportation. Health club privileges. Cr cds: A, C, D, DS, JCB, MC, V.

D SC

✓★ **VAGABOND INN.** *3580 El Camino Real (95051), at jct CA 82, Lawrence Expy. 408/241-0771; FAX 408/247-3386; res: 800/522-1555.* 70 rms, 2 story. S, D $89; each addl $5; under 18 free. Crib $5. Pet accepted; $5. TV; cable (premium). Heated pool. Complimentary continental bkfst. Coffee in rms. Restaurant nearby. Ck-out noon. Coin Indry. Business servs avail. In-rm modem link. Valet serv. Some refrigerators, microwaves. Cr cds: A, C, D, DS, MC, V.

SC

Motor Hotel

★★★ **QUALITY SUITES SILICON VALLEY.** *3100 Lakeside Dr (95054). 408/748-9800; FAX 408/748-1476; res: 800/638-7949.* 220 suites, 7 story. S, D $209-$219; each addl $10; under 18 free; lower rates wkends. Crib free. TV; cable (premium), VCR avail (movies). Heated pool. Complimentary full bkfst. Complimentary coffee in rms. Restaurant nearby. Ck-out noon. Coin Indry. Meeting rms. Business center. Bellhops. Sundries. Gift shop. Free garage parking. Free airport, RR station, bus depot transportation. Exercise equipt. Minibars. Cr cds: A, C, D, DS, JCB, MC, V.

D SC

Hotels

★★★ **MARRIOTT.** *2700 Mission College Blvd (95054), 5 mi N, ½ mi E of US 101 at Great America Pkwy exit. 408/988-1500; FAX 408/727-4353; res: 800/228-9290.* 754 rms, 2-14 story. S, D $239; suites $400; under 18 free; wkend plans. Crib free. Pet accepted, some restrictions. TV; cable (premium), VCR avail. Indoor/outdoor pool; whirlpool, poolside serv. Restaurants 6 am-11 pm. Rm serv to midnight. Bar 11:30-2 am. Ck-out 11 am. Convention facilities. Business center. Gift shop. Airport transportation. Lighted tennis. Exercise equipt. Some refrigerators; bathrm phone in suites. Some private patios, balconies. Luxury level. Cr cds: A, C, D, DS, ER, JCB, MC, V.

D SC

★★★ **WESTIN HOTEL.** *5101 Great America Pkwy (95054), near Great America Theme Park. 408/986-0700; FAX 408/980-3990; res: 800/937-8461.* 505 rms, 14 story. S $265; D $285; each addl $20; suites $450-$650; under 18 free; wkend, hol rates. Crib free. Pet accepted, some restrictions. Valet parking $11. TV; cable (premium). Heated pool; whirlpool, poolside serv. Restaurant 6 am-10 pm. Rm serv 24 hrs. Bar 11 am-midnight. Ck-out noon. Convention facilities. Business center. In-rm modem link. Concierge. Gift shop. Exercise equipt; sauna. Health club privileges. Tennis privileges. Golf privileges. Minibars; refrigerators avail. Balconies. Picnic tables. Near airport. Cr cds: A, C, D, DS, ER, JCB, MC, V.

D SC

★★★ **WOODCREST HOTEL.** *5415 Stevens Creek Blvd (95051), at I-280. 408/446-9636; FAX 408/446-9739; res: 800/862-8282.* 60 rms, 4 story. S, D $145-$165; each addl $15; suites $165-$300; under 12 free; wkend rates. Crib free. TV; cable (premium), VCR (free movies). Complimentary bkfst buffet. Coffee in rms. Bar 5:30-10:30 pm; closed Fri-Sun. Ck-out noon. Meeting rms. Business servs avail. Covered parking. Health club privileges. Bathrm phones; some fireplaces; refrigerator, wet bar in suites. Resembles French country estate with courtyard. Cr cds: A, C, D, MC, V.

D

Inn

✓★★ **MADISON STREET INN.** *1390 Madison St (95050). 408/249-5541; FAX 408/249-6676; res: 800/491-5541.* 6 rms, 4 baths. S, D $75-$115. TV avail. Pool. Complimentary full bkfst. Ck-out noon, ck-in 4 pm. Health club privileges. Picnic tables, grills. Victorian furnishings (1895); library, antiques, bearclaw tubs. Garden. Totally nonsmoking. Cr cds: A, C, D, DS, MC, V.

SC

Restaurants

★★ **LA GALLERIA.** *2798 El Camino Real (95051). 408/296-6800.* Hrs: 11:30 am-9 pm; Fri to 9:30 pm; Sat 5-9:30 pm. Closed Sun; Thanksgiving, Dec 25. Res accepted. Northern Italian menu. Wine, beer. Semi-a la carte: lunch $7.95-$16.95, dinner $8.50-$17.95. Specialties: osso bucco Milanese, fettucine alla Galleria. Parking. Cr cds: A, C, D, DS, JCB, MC, V.

D

✓★ **LA PALOMA.** *2280 El Camino Real (95050). 408/247-0990.* Hrs: 11 am-9:30 pm; Fri, Sat to 10 pm; Sun 4-9 pm. Closed July 4, Thanksgiving, Dec 25. Res accepted. Mexican menu. Bar. Semi-a la carte: lunch, dinner $6.50-$11.95. Child's meals. Specialties: pollo al cilantro, burrito ranchero. Parking. Mexican village decor. Cr cds: A, C, D, DS, MC, V.

D

Santa Cruz (F-1)

(See also Los Gatos, Santa Clara)

Founded 1840 **Pop** 49,040 **Elev** 20 ft **Area Code** 831 **Web** www.scccvc.org

Information Santa Cruz County Conference & Visitors Council, 701 Front St, 95060; 831/425-1234 or 800/833-3494

Santa Cruz is a bustling seaside resort and arts and crafts center with 29 miles of public beaches. The county is home to a wide variety of agricultural products such as strawberries, apples and begonias. The present town is predated by the village of Branciforte, which it has now assimilated. Branciforte was founded in 1797 as a colonial venture of the Spanish government. Lacking financial support, the village failed to develop, and its shiftless colonists made much trouble for the nearby mission. The Santa Cruz Valley was given its name, Holy Cross, by Don Gaspar de Portola and Father Crespi, who discovered it in 1769.

What to See and Do

Bargetto Winery. Family winery with tours and tasting (daily; closed most major hols). 3535 N Main St, E on CA 1, exit Capitola/Soquel exit, right on Main St in Soquel. Tasting rm, 700 Cannery Row, Suite L, Monterey 93940; phone 831/475-2258. **Free**

Felton covered bridge. Built in 1892; spans San Lorenzo River 80 ft above the water.

Municipal Wharf. Extends ½ mi into Monterey Bay. One of few piers of this type to permit auto traffic. Restaurants, gift shops, fish markets, charter boats; free fishing area.

Roaring Camp & Big Trees Narrow-Gauge Railroad. Authentic 19th-century narrow-gauge steam locomotives carry passengers up North America's steepest railroad grades through groves of giant redwoods. Stopover at Bear Mt for picnicking, hiking; round trip 6 mi, 1¼ hrs. Historic townsite with 1880s depot, old-time general store, covered bridge. Trains leave Roaring Camp depot, ½ mi SE of Felton at jct Graham Hill & Roaring Camp Rds. (Schedule varies; additional trains wkends, hols and in summer) Chuckwagon barbecue (May-Oct, wkends). 6 mi N on Graham Hill Rd in Felton. For additional information and schedule Phone 831/335-4400. **¢¢¢¢** Also here is

Santa Cruz, Big Trees & Pacific Railway. 1920s-era railroad operating vintage passenger coaches over spectacular rail route between redwoods at Roaring Camp and beach and boardwalk at Santa Cruz. A 2½-hr round trip excursion through tunnel, over trestles and along rugged San Lorenzo River Canyon on its way to the beach at Santa Cruz. Historic railroad dates back to 1875. (June-Sept, daily; May & Oct, wkends & hols) For information and schedule phone 831/335-4400. **¢¢¢¢**

Santa Cruz Beach Boardwalk. Half-mile long. Only remaining beachside amusement park on the West Coast. Includes famous Cocoanut Grove ballroom, Neptune's Kingdom with entertainment and attractions, restaurants, shops, outdoor shows at beach bandstand, miniature golf, arcades, games & rides and the Giant Dipper roller coaster and 1911 Looff carousel. Boardwalk (Memorial Day-Labor Day, daily; rest of yr, wkends & hols; closed Dec 25, 26). Neptune's Kingdome (daily; closed Dec 24 & 25). For hrs phone 831/426-7433. All-day unlimited ride pass **¢¢¢¢¢**

Santa Cruz City Museum of Natural History. Natural and cultural history of the northern Monterey Bay region. California Native American exhibits; tidepool aquarium. (Daily exc Mon; closed major hols) 1305 E Cliff Dr. Phone 831/429-3773. **Free**

Santa Cruz Mission State Historical Park. Casa Adobe (Neary-Rodriguez Adobe) is the only remaining building of the old Santa Cruz Mission; the date of construction is between 1822 and 1824; displays. (Thurs-Sun by appt) 144 School St. Phone 831/425-5849. **¢**

State parks.

Big Basin Redwoods (see). 23 mi N via CA 9, 236.

Forest of Nisene Marks. Seismologists identified the epicenter of the Oct 1989 earthquake (7.1 magnitude) in this 10,000-acre state park. Diagonal fault ridges are evident although the earthquake epicenter can barely be distinguished. Hiking, bicycling. Picnicking. Primitive camping (fee; 6-mi hike to campsite). 6 mi SE on CA 1 to Aptos, then N on Aptos Creek Rd. Phone 831/335-4598.

Henry Cowell Redwoods. These 1,737 acres contain some of the finest specimens of coastal redwood in the world, including one tree that has a base large enough to shelter several people. Self-guided nature trail, hiking, bridle trails. Picnicking. Camping. Some campfire programs and guided walks conducted by rangers. 5 mi N on CA 9. Phone 831/335-4598. **¢¢**

Natural Bridges Beach. Ocean-formed sandstone arch; winter site for monarch butterflies. Fishing. Nature trail. Picnicking. Displays of local tidepool life. Day use only. W of city limits on W Cliff Dr. Phone 831/423-4609. **¢¢¢**

Seacliff Beach. Fishing pier leads to *"The Cement Ship,"* sunk here in 1929 to serve as an amusement center. Swimming beach, seasonal lifeguards; fishing. Picnicking. Campsites (full hookups); no tents. 5 mi S on CA 1. Phone 831/688-3222; for reservations phone 800/444-7275. **¢¢¢**

Wilder Ranch. Coastal terraces, pocket beaches and historic farm on 3,000 acres. Nature, hiking, biking, bridle trails. Interpretive displays. Farm and blacksmith demonstrations. Day use only. 3 mi NW on CA 1. Phone 831/426-0505. **¢¢¢**

The Mystery Spot. Area 150 ft in diameter that "defies" conventional laws of gravity, perspective; balls roll uphill, trees grow sideways. Discovered in 1939. Guided tours. (Daily) 1953 Branciforte Dr, 2½ mi N. Phone 831/423-8897. **¢¢**

University of California, Santa Cruz (1965). (10,000 students) Made up of 8 colleges on a 2,000-acre campus overlooking Monterey Bay. The Institute of Marine Sciences offers guided tours of the Long Marine Laboratory. Art galleries, astronomical exhibits, agroecology farm and arboretum. NW section of town. Phone 831/459-2495.

West Cliff Drive. One of the most renowned ocean drives in the state. On N shoreline of Santa Cruz Beach.

Annual Events

Santa Cruz County Fair. Santa Cruz County Fairgrounds. Phone 831/724-5671. Early-mid-Sept.

Capitola Begonia Festival. 5 mi E, in Capitola. Height of blooming season. Fishing derbies, parade. Sept.

Mountain Man Rendezvous. Re-enactment of an early day rendezvous with participants authentically costumed as trappers and traders as they gather to exchange products, swap tales and engage in old-time games. Thanksgiving wkend.

Seasonal Event

Shakespeare/Santa Cruz Festival. UCSC Campus. Presentation of Shakespearean and contemporary plays by professional actors; indoor and outdoor performances. Phone 831/459-2121. Thurs-Sun, mid-July-late Aug.

Motels

★★ **BEST WESTERN INN.** *7500 Old Dominion Ct (95003), 5 mi S on CA 1, exit Seacliff Beach, 1 blk E then left. 831/688-7300; FAX 408/685-3603; res: 800/367-2003.* E-mail info@seacliffinn.com; web www.seacliffinn.com. 140 rms, 2 story. Mid-Mar-mid-Oct: S, D $99-$149; each addl $10; suites $179-$239; under 18 free; higher rates: hols, special events; lower rates rest of yr. Crib free. TV; cable (premium). Heated pool; whirlpool, poolside serv. Complimentary continental bkfst (Mon-Fri). Complimentary coffee in rms. Restaurant 6:30 am-9 pm. Rm serv. Bar 11 am-midnight; entertainment. Ck-out noon. Meeting rms. Business servs avail. Bellhops. Refrigerator in suites. Balconies. Beach ¼ mi. Cr cds: A, C, D, DS, MC, V.

D SC

✓★ **CAROUSEL MOTEL.** *110 Riverside Ave (95060). 831/425-7090; FAX 408/423-4801; res: 800/214-7400.* Web www.beachboardwalk.com. 34 rms, 3 story. No A/C. Late Mar-early Sept: S, D $59-$159; under 16 free; vacation packages; higher rates: spring break, Easter, some hols; lower rates rest of yr. Crib $10. TV; cable. Complimentary continental bkfst. Restaurant nearby. Ck-out 11 am. Many refrigerators, microwaves. Balconies. Ocean nearby. Boardwalk view. Cr cds: A, C, D, DS, MC, V.

D SC

★★ **HOLIDAY INN EXPRESS.** *600 Riverside Ave (95060). 831/458-9660; FAX 831/426-8775; res: 800/527-3833.* Web www.holidayinnexsantacruz.com. 79 rms, 3 story, 9 suites. Mid-June-Sept: S, D $99-$138; each addl $10; suites $127-$250; under 19 free; higher rates wkends; lower rates rest of yr. Crib free. TV; cable. Pool; whirlpools. Complimentary continental bkfst. Ck-out 11 am. Meeting rm. Business servs avail. Private patios, balconies. Beach, boardwalk 4 blks. Cr cds: A, C, D, DS, JCB, MC, V.

D SC

★★ **SEA & SAND INN.** *201 W Cliff Dr (95060). 831/427-3400; FAX 831/427-3400.* Web www.beachboardwalk.com. 18 rms, 2 story, 2 kit. cottages. Memorial Day-Labor Day: S, D $119-$239; each addl $10; kit. cottages $229-$299; under 12 free; Sat (2-day min); lower rates rest of yr. Crib $10. TV; cable, VCR (movies $3). Complimentary continental bkfst; afternoon refreshments. Ck-out 11 am. Some in-rm whirlpools. On cliffs overlooking Monterey Bay. Ocean swimming, beach. Cr cds: A, C, D, DS, MC, V.

SC

Motor Hotel

★★ **WEST COAST SANTA CRUZ HOTEL.** *175 W Cliff Dr (95060), adj to boardwalk amusement park, exit S on Bay St from Hwy 1. 831/426-4330; FAX 831/427-2025; res: 800/426-0670.* 163 rms, 1-10 story. Mid-June-mid-Sept: S, D $179-$199; suites $249-$329; under 18 free; lower rates rest of yr. Crib free. TV; cable (premium). Heated pool; whirlpools, poolside serv. Coffee in rms. Restaurants 7 am-10 pm. Rm serv. Bar to midnight. Ck-out noon. Meeting rms. Business servs avail. Bellhops. Refrigerators. Private balconies. Overlooks beach. Cr cds: A, C, D, DS, MC, V.

D SC

Inns

★★★ **BABBLING BROOK INN.** *1025 Laurel St (95060). 831/427-2437; FAX 831/427-2457; res: 800/866-1131.* E-mail lodging@babblingbrookinn.com; web www.babblingbrookinn.com. 14 rms. S, D $145-$195; each addl $20. Adults preferred. TV; cable. Complimentary full bkfst buffet; afternoon refreshments. Ck-out 11:30 am, ck-in 3 pm. Many wood-burning stoves. Some in-rm whirlpools. Many balconies. Former gristmill & tannery. Country French decor. Garden walkways, waterfalls, avail for weddings. Boardwalk 7 blks. Totally nonsmoking. Cr cds: A, C, D, DS, MC, V.

D

★★ **BAYVIEW HOTEL.** *8041 Soquel Dr (95003), 5 mi S on CA 1, exit Seacliff/Aptos. 831/688-8654; FAX 408/688-5128; res: 800/422-9843.* E-mail lodging@bayviewhotel.com; web www.bayviewhotel.com. 11 rms, 7 with shower only, 3 story, 1 suite. No A/C. S, D $90-$160; each addl $20; suite $150; wkends, hols (2-day min). TV; cable. Complimentary contintental bkfst. Restaurant 11 am-10 pm. Rm serv. Ck-out 11:30, ck-in 3 pm. Luggage handling. Concierge serv. Built in 1878; antiques. Totally nonsmoking. Cr cds: A, C, MC, V.

SC

★★ **CHATEAU VICTORIAN.** *118 1st St (95060). 831/458-9458.* Web www.travelguides.com/bb/chateauvictorian. 7 rms, 2 story. No A/C. No rm phones. D $110-$140. Adults only. Complimentary bkfst, evening refreshments. Restaurant nearby. Ck-out noon, ck-in 3:30-6:30 pm. Victorian house; fireplaces. 1 blk to beach. Totally nonsmoking. Cr cds: C, MC, V.

★★★ **INN AT DEPOT HILL.** *250 Monterey Ave (95010), S via CA 1, Park Ave exit, left on Monterey Ave. 831/462-3376; FAX 831/462-3697; res: 800/572-2632.* E-mail lodging@innatdepothill.com; web www.innatdepothill.com. 12 rms, 2 story, 5 suites. Some A/C. S, D $195-$275; each addl $20; suites $210-$275. TV; cable, VCR (movies). Complimentary full bkfst; afternoon refreshments, complimentary evening wine and hors d'oeuvres, complimentary coffee in rms. 22 Restaurants nearby. Limited rm serv. Ck-out 11:30 am, ck-in 3 pm. Meeting rm. Business servs avail. In-rm modem link. Concierge serv. Health club privileges. Fireplaces; some in-rm whirlpools. Ocean 2 blks; swimming beach. Most rms w/private patios and hot tubs. Cr cds: A, C, DS, MC, V.

D

Restaurants

★★ **BITTERSWEET BISTRO.** *787 Rio Del Mar Blvd (95003), W on CA 1 exit Rio Del Mar. 408/662-9799.* E-mail vinolus@got.net; web www.bittersweetbistro.com. Hrs: 11 am-2 pm, 3-9 pm; Tues from 3 pm; Fri to 10 pm; Sat 3-10 pm; Sun brunch 11 am-2 pm. Closed Mon; also Jan 1, Dec 25. Res accepted. Contemporary Amer menu. Bar. A la carte entrees: bkfst, lunch $6-$14, dinner $12-$21. Sun brunch $6-$14. Child's meals. Specialties: halibut en papillote, goat cheese salad, chocolate trio. Parking. Outdoor dining. Bistro atmosphere. Totally nonsmoking. Cr cds: A, C, MC, V.

D

★★ **CAFE SPARROW.** *8042 Soquel Dr (95003), 5 mi S on CA 1, exit Seacliff Beach. 831/688-6238.* Hrs: 11 am-2 pm, 5:30-9 pm; Sun brunch 9 am-2 pm. Closed some major hols; also Halloween. Res accepted. French menu. Wine, beer. Semi-a la carte: lunch $7.95-$12.95, dinner $17-$22. Sun brunch $8-$15. Specializes in Country French cooking. Country French theme. Totally nonsmoking. Cr cds: C, MC, V.

★★★ **CHEZ RENEE.** *9051 Soquel Dr (95003), 8 mi E on CA 1 to Rio del Mar exit, then ¼ mi W on Soquel Dr. 831/688-5566.* Hrs: 11:30 am-2 pm, 5:30-10 pm. Closed Sun, Mon; Jan 1, Thanksgiving, Dec 25; also 1st wk Jan, last wk Oct. California French, Italian menu. Bar. Wine cellar. Semi-a la carte: lunch $6.95-$11.95, dinner $18.95-$25.95. Specializes in duck, lamb, fresh fish. Own pastries. Outdoor dining. French country atmosphere; antiques, Steuben glass. Totally nonsmoking. Cr cds: C, MC, V.

D

★★ **CROW'S NEST.** *2218 E Cliff Dr (95062). 831/476-4560.* E-mail crow@scruznet.com; web www.crowsnest-santacruz.com. Hrs: 11:30 am-2:30 pm, 5:30-9:30 pm; Sat 11 am-3 pm, 5-10 pm; Sun 11 am-3 pm, 5-9 pm. Closed Dec 25. Res accepted. Bar. A la carte entrees: lunch $6.95-$14.95, dinner $8.95-$17.95. Child's meals. Specializes in fresh seafood, steak. Salad bar. Entertainment. Outdoor dining. On beach, at yacht harbor; view of bay. Cr cds: A, C, D, DS, MC, V.

D

★★ **GILBERTS SEAFOOD GRILL.** *Municipal Wharf #25 (95060). 831/423-5200.* Hrs: 11:30 am-10 pm; Fri & Sat to 11 pm. Res accepted. Bar. Semi-a la carte: lunch $7.95-$14.95, dinner $7.95-$29.95. Child's meals. Specializes in fresh local fish, seafood, pasta. View of Monterey Bay and beach from wharf. Totally nonsmoking. Cr cds: A, C, D, DS, JCB, MC, V.

D

★★ **OSWALD'S.** *1547 E Pacific Ave (95060). 408/423-7427.* Web www.oswald.com. Hrs: 5:30-10 pm. Closed Thanksgiving, Dec 24 25. Res required Fri, Sat. French menu. Wine, beer. A la carte entrees: dinner $10-$20. Specializes in fish, vegetarian, beef. Parking. Outdoor dining. California bistro decor and atmosphere. Totally nonsmoking. Cr cds: A, C, D, MC, V.

★★★ **SHADOWBROOK.** *1750 Wharf Rd (95010), 4 mi S on CA 1, ½ mi S on 41st Ave, ½ mi E on Capitola Rd. 831/475-1511.* E-mail tedburke@shadowbrook-capitola.com; web shadowbrook-captiola.com. Hrs: 5:30-9 pm; Sat 4-10 pm; Sun 4-9 pm; Sun brunch 10 am-2:30 pm. Res accepted. Bar from 5 pm. Complete meals: dinner $13.95-$24.95. Sun brunch $7.95-$16.95. Child's meals. Specializes in seafood, prime rib. Own baking. Free parking. Small dining rm on rooftop. Garden stairway to restaurant; garden decor. Overlooks river. Cable car from parking lot to restaurant. Totally nonsmoking. Cr cds: A, C, D, DS, MC, V.

D

★★★ **THEO'S FRENCH RESTAURANT.** *3101 N Main St (95073), W on CA 1 Porter St/Bay Ave, N on Main St. 831/462-3657.* Hrs: 5:30-9:30 pm, closed Sun, Mon. Res accepted. California-French menu. Wine cellar. Semi-a la carte: dinner $14-$24. Specializes in duck, lamb, fresh seafood. Own baking. Outdoor dining, garden patio for receptions. French country decor. Organic garden. Uses locally grown produce. Cr cds: A, C, D, MC, V.

D

Santa Maria (H-2)

(See also Lompoc, San Luis Obispo, Solvang)

Pop 61,284 **Elev** 216 ft **Area Code** 805 **E-mail** smvcc@santamaria.com **Web** www.santamaria.com

Information Chamber of Commerce, 614 S Broadway, 93454; 805/925-2403 or 800/331-3779

A Ranger District office of the Los Padres National Forest (see KING CITY, SANTA BARBARA) is located in Santa Maria.

What to See and Do

Santa Maria Historical Museum. Early settler and Chumash artifacts. (Tues-Sat; closed major hols) 614 S Broadway. Phone 805/922-3130. **Free**

Annual Events

Elks Rodeo & Parade. Elks Event Center. 1st wkend June.

Santa Barbara County Fair. Santa Maria Fairgrounds. June-early July.

Motel

★★★ **BEST WESTERN BIG AMERICA.** *1725 N Broadway (93454). 805/922-5200; FAX 805/922-9865; res: 800/528-1234.* E-mail info@bigamerica.com; web www.bigamerica.com. 106 units, 2 story, 16 suites. S $55-$85; D $60-$90; suites $75-$130; under 18 free; wkly rates. Crib free. TV; cable (premium), VCR avail (movies). Heated pool; whirlpool. Complimentary continental bkfst. Restaurant 6 am-9 pm. Rm serv. Bar. Ck-out noon. Meeting rms. Business servs avail. Valet serv. Free airport, bus depot transportation. Refrigerators, wet bars. Cr cds: A, C, D, DS, MC, V.

D SC

Motor Hotel

★★★ **SANTA MARIA INN.** *801 S Broadway (93454). 805/928-7777; FAX 805/928-5690; res: 800/462-4276.* 166 rms, 2-6 story. S, D $89-$160; each addl $15; suites $150-$340; under 12 free; golf plan. Crib free. TV; cable, VCR avail (movies $4). Pool; whirlpool, poolside serv in season. Coffee in rms. Restaurant (see SANTA MARIA INN). Rm serv. Bar 10:30-2 am; entertainment. Ck-out noon. Business servs avail. Bellhops. Valet serv. Shopping arcade. Barber, beauty shop. Airport transportation. Pitch and putt course. Exercise equipt; sauna. Refrigerators; some bathrm phones, fireplaces. Private patios, balconies. 1917 inn; antique fountain, English antiques, stained glass. Cr cds: A, C, D, DS, JCB, MC, V.

D SC

Restaurant

★★★ **SANTA MARIA INN.** *(See Santa Maria Inn motor hotel) 805/928-7777.* Hrs: 6:30 am-10 pm; early-bird dinner 5-6:30 pm; Sun brunch 10:30 am-2 pm. Res accepted. Bar. Semi-a la carte: bkfst $5.95-$9.25, lunch $6.95-$9.95, dinner $10.95-$20.95. Sun brunch $16.95. Child's meals. Specializes in prime rib, fresh seafood, Santa Maria barbecue. Parking. Outdoor dining. Totally nonsmoking. Cr cds: A, C, D, DS, JCB, MC, V.

D SC

Santa Monica (J-3)

(See also Beverly Hills, Buena Park, Fullerton, Los Angeles, Malibu, Marina del Rey)

Founded 1875 **Pop** 86,905 **Elev** 101 ft **Area Code** 310 **Web** www.santamonica.com

Information Visitor Center, 1400 Ocean Ave, 90401; 310/393-7593

With its wide, white beaches, continual sunshine and casual ambience, Santa Monica is one of southern California's undiscovered beachside resorts. Located at the end of famed Wilshire Boulevard, Santa Monica is perhaps best known for its popular bay. Here the scenery of palm trees, beach and mountains has been popular for years in snapshots, movies and postcards.

What to See and Do

California Heritage Museum. Built along palisades in 1894. Moved to present site and restored. Houses changing history exhibits; contemporary art and photo gallery. (Wed-Sun; closed hols) 2612 Main St. Phone 310/392-8537. ¢

Museum of Flying. Historical and current aviation exhibits, models and memorabilia; Donald Douglas Library and Archives. Most aircraft on display are in fully operational condition. Special events, exhibitions. (Wed-Sun; closed hols) At Santa Monica Airport. Phone 310/392-8822. ¢¢¢

★ **Palisades Park.** Parks, paths and gardens on 26 acres overlooking the ocean. Senior recreation center (all yr). Ocean Ave from Colorado Ave to Adelaide Dr. Phone 310/458-8310. **Free**

Santa Monica Pier. Restaurants, shops; also antique carousel with 46 hand-carved horses housed in restored building (1916). On Ocean Ave at the foot of Colorado Ave. Phone 310/458-8900. **Free** Also here are

Pacific Park. Two-acre amusement park with 11 rides, including a 9-story Ferris wheel and roller coaster. (Summer, daily; winter, schedule varies) Phone 310/458-8900. **Free**

UCLA Ocean Discovery Center. Innovative, interactive aquarium, Wet Lab, Pier Tank. (Sat & Sun) Phone 310/393-6149. ¢¢

Santa Monica State Beach. Considered one of the best in Los Angeles area; 3.3 mi long; lifeguards, surfing, volleyball, bike path, play equipment, snack bars. Phone 310/458-8310. Parking ¢¢¢

Motel

✓★★ **COMFORT INN.** *2815 Santa Monica Blvd (90404). 310/828-5517; FAX 310/829-6084.* 108 rms, 3 story. June-Sept: S $69-$79; D $79-$89; each addl $10; under 18 free; lower rates rest of yr. Crib $10. TV, cable (premium). Heated pool. Complimentary coffee. Ck-out noon. Health club privileges. Refrigerators. Cr cds: A, C, D, DS, MC, V.

D SC

★ **TRAVELODGE.** *3102 Pico Blvd (90405). 310/450-5766; FAX 310/450-8843; res: 800/578-7878.* 85 rms, 6 with shower only, 2 story. Mid-May-Sept: S $79; D $89; each addl $6; under 12 free; wkly rates; lower rates rest of yr. Crib free. TV; cable (premium). Complimentary continental bkfst. Complimentary coffee in rms. Restaurant nearby. Ck-out 11 am. Business servs avail. Airport, RR station transportation. Many refrigerators; some microwaves. Picnic tables, grills. Cr cds: A, C, D, DS, JCB, MC, V.

D

Motor Hotels

★★ **BEST WESTERN.** *1920 Santa Monica Blvd (90404). 310/829-9100; FAX 310/829-9211; res: 800/528-1234.* E-mail gatewaysm@aol.com; web www.gatewayhotel.com. 122 rms, 4 story. Mid-June-mid-Sept: S $79; D $140; each addl $5; under 18 free; higher rates special events; lower rates rest of yr. Crib free. TV; cable. Restaurant 6:30 am-10 pm. Rm serv 7 am-9 pm. Ck-out noon. Meeting rms. Business servs avail. In-rm modem link. Bellhops. Valet serv. Exercise equipt. Cr cds: A, C, D, DS, MC, V.

D SC

★ **BEST WESTERN OCEAN VIEW HOTEL.** *1447 Ocean Ave (90401). 310/458-4888; FAX 310/458-0848; res: 800/528-1234; res: 800/452-4888.* Web www.travelweb.com. 69 rms, 4 story. Mid-June-mid-Sept: S, D $149-$199; each addl $10; under 18 free; 2-day min wkends; lower rates rest of yr. Crib free. Garage parking in/out $7. TV; cable (premium), VCR avail. Complimentary coffee in lobby. Restaurant adj 10 am-11 pm. Ck-out noon. Business servs avail. In-rm modem link. Bellhops. Valet serv. Concierge. Some refrigerators. Microwaves avail. Cr cds: A, C, D, DS, ER, JCB, MC, V.

D SC

Hotels

★★ **DOUBLETREE GUEST QUARTERS SUITES HOTEL.** *1707 4th St (90401), CA 1 to Lincoln Blvd. 310/395-3332; FAX 310/452-7399; res: 800/222-8733.* 253 suites, 8 story. July-Sept: S, D $175-$225; each addl $20; under 18 free; wkly rates; package plans; lower rates rest of yr. Crib free. Garage parking $12, valet $15. TV; cable (premium), VCR avail. Pool; whirlpool; poolside serv. Complimentary coffee in rms. Restaurant 6:30 am-10 pm. Bar 5 pm-12:30 am. Ck-out noon. Coin Indry. Convention facilities. Business center. In-rm modem link. Gift shop. Airport transportation. Exercise equipt; sauna. Refrigerators, minibars; microwaves avail. Some rms with ocean view. Cr cds: A, C, D, DS, JCB, MC, V.

D SC

★★ **FOUR POINTS SHERATON.** *530 W Pico Blvd (90405). 310/399-9344; FAX 310/399-2504; res: 800/465-4329; res: 800/495-7776.* 309 rms, 9 with shower only, 9 story. S $145-$185; D $165-$205; each addl $10; suites $350; under 12 free. Crib free. TV; cable (premium). 2 pools; whirlpools, poolside serv. Complimentary coffee in rms. Restaurant 6:30 am-11 pm. Ck-out noon. Coin Indry. Convention facilities. Business servs avail. In-rm modem link. Gift shop. Exercise equipt. Cr cds: A, C, D, DS, JCB, MC, V.

D SC

★ **GEORGIAN HOTEL.** *1415 Ocean Ave (90401). 310/395-9945; FAX 310/656-0904; res: 800/538-8147.* E-mail sales@georgianhotel.com; web www.georgianhotel.com. 84 rms, 8 story, 28 suites. July-Aug: S $175-$210; D $200-$235; each addl $25; suites $295-$350; family, wkly rates; pkg plans; lower rates rest of yr. Crib free. Pet accepted; $250. Valet parking $12. TV; cable (premium), VCR avail. Complimentary coffee in rms. Restaurant 6:30-10:30 am. Ck-out noon. Meeting rms. Business servs avail. In-rm modem link. Concierge. Health club privileges. Minibars. Opp ocean. Cr cds: A, C, D, JCB, MC, V.

D SC

★ **HOLIDAY INN.** *120 Colorado Ave (90401). 310/451-0676; FAX 310/393-7145; res: 800/465-4329.* 132 rms, 7 story. Apr-Oct: S $159-$189; D $174-$204; each addl $15; under 18 free; higher rates Rose Bowl, other special events; lower rates rest of yr. Crib free. Pet accepted; $50 deposit. Valet parking $6.60, in/out $6.60. TV; cable (premium), VCR avail (movies). Pool. Restaurant 6:30-11 am, 5-10 pm. Ck-out noon. Coin Indry. In-rm modem link. Concierge. Gift shop. Health club privileges. Some refrigerators. Cr cds: A, C, D, DS, JCB, MC, V.

D SC

★★★ **LOEWS SANTA MONICA BEACH HOTEL.** *1700 Ocean Ave (90401), west of downtown. 310/458-6700; FAX 310/458-6761; res: 800/23-LOEWS.* E-mail loewssantamonicabeach@loewshotels.com; web www.loweshotels.com. 345 rms, 8 story, 35 suites. S, D $290-$475; each addl $20; suites $575-$2,500; under 18 free. Valet parking $18; self-park $15.40. TV; cable (premium), VCR avail (movies). Indoor/outdoor pool; whirlpool, poolside serv. Supervised child's activities; ages 5-12. Crib free. Restaurants 6 am-10 pm (also see LAVANDE). Rm serv 24 hrs. Bar 10-1 am; entertainment. Ck-out noon. Convention facilities. Business center. In-rm modem link. Concierge. Gift shop. Barber, beauty shop. Tennis privileges. Golf privileges. Exercise rm; sauna, steam rm. Massage. Bicycle and roller skate rentals. Bathrm phones, minibars; some wet bars. Balconies. Atrium. Beach approx 50 yds. Cr cds: A, C, D, DS, JCB, MC, V.

D SC

★★★ **MIRAMAR SHERATON HOTEL.** *101 Wilshire Blvd (90401). 310/576-7777; FAX 310/458-7912; res: 800/325-3535.* Web www.sheraton.com. 302 rms, 10 story. S, D $280-$295; each addl $20; suites $365-$900; under 17 free; wkend rates. Crib free. TV; cable (premium), VCR avail (movies). Pool; whirlpool; poolside serv. Coffee in rms. Restaurants 6:30 am-11 pm. Rm serv 24 hrs. Bar; pianist. Ck-out noon. Meeting rms. Business servs avail. In-rm modem link. Concierge. Gift shop. Barber, beauty shop. Exercise rm; sauna. Massage. Bathrm phones, minibars. Beach opp. Cr cds: A, C, D, DS, ER, JCB, MC, V.

D SC

★★ **RADISSON HOTEL.** *1111 2nd St (90403). 310/394-5454; FAX 310/458-9776; res: 800/333-3333.* 213 rms, 18 story. June-Oct: S, D $179-$259; each addl $20; suite $450; under 17 free; lower rates rest of yr. Crib free. Valet parking $8.50, in/out $8.50. TV; cable, VCR avail (movies). Restaurant 6-2 am. Ck-out noon. Meeting rms. Business servs avail. In-rm modem link. Concierge. Gift shop. Barber, beauty shop. Exercise equipt. Minibars; some refrigerators, microwaves. Cr cds: A, C, D, DS, ER, JCB, MC, V.

D SC

★★ **SHANGRI-LA HOTEL.** *1301 Ocean Ave (90401). 310/394-2791; FAX 310/451-3351; res: 800/345-7829.* E-mail nanniluigi@aol.com; web www.shangrila-hotel.com. 55 units, 7 story, 47 kits. S, D $130-$255; each addl $15; suites $170-$470. Crib $15. TV; cable (premium). Complimentary continental bkfst; afternoon refreshments. Ck-out noon. Balconies. Large terrace, tropical grounds. Beach opp. Cr cds: A, C, D, DS, JCB, MC, V.

★★★ **SHUTTERS ON THE BEACH.** *1 Pico Blvd (95403). 310/458-0030; FAX 310/587-1789; res: 800/334-9000.* Web www.shuttersonthebeach.com. 196 rms in 2 bldgs, 7 story. S, D $325-$525; each addl $50; suites $750-$2,500; under 5 free; wkend plans. Valet parking $18. TV; cable (premium), VCR (movies). Pool; whirlpool, poolside serv. Restaurants 6:30 am-11 pm (also see 1 PICO). Rm serv 24 hrs. Bar 11-2 am. Ck-out noon. Meeting rms. Business center. In-rm modem link. Concierge. Gift shop. Exercise equipt; sauna, steam rm. Massage. Minibars; microwaves avail. Balconies. Oceanfront boardwalk. Named for distinctive sliding shutter doors of each guest rm. Cr cds: A, C, D, DS, JCB, MC, V.

D

Inns

★★ **CHANNEL ROAD INN.** *219 W Channel Rd (90402). 310/459-1920; FAX 310/454-9920.* E-mail channelinn@aol.com; web www.innaccess.com/cha. 14 rms, 3 story, 2 suites. S, D $125-$275; suites $245-$275. Crib free. TV; cable (premium), VCR avail (free movies). Complimentary full bkfst. Restaurants opp 7 am-11 pm. Ck-out noon, ck-in 3 pm. Business servs avail. In-rm modem link. Whirlpool. Bicycles. Colonial-revival house built in 1910; library, fireplace, antiques. 1 blk from beach, bike path. Cr cds: A, C, MC, V.

D

✓★ **VENICE BEACH HOUSE.** *15 30th Ave (90291). 310/823-1966; FAX 310/823-1842.* 9 units, 5 baths, 4 share bath, 2 story. Shared bath $85-$95; private bath $120-$165. TV; cable. Complimentary continental bkfst; afternoon refreshments. Ck-out 11 am, ck-in 2-8 pm. Some private patios, balconies. 1911 California Craftsman house. Venice beach ¼ blk. Totally nonsmoking. Cr cds: A, C, MC, V.

Restaurants

★★★ **1 PICO.** *(See Shutters on the Beach) 310/458-0030.* Web www.shuttersonthebeach.com. Hrs: 11:30 am-3 pm, 6-11 pm; Sun brunch 11 am-3 pm. Res accepted. Bar 12:30 pm-1:30 am. Wine list. A la carte entrees: lunch $11.75-$17.75, dinner $14.50-$29. Sun brunch $10.25-$17.50. Specializes in pasta, seafood. Valet parking. Floor to ceiling windows give view of ocean. Totally nonsmoking. Cr cds: A, C, D, DS, JCB, MC, V.

D

★★★ **72 MARKET ST. OYSTER BAR & GRILL.** *72 Market St (90291). 310/392-8720.* Web www.72marketst.com. Hrs: 11:30 am-2:30 pm, 6-10 pm; Fri to 11 pm; Sat 6-11 pm; Sun 5:30-9 pm. Res accepted. Bar. A la carte entrees: lunch $8-$12, dinner $15-$24. Specialties: tuna tartare, meat loaf, chili. Oyster bar. Own baking. Pianist. Valet parking. Two dining rms: high-tech; chic supper club. Celebrity haunt. Rotating art exhibit. Cr cds: A, C, D, JCB, MC, V.

D ♥

★★ **BOB BURNS.** *202 Wilshire Blvd (90401). 310/393-6777.* Hrs: 11:30 am-11 pm; Fri, Sat to midnight; Sun brunch to 3 pm. Closed Dec 25. Res accepted. Continental menu. Bar to midnight, Fri, Sat to 2 am. Semi-a la carte: lunch $8-$16, dinner $13-$29. Sun brunch $9.50-$15.95. Child's meals. Specializes in fresh fish, lamb chops, roast duckling. Jazz pianist. Valet parking. Fireplace. Cr cds: A, C, D, DS, MC, V.

D

★★ **BORDER GRILL.** *1445 4th St (90401). 310/451-1655.* E-mail mail@bordergrill.com; web www.bordergrill.com. Hrs: noon-3 pm, 5:30-10 pm; Mon from 5:30 pm. Closed Jan 1, Thanksgiving, Dec 25. Res accepted. Mexican menu. Bar. A la carte entrees: lunch $8-$12, dinner $10-$22. Own desserts. 2-story murals. Cr cds: A, C, DS, MC, V.

★ **BROADWAY BAR & GRILL.** *1460 3rd St Promenade (90401). 310/393-4211.* Hrs: 11:30 am-10:30 pm; wkends to midnight; Sun brunch 11:30 am-3 pm. Res accepted. Bar Fri, Sat to 2 am. A la carte entrees: lunch $7.95-$12.95, dinner $8.95-$18.95. Sun brunch $7.95-$13.95. Specializes in pork chops, steak, fresh fish. Entertainment Tues evenings. Outdoor dining. Antique oak bar. Cr cds: A, C, DS, MC, V.

✓★ **BROADWAY DELI.** *1457 3rd St Promenade (90401). 310/451-0616.* Hrs: 7 am-midnight; Fri to 1 am; Sat 8-1 am; Sun 8 am-midnight. International menu. Bar. A la carte entrees: bkfst $5-$8, lunch $6-$12, dinner $12-$16. Specialties: rotisserie-cooked herb chicken, creme brulee, fruit cobbler. Valet parking. Contemporary decor. Gourmet market on premises. Cr cds: A, C, DS, MC, V.

★★ **CHINOIS ON MAIN.** *2709 Main St (90405). 310/392-3037.* Hrs: 6-10:30 pm; Wed-Fri 11:30 am-2 pm; Sun 5:30-10 pm. Closed some major hols. Res required. Chinese, French menu. Bar. A la carte entrees: lunch $9.50-$18.50, dinner $19.50-$29.50. Specialties: sizzling catfish, curried oysters. Valet parking. Cr cds: A, C, D, DS, MC, V.

D

★★ **DRAGO RESTAURANT.** *2628 Wilshire Blvd (90403), I-405 exit Wilshire Blvd W. 310/828-1585.* E-mail drago@gte.net. Cuisine: Italian. Hrs: 11:30 am-3 pm, 5:30-11 pm. Closed some major hols. Res accepted; required Thurs-Sat (dinner). Italian menu. Bar. A la carte entrees: lunch, dinner $9-$24. Specialties: loin of venison with red wine & cherries, Sicilian swordfish with caponata. Valet parking. Cr cds: A, C, D, DS, MC, V.

D

✓★★ **FISH COMPANY.** *174 Kinney St (90405). 310/392-8366.* Hrs: 11:30 am-10 pm; Fri & Sat to 11 pm. Closed Thanksgiving, Dec 25. Res accepted. Bar. Semi-a la carte: lunch $7-$10, dinner $10-$17. Child's meals. Specializes in fresh fish, Alaskan king crab legs, oyster bar. Sushi bar. Patio dining. In restored railroad warehouse (ca 1910). Nautical decor; large salt water aquarium. Cr cds: A, C, D, MC, V.

D

★★★ **JIRAFFE.** *502 Santa Monica Blvd (90401). 310/917-6671.* French, American menu. Specializes in chicken, fish, seasonal game. Valet parking. Hrs: noon-2 pm, 6-10 pm; Fri, Sat 6-11 pm; Sun 5:30-9 pm. Closed Mon; most major hols. Res required. Wine cellar. A la carte entrees: lunch $7-$14, dinner $17-$26. Totally nonsmoking. Cr cds: A, C, D, MC, V.

D

✓★★ **JOES RESTAURANT.** *1023 Abbot Kinney Blvd (90291), S on Main St. 310/399-5811.* E-mail joeslp@aol.com. Hrs: 11 am-3 pm, 6-11 pm. Closed Mon; Jan 1, Dec 25. Res accepted. Wine, beer. A la carte entrees: lunch $9-$11, dinner $15-$18. Specialties: grilled salmon, chicken ravioli with tomato coulis. Own pastas, pastries. Patio dining. Contemporary artwork. Cr cds: A, C, MC, V.

★★★ **KNOLL'S BLACK FOREST INN.** *2454 Wilshire Blvd (90403). 310/395-2212.* Web www.ladining.com/knollsblackforest. Hrs: 11:30 am-2:30 pm, 5-10:30 pm; Sat & Sun from 5 pm. Closed Mon; Dec 25. Res accepted. German, continental menu. Bar. Wine cellar. Semi-a la carte: lunch $8.50-$15, dinner $11.50-$23.50. Prix fixe $26.50. Specializes in venison, fresh fish, Wienerschnitzel. Valet parking. Patio dining. Casual atmosphere in elegant surroundings. Family-owned. Cr cds: A, C, D, DS, MC, V.

D

★★★ **LAVANDE.** *(See Loews Santa Monica Beach Hotel) 310/576-3181.* E-mail loewssantamonicabeach@loewshotels; web www.loweshotels.com. Hrs: 11 am-2:30 pm, 5:30-10 pm; Sun (brunch) 10:30 am-2:30 pm. Res accepted. French menu. Bar 11-1 am. A la carte entrees: lunch $12-$16, dinner $19-$27. Prix fixe: lunch $19, dinner $55. Sun brunch $41. Child's meals. Specialties: veal daube, fish soup, vacherin glace with lavender ice cream. Jazz. Valet parking. Outdoor dining. View of ocean. Totally nonsmoking. Cr cds: A, C, D, DS, ER, JCB, MC, V.

D

★★★ **MICHAEL'S.** *1147 3rd St (90403). 310/451-0843.* Hrs: 11:30 am-2:30 pm; 5:30-10:30 pm. Closed Sun, Mon; most major hols. Res accepted. French, Amer menu. Bar. Wine cellar. A la carte entrees: lunch $16.50-$19.75, dinner $19.50-$29.95. Prix fixe: lunch $16.50, dinner $26.50. Serv charge 15%. Specializes in fresh fish, seafood, fine meats. Own pastries. Valet parking. Outdoor, private dining with fireplace. Contemporary decor; modern art collection. Garden. Cr cds: A, C, D, MC, V.

D

★★★ **ROCKENWAGNER.** *2435 Main St (90405). 310/399-6504.* Hans Rockenwagner's cutting-edge California cooking seem at home in a building designed by Frank Gehry. Drawing on his German background, his French training, and his West Coast home, his seasonal cooking is exciting and delicious.Specialties: crab souffle; napoleon of salmon, potatoes, tomatoes and spinach. Hrs: 11:30 am-2:30 pm, 6-9:45 pm; Mon from 6 pm; Sat 5:30-10:30 pm; Sun 5:30-9:30 pm; Sat, Sun brunch 9 am-2:30 pm. Closed Dec 25. Res accepted. Serv bar. A la carte entrees: lunch $8.50-$12.50, dinner $17.50-$23. Sat, Sun brunch $7.50-$12.50. Valet parking. Outdoor dining. Modern decor. Totally nonsmoking. Cr cds: A, C, D, MC, V.

D

✓★★ **TEASERS.** *1351 3rd St Promenade (90401). 310/394-8728.* Hrs: 11:30 am-midnight; Fri-Sun to 1 am; early-bird dinner 4:30-6 pm. Closed Thanksgiving, Dec 25. Res accepted. Bar. Semi-a la carte: lunch $6.50-$9, dinner $6.50-$14.95. Child's meals. Specialties: southwest chicken platter, Alfredo pasta, sun-pot roast. Own breads. Entertainment Tues, Wed, Fri-Sun. Sports bar. Casual atmosphere. Cr cds: A, C, D, DS, MC, V.

D ♥

★★★★ **VALENTINO.** *3115 Pico Blvd (90405). 310/829-4313.* Piero Selvaggio, the charming owner of this wonderful Italian restaurant, welcomes each guest in person. The elegance of the modern California design is matched by the superb traditional and contemporary food and the award-winning wine list. The close quarters create a congenial atmosphere. Hrs: 5:30-11:30 pm; Fri also noon-3 pm. Closed Sun; most major hols. Res accepted. Contemporary Italian menu. Bar. Wine list. A la carte entrees: dinner $20-$29.50. Prix fixe: dinner $65. Own baking, pasta. Valet parking. Cr cds: A, C, D, MC, V.

D

★★ **WOLFGANG PUCK CAFE.** *1323 Montana Ave (90403), Hwy 10 exit Lincoln, E at Montana Ave. 310/393-0290.* Hrs: 11:30 am-10 pm; Fri, Sat to 11 pm; Sun to 9:30 pm. Closed Nov 26, Dec 25. Res accepted. Bar. A la carte entrees: lunch, dinner $8.50-$18.95. Child's meals. Specialties: chinois chicken salad, smoked salmon, wild mushroom tortellini. Modern decor. Totally nonsmoking. Cr cds: A, C, D, MC, V.

D

Santa Nella (F-2)

Pop summer (est) 500 **Area Code** 209 **Zip** 95322

Motels

★★ **BEST WESTERN ANDERSEN'S INN.** *12367 S Hwy 33 (95322), at jct I-5, CA 33. 209/826-5534; FAX 209/826-4353; res: 800/528-1234.* 94 rms, 2 story. S $61; D $72; each addl $7; under 18 free. Crib free. Pet accepted, some restrictions. TV; cable (premium). Heated pool. Complimentary continental bkfst. Restaurant adj 7 am-10 pm. Ck-out 11 am. Private patios, balconies. Cr cds: A, C, D, DS, MC, V.

D SC

✓★ **RAMADA INN MISSION DE ORO.** *13070 S CA 33 (65322), jct I-5. 209/826-4444; FAX 209/826-8071; res: 800/546-5697.* 159 rms, 2 story. S $39.95-$59.95; D $49.95-$64.95; each addl $10; under 13 free. Pet accepted; $10. TV; cable (premium). Heated pool; whirlpool. Playground. Restaurant 6:30 am-10 pm. Rm serv. Bar 2 pm-2 am. Ck-out noon. Coin Indry. Meeting rms. Sundries. Some private patios, balconies. Spanish-style mission structure. Cr cds: A, C, D, DS, JCB, MC, V.

D SC

Restaurant

★ **PEA SOUP ANDERSEN'S.** *12411 S CA 33 (95322), off jct I-5 & CA 33. 209/826-1685.* Hrs: 7 am-10 pm; Fri-Sun to 11 pm; Sun brunch 10 am-2 pm. Res accepted. Bar. Semi-a la carte: bkfst $3.45-$9.50, lunch, dinner $7-$16. Sun brunch $9.95. Child's meals. Specializes in pea soup, salads, sandwiches. Gift and wine shop. Danish decor, windmill, heraldic flags. Cr cds: A, C, D, DS, MC, V.

D

Santa Rosa (D-2)

(See also Calistoga, Healdsburg, Petaluma, Sonoma)

Settled 1829 **Pop** 113,313 **Elev** 167 ft **Area Code** 707 **E-mail** tour@visitsonoma.com **Web** www.visitsonoma.com

Information Sonoma County Convention and Visitors Bureau, 2300 County Center Dr, Suite B260, 95403; 707/565-2146 or 800/5-SONOMA

Surrounded by vineyards and mountains, the county seat of Sonoma County is within minutes of more than 150 wineries. The rich soil and even climate of the Sonoma Valley lured famed horticulturist Luther Burbank here to develop innumerable new and better plants. Many farm and ranch products originate from the area today.

What to See and Do

Luther Burbank Home & Gardens. Features work of the famous horticulturist who lived and worked in Santa Rosa. Site includes greenhouse, gardens, carriage house exhibits. Gift shop. Home tours (Apr-Oct, Wed-Sun). Gardens (daily, all yr; free). Santa Rosa & Sonoma Aves. Phone 707/524-5445. Home tours ¢

Snoopy's Gallery. Houses a museum of Charles Schulz's original drawings of the *Peanuts* characters; awards and trophies. Gift shop. (Daily; closed some hols) 1665 W Steele Ln. Phone 707/546-3385. **Free**

Sonoma County Museum. Regional history and art museum of Sonoma County and northern California. Changing exhibits. Guided tours (by appt). Special events throughout the yr. (Wed-Sun; closed hols) 425 7th St. Phone 707/579-1500. ¢

Annual Events

Luther Burbank Rose Festival. 3 days of art and flower shows, parade. Mid-May.

Sonoma County Fair. Horse racing daily exc Sun, exhibits, stock shows, rodeos, entertainment. Phone 707/545-4200. Late July-early Aug.

Motels

★★ **BEST WESTERN GARDEN INN.** *1500 Santa Rosa Ave (95404), off US 101. 707/546-4031; FAX 707/526-4903; res: 800/929-2771.* 78 rms. June-Oct: S, D $69-$89; suites $140-$150; each addl $6; under 12 free; lower rates rest of yr. Crib free. Pet accepted, some restrictions; $10. TV; cable (premium). 2 pools. Coffee in rms. Restaurant 6:30-11 am. Coin Indry. Business servs avail. Health club privileges. Some refrigerators. Some patios. Cr cds: A, C, D, DS, MC, V.

D SC

★ **LOS ROBLES LODGE.** *1985 Cleveland Ave (95401). 707/545-6330; FAX 707/575-5826; res: 800/255-6330.* 104 units, 2 story. May-Oct: S $75-$90; D $85-$105; each addl $10; under 16 free; lower rates rest of yr. Crib free. Pet accepted, some restrictions. TV; cable, VCR avail. Heated pool; wading pool, whirlpool, poolside serv. Complimentary coffee in rms. Restaurant 6 am-10 pm. Rm serv. Bar 11 am-midnight; entertainment. Ck-out noon. Coin Indry. Meeting rms. Business servs avail.

In-rm modem link. Valet serv. Exercise equipt. Refrigerators; microwaves avail. Private patios, balconies; many overlook pool. Cr cds: A, C, D, DS, JCB, MC, V.

D SC

✓★ **SUPER 8 MOTEL.** *2632 N Cleveland Ave (95403). 707/542-5544; FAX 707/542-9738; res: 800/800-8000.* 100 rms, 3 story. Apr-Oct: S $50-$60; D $54-$65; suites $85-$90; under 12 free; lower rates rest of yr. Crib free. TV; cable. Pool. Restaurant 6 am-10 pm. Ck-out 11 am. Business servs avail. Health club privileges. Microwaves avail. Cr cds: A, C, D, DS, MC, V.

D SC

Motor Hotels

★★★ **FLAMINGO RESORT HOTEL.** *2777 4th St (95405). 707/545-8530; FAX 707/528-1404; res: 800/848-8300.* E-mail info@flamingoresort.com; web www.flamingoresort.com. 170 rms, 2 story. Apr-Oct: S, D $99-$149; each addl $10; suites $149-$199; under 12 free (up to 2); monthly rates; lower rates rest of yr. Crib free. TV; cable (premium), VCR avail. Pool; wading pool, whirlpool, poolside serv. Restaurant 6:30 am-10 pm. Rm serv. Bar. Ck-out 11 am. Meeting rms. Business center. In-rm modem link. Beauty shop. 5 tennis courts. Golf privileges. Exercise rm; steam rm, sauna. Lawn games. Refrigerators. Microwaves avail. Balconies. Gardens. Totally nonsmoking. Cr cds: A, C, D, MC, V.

D SC

★★★ **HILTON SONOMA COUNTY.** *3555 Round Barn Blvd (95403), US 101 exit at Mendocino Ave. 707/523-7555; FAX 707/545-2807; res: 800/445-8667.* Web www.hilton.com. 246 rms, 3 story. S $149; D $159; each addl $15; suites $250-$300; under 18 free. Crib free. TV; cable (premium). Pool; whirlpool. Coffee in rms. Restaurant 6:30 am-10 pm. Rm serv. Bar 2:30 pm-1:30 am. Ck-out noon. Valet serv. Tennis privileges. 18-hole golf privileges, pro, greens fee $45-$70. Exercise equipt. Health club privileges. Bathrm phones; some refrigerators; microwaves avail. Cr cds: A, C, D, DS, ER, JCB, MC, V.

D SC

★★★ **VINTNERS INN.** *4350 Barnes Rd (95403). 707/575-7350; FAX 707/575-1426; res: 800/421-2584.* Web www.vintnersinn.com. 44 rms, 2 story. S, D $148-$225; each addl $20; under 6 free. Crib $6. TV; VCR avail (movies). Complimentary continental bkfst. Restaurant (see JOHN ASH & CO). Rm serv. Bar. Ck-out noon. Meeting rms. Business servs avail. In-rm modem link. Valet serv. Bellhops. Concierge. Tennis privileges. Golf privileges, greens fee $32-$55 (incl cart), pro. Whirlpool. Health club privileges. Refrigerators; many fireplaces. Private patios, balconies. Views of vineyards, courtyard with fountain. Cr cds: A, C, D, MC, V.

D

Hotels

★★★ **FOUNTAINGROVE INN.** *101 Fountain Grove Pkwy (95403), exit US 101 at Mendocino Ave. 707/578-6101; FAX 707/544-3126; res: 800/222-6101.* E-mail fgi@FountaingroveInn.com; web www.FountaingroveInn.com. 126 units, 2 story. S, D $109-$159; each addl $10; suites $165-$275; under 13 free. Crib free. TV; cable, VCR avail. Heated pool; whirlpool, poolside serv. Complimentary bkfst buffet. Restaurant (see EQUUS). Rm serv from 6 am. Entertainment. Ck-out noon. Meeting rms. Business center. In-rm modem link. Valet serv. Sundries. Free local airport, bus depot transportation. Tennis privileges. 18-hole golf privileges, greens fee $75-$110. Health club privileges. Refrigerators. Redwood sculpture, waterfall in lobby. Equestrian theme. Cr cds: A, C, D, DS, JCB, MC, V.

D SC

★★ **HOTEL LA ROSE.** *308 Wilson St (95401). 707/579-3200; FAX 707/579-3247; res: 800/527-6738.* E-mail concierge@hotellarose.com; web www.hotellarose.com. 49 rms, 4 story, 11 suites. May-Oct: S $139-$159; D $154-$174; each addl $15; suites $219; lower rates rest of yr. Crib $10. TV; cable, VCR avail. Complimentary bkfst. Restaurant (see JOSEF'S). Rm serv 24 hrs. Bar. Ck-out noon. Lndry facilities. Meeting rms. Business center. In-rm modem link. Health club privileges. Microwaves avail. In historic Railroad Square. Cr cds: A, C, D, DS, MC, V.

D

Inns

★★★ **GABLES INN.** *4257 Petaluma Hill Rd (95404). 707/585-7777.* Web www.thegablesinn.com. 3 rms, 4 suites, 1 cottage. No rm phones. S, D $135; each addl $25; suites $135-$225. Complimentary full bkfst. Ck-out 11 am, ck-in 3-6 pm. Picnic tables. House of 15 gables in Gothic-revival style (1877) with unusual keyhole window in each gable. Interior boasts 12-ft ceilings, Italian marble fireplaces and mahogany spiral staircase. Antique furnishings & fixtures. Whirlpool in cottage. Totally nonsmoking. Cr cds: A, C, DS, MC, V.

D

★★★ **KENWOOD.** *10400 Sonoma Hwy (95452), 9 mi SE on CA 12. 707/833-1293; FAX 707/833-1247; res: 800/353-6966.* Web www.sterba.com/kenwood/inn. 12 rms, 2 story. No rm phones. Apr-Oct: S, D $325-$350; each addl $35; suite $425; spa plans; 2-day min wkends; lower rates rest of yr. Adults only. Pool; whirlpool. Sauna. Complimentary full bkfst. Restaurant nearby. Ck-out 11 am, ck-in 3 pm. Luggage handling. Concierge serv. Business servs avail. Spa. Balconies. Totally nonsmoking. Cr cds: A, C, D, MC, V.

D

Restaurants

★★ **CA BIANCA ITALIAN RESTAURANT.** *835 2nd St (95404). 707/542-5800.* Hrs: 11 am-2:30 pm, 5-10 pm; Italian menu. Wine, beer. A la carte entrees: lunch $7-$15, dinner $9-$15. Specializes in homemade bread and pasta. Outdoor dining. In Victorian house built 1876. Cr cds: A, C, MC, V.

D

✓★ **CAFE CITTI.** *9049 Sonoma Hwy (95452), Approx 8 mi S on CA 12. 707/833-2690.* Hrs: 11 am-3:30 pm, 5-9 pm ; Fri, Sat to 9:30 pm. Closed some major hols. Italian menu. Wine, beer. A la carte entrees: lunch $5-$12, dinner $9-$16. Specialties: rotisserie chicken, homemade pasta, dessert. Parking. Outdoor dining. Totally nonsmoking. Cr cds: C, MC, V.

D

★★ **CAFE LOLO.** *620 5th St (95404). 707/576-7822.* Hrs: 11:30 am-2 pm, 5:30-10 pm; Sat from 5:30 pm. Closed Sun; most major hols. Res accepted. Continental menu. Wine, beer. A la carte entrees: lunch $6.95-$8.95, dinner $8.95-$16.95. Child's meals. Totally nonsmoking. Cr cds: A, C, D, MC, V.

D

★★ **CRICKLEWOOD.** *4618 Old Redwood Hwy (95403). 707/527-7768.* Hrs: 11:30 am-2:30 pm, 5-9:30 pm; Fri to 10 pm; Sat, Sun 5-10 pm. Closed Easter, Thanksgiving, Dec 25. Bar to 10 pm. Semi-a la carte: lunch $4.95-$7.95, dinner $8.95-$20. Specializes in prime rib, steak, seafood. Salad bar. Parking. Outdoor dining. Cr cds: A, C, MC, V.

★★★ **EQUUS.** *(See Fountaingrove Inn) 707/578-0149.* E-mail fgi@wco.com; web www.FountaingroveInn.com. Hrs: 11:30 am-2:30 pm, 5:30-9:30 pm; Fri to 10 pm; Sat 5:30-10 pm; Sun brunch 10 am-2 pm. Res accepted. Wine country cuisine. Bar. Wine list. Semi-a la carte: lunch $7.95-$11.95, dinner $15.95-$25. Specializes in dishes made from local meats & produce. Pianist wkends. Parking. Elegant dining; equine mural and original oils. Totally nonsmoking. Cr cds: A, C, D, DS, JCB, MC, V.

D

✓★★ **FABIANI RESTAURANT.** *75 Montgomery Dr (95404). 707/579-2682.* Hrs: 11 am-2 pm, 5-10 pm; Sat from 5 pm. Closed Sun; Jan 1, Thanksgiving, Dec 25. Res accepted. Italian menu. Wine, beer. A la carte entrees: lunch $6.50-$13, dinner $7.50-$14.50. Specializes in pasta, seafood. Parking. Patio dining. Totally nonsmoking. Cr cds: C, MC, V.

D

✓★★ **GARY CHU'S.** *611 5th St (95404). 707/526-5840.* Web www.sterba.com/sro/garychu. Hrs: 11:30 am-9:30 pm. Closed Mon; July 4, Thanksgiving, Dec 25. Chinese menu. Wine, beer. A la carte entrees: lunch $6.75-$7.25, dinner $7.50-$10.95. Specialties: orange-peel beef, walnut prawns, sweet basil chicken. Chinese decor. Totally nonsmoking. Cr cds: A, C, D, DS, MC, V.

D

★★★ **JOHN ASH & CO.** *(See Vintners Inn) 707/527-7687.* Web www.johnashco.com. Hrs: 11:30 am-2 pm, 5:30-9:30 pm; Mon from 5:30 pm; Fri, Sat to 10 pm; Sun from 10:30 am. Res accepted. Bar. Wine cellar. A la carte entrees: lunch $9.95-$15.95, dinner $15.95-$26.95. Sun brunch $9.95-$15.95. Specializes in wine country cuisine. Parking. Outdoor dining. View of vineyards. Totally nonsmoking. Cr cds: A, C, MC, V.

D

★★ **JOSEF'S.** *(See Hotel La Rose) 707/571-8664.* E-mail http://www.josefs.com. Hrs: 11:30 am-2 pm, 5:30-9 pm; Mon from 5:30 pm; Fri, Sat to 9:30 pm. Closed Sun; some major hols. Res accepted. Continental menu. Bar. Semi-a la carte: lunch $8.50-$12.50, dinner $14.50-$22. Specializes in fresh fish, veal, spaetzle. Patio dining. Intimate, European-style restaurant with mahogany bar. Totally nonsmoking. Cr cds: A, C, MC, V.

D

★★ **KENWOOD RESTAURANT & BAR.** *9900 Sonoma Hwy (95452), 9 mi SE on CA 12. 707/833-6326.* Hrs: 11:30 am-9 pm. Closed Mon, Tues; Jan 1, Thanksgiving, Dec 25. Res accepted. Continental menu. Bar. A la carte entrees: lunch, dinner $4.75-$25. Specializes in California cuisine with French influence. Parking. Outdoor dining. Extensive Sonoma Valley wine selection. Totally nonsmoking. Cr cds: C, MC, V.

D

✓★★ **LA GARE.** *208 Wilson St (95401), at Railroad Square. 707/528-4355.* Hrs: 5:30-10 pm; Fri, Sat from 5 pm; Sun 5-9 pm. Closed Mon, Tues; Jan 1, Thanksgiving, Dec 25. Res accepted. French, Continental menu. Semi-a la carte: dinner $11.25-$18.95. Child's meals. Specializes in baked salmon, beef Wellington. Totally nonsmoking. Cr cds: A, C, D, DS, MC, V.

D

★★★ **LISA HEMENWAY'S.** *714 Village Court Mall (95405), in Montgomery Village. 707/526-5111.* Web www.sterba.com. Hrs: 11:30 am-2:30 pm, 5:30-9:30 pm; Sun brunch 11 am-2:30 pm. Closed Jan 1, Dec 25. Res accepted. Semi-a la carte: lunch $7.95-$13.95, dinner $15.95-$23. Sun brunch $6.95-$16.95. Specializes in Sonoma County cuisine, seafood, pasta. Outdoor dining. Totally nonsmoking. Cr cds: A, C, D, DS, MC, V.

D

★★ **MARK WEST LODGE.** *2520 Mark West Springs Rd (95404). 707/546-2592.* Hrs: 5-10 pm; Sun 10:30 am-9 pm; Sun brunch to 2:30 pm. Closed Mon; Jan 1, Dec 25; also Tues Oct-May. Res accepted; required hols. European cuisine. Bar. A la carte entrees: dinner $14.95-$24.75. Sun brunch buffet $13.95. Jazz pianist. Outdoor dining. In former stagecoach stop. Cr cds: A, C, MC, V.

D

✓★★ **MISTRAL.** *1229 N Dutton Ave (95401). 707/578-4511.* E-mail mistral@sonic.net; web www.sterba.com/sro/mistral. Hrs: 11:30 am-9:30 pm; Sat 5:30-10 pm; Sun 5-9 pm. Closed most major hols. Res accepted. Mediterranean menu. Beer. Wine list. A la carte entrees: lunch $7.75-$11.75, dinner $8.75-$15.75. Child's meals. Specializes in grilled seafood, homemade pasta, fresh local produce. Outdoor dining on brick terrace with stone fountain. Totally nonsmoking. Cr cds: A, C, D, DS, JCB, MC, V.

D

★★★ **MIXX-AN AMERICAN BISTRO.** *135 4th St (95401). 707/573-1344.* Hrs: 11:30 am-2 pm, 5:30-9:30 pm; Fri to 10:30 pm; Sat from 5:30 pm. Closed Sun, Dec 25. Res accepted. Bar from 5 pm. Wine list. Semi-a la carte: lunch $4-$19, dinner $3.95-$25. Child's meals. Specializes in fresh fish, local lamb, pasta. Own desserts. Art deco decor. Totally nonsmoking. Cr cds: A, C, D, MC, V.

D ♥

✓★ **OLD MEXICO EAST.** *4501 Montgomery Dr (95409). 707/539-2599.* Hrs: 11 am-10 pm; Fri, Sat to 11 pm; Sun to 9 pm. Res accepted. Mexican, Amer menu. Bar to 2 am. Semi-a la carte: lunch $5, dinner $6.50-$14. Child's meals. Specialties: prawns rancheros, chimichangas, quesadillas. Parking. Outdoor dining. Family-owned. Cr cds: A, C, D, DS, MC, V.

D

★★ **RUSSIAN RIVER VINEYARDS.** *5700 Gravenstein Hwy (95436), 8 mi W on Guerneville Rd, 1 mi N on CA 116. 707/887-1562.* E-mail alibou@ix.netcom.com. Hrs: 11:30 am-2:30 pm, 5:30-9:30 pm; Sun brunch 10:30 am-2:30 pm; off-season days vary. Res accepted. No A/C. California, Greek menu. Complete meals: lunch $7.50-$10.50, dinner $10-$20. Sun brunch $8-$10.50. Child's meals. Specializes in Greek dishes, seafood. Entertainment. Parking. Outdoor dining. Own herb garden. Garden area with many native plants. Family-operated winery and restaurant. Totally nonsmoking. Cr cds: A, C, D, DS, MC, V.

★★ **WILLOWSIDE CAFE.** *3535 Guerneville Rd (95401). 707/523-4814.* E-mail mikehale@ap.net. Hrs: 5:30-9 pm. Closed Mon, Tues; also 3 wks Jan. Res accepted. Wine, beer. A la carte entrees: dinner $11.95-$17.95. Parking. Eclectic decor. Totally nonsmoking. Cr cds: C, MC, V.

D

Saratoga
(F-4 see San Francisco map)

(See also Palo Alto, Redwood City, San Jose, Santa Clara, Sunnyvale)

Pop 28,061 **Elev** 455 ft **Area Code** 408 **Zip** 95070 **Web** www.saratoga-ca.com

Information Chamber of Commerce, 20460 Saratoga-Los Gatos Rd; 408/867-0753

An early California lumber town nestled in the lush, redwood-covered foothills of the Santa Cruz Mountains, Saratoga was named after Saratoga, New York, when mineral springs were found nearby. Located just 26 miles east of the Pacific Coast, this quaint town offers many restaurants and cultural activities in the tranquillity of the romantic Santa Clara Valley. Visitors enjoy strolling through the village Main Street with its historic homes and intriguing shops.

What to See and Do

Big Basin Redwoods State Park (see). 18 mi W on CA 9.

Hakone Gardens. Japanese gardens, pond, bridge, Japanese-style houses, waterfall, picnic area. (Daily; closed legal hols) 21000 Big Basin Way. Phone 408/741-4994. ¢¢

Villa Montalvo (1912). Mediterranean-style summer house of Senator James D. Phelan. Now a cultural center with art galleries, concerts, plays, lectures, poetry readings, artists in residence. Formal gardens with hiking trails, arboretum, outdoor amphitheater and Carriage House Theatre. Grounds (daily; free). Galleries (Thurs & Fri, afternoons, also Sat & Sun;

closed Jan 1, Thanksgiving, Dec 25). 15400 Montalvo Rd, ½ mi S, just off CA 9. Phone 408/961-9800. **Free**

Seasonal Event

Villa Montalvo Performing Arts. Winter & summer series. Phone 408/961-9898. Jan-Oct.

Inn

★★★ **THE INN AT SARATOGA.** *20645 4th St (95070), downtown. 408/867-5020; FAX 408/741-0981; res: 800/338-5020.* 45 rms, 5 story, 4 suites. S, D $175-$195; suites $435-$475; under 18 free. Crib free. TV; cable (premium), VCR (free movies). Complimentary continental bkfst; afternoon refreshments. Restaurants nearby. Ck-out noon, ck-in 3 pm. Meeting rms. Business servs avail. In-rm modem link. Valet serv. Concierge. Bathrm phones, refrigerators. Balconies. Patio. All rms are oversized, each overlooking Saratoga Creek and a wooded park. Totally nonsmoking. Cr cds: A, C, D, MC, V.

D SC

Restaurants

★★ **BELLA SARATOGA.** *14503 Big Basin Way (95070). 408/868-9774.* Web www.saratoga-ca.com/bella. Hrs: 11:30 am-8:30 pm; Wed, Thurs to 9:30 pm; Fri to 10 pm; Sat 10 am-10 pm; Sat brunch 10 am-1 pm; Sun brunch 10 am-3 pm. Closed Thanksgiving, Dec 25. Res accepted. Italian menu. Bar. Semi-a la carte: lunch $6.95-$17.95, dinner $10.95-$20.95. Sat, Sun brunch $10.50-$13.95. Child's meals. Specialty: salmon ravioli. Parking. Outdoor dining. Victorian home in European-style village atmosphere. Totally nonsmoking. Cr cds: A, C, D, DS, MC, V.

★★★ **LA MERE MICHELLE.** *14467 Big Basin Way (95070). 408/867-5272.* Hrs: 11:30 am-2 pm, 6-9:30 pm; Fri, Sat 6-10 pm; Sun 11 am-2 pm (brunch), 5:30-9 pm. Closed Mon; major hols. Res accepted. French, continental menu. Bar. Wine list. A la carte entrees: lunch $7.50-$13.50, dinner $17.50-$24.50. Sun brunch $8.50-$13.50. Specializes in veal, beef, seafood. Own pastries. Entertainment Fri, Sat. Elegant French decor. Family-owned. Patio dining. Cr cds: A, C, D, DS, JCB, MC, V.

D

★★★ **LE MOUTON NOIR.** *14560 Big Basin Way (95070). 408/867-7017.* Web www.lemoutonnoir.com. Hrs: 5-9 pm; Sat 11:30 am-2 pm, 5-9 pm. Closed Jan 1, Thanksgiving, Dec 25. Res accepted. French menu. Wine list. A la carte entrees: lunch $10.95-$18.95, dinner $20.95-$28.95. Complete meal: dinner $69.95. Specialties: duck confit, Grand Marnier souffle. Valet parking. Outdoor dining. French country atmosphere. Fireplace. Totally nonsmoking. Cr cds: A, C, D, MC, V.

D

★★★ **PLUMED HORSE.** *14555 Big Basin Way (95070). 408/867-4711.* Hrs: 6-10 pm. Closed Sun; hols. Res accepted. Country French menu. Bar 4 pm-2 am. Wine cellar. A la carte entrees: dinner $17-$34. Prix-fixe: dinner $25-$42. Specializes in fresh game birds, venison, rack of lamb. Own pastries. Jazz trio. Elegant country decor; originally a stable (1883). Cr cds: A, C, D, JCB, MC, V.

D

★★★ **SENT SOVI.** *14583 Big Basin Way (95070). 408/867-3110; FAX 408/867-5545.* Specialties: braised lamb shank, wild mushroom & black truffle soup. Hrs: 5:30-9:30 pm; Sun 5-9 pm. Closed Mon; major hols; also 1st 2 wks Jan. Res accepted. Contemporary French menu. Wine list. A la carte entrees: dinner $24-$30. Street parking. Outdoor dining. Totally nonsmoking. Cr cds: A, C, D, MC, V.

Sausalito (C-2 see San Francisco map)

(See also San Francisco, Tiburon)

Settled 1800 **Pop** 7,152 **Elev** 14 ft **Area Code** 415 **Zip** 94965
E-mail scoc@ix.netcom.com **Web** www.sausalito.org

Information Chamber of Commerce, PO Box 566, 94966; 415/332-0505 or 415/331-7262

Sausalito, a picturesque town above San Francisco Bay, is an art colony and residential suburb in the shadow of the Golden Gate Bridge. Whalers first used the cove here. The town's name is a corruption of the Spanish for willows, which flourished here at one time. Sausalito's springs were San Francisco's major source of water for many years.

What to See and Do

San Francisco Bay & Delta Hydraulic Model. Hydraulic model reproduces tidal action, currents and mixing of salt and fresh water and indicates trends in sediment deposition; the 850-sq-mi bay-delta area is duplicated in a 3-acre building. Interactive exhibits, 9-min orientation video and 45-min general information audio tour. Self-guided tour; audio tours avail in 6 languages: English, French, German, Japanese, Spanish and Russian. (Memorial Day-Labor Day, daily exc Mon; rest of yr, Tues-Sat) 2100 Bridgeway. Model in operation only during testing; for schedule Phone 415/332-3870 (recording). **Free**

Village Fair. Fascinating and colorful 3-story complex of specialty shops selling unusual crafts, artifacts & imports. The building was once a Chinese gambling hall, opium den and a distillery for bootleg whiskey. Cafeteria. (Daily; closed Thanksgiving, Dec 25) 777 Bridgeway, opp Yacht Harbor. Phone 415/332-1902.

Annual Event

Sausalito Art Festival. Labor Day wkend.

Motel

★★ **ALTA MIRA HOTEL.** *125 Bulkley Ave (94966). 415/332-1350; FAX 415/331-3862.* 35 rms, 2 story, 14 cottages. No A/C. S, D, cottages $90-$200; each addl $10. TV; cable. Restaurant 7 am-11 pm. Rm serv. Bar. Ck-out noon. Meeting rm. Business servs avail. Bellhops. Valet parking. Fireplace in cottages. Some balconies. On hillside above city; view of bay from many rms. Cr cds: A, C, D, JCB, MC, V.

Inns

★★★ **CASA MADRONA HOTEL.** *801 Bridgeway (94965). 415/332-0502; FAX 415/332-2537; res: 800/567-9524.* E-mail casa@casamadrona.com; web www.casamadrona.com. 29 rms, 5 cottages, 2 with kit. S, D $138-$260; cottages $188-$205. TV; VCR avail (free movies). Parking $7. Complimentary bkfst. Restaurant (see MIKAYLA). Rm serv. Ck-out noon, ck-in 3 pm. Meeting rm. Business servs avail. Luggage handling. Valet serv. Concierge serv. Whirlpool. Refrigerators, fireplaces. Many balconies, decks. Victorian house (1885); antiques. Cr cds: A, C, D, DS, MC, V.

D

★★★ **THE INN ABOVE TIDE.** *30 El Portal (94965). 415/332-9535; FAX 415/332-6714; res: 800/893-8433.* E-mail inntide@ix.net com.com. 30 rms, 3 story. S, D $195-$285; suites $325-$445; 2-day min wkends. Crib free. TV; cable (premium), VCR avail. Complimentary continental bkfst; afternoon refreshments. Restaurant adj 7 am-9 pm. Ck-out noon, ck-in 3 pm. Luggage handling. Concierge serv. Massage. Business servs avail. In-rm modem link. Parking $8. Minibars. Balconies. Picnic table. Built over water, rooms provide view of bay and San Francisco. Totally nonsmoking. Cr cds: A, C, D, MC, V.

D

Restaurants

★★ **ANGELINO.** *621 Bridgeway (94965). 415/331-5225.* Hrs: 11:30 am-9:30 pm; Fri, Sat to 10 pm. Closed Thanksgiving, wk before Dec 25. Res accepted; required wkends. Italian menu. Bar. A la carte entrees: lunch $14-$25, dinner $18-$28. Specializes in seafood, pasta dishes. Cr cds: A, C, MC, V.

D

★★ **HORIZONS.** *558 Bridgeway (94965). 415/331-3232.* Hrs: 11 am-10 pm; Fri to 11 pm; Sat, Sun 10 am-10 pm. Closed Thanksgiving, Dec 25. No A/C. Bar. Semi-a la carte: lunch, dinner $6.50-$25. Daily brunch $7.25-$14. Specializes in fresh seafood. Entertainment Fri, Sat evenings. Valet parking. Outdoor dining. View of San Francisco, East Bay. Family-owned. Cr cds: A, C, D, DS, MC, V.

D

★★★ **MIKAYLA.** *(See Casa Madrona Hotel Inn) 415/331-5888.* E-mail casa@casamadrona.com; web www.mikayla.com. Hrs: 6-10 pm; Sun brunch 10 am-2:30 pm. Res accepted. Wine list. A la carte entrees: dinner $14.95-$21.50. Sun brunch $24.50. Specializes in American cuisine with west coast influence. Own baking. Valet parking $3. Outdoor dining. View of bay. Cr cds: A, C, D, DS, MC, V.

★★ **SCOMA'S.** *588 Bridgeway (94965). 415/332-9551.* Hrs: 11:30 am-9:30 pm; Tues, Wed from 5:30 pm. Closed Thanksgiving, Dec 25-Jan 1. Seafood menu. Bar. Semi-a la carte: lunch $7-$15, dinner $15-$32. Child's meals. Specializes in seafood, pasta. Landmark Victorian building at end of wharf; view of bay. Family-owned. Cr cds: A, C, D, DS, JCB, MC, V.

D

★★ **SPINNAKER.** *100 Spinnaker Dr (94965), at end of Anchor St. 415/332-1500.* Hrs: 11 am-11 pm; Sun brunch to 3 pm. Closed Thanksgiving, Dec 24-25. Res accepted. Bar. A la carte entrees: lunch $7.95-$16.95, dinner $9.95-$18.95. Sun brunch $6.75-$12. Child's meals. Specializes in fresh seafood, fresh pasta. Valet parking. View of bridges and bay. Family-owned. Cr cds: A, C, D, DS, MC, V.

D

✓★ **WINSHIPS.** *670 Bridgeway (94965). 415/332-1454.* Web www.winships.com. Hrs: 8 am-3 pm; Sun brunch to 1 pm. Closed Thanksgiving, Dec 25. Res accepted. Bar. Semi-a la carte: bkfst $5.95-$11.95, lunch $5.95-$15.95. Sun brunch $3.50-$12.95. Child's meals. Specializes in soups, fresh seafood, pasta. Nautical decor; ship models, marine artifacts. Family-owned. Totally nonsmoking. Cr cds: A, C, D, DS, JCB, MC, V.

D

Sequoia & Kings Canyon National Parks (F-3)

(See also Porterville, Three Rivers)

(55 mi E of Fresno on CA 180; 35 mi E of Visalia on CA 198)

Although independently established, Sequoia and Kings Canyon National Parks are geographically and administratively one. Lying across the heart of the Sierra Nevada in eastern central California, they comprise more than 1,300 square miles and include more than 25 isolated groves of spectacular giant sequoias, towering granite peaks, deep canyons and hundreds of alpine lakes. Giant sequoias reach their greatest size and are found in the largest numbers here. Mount Whitney, 14,495 feet, is the highest point in the lower 48 states. Some rocks of the foothill and summit area indicate that this whole region once lay under the ocean.

Allow plenty of driving time due to the gradient into and out of the mountains. Limited groceries are available all year in both parks. Gasoline may not be available; inquire before entering. Camping (no trailer hookups) is restricted to designated areas. Many of the campgrounds are closed by snow, October-late May. Routes to Sequoia and Kings Canyon National Parks involve some travel over steep grades, which may extend driving times. Winter visitors should carry tire chains. Entry fee valid for 7 days. For information contact Sequoia and Kings Canyon National Parks, Three Rivers 93271; 559/565-3134.

What to See and Do

Boyden Cavern. A 45-min tour on lighted, handrail-equipped trail through ornate chambers with massive stalagmites, stalactites and columns. (May-Oct; daily) Located in King's River Canyon, in Sequoia National Forest between Grant Grove and Cedar Grove. For further information contact PO Box 78, Vallecito 95251; Phone 559/736-2708. ¢¢¢

Cedar Grove. Towering peaks rise a mile high above the stream. Horses, pack animals. Hiking trails. Road closed Nov-Apr. In canyon of S Fork of Kings River.

Fishing for trout is excellent in a few lakes and streams; the most popular spots are along Kings River and the forks of the Kaweah River. Some stores in the park sell state fishing licenses.

Foothills, Lodgepole and Grant Grove Visitor Centers. Exhibits, photos, data about the parks; expert advice on how to organize sightseeing. Schedules of campfire talks and guided trips are posted here. Foothills & Grant Grove (daily), Lodgepole (May-Oct, daily). Phone 559/565-3134; Lodgepole 559/565-3782; Grant Grove 559/335-2856.

General Grant Grove. Includes the General Grant Tree, 267 ft tall with a circumference of 108 ft. Saddle rides. Hiking trails.

★ **Giant Forest.** One of the finest groves of giant sequoias. The General Sherman Tree is the largest living thing on earth. At 275 ft high and 103 ft in circumference, it is estimated to be 2,300-2,700 yrs old. Moro Rock, Crescent Meadow, Crystal Cave and Tokopah Valley are in this section of the park. Horses, pack animals available at Wolverton Pack Station. Hiking trails.

The high country. Vast region of wilderness, mountains, canyons, rivers, lakes and meadows, accessible by trail. The Sierra Crest forms the eastern boundary.

Redwood Mountain Grove. Includes the Hart Tree, a large sequoia; accessible by trail.

Motels

★ **CEDAR GROVE LODGE.** *Hwy 180 (93633), at end of CA 180, 30 mi E of General Grant Grove. 559/565-0100; FAX 559/565-0101.* 21 rms, 2 story. No rm phones. Late Apr-Oct: S, D $93.25; each addl $6; under 12 free. Closed rest of yr. Crib free. Restaurant 7 am-8 pm. Ck-out 11 am. Coin Indry. Gift shop. Picnic tables, grills. Cr cds: C, MC, V.

D

✓★ **GRANT GROVE VILLAGE.** *Hwy 180 (93633), 4 mi E on CA 180. 559/561-3314; FAX 559/561-3135; res: 888/252-5757.* 63 rms, 24 cottages. No A/C. No elvtrs. No rm phones. S, D $80-$85; each addl $8; cottages w/o kit. unit $35-$55; under 12 free. Crib free. Restaurant 7 am-9 pm. Ck-out 11 am. Sundries. Gift shop. X-country ski on-site. Fireplace in cottages. Picnic tables. Totally nonsmoking. Cr cds: C, MC, V.

Solvang (H-2)

(See also Lompoc, Santa Barbara)

Founded 1911 **Pop** 4,741 **Elev** 495 ft **Area Code** 805 **Zip** 93463
E-mail solvangusa@syv.com **Web** www.solvangusa.com

Information Information Center, 1511-A Mission Dr, PO Box 70, 93464; 800/468-6765

Founded by Danes from the Midwest in 1911, a corner of Denmark has been re-created here. Solvang is a community of picturesque Danish-style buildings, which include four windmills. Rich Danish pastries and Danish imports are featured in its shops.

What to See and Do

Lake Cachuma Recreation Area. Swimming pool (summer); fishing; boating (rentals). General store. Camping (hookups). Fees for some activities. (Daily) 6 mi E on CA 246, then 6 mi S on CA 154. Phone 805/688-4658 (recording). Per vehicle day-use ¢¢

Old Mission Santa Inés (1804). Established by Fray Estevan Tapis as the 19th mission. A gold adobe building with red-tiled roof, garden and arched colonnade in front. Used as a church; many artifacts, manuscripts and vestments on exhibit; recorded tour. (Daily; closed hols) 1760 Mission Dr. Phone 805/688-4815. ¢¢

Annual Event

Danish Days Festival. Danish folk dancing, singing, band concerts; parade on Sat. 3rd wkend Sept.

Seasonal Event

Solvang Theaterfest. 420 Second St. The Pacific Conservatory of the Performing Arts (PCPA) presents musicals, dramas, new works and classics in an outdoor theater. Contact PCPA Theaterfest, PO Box 1700, Santa Maria 93456; 805/922-8313. Early June-early Oct.

Motels

✓★★ **ANDERSON BEST WESTERN.** *51 E Hwy 246 (93427), on CA 246, just W of US 101. 805/688-3216; FAX 805/688-9767; res: 800/528-1234.* 97 rms, 2 story. May-Sept: S, D $59-$89; each addl $10; under 12 free; lower rates rest of yr. Crib $5. TV; cable (premium). Heated pool; whirlpool. Complimentary continental bkfst. Coffee in rms. Restaurant 7 am-10 pm. Bar from 11 am. Ck-out noon. Business servs avail. Sundries. Putting green. Some refrigerators; microwaves avail. Private patios. Grill, picnic area, gazebo. Cr cds: A, C, D, DS, MC, V.

D SC

★★ **CHIMNEY SWEEP INN.** *1554 Copenhagen Dr (95476). 805/688-2111; FAX 805/688-8824; res: 800/824-6444.* 56 units, 1-2 story, 6 kit. cottages. S, D $85-$145; each addl $10; suites $115-$165; kit. cottages $155-$275; wkends (2-day min). Crib $5. TV; cable (premium). Whirlpool. Complimentary continental bkfst. Coffee in rms. Ck-out 11 amnoon. Business servs avail. Health club privileges. Swimming privileges. Microwaves; many in-rm whirlpools in kit. cottages. Cr cds: A, C, DS, MC, V.

D SC

★★★ **DANISH COUNTRY INN.** *1455 Mission Dr (93463), 3 mi E of jct CA 246, I-101. 805/688-2018; FAX 805/688-1156; res: 800/447-3529.* 82 rms, 3 story, 9 suites. S, D $148-$158; each addl $10; suites $185; under 12 free; golf plans. Crib free. Pet accepted; $25. TV; cable, VCR (movies $4). Heated pool; whirlpool. Complimentary full bkfst. Restaurant 6:30-9:30 am. Ck-out noon. Meeting rms. Business servs avail. In-rm modem link. Garage parking. Refrigerators. Balconies. Country inn elegance. Sitting rm. Antiques. Cr cds: A, C, D, DS, JCB, MC, V.

D SC

★★ **IMA SVENDSGAARD'S DANISH LODGE.** *1711 Mission Dr (93463). 805/688-3277; FAX 805/688-3277; res: 800/341-8000.* 48 rms, 3 story, 4 kits. S, D $58-$103; each addl $6; suites, kit. units $66-$107; golf plan. Crib free. TV; cable. Heated pool; whirlpool. Complimentary continental bkfst. Coffee in rms. Restaurant nearby. Ck-out 11 am. Business servs avail. Refrigerators; some microwaves, fireplaces. Private balconies. Sun deck. Mission opp. Cr cds: A, C, D, DS, JCB, MC, V.

SC

★★ **ROYAL COPENHAGEN MOTEL.** *1579 Mission Dr (93463). 805/688-5561; FAX 805/688-7029; res: 800/624-6604.* 48 units, 1-2 story. S, D $80-$90; each addl $5; suites $110. TV; cable. Heated pool. Complimentary continental bkfst. Restaurant nearby. Ck-out 11 am. Business servs avail. Danish motif. Large rose garden. Cr cds: A, C, DS, MC, V.

D SC

✓★★ **WINDMILL MOTOR INN.** *114 E Hwy 246 (93427), jct US 101 & CA 246. 805/688-8448; FAX 805/686-1338; res: 800/946-3466.* 108 rms, 2 story. Mar-Aug: S $42-$86; D $48-$92; each addl $8; suites $98-$156; under 12 free; lower rates rest of yr. Crib free. TV; cable. Heated pool; whirlpool. Complimentary continental bkfst wkends. Bar 4 pm-2 am. Ck-out noon. Coin Indry. Meeting rms. Business servs avail. Sundries. Microwaves avail. Patios, balconies. Danish-style architecture. Cr cds: A, C, D, DS, JCB, MC, V.

D SC

Hotels

★★★ **MARRIOTT RANCHO SANTA BARBARA.** *555 Mcmurray Rd (93427), at jct US 101 & CA 246. 805/688-1000; FAX 805/688-0380; res: 800/638-8882.* Web www.marriott.com. 149 units, 4 story. S, D $79-$159; each addl $10; suites $119-$250; family rates. Crib free. TV; cable (premium). Heated pool; whirlpool, poolside serv in summer. Coffee in rms. Restaurants 6:30 am-10 pm. Bar 4-10 pm. Ck-out noon. Coin Indry. Meeting rms. Business servs avail. In-rm modem link. Airport, bus depot transportation. Tennis. Exercise equipt. Game rm. Rec rm. Refrigerators, microwaves avail. Balconies. Elaborate landscaping; fountains. 5 movie theaters. Cr cds: A, C, D, DS, JCB, MC, V.

D SC

★★★ **SOLVANG ROYAL SCANDINAVIAN INN.** *400 Alisal Rd (93463), I-101 exit CA 246E, S on Mission. 805/688-8000; FAX 805/688-0761; res: 800/624-5572.* E-mail sroyal@silicon.com. 133 rms, 3 story. June-Sept: S, D $111-$151; each addl $10; suites $135-$245; under 18 free; golf plan; lower rates rest of yr. Crib free. TV; cable (premium), VCR avail. Heated pool; whirlpool. Restaurant (see ROYAL SCANDIA). Bar 11-1:30 am; entertainment. Ck-out 11 am. Meeting rms. Business servs avail. Valet serv. Refrigerator, wet bar in suites. Many patios, balconies. Custom-made Danish furniture. Cr cds: A, C, D, DS, ER, JCB, MC, V.

D SC

Inns

★★★ **BALLARD INN.** *2436 Baseline Ave (93463), E on CA 246 to Alamo Pintado Rd, then 2 mi N. 805/688-7770; FAX 805/688-9560; res: 800/638-2466.* 15 rms, 1-2 story. Rm phones avail. S, D $170-$250; each addl $50; golf plan; wkends, hols (2-day min). TV & VCR in sitting rm. Complimentary full bkfst; afternoon refreshments. Dining rm 6-9 pm; closed Mon, Tues. Ck-out noon, ck-in 3 pm. Luggage handling. Business servs avail. 18-hole golf privileges. Mountain bikes avail. Games in parlor. Individually decorated rms, each with theme of local history. Totally nonsmoking. Cr cds: A, C, MC, V.

D SC

★★★ **FESS PARKER'S WINE COUNTRY INN.** *2860 Grand Ave (93441), 2 mi E of US 101 on CA 154. 805/688-7788; FAX 805/688-1942; res: 800/446-2455.* Web www.foursisters.com. 21 rms, 2 story. S, D $225-$270; suite $340; package plans. Crib free. TV; cable, VCR avail.

Heated pool; whirlpool, poolside serv. Complimentary full bkfst; afternoon refreshments. Dining rm 8 am-2:30 pm, 5:30-9 pm; Sat, Sun 8 am-3 pm, 5:30-10 pm. Rm serv. Ck-out noon, ck-in 2 pm. Meeting rms. Business servs avail. Luggage handling. Golf privileges. Health club privileges. Bicycles avail. Fireplaces. Library. Elegant decor with many antiques; extensive landscaping. Totally nonsmoking. Cr cds: A, C, D, DS, MC, V.

D

★★★ **PETERSEN VILLAGE INN.** *1576 Mission Dr (93464). 805/688-3121; FAX 805/688-5732; res: 800/321-8985.* Web www.peterseninn.com. 42 rms, 3 story. S, D $125-$195; suites $195-$235. Children over 7 yrs only. TV; cable (premium), VCR avail. Complimentary bkfst buffet. Complimentary coffee in rms. Restaurants nearby. Ck-out 1 pm, ck-in 3 pm. Business servs avail. In-rm modem link. Luggage handling. Health club privileges. Whirlpool, fireplace in suites. Some private patios, balconies. Replica of old Danish village; 28 shops on premises; garden area. Cr cds: A, C, MC, V.

D

Guest Ranch

★★★ **ALISAL GUEST RANCH & RESORT.** *1054 Alisal Rd (93463), 2½ mi S of CA 246. 805/688-6411; FAX 805/688-2510; res: 800/425-4725.* E-mail info@alisal.com; web www.alisal.com. 73 units. No A/C. No rm phones. MAP (2-day min): D $335-$415; each addl: 3-6 yrs $40, over 6 yrs $65; under 3 free; package plans. Crib free. TV in lounge; cable, VCR avail. Heated pool; whirlpool, poolside serv in season, lifeguard in summer. Supervised child's activities (June-Labor Day, hols). Coffee in rms. Restaurant 7:30-10 am, 6:30-9 pm (jacket dinner); closed to public. Cookouts in season, picnic lunches, bkfst rides. Snack bar at golf course. Bars 11 am-midnight. Ck-out 1 pm, ck-in 4 pm. Guest lndry. Meeting rm. Business servs avail. Bellhops. Tennis, pro. 36-hole golf, greens fee $75, cart $26, pro, putting green. Fly fishing, canoes, kayaks, sailboats, rowboats, windsurfing. Indoor, outdoor games. Hayrides. Horseback trail rides. Bicycle rentals. Health club privileges. Adult, child rec rms. Entertainment nightly. Winery tours. Fireplaces, refrigerators. Library. 10,000-acre working ranch, up to 2,000 head of cattle, petting zoo. Large private lake. Cr cds: A, C, D, MC, V.

D

Restaurants

★★ **ANDERSEN'S RESTAURANT.** *376 Ave of the Flags (93427), 4 mi W on US 101. 805/688-5581.* Web www.silcom.com/~splitpea. Hrs: 7 am-10 pm; early-bird dinner (Mon-Thurs) 4-7 pm. Danish, Amer menu. Bar. A la carte entrees: $3.95-$6.95, lunch $5.95-$7.95, dinner $7.95-$16.95. Child's meals. Specialties: split pea soup, Danish sausage sandwich, pot roast. Parking. Outdoor dining. Totally nonsmoking. Cr cds: A, C, D, DS, MC, V.

D SC

✓★★ **MOLLEKROEN.** *435 Alisal Rd (93463). 805/688-4555.* Hrs: 11:30 am-9 pm. Closed Dec 25. Res accepted. Danish, Amer menu. Bar to midnight. Semi-a la carte: lunch $3.95-$9.95. Complete meals: dinner $9.50-$18.95. Child's meals. Specializes in open-face Danish sandwiches, smorgasbord. Family-owned since 1973. Cr cds: A, C, D, DS, ER, JCB, MC, V.

✓★ **MUSTARD SEED.** *1655 Mission Dr (93463). 805/688-1318.* Hrs: 7 am-2:30 pm, 4:30-9 pm. Closed Thanksgiving, Dec 25. Res accepted. Wine, beer. Semi-a la carte: bkfst $3.25-$6.25, lunch $3.95-$6.95, dinner $6.95-$10.95. Child's meals. Specializes in omelets, soup, salad. Parking. Outdoor dining. Casual dining. Cr cds: C, MC, V.

★★ **ROYAL SCANDIA.** *(See Solvang Royal Scandinavian Inn Hotel) 805/688-8000.* E-mail sroyal@silicon.com. Hrs: 7 am-9 pm; Sun brunch 11 am-2 pm. Res accepted, required hols. Danish, Amer menu. Bar 11 am-midnight. Semi-a la carte: bkfst $4.95-$7.25, lunch $5.25-$9.25, dinner $10.95-$19.95. Sun brunch $12.95. Child's meals. Specializes in fresh salmon, prime rib, smorgasbord. Salad bar. Entertainment. Outdoor dining. Scandinavian decor. Totally nonsmoking. Cr cds: A, C, D, DS, ER, JCB, MC, V.

D

Sonoma (D-2)

(See also Calistoga, Napa, Petaluma, Santa Rosa , St Helena)

Founded 1823 **Pop** 8,121 **Elev** 84 ft **Area Code** 707 **Zip** 95476
E-mail svvb@wco.com **Web** www.sonomavalley.com

Information Sonoma Valley Visitors Bureau, 453 First St E; 707/996-1090

Mission San Francisco Solano (1823) was secularized under Mariano Guadalupe Vallejo in 1834. Vallejo had been sent by Governor Figueroa to investigate Russian activities at Fort Ross (see FORT ROSS STATE HISTORIC PARK). This mission was the last and most northerly of the 21 Franciscan missions in California and the only one established under Mexican rule. On June 14, 1846, Sonoma was the scene of the Bear Flag Revolt—establishing the California Republic, which lasted until July 9.

Sonoma Valley is the birthplace of the California wine industry. More than 40 premium wineries can be found here amongst 18,000 acres of vineyards.

What to See and Do

Haraszthy Villa. Villa built in 1861 by Count Agoston Haraszthy has been re-created; also vineyard and gazebo. Picnicking. (Wed, Sat & Sun) E via Napa St, then N on Old Winery Rd, in Bartholomew Memorial Park. Phone 707/938-2244. **Free**

Jack London State Historic Park. Memorial, "House of Happy Walls," and grave of author. Wolf House ruins, Jack London cottage; farm building; winery structure ruins located in beautiful Valley of the Moon. Hiking trails. Park (daily). Museum (daily; closed Jan 1, Thanksgiving, Dec 25). 2400 London Ranch Rd. 8½ mi W on CA 12, then 1½ mi W of Glen Ellen on London Ranch Rd. Phone 707/938-5216. Per vehicle **¢¢**

Sears Point Raceway. Motor sports entertainment, including NASCAR Cup, NHRA drag racing, SCCA pro and amateur road races, AMA and AFM motorcycle events, vintage car races, amateur drag racing, car clubs. Under 12 yrs with adult only. (Daily; closed Dec 25) CA 37 & CA 121. Phone 800/870-RACE. **¢¢¢¢¢**

Sonoma State Historic Park. General Vallejo's house (1851-1880), W Spain St & 3rd St W; Mission San Francisco Solano (1823-1846), barracks (1840-1846), E Spain St & 1st St E; other buildings on and near Sonoma Plaza. Picnicking. (Daily; closed Jan 1, Thanksgiving, Dec 25) phone 707/938-1519. **¢**

Train Town. Steam- or diesel-powered miniature railroad makes 20-min run through landscaped park with animals, waterfalls and historic replica structures. (June-Sept, daily; rest of yr, Fri-Sun) 20264 Broadway. Phone 707/938-3912. **¢¢**

Wineries.

Buena Vista Winery. Cellars built in 1857. Historical panels; tasting rm; art gallery; picnic area. Concerts in summer; special events. Tours (daily; closed Jan 1, Thanksgiving, Dec 25). 18000 Old Winery Rd, 1½ mi E. Phone 707/938-1266 or 800/926-1266. **Free**

Gloria Ferrer Champagne Caves. Guided tours through "champagne caves" (inquire for schedule); wine tasting. (Daily; closed Thanksgiving, Dec 25, also early Jan) 23555 CA 121, 6 mi S. Phone 707/996-7256. **Free**

Sebastiani Sonoma Cask Cellars. Large collection of carved casks. Guided tours; tasting rm and aging cellars may be visited. Free tram ride to winery from Sonoma Plaza. (Daily; closed major hols) 389 4th St E. Phone 707/938-5532 or 800/888-5532. **Free**

Annual Event

Valley of the Moon Vintage Festival. Sonoma Plaza. California's oldest wine festival. Parades, wine tasting, folk dancing. Phone 707/996-2109 Usually last full wkend Sept.

Motels

★★ **BEST WESTERN SONOMA VALLEY INN.** *550 2nd St W (95476). 707/938-9200; FAX 707/938-0935; res: 800/334-5784.* E-mail sviwine@pacbell.net; web www.sonoma.com.svi. 75 rms, 2 story. Apr-Dec: S, D $119-$249; each addl $10; under 12 free; lower rates rest of yr. Crib free. Pet accepted; $15/day. TV; cable (premium). Pool; whirlpool. Complimentary continental bkfst in rms. Restaurant nearby. Ck-out noon. Free guest lndry facilities. Business servs avail. Valet serv. Exercise equipt. Refrigerators; many fireplaces; some in-rm whirlpools; microwaves avail. Private patios, balconies. Totally nonsmoking. Cr cds: A, C, D, DS, ER, JCB, MC, V.

D SC

✓★ **EL PUEBLO MOTEL.** *896 W Napa St (95476). 707/996-3651; FAX 707/935-5988; res: 800/900-8844.* 38 units, 2 story. Apr-Oct: S, D $75-$90; each addl $10; lower rates rest of yr. Crib $5. TV; cable. Heated pool. Complimentary coffee in rms. Restaurant nearby. Ck-out noon. Business servs avail. Microwaves avail. Cr cds: A, C, DS, MC, V.

D

Hotel

SONOMA MISSION INN & SPA. *896 W Napa St (95476), Sonoma Hwy, Valley of the Moon area. 707/938-9000; FAX 707/938-4250; res: 800/862-4945.* Web www.sonomamissioninn.com. Unrated for 2000. Cr cds: A, C, D, MC, V.

D SC

Inns

★★★ **GAIGE HOUSE INN.** *13540 Arnold Dr (95442), 7 mi N on CA 12. 707/935-0237; FAX 707/935-6411.* E-mail gaige@sprynet.com; web www.gaige.com. 13 rms, 2 with shower only, 3 story. Apr-Oct: S, D $170-$325; each addl $25; lower rates rest of yr. Children over 12 yrs only. TV in parlor. Pool; whirlpool. Complimentary full bkfst; afternoon refreshments. Restaurant nearby. Ck-out 11 am, ck-in 3-7 pm. Concierge serv. Twin parlors. Built in the late 1890s; antiques. Totally nonsmoking. Cr cds: A, C, DS, MC, V.

★★ **THISTLE DEW INN.** *171 W Spain St (95476). 707/938-2909; FAX 707/996-8413; res: 800/382-7895.* Web www.thistledew.com. 6 rms, 3 with shower only, 1 suite. Mar-Nov: S, D $100-$180; each addl $30; suite $180; lower rates rest of yr. Complimentary full bkfst. Restaurant nearby. Ck-out noon, ck-in 3 pm. Luggage handling. Concierge serv. Bicycle. Many fireplaces. Many balconies. Picnic tables, grills. Built in 1869. Antique furniture. Totally nonsmoking. Cr cds: A, C, MC, V.

D

★★ **TROJAN HORSE INN.** *19455 Sonoma Hwy (95476). 707/996-2430; FAX 707/996-9185; res: 800/899-1925.* E-mail trojaninn@aol.com; web www.trojanhorseinn.com. 6 rms. No rm phones. Apr-mid-Nov: S, D $135-$170; each addl $20; lower rates rest of yr. Crib $20. Complimentary full bkfst, evening refreshments. Restaurant nearby. Ck-out 11 am, ck-in 3 pm. Business servs avail. Whirlpool. Picnic tables. Restored pioneer family home (1887); period antiques. Totally nonsmoking. Cr cds: A, C, D, DS, MC, V.

D

★★ **VICTORIAN GARDEN INN.** *316 E Napa St (95476). 707/996-5339; res: 800/539-5339.* Web www.victoriangardeninn.com. 4 rms, 2 story. No rm phones. D $95-$175. Complimentary full bkfst. Ck-out noon, ck-in 2-5 pm. Business servs avail. Exercise equipt. Whirlpool. Private patios. Picnic tables. Former farmhouse (1870); gardens. Totally nonsmoking. Cr cds: A, C, D, ER, JCB, MC, V.

Restaurants

★★ **BABETTE'S.** *464 First St E (95476). 707/939-8921.* Hrs: 6-9:30 pm; Fri, Sat from 5:30 pm. Closed Sun, Mon; most major hols. Res required. Contemporary French menu. Bar. Complete 6 course meal: dinner $63. Specialties: eggshell filled with Beluga caviar, sauteed foie gras medallion, pico picandine. Street parking. Intimate dining. Totally nonsmoking. Cr cds: C, MC, V.

D

✓★★ **CAFE AT SONOMA MISSION INN.** *(See Sonoma Mission Inn & Spa) 707/938-9000.* Web www.sonomamissioninn.com. Hrs: 7 am-9:30 pm; Sun brunch to 3 pm. Res accepted. Bar. A la carte entrees: bkfst $6.50-$12.50, lunch $8-$14, dinner $9-$21. Sun brunch $7-$14. Child's meals. Specialties: apple oatcakes, pizza from wood-burning oven. Casual atmosphere. Totally nonsmoking. Cr cds: A, C, D, MC, V.

D

✓★ **CAFE LAHAYE.** *140 E Napa St (95476). 707/935-5994.* Hrs: 5:30-9:30 pm; Sat 11:30 am-2:30 pm, 5:30-9:30 pm; Sun 10 am-2 pm. Closed Mon; also many major hols. Res accepted (dinner only). Eclectic menu. Wine, beer. Semi-a la carte: lunch $5.95-$8.95, dinner $11.95-$16.95. Specialty: seared black pepper-lavender filet of beef with gorgonzola potato gratin. Street parking. Original art. Totally nonsmoking. Cr cds: A, C, MC, V.

★★ **DELLA SANTINA'S.** *133 E Napa St (95476). 707/935-0576.* Hrs: 11 am-9:30 pm. Closed some major hols. Res accepted. Italian menu. Wine, beer. A la carte entrees: lunch $4.75-$13.25, dinner $4.75-$16.25. Child's meals. Specializes in Tuscan cuisine, rotisserie. Own pasta, desserts. Street parking. Outdoor dining. Fountain on patio. Totally nonsmoking. Cr cds: A, C, DS, MC, V.

D

★★ **DEUCE.** *691 Broadway (95476). 707/933-3823.* Hrs: 11:30 am-9 pm. Closed Dec 25. Res accepted. Contemporary Amer menu. Bar. A la carte entrees: lunch $4.95-$11.95, dinner $4.95-$19.95. Child's meals. Specialties: beet salad, onion-crusted chicken breast, club steak. Outdoor dining. Unique woodwork. Totally nonsmoking. Cr cds: A, C, MC, V.

D

★★ **FREESTYLE.** *522 Broadway (95476). 707/996-9916.* Hrs: 11:30 am-2:30 pm, 5:30-9:30 pm; Sun brunch 11:30 am-2:30 pm. Closed Tues. Res accepted. Bar. A la carte entrees: lunch $8-$13, dinner $14-$21. Complete meal: dinner $28-$48. Sun brunch $8-$12. Child's meals. Specialties: grilled pork chop with jalapeño mashed potatoes, daily changing trio appetizer, Valrhona devil's food cake with espresso ice-cream. Street parking. Outdoor dining. Totally nonsmoking. Cr cds: A, C, D, MC, V.

D

★★★ **GENERAL'S DAUGHTER.** *400 W Spain St (95476). 707/938-4004.* Hrs: 11:30 am-9:30 pm; Fri & Sat to 10:30 pm; Sun brunch 11 am-2:30 pm. Closed Dec 25. Res accepted. Bar. Wine list. Semi-a la carte: lunch, dinner $8-$22.50. Sun brunch $8-$15. Specializes in lamb chops, flatbread, local produce. Parking. Casual elegance in 1874 bldg; patio dining with views of landscaped grounds. Totally nonsmoking. Cr cds: C, MC, V.

D

★★ **GLEN ELLEN INN.** *13670 Arnold Dr (95442), 7 mi N on CA 12. 707/996-6409.* Hrs: 5:30-9:30 pm. Closed Wed in winter. Res accepted. Wine, beer. A la carte entrees: dinner $11.95-$23.95. Specialties: smokin' chicken Napoleon, wild mushroom and sausage purse, grilled filet mignon. Outdoor dining. Intimate cottage. Totally nonsmoking. Cr cds: A, C, MC, V.

✓★ **LA CASA RESTAURANT.** *121 E Spain St (95476). 707/996-3406.* Hrs: 11:30 am-10 pm. Closed Thanksgiving, Dec 25. Res accepted. Mexican menu. Bar. Semi-a la carte: lunch, dinner $4-$13. Child's meals. Specialties: fresh snapper Veracruz, tamales, chimichangas. Mexican decor. Outdoor dining. Cr cds: A, C, D, MC, V.

D

★ **LA SALETTE.** *18625 Sonoma Hwy 12 (95476). 707/938-1926.* Hrs: 11 am-9 pm. Closed Mon. Res accepted. International menu. A la carte entrees: lunch, dinner $4.50-$15.75. Specialties: house smoked swordfish, grilled salted cod, salmon teijoada. Parking. Outdoor dining. Small cottage; casual dining. Totally nonsmoking. Cr cds: C, MC, V.

D

★ **MES TROIS FILLES.** *13648 Arnold Dr (95442), 7 mi N of Sonoma off CA 12. 707/938-4844.* Hrs: 5-9:30 pm. Closed Mon, Tues. Res accepted. Country French, continental menu. Wine, beer. A la carte entrees: dinner $14.50-$20.50. Child's meals. Specialties: smoked salmon terrine & cilantro cream in wasabi-dill, wild mushroom ravioli. Street parking. Intimate dining. Totally nonsmoking. Cr cds: A, C, DS, MC, V.

D

★★ **PIATTI.** *405 First St W (95476). 707/996-2351.* Hrs: 11:30 am-10 pm; Fri & Sat to 11 pm. Res accepted. Italian menu. Bar. A la carte entrees: lunch $9.95-$16.95, dinner $11.95-$22.95. Child's meals. Specialties: ravioli with lemon cream, lasagne al pesto. Outdoor dining. Italian country atmosphere. Totally nonsmoking. Cr cds: A, C, D, MC, V.

D

★★ **THE DEPOT HOTEL CUCINA RUSTICA.** *241 1st St W (95476). 707/938-2980.* E-mail depotel@interx.net; web www.depotal.com. Hrs: 11:30 am-2 pm, 5-9:30 pm; Sat, Sun from 5 pm. Closed Mon, Tues; Jan 1, Dec 25. Res accepted. Northern Italian menu. Beer, wine. A la carte entrees: lunch $6.75-$14.50, dinner $7.75-$18.50. Child's meals. Parking. Outdoor dining around pool. Historic stone building (1870); originally a hotel, later a saloon and private residence. Restored in 1962. Herb & vegetable garden. Chef-owned. Cr cds: A, C, D, DS, MC, V.

D

★★ **THE GIRL & THE FIG.** *13690 Arnold Dr (95442), 7 mi N on CA 12. 707/938-3634.* Web www.thegirlandthefig.com. Hrs: 5:30-9 pm; Sat, Sun brunch 10 am-2:30 pm. Closed Thanksgiving, Dec 25. Res accepted. Country French bistro menu. Wine, beer. A la carte entrees: dinner $12.95-$19.95. Sat, Sun brunch $6.50-$15.95. Child's meals. Specializes in fresh local meats, seafood, cheese. Parking. Outdoor dining. Art changes every 6 wks. Totally nonsmoking. Cr cds: A, C, MC, V.

D

★★ **THE GRILLE.** *(See Sonoma Mission Inn & Spa Hotel) 707/938-9000.* Web www.sonomamissioninn.com. Hrs: 6-9:30 pm; Sun brunch 10 am-2 pm. Res accepted. Bar 11am-11pm. Wine cellar. A la carte entrees: dinner $22-$29. Sun brunch $7-$20. Complete meals: dinner $40. Specializes in wine country cuisine featuring local seafood, game, produce. Own baking. Pianist. Valet parking. Totally nonsmoking. Cr cds: A, C, D, MC, V.

D

★ **ZINOS RESTAURANTE ON THE PLZ.** *420 1st St E (95476). 707/996-4466.* E-mail zinoristorante@msn.com. Hrs: 11 am-10 pm. Res accepted; required wkends. Italian menu. Semi-a la carte: lunch $7.50-$12.50, dinner $9.50-$16. Specializes in pasta, seafood. Bistro-style dining in converted storefront. Patio dining. Totally nonsmoking. Cr cds: A, C, D, MC, V.

D SC

Sonora (E-3)

(See also Modesto, Oakdale)

Settled 1848 **Pop** 4,153 **Elev** 1,825 ft **Area Code** 209 **Zip** 95370
E-mail tcvb@mlode.com

Information Tuolumne County Visitors Bureau, 55 W Stockton Rd, PO Box 4020; 209/533-4420 or 800/446-1333

Mexican miners named this the Sonoran Camp for their home state. Mexicans, Chileans and Americans did not mix well and the camp became peaceful only after the varied groups dispersed. At the Big Bonanza, richest pocket mine in the Mother Lode, $160,000 in nearly pure gold was harvested in a single day. Stretching across seven hills, this colorful town, the seat of Tuolumne County, was the setting for several tales by Mark Twain and Bret Harte.

What to See and Do

Columbia State Historic Park. The 1850 gold town of Columbia is restored to its early glory. The gold boom brought stages, freight wagons, brick stores, all the facilities of civilization and thousands of gold-hungry miners. Operating gold mine tour; gold panning; stagecoach ride; concessions (fees). Free slide show in museum. Guided tours (summer, wkends). Most of the buildings are open (daily; closed Thanksgiving, Dec 25; some shops closed wkdays in winter). 4 mi N via CA 49 & Parrotts Ferry Rd. Phone 209/532-4301 or 209/532-0150. **Free** Among the 40 buildings on the self-guided tour are

City Hotel. Refitted as period restaurant and hotel.

Eagle Cotage *(sic).* Reconstructed boardinghouse. Outside viewing only.

Firehouse. Tuolumne Engine Co #1 and pumper "Papeete." **Free**

Schoolhouse (1860). One of the oldest of its kind in the state; in use until 1937; authentically refurnished. **Free**

Don Pedro Lake Recreation Area. A 26-mi-long lake impounded by 580-ft dam. Swimming (fee); fishing; boat launching (marinas). Picnicking. Camping (fee; hookups). No pets. (Daily) Fee for activities. 13 mi S off CA 120. Phone 209/852-2396. Per vehicle **¢¢**

Mercer Caverns. Stalagmites, stalactites, aragonite, other formations in caves discovered in 1885. Ten rms; lighted walkways; 55°F; 45-min guided tours. Picnic area. (June-Sept, daily; rest of yr, wkends & school hols; closed Thanksgiving, Dec 25) 10 mi N on CA 49, then 5 mi NE on CA 4. Phone 209/728-2101. **¢¢**

Moaning Cavern. Discovered in 1849. View formations from 100-ft spiral staircase. Walking tour (45 min). Visitors may also descend into the cavern via 180-ft rope rappel; or take a 3-hr tour into the undeveloped cavern depths (by appt). Display of Native American and mining artifacts. (Daily) 5350 Moaning Cave Rd, 12 mi N near Vallecito. Phone 209/736-2708. **¢¢¢**

New Melones Lake Recreation Area. When full, the lake offers more than 100 mi of shoreline for water and fishing sports, as well as 7-lane launch ramps, fish cleaning facilities and a marina. During low lake levels, river rafting is popular on the Stanislaus River. Improved camping & day use facilities avail in the Glory Hole and Tuttletown recreation areas. (All yr, daily; some sections of day-use areas & campgrounds may be closed during winter) 10 N via CA 49, situated between Angels Camp, Sonora & Columbia. Phone 209/536-9094. **Free** Camping **¢¢¢**

Railtown 1897 State Historic Park. Steam passenger train rides (daytime, 1 hr; evening, 2 hrs) over the Sierra foothills. Roundhouse tour. Park (daily). Rides (Mar-Nov, Sat, Sun & hols). Res necessary for evening rides. Combination tickets avail. 3 mi S in Jamestown, at 5th Ave & Reservoir Rd. For information contact Railtown, PO Box 1250, Jamestown 95327; phone 209/984-3953. Tours **¢¢**; Rides **¢¢¢**

Skiing.

Bear Valley. Two triple, 7 double chairlifts, 2 surface lifts; patrol, school, rentals; restaurant, cafeteria, concession area, bar; lodging. Longest run 3 mi; vertical drop 1,900 ft. (Nov-Apr, daily) 17 mi NW on CA 49, then 50 mi E on CA 4. Cross-country skiing also avail in area (Phone

209/753-2834). Half-day rates. Phone 209/753-2301, 209/753-2308 (snow conditions). ¢¢¢¢¢

Dodge Ridge. Two triple, 5 double chairlifts, 4 rope tows; patrol, school, rentals; cafeteria, bar; day-lodge, nursery. 28 runs; longest run 2¼ mi; vertical drop 1,600 ft. Snowboarding. (Mid-Nov-mid-Apr, daily) 30 mi E on CA 108. Phone 209/965-3474 or -4444 (snow conditions, 24 hrs). ¢¢¢¢¢

Stanislaus National Forest. More than 890,000 acres; contains Emigrant Wilderness, Carson-Iceberg Wilderness and a portion (22,917 acres) of the Mokelumne Wilderness. The forest has many developed recreation sites with swimming; fishing; boating, rafting. Hiking, bridle trails. Winter sports. Picnicking. More than 40 developed campgrounds (fee). NE & SE of town. For further information contact the Forest Supervisor's Office, 19777 Greenley Rd; phone 209/532-3671 or the Summit Ranger District Office at 209/965-3434.

Annual Events

Fireman's Muster. Columbia State Historic Park. Antique fire engines, parade, pumping contests. Early May.

Mother Lode Roundup Parade and Rodeo. Mother Lode Fairgrounds on CA 108. Mother's Day wkend.

Mother Lode Fair. Fairgrounds. 4 days mid-July.

Wild West Film Fest & Rodeo. Fairgrounds. Celebration of all things Western. Last wkend Sept.

Motor Hotels

✓★ **DAYS INN.** *160 S Washington St (95370). 209/532-2400; FAX 209/532-4542; res: 800/580-4667.* 64 rms, 3 story. S, D $49-$79; each addl $5; suites $99-$169; under 18 free; ski plans. Crib avail. Pet accepted; $10. TV; cable (premium). Pool. Complimentary coffee in rms. Restaurant 6 am-10 pm. Bar 4 pm-2 am. Ck-out 11 am. Meeting rms. Some refrigerators. Cr cds: A, C, D, DS, MC, V.

SC

★★ **MURPHYS HISTORIC HOTEL.** *457 Main St (95247), 15 mi N, Parrot's Ferry N to CA 4 E. 209/728-3444; FAX 209/728-1590; res: 800/532-7684; res: 800/532-7684.* 29 rms, 20 with A/C, 20 with bath, 20 with rm phones, 1-2 story, 2 suites. S, D $70-$80; each addl $6; suites $75-$90; under 12 free; ski, golf plans. Crib $6. Cable TV in many rms. Complimentary continental bkfst. Restaurant 7 am-9 pm. Rm serv. Bar; entertainment Fri, Sat. Ck-out 11 am. Meeting rms. Business servs avail. Downhill/x-country ski 20 mi. Some balconies. Cr cds: A, C, D, DS, MC, V.

SC

Inns

★★ **BARRETTA GARDENS INN.** *700 S Baretta St (95370). 209/532-6039; FAX 209/532-8257; res: 800/206-3333.* E-mail barretta@mlode.com; web www.sonnet.com/dancers/bandb/barretta. 5 rms, 2 story. S, D $95-$105. Crib free. TV. Complimentary full bkfst; refreshments. Ck-out 11 am, ck-in 3-5 pm. Antiques. 3 parlors, one with fireplace. Solarium, porches looking out on acre of lawns and gardens. Victorian house (1903). Totally nonsmoking. Cr cds: A, C, MC, V.

SC

★★ **CITY HOTEL.** *22768 Main St (95310), N on CA 49, on Main St. 209/532-1470; FAX 209/532-7027; res: 800/532-1479.* E-mail info@cityhotel.com; web www.cityhotel.com. 10 rms, 2 story. No rm phones. S $80-$100; D $85-$105; each addl $10; package plans. Crib free. Complimentary continental bkfst; afternoon refreshments. Restaurant. Bar. Ck-out noon, ck-in 2 pm. Meeting rm. Business servs avail. Concierge serv. Balconies. Restored Gold Rush-era hotel (1856). Many antiques. Totally nonsmoking. Cr cds: A, C, DS, MC, V.

✓★★ **FALLON HOTEL.** *11175 Washington St (95310), 3 mi N on CA 49. 209/532-1470; FAX 209/532-7027; res: 800/532-1479.* E-mail info@cityhotel.com; web www.cityhotel.com. 14 rms, 2 story. No rm phones. S, D $55-$105; suite $155; package plans. Crib free. Continental bkfst. Ck-out noon, ck-in 2 pm. Meeting rms. Business servs avail. Concierge serv. Balconies. Established 1857; in Columbia State Historic Park. Totally nonsmoking. Cr cds: A, C, DS, MC, V.

D

★★ **JAMESTOWN HOTEL.** *18153 Main St (95370), on Main St, 3 mi W on CA 108. 209/984-3902; FAX 209/984-4149; res: 800/205-4901.* E-mail jthotel@sonnet.com; web www.sonnet.com/jthotel. 11 rms, 2 story. S, D $80-$135; lower rates Oct-Apr (Sun-Thurs). TV; cable. Complimentary full bkfst. Restaurant (see JAMESTOWN HOTEL). Bar 10 am-10 pm. Ck-out noon, ck-in 2 pm. Balconies. Antique furnishings, lace curtains. Some in-rm whirlpools. Totally nonsmoking. Cr cds: A, C, D, DS, JCB, MC, V.

D SC

✓★ **LAVENDER HILL BED AND BREAKFAST.** *683 Barretta St (95370). 209/532-9024; res: 800/446-1333.* E-mail lavender@sonnet.com; web www.lavenderhill.com. 4 rms, 2 story. No rm phones. S $65-$85; D $75-$85; each addl $15; package plans; hols (2-day min). Cable TV in common rm. Complimentary full bkfst; refreshments. Restaurant nearby. Ck-out 11 am, ck-in 2 pm. Luggage handling. Concierge serv. Built in 1900. Totally nonsmoking. Cr cds: A, C, MC, V.

SC

★★★ **MCCAFFREY HOUSE BED & BREAKFAST INN.** *23251 Hwy 108 (95383), 10 mi E on CA 108, 500 ft past 4000 ft elevation marker. 209/586-0757; FAX 209/586-3689; res: 888/586-0757.* E-mail innkeeper@sierragetaway.com; web www.sierragetaway. com. 7 rms, 3 story. No elvtr. S, D $95-$120; each addl $10; package plans; hols, wkends 2-day min. Crib free. TV; cable, VCR (movies). Complimentary afternoon refreshments. Restaurant nearby. Ck-out 11 am, ck-in 2 pm. Business servs avail. In-rm modem link. Luggage handling. Concierge serv. Downhill ski 19 mi; x-country ski 15 mi. Lawn games. Fireplaces. Many balconies. Picnic tables, grills. Adj to forest. Original art. Totally nonsmoking. Cr cds: A, C, MC, V.

★★ **NATIONAL HOTEL.** *18183 Main St (95327), on Main St, 3 mi W on CA 108. 209/984-3446; FAX 209/984-5620; res: 800/894-3446.* E-mail info@national-hotel.com; web www.national-hotel.com. 9 rms, 2 story. No rm phones. S, D $80-$100; each addl $10. Children over 10 yrs only. Pet accepted, some restrictions; $50 deposit. TV avail. Complimentary bkfst. Dining rm 11 am-10 pm; Sun to 9 pm. Rm serv. Bar 9 am-10 pm. Ck-out noon, ck-in 2 pm. Balconies. Continuously operated since 1859. Totally nonsmoking. Cr cds: A, C, DS, MC, V.

★★ **PALM HOTEL BED & BREAKFAST.** *10382 Willow St (95327), 3 mi W on CA 108. 209/984-3429; FAX 209/984-4929; res: 800/446-7256; res: 888/551-1852.* E-mail innkeeper@palmhotel.com; web www.palmhotel.com. 9 rms, 2 story. No rm phones. S, D $85-$145. TV; cable. Complimentary full bkfst; refreshments. Restaurant nearby. Ck-out 11 am, ck-in 3-6 pm. Business servs avail. Concierge serv. Lawn games. Picnic tables. Built in 1890, remodeled in 1982. Totally nonsmoking. Cr cds: A, C, MC, V.

D

★★ **REDBUD INN.** *402 Main St (95247), Parrot's Ferry N to CA 4 E. 209/728-8533; FAX 209/728-8132; res: 800/827-8533.* Web www.redbudinn.com. 13 rms, 2 story, 3 suites. No rm phones. Apr-Nov: S, D $90-$160; each addl $15; suites $175-$245; ski, golf plans; hols (2-day min). Crib free. Complimentary full bkfst; afternoon refreshments. Restaurant 11:30 am-10 pm. Ck-out 11 am, ck-in 2-3 pm. Business servs avail.

Luggage handling. Street parking. Downhill/x-country ski 20 mi. Massage. Many fireplaces; some in-rm whirlpools, refrigerators, wet bars. Many balconies. Totally nonsmoking. Cr cds: C, DS, MC, V.

D

★ **RYAN HOUSE 1855.** *153 S Shepherd St (95370). 209/533-3445; res: 800/831-4897.* Web www.ryanhouse.com. 4 rms, 3 with shower only, 2 story, 1 suite. S, D $87-$90; suite $155. TV, VCR in sitting rm. Complimentary full bkfst; afternoon refreshments. Restaurant nearby. Ck-out 11 am, ck-in 3 pm. 1850s Gold Rush house furnished with antiques and reproductions. Totally nonsmoking. Cr cds: A, C, MC, V.

★★ **SERENITY.** *15305 Bear Cub Dr (95370). 209/533-1441; res: 800/426-1441.* E-mail serenity@mlode.com; web www.serenity-inn.com. 4 rms, 2 story. No rm phones. S $75-$100; D $95-$120; package plans. Complimentary full bkfst; refreshments. Restaurant nearby. Ck-out noon, ck-in 3 pm. Concierge serv. Lawn games. Some fireplaces. Grills. ½ mi opp lake. Custom-built home; unique kitchen; antiques. Totally nonsmoking. Cr cds: A, C, DS, MC, V.

Restaurants

★★★ **CITY HOTEL.** *(See Fallon Hotel) 209/532-1479; FAX 209/532-7027.* E-mail info@cityhotel.com; web www.cityhotel.com. Hrs: 5-9 pm; Sun brunch 11 am-2 pm. Closed Mon; Dec 24-25. Res accepted. Contemporary French menu. Bar to 11 pm. A la carte entrees: dinner $15-$23. Complete meals: dinner $30-$38. Sun brunch $6-$15. Specializes in California French cuisine. Own baking. Restored Gold Rush-era hotel (1856). Totally nonsmoking. Cr cds: A, C, DS, MC, V.

★★★ **HEMINGWAY'S.** *362 S Stewart St (95370). 209/532-4900.* E-mail hemnway@lodelink.com. Hrs: 5 pm-closing. Closed Mon; Jan 1. Res accepted. Continental menu. Beer. Wine list. Semi-a la carte: dinner $20-$25. Complete meals: dinner $39. Specialties: Mahagony duckling, tournedos of veal. Own desserts. Entertainment Fri, Sat. Outdoor dining. Rotating menu. Country European cafe. Ernest Hemingway theme. Totally nonsmoking. Cr cds: A, C, DS, JCB, MC, V.

D

✓★★ **JAMESTOWN HOTEL.** *(See Jamestown Hotel Inn) 209/984-3902.* E-mail jthotel@sonnet.com; web www.sonnet.com/jthotel. Hrs: 11 am-3 pm, 5-9 pm; Fri, Sat to 10 pm; Sun 4-9 pm; Sun brunch 10 am-3 pm. Res accepted. Bar 10 am-10 pm. Semi-a la carte: lunch $4.95-$9.95, dinner $8.50-$16.95. Sun brunch $4.95-$8.95. Specialty: Gorgonzola stuffed filet mignon. Outdoor dining. Historic building (1859); 19th-century bar. Victorian decor; antiques. Totally nonsmoking. Cr cds: A, C, D, DS, JCB, MC, V.

D

South Lake Tahoe (Lake Tahoe Area) (D-4)

Pop 21,586 **Elev** 6,260 ft **Area Code** 530

Motels

★★★ **BEST WESTERN STATION HOUSE INN.** *901 Park Ave (96150). 530/542-1101; FAX 530/542-1714; res: 800/822-5953.* E-mail stationhouse@nanosecond.com. 102 rms, 2 story. June-Oct, hols: S, D $88-$108; each addl $10; suites $125-$200; under 12 free; ski plan; lower rates rest of yr. TV; cable. Heated pool; whirlpool, poolside serv. Complimentary full bkfst. Restaurant 7:30-10:30 am, 5:30-10 pm; Wed to 10:30 am. Bar from 5 pm. Ck-out noon. Meeting rms. Business servs avail. Valet serv. Downhill ski 1 mi; x-country ski 14 mi. Microwaves avail. Private beach 1½ blks. Cr cds: A, C, D, DS, MC, V.

SC

★★★ **BEST WESTERN TIMBER COVE LODGE.** *3411 Lake Tahoe Blvd (96150). 530/541-6722; FAX 530/541-7959; res: 800/528-1234.* 262 rms, 192 with shower only, 3 story. Mid-June-Sept: S, D $100-$160; each addl $10; under 17 free; family rates; ski plans; wkends, hols (2-day min); higher rates special events; lower rates rest of yr. Crib free. TV; cable. Complimentary coffee in rms. Restaurant 6:30 am-2 pm, 5:30-10 pm. Rm serv. Bar 4 pm-midnight. Ck-out noon. Meeting rms. Business servs avail. Bellhops. Concierge. Sundries. Gift shop. Coin lndry. Downhill ski 1 mi; x-country ski 5 mi. Pool; whirlpool, poolside serv. Some fireplaces. Some balconies. On lake. Cr cds: A, C, D, DS, JCB, MC, V.

SC

✓★ **CEDAR LODGE.** *4069 Cedar Ave (96150). 530/544-6453; FAX 530/542-1290; res: 800/222-1177.* 34 rms, 2 story. No A/C. Mid-June-mid-Sept, wkends, hols: S, D $58-$98; each addl $10; ski plans; lower rates rest of yr. TV; cable. Pool; whirlpool (winter). Complimentary coffee in rms. Restaurant nearby. Ck-out noon. Downhill ski 1 mi; x-country ski 15 mi. Some fireplaces. Beach privileges 4 blks. Cr cds: A, C, DS, MC, V.

SC

★ **DAYS INN.** *3530 Lake Tahoe Blvd (96150). 530/544-3445; FAX 530/544-3466; res: 800/350-3446.* 42 rms. S, D $49-$99; under 12 free; higher rates wkends, hols. Crib $10. TV; cable. Pool. Complimentary continental bkfst. Restaurant nearby. Ck-out 11 am. Downhill ski 2 mi; x-country 14 mi. Microwaves avail. 4 blks to lake. Cr cds: A, C, D, DS, JCB, MC, V.

SC

★★ **FANTASY INN & WEDDING CHAPEL.** *3696 Lake Tahoe Blvd (96150). 530/541-4200; FAX 530/541-6798; res: 800/367-7736.* E-mail fantasy@sierra.net. 53 rms, 2 story, 15 suites. Mid-Mar-mid-Oct: S, D $98-$259; suites $98-$299; ski, golf plans; wkends, hols (2-day min); higher rates special events; lower rates rest of yr. TV. Complimentary coffee in rms. Restaurant nearby. Ck-out 11 am. Business servs avail. Downhill ski 2 mi; x-country ski 10 mi. In-rm whirlpool; some refrigerators, fireplaces. Opp lake. Open courtyard wedding chapel. Cr cds: A, C, D, DS, ER, JCB, MC, V.

SC

★★ **FOREST INN SUITES.** *1 Lake Pkwy (96150). 530/541-6655; FAX 530/544-3135; res: 800/822-5950.* 118 rms, 3 story, 101 suites. Jan-mid-Apr, mid-June-mid-Sept: S, D $140-$175; suites $130-$225; under 17 free; lower rates rest of yr. Crib free. TV; cable. 2 pools; whirlpool. Complimentary continental bkfst. Coffee in rms. Restaurant nearby. Bar 4-10 pm. Ck-out noon. Meeting rms. Business servs avail. Coin lndry. Downhill ski 2 mi; x-country 5 mi. Exercise equipt; sauna. Game rm. Microwaves; refrigerators in suites. Cr cds: A, C, D, DS, MC, V.

SC

★★ **HOLIDAY INN EXPRESS.** *3961 Lake Tahoe Blvd (96150). 530/544-5900; FAX 530/544-5333; res: 800/544-5288.* E-mail holiday@sierra.net; web virtualtahoe.com/holidayinnexpress. 89 rms, 2 story. Mid-June-Aug: S, D $89-$99; kit. suites $129-$179; under 19 free; ski plan; higher rates: wkends, hols; lower rates rest of yr. Crib free. TV; cable (premium). Heated pool in season; whirlpools. Sauna. Complimentary continental bkfst. Coffee in rms. Restaurant adj 6:30 am-midnight. Ck-out noon. Coin lndry. Business servs avail. Downhill ski 1 mi; x-country ski 5 mi. Refrigerators; microwaves avail; some wet bars. Cr cds: A, C, D, DS, JCB, MC, V.

SC

★★★ **INN BY THE LAKE.** *3300 Lake Tahoe Blvd (96150). 530/542-0330; FAX 530/541-6596; res: 800/877-1466.* E-mail ibl@sierra.net; web www.innbythelake.com. 100 rms, 3 story. June-Sept: S, D $98-$165; suites $175-$395; ski, golf plans; lower rates rest of yr. TV;

cable (premium). Heated pool; whirlpool. Sauna. Complimentary continental bkfst. Coffee in rms. Restaurant adj 24 hrs. Ck-out noon. Coin Indry. Meeting rm. Business servs avail. In-rm modem link. Valet serv. Sundries. Downhill ski 1½ mi; x-country ski 10 mi. Some refrigerators, wet bars, bathrm phones. Balconies. Picnic area. Lake opp. Cr cds: A, C, D, DS, MC, V.

D SC

✓★ **MATTERHORN MOTEL.** *2187 Lake Tahoe Blvd (96150). 530/541-0367; FAX 530/541-0367; res: 800/821-7335.* 18 rms, 2 story. No A/C. Mid-June-mid-Sept, wkends, hols: S, D $49-$79; kit. units $10 addl; lower rates rest of yr. Pet accepted; $10 per day. TV; cable. Pool; whirlpool. Complimentary coffee in lobby. Ck-out 11 am. Business servs avail. Downhill ski 3 mi; x-country ski 10 mi. Microwaves avail. Near marina. Cr cds: A, C, D, DS, MC, V.

SC

★ **QUALITY INN.** *3838 Lake Tahoe Blvd (92263). 530/541-5400; FAX 530/541-7170.* 121 rms, 2 story. S, D $58-$88; kits. $110-$130; under 12 free; higher rates: wkends, hols. Crib free. TV; cable. Pool. Complimentary coffee in rms. Restaurant. Bar. Ck-out 11 am. Coin Indry. Meeting rms. Business servs avail. Downhill ski 1 mi; x-country ski 13 mi. Lake 4 blks. Cr cds: A, C, D, DS, ER, JCB, MC, V.

SC

★ **ROYAL VALHALLA LODGE.** *4104 Lakeshore Blvd (96157). 530/544-2233; FAX 530/544-1436; res: 800/999-4104.* 80 rms, 3 story, 30 kits. (some equipt). No A/C. June-Sept: S, D $100-$105; each addl $10; suites $112-$212; kit. units $5 addl; under 12 free; higher rates some hols; lower rates rest of yr. TV; cable. Heated pool; whirlpool. Complimentary continental bkfst. Complimentary coffee in rms. Restaurant nearby. Ck-out 11 am. Coin Indry. Business servs avail. Sundries. Downhill ski 1½ mi; x-country ski 14 mi. Many private patios, balconies. Private beach. Cr cds: A, C, D, MC, V.

SC

✓★ **STATELINE TRAVELODGE.** *4011 Lake Tahoe Blvd (96157). 530/544-6000; FAX 530/544-6869; res: 800/578-7878.* 50 rms, 49 with shower only, 2 story. S, D $49-$110; each addl $5; under 18 free; higher rates: hols, special events. TV; cable (premium). Complimentary coffee in rms. Restaurant nearby. Ck-out noon. Pool. Refrigerators. Cr cds: A, C, D, DS, MC, V.

SC

★ **TAHOE CHALET INN.** *3860 Lake Tahoe Blvd (96156). 530/544-3311; FAX 530/544-4069; res: 800/821-2656.* 66 units, 2 story, 14 suites, 6 kits. Some A/C. Mid-June-Sept & mid-Dec-Mar: S $58-$82; D $82-$88; suites $98-$220; higher rates some hols; lower rates rest of yr. TV; cable (premium), VCR avail (movies). Heated pool; whirlpool. Sauna. Complimentary continental bkfst. Restaurant nearby. Ck-out 11 am. Coin Indry. Meeting rms. Business servs avail. Downhill ski 2½ mi. Many refrigerators. Some bathrm phones, wet bars. Some rms with in-rm whirlpool, fireplace. ½ mi to lake. Cr cds: A, C, D, DS, MC, V.

SC

✓★ **TAHOE COLONY INN.** *3794 Montreal Rd (96150). 530/544-6481; FAX 530/544-2775; res: 800/338-5552.* E-mail colony@tahoe.net.com; web www.americana-inns.com. 86 rms, 2 story. No A/C. Mid-June-Sept: S, D $59; wkend rates; hols (2-day min); lower rates rest of yr. Crib free. Pet accepted, some restrictions. TV; cable. Complimentary continental bkfst. Restaurant opp open 24 hrs. Ck-out noon. Meeting rms. Business servs avail. Pool; whirlpool. Some balconies. Grills. Cr cds: A, C, D, MC, V.

SC

✓★ **TRAVELODGE.** *4003 Lake Tahoe Blvd (96150). 530/541-5000; FAX 530/544-6910; res: 800/578-7878.* 66 rms, all with shower only, 2 story. S, D $49-$110; each addl $5; under 18 free; higher rates: wkends, hols. TV; cable (premium). Complimentary coffee in rms. Restaurant nearby. Ck-out noon. Pool. Refrigerators. Lake 3 blks. Cr cds: A, C, D, DS, MC, V.

SC

✓★ **TRAVELODGE.** *3489 Lake Tahoe Blvd (96156). 530/544-5266; FAX 530/544-6985; res: 800/578-7878.* 59 rms, 2 story. S, D $49-$110; each addl $5; under 18 free; higher rates: wkends, hols. TV; cable (premium). Heated pool. Complimentary coffee in rms. Restaurant adj 7 am-2 pm. Ck-out noon. Business servs avail. Downhill ski 1 mi; x-country ski 11 mi. Cr cds: A, C, D, DS, ER, JCB, MC, V.

SC

Motor Hotel

★★ **LAKELAND VILLAGE BEACH & SKI RESORT.** *3535 Lake Tahoe Blvd (96150), 1 mi SW of CA-NV state line on US 50. 530/544-1685; FAX 530/544-0193; res: 800/822-5969.* E-mail lakeland@sierra.net; web www.lakeland-village.com. 212 kit. units, 1-3 story. July-Aug, mid-Dec-Mar, hols (2-day min): S, D $75-$175; town houses $170-$530; ski plans; lower rates rest of yr. Crib free. TV; cable (premium). 2 pools, heated; wading pool, 2 whirlpools, sauna. Playground. Coffee in rms. Restaurant adj 7 am-10 pm. Ck-out 11 am. Coin Indry. Meeting rms. Business servs avail. Some garage parking. Tennis, pro. Downhill ski 1½ mi; x-country ski 15 mi. 1½-2 baths in most units. Refrigerators, microwaves, fireplaces. Private patios, balconies. Pier; dock. Private sand beach. Spacious grounds, 19 acres. Cr cds: A, C, MC, V.

SC

Hotel

★★★ **EMBASSY SUITES RESORT.** *4130 Lake Tahoe Blvd (96150). 530/544-5400; FAX 530/544-4900; res: 800/362-2779.* E-mail sales2@embassytahoe.com; web www.embassytahoe.com. 400 suites, 9 story. Jan-Mar & July-Aug: S, D $149-$359; under 12 free; ski, golf plans; higher rates hols; lower rates rest of yr. Crib free. Valet parking $2. TV; cable (premium), VCR (movies). Indoor pool; whirlpool, poolside serv. Complimentary full bkfst. Complimentary coffee in rms. Restaurant 11 am-11 pm. Bar to 2 am; entertainment. Ck-out noon. Coin Indry. Convention facilities. Business servs avail. Concierge. Gift shop. Downhill ski 1 mi; x-country ski 5 mi. Exercise equipt; sauna. Refrigerators, microwaves, minibars, wet bars; some bathrm phones. Some balconies. Cr cds: A, C, D, DS, ER, JCB, MC, V.

D SC

Inn

★★★ **TAHOE VISTA INN AND MARINA.** *7220 N Lake Blvd (96148), ¾ mi W of jct CA 267 & CA 28. 530/546-7662; FAX 530/546-0667; res: 800/521-6656.* 6 suites, 5 A/C. Jan-Mar & mid-June-Sept: S, D $160-$240; lower rates rest of yr. TV; cable. Complimentary coffee in rms. Restaurant (see CAPTAIN JON'S under Tahoe Vista listing). Ck-out noon, ck-in 3 pm. Business servs avail. Downhill/x-country ski 15 mi. Microwaves, whirlpools, fireplaces. Balconies. On Lake Tahoe. Cr cds: C, MC, V.

Restaurants

★★★ **EVANS AMERICAN GOURMET CAFE.** *536 Emerald Bay Rd (96150). 530/542-1990.* Hrs: 6-10 pm. Closed Sun; Easter, Thanksgiving, Dec 25. Res accepted. Wine list. A la carte entrees: dinner $15.95-$22.95. Specializes in veal, venison, seafood. Small clapboard house with French country atmosphere. Totally nonsmoking. Cr cds: C, MC, V.

★★ **FRESH KETCH.** *2433 Venice Dr E (96150). 530/541-5683.* Hrs: 11:30-10:30 pm. Closed Thanksgiving, Dec 25. Res accepted. Bar 11:30-1:30 am. A la carte entrees: dinner $13.95-$30. Child's meals. Specializes in seafood, rack of lamb. Valet parking (summer). Outdoor dining. View of marina. Cr cds: A, C, D, DS, JCB, MC, V.

D

★★★ **LLEWELLYN.** *775/588-2411.* International. Specialties: Wild Boar, Abalone, rack of lamb; buffalo. Hrs: Wed-Sat 11:30 am- 2 pm; Mon-Thurs 6 pm-9:30 pm; Fri 6-10pm; Sat 5pm-10pm; Sun brunch 9:45am-2pm $22.95. Entertainment. Bar. Valet. Cr cds: C.

★★ **NEPHELE'S RESTAURANT.** *1169 Ski Run Blvd (96150). 530/544-8130.* Hrs: 5-10 pm. Res accepted. Bar 2 pm-2 am. Semi-a la carte: dinner $15-$25. Child's meals. Specializes in fresh fish and game. Own pasta. Mountain house and cabins converted into restaurant and boutique shops. Casual dining. Totally nonsmoking. Cr cds: A, C, D, DS, ER, JCB, MC, V.

D

★★★ **SWISS CHALET.** *2544 Lake Tahoe Blvd (96150), 4 mi W of CA-NV state line on US 50. 530/544-3304.* Hrs: 5-10 pm. Closed Mon; Easter, Thanksgiving, Dec 25; also 3 wks in Nov. Res accepted. Continental menu. Bar from 4 pm. Semi-a la carte: dinner $13.50-$21. Child's meals. Specializes in veal dishes, fondues, fresh seafood. Own baking. Swiss decor. Family-owned. Cr cds: A, C, MC, V.

D

South San Francisco

(see San Francisco Airport Area)

Squaw Valley

(see Lake Tahoe Area)

St Helena (D-2)

(See also Calistoga, Napa, Santa Rosa, Yountville)

Founded 1853 **Pop** 4,990 **Elev** 257 ft **Area Code** 707 **Zip** 94574
E-mail shchbr2@napanet.net **Web** www.sthelena.com

Information Chamber of Commerce, 1010A Main St, PO Box 124; 707/963-4456

What to See and Do

Lake Berryessa. Man-made lake formed by Monticello Dam; 165 mi of shoreline. Swimming, waterskiing; fishing. Picnicking, concession areas. Camping. Oak Shores has car top boat launch (fee). 4 mi S on CA 29 to Rutherford, then E on CA 128. Contact Lake Berryessa Recreation Office, Bureau of Reclamation, 5520 Knoxville Rd, Spanish Flat Station, Napa 94558; phone 707/966-2111.

Silverado Museum. Approx 8,500 items of Robert Louis Stevenson memorabilia; first and variant editions of author's works, original letters and manuscripts; paintings, sculptures, photographs. Special exhibits. (Daily exc Mon, afternoons; closed major hols) 1490 Library Ln. Phone 707/963-3757. **Free**

Wineries.

Beaulieu Vineyard. Winery founded at the turn of the century. Tours and tastings (daily; closed major hols). Select tasting rm (fee). 4 mi S on CA 29, at 1960 S St Helena Hwy, in Rutherford. Phone 707/963-2411. **Free**

Beringer Vineyards. Established 1876. Underground cellars; Rhine House (1883). Tours with wine tasting (daily; closed major hols). 2000 Main St, N on CA 29. Phone 707/963-4812 or 707/963-7115. **Free**

Charles Krug Winery. Established 1861. Tours and wine tasting. Select tasting rm (fee). (Daily; closed major hols) 2800 Main St. Phone 707/963-5057. **¢¢**

Franciscan Vineyards. Wine tasting and sales. (Daily; closed some hols) 15 mi N via CA 29 in Rutherford, at 1178 Galleron Rd. Phone 707/963-7111. Tastings **¢¢**

Louis M. Martini Winery. Guided tours. Wine tasting. (Daily; closed major hols) 254 S St Helena Hwy. Phone 707/963-2736 or 800/321-9463. **Free**

Merryvale Vineyards. Tasting rm within restored 1930s building; 2,000- and 3,000-gallon oak casks on display. Merryvale produces distinct Chardonnays as well as Bordeaux-style red wine. Tours (daily, by appt; closed some major hols). 1000 Main St. Phone 707/963-7777 or 707/963-2225. **¢¢**

Motel

★★ **EL BONITA MOTEL.** *195 Main St (94574). 707/963-3216; FAX 707/963-8838; res: 800/541-3284.* E-mail elbonita@aol.com; web www.napavalley.com/napavalley/lodgings/hotels/elbonita/index.html. 42 rms, 27 kits. June-Oct: S, D $95-$165; suites $199-$219; lower rates rest of yr. Crib $5. Pet accepted, some restrictions; $5. TV; cable (premium). Pool; whirlpool, sauna. Complimentary continental bkfst. Complimentary coffee in rms. Restaurant nearby. Ck-out 11:30 am. Business servs avail. Refrigerators; some in-rm whirlpools. Cr cds: A, C, D, DS, MC, V.

D

Hotel

★★★★ **AUBERGE DU SOLEIL.** *180 Rutherford Hill Rd (94573), N via CA 29 to Rutherford, E on CA 128 to Silverado Trail, then N to Rutherford Hill Rd. 707/963-1211; FAX 707/963-8764; res: 800/348-5406.* E-mail aubergedusoleil@aol.com; web www.aubergedusoleil.com. The adobe-style buildings of this elegant wine-country inn are set in a 33-acre hillside olive grove overlooking Napa Valley. In true European style, the service can be cold, but the overall experience is delightful. 52 rms, 2 story, 2 in-house rooms, private cottages. Apr-Nov: S, D $300-$1500; cottages from $525-$2000; lower rates rest of yr. TV; cable (premium), VCR (movies). Pool; poolside serv. Dining rm (AUBERGE DU SOLEIL). Rm serv 24 hrs. Bar 11 am-11pm with light menu. Ck-out noon, ck-in 3 pm. Meeting rm. Business servs avail. In-rm modem link. Luggage handling. Valet serv. Gift shop. Beauty shop. Tennis, pro. Bicycles avail. Exercise equipt; steam rm. Massage. Refrigerators, fireplaces. Private patios, balconies. Cr cds: A, C, D, DS, MC, V.

D

Resort

★★★★ **MEADOWOOD.** *900 Meadowood Lane (94574), off Silverado Trail at Howell Mt Rd, Napa Valley area. 707/963-3646; FAX 707/963-3532; res: 800/458-8080.* Web www.placestostay.com; www.relais chateaux.fr/meadowood. This wine-country resort sits on 256 private wooded acres with golf, tennis, and croquet facilities. Minutes from many of the state's best wineries. 99 units, 51 suites. July-mid-Nov: S, D $335-$525; each addl $25; suites $570-$2,175; under 12 free; lower rates rest of yr. Crib free. TV; cable (premium), VCR avail (movies). 2 pools; whirlpool, poolside serv. Coffee in rms. Dining rm (see THE RESTAURANT AT MEADOWOOD). Rm serv. 3 bars 10:30 am-midnight. Ck-out noon, ck-in 4 pm. Meeting rms. Business center. 7 tennis courts, pro. 9-hole golf, pro, putting green. Hiking, swimming. World-class croquet facilities, pro. Bicycle rentals. Exercise rm; sauna, steam rm. Spa. Refrigerators, minibars; many fireplaces; microwaves avail. Private patios, balconies. Cr cds: A, C, D, DS, MC, V.

D

Inns

★★ **CHESTELSON HOUSE.** *1417 Kearney St (94574). 707/963-2238.* E-mail diane@chestelson.com; web www.chelston.com. 4 rms, 2 story, 1 suite. May-mid-Nov: S, D $139-$195; each addl $30; wkends (2-day min); wkly rates; lower rates rest of yr. TV; VCR. Complimentary full bkfst, afternoon refreshments. Restaurant nearby. Ck-out 11 am, ck-in 4 pm. Business servs avail. Street parking. Victorian house (1904) with wrap-around porch; library/sitting rm furnished with antiques. Totally nonsmoking. Cr cds: C, D, JCB, MC, V.

★★★ **HARVEST INN.** *1 Main St (94574). 707/963-9463; FAX 707/963-4402; res: 800/950-8466.* E-mail innkeeper@harvestinn.com; web www.harvestinn.com. 54 rms, 1-2 story. Apr-Oct: S, D $189-$319; suites $319-$499; wkends (2-day min); lower rates rest of yr. Crib free. Pet accepted, some restrictions; $75. TV; cable, VCR avail (movies). 2 heated pools; whirlpools. Complimentary continental bkfst. Complimentary coffee in rms. Ck-out 11 am, ck-in after 4 pm. Meeting rms. Business servs avail. In-rm modem link. Refrigerators, bathrm phones, fireplaces, wet bars. Some private patios, balconies. Overlooks vineyards. Cr cds: A, C, D, DS, MC, V.

★★ **HOTEL SAINT HELENA.** *1309 Main St (94574). 707/963-4388; FAX 707/963-5402; res: 888/438-4355; res: 888/478-4355.* Web napavalley.com/napavalley/lodging/hotels/sthelena. 18 units, 14 with bath, 2 story (no ground floor units). S, D $145-$275; each addl $20; mid-wk rates. TV in most rms; cable (premium). Complimentary continental bkfst. Restaurant adj 8:30 am-10 pm. Ck-out noon, ck-in 3 pm. Business servs avail. Victorian structure (1881). Cr cds: A, C, D, DS, JCB, MC, V.

★★ **OLIVER HOUSE.** *2970 Silverado Trl N (95474). 707/963-4089; FAX 707/963-5566; res: 800/682-7888.* 4 suites, 2 story. Rm phones avail. Apr-Nov: suites $135-$285; each addl $15; wkends (2-day min); lower rates rest of yr. Complimentary full bkfst. Ck-out 11 am, ck-in 3-6 pm. Business servs avail. Lawn games. Balconies. Country-Swiss house with antique furnishings; fireplaces. Totally nonsmoking. Cr cds: A, C, MC, V.

SC

★★ **RANCHO CAYMUS INN.** *1140 Rutherford Rd (94573), jct CA 29 & 128. 707/963-1777; FAX 707/963-5387; res: 800/845-1777.* 26 suites, 2 story, 5 kits. Apr-Nov: suites $165-$195; kit. units $265-$315; wkends (2-day min); lower rates rest of yr. TV. Complimentary continental bkfst. Ck-out noon, ck-in 3 pm. Business servs avail. Health club privileges. Refrigerators; some in-rm whirlpools, fireplaces. Private patios, balconies. Spanish-style architecture. Cr cds: A, C, MC, V.

D SC

★★ **VINEYARD COUNTRY INN.** *201 Main St (94574), on CA 29. 707/963-1000; FAX 707/963-1794.* 21 suites, 2 story. Mid-May-mid-Nov: S, D $205; each addl $15; under 5 free; wkends (2-day min), hols (3-day min). TV. Heated pool; whirlpool. Complimentary buffet bkfst. Restaurant nearby. Ck-out noon. Business servs avail. Refrigerators. Some balconies, patios. Cr cds: A, C, D, MC, V.

D

✓★ **WHITE SULPHUR SPRING RESORT SPA.** *3100 White Sulphur Spr Rd (94574). 707/963-8588; FAX 707/963-2890; res: 800/593-8873.* Web www.whitesilversprings.com. 28 rms in 2 bldgs, 14 share bath, 14 full baths, 9 cottages, 4 with kit. No A/C (5 cottages with A/C). No rm phones. S, D $95-$115; each addl $15; cottages $135; kit. cottages $185; wkend rates. Crib free. Pool; whirlpool. Complimentary continental bkfst. Ck-out 11 am, ck-in 3 pm. Meeting rms. Business servs avail. Hiking. Massage. Lawn games. Microwaves avail. Picnic tables, grills. Rustic inn in secluded canyon surrounded by forests; a hot sulphur spring (87°F) flows out of the mountains into a rock-lined outdoor soaking pool. Totally nonsmoking. Cr cds: C, MC, V.

★★★ **WINE COUNTRY INN.** *1152 Lodi Ln (94574). 707/963-7077; FAX 707/963-9018; res: 800/473-3463.* E-mail romance@winecountryinn.com; web www.winecountryinn.com. 24 units, 2-3 story. Mid-Apr-mid-Oct: S $125-$248; D $145-$268; each addl $20; suites $206-$268; lower rates rest of yr. Closed Dec 25. Pool; whirlpool. Complimentary full bkfst; afternoon refreshments. Ck-out noon, ck-in 3 pm. Gift shop. Many fireplaces; some in-rm whirlpools, refrigerators. Private patios, balconies. Handmade quilts in many rms; antiques. View of vineyards. Cr cds: C, MC, V.

Restaurants

★★ **BRAVA TERRACE.** *3010 Saint Helena Hwy N (94574). 707/963-9300.* Hrs: noon-9 pm. Closed Wed Nov-Apr; Thanksgiving, Dec 25; also 10 days Jan. Res accepted. Contemporary Amer menu. Bar. A la carte entrees: lunch, dinner $7.95-$22. Specialties: cassoulet, penne pasta, coq au vin. Parking. Outdoor dining. Large stone fireplace. Totally nonsmoking. Cr cds: A, C, D, DS, MC, V.

D

★★★ **GREYSTONE.** *2555 Main St (94574). 707/967-1010.* Hrs: 11:30 am-9 pm; Fri, Sat to 10 pm. Closed most major hols; Jan 1-15; also Tues, Wed Dec-Mar. Res accepted. Mediterranean menu. Bar. Wine cellar. A la carte entrees: lunch, dinner $15-$23. Child's meals. Specialties: greystone paella, tapas. Outdoor dining. View of vineyard. Totally nonsmoking. Cr cds: A, C, D, DS, MC, V.

D

★★ **PINOT BLANC.** *641 Main St (94574). 707/963-6191.* Hrs: 11:30 am-10 pm. Country French menu. Bar. A la carte entrees: lunch $8.25-$19.95, dinner $14.50-$22.95. Child's meals. Daily menu and specials. Own baking. Outdoor dining. Fireplace. Totally nonsmoking. Cr cds: A, C, D, DS, JCB, MC, V.

D

★★ **SHOWLEY'S AT MIRAMONTE.** *1327 Railroad Ave (94574), 1 blk E of Main St. 707/963-1200.* Hrs: 11:30 am-3 pm, 6-9 pm. Closed Mon; most major hols. Res accepted; required wkends. Eclectic cuisine. A la carte entrees: lunch $8-$15, dinner $14-$22. Child's meals. Specialties: grilled duck breast, lamb shanks. Jazz Fri. Outdoor dining. Landmark building (1858). Cr cds: A, C, DS, MC, V.

D

★★★★ **TERRA.** *1345 Railroad Ave (94574). 707/963-8931.* Chef Hiro Sone serves up Mediterranean accented dishes (of French and Italian inspiration) in this century-old converted foundry. Rough hewn wood beams and tile floors set a casual stage for an elegant dining experience. Save room for dessert. Southern French, northern Italian menu. Specialties: petit ragout of sweetbreads with prosciutto, broiled sake-marinated sea bass with shrimp dumplings. Own pastries. Hrs: 6-9:30 pm; Fri, Sat to 10 pm. Closed Tues; some major hols. Res required. Wine, beer. A la carte entrees: dinner $15-$25. Street parking. Totally nonsmoking. Cr cds: C, D, MC, V.

D

★★★ **THE RESTAURANT AT MEADOWOOD.** *(See Meadowood Resort) 707/963-3646.* Web www.placestostay.com. Hrs: 6-9:30 pm; Sun brunch 10 am-2 pm. Res accepted. French, Amer menu. Bar open 5:30-12pm on weekends. Wine cellar. A la carte entrees: dinner $26-

$32. Complete meals: dinner $45-$75. Sun brunch $34. Specializes in vegetarian items, seafood. Own baking. Valet parking on weekends. Outdoor dining. Jacket required. Cr cds: A, C, D, DS, MC, V.

D

★ **TOMATINA.** *1020 Main St (94574). 707/967-9999.* Hrs: 11:30 am-10 pm. Closed Dec 25. Italian menu. Bar. A la carte entrees: lunch, dinner $6.95-$19.95. Child's meals. Specialty: pizza wraps. Parking. Outdoor dining. Modern artwork. Totally nonsmoking. Cr cds: C, D, DS, JCB, MC, V.

D

✓★★★ **TRA VIGNE.** *1050 Charter Oak Ave (94574). 707/963-4444.* Hrs: 11:30 am-10:30 pm; Fri, Sat to 11 pm. Closed July 4, Thanksgiving, Dec 25. Res accepted. Northern Italian menu. Bar. A la carte entrees: lunch, dinner $4.95-$17.50. Specializes in fresh pasta, grilled dishes. Own desserts. Parking. Outdoor dining. Patio. Totally nonsmoking. Cr cds: C, D, DS, JCB, MC, V.

D

★★ **TRILOGY.** *1234 Main St (94574). 707/963-5507.* Hrs: 6 pm to closing. Closed Sun, Mon; Thanksgiving, Dec 25. Res accepted. California, French menu. Wine, beer. Prix fixe: dinner $33. Specializes in beef, seafood, lamb. Outdoor dining. Cr cds: C, MC, V.

D

Stockton (E-3)

(See also Lodi, Modesto)

Founded 1849 **Pop** 210,943 **Elev** 13 ft **Area Code** 209 **E-mail** ssjcvb@ssjcvb.com **Web** www.ssjcvb.org

Information Stockton/San Joaquin Convention and Visitors Bureau, 46 W Fremont St, 95202; 209/943-1987 or 800/350-1987

Connected to San Francisco Bay by a 78-mile deepwater channel, Stockton is an important inland port with giant ore-loading facilities and grain terminals accessible to large ships. In its early days as the gateway to the Mother Lode country, it became a "city of a thousand tents." Many of the 49ers settled here and became rich when irrigation systems turned the surrounding countryside into fertile grain fields.

What to See and Do

Children's Museum. Interactive displays covering 24,000 sq ft; special events. (Tues-Sat, also Sun afternoon; closed some major hols) 402 W Weber Ave. Phone 209/465-4386. ¢¢

Haggin Museum. State and local historical exhibits; 19th-century European and American paintings and decorative arts; Native American arts. Guided tours (Sat or by appt); changing exhibits. (Daily exc Mon, afternoons; closed Jan 1, Thanksgiving, Dec 25) 1201 N Pershing Ave, at Rose St in Victory Park. Phone 209/462-4116 or 209/462-1566. **Donation**

Municipal recreation facilities. The city maintains 50 parks, tennis courts, playgrounds, swimming pools, picnic areas; 2 golf courses; boat launching facilities and berths; ice arena; community and senior citizen centers. Fee for activities. Phone 209/937-8206.

Pixie Woods. Mother Goose and Fairyland characters; puppet shows in Toadstool Theatre; train, boat and merry-go-round rides. (June-Labor Day, Wed-Sun; late Feb-May & after Labor Day-late Oct, Sat, Sun & hols, including Easter wk) In Louis Park, W end of Monte Diablo Blvd. Phone 209/937-8206. ¢

World Wildlife Museum. Over 2,000 mounted zoological specimens represent wildlife from every continent. Include deer, elk, African animals, wolves, antelope, bears, crocodiles and alligators, birds, Arctic animals. (Wed-Sun) 1245 W Weber Ave. Phone 209/465-2834. ¢¢

Annual Events

Asparagus Festival. Musical entertainment, asparagus food dishes, car show, wagon rides. Phone 800/350-1987. Late Apr.

San Joaquin County Fair. Horse racing, agricultural and livestock displays, entertainment. Phone 209/466-5041. June.

Obon Festival and Bazaar. Street dance, food, exhibits, authentic Japanese costumes, colorful decorations at the Buddhist Temple. Phone 209/466-6701. Late July.

Greek Festival. Food, music, dancing. Phone 209/478-7564. Sept.

Motels

✓★ **HOWARD JOHNSON EXPRESS INN.** *1672 Herndon Rd (95307), 3 mi S on CA 99 exit Hatch Rd S. 209/537-4821; FAX 209/537-1040; res: 800/446-4656.* 50 rms, 25 with shower only, 1-2 story. Apr-Sept: S $55-$65; D $60-$80; each addl $10; under 18 free. Crib free. Pet accepted, some restrictions. TV; cable (premium), VCR avail (movies). Complimentary continental bkfst. Complimentary coffee in rms. Restaurant nearby. Ck-out 11 am. Meeting rms. Business servs avail. In-rm modem link. Valet serv. Pool. Some refrigerators, microwaves. Cr cds: A, C, D, DS, MC, V.

D SC

★ **RED ROOF INN.** *2654 W March Ln (95207). 209/478-4300; FAX 209/478-1872.* 123 rms, 3 story. S $52; D $59; each addl $4; suites $80-$100; under 11 free. Crib free. TV; cable (premium). Pool; whirlpool. Complimentary coffee in lobby. Restaurant adj open 24 hrs. Ck-out 11 am. Meeting rms. Business servs avail. In-rm modem link. Refrigerator, wet bar in suites. Cr cds: A, C, D, DS, MC, V.

D SC

Hotel

★★ **RADISSON HOTEL.** *2323 Grand Canal Blvd (95207), I-5 March Lane exit. 209/957-9090; FAX 209/473-0739; res: 800/932-3322.* 198 rms, 5 story. S $86-$106; D $98-$118; each addl $21; suites $250-$350; under 21 free; wkend rates. Crib free. TV; cable (premium), VCR avail. Pool. Restaurant 6:30 am-11 pm. Bar noon-midnight. Ck-out 11 am. Meeting rms. Business servs avail. In-rm modem link. Health club privileges. Some balconies. Cr cds: A, C, D, DS, MC, V.

D SC

Restaurant

★★ **LE BISTRO.** *3121 W Benjamin Holt Dr (95219), in Marina Shopping Ctr. 209/951-0885.* Hrs: 11:30 am-3 pm, 5-9 pm; Fri, Sat to 10 pm. Closed some major hols. Res accepted. Continental menu. Bar. Semi-a la carte: lunch $10.50-$13.95, dinner $19.95-$25. Specializes in fresh fish, souffles, European-style cuisine. Own desserts. Totally nonsmoking. Cr cds: A, C, D, DS, MC, V.

D

Studio City (L.A.) (B-3 see Los Angeles map)

Area Code 818 **Zip** 91604

This community, located in the San Fernando Valley, is a neighborhood of Los Angeles, but is regarded by many as a separate entity.

Motor Hotel

★★★ **SPORTSMEN'S LODGE HOTEL.** *12825 Ventura Blvd (91604). 818/769-4700; FAX 213/769-4798; res: 800/821-8511.* E-mail information@slhotel.com; web www.slhotel.com. 198 rms, 2-5 story. S, D $105-$138; each addl $10; suites $180-$290; under 18 free. Crib free. TV; cable (premium). Heated pool; whirlpool, poolside serv. Restaurants 6:30 am-10 pm. Rm serv. Bars 11 am-midnight. Ck-out noon. Coin lndry. Meeting rms. Business servs avail. Bellhops. Valet serv. Gift shop. Beauty salon. Free airport transportation. Exercise equipt. Private patios, balconies. Gardens; ponds. Cr cds: A, C, D, DS, ER, JCB, MC, V.

D SC

Hotel

★★★ **RADISSON VALLEY CENTER HOTEL.** *15433 Ventura Blvd (91403), 4 mi W at Jct US 101 & I-405. 818/981-5400; FAX 818/981-3175; res: 800/333-3333.* E-mail radissonvalleycenterla@msn.com; web www.radisson.com. 198 rms, 13 story. S, D $140-$170; suites $165-$495; under 18 free. Crib free. Garage parking $5.50. TV; cable (premium), VCR avail. Heated pool; whirlpool, poolside serv. Complimentary continental bkfst. Restaurant 6:30 am-10 pm. Rm serv 24 hrs. Bar 11-2 am. Ck-out noon. Meeting rms. Business servs avail. Gift shop. Barber, beauty shop. Valet serv. Health club privileges. Cr cds: A, C, D, DS, ER, JCB, MC, V.

D SC

Restaurants

★★ **CAFE BIZOU.** *14016 Ventura Blvd (91423), W on US 101, exit Woodman Ave, S to Ventura Blvd, then W. 818/788-3536.* Hrs: 11:30 am-2:30 pm, 5:30-10 pm; Fri to 11 pm; Sat, Sun 11 am-2:30 pm, 5-11 pm. Closed Jan 1, Dec 25. Res required (dinner). California, French menu. Bar. A la carte entrees: lunch $5.50-$9.95, dinner $5.95-$15.95. Sat, Sun brunch $6.50-$8.95. Specialties: sauteed sesame-seed-coated salmon in a red wine sauce, steak au poivre in a peppered veal sauce. Valet parking. Outdoor dining. Casual French cafe. Totally nonsmoking. Cr cds: A, C, D, MC, V.

D

✓★★ **LA LOGGIA.** *11814 Ventura Blvd (91604), US 101 exit Laurel Canyon Blvd S. 818/985-9222.* Web www.ladining.com/laloggia/. Hrs: 11:30 am-2:30 pm, 5:30-10:30 pm; Fri to 11 pm; Sat 5:30-11 pm; Sun 5-10 pm. Closed most major hols. Res accepted. Italian menu. Bar. A la carte entrees: lunch, dinner $8.25-$17.95. Specializes in fresh pasta, Northern Italian dishes. Own pasta. Valet parking. Menu changes quarterly. Trattoria setting. Totally nonsmoking. Cr cds: A, C, D, MC, V.

D

★★ **PERROCHE.** *11929 Ventura Blvd (91604). 818/766-1179.* E-mail perroche@aol.com. Hrs: noon-2 pm, 6-10 pm. Closed Sun; also major hols. Res required (dinner). Continental menu. Bar. A la carte entrees: lunch $12-$18, dinner $13-$22. Specialties: Perroche smoked trout with horseradish; roasted Kendor farm young chicken, asparagus and morels; creme caramel. Valet parking. Outdoor dining. Provincial country decor; casual dining. Cr cds: A, C, D, DS, MC, V.

D

★★ **PINOT BISTRO.** *12969 Ventura Blvd (91604), US 101 exit Coldwater Canyon Ave S. 818/990-0500.* Hrs: 11:30 am-2:30 pm, 6-9:30 pm; Fri to 10:30 pm; Sat 5:30-10:30 pm; Sun 5:30-9:30 pm. Closed Jan 1, July 4, Dec 25. Res accepted. California, French menu. Bar. A la carte entrees: lunch $10.50-$14.95, dinner $13.95-$21.95. Prix fixe: lunch $19.98. Specialties: crispy duck leg confit, oysters on the half shell, endive salad. Valet parking. Outdoor dining. Several dining areas. Bistro decor; original artwork, photographs of celebrities. Cr cds: A, C, D, DS, JCB, MC, V.

D ♥

✓★★ **THE GREAT GREEK.** *13362 Ventura Blvd (91423). 818/905-5250.* Hrs: 11:30 am-11 pm; Fri, Sat to midnight. Res accepted. Greek menu. Bar. Semi-a la carte: lunch $6.45-$14.95, dinner $9.95-$20.95. Specialties: oven-roasted spring lamb, stuffed grape leaves, moussaka. Own desserts. Greek music, dancing. Greek decor. Totally nonsmoking. Cr cds: A, C, D, DS, MC, V.

★★ **WINE BISTRO.** *11915 Ventura Blvd (91604), US 101 exit Laurel Canyon Blvd S. 818/766-6233.* Hrs: 11:30 am-10:30 pm; Sat from 5:30 pm. Closed Sun; major hols. Res accepted. French, continental menu. Bar. Semi-a la carte: lunch $9.95-$13.95, dinner $10.95-$19.95. Prix fixe: dinner $28.95. Specializes in bouillabaisse, duck. Valet parking. Outdoor dining. Cr cds: A, C, D, DS, MC, V.

Sunnyvale (E-2)

(See also Santa Clara)

Pop 117,229 **Elev** 130 ft **Area Code** 408

Information Chamber of Commerce, 499 S Murphy Ave, 94086; 408/736-4971

What to See and Do

Sunnyvale Historical Museum. Houses historical artifacts and pictures of area as well as information on pioneering families. (Tues, Thurs & Sun; closed major hols) 235 E California Ave, in Martin Murphy Jr Park. Phone 408/749-0220. **Free**

Motels

✓★★ **MAPLE TREE INN.** *711 E El Camino Real (94087). 408/720-9700; FAX 408/738-5665; res: 800/423-0243.* 181 rms, 2-3 story. S $125-$145; D $135-$155; each addl $10; suites, kit. unit $150-$175; under 12 free; wkend, hol rates; higher rates Stanford graduation. Crib free. Pet accepted, some restrictions. TV; cable (premium). Pool. Complimentary continental bkfst. Restaurant nearby. Ck-out noon. Coin lndry. Meeting rm. Business servs avail. In-rm modem link. Valet serv. Health club privileges. Some refrigerators. Cr cds: A, C, D, DS, ER, JCB, MC, V.

D SC

★★ **RAMADA INN SILICON VALLEY.** *1217 Wildwood Ave (94089). 408/245-5330; FAX 408/732-2628; res: 800/272-6232.* 176 rms, 2 story. S $104-$124; D $114-$134; each addl $10; under 18 free; wkend rates; special package plans. Crib free. TV; cable (premium), VCR avail. Pool; whirlpool, poolside serv. Coffee in rms. Restaurants 6 am-10 pm; Sat, Sun from 7 am. Rm serv. Bars. Ck-out noon. Coin lndry. Meeting rms. Business center. Bellhops. Valet serv. Concierge. Free airport transportation. Health club privileges. Cr cds: A, C, D, DS, JCB, MC, V.

D SC

★★ **RESIDENCE INN.** *750 Lakeway Dr (96145). 408/720-1000; FAX 408/737-9722; res: 800/331-3131.* 231 kit. units, 2 story. S $179; D $199. Pet accepted; $10/day. TV; cable (premium). Pool; 2 whirlpools. Complimentary continental bkfst. Restaurant nearby. Ck-out noon. Coin lndry. Meeting rm. Business servs avail. Valet serv. Free airport transportation. Tennis. Exercise equipt. Lawn games. Picnic tables, grills. Small lake. Cr cds: A, C, D, DS, JCB, MC, V.

D SC

★★★ **SHERATON INN.** *1100 N Mathilda Ave (94089). 408/745-6000; FAX 408/734-8276; res: 800/544-5064.* 174 units, 2 story. S, D $189-$219; each addl $15; under 18 free; wkend rates. Crib free. TV; cable (premium). Heated pool; whirlpool, poolside serv. Complimentary coffee in rms. Restaurant 6:30 am-10 pm; Sat & Sun from 7:30 am. Bar noon-10 pm. Ck-out 1 pm. Meeting rms. Business servs avail. Bellhops. Valet serv.

Free airport transportation. Exercise equipt. Bathrm phones. Refrigerators avail. Garden with gazebo for special events. Cr cds: A, C, D, DS, ER, JCB, MC, V.

D SC

★★ **SUMMERFIELD SUITES HOTEL.** *900 Hamlin Ct (94089), just E of US 101 Mathilda Ave (N) exit. 408/745-1515; FAX 408/745-0540; res: 800/833-4353.* 138 kit. suites, 2-3 story. S $209; D $259; wkend rates. Crib free. Pet accepted, some restrictions; $10/day. TV; cable (premium), VCR (movies $3). Pool; whirlpool. Complimentary bkfst buffet. Complimentary coffee in rms. Restaurant nearby. Ck-out noon. Coin lndry. Meeting rms. Business servs avail. In-rm modem link. Valet serv. Sundries. Free airport transportation. Exercise equipt. Health club privileges. Some fireplaces. Grills. Cr cds: A, C, D, DS, JCB, MC, V.

D SC

★★★ **SUNDOWNER INN.** *504 Ross Dr (94089). 408/734-9900; FAX 408/747-0580; res: 800/223-9901.* 105 units, 2 story. S, D $176-$196; each addl $10; suites $200-$260; wkend rates. Crib free. TV; cable (premium), VCR avail (free movies). Heated pool. Complimentary continental bkfst. Restaurant 6 am-10:45 pm; Sat, Sun from 9 am. Bar to 2 am; entertainment Tues-Sat. Ck-out noon. Meeting rms. Business servs avail. Valet serv. Exercise equipt; sauna. Health club privileges. Library. Refrigerators. Cr cds: A, C, D, DS, JCB, MC, V.

SC

Motor Hotels

★★★ **HILTON.** *1250 Lakeside Dr (94086). 408/738-4888; FAX 408/737-7147; res: 800/932-3322.* 372 rms, 2-3 story. S, D $199-$269; each addl $15; suites $350; family, wkend rates. Crib free. TV; cable (premium). Heated pool; poolside serv, whirlpool. Coffee in rms. Restaurants 6 am-10 pm. Rm serv. Bar 10-2 am. Ck-out noon. Bellhops. Convention facilities. Business servs avail. Gift shop. Free airport transportation. Health club privileges. Bathrm phones. Park, duck pond, small beach. Cr cds: A, C, D, DS, ER, JCB, MC, V.

D SC

★★★ **RADISSON HOTEL.** *1085 E El Camino Real (94087). 408/247-0800; FAX 408/984-7120; res: 800/333-3333.* 136 rms, 3 story. S, D $180-190; each addl $10; suites $200-$210; under 13 free; wkend rates. Crib free. TV; cable (premium). Pool. Complimentary bkfst buffet. Restaurant 6 am-10 pm; Sat, Sun from 7 am. Rm serv 6-10 pm. Bar from 4 pm. Ck-out noon. Meeting rms. Business servs avail. Bellhops. Valet serv. Free garage parking. Free airport transportation. Exercise equipt. Health club privileges. Minibars. Atrium. Cr cds: A, C, D, DS, JCB, MC, V.

D SC

Susanville (B-3)

Settled 1853 **Pop** 7,279 **Elev** 4,258 ft **Area Code** 530 **Zip** 96130
E-mail lassenco@psln.com

Information Lassen County Chamber of Commerce, 84 N Lassen St, PO Box 338; 530/257-4323

Susanville is currently a trading center for an area producing livestock, lumber, alfalfa, garlic and strawberries. There is fine hunting for deer, bear, antelope, pheasant, grouse, quail, ducks and geese, and fishing in many lakes and rivers in the surrounding hills and mountains. Lassen National Forest headquarters and a Ranger District office are located here. In 1856, Susanville was the capital of the Republic of Nataqua, an area of 50,000 square miles. Isaac Roop, the town's first settler, helped establish the republic, which later joined the Nevada Territory. Roop was first Provisional Governor of Nevada and later senator. California surveys showed the area was part of Plumas County. The locals refused to join and holed up in Roop's house in 1864. After a day of gunfighting, California won back what is now Lassen County. Susanville was named by Roop in honor of his only daughter.

What to See and Do

Bizz Johnson Trail. Multipurpose trail winding 25.4 mi from Susanville to Mason Station, 4 mi N of Westwood. Transverses rugged Susan River Canyon on former railroad route. Fishing on river. Hiking, bicycling, horseback riding. Cross-country skiing. Camping. Begins ½ mi S via S Weatherlow St, left on Richmond Rd to Susanville Depot Trailhead; parking avail. Phone 530/257-3252. **Free**

Eagle Lake. Called by scientists "the lake that time forgot," this 26,000-acre lake was formed by the receding waters of a primeval lake larger than Lake Erie. It is the second-largest natural lake in California and home to Eagle Lake trout, a species averaging 3-5 lbs that has adapted to living in the lake's alkaline water. Gallatin Beach, at S end of lake, provides swimming, waterskiing, five campgrounds avail (fee). Marina has boat rentals. 2 mi W on CA 36, then 15 mi N on County A1, in Lassen National Forest. For additional information contact Supervisor, Lassen National Forest, 55 S Sacramento St; Phone 530/257-4188.

Gallatin Marina, adj to Lassen National Forest Campgrounds. Fishing, boating (ramps, rentals); groceries. (Late May-mid-Oct) Phone 530/257-2151.

Lassen National Forest. More than 1 million acres. Swimming; excellent trout fishing in lakes and streams, hunting. Cross-country and downhill skiing, snowmobiling. 7 mi W on CA 36. For further information contact the Forest Supervisor, 55 S Sacramento St; phone 530/257-2151. Includes

Wilderness Areas. All offer backpacking, primitive camping. (Daily) 35 mi W via CA 36 & County A21. Phone 530/257-2151. **Caribou Peak.** Gentle rolling forested terrain with many small crystal lakes. Many small cinder cones. **Thousand Lakes.** Contrasting topography; hiking trails. 25 mi E & S of Burney via CA 299, 89, Forest Road 26. **Ishi Wilderness.** Dotted with rock outcroppings and bizarre pillar lava formations. Ishi. 35 mi W & S of Chester via CA 36, 32.

Roop's Fort & Lassen Historical Museum. Fort (1854), built by Isaac Roop, was the state capitol of the Nataqua Republic. (May-Oct, Mon-Fri) N Weatherlow St. Phone 530/257-3292. **Free**

Annual Event

Lassen County Fair. Fairgrounds, off Russell Ave & Main St. Livestock and horse shows; rodeos; parade, livestock auction; entertainment. Phone 530/257-4104. 3rd wkend July.

Motel

★★ **BEST WESTERN TRAILSIDE INN.** *2785 Main St (96130). 530/257-4123; FAX 530/257-2665; res: 800/528-1234.* 108 rms, 2 story. Apr-Oct: S, D $49-$85; each addl $5; suites $90; lower rates rest of yr. TV; cable (premium). Heated pool. Restaurant open 24 hrs. Rm serv 6 am-10 pm. Ck-out 11 am. Meeting rm. Business servs avail. Health club privileges. X-country ski 2 mi. Some refrigerators. Microwaves avail. Cr cds: A, C, D, DS, MC, V.

SC

Tahoe City (Lake Tahoe Area) (D-3)

Pop 2,500 (est) **Elev** 6,240 ft **Area Code** 530 **Zip** 95730

At north end of Lake Tahoe.

Motel

★★ **TRAVELODGE.** *455 N Lake Blvd (96145). 530/583-3766; FAX 530/583-8045; res: 800/578-7878.* 47 rms, 2 story. No A/C. July-Labor Day: S $69-$101; D $81-$106; each addl $5; under 17 free; higher rates: wkends, hols; lower rates rest of yr. Crib free. TV; cable. Pool; whirlpool. Sauna. Complimentary coffee, tea in rms. Restaurant nearby. Ck-out 11 am. Business servs avail. Tennis privileges. Golf privileges. Downhill ski 5 mi; x-country ski 2 mi. Sun deck. Microwaves; some balconies. Lake opp. Cr cds: A, C, D, DS, ER, JCB, MC, V.

SC

Resorts

★★ **GRANLIBAKKEN RESORT & CONFERENCE CENTER.** *Granlibakken Rd (96145), 1 mi W, at end of Granlibakken Rd. 530/583-4242; FAX 530/583-7641; res: 800/543-3221.* E-mail granresv@sierra.net; web www.granlibakken.com. 76 kit. units, 3 story. No elvtr. Late Dec-early Jan: S, D $109-$125; each addl $25; 2-5-bedrm units $230-$727. Crib $5. TV; cable. Heated pool (seasonal); wading pool, whirlpool. Sauna. Complimentary full bkfst. Snack bar (winter). Ck-out 11 am, ck-in 4 pm. Grocery, package store 1 mi. Coin lndry. Convention facilities. Business servs avail. Airport, RR station, bus depot transportation. Tennis. Downhill/x-country ski on site. Rental equipt. Sledding. Hiking. Many fireplaces; microwaves avail. Many balconies. Cr cds: A, C, D, DS, JCB, MC, V.

D

★★★ **RESORT AT SQUAW CREEK.** *400 Squaw Creek Rd (96146), 6 mi N on CA 89, Squaw Valley exit. 530/583-6300; FAX 530/581-5407; res: 800/327-3353.* E-mail squawcreek@thegrid.net; web www.squawcreek.com. 405 units, 9 story, 205 suites. Mid-Dec-Jan: S, D $375; suites $425-$1,800; under 17 free; lower rates rest of yr. Crib free. TV; cable, VCR avail. 3 heated pools; wading pool, whirlpool, poolside serv, lifeguard. Supervised child's activities; ages 3-13. Coffee in rms. Dining rms 6:30 am-11 pm (also see GLISSANDI). Rm serv. Bar 11-1 am. Ck-out 11 am, ck-in 4 pm. Package store. Grocery 2 mi. Coin lndry 6 mi. Convention facilities. Business center. Bellhops. Valet serv. Concierge. Gift shop. Beauty shop. Valet parking. Airport transportation. Sports dir. Lighted tennis, pro. Golf, greens fee (incl cart) $110, pro. Aquatic center; 250-ft waterfall, waterslide, stream. Downhill/x-country ski on site. Rental equipt. Ice skating. 7 mi of landscaped hiking & bicycle paths; bicycle rentals. Exercise rm; saunas. Massage. Microwaves avail. Cr cds: A, C, D, DS, MC, V.

D SC

Inns

★★★ **CHANEY HOUSE.** *400 Squaw Creek Rd (96145), 5½ mi S on US 89. 916/525-7333.* Web www.chaneyhouse.com. 4 rms, 2 story, 3 suites. No A/C. S, D $110; each addl $20; suites $120-$195; ski plans; wkends, hols (2-3 day min); lower rates rest of yr. Complimentary full bkfst; afternoon refreshments. Restaurant nearby. Ck-out 11 am, ck-in 2 pm. Concierge serv. Downhill ski 1 mi; x-country ski on site. Picnic tables, grills. Built in 1928; original stone construction. Totally nonsmoking. Cr cds: C, MC, V.

★★★ **COTTAGE INN.** *1690 W Lake Blvd (96145), 2 mi S of CA 89. 530/581-4073; FAX 530/581-0226; res: 800/581-4073.* 15 units. No A/C. No rm phones. S, D $140-$210. Children over 12 yrs only. TV; cable, VCR (free movies). Complimentary full bkfst; afternoon refreshments. Restaurant nearby. Ck-out 11 am, ck-in 3 pm. Business servs avail. Downhill/x-country ski 3 mi. Sauna. Lawn games. Microwaves avail. Picnic tables. Library. Rustic cabins in the woods. Totally nonsmoking. Cr cds: C, MC, V.

SC

Restaurants

★★★ **GLISSANDI.** *(See Resort at Squaw Creek) 530/581-6621.* Hrs: 6-10 pm. Closed Sun. Res required. Continental menu. Serv bar. Wine cellar. Semi-a la carte: dinner $22-$32. Prix fixe: dinner $49. Specialties: wild game, filet mignon, rack of lamb. Valet parking. Elegant dining with view of mountains. Totally nonsmoking. Cr cds: A, C, D, DS, ER, JCB, MC, V.

D SC

★★★ **SWISS LAKEWOOD RESTAURANT.** *5055 W Lake Blvd (96141), 6 mi S on CA 89. 530/525-5211.* Hrs: 5:30-10 pm. Closed Mon exc hols. Res required. French, continental menu. Bar. Semi-a la carte: dinner $18.50-$26.50. Swiss, European decor; many antiques; wagon wheel chandeliers. Totally nonsmoking. Cr cds: A, C, MC, V.

D

★ **WOLFDALE'S.** *640 N Lake Blvd (96145). 530/583-5700.* Hrs: 5:30-10 pm; wkends from 6 pm. Closed Tues Sept-June. Res accepted. Bar to midnight. A la carte entrees: dinner $16-$21. Specializes in seafood. Outdoor dining. Local artwork. Cr cds: C, MC, V.

D SC

Tahoe Vista (Lake Tahoe Area) (D-4)

Pop 1,144 **Elev** 6,232 ft **Area Code** 530

At north end of Lake Tahoe.

Motels

★★ **CAL NEVA INN.** *9937 N Lake Blvd (96143), E on CA 28, at state line. 530/546-3341; FAX 530/546-2922.* 94 rms, 70 with shower only, 2 story. Mid-May-Sept: S, D $69-$89; each addl $10; under 10 free; ski plans; wkend rates; 2-day min hols; lower rates rest of yr. Crib $10. TV; cable. Pool; whirlpool. Complimentary coffee in lobby. Restaurant opp open 24 hrs. Ck-out 11 am. Meeting rm. Downhill/x-country ski 5 mi. Microwaves avail. Cr cds: A, C, D, DS, MC, V.

SC

✓★ **CEDAR GLEN LODGE.** *6589 N Lake Blvd (96148), 1½ mi W of CA 267 on CA 28. 530/546-4281; FAX 530/546-2250; res: 800/341-8000.* E-mail cglodge@sierra.net; web www.go-tahoe.com/go/cedarglen. 31 rms in 2-story motel, cottages, 14 kits. No A/C. Mid-June-mid-Sept, Dec-Apr: S, D $45-$65; each addl $5; kit. units, cottages $80-$129; wkly rates; lower rates rest of yr. Crib free. TV; cable, VCR avail (movies). Pool; whirlpools. Sauna. Playground. Complimentary continental bkfst. Complimentary coffee in rms. Restaurant nearby. Ck-out 11 am. Business servs avail. Downhill ski 8 mi; x-country ski 4 mi. Some refrigerators; microwaves avail. Private patios. Picnic tables, grills. Beach opp. Cr cds: A, C, DS, MC, V.

SC

★ **VISTA VILLA RESORT.** *6750 N Lake Blvd (96148). 530/546-1550; FAX 530/546-4100.* 13 rms, 10 kits. No A/C. S, D $75; each addl $10; studio rms $85-$165; kit. units for 1-4, $85-$165; wkly rates in summer. TV; cable, VCR avail (movies). Pool. Coffee in rms. Ck-out 11 am. Coin lndry. Business servs avail. Downhill ski 15 mi; x-country ski 10 mi. Refrigerators, microwaves. Private patios. Picnic tables, grill. Sun deck. On private sand beach; moorage. Cr cds: A, C, DS, MC, V.

Inn

★★★ **SHORE HOUSE AT LAKE TAHOE.** *7170 N Lake Blvd (96148). 530/546-7270; FAX 530/546-7130; res: 800/207-5160.* E-mail shorehse@inntahoe.com; web www.inntahoe.com. 9 rms, 4 with shower only, 2 story. No A/C. No rm phones. S, D $130-$190; each addl $20; wkends, hols (2-day min); higher rates special events. Complimentary full bkfst. Restaurant adj 11 am-10 pm. Ck-out 11 am, ck-in 4 pm. Concierge serv. Business servs avail. Whirlpool. Downhill ski 8 mi, x-country ski 1 mi. Refrigerators, fireplaces. Picnic tables. On lake. Totally nonsmoking. Cr cds: C, DS, MC, V.

Restaurants

★★ **CAPTAIN JON'S.** *(See Tahoe Vista Inn & Marina) 530/546-4819.* Hrs: 10:30 am-10 pm (summer), 5:30-10:30 pm (winter). Res accepted. Country French seafood menu. Bar 3 pm-2 am, summer from 11 am. Semi-a la carte: lunch $8-$12, dinner $16-$23. Specializes in seafood. Pianist Thurs-Sat 5:30-11 pm. Valet parking. Nautical decor. Outdoor dining. On lakefront. Cr cds: A, C, D, DS, MC, V.

D

★★ **GAR WOODS GRILL & PIER.** *5000 N Lake Blvd (96140), W on CA 28. 530/546-3366.* E-mail garwoods@sierra.net; web www.garwoods.com. Hrs: 10:30 am-10 pm; winter from 4 pm; wkends from 11:30 am; Sun brunch 9:30 am-2 pm. Res accepted. No A/C. Bar. A la carte entrees: bkfst $7-$10, lunch $8-$13.95, dinner $12-$22. Sun brunch $18.95-$22.95. Child's meals. Specializes in fresh seafood, steak. Acoustic duo Fri, Sat. Outdoor dining. View of lake and sunsets. Cr cds: A, C, MC, V.

D

★★★ **LE PETIT PIER.** *7238 N Lake Blvd (96148). 530/546-4464.* Hrs: 6-10 pm. Closed Tues. Res accepted. French menu. Bar. Wine cellar. A la carte entrees: dinner $19-$26. Complete meal: dinner $50. Child's meals. Specialties: asparagus shiitake feuilletage, baked oysters, noisette of lamb en croute. Valet parking. Family-owned since 1972. Many separate dining areas with lake views. Intimate dining. Totally nonsmoking. Cr cds: A, C, D, DS, ER, JCB, MC, V.

D

Tehachapi (H-3)

(See also Bakersfield)

Pop 5,791 **Elev** 3,973 ft **Area Code** 805 **Zip** 93581 **E-mail** chamber@tminet.com **Web** www.tehachapi.com/chamber

Information Greater Tehachapi Chamber of Commerce, PO Box 401; 805/822-4180

Tehachapi was founded when the railroad made its way through the pass between the San Joaquin Valley and the desert to the east. The Tehachapi Pass, east of town, is one of the windiest areas in the world; of the approximately 15,000 wind turbines located in the state, 5,000 are located here. The best time to see the turbines spinning is late afternoon, when heat on the nearby Mojave Desert is greatest. Historians believe the name Tehachapi is derived from a Native American word meaning "sweet water and many acorns," but others believe it means "windy place." Both are true of the area.

What to See and Do

Tehachapi Loop. Visitors and railroad buffs enjoy watching trains (with 85 or more boxcars) pass over themselves when rounding the "Tehachapi Loop." Built in 1875-1876, the loop makes it possible for trains to gain the needed elevation in a short distance. It can be seen by taking Woodford-Tehachapi Rd to a viewpoint just above the loop. NW of town.

Annual Events

Indian Pow Wow. Native American cultural and religious gathering of various tribes. Open to public viewing: dance competition, arts & crafts, museum display of artifacts. Usually last wkend June.

Windfair. Windmill demonstrations, arts & crafts, entertainment, food, electric car races. July.

Mountain Festival and PRCA Rodeo. Includes arts & crafts, food booths, parade, events. 3rd wkend Aug.

Motels

✓★ **BEST WESTERN.** *416 W Tehachapi Blvd (93561). 805/822-5591; FAX 805/822-6197; res: 800/528-1234.* 74 rms, 2 story. S $55-$65; D $65-$75; each addl $3; under 18 free. Crib free. Pet accepted. TV; cable (premium). Pool. Restaurant 5:30 am-midnight. Ck-out noon. Coin lndry. Refrigerators; microwaves avail. Cr cds: A, C, D, DS, MC, V.

D SC

★★ **SUMMIT TRAVELODGE.** *500 Steuber Rd (93561), Hwy 58 at East Tehachapi Blvd. 805/823-8000; FAX 805/823-8006; res: 800/578-7878.* 76 units, 2 story. S $49-$52; D $56-$59; each addl $7; suites $61-$64; kit. unit $90; under 18 free. Crib free. Pet accepted. TV; cable (premium). Heated pool; whirlpool. Complimentary coffee in rms. Restaurant. Bar 2-10 pm. Ck-out 11 am. Meeting rms. Business servs avail. In-rm modem link. Gift shop. Some refrigerators. Balconies. Cr cds: A, C, D, DS, JCB, MC, V.

D SC

Lodge

★★★ **STALLION SPRINGS.** *18100 Lucaya Way (90746), 15 mi W on CA 202 to Cummings Valley, then follow signs to Stallion Springs. 805/822-5581; FAX 805/822-4055; res: 800/244-0864.* 63 rms in main bldg, 2 story, 21 kit. cottages (1-2 bedrms). S, D, suites $72-$195; each addl $10; kit. cottages $150-$185; golf plans. Crib free. Pet accepted; $20 deposit. TV; cable (premium). Heated pool; whirlpool. Playground. Dining rm 7:30 am-1:30 pm, 6-8:30 pm. Bar 5-9 pm, wkend hrs vary; entertainment. Ck-out noon, ck-in 3 pm. Meeting rms. Sports dir. Lighted tennis, pro. 18-hole golf, greens fee $22-$32, pro, 2 putting greens, driving range. Hiking. Lawn games. Exercise equipt; sauna. Balconies. Situated atop hill; overlooks golf course, lakes, forests. Cr cds: A, C, D, DS, MC, V.

D SC

Temecula (J-4)

(See also Fallbrook)

Pop 27,099 **Elev** 1,006 ft **Area Code** 909 **E-mail** info@temecula.org **Web** www.temecula.org

Information Temecula Valley Chamber of Commerce, 27450 Ynez Rd, #104, 92591; 909/676-5090

The Temecula Valley, bordered on the west by Camp Pendleton Marine Corps Base and the Cleveland National Forest, is approximately mid-way between Los Angeles and San Diego. This area offers activities for everyone, from tours of 12 local wineries to golfing on any of five championship courses.

Annual Event

Balloon and Wine Festival. Wine tasting, hot air balloon race, musical entertainment, children's activities. Phone 909/676-4713 or 909/676-6713. Late Apr.

Motel

★★ **RAMADA INN.** *28980 Front St (92590). 909/676-8770; FAX 909/699-3400; res: 800/272-6232.* Web www.ramada.com/ramada.html. 70 rms, 2 story. S, D $54-$64; each addl $5; under 17 free. Crib free. TV; cable (premium). Pool; whirlpool. Complimentary continental bkfst. Complimentary coffee in rms. Restaurant adj 6 am-10 pm. Ck-out noon. Meeting rm. Business servs avail. Refrigerators; some wet bars, microwaves. Cr cds: A, C, D, DS, MC, V.

D SC

Lodge

★★★ **TEMECULA CREEK INN.** *44501 Rainbow Canyon Rd (92592). 909/694-1000; FAX 909/676-3422; res: 800/962-7335.* 80 rms in 5 bldgs, 2 story. S, D $130-$205; each addl $20; package plans; under 12 free. Crib free. TV; cable. Heated pool; whirlpool, poolside serv. Complimentary coffee in rms. Dining rm 6:30 am-10 pm. Bar 9:30 am-11 pm; entertainment Fri, Sat. Ck-out noon, ck-in 4 pm. Meeting rms. Business servs avail. Tennis. 27-hole golf, greens fee $55-$90, pro, putting green, driving range. Lawn games. Bicycle rental. Refrigerators, minibars. Balconies. Picnic tables. Cr cds: A, C, D, DS, MC, V.

D SC

Hotel

★★ **EMBASSY SUITES.** *29345 Rancho California Rd (92591). 909/676-5656; FAX 909/699-3928; res: 800/362-2779.* Web www.embassy-suites.com. 136 suites, 4 story. S, D $109-$149; each addl $10; under 18 free. Crib free. TV; cable (premium), VCR. Heated pool; whirlpool, poolside serv. Complimentary full bkfst. Coffee in rms. Restaurant 6:30-9:30 am, 11 am-2 pm, 5-10 pm. Rm serv. Bar noon-10 pm. Ck-out noon. Coin Indry. Meeting rms. Business servs avail. Valet serv. Gift shop. Exercise equipt. Refrigerators, microwaves, wet bars. Many balconies. Cr cds: A, C, D, DS, MC, V.

D SC

Inn

★★ **LOMA VISTA BED & BREAKFAST.** *33350 La Serena Way (92591). 909/676-7047; FAX 909/676-0077.* 6 rms, 2 story. No rm phones. S, D $100-$150; each addl $25; some 2-day min wkends. TV in sitting rm. Complimentary full bkfst; evening refreshments. Restaurant opp 11 am-9 pm. Ck-out 11 am, ck-in 3-8 pm. Whirlpool. Some balconies. Mission-style house surrounded by citrus groves and vineyards. Totally nonsmoking. Cr cds: C, MC, V.

Restaurants

★★ **BAILY WINE COUNTRY CAFE.** *27644 Ynez Rd M-11 (92591). 909/676-9567.* Web www.baily.com. Hrs: 11 am-2:30 pm, 5-9 pm; Fri to 9:30 pm; Sat 11 am-9:30 pm; Sun 11 am-9 pm; Sun brunch 11 am-2 pm. Closed some major hols. Res accepted. Continental menu. Wine, beer. Semi-a la carte: lunch $7.95-$10.95, dinner $12.95-$21.95. Sun brunch $7.95-$8.95. Specialties: sauteed crab cakes, salmon Wellington, southwestern pork tenderloin. Parking. Outdoor dining. Casual decor; modern artwork, silk trees. Cr cds: A, C, D, MC, V.

D

✓★ **BANK OF MEXICAN FOOD.** *28645 Front St (92590). 909/676-6160.* Hrs: 11 am-9 pm. Closed Easter, Thanksgiving, Dec 25. Res accepted. Mexican menu. Wine, beer. Complete meals: lunch $4.50-$8.95, dinner $5.95-$8.95. Specialties: homemade chile relleno, crab enchiladas. Child's meals. Patio dining. In refurbished bank building (1913). Family-owned since 1978. Cr cds: C, D, DS, MC, V.

D

★★ **CAFE CHAMPAGNE.** *32575 Rancho California Rd (92591). 909/699-0088.* E-mail gr8wine@ix.netcom.com; web www.temelink.com/thornton. Hrs: 11 am-9 pm; Mon to 4 pm; Sun brunch to 4 pm. California eclectic menu. Bar. A la carte entrees: lunch $12.95-$23.95, dinner $18.95-$27.95. Sun brunch $12.95-$23.95. Specializes in mesquite-grilled foods, award-winning sparkling wines. Own baking. Parking. Outdoor dining. View of vineyard. Herb garden. Cr cds: A, C, D, DS, MC, V.

D

Thousand Oaks (J-3)

(See also Los Angeles)

Pop 104,352 **Elev** 800 ft **Area Code** 805 **E-mail** chamber@cvcc.com **Web** www.cvcc.com/chamber

Information Thousand Oaks/Westlake Village Regional Chamber of Commerce, 600 Hampshire Rd, Suite 200, Westlake Village, 91361; 805/370-0035

What to See and Do

Stagecoach Inn Museum Complex. Reproduction of 1876 building with Victorian furnishings; contains Chumash display; pioneer artifacts; changing exhibits; carriage house with antique vehicles; gift shop. Tri-Village consists of Chumash hut, Spanish adobe and pioneer house representing 3 early cultures in Conejo Valley. One-rm schoolhouse. Nature trail. (Wed-Sun afternoons; closed Easter, Thanksgiving, Dec 25) 51 S Ventu Park Rd, ½ mi S of US 101 in Newbury Park. Phone 805/498-9441. ¢

Motel

★★★ **CLARION HOTEL.** *1775 Madera Rd (93065), N on CA 23, E on Olsen to Madera Rd. 805/584-6300; FAX 805/527-9969; res: 800/228-5050.* 120 rms, 2 story. S, D $84-$104; each addl $10; suites $150-$400; under 18 free; wkly, monthly rates. TV; cable (premium). Heated pool; whirlpool. Complimentary full bkfst. Complimentary coffee in rms. Restaurant 6:30-9 am. Rm serv. Bar 5-10 pm. Ck-out noon. Coin Indry. Meeting rms. Business servs avail. In-rm modem link. Bellhops. Valet serv. Airport transportation. Health club privileges. Some refrigerators. Private patios, balconies. Garden courtyard with waterfall. Cr cds: A, C, D, DS, ER, JCB, MC, V.

D SC

Motor Hotel

★★★ **WESTLAKE VILLAGE INN.** *31943 Agoura Rd (91361), ¼ mi S of Ventura Frwy (US 101), Westlake Blvd (E), Lindero Cyn Rd (W) exit. 818/889-0230; FAX 818/879-0812; res: 800/535-9978.* Web www.wvinn.com. 141 units, 2 story. S, D $96-$350; each addl $10; suites $165-$350; under 12 free; golf plan. Crib free. TV; cable (premium), VCR (movies $6). Heated pool; whirlpool. Complimentary continental bkfst. Coffee in rms. Restaurant 7 am-10 pm; Sun 10 am-2:30 pm, 5-9 pm. Rm serv. Bar 11:30-2 am; entertainment. Ck-out noon. Meeting rms. Business servs avail. In-rm modem link. Concierge. Gift shop. Valet serv. Lighted tennis. 18-hole golf, greens fee $25, cart $17, pro. Exercise equipt. Minibars. Fireplace in suites. Private patios, courtyards. Balconies overlook lake. Spacious grounds include waterfalls and a rose garden. Cr cds: A, C, D, DS, MC, V.

D SC

Hotel

★★★ **HYATT PLAZA.** *880 S Westlake Blvd (91361), off Ventura Frwy (US 101), Westlake Blvd exit. 805/497-9991; FAX 805/379-9392; res: 800/233-1234.* Web www.hyattwestlake.com. 262 rms, 5 story. S $99-$180; D $180; each addl $25; suites $200-$500; under 18 free; wkend rates; package plans. Crib free. TV; cable (premium), VCR avail (movies). Heated pool; whirlpool, poolside serv. Restaurant 6:30 am-10:30 pm. Bar 11-1 am; entertainment. Ck-out noon. Meeting rms. Business center. In-rm modem link. Concierge. Gift shop. Valet parking. Tennis privileges. Golf privileges. Exercise equipt. Bicycle rentals. Refrigerators avail. Private patios, balconies. Garden atrium. Spanish mission-style architecture. Cr cds: A, C, D, DS, ER, JCB, MC, V.

D SC

Restaurant

★ **CORRIGAN'S STEAK HOUSE.** *556 E Thousand Oaks Blvd (91360). 805/495-5234.* Hrs: 11 am-10:30 pm; Sat, Sun from 9 am. Closed Thanksgiving, Dec 25. Res accepted. Bar to midnight. Semi-a la carte: bkfst $3.75-$10.50, lunch $5.75-$10.95, dinner $8.95-$20.95. Specializes in steak, seafood, chili. Old time Western decor; Western movies memorabilia. Totally nonsmoking. Cr cds: C, MC, V.

Three Rivers (G-3)

(See also Sequoia & Kings Canyon National Parks)

Pop 2,000 (est) **Elev** 1,200 ft **Area Code** 209 **Zip** 93271

Motels

★★ **BEST WESTERN.** *40105 Sierra Dr (93271), 8 mi W of Sequoia & Kings Canyon National parks' entrance, on CA 198. 559/561-4119; FAX 559/561-3427; res: 888/523-9909.* E-mail bestwest@theworks.com. 54 rms, 1-2 story. May-Oct: S $75; D $89; each addl $4; suites $77-$91; lower rates rest of yr. Crib $4. Pet accepted. TV; cable. Pool; whirlpool. Playground. Continental bkfst. Complimentary coffee in rms. Ck-out 11 am. Refrigerators; some microwaves, fireplaces. Balconies. Grills. Cr cds: A, C, D, DS, JCB, MC, V.

D SC

★★ **HOLIDAY INN EXPRESS.** *40820 Sierra Dr; Hwy 198 (93271). 209/561-9000; FAX 209/561-9010; res: 800/331-2140.* E-mail express@lightspeed.net; web www.3riversholidayinn.com. 62 rms, 2 story, 16 suites. Apr-Oct: S $99; D $99-$129; each addl $10; suites $109-$149; under 18 free; family rates; higher rates Jazzfest; lower rates rest of yr. Crib free. TV; cable (premium), VCR avail. Complimentary continental bkfst. Complimentary coffee in rms. Restaurant adj 6 am-11 pm. Ck-out 11 am. Meeting rms. Business servs avail. In-rm modem link. Sundries. Coin lndry. X-country ski 15 mi. Exercise equipt; sauna. Heated pool; whirlpool. Refrigerators, microwaves; some in-rm whirlpools, fireplaces. Cr cds: A, C, D, DS, ER, JCB, MC, V.

D SC

★★ **LAZY J RANCH MOTEL.** *39625 Sierra Dr (93271), on Hwy 198. 559/561-4449; FAX 559/561-4889; res: 800/341-8000.* 20 rms, 12 with shower only. S $45-$60; D $46-$70; suites $150-$170; kit. units $88-$98; wkly rates; some hols (3-day min). Crib free. Pet accepted, some restrictions. TV; cable. Pool. Playground. Complimentary coffee in rms. Ck-out 11 am. Coin lndry. X-country ski 20 mi. Refrigerators; some fireplaces. Picnic tables. On river. Cr cds: A, C, D, DS, MC, V.

D

✓★ **SIERRA LODGE.** *43175 Sierra Dr (93271). 559/561-3681; FAX 559/561-3264; res: 800/367-8879.* Web www.threerivers.com. 22 units, 1-3 story, 5 kit. suites. No elvtr. May-Sept: S, D $49-$72; each addl $3; suites $85-$165; lower rates rest of yr. Pet accepted, some restrictions. TV; cable (premium). Pool. Complimentary continental bkfst. Complimentary coffee in rms. Restaurant nearby. Ck-out 11 am. Meeting rm. Business servs avail. Sundries. Refrigerators; some fireplaces. Balconies. Cr cds: A, C, D, DS, MC, V.

SC

Tiburon (C-2 see San Francisco map)

(See also Mill Valley, San Francisco, San Rafael, Sausalito)

Pop 7,532 **Elev** 90 ft **Area Code** 415 **Zip** 94920

What to See and Do

China Cabin. Elegant social saloon of the 19th-century transpacific steamship SS *China.* The 20-by-40-ft cabin was removed in 1886 and used as a waterfront cottage until 1978. Completely restored; intricate woodwork, gold leaf, cut glass windows, brass & crystal chandeliers; period furnishings. Tours (Apr-Oct, Wed & Sun afternoons or by appt) 54 Beach Rd, Belvedere Cove, near jct Tiburon Blvd. Phone 415/435-1853. **Donation**

Motel

★★ **TIBURON LODGE.** *1651 Tiburon Blvd (94920), on CA 131. 415/435-3133; FAX 415/435-2451; res: 800/762-7770.* 101 rms, 3 story. May-Oct: S $159-$299; D $204-$339; each addl $15; kit. suites $260-$290; under 12 free; lower rates rest of yr. Crib free. TV; cable, VCR avail (free movies). Heated pool. Restaurant 7-10 am. Ck-out noon. Meeting rms. Business servs avail. In-rm modem link. Bellhops. Valet serv. Some in-rm whirlpools. Some private patios, balconies. San Francisco ferry 1 blk. Cr cds: A, C, D, DS, ER, JCB, MC, V.

D SC

Restaurants

✓★★ **GUAYMAS.** *5 Main St (94920). 415/435-6300.* Hrs: 11:30 am-10 pm; Fri, Sat to 11 pm; Sun 10:30 am-10 pm. Closed Thanksgiving, Dec 25. Res accepted. Mexican menu. Bar. Semi-a la carte: lunch, dinner $8.95-$18.95. Specializes in authentic Mexican cuisine. Mariachi Sun. Outdoor dining. On bay. Totally nonsmoking. Cr cds: A, C, D, MC, V.

D

★★★ **TUTTO MARE.** *9 Main St (94920). 415/435-4747.* Web www.spectrumfoods.com. Hrs: 11:30 am-10:30 pm; Fri to 11 pm; Sat 11 am-11 pm; Sun 11 am-10:30 pm; Sun brunch to 2:30 pm. Closed Thanksgiving. Res accepted. Bar. A la carte entrees: lunch, dinner $10-$18.50. Sun brunch $10-$12. Child's meals. Specializes in fresh fish, oysters. Jazz Sat. Outdoor dining on deck with view of San Francisco. Totally nonsmoking. Cr cds: A, C, D, MC, V.

D

Tijuana, Baja California, Mexico (K-4)

Pop 1,500,000 (est) **Elev** 15 ft **E-mail** impamexicoinfo@worldnet.att.net

Information Tijuana & Baja Tourism and Convention Bureau, 7860 Mission Center Court, Suite 202, San Diego 92108; 619/298-4105 or 800/225-2786

Tijuana has all the characteristics of a Mexican border town: recreation that is Latin in flavor, yet tailored to North American desires; a mixture of two cultures resulting in a spirited vitality. A great deal of enjoyment can be found here, as is indicated by the host of people who cross the border from Los Angeles and San Diego daily. Trolley and tour bus transportation to the border is available from San Diego (see). (For Border Crossing Regulations see MAKING THE MOST OF YOUR TRIP.)

What to See and Do

Jai Alai. Ancient Basque game with parimutuel betting; restaurant. Games (Mon & Tues, afternoons; Thurs-Tues, evenings). Admission charged. Downtown at Fronton Palacio, Revolucion Ave & 7th St. Phone 619/231-1910.

Mexitlan. Mexico's miniature museum, with over 150 scale models of Mexican cathedrals, pyramids, monuments, buildings and colonial towns. Entertainment stage features Mexican musicians and dancers. Also shopping and dining avail. (Daily exc Mon) Ocampo & 2nd Ave, downtown. Phone 011-52-66/38-41-01 or 619/685-3628. ¢¢

Tijuana Cultural Center. Complex housing Omnitheater (fee) with film presentations on Mexico, museum, concert hall, open-air shows with mariachis, regional dancers, Papantla Fliers. Gift shop. Tours. (Daily) Paseo de los Héroes. Phone 011-52-66/84-11-11. ¢¢

Seasonal Event

Bullfights. Plaza Monumental, Calle Segunda, W side of town in Playas de Tijuana section. El Toreo de Tijuana, Agua Caliente Blvd, S side of town. Admission charged. Sun, May-Sept.

Motor Hotel

★★ **BAJA INN HACIENDA DEL RIO.** *Blvd. Rodolfo Sanchez Taboada #10606 Zona Rìo (22320); res: 800/303-2684.* 131 rms, 3 story. S, D $55-$65; each addl $9; suites $75-$85; wkly rates. TV; cable (premium). Pool. Restaurant 7 am-10:30 pm. Rm serv to 3 am. Ck-out 1 pm. Meeting rms. In-rm modem link. Sundries. Exercise equipt. Cr cds: A, C, MC, V.

Hotels

★★★ **GRAND HOTEL TIJUANA.** *4500 Blvd Agua Caliente (22180); res: 800/GRAND-TJ.* 422 rms, 23 story. S, D $70-$90; each addl $11; under 12 free. Crib free. Covered parking $2. TV; cable (premium). Pool; whirlpool. Restaurant 6-1 am. Rm serv 24 hrs. Bar noon-1 am. Ck-out 1 pm. Convention facilities. Business center. Concierge. Shopping arcade. Barber, beauty shop. 2 tennis courts. Golf privileges, greens fee $30-$40, pro. Health club privileges. Sauna. Refrigerators. Luxury level. Cr cds: A, C, MC, V.

SC

★★ **PLAZA LAS GLORIAS-TIJUANA.** *Blvd Agua Caliente #11553 (22420); res: 800/748-8785.* 192 rms, 10 story. S, D $75-$85; each addl $10; suites $183-$305; under 12 free. Crib free. TV; cable (premium), VCR avail. Heated pool; whirlpool. Restaurant 7 am-11 pm. Bar; entertainment Wed-Sat. Ck-out 1 pm. Business center. Exercise equipt. Some refrigerators. Balconies. Cr cds: A, C, D, MC, V.

SC

Resort

★★★ **RESIDENCE INN BY MARRIOTT.** *Km 19.5 Toll Rd (22605); res 800/803-6038.* 75 kit. suites, 3 story. S $99-$109; D $109-$149; each addl $10; under 15 free; wkly rates; golf plans; 3-day min hols, 2-day min wkends. Crib free. TV; cable (premium). Pool; whirlpool. Playground. Supervised child's activities; ages 2-10. Complimentary continental bkfst. Complimentary coffee in rms. Restaurant (see PEDRIN'S AT REAL DEL MAR). Rm serv. Bar 10 am-11 pm; entertainment Fri-Sun. Ck-out noon, ck-in 3 pm. Coin lndry. Meeting rms. Business servs avail. Bellhops. Sundries. Gift shop. Beauty shop. Tennis. 18-hole golf course, greens fee $69-$75, pro, putting green, driving range. Exercise equipt; sauna. Massage. Refrigerators, microwaves. Some balconies. Overlooks ocean. Cr cds: A, C, MC, V.

SC

Restaurants

★★ **LA COSTA.** *81-31 7th St, Galeana, Baja California, Mexico 011-52-66/85-8494.* Hrs: 10 am-midnight. Bar. Semi-a la carte: lunch, dinner $7.50-$28. Specializes in seafood. Parking. Nautical decor. Cr cds: C, MC, V.

D

★★ **LA ESPADANA.** *10813 Blvd Sanchez Taboada. 011-52-66/34-14-88.* Hrs: 7:30 am-11 pm; Sun to 10 pm. Closed Jan 1, Dec 25; also Thurs, Fri before Easter. Mexican menu. Bar. Semi-a la carte: bkfst $3-$6, lunch, dinner $7-$15. Specializes in steak, shrimp, spare ribs. Parking. Old hacienda atmosphere; wooden beam ceilings, adobe walls. Antiques. Cr cds: A, C, MC, V.

★★★ **PEDRIN'S AT REAL DEL MAR.** *(See Residence Inn by Marriott) 011-52-661/3-33-80.* Hrs: 11 am-midnight; Sat, Sun from 8 am. Res accepted. Continental menu. Bar. Buffet: bkfst $7.95. Semi-a la carte: lunch, dinner $6.95-$24.95. Specialties: prime rib, tortilla soup, pasta Pedrin's. Jazz band, singer Thurs-Sun. Valet parking. Outdoor dining. View of golf course. Cr cds: C, MC, V.

★★★ **TOUR DE FRANCE.** *Gobernador Ibarra #252. 011-52-66/81-75-42.* Hrs: 8 am-10:30 pm; Fri, Sat to 11:30 pm. Closed Sun; some major hols; also May 1, Sept 16. Res accepted Fri, Sat. French menu. Bar. A la carte entrees: bkfst $5-$10, lunch, dinner $8-$28. Specialties: duck in garlic & honey sauce, filet of beef with escargots. Pianist Wed-Sat. Valet parking. Outdoor dining. Elegant dining in chateau-style restaurant. Original art. Chef-owned. Cr cds: C, MC, V.

Torrance (J-3)

Pop 133,107 **Elev** 84 ft **Area Code** 310 **E-mail** barbara@torrance.uucp.netcom.com **Web** www.torrance.ca.us

Information Chamber of Commerce, 3400 Torrance Blvd, Ste 100, 90503; 310/540-5858

Motels

★★ **PLAZA DEL AMO COURTYARD BY MARRIOTT.** *2633 Sepulveda Blvd (90505), I-405, Crenshaw Blvd exit. 310/533-8000; FAX 310/533-0564; res: 800/321-2211.* Web www.courtyard.com. 149 rms, 3 story. S, D $74-$99; suites $119; under 18 free; wkend rates. Crib free. TV; cable (premium), VCR avail. Heated pool; whirlpool. Complimentary coffee in rms. Ck-out 1 pm. Coin Indry. Meeting rms. Business servs avail. In-rm modem link. Valet serv. Free parking. Exercise equipt. Balconies. Cr cds: A, C, D, DS, MC, V.

D SC

✓★ **RAMADA INN.** *850 E Dominguez St (95570), 1 blk off San Diego Frwy (I-405), Avalon Blvd exit. 310/538-5500; FAX 310/715-2957; res: 800/272-6232.* 167 rms, 2 story. S $109-$119; D $119-$129; each addl $10; suites $125-$275; under 18 free. Crib free. TV; cable (premium). Pool. Restaurant 7 am-10 pm. Rm serv. Bar 11-2 am. Ck-out 1 pm. Coin Indry. Meeting rms. Valet serv. Beauty shop. Exercise equipt. Microwaves avail. Cr cds: A, C, D, DS, JCB, MC, V.

D SC

★★ **SUMMERFIELD SUITES HOTEL.** *19901 Prairie Ave (90503), I-405 to Redondo Beach Blvd. 310/371-8525; FAX 310/542-9628; res: 800/833-4353.* 144 kit. suites, 3 story. Kit. suites $184-$230; under 12 free. Crib avail. Pet accepted. TV; cable. Heated pool; whirlpool. Complimentary continental bkfst. Complimentary coffee in rms. Restaurant nearby. Ck-out noon. Coin Indry. Meeting rm. Airport transportation. Exercise equipt. Microwaves. Lawn games. Picnic tables, grills. Cr cds: A, C, D, DS, JCB, MC, V.

D SC

Hotels

★★★ **HILTON TORRANCE.** *21333 Hawthorne Blvd (90503). 310/540-0500; FAX 310/540-2065; res: 800/932-3322; res: 800/552-0852.* E-mail hhonors@hilton.com; web www.hilton.com. 371 rms, 12 story. S $129-$179; D $139-$189; each addl $10; suites $295-$650; under 18 free; wkend rates. Crib free. TV; cable (premium), VCR avail. Pool; whirlpool. Complimentary coffee in rms. Restaurant 6 am-10 pm. Bar 11-1 am; entertainment Tues-Sat. Ck-out noon. Convention facilities. Business servs avail. In-rm modem link. Concierge. Gift shop. Coin Indry. Exercise equipt; sauna. Many refrigerators. Some balconies. Luxury level. Cr cds: A, C, D, DS, ER, JCB, MC, V.

D SC

★★★ **MARRIOTT.** *3635 Fashion Way (90503), I-405 S exit Hawthorne to Torrance Blvd. 310/316-3636; FAX 310/543-6076; res: 800/228-9290.* Web www.marriott.com. 487 rms, 17 story. S, D $134-$169; suites from $275; under 18 free; wkend rates. Crib free. Valet parking $8/day; self-park free. TV; cable (premium), VCR avail. Indoor/outdoor pool; whirlpool, poolside serv. Restaurant 6:30 am-10 pm; Fri, Sat to 11 pm. Bars 11-2 am. Ck-out 1 pm. Coin Indry. Meeting rms. Business center. In-rm modem link. Concierge. Gift shop. Barber, beauty shop. Tennis privileges. Golf privileges. Exercise equipt; sauna. Some bathrm phones. Balconies. Opp shopping center. Luxury level. Cr cds: A, C, D, DS, ER, JCB, MC, V.

D SC

Restaurants

★★ **CHRISTINE.** *24530 Hawthorne Blvd (90505). 310/373-1952.* Web www.chezmelange.com. Hrs: 11 am-2 pm, 5:30-9 pm; Sat 5-10 pm; Sun 5-9 pm. Closed most major hols. Res accepted. Eclectic menu. Bar. A la carte entrees: lunch $7.95-$12.95, dinner $8.95-$19.95. Child's meals. Specialties: portabella mushroom, peppered-crusted filet mignon, Asian grazing sampler. Parking. Outdoor dining. Tuscan villa atmosphere. Totally nonsmoking. Cr cds: A, C, MC, V.

D

★★★ **DEPOT.** *1250 Cabrillo Ave (90501), I-405 exit Western Ave. 310/787-7501.* Web www.chezmelange.com. Hrs: 11 am-2 pm, 5:30-10 pm; Fri to 10:30 pm; Sat 5-10:30 pm. Closed Sun; some major hols. Res accepted. Continental menu. Bar. Wine list. Semi-a la carte: lunch $7.95-$12.95, dinner $8.95-$20. Child's meals. Specialties: Thai barbecue chicken over stir-fry orzo, rock shrimp sausage with garlic, mushroom-crusted lamb chops. Valet parking. Outdoor dining. Elegant dining in casual atmosphere; original art displayed. Cr cds: A, C, D, MC, V.

D ♥

Trinidad (B-1)

(See also Eureka)

Pop 362 **Elev** 40 ft **Area Code** 707 **Zip** 95570

Information Chamber of Commerce, PO Box 356, 95570; 707/677-1610

When leaders of a Spanish expedition landed here on June 18, 1775, it was Trinity Sunday, so the leaders named the area Trinidad. The city was founded in 1850 and was a port of entry for supplies packed into the upriver gold country. Offshore is Prisoner Rock; in the old days, constables took drunks here and gave them two options: swim the sobering length ashore or dry here.

What to See and Do

Patrick's Point State Park. On 650 acres. Ocean fishing, beachcombing, tidepooling. Hiking trails. Picnicking. Camping facilities in unusual rain-forest type of growth; res suggested. Museum exhibits, naturalist programs, Yorok Village. Standard fees. 5 mi N on US 101. Phone 707/677-3570.

Telonicher Marine Laboratory. Marine teaching and research facility of Humboldt State Univ. Touch-tank with local tidepool marine life; display aquariums. Self-guided tours of hallway exhibits. (Sept-May, daily; rest of yr, Mon-Fri; schedule may vary; closed academic hols) 570 Ewing St, at Edwards St. Phone 707/677-3671. **Free**

Motel

★★ **BISHOP PINE LODGE.** *1481 Patricks Point Dr (95570). 707/677-3314; FAX 707/677-3444.* 12 cottage units (1-2-rm), 10 kits. No A/C. Apr-mid-Oct, hols: S, D $60-$100; each addl $8; kit. units $8 addl; wkly rates mid-Oct-Mar; lower rates rest of yr. Crib $8. TV; cable (premium). Playground. Complimentary coffee. Ck-out 11 am. Business servs avail. In-rm modem link. Free airport transportation. Exercise equipt. Picnic tables, grills. Fish storage. Gazebo. Rustic cottages surrounded by wild azaleas, wooded grounds. Totally nonsmoking. Cr cds: A, C, DS, MC, V.

Inn

★★ **LOST WHALE BED & BREAKFAST INN.** *3452 Patricks Point Dr (95570). 707/677-3425; FAX 707/677-0284; res: 800/677-7859.* E-mail miller@lost-whale-inn.com; web www.lost-whale-inn.com. 8 rms. No A/C. No rm phones. May-Oct: S $120-$150; D $130-$160; each addl $15-$20; mid-June-mid-Sept (2-day min); lower rates rest of yr. Crib free. Playground. Complimentary full bkfst; afternoon refreshments. Ck-out 11 am, ck-in 3-6 pm. Business servs avail. Whirlpool. Balconies. Ocean view. Private beach. Greenhouse. On four acres. Totally nonsmoking. Cr cds: A, C, DS, MC, V.

SC

Restaurant

★★ **MERRYMAN'S.** *100 Moonstone Beach Rd (95570), 3 mi S, US 101 Westhaven (N), 6th Ave (S) exits. 707/677-3111.* Hrs: 5-9 pm; Sun from 4 pm. Closed major hols; also Mon, Tues in summer, wkdays Oct-mid-Apr. No A/C. Bar. Complete meal: dinner $15.50-$22. Specializes in seafood, beef, pasta. Ocean view. Totally nonsmoking. Cr cds: C.

Truckee (C-3)

(See also Tahoe City, Tahoe Vista)

Pop 3,484 **Elev** 5,820 ft **Area Code** 916 **Zip** 96161

Information Truckee-Donner Chamber of Commerce, 12036 Donner Pass Rd; 916/587-2757

Once a lumbering camp, now a railroad and recreation center, Truckee becomes important in winter as the gateway to one of California's best winter sports areas. In 1913 the first California ski club was organized; today more than 20 ski clubs make their headquarters here. Truckee is surrounded by Tahoe National Forest; a Ranger District office of the forest is located here.

What to See and Do

Donner Lake. Sparkling blue lake surrounded by mountain slopes of Sierras. Fishing; water sports. Nearby is Donner Pass, main route into California for more than a century. 3 mi W on US 40.

Donner Memorial State Park. A 353-acre area that serves as monument to Donner Party, stranded here in Oct 1846 by early blizzards. Of a party of 81 who pitched camp, only 48 survived. Emigrant Trail Museum has exhibits on Donner Party, construction of first transcontinental railroad, geology of the Sierra Nevada, wildlife and Native Americans (daily; closed Jan 1, Thanksgiving, Dec 25; fee). Swimming, fishing. Nature trail. Cross-country ski trail. Picnicking. Camping (Memorial Day-Labor Day). Ranger, naturalist programs (seasonal). Park (daily). Standard fees. 2 mi W on Donner Pass Rd. Phone 916/582-7892.

Skiing.

Boreal. 2 quad, 2 triple, 6 double chairlifts; patrol, school, rentals; snowmaking; cafeteria, bar; lodge. 41 runs, longest run 1 mi; vertical drop 600 ft. (Nov-May, daily) Night skiing. 10 mi W on I-80, Castle Peak exit. Phone 916/426-3666 for snow conditions. ¢¢¢¢¢

Donner Ski Ranch. Triple, 3 double chairlifts; patrol, school, rentals; bar, restaurant, cafeteria. Longest run 1 mi; vertical drop 720 ft. (Nov-May, daily) 10 mi W, 3½ mi off I-80 at Soda Springs exit. Phone 916/426-3635. ¢¢¢¢-¢¢¢¢¢

Northstar. 2 quad, 3 triple, 3 double chairlifts, gondola; patrol, school, rentals; snowmaking; cafeteria, restaurants, bars; lodging. Longest run 3 mi; vertical drop 2,200 ft. Cross-country skiing; rentals. (Nov-Apr, daily) Half-day rates. Summer activities include tennis, 18-hole golf, mountain biking, horseback riding and swimming. 6 mi S on CA 267 via I-80. Phone 916/562-1010 or 800/533-6787. ¢¢¢¢¢

Royal Gorge Cross Country Ski Resort. Approx 80 cross-country trails over 200 mi of rolling terrain. Patrol, school, rentals; restaurants; 2 lodges. Longest trail 14 mi. (Mid-Nov-mid-May) 12 mi W on I-80. Phone 916/426-3871. ¢¢¢¢¢

Sugar Bowl. Quad, 6 double chairlifts, gondola; patrol, school, rentals; restaurant, cafeterias, bar; nursery, lodging. 47 runs, longest run 1.5 mi; vertical drop 1,500 ft. (Nov-Apr, daily) 11 mi W on I-80. Phone 916/426-3651 or 916/426-3847 (snow conditions). ¢¢¢¢¢

Tahoe Donner. 2 double chairlifts, rope tow; patrol, school, rentals; cafeteria, restaurant, bar. (Dec-Apr, daily; closed Easter) Cross-country trails (fee). 6 mi NW off I-80. Phone 916/587-9444 or 916/587-9494 (snow conditions). ¢¢¢¢¢

Annual Events

Truckee-Tahoe Airshow. Mid-June.

Truckee Rodeo. 2nd wkend Aug.

Donner Party Hike. 1st wkend Oct.

Motels

★★ **BEST WESTERN TAHOE INN.** *11331 Sr 267 (96161). 530/587-4525; FAX 530/587-8173; res: 800/824-6385.* E-mail bwtti@mail.telis.org. 100 rms, 2 story. S $77; D $84; each addl $7; under 12 free; golf, fishing, ski packages; higher rates hol wkends. Crib free. TV; VCR avail (free movies). Pool; whirlpool. Complimentary continental bkfst. Restaurant nearby. Ck-out 11 am. Meeting rms. Business servs avail. Downhill ski 5 mi. Exercise equipt; sauna. Microwaves avail. Cr cds: A, C, D, DS, MC, V.

SC

★★ **DONNER LAKE VILLAGE RESORT.** *15695 Donner Pass Rd (96161). 916/587-6081; FAX 916/587-8782; res: 800/621-6664.* 66 rms, 2 story. No A/C. July-Sept, mid-Dec-Apr: S, D $100-$135; each addl $10; suites $135-$180; under 12 free; higher rates hols; lower rates rest of yr. Crib free. TV; cable. Complimentary coffee in rms. Ck-out 11 am. Meeting rms. Business servs avail. Downhill ski 4 mi; x-country ski 7 mi. Sauna. Balconies, grills. On lake; marina. Cr cds: A, C, D, DS, MC, V.

SC

Resort

★★ **NORTHSTAR AT TAHOE.** *Hwy 267 & Northstar Dr (96160), 6 mi S on CA 267. 530/562-1010; FAX 530/562-2215; res: 800/466-6784.* Web www.skinorthstar.com. 30 rms in 3-story lodge, 205 condos, 27 houses (3-5-bedrm). No A/C. Mid-Nov-mid-Apr: S, D $149-$454; condos $149-$454; houses $366-$599; ski, golf plans; higher rates: Dec 25, hols; lower rates rest of yr. TV; cable. 2 heated pools; whirlpool, wading pool. Playgrond. Coffee in rms. Bar. Ck-out 11 am, ck-in 5 pm. Grocery, delicatessen. Coin Indry. Meeting rms. Business center. Free RR station, bus depot transportation. Tennis, pro. 18-hole golf, pro, greens fee $67 (incl cart), putting green, driving range. Downhill/x-country ski on site. Game rm. Exercise equipt; sauna. Many fireplaces. Private decks, balconies. Picnic tables. Cr cds: A, C, DS, MC, V.

Inn

★ **TRUCKEE HOTEL.** *10007 Branch St (96160). 530/587-4444; FAX 530/587-1599; res: 800/659-6921.* E-mail truckee.sierra@aol.com; web www.truckeetahoe.com/truckeehotel. 37 rms, 29 with shower only, 4 story, 5 suites. No A/C. No elvtr. No rm phones. Thanksgiving-Mar: S, D $85-$125; each addl $15; suites $110-$125; under 5 free; hols (2-day min); lower rates rest of yr. Crib free. Street parking. Complimentary continental bkfst. Complimentary coffee in rms. Bar. Ck-out 11 am, ck-in 3 pm. Meeting rms. Business servs avail. Gift shop. Sundries. Airport, RR station transportation. Game rm. Opp river. Totally nonsmoking. Cr cds: A, C, MC, V.

Restaurant

✓★ **O'B'S PUB & RESTAURANT.** *10046 Donner Pass Rd (96160). 530/587-4164.* E-mail innett@sierra.net. Hrs: 11:30 am-10:30 pm. Bar. Semi-a la carte: lunch $3.95-$7.95. A la carte entrees: dinner $10.95-$16. Specializes in seafood, beef. Built in early 1900s; many antiques, wood-burning stove. Cr cds: C, D, DS, MC, V.

D

Ukiah (D-1)

(See also Clear Lake Area)

Settled 1855 **Pop** 14,599 **Elev** 639 ft **Area Code** 707 **Zip** 95482

Information Greater Ukiah Chamber of Commerce, 200 S School St; 707/462-2088

In the center of a valley that Native Americans called Ukiah, or Deep Valley, this is the seat of Mendocino County. It is the trading place of an agricultural area that produces a $75-million annual crop of pears, grapes and other products. Recreational activities include golf, tennis and fishing.

What to See and Do

Grace Hudson Museum. Permanent exhibits on Pomo people; regional artists and photographers; early 20th-century paintings by Mendocino County artist Grace Hudson. Changing exhibits. **The Sun House** (1911) is the 6-rm craftsman house of Grace and John Hudson. Tours. (July 4-Labor Day, daily exc Mon; rest of yr, Wed-Sun) 431 S Main St. Phone 707/462-3370. **Free**

Lake Mendocino. Artificial lake produced by Coyote Dam, which controls Russian River. Dedicated in 1959, the lake provides swimming, waterskiing; fishing; boating (ramps, docks). Hiking. Picnicking. Camping (fee). Interpretive programs. (Apr-Sept, daily; closed rest of yr exc some campgrounds) Pets on leash only. No camping res accepted. 3 mi NE, off US 101. Phone 707/462-7581 or 707/462-7582. **Free**

Wineries.

Dunnewood Vineyards. Winery tours (by appt). Tasting rm (daily; closed hols). Picnic area. 2399 N State St. Phone 707/462-2985. **Free**

Parducci Wine Cellars. Guided tours; wine tasting (daily; closed hols). 501 Parducci Rd. Phone 707/462-WINE. **Free**

Annual Event

Mendocino County Fair & Apple Show. Boonville. 3 days mid- or late Sept.

Motels

★★ **BEST WESTERN INN.** *601 Talmage Rd (95482). 707/462-8868; FAX 707/468-9043; res: 800/272-6232.* 40 rms, 2 story. May-Sept: S, D $55-$75; each addl $5; lower rates rest of yr. TV; cable (premium). Pool. Complimentary continental bkfst. Complimentary coffee in rms. Restaurant nearby. Ck-out 11 am. Business servs avail. In-rm modem link. Refrigerators. Cr cds: A, C, D, DS, JCB, MC, V.

SC

★★★ **DISCOVERY INN.** *1340 N State St (95482). 707/462-8873; FAX 707/462-1249.* 177 rms, 2 story. May-Sept: S $58-$65; D $62-$78; each addl $5; suites $65-$80; kit. units $85; lower rates rest of yr. Crib free. TV; cable (premium). Complimentary continental bkfst. 2 heated pools; whirlpools. Restaurant 6 am-11 pm. Ck-out noon. Coin lndry. Meeting rms. Business servs avail. In-rm modem link. Refrigerators. Redwood theme park on grounds. Cr cds: A, C, D, DS, MC, V.

D SC

✓★ **ECONOMY INN.** *406 S State St (95482). 707/462-8611; FAX 707/468-9476; res: 800/578-7878.* 40 rms, 2 story. May-Sept: S, D $55-$65; each addl $5; higher rates: hols, special events; lower rates rest of yr. TV; cable (premium). Pool. Complimentary coffee in rms. Restaurant opp 9 am-10 pm. Ck-out 11 am. Business servs avail. Some refrigerators. Cr cds: A, C, D, DS, MC, V.

SC

Inns

★★★ **THATCHER INN.** *13401 S Hwy 101 (95449), 12 mi S on US 101. 707/744-1890; FAX 707/744-1219; res: 800/266-1891.* E-mail info@thatcherinn.com; web www.thatcherinn.com. 20 rms, 3 story, 2 suites. 3 A/C. D $115-$130; each addl $25; suites $150-$165; under 10 free. TV in game rm. Pool. Complimentary full bkfst. Dining rm 11:30 am-2 pm, 5:30-9:30 pm. Bar 11 am-10 pm. Ck-out noon, ck-in 3 pm. Business servs avail. In-rm modem link. Victorian inn (1890) with period furnishings. Totally nonsmoking. Cr cds: A, C, MC, V.

SC

★★★ **VICHY MINERAL SPRINGS RESORT.** *2605 Vichy Springs Rd (95482). 707/462-9515; FAX 707/462-9516.* E-mail vichy@pacific.net; web www.vichysprings.com. 20 rms, 3 cottages. S $99-$130; D $135-$155; each addl $35; cottages $195; hols (2-day min). TV avail; VCR avail. Complimentary full bkfst. Restaurant nearby. Ck-out noon, ck-in 3 pm. Business servs avail. Luggage handling. Free RR station, bus depot transportation. Lighted tennis privileges. 18-hole golf privileges. Pool; whirlpool. Refrigerator, microwave, fireplace in cottage. Balconies. Picnic tables, grills. Built between 1854-1870; country decor. Totally nonsmoking. Cr cds: A, C, D, JCB, MC, V.

D

Vacaville (D-2)

(See also Fairfield)

Pop 71,479 **Elev** 179 ft **Area Code** 707 **Zip** 95688

What to See and Do

Factory Stores at Vacaville. Approx 120 outlet stores. (Daily) I-80, Orange Dr exit, 321-2 Nut Tree Rd. Phone 707/447-5755.

Motels

★ **BEST WESTERN HERITAGE INN.** *1420 E Monte Vista Ave (95688). 707/448-8453; FAX 707/447-8649; res: 800/528-1234.* 41 rms, 2 story. S $63; D $70; each addl $5; suites $90; under 12 free. Crib $5. TV; cable. Pool. Complimentary continental bkfst. Restaurant adj open 24 hrs. Ck-out 11 am. Business servs avail. Refrigerators, microwaves avail. Cr cds: A, C, D, DS, MC, V.

SC

★★ **COURTYARD BY MARRIOTT.** *120 Nut Tree Pkwy (95687). 707/451-9000; FAX 707/449-3952; res: 800/451-8000.* 127 rms, 2 story. S, D $84-$130; each addl $10; suites $120-$150; under 18 free; wkend rates. Crib free. TV; cable. Complimentary coffee in rms. Restaurant 6:30-10 am; Sat, Sun 7-11 am. Rm serv 5-10 pm. Bar 5-10 pm. Ck-out noon. Meeting rms. Business servs avail. In-rm modem link. Coin lndry. Exercise equipt. Health club privileges. Pool; whirlpool. Refrigerators, microwaves avail. Cr cds: A, C, D, DS, MC, V.

D SC

★ **QUALITY INN.** *950 Leisure Town Rd (95687), just off I-80. 707/446-8888; FAX 707/449-0109; res: 800/638-7949.* 120 rms, 2 story. S $50-$55; D $60-$65; each addl $5; under 18 free. Crib free. TV; cable. Pool; whirlpool. Complimentary continental bkfst. Restaurant opp 7 am-9 pm. Ck-out 11 am. Business servs avail. In-rm modem link. Cr cds: A, C, D, DS, MC, V.

D SC

Restaurant

✓★ **COFFEE TREE.** *100 Nut Tree Pkwy (95687), just N off I-80. 707/448-8435.* Hrs: 6 am-9 pm. Closed Dec 25. Semi-a la carte: bkfst $3.95-$8.55, lunch, dinner $3.95-$14.95. Child's meals. Own desserts. Colorful decor; art display. Family-owned. Totally nonsmoking. Cr cds: A, C, D, DS, MC, V.

D

Valencia (H-3)

(See also Los Angeles)

Pop 30,000 (est) **Area Code** 805 **Zip** 91355

Information Santa Clarita Valley Chamber of Commerce, 23920 Valencia Blvd, Ste 100, Santa Clarita 91355-2175; 805/259-4787 or 800/718-TOUR, ext 123

What to See and Do

Pyramid Lake Recreation Area. Lake with swimming, waterskiing, windsurfing; fishing; boating (rentals, ramp). Picnicking, concession. Camping (fee). (Daily; closed major hols) 20 mi N on I-5. Phone 805/257-2892 or 805/295-1245. Per vehicle ¢¢¢

Six Flags California. Includes Magic Mountain theme park and Hurricane Harbor water park. Theme park features over 100 rides, shows and attractions, including Superman The Escape—the first ride ever to break the 100-mph speed barrier; Batman & Robin Live Action Show; 8 major roller coasters; children's play area with scaled-down rides, animal farm, petting zoo. Theme park (late Mar-late Oct, daily). Water park features 75-ft-tall enclosed speed slides; adult activities pool & body slides; 7,000-sq-ft lagoon with water sports; children's Castaway Cove. Water park (June-Labor Day, daily; mid-late May & mid-late Sept, wkends). 26101 Magic Mt Pkwy, off I-5. Phone 805/255-4111. ¢¢¢¢¢

Motels

★ **BEST WESTERN INN.** *27413 N Tourney Rd (91355), opp Six Flags California. 805/255-0555; FAX 805/255-2216; res: 800/528-1234.* E-mail rhi@scvnet.com; web www.bestwestern.com. 182 rms, 2 suites in 4 buildings, 2 story. S, D $80-$110; each addl $10; suites $175; under 18 free. Crib free. TV; cable (premium). 2 heated pools; wading pool, whirlpool. Complimentary coffee in rms. Restaurant 7 am-10 pm. Rm serv. Bar 4-10 pm. Ck-out noon. Coin Indry. Meeting rms. Business servs avail. Refrigerators avail. Some patios. Cr cds: A, C, D, DS, MC, V.

D SC

★★ **HAMPTON INN.** *25259 The Old Rd (91381), I-5 exit Lyons Ave W to Chiquella Lane, then S. 805/253-2400; FAX 805/253-1683; res: 800/426-7866.* 130 rms, 4 story. S, D $99-$109. Crib free. TV; cable (premium). Heated pool; whirlpool. Complimentary continental bkfst. Coffee in rms. Restaurant opp open 24 hrs. Ck-out noon. Coin Indry. Meeting rm. Business center. Valet serv. Sundries. Health club privileges. Some refrigerators; microwaves avail. Some balconies. Cr cds: A, C, D, DS, MC, V.

D SC

★★★ **HILTON.** *27710 The Old Rd (91355), opp Six Flags California. 805/254-8800; FAX 805/254-9399; res: 800/445-8667.* 152 rms, 2 story. S $89-$129; D $99-$139; each addl $10; suites $198-$250; under 18 free; family rates. Crib free. TV; cable (premium). Heated pool; whirlpool, poolside serv. Complimentary coffee in rms. Restaurant 6:30 am-10 pm. Rm serv 5:30-10:30 pm. Bar 5-10:30 pm. Ck-out noon. Sundries. Coin Indry. Meeting rms. Business center. In-rm modem link. Exercise equipt. Refrigerators, microwaves; some bathrm phones. Some balconies. Cr cds: A, C, D, DS, ER, JCB, MC, V.

D SC

Vallejo (E-2)

(See also Berkeley, Fairfield, Martinez, Oakland)

Founded 1851 **Pop** 109,199 **Elev** 50 ft **Area Code** 707 **E-mail** vjocvb@visitvallejo.com **Web** www.visitvallejo.com

Information Convention & Visitors Bureau, 495 Mare Island Way, 94590; 707/642-3653 or 800/4-VALLEJO

This was California's capital in 1852 for about a week; and again, a year later, for just over one month. Despite the departure of the legislature in 1853 for Benicia, the town prospered because the United States purchased Mare Island for a Navy yard in 1854. The former Mare Island Naval Shipyard is a 2,300-acre spread of land between the Mare Island Strait and San Pablo Bay.

What to See and Do

Benicia Capitol State Historic Park. Building has been restored and furnished in style of 1853-1854, when it served as state capitol. (Daily; closed Jan 1, Thanksgiving, Dec 25) 1st & G Sts, 6 mi SE, in Benicia. Phone 707/745-3385. ¢

Marine World. Wildlife theme park. Major shows featuring killer whales, dolphins, sea lions, tigers, exotic and predatory birds and waterski/boat show. Rides and attractions include 2 roller coasters. Participatory exhibits include Elephant Encounter, Butterfly World, giraffe feedings and lorikeet feedings. (Memorial Day-Labor Day, daily; Apr-Memorial Day & Labor Day-Oct, Fri-Sun) Jct I-80 & CA 37, Marine World Pkwy. Phone 707/643-ORCA (recording). ¢¢¢¢¢

Vallejo Ferry. One-hr direct ferry service between Vallejo and San Francisco. Also to Angel Island State Park (Apr-Oct). Ferry packages include Marine World Package, Napa Valley Wine Tour and Napa Valley Wine Train (schedules vary; fee). (Daily; closed Jan 1, Thanksgiving, Dec 25) 495 Mare Island Way. Phone 707/643-3779. One-way ¢¢¢

Vallejo Naval and Historical Museum. Two galleries house changing exhibits on local history. Two additional galleries house permanent exhibits on Navy and Mare Island Naval Shipyard history. Naval exhibits include models, murals and a functioning submarine periscope. Also here is a local history research library (by appt) and a book/gift shop. (Tues-Sat; closed some major hols) 734 Marin St, located in the old City Hall building. Phone 707/643-0077. ¢

Annual Events

Solano County Fair. Fairgrounds, Fairgrounds Dr, N off I-80. Phone 707/648-3247. July.

Jazz & Art Festival. Waterfront at Mare Island Way. Late Aug.

Whaleboat Regatta. Marina Vista Park. Early Oct.

Motels

★★ **BEST WESTERN HERITAGE INN.** *1955 E 2nd St (94510), 6 mi E off I-780. 707/746-0401; FAX 707/745-0842; res: 800/528-1234.* 100 rms, 3 story. S, D $65-$85; each addl $5; suites $85-$100; kit. units $75-$85; under 12 free; wkly, monthly rates. Crib free. Pet accepted, some restrictions; $25 refundable. TV; cable (premium). Pool; whirlpool. Complimentary continental bkfst. Coffee in rms. Restaurant nearby. Ck-out 11 am. Meeting rms. Business servs avail. Valet serv. In-rm whirlpools; some refrigerators, wet bars; microwaves avail. Cr cds: A, C, D, DS, MC, V.

D SC

★ **RAMADA INN.** *1000 Admiral Callaghan Ln (91355), I-80 at Columbus Pkwy exit. 707/643-2700; FAX 707/642-1148; res: 800/677-4466.* 130 rms, 3 story, 36 suites. May-Sept: S $95-$100; D $110; each addl $15; suites $105-$130; under 18 free. Crib free. TV; cable (premium). Pool; whirlpool. Complimentary continental bkfst. Complimentary coffee in rms. Restaurant nearby. Ck-out noon. Coin Indry. Meeting rms. Business servs avail. In-rm modem link. Valet serv. Health club privileges. Refrigerators, microwaves. Picnic tables, grill. Cr cds: A, C, D, DS, ER, JCB, MC, V.

D SC

Van Nuys (L.A.)

(B-3 see Los Angeles map)

Area Code 818

This community in the San Fernando Valley is an integral part of Los Angeles, but is regarded by many as a separate entity.

Motel

✓★ **TRAVELODGE AT VAN NUYS.** *6909 Sepulveda Blvd (91405), I-405 exit Sherman Way E. 818/787-5400; FAX 818/782-0239; res: 800/578-7878.* Web www.travelodge.com. 74 rms, 3 story. S, D $49-$79; each addl $6; under 12 free. TV; cable (premium). Pool. Complimentary continental bkfst. Complimentary coffee in rms. Restaurant nearby. Ck-out noon. Meeting rm. Refrigerators. Cr cds: A, C, D, DS, ER, JCB, MC, V.

D SC

Motor Hotel

★★★ **AIRTEL PLAZA HOTEL.** *7277 Valjean Ave (91406), I-405 Sherman Way W exit. 818/997-7676; FAX 818/785-8864; res: 800/224-7835.* E-mail airtel@airtelplaza.com; web www.airtelplaza.com. 268 rms, 3-5 story. S, D $119-$129; each addl $10; suites $165-$600; under 18 free. Crib free. TV; cable (premium). Heated pool; whirlpools, poolside serv. Restaurants 6 am-10 pm. Rm serv. Bar 10-2 am. Ck-out noon. Convention facilities. Business servs avail. In-rm modem link. Bellhops. Gift shop. Exercise equipt. Some refrigerators. Some private patios, balconies. Cr cds: A, C, D, DS, ER, JCB, MC, V.

D SC

Ventura

(J-3)

(See also Ojai, Oxnard, Santa Barbara, Thousand Oaks)

Founded 1782 **Pop** 93,483 **Elev** 50 ft **Area Code** 805 **E-mail** vcb@ventura-usa.com **Web** www.ventura-usa.com

Information Visitor & Convention Bureau Information Center, 89 S California St, Ste C, 93001; 805/648-2075 or 800/333-2989

What was once a little mission surrounded by huge stretches of sagebrush and mustard plants is now the busy city of Ventura. The sagebrush and mustard have been replaced by citrus, avocado and other agriculture, but the mission still stands. With the Pacific shore at its feet and rolling foothills at its back, Ventura attracts a steady stream of vacationers. It is in the center of the largest lemon-producing county in the US.

What to See and Do

Albinger Archaeological Museum. Preserved archaeological exploration site and visitor center in downtown area. Evidence of Native American culture 3,500 yrs old; Chumash village site, settled approx A.D. 1500; foundation of original mission; Chinese and Mexican artifacts; audiovisual programs. (Wed-Sun; closed some hols) 113 E Main St. Phone 805/648-5823. **Free**

Camping. Emma Wood State Beach. North Beach. Swimming, surfing; fishing. 2 RV group camping sites, 61 primitive camp sites. Standard fees. Access from W Pacific Coast Hwy, state beaches exit northbound US 101. Phone 805/968-1033. **McGrath State Beach.** Swimming; fishing. Nature trail. 170 developed campsites. 3 mi S off Harbor Blvd. Standard fees. Phone 800/444-7275.

Channel Islands National Park (see).

Channel Islands National Park Visitor's Center. Displays, exhibits and scale models of the 5 islands; marine life exhibit; observation tower; film of the islands (25 min). (Daily; closed Thanksgiving, Dec 25) 1901 Spinnaker Dr. Phone 805/658-5730. **Free**

Island Packer Cruises. Boat leaves Ventura Harbor for picnic, sightseeing and recreational trips to Channel Islands National Park. Res required. (Memorial Day-Sept, 5 islands; rest of yr, 2 islands) For details contact 1867 Spinnaker Dr, 93001; phone 805/642-7688 (recording) or 805/642-1393 (res). **¢¢¢¢¢**

Olivas Adobe (1847). Restored with antique furnishings; displays; gardens; visitor center, video. Tours (by appt). House open for viewing (Sat, Sun). Grounds (daily; closed some hols). Special programs monthly. 4200 Olivas Park Dr, off US 101 Victoria Ave exit. Phone 805/644-4346. **Free**

Ortega Adobe (1857). Restored and furnished adobe built on the Camino Real. Furnished with rustic handmade furniture from the 1850s. Tours (by appt). Grounds (daily). 100 W Main St. Phone 805/658-4728. **Free**

San Buenaventura Mission (1782). Ninth California mission and the last founded by Fray Junipero Serra. Massive, with a striped rib dome on the bell tower; restored. Garden with fountain. Museum (enter through gift shop at 225 E Main St) features original wooden bell. Museum (daily; closed major hols). Church and gardens (daily). 211 E Main St, off US 101. Phone 805/643-4318 or 805/648-4496 (gift shop). **¢**

San Buenaventura State Beach. Approx 115 acres on a sheltered sweep of coast. Offers swimming, lifeguard (summer); surf fishing. Coastal bicycle trail access point. Picnicking, concession. Standard fees. (Daily) Phone 805/968-1033. Per vehicle **¢¢**

Ventura County Museum of History and Art. Collection of Native American, Spanish and pioneer artifacts; George Stuart Collection of Historical Figures; changing exhibits of local history and art; outdoor areas depicting the county's agricultural history; educational programs, research library; gift shop. (Daily exc Mon; closed Jan 1, Thanksgiving, Dec 25) 100 E Main St. Phone 805/653-0323. **¢**

Ventura Harbor. Accommodates more than 1,500 boats; 3 marinas, launch ramp, mast up dry storage boat yard, drydock and repair facilities, fuel docks, guest slips. Sportfishing and island boats; sailboat rentals; cruises. Swimming, fishing; hotel, shops, restaurants; Channel Islands National Park headquarters. 1603 Anchors Way Dr. Phone 805/642-8538 or 805/644-0169.

Annual Event

Ventura County Fair. Seaside Park. Parade, rodeo, carnival, entertainment, livestock auction. Aug.

Seasonal Event

Whale watching. Gray whales, Dec-Mar; blue whales, July-Sept.

Motels

★★★ **COUNTRY INN.** *298 S Chestnut St (93001). 805/653-1434; FAX 805/648-7126; res: 800/447-3529.* 120 kit. units, 3 story. S, D $148-$158; each addl $10; suites $209; under 12 free. Garage parking. Pet accepted. TV; cable, VCR (movies $4). Heated pool; whirlpool. Complimentary full bkfst. Ck-out noon. Coin Indry. Meeting rm. Business servs avail. In-rm modem link. Valet serv. Bathrm phones; some fireplaces. Private patios, balconies. Country decor. Opp ocean. Cr cds: A, C, D, DS, JCB, MC, V.

D SC

★★★ **PIERPONT INN.** *550 Sanjon Rd (93001). 805/643-6144; FAX 805/641-1501; res: 800/285-4667.* E-mail info@pierpontinn.com; web www.pierpontinn.com. 72 rms, 2-3 story. No A/C. No elvtr. S, D $99-$109; each addl $10; suites $169; cottages $189-$289; under 12 free. Crib free. TV; cable (premium), VCR avail (movies). Pool. Complimentary continental bkfst. Coffee in rms. Restaurant 6:30-9 am, 11:30 am-closing. Rm serv. Bar 11 am-midnight. Ck-out noon. Meeting rms. Business servs avail. Valet serv. Tennis privileges. Health club privileges. Some fireplaces. Many private verandas, balconies. Established in 1908. Overlooks Pierpont Bay. Cr cds: A, C, D, DS, ER, MC, V.

D SC

★★★ **RAMADA INN CLOCKTOWER.** *181 E Santa Clara St (93001). 805/652-0141; FAX 805/643-1432; res: 800/272-6232; res: 800/727-1027.* 49 rms, 2 story. S, D $70-$100; each addl $10; under 12 free. TV; cable (premium), VCR avail. Complimentary continental bkfst. Restaurant 11 am-2:30 pm, 5-9:30 pm; Fri-Sun to 10 pm. Rm serv. Ck-out noon. Meeting rms. Business servs avail. In-rm modem link. Some fireplaces. Private patios, balconies. Near beach, downtown. Southwestern decor. Renovated firehouse in park setting; atrium. Cr cds: A, C, D, DS, ER, JCB, MC, V.

D SC

✓★ **VAGABOND INN.** *756 E Thompson Blvd (93001). 805/648-5371; FAX 805/648-5613; res: 800/522-1555.* 82 rms, 2 story. S $45-$68; D $50-$80; each addl $5; higher rates special events. Crib free. Pet accepted; $5. TV; cable (premium). Heated pool; whirlpool. Complimentary continental bkfst. Complimentary coffee in rms. Restaurant open 5 am-10 pm. Ck-out noon. Business servs avail. Cr cds: A, C, D, DS, MC, V.

SC

Hotel

★★ **DOUBLETREE HOTEL.** *2055 Harbor Blvd (93001). 805/643-6000; FAX 805/643-7137; res: 800/222-8733.* 284 rms, 4 story. July-Labor Day: S, D $75-$99; each addl $10; suites $139; under 18 free; package plans; lower rates rest of yr. TV; cable (premium), VCR avail. Heated pool; whirlpool. Coffee in rms. Restaurant 6:30 am-10 pm; Sat, Sun 7 am-10:30 pm. Bar 3-11 pm. Ck-out noon. Convention facilities. Business servs avail. In-rm modem link. Valet serv. Gift shop. Exercise equipt; sauna. Balconies. Beach 1 blk. Cr cds: A, C, D, DS, ER, JCB, MC, V.

D SC

Inn

★★ **LA MER EUROPEAN BED & BREAKFAST.** *411 Poli St (93001). 805/643-3600; FAX 805/653-7329.* Web www.vcol./lamer. 5 rms, 2 story, 1 suite. No A/C. No rm phones. S $80-$150; D $85-$155; suite $150-$155; mid-wk rates, packages avail. Children over 13 yrs only. Complimentary buffet bkfst; afternoon refreshments. Ck-out noon, ck-in 4 pm. Business servs avail. Massage. Antique horse-drawn carriage rides. 1890 bldg, library. Antiques. Each rm individually decorated to represent a European country. Private patios. Overlooks ocean. Totally nonsmoking. Cr cds: A, C, MC, V.

Victorville (H-4)

(See also Barstow, Big Bear Lake, Lake Arrowhead)

Founded 1878 **Pop** 40,674 **Elev** 2,715 ft **Area Code** 760

Information Chamber of Commerce, 14174 Green Tree Blvd, 92392; 760/245-6506

You may never have been in Victorville, but you've probably seen the town before—it has been the setting for hundreds of cowboy movies. This aspect of the town's economy has waned, replaced by light industry. On the edge of the Mojave Desert, the town serves as a base for desert exploration. The presence of lime has attracted four major cement plants to the vicinity.

What to See and Do

California Route 66 Museum. A tribute to the first national highway to connect Chicago with Los Angeles. Exhibits on different artists' views of Route 66 and its history. (Thurs-Mon) 16849 Route 66 "D" St. Phone 760/261-8766. **Free**

Mojave Narrows Regional Park. Fishing, boating. Hiking, bridle trails. Picnicking, snack bar. Camping (fee). Park (daily; closed Dec 25). 2 mi S on I-15, then 4 mi E on Bear Valley Rd, 3 mi N on Ridgecrest. Contact PO Box 361, 92393; Phone 760/245-2226. Per vehicle **¢¢**

Roy Rogers-Dale Evans Museum. Western-style fort depicting the personal and professional lives of the Rogers. (Daily; closed Easter, Thanksgiving, Dec 25) 15650 Seneca Rd. Phone 760/243-4547 or 760/243-4548. **¢¢¢**

Annual Events

Huck Finn Jubilee. At Mojave Narrows Regional Park. River-raft building, fence painting, bluegrass and clogging activities; food. Father's Day wkend.

San Bernardino County Fair. 14800 7th St. Rodeo, livestock and agricultural exhibits, carnival. Phone 760/951-2200. Late spring or early summer.

Motels

★ **BEST WESTERN GREEN TREE INN.** *14173 Green Tree Blvd (92392). 760/245-3461; FAX 760/245-7745; res: 800/528-1234; res: 800/877-3644.* 168 rms, 2-3 story. S $60-$64; D $64-$68; each addl $4; suites $70-$80; kit. units, studio rms $64-$70; under 12 free. Crib free. TV; cable. Heated pool; wading pool, whirlpool, poolside serv. Complimentary coffee in rms. Restaurant open 24 hrs. Rm serv 7 am-10 pm. Bar 10-2 am; entertainment. Ck-out 1 pm. Meeting rms. Business center. Shopping arcade. Beauty shop. Health club privileges. Refrigerators. View of desert, mountains. Cr cds: A, C, D, DS, ER, JCB, MC, V.

D SC

✓★ **TRAVELODGE.** *16868 Stoddard Wells Rd (92392), I-15, exit Stoddard Wells Rd. 760/243-7700; FAX 760/243-4432; res: 888/315-2225; res: 800/315-2225.* Web www.expedia.com. 101 rms, 2 story. S $27-$36; D $36-$58; each addl $5; suites $65-$85; under 17 free. Crib free. TV; cable (premium). Pool. Complimentary coffee in lobby. Restaurant opp open 24 hrs. Ck-out noon. Coin lndry. Business servs avail. Some in-rm whirlpools. Cr cds: A, C, D, DS, MC, V.

D SC

Restaurant

★★ **CHATEAU CHANG.** *15425 Anacapa Rd (92392). 760/241-3040.* Hrs: 11:30 am-2:30 pm, 5-9:30 pm; Fri, Sat to 10:30 pm. Closed Sun; some major hols. Res accepted. French, continental menu. Bar. Semi-a la carte: lunch $6-$6.50. Complete meals: dinner $9.95-

$33.95. Specialties: flaming filet mignon, roast duck with orange sauce, whole lobster Thermidor. Contemporary decor; gray marble floors; saltwater aquarium. Cr cds: A, C, DS, MC, V.

D

Visalia (G-3)

(See also Hanford, Porterville, Three Rivers)

Pop 75,636 **Elev** 331 ft **Area Code** 559 **E-mail** www.cvb123@lightspeed.net **Web** www.cvbvisalia.com

Information Convention & Visitors Bureau, 301 E Acequia St; 559/738-3435 or 800/524-0303

What to See and Do

Chinese Cultural Center. Chinese artifacts, paintings, rare archaeological findings. Chinese garden. Confucius Temple. (Wed-Sun; closed major hols) 500 S Akers Rd. Phone 559/625-4545. **Free**

Sequoia & Kings Canyon National Parks (see). Due to gradient into and from the mountains, allow minimum of 1-5 hrs driving time to the visitors center. Approx 50 mi E on CA 198.

Tulare County Museum. Ten buildings set in a 140-acre park house historical exhibits. Park features *End of the Trail* statue by James Earl Fraser. Museum has Native American artifacts, early farm equipment, antique guns, clocks, dolls; log cabin. (Thurs-Mon; closed some hols) Mooney Grove, 27000 S Mooney Blvd. Phone 559/733-6616. Park entry (per vehicle) ¢¢; Museum ¢

Motel

✓★ **ECONO LODGE.** *1400 S Mooney Blvd (93277). 559/732-6641; FAX 559/739-7520; res: 800/228-5050; res: 800/242-4261.* E-mail pointer@prodigy.com. 49 rms, 2 story. S $55; D $61; each addl $5. Crib $4. TV; cable (premium). Pool. Complimentary continental bkfst. Complimentary coffee in rms. Restaurant 5:30-10 pm. Ck-out 11 am. Some refrigerators, microwaves. Cr cds: A, C, D, DS, ER, JCB, MC, V.

SC

Hotel

★★★ **RADISSON HOTEL.** *300 S Ct St (93291). 559/636-1111; FAX 559/636-8224; res: 800/333-3333.* 201 rms, 8 story. S, D $138-$148; each addl $10; suites $200-$450; family rates. Crib free. TV; cable. Pool; whirlpool; poolside serv. Complimentary coffee in rms. Restaurant 6 am-10 pm. Bar 11-2 am. Ck-out noon. Meeting rms. Business servs avail. In-rm modem link. Concierge. Valet parking. Free airport, RR station transportation. Exercise equipt. Minibars. Wet bar in suites. Cr cds: A, C, D, DS, JCB, MC, V.

D SC

Inn

★★ **SPALDING HOUSE.** *631 N Encina St (93291). 559/739-7877; FAX 559/625-0902.* 3 suites, 2 story. No rm phones. S $75; D $85. TV in living rm; VCR avail. Complimentary full bkfst. Restaurant nearby. Ck-out noon, ck-in 3 pm. Historic Colonial-revival house built 1901; fully restored. Elegant furnishings; some fireplaces, antiques. Library; piano in music rm; sitting rm. Totally nonsmoking. Cr cds: C, MC, V.

Restaurant

★★★ **THE VINTAGE PRESS.** *216 N Willis (93291). 559/733-3033.* Hrs: 11:30 am-2 pm, 6-10:30 pm; Fri, Sat to 11 pm; Sun 10 am-2 pm, 5-9 pm. Closed Dec 25. Res accepted. California menu. Bar 11-2 am. Semi-a la carte: lunch $6.95-$12.95, dinner $15.95-$37. Child's meals. Outdoor dining. Antiques. Family-owned. Cr cds: A, C, D, MC, V.

D

Walnut Creek (B-4 see San Francisco map)

(See also Berkeley, Concord, Oakland)

Pop 60,569 **Elev** 135 ft **Area Code** 510

Motor Hotel

★★★ **LAFAYETTE PARK HOTEL.** *3287 Mt Diablo Blvd (94549), 2 mi W on CA 24 to Pleasant Hill Rd S exit, then 1 blk to Mt Diablo Blvd. 925/283-3700; FAX 925/284-1621; res: 800/368-2468.* Web www.woodsidehotels.com. 139 rms, 4 story. S, D $180-$260; suites $250-$450. TV; cable (premium), VCR avail. Heated pool; whirlpool, poolside serv. Restaurant (see DUCK CLUB). Rm serv 24 hrs. Bar 11 am-midnight. Ck-out noon. Meeting rms. Business servs avail. In-rm modem link. Valet serv. Concierge. Covered parking. Exercise equipt; sauna. Health club privileges. Bathrm phones, refrigerators, minibars; microwaves avail. Some private patios. Cr cds: A, C, D, DS, MC, V.

D SC

Hotels

★★ **EMBASSY SUITES HOTEL.** *1345 Treat Blvd (94596), I-680 to Treat exit. 925/934-2500; FAX 925/256-7233; res: 800/362-2779.* Web www.embassy-suites.com. 249 suites, 8 story. S $129-$179; D $144-$194; each addl $15; under 18 free. Crib free. Pet accepted; $100. In/out parking $7. TV; cable (premium), VCR avail. Complimentary full bkfst. Complimentary coffee in rms. Restaurant 11:30 am-2:30 pm, 5-10 pm. Rm serv 11 am-11 pm. Bar 11 am-midnight. Ck-out 1 pm. Meeting rms. Business servs avail. In-rm modem link. Gift shop. Coin Indry. Exercise equipt. Heated indoor pool; whirlpool. Refrigerators, microwaves, wet bars. Cr cds: A, C, D, DS, JCB, MC, V.

D SC

★★★ **MARRIOTT.** *2600 Bishop Drive (94583), I-680 exit Bollinger Canyon Rd, 5 mi N of I-580 interchange at Bishop Ranch. 925/867-9200; FAX 925/830-9326.* Web www.marriott.com. 368 rms, 6 story. S, D $159; suites $300-$600; under 18 free; wkend rates. Crib free. Pet accepted. TV; cable (premium), VCR avail. Pool; whirlpool. Restaurant 6:30 am-10 pm. Bar 11:30 am-midnight. Ck-out noon. Coin Indry. Convention facilities. Business servs avail. In-rm modem link. Concierge. Sundries. Exercise equipt; sauna. Health club privileges. Microwaves avail; wet bar in suites. View of Mt Diablo. Luxury level. Cr cds: A, C, D, DS, ER, JCB, MC, V.

D SC

★★★ **MARRIOTT.** *2355 N Main (95338). 925/934-2000; FAX 925/934-6374; res: 800/228-9290.* Web www.marriott.com. 338 rms, 6 story. S $149; D $159; suites $184-$450; under 18 free; wkend rates. Crib free. TV; cable, VCR avail. Pool; whirlpool. Coffee in rms. Restaurant 6:30 am-10 pm; Fri, Sat to 11 pm. Bar 11 am-midnight. Ck-out noon. Meeting rms. Business servs avail. In-rm modem link. Concierge. Gift shop. Exercise equipt. Bathrm phones; some refrigerators. Balconies. Luxury level. Cr cds: A, C, D, DS, ER, JCB, MC, V.

D SC

Restaurants

★★★ **BRIDGES RESTAURANT & BAR.** *44 Church St (94526), I-680, Diablo W exit to Hartz Ave, left to Church St. 975/820-7200.* Hrs: 5:30-9:30 pm; Fri 11:30 am-2 pm, 5:30-10 pm; Sat to 10 pm. Closed most major hols. Res accepted. Eclectic menu. Bar from 5 pm. A la carte entrees: lunch $6-$15, dinner $17-$30. Child's meals. Menu changes daily. Guitarist Wed. Valet parking. Outdoor dining. Heated garden patio. Totally nonsmoking. Cr cds: A, C, MC, V.

D

★★★ **DUCK CLUB.** *(See Lafayette Park Hotel) 925/283-7108.* Web www.woodsidehotels.com. Hrs: 6:30 am-2 pm, 6-9:30 pm; wkend hrs vary. Closed Jan 1 (eve). Res accepted. French bistro cuisine. Bar 11:30 am-midnight. Wine cellar. Semi-a la carte: bkfst $6-$12, lunch $8.95-$14.95, dinner $11.95-$26. Child's meals. Specialties: roast duck, five-onion soup, crab cakes. Valet parking. Outdoor dining. Overlooks courtyard and fountain. Rotisserie oven. Totally nonsmoking. Cr cds: A, C, D, DS, MC, V.

D

★★ **LARK CREEK CAFE.** *1360 Locust St (94596). 925/256-1234.* Hrs: 11:30 am-9 pm; Fri, Sat to 10 pm; Sun 4:30-9 pm; Sat, Sun brunch 10 am-3 pm. Closed Jan 1, Dec 25. Res accepted. Bar. Semi-a la carte: lunch $7.95-$14.50, dinner $8.95-$23.95. Child's meals. Specialties: pot roast, tamale pancake, meatloaf. Street, garage parking. Outdoor dining. Casual decor. Totally nonsmoking. Cr cds: A, C, D, MC, V.

D ♥

★★ **MUDD'S RESTAURANT.** *10 Boardwalk (94583), I-680 exit Crow Canyon Rd W to Park Place. 925/837-9387.* Web www.mudds.com. Hrs: 11:30 am-2:30 pm, 5:30-9 pm; Sat 5-10 pm; Sun 5-9 pm; Sun brunch 10 am-2 pm. Res accepted; required wkends, hols. Bar 11:30 am-10:30 pm. Semi-a la carte: lunch $9.50-$15, dinner $14.50-$27.95. Sun brunch $8-$14. Specializes in fresh salads, homemade pasta, loin chops. Outdoor dining. Cedarwood ceilings. 2-acre garden. Totally nonsmoking. Cr cds: A, C, D, MC, V.

D

★★★ **POSTINO.** *3565 Mt Diablo Blvd (94549), 3 mi W via CA 24. 925/299-8700.* Hrs: 5:30-10 pm; Fri, Sat 5-10:30 pm; Sun from 5 pm. Closed some major hols. Res accepted. Italian menu. Bar. A la carte entrees: dinner $10.95-$22.50. Child's meals. Outdoor dining. Cr cds: C, D, DS, JCB, MC, V.

D

★★ **PRIMA TRATTORIA E NEGOZIO-VINI.** *1522 N Main St (94596). 925/935-7780.* Hrs: 11:30 am-3 pm, 5-9 pm; Fri, Sat 11:30 am-11 pm; Sun from 5 pm. Closed major hols. Res accepted. Italian menu. Bar. Semi-a la carte: lunch $8-$16, dinner $12-$25. Specializes in Italian cuisine. Pianist Wed-Sat. Valet parking. Outdoor dining. Mediterranean atmosphere. Wine shop on premises. Family-owned. Cr cds: A, C, MC, V.

D

★★ **SPIEDINI.** *101 Ygnacio Valley Rd (94596). 925/939-2100.* Hrs: 11:30 am-10 pm; Fri to 11 pm; Sat 5-11 pm; Sun 5-9:30 pm. Closed Jan 1, Thanksgiving, Dec 25. Res accepted. Italian menu. Bar. A la carte entrees: lunch $8.50-$17.75, dinner $9.95-$18.95. Specializes in rotisserie grilled meats. Own pasta. Parking. Outdoor dining. Upscale dining. Totally nonsmoking. Cr cds: A, C, D, MC, V.

D

✓★★ **WALNUT CREEK HOFBRAU HOUSE.** *1401 Mt Diablo Blvd (94596). 925/947-2928.* E-mail wcyc@aol.com. Hrs: 11:30 am-10 pm; Sun 5-10 pm. Closed Jan 1, Thanksgiving, Dec 25. Res accepted. Seafood menu. Bar. Semi-a la carte: lunch, dinner $10.50-$19.50. Child's meals. Specializes in raw bar, fresh grilled fish. Parking. Outdoor dining. Totally nonsmoking. Cr cds: A, C, MC, V.

Weaverville (B-2)

(See also Redding)

Founded 1849 **Pop** 3,370 **Elev** 2,011 ft **Area Code** 530 **Zip** 96093 **E-mail** chamber@trinitycounty.com **Web** www.trinitycounty.com

Information Trinity County Chamber of Commerce, 210 N Main St, PO Box 517; 530/623-6101 or 800/487-4648

Weaverville's birth was linked with the discovery of gold. Within a few years the town's population had jumped to 3,000—half of it composed of Chinese miners. A Ranger District office of the Shasta-Trinity National Forest (see REDDING) is located here.

What to See and Do

Highland Art Center. Exhibits by local and other artists include paintings, photography, sculpture, textiles and pottery. (Daily) 503 Main St. Phone 530/623-5111. **Free**

J.J. Jackson Memorial Museum. Local historical exhibits. (Apr-Nov, daily; rest of yr, Tues & Sat) 508 Main St, on CA 299. Phone 530/623-5211. **Donation**

Trinity Alps Wilderness Area. Reached from Canyon Creek, Stuart Fork, Swift Creek, North Fork, New River or Coffee Creek. Unsurpassed alpine scenery, called US counterpart of Swiss Alps. Backpack, fishing, pack trips. 15 mi N in Shasta-Trinity National Forest (see REDDING). Resort areas on fringes. Wilderness permit necessary (free); obtain at Ranger District Office, PO Box 1190; Phone 530/623-2121. **Free**

Weaverville Joss House State Historic Park. Temple, built in 1874 by Chinese during gold rush, contains priceless tapestries and gilded wooden scrollwork. Hrly guided tours (Wed-Sun; closed Jan 1, Thanksgiving, Dec 25). Main & Oregon Sts, on CA 299. Phone 530/623-5284. ¢

West Covina (B-6 see Los Angeles map)

(See also Pomona)

Pop 96,086 **Elev** 381 ft **Area Code** 626

Motels

★ **COMFORT INN.** *2804 E Garvey Ave (91791). 626/915-6077; FAX 626/339-4587; res: 800/438-4116.* Web www.comfortinn.com. 58 rms, 3 story. S $49-$79; D $54-$84; each addl $5; under 18 free. Crib $5. TV; cable, (premium). Heated pool; whirlpool. Complimentary continental bkfst. Restaurant nearby. Ck-out 11 am. Meeting rm. Refrigerators; some in-rm whirlpools. Cr cds: A, C, D, DS, ER, JCB, MC, V.

SC

✓★ **EL DORADO MOTOR INN.** *140 N Azusa Ave (91791), I-10 exit Azusa Ave N. 626/331-6371.* 82 rms, 2 story. S, D $39; suites $45-$90; wkly rates. Crib free. TV; cable (premium). Pool. Restaurant nearby. Ck-out 11 am. Private patios, balconies. Cr cds: A, C, D, DS, MC, V.

SC

Motor Hotel

★★ **HOLIDAY INN.** *3223 E Garvey Ave N (91791), I-10 exit Barranca or Grand Ave N. 626/966-8311; FAX 818/339-2850; res: 800/638-9938.* Web www.holidayinnwestcovina.com. 134 rms, 5 story. S, D $79-$120; each addl $10; under 18 free. Crib free. Pet accepted. TV; cable (premium). Heated pool. Complimentary full bkfst. Complimentary coffee in rms. Restaurant 6 am-2 pm, 5-10 pm. Rm serv. Bar from 5 pm. Ck-out noon. Coin Indry. Meeting rms. Business servs avail. Valet serv. Refrigerators. Cr cds: A, C, D, DS, ER, JCB, MC, V.

D SC

Hotel

★★★ **SHERATON RESORT & CONFERENCE CENTER.** *1 Industry Hills Pkwy (91744), CA 60, exit Azusa Ave, then 1½ mi N to Industry Hills Pkwy. 626/810-4455; FAX 626/854-3205; res: 800/325-3535; res: 800/524-4557.* 294 rms, 11 story. S $150-$165; D $165-$175; each addl $15; suites $295-$375; under 17 free; wkend rates; package plans. Crib free. TV; cable (premium), VCR avail. 2 heated pools; whirlpools. Coffee in rms. Restaurants 6 am-11 pm. Bars 11-2 am; entertainment. Ck-out noon. Convention facilities. Business servs avail. Concierge. Gift shop. Lighted tennis, 17 courts, pro. Two 18-hole golf courses, pro, driving range. Exercise equipt; sauna. Some refrigerators, wet bars. Many balconies. Cr cds: A, C, D, DS, ER, JCB, MC, V.

D SC

Restaurant

★★ **MONTEREY BAY CANNERS.** *3057 E Garvey Ave (91791), I-10 exit Barranca Ave N. 626/915-3474.* E-mail mbcwc@juno.com. Hrs: 11 am-10 pm; Fri, Sat to 11 pm. Closed Thanksgiving, Dec 25. Res accepted. Bar. Semi-a la carte: lunch $6.50-$12.95, dinner $7.95-$18.95. Child's meals. Specializes in mesquite-grilled seafood, chowders. Oyster bar. Rustic, nautical decor. Totally nonsmoking. Cr cds: A, C, DS, MC, V.

D SC

Westwood Village (L.A.)

(C-3 see Los Angeles map)

Area Code 310

This community is an integral part of Los Angeles, but is regarded by many as a separate entity.

What to See and Do

Westwood Memorial Cemetery. Graves of movie stars Marilyn Monroe, Peter Lorre and Natalie Wood. (Daily) Glendon Ave, 1 blk E of Westwood Blvd.

Motel

★★ **HOTEL DEL CAPRI.** *10587 Wilshire Blvd (90024). 310/474-3511; FAX 310/470-9999; res: 800/444-6835.* 80 units, 2-4 story, 46 kit. suites. S $95; D $105-$115; each addl $10; kit. suites $120-$150. Crib $10. Pet accepted, some restrictions; fee. TV; cable (premium), VCR avail. Heated pool. Complimentary continental bkfst. Restaurants nearby. Ck-out noon. Guest Indry. Business servs avail. Bellhops. Valet serv. Health club privileges. Bathrm phones, refrigerators; many in-rm whirlpools. Cr cds: A, C, D, MC, V.

SC

Hotels

★★★ **DOUBLETREE HOTEL.** *10740 Wilshire Blvd (90024), I-405 exit Wilshire Blvd. 310/475-8711; FAX 310/475-5220; res: 800/472-8556.* 295 rms, 19 story. S $119-$165; D $129-$170; each addl $10; suites $200-$230; under 18 free. Crib free. TV; cable (premium). Pool; whirlpool, poolside serv. Restaurant 6:30 am-11 pm. Bar 4 pm-midnight. Ck-out noon. Meeting rms. Business center. In-rm modem link. Concierge. Gift shop. Valet parking. Exercise equipt; sauna. Refrigerators avail. Cr cds: A, C, D, DS, MC, V.

D SC

★★ **HILGARD HOUSE HOTEL.** *927 Hilgard Ave (90024), I-405 exit Wilshire Blvd E. 310/208-3945; FAX 310/208-1972; res: 800/826-3934.* E-mail reservations@hilgardhouse.com; web www.hilgardhouse.com. 47 rms, 4 story. S $104-$114; D $114-$124; each addl $10; under 18 free. Crib free. TV; cable (premium). Complimentary continental bkfst. Ck-out noon. Guest Indry. Free covered parking. Refrigerators avail. Cr cds: A, C, D, DS, JCB, MC, V.

D SC

★★★ **WESTWOOD MARQUIS HOTEL & GARDENS.** *930 Hilgard Ave (90024). 310/208-8765; FAX 310/824-0355; res: 800/421-2317.* E-mail padavis@earthlink.net. 257 suites (1-3 bedrm), 16 story. S, D $235-$650; wkend rates. Crib free. Pet accepted. Garage; valet parking, in/out $18. TV; cable (premium), VCR avail (movies). 2 heated pools. Restaurants 6:30 am-11 pm (also see DYNASTY ROOM). Rm serv 24 hrs. Bar 10-2 am; entertainment Fri-Sun. Ck-out noon. Meeting rms. Business servs avail. In-rm modem link. Concierge. Gift shop. Exercise equipt. Massage. Health club privileges. Refrigerators, minibars; microwaves avail. Cr cds: A, C, D, DS, JCB, MC, V.

D

Restaurants

★★★ **DYNASTY ROOM.** *(See Westwood Marquis Hotel Gardens) 310/208-8765.* E-mail padavis@earthlink.net. Hrs: 6-10:30 pm. Res accepted. California menu. Bar 10-1:30 am. A la carte entrees: dinner $22-$34. Child's meals. Specialties: potato pancake with smoked salmon and cavier, rack of lamb. Valet parking. Elegant setting; with exclusive collection of objets d'art from the Tang dynasty. Cr cds: A, C, D, DS, JCB, MC, V.

D

★★ **MONTY'S STEAK HOUSE.** *1100 Glendon Ave (90024), I-405 exit Wilshire Blvd E. 310/208-8787.* Hrs: 11 am-3 pm, 5 pm-1 am; Sat, Sun 5 pm-midnight. Closed Thanksgiving. Res accepted. Bar to 2 am; Sat, Sun from 5 pm. Semi-a la carte: lunch $8-$20, dinner $15-$80. Specializes in steak, seafood, prime rib. Entertainment. Valet parking. Located on 21st floor of building; panoramic view. Cr cds: A, C, D, MC, V.

D

Whittier

(C-5 see Los Angeles map)

(See also Anaheim, Buena Park, West Covina)

Founded 1887 **Pop** 77,671 **Elev** 365 ft **Area Code** 562

Information Chamber of Commerce, 8158 Painter Ave, 90602; 562/698-9554

This Quaker-founded community was named for John Greenleaf Whittier, the Quaker poet. At the foot of the rolling Puente Hills, this residential city was once a citrus empire. It is the home of Whittier College.

What to See and Do

Richard Nixon Library & Birthplace. Archives, original home and burial place of the 37th president of the United States. Nine-acre grounds include the library's main hall with display of gifts from world leaders, life-size statues; video forum allows guests to ask questions via "touchscreen"; 75-seat amphitheater; reflecting pool; First Lady's garden. Only privately-funded presidential library in the country. Nixon grew up in Yorba Linda before moving to Whittier and graduating from Whittier College. (Daily; closed Jan 1, Thanksgiving, Dec 25) 18001 Yorba Linda Blvd, in Yorba Linda. Phone 714/993-3393. ¢¢

Rose Hills Memorial Park. Gardens and cemetery covering 2,500 acres. Pageant of Roses Garden has more than 7,000 rose bushes of over 600 varieties in bloom most of the yr; Japanese gardens with a lake, arched bridge and meditation house. (Daily) 3888 S Workman Mill Rd. Phone 562/692-1212 or 562/699-0921. **Free**

Motel

✓★ **VAGABOND INN.** *14125 E Whittier Blvd (90605), I-605 exit Whittier Blvd E. 562/698-9701; FAX 562/698-8716; res: 800/522-1555.* Web www.vagabondinn.com. 48 rms, 3 story. S, D $60-$70; each addl $5; under 18 free. Crib free. Pet accepted, some restrictions; $5/day. TV; cable. Heated pool. Complimentary continental bkfst. Coffee in rms. Restaurant opp 7 am-11 pm. Ck-out noon. Refrigerators avail. Cr cds: A, C, D, DS, MC, V.

SC

Hotel

★★ **HILTON.** *7320 Greenleaf Ave (90602), I-605 exit Whittier Blvd E. 562/945-8511; FAX 562/945-6018; res: 800/667-4400.* Web www.hilton.com. 202 units, 8 story, 9 suites. S $109-$135; D $119-$145; each addl $10; suites $195-$475; under 18 free; family, wkly, wkend rates. Crib free. TV; cable (premium). Heated pool; whirlpool, poolside serv. Coffee in rms. Restaurant 6 am-10 pm. Bar 11-1 am; entertainment Fri, Sat. Ck-out noon. Meeting rms. Business servs avail. Gift shop. Exercise equipt. Health club privileges. Some refrigerators, microwaves. Some private patios. Cr cds: A, C, D, DS, JCB, MC, V.

D SC

Restaurant

✓★ **SEAFARE INN.** *16363 E Whittier Blvd (90603). 562/947-6645.* Hrs: 11:30 am-9 pm; Fri 11 am-10 pm. Closed Mon; major hols. Wine, beer. Semi-a la carte: lunch $3.25-$5.95, dinner $5.95-$12.75. Child's meals. Specializes in seafood. Own desserts. Nautical decor. Family-owned since 1961. Totally nonsmoking. Cr cds: C, MC, V.

♥

Willits (C-1)

(See also Fort Bragg, Mendocino, Ukiah)

Pop 5,027 **Elev** 1,364 ft **Area Code** 707 **Zip** 95490 **E-mail** willits@mcn.org

Information Chamber of Commerce, 239 S Main St; 707/459-7910

Nestled in the Little Lake Valley, Willits is the hub of three railroads: the California Western "Skunk Train" (see FORT BRAGG), the North Coast Railroad and the Northwestern Pacific.

What to See and Do

Mendocino County Museum. History of area depicted by artifacts, including unique collection of Pomo baskets; stagecoaches, redwood logging tools, antique steam engines; contemporary art shows. Special programs. (Wed-Sun; closed major hols exc July 4) 400 E Commercial St. Phone 707/459-2736. **Free**

Willits Community Theatre. 37 W Van Lane. For current performance schedule phone 707/459-2281.

Motels

★★ **BAECHTEL CREEK INN.** *101 Gregory Ln (95490). 707/459-9063; FAX 707/459-0226; res: 800/459-9911.* 46 rms, 2 story. June-Oct: S, D $65-$105; each addl $3; under 12 free; lower rates rest of yr. Crib free. Pet accepted; $10. TV; cable. Pool; whirlpool. Complimentary continental bkfst. Restaurant adj 6 am-11 pm. Ck-out 11 am. Meeting rms. Some refrigerators. Cr cds: A, C, DS, MC, V.

SC

★ **HOLIDAY LODGE MOTEL.** *1540 S Main St (95490). 707/459-5361; FAX 707/459-2334; res: 800/835-3972.* 16 rms. Mid-May-mid-Oct: S $42-$52; D $48-$62; each addl $5; lower rates rest of yr. Crib free. Pet accepted, some restrictions. TV; cable (premium). Pool. Complimentary continental bkfst. Complimentary coffee in rms. Restaurant opp 8 am-11 pm. Ck-out 11 am. Business servs avail. Refrigerators. Cr cds: A, C, DS, MC, V.

SC

Willows (C-2)

Pop 5,988 **Elev** 135 ft **Area Code** 530 **Zip** 95988

Information Willows Area Chamber of Commerce, 130-H N Butte St; 530/934-8150

What to See and Do

Mendocino National Forest. More than 1 million acres. Swimming; fishing for steelhead and trout; boating at 2,000-acre Pillsbury Lake. Hiking, bridle and off-road vehicle trails. Camping (fee at more developed sites; some water; high elevation sites closed in winter). Hang gliding. Approx 25 mi W via CA 162. Contact the Forest Supervisor, 420 E Laurel St; Phone 530/934-3316. For recorded information on road conditions and recreation phone 530/934-2350.

Motels

★★★ **BEST WESTERN GOLDEN PHEASANT INN.** *249 N Humboldt Ave (95988). 530/934-4603; FAX 530/934-4275; res: 800/838-1387.* 104 rms. S $55-$69; D $69-$89; each addl $10; suites $90. Crib $6. Pet accepted; $10. TV; cable, VCR avail (movies $3.50). 2 heated pools. Complimentary continental bkfst. Coffee in rms. Restaurant 6-10 am, 11:30 am-9 pm. Rm serv. Bar from 10 am. Ck-out 11 am. Coin Indry. Meeting rms. Business servs avail. Free airport, bus depot transportation. 7 acres of gardens and park. Cr cds: A, C, D, DS, ER, JCB, MC, V.

D SC

✓★ **CROSS ROADS WEST INN.** *452 N Humboldt Ave (95988). 530/934-7026; FAX 530/934-7028; res: 800/814-6301.* 41 rms, 2 story. S $37.33; D $41.96-$46.59; each addl $6; under 6 free. Pet accepted. TV; cable (premium). Pool. Restaurant adj 7 am-9 pm. Ck-out 11 am. Cr cds: A, C, DS, MC, V.

SC

★ **WOODCREST INN.** *400 C St (95987), Approx 30 mi S on I-5. 530/473-2381; FAX 530/473-2418.* 60 rms, 2 story. S $50; D $55; each addl $5. Crib free. Pet accepted; $5. TV; cable. Pool; whirlpool. Complimentary continental bkfst. Restaurant nearby. Ck-out noon. Business servs avail. Refrigerators avail. Cr cds: A, C, D, DS, ER, MC, V.

D SC

Woodland Hills (L.A.)

(B-2 see Los Angeles map)

Elev 460 ft **Area Code** 818

This community, located in the San Fernando Valley, is a neighborhood of Los Angeles, but is regarded by many as a separate entity.

Motels

★★ **CLARION SUITES HOTEL.** *20200 Sherman Way (91306), 2 mi N of US 101, off Winnetka Ave. 818/883-8250; FAX 818/883-8268; res: 800/252-7466.* Web www.clarioninn.com. 99 rms, 3 story, 88 kit. suites. S, D $99-$119; each addl $10; kit. suites $119-$149; under 18 free; monthly rates. Crib free. Pet accepted. TV; cable (premium). Heated pool. Complimentary continental bkfst. Complimentary coffee in rms. Restaurant nearby. Ck-out noon. Coin lndry. Meeting rm. Valet serv. Lighted tennis. Health club privileges. Refrigerators, microwaves. Some balconies. Cr cds: A, C, D, DS, ER, JCB, MC, V.

SC

★★★ **COUNTRY INNS & SUITES BY CARLSON.** *23627 Calabasas Rd (91302), 2 mi W on US 101, Pkwy Calabasas exit. 818/222-5300; FAX 818/591-0870; res: 800/456-4000.* 122 rms, 3 story. S, D $148; each addl $10; kit. suites $275-$300; under 12 free. Crib free. Pet accepted; $25. TV; VCR (movies $4). Heated pool; whirlpool. Complimentary full bkfst. Restaurant nearby. Ck-out noon. Coin lndry. Meeting rm. Business servs avail. In-rm modem link. Valet serv. Health club privileges. Refrigerators, microwaves, wet bars. Cr cds: A, C, D, DS, JCB, MC, V.

D SC

★ **VAGABOND INN.** *20157 Ventura Blvd (91364), US 101 Winnetka Ave exit, S to Ventura Blvd. 818/347-8080; FAX 818/716-5333; res: 800/522-1555.* E-mail saleswoodlandhills@vagabondinns.com; web www.vagabondinns.com. 99 rms, 3 story. S $60-$75; D $65-$85; each addl $5; under 19 free. Crib free. Pet accepted, some restrictions; $5. TV; cable (premium). Heated pool; whirlpool. Complimentary continental bkfst. Restaurant adj open 24 hrs. Ck-out noon. Meeting rm. Business servs avail. Cr cds: A, C, D, DS, MC, V.

D SC

✓★ **WARNER GARDENS MOTEL.** *21706 Ventura Blvd (91364), US 101, Canoga Ave exit, S to Ventura Blvd. 818/992-4426; FAX 818/704-1062; res: 800/824-9292.* 42 rms, 2 story. S, D $46-$54; suites $58-$65; under 17 free; wkly rates. Crib free. TV; cable (premium). Pool; whirlpool. Complimentary continental bkfst. Restaurant adj 8 am-8 pm. Ck-out 11 am. Valet serv. Cr cds: A, C, D, DS, MC, V.

D SC

Hotels

★★★ **WARNER CENTER MARRIOTT HOTEL.** *21850 Oxnard St (91367), US 101, Topanga Canyon Blvd exit N to Oxnard. 818/887-4800; FAX 818/340-5893; res: 800/228-9290.* E-mail wcmarriott@aol.com; web www.marriott.com/marriott/laxwc. 463 rms, 16 story. S, D $150-$165; suites $250-$500; under 18 free; wkend rates. Crib free. Garage $5; valet parking $9. TV; cable (premium). Heated indoor/outdoor pools; whirlpool, poolside serv. Restaurant 6:30 am-11 pm. Bar 11-1 am. Ck-out noon. Convention facilities. Business servs avail. Gift shop. Airport transportation. Exercise equipt; sauna. Balconies. Luxury level. Cr cds: A, C, D, DS, JCB, MC, V.

D SC

★★★ **WOODLAND HILLS HILTON.** *6360 Canoga Ave (91367), US 101, Canoga Ave exit, N 1 mi. 818/595-1000; FAX 818/596-4578; res: 800/922-2400.* Web www.hilton.com. 330 rms, 14 story. S, D $159; each addl $10; suites $195-$550; family; wkend rates. Crib free. Garage $5; valet parking $8. TV; cable (premium). Heated pool; whirlpool. Coffee in rms. Restaurant 6 am-10:30 pm. Bar 3 pm-1 am. Ck-out noon. Convention facilities. Business servs avail. Concierge. Airport transportation. Lighted tennis. Health club privileges. Some balconies. Luxury level. Cr cds: A, C, D, DS, JCB, MC, V.

D SC

Restaurants

✓★★ **BACIO TRATTORIA.** *23663 Calabasas Rd (91302), 2 mi W on US 101, exit Calabasas Pkwy. 818/591-1355.* Hrs: 11:30 am-10 pm; Fri to 11 pm; Sat 5-11 pm; Sun 5-10 pm. Closed Jan 1, Thanksgiving, Dec 25. Northern Italian menu. Wine, beer. A la carte entrees: lunch, dinner $3.95-$15.95. Child's meals. Specialties: fettuccine bacio, cioppino, tortini risotto. Parking. Outdoor dining. Italian cafe; casual dining. Cr cds: A, C, D, MC, V.

D

★ **CAPRI RISTORANTE ITALIANO.** *21926 Ventura Blvd (91364), US 101, Topanga Canyon Blvd exit S to Ventura Blvd. 818/883-3401.* Hrs: 11:30 am-10 pm; Sat, Sun 5:30-10:30 pm. Res accepted. Italian menu. A la carte entrees: lunch $5.95-$9.95, dinner $7-$18. Specializes in traditional Italian pizza. Outdoor dining. Cr cds: A, C, DS, MC, V.

D

★★ **COSMOS GRILL & ROTISSERIE.** *23631 Calabasas Rd (91302), 2 mi W on US 101, exit Pkwy Calabasas. 818/591-2211.* Hrs: 11:30 am-10 pm; Fri, Sat to 11 pm; Sun from 4:30 pm. Closed July 4, Thanksgiving, Dec 25. Res accepted. Beer, wine. A la carte entrees: lunch, dinner $4.50-$17.95. Child's meals. Specialties: marinated skirt steak, penne country chicken. Outdoor dining. Modern artwork. Cr cds: A, C, D, JCB, MC, V.

D

★★ **LE SANGLIER FRENCH RESTAURANT.** *18760 Ventura Blvd (91356), US 101, Reseda exit then 4 blks W on Ventura Blvd. 818/345-0470.* Hrs: 5:30-9:30 pm; Fri, Sat to 10:30 pm. Closed Mon; major hols. Res accepted. French menu. Bar. Semi-a la carte: dinner $18.95-$24.95. Prix fixe: dinner $35. Specializes in French country cuisine. French hunting lodge interior. Totally nonsmoking. Cr cds: A, C, D, DS, MC, V.

Yosemite National Park

(E-4)

(See also Lee Vining)

Area Code 209 **Zip** 95389

(67 mi NE of Merced on CA 140; 62 mi N of Fresno on CA 41; 13 mi W of Lee Vining on CA 120)

John Muir, the naturalist instrumental in the founding of this national park, wrote that here are "the most songful streams in the world. the noblest forests, the loftiest granite domes, the deepest ice sculptured canyons." More than 4 million people visit Yosemite year round, and most agree with Muir. An area of 1,169 square miles, it is a park of lofty waterfalls, sheer cliffs, high wilderness country, alpine meadows, lakes, snowfields, trails, streams and river beaches. There are magnificent waterfalls during spring and early summer. Yosemite's granite domes are unsurpassed in number and diversity. Entrance fee is $20 per car. Routes to Yosemite National Park involve some travel over steep grades, which may extend driving times. Tioga Rd (CA 120) is closed in winter. For general park information contact Public Information Office, PO Box 577, Yosemite National Park; 209/372-0200. For lodging information contact Yosemite Concession Services, Yosemite National Park; 209/252-4848. For recorded camping information phone 209/372-0200. Camping reservations taken by NPRS, the National Park Reservation System for Yosemite Valley (800/436-7275) and other campgrounds.

What to See and Do

Boating. No motors permitted.

Campfire programs. At several campgrounds; in summer, naturalists present nightly programs on park-related topics and provide tips on how to enjoy the park. Evening programs all yr in the Valley only.

Camping. Limited to 30 days in a calendar yr; May-mid-Sept, camping is limited to 7 days in Yosemite Valley, in the rest of the park to 14 days. Campsites in the Valley campgrounds, Hodgdon Meadow, Crane Flat, Wawona and half of Tuolumne Meadows campgrounds may be reserved through NPRS. Other park campgrounds are on a first-come, first-served basis. Winter camping in the Valley, Hodgdon Meadow and Wawona only.

Fishing. California fishing regulations pertain to all waters. State license, inland waters stamp and trout stamp are required. Special regulations for Yosemite Valley also apply.

Glacier Point. Offers one of the best panoramic views in Yosemite. From here the crest of the Sierra Nevada can be viewed, as well as Yosemite Valley 3,214 ft below. Across the valley are Yosemite Falls, Royal Arches, North Dome, Basket Dome, Mt Watkins and Washington Column; up the Merced Canyon are Vernal and Nevada Falls; Half Dome, Grizzly Peak, Liberty Cap and the towering peaks along the Sierran crest and the Clark Range mark the skyline. (Road closed in winter)

Hiking and backpacking on 840 mi of maintained trails. Wilderness permits are required for all overnight backcountry trips. Advance res for permits may be made up to 24 wks in advance; phone 209/372-0740.

Pioneer Yosemite History Center. A few miles from Mariposa Grove in Wawona. Has a covered bridge, historic buildings, wagons and other exhibits. Living history program in summer.

Swimming. Prohibited at Hetch Hetchy Reservoir and in some areas of the Tuolumne River watershed. Swimming pools are maintained at Camp Curry, Yosemite Lodge and Wawona.

The Giant Sequoias. Located principally in 3 groves. Mariposa Grove is near the south entrance to the park; toured on foot or by 50-passenger trams (May-early Oct; fee). Merced and Tuolumne groves are near Crane Flat, northwest of Yosemite Valley. The Grizzly Giant in Mariposa Grove is estimated to be 2,700 yrs old and is 209 ft high and 34.7 ft in diameter at its base.

The High Country. The Tioga Rd (closed in winter) crosses the park and provides the threshold to a vast wilderness accessible via horseback, or on foot to mountain peaks, passes and lakes. Tuolumne Meadows is the major trailhead for this activity; one of the most beautiful and largest of the subalpine meadows in the High Sierra, 55 mi from Yosemite Valley by way of Big Oak Flat and Tioga Rds. Organized group horse and hiking trips start from Tuolumne Meadows (exc winter), follow the High Sierra Loop, and fan out to mountain lakes and peaks. Each night's stop is at a High Sierra Camp; the pace allows plenty of time to explore at each camp. For res information phone 209/253-5674.

The Nature Center at Happy Isles. Exhibits on ecology and natural history. (Summer, daily) E end of Yosemite Valley.

Visitor Center. Orientation slide program on Yosemite (daily). Exhibits on geology and ecology; naturalist-conducted walks and evening programs offered throughout the yr on varying seasonal schedules. Native American cultural demonstrators (summer, daily). At Park Headquarters in Yosemite Valley. Phone 209/372-0200.

Indian Village (Ahwahnee). Reconstructed Miwok-Paiute Village behind Visitor Center has self-guided trail.

The Indian Cultural Museum, located in the building west of the Valley visitor center, portrays the cultural history of the Yosemite Native Americans. Consult *Yosemite Guide* for hrs. Adj is

Yosemite Fine Arts Museum. Gallery featuring contemporary art exhibits and the Yosemite Centennial. Consult *Yosemite Guide* for hrs.

Walks and hikes. Conducted all yr in the Valley and, during summer, at Glacier Point, Mariposa Grove, Tuolumne Meadows, Wawona, White Wolf and Crane Flat.

Waterfalls. Reaching their greatest proportions in mid-May, they may, in dry years, dwindle to trickles or disappear completely by late summer. The Upper Yosemite Fall drops 1,430 ft; the lower fall drops 320 ft. With the middle Cascade they have a combined height of 2,425 ft and are the fifth-highest waterfall in the world. Others are Ribbon Fall, 1,612 ft; Vernal Fall, 317 ft; Bridalveil Fall, 620 ft; Nevada Fall, 594 ft; and Illilouette Fall, 370 ft.

Winter sports are centered around the **Badger Pass Ski Area**, 23 mi from Yosemite Valley on Glacier Point Rd. Four chairlifts, rope tow; patrol, rentals; snack stand; sun deck; nursery (min age 3 yrs); instruction (over 4 yrs). (Thanksgiving-mid-Apr, daily, weather permitting) Cross-country skiing. Ice-skating (fee) in Yosemite Valley; scheduled competitions. Naturalists conduct snowshoe tours (fee) in the Badger Pass area. Phone 209/372-8444 or 209/372-1000 for snow conditions. Lift ticket. ¢¢¢¢¢

Yosemite Mountain-Sugar Pine Railroad. Four-mi historic narrow-gauge steam train excursion through scenic Sierra National Forest. Picnic area. Museum; gift shops. Logger steam train (mid-May-Sept, daily; early May & Oct, wkends). Jenny Railcars (Mar-Oct, daily). Evening steam train, outdoor barbecue, live entertainment (late May-early Oct, Sat evenings; res advised). 4 mi S of S park entrance on CA 41. For res and information phone 209/683-7273. ¢¢¢-¢¢¢¢¢

Yosemite Valley. Surrounded by sheer walls, waterfalls, towering domes and peaks. One of the most spectacular views is from Tunnel View, looking up the Valley to Clouds Rest. El Capitan (7,569 ft) on the left, Bridalveil Falls on the right. The east end of the Valley, beyond Camp Curry, is closed to automobiles, but is accessible by foot, bicycle and, in summer, shuttle bus (free); special placards permit the disabled to drive in restricted area when the route is drivable. The placards are avail at visitor centers and entrance stations.

Motels

★★ **CEDAR LODGE.** *9966 Hwy 140 (95318), 22 mi W on CA 140. 209/379-2612; FAX 209/379-2712; res: 800/321-5261.* E-mail reservations@yosemite-hotels.com; web www.yosemite-hotels.com. 224 rms, 1-2 story. Mar-Nov: S $85; D $99; suites $120-$400; kit. units $104; hols (2-day min); lower rates rest of yr. Crib $5. TV; cable (premium), VCR avail (movies). Complimentary coffee in lobby. Restaurant adj 7 am-10 pm. Bar. Ck-out 11 am. Meeting rms. Business servs avail. In-rm modem link. Sundries. Gift shop. 2 pools, 1 indoor; whirlpool. Many refrigerators, microwaves; some in-rm whirlpools. Some balconies. Picnic tables, grills. On river. Cr cds: A, C, MC, V.

D

✓★ **COMFORT INN.** *4994 Bullion St (95338), 35 mi W on CA 140. 209/966-4344; FAX 209/966-4655; res: 800/228-5150; res: 800/221-2222.* E-mail reservations@yosemite-motels.com; web www.yosemite-motels.com/. 61 rms, 2-3 story. Apr-Oct: S $75-$80; D $85-$90; each addl $6; suite $96-$185; kit. units $140-$185; under 18 free; lower rates rest of yr. Crib free. TV; cable (premium). Complimentary continental bkfst. Restaurant nearby. Ck-out 11 am. Meeting rms. Business servs avail. In-rm modem link. Pool; whirlpool. Cr cds: A, C, D, DS, MC, V.

D SC

★ **IMA MARIPOSA LODGE.** *5052 State Hwy 140 (95338), at jct CA 140, CA 49. 209/966-3607; FAX 209/742-7038; res: 800/341-8000.* E-mail marlodge@yosemite.net; web member.yosemite.net/frame/. 44 rms, 13 rms with shower only. Apr-Oct: S, D $65-$76; each addl $6; lower rates rest of yr. Crib $6. Pet accepted, some restrictions; $6. TV; cable (premium), VCR avail. Heated pool; whirlpool. Complimentary coffee in rms. Restaurant adj 7 am-9 pm. Ck-out 11 am. Free airport transportation. Gazebo. Cr cds: A, C, D, DS, JCB, MC, V.

D

★ **MINERS INN.** *5181 Hwy 49 N (95338), jct of CA 49 & CA 140, 45 mi W on CA 140. 209/742-7777; FAX 209/966-2343; res: 888/646-2244; res: 800/321-5261.* E-mail reservations@yosemite-hotels.com; web www.yosemite-hotels.com. 78 rms, 2 story. Apr-Oct: S, D $79; each addl $6; suites $149; kit. units $125; under 6 free; lower rates rest of yr. Crib free. Pet accepted; $6. TV; cable (premium). Complimentary coffee in rms. Restaurant 6:30 am-10 pm. Bar; entertainment Fri, Sat. Ck-out 11 am. Business servs avail. Sundries. Gift shop. Pool; whirlpool. Some bathrm phones, in-rm whirlpools, refrigerators, microwaves, fireplaces. Many balconies. Cr cds: A, C, D, DS, MC, V.

SC

★★ **PINES RESORT.** *54449 Rd 432 (93604), 14 mi S of entrance, 5 mi off CA 41 on North Shore Rd at lakefront. 559/642-3121; FAX 559/642-3902; res: 800/350-7463.* E-mail pines@basslake.com; web www.basslake.com. 104 units, 2 story. Apr-Oct: S, D $159-$279; family rates; wkends, hols (2-3 day min); higher rates special events; lower rates rest of yr. Crib free. TV; cable (premium), VCR (movies avail). Heated pool; whirlpool, poolside serv. Complimentary continental bkfst. Complimentary coffee in rms. Restaurant 11 am-midnight. Rm serv. Bar; entertainment Fri, Sat. Ck-out noon. Coin Indry. Meeting rms. Business servs avail. Tennis. X-country ski 5 mi. Refrigerators. Balconies. Split-level units on lake. Cr cds: A, C, D, DS, ER, JCB, MC, V.

D SC

✓★ **YOSEMITE LODGING: LEE'S MIDDLE FORK RESORT-MOTEL.** *11399 Cherry Lake Rd (95321), 14 mi E of Groveland & 10 mi W of Yosemite Park entrance on CA 120, N on Cherry Lake Rd. 209/962-7408; FAX 209/962-7400; res: 800/626-7408.* E-mail lmr@sonnet.com; web www.sonnet.com/usr/yosemite/. 18 rms, 2 kit units. No rm phones. May-Sept: S $39-$89; D $59-$89; each addl $10; kit units $79-$89; under 5 free; wkly rates; lower rates rest of yr. Crib free. TV. Pool privileges. Complimentary continental bkfst. Ck-out 11 am. Refrigerators avail. Balconies. Picnic tables. On stream. Cr cds: A, C, D, DS, JCB, MC, V.

D SC

★★ **YOSEMITE VIEW LODGE.** *11136 Hwy 140 (95318), CA 140. 209/379-2681; FAX 209/379-2704; res: 800/321-5261.* E-mail reservations@yosemite-motels.com; web www.yosemite-motels.com. 280 kit. units, 2-3 story. Apr-Oct: S $99-$129; D $99-$139; each addl $10; ski plans; hols (2-day min); lower rates rest of yr. Crib $5. Pet accepted; $5. TV; cable (premium). Complimentary coffee in rms. Restaurant 7 am-10 pm. Bar. Ck-out 11 pm. Meeting rms. Business servs avail. Sundries. Gift shop. Grocery store. Coin Indry. Downhill/x-country ski 20 mi. 2 pools, 1 indoor; whirlpool. Many in-rm whirlpools, fireplaces. Many balconies. On river. Cr cds: C, MC, V.

D SC

Lodges

★★★ **TENAYA LODGE AT YOSEMITE.** *1122 Hwy 41 (93623), 2 mi S of Yosemite Natl Park south gate on CA 41, near Fish Camp. 559/683-6555; FAX 559/683-8684; res: 800/635-5807.* Web www.tenayalodge.com. 244 rms, 3-4 story, 20 suites. Mid-May-mid-Sept: S, D $189-$259; suites $229-$339; under 18 free; package plans; lower rates rest of yr. Crib free. Pet accepted, some restrictions. TV; cable (premium), VCR avail. 2 pools, 1 indoor; whirlpool. Supervised child's activities; ages 3-12. Complimentary coffee in rms. Dining rm 6:30-11 am, 5:30-10 pm. Rm serv. Ck-out noon, ck-in 3 pm. Coin Indry. Convention facilities. Business center. In-rm modem link. Bellhops. Valet serv. Concierge. Gift shop. X-country ski on site. Exercise equipt; saunas, steam rm. Massage. Game rm. Guided hikes and tours. Bicycle rentals. Bathrm phones, minibars; wet bar in suites. On river; water sports. Southwest, Native American decor; rustic with an elegant touch. June-Sept Western jamboree cookouts, wagon rides. Totally nonsmoking. Cr cds: A, C, D, DS, JCB, MC, V.

D SC

★ **WAWONA HOTEL.** *Yosemite National Park (95389), 4 mi NE of S entrance on CA 41, 27 mi from Park HQ. 209/375-6556; FAX 209/375-6601.* 104 rms, 50 with bath, 1-2 story. No A/C. No rm phones. Mid-Apr-late Dec: S, D $80-$110.55; each addl $13.75. Crib avail. TV in lounge; VCR. Heated pool. Dining rm 7:30-10:30 am, noon-1:30 pm, 5:30-9 pm. Ck-out 11 am. Meeting rm. Tennis. 9-hole golf, greens fee $13.75-$22, putting green. Saddle trips, stagecoach rides. Historic summer hotel. Cr cds: C, D, DS, JCB, MC, V.

D

Motor Hotel

★★ **YOSEMITE LODGE.** *On Ca 41/140 (95389), 1 mi W of Park HQ. 209/252-4848; FAX 209/372-1444.* Web www.yosemitepark.com. 226 rms, 2 story. No A/C. Apr-Oct: S, D $76-$90; each addl $6-$12; lower rates rest of yr. Crib $5. Pool; lifeguard. Supervised child's activities (June-Aug); ages over 3. Restaurant 6:30 am-7 pm. Bar noon-10 pm. Ck-out 11 am. Meeting rms. Sundries. Gift shop. Valley tours. Cr cds: C, D, DS, JCB, MC, V.

D

Hotel

★★★ **THE AHWAHNEE HOTEL.** *Yosemite Valley (95389), ½ mi E of Yosemite Village. 209/372-1000; FAX 209/372-1463.* Web www.yosemitepark.com. 99 rms, 4 suites, 6 story, 24 cottages. S, parlor $212.75; D $238.50; each addl $20; suites $286-$510; 3-12 yrs free. TV; VCR avail. Heated pool. Restaurant (res required). Rm serv 6 am-11 pm. Bar noon-10:30 pm; entertainment. Ck-out noon. Meeting rms. Concierge. Gift shops. Free valet parking. Tennis. Some fireplaces. Some balconies. Stone building with natural wood interior, Native American decor. Tire chains may be required by Park Service Nov-Mar to reach lodge. Cr cds: C, D, DS, JCB, MC, V.

D

Inns

★★ **GROVELAND HOTEL.** *18767 Main St (95321). 209/962-4000; FAX 209/962-6674; res: 800/273-3314.* E-mail peggy@groveland.com; web www.groveland.com. 17 rms, 2 separate two-story buildings (one is Ca. Resource Adobe), 3 suites. Open year-round. May-Sept: S,D $125-$145; each addl $15 for 12 under and $25 for over 12 years; suites $200. Crib free. Pet accepted. TV in common rm/bar; cable, VCR avail (movies). Complimentary innkeeper bkfst. Complimentary coffee in rms. Restaurant (see THE VICTORIAN ROOM). Ck-out noon, ck-in 2 pm. Conference/Business servs avail. In-rm modem link with dataports and voice. Concierge serv. Downhill/x-country ski 20 mi. In-rm whirlpool, fireplace in suites. Picnic tables. Built in 1849; European antiques. Down comforters. Robes. Hairdryers. Iron/board available. Totally nonsmoking. Special events. Cr cds: A, C, D, DS, MC, V.

★★ **LARRY ENDS & CINDY BROOKS.** *41110 Rd 600 (93601), W on CA 49 to Road 600, then S. 559/683-0495; FAX 559/683-8165.* E-mail homestd@sierranet.net; web www.sierranet.net/~homestead. 5 kit. cottages, shower only. No rm phones. S, D $149; wkly rates. TV; cable (premium). Complimentary continental bkfst. Ck-out 11 am, ck-in 3-6 pm. On 160-acres bordering Fresno River. Totally nonsmoking. Cr cds: A, C, DS, MC, V.

D

★ **LITTLE VALLEY INN.** *3483 Brooks Rd (95338), 8 mi S of Mariposa, off CA 49. 209/742-6204; FAX 209/742-5099.* E-mail innkeeper@littlevalley.com; web www.littlevalley.com. 3 rms. No rm phones. S, D $90; kit. units $115; each addl $15. TV; VCR (movies). Complimentary full bkfst. Complimentary coffee in rms. Ck-out noon, ck-in 4 pm. Concierge serv. Luggage handling. Picnic tables. Smoking on deck only. Cr cds: A, C, JCB, MC, V.

D SC

Restaurants

★★ **CHARLES STREET DINNER HOUSE.** *5043 Charles St. (95338), on CA 140 at 7th St. 209/966-2366.* Web mariposa.yosemite.net/csdh/. Hrs: from 5 pm. Closed Mon, Tues; Thanksgiving, Dec 24, 25; also Jan. Res accepted. Beer. Semi-a la carte: dinner $10-$30. Specializes in steak, fresh seafood. Own desserts. 19th-century house. Cr cds: A, C, DS, MC, V.

SC

★★ **THE VICTORIAN ROOM.** *(See Groveland Hotel Inn) 209/962-4000.* E-mail peggy@groveland.com; web www.groveland.com. Hrs: 6-11 pm. Res accepted. Contemporary Amer menu. Bar from noon.

Semi-a la carte: dinner $13.50-$27. Specialties: baby back ribs, rack of lamb. Parking. Outdoor dining. Victorian decor. Totally nonsmoking. Cr cds: A, C, D, DS, MC, V.

D

Yountville (D-2)

(See also Napa, St Helena)

Settled 1831 **Pop** 3,259 **Elev** 97 ft **Area Code** 707 **Zip** 94599

Information Chamber of Commerce, PO Box 2064; 707/944-0904

In the heart of the Napa Valley, Yountville has retained the turn-of-the-century charm of a quiet farming community. The town dates from 1831 with the settlement of George Yount, a North Carolina trapper. Although now a major tourist destination, surrounded by world-famous wineries, the town has successfully protected its rural atmosphere and historic character, reflected in its quaint hotels, restaurants and shops.

What to See and Do

Vintage 1870. Restored brick winery complex houses 5 restaurants, a bakery and more than 40 specialty shops. Wine tasting cellar. Entertainment and holiday demonstrations in Dec. Picnic areas. (Daily; closed Jan 1, Easter, Thanksgiving, Dec 25) 6525 Washington St. Phone 707/944-2451. **Free**

Wineries.

Domaine Chandon. Subsidiary of French producers of champagne and cognac. Visitors observe all phases of the *méthode champenoise*, the classic French method of producing champagnes. Guided tours, salon, retail sales, restaurant. Tasting (fee). (May-Oct, daily; rest of yr, Wed-Sun) W of CA 29, California Dr. Phone 707/944-2280 (tour) or 707/944-2892 (restaurant). **Free**

Robert Mondavi. Graceful, mission-style building. Guided tours, wine tasting. Res recommended. (Daily; closed some hols) 7801 St Helena Hwy, N in Oakville. Phone 707/963-9611. **Free**

Motor Hotels

★★★ **NAPA VALLEY LODGE.** *2230 Madison St (94599), ½ blk E of CA 29. 707/944-2468; FAX 707/944-9362; res: 800/368-2468.* E-mail napavalleylodge@woodsidehotels.com; web www.woodsidehotels.com. 55 rms, 2 story. S, D $172-$232; each addl $25; suites $212-$325. Crib free. TV; cable. Heated pool; whirlpool. Complimentary continental bkfst. Complimentary coffee in rms. Restaurant nearby. Ck-out noon. Meeting rms. Business servs avail. In-rm modem link. Bellhops. Valet serv. Exercise equipt; sauna. Refrigerators, minibars, fireplaces. Private patios, balconies. Park opp. Cr cds: A, C, D, DS, MC, V.

D SC

★★★ **VINTAGE INN.** *6541 Washington St (94599). 707/944-1112; FAX 707/944-1617; res: 800/531-1133.* 80 rms in 9 buildings, 1-2 story. S, D $200-$275; each addl $25; suites, villas $225-$275; under 12 free. Crib $25. Pet accepted; $25. TV; cable, VCR avail (movies). Heated pool; whirlpool. Complimentary continental bkfst; afternoon refreshments. Coffee in rms. Restaurant adj 11:30 am-10 pm. Bar 10 am-10 pm. Ck-out noon. Meeting rms. Business servs avail. Concierge. Bellhops. Valet serv exc Sun. Tennis. Health club privileges. Refrigerators, fireplaces. Verandas. Vineyard, mountain views. Cr cds: A, C, D, MC, V.

D SC

Hotel

★★★ **VILLAGIO INN AND SPA.** *6481 Washington St (94599). 707/944-8877; FAX 707/944-8855; res: 800/351-1133.* Web www.villagio.com. Rms 112, 2 FL. Prices $225-$335; weekends $250-$360. Ck-in: 3 pm. Ck-out: 12 pm. Bar. No restaurant. TV/VCR. Cribs. Full health spa. Tennis. Pool. Massages. Cr cds: A, C, D, MC, V.

D

Inns

★★★ **MAISON FLURIE FOUR SISTERS INN.** *6529 Yount St (94599). 707/944-2056; FAX 707/944-9342; res: 800/788-0369.* 13 rms, 6 with shower only, 2 story. Apr-Oct: S, D $110-$230; each addl $15; lower rates rest of yr. Crib free. TV; cable. Complimentary full bkfst; afternoon refreshments. Restaurant adj 11:30 am-10 pm. Ck-out noon, ck-in 2 pm. Luggage handling. Concierge serv. Bicycles. Pool; whirlpool. Some in-rm whirlpools, fireplaces. Some balconies. Picnic tables. Built in 1876. French country ambience. Totally nonsmoking. Cr cds: A, C, D, MC, V.

D

★ **NAPA VALLEY RAILWAY INN.** *6503 Washington St (94599). 707/944-2000; FAX 707/944-8710.* 9 rms. No rm phones. Apr-Oct: S, D $95-$130; each addl $10; under 5 free; lower rates rest of yr. TV. Complimentary coffee. Restaurant nearby. Ck-out 11 am, ck-in 2 pm. Health club privileges. Unique lodging in restored turn-of-the-century railroad cars; bay windows, skylights; private entrance. Vineyards nearby. Cr cds: C, MC, V.

D SC

★★ **OLEANDER HOUSE.** *7433 St Helena Hwy (CA 29) (94599). 707/944-8315; FAX 707/944-0980; res: 800/788-0357.* E-mail oleanderhs@aol.com; web www.oleanderhs.com. 5 rms, 2 story. No rm phones. S, D $145-$175; each addl $25; wkends, hols (2-day min). Complimentary full bkfst; afternoon refreshments. Restaurant adj 11 am-10 pm. Ck-out 11 am, ck-in 1 pm. Business servs avail. Whirlpool. Balconies. Individually decorated rms; wood-burning fireplaces. Rose garden. Totally nonsmoking. Cr cds: A, C, MC, V.

D

Restaurants

★★ **BISTRO JEANTY.** *6510 Washington St (94599). 707/944-0103.* Hrs: 11:30 am-10:30 pm. Res accepted. French menu. Bar. A la carte entrees: dinner $9.50-$16.50. Specialties: rabbit & sweetbread ragout, mussels steamed in red wine. Parking. Outdoor dining. French bistro atmosphere. Totally nonsmoking. Cr cds: C, MC, V.

D

★★★ **BRIX RESTAURANT.** *7377 St Helena Hwy (94599). 707/944-2749.* Hrs: 11:30 am-9:30 pm; Fri, Sat to 10 pm. Res accepted. Contemporary Amer menu. Bar to midnight. A la carte entrees: lunch $7-$12.95, dinner $14-$24. Child's meals. Specialties: Thai pesto smoked rack of lamb, black and blue seared ahi tuna. Own baking. Totally nonsmoking. Cr cds: A, C, MC, V.

D

✓★ **CAFE KINYON.** *6525 Washington St (94599), in Vintage 1870 shopping complex. 707/944-2788.* Hrs: 11:30 am-2 pm. Closed Jan 1, Easter, Dec 25. Res accepted. Bar. Semi-a la carte: lunch $3.50-$9.75. Specialty: peanut chicken salad. Original art. Totally nonsmoking. Cr cds: A, C.

D

★ **COMPADRES MEXICAN BAR & GRILL.** *6539 Washington St (94599). 707/944-2406.* Hrs: Sun-Thurs 8 am-10 pm; Fri, Sat to 11 pm. Closed Thanksgiving, Dec 25. Mexican grill menu. Bar. Semi-a la carte: lunch, dinner $6.99-$16.99. Specializes in grilled meat & seafood. Parking. Outdoor dining. Atrium; fireplace. Cr cds: A, C, JCB, MC, V.

D

★★★ **DOMAINE CHANDON.** *1 California Dr (94599), just W of CA 29. 707/944-2892.* Specialties: carmelized scallops with sweet pea sauce, pan seared yellowfin tuna, Monterey Bay sardines on basil potatoes. Menu changes wkly. Hrs: M-Sun 11:30 am-2:30 pm, Wed-Sun dinner only 6-9:00 pm. May-Oct open for lunch, also 2 wks Jan. Res accepted. French, California menu. Wine list. A la carte entrees: lunch $15-$21, dinner $24-$38. Own desserts. Outdoor dining at lunch, (May-Nov). Totally nonsmoking. Cr cds: A, C, D, DS, MC, V.

D

★★★ **MUSTARD'S GRILL.** *7399 St Helena Hwy (94599). 707/944-2424.* Hrs: 11:30 am-10 pm; Nov-Apr to 9 pm. Closed Thanksgiving, Dec 25. Res accepted. Bar. A la carte entrees: lunch, dinner $7.95-$17.95. Specializes in smoked and grilled fish, fowl, beef. Parking. Totally nonsmoking. Cr cds: C, D, DS, MC, V.

D

★★ **NAPA VALLEY GRILLE.** *6795 Washington St (94599). 707/944-8686.* Hrs: 11:30 am-9:30 pm; Fri, Sat to 10:30 pm; Sun from 10:30 am; Sun brunch to 2:30 pm. Closed Dec 25. Res accepted. Contemporary Amer menu. Bar. Semi-a la carte: lunch $7.95-$15.95, dinner $9.95-$25. Sun brunch $8.95-$16.95. Child's meals. Specialty: homemade focaccia. Jazz Fri (summer). Outdoor dining. Contemporary decor; over 600 wines avail. Totally nonsmoking. Cr cds: A, C, D, DS, MC, V.

D

★ **OAKVILLE GROCERY CAFE.** *7848 St Helena Hwy (94562), 2 mi on Hwy 29 N. 707/944-0111.* Hrs: 7 am-9 pm; Tues, Wed to 4 pm. Closed Thanksgiving, Dec 25. Res accepted (dinner). Mediterranean menu. Wine, beer. A la carte entrees: lunch $6.95-$9.95, dinner $6.95-$14.95. Specialties: roast leg of lamb sandwich, charcuterie plate. Own baking. Parking. Outdoor dining. Casual dining; artwork. Totally nonsmoking. Cr cds: A, C, MC, V.

D

★ **THE DINER.** *6476 Washington St (94599). 707/944-2626.* Hrs: 8 am-3 pm, 5:30-9 pm. Closed Mon; Thanksgiving, Dec 25. Mexican, Amer menu. Wine, beer. Complete meals: bkfst, lunch $4-$9.95, dinner $6-$13.25. Child's meals. Specialties: cornmeal pancakes, huevos rancheros. Organic bakery on premises. Cr cds: C.

D

★★★★★ **THE FRENCH LAUNDRY.** *6640 Washington Ave (94599), at Creek St. 707/944-2380.* If you can manage to get a reservation at this small restaurant, hidden without a sign on a quiet road, you will be in for one of the most exciting culinary journeys in the country. Chef/owner Thomas Keller is known for small, intensely creative and witty dishes, that issue forth in a parade of flavors and intricate presentations. An impressive wine list features both local and imported labels. Competent service is better if you are known. Specializes in American fare with French influence. Hrs: Fri, Sat, Sun (lunch) 11 am-1 pm; Mon-Sun (dinner) 5:30-10:30 pm; Closed Mon (Nov-May); Dec 25; also 1st 3 wks Jan. Res accepted. Wine, beer. Complete meals: lunch & dinner 5-course $80, 9-course $95. Parking. Totally nonsmoking. Cr cds: A, C, MC, V.

D

Yreka (A-2)

(See also Mount Shasta)

Founded 1851 **Pop** 6,948 **Elev** 2,625 ft **Area Code** 530 **Zip** 96097
E-mail a-yreka@inreach.com **Web** www.yrekachamer.com

Information Chamber of Commerce, 117 W Miner St; 530/842-1649 or 800/ON-YREKA (recording)

Yreka (Why-RE-ka) was known in gold rush days as Thompson's Dry Diggings, later as Shasta Butte City, and finally, since 1852, as Yreka. Yreka today is the seat of Siskiyou County and a trade center for ranchers, lumbermen and miners. Many historic buildings may be seen in the Historic Preservation District, in the vicinity of Miner and Third streets. Hunting and fishing are popular in the area.

What to See and Do

County Gold Exhibit. Extensive display of gold nuggets taken from mines in Siskiyou County. (Mon-Fri; closed hols) County Courthouse, 311 4th St. Phone 530/842-8340. **Free**

Iron Gate Dam and Lake. Water sports, fishing, boating (ramps, launching facilities). Picnicking. Camping. 13 mi NE on I-5, then 6 mi E on Klamath River Road.

Klamath National Forest. Approx 1.72 million acres, of which 1.69 million acres are in California and the remainder in Oregon. Within the forest are the Klamath, Scott, Salmon, Siskiyou and Marble mountain ranges and the Klamath, Scott and Salmon rivers. Camping; hunting, hiking; fishing, white water boating on the 3 rivers; cross-country skiing. E & W of town via CA 263, turn left onto CA 96. The western section of the forest also includes the

Marble Mountain Wilderness. 241,000 acres. Once part of the flat bottom of a shallow ocean, volcanic upheaval and the erosive action of rivers and glaciers have since combined to form what is now one of the most attractive wilderness areas in California. Marble Mountain itself is composed primarily of prehistoric marine invertebrate fossils. Camping, hiking; fishing in many streams and 79 trout-stocked lakes. Fire permit for this wilderness area is required and may be obtained at the Supervisor's office or any Ranger District Office. Access off CA 96. Contact the Forest Supervisor, 1312 Fairlane Rd; phone 530/842-6131. Also at the Supervisor's office is the

Northwest Interpretive Museum. Lookout model; displays of wildlife, mining, timber production, fire management. (Mon-Fri; closed hols) **Free**

Siskiyou County Museum. Exhibits of Siskiyou County from prehistoric era, Native Americans, trappers, gold rush, transportation, logging, agriculture. First and second floors include period rms and environments. Research library on premises. (Tues-Sat) 530 S Main St. Phone 916/842-3836. **¢** Also on grounds is

Outdoor Museum. On 2½ acres with pioneer cabin, school house, blacksmith shop, logging skid shack, miner's cabin, church, operating general store. (Tues-Sat) **Free**

Yreka Western Railroad. Steam engine-powered 1915 historic train takes visitors on a 3-hr tour of the Shasta Valley. (Memorial Day-mid-June, wkends; mid-June-Labor Day, Wed-Sun; 1 departure mid-morning) 300 E Miner St. Phone 530/842-4146 or 800/YREKA-RR. **¢¢¢**

Motel

✓★★ **KLAMATH MOTOR LODGE.** *1111 S Main St (96097). 530/842-2751; FAX 530/842-4703.* 28 rms, 1-2 story. S $43; D $46-$50; each addl $4; suites $74-$84. TV; cable (premium). Heated pool. Coffee in rms. Restaurant nearby. Ck-out 11 am. Business servs avail. In-rm modem link. Refrigerators. Picnic table. Gardens. Cr cds: A, C, D, DS, MC, V.

SC

Nevada

Population: 1,201,833
Land area: 109,895 square miles
Elevation: 470-13,143 feet
Highest point: Boundary Peak (Esmeralda County)
Entered union: October 31, 1864 (36th state)
Capital: Carson City
Motto: All for our country
Nickname: Silver State
State flower: Sagebrush
State bird: Mountain bluebird
State tree: Piñon and bristlecone pine
State fair: August 23-27, 2000, in Reno
Time zone: Pacific
Web: www.travelnevada.com

Famous for gambling and glamorous nightlife, Nevada also has a rich history and tradition, magnificent scenery and some of the wildest desert country on the continent. Tourism is still the lifeblood of Nevada, with some 42 million visitors a year coming for a vacation or convention. Because of its central location and lack of inventory tax on goods bound out of state, Nevada is becoming increasingly important as a warehousing center for the western states.

Gambling (Nevadans call it "gaming") was first legalized in the Depression year of 1931, the same year residency requirements for obtaining a divorce were relaxed. Gaming is strictly controlled and regulated in Nevada, and casinos offer each bettor a fair chance to win. Taxes derived from the casinos account for nearly half of the state's revenue.

Most Nevadans feel it is preferable to license, tax and regulate gambling strictly than to tolerate the evils of bribery and corruption that inevitably accompany illegal gambling activities. While the state enforces numerous regulations, such as those barring criminals and prohibiting cheating, it *does not* control odds on the various games.

Although Nevada has little rainfall and few rivers, water sports are popular on a few large lakes, both natural and man-made. These include Lakes Tahoe, Mead, Lahontan, Pyramid Lake and Walker Lake.

Mining and ranching have always been important facets of Nevada's economy. Sheep raising became important when millions of sheep were needed to feed the hungry miners working Nevada's Comstock Lode and California's Mother Lode. Most of these sheepherders were Basque. Although today's sheepherder is more likely Peruvian or Mexican, the Basques are still an important influence in the state.

Because of Nevada's arid land, cattle have to roam over a wide area; therefore, ranches average more than 2,000 acres in size. Most Nevada beef cattle are shipped to California or the Midwest for fattening prior to marketing.

Known for its precious metals, Nevada produces more than $2.6 billion worth of gold and silver a year. Eerie ghost towns still hint at the romantic early days of fabulous gold and silver strikes that made millionaires overnight and generated some of the wildest history in the world. In the southern part of the state, the deserted mining camps of Rhyolite, Berlin, Belmont, Goodsprings and Searchlight, to name a few, still delight explorers. Industrial metals and minerals also have an impact on the economy.

The fur traders of the 1820s and 1830s, Jedediah Smith, Peter Ogden and Joseph Walker and the Frémont expeditions, guided by Kit Carson in 1848, were the first to report on the area that is now Nevada.

The Mormons established a trading post in 1851. Now called Genoa, this was Nevada's first non-Indian settlement. Gold was found along the Carson River in Dayton Valley in May of 1850. A decade later the fabulous Comstock Lode (silver and gold ore) was discovered. The gold rush was on and Virginia City mushroomed into a town of 20,000. Formerly a part of Utah and New Mexico Territory, ceded by Mexico in 1848, Nevada became a territory in 1861, a state in 1864. Before Europeans arrived, Nevada was the home of the Paiute, the Shoshone and the Washoe, and even earlier, the Basketmakers.

Note: It is illegal to pick many types of wildflowers in Nevada, as well as gathering rocks. It is also illegal in this dry land to toss away lighted cigarette butts.

When to Go/Climate

Temperatures vary greatly in Nevada—from scorching desert days in Death Valley to bone-chilling night freezes in the Sierra Nevada. The entire state is arid. You may want to avoid visiting Nevada in the hot summer months of June, July and August, when daytime temperatures can remain above 100 degrees in many parts of the state.

AVERAGE HIGH/LOW TEMPERATURES (°F)

ELKO

Jan 37/13	**May** 69/37	**Sept** 78/39
Feb 43/20	**June** 80/47	**Oct** 66/30
Mar 50/25	**July** 91/50	**Nov** 49/23
Apr 60/30	**Aug** 89/39	**Dec** 37/14

LAS VEGAS

Jan 57/34	**May** 88/60	**Sept** 95/66

Feb 63/39	**June** 100/69	**Oct** 82/54
Mar 69/44	**July** 106/76	**Nov** 67/43
Apr 78/51	**Aug** 103/74	**Dec** 58/34

Parks and Recreation Finder

Directions to and information about the parks and recreation areas below are given under their respective town/city sections. Please refer to those sections for details.

NATIONAL PARK AND RECREATION AREAS

Key to abbreviations. I.H.S. = International Historic Site; I.P.M. = International Peace Memorial; N.B. = National Battlefield; N.B.P. National Battlefield Park; N.B.C. = National Battlefield & Cemetery; N.C. = National Conservation Area; N.E.M. = National Expansion Memorial; N.F. = National Forest; N.G. = National Grassland; N.H. = National Historical Park; N.H.C. = National Heritage Corridor; N.H.S. National Historic Site; N.L. = National Lakeshore; N.M. = National Monument; N.M.P. National Military Park; N.Mem. = National Memorial; N.P. = National Park; N.Pres. = National Preserve; N.R. = National Recreational Area; N.R.R. = National Recreational River; N.Riv. = National River; N.S. = National Seashore; N.S.R. = National Scenic Riverway; N.S.T. = National Scenic Trail; N.Sc. = National Scientific Reserve; N.V.M. = National Volcanic Monument.

Place Name	Listed Under
Great Basin N.P.	same
Humboldt N.F.	ELKO
Lake Mead N.R.	same
Toiyabe N.F.	RENO

STATE PARK AND RECREATION AREAS

Key to abbreviations. I.P. = Interstate Park; S.A.P. = State Archaeological Park; S.B. = State Beach; S.C. = State Conservation Area; S.C.P. = State Conservation Park; S.Cp. = State Campground; S.F. = State Forest; S.G. = State Garden; S.H.A. = State Historic Area; S.H.P. = State Historic Park; S.H.S. = State Historic Site; S.M.P. = State Marine Park; S.N.A. = State Natural Area; S.P. = State Park; S.P.C. = State Public Campground; S.R. = State Reserve; S.R.A. = State Recreation Area; S.Res. = State Reservoir; S.Res.P. = State Resort Park; S.R.P. = State Rustic Park.

Place Name	Listed Under
Beaver Dam S.P.	CALIENTE
Berlin-Ichthyosaur S.P.	AUSTIN
Cathedral Gorge S.P.	CALIENTE
Cave Lake S.P.	ELY
Echo Canyon S.P.	CALIENTE
Floyd Lamb S.P.	LAS VEGAS
Fort Churchill S.H.P.	YERINGTON
Lahontan S.R.A.	FALLON
Lake Tahoe Nevada S.P.	INCLINE VILLAGE
Rye Patch S.R.A.	LOVELOCK
Spring Mountain Ranch S.P.	LAS VEGAS
Spring Valley S.P.	CALIENTE
Valley of Fire S.P.	same
Walker Lake S.R.A.	HAWTHORNE
Ward Charcoal Ovens Historic State Monument	ELY

Water-related activities, hiking, riding, various other sports, picnicking and visitor centers, as well as camping, are available in many of these areas. "Roughing it" may be necessary in remote areas. Camping on a first-come, first-served basis; $3-$9/night. Boat launching $2-$6, except Lake Tahoe; (covers all fees, including boat launching). Inquire locally about road conditions for areas off paved highways. Carry drinking water in remote areas. Pets on leash only. For detailed information contact Nevada Division of State Parks, 1300 S Curry St, Carson City 89703-5202; 775/687-4384.

SKI AREAS

Place Name	Listed Under
Diamond Peak Ski Resort	INCLINE VILLAGE
Mt Rose Ski Area	INCLINE VILLAGE

FISHING & HUNTING

Nevada's streams and lakes abound with trout, bass, mountain whitefish and catfish. Most fishing areas are open year-round. There are some exceptions; inquire locally. Nonresident license: $51 for 1 year or $12 for 1 day. Special use stamp ($3) for Lake Mead, Lake Mohave and the Colorado River; $5 annual trout stamp required to take or possess trout.

There is an abundance of wildlife—mule deer, quail, ducks, geese and partridges. Deer hunting season lasts 4 to 5 weeks from the first 2 weekends in October; season varies in some counties. Nonresident hunting license: $111 plus $155 for deer tag and processing. Deer hunting with bow and arrow: nonresidents $111 for license and $155 for tag and processing. Archery hunts usually held August 8 through September 4, prior to rifle season.

For digest of fishing and hunting regulations write to the Nevada Division of Wildlife, PO Box 10678, Reno 89520; 775/688-1500.

CALENDAR HIGHLIGHTS

JANUARY

Cowboy Poetry Gathering (Elko). Working cowpersons participate in storytelling verse. Demonstrations; country music. Phone 800/428-7143.

MAY

Fallon Air Show (Fallon). Fallon Naval Air Station. Military exhibition flying, civilian aerobatics, aircraft displays; Blue Angels Demonstration Team. Phone 775/423-2544.

Laughlin Riverdays (Laughlin). World's longest line dance, carnival, golf tournament. Contact Laughlin Chamber of Commerce 800/227-5245.

JUNE

Helldorado Days (Las Vegas). Rodeos, parades, carnival, street dance, chili cook-off; Western theme throughout. Phone 702/870-1221.

Kit Carson Rendezvous (Carson City). Mountain man encampment, Civil War camp, Native American village with competition dancing, music, arts & crafts and food vendors. Contact Carson City Convention & Visitors Bureau 775/687-7410 or 800/638-2321.

JULY

National Basque Festival (Elko). Contests in weightlifting, sheephooking, other skills of mountaineers; dancing, feast. Phone 775/623-5071.

AUGUST

Nevada State Fair (Reno). Fairgrounds. Exhibits, entertainment, rides, games and more. Phone 775/688-5767.

SEPTEMBER

National Championship Air Races (Reno). Stead Air Field. The world's longest-running air race, featuring four race classes—Unlimited, Formula One, AT-6 and Biplane. Skywriting, aerobatics and displays. Phone 775/972-6663.

OCTOBER

Las Vegas Invitational (Las Vegas). PGA tournament with more than $1 million in prize money.

DECEMBER

National Finals Rodeo (Las Vegas). Thomas and Mack Center. Nation's richest professional rodeo, featuring 15 finalists in 7 rodeo disciplines. Phone 702/731-2115.

Driving Information

Safety belts are mandatory for all persons anywhere in vehicle. Children under 5 years and under 40 pounds in weight must be in an approved safety seat anywhere in vehicle. For further information phone 775/687-5300.

INTERSTATE HIGHWAY SYSTEM

Use the following list as a guide to access interstate highways in Nevada. You should always consult a map to confirm driving routes.

Highway Number	Cities/Towns within 10 miles
Interstate 15	Las Vegas, Overton.
Interstate 80	Battle Mountain, Elko, Lovelock, Reno, Winnemucca.

Additional Visitor Information

Nevada Magazine, an illustrated bimonthly magazine, and *Nevada's Events Guide* (free), may be obtained by contacting the Nevada Commission on Tourism, 401 N Carson St, Carson City 89710; 775/687-4322 or 800/NEVADA-8.

For information about the Lake Mead area write the Public Affairs Officer, Lake Mead National Recreation Area, Boulder City 89005.

Information on camping, fishing and hunting, water sports, gambling, ghost towns, mining, agriculture, the state capitol and museum may also be obtained from the Commission on Tourism (see above).

Gambling

Gambling is limited to those 21 or over. Children are welcome in restaurants, and many casinos have child-care facilities.

Austin (D-3)

(See also Battle Mountain)

Settled 1862 **Pop** 350 (est) **Elev** 6,525 ft **Area Code** 775 **Zip** 89310

Information Chamber of Commerce, PO Box 212; 775/964-2200

Austin was the mother town of central and eastern Nevada mining. For a time its strike did not attract hordes because of the phenomenal character of the Comstock Lode in booming Virginia City. By 1867, however, the number of ore-reduction mills had increased to 11, and 6,000 claims had been filed.

Many of its old buildings have deteriorated and fallen down, but Austin firmly denies that it is a ghost town. Rather, it is a relic of Nevada's greatest days of fame and glory looking toward a future of renewed mining activity made possible through improved methods for using low-grade ore.

A Ranger District office of the Toiyabe National Forest (see RENO) is located here.

What to See and Do

Berlin-Ichthyosaur State Park. Approx 1,070 acres. Fossilized remains of marine reptiles, some up to 50 ft long, with fish-shaped bodies and long narrow snouts. The ghost town of Berlin is also here. Hiking, nature trail. Picnicking. Camping facilities (fee, dump station). (Daily) Standard fees. 50 mi SW via US 50, then 30 mi S on NV 361 to Gabbs, then 22 mi E on NV 844, in Toiyabe National Forest. Phone 775/964-2440.

Hickison Petroglyph Recreation Site. Native American drawings carved in stone (ca 1000 B.C.-A.D. 1500); near former pony express trail. Picnicking. Camping; no drinking water avail. (Daily) 24 mi E on US 50. Phone 775/635-4000. **Free**

Mountain biking. Many miles of biking trails through central Nevada's varied terrain. Brochure describing designated trails avail from Chamber of Commerce, phone 775/964-2200; or Tyrannosaurus Rex Mountain Bike & Specialties, PO Box 504, phone 775/964-1212.

Other old buildings. Stores, churches, hotels and saloons. Stokes Castle is a century-old, three-story stone building that can be seen for miles.

The Lander County Courthouse. Oldest county courthouse in the state and one of the plainest. Its sturdy construction, without frills, suited the early residents.

The Reese River *Reveille*. Published from May 16, 1863, to 1993; complete files are preserved.

Battle Mountain (C-4)

Settled 1868 **Pop** 3,542 **Elev** 4,512 ft **Area Code** 775 **Zip** 89820

Motels

✓★ **BEST INN & SUITES.** *650 W Front St (89820), on I-80 Business. 775/635-5424; FAX 775/635-5699; res: 800/343-0085.* 72 rms, 2 story. S $35-$44; D $42-$51; each addl $5; under 12 free. Pet accepted. TV; cable (premium). Coffee in lobby. Restaurant adj open 24 hrs. Ck-out 11 am. Business servs avail. Some refrigerators. Picnic table, grill. Western theme. Cr cds: A, C, DS, MC, V.

D SC

★★ **COMFORT INN.** *521 E Front St (89820), on I-80 Business. 775/635-5880; FAX 775/635-5788; res: 800/626-1900.* 72 rms, 3 story. June-Aug: S, D $56-$61; each addl $5; under 6 free. Crib $5. Pet accepted; $20 deposit. TV; cable (premium). Heated pool; whirlpool. Complimentary continental bkfst. Restaurant adj 11 am-9 pm. Ck-out 11 am. Coin lndry. Meeting rms. Business servs avail. Refrigerators. Cr cds: A, C, D, DS, MC, V.

SC

★ **OWL HOTEL & CASINO.** *8 E Front St (89820). 775/635-5155; FAX 775/635-8012.* 18 rms, 2 story. S, D $32.40. TV; cable (premium). Restaurant adj open 24 hrs. Ck-out 11 am. Cr cds: A, C, DS, MC, V.

Boulder City (J-5)

(See also Henderson, Lake Mead National Recreation Area, Las Vegas)

Founded 1931 **Pop** 12,567 **Elev** 2,500 ft **Area Code** 702

Information Chamber of Commerce, 1305 Arizona St; 702/293-2034

Boulder City owes its birth to the construction of the mighty Hoover Dam, which spans the Colorado River. A movie on the project can be seen daily at the Hoover Dam Museum; for information phone 702/294-1988.

This is a well-planned model city built by the federal government to house personnel and serve as headquarters for Reclamation, Park Service and Bureau of Mines forces operating in the area. It also serves as a gateway to the Lake Mead National Recreation Area (see).

Annual Events

Boulder Damboree. Central Park. July 4.

Art in the Park. Wilbur Square, Bicentennial & Escalante parks. 1st full wkend Oct.

Motels

★ **EL RANCHO BOULDER MOTEL.** *725 Nevada Hwy (89005). 702/293-1085; FAX 702/293-3021.* 39 rms. S, D $60-$150; family, wkly rates. TV; cable (premium). Pool. Complimentary coffee in lobby.

Restaurant adj 6 am-midnight. Ck-out 11 am. Meeting rms. Airport transportation. Refrigerators. Cr cds: A, C, D, DS, ER, MC, V.

D SC

✓★ **GOLD STRIKE INN & CASINO.** *US Hwy 93 (89005), 3 mi W of Hoover Dam. 702/293-5000; FAX 702/293-5608; res: 800/245-6380.* 378 rms, 17 story. S, D $29-$69; each addl $3.27; under 12 free. Crib $3. TV. Heated pool. Restaurant open 24 hrs. Bar; entertainment Thurs-Sun. Ck-out 11 am. Gift shop. Casino. Some private patios, balconies. View of Lake Mead. Cr cds: A, C, D, DS, MC, V.

D

★ **SUPER 8 MOTEL.** *704 Nevada Hwy (89005). 702/294-8888; FAX 702/293-4344; res: 800/800-8000.* 114 rms, 3 story. S, D $42.88-$79.88; suites $75.88-$200.88; wkly, monthly rates. Crib $5. TV; cable (premium). Indoor pool; whirlpool. Restaurant 7 am-10 pm. Bar. Ck-out noon. Meeting rms. Airport transportation. Game rm. Picnic tables. Cr cds: A, C, D, DS, MC, V.

D SC

Caliente (G-6)

(See also Las Vegas, Overton)

Pop 1,111 **Elev** 4,395 ft **Area Code** 702 **Zip** 89008

Information Chamber of Commerce, PO Box 553; 702/726-3129

This is a ranch and recreation center situated in a fertile valley.

What to See and Do

State parks and recreation areas.

Beaver Dam. (Check conditions locally; trailers over 24 ft not recommended.) More than 2,200 acres set amid pine forests and lofty cliffs. Fishing. Hiking. Picnicking. Camping. (Apr-Oct) 6 mi N on US 93, then 28 mi E on improved gravel road. Phone 702/728-4460. Day use **¢¢**; Camping **¢¢¢**

Cathedral Gorge. This 1,633-acre park is a long, narrow valley cut into tan bentonite clay formations. Peculiar erosion has created unique patterns, fluting the gorge walls and forming isolated towers that resemble cathedral spires. Hiking. Picnicking. Camping facilities. 14 mi N on US 93. Phone 702/728-4460. Day use **¢¢**; Camping **¢¢¢**

Echo Canyon. A 920-acre park. Swimming; fishing on 65-acre reservoir (daily); boat launching. Picnicking. Camping (dump station). 25 mi N on US 93, then 4 mi E on NV 322, then 10 mi SE on NV 323. Phone 702/728-4460. Day use **¢¢**; Camping **¢¢¢**

Spring Valley. A 1,630-acre park. Boating and fishing on Eagle Valley Reservoir. Picnicking. Camping (dump station). (Daily) 26 mi N on US 93 to Pioche, then 18 mi E on NV 322. Phone 702/728-4460. Day use **¢¢**; Camping **¢¢¢**

Annual Events

Lincoln County Homecoming. Barbecue, celebrity auction, art show. Memorial Day wkend.

Lincoln County Fair and Rodeo. Mid-Aug.

Meadow Valley Western Days. Hayrides, rodeo, talent show. 3rd wkend Sept.

Carson City (E-1)

(See also Incline Village, Reno, Stateline, Virginia City; also see Lake Tahoe Area, CA)

Founded 1858 **Pop** 40,443 **Elev** 4,687 ft **Area Code** 775 **Zip** 89701

Information Convention & Visitors Bureau, 1900 S Carson St, Suite 200; 775/687-7410 or 800/638-2321

State capital and a county itself, Carson City is situated near the edge of the forested eastern slope of the Sierra Nevada in Eagle Valley. It was first called Eagle Ranch and later renamed for Kit Carson. It became the social center for nearby settlements and shared Wild West notoriety in the silver stampede days of the last century. Fitzsimmons knocked out Corbett here in 1897. Movies of the event (first of their kind) grossed $1 million.

A Ranger District office of the Toiyabe National Forest (see RENO) is located here.

What to See and Do

Bowers Mansion (1864). The Bowers built this $200,000 granite house with the profits from a gold and silver mine. Their resources were soon depleted, leaving them penniless and forcing Mrs. Bower to become the "Washoe seeress," telling fortunes for a living. Half-hr guided tours of 16 rms with many original furnishings. (Memorial Day-Labor Day, daily; May, Sept & Oct, wkends). Swimming pool (Memorial Day-Labor Day; fee) and picnicking in adj park. 10 mi N in Washoe Valley. Phone 775/849-0201. Tours **¢¢**

Skiing. (See LAKE TAHOE AREA, CA)

State Capitol (1871). Large stone structure with Doric columns and a silver dome. Houses portraits of past Nevada governors. (Mon-Fri) N Carson St. Phone 775/687-5000. Near the capitol are

State Library Building. Files of Nevada newspapers and books about the state. (Mon-Fri; closed hols) 401 N Carson St. **Free**

Nevada State Museum. Former US Mint. Exhibits of coins, guns, minerals, pioneer memorabilia, mining operations; life-size displays of Nevada ghost town, Native American camp with artifacts and walk-through "Devonian sea." A 300-ft mine tunnel with displays runs beneath the building. (Daily; closed Jan 1, Thanksgiving, Dec 25) 600 N Carson St. Phone 775/687-4810. **¢¢**

Warren Engine Company No. 1 Fire Museum. Currier and Ives series "The Life of a Fireman," old photographs, antique fire-fighting equipment, state's first fire truck (restored), 1863 Hunneman handpumper, 1847 4-wheel cart. Children under 18 must be accompanied by adult. 777 S Stewart St. For schedule, phone 775/887-2210. **Free**

Nevada State Railroad Museum. Exhibits 22 freight and passenger cars, as well as 3 steam locomotives that once belonged to the Virginia and Truckee RR. Houses pictorial history gallery and artifacts of the famed Bonanza Road. Motor-rail car rides (summer wkends; fee) and steam-engine rides (summer hols & some wkends; fee). Museum (Daily). S Carson at Fairview Dr. Phone 775/687-6953. Museum **¢**

Annual Events

Kit Carson Rendezvous. Mountain man encampment, Civil War camp, Native American village with competition dancing, music, arts & crafts and food vendors. Early June.

Nevada Day Celebration. Commemorates admission to the Union. Grand Ball, parades, exhibits. 4 days late Oct.

Motels

★ **HARDMAN HOUSE MOTOR INN.** *917 N Carson St (89701). 775/882-7744; FAX 775/887-0321; res: 800/626-0793.* 62 rms, 3 story. May-Oct: S $40-$60; D $45-$65; each addl $6; suites $80-$100; higher rates: wkends, hols, air races; lower rates rest of yr. Crib free. TV; cable. Complimentary coffee in lobby. Restaurant nearby. Ck-out noon.

Business servs avail. Garage parking. Some refrigerators; some wet bars. Cr cds: A, C, D, DS, MC, V.

D SC

★ **MILL HOUSE INN MOTEL.** *3251 S Carson St (89701). 775/882-2715; FAX 775/882-2415.* 24 rms. May-Oct: S $40-$50; D $45-$55; each addl $5; under 12 free; higher rates: wkends, hols; lower rates rest of yr. Crib $5. TV; cable. Heated pool (seasonal). Complimentary coffee in lobby. Restaurant nearby. Ck-out 11 am. Picnic tables. Cr cds: A, C, DS, MC, V.

SC

✓★ **NUGGET MOTEL.** *651 N Stewart St (89701). 775/882-7711; FAX 775/882-5197; res: 800/948-9111.* 60 rms, 2 story. S $35-$45; D $43-$60; each addl $5; under 6 free. TV; cable. Complimentary coffee in lobby. Restaurant nearby. Ck-out noon. Cr cds: A, C, DS, MC, V.

SC

Restaurants

★★ **ADELE'S RESTAURANT & LOUNGE.** *1112 N Carson St (89701). 775/882-3353.* Hrs: 11 am-midnight. Closed Sun; also wk of Dec 31-mid-Jan. Res accepted. Complete meals: lunch $7.95-$18.95, dinner $17.95-$44.95. Specializes in seafood, steak, roast duck. Comstock Victorian decor in Second Empire house. Cr cds: A, C, MC, V.

D

✓★★ **CARSON NUGGET STEAK HOUSE.** *507 N Carson St (89702). 775/882-1626.* Hrs: 5-10 pm. Res accepted. Bar open 24 hrs. Semi-a la carte: dinner $9.95-$17.95. Child's meals. Specializes in seafood, prime rib, steak. Valet parking. Western decor. Also on premises are buffet dining rm & coffee shop open 24 hrs. Cr cds: A, C, D, DS, MC, V.

D SC

★ **SILVANA'S.** *1301 N Carson St (89701). 775/883-5100.* Hrs: 5-10 pm. Closed Sun, Mon; Dec 25. Res accepted. Italian menu. Bar. Semi-a la carte: dinner $10.95-$19.95. Specializes in pasta, seafood, steak. European decor. Cr cds: A, C, D, MC, V.

D

Crystal Bay

(see Incline Village)

Elko (C-5)

Settled ca 1870 **Pop** 14,736 **Elev** 5,067 ft **Area Code** 775 **Zip** 89801
E-mail elkocc@sierra.net **Web** www.elkonevada.com

Information Chamber of Commerce, 1601 Idaho St; 775/738-7135 or 800/428-7143

On the Humboldt River, Elko is the center of a large ranching area. Originally a stopping point for wagon trains headed for the West Coast, its main sources of revenue today are tourism, ranching, gold mining, gaming and a large service industry.

What to See and Do

Humboldt National Forest. Some of the features of this more than 2 million-acre forest are its 8 wilderness areas, spectacular canyons, streams and old mining camps. Fishing; hunting. Picnicking. Camping (May-Oct; fee). 20 mi SE on NV 228 (Ruby Mountain District), or 70 mi N on NV 225 (Mountain City & Jarbridge Districts). For further information contact Supervisor, 976 Mountain City Hwy; phone 775/738-5171. **¢¢-¢¢¢**

Licensed casinos, nightclubs. Particularly along Idaho St.

Northeastern Nevada Museum. Three galleries feature art, historical, Native American and nature exhibits of area. Pioneer vehicles and original 1860 pony express cabin on grounds. (Daily; closed Jan 1, Thanksgiving, Dec 25) 1515 Idaho St. Phone 775/738-3418. **Free**

Annual Events

Cowboy Poetry Gathering. Working cowpersons participate in storytelling verse. Demonstrations; music. Last full wk Jan.

National Basque Festival. Contests in weightlifting, sheephooking, other skills of mountaineers; dancing, feast. Wkend early July.

County Fair and Livestock Show. Horse racing. 4 days Labor Day wkend.

Motels

✓★ **BEST WESTERN INN EXPRESS.** *837 Idaho St (89801). 775/738-7261; FAX 775/738-0118; res: 800/600-1234.* 49 rms, 2 story. Mid-May-Sept: S $44-$54; D $54-$64; each addl $5; suites $79; higher rates special events; varied lower rates rest of yr. Crib $5. TV; cable (premium). Heated pool. Complimentary continental bkfst. Ck-out noon. Business servs avail. Cr cds: A, C, D, DS, MC, V.

SC

★★ **HIGH DESERT INN.** *3015 E Idaho St (89801). 775/738-8425; FAX 775/753-7906; res: 888/394-8303.* 170 rms, 4 story. Apr-Oct: S $64-$84, D $74-$94; each addl $10; higher rates: Cowboy Poetry Gathering, Mining Exposition; lower rates rest of yr. Crib free. Pet accepted. TV; cable. Indoor pool; whirlpool. Coffee in rms. Restaurant 6 am-10 pm. Rm serv. Bar 4 pm-midnight. Ck-out noon. Coin lndry. Meeting rms. Valet serv. Free airport, RR station, bus depot transportation. Exercise equipt. Cr cds: A, C, D, DS, JCB, MC, V.

D SC

★★ **RED LION INN & CASINO.** *2065 E Idaho St (89801). 775/738-2111; FAX 775/753-9859; res: 800/545-0044.* 223 rms, 3 story. S $69-$79; D $79-$89; each addl $10; suites $259; under 18 free. Crib free. Pet accepted. TV; cable (premium). Heated pool. Coffee in rms. Restaurant open 24 hrs. Bar; entertainment. Ck-out noon. Business servs avail. Gift shop. Barber, beauty shop. Free airport transportation. Game rm. Casino. Cr cds: A, C, D, DS, ER, MC, V.

D SC

★★ **SHILO INN.** *2401 Mountain City Hwy (89801), near JC Harris Airport. 775/738-5522; FAX 775/738-6247; res: 800/222-2244.* 70 rms, 2 story, 16 kit. units. S, D $69-$89; kit. units $69-$119; under 12 free; wkly rates; higher rates special events. Crib free. Pet accepted; $7. TV; cable (premium), VCR avail. Indoor pool; whirlpool. Complimentary continental bkfst. Restaurant nearby. Ck-out noon. Coin lndry. Meeting rm. Business servs avail. In-rm modem link. Sundries. Free airport, RR station, bus depot transportation. Exercise equipt; sauna. Bathrm phones, refrigerators, wet bars. Cr cds: A, C, D, DS, ER, JCB, MC, V.

D SC

✓★ **SUPER 8 MOTEL.** *1755 Idaho St (89801). 775/738-8488; FAX 775/738-4637; res: 800/800-8000.* 75 rms, 2 story. Late May-Sept: S,D $40.88-$55.88; each addl $3; under 12 free; higher rates special events; lower rates rest of yr. Crib free. TV; cable (premium). Complimentary coffee in lobby. Restaurant nearby. Ck-out 11 am. Business servs avail. Cr cds: A, C, D, DS, MC, V.

D SC

Ely (E-5)

Settled 1868 **Pop** 4,756 **Elev** 6,427 ft **Area Code** 775 **Zip** 89301

Information White Pine Chamber of Commerce, 636 Aultman St; 775/289-8877

Although founded in 1868 as a silver mining camp, Ely's growth began in 1906 with the arrival of the Nevada Northern Railroad, which facilitated the development, in 1907, of large-scale copper mining. Gold and silver are still mined in Ely. The seat of White Pine County, it is the shopping and recreational center of a vast ranching and mining area. The city is surrounded by mountains that offer deer hunting, trout fishing and winter skiing. High elevation provides a cool, sunny climate.

A Ranger District office of the Humboldt National Forest (see ELKO) is located here.

What to See and Do

Cave Lake State Park. A 1,240-acre area; 32-acre reservoir provides swimming; fishing (trout); boating. Picnicking. Camping (dump station). (Daily; access may be restricted in winter) Standard fees. 8 mi S on US 93, then 7 mi E on Success Summit Rd, NV 486. Phone 775/728-4467.

Humboldt National Forest (see ELKO).

Nevada Northern Railway Museum. Located in the historic Nevada Northern Railway Depot (1906). Original oak furniture, filing cabinets and tele Phone 775/289-2085. Museum ¢¢; Train excursions ¢¢¢¢

Ward Charcoal Ovens State Historic Park. Six stone beehive charcoal ovens used during the 1870 mining boom. Hunting in season. Picnicking. 7 mi SE on US 6/50/93, then 11 mi W on Cave Valley Rd, a gravel road.

White Pine Public Museum. 1905 coach and 1909, 1917 steam locomotives, early-day relics and mementos, mineral display. (Daily) 2000 Aultman St. Phone 775/289-4710. **Free**

Annual Events

Auto races. Open road auto races. 3rd wkend May & Sept.

Pony Express Days. Horse racing, parimutuel betting. Last 2 wkends Aug.

White Pine County Fair. Last wkend Aug.

Motels

✓★ **JAIL HOUSE MOTEL.** *211 5th St (89301). 775/289-3033; FAX 775/289-8709; res: 800/841-5430.* 47 rms, 2 story. S $42; D $46-$51; each addl $5. Crib free. TV; cable (premium). Restaurant 5 am-9 pm. Ck-out 11 am. Casino. Cr cds: A, C, D, DS, MC, V.

D SC

★★ **RAMADA INN.** *805 Great Basin Blvd (89301), at jct US 50, US 93 & US 6. 775/289-4884; FAX 775/289-1492; res: 800/851-9526.* 65 rms, 2 story. S $49-$60; D $54-$65; each addl $5. Crib free. Indoor pool; whirlpool. TV; cable (premium). Complimentary continental bkfst. Restaurant 11 am-10 pm. Bar. Ck-out noon. Business servs avail. Free airport transportation. Some refrigerators. Casino. Cr cds: A, C, D, MC, V.

SC

Fallon (D-2)

Pop 6,438 **Elev** 3,963 ft **Area Code** 775 **Zip** 89406
Web www.fallonchamber.com

Information Chamber of Commerce, 65 S Maine St, Ste B; 775/423-2544

What to See and Do

Lahontan State Recreation Area. Approx 30,000 acres with a 16-mi-long reservoir. Water sports; fishing; boating (launching, ramps). Picnicking. Camping (dump station). Standard fees. 18 mi W on US 50. Phone 775/867-3500.

Annual Events

Fallon Air Show. Fallon Naval Air Station. Military exhibition flying, civilian aerobatics, aircraft displays; Blue Angels Demonstration Team. Mid-May.

All Indian Rodeo. Rodeo events, parade, powwow, Native American dances, arts, games. Phone 775/423-2544. 3rd wkend July.

Motels

★ **BONANZA INN & CASINO.** *855 W Williams Ave (89406). 775/423-6031; FAX 775/423-6282.* 75 rms, 2 story. S $40; D $46; each addl $5; suite $59-$76; under 12 free. Crib $5. Pet accepted; $20. TV; cable (premium). Restaurant open 24 hrs. Bar. Ck-out 11 am. Business servs avail. Casino. RV park. Cr cds: A, C, D, DS, MC, V.

D SC

★ **COMFORT INN.** *1830 W Williams Ave (89406). 775/423-5554; FAX 775/423-0663; res: 888/691-6388.* 82 rms, 2 story. Apr-Oct: S, D $51-$65; suites $75-$100; under 18 free; lower rates rest of yr. Crib free. TV; cable, VCR avail. Indoor pool. Complimentary continental bkfst. Ck-out noon. Business servs avail. Sundries. Coin Indry. Some refrigerators, microwaves, in-rm whirlpools. Cr cds: A, C, D, DS, ER, JCB, MC, V.

D SC

✓★ **WESTERN MOTEL.** *125 S Carson St (89407). 775/423-5118; FAX 775/423-6065.* 22 rms, 2 story. S $39; D $43; each addl $5. Crib $4. Pet accepted, some restrictions; $3. TV. Heated pool. Complimentary continental bkfst. Restaurant nearby. Ck-out 11 am. Refrigerators. Cr cds: A, C, D, MC, V.

SC

Gardnerville (E-1)

(See also Carson City, Stateline; also see Lake Tahoe Area, CA)

Pop 2,177 **Elev** 4,746 ft **Area Code** 775 **Zip** 89410
E-mail info@ carsonvalleynv.org **Web** www.carsonvalleynv.org

Information Carson Valley Chamber of Commerce & Visitors Authority, 1512 US 395, Suite 1; 775/782-8144 or 800/727-7677

Gardnerville lies just southeast of Minden, seat of Douglas County. The two are considered contiguous towns.

What to See and Do

Mormon Station State Historic Park. Fort/stockade. Museum exhibits relics of the early pioneer days and the first white settlement in state. Also picnicking, tables, stoves. (Mid-May-mid-Oct, daily) 4 mi N via US 395, then 4 mi W on NV 57 in Genoa. Phone 775/782-2590.

Annual Events

Carson Valley Days. Parade, arts & crafts, rodeo, sport tournaments. 2nd wkend June.

Carson Valley Fine Arts & Crafts Street Celebration. Street celebration with hundreds of crafters, treasures, entertainment and food. Mid-Aug.

Motel

★ **CARSON VALLEY INN.** *1627 Hwy 395 N (89423), 2 mi N on US 395. 775/782-9711; FAX 775/782-7472; res: 800/321-6983.* 76 rms, 2 story. S, D $39-$59; suites $62-$80; under 12 free; higher rates hols.

Crib avail. TV; cable. Complimentary coffee in lobby. Ck-out noon. Meeting rms. Cr cds: A, C, D, DS, MC, V.

D SC

Motor Hotel

★★★ **CARSON VALLEY INN.** *1627 Hwy 395 (89423), N on US 395. 775/782-9711; FAX 775/782-7472; res: 800/321-6983.* E-mail cvinn@aol.com; web www.cvinn.com. 154 rms, 4 story. Registration in rear bldg. June-Oct: S, D $59-$89; each addl $6; suites $129-$159; under 12 free; ski, golf packages; higher rates: wkends, hols; lower rates rest of yr. Crib free. TV. Supervised child's activities; ages 4-12. Restaurant open 24 hrs. Rm serv 6 am-10 pm. Bar; entertainment. Ck-out noon. Meeting rms. Business servs avail. Bellhops. Gift shop. Valet serv. Downhill ski 15 mi; x-country ski 18 mi. Health club privileges. Whirlpool. Game rm. Some bathrm phones, refrigerators. Casino. Stained-glass wedding chapel. Cr cds: A, C, D, DS, MC, V.

D SC

Inn

★★ **JENSEN MANSION.** *1431 Ezell St (89410). 775/782-7644.* 4 air-cooled rms, 2 share bath, 3 story. No rm phones. S, D $85-$130; each addl $10; family & wkly rates. Crib free. Pet accepted. TV in sitting rm; cable. Complimentary full bkfst. Restaurant nearby. Ck-out 11 am, ck-in 3 pm. Downhill ski 18 mi; x-country ski 20 mi. Exercise equipt. Picnic tables, grills. Built 1910; period furnishings. Cr cds: C, MC, V.

SC

Great Basin National Park (E-6)

(5 mi W of Baker on NV 488)

Established as a national park in 1986, Great Basin includes Lehman Caves (formerly Lehman Caves National Monument), Wheeler Peak (elev 13,063 ft), the park's only glacier, and Lexington arch, a natural limestone arch more than six stories tall. The park consists of 77,092 acres of diverse scenic, ecologic and geologic attractions. Of particular interest in the park is Lehman Caves, a large limestone solution cavern. The cave contains numerous limestone formations, including shields and helictites. Temperature in the cave is 50°F; jackets are recommended.

The 12-mile Wheeler Peak Scenic Drive reaches to the 10,000-foot elevation mark of Wheeler Peak. From there, hiking is possible to the summit. Backcountry hiking and camping are permitted. The Lexington Arch is located at the south end of the park.

Camping is allowed at three campgrounds located along the Wheeler Peak Scenic Drive: the Wheeler Peak Campground, the Upper Lehman Creek Campground and the Lower Lehman Campground. Baker Creek Campground is located approximately five miles from park headquarters. Picnic facilities are available near park headquarters.

Park headquarters and the Visitor Center are located at Lehman Caves (daily; closed Jan 1, Thanksgiving, Dec 25; extended hrs in summer). Also here is a souvenir and snack shop (early Apr-mid-Oct; daily). For further information contact the Superintendent, Great Basin National Park, Baker 89311; 775/234-7331.

Hawthorne (E-2)

Pop 4,162 **Elev** 4,320 ft **Area Code** 775 **Zip** 89415
Information Chamber of Commerce, 932 E St, PO Box 1635; 775/945-5896

Hawthorne, seat of Mineral County, is a truly Western desert town on a broad plain rimmed by beautiful mountains where gold has been mined. The area is inviting to people who like to explore the "old" Nevada.

What to See and Do

Walker Lake. Named for the trapper and scout Joseph Walker, this is a remnant of ancient Lake Lahontan. It is 15 mi long and 5 mi wide. Swimming, water skiing. Fishing is good for cutthroat trout in these alkaline and saline waters. Boating (landing). Camping sites. The US Bureau of Land Management maintains one recreational area: Sportsman's Beach (boat launching, camping; free). 12 mi N on US 95. Phone 775/885-6000 or 775/867-3001. Also here is

Walker Lake State Recreation Area. Approx 280 acres. Swimming; fishing; boating (launching ramp). Picnicking, shade structures.

Motels

★ **EL CAPITAN MOTOR LODGE.** *540 F St (89415), 1 blk E of US 95. 775/945-3321; FAX 775/945-2193; res: 800/922-2311.* Web www.elcapitancasino.com. 103 rms, 1-2 story. S $33-$45; D $39-$50; each addl $7; under 12 free. Crib free. Pet accepted; $10 deposit. TV; cable. Heated pool. Restaurant open 24 hrs. Bar. Ck-out 1 pm. Meeting rms. Sundries. Game rm. Refrigerators. Casino. Cr cds: A, C, D, DS, MC, V.

SC

✓★ **SAND N SAGE LODGE.** *1301 E 5th St (89415), 1 blk NE of US 95. 775/945-3352; FAX 775/945-3353.* 37 rms, 2 story. S $29.95; D $34.95; each addl $5; kit. units $6 addl. Crib free. Pet accepted, some restrictions. TV; cable (premium). Pool. Complimentary coffee in lobby. Restaurant nearby. Ck-out 11 am. Refrigerators, microwaves. Cr cds: A, C, DS, MC, V.

Henderson (J-5)

(See also Boulder City, Lake Mead National Recreation Area, Las Vegas)

Settled 1942 **Pop** 64,942 **Elev** 1,960 ft **Area Code** 702 **Zip** 89015
Information Chamber of Commerce, 590 S Boulder Hwy; 702/565-8951

The industrial center of Nevada, Henderson is on level desert terrain, midway between Boulder City (see) and Las Vegas (see). It was originally created to provide housing for the employees of a wartime magnesium plant. The fastest growing city in Nevada, it has become the third-largest city in the state.

What to See and Do

Clark County Heritage Museum. Exhibit Center with county "timeline." Railroad, early residence exhibits; commercial print shop, outdoor mining, farming display; gift shop. (Daily; closed Jan 1, Dec 25) 1830 S Boulder Hwy. Phone 702/455-7955. ¢

Ethel M Chocolates Factory & Cactus Garden. Self-guided tours of famous chocolate factory and adj cactus garden. Free samples. Shops. (Daily, hrs vary) 1 Sunset Way, at jct Mt Vista. Phone 702/433-2500. **Free**

Annual Event

Heritage Days. 5 days Apr.

Motel

✓★ **BEST WESTERN.** *85 W Lake Mead Dr (89015). 702/564-1712; FAX 702/564-7642; res: 800/528-1234; res: 800/446-2944.* 59 rms, 2 story. S $50-$99; D $56-$99; under 12 free; higher rates: hols, special events. Crib free. TV; cable (premium). Complimentary continental bkfst. Restaurant nearby. Ck-out 11 am. Pool. Refrigerators. Cr cds: A, C, D, DS, MC, V.

D SC

Hotels

✓★★ **SUNSET STATION CASINOS INC.** *1301 W Sunset Rd (89014). 702/547-7777; FAX 702/547-7774; res: 888/786-7389.* Web www.sunsetstation.com. 450 rms, 20 story, 52 suites. S, D $49-$219; each addl $10; suites $69-$119; under 12 free; wkend, hol rates; higher rates special events. Crib $10. TV; cable (premium). Complimentary coffee in rms. Restaurant open 24 hrs. Entertainment. Ck-out noon. Meeting rms. Business servs avail. Concierge. Shopping arcade. Barber, beauty shop. Pool; poolside serv. Cr cds: A, C, D, DS, ER, MC, V.

D

✓★★ **THE RESERVE HOTEL CASINO.** *777 W Lake Mead Dr (89015). 702/558-7000; FAX 702/567-7373; res: 888/899-7770.* Web www.ameristars.com. 224 rms, 10 story. S, D $29-$99; suites $100-$150; under 12 free. Crib avail. TV; cable (premium), VCR avail. Restaurant open 24 hrs. Rm serv 24 hrs. Bar. Ck-out noon. Meeting rms. Business center. Concierge. Shopping arcade. Barber, beauty shop. Heated pool. Cr cds: A, C, D, DS, ER, MC, V.

D SC

Restaurants

★★★ **CARVER'S.** *2061 W Sunset Rd (89014). 702/433-5801.* Hrs: 5-9:30 pm; Fri, Sat to 11 pm; Sun to 9 pm. Closed Dec 25. Res accepted. Semi-a la carte: dinner $16.50-$24. Specializes in top sirloin, veal, lamb. Art Deco decor; fireplace. Cr cds: A, C, D, DS, ER, MC, V.

D

★★ **D'ANGELO.** *2895 Green Valley Pkwy (89014). 702/451-8886.* Hrs: 11 am-10 pm; Fri to 11 pm; Sat 4-11 pm; Sun 4-10 pm. Closed Thanksgiving, Dec 25. Res accepted. Italian menu. Bar. A la carte entrees: lunch $7.50-$11.95, dinner $10.25-$18. Child's meals. Specialties: fettuccine, pasta osso bucco, filet mignon. Salad bar. Parking. Outdoor dining. Italian decor. Cr cds: A, C, D, ER, JCB, MC, V.

D SC

✓★ **RAINBOW CLUB.** *122 Water St (89015). 702/565-9777.* Open 24 hrs. Bar. Semi-a la carte: bkfst $.99-$4.50, lunch $3.50-$4.10, dinner $4.95-$6.45. Specializes in steak, chicken, seafood. In casino. Cr cds: C, MC, V.

D

Incline Village (D-1)

(See also Stateline; also see Lake Tahoe Area, CA)

Pop 7,1119 **Elev** 6,360 ft **Area Code** 775 **Zip** 89451
E-mail info@ gotahoe.com **Web** www.gotahoe.com

Information Lake Tahoe Incline Village/Crystal Bay Visitors Bureau, 969 Tahoe Blvd; 775/832-1606 or 800/GO-TAHOE

What to See and Do

Lake Tahoe Nevada State Park. Approx 14,200 acres on the eastern shore of beautiful Lake Tahoe consisting of five management areas. Gently sloping sandy beach, swimming; fishing; boating (ramp). Hiking. Mountain biking. X-country skiing. Picnic tables, stoves. No camping. Standard fees. (Daily) On NV 28. Phone 775/831-0494.

Ponderosa Ranch and Western Theme Park. Cartwright House seen in the *Bonanza* television series. Frontier town with 1870 country church; vintage autos; bkfst hayrides (fee); amusements May-Oct. Convention facilities. (Daily) On Tahoe Blvd (NV 28). Phone 775/831-0691. ¢¢¢

Skiing.

Diamond Peak Ski Resort. Three quads, 3 double chairlifts; patrol, school, rentals, snowmaking; cafeteria, bar; lodge. 35 runs; longest run approx 2.5 mi; vertical drop 1,840 ft. (Mid-Nov-mid-Apr, daily) Jct NV 28 & Country Club Dr. Phone 775/832-1177 for fees, 775/831-3211 for snow conditions. ¢¢¢¢¢

Mount Rose Ski Area. Two quads, 3 triple, double chairlifts; patrol, rentals, school; bar, cafeteria and deli; sport shop. Longest run 2½ mi; vertical drop 1,440 ft. (Mid-Nov-mid-Apr, daily) 12 mi NE on NV 431. Phone 775/849-0704 or 800/SKI-ROSE (exc NV). ¢¢¢¢¢

Annual Events

Lake Tahoe Winter Games Festival. Diamond Peak Ski Resort (see). Early Mar.

Native American Snow Dance. Preston Field. Original native crafts and jewelry, more than 100 performances. 2 days mid-Oct.

Motel

★ **INN AT INCLINE & CONDOMINIUMS.** *1003 Tahoe Blvd (NV 28) (89451). 775/831-1052; FAX 775/831-3016; res: 800/824-6391.* E-mail info@innatincline.com; web www.innatincline.com. 38 rms, 2 story. No A/C. Mid-June-late Sept: S, D $89-$135; each addl $10; under 18 free; lower rates rest of yr. TV; cable (premium). Indoor pool; whirlpool. Sauna. Complimentary continental bkfst. Restaurant nearby. Ck-out 11 am. Business servs avail. Downhill ski 1 mi; x-country ski 6 mi. Some refrigerators. Some balconies. Cr cds: A, C, DS, MC, V.

SC

Hotels

★★★ **CAL-NEVA RESORT HOTEL/SPA & CASINO.** *2 Stateline Rd (89402), W on NV 28. 775/832-4000; FAX 775/831-9007; res: 800/225-6382.* E-mail calnevaresort@worldnet.att.net; web www.calnevaresort.com. 200 rms, 9 story. S, D $69-$169; suites $199-$269; under 10 free; higher rates hols (2-4-day min). Crib $10. TV; cable. Heated pool; whirlpool. Complimentary coffee in rms. Restaurant 7 am-11 pm; summer to 2 am. Bar. Ck-out noon. Meeting rms. Business servs avail. Concierge. Shopping arcade. Barber, beauty shop. Tennis. Exercise equipt; sauna. Massage. Balconies. On lake. Cr cds: A, C, D, DS, ER, JCB, MC, V.

D SC

★★★ **HYATT REGENCY LAKE TAHOE.** *111 Country Club Dr (89450), Lakeshore Blvd & Country Club Dr. 775/832-1234; FAX 775/831-7508.* 458 rms, 12 story. June-Sept, wkends, hols: S, D $205-$280; each addl $30; suites $500-$650; cottages $700-$850; under 18 free; ski plans; lower rates rest of yr. Crib free. TV; cable (premium). Heated pool; whirlpool, poolside serv. Supervised child's activities (daily in season; Fri, Sat evenings off-season); ages 3-12. Restaurant open 24 hrs. Rm serv. Bar. Ck-out 11 am. Convention facilities. Business center. Concierge. Shopping arcade. Free valet parking. Downhill ski 1½ mi; x-country ski 6 mi. Exercise rm; sauna, steam rm. Massage. Arcade Rec rm. Lawn games. Bicycles avail. Minibars; some refrigerators. Wet bar in cottages. Cottages have balconies. Casino. Private beach. Luxury level. Cr cds: A, C, D, DS, ER, JCB, MC, V.

D SC

★★ **TAHOE BILTMORE LODGE & CASINO.** *5 Hwy 28 (89402). 775/831-0660; FAX 775/833-6715; res: 800/245-8667.* E-mail fun@tahoebiltmore.com.; web www.tahoebiltmore. com. 92 rms, 4 story. June-Sept: S $39-$99; D $49-$109; hols (2-day min); lower rates rest of yr. Crib $10. TV; cable (premium). Complimentary full bkfst. Restaurant open 24 hrs. Bar; entertainment. Ck-out 11 am. Meeting rms. Business servs avail. Downhill/x-country ski 5 mi. Pool. Some refrigerators, microwaves. Some balconies. Opp beach. Cr cds: A, C, D, DS, MC, V.

D SC

Restaurants

★ **LAS PANCHITAS.** *930 Tahoe Blvd NV 28 (89451), in Raley's Shopping Center. 702/831-4048.* Hrs: 11 am-10 pm; Sat, Sun from noon. Closed Thanksgiving, Dec 25. Mexican menu. Bar. Semi-a la carte: lunch $5.25-$11.95, dinner $7.55-$11.95. Specialties: fajitas, chile rellenos. Outdoor dining. Rustic Mexican decor. Cr cds: A, C, MC, V.

★★★ **LONE EAGLE GRILLE ON THE LAKE.** *(See Hyatt Regency Lake Tahoe) 775/832-3250.* Hrs: 11:30 am-2:30 pm, 6-10 pm; Sun brunch 10:30 am-2:30 pm. Res accepted. Bar 11 am-midnight. Wine cellar. Semi-a la carte: lunch $12-$16, dinner $30-$40. Sun brunch $25. Child's meals. Specialties: prime rib, eagle-rubbed chicken. Guitarist & vocalist Fri, Sat. Valet parking. Outdoor dining. Cr cds: A, C, D, DS, ER, JCB, MC, V.

D

Lake Mead National Recreation Area (J-6 - H-6)

(See also Boulder City, Overton)

(4 mi NE of Boulder City on US 93)

This 2,627-square-mile tract extends along the Colorado River from Grand Canyon National Park to a point below Davis Dam. It is a land of colorful deserts, high plateaus, narrow canyons and two magnificent lakes. Lake Mead, impounded by Hoover Dam (726 feet high), is by volume the largest man-made reservoir; 110 miles long, with a shoreline of 550 miles when full, with a maximum depth of 500 feet. Lake Mohave, formed behind Davis Dam, is 67 miles long with a shoreline of 150 miles. The dams are part of an irrigation, reclamation and power project of the federal government. More than ten million people use the recreational facilities yearly. The Alan Bible Visitor Center on US 93 is open daily except Jan 1, Thanksgiving and Dec 25.

What to See and Do

Davis Dam (see BULLHEAD CITY, AZ).

Hoover Dam. Tour of dam and powerhouse (daily; closed Dec 25). Exhibit building houses model of a generating unit and topographical model of Colorado River Basin. About 8 mi E of Boulder City on US 93. Phone 702/293-8421 or 702/294-3523. Tour ¢¢¢

Lake Mead Cruises. One-and-one-half-hr sightseeing cruise to Hoover Dam on paddlewheeler *Desert Princess.* Bkfst and dinner cruises avail. (Daily exc Dec 25) Concessioner of National Park Service. Lake Mead Marina. 7 mi E of Boulder City on Lakeshore Dr, at Lake Mead Resort Area. For details phone 702/293-6180. ¢¢¢¢

Swimming, fishing, boating, camping, hiking. Developed areas in Arizona: Willow Beach on Lake Mohave, 18 mi S of Hoover Dam (no camping); Temple Bar on Lake Mead, 50 mi E of Hoover Dam; Katherine on Lake Mohave, 3 mi N of Davis Dam (campgrounds, stores, restaurants, motels, marinas, boat ramps in these areas). Developed areas in Nevada: Boulder Beach on Lake Mead, 6 mi NE of Boulder City; Las Vegas Bay, 10 mi NE of Henderson; Callville Bay, 24 mi NE of Henderson; Overton Beach, 9 mi S of Overton; Echo Bay, 23 mi S of Overton; Cottonwood Cove, 14 mi E of Searchlight. (All these sites, except Willow Beach and Overton Beach, have campgrounds, $10/site/night; stores, restaurants, marinas and boat ramps.) For information contact Superintendent, Lake Mead National Recreation Area, 601 Nevada Hwy, Boulder City 89005-2426; phone 702/293-8906.

Lake Tahoe

(see Lake Tahoe Area, CA)

Las Vegas (H-5)

(See also Boulder City, Henderson)

Settled 1905 **Pop** 258,295 **Elev** 2,020 ft **Area Code** 702
Web www.lasvegas24hours.com

Information Las Vegas Convention/Visitors Authority, Convention Center, 3150 Paradise Rd, 89109; 702/892-0711

Las Vegas, Nevada's largest city, became a major entertainment center after World War II. Near Hoover Dam and Lake Mead National Recreation Area (see), the city has public buildings and entertainment facilities designed to attract vacationers. Famous for glittering nightclubs, bars, gambling casinos and plush hotels, Las Vegas also offers tennis, racquetball, bowling, water sports, snow skiing, golf, fishing and hunting, hiking and riding trails, and tours to nearby points of interest. The townsite covers 53 square miles on a plain encircled by distant mountains. Beyond its suburban fringe lies the desert.

Two natural springs and green meadows made the Las Vegas valley a favorite camping place in the 1840s for caravans following the Old Spanish Trail from Santa Fe to California. It was first settled by the Spanish in 1829. American settlement began in 1855 when Brigham Young sent 30 settlers to build a fort and stockade here. The Mormons tried mining in the area but found that the ore was hard to smelt and the metal made poor bullets. Later this "lead" was discovered to be a galena ore carrying silver.

The Mormons abandoned the settlement in 1857; from 1862 to 1899 it was operated as a ranch. Las Vegas was really born in 1905 with the advent of the railroad. A tent town sprang up; streets were laid out, and permanent buildings followed. In 1911 the city of Las Vegas was created by an act of the legislature.

A Ranger District office of the Toiyabe National Forest (see RENO) is located here.

Transportation

Las Vegas McCarran Intl Airport. Information 702/261-5733; weather 702/248-4800.

Car Rental Agencies. See IMPORTANT TOLL-FREE NUMBERS.

Public Transportation. Citizens Area Transit, 702/228-7433.

Rail Passenger Service. Amtrak 800/872-7245.

What to See and Do

Air Nevada Airlines. Day trips to Grand Canyon. For schedule and information contact PO Box 11105, 89111; Phone 702/736-8900 or 800/634-6377. ¢¢¢¢¢

Bonnie Springs Old Nevada. Historic Western mining town features narrow-gauge railroad, museums, shops, entertainment; 1890 melodramas. Also restaurants, motel, riding stables and petting zoo. (Daily) 20 mi W via W Charleston Blvd. Phone 702/875-4191. ¢¢¢

Convention Center. The largest single-level convention center in the country; 1.3 million sq ft of exhibit and meeting space. Paradise Rd, S of town. Phone 702/892-0711.

Factory Stores of America. More than 50 outlet stores. (Daily) 9155 S Las Vegas Blvd. Phone 702/897-9090.

Floyd Lamb State Park. Approx 2,000 acres. Small lakes; fishing. Picnicking. No overnight camping. 10 mi N via US 95. Phone 702/486-5413. Per vehicle ¢¢

Guinness World of Records Museum. Interactive computers bring the famous Guinness book to life. Displays; rare videos; special exhibit on Las

Vegas. Gift shop. (Daily) 2780 Las Vegas Blvd S. Phone 702/792-3766. ¢¢

Imperial Palace Auto Collection. More than 200 antique and classic cars on display. Large collection of Duesenbergs. Also cars belonging to Adolf Hitler, the King of Siam, Eleanor Roosevelt, Howard Hughes, Al Capone. (Daily) 3535 Las Vegas Blvd, on 5th-floor parking area of hotel. Phone 702/731-3311 or 702/794-3174. ¢¢¢

Las Vegas Art Museum. The main gallery features local, national and international artists. Changing monthly exhibits. (Daily exc Mon; closed hols) 9600 W Sahara Ave. Phone 702/360-8000. ¢¢

Las Vegas Motor Speedway. Motorsports complex covers 1,500 acres and features a 1½-mi superspeedway, 2½-mi road course, ½-mi dirt oval, drag strip, Go-Kart tracks, racing schools and fantasy camps and other attractions. Home to NASCAR, IRL & AMA racing. Tours. (Daily; event schedule varies) 7000 Las Vegas Blvd N. Phone 702/644-4444 (information) or -4443 (tickets).

Las Vegas Natural History Museum. Wildlife collection featuring animated dinosaurs and shark exhibits. (Daily; closed Thanksgiving, Dec 25) 900 Las Vegas Blvd N. Phone 702/384-3466. ¢¢

Liberace Museum. Displays memorabilia of Liberace's career, including antique and custom cars, miniature and full-size pianos, the world's largest rhinestone and a portion of his million-dollar wardrobe. Showcases contain awards, gifts from fans and dignitaries and personal items. (Daily; closed Jan 1, Dec 25) 1775 E Tropicana Ave, 2½ mi E of Strip. Phone 702/798-5595. ¢¢¢

Mt Charleston Recreation Area. Picnicking. Camping (fee). 15 mi NW on US 95, then 21 mi W on NV 157, which leads to Toiyabe National Forest (see RENO). Phone 702/873-8800. Per vehicle ¢¢

Nevada State Museum and Historical Society. Exhibits explore the growth of southern Nevada from Spanish explorers to present. The natural history of the area is presented in the Hall of Biological Science. Changing exhibits on art, history of the region. (Daily; closed Jan 1, Thanksgiving, Dec 25) 700 Twin Lakes Dr, in Lorenzi Park. Phone 702/486-5205. ¢

★ **Red Rock Canyon National Conservation Area.** Spectacular view of the area's steep canyons and red and white hues of the Aztec sandstone formation. Picnicking, hiking trails, rock climbing; 13-mi scenic drive (daylight hrs only); limited primitive camping. Visitor center; nature walks led by Bureau of Land Management ranger-naturalists. 18 mi W on W Charleston Blvd. Phone 702/363-1921. Per vehicle ¢¢ Nearby is

Spring Mountain Ranch State Park. Visitor center at main ranch house (daily; closed Jan 1, Thanksgiving, Dec 25) has brochures with self-guided tours of park and interpretive trails. Guided tours of ranch buildings (wkends & hols). Picnicking. (Daily) Approx 18 mi W on W Charleston Blvd. Phone 702/875-4141. Per vehicle ¢¢

Southern Nevada Zoological Park. Apes, monkeys; tiger; ostriches, exotic bird collection and Southwestern desert animals. Also here is an endangered species breeding program. (Daily; closed Jan 1, Thanksgiving, Dec 25) 1775 N Rancho Dr. Phone 702/647-4685. ¢¢

★ **The Strip.** Las Vegas's biggest attraction, with dazzling casinos, roulette wheels, luxurious hotels, glamorous chorus lines and top entertainers. Some shows are free; some require buying food or drink. Make reservations. Las Vegas Blvd, S of town.

University of Nevada, Las Vegas (1957). (19,500 students) Campus tours arranged in advance by calling 702/895-3443. 4505 Maryland Pkwy, 1½ mi E of Strip. For university activities open to the public, phone 702/895-3131. On campus are

Artemus W. Ham Concert Hall. A 1,900-seat theater featuring yrly Charles Vanda Master Series of symphony, opera and ballet. Jazz and popular music concerts also performed here. Box office phone 702/895-3801.

Donna Beam Fine Art Gallery. Exhibits by professional artists, faculty, students; emphasis on contemporary art. (Mon-Fri; closed major hols) Phone 702/895-3893. **Free**

The Flashlight. A 38-ft-tall steel sculpture by Claes Oldenburg and Coosje von Bruggen.

Judy Bayley Theatre. Varied theatrical performances all yr. Box office phone 702/895-3801.

Marjorie Barrick Museum of Natural History. Exhibits of the biology, geology and archaeology of the Las Vegas area, including live desert animals. (Daily exc Sun; closed major hols) Phone 702/895-3381. **Free**

Thomas and Mack Center. 18,500-seat events center features concerts, ice shows, rodeos, sporting events. Phone 702/895-3900.

Wet 'n Wild. Aquatic amusement park featuring 75-ft water slide; rafting (rentals), flumes, water cannons, whirlpools, whitewater rapids, waterfalls, pools, lagoon, 4-ft waves and children's activities. Picnicking; snack bars. (May-Sept, daily) 2601 Las Vegas Blvd S. Phone 702/737-3819. ¢¢¢¢¢

Annual Events

Helldorado Days. Rodeos, parades, carnival, street dance, chili cook-off; Western theme throughout. Phone 702/870-1221. May or June.

Las Vegas Invitational. PGA tournament with more than $1 million in prize money. Oct.

National Finals Rodeo. Thomas and Mack Center. Nation's richest professional rodeo, featuring 15 finalists in 7 rodeo disciplines. Dec.

Motels

✓★ **ARIZONA CHARLIE'S HOTEL & CASINO.** *740 S Decatur Ave (89107), west of the Strip. 702/258-5200; FAX 702/258-5196; res: 800/342-2695.* Web www.azcharlies.com. 257 rms, 7 story. S, D $38-$69; suites $95-$115. Crib free. TV. Pool; lifeguard. Restaurant open 24 hrs. Bar. Ck-out 11 am. Bellhops. Business servs avail. Valet serv. Gift shop. Airport transportation. Casino. Cr cds: A, C, D, DS, MC, V.

D SC

★★ **BEST WESTERN MCCARRAN INN.** *4970 Paradise Rd (89119), near McCarran Intl Airport, east of the Strip . 702/798-5530; FAX 702/798-7627; res: 800/626-7575.* Web www.bestwestern.com/thisco/bw/29058/29058b.html. 99 rms, 3 story. S, D $49-$129; each addl $7; suites $90-$179; under 17 free; higher rates: national hols, major events. TV. Pool. Complimentary continental bkfst. Coffee in rms. Restaurant nearby. Coin Indry. Ck-out noon. Business servs avail. Free airport transportation. Cr cds: A, C, D, DS, ER, JCB, MC, V.

D SC

✓★ **CENTER STRIP INN.** *3688 Las Vegas Blvd S (89109), on the Strip. 702/739-6066; FAX 702/736-2521; res: 800/777-7737.* 156 rms, 5 story, 44 suites. S, D $29.95-$89.95; each addl $10; suites $69-$189; under 18 free. Pet accepted. TV; cable (premium), VCR (movies $3). Pool. Complimentary continental bkfst. Ck-out 11 am. Business servs avail. In-rm modem link. Refrigerators; whirlpool in suites. Cr cds: A, C, D, DS, ER, JCB, MC, V.

D SC

★ **COMFORT INN.** *211 East Flamingo Rd (89109), east of the Strip. 702/733-7800; FAX 702/733-7353; res: 800/634-6774.* 121 rms, 2 story. S, D $55-$125; under 12 free. TV; cable (premium). Pool. Complimentary continental bkfst. Ck-out 11 am. Cr cds: A, C, D, DS, MC, V.

D SC

✓★ **COMFORT INN.** *5075 Koval Ln (89119), near McCarran Intl Airport, east of the Strip. 702/736-3600; FAX 702/736-0726; res: 888/844-3131.* 106 rms, 2 story. S, D $42-$160; under 18 free. Crib free. TV; cable (premium). Pool. Complimentary continental bkfst. Restaurant adj open 24 hrs. Ck-out 11 am. Business servs avail. Cr cds: A, C, D, DS, ER, JCB, MC, V.

D SC

★ **DAYS INN.** *707 E Fremont St (89101). 702/388-1400; FAX 702/388-9622; res: 800/325-2344.* 147 units, 3 story. Feb-Nov: S $28-$120; D $32-$120; each addl $10; suites $60-$200; under 18 free; lower rates rest of yr. Crib free. TV. Pool. Restaurant 7 am-7 pm. Ck-out noon. Cr cds: A, C, D, DS, JCB, MC, V.

D SC

★★ **FAIRFIELD INN BY MARRIOTT.** *3850 Paradise Rd (89109), near McCarran Intl Airport, east of the Strip. 702/791-0899; FAX 702/791-2705; res: 800/228-2800.* 129 rms, 4 story. S, D $62-$175; under 18 free. Crib free. TV; cable (premium). Heated pool; whirlpool. Complimentary continental bkfst. Restaurants nearby. Ck-out noon. Meeting rms. In-rm modem link. Free airport transportation. Cr cds: A, C, D, DS, JCB, MC, V.

D SC

★ **LA QUINTA INN.** *3782 Las Vegas Blvd S (89109), on the Strip. 702/739-7457; FAX 702/736-1129; res: 800/687-6667.* 114 rms, 3 story. S $69-$89; D $79-$99; each addl $10; under 18 free. Crib free. TV; cable. Pool. Complimentary continental bkfst. Restaurant nearby. Ck-out noon. Business servs avail. Free airport transportation. Cr cds: A, C, D, DS, MC, V.

D SC

★★ **RESIDENCE INN BY MARRIOTT.** *3225 Paradise Rd (89109), near McCarran Intl Airport, east of the Strip . 702/796-9300; FAX 702/796-9562; res: 800/331-3131.* 192 kit. units, 1-2 story. S, D $95-$219. Crib free. Pet accepted, some restrictions; $7/day. TV; cable (premium), VCR (movies $3.50). Heated pool; whirlpool. Complimentary continental bkfst. Restaurant adj 6:30 am-9 pm. Ck-out noon. Coin lndry. Meeting rms. Business servs avail. Free airport transportation. Balconies. Picnic tables, grills. Cr cds: A, C, D, DS, JCB, MC, V.

D SC

★★★ **ST. TROPEZ HOTEL.** *455 E Harmon Ave (89109), near McCarran Intl Airport, west of the Strip. 702/369-5400; FAX 702/369-1150; res: 800/666-5400.* 149 suites, 2 story. Suites $95-$250; family rates. Crib free. TV; VCR. Heated pool; poolside serv. Complimentary continental bkfst. Complimentary coffee in rms. Restaurant adj 11-3 am. Bar. Ck-out noon. Meeting rms. Business servs avail. In-rm modem link. Bellhops. Concierge. Shopping arcade. Airport transportation. Exercise equipt. Refrigerators, minibars. Cr cds: A, C, D, DS, ER, JCB, MC, V.

D SC

✓★ **TRAVELODGE.** *2028 E Fremont St (89101). 702/384-7540; FAX 702/384-0408; res: 800/578-7878.* 58 rms, 2 story. S, D $30-$70; each addl $5; family rates. Crib free. TV; cable. Pool. Complimentary coffee in rms. Restaurant nearby. Ck-out 11 am. Cr cds: A, C, D, DS, ER, JCB, MC, V.

SC

✓★ **TRAVELODGE INN.** *1501 W Sahara Ave (89102), west of the Strip. 702/733-0001; FAX 702/733-1571; res: 800/554-4092.* 223 rms, 4 story. S, D $39-$199; under 18 free. TV; cable (premium). Pool. Complimentary continental bkfst. Ck-out noon. Business servs avail. Gift shop. Cr cds: A, C, D, DS, ER, MC, V.

D SC

Motor Hotels

★★ **COURTYARD BY MARRIOTT.** *3275 Paradise Rd (89109), near McCarran Intl Airport, east of the Strip. 702/791-3600; FAX 702/796-7981; res: 800/244-3364.* 137 rms, 3 story, 12 suites. S, D $89-$119; higher rates: conventions, hol wkends. Crib free. TV; cable (premium). Heated pool; whirlpool. Complimentary coffee in rms. Restaurant 6:30 am-2 pm; 5-10 pm. Bar 5-11 pm. Ck-out noon. Coin lndry. Meeting rms. Business servs avail. In-rm modem link. Valet serv. Free airport transportation. Exercise equipt. Some refrigerators. Balconies. Cr cds: A, C, D, DS, ER, JCB, MC, V.

D SC

★★ **HOLIDAY INN.** *325 E Flamingo Rd (89109), near McCarran Intl Airport, east of the Strip. 702/732-9100; FAX 702/731-9784; res: 800/732-7889.* 150 units, 3 story, 140 suites. Mid-Sept-May: S, D $69-$175; each addl $15; suites $99-$165; under 19 free; higher rates: hols, special events; lower rates rest of yr. Crib free. TV; cable (premium), VCR avail. Heated pool; whirlpool, poolside serv. Complimentary coffee in rms. Restaurant 6:30 am-11 pm. Bar noon-2 am. Ck-out noon. Meeting rms. Concierge. Free airport transportation. Exercise equipt. Refrigerators; wet bars. Cr cds: A, C, D, DS, JCB, MC, V.

D SC

★★ **LA QUINTA INN.** *3970 Paradise Rd (89109), near McCarran Intl Airport, east of the Strip. 702/796-9000; FAX 702/796-3537; res: 800/687-6667.* 228 units, 3 story, 21 kits. S, D $75-$250; under 18 free. Crib free. TV; cable (premium). Pool. Complimentary continental bkfst. Ck-out noon. Coin lndry. Meeting rms. Business servs avail. In-rm modem link. Bellhops. Free airport transportation. In-rm whirlpools, refrigerators. Private patios, balconies. Cr cds: A, C, D, DS, ER, MC, V.

D SC

★★ **SILVERTON HOTEL CASINO.** *3333 Blue Diamond Rd (89139), S of the Strip. 702/263-7777; FAX 702/896-5635; res: 800/588-7711.* E-mail silverton@earthlink.net. 300 rms, 4 story. S, D $49-$70; suites $150-$200; under 12 free; higher rates hols. Crib avail. TV; cable (premium). 2 pools; wading pool, whirlpool, poolside serv, lifeguard. Restaurant open 24 hrs. Rm serv. Ck-out noon. Coin lndry. Meeting rms. Business servs avail. In-rm modem link. Shopping arcade. RV park. Cr cds: A, C, D, DS, ER, JCB, MC, V.

D SC

★ **WESTWARD HO CASINO & HOTEL.** *2900 Las Vegas Blvd S (89109), on the Strip. 702/731-2900; FAX 702/731-3544; res: 800/634-6803.* 777 rms, 2-4 story. S, D $37-$67; each addl $15; 2-bedrm apt $81-$111; package plan. Crib $15. TV. 4 pools, 1 heated; whirlpools. Restaurant open 24 hrs. Rm serv. Bars; entertainment. Ck-out 11 am. Free airport transportation. Some refrigerators; microwaves avail. Casino. Cr cds: A, C, MC, V.

D

Hotels

★★★ **ALEXIS PARK RESORT HOTEL.** *375 E Harmon Ave 89101 (89109), near McCarran Intl Airport, 1 mi E of the Strip. 702/796-3300; FAX 702/796-4334; res: 800/582-2228.* 500 suites, 2 story. 1-bedrm $85-$500; 2-bedrm $300-$1,150; each addl $15; under 12 free. Crib free. Pet accepted, some restrictions; $60. TV; cable (premium). 3 pools, 1 heated; whirlpool; poolside serv. Restaurant 6 am-3 pm, 6-11 pm (also see PEGASUS). Bar 4 pm-midnight; entertainment. Ck-out 11 am. Convention facilities. Business center. In-rm modem link. Concierge. Gift shop. Barber, beauty shop. Exercise equipt; sauna, steam rm. Refrigerators, minibars; some bathrm phones, in-rm whirlpools. Cr cds: A, C, D, DS, JCB, MC, V.

D

★★★ **BALLY'S.** *3645 Las Vegas Blvd (89109), on the Strip. 702/739-4111; FAX 702/967-4405; res: 800/634-3434.* Web www.ballys.com. 2,814 rms, 26 story. S, D $101-$191; each addl $15; suites $191-$2,600; under 18 free; package plans. Crib free. TV; cable (premium), VCR avail. Heated pool; whirlpool, poolside serv. Restaurant open 24 hrs. Bars; entertainment. Ck-out 11 am. Convention facilities. Business servs avail. In-rm modem link. Shopping arcade. Barber, beauty shop. Lighted tennis, pro. Exercise equipt; sauna. Game rm. Some bathrm phones, refrigerators. Casino, wedding chapel. Cr cds: A, C, D, DS, JCB, MC, V.

D SC

★★ **BARBARY COAST HOTEL.** *3595 Las Vegas Blvd S (89109), on the Strip. 702/737-7111; FAX 702/894-9954; res: 800/634-6755.* E-mail coastres@aol.com; web www.barbarycoastcasino.com. 200 rms, 8 story. S, D $39-$125; each addl $10; suites $200-$500; under 12 free. TV; cable (premium). Restaurant (see DRAI'S OF LAS VEGAS). Bar. Ck-out noon. Gift shop. Free valet, covered parking. Casino. Cr cds: A, C, D, DS, JCB, MC, V.

D

✓★ **BINIONS HORSESHOE HOTEL & CASINO.** *128 East Fremont 89101 702/382-1600; FAX 702/382-1574; res: 800/237-6537.* 369

rms, 22 story. S, D $40-$60. Crib $8. TV; cable (premium). Pool; lifeguard. Restaurant open 24 hrs. Bar. Ck-out noon. Gift shop. Casino. Cr cds: A, C, D, DS, ER, JCB, MC, V.

D

★★★ **BOULDER STATION HOTEL & CASINO.** *4111 Boulder Hwy (89112), off I-515, east of the Strip. 702/432-7777; FAX 702/432-7744; res: 800/683-7777.* Web www.boulderstation.com. 300 rms, 16 story. S, D $49-$109; suites $125-$250; under 12 free. Crib free. TV; cable. Pool. Restaurant open 24 hrs. Ck-out noon. Business servs avail. In-rm modem link. Shopping arcade. Victorian-era railroad decor. Cr cds: A, C, D, DS, ER, MC, V.

D

★ **BOURBON STREET HOTEL & CASINO.** *120 E Flamingo Rd (91761), W of the Strip. 702/737-7200; FAX 702/794-3490; res: 800/634-6956.* 166 rms, 9 story. S, D $39-$99; under 17 free. TV. Pool privileges. Restaurant open 24 hrs. Ck-out noon. Meeting rms. Concierge. Gift shop. Near airport. Cr cds: A, C, D, DS, MC, V.

D SC

★★★★ **CAESARS PALACE.** *3570 Las Vegas Blvd S (89109), 1 blk E of I-15 Dunes/Flamingo exit, on the Strip. 702/731-7110; FAX 702/731-6636; res: 800/634-6001.* E-mail guest@lv.caesars.com; web www.caesars.com. A cross between Ancient Rome and Disney World, this gigantic casino hotel is classic Vegas. The amenities—pools, shopping mall, meeting rooms, entertainment—are exceptional. Service is efficient. 2,500 rms, 14-32 story. S, D $79-$500; each addl $15; suites $275-$5,000; under 13 free. TV; cable (premium), VCR avail (movies). 3 pools; 2 whirlpools, lifeguard. Restaurant open 24 hrs (also see EMPRESS COURT and PALACE COURT). Bars. Circus Maximus, star entertainment. Ck-out noon. Convention facilities. Business center. In-rm modem link. Concierge. Shopping arcade. Barber, beauty shop. Free parking. Exercise rm; sauna, steam rm. Massage. Solarium. Racquetball. Handball. Game rm. Casino. Bathrm phones; many whirlpools; some refrigerators. Many bi-level suites with wet bar. Cr cds: A, C, D, DS, JCB, MC, V.

D

✓★★ **CALIFORNIA HOTEL & CASINO.** *12 Ogden St (89101), I-95 Casino Center exit. 702/385-1222; FAX 702/388-2670; res: 800/634-6255.* 781 rms, 11 story. S, D $40-$60; each addl $10; under 12 free; package plans. Crib free. TV. Pool. Restaurant open 24 hrs. Bar. Ck-out noon. Gift shop. Refrigerators. Casino. Cr cds: A, C, D, DS, JCB, MC, V.

D

★★ **CARRIAGE HOUSE.** *105 E Harmon Ave (89109), east of the Strip. 702/798-1020; FAX 702/798-1020; res: 800/221-2301.* 154 kit. suites, 9 story. S, D $125-$275; children free; wkly rates; higher rates: special events, hols. Crib free. TV; cable (premium). Heated pool; whirlpool. Complimentary coffee in rms. Restaurant 7-10 am, 5-11 pm. Bar from 5 pm. Ck-out 11 am. Coin lndry. Business servs avail. In-rm modem link. Free airport transportation. Tennis. Microwaves. Cr cds: A, C, D, DS, ER, MC, V.

D SC

✓★★ **CIRCUS CIRCUS HOTEL & CASINO.** *2880 Las Vegas Blvd S (89109), S on the Strip. 702/734-0410; FAX 702/734-5897; res: 800/634-3450.* Web www.circuscircus-lasvegas.com. 3,744 rms, 3-29 story. S, D $39-$99; each addl $10; suites $99-$650; under 12 free. Crib $10. TV. 3 pools, 1 heated; poolside serv, lifeguard. Restaurants open 24 hrs (also see THE STEAK HOUSE). Bars; entertainment. Ck-out 11 am. Meeting rms. Business servs avail. In-rm modem link. Shopping arcade. Barber, beauty shop. Health club privileges. Casino, performing circus and midway housed together in tent-like structure. Cr cds: A, C, D, DS, MC, V.

D

★★ **CROWNE PLAZA HOTEL.** *4255 S Paradise Rd (89109), near McCarran Intl Airport, east of the Strip. 702/369-4400; FAX 702/369-3770; res: 800/227-6963.* Web www.crowneplaza.com. 201 suites, 6 story. S, D $145-$250; each addl $20; under 18 free. Crib free. Pet accepted. TV; cable (premium), VCR avail. Heated pool; whirlpool, poolside serv. Complimentary coffee in rms. Restaurant 6 am-2 pm, 5-10 pm. Bar 11 am-midnight. Ck-out noon. Meeting rms. Business center. In-rm modem link. Concierge. Gift shop. Free airport transportation. Exercise equipt; sauna. Minibars. Cr cds: A, C, D, DS, ER, JCB, MC, V.

D

★★★ **DESERT INN.** *3145 Las Vegas Blvd S (89109), on the Strip. 702/733-4444; FAX 702/733-4790; res: 800/634-6909.* 715 rms, 7-15 story. S, D $100-$390; each addl $35; suites $350-$10,000. Crib free. TV; cable (premium), VCR avail (movies). Heated pool; whirlpool, poolside serv, lifeguard. Restaurant (see MONTE CARLO). Rm serv 24 hrs. Bars open 24 hrs; Crystal Room, theater, star entertainment. Ck-out noon. Convention facilities. Business center. In-rm modem link. Concierge. Shopping arcade. Free valet parking. Lighted tennis, pro. 18-hole golf, greens fee, putting green, driving range. Exercise rm; sauna, steam rm. Bathrm phones, refrigerators; wet bar in suites. Private patios, balconies. Casino. Resort hotel on 160 acres. Cr cds: A, C, D, DS, JCB, MC, V.

D

✓★ **EL CORTEZ HOTEL & CASINO.** *600 E Fremont St (89125). 702/385-5200; FAX 702/385-9765; res: 800/634-6703.* 303 rms, 15 story. S, D $18-$40; each addl $3. Crib free. TV; cable (premium). Restaurant 4:30-11 pm. Rm serv 7 am-7 pm. Bar open 24 hrs. Ck-out noon. Meeting rms. Shopping arcade. Barber, beauty shop. Free valet parking. Casino. Cr cds: A, C, DS, JCB, MC, V.

D

★★ **EXCALIBUR HOTEL & CASINO.** *3850 Las Vegas Blvd S (89109), on the Strip. 702/597-7777; FAX 702/597-7009; res: 800/937-7777.* Web www.excalibur-casino.com. 4,008 rms, 28 story. S, D $55-$89; each addl $12; suites $275; higher rates: wkends, hols. Crib $10. TV; cable (premium). 2 heated pools; poolside serv, lifeguard. Restaurants open 24 hrs (also see CAMELOT and SIR GALLAHAD'S). Dinner theater. Bar open 24 hrs; entertainment. Ck-out 11 am. Business servs avail. In-rm modem link. Health club privileges. Shopping arcade. Barber, beauty shop. Whirlpool in suites. Casino. Castle-like structure with medieval/old English interiors based upon legend of King Arthur and Round Table. Cr cds: A, C, D, DS, MC, V.

D

★ **FIESTA HOTEL/CASINO.** *2400 N Rancho Dr (89130). 702/631-7000; FAX 702/631-6588; res: 800/731-7333.* 100 rms, 5 story. S, D $49-$129; under 18 free. Crib free. TV; cable. Restaurant open 24 hrs (also see GARDUÑOS). No rm serv. Ck-out noon. Meeting rms. Gift shop. Heated pool. Casino. Near North Las Vegas Airport. Cr cds: A, C, D, DS, ER, MC, V.

D

✓★★ **FITZGERALDS CASINO HOLIDAY HOTEL.** *301 Fremont St (89101), west of the Strip. 702/388-2400; FAX 702/388-2181; res: 800/274-5825.* Web www.fitzgeralds.comm. 638 rms, 34 story, 14 suites. S, D $40-$90; suites $150-$450; under 18 free. Crib $10. TV. Restaurant open 24 hrs. Rm serv. Bar. Ck-out noon. Business servs avail. Concierge. Gift shop. Casino. Cr cds: A, C, D, DS, ER, JCB, MC, V.

D

★★★ **FLAMINGO HILTON.** *3555 Las Vegas Blvd S (89109), on the Strip. 702/733-3111; FAX 702/733-3528; res: 800/732-2111.* 3,642 rms, 28 story. S, D $69-$205; each addl $16; suites $250-$580; family rates; package plan. Crib free. TV; cable (premium). 5 pools; whirlpools, poolside serv, lifeguard. Restaurant open 24 hrs. Bar; stage show. Ck-out noon. Convention center. Business center. In-rm modem link. Shopping arcade. Barber, beauty shop. Free valet parking. Tennis privileges. Exercise equipt; sauna, steam rm. Some bathrm phones; refrigerators avail. Casino. Cr cds: A, C, D, DS, ER, JCB, MC, V.

D SC

★★ **FOUR QUEENS HOTEL & CASINO.** *202 E Fremont (89101), at Casino Center Blvd. 702/385-4011; FAX 702/387-5133; res: 800/634-6045.* Web www.fourqueens.comm. 700 rms, 19 story. S, D $45-$125; each addl $15; suites $99-$200; under 2 free. TV. Restaurant open

24 hrs (also see FOUR QUEENS); dining rm 6 pm-midnight. Bar; entertainment. Ck-out noon. Meeting rms. Business servs avail. Garage parking. Wet bar in suites. Casino. Cr cds: A, C, D, DS, MC, V.

D SC

✓★★★★ **FOUR SEASONS HOTEL LAS VEGAS.** *3960 Las Vegas Blvd S (89119). 702/632-5000; FAX 702/632-5195; res: 877/639-5000.* This welcome respite from the casino din actually comprises the top floors of the Mandalay Bay Resort. A separate lobby, restaurant, and pool ensure privacy. The service is friendly and attentive. 424 rooms, 5 floors. $200 Sun-Thurs $300 Fri & Sat; Presidential suite $3,000-$3,100. Children under 18 free. Cribs. Pet allowed; restrictions; TV. Exercise room. Pool. Conceirge. Valet; 24 hr room service. First floor grill. Bar 5 pm-midnight. Handicap accessible. Airport 2 mi. Cr cd: C.

✓★ **FREMONT HOTEL & CASINO.** *200 E Fremont St (89101). 702/385-3232; FAX 702/385-6229; res: 800/634-6182.* 423 rms, 14 story. S, D $46-$150; suites $80-$150; package plan. TV. Restaurant open 24 hrs. Bars. Ck-out noon. Gift shop. Casino. Cr cds: A, C, D, DS, JCB, MC, V.

✓★★ **FRONTIER HOTEL & GAMBLING HALL.** *3120 Las Vegas Blvd S (89109). 702/794-8200; FAX 702/735-8200; res: 800/421-7806; res: 800/634-6966.* 980 rms, 16 story, 384 suites. S $35-$65; D $55-$95; suites $65-$95; under 12 free; wkends, hols (min stay required); higher rates special events. Crib free. TV. Restaurant open 24 hrs. Bar. Ck-out noon. Meeting rms. Business center. In-rm modem link. Concierge. Shopping arcade. Barber, beauty shop. Lighted tennis. Pool; whirlpool, poolside serv, lifeguard. Some bathrm phones. Cr cds: A, C, D, DS, ER, MC, V.

D

★★ **GOLD COAST HOTEL & CASINO.** *4000 W Flamingo Rd (89103), at Valley View Blvd, west of the Strip. 702/367-7111; FAX 702/367-8575; res: 888/402-6278.* 711 rms, 10 story. S, D $55-$75; suites $125-$400; family rates; package plan. TV; cable (premium). Pool. Supervised child's activities. Restaurant open 24 hrs. Bars; entertainment. Ck-out noon. Convention facilities. Business servs avail. Barber, beauty shop. Free valet parking. Game rm. Bowling. Some bathrm phones. Casino. Movie theaters. Dance hall. Cr cds: A, C, D, DS, ER, JCB, MC, V.

D SC

✓★ **GOLD SPIKE HOTEL & CASINO.** *400 E Ogden Ave (89101). 702/384-8444; FAX 702/384-8768; res: 800/634-6703.* 109 rms, 7 story. S, D $22; suites $33; under 12 free. TV. Restaurant open 24 hrs. Ck-out noon. Business servs avail. Cr cds: A, C, D, DS, ER, MC, V.

D

★★★ **GOLDEN NUGGET.** *129 E Fremont St (89101), at Casino Center. 702/385-7111; FAX 702/386-8362; res: 800/634-3454.* Web www.goldennugget.com. 1,907 rms, 18-22 story. S, D $59-$129; each addl $20; suites $275-$750. Crib free. TV; cable, VCR avail. Heated pool; whirlpool, poolside serv, lifeguard. Restaurants open 24 hrs (also see LILY LANGTRY'S and STEFANO'S). Bar; entertainment. Ck-out noon. Convention facilities. Business center. In-rm modem link. Gift shop. Barber, beauty shop. Exercise rm; sauna, steam rm. Massage. Casino. Some bathrm phones. Cr cds: A, C, D, DS, JCB, MC, V.

D

★★★ **HARD ROCK.** *4455 Paradise Rd (89109). 702/693-5000; FAX 702/693-5010; res: 800/473-7625.* Web www.hardrock.com. 340 rms, 11 story. S, D $75-$300; suites $250-$500. Crib free. TV; cable (premium). Pool; lifeguard. Restaurants (see MORTONI'S, and see HARD ROCK CAFE, Unrated Dining). Ck-out noon. Concierge. Sundries. Gift shop. Exercise rm. Cr cds: A, C, D, DS, ER, JCB, MC, V.

D

★★★ **HARRAH'S CASINO HOTEL.** *3475 Las Vegas Blvd S (89109), on the Strip. 702/369-5000; FAX 702/369-5040; res: 800/427-7247.* Web harrahs.com. 2,673 rms, 35 story. S, D $50-$300; each addl $15; suites $395-$1,800; under 12 free; higher rates special events. Crib $10. TV; cable. Pool; whirlpool, poolside serv, lifeguard. Restaurant (see THE RANGE STEAKHOUSE). Bar; entertainment exc Sun. Ck-out noon. Coin lndry. Convention facilities. Business servs avail. Shopping arcade. Barber, beauty shop. Valet parking; covered parking free. Exercise equipt; sauna. Massage. Game rm. Balconies. Casino. Wedding chapel. Cr cds: A, C, D, DS, JCB, MC, V.

D

★★★ **HILTON.** *3000 Paradise Rd (89109), east of the Strip. 702/732-5111; FAX 702/794-3611; res: 800/732-7117.* Web www.lv/hilton.com. 3,170 rms, 30 story. S, D $99-$349; each addl $25; 1-2 bedrm suites $340-$835; lanai suites $330-$350. Crib free. TV. Rooftop pool; whirlpool, poolside serv, lifeguard. Restaurant open 24 hrs (also see LE MONTRACHET). Bars; entertainment. Ck-out noon. Convention facilities. Business center. In-rm modem link. Shopping arcade. Barber, beauty shop. Free valet parking. Lighted tennis, pro. Golf privileges, greens fee $80, putting green. Exercise rm; sauna. Massage. Game rm. Some bathrm phones, refrigerators. Private patios, balconies. Casino. Cr cds: A, C, D, DS, JCB, MC, V.

D

★★ **HOTEL SAN REMO.** *115 E Tropicana Ave (89109), near McCarran Intl Airport, east of the Strip. 702/739-9000; FAX 702/736-1120; res: 800/522-7366.* E-mail hotelsanremo@mindspring.com; web www.sanremolasvegas.com. 711 rms, 19 story. S, D $59-$199; each addl $15; suites $125-$500; higher rates: hols, conventions. Crib $15. TV. Heated pool; poolside serv. Restaurant open 24 hrs, dining rm 5-11 pm. Bar; entertainment. Ck-out 11 am. Meeting rms. Business servs avail. In-rm modem link. Gift shop. Free garage parking. Casino. Cr cds: A, C, D, DS, ER, JCB, MC, V.

D

★ **IMPERIAL PALACE HOTEL AND CASINO.** *3535 Las Vegas Blvd S (89109), on the Strip. 702/731-3311; FAX 702/735-8328; res: 800/634-6441.* Web www.imperialpalace.com. 2,700 rms, 19 story. S, D $39-$99; each addl $15; suites $159-$499; package plan; higher rates hols. Crib $15. TV; cable (premium). Pool; whirlpool. Restaurant open 24 hrs. Bar; entertainment. Ck-out noon. Convention facilities. Business servs avail. In-rm modem link. Shopping arcade. Barber, beauty shop. Free valet, covered parking. Exercise equipt. Some bathrm phones, refrigerators. Private balconies. Casino. Antique auto exhibit. Cr cds: A, C, D, DS, JCB, MC, V.

D

★★ **LADY LUCK CASINO HOTEL.** *206 N 3rd St (89101). 702/477-3000; FAX 702/477-7021; res: 800/523-9582.* Web www.ladyluck.com/ladyluck. 792 rms, 17 & 25 story. Feb-Mar, Sept-Oct: S, D $39-$99; suites $49-$100; package plans; lower rates rest of yr. TV. Pool. Restaurant open 24 hrs. Bar. Ck-out noon. Free garage parking. Airport transportation. Refrigerators. Casino. Cr cds: A, C, D, DS, JCB, MC, V.

D

✓★★ **LAS VEGAS CLUB HOTEL & CASINO.** *18 E Fremont St (89109). 702/385-1664; FAX 702/380-5789; res: 800/634-6532.* 410 rms, 16 story. S, D $40-$55; under 12 free; higher rates: hols, special events. Crib free. TV; cable. Restaurant open 24 hrs. Ck-out noon. Business servs avail. Shopping arcade. Cr cds: C.

★★★ **LUXOR HOTEL & CASINO.** *3900 Las Vegas Blvd S (89119), near McCarran Intl Airport, on the Strip. 702/262-4000; FAX 702/262-4857; res: 800/288-1000.* Web www.luxor.com. 4,407 rms, 30 story, 473 suites. S, D $59-$359; suites $159-$800; under 12 free. Crib $10. TV; cable (premium), VCR avail. 5 pools, 1 heated; wading pool, poolside serv, lifeguard. Restaurants open 24 hrs (also see SACRED SEA). Bar; entertainment. Ck-out 11 am. Business center. Concierge. Shopping arcade. Barber, beauty shop. Massage. Exercise equipt; sauna. Casino. Pyramid-shaped hotel with replica of the Great Sphinx of Giza. Extensive landscaping with Egyptian theme. Cr cds: A, C, D, DS, JCB, MC, V.

D

✓★★★ **MAIN STREET STATION.** *200 N Main St (89101). 702/387-1896; FAX 702/388-4421; res: 800/713-8933.* 406 rms, 15 story.

S, D $45-$105; suites $80-$105; higher rates hols. Crib free. TV; cable (premium). Restaurant open 24 hrs. Ck-out noon. Meeting rms. Business center. In-rm modem link. Concierge. Shopping arcade. Cr cds: A, C, D, DS, ER, MC, V.

★ **MAXIM HOTEL 7 CASINO.** *160 E Flamingo (89109), W of the Strip. 702/731-4300; FAX 702/735-3252; res: 800/634-6987.* E-mail maxim@anu.net; web www.maximhotel.com. 795 rms, 17 story. S, D $39-$98; suites $175-$305. Crib $10. TV. Pool; poolside serv, lifeguard. Restaurants. Ck-out noon. Meeting rms. Business servs avail. Gift shop. Barber, beauty shop. Cr cds: A, C, D, DS, ER, JCB, MC, V.

D SC

✓★★★ **MGM GRAND HOTEL.** *3799 Las Vegas Blvd S (89109), near McCarran Intl Airport, on the Strip. 702/891-1111; FAX 702/891-1030; res: 800/929-1111.* Web www.mgmgrand.com. 5,005 rms, 30 story, 740 suites. S, D $69-$399; suites $109-$750; under 12 free; higher rates hols. Crib free. TV; cable (premium). Pools; poolside serv, lifeguard. Supervised child's activities; ages 3-12. Restaurants open 24 hrs (also see BROWN DERBY, COYOTE CAFE, EMERIL'S NEW ORLEANS, GATSBY'S and WOLFGANG PUCK'S CAFE). Bars; entertainment. Ck-out 11 am. Convention facilities. Business center. In-rm modem link. Concierge. Shopping arcade. Barber, beauty shop. Exercise rm; steam rm. Spa. Game rm. Cr cds: A, C, D, DS, ER, JCB, MC, V.

D

★★★ **MIRAGE RESORT & CASINO.** *3400 Las Vegas Blvd S (89177), on the Strip. 702/791-7111; FAX 702/791-7446; res: 800/627-6667.* Web www.mirage.com. 3,044 rms, 30 story. S, D $79-$399; each addl $30; suites $375-$3,000. Crib $30. TV; VCR avail. Pool. Restaurant open 24 hrs (also see MELANGE). Bar; entertainment. Ck-out noon. Convention facilities. Business center. In-rm modem link. Concierge. Shopping arcade. Barber, beauty shop. Valet parking. Exercise rm. Massage. Bathrm phone, refrigerator, wet bar in suites. Casino. Atrium features tropical rain forest; behind front desk is 20,000-gallon aquarium with sharks and tropical fish. On 100 acres with dolphin and white tiger habitats. Cr cds: A, C, D, DS, ER, JCB, MC, V.

D

★★★ **MONTE CARLO RESORT & CASINO.** *3770 S Las Vegas Blvd (89030), on the Strip. 702/730-7777; FAX 702/730-7250; res: 800/311-8999.* Web www.montecarlo.com. 3,002 rms, 32 story. S, D $59-$249; suites $250-$1,000; under 12 free. Crib free. TV; cable (premium), VCR avail. Pool; poolside serv, lifeguard. Restaurant open 24 hrs. Ck-out 11 am. Gift shop. Concierge. Convention facilities. Business center. In-rm modem link. Tennis. Exercise rm. Cr cds: A, C, D, DS, ER, JCB, MC, V.

D

★★★ **NEW YORK-NEW YORK HOTEL & CASINO.** *3790 Las Vegas Blvd S (89109). 702/740-6969; FAX 702/740-6920; res: 800/693-6763.* Web www.nynyhotelcasino.com. 2,033 rms, 45 story. S, D $69-$200; each addl $20; under 12 free; wkends, hols (min stay required). Crib free. TV; cable (premium). Restaurant open 24 hrs (also see IL FORNAIO and MOTOWN CAFE). Bar. Ck-out noon. Convention facilities. Business center. In-rm modem link. Concierge. Shopping arcade. Barber, beauty shop. Free garage parking. Pool; whirlpool, poolside serv, lifeguard. Rec rm. Some bathrm phones. Hotel re-creates New York City's famous landmarks and attractions including the Statue of Liberty and the Manhattan Express. Cr cds: A, C, D, DS, MC, V.

D

★★ **ORLEANS HOTEL & CASINO.** *4500 W Tropicana Ave (89103). 702/365-7111; FAX 702/365-7500; res: 888/365-7111; res: 800/675-3267.* 840 rms, 21 story. S, D $49-$1,000; each addl $10; under 12 free; wkends (2-day min); higher rates hols. Crib free. TV; cable (premium). Restaurants open 24 hrs. Bar; entertainment. Ck-out noon. Meeting rms. Business center. Shopping arcade. Barber, beauty shop. Pool; poolside serv. Cr cds: C.

★★★ **PALACE STATION HOTEL & CASINO.** *2411 W Sahara Ave (89102), at I-15, west of the Strip. 702/367-2411; FAX 702/367-2478; res: 800/634-3101.* 1,029 rms, 21 story. S, D $59-$169; each addl $10; suites $250-$1,000; under 12 free. Crib free. TV. 2 pools; whirlpools. Restaurants open 24 hrs. Bars; entertainment. Ck-out noon. Business servs avail. Gift shop. Garage parking. Game rm. Casino, bingo. Cr cds: A, C, D, DS, ER, MC, V.

D

★★★ **RIO SUITE HOTEL & CASINO.** *3700 W Flamingo Rd (89103), I-15 at Flamingo Rd, west of the Strip. 702/252-7777; FAX 702/579-6565; res: 888/746-7482.* Web www.playrio.com. 2,563 suites, 41 story. Suites $95-$149; each addl $25; mid-wk rates. TV; cable (premium). 3 pools; whirlpools. Complimentary coffee in rms. Restaurant open 24 hrs (also see ANTONIO'S and NAPA). Bar; entertainment. Ck-out noon. Convention facilities. Business servs avail. Concierge. Shopping arcade. Barber, beauty shop. Exercise equipt. Massage. Refrigerators. Building facade of red and blue glass trimmed in neon. Casino. Cr cds: A, C, D, DS, JCB, MC, V.

D

★★ **RIVIERA HOTEL AND CASINO.** *2901 Las Vegas Blvd S (89109), on the Strip. 702/734-5110; FAX 702/794-9483; res: 800/634-6753.* Web www.theriviera.com. 2,100 rms, 6-24 story. S, D $59-$99; each addl $20; suites $125-$500; package plan. Crib free. TV; cable (premium). Heated pool; whirlpool, poolside serv, lifeguard. Restaurant open 24 hrs. Bar; Versailles Room, name entertainment. Ck-out 11 am. Convention facilities. Business center. In-rm modem link. Shopping arcade. Barber, beauty shop. Lighted tennis. Exercise equipt; sauna, steam rm. Some refrigerators. Bathrm phone in some suites. Some balconies. Casino. Cr cds: A, C, D, DS, MC, V.

D

★★ **SAHARA HOTEL & CASINO.** *2535 Las Vegas Blvd S (89109), on the Strip. 702/737-2111; FAX 702/791-2027; res: 888/696-2121.* 1,708 rms, 2-27 story. S, D $55-$95; each addl $12; suites $200-$300; under 12 free; package plans. Crib $10. TV. Heated pool; poolside serv, lifeguard. Restaurant open 24 hrs. Bar; Congo Theatre, star entertainment. Ck-out noon. Convention facilities. Business center. In-rm modem link. Shopping arcade. Barber, beauty shop. Free covered parking. Health club privileges. Many bathrm phones. Private patios, balconies. Casino. Cr cds: A, C, D, DS, JCB, MC, V.

D SC

★★★ **SAM'S TOWN HOTEL AND GAMBLING HALL.** *5111 Boulder Hwy (89109), E of the Strip. 702/456-7777; FAX 702/454-8107; res: 800/897-8696.* E-mail roomres@samstown.boydnet. 648 rms, 9 story. S, D $40-$95; suites $165-$265; under 12 free. Crib free. TV; cable. Heated pool. 10 restaurants (some open 24 hrs). Ck-out noon. Coin Indry. Convention facilities. Business servs avail. In-rm modem link. Shopping arcade. Casino, bowling center. Old West decor; atrium. Cr cds: A, C, D, DS, ER, MC, V.

D

✓★★ **SANTA FE HOTEL & CASINO.** *4949 N Rancho Dr (89130). 702/658-4900; FAX 702/658-4919; res: 800/872-6823.* 200 rms, 5 story. S, D $49-$89; each addl $5; under 13 free; higher rates some hols. TV; cable. Supervised child's activities. Restaurant open 24 hrs (also see SUZETTE'S). Bar; entertainment. Ck-out noon. Meeting rm. Business servs avail. Gift shop. Game rm. Bowling lanes. Ice rink. Cr cds: A, C, D, DS, MC, V.

D

✓★★ **SHOWBOAT HOTEL & CASINO.** *2800 E Fremont St (89116). 702/385-9123; FAX 702/383-9238; res: 800/634-6484.* Web www.showboat-lv.com. 453 rms, 19 story. S, D $29-$89; suites $149-$195; under 12 free. Crib $5. TV. Heated pool; lifeguard. Restaurants open 24 hrs. Bar. Ck-out noon. Meeting rms. Business servs avail. Gift shop. Barber, beauty shop. Free airport transportation. Game rm. Casino; bingo parlor. 106-lane bowling. Cr cds: A, C, D, DS, MC, V.

D

✓★★ **STARDUST RESORT & CASINO.** *3000 Las Vegas Blvd S (89109), on the Strip. 702/732-6111; FAX 702/732-6296; res: 800/825-6033.* E-mail roomres@stardust.com; web www.vegas.com. 2,341 rms, 2-32 story. Jan-May, Oct-Nov: S, D $38-$150; suites $150-$500. Crib free. TV. 2 pools; lifeguard, poolside serv. Restaurants open 24 hrs. Bar; entertainment. Ck-out noon. Convention facilities. Business servs avail. In-rm modem link. Shopping arcade. Barber, beauty shop. Health club privileges. Game rm. Some bathrm phones, refrigerators. Some private patios, balconies. Casino. Cr cds: A, C, D, DS, ER, JCB, MC, V.

D

★★ **STRATOSPHERE HOTEL & CASINO.** *2000 Las Vegas Blvd S (89104), on the Strip. 702/380-7777; FAX 702/380-7732; res: 800/998-6937.* Web www.stratlv.com. 1,444 rms, 24 story. S, D $49-$249; under 13 free. McCarran Intl Airport, east of the Strip. Cr cds: C, D, DS, ER, JCB, V.

D SC

★★ **TEXAS GAMBLING HALL & HOTEL INC.** *2101 Texas Star Ln (85719), N on Rancho Dr. 702/631-1000; FAX 702/631-1087; res: 800/654-8888.* 200 rms, 6 story. S $49-$189; D $69-$225; under 12 free. Crib free. TV; cable. Pool; poolside serv, lifeguard. Coffee in rms. Restaurants open 24 hrs (also see LAREDO CANTINA). Ck-out noon. Gift shop. Cr cds: A, C, D, DS, ER, JCB, MC, V.

D

★★★ **TREASURE ISLAND AT THE MIRAGE.** *3300 Las Vegas Blvd S (89109), on the Strip. 702/894-7111; FAX 702/894-7411; res: 800/944-7444.* Web www.treasureislandlasvegas.com. 2,679 rms, 36 story. S, D $49-$359; suites $100-$600. Crib $25. TV; cable, VCR avail. Heated pools; wading pool, poolside serv, lifeguard. Restaurants open 24 hrs (see BUCCANEER BAY CLUB). Bars; entertainment. Ck-out noon. Convention facilities. Business center. In-rm modem link. Shopping arcade. Barber, beauty shop. Exercise equipt. Refrigerators. Casino. Arcade entertainment complex. Buccaneer Bay Village adventure attraction. Cr cds: A, C, D, DS, JCB, MC, V.

D

★★★ **TROPICANA RESORT & CASINO.** *3801 Las Vegas Blvd S (89193), near McCarran Intl Airport, on the Strip. 702/739-2222; FAX 702/739-2469; res: 800/634-4000.* 1,874 rms, 22 story. S, D $55-$169; each addl $15. TV; cable (premium). Pool; whirlpool, poolside serv, lifeguard. Restaurant open 24 hrs. Bar; Tiffany Theatre, entertainment. Ck-out noon. Convention facilities. Business center. In-rm modem link. Shopping arcade. Barber, beauty shop. Exercise equipt; sauna. Some bathrm phones, refrigerators. Private patios, balconies. Casino. Cr cds: A, C, D, DS, JCB, MC, V.

D

★★ **UNION PLAZA HOTEL & CASINO.** *1 Main St (89125), east of the Strip. 702/386-2110; FAX 702/382-8281; res: 800/634-6575.* 1,037 rms, 25 story. S, D $30-$90; suites $60-$150; under 12 free. Crib $8. TV; VCR avail. Heated pool; wading pool. Restaurant open 24 hrs. Bar. Ck-out noon. Coin lndry. Convention facilities. Business servs avail. Shopping arcade. Barber. Tennis. Casino. Cr cds: A, C, D, DS, ER, MC, V.

D

Resorts

✓★★★ **MANDALAY BAY RESORT & CASINO.** *3950 Las Vegas Blvd S (89119). 702/632-7777; FAX 702/632-7108; res: 877/632-7000.* 3,700 rms. $99-$429. $35 each addl. Call for weekend and promo rates. Cribs $20. Handicap accessible. 15 restaurants. 4 lounges. Entertainment. House of Blues. 24-hr rm serv. Airport 1 mi. Exercise room, spa, massage, 3 pools, wade pool & beach, modem & fax link in rooms; TV, bathroom phones. Cr cds: C.

✓★★★★ **THE BELLAGIO RESORT.** *3600 Las Vegas Blvd S (89109). 702/693-7111; FAX 702/693-8585.* Web www.bellagioresort.com. Steve Wynn wanted to bring class to Las Vegas and he did it with this $2 billion Italianate tribute to the finer things in life—and gambling. Extraordinary restaurants, a luxurious day spa, exquisite shopping, museum-quality art, and an obsessive attention to design and service details set Bellagio apart from the other hotels and casinos in the area. 3,000 rms. Dlx $129-$499; suites $250-$525; penthouse suites $525-$1,250. $35 per person. Children under 18 not allowed. TV, radio, suites stereo; bathroom phone; in line modem. 12 restaurants, beauty salon, shopping (Chanel No 5, Tiffany & Co, Armani, etc.) Live entertainment. Swimming. Exercise room. Massage. Golf and tennis privileges. Cr cds: C.

Restaurants

★★★ **ANTONIO'S.** *(See Rio Suite Hotel & Casino) 702/252-7737.* Hrs: 5-11 pm. Res accepted. Italian menu. Bar. Semi-a la carte: dinner $16.95-$35. Specialties: aragosta sardinia, cioppino, scaloppine piccata. Guitarist. Valet parking. Elegant dining; crystal chandeliers, marble columns. Cr cds: A, C, D, DS, ER, JCB, MC, V.

D

★★★★ **AQUA.** *3600 Las Vegas Blvd. (89109). 702/693-7223.* This Las Vegas outpost of San Francisco's premier seafood restaurant serves the same high-styled preparations in a similarly elegant setting at the Bellagio hotel. Service is professional and desserts are top-notch. Cuisine: contemporary seafood. Specialties: caviar tableside; whole foie gras Hrs: 5:30-11pm Mon-Sun. Reserv reqd. Jackets pref. Prices $28-$40. Valet. Cr cds: C.

★ **BATTISTA'S HOLE IN THE WALL.** *4041 Audrie St (89109), east of the Strip. 702/732-1424.* Hrs: 4:30-11 pm. Closed Thanksgiving, Dec 24 & 25. Res accepted. Italian menu. Bar. Complete meals: dinner $15.95-$29.95. Specializes in fresh pasta. Parking. Casual atmosphere. Family-owned. Cr cds: A, C, D, DS, MC, V.

D

★★ **BERTOLINI'S.** *3500 Las Vegas Blvd S (89109). 702/735-4663.* Hrs: 11 am-midnight; Fri, Sat to 1 am. Italian menu. Bar. A la carte entrees: lunch, dinner $5.25-$18.95. Specializes in pasta. Conservative Italian decor. Cr cds: A, C, D, JCB, MC, V.

D

★★★ **BROWN DERBY.** *(See MGM Grand) 702/891-1111.* Web www.mgm.com. Hrs: 5:30-11 pm. Res accepted. Bar. Wine list. Complete meals: dinner $30-$52. Specializes in prime steak. Pianist, vocalist Tues-Sun. Elegant surroundings. Cr cds: A, C, D, DS, ER, MC, V.

D

★★★ **BUCCANEER BAY CLUB.** *(See Treasure Island) 702/894-7350.* Hrs: 5-10:30 pm. Res accepted. Continental menu. Bar. Wine list. Semi-a la carte: dinner $16.95-$27.50. Specialties: veal scallopine, duck melba, venison royale. Valet parking. Arched windows with view of pirate ship in front of hotel. Cr cds: A, C, D, DS, ER, MC, V.

D

★★ **CAFE NICOLLE.** *4760 W Sahara Ave (89102). 702/870-7675.* Hrs: 11 am-midnight. Closed major hols. Res accepted. French menu. Bar. Semi-a la carte: lunch $7.50-$12.50, dinner $18-$26.95. Specializes in lamb chops, steak, seafood. Entertainment. Outdoor dining. Casual decor. Cr cds: A, C, DS, MC, V.

★★★ **CAMELOT.** *(See Excalibur) 702/597-7700.* Hrs: 6-11 pm. Closed Mon, Tues. Res accepted. Continental menu. Bar. Wine cellar. A la carte entrees: dinner $15.95-$24.95. Child's meals. Specializes in fish, steak, veal. Valet parking. Large fireplace. Jacket. Cr cds: A, C, D, DS, ER, JCB, MC, V.

D

✓★★ **CATHAY HOUSE.** *5300 W Spring Mountain Rd (89102). 702/876-3838.* Hrs: 11 am-11 pm. Chinese menu. Bar. Semi-a la carte: lunch $8.25-$15.95, dinner $8.25-$26. Specialties: strawberry chicken, orange flavored beef. Chinese decor. Cr cds: A, C, D, DS, MC, V.

D

✓★ **CHAPALA.** *2101 S Decatur Blvd (89102), in shopping center. 702/871-7805.* Hrs: 11 am-11 pm; Fri, Sat to midnight. Closed some major hols. Res accepted. Mexican menu. Bar. Semi-a la carte: lunch, dinner $2.50-$10.25. Specialties: fajitas, enchilada ranchero. Cr cds: C, MC, V.

D

★★★ **CHIN'S.** *3200 Las Vegas Blvd S (89109), on the Strip. 702/733-8899.* Hrs: 11:30 am-10 pm; Sun from noon. Closed Thanksgiving, Dec 24 & 25. Res accepted. Cantonese menu. Bar. Wine cellar. A la carte entrees: lunch $9.95-$16, dinner $6-$28. Complete meals: lunch $14.50-$15, dinner $29.50-$50. Specialties: Chin's beef, strawberry chicken, shrimp puffs. Pianist Thurs-Sun. Valet parking. Cr cds: A, C, MC, V.

D

★★★ **CHINOIS.** *3500 Las Vegas Blvd (89109), in the Forum Shops at Caesars Palace. 702/737-9700.* Hrs: 11 am-11 pm; Fri-Sun to midnight. Res required. Asian menu. Bar. Wine list. Semi-a la carte: lunch, dinner $11.50-$28. Specializes in seafood, chicken, sushi. Valet parking. Oriental decor; waterfall, Oriental garden. Cr cds: A, C, D, DS, ER, JCB, MC, V.

D

★★★ **CIPRIANI.** *2790 E Flamingo Rd (89121). 702/369-6711.* Web www.vegas.com/restaurants/cipriani. Hrs: 11:30 am-2 pm, 5:30-10 pm. Closed Sun, Mon. Res accepted. Italian menu. Serv bar. Semi-a la carte: lunch $8.95-$15, dinner $15-$32. Specialties: scaloppina Monte Bianco, medallion of beef Piemontese, fresh seafood. Pianist, vocalist 6-10 pm. Florentine atmosphere. Cr cds: A, C, D, MC, V.

D

★★★ **CIRCO, OSTERIA DEL.** *3600 Las Vegas Blvd (89109). 702/693-8150.* Cuisine Italian. Hrs 11:30 am-2:30 pm; 5:30-11 pm. Dinner $19-$26. Jackets. Reserv. 60 days in advance. Cr cds: C.

✓★ **COUNTRY INN.** *1401 Rainbow Blvd. 702/254-0520.* Hrs: 7 am-10 pm; wkends to 11 pm. Closed Dec 25. Wine, beer. Semi-a la carte: bkfst $2.25-$6.50, lunch, dinner $6.95-$12.95. Child's meals. Specializes in turkey, fish, steak. Cr cds: A, C, D, DS, MC, V.

D

★★ **COYOTE CAFE.** *(See MGM Grand) 702/891-7349.* Hrs: 7:30 am-11 pm. Res accepted. Southwestern menu. Bar. Semi-a la carte: bkfst $3-$8, lunch $5-$16, dinner $20-$32. Specialties: chicken tostada, beef fajita tostada. Valet parking. Southwestern decor; artwork, cacti. Cr cds: A, C, D, DS, ER, MC, V.

D

★★★ **DRAI'S OF LAS VEGAS.** *(See Barbary Coast) 702/737-0555.* Hrs: 5:30-11 pm; Sat, Sun to midnight. Res required. Bar. A la carte entrees: dinner $14-$35. Specializes in lobster, steak, seafood. Jazz Fri, Sat. Valet parking. Intimate atmosphere; unique oil paintings. Jacket. Cr cds: A, C, D, DS, ER, JCB, MC, V.

★★★ **EMERIL'S NEW ORLEANS.** *(See MGM Grand) 702/891-1111.* Hrs: 11 am-2:30 pm, 5:30-10:30 pm. Res accepted. French menu. Bar. Complete meals: lunch $15-$25, dinner $17-$28. Specializes in seafood. French Quarter decor. Pictures of New Orleans. Cr cds: A, C, D, DS, ER, MC, V.

D

★★★ **EMPRESS COURT.** *(See CAESARS PALACE) 702/731-7110.* Hrs: 6-11 pm. Res accepted. Cantonese menu. Bar. Complete meals: dinner $30-$80. Specializes in shark fin dishes. Valet parking. Elegant dining. Jacket. Cr cds: A, C, D, MC, V.

D

✓★★ **FASOLINI'S PIZZA CAFE.** *222 Decatur Blvd (89107). 702/877-0071.* Hrs: noon-10 pm; Sun to 5 pm. Closed Jan 1, Easter, Dec 25. Italian menu. Beer, wine. Semi-a la carte: lunch $5.95-$9.95, dinner $9.95-$12.95. Specialties: chicken cacciatore, spaghetti. Art Deco decor; posters of famous movies. Cr cds: A, C, D, DS, ER, MC, V.

D

★★ **FERRARO'S RESTAURANT.** *5920 W Flamingo Rd (89103). 702/364-8867.* Hrs: 5:30-11 pm. Closed Dec 25. Res accepted. Italian menu. Bar. Semi-a la carte: dinner $12-$32.50. Specializes in pasta, seafood, steak. Pianist. Parking. Patio dining. Italian decor. Cr cds: A, C, D, DS, MC, V.

D

★★ **FOUR QUEENS HOTEL.** *(See Four Queens) 702/385-4011.* Hrs: 5:30-11 pm. Res accepted. Bar. Complete meals: dinner $24-$49. Specialties: Australian lobster tails, filet mignon. Intimate dining; original artwork. Jacket. Cr cds: A, C, D, DS, ER, MC, V.

D

✓★ **GARDUÑOS.** *(See Fiesta) 702/631-7000.* Hrs: 11 am-10 pm; Fri, Sat to 11 pm. Closed Thanksgiving, Dec 25. Mexican menu. Bar. Semi-a la carte: lunch $7.50-$12.50, dinner $10-$12.50. Specializes in pollo, carnes, fajitas. Old Mexican village decor. Cr cds: A, C, D, DS, ER, MC, V.

D

★★★ **GATSBY'S.** *(See MGM Grand) 702/891-1111.* Web www.mgm.com. Hrs: 5:30-11 pm. Closed Tues. French menu. Bar. Complete meal: dinner $22.50-$90. Specialties: seared breast of duck, Colorado rack of lamb. Pianist, singer exc Sun. Formal decor. Cr cds: A, C, D, DS, ER, MC, V.

D

★★ **GIO'S CAFE MILANO.** *3900 Paradise Rd (89109). 702/732-2777.* Hrs: noon-3 pm, 5-10 pm. Closed Sun. Res accepted. Italian menu. Wine. Semi-a la carte: lunch $5.95-$10.95, dinner $9.50-$27.50. Specializes in chicken, beef, pasta. Parking. Outdoor dining. Cr cds: A, C, D, DS, ER, JCB, MC, V.

D

★★ **GOLDEN STEER STEAK HOUSE.** *308 W Sahara Ave (89109), west of the Strip. 702/384-4470.* Hrs: 4:30 pm-midnight. Closed Thanksgiving, Dec 25. Res accepted. Bar. Semi-a la carte: dinner $19.95-$50. Specializes in steak, seafood. Valet parking. 1890s Western decor. Family-owned. Cr cds: A, C, D, DS, MC, V.

D

★★ **HAMADA OF JAPAN.** *598 E Flamingo Rd (89119), 5 mi SE on I-15, E Flamingo exit. 702/733-3005.* Hrs: 5 pm-midnight. Res accepted. Japanese menu. Bar. Semi-a la carte: dinner $6.95-$39. Specializes in traditional Japanese cuisine. Artwork, aquarium. Cr cds: A, C, D, DS, ER, MC, V.

D

★★ **IL FORNAIO ITALIAN RESTAURANT.** *(See New York-New York) 702/650-6500.* Hrs: 11:30 am-midnight; Fri, Sat to 1 am. Res accepted. Italian menu. Bar. A la carte entrees: lunch $4.95-$8.50, dinner $9.50-$12. Specialties: antipasto, minestrone. Valet parking. Cr cds: A, C, D, DS, ER, JCB, MC, V.

D

✓★★ **LANDRYS SEAFOOD RESTAURANT.** *2610 W Sahara (89102). 702/251-0101.* Hrs: 11 am-10 pm; Fri, Sat to 11 pm. Closed Dec 25. Res accepted. Bar. Semi-a la carte: lunch $6.99-$9.99, dinner $9.99-$26.99. Specializes in seafood, pasta, beef. Contemporary decor. Cr cds: A, C, D, DS, MC, V.

D

★ **LAREDO CANTINA & CAFE.** *(See Texas) 702/631-1044.* Hrs: 5-11 pm. Closed Tues. Res accepted. Mexican menu. Bar. Semi-a la carte: dinner $7.25-$25. Specializes in fajitas, burritos, chimichangas. Mexican decor. Cr cds: A, C, D, DS, ER, MC, V.

★★★ **LAWRY'S THE PRIME RIB.** *4043 Howard Hughes Pkwy (89109), 5 mi SE on I-15 to E Flamingo Rd exit, E on Flamingo Rd, N on Paradise Rd to Howard Hughes Pkwy. 702/893-2223.* Hrs: 5-10 pm; Fri, Sat to 11 pm. Res accepted. Bar. Wine cellar. Semi-a la carte: $20-$40. Specializes in prime rib, lobster. Art Deco decor; red velvet booths, fireplace. Meats carved tableside. Cr cds: A, C, D, DS, ER, MC, V.

D

★★★★ **LE CIRQUE.** *3600 Las Vegas Blvd. (89109). 702/693-8100.* This intimate, plush restaurant sits just off the main casino (see Bellagio). All of the glamour and flash of the New York original has been well received in Vegas. The contemporary French food and doting service make for an exhilarating dining experience. French cuisine. Hrs 5:30-10:30 pm. Reserv reqd. Jacket. Prices $28-$39; tasting menu $50-$120. Cr cds: C.

★★★ **LE MONTRACHET.** *(See Hilton) 702/732-5111.* Hrs: 6-10 pm. Closed Tues. Res accepted. French menu. Bar. Wine cellar. A la carte entrees: dinner $16-$46. Specialties: salmon medallions, sauteed lobster tails, roasted breast of Muscovy duck. Parking. Cr cds: A, C, D, DS, JCB, MC, V.

D

★★★ **LILY LANGTRY'S.** *(See Golden Nugget Hotel) 702/385-7111.* Hrs: 5-11 pm. Res accepted. Cantonese menu. Bar. Wine cellar. A la carte entrees: dinner $9-$30. Specialties: lobster Cantonese, Chinese pepper steak, moo goo gai pan. Own baking. Valet parking. Oriental decor. Cr cds: A, C, D, DS, JCB, MC, V.

D

★★★ **MANHATTAN OF LAS VEGAS.** *2600 E Flamingo Rd (89121), E of Las Vegas Blvd. 702/737-5000.* Hrs: 4 pm-1 am. Res accepted. Bar. Wine list. Complete meals: dinner $25-$50. Specializes in beef, veal, lamb. Entertainment. Marble entry leads to intimate dining area with French windows and crystal chandeliers. Cr cds: A, C, D, DS, ER, MC, V.

D

★ **MARRAKECH.** *3900 Paradise Rd (89109). 702/737-5611.* Hrs: 5:30-11 pm. Closed Dec 25. Res accepted. Moroccan menu. Bar. Complete six-course meal: dinner $24.95. Specialties: shish kebab, chicken in light lemon sauce, shrimp scampi. Belly dancers. French Moroccan decor. Cr cds: A, C, MC, V.

D

★★ **MAYFLOWER CUISINIER.** *4750 W Sahara Ave (89102), at Decatur. 702/870-8432.* Hrs: 11 am-3 pm, 5-10 pm; Sat 5-11 pm. Closed Sun; major hols. Res accepted. Chinese menu. Bar. Semi-a la carte: lunch $7.25-$10.95, dinner $8.95-$21.95. Specialties: roast duck, boneless chicken, Thai shrimp. Outdoor dining. Oil paintings. Totally nonsmoking. Cr cds: A, C, D, DS, MC, V.

D

★★★ **MELANGE.** *(See Mirage) 702/791-7111.* Hrs: 5:30-11 pm. Res accepted. French menu. Wine list. Semi-a la carte: dinner $24-$45. Specialties: trio of venison, pecan-crusted rack of lamb. Original Picasso paintings. Cr cds: A, C, D, DS, ER, MC, V.

D

★★★ **MONTE CARLO.** *(See Desert Inn) 702/733-4524.* Hrs: 6-11 pm. Closed Sun, Mon. Res accepted. French menu. Serv bar. Wine cellar. Semi-a la carte: dinner $60-$90. Specializes in boneless roast duckling, stuffed veal chop, sea bass Kiev. Own baking. Valet parking. Jacket. Cr cds: A, C, D, DS, JCB, MC, V.

D

★★ **MORTONI'S.** *(See Hard Rock) 702/693-5047.* Web www.hardrock.com. Hrs: 6-11 pm. Res accepted. Italian menu. Bar. Semi-a la carte: dinner $9-$59. Specializes in pasta, seafood, chicken. Outdoor dining. Italian decor. Cr cds: A, C, D, DS, ER, JCB, MC, V.

★★ **MOTOWN CAFE.** *(See New York-New York) 702/740-6440.* Hrs: 7 am-midnight; Sat to 2 am; Sun to 3 am. Bar. Semi-a la carte: bkfst $2.25-$10.25, lunch, dinner $8-$18. Specializes in waffles, New York-style sandwiches. Entertainment. Outdoor dining. Features Motown music; bronze statues of musical celebrities. Cr cds: A, C, D, DS, ER, MC, V.

D

★★★★ **NAPA.** *(See Rio Suite Hotel & Casino) 702/252-7737.* The first high-profile chef to relocate to Vegas, Jean-Louis Palladin has a reputation for cutting-edge French cooking that has inspired a generation of chefs. When his is on, no one is better. Though the restaurant is nondescript, the attentive service, exceptional wine list, and Jean-Louis's food make the experience delightful.Hrs: 6-11 pm. Closed Sun, Mon. French menu. Bar. Wine cellar. Semi-a la carte: dinner $26-$48. Specialties: Atlantic salmon, roast rack of veal, duck pithivier. Modern sculpture in center of restaurant highlighted by skylight; oil paintings. Cr cds: A, C, D, DS, ER, JCB, MC, V.

★★★ **NICKY BLAIR'S.** *3925 Paradise Rd (89109). 702/792-9900.* Hrs: 4-11 pm. Closed Sun; Dec 25. Res required. Northern Italian menu. Bar. Semi-a la carte: dinner $13.50-$28. Specialties: petti di pollo, osso bucco, prime filet mignon. Italian decor; extensive wall murals. Cr cds: A, C, D, DS, ER, MC, V.

★★ **NORTH BEACH CAFE.** *2605 S Decatur Blvd (89102), I-15 exit Sahara. 702/247-9530.* Hrs: 11:30 am-4 pm, 5-10 pm; Sat, Sun from 5 pm. Closed July 4, Dec 25. Res accepted. Italian menu. Bar. Semi-a la carte: lunch $4.95-$8.95, dinner $10.75-$16. Specialties: eggplant parmigiana, fettucine salmone, lasagna Bolognese. Pianist Wed-Sun eves. Outdoor dining. Intimate atmosphere; northern Italian decor, original art. Cr cds: A, C, D, DS, ER, JCB, MC, V.

★★★ **PALACE COURT.** *(See Caesars Palace Hotel) 702/731-7110.* Hrs: 6-11 pm; Closed Tues, Wed. Res accepted. French, continental menu. Extensive wine list. A la carte entrees: dinner $28-$65. Specializes in French gourmet dishes, lobster, veal. Own baking. Pianist Thurs-Sun. Valet parking. Jacket. Cr cds: A, C, D, MC, V.

D

★★★ **PALM RESTAURANT.** *3500 Las Vegas Blvd S Suite A (89109), in Forum Shops At Caesars, on the Strip. 702/732-7256.* Hrs: 11:30 am-11 pm. Res accepted. Bar. Wine list. A la carte entrees: lunch $10-$14, dinner $15-$60. Specializes in prime beef, seafood, chops. Valet parking. Counterpart of famous New York restaurant. Caricatures of celebrities on walls. Cr cds: A, C, D, MC, V.

D

★★★ **PEGASUS RESTAURANT.** *(See Alexis Park Resort) 702/796-3353.* Hrs: 6 am-10 pm. Res accepted. Bar. Wine cellar. A la carte entrees: bkfst $6-$10, lunch $8.95-$15.95, dinner $12.95-$18.95. Bkfst buffet $10. Specialties: filet mignon, prime steak. Valet parking. Outdoor dining. Cr cds: A, C, D, DS, ER, JCB, MC, V.

D

★★ **PHILIPS SUPPER HOUSE.** *4545 W Sahara (89102). 702/873-5222.* Hrs: 4:30-11 pm; early-bird dinner 4:30-6:30 pm. Res accepted. Continental menu. Bar. Complete meals: dinner $14.95-$28.95. Specializes in prime aged beef. Parking. Victorian decor. Cr cds: A, C, D, DS, ER, MC, V.

D

★★★★★ **PICASSO.** *3600 Las Vegas Blvd (89109). 702/693-7223.* The only reason to take your eyes off the dazzling Picasso paintings and ceramics on the walls and around the room (all originals) is to study chef Julian Serrano's spectacular cooking on the plate. Like the master himself, Serrano is Spanish born and French trained. His food is understated, elegant, and exceptional. Cuisine: French with Spanish flair. Hrs: Sun-Thurs 6-10 pm; Fri-Sat to 11 pm. Closed on Wed. Reservations reqd 60 days in advance. Price fixe $70. Degustation menu $80. Valet. Jackets reqd. Cr cds: C.

★★★ **PRIME.** *3600 Las Vegas Blvd. 702/693-7223.* Specialties: prime meat, seafood & chops. Hrs: Mon-Sun 5:30-10 pm. $18-$54. Jackets pref. Reserv 60 days in advance. Cr cds: C.

★★★★★ **RENOIR.** *3600 Las Vegas Blvd. 702/791-7444.* French cuisine. Specialties; Foie gras with peppered pineapple and aged balsamic vinegar, asparagus cannelloni, Maui onions and puffy pastry, Seasonal menu. Hrs: Open every night except Wed. 6-10:15 pm. Prices: Tasting menu & vegetable tasting $95. A la carte: $29-$44. No less than nine original Renoir paintings are the focal point of this jewel box of a dining room in the Mirage hotel; patterned fabric walls and splendid floral arrangements enhance the bold decor. Chef Alex Stratta's superb blend of contemporary French and southwestern cuisines is exquisitely presented and the doting service makes everyone feel like a high roller. Jackets sugg. Resv reqd. Valet. Nonsmoking. Cr cds: C.

✓★★ **RICARDO'S.** *2380 E Tropicana (89119), east of the Strip. 702/798-4515.* Hrs: 11 am-11 pm; Sun noon-10 pm. Closed Jan 1, Thanksgiving, Dec 25. Res accepted. Mexican menu. Bar. Semi-a la carte: lunch, dinner $6.75-$19.75. Buffet lunch $6.75. Specialty: chicken Ricardo's. Guitarist, vocalist daily exc Mon. Old Mexican decor. Cr cds: A, C, D, DS, MC, V.

D

✓★★ **ROMANO'S MACARONI GRILL.** *2400 W Sahara Ave (89102). 702/248-9500.* Hrs: 11 am-10 pm; Fri, Sat to 11 pm. Closed Thanksgiving, Dec 25. Italian menu. Bar. Semi-a la carte: lunch $7-$9, dinner $6.50-$17.95. Specializes in pizza, pasta, seafood. Italian country decor. Cr cds: A, C, D, DS, ER, JCB, MC, V.

D

★★★ **RUTH'S CHRIS STEAK HOUSE.** *3900 Paradise Rd (89109), east of the Strip. 702/791-7011.* Hrs: 11 am-10:30 pm; Fri, Sat from 4:30 pm. Closed Thanksgiving, Dec 25. Res accepted. Bar. Wine list. A la carte entrees: dinner $18.95-$34. Specializes in steak. 3 dining rms, contemporary decor. Cr cds: A, C, D, DS, ER, MC, V.

D

★★★ **SACRED SEA.** *(See Luxor) 702/262-4772.* Hrs: 5-11 pm. Res accepted. Bar. Semi-a la carte: dinner $24-$28. Specialties: Alaskan king crab, lobster tail. Own pasta. Valet parking. Egyptian decor, artwork. Cr cds: A, C, D, DS, ER, MC, V.

★ **SAM WOO BBQ.** *4215 Spring Mountain Rd (89102), in Chinatown Mall. 702/368-7628.* Hrs: 10-5 am. Chinese menu. Semi-a la carte: lunch $5-$10, dinner $10-$24. Specializes in barbeque, fried rice, seafood. Chinese decor. Cr cds: A, C, D, DS, ER, JCB, MC, V.

D

★★★ **SEASONS.** *(See Bally's) 702/795-3990.* Hrs: 6-11 pm. Res required. Contemporary Amer menu. Bar. Wine cellar. Semi-a la carte: dinner $25-$60. Specializes in steak, salmon, chicken. Valet parking. Elegant dining; crystal chandeliers, elaborate wall murals. Cr cds: A, C, D, DS, ER, MC, V.

★★ **SFUZZI.** *3200 Las Vegas Blvd S (89109), 5 mi S on I-15 to Spring Mountain Rd exit, W to Las Vegas Blvd. 702/699-5777.* Hrs: 11:30 am-11 pm; Sun from 11 am. Res accepted. Northern Italian menu. Bar. Semi-a la carte: lunch $4-$12, dinner $12-$20. Specialties: skillet-roasted sea bass, osso bucco, grilled Atlantic salmon. Outdoor dining. Exterior features Italian village facade. Cr cds: A, C, D, DS, ER, MC, V.

D

✓★ **SHALIMAR.** *3900 Paradise Rd (89109), in shopping mall, east of the Strip. 702/796-0302.* Hrs: 11:30 am-2 pm, 5:30-10 pm; Sat, Sun from 5:30 pm. Res accepted. Northern Indian menu. Serv bar. Buffet: lunch $6.95. A la carte entrees: dinner $10.50-$15.95. Specialties: chicken tandoori, lamb Shalimar, lamb & seafood curries. Contemporary decor. Cr cds: A, C, D, DS, MC, V.

D

✓★★ **SIR GALLAHAD'S.** *(See Excalibur) 702/597-7700.* Hrs: 5-10 pm; Fri-Sat to 11 pm. Res accepted. English menu. Bar. Complete meal: dinner $14.95-$24.95. Specialty: prime rib. Medieval decor with suits of armor and cast iron chandeliers. Cr cds: A, C, D, DS, ER, MC, V.

D

★★★ **SPAGO.** *3500 Las Vegas Blvd S (89109), in Forum Shops at Caesars Palace Hotel. 702/369-6300.* Hrs: 11-12:30 am. Res accepted. Varied menu. Bar. Wine cellar. A la carte entrees: lunch $9.50-$18.50. Complete meals: dinner $17-$30. Specialties: pizza, chicken salad. Jazz pianist Sun. Parking. Modern artwork. Art deco, wrought iron design. Counterpart of famous restaurant in West Hollywood. Cr cds: A, C, D, DS, ER, MC, V.

D

✓★ **STAGE DELI.** *3500 Las Vegas Blvd S (89109), in Forum Shops At Caesars Palace, on the Strip. 702/893-4045.* Hrs: 7:30 am-11 pm. Res accepted. Wine, beer. Semi-a la carte: bkfst $4.95-$7.95, lunch $4.75-$12.95, dinner $9.95-$13.95. Specializes in deli fare. New York deli atmosphere; posters of Broadway shows. Cr cds: A, C, D, DS, ER, MC, V.

D

★★★ **STEFANO'S.** *(See Golden Nugget) 702/385-7111.* Hrs: 6-11 pm; wkends from 5:30 pm. Italian menu. Bar. Wine cellar. A la carte entrees: dinner $9.95-$27.95. Specializes in Northern Italian food. Parking. Singing waiters. Murals of Italy. Cr cds: A, C, D, DS, JCB, MC, V.

D

★★★ **SUZETTE'S.** *(See Santa Fe) 702/658-4900.* Hrs: 5-10 pm. Res accepted. French menu. Bar. Wine list. Semi-a la carte: dinner $28-$56. Specialties: chicken breast stuffed with wild mushrooms, medallions of lobster. French decor. Jacket. Totally nonsmoking. Cr cds: A, C, D, DS, MC, V.

D

★★ **THE DIVE.** *3200 Las Vegas Blvd S (89109), S on I-15 to Spring Mountain Rd exit, W to Las Vegas Blvd. 702/369-2270.* Hrs: 11:30 am-10 pm; Fri, Sat to 11 pm. Res accepted. Bar. Semi-a la carte: lunch $6-$14, dinner $10.95-$17.95. Specialties: bouillabaisse, baby back ribs. Nautical decor; shaped to look like submarine. Cr cds: A, C, D, DS, ER, MC, V.

D

★★★★ **THE FIRST FLOOR GRILL.** *(See Four Seasons Hotel) 702/632-5000.* The spacious dining room with vaulted ceilings and atmospheric lighting has the feel of a Medieval castle. And the creative American cuisine and attentive service are fit for a king. Like the hotel itself, a welcome respite from the sound of slot machines. American French Cuisine. Specialties: Hawaiian fish & steaks. Hrs: 5:30-11 pm; Closed Sun & Mon. Prices $25-$35. Reserv pref. Wine cellar. Children meals. Lounge. Valet. Cr cds: C.

★★★ **THE RANGE STEAKHOUSE.** *(See Harrah's) 702/369-5000.* Web www.harrahs.com. Hrs: 5:30-10:30 pm, Fri-Sun to 11:30 pm. Res accepted. Bar. A la carte entrees: dinner $25-$35. Specializes in steak, lamb, veal. Valet parking. Cr cds: A, C, D, DS, ER, JCB, MC, V.

★★ **THE STEAK HOUSE.** *(See Circus-Circus Hotel & Casino) 702/734-0410.* Hrs: 5-11 pm; Sun brunch 10 am-2 pm. Res accepted. Bar. Semi-a la carte: dinner $14.95-$25. Sun brunch $19.95. Specializes in top sirloin, crab legs, halibut. Western decor. Cr cds: A, C, D, DS, ER, JCB, MC, V.

★★★ **TILLERMAN.** *2245 E Flamingo (89109), east of the Strip. 702/731-4036.* Hrs: 5-11 pm. Closed major hols. Wine list. Semi-a la carte: dinner $19.95-$36.95. Specializes in fresh fish, steak, pasta. Atrium, garden, loft dining areas. Cr cds: A, C, D, DS, MC, V.

D

★★★ **TOP OF THE WORLD.** *(See Stratosphere Hotel) 702/380-7711.* Hrs: 5-11 pm; Sat, Sun to midnight. Res required. Bar. Extensive wine list. Semi-a la carte: dinner $25-$48. Specializes in steak, salmon, lobster. Entertainment. Rotating restaurant from 1,000-ft elevation. Totally nonsmoking. Cr cds: A, C, D, DS, ER, JCB, MC, V.

D

★ **VIVA MERCADOS MEXICAN RESTAURANT.** *6182 W Flamingo (89103), 2 mi W of I-15, in shopping center. 702/871-8826.* Hrs: 11 am-10 pm; Fri, Sat to 11 pm. Closed Sun; Thanksgiving, Dec 25. Res accepted (dinner). Mexican menu. Bar. Semi-a la carte: lunch $5.75-$12.75, dinner $11.95-$16.95. Specialties: orange roughy, camerones rancheros, mariscos vallarta. Mexican decor. Cr cds: A, C, D, DS, MC, V.

D

★★★ **WOLFGANG PUCK'S CAFE.** *(See MGM Grand) 702/895-9653.* Hrs: 8 am-11 pm; Fri, Sat to midnight. Bar. A la carte entrees: breakfast, lunch, dinner $4.95-$19.95. Specialties: wood-burning oven pizza, rotisserie chicken. Ultra modern decor. Cr cds: A, C, D, MC, V.

D

★ **XINH-XINH.** *220 W Sahara Ave (89102), W of the Strip. 702/471-1572.* Hrs: 11 am-11 pm. Res accepted. Vietnamese menu. Wine, beer. Semi-a la carte: lunch $5.95-$7.95, dinner $8.95-$16.95. Specializes in Vietnamese cuisine. Cr cds: A, C, MC, V.

D SC

★ **YOLIE'S BRAZILIAN STEAKHOUSE.** *3900 Paradise Rd (89109), east of the Strip. 702/794-0700.* Hrs: 11 am-11 pm; Sat from 5 pm. Res required. Brazilian menu. Bar. Semi-a la carte: lunch $6.95-$12.95, dinner $14.95-$22.95. Child's meals. Specializes in steak, lamb. Outdoor dining. Cr cds: A, C, D, DS, MC, V.

D

✓★★★ **Z' TEJAS GRILL.** *3824 Paradise Rd (89109). 702/732-1660.* Hrs: 11 am-11 pm. Closed Thanksgiving, Dec 25. Res accepted. Southwestern menu. Bar. Semi-a la carte: lunch $9.75-$11.95, dinner $8.95-$16.95. Specialties: crab-stuffed shrimp, pork roast vera cruz. Southwestern decor. Totally nonsmoking. Cr cds: A, C, D, DS, ER, MC, V.

D

Unrated Dining Spots

AUREOLE. *3950 Las Vegas Blvd (89119). 702/632-7401.* Progressive American. Hrs: 5-10:30 pm. Price $25-$40. Complete meals $50-$60. Res pref. Valet. Bar until 1 am. Cr cds: C.

HARD ROCK CAFE. *(See Hard Rock) 702/733-8400.* Hrs: 11 am-11:30 pm. Bar. Semi-a la carte: lunch, dinner $5.50-$13.95. Specializes in chicken, ribs. Entertainment Fri. Valet parking. Rock & roll memorabilia. Cr cds: A, C, D, MC, V.

D

PLANET HOLLYWOOD. *3500 Las Vegas Blvd (89109). 702/791-7827.* Hrs: 11 am-midnight; Fri, Sat to 1 am. Bar. A la carte entrees: lunch, dinner $7.95-$17.95. Specializes in California cuisine. Parking. Hollywood artifacts and television memorabilia. Cr cds: A, C, D, DS, ER, MC, V.

D

Laughlin (K-6)

(See also Bullhead City, AZ, Kingman, AZ; also see Needles, CA)

Pop 4,791 **Elev** 520 ft **Area Code** 702 **Zip** 89029

Information Chamber of Commerce, PO Box 77777; 800/227-5245

This resort community offers a pleasant change of pace from the dazzle of Las Vegas. In many ways, it resembles Las Vegas in its earlier days. Many hotels and casinos line the Colorado River; some provide ferry service to and from parking facilities on the Arizona side. But Laughlin offers other diversions as well; water sports such as fishing, waterskiing and swimming in nearby Lake Mohave are popular.

Annual Events

Laughlin Riverdays. World's longest line dance, carnival, golf tournament. Mid-May.

River Flight. Hot air balloon event. Oct.

Motor Hotel

✓★★ **PIONEER HOTEL & GAMBLING HALL.** *2200 S Casino Dr (89028), 3 mi S of Davis Dam. 702/298-2442; FAX 702/298-3054; res: 800/634-3469.* 415 rms, 2 story. S, D $28-$75. TV. Pool. Restaurants open 24 hrs. Bar. Ck-out 11 am. Business servs avail. Gift shop. Free airport transportation. Game rm. Some refrigerators. On river; some riverfront rms. Cr cds: A, C, DS, MC, V.

D

Hotels

✓★★ **COLORADO BELLE HOTEL & CASINO.** *2100 S Casino Dr (89029). 702/298-4000; FAX 702/298-2597; res: 800/477-4837.* E-mail cbres@ccei.com; web www.colobelle.com. 1,223 rms, 6 story. S, D $18-$100; each addl $4. Crib $7. TV. 2 heated pools; whirlpool. Restaurant open 24 hrs. Limited rm serv. Bar; entertainment. Ck-out 11 am. Business servs avail. Shopping arcade. Free airport transportation. Casino. Adj to replica of three-deck Mississippi paddlewheeler. Cr cds: A, C, D, DS, MC, V.

D

★★ **DON LAUGHLIN'S RIVERSIDE HOTEL.** *1650 Casino Dr (89029), 2 mi NW on AZ 68, 2 mi S of Davis Dam. 702/298-2535; FAX 702/298-2695; res: 800/227-3849.* Web www.riverside.com. 1,404 rms, 28 story. S, D $43-$75; suites $85-$300; higher rates wkends. Crib $8. TV; cable. 2 pools. Restaurant open 24 hrs. Bars; entertainment. Ck-out 11 am. Convention facilities. Business center. In-rm modem link. Free airport transportation. Bathrm phones. Balconies. Movie theaters. Casino. Bus depot on premises. Boat dockage on Colorado River; RV spaces. Cr cds: A, C, D, DS, MC, V.

D

★ **EDGEWATER HOTEL & CASINO.** *2020 S Casino Dr (89029). 702/298-2453; FAX 702/298-4271; res: 800/677-4837.* E-mail edgeres@laughlin; web www.edgewater-casino.com. 1,446 rms, 6-26 story. S, D $18-$150; each addl $4; suites $75-$125; higher rates hols; under 12 free. Crib $7. TV. Pool; whirlpool. Restaurant open 24 hrs. Bar; entertainment. Ck-out 11 am. Gift shop. Covered parking. Free airport transportation. Some balconies. On river. Cr cds: A, C, D, DS, MC, V.

D SC

★ **GOLD RIVER RESORT & CASINO.** *2700 S Casino Dr (89029). 702/298-2242; FAX 702/298-2196; res: 800/835-7903.* Web www.goldrivercasino.com. 1,003 rms, 3-25 story. S, D $18-$60; suites $125-$300. Crib free. TV. Heated pool; whirlpool. Restaurant open 24 hrs. Bar; entertainment. Ck-out 11 am. Convention facilities. Business servs avail. Shopping arcade. Free valet parking. Free airport transportation. Exercise equipt. Game rm. Cr cds: A, C, D, DS, JCB, MC, V.

D

✓★★★ **GOLDEN NUGGET.** *2300 Casino Dr (89028). 702/298-7222; FAX 702/298-7122; res: 800/950-7700.* 300 rms, 4 story. S, D $21-$95; suites $150; under 12 free; higher rates wkends. Crib free. TV; cable. Pool; whirlpool, poolside serv. Restaurants open 24 hrs. Bar. Ck-out noon.

Business servs avail. Shopping arcade. Free airport transportation. On Colorado River. Cr cds: A, C, DS, MC, V.

D SC

★★ **HILTON FLAMINGO-LAUGHLIN.** *1900 S Casino Dr (89029). 702/298-5111; FAX 702/298-5116; res: 800/352-6464.* 1,900 rms, 18 story, 60 suites. Mar-Oct: S, D $19-$119; each addl $9; suites $200-$325; family rates; higher rates: wkends, hols; lower rates rest of yr. Crib free. TV; cable (premium). Heated pool. Restaurant open 24 hrs. Rm serv 6 am-midnight. Bar; entertainment. Ck-out 11 am. Meeting rms. Business servs avail. Shopping arcade. Free garage parking. Free airport transportation. Lighted tennis. Game rm. Wet bar in suites. Casino. On 18-acre site along Colorado River. Cr cds: A, C, D, DS, ER, JCB, MC, V.

D

★★ **RAMADA INN.** *2121 S Casino Dr (89029). 702/298-4200; FAX 702/298-6403; res: 800/243-6846.* Web www.ramadaexp.com. 1,501 rms, 24 story. S, D $18-$59; suites $65-$200; higher rates: hols, gaming tournaments. Crib free. TV; cable. Heated pool; poolside serv. Restaurant open 24 hrs. Bar; entertainment. Ck-out 11 am. Gift shop. Valet parking. Free airport transportation. Game rm. Refrigerator, wet bar in suites. Opp river. Railroad station theme; full-size train runs around hotel. Cr cds: A, C, D, DS, MC, V.

D

Lovelock (C-2)

Settled early 1840s **Pop** 2,069 **Elev** 3,977 ft **Area Code** 775 **Zip** 89419

Information Pershing County Chamber of Commerce, 25 W Marzen Lane, PO Box 821; 775/273-7213

The 49ers stopped in Lovelock Valley on their way west. There was plenty of feed for weary oxen and horses because beavers had dammed the Humboldt River, thus providing a steady water supply. The travelers mended their wagons and made other preparations for the 36-hour dash across the dreaded 40-mile desert to Hot Springs.

A deep layer of rich, black loam, left in the Lovelock Valley as the waters of an ancient lake receded, spreads over more than 40,000 acres. This soil, irrigated from the Rye Patch Reservoir, supports rich farms and productive ranches. Lovelock, the seat of Pershing County, was named for an early settler, George Lovelock, across whose ranch the original Central Pacific Railroad was built. Ore mines, mineral deposits and a seed-processing plant in the area contribute to the growth of modern Lovelock.

What to See and Do

Courthouse Park. The only round courthouse still in use. Shaded picnic grounds; swimming pool. (May-Aug, daily) ¢

Rye Patch State Recreation Area. Approx 27,500 acres on 200,000-acre reservoir; swimming, waterskiing; fishing; boating (launching ramps). Picnicking. Camping (dump station). Standard fees. 23 mi N on I-80. Phone 775/538-7321.

Annual Event

Frontier Days. Parade, races, rodeo. Late July or early Aug.

Lunar Crater (F-4)

(Near US 6 between Tonopah and Ely)

This is a vast field of cinder cones and frozen lava. The crater is a steep-walled pit, 400 feet deep and three-quarters of a mile in diameter, created by volcanic action about 1,000 years ago. The earth exploded violently, heaving cinders, lava and rocks the size of city blocks high into the air. Awed by the remains, pioneers named the pit Lunar Crater.

Overton (H-6)

(See also Las Vegas)

Pop 3,000 (est) **Elev** 1,270 ft **Area Code** 702 **Zip** 89040

An old Mormon settlement, Overton is located at the site of an ancient civilization that, 1,200 years ago, extended for 30 miles along the Muddy River. Some of this area is now covered by Lake Mead.

What to See and Do

Lake Mead National Recreation Area (see). SE via NV 169.

Lost City Museum of Archaeology. An agency of the state of Nevada, the museum is located on a restored portion of Pueblo Grande de Nevada. The museum has an extensive collection of ancient Native American artifacts, fossils and semiprecious gems. There is also a picnic area. The curator and staff have travel tips and information on the area; gift shop. (Daily; closed Jan 1, Thanksgiving, Dec 25) 1 mi S on NV 169. Phone 702/397-2193. ¢

Valley of Fire State Park (see). Approx 15 mi SW via NV 169.

Pyramid Lake (C-1 - D-1)

(See also Reno)

(36 mi N of Reno on NV 445)

Surrounded by rainbow-tinted, eroded hills, this is a remnant of prehistoric Lake Lahontan, which once covered 8,400 square miles in western Nevada and northeastern California. The largest natural lake in the state, Pyramid is about 30 miles long and from 7 to 9 miles wide, with deep-blue sparkling waters. It is fed by scant water from the diverted Truckee River and by brief floods in other streams. Since the Newlands Irrigation Project deprives it of water, its level is receding.

General John C. Frémont gave the lake its name when he visited the area in 1844, apparently taking it from the tufa (porous rock) islands that jut up from the water. One, 475 feet high, is said by Native Americans to be a basket inverted over an erring woman. Though turned to stone, her "breath" (wisps of steam from a hot spring) can still be seen. Another is called Stone Mother and Basket. At the north end there is a cluster of sharp spires known as the Needles. Anahoe Island, in the lake, is a sanctuary and breeding ground for more than 10,000 huge white pelicans.

An air of mystery surrounds the area, bred by the murmuring waves, the spires and domes with their wisps of steam, and the ever-changing tints of the folded, eroded hills. At nearby Astor Pass, railroad excavations uncovered a horse skull, fragmentary remains of an elephant, bison and camel, all believed to have lived on the lakeshore in prehistoric times.

Pyramid Lake abounds with Lahonton cutthroat trout; it is one of the top trophy trout lakes in the United States. All rights belong to the Native Americans. For information about roads, fishing and boat permits, contact the Sutcliffe Ranger Station or Pyramid Lake Fisheries, Star Rte, Sutcliffe 89510; 775/476-0500. Camping, boating and fishing at Pyramid Lake is considered by many to be the best in the state. Day use ¢¢¢

Visitor centers, located in the hatcheries at Sutcliffe and between Nixon and Wadsworth, describe the land, lake and people through photographs and displays (daily).

Reno (D-1)

(See also Carson City, Incline Village, Virginia City)

Founded 1868 **Pop** 133,850 **Elev** 4,498 ft **Area Code** 775
E-mail info@reno-sparkschamber.org
Web www.reno-sparkschamber.org

Information Chamber of Commerce, 405 Marsh Ave, PO Box 3499, 89505; 775/686-3030. For information on cultural events contact the Sierra Arts Foundation, 200 Flint St, 89501; 775/329-2787

Reno, "the biggest little city in the world," renowned as a gambling and vacation center, is an important distribution and merchandising area, the home of the University of Nevada-Reno and a residential city. Between the steep slopes of the Sierra and the low eastern hills, Reno spills across the Truckee Meadows. The neon lights of the nightclubs, gambling casinos and bars give it a glitter that belies its quiet acres of fine houses, churches and schools. The surrounding area is popular for sailing, boating, horseback riding and deer and duck hunting.

Reno was known as Lake's Crossing and was an overland travelers' camping place even before the gold rush. It grew with the exploitation of the Comstock Lode and became a city in May 1868, with a public auction of real estate by a railway agent. Within a month there were 100 houses. A railroad official named the town in honor of a Union officer of the Civil War, General Jesse Lee Reno. In 1871 it became the seat of Washoe County.

Many Nevadans resent Reno's reputation as a divorce capital. They point out that many more couples are married than divorced at the Washoe County Courthouse. A six-month divorce law had been on the books since 1861, before Nevada became a state. The six-week law became effective in the 1930s.

What to See and Do

Gray Line bus tours. To Virginia City, Ponderosa Ranch, Lake Tahoe and other nearby points. For information contact 2050 Glendale Ave, Sparks 89431; phone 775/331-1147 or 800/822-6009.

National Automobile Museum. More than 200 vehicles on display. Theater presentation; period street scenes. (Daily; closed Thanksgiving, Dec 25) 10 S Lake St. Phone 775/333-9300. **¢¢¢**

Nevada Museum of Art. Changing art exhibits by international, national, regional and local artists. (Daily exc Mon; closed hols) 160 W Liberty St. Phone 775/329-3333. **¢¢**

Pyramid Lake (see). 36 mi N on NV 445.

Toiyabe National Forest. Approx 3 million acres, partly in California. Big-game hunting, saddle and pack trips, trout fishing, campsites (fees vary), picnicking, winter sports. Berlin-Ichthyosaur State Park (see AUSTIN), Lake Tahoe (see CALIFORNIA) and Mt Charleston Recreation Area (see LAS VEGAS) are in the forest. (Daily) 10 mi W on I-80, then W on NV 27. For further information contact Public Affairs Officer, 1200 Franklin Way, Sparks 89431; phone 775/331-6444. **Free**

University of Nevada-Reno (1874). (12,000 students) The campus covers 200 acres on a plateau overlooking the Truckee Meadows, in the shadow of the Sierra Nevada Mountains. Opened in Elko, it was moved to Reno and reopened in 1885. Tours of campus. 9th & N Virginia Sts. Phone 775/784-4865. On campus are

Fleischmann Planetarium. Northern Nevada's only planetarium, this facility features star shows, movies, astronomy museum, telescope viewing (Fri eves) and more. (Daily; closed Jan 1, Thanksgiving, Dec 25) Phone 775/784-4812. **¢¢¢**

Mackay School of Mines Museum. Minerals, rocks, fossils and mining memorabilia. (Mon-Fri; closed hols) Phone 775/784-6052. **Free**

Nevada Historical Society Museum. Prehistoric and modern Native American artifacts; ranching, mining and gambling artifacts. Carson City Mint materials; audiovisual programs; museum tours; research and genealogy library (daily exc Sun). Museum (daily exc Sun; closed hols, Oct 31). 1650 N Virginia St. Phone 775/688-1190. **Donation**

Annual Events

Rodeo. Reno Livestock Events Center. Downtown contests and celebrations on closed streets. Phone 775/329-3877. Mid-June.

Nevada State Fair. Fairgrounds, Wells St. Phone 775/688-5767. Aug 23-27.

National Championship Air Races. Reno/Stead Airport. 775/972-6663. 4 days mid-Sept.

Motels

★★ **LA QUINTA INN.** *4001 Market St (89502), US 395 exit Villanova & Plumb Ln, near Reno Tahoe Intl Airport. 775/348-6100; FAX 775/348-8794; res: 800/687-6667; res: 800/531-5900.* Web www.laquinta.com. 130 rms, 2 story. S $61-$69; D $61-$77; each addl $8; under 18 free. Crib free. Pet accepted. TV; cable. Pool. Complimentary continental bkfst. Coffee in rms. Restaurant adj open 24 hrs. Ck-out noon. Business servs avail. Free airport transportation. Cr cds: A, C, D, DS, MC, V.

★ **TRAVELODGE.** *2050 Market St (89502), US 395S exit Mill St W, near Reno-Tahoe Intl Airport. 775/786-2500; FAX 775/786-3884; res: 800/648-3800.* 211 units, 4 story, 70 kits. (no equipt). Late May-Oct: S $49, D $157; each addl $9; kit. suites $64-$157; under 18 free; wkly rates; higher rates: wkends, hols, special events; lower rates rest of yr. Crib free. Pet accepted; $5/day. TV; cable. Pool; whirlpool. Sauna. Complimentary continental bkfst. Restaurant nearby. Ck-out noon. Coin Indry. Business servs avail. Airport, casino transportation. Microwaves in kit. units. Cr cds: A, C, D, DS, JCB, MC, V.

✓★ **VAGABOND INN.** *3131 S Virginia St (89502). 775/825-7134; FAX 702/825-3096; res: 800/522-1555.* 129 rms, 2 story. May-Oct: S $45-$65; D $49-$69; each addl $5; under 18 free; higher rates special events, hols; lower rates rest of yr. Crib free. Pet accepted, some restrictions; $5/day. TV; cable (premium). Pool. Complimentary continental bkfst. Restaurant adj 11-4 am. Ck-out 11 am. Meeting rm. Business servs avail. Airport, RR station, bus depot transportation. Health club privileges. Some private patios, balconies. Cr cds: A, C, D, DS, MC, V.

Motor Hotels

★★ **BEST WESTERN PLAZA.** *1981 Terminal Way (89502), at Reno Cannon Intl Airport. 775/348-6370; FAX 775/348-9722; res: 800/648-3525.* E-mail applaza@worldnet.att.net. 270 rms, 3 story. S $69-$99; D $69-$119; each addl $10; suites $125-$250; kit. unit $275; under 12 free; higher rates: hols, special events. Crib free. TV; cable (premium), VCR avail. Pool; whirlpool. Restaurant 5:30 am-11 pm. Rm serv. Bar 11-1 am. Ck-out noon. Meeting rms. Business center. In-rm modem link. Bellhops. Valet serv. Airport transportation. Putting green. Exercise equipt; sauna. Health club privileges. Refrigerators avail. Some fireplaces. Mini-casino. Cr cds: A, C, D, DS, MC, V.

★★ **JOHN ASCUAGA'S NUGGET COURTYARD.** *1100 Nugget Ave (89431), adj to John Ascuaga's Nugget Tower, 3 mi E off I-80, exit 17. 775/356-3300; FAX 775/356-4198; res: 800/648-1177.* E-mail janugget.com; web janugget.com. 157 rms, 5 story. S, D $79-$89; under 18 free. Crib free. TV; cable. Heated pool; poolside serv. Complimentary coffee in lobby. Ck-out 11 am. Business servs avail. Free parking. Sundries. Free airport transportation. Health club privileges. Some balconies. Wedding chapel. Cr cds: A, C, D, DS, MC, V.

Hotels

★★★ **ATLANTIS CASINO RESORT.** *3800 S Virginia St (89502). 775/825-4700; FAX 775/826-7860.* E-mail mkt@atlantis.reno.nv.us; web www.atlantiscasino.com. 600 rms, 18 story. May-Sept: S, D $59-$79; each addl $10; suites $145-$195; under 18 free; ski, golf rates; higher rates: wkends, hols, special events; lower rates rest of yr. Crib free. TV; cable. Heated pool; whirlpool. Restaurant open 24 hrs (also see ATLANTIS). Bar; entertainment. Ck-out 11 am. Convention facilities. Business servs avail. Free valet parking. Free airport transportation. Exercise equipt; sauna. Massage. Some in-rm whirlpools. Casino. Cr cds: A, C, D, DS, ER, JCB, MC, V.

✓★★★ **CIRCUS CIRCUS HOTEL & CASINO.** *500 N Sierra St (89513). 775/329-0711; FAX 775/328-9652; res: 800/648-5010.* E-mail circus@circus.reno.nv.us; web www.circuscircus.org. 1,572 rms, 23 & 28 story. S, D $39-$59; each addl $10; minisuites $59-$79; under 13 free; ski plans; higher rates: wkends, hols, special events. Crib $6. TV; cable. Restaurant open 24 hrs. Bar; entertainment. Ck-out noon. Business servs avail. Gift shop. Free covered valet parking. Airport transportation. Health club privileges. Rec rm. Casino. Midway, arcade games. Free circus acts. Cr cds: A, C, D, DS, MC, V.

✓★★ **COMSTOCK HOTEL & CASINO.** *200 W 2nd St (89501), downtown. 775/329-1880; FAX 775/348-0539; res: 800/266-7862.* 310 rms, 16 story. Mid-Apr-mid-Nov: S, D $47-$69; each addl $8; suites $110-$300; under 12 free; higher rates: wkends, special events; lower rates rest of yr. Crib free. TV. Heated pool; whirlpool. Restaurant open 24 hrs. Bar open 24 hrs. Ck-out 11 am. Meeting rms. Business servs avail. Free valet parking. Airport transportation. Exercise equipt; sauna. Whirlpool in some suites. Casino. Cr cds: A, C, D, DS, ER, MC, V.

★★★ **ELDORADO HOTEL CASINO.** *345 N Virginia St (89505), at 4th St. 775/786-5700; FAX 775/322-7124; res: 800/648-5966.* Web www.eldoradoreno.com. 817 rms, 26 story. July-Oct: S, D $69-$89; each addl $10; suites $110-$495; under 12 free; higher rates: wkends, hols; lower rates rest of yr. Crib free. TV; cable. Heated pool; whirlpool, poolside serv. Restaurants open 24 hrs. Rm serv 24 hrs. Bar; entertainment. Ck-out noon. Convention facilities. Business servs avail. In-rm modem link. Concierge. Gift shop. Airport transportation. Garage; free valet parking. Health club privileges. Wet bar in some suites; some bathrm phones, refrigerators. Casino. Cr cds: A, C, D, DS, ER, MC, V.

✓★★ **FITZGERALD'S CASINO HOTEL.** *255 N Virginia St (89501). 775/785-3300; FAX 775/786-3686; res: 800/648-5022.* Web www.fitzgerald.com. 351 rms, 16 story. May-Oct: S, D $36-$88; each addl $10; suites $90-$140; under 13 free; higher rates: wkends, hols; lower rates rest of yr. TV; cable. Restaurants open 24 hrs. Rm serv 6 am-9 pm. Bars; entertainment. Ck-out noon. Free valet parking. Casino. Cr cds: A, C, D, DS, MC, V.

★★ **FLAMINGO HILTON.** *255 N Sierra St (89501), downtown. 775/322-1111; FAX 775/785-7086; res: 888/648-4882; res: 800/648-4882.* 604 rms, 20 story. May-Sept: S, D $59-$159; each addl $10; suites $145-$395; under 19 free; higher rates hols; lower rates rest of yr. Crib free. TV; cable. Restaurants open 24 hrs. Bars; entertainment. Ck-out 11 am. Convention facilities. Business servs avail. In-rm modem link. Gift shop. Barber, beauty shop. Free valet parking. Airport transportation. Exercise equipt. Casino. Cr cds: A, C, D, DS, ER, JCB, MC, V.

★★ **HARRAH'S.** *219 Center St (89054). 775/788-2300; FAX 775/788-2815; res: 800/427-7247.* 408 rms, 26 story. May-Oct: S, D $69-$84; each addl $10; under 12 free; lower rates rest of yr. Crib free. Pet accepted. TV; cable (premium). Pool. Complimentary continental bkfst. Restaurant adj open 24 hrs. Bar. Ck-out noon. Meeting rms. Business servs avail. In-rm modem link. Sundries. Shopping arcade. Barber, beauty shop. Valet serv. Free airport transportation. Exercise equipt. Health club privileges. Cr cds: A, C, D, DS, JCB, MC, V.

★★★ **HARRAH'S.** *219 N Center St (89504), at 2nd St, downtown. 775/786-3232; FAX 775/788-3274; res: 800/427-7247.* 565 rms, 24 story, no rms on 1st 5 floors. May-Oct: S, D $79-$89; each addl $10; suites $210-$425; under 15 free; higher rates wkends; lower rates rest of yr. Crib free. Pet accepted, some restrictions. TV; cable. Heated pool; whirlpool, lifeguard in season. Restaurant open 24 hrs. Bars; entertainment. Ck-out noon. Convention facilities. Business servs avail. In-rm modem link. Shopping arcade. Barber, beauty shop. Covered parking; valet. Free airport, bus depot transportation. Exercise rm; sauna, steam rm. Massage. Game rm. Rec rm. Casino. Some bathrm phones. Some private patios. Cr cds: A, C, D, DS, JCB, MC, V.

★★★ **JOHN ASCUAGA'S NUGGET COURTYARD.** *1100 Nugget Ave (89431), 3 mi E off I-80, exit 17. 775/356-3300; FAX 775/356-4198; res: 800/648-1177.* E-mail janugget.com; web janugget.com. 1,407 rms, 29 story. S, D $99-$125; each addl $10; suites $145-$450; under 18 free. Crib free. TV; cable. Indoor/outdoor pool; whirlpool, poolside serv. Restaurants open 24 hrs. Bars; entertainment. Ck-out 11 am. Convention facilities. Business center. Concierge. Gift shop. Beauty shop. Free valet parking. Free airport transportation. Exercise equipt. Massage. Casino. Cr cds: C.

★★★ **PEPPERMILL HOTEL & CASINO.** *2707 S Virginia St (89502), 2 mi W of Reno Tahoe Intl Airport. 775/826-2121; FAX 775/689-7178; res: 800/648-6992.* 1,670 rms, 16 story. S, D $49-$100; suites $200-$500; under 15 free. Crib free. Valet parking. TV; cable. 2 heated pools; whirlpool. Restaurant open 24 hrs. Bars; entertainment. Ck-out noon. Meeting rms. Business servs avail. Gift shop. Barber, beauty shop. Free airport transportation. Exercise equipt; sauna. Minibars. Casino. Cr cds: A, C, D, DS, MC, V.

★★★ **RENO HILTON RESORT & CASINO.** *2500 E 2nd St (89595), near Reno Tahoe Intl Airport. 775/789-2000; FAX 775/789-2418; res: 800/648-5080.* E-mail room_reservation@hilton.com; web www.renohilton.com. 2,000 rms, 27 story. S, D $69-$149; each addl $10; suites $149-$900; package plans. Crib free. TV; cable. Pool; whirlpool, poolside serv, lifeguard. Restaurants open 24 hrs (also see THE STEAK HOUSE). Bars; entertainment. Ck-out 11 am. Convention facilities. Meeting rms. Business center. Shopping arcade. Barber, beauty shop. Free valet parking. Free airport transportation. Lighted indoor & outdoor tennis, pro. Driving range. Exercise rm; sauna, steam rm. Spa. Massage. Rec rm. Bowling. Some bathrm phones, refrigerators; wet bars. Movie theaters. Casino. Cr cds: A, C, D, DS, ER, JCB, MC, V.

★★★ **SILVER LEGACY RESORT & CASINO.** *407 N Virginia St (89501). 775/329-4777; FAX 775/325-7470; res: 800/687-8733.* E-mail resv@silverlegacy.com; web www.silverlegacy.com. 1,720 rms, 38 story. July-Oct: S, D $59-$119; each addl $10; suites $100-$200; under 12 free; lower rates rest of yr. TV; cable. Pool; whirlpool, poolside serv. Restaurant open 24 hrs. Bar. Ck-out 11 am. Convention facilities. Business servs avail. Shopping arcade. Barber, beauty shop. Valet serv. Free airport transportation. Exercise rm; sauna. Cr cds: A, C, D, DS, MC, V.

Restaurants

★★★ **ATLANTIS.** *(See Atlantis Casino Resort) 702/825-4700.* E-mail mkt@atlantis.reno.nv.us; web www.atlantis.reno.nv.us. Hrs: 5-10 pm; Fri, Sat to 10:30 pm; early-bird dinner to 6 pm. Res accepted. Continental menu. Semi-a la carte: dinner $14.95-$26.95. Specialties: flaming coconut prawns, double-cut lamb chops, Alaskan king crab. Valet parking. Brightly decorated interior resembles underwater terrain; large saltwater aquarium completes illusion. Cr cds: A, C, D, DS, ER, JCB, MC, V.

★★ **BRICKS RESTAURANT & WINE BAR.** *1695 S Virginia St (89502). 775/786-2277.* Hrs: 11:30 am-2 pm, 5-10 pm; Sat from 5 pm. Closed Sun; major hols. Res accepted. Continental menu. Bar 4-11 pm.

Semi-a la carte: lunch $6.95-$12.95, dinner $11.95-$21.95. Specialties: shrimp scampi risotto, pork tenderloin, chicken pesto. Intimate atmosphere. Cr cds: A, C, D, DS, MC, V.

D

★★ **FAMOUS MURPHYS.** *3127 S Virginia St (89502). 775/827-4111.* Web www.famousmurphys.com. Hrs: 11 am-2 pm, 5-10 pm; Sat, Sun 10 am-2 pm, 5-10 pm. Res accepted. Bar to 3:30 am. Semi-a la carte: lunch $4.95-$12.95, dinner $10.95-$22.95. Child's meals. Specializes in steak, seafood, pasta. Oyster bar. Pub atmosphere. Cr cds: A, C, DS, JCB, MC, V.

D

★★ **GLORY HOLE RESTAURANTE.** *4201 W 4th St (89503). 702/786-1323.* Hrs: 5-10:30 pm. Closed Thanksgiving. Bar. Semi-a la carte: dinner $10-$42.95. Specializes in steak, fresh seafood, chicken. Salad bar. Old West saloon, mining camp decor. Cr cds: A, C, D, DS, MC, V.

D

★★★ **ICHIBAN JAPANESE STEAK HOUSE.** *210 N Sierra St Fl 2 (89501), downtown. 775/323-5550.* Hrs: 4:30-10 pm; Fri, Sat to 11 pm. Res accepted. Japanese menu. Bar. A la carte entrees: dinner $8.95-$15.95. Complete meals: $14.95-$26.95. Child's meals. Specializes in steak, seafood, chicken. Sushi bar. Cr cds: A, C, D, DS, MC, V.

D SC

✓★★ **PALAIS DE JADE.** *960 W Moana Lane #107 (89509), in Lakeside Crossing Shopping Ctr. 775/827-5233.* Hrs: 11 am-10 pm. Closed most maj hols. Res accepted. Bar. Semi-a la carte: lunch $5.50-$7.50, dinner $5.50-$17.95. Specialties: jade crispy shrimp, sesame chicken, orange-flavored beef. Chinese decor. Cr cds: A, C, MC, V.

D

★★★ **PIMPAREL'S LA TABLE FRANÇAISE.** *3065 W 4th St (89503), 2 mi west of downtown. 702/323-3200.* Hrs: 6-10 pm. Closed Sun, Mon; Jan 1, Thanksgiving, Dec 25. Res accepted. French menu. Bar. Wine list. A la carte entrees: dinner $12-$33.50. Menu changes bimonthly; based on seasonal ingredients. Own baking. Cr cds: A, C, MC, V.

D

✓★★ **RAPSCALLION.** *1555 S Wells Ave (89502). 702/323-1211.* Hrs: 11:30 am-10 pm; Fri, Sat 5-10:30 pm; Sun brunch 10 am-2 pm. Closed Thanksgiving, Dec 25. Res accepted. Bar 11-1 am; Sat to 2 am; Sun from 10 am. A la carte entrees: lunch, dinner $5.95-$18.95. Sun brunch $4.95-$7.95. Specializes in seafood. Parking. Outdoor dining. 1890s San Francisco decor. Cr cds: A, C, MC, V.

D

★★★ **THE STEAK HOUSE.** *(See Reno Hilton) 702/789-2270.* Web www.renohilton.net. Hrs: 5-10 pm; early-bird dinner to 6 pm. Res accepted. Setups. Wine list. A la carte entrees: $14.25-$27.95. Specialties: Winnemucca potatoes, broiled swordfish. Valet parking. Cr cds: A, C, MC, V.

D

South Lake Tahoe

(see South Lake Tahoe, CA)

Sparks

(see Reno)

Stateline (E-1)

Pop 1,379 **Elev** 6,360 ft **Area Code** 775 **Zip** 89449

This area is best known for its famous high-rise casino/hotels, cabarets and fine dining, but as an integral part of Tahoe's "south shore," it is also appreciated for its spectacular natural beauty. Alpine beaches and Sierra forests afford visitors an endless variety of year-round recreation. There are several excellent public golf courses in the area.

Motel

★★ **LAKESIDE INN & CASINO.** *Hwy 50 Kingsbury Grade (89449), ½ mi NE on US 50, at Kingsbury Grade. 775/588-7777; FAX 775/588-4092; res: 800/624-7980.* Web www.lakesideinn.com. 124 rms, 2 story. Mid-June-mid-Oct: S, D $69-$99; each addl $10; suites $120-$235; package plans in winter; under 16 free; lower rates rest of yr. Crib free. TV; cable. Pool. Complimentary coffee in rms. Restaurant open 24 hrs. Bars. Ck-out noon. Meeting rms. Business servs avail. Sundries. Downhill ski 2 mi; x-country ski 16 mi. Game rm. Wet bar in suites. Casino. Cr cds: A, C, D, DS, MC, V.

SC

Hotels

★★★ **CAESARS TAHOE.** *55 Highway 50 (89449), 1 blk N on US 50. 775/588-3515; FAX 775/586-4694; res: 800/648-3353.* Web www.caesars.com. 440 rms, 15 story. Mid-June-Sept: S, D $99-$220; each addl $10; suites $300-$990; under 12 free; ski, golf packages; lower rates rest of yr. Crib free. TV; cable (premium), VCR avail. Indoor pool; whirlpools. Coffee in rms. Restaurant open 24 hrs. Bar; entertainment. Ck-out noon. Convention facilities. Business servs avail. In-rm modem link. Concierge. Shopping arcade. Barber, beauty shop. Free valet parking. Lighted tennis. Exercise equipt; steam rm, sauna. Massage. Racquetball. Game rm. Bathrm phones; some refrigerators, in-rm whirlpools; microwaves avail. Casino. Cr cds: A, C, D, DS, JCB, MC, V.

D SC

★★★★ **HARRAH'S HOTEL CASINO.** *US 50 (89449), on US 50, downtown. 775/588-6611; FAX 702/586-6607; res: 800/648-3773.* Web harrahstahoe.com. The spacious and tastefully decorated rooms are what distinguish this casino from the others in the area. Some offer views of the lake and the mountains. 532 rms, 18 story. Mid-June-mid-Sept: S, D $149-$209; each addl $20; suites $199-$950; under 15 free; ski plans; higher rates wkends, hols; lower rates rest of yr. Crib free. Pet accepted. TV; cable, VCR avail. Indoor pool; whirlpool, poolside serv. 7 restaurants w/1 open 24 hrs (also see FRIDAY'S STATION and SUMMIT). Rm serv 24 hrs. Bars; theater-restaurant; entertainment. Ck-out noon. Convention facilities. Business servs avail. Concierge. Shopping arcade. Barber, beauty shop. Free covered valet parking. Exercise equipt; sauna, steam rm. Massage. Game rm. Casino. Microwaves avail. Butler serv in suites. Cr cds: A, C, D, DS, ER, JCB, MC, V.

D SC

★★★ **HARVEY'S RESORT HOTEL CASINO.** *Stateline Ave (US 50) (89449), on US 50, downtown. 775/588-2411; FAX 775/588-6643; res: 800/427-8397.* Web www.harveys.com/reservations.html. 740 rms, 19 story. July-Aug: S, D $115-$185; each addl $20; suites $275-$725; package plans; higher rates wkends, hols; lower rates rest of yr. Crib free. TV; cable. Pool; whirlpool. Complimentary continental bkfst. 8 restaurants (also see LEWELLYN'S and SAGE ROOM). Rm serv 24 hrs. 6 bars open 24 hrs; entertainment. Ck-out noon. Convention facilities. Business servs avail. Concierge. Shopping arcade. Barber, beauty shop. Covered parking; free valet, self-park. Airport transportation. Exercise rm; sauna. Massage. Game rm. Rec rm. Casino. Bathrm phones; many minibars; wet bar in suites. Tahoe's first gaming establishment (1944). Cr cds: A, C, D, DS, JCB, MC, V.

D SC

★ **HORIZON CASINO RESORT.** *50 Hwy 50 (89449), 1 blk NE on US 50. 775/588-6211; FAX 775/588-1344; res: 800/322-7723.* E-mail horizoncasino@oakweb; web www.horizoncasino.com. 539 rms, 15 story. Mid-June-mid-Sept: S, D $79-$164; each addl $10; suites $300-$400; higher rates: hols, special events; lower rates rest of yr. Crib free. TV; cable. Heated pool (seasonal); whirlpools, poolside serv, lifeguard. Restaurants open 24 hrs. Bars; entertainment. Ck-out noon. Convention facilities. Business servs avail. Concierge. Shopping arcade. Barber, beauty shop. Free garage parking. Downhill ski 1 mi; x-country ski 15 mi. Exercise equipt. Massage. Game rm. Wet bar in suites. Some balconies. Casino. Cr cds: A, C, D, DS, JCB, MC, V.

D SC

Restaurants

★★ **CHART HOUSE.** *392 Kingsbury Grade (89449), 2 mi E off US 50, on Kingsbury grade (NV 28). 775/588-6276.* Hrs: 5:30-10 pm; Sat 5-10:30 pm. Res accepted. Bar from 5 pm; Sat from 4:30 pm. Semi-a la carte: dinner $15.50-$31.95. Child's meals. Specialties: teriyaki sirloin, prime rib. Salad bar. Outdoor dining. View of lake. Cr cds: A, C, D, DS, MC, V.

D

★★★ **FRIDAY'S STATION.** *(See Harrah's Hotel Casino) 775/588-6611.* Hrs: 5:30-9:30 pm; Fri to 10 pm; Sat to 10:30 pm. Res accepted. Bar. A la carte entrees: dinner $16-$32. Specializes in hardwood-grilled seafood and steak. Overlooks Lake Tahoe. Cr cds: A, C, D, DS, MC, V.

D

★★★ **LEWELLYN'S.** *(See Harvey's Resort) 702/588-2411.* Hrs: 11:30 am-2:30 pm, 6-9:30 pm; Sun-Tues from 6 pm; Fri to 10 pm; Sat 11:30 am-2:30 pm, 5-10 pm. Res accepted. International menu. Bar 11 am-10:30 pm. Wine list. Semi-a la carte: lunch $8-$14, dinner $18-$28. Specialties: abalone, rack of lamb, wild boar. Pianist Wed-Sun. Valet parking. Elegant dining rm; view of Lake Tahoe. Totally nonsmoking. Cr cds: A, C, D, DS, JCB, MC, V.

D

★★★ **SAGE ROOM.** *(See Harvey's Resort Hotel) 702/588-2411.* E-mail info@harveys.com; web www.harveys.com. Hrs: 6-10 pm; Sat to 11 pm. Res accepted. Continental, Amer menu. Bar. Wine cellar. Semi-a la carte: dinner $18-$28. Specializes in steak, fresh seafood, game (in season). Own baking. Valet parking. Dining rm interior is part of original Wagon Wheel Saloon & Gambling Hall; hand-hewn beams, redwood ceilings, Remington bronzes, Western decor. Cr cds: A, C, D, DS, JCB, MC, V.

D

★★★ **SUMMIT.** *(See Harrah's Hotel Casino) 702/588-6611.* Hrs: 5:30-10 pm; Fri to 10:30 pm; Sat to 11 pm. Res accepted. Continental menu. Bar. Wine list. Semi-a la carte: dinner $26-$65. Specialties: rack of lamb, lobster thermidor, abalone. Pianist exc Mon. Valet parking. Formal atmosphere; glass wine cases, views of lake. Totally nonsmoking. Cr cds: A, C, D, DS, MC, V.

D

Tonopah (F-3)

Settled 1900 **Pop** 3,616 **Elev** 6,030 ft **Area Code** 775 **Zip** 89049
E-mail tonopahc@sierra.net

Information Chamber of Commerce, 301 Brougher St, PO Box 869; 775/482-3859

Founded by prospector Jim Butler in 1900 and named by his wife, Tonopah was a high-spirited but unusually orderly camp in its early days. "Tono" is a shrub of the greasewood family, the roots of which can be eaten; "pah" means water in the Shoshone language. There are a couple of gold mines and a silver mine in the vicinity. The Tonopah Test Range is approximately 35 miles east. A Ranger District office of the Toiyabe National Forest (see RENO) is located here, as well as a detached area office of the Bureau of Land Management.

What to See and Do

Central Nevada Museum. Historical, mining and gem displays. (Daily, afternoons; closed Dec 25) Logan Field Rd. Phone 775/482-9676. **Donation**

Mizpah Hotel (1907). Old mining hotel completely restored to its original Victorian style. 100 Main St. Phone 775/482-6202.

Rock collecting. Rich variety of minerals.

Motels

★★ **BEST WESTERN HI DESERT INN.** *320 Main St (us 95) (89049). 775/482-3511; FAX 775/482-3300; res: 877/286-2208.* 62 rms, 2 story. S $45-$49; D $59-$69; each addl $6. Crib $8. Pet accepted, some restrictions. TV; cable (premium). Pool; whirlpool. Complimentary continental bkfst. Restaurant nearby. Ck-out 11 am. Cr cds: C.

★ **JIM BUTLER MOTEL.** *100 S Main St (89049). 775/482-3577; FAX 775/482-5240; res: 800/635-9455.* 24 rms, 2 story. S, D $34-$42. Crib $5. Pet accepted, some restrictions. TV; cable (premium). Complimentary coffee in lobby. Restaurant adj 24 hrs. Ck-out 11 am. Some refrigerators. Cr cds: A, C, D, DS, MC, V.

SC

✓★ **SILVER QUEEN MOTEL.** *255 Erie Main (89049). 775/482-6291; FAX 775/482-3190; res: 800/210-9218.* 85 rms, 1-2 story. No elvtr. S $33; D $33-$36; kit. units $45. Crib $4. Pet accepted. TV; cable (premium), VCR avail (movies). Pool. Restaurant adj 6 am-10 pm. Bar 11 am-midnight. Ck-out 11 am. Some refrigerators, microwaves. Cr cds: A, C, D, DS, MC, V.

SC

Motor Hotel

★ **STATION HOUSE HOTEL & CASINO.** *1100 Erie Main St (89049). 775/482-9777; FAX 775/482-8762.* 78 rms, 3 suites, 2 story. S $36; D $39; each addl $2; suites $58-$80; under 11 free. Crib free. TV; cable (premium). Complimentary coffee in rms. Restaurant open 24 hrs. Bar; entertainment exc Mon. Ck-out 11 am. Meeting rms. Shopping arcade. Free bus depot transportation. Cr cds: A, C, D, DS, MC, V.

SC

Valley of Fire State Park (H-6)

(See also see Las Vegas, Overton)

(37 mi NE of Las Vegas on I-15, then 18 mi SE on NV 169)

This park offers a geologically incredible 38,480-acre area that gains its name from the red, Jurassic-period sandstone formed 150 million years ago. Fine examples of Native American petroglyphs can be seen throughout the park. Picnicking. Camping (dump station). Group use areas, visitor center. Standard fees. Phone 702/397-2088.

Virginia City (D-1)

(See also Carson City, Reno)

Settled 1859 **Pop** 750 **Elev** 6,220 ft **Area Code** 775 **Zip** 89440

Information Chamber of Commerce, South C Street, PO Box 464; phone 775/847-0311

Nevada's most famous mining town, Virginia City once had a population of about 35,000 people and was one of the richest cities in North America. Its dazzling career coincided with the life of the Comstock Lode, which yielded more than $1 billion worth of silver and gold. In the 1870s Virginia City had 4 banks, 6 churches, 110 saloons, an opera house, numerous theaters and the only elevator between Chicago and San Francisco. Great fortunes, including those of Hearst and Mackay, were founded here.

Virginia City is perched on the side of Mt Davidson, where a diagonal slit marks the Comstock Lode. The site is beautiful, and the air is so clear that the blue and purple masses of the Stillwater Range can be seen 120 miles away. Nearer are the green fields and cottonwoods along the Carson River and the white sands of Forty Mile Desert. Gold was found in this area in 1848, but the big silver strike was made in 1859.

Visitors can tour mines and old mansions, some of which have been restored (Easter week, Memorial Day-Oct, daily); visit several museums and saloons (daily); stroll through the local shops and ride on the steam-powered V&T Railroad (May-Sept).

What to See and Do

The Castle (1868). Built by Robert N. Graves, a mine superintendent of the Empire Mine, this Victorian mansion was once referred to as the "house of silver door knobs." Filled with international riches; original furnishings. (Memorial Day wkend-Oct; daily) 70 South B Street. Phone 775/847-0275. **¢¢**

Annual Event

Camel Races. Mid-Sept.

Wendover

(see Wendover, UT)

Winnemucca (B-3)

Settled ca 1850 **Pop** 6,134 **Elev** 4,299 ft **Area Code** 775 **Zip** 89445

Information Humboldt County Chamber of Commerce, 30 W Winnemucca Blvd; 775/623-2225

Originally called French Ford, the town was renamed for the last great chief of the Paiutes, who ruled the area. Winnemucca was first settled by a Frenchman who set up a trading post. Many Basques live here. A Ranger District office of the Humboldt National Forest (see ELKO) is located here.

What to See and Do

Humboldt Museum. Historical museum features Native American artifacts; bottles; pioneers' home items, tools, utensils; local history; antique auto display; old country store. (Mon-Fri, also Sat afternoons; closed major hols) Jungo Rd & Maple Ave. Phone 775/623-2912. **Donation**

Motels

★★ **BEST WESTERN GOLD COUNTRY INN.** *921 W Winnemucca Blvd (89445). 775/623-6999; FAX 775/623-9190; res: 800/346-5306.* 71 rms, 2 story. June-Labor Day: S, D $65-$75; each addl $10; under 12 free; lower rates rest of yr. Crib $5. Pet accepted, some restrictions. TV; cable (premium). Heated pool. Complimentary coffee in lobby. Restaurant adj open 24 hrs. Ck-out noon. Business servs avail. In-rm modem link. Airport transportation. Cr cds: A, C, D, DS, ER, MC, V.

D SC

★ **DAYS INN.** *511 W Winnemucca Blvd (89445). 775/623-3661; FAX 775/623-4234; res: 800/329-7466.* 50 rms, 2 story. June-Labor Day: S $60; D $65; each addl $5; lower rates rest of yr. Crib $5. Pet accepted. TV; cable (premium). Heated pool. Coffee in lobby. Restaurant nearby. Ck-out noon. Cr cds: A, C, D, DS, MC, V.

SC

★★ **RED LION INN & CASINO.** *741 W Winnemucca Blvd (89445). 775/623-2565; FAX 775/623-2527; res: 800/633-6435.* 107 units, 2 story. June-Oct: S, D $79-$89; each addl $10; suites $99-$150; under 12 free; lower rates rest of yr. Crib $5. Pet accepted, some restrictions; $50 deposit. TV; cable (premium), VCR avail. Heated pool. Restaurant open 24 hrs. Bar. Ck-out noon. Business servs avail. Airport transportation. Game rm. Some balconies. Casino. Cr cds: A, C, D, DS, MC, V.

D SC

★ **VAL-U INN.** *125 E Winnemucca Blvd (89445). 775/623-5248; FAX 775/623-4722; res: 800/443-7777.* 80 rms, 3 story. No elvtr. Mid-May-Sept: S $45-$50; D $48-$57; each addl $5; lower rates rest of yr. Crib $4. Pet accepted; $5. TV; cable (premium), VCR avail. Heated pool. Sauna, steam rm. Continental bkfst. Restaurant nearby. Ck-out noon. Business servs avail. Cr cds: A, C, D, DS, MC, V.

SC

✓★ **WINNERS HOTEL & CASINO.** *185 W Winnemucca Blvd (89445). 775/623-2511; FAX 775/623-3976; res: 800/648-4770.* 37 rms, 2 story. May-Labor Day: S $45; D $50-$65; each addl $5; suites $70; lower rates rest of yr. Pet accepted. TV; cable (premium). Continental bkfst in lobby. Restaurant nearby. Ck-out 11 am. Coin lndry. Cr cds: A, C, DS, MC, V.

D SC

Restaurant

★ **ORMACHEA'S.** *180 Melarky St (89445). 775/623-3455.* Hrs: 4-10 pm. Closed Mon; some major hols. Basque, Amer menu. Bar. Complete meals: dinner $10.25-$17. Child's meals. Specializes in Basque dishes. Cr cds: C, D, DS, MC, V.

Yerington (E-1)

Pop 2,367 **Elev** 4,384 ft **Area Code** 775 **Zip** 89447
E-mail lceda@tele-net.net **Web** www.tele-net.net/lceda

Information Mason Valley Chamber of Commerce, 227 S Main St; 775/463-2245

The town was once named Pizen Switch, presumably because of the bad whiskey being sold in a saloon. Wovoka, the Paiute messiah, grew up in this area. In 1889 Wovoka claimed to have had a vision in which he was instructed to teach a new dance that would oust the white intruders and restore to the Native Americans their lands and old way of life.

In 1894, the citizens saw the economic value of being on the route of the Carson and Colorado Railway. They decided to rename their town after the man with the power to decide the route—Henry Marvin Yerington. The railroad never did come to Yerington, instead established at nearby Wabuska.

What to See and Do

Fort Churchill State Historic Park. This post was established when the rush to the Comstock began, as protection against the Paiutes. It was garrisoned from 1860 to 1869. Adobe walls of the old buildings exist in a state of arrested decay. The visitor center has displays. Picnicking. Trails. Camping facilities on 1,232 acres. 25 mi N on US 95A, then 1 mi W on Old Fort Churchill Rd. Phone 775/577-2345. Camping **¢¢¢**; Day use **Free**

Utah

Population: 1,722,850
Land area: 84,990 square miles
Elevation: 2,200-13,528 feet
Highest point: Kings Peak (Duchesne County)
Entered union: January 4, 1896 (45th state)
Capital: Salt Lake City
Motto: Industry
Nickname: Beehive State
State flower: Sego lily
State bird: California gull
State tree: Blue spruce
State fair: September 7-17, 2000, in Salt Lake City
Time zone: Mountain

Utah is named for the Ute people, a nomadic tribe that populated these regions before the days of westward expansion. The state presents many natural faces, with arid desert and the deep, jagged canyons of the Colorado and Green rivers dominating the west and south, and high, rugged mountains in the east and north. Utah contains examples of almost all water and land forms, many unique to the state. This natural diversity, although stimulating to the artistic eye, created an environment inhospitable to early settlers. Tribes of Ute, Piute and Shoshone were the only people living in the region when the first white men, two Franciscan priests, passed through the area in 1776 en route to California from New Mexico. In 1819, British fur trappers began voyaging into northern Utah; by 1824 mountain men—people like Canadians Étienne Provost and Peter Skene Ogden, for whom some of Utah's towns and rivers are named—were venturing into Utah's wilds. Although these men traversed and explored much of the state, it took the determination and perseverance of a band of religious fugitives, members of the Church of Jesus Christ of Latter-day Saints, to conquer the wilderness that was Utah and permanently settle the land.

Brigham Young, leader of the Mormon followers, once remarked, "If there is a place on this earth that nobody else wants, that's the place I am hunting for." On July 24, 1847, upon entering the forbidding land surrounding the Great Salt Lake, Young exclaimed, "This is the place!" Immediately the determined settlers began to plow the unfriendly soil and build dams for irrigation. Hard work and tenacity were put to the test as the Mormons struggled to convert the Utah wilderness into productive land. With little to work with—what the settlers did not have, they did without—the Mormons gradually triumphed over the land, creating the safe haven they were searching for.

The Mormon church was founded by Joseph Smith on April 6, 1830, in New York state. The religion, based on writings inscribed on golden plates said to have been delivered to Smith by an angel and translated by him into *The Book of Mormon,* drew a large following. Moving from New York to Ohio and Missouri, and then driven from Missouri and later Illinois, the church grew despite persecution and torture. When Smith was killed in Illinois, Young took over. With a zealot's determination, he headed farther west in search of a place of refuge. He found it in the Salt Lake area of Utah. Growing outward from their original settlement, Mormon pioneers and missionaries established colonies that were to become many of Utah's modern-day cities. During 1847, as many as 1,637 Mormons came to Utah, and by the time the railroad penetrated the region, more than 6,000 had settled in the state. Before his death in 1877, 30 years after entering the Salt Lake Valley, Brigham Young had directed the founding of more than 350 communities.

While the Mormon church undoubtedly had the greatest influence on the state—developing towns in an orderly fashion with wide streets, planting straight rows of poplar trees to provide wind breaks and introducing irrigation throughout the desert regions—the church members were not the only settlers. In the latter part of the 19th century, the West's fabled pioneer era erupted. The gold rush of 1849-1850 sent gold seekers pouring through Utah on their way to California. The arrival of the Pony Express in Salt Lake City in 1860 brought more immigrants, and when the mining boom hit the state in the 1870s and 1880s, Utah's mining towns appeared almost overnight. In 1900 there were 277,000 Utahns; now the population stands at more than 1,700,000, with more than 75 percent living within 50 miles of Salt Lake City. The Mormon Church continues to play an important role, with close to 60 percent of the state's population being members of the Church.

Utah's natural diversity has made it a state of magnificent beauty, with more than 3,000 lakes, miles of mountains, acres upon acres of forests and large expanses of deserts. Its main heights, 13,000 feet or more, are reached by plateaus and mountains lifted during the Cascade disturbance of the Cenozoic period. In northern Utah, the grandeur of the Wasatch Range, one of the most rugged mountain ranges in the United States, cuts across the state north to south; the Uinta Range, capped by the white peaks of ancient glaciers, is the only major North American range that runs east to west. In the western third of the state lies the Great Basin, a landlocked drainage area that, at one time, was half covered by a large, ancient sea. At its peak, Lake Bonneville was 1,050 feet deep, 145 miles wide and 346 miles long. The Great Salt Lake and Sevier Lake are saltwater remnants of Bonneville, and Utah Lake is a freshwater remnant. To the east, the Bonneville Salt Flats lie where the ancient lake had retreated. To the east and west extends the Colorado River Plateau, or Red Plateau. This red rock country, renowned for its brilliant coloring and fantastic rock formations, is also home to one of the largest concentrations of national parks and monuments. With its many aspects, Utah is a land designed for the traveler who loves the Western outdoors and can appreciate the awesome accomplishments of the pioneers who developed it.

When to Go/Climate

Temperatures vary across the state, but in general, summer days are hot, summer nights cool; winters are cold and snowy, except in the southwestern part of the state. The best time to visit Utah is in the spring or fall when temperatures are milder and tourist crowds have thinned out.

AVERAGE HIGH/LOW TEMPERATURES (°F)

ST GEORGE

Jan 54/27	**May** 86/52	**Sept** 93/57
Feb 61/32	**June** 96/61	**Oct** 81/45
Mar 67/37	**July** 102/68	**Nov** 65/38
Apr 76/44	**Aug** 99/66	**Dec** 55/27

SALT LAKE CITY

Jan 37/19	**May** 72/46	**Sept** 79/51
Feb 44/25	**June** 83/55	**Oct** 66/40
Mar 52/31	**July** 92/64	**Nov** 51/31
Apr 61/38	**Aug** 89/62	**Dec** 38/22

CALENDAR HIGHLIGHTS

JANUARY

Sundance Film Festival (Park City). Week-long festival for independent filmmakers. Workshops, screenings and special events.

JUNE

Utah Summer Games (Cedar City). Olympic-style athletic events for amateur athletes. Phone 435/865-8421.

Utah Arts Festival (Salt Lake City). Downtown. More than 1,000 participants, 90 performing groups; Children's Art Yard, juried show with demonstrations. Ethnic food. Phone 801/322-2428.

JULY

Renaissance Fair (Cedar City). Main St City Park. Entertainment, food and games in Renaissance style. Held in conjunction with the opening of Utah Shakespearean Festival.

Ute Stampede Rodeo (Nephi). Three-day festival featuring horse and mammoth parades, carnival, PRCA rodeo, contests, arts and crafts, concessions. Phone 435/623-7102.

Festival of the American West (Logan). Ronald V. Jensen Living Historical Farm. Historical pageant; pioneer and Native American crafts fair, art exhibition, antique quilt show; frontier town; medicine man show; log construction; Dutch-oven cook-off. Phone 435/797-1143 or 800/225-FEST.

AUGUST

Novell Showdown (Park City). PGA invitational golf tournament. Contact Park Meadows Golf Club 801/531-7029.

Railroaders Festival (Brigham City). Golden Spike National Historic Site. Relive the rush to complete transcontinental railroad. Professional railroaders pursue world record in spike driving. Contact Golden Spike National Historic Site 435/471-2209.

Bonneville National Speed Trials (Wendover). Bonneville Speedway. Held since 1914 on the Bonneville Salt Flats, which has been used as a track for racing the world's fastest cars. Car racing in competition and against the clock. Phone 805/526-1805.

SEPTEMBER

Utah State Fair (Salt Lake City). State Fair Park. Arts & crafts, live entertainment, horse show and rodeo. Phone 801/538-FAIR.

Parks and Recreation Finder

Directions to and information about the parks and recreation areas below are given under their respective town/city sections. Please refer to those sections for details.

NATIONAL PARK AND RECREATION AREAS

Key to abbreviations. I.H.S. = International Historic Site; I.P.M. = International Peace Memorial; N.B. = National Battlefield; N.B.P. = National Battlefield Park; N.B.C. = National Battlefield & Cemetery; N.C. = National Conservation Area; N.E.M. = National Expansion Memorial; N.F. = National Forest; N.G. = National Grassland; N.H. = National Historical Park; N.H.C. = National Heritage Corridor; N.H.S. = National Historic Site; N.L. = National Lakeshore; N.M. = National Monument; N.M.P. = National Military Park; N.Mem. = National Memorial; N.P. = National Park; N.Pres. = National Preserve; N.R. = National Recreational Area; N.R.R. = National Recreational River; N.Riv. = National River; N.S. = National Seashore; N.S.R. = National Scenic Riverway; N.S.T. = National Scenic Trail; N.Sc. = National Scientific Reserve; N.V.M. = National Volcanic Monument.

Place Name	Listed Under
Arches N.P.	same
Ashley N.F.	VERNAL
Bryce Canyon N.P.	same
Canyonlands N.P.	same
Capitol Reef N.P.	same
Cedar Breaks N.M.	same
Dinosaur N.M.	same
Dixie N.F.	CEDAR CITY
Fishlake N.F.	RICHFIELD
Glen Canyon N.R.	LAKE POWELL
Golden Spike N.H.S.	BRIGHAM CITY
Hovenweep N.M.	BLANDING
Manti-LaSal N.F.	MOAB, MONTICELLO, PRICE
Natural Bridges N.M.	same
Rainbow Bridge N.M.	same
Timpanogos Cave N.M.	same
Uinta N.F.	PROVO
Wasatch-Cache N.F.	LOGAN, SALT LAKE CITY
Zion N.P.	same

STATE PARK AND RECREATION AREAS

Key to abbreviations. I.P. = Interstate Park; S.A.P. = State Archaeological Park; S.B. = State Beach; S.C. = State Conservation Area; S.C.P. = State Conservation Park; S.Cp. = State Campground; S.F. = State Forest; S.G. = State Garden; S.H.A. = State Historic Area; S.H.P. = State Historic Park; S.H.S. = State Historic Site; S.M.P. = State Marine Park; S.N.A. = State Natural Area; S.P. = State Park; S.P.C. = State Public Campground; S.R. = State Reserve; S.R.A. = State Recreation Area; S.Res. = State Reservoir; S.Res.P. = State Resort Park; S.R.P. = State Rustic Park.

Place Name	Listed Under
Bear Lake S.P.	GARDEN CITY
Coral Pink Sand Dunes S.P.	KANAB
Dead Horse Point S.P.	MOAB
Deer Creek S.P.	HEBER CITY
Escalante S.P.	LOA
Goblin Valley S.P.	GREEN RIVER
Gunlock S.P.	ST GEORGE
Hyrum S.P.	LOGAN
Palisade S.P.	SALINA
Rockport S.P.	PARK CITY
Scofield S.P.	PRICE
Snow Canyon S.P.	ST GEORGE
Steinaker S.P.	VERNAL
Utah Lake S.P.	PROVO

Place Name	Listed Under
Wasatch Mountain S.P.	HEBER CITY
Willard Bay S.P.	OGDEN
Yuba S.P.	NEPHI

Water-related activities, hiking, riding, various other sports, picnicking and visitor centers, as well as camping, are available in many of these areas. Day-use fee, including picnicking, boat launching and museums: $4-$6 per vehicle. Camping (mid-Apr-Oct; some sites available rest of yr), $7-$16/site/night; most sites 14-day max. Advance reservations may be obtained at most developed state parks; phone 801/322-3770 (Salt Lake City) or 800/322-3770. Pets on leash only. Sr citizen and disabled permit (free; UT residents only). For information on park facilities and permits, contact Utah State Parks & Recreation, 1594 W North Temple, Salt Lake City 84114; 801/538-7220.

SKI AREAS

Place Name	Listed Under
Alta Ski Area	ALTA
Beaver Mt	GARDEN CITY
Brian Head Ski Area	CEDAR CITY
Brighton Resort	SALT LAKE CITY
Deer Valley Resort	PARK CITY
Elk Meadows	BEAVER
Mt Holly	BEAVER
Nordic Valley	OGDEN
Park City Ski Area	PARK CITY
Powder Mountain	OGDEN
Snow Basin	OGDEN
Snowbird Ski and Summer Resort	SNOWBIRD
Solitude	SALT LAKE CITY
Sundance	PROVO
The Canyons	PARK CITY
White Pine Touring Center	PARK CITY

A booklet and further information may be obtained from Utah Travel Council, Council Hall, Capitol Hill, 300 N State St, Salt Lake City 84114; 801/538-1030.

FISHING & HUNTING

Wildlife habitat authorization $6; nonresident deer permit $198; permit for bull elk $328; once-in-a-lifetime permit for moose, bison, desert bighorn sheep, Rocky Mountain goat $1,003. For special permits write for information and apply from early-late January (bucks, bulls, and once-in-a-lifetime draw) and early June (antlerless draw). Small game licenses $41. Deer, elk, ducks, geese, pheasants, mourning doves and grouse are favorite quarry.

More than 3,000 lakes and hundreds of miles of mountain streams are filled with rainbow, German brown, cutthroat, Mackinaw and brook trout; there are also catfish, walleyed pike, bass, crappie and bluegill. Nonresident season fishing license (14 years and over) $42; 7-day fishing license $17; 1-day fishing license $7.

Further information may be obtained from the Division of Wildlife Resources, 1594 W North Temple, Box 146301, Salt Lake City 84114-6301; 801/538-4700.

River Expeditions

See Bluff, Green River, Moab, Salt Lake City, Vernal. For a directory of professional outfitters and river runners write Utah Travel Council, Council Hall, Capitol Hill, 300 N State St, Salt Lake City 84114; 801/538-1030 or 800/200-1160.

Driving Information

Safety belts are mandatory for all persons in front seat of vehicle. Children under age 8 must be in an approved passenger restraint anywhere in the vehicle: ages 2-7 may use a regulation safety belt; under age 2 must use an approved safety seat.

INTERSTATE HIGHWAY SYSTEM

Use the following list as a guide to access interstate highways in Utah. You should always consult a map to confirm driving routes.

Highway Number	Cities/Towns within 10 miles
Interstate 15	Beaver, Brigham City, Cedar City, Fillmore, Nephi, Ogden, Payson, Provo, St George, Salt Lake City.
Interstate 70	Green River, Salina.
Interstate 80	Salt Lake City, Wendover.

Additional Visitor Information

Utah Travel Council, Council Hall, Capitol Hill, 300 N State St, Salt Lake City 84114, will furnish excellent, extensive information on every section of the state and on special and annual events; phone 801/538-1030 or 800/200-1160.

There are several visitor centers in Utah, with information and brochures about points of interest. Major centers may be found at the following locations: Utah Field House of Natural History, 235 E Main St, Vernal; St George Information Center, Dixie Center; Echo Information Center, 2 mi E of jct I-80E, I-80N; Thompson Information Center, on I-70, 45 mi W of Utah-Colorado border; Brigham City Information Center, I-15, 5 mi N.

The Utah Fine Arts Council, 617 E South Temple, Salt Lake City 84102, phone 801/236-7555, provides information on local and statewide artists, museums, galleries and exhibits.

Alta (C-3)

(See also Heber City, Park City, Salt Lake City)

Pop 397 **Elev** 8,600 ft **Area Code** 435 **Zip** 84092

Founded around silver mines in the 1870s, Alta was notorious for constant shoot-outs in its 26 saloons. The town became the center of a noted ski area in 1937, with the opening of Utah's first ski resort. Historic markers identify the original townsite, and unusual wildflowers are found in Albion Basin.

What to See and Do

Alta Ski Area. Two triple, 6 double chairlifts, 4 rope tows; patrol, school, rentals; lodges, restaurant, cafeteria. Longest run 3½ mi, vertical drop 2,000 ft. (Mid-Nov-Apr, daily) Half-day rates. On UT 210 in Little Cottonwood Canyon. Phone 435/742-3333 or 435/572-3939 (snow conditions). ¢¢¢¢¢

Motels

★ **ALTA LODGE.** *Main St (84092), in Little Cottonwood Canyon. 801/742-3500; FAX 801/742-3504; res: 800/707-2582.* E-mail info@altalodge.com; web www.altalodge.com. 57 rms, 3 story. No elvtr. MAP, Nov-Apr: S $155-$324; D $114-$198/person; each addl $84-$93; men's, women's dorms $98-$108; under 4 free; EP avail in summer; lower rates June-early-Oct. Closed rest of yr. TV in common area; cable, VCR avail (free movies). Supervised child's activities (Nov-Apr); ages 3-12. Restaurant 6:30-9 pm. Bar (winter). Ck-out 11 am. Meeting rms. Business servs avail. Coin lndry. Downhill/x-country ski on site. Health club privileges. Whirlpool. Sauna. Some fireplaces. Some balconies. Sun deck. Accept cr cds (summer). Cr cds: C, DS, MC, V.

★★ **RUSTLER LODGE.** *Little Cottonwood Canyon (84092), atop Little Cottonwood Canyon. 801/742-2200; FAX 801/742-3832; res: 888/532-2582.* 85 rms, 5 story. No A/C. MAP: S, D $100-$520/person; each addl $80; suites $520-$650/rm; under 5 free; higher rates: Dec 19, mid-Mar. Closed May-Oct. Crib avail. TV in rec rm; cable. Heated pool; whirlpool. Restaurant 7:30-9:45 am, 12:30-2 pm, 6:30-9 pm. Private club 3-

11 pm. Ck-out 1 pm. Coin lndry. Meeting rms. Bellhops. Downhill/x-country ski on site. Exercise equipt. Rec rm. Cr cds: C.

D

Arches National Park (F-6)

(See also Moab)

(5 mi NW of Moab on US 191 to paved entrance road)

This timeless, natural landscape of giant stone arches, pinnacles, spires, fins and windows was once the bed of an ancient sea. Over time, erosion laid bare the skeletal structure of the earth, making this 114-square-mile area a spectacular outdoor museum. This wilderness, which contains the greatest density of natural arches in the world, was named a national monument in 1929 and a national park in 1971. More than 2,000 arches have been cataloged, ranging in size from three feet wide to the 105-foot-high, 306-foot-wide Landscape Arch.

The arches, other rock formations and views of the Colorado River canyon with the peaks of the LaSal Mountains in the distance, can be reached by car, but hiking is suggested as the best way to explore. Petroglyphs from the primitive peoples who roamed this section of Utah from A.D. 700-1200 can be seen at the Delicate Arch trailhead. This is a wildlife sanctuary; no hunting is permitted. Hiking, rock climbing or camping in isolated sections should not be undertaken unless first reported to a park ranger at the visitor center (check locally for hours). Twenty-four miles of paved roads are open year round. Graded and dirt roads should not be attempted in wet weather. Devils Garden Campground, 18 miles north of the visitor center off US 191, provides 52 individual and 2 group camp sites (yr-round; fee; water available only March-mid-October). There is an entrance fee of $10/7-day permit; Golden Eagle, Golden Age and Golden Access passports accepted (see MAKING THE MOST OF YOUR TRIP). For further information contact the Superintendent, PO Box 907, Moab 84532; 435/259-8161 or -5279 (TTY).

Beaver (G-2)

(See also Cedar City, Richfield)

Settled 1856 **Pop** 1,998 **Elev** 5,898 ft **Area Code** 435 **Zip** 84713
Information Chamber of Commerce, 1603 S Campground Rd, PO Box 760; 435/438-2975

Seat of Beaver County, this town is a national historic district with more than 200 houses of varied architectural styles and periods. It is also the birthplace of Butch Cassidy (1866).

Problems arose in Beaver's early days when tough gentile prospectors (in Utah, anyone not a Mormon was called a "gentile"), who came with a mining boom, derided the Mormons, who owned woolen mills. There was little harmony until the boom was over, but millions in gold, silver, lead, copper, tungsten, zinc, bismuth and sulphur had been mined by then. Now, irrigation has brought farming to Beaver. Dairying and stock-raising, as well as recreation, hunting and fishing, are important to the economy.

What to See and Do

Elk Meadows and Mt Holly Ski Area. Triple, double chairlifts. School; rentals; shops, cafe, lodging. Longest run 2 mi; vertical drop 1,200 ft. (Mid-Dec-Mar, daily) 18 mi E on UT 153. Phone 435/438-5433. ¢¢¢¢¢

Fishlake National Forest. (See RICHFIELD) A Ranger District office of the forest is located in Beaver. E on UT 153.

Annual Event

Pioneer Days. Features parade, entertainment, horse racing; other events. Late July.

Motels

★★ **BEST WESTERN PAICE INN.** *161 S Main St (84713). 435/438-2438; FAX 435/438-1053; res: 800/528-1234.* 24 rms, 2 story. Mid-May-Oct: S $49; D $54-$59; lower rates rest of yr. Crib $3. Pet accepted, some restrictions. TV; cable (premium). Heated pool; whirlpool. Coffee in rms. Restaurant 7 am-10 pm. Ck-out 11 am. Business servs avail. In-rm modem link. Downhill ski 18 mi. Sauna. Cr cds: A, C, D, DS, MC, V.

SC

✓★ **DE LANO MOTEL.** *480 N Main St (84713). 435/438-2418; FAX 435/438-2115; res: 800/537-2165.* 10 rms. May-Oct: S $34-$36; D $36-$39; each addl $4; wkly rates; lower rates rest of yr. Crib $3. Pet accepted. TV; cable (premium). Restaurant nearby. Ck-out 11 am. Business servs avail. Covered parking. Downhill ski 15 mi. Some refrigerators, microwaves. Cr cds: A, C, DS, MC, V.

SC

★★ **QUALITY INN.** *781 W 1800 S (84713). 435/438-5426; FAX 435/438-2493; res: 800/228-5050.* 52 rms, 2 story. June-Oct: S $45-$50; D $52; each addl $6; suites $60; under 18 free; ski plans; lower rates rest of yr. Crib $5. TV; cable. Indoor pool; whirlpool. Restaurant adj 6 am-10 pm. Ck-out 11 am. Business servs avail. Downhill/x-country ski 18 mi. Cr cds: A, C, D, DS, MC, V.

D SC

★ **SLEEPY LAGOON MOTEL.** *882 S Main St (84713), ¼ mi N of I-15, South Beaver exit. 435/438-5681; FAX 435/438-1251.* 20 rms. May-Sept: S, D $39-$54; each addl $2; lower rates rest of yr. Crib free. TV; cable. Heated pool. Complimentary continental bkfst (summer). Coffee in rms (winter). Restaurant nearby. Ck-out 11 am. Small pond. Cr cds: A, C, DS, MC, V.

SC

Restaurants

✓★ **ARSHEL'S CAFE.** *711 N Main St (84713). 435/438-2977.* Hrs: 6 am-10 pm; Nov-Mar to 9 pm. Closed Thanksgiving, Dec 25. Res accepted. Semi-a la carte: bkfst $2.60-$5.60, lunch, dinner $3.70-$10. Specialties: chicken-fried steak, honey pecan chicken & shrimp. Cr cds: A, C, MC, V.

D

★★ **COTTAGE INN.** *171 S Main St (84713). 435/438-5855.* Hrs: 7 am-10 pm. Closed Dec 25. Res accepted. Semi-a la carte: bkfst $2.95-$7.95, lunch $3.95-$9.95, dinner $3.95-$14.95. Child's meals. Specializes in prime rib (Fri, Sat), chicken-fried steak. Victorian-style interior with handcrafted doll case, antiques, carvings. Cr cds: C, MC, V.

D

Blanding (H-6)

(See also Bluff, Monticello)

Settled 1905 **Pop** 3,162 **Elev** 6,105 ft **Area Code** 435 **Zip** 84511
Web www.edonnet.com/fourcorners/sjcu
Information San Juan County Visitor Center, 117 S Main St, Box 490, Monticello 84535; 435/587-3235 or 800/574-4386

In 1940, with a population of 600, Blanding was the largest town in a county the size of Connecticut, Rhode Island and Delaware combined.

Although surrounded by ranches and grazing areas, the city is a gateway to hunting and fishing grounds and national monuments. The sites can be explored by jeep or horseback along the many trails, or by boat through the waters of Glen Canyon National Recreation Area. A Pueblo ruin, inhabited between A.D. 800-1200, is now a state park within the city limits.

What to See and Do

Edge of the Cedars State Park. Excavated remnants of ancient dwellings and ceremonial chambers fashioned by the ancient Pueblo people. Artifacts and pictographs; museum of Native American history and culture. Visitor center. (Daily) 1 mi NW off US 191. Phone 435/678-2238. **¢**

Glen Canyon National Recreation Area/Lake Powell. 4 mi S on US 191, then 85 mi W on UT 95 & UT 276. (See LAKE POWELL)

★ **Hovenweep National Monument.** Monument consists of six units of prehistoric ruins; the best preserved are the remains of pueblos (small cliff dwellings) and towers at Square Tower. Self-guided trail; park ranger on duty; visitor area (daily). Approx 13 mi S on US 191, then 9 mi E on UT 262 and 6 mi E on county roads to Hatch Trading Post, follow signs 16 mi to Hovenweep. **¢¢¢**

Natural Bridges National Monument (see). 4 mi S on US 191, then 40 mi W on UT 95.

Bluff (H-6)

(See also Blanding)

Founded 1880 **Pop** 360 (est) **Elev** 4,320 ft **Area Code** 435 **Zip** 84512
Web www.edonnet.com/fourcorners/sjcu

Information San Juan County Visitor Center, 117 S Main St, Box 490, Monticello 84535; 435/587-3235 or 800/574-4386

Bluff's dramatic location between the sandstone cliffs along the San Juan River, its Anasazi ruins among the canyon walls and its Mormon pioneer past all combine to make it an interesting stop along scenic US 163 between the Grand Canyon and Mesa Verde national parks.

What to See and Do

★ **Tours of the Big Country.** Trips to Monument Valley, the Navajo Reservation and into canyons of southeastern Utah explore desert plant and wildlife, history, geology and Anasazi archaeology of this area. Naturalist-guided walking or four-wheel-drive tours. Half-day, full-day or overnight trips. (Apr-Oct) Contact Recapture Lodge, phone 435/672-2281. **¢¢¢¢¢**

Wild Rivers Expeditions. Fun and educational trips on the archaeologically rich San Juan River through Glen Canyon National Recreation Area (see LAKE POWELL) and Cataract Canyon of the Colorado River. Geological formations, fossil beds and sites of 12,000-yr-old early Paleo-Indians, through the Pueblo culture to modern Navajo villages. (Apr-Oct) Phone 435/672-2244 or 800/422-7654 (exc UT). **¢¢¢¢¢**

Annual Event

Utah Navajo Fair. 3rd wkend Sept.

Motel

✓★ **RECAPTURE LODGE.** *US 191 (84512). 435/672-2281; FAX 435/672-2281.* 28 air-cooled rms, 1-2 story, 3 kits. (equipt avail). S $30-$42; D $32-$48; each addl $3-$6. Crib free. TV; VCR avail. Heated pool; whirlpool. Playground. Continental bkfst. Restaurants opp 7 am-9 pm. Ck-out 11 am. Coin lndry. Business servs avail. Airport transportation. Lawn games. Some refrigerators. Balconies. Picnic tables, grills. Sun decks. Also units for groups, families at Pioneer House (historic building). Geologist-guided tours; slide shows. ½ mi to San Juan River. Cr cds: A, C, DS, MC, V.

Brigham City (B-3)

(See also Logan, Ogden)

Settled 1851 **Pop** 15,644 **Elev** 4,439 ft **Area Code** 435 **Zip** 84302
E-mail chamber@brigham.net **Web** www.northernutah.com/bec

Information Chamber of Commerce, 6 N Main St, PO Box 458; 435/723-3931

Renamed for Brigham Young in 1877, when he made his last public address here, this community was first known as Box Elder because of the many trees of that type that grew in the area. Main Street, which runs through the center of this city situated at the base of the towering Wasatch Mountains, is still lined with these leafy trees.

What to See and Do

Brigham City Museum-Gallery. Permanent history exhibits, rotating art exhibits; displays include furniture, clothing, books, photographs and documents reflecting the history of the Brigham City area since 1851. (Tues-Fri, also Sat afternoons) 24 N 3rd W. Phone 435/723-6769. **Free**

★ **Golden Spike National Historic Site.** Site where America's first transcontinental railroad was completed on May 10, 1869. Visitor center, movies, exhibits (daily; closed Jan 1, Thanksgiving, Dec 25). Self-guided auto tour along old railroad bed. Summer interpretive program includes presentations and operating replicas of steam locomotives "Jupiter" and "119" (May-early Oct, daily). (See ANNUAL EVENTS) Golden Eagle, Golden Age, Golden Access passports accepted (see MAKING THE MOST OF YOUR TRIP). 30 mi W via UT 83 & County Road. Contact Chief Ranger, PO Box 897; phone 435/471-2209. Per person **¢¢**; Per vehicle **¢¢¢**

Tabernacle (1881). The tabernacle, one of the most architecturally interesting buildings in Utah, has been in continuous use since 1881. Guided tours (May-Sept, daily). 251 S Main St. Phone 435/723-5376. **Free**

Annual Events

Driving of Golden Spike. At Promontory, site where the Central Pacific and Union Pacific met. Re-enactment of driving of golden spike in 1869. Locomotive replicas used. Mid May.

Railroaders Festival. Golden Spike National Historic Site. Relive the rush to complete transcontinental railroad. Professional railroaders pursue world record in spike driving. 2nd Sat Aug.

Box Elder County Fair. Late Aug.

Peach Days Celebration. Parade; arts & crafts; carnival; car show; entertainment. 1st wkend after Labor Day.

Motel

✓★ **HOWARD JOHNSON.** *1167 S Main St (84302). 435/723-8511; FAX 435/723-8511; res: 800/446-4656.* 44 rms, 2 story. S $40-$45; D $49-$56; each addl $5; under 18 free. Crib free. Pet accepted, some restrictions. TV; cable (premium). Indoor pool; whirlpool. Complimentary continental bkfst. Restaurant adj 7 am-9 pm; closed Sun. Business servs avail. Ck-out noon. Cr cds: A, C, D, DS, ER, JCB, MC, V.

D SC

Restaurant

★★ **MADDOX RANCH HOUSE.** *1900 S US 89 (84302), 1 mi S on US 89/91. 435/723-8545.* Hrs: 11 am-9:30 pm. Closed Sun, Mon; Thanksgiving, Dec 25. Res accepted. Semi-a la carte: lunch, dinner $6.95-$17.95. Child's meals. Specializes in chicken, beef, seafood. Western decor. Family-owned. Cr cds: A, C, D, DS, MC, V.

D

Bryce Canyon National Park (H-3)

(7 mi S of Panguitch on US 89, then 17 mi SE on UT 12 to UT 63, 3 mi to entrance)

Bryce Canyon is a 56-square-mile area of colorful, fantastic cliffs created by millions of years of erosion. Towering rocks worn to odd, sculptured shapes stand grouped in striking sequences. The Paiute, who once lived nearby, called this "the place where red rocks stand like men in a bowl-shaped canyon." Although termed a canyon, Bryce is actually a series of "breaks" in 12 large amphitheaters—some plunging as deep as 1,000 feet into the multicolored limestone. The formations appear to change color as the sunlight strikes from different angles and seem incandescent in the late afternoon. The famous Pink Cliffs were carved from the Claron Formation; shades of red, orange, white, gray, purple, brown and soft yellow appear in the strata. Park Road follows 17 miles along the eastern edge of the Paunsaugunt Plateau, where the natural amphitheaters are spread out below; plateaus covered with evergreens and valleys filled with sagebrush stretch away into the distance.

The visitor center at the entrance station has complete information on the park, including orientation shows, geologic displays and detailed maps (daily; closed Jan 1, Thanksgiving, Dec 25). Park is open year round; in winter, park road is open to most viewpoints. Lodging is also available April-October. There is an entrance fee of $10 per vehicle; Golden Eagle, Golden Age and Golden Access passports are accepted (see MAKING THE MOST OF YOUR TRIP). Shuttle system (fee, phone for information). For further information contact the Superintendent, PO Box 170001, Bryce Canyon 84717; 435/834-5322.

What to See and Do

Camping. North Campground, E of park headquarters; Sunset Campground, 2 mi S of park headquarters. 14-day limit at both sites; fireplaces, picnic tables, rest rms, water avail. (Apr-Oct) ¢¢¢

Hikes with ranger naturalists into canyon. (June-Aug)

Riding. Horses & mules avail, guided trips early morning, afternoon (spring, summer & fall). Fee.

Talks by rangers about history, geology, fauna, flora at campgrounds in the evening. (June-Aug)

Motels

★★★ **BEST WESTERN RUBY'S INN.** *Utah Hwy 63 (84764), ½ mi N of park entrance on UT 63. 435/834-5341; FAX 435/834-5265; res: 800/528-1234.* E-mail bob@rubysinn.com; web www.rubysinn.com. 369 rms, 1-3 story. June-Sept: S, D $83; each addl $5; suites, $125; lower rates rest of yr. Crib free. Pet accepted, some restrictions; $100 deposit. TV; cable, VCR (movies). Indoor pool; outdoor whirlpool. Restaurant 6:30 am-9 pm; winter hrs vary. Private club, setups. Ck-out 11 am. Coin Indry. Business servs avail. Shopping arcade. Game rm. X-country ski opp. Picnic tables. Rodeo in summer; general store. Lake on property. Trailer park. Cr cds: A, C, D, DS, MC, V.

D SC

★★ **BRYCE CANYON LODGE.** *1 Bryce Canyon Lodge (84717), on UT 63, 3 mi S of UT 12. 435/834-5361; FAX 435/834-5464; res: 303/297-2757.* Web www.amfac.com. 114 units in cabins, motel. Apr-Nov: motel units $83; cabin units $93; each addl $5; suites $115; each addl $5. Closed rest of yr. Crib $5. Restaurant 6:30 am-4 pm, 5:30-9:30 pm. Ck-out 11 am. Coin Indry. Business servs avail. Bellhops. Sundries. Gift shop. Trail rides on mules, horses avail. Private patios, balconies. Original 1925 building. Cr cds: A, C, D, DS, MC, V.

D

✓★★ **BRYCE CANYON PINES MOTEL.** *Hwy 12 (84764), 6 mi NW of park entrance on UT 12. 435/834-5441; FAX 801/834-5330; res: 800/892-7923.* 50 rms, 1-2 story. May-Oct: S, D $65-$75; each addl $5; suites $85-$110; kit. cottage $95; lower rates rest of yr. Crib $5. TV; cable. Heated pool. Restaurant 6:30 am-9:30 pm. Ck-out 11 am. Business servs avail. Some fireplaces. Early American decor. Cr cds: A, C, D, DS, MC, V.

D SC

Restaurant

★ **FOSTER'S STEAK HOUSE.** *(84764), 3 mi NW of park entrance on UT 12. 435/834-5227.* Hrs: 7 am-10 pm; Dec-Mar from 2 pm. Beer. Semi-a la carte: bkfst $1.75-$5.99, lunch $3.99-$4.99, dinner $8.99-$18.99. Child's meals. Specializes in seafood, prime rib. Salad bar. Bakery adj. Cr cds: A, C, D, DS, MC, V.

D

Canyonlands National Park (G-5)

(See also Moab, Monticello)

(N district: 12 mi N of Moab on US 191, then 21 mi SW on UT 313; S district: 12 mi N of Monticello on US 191, then 38 mi W on UT 211)

Spectacular rock formations, canyons, arches, spires, pictograph panels, ancestral Puebloan ruins and desert flora are the main features of this 337,570-acre area. Set aside by Congress in 1964 as a national park, the area is largely undeveloped. Road conditions vary; primary access roads are paved and maintained, others are safe only for high clearance four-wheel-drive vehicles. For backcountry road conditions and information phone 801/259-7164.

Island in the Sky, North District, south and west of Dead Horse Point State Park (see MOAB) has Grand View Point, Upheaval Dome and Green River Overlook. This section is accessible by passenger car via UT 313; also accessible by four-wheel-drive vehicles and mountain bikes on dirt roads.

Needles, South District, has hiking trails and four-wheel-drive roads to Angel Arch, Chesler Park and the confluence of the Green and Colorado rivers. Also here are prehistoric ruins and rock art. This section is accessible by passenger car via UT 211, by four-wheel-drive vehicle on dirt roads and by mountain bike.

Maze, West District, is accessible by hiking or by four-wheel-drive vehicles using unimproved roads. The most remote and least-visited section of the park, this area received its name from the many maze-like canyons. Horseshoe Canyon, a separate unit of the park nearby, is accessible via UT 24 and 30 miles of two-wheel-drive dirt road. Roads are usually passable only mid-March through mid-November.

Canyonlands is excellent for calm-water and whitewater trips down the Green and Colorado rivers. Permits are required for private trips (fee; contact Reservation Office, 435/259-4351); commercial trips (see MOAB). Campgrounds, with tent sites, are located at Island in the Sky (free) and Needles (fee); water is available only at Needles. Visitor centers are in each district (daily). There is an entrance fee of $10 per vehicle. Golden Eagle, Golden Age, Golden Access passports accepted (see MAKING THE MOST OF YOUR TRIP). For further information contact Canyonlands NP, 2282 S West Resource Blvd, Moab 84532; 435/259-7164.

Capitol Reef National Park (G-4)

(See also Loa)

(10 mi E of Richfield on UT 119, then 65 mi SE on UT 24)

Capitol Reef, at an elevation ranging from 3,900-8,800 feet, is composed of red sandstone cliffs capped with domes of white sandstone. Located in the heart of Utah's slickrock country, the park is actually a 100-mile section of the Waterpocket Fold, an upthrust of sedimentary rock created during the formation of the Rocky Mountains. Pockets in the rocks collect thousands of gallons of water each time it rains. Capitol Reef was so named because the rocks formed a natural barrier to pioneer travel and the white sandstone domes resemble the dome of the US Capitol.

This 378-square-mile area was the home from A.D. 700-1350 of an ancient people who grew corn along the Fremont River. Petroglyphs can be seen on some of the sandstone walls. A schoolhouse, farmhouse and orchards, established by early Mormon settlers, are seasonally open to the public.

The park can be approached from either east or west via UT 24, a paved road. There is a visitor center on this road about seven miles from the west boundary and eight miles from the east (daily; closed Dec 25). A 25-mile round-trip scenic drive starts from this point (some parts unpaved). There are evening programs and guided walks (Memorial Day-Labor Day; free). Three campgrounds are available: Fruita, approximately 1 mi S off UT 24, provides 70 tent and trailer sites year round (fee); Cedar Mesa, 23 mi S off UT 24, and Cathedral, 28 mi N off UT 24, offer 5 primitive sites with access depending on weather (free; no facilities). There is an entrance fee of $4 per vehicle. Golden Eagle, Golden Age, Golden Access passports accepted (see MAKING THE MOST OF YOUR TRIP). For further information contact the Superintendent, HC 70, Box 15, Torrey 84775; 435/425-3791.

Motels

★ **CAPITOL REEF INN & CAFE.** *360 W Main St (84775), 7 mi W of park on UT 24, ½ mi W of Torrey. 435/425-3271.* 10 rms. Apr-Oct: S $40, D $44; each addl $4. Closed rest of yr. Pet accepted. TV; cable (premium). Whirlpool. Playground. Restaurant 7-11 am, 5-9 pm. Ck-out 11 am. Gift shop. Cr cds: C, DS, MC, V.

✓★ **SUNGLOW MOTEL.** *63 E Main (84715), W of park on UT 24. 435/425-3821; FAX 435/425-3821.* 18 rms, 10 A/C. Mar-mid-Nov: S $25-$28; D $36; each addl $2-$4. Closed rest of yr. Crib $2. TV; cable. Restaurant 6:30 am-10 pm. Ck-out 11 am. Cr cds: A, C, DS, MC, V.

Cedar Breaks National Monument (H-2)

(See also Cedar City)

(23 mi E of Cedar City via UT 14)

Cedar Breaks National Monument's major formation is a spectacular, multicolored, natural amphitheater created by the same forces that sculpted Utah's other rock formations. The amphitheater, shaped like an enormous coliseum, is 2,000 feet deep and more than three miles in diameter. It is carved out of the Markagunt Plateau and is surrounded by Dixie National Forest (see CEDAR CITY). Cedar Breaks, at an elevation of more than 10,000 feet, was established as a national monument in 1933. It derives its name from the surrounding cedar trees and the word "breaks," which means "badlands." Although similar to Bryce Canyon National Park, Cedar Breaks's formations are fewer but more vivid and varied in color. Young lava beds, resulting from small volcanic eruptions and cracks in the earth's surface, surround the Breaks area; the heavy forests include bristlecone pines, one of the oldest trees on the earth. Here, as soon as the snow melts, wildflowers bloom profusely and continue to bloom throughout the summer.

Rim Drive, a five-mile scenic road through the Cedar Breaks High Country, provides views of the monument's formations from four different overlooks. The area is open late May-mid-October, weather permitting. Point Supreme Campground, two miles north of south entrance, provides 30 tent and trailer sites (mid-June-mid-Sept, fee; water, rest rms). The visitor center offers geological exhibits (June-mid-Oct, daily); interpretive activities (mid-June-Labor Day). There is an entrance fee of $4 per vehicle. Golden Eagle, Golden Age, Golden Access passports accepted (see MAKING THE MOST OF YOUR TRIP). For further information contact the Superintendent, 2390 W Hwy 56, Suite 11, Cedar City 84720; 435/586-9451.

Cedar City (H-2)

Settled 1851 **Pop** 13,443 **Elev** 5,834 ft **Area Code** 801 **Zip** 84720
E-mail tourism@tcd.net

Information Chamber of Commerce, 286 N Main St; 801/586-4484

In 1852, Cedar City produced the first iron made west of the Mississippi. The blast furnace operation was not successful, however, and stock-raising soon overshadowed it, although iron is still mined west of the city on a limited basis. A branch line of the Union Pacific entered the region in 1923 and helped develop the area. Now a tourist center because of its proximity to Bryce Canyon and Zion national parks (see both), Cedar City takes pride in its abundant natural wonders; streams and lakes have rainbow trout and the Markagunt Plateau provides deer and mountain lion hunting. Headquarters and a Ranger District office of the Dixie National Forest is located here.

What to See and Do

Brian Head Ski Resort. Five triple, 1 double chairlift; patrol; school, lessons, rentals; restaurants, cafeterias, bars; nursery; ski shops, grocery, gift shops; lodging. Longest run ½ mi, vertical drop 1,400 ft. (Mid-Nov-late Apr, daily) Cross-country trails, rentals. Snowmobiling. Mountain biking (summer). 19 mi NE on I-15 to Parowan, then 11 mi SE on UT 143, in Dixie National Forest. Phone 435/677-2035. **¢¢¢¢¢**

Cedar Breaks National Monument (see). 23 mi E via UT 14.

Dixie National Forest. Table Cliff Point offers a view of four states—Colorado, Arizona, Nevada and Utah. Camping, picnicking, hiking, mountain biking, winter sports, lake and stream fishing, boating, hunting for deer, elk and cougar on 1.9 acres. (Daily) 12 mi E on UT 14 to forest boundary or 17 mi SW on I-15, then W. For information contact the Supervisor, PO Box 580, 84721; phone 435/865-3200. **Free**

Iron Mission State Park. Museum dedicated to the first pioneer iron foundry west of the Mississippi; extensive collection of horse-drawn vehicles and wagons from Utah pioneer days, Native American artifacts. (Daily; closed Jan 1, Thanksgiving, Dec 25) 585 N Main. Phone 435/586-9290. **¢**

Kolob Canyons Visitor Center. This section of Zion National Park (see) provides a 7-mi hike to the Kolob Arch, world's largest, with a span of 310 ft. A 5-mi scenic drive offers spectacular views of rugged peaks and sheer canyon walls 1,500 ft high. (Daily; closed Jan 1, Dec 25) 17 mi S on I-15. Phone 801/586-9548. **Free**

Sightseeing trips. Cedar City Air Service. Trips include Cedar Breaks National Monument and Grand Canyon, Zion and Bryce Canyon national parks (see all); other trips avail. (Daily) Phone 435/586-3881. **¢¢¢¢¢**

Southern Utah University (1897). (5,500 students) Braithwaite Fine Arts Gallery (daily exc Sun; free). (See SEASONAL EVENTS) 351 W Center. Phone 435/586-7700.

Zion National Park (see). 60 mi SE via I-15 & UT 9.

Annual Events

Utah Summer Games. Olympic-style athletic events for amateur athletes. Phone 435/586-7228. June.

Renaissance Fair. Main St City Park. Entertainment, food and games, all in the style of the Renaissance. Held in conjunction with opening of Utah Shakespearean Festival (see SEASONAL EVENTS). Early July.

Seasonal Events

Utah Shakespearean Festival. Southern Utah University campus. Shakespeare presented on outdoor stage that is replica of 16th-century Tiring House and 750-seat indoor facility. Nightly exc Sun; preplay activities. Children over 5 yrs only; babysitting at festival grounds. Phone 435/586-7878 (box office). Late June-early Sept.

American Folk Ballet Summer Festival. Southern Utah University Centrum. Matinee and nightly performances. Phone 435/586-7872 (box office). Mid-July.

Motels

★★ **ABBEY INN.** *940 W 200 N (01453). 435/586-9966; FAX 435/586-6522; res: 800/325-5411.* Web www.abbeyinncedar.com. 81 rms, 2 story. June-mid-Sept: S, D $68-$80; suites $95-$150; under 12 free; lower rates rest of yr. Crib $5. TV; cable (premium), VCR avail. Indoor pool; whirlpool. Complimentary continental bkfst. Coffee in rms. Restaurant adj 6 am-10 pm. Ck-out 11 am. Coin lndry. Business servs avail. In-rm modem link. Airport transportation. Refrigerators, microwaves. Near airport. Cr cds: A, C, D, DS, MC, V.

★★ **BEST WESTERN TOWN & COUNTRY INN.** *189 N Main St (84720), near Municipal Airport. 435/586-9900; FAX 435/586-1664; res: 800/528-1234.* E-mail reserv@bwtowncounty.com. 160 rms, 2 story. S $60-$81; D $69-$99; each addl $4; suites $82-$150. Crib $4. TV. 2 pools, 1 indoor; whirlpool. Restaurant 7 am-10 pm. Ck-out 11 am. Coin lndry. Meeting rm. Business servs avail. Free airport transportation. Game rm. Many refrigerators, microwaves. Cr cds: A, C, D, DS, MC, V.

★★ **COMFORT INN.** *250 N 1100 W (84720). 435/586-2082; FAX 801/586-3193; res: 800/627-0374.* 94 rms, 2 story. June-Sept: S $63; D $72; each addl $5; under 12 free; lower rates rest of yr. Crib free. Pet accepted. TV; cable. Indoor pool. Complimentary continental bkfst. Restaurant open 24 hrs. Ck-out 11 am. Business servs avail. Free airport transportation. Exercise equipt. Cr cds: A, C, D, DS, ER, MC, V.

★★ **HOLIDAY INN.** *1575 W 200 N (84720), near Municipal Airport. 435/586-8888; FAX 801/586-1010; res: 800/465-4329; res: 800/432-8828.* Web www.holidayinncedar.com. 100 rms, 2 story. June-Sept: S $83; D $93; each addl $10; suites $135; under 18 free; ski plan; lower rates rest of yr. Crib free. Pet accepted. TV; cable (premium). Heated pool; whirlpool. Restaurant 7 am-10 pm. Rm serv. Ck-out noon. Coin lndry. Meeting rms. Business servs avail. Free airport, bus depot transportation. Exercise equipt; sauna. Cr cds: A, C, D, DS, MC, V.

★★ **QUALITY INN.** *18 S Main St (84721). 435/586-2433; FAX 435/586-4425; res: 800/638-7949.* 50 rms, 3 story. No elvtr. June-Sept: S, D $79-$99; each addl $4; under 19 free; lower rates rest of yr. Crib $4. TV; cable. Pool. Complimentary continental bkfst. Restaurant adj 6 am-11 pm. Ck-out 11 am. Free airport transportation. Cr cds: A, C, D, DS, JCB, MC, V.

✓★ **RODEWAY INN.** *281 S Main St (84720). 435/586-9916; FAX 435/586-9916; res: 800/228-2000.* 48 rms, 2 story. June-Sept: S $54; D $70; suites $66-$74; under 18 free; lower rates rest of yr. Crib free. Pet accepted. TV; cable (premium). Heated pool. Sauna. Coffee in rms. Restaurant adj 6 am-10 pm; winter to 9:30 pm. Ck-out noon. Meeting rm. Business servs avail. Free airport transportation. Game rm. Cr cds: A, C, D, DS, ER, JCB, MC, V.

Resort

✓★★ **LODGE AT BRIAN HEAD.** *314 W Hunter Ridge Dr (84719), 28 mi NE of Cedar City exit 75. 435/677-3222; FAX 435/677-2506; res: 800/386-5634.* 72 rms, 3 story. Nov-mid-Apr: S, D $69-$99; suites $89-$119; family plans; package plans; higher rates hols; lower rates rest of yr. Crib avail. Pet accepted; $50. TV; cable. Complimentary continental bkfst. Restaurant 5-10 pm. Box lunches. Private club 5 pm-1 am. Ck-out 11 am. Grocery nearby. Coin lndry nearby. Meeting rms. Business servs avail. Shopping arcade. Downhill/x-country ski on site. Snowmobiles. Rec rm. Game rm. Exercise equipt; sauna. Spa. Indoor pool; whirlpool. Cr cds: A, C, DS, MC, V.

Restaurant

★ **MILT'S STAGE STOP.** *Cedar Canyon Rd (84720), 5 mi E on UT 14 in Cedar Canyon. 435/586-9344.* Hrs: 6-10 pm. Closed Thanksgiving, Dec 25. Res accepted. Bar. Semi-a la carte: dinner $11.75-$30. Child's meals. Specializes in steak, seafood. Salad bar. Rustic decor. Cr cds: A, C, D, DS, MC, V.

Dinosaur National Monument (D-6)

(See also Vernal)

(7 mi N of Jensen on UT 149)

On August 17, 1909, paleontologist Earl Douglass discovered dinosaur bones in this area, several of them nearly complete skeletons. Since then, this location has provided more skeletons, skulls and bones of Jurassic-period dinosaurs than any other dig in the world. The dinosaur site comprises only 80 acres of this 325-square-mile area, which lies at the border of Utah and Colorado. The back country section, most of which is in Colorado, is a land of fantastic and deeply eroded canyons of the Green and Yampa rivers. The entire area was named a national monument in 1915.

Utah's Dinosaur Quarry section can be entered from the junction of US 40 and UT 149, north of Jensen, 13 miles east of Vernal; approximately 7 miles north on UT 149 is the fossil exhibit. Another 5 miles north is Green River Campground, with 90 tent & trailer sites available mid-May-mid-September. A smaller campground, Rainbow Park, provides a small number of tent sites from May-November. Lodore, Deerlodge and Echo Park campgrounds are available in Colorado. A fee is charged at Green River, Echo Park and Lodore (water and rest rooms available). Access to the Colorado back country section is via Harpers Corner Road, starting at monument headquarters on US 40, 2 miles east of Dinosaur, Colorado. This 32-mile surfaced road ends at Harpers Corner. From there a 1-mile foot trail leads to a promontory overlooking the Green and Yampa rivers, more than 2,500 feet below.

Because of snow, some areas of the monument are closed approximately mid-November-mid-April. There is an entrance fee of up to $10 per vehicle. Golden Eagle, Golden Age, Golden Access passports accepted (see MAKING THE MOST OF YOUR TRIP). For further information contact the Superintendent, 4545 E Hwy 40, Dinosaur, CO 81610; 970/374-3000 (headquarters).

What to See and Do

Backpacking. By permit obtainable at visitor centers; few marked trails.

Dinosaur Quarry Information Center. Remarkable fossil deposit exhibit of 150-million-yr-old dinosaur remains; preparation laboratory on display. (Daily; closed Jan 1, Thanksgiving, Dec 25)

Picnicking, hiking, fishing. Harpers Corner area has picnic facilities, also picnicking at campgrounds. Self-guided nature trails (all-yr), guided nature walks. State fishing license required; boating permit required (obtainable by advance lottery at the Headquarters Boating Office).

River rafting. On Green and Yampa rivers, by advance permit from National Park Service or with concession-operated guided float trips. Information at Superintendent's office.

Fillmore (F-3)

(See also Nephi, Richfield)

Settled 1856 **Pop** 1,956 **Elev** 5,135 ft **Area Code** 435 **Zip** 84631

Information Chamber of Commerce, City of Fillmore, 75 W Center, PO Box 687; 435/743-5233

Fillmore, the seat of Millard County and Utah's territorial capital until 1856, is today a trading center for the surrounding farm and livestock region. It is a popular hunting and fishing area. A Ranger District office of the Fishlake National Forest is located here.

What to See and Do

Fishlake National Forest. E on improved gravel road (see RICHFIELD).

Territorial Statehouse State Park. Utah's first territorial capitol, built in the 1850s of red sandstone, is now a museum with extensive collection of pioneer furnishings, pictures, Native American artifacts and early documents; also rose garden. (Daily; closed Jan 1, Thanksgiving, Dec 25) 50 W Capitol Ave. Phone 435/743-5316. ¢

Motel

✓★ **BEST WESTERN PARADISE INN.** *905 N Main St (84631). 435/743-6895; FAX 435/743-6892; res: 800/528-1234.* 80 rms, 2 story. Mid-May-Oct: S $49; D $51; each addl $2; lower rates rest of yr. Crib $6. Pet accepted. TV; cable (premium). Heated pool; whirlpool. Restaurant 6 am-10 pm; summer to 11 pm. Ck-out 11 am. Business servs avail. Cr cds: A, C, D, DS, MC, V.

SC

Garden City (A-4)

(See also Logan)

Settled 1875 **Pop** 193 **Elev** 5,960 ft **Area Code** 435 **Zip** 84028

Information Bear Lake Convention & Visitors Bureau, PO Box 26, Fish Haven, ID 83287; 208/945-2333 or 800/448-2327

As was the case with many of Utah's towns, Garden City was settled by Mormon pioneers sent here from Salt Lake City. Today, it is a small resort town on the western shore of Bear Lake.

What to See and Do

Bear Lake. Covering 71,000 acres on the border of Utah and Idaho, this body of water is the state's second-largest freshwater lake. Approx 20 mi long and 200 ft deep, it offers good fishing for mackinaw, rainbow trout and the rare Bonneville Cisco. Boat rentals at several resorts. On the W shore is

Bear Lake State Park. Three park areas include state marina on west shore of lake, Rendezvous Beach on south shore and Eastside area on east shore. Swimming, beach, waterskiing; fishing, ice fishing; boating (ramp, dock), sailing. Hiking, mountain biking. Cross-country skiing, snowmobiling. Picnicking. Tent & trailer sites (rest rms, showers, hookups, dump station; fee). Visitor center. (Daily) 2 mi N on US 89. Phone 435/946-3343. Per vehicle ¢¢

Beaver Mt Ski Area. Three double chairlifts; patrol, school, rentals; day lodge, cafeteria. 16 runs; vertical drop 1,600 ft. Half-day rates. (Dec-early Apr, daily) 15 mi W via US 89. Phone 435/753-0921 or 435/753-4822 (snow conditions). ¢¢¢¢¢

Green River (F-5)

Settled 1878 **Pop** 866 **Elev** 4,079 ft **Area Code** 435 **Zip** 84525

Information Green River Travel Council, 885 E Main St; 435/564-3526

Originally a mail relay station between Ouray, Colorado, and Salina, Utah, Green River now produces premium watermelons and cantaloupes on land irrigated by the Green River, one of Utah's largest rivers.

What to See and Do

Arches National Park (see). 23 mi E on I-70 (US 50), then 54 mi S on US 191.

Goblin Valley State Park. Mile-wide basin filled with intricately eroded sandstone formations. Hiking, camping (rest rms, showers, dump station). (Daily) 12 mi W on I-70 (US 50), then 30 mi S on UT 24. Phone 435/564-3633. ¢¢

John Wesley Powell River History Museum. 20,000-sq-ft museum sits on the banks of the Green River. Contains exhibits exploring geology & geography of area; auditorium with 20-min multi-media presentation; river runner Hall of Fame. Green River Visitor Center (daily). Gift shop. Picnic area. (Daily; closed Jan 1, Thanksgiving, Dec 25) 885 E Main St. Phone 435/564-3427. ¢

River trips. On the Colorado, Green, San Juan and Dolores rivers.

Adventure River Expeditions. PO Box 96; phone 801/564-3454 or 800/331-3324. ¢¢¢¢¢

Colorado River & Trail Expeditions, Inc. PO Box 57575, Salt Lake City 84157-0575; phone 801/261-1789 or 800/253-7328. ¢¢¢¢¢

Holiday River and Bike Expeditions. 544 E 3900 South, Salt Lake City 84107; phone 801/266-2087 or 800/624-6323 (exc UT). ¢¢¢¢¢

Moki Mac River Expeditions. PO Box 21242, Salt Lake City 84121; phone 801/268-6667 or 800/284-7280. ¢¢¢¢¢

Western River Expeditions. 7258 Racquet Club Dr, Salt Lake City 84121; phone 801/259-7019 or 800/453-7450. ¢¢¢¢¢

Annual Event

Melon Days. 3rd wkend Sept.

Motels

★★ **BEST WESTERN RIVER TERRACE MOTEL.** *880 E Main St (84525). 435/564-3401; FAX 435/564-3403; res: 800/528-1234.* 51 rms, 2-3 story. No elvtr. May-Oct: S $79; D $79-$120; higher rates some hols & special events; lower rates rest of yr. TV; cable (premium). Heated pool; whirlpool. Restaurant adj 6 am-10 pm. Ck-out 11 am. Private patios, balconies. On river. Cr cds: A, C, D, DS, MC, V.

SC

✓★ **RODEWAY INN.** *525 E I-70 Business Loop (84525). 435/564-3421; FAX 435/564-8162; res: 800/228-2000.* 42 rms, 2 story. May-Oct: S, D $55-$65; each addl $5; suites $55-$65; under 18 free; lower rates rest of yr. Crib free. TV; cable (premium). Restaurant adj open 24 hrs. Ck-out 11 am. Coin lndry. Meeting rms. Cr cds: A, C, D, DS, ER, JCB, MC, V.

D SC

Restaurant

✓★ **TAMARISK.** *870 E Main St (84525). 435/564-8109.* Hrs: 6 am-10 pm. Closed Thanksgiving, Dec 25. Semi-a la carte: bkfst $2.20-$6.95, lunch, dinner $2.95-$13.95. Buffet: bkfst $5.25, lunch $6.95, dinner $10.95. Child's meals. Specializes in chicken, steak, fish. Salad bar. Country-style cafe; view of Green River. Totally nonsmoking. Cr cds: A, C, D, DS, MC, V.

D

Heber City (D-4)

(See also Alta, Park City, Provo, Salt Lake City)

Settled 1859 **Pop** 4,782 **Elev** 5,595 ft **Area Code** 435 **Zip** 84032
E-mail heberc@shadowlink.net **Web** www.hebervalleycc.org

Information Heber Valley Chamber of Commerce, 475 N Main St, PO Box 427; 435/654-3666

In a fertile mountain-ringed valley, Heber City was once a commercial and livestock shipping center. Unusual crater mineral springs, called hot pots, are located four miles west near Midway. Mt Timpanogos, one of the most impressive mountains in the state, is to the southwest in the Wasatch Range. Good picnicking, fishing and hunting areas abound. A Ranger District office of the Uinta National Forest (see PROVO) is located here.

What to See and Do

Deer Creek State Park. Swimming; fishing; boating (ramp). Camping (fee; rest rms, showers; dump and fish cleaning stations). (Daily) 8 mi SW on US 189. Phone 435/654-0171. Day-use per vehicle ¢¢

Heber Valley Railroad. 90-yr-old steam-powered excursion train takes passengers through the farmlands of Heber Valley, along the shore of Deer Creek Lake and into Provo Canyon on various 1-hr to 4-hr trips. Restored coaches & open-air cars. Special trips some Sat eves. Res required. (May-mid-Oct, daily; mid-Oct-Nov, schedule varies; Dec-Apr, daily exc Sun) For schedule and fee information, contact 450 S 600 W, PO Box 609. Phone 435/654-5601 or 801/581-9980 (in Salt Lake City). ¢¢¢–¢¢¢¢¢

State Fish Hatchery. Children with adult only. (Daily) 4 mi W on UT 113, then S, near Midway. Phone 435/654-0282. **Free**

Timpanogos Cave National Monument (see). 16 mi SW on US 189, then 12 mi NW on UT 92.

Wasatch Mountain State Park. Approx 25,000 acres in Heber Valley. Fishing; boating. Hiking; 27-hole golf. Snowmobiling, cross-country skiing. Picnicking, restaurant. Camping (fee; hookups, dump station). Visitor center. (Daily) Standard fees. 2 mi NW off UT 220 or 224. Phone 435/654-0532.

Annual Events

Cutter, snowmobile and dog sled races. 1st wkend Feb.

Wasatch County Fair. Parades, exhibits, livestock shows, rodeos, dancing. 1st wkend Aug.

Swiss Days. 4 mi W in Midway. "Old country" games, activities, costumes. Fri & Sat before Labor Day.

Motels

✓★ **DANISH VIKING LODGE.** *989 S Main St (84032). 435/654-2202; FAX 435/654-2770; res: 800/544-4066.* 34 rms, 1-2 story, 3 kits. Mid-May-mid-Sept & Christmas season: S $40-$49; D $49-$65; each addl $5; suite $99-$150; kit. units $65-$95; under 18 free; package plans; lower rates rest of yr. Crib $3. Pet accepted, some restrictions. TV; cable (premium), VCR avail. Pool; whirlpool. Sauna. Playground. Complimentary continental bkfst. Restaurant nearby. Ck-out 11 am. Coin lndry. Downhill ski 12 mi; x-country ski 7 mi. Health club privileges. Refrigerators, microwaves. Picnic tables, grills. Cr cds: A, C, D, DS, MC, V.

SC

★ **HIGH COUNTRY INN & RV PARK.** *1000 S Main St. (84032). 435/654-0201; res: 800/345-9198.* E-mail nci@causefx.com. 38 rms. S $45-$50; D $50-$55; each addl $5; lower rates rest of yr. Crib $5. TV; cable (premium), VCR avail. Heated pool; whirlpool. Playground. Complimentary continental bkfst. Restaurant adj. Ck-out 11 am. Coin lndry. Downhill ski 20 mi; x-country ski 5 mi. Refrigerators, microwaves. Picnic table. View of mountains. Cr cds: A, C, DS, MC, V.

SC

Resort

★★★ **THE HOMESTEAD.** *700 N Homestead Dr (84049), 5 mi W of US 40. 435/654-1102; FAX 435/654-5087; res: 800/327-7220.* E-mail homeut@aol.com; web www.homestead-ut.com. 140 rms, 1-2 story, 26 suites. S, D $109-$149; suites $179-$324; condos $249-$600; ski, golf plans. TV; cable (premium), VCR avail (movies). 2 pools, 1 indoor; whirlpool. Restaurant (see SIMON'S FINE DINING). Bar. Ck-out noon, ck-in 4 pm. Meeting rms. Business center. Gift shop. Lighted tennis. 18-hole golf. X-country ski 10 mi. Exercise equipt; sauna. Massage. Horse stables. Wagon & buggy rides. Lawn games. Historic country inn (1886); spacious grounds, gardens, duck ponds. Cr cds: A, C, D, DS, MC, V.

D SC

Restaurant

★★★ **SIMON'S FINE DINING.** *(See Homestead Resort) 435/654-1102.* Web www.homestead-ut.com. Hrs: 5:30-9:30 pm; Sun brunch 10 am-2:30 pm; closed Mon, Tues. Res accepted. Wine list. Complete meals: dinner $23-$34. Sun brunch $16.95. Child's meals. Daily specials. Pianist. Outdoor dining. Fireplaces. View of valley. Cr cds: A, C, D, DS, MC, V.

Kanab (J-2)

Founded 1870 **Pop** 3,289 **Elev** 4,909 ft **Area Code** 435 **Zip** 84741
E-mail kanetrav@xpressweb.com

Information Kane County Office of Tourism, 78 S 100 E; 435/644-5033 or 800/733-5263

Located at the base of the Vermilion Cliffs, this city began around Fort Kanab, built in 1864. Native Americans, however, forced the abandonment of the fort. Later, Mormon missionaries made Kanab a permanent settlement. The city's regular economy revolves around tourism. Since 1922, more than 200 Hollywood productions have used the sand dunes, canyons and lakes surrounding Kanab as their settings. Some movie-set towns can still be seen. Kanab is within a 1½-hour drive from the north rim of the Grand Canyon, Zion and Bryce Canyon national parks, Cedar Breaks and Pipe Spring national monuments and Glen Canyon National Recreation Area.

What to See and Do

Coral Pink Sand Dunes State Park. Six sq mi of very colorful, windswept sandhills. Hiking. Picnicking. Tent & trailer sites (fee; showers, dump station). Off-hwy vehicles allowed; exploring, photography. (Daily) 8 mi NW on US 89, then 12 mi SW on county road. Phone 435/874-2408. Day-use per vehicle ¢¢

Glen Canyon National Recreation Area/Lake Powell. 68 mi E via US 89, at Wahweap Basin Marina (see PAGE, AZ); access in Utah at Bullfrog Marina (see LAKE POWELL).

Grand Canyon Scenic Flights. Flights to Grand Canyon during daylight hrs; flight covering Bryce Canyon and Zion national parks, Lake Powell and Coral Pink Sand Dunes. (All-yr, by res) 2½ mi S on US 89 A. Phone 435/644-2904. ¢¢¢¢¢

Pipe Spring National Monument (see ARIZONA). 7 mi S on US 89, then 14 mi W on AZ 389, in Arizona.

Zion National Park (see). 17 mi NW on US 89, then 25 mi W on UT 9.

Seasonal Event

Melodrama. Old Barn Theater. Phone 435/644-2601. Late May-late Sept.

Motels

★★ **BEST WESTERN RED HILLS.** *124 W Center St (84741). 435/644-2675; FAX 435/644-5919; res: 800/528-1234.* 75 rms, 2 story. May-Oct: S, D $76; each addl $5; lower rates rest of yr. Crib $5. TV; cable, VCR (movies). Heated pool; whirlpool. Restaurant opp 6 am-10 pm. Ck-out 11 am. Meeting rm. Business servs avail. Refrigerators. Some balconies. Cr cds: A, C, D, DS, MC, V.

D SC

★ **FOUR SEASONS INN.** *36 N 300 W (84741). 435/644-2635; FAX 435/644-5895.* 41 rms, 2 story. Apr-Oct: S $74; D $78; each addl $5; lower rates rest of yr. Crib $5. TV; cable. Pool; wading pool. Restaurant 6:30 am-10 pm. Ck-out 11 am. Business servs avail. Gift shop. Cr cds: A, C, D, DS, MC, V.

SC

✓★★ **PARRY LODGE & RESTAURANT.** *89 E Center St (84741). 435/644-2601; FAX 435/644-2605; res: 800/748-4104.* 89 rms, 1-2 story. May-Oct: S $43-$57; D $57-$65; each addl $6; family rates; lower rates rest of yr. Pet accepted. TV; cable. Heated pool. Restaurant 7 am-noon, 5-10 pm. Ck-out 11 am. Coin Indry. Business servs avail. Autographed pictures of movie stars displayed in lobby. Cr cds: A, C, DS, MC, V.

SC

★★ **SHILO INN.** *296 W 100 N (84741). 435/644-2562; FAX 435/644-5333; res: 800/222-2244.* 119 rms, 2-3 story. Mid-Apr-Sept: S, D $68-$88; each addl $10; lower rates rest of yr. Crib $10. TV; cable, VCR avail (movies). Heated pool; whirlpool. Complimentary continental bkfst. Restaurant opp 7 am-9 pm. Ck-out noon. Coin Indry. Meeting rms. Business servs avail. Sundries. Gift shop. Free airport transportation. Many refrigerators. Cr cds: A, C, D, DS, MC, V.

D SC

Restaurants

★ **CHEF'S PALACE.** *176 W Center St (84741). 435/644-5052.* Hrs: 6 am-11 pm; winter to 9 pm. Closed Dec 25. Res accepted. Semi-a la carte: bkfst $2.90-$8.40, lunch $3.15-$6.25, dinner $5-$38. Child's meals. Specializes in prime rib, broiled steak. Salad bar. Cr cds: A, C, DS, MC, V.

D

✓★ **HOUSTON'S TRAIL'S END.** *32 E Center St (84741). 435/644-2488.* Hrs: 6 am-10:30 pm. Closed Thanksgiving, Dec 25; also Jan & Feb. Semi-a la carte: bkfst $2.65-$5.75, lunch $4.50-$6.75, dinner $5-$13.50. Child's meals. Specializes in chicken-fried steak, shrimp. Salad bar. Rustic, Western decor; "burned-wood" walls, wagon wheel lamps. Cr cds: A, C, DS, MC, V.

Lake Powell (H-4)

(See also Page, AZ)

E-mail chamber@page-lakepowell.com

Information Powell Resorts & Marinas/ARAMARK, Box 56909, Phoenix, AZ 85079, phone 800/528-6154; or the Page/Lake Powell Chamber of Commerce, 644 N Navajo, Tower Plaza, PO Box 727, Page, AZ 86040, phone 520/645-2741 or 888/261-PAGE

Lake Powell, formed by the Glen Canyon Dam on the Colorado River, is located in Glen Canyon National Recreation Area. It stretches 186 miles, has more than 1,900 miles of shoreline, is the second-largest man-made lake in the US and is located in the second-largest canyon in the US. The lake is named for John Wesley Powell, the one-armed explorer who, in 1869, successfully navigated the Colorado River through Glen Canyon and the Grand Canyon and later became director of the US Geological Survey.

What to See and Do

Boat trips on Lake Powell. Trips include Canyon Explorer tour (2½ hrs) and all-day Rainbow Bridge National Monument tour; also houseboat and powerboat rentals. Res advised. (Daily) From Bullfrog or Halls Crossing marinas, both on UT 276. Phone 800/528-6154.

Glen Canyon National Recreation Area (Bullfrog Marina). This 1.2-million-acre, yr-round recreation area offers swimming; fishing; boating, boat tours & trips, boat rentals & repairs; picnicking; camping, tent & trailer sites (full hookups; fee); lodgings. A ranger station and visitors center offering summer campfire programs is located in Bullfrog on UT 276 (Apr-Oct, daily); phone 435/684-2243. Additional access and recreational activities avail at Hite Marina, north end of lake, just off UT 95; Halls Crossing Marina, across lake from Bullfrog on UT 276, accessible by ferry; Dangling Rope Marina, 5 mi downlake (south) from Bullfrog, accessible only by boat; and Wahweap Lodge and Marina, at far south end of lake near Page, AZ (see). A visitors center and headquarters for the recreation area are located in Page, AZ. (Daily) Access from the north via UT 95 to UT 276. Phone 520/608-6404.

Lake Powell Ferry. Approx 3-mi trip between Bullfrog and Hall's Crossing saves 130 mi driving around lake. (Daily; reduced hrs in winter) Contact Utah Travel Council, Council Hall/Capitol Hill, Salt Lake City 84114; phone 801/538-1030 or 435/684-7000 (Lake Powell). Passenger vehicles. ¢¢¢-¢¢¢¢¢; Passengers on foot ¢

Rainbow Bridge National Monument (see). On E shore of Lake Powell, 50 mi by boat from Bullfrog Marina, Halls Crossing Marina and Wahweap Lodge and Marina.

Lodge

★★ **DEFIANCE HOUSE.** *1000 Main St (84533), ¼ mi from Bullfrog Marina, at top of hill. 435/684-2233; FAX 435/684-2312; res: 800/528-6154.* 56 units, 2 story, 8 cottages. Many rm phones. Mid-May-Sept: S, D $87-$100; each addl $10; suites $95-$105; cottages $107; under 18 free; boating tour plans; lower rates rest of yr. Crib free. TV; cable. Playground. Dining rm 7 am-8 pm; summer to midnight. Bar 5-9 pm; summer to midnight. Ck-out 11 am. Coin Indry. Sundries. Gift shop. Balconies. Anasazi motif; decor, artifacts. On lake; swimming. Cr cds: A, C, D, DS, MC, V.

D

Loa (G-3)

Pop 444 **Elev** 7,060 ft **Area Code** 435 **Zip** 84747

This town was named Loa because of the volcano-like appearance of a nearby mountain. A Ranger District office of the Fishlake National Forest (see RICHFIELD) is located here.

What to See and Do

Capitol Reef National Park (see). Approx 23 mi E via UT 24.

Escalante State Park. Petrified forest; mineralized wood and dinosaur bones. Swimming; fishing; boating (ramps) at reservoir. Hiking; bird watching. Picnicking. Camping (fee; rest rms, showers, dump station). (Daily) Standard fees. 65 mi S via UT 12, then 1 mi W, near Escalante. Phone 435/826-4466. Per vehicle ¢¢

Lodge

★★★ **ROAD CREEK INN.** *90 S Main (84747). 435/836-2485; FAX 435/836-2490; res: 800/388-7688.* 13 rms, 3 story, 2 suites. May-Oct: S, D $69-$75; each addl $6; suites $98-$122; under 12 $4; lower rates rest of yr. Crib free. TV; cable (premium), VCR avail. Complimentary full bkfst. Restaurant 5-9:30 pm. Ck-out 11 am. Meeting rm. Business servs avail. Gift shop. Free airport transportation. Whirlpool. Sauna. Rec rm. Fish/hunt guides. Restored 1912 general store building; inn-like amenities. Totally nonsmoking. Cr cds: A, C, DS, MC, V.

D

Logan (B-3)

(See also Brigham City, Garden City)

Founded 1856 **Pop** 32,762 **Elev** 4,535 ft **Area Code** 435 **Zip** 84321
E-mail btr@sunrem.com **Web** bridgerland.com

Information Cache Chamber of Commerce/Bridgerland Travel Region, 160 N Main; 435/752-2161 or 800/882-4433

Logan, situated in the center of beautiful Cache Valley, is surrounded by snowcapped mountains. The city received its name from an early trapper, Ephraim Logan. Begun by Mormons who were dedicated to living from fruits of the soil, little else was sold in Logan's early days except timber and farm produce. The change to a more industrialized economic base came about slowly. Now the city of Logan is the location of Utah State University, five electronics plants, space technology, book printing, plastics, baking and meat packing plants, as well as specialized woodworking and locally made craft and collectible shops.

What to See and Do

Daughters of the Utah Pioneers Museum. Exhibits depict Utah's past. 160 N Main, in Chamber of Commerce Bldg. (Mon-Fri) Phone 435/752-5139. **Free**

Hyrum State Park. A 450-acre reservoir with beach swimming, waterskiing; fishing; boating (ramp, dock), sailing. Picnicking. Camping (trailer parking). (Apr-Oct) Standard fees. 12 mi S, off US 89/90. Phone 435/245-6866. Day-use per vehicle ¢¢

Mormon Tabernacle (1891). Gray limestone example of early Mormon building; seats 2,000. Genealogy library. (Mon-Fri) 100 N Main. Phone 435/755-5598.

Mormon Temple (1884). The site for this massive, castellated limestone structure was chosen by Brigham Young, who also broke ground for it in 1877. Grounds are open all yr, but the temple is closed to the general public. 175 N 300 East. Phone 435/752-3611.

Ronald V. Jensen Living Historical Farm. Agricultural museum with typical Mormon family farm of World War I era; 120 acres of fields, meadows, orchards and gardens; artifacts and machinery; costumed interpreters. (June-Sept, Tues-Sat) (See ANNUAL EVENTS) 5 mi S on US 89/91, in Wellsville. Phone 435/245-4064. ¢

Utah State University (1888). (20,100 students) On campus is the Nora Eccles Harrison Museum of Art (Mon-Fri; closed hols, also Thanksgiving wkend, Dec 22-Jan 2; free). 5th North & 7th East Sts. For tours of campus Phone 435/797-1129.

Wasatch-Cache National Forest, Logan Canyon. Fishing. Back country trails, hunting. Winter sports. Picnicking. Camping. Fees charged at most recreation sites. (Daily) E on US 89 Natl Forest (scenic byway). A Ranger District office is located in Logan at 1500 E US 89; phone 435/755-3620.

Annual Events

Utah Festival Opera Company. July-Aug.

Festival of the American West. Ronald V. Jensen Living Historical Farm. Historical pageant; pioneer and Native American crafts fair, art exhibition, antique quilt show; frontier town; medicine man show; log construction; Dutch-oven cook-off. Phone 435/797-1143. Late July-early Aug.

Cache County Fair. Rodeo, horse races, exhibits. Early Aug.

Motels

✓★★ **BEST WESTERN BAUGH MOTEL.** *153 S Main St (84321). 435/752-5220; FAX 801/752-3251; res: 800/462-4154.* E-mail baugh @sisna.com. 77 rms, 1-2 story. S $46-$70; D $50-$74; each addl $6. Crib $4. TV; cable (premium), VCR avail (movies). Heated pool. Restaurant 6 am-10 pm; Sun 8 am-2 pm. Rm serv. Ck-out noon. Meeting rm. Business servs avail. Health club privileges. Some fireplaces, refrigerators; microwaves avail. Sun deck. Cr cds: A, C, D, DS, MC, V.

SC

★★ **COMFORT INN.** *447 N Main St (84321). 435/752-9141; FAX 435/752-9723; res: 800/228-5150.* E-mail gowest478@aol.com. 83 rms, 2 story. S $50; D $52; each addl $4; suites $60; under 18 free. Crib $5. TV; cable. Indoor pool; whirlpool. Complimentary continental bkfst. Restaurant adj 6-1 am; wkends to 2 am. Ck-out noon. Coin Indry. Meeting rms. Business servs avail. In-rm modem link. Valet serv. X-country ski 20 mi. Exercise equipt. Refrigerator in suites. Cr cds: A, C, D, DS, ER, JCB, MC, V.

D SC

✓★ **DAYS INN.** *364 S Main St (84321). 435/753-5623; FAX 435/753-3357; res: 800/329-7466.* 64 rms, 2 story, 20 kit. units. S $36-$38; D $44-$52; each addl $4; kit. units $48-$56; under 12 free; wkly rates Sept-May. Crib free. TV; cable, VCR (movies $2). Indoor pool. Complimentary continental bkfst. Restaurant nearby. Ck-out 11 am. Coin Indry. X-country ski 20 mi. Many refrigerators; some in-rm whirlpools. Cr cds: A, C, D, DS, MC, V.

D SC

Inns

★★★ **INN ON CENTER STREET.** *169 E Center St (84321). 435/752-3443; FAX 435/752-8550; res: 800/574-7605.* Web www.centerstreetinn.com. 18 rms in 4 buildings, 5 A/C, 8 air-cooled, 3 story, 16 suites. S, D $25-$57; suites $57-$180. Adults only. TV; cable, VCR avail (movies). Pool. Complimentary continental bkfst. Restaurant nearby. Ck-out 11 am, ck-in 3 pm. Downhill/x-country ski 20 mi. Microwaves avail. Lobby in historic mansion (1879); Oriental rugs, period furniture. Special theme suites, such as penthouse suite and space odyssey, are uniquely decorated. Totally nonsmoking. Cr cds: A, C, DS, MC, V.

D

★★★ **LOGAN HOUSE INN.** *168 N 100 East (84321), in Historical District. 435/752-7727; FAX 435/752-0092; res: 800/478-7459.* 6 rms, 2 story. S, D $79-$165; each addl $20; golf, ski plans. TV; cable, VCR (movies). Complimentary full bkfst; afternoon refreshments. Restaurant opp Wed-Sat 5:30-10 pm. Ck-out 10:30 am, ck-in 3 pm. Business serv avail. In-rm modem link. Luggage handling. Concierge serv. Guest Indry.

In-rm whirlpools, fireplaces. Built in 1898; antiques. Totally nonsmoking. Cr cds: A, C, D, DS, MC, V.

D

★★★ **PROVIDENCE INN BED & BREAKFAST.** *10 S Main (84332). 435/752-3432; FAX 435/752-3482; res: 800/480-4943.* E-mail provinn@providenceinn.com; web www.providenceinn.com. 14 rms, 2 with shower only, 3 story, 1 suite. June-Sept: S $45-$139; D $55-$149; each addl $10; suite $119-$149; under 5 free; golf plans. TV; cable, VCR (movies). Complimentary full bkfst. Complimentary coffee in rms. Restaurant nearby. Ck-out 11 am, ck-in 4 pm. Business servs avail. In-rm modem link. Coin lndry. X-country ski 5 mi. Many in-rm whirlpools. Picnic tables. Built in 1869; accurately restored. Totally nonsmoking. Cr cds: A, C, D, DS, MC, V.

D

Restaurant

★★ **GIA'S RESTAURANT & DELI.** *119 S Main St (84321). 435/752-8384.* Hrs: 10 am-9:30 pm; Fri, Sat to 10 pm. Closed Dec 25. Res accepted. Italian menu. Serv bar. Semi-a la carte: lunch, dinner $6-$14.75. Child's meals. Specialties: chicken Marsala, manicotti. Italian tapestry and pictures, European decor. Family-owned. Cr cds: A, C, D, DS, MC, V.

D SC

Unrated Dining Spot

BLUEBIRD. *19 N Main St (84321). 435/752-3155.* Hrs: 11 am-9:30 pm; Fri, Sat to 10 pm. Closed Sun; most major hols. Res accepted. Semi-a la carte: bkfst $2-$6.50, lunch $3-$10.45, dinner $7.50-$11. Child's meals. Limited menu. 1920s decor; ice cream, candy factory. Cr cds: A, C, DS, MC, V.

Moab (F-6)

Founded 1879 **Pop** 3,971 **Elev** 4,025 ft **Area Code** 435 **Zip** 84532
E-mail pseep@grand.state.ut.us **Web** www.canyonlands-utah.com

Information Grand County Travel Council, PO Box 550; 435/259-8825, 435/259-1370 or 800/635-6622

The first attempt to settle this valley was made in 1855, but Moab, named after an isolated area in the Bible, was not permanently settled until 1880. Situated on the Colorado River at the foot of the LaSal Mountains, Moab was a sleepy agricultural town until after World War II, when uranium exploration and production and oil and potash development made it boom. Today, tourism and moviemaking help make it a thriving community. A Ranger District office of the Manti-LaSal National Forest is located here, as are headquarters for Canyonlands and Arches national parks.

What to See and Do

Arches National Park (see). 5 mi NW on US 191.

Canyonlands Field Institute. Educational seminars/trips featuring geology, natural and cultural history, endangered species, Southwestern literature and landscape photography. Many programs use Canyonlands and Arches national parks as outdoor classrooms. (Mon-Fri) For information contact PO Box 68, 84532; phone 435/259-7750. ¢¢¢¢-¢¢¢¢¢

Canyonlands National Park (see). N district: 9 mi N on US 191, then 21 mi SW on UT 313.

Dan O'Laurie Canyon Country Museum. Exhibits on local history, archaeology, geology, uranium, minerals of the area. Walking tour information. (Daily exc Sun; closed Jan 1, July 4, Thanksgiving, Dec 25) 118 E Center St. Phone 435/259-7985. **Donation**

Dead Horse Point State Park. Named for promontory rising 2,000 ft above the Colorado River, this island mesa offers views of the LaSal Mountains, Canyonlands National Park and the Colorado River. Approx 5,200 acres in region of gorges, cliffs, buttes and mesas. Visitor center, museum. Picnicking; limited drinking water. Camping (fee; electricity, dump station). Trailer parking. (Daily) 9 mi NW on US 191, then 22 mi SW on UT 313. Phone 435/259-2614. Day use ¢¢

Hole 'n the Rock. A 5,000-sq-ft dwelling carved into huge sandstone rock. Picnic area with stone tables and benches. (Daily; closed Jan 1, Thanksgiving, Dec 25) 15 mi S via US 191. Phone 435/686-2250. Tours ¢¢

Manti-LaSal National Forest, LaSal Division. The land of the forest's LaSal Division is similar in color and beauty to some parts of the Grand Canyon, but also includes high mountains nearing 13,000 ft and pine and spruce forests. Swimming; fishing. Hiking, hunting. (See MONTICELLO, PRICE) 8 mi S on US 191, then 5 mi E. For information contact the Ranger District office, 125 W 200 South, phone 435/259-7155; or the Forest Supervisor, 599 W Price River Dr, Price 84501, phone 435/637-2817. **Free**

River trips. On the Green and Colorado rivers, including Canyonlands National Park, Lake Powell (see both) and Cataract Canyon.

Adrift Adventures. Oar, paddle and motorized trips avail; 1-7-days. (Early Apr-late Oct) Phone 435/259-8594 or 800/874-4483. ¢¢¢¢¢

Canyon Voyages. (Early Apr-Oct)Phone 435/259-6007 or 800/733-6007.

Colorado River & Trail Expeditions, Inc. Phone 435/261-1789 or 800/253-7328. ¢¢¢¢¢

Sheri Griffith River Expeditions. Choice of rafts: oarboats, motorized rafts, paddleboats, inflatable kayaks or whitewater canoes; 1-6-day trips; instruction avail. (May-Sept) PO Box 1324. Phone 435/259-8229 or 800/332-2439. ¢¢¢¢¢

Tex's Riverways. Flatwater canoe trips, 4-10 days. Confluence pick-ups avail, jet boat cruises, all river services. (Mar-Oct) PO Box 67. Phone 435/259-5101. ¢¢¢¢¢

Sightseeing tours.

Canyonlands By Night. Two-hr boat trip with sound-and-light presentation highlights history of area. (May-mid-Oct, daily, leaves at sundown, weather permitting) Res required; tickets must be purchased at office, 1861 N US 191. PO Box 328. Leaves dock at bridge, 2 mi N on US 191. Phone 435/259-5261. ¢¢¢¢¢

Lin Ottinger's Scenic Tours. Full- and half-day tours of Canyonlands and Arches national parks, Dead Horse Point State Park and other areas; rockhounding and geology offered. Tours may involve some hiking (sturdy shoes recommended), minimum fare required. Free evening slide show at tour headquarters. (Mid-Apr-Oct, daily) Res suggested. Moab Rock Shop, 600 N Main St. Phone 435/259-7312. ¢¢¢¢¢

Rim Tours. Guided mountain bike tours in canyon country and the Colorado Rockies. Vehicle support for camping tours. Daily and overnight trips; combination bicycle/river trips avail. 94 W 1st N. Phone 435/259-5223 or 800/626-7335. ¢¢¢¢¢

Scenic Air Tours. Flights over Canyonlands National Park and various other tours. (All-yr; closed Jan 1, Thanksgiving, Dec 25) 18 mi N on US 191, at Canyonlands Field. Contact Redtail Aviation, phone 435/259-7421 or 435/564-3412. ¢¢¢¢¢

Tag-A-Long Expeditions. One- to seven-day whitewater rafting trips on the Green and Colorado rivers; jetboat trips on the Colorado River; jetboat trips and four-wheel-drive tours into Canyonlands National Park; winter four-wheel-drive tours (Nov-Feb). Also Canyon Classics, one-day jetboat trips with cultural performing arts programs. Most trips (Apr-mid-Oct). 452 N Main St. Phone 435/259-8946 or 800/453-3292. ¢¢¢¢¢

Trail rides. Pack Creek Ranch. Horseback rides, ranging from one to six hrs, in red rock canyons including Arches and Canyonlands national parks. Guided tours for small groups; also overnight trips. (Mar-Oct; upon availability) PO Box 1270. Phone 435/259-5505. Per hr ¢¢¢¢¢

Annual Events

Jeep Safari. Easter wk & wkend.

Butch Cassidy Days PRCA Rodeo. Mid-June.

Moab Music Festival. Mid-Sept.

Motels

★ **BEST WESTERN INN.** *105 S Main St (84532). 435/259-6151; FAX 435/259-4397; res: 800/528-1234.* E-mail bwgreenwell@juno.com. 72 rms, 1-2 story. Mar-Oct: S, D $45-$121; each addl $8; lower rates rest of yr. Crib free. TV; cable (premium). Heated pool. Coffee in lobby. Restaurant 7 am-9 pm. Ck-out 11 am. Exercise equipt. Cr cds: A, C, D, DS, MC, V.

SC

★★ **BEST WESTERN INN.** *16 S Main St (84532). 435/259-2300; FAX 435/259-2301; res: 800/528-1234.* 77 rms, 2 story, 46 suites. Early Apr-Oct: S, D $99; each addl $8; suites $199; under 12 free; golf plan; higher rates Jeep Safari; lower rates rest of yr. Crib $20. TV; cable (premium). Indoor/outdoor pool. Complimentary bkfst. Restaurant adj noon-11 pm. Ck-out 11 am. Coin Indry. Meeting rms. Business servs avail. Exercise equipt; sauna. Game rm. Refrigerators. Cr cds: A, C, D, DS, MC, V.

D SC

✓★ **BOWEN MOTEL.** *169 N Main St (84532). 435/259-7132; FAX 801/259-6144; res: 800/874-5439.* E-mail bowen@moab-utah.com; web www.moab-utah.com/bowen/motel.html. 40 rms, 2 story. Mar-Oct: S $65; D $70-$75; each addl $4. Crib $4; under 12 free. TV; cable (premium). Heated pool. Complimentary coffee in lobby. Restaurants nearby. Ck-out 11 am. Cr cds: A, C, D, DS, MC, V.

★ **LANDMARK MOTEL.** *168 N Main St (84532). 435/259-6147; FAX 435/259-5556; res: 800/441-6147.* 35 rms, 2 story. Mid-Mar-Oct: S $70-$76; D $80-$84; each addl $4; family rates; lower rates rest of yr. Crib free. TV; cable. Heated pool; wading pool, whirlpool. Complimentary coffee in lobby. Restaurant adj 7 am-midnight. Ck-out 11 am. Coin Indry. Cr cds: A, C, D, DS, MC, V.

Inns

★★★ **CASTLE VALLEY INN.** *424 Amber Ln; Hwy 64 Box 2602 (84532). 435/259-6012; FAX 435/259-1501.* 8 rms, 3 kit. cabins. No rm phones. Apr-late Nov: S, D $90-$130; cabins $155; lower rates Feb-Mar. Closed Dec-Jan. Children over 15 yrs only. Complimentary full bkfst; afternoon refreshments. Ck-out 11 am, ck-in 3-9 pm. Lawn games. Refrigerators. Cr cds: C, DS, MC, V.

★★ **SUNFLOWER HILL BED & BREAKFAST.** *185 N 300 E (84532). 435/259-2974; FAX 435/259-2470; res: 800/662-2786.* E-mail innkeeper@sunflowerhill.com; web www.sunflowerhill.com. 11 rms, 2 story, 2 suites. No rm phones. Mar-Oct: S, D $85-$155; each addl $20; suites $135. Children over 8 yrs only. TV; cable. Whirlpool. Complimentary full bkfst; afternoon refreshments. Ck-out 11 am, ck-in 3-6 pm. Turn-of-the-century adobe farm house, cottage amid gardens. Totally nonsmoking. Cr cds: C, DS, MC, V.

SC

Guest Ranch

★★ **PACK CREEK RANCH.** *Lasal Mountain Loop Rd (84532), 8 mi S on US 191 to La Sal Mt Loop Rd, head E to "T" intersection, then right 6 mi to Pack Creek turnoff. 435/259-5505; FAX 435/259-8879.* 10 kit. cottages (1, 2 & 3 bedrm). No rm phones. Apr-Oct, AP: $125 per person; lower rates rest of yr. Crib $10 (one-time fee). Pet accepted. Pool; whirlpool. Sauna. Dining rm 7-10 am, 6:30-8:30 pm. Ck-out 11 am, ck-in 3 pm. Grocery, package store 16 mi. X-country ski on site. Hiking. Picnic tables. A 300-acre ranch at foot of La Sal Mts; features trail rides, pack trips. Cr cds: A, C, DS, MC, V.

Restaurants

★★ **CENTER CAFE.** *92 E Center St (84532). 435/259-4295.* Hrs: 5:30-10 pm. Closed Jan. Res accepted. Continental menu. Serv bar. A la carte entrees: dinner $12-$26. Specializes in fresh fish, grilled meats. Own pastries. Original artwork. Totally nonsmoking. Cr cds: C.

★★ **GRAND OLD RANCH HOUSE.** *1266 N US 191 (84532). 435/259-5753.* Hrs: 5-10:30 pm. Closed Dec 25. Res accepted. German, Amer menu. Serv bar. A la carte: dinner $8-$28.95. Specialties: jaegerschnitzel, prime rib. Outdoor dining. Historic building (1896). Antiques, old photos. Cr cds: A, C, D, DS, MC, V.

★★ **SUNSET GRILL.** *900 N US 191 (84532). 453/259-7146.* Hrs: 5-10 pm. Closed Dec 25. Serv bar. Semi-a la carte: dinner $9.95-$18.95. Specializes in prime rib, steak, fresh seafood. Outdoor dining. In house of prospector Charlie Steen, whose strike started the uranium boom of the 1950s. View of Colorado River; historic items from the boom days. Cr cds: A, C, DS, MC, V.

Monticello (G-6)

(See also Blanding)

Founded 1887 **Pop** 1,806 **Elev** 7,066 ft **Area Code** 435 **Zip** 84535
Web www.edonnet.com/fourcorners/sjcu

Information San Juan County Visitor Center, 117 S Main St, PO Box 490; 435/587-3235 or 800/574-4386

Highest county seat in Utah (San Juan County), Monticello was named for Thomas Jefferson's Virginia home. On the east slope of the Abajo Mountains, the elevation makes the weather delightful but the growing season short. Livestock raising, dry farming and tourism are the chief industries.

What to See and Do

Canyon Rims Recreation Area. Anticline and Needles overlooks into Canyonlands National Park are located here, as are Wind Whistle & Hatch campgrounds. 20 mi N on US 191.

Canyonlands National Park (see). Beyond this point are primarily foot trails and four-wheel drive areas. S district: 14 mi N on US 191, then 35 mi W on UT 211 to Squaw Flats Campground Area.

Manti-LaSal National Forest, LaSal Division. (See MOAB, PRICE) The forest land of this division ranges from red rock canyons to high alpine terrain. Ancient ruins and rock art contrast with pine and spruce forests and aspen-dotted meadows. Fishing, hiking, snowmobiling, cross-country skiing, hunting, camping (fee). 2½ mi W. For further information contact the Ranger District Office, 496 E Central, phone 435/587-2041; or the Forest Supervisor, 599 W Price River Dr, Price 84501, phone 435/637-2817. **Free**

Annual Events

Monticello Pioneer Days. Parade, booths, food, games, sports. Wkend nearest July 24.

San Juan County Fair & Rodeo. 2nd wkend Aug.

Motels

★★ **BEST WESTERN WAYSIDE INN.** *197 E Central Ave (84535), 2 blks E of US 191. 435/587-2261; FAX 435/587-2920; res: 800/633-9700.* 38 rms. May-late Oct: S, D $64-$69; each addl $5; suites $64-$85; under 12 free; lower rates rest of yr. Crib $4. TV; cable. Pool. Restaurant opp 6 am-10 pm. Ck-out 11 am. X-country ski 6 mi. Picnic tables. Cr cds: A, C, D, DS, MC, V.

SC

✓★ **TRIANGLE HOTEL.** *164 E Hwy 666 (84535), on US 666E, 2 blks E of US 191. 435/587-2274; FAX 435/587-2175; res: 800/657-6622.* 26 rms. S $24-$42; D $24-$66; each addl $3; suite $46-

$88. Crib $3. TV; cable. Restaurant nearby. Ck-out 11 am. X-country ski 3 mi. Refrigerators avail. Cr cds: A, C, D, MC, V.

SC

Monument Valley

(see Kayenta, AZ)

Natural Bridges National Monument (H-5)

(4 mi S of Blanding on US 191, then 36 mi W on UT 95, then 4 mi N on UT 275)

This 7,439-acre area of fantastically eroded and colorful terrain, made a national monument in 1908, features three natural bridges, all with Hopi names: Sipapu, a 268-foot span, and Kachina, a 204-foot span, are in White Canyon, a major tributary gorge of the Colorado River; Owachomo, a 180-foot span, is near Armstrong Canyon, which joins White Canyon. Sipapu is the second-largest natural bridge in the world. From 650 to 2,000 years ago, the ancestral Puebloan people lived in this area, leaving behind cliff dwelling ruins and pictographs, which can be viewed today. Bridge View Drive, a nine-mile loop road, provides views of the three bridges from rim overlooks. There are hiking trails to each bridge within the canyon. In the park is a visitor center (daily; closed hols in winter) and a primitive campground with 13 tent & trailer sites (all-yr, fee; 26-ft combined-length limit). Car and passenger ferry service across Lake Powell is available (see LAKE POWELL). There is a $6 per vehicle entrance fee; Golden Eagle, Golden Age, Golden Access passports accepted (see MAKING THE MOST OF YOUR TRIP). For further information contact the Superintendent, Box 1, Lake Powell 84533; 435/692-1234.

Nephi (E-3)

(See also Fillmore, Payson)

Settled 1851 **Pop** 3,515 **Elev** 5,133 ft **Area Code** 435 **Zip** 84648
Web www.utahreach.usu.edu

Information Juab Travel Council, 4 S Main, PO Box 71, 84648; 435/623-5203 or 435/623-2411

What to See and Do

Yuba State Park. Waterskiing and walleyed pike fishing are the big attractions of this lake, as well as sandy beaches. Swimming, waterskiing; fishing, boating (ramps). Picnicking. Camping (fee; rest rms, showers, dump station). (Daily) 30 mi S via I-15, near Scipio. Phone 435/758-2611. Day-use per vehicle **¢¢**

Annual Event

Ute Stampede Rodeo. Three-day festival featuring horse and mammoth parades, carnival, PRCA rodeo, contests, arts & crafts, concessions. Phone 435/623-4407. 2nd wkend July.

Motels

★ **BEST WESTERN PARADISE INN.** *1025 S Main (84648). 435/623-0624; FAX 435/623-0624; res: 800/528-1234.* 40 rms, 2 story. Mid-May-Oct: S $49; D $55; each addl $2; lower rates rest of yr. Crib $6. Pet accepted, some restrictions. TV; cable (premium). Heated pool; whirlpool. Complimentary continental bkfst. Restaurant nearby. Ck-out 11 am. Exercise equipt. Cr cds: A, C, D, DS, MC, V.

SC

✓★ **ROBERTA'S COVE MOTOR INN.** *2250 S Main (84648). 435/623-2629; FAX 435/623-2245; res: 800/456-6460.* 43 air-cooled rms, 2 story. S $36-$44; D $40-$50; each addl $5; higher rates Ute Stampede. Crib $4. TV; cable (premium). Pool; whirlpool. Coffee in rms. Restaurant opp 6 am-9:30 pm. Ck-out 11 am. Coin lndry. Free bus depot transportation. Cr cds: A, C, D, DS, MC, V.

Inn

★★ **WHITMORE MANSION.** *110 S Main St (84648). 435/623-2047.* 9 rms, 5 with shower only, 3 story, 2 suites. No rm phones. S, D $75-$125; each addl $10; suites $100-$110. TV in common rm, VCR avail (movies). Complimentary continental bkfst. Restaurant nearby. Ck-out 11 am, ck-in 4-8 pm. Business servs avail. Street parking. X-country ski 10 mi. Rec rm. Built in 1898; antiques. Totally nonsmoking. Cr cds: A, C, DS, MC, V.

SC

Ogden (C-3)

(See also Brigham City, Salt Lake City)

Settled 1844 **Pop** 63,909 **Elev** 4,300 ft **Area Code** 801
E-mail info@ogdencvb.org **Web** www.ogdencvb.org

Information Convention & Visitors Bureau, 2501 Wall Ave, 84401; 801/627-8288 or 800/255-8824

The streets of Ogden, fourth-largest city in Utah, were laid out by Brigham Young in traditional Mormon geometrical style: broad, straight and bordered by poplar, box elder, elm and cottonwood trees. In the 1820s and 1830s, Ogden was a rendezvous and wintering place for trappers, who wandered as far afield as California and Oregon. In 1846, Miles Goodyear, the first white settler, built a cabin and trading post, Fort Buenaventura, here. The next year he sold out to the Mormons. During the last 30 years of the 19th century, Ogden was an outfitting center for trappers and hunters heading north. Its saloons and gambling halls were typical of a frontier town, and there was considerable friction between the Mormons and the "gentiles." With the coming of the railroad, however, Ogden became one of the few cities in Utah whose inhabitants were not primarily Mormons.

Today, Ogden is a commercial and industrial center. Hill Air Force Base is nearby. Bernard DeVoto—American novelist, journalist, historian and critic, best known for his history of the western frontier—was born in Ogden, as was John M. Browning, inventor of the automatic rifle. Mt Ben Lomond, north of the city in the Wasatch Range, was the inspiration for the logo of Paramount Pictures. A Ranger District office of the Wasatch-Cache National Forest (see SALT LAKE CITY) is located in Ogden.

What to See and Do

Daughters of Utah Pioneers Museum & Relic Hall. Old handicrafts, household items, pioneer clothing and furniture and portraits of those who came to Utah prior to the railroad of 1869. Also Miles Goodyear's cabin, the first permanent house built in Utah. (Mid-May-mid-Sept, daily exc Sun) 2148 Grant Ave, in Tabernacle Square. Phone 801/393-4460 or 801/621-5224. **Free**

Fort Buenaventura State Park. The exciting era of mountain men is brought to life on this 32-acre site, where the actual fort, Ogden's first settlement, was built in 1846 by Miles Goodyear. The fort has been reconstructed according to archaeological and historical research: no nails have been used in building the stockade; wooden pegs and mortise and tenon joints hold the structure together. (Apr-Nov) 2450 A Ave. Phone 801/621-4808. Per vehicle ¢¢

Hill Air Force Base Museum. More than 55 aircraft on display, some indoors and suspended from ceiling. Planes include B-29 Superfortress, SR-71 "Blackbird" reconnaissance plane, B-52 bomber, PT-71 Stearman; helicopters, jet engines, missiles; uniforms and other memorabilia. (Daily exc Mon, limited hrs Tues-Fri; closed Jan 1, Thanksgiving, Dec 25) 7961 Wardleigh Rd. 4 mi S on I-15 exit 341, in Roy. Phone 801/777-6868. **Free**

Lagoon Pioneer Village. Amusement park. Thrill rides, musical entertainment, water park, food; campground. (June-Aug, daily; late Apr-Memorial Day & Labor Day-Oct, wkends) Approx 20 mi S on I-15, in Farmington. Phone 801/451-8000 or 800/748-5246, ext 5035. ¢¢¢¢¢

Pine View Reservoir. Boating, fishing, waterskiing. Camping, picnicking. Fees for activities. 9 mi E on UT 39 in Ogden Canyon in Wasatch-Cache National Forest (see SALT LAKE CITY).

Skiing.

Nordic Valley. Two chairlifts; patrol, school, rentals; snack bar. Longest run 1½ mi, vertical drop 1,000 ft. (Dec-Apr, daily) 7 mi E on UT 39, then N on UT 162. Phone 801/745-3511. ¢¢¢¢¢

Powder Mountain. Three chairlifts, 3 surface tows; patrol, school, rentals; food service, lodging. (Mid-Nov-Apr, daily) Night skiing. 7 mi E on UT 39, then 4½ mi N on UT 158, in Eden. Phone 801/745-3772. ¢¢¢¢¢

Snowbasin. 4 triple, double chairlifts; patrol, school, rentals; food service. Longest run 3 mi, vertical drop 2,400 ft. (Late Nov-mid-Apr, daily) 10 mi E on UT 39, then S on UT 226 in Wasatch-Cache National Forest (see SALT LAKE CITY). Phone 801/399-1135 or 801/399-0198 (snow conditions). ¢¢¢¢¢

Union Station-the Utah State Railroad Museum. Spencer S. Eccles Railroad Center features some of the world's largest locomotives, model railroad, films, gem and mineral displays, guided tours by "conductors." **Browning-Kimball Car Museum** has classic American cars. **Browning Firearms Museum** contains the reconstructed original Browning gun shop and inventor's models. Also here is 500-seat theater for musical and dramatic productions and an art gallery; restaurant. Visitors Bureau for northern Utah located here. (June-Sept, daily; rest of the yr, daily exc Sun; closed Jan 1, Thanksgiving, Dec 25) 2501 Wall Ave, center of Ogden. Phone 801/629-8444. ¢

Weber State University (1889). (15,000 students) On campus are Layton P. Ott Planetarium, with natural science museum and Foucault pendulum, shows (Wed; no shows Aug; fee); and Stewart Bell Tower, with 183-bell electronic carillon, performances (daily; free). Campus tours. Harrison Blvd, off US 89. Phone 801/626-6000.

Willard Bay State Park. This park features a 9,900-acre lake. Swimming; fishing; boating (ramps), sailing. Picnicking. Tent & trailer sites (fee; showers, dump station). (Daily) 15 mi N via I-15, exit 360, near Willard. Phone 801/734-9494. Day-use per vehicle ¢¢

Annual Events

Pioneer Days. Ogden Pioneer Stadium. Rodeo; concerts; vintage car shows; fireworks; chili cookoff. Nightly exc Sun. Mid-late July.

Utah Symphony Pops Concert. Lindquist Fountain/Plaza. Music enhanced by fireworks display. Late July.

Motel

✓★ **MOTEL 6.** *1500 W Riverdale Rd (84405). 801/627-2880; FAX 801/392-1713; res: 800/466-8356.* 109 rms, 2 story. June-Aug: S, D $39.99-$45.99; each addl $6; suites $79.98; under 17 free; lower rates rest of yr. Crib free. Pet accepted, some restrictions. TV; cable (premium). Heated pool. Restaurant 8 am-10 pm. Bar 5:30 pm-1 am Tues-Sat; private club Sun, Mon. Ck-out noon. Coin lndry. Business servs avail. Some in-rm whirlpools. Cr cds: A, C, D, DS, MC, V.

D

Motor Hotel

★★ **DAYS INN.** *3306 Washington Blvd (84401). 801/399-5671; FAX 801/621-0321; res: 800/999-6841.* 109 rms, 2 story. S $65-$70; D $80-$88; each addl $8; under 18 free. Crib free. TV; cable (premium). Indoor pool; whirlpool. Complimentary continental bkfst. Ck-out noon. Coin lndry. Business servs avail. In-rm modem link. Downhill/x-country ski 15 mi. Microwaves avail. Cr cds: A, C, D, DS, MC, V.

D SC

Hotels

★★★ **MARRIOTT.** *247 24th St (84401). 801/627-1190; FAX 801/394-6312; res: 800/421-7599.* 292 rms, 8 story. S $85-$95; D $95-$105; suites $150-$350; wkend rates; ski plans. TV; cable. Indoor pool; whirlpool. Coffee in rms. Restaurant 6 am-10 pm. Private club 2 pm-midnight. Ck-out noon. Coin lndry. Convention facilities. Business servs avail. Gift shop. Free parking. Exercise equipt. Massage. Refrigerator in suites. Cr cds: A, C, D, DS, JCB, MC, V.

D SC

★★★ **RADISSON SUITE HOTEL.** *2510 Washington Blvd (84401). 801/627-1900; FAX 801/394-5342; res: 800/333-3333.* 122 suites, 11 story. S $139-$159; D $149-$169; each addl $12; suites $129-$169; under 12 free; ski packages. Crib free. Pet accepted, some restrictions. TV; cable (premium). Complimentary full bkfst. Complimentary coffee in rms. Restaurant 6 am-9 pm; Sat 6:30 am-10 pm; Sun 7 am-11 pm. Ck-out noon. Coin lndry. Meeting rms. Business center. Free covered parking. Downhill/x-country ski 16 mi. Exercise equipt. Health club privileges. Refrigerator, microwave, wet bar in suites. Cr cds: A, C, D, DS, ER, JCB, MC, V.

D SC

Restaurants

★★ **BAVARIAN CHALET.** *4387 Harrison Blvd (84403). 801/479-7561.* Hrs: 5-10 pm. Closed Sun, Mon; some major hols; also July. Res accepted. German menu. Serv bar. Semi-a la carte: dinner $8.95-$17.95. Child's meals. Specialties: Wienerschnitzel, jagerschnitzel. Outdoor dining. German art, wall hangings and background music create a distinctive German atmosphere. Totally nonsmoking. Cr cds: A, C, D, MC, V.

D

★★ **GRAY CLIFF LODGE.** *508 Ogden Canyon (84401). 801/392-6775.* Hrs: 5-10 pm; Sat to 11 pm; Sun 3-8 pm; Sun brunch 10 am-2 pm. Closed Mon; most major hols. Res accepted; required some hols. Bar. Complete meal: dinner $9.95-$25.95. Sun brunch $8.95. Child's meals. Specialties: prime rib, fresh mountain trout, lamb chops. Own baking. Converted summer home with country atmosphere. Family-owned. Totally nonsmoking. Cr cds: A, C, D, DS, MC, V.

D SC

★★ **YE LION'S DEN.** *3607 Washington Blvd (84403). 801/399-5804.* Hrs: 11:30 am-2 pm, 5-9:30 pm; Fri to 10 pm; Sat 5-10 pm; Sun noon-7 pm. Closed Jan 1, Dec 24, 25. Res accepted. Serv bar. Complete meals: lunch $4.25-$6.95, dinner $9.95-$29.95. Specializes in prime rib, steak, seafood. Open-hearth grill. Cr cds: A, C, DS, MC, V.

D

Panguitch (G-3)

(See also Cedar City)

Settled 1864 **Pop** 1,444 **Elev** 6,624 ft **Area Code** 435 **Zip** 84759
Web www.infowest.com/panguitch

Information City of Panguitch, 25 S 200 E, PO Box 75; 435/676-8585

A livestock, lumbering and farm town, Panguitch is also a center for summer tourists who come to see nearby Bryce Canyon National Park and Cedar Breaks National Monument. The Paiutes named the city, which means "big fish," because of the large fish they caught in nearby Panguitch Lake. A Ranger District office of the Dixie National Forest (see CEDAR CITY) is located here.

What to See and Do

Anasazi Indian Village State Park. Partially excavated village, believed to have been occupied from A.D. 1050-1200, is one of the largest ancient communities west of the Colorado River. Picnicking. Visitor center & museum (daily; closed Jan 1, Thanksgiving, Dec 25). (Daily) 98 mi E on UT 12, near Boulder. Phone 435/335-7308. ¢

Bryce Canyon National Park (see). 7 mi S on US 89, then 19 mi SE on UT 12.

Cedar Breaks National Monument (see). 35 mi SW on UT 143 through Dixie National Forest (see CEDAR CITY).

Panguitch Lake. This 8,000-ft-high lake, which fills a large volcanic basin, has fishing, resorts, public campgrounds (developed sites, fee); ice fishing, snowmobiling, cross-country skiing. 17 mi SW on paved road in Dixie National Forest (see CEDAR CITY). Phone 435/676-2649.

Paunsagaunt Wildlife Museum. More than 300 animals from North America in their natural habitat can be viewed here. Also exotic game animals from Africa, India and Europe. (Apr-Oct, daily) 250 E Center St. Phone 435/676-2500. ¢¢

Motel

✓★ **BEST WESTERN NEW WESTERN MOTEL.** *180 E Center St (84759). 435/676-8876; FAX 435/676-8876; res: 800/528-1234.* 55 rms. Apr-Oct: S $60; D $75; each addl $5; suites $85-$125; lower rates rest of yr. Crib free. TV; cable. Heated pool; whirlpool. Restaurant nearby. Ck-out 11 am. Coin lndry. Business servs avail. Some refrigerators. Some rms across street. Cr cds: A, C, D, DS, MC, V.

D SC

Restaurant

✓★ **FOY'S COUNTRY CORNER.** *80 N Main (84759). 435/676-8851.* Hrs: 6 am-9:30 pm. Closed Dec 25. Semi-a la carte: bkfst $2.25-$5, lunch $4-$7, dinner $6-$13. Specializes in steak, trout, chicken. Cr cds: A, C, DS, MC, V.

D

Park City (C-4)

(See also Alta, Heber City, Salt Lake City)

Founded 1868 **Pop** 4,468 **Elev** 7,080 ft **Area Code** 435 **Zip** 84060
Web www.parkcityinfo.com

Information Park City Chamber/Visitors Bureau, 1910 Prospector Ave, PO Box 1630; or the Visitor Information Center, 750 Kearns Ave; 435/649-6100, 435/649-6104 or 800/453-1360

Soldiers struck silver here in 1868, starting one of the nation's largest silver mining camps, which reached a population of 10,000 before declining to a near ghost town when the silver market collapsed. Since then, however, Park City has been revived as a four-season resort area with skiing, snowboarding, golf, tennis, water sports and mountain biking.

What to See and Do

Egyptian Theatre (1926). Originally built as a silent movie and vaudeville house, now a yr-round performing arts center with a full semi-professional theater season. (Thurs-Sat; some performances other days) 328 Main St. Phone 435/649-9371.

Factory Stores at Park City. More than 45 outlet stores. (Daily) I-80 & UT 224 at Kimball Junction. Phone 435/645-7078.

Kimball Art Center. Exhibits in various media by local and regional artists. (Daily) 638 Park Ave. Phone 435/649-8882. **Free**

Park City Silver Mine Adventure. Mine tour 1,500 ft into the depths of the city's mountains. Also interactive museum. (Daily) Ontario Mine, UT 224. Phone 435/655-7444 or 800/467-3828. ¢¢¢¢

Rockport State Park. Approx 1,000-acre park along east side of Rockport Lake. Opportunity for viewing wildlife, including bald eagles (winter) and golden eagles. Swimming, waterskiing, sailboarding; fishing; boating (rentals, launch). Picnicking; restaurant, concession. Cross-country ski trail (6 mi). Camping, tent & trailer sites. (Daily) Standard fees. N on UT 248 & US 40, then 8 mi NE on I-80, Wanship exit. Phone 435/336-2241.

Skiing.

Brighton Resort. Approx 10 mi SW via UT 190 in Big Cottonwood Canyon (see SALT LAKE CITY).

The Canyons. Three high-speed quad, 3 fixed-grip quad, 2 double chairlifts; gondola; patrol, school, rentals; restaurant, cafeteria, bar. 74 trails. (Dec-Apr, daily) Phone 435/649-5400. ¢¢¢¢¢

Deer Valley Resort. Three high-speed quad, 9 triple, 2 double chairlifts; rental, patrol, school; snowmaking; restaurants, lounge; lodge, nursery. Approx 1,750 skiable acres. (Dec-mid-Apr, daily) Summer activities include mountain biking, hiking, horseback riding and scenic chairlift rides (fee). 1 mi SE on Deer Valley Dr. Phone 435/649-1000. ¢¢¢¢¢

Park City Mountain Resort. Two quad, 4 double, 5 triple, 3 six-passenger chairlifts; patrol, school, rentals; snowmaking; restaurants, cafeteria, bar. Approx 2,200 acres; 93 novice, intermediate, expert slopes and trails; 650 acres of open-bowl skiing. Lighted snowboarding. (Mid-Nov-mid-Apr, daily) Alpine slide, children's park, miniature golf in summer (fees). Phone 435/649-8111 or 435/647-5335 (snow report). Summer ¢¢¢; Winter ¢¢¢¢¢

Solitude Resort. Approx 12 mi SW via UT 190 in Big Cottonwood Canyon (see SALT LAKE CITY).

White Pine Touring Center. Groomed cross-country trails (18 km) school, rentals; guided tours. (Nov-Apr, daily) Summer mountain biking; rentals. Approx 1 mi N via UT 224 to Park City Golf Course. Phone 435/649-8710 or 435/649-8701 (winter). Winter ¢¢¢; Summer ¢¢¢¢¢

Utah Winter Sports Park. Recreational ski jumping in $25-million park built for 2002 Olympic Winter Games. Nordic, competition, freestyle and training jumps. Lessons followed by 2-hr jumping session. Also Olympic bobsled and luge track (high-speed rides avail). Day lodge, snack bar, gift shop. (Dec-late Mar, Wed-Sun) 4 mi N on Bear Hollow Dr. Phone 435/658-4200. Ski jumping ¢¢¢¢¢

Annual Events

Sundance Film Festival. Wk-long festival for independent filmmakers. Workshops, screenings and special events. Mid-Jan.

Snow Sculpture Contest. City Park. Late Feb.

Franklin Quest Championship Senior PGA Tournament. 8 mi N on UT 224, then W on I-80, at Park Meadows. PGA Invitational Golf tournament. Mid-late July.

Art Festival. Main St. Open-air market featuring work of more than 200 visual artists. Also street entertainment. 1st wkend Aug.

Motel

★ **EDELWEISS HAUS HOTEL.** *1482 Empire Ave (84060). 435/649-9342; FAX 435/649-4049; res: 800/245-6417.* Web www.pclodge.com. 45 kit. units, 4 story. Nov-Mar: S, D $100-$118; each addl $10; suites, kit. units $225-$290; higher rates Christmas wk; lower rates rest of yr. Crib $10. TV; cable. Heated pool; whirlpool. Restaurant nearby. Ck-out 10 am. Coin lndry. Underground parking. Downhill/x-country ski opp. Exercise equipt; saunas. Microwaves. Balconies, patios. Cr cds: A, C, DS, MC, V.

Lodge

★★ **THE LODGE AT MOUNTAIN VILLAGE.** *1415 Lowell Ave (84060). 435/649-0800; FAX 435/649-1464; res: 800/754-2002.* E-mail david@davidhollands.com; web www.davidhollands.com. 123 rms, 3 story, 98 suites. Some A/C. Mid-Jan-Mar: S, D $160-$455; suites $225-$1,500; higher rates: Christmas, Presidents' Week; lower rates rest of yr. Crib free. TV; cable (premium), VCR avail (movies). Indoor/outdoor pool; whirlpool. Sauna. Bar. Ck-out 10 am. Meeting rms. Business servs avail. Downhill ski on site; x-country ski 1 mi. Refrigerators, some microwaves. Balconies. Cr cds: A, C, D, DS, MC, V.

Motor Hotels

★★★ **OLYMPIA PARK HOTEL.** *1895 Sidewinder Dr (84060). 435/649-2900; FAX 435/649-4852; res: 800/234-9003.* E-mail olysales @pc; web www.olympiahotel.com. 200 rms, 1-4 story. S, D $155-$209; each addl $10; suites $239-$359; under 18 free; ski, golf packages. Crib free. Pet accepted; fee. TV; cable (premium). Indoor pool; whirlpool. Restaurant 7 am-9:30 pm; off season hrs vary. Rm serv 11 am-10 pm. Bar. Ck-out 11 am. Meeting rms. Business center. In-rm modem link. Bellhops. Concierge. Gift shop. Garage parking. Downhill/x-country ski ½ mi. Exercise equipt; sauna. Game rm. Balconies. Cr cds: A, C, D, DS, MC, V.

★★★ **SHADOW RIDGE.** *50 Shadow Ridge St (84060). 435/649-4300; FAX 435/649-5951; res: 800/754-2002.* E-mail david@ holland.com. 150 rms, 4 story, 50 suites. Mid-Jan-late-Mar: S $150-$190; D $185-$215; condos $300-$630; family rates; ski, golf plans; higher rates mid-Dec-early Jan; lower rates rest of yr. Crib free. TV; cable, VCR avail (movies). Heated pool; whirlpool. Restaurant (seasonal). Ck-out 10 am. Lndry facilities. Meeting rms. Business servs avail. Bellhops in season. Valet serv. Downhill ski opp; x-country ski ½ mi. Exercise equipt; sauna. Some refrigerators, fireplaces; microwaves avail. Balconies. Golf course adj. Cr cds: A, C, D, DS, JCB, MC, V.

★★★ **YARROW HOTEL.** *1800 Park Ave (84060). 435/649-7000; FAX 435/645-7007; res: 800/927-7694.* Web www.yarrowresort.com. 181 rms, 2 story. S, D $129-$249; each addl $30; suites $189-$309; under 13 free; package plan; higher rates mid-Dec-Mar. Crib free. TV; cable (premium). Heated pool; whirlpools. Coffee in rms. Restaurant 6:30 am-10 pm. Rm serv. Bar. Ck-out 11 am. Coin lndry. Meeting rms. Business center. Bellhops. Concierge. Downhill ski ¼ mi; x-country ski ½ mi. Exercise equipt. Refrigerators; microwaves avail. Balconies. Golf course opp. Cr cds: A, C, D, DS, JCB, MC, V.

Hotels

★★★ **GOLDENER HIRSCH INN.** *7570 Royal St E (84060). 435/649-7770; FAX 435/649-7901; res: 800/252-3373.* 20 rooms, 4 fl; $100-$340; $1,080 PH suite. $25 addl person. Crib free. The Golderner Hirsch Restaurant. Bar. Lounge. Entertainment winter 5 nights & Summer weekend evenings. Room service limited. Exercise equipment. Business center/facility. TV, VCR, fireplaces, bathroom phones. Valet. Conceirge. Gift shop. Cr cds: C.

★★★ **SILVER KING HOTEL.** *1485 Empire Ave (84060). 435/649-5500; FAX 435/649-6647; res: 800/331-8652.* 64 kit. suites, 5 story. Nov-Apr: S, D $155-$660; higher rates Sundance film festival; lower rates rest of yr. Crib free. Garage parking free. TV; cable (premium), VCR (movies). Complimentary coffee in rms. Restaurant nearby. Ck-out 11 am. Meeting rms. Business servs avail. Downhill/x-country ski 1 mi. Sauna. Health club privileges. Indoor/outdoor pool; whirlpool. Refrigerators, microwaves, fireplaces. Some in-rm whirlpools. Picnic tables, grills. Cr cds: A, C, DS, MC, V.

Resorts

★★ **INN AT PROSPECTOR SQUARE.** *2200 Sidewinder Dr (84060). 435/649-7100; FAX 435/649-8377; res: 800/453-3812.* Web www.thelodgingcompany.com. 230 units, 2-3 story, 125 kits. Late Nov-mid-Apr: S, D $127-$207; kit. studio rms $167-$187; 1-2-3-bedrm condos $175-$400; under 12 free; ski plan; lower rates rest of yr. TV; VCR avail. Pool. Coffee in rms. Ck-out 11 am, ck-in 4 pm. Convention facilities. Business servs avail. In-rm modem link. Valet serv. Downhill ski ½ mi; x-country ski ¼ mi. Health club privileges. 2 whirlpools. Bicycle rentals. Refrigerators, microwaves. Some balconies. Picnic tables, grills. Cr cds: A, C, D, DS, MC, V.

★★★★ **STEIN ERIKSEN LODGE.** *7700 Stein Way (84060), 4 mi SW on UT 224 to Park Ave, then Deer Valley Dr to Royal St. 435/649-3700; FAX 435/649-5825; res: 800/453-1302.* Web www.steinlodge.com. You can ski in or ski out of this luxurious Norwegian-style mountain lodge. The dramatic two-story stone lobby fireplace will take the chill off before you retire to your spacious room. 129 rms, 13 rms in main lodge, 2 story, 40 kit. suites. Early Dec-early Apr: S, D from $450; each addl $25; kit. suites from $925; under 12 free; summer rates; ski plans; higher rates hol seasons; lower rates rest of yr. Crib free. TV; cable (premium), VCR. Heated pool; whirlpool, poolside serv. Complimentary full bkfst (winter only). Dining rms (see GLITRETIND); 2nd dining rm open winter only. Rm serv 6:30 am-11 pm. Box lunches. Bar; pianist in winter. Ck-out 11 am, ck-in 4 pm. Grocery 4 mi. Meeting rms. Business center. In-rm modem link. Concierge. Boutique. Underground parking. Golf privileges. Downhill ski on site; x-country ski 3 mi. Sleighing. Snowmobiles. Hot air balloons; mountain bikes avail. Lawn games. Exercise equipt; sauna. Massage. Health club privileges. Refrigerators. Bathrm phone, whirlpool, washer, dryer in most rms. Some fireplaces; microwaves avail. Many balconies. Cr cds: A, C, D, DS, MC, V.

Inns

★★ **1904 IMPERIAL HOTEL BED & BREAKFAST.** *221 Historic Main Street (84060). 435/649-1904; FAX 435/645-7421; res: 800/669-8824.* E-mail stay@1904imperial; web www.1904imperial.com. 10 rms, 3 story, 2 suites. No A/C. Mid-Nov-mid-Apr: S, D $140-$175; suite $190-$195; higher rates: hols, film festival; lower rates rest of yr. TV; cable. Complimentary full bkfst. Ck-out 11 am, ck-in 4 pm. Downhill ski ½ mi; x-country ski 2 mi. Whirlpool. Restored boarding house (1904) in historic area. Cr cds: A, C, DS, MC, V.

★★★ **OLD MINERS LODGE.** *615 Woodside Ave (84060). 435/645-8068; FAX 435/645-7420; res: 800/648-8068.* 12 rms, 2 story, 3 suites. No A/C. Mid-Nov-mid-Apr: S, D $100-$225; each addl $15; suites $185-$225; higher rates mid-Dec-early Jan; lower rates rest of yr. Crib $5. Complimentary full bkfst. Restaurant nearby. Ck-out noon, ck-in 2 pm. Business servs avail. Street parking. Downhill ski 1½ blks; x-country ski 1½ mi. Whirlpool. Picnic tables. Renovated lodging house used by miners

(1889); early Western decor, fireplace, antiques. Totally nonsmoking. Cr cds: A, C, D, DS, MC, V.

★★★ **WASHINGTON SCHOOL INN.** *543 Park Ave (84060). 435/649-3800; FAX 435/649-3802; res: 800/824-1672.* Web www.bbiu.org. 12 rms, 3 story, 3 suites. No A/C. Mid-Dec-Mar: S, D $129-$235; suites $195-$365; lower rates rest of yr. TV in some rms; cable. Complimentary full bkfst; afternoon refreshments. Restaurant nearby. Ck-out 11 am, ck-in 4 pm. Meeting rms. Business servs avail. Street parking. Downhill ski 1½ blks; x-country ski 1½ mi. Exercise equipt; sauna. Whirlpool. Historic, stone schoolhouse (1889); antiques, sitting rm with stone and carved wood fireplace, library, bell tower, turn-of-the-century country decor. Cr cds: A, C, D, DS, ER, MC, V.

SC

Restaurants

★★★★ **GLITRETIND RESTAURANT.** *(See Stein Eriksen Lodge Resort) 435/649-3700.* Web www.steinlodge.com. New American cuisine served by an accommodating well-informed staff in a delightful alpine setting. The understated elegance of the restaurant and spectacular views of the surrounding mountains are a fitting setting for the well executed dishes. Alfresco dining is an option during the summer. Hrs: 7 am-10 pm; Sun brunch 10:30 am-2:30 pm. Res accepted. Bar from 11 am. Wine cellar. Semi-a la carte: bkfst $5-$15, lunch $6-$15, dinner $18-$34. Sun brunch $29. Child's meals. Specializes in fresh seafood. Own baking. Valet parking. Outdoor dining. Cr cds: A, C, D, DS, MC, V.

D

★★★ **GRAPPA.** *151 Main St (84060). 435/645-0636.* Hrs: 5-10 pm. Closed Dec 24; also mid-Apr-mid-May. Res accepted. Italian menu. Serv bar. A la carte entrees: dinner $17-$29. Child's meals. Seasonal menu. Specializes in pasta. Outdoor dining. Rustic decor, stained glass windows. Totally nonsmoking. Cr cds: A, C, DS, MC, V.

★★ **KAMPAI.** *586 Main St (84060). 435/649-0655.* Hrs: 6-10 pm. Closed Thanksgiving, Dec 25; also 10 days in spring. Japanese menu. Serv bar. Semi-a la carte: dinner $12.95-$24. Specializes in sushi, sashimi, tempura. Outdoor dining. Casual Japanese decor; extensive sushi bar. Totally nonsmoking. Cr cds: A, C, MC, V.

D

✓★ **MAINSTREET PIZZA & NOODLE.** *530 Main St (84060). 435/645-8878.* Hrs: 11:30 am-10 pm; Fri, Sat to 11 pm. Closed Thanksgiving. Italian, Amer menu. Bar. Semi-a la carte: lunch $5-$8, dinner $8-$12. Specializes in pizza, pasta. Casual decor. Totally nonsmoking. Cr cds: A, C, D, DS, MC, V.

★★★★ **RIVERHORSE CAFE.** *540 Main St (84060). 435/649-3536.* This second-story restaurant features a variety of dining rooms with eclectic decor. Al fresco dining in the summer and jazz on the weekends are only a prelude to the well-executed contemporary American menu and pampering service in the heart of Park City's tourist and shopping district. Hrs: 5:30-10 pm; summer hrs vary. Closed Thanksgiving. Res accepted. Bar. Wine list. Semi-a la carte: dinner $18.50-$29.50. Child's meals. Specialties: Macadamia-crusted halibut, seared ahi tuna, Utah rack of lamb. Own baking, pasta. Entertainment Fri, Sat. Outdoor dining. Cr cds: A, C, DS, MC, V.

✓★ **TEXAS RED'S PIT BARBECUE AND C.** *440 Main St (84060). 435/649-7337.* Hrs: 11:30 am-10 pm. Bar. Semi-a la carte: lunch $3.95-$5.95, dinner $5.95-$16.95. Child's meals. Specializes in pit-barbecued ribs. Restored storefront (1910); Rustic western decor. Cr cds: A, C, DS, MC, V.

★★ **ZOOM ROADHOUSE GRILL.** *660 Main St (84060). 435/649-9108.* Hrs: 11:30 am-2:30 pm, 5:30-10 pm. Res accepted (dinner). Bar. Semi-a la carte: lunch $6-$11, dinner $9-$23. Child's meals. Specialties: Belle Isle ribs, roasted corn risotto with grilled shrimp. Own baking. Outdoor dining. Former train depot with original wood floor, high ceiling, fireplace. Cr cds: A, C, D, DS, MC, V.

D

Payson (D-3)

(See also Nephi, Provo)

Settled 1850 **Pop** 9,510 **Elev** 4,648 ft **Area Code** 801 **Zip** 84651

Information Chamber of Commerce, 439 West Utah Ave; 801/465-5200 or 801/465-2634

Payson sits at the foot of the Wasatch Mountains, near Utah Lake. Mormons first settled the area after spending a night on the banks of Peteneet Creek. The surrounding farmlands produce fruit, milk, grain and row crops; livestock is raised. Limestone and dolomite are dug in the vicinity for use in smelting iron.

What to See and Do

Mt Nebo Scenic Loop Drive. This 45-mi drive around the eastern shoulder of towering Mt Nebo (elevation 11,877 ft) is one of the most thrilling in Utah; Mt Nebo's three peaks are the highest in the Wasatch range. The road travels south through Payson and Santaquin canyons and then climbs 9,000 ft up Mt Nebo, offering a view of Devil's Kitchen, a brilliantly colored canyon. (This section of the drive not recommended for those who dislike heights.) The forest road continues S to UT 132; take UT 132 E to Nephi and then drive N on I-15 back to Payson.

Payson Lake Recreation Area. Fishing, camping, swimming, hiking, backpacking. 12 mi SE on unnumbered road in Uinta National Forest (see PROVO).

Annual Event

Golden Onion Days. Includes community theater presentations, marathon, horse races, parade, fireworks and picnic. Labor Day wkend.

Motel

★★ **COMFORT INN.** *830 N Main St (84651). 801/465-4861; FAX 801/465-4861; res: 800/228-5150.* 62 rms, 2 story, 6 kits. (no equipt). S $66-$76; D $75-$85; each addl $6; suites $120; under 18 free. Crib free. Pet accepted; $10 deposit. TV; cable (premium), VCR avail (movies). Indoor pool; whirlpool. Complimentary continental bkfst. Restaurant adj open 24 hrs. Ck-out 11 am. Coin Indry. Meeting rms. Business servs avail. Exercise equipt; sauna. Cr cds: A, C, D, DS, ER, JCB, MC, V.

D SC

Price (E-4)

Settled 1879 **Pop** 8,712 **Elev** 5,567 ft **Area Code** 435 **Zip** 84501

Information Carbon County Chamber of Commerce, 31 N 200 East, PO Box 764; 435/637-2788 or 435/637-8182

Price, the seat of Carbon County, bases its prosperity on coal; more than 30 mine properties, as well as oil and natural gas fields, are within 30 miles. Farming and livestock are also important. Price was one of the stopping places for the Robbers Roost gang in the 1930s. Headquarters and a Ranger District office of the Manti-LaSal National Forest are located here.

What to See and Do

Cleveland-Lloyd Dinosaur Quarry. Since 1928, more than 12,000 dinosaur bones, representing at least 70 different animals, have been excavated on this site. Visitor center, nature trail, picnic area. (Memorial Day-Labor Day, daily; Easter-Memorial Day, wkends only) 22 mi S on UT 10, then approx 15 mi E on unnumbered road. Phone 435/637-5060. **Free**

College of Eastern Utah Prehistoric Museum. Dinosaur displays, archaeology exhibits; geological specimens. (Memorial Day-Labor Day, daily; rest of yr, daily exc Sun; closed major hols) 155 E Main St. Phone 435/637-5060. **Donation**

Geology tours. Self-guided tours of wilderness area, Nine Mile Canyon, Native American dwellings, paintings, San Rafael Desert, Dinosaur Pit, Little Grand Canyon. Maps avail at Chamber of Commerce office or the Carbon County Travel Bureau, 625 E 100 North; phone 435/637-3009. **Free**

Manti-LaSal National Forest, Manti Division. (See MOAB, MONTICELLO) Originally two forests—the Manti in central Utah and the LaSal section in southeastern Utah—now under single supervision. A 1,327,631-acre area partially in Colorado, this forest has among its attractions high mountain scenic drives, deep canyons, riding trails, campsites, winter sports, fishing, and deer and elk hunting. Joe's Valley Reservoir on UT 29 and Electric Lake on UT 31 have fishing and boating. Areas of geologic interest, developed as a result of massive landslides, are near Ephraim. Some fees in developed areas. 21 mi SW on UT 10, then NW on UT 31. For further information contact the Ranger District office or the Forest Supervisor at 599 W Price River Dr; phone 435/637-2817. **Free**

Price Canyon Recreation Area. Scenic overlooks; hiking; picnicking; camping (fee). Roads have steep grades. (May-mid-Oct, daily) 15 mi N on US 6, then 3 mi W on unnumbered road. Phone 435/637-4584. **Free**

Scofield State Park. Utah's highest state park has a 2,800-acre lake that lies at an altitude of 7,616 ft. Fishing; boating (docks, ramps); camping (rest rms, showers). Snowmobiling, ice fishing, cross-country skiing in winter. (May-Oct) Standard fees. 24 mi N on US 6, then 10 mi W & S on UT 96. Phone 435/448-9449. Camping **¢¢¢**

Motels

✓★ **BEST WESTERN CARRIAGE HOUSE INN.** *590 E Main St. (84501). 435/637-5660; FAX 435/637-5660; res: 800/528-1234.* 41 rms, 2 story. S $46-$70; D $50-$76; each addl $6; suites $59-$89. Crib free. TV; cable. Indoor pool; whirlpool. Complimentary continental bkfst. Restaurant nearby. Ck-out noon. Airport transportation. Cr cds: A, C, D, DS, MC, V.

D SC

✓★ **GREENWELL INN.** *655 E Main St (84501). 435/637-3520; FAX 435/637-4858; res: 800/666-3520.* E-mail greenwel@castlenet.com; web castlenet.com/greenwell. 125 rms, 1-2 story. May-Sept: S $32-$42; D $43-$58; each addl $5; suites $46.50-$51.50; under 18 free; lower rates rest of yr. Crib $6. Pet accepted. TV; cable. Indoor pool. Complimentary continental bkfst. Restaurant adj 6 am-9 pm. Ck-out 11 am. Meeting rm. Lndry facilities. Gift shop. Exercise equipt. Health club privileges. Refrigerators avail. Cr cds: A, C, D, DS, ER, MC, V.

SC

★★ **HOLIDAY INN.** *838 Westwood Blvd (84501). 435/637-8880; FAX 435/637-7707; res: 800/465-4329.* E-mail hiprice@castlenet.com. 151 rms, 2 story. S $65-$75; D $71-$81; each addl $6; suites $75-$125; under 17 free. Crib free. TV. Indoor pool. Restaurant 6 am-10 pm. Rm serv. Bar. Ck-out noon. Meeting rms. Exercise equipt. Health club privileges. Refrigerators avail. Cr cds: A, C, D, DS, MC, V.

D SC

Restaurant

✓★ **CHINA CITY CAFE.** *350 E Main St (84501). 435/637-8211.* Hrs: 11 am-10 pm. Closed Thanksgiving, Dec 25; also July. Res accepted. Chinese, Amer menu. Complete meals: lunch $4.25-$4.95, dinner $5.45-$6.45. Child's meals. Specialty: cashew chicken. Cafe atmosphere with Chinese decor. Cr cds: A, C, D, DS, MC, V.

Unrated Dining Spot

CASTLE ROCK CAFE. *700 W Price River Dr (84501), in Creekview Shopping Center. 435/637-6907.* Hrs: 9:30 am-10 pm. Closed Thanksgiving, Dec 25. Res accepted. Italian, Amer menu. Semi-a la carte: bkfst $2.50-$4.89, lunch $2-$10, dinner $4-$10. Specializes in pizza, sandwiches. Salad bar. Cr cds: A, C, D, DS, MC, V.

Provo (D-3)

(See also Heber City, Payson, Salt Lake City)

Settled 1849 **Pop** 86,835 **Elev** 4,549 ft **Area Code** 801

Information Utah Valley Convention & Visitors Bureau, 51 S University Ave, PO Box 912, 84601; 801/370-8393 or 800/222-8824

Provo received its name from French-Canadian trapper Etienne Provost, who arrived in the area in 1825. Provost and his party of mountain men set up camp near the mouth of the Provo River, but skirmishes with Native Americans forced them to escape to the mountains. It wasn't until 1849 that the first permanent settlement, begun by a party of Mormons, was established. The Mormon settlers erected Fort Utah as their first building, and despite famine, drought, hard winters and the constant danger of attack, they persisted and the settlement grew. Today, Provo is the seat of Utah County and the state's third-largest city.

An important educational and commercial center, Provo's largest employer is Brigham Young University. Beyond that, the city boasts major steel and electronic component manufacturers, health care and municipal employers and other educational facilities. Provo lies in the middle of a lush, green valley: to the north stands 12,008-foot Mount Timpanogos; to the south is the perpendicular face of the Wasatch Range; to the east Provo Peak rises 11,054 feet; and to the west lies Utah Lake, backed by more mountains. Provo is the headquarters of the Uinta National Forest, and many good fishing, boating, camping and hiking spots are nearby.

What to See and Do

Brigham Young University (1875). (27,000 students) Founded by Brigham Young and operated by the Church of Jesus Christ of Latter-day Saints. This is one of the world's largest church-related institutions of higher learning, with students from every state and more than 90 foreign countries. One-hr, free guided tours arranged at Hosting Center (Mon-Fri; also by appt, phone 801/378-4678). Phone 801/378-1211. Buildings on campus (Mon-Fri; closed hols) include

Eyring Science Center. Geological collection, extensive series of minerals and fossils. **Free**

Harris Fine Arts Center. Houses B.F. Larsen Gallery and Gallery 303; periodic displays of rare instruments and music collection. Concert, theater performances. Phone 801/378-HFAC. **Free** Adj is

Monte L. Bean Life Science Museum. Exhibits and collections of insects, fish, amphibians, reptiles, birds, animals and plants. Phone 801/378-5051. **Free**

Museum of Art. Exhibits from the BYU Permanent Collection; traveling exhibits (some fees). Phone 801/378-2787. **¢¢¢**

Museum of Peoples and Cultures. Material from South America, the Near East and the southwestern US. Allen Hall, 710 N 100 East. Phone 801/378-6112. **Free**

Camp Floyd and Stagecoach Inn state parks. Only the cemetery remains as evidence of the pre-Civil War post that quartered the largest troop concentration in the US here between 1858-1861. Approx 400 buildings were constructed for troops deployed to the west in expectation of a Mormon rebellion. The nearby Stagecoach Inn has been restored with original period furnishings. Visitor center. Museum. (Easter wkend-mid-Oct; daily) Standard fees. 13 mi N on I-15 to Lehi, then 21 mi W on UT 73, in Cedar Valley. Phone 801/768-8932. Museum **¢**

John Hutchings Museum. Six main collections include archaeology, ornithology and oology, paleontology, mineralogy and pioneer artifacts. Most of the items are from the Great Basin area. Rare sea shells, fossils, Native American artifacts. (Daily exc Sun; closed most hols) 17 mi NW via I-15 or UT 89/91, at 55 N Center St, in Lehi. Phone 801/768-7180. **¢¢**

McCurdy Historical Doll Museum. More than 3,000 dolls of many varieties on exhibit; antique toys, miniatures and doll shop. Documentary film.

Doll hospital. (Tues-Sat afternoons) 246 N 100 East. Phone 801/377-9935. ¢

Pioneer Museum. Outstanding collection of Utah pioneer relics and Western art. Pioneer Village. (June-early Sept, Wed, Fri, Sat afternoons; rest of yr, by appt) 500 W 500 North, on US 89. Phone 801/852-6609. **Free**

Springville Museum of Art. Utah art history from 1852 to present, including paintings, drawings, sculpture. State competition in Apr, quilt show in June. Guided tours. (Hrs vary with exhibit; closed Jan 1, Easter, Dec 25) 7 mi SE via I-15 exit 263, at 126 E 400 South, in Springville. Phone 801/489-2727. **Free**

Sundance Ski Area. Four chairlifts; patrol, school, rentals; warming hut, 4 restaurants. Longest run 2 mi, vertical drop 2,150 ft. (Dec-Apr, daily) Cross-country trails. 15 mi NE on US 189, North Fork Provo Canyon. Phone 801/225-4107 or 800/892-1600 (exc UT). ¢¢¢¢¢

Timpanogos Cave National Monument (see). 15 mi NE on UT 146 (State St), then 2 mi E on UT 29.

Uinta National Forest. Scenic drives through the 950,000-acre forest; areas include Provo Canyon, Bridal Veil Falls, Deer Creek Dam and Reservoir, Diamond Fork Canyon, Hobble Creek Canyon, Strawberry Reservoir and the Alpine and Mt Nebo Scenic Loop (see PAYSON); roads give an unsurpassed view of colorful landscapes, canyons, waterfalls. Stream and lake fishing, hunting for deer and elk, camping and picnicking. Camping fee. Res accepted. S & E of town. For further information contact the Supervisor, 88 W 100 North, PO Box 1428, 84601; phone 801/377-5780.

Utah Lake State Park. Park situated on the eastern shore of Utah Lake, a 150-sq-mi, freshwater remnant of ancient Lake Bonneville, which created the Great Salt Lake. Fishing (cleaning station); boating (ramp, dock). Ice-skating (winter), roller skating (summer). Picnicking, play area. Camping (dump station). Visitor center. (Daily) Standard fees. 2 mi W on Center St, off I-15. Phone 801/375-0733 or -0731.

Annual Event

Freedom Festival. Bazaar, carnival, parades. Early July.

Motels

★★ **BEST WESTERN COTTONTREE INN.** *2230 N University Pkwy (84604). 801/373-7044; FAX 801/375-5240; res: 800/662-6886.* 80 rms, 2 story. S $66-$76; D $70-$80; each addl $5; suites $150; under 18 free. Crib free. TV; cable. 2 heated pools, 1 indoor; whirlpool. Complimentary continental bkfst. Restaurant nearby. Ck-out noon. Meeting rms. Business servs avail. Valet serv. Beauty shop. Downhill ski 15 mi. Health club privileges. Microwaves avail. Balconies. View of river. Cr cds: A, C, D, DS, ER, MC, V.

SC

✓★ **COLONY INN NATIONAL 9.** *1380 S University Ave (84601). 801/374-6800; FAX 801/374-6803; res: 800/524-9999.* 80 kit. suites, 2 story. May-Oct: S $42-$52; D $58-$72; each addl $5; wkly, monthly rates; lower rates rest of yr. Crib $5. Pet accepted, some restrictions; $15 refundable & $5/day. TV; cable (premium). Heated pool. Complimentary continental bkfst. Restaurant adj. Ck-out noon. Coin Indry. Business servs avail. In-rm modem link. Downhill ski 20 mi. Cr cds: A, C, DS, MC, V.

SC

★★ **COMFORT INN.** *1555 N Canyon Rd (84604). 801/374-6020; FAX 801/374-0015; res: 800/228-5150.* E-mail comfortu@enol.com; web www.nwhotels.com. 100 rms, 2 story, 6 suites. S, D $79; suites $99-$149; kit. unit $139; under 18 free. Crib free. Pet accepted, some restrictions. TV; cable (premium), VCR avail (movies $7). Indoor pool; whirlpool. Complimentary continental bkfst. Restaurant nearby. Ck-out 1 pm. Coin Indry. Meeting rms. Business servs. In-rm modem link. Sundries. Downhill/x-country ski 15 mi. Exercise equipt. Some refrigerators, microwaves. Cr cds: A, C, D, DS, ER, JCB, MC, V.

D SC

★ **DAYS INN.** *1675 N 200 W (84604). 801/375-8600; FAX 801/374-6654; res: 800/329-7466.* 49 rms, 2 story. S $54; D $59; each addl $5; kit. unit $65-$70; under 18 free. Crib free. Pet accepted, some restrictions. TV; cable. Heated pool. Complimentary continental bkfst. Coffee in rms. Restaurant 11 am-11 pm. Ck-out noon. Business servs avail. In-rm modem link. Downhill/x-country ski 15 mi. Some refrigerators, microwaves. Cr cds: A, C, D, DS, MC, V.

D SC

★★★ **HOLIDAY INN.** *1460 S University Ave (84601). 801/374-9750; FAX 801/377-1615; res: 800/465-4329.* 78 rms, 2 story. S, D $65-$90; under 18 free. Crib free. TV; cable (premium). Pool. Complimentary continental bkfst. Restaurant 11 am-10 pm. Rm serv. Ck-out noon. Meeting rms. Business center. Downhill ski 20 mi. Exercise equipt. Cr cds: A, C, D, DS, JCB, MC, V.

D SC

✓★★ **HOWARD JOHNSON HOTEL.** *1292 S University Ave (84601). 801/374-2500; FAX 801/373-1146; res: 800/326-0025.* 116 rms, 2 story. Apr-mid-Sept: S $49-$79; D $54-$85; each addl $6; suites $70-$75; cabin suite $195; family rates; lower rates rest of yr. Crib free. TV; cable (premium). Heated pool; whirlpool. Restaurant. Ck-out noon. Coin Indry. Meeting rms. Business servs avail. Downhill ski 20 mi. Exercise equipt. Game rm. Microwaves avail. Cr cds: A, C, D, DS, MC, V.

SC

Hotel

★★★ **MARRIOTT.** *101 W 100 N (84601). 801/377-4700; FAX 801/377-4708; res: 800/777-7144.* E-mail marriott@itsnet.com; web www.marriott.com. 331 rms, 9 story. S $89-$125; D $89-$130; each addl $8; suites $99-$275; under 18 free; ski, honeymoon packages. Crib free. TV; cable (premium). Heated pool; whirlpool. Complimentary coffee in rms. Restaurant 6:30 am-10 pm. Private club 4 pm-midnight. Ck-out noon. Meeting rms. Business center. In-rm modem link. Gift shop. Free covered parking. Airport transportation; free RR station, bus depot transportation. Downhill ski 14 mi. Exercise equipt; sauna. Some refrigerators, microwaves, wet bars. Cr cds: A, C, D, DS, JCB, MC, V.

D SC

Resort

★★★ **SUNDANCE RESORT.** *N Fork Provo Canyon (84604), 14 mi NE on US 189, NW on UT 92, in North Fork Provo Canyon. 801/225-4107; FAX 801/226-1937; res: 800/892-1600.* Web www.sundance-utah.com. 93 kit. units. Mid-Dec-Mar: S, D $195-$425; suites $425; 2-3-bedrm cottages $750-$950; ski plans; lower rates rest of yr. TV; cable (premium), VCR avail (free movies). Supervised child's activities (June-Sept); ages 6-12. Dining rms (see FOUNDRY GRILL). Ck-out 11 am, ck-in 3 pm. Meeting rms. Business servs avail. Concierge. Downhill/x-country ski on site. Exercise equipt. Some fireplaces; microwaves avail. Private patios. Handmade wooden furniture; Native American art. Rustic retreat surrounded by pristine wilderness. Cr cds: A, C, D, DS, MC, V.

Restaurants

★ **BOMBAY HOUSE.** *463 N University Ave (84601). 801/373-6677.* Hrs: 4-10:30 pm. Closed Sun; Dec 25. Res accepted. Indian menu. A la carte entrees: dinner $6.95-$16. Specializes in tandoori, lamb, seafood. Indian atmosphere. Cr cds: A, C, D, DS, MC, V.

★★ **FOUNDRY GRILL.** *(See Sundance) 801/225-4107.* Web www.sundance-utah.com. Hrs: 7 am-10 pm; Sun 9 am-10:30 pm; Sun brunch to 3 pm. Res accepted; required Thurs-Sun dinner. Southwestern, Amer menu. Serv bar. Semi-a la carte: bkfst $1.75-$12.95, lunch, dinner $6.95-$18.95. Sun brunch $22.95. Child's meals. Specialties: chicken pizza, Sundance sandwich, rotisserie. Outdoor dining. Rustic, western decor; fireplace, bare wood floors. Totally nonsmoking. Cr cds: A, C, D, DS, MC, V.

D

★ **MAGLEBY'S.** *1675 N 200 West (84604), on Freedom Blvd. 801/374-6249.* Hrs: 11 am-10 pm; Fri, Sat 4-11 pm. Closed Sun; Thanksgiving, Dec 24 & 25. Res accepted. Semi-a la carte: lunch $5.95-$10.95, dinner $11.95-$21.95. Specializes in steak, seafood, deep-dish apple pie. Salad bar. Street lamps and high windows with flower boxes; artwork for sale. Totally nonsmoking. Cr cds: A, C, DS, MC, V.

D

Rainbow Bridge National Monument (J-4)

(NW of Navajo Mountain, approachable from Arizona)

Rising from the eastern shore of Lake Powell, Rainbow Bridge, the largest natural rock bridge in the world, was named a national monument in 1910, one year after its sighting was documented. Carved by a meander of Bridge Creek, this natural bridge stands 290 feet tall, spans 275 feet and stretches 33 feet at the top. One of the seven natural wonders of the world, Rainbow Bridge is higher than the nation's capitol dome and nearly as long as a football field. The monument is predominantly salmon pink in color, modified by streaks of iron oxide and manganese. In the light of the late afternoon sun, the bridge becomes brilliant to see. Native Americans consider the area a sacred place; legend holds that the bridge is a rainbow turned to stone.

The easiest way to reach Rainbow Bridge is a half-day round-trip boat ride across Lake Powell from Page, AZ (see) or a full-day round-trip boat ride from Bullfrog and Halls Crossing marinas (see LAKE POWELL). The bridge also can be reached on foot or horseback via the Rainbow Trail through the Navajo Indian Reservation (see ARIZONA; permit required). Fuel and camp supplies are available at Dangling Rope Marina, accessible by boat only, 10 miles downlake (south). For further information contact the Superintendent, Glen Canyon National Recreation Area, PO Box 1507, Page, AZ 86040; 520/608-6404.

Richfield (F-3)

(See also Beaver, Fillmore, Salina)

Settled 1863 **Pop** 5,593 **Elev** 5,330 ft **Area Code** 435 **Zip** 84701
Web www.racoc@inquo.net
Information Chamber of Commerce, PO Box 327; 435/896-4241

Brigham Young sent members of his church here to settle the area, but problems with Native Americans forced abandonment of the fledgling town for almost a year before the pioneers were able to regain their settlement. Located in the center of Sevier Valley, Richfield has become the commercial hub of the region. Today, some of the world's best beef is raised in and shipped from this area. Headquarters and a Ranger District Office of the Fishlake National Forest is located here.

What to See and Do

Big Rock Candy Mountain. Multicolored mountain that Burl Ives popularized in song. 25 mi S on US 89, in Marysvale Canyon.

Capitol Reef National Park (see). 10 mi E on UT 119, then 76 mi SE on UT 24.

Fishlake National Forest. This 1,424,000-acre forest offers fishing, hunting, hiking, picnicking and camping (fee). Fish Lake, 33 mi SE via UT 119 & UT 24, then 7 mi NE on UT 25, offers high-altitude angling on 6-mi-long lake covering 2,600 acres. Also campgrounds (mid-May-late Oct) and resorts (yr-round). Contact the Supervisor's Office, 115 East 900 North; phone 435/896-9233.

Fremont Indian State Park. Museum and trails feature the Fremont people, who lived in the area from A.D. 300-1300 and then vanished. There is no explanation, only speculation, for their disappearance. Interpretive center highlights evolution of their culture; artifacts from nearby Five Fingers Hill; nature trails lead to panels of rock art and a reconstructed pit house dwelling and granary. Fishing. Camping (fee). Picnicking. (Daily; closed Jan 1, Thanksgiving, Dec 25) Standard fees. 20 mi SW via I-70, at 11550 W Clear Creek Canyon Rd, in Sevier. Phone 435/527-4631.

Motels

★ **BEST WESTERN APPLE TREE INN.** *145 S Main St (84701). 435/896-5481; FAX 435/896-9465; res: 800/528-1234.* 62 rms, 1-2 story. May-Oct: S, D $49-$65; each addl $5; suites $58-$102; lower rates rest of yr. Crib $4. TV; cable. Heated pool; whirlpool. Complimentary continental bkfst. Restaurant nearby. Ck-out noon. Business servs avail. Cr cds: C.

★★ **DAYS INN.** *333 N Main St (84701). 435/896-6476; FAX 435/896-6476; res: 800/329-7466; res: 888/275-8513.* 51 rms, 3 story. No elvtr. May-Oct: S $50-$65; D $60-$95; each addl $5; suites $85-$110; under 12 free; lower rates rest of yr. Crib free. Pet accepted; $50 refundable. TV; cable (premium). Heated pool; whirlpool. Sauna. Restaurant 6 am-10 pm. Ck-out 11 am. Meeting rms. Business servs avail. In-rm modem link. Sundries. Refrigerators. Cr cds: A, C, D, DS, JCB, MC, V.

SC

★★ **QUALITY INN.** *540 S Main St (84701). 435/896-5465; FAX 435/896-5465; res: 800/228-5151.* 79 rms, 2 story. Mid-May-Oct: S, D $55-$80; suites $80-$110; under 18 free; lower rates rest of yr. Crib free. TV; cable. Heated pool. Complimentary continental bkfst. Restaurant adj 6 am-11 pm. Ck-out noon. Meeting rms. Exercise equipt. Whirlpool in suites. Cr cds: A, C, D, DS, JCB, MC, V.

D SC

✓★ **ROMANICO INN.** *1170 S Main St (84701). 435/896-8471; res: 800/948-0001; res: 800/948-2665.* 29 rms, 2 story. S, D $36-$64; each addl $4; under 12 free. Crib free. Pet accepted. TV; cable. Restaurant adj 5:30-10 pm. Ck-out noon. Coin Indry. Whirlpool. Refrigerators, microwaves. Cr cds: A, C, D, DS, MC, V.

D SC

★★ **WESTON INN.** *647 S Main St (84701). 435/896-9271; FAX 435/896-6864; res: 800/255-9840.* 40 rms, 2 story. June-Sept: S, D $38-$48; each addl $4; under 12 free; lower rates rest of yr. Crib free. Pet accepted. TV; cable. Indoor pool; whirlpool. Restaurant 6 am-9 pm. Rm serv. Ck-out noon. Meeting rms. Business servs avail. Sundries. Cr cds: A, C, D, DS, MC, V.

D SC

Restaurant

★★ **TOPSFIELD LODGE STEAKHOUSE.** *1200 S Main St (84701), behind Richfield Plaza shopping center. 435/896-5437.* Hrs: 5:30-10 pm. Closed Sun; Thanksgiving, Dec 25. Serv bar. Semi-a la carte: dinner $6.95-$18.95. Child's meals. Specializes in steak, shrimp, local seafood. Salad bar. Own spice cake. Country decor; fireplace, tole-painted wall hangings. Antiques. Cr cds: C, MC, V.

D

Roosevelt (D-5)

(See also Vernal)

Settled 1905 **Pop** 3,915 **Elev** 5,182 ft **Area Code** 435 **Zip** 84066
E-mail dcac@ubtanet.com

Information Chamber of Commerce, 50 E 200 S 35-11, PO Box 1417; 435/722-4598

Roosevelt, in the geographical center of Utah's "dinosaur land," was settled when the opening of reservation lands prompted a flood of homesteaders to stake claims in the area. The town was named after Theodore Roosevelt, who had once camped on the banks of a nearby river. Nine Mile Canyon, with its Native American petroglyphs, can be reached from here. A Ranger District office of the Ashley National Forest (see VERNAL) is located in the town.

Motels

★ **BEST WESTERN INN.** *E Hwy 40 (84066). 435/722-4644; FAX 801/722-0179; res: 800/528-1234.* 40 rms, 2 story. May-mid-Nov: S $50; D $55; lower rates rest of yr. Crib $5. TV; cable (premium). Heated pool; whirlpool. Restaurant adj 6 am-11:30 pm. Ck-out 11 am. Business servs avail. Sundries. Exercise equipt. Cr cds: A, C, D, DS, MC, V.

SC

✓★ **FRONTIER MOTEL INC.** *75 S 200 E (98624). 435/722-2201; FAX 435/722-2212.* 54 units, 2 kits. S $35-$45; D $42-$60; each addl $3; kit. units $40-$50. Crib $3. Pet accepted. TV; cable (premium). Pool. Restaurant 6 am-9:30 pm; Sun to 9 pm. Ck-out 11 am. Business servs avail. Cr cds: A, C, D, DS, MC, V.

SC

Salina (F-3)

(See also Richfield)

Settled 1863 **Pop** 1,943 **Elev** 5,150 ft **Area Code** 435 **Zip** 84654

What to See and Do

Palisade State Park. Approx 200 acres. Swimming beaches, showers; fishing; nonmotorized boating, canoe rentals. Nature trail, hiking. 9-hole golf. Picnicking. Camping (fee; dump station). Six Mile Canyon adj. 20 mi N via US 89, then 2 mi E, near Sterling. Phone 435/835-7275 or 800/322-3770 (camping res). Day use ¢¢

Annual Event

Mormon Miracle Pageant. 30 mi N via US 89 in Manti, on Temple grounds. Portrays historical events of the Americas; cast of 600. Phone 435/835-3000. Early-mid-June.

Motels

★★ **BEST WESTERN SHAHEEN'S.** *1225 S State St (84654). 435/529-7455; FAX 435/529-7257; res: 800/528-1234.* 40 rms, 2 story. May-Nov: S $60; D $66-$70; each addl $6; lower rates rest of yr. Crib $4. TV; cable (premium). Heated pool. Restaurant 6 am-10 pm. Ck-out 11 am. Meeting rm. Business servs avail. Sundries. Cr cds: A, C, D, DS, MC, V.

D SC

★ **SENIC HILLS MOTEL.** *1425 S State St (84654). 435/529-7483.* 28 rms, 2 story. June-mid-Oct: S $44-$56; D $52-$56; each addl $6; under 12 free; lower rates rest of yr. Crib $6. Pet accepted. TV; cable. Heated pool. Restaurant 6 am-10 pm. Ck-out 11 am. Business servs avail. Cr cds: A, C, D, DS, MC, V.

SC

Restaurant

✓★ **MOM'S CAFE.** *10 E Main St (84654). 435/529-3921.* Hrs: 7 am-10 pm. Closed Thanksgiving, Dec 25. Semi-a la carte: bkfst $2.50-$8.95, lunch $5.20-$8.50, dinner $6.25-$11.75 Child's meals. Specialties: fish & chips, liver & onions, spare ribs. Salad bar. Own pies. Homey atmosphere. Family-owned. Cr cds: C, DS, MC, V.

D

Salt Lake City (C-3)

(See also Heber City, Ogden, Park City, Provo)

Founded 1847 **Pop** 159,936 **Elev** 4,330 ft **Area Code** 801
E-mail slcvb@saltlake.org **Web** www.saltlake.org

Information Convention & Visitor's Bureau, 90 S West Temple, 84101-1406; 801/521-2822 or 801/534-4900

On a hill at the north end of State Street stands Utah's classic capitol building. Three blocks south is Temple Square, with the famed Mormon Temple and Tabernacle. The adjacent block houses the headquarters of the Church of Jesus Christ of Latter-day Saints, whose members are often called Mormons. Salt Lake City, with its 10-acre blocks, 132-foot-wide, tree-lined streets and mountains rising to the east and west, is one of the most beautifully planned cities in the country.

Once a desert wilderness, Salt Lake City was built by Mormon settlers who sought refuge from religious persecution. Neither the barrenness of the land, drought nor a plague of crickets swerved these people from their purpose. Followers of Brigham Young arrived and named their new territory "Deseret." In these early days the Mormons began a variety of experiments in farming, industry and society, many of which were highly successful. Today, Salt Lake City is an industrious, businesslike city, a center for electronics, steel, missiles and a hundred other enterprises.

West of the city is the enormous Great Salt Lake, stretching 48 miles one way and 90 miles the other. It is less than 35 feet deep and between 15 and 20 percent salt—almost five times as salty as the ocean—humans bob like a cork and cannot sink in the water. The lake is what remains of ancient Lake Bonneville, once 145 miles wide, 350 miles long and 1,000 feet deep. As Lake Bonneville water evaporated over thousands of years, a large expanse of perfectly flat, solid salt was left. Today the Bonneville Salt Flats stretch west almost to Nevada.

Headquarters and a Ranger District office of the Wasatch-Cache National Forest is located in Salt Lake City.

Salt Lake City was laid out in grid fashion, with Temple Square at the center. Most street names are coordinates on this grid: 4th South St is four blocks south of Temple Square, 7th East is seven blocks east. These are written as 400 South and 700 East.

Transportation

Car Rental Agencies. See IMPORTANT TOLL-FREE NUMBERS.

Public Transportation. Buses (Utah Transit Authority), phone 801/287-4636.

Rail Passenger Service. Amtrak 800/872-7245.

Airport Information

Salt Lake City Intl Airport. Information 801/575-2400 or -2401; lost and found 801/575-2427; weather 801/524-5133; cash machines, Terminal Unit 2, near gift shop opp entrance to Concourse C.

What to See and Do

Arrow Press Square. Once the city's printing district, now buildings such as Arrow Press Bldg (1890), Upland Hotel (1910) and Midwest Office Bldg Supply (1910) have been reconstructed into a retail/restaurant complex. 165 S West Temple St. Phone 801/531-9700.

Brigham Young Monument (1897). Intersection of Main & South Temple Sts, at north side of intersection.

Bus tours.

Gray Line. 553 W 100 South ST, 84101. Phone 801/521-7060.

InnsBrook Tours. 3353 S Main, Suite 804, 84115. Phone 801/534-1001.

Council Hall (1864-1866). Meeting place of territorial legislature and city hall for 30 yrs was dismantled and then reconstructed in 1963 at present location; Federal/Greek-revival style architecture. Visitor information center and office; memorabilia. (Daily; closed Jan 1, Thanksgiving, Dec 25) Capitol Hill, 300 N State St, 84114. Phone 801/538-1467. **Free**

Ft Douglas Military Museum. Army museum features history of military in Utah from arrival of Johnston's Army during the 1857 "Utah War" through Vietnam. Also tours of fort (self-guided or guided, by appt). (Tues-Sat; closed most hols) 3 mi NE, Bldg 32 Potter St. Phone 801/581-1710. **Free**

Governor's Mansion (1902). Restored mansion of Thomas Kearns, wealthy Utah senator of early 1900s; decorated with Russian mahogany, Italian marble. Tours. (Apr-Dec, Tues & Thurs afternoons; closed hols) 603 E South Temple St. Phone 801/538-1005. **Free**

Hansen Planetarium. Space science museum and library. Seasonal star shows, stage plays (fee; schedule varies). (Daily; closed hols) 15 S State St. Phone 801/538-2098. **Free**

Hogle Zoological Garden. Wildlife exhibits; Discovery Land; animal demonstrations; miniature train (summer). Picnicking, concession. (Daily; closed Jan 1, Dec 25) 2600 E Sunnyside Ave. Phone 801/582-1631. **¢¢**

Kennecott Bingham Canyon Mine. Open-pit copper mine 2½ mi wide and ½-mi deep. Visitor center, observation deck and audio presentation explain mining operations, which date from 1906. (Apr-mid-Oct, daily) 8400 W Hwy U 111. Phone 801/569-6248. Per vehicle **¢**

Lagoon Amusement Park, Pioneer Village and Water Park. Rides; water slides; re-creation of 19th-century Utah town; stagecoach and steam-engine train rides. Camping. Picnicking. (Memorial Day-Aug, daily; mid-Apr-late May & Sept, Sat & Sun only) Parking (fee). 17 mi N on I-15 exit 325, then N to Lagoon Dr. Phone 800/748-5246. Entrance only **¢¢¢**; All-day passport **¢¢¢¢¢**

Liberty Park. In 100-acre park are Chase Mill (1852), Tracy Aviary, children's garden playground (Apr-Sept), amusement park. Swimming. Lighted tennis, horseshoe courts. Picnicking. (Daily) 1300 South & 600 East Sts. Phone 801/972-7800 (park) or 801/596-8500 (aviary). Park. **Free**; Aviary **¢¢**

Lion House (1856) and **Beehive House** (1854). Family residences, offices and social centers for Brigham Young and his wives and children. Guided tours of Beehive House. (Daily; closed Jan 1, Thanksgiving, Dec 25) 63 & 67 E South Temple. Phone 801/363-5466 (Lion House) or 801/240-2671 (Beehive House). **Free**

Maurice Abravanel Concert Hall. The home of the Utah Symphony, this building is adorned with more than 12,000 sq ft of 24-karat gold leaf and a mile of brass railing. It has been rated one of the acoustically best halls in the US. Free tours (by appt). The symphony has performances most weekends. 123 W South Temple. Phone 801/533-6683 or 801/533-6407 (box office).

Pioneer Memorial Museum. Manuscripts, pioneer relics. Also here is **Carriage House,** with exhibits relating to transportation, including Brigham Young's wagon, mule-drawn vehicles, Pony Express items. One-hr guided tours (by appt). (Daily exc Sun; closed hols) 300 N Main St, W side of capitol grounds. Phone 801/538-1050. **Free**

Professional sports.

NBA (Utah Jazz). Delta Center, 301 S West Temple. Phone 801/355-3865.

River trips. Moki Mac River Expeditions. Offers 1-14-day whitewater trips on the Green and Colorado rivers. Contact PO Box 71242, 84171; phone 801/268-6667 or 800/284-7280. **¢¢¢¢¢**

Salt Lake Art Center. Changing exhibits; school; lectures, seminars, films. (Daily; closed major hols) 20 S West Temple. Phone 801/328-4201. **Donation**

Skiing.

Alta. 26 mi SE on UT 210 in Little Cottonwood Canyon in Alta (see).

Brighton Resort. Two high-speed quad, 2 triple, 3 double chairlifts; patrol, school, rentals; lodge, restaurant, cafeteria. 61 runs; longest run 3 mi, vertical drop 1,745 ft. (Mid-Nov-mid-Apr, daily) Night skiing (nightly exc Sun). Half-day rates. Cross-country skiing. 25 mi SE via I-215, exit 6 in Big Cottonwood Canyon. Phone 801/532-4731. **¢¢¢¢¢**

Deer Valley. 34 mi E & S via I-80, UT 224 in Park City (see).

Park City Mountain Resort. 32 mi E & S via I-80, UT 224 in Park City (see).

The Canyons. 28 mi E & S via I-80, UT 224 in Park City (see).

Snowbird. 25 mi E & S via I-215, UT 210 in Little Cottonwood Canyon (see SNOWBIRD).

Solitude Resort. Detachable quad, 2 triple, 4 double chairlifts; race course, patrol, school, rentals; day lodge, cafeteria, restaurants, bar. Longest run 2½ mi, vertical drop 2,030 ft. (Thanksgiving-mid-Apr, daily) Cross-country center. SE via I-215, in Big Cottonwood Canyon. Phone 801/534-1400. **¢¢¢¢¢**

State Capitol (1914). Constructed of Utah granite and Georgia marble, with a modern annex, capitol has a commanding view of the valley and Wasatch Mountains. Gold Room is decorated with bird's-eye marble and gold from Utah mines; ground floor has exhibits. Guided tours every 30 min (Mon-Fri; hrs vary). 350 N Main St. Phone 801/538-3000. **Free**

★ **Temple Square.** (Daily) Visitor centers provide information, exhibits and guided tours (½- to 1-hr; daily, every 15 min). North, South & West Temple Sts & Main St. Phone 801/240-2534. **Free** Tour includes

Assembly Hall (1880). Tours (daily), concerts (Fri, Sat eves).

Family History Library. Largest genealogy library in the world aids in compilation of family histories. (Daily exc Sun) 35 N West Temple. Phone 801/240-2331. **Free**

Museum of Church History and Art. Exhibits of Latter-day Saints church history from 1820 to present. (Daily; closed Jan 1, Easter, Thanksgiving, Dec 25) 45 N West Temple St. Phone 801/240-3310. **Free**

Seagull Monument (1913). Commemorates saving of the crops from crickets in 1848.

Tabernacle (1867). The self-supporting roof, an elongated dome, is 250 ft long and 150 ft wide. The tabernacle organ has 11,623 pipes, ranging from ⅝ inch to 32 ft in length. The world-famous Tabernacle Choir may be heard at rehearsal (Thurs eve) or at broadcast time (Sun morning). Organ recitals (Mon-Sat, noon or Sun, afternoon). **Free**

Temple (1893). Used for sacred ordinances, such as baptisms and marriages. Closed to non-Mormons.

This is the Place State Park. Day-use museum park at mouth of Emigration Canyon, where Mormon pioneers first entered the valley. In park are **"This Is the Place" Monument** (1947), commemorating Brigham Young's words upon first seeing the Salt Lake City site; visitor center with audio presentation and murals of the Mormon migration; and **Old Deseret Pioneer Village**, a living museum that depicts the 1847-1869 era and pioneer life. (June-Sept, daily) 2601 Sunnyside Ave. Phone 801/584-8392. **¢¢**

Timpanogos Cave National Monument (see). 26 mi S on I-15, then 10 mi E on UT 92.

Trolley Square. Ten-acre complex of trolley barns converted into entertainment/shopping/dining center. (Daily) Bounded by 500 & 600 South Sts and 600 & 700 East Sts. Phone 801/521-9877.

University of Utah (1850). (25,900 students) 2½ mi E, at head of 200 South St. Phone 801/581-7200. On campus are

Marriott Library. Western Americana collection, rare books, manuscripts. (Daily; closed major hols, also July 24) Phone 801/581-8558. **Free**

Pioneer Theatre Company. Two auditoriums; dramas, musicals, comedies. (Sept-May; closed major hols) 300 South & 1400 E Sts. Phone 801/581-6270 or 801/581-6961 (box office).

Red Butte Garden and Arboretum. More than 9,000 trees on 150 acres, representing 350 species; conservatory. Self-guided tours. Special events in summer. (Daily; closed Dec 25) On campus. Phone 801/581-5322. **Free**

Utah Museum of Fine Arts. Representations of artistic styles from Egyptian antiquities to contemporary American paintings; 19th-century French and American paintings, furniture. (Daily; closed hols) Art & Architecture Center, S of library. Phone 801/581-7332. **Free**

Utah Museum of Natural History. Halls of anthropology, biology, mineralology, paleontology, geology; traveling exhibits. (Daily; closed some major hols, also July 24) Phone 801/581-4303. **¢¢**

Utah Fun Dome. Enclosed mall with entertainment, rides, bowling, roller skating, baseball, arcades, miniature golf; cafes. Fee for activities. (Daily) S on I-15, 53rd St S exit, W to 700 West, then N to 4998 S 360 West, in Murray. Phone 801/293-0800.

Utah Opera Company. Grand opera. (Oct-May) 50 W 200 South St. Phone 801/736-6868 or 801/355-ARTS (tickets).

Wasatch-Cache National Forest. High Uintas Wilderness Area has alpine lakes and rugged peaks; Big Cottonwood, Little Cottonwood and Logan canyons. Forest (1 million acres) has fishing; deer and elk hunting; boating. Winter sports. Picnicking. Camping (fees). E via I-80; or N via US 89; Lone Peak Wilderness Area, 20 mi SE. Contact the Supervisor, 8230 Federal Bldg, 125 S State St, 84138; phone 801/524-3900. **Free**

Wheeler Historic Farm. Living history farm (75 acres) depicts rural life from 1890 to 1918. Farmhouse, farm buildings; animals, crops; hay rides (fee). Tour (fee). Visitors can feed animals, gather eggs, milk cows. (Daily; no rides Sun) 6351 S 900 East St, 15 mi SE on I-15, exit I-215. Phone 801/264-2241. **¢¢**

ZCMI (Zion's Co-operative Mercantile Institution) Center. Department store established in 1868 by Brigham Young anchors this 85-store, enclosed, downtown shopping mall. (Daily exc Sun) 36 S State St. Phone 801/321-8743. **Free**

Annual Events

Utah Arts Festival. Downtown. More than 1,000 participants, 90 performing groups; Children's Art Yard, juried show with demonstrations. Ethnic food. Last wk June.

"Days of '47" Celebration. Mid-July.

Utah State Fair. State Fair Park. Phone 801/538-FAIR. Sept 7-17.

Temple Square Christmas. Includes Handel's *Messiah* sung by the Oratorio Society of Utah. Lighting ceremony Fri after Thanksgiving. Phone 801/240-2534. Early Dec.

Additional Visitor Information

For additional information contact the Salt Lake Convention & Visitors Bureau, 90 S West Temple, 84101-1406, phone 801/521-2822; or the Utah Travel Council and Visitor Information Center, Council Hall, 300 N State St, 84114, phone 801/538-1030.

City Neighborhoods

Many of the restaurants, unrated dining establishments and some lodgings listed under Salt Lake City include neighborhoods as well as exact street addresses. Geographic descriptions of Downtown and Trolley Square are given.

Downtown. South of 9th Ave, west of A St and 300 East St, north of 700 South St and east of 400 West St. **East of Downtown:** East of 9th East St.

Trolley Square. South of 500 South St, west of 700 East St, north of 600 South St and east of 600 East St.

Motels

★★ **BEST WESTERN EXECUTIVE INN.** *280 W 7200 S (84047), 8 mi S on I-15, exit 301. 801/566-4141; FAX 801/566-5142; res: 800/528-1234.* Web www.travelweb.com/thisco/bw/45063/45063_b.html. 92 rms, 2 story. Late Dec-Mar: S, D $79-$89; each addl $5; suites $79-$149; under 18 free; lower rates rest of yr. Crib $4. TV. Heated pool; whirlpool. Complimentary coffee in lobby. Restaurant adj 6 am-midnight. Ck-out noon. Meeting rms. Business servs avail. In-rm modem link. Downhill ski 15 mi; x-country ski 20 mi. Health club privileges. Many refrigerators; microwaves avail. Balconies. Cr cds: A, C, D, DS, ER, JCB, MC, V.

SC

★ **BRIGHTON SKI RESORT.** *Hwy 30 (84121), approx 15 mi W via UT 190. 801/532-4731; FAX 435/649-1787; res: 800/873-5512.* 22 rms, 2 story. Mid-Nov-mid-Apr: S, D $50-$120; lower rates rest of yr. TV rm. Heated pool; whirlpool. Bar. Ck-out 11:30 am. Downhill/x-country ski on site. Refrigerators. Picnic tables, grills. On creek. Cr cds: A, C, DS, MC, V.

SC

★★ **COMFORT INN.** *8955 S 255 W (84070), south of downtown. 801/255-4919; FAX 801/255-4998; res: 800/228-5150.* E-mail reservations@comfortinnsandy; web comfortinn-sandy.com. 98 rms, 2 story. S, D $70-$150; each addl $5; under 18 free. Crib free. TV; cable (premium), VCR (movies $4). Indoor pool; whirlpool. Complimentary continental bkfst. Ck-out noon. Meeting rm. Business servs avail. In-rm modem link. Game rm. Cr cds: A, C, D, DS, JCB, MC, V.

SC

✓★★ **COUNTRY INN & SUITES.** *3422 S Decker Lake Dr (84119). 801/908-0311; FAX 801/908-0315; res: 800/456-4000.* Web www.countryinns.com. 82 rms, 3 story, 49 suites. S $79-$89; D $79-$97; each addl $8; suites $89-$97; under 18 free; wkend rates. Crib free. TV; cable. Complimentary continental bkfst. Complimentary coffee in rms. Restaurant adj 11 am-11 pm. Ck-out noon. Meeting rms. Business servs avail. In-rm modem link. Coin lndry. Free airport transportation. Indoor pool; whirlpools. Refrigerator, microwave in suites. Cr cds: A, C, D, DS, ER, JCB, MC, V.

D SC

★★ **COURTYARD BY MARRIOTT.** *10701 S Holiday Park Dr (93515), 15 mi S on I-15, exit 297. 801/571-3600; FAX 801/572-1383; res: 800/321-2211.* Web www.courtyard.com. 124 rms, 4 story. S $79-$99; D $89-$109; each addl $10; suites $135-$145; under 18 free; wkend, hol rates; ski plan. Crib free. TV; cable (premium). Indoor pool; whirlpool. Complimentary coffee in rms. Restaurant 6:30-10:30 am, 5-10 pm. Rm serv. Bar 5-10 pm. Ck-out noon. Coin lndry. Meeting rms. Business servs avail. Downhill/x-country ski 12 mi. Exercise equipt. Health club privileges. Microwaves avail. Some balconies. Cr cds: A, C, D, DS, MC, V.

D SC

✓★★ **CRYSTAL INN.** *2254 W City Center Court (84119), 10 mi on I-215, 3300 SW to Decker Lake Dr. 801/736-2000; FAX 801/736-2001; res: 888/977-9400.* 122 rms, 3 story. S, D $79-$89; each addl $10; suites $119; under 18 free; wkend rates. Crib free. TV; cable (premium), VCR (movies). Complimentary full bkfst. Complimentary coffee in rms. Ck-out 2 pm. Meeting rms. Business servs avail. In-rm modem link. Coin lndry. Free airport, RR station transportation. Indoor pool. Bathrm phones, refrigerators, microwaves. Cr cds: A, C, D, DS, MC, V.

D SC

✓★★ **DAYS INN AIRPORT.** *1900 W North Temple (84116), west of downtown. 801/539-8538; FAX 801/595-1041; res: 800/329-7466.* 110 rms, 2 story. S, D $58-$105; each addl $7; suites $98-$125; under 17 free. Crib free. Pet accepted. TV; cable (premium). Indoor pool. Complimentary continental bkfst. Restaurant nearby. Ck-out 11 am. Business servs avail. In-rm modem link. Valet serv. Guest lndry. Free airport, RR station, bus depot transportation. Exercise equipt. Health club privileges. Refrigerators, microwaves. Cr cds: A, C, D, DS, JCB, MC, V.

D SC

★★ **HAMPTON INN.** *10690 S Holiday Park Dr (84070), S via I-15, exit 10600 South St, then ½ blk E. 801/571-0800; FAX 801/572-0708; res: 800/426-7866.* Web www.hamptoninn.com. 131 rms, 4 story. S, D $78-$88; under 18 free; wkly rates, ski plans. Crib free. TV; cable (premium). Indoor pool; whirlpool. Complimentary continental bkfst. Restaurant adj 6 am-11 pm. Ck-out noon. Coin lndry. Meeting rms. Business servs avail. In-rm modem link. Sundries. Free bus depot transportation. Downhill ski 14 mi. Exercise equipt. Health club privileges. Microwaves avail. Shopping center adj. Cr cds: A, C, D, DS, MC, V.

D SC

★★ **HAMPTON INN.** *2393 S 800 W (84087). 801/296-1211; FAX 801/296-1222; res: 800/426-7866.* 60 rms, 3 story. S, D $69-$85; suites $159; under 18 free. Crib free. Pet accepted. TV; cable (premium). Indoor pool; whirlpool. Complimentary continental bkfst. Restaurant nearby. Ck-out noon. Meeting rms. Business servs avail. In-rm modem link. Coin lndry. Free airport transportation. Health club privileges. Microwaves avail. Cr cds: A, C, D, DS, MC, V.

D SC

✓★★ **LA QUINTA INN.** *7231 S Catalpa Rd (84047), 8 mi S on I-15, 72nd South St exit, E to Catalpa Rd. 801/566-3291; FAX 801/562-5943; res: 800/687-6667.* 122 rms, 2 story. S $69; D $77; each addl $8; under 18 free. Crib free. Pet accepted. TV; cable (premium). Heated pool. Continental bkfst. Complimentary coffee in rms. Restaurant adj open 24 hrs. Ck-out noon. Coin lndry. Business servs avail. In-rm modem link. Downhill ski 15 mi; x-country ski 20 mi. Health club privileges. Microwaves avail. Cr cds: A, C, D, DS, MC, V.

D SC

★★ **QUALITY INN.** *4465 Century Dr South (84123), south of downtown. 801/268-2533; FAX 801/266-6206; res: 800/268-5801.* 132 rms, 2 story. Feb-Mar, July-Sept: S $69-$89; D $79-$109; under 18 free; ski plan; lower rates rest of yr. Crib free. Pet accepted; $7/day. TV; cable (premium). Pool; whirlpool. Complimentary continental bkfst. Complimentary coffee. Restaurant adj open 24 hrs. Ck-out noon. Coin lndry. Business servs avail. In-rm modem link. Balconies. Cr cds: A, C, D, DS, ER, JCB, MC, V.

D SC

★ **RAMADA INN.** *230 W 600 S (84101), downtown. 801/364-5200; FAX 801/359-2542; res: 800/595-0505.* Web www.ramadainnslc.com. 160 rms, 2 story. S, D $59-$79; each addl $10; under 19 free. Crib free. Pet accepted, some restrictions; $10 deposit. TV; cable. Indoor pool; whirlpool. Restaurant 6 am-10 pm; Sun 6:30 am-9 pm. Rm serv. Private club from 5 pm. Ck-out noon. Coin lndry. Meeting rms. Business servs avail. In-rm modem link. Valet serv. Free airport, RR station, bus depot transportation. Exercise equipt; sauna. Game rm. Rec rm. Microwaves avail. Cr cds: A, C, D, DS, MC, V.

D SC

★★ **RESIDENCE INN BY MARRIOTT.** *765 East 400 S (84102), east of downtown. 801/532-5511; FAX 801/531-0416; res: 800/331-3131.* Web residenceinn.slc.com. 128 kit. suites (1-2-bedrm), 2 story. Suites $159-$199; wkly, monthly rates; ski packages. Pet accepted. TV; cable (premium), VCR avail (movies). Heated pool. Complimentary continental bkfst. Ck-out noon. Coin lndry. Business servs avail. In-rm modem link. Bellhops. Valet serv. Free airport, RR station, bus depot transportation. Exercise equipt. Microwaves; many fireplaces. Sport court. Cr cds: A, C, D, DS, JCB, MC, V.

D SC

★ **SLEEP INN.** *10626 S 300 W (84095), S on I-15, exit 10600 South, then ½ blk W. 801/572-2020; FAX 801/572-2459; res: 800/62 SLEEP.* E-mail sleep-saltlake@travelbase.com. 68 rms, shower only, 2 story. S $59-$69; D $65-$75; each addl $5; family rates. Crib free. TV; cable (premium), VCR (movies). Indoor pool. Complimentary continental bkfst. Coffee in lobby. Restaurant nearby. Ck-out noon. Coin lndry. Business servs avail. In-rm modem link. Downhill ski 20 mi. Health club privileges. Cr cds: A, C, D, DS, ER, JCB, MC, V.

D SC

✓★ **SUPER 8 MOTEL.** *616 S 200 W (84101), south of downtown. 801/534-0808; FAX 801/355-7735; res: 800/800-8000.* 120 rms, 4 story. S $64.99; D $69.99; under 13 free; package plans; higher rates special events. Crib free. Pet accepted; $25 deposit. TV; cable (premium). Complimentary coffee in lobby. Restaurant nearby. Ck-out 11 am. Business servs avail. Sundries. Coin lndry. Some refrigerators, microwaves. Cr cds: A, C, D, DS, MC, V.

D SC

★ **TRAVELODGE.** *524 SW Temple St (84101), downtown. 801/531-7100; FAX 801/359-3814; res: 800/578-7878.* E-mail travelodgecitycenter@travelbase.com. 60 rms, 3 story. S $50-$72; D $58-$79; each addl $6; under 18 free. Crib free. Pet accepted. TV; cable (premium). Heated pool; whirlpool. Complimentary coffee in rms. Restaurant nearby. Ck-out noon. Business servs avail. Cr cds: A, C, D, DS, MC, V.

SC

Motor Hotels

★★ **BEST WESTERN SALT LAKE PLAZA.** *122 W South Temple St (84101), downtown. 801/521-0130; FAX 801/322-5057; res: 800/366-3684.* E-mail rooms@plaza-hotel.com; web www.plaza-hotel.com. 226 rms, 13 story. S $89-$169; D $99-$169; each addl $10; suites $269; under 18 free. Crib free. Pet accepted; $10. TV; cable. Heated pool; whirlpool. Restaurant 6 am-11 pm. Rm serv. Ck-out 11 am. Lndry facilities. Meeting rms. Business servs avail. In-rm modem link. Gift shop. Exercise equipt. Some refrigerators. Cr cds: A, C, D, DS, ER, JCB, MC, V.

D SC

★★ **COMFORT INN.** *200 N Admiral Byrd Rd (84116), in Salt Lake Intl Center, near Intl Airport, west of downtown. 801/537-7444; FAX 801/532-4721; res: 800/228-5150.* Web www.citysearch.com/airportcomfort. 154 rms, 4 story. S, D $69-$139; each addl $10; under 18 free. Crib free. Pet accepted; $25 deposit. TV. Heated pool; whirlpool. Restaurant 6 am-2 pm, 5 pm-midnight. Rm serv. Ck-out 11 am. Meeting rms. Business servs avail. Valet serv. Free airport transportation. Exercise equipt. Some refrigerators; microwaves avail. Some balconies. Cr cds: A, C, D, DS, JCB, MC, V.

D SC

★★ **CRYSTAL INN.** *230 W 500 S (84101), downtown. 801/328-4466; FAX 801/328-4072; res: 800/366-4466.* 175 rms, 4 story. S, D $90-$150; each addl $10; under 18 free; ski plan. Crib free. TV; cable. Indoor pool; whirlpool. Complimentary full bkfst. Restaurant adj open 24 hrs. Ck-out noon. Coin lndry. Meeting rms. Business servs avail. In-rm modem link. Sundries. Valet serv. Free airport transportation. Exercise equipt; sauna. Refrigerators, microwaves; some wet bars. Cr cds: A, C, D, DS, JCB, MC, V.

D SC

★★★ **HOLIDAY INN.** *999 S Main St (84111), south of downtown. 801/359-8600; FAX 801/359-7186; res: 800/465-4329.* 292 rms, 3 story, 14 suites. S, D $98-$179; each addl $10; under 18 free; ski plans. Crib free. TV; cable, VCR avail. Indoor/outdoor pool; whirlpool. Playground. Restaurants 6 am-2 pm, 5-10 pm. Rm serv. Bar. Ck-out noon. Coin lndry. Convention facilities. Business center. Bellhops. Concierge. Gift shop. Free airport, RR station, bus depot transportation. Tennis. Exercise equipt; sauna. Basketball court. Lawn games. Some refrigerators. Wet bar in suites. Cr cds: A, C, D, DS, JCB, MC, V.

D SC

★★★ **RADISSON HOTEL AIRPORT.** *2177 W North Temple St (84116), near Intl Airport, west of downtown. 801/364-5800; FAX 801/364-5823; res: 800/333-3333.* E-mail sala@radisson.com; web www.radisson.com. 127 rms, 3 story, 46 suites. S, D $89-$169; each addl $10; suites $109-$159; under 18 free; ski, golf plans. Crib free. TV; cable (premium). Heated pool. Complimentary continental bkfst. Complimentary coffee in rms. Restaurant 6:30-10 am, 11:30 am-2 pm, 5-10 pm; Sat, Sun 6:30-11 am. Rm serv. Ck-out noon. Meeting rms. Business servs avail. Bellhops. Free garage parking. Free airport, RR station, bus depot transportation. Exercise equipt. Bathrm phones, refrigerators, wet bars; some fireplaces; microwaves avail. Balconies. Cr cds: A, C, D, DS, ER, JCB, MC, V.

D SC

Hotels

★★★ **CAVANAUGH'S OLYMPUS MOTEL.** *161 W 600 S (84101), downtown. 801/521-7373; FAX 801/524-0354; res: 800/325-4000.* Web www.cavanaughs.com. 393 rms, 13 story. S, D $109-$169; suites $250; under 18 free; wkend rates; ski plan. Crib free. TV; cable. Pool; whirlpool. Restaurant 6 am-11 pm. Ck-out noon. Convention facilities. Business servs avail. Barber shop. Free airport transportation. Exercise equipt. Some refrigerators; microwaves avail. Balconies. Cr cds: A, C, D, DS, ER, JCB, MC, V.

★★★ **DOUBLETREE HOTEL.** *255 S West Temple (84101). 801/328-2000; FAX 801/532-1953; res: 800/547-8010.* Web www.citysearch.com/slc/doubletree. 500 rms, 18 story. S, D $129-$160; each addl $20; suites $295-$495; under 18 free; wkend rates; ski package. Crib free. Pet accepted. TV; VCR avail. Indoor pool; whirlpool, poolside serv. Complimentary coffee in rms. Restaurant (see SPENCER'S). Private club; entertainment. Ck-out noon. Convention facilities. Business center. In-rm modem link. Concierge. Gift shop. Covered parking; valet. Free airport, RR station, bus depot transportation. Exercise equipt; sauna. Some refrigerators. Luxury level. Cr cds: A, C, D, DS, ER, JCB, MC, V.

★★★ **EMBASSY SUITES.** *110 West 600 South St (84101), downtown. 801/359-7800; FAX 801/359-3753; res: 800/325-7643.* 241 suites, 9 story. S $139-$149; D $151-$161; each addl $15; under 18 free; wkend, ski rates. Crib free. TV; cable (premium). Indoor pool; whirlpool. Complimentary full bkfst. Complimentary coffee in rms. Restaurant 11 am-11 pm. Private club to 1 am. Ck-out noon. Coin Indry. Meeting rms. In-rm modem link. Gift shop. Covered parking. Free airport, RR station, bus depot transportation. Exercise equipt; sauna. Refrigerators, wet bars, microwaves. Atrium lobby. Cr cds: A, C, D, DS, ER, JCB, MC, V.

★★★ **HILTON.** *150 W 500 S (84101), downtown. 801/532-3344; FAX 801/531-0705; res: 800/421-7602.* 362 rms, 10 story. S, D $89-$159; each addl $10; suites $195-$399; ski plans. Crib free. Pet accepted, some restrictions; $50 deposit. TV; cable (premium), VCR avail. Pool; whirlpool, poolside serv. Restaurant 6 am-11:30 pm. Private club 11:30 am-midnight, Sun 5-10 pm. Ck-out noon. Convention facilities. Business center. In-rm modem link. Barber, beauty shop. Free airport transportation. Exercise equipt; sauna. Health club privileges. Ski rentals avail. Balconies. Luxury level. Cr cds: A, C, D, DS, ER, JCB, MC, V.

★★★ **HILTON AIRPORT.** *5151 Wiley Post Way (84116), west of downtown. 801/539-1515; FAX 801/539-1113; res: 800/999-3736.* Web www.citysearch.comslcairporthilton. 287 rms, 5 story. Jan-Oct: S $79-$169; D $89-$179; each addl $10; suites $189-$299; under 18 free; family rates; package plans; lower rates rest of yr. Crib free. Pet accepted; $50 deposit. TV; cable (premium), VCR avail (movies). Complimentary coffee in rms. Restaurant 6:30 am-midnight. Bar 4:30 pm-midnight. Ck-out 1 pm. Convention facilities. Business center. Concierge. Gift shop. Coin Indry. Free airport, RR station transportation. 9-hole golf, putting green. Exercise equipt. 2 pools, 1 indoor; whirlpool. Some in-rm whirlpools; refrigerators avail. Balconies avail. Picnic tables. Luxury level. Cr cds: A, C, D, DS, ER, JCB, MC, V.

✓★★★ **LITTLE AMERICA HOTEL & TOWERS.** *500 S Main St (84101), downtown. 801/363-6781; FAX 801/596-5911; res: 800/453-9450.* E-mail lahinfo@lamerica.com; web www.lamerica.com. 850 rms, 17 story. S $75-$149; D $85-$164; suites $800; under 13 free. Crib free. TV; cable (premium). 2 pools, 1 indoor; wading pool, whirlpool. Restaurant 5 am-midnight; dining rm 7-10 am, 11 am-2 pm, 5-11 pm. Bar noon-midnight; entertainment. Ck-out 1 pm. Convention facilities. Business servs avail. Barber, beauty shop. Free covered parking. Free airport, RR station, bus depot transportation. Exercise equipt; sauna. Health club privileges. Many bathrm phones, refrigerators. Garden setting on 10 acres. Cr cds: A, C, D, DS, MC, V.

★★★ **MARRIOTT.** *75 S West Temple (84101), downtown. 801/531-0800; FAX 801/532-4127.* 515 rms, 15 story. S, D $109-$205; suites $250-$850; family rates; package plans. Crib free. TV; cable (premium), VCR avail. Heated indoor/outdoor pool; whirlpool, poolside serv. Complimentary coffee in rms. Restaurant 6:30 am-11 pm; Fri, Sat to midnight. Private club. Ck-out noon. Coin Indry. Convention facilities. Business center. In-rm modem link. Concierge. Covered valet parking. Free airport, RR station, bus depot transportation. Exercise equipt; sauna. Balconies. Inside access to shopping mall. Luxury level. Cr cds: A, C, D, DS, ER, JCB, MC, V.

★★★ **MARRIOTT UNIVERSITY PARK.** *480 Wakara Way (84108), east of downtown. 801/581-1000; FAX 801/584-3321; res: 800/637-4390.* Web www.uparkhotel.com. 218 rms, 7 story, 29 suites. S, D $125-$195; suites $145-$205; under 12 free. Crib free. TV; cable (premium). Indoor pool; whirlpool. Restaurant 6:30 am-10 pm. Bar 11 am-midnight. Ck-out noon. Meeting rms. Business center. Gift shop. Free airport, RR station, bus depot transportation. Downhill/x-country ski 15 mi. Exercise equipt. Rec rm. Refrigerators, wet bar; microwave in suites. Cr cds: A, C, D, DS, MC, V.

✓★★ **PEERY HOTEL.** *110 W 300 S (84101), downtown. 801/521-4300; FAX 801/575-5014; res: 800/331-0073.* Web www.citysearchslc.peery. 77 rms, 3 story. S, D $99-$149; under 16 free; wkend rates. TV; cable (premium). Whirlpool. Complimentary continental bkfst. Restaurant (see PEERY WASATCH PUB & BISTRO). Bar. Ck-out 11 am. Meeting rms. Concierge. Gift shop. Free airport transportation. Exercise equipt. Historic building (1910). Cr cds: A, C, DS, MC, V.

★★★ **SHILO INN.** *206 SW Temple St. (84101), downtown. 801/521-9500; FAX 801/359-6527; res: 800/222-2244.* 200 rms, 12 story. S, D $105-$129; each addl $12; suites $265-$425; under 12 free. Crib free. TV; cable (premium), VCR (movies $3). Heated pool; whirlpool. Complimentary full bkfst. Coffee in rms. Restaurant 6 am-10 pm. Ck-out noon. Coin Indry. Meeting rms. Business servs avail. Gift shop. Free airport transportation. Exercise equipt; sauna. Game rm. Wet bars, refrigerators, microwaves; some bathrm phones. Cr cds: A, C, D, DS, MC, V.

★★★ **WYNDHAM HOTEL.** *215 W S Temple (84101), downtown. 801/531-7500; FAX 801/328-1289; res: 800/996-3426.* Web www.travelweb.com. 381 rms, 15 story. S, D $79-$179; each addl $10; suites $179-$550; under 18 free; wkend, hol rates; ski packages. TV; cable (premium). Indoor pool; whirlpool. Coffee in rms. Restaurant 6 am-10:30 pm. Bar 11 am-midnight. Ck-out noon. Convention facilities. Business center. In-rm modem link. Concierge. Gift shop. Free airport, RR station transportation. Exercise equipt; sauna. Health club privileges. Microwaves avail. Adj to Delta Center. Cr cds: A, C, D, DS, ER, JCB, MC, V.

Inns

★★★ **ARMSTRONG MANSION.** *667 E 100 S (84102), downtown. 801/531-1333; FAX 801/531-0282; res: 800/708-1333.* E-mail armstrong@vii.com; web www.armstrong-bb.com. 13 rms, 4 with shower only, 3 story. S, D $99-$209; suites $169-$229. TV; cable, VCR. Complimentary full bkfst. Restaurant nearby. Ck-out 11 am, ck-in 3 pm. Luggage handling. Downhill/x-country ski 20 mi. Built in 1893; antiques. Totally nonsmoking. Cr cds: A, C, D, DS, MC, V.

★★★★ **BRIGHAM STREET INN.** *1135 E South Temple St (84102), 2 mi E of Main St, east of downtown. 801/364-4461; FAX*

801/521-3201; res: 800/417-4461. Conveniently located between the University of Utah and the downtown business district, this restored Victorian mansion offers a variety of attractively furnished guestrooms and public areas. 9 rms, 3 story. S, D $85-$185; each addl $10. Crib free. TV; cable, VCR avail. Complimentary continental bkfst. Setups. Ck-out 11 am, ck-in 3 pm. Business servs avail. X-country ski 15 mi. Fireplace in 5 rms. Cr cds: A, C, MC, V.

★★★ **INN AT TEMPLE SQUARE.** *71 W S Temple (84101), downtown. 801/531-1000; FAX 801/536-7272; res: 800/843-4668.* Web www.theinn.com. 90 rms, 7 story, 10 suites. S, D $130-$155; each addl $10; suites $170-$240; under 18 free. Crib free. TV; cable, VCR avail. Pool privileges. Complimentary bkfst buffet. Dining rm 6:30-9:30 am, 11:30 am-2:30 pm, 5-10 pm. Rm serv. Ck-out noon, ck-in 3 pm. Business servs avail. Bellhops. Valet serv. Concierge. Free airport, RR station, bus depot transportation. Health club privileges. Bathrm phones, refrigerators. Elegant inn built in 1930; antiques from old Hotel Utah. Opp Temple Square. Totally nonsmoking. Cr cds: A, C, D, DS, MC, V.

D SC

★★★ **SALTAIR BED & BREAKFAST.** *164 S 900 E (84102), east of downtown. 801/533-8184; FAX 801/595-0332; res: 800/733-8184.* E-mail saltair@travelbase.com; web travelbase.com/ destinations/salt-lake-city/saltair. 8 rms, 3 share baths, 2 with shower only, 2 story, 3 suites. Some rm phones. S $55-$104; D $75-$149; each addl $15; suites $129-$225. TV in some rms; cable (premium), VCR avail (movies). Complimentary full bkfst; afternoon refreshments. Restaurant nearby. Ck-out 11 am, ck-in 3:30 pm. X-country ski 15 mi. Health club privileges. Whirlpool. Some refrigerators, microwaves, fireplaces. Built in 1903; antiques. Totally nonsmoking. Cr cds: A, C, D, DS, MC, V.

SC

✓★★ **SPRUCES INN.** *6151 South 900 East (84121), south of downtown. 801/268-8762; FAX 801/268-6652; res: 877/777-8237.* 4 rms, air-cooled, 2 story, 2 kit. units. S, D $55-$150; under 12 free. TV; VCR avail. Complimentary full bkfst. Restaurant nearby. Ck-out 11 am, ck-in 2 pm. Downhill/x-country ski 15 mi. Balconies. Picnic tables. Surrounded by spruce trees. Built in 1902 by a Norwegian carpenter; folk art and Southwestern decor. Totally nonsmoking. Cr cds: A, C, DS, MC, V.

SC

★★ **WILDFLOWERS BED & BREAKFAST.** *936 E 1700 S (84105), east of downtown. 801/466-0600; FAX 801/466-4728; res: 800/569-0009.* E-mail lark2spur@aol.com; web wildflowersbb.com. 5 rms, 3 story. No elvtr. S $80-$105; D $85-$120; kit. unit $130-$175; under 12 free. TV; cable (premium), VCR avail. Crib free. Complimentary full bkfst. Restaurant nearby. Ck-out 11 am, ck-in 3 pm. Business servs avail. Built in 1891; antiques. Totally nonsmoking. Cr cds: A, C, DS, MC, V.

SC

Restaurants

✓★★ **BABA AFGHAN.** *55 E 400 S (84111), downtown. 801/596-0786.* Hrs: 11:30 am-2:30 pm, 5-9:30 pm; Mon to 2:30 pm; Sat, Sun from 5 pm. Closed some hols. Res accepted (dinner). Afghan menu. Buffet: lunch $6.50. Semi-a la carte: dinner $7.95-$14.95. Specializes in lamb, beef, chicken. Own baking. Street parking. Afghani clothing display. Totally nonsmoking. Cr cds: A, C, D, DS, MC, V.

D

★★ **BACI TRATTORIA.** *134 W Pierpont Ave (84101), downtown. 801/328-1500.* Web www.gastronomy.com. Hrs: 11:30 am-3 pm, 5-10 pm; Fri, Sat to 11 pm. Closed Sun; major hols. Italian menu. Bar. A la carte entrees: lunch $6.99-$16.99, dinner $7.99-$26.99. Specializes in fresh pasta, fresh seafood. Outdoor dining (summer). Large stained-glass partitions. Wood-burning pizza oven. Cr cds: A, C, D, DS, MC, V.

D

✓★★ **BARKING FROG GRILLE.** *39 Market St (84101), downtown. 801/322-3764.* Hrs: 5-10 pm. Closed major hols; also July 24. Res accepted. Southwestern menu. Bar. Semi-a la carte: dinner $8.95-$20.95. Child's meals. Specializes in ribs, game, fish. Parking. Southwest decor; art. Totally nonsmoking. Cr cds: A, C, DS, MC, V.

D

★★ **BENIHANA OF TOKYO.** *165 S West Temple St (84101), near Salt Lake Convention Center, on Arrow Press Sq, downtown. 801/322-2421.* Hrs: 11:30 am-2 pm, 5-9:30 pm; Fri, Sat 5-10:30 pm; Sun, hols to 9 pm. Res accepted. Japanese menu. Bar. Semi-a la carte: lunch $5.50-$14, dinner $12.50-$27.50. Child's meals. Specializes in seafood, steak, chicken. Tableside cooking. Japanese decor. Cr cds: A, C, D, DS, JCB, MC, V.

✓★ **BUFFALO JOE'S SMOKEHOUSE.** *5927 S State St (84107), downtown. 801/261-3537.* Hrs: 11 am-10 pm; Sat to 10:30 pm; Sun noon-9:30 pm; early-bird dinner 4-6 pm. Closed Thanksgiving, Dec 25. Bar. Semi-a la carte: lunch $5-$8, dinner $8-$16. Child's meals. Specializes in steak, ribs, chicken. Outdoor dining. Casual, Texas-barbecue atmosphere. Totally nonsmoking. Cr cds: A, C, DS, MC, V.

★★★ **CAPITOL CAFE.** *54 W 200 S (84101), downtown. 801/532-7000.* Web www.citysearch.com/sic/capitolcafe. Hrs: 11:30 am-10 pm; Fri to 11 pm; Sat 5-11 pm. Closed Sun; also most major hols. Res accepted. Contemporary Amer menu. Wine cellar. A la carte entrees: lunch $5.25-$13.95, dinner $10.95-$26.95. Specialties: Sonoma smoked chicken salad, balsamic glazed pork chop, creme brulee. Parking. Outdoor dining. Paintings by local artists. Totally nonsmoking. Cr cds: A, C, DS, MC, V.

D

✓★ **COWBOY GRUB.** *2350½ Foothill Blvd (84109), I-80 to Foothill Dr, exit N, east of downtown. 801/466-8334.* E-mail summi@ix.netcom.com. Hrs: 11 am-10 pm; Fri, Sat to 11 pm. Closed Sun; major hols; also July 24. Semi-a la carte: lunch, dinner $5-$15. Child's meals. Specializes in pot roast, Mexican dishes. Salad bar. Western decor. Cr cds: A, C, D, DS, MC, V.

D

★★ **CREEKSIDE AT SOLITUDE.** *12000 Big Cottonwood Canyon (84121), 20 mi E at Creekside Condominiums. 435/649-8400.* Hrs: 11:30 am-9 pm; Sat, Sun brunch 9 am-3 pm. Res accepted (dinner). Continental menu. Semi-a la carte: lunch $7-$12, dinner $12-$20. Sat, Sun brunch $7-$10. Child's meals. Specializes in fresh seafood, pasta, wood-burning dishes. Own pasta. Jazz Fri. Outdoor dining. Mediterranean decor; windows overlook pond, ski slopes. Cr cds: A, C, D, DS, MC, V.

D

★★ **DELLA FONTANA RISTORANTE.** *336 S 400 East St (84111), downtown. 801/328-4243.* Hrs: 11 am-10 pm. Closed Sun; some major hols; also July 24. Res accepted. Italian, Amer menu. Semi-a la carte: lunch $6.85-$13.95, dinner $10.95-$17.95. Child's meals. Specializes in pasta, veal, Cordon Bleu. Historic converted church, stained-glass windows, antique chandeliers. Waterfall in dining rm. Cr cds: A, C, D, DS, MC, V.

♥

✓★★ **DESERT EDGE PUB.** *602 E 500 S (84102), downtown. 801/521-8918.* Hrs: 11 am-midnight; Thurs-Sat to 1 am; Sun noon-10 pm. Closed Dec 25. Contemporary Amer menu. Bar. Semi-a la carte: lunch, $2.25-$7.95, dinner $2.25-$10.95. Specializes in pasta, sandwiches, salads. Own pastas, beer. Outdoor dining. Informal, casual atmosphere; microbrewery. Cr cds: A, C, DS, MC, V.

D

★★ **HELEN'S.** *3693 Brighton Point Dr (84121), east of downtown. 801/265-0205.* Hrs: 11:30 am-3 pm, 5:30-9 pm; Fri to 10:30 pm; Sun 10 am-9 pm. Res accepted. Continental menu. Wine, beer. Semi-a la carte: lunch $7-$9, dinner $18-$23. Specialties: potato-crusted salmon, blackberry brandy chicken, Vienese breaded pork. Outdoor dining. Country home atmosphere. Totally nonsmoking. Cr cds: A, C, D, DS, MC, V.

★★ **HUNGRY I.** *1440 S Foothill Blvd (84108), east of downtown. 801/582-8600.* Hrs: 11 am-3 pm, 5-10 pm; Sat noon-11 pm; Sun 9 am-9 pm; Sun brunch 10 am-3 pm. Closed Thanksgiving, Dec 25. Res accepted (dinner). Greek menu. Bar. Semi-a la carte: bkfst $4.95-$10.95, lunch $6.95-$11.95, dinner $11.95-$31.95. Buffet: lunch $7.95. Sun brunch $11.99. Child's meals. Specialties: filet mignon, halibut, mousaka. Jazz pianist Fri, Sat. Valet parking. Outdoor dining. Cr cds: A, C, D, DS, MC, V.

D

★★★ **IL SANSOVINO.** *299 S Main St (84111), downtown. 801/533-9999.* Hrs: 11 am-2 pm, 5:30-10 pm; Sat 5:30-10:30 pm. Closed major hols. Res accepted. Italian menu. Bar. Wine cellar. A la carte entrees: lunch, dinner $6-$16. Complete meal: 7-9 course dinner $50-$125. Specialties: Tuscan grilled marinated chicken, grilled baby calamari with spinach, pasta Sansovino. Pianist Fri, Sat (winter). Valet parking. Outdoor dining. In skyscraper. Totally nonsmoking. Cr cds: A, C, DS, MC, V.

D

★★★ **LOG HAVEN.** *6451 E 3800 S (84109), 15 mi SE to Millcreek Canyon, off I-215, exit 3900S, east of downtown. 801/272-8255.* Web www.log-haven.com. Hrs: 5:30-9 pm; Sun 4:30-8:30 pm. Closed Jan 1, July 4, Dec 25. Res accepted. Continental menu. Bar. Wine list. Semi-a la carte: dinner $14-$27. Child's meals. Specialties: seared rare ahi tuna, Mediterranean seasoned top sirloin, filet mignon. Own baking. Valet parking. Outdoor dining. Renovated 1920 log mansion nestled among pine trees; views of waterfall, natural surroundings. Cr cds: A, C, D, DS, MC, V.

D

✓★★ **MANDARIN.** *348 E 900 N (84010), 9 blks N on I-15 exit 321. 801/298-2406.* E-mail agskedros@msn.com; web www.citysearch.com/slc/skedros. Hrs: 5-9:30 pm; Fri, Sat to 10:30 pm. Closed Sun; most major hols. Res accepted. Chinese menu. Wine, beer. Semi-a la carte: dinner $7-$13. Specialties: Szechwan shrimp, almond chicken, seasonal beef and beans. Parking. Elegant atmosphere. Unique Chinese decor; murals. Glass atrium in garden rm. Totally nonsmoking. Cr cds: A, C, MC, V.

D

★★ **MARKET STREET BROILER.** *260 S 1300 E (84102), east of downtown. 801/583-8808.* Web www.gastronomy.com. Hrs: 11 am-10 pm; Sun 4-9 pm; early-bird dinner 4-6 pm. Bar from noon. Semi-a la carte: lunch $4.99-$16.99, dinner $7.99-$29.99. Child's meals. Specializes in fresh fish, barbecued ribs. Outdoor dining. Modern decor in historic former fire station. Cr cds: A, C, D, DS, MC, V.

D

★★ **MARKET STREET GRILL.** *54 Market St (84101), downtown. 801/531-6044.* Web citysearch.com. Hrs: 6:30 am-10 pm; Sat 7 am-11 pm; Fri, Sat to 11 pm; Sun 9 am-10 pm; early-bird dinner 3-7 pm; Sun brunch 9 am-3 pm. Closed Labor Day, Thanksgiving, Dec 25. Bar 11:30 am-11:30 pm. Semi-a la carte: bkfst $3.99-$7.99, lunch $5.99-$14.99, dinner $13.99-$29.99. Sun brunch $5.99-$12.99. Child's meals. Specializes in steak, seafood. In renovated 1906 hotel. Cr cds: A, C, D, DS, MC, V.

★★★ **METROPOLITAN.** *173 W Broadway (84110), downtown. 801/364-3472.* Hrs: 5-10 pm; Fri, Sat to 11 pm. Closed Mon, Sun; also Jan 1, Thanksgiving, Dec 25. Res accepted. Contemporary Amer menu. Bar. Wine cellar. A la carte entrees: dinner $7-$28. Complete meal: dinner $55. Specializes in fish, wild game. Own pasta. Own desserts. Street parking. Totally nonsmoking. Cr cds: A, C, D, MC, V.

D

★★ **MIKADO JAPANESE RESTAURANT.** *67 West 100 South St (84101), downtown. 801/328-0929.* Hrs: 5:30-9:30 pm; Fri, Sat to 10 pm; summer: 6-9:30 pm; Sun to 9 pm. Closed major hols. Res accepted. Japanese menu. Semi-a la carte: dinner $11-$21. Child's meals. Specialties: shrimp tempura, chicken teriyaki, beef sukiyaki. Sushi bar. Zashiki rms. Cr cds: A, C, D, DS, JCB, MC, V.

D

★★★ **NEW YORKER CLUB.** *60 W Market St (84101), between Main St & W Temple at 350 S, downtown. 801/363-0166.* Hrs: 11:30 am-10 pm; Fri to 11 pm; Sat 5-11 pm. Closed Sun; major hols; July 24. Res accepted. Continental menu. Bar. Wine cellar. Semi-a la carte: lunch $6.95-$15.95, dinner $14.95-$29.95. Specializes in fresh seafood, beef, veal. Own desserts. Valet parking. Cr cds: A, C, D, DS, MC, V.

★★ **OLD SALT CITY JAIL RESTAURANT.** *460 S 1000 E (84102), east of downtown. 801/355-2422.* Hrs: 5-9 pm; Fri 4:30-10 pm; Sat 4-10 pm; Sun 4-9 pm. Res accepted. Bar. Semi-a la carte: dinner $9.95-$18.95. Child's meals. Specializes in prime rib, steak, seafood. Salad bar. Entertainment Thurs-Sat. Early brewery re-created as an old country jail. Totally nonsmoking. Cr cds: A, C, D, DS, MC, V.

D

★★ **PEERY WASATCH PUB & BISTRO.** *(See Peery) 801/521-5037.* Hrs: 11:30 am-10 pm. Closed Sun; Easter, Dec 25. Res accepted. Continental menu. Bar. Semi-a la carte: lunch $4.95-$7.95, dinner $9.95-$15.95. Specializes in pasta, seafood, beef. Casual decor. Totally nonsmoking. Cr cds: A, C, DS, MC, V.

D

★★ **PIERPONT CANTINA.** *122 W Pierpont Ave (84101), downtown. 801/364-1222.* Hrs: 11:30 am-10 pm; Sat 4-11 pm, Sun 10 am-10 pm; early bird 4-7 pm. Closed Jan 1, Thanksgiving, Dec 25. Res accepted. Mexican menu. Bar. Semi-a la carte: lunch $6.99-$14.99, dinner $7.99-$19. Buffet: $4.99. Child's meals. Specializes in carnitas, seafood. Outdoor dining. Mexican decor. Totally nonsmoking. Cr cds: A, C, D, DS, MC, V.

D

★★ **POMODORO RESTAURANT.** *2440 E Ft Union Blvd (84121), downtown. 801/944-1895.* Hrs: 5:30-10 pm; Fri, Sat 5-11 pm. Closed Mon; most major hols. Res accepted. Italian menu. Bar. Semi-a la carte: dinner $10.50-$21.50. Specializes in seafood, pasta, garlic mashed potatoes. Own pastas, desserts. Cozy atmosphere; fireplace. Totally nonsmoking. Cr cds: A, C, D, DS, MC, V.

D

✓★ **QUILA'S.** *935 E Fort Union Blvd (84047), 9 mi S on I-15. 801/566-9313.* Hrs: 11 am-10 pm; Fri, Sat to 11 pm; Sun from 10 am; Sun brunch to 2:30 pm. Closed Thanksgiving, Dec 25. Res accepted. Mexican menu. Bar. Buffet: lunch $6.95. Semi-a la carte: lunch $4.99-$7.99, dinner $6.99-$10.99. Sun brunch $10.95. Child's meals. Specialties: fajitas with homemade tortillas, shrimp & fish tacos. Own baking. Guitarist Fri, Sat, Sun brunch. 1940s Mexican roadhouse decor. Totally nonsmoking. Cr cds: A, C, D, DS, JCB, MC, V.

D

✓★ **RAFAEL'S MEXICAN RESTAURANT.** *889 E 9400 S (84094), S on I-15, exit 9000 South St, then 2 mi E, in Aspen Plaza. 801/561-4545.* Hrs: 11:30 am-9 pm; Fri, Sat to 10 pm. Closed Sun; some major hols. Mexican menu. Semi-a la carte: lunch, dinner $4.50-$10. Specializes in enchiladas, fajitas. Mexican, Indian and Aztec artwork. Cr cds: C, DS, MC, V.

D

✓★ **REDBONES.** *2207 S 700 East St (84106), east of downtown. 801/463-4800.* Web www.redbones.com. Hrs: 11:30 am-9 pm; Fri, Sat to 10 pm; Sun noon-8 pm. Closed most major hols; July 24. Barbecue menu. Beer. Semi-a la carte: lunch, dinner $4.95-$14.95. Specializes in spare ribs, pulled pork, chicken. Outdoor dining. Features architecture of Southern Utah. Separate motorcycle parking; motorcycle on display indoors. Totally nonsmoking. Cr cds: A, C, D, DS, MC, V.

D

★★ **RINO'S ITALIAN RISTORANTE.** *2302 Parleys Way (84109), east of downtown. 801/484-0901.* Hrs: 6-10 pm; Fri, Sat 5:30-10:30 pm; Sun 5-9 pm. Closed major hols. Res accepted. Italian, continental menu. Serv bar. Semi-a la carte: dinner $9.99-$24.99. Patio dining. Bistro-style cafe. Cr cds: A, C, MC, V.

D

✓★★ **RIO GRANDE CAFE.** *270 S Rio Grande St (84101), downtown. 801/364-3302.* Hrs: 11 am-2:30 pm, 5-9:30 pm; Fri to 10:30 pm; Sat 11:30 am-2:30 pm, 5-10:30 pm; Sun 4-9 pm. Closed major hols. Mexican menu. Bar. Semi-a la carte: lunch, dinner $5-$9. Child's meals. Specializes in carnitas, traditional Mexican dishes. Outdoor dining. In historic Rio Grande Depot also housing RR museum and displays. Totally nonsmoking. Cr cds: A, C, D, DS, MC, V.

D

★★★ **SPENCER'S FOR STEAKS & CHOPS.** *(See Doubletree) 801/238-4748.* Hrs: 11:30-1:30 am; Sat, Sun from 4 pm. Res accepted. Bar. Wine cellar. A la carte entrees: lunch $6.95-$19.95, dinner $12.95-$29.95. Child's meals. Specializes in steaks, seafood, desserts. Valet parking. Classic Chicago-style steakhouse. Cr cds: A, C, D, DS, MC, V.

D

✓★ **SQUATTERS PUB BREWERY.** *147 W 300 S (84101), downtown. 801/363-2739.* E-mail callen@squatters.com; web www.squatters.com. Hrs: 11:30-12:30 am; Sun to 11:30 pm. Closed Thanksgiving, Dec 25. Bar. Semi-a la carte: lunch, dinner $6.99-$13.99. Child's meals. Specializes in burgers, sandwiches. Own baking, pasta. Guitarist Wed-Sat. Turn-of-the-century bldg; microbrewery. Totally nonsmoking. Cr cds: A, C, D, DS, MC, V.

D

★★ **TUCCI'S CUCINA ITALIANA.** *4835 S Highland Dr (84117), downtown. 801/277-8338.* Hrs: 11:30 am-10 pm; Fri, Sat to 11 pm; Sun noon-9 pm. Closed Thanksgiving, Dec 25. Italian menu. Bar. Semi-a la carte: lunch $5.95-$9.95, dinner $5.95-$18.95. Child's meals. Specialties: pizza tradizionale, farfalle con sugo blanco, picatta. Outdoor dining. Colorful decor. Totally nonsmoking. Cr cds: A, C, D, DS, MC, V.

D

★★★ **TUSCANY.** *2832 E 6200 S (84121), I-215 to Holladay, east of downtown . 801/277-9919.* Web www.citysearch.com. Hrs: 11:30 am-2:30 pm, 5-10 pm; Fri to 10:30 pm; Sat 5-10:30 pm; Sun 5-9 pm. Closed most major hols. Res accepted. Italian menu. Bar. Wine list. Semi-a la carte: lunch $7-$13, dinner $11-$23. Child's meals. Specialties: linguini with clams, pesto-crusted salmon, double-cut pork chop. Own baking, pasta. Valet parking. Outdoor dining. Italian villa decor with several unique dining rms; landscaped, wooded grounds near Big Cottonwood Canyon. Cr cds: A, C, D, MC, V.

D

★★ **XIAO LI.** *307 W 200 S #1000 (84101), downtown. 801/328-8688.* Web www.citysearch.com. Hrs: 11:30 am-2:30 pm, 4:30-10 pm; Fri to 11 pm; Sat 4:30-11 pm; Sun 4:30-10 pm. Closed July 4, Dec 25. Chinese menu. Serv bar. A la carte entrees: lunch, dinner $7-$12. Buffet: lunch $8. Specialties: salt & pepper shrimp, house special tofu, eggplant in garlic sauce. Parking. Oriental decor. Totally nonsmoking. Cr cds: A, C, D, DS, MC, V.

D

Unrated Dining Spot

LITZA'S FOR PIZZA. *716 E 400 South St, downtown. 801/359-5352.* Hrs: 11 am-11 pm; Fri, Sat to 12:30 am. Closed Sun; Thanksgiving, Dec 25. Italian menu. Semi-a la carte: lunch $5.15-$11, dinner $8-$15, specializes in pizza. Cr cds: C.

Snowbird (C-3)

(See also Alta, Park City, Salt Lake City)

Pop 150 (est) **Area Code** 435 **Zip** 84092

In 1971, a Texas oil man recognized the potential of Little Cottonwood Canyon in the Wasatch National Forest and developed the area as a ski resort. At one time home to thriving mining communities, today the resort village of Snowbird, 29 miles east of Salt Lake City, offers year-round recreational activities.

What to See and Do

Snowbird Ski and Summer Resort. Seven double chairlifts; high-speed quad; 125-passenger aerial tram; patrol, school, rentals; restaurants, cafeteria, bar, children's center, 4 lodges. Elevations of 7,900-11,000 ft. (Mid-Nov-early-May, daily) Summer activities (June-Oct, daily) include rock climbing, hiking, mountain biking (rentals), tennis; tram rides; concerts (see SEASONAL EVENTS). On UT 210. Contact PO Box 929000; phone 435/742-2222 or 800/453-3000 (res). Lifts ¢¢¢¢¢; Summer tram ¢¢¢

Seasonal Event

Utah Symphony. Snowbird Ski and Summer Resort (see). Summer home of the orchestra. Several Sun afternoon concerts. July-Aug.

Motor Hotels

★★★ **CLIFF LODGE.** *716 E 400 South St (84092), 2 blks W of Snowbird Plaza Ctr. 801/742-2222; FAX 801/933-2119; res: 800/453-3000.* 159 rms, 11 story, 125 kits. Mid-Dec-Mar: S, D $179; kit. suites $194-$532; each addl $10; lower rates rest of yr. Closed 1 wk Nov, 1 wk May. Crib $10/wk. TV; cable (premium), VCR avail. 2 heated pools; whirlpool. Supervised child's activities (May-Oct). Restaurant 6-10 pm. Ck-out 10 am. Coin Indry. Meeting rm. Business servs avail. Bellhops. Valet serv. Tennis, pro (summer). Airport transportation. Downhill ski on site; x-country ski 1 mi. Exercise equipt; sauna, steam rm. Rec rm. Fireplaces. Balconies. Scenic views. Cr cds: A, C, D, DS, JCB, MC, V.

D SC

★★★ **LODGE AT SNOWBIRD.** *Cliff Lodge Entry Level 4 (84092), opp Snowbird Plaza Ctr. 801/742-2222; FAX 801/933-2119; res: 800/453-3000.* Web www.snowbird.com. 120 rms, 7 story, 61 kits. No A/C. Late Nov-early May: S, D $229; suites $498; kit. studio rms $269; package plans. Crib free. TV; cable (premium), VCR avail. Heated pool; whirlpool. Saunas. Playground. Supervised child's activities (Nov-May). Restaurant 4-10 pm (winter). Bar 3 pm-1 am. Ck-out 11 am. Coin Indry. Business servs avail. Bellhops. Valet serv. Downhill ski on site; x-country ski 1 mi. Fireplaces. Balconies. Cr cds: A, C, D, DS, JCB, MC, V.

SC

Hotel

★★★ **CLIFF LODGE.** *Cliff Lodge Entry # 4 (UT 210) (84092), just E of Snowbird Plz Ctr. 801/742-2222; FAX 801/933-2119; res: 800/453-3000.* Web www.snowbird.com. 370 rms, 13 story. Dec-Mar: S, D $229-$289; suites $389-$939; under 12 free; ski packages; lower rates rest of yr. TV; cable, VCR avail. 2 heated pools, 1 rooftop; whirlpool, poolside serv. Supervised child's activities; ages infant-13. Restaurant. Private club noon-1 am; entertainment. Ck-out 11 am. Coin Indry. Convention facilities. Business center. Concierge. Gift shop. Barber, beauty shop. Free garage; free valet parking. Airport transportation. Tennis. Downhill ski on site; x-country ski 1 mi. Exercise rm; sauna, steam rm. Game rm. Rec rm. Some refrigerators. Some private patios. Picnic tables. Tram allows bicycles. Cr cds: A, C, D, DS, JCB, MC, V.

D

Restaurant

★★ **STEAK PIT.** *Snowbird Ctr (84092), in Snowbird Plaza Ctr. 801/933-2260.* Web www.snowbird.com. Hrs: 6-10 pm. No A/C. Serv bar. Semi-a la carte: dinner $14-$42. Child's meals. Specializes in steak, seafood, chicken. Mountain view. Cr cds: A, C, D, DS, JCB, MC, V.

D SC

St George (H-1)

Founded 1861 **Pop** 28,502 **Elev** 2,761 ft **Area Code** 435 **Zip** 84770

Information Washington County Travel & Convention Bureau, 425 S 700 East, Dixie Center, 84770; 435/634-5747 or 800/869-6635

Extending themselves to this hot, arid corner of southwest Utah, members of the Mormon Church built their first temple here and struggled to survive by growing cotton—hence the nickname "Dixie." With determination and persistence, members of the Church struggled against odds to construct the temple. The site, chosen by Brigham Young, turned out to be a bog, but another site was not selected. Instead, hundreds of tons of rocks were pounded into the mud until a stable foundation could be laid. Mormons from the north worked 40-day missions, and southern church members gave one day's labor in 10 until the temple was complete. The workers quarried 17,000 tons of rock by hand. A team of oxen hauled the stones to the construction site, and for seven straight days, timber was hauled more than 80 miles from Mount Trumbull to construct the structure. Made of red sandstone plastered to a gleaming white, the Mormon temple is not only the town's landmark, but also a beacon for passing aircraft.

In St George, warm summers are balanced by mild winters and a long growing season. Tourists and sportsmen bring in important business. The seat of Washington County, St George is the closest town of its size to Zion National Park (see). A Ranger District office of the Dixie National Forest (see CEDAR CITY) is located here.

What to See and Do

Brigham Young Winter Home (1873). Two-story adobe house where the Mormon leader spent the last four winters of his life; period furnishings, garden. (Daily; closed Dec 25) 200 North & 100 West Sts. Phone 435/673-2517 or 435/673-5181. **Free**

Daughters of Utah Pioneers Collection. Regional memorabilia. (Daily exc Sun; closed hols) Memorial Bldg, 143 N 100 East. Phone 435/628-7274. **Donation**

Jacob Hamblin Home (1863). Native sandstone house of Hamblin, Mormon missionary to Native Americans for 32 yrs; pioneer furnishings. (Daily; closed Dec 25) 5 mi W off I-15, in Santa Clara. Phone 435/673-2161 or 435/673-5181. **Free**

Pine Valley Chapel. White frame meeting house built in 1868 as an upside-down ship by Ebenezer Bryce, a shipbuilder by trade. The walls were completed on the ground, then raised and joined with wooden pegs and rawhide. Still in use, the chapel served as both church and schoolhouse until 1919. (Memorial Day-Labor Day, daily) 30 mi N via UT 18, Central exit, in Dixie National Forest. **Free**

State parks.

Gunlock. Approx 450 undeveloped acres in scenic red rock country. A dam across the Santa Clara River has created a 240-acre lake, which offers swimming, waterskiing; fishing; boating (ramp). Picnicking. Primitive camping; no drinking water. (Daily) 16 mi NW on Old Hwy 91. Phone 435/628-2255. **Free**

Snow Canyon. Flat-bottomed gorge cut into multicolored Navajo sandstone; massive erosional forms, sand dunes, Native American petroglyphs. Hiking. Picnicking. Improved camping areas (some hookups, dump station), trailer parking. (Daily) Standard fees. 10 mi N on UT 18. Phone 435/628-2255 or 800/322-3770 (reservations).

Tabernacle. Red sandstone structure built 1863-1876 with local materials; resembles colonial New England church. (Daily; closed Dec 25) Main & Tabernacle Sts. Phone 435/628-4072. **Free**

Temple Visitor Center. On grounds of temple; guided tour of center explains local history and beliefs of the Latter-day Saints; audiovisual program. (Daily; closed Dec 25) 490 S 300 East. Phone 435/673-5181. **Free**

Zion National Park (see). 42 mi NE on UT 9.

Motels

✓★ **AMBASSADOR INN.** *1481 S Sunland Dr (84770), near Municipal Airport. 435/673-7900; FAX 435/673-8325; res: 800/221-2222.* 68 rms, shower only, 2 story. Apr-Nov: S $38-$45; D $45-$55; under 18 free; higher rates Easter; lower rates rest of yr. Crib free. TV; cable. Heated pool; whirlpool. Restaurant nearby. Ck-out noon. Business servs avail. Cr cds: A, C, D, DS, JCB, MC, V.

D SC

★★ **BEST WESTERN CORAL HILLS.** *125 E St George Blvd (84770). 435/673-4844; FAX 435/673-5352; res: 800/528-1234; res: 800/542-7733.* Web www.coralhills.com. 98 rms, 2 story. Feb-Oct: S $42-$58; D $49-$60; each addl $4; suites $69-$99; under 18 free; lower rates rest of yr. Crib $4. TV; cable. 2 pools, 1 indoor; wading pool, whirlpool. Complimentary continental bkfst. Restaurant opp 6 am-9:30 pm. Ck-out 11 am. Meeting rms. Business servs avail. Exercise equipt. Putting green. Rec rm. Refrigerators. Some balconies. Cr cds: C.

✓★ **CLARIDGE INN.** *1187 S Bluff St (84770). 435/673-7222; FAX 435/634-0773; res: 800/367-3790.* 50 rms, 2 story. S, D $34-$54. Crib $3. TV; cable. Heated pool; whirlpool. Restaurant adj open 24 hrs. Ck-out 11 am. Business servs avail. Totally nonsmoking. Cr cds: A, C, DS, MC, V.

D

★★ **COMFORT SUITES.** *1239 S Main St. (84770). 435/673-7000; FAX 435/628-4340; res: 800/245-8602.* E-mail comfort@infowest.com; web www.comfortsuites.net. 122 units, 2 story. Feb-Aug: S, D $59-$89; under 18 free; higher rates: Easter, early Oct; lower rates rest of yr. Crib free. TV; cable. Heated pool; whirlpool. Complimentary continental bkfst. Restaurant opp open 24 hrs. Ck-out 11 am. Meeting rms. Business servs avail. Refrigerators, microwaves. Cr cds: A, C, D, DS, MC, V.

D SC

★★ **FOUR SEASONS HOWARD JOHNSON.** *747 E Saint George (84771). 435/673-6111; FAX 435/673-0994; res: 800/635-4441.* 95 rms, 2 story. S, D $45-$75; each addl $5; suites $80-$135; under 12 free. TV; cable (premium). Indoor/outdoor pool; whirlpool. Complimentary continental bkfst. Restaurant 5-10 pm. Ck-out 11 am. Meeting rms. Sun deck. Cr cds: A, C, DS, MC, V.

SC

★★★ **HOLIDAY INN.** *850 S Bluff St (84770), near Municipal Airport. 435/628-4235; FAX 435/628-8157; res: 800/457-9800.* E-mail sgeut@infowest.com; web www.infowest.com/holidayinn/. 164 rms, 2 story. S, D $64-$99; each addl $8; suites $100-$140; under 19 free. Crib free. TV; cable (premium). Indoor/outdoor pool; whirlpool. Restaurant 6 am-10 pm. Rm serv. Ck-out 11 am. Coin lndry. Meeting rms. Business servs avail. In-rm modem link. Bellhops. Shopping arcade. Airport transportation. Lighted tennis. Putting green. Exercise equipt. Game rm. Some refrigerators. Balconies. Cr cds: A, C, D, DS, JCB, MC, V.

D SC

★★ **SINGLETREE INN.** *260 E St George Blvd (84770). 435/673-6161; FAX 435/674-2406; res: 800/528-8890.* 48 rms, 2 story. S, D $46-$56. Crib free. Pet accepted; $5. TV; cable. Heated pool; whirlpool. Continental bkfst. Restaurant adj 11:30 am-10 pm. Ck-out 11 am. Business servs avail. Cr cds: A, C, DS, MC, V.

D SC

✓★ **SUN TIME INN.** *420 E St George Blvd (84770). 435/673-6181; res: 800/237-6253.* 46 rms, 2 story. S $28-$60; D $39-$85; each addl $4; under 16 free; wkly rates. Crib free. TV; cable. Heated pool. Restaurant adj 10 am-9:30 pm. Ck-out 11 am. Some refrigerators. Cr cds: A, C, DS, MC, V.

D SC

✓★ **TRAVELODGE.** *175 N 1000 E (84770). 435/673-4621; FAX 435/675-2635.* 40 rms, 2 story. S $36-$49; D $44-$59; each addl $6; suites $76; under 18 free. Crib free. Pet accepted; $5. TV; cable. Heated pool. Coffee in rms. Restaurant adj open 24 hrs. Ck-out noon. Business servs avail. Some refrigerators. Cr cds: A, C, D, DS, ER, JCB, MC, V.

SC

Inn

★★★ **GREENE GATE VILLAGE.** *76 W Tabernacle St (84770). 435/628-6999; FAX 435/628-6989; res: 800/350-6999.* E-mail stay@greenegate.net; web www.greenegate.com. 20 rms, 1-2 story, 7 suites, 1 full house, 3 kit. units. S, D, suites $55-$125; each addl $10-$25; kit. units $65-$125; wkly, monthly rates. Crib free. TV; cable (premium), VCR avail (movies $2). Pool; whirlpool. Complimentary full bkfst. Dining rm Thurs-Sat 6-8 pm. Ck-out 11 am, ck-in 3 pm. Business servs avail. Free airport, bus depot transportation. Balconies; some fireplaces. Picnic tables, grills. Consists of 8 Victorian and pioneer houses from late 1800s; library, sitting rm, antiques, tole-painted furnishings. Totally nonsmoking. Cr cds: A, C, D, DS, MC, V.

D

Restaurants

★★★ **ANDELIN'S GABLE HOUSE.** *290 E St George Blvd (84770). 435/673-6796.* Hrs: 11:30 am-10 pm. Closed Sun; Jan 1, Thanksgiving, Dec 24 eve, Dec 25. Res accepted. Semi-a la carte: lunch $5.95-$9.95. Complete meals: dinner $6.95-$24.95. Child's meals. Specializes in prime rib, rack of pork, fresh fish. Own baking. Old English decor, antiques. Old family recipes. Totally nonsmoking. Cr cds: A, C, DS, MC, V.

★ **DICK'S CAFE.** *114 E St George Blvd (84770). 435/673-3841.* Hrs: 6:30 am-8:30 pm; Fri, Sat to 9 pm; Sun to 2 pm. Semi-a la carte: bkfst $2-$7; lunch $3.50-$6, dinner $5-$12. Child's meals. Specializes in steak, chicken, seafood. Western decor. Since 1935. Gift shop. Cr cds: A, C, DS, MC, V.

Timpanogos Cave National Monument (D-3)

(See also Heber City, Park City, Provo)

(26 mi S of Salt Lake City on I-15, then 10 mi E on UT 92)

Timpanogos (Tim-pa-NOH-gos) Cave National Monument consists of three small, beautifully decorated underground chambers within limestone beds. The cave entrance is on the northern slope of Mt Timpanogos, monarch of the Wasatch Range. Much of the cave interior is covered by a filigree of colorful crystal formations where stalactities and stalagmites are common. However, what makes Timpanogos unique is its large number of helictites—formations that appear to defy gravity as they grow outward from the walls of the cave. Temperature in Timpanogos Cave is a constant 45°F, and the interior is electrically lighted.

The cave's headquarters are located on UT 92, 8 mi E of American Fork. There is picnicking at Swinging Bridge Picnic Area, ¼ mi from the headquarters. The cave entrance is 1½ miles from headquarters via a paved trail with a vertical rise of 1,065 feet. Allow 3-5 hours for guided tour. No pets; no strollers; walking shoes advised; jackets and sweaters needed. Tours limited to 20 people (late May-early Sept, daily). Purchase tickets in advance by calling 801/756-5238 or 801/756-1679, or at the Visitor Center. Golden Age and Golden Access passports accepted (see MAKING THE MOST OF YOUR TRIP). For information contact the Superintendent, RR 3, Box 200, American Fork 84003; 435/756-5238. Cave tours ¢¢¢

Vernal (D-6)

(See also Roosevelt)

Pop 6,644 **Elev** 5,336 ft **Area Code** 435 **Zip** 84078
E-mail dinoland@ubtanet.com **Web** www.dinoland.com

Information Dinosaurland Travel Board, 25 E Main St; 435/789-6932 or 800/477-5558

This is the county seat of Uintah County in northeastern Utah, which boasts oil, natural gas and many mineral deposits. A trading center for sheep and cattle, Vernal is in an area of ancient geologic interest. Nearby are beautiful canyons, striking rock formations and majestic peaks. Headquarters and a Ranger District office of the Ashley National Forest is located here.

What to See and Do

Ashley National Forest. The High Uinta Mountains—the only major east-west range in the US—runs through the heart of this nearly 1.5 million-acre forest. The 1,500-ft-deep Red Canyon, the 13,528-ft Kings Peak and Sheep Creek Geological Area are also here. Swimming; fishing; boating (ramps, marinas), whitewater rafting and canoeing. Hiking and nature trails. Cross-country skiing, snowmobiling. Improved or back country campgrounds (fee). Visitor centers. 15 mi N on US 191. For further information contact the Supervisor, 355 N Vernal Ave; phone 435/789-1181. **Free**

Daughters of Utah Pioneers Museum. Relics and artifacts dating from before 1847, when pioneers first settled in Utah; period furniture, quilts, clothing; dolls; early doctor's, dentist's and undertaker's instruments; restored Little Rock tithing office (1887). (June-wkend before Labor Day, daily exc Sun) 500 West 200 South. Phone 435/789-3890. **Donation**

Dinosaur National Monument (see). 13 mi SE on US 40, then 7 mi N on UT 149.

Flaming Gorge Dam and National Recreation Area. Area surrounds 91-mi-long Flaming Gorge Reservoir and 502-ft-high Flaming Gorge Dam. Fishing on reservoir & river (all yr); marinas, boat ramps, waterskiing; lodges; campgrounds (fee). River rafting below dam. Visitor centers at dam and Red Canyon (on secondary paved road 3 mi off UT 44). 42 mi N on US 191, in Ashley National Forest. For information contact the Ranger District office, PO Box 279, Manila 84046; phone 435/784-3445.

Ouray National Wildlife Refuge. Waterfowl nesting marshes; desert scenery; self-guided auto tour (limited route during hunting season). (Daily) 30 mi SW on UT 88. Phone 435/789-0351. **Free**

River trips. Guided whitewater trips on the Green and Yampa rivers.

Adrift Adventures of Dinosaur. Phone 800/824-0150. ¢¢¢¢¢

Hatch River Expeditions. Phone 435/789-4316 or 800/342-8243. ¢¢¢¢¢

Holiday River and Bike Expeditions. Phone 435/266-2087 or 800/624-6323 (exc UT). ¢¢¢¢¢

Steinaker State Park. Approx 2,200 acres on west shore of Steinaker Reservoir. Swimming, waterskiing; fishing; boating (ramp, dock). Picnicking. Tent & trailer sites (fee). (Apr-Nov; fishing all yr) 7 mi N off US 191. Phone 435/789-4432. Per vehicle ¢¢

Utah Field House of Natural History and Dinosaur Gardens. Guarded outside by 3 life-size cement dinosaurs, this museum has exhibits of fossils, archaeology, life zones, geology and fluorescent minerals of the region. Adj Dinosaur Gardens contain 18 life-size model dinosaurs in natural surroundings. (Daily; closed Jan 1, Thanksgiving, Dec 25) 235 Main St. Phone 435/789-3799. ¢

Western Heritage Museum. Houses memorabilia from Uintah County's "outlaw" past as well as other artifacts dealing with a western theme. Includes the Thorne Collection, a collection of photographs and artifacts of the ancient people of Utah. (Daily exc Sun; closed hols) 302 E 200 S. Phone 435/789-7399. **Free**

Annual Events

Outlaw Trail Festival. Festivals, sporting events, entertainment, theatrical events. Late June-mid Aug.

Dinosaur Roundup Rodeo. Mid-July.

Uintah County Fair. Aug.

Motels

★ **WESTON PLAZA HOTEL.** *1684 W Hwy 40 (84078). 435/789-9550; FAX 435/789-4874.* 102 rms, 3 story. S, D $48-$56; each addl $8; suites $95; under 12 free; wkend rates. TV; cable (premium). Indoor pool; whirlpool. Continental bkfst. Restaurant 5-9 pm. Bar to 1 am; entertainment exc Sun (summer). Ck-out 11 am. Meeting rms. Business servs avail. Airport, bus depot transportation. Cr cds: A, C, D, MC, V.

D SC

✓★ **WESTONS LAMPLIGHTER INN.** *120 E Main St (84078). 435/789-0312; FAX 435/781-1480.* 167 rms, 2 story. May-Aug: S $36; D $46; each addl $8; under 12 free; lower rates rest of yr. TV; cable (premium). Heated pool. Playground. Restaurant hrs vary. Ck-out 11 am. Business servs avail. Beauty shop. Airport transportation. Picnic tables, grills. Cr cds: A, C, D, MC, V.

SC

Restaurant

★ **7-11 RANCH.** *77 E Main St (84078), on US 40. 435/789-1170.* E-mail ranch711@easlink.com. Hrs: 6 am-11 pm. Closed Sun; Jan 1, Thanksgiving, Dec 25. Res accepted. Semi-a la carte: bkfst $2-$6.45, lunch $4-$7, dinner $7.50-$12.50. Child's meals. Specializes in roasted chicken, barbecue ribs. Western motif; gift shop. Family-owned. Totally nonsmoking. Cr cds: C, MC, V.

D

Wendover (C-1)

Founded 1907 **Pop** 1,127 **Elev** 4,232 ft **Area Code** 435 **Zip** 84083

Half in Utah, half in Nevada, Wendover lies on the western edge of the Great Salt Lake Desert. The town was settled to serve the Western Pacific Railroad, which cut a historic route through here across the Bonneville Salt Flats. Accommodations can be found on both sides of the state line, but gambling is allowed only in Nevada. Blue Lake, 30 miles south, provides water at a constant temperature of 75° F for scuba diving and is open to the public (no facilities).

What to See and Do

Bonneville Salt Flats. This approx 100-sq-mi area of perfectly flat salt, packed as solid as cement, is what remained after ancient Lake Bonneville, which once covered the entire area, retreated to the present-day Great Salt Lake. The area is part of the Great Salt Lake Desert. E of town.

Annual Event

Bonneville National Speed Trials. Bonneville Speedway, approx 15 mi E, then N. Held since 1914 on the Bonneville Salt Flats (see), which has been used as a track for racing the world's fastest cars. Car racing in competition and against the clock. Phone 805/526-1805. Aug or Sept.

Hotel

✓★★ **STATE LINE/SILVER SMITH HOTEL-CASINO.** *100 Wendover Blvd (84083), 1 mi W on I-80 Business (Wendover Blvd). 702/664-2221; FAX 702/531-4090; res: 800/848-7300.* 500 rms, 5 story. S, D $39-$54; each addl $5; suites $50-$130; under 12 free; higher rates wkends. Crib free. TV; cable, VCR avail. Heated pool. Restaurant open 24 hrs. Bars; entertainment. Ck-out noon. Meeting rms. Business servs avail. Gift shop. Free airport transportation. Tennis privileges. Game rm. Casinos. Cr cds: A, C, D, DS, MC, V.

D

Zion National Park (H-2)

(See also Cedar City, Kanab, St George)

(42 mi NE of St George on UT 9)

The spectacular canyons and enormous rock formations in this 147,551-acre national park are the result of powerful upheavals of the earth and erosion by flowing water and frost. Considered the "grandfather" of Utah's national parks, Zion is one of the nation's oldest national parks and one of the state's wildest, with large sections virtually inaccessible. The Virgin River runs through the interior of the park, and Zion Canyon, with its deep, narrow chasm and multicolored, vertical walls, cuts through the middle, with smaller canyons branching from it like fingers. A paved roadway following the bottom of Zion Canyon is surrounded by massive rock formations in awe-inspiring colors that change with the light. The formations, described as temples, cathedrals and thrones, rise to great heights, the loftiest reaching 8,726 feet. The canyon road runs seven miles to the Temple of Sinawava, a natural amphitheater surrounded by cliffs. Another route, an extension of UT 9, cuts through the park in an east-west direction, taking visitors through the mile-long Zion-Mt Carmel Tunnel, then descends through a series of switchbacks with viewpoints above Pine Creek Canyon. **Note:** An escort fee is charged for large vehicles to pass through tunnel.

Zion's main visitor center is near the south entrance (daily). Check here for maps, information on the park and schedules of naturalist activities and evening programs. Each evening, spring through fall, park naturalists give illustrated talks on the natural and human history of the area. Pets must be kept on leash and are not permitted on trails. Vehicle lights should be checked; they must be in proper condition for driving through highway tunnel. The park is open year round. There is an admission fee of $10/7-day stay per vehicle; Golden Eagle Passport is accepted (see MAKING THE MOST OF YOUR TRIP). For further information contact Superintendent, Springdale 84767-1099; 435/772-3256.

What to See and Do

Bicycling is permitted on roads in park, except through Zion-Mt Carmel Tunnel. Roads are narrow and no designated bicycle routes exist.

Camping. At south entrance to park: South Campground provides 140 tent or trailer sites (mid-Apr-mid-Sept); Watchman Campground provides 229 tent sites and 185 trailer sites (all yr). Lava Point Campground, 26 mi N of Virgin off UT 9, provides a minimal number of tent sites (free; no facilities). South & Watchman campgrounds **¢¢¢**

Escorted horseback trips. (Mar-Oct, daily) Special guide service may be obtained for other trips not regularly scheduled. Contact Bryce/Zion Trail Rides at Zion Lodge. Phone 435/772-3967 or 435/679-8665 (off-season).

"Grand Circle: A National Park Odyssey." Multimedia presentation encompassing 4 states, 14 national parks and monuments and numerous state parks and historic sites, plus Glen Canyon National Recreation Area (see PAGE, AZ and LAKE POWELL, UT) and Monument Valley Navajo Tribal Park (see KAYENTA, AZ). One-hr show (Memorial Day-Labor Day). O.C. Tanner Amphitheatre in Springdale. Phone 435/673-4811, ext 276. **¢¢**

Guided trips, hiking tours conducted by ranger naturalists, who explain geology, plant life and history.

Kolob Canyons Visitor Center (see CEDAR CITY).

Mountain climbing should be undertaken with great care due to unstable sandstone. Climbers should consult with a ranger at the park Visitor Center.

Park trails lead to otherwise inaccessible areas: the Narrows (walls of this canyon are 2,000 ft high and as little as 50 ft apart at the stream), the Hanging Gardens of Zion, Weeping Rock, the Emerald Pools. Trails range from ½-mi trips to day-long treks, some requiring tested stamina. Trails in less traveled areas should not be undertaken without first obtaining information from a park ranger. Back country permits required for travel through the Virgin River Narrows and other canyons, and on all overnight trips (fee/person/night).

Zion Nature Center. Junior Ranger program for children ages 6-12. (Memorial Day-Labor Day, Mon-Fri) Adj to South Campground. ¢

Motels

★★ **CLIFFROSE LODGE & GARDENS.** *281 Zions Park Bl (84767). 435/772-3234; FAX 435/772-3900; res: 800/243-8824.* 36 rms, 2 story. May-mid-Oct: S, D $119-$145; suites $145; each addl $10; under 18 free; lower rates rest of yr. Crib $6. Pet accepted; $10. TV; cable (premium), VCR avail. Pool. Playground. Complimentary coffee in lobby. Restaurant nearby. Ck-out 11 am. Picnic tables. Cr cds: A, C, DS, MC, V.

D

★★ **DRIFTWOOD LODGE.** *1515 Zion Park Blvd (84767), on SR 9, 2 mi S of park entrance. 435/772-3262; FAX 435/772-3702; res: 888/801-8811.* E-mail drftwood@infowest.com; web www.drftwood-lodge.net. 47 rms, 1-2 story. S $70; D $80; each addl $4. Crib $2. Pet accepted. TV. Heated pool; whirlpool. Complimentary continental bkfst. Ck-out 11 am. Business servs avail. Gift shop. Private patios, balconies. Shaded grounds; good views of park. Cr cds: A, C, D, DS, MC, V.

D SC

★★ **FLANIGAN'S INN.** *428 Zion Park Blvd (84767), on UT 9, ¼ mi S of park entrance. 435/772-3244; FAX 435/772-3396; res: 800/765-7787.* E-mail info@flanigans.com; web www.flanigans.com. 32 rms, 1-2 story. Mid-Mar-mid-Nov: S, D $79-$139; each addl $5; lower rates rest of yr. Crib free. TV; cable (premium). Pet accepted; $25. Heated pool. Complimentary continental bkfst. Restaurant 5-10 pm. Ck-out 11 am. Small local artists' gallery. Cr cds: A, C, DS, MC, V.

D

★ **TERRACE BROOK LODGE.** *990 Zion Park Blvd (84767), on UT 9, 1 mi S of park entrance. 435/772-3932; FAX 435/772-3596; res: 800/542-6779.* 27 rms, 2 story. Apr-Oct: S $49; D $49-$55; each addl $4; lower rates rest of yr. Crib $4. TV; cable (premium). Heated pool. Restaurant nearby. Ck-out 11 am. Picnic tables, grills. Cr cds: C, DS, MC, V.

★★ **ZION LODGE.** *Zion National Park (84767), on UT 9, 5 mi N of park entrance. 435/772-2313; FAX 435/772-2001; res: 800/253-5896; res: 303/297-2757.* 75 rms in motel, 1-2 story, 40 cabins. S, D $83; each addl $5; suites $112; cabins $93. Crib $5. Restaurant 6:30-10 am, 11:30 am-3 pm, 6-10 pm. Ck-out 11 am. Business servs avail. Bellhops. Sundries. Gift shop. Private porches. Cr cds: A, C, D, DS, MC, V.

D

★ **ZION PARK MOTEL.** *855 Zion Park Blvd (84767), on UT 9, 1 mi W of park entrance. 435/772-3251.* 21 rms. S $45-$50; D $56-$66; kit. units $99; lower rates off-season. Crib $2. TV; cable. Heated pool. Playground. Restaurant adj 7 am-10 pm. Ck-out 11 am. Sundries. Picnic tables, grill. Cr cds: A, C, DS, MC, V.

Inns

★★★ **NOVEL HOUSE INN.** *73 Paradise Rd (84767). 435/772-3650; FAX 435/772-3651; res: 800/711-8400.* Web www.novelhouse.com. 10 rms, 2 story. S $75; D $85-$105. Children over 12 yrs only. TV; cable. Complimentary full bkfst. Cr cds: A, C, D, JCB, MC.

D SC

★★ **RED ROCK INN.** *998 Zion Park Blvd (84767), 1 mi SW of Zion National Park entrance. 435/772-3139; FAX 435/772-3697.* E-mail rrinn@infowest.com; web redrockinn.com. 5 cottages, 1 story. No rm phones. Apr-Oct: S $71-$115; D $75-$120; each addl $10; suites $115-$140; under 10 free; hols 2-day min; lower rates rest of yr. TV; cable (premium), VCR avail (movies). Complimentary full bkfst. Restaurant nearby. Ck-out 11 am, ck-in 4 pm. Business servs avail. Concierge serv. Gift shop. Massage. Some in-rm whirlpools; microwaves avail. View of canyon. Totally nonsmoking. Cr cds: A, C, DS, MC, V.

D

Appendix A

Restaurant List

Establishment names are listed in alphabetical order followed by a symbol identifying their classification, and then city and state. Establishments affiliated with a chain appear alphabetically under their chain name, followed by the state and city. The symbols for classification are: [R] for restaurants and [U] for unrated dining spots.

1 PICO [R] *Santa Monica, CA*
150 GRAND CAFE [R] *Escondido, CA*
21 OCEANFRONT [R] *Newport Beach, CA*
22ND STREET LANDING SEAFOOD [R] *San Pedro (L.A.), CA*
42 DEGREES [R] *San Francisco, CA*
7-11 RANCH [R] *Vernal, UT*
72 MARKET ST. OYSTER BAR & GRILL [R] *Santa Monica, CA*
A CELADON THAI RESTAURANT [R] *San Diego, CA*
A LA CARTE [R] *Laguna Beach, CA*
A. SABELLA'S [R] *San Francisco, CA*
A TOUCH OF MAMA'S [R] *Palm Desert, CA*
ABALONETTI SEAFOOD TRATTORIA [R] *Monterey, CA*
ACE WASABI'S ROCK & ROLL SUSHI [R] *San Francisco, CA*
ACQUERELLO [R] *San Francisco, CA*
ADELE'S RESTAURANT & LOUNGE [R] *Carson City, NV*
ADRIANA'S RISTORANTE [R] *San Rafael, CA*
AESOP'S TABLES [R] *San Diego, CA*
AFGHANISTAN KHYBER PASS [R] *San Diego, CA*
AJANTA RESTAURANT [R] *Berkeley, CA*
AL AMIR [R] *Los Angeles, CA*
ALAMO SQUARE SEAFOOD GRILL [R] *San Francisco, CA*
ALBION RIVER INN [R] *Mendocino, CA*
ALBONA RISTORANTE ISTRIANO [R] *San Francisco, CA*
ALDO'S [R] *Sacramento, CA*
ALEGRIA'S FOODS FROM SPAIN [R] *San Francisco, CA*
ALEX'S RESTAURANT & PUB [R] *Calistoga, CA*
ALL SEASONS CAFE [R] *Calistoga, CA*
ALTO PALATO TRATTORIA [R] *Hollywood (L.A.), CA*
AMARIN THAI CUISINE [R] *Monterey, CA*
AMBER INDIA [R] *Mountain View, CA*
AMELIA'S SEAFOOD & ITALIAN [R] *Newport Beach, CA*
AMERICAN GRILL [R] *Mesa, AZ*
ANDELIN'S GABLE HOUSE [R] *St George, UT*
ANDERSEN'S RESTAURANT [R] *Solvang, CA*
ANDRIA'S HARBORSIDE [R] *Santa Barbara, CA*
ANGELINO [R] *Sausalito, CA*
ANJOU [R] *San Francisco, CA*
ANNA'S ITALIAN RESTAURANT [R] *Los Angeles, CA*
ANNABELLE'S BAR & BISTRO [R] *San Francisco, CA*
ANNELIESE'S BAVARIAN INN [R] *Long Beach, CA*
ANTHONY'S FISH GROTTO [R] *San Diego, CA*
ANTHONY'S STAR OF THE SEA ROOM [R] *San Diego, CA*
ANTICA TRATTORIA [R] *San Francisco, CA*
ANTON & MICHEL [R] *Carmel, CA*
ANTONELLO [R] *Santa Ana, CA*
ANTONIO'S, *CA*
[R] *Hollywood (L.A.)*
ANTONIO'S, *NV*
[R] *Las Vegas*
ANTONIO'S PIZZERIA & CATALINA [R] *Avalon (Catalina Island), CA*
APPLE FARM [R] *San Luis Obispo, CA*
APPLEWOOD [R] *Guerneville, CA*
AQUA, *CA*
[R] *San Francisco*
AQUA, *NV*
[R] *Las Vegas*
ARIZONA KITCHEN [R] *Litchfield Park, AZ*
ARMSTRONG'S FISH MARKET & SEAFOOD [R] *Avalon (Catalina Island), CA*
ARNIE MORTON'S OF CHICAGO [R] *Los Angeles, CA*
ARSHEL'S CAFE [R] *Beaver, UT*
ASHOKA CUISINE OF INDIA [R] *La Jolla (San Diego), CA*
ATHENS MARKET TAVERNA [R] *San Diego, CA*
ATLANTIS [R] *Reno, NV*
ATRIUM, *AZ*
[R] *Sedona*
ATRIUM, *CA*
[R] *Corte Madera*
AUREOLE [R] *Las Vegas, NV*
AVANTI OF PHOENIX [R] *Phoenix, AZ*
AVANTI'S OF SCOTTSDALE [R] *Scottsdale, AZ*
AVENUE 9 [R] *San Francisco, CA*
AZZURA POINT [R] *Coronado, CA*
BABA AFGHAN [R] *Salt Lake City, UT*
BABETTE'S [R] *Sonoma, CA*
BABY KAY'S CAJUN KITCHEN [R] *Phoenix, AZ*
BACI RISTORANTE [R] *San Diego, CA*
BACI TRATTORIA [R] *Salt Lake City, UT*
BACIO TRATTORIA [R] *Woodland Hills (L.A.), CA*
BAILY WINE COUNTRY CAFE [R] *Temecula, CA*
BAKER STREET BISTRO [R] *San Francisco, CA*
BALBOA CAFE [R] *San Francisco, CA*
BANDERA [R] *Scottsdale, AZ*
BANK OF MEXICAN FOOD [R] *Temecula, CA*
BARBARA WORTH GOLF RESORT & CONVENTION CENTER [R] *El Centro, CA*
BARKING FROG GRILLE [R] *Salt Lake City, UT*
BASIL THAI RESTAURANT & BAR [R] *San Francisco, CA*
BASTA PASTA [R] *San Francisco, CA*
BATTISTA'S HOLE IN THE WALL [R] *Las Vegas, NV*
BAVARIAN CHALET [R] *Ogden, UT*
BAY CLUB [R] *Pebble Beach, CA*
BAY VIEW RESTAURANT [R] *Bodega Bay, CA*
BAY WOLF [R] *Oakland, CA*
BAYOU BAR & GRILL [R] *San Diego, CA*
BEACH HOUSE INN [R] *Laguna Beach, CA*
BECKHAM PLACE [R] *Pasadena, CA*
BELGIAN LION [R] *San Diego, CA*
BELLA LUNA [R] *San Diego, CA*
BELLA NAPOLI [R] *Page, AZ*
BELLA SARATOGA [R] *Saratoga, CA*
BELLEFLEUR [R] *Carlsbad, CA*
BELVEDERE, THE [R] *Beverly Hills, CA*
BENBOW INN [R] *Garberville, CA*
BENIHANA [R] *San Diego, CA*
BENIHANA OF TOKYO [R] *Salt Lake City, UT*
BERNARD'S, *CA*
[R] *Borrego Springs*, [R] *Los Angeles*
BERTOLINI'S [R] *Las Vegas, NV*
BETELNUT PEJIU WU [R] *San Francisco, CA*
BIBA [R] *Sacramento, CA*
BIG FOUR RESTAURANT [R] *San Francisco, CA*
BIG NOSE KATE'S SALOON [R] *Tombstone, AZ*
BIG YELLOW HOUSE [R] *Santa Barbara, CA*
BIRD ROCK CAFE [R] *La Jolla (San Diego), CA*
BISCUITS & BLUES [R] *San Francisco, CA*
BISTRO 201 [R] *Newport Beach, CA*
BISTRO 24 [R] *Phoenix, AZ*
BISTRO 45 [R] *Pasadena, CA*
BISTRO ALSACIENNE [R] *Mill Valley, CA*
BISTRO DON GIOVANNI [R] *Napa, CA*
BISTRO JEANTY [R] *Yountville, CA*
BISTRO RALPH [R] *Healdsburg, CA*
BITTERSWEET BISTRO [R] *Santa Cruz, CA*
BIX [R] *San Francisco, CA*
BIZOU [R] *San Francisco, CA*
BLUE CHALK CAFE [R] *Palo Alto, CA*
BLUE COYOTE [R] *Palm Springs, CA*
BLUE PARROT [R] *Avalon (Catalina Island), CA*
BLUE POINT, *CA*
[R] *San Diego*, [R] *San Francisco*
BLUE SHARK BISTRO [R] *Santa Barbara, CA*
BLUE WHALE LAKESIDE RESTAURANT [R] *Big Bear Lake, CA*
BLUE WILLOW [R] *Tucson, AZ*
BLUEBIRD [R] *Logan, UT*
BOB BURNS [R] *Santa Monica, CA*
BOBBY RUBINO'S [R] *San Francisco, CA*
BOCCA ROTIS RESTAURANT [R] *San Francisco, CA*
BOMBAY HOUSE [R] *Provo, UT*
BONTA RISTORANTE [R] *San Francisco, CA*
BOOK SOUP BISTRO [R] *Hollywood (L.A.), CA*
BORDER GRILL [R] *Santa Monica, CA*
BORREGO'S KITCHEN [R] *Borrego Springs, CA*
BOULEVARD [R] *San Francisco, CA*
BRAMBLES [R] *Cambria, CA*
BRANDING IRON STEAK HOUSE [R] *Show Low, AZ*
BRANNAN'S GRILL [R] *Calistoga, CA*
BRASSERIE [AT] LA COSTA RESORT [R] *Carlsbad, CA*
BRASSERIE SAVOY [R] *San Francisco, CA*
BRAVA TERRACE [R] *St Helena, CA*
BRICKS RESTAURANT & WINE BAR [R] *Reno, NV*
BRIDGES RESTAURANT & BAR [R] *Walnut Creek, CA*
BRIGANTINE [R] *Coronado, CA*
BRIGITTE'S RESTAURANT CAFE [R] *Santa Barbara, CA*
BRIX RESTAURANT [R] *Yountville, CA*
BROADWAY BAR & GRILL [R] *Santa Monica, CA*

BROADWAY DELI [R] *Santa Monica, CA*
BROCKTON VILLA [R] *La Jolla (San Diego), CA*
BROOKFIELD'S [R] *Rancho Cordova, CA*
BROWN DERBY [R] *Las Vegas, NV*
BUCCANEER BAY CLUB [R] *Las Vegas, NV*
BUCKEYE ROADHOUSE [R] *Mill Valley, CA*
BUDDY'S GRILL [R] *Tucson, AZ*
BUFFALO JOE'S SMOKEHOUSE [R] *Salt Lake City, UT*
BUNGALOW, THE [R] *Corona del Mar, CA*
BUON GIORNO [R] *Chula Vista, CA*
BUONA SERA [R] *Petaluma, CA*
BUSALACCHI'S [R] *San Diego, CA*
BUSTER'S RESTAURANT & BAR [R] *Flagstaff, AZ*
BUSTER'S RESTAURANT GRILL [R] *Scottsdale, AZ*
BUTCHER SHOP [R] *Chula Vista, CA*
BYBLOS RESTAURANT [R] *Tempe, AZ*
C-FU GOURMET [R] *Chandler, AZ*
CA BIANCA ITALIAN RESTAURANT [R] *Santa Rosa, CA*
CA'BREA [R] *Hollywood (L.A.), CA*
CACTI RESTAURANT [R] *San Rafael, CA*
CAFE AKIMBO [R] *San Francisco, CA*
CAFE AT SONOMA MISSION INN [R] *Sonoma, CA*
CAFE BASTILLE [R] *San Francisco, CA*
CAFE BEAUJOLAIS [R] *Mendocino, CA*
CAFE BERLIN [R] *Carmel, CA*
CAFE BERNARDO [R] *Davis, CA*
CAFE BIZOU [R] *Studio City (L.A.), CA*
CAFE CHAMPAGNE [R] *Temecula, CA*
CAFE CITTI [R] *Santa Rosa, CA*
CAFE COYOTE [R] *San Diego, CA*
CAFE FINA [R] *Monterey, CA*
CAFE JAPENGO [R] *La Jolla (San Diego), CA*
CAFE KATI [R] *San Francisco, CA*
CAFE KINYON [R] *Yountville, CA*
CAFE LAHAYE [R] *Sonoma, CA*
CAFE LATTE [R] *San Francisco, CA*
CAFE LOLO [R] *Santa Rosa, CA*
CAFE MARIMBA [R] *San Francisco, CA*
CAFE NICOLLE [R] *Las Vegas, NV*
CAFE PACIFICA [R] *San Diego, CA*
CAFE PESCATORE [R] *San Francisco, CA*
CAFE PINOT [R] *Los Angeles, CA*
CAFE POCA COSA [R] *Tucson, AZ*
CAFE RIGGIO [R] *San Francisco, CA*
CAFE ROMA [R] *San Luis Obispo, CA*
CAFE ROUGE [R] *Berkeley, CA*
CAFE SANTORINI [R] *Pasadena, CA*
CAFE SPARROW [R] *Santa Cruz, CA*
CAFE SWEETWATER [R] *Tucson, AZ*
CAFE TERRA COTTA, *AZ*
[R] *Scottsdale*, [R] *Tucson*
CAFE TIRAMISU [R] *San Francisco, CA*
CAFFE NAPOLI [R] *Carmel, CA*
CAIOTI [R] *Hollywood (L.A.), CA*
CALIFORNIA CAFE [R] *Corte Madera, CA*
CALIFORNIA CUISINE [R] *San Diego, CA*
CALISTOGA INN [R] *Calistoga, CA*
CAMELOT [R] *Las Vegas, NV*
CAMPANILE [R] *Los Angeles, CA*
CAMPTON PLACE DINING ROOM [R] *San Francisco, CA*
CANNERY RESTAURANT [R] *Newport Beach, CA*
CANTINA DEL PEDREGAL [R] *Carefree, AZ*
CAPITAL GRILLE, THE [R] *San Francisco, CA*
CAPITOL CAFE [R] *Salt Lake City, UT*
CAPRI RISTORANTE ITALIANO [R] *Woodland Hills (L.A.), CA*
CAPRICCIO [R] *Tucson, AZ*
CAPTAIN JON'S [R] *Tahoe Vista (Lake Tahoe Area), CA*
CARNELIAN ROOM [R] *San Francisco, CA*
CARSON NUGGET STEAK HOUSE [R] *Carson City, NV*
CARTA [R] *San Francisco, CA*
CARVER'S [R] *Henderson, NV*
CASA DE BANDINI [R] *San Diego, CA*
CASA MANANA [R] *Safford, AZ*
CASAMAR [R] *Ensenada, Baja California, Mexico, CA*
CASANOVA RESTAURANT [R] *Carmel, CA*
CASINO ROYAL [R] *Ensenada, Baja California, Mexico, CA*
CASK 'N CLEAVER [R] *Fallbrook, CA*
CASSELL'S [R] *Los Angeles, CA*
CASTLE ROCK CAFE [R] *Price, UT*
CAT & THE CUSTARD CUP [R] *La Habra, CA*
CATAHOULA [R] *Calistoga, CA*
CATALINA GRILLE [R] *Tucson, AZ*
CATCH, THE [R] *Anaheim, CA*
CATELLI'S THE REX [R] *Healdsburg, CA*
CATHAY HOUSE [R] *Las Vegas, NV*
CATTLEMAN'S WHARF [R] *Anaheim, CA*
CAVA RESTAURANT [R] *Los Angeles, CA*
CEDAR CREEK INN, *CA*
[R] *Laguna Beach*, [R] *Palm Desert*, [R] *Palm Springs*
CELADON [R] *Napa, CA*
CELLAR THE CUISINE FRANCAISE [R] *Fullerton, CA*
CENTER CAFE [R] *Moab, UT*
CHA CHA CHA [R] *San Francisco, CA*
CHAD'S STEAKHOUSE [R] *Tucson, AZ*
CHALET RESTAURANT & LOUNGE [R] *Pinetop, AZ*
CHAMELEON CAFE [R] *Coronado, CA*
CHANNEL HOUSE [R] *Avalon (Catalina Island), CA*
CHANTECLAIR [R] *Irvine, CA*
CHANTERELLE [R] *Sacramento, CA*
CHANTERELLE RESTAURANT [R] *Napa, CA*
CHAPALA [R] *Las Vegas, NV*
CHAPARRAL DINING ROOM [R] *Scottsdale, AZ*
CHARISMA CAFE [R] *Los Angeles Intl Airport Area, CA*
CHARLES [R] *Tucson, AZ*
CHARLES NOB HILL [R] *San Francisco, CA*
CHARLES STREET DINNER HOUSE [R] *Yosemite National Park, CA*
CHARLIE CLARK'S STEAK HOUSE [R] *Pinetop, AZ*
CHART HOUSE, *AZ*
[R] *Scottsdale*
CHART HOUSE, *CA*
[R] *Monterey*
CHART HOUSE, *NV*
[R] *Stateline*
CHATEAU CHANG [R] *Victorville, CA*
CHATEAU ORLEANS [R] *Pacific Beach (San Diego), CA*
CHATEAU SOUVERAIN [R] *Healdsburg, CA*
CHATTER BOY CAFE [R] *Jackson, CA*
CHECKERS [R] *Los Angeles, CA*
CHEF PAUL'S [R] *Oakland, CA*
CHEF'S PALACE [R] *Kanab, UT*
CHEZ LOMA [R] *Coronado, CA*
CHEZ MARC BISTRO [R] *Flagstaff, AZ*
CHEZ MELANGE [R] *Redondo Beach, CA*
CHEZ MICHEL [R] *San Francisco, CA*
CHEZ PANISSE RESTAURANT & CAFE [R] *Berkeley, CA*
CHEZ RENEE [R] *Santa Cruz, CA*
CHEZ SATEAU [R] *Arcadia, CA*
CHEZ T.J. [R] *Mountain View, CA*
CHIANTI RISTORANTE & CUCINA [R] *Hollywood (L.A.), CA*
CHIC'S SEAFOOD [R] *San Francisco, CA*
CHICAGO JOE'S [R] *Irvine, CA*
CHIEU-ANH [R] *San Diego, CA*
CHIMAYO GRILL [R] *Newport Beach, CA*
CHIN'S [R] *Las Vegas, NV*
CHINA CITY CAFE [R] *Price, UT*
CHINOIS [R] *Las Vegas, NV*
CHINOIS ON MAIN [R] *Santa Monica, CA*
CHOMPIE'S, *AZ*
[R] *Phoenix*, [R] *Scottsdale*
CHRISTINE [R] *Torrance, CA*
CHRISTOPHER'S BISTRO [R] *Phoenix, AZ*
CIAO BELLA [R] *Riverside, CA*
CIAO TRATTORIA [R] *Los Angeles, CA*
CIBO RISTORANTE ITALIANO [R] *Monterey, CA*
CIELO [R] *Big Sur, CA*
CILANTROS [R] *Del Mar, CA*
CINDY BLACK'S [R] *La Jolla (San Diego), CA*
CIPRIANI [R] *Las Vegas, NV*
CIRCO, OSTERIA DEL [R] *Las Vegas, NV*
CITRONELLE [R] *Santa Barbara, CA*
CITRUS RESTAURANT [R] *Hollywood (L.A.), CA*
CITY DELICATESSEN [R] *San Diego, CA*
CITY GRILL [R] *Tucson, AZ*
CITY HOTEL [R] *Sonora, CA*
CLEARMAN'S STEAK 'N STEIN INN [R] *San Gabriel, CA*
CLOCK GARDEN [R] *Monterey, CA*
CLUB 74 [R] *Palm Desert, CA*
CLUB XIX [R] *Pebble Beach, CA*
COFFEE TREE [R] *Vacaville, CA*
COLONIAL KITCHEN [R] *San Marino, CA*
COMPADRES MEXICAN BAR & GRILL [R] *Yountville, CA*
COMPASS ATOP HYATT REGENCY [R] *Phoenix, AZ*
CORRIGAN'S STEAK HOUSE [R] *Thousand Oaks, CA*
CORVETTE DINER BAR & GRILL [R] *San Diego, CA*
COSMOS GRILL & ROTISSERIE [R] *Woodland Hills (L.A.), CA*
COTTAGE, THE [R] *Laguna Beach, CA*
COTTAGE INN [R] *Beaver, UT*
COTTAGE PLACE [R] *Flagstaff, AZ*
COTTAGE RESTAURANT [R] *Carmel, CA*
COTTONWOOD CAFE [R] *Tucson, AZ*
COUGAN'S AT ARROWHEAD [R] *Glendale, AZ*
COUNTRY INN [R] *Las Vegas, NV*
COWBOY CLUB [R] *Sedona, AZ*
COWBOY GRUB [R] *Salt Lake City, UT*
COYOTE CAFE [R] *Las Vegas, NV*
CRAB CATCHER [R] *La Jolla (San Diego), CA*
CREEKSIDE AT SOLITUDE [R] *Salt Lake City, UT*
CRESCENT SHORES GRILL [R] *La Jolla (San Diego), CA*
CRICKLEWOOD [R] *Santa Rosa, CA*
CROCE'S [R] *San Diego, CA*
CROCODILE CAFE [R] *Pasadena, CA*
CROCODILE GRILL [R] *Pacific Grove, CA*
CROSSING, THE [R] *Yuma, AZ*
CROW'S NEST [R] *Santa Cruz, CA*
CROWN ROOM [R] *Coronado, CA*
CRUSTACEAN [R] *Beverly Hills, CA*
CUCINA PARADISO [R] *Redondo Beach, CA*
CUISTOT [R] *Palm Desert, CA*
CYPRESS CLUB [R] *San Francisco, CA*
CYPRESS GROVE [R] *Pacific Grove, CA*
D A PASQUALE CAFE [R] *Beverly Hills, CA*
D & E'S [R] *Borrego Springs, CA*
D.Z. AKIN'S [R] *San Diego, CA*
D'ANGELO [R] *Henderson, NV*
D'ANTONIO'S RISTORANTE [R] *Pomona, CA*
DA VINCI [R] *Beverly Hills, CA*
DAILY'S FIT AND FRESH [R] *La Jolla (San Diego), CA*
DAISY MAE'S STEAK HOUSE [R] *Tucson, AZ*
DAKOTA GRILL & SPIRITS [R] *San Diego, CA*
DAME A RESTAURANT [R] *San Francisco, CA*
DAN TANA'S [R] *Hollywood (L.A.), CA*
DANIEL'S TRATTORIA [R] *Tucson, AZ*
DATTILO RISTORANTE [R] *Hemet, CA*
DAVID'S [R] *San Francisco, CA*
DE SCHMIRE [R] *Petaluma, CA*
DELANEY'S [R] *Laguna Beach, CA*
DELECTABLES [R] *Tucson, AZ*
DELICIAS [R] *Rancho Santa Fe, CA*
DELLA FONTANA RISTORANTE [R] *Salt Lake City, UT*
DELLA SANTINA'S [R] *Sonoma, CA*
DEPOT, *CA*
[R] *Oroville*, [R] *Torrance*
DEPOT HOTEL CUCINA RUSTICA, THE [R] *Sonoma, CA*
DERBY, THE [R] *Arcadia, CA*
DESERT EDGE PUB [R] *Salt Lake City, UT*
DEUCE [R] *Sonoma, CA*
DIAGHILEV [R] *Los Angeles, CA*
DICK'S CAFE [R] *St George, UT*
DICK'S LAST RESORT [R] *San Diego, CA*
DIFFERENT POINTE OF VIEW [R] *Phoenix, AZ*
DINER, THE [R] *Yountville, CA*
DINING ROOM, THE, *CA*
[R] *Del Mar*, [R] *Laguna Beach*, [R] *Marina del Rey*, [R] *Palm Springs*, [R] *San Francisco*
DINING ROOM - BEVERLY WILSHIRE, THE [R] *Beverly Hills, CA*
DIVA RESTAURANT [R] *Costa Mesa, CA*

DIVE, THE [R] *Las Vegas, NV*
DOBSON'S BAR & RESTAURANT [R] *San Diego, CA*
DOMAINE CHANDON [R] *Yountville, CA*
DOMENICO'S [R] *Monterey, CA*
DON & CHARLIE'S AMERICAN RIB & CHOP HOUSE [R] *Scottsdale, AZ*
DONA ESTHER MEXICAN RESTAURANT [R] *San Juan Bautista, CA*
DOTTIE'S TRUE BLUE CAFE [R] *San Francisco, CA*
DOWNEY'S [R] *Santa Barbara, CA*
DRAGO RESTAURANT [R] *Santa Monica, CA*
DRAI'S [R] *Hollywood (L.A.), CA*
DRAI'S OF LAS VEGAS [R] *Las Vegas, NV*
DUCK AND DECANTER [R] *Phoenix, AZ*
DUCK CLUB, *CA*
[R] *Menlo Park*, [R] *Monterey*, [R] *Walnut Creek*
DUCK CLUB RESTAURANT [R] *Bodega Bay, CA*
DYLAN'S [R] *Sedona, AZ*
DYNASTY ROOM [R] *Westwood Village (L.A.), CA*
EAGLES NEST [R] *Merced, CA*
ED DEBEVIC'S, *AZ*
[R] *Phoenix*
ED DEBEVIC'S, *CA*
[R] *Beverly Hills*
EDDIE'S GRILL [R] *Phoenix, AZ*
EDGEWATER GRILL [R] *San Diego, CA*
EIGHT FORTY NORTH FIRST RSTRNT [R] *San Jose, CA*
EL ADOBE DE CAPISTRANO [R] *San Juan Capistrano, CA*
EL BIZCOCHO [R] *San Diego, CA*
EL CHARRO [R] *Tucson, AZ*
EL CHOLO RESTAURANT [R] *Los Angeles, CA*
EL CHORRO LODGE [R] *Scottsdale, AZ*
EL EMBARCADERO [R] *San Diego, CA*
EL ENCANTO DINING ROOM [R] *Santa Barbara, CA*
EL ENCANTO MEXICAN RESTAURANT [R] *Bullhead City, AZ*
EL FAROLITO [R] *Healdsburg, CA*
EL INDIO MEXICAN [R] *San Diego, CA*
EL PASEO RESTAURANT [R] *Santa Barbara, CA*
EL REY SOL [R] *Ensenada, Baja California, Mexico, CA*
EL RINCON RESTAURANTE MEXICANO [R] *Sedona, AZ*
EL TAPATIO [R] *Lancaster, CA*
EL TECOLOTE MEXICAN RESTAURANT [R] *San Diego, CA*
EL TOREADOR [R] *San Francisco, CA*
EL TORITO, *CA*
[R] *Huntington Beach*, [R] *Monterey*, [R] *Oakland*
EL TORITO GRILL, *CA*
[R] *Costa Mesa*, [R] *Newport Beach*
EL TOVAR DINING ROOM [R] *South Rim (Grand Canyon National Park), AZ*
ELEVEN [R] *San Francisco, CA*
ELIZA RESTAURANT [R] *San Francisco, CA*
EMERIL'S NEW ORLEANS [R] *Las Vegas, NV*
EMILE'S [R] *San Jose, CA*
EMPRESS COURT [R] *Las Vegas, NV*
EMPRESS OF CHINA [R] *San Francisco, CA*
ENRICO'S SIDEWALK CAFE [R] *San Francisco, CA*
EOS [R] *San Francisco, CA*
EPAZOTE [R] *Del Mar, CA*
EQUUS [R] *Santa Rosa, CA*
ERNA'S ELDERBERRY HOUSE [R] *Oakhurst, CA*
EULIPIA [R] *San Jose, CA*
EUROPA RESTAURANT [R] *Palm Springs, CA*
EVANS AMERICAN GOURMET CAFE [R] *Lake Tahoe Area, CA*
EVIVA [R] *Palo Alto, CA*
F. MCLINTOCKS [R] *Pismo Beach, CA*
F. MCLINTOCKS SALOON [R] *Paso Robles, CA*
FABIANI RESTAURANT [R] *Santa Rosa, CA*
FAIROUZ CAFE & GALLERY [R] *San Diego, CA*
FALCON RESTAURANT [R] *Winslow, AZ*
FAMOUS MURPHYS [R] *Reno, NV*
FANDANGO [R] *Pacific Grove, CA*
FAR NIENTE RISTORANTE [R] *Glendale, CA*
FARALLON [R] *San Francisco, CA*
FASOLINI'S PIZZA CAFE [R] *Las Vegas, NV*
FATTOUSH [R] *San Francisco, CA*
FAZ RESTAURANT & BAR [R] *San Francisco, CA*
FELIX & LOUIE'S [R] *Healdsburg, CA*
FENIX [R] *Hollywood (L.A.), CA*
FERRARO'S RESTAURANT [R] *Las Vegas, NV*
FIDDLER'S [R] *Flagstaff, AZ*
FIGARO [R] *San Francisco, CA*
FIGARO'S [R] *Carlsbad, CA*
FINO CUCINA ITALIANA [R] *Petaluma, CA*
FINO RESTAURANT [R] *San Francisco, CA*
FIO'S [R] *San Diego, CA*
FIOR D'ITALIA [R] *San Francisco, CA*
FIREFLY RESTAURANT [R] *San Francisco, CA*
FIREHOUSE [R] *Sacramento, CA*
FIREHOUSE GRILL [R] *Bishop, CA*
FIRST FLOOR GRILL, THE [R] *Las Vegas, NV*
FISH COMPANY [R] *Santa Monica, CA*
FISH MARKET [R] *Phoenix, AZ*
FISHWIFE [R] *Pacific Grove, CA*
FIVE CROWNS RESTAURANT [R] *Corona del Mar, CA*
FIVE FEET [R] *Laguna Beach, CA*
FLEUR DE LYS [R] *San Francisco, CA*
FLOWER DRUM [R] *Palm Springs, CA*
FLY TRAP RESTAURANT [R] *San Francisco, CA*
FLYING FISH CAFE-KENNYS [R] *Carmel, CA*
FOG CITY DINER [R] *San Francisco, CA*
FORGE IN THE FOREST AND GENERAL STORE, THE [R] *Carmel, CA*
FORTUNE COOKIE [R] *San Diego, CA*
FOSTER'S STEAK HOUSE [R] *Bryce Canyon National Park, UT*
FOUNDRY GRILL [R] *Provo, UT*
FOUNTAIN COURT [R] *San Francisco, CA*
FOUNTAINBLEU [AT] WESTGATE HOTEL [R] *San Diego, CA*
FOUR OAKS [R] *Los Angeles, CA*
FOUR QUEENS HOTEL [R] *Las Vegas, NV*
FOURNOU'S OVENS [R] *San Francisco, CA*
FOXFIRE [R] *Anaheim, CA*
FOY'S COUNTRY CORNER [R] *Panguitch, UT*
FRANCISCAN [R] *San Francisco, CA*
FRANK FAT'S [R] *Sacramento, CA*
FRANTOIO [R] *Mill Valley, CA*
FRASCATI [R] *San Francisco, CA*
FREESTYLE [R] *Sonoma, CA*
FRENCH LAUNDRY, THE [R] *Yountville, CA*
FRENCH MARKET GRILLE [R] *San Diego, CA*
FRENCH PASTRY SHOP [R] *La Jolla (San Diego), CA*
FRENCH POODLE RESTAURANT [R] *Carmel, CA*
FRENCH ROOM [R] *San Francisco, CA*
FRESH CREAM [R] *Monterey, CA*
FRESH KETCH [R] *Lake Tahoe Area, CA*
FRIAR TUCK'S [R] *Nevada City, CA*
FRIDAY'S STATION [R] *Stateline, NV*
FRINGALE [R] *San Francisco, CA*
FRUIT BASKET [R] *Madera, CA*
FUEGO RESTAURANT BAR & GRILL [R] *Tucson, AZ*
FUNG LUM [R] *San Jose, CA*
FUSILLI RISTORANTE [R] *Fairfield, CA*
GABBIANOS [R] *San Francisco, CA*
GALLEY RESTAURANT [R] *Morro Bay, CA*
GAR WOODS GRILL & PIER [R] *Tahoe Vista (Lake Tahoe Area), CA*
GARDEN COURT [R] *San Francisco, CA*
GARDENS [R] *Los Angeles, CA*
GARDUÑOS [R] *Las Vegas, NV*
GARY CHU'S [R] *Santa Rosa, CA*
GARY DANKO'S [R] *San Francisco, CA*
GASTROGNOME [R] *Idyllwild, CA*
GATSBY'S [R] *Las Vegas, NV*
GAYLORD INDIA [R] *San Francisco, CA*
GENERAL'S DAUGHTER [R] *Sonoma, CA*
GEOFFREY'S [R] *Malibu, CA*
GEORGE & DRAGON [R] *Phoenix, AZ*
GEORGE'S [R] *Fresno, CA*
GEORGE'S AT THE COVE [R] *La Jolla (San Diego), CA*
GERARDS FRENCH RSTRNT [R] *Riverside, CA*
GERMANIA AT THE HOCHBURG [R] *San Jose, CA*
GERNOT'S VICTORIA HOUSE [R] *Pacific Grove, CA*
GHIRARDELLI CHOCOLATE MANUFACTORY [R] *San Francisco, CA*
GIA'S RESTAURANT & DELI [R] *Logan, UT*
GILBERTS SEAFOOD GRILL [R] *Santa Cruz, CA*
GINGER ISLAND [R] *Berkeley, CA*
GINZA SUSHIKO [R] *Beverly Hills, CA*
GIO'S CAFE MILANO [R] *Las Vegas, NV*
GIORDANO'S [R] *Mesa, AZ*
GIRASOLE [R] *Pleasanton, CA*
GIRL & THE FIG, THE [R] *Sonoma, CA*
GLEN ELLEN INN [R] *Sonoma, CA*
GLISSANDI [R] *Tahoe City (Lake Tahoe Area), CA*
GLITRETIND RESTAURANT [R] *Park City, UT*
GLOBE [R] *San Francisco, CA*
GLORY HOLE RESTAURANTE [R] *Reno, NV*
GOLD ROOM [R] *Tucson, AZ*
GOLDEN GATE PARK BREWERY [R] *San Francisco, CA*
GOLDEN STEER STEAK HOUSE [R] *Las Vegas, NV*
GOLDEN SWAN [R] *Scottsdale, AZ*
GOLDEN TRUFFLE [R] *Costa Mesa, CA*
GRAND CAFE, *CA*
[R] *Los Angeles*, [R] *San Francisco*
GRAND OLD RANCH HOUSE [R] *Moab, UT*
GRANITA [R] *Malibu, CA*
GRAPPA [R] *Park City, UT*
GRAY CLIFF LODGE [R] *Ogden, UT*
GRAY WHALE PUB & PIZZERIA [R] *Inverness, CA*
GRAZIANO'S [R] *Petaluma, CA*
GREAT GREEK, THE [R] *Studio City (L.A.), CA*
GREAT WALL [R] *Palm Springs, CA*
GREAT WALL CHINA [R] *Tucson, AZ*
GREEK CORNER [R] *San Diego, CA*
GREEKFEST [R] *Phoenix, AZ*
GREEN FLASH [R] *Pacific Beach (San Diego), CA*
GREENS [R] *San Francisco, CA*
GREYSTONE [R] *St Helena, CA*
GRILL, THE, *CA*
[R] *Beverly Hills*, [R] *Pasadena*
GRILL ON OCEAN AVENUE [R] *Carmel, CA*
GRILL ON THE ALLEY, *CA*
[R] *Los Angeles*, [R] *San Jose*
GRILLE, THE [R] *Sonoma, CA*
GRINGO'S [R] *Mammoth Lakes, CA*
GUAYMAS [R] *Tiburon, CA*
GURLEY STREET GRILL [R] *Prescott, AZ*
GUSTAF ANDERS [R] *Santa Ana, CA*
GUSTAV'S JAGERHAUS [R] *Anaheim, CA*
HABANA [R] *Costa Mesa, CA*
HALIOTIS [R] *Ensenada, Baja California, Mexico, CA*
HAMADA OF JAPAN [R] *Las Vegas, NV*
HAMILTON'S [AT] THE HYATT [R] *Palm Desert, CA*
HANSA HOUSE SMORGASBORD [R] *Anaheim, CA*
HARBOR AND LONGBOARD'S GRILL [R] *Santa Barbara, CA*
HARBOR HOUSE [R] *San Diego, CA*
HARBOR VIEW GROTTO [R] *Crescent City, CA*
HARD ROCK CAFE, *AZ*
[R] *Phoenix*
HARD ROCK CAFE, *CA*
[R] *Los Angeles*
HARD ROCK CAFE, *NV*
[R] *Las Vegas*
HARRIS', *AZ*
[R] *Phoenix*
HARRIS', *CA*
[R] *San Francisco*
HARRY DENTON'S [R] *San Francisco, CA*
HAVANA CAFE [R] *Phoenix, AZ*
HAWTHORNE LANE [R] *San Francisco, CA*
HAYES STREET GRILL [R] *San Francisco, CA*
HEADQUARTER HOUSE [R] *Auburn, CA*
HEARTLINE CAFE [R] *Sedona, AZ*
HELEN'S [R] *Salt Lake City, UT*
HELMAND RESTAURANT [R] *San Francisco, CA*
HEMINGWAY'S [R] *Sonora, CA*
HIDEAWAY [R] *Sedona, AZ*
HOB NOB HILL [R] *San Diego, CA*
HOBBIT [R] *Orange, CA*
HOG'S BREATH [R] *Carmel, CA*
HONG KONG FLOWER LOUNGE RSTRNT [R] *San Francisco, CA*
HOPS! BISTRO & BREWERY, *AZ*
[R] *Phoenix*, [R] *Scottsdale*
HORIZONS [R] *Sausalito, CA*
HOUSE [R] *San Francisco, CA*

HOUSE OF CHAN [R] *Kingman, AZ*
HOUSE OF PRIME RIB [R] *San Francisco, CA*
HOUSE OF TRICKS [R] *Tempe, AZ*
HOUSTON'S, *AZ*
[R] *Phoenix*, [R] *Scottsdale*
HOUSTON'S TRAIL'S END [R] *Kanab, UT*
HUMPHREY'S BY THE BAY [R] *San Diego, CA*
HUNAN RESTAURANT [R] *San Francisco, CA*
HUNGRY BEAR [R] *Needles, CA*
HUNGRY I [R] *Salt Lake City, UT*
HUNTER STEAKHOUSE, *AZ*
[R] *Tempe*, [R] *Yuma*
HYDRO BAR & GRILL [R] *Calistoga, CA*
I FRATELLI [R] *San Francisco, CA*
ICHIBAN JAPANESE STEAK HOUSE [R] *Reno, NV*
IDLE SPURS STEAK HOUSE [R] *Barstow, CA*
IL CIELO [R] *Beverly Hills, CA*
IL FORNAIO [R] *Del Mar, CA*
IL FORNAIO CUCINA ITALIANA [R] *Corte Madera, CA*
IL FORNAIO ITALIAN RESTAURANT [R] *Las Vegas, NV*
IL PASTAIO [R] *Beverly Hills, CA*
IL PESCATORE [R] *Oakland, CA*
IL SANSOVINO [R] *Salt Lake City, UT*
IMPERIAL DYNASTY [R] *Hanford, CA*
IMPERIAL HOUSE [R] *San Diego, CA*
INFUSION BAR & RESTAURANT [R] *San Francisco, CA*
INN DINING ROOM [R] *Death Valley National Monument, CA*
INYO COUNTRY STORE & RESTAURANT [R] *Bishop, CA*
ISOBUNE [R] *San Francisco, CA*
ITRI ITALIAN RESTAURANT [R] *San Diego, CA*
IZZY ORTEGA'S [R] *San Luis Obispo, CA*
JACK & GIULIO [R] *San Diego, CA*
JACK'S WATERFRONT RESTAURANT [R] *Oakland, CA*
JAKE'S DEL MAR [R] *Del Mar, CA*
JAMESTOWN HOTEL [R] *Sonora, CA*
JANOS [R] *Tucson, AZ*
JAPENGO [R] *La Jolla (San Diego), CA*
JARDIENERE [R] *San Francisco, CA*
JARDINES DE SAN JUAN [R] *San Juan Bautista, CA*
JASMINE [R] *San Diego, CA*
JASMINE HOUSE [R] *San Francisco, CA*
JILLIAN'S [R] *Palm Desert, CA*
JIMMY'S [R] *Beverly Hills, CA*
JIRAFFE [R] *Santa Monica, CA*
JOE GREENSLEEVES [R] *Redlands, CA*
JOES RESTAURANT [R] *Santa Monica, CA*
JOEY BISTRO [R] *Sedona, AZ*
JOHN ASH & CO [R] *Santa Rosa, CA*
JOHN PISTO'S WHALING STATION [R] *Monterey, CA*
JOHNNY MCNALLY'S FAIRVIEW LODGE [R] *Kernville, CA*
JONESY'S FAMOUS STEAK HOUSE [R] *Napa, CA*
JOSEF'S [R] *Santa Rosa, CA*
JOZU [R] *Hollywood (L.A.), CA*
JT'S BRANDING IRON [R] *San Juan Bautista, CA*
JULIUS CASTLE [R] *San Francisco, CA*
JUST DESSERTS [R] *San Francisco, CA*
KABUTO SUSHI [R] *San Francisco, CA*
KACHINA DOWNTOWN [R] *Flagstaff, AZ*
KAISER GRILLE [R] *Palm Desert, CA*
KAMPAI [R] *Park City, UT*
KARL STRAUSS' BREWERY & GRILL [R] *San Diego, CA*
KASBAH MOROCCAN RESTAURANT [R] *San Rafael, CA*
KATIA'S RUSSIAN TEA ROOM [R] *San Francisco, CA*
KELLY'S STEAKHOUSE [R] *San Diego, CA*
KEN'S OLD WEST [R] *Page, AZ*
KENWOOD RESTAURANT & BAR [R] *Santa Rosa, CA*
KHAN TOKE THAI HOUSE [R] *San Francisco, CA*
KING'S FISH HOUSE [R] *Long Beach, CA*
KINGFISHER [R] *Tucson, AZ*
KIRBY'S CREEKSIDE [R] *Nevada City, CA*
KNOLL'S BLACK FOREST INN [R] *Santa Monica, CA*
KOBE JAPANESE STEAK HOUSE [R] *Palm Springs, CA*
KOTO JAPANESE RESTAURANT [R] *Newport Beach, CA*
KULETO'S RESTAURANT [R] *San Francisco, CA*
KYO YA [R] *San Francisco, CA*
KYOTO JAPANESE RESTAURANT [R] *Scottsdale, AZ*
L.J. QUINN'S LIGHTHOUSE [R] *Oakland, CA*
L'AMIE DONIA [R] *Palo Alto, CA*
L'ANGOLO RISTORANTE [R] *Hollywood (L.A.), CA*
L'AUBERGE, *AZ*
[R] *Sedona*
L'AUBERGE, *CA*
[R] *Ojai*
L'ECOLE RESTAURANT [R] *Scottsdale, AZ*
L'ERMITAGE [R] *Beverly Hills, CA*
L'HIRONDELLE [R] *San Juan Capistrano, CA*
L'ORANGERIE [R] *Hollywood (L.A.), CA*
LA BODEGA [R] *San Francisco, CA*
LA BOHEME RESTAURANT [R] *Carmel, CA*
LA BOUCANE [R] *Napa, CA*
LA BRASSERIE [R] *Orange, CA*
LA BRUSCHETTA [R] *La Jolla (San Diego), CA*
LA CACHETTE RESTAURANT [R] *Los Angeles, CA*
LA CASA PEQUENA [R] *Payson, AZ*
LA CASA RESTAURANT [R] *Sonoma, CA*
LA COSTA [R] *Tijuana, Baja California, Mexico, CA*
LA EMBOTELLADORA VIEJA [R] *Ensenada, Baja California, Mexico, CA*
LA ESPADANA [R] *Tijuana, Baja California, Mexico, CA*
LA FAYETTE [R] *Garden Grove, CA*
LA FOLIE [R] *San Francisco, CA*
LA FONTANELLA [R] *Phoenix, AZ*
LA FUENTE [R] *Tucson, AZ*
LA GALLERIA [R] *Santa Clara, CA*
LA GARE [R] *Santa Rosa, CA*
LA GOLONDRINA MEXICAN CAFE [R] *Los Angeles, CA*
LA HACIENDA [R] *Scottsdale, AZ*
LA LOGGIA [R] *Studio City (L.A.), CA*
LA MARINA [R] *Santa Barbara, CA*
LA MASIA [R] *Hollywood (L.A.), CA*
LA MERE MICHELLE [R] *Saratoga, CA*
LA PALOMA, *CA*
[R] *Oceanside*, [R] *Santa Clara*
LA PARISIENNE [R] *Arcadia, CA*
LA PASTAIA [R] *San Jose, CA*
LA PAVILLION AT RAMS HILL [R] *Borrego Springs, CA*
LA PLACITA CAFE [R] *Tucson, AZ*
LA QUINTA CLIFFHOUSE [R] *Palm Desert, CA*
LA SALETTE [R] *Sonoma, CA*
LA SCALA RESTAURANT [R] *Beverly Hills, CA*
LA VACHE & CO [R] *San Diego, CA*
LA VIE EN ROSE [R] *Fullerton, CA*
LA VIE VIETNAMESE RESTAURANT [R] *San Francisco, CA*
LAGHI [R] *San Francisco, CA*
LALIME'S CAFE [R] *Berkeley, CA*
LAMONT ST GRILL [R] *Pacific Beach (San Diego), CA*
LANDMARK [R] *Mesa, AZ*
LANDMARK CAFE [R] *Tucson, AZ*
LANDRY'S PACIFIC FISH COMPANY [R] *Scottsdale, AZ*
LANDRYS SEAFOOD RESTAURANT [R] *Las Vegas, NV*
LAREDO CANTINA & CAFE [R] *Las Vegas, NV*
LARK CREEK CAFE [R] *Walnut Creek, CA*
LARK CREEK INN [R] *Corte Madera, CA*
LAS BRISAS DE LAGUNA [R] *Laguna Beach, CA*
LAS CASUELAS NUEVAS [R] *Palm Springs, CA*
LAS CASUELAS TERRAZA [R] *Palm Springs, CA*
LAS PANCHITAS [R] *Incline Village, NV*
LAST TERRITORY [R] *Tucson, AZ*
LATILLA [R] *Carefree, AZ*
LAUREL [R] *San Diego, CA*
LAVANDE [R] *Santa Monica, CA*
LAWRY'S THE PRIME RIB, *CA*
[R] *Beverly Hills*
LAWRY'S THE PRIME RIB, *NV*
[R] *Las Vegas*
LE BEAUJOLAIS [R] *Redondo Beach, CA*
LE BISTRO, *AZ*
[R] *Tucson*
LE BISTRO, *CA*
[R] *Stockton*
LE CHARM FRENCH BISTRO [R] *San Francisco, CA*
LE CIRQUE [R] *Las Vegas, NV*
LE COQ D'OR [R] *Carmel, CA*
LE DOME [R] *Hollywood (L.A.), CA*
LE DONNE CUCINA ITALIANA [R] *Palm Desert, CA*
LE FONTAINEBLEAU [R] *San Diego, CA*
LE MONTRACHET [R] *Las Vegas, NV*
LE MOUTON NOIR [R] *Saratoga, CA*
LE PAON [R] *Palm Desert, CA*
LE PETIT FOUR [R] *Hollywood (L.A.), CA*
LE PETIT PIER [R] *Tahoe Vista (Lake Tahoe Area), CA*
LE POT AU FEU [R] *Menlo Park, CA*
LE RENDEZ-VOUS [R] *Tucson, AZ*
LE RHONE RESTAURANT BAR & CLUB [R] *Phoenix, AZ*
LE RHONE'S BISTRO [R] *Litchfield Park, AZ*
LE SAINT GERMAIN [R] *Palm Desert, CA*
LE SANGLIER FRENCH RESTAURANT [R] *Woodland Hills (L.A.), CA*
LE VALLAURIS [R] *Palm Springs, CA*
LEFT AT ALBUQUERQUE [R] *Santa Barbara, CA*
LEMON GRASS [R] *Sacramento, CA*
LEWELLYN'S [R] *Stateline, NV*
LG'S PRIME STEAKHOUSE [R] *Palm Desert, CA*
LHASA MOON [R] *San Francisco, CA*
LIDO DI [R] *Los Angeles Intl Airport Area, CA*
LILY LANGTRY'S [R] *Las Vegas, NV*
LINO'S [R] *San Diego, CA*
LISA HEMENWAY'S [R] *Santa Rosa, CA*
LITTLE JOE'S [R] *Los Angeles, CA*
LITTLE NAPOLI [R] *Carmel, CA*
LITZA'S FOR PIZZA [R] *Salt Lake City, UT*
LLEWELLYN [R] *Lake Tahoe Area, NV*
LO CASCIO [R] *Tempe, AZ*
LOCANDA VENETA [R] *Los Angeles, CA*
LOG HAVEN [R] *Salt Lake City, UT*
LOLA'S [R] *Hollywood (L.A.), CA*
LOLLI'S CASTAGNOLA [R] *San Francisco, CA*
LOMBARDI'S AT THE ARIZONA CENT [R] *Phoenix, AZ*
LON'S AT THE HERMOSA INN [R] *Scottsdale, AZ*
LONE EAGLE GRILLE ON THE LAKE [R] *Incline Village, NV*
LONGHORN [R] *Tombstone, AZ*
LORD FLETCHER INN [R] *Palm Springs, CA*
LORNA'S ITALIAN KITCHEN [R] *San Diego, CA*
LOS GATOS BREWING CO [R] *Los Gatos, CA*
LOTUS GARDEN, *AZ*
[R] *Tucson*
LOTUS GARDEN, *CA*
[R] *San Bernardino*
LOTUS THAI RESTAURANT [R] *Healdsburg, CA*
LOU LA BONTE'S [R] *Auburn, CA*
LOU'S VILLAGE [R] *San Jose, CA*
LOUISE'S PANTRY [R] *Palm Desert, CA*
LUCAS WHARF [R] *Bodega Bay, CA*
LUCQUES [R] *Los Angeles, CA*
LUGANO SWISS BISTRO [R] *Carmel, CA*
LULU [R] *San Francisco, CA*
LYON'S RESTAURANT [R] *Placerville, CA*
LYONS ENGLISH GRILLE [R] *Palm Springs, CA*
M POINT BAR-SUSHI & GRILL [R] *San Francisco, CA*
MAC ARTHUR PARK [R] *San Francisco, CA*
MACAYO MEXICAN RESTAURANT [R] *Tempe, AZ*
MADDOX RANCH HOUSE [R] *Brigham City, UT*
MADEO RESTAURANT [R] *Los Angeles, CA*
MADRONA MANOR [R] *Healdsburg, CA*
MAGIC LAMP INN [R] *Rancho Cucamonga, CA*
MAGLEBY'S [R] *Provo, UT*
MAINSTREET PIZZA & NOODLE [R] *Park City, UT*
MAMA TOSCA'S [R] *Bakersfield, CA*
MAMMA LUISA ITALIAN RISTORANTE [R] *Flagstaff, AZ*
MANCUSO'S [R] *Scottsdale, AZ*
MANDARIN, THE [R] *Beverly Hills, CA*

MANDARIN, *CA*
[R] *San Francisco*
MANDARIN, *UT*
[R] *Salt Lake City*
MANDARIN PALACE [R] *Yuma, AZ*
MANGIA BENE [R] *Healdsburg, CA*
MANGIAFUCCO [R] *San Francisco, CA*
MANGIAMO [R] *Los Angeles Intl Airport Area, CA*
MANHATTAN BAR & GRILL [R] *Los Angeles Intl Airport Area, CA*
MANHATTAN OF LAS VEGAS [R] *Las Vegas, NV*
MANKA'S INVERNESS LODGE [R] *Inverness, CA*
MANZELLA'S SEAFOOD LOFT [R] *Hayward, CA*
MAPLE DRIVE [R] *Beverly Hills, CA*
MARC'S CAFE AMERICAIN [R] *Flagstaff, AZ*
MARCELLO'S PASTA GRILL [R] *Tempe, AZ*
MARCO POLO SUPPER CLUB [R] *Scottsdale, AZ*
MARIA'S WHEN IN NAPLES [R] *Scottsdale, AZ*
MARILYN'S [R] *Phoenix, AZ*
MARINE ROOM [R] *La Jolla (San Diego), CA*
MARIO'S RESTAURANT [R] *Payson, AZ*
MARK WEST LODGE [R] *Santa Rosa, CA*
MARK'S RESTAURANT [R] *Laguna Beach, CA*
MARKET BROILER [R] *Riverside, CA*
MARKET STREET BROILER [R] *Salt Lake City, UT*
MARKET STREET GRILL [R] *Salt Lake City, UT*
MARQUESA [R] *Scottsdale, AZ*
MARRAKECH [R] *Las Vegas, NV*
MARRAKECH MOROCCAN [R] *San Francisco, CA*
MARY ELAINE'S [R] *Scottsdale, AZ*
MASA'S [R] *San Francisco, CA*
MATSUHISA [R] *Beverly Hills, CA*
MATTA'S [R] *Mesa, AZ*
MATTERHORN SWISS [R] *San Francisco, CA*
MAYFLOWER CUISINIER [R] *Las Vegas, NV*
MC CORMICK & SCHMICK'S SEAFOOD [R] *Irvine, CA*
MC2 [R] *San Francisco, CA*
MCCORMICK & KULETO'S [R] *San Francisco, CA*
MCCORMICK & SCHMICK'S, *CA*
[R] *Corte Madera*, [R] *Los Angeles Intl Airport Area*
MECCA [R] *San Francisco, CA*
MEDIEVAL TIMES DINNER & TOURNAMENT [R] *Buena Park, CA*
MEETING HOUSE [R] *San Francisco, CA*
MELANGE [R] *Las Vegas, NV*
MELVYN'S AT THE INGLESIDE [R] *Palm Springs, CA*
MEMPHIS SOUL CAFE [R] *Costa Mesa, CA*
MERRYMAN'S [R] *Trinidad, CA*
MES TROIS FILLES [R] *Sonoma, CA*
MESA ITALIANA [R] *Holbrook, AZ*
MESQUITE TREE RESTAURANT [R] *Sierra Vista, AZ*
METROPOLITAN [R] *Salt Lake City, UT*
METROPOLITAN GRILL [R] *Tucson, AZ*
MEXICAN VILLAGE RESTAURANTE [R] *Coronado, CA*
MI FAMILIA [R] *Hollywood (L.A.), CA*
MI PIACE [R] *Pasadena, CA*
MI PLACE [R] *Burbank, CA*
MICHAEL'S, *AZ*
[R] *Scottsdale*
MICHAEL'S, *CA*
[R] *Santa Monica*
MIFUNE [R] *San Francisco, CA*
MIKADO JAPANESE RESTAURANT [R] *Salt Lake City, UT*
MIKAYLA [R] *Sausalito, CA*
MILLE FLEURS [R] *Rancho Santa Fe, CA*
MILLIE'S WEST PANCAKE HAUS [R] *Tucson, AZ*
MILT'S STAGE STOP [R] *Cedar City, UT*
MISSION RANCH [R] *Carmel, CA*
MISTER A'S [R] *San Diego, CA*
MISTRAL [R] *Santa Rosa, CA*
MIXX [R] *San Diego, CA*
MIXX-AN AMERICAN BISTRO [R] *Santa Rosa, CA*
MIYAKO RESTAURANT [R] *Pasadena, CA*
MO'S GOURMET HAMBURGERS [R] *San Francisco, CA*
MOLLEKROEN [R] *Solvang, CA*
MOLLY BUTLER [R] *Greer, AZ*
MOM'S CAFE [R] *Salina, UT*
MONEY PANCHO, *CA*
[R] *Camarillo*, [R] *Oxnard*
MONTANA'S AMERICAN GRILL [R] *San Diego, CA*
MONTE CARLO [R] *Las Vegas, NV*
MONTEREY BAY CANNERS [R] *West Covina, CA*
MONTI'S [R] *Phoenix, AZ*
MONTRIO [R] *Monterey, CA*
MONTY'S STEAK HOUSE [R] *Westwood Village (L.A.), CA*
MOON'S RESTAURANT [R] *Quincy, CA*
MOONSHADOWS [R] *Malibu, CA*
MOOSE'S [R] *San Francisco, CA*
MORTON'S OF CHICAGO, *CA*
[R] *Sacramento*, [R] *San Francisco*
MORTONI'S [R] *Las Vegas, NV*
MORTONS RESTAURANT [R] *Hollywood (L.A.), CA*
MOSS BEACH DISTILLERY RSTRNT [R] *Half Moon Bay, CA*
MOTOWN CAFE [R] *Las Vegas, NV*
MOUNTAIN HOME INN [R] *Mill Valley, CA*
MR C'S [R] *Nogales, AZ*
MR. STOX [R] *Anaheim, CA*
MUDD'S RESTAURANT [R] *Walnut Creek, CA*
MULBERRY STREET [R] *Fullerton, CA*
MUM'S [R] *Long Beach, CA*
MUMS VEGETARIAN RESTAURANT [R] *Sacramento, CA*
MURPHY'S, *AZ*
[R] *Prescott*
MURPHY'S, *CA*
[R] *San Francisco*
MUSSO & FRANK GRILL [R] *Hollywood (L.A.), CA*
MUSTARD SEED [R] *Solvang, CA*
MUSTARD'S GRILL [R] *Yountville, CA*
NAPA [R] *Las Vegas, NV*
NAPA VALLEY GRILLE [R] *Yountville, CA*
NAPA VALLEY WINE TRAIN [R] *Napa, CA*
NATI'S MEXICAN RESTAURANT [R] *San Diego, CA*
NATIONAL HOTEL VICTORIAN DINING ROOM [R] *Nevada City, CA*
NELLIE CASHMAN'S RESTAURANT [R] *Tombstone, AZ*
NEPENTHE [R] *Big Sur, CA*
NEPHELE'S RESTAURANT [R] *Lake Tahoe Area, CA*
NEST [R] *Palm Desert, CA*
NEW GOLDEN TURTLE RESTAURANT [R] *San Francisco, CA*
NEW JOE'S [R] *San Francisco, CA*
NEW YORKER CLUB [R] *Salt Lake City, UT*
NEWPORT BEACH BREWING CO [R] *Newport Beach, CA*
NICK'S AT THE BEACH [R] *San Diego, CA*
NICKY BLAIR'S [R] *Las Vegas, NV*
NOB HILL [R] *San Francisco, CA*
NORTH BEACH [R] *San Francisco, CA*
NORTH BEACH CAFE [R] *Las Vegas, NV*
NORTH INDIA [R] *San Francisco, CA*
O'B'S PUB & RESTAURANT [R] *Truckee, CA*
O'REILLY'S [R] *San Francisco, CA*
OAKVILLE GROCERY CAFE [R] *Yountville, CA*
OBACHINE [R] *Beverly Hills, CA*
ODESSA RESTAURANT & BAR [R] *Laguna Beach, CA*
OLD BATH HOUSE [R] *Pacific Grove, CA*
OLD MEXICO EAST [R] *Santa Rosa, CA*
OLD OX [R] *Pacific Beach (San Diego), CA*
OLD SALT CITY JAIL RESTAURANT [R] *Salt Lake City, UT*
OLD SAN FRANCISCO EXPRESS [R] *Fairfield, CA*
OLD TOWN MEXICAN CAFE & CANTINA [R] *San Diego, CA*
OLEMA INN [R] *Inverness, CA*
OLIVE TREE [R] *Tucson, AZ*
OLIVETO [R] *Oakland, CA*
OLSEN'S CABIN RESTAURANT [R] *Quincy, CA*
OLYMPIC FLAME [R] *Tucson, AZ*
ONE MARKET [R] *San Francisco, CA*
ORIGINAL JOE'S [R] *San Jose, CA*
ORMACHEA'S [R] *Winnemucca, NV*
OSAKA GRILL [R] *San Francisco, CA*
OSTERIA PANEVINO [R] *San Diego, CA*
OSWALD'S [R] *Santa Cruz, CA*
OTTAVIO'S [R] *Camarillo, CA*
OVERLAND HOUSE GRILL [R] *Oakland, CA*
OYE RESTAURANT [R] *Pasadena, CA*
P.F. CHANG'S CHINA BISTRO [R] *Scottsdale, AZ*
PACIFIC [R] *San Francisco, CA*
PACIFIC COAST GRILL [R] *Del Mar, CA*
PACIFIC'S EDGE [R] *Carmel, CA*
PACIFICO [R] *Calistoga, CA*
PACKING HOUSE RESTAURANT [R] *Fallbrook, CA*
PALACE COURT [R] *Las Vegas, NV*
PALACE GRILL [R] *Santa Barbara, CA*
PALAIS DE JADE [R] *Reno, NV*
PALAZZIO [R] *Santa Barbara, CA*
PALAZZIO-DOWNTOWN [R] *Santa Barbara, CA*
PALIO D'ASTI [R] *San Francisco, CA*
PALM [R] *Hollywood (L.A.), CA*
PALM COURT [R] *Scottsdale, AZ*
PALM RESTAURANT [R] *Las Vegas, NV*
PALMIE FRENCH RESTAURANT [R] *Palm Springs, CA*
PALOMINO EURO BISTRO [R] *Palm Desert, CA*
PANDA INN [R] *San Diego, CA*
PANE E VINO RESTAURANT [R] *San Francisco, CA*
PANGAEA [R] *Los Angeles, CA*
PARADISO TRATTORIA [R] *Monterey, CA*
PARK GRILL, *CA*
[R] *Los Angeles*, [R] *San Francisco*
PARKER'S LIGHTHOUSE [R] *Long Beach, CA*
PARTNERS BISTRO [R] *Laguna Beach, CA*
PASCAL FRENCH PROVENCAL [R] *Newport Beach, CA*
PASTA ITALIA [R] *Palm Desert, CA*
PASTA MOON [R] *Half Moon Bay, CA*
PASTIS [R] *San Francisco, CA*
PATINA RESTAURANT [R] *Hollywood (L.A.), CA*
PATINETTE AT MOCA [R] *Los Angeles, CA*
PATISSERIE BOISSIERE [R] *Carmel, CA*
PAVILION [R] *Newport Beach, CA*
PEA SOUP ANDERSEN'S [R] *Santa Nella, CA*
PEAKS AT PINNACLE PEAK [R] *Scottsdale, AZ*
PEDRIN'S AT REAL DEL MAR [R] *Tijuana, Baja California, Mexico, CA*
PEERY WASATCH PUB & BISTRO [R] *Salt Lake City, UT*
PEGASUS RESTAURANT [R] *Las Vegas, NV*
PEKING CHINESE RESTAURANT [R] *Red Bluff, CA*
PENELOPE'S [R] *Tucson, AZ*
PEOHE'S [R] *Coronado, CA*
PEPPER MILL [R] *Pasadena, CA*
PEPPERS MEXICALI CAFE [R] *Pacific Grove, CA*
PERROCHE [R] *Studio City (L.A.), CA*
PERRY'S [R] *San Francisco, CA*
PERRY'S DOWNTOWN [R] *San Francisco, CA*
PF CHANG'S CHINA BISTRO [R] *Newport Beach, CA*
PHILIPPE THE ORIGINAL [R] *Los Angeles, CA*
PHILIPS SUPPER HOUSE [R] *Las Vegas, NV*
PIATTI [R] *Sonoma, CA*
PIATTI RISTORANTE [R] *La Jolla (San Diego), CA*
PICASSO [R] *Las Vegas, NV*
PICKLED GINGER [R] *San Francisco, CA*
PIEMONT RESTAURANT [R] *Mt Shasta, CA*
PIERPONT CANTINA [R] *Salt Lake City, UT*
PIETRO'S ITALIAN RESTAURANT [R] *Sedona, AZ*
PILOTHOUSE [R] *Sacramento, CA*
PIMPAREL'S LA TABLE FRANÇAISE [R] *Reno, NV*
PINE CONE INN [R] *Prescott, AZ*
PINNACLE PEAK [R] *Tucson, AZ*
PINOT [R] *Pasadena, CA*
PINOT BISTRO [R] *Studio City (L.A.), CA*
PINOT BLANC [R] *St Helena, CA*
PINOT HOLLYWOOD [R] *Los Angeles, CA*
PISCES [R] *Carlsbad, CA*
PISCHKE'S PARADISE [R] *Scottsdale, AZ*
PIZZERIA BIANCO [R] *Phoenix, AZ*
PLANET HOLLYWOOD, *AZ*
[R] *Phoenix*
PLANET HOLLYWOOD, *CA*
[R] *Beverly Hills*
PLANET HOLLYWOOD, *NV*
[R] *Las Vegas*
PLEASANTON HOTEL [R] *Pleasanton, CA*
PLOUF [R] *San Francisco, CA*
PLUMED HORSE [R] *Saratoga, CA*
PLUMPJACK CAFE [R] *San Francisco, CA*

POLO LOUNGE [R] Beverly Hills, CA
POMODORO RESTAURANT [R] Salt Lake City, UT
PORTERHOUSE, THE [R] Prescott, AZ
POSTINO [R] Walnut Creek, CA
POSTO RESTAURANT [R] Los Angeles, CA
POSTRIO RESTAURANT [R] San Francisco, CA
POT STICKER [R] San Francisco, CA
PREGO, CA
[R] Beverly Hills, [R] San Diego
PREGO RISTORANTE [R] San Francisco, CA
PRESIDIO AT LA CASA DEL ZORRO [R] Borrego Springs, CA
PRESIDIO GRILL [R] Tucson, AZ
PRIMA TRATTORIA E NEGOZIO-VINI [R] Walnut Creek, CA
PRIMAVERA [R] Coronado, CA
PRIME [R] Las Vegas, NV
PRIMI RISTORANTE [R] Los Angeles, CA
PRINCE OF WALES [R] Coronado, CA
PRONTO RISTORANTE [R] Phoenix, AZ
PUB'S PRIME RIB [R] Salinas, CA
PUCCINI & PINETTI [R] San Francisco, CA
PUNTA MORRO [R] Ensenada, Baja California, Mexico, CA
QUIET WOMAN [R] Corona del Mar, CA
QUILA'S [R] Salt Lake City, UT
QUILTED BEAR [R] Scottsdale, AZ
R J'S THE RIB JOINT [R] Beverly Hills, CA
RAFAEL'S MEXICAN RESTAURANT [R] Salt Lake City, UT
RAFFAELE'S [R] Phoenix, AZ
RAFFAELLO CARMEL RESTAURANT [R] Carmel, CA
RAINBOW CLUB [R] Henderson, NV
RAINWATER'S [R] San Diego, CA
RAJDOOT INDIAN CUISINE [R] Buena Park, CA
RANCH HOUSE [R] Ojai, CA
RANCHO PINOT GRILL [R] Scottsdale, AZ
RANGE STEAKHOUSE, THE [R] Las Vegas, NV
RAPPA'S SEAFOOD RESTAURANT [R] Monterey, CA
RAPSCALLION [R] Reno, NV
RAVENOUS [R] Healdsburg, CA
RAYMOND RESTAURANT [R] Pasadena, CA
RAZZ'S RESTAURANT & BAR [R] Scottsdale, AZ
RED LION TAVERN [R] Carmel, CA
RED SAILS INN [R] San Diego, CA
REDBONES [R] Salt Lake City, UT
REEDS RESTAURANT [R] Los Angeles Intl Airport Area, CA
REMINGTON [R] Scottsdale, AZ
RENDEZVOUS [R] Fort Bragg, CA
RENE AT TLAQUEPAQUE [R] Sedona, AZ
RENOIR [R] Las Vegas, NV
RESTAURANT [R] Fort Bragg, CA
RESTAURANT, THE [R] Los Angeles, CA
RESTAURANT 301 [R] Eureka, CA
RESTAURANT AT MEADOWOOD, THE [R] St Helena, CA
RESTAURANT AT SHERMAN HOUSE [R] San Francisco, CA
RESTAURANT HAPA [R] Scottsdale, AZ
RESTAURANT OCEANA [R] Scottsdale, AZ
RICARDO'S [R] Las Vegas, NV
RICK'S DESSERT DINER [R] Sacramento, CA
RINO'S ITALIAN RISTORANTE [R] Salt Lake City, UT
RIO GRANDE CAFE [R] Salt Lake City, UT
RIO GRILL [R] Carmel, CA
RIPE TOMATO [R] Fresno, CA
RISTORANTE IDEALE [R] San Francisco, CA
RISTORANTE MAMMA GINA [R] Palm Desert, CA
RISTORANTE PIATTI [R] Sacramento, CA
RITZ, THE [R] Newport Beach, CA
RIVER ROCK CAFE [R] Idyllwild, CA
RIVERHORSE CAFE [R] Park City, UT
RIVOLI [R] Berkeley, CA
ROARING FORK [R] Scottsdale, AZ
ROAST TO GO [R] Los Angeles, CA
ROBATA GRILL & SAKE BAR [R] Carmel, CA
ROBATA GRILL & SUSHI [R] Mill Valley, CA
ROBERT KINCAID'S BISTRO [R] Carmel, CA
ROBIN'S RESTAURANT [R] Cambria, CA
ROCCO'S SEAFOOD GRILL [R] San Francisco, CA
ROCK GARDEN CAFE [R] Palm Springs, CA
ROCKENWAGNER [R] Santa Monica, CA
ROCKY POINT [R] Carmel, CA
ROD'S STEAK HOUSE [R] Williams (Coconino Co), AZ
ROMANO'S MACARONI GRILL [R] Las Vegas, NV
ROPPONGI [R] La Jolla (San Diego), CA
ROSA'S ITALIAN RESTAURANT, CA
[R] Bakersfield, [R] Pismo Beach
ROSA'S RESTAURANT [R] Ontario, CA
ROSE PISTOLA [R] San Francisco, CA
ROSE'S CAFE [R] San Francisco, CA
ROSE'S LANDING [R] Morro Bay, CA
ROSEBUD'S CLASSIC CAFE [R] Jackson, CA
ROSEBUDS RESTAURANT [R] Sedona, AZ
ROSTI RESTAURANTS [R] San Francisco, CA
ROSY'S [R] Roseville, CA
ROTI RESTAURANT [R] San Francisco, CA
ROXSAND [R] Phoenix, AZ
ROY'S AT PEBBLE BEACH [R] Pebble Beach, CA
ROYAL KHYBER [R] Newport Beach, CA
ROYAL OAK [R] Lake Arrowhead, CA
ROYAL SCANDIA [R] Solvang, CA
RUBICON RESTAURANT [R] San Francisco, CA
RUE DE MAIN [R] Hayward, CA
RUE LEPIC [R] San Francisco, CA
RUFFINO'S [R] Napa, CA
RUMARI RESTAURANT [R] Laguna Beach, CA
RUMPUS [R] San Francisco, CA
RUSSIAN RIVER VINEYARDS [R] Santa Rosa, CA
RUSTLER'S ROOSTE [R] Phoenix, AZ
RUSTY DUCK [R] Sacramento, CA
RUTH'S CHRIS STEAK HOUSE, AZ
[R] Phoenix, [R] Scottsdale
RUTH'S CHRIS STEAK HOUSE, CA
[R] San Diego, [R] San Francisco
RUTH'S CHRIS STEAK HOUSE, NV
[R] Las Vegas
SACRED SEA [R] Las Vegas, NV
SAFFRON [R] San Diego, CA
SAGE ROOM [R] Stateline, NV
SAGUARO CORNERS [R] Tucson, AZ
SAJI JAPANESE CUISINE [R] San Francisco, CA
SAKURA [R] Flagstaff, AZ
SALADANG [R] Pasadena, CA
SALLY'S [R] San Diego, CA
SALSA BRAVA [R] Flagstaff, AZ
SALT CELLAR [R] Scottsdale, AZ
SALVATORE'S [R] San Diego, CA
SAM WOO BBQ [R] Las Vegas, NV
SAM'S GRILL [R] San Francisco, CA
SAMMY'S CALIFORNIA WOODFIRED P [R] La Jolla (San Diego), CA
SAN DIEGO PIER CAFE [R] San Diego, CA
SAN SHI GO [R] Laguna Beach, CA
SANDBAR & GRILL [R] Monterey, CA
SANDCRAB CAFE [R] Escondido, CA
SANS SOUCI RESTAURANT [R] Carmel, CA
SANTA FE BAR & GRILL [R] Berkeley, CA
SANTA MARIA INN [R] Santa Maria, CA
SANTAS KITCHEN [R] Santa Barbara, CA
SANTE RESTAURANT [R] La Jolla (San Diego), CA
SAPORI [R] Newport Beach, CA
SARDINE FACTORY [R] Monterey, CA
SARDUCCI'S CAFE & GRILL [R] San Juan Capistrano, CA
SAU-HY'S CHINESE CUISINE [R] Fallbrook, CA
SAVANNAH CHOP HOUSE [R] Laguna Beach, CA
SCALA'S BISTRO [R] San Francisco, CA
SCHEIDEL'S [R] Grass Valley, CA
SCHROEDER'S [R] San Francisco, CA
SCOMA'S, CA
[R] San Francisco, [R] Sausalito
SCORDATO'S [R] Tucson, AZ
SCOTT'S SEAFOOD GRILL [R] Costa Mesa, CA
SCOTT'S SEAFOOD GRILL & BAR, CA
[R] Oakland, [R] Palo Alto
SCRIBBLES [R] El Centro, CA
SEA GRILL [R] Eureka, CA
SEAFARE INN [R] Whittier, CA
SEARS FINE FOODS [R] San Francisco, CA
SEASONS [R] Las Vegas, NV
SEDONA SWISS RESTAURANT & CAFE [R] Sedona, AZ
SENT SOVI [R] Saratoga, CA
SEOUL JUNG [R] Los Angeles, CA
SERI MELAKA [R] Tucson, AZ
SESAME RESTAURANT [R] Palm Desert, CA
SFUZZI [R] Las Vegas, NV
SHADOWBROOK [R] Santa Cruz, CA
SHALIMAR [R] Las Vegas, NV
SHIRO [R] Pasadena, CA
SHOWLEY'S AT MIRAMONTE [R] St Helena, CA
SHUGRUE'S [R] Lake Havasu City, AZ
SHUGRUE'S HILLSIDE GRILL [R] Sedona, AZ
SHUGRUE'S WEST [R] Sedona, AZ
SIAMESE CAT THAI RESTAURANT [R] Tempe, AZ
SIERRA INN [R] June Lake, CA
SIERRA MAR RESTAURANT [R] Big Sur, CA
SILKS [R] San Francisco, CA
SILVA'S SHELDON INN [R] Sacramento, CA
SILVANA'S [R] Carson City, NV
SILVER DRAGON [R] Oakland, CA
SIMON'S [R] San Pedro (L.A.), CA
SIMON'S FINE DINING [R] Heber City, UT
SIR GALLAHAD'S [R] Las Vegas, NV
SIRINO'S RESTORANTE [R] Escondido, CA
SIROCCO [R] Palm Desert, CA
SISLEY ITALIAN KITCHEN [R] Los Angeles, CA
SKATES ON THE BAY [R] Berkeley, CA
SLANTED DOOR [R] San Francisco, CA
SLOCUM HOUSE [R] Rancho Cordova, CA
SMALLEY'S ROUNDUP [R] Salinas, CA
SOCCA RESTAURANT [R] San Francisco, CA
SOGA'S RESTAURANT [R] Davis, CA
SOIZIC RESTAURANT [R] Oakland, CA
SOLARIUM [R] Tucson, AZ
SONORA CAFE [R] Hollywood (L.A.), CA
SORRENTINO'S SEAFOOD HOUSE [R] Palm Springs, CA
SPADO'S [R] Salinas, CA
SPAGO, CA
[R] Beverly Hills, [R] Hollywood (L.A.), [R] Palo Alto
SPAGO, NV
[R] Las Vegas
SPENCER'S FOR STEAKS & CHOPS [R] Salt Lake City, UT
SPIEDINI [R] Walnut Creek, CA
SPINNAKER [R] Sausalito, CA
SPIRITO'S [R] Carlsbad, CA
SPLENDIDO [R] San Francisco, CA
SQUATTERS PUB BREWERY [R] Salt Lake City, UT
ST JAMES AT THE VINEYARD [R] Palm Springs, CA
ST JAMES BAR [R] La Jolla (San Diego), CA
ST ORRES [R] Gualala, CA
STACKS' [R] San Francisco Airport Area, CA
STAGE DELI [R] Las Vegas, NV
STARS [R] San Francisco, CA
STATE & A BAR & GRILL [R] Santa Barbara, CA
STATION HOUSE CAFE [R] Inverness, CA
STEAK HOUSE, THE, NV
[R] Las Vegas, [R] Reno
STEAK PIT [R] Snowbird, UT
STEAKHOUSE AT THE GRAND CANYON [R] South Rim (Grand Canyon National Park), AZ
STEAMERS OYSTER GRILL [R] Phoenix, AZ
STEAMERS SEAFOOD & RAW BAR [R] Phoenix, AZ
STEFANO'S [R] Las Vegas, NV
STEWART HOUSE [R] Grass Valley, CA
STILLWATER BAR AND GRILL [R] Pebble Beach, CA
STINKING ROSE [R] Beverly Hills, CA
STOKES ADOBE [R] Monterey, CA
STONEHOUSE [R] Santa Barbara, CA
SUCH IS LIFE [R] Phoenix, AZ
SUMMIT [R] Stateline, NV
SUMMIT HOUSE [R] Fullerton, CA
SUNNY JIM'S [R] San Francisco, CA
SUNSET GRILL [R] Moab, UT
SUSHI ON SHEA [R] Scottsdale, AZ
SUZETTE'S [R] Las Vegas, NV
SWAN OYSTER DEPOT [R] San Francisco, CA
SWISS CHALET [R] Lake Tahoe Area, CA

SWISS LAKEWOOD RESTAURANT [R] *Tahoe City (Lake Tahoe Area), CA*
SWISS LOUIS [R] *San Francisco, CA*
SYCAMORE INN [R] *Rancho Cucamonga, CA*
T. COOK'S [R] *Phoenix, AZ*
TACK ROOM, THE [R] *Tucson, AZ*
TACO AUCTIONEERS [R] *Del Mar, CA*
TADICH GRILL [R] *San Francisco, CA*
TAIX [R] *Los Angeles, CA*
TAKA RESTAURANT [R] *San Diego, CA*
TALE OF THE WHALE [R] *Newport Beach, CA*
TALIA'S ITALIAN RESTAURANT [R] *Los Angeles Intl Airport Area, CA*
TAM-O-SHANTER INN [R] *Los Angeles, CA*
TAMARISK [R] *Green River, UT*
TAPENADE [R] *La Jolla (San Diego), CA*
TARBELL'S [R] *Phoenix, AZ*
TARPY'S ROADHOUSE [R] *Monterey, CA*
TASTE CAFE & BISTRO [R] *Pacific Grove, CA*
TEA & SYMPATHY [R] *Costa Mesa, CA*
TEASERS [R] *Santa Monica, CA*
TEE OFF [R] *Santa Barbara, CA*
TERRA [R] *St Helena, CA*
TERRA NOVA [R] *Tucson, AZ*
TERRACE, THE, *AZ*
[R] *Scottsdale*
TERRACE, THE, *CA*
[R] *Los Angeles*
TEXAS RED'S PIT BARBECUE AND C [R] *Park City, UT*
THEE BUNGALOW [R] *San Diego, CA*
THEE WHITE HOUSE RESTAURANT [R] *Anaheim, CA*
THEO'S FRENCH RESTAURANT [R] *Santa Cruz, CA*
THUNDERBIRD BOOKSHOP CAFE [R] *Carmel, CA*
TILLERMAN [R] *Las Vegas, NV*
TIMBERHILL RANCH [R] *Fort Ross State Historic Park, CA*
TIMOTHY'S [R] *Phoenix, AZ*
TINNERY AT THE BEACH [R] *Pacific Grove, CA*
TITANIC CAFE [R] *San Francisco, CA*
TOHONO CHUL TEA ROOM [R] *Tucson, AZ*
TOM HAM'S LIGHTHOUSE [R] *San Diego, CA*
TOMASO'S [R] *Phoenix, AZ*
TOMATINA [R] *St Helena, CA*
TOMMY TOY'S [R] *San Francisco, CA*
TOP O' THE COVE [R] *La Jolla (San Diego), CA*
TOP OF THE MARKET, *AZ*
[R] *Phoenix*
TOP OF THE MARKET, *CA*
[R] *San Diego*
TOP OF THE ROCK [R] *Tempe, AZ*
TOP OF THE WORLD [R] *Las Vegas, NV*
TOPAZ CAFE [R] *Santa Ana, CA*
TOPSFIELD LODGE STEAKHOUSE [R] *Richfield, UT*
TORREY PINES CAFE [R] *Del Mar, CA*
TORREYANA GRILLE [R] *La Jolla (San Diego), CA*
TOUR DE FRANCE [R] *Tijuana, Baja California, Mexico, CA*
TOWER, THE [R] *Los Angeles, CA*
TRA VIGNE [R] *St Helena, CA*
TRADER VIC'S [R] *Oakland, CA*
TRATTORIA FANTASTICA [R] *San Diego, CA*
TRATTORIA LA STRADA [R] *San Diego, CA*
TRATTORIA POSITANO [R] *Del Mar, CA*
TRATTORIA SPIGA [R] *Costa Mesa, CA*
TRILOGY [R] *St Helena, CA*
TRILUSSA [R] *Palm Springs, CA*
TRIO CAFE [R] *San Francisco, CA*
TRIPLES [R] *Monterey, CA*
TROQUET [R] *Huntington Beach, CA*
TUBA GARDEN [R] *San Francisco, CA*
TUCCHETTI [R] *Phoenix, AZ*
TUCCI'S CUCINA ITALIANA [R] *Salt Lake City, UT*
TUSCANY, *CA*
[R] *Palm Desert*
TUSCANY, *UT*
[R] *Salt Lake City*
TUSCANY RISTORANTE-BAR-CAFE [R] *Carlsbad, CA*
TUTTO MARE, *CA*
[R] *La Jolla (San Diego)*, [R] *Newport Beach*, [R] *Tiburon*
TWIN PALMS, *CA*
[R] *Newport Beach*, [R] *Pasadena*
UNCLE BILL'S PANCAKE HOUSE [R] *Los Angeles, CA*
UNIVERSAL CAFE [R] *San Francisco, CA*
VALENCIA [R] *Rancho Santa Fe, CA*
VALENTINO [R] *Santa Monica, CA*
VENTANA ROOM [R] *Tucson, AZ*
VERTIGO RESTAURANT [R] *San Francisco, CA*
VICTORIAN ROOM, THE [R] *Yosemite National Park, CA*
VIGILUCCI'S TRATTORIA ITALIANA [R] *Carlsbad, CA*
VILLA NOVA [R] *Newport Beach, CA*
VINCENT GUERITHAULT ON CAMELBAK [R] *Phoenix, AZ*
VINCINO MARE [R] *San Diego, CA*
VINTAGE PRESS, THE [R] *Visalia, CA*
VINTNERS COURT [R] *Napa, CA*
VITO'S ITALIAN RESTAURANT [R] *Pacific Grove, CA*
VIVA MERCADOS MEXICAN RESTAURANT [R] *Las Vegas, NV*
VIVACE AT THE FOUR SEASONS [R] *Carlsbad, CA*
WALLY'S DESERT TURTLE [R] *Palm Springs, CA*
WALNUT CREEK HOFBRAU HOUSE [R] *Walnut Creek, CA*
WALNUT GROVE [R] *San Juan Capistrano, CA*
WAPPO BAR & BISTRO [R] *Calistoga, CA*
WATER GRILL [R] *Los Angeles, CA*
WATERFRONT [R] *San Francisco, CA*
WENTE BROTHERS [R] *Livermore, CA*
WENTE VINEYARDS [R] *Livermore, CA*
WESTERN BOOT STEAK HOUSE [R] *Healdsburg, CA*
WHARF, THE [R] *Fort Bragg, CA*
WHISKEY CREEK [R] *Bishop, CA*
WILD TOUCAN [R] *Sedona, AZ*
WILDE GOOSE [R] *Palm Springs, CA*
WILL'S FARGO RESTAURANT [R] *Carmel, CA*
WILLOWSIDE CAFE [R] *Santa Rosa, CA*
WINDOWS ON THE BAY [R] *Newport Beach, CA*
WINDOWS ON THE GREEN [R] *Scottsdale, AZ*
WINE BISTRO [R] *Studio City (L.A.), CA*
WINE CASK [R] *Santa Barbara, CA*
WINE & ROSES [R] *Lodi, CA*
WINESELLAR & BRASSERIE [R] *San Diego, CA*
WINSHIPS [R] *Sausalito, CA*
WOLFDALE'S [R] *Tahoe City (Lake Tahoe Area), CA*
WOLFGANG PUCK CAFE, *CA*
[R] *Los Angeles Intl Airport Area*, [R] *North Hollywood (L.A.)*, [R] *Santa Monica*
WOLFGANG PUCK'S CAFE [R] *Las Vegas, NV*
WOOL GROWERS [R] *Bakersfield, CA*
WRIGHT'S [R] *Phoenix, AZ*
XIAO LI [R] *Salt Lake City, UT*
XINH-XINH [R] *Las Vegas, NV*
XIOMARA [R] *Pasadena, CA*
YABBIES COASTAL KITCHEN [R] *San Francisco, CA*
YAKINIKU HOUSE JUBAN [R] *San Francisco Airport Area, CA*
YAMABUKI [R] *Anaheim, CA*
YAMAKASA RESTAURANT [R] *Chandler, AZ*
YANK SING [R] *San Francisco, CA*
YARD HOUSE, THE [R] *Long Beach, CA*
YAVAPAI [R] *Sedona, AZ*
YE LION'S DEN [R] *Ogden, UT*
YEN CHING [R] *Orange, CA*
YIANNIS GREEK RESTAURANT [R] *Claremont, CA*
YOLIE'S BRAZILIAN STEAKHOUSE [R] *Las Vegas, NV*
YOSHIDA-YA [R] *San Francisco, CA*
YOYO BISTRO [R] *San Francisco, CA*
YUJEAN KANG'S, *CA*
[R] *Hollywood (L.A.)*, [R] *Pasadena*
Z' TEJAS GRILL [R] *Las Vegas, NV*
ZARZUELA [R] *San Francisco, CA*
ZAX [R] *San Francisco, CA*
ZIBIBBO [R] *Palo Alto, CA*
ZINGARI [R] *San Francisco, CA*
ZINOS RESTAURANTE ON THE PLZ [R] *Sonoma, CA*
ZOOM ROADHOUSE GRILL [R] *Park City, UT*
ZORBA'S GREEK RESTAURANT [R] *Palm Springs, CA*
ZUNI CAFE [R] *San Francisco, CA*

Appendix B

Lodging List

Establishment names are listed in alphabetical order followed by a symbol identifying their classification, and then city and state. Establishments affiliated with a chain appear alphabetically under their chain name, followed by the state and city. The symbols for classification are: [H] for hotels; [I] for inns; [M] for motels; [L] for lodges; [MH] for motor hotels; [RO] for resorts, guest ranches and cottage colonies.

1904 IMPERIAL HOTEL BED & BREAKFAST [I] *Park City, UT*
ABBEY INN [M] *Cedar City, UT*
ADELAIDE MOTOR INN [M] *Paso Robles, CA*
ADOBE INN, *CA*
[M] *Carmel*, [I] *San Luis Obispo*
ADOBE ROSE INN BED & BREAKFAST [I] *Tucson, AZ*
AHWAHNEE HOTEL, THE [H] *Yosemite National Park, CA*
AIRTEL PLAZA HOTEL [MH] *Van Nuys (L.A.), CA*
ALAMO SQUARE INN [I] *San Francisco, CA*
ALBION HOUSE INN BED & BREAKFAST [I] *San Francisco, CA*
ALBION RIVER INN [I] *Mendocino, CA*
ALEXIS PARK RESORT HOTEL [H] *Las Vegas, NV*
ALISAL GUEST RANCH & RESORT [RO] *Solvang, CA*
ALISO CREEK INN [M] *Laguna Beach, CA*
ALTA LODGE [M] *Alta, UT*
ALTA MIRA HOTEL [M] *Sausalito, CA*
AMBASSADOR INN [M] *St George, UT*
AMBER HOUSE BED & BREAKFAST INN [I] *Sacramento, CA*
AMERICANA INN & SUITES [M] *San Ysidro (San Diego), CA*
AMERICINN [M] *Wickenburg, AZ*
AMERISUITES [MH] *Flagstaff, AZ*
AMSTERDAM HOTEL [I] *San Francisco, CA*
AN ELEGANT VICTORIAN MANSION [I] *Eureka, CA*
ANCHORAGE INN [M] *Clear Lake Area (Lake Co), CA*
ANDREA VILLA INN [M] *La Jolla (San Diego), CA*
ANDREWS HOTEL, THE [I] *San Francisco, CA*
ANDRUSS MOTEL [M] *Coleville, CA*
APPLE FARM TRELLIS COURT [M] *San Luis Obispo, CA*
APPLE FARM TRELLIS COURT AND INN [I] *San Luis Obispo, CA*
APPLE ORCHARD INN [I] *Sedona, AZ*
APPLE WOOD [I] *Guerneville, CA*
ARCHBISHOP'S MANSION [I] *San Francisco, CA*
ARGENT HOTEL [H] *San Francisco, CA*
ARGYLE, THE [H] *Hollywood (L.A.), CA*
ARIZONA BILTMORE RESORT & SPA [RO] *Phoenix, AZ*
ARIZONA CHARLIE'S HOTEL & CASINO [M] *Las Vegas, NV*
ARIZONA GOLF RESORT & CONFERENCE CENTER [RO] *Mesa, AZ*
ARIZONA INN [I] *Tucson, AZ*
ARIZONA MOUNTAIN INN [M] *Flagstaff, AZ*
ARMSTRONG MANSION [I] *Salt Lake City, UT*
ARTIST'S INN [I] *Pasadena, CA*
ASCOT INN & SUITES [M] *Morro Bay, CA*
ATHERTON HOTEL [H] *San Francisco, CA*
ATLANTIS CASINO RESORT [H] *Reno, NV*
ATRIUM HOTEL AT ORANGE COUNTY AIRPORT [MH] *Irvine, CA*
AUBERGE DU SOLEIL [H] *St Helena, CA*
AUBURN BEST INN [M] *Auburn, CA*
BABBLING BROOK INN [I] *Santa Cruz, CA*
BAECHTEL CREEK INN [M] *Willits, CA*
BAJA INN COUNTRY CLUB [MH] *Tijuana, Baja California, Mexico*
BAJA INN HACIENDA DEL RIO [MH] *Tijuana, Baja California, Mexico*
BAJAMAR OCEAN FRONT GOLF RESORT [RO] *Ensenada, Baja California, Mexico*
BALBOA PARK INN [M] *San Diego, CA*
BALLARD INN [I] *Solvang, CA*
BALLY'S [H] *Las Vegas, NV*
BANCROFT HOTEL [I] *Berkeley, CA*
BARBARA WORTH GOLF RESORT & CONVETION CENTER [M] *El Centro, CA*
BARBARY COAST HOTEL [H] *Las Vegas, NV*
BARNABEY'S HOTEL [H] *Los Angeles Intl Airport Area, CA*
BARRETTA GARDENS INN [I] *Sonora, CA*
BAY CLUB HOTEL AND MARINA [MH] *San Diego, CA*
BAY HILL MANSION BED & BREAKFAST [I] *Bodega Bay, CA*
BAY PARK HOTEL [M] *Monterey, CA*
BAY VIEW LODGE [M] *Morro Bay, CA*
BAYVIEW HOTEL [I] *Santa Cruz, CA*
BAYVIEW INN [M] *Crescent City, CA*
BEACHCOMBER INN [M] *Santa Barbara, CA*
BEACHWALKER INN [I] *Morro Bay, CA*
BEAZLEY HOUSE [I] *Napa, CA*
BED & BREAKFAST AT SADDLE ROCK RANCH [I] *Sedona, AZ*
BED & BREAKFAST INN AT LA JOLLA [I] *La Jolla (San Diego), CA*
BELLAGIO RESORT, THE [RO] *Las Vegas, NV*
BELLE DEJOUR INN [I] *Healdsburg, CA*
BENBOW INN [I] *Garberville, CA*
BERESFORD ARMS HOTEL [H] *San Francisco, CA*
BERESFORD HOTEL [H] *San Francisco, CA*
BERKELEY CAMPUS MOTEL [M] *Berkeley, CA*
BERNARDUS LODGE [H] *Carmel Valley, CA*
BEST INN & SUITES [M] *Battle Mountain, NV*
BEST WESTERN, *AZ*
[M] *Bullhead City*, [M] *Canyon de Chelly National Monument*, [M] *Cottonwood*, [M] *Flagstaff*, [M] *Gila Bend*, [M] *Glendale*, [M] *Holbrook*, [M] *Kingman*, [M] *Mesa*, [M] *Page*, [M] *Payson*, [MH] *Phoenix*, [H] *Phoenix*, [M] *Pinetop*, [M] *Prescott*, [M] *Safford*, [M] *Scottsdale*, [M] *Sedona*, [MH] *Sedona*, [RO] *Show Low*, [M] *South Rim (Grand Canyon National Park)*, [M] *Tombstone*, [M] *Tucson*, [MH] *Tucson*, [M] *Wickenburg*, [M] *Willcox*, [M] *Williams (Coconino Co)*, [M] *Winslow*, [M] *Yuma*
BEST WESTERN, *CA*
[M] *Alturas*, [M] *Anaheim*, [M] *Antioch*, [M] *Bakersfield*, [M] *Barstow*, [M] *Beaumont*, [M] *Bishop*, [M] *Blythe*, [M] *Buena Park*, [M] *Camarillo*, [M] *Cambria*, [M] *Carmel*, [I] *Carmel*, [M] *Chico*, [MH] *Clear Lake Area (Lake Co)*, [M] *Concord*, [M] *Corona*, [M] *Corte Madera*, [M] *Costa Mesa*, [M] *Crescent City*, [M] *Davis*, [M] *Del Mar*, [M] *El Cajon*, [M] *Eureka*, [M] *Fairfield*, [M] *Fallbrook*, [M] *Fremont*, [M] *Fresno*, [M] *Garden Grove*, [M] *Glendale*, [M] *Healdsburg*, [M] *Hemet*, [M] *Hollywood (L.A.)*, [M] *Indio*, [M] *Jackson*, [M] *Joshua Tree National Monument*, [MH] *La Jolla (San Diego)*, [M] *Laguna Beach*, [M] *Lake Tahoe Area*, [M] *Lancaster*, [M] *Lodi*, [MH] *Long Beach*, [MH] *Madera*, [M] *Marysville*, [M] *Merced*, [M] *Modesto*, [MH] *Monterey*, [M] *Morro Bay*, [M] *Mountain View*, [M] *Mt Shasta*, [MH] *Napa*, [M] *Newport Beach*, [MH] *North Hollywood (L.A.)*, [M] *Oakhurst*, [M] *Oakland*, [M] *Oceanside*, [M] *Ojai*, [M] *Ontario*, [M] *Oroville*, [M] *Palm Springs*, [MH] *Palm Springs*, [M] *Pasadena*, [M] *Paso Robles*, [M] *Petaluma*, [M] *Pismo Beach*, [M] *Placerville*, [M] *Pomona*, [M] *Rancho Cordova*, [MH] *Rancho Cucamonga*, [M] *Redding*, [M] *Redlands*, [M] *Redondo Beach*, [M] *Redwood City*, [M] *Sacramento*, [M] *San Diego*, [MH] *San Diego*, [H] *San Diego*, [M] *San Francisco*, [MH] *San Francisco*, [MH] *San Francisco Airport Area*, [M] *San Jose*, [M] *San Juan Capistrano*, [M] *San Luis Obispo*, [M] *San Pedro (L.A.)*, [MH] *San Rafael*, [M] *San Simeon*, [M] *Santa Barbara*, [MH] *Santa Barbara*, [M] *Santa Clara*, [M] *Santa Cruz*, [M] *Santa Maria*, [MH] *Santa Monica*, [M] *Santa Nella*, [M] *Santa Rosa*, [M] *Solvang*, [M] *Sonoma*, [M] *Susanville*, [M] *Tehachapi*, [M] *Three Rivers*, [M] *Truckee*, [M] *Ukiah*, [M] *Vacaville*, [M] *Valencia*, [M] *Vallejo*, [M] *Victorville*, [M] *Willows*
BEST WESTERN, *NV*
[M] *Elko*, [M] *Henderson*, [M] *Las Vegas*, [MH] *Reno*, [M] *Tonopah*, [M] *Winnemucca*
BEST WESTERN, *UT*
[M] *Beaver*, [M] *Bryce Canyon National Park*, [M] *Cedar City*, [M] *Fillmore*, [M] *Green River*, [M] *Kanab*, [M] *Logan*, [M] *Moab*, [M] *Monticello*, [M] *Nephi*, [M] *Panguitch*, [M] *Price*, [M] *Provo*, [M] *Richfield*, [M] *Roosevelt*, [M] *Salina*, [M] *Salt Lake City*, [MH] *Salt Lake City*, [M] *St George*
BEST WESTERN TUSCAN INN [H] *San Francisco, CA*
BEVERLY HERITAGE HOTEL [H] *San Jose, CA*
BEVERLY HILLS HOTEL [H] *Beverly Hills, CA*
BEVERLY HILLS PLAZA HOTEL, THE [H] *Beverly Hills, CA*

BEVERLY PLAZA HOTEL, THE [H] *Los Angeles, CA*
BIDWELL HOUSE BED & BREAKFAST [I] *Chester, CA*
BIG BEAR LAKE INN [M] *Big Bear Lake, CA*
BINIONS HORSESHOE HOTEL & CASINO [H] *Las Vegas, NV*
BISHOP PINE LODGE [M] *Trinidad, CA*
BISHOP THUNDERBIRD MOTEL [M] *Bishop, CA*
BLACKBERRY INN [I] *Mendocino, CA*
BLACKTHORNE [I] *Inverness, CA*
BLUE LANTERN INN [I] *Laguna Beach, CA*
BLUE SAIL INN [M] *Morro Bay, CA*
BODEGA BAY LODGE RESORT & SPA [MH] *Bodega Bay, CA*
BODEGA COAST INN [M] *Bodega Bay, CA*
BONANZA INN & CASINO [M] *Fallon, NV*
BORREGO SPRINGS RESORT HOTEL [M] *Borrego Springs, CA*
BORREGO VALLEY INN [I] *Borrego Springs, CA*
BOULDER LODGE MOTEL [M] *June Lake, CA*
BOULDER STATION HOTEL & CASINO [H] *Las Vegas, NV*
BOULDERS, THE [RO] *Carefree, AZ*
BOURBON STREET HOTEL & CASINO [H] *Las Vegas, NV*
BOWEN MOTEL [M] *Moab, UT*
BRANNAN COTTAGE INN [I] *Calistoga, CA*
BREAKERS INN [I] *Gualala, CA*
BREAKERS MOTEL [M] *Morro Bay, CA*
BRIAR PATCH INN [I] *Sedona, AZ*
BRIAR ROSE BED & BREAKFAST [I] *San Jose, CA*
BRIARWOOD [I] *Carmel, CA*
BRIDGE BAY RESORT [M] *Redding, CA*
BRIGHAM STREET INN [I] *Salt Lake City, UT*
BRIGHT ANGEL LODGE [M] *South Rim (Grand Canyon National Park), AZ*
BRIGHTON SKI RESORT [M] *Salt Lake City, UT*
BRYCE CANYON LODGE [M] *Bryce Canyon National Park, UT*
BRYCE CANYON PINES MOTEL [M] *Bryce Canyon National Park, UT*
BUENA PARK HOTEL [H] *Buena Park, CA*
BUENA VISTA MOTOR INN [M] *San Francisco, CA*
CAESARS PALACE [H] *Las Vegas, NV*
CAESARS TAHOE [H] *Stateline, NV*
CAIN HOUSE [I] *Bridgeport, CA*
CAL NEVA INN [M] *Tahoe Vista (Lake Tahoe Area), CA*
CAL-NEVA RESORT HOTEL/SPA & CASINO [H] *Incline Village, NV*
CALIFORNIA HOTEL & CASINO [H] *Las Vegas, NV*
CALIFORNIA INN [M] *Bakersfield, CA*
CALIPATRIA INN [M] *El Centro, CA*
CALISTOGA INN [I] *Calistoga, CA*
CALISTOGA SPA HOT SPRINGS [M] *Calistoga, CA*
CALUMET & ARIZONA GUEST HOUSE [I] *Bisbee, AZ*
CAMBRIA SHORES MOTEL [M] *Cambria, CA*
CAMELLIA INN [I] *Healdsburg, CA*
CAMPBELL INN [MH] *San Jose, CA*
CAMPBELL RANCH INN [I] *Healdsburg, CA*
CAMPTON PLACE HOTEL [H] *San Francisco, CA*
CANDLE LIGHT INN [M] *Carmel, CA*
CANDLEWOOD SUITES [MH] *Pleasanton, CA*
CANYON PORTAL MOTEL [M] *Sedona, AZ*
CANYON VILLA BED & BREAKFAST INN [I] *Sedona, AZ*
CAPITOL REEF INN & CAFE [M] *Capitol Reef National Park, UT*
CAR-MAR'S SOUTHWEST BED & BREAKFAST [I] *Tucson, AZ*
CARLSBAD INN BEACH RESORT [M] *Carlsbad, CA*
CARLTON HOTEL [H] *San Francisco, CA*
CARLYLE INN [I] *Beverly Hills, CA*
CARMEL GARDEN COURT INN [I] *Carmel, CA*
CARMEL RESORT INN [M] *Carmel, CA*
CARMEL VALLEY LODGE [I] *Carmel Valley, CA*
CARMEL VALLEY RANCH [RO] *Carmel Valley, CA*
CAROUSEL INN & SUITES [M] *Anaheim, CA*
CAROUSEL MOTEL [M] *Santa Cruz, CA*
CARRIAGE HOUSE [H] *Las Vegas, NV*
CARRIAGE HOUSE INN [I] *Carmel, CA*
CARSON VALLEY INN, *NV*
[M] *Gardnerville*, [MH] *Gardnerville*
CARTER INN AND CARTER HOUSE BED & BREAKFAST [I] *Eureka, CA*
CARTWRIGHT HOTEL [H] *San Francisco, CA*
CASA ALEGRE BED & BREAKFAST INN [I] *Tucson, AZ*
CASA CODY BED & BREAKFAST COUNTRY INN [I] *Palm Springs, CA*
CASA DEL MAR [M] *Santa Barbara, CA*
CASA DEL MAR CORPORATION [I] *Mill Valley, CA*
CASA LAGUNA INN [I] *Laguna Beach, CA*
CASA MADRONA HOTEL [I] *Sausalito, CA*
CASA MALIBU INN ON THE BEACH [M] *Malibu, CA*
CASA SEDONA BED & BREAKFAST [I] *Sedona, AZ*
CASA SIRENA HOTEL & MARINA [MH] *Oxnard, CA*
CASTLE CREEK INN RESORT & SPA [I] *Escondido, CA*
CASTLE INN BY SEA [M] *Cambria, CA*
CASTLE INN & SUITES [M] *Anaheim, CA*
CASTLE VALLEY INN [I] *Moab, UT*
CATALINA ISLAND SEACREST INN [I] *Avalon (Catalina Island), CA*
CATALINA PARK INN [I] *Tucson, AZ*
CATAMARAN RESORT HOTEL [H] *Pacific Beach (San Diego), CA*
CATHEDRAL HILL HOTEL [H] *San Francisco, CA*
CATHEDRAL ROCK LODGE [I] *Sedona, AZ*
CAVANAUGH'S OLYMPUS MOTEL [H] *Salt Lake City, UT*
CEDAR GLEN LODGE [M] *Tahoe Vista (Lake Tahoe Area), CA*
CEDAR GROVE LODGE [M] *Sequoia & Kings Canyon National Parks, CA*
CEDAR LODGE, *CA*
[M] *Lake Tahoe Area*, [M] *Yosemite National Park*
CEDAR LODGE MOTEL [M] *Dunsmuir, CA*
CENTER STRIP INN [M] *Las Vegas, NV*
CENTRELLA INN [I] *Pacific Grove, CA*
CHABLIS INN [M] *Napa, CA*
CHALFANT HOUSE BED & BREAKFAST [I] *Bishop, CA*
CHANCELLOR HOTEL [H] *San Francisco, CA*
CHANDLER INN [M] *Palm Springs, CA*
CHANEY HOUSE [I] *Tahoe City (Lake Tahoe Area), CA*
CHANNEL ROAD INN [I] *Santa Monica, CA*
CHASE SUITE HOTEL [H] *Fullerton, CA*
CHATEAU DU LAC [I] *Lake Arrowhead, CA*
CHATEAU DU SUREAU HOTEL [I] *Oakhurst, CA*
CHATEAU HOTEL [MH] *Napa, CA*
CHATEAU INN BY PICCADILLY INNS [M] *Fresno, CA*
CHATEAU MARMOUNT HOTEL [H] *Los Angeles, CA*
CHATEAU VICTORIAN [I] *Santa Cruz, CA*
CHELSEA MOTOR INN [M] *San Francisco, CA*
CHESHIRE CAT INN [I] *Santa Barbara, CA*
CHESTELSON HOUSE [I] *St Helena, CA*
CHIMNEY SWEEP INN [M] *Solvang, CA*
CHIRICAHUA FOOTHILLS [I] *Willcox, AZ*
CHRISTOPHER'S INN [I] *Calistoga, CA*
CHUCKAWALLA MANOR [M] *Palm Springs, CA*
CINNAMON BEAR INN [I] *Mammoth Lakes, CA*
CIRCLE C LODGE [M] *Joshua Tree National Monument, CA*
CIRCUS CIRCUS HOTEL & CASINO, *NV*
[H] *Las Vegas*, [H] *Reno*
CITY HOTEL [I] *Sonora, CA*
CLARIDGE INN [M] *St George, UT*
CLARION, *AZ*
[M] *Tucson*, [MH] *Tucson*, [H] *Tucson*
CLARION, *CA*
[M] *Del Mar*, [H] *Hollywood (L.A.)*, [H] *Oakland*, [MH] *Sacramento*, [H] *San Diego*, [H] *San Francisco*, [M] *Thousand Oaks*, [M] *Woodland Hills (L.A.)*
CLEONE LODGE INN [I] *Fort Bragg, CA*
CLIFF DWELLERS LODGE [M] *Marble Canyon, AZ*
CLIFF LODGE, *UT*
[MH] *Snowbird*, [H] *Snowbird*
CLIFFROSE LODGE & GARDENS [M] *Zion National Park, UT*
CLIFFS AT SHELL BEACH [H] *Pismo Beach, CA*
CLIFT HOTEL, THE [H] *San Francisco, CA*
COAST VILLAGE INN [M] *Santa Barbara, CA*
COBBLESTONE INN [I] *Carmel, CA*
COLOMA COUNTRY INN [I] *Coloma, CA*
COLONY INN [M] *Buena Park, CA*
COLORADO BELLE HOTEL & CASINO [H] *Laughlin, NV*
COLUMBUS MOTOR INN [M] *San Francisco, CA*
COMFORT INN, *AZ*
[M] *Flagstaff*, [M] *Holbrook*, [M] *Pinetop*, [M] *Prescott*, [M] *Safford*, [M] *Scottsdale*
COMFORT INN, *CA*
[M] *Anaheim*, [M] *Bishop*, [M] *Blythe*, [M] *Calistoga*, [M] *Concord*, [M] *Escondido*, [M] *Hayward*, [M] *Huntington Beach*, [M] *Indio*, [M] *Oakhurst*, [M] *Pasadena*, [M] *Rancho Cordova*, [M] *Redwood City*, [M] *Salinas*, [M] *San Diego*, [H] *San Francisco*, [M] *San Francisco Airport Area*, [M] *San Jose*, [MH] *Santa Ana*, [M] *Santa Monica*, [M] *West Covina*, [M] *Willows*, [M] *Yosemite National Park*
COMFORT INN, *NV*
[M] *Fallon*, [M] *Las Vegas*
COMFORT INN, *UT*
[M] *Cedar City*, [M] *Logan*, [M] *Payson*, [M] *Provo*, [M] *Salt Lake City*, [MH] *Salt Lake City*, [M] *St George*
COMMODORE INTERNATIONAL HOTEL SAN FRANCISCO [H] *San Francisco, CA*
COMSTOCK HOTEL & CASINO [H] *Reno, NV*
CONVENTION CENTER INN [M] *Anaheim, CA*
COPPER QUEEN HOTEL [H] *Bisbee, AZ*
CORAL REEF MOTEL & SUITES [M] *Oakland, CA*
CORONA [H] *Ensenada, Baja California, Mexico*
COTTAGE GROVE INN CALISTOGA [I] *Calistoga, CA*
COTTAGE INN [I] *Tahoe City (Lake Tahoe Area), CA*
COUNTRY GARDEN INN [I] *Napa, CA*
COUNTRY INN, THE [M] *Corona, CA*
COUNTRY INN [M] *Ventura, CA*
COUNTRY INN AT CAMARILLO, THE [M] *Camarillo, CA*
COUNTRY INN AT PORT HUENEME, THE [M] *Oxnard, CA*
COUNTRY INN MOTEL [M] *Palo Alto, CA*
COUNTRY INNS & SUITES BY CARLSON [M] *Woodland Hills (L.A.), CA*
COUNTRY SIDE INN [M] *Del Mar, CA*
COUNTRY SIDE INN & SUITES [MH] *Costa Mesa, CA*
COUNTRY SIDE SUITES [MH] *Anaheim, CA*
COUNTRY SUITES [MH] *Ontario, CA*
COUNTRY SUITES BY CARLSON, *AZ*
[M] *Scottsdale*, [M] *Tempe*, [M] *Tucson*
COUNTRY SUITES BY CARLSON, *UT*
[M] *Salt Lake City*
COUNTRYSIDE INN [M] *Ontario, CA*
COUNTY INN [M] *Mountain View, CA*
COUNTYSIDE INN [MH] *Orange, CA*
COURTESY INN [M] *King City, CA*
COURTYARD BY MARRIOTT, *AZ*
[M] *Mesa*, [M] *Phoenix*, [M] *Scottsdale*, [MH] *Tempe*, [M] *Tucson*
COURTYARD BY MARRIOTT, *CA*
[M] *Bakersfield*, [M] *Buena Park*, [M] *Fremont*, [MH] *Laguna Beach*, [MH] *Long Beach*, [MH] *Los Angeles*, [M] *Palm Springs*, [M] *Pleasanton*, [M] *Rancho Cordova*, [H] *Riverside*, [M] *San Francisco Airport Area*, [M] *San Jose*, [M] *Torrance*, [M] *Vacaville*
COURTYARD BY MARRIOTT, *NV*
[MH] *Las Vegas*
COURTYARD BY MARRIOTT, *UT*
[M] *Salt Lake City*
COVENTRY MOTOR INN [M] *San Francisco, CA*
COW HOLLOW MOTOR INN & SUITES [M] *San Francisco, CA*
COWPER INN [I] *Palo Alto, CA*
COZY INN [M] *Costa Mesa, CA*
CREEKSIDE INN [MH] *Palo Alto, CA*
CROSS ROADS WEST INN [M] *Willows, CA*
CROWN CITY INN [M] *Coronado, CA*
CROWNE PLAZA, *CA*
[H] *Los Angeles Intl Airport Area*, [H] *Palm Springs*, [H] *Pleasanton*, [H] *Redondo Beach*, [H] *San Francisco Airport Area*, [MH] *San Jose*
CRYSTAL INN, *UT*
[M] *Salt Lake City*, [MH] *Salt Lake City*
CRYSTAL ROSE INN, THE [I] *Pismo Beach, CA*
CRYSTAL TERRACE INN [I] *Carmel, CA*

CULVER'S [I] *Calistoga, CA*
CURLY REDWOOD LODGE [M] *Crescent City, CA*
CYPRESS GARDENS INN [M] *Monterey, CA*
CYPRESS INN, *CA*
[I] *Carmel*, [I] *Half Moon Bay*
CYPRESS TREE INN [M] *Monterey, CA*
DALY INN [I] *Eureka, CA*
DANA INN & MARINA [M] *San Diego, CA*
DANISH COUNTRY INN [M] *Solvang, CA*
DANISH VIKING LODGE [M] *Heber City, UT*
DAYS INN, *AZ*
[M] *Flagstaff*, [M] *Kingman*, [M] *Mesa*, [M] *Prescott*, [M] *Show Low*, [M] *Willcox*
DAYS INN, *CA*
[M] *Anaheim*, [M] *Barstow*, [M] *Clear Lake Area (Lake Co)*, [M] *Lake Tahoe Area*, [M] *Morro Bay*, [M] *Oceanside*, [M] *Pacific Grove*, [M] *Palm Springs*, [M] *Redwood City*, [M] *Sacramento*, [M] *San Diego*, [M] *San Francisco*, [MH] *Sonora*
DAYS INN, *NV*
[M] *Las Vegas*, [M] *Winnemucca*
DAYS INN, *UT*
[M] *Logan*, [MH] *Ogden*, [M] *Provo*, [M] *Richfield*, [M] *Salt Lake City*
DE LANO MOTEL [M] *Beaver, UT*
DEER HAVEN INN [M] *Pacific Grove, CA*
DEFIANCE HOUSE [RO] *Lake Powell, UT*
DESERT HOT SPRINGS SPA HOTEL [M] *Desert Hot Springs, CA*
DESERT INN [H] *Las Vegas, NV*
DESERT QUAIL INN [M] *Sedona, AZ*
DESERT VIEW MOTEL [M] *Joshua Tree National Monument, CA*
DINAH'S GARDEN HOTEL [MH] *Palo Alto, CA*
DISCOVERY INN [M] *Ukiah, CA*
DISNEYLAND HOTEL [H] *Anaheim, CA*
DISNEYLAND PACIFIC HOTEL [H] *Anaheim, CA*
DOC'S GETAWAY & GOLDMINE LODGE [M] *Big Bear Lake, CA*
DOLPHIN INN [M] *Carmel, CA*
DOLPHIN'S COVE RESORT [M] *Anaheim, CA*
DON LAUGHLIN'S RIVERSIDE HOTEL [H] *Laughlin, NV*
DONATELLO, THE [H] *San Francisco, CA*
DONNER LAKE VILLAGE RESORT [M] *Truckee, CA*
DORYMAN'S OCEANFRONT INN [I] *Newport Beach, CA*
DOUBLETREE, *AZ*
[H] *Phoenix*, [MH] *Scottsdale*, [MH] *Tucson*, [H] *Tucson*
DOUBLETREE, *CA*
[MH] *Costa Mesa*, [MH] *Eureka*, [H] *Fresno*, [H] *Laguna Beach*, [H] *Los Angeles Intl Airport Area*, [H] *Modesto*, [H] *Monterey*, [MH] *Ontario*, [H] *Ontario*, [H] *Orange*, [RO] *Palm Springs*, [H] *Pasadena*, [MH] *Redding*, [MH] *Sacramento*, [MH] *San Diego*, [H] *San Diego*, [RO] *San Diego*, [H] *San Francisco Airport Area*, [H] *San Jose*, [H] *Santa Ana*, [H] *Santa Barbara*, [H] *Santa Monica*, [H] *Ventura*, [H] *Westwood Village (L.A.)*
DOUBLETREE, *UT*
[H] *Salt Lake City*
DOW VILLA MOTEL [M] *Lone Pine, CA*
DOWNTOWN MOTEL [M] *Hanford, CA*
DR WILKINSON'S HOT SPRINGS [M] *Calistoga, CA*
DRIFTWOOD LODGE [M] *Zion National Park, UT*
DYNASTY SUITES, *CA*
[M] *Buena Park*, [M] *Corona*, [M] *Riverside*
EAGLES NEST BED & BREAKFAST [I] *Big Bear Lake, CA*
ECONO LODGE, *AZ*
[M] *Holbrook*, [M] *Winslow*
ECONO LODGE, *CA*
[M] *Mammoth Lakes*, [M] *San Luis Obispo*, [M] *Visalia*
ECONO LODGE MAINGATE [M] *Anaheim, CA*
ECONOMY INN, *CA*
[M] *San Ysidro (San Diego)*, [M] *Ukiah*
ECONOMY INNS OF AMERICA, *CA*
[M] *Carlsbad*, [M] *Fresno*, [M] *Rancho Cordova*
ECONOMY INNS OF AMERICA, *NV*
[M] *Las Vegas*
EDELWEISS HAUS HOTEL [M] *Park City, UT*
EDGEWATER HOTEL & CASINO [H] *Laughlin, NV*

EILERS INN [I] *Laguna Beach, CA*
EL ADOBE INN [M] *Monterey, CA*
EL BONITA MOTEL [M] *St Helena, CA*
EL CAPITAN MOTOR LODGE [M] *Hawthorne, NV*
EL CORDOVA HOTEL [M] *Coronado, CA*
EL CORTEZ HOTEL & CASINO [H] *Las Vegas, NV*
EL DORADO MOTOR INN [M] *West Covina, CA*
EL ENCANTO HOTEL [RO] *Santa Barbara, CA*
EL PRADO INN [M] *Santa Barbara, CA*
EL PRESIDIO BED & BREAKFAST INN [I] *Tucson, AZ*
EL PUEBLO MOTEL [M] *Sonoma, CA*
EL RANCHO BOULDER MOTEL [M] *Boulder City, NV*
EL RANCHO LODGE [M] *Palm Springs, CA*
EL RANCHO MOTEL [M] *Williams (Coconino Co), AZ*
EL TERADO TERRACE HOTEL [M] *Avalon (Catalina Island), CA*
EL TOVAR [H] *South Rim (Grand Canyon National Park), AZ*
ELDORADO HOTEL CASINO [H] *Reno, NV*
ELK COVE INN [I] *Mendocino, CA*
ELMS BED & BREAKFAST, THE [I] *Calistoga, CA*
ELSBREE HOUSE BED & BREAKFAST [I] *San Diego, CA*
EMBASSY SUITES, *AZ*
[MH] *Flagstaff*, [MH] *Phoenix*, [H] *Phoenix*, [H] *Scottsdale*, [H] *Tempe*, [MH] *Tucson*, [H] *Tucson*
EMBASSY SUITES, *CA*
[H] *Anaheim*, [H] *Arcadia*, [MH] *Buena Park*, [H] *Irvine*, [H] *La Jolla (San Diego)*, [H] *Lake Tahoe Area*, [H] *Lompoc*, [H] *Los Angeles Intl Airport Area*, [H] *Monterey*, [H] *Napa*, [H] *Oxnard*, [MH] *Palm Desert*, [H] *San Diego*, [H] *San Francisco Airport Area*, [H] *San Jose*, [H] *San Luis Obispo*, [H] *Santa Ana*, [H] *Temecula*, [H] *Walnut Creek*
EMBASSY SUITES, *UT*
[H] *Salt Lake City*
EMMA NEVADA HOUSE [I] *Nevada City, CA*
EMPRESS HOTEL [H] *La Jolla (San Diego), CA*
ENCHANTMENT RESORT [RO] *Sedona, AZ*
ESCAPE FOR ALL SEASONS [M] *Big Bear Lake, CA*
ESSEX HOTEL [H] *San Francisco, CA*
ESTERO BEACH RESORT [MH] *Ensenada, Baja California, Mexico, Mexico*
ESTRELLA INN [I] *Palm Springs, CA*
EUREKA INN [H] *Eureka, CA*
EVERGREEN BED & BREAKFAST [I] *Pleasanton, CA*
EXCALIBUR HOTEL & CASINO [H] *Las Vegas, NV*
EXECUTIVE INN, *CA*
[M] *El Centro*, [M] *Hayward*
FAIRFIELD INN BY MARRIOTT, *AZ*
[M] *Chandler*, [M] *Flagstaff*, [M] *Glendale*, [M] *Mesa*, [M] *Scottsdale*
FAIRFIELD INN BY MARRIOTT, *CA*
[MH] *Anaheim*, [M] *Buena Park*, [M] *Ontario*
FAIRFIELD INN BY MARRIOTT, *NV*
[M] *Las Vegas*
FAIRMONT, THE [H] *San Jose, CA*
FAIRMONT HOTEL [H] *San Francisco, CA*
FALLON HOTEL [I] *Sonora, CA*
FANTASY INN & WEDDING CHAPEL [M] *Lake Tahoe Area, CA*
FERN VALLEY INN [I] *Idyllwild, CA*
FESS PARKER'S WINE COUNTRY INN [I] *Solvang, CA*
FIESTA HOTEL/ CASINO [H] *Las Vegas, NV*
FIESTA INN [MH] *Tempe, AZ*
FINLANDIA MOTEL [M] *Mt Shasta, CA*
FIRESIDE INN [I] *Idyllwild, CA*
FIRST CHOICE INN [MH] *Roseville, CA*
FITZGERALD'S CASINO HOTEL [H] *Reno, NV*
FITZGERALDS CASINO HOLIDAY HOTEL [H] *Las Vegas, NV*
FLAMINGO RESORT HOTEL [MH] *Santa Rosa, CA*
FLANIGAN'S INN [M] *Zion National Park, UT*
FLUMES END BED & BREAKFAST [I] *Nevada City, CA*
FLYING E RANCH [RO] *Wickenburg, AZ*
FOGHORN HOTEL [M] *Marina del Rey, CA*
FOOTHILL BED & BREAKFAST [I] *Calistoga, CA*
FOREST INN SUITES [M] *Lake Tahoe Area, CA*
FOREST VILLAS HOTEL [H] *Prescott, AZ*
FOUNTAINGROVE INN [H] *Santa Rosa, CA*

FOUR QUEENS HOTEL & CASINO [H] *Las Vegas, NV*
FOUR SEASONS, *CA*
[RO] *Carlsbad*, [H] *Los Angeles*, [H] *Newport Beach*, [H] *Santa Barbara*
FOUR SEASONS HOTEL LAS VEGAS [H] *Las Vegas, NV*
FOUR SEASONS INN [M] *Kanab, UT*
FOX ENTERPRISES INC [I] *Jackson, CA*
FRANCISCAN INN [M] *Santa Barbara, CA*
FRANCISCO BAY MOTEL [M] *San Francisco, CA*
FRANCISCO GRANDE RESORT & GOLF CLUB [RO] *Casa Grande, AZ*
FRAY MARCOS HOTEL [MH] *Williams (Coconino Co), AZ*
FREMONT HOTEL & CASINO [H] *Las Vegas, NV*
FRONTIER HOTEL & GAMBLING HALL [H] *Las Vegas, NV*
FRONTIER MOTEL INC [M] *Roosevelt, UT*
FURAMA HOTEL LOS ANGELES [H] *Los Angeles Intl Airport Area, CA*
FURNACE CREEK INN [RO] *Death Valley National Monument, CA*
FURNACE CREEK RANCH [H] *Death Valley National Monument, CA*
GABLES INN [I] *Santa Rosa, CA*
GAIGE HOUSE INN [I] *Sonoma, CA*
GALLERIA PARK HOTEL, THE [H] *San Francisco, CA*
GARDEN COURT HOTEL [H] *Palo Alto, CA*
GARDEN STREET INN [I] *San Luis Obispo, CA*
GARRATT MANSION [I] *Oakland, CA*
GATE HOUSE INN [I] *Jackson, CA*
GATEHOUSE INN [I] *Pacific Grove, CA*
GEORGIAN HOTEL [H] *Santa Monica, CA*
GERSTLE PARK INN [I] *San Rafael, CA*
GEYSERVILLE INN [M] *Healdsburg, CA*
GINGERBREAD MANSION [I] *Eureka, CA*
GLENBOROUGH INN [I] *Santa Barbara, CA*
GLENMORE PLAZA HOTEL [H] *Avalon (Catalina Island), CA*
GLORIETTA BAY INN [M] *Coronado, CA*
GOLD CANYON GOLF RESORT LP [RO] *Mesa, AZ*
GOLD COAST HOTEL & CASINO [H] *Las Vegas, NV*
GOLD RIVER RESORT & CASINO [H] *Laughlin, NV*
GOLD SPIKE HOTEL & CASINO [H] *Las Vegas, NV*
GOLD STRIKE INN & CASINO [M] *Boulder City, NV*
GOLDEN NUGGET, *NV*
[H] *Las Vegas*, [H] *Laughlin*
GOLDENER HIRSCH INN [H] *Park City, UT*
GOOD NITE INN, *CA*
[M] *Chula Vista*, [M] *San Diego*
GOOSE & TURRETS BED & BREAKFAST INN [I] *Half Moon Bay, CA*
GOSBY HOUSE INN [I] *Pacific Grove, CA*
GOTLANDS INN CAVE CREEK [I] *Carefree, AZ*
GOULDING LODGE [M] *Kayenta, UT*
GOVERNORS INN [MH] *Sacramento, CA*
GRAHAM BED & BREAKFAST INN & ADOBE VILLAGE, THE [I] *Sedona, AZ*
GRANADA INN [M] *Anaheim, CA*
GRAND CANYON LODGE [M] *North Rim (Grand Canyon National Park), AZ*
GRAND CANYON PARK NATIONAL LODGES [M] *South Rim (Grand Canyon National Park), AZ*
GRAND COLONIAL, THE [H] *La Jolla (San Diego), CA*
GRAND HOTEL TIJUANA [H] *Tijuana, Baja California, Mexico*
GRANDMERES BED & BREAKFAST INN [I] *Nevada City, CA*
GRANLIBAKKEN RESORT & CONFERENCE CENTER [RO] *Tahoe City (Lake Tahoe Area), CA*
GRANT GROVE VILLAGE [M] *Sequoia & Kings Canyon National Parks, CA*
GRANT PLAZA HOTEL [H] *San Francisco, CA*
GRAPE LEAF INN [I] *Healdsburg, CA*
GREEN GABLES INN [I] *Pacific Grove, CA*
GREENE GATE VILLAGE [I] *St George, UT*
GREENWELL INN [M] *Price, UT*
GREER LODGE [RO] *Greer, AZ*

GREY GABLES BED & BREAKFAST INN [I] Jackson, CA
GREY WHALE INN BED & BREAKFAST [I] Fort Bragg, CA
GROVELAND HOTEL [I] Yosemite National Park, CA
GUEST HOUSE [M] Long Beach, CA
GUEST HOUSE INN [I] Organ Pipe Cactus National Monument, AZ
GUESTHOUSE INN AND SUITES [M] San Luis Obispo, CA
GUESTHOUSE INN & SUITE [M] Santa Clara, CA
HACIENDA MOTEL [M] Alturas, CA
HALF MOON BAY LODGE & CONFERENCE CENTER [MH] Half Moon Bay, CA
HALLMARK INN [M] Davis, CA
HALLMARK SUITES [MH] Rancho Cordova, CA
HAMPTON INN, AZ
[MH] Chandler, [M] Flagstaff, [MH] Flagstaff, [MH] Glendale, [M] Mesa, [M] Phoenix, [M] Scottsdale, [M] Sedona, [M] Tucson
HAMPTON INN, CA
[M] Arcadia, [M] Blythe, [M] Fairfield, [M] Los Angeles Intl Airport Area, [M] Oakland, [M] Palm Springs, [M] Riverside, [M] San Diego, [M] Valencia
HAMPTON INN, NV
[H] Reno
HAMPTON INN [M] Salt Lake City, UT
HANDLERY HOTEL RESORT [MH] San Diego, CA
HANDLERY UNION SQUARE HOTEL [H] San Francisco, CA
HANFORD HOTEL [M] Anaheim, CA
HANFORD HOUSE [I] Jackson, CA
HAPPY LANDING INN [I] Carmel, CA
HARBOR COURT MOTEL, THE [H] San Francisco, CA
HARBOR HOUSE INN, THE [I] Mendocino, CA
HARBOR LITE LODGE [M] Fort Bragg, CA
HARBOR SIDE INN [M] Santa Barbara, CA
HARBOR VIEW INN [M] Santa Barbara, CA
HARDMAN HOUSE MOTOR INN [M] Carson City, NV
HARD ROCK [H] Las Vegas, NV
HARMONY HOUSE INN [I] Phoenix, AZ
HARRAH'S [H] Reno, NV
HARRAH'S CASINO HOTEL [H] Las Vegas, NV
HARRAH'S HOTEL CASINO [H] Stateline, NV
HARVEST INN [I] St Helena, CA
HARVEY'S RESORT HOTEL CASINO [H] Stateline, NV
HASSAYAMPA INN [H] Prescott, AZ
HAWTHORN SUITES, AZ
[MH] Scottsdale, [M] Tucson
HAWTHORN SUITES, CA
[M] Orange
HAWTHORN SUITES HOTEL [MH] Sacramento, CA
HAYDON STREET [I] Healdsburg, CA
HAYES CONFERENCE CENTER [H] San Jose, CA
HEADLANDS INN [I] Mendocino, CA
HERITAGE HOUSE [I] Mendocino, CA
HERITAGE PARK INN [I] San Diego, CA
HERMOSA HOTEL [M] Redondo Beach, CA
HERMOSA INN [I] Scottsdale, AZ
HIGH DESERT INN [M] Elko, NV
HIGHLAND DELL INN [I] Guerneville, CA
HIGHLANDS INN [H] Carmel, CA
HILGARD HOUSE HOTEL [H] Westwood Village (L.A.), CA
HILL HOUSE INN [I] Mendocino, CA
HILL TOP MOTEL [M] Kingman, AZ
HILTON, AZ
[M] Flagstaff, [H] Mesa, [MH] Phoenix, [H] Phoenix, [RO] Phoenix, [H] Tucson
HILTON, CA
[H] Anaheim, [H] Beverly Hills, [H] Burbank, [H] Concord, [H] Del Mar, [H] Fremont, [H] Huntington Beach, [H] Long Beach, [H] Los Angeles Intl Airport Area, [MH] Monterey, [H] North Hollywood (L.A.), [MH] Oakland, [H] Ontario, [H] Orange, [H] Oxnard, [H] Palm Springs, [H] Pasadena, [H] Pleasanton, [H] Sacramento, [H] San Bernardino, [H] San Diego, [H] San Francisco, [H] San Jose, [H] San Pedro (L.A.), [MH] Santa Rosa, [MH] Sunnyvale, [H] Torrance, [M] Valencia, [H] Whittier, [H] Woodland Hills (L.A.)
HILTON, NV
[H] Las Vegas, [H] Laughlin, [H] Reno
HILTON [H] Salt Lake City, UT
HOFSAS HOUSE [M] Carmel, CA
HOLIDAY INN, AZ
[MH] Canyon de Chelly National Monument, [MH] Flagstaff, [M] Glendale, [M] Globe, [M] Holbrook, [M] Kayenta, [M] Kingman, [MH] Lake Havasu City, [M] Litchfield Park, [M] Payson, [H] Phoenix, [M] Prescott, [MH] Scottsdale, [RO] Scottsdale, [M] Tempe, [MH] Tempe, [MH] Tucson, [H] Tucson, [MH] Williams (Coconino Co)
HOLIDAY INN, CA
[MH] Anaheim, [MH] Arcadia, [M] Bakersfield, [MH] Big Bear Lake, [MH] Buena Park, [M] Carlsbad, [MH] Chico, [M] Chula Vista, [MH] Costa Mesa, [M] Crescent City, [MH] Fairfield, [H] Fresno, [MH] Fullerton, [M] Half Moon Bay, [H] Huntington Beach, [H] Irvine, [M] Laguna Beach, [MH] Laguna Beach, [M] Lake Tahoe Area, [M] Lodi, [MH] Los Angeles, [H] Los Angeles, [M] Mill Valley, [MH] Modesto, [M] Monterey, [M] Mountain View, [MH] North Hollywood (L.A.), [MH] Oakland, [MH] Ontario, [M] Palm Desert, [MH] Palo Alto, [MH] Pasadena, [H] Pomona, [H] Riverside, [H] Sacramento, [MH] San Clemente, [MH] San Diego, [H] San Diego, [MH] San Francisco, [H] San Francisco, [MH] San Jose, [MH] San Luis Obispo, [M] San Mateo, [MH] Santa Ana, [MH] Santa Barbara, [M] Santa Cruz, [H] Santa Monica, [M] Three Rivers, [MH] West Covina
HOLIDAY INN, NV
[M] Battle Mountain, [MH] Las Vegas, [H] Las Vegas
HOLIDAY INN, UT
[M] Cedar City, [M] Price, [M] Provo, [MH] Salt Lake City, [M] St George
HOLIDAY LODGE, CA
[M] Grass Valley, [MH] San Francisco
HOLIDAY LODGE MOTEL [M] Willits, CA
HOMESTEAD, THE [RO] Heber City, UT
HOMEWOOD SUITES, AZ
[M] Phoenix, [M] Scottsdale
HONOR MANSION [I] Healdsburg, CA
HORIZON CASINO RESORT [H] Stateline, NV
HORIZON INN [M] Carmel, CA
HORTON GRAND HOTEL [H] San Diego, CA
HOSPITALITY SUITE RESORT [M] Scottsdale, AZ
HOTEL BEL-AIR [H] Los Angeles, CA
HOTEL BIJOU [H] San Francisco, CA
HOTEL BOHEME [I] San Francisco, CA
HOTEL BRITTON [H] San Francisco, CA
HOTEL CORAL & MARINA [H] Ensenada, Baja California, Mexico, Mexico
HOTEL DE ANZA [H] San Jose, CA
HOTEL DEL CAPRI [M] Westwood Village (L.A.), CA
HOTEL DEL CORONADO [RO] Coronado, CA
HOTEL DIVA [H] San Francisco, CA
HOTEL DURANT [H] Berkeley, CA
HOTEL GRIFFON [H] San Francisco, CA
HOTEL INTER-CONTINENTAL [H] Los Angeles, CA
HOTEL LA JOLLA [H] La Jolla (San Diego), CA
HOTEL LA ROSE [H] Santa Rosa, CA
HOTEL LAGUNA [H] Laguna Beach, CA
HOTEL LAMORE BISBEE INN [I] Bisbee, AZ
HOTEL MAJESTIC, THE [H] San Francisco, CA
HOTEL METROPOLE [H] Avalon (Catalina Island), CA
HOTEL MILANO [H] San Francisco, CA
HOTEL MONACO [H] San Francisco, CA
HOTEL NIKKO [H] San Francisco, CA
HOTEL NIKKO AT BEVERLY HILLS [H] Los Angeles, CA
HOTEL PACIFIC [I] Monterey, CA
HOTEL PARAISO LAS PALMAS [M] Ensenada, Baja California, Mexico
HOTEL REX [H] San Francisco, CA
HOTEL SAINT HELENA [I] St Helena, CA
HOTEL SAN CARLOS [H] Phoenix, AZ
HOTEL SAN REMO [H] Las Vegas, NV
HOTEL SANTA BARBARA [MH] Santa Barbara, CA
HOTEL ST LAUREN [MH] Avalon (Catalina Island), CA
HOTEL TRITON [H] San Francisco, CA
HOTEL UNION SQUARE [H] San Francisco, CA
HOTEL VENDOME - CLARION CARRIAGE HOUSE INN [M] Prescott, AZ
HOTEL VILLA PORTOFINO [M] Avalon (Catalina Island), CA
HOTEL VINTAGE COURT [H] San Francisco, CA
HOTEL VISTA DEL MAR [M] Avalon (Catalina Island), CA
HOUNDS TOOTH INN [I] Oakhurst, CA
HOWARD JOHNSON, AZ
[MH] Flagstaff
HOWARD JOHNSON, CA
[MH] Anaheim, [M] Fullerton, [M] Palm Springs, [M] Santa Clara, [M] Stockton
HOWARD JOHNSON, UT
[M] Brigham City, [M] Provo, [M] St George
HUMBOLDT REDWOODS INN [M] Garberville, CA
HUMPHREY'S HALF MOON INN [M] San Diego, CA
HUNTINGTON HOTEL [H] San Francisco, CA
HYATT, AZ
[H] Phoenix, [RO] Scottsdale
HYATT, CA
[H] Anaheim, [H] Irvine, [H] La Jolla (San Diego), [H] Long Beach, [H] Los Angeles, [H] Monterey, [RO] Newport Beach, [RO] Palm Desert, [H] Palm Springs, [H] Palo Alto, [H] Sacramento, [H] San Diego, [H] San Francisco, [H] San Francisco Airport Area, [H] San Jose, [H] Thousand Oaks
HYATT, NV
[H] Incline Village
IMA MARIPOSA LODGE [M] Yosemite National Park, CA
IMA NORRIS MOTEL [M] Williams (Coconino Co), AZ
IMA SVENDSGAARD'S DANISH LODGE [M] Solvang, CA
IMPERIAL HOTEL [I] Jackson, CA
IMPERIAL PALACE HOTEL AND CASINO [H] Las Vegas, NV
INDIAN WELLS RESORT HOTEL [RO] Palm Desert, CA
INGLESIDE INN [I] Palm Springs, CA
INN ABOVE TIDE, THE [I] Sausalito, CA
INN AT 410 BED & BREAKFAST [I] Flagstaff, AZ
INN AT CITADEL [I] Scottsdale, AZ
INN AT DEEP CANYON [M] Palm Desert, CA
INN AT DEPOT HILL [I] Santa Cruz, CA
INN AT HARRIS RANCH [MH] Hanford, CA
INN AT INCLINE & CONDOMINIUMS [M] Incline Village, NV
INN AT LA JOLLA [M] La Jolla (San Diego), CA
INN AT LAGUNA BEACH [MH] Laguna Beach, CA
INN AT MORRO BAY [H] Morro Bay, CA
INN AT OCCIDENTAL [I] Bodega Bay, CA
INN AT PARKSIDE, THE [I] Sacramento, CA
INN AT PLAYA DEL REY [I] Marina del Rey, CA
INN AT PROSPECTOR SQUARE [RO] Park City, UT
INN AT RANCHO SANTA FE [RO] Rancho Santa Fe, CA
INN AT SARATOGA, THE [I] Saratoga, CA
INN AT SCHOOLHOUSE CREEK [I] Mendocino, CA
INN AT SPANISH BAY [RO] Pebble Beach, CA
INN AT TEMPLE SQUARE [I] Salt Lake City, UT
INN AT THE OPERA [H] San Francisco, CA
INN AT THE TIDES [MH] Bodega Bay, CA
INN AT UNION SQUARE [I] San Francisco, CA
INN BY THE LAKE [M] Lake Tahoe Area, CA
INN OF LONG BEACH, THE [M] Long Beach, CA
INN OF PAYSON [M] Payson, AZ
INN ON CENTER STREET [I] Logan, UT
INN ON MT ADA [I] Avalon (Catalina Island), CA
INN ON OAK CREEK, THE [I] Sedona, AZ
INN ON SUMMER HILL [I] Santa Barbara, CA
INN SAN FRANCISCO [I] San Francisco, CA
INN SUITES HOTEL [MH] Tempe, AZ
INN SUITES HOTEL SCOTTSDALE RESORT [MH] Scottsdale, AZ
INN SUITES HOTELS [M] Buena Park, CA

INNS BY THE SEA- SVENDSGAARD'S INN [M] *Carmel, CA*
INTERNATIONAL LODGE [M] *Palm Desert, CA*
INTERNATIONAL MOTOR INN [M] *San Ysidro (San Diego), CA*
INTERSTATE 8 INN [M] *Yuma, AZ*
INVERNESS LODGE [I] *Inverness, CA*
IRWIN STREET INN [I] *Hanford, CA*
J PATRICK HOUSE BED & BREAKFAST INN [I] *Cambria, CA*
J STREET INN [H] *San Diego, CA*
JABBERWOCK [I] *Monterey, CA*
JACKSON COURT [I] *San Francisco, CA*
JACKSON LODGE [M] *Jackson, CA*
JAIL HOUSE MOTEL [M] *Ely, NV*
JAMESTOWN HOTEL [I] *Sonora, CA*
JENSEN MANSION [I] *Gardnerville, NV*
JETER VICTORIAN INN [I] *Red Bluff, CA*
JIM BUTLER MOTEL [M] *Tonopah, NV*
JOHN ASCUAGA'S NUGGET COURTYARD, *NV*
[MH] *Reno*, [H] *Reno*
JOHN MUIR INN [MH] *Napa, CA*
JOLLY ROGERS HOTEL [MH] *Anaheim, CA*
JOSHUA GRINDLE INN [I] *Mendocino, CA*
JOSHUA TREE INN [I] *Joshua Tree National Monument, CA*
JULIAN GOLDRUSH HOTEL INC [I] *San Diego, CA*
JULIAN WHITE HOUSE BED & BREAKFAST [I] *San Diego, CA*
JULIANA HOTEL [H] *San Francisco, CA*
KACHINA LODGE [M] *South Rim (Grand Canyon National Park), AZ*
KEEFER'S INN [M] *King City, CA*
KENSINGTON PARK HOTEL [H] *San Francisco, CA*
KENWOOD [I] *Santa Rosa, CA*
KERN RIVER INN BED & BREAKFAST [I] *Kernville, CA*
KERNVILLE INN [M] *Kernville, CA*
KING GEORGE HOTEL [H] *San Francisco, CA*
KLAMATH MOTOR LODGE [M] *Yreka, CA*
KOFA INN [M] *Parker, AZ*
KOKOPELLI SUITES [M] *Sedona, AZ*
KON TIKI INN [MH] *Pismo Beach, CA*
KORAKIA PENSIONE [I] *Palm Springs, CA*
L'AUBERGE DE SEDONA [H] *Sedona, AZ*
L'AUBERGE DEL MAR RESORT & SPA [RO] *Del Mar, CA*
L'ERMITAGE [H] *Beverly Hills, CA*
L'HORIZON GARDEN HOTEL [M] *Palm Springs, CA*
LA AVENIDA INN [M] *Coronado, CA*
LA CASA DEL ZORRO [RO] *Borrego Springs, CA*
LA COSTA RESORT & SPA [RO] *Carlsbad, CA*
LA ESTANCIA BED AND BREAKFAST [I] *Phoenix, AZ*
LA FUENTE INN [M] *Yuma, AZ*
LA HACIENDA INN HOTEL [M] *Los Gatos, CA*
LA JOLLA COVE SUITES [M] *La Jolla (San Diego), CA*
LA JOLLA SHORES INN [M] *La Jolla (San Diego), CA*
LA MANCHA PRIVATE CLUB & VILLAS [RO] *Palm Springs, CA*
LA MER EUROPEAN BED & BREAKFAST [I] *Ventura, CA*
LA PLAYA HOTEL [H] *Carmel, CA*
LA POSADA DEL VALLE BED & BREAKFAST [I] *Tucson, AZ*
LA QUINTA, *AZ*
[MH] *Glendale*, [M] *Mesa*, [M] *Phoenix*, [M] *Scottsdale*, [M] *Tempe*, [M] *Tucson*
LA QUINTA, *CA*
[M] *Bakersfield*, [MH] *Redding*, [M] *Sacramento*, [M] *San Bernardino*, [M] *San Diego*
LA QUINTA, *NV*
[M] *Las Vegas*, [MH] *Las Vegas*, [M] *Reno*
LA QUINTA, *UT*
[M] *Salt Lake City*
LA RESIDENCE COUNTRY INN [I] *Napa, CA*
LA SERENA INN [M] *Morro Bay, CA*
LA SIESTA VILLAS [M] *Palm Springs, CA*
LA VALENCIA [H] *La Jolla (San Diego), CA*
LADY LUCK CASINO HOTEL [H] *Las Vegas, NV*
LAFAYETTE PARK HOTEL [MH] *Walnut Creek, CA*
LAGUNA HOUSE [I] *Laguna Beach, CA*
LAGUNA RIVERA HOTEL [M] *Laguna Beach, CA*
LAKE ARROWHEAD RESORT [MH] *Lake Arrowhead, CA*
LAKE ARROWHEAD TREE TOP LODGE [M] *Lake Arrowhead, CA*
LAKE MARY BED & BREAKFAST [I] *Flagstaff, AZ*
LAKE MOHAVE RESORT [M] *Bullhead City, AZ*
LAKE OROVILLE BED & BREAKFAST [I] *Oroville, CA*
LAKELAND VILLAGE BEACH & SKI RESORT [MH] *Lake Tahoe Area, CA*
LAKESIDE INN & CASINO [M] *Stateline, NV*
LAMPLIGHTER LODGE [M] *Red Bluff, CA*
LANDMARK MOTEL [M] *Moab, UT*
LARCHWOOD-DEER HAVEN INN, THE [M] *Pacific Grove, CA*
LARIAT LODGE [M] *Quincy, CA*
LARRY ENDS & CINDY BROOKS [I] *Yosemite National Park, CA*
LAS ROSAS BY THE SEA [H] *Ensenada, Baja California, Mexico*
LAS VEGAS CLUB HOTEL & CASINO [H] *Las Vegas, NV*
LAUREL INN MOTEL [M] *Salinas, CA*
LAVENDER HILL BED AND BREAKFAST [I] *Sonora, CA*
LAZY J RANCH MOTEL [M] *Three Rivers, CA*
LAZY K BAR GUEST RANCH [RO] *Tucson, AZ*
LE MONTROSE HOTEL [H] *Hollywood (L.A.), CA*
LE PALMIER INN [M] *Palm Springs, CA*
LEISURE INN & SUITES [M] *San Bernardino, CA*
LEXINGTON HOTEL & SPORTS CLUB [H] *Phoenix, AZ*
LITTLE AMERICA HOTEL [MH] *Flagstaff, AZ*
LITTLE AMERICA HOTEL & TOWERS [H] *Salt Lake City, UT*
LITTLE VALLEY INN [I] *Yosemite National Park, CA*
LOBOS LODGE [M] *Carmel, CA*
LODGE AT BRIAN HEAD [RO] *Cedar City, UT*
LODGE AT MOUNTAIN VILLAGE, THE [RO] *Park City, UT*
LODGE AT NOYO RIVER [I] *Fort Bragg, CA*
LODGE AT PEBBLE BEACH, THE [RO] *Pebble Beach, CA*
LODGE AT SEDONA [I] *Sedona, AZ*
LODGE AT SKYLONDA, THE [RO] *Redwood City, CA*
LODGE AT SNOWBIRD [MH] *Snowbird, UT*
LODGE AT VENTANA CANYON, THE [RO] *Tucson, AZ*
LODGE AT VILLA FELICE [M] *Los Gatos, CA*
LODGE ON THE RIVER [M] *Bullhead City, AZ*
LOEWS, *AZ*
[RO] *Tucson*
LOEWS, *CA*
[RO] *Coronado*, [H] *Santa Monica*
LOGAN HOUSE INN [I] *Logan, UT*
LOMA VISTA BED & BREAKFAST [I] *Temecula, CA*
LOMBARD MOTOR INN [M] *San Francisco, CA*
LORD BRADLEY'S INN [I] *Fremont, CA*
LOS ABRIGADOS RESORT [RO] *Sedona, AZ*
LOS GATOS LODGE [MH] *Los Gatos, CA*
LOS LAURELES [I] *Carmel Valley, CA*
LOS OLIVOS HOTEL AND SUITES [MH] *Phoenix, AZ*
LOS PADRES INN [M] *Ojai, CA*
LOS ROBLES LODGE [M] *Santa Rosa, CA*
LOST WHALE BED & BREAKFAST INN [I] *Trinidad, CA*
LUXOR HOTEL & CASINO [H] *Las Vegas, NV*
MADISON STREET INN [I] *Santa Clara, CA*
MADONNA INN [MH] *San Luis Obispo, CA*
MADRONA MANOR [I] *Healdsburg, CA*
MAIN STREET DUPLEX [I] *Healdsburg, CA*
MAIN STREET STATION [H] *Las Vegas, NV*
MAISON FLURIE FOUR SISTERS INN [I] *Yountville, CA*
MAJESTIC MOUNTAIN INN [M] *Payson, AZ*
MALIBU BEACH INN [MH] *Malibu, CA*
MALIBU COUNTRY INN [M] *Malibu, CA*
MAMMOTH MOUNTAIN INN [RO] *Mammoth Lakes, CA*
MANDALAY BAY RESORT & CASINO [RO] *Las Vegas, NV*
MANDARIN ORIENTAL [H] *San Francisco, CA*
MANSIONS HOTEL [I] *San Francisco, CA*
MAPLE TREE INN [M] *Sunnyvale, CA*
MARBLE CANYON LODGE [M] *Marble Canyon, AZ*
MARIANI'S INN [M] *Santa Clara, CA*
MARICOPA MANOR [I] *Phoenix, AZ*
MARIN SUITES HOTEL [H] *Corte Madera, CA*
MARINA DEL REY HOTEL [MH] *Marina del Rey, CA*
MARINA INN [I] *San Francisco, CA*
MARINA RIVIERA RESORT [M] *Big Bear Lake, CA*
MARINA VILLAGE INN [M] *Oakland, CA*
MARIPOSA INN [M] *Monterey, CA*
MARK HOPKINS INTER-CONTINENTAL [H] *San Francisco, CA*
MARKS HOUSE VICTORIAN BED & BREAKFAST, THE [I] *Prescott, AZ*
MARRIOTT, *AZ*
[M] *Phoenix*, [M] *Scottsdale*, [H] *Scottsdale*, [RO] *Scottsdale*, [H] *Tucson*
MARRIOTT, *CA*
[H] *Anaheim*, [H] *Buena Park*, [R] *Coronado*, [H] *Costa Mesa*, [H] *Fullerton*, [H] *Irvine*, [H] *La Jolla (San Diego)*, [RO] *Laguna Beach*, [H] *Long Beach*, [H] *Los Angeles Intl Airport Area*, [MH] *Marina del Rey*, [H] *Marina Del Rey*, [H] *Monterey*, [MH] *Napa*, [H] *Newport Beach*, [H] *Oakland*, [H] *Ontario*, [RO] *Palm Desert*, [RO] *Palm Springs*, [H] *San Diego*, [H] *San Francisco*, [H] *San Francisco Airport Area*, [H] *Santa Clara*, [H] *Solvang*, [H] *Torrance*, [H] *Walnut Creek*, [H] *Woodland Hills (L.A.)*
MARRIOTT, *UT*
[H] *Ogden*, [H] *Provo*, [H] *Salt Lake City*
MARTINE INN, THE [I] *Pacific Grove, CA*
MATLICK HOUSE BED & BREAKFAST, THE [I] *Bishop, CA*
MATTERHORN MOTEL [M] *Lake Tahoe Area, CA*
MAUINA BEACH MOTEL [M] *Santa Barbara, CA*
MAXIM HOTEL 7 CASINO [H] *Las Vegas, NV*
MAXWELL HOTEL [H] *San Francisco, CA*
MCCAFFREY HOUSE BED & BREAKFAST INN [I] *Sonora, CA*
MCCLOUD HOTEL BED & BREAKFAST [I] *Mt Shasta, CA*
MEADOWLARK COUNTRY HOUSE AND INN [I] *Calistoga, CA*
MEADOWOOD [RO] *St Helena, CA*
MELODY RANCH MOTEL [M] *Paso Robles, CA*
MENDOCINO [I] *Mendocino, CA*
MENLO PARK INN [M] *Menlo Park, CA*
MERRITT HOUSE INN [I] *Monterey, CA*
MERV GRIFFINS WICKENBURG INN & DUDE RANCH [RO] *Wickenburg, AZ*
MGM GRAND HOTEL [H] *Las Vegas, NV*
MILL HOUSE INN MOTEL [M] *Carson City, NV*
MILL ROSE INN [I] *Half Moon Bay, CA*
MILL VALLEY INN [I] *Mill Valley, CA*
MILLWOOD INN [M] *San Francisco Airport Area, CA*
MINE MANAGERS HOUSE BED & BREAKFAST [I] *Organ Pipe Cactus National Monument, AZ*
MINERS INN [M] *Yosemite National Park, CA*
MIRA LOMA HOTEL [M] *Palm Springs, CA*
MIRAGE RESORT & CASINO [H] *Las Vegas, NV*
MISSION INN [H] *Riverside, CA*
MISSION RANCH [I] *Carmel, CA*
MONDRIAN HOTEL [H] *Hollywood (L.A.), CA*
MONTE CARLO RESORT & CASINO [H] *Las Vegas, NV*
MONTECITO INN [H] *Santa Barbara, CA*
MONTEREY BAY INN [M] *Monterey, CA*
MONTEREY HOTEL, THE [I] *Monterey, CA*
MONTEREY PLAZA HOTEL [H] *Monterey, CA*
MONTICELLO INN [H] *San Francisco, CA*
MOONSTONE INN [I] *Cambria, CA*
MOTEL 6, *AZ*
[M] *Williams (Coconino Co)*
MOTEL 6, *CA*
[M] *Bishop*, [M] *Palm Springs*
MOTEL 6, *UT*
[M] *Ogden*
MOUNT SHASTA RESORT [RO] *Mt Shasta, CA*
MOUNT VERNON INN [I] *Prescott, AZ*
MOUNT VIEW HOTEL & SPA [H] *Calistoga, CA*
MOUNTAIN HOME INN [I] *Mill Valley, CA*
MURPHYS HISTORIC HOTEL [MH] *Sonora, CA*

NAPA VALLEY LODGE [MH] Yountville, CA
NAPA VALLEY RAILWAY INN [I] Yountville, CA
NATIONAL 9, UT
[M] Heber City, [M] Provo
NATIONAL HOTEL [I] Sonora, CA
NEW OTANI HOTEL & GARDEN [H] Los Angeles, CA
NEW YORK-NEW YORK HOTEL & CASINO [H] Las Vegas, NV
NOB HILL LAMBOURNE HOTEL [H] San Francisco, CA
NOB HILL MOTEL [M] San Francisco, CA
NORMANDY INN [I] Carmel, CA
NORTH COAST COUNTRY INN [I] Gualala, CA
NORTHSTAR AT TAHOE [RO] Truckee, CA
NORTHWOODS RESORT [MH] Big Bear Lake, CA
NOVEL HOUSE INN [I] Springdale, UT
NUGGET MOTEL [M] Carson City, NV
OASIS OF EDEN INN & SUITES [M] Joshua Tree National Monument, CA
OBRIEN MOUNTIAN INN [I] Redding, CA
OCEAN PALMS BEACH RESORT [M] Carlsbad, CA
OCEAN PARK INN [M] Pacific Beach (San Diego), CA
OJAI VALLEY INN [RO] Ojai, CA
OLD MINERS LODGE [I] Park City, UT
OLD MONTEREY INN [I] Monterey, CA
OLD SAW MILL LODGE [I] Half Moon Bay, CA
OLD THYME INN [I] Half Moon Bay, CA
OLD TOWN BED & BREAKFAST INN [I] Eureka, CA
OLD TOWN INN [M] San Diego, CA
OLD WORLD INN [I] Napa, CA
OLD YACHT CLUB INN [I] Santa Barbara, CA
OLEANDER HOUSE [I] Yountville, CA
OLEMA INN [I] Inverness, CA
OLIVE HOUSE [I] Santa Barbara, CA
OLIVER HOUSE [I] St Helena, CA
OLYMPIA PARK HOTEL [MH] Park City, UT
OMNI, AZ
[RO] Tucson
OMNI, CA
[H] Los Angeles
ORANGE TREE GOLF & CONFERENCE RESORT [RO] Scottsdale, AZ
ORCHARD HILL COUNTRY INN [I] San Diego, CA
ORCHID TREE INN [I] Palm Springs, CA
ORLEANS HOTEL & CASINO [H] Las Vegas, NV
OTTER INN [M] Monterey, CA
OWL HOTEL & CASINO [M] Battle Mountain, NV
OXFORD INN [M] Bakersfield, CA
OXFORD PALACE [H] Los Angeles, CA
OXFORD SUITES RESORT [MH] Pismo Beach, CA
PACIFIC GROVE INN [I] Pacific Grove, CA
PACIFIC HEIGHTS INN [M] San Francisco, CA
PACIFIC MOTOR HOTEL [M] Crescent City, CA
PACIFIC TERRACE INN [MH] Pacific Beach (San Diego), CA
PACIFICA SUITES [M] Santa Barbara, CA
PACK CREEK RANCH [RO] Moab, UT
PALA MESA RESORT [RO] Fallbrook, CA
PALACE HOTEL [H] San Francisco, CA
PALACE STATION HOTEL & CASINO [H] Las Vegas, NV
PALM CANYON RESORT [M] Borrego Springs, CA
PALM HOTEL BED & BREAKFAST [I] Sonora, CA
PALM SPRINGS RIVERIA RESORT [MH] Palm Springs, CA
PALMS AT INDIAN HEAD [I] Borrego Springs, CA
PALOS VERDES INN [MH] Redondo Beach, CA
PAN PACIFIC [H] San Francisco, CA
PARK PLAZA HOTEL SAN FRANCISCO [H] San Francisco Airport Area, CA
PARRY LODGE & RESTAURANT [M] Kanab, UT
PEACOCK SUITES HOTEL [MH] Anaheim, CA
PEERY HOTEL [H] Salt Lake City, UT
PENINSULA, THE [H] Beverly Hills, CA
PENNY SLEEPER INN [M] Anaheim, CA
PEPPERMILL HOTEL & CASINO [H] Reno, NV
PEPPERTREES BED & BREAKFAST INN [I] Tucson, AZ
PETERSEN VILLAGE INN [I] Solvang, CA
PHOENICIAN RESORT [RO] Scottsdale, AZ
PHOENIX INN [MH] Phoenix, AZ
PHOENIX INN, THE [M] San Francisco, CA
PICCADILLY INNS, CA
[M] Fresno, [MH] Fresno
PIERPONT INN [M] Ventura, CA
PINE BEACH INN & SUITES [M] Fort Bragg, CA
PINE COVE INN [I] Idyllwild, CA
PINE INN [H] Carmel, CA
PINES RESORT [M] Yosemite National Park, CA
PINK MANSION [I] Calistoga, CA
PIONEER HOTEL & GAMBLING HALL [MH] Laughlin, NV
PLACE IN THE SUN [M] Palm Springs, CA
PLAZA HOTEL & CONFERENCE CENTER [MH] Tucson, AZ
PLAZA LAS GLORIAS-TIJUANA [H] Tijuana, Baja California, Mexico
PLEASANT STREET INN [I] Prescott, AZ
POCO DIABLO RESORT [RO] Sedona, AZ
POINT REYES SEASHORE LODGE [I] Inverness, CA
PORTOFINO BEACH HOTEL [I] Newport Beach, CA
PORTOFINO HOTEL & YACHT CLUB, THE [MH] Redondo Beach, CA
POST RANCH INN [RO] Big Sur, CA
PREMIER INNS OF METRO CENTER [M] Phoenix, AZ
PRESCOTT COUNTRY INN [I] Prescott, AZ
PRESCOTT HOTEL [I] San Francisco, CA
PRESCOTT RESORT CONFERENCE CTR & CASINO [H] Prescott, AZ
PROSPECT PARK INN [I] La Jolla (San Diego), CA
PROVIDENCE INN BED & BREAKFAST [I] Logan, UT
PRUFROCKS GARDEN BED & BREAKFAST [I] Santa Barbara, CA
PRUNEYARD INN [MH] San Jose, CA
PUNTA MORRO HOTEL SUITES [M] Ensenada, Baja California, Mexico
QUAIL LODGE RESORT & GOLF CLUB [RO] Carmel, CA
QUAIL RIDGE RESORT [M] Sedona, AZ
QUAILS INN HOTEL [MH] Escondido, CA
QUALITY INN, AZ
[M] Cottonwood, [M] Flagstaff, [M] Kingman, [M] Mesa, [MH] Phoenix, [M] South Rim (Grand Canyon National Park)
QUALITY INN, CA
[MH] Anaheim, [M] Bakersfield, [MH] Calexico, [MH] Camarillo, [M] Eureka, [MH] Laguna Beach, [M] Lake Tahoe Area, [MH] Lompoc, [H] Los Angeles Intl Airport Area, [M] Mammoth Lakes, [M] Monterey, [M] Pacific Grove, [M] Palm Springs, [M] Petaluma, [MH] San Diego, [MH] San Luis Obispo, [MH] Santa Ana, [MH] Santa Clara, [M] Vacaville
QUALITY INN, UT
[M] Beaver, [M] Cedar City, [M] Richfield, [M] Salt Lake City
QUEEN ANNE HOTEL [I] San Francisco, CA
QUIET CREEK INN [M] Idyllwild, CA
RADISSON, AZ
[MH] Flagstaff, [MH] Phoenix, [H] Phoenix, [RO] Scottsdale, [M] Yuma
RADISSON, CA
[MH] Anaheim, [MH] Berkeley, [H] La Jolla (San Diego), [H] Los Angeles, [MH] Sacramento, [H] San Bernardino, [H] San Diego, [H] San Francisco, [H] San Jose, [H] Santa Barbara, [H] Santa Monica, [H] Stockton, [H] Studio City (L.A.), [MH] Sunnyvale, [H] Visalia
RADISSON, UT
[H] Ogden, [MH] Salt Lake City
RAILROAD PARK RESORT [M] Dunsmuir, CA
RAMADA, AZ
[M] Flagstaff, [M] Mesa, [MH] Page, [MH] Phoenix, [MH] Tempe, [M] Tucson, [M] Williams (Coconino Co)
RAMADA, CA
[M] Anaheim, [MH] Anaheim, [M] Antioch, [M] Carlsbad, [M] Chula Vista, [M] Claremont, [M] Costa Mesa, [H] Culver City, [M] El Centro, [MH] Hollywood (L.A.), [H] Hollywood (L.A.), [M] Huntington Beach, [M] Oakdale, [H] Palm Springs, [MH] Palmdale, [M] San Diego, [MH] San Diego, [H] San Diego, [MH] San Francisco, [M] San Francisco Airport Area, [M] Santa Barbara, [M] Santa Nella, [M] Sunnyvale, [M] Temecula, [M] Torrance, [M] Vallejo, [M] Ventura
RAMADA, NV
[M] Ely, [H] Laughlin
RAMADA, UT
[M] Salt Lake City
RAMADA LTD [M] Globe, AZ
RAMSEY CANYON INN [I] Sierra Vista, AZ
RANCHITO MOTEL [M] Quincy, CA
RANCHO BERNARDO INN [RO] San Diego, CA
RANCHO CAYMUS INN [I] St Helena, CA
RANCHO DE LOS CABALLEROS [RO] Wickenburg, AZ
RANCHO SAN GREGORIO [I] Half Moon Bay, CA
RANCHO SONORA INN [I] Florence, AZ
RANCHO VALENCIA [RO] Rancho Santa Fe, CA
RANKIN RANCH [RO] Bakersfield, CA
RECAPTURE LODGE [M] Bluff, UT
RED CASTLE [I] Nevada City, CA
RED LION HOTELS AND INNS, CA
[MH] Sacramento
RED LION HOTELS AND INNS, NV
[M] Elko, [M] Winnemucca
RED ROCK INN [I] Zion National Park, UT
RED SETTER INN [I] Greer, AZ
REDBUD INN [I] Sonora, CA
REGAL INNS [H] Los Angeles, CA
REGAL MCCORMICK RANCH [RO] Scottsdale, AZ
REGENCY PLAZA HOTEL [H] San Diego, CA
REGENT BEVERLY WILSHIRE, THE [H] Beverly Hills, CA
RENAISSANCE, CA
[H] Long Beach, [H] Los Angeles Intl Airport Area, [RO] Palm Desert, [H] San Francisco
RENAISSANCE BEVERLY HOUSE HOTEL [H] Beverly Hills, CA
RENAISSANCE COTTONWOOD RESORT [RO] Scottsdale, AZ
RENAISSANCE STANFORD COURT HOTEL [H] San Francisco, CA
RESERVE HOTEL CASINO, THE [H] Henderson, NV
RESIDENCE INN BY MARRIOTT, AZ
[M] Scottsdale
RESIDENCE INN BY MARRIOTT, CA
[M] Arcadia, [M] Fremont, [M] La Jolla (San Diego), [M] Los Angeles, [M] Mountain View, [M] Ontario, [M] Orange, [H] Oxnard, [M] Sacramento, [M] San Jose, [M] Sunnyvale
RESIDENCE INN BY MARRIOTT, NV
[M] Las Vegas
RESIDENCE INN BY MARRIOTT, UT
[M] Salt Lake City
RESIDENCE INN BY MARRIOTT, Mexico
[RO] Tijuana, Baja California, Mexico
RESORT AT SQUAW CREEK [RO] Tahoe City (Lake Tahoe Area), CA
RESORT SUITES [MH] Scottsdale, AZ
RIDENHOUR RANCH HOUSE INN [I] Guerneville, CA
RIO RICO RESORT & COUNTRY CLUB [RO] Nogales, AZ
RIO SUITE HOTEL & CASINO [H] Las Vegas, NV
RITZ-CARLTON, AZ
[H] Phoenix
RITZ-CARLTON, CA
[RO] Laguna Beach, [H] Marina del Rey, [RO] Palm Springs, [H] Pasadena, [H] San Francisco
RIVER INN MOTOR HOTEL [M] Redding, CA
RIVIERA HOTEL AND CASINO [H] Las Vegas, NV
ROAD CREEK INN [RO] Loa, UT
ROBERTA'S COVE MOTOR INN [M] Nephi, UT
ROBIN HOOD INN [M] Big Bear Lake, CA
ROCKLIN PARK HOTEL [H] Roseville, CA
RODEWAY INN, AZ
[M] Scottsdale, [M] South Rim (Grand Canyon National Park), [M] Tempe, [M] Tucson
RODEWAY INN, CA
[M] Chula Vista, [MH] San Diego
RODEWAY INN, UT
[M] Cedar City, [M] Green River
ROMANICO INN [M] Richfield, UT
ROMANTIQUE LAKEVIEW LODGE [I] Lake Arrowhead, CA
ROSE GARDEN INN [I] Berkeley, CA
ROSEDALE INN [M] Pacific Grove, CA
ROYAL COPENHAGEN MOTEL [M] Solvang, CA

ROYAL PACIFIC MOTOR INN [M] San Francisco, CA
ROYAL PALMS HOTEL & CASITAS [RO] Phoenix, AZ
ROYAL VALHALLA LODGE [M] Lake Tahoe Area, CA
RUSTLER LODGE [M] Alta, UT
RYAN HOUSE 1855 [I] Sonora, CA
SAFARI INN [M] Burbank, CA
SAFARI RESORT [M] Scottsdale, AZ
SAGA MOTOR HOTEL [M] Pasadena, CA
SAHARA HOTEL & CASINO [H] Las Vegas, NV
SALT POINT LODGE [M] Fort Ross State Historic Park, CA
SALTAIR BED & BREAKFAST [I] Salt Lake City, UT
SAM'S TOWN HOTEL AND GAMBLING HALL [H] Las Vegas, NV
SAN DIEGO PARADISE POINT RESORT [RO] San Diego, CA
SAN JOAQUIN SUITE HOTEL, THE [M] Fresno, CA
SAN JUAN INN [M] San Juan Bautista, CA
SAN NICOLAS RESORT HOTEL [H] Ensenada, Baja California, Mexico
SAN REMO HOTEL [I] San Francisco, CA
SAN SIMEON PINES RESORT [M] San Simeon, CA
SAN YSIDRO RANCH [RO] Santa Barbara, CA
SAND DOLLAR INN [M] Monterey, CA
SAND N SAGE LODGE [M] Hawthorne, NV
SANDCASTLE INN [MH] Pismo Beach, CA
SANDPIPER INN AT THE BEACH CARMEL [I] Carmel, CA
SANDS MOTEL & SUITES [M] San Luis Obispo, CA
SANDY COVE INN [I] Inverness, CA
SANTA BARBARA INN [H] Santa Barbara, CA
SANTA FE HOTEL & CASINO [H] Las Vegas, NV
SANTA MARIA INN [MH] Santa Maria, CA
SAVOY HOTEL [H] San Francisco, CA
SCHOOL HOUSE INN [I] Bisbee, AZ
SCOTT COURTYARD [I] Calistoga, CA
SCOTTSDALE PLAZA RESORT [RO] Scottsdale, AZ
SCOTTSDALE PRINCESS HOTEL [RO] Scottsdale, AZ
SEA CREST RESORT MOTEL [M] Pismo Beach, CA
SEA GYPSY MOTEL [M] Pismo Beach, CA
SEA LODGE OCEANFRONT HOTEL [MH] La Jolla (San Diego), CA
SEA RANCH LODGE & GOLF LINKS [M] Gualala, CA
SEA & SAND INN [M] Santa Cruz, CA
SEA VENTURE RESORT [M] Pismo Beach, CA
SEAL BEACH COUNTRY INN & GARDENS [I] Long Beach, CA
SEAL COVE INN [I] Half Moon Bay, CA
SEDONA REAL INN [M] Sedona, AZ
SENIC HILLS MOTEL [M] Salina, UT
SERENITY [I] Sonora, CA
SEVEN GABLES INN [I] Pacific Grove, CA
SHADOW MOUNTAIN RESORT [RO] Palm Desert, CA
SHADOW RIDGE [MH] Park City, UT
SHANGRI-LA HOTEL [H] Santa Monica, CA
SHATTUCK HOTEL [H] Berkeley, CA
SHEEHAN HOTEL [H] San Francisco, CA
SHELTER POINTE HOTEL & MARINA [H] San Diego, CA
SHERATON, AZ
[RO] Chandler, [H] Mesa, [H] Phoenix, [H] Tucson, [RO] Tucson
SHERATON, CA
[MH] Anaheim, [M] Bakersfield, [H] Buena Park, [H] Concord, [MH] Fresno, [MH] Fullerton, [H] La Jolla (San Diego), [H] Los Angeles Intl Airport Area, [H] Newport Beach, [H] North Hollywood (L.A.), [H] Rancho Cordova, [H] San Diego, [MH] San Francisco, [H] San Jose, [H] San Pedro (L.A.), [H] Santa Monica, [M] Sunnyvale, [H] West Covina
SHERIDAN INN [M] Escondido, CA
SHERMAN HOUSE, THE [I] San Francisco, CA
SHERWOOD FOREST MOTEL [M] Garberville, CA
SHILO INN, AZ
[MH] Yuma
SHILO INN, CA
[M] Mammoth Lakes, [M] Oakhurst, [M] Palm Springs, [MH] Pomona
SHILO INN, NV
[M] Elko
SHILO INN, UT
[M] Kanab, [H] Salt Lake City
SHORE HOUSE AT LAKE TAHOE [I] Tahoe Vista (Lake Tahoe Area), CA
SHOWBOAT HOTEL & CASINO [H] Las Vegas, NV
SHUTTERS ON THE BEACH [H] Santa Monica, CA
SIERRA LODGE [M] Three Rivers, CA
SILVER KING HOTEL [H] Park City, UT
SILVER LEGACY RESORT & CASINO [H] Reno, NV
SILVER MAPLE INN [M] Bridgeport, CA
SILVER QUEEN MOTEL [M] Tonopah, NV
SILVER ROSE INN & SPA [I] Calistoga, CA
SILVERADO COUNTRY CLUB RESORT [RO] Napa, CA
SILVERTON HOTEL CASINO [MH] Las Vegas, NV
SIMPSON HOUSE INN [I] Santa Barbara, CA
SINGING HILLS RESORT [RO] El Cajon, CA
SINGLETREE INN [M] St George, UT
SIR FRANCIS DRAKE HOTEL [H] San Francisco, CA
SKY RANCH LODGE [M] Sedona, AZ
SLEEP INN [M] Salt Lake City, UT
SLEEPY LAGOON MOTEL [M] Beaver, UT
SMUGGLERS INN [M] Tucson, AZ
SNOW GOOSE INN [I] Mammoth Lakes, CA
SOFITEL, CA
[H] Los Angeles, [H] Redwood City
SOLVANG ROYAL SCANDINAVIAN INN [H] Solvang, CA
SONOMA COAST VILLA INC [I] Bodega Bay, CA
SONOMA MISSION INN & SPA [H] Sonoma, CA
SOUTHWEST INN [M] Sedona, AZ
SOUTHWEST INN AT EAGLE MOUNTAIN [M] Scottsdale, AZ
SPA HOTEL & CASINO RESORT & MINERAL SPRINGS [MH] Palm Springs, CA
SPALDING HOUSE [I] Visalia, CA
SPENCER HOUSE [I] San Francisco, CA
SPINDRIFT INN [I] Monterey, CA
SPORTSMEN'S LODGE HOTEL [MH] Studio City (L.A.), CA
SPRUCES INN [I] Salt Lake City, UT
SPYGLASS INN SHELL BEACH [MH] Pismo Beach, CA
SQUIBB HOUSE [I] Cambria, CA
ST ORRES RESTAURANT & INN [I] Gualala, CA
ST. TROPEZ HOTEL [M] Las Vegas, NV
STAGE STOP INN [M] Patagonia, AZ
STALLION SPRINGS [RO] Tehachapi, CA
STANFORD INN BY THE SEA [I] Mendocino, CA
STANFORD PARK [MH] Menlo Park, CA
STANFORD TERRACE INN [M] Palo Alto, CA
STANYAN PARK HOTEL [I] San Francisco, CA
STARDUST RESORT & CASINO [H] Las Vegas, NV
STATE LINE/SILVER SMITH HOTEL-CASINO [H] Wendover, UT
STATION HOUSE HOTEL & CASINO [MH] Tonopah, NV
STEIN ERIKSEN LODGE [RO] Park City, UT
STERLING HOTEL, THE [I] Sacramento, CA
STONEHOUSE INN [I] Carmel, CA
STONEPINE ESTATE RESORT [I] Carmel Valley, CA
STOVE PIPE WELLS VILLAGE [M] Death Valley National Monument, CA
STRATOSPHERE HOTEL & CASINO [H] Las Vegas, NV
STRAWBERRY CREEK INN [I] Idyllwild, CA
STRAWBERRY VALLEY INN [M] Mt Shasta, CA
SUITES AT FISHERMANS WHARF, THE [MH] San Francisco, CA
SUMMERFIELD SUITES, CA
[H] Los Angeles, [H] Los Angeles Intl Airport Area, [M] San Jose, [M] Sunnyvale, [M] Torrance
SUMMIT HOTEL BEL AIR [H] Los Angeles, CA
SUMMIT HOTEL RODEO DRIVE [H] Beverly Hills, CA
SUN TIME INN [M] St George, UT
SUNBURST RESORT [RO] Scottsdale, AZ
SUNCATCHER BED & BREAKFAST TUSCON DESERT RETREAT [I] Tucson, AZ
SUNDANCE RESORT [RO] Provo, UT
SUNDANCE VILLAS [M] Palm Springs, CA
SUNDIAL LODGE & RESTAURANT [M] Modesto, CA
SUNDOWNER INN [M] Sunnyvale, CA
SUNFLOWER HILL BED & BREAKFAST [I] Moab, UT
SUNGLOW MOTEL [M] Capitol Reef National Park, UT
SUNSET HOUSE [I] Carmel, CA
SUNSET MARQUIS HOTEL & VILLAS [H] Hollywood (L.A.), CA
SUNSET STATION CASINOS INC [H] Henderson, NV
SUPER 8, AZ
[M] Nogales, [M] Sierra Vista
SUPER 8, CA
[M] Anaheim, [M] Bakersfield, [M] Buena Park, [M] Crescent City, [M] Hemet, [M] Hollywood (L.A.), [M] Ontario, [M] Palm Springs, [M] Redlands, [M] Sacramento, [H] San Francisco, [M] Santa Rosa
SUPER 8, NV
[M] Boulder City, [M] Elko
SUPER 8, UT
[M] Salt Lake City
SURF MOTEL [M] Fort Bragg, CA
SURF & SAND HOTEL [H] Laguna Beach, CA
SUTTER CREEK INN [I] Jackson, CA
SUTTON PLACE HOTEL, THE [H] Newport Beach, CA
SWISS HOLIDAY LODGE [M] Mt Shasta, CA
SWITZERLAND HAUS BED & BREAKFAST [I] Big Bear Lake, CA
SYLVIA'S BURTON DRIVE INN [I] Cambria, CA
TAHOE BILTMORE LODGE & CASINO [H] Incline Village, NV
TAHOE CHALET INN [M] Lake Tahoe Area, CA
TAHOE COLONY INN [M] Lake Tahoe Area, CA
TAHOE VISTA INN AND MARINA [I] Lake Tahoe Area, CA
TALLY HO INN [M] Carmel, CA
TANQUE VERDE GUEST RANCH [RO] Tucson, AZ
TEMECULA CREEK INN [RO] Temecula, CA
TEMPE MISSION PALMS HOTEL [H] Tempe, AZ
TEN INVERNESS WAY [I] Inverness, CA
TENAYA LODGE AT YOSEMITE [RO] Yosemite National Park, CA
TERRACE BROOK LODGE [M] Zion National Park, UT
TERRITORIAL HOUSE BED & BREAKFAST [I] Sedona, AZ
TERRY RANCH BED & BREAKFAST [I] Williams (Coconino Co), AZ
TEXAS GAMBLING HALL & HOTEL INC [H] Las Vegas, NV
THATCHER INN [I] Ukiah, CA
THISTLE DEW INN [I] Sonoma, CA
THRIFTLODGE, CA
[M] El Cajon, [M] San Francisco
THUNDERBIRD LODGE, AZ
[M] Canyon de Chelly National Monument, [M] South Rim (Grand Canyon National Park)
TIBURON LODGE [M] Tiburon, CA
TICKLE PINK COUNTRY INN CARMEL [M] Carmel, CA
TIFFANY INN [I] Santa Barbara, CA
TIMBER COVE INN [M] Fort Ross State Historic Park, CA
TIMBERHILL RANCH [I] Fort Ross State Historic Park, CA
TOLL HOUSE HOTEL [MH] Los Gatos, CA
TOUCH OF SEDONA BED & BREAKFAST, A [I] Sedona, AZ
TOWN & COUNTRY HOTEL [H] San Diego, CA
TOWN HOUSE INN [M] Palo Alto, CA
TRADEWINDS LODGE [M] Fort Bragg, CA
TRAVELERS INN, CA
[M] Buena Park, [M] Palm Desert, [M] Stockton
TRAVELERS REPOSE BED & BREAKFAST [I] Desert Hot Springs, CA
TRAVELODGE, AZ
[M] Mesa, [M] Tempe, [M] Tucson, [M] Yuma
TRAVELODGE, CA
[M] Anaheim, [M] Bakersfield, [M] Blythe, [M] Buena Park, [M] El Cajon, [M] El Centro, [M] Eureka, [M] Fallbrook, [M] Hemet, [M] La Jolla (San Diego), [M] Lake Tahoe Area, [M] Los Angeles Intl Airport Area, [MH] Mammoth Lakes,

[M] *Morro Bay*, [M] *Palm Springs*, [M] *Redondo Beach*, [M] *San Clemente*, [M] *San Diego*, [H] *San Diego*, [M] *San Francisco Airport Area*, [M] *Santa Barbara*, [M] *Santa Monica*, [M] *Tahoe City (Lake Tahoe Area)*, [M] *Tehachapi*, [M] *Van Nuys (L.A.)*, [M] *Victorville*
TRAVELODGE, *NV*
[M] *Las Vegas*, [M] *Reno*
TRAVELODGE, *UT*
[M] *Salt Lake City*, [M] *St George*
TRAVELODGE, *Mexico*
[M] *Ensenada, Baja California, Mexico*
TREASURE ISLAND AT THE MIRAGE [H] *Las Vegas, NV*
TRES PALMAS BED & BREAKFAST [I] *Palm Desert, CA*
TRIANGLE HOTEL [M] *Monticello, UT*
TROJAN HORSE INN [I] *Sonoma, CA*
TROPICANA INN & SUITES [M] *Santa Barbara, CA*
TROPICANA RESORT & CASINO [H] *Las Vegas, NV*
TRUCKEE HOTEL [I] *Truckee, CA*
TUBAC GOLF RESORT [M] *Tumacacori National Historical Park, AZ*
TURRET HOUSE VICTORIAN BED & BREAKFAST, THE [I] *Long Beach, CA*
TWIN DOLPHIN [M] *Morro Bay, CA*
TWIN PALMS HOTEL [H] *Tempe, AZ*
TWO BUNCH PALMS RESORT & SPA [RO] *Desert Hot Springs, CA*
U S GRANT HOTEL [H] *San Diego, CA*
UNION PLAZA HOTEL & CASINO [H] *Las Vegas, NV*
UPHAM HOTEL [I] *Santa Barbara, CA*
VACATION INN, *CA*
[M] *El Centro*, [M] *Palm Desert*
VACATION VILLAGE HOTEL [MH] *Laguna Beach, CA*
VAGABOND INN, *CA*
[M] *Chico*, [M] *Costa Mesa*, [M] *Glendale*, [M] *Modesto*, [M] *Palm Springs*, [M] *Sacramento*, [M] *Salinas*, [M] *San Diego*, [M] *San Francisco*, [M] *Santa Clara*, [M] *Ventura*, [M] *Whittier*, [M] *Woodland Hills (L.A.)*
VAGABOND INN, *NV*
[M] *Reno*
VAGABOND'S HOUSE INN [I] *Carmel, CA*
VAL-U INN [M] *Winnemucca, NV*
VENICE BEACH HOUSE [I] *Santa Monica, CA*
VENTANA [I] *Big Sur, CA*
VICHY MINERAL SPRINGS RESORT [I] *Ukiah, CA*
VICTORIAN GARDEN INN [I] *Sonoma, CA*
VICTORIAN INN ON THE PARK [I] *San Francisco, CA*
VILLA FLORENCE [H] *San Francisco, CA*
VILLA HOTEL [MH] *San Mateo, CA*
VILLA INN [M] *San Rafael, CA*
VILLA MOTEL, *CA*
[M] *Oroville*, [M] *San Luis Obispo*
VILLA ROSA INN [I] *Santa Barbara, CA*
VILLA ROYALE BED & BREAKFAST INN [I] *Palm Springs, CA*
VILLAGE INN [M] *Carmel, CA*
VILLAGIO INN AND SPA [H] *Yountville, CA*
VINEYARD COUNTRY INN [I] *St Helena, CA*
VINTAGE INN [MH] *Yountville, CA*
VINTNERS INN [MH] *Santa Rosa, CA*
VISTA VILLA RESORT [M] *Tahoe Vista (Lake Tahoe Area), CA*
VIZCAYA [I] *Sacramento, CA*
W HOTEL [H] *San Francisco, CA*
WAHWEAP LODGE & MARINA [MH] *Page, AZ*
WAHWEAP LODGE/LAKE POWELL MOTEL [M] *Page, AZ*
WALKER RIVER LODGE [M] *Bridgeport, CA*
WARNER GARDENS MOTEL [M] *Woodland Hills (L.A.), CA*
WARWICK REGIS HOTEL [H] *San Francisco, CA*
WASHINGTON INN [H] *Oakland, CA*
WASHINGTON SCHOOL INN [I] *Park City, UT*
WASHINGTON SQUARE INN [I] *San Francisco, CA*
WATERFRONT PLAZA HOTEL [H] *Oakland, CA*
WAWONA HOTEL [RO] *Yosemite National Park, CA*
WAY STATION MOTEL [M] *Monterey, CA*
WAYSIDE INN [M] *Carmel, CA*
WEDGEWOOD INN [I] *Jackson, CA*
WELK RESORT CENTER [RO] *Escondido, CA*
WEST COAST SANTA CRUZ HOTEL [MH] *Santa Cruz, CA*
WESTCOAST HOTELS LONG BEACH [H] *Long Beach, CA*
WESTERN MOTEL, *NV*
[M] *Fallon*, [M] *Socorro*
WESTGATE HOTEL, THE [H] *San Diego, CA*
WESTIN, *AZ*
[RO] *Tucson*
WESTIN, *CA*
[H] *Costa Mesa*, [H] *Long Beach*, [H] *Los Angeles*, [H] *Los Angeles Intl Airport Area*, [RO] *Palm Springs*, [H] *San Diego*, [H] *San Francisco*, [H] *San Francisco Airport Area*, [H] *Santa Clara*
WESTLAKE VILLAGE INN [MH] *Thousand Oaks, CA*
WESTON EMPIRE HOUSE MOTEL & RESTAURANT [M] *Page, AZ*
WESTON INN [M] *Richfield, UT*
WESTON PLAZA HOTEL [M] *Vernal, UT*
WESTONS LAMPLIGHTER INN [M] *Vernal, UT*
WESTWARD HO CASINO & HOTEL [MH] *Las Vegas, NV*
WESTWARD LOOK RESORT [RO] *Tucson, AZ*
WESTWOOD MARQUIS HOTEL & GARDENS [H] *Westwood Village (L.A.), CA*
WHALE WATCH INN BY THE SEA [I] *Gualala, CA*
WHARF INN [M] *San Francisco, CA*
WHISPERING PINES LODGE [M] *Kernville, CA*
WHITE STALLION RANCH [RO] *Tucson, AZ*
WHITE SULPHUR SPRING RESORT SPA [I] *St Helena, CA*
WHITEGATE INN [I] *Mendocino, CA*
WHITMORE MANSION [I] *Nephi, UT*
WIGWAM, THE [RO] *Litchfield Park, AZ*
WILDFLOWERS BED & BREAKFAST [I] *Salt Lake City, UT*
WILDWOOD RESORT [M] *Big Bear Lake, CA*
WILLOWS, THE [I] *Palm Springs, CA*
WINDMILL INN AT SUN CITY WEST [M] *Glendale, AZ*
WINDMILL INN AT TUCSON [MH] *Tucson, AZ*
WINDMILL MOTOR INN [M] *Solvang, CA*
WINE COUNTRY INN [I] *St Helena, CA*
WINE & ROSES COUNTRY INN [I] *Lodi, CA*
WINE WAY INN [I] *Calistoga, CA*
WINNEDUMAH COUNTRY INN [I] *Lone Pine, CA*
WINNERS HOTEL & CASINO [M] *Winnemucca, NV*
WOODCREST HOTEL [H] *Santa Clara, CA*
WOODLAND PARK MANOR [M] *Idyllwild, CA*
WYNDEMERE HOTEL [MH] *Sierra Vista, AZ*
WYNDHAM, *AZ*
[MH] *Chandler*, [MH] *Phoenix*, [H] *Phoenix*, [H] *Tempe*
WYNDHAM, *CA*
[H] *Costa Mesa*, [H] *Hollywood (L.A.)*, [H] *Los Angeles*, [H] *Los Angeles Intl Airport Area*, [H] *Palm Springs*, [H] *Pleasanton*, [H] *San Diego*, [H] *San Jose*, [H] *San Rafael*
WYNDHAM, *UT*
[H] *Salt Lake City*
YARROW HOTEL [MH] *Park City, UT*
YAVAPAI LODGE [M] *South Rim (Grand Canyon National Park), AZ*
YORK HOTEL [H] *San Francisco, CA*
YOSEMITE GATEWAY MOTEL [M] *Lee Vining, CA*
YOSEMITE LODGE [MH] *Yosemite National Park, CA*
YOSEMITE LODGING: LEE'S MIDDLE FORK RESORT-MOTEL [M] *Yosemite National Park, CA*
YOSEMITE VIEW LODGE [M] *Yosemite National Park, CA*
ZABALLA HOUSE [I] *Half Moon Bay, CA*
ZION LODGE [M] *Zion National Park, UT*
ZION PARK MOTEL [M] *Zion National Park, UT*
ZOSA GARDENS BED & BREAKFAST [I] *Escondido, CA*

City Index

Alta UT, 352
Alturas CA, 67
Anaheim CA, 67
Antioch CA, 71
Anza-Borrego Desert State Park CA, 71
Arcadia CA, 71
Arches National Park UT, 353
Atascadero CA, 72
Auburn CA, 72
Austin NV, 327
Avalon (Catalina Island) CA, 73
Bakersfield CA, 74
Barstow CA, 75
Battle Mountain NV, 327
Beaumont CA, 76
Beaver UT, 353
Berkeley CA, 76
Beverly Hills CA, 78
Big Basin Redwoods State Park CA, 81
Big Bear Lake CA, 81
Big Sur CA, 82
Bisbee AZ, 3
Bishop CA, 83
Blanding UT, 353
Bluff UT, 354
Blythe CA, 83
Bodega Bay CA, 84
Borrego Springs CA, 85
Boulder City NV, 327
Bridgeport CA, 86
Brigham City UT, 354
Bryce Canyon National Park UT, 355
Buena Park CA, 86
Bullhead City AZ, 3
Burbank CA, 88
Burney CA, 88
Calexico CA, 88
Caliente NV, 328
Calistoga CA, 88
Camarillo CA, 90
Cambria CA, 91
Canyon de Chelly National Monument AZ, 4
Canyonlands National Park UT, 355
Capitol Reef National Park UT, 356
Carefree AZ, 4
Carlsbad CA, 92
Carmel CA, 93
Carmel Valley CA, 97
Carson City NV, 328
Casa Grande AZ, 5
Casa Grande Ruins National Monument AZ, 5
Cedar Breaks National Monument UT, 356
Cedar City UT, 356
Chandler AZ, 6
Channel Islands National Park CA, 98
Chester CA, 98
Chico CA, 98
Chiricahua National Monument AZ, 6
Chula Vista CA, 99
Claremont CA, 100
Clear Lake Area (Lake Co) CA, 100
Clifton AZ, 6
Coleville CA, 100
Concord CA, 101
Corona CA, 101
Corona del Mar CA, 102
Coronado CA, 102
Corte Madera CA, 103
Costa Mesa CA, 104
Cottonwood AZ, 7
Crescent City CA, 105
Crestline CA, 106
Culver City CA, 106
Davis CA, 107
Death Valley National Park CA, 107
Del Mar CA, 108
Desert Hot Springs CA, 109
Devils Postpile National Monument CA, 110
Dinosaur National Monument UT, 357
Disneyland CA, 110
Douglas AZ, 7
Dunsmuir CA, 110
El Cajon CA, 111
El Centro CA, 111
Elko NV, 329
Ely NV, 330
Ensenada MEX, 112
Escondido CA, 113
Eureka CA, 114
Fairfield CA, 116
Fallbrook CA, 116
Fallon NV, 330
Fillmore UT, 358
Flagstaff AZ, 7
Florence AZ, 10
Fort Bragg CA, 117
Fort Ross State Historic Park CA, 118
Fremont CA, 118
Fresno CA, 119
Fullerton CA, 121
Ganado AZ, 10
Garberville CA, 122
Garden City UT, 358
Garden Grove CA, 122
Gardnerville NV, 330
Gila Bend AZ, 11
Gilroy CA, 122
Glendale AZ, 11
Glendale CA, 123
Globe AZ, 11
Grand Canyon National Park AZ, 12
Grass Valley CA, 123
Great Basin National Park NV, 331
Green River UT, 358
Greer AZ, 14
Gualala CA, 123
Guerneville CA, 124
Half Moon Bay CA, 125
Hanford CA, 126
Hawthorne NV, 331
Hayward CA, 126
Healdsburg CA, 127
Hearst-San Simeon State Historical Monument (Hearst Castle) CA, 128
Heber City UT, 359
Hemet CA, 129
Henderson NV, 331
Holbrook AZ, 14
Hollywood (L.A.) CA, 129
Hopi Indian Reservation AZ, 15
Humboldt Redwoods State Park CA, 132
Huntington Beach CA, 133
Idyllwild CA, 133
Incline Village NV, 332
Indio CA, 134
Inverness CA, 134
Inyo National Forest CA, 135
Irvine CA, 136
Jackson CA, 137
Joshua Tree National Monument CA, 137
June Lake CA, 138
Kanab UT, 359
Kayenta AZ, 15
Kernville CA, 138
King City CA, 139
Kingman AZ, 15
La Habra CA, 142
La Jolla (San Diego) CA, 142
Laguna Beach CA, 139
Lake Arrowhead CA, 145
Lake Havasu City AZ, 16
Lake Mead National Recreation Area NV, 333
Lake Powell UT, 360
Lake Tahoe Area CA, 146
Lancaster CA, 147
Las Vegas NV, 333
Lassen Volcanic National Park CA, 147
Laughlin NV, 343
Lava Beds National Monument CA, 148
Lee Vining CA, 148
Litchfield Park AZ, 16
Livermore CA, 148
Loa UT, 361
Lodi CA, 149
Logan UT, 361
Lompoc CA, 149
Lone Pine CA, 150
Long Beach CA, 150
Los Angeles CA, 153
Los Angeles Area CA, 152
Los Angeles Intl Airport Area CA, 161
Los Gatos CA, 163
Lovelock NV, 344
Lunar Crater NV, 344
Madera CA, 164
Malibu CA, 164
Mammoth Lakes CA, 165
Marble Canyon AZ, 17
Marina del Rey CA, 166
Martinez CA, 167
Marysville CA, 167
McNary AZ, 17
Mendocino CA, 167
Menlo Park CA, 169
Merced CA, 169
Mesa AZ, 18
Mill Valley CA, 170

Moab UT, 362
Modesto CA, 171
Monterey CA, 172
Montezuma Castle National Monument AZ, 20
Monticello UT, 363
Morro Bay CA, 176
Mother Lode Country CA, 177
Mount Shasta CA, 177
Mountain View CA, 178
Mt Diablo State Park CA, 179
Muir Woods National Monument CA, 179
Napa CA, 179
Natural Bridges National Monument UT, 364
Navajo Indian Reservation AZ, 20
Navajo National Monument AZ, 20
Needles CA, 180
Nephi UT, 364
Nevada City CA, 181
Newport Beach CA, 182
Nogales AZ, 20
North Hollywood (L.A.) CA, 184
North Rim (Grand Canyon National Park) AZ, 12
Oakdale CA, 185
Oakhurst CA, 185
Oakland CA, 186
Oceanside CA, 188
Ogden UT, 364
Ojai CA, 189
Ontario CA, 190
Orange CA, 191
Organ Pipe Cactus National Monument AZ, 21
Oroville CA, 192
Overton NV, 344
Oxnard CA, 193
Pacific Beach (San Diego) CA, 193
Pacific Grove CA, 194
Page AZ, 21
Palm Desert CA, 196
Palm Springs CA, 198
Palm Springs Area CA, 198
Palmdale CA, 204
Palo Alto CA, 204
Panguitch UT, 366
Park City UT, 366
Parker AZ, 22
Pasadena CA, 205
Paso Robles CA, 207
Patagonia AZ, 23
Payson AZ, 23
Payson UT, 368
Pebble Beach CA, 208
Petaluma CA, 209
Petrified Forest National Park AZ, 24
Phoenix AZ, 24
Pine Valley CA, 209
Pinetop AZ, 32
Pinnacles National Monument CA, 209
Pipe Spring National Monument AZ, 32
Pismo Beach CA, 210
Placerville CA, 211
Pleasanton CA, 212
Pomona CA, 213
Porterville CA, 213
Prescott AZ, 32
Price UT, 368
Provo UT, 369
Pyramid Lake NV, 344
Quincy CA, 214
Rainbow Bridge National Monument UT, 371
Rancho Cordova CA, 214
Rancho Cucamonga CA, 215
Rancho Santa Fe CA, 215
Red Bluff CA, 216
Redding CA, 216
Redlands CA, 218
Redondo Beach CA, 218
Redwood City CA, 219
Redwood Highway CA, 220
Reno NV, 345
Richardson Grove State Park CA, 220
Richfield UT, 371
Riverside CA, 220
Roosevelt UT, 372
Roseville CA, 221
Sacramento CA, 222
Safford AZ, 34
Saguaro National Park AZ, 34
Salina UT, 372
Salinas CA, 225
Salt Lake City UT, 372
Salton Sea State Recreation Area CA, 226
San Bernardino CA, 226
San Carlos AZ, 34
San Clemente CA, 227
San Diego CA, 227
San Fernando CA, 240
San Fernando Valley Area CA, 240
San Francisco CA, 240
San Francisco Airport Area CA, 265
San Gabriel CA, 266
San Jose CA, 266
San Juan Bautista CA, 270
San Juan Capistrano CA, 270
San Luis Obispo CA, 271
San Marino CA, 273
San Mateo CA, 273
San Pedro (L.A.) CA, 274
San Rafael CA, 274
San Simeon CA, 275
San Ysidro (San Diego) CA, 275
Santa Ana CA, 276
Santa Barbara CA, 277
Santa Clara CA, 281
Santa Cruz CA, 283
Santa Maria CA, 285
Santa Monica CA, 285
Santa Nella CA, 288
Santa Rosa CA, 288
Saratoga CA, 290
Sausalito CA, 291
Scottsdale AZ, 35
Sedona AZ, 41
Seligman AZ, 45
Sells AZ, 45
Sequoia & Kings Canyon National Parks CA, 292
Show Low AZ, 45
Sierra Vista AZ, 46
Snowbird UT, 379
Solvang CA, 293
Sonoma CA, 294
Sonora CA, 296
South Lake Tahoe (Lake Tahoe Area) CA, 298
South Rim (Grand Canyon National Park) AZ, 12
Springerville AZ, 46
St George UT, 380
St Helena CA, 300
Stateline NV, 347
Stockton CA, 302
Studio City (L.A.) CA, 302
Sunnyvale CA, 303
Sunset Crater Volcano National Monument AZ, 47
Susanville CA, 304
Tahoe City (Lake Tahoe Area) CA, 304
Tahoe Vista (Lake Tahoe Area) CA, 305
Tehachapi CA, 306
Temecula CA, 306
Tempe AZ, 47
Thousand Oaks CA, 307
Three Rivers CA, 308
Tiburon CA, 308
Tijuana MEX, 309
Timpanogos Cave National Monument UT, 381
Tombstone AZ, 49
Tonopah NV, 348
Torrance CA, 309
Trinidad CA, 310
Truckee CA, 311
Tucson AZ, 50
Tumacacori National Historical Park AZ, 58
Ukiah CA, 312
Vacaville CA, 312
Valencia CA, 313
Vallejo CA, 313
Valley of Fire State Park NV, 348
Van Nuys (L.A.) CA, 314
Ventura CA, 314
Vernal UT, 381
Victorville CA, 315
Virginia City NV, 348
Visalia CA, 316
Walnut Creek CA, 316
Weaverville CA, 317
Wendover UT, 382
West Covina CA, 317
Westwood Village (L.A.) CA, 318
Whittier CA, 318
Wickenburg AZ, 58
Willcox AZ, 59
Williams (Coconino Co) AZ, 60
Willits CA, 319
Willows CA, 319
Window Rock AZ, 61
Winnemucca NV, 349
Winslow AZ, 61
Woodland Hills (L.A.) CA, 320
Wupatki National Monument AZ, 62
Yerington NV, 349
Yosemite National Park CA, 320
Yountville CA, 323
Yreka CA, 324
Yuma AZ, 62
Zion National Park UT, 382

Mobil Travel Guide

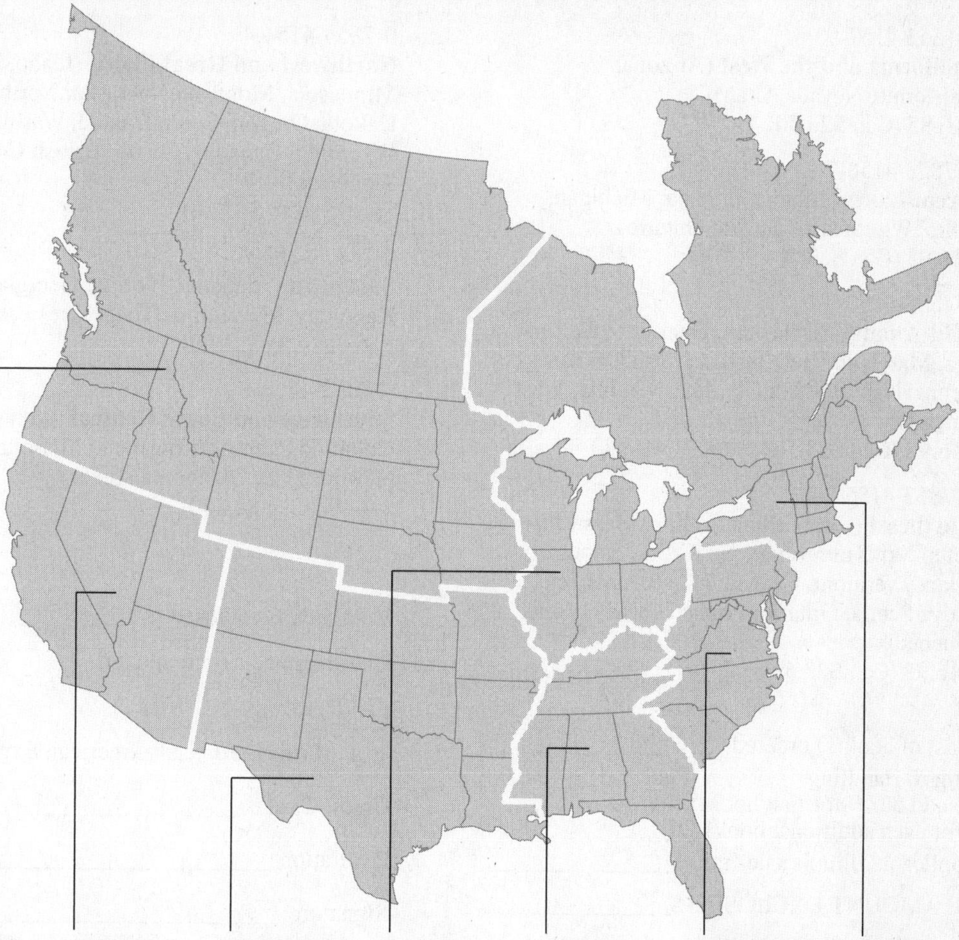

Northwest & Great Plains
Idaho
Iowa
Minnesota
Montana
Nebraska
North Dakota
Oregon
South Dakota
Washington
Wyoming

Canada:
Alberta
British Columbia
Manitoba

California & the West
Arizona
California
Nevada
Utah

Southwest & South Central
Arkansas
Colorado
Kansas
Louisiana
Missouri
New Mexico
Oklahoma
Texas

Great Lakes
Illinois
Indiana
Michigan
Ohio
Wisconsin

Canada:
Ontario

Southeast
Alabama
Florida
Georgia
Kentucky
Mississippi
Tennessee

Mid-Atlantic
Delaware
District of Columbia
Maryland
New Jersey
North Carolina
Pennsylvania
South Carolina
Virginia
West Virginia

Northeast
Connecticut
Maine
Massachusetts
New Hampshire
New York
Rhode Island
Vermont

Canada:
New Brunswick
Nova Scotia
Ontario
Prince Edward Island
Quebec

YOU CAN HELP MAKE THE *MOBIL TRAVEL GUIDE* MORE ACCURATE AND USEFUL

ALL INFORMATION WILL BE KEPT CONFIDENTIAL

Your Name ______________ (Please Print)	Were children with you on trip? ❑ Yes ❑ No
Street ______________	Number of people in your party ______________
City, State, Zip ______________	Your occupation ______________

1. Establishment Name ______________ Hotel ❑ Resort ❑ Other ❑ Motel ❑ Inn ❑ Restaurant ❑

Street ______________ City ______________ State ______________

Do you agree with our description? ❑ Yes ❑ No; if not, give reason ______________

Please give us your opinion of the following:

DECOR	CLEANLINESS	SERVICE	FOOD
❑ Excellent	❑ Spotless	❑ Excellent	❑ Excellent
❑ Good	❑ Clean	❑ Good	❑ Good
❑ Fair	❑ Unclean	❑ Fair	❑ Fair
❑ Poor	❑ Dirty	❑ Poor	❑ Poor

2000 *GUIDE* RATING ______ ★

CHECK YOUR SUGGESTED RATING BELOW:

❑ ★ good, satisfactory ❑ ★★★★ outstanding
❑ ★★ very good ❑ ★★★★★ one of best in country
❑ ★★★ excellent
❑ ✓ unusually good value

Comments: ______________

Date of visit ______________ First visit? ❑ Yes ❑ No

2. Establishment Name ______________ Hotel ❑ Resort ❑ Other ❑ Motel ❑ Inn ❑ Restaurant ❑

Street ______________ City ______________ State ______________

Do you agree with our description? ❑ Yes ❑ No; if not, give reason ______________

Please give us your opinion of the following:

DECOR	CLEANLINESS	SERVICE	FOOD
❑ Excellent	❑ Spotless	❑ Excellent	❑ Excellent
❑ Good	❑ Clean	❑ Good	❑ Good
❑ Fair	❑ Unclean	❑ Fair	❑ Fair
❑ Poor	❑ Dirty	❑ Poor	❑ Poor

2000 *GUIDE* RATING ______ ★

CHECK YOUR SUGGESTED RATING BELOW:

❑ ★ good, satisfactory ❑ ★★★★ outstanding
❑ ★★ very good ❑ ★★★★★ one of best in country
❑ ★★★ excellent
❑ ✓ unusually good value

Comments: ______________

Date of visit ______________ First visit? ❑ Yes ❑ No

3. Establishment Name ______________ Hotel ❑ Resort ❑ Other ❑ Motel ❑ Inn ❑ Restaurant ❑

Street ______________ City ______________ State ______________

Do you agree with our description? ❑ Yes ❑ No; if not, give reason ______________

Please give us your opinion of the following:

DECOR	CLEANLINESS	SERVICE	FOOD
❑ Excellent	❑ Spotless	❑ Excellent	❑ Excellent
❑ Good	❑ Clean	❑ Good	❑ Good
❑ Fair	❑ Unclean	❑ Fair	❑ Fair
❑ Poor	❑ Dirty	❑ Poor	❑ Poor

2000 *GUIDE* RATING ______ ★

CHECK YOUR SUGGESTED RATING BELOW:

❑ ★ good, satisfactory ❑ ★★★★ outstanding
❑ ★★ very good ❑ ★★★★★ one of best in country
❑ ★★★ excellent
❑ ✓ unusually good value

Comments: ______________

Date of visit ______________ First visit? ❑ Yes ❑ No

FOLD AND TAPE (OR SEAL) FOR MAILING—PLEASE DO NOT STAPLE

POSTAGE
REQUIRED

00

Mobil Travel Guide
7373 North Cicero Avenue
Lincolnwood, IL 60712

Revised editions are now being prepared for publication next year:

California and the West: Arizona, California, Nevada, Utah.

Great Lakes: Illinois, Indiana, Michigan, Ohio, Wisconsin; Ontario, Canada.

Mid-Atlantic: Delaware, District of Columbia, Maryland, New Jersey, North Carolina, Pennsylvania, South Carolina, Virginia, West Virginia.

Northeast: Connecticut, Maine, Massachusetts, New Hampshire, New York, Rhode Island, Vermont; Eastern Canada.

Northwest and Great Plains: Idaho, Iowa, Minnesota, Montana, Nebraska, North Dakota, Oregon, South Dakota, Washington, Wyoming; Western Canada.

Southeast: Alabama, Florida, Georgia, Kentucky, Mississippi, Tennessee.

Southwest and South Central: Arkansas, Colorado, Kansas, Louisiana, Missouri, New Mexico, Oklahoma, Texas.

The **Mobil Travel Guide** is available at bookstores or by mail from Mobil Travel Guide, 7373 North Cicero Avenue, Lincolnwood, IL 60712, or call toll-free, 1-800-653-0220 (8am - 5pm CST).

HOW CAN WE IMPROVE THE *MOBIL TRAVEL GUIDE*?

Mobil Travel Guides are constantly being revised and improved. All attractions are updated and all listings are revised and evaluated annually. You can contribute to the accuracy and usefulness of the guides by sending us your reactions to the places you have visited. Your suggestions for improving the guides are also welcome. Just complete this form or address letters to: Mobil Travel Guide, 7373 North Cicero Avenue, Lincolnwood, IL 60712. The editors appreciate your comments.

Have you sent us one of these forms before? ❑ Yes ❑ No

Please make any general comment here. Thanks! ______________________________

____

____

____